U.S. and CANADA LITERATU

NAME: ______________________

COMPANY: ______________________

ADDRESS: ______________________

CITY: ______________ STATE: ________ ZIP: ________

COUNTRY: ______________________

PHONE NO.: ( )______________________

ORDER NO.	TITLE	QTY.		PRICE	TOTAL
			×		=
			×		=
			×		=
			×		=
			×		=
			×		=
			×		=
			×		=
			×		=
			×		=

Subtotal ________

Must Add Your Local Sales Tax ________

Include postage:
Must add 15% of Subtotal to cover U.S. and Canada postage. (20% all other.) → Postage ________

Total ________

Pay by check, money order, or include company purchase order with this form ($200 minimum). We also accept VISA, MasterCard or American Express. Make payment to Intel Literature Sales. Allow 2-3 weeks for delivery.

☐ VISA ☐ MasterCard ☐ American Express Expiration Date ______________

Account No. ______________________

Signature ______________________

Mail To: Intel Literature Sales
P.O. Box 7641
Mt. Prospect, IL 60056-7641

International Customers outside the U.S. and Canada should use the International order form on the next page or contact their local Sales Office or Distributor.

For phone orders in the U.S. and Canada, call Toll Free: (800) 548-4725 or FAX to (708) 296-3699. Please print clearly in ink to expedite your order.

Prices good until 12/31/94.
Source HB

LOFUS1/100693

INTERNATIONAL LITERATURE ORDER FORM

NAME: ______________________________

COMPANY: ______________________________

ADDRESS: ______________________________

CITY: ______________ STATE: ________ ZIP: ________

COUNTRY: ______________________________

PHONE NO.: (   ) ______________________________

ORDER NO.	TITLE	QTY.		PRICE		TOTAL
			×		=	
			×		=	
			×		=	
			×		=	
			×		=	
			×		=	
			×		=	
			×		=	
			×		=	
			×		=	

Subtotal ________

Must Add Your Local Sales Tax ________

Total ________

PAYMENT

Cheques should be made payable to your ***local*** Intel Sales Office (see inside back cover).

Other forms of payment may be available in your country. Please contact the Literature Coordinator at your ***local*** Intel Sales Office for details.

The completed form should be marked to the attention of the LITERATURE COORDINATOR and returned to your ***local*** Intel Sales Office.

LOFINT1/100693

intel®

PERIPHERAL COMPONENTS

1994

Additional copies of this document or other Intel literature may be obtained from:

Intel Corporation
Literature Sales
P.O. Box 7641
Mt. Prospect, IL 60056-7641

or call 1-800-879-4683

LGCPY1/100693

CUSTOMER SUPPORT

FaxBACK SYSTEM

Order documents by phone for prompt delivery to your fax machine. You can rely on FaxBACK for the following types of information.

- Product Literature
- Tools and technical support material
- Application articles
- New product announcements
- Design recommendations
- Stepping and errata notification

Just dial 1-800-628-2283 or 916-356-3105 and the user-friendly system will prompt you along. Just have your fax number ready. Available 24 hours a day.

APPLICATIONS SUPPORT HOTLINE

The Technical Hotline is manned by applications personnel during normal business hours. You can leave a message during off hours or when applications personnel are already handling calls. The number (U.S. and Canada) is 1-800-628-8686. Assistance is also available through your local distributor or sales office.

INTEL'S APPLICATION BULLETIN BOARD SYSTEM

Key into our centralized Intel Applications Bulletin Board System and pull up all the latest information in Intel's product line. The BBS can provide you with the following type of information:

- software drivers
- documentation
- new products
- tools information
- firmware upgrades
- presentations
- revised sofrware

Intel's Application Bulletin Board System enables file retrieval and message/file exchange with our System Operator (Sysop) and File Operators (Fileops).

Just dial 916-356-3600 on your modem, and the user-friendly system will prompt you along.

For new users, the first log-in allows you to register with the system operator by entering your name and location. To access files on the BBS, log in again 24 hours later.

For immediate file access, call 1-800-628-8686 or 916-356-3104. For a listing of files available on the BBS, call FaxBACK at 1-800-628-2283 or 916-356-3105, order catalog #6.

- Settings: 9600 baud, N, 8, 1
- Auto configuration supports 1200 through 9600 baud MODEMs

October 1993
Order Number: 297389-001

DATA SHEET DESIGNATIONS

Intel uses various data sheet markings to designate each phase of the document as it relates to the product. The marking appears in the upper, right-hand corner of the data sheet. The following is the definition of these markings:

Data Sheet Marking	Description
Product Preview	Contains information on products in the design phase of development. Do not finalize a design with this information. Revised information will be published when the product becomes available.
Advanced Information	Contains information on products being sampled or in the initial production phase of development.*
Preliminary	Contains preliminary information on new products in production.*
No Marking	Contains information on products in full production.*

*Specifications within these data sheets are subject to change without notice. Verify with your local Intel sales office that you have the latest data sheet before finalizing a design.

Table of Contents

Table of Contents (Continued)

CHAPTER 5
Support Peripherals
DATA SHEETS

Alphanumeric Index

DATA-ON-DEMAND LITERATURE

The following documents are maintained on Intel's "Data-on-Demand" CD-ROM system.

To obtain a copy of the following documents, contact your local Intel field sales office. Intel technical distributor or call 1-800-548-4725 (U.S. and Canada).

Order Number	Title
230809-001	AP-167 Interfacing the 8207 Dynamic RAM Controller to the iAPX 186
230862-001	AP-168 Interfacing the 8207 Advanced Dynamic RAM Controller to the iAPX 286
292018-001	AP-281 UPI-452 Accelerates iAPX 286 Bus Performance

October 1993
Order Number: 297386-001

Chip Sets

1

1

82430 PCIset FOR THE Pentium™ PROCESSOR

- **Supports the Pentium™ Processor at 60 MHz or 66 MHz**
- **Interfaces the Host and Standard Buses to the Peripheral Component Interconnect (PCI) Local Bus Operating at 30 MHz or 33 MHz**
  - **Up to 132 Mbytes/sec Transfer Rate**
  - **Full Concurrency between CPU Host Bus and PCI Bus Transactions**
- **Integrated Cache Controller Provided for Optional Second Level Cache**
  - **256 Kbyte or 512 Kbyte Cache**
  - **Write-Back or Write-Through Policy**
  - **Standard or Burst SRAM**
- **Integrated Tag RAM for Cost Savings on Second Level Cache**
- **Provides a 64-Bit Interface to DRAM Memory**
  - **From 2 Mbytes to 192 Mbytes of Main Memory**
  - **70 ns and 60 ns DRAMs Supported**
- **Supports the Pipelined Address Mode of the Pentium Processor for Higher Performance**
- **Optional ISA or EISA Standard Bus Interface**
  - **Single Component ISA Controller**
  - **Two Component EISA Bus Interface**
  - **Minimal External Logic Required**
- **Supports Burst Read and Writes of Memory from the Host and PCI Buses**
- **Five Integrated Write Posting and Read Prefetch Buffers Increase CPU and PCI Master Performance**
- **Host CPU Writes to PCI in Zero Wait State PCI Bursts with Optional TRDY# Connection**
- **Integrated Low Skew Host Bus Clock Driver for Cost and Board Space Savings**
- **PCIset Operates Synchronous to the 66 MHz CPU and 33 MHz PCI Clocks**
- **Byte Parity Support for the Host/PCI and Main Memory Buses**
  - **Optional Parity on the Second Level Cache**

1

The 82430 PCIset provides the Host/PCI bridge, cache/main memory controller, and an I/O subsystem core (either PCI/EISA or PCI/ISA bridge) for the next generation of high-performance personal computers based on the Pentium Processor. System designers can take advantage of the power of the PCI (Peripheral Component Interconnect) bus for the local I/O while maintaining access to the large base of EISA and ISA expansion cards, and corresponding software applications. Extensive buffering and buffer management within the bridges ensures maximum efficiency in all three bus environments (Host CPU, PCI, and EISA/ISA Buses).

The 82430 PCIset consists of the 82434LX PCI/Cache/Memory Controller (PCMC) and the 82433LX Local Bus Accelerator (LBX) components, plus, either a PCI/ISA bridge or a PCI/EISA bridge. The PCMC and LBX provide the core cache and main memory architecture and serve as the Host/PCI bridge. For an ISA-based system, the 82430 PCIset includes the 82378 System I/O (SIO) component as the PCI/ISA bridge. For an EISA-based system, the 82430 PCIset includes the 82375EB PCI/EISA Bridge (PCEB) and the 82374EB EISA System Component (ESC). The PCEB and ESC work in tandem to form the complete PCI/EISA bridge. Both the ISA and EISA-based systems are shown on the following pages.

For complete data sheets on all these devices, refer to Order Number 290482 and 290483.

October 1993
Order Number: 290481-002

82430 PCIset ISA Block Diagram

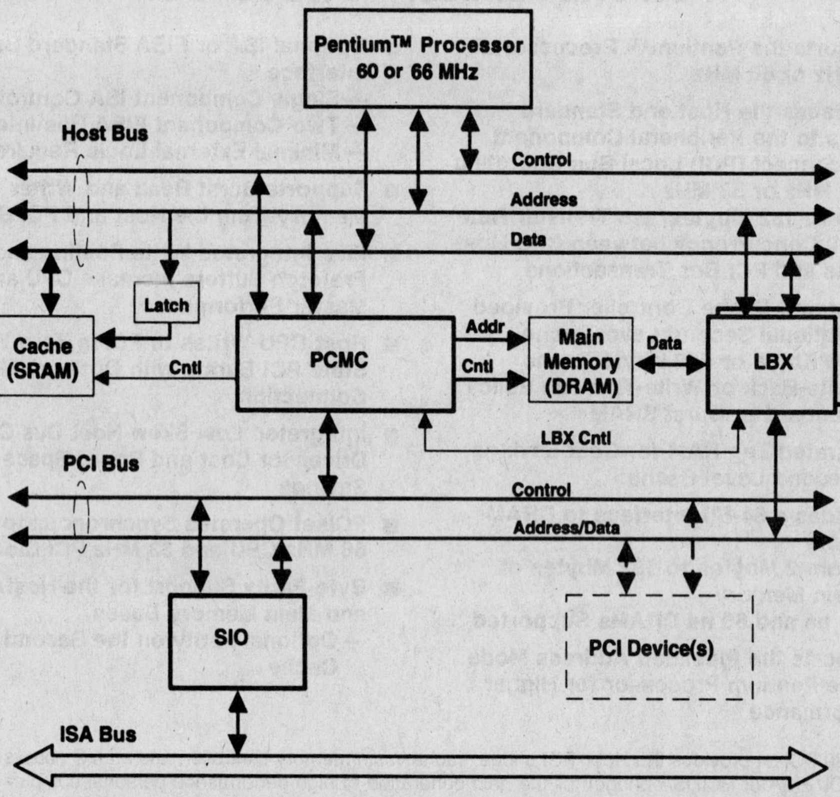

Pentium™ Processor
60 or 66 MHz

Host Bus
Control
Address
Data

Latch
Cache (SRAM)
Cntl
PCMC
Addr
Cntl
Main Memory (DRAM)
Data
LBX
LBX Cntl

PCI Bus
Control
Address/Data

SIO
PCI Device(s)

ISA Bus

290481–1

1

82430 PCIset EISA Block Diagram

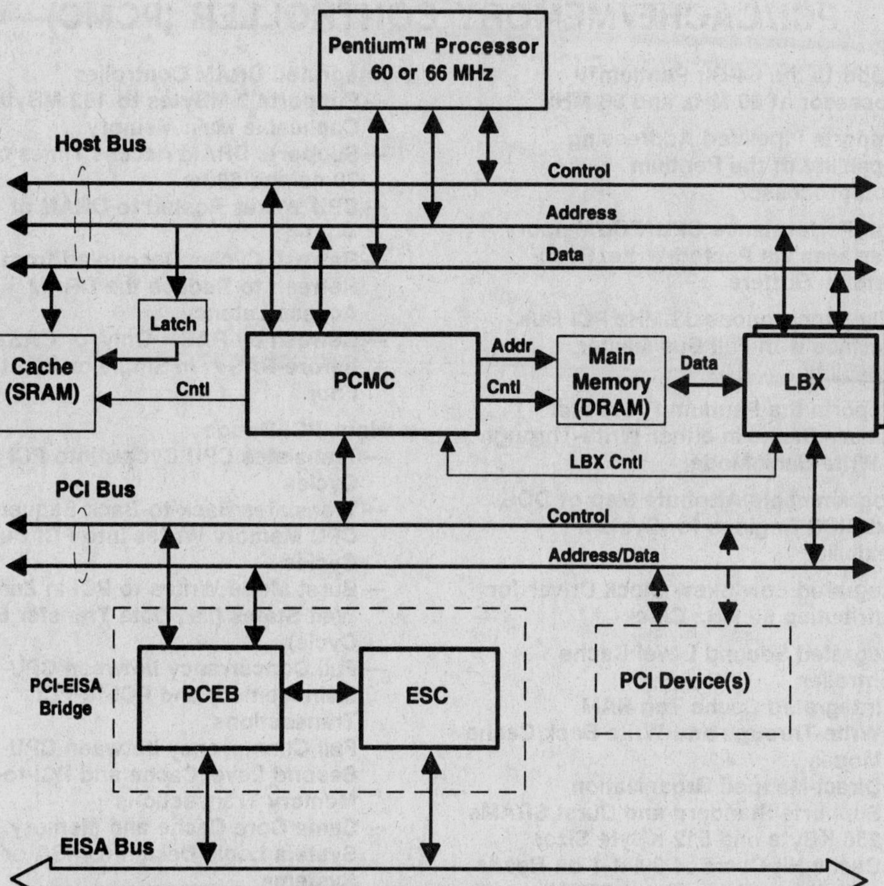

Pentium™ Processor
60 or 66 MHz

Host Bus

Control

Address

Data

Latch

Cache
(SRAM)

Cntl

PCMC

Addr

Cntl

Main
Memory
(DRAM)

Data

LBX

LBX Cntl

PCI Bus

Control

Address/Data

PCI-EISA
Bridge

PCEB

ESC

PCI Device(s)

EISA Bus

290481-2

82434LX
PCI/CACHE/MEMORY CONTROLLER (PCMC)

- **Supports the 64-Bit Pentium™ Processor at 60 MHz and 66 MHz**
- **Supports Pipelined Addressing Capability of the Pentium Microprocessor**
- **High Performance CPU/PCI/Memory Interfaces via Posted-Write/Read-Prefetch Buffers**
- **Fully Synchronous 33 MHz PCI Bus Interface with Full Bus Master Capability**
- **Supports the Pentium Processor Primary Cache in either Write-Through or Write-Back Mode**
- **Programmable Attribute Map of DOS and BIOS Regions for System Flexibility**
- **Integrated Low Skew Clock Driver for Distributing 66 MHz Clock**
- **Integrated Second Level Cache Controller**
  - **—Integrated Cache Tag RAM**
  - **—Write-Through and Write-Back Cache Modes**
  - **—Direct-Mapped Organization**
  - **—Supports Standard and Burst SRAMs**
  - **—256 KByte and 512 KByte Sizes**
  - **—Cache Hit Cycle of 3-1-1-1 on Reads and Writes Using Burst SRAMs**
  - **—Cache Hit Cycle of 3-2-2-2 on Reads and 4-2-2-2 on Writes Using Standard SRAMs**
- **Integrated DRAM Controller**
  - **—Supports 2 MBytes to 192 MBytes of Cacheable Main Memory**
  - **—Supports DRAM Access Times of 70 ns and 60 ns**
  - **—CPU Writes Posted to DRAM at 4-1-1-1**
  - **—Refresh Cycles Decoupled from ISA Refresh to Reduce the DRAM Access Latency**
  - **—Refresh by RAS#-Only, or CAS#-before-RAS#, in Single or Burst of Four**
- **Host/PCI Bridge**
  - **—Translates CPU Cycles into PCI Bus Cycles**
  - **—Translates Back-to-Back Sequential CPU Memory Writes into PCI Burst Cycles**
  - **—Burst Mode Writes to PCI in Zero PCI Wait States (i.e., Data Transfer Every Cycle)**
  - **—Full Concurrency between CPU-to-Main Memory and PCI-to-PCI Transactions**
  - **—Full Concurrency between CPU-to-Second Level Cache and PCI-to-Main Memory Transactions**
  - **—Same Core Cache and Memory System Logic Design for ISA or EISA Systems**
  - **—Cache Snoop Filter Ensures Data Consistency for PCI-to-Main Memory Transactions**
- **PCMC (208-Pin QFP Package) Uses 5V CMOS Technology**

The 82434LX PCI, Cache, Memory Controller (PCMC) integrates the cache and main memory DRAM control functions and provides the bus control for transfers between the CPU, cache, main memory, and the Peripheral Component Interconnect (PCI) Local Bus. The cache controller supports both write-through and write-back cache policies and cache sizes of 256 KBytes and 512 KBytes. The cache memory can be implemented with either standard or burst SRAMs. The PCMC cache controller integrates a high-performance Tag RAM to reduce system cost. Up to twelve single-sided SIMMs or six double-sided SIMMs provide a maximum of 192 MBytes of main memory. The PCMC is intended to be used with the 82433LX Local Bus Accelerator (LBX). The LBX provides the Host-to-PCI address path and data paths between the CPU/cache, main memory, and PCI. The LBX also contains posted write buffers and read-prefetch buffers. Together, these two components provide a full function data path to main memory and form a PCI bridge to the CPU/Cache and DRAM subsystem.

PCMC Block Diagram

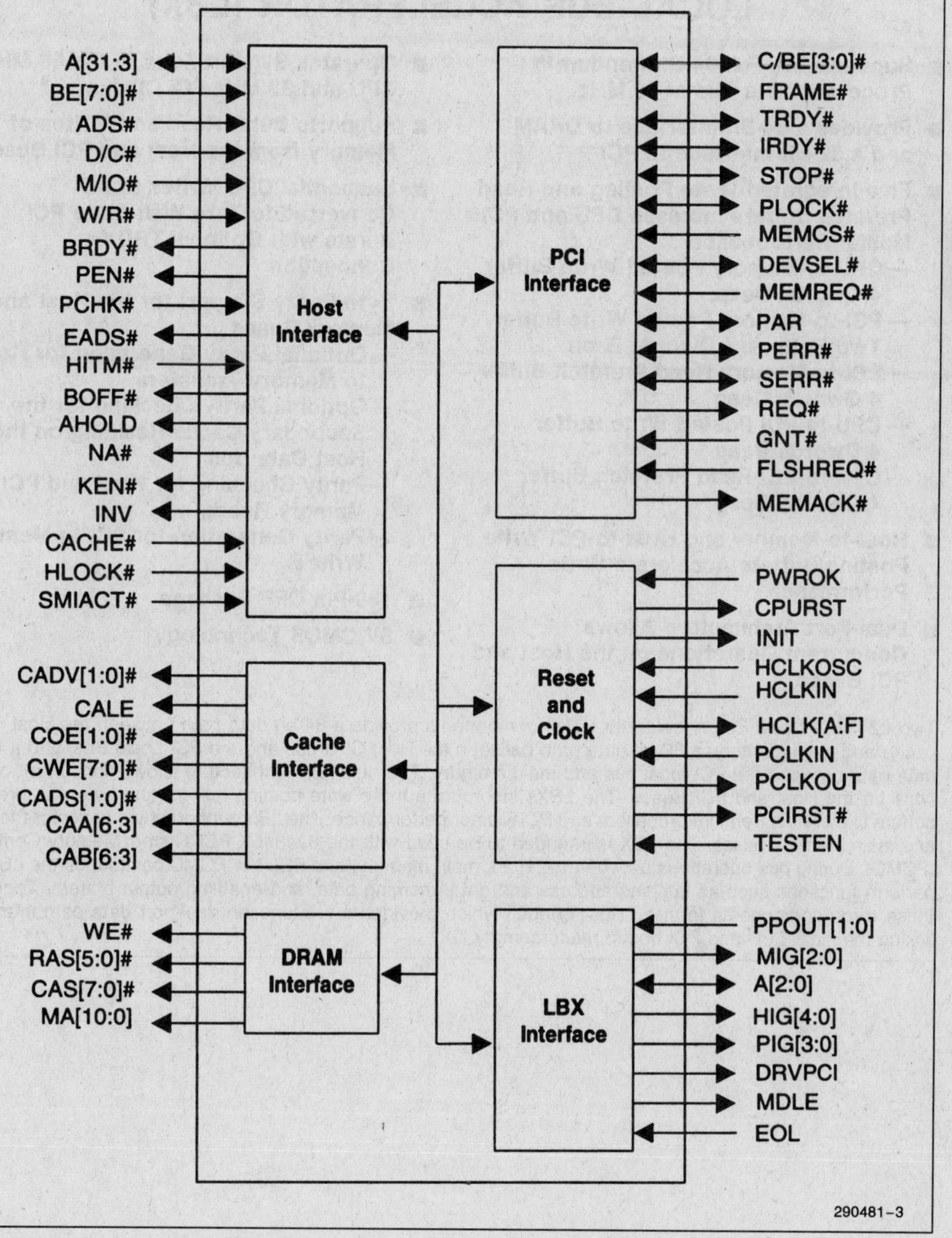

82433LX
LOCAL BUS ACCELERATOR (LBX)

- **Supports the Full 64-Bit Pentium™ Processor Data Bus at 66 MHz**
- **Provides a 64-Bit Interface to DRAM and a 32-Bit Interface to PCI**
- **Five Integrated Write Posting and Read Prefetch Buffers Increase CPU and PCI Master Performance**
  - **—CPU-to-Memory Posted Write Buffer 4 Qwords Deep**
  - **—PCI-to-Memory Posted Write Buffer Two Buffers, 4 Dwords Each**
  - **—PCI-to-Memory Read Prefetch Buffer 4 Qwords Deep**
  - **—CPU-to-PCI Posted Write Buffer 4 Dwords Deep**
  - **—CPU-to-PCI Read Prefetch Buffer 4 Dwords Deep**
- **Host-to-Memory and Host-to-PCI Write Posting Buffers Accelerate Write Performance**
- **Dual-Port Architecture Allows Concurrent Operations on the Host and PCI Buses**
- **Operates Synchronous to the 66 MHz CPU and 33 MHz PCI Clocks**
- **Supports Burst Read and Writes of Memory from the Host and PCI Buses**
- **Sequential CPU Writes to PCI Converted to Zero Wait State PCI Bursts with Optional TRDY# Connection**
- **Byte Parity Support for the Host and Memory Buses**
  - **—Optional Parity Generation for Host to Memory Transfers**
  - **—Optional Parity Checking for the Secondary Cache Residing on the Host Data Bus**
  - **—Parity Checking for Host and PCI Memory Reads**
  - **—Parity Generation for PCI to Memory Writes**
- **160-Pin QFP Package**
- **5V CMOS Technology**

Two 82433LX Local Bus Accelerator (LBX) components provide a 64-bit data path between the Host CPU/cache and main memory, a 32-bit data path between the Host CPU bus and the PCI Local Bus, and a 32-bit data path between the PCI local bus and main memory. The dual-port architecture allows concurrent operations on the Host and PCI Buses. The LBXs incorporate three write posting buffers and two read prefetch buffers to increase Pentium processor and PCI Master performance. The LBX supports byte parity for the Host and main memory buses. The LBX is intended to be used with the 82434LX PCI/Cache/Memory Controller (PCMC). During bus operations between the Host, main memory, and PCI, the PCMC commands the LBXs to perform functions such as latching address and data, merging data, and enabling output buffers. Together, these three components form a "Host Bridge" which provides a full function dual-port data path interface, linking the Host CPU and PCI bus to main memory.

LBX Block Diagram

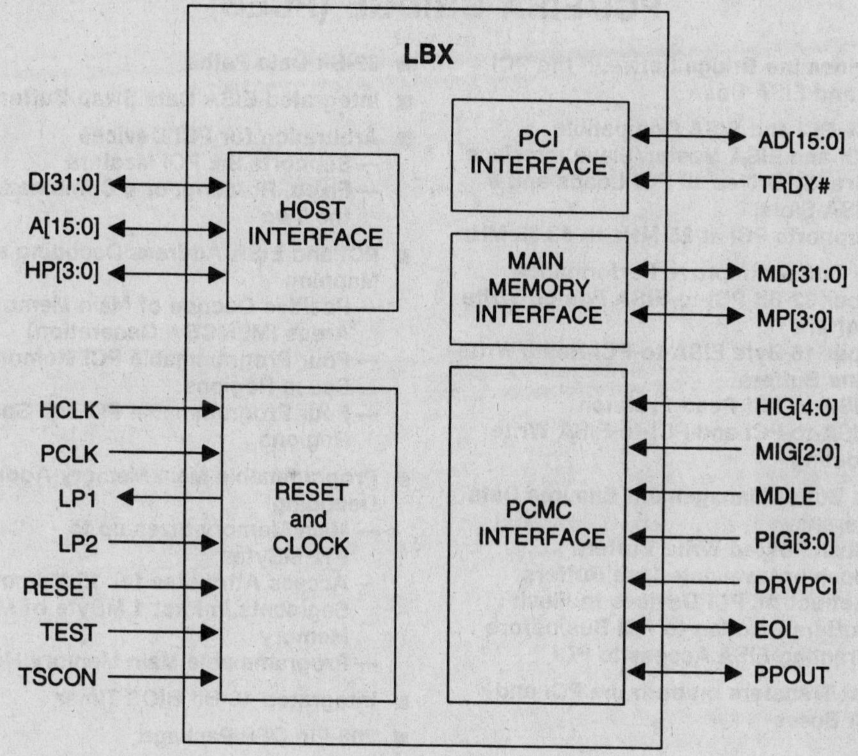

290481–4

1

82375EB PCI/EISA BRIDGE (PCEB)

- Provides the Bridge between the PCI Bus and EISA Bus
- 100% PCI and EISA Compatible
  - PCI and EISA Master/Slave Interface
  - Directly Drives 10 PCI Loads and 8 EISA Slots
  - Supports PCI at 25 MHz to 33.33 MHz
- Data Buffers Improve Performance
  - Four 32-Bit PCI-to-EISA Posted Write Buffers
  - Four 16-Byte EISA-to-PCI Read/Write Line Buffers
  - EISA-to-PCI Read Prefetch
  - EISA-to-PCI and PCI-to-EISA Write Posting
- Data Buffer Management Ensures Data Coherency
  - Flush Posted Write Buffers
  - Flush or Invalidate Line Buffers
  - Instruct All PCI Devices to Flush Buffers Pointing to PCI Bus before Granting EISA Access to PCI
- Burst Transfers on both the PCI and EISA Buses
- 32-Bit Data Paths
- Integrated EISA Data Swap Buffers
- Arbitration for PCI Devices
  - Supports Six PCI Masters
  - Fixed, Rotating, or a Combination of the Two
- PCI and EISA Address Decoding and Mapping
  - Positive Decode of Main Memory Areas (MEMCS# Generation)
  - Four Programmable PCI Memory Space Regions
  - Four Programmable PCI I/O Space Regions
- Programmable Main Memory Address Decoding
  - Main Memory Sizes up to 512 MBytes
  - Access Attributes for 15 Memory Segments in First 1 MByte of Main Memory
  - Programmable Main Memory Hole
- Integrated 16-Bit BIOS Timer
- 208-Pin QFP Package
- 5V CMOS Technology

The 82375EB PCI-EISA Bridge (PCEB) provides the master/slave functions on both the Peripheral Component Interconnect (PCI) Local Bus and the EISA Bus. Functioning as a bridge between the PCI and EISA buses, the PCEB provides the address and data paths, bus controls, and bus protocol translation for PCI-to-EISA and EISA-to-PCI transfers. Extensive data buffering in both directions increases system performance by maximizing PCI and EISA Bus efficiency and allowing concurrency on the two buses. The PCEB's buffer management mechanism ensures data coherency. The PCEB integrates central bus control functions including a programmable bus arbiter for the PCI Bus and EISA data swap logic for the EISA Bus. Integrated system functions include PCI parity generation, system error reporting, and programmable PCI and EISA memory and I/O address space mapping and decoding. The PCEB also contains a BIOS Timer that can be used to implement timing loops. The PCEB is intended to be used with the EISA System Component (ESC) to provide an EISA I/O subsystem interface.

PCEB Block Diagram
PCICLK
PCIRST#
AD[31:0]
C/BE[3:0]#
FRAME#
TRDY#
IRDY#
STOP#
PLOCK#
IDSEL
DEVSEL#
PAR
PERR#
MEMCS#
PIODEC#
CPUREQ#
CPUGNT#
REQ1#
GNT1#/RESUME#
REQ0#/PCEBGNT#
GNT0#/PCEBREQ#
REQ[3:2]#
GNT[3:2]#
MEMREG#
FLSHREQ#
MEMACK#
TEST#
PCI Interface
Data Buffers
EISA Address Decoder
PCI Address Decoder
BIOS Timer
PCI Arbiter
Test
EISA Interface
EISA Data Swap Logic
PCEB/ ESC Interface
ISA Interface
BCLK
START#
CMD#
M/IO#
W/R#
EXRDY
EX32#
EX16#
MSBURST#
SLBURST#
LOCK#
BE[3:0]#
LA[23:2]
LA[31:24]
REFRESH#
SD[31:0]
EISAHOLD
EISAHOLDA
PEREQ#/INTA#
NMFLUSH#
SDCPYEN01#
SDCPYEN02#
SDCPYEN03#
SDCPYEN13#
SDCPYUP
SDOE[2:0]#
SDLE[3:0]#
INTCHIP0
IO16#

290481–5

1

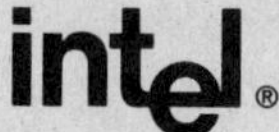

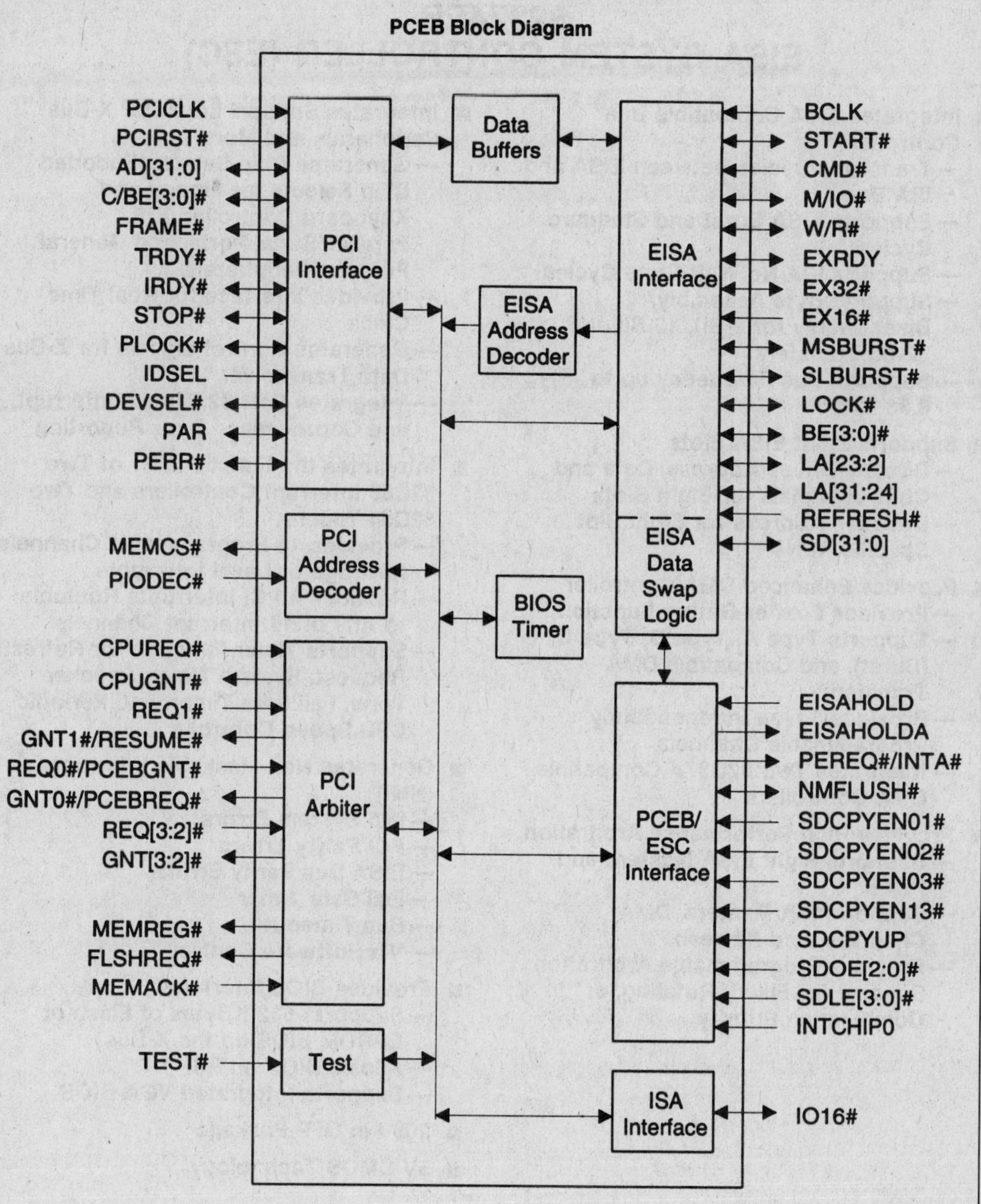

82374EB
EISA SYSTEM CONTROLLER (ESC)

- **Integrates EISA Compatible Bus Controller**
  - **— Translates Cycles between EISA and ISA Bus**
  - **— Supports EISA Burst and Standard Cycles**
  - **— Supports ISA No Wait State Cycles**
  - **— Supports Byte Assembly/ Disassembly for 8-Bit, 16-Bit and 32-Bit Transfers**
  - **— Supports Bus Frequency up to 8.33 MHz**
- **Supports Eight EISA Slots**
  - **— Directly Drives Address, Data and Control Signals for Eight Slots**
  - **— Decodes Address for Eight Slot Specific AENs**
- **Provides Enhanced DMA Controller**
  - **— Provides Scatter-Gather Function**
  - **— Supports Type A, Type B, Type C (Burst), and Compatible DMA Transfers**
  - **— Provides Seven Independently Programmable Channels**
  - **— Integrates Two 82C37A Compatible DMA Controllers**
- **Provides High Performance Arbitration**
  - **— Supports Eight EISA Masters and PCEB**
  - **— Supports ISA Masters, DMA Channels, and Refresh**
  - **— Provides Programmable Arbitration Scheme for Fixed, Rotating, or Combination Priority**
- **Integrates Support Logic for X-Bus Peripherals and More**
  - **— Generates Chip Selects/Encoded Chip Selects for Floppy and Keyboard Controller, IDE, Parallel/Serial Ports, and General Purpose Peripherals**
  - **— Provides Interface for Real Time Clock**
  - **— Generates Control Signals for X-Bus Data Transceiver**
  - **— Integrates Port 92, Mouse Interrupt, and Coprocessor Error Reporting**
- **Integrates the Functionality of Two 82C59 Interrupt Controllers and Two 82C54 Timers**
  - **— Provides 14 Programmable Channels for Edge or Level Interrupts**
  - **— Provides 4 PCI Interrupts Routable to Any of 11 Interrupt Channels**
  - **— Supports Timer Function for Refresh Request, System Timer, Speaker Tone, Fail Safe Timer, and Periodic CPU Speed Control**
- **Generates Non-Maskable Interrupts (NMI)**
  - **— PCI System Errors**
  - **— PCI Parity Errors**
  - **— EISA Bus Parity Errors**
  - **— Fail Safe Timer**
  - **— Bus Timeout**
  - **— Via Software Control**
- **Provides BIOS Interface**
  - **— Supports 512 KBytes of Flash or EPROM BIOS on the X-Bus**
  - **— Allows BIOS on PCI**
  - **— Supports Integrated VGA BIOS**
- **208-Pin QFP Package**
- **5V CMOS Technology**

The 82374EB EISA System Component (ESC) provides all the EISA system compatible functions. The ESC, with the PCEB, provides all the functions to implement an EISA to PCI bridge and EISA I/O subsystem. The ESC integrates the common I/O functions found in today's EISA based PC systems. The ESC incorporates the logic for an EISA (master and slave) interface, EISA Bus Controller, enhanced seven channel DMA controller with Scatter-Gather support, EISA arbitration, 14 channel interrupt controller, five programmable timer/counters, and non-maskable interrupt (NMI) control logic. The ESC also integrates support logic to decode peripheral devices such as the Flash BIOS, Real Time Clock, Keyboard/Mouse Controller, Floppy Controller, two Serial Ports, one Parallel Port, and IDE Hard Disk Drive.

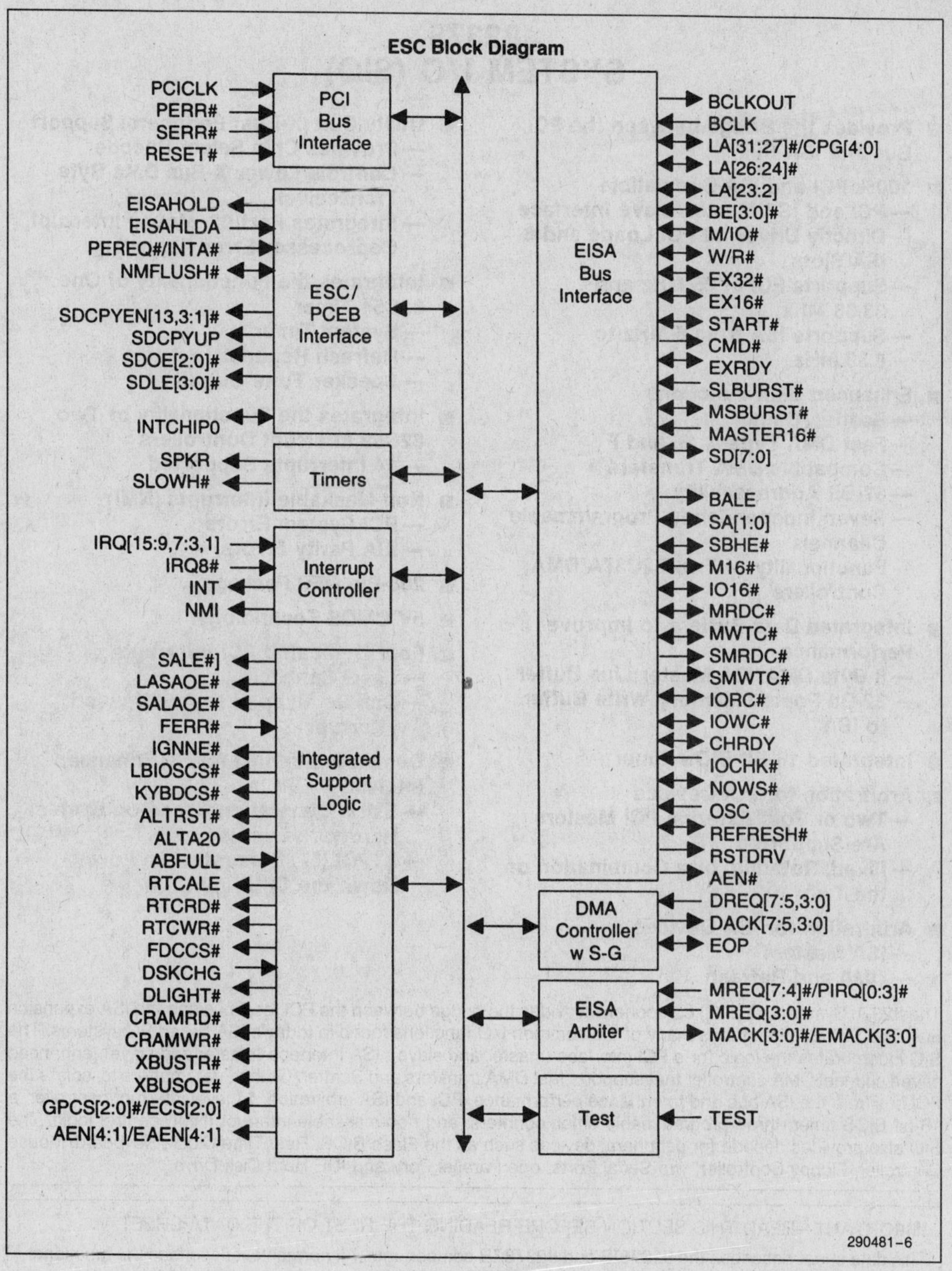

ESC Block Diagram

PCICLK
PERR#
SERR#
RESET#
PCI Bus Interface
EISAHOLD
EISAHLDA
PEREQ#/INTA#
NMFLUSH#
SDCPYEN[13,3:1]#
SDCPYUP
SDOE[2:0]#
SDLE[3:0]#
INTCHIP0
ESC/ PCEB Interface
SPKR
SLOWH#
Timers
IRQ[15:9,7:3,1]
IRQ8#
INT
NMI
Interrupt Controller
SALE#]
LASAOE#
SALAOE#
FERR#
IGNNE#
LBIOSCS#
KYBDCS#
ALTRST#
ALTA20
ABFULL
RTCALE
RTCRD#
RTCWR#
FDCCS#
DSKCHG
DLIGHT#
CRAMRD#
CRAMWR#
XBUSTR#
XBUSOE#
GPCS[2:0]#/ECS[2:0]
AEN[4:1]/EAEN[4:1]
Integrated Support Logic
EISA Bus Interface
BCLKOUT
BCLK
LA[31:27]#/CPG[4:0]
LA[26:24]#
LA[23:2]
BE[3:0]#
M/IO#
W/R#
EX32#
EX16#
START#
CMD#
EXRDY
SLBURST#
MSBURST#
MASTER16#
SD[7:0]
BALE
SA[1:0]
SBHE#
M16#
IO16#
MRDC#
MWTC#
SMRDC#
SMWTC#
IORC#
IOWC#
CHRDY
IOCHK#
NOWS#
OSC
REFRESH#
RSTDRV
AEN#
DMA Controller w S-G
DREQ[7:5,3:0]
DACK[7:5,3:0]
EOP
EISA Arbiter
MREQ[7:4]#/PIRQ[0:3]#
MREQ[3:0]#
MACK[3:0]#/EMACK[3:0]
Test
TEST

290481-6

82378
SYSTEM I/O (SIO)

- **Provides the Bridge between the PCI Bus and ISA Bus**
- **100% PCI and ISA Compatible**
  - **— PCI and ISA Master/Slave Interface**
  - **— Directly Drives 10 PCI Loads and 6 ISA Slots**
  - **— Supports PCI at 25 MHz and 33.33 MHz**
  - **— Supports ISA from 6 MHz to 8.33 MHz**
- **Enhanced DMA Functions**
  - **— Scatter/Gather**
  - **— Fast DMA Type A, B, and F**
  - **— Compatible DMA Transfers**
  - **— 32-Bit Addressability**
  - **— Seven Independently Programmable Channels**
  - **— Functionality of Two 82C37A DMA Controllers**
- **Integrated Data Buffers to Improve Performance**
  - **— 8-Byte DMA/ISA Master Line Buffer**
  - **— 32-Bit Posted Memory Write Buffer to ISA**
- **Integrated 16-Bit BIOS Timer**
- **Arbitration for PCI Devices**
  - **— Two or Four External PCI Masters Are Supported**
  - **— Fixed, Rotating, or a Combination of the Two**
- **Arbitration for ISA Devices**
  - **— ISA Masters**
  - **— DMA and Refresh**
- **Utility Bus (X-Bus) Peripheral Support**
  - **— Provides Chip Select Decode**
  - **— Controls Lower X-Bus Data Byte Transceiver**
  - **— Integrates Port 92, Mouse Interrupt, Coprocessor Error Reporting**
- **Integrates the Functionality of One 82C54 Timer**
  - **— System Timer**
  - **— Refresh Request**
  - **— Speaker Tone Output**
- **Integrates the Functionality of Two 82C59 Interrupt Controllers**
  - **— 14 Interrupts Supported**
- **Non-Maskable Interrupts (NMI)**
  - **— PCI System Errors**
  - **— ISA Parity Errors**
- **208-Pin QFP Package**
- **5V CMOS Technology**
- **Four Dedicated PCI Interrupts**
  - **— Level Sensitive**
  - **— Can Be Mapped to Any Unused Interrupt**
- **Complete Support for SL Enhanced Intel486™ CPU's**
  - **— SMI# Generation Based on System Hardware Events**
  - **— STPCLK# Generation to Power-Down the CPU**

The 82378 System I/O (SIO) component provides the bridge between the PCI local bus and the ISA expansion bus. The SIO also integrates many of the common I/O functions found in today's ISA based PC systems. The SIO incorporates the logic for a PCI interface (master and slave), ISA interface (master and slave), enhanced seven channel DMA controller that supports fast DMA transfers and Scatter/Gather, data buffers to isolate the PCI bus from the ISA bus and to enhance performance, PCI and ISA arbitration, 14 level interrupt controller, a 16-bit BIOS timer, three programmable timer/counters, and non-maskable-interrupt (NMI) control logic. The SIO also provides decode for peripheral devices such as the Flash BIOS, Real Time Clock, Keyboard/Mouse Controller, Floppy Controller, two Serial Ports, one Parallel Port, and IDE Hard Disk Drive.

IMPORTANT—READ THIS SECTION BEFORE READING THE REST OF THE DATA SHEET.

This data sheet describes the 82378IB and 82378ZB components. All normal text describes the functionality for both components. All features that exist on the 82378ZB are shaded as shown below.

This is an example of what the shaded sections that apply only to the 82378ZB component look like.

SIO Block Diagram

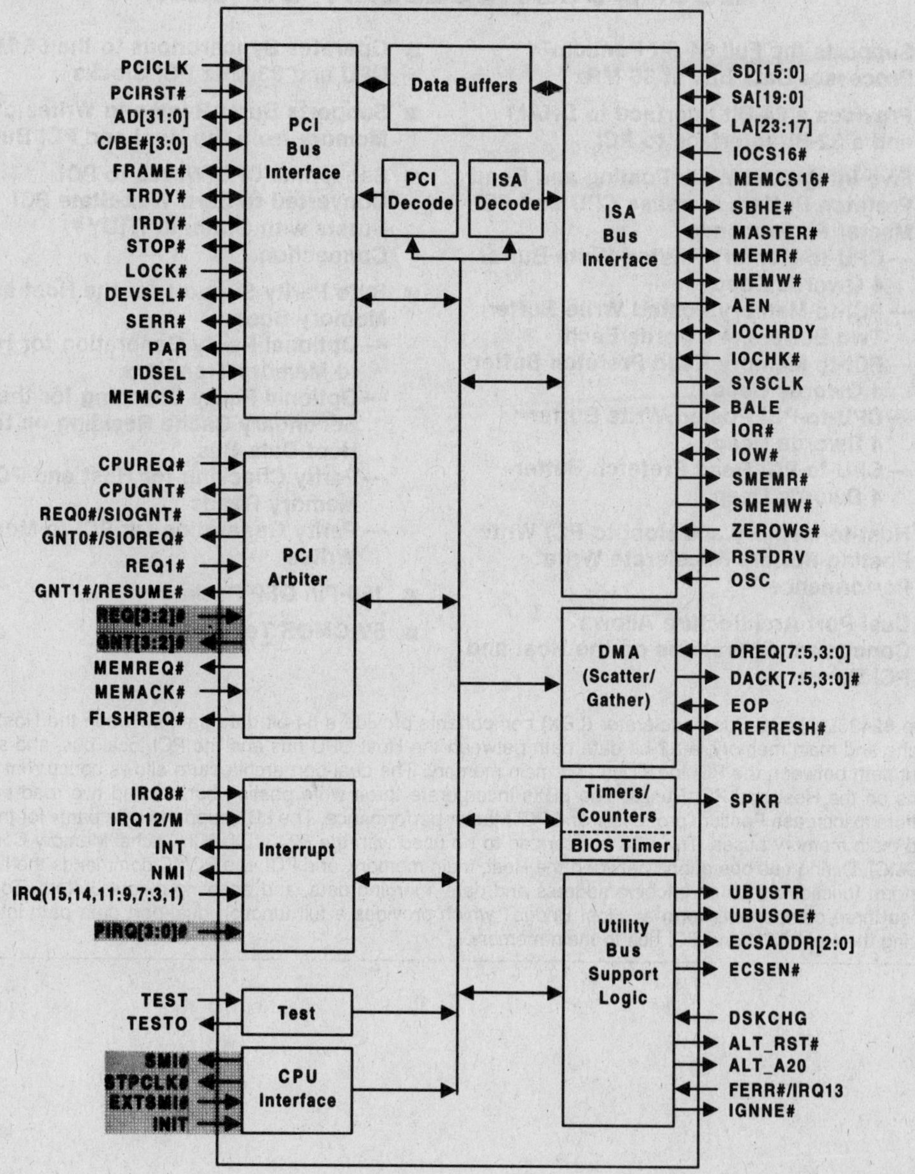

PCICLK
PCIRST#
AD[31:0]
C/BE#[3:0]
FRAME#
TRDY#
IRDY#
STOP#
LOCK#
DEVSEL#
SERR#
PAR
IDSEL
MEMCS#

PCI Bus Interface

Data Buffers

PCI Decode

ISA Decode

ISA Bus Interface

SD[15:0]
SA[19:0]
LA[23:17]
IOCS16#
MEMCS16#
SBHE#
MASTER#
MEMR#
MEMW#
AEN
IOCHRDY
IOCHK#
SYSCLK
BALE
IOR#
IOW#
SMEMR#
SMEMW#
ZEROWS#
RSTDRV
OSC

CPUREQ#
CPUGNT#
REQ0#/SIOGNT#
GNT0#/SIOREQ#
REQ1#
GNT1#/RESUME#
REQ[3:2]#
GNT[3:2]#
MEMREQ#
MEMACK#
FLSHREQ#

PCI Arbiter

DMA (Scatter/Gather)

DREQ[7:5,3:0]
DACK[7:5,3:0]#
EOP
REFRESH#

IRQ8#
IRQ12/M
INT
NMI
IRQ(15,14,11:9,7:3,1)
PIRQ[3:0]#

Interrupt

Timers/Counters

BIOS Timer

SPKR

Utility Bus Support Logic

UBUSTR
UBUSOE#
ECSADDR[2:0]
ECSEN#
DSKCHG
ALT_RST#
ALT_A20
FERR#/IRQ13
IGNNE#

TEST
TESTO

Test

SMI#
STPCLK#
EXTSMI#
INIT

CPU Interface

290481–7

1

82433LX LOCAL BUS ACCELERATOR (LBX)

- **Supports the Full 64-Bit Pentium™ Processor Data Bus at 66 MHz**
- **Provides a 64-Bit Interface to DRAM and a 32-Bit Interface to PCI**
- **Five Integrated Write Posting and Read Prefetch Buffers Increase CPU and PCI Master Performance**
  - **CPU-to-Memory Posted Write Buffer 4 Qwords Deep**
  - **PCI-to-Memory Posted Write Buffer Two Buffers, 4 Dwords Each**
  - **PCI-to-Memory Read Prefetch Buffer 4 Qwords Deep**
  - **CPU-to-PCI Posted Write Buffer 4 Dwords Deep**
  - **CPU-to-PCI Read Prefetch Buffer 4 Dwords Deep**
- **Host-to-Memory and Host-to-PCI Write Posting Buffers Accelerate Write Performance**
- **Dual-Port Architecture Allows Concurrent Operations on the Host and PCI Buses**
- **Operates Synchronous to the 66 MHz CPU and 33 MHz PCI Clocks**
- **Supports Burst Read and Writes of Memory from the Host and PCI Buses**
- **Sequential CPU Writes to PCI Converted to Zero Wait-State PCI Bursts with Optional TRDY# Connection**
- **Byte Parity Support for the Host and Memory Buses**
  - **Optional Parity Generation for Host to Memory Transfers**
  - **Optional Parity Checking for the Secondary Cache Residing on the Host Data Bus**
  - **Parity Checking for Host and PCI Memory Reads**
  - **Parity Generation for PCI to Memory Writes**
- **160-Pin QFP Package**
- **5V CMOS Technology**

Two 82433LX Local Bus Accelerator (LBX) components provide a 64-bit data path between the Host CPU/cache and main memory, a 32-bit data path between the Host CPU bus and the PCI local bus, and a 32-bit data path between the PCI local bus and main memory. The dual-port architecture allows concurrent operations on the Host and PCI Buses. The LBXs incorporate three write posting buffers and two read prefetch buffers to increase Pentium processor and PCI Master performance. The LBX supports byte parity for the Host and main memory buses. The LBX is intended to be used with the 82434LX PCI/Cache/Memory Controller (PCMC). During bus operations between the Host, main memory, and PCI, the PCMC commands the LBXs to perform functions such as latching address and data, merging data, and enabling output buffers. Together, these three components form a "Host Bridge" which provides a full function dual-port data path interface, linking the Host CPU and PCI bus to main memory.

Pentium™ is a trademark of Intel Corporation.
Manufactured and tested for Intel Corporation by LSI Logic in accordance with LSI's internal standards.

October 1993
Order Number: 290478-002

82433LX Local Bus Accelerator (LBX)

CONTENTS

PAGE

CONTENTS

PAGE

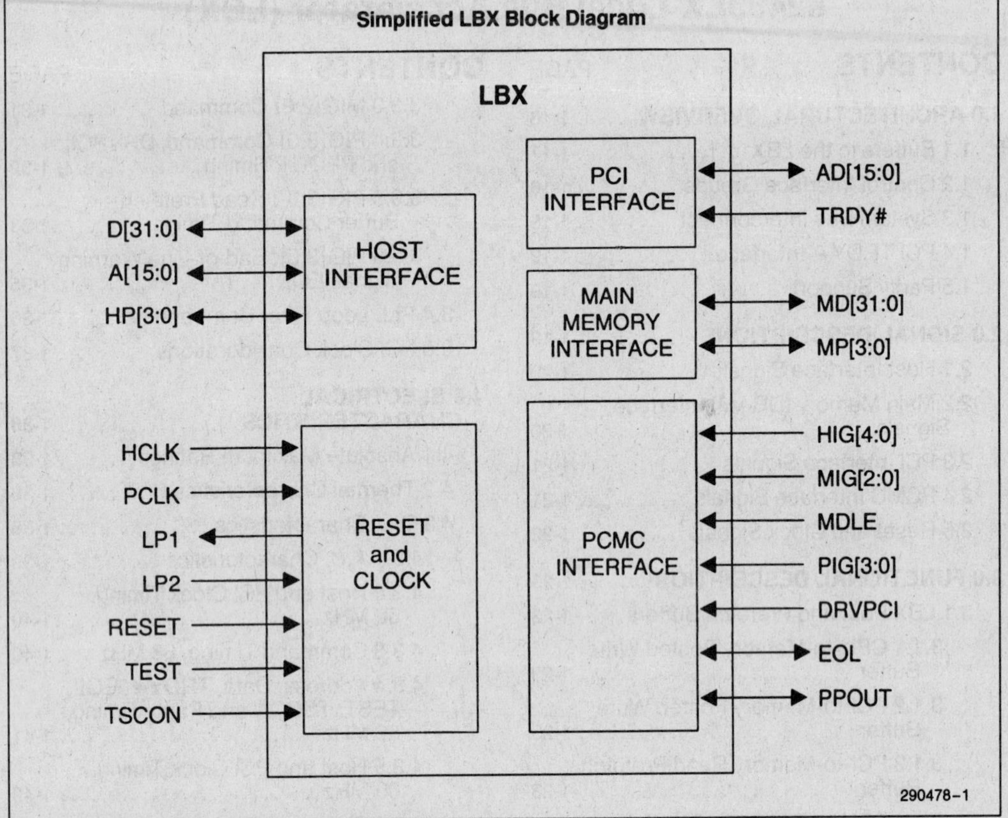

Simplified LBX Block Diagram

LBX

HOST INTERFACE
D[31:0]
A[15:0]
HP[3:0]

RESET and CLOCK
HCLK
PCLK
LP1
LP2
RESET
TEST
TSCON

PCI INTERFACE
AD[15:0]
TRDY#

MAIN MEMORY INTERFACE
MD[31:0]
MP[3:0]

PCMC INTERFACE
HIG[4:0]
MIG[2:0]
MDLE
PIG[3:0]
DRVPCI
EOL
PPOUT

290478–1

1.0 ARCHITECTURAL OVERVIEW

The Local Bus Accelerator (LBX) provides a high performance data and address path for the 82430 PCIset. The LBX incorporates five integrated buffers to increase the performance of the Pentium processor and PCI Master devices. Two LBXs in the system support the following areas:

1. 64-bit data and 32-bit address bus of the Pentium processor,
2. 32-bit multiplexed address/data bus of PCI, and
3. 64-bit data bus of the main memory.

In addition, the LBXs provide parity support for the three areas noted above (discussed further in Section 1.4).

1.1 Buffers in the LBX

The Local Bus Accelerator (LBX) components have five integrated buffers designed to increase the performance of the Host and PCI Interfaces of the 82430 PCIset. The five buffers numbered in Figure 1-1 are described in the following section.

1. **CPU-to-Memory Posted Write Buffer**—This buffer is 4 Qwords deep, enabling the Pentium processor to write-back a whole cache line in 4-1-1-1 timing, a total of 7 CPU clocks.
2. **PCI-to-Memory Posted Write Buffer**—A PCI Master can post two consecutive sets of 4 Dwords (total of one cache line) or two single non-consecutive transactions.
3. **PCI-to-Memory Read Prefetch Buffer**—A PCI Master to memory read transaction will cause this prefetch buffer to read up to 4 Qwords of data from memory, allowing up to 8 Dwords to be read onto PCI in a single burst transaction.
4. **CPU-to-PCI Posted Write Buffer**—The Pentium processor can post up to 4 Dwords into this buffer. The TRDY# connect option allows zero wait-state burst writes to PCI, making this buffer especially useful for graphic write operations.
5. **CPU-to-PCI Read Prefetch Buffer**—This prefetch buffer is 4 Dwords deep, enabling faster sequential Pentium processor reads when targeting PCI.

With the exception of the PCI-to-Memory write buffer and the CPU-to-PCI write buffer, the buffers in the LBX store data only, addresses are stored in the PCMC component.

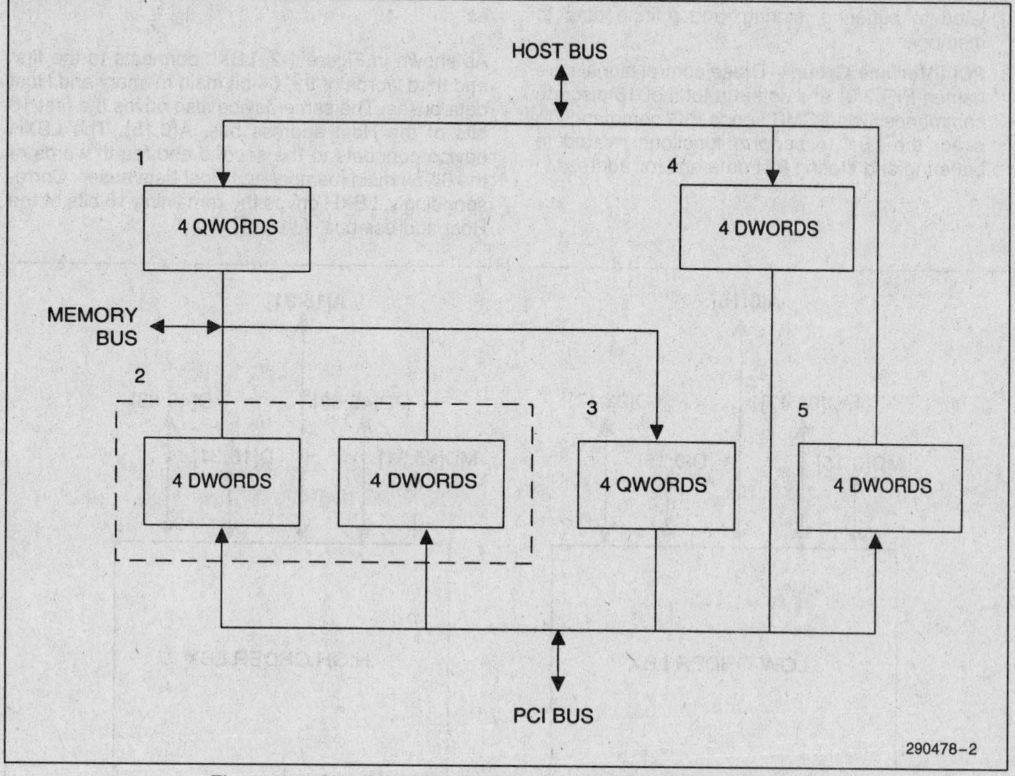

Figure 1-1. Simplified Block Diagram of the LBX Data Buffers

1.2 Control Interface Groups

The LBX is controlled by the PCMC via the control interface group signals. There are three interface groups; Host, Memory, and PCI. These control groups are signal lines that carry binary codes which the LBX internally decodes in order to implement specific functions such as latching data and steering data from PCI to memory. The control interfaces are described below.

1. **Host Interface Group**—These control signals are named HIG[4:0] and define a total of 29 discrete commands. The PCMC sends HIG commands to direct the LBX to perform functions related to buffering and storing Host data and/or address.
2. **Memory Interface Group**—These control signals are named MIG[2:0] and define a total of 7 discrete commands. The PCMC sends MIG commands to direct the LBX to perform functions related to buffering, storing, and retiring data to memory.
3. **PCI Interface Group**—These control signals are named PIG[3:0] and define a total of 15 discrete commands. The PCMC sends PIG commands to direct the LBX to perform functions related to buffering and storing PCI data and/or address.

1.3 System Bus Interconnect

The architecture of the 82430 PCIset splits the 64-bit memory and host data buses into logical halves in order to manufacture LBX devices with manageable pin counts. The two LBXs interface to the 32-bit PCI AD[31:0] bus with 16 bits each. Each LBX connects to 16 bits of the AD[31:0] bus and 32 bits of both the MD[0:63] bus and the D[0:63] bus. The lower order LBX (LBXL) connects to the low word of the AD[31:0] bus, while the high order LBX (LBXH) connects to the high word of the AD[31:0] bus.

Since the PCI connection for each LBX falls on 16-bit boundaries, each LBX does *not* simply connect to either the low Dword or high Dword of the Qword memory and Host buses. Instead, the low order LBX buffers the first and third words of each 64-bit bus while the high order LBX buffers the second and fourth words of the memory and Host buses.

As shown in Figure 1-2, LBXL connects to the first and third words of the 64-bit main memory and Host data buses. The same device also drives the first 16 bits of the Host address bus, A[0:15]. The LBXH device connects to the second and fourth words of the 64-bit main memory and Host data buses. Correspondingly, LBXH drives the remaining 16 bits of the Host address bus, A[16:31].

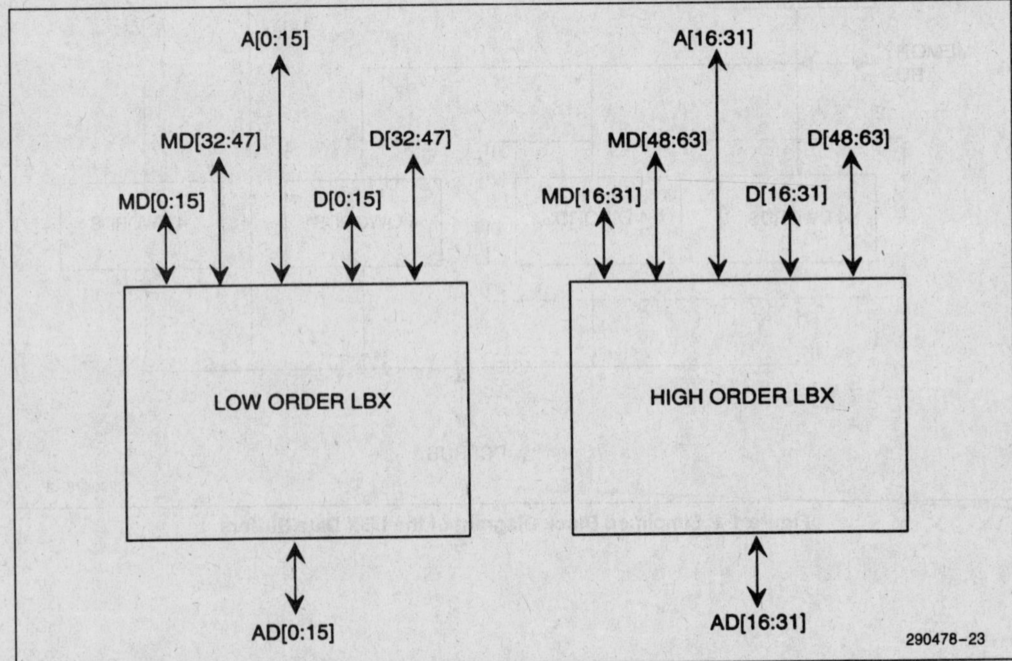

Figure 1-2. Simplified Interconnect Diagram of LBXs to System Buses

1.4 PCI TRDY# Interface

The PCI control signals do not interface to the LBXs, instead these signals connect to the 82434LX PCMC component. The main function of the LBXs PCI interface is to drive address and data onto PCI when the CPU targets PCI and to latch address and data when a PCI Master targets main memory.

The TRDY# option provides the capability for zero-wait state performance on PCI when the Pentium processor performs sequential writes to PCI. This option requires that PCI TRDY# be connected to each LBX, for a total of two additional connections in the system. These two TRDY# connections are in addition to the single TRDY# connection that the PCMC requires.

1.5 Parity Support

The LBXs support byte parity on the Host bus (CPU and second level cache) and main memory buses (local DRAM). The LBXs support parity during the address and data phases of PCI transactions to/from the Host Bridge.

2.0 SIGNAL DESCRIPTIONS

This section provides a detailed description of each signal. The signals (Figure 2-1) are arranged in functional groups according to their associated interface.

The "#" symbol at the end of a signal name indicates that the active, or asserted state occurs when the signal is at a low voltage level. When "#" is not present after the signal name, the signal is asserted when at the high voltage level.

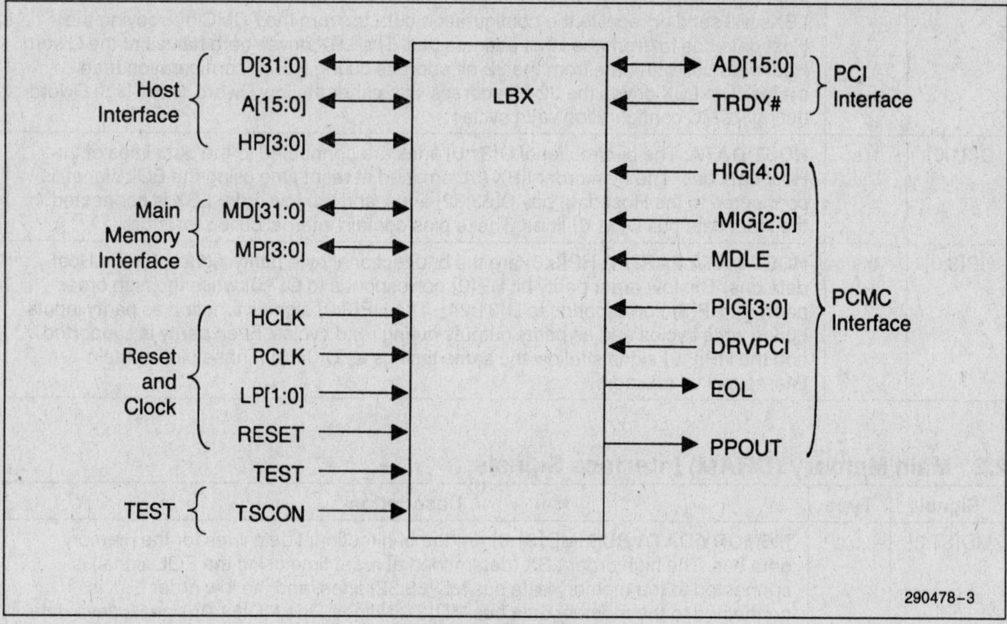

Figure 2-1. LBX Signals

The terms assertion and negation are used extensively. This is done to avoid confusion when working with a mixture of "active-low" and "active-high" signals. The term **assert**, or **assertion** indicates that a signal is active, independent of whether that level is represented by a high or low voltage. The term **negate**, or **negation** indicates that a signal is inactive.

The following notations are used to describe the signal type.

in Input is a standard input-only signal.

out Totem Pole output is a standard active driver.

t/s Tri-State is a bi-directional, tri-state input/output pin.

2.1 Host Interface Signals

Signal	Type	Description
A[15:0]	t/s	**ADDRESS BUS:** The bi-directional A[15:0] lines are connected to the address lines of the Host bus. The high order LBX (determined at reset time using the EOL signal) is connected to A[31:16], and the low order LBX is connected to A[15:0]. The host address bus is common with the Pentium processor, second level cache (L2), PCMC and the two LBXs. During CPU cycles A[31:3] are driven by the CPU and A[2:0] are driven by the PCMC, all are inputs to the LBXs. During inquire cycles the LBX drives the PCI Master address onto the Host address lines A[31:0]. This snoop address is driven to the CPU and the PCMC by the LBXs to snoop L1 and the integrated second level tags, respectively. During PCI configuration cycles bound for the PCMC, the LBXs will send or receive the configuration data to/from the PCMC by copying the Host data bus to/from the Host address bus. The LBX drives both halves of the Qword Host data bus with data from the 32-bit address during PCMC configuration read cycles. The LBX drives the 32-bit address with either the low Dword or the high Dword during PCMC configuration write cycles.
D[31:0]	t/s	**HOST DATA:** The bi-directional D[31:0] lines are connected to the data lines of the Host data bus. The high order LBX (determined at reset time using the EOL signal) is connected to the Host data bus D[63:32] lines, and the low order LBX is connected to the Host data bus D[31:0] lines. These pins contain internal pullup resistors.
HP[3:0]	t/s	**HOST DATA PARITY:** HP[3:0] are the bi-directional byte parity signals for the Host data bus. The low order parity bit HP[0] corresponds to D[7:0] while the high order parity bit HP[3] corresponds to D[31:24]. The HP[3:0] signals function as parity inputs during write cycles and as parity outputs during read cycles. Even parity is supported and the HP[3:0] signals follow the same timings as D[31:0]. These pins contain internal pullup resistors.

2.2 Main Memory (DRAM) Interface Signals

Signal	Type	Description
MD[31:0]	t/s	**MEMORY DATA BUS:** MD[31:0] are the bi-directional data lines for the memory data bus. The high order LBX (determined at reset time using the EOL signal) is connected to the memory data bus MD[63:32] lines, and the low order LBX is connected to the memory data bus MD[31:0] lines. The MD[31:0] signals drive data destined for either the Host data bus or the PCI bus. The MD[31:0] signals input data that originated from either the Host data bus or the PCI bus. These pins contain internal pullup resistors.
MP[3:0]	t/s	**MEMORY PARITY:** MP[3:0] are the bi-directional byte enable parity signals for the memory data bus. The low order parity bit MP[0] corresponds to MD[7:0] while the high order parity bit MP[3] corresponds to MD[31:24]. The MP[3:0] signals are parity outputs during write cycles to memory and parity inputs during read cycles from memory. Even parity is supported and the MP[3:0] signals follow the same timings as MD[31:0]. These pins contain internal pullup resistors.

2.3 PCI Interface Signals

Signal	Type	Description
AD[15:0]	t/s	**ADDRESS AND DATA:** AD[15:0] are bi-directional data lines for the PCI bus. The AD[15:0] signals sample or drive the address and data on the PCI bus. The high order LBX (determined at reset time using the EOL signal) is connected to the PCI bus AD[31:16] lines, and the low order LBX is connected to the PCI AD[15:0] lines.
TRDY#	in	**TARGET READY:** TRDY# indicates the selected (targeted) device's ability to complete the current data phase of the bus operation. For normal operation TRDY# is tied asserted low. When the TRDY# option is enabled in the PCMC (for zero wait state PCI burst writes), TRDY# should be connected to the PCI bus.

2.4 PCMC Interface Signals

Signal	Type	Description
HIG[4:0]	in	**HOST INTERFACE GROUP:** These signals are driven from the PCMC and control the Host interface of the LBX. The LBX decodes the binary pattern of these lines to perform 29 unique functions. These signals are synchronous to the rising edge of HCLK.
MIG[2:0]	in	**MEMORY INTERFACE GROUP:** These signals are driven from the PCMC and control the memory interface of the LBX. The LBX decodes the binary pattern of these lines to perform 7 unique functions. These signals are synchronous to the rising edge of HCLK.
PIG[3:0]	in	**PCI INTERFACE GROUP:** These signals are driven from the PCMC and control the PCI interface of the LBX. The LBX decodes the binary pattern of these lines to perform 15 unique functions. These signals are synchronous to the rising edge of HCLK.
MDLE	in	**MEMORY DATA LATCH ENABLE:** During CPU reads from DRAM, the LBX uses a clocked register to transfer data from the MD[31:0] and MP[3:0] lines to the D[31:0] and HP[3:0] lines. MDLE is the clock enable for this register. Data is clocked into this register when MDLE is asserted. The register retains its current value when MDLE is negated. During CPU reads from main memory, the LBX tri-states the D[31:0] and HP[3:0] lines on the rising edge of MDLE when HIG[4:0] = NOPC.
DRVPCI	in	**DRIVE PCI BUS:** This signal enables the LBX to drive either address or data information onto the PCI AD[15:0] lines.
EOL	t/s	**END OF LINE:** This signal is asserted when a PCI master read or write transaction is about to overrun a cache line boundary. The low order LBX will have this pin connected to the PCMC (internally pulled up in the PCMC). The high order LBX connects this pin to a pull-down resistor. With one LBX EOL line being pulled down and the other LBX EOL pulled up, the LBX samples the value of this pin on the negation of the RESET signal to determine if it's the high or low order LBX.

2.4 PCMC Interface Signals (Continued)

Signal	Type	Description
PPOUT	t/s	**LBX PARITY:** This signal reflects the parity of the 16 AD lines driven from or latched into the LBX, depending on the command driven on PIG[3:0]. The PCMC uses PPOUT from both LBXs (called PPOUT[1:0]) to calculate the PCI parity signal in (PAR) for CPU to PCI transactions during the address phase of the PCI cycle. The LBX uses PPOUT to check the PAR signal for PCI Master transactions to memory during the address phase of the PCI cycle. When transmitting data to PCI the PCMC uses PPOUT to calculate the proper value for PAR. When receiving data from PCI the PCMC uses PPOUT to check the value received on PAR. If the L2 cache does not implement parity, the LBX will calculate parity so the PCMC can drive the correct value on PAR during L2 reads initiated by a PCI Master. The LBX samples the PPOUT signal at the negation of reset and compares that state with the state of EOL to determine whether the L2 cache implements parity. The PCMC internally pulls down PPOUT[0] and internally pulls up PPOUT[1]. The L2 supports parity if PPOUT[0] is connected to the high order LBX and PPOUT[1] is connected to the low order LBX. The L2 is defined to not support parity if these connections are reversed, and for this case, the LBX will calculate parity. For normal operations either connection allows proper parity to be driven to the PCMC.

2.5 Reset and Clock Signals

Signal	Type	Description
HCLK	in	**HOST CLOCK:** HCLK is input to the LBX to synchronize command and data from the host and memory interfaces. This input is derived from a buffered copy of the PCMC HCLKx output.
PCLK	in	**PCI CLOCK:** All timing on the LBX PCI interface is referenced to the PCLK input. All output signals on the PCI interface are driven from PCLK rising edges and all input signals on the PCI interface are sampled on PCLK rising edges. This input is derived from a buffered copy of the PCMC PCLK output.
RESET	in	**RESET:** Assertion of this signal resets the LBX component. After reset has been negated the LBX configures itself by sampling the EOL and PPOUT pins.
LP1	out	**LOOP 1:** Phase Lock Loop Filter pin. The filter components required for the LBX are connected to these pins.
LP2	in	**LOOP 2:** Phase Lock Loop Filter pin. The filter components required for the LBX are connected to these pins.
TEST	in	**TEST:** The TEST pin must be tied low for normal system operation.
TSCON	in	**TRI-STATE CONTROL:** This signal enables the output buffers on the LBX. This pin must be held high for normal operation. If TSCON is negated, all LBX outputs will tri-state.

3.0 FUNCTIONAL DESCRIPTION

3.1 LBX Post and Prefetch Buffers

This section describes the five write posting and read prefetching buffers implemented in the LBX. The discussion in this section refers to the operation of both LBXs in the system.

3.1.1 CPU-TO-MEMORY POSTED WRITE BUFFER

The write buffer is a queue 4 Qwords deep, it loads Qwords from the CPU and stores Qwords to memory. It is 4 Qwords deep to accommodate write-backs from the first or second level caches. It is organized as a simple FIFO. Commands driven on the HIG[4:0] lines store Qwords into the buffer, while commands on the MIG[2:0] lines retire Qwords from the buffer. While retiring Qwords to memory, the DRAM controller unit of the PCMC will assert the appropriate MA, CAS[7:0]#, and WE# signals. The PCMC keeps track of full/empty states, status of the data and address.

Byte parity for data to be written to memory is either propagated from the host bus or generated by the LBX. The LBX generates parity for data from the second level cache when the second level cache does not implement parity.

3.1.2 PCI-TO-MEMORY POSTED WRITE BUFFER

The buffer is organized as 2 buffers (4 Dwords each). There is an address storage register for each buffer. When an address is stored one of the two buffers is allocated and subsequent Dwords of data are stored beginning at the first location in that buffer. Buffers are retired to memory strictly in order, Qword at a time.

Commands driven on the PIG[3:0] lines post addresses and data into the buffer. Commands driven on HIG[4:0] result in addresses being driven on the Host address bus. Commands driven on MIG[2:0] result in data being retired to DRAM.

For cases where the address targeted by the first Dword is odd, i.e., A[2] = 1, and the data is stored in an even location in the buffer, the LBX correctly aligns the Dword when retiring the data to DRAM. In other words the buffer is capable of retiring a Qword to memory where the data in the buffer is shifted by 1 Dword (Dword is position 0 shifted to 1, 1 shifted to 2 etc.). The DRAM controller of the PCMC asserts the correct CAS[7:0]# signals depending on the PCI C/BE[3:0]# signals stored in the PCMC for that Dword.

The End Of Line (EOL) signal is used to prevent PCI master writes from bursting past the cache line boundary. The device that provides "warning" to the PCMC is the low order LBX. This device contains the PCI master write low order address bits necessary to determine how many Dwords are left to the end of the line. Consequently, the LBX protocol uses the EOL signal from the low order LBX to provide this "end-of-line" warning to the PCMC, so that it may retry a PCI master write when it bursts past the cache line boundary. This protocol is described fully in Section 3.3.6.

The LBX calculates Dword parity on PCI write data, sending the proper value to the PCMC on PPOUT. The LBX generates byte parity on the MP signals for writing into DRAM.

1

3.1.3 PCI-TO-MEMORY READ PREFETCH BUFFER

This buffer is organized as a line buffer (4 Qwords) for burst transfers to PCI. The data is transferred into the buffer a Qword at a time and read out a Dword at a time. The LBX then effectively decouples the memory read rate from the PCI rate to increase concurrence.

Each new transaction begins by storing the first Dword in the first location in the buffer. The starting Dword for reading data out of the buffer onto PCI must be specified within a Qword boundary; that is the first requested Dword on PCI could be an even or odd Dword. If the snoop for a PCI master read results in a write-back from the first or second level cache this write-back is sent directly to PCI and Memory. The following two paragraphs describe this process for cache line write-backs.

Since the write-back data from the primary cache is in linear order, writing into the buffer is straightforward. Only those Qwords to be transferred onto PCI are latched into the PCI-to-Memory read buffer. For example, if the address targeted by PCI is in the 3rd or 4th Qword in the line, the first 2 Qwords of write-back data are discarded and not written into the read buffer. The primary cache write-back is always written completely to the CPU-to-Memory posted write buffer.

If the PCI master read data is read from the second level cache, it is not written back to memory. Write-backs from the second level cache when using burst SRAMs are in Pentium processor burst order, the order depending on which Qword of the line is targeted by the PCI read. The buffer is directly ad-

dressed when latching second level cache write-back data to accommodate this burst order. For example, if the requested Qword is Qword 1, then the burst order is 1-0-3-2. Qword 1 is latched in buffer location 0, Qword 0 is discarded, Qword 3 is latched into buffer location 2 and Qword 2 is latched into buffer location 1.

Commands driven on MIG[2:0] and HIG[4:0] enter data into the buffer from the DRAM interface and the Host interface (i.e., the caches), respectively. Commands driven on the PIG[3:0] lines drive data from the buffer onto the PCI AD[31:0] lines.

Parity driven on the PPOUT signal is calculated from the byte parity received on the Host bus or the memory bus, whichever is the source. If the second level cache is the source of the data and it does not implement parity, the parity driven on PPOUT is generated by the LBX from the second level cache data.

3.1.4 CPU-TO-PCI POSTED WRITE BUFFER

The CPU-to-PCI posted write buffer is 4 Dwords deep. The buffer is constructed as a simple FIFO, with some performance enhancements. An address is stored in the LBX with each Dword of data. The structure of the buffer accommodates the packetization of writes to be burst on PCI. This is accomplished by effectively discarding addresses of data Dwords driven within a burst. Thus, while an address is stored for each Dword, an address is not necessarily driven on PCI for each Dword. The PCMC determines when a burst write may be performed based on consecutive addresses. The buffer also enables consecutive bytes to be merged within a single Dword, accommodating byte, word, and misaligned Dword string store and string move operations. Qword writes on the Host bus are stored within the buffer as two individual Dword writes, with separate addresses.

The storing of an address with each Dword of data allows burst writes to be retried easily. In order to retry transactions, the FIFO is effectively "backed up" by one Dword. This is accomplished by making the FIFO physically one entry larger than it is logically. Thus, the buffer is physically 5 entries deep (an entry consists of an address and a Dword of data), while logically it is considered full when 4 entries have been posted. This design allows the FIFO to be backed up one entry when it is logically full.

Commands driven on HIG[4:0] post addresses and data into the buffer, and commands driven on PIG[3:0] retire addresses and data from the buffer and drive them onto the PCI AD[31:0] lines. As discussed previously, when bursting, not all addresses are driven onto PCI.

Data parity driven on the PPOUT signal is calculated from the byte parity received on the Host bus. Address parity driven on PPOUT is calculated from the address received on the Host bus.

3.1.5 CPU-TO-PCI READ PREFETCH BUFFER

This prefetch buffer is organized as a single buffer 4 Dwords deep. The buffer is organized as a simple FIFO. Reads from the buffer are sequential; the buffer does not support random access of its contents. To support reads of less than a Dword the FIFO read pointer can function with or without a pre-increment. The pointer can also be reset to the first entry before a Dword is driven. When a Dword is read, it is driven onto both halves of the Host data bus.

Commands driven on the HIG[4:0] lines enable read addresses to be sent onto PCI, the addresses are driven using PIG[3:0] commands. Read data is latched into the LBX by commands driven on the PIG[3:0] lines and the data is driven onto the host data bus using commands driven on the HIG[4:0] lines.

The LBX calculates Dword parity on PCI read data, sending the proper value to the PCMC on PPOUT. The LBX does not generate byte parity on the Host data bus when the CPU reads PCI.

3.2 LBX Interface Command Descriptions

This section describes the functionality of the HIG, MIG and PIG commands driven by the PCMC to the LBXs.

3.2.1 HOST INTERFACE GROUP: HIG[4:0]

The Host Interface commands are shown in Table 3-1. These commands are issued by the Host interface of the PCMC to the LBXs in order to perform the following functions:

- Reads from CPU-to-PCI read prefetch buffer when the CPU reads from PCI.
- Stores write-back data to PCI-to-Memory read prefetch buffer when PCI read address results in a hit to a modified line in the first or second level caches.
- Posts data to CPU-to-Memory write buffer in the case of a CPU to memory write.
- Posts data to CPU-to-PCI write buffer in the case of a CPU to PCI write.
- Drives Host address to data lines and data to address lines for programming the PCMC configuration registers.

Table 3-1. HIG Command

Command	Code	Description
NOPC	00000b	No Operation on CPU Bus
CMR	11100b	CPU Memory Read
CPRF	00100b	CPU Read First Dword from CPU-to-PCI Read Prefetch Buffer
CPRA	00101b	CPU Read Next Dword from CPU-to-PCI Read Prefetch Buffer, Toggle A
CPRB	00110b	CPU Read Next Dword from CPU-to-PCI Read Prefetch Buffer, Toggle B
CPRQ	00111b	CPU Read Qword from CPU-to- PCI Read Prefetch Buffer
SWB0	01000b	Store Write-back Data Qword 0 to PCI-to-Memory Read Buffer
SWB1	01001b	Store Write-back Data Qword 1 to PCI-to-Memory Read Buffer
SWB2	01010b	Store Write-back Data Qword 2 to PCI-to-Memory Read Buffer
SWB3	01011b	Store Write-back Data Qword 3 to PCI-to-Memory Read Buffer
PCMWQ	01100b	Post to CPU-to-Memory Write Buffer Qword
PCMWFQ	01101b	Post to CPU-to-Memory Write and PCI-to-Memory Read Buffer First Qword
PCMWNQ	01110b	Post to CPU-to-Memory Write and PCI-to-Memory Read Buffer Next Qword
PCPWL	10000b	Post to CPU-to-PCI Write Low Dword
MCP3L	10011b	Merge to CPU-to-PCI Write Low Dword 3 Bytes
MCP2L	10010b	Merge to CPU-to-PCI Write Low Dword 2 Bytes
MCP1L	10001b	Merge to CPU-to-PCI Write Low Dword 1 Byte
PCPWH	10100b	Post to CPU-to-PCI Write High Dword
MCP3H	10111b	Merge to CPU-to-PCI Write High Dword 3 Bytes
MCP2H	10110b	Merge to CPU-to-PCI Write High Dword 2 Bytes
MCP1H	10101b	Merge to CPU-to-PCI Write High Dword 1 Byte
LCPRAD	00001b	Latch CPU to PCI Read Address
DPRA	11000b	Drive Address from PCI A/D Latch to CPU Address Bus
DPWA	11001b	Drive Address from PCI-to-Memory Write Buffer to CPU Address Bus
ADCPY	11101b	Address to Data Copy in the LBX
DACPYH	11011b	Data to Address Copy in the LBX High Dword
DACPYL	11010b	Data to Address Copy in the LBX Low Dword
PSCD	01111b	Post Special Cycle Data
DRVFF	11110b	Drive FF..FF (All 1's) onto the Host Data Bus

NOTE:
All other patterns are reserved.

NOPC: No Operation is performed on the Host bus by the LBX hence it tri-states its Host bus drivers.

CMR: This command effectively drives DRAM data onto the Host data bus. The LBX acts as a transparent latch in this mode, depending on MDLE for latch control. With the MDLE signal high the CMR command will cause the LBXs to buffer memory data onto the Host bus. When MDLE is low, the LBX will drive onto the Host bus whatever memory data that was latched when MDLE was negated.

CPRF: This command reads the first Dword of the CPU-to-PCI read prefetch buffer. The read pointer of the FIFO is set to point to the first Dword. The Dword is driven onto the upper and lower halves of the Host data bus.

CPRA: This command increments the read pointer of the CPU-to-PCI read prefetch buffer FIFO and drives that Dword onto the Host bus when it is driven after a CPRF or CPRB command. If driven after another CPRA command, the LBX drives the current Dword while the read pointer of the FIFO is not incremented. The Dword is driven onto the upper and lower halves of the Host data bus.

CPRB: This command increments the read pointer of the CPU-to-PCI read prefetch buffer FIFO and drives that Dword onto the Host bus when it is driven after a CPRA command. If driven after another CPRB command, the LBX drives the current Dword while the read pointer of the FIFO is not incremented. The Dword is driven onto the upper and lower halves of the Host data bus.

CPRQ: This command drives the first Dword stored in the CPU-to-PCI read prefetch buffer onto the lower half of the Host data bus, and drives the second Dword onto the upper half of the Host data bus, regardless of the state of the read pointer. The read pointer is not affected by this command.

SWB0: This command stores a Qword from the host data lines into location 0 of the PCI-to-Memory read buffer. Parity is either generated for the data or propagated from the Host bus based on the state of the PPOUT signals sampled at the negation of RESET when the LBXs were initialized.

SWB1: This command (similar to SWB0) stores a Qword from the host data lines into location 1 of the PCI-to-Memory read buffer. Parity is either generated for the data or propagated from the Host Bus based on the state of the PPOUT signal sampled at the falling edge of RESET.

SWB2: This command, (similar to SWB0), stores a Qword from the host data lines into location 2 of the PCI-to-Memory read buffer. Parity is either generated for the data or propagated from the Host Bus based on the state of the PPOUT signal sampled at the falling edge of RESET.

SWB3: This command stores a Qword from the host data lines into location 3 of the PCI-to-Memory read buffer. Parity is either generated for the data or propagated from the Host Bus based on the state of the PPOUT signal sampled at the falling edge of RESET.

PCMWQ: This command posts one Qword of data from the host data lines to the CPU-to-Memory write buffer.

PCMWFQ: If the PCI Memory read address leads to a hit on a modified line in the first level cache, a write-back is scheduled and this data has to be written into the CPU-to-Memory write buffer and PCI-to-Memory read buffer at the same time. The write-back of the first Qword is done by this command to both the buffers.

PCMWNQ: This command follows the previous command to store or post subsequent write-back Qwords.

PCPWL: This command posts the low Dword of a CPU to PCI write. The CPU-to-PCI write buffer stores a Dword of PCI address for every Dword of data, hence this command also stores the address of the low Dword in the address location for the data. Address bit [2] is not stored directly; this command assumes a value of 0 for A[2] and this is what is stored.

MCP3L: This command merges the 3 most significant bytes of the low Dword of the Host data bus into the last Dword posted to the CPU-to-PCI write buffer. The address is not modified.

MCP2L: This command merges the 2 most significant bytes of the low Dword of the Host data bus into the last Dword posted to the CPU-to-PCI write buffer. The address is not modified.

MCP1L: This command merges the most significant byte of the low Dword of the Host data bus into the last Dword posted to the CPU-to-PCI write buffer. The address is not modified.

PCPWH: This command Posts the high Dword of a CPU to PCI write, with its address, into the address location. Hence, to do a Qword write PCPWL has to be followed by a PCPWH. Address bit [2] is not stored directly; this command forces a value of 1 for A[2] and this is what is stored.

MCP3H: This command merges the 3 most significant bytes of the high Dword of the Host data bus into the last Dword posted to the CPU-to-PCI write buffer. The address is not modified.

MCP2H: This command merges the 2 most significant bytes of the high Dword of the Host data bus into the last Dword posted to the CPU-to-PCI write buffer. The address is not modified.

MCP1H: This command merges the most significant byte of the high Dword of the Host data bus into the last Dword posted to the CPU-to-PCI write buffer. The address is not modified.

LCPRAD: This command latches the Host address to drive on PCI for a CPU to PCI read. It is necessary to latch the address in order to drive inquire addresses on the Host address bus before the CPU address is driven onto PCI.

DPRA: The PCI Memory read address is latched in the PCI A/D latch by a PIG command LCPRAD, this address is driven onto the Host address bus by DPRA. Used in PCI to memory read transaction.

DPWA: The DPWA command drives the address of the current PCI master write buffer onto the Host address bus. This command is potentially driven for multiple cycles. When it is no longer driven, the read pointer will increment to point to the next buffer, and a subsequent DPWA command will read the address from that buffer.

ADCPY: This command drives the Host data bus with the Host address. The address is copied on the high and low halves of the Qword data bus; i.e., A[31:0] is copied onto D[31:0] and D[63:32]. This command is used when the CPU reads from the PCMC configuration registers.

DACPYH: This command drives the Host address bus with the high Dword of Host data. This command is used when the CPU writes to the PCMC configuration registers.

DACPYL: This command drives the Host address bus with the low Dword of host data. This command is used when the CPU writes to the PCMC configuration registers.

PSCD: This command is used to post the value of the Special Cycle code into the CPU-to-PCI posted write buffer. The value is driven onto the A[31:0] lines by the PCMC, after acquiring the address bus by asserting AHOLD. The value on the A[31:0] lines is posted into the DATA location in the CPU-to-PCI posted write buffer.

DRVFF: This command causes the LBX to drive FFFFFFFFh onto the Host data bus. It is used for CPU reads from PCI that terminate with master abort.

3.2.2 MEMORY INTERFACE GROUP: MIG[2:0]

The Memory Interface commands are shown in Table 3-2. These commands are issued by the DRAM controller of the PCMC to perform the following functions:

- Retires data from CPU-to-Memory write buffer to DRAM.
- Stores data into PCI-to-Memory read buffer when the PCI read address is targeted to DRAM.
- Retires PCI-to-Memory write buffer to DRAM.

1

Table 3-2. MIG Commands

Command	Code	Description
NOPM	000b	No Operation on Memory Bus
PMRFQ	001b	Place into PCI-to-Memory Read Buffer First Qword
PMRNQ	010b	Place into PCI-to-Memory Read Buffer Next Qword
RCMWQ	100b	Retire CPU-to-Memory Write Buffer Qword
RPMWQ	101b	Retire PCI-to-Memory Write Buffer Qword
RPMWQS	110b	Retire PCI-to-Memory Write Buffer Qword Shifted
MEMDRV	111b	Drive Latched Data onto Memory Bus for 1 Clock Cycle

NOTE:
All other patterns are reserved.

NOPM: No Operation on the Memory bus. The LBX tri-states its drivers driving the memory bus.

PMRFQ: The PCI to Memory read address targets memory if there is a miss on L1 and L2 caches, this command stores the first Qword of data starting at the first location in the buffer. This buffer is 8 Dwords or 1 cache line deep.

PMRNQ: This command stores subsequent Qwords from memory starting at the next available location in the PCI-to-Memory read buffer. It is always used after PMRFQ.

RCMWQ: This command retires one Qword from the CPU-to-Memory write buffer to DRAM. The address is stored in the address queue for this buffer in the PCMC.

RPMWQ: This command retires one Qword of data from one line of the PCI-to-Memory write buffer to DRAM. When all the valid data in one buffer is retired, the next RPMWQ (or RPMWQS) will read data from the next buffer.

RPMWQS: This command retires one Qword of data from one line of PCI-to-Memory write buffer to DRAM. For this command the data in the buffer is shifted by one Dword (Dword in position 0 is shifted to 1, 1 to 2 etc.). This is because the address targeted by the first Dword of the write could be an odd Dword (i.e., address bit [2] is a 1). To retire a misaligned line this command has to be used for all the data in the buffer. When all the valid data in one buffer is retired, the next RPMWQ (or RPMWQS) will read data from the next buffer.

MEMDRV: For a memory write operation the data on the memory bus is required for more than one clock cycle hence all DRAM retires are latched and driven to the memory bus in subsequent cycles by this command.

3.2.3 PCI INTERFACE GROUP: PIG[3:0]

The PCI Interface commands are shown in Table 3-3. These commands are issued by the PCI Master/Slave interface of the PCMC to perform the following functions:

- Slave Posts address and data to PCI-to-Memory Write Buffer.
- Slave Sends PCI-to-Memory read data on the AD bus.
- Slave Latches PCI Master Memory address so that it can be gated to the host address bus.
- Master Latches CPU-to-PCI read data from the AD bus.
- Master Retires CPU-to-PCI write buffer.
- Master sends CPU-to-PCI address to the AD bus.

The PCI AD[31:0] lines are driven by asserting the signal DRVPCI. This signal is used for both master and slave transactions.

Parity is calculated on either the value being driven onto PCI or the value being received on PCI, depending on the command. In Table 3-3, the PAR column has been included to indicate the value that the PPOUT signals are based on. An "I" indicates that the PPOUT signals reflect the parity of the AD lines as inputs to the LBX. An "O" indicates that the PPOUT signals reflect the value being driven on the PCI AD lines. See Section 3.3.4 for the timing relationship between the PIG[3:0] command, the AD[31:0] lines, and the PPOUT signals.

Table 3-3. PIG Commands

Command	Code	PAR	Description
PPMWA	1000b	I	Post to PCI-to-Memory Write Buffer Address
PPMWD	1001b	I	Post to PCI-to-Memory Write Buffer Data
SPMRH	1101b	O	Send PCI Master Read Data High Dword
SPMRL	1100b	O	Send PCI Master Read Data Low Dword
SPMRN	1110b	O	Send PCI Master Read Data Next Dword
LCPRF	0000b	I	Latch CPU Read from PCI into Read Prefetch Buffer First Dword
LCPRA	0001b	I	Latch CPU Read from PCI into Prefetch Buffer Next Dword, A Toggle
LCPRB	0010b	I	Latch CPU Read from PCI into Prefetch Buffer Next Dword, B Toggle
DCPWA	0100b	O	Drive CPU-to-PCI Write Buffer Address
DCPWD	0101b	O	Drive CPU-to-PCI Write Buffer Data
DCPWL	0110b	O	Drive CPU-to-PCI Write Buffer Last Data
DCCPD	1011b	O	Discard Current CPU-to-PCI Write Buffer Data
BCPWR	1010b	O	Backup CPU-to-PCI Write Buffer for Retry
SCPA	0111b	O	Send CPU to PCI Address
LPMA	0011b	I	Latch PCI Master Address

NOTE:
All other patterns are reserved.

PPMWA: This command selects a new buffer and places the PCI Master address latch value into the address register for that buffer. The next PPMWD command posts write data in the first location of this newly selected buffer. This command also causes the EOL logic to decrement the count of Dwords remaining in the line.

PPMWD: This command stores the value in the AD latch into the next data location in the currently selected buffer. This command also causes the EOL logic to decrement the count of Dwords remaining in the line.

SPMRH: This command sends the high order Dword from the first Qword of the PCI-to-Memory read buffer onto PCI. This command also causes the EOL logic to decrement the count of Dwords remaining in the line.

SPMRL: This command sends the low order Dword from the first Qword of the PCI-to-Memory read buffer onto PCI. This command also selects the Dword alignment for the transaction and causes the EOL logic to decrement the count of Dwords remaining in the line.

SPMRN: This command sends the next Dword from the PCI-to-Memory read buffer onto PCI. This command also causes the EOL logic to decrement the count of Dwords remaining in the line. This command is used for the second and all subsequent Dwords of the current transaction.

LCPRF: This command acquires the value of the AD[31:0] lines into the first location in the CPU-to-PCI read prefetch buffer until a different command is driven.

LCPRA: When driven after a LCPRF or LCPRB command, this command latches the value of the AD[31:0] lines into the next location into the CPU-to-PCI read prefetch buffer. When driven after another LCPRA command, this command latches the value on AD[31:0] into the same location in the CPU-to-PCI read prefetch buffer, overwriting the previous value.

LCPRB: When driven after a LCPRA command, this command latches the value of the AD[31:0] lines into the next location into the CPU-to-PCI read prefetch buffer. When driven after another LCPRB command, this command latches the value on AD[31:0] into the same location in the CPU-to-PCI read prefetch buffer, overwriting the previous value.

DCPWA: This command drives the next address in the CPU-to-PCI write buffer onto PCI. The read pointer of the FIFO is not incremented.

DCPWD: This command drives the next data Dword in the CPU-to-PCI write buffer onto PCI. The read pointer of the FIFO is incremented on the next PCLK if TRDY# is asserted.

DCPWL: This command drives the previous data Dword in the CPU-to-PCI write buffer onto PCI. This is the data which was driven by the last DCPWD command. The read pointer of the FIFO is not incremented.

DCCPD: This command discards the current Dword in the CPU-to-PCI write buffer. This is used to clear write data when the write transaction terminates with Master Abort, where TRDY# is never asserted.

BCPWR: For this command the CPU-to-PCI write buffer is "backed up" one entry such that the address/data pair last driven with the DCPWA and DCPWD commands will be driven again on the AD[31:0] lines when the commands are driven again. This command is used when the target has retried the write cycle.

SCPA: This command drives the value on the Host address bus onto PCI.

LPMA: This command stores the previous AD[31:0] value into the PCI master address latch. If the EOL logic determines that the requested Dword is the last Dword of a line, then the EOL signal will be asserted; otherwise the EOL signal will be negated.

3.3 LBX Timing Diagrams

This section describes the timing relationship between the LBX control signals and the interface buses.

3.3.1 HIG[4:0] COMMAND TIMING

The commands driven on HIG[4:0] can cause the Host address bus and/or the Host data bus to be driven and latched. The following timing diagram illustrates the timing relationship between the driven command and the buses. The "Host bus" in the diagram could be address and/or data.

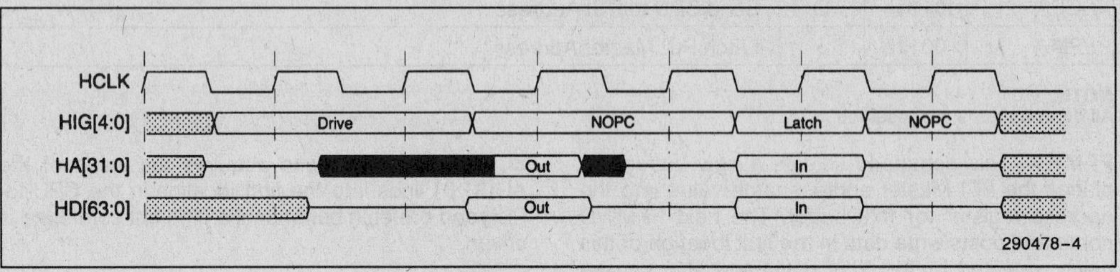

Figure 3-1. HIG[4:0] Command Timing

Note that the Drive command takes two cycles to drive the Host data bus, but only one to drive the address. When the NOPC command is sampled, the LBX takes only one cycle to release the Host bus.

The Drive commands in Figure 3-1 are any of the following:

CMR	**CPRF**	**CPRA**	**CPRB**
CPRQ	**DPRA**	**DPWA**	**ADCPY**
DACPYH	**DACPYL**	**DRVFF**	

The Latch command in Figure 3-1 is any of the following:

SWB0	**SWB1**	**SWB2**	**SWB3**
PCMWQ	**PCMWFQ**	**PCMWNQ**	**PCPWL**
MCP3L	**MCP2L**	**MCP1L**	**PCPWH**
MCP3H	**MCP2H**	**LCPRAD**	**PSCD**

3.3.2 HIG[4:0] MEMORY READ TIMING

Figure 3-2 illustrates the timing relationship between the HIG[4:0], MIG[2:0], CAS[7:0]#, and MDLE signals for DRAM memory reads. The delays shown in Figure 3-2 do not represent the actual A.C. timings, but are intended only to show how the delay affects the sequencing of the signals.

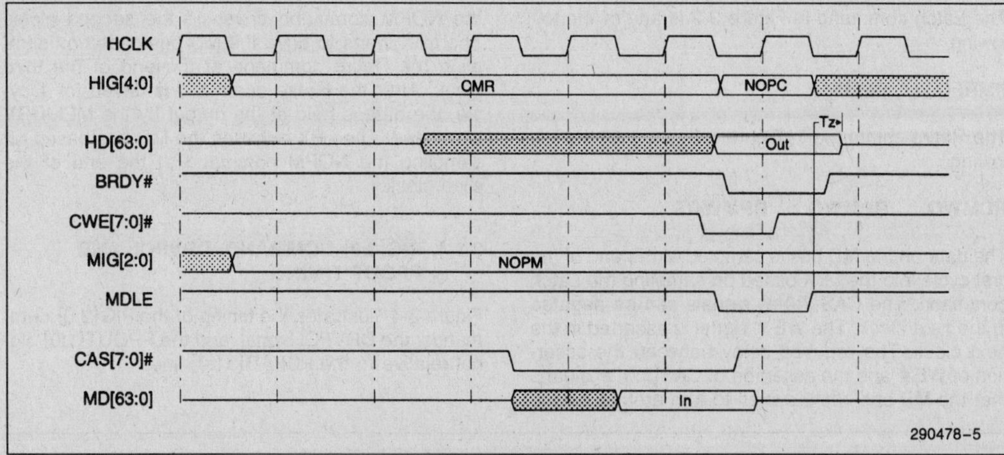

Figure 3-2. CPU Read from Memory

When the CPU is reading from DRAM, the HIG[4:0] lines are driven with the CMR command which causes the LBX to drive memory data onto the HD bus. Until the MD bus is valid, the HD bus will be driven with invalid data. When CAS[7:0]# assert, the MD bus becomes valid after the DRAM CAS[7:0]# access time. The MD and MP lines are directed through a synchronous register inside the LBX to the HD and HP lines. MDLE acts as a clock enable for this register. When MDLE is asserted, the LBX samples the MD and MP lines. When MDLE is negated, the MD and HD register retains its current value.

The LBX releases the HD bus based on sampling the NOPC command on the HIG[4:0] lines and MDLE being asserted. By delaying the release of the HD bus until MDLE is asserted, the LBX provides hold time for the data with respect to the write enable strobes (CWE[7:0]#) of the second level cache.

3.3.3 MIG[2:0] COMMAND

Figure 3-3 illustrates the timing of the MIG[2:0] commands with respect to the MD bus, CAS[7:0]#, and WE#. Figure 3-3 shows the MD bus transitioning from a read to a write cycle.

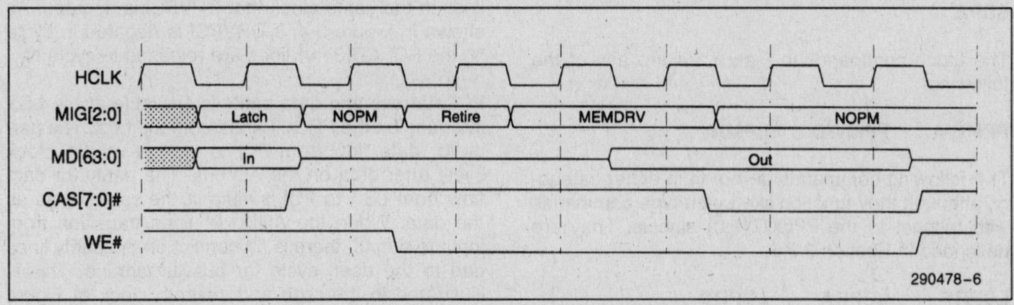

Figure 3-3. MIG[2:0] Command Timing

The Latch command in Figure 3-3 is any of the following:

PMRFQ PMRNQ

The Retire command in Figure 3-3 is any of the following:

RCMWQ RPMWQ RPMWQS

The data on the MD bus is sampled at the end of the first cycle into the LBX based on sampling the Latch command. The CAS[7:0]# signals can be negated in the next clock. The WE# signal is asserted in the next clock. The required delay between the assertion of WE# and the assertion of CAS[7:0]# means that the MD bus has 2 cycles to turn around; hence the NOPM command driven in the second clock. The LBX starts to drive the MD bus based on sampling the Retire command at the end of the third clock. After the Retire command is driven for 1 cycle, the data is held at the output by the MEMDRV command. The LBX releases the MD bus based on sampling the NOPM command at the end of the sixth clock.

3.3.4 PIG[3:0] COMMAND, DRVPCI, AND PPOUT TIMING

Figure 3-4 illustrates the timing of the PIG[3:0] commands, the DRVPCI signal, and the PPOUT[1:0] signal relative to the PCI AD[31:0] lines.

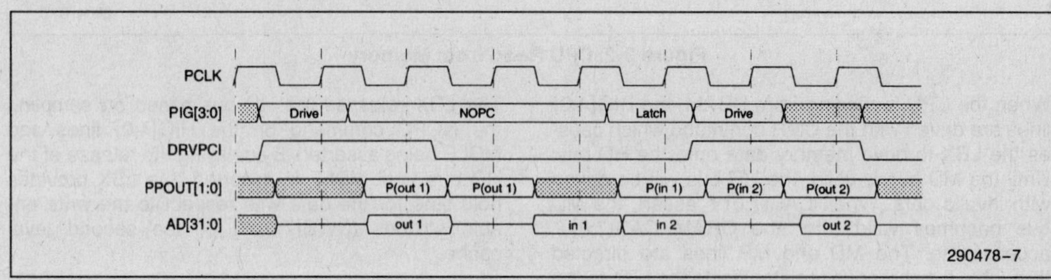

Figure 3-4. PIG[3:0] Command Timing

The Drive commands in Figure 3-4 are any of the following:

SPMRH SPMRL SPMRN
DCPWA DCPWD DCPWL
SCPA

The Latch commands in Figure 3-4 are any of the following:

PPMWA PPMWD LPMA

The following commands do not fit in either category, although they function like Latch type commands with respect to the PPOUT[1:0] signals. They are described in Section 3.3.5.

LCPRF LCPRA LCPRB

The DRVPCI signal is driven synchronous to the PCI bus, enabling the LBXs to initiate driving the PCI AD[31:0] lines one clock after DRVPCI is asserted.

As shown in Figure 3-4, if DRVPCI is asserted in cycle N, the PCI AD[31:0] lines are driven in cycle N+1. The negation of the DRVPCI signal causes the LBXs to asynchronously release the PCI bus, enabling the LBXs to cease driving the PCI AD[31:0] lines in the same clock that DRVPCI is negated. As shown in Figure 3-4, if DRVPCI is negated in cycle N, the PCI AD[31:0] lines are released in cycle N.

PCI address and data parity is available at the LBX interface on the PPOUT lines from the LBX. The parity for data flow from PCI to LBX is valid 1 clock cycle after data on the AD bus. The parity for data flow from LBX to PCI is valid in the same cycle as the data. When the AD[31:0] lines transition from input to output, there is no conflict on the parity lines due to the dead cycle for bus turnaround. This is illustrated in the sixth and seventh clock of Figure 3-4.

3.3.5 PIG[3:0]: READ PREFETCH BUFFER COMMAND TIMING

The structure of the CPU-to-PCI read prefetch buffer required special considerations due to the partition of the PCMC and LBX. The PCMC interfaces only to the PCI control signals, while the LBXs interface only to the data. Therefore, it is not possible to latch a Dword of data into the prefetch buffer after it is qualified by TRDY#: instead, the data is repetitively latched into the same location until TRDY# is sampled asserted. Only after TRDY# is sampled asserted is data valid in the buffer. A toggling mechanism is implemented to advance the write pointer to the next Dword after the current Dword has been qualified by TRDY#.

Other considerations of the partition are taken into account on the Host side as well. When reading from the buffer, the command to drive the data onto the Host bus is sent before it is known that the entry is valid. This method avoids the wait state that would be introduced by waiting for an entry's TRDY# to be asserted before sending the command to drive the entry onto the Host bus. The FIFO structure of the buffer also necessitates a toggling scheme to advance to the next buffer entry after the current entry has been successfully driven. Also, this method gives the LBX the ability to drive the same Dword twice, enabling reads of less than a Dword to be serviced by the buffer; reads of individual bytes of a Dword would read the same Dword 4 times.

The HIG[4:0] and PIG[3:0] lines are defined to enable the features described previously. The LCPRF PIG[3:0] command latches the first PCI read Dword into the first location in the CPU-to-PCI read prefetch buffer. This command is driven until TRDY# is sampled asserted. The valid Dword would then be in the first location of the buffer. The cycle after TRDY# is sampled asserted, the PCMC drives the LCPRA command on the PIG[3:0] lines. This action latches the value on the PCI AD[31:0] lines into the *next* Dword location in the buffer. Again, the LCPRA command is driven until TRDY# is sampled asserted. Each cycle the LCPRA command is driven, data is latched into the same location in the buffer. When TRDY# is sampled asserted, the PCMC drives the LCPRB command on the PIG[3:0] lines. This latches the value on the AD[31:0] lines into the next location in the buffer, the one *after* the location that the previous LCPRA command latched data into. After TRDY# has been sampled asserted again, the command switches back to LCPRA. In this way, the same location in the buffer can be filled repeatedly until valid, and when it is known that the location is valid, the next location can be filled.

The commands for the HIG[4:0], CPRF, CPRA, and CPRB, work exactly the same way. If the same command is driven, the same data is driven. Driving an appropriately different command results in the next data being driven. Figure 3-5 illustrates the usage of these commands.

1

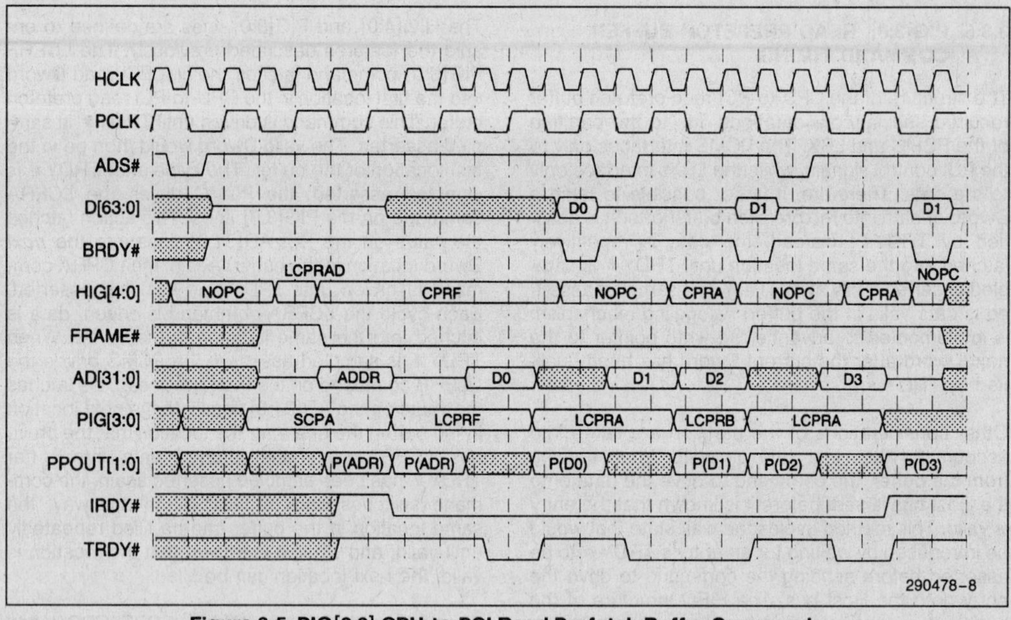

Figure 3-5. PIG[3:0] CPU-to-PCI Read Prefetch Buffer Commands

Figure 3-5 shows an example of how the PIG commands function on the PCI side of the LBX. The LCPRF command is driven on the PIG[3:0] lines until TRDY# is sampled asserted at the end of the fifth PCI clock. The LCPRA command is then driven until TRDY# is again sampled asserted at the end of the seventh PCI clock. TRDY# is sampled asserted again at the end of the eighth PCI clock so LCPRB is driven only once. Finally, LCPRA is driven again until the last TRDY# is asserted, at the end of the tenth PCI clock. In this way, 4 Dwords are latched in the CPU-to-PCI read prefetch buffer.

Figure 3-5 also shows an example of how the HIG commands function on the Host side of the LBX. Two clocks after sampling the CPRF command, the LBX drives the host data bus. The data takes two cycles to become stable. The first data driven in this case is invalid, since the data has not arrived on PCI. The data driven on the Host bus changes in the seventh Host clock, since the LCPRF command has been driven on the HIG[3:0] lines the previous cycle, latching a new value into the first location of the read prefetch buffer. At this point the data is not the correct value, since TRDY# has not yet been asserted on PCI. The LCPRF command is driven again in the fifth PCI clock while TRDY# is sampled asserted at the end of this clock. The requested data for the read is then latched into the first location of the read prefetch buffer and driven onto the Host data bus, becoming valid at the end of the twelfth CPU clock. The BRDY# signal can therefore be driven asserted in this clock. The following read transaction (issued in CPU clock 15) requests the next Dword, and so the CPRA command is driven on the HIG[4:0] lines, advancing to read the next location in the read prefetch buffer. As the correct data is already there, the command is driven only once for this transaction. The next read transaction requests data in the same Dword as the previous. Therefore, the CPRA command is driven again, the buffer is not advanced, and the same Dword is driven onto the Host bus.

3.3.6 PIG[3:0]: END-OF-LINE WARNING SIGNAL: EOL

When posting PCI master writes, the PCMC must be informed when the line boundary is about to be overrun, as it has no way of determining this itself (recall that the PCMC does not receive any address bits from PCI). The low order LBX determines this, as it contains the low order bits of the PCI master write address and also tracks how many Dwords of write data have been posted. Therefore, the low order LBX component sends the "end-of-line" warning to the PCMC. This is accomplished with the EOL signal driven from the low order LBX to the PCMC. Figure 3-6 illustrates the timing of this signal:

1. The FRAME# signal is sampled asserted in the first clock. The LPMA command is driven on the PIG[3:0] signals to hold the address while it is being decoded (e.g., in the MEMCS# decode circuit of the 82378IB SIO). The first data (D0) remains on the bus until TRDY# is asserted in response to MEMCS# being sampled asserted in the third clock.
2. The PPMWA command is driven in response to sampling MEMCS# asserted. TRDY# is asserted in this cycle indicating that D0 has been latched at the end of the fourth clock. The action of the PPMWA command is to transfer the PCI address captured in the PCI AD latch at the end of the first clock to the posting buffer, and open the PCI AD latch in order to capture the data. This data will be posted to the write buffer in the following cycle by the PPMWD command.
3. The EOL signal is first negated when the LPMA command is driven on the PIG[3:0] signals. However, if the first data Dword accepted is also the last that should be accepted, the EOL signal will be asserted in the third clock. This is the "end-of-line" indication. In this case, the EOL signal is asserted as soon as the LPMA command has been latched. The action by the PCMC in response is to deassert TRDY# and assert STOP# in the fifth clock. Note that the EOL signal is asserted even before the MEMCS# signal is sampled asserted in this case. The EOL signal will remain asserted until the next time the LPMA command is driven.
4. If the second Dword is the last that should be accepted, the EOL signal will be asserted in the fifth clock to deassert TRDY# and assert STOP# on the following clock. The EOL signal is asserted in response to the PPMWA command being sampled, and relies on the knowledge that TRDY# for the first Dword of data will be sampled asserted by the master in the same cycle (at the end of the fourth clock). Therefore, to prevent a third assertion of TRDY# in the sixth clock, the EOL signal must be asserted in the fifth clock.

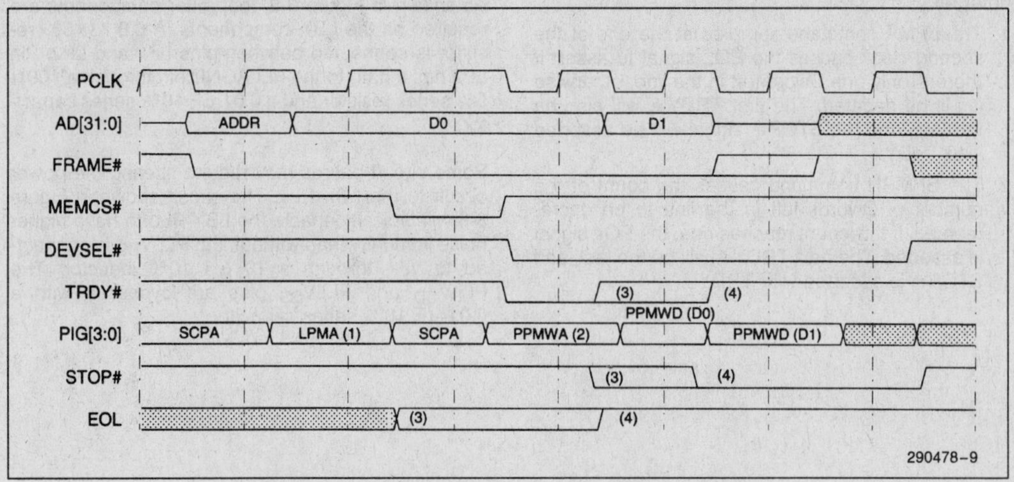

Figure 3-6. EOL Signal Timing for PCI Master Writes

A similar sequence is defined for PCI Master Reads. While it is possible to know when to stop driving read data due to the fact that the read address is latched into the PCMC before any read data is driven on PCI, the use of the EOL signal for PCI master reads simplifies the logic internal to the PCMC. The following diagram illustrates the timing of EOL with respect to the PIG[3:0] commands to drive out PCI read data:

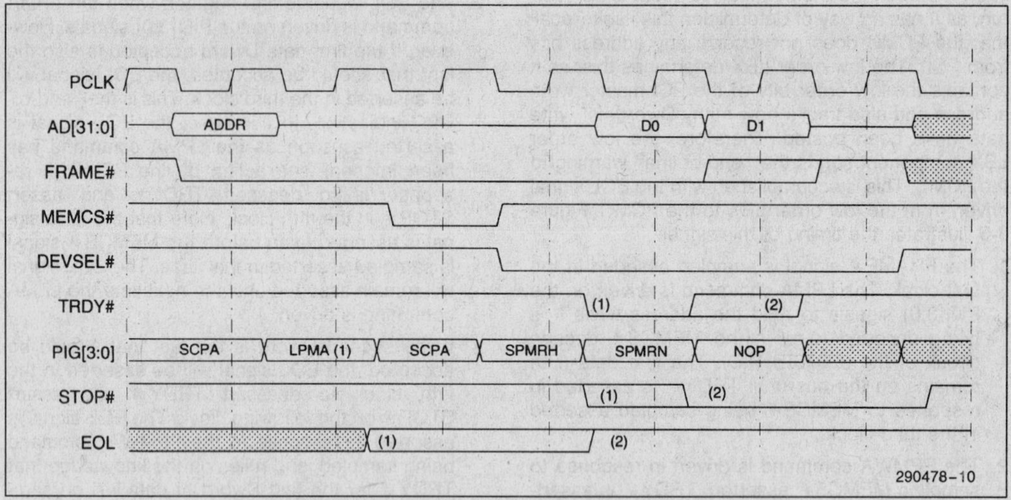

Figure 3-7. EOL Signal Timing for PCI Master Reads

Note that unlike the PCI master write sequence, the STOP# signal is asserted with the last data transfer, not after.

1. The LPMA command sampled at the end of the second clock causes the EOL signal to assert if there is only one Dword left in the line, otherwise it will be negated. The first TRDY# will also be the last, and the STOP# signal will be asserted with TRDY#.
2. The SPMRH command causes the count of the number of Dwords left in the line to be decremented. If this count reaches one, the EOL signal is asserted. The next TRDY# will be the last, and STOP# is asserted with TRDY#.

3.4 PLL Loop Filter Components

As shown in Figure 3-8, loop filter components are required on the LBX components. A 6.8 KΩ 5% resistor is connected between pins LP1 and LP2. Pin LP2 has a path to the PLLAGND pin through a 100Ω 5% series resistor and a 0.01 μF 10% series capacitor.

Some circuit boards may require filtering the power circuit to the LBX PLL. The circuit shown in Figure 3-8 will typically enable the LBX PLL to have higher noise immunity than without. Pin $PLLV_{DD}$ is connected to V_{CC} through a 10 μH 10% inductor. The $PLLV_{DD}$ and $PLLV_{SS}$ pins are bypassed with a 0.01 μF 10% series capacitor.

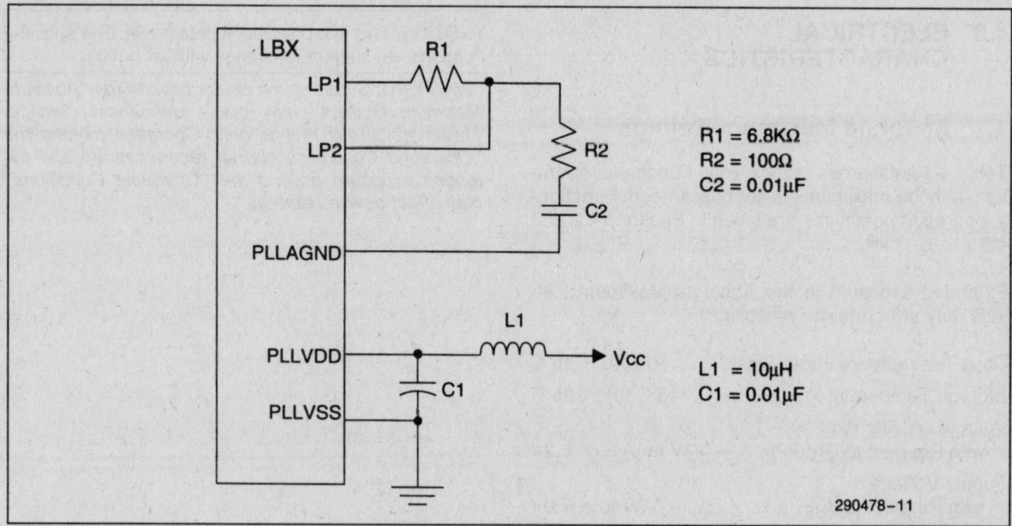

Figure 3-8. Loop Filter Circuit

3.5 PCI Clock Considerations

There is a 1.25 ns clock skew specification between the PCMC and the LBX that must be adhered to for proper operation of the PCMC/LBX timing. As shown in Figure 3-9 below, the PCMC drives PCLKOUT to an external clock driver which supplies copies of PCLK to PCI devices, the LBXs, and back to the PCMC. The skew specification is defined as the difference in timing between the signal that appears at the PCMC PCLKIN input pin and the signal that appears at the LBX PCLK input pin. For both the low order LBX and the high order LBX, the PCLK rising and falling edges must not be more than 1.25 ns apart from the rising and falling edge of the PCMC PCLKIN signal.

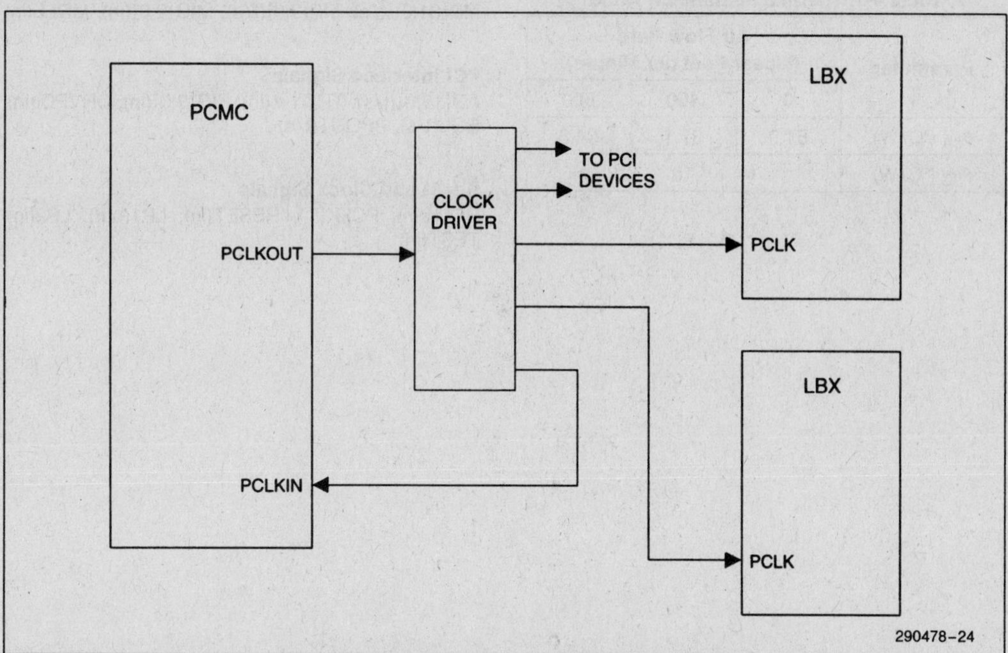

Figure 3-9. PCI Clock Circuit of PCMC and LBX

4.0 ELECTRICAL CHARACTERISTICS

4.1 Absolute Maximum Ratings

Table 4-1 lists stress ratings only. Functional operation at these maximums is not guaranteed. Functional operation conditions are given in Sections 4.2 and 4.3.

Extended exposure to the Absolute Maximum Ratings may affect device reliability.

Case Temperature under Bias .... 0°C to +85°C

Storage Temperature .... −40°C to +125°C

Voltage on Any Pin
with Respect to Ground ... −0.3V to V_{CC} + 0.3V

Supply Voltage
with Respect to V_{SS} .... −0.3V to +7.0V

Maximum Power Dissipation 1.4W

NOTICE: This is a production data sheet. The specifications are subject to change without notice.

**WARNING: Stressing the device beyond the "Absolute Maximum Ratings" may cause permanent damage. These are stress ratings only. Operation beyond the "Operating Conditions" is not recommended and extended exposure beyond the "Operating Conditions" may affect device reliability.*

4.2 Thermal Characteristics

The LBX is designed for operation at case temperatures between 0°C and +85°C. The thermal resistances of the package are given in the following tables.

Table 4-1. Thermal Resistance Table

Parameter	Air Flow Rate (Linear Feet per Minute)		
	0	400	600
θ_{JA} (°C/W)	51.9	37.1	34.8
θ_{JC} (°C/W)	10		

4.3 D.C. Characteristics

Host Interface Signals
A[15:0](t/s), D[31:0](t/s), HIG[4:0](t/s), HP[3:0](in)

Main Memory (DRAM) Interface Signals
MD[31:0](t/s), MP[3:0](t/s), MIG[2:0](in), MDLE(in)

PCI Interface Signals
AD[15:0](t/s), TRDY#(in), PIG[3:0](in), DRVPCI(in), EOL(t/s), PPOUT(t/s)

Reset and Clock Signals
HCLK(in), PCLK(in), RESET(in), LP1(out), LP2(in), TEST(in)

1

Table 4-2. LBX D.C. Characteristics

Functional Operating Range: V_{CC} = 5V ±5%; T_C = 0°C to +85°C

Symbol	Parameter	Min	Typical	Max	Units	Notes
V_{IL1}	Input Low Voltage	−0.3		0.8	V	1
V_{IH1}	Input High Voltage	2.0		V_{CC} + 0.3	V	1
V_{IL2}	Input Low Voltage	−0.3		0.3 × V_{CC}	V	2
V_{IH2}	Input High Voltage	0.7 × V_{CC}		V_{CC} + 0.3	V	2
V_{OL1}	Output Low Voltage			0.4	V	3
V_{OH1}	Output High Voltage	2.4			V	3
V_{OL2}	Output Low Voltage			0.5	V	4
V_{OH2}	Output High Voltage	V_{CC} − 0.5			V	4
I_{OL1}	Output Low Current			1	mA	5
I_{OH1}	Output High Current	−1			mA	5
I_{OL2}	Output Low Current			3	mA	6
I_{OH2}	Output High Current	−2			mA	6
I_{OL3}	Output Low Current			3	mA	7
I_{OH3}	Output High Current	−1			mA	7
I_{IH}	Input Leakage Current			+10	μA	
I_{IL}	Input Leakage Current			−10	μA	
C_{IN}	Input Capacitance		4.6		pF	
C_{OUT}	Output Capacitance		4.3		pF	
$C_{I/O}$	I/O Capacitance		4.6		pF	

NOTES:
1. V_{IL1} and V_{IH1} apply to the following signals: AD[15:0], A[15:0], D[31:0], HP[3:0], MD[31:0], MP[3:0], TRDY#, RESET, HCLK, PCLK.
2. V_{IL2} and V_{IH2} apply to the following signals: HIG[4:0], PIG[3:0], MIG[2:0], MDLE, DRVPCI.
3. V_{OL1} and V_{OH1} apply to the following signals: AD[15:0], A[15:0], D[31:0], HP[3:0], MD[31:0], MP[3:0].
4. V_{OL2} and V_{OH2} apply to the following signals: PPOUT, EOL.
5. I_{OL1} and I_{OH1} apply to the following signals: PPOUT, EOL.
6. I_{OL2} and I_{OH2} apply to the following signals: AD[15:0].
7. I_{OL3} and I_{OH3} apply to the following signals: A[15:0], D[31:0], HP[3:0], MD[31:0], MP[3:0].

4.3.1 A.C. CHARACTERISTICS

The A.C. specifications given in this section consist of propagation delays, valid delays, input setup requirements, input hold requirements, output float delays, output enable delays, clock high and low times and clock period specifications. Figures 4-1 through 4-9 define these specifications. Sections 4.3.1 through 4.3.3 list the A.C. Specifications.

In Figures 4-1 through 4-9, V_T = 1.5V for the following signals: MD[31:0], MP[3:0], D[31:0], HP[3:0], A[15:0], AD[15:0], TRDY#, HCLK, PCLK, RESET, TEST.

V_T = 2.5V for the following signals: HIG[4:0], PIG[3:0], MIG[2:0], MDLE, DRVPCI, PPOUT, EOL.

4.3.2 HOST AND PCI CLOCK TIMING, 66 MHz

Functional Operating Range: V_{CC} = 4.9V–5.25V; T_C = 0°C to +70°C

Symbol	Parameter	Min	Max	Figures	Notes
t1a	HCLK Period	15	20	4-6	
t1b	HCLK High Time	5		4-6	
t1c	HCLK Low Time	5		4-6	
t1d	HCLK Rise Time		1.5	4-7	
t1e	HCLK Fall Time		1.5	4-7	
t1f	HCLK Period Stability		100 ps(1)		
t2a	PCLK Period	30		4-6	
t2b	PCLK High Time	12		4-6	
t2c	PCLK Low Time	12		4-6	
t2d	PCLK Rise Time		3	4-7	
t2e	PCLK Fall Time		3	4-7	
t3	HCLK to PCLK Skew	−7.2	5.8	4-9	

NOTE:
1. Measured on rising edge of adjacent clocks at 1.5V.

4.3.3 COMMAND TIMING, 66 MHz

Functional Operating Range: V_{CC} = 4.9V–5.25V; T_C = 0°C to +70°C

Symbol	Parameter	Min	Max	Figures	Notes
t10a	HIG[4:0] Setup Time to HCLK Rising	5.4		4-3	
t10b	HIG[4:0] Hold Time from HCLK Rising	0		4-3	
t11a	MIG[2:0] Setup Time to HCLK Rising	5.4		4-3	
t11b	MIG[2:0] Hold Time from HCLK Rising	0		4-3	
t12a	PIG[3:0] Setup Time to PCLK Rising	15.6		4-3	
t12b	PIG[3:0] Hold Time from PCLK Rising	−1.0		4-3	
t13a	MDLE Setup Time to HCLK Rising	5.7		4-3	
t13b	MDLE Hold Time to HCLK Rising	−0.3		4-3	
t14a	DRVPCI Setup Time to PCLK Rising	6.5		4-3	
t14b	DRVPCI Hold Time from PCLK Rising	−0.5		4-3	
t15a	RESET Setup Time to HCLK Rising	3.1		4-3	
t15b	RESET Hold Time from HCLK Rising	0.3		4-3	

4.3.4 ADDRESS, DATA, TRDY#, EOL, TEST, TSCON AND PARITY TIMING, 66 MHz

Functional Operating Range: V_{CC} = 4.9V–5.25V; T_C = 0°C to +70°C

Symbol	Parameter	Min	Max	Figures	Notes
t20a	AD[15:0] Output Enable Delay from PCLK Rising	2		4-5	
t20b	AD[15:0] Valid Delay from PCLK Rising	2	11	4-2	1
t20c	AD[15:0] Setup Time to PCLK Rising	7		4-3	
t20d	AD[15:0] Hold Time from PCLK Rising	0		4-3	
t20e	AD[15:0] Float Delay from DRVPCI Falling	2	10	4-4	
t21a	TRDY# Setup Time to PCLK Rising	7		4-3	
t21b	TRDY# Hold Time from PCLK Rising	0		4-3	
t22a	D[31:0], HP[3:0] Output Enable Delay from HCLK Rising	0	7.7	4-5	2
t22b	D[31:0], HP[3:0] Float Delay from HCLK Rising	3.1	15.5	4-4	
t22c	D[31:0], HP[3:0] Float Delay from MDLE Rising	2	11.0	4-4	3
t22d	D[31:0], HP[3:0] Valid Delay from HCLK Rising	0	7.7	4-2	2
t22f	D[31:0],HP[3:0] Setup Time to HCLK Rising	2.7		4-3	
t22g	D[31:0], HP[3:0] Hold Time from HCLK Rising	0.3		4-3	
t23a	HA[15:0] Output Enable Delay from HCLK Rising	0	15.2	4-5	
t23b	HA[15:0] Float Delay from HCLK Rising	0	15.2	4-4	
t23c	HA[15:0] Valid Delay from HCLK Rising	0	16.0	4-2	7
t23cc	HA[15:0] Valid Delay from HCLK Rising	0	14.5		8
t23d	HA[15:0] Setup Time to HCLK Rising	15		4-3	4
t23e	HA[15:0] Setup Time to HCLK Rising	4.1		4-3	5
t23f	HA[15:0] Hold Time from HCLK Rising	0.3		4-3	
t24a	MD[31:0], MP[3:0] Valid Delay from HCLK Rising	0	12.0	4-2	6
t24b	MD[31:0], MP[3:0] Setup Time to HCLK Rising	4.0		4-3	
t24c	MD[31:0], MP[3:0] Hold Time from HCLK Rising	0.4		4-3	
t25	EOL, PPOUT Valid Delay from PCLK Rising	2.3	17.2	4-2	2
t26a	All Outputs Float Delay from TSCON Falling	0	30	4-4	
t26b	All Outputs Enable Delay from TSCON Rising	0	30	4-5	

NOTES:
1. Min: 0 pF, Max: 50 pF.
2. 0 pF.
3. When NOPC command sampled on previous rising HCLK on HIG[4:0].
4. CPU to PCI Transfers.
5. When ADCPY command is sampled on HIG[4:0].
6. 50 pF.
7. When DACPYL or DACPYH command is sampled on HIG[4:0].
8. Inquire cycle.

1

4.3.5 HOST AND PCI CLOCK TIMING, 60 MHz

Functional Operating Range: V_{CC} = 5V ±5%; T_C = 0°C to +85°C

Symbol	Parameter	Min	Max	Figures	Notes
t1a	HCLK Period	16.6	20	4-6	
t1b	HCLK High Time	5.5		4-6	
t1c	HCLK Low Time	5.5		4-6	
t1d	HCLK Rise Time		1.5	4-7	
t1e	HCLK Fall Time		1.5	4-7	
t1f	HCLK Period Stability		100 ps(1)		
t2a	PCLK Period	33.33		4-6	
t2b	PCLK High Time	13		4-6	
t2c	PCLK Low Time	13		4-6	
t2d	PCLK Rise Time		3	4-7	
t2e	PCLK Fall Time		3	4-7	
t3	HCLK to PCLK Skew	−7.2	5.8	4-9	

NOTE:
1. Measured on rising edge of adjacent clocks at 1.5V.

4.3.6 COMMAND TIMING, 60 MHz

Functional Operating Range: V_{CC} = 5V ±5%; T_C = 0°C to +85°C

Symbol	Parameter	Min	Max	Figures	Notes
t10a	HIG[4:0] Setup Time to HCLK Rising	6.0		4-3	
t10b	HIG[4:0] Hold Time from HCLK Rising	0		4-3	
t11a	MIG[2:0] Setup Time to HCLK Rising	6.0		4-3	
t11b	MIG[2:0] Hold Time from HCLK Rising	0		4-3	
t12a	PIG[3:0] Setup Time to PCLK Rising	16.0		4-3	
t12b	PIG[3:0] Hold Time from PCLK Rising	0		4-3	
t13a	MDLE Setup Time to HCLK Rising	5.9		4-3	
t13b	MDLE Hold Time to HCLK Rising	−0.3		4-3	
t14a	DRVPCI Setup Time to PCLK Rising	7.0		4-3	
t14b	DRVPCI Hold Time from PCLK Rising	−0.5		4-3	
t15a	RESET Setup Time to HCLK Rising	3.4		4-3	
t15b	RESET Hold Time from HCLK Rising	0.4		4-3	

4.3.7 ADDRESS, DATA, TRDY#, EOL, TEST, TSCON AND PARITY TIMING, 60 MHz

Functional Operating Range: V_{CC} = 5V ±5%; T_C = 0°C to +85°C

Symbol	Parameter	Min	Max	Figures	Notes
t20a	AD[15:0] Output Enable Delay from PCLK Rising	2		4-5	
t20b	AD[15:0] Valid Delay from PCLK Rising	2	11	4-2	1
t20c	AD[15:0] Setup Time to PCLK Rising	7		4-3	
t20d	AD[15:0] Hold Time from PCLK Rising	0		4-3	
t20e	AD[15:0] Float Delay from DRVPCI Falling	2	10	4-4	
t21a	TRDY# Setup Time to PCLK Rising	7		4-3	
t21b	TRDY# Hold Time from PCLK Rising	0		4-3	
t22a	D[31:0], HP[3:0] Output Enable Delay from HCLK Rising	0	7.9	4-5	2
t22b	D[31:0], HP[3:0] Float Delay from HCLK Rising	3.1	15.5	4-4	
t22c	D[31:0], HP[3:0] Float Delay from MDLE Rising	2	11.0	4-4	3
t22d	D[31:0], HP[3:0] Valid Delay from HCLK Rising	0	7.8	4-2	2
t22f	D[31:0],HP[3:0] Setup Time to HCLK Rising	3.4		4-3	
t22g	D[31:0], HP[3:0] Hold Time from HCLK Rising	0.3		4-3	
t23a	HA[15:0] Output Enable Delay from HCLK Rising	0	15.2	4-5	
t23b	HA[15:0] Float Delay from HCLK Rising	0	15.2	4-4	
t23c	HA[15:0] Valid Delay from HCLK Rising	0	18.5	4-2	7
t23cc	HA[15:0] Valid Delay from HCLK Rising	0	15.5		8
t23d	HA[15:0] Setup Time to HCLK Rising	15.0		4-3	4
t23e	HA[15:0] Setup Time to HCLK Rising	4.1		4-3	5
t23f	HA[15:0] Hold Time from HCLK Rising	0.3		4-3	
t24a	MD[31:0], MP[3:0] Valid Delay from HCLK Rising	0	12.0	4-2	6
t24b	MD[31:0], MP[3:0] Setup Time to HCLK Rising	4.4		4-3	
t24c	MD[31:0], MP[3:0] Hold Time from HCLK Rising	1.0		4-3	
t25	EOL, PPOUT Valid Delay from PCLK Rising	2.3	17.2	4-2	2
t26a	All Outputs Float Delay from TSCON Falling	0	30	4-4	
t26b	All Outputs Enable Delay from TSCON Rising	0	30	4-5	

NOTES:
1. Min: 0 pF, Max: 50 pF.
2. 0 pF.
3. When NOPC command sampled on previous rising HCLK on HIG[4:0].
4. CPU to PCI Transfers.
5. When ADCPY command is sampled on HIG[4:0].
6. 50 pF.
7. When DACPYL or DACPYH command is sampled on HIGH[4:0].
8. Inquire cycle.

4.3.8 TEST TIMING

Functional Operating Range: V_{CC} = 5V ±5%; T_C = 0°C to +85°C

Symbol	Parameter	Min	Max	Figures	Notes
t30	All Test Signals Setup Time to HCLK/PCLK Rising	10.0			In PLL Bypass Mode
t31	All Test Signals Hold Time to HCLK/PCLK Rising	12.0			In PLL Bypass Mode
t32	TEST Setup Time to HCLK/PCLK Rising	15.0			
t33	TEST Hold Time to HCLK/PCLK Rising	5.0			
t34	PPOUT Valid Delay from PCLK Rising	0.0	500		In PLL Bypass Mode

4.3.9 TIMING DIAGRAMS

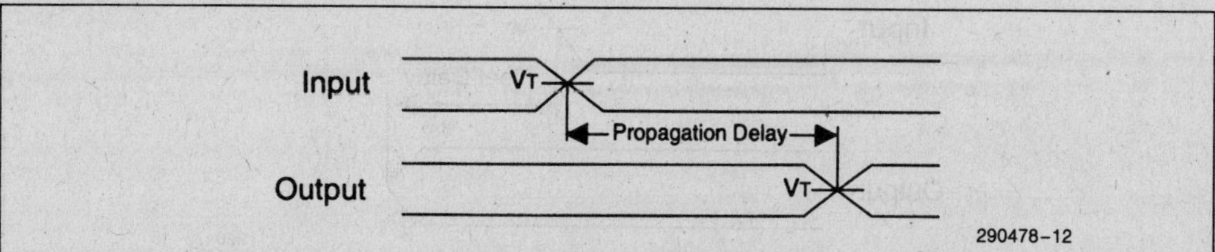

Figure 4-1. Propagation Delay

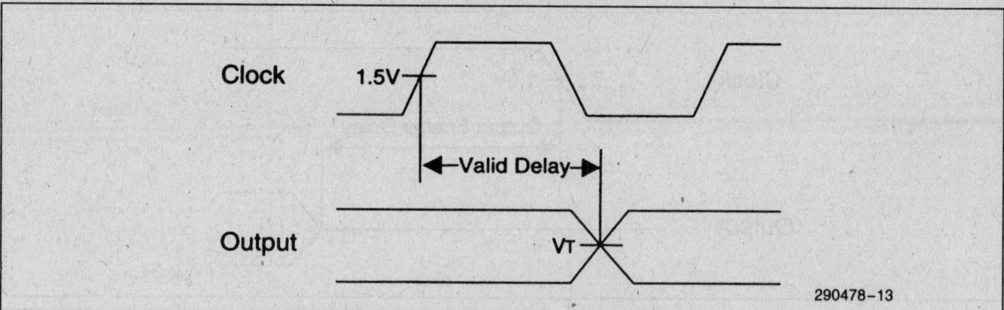

Figure 4-2. Valid Delay from Rising Clock Edge

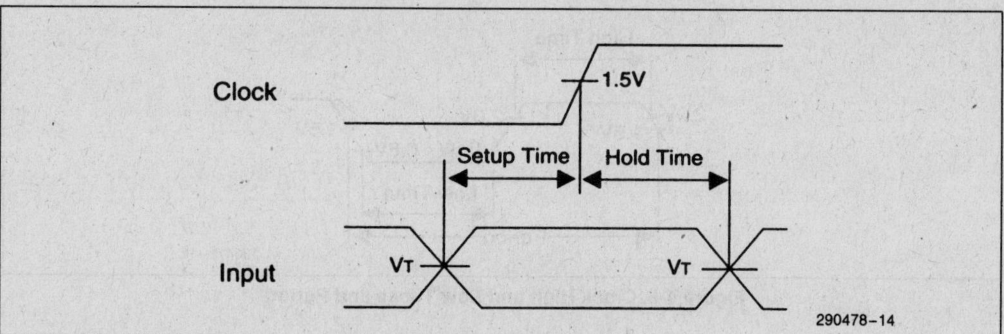

Figure 4-3. Setup and Hold Times

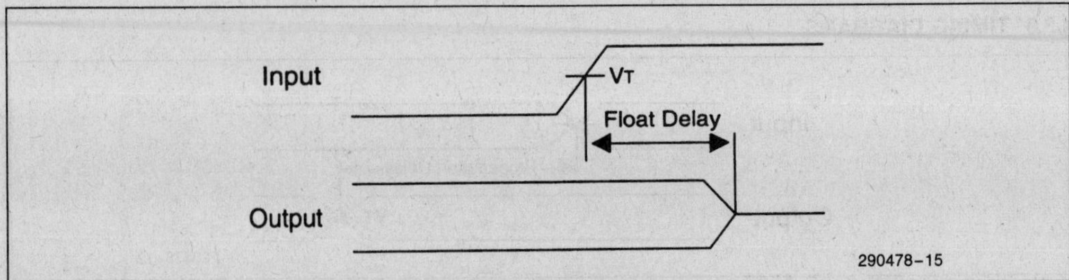

Figure 4-4. Float Delay

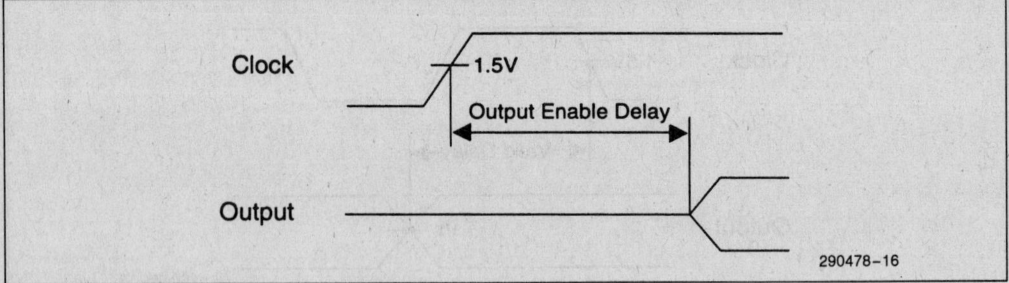

Figure 4-5. Output Enable Delay

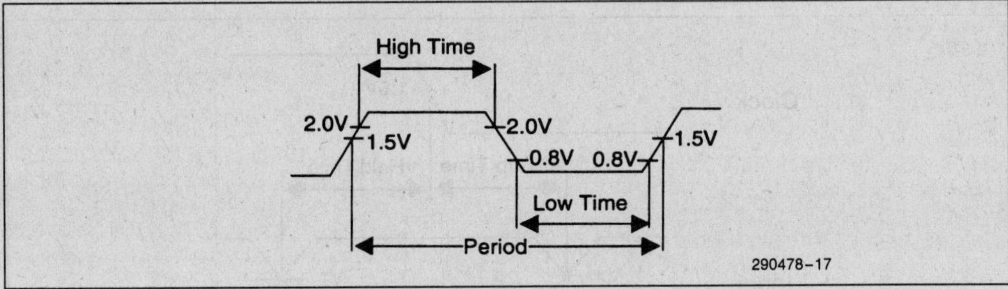

Figure 4-6. Clock High and Low Times and Period

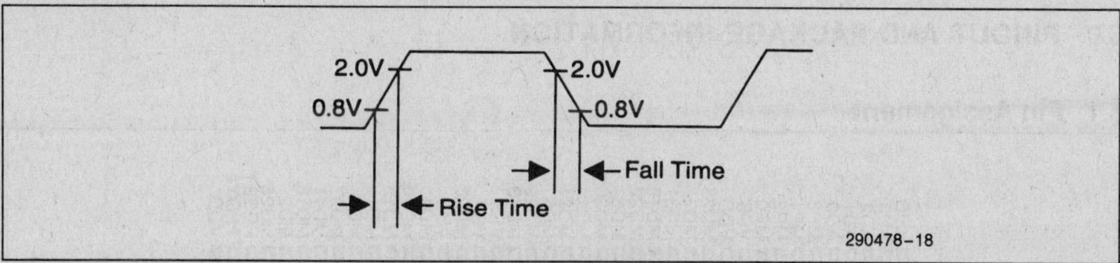

Figure 4-7. Clock Rise and Fall Times

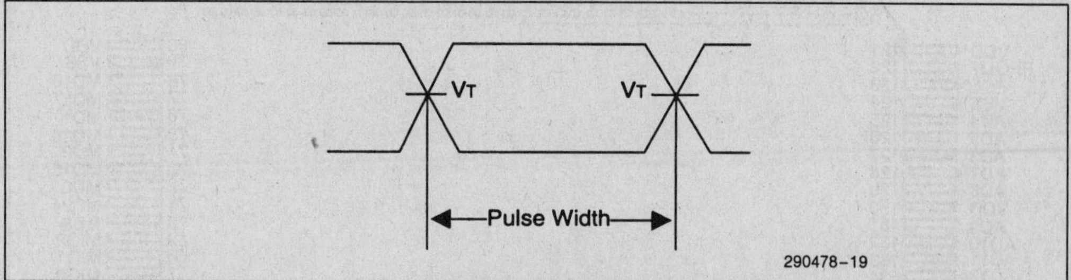

Figure 4-8. Pulse Width

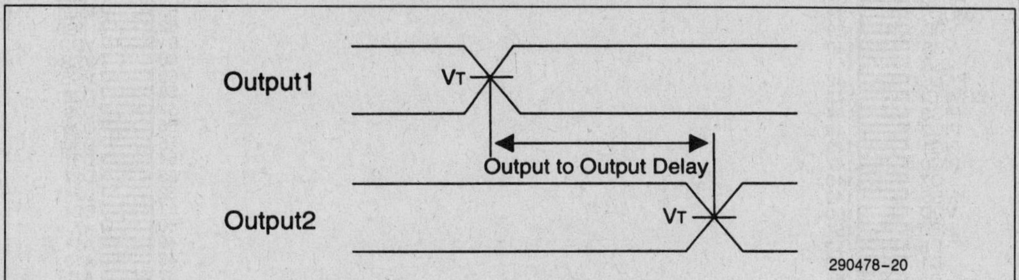

Figure 4-9. Output to Output Delay

5.0 PINOUT AND PACKAGE INFORMATION

5.1 Pin Assignment

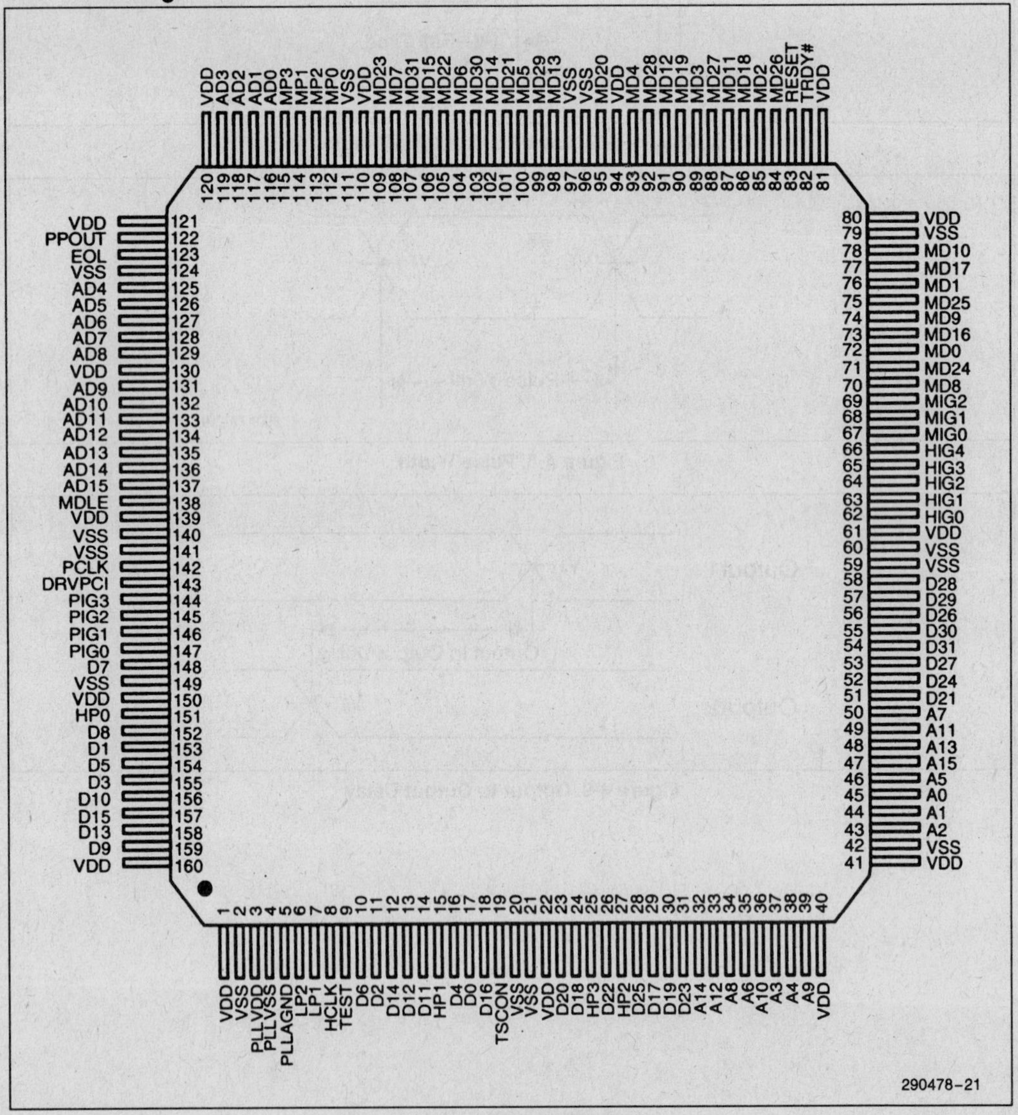

Pin	Signal	Pin	Signal	Pin	Signal	Pin	Signal
1	VDD	41	VDD	81	VDD	121	VDD
2	VSS	42	VSS	82	TRDY#	122	PPOUT
3	PLLVDD	43	A2	83	RESET	123	EOL
4	PLLVSS	44	A1	84	MD26	124	VSS
5	PLLAGND	45	A0	85	MD2	125	AD4
6	LP2	46	A5	86	MD18	126	AD5
7	LP1	47	A15	87	MD11	127	AD6
8	HCLK	48	A13	88	MD27	128	AD7
9	TEST	49	A11	89	MD3	129	AD8
10	D6	50	A7	90	MD19	130	VDD
11	D2	51	D21	91	MD12	131	AD9
12	D14	52	D24	92	MD28	132	AD10
13	D12	53	D27	93	MD4	133	AD11
14	D11	54	D31	94	VDD	134	AD12
15	HP1	55	D30	95	MD20	135	AD13
16	D4	56	D26	96	VSS	136	AD14
17	D0	57	D29	97	VSS	137	AD15
18	D16	58	D28	98	MD13	138	MDLE
19	TSCON	59	VSS	99	MD29	139	VDD
20	VSS	60	VSS	100	MD5	140	VSS
21	VSS	61	VDD	101	MD21	141	VSS
22	VDD	62	HIG0	102	MD14	142	PCLK
23	D20	63	HIG1	103	MD30	143	DRVPCI
24	D18	64	HIG2	104	MD6	144	PIG3
25	HP3	65	HIG3	105	MD22	145	PIG2
26	D22	66	HIG4	106	MD15	146	PIG1
27	HP2	67	MIG0	107	MD31	147	PIG0
28	D25	68	MIG1	108	MD7	148	D7
29	D17	69	MIG2	109	MD23	149	VSS
30	D19	70	MD8	110	VDD	150	VDD
31	D23	71	MD24	111	VSS	151	HP0
32	A14	72	MD0	112	MP0	152	D8
33	A12	73	MD16	113	MP2	153	D1
34	A8	74	MD9	114	MP1	154	D5
35	A6	75	MD25	115	MP3	155	D3
36	A10	76	MD1	116	AD0	156	D10
37	A3	77	MD17	117	AD1	157	D15
38	A4	78	MD10	118	AD2	158	D13
39	A9	79	VSS	119	AD3	159	D9
40	VDD	80	VDD	120	VDD	160	VDD

290478-21

Figure 5-1. Pin Assignment

Table 5-1. LBX Numerical Pin Assignment List

Pin #	Name	Type	Pin #	Name	Type	Pin #	Name	Type	Pin #	Name	Type
1	V_{DD}	V	21	V_{SS}	V	41	V_{DD}	V	61	V_{DD}	V
2	V_{SS}	V	22	V_{DD}	V	42	V_{SS}	V	62	HIG0	I
3	$PLLV_{DD}$	V	23	D20	t/s	43	A2	t/s	63	HIG1	I
4	$PLLV_{SS}$	V	24	D18	t/s	44	A1	t/s	64	HIG2	I
5	PLLAGND	V	25	HP3	t/s	45	A0	t/s	65	HIG3	I
6	LP2	I	26	D22	t/s	46	A5	t/s	66	HIG4	I
7	LP1	O	27	HP2	t/s	47	A15	t/s	67	MIG0	I
8	HCLK	I	28	D25	t/s	48	A13	t/s	68	MIG1	I
9	TEST	I	29	D17	t/s	49	A11	t/s	69	MIG2	I
10	D6	t/s	30	D19	t/s	50	A7	t/s	70	MD8	t/s
11	D2	t/s	31	D23	t/s	51	D21	t/s	71	MD24	t/s
12	D14	t/s	32	A14	t/s	52	D24	t/s	72	MD0	t/s
13	D12	t/s	33	A12	t/s	53	D27	t/s	73	MD16	t/s
14	D11	t/s	34	A8	t/s	54	D31	t/s	74	MD9	t/s
15	HP1	t/s	35	A6	t/s	55	D30	t/s	75	MD25	t/s
16	D4	t/s	36	A10	t/s	56	D26	t/s	76	MD1	t/s
17	D0	t/s	37	A3	t/s	57	D29	t/s	77	MD17	t/s
18	D16	t/s	38	A4	t/s	58	D28	t/s	78	MD10	t/s
19	TSCON	I	39	A9	t/s	59	V_{SS}	V	79	V_{SS}	V
20	V_{SS}	V	40	V_{DD}	V	60	V_{SS}	V	80	V_{DD}	V

Table 5-1. LBX Numerical Pin Assignment List (Continued)

Pin #	Name	Type	Pin #	Name	Type	Pin #	Name	Type	Pin #	Name	Type
81	V_{DD}	V	101	MD21	t/s	121	V_{DD}	V	141	V_{SS}	V
82	TRDY#	I	102	MD14	t/s	122	PPOUT	t/s	142	PCLK	I
83	RESET	I	103	MD30	t/s	123	EOL	t/s	143	DRVPCI	I
84	MD26	t/s	104	MD6	t/s	124	V_{SS}	V	144	PIG3	I
85	MD2	t/s	105	MD22	t/s	125	AD4	t/s	145	PIG2	I
86	MD18	t/s	106	MD15	t/s	126	AD5	t/s	146	PIG1	I
87	MD11	t/s	107	MD31	t/s	127	AD6	t/s	147	PIG0	I
88	MD27	t/s	108	MD7	t/s	128	AD7	t/s	148	D7	t/s
89	MD3	t/s	109	MD23	t/s	129	AD8	t/s	149	V_{SS}	V
90	MD19	t/s	110	V_{DD}	V	130	V_{DD}	V	150	V_{DD}	V
91	MD12	t/s	111	V_{SS}	V	131	AD9	t/s	151	HP0	t/s
92	MD28	t/s	112	MP0	t/s	132	AD10	t/s	152	D8	t/s
93	MD4	t/s	113	MP2	t/s	133	AD11	t/s	153	D1	t/s
94	V_{DD}	V	114	MP1	t/s	134	AD12	t/s	154	D5	t/s
95	MD20	t/s	115	MP3	t/s	135	AD13	t/s	155	D3	t/s
96	V_{SS}	V	116	AD0	t/s	136	AD14	t/s	156	D10	t/s
97	V_{SS}	V	117	AD1	t/s	137	AD15	t/s	157	D15	t/s
98	MD13	t/s	118	AD2	t/s	138	MDLE	I	158	D13	t/s
99	MD29	t/s	119	AD3	t/s	139	V_{DD}	V	159	D9	t/s
100	MD5	t/s	120	V_{DD}	V	140	V_{SS}	V	160	V_{DD}	V

Table 5-2. LBX Alphabetical Pin Assignment List

Name	Pin #	Type
A0	45	t/s
A1	44	t/s
A2	43	t/s
A3	37	t/s
A4	38	t/s
A5	46	t/s
A6	35	t/s
A7	50	t/s
A8	34	t/s
A9	39	t/s
A10	36	t/s
A11	49	t/s
A12	33	t/s
A13	48	t/s
A14	32	t/s
A15	47	t/s
AD0	116	t/s
AD1	117	t/s
AD2	118	t/s
AD3	119	t/s
AD4	125	t/s
AD5	126	t/s
AD6	127	t/s
AD7	128	t/s
AD8	129	t/s
AD9	131	t/s
AD10	132	t/s
AD11	133	t/s
AD12	134	t/s
AD13	135	t/s
AD14	136	t/s
AD15	137	t/s
D0	17	t/s
D1	153	t/s
D2	11	t/s
D3	155	t/s
D4	16	t/s
D5	154	t/s
D6	10	t/s
D7	148	t/s
D8	152	t/s
D9	159	t/s
D10	156	t/s
D11	14	t/s
D12	13	t/s
D13	158	t/s
D14	12	t/s
D15	157	t/s
D16	18	t/s
D17	29	t/s
D18	24	t/s
D19	30	t/s
D20	23	t/s
D21	51	t/s
D22	26	t/s
D23	31	t/s
D24	52	t/s
D25	28	t/s
D26	56	t/s
D27	53	t/s
D28	58	t/s
D29	57	t/s
D30	55	t/s
D31	54	t/s
DRVPCI	143	I
EOL	123	t/s
HCLK	8	I
HIG0	62	I
HIG1	63	I
HIG2	64	I
HIG3	65	I
HIG4	66	I
HP0	151	t/s
HP1	15	t/s
HP2	27	t/s
HP3	25	t/s
LP1	7	O
LP2	6	I
MD0	72	t/s
MD1	76	t/s

Table 5-2. LBX Alphabetical Pin Assignment List (Continued)

Name	Pin #	Type	Name	Pin #	Type	Name	Pin #	Type	Name	Pin #	Type
MD2	85	t/s	MD22	105	t/s	PIG1	146	I	V_{DD}	120	V
MD3	89	t/s	MD23	109	t/s	PIG2	145	I	V_{DD}	121	V
MD4	93	t/s	MD24	71	t/s	PIG3	144	I	V_{DD}	130	V
MD5	100	t/s	MD25	75	t/s	PLLAGND	5	V	V_{DD}	139	V
MD6	104	t/s	MD26	84	t/s	PLLV$_{DD}$	3	V	V_{DD}	150	V
MD7	108	t/s	MD27	88	t/s	PLLV$_{SS}$	4	V	V_{DD}	160	V
MD8	70	t/s	MD28	92	t/s	PPOUT	122	t/s	V_{SS}	2	V
MD9	74	t/s	MD29	99	t/s	RESET	83	I	V_{SS}	20	V
MD10	78	t/s	MD30	103	t/s	TEST	9	I	V_{SS}	21	V
MD11	87	t/s	MD31	107	t/s	TRDY#	82	I	V_{SS}	42	V
MD12	91	t/s	MDLE	138	I	TSCON	19	I	V_{SS}	59	V
MD13	98	t/s	MIG0	67	I	V_{DD}	1	V	V_{SS}	60	V
MD14	102	t/s	MIG1	68	I	V_{DD}	22	V	V_{SS}	79	V
MD15	106	t/s	MIG2	69	I	V_{DD}	40	V	V_{SS}	96	V
MD16	73	t/s	MP0	112	t/s	V_{DD}	41	V	V_{SS}	97	V
MD17	77	t/s	MP1	114	t/s	V_{DD}	61	V	V_{SS}	111	V
MD18	86	t/s	MP2	113	t/s	V_{DD}	80	V	V_{SS}	124	V
MD19	90	t/s	MP3	115	t/s	V_{DD}	81	V	V_{SS}	140	V
MD20	95	t/s	PCLK	142	I	V_{DD}	94	V	V_{SS}	141	V
MD21	101	t/s	PIG0	147	I	V_{DD}	110	V	V_{SS}	149	V

5.2 Package Information

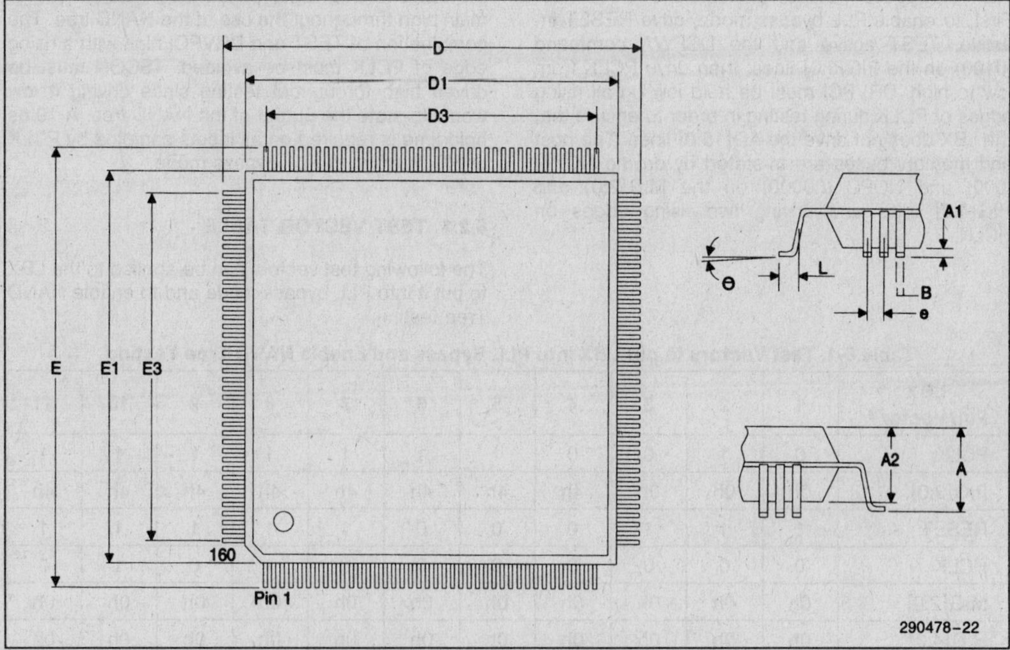

Table 5-3. Package Information Values

Symbol	Min Value (mm)	Max Value (mm)
A		4.01
A1	0.25	0.36
A2	3.43	3.66
B	0.25	0.35
D	31.60	32.40
D1	27.90	28.10
D3		25.35
E		32.40
E1	27.90	28.10
E3		25.35
e		0.65
L	0.60	1.00
θ	0°	10°

6.0 TESTABILITY

6.1 Tri-State Control

The TSCON pin may be used to help test circuits surrounding the LBX. During normal operations, the TSCON pin must be tied to V_{CC} or connected to V_{CC} through a pullup resistor. All LBX outputs are tri-stated when the TSCON pin is held low or grounded.

6.2 NAND Tree

A NAND tree is provided in the LBX for Automated Test Equipment (ATE) board level testing. The NAND tree allows the tester to set the connectivity of each of the LBX signal pins.

The following steps must be taken to put the LBX into PLL bypass mode and enable the NAND tree. First, to enable PLL bypass mode, drive RESET inactive, TEST active and the DCPWA command (0100) on the PIG[3:0] lines, then drive PCLK from low to high. DRVPCI must be held low on all rising edges of PCLK during testing in order to ensure that the LBX does not drive the AD[15:0] lines. The host and memory buses are tri-stated by driving NOPM (000) and NOPC (00000) on the MIG[2:0] and HIG[4:0] lines and driving two rising edges on HCLK.

A rising edge on PCLK with RESET high will cause the LBXs to exit PLL bypass mode. TEST must remain high throughout the use of the NAND tree. The combination of TEST and DRVPCI high with a rising edge of PCLK must be avoided. TSCON must be driven high throughout testing since driving it low would tri-state the output of the NAND tree. A 10 ns hold time is required on all inputs sampled by PCLK or HCLK when in PLL bypass mode.

6.2.1 TEST VECTOR TABLE

The following test vectors can be applied to the LBX to put it into PLL bypass mode and to enable NAND Tree testing.

Table 6-1. Test Vectors to put LBX into PLL Bypass and Enable NAND Tree Testing

LBX Pin/Vector #	1	2	3	4	5	6	7	8	9	10	11
PCLK	0	1	0	0	1	1	1	1	1	1	1
PIG[3:0]	0h	0h	0h	4h	4h	4h	4h	4h	4h	4h	4h
RESET	1	1	1	0	0	0	1	1	1	1	1
HCLK	0	0	0	0	0	0	0	1	0	1	0
MIG[2:0]	0h	0h	0h	0h	0h	0h	0h	0h	0h	0h	0h
HIG[4:0]	0h	0h	0h	0h	0h	0h	0h	0h	0h	0h	0h
TEST	1	1	1	1	1	1	1	1	1	1	1
DRVPCI	0	0	0	0	0	0	0	0	0	0	0

6.2.2 NAND TREE TABLE

Table 6-2 shows the sequence of the NAND tree in the LBX. Non-inverting inputs are driven directly into the input of a NAND gate in the tree. Inverting inputs are driven into an inverter before going into the NAND tree. The output of the NAND tree is driven on the PPOUT pin.

1

Table 6-2. NAND Tree Sequence

Order	Pin#	Signal	Non-Inverting
1	10	D6	Y
2	11	D2	Y
3	12	D14	Y
4	13	D12	Y
5	14	D11	Y
6	15	HP1	Y
7	16	D4	Y
8	17	D0	Y
9	18	D16	Y
10	23	D20	Y
11	24	D18	Y
12	25	HP3	Y
13	26	D22	Y
14	27	HP2	Y
15	28	D25	Y
16	29	D17	Y
17	30	D19	Y
18	31	D23	Y
19	32	A14	Y
20	33	A12	Y
21	34	A8	Y
22	35	A6	Y
23	36	A10	Y
24	37	A3	Y
25	38	A4	Y
26	39	A9	Y
27	43	A2	Y
28	44	A1	Y
29	45	A0	Y
30	46	A5	Y
31	47	A15	Y
32	48	A13	Y

Order	Pin#	Signal	Non-Inverting
33	49	A11	Y
34	50	A7	Y
35	51	D21	Y
36	52	D24	Y
37	53	D27	Y
38	54	D31	Y
39	55	D30	Y
40	56	D26	Y
41	57	D29	Y
42	58	D28	Y
43	62	HIG0	Y
44	63	HIG1	Y
45	64	HIG2	Y
46	65	HIG3	Y
47	66	HIG4	Y
48	67	MIG0	N
49	68	MIG1	N
50	69	MIG2	N
51	70	MD8	N
52	71	MD24	N
53	72	MD0	N
54	73	MD16	N
55	74	MD9	N
56	75	MD25	N
57	76	MD1	N
58	77	MD17	N
59	78	MD10	N
60	82	TRDY#	Y
61	83	RESET	N
62	84	MD26	N
63	85	MD2	N
64	86	MD18	N

Table 6-2. NAND Tree Sequence (Continued)

Order	Pin #	Signal	Non-Inverting
65	87	MD11	N
66	88	MD27	N
67	89	MD3	N
68	90	MD19	N
69	91	MD12	N
70	92	MD28	N
71	93	MD4	N
72	95	MD20	N
73	98	MD13	N
74	99	MD29	N
75	100	MD5	N
76	101	MD21	N
77	102	MD14	N
78	103	MD30	N
79	104	MD6	N
80	105	MD22	N
81	106	MD15	N
82	107	MD31	N
83	108	MD7	N
84	109	MD23	N
85	112	MP0	N
86	113	MP2	N
87	114	MP1	N
88	115	MP3	N
89	116	AD0	Y
90	117	AD1	Y
91	118	AD2	Y
92	119	AD3	Y
93	123	EOL	Y

Order	Pin #	Signal	Non-Inverting
94	125	AD4	Y
95	126	AD5	Y
96	127	AD6	Y
97	128	AD7	Y
98	129	AD8	Y
99	131	AD9	Y
100	132	AD10	Y
101	133	AD11	Y
102	134	AD12	Y
103	135	AD13	Y
104	136	AD14	Y
105	137	AD15	Y
106	138	MDLE	Y
107	143	DRVPCI	N
108	144	PIG3	N
109	145	PIG2	N
110	146	PIG1	N
111	147	PIG0	N
112	148	D7	Y
113	151	HP0	Y
114	152	D8	Y
115	153	D1	Y
116	154	D5	Y
117	155	D3	Y
118	156	D10	Y
119	157	D15	Y
120	158	D13	Y
121	159	D9	Y

7.0 REVISION HISTORY

The following list represents the key differences between version 001 and version 002 of the 82433LX Local Bus Accelerator (LBX) Data Sheet.

Section 2.1	Notes added to indicate that the D[31:0] and HP[3:0] lines contain internal pull-up resistors.
Section 2.2	Notes added to indicate that the MD[31:0] and MP[3:0] lines contain internal pull-up resistors.
Section 2.4	MDLE pin discription has been rewritten.
Section 3.3.2	Figure 3.2 and the discussion on MDLE functionality has been modified to reflect the synchronous path from the memory data bus to the host data bus.
Section 4.3	The AC Specifications have been separated for 60 MHz and 66 MHz operation. Several changes have been made to AC Specifications. Test timings have been added for operation in PLL bypass mode. The 66 MHz AC Specifications have a different Functional Operating Range than the 60 MHz AC Specifications. For 66 MHz operation, V_{CC} ranges between 4.9V and 5.45V and the maximum case temperature is 70°C.
Section 6.0	This section has been split into Sections 6.1 and 6.2. Section 6.1 describes the Tri-State Control function. Section 6.2 is entirely new and describes the details of the NAND Tree in the LBX.

1

82434LX
PCI, CACHE, AND MEMORY CONTROLLER (PCMC)

- Supports the Full 64-Bit Pentium™ Processor at 60 MHz and 66 MHz
- Supports Pipelined Addressing Capability of the Pentium Processor
- High Performance CPU/PCI/Memory Interfaces Via Posted-Write/Read-Prefetch Buffers
- Fully Synchronous 33 MHz PCI Bus Interface with Full Bus Master Capability
- Supports the Pentium Processor Primary Cache in either Write-Through or Write-Back Mode
- Programmable Attribute Map of DOS and BIOS Regions for System Flexibility
- Integrated Low Skew Clock Driver for Distributing Host Clock
- Integrated Second Level Cache Controller
  - Integrated Cache Tag RAM
  - Write-Through and Write-Back Cache Modes
  - Direct-Mapped Organization
  - Supports Standard and Burst SRAMs
  - 256 KByte and 512 KByte Sizes
  - Cache Hit Cycle of 3-1-1-1 on Reads and Writes Using Burst SRAMs
  - Cache Hit Cycle of 3-2-2-2 on Reads and 4-2-2-2 on Writes Using Standard SRAMs
- Integrated DRAM Controller
  - Supports 2 MByte to 192 MByte of Cacheable Main Memory
  - Supports DRAM Access Times of 70 ns and 60 ns
  - CPU Writes Posted to DRAM at 4-1-1-1
  - Refresh Cycles Decoupled from ISA Refresh to Reduce the DRAM Access Latency
  - Refresh by RAS#-Only, or CAS#-Before-RAS#, in Single or Burst of Four
- Host/PCI Bridge
  - Translates CPU Cycles into PCI Bus Cycles
  - Translates Back-To-Back Sequential CPU Memory Writes into PCI Burst Cycles
  - Burst Mode Writes to PCI in Zero PCI Wait States (i.e. data transfer every cycle)
  - Full Concurrency between CPU-to-Main Memory and PCI-to-PCI Transactions
  - Full Concurrency between CPU-to-Second Level Cache and PCI-to-Main Memory Transactions
  - Same Core Cache and Memory System Logic Design for ISA or EISA Systems
  - Cache Snoop Filter Ensures Data Consistency for PCI-to-Main Memory Transactions
- PCMC (208-Pin QFP Package) uses 5V CMOS Technology

The 82434LX PCI, Cache, Memory Controller (PCMC) integrates the cache and main memory DRAM control functions and provides the bus control for transfers between the CPU, cache, main memory, and the Peripheral Component Interconnect (PCI) Bus. The cache controller supports both write-through and write-back cache policies and cache sizes of 256 KBytes and 512 KBytes. The cache memory can be implemented with either standard or burst SRAMs. The PCMC cache controller integrates a high-performance Tag RAM to reduce system cost. Up to twelve single-sided SIMMs or six double-sided SIMMs provide a maximum of 192 MBytes of main memory. The PCMC is intended to be used with the 82433LX Local Bus Accelerator (LBX). The LBX provides the Host-to-PCI address path and data paths between the CPU/cache, main memory, and PCI. The LBX also contains posted write buffers and read-prefetch buffers. Together, these two components provide a full function data path to main memory and form a PCI bridge to the CPU/cache and DRAM subsystem.

November 1993
Order Number: 290479-002

82434LX PCI, Cache, and Memory Controller (PCMC)

CONTENTS PAGE

CONTENTS PAGE

1

CONTENTS PAGE

Simplified Block Diagram of the PCMC

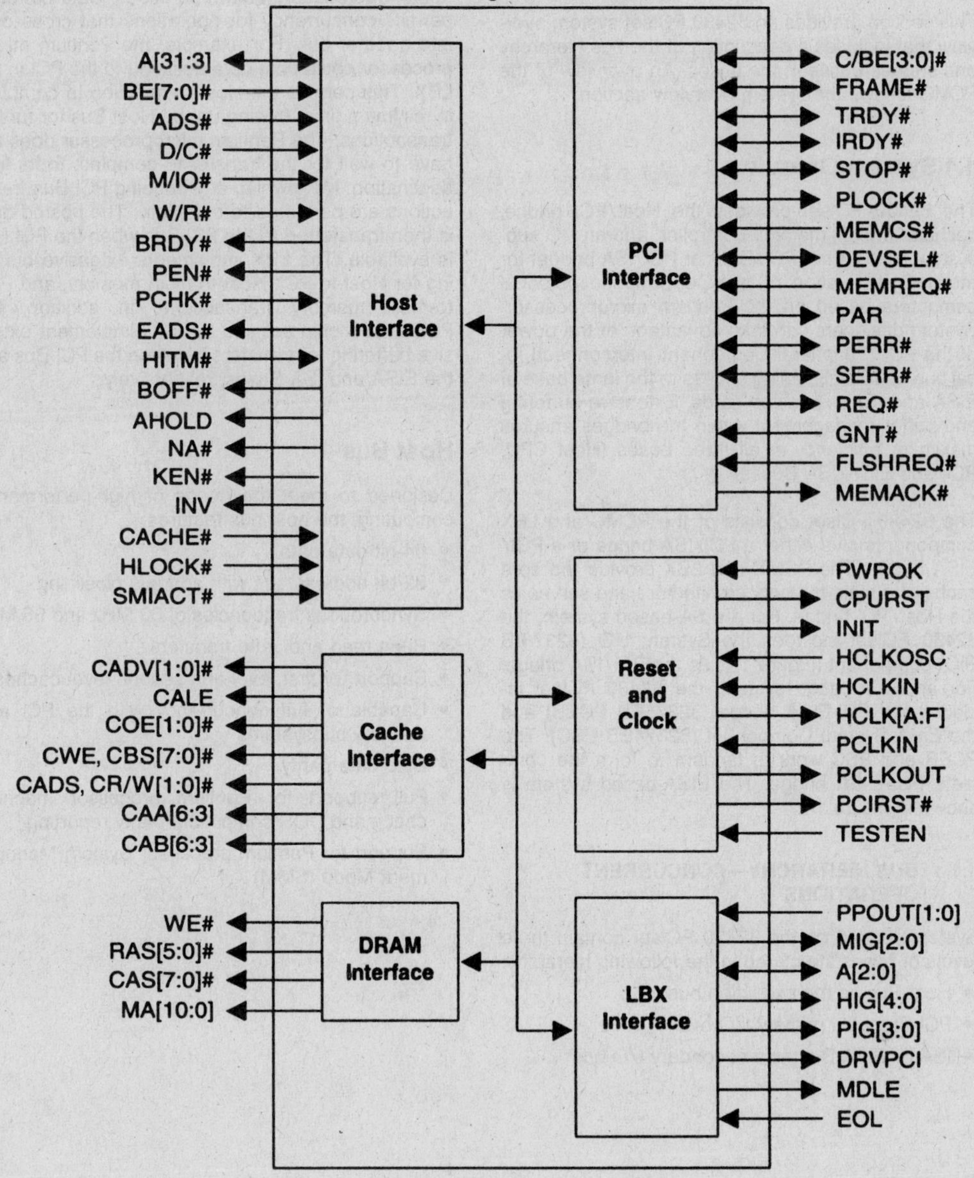

Host Interface

A[31:3]
BE[7:0]#
ADS#
D/C#
M/IO#
W/R#
BRDY#
PEN#
PCHK#
EADS#
HITM#
BOFF#
AHOLD
NA#
KEN#
INV
CACHE#
HLOCK#
SMIACT#

Cache Interface

CADV[1:0]#
CALE
COE[1:0]#
CWE, CBS[7:0]#
CADS, CR/W[1:0]#
CAA[6:3]
CAB[6:3]

DRAM Interface

WE#
RAS[5:0]#
CAS[7:0]#
MA[10:0]

PCI Interface

C/BE[3:0]#
FRAME#
TRDY#
IRDY#
STOP#
PLOCK#
MEMCS#
DEVSEL#
MEMREQ#
PAR
PERR#
SERR#
REQ#
GNT#
FLSHREQ#
MEMACK#

Reset and Clock

PWROK
CPURST
INIT
HCLKOSC
HCLKIN
HCLK[A:F]
PCLKIN
PCLKOUT
PCIRST#
TESTEN

LBX Interface

PPOUT[1:0]
MIG[2:0]
A[2:0]
HIG[4:0]
PIG[3:0]
DRVPCI
MDLE
EOL

290479–1

1

1.0 ARCHITECTURAL OVERVIEW

This section provides an 82430 PCIset system overview that includes a description of the bus hierarchy and bridges between the buses. An overview of the PCMC follows the system overview section.

1.1 System Overview

The 82430 PCIset provides the Host/PCI bridge, cache and main memory controller, and an I/O subsystem core (either PCI/EISA or PCI/ISA bridge) for the next generation of high-performance personal computers based on the Pentium microprocessor. System designers can take advantage of the power of the PCI (Peripheral Component Interconnect) local bus while maintaining access to the large base of EISA and ISA expansion cards. Extensive buffering and buffer management within the bridges ensures maximum efficiency in all three buses (Host CPU, PCI, and EISA/ISA Buses).

The 82430 PCIset consists of the PCMC and LBX components plus either a PCI/ISA bridge or a PCI/EISA bridge. The PCMC and LBX provide the core cache and main memory architecture and serves as the Host/PCI bridge. For an ISA-based system, the 82430 PCIset includes the System I/O (82378IB SIO) component (Figure 1-1) as the PCI/ISA bridge. For an EISA-based system, the 82430 PCIset includes the PCI-EISA bridge (82375EB PCEB) and the EISA System Component (82374EB ESC). The PCEB and ESC work in tandem to form the complete PCI/EISA bridge. The EISA-based system is shown in Figure 1-2.

1.1.1 BUS HIERARCHY—CONCURRENT OPERATIONS

Systems based on the 82430 PCIset contain three levels of buses structured in the following hierarchy:

- Host Bus as the execution bus
- PCI Bus as a primary I/O bus
- ISA or EISA Bus as a secondary I/O bus

This bus hierarchy allows concurrency for simultaneous operations on all three buses. Data buffering permits concurrency for operations that cross over into another bus. For example, the Pentium microprocessor could post data destined to the PCI in the LBX. This permits the Host transaction to complete in minimum time, freeing up the Host Bus for further transactions. The Pentium microprocessor does not have to wait for the transfer to complete to its final destination. Meanwhile, any ongoing PCI Bus transactions are permitted to complete. The posted data is then transferred to the PCI Bus when the PCI Bus is available. The LBX implements extensive buffering for Host-to-PCI, Host-to-main memory, and PCI-to-main memory transactions. In addition, the PCEB/ESC chip set and the SIO implement extensive buffering for transfers between the PCI Bus and the EISA and ISA Buses, respectively.

Host Bus

Designed to meet the needs of high-performance computing, the host bus features:

- 64-bit data path
- 32-bit address bus with address pipelining
- Synchronous frequencies of 60 MHz and 66 MHz
- Burst read and write transfers
- Support for first level and second level caches
- Capable of full concurrency with the PCI and memory subsystems
- Byte data parity
- Full support for Pentium processor machine check and DOS compatible parity reporting
- Support for Pentium processor System Management Mode (SMM)

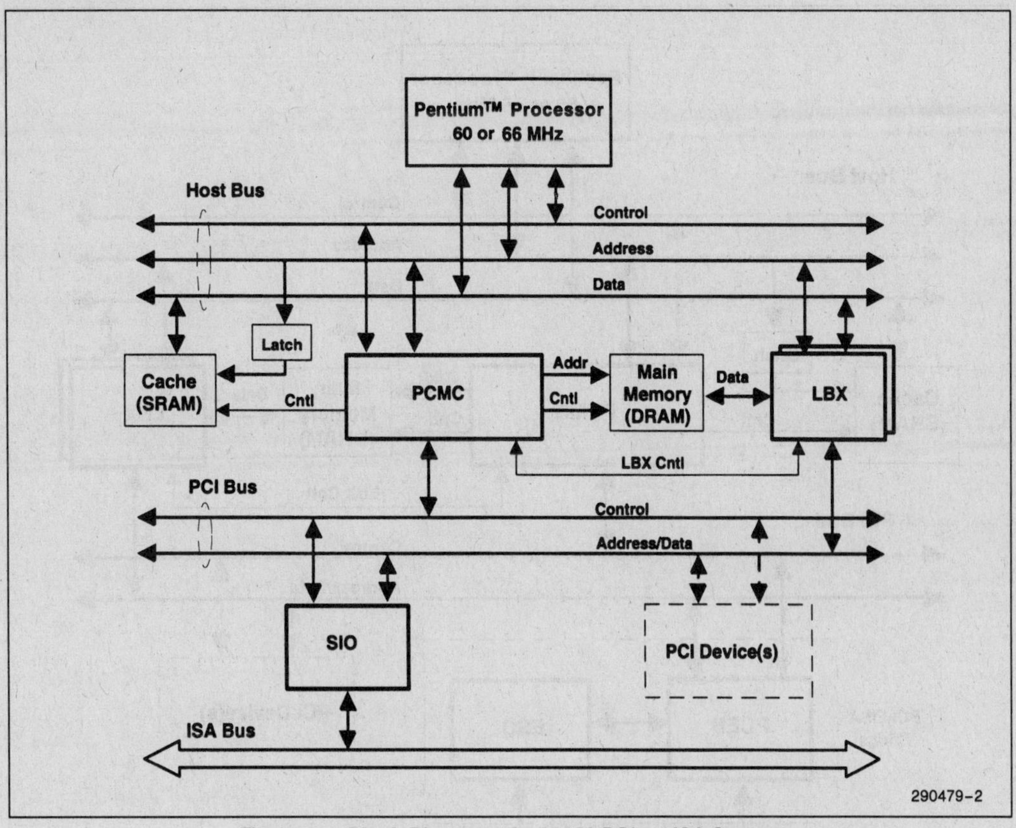

290479-2

Figure 1-1. Block Diagram of a 82430 PCIset ISA System

PCI Bus

The PCI Bus is designed to address the growing industry needs for a standardized *local bus* that is not directly dependent on the speed and the size of the processor bus. New generations of personal computer system software such as Windows and Win-NT with sophisticated graphical interfaces, multi-tasking, and multi-threading bring new requirements that traditional PC I/O architectures cannot satisfy. In addition to the higher bandwidth, reliability and robustness of the I/O subsystem are becoming increasingly important. PCI addresses these needs and provides a future upgrade path. PCI features include:

- Processor independent
- Multiplexed, burst mode operation
- Synchronous at frequencies up to 33 MHz
- 120 MByte/sec usable throughput (132 MByte/sec peak) for a 32-bit data path
- Low latency random access (60 ns write access latency to slave registers from a master parked on the bus)
- Capable of full concurrency with the processor/memory subsystem
- Full multi-master capability allowing any PCI master peer-to-peer access to any PCI slave
- Hidden (overlapped) central arbitration
- Low pin count for cost effective component packaging (multiplexed address/data)
- Address and data parity
- Three physical address spaces: memory, I/O, and configuration
- Comprehensive support for autoconfiguration through a defined set of standard configuration functions.

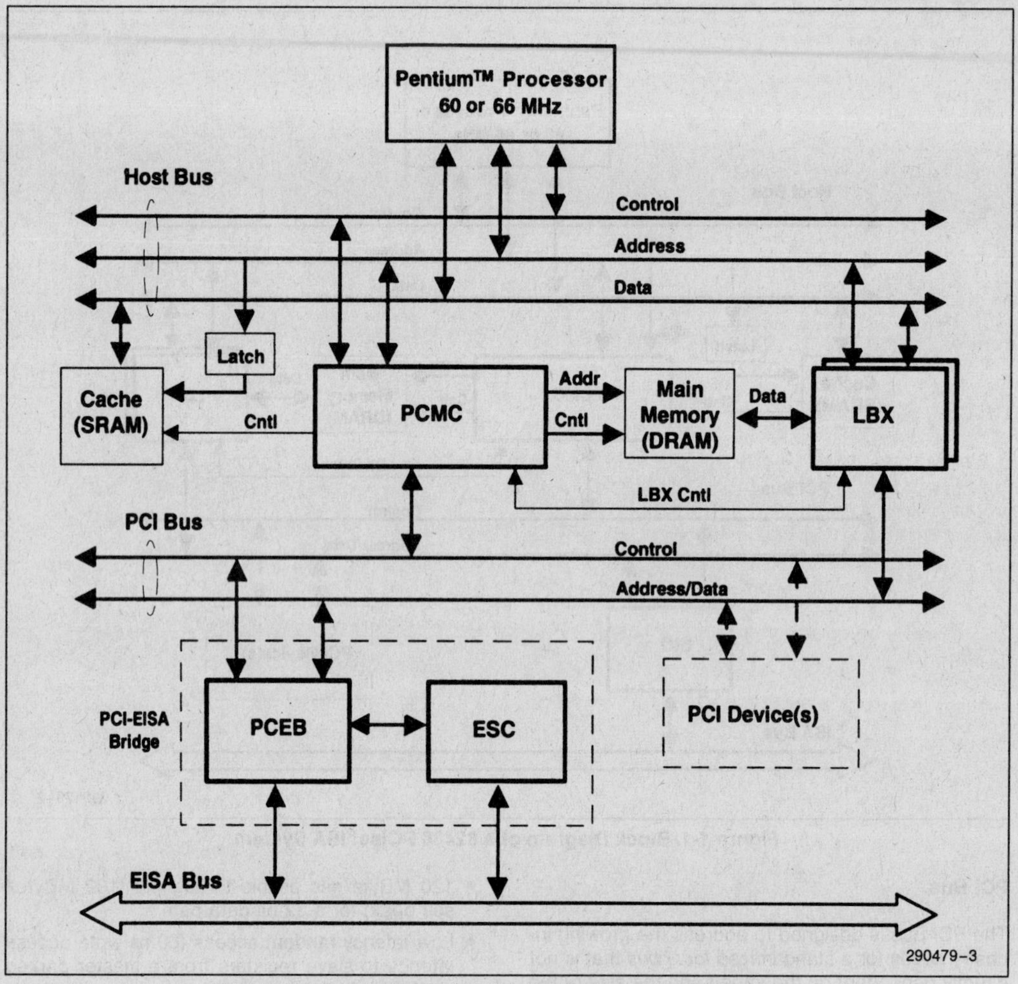

Figure 1-2. Block Diagram of the 82430 PCIset EISA System

ISA Bus

Figure 1-1 represents a system using the ISA Bus as the second level I/O bus. It allows personal computer platforms built around the PCI as a primary I/O bus to leverage the large ISA product base. The ISA Bus has 24-bit addressing and a 16-bit data path.

EISA Bus

Figure 1-2 represents a system using the EISA Bus as the second level I/O bus. It allows personal computer platforms built around the PCI as a primary I/O bus to leverage the large EISA/ISA product base. Combinations of PCI and EISA buses, both of which can be used to provide expansion functions, will satisfy even the most demanding applications.

Along with compatibility for 16-bit and 8-bit ISA hardware and software, the EISA bus provides the following key features:

- 32-bit addressing and 32-bit data path
- 33 MByte/sec bus bandwidth
- Multiple bus master support through efficient arbitration
- Support for autoconfiguration

1.1.2 BUS BRIDGES

Host/PCI Bridge Chip Set (PCMC and LBX). The PCMC and LBX enhance the system performance by allowing for concurrency between the Host CPU Bus and PCI Bus, giving each greater bus throughput and decreased bus latency. The LBX contains posted write buffers for Host-to-PCI, Host-to-main memory, and PCI-to-main memory transfers. The LBX also contains read prefetch buffers for Host reads of PCI, and PCI reads of main memory. There are two LBXs per system. The LBXs are controlled by commands from the PCMC. The PCMC/LBX Host/PCI bridge chip set is covered in more detail in Section 1.2, PCMC Overview.

PCI-EISA Bridge Chip Set (PCEB and ESC): The PCEB provides the master/slave functions on both the PCI Bus and the EISA Bus. Functioning as a bridge between the PCI and EISA buses, the PCEB provides the address and data paths, bus controls, and bus protocol translation for PCI-to-EISA and EISA-to-PCI transfers. Extensive data buffering in both directions increase system performance by maximizing PCI and EISA Bus efficiency and allowing concurrency on the two buses. The PCEB's buffer management mechanism ensures data coherency. The PCEB integrates central bus control functions including a programmable bus arbiter for the PCI Bus and EISA data swap buffers for the EISA Bus. Integrated system functions include PCI parity generation, system error reporting, and programmable PCI and EISA memory and I/O address space mapping and decoding. The PCEB also contains a BIOS Timer that can be used to implement timing loops. The PCEB is intended to be used with the ESC to provide an EISA I/O subsystem interface.

The ESC integrates the common I/O functions found in today's EISA-based PCs. The ESC incorporates the logic for an EISA Bus controller, enhanced seven channel DMA controller with scatter-gather support, EISA arbitration, 14 level interrupt controller, five programmable timer/counters, and non-maskable-interrupt (NMI) control. The ESC also integrates support logic to decode peripheral devices (e.g., the flash BIOS, real time clock, keyboard/mouse controller, floppy controller, two serial ports, one parallel port, and IDE hard disk drive).

PCI/ISA Bridge (SIO): The SIO component provides the bridge between the PCI Bus and the ISA Bus. The SIO also integrates many of the common I/O functions found in today's ISA-based PCs. The SIO incorporates the logic for a PCI interface (master and slave), ISA interface (master and slave), enhanced seven channel DMA controller that supports fast DMA transfers and scatter-gather, data buffers to isolate the PCI Bus from the ISA Bus and to enhance performance, PCI and ISA arbitration, 14 level interrupt controller, a 16-bit BIOS timer, three programmable timer/counters, and non-maskable-interrupt (NMI) control logic. The SIO also provides decode for peripheral devices (e.g., the flash BIOS, real time clock, keyboard/mouse controller, floppy controller, two serial ports, one parallel port, and IDE hard disk drive).

1.2 PCMC Overview

The PCMC (along with the LBX) provides three basic functions: a cache controller, a main memory DRAM controller, and a Host/PCI bridge. This section provides an overview of these functions. Note that, in this document, operational descriptions assume that the PCMC and LBX components are used together.

1.2.1 CACHE OPERATIONS

The PCMC provides the control for a second level cache memory array implemented with either standard asynchronous SRAMs or synchronous burst SRAMs. The data memory array is external to the PCMC and located on the Host address/data bus. Since the Pentium microprocessor contains an internal cache, there can be two separate caches in a Host subsystem. The cache inside the Pentium microprocessor is referred to as the first level cache (also called primary or L1 cache). A detailed description of the first level cache is beyond the scope of this document. The PCMC cache control circuitry and associated external memory array is referred to as the second level cache (also called secondary or L2 cache). The second level cache is unified, meaning that both CPU data and instructions are stored in the cache. The PCMC supports both write-through and write-back caching policies.

The optional second level cache memory array can be either 256 KBytes or 512 KBytes in size. The cache is direct-mapped and is organized as either 8K or 16K cache lines of 32 bytes per line.

In addition to the cache data RAM, the second level cache contains a 4K set of cache tags that are internal to the PCMC. Each tag contains an address that is associated with the corresponding data sector (2 lines for a 256 KByte cache and 4 lines for a 512 KByte cache) and two status bits for each line in the sector.

During a main memory read or write operation, the PCMC first searches the cache. If the addressed code or data is in the cache, the cycle is serviced by the cache. If the addressed code or data is not in the cache, the cycle is forwarded to main memory.

The PCMC second level cache can be configured for either a write-through or write-back caching policies. For these two policies, the cache operation is determined by the CPU read or write cycle as follows:

Write cycle: If the caching policy is write-through and the write cycle hits in the cache, both the cache and main memory are updated. Upon a cache miss, only main memory is updated. A new cache line is not allocated on a write miss.

If the caching policy is write-back and the write cycle hits in the cache, only the cache is updated; main memory is not affected. Upon a cache miss, only main memory is updated. A new cache line is not allocated on a write miss.

Read cycle: Upon a cache hit, the cache operation is the same for both write-through and write-back. In this case, data is transferred from the cache to the CPU. Main memory is not accessed.

If the read cycle causes a cache miss, the line containing the requested data is transferred from the main memory to the cache and to the CPU. In the case of a write-back cache, if the cache line fill is to a sector containing one or more modified lines, the modified lines are written back to main memory and the new line is brought into the cache. For a modified line write-back operation, the PCMC transfers the modified cache lines to main memory via a write buffer in the LBX. Before writing the last modified line from the write buffer to main memory, the PCMC updates the first and second level caches with the new line, allowing the CPU access to the requested data with minimum latency.

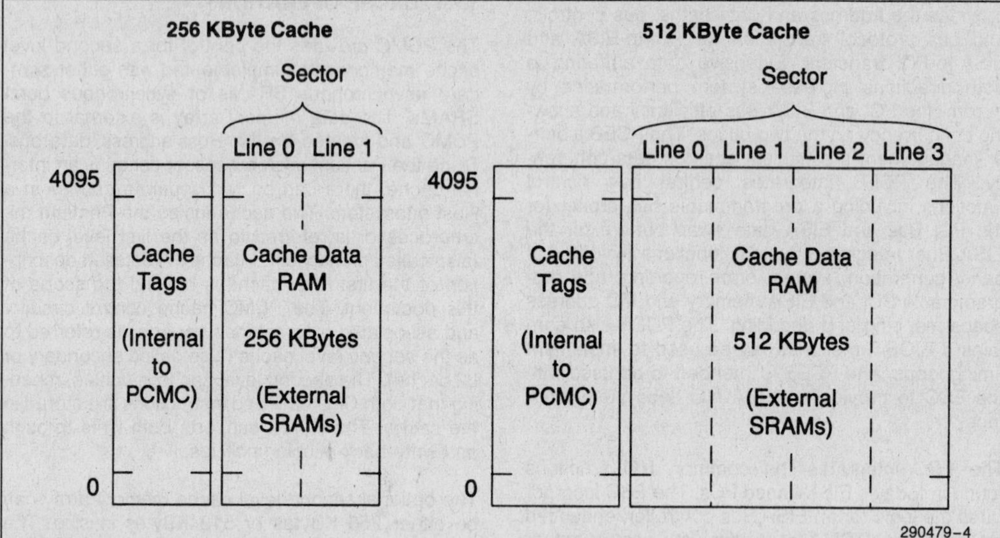

NOTES:

1. Cache tags contain an address tag and two status bits for each line in the associated sector.
2. For the 256 KByte cache, A[17:6] select a particular tag and associated data sector. Host address line A5 selects a particular line within a sector.
3. For a 512 KByte cache, A[18:7] selects a particular tag and associated data sector. Host address lines A[6:5] select a particular line within a sector.

Figure 1-3. Second Level Cache Organization

1.2.1.1 Cache Consistency

The snoop mechanism in the PCMC ensures data consistency between cache (both first level and second level) and main memory. The PCMC monitors PCI master accesses to main memory and when needed, initiates an inquire (snoop) cycle to the first and second level caches. The snoop mechanism guarantees that consistent data is always delivered to both the host CPU and PCI masters.

1.2.2 ADDRESS/DATA PATHS

Address paths between the CPU/cache and PCI and data paths between the CPU/cache, PCI, and main memory are supplied by two LBX components. The LBX is a companion component to the PCMC. Together, they form a Host/PCI bridge. The PCMC (via the PCMC/LBX interface signals), controls the address and data flow through the LBX's. Refer to the LBX data sheet for more details on the address and data paths.

Data is transferred to and from the PCMC internal registers via the PCMC address lines. When the Host CPU performs a write operation, the data is sent to the LBXs. When the PCMC decodes the cycle as an access to one of its internal registers, it asserts AHOLD to the CPU and instructs the LBX to copy the data onto the Host address lines. When the PCMC decodes a Host read as an access to a PCMC internal register, it asserts AHOLD to the CPU. The PCMC then places the register data on its address lines and instructs the LBX's to copy the data on the Host address bus to the Host data bus. When the register data is on the Host data bus, the PCMC negates AHOLD and completes the cycle.

1.2.2.1 Read/Write Buffers

The LBX provides an interface for the CPU address and data buses, PCI Address/Data bus, and the main memory DRAM data bus. There are three posted write buffers and two read-prefetch buffers implemented in the LBXs to increase performance and to maximize concurrency. The buffers are:

- CPU-to-Main Memory Posted Write Buffer (4 Qwords)
- CPU-to-PCI Posted Write Buffer (4 Dwords)
- PCI-to-Main Memory Posted Write Buffer (2 x 4 Dwords)
- PCI-to-Main Memory Read Prefetch Buffer (line buffer, 4 Qwords)
- CPU-to-PCI Read Prefetch Buffer (4 Dword FIFO)

Refer to the LBX data sheet for details on the operation of these buffers.

1.2.3 HOST/PCI BRIDGE OPERATIONS

The PCMC permits the Host CPU to access devices on the PCI Bus. These accesses can be to PCI I/O space, PCI memory space, or PCI configuration space.

As a PCI device, the PCMC can be either a master initiating a PCI Bus operation or a target responding to a PCI Bus operation. The PCMC is a PCI Bus master for Host-to-PCI cycles and a target for PCI-to-main memory transfers. Note that the PCMC does not permit peripherals to be located on the Host Bus. CPU I/O cycles, other than to PCMC internal registers, are forwarded to the PCI Bus and PCI Bus accesses to the Host Bus are not supported.

When the CPU initiates a bus cycle to a PCI device, the PCMC becomes a PCI Bus master and translates the CPU cycle into the appropriate PCI Bus cycle. The Host/PCI Posted write buffer in the LBXs permits the CPU to complete CPU-to-PCI Dword memory writes in three CPU clocks (1 wait state), even if the PCI Bus is currently busy. The posted data is written to the PCI device when the PCI Bus is available.

When a PCI Bus master initiates a main memory access, the PCMC (and LBXs) become the target of the PCI Bus cycle and responds to the read/write access. During PCI-to-main memory accesses, the PCMC automatically performs cache snoop operations on the Host Bus, when needed, to maintain data consistency.

As a PCI device, the PCMC contains all of the required PCI configuration registers. The Host CPU reads and writes these registers as described in Section 3.0, Register Description.

1.2.4 DRAM MEMORY OPERATIONS

The PCMC contains a DRAM controller that supports CPU and PCI master accesses to main memory. The PCMC DRAM interface supplies the control signals and address lines and the LBXs supply the data path.

The memory array is 64-bits wide and ranges in size from 2 MBytes to 192 MBytes. The array can be implemented with either single-sided or double-sided SIMMs. DRAM SIMM sizes of 256K x 36, 1M x 36 and 4M x 36 are supported. DRAM parity is generated for main memory writes and checked for memory reads.

To provide optimum support for the various cache configurations, and the resultant mix of bus cycles, the system designer can select between 0-active RAS# and 1-active RAS# modes. These modes affect the behavior of the RAS# signal following either Host-to-main memory cycles or PCI-to-main memory cycles.

The PCMC also provides programmable memory and cacheability attributes on 14 memory segments of various sizes in the ISA compatibility range (512 KByte to 1 MByte address range). Access rights to these memory segments from the PCI Bus are controlled by the expansion bus bridge.

The PCMC permits a gap to be created in main memory within the 1 MByte to 16 MByte address range, accommodating ISA devices which are mapped into this range (e.g., ISA LAN card or an ISA frame buffer).

2.0 SIGNAL DESCRIPTIONS

This section provides a detailed description of each signal. The signals are arranged in functional groups according to their associated interface. The states of all of the signals during hard reset are provided in Section 8.0, System Clocking and Reset.

The "#" symbol at the end of a signal name indicates that the active, or asserted state occurs when the signal is at a low voltage level. When "#" is not present after the signal name, the signal is asserted when at the high voltage level.

The terms assertion and negation are used extensively. This is done to avoid confusion when working with a mixture of "active-low" and "active-high" signals. The term **assert**, or **assertion** indicates that a signal is active, independent of whether that level is represented by a high or low voltage. The term **negate**, or **negation** indicates that a signal is inactive.

The following notations are used to describe the signal type.

in Input is a standard input-only signal.

out Totem pole output is a standard active driver.

o/d Open drain

t/s Tri-State is a bi-directional, tri-state input/output pin.

s/t/s Sustained tri-state is an active low tri-state signal owned and driven by one and only one agent at a time. The agent that drives a s/t/s pin low must drive it high for at least one clock before letting it float. A new agent can not start driving a s/t/s signal any sooner than one clock after the previous owner tri-states it. An external pull-up is required to sustain the inactive state until another agent drives it and must be provided by the central resource.

2.1 Host Interface

<table>
<tr><th>Signal</th><th>Type</th><th>Description</th></tr>
<tr><td>A[31:0]</td><td>t/s</td><td>ADDRESS BUS: A[31:0] are the address lines of the Host Bus. A[31:3] are connected to the CPU A[31:3] lines and to the LBXs. A[2:0] are only connected to the LBXs. A[18:7] are connected to an external cache SRAM address latch. Along with the byte enable signals, the A[31:3] lines define the physical area of memory or I/O being accessed.

During CPU cycles, the A[31:3] lines are inputs to the PCMC. They are used for address decoding and second level cache tag lookup sequences. Also during CPU cycles, A[2:0] are outputs and are generated from BE[7:0]#.

During inquire cycles, A[31:5] are inputs from the LBXs to the CPU and the PCMC to snoop the first and the second level cache tags, respectively. In response to a Flush or Flush Acknowledge Special Cycle, the PCMC asserts AHOLD and drives the addresses of the second level cache lines to be written back to main memory on A[18:7].

During CPU to PCI configuration cycles, the PCMC drives A[31:0] with the PCI configuration space address that is internally derived from the CPU physical I/O address. All PCMC internal configuration registers are accessed via A[31:0]. During CPU reads from PCMC internal configuration registers, the PCMC asserts AHOLD and drives the contents of the addressed register on A[31:0]. The PCMC then signals the LBXs to copy this value from the address lines onto the host data lines. During writes to PCMC internal configuration registers, the PCMC asserts AHOLD and signals the LBXs to copy the write data onto the A[31:0] lines.

Finally, when in deturbo mode, the PCMC periodically asserts AHOLD and then drives A[31:0] to valid logic levels to keep these lines from floating for an extended period of time.

A[31:28] provide hardware strapping options at powerup. For more details on strapping options, refer to Section 8.0, System Clocking and Reset.</td></tr>
<tr><td>BE[7:0]#</td><td>in</td><td>BYTE ENABLES: The byte enables indicate which byte lanes on the CPU data bus carry valid data during the current bus cycle. In the case of cacheable reads, all 8 bytes of data are driven to the Pentium CPU, regardless of the state of the byte enables. The byte enable signals indicate the type of special cycle when M/IO# = D/C# = 0 and W/R# = 1. During special cycles, only one byte enable is asserted by the CPU. The following table depicts the special cycle types and their byte enable encodings:

Special Cycle Type — Asserted Byte Enable
Shutdown — BE0#
Flush — BE1#
Halt — BE2#
Write Back — BE3#
Flush Acknowledge — BE4#
Branch Trace Message — BE5#

When the PCMC decodes a shutdown special cycle, it asserts AHOLD, drives 000 . . . 000 (the PCI shutdown special cycle encoding) on the A[31:0] lines and signals the LBXs to latch the host address bus. The PCMC then drives a special cycle on PCI, signaling the LBXs to drive the latched address (00 . . . 00) on the AD[31:0] lines during the data phase. The PCMC then asserts INIT for 16 HCLKs.

In response to flush and flush acknowledge special cycles, the PCMC internally inspects the Valid and Modified bits for each of the Second Level Cache Sectors. If a line is both valid and modified, the PCMC drives the cache address of the line on the A[18:7] and CAA/CAB[6:3] lines and writes the line back to main memory. The valid and modified bits are both reset to 0. All valid and unmodifed lines are simply marked invalid.</td></tr>
</table>

1

2.1 Host Interface (Continued)

Signal	Type	Description
BE[7:0]#	in	**BYTE ENABLES:** (Continued) In response to a write back special cycle, the PCMC simply returns BRDY# to the CPU. The second level cache will be written back to main memory in response to the following flush special cycle. In response to a halt special cycle, the PCMC asserts AHOLD, drives 000 . . . 001 (the PCI halt special cycle encoding) on the A[31:0] lines, and signals the LBXs to latch the host address bus. The PCMC then drives a special cycle on PCI, signaling the LBXs to drive the latched address (00 . . . 01) on the AD[31:0] lines during the data phase.
ADS#	in	**ADDRESS STROBE:** The Pentium microprocessor asserts ADS# to indicate that a new bus cycle is beginning. ADS# is driven active in the same clock as the address, byte enable, and cycle definition signals. The PCMC ignores a floating low ADS# that may occur when BOFF# is asserted as the CPU is asserting ADS#.
BRDY#	out	**BURST READY:** BRDY# indicates that the system has responded in one of three ways: 1) valid data has been placed on the Pentium CPU data pins in response to a read, 2) CPU write data has been accepted by the system, or 3) the system has responded to a special cycle.
NA#	out	**NEXT ADDRESS:** The PCMC asserts NA# for one clock when the memory system is ready to accept a new address from the CPU, even if all data transfers for the current cycle have not completed. The CPU may drive out a pending cycle two clocks after NA# is asserted and has the ability to support up to two outstanding bus cycles.
AHOLD	out	**ADDRESS HOLD:** The PCMC asserts AHOLD to force the Pentium microprocessor to stop driving the address bus so that either the PCMC or LBXs can drive the bus. During PCI master cycles, AHOLD is asserted to allow the LBXs to drive a snoop address onto the address bus. If the PCI master locks main memory, AHOLD remains asserted until the PCI master locked sequence is complete and the PCI master negates PLOCK#. AHOLD is asserted during all accesses to PCMC internal configuration registers to allow configuration register accesses to occur over the A[31:0] lines. When in deturbo mode, the PCMC periodically asserts AHOLD to prevent the processor from initiating bus cycles in order to emulate a slower system. The duration of AHOLD assertion in deturbo mode is controlled by the Deturbo Frequency Control Register (offset 51h). When PWROK is negated, the PCMC asserts AHOLD to allow the strapping options on A[31:28] to be read. For more details on strapping options, see Section 8.0, System Clocking and Reset Logic.
EADS#	out	**EXTERNAL ADDRESS STROBE:** The PCMC asserts EADS# to indicate to the Pentium microprocessor that a valid snoop address has been driven onto the CPU address lines to perform an inquire cycle. During PCI master cycles, the PCMC signals the LBXs to drive a snoop address onto the host address lines and then asserts EADS# to initate a snoop cycle to the primary cache.
INV	out	**INVALIDATE:** The INV signal specifies the final state (invalid or shared) that a first level cache line transitions to in the event of a cache line hit during a snoop cycle. When snooping the caches during a PCI master write, the PCMC asserts INV with EADS#. When INV is asserted with EADS#, an inquire hit results in the line being invalidated. When snooping the caches during a PCI master read, the PCMC does not assert INV with EADS#. In this case, an inquire cycle hit results in a line transitioning to the shared state.
BOFF#	out	**BACKOFF:** The PCMC asserts BOFF# to force the Pentium CPU to abort all outstanding bus cycles that have not been completed and float its bus in the next clock. The PCMC uses this signal to force the CPU to re-order a write-back due to a snoop cycle around a currently outstanding bus cycle. The CPU remains in bus hold until BOFF# is negated.

1

2.1 Host Interface (Continued)

Signal	Type	Description
HITM#	in	**HIT MODIFIED:** The Pentium processor asserts HITM# to inform the PCMC that the current inquire cycle hit a modified line. HITM# is asserted by the Pentium microprocessor two clocks after the assertion of EADS# if the inquire cycle hits a modified line in the primary cache.
M/IO# D/C# W/R#	in	**BUS CYCLE DEFINITION (MEMORY/INPUT-OUTPUT, DATA/CONTROL, WRITE/READ):** M/IO, D/C# and W/R# define Host Bus cycles as shown in the table below. **M/IO# D/C# W/R# Bus Cycle Type** Low Low Low Interrupt Acknowledge Low Low High Special Cycle Low High Low I/O Read Low High High I/O Write High Low Low Code Read High Low High Reserved High High Low Memory Read High High High Memory Write Interrupt acknowledge cycles are forwarded to the PCI Bus as PCI interrupt acknowledge cycles (i.e. C/BE[3:0]# = 0000 during the address phase). All I/O cycles and any memory cycles that are not directed to memory controlled by the PCMC DRAM controller are forwarded to PCI. The Pentium microprocessor generates six different types of special cycles. The special cycle type is encoded on the BE[7:0]# lines.
HLOCK#	in	**HOST BUS LOCK:** The Pentium processor asserts HLOCK# to indicate the current bus cycle is locked. HLOCK# is asserted in the first clock of the first locked bus cycle and is negated after the BRDY# is returned for the last locked bus cycle. The Pentium microprocessor guarantees HLOCK# to be negated for at least one clock between back-to-back locked operations. When a CPU locked cycle is directed to main memory, the PCMC guarantees that once the locked operation begins in main memory, the CPU has exclusive access to main memory (i.e., PCI master accesses to main memory will not be initiated until the CPU locked operation completes). When a CPU locked cycle is directed to PCI, the PCMC arbitrates for PLOCK# (PCI LOCK#) before initiating the cycle on PCI, except when the cycle is to the memory range defined by the Frame Buffer Range Register and the No Lock Requests bit in that register is set to 1.
CACHE#	in	**CACHEABILITY:** The Pentium processor asserts CACHE# to indicate the internal cacheability of a read cycle or that a write cycle is a burst write-back cycle. If the CPU drives CACHE# inactive during a read cycle, the returned data is not cached, regardless of the state of KEN#. The CPU asserts CACHE# for cacheable data reads, cacheable code fetches, and cache line write-backs. CACHE# is driven along with the cycle definition pins.
KEN#	out	**CACHE ENABLE:** The PCMC asserts KEN# to indicate to the CPU that the current cycle is cacheable. KEN# is asserted for all accesses to memory ranges 0 KBytes–512 KBytes and 1024 KBytes to the top of main memory controlled by the PCMC when the Primary Cache Enable bit is set to 1, except in the following case: KEN# is not asserted for accesses to the top 64 KByte of main memory controlled by the PCMC when the SMRAM Enable bit in the DRAM Control Register (Offset 57h) is set to 1. KEN# is asserted for any CPU access within the range of 512 KBytes–1024 KBytes if the corresponding Cache Enable bit in the PAM[6:0] Registers (offsets 59h–5Fh) is set to 1 and the area is not write protected. If the area is write protected and cacheable, KEN# is asserted for code read cycles, but is not asserted during data read cycles. When the Pentium processor indicates that the current read cycle can be cached by asserting CACHE# and the PCMC responds with KEN#, the cycle is converted into a burst cache line fill. The CPU samples KEN# with the first of either BRDY# or NA#.

2.1 Host Interface (Continued)

Signal	Type	Description
SMIACT#	in	**SYSTEM MANAGEMENT INTERRUPT ACTIVE:** The Pentium processor asserts SMIACT# to indicate that the processor is operating in System Management Mode (SMM). When the SMRAM Enable bit in the DRAM Control Register (offset 57h) is set to 1, the PCMC allows CPU accesses to SMRAM as permitted by the SMRAM Space Register at configuration space offset 72h.
PEN#	out	**PARITY ENABLE:** The PEN# signal, along with the MCE bit in CR4 of the Pentium microprocessor, determines whether a machine check exception will be taken by the CPU as a result of a parity error on a read cycle. The PCMC asserts PEN# during DRAM read cycles if the MCHK on DRAM/L2 Cache Data Parity Error Enable bit in the Error Command Register (offset 70h) is set to 1. The PCMC asserts PEN# during CPU second level cache read cycles if the MCHK on DRAM/L2 Cache Data Parity Error Enable and the L2 Cache Parity Enable bits in the Error Command Register (offset 70h) are both set to 1.
PCHK#	in	**DATA PARITY CHECK:** PCHK# is sampled by the PCMC to detect parity errors on CPU read cycles from main memory if the Parity Error Mask Enable bit in the DRAM Control Register (offset 57h) is reset to 0. PCHK# is sampled by the PCMC to detect parity errors on CPU read cycles from the second level cache if the L2 Cache Parity Enable bit in the Error Command Register (offset 70h) is set to 1. If incorrect parity was detected on a data read, the PCHK# signal is asserted by the Pentium microprocessor two clocks after BRDY# is returned. PCHK# is asserted for one clock for each clock in which a parity error was detected.

2.2 DRAM Interface

Signal	Type	Description
RAS[5:0]#	out	**ROW ADDRESS STROBES:** The RAS[5:0]# signals are used to latch the row address on the MA[10:0] lines into the DRAMs. Each RAS[5:0]# signal corresponds to one DRAM row. The PCMC supports up to 6 rows in the DRAM array. Each row is eight bytes wide. These signals drive the RAS# lines of the DRAM array directly, without external buffers.
CAS[7:0]#	out	**COLUMN ADDRESS STROBES:** The CAS[7:0]# signals are used to latch the column address on the MA[10:0] lines into the DRAMs. Each CAS[7:0]# signal corresponds to one byte of the eight byte-wide array. These signals drive the CAS# lines of the DRAM array directly, without external buffers. In a minimum configuration, each CAS[7:0]# line only has one SIMM load, while the maximum configuration has 6 SIMM loads.
WE#	out	**DRAM WRITE ENABLE:** WE# is asserted during both CPU and PCI master writes to main memory. During burst writes to main memory, WE# is asserted before the first assertion of CAS[7:0]# and is negated with the last CAS[7:0]#. The WE# signal is externally buffered to drive the WE# inputs on the DRAMs.
MA[10:0]	out	**DRAM MULTIPLEXED ADDRESS:** MA[10:0] provide the row and column address to the DRAM array. The MA[10:0] lines are externally buffered to drive the multiplexed address lines of the DRAM array.

2.3 Cache Interface

Signal	Type	Description
CALE	out	**CACHE ADDRESS LATCH ENABLE:** CALE controls the external latch between the host address lines and the cache address lines. CALE is asserted to open the external latch, allowing the host address lines to propagate to the cache address lines. CALE is negated to latch the cache address lines.
CADS[1:0]#, CR/W[1:0]#	out	These pins serve one of two purposes depending on the type of SRAMs used for the second level cache. **CACHE ADDRESS STROBE:** CADS[1:0]# are used with burst SRAMs. When asserted, CADS[1:0]# cause the burst SRAMs to latch the cache address on the rising edge of HCLK. CADS[1:0]# are glitch-free synchronous signals. CADS[1:0]# functionality is provided when the SRAM type bit in the Secondary Cache Control register is set to 1. Two copies of this signal are provided for timing reasons only. **CACHE READ/WRITE:** CR/W[1:0]# provide read/write control to the second level cache when using asynchronous dual-byte select SRAMs. This functionality is provided when the SRAM Type and Cache Byte Control bits in the Secondary Cache Control register are both reset to 0. The two copies of this signal are always driven to the same logic level.
CADV[1:0]#	out	**CACHE ADVANCE:** CADV[1:0]# are used with burst SRAMs to advance the internal two bit address counter inside the SRAMs to the next address of the burst sequence. Two copies of this signal are provided for timing reasons only. The two copies are always driven to the same logic level.
CAA[6:3] CAB[6:3]	out	**CACHE ADDRESS [6:3]:** CAA[6:3] and CAB[6:3] are connected to address lines A[3:0] on the second level cache SRAMs. CAA[4:3] and CAB[4:3] are used with standard SRAMs to advance through the burst sequence. CAA[6:5] and CAB[6:5] are used during second level cache write-back cycles to address the modified lines within the addressed sector. Two copies of these signals are provided for timing reasons only. The two copies are always driven to the same logic level.
COE[1:0]#	out	**CACHE OUTPUT ENABLE:** COE[1:0]# are asserted when data is to be read from the second level cache and are negated at all other times. Two copies of this signal are provided for timing reasons only. The two copies are always driven to the same logic level.
CWE[7:0]#, CBS[7:0]#	out	These pins serve one of two purposes depending on the type of SRAMs used for the second level cache. **CACHE WRITE ENABLES:** CWE[7:0]# are asserted to write data to the second level cache SRAMs on a byte-by-byte basis. CWE7# controls the most significant byte while CWE0# controls the least significant byte. These pins act as Cache Write Enables (CWE[7:0]#) when using burst SRAMs (SRAM Type bit in SCC register is set to 1) or when using asynchronous SRAMs (SRAM Type bit in SCC is reset to 0) and the Cache Byte Control bit in the SCC register is set to 1. **CACHE BYTE SELECTS:** The CBS[7:0]# lines provide byte control to the secondary cache when using dual-byte select asynchronous SRAMs. These pins act as Cache Byte Select lines when the SRAM Type and Cache Byte Control bits in the SCC register are both reset to 0.

2.4 PCI Interface

<table>
<tr><th>Signal</th><th>Type</th><th>Description</th></tr>
<tr><td>C/BE[3:0]#</td><td>t/s</td><td>PCI BUS COMMAND AND BYTE ENABLES: C/BE[3:0]# are driven by the current bus master during the address phase of a PCI cycle to define the PCI command, and during the data phase as the PCI byte enables. The PCI commands indicate the current cycle type, and the PCI byte enables indicate which byte lanes carry meaningful data. C/BE[3:0]# are outputs of the PCMC during CPU cycles that are directed to PCI. C/BE[3:0]# are inputs when the PCMC acts as a slave. The command encodings and types are listed below.

C/BE[3:0]# — Command
0000 — Interrupt Acknowledge
0001 — Special Cycle
0010 — I/O Read
0011 — I/O Write
0100 — Reserved
0101 — Reserved
0110 — Memory Read
0111 — Memory Write
1000 — Reserved
1001 — Reserved
1010 — Configuration Read
1011 — Configuration Write
1100 — Memory Read Multiple
1101 — Reserved
1110 — Memory Read Line
1111 — Memory Write and Invalidate</td></tr>
<tr><td>FRAME#</td><td>s/t/s</td><td>CYCLE FRAME: FRAME# is driven by the current bus master to indicate the beginning and duration of an access. FRAME# is asserted to indicate that a bus transaction is beginning. While FRAME# is asserted, data transfers continue. When FRAME# is negated, the transaction is in the final data phase. FRAME# is an output of the PCMC during CPU cycles which are directed to PCI. FRAME# is an input to the PCMC when the PCMC acts as a slave.</td></tr>
<tr><td>IRDY#</td><td>s/t/s</td><td>INITIATOR READY: The assertion of IRDY# indicates the current bus master's ability to complete the current data phase. IRDY# works in conjunction with TRDY# to indicate when data has been transferred. On PCI, data is transferred on each clock that both IRDY# and TRDY# are asserted. During read cycles, IRDY# is used to indicate that the master is prepared to accept data. During write cycles, IRDY# is used to indicate that the master has driven valid data on the AD[31:0] lines. Wait states are inserted until both IRDY# and TRDY# are asserted together. IRDY# is an output of the PCMC when the PCMC is the PCI master. IRDY# is an input to the PCMC when the PCMC acts as a slave.</td></tr>
<tr><td>TRDY#</td><td>s/t/s</td><td>TARGET READY: TRDY# indicates the target device's ability to complete the current data phase of the transaction. It is used in conjunction with IRDY#. A data phase is completed on each clock that TRDY# and IRDY# are both sampled asserted. During read cycles, TRDY# indicates that valid data is present on AD[31:0] lines. During write cycles, TRDY# indicates the target is prepared to accept data. Wait states are inserted on the bus until both IRDY# and TRDY# are asserted together. TRDY# is an output of the PCMC when the PCMC is the PCI slave. TRDY# is an input to the PCMC when the PCMC is a master.</td></tr>
</table>

2.4 PCI Interface (Continued)

Signal	Type	Description
DEVSEL#	s/t/s	**DEVICE SELECT:** When asserted, DEVSEL# indicates that the driving device has decoded its address as the target of the current access. DEVSEL# is an output of the PCMC when PCMC is a PCI slave and is derived from the MEMCS# input. MEMCS# is generated by the expansion bus bridge as a decode to the main memory address space. During CPU to PCI cycles, DEVSEL# is an input. It is used to determine if any device has responded to the current bus cycle, and to detect a target abort cycle. Master-abort termination results if no subtractive decode agent exists in the system, and no one asserts DEVSEL# within a programmed number of clocks.
STOP#	s/t/s	**STOP:** STOP# indicates that the current target is requesting the master to stop the current transaction. This signal is used in conjunction with DEVSEL# to indicate disconnect, target-abort, and retry cycles. When the PCMC is acting as a master on PCI, if STOP# is sampled active on a rising edge of PCLKIN, FRAME# is negated within a maximum of 3 clock cycles. STOP# may be asserted by the PCMC in three cases. If a PCI master attempts to access main memory when another PCI master has locked main memory, the PCMC asserts STOP# to signal retry. The PCMC detects this condition when sampling FRAME# and LOCK# both active during an address phase. When a PCI master is reading from main memory, the PCMC asserts STOP# when the burst cycle is about to cross a cache line boundary. When a PCI master is writing to main memory, the PCMC asserts STOP# upon filling either of the two PCI-to-main memory posted write buffers. Once asserted, STOP# remains asserted until FRAME# is negated.
PLOCK#	s/t/s	**PCI LOCK:** PLOCK# is used to indicate an atomic operation that may require multiple transactions to complete. PCI provides a mechanism referred to as "resource lock" in which only the target of the PCI transaction is locked. The assertion of GNT# on PCI does not guarantee control of the PLOCK# signal. Control of PLOCK# is obtained under its own protocol. When the PCMC is the PCI slave, PLOCK# is sampled as an input on the rising edge of PCLKIN when FRAME# is sampled active. If PLOCK# is sampled asserted, the PCMC enters into a locked state and remains in the locked state until PLOCK# is sampled negated on a following rising edge of PCLKIN, when FRAME# is sampled asserted.
REQ#	out	**REQUEST:** The PCMC asserts REQ# to indicate to the PCI bus arbiter that the PCMC is requesting use of the PCI Bus in response to a CPU cycle directed to PCI.
GNT#	in	**GRANT:** When asserted, GNT# indicates that access to the PCI Bus has been granted to the PCMC by the PCI Bus arbiter.
MEMCS#	in	**MAIN MEMORY CHIP SELECT:** When asserted, MEMCS# indicates to the PCMC that a PCI master cycle is targeting main memory. MEMCS# is generated by the expansion bus bridge. MEMCS# is sampled by the PCMC on the rising edge of PCLKIN on the first and second cycle after FRAME# has been asserted.
FLSHREQ#	in	**FLUSH REQUEST:** When asserted, FLSHREQ# instructs the PCMC to flush the CPU-to-PCI posted write buffer in the LBXs and to disable further posting to this buffer as long as FLSHREQ# remains active. The PCMC acknowledges completion of the CPU-to-PCI write buffer flush operation by asserting MEMACK#. MEMACK# remains asserted until FLSHREQ# is negated. FLSHREQ# is driven by the expansion bus bridge and is used to avoid deadlock conditions on the PCI Bus.
MEMREQ#	in	**MEMORY REQUEST:** When asserted, MEMREQ# instructs the PCMC to flush the CPU-to-PCI and CPU-to-main memory posted write buffers and to disable posting in these buffers as long as MEMREQ# is active. The PCMC acknowledges completion of the flush operations by asserting MEMACK#. MEMACK# remains asserted until MEMREQ# is negated. MEMREQ# is driven by the expansion bus bridge.

2.4 PCI Interface (Continued)

Signal	Type	Description
MEMACK#	out	**MEMORY ACKNOWLEDGE:** When asserted, MEMACK# indicates the completion of the operations requested by an active FLSHREQ# and/or MEMREQ#.
PAR	t/s	**PARITY:** PAR is an even parity bit across the AD[31:0] and C/BE[3:0]# lines. Parity is generated on all PCI transactions. As a master, the PCMC generates even parity on CPU writes to PCI, based on the PPOUT[1:0] inputs from the LBXs. During CPU read cycles from PCI, the PCMC checks parity by checking the value sampled on the PAR input with the PPOUT[1:0] inputs from the LBXs. As a slave, the PCMC generates even parity on PAR, based on the PPOUT[1:0] inputs during PCI master reads from main memory. During PCI master writes to main memory, the PCMC checks parity by checking the value sampled on PAR with the PPOUT[1:0] inputs.
PERR#	s/t/s	**PARITY ERROR:** PERR# may be pulsed by any agent that detects a parity error during an address phase, or by the master or the selected target during any data phase in which the AD lines are inputs. The PERR# signal is enabled when the PERR# on Receiving Data Parity Error bit in the Error Command Register (offset 70h) and the Parity Error Enable bit in the PCI Command Register (offset 04h) are both set to 1. When enabled, CPU-to-PCI write data is checked for parity errors by sampling the PERR# signal two PCI clocks after data is driven. Also, when enabled, PERR# is asserted by the PCMC when it detects a data parity error on CPU read data from PCI and PCI master write data to main memory. PERR# is neither sampled nor driven by the PCMC when either the PERR# on Receiving Data Parity Error bit in the Error Command Register or the Parity Error Enable bit in the PCI Command Register is reset to 0.
SERR#	o/d	**SYSTEM ERROR:** SERR# may be pulsed by any agent for reporting errors other than parity. SERR# is asserted by the PCMC whenever a serious system error (not necessarily a PCI error) occurs. The intent is to have the PCI central agent (for example, the expansion bus bridge) assert NMI to the processor. Control over the SERR# signal is provided via the Error Command Register (offset 70h) when the Parity Error Enable bit in the PCI Command Register (offset 04h) is set to 1. When the SERR# DRAM/L2 Cache Data Parity Error bit is set to 1, SERR# is asserted upon detecting a parity error on CPU read cycles from DRAM. If the L2 Cache Parity bit is also set to 1, SERR# will be asserted upon detecting a parity error on CPU read cycles from the second level cache. The Pentium microprocessor indicates these parity errors to the PCMC via the PCHK# signal. When the SERR# on PCI Address Parity Error bit is set to 1, the PCMC asserts SERR# if a parity error is detected during the address phase of a PCI master cycle. When the SERR# on Received PCI Data Parity bit is set to 1, the PCMC asserts SERR# if a parity error is detected on PCI during a CPU read from PCI. During CPU to PCI write cycles, when the SERR# on Transmitted PCI Data Parity Error bit is set to 1, the PCMC asserts SERR# in response to sampling PERR# active. When the SERR# on Received Target Abort bit is set to 1, the PCMC asserts SERR# when the PCMC receives a target abort on a PCMC initiated PCI cycle. If the Parity Error Enable bit in the PCI Command Register is reset to 0, SERR# is disabled and is never asserted by the PCMC.

2.5 LBX Interface

Signal	Type	Description
HIG[4:0]	out	**HOST INTERFACE GROUP:** HIG[4:0] are outputs of the PCMC used to control the LBX HA (Host Address) and HD (Host Data) buses. Commands driven on HIG[4:0] cause the host data and/or address lines to be either driven or latched by the LBXs. See the 82433LX (LBX) Local Bus Accelerator Data Sheet for a listing of the HIG[4:0] commands.
MIG[2:0]	out	**MEMORY INTERFACE GROUP:** MIG[2:0] are outputs of the PCMC used to control the LBX MD (Memory Data) bus. Commands driven on the MIG[2:0] lines cause the memory data lines to be either driven or latched by the LBXs. See the 82433LX (LBX) Local Bus Accelerator Data Sheet for a listing of the MIG[2:0] commands.
MDLE	out	**MEMORY DATA LATCH ENABLE:** During CPU reads from main memory, MDLE is used to control the latching of memory read data on the CPU data bus. MDLE is negated as CAS[7:0]# are negated to close the latch between the memory data bus and the host data bus. During CPU reads from main memory, the PCMC closes the memory data to host data latch in the LBXs as BRDY# is asserted and opens the latch after the CPU has sampled the data.
PIG[3:0]	out	**PCI INTERFACE GROUP:** PIG[3:0] are outputs of the PCMC used to control the LBX AD (PCI Address/Data) bus. Commands driven on the PIG[3:0] lines cause the AD lines to be either driven or latched. See the 82433LX (LBX) Local Bus Accelerator Data Sheet for a listing of the PIG[3:0] commands.
DRVPCI	out	**DRIVE PCI:** DRVPCI acts as an output enable for the LBX AD lines. When sampled asserted, the LBXs begin driving the PCI AD lines. When negated, the AD lines on the LBXs are tri-stated. The LBX AD lines are tri-stated asynchronously from the falling edge of DRVPCI.
EOL	in	**END OF LINE:** EOL is asserted by the low order LBX when a PCI master read or write transaction is about to overrun a cache line boundary. EOL has an internal pull-up resistor inside the PCMC. The low order LBX EOL signal connects to this PCMC input. The high order LBX EOL signal is connected to ground through an external pull-down resistor.
PPOUT[1:0]	in	**PCI PARITY OUT:** These signals reflect the parity of the 32 AD lines driven from or latched in the LBXs, depending on the command driven on PIG[3:0]. The PPOUT0 pin has a weak internal pull-down resistor. The PPOUT1 pin has a weak internal pull-up resistor.

2.6 Reset and Clock

Signal	Type	Description
HCLKOSC	in	**HOST CLOCK OSCILLATOR:** The HCLKOSC input is driven externally by either a 60 MHz or 66.667 MHz crystal oscillator. The PCMC generates six copies of HCLK from HCLKOSC (HCLKA–HCLKF). During power-up, HCLKOSC must stabilize for 1 ms before PWROK is asserted. If an external clock driver is used to clock the CPU, PCMC, LBXs and second level cache SRAMs instead of the HCLKA–HCLKF outputs, HCLKOSC must be tied either high or low.
HCLKA–HCLKF	out	**HOST CLOCK OUTPUTS:** HCLKA–HCLKF are six low skew copies of the host clock. These outputs eliminate the need for an external low skew clock driver. One of these outputs drives both the CPU and the PCMC. Thus, the clock skew between the CPU and PCMC is kept lower than the skew between the PCMC and other components. Another HCLK output drives both of the LBXs. The remaining four are used to drive the second level cache SRAMs.

1

2.6 Reset and Clock (Continued)

Signal	Type	Description
HCLKIN	in	**HOST CLOCK INPUT:** All timing on the host, DRAM and second level cache interfaces is based on HCLKIN. If an external clock driver is used to clock the CPU, PCMC, LBXs and second level cache SRAMs, the externally generated clock must be connected to HCLKIN. During power-up HCLKIN must stabilize for 1 ms before PWROK is asserted.
CPURST	out	**CPU HARD RESET:** The CPURST pin is asserted in response to one of two conditions. First, during power-up the PCMC asserts CPURST when PWROK is negated. When PWROK is asserted, the PCMC first ensures that it has been initialized before negating CPURST. CPURST is also asserted when the System Hard Reset Enable bit in the Turbo-Reset Control Register (I/O address 0CF9h) is set to 1 and the Reset CPU bit toggles from 0 to 1. CPURST is driven synchronously to the rising edge of HCLKIN.
INIT	out	**INITIALIZATION:** INIT is asserted in response to any one of three conditions. When the System Hard Reset Enable bit in the Turbo-Reset Control Register is reset to 0 and the Reset CPU bit toggles from 0 to 1, the PCMC initiates a soft reset by asserting INIT. The PCMC also initiates a soft reset by asserting INIT in response to a shutdown special cycle. In both cases, INIT is asserted for a minimum of 16 Host clocks. If the BIST Enable bit and the System Hard Reset Enable bit in the Turbo-Reset Control Register are both set to 1, and the Reset CPU bit toggles from 0 to 1, the PCMC will assert INIT along with CPURST and will negate INIT one clock after negating CPURST. This will force the CPU to execute a Built In Self Test (BIST) prior to the start of program execution.
PWROK	in	**POWER OK:** When asserted, PWROK is an indication to the PCMC that power and HCLKIN have stabilized for at least 1 ms. PWROK can be driven asynchronously. When PWROK is negated, the PCMC asserts both CPURST and PCIRST#. When PWROK is driven high, the PCMC ensures that it is initialized before negating CPURST and PCIRST#.
PCLKOUT	out	**PCI CLOCK OUTPUT:** PCLKOUT is internally generated by a Phase Locked Loop (PLL) that divides the frequency of HCLKIN by 2. This output must be buffered externally to generate multiple copies of the PCI Clock. One of the copies must be connected to the PCLKIN pin.
PCLKIN	in	**PCI CLOCK INPUT:** An internal PLL locks PCLKIN in phase with HCLKIN. All timing on the PCMC PCI interface is referenced to the PCLKIN input. All output signals on the PCI interface are driven from PCLKIN rising edges and all input signals on the PCI interface are sampled on PCLKIN rising edges.
PCIRST#	out	**PCI RESET:** PCIRST# is asserted to initiate hard reset on PCI. PCIRST# is asserted in response to one of two conditions. First, during power-up the PCMC asserts PCIRST# when PWROK is negated. When PWROK is asserted the PCMC will first ensure that it has been initialized before negating PCIRST#. PCIRST# is also asserted when the System Hard Reset Enable bit in the Turbo/Reset Control Register is set to 1 and the Reset CPU bit toggles from 0 to 1. PCIRST# is driven asynchronously.
TESTEN	in	**TEST ENABLE:** TESTEN must be tied low for normal system operation.

3.0 REGISTER DESCRIPTION

The PCMC contains two sets of software accessible registers. These registers are accessed via the Host CPU I/O address space. The I/O mapped register set contains two control registers that reside in the CPU I/O space and are used to reset the CPU, enable/disable the CPU deturbo mode, and enable/disable access to the PCI configuration space (see Section 3.1, I/O Mapped Registers). The PCMC also contains a set of configuration registers that reside in PCI configuration space and are used to specify PCI configuration, DRAM configuration, cache configuration, operating parameters and optional system features (see Section 3.2, PCI Configuration Space). The PCMC internal registers (both I/O Mapped and Configuration registers) are only accessible by the Host CPU and cannot be accessed by PCI masters. The registers can be accessed as byte, word (16-bit), or Dword (32-bit) quantities. All multi-byte numeric fields use "little-endian" ordering (i.e., lower addresses contain the least significant parts of the field).

Some of the PCMC registers described in this section contain reserved bits. These bits are labeled "R". Software must deal correctly with fields that are reserved. On reads, software must use appropriate masks to extract the defined bits and not rely on reserved bits being any particular value. On writes, software must ensure that the values of reserved bit positions are preserved. That is, the values of reserved bit positions must first be read, merged with the new values for other bit positions and then written back.

In addition to reserved bits within a register, the PCMC contains address locations in the PCI configuration space that are marked "Reserved" (Table 3-1). The PCMC responds to accesses to these address locations by completing the Host cycle. When a reserved register location is read, 0000h is returned. Writes to reserved registers have no affect on the PCMC.

Upon receiving a hard reset via the PWROK signal, the PCMC sets its internal configuration registers to predetermined default states. The default state represents the minimum functionality feature set required to successfully bring up the system. Hence, it does not represent the optimal system configuration. It is the responsibility of the system initialization software (usually BIOS) to properly determine the DRAM configurations, cache configuration, operating parameters and optional system features that are applicable, and to program the PCMC registers accordingly.

3.1 I/O Mapped Registers

The PCMC contains three registers that reside in the CPU I/O address space the Configuration Space Enable (CSE) Register, the Turbo-Reset Control (TRC) Register and the Forward Address Register. These registers can not reside in PCI configuration space because of the special functions they perform. The Configuration Space Enable (CSE) Register enables/disables the configuration space and, hence, can not reside in that space. The TRC Register enables/disables deturbo mode which effectively slows the processor to accommodate software programs that rely on the slow speed of PC/XT systems to time certain events. The Forward Address Register determines to which of the possible hierarchical PCI buses a cycle is directed.

3.1.1 CSE—CONFIGURATION SPACE ENABLE REGISTER

I/O Address: 0CF8h

Default Value: 00h

Attribute: Read/Write

Size: 8 Bits

CSE is an 8-bit read/write register used to enable/disable configuration space access and to access specific functions within a PCI agent. The PCMC, as a Host/PCI Bridge, supports multi-function devices on the PCI Bus. The function number permits individual configuration spaces for up to eight functions within an agent. The register is located in the CPU I/O address space. The CSE Register fields are shown in Figure 3-1 and described in Table 3-1.

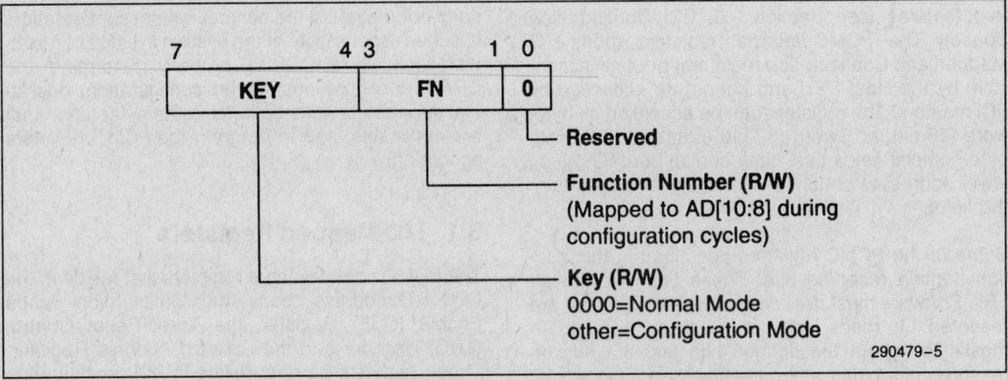

Figure 3-1. Configuration Space Enable Register

Table 3-1. Configuration Space Enable Register

Bit	Description
7:4	**KEY**: Configuration space is mapped into I/O space by writing to the Configuration Space Enable (CSE) Register. The KEY field selects between normal mode and configuration mode as follows: **KEY** **Description** 0000 Normal mode. In this mode, the PCMC translates CPU I/O read/write cycles in the C000h–CFFFh address range to PCI I/O cycles. 1000 Configuration mode. In this mode, the PCMC translates CPU I/O read/write cycles in the C000h–CFFFh address range to PCI configuration read/write cycles.
3:1	**FN (FUNCTION NUMBER):** For multi-function devices, this field selects a particular function within a PCI device. During a configuration cycle, bits [3:1] become part of the PCI Bus address and correspond to AD[10:8].
0	**RESERVED**

3.1.2 TRC—TURBO-RESET CONTROL REGISTER

I/O Address: 0CF9h
Default Value: 00h
Attribute: Read/Write
Size: 8 Bits

The TRC Register is an 8-bit read/write register that selects turbo/deturbo mode of the CPU, initiates PCI Bus and CPU reset cycles, and initiates the CPU Built In Self Test (BIST). TRC is located in CPU I/O address space.

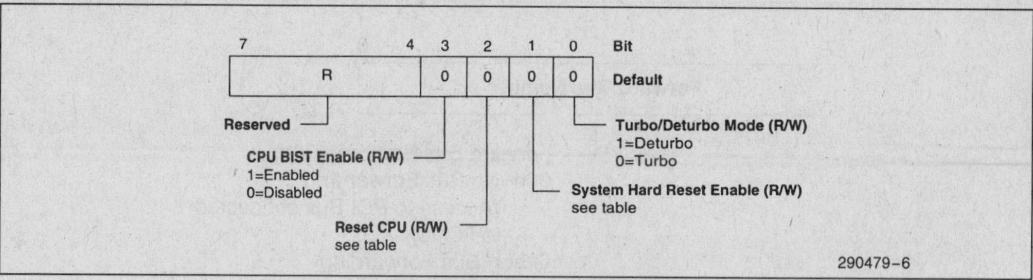

Figure 3-2. Turbo-Reset Register

Table 3-2. Turbo-Reset Register

Bit	Description
7:3	**Reserved.**
2	**Reset CPU (RCPU):** RCPU is used to initiate a hard reset or soft reset to the CPU. During a hard reset, the PCMC asserts CPURST and PCIRST#. The PCMC initiates a hard reset when this register is programmed for a hard reset or when the PWROK signal is asserted. During a soft reset, the PCMC asserts INIT. The PCMC initiates a soft reset when this register is programmed for a soft reset and in response to a shutdown special cycle. This bit is used in conjunction with bit 3 and bit 1 of this register. Bit 3 and bit 1 must be set up prior to writing a 1 to this register. Thus, two write operations are required to initiate a reset using this bit. The first write operation programs bit 3 and bit 1 to the appropriate state while setting this bit to 0. The second write operation keeps the bit 3 and bit 1 at their programmed state (1 or 0) while setting this bit to a 1. When RCPU transitions from a 0 to a 1, a hard reset is initiated if bit 1 = 1 and a soft reset is initiated if bit 1 = 0. In addition, if bit 3 = 1 during a hard reset, the CPU Built In Self Test is invoked.
1	**System Hard Reset Enable (SHRE):** This bit is used in conjunction with bit 2 of this register to initiate either a hard or soft reset. When SHRE = 1, the PCMC initiates a hard reset to the CPU when bit 2 transitions from 0 to 1. When SHRE = 0, the PCMC initiates a soft reset when bit 2 transitions from 0 to 1.
0	**Deturbo Mode (DM):** This bit enables and disables deturbo mode. When DM = 1, the PCMC is in the deturbo mode. In this mode, the PCMC periodically asserts the AHOLD signal to slow down the effective speed of the CPU. The AHOLD duty cycle is programmable through the Deturbo Frequency Control (DFC) Register. When DM = 0, the deturbo mode is disabled. Deturbo mode can be used to maintain backward compatibility with older software packages that rely on the operating speed of older processors. For accurate speed emulation, caching should be disabled. If caching is disabled during runtime, the following steps should be performed to make sure that modified lines have been flushed from the cache to main memory before entering deturbo mode. Disable the primary cache via the PCE bit in the HCS Register. This prevents the KEN# signal from being asserted, which prevents any further first and second level cache line fills. At this point, software executes the WBINVD instruction to flush the caches, and then sets DM to 1. When exiting the deturbo mode, the system software must first set DM to 0, then enable first and second level caching by writing to the HCS Register.

3.1.3 FORW—FORWARD REGISTER

I/O Address: 0CFAh

Default Value: 00h

Attribute: Read/Write

Size: 8 Bits

This 8-bit register specifies which PCI Bus configuration space is enabled in a multiple PCI Bus configuration. The default value for the FORW Register enables the configuration space of the PCI Bus connected to the PCMC. The register field is shown in Figure 3-3 and described in Table 3-3.

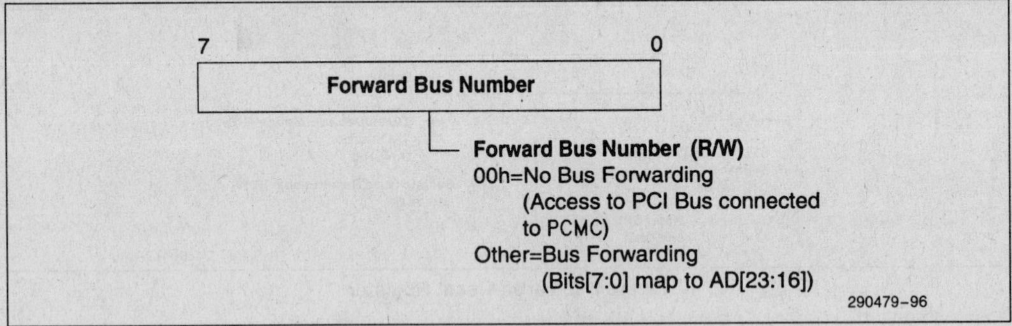

Figure 3-3. Forward Register

Table 3-3. Forward Register

Bit	Description
7:0	**FORWARD BUS NUMBER:** When this register is set to 00h, the configuration space of the PCI Bus connected to the PCMC is enabled and the PCMC initiates a type 0 configuration cycle. If the value of this register is not 00h, the PCMC initiates a type 1 configuration cycle to forward the cycle (via one or more PCI/PCI Bridges) to the PCI Bus specified by the contents of this register. For non-zero values, bits [7:0] are mapped to AD[23:16], respectively. The default value for this register is 00h.

3.2 PCI Configuration Space Mapped Registers

The PCI Bus defines a slot based "configuration space" that allows each device to contain up to 256 8-bit configuration registers. The PCI specification defines two bus cycles to access the PCI configuration space—**Configuration Read** and **Configuration Write**. While memory and I/O spaces are supported by the Pentium microprocessor, configuration space is not supported. The PCMC provides the mechanism that allows the Host CPU to access the PCI configuration space. The bus cycles used to access PCMC internal configuration registers are described in Section 7.0, PCI Interface.

3.2.1 HOST CPU I/O SPACE TO PCI CONFIGURATION SPACE TRANSLATION

The PCI specification defines two bus cycles to access the PCI configuration space: **Configuration Read** and **Configuration Write**. However, today's CPUs do not generate these bus cycles. Therefore, Host/PCI bridges (e.g., the PCMC) must translate either memory or I/O read/write cycles of certain address ranges into PCI configuration cycles.

The PCMC translates CPU I/O read/write cycles to the C000h-CFFFh address range into PCI configuration read/write cycles. A brief description of the translation map is provided in the following paragraphs.

When PCI configuration space is enabled through the CSE Register, all I/O read/write cycles to the C000h–CFFFh address range of the I/O space are translated to PCI configuration read/write cycles. There are two types of configuration cycles (type 0 and type 1) that differ by the type of address mapping used to translate the Host I/O cycle to a PCI configuration cycle. Type 0 cycles access the configuration space of the PCI Bus that is connected to the PCMC. Type 1 cycles are used in multiple PCI Bus systems to access the configuration space of PCI Buses that are not directly connected to the PCMC. The value programmed into the PCMC's Forward Register determines whether the PCMC generates a type 0 or type 1 configuration cycle.

In a multiple PCI Bus system each bus is assigned a bus number. The bus number for the PCI Bus connected to the PCMC is hardwired to 0. The PCMC uses the Forward Register, Bus Number Register, and Subordinate Bus Number Register to forward configuration cycles to the appropriate PCI/PCI Bridge. The PCMC's Forward Register must be programmed with the desired PCI Bus number. During a type 1 configuration cycle, this number is mapped into the address of the PCI Bus configuration cycle. PCI/PCI Bridges compare this number with the values programmed into their Bus Number and Subordinate Bus Number Registers to determine if the configuration cycle is intended for a bus behind that particular bridge. If the bridge accepts the cycle, it may, in turn, generate either a type 0 or type 1 configuration cycle, depending on where the bus is located in its bus hierarchy.

Type 0 Configuration Cycles

For type 0 configuration cycles, AD[1:0] = 00 (Figure 3-4). Host CPU address bits A[7:2] are not translated and become AD[7:2] on the PCI Bus. AD[7:2] select one of the 256 8-bit I/O locations in the PCI configuration space. The FN field (AD[10:8]) is a function number for multi-function devices and corresponds to bits [3:1] of the Configuration Space Enable Register. Host CPU address bits A[11:8] are mapped to an IDSEL input for each of the 16 possible PCI devices. The IDSEL input for each PCI device must be hard-wired to one of the AD[31:16] signals on the PCI Bus. AD16 is reserved for the PCMC. While the PCMC does not have an external IDSEL input pin, this signal is internally hard-wired to AD16. Other devices on the PCI bus should not use AD16.

Type 1 Configuration Cycles

For type 1 configuration cycles, AD[1:0] = 01 (Figure 3-5). AD[10:2] are generated the same as for the type 0 configuration cycle. Host CPU address bits A[11:8] contain the specific device number and are mapped to AD[14:11]. AD[23:16] contain the bus number of the PCI Bus that is to be accessed and corresponds to the Forward Register bits [7:0].

15
12 11
8 7
2
Host Address
A[15:2]
1 1 0 0
1 of 16
Agents
Conf. Reg.
Offset
PCI Address
AD[31:0]
IDSEL# Select
R
FN
Conf. Reg.
Offset
0 0
31
16 15
11 10
8 7
2 1 0
IDSEL# Select
(Only one "1" and
AD16 must be 0)
Reserved
Function Number
(CSE Register Bits [3:1])
Configuration Register Offset
(Selects one of 256 8-bit I/O locations)
290479-7

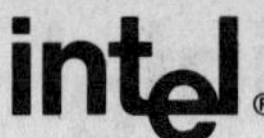

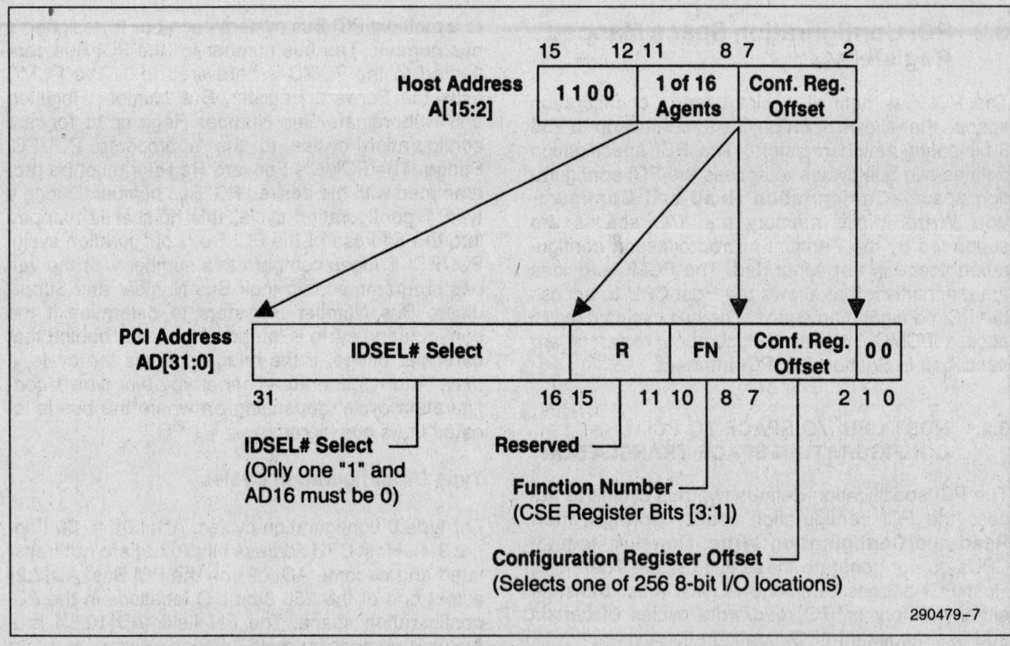

Figure 3-4. Host-to-PCI Address Mapping for a Type 0 Configuration Cycle

15
12 11
8 7
2
Host Address
A[15:2]
1 1 0 0
1 of 16
Agents
Conf. Reg.
Offset
PCI Address
AD[31:0]
R
FBN
0
1 of 16
Agents
FN
Conf. Reg.
Offset
0 1
31
24 23
16 15 14
11 10
8 7
2 1 0
Reserved
Forward Bus Number
(FORW Register Bits [7:0])
Function Number
(CSE Register Bits [3:1])
Configuration Register Offset
(Selects one of 256 8-bit I/O locations)
290479-97

Figure 3-5. Host-to-PCI Address Mapping for a Type 1 Configuration Cycle

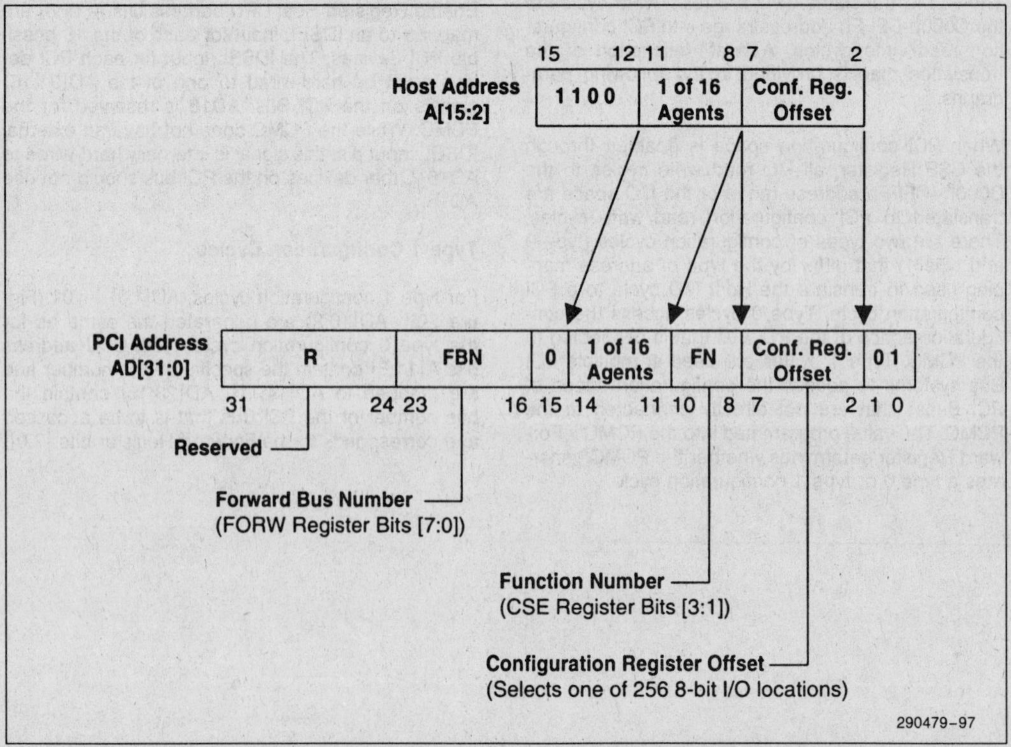

Table 3-4 shows the PCMC configuration space. The following nomenclature is used for access attributes.

RO **Read Only.** If a register is read only, writes to this register have no effect.

R/W **Read/Write.** A register with this attribute can be read and written.

R/WC **Read/Write Clear.** A register bit with this attribute can be read and written. However, a write of a 1 clears (sets to 0) the corresponding bit and a write of a 0 has no effect.

Table 3-4. PCMC Configuration Space

Address Offset	Register Symbol	Register Name	Access
00–01h	VID	Vendor Identification	RO
02–03h	DID	Device Identification	RO
04–05h	PCICMD	Command Register	R/W
06–07h	PCISTS	Status Register	RO, R/WC
08h	RID	Revision Identification	RO
09h	RLPI	Register-Level Programming Interface	RO
0Ah	SCCD	Sub-Class Code	RO
0Bh	BCCD	Base Class Code	RO
0Ch		Reserved	—
0Dh	MLT	Master Latency Timer	R/W
0Eh		Reserved	—
0Fh	BIST	BIST Register	RO
10–4Fh		Reserved	—
50h	HCS	Host CPU Selection	R/W
51h	DFC	Deturbo Frequency Control	R/W
52h	SCC	Secondary Cache Control	R/W
53h	HBC	Host Read/Write Buffer Control	R/W
54h	PBC	PCI Read/Write Buffer Control	R/W
55–56h		Reserved	—
57h	DRAMC	DRAM Control	R/W
58h	DT	DRAM Timing	R/W
59–5Fh	PAM[6:0]	Programmable Attribute Map (7 registers)	R/W
60–65h	DRB[5:0]	DRAM Row Boundary (6 registers)	R/W
66–6Fh		Reserved	—
70h	ERRCMD	Error Command	R/W
71h	ERRSTS	Error Status	R/WC
72h	SMRS	SMRAM Space	R/W
73–77h		Reserved	—
78–79h	MSG	Memory Space Gap	R/W
7C–7Fh	FBR	Frame Buffer Range	R/W
80–FFh		Reserved	—

1

3.2.2 VID—VENDOR IDENTIFICATION REGISTER

Address Offset: 00–01h
Default Value: 8086h
Attribute: Read Only
Size: 16 Bits

The VID Register contains the vendor identification number. This 16-bit register combined with the Device Identification Register uniquely identifies any PCI device. Writes to this register have no effect.

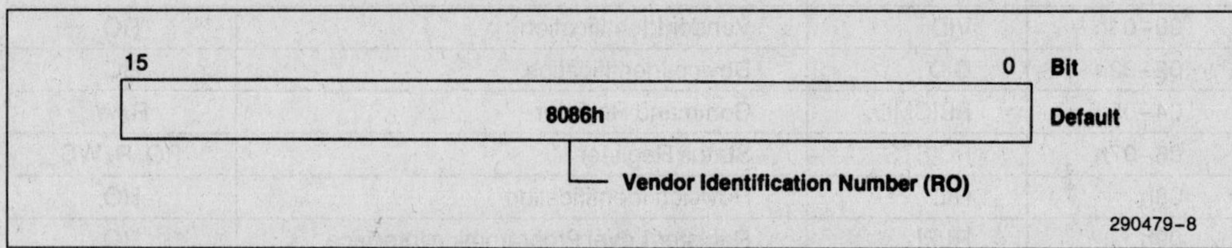

Figure 3-6. Vendor Identification Register

Table 3-5. Vendor Identification Register

Bit	Description
15:0	**Vendor Identification Number:** This is a 16-bit value assigned to Intel.

3.2.3 DID—DEVICE IDENTIFICATION REGISTER

Address Offset: 02–03h
Default Value: 04A3h
Attribute: Read Only
Size: 16 Bits

This 16-bit register combined with the Vendor Identification Register uniquely identifies any PCI device. Writes to this register have no effect.

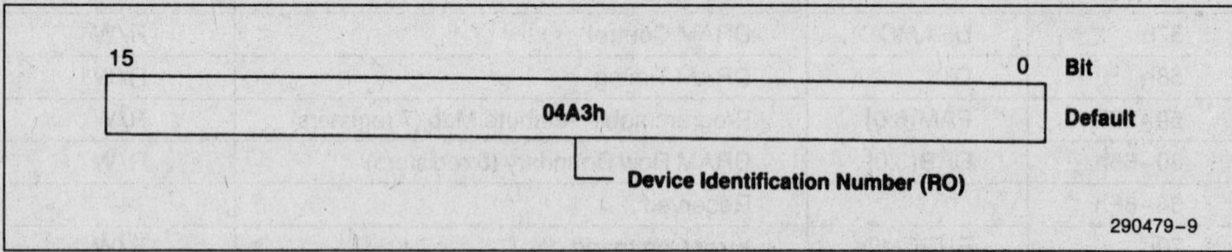

Figure 3-7. Device Identification Register

Table 3-6. Device Identification Register

Bit	Description
15:0	**Device Identification Number:** This is a 16-bit value assigned to the PCMC.

3.2.4 PCICMD—PCI COMMAND REGISTER

Address Offset: 04-05h
Default: 06h
Attribute: Read/Write
Size: 16 Bits

This 16-bit register provides basic control over the PCMC's ability to respond to PCI cycles. The PCICMD Register enables and disables the SERR# signal, the parity error signal (PERR#), PCMC response to PCI special cycles, and enables and disables PCI master accesses to main memory.

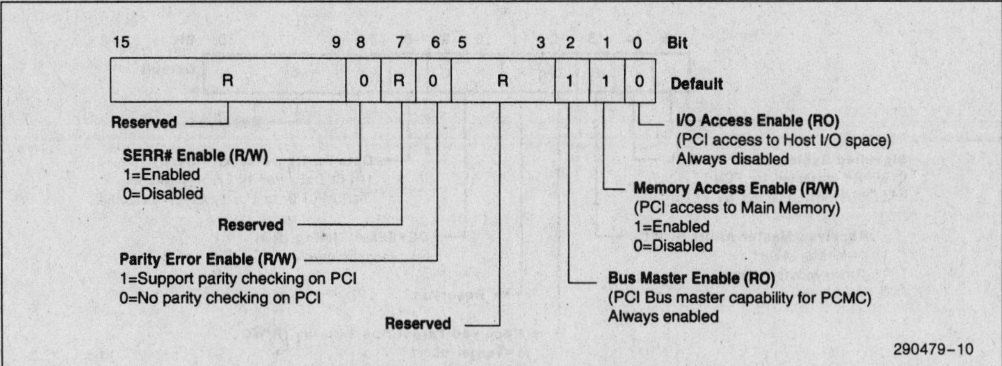

Figure 3-8. PCI Command Register

Table 3-7. PCI Command Register

Bit	Description
15:9	**Reserved.**
8	**SERR# Enable (SERRE):** SERRE enables/disables the SERR# signal. When SERRE = 1 and PERRE = 1, SERR# is asserted if the PCMC detects a PCI Bus address/data parity error, main memory (DRAM) or cache parity error, or a target abort on a PCMC-initiated PCI cycle and the corresponding errors are enabled in the Error-Command Register. When SERRE = 0, SERR# is never asserted.
7	**Reserved.**
6	**Parity Error Enable (PERRE):** PERRE controls the PCMC's response to PCI parity errors. This bit is a master enable for bit 3 of the ERRCMD Register. This bit must be set to 1 to enable bit 8 (SERRE) of this register.
5:3	**Reserved.**
2	**Bus Master Enable (BME):** The PCMC does not support disabling of its bus master capability on the PCI Bus. This bit is always set to 1, permitting the PCMC to function as a PCI Bus master. Writes to this bit position have no affect.
1	**Memory Access Enable (MAE):** This bit enables/disables PCI master access to main memory (DRAM). When MAE = 1, the PCMC permits PCI masters to access main memory if the MEMCS# signal is asserted. When MAE = 0, the PCMC does not respond to main memory accesses (MEMCS# asserted).
0	**I/O Access Enable (IOAE):** The PCMC does not respond to PCI I/O cycles, hence this command is not supported. PCI master access to I/O space on the Host Bus is always disabled.

3.2.5 PCISTS—PCI STATUS REGISTER

Address Offset: 06-07h
Default Value: 40h
Attribute: Read Only, Read/Write Clear
Size: 16 Bits

PCISTS is a 16-bit status register that reports the occurrence of a PCI master abort, PCI target abort, and DRAM or cache parity error. PCISTS also indicates the DEVSEL# timing that has been set by the PCMC hardware. Bits [15:12] are read/write clear and bits [10:9] are read only.

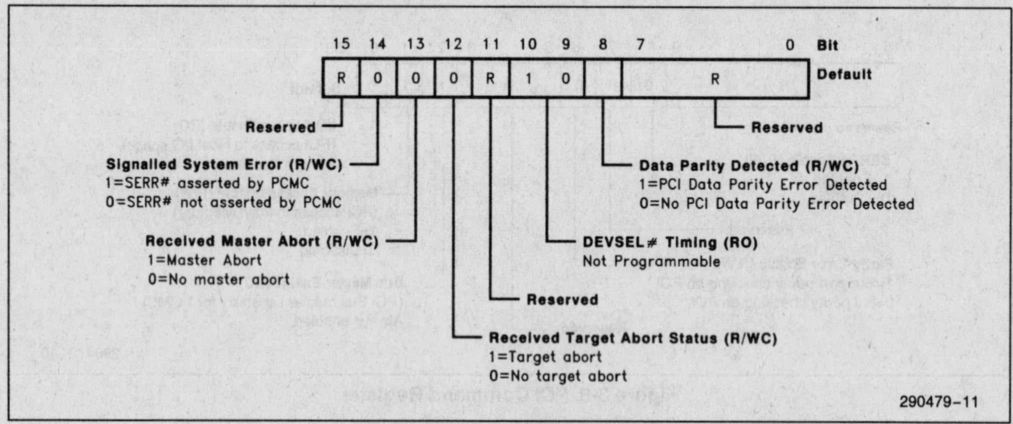

Figure 3-9. PCI Status Register

Table 3-8. PCI Status Register

Bit	Description
15	**Reserved.**
14	**Signaled System Error (SSE):** When the PCMC asserts the SERR# signal, this bit is also set to 1. Software sets SSE to 0 by writing a 1 to this bit.
13	**Received Master Abort Status (RMAS):** When the PCMC terminates a Host-to-PCI transaction (PCMC is a PCI master) which is not a special cycle with a master abort, this bit is set to 1. Software resets this bit to 0 by writing a 1 to it.
12	**Received Target Abort Status (RTAS):** When a PCMC-initiated PCI transaction is terminated with a target abort, RTAS is set to 1. The PCMC also asserts SERR# if the SERR# Target Abort bit in the ERRCMD Register is 1. Software resets RTAS to 0 by writing a 1 to it.
11	**Reserved.**
10:9	**DEVSEL# Timing (DEVT):** This 2-bit field indicates the timing of the DEVSEL# signal when the PCMC responds as a target. The PCI specification defines three allowable timings for assertion of DEVSEL#: 00 = fast, 01 = medium, and 10 = slow (DEVT = 11 is reserved). DEVT indicates the slowest time that a device asserts DEVSEL# for any bus command, except configuration read and write cycles. Note that these two bits determine the slowest time that the PCMC asserts DEVSEL#. However, the PCMC can also assert DEVSEL# in medium time. The PCMC asserts DEVSEL# in response to sampling MEMCS# active. The PCMC samples MEMCS# one and two clocks after FRAME# is sampled asserted. If MEMCS# is sampled active one PCI clock after FRAME# is sampled active, then the PCMC will respond with DEVSEL# in medium time. If MEMCS# is sampled active two PCI clocks after FRAME# is sampled active, then the PCMC will respond with DEVSEL# in slow time.

Table 3-8. PCI Status Register (Continued)

Bit	Description
8	**Data Parity Detected (DPD):** This bit is set when all of the following conditions are met: 1. The PCMC asserted PERR# or sampled PERR# asserted, 2. The PCMC was the bus master for the operation in which the error occurred, and, 3. The parity Error Response bit (Command Register bit 6) is set.
7:0	**Reserved.**

3.2.6 RID—REVISION IDENTIFICATION REGISTER

Address Offset: 08h
Default Value: 03h for A-3 Stepping
Attribute: Read Only
Size: 8 Bits

This register contains the revision number of the PCMC. These bits are read only and writes to this register have no effect. For A-3 Stepping, this value is 03h.

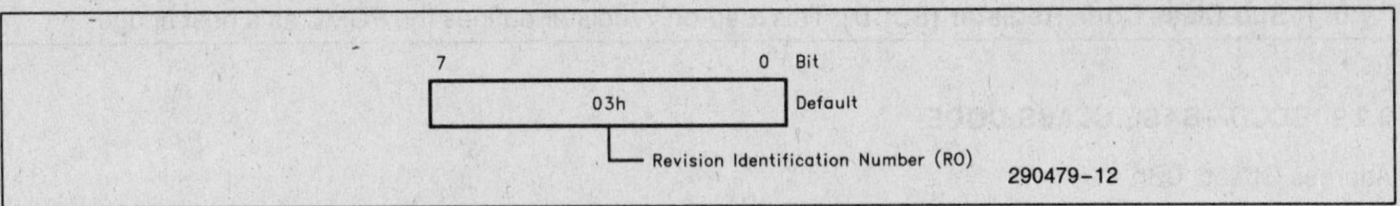

Figure 3-10. Revision Identification Register

Table 3-9. Revision Identification Register

Bit	Description
7:0	**Revision Identification Number:** This is an 8-bit value that indicates the revision identification number for the PCMC.

3.2.7 RLPI—REGISTER-LEVEL PROGRAMMING INTERFACE REGISTER

Address Offset: 09h
Default Value: 00h
Attribute: Read Only
Size: 8 Bits

This read-only register defines the PCMC as having no defined register-level programming interface.

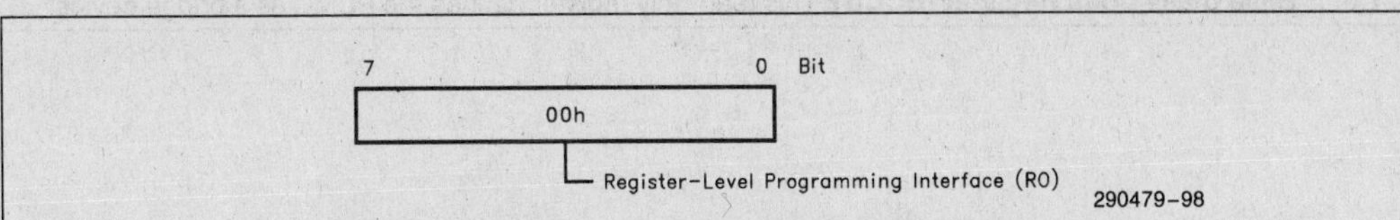

Figure 3-11. Register Level Programming Interface Register

Table 3-10. Register Level Programming Interface Register

Bit	Description
7:0	**Register-Level Programming Interface (RLPI):** This read-only register defines the PCMC as having no defined register-level programming interface.

3.2.8 SCCD—SUB-CLASS CODE REGISTER

Address Offset: 0Ah
Default Value: 00h
Attribute: Read Only
Size: 8 Bits

This read-only register defines the PCMC as a host bridge.

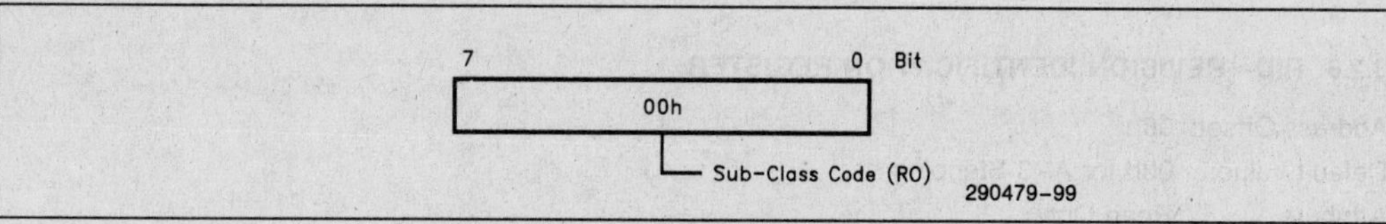

Figure 3-12. Sub-Class Code Register

Table 3-11. Sub-Class Code Register

Bit	Description
7:0	**Sub-Class Code Register (SCCD):** This read-only register defines the PCMC as a host bridge.

3.2.9 BCCD—BASE CLASS CODE

Address Offset: 0Bh
Default Value: 06h
Attribute: Read Only
Size: 8 Bits

This read-only register defines the PCMC as a bridge device.

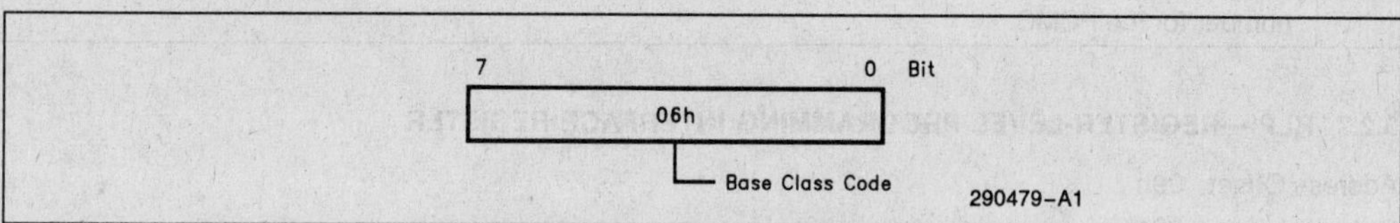

Figure 3-13. Base Class Code Register

Table 3-12. Base Class Code Register

Bit	Description
7:0	**Base Class Code Register (BCCD):** This read-only register defines the PCMC as a bridge device.

3.2.10 MLT—MASTER LATENCY TIMER REGISTER

Address Offset: 0Dh
Default Value: 20h
Attribute: Read/Write
Size: 8 Bits

MLT is an 8-bit register that controls the amount of time the PCMC, as a bus master, can burst data on PCI. MLT is used when the PCMC becomes the PCI Bus master and is cleared and suspended when the PCMC is not asserting FRAME#. When the PCMC asserts FRAME#, the counter is enabled and begins counting. If the PCMC finishes its transaction before the count expires, the MLT count is ignored. If the count expires before the transaction completes the PCMC initiates a transaction termination as soon as its GNT# is removed. The number of clocks programmed in the MLT represents the guaranteed time slice (measured in PCI clocks) allotted to the PCMC, after which it must surrender the bus as soon as its GNT# is taken away. The number of clocks in the Master Latency Timer is the count value field multiplied by 16.

1

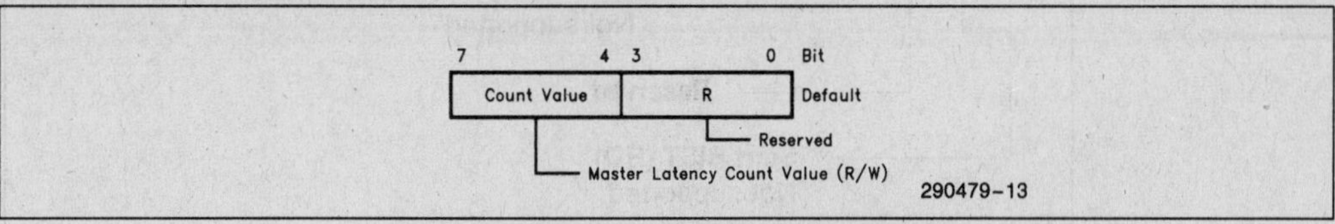

Figure 3-14. Master Latency Timer Register

Table 3-13. Master Latency Timer Register

Bit	Description
7:4	**Master Latency Timer Count Value:** If GNT# is negated during a PCMC-initiated PCI burst cycle, the PCMC limits the duration of the burst cycle to the number of PCI Bus clocks specified by this field, multiplied by 16.
3:0	**Reserved.**

3.2.11 BIST—BIST REGISTER

Offset: 0Fh
Default: 0h
Attribute: Read Only
Size: 8 Bits

The BIST function is not supported by the PCMC. Writes to this register have no affect.

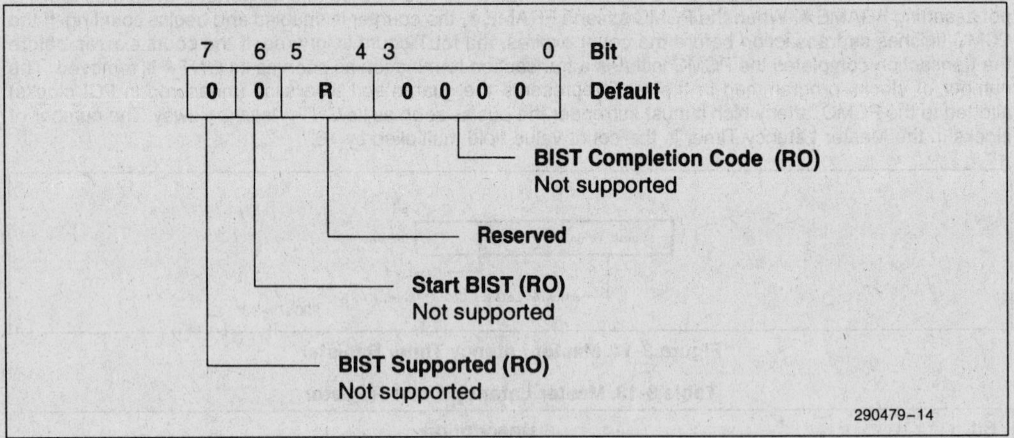

Figure 3-15. BIST Register

Table 3-14. BIST Register

Bit	Description
7	**BIST Supported:** This read only bit is always set to 0, disabling the BIST function. Writes to this bit position have no affect.
6	**Start BIST:** This function is not supported and writes have no affect.
5:4	**Reserved.**
3:0	**Completion Code:** This read only field always returns 0 when read and writes have no affect.

3.2.12 HCS—HOST CPU SELECTION REGISTER

Address Offset: 50h
Default Value: 82h
Attribute: Read/Write
Size 8 Bits

The HCS Register is used to specify the Host CPU type and speed. This 8-bit register is also used to enable and disable the first level cache. A hard reset selects the Pentium microprocessor as the Host CPU Type (bits[7:5] = 100), disables the first level cache, and selects 60 MHz as the Host CPU frequency.

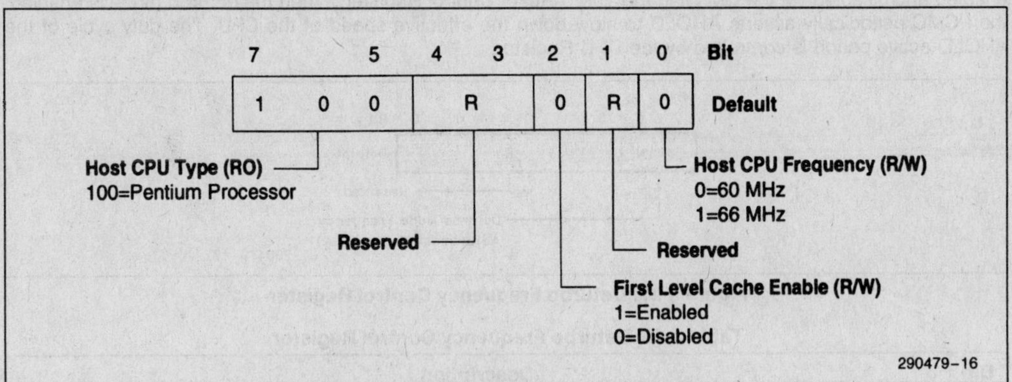

Figure 3-16. Host CPU Selection Register

Table 3-15. Host CPU Selection Register

Bit	Description
7:5	**Host CPU Type (HCT):** This field defines the Host CPU Type. These bits are hardwired to 100, which selects the Pentium microprocessor. All other combinations are reserved.
4:3	**Reserved.**
2	**First Level Cache Enable (FLCE):** FLCE enables and disables the first level cache. When FLCE = 1, the PCMC responds to CPU cycles with KEN# asserted for cacheable memory cycles. When FLCE = 0, KEN# is always negated. This prevents new cache line fills to either the first level or second level caches.
1	**Reserved.**
0	**Host Operating Frequency (HOF):** If this bit is 1, the PCMC supports a 66 MHz CPU. If this bit is reset to 0, the PCMC supports a 60 MHz CPU. The DRAM refresh rate is adjusted according to the frequency selected by this field.

3.2.13 DFC—DETURBO FREQUENCY CONTROL REGISTER

Address Offset: 51h

Default Value: 80h

Attribute: Read/Write

Size: 8 Bits

Some software packages rely on the operating speed of the processor to time certain system events. To maintain backward compatibility with these software packages, the PCMC provides a mechanism to emulate a slower operating speed. This emulation is achieved with the PCMC's deturbo mode. The deturbo mode is enabled and disabled via the DM bit in the Turbo-Reset Control Register. When the deturbo mode is enabled, the PCMC periodically asserts AHOLD to slow down the effective speed of the CPU. The duty cycle of the AHOLD active period is controlled by the DFC Register.

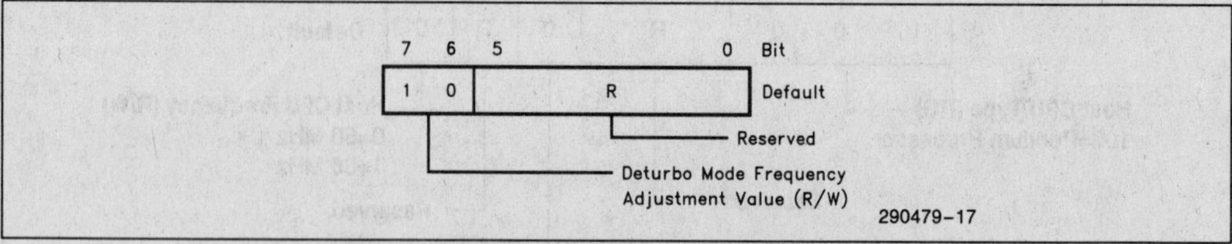

Figure 3-17. Deturbo Frequency Control Register

Table 3-16. Deturbo Frequency Control Register

Bit	Description
7:6	**Deturbo Mode Frequency Adjustment Value:** This 2-bit value effectively defines the duty cycle of the AHOLD signal. The value programmed into this register is compared against a free running 8-bit counter running at ⅛ the CPU clock. When the counter is greater than the value specified in this register, AHOLD is asserted. AHOLD is negated when the counter value is equal to or smaller than the contents of this register. AHOLD is negated when the counter rolls over to 00h. The deturbo emulation speed is directly proportional to the value in this register. Smaller values in this register yield slower deturbo emulation speed. Valid combinations for bits [7:6] are 01, 10, and 11. A value of 00 is reserved and must be written to this field.
5:0	**Reserved.**

3.2.14 SCC—SECONDARY CACHE CONTROL REGISTER

Address Offset: 52h
Default: SSS01*10 S = Strapping option
Attribute: Read/Write
Size: 8 Bits

This 8-bit register defines the secondary cache operations. The SCC register enables and disables the second level cache, adjusts cache size, selects the cache write and allocation policies, and defines the cache SRAM type.

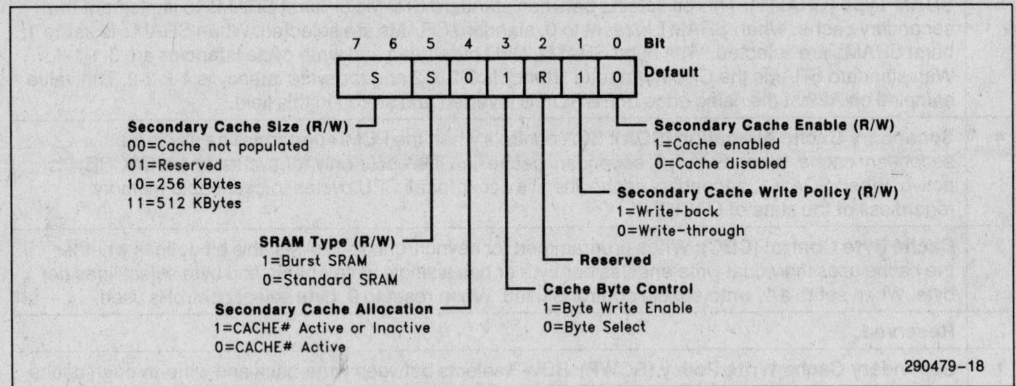

Figure 3-18. Secondary Cache Control Register

Table 3-17. Secondary Cache Control Register

Bit	Description
7:6	**Secondary Cache Size (SCS):** This field defines the size of the second level cache. The values sampled on the A[31:30] lines at the rising edge of PWROK are inverted and stored in this field. **Bits[7:6] Secondary Cache Size** 0 0 Cache not populated 0 1 Reserved 1 0 256 KBytes 1 1 512 KBytes
5	**SRAM Type (SRAMT):** This bit selects between standard SRAMs or burst SRAMs to implement the secondary cache. When SRAMT is reset to 0, standard SRAMs are selected. When SRAMT is set to 1, burst SRAMs are selected. With burst SRAMs, CPU burst read and write cycle latencies are 3-1-1-1. With standard SRAMs the CPU burst read latency is 3-2-2-2 and the write latency is 4-2-2-2. The value sampled on A29 at the rising edge of PWROK is inverted and stored in this field.
4	**Secondary Cache Allocation (SCA):** SCA controls when the PCMC performs line fills in the secondary cache. When SCA=0, secondary cache line fills occur only for cycles where CACHE# is active. When SCA=1, secondary cache line fills occur for all CPU cycles to cacheable memory regardless of the state of CACHE#.
3	**Cache Byte Control (CBC):** When programmed for asynchronous SRAMs, this bit defines whether the cache uses individual write enables per byte or has a single write enable and byte select lines per byte. When set to a 1, write enable control is used. When reset to 0, byte select control is used.
2	**Reserved.**
1	**Secondary Cache Write Policy (SCWP):** SCWP selects between write-back and write-through cache policies for the secondary cache. When SCWP = 0 and the secondary cache is enabled (bit 0 = 1), the secondary cache is configured for write-through mode. When SCWP = 1 and the secondary cache is enabled (bit 0 = 1), the secondary cache is configured for write-back mode.
0	**Secondary Cache Enable (SCE):** SCE enables and disables the secondary cache. When SCE = 1, the secondary cache is enabled. When SCE = 0, the secondary cache is disabled. When the secondary cache is disabled, the PCMC forwards all main memory cycles to the DRAM interface. Note that setting this bit to 0 does not affect existing valid cache lines. If a cache line contains modified data, the data is not written back to memory. Valid lines in the cache remain valid. When the secondary cache is disabled, the CWE[7:0]# lines will remain inactive. COE[1:0]# may still toggle. When system software disables secondary caching through this register during run-time, the software should first flush the second level cache. This process is accomplished by first disabling first level caching via the PCE bit in the HCS Register. This prevents the KEN# signal from being asserted, which disables any further line fills. At this point, software executes the WBINVD instruction to flush the caches. When the instruction completes, bit 0 of this register can be reset to 0, disabling the secondary cache. The first level cache can then be enabled by writing the PCE bit in the HCS Register.

3.2.15 HBC—HOST READ/WRITE BUFFER CONTROL

Offset: 53h

Default: 00h

Attribute: Read/Write

Size: 8 Bits

The HBC Register enables and disables Host-to-main memory and Host-to-PCI posting of write cycles. When posting is enabled, the write buffers in the LBX devices post the data that is destined for either main memory or PCI. This register also permits a CPU-to-main memory read cycle to be performed before any pending posted write data is written to memory.

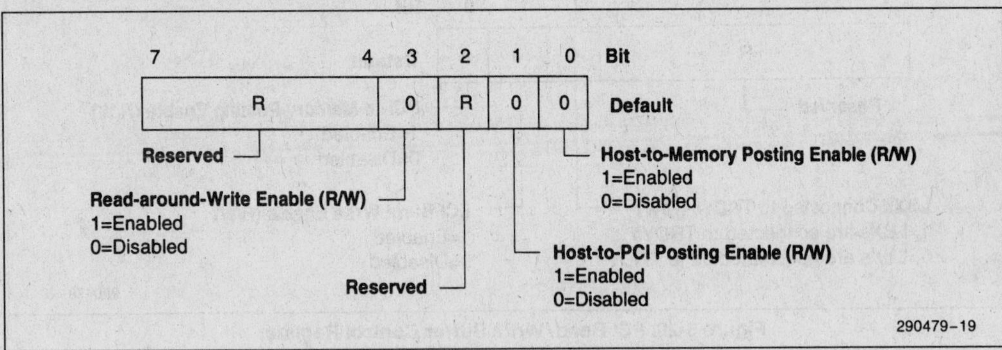

Figure 3-19. Host Read/Write Buffer Control

Table 3-18. Host Read/Write Buffer Control

Bit	Description
7:4	**Reserved.**
3	**Read-Around-Write Enable (RAWCM):** If enabled, the PCMC, during a CPU read cycle to memory where posted write cycles are pending, internally snoops the write buffers. If the address of the read differs from the posted write addresses, the PCMC initiates the memory read cycle ahead of the pending posted memory write. When RAWCM = 0, the pending posted write is written to memory before the memory read is performed. When RAWCM = 1, the PCMC initiates the memory read ahead of the pending posted memory writes.
2	**Reserved.**
1	**Host-to-PCI Posting Enable (HPPE):** This bit enables and disables the posting of Host-to-PCI write data in the LBX posting buffers. When HPPE = 1, up to 4 Dwords of data can be posted to PCI. When HPPE = 0, buffering is disabled and each CPU write does not complete until the PCI transaction completes (TRDY# is asserted).
0	**Host-to-Memory Posting Enable (HMPE):** This bit enables and disables the posting of Host-to-main memory write data in the LBX posting buffers. When HMPE = 1, the CPU can post a single write or a burst write (4 Qwords). The CPU burst write completes at 4-1-1-1 when the second level cache is in write-back mode and at 3-1-1-1 when the second level cache is either disabled or in write-through mode. When HMPE = 0, Host-to-main memory posting is disabled and CPU write cycles do not complete until the data is written to memory.

3.2.16 PBC—PCI READ/WRITE BUFFER CONTROL REGISTER

Address Offset: 54h
Default Value: 00h
Attribute: Read/Write
Size: 8 Bits

The PBC Register enables and disables PCI-to-main memory write posting and permits single CPU-to-PCI writes to be assembled into PCI burst cycles.

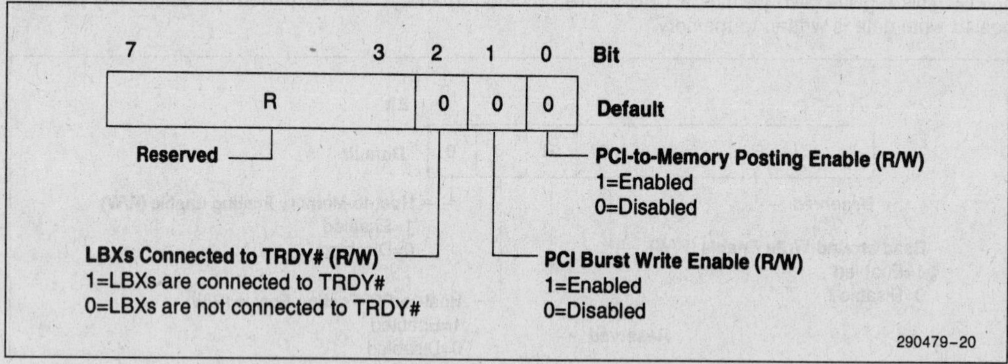

Figure 3-20. PCI Read/Write Buffer Control Register

Table 3-19. PCI Read/Write Buffer Control Register

Bit	Description
7:3	**Reserved.**
2	**LBXs Connected to TRDY#:** The TRDY# pin on the LBXs can be connected either to the PCI TRDY# signal or to ground. The cycle time for CPU-to-PCI writes is improved if TRDY# is connected to the LBXs. Since there are two LBXs used in a system, connecting this signal to the LBXs increases the electrical loading of TRDY# by two loads. When this bit is set to 1, the LBXs are externally hardwired to TRDY#. This enables the capability of CPU-to-PCI writes at 2-1-1-1... (PCI clocks). When this bit is reset to 0, the LBXs are not connected to TRDY# and CPU-to-PCI writes are completed at 2-2-2-2... timing. For designs where the LBXs TRDY# pin is connected to the PCI TRDY# signal, this bit must be set to 1 before the CPU writes to PCI.
1	**PCI Burst Write Enable (PBWE):** This bit enables and disables PCI Burst memory write cycles for back-to-back sequential CPU memory write cycles to PCI. When PBWE is set to 1, PCI burst writes are enabled. When PBWE is reset to 0, PCI burst writes are disabled and each single CPU write to PCI invokes a single PCI write cycle (each cycle has an associated FRAME# sequence).
0	**PCI-to-Memory Posting Enable (PMPE):** This bit enables and disables posting of PCI-to-memory write cycles. The posting occurs in a pair of four Dword-deep buffers in the LBXs. When PMPE is set to 1, these buffers are used to post PCI-to-main memory write data. When PMPE is reset to 0, PCI write transactions to main memory are limited to single transfers. The PCMC asserts STOP# with the first TRDY# to disconnect the PCI Master.

3.2.17 DRAMC—DRAM CONTROL REGISTER

Address Offset: 57h
Default Value: 31h
Attribute: Read/Write
Size: 8 Bits

This 8-bit register controls main memory DRAM operating modes and features.

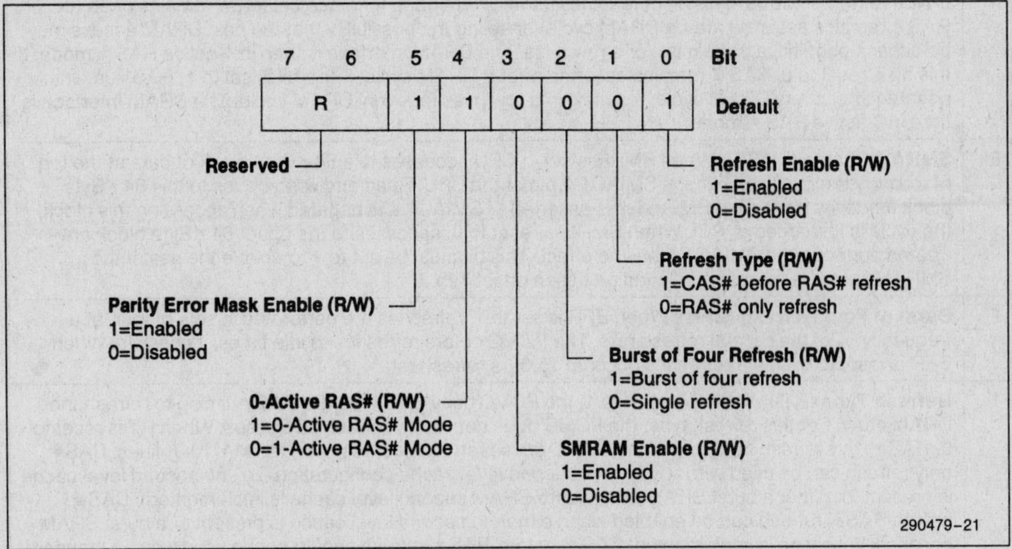

Figure 3-21. DRAM Control Register

Table 3-20. DRAM Control Register

Bit	Description
7:6	**Reserved.**
5	**Parity Error Mask (PERRM):** When PERRM = 1, parity errors generated during DRAM read cycles initiated by either the CPU request or a PCI Master are masked. This bit affects bits 0 and 1 of the Error Command Register and the ability of the PCMC to respond to PCHK# and assert SERR# when a DRAM parity error occurs. When PERRM is reset to 0, parity errors are not masked.
4	**0-Active RAS# Mode:** This bit determines if the DRAM page for a particular row remains open (i.e. RAS# remains asserted after a DRAM cycle) enabling the possibility that the next DRAM access may be either a page hit, a page miss, or a row miss. The DRAM interface is then in 1-active RAS# mode. If this bit is reset to 0, RAS# remains asserted after a DRAM cycle. If this bit is set to 1, RAS# is negated after every DRAM cycle, resulting in a row miss for every DRAM cycle. The DRAM interface is then in 0-active RAS# mode.
3	**SMRAM Enable (SMRE):** When SMRE is set 1, CPU accesses to a 64 KByte block of data at the top of memory are qualified with the SMIACT# pin of the CPU. Read and write cycles to this 64 KByte block functions normally if SMIACT# is asserted. If SMIACT# is negated when accessing this block, the cycle is forwarded to PCI. When SMRE is reset to 0, accesses to the upper 64 KByte block are treated normally and SMIACT# has no effect. This bit must be set to 1 to enable the use of the SMRAM space register at configuration space offset 72h.
2	**Burst of Four Refresh (BFR):** When BFR is set to 1, refreshes are performed in sets of four, at a frequency ¼ of the normal refresh rate. The PCMC defers refreshes to idle times, if possible. When BFR is reset to 0, single refreshes occur at 15.6 μs refresh rate.
1	**Refresh Type (RT):** When RT is set to 1, the PCMC uses CAS# before RAS# timing to refresh the DRAM array. For this refresh type, the PCMC does not supply refresh addresses. When RT is reset to 0, RAS# only refresh is used and the PCMC drives refresh addresses on the MA[10:0] lines. RAS# only refresh can be used with any type of second level cache configuration (i.e., no second level cache is present, or either a burst SRAM or standard SRAM second level cache is implemented). CAS#-before-RAS# refresh can be enabled when either no second level cache is present or a burst SRAM second level cache is implemented. CAS#-before-RAS# refresh should not be used when a standard SRAM second level cache is implemented.
0	**Refresh Enable (RE):** When RE is set to 1, the main memory array is refreshed as configured via bits 1 and 2 of this register. When RE is reset to 0, DRAM refresh is disabled. Note that disabling refresh results in the loss of DRAM data.

3.2.18 DT—DRAM TIMING REGISTER

Address Offset: 58h

Default Value: 00h

Attribute: Read/Write

Size: 8 Bits

This register controls the leadoff latency for CPU DRAM accesses.

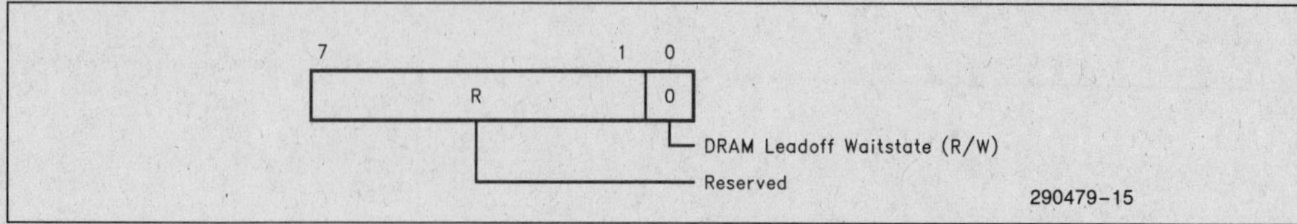

Figure 3-22. DRAM Timing Register

Table 3-21. DRAM Timing Register

Bit	Description
7:1	**Reserved.**
0	**DRAM Leadoff Waitstate (DLW):** When set, the PCMC will add an extra wait state to all CPU DRAM accesses. An extra clock is inserted between when the PCMC drives the column addresses and when CAS[7:0] # are asserted.

3.2.19 PAM—PROGRAMMABLE ATTRIBUTE MAP REGISTERS (PAM[6:0])

Address Offset: 59h–5Fh
Default Value: PAM0 = 0Fh, PAM[1:6] = 0h
Attribute: Read/Write

1

The PCMC allows programmable memory and cacheability attributes on 14 memory segments of various sizes in the 512 KByte to 1 MByte address range. Seven Programmable Attribute Map (PAM) Registers are used to support these features. Three bits are used to specify cacheability and memory attributes for each memory segment. These attributes are:

RE— **Read Enable:** When RE = 1, the CPU read accesses to the corresponding memory segment are directed to main memory. Conversely, when RE = 0, the CPU read accesses are directed to PCI.

WE— **Write Enable:** When WE = 1, the CPU write accesses to the corresponding memory segment are directed to main memory. Conversely, when WE = 0, the CPU write accesses are directed to PCI.

CE— **Cache Enable:** When CE = 1, the corresponding memory segment is cacheable. CE must not be set to 1 when RE is reset to 0 for any particular memory segment. When CE = 1 and WE = 0, the corresponding memory segment is cached in the first and second level caches only on CPU code read cycles.

The RE and WE attributes permit a memory segment to be Read Only, Write Only, Read/Write, or disabled. For example, if a memory segment has RE = 1 and WE = 0, the segment is Read Only. The characteristics for memory segments with these read/write attributes are described in Table 3-22.

Table 3-22. Attribute Definition

Read/Write Attribute	Definition
Read Only	Read cycles: CPU cycles are serviced by the DRAM in a normal manner. Write cycles: CPU initiated write cycles are ignored by the DRAM interface as well as the cache. Instead, the cycles are passed to PCI for termination. Areas marked as Read Only are cacheable for Code accesses only. These regions may be cached in the second level cache, however as noted above, writes are forwarded to PCI, effectively write protecting the data.
Write Only	Read cycles: All read cycles are ignored by the DRAM interface as well as the second level cache. CPU-initiated read cycles are passed onto PCI for termination. The write only state can be used while copying the contents of a ROM, accessible on PCI, to main memory for shadowing, as in the case of BIOS shadowing. Write cycles: CPU write cycles are serviced by the DRAM and cache in a normal manner.
Read/Write	This is the normal operating mode of main memory. Both read and write cycles from the CPU and PCI are serviced by the DRAM and cache interface.
Disabled	All read and write cycles to this area are ignored by the DRAM and cache interface. These cycles are forwarded to PCI for termination.

Each PAM Register controls two regions, typically 16 KByte in size. Each of these regions have a 4-bit field. The four bits that control each region have the same encoding and are defined in Table 3-23.

Table 3-23. Attribute Bit Assignment

Bits [7,3] Reserved	Bits [6,2] Cache Enable	Bits [5,1] Write Enable	Bits [4,0] Read Enable	Description
x	x	0	0	DRAM disabled, accesses directed to PCI
x	0	0	1	read only, DRAM write protected, non-cacheable
x	1	0	1	read only, DRAM write protected, cacheable for code accesses only
x	0	1	0	write only
x	0	1	1	read/write, non-cacheable
x	1	1	1	read/write, cacheable

NOTE:

To enable PCI master access to the DRAM address space from C0000h to FFFFFh the MEMCS# configuration registers of the ISA or EISA bridge must be properly configured. These registers must correspond to the PAM Registers in the PCMC.

As an example, consider a BIOS that is implemented on the expansion bus. During the initialization process the BIOS can be shadowed in main memory to increase the system performance. When a BIOS is shadowed in main memory, it should be copied to the same address location. To shadow the BIOS, the attributes for that address range should be set to write only. The BIOS is shadowed by first doing a read of that address. This read is forwarded to the expansion bus. The CPU then does a write of the same address, which is directed to main memory. After the BIOS is shadowed, the attributes for that memory area are set to read only so that all writes are forwarded to the expansion bus.

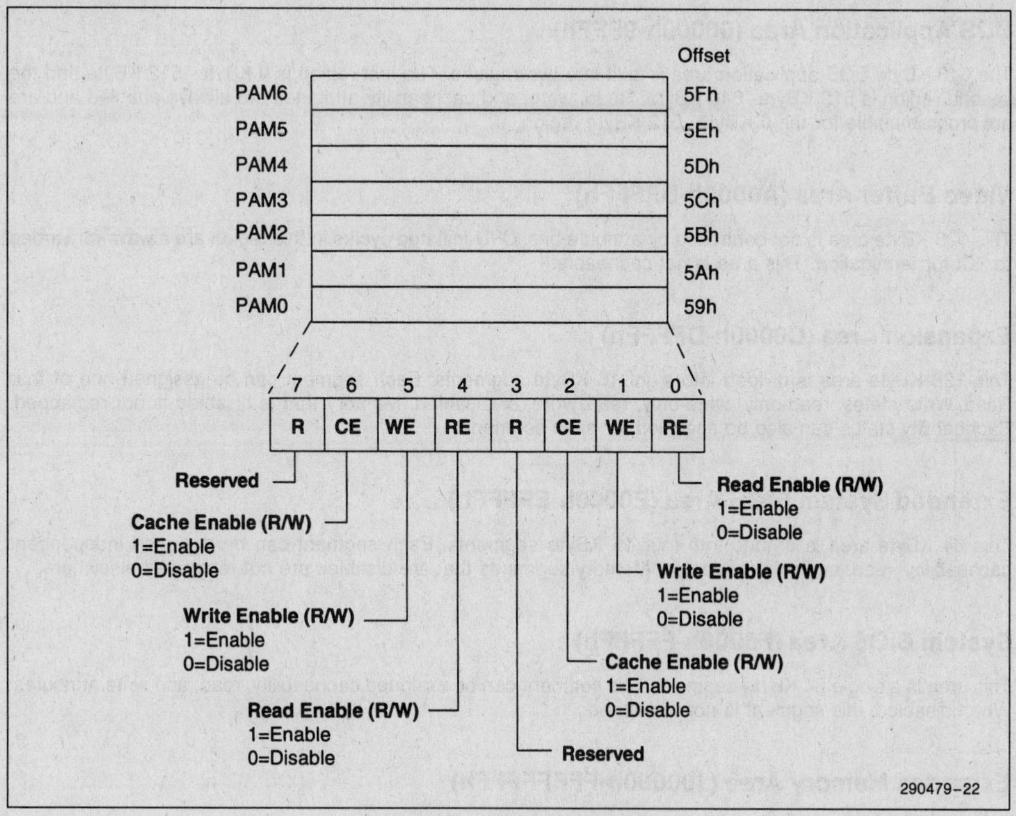

Figure 3-23. PAM Registers

Table 3-24. PAM Registers and Associated Memory Segments

PAM Reg	Attribute Bits				Memory Segment	Comments	Offset
PAM0[3:0]	R	CE	WE	RE	080000h–09FFFFh	512K to 640K	59h
PAM0[7:4]	R	CE	WE	RE	0F0000h–0FFFFFh	BIOS Area	59h
PAM1[3:0]	R	CE	WE	RE	0C0000h–0C3FFFh	ISA Add-on BIOS	5Ah
PAM1[7:4]	R	CE	WE	RE	0C4000h–0C7FFFh	ISA Add-on BIOS	5Ah
PAM2[3:0]	R	CE	WE	RE	0C8000h–0CBFFFh	ISA Add-on BIOS	5Bh
PAM2[7:4]	R	CE	WE	RE	0CC000h–0CFFFFh	ISA Add-on BIOS	5Bh
PAM3[3:0]	R	CE	WE	RE	0D0000h–0D3FFFh	ISA Add-on BIOS	5Ch
PAM3[7:4]	R	CE	WE	RE	0D4000h–0D7FFFh	ISA Add-on BIOS	5Ch
PAM4[3:0]	R	CE	WE	RE	0D8000h–0DBFFFh	ISA Add-on BIOS	5Dh
PAM4[7:4]	R	CE	WE	RE	0DC000h–0DFFFFh	ISA Add-on BIOS	5Dh
PAM5[3:0]	R	CE	WE	RE	0E0000h–0E3FFFh	BIOS Extension	5Eh
PAM5[7:4]	R	CE	WE	RE	0E4000h–0E7FFFh	BIOS Extension	5Eh
PAM6[3:0]	R	CE	WE	RE	0E8000h–0EBFFFh	BIOS Extension	5Fh
PAM6[7:4]	R	CE	WE	RE	0EC000h–0EFFFFh	BIOS Extension	5Fh

1

DOS Application Area (00000h-9FFFh)

The 640 KByte DOS application area is split into two regions. The first region is 0 KByte–512 KByte and the second region is 512 KByte–640 KByte. Read, write, and cacheability attributes are always enabled and are not programmable for the 0 KByte–512 KByte region.

Video Buffer Area (A0000h-BFFFFh)

This 128 KByte area is not controlled by attribute bits. CPU-initiated cycles in this region are always forwarded to PCI for termination. This area is not cacheable.

Expansion Area (C0000h-DFFFFh)

This 128 KByte area is divided into eight 16 KByte segments. Each segment can be assigned one of four Read/Write states: read-only, write-only, read/write, or disabled. Memory that is disabled is not remapped. Cacheability status can also be specified for each segment.

Extended System BIOS Area (E0000h-EFFFFh)

This 64 KByte area is divided into four 16 KByte segments. Each segment can be assigned independent cacheability, read, and write attributes. Memory segments that are disabled are not remapped elsewhere.

System BIOS Area (F0000h-FFFFFh)

This area is a single 64 KByte segment. This segment can be assigned cacheability, read, and write attributes. When disabled, this segment is not remapped.

Extended Memory Area (100000h-FFFFFFFFh)

The extended memory area can be split into several parts;

- Flash BIOS area from 4 GByte to 4 GByte–512 KByte (aliased on ISA at 16 MByte–15.5 MByte)
- DRAM Memory from 1 MByte to a maximum of 192 MBytes
- PCI Memory space from the top of DRAM to 4 GByte–512 KByte
- Memory Space Gap between the range of 1 MByte up to 15.5 MByte
- Frame Buffer Range mapped into PCI Memory Space or the Memory Space Gap.

On power-up or reset the CPU vectors to the Flash BIOS area, mapped in the range of 4 GByte to 4 GByte–512 KByte. This area is physically mapped on the expansion bus. Since these addresses are in the upper 4 GByte range, the request is directed to PCI.

The DRAM memory space can occupy extended memory from a minimum of 2 MByte up to 192 MBytes. This memory is cacheable.

The address space on PCI between the Flash BIOS (4 GByte to 4 GByte–512 KByte) and the top of DRAM (including any remapped memory) may be occupied by PCI memory. This memory space is not cacheable.

3.2.20 DRB—DRAM ROW BOUNDARY REGISTERS

Address Offset: 60-65h
Default Value: 02h
Attribute: Read/Write
Size: 8 Bits

The PCMC supports 6 rows of DRAM. Each row is 64 bits wide. The DRAM Row Boundary Registers define upper and lower addresses for each DRAM row. Contents of these 8-bit registers represent the boundary addresses in MBytes.

DRB0 = Total amount of memory in row 0 (in MBytes)
DRB1 = Total amount of memory in row 0 + row 1 (in MBytes)
DRB2 = Total amount of memory in row 0 + row 1 + row 2 (in MBytes)
DRB3 = Total amount of memory in row 0 + row 1 + row 2 + row 3 (in MBytes)
DRB4 = Total amount of memory in row 0 + row 1 + row 2 + row 3 + row 4 (in MBytes)
DRB5 = Total amount of memory in row 0 + row 1 + row 2 + row 3 + row 4 + row 5 (in MBytes)

The DRAM array can be configured with 256K x 36, 1M x 36 and 4M x 36 SIMMs. Each register defines an address range that will cause a particular RAS# line to be asserted (e.g. if the first DRAM row is 2 MBytes in size then accesses within the 0 to 2 MBytes range will cause RAS0# to be asserted). The DRAM Row Boundary (DRB) Registers are programmed with an 8-bit upper address limit value. This upper address limit is compared to A[27:20] of the Host address bus, for each row, to determine if DRAM is being targeted. Since this value is 8 bits and the resolution is 1 MByte, the total bits compared span a 256 MByte space. However, only 192 MBytes of main memory is supported.

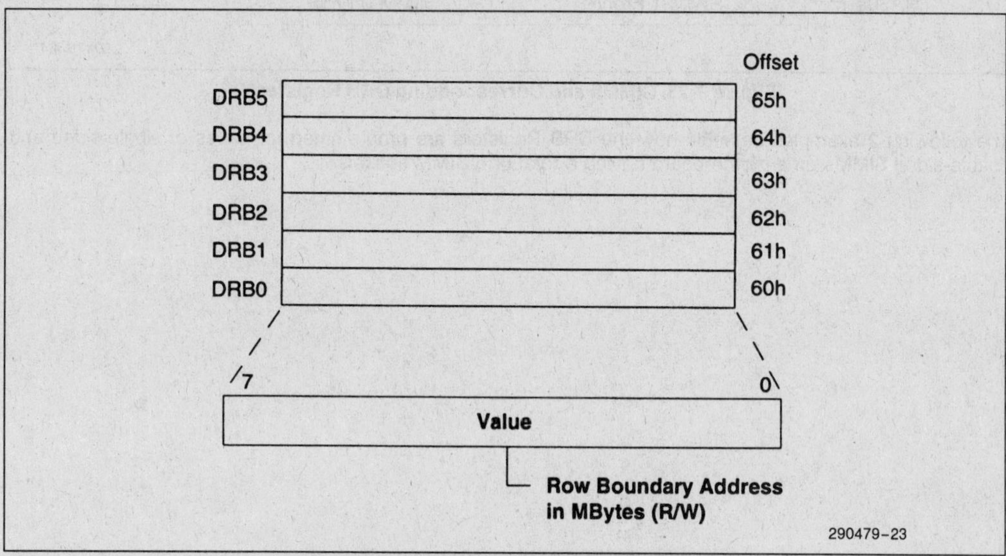

Figure 3-24. DRAM Row Boundary Register

Table 3-25. DRAM Row Boundary Register

Bit	Description
7:0	**Row Boundary Address in MBytes:** This 8-bit value is compared against address lines A[27:20] to determine the upper address limit of a particular row, i.e., this DRB − previous DRB = row size. Bits 7, 6, 4, 2 and 0 of DRB0 are reserved. Bits 7 and 0 of DRB1 are reserved and Bit 0 is reserved in DRB2 through DRB5.

Row Boundary Address in MBytes

These 8-bit values represent the upper address limits of the six rows (i.e., this row − previous row = row size). Unpopulated rows have a value equal to the previous row (row size = 0). The value programmed into DRB5 reflects the maximum amount of DRAM in the system. Memory remapped at the top of DRAM, as a result of setting the Memory Space Gap Register, is not reflected in the DRB Registers. The top of memory is always determined by the value written into DRB5 added to the memory space gap size (if enabled).

As an example of a general purpose configuration where 3 physical rows are configured for either single-sided or double-sided SIMMs, the memory array would be configured like the one shown in Figure 3-25. In this configuration, the PCMC drives two RAS# signals directly to the SIMM rows. If single-sided SIMMs are populated, the even RAS# signal is used and the odd RAS# is not connected. If double-sided SIMMs are used, both RAS# signals are used.

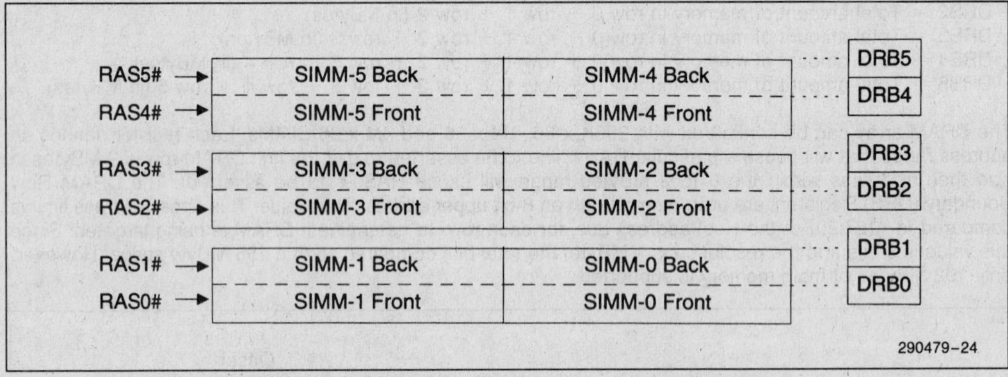

Figure 3-25. SIMMs and Corresponding DRB Registers

The following 2 examples describe how the DRB Registers are programmed for cases of single-sided and double-sided SIMMs on a motherboard having a total of 6 SIMM sockets.

Example #1

The memory array is populated with six single-sided 256 KByte x 36 SIMMs. Two SIMMs are required for each populated row making each populated row 2 MBytes in size. Filling the array yields 6 MBytes total DRAM. The DRB Registers are programmed as follows:

DRB0 = 02h populated

DRB1 = 02h empty row, not double-sided SIMMs

DRB2 = 04h populated

DRB3 = 04h empty row, not double-sided SIMMs

DRB4 = 06h populated

DRB5 = 06h empty row, not double-sided SIMMs, maximum memory = 6 MBytes

1

Example #2

As an another example, if the first four SIMM sockets are populated with 2M x 36 double-sided SIMMs and the last two SIMM sockets are populated with 4M x 36 single-sided SIMMs then filling the array yields 64 MBytes total DRAM. The DRB Registers are programmed as follows:

DRB0 = 08h populated with 8 MBytes, ½ of the double-sided SIMMs

DRB1 = 10h the other 8 MBytes of the double-sided SIMMs

DRB2 = 18h populated with 8 MBytes, ½ of the double-sided SIMMs

DRB3 = 20h the other 8 MBytes of the double-sided SIMMs

DRB4 = 40h populated with 32 MBytes

DRB5 = 40h empty row, not double-sided SIMMs, maximum memory = 64 MBytes

3.2.21 ERRCMD—ERROR COMMAND REGISTER

Address Offset: 70h
Default Value: 00h
Attribute: Read/Write
Size: 8 Bits

The Error Command Register controls the PCMC responses to various system errors. Bit 6 of the PCICMD Register in the master enable for bit 3 of this register. Bit 6 of the PCICMD Register must be set to 1 to enable the error reporting function defined by bit 3 of this register. Bits 6 and 8 of the PCICMD Register are the master enables for bits 7, 6, 5, 4 and 1 of this register. Both bits 6 and 8 of the PCICMD Register must be set to 1 to enable the error reporting functions defined by bits 7, 6, 5, 4 and 1 of this register.

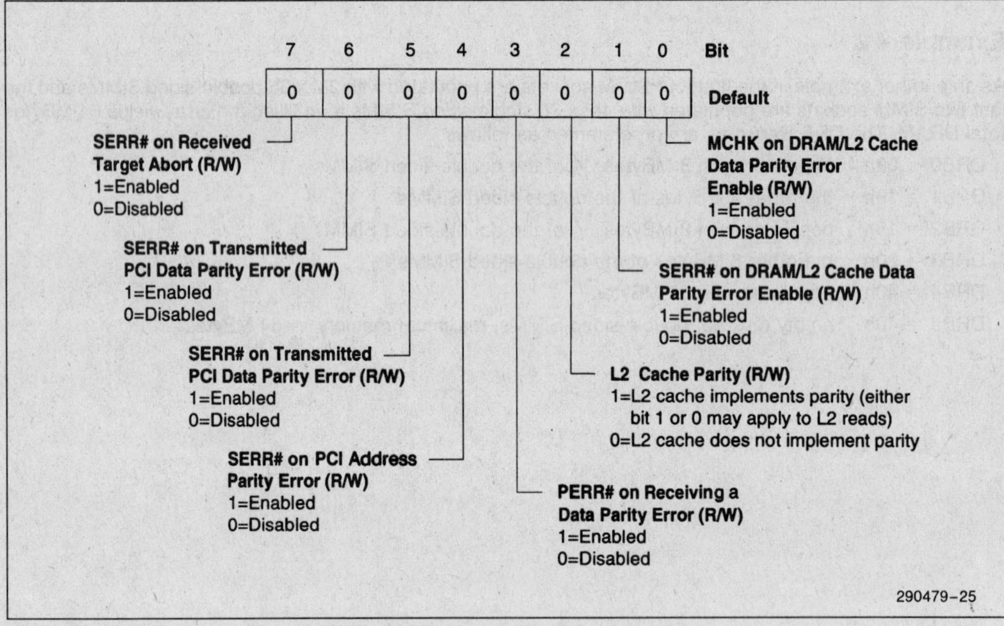

Figure 3-26. Error Command Register

Table 3-26. Error Command Register

Bit	Description
7	**SERR# on Received Target Abort:** When this bit is set to 1 (and bits 6 and 8 of the PCICMD Register are set to 1), the PCMC asserts SERR# upon receiving a target abort. When this bit is reset to 0, the PCMC is disabled from asserting SERR# upon receiving a target abort.
6	**SERR# on Transmitted PCI Data Parity Error:** When this bit is set to 1 (and bits 6 and 8 of the PCICMD Register are set to 1), the PCMC asserts SERR# when it detects a data parity error as a result of a CPU-to-PCI write (PERR# detected asserted). When this bit is reset to 0 the PCMC is disabled from asserting SERR# when data parity errors are detected via PERR#.
5	**SERR# on Received PCI Data Parity Error:** When this bit is set to 1 (and bits 6 and 8 of the PCICMD Register are set to 1), the PCMC asserts SERR# when it detects a data parity error as a result of a CPU-to-PCI read (PAR incorrect with received data). In this case, the SERR# signal is asserted when parity errors are detected on PCI return data. When this bit is reset to 0, the PCMC is disabled from asserting SERR# when data parity errors are detected during a CPU-to-PCI read.
4	**SERR# on PCI Address Parity Error:** When this bit is set to 1 (and bits 6 and 8 of the PCICMD Register are set to 1), the PCMC asserts SERR# when an address parity error is detected on PCI transactions. When this bit is reset to 0, the PCMC is disabled from asserting SERR# when address parity errors are detected on PCI transactions.
3	**PERR# on Receiving a Data Parity Error:** This bit indicates whether the PERR# signal is implemented in the system. When this bit is set to 1 (and bit 6 of the PCICMD Register is also set to 1), the PCMC asserts PERR# when it detects a data parity error (PAR incorrect with received data), either from a CPU-to-PCI read or a PCI master write to memory. When this bit is reset to 0 (or bit 6 of the PCICMD Register is reset to 0), the PERR# signal is not asserted by the PCMC.
2	**L2 Cache Parity Enable:** This bit indicates that the second level cache implements parity. When this bit is set to 1, bit 0 and bit 1 of this register control the checking of parity errors during CPU reads from the second level cache. If this bit is 0, parity is not checked when the CPU reads from the second level cache (PCHK# ignored) and neither bit 1 nor bit 0 apply.
1	**SERR# on DRAM/L2 Cache Data Parity Error Enable:** This bit enables and disables the SERR# signal for parity errors on reads from main memory or the second level cache. When this bit is set to 1 (and bits 6 and 8 of the PCICMD Register are set to 1), and bit 0 of this register is set 1, SERR# is enabled upon a PCHK# assertion from the CPU when reading from main memory or the second level cache. The processor indicates that a parity error was received by asserting PCHK#. The PCMC then latches status information in the Error Status register and asserts SERR#. When this bit is reset to 0, SERR# is not asserted upon detecting a parity error. 10 is a reserved combination of bits [1:0] of this register. 0 = Disable assertion of SERR# upon detecting a DRAM/second level cache read parity error. 1 = Enable assertion of SERR# upon detecting a DRAM/second level cache read parity error.
0	**MCHK on DRAM/L2 Cache Data Parity Error Enable:** When this bit is set to 1, PEN# is asserted for data returned from main memory or the second level cache. The processor indicates that a parity error was received by asserting the PCHK# signal. In addition, the processor invokes a machine check exception if enabled via the MCE bit in CR4 in the Pentium processor. The PCMC then latches status information in the Error Status Register. When this bit is reset to 0, PEN# is not asserted. 10 is a reserved combination of bits [1:0] of this register.

3.2.22 ERRSTS—ERROR STATUS REGISTER

Address Offset: 71h
Default Value: 00h
Attribute: Read/Write Clear
Size: 8 Bits

The Error Status Register is an 8-bit register that reports the occurrence of PCI, second level cache, and DRAM parity errors. This register also reports the occurrence of a CPU shutdown cycle.

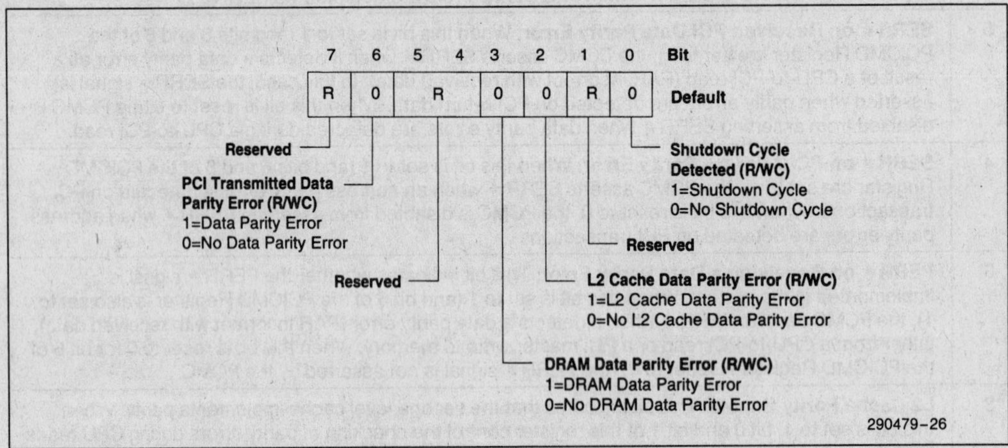

Figure 3-27. Error Status Register

Table 3-27. Error Status Register

Bit	Description
7	**Reserved.**
6	**PCI Transmitted Data Parity Error:** The PCMC sets this bit to a 1 when it detects a data parity error (PERR# asserted) as a result of a CPU-to-PCI write. Software resets this bit to 0 by writing a 1 to it.
5:4	**Reserved.**
3	**DRAM Data Parity Error:** The PCMC sets this bit to a 1 when it detects a parity error from the CPU PCHK# signal resulting from a CPU-to-main memory read. Software resets this bit to 0 by writing a 1 to it.
2	**L2 Cache Data Parity Error:** The PCMC sets this bit to a 1 when it detects a parity error from the CPU PCHK# signal resulting from a CPU read access that hit in the second level cache. Software resets this bit to 0 by writing a 1 to it.
1	**Reserved.**
0	**Shutdown Cycle Detected:** The PCMC sets this bit to a 1 when it detects a shutdown special cycle on the Host Bus. Under this condition the PCMC drives a shutdown special cycle on PCI and asserts INIT. Software resets this bit to 0 by writing a 1 to it.

3.2.23 SMRS—SMRAM SPACE REGISTER

Address Offset: 72h

Default Value: 00h

Attribute: R/W

Size: 8 Bits

The PCMC supports a 64 KByte SMRAM space which can be selected to reside at the top of main memory, A0000–AFFFFh or B0000–BFFFFh. The SMRAM space defined by this register is not cacheable. This register defines a mechanism which allows the CPU to execute code out of the SMRAM space at either A0000h or B0000h while accessing the frame buffer on PCI. The SMRAM Enable bit in the DRAM Control register must be set to 1 to enable the features defined by this register.

1

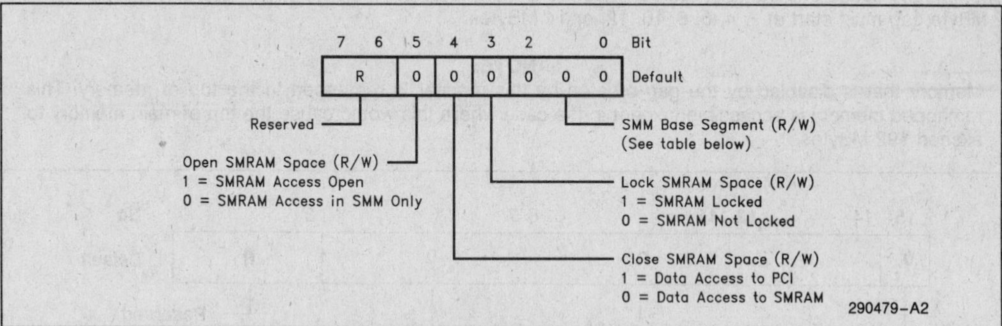

Figure 3-28. SMRAM Space Register

Table 3-28. SMRAM Space Register

Bit	Description
7:6	**Reserved.**
5	**Open SMRAM Space (OSS):** When set to 1, the CPU can access SMRAM space without being in SMM mode. That is, access to SMRAM are permitted even with SMIACT# inactive. This bit is intended to be used during POST to allow the CPU to initialize SMRAM space before the first SMI# interrupt is issued.
4	**Close SMRAM SPACE (CSS):** When this bit is set to 1 and SMRAM is enabled, CPU code accesses to the SMRAM memory range are directed to SMRAM in main memory and data accesses are forwarded to PCI. This bit allows the CPU to read and write the frame buffer on PCI while executing SMM code. When reset to 0, and SMRAM is enabled, all accesses to the SMRAM memory range, both code and data, are directed to SMRAM (main memory).
3	**Lock SMRAM Space (LSS):** When set to 1, this bit prevents the SMRAM space from being manually opened, effectively disabling bit 5 of this register. Only a power-on reset can reset this bit to 0.
2:0	**SMM Base Segment (SBS):** This field defines the 64 KByte base segment where SMRAM is located. The memory area defined by this field is non-cacheable. **Bits** **SMRAM Location** 000 Top of Main Memory 001 Reserved 010 A0000–AFFFFh 011 B0000–BFFFFh 100 Reserved 101 Reserved 110 Reserved 111 Reserved

3.2.24 MSG—MEMORY SPACE GAP REGISTER

Address Offset: 78–79h
Default Value: 00h
Attribute: Read/Write
Size: 16 Bits

The Memory Space Gap Register defines the starting address and size of a gap in main memory. This register accommodates ISA devices that have their memory mapped into the 1 MByte to 15.5 MByte range (e.g., an ISA LAN card or an ISA frame buffer). The Memory Space Gap register defines a hole in main memory that transfers the cycles in this address space to the PCI Bus instead of main memory. This area is not cacheable.

The memory space gap starting address must be a multiple of the memory space gap size. For example, a 2 MByte gap must start at 2, 4, 6, 8, 10, 12, or 14 MBytes.

NOTE:
Memory that is disabled by the gap created by this register is remapped to the top of memory. This remapped memory is accessible, except in the case where this would cause the top of main memory to exceed 192 MBytes.

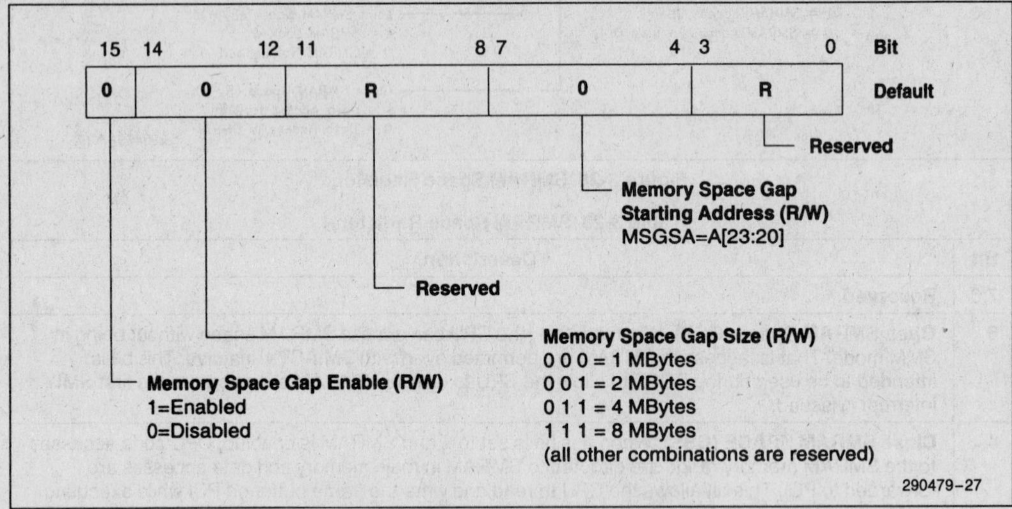

Figure 3-29. Memory Space Gap Register

Table 3-29. Memory Space Gap Register

Bit	Description
15	**Memory Space Gap Enable (MSGE):** MSGE enables and disables the memory space gap. When MSGE is set to 1, the CPU accesses to the address range defined by this register are forwarded to PCI bus. The size of the gap created in main memory causes a corresponding amount of DRAM to be remapped at the top of main memory (top specified by DRB Registers). If the Frame Buffer Range is programmed below 16 MBytes and within main memory space, the MSG register must include the Frame Buffer Range. When MSGE is reset to 0, the memory space gap is disabled.
14:12	**Memory Space Gap Size (MSGS):** This 3-bit field defines the size of the memory space gap. If the Frame Buffer Range is programmed below 16 MBytes and within main memory space, this register must include the frame buffer range. The amount of main memory specified by these bits is remapped to the top of main memory. **Bit[14:12]** Memory Gap Size 0 0 0 1 MBytes 0 0 1 2 MBytes 0 1 1 4 MBytes 1 1 1 8 MBytes (all other combinations are reserved)
11:8	**Reserved.**
7:4	**Memory Space Gap Starting Address (MSGSA):** These 4 bits define the starting address of the memory space gap in the space from 1 MByte to 16 MByte. These bits are compared against A[23:20]. The memory space gap starting address must be a multiple of the memory space gap size. For example, a 2 MByte gap must start at 2, 4, 6, 8, 10, 12, or 14 MBytes.
3:0	**Reserved.**

1

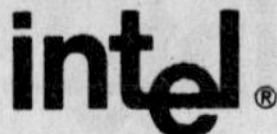

3.2.25 FBR—FRAME BUFFER RANGE REGISTER

Address Offset: 7C-7Fh
Default Value: 0000h
Attribute: Read/Write
Size: 32 Bits

This 32-bit register enables and disables a frame buffer area and provides attribute settings for the frame buffer area. The attributes defined in this register are intended to increase the performance of the frame buffer. The FBR Register can be used to accommodate PCI devices that have their memory mapped onto PCI from the top of DRAM to 4 GByte−512 KByte range (e.g., a linear frame buffer). If the Frame Buffer Range is located within the 1 MByte to 16 MByte main memory region where DRAM is populated, the Memory Space Gap Register must be programmed to include the Frame Buffer Range.

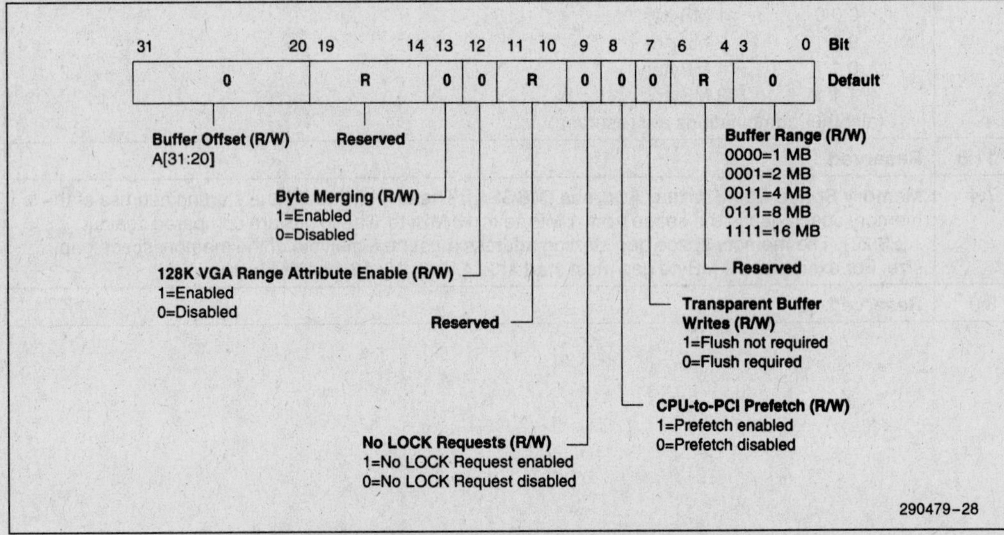

Figure 3-30. Frame Buffer Range Register

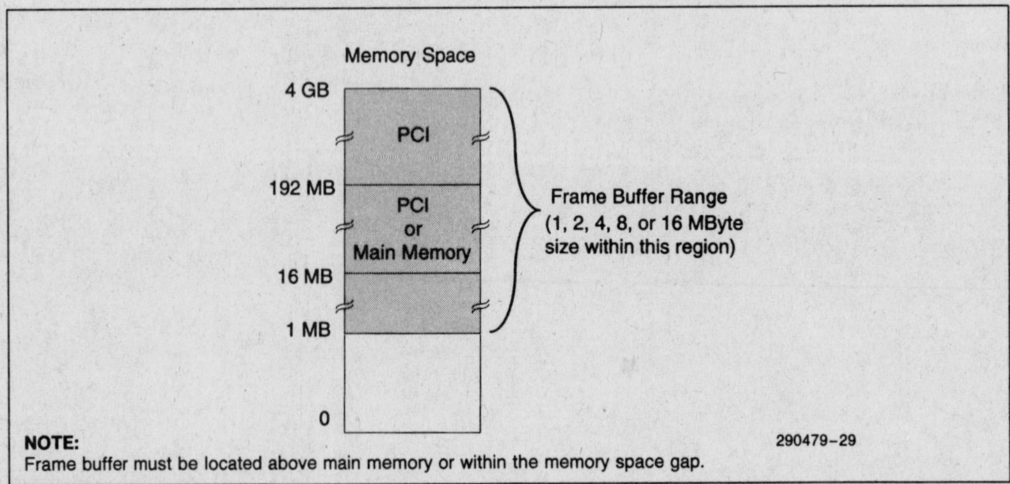

NOTE:
Frame buffer must be located above main memory or within the memory space gap.

Figure 3-31. Frame Buffer Range

Table 3-30. Frame Buffer Range Register

Bit	Description
31:20	**Buffer Offset (BO):** BO defines the starting address of the frame buffer address space in increments of 1 MByte. This 12-bit field is compared directly against A[31:20]. The frame buffer range can either be located at the top of memory, including remapped memory or within the memory space gap (i.e., frame buffer range programmed below 16 MByte and within main memory space. When these bits are reset to 000h and bit 12 is reset to 0, all features defined by this register are disabled.
19:14	**Reserved.**
13	**Byte Merging (BM):** Byte merging permits CPU-to-PCI byte writes to the LBX posted write buffer to be combined into a single transfer on the PCI Bus, when appropriate. When BM is set to 1, byte merging on CPU-to-PCI posted write cycles is enabled. When BM is reset to 0, byte merging is disabled.
12	**128K VGA Range Attribute Enable (VRAE):** When VRAE = 1, the attributes defined in this register (bits [13, 10:7]) also apply to the VGA memory range of A0000h–BFFFFh regardless of the value programmed in the Buffer Offset field. When VRAE = 0, the attributes do not apply to the VGA memory range. Note that this bit only affects the mentioned attributes of the VGA memory range and does not enable or disable accesses to the VGA memory range.
11:10	**Reserved.**
9	**No LOCK Requests (NLR):** When NLR is set to 1, the PCMC never requests exclusive access to a PCI resource via the PCI LOCK# signal in the range defined by this register. When NLR is reset to 0, exclusive access via the PCI LOCK# signal in the range defined by this register is enabled.
8	**CPU-to-PCI Prefetch (CPP):** This bit enables and disables CPU-to-PCI read prefetch. When CPP is set to 1, CPU-to-PCI reads cause read prefetching into the 4 Dword-deep buffer in the LBX. When CPP is reset to 0, prefetching is disabled.
7	**Transparent Buffer Writes (TBW):** When set to 1, this bit indicates that writes to the Frame Buffer Range need not be flushed for deadlock or coherence reasons on synchronization events (i.e., PCI master reads, and the FLSHBUF#/MEMREQ# protocol). When reset to 0, this bit indicates that upon synchronization events flushing is required for Frame Buffer writes posted in the CPU-to-PCI Write Buffer in the LBX.
6:4	**Reserved.**
3:0	**Buffer Range (BR):** These bits define the size of the frame buffer address space, allowing up to 16 MBytes of frame buffer. If the frame buffer range is within the memory space gap, the buffer range is limited to 8 MBytes and must be included within the memory space gap size. The bits listed below in the Reserved Buffer Offset (BO) Bits column are ignored by the PCMC for the corresponding buffer sizes. **Bits[3:0] / Buffer Size / Reserved Buffer Offset (BO) Bits** 0 0 0 0 / 1 MBytes / None 0 0 0 1 / 2 MBytes / [20] 0 0 1 1 / 4 MBytes / [21:20] 0 1 1 1 / 8 MBytes / [22:20] 1 1 1 1 / 16 MBytes / [23:20] (all other combinations are reserved)

4.0 PCMC ADDRESS MAP

The Pentium processor has two distinct physical address spaces: Memory and I/O. The memory address space is 4 GBytes and the I/O address space is 64 KBytes. The PCMC maps accesses to these address spaces as described in this section.

4.1 CPU Memory Address Map

Figure 4-1 shows the address map for the 4 GByte Host CPU memory address space. Depending on the address range and whether a memory gap is enabled via the MSG Register, the PCMC forwards CPU memory accesses to either main memory or PCI memory. Accesses forwarded to main memory invoke operations on the DRAM interface and accesses forwarded to PCI memory invoke operations on PCI. Mapping to the PCI Bus permits PCI or EISA/ISA Bus-based memory.

The main memory size ranges from 2 to 192 MBytes. Memory accesses above 192 MBytes are always forwarded to PCI. In addition, a memory gap can be created in the 1 MByte to 16 MByte region that provides a window to PCI-based memory. The location and size of the gap is programmable. Accesses to addresses in the gap are ignored by the DRAM controller and forwarded to PCI. Note that CPU memory accesses that are forwarded to PCI (including the Memory Space Gap) are not cacheable. Only main memory controlled by the PCMC DRAM interface is cacheable.

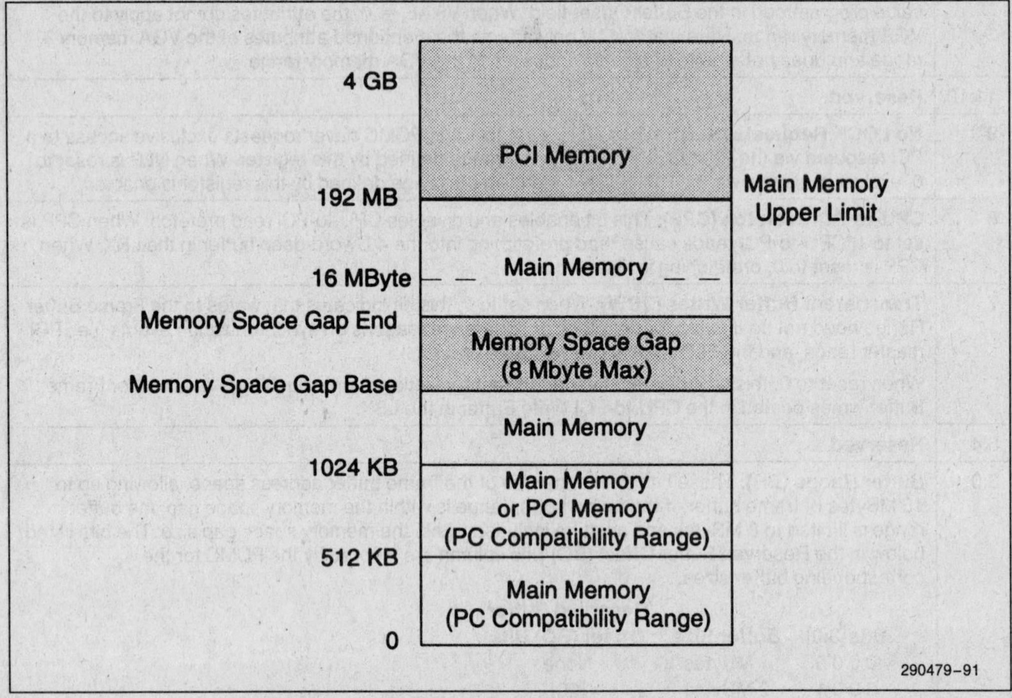

Figure 4-1. CPU Memory Address Map—Full Range

4.2 System Management RAM—SMRAM

The PCMC supports the use of main memory as System Management RAM (SMRAM) enabling the use of System Management Mode. This function is enabled and disabled via the DRAM Control Register. When this function is disabled, the PCMC memory map is defined by the DRB and PAM Registers. When SMRAM is enabled, the PCMC reserves the top 64 KBytes of main memory for use as SMRAM.

SMRAM can also be placed at A0000h through AFFFFh or B0000h through BFFFFh via the SMRAM Space Register at configuration space offset 72h. Enhanced SMRAM features can also be enabled via the SMRAM Space Register.

4.3 PC Compatibility Range

The PC Compatibility Range is the first MByte of the Memory Map. The 512 KByte to 1 MByte range is subdivided into several regions as shown in Figure 4-2. Each region is provided with programmable attributes in the PAM Registers. The attributes are Read Enable (RE), Write Enable (WE) and Cache Enable (CE). The attributes determine readability, writeability and cacheability of the corresponding memory region. When the associated bit in the PAM Register is set to a 1, the attribute is enabled and when set to a 0 the attribute is disabled. The following rules apply for cacheability in the first level and second level caches:

1. If RE = 1, WE = 1, and CE = 1, the region is cacheable in the first level and second level caches.
2. If RE = 1, WE = 0, and CE = 1, the region is cacheable only on code reads (i.e., D/C# = 0). Data reads do not result in a line fill. Writes to the region are not serviced by the secondary cache, but are forwarded to PCI.

The RE and WE bits for each region are used to shadow BIOS ROM in main memory for improved system performance. To shadow BIOS area, RE is reset to 0 and WE is set to 1. RE is set to 1 and WE is reset to 0. Any writes to the BIOS area are forwarded to PCI.

1

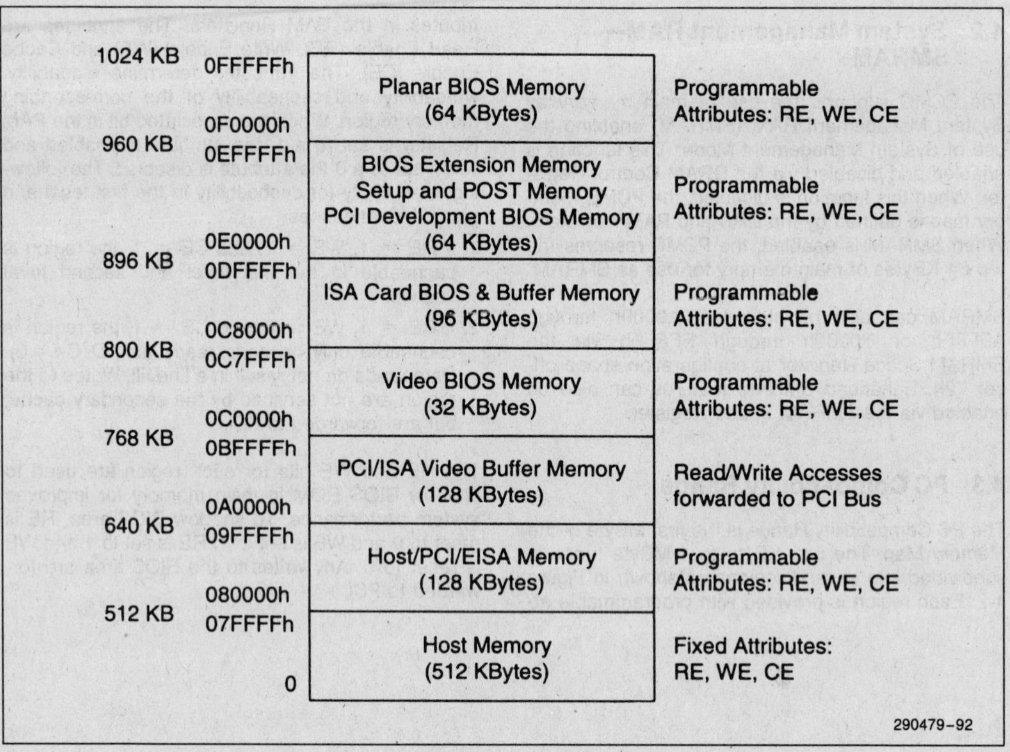

Size	Address Range	Memory Region	Attributes
1024 KB – 960 KB	0FFFFFh – 0F0000h	Planar BIOS Memory (64 KBytes)	Programmable Attributes: RE, WE, CE
960 KB – 896 KB	0EFFFFh – 0E0000h	BIOS Extension Memory Setup and POST Memory PCI Development BIOS Memory (64 KBytes)	Programmable Attributes: RE, WE, CE
896 KB – 800 KB	0DFFFFh – 0C8000h	ISA Card BIOS & Buffer Memory (96 KBytes)	Programmable Attributes: RE, WE, CE
800 KB – 768 KB	0C7FFFh – 0C0000h	Video BIOS Memory (32 KBytes)	Programmable Attributes: RE, WE, CE
768 KB – 640 KB	0BFFFFh – 0A0000h	PCI/ISA Video Buffer Memory (128 KBytes)	Read/Write Accesses forwarded to PCI Bus
640 KB – 512 KB	09FFFFh – 080000h	Host/PCI/EISA Memory (128 KBytes)	Programmable Attributes: RE, WE, CE
512 KB – 0	07FFFFh – 0	Host Memory (512 KBytes)	Fixed Attributes: RE, WE, CE

290479–92

Figure 4-2. CPU Memory Address Map—PC Compatibility Range

4.4 I/O Address Map

I/O devices (other than the PCMC) are not supported on the Host Bus. The PCMC generates PCI Bus cycles for all CPU I/O accesses, except to the PCMC internal registers. Figure 4-3 shows the mapping for the CPU I/O address space. Two PCMC registers are located in the CPU I/O address space. They are the Configuration Space Enable (CSE) Register located at 0CF8h and the Turbo-Reset Control (TRC) Register located at 0CF9h.

Except for the two above mentioned I/O locations, all other CPU I/O accesses are mapped to either PCI I/O space or PCI configuration space. If the access is to PCI I/O space, the PCI address is the same as the CPU address. If the access is to PCI configuration space, the CPU address is mapped to a configuration space address as described in Section 3.0, Register Description.

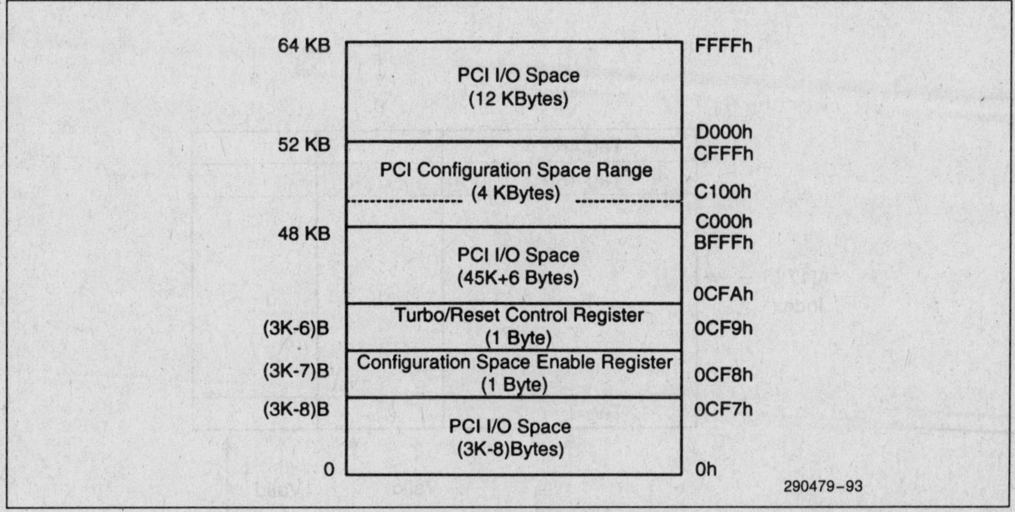

Figure 4-3. CPU I/O Address Map

If configuration space is enabled via the CSE Register, the PCMC maps accesses in the address range of C100h to CFFFh to PCI configuration space. Accesses to the PCMC configuration register range (C000h to C0FFh) are intercepted by the PCMC and not forwarded to PCI. If the configuration space is disabled in the CSE Register, CPU accesses to the configuration address range (C000h to CFFFh) are forwarded to PCI I/O space.

5.0 SECOND LEVEL CACHE INTERFACE

5.1 Cache Overview

The PCMC integrates a high performance write-back/write-through second level cache controller providing integrated tags and a full first level and second level cache coherency mechanism. The second level cache controller can be configured to support either a 256 KByte cache or a 512 KByte cache using either synchronous burst SRAMs or standard asynchronous SRAMs. The cache is direct mapped and can be configured to support either a write-back or write-through write policy. Parity on the second level cache data SRAMs is optional.

The PCMC contains 4096 address tags. Each tag represents a *sector* in the second level cache. If the second level cache is 256 KByte, each tag represents two cache lines. If the second level cache is 512 KByte, each tag represents four cache lines. Thus, in the 256 KByte configuration each sector contains two lines. In the 512 KByte configuration, each sector contains four lines. *Valid* and *modified* status bits are kept on a per line basis. Thus, in the case of a 256 KByte cache each tag has two valid bits and two modified bits associated with it. In the case of a 512 KByte cache each tag has four valid and four modified bits associated with it. Upon a CPU read cache miss, the PCMC inspects the valid and modified bits within the addressed sector and writes back to main memory only the lines marked both valid and modified. All of the lines in the sector are then invalidated. The line fill will then occur and the valid bit associated with the allocated line will be set. Only the requested line will be fetched from main memory and written into the cache. If no write back is required, all of the lines in the sector are marked invalid. The line fill then occurs and the valid bit associated with the allocated line will be set. Lines are not allocated on write misses. When a CPU write hits a line in the second level cache, the modified bit for the line is set.

The second level cache is optional to allow the PCMC to be used in a low cost configuration. A 256 KByte cache is implemented with a single bank of eight 32K x 9 SRAMs if parity is supported or 32K x 8 SRAMs if parity is not supported on the cache. A 512 KByte cache is implemented with four 64K x 18 SRAMs if parity is supported or 64K x 16 SRAMs if parity is not supported on the cache. Two 74AS373 latchs complete the cache. Only main memory controlled by the PCMC DRAM interface is cached. Memory on PCI is not cached.

Figures 5-1 and 5-2 depict the organization of the internal tags in the PCMC configured for a 256 KByte cache and a 512 KByte cache.

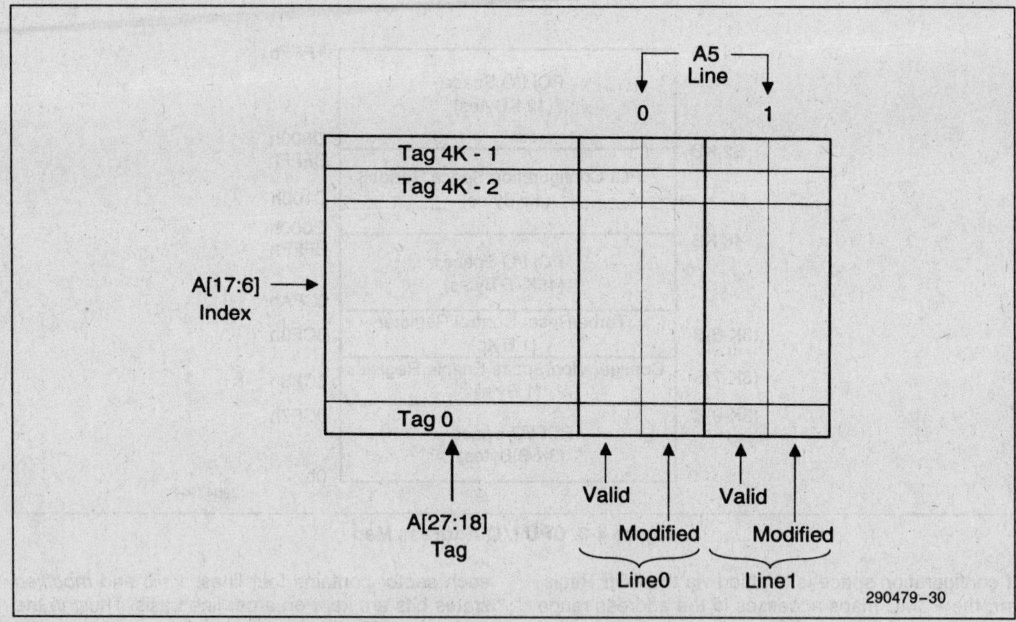

Figure 5-1. PCMC Internal Tags with 256 KByte Cache

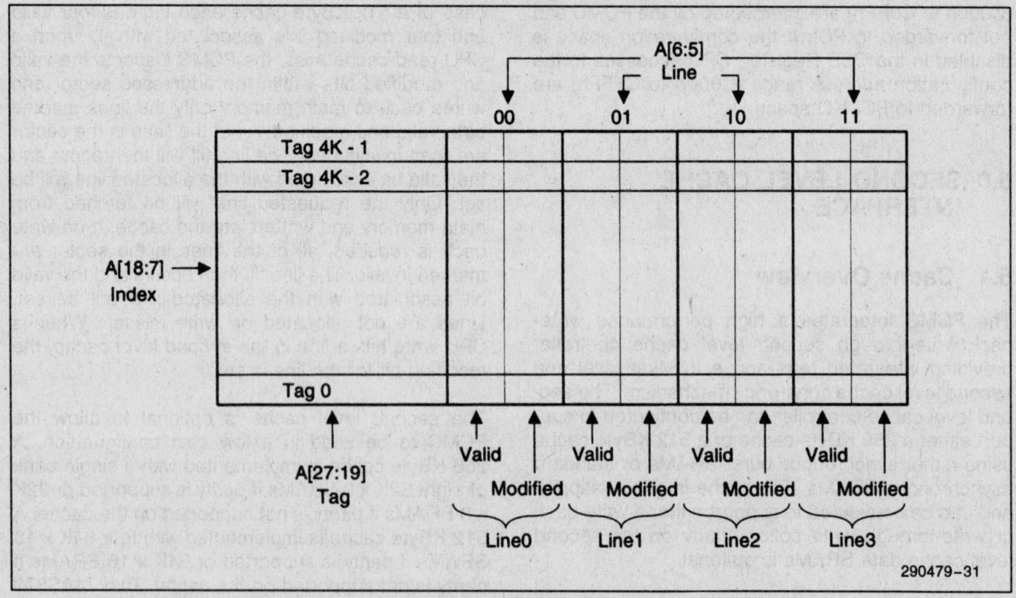

Figure 5-2. PCMC Internal Tags with 512 KByte Cache

In the 256 KByte cache configuration A[17:6] form the tag RAM index. The ten tag bits read from the tag RAM are compared against A[27:18] from the host address bus. Two valid bits and two modified bits are kept per tag in this configuration. Host address bit 5 is used to select between lines 0 and 1 within a sector. In the 512 KByte cache configuration A[18:7] form the tag RAM index. The nine bits read from the tag RAM are compared against A[27:19] from the host bus. Four valid bits and four modified bits are kept per tag. Host address bits 5 and 6 are used to select between lines 0, 1, 2 and 3 within a sector.

The Secondary Cache Controller Register at offset 52h in configuration space controls the secondary cache size, write and allocation policies, and SRAM type. The cache can also be enabled and disabled via this register.

Figures 5-3 through 5-7 show the connections between the PCMC and the external cache data SRAMs and latches.

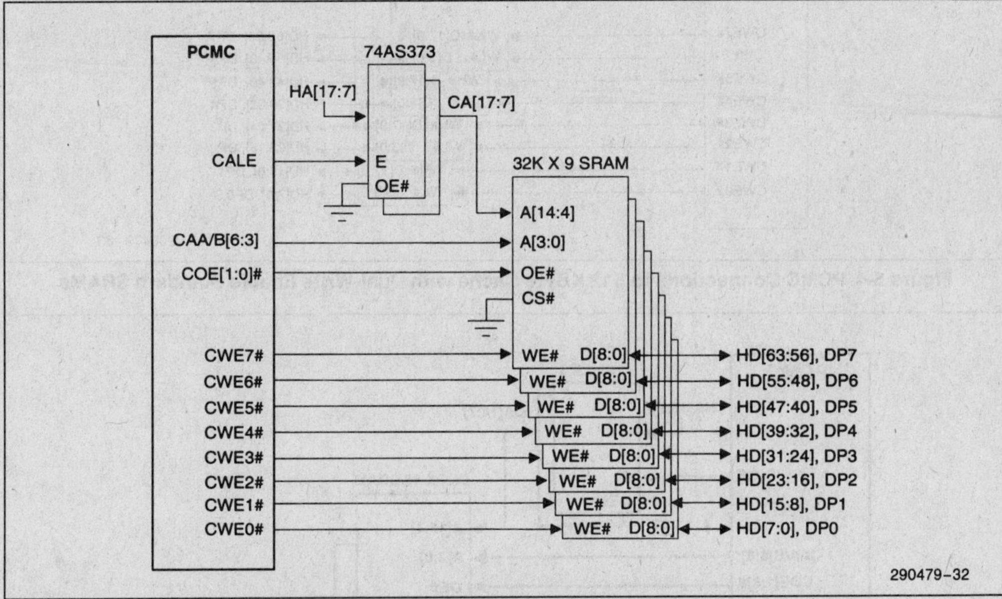

Figure 5-3. PCMC Connections to 256 KByte Cache with Standard SRAMs

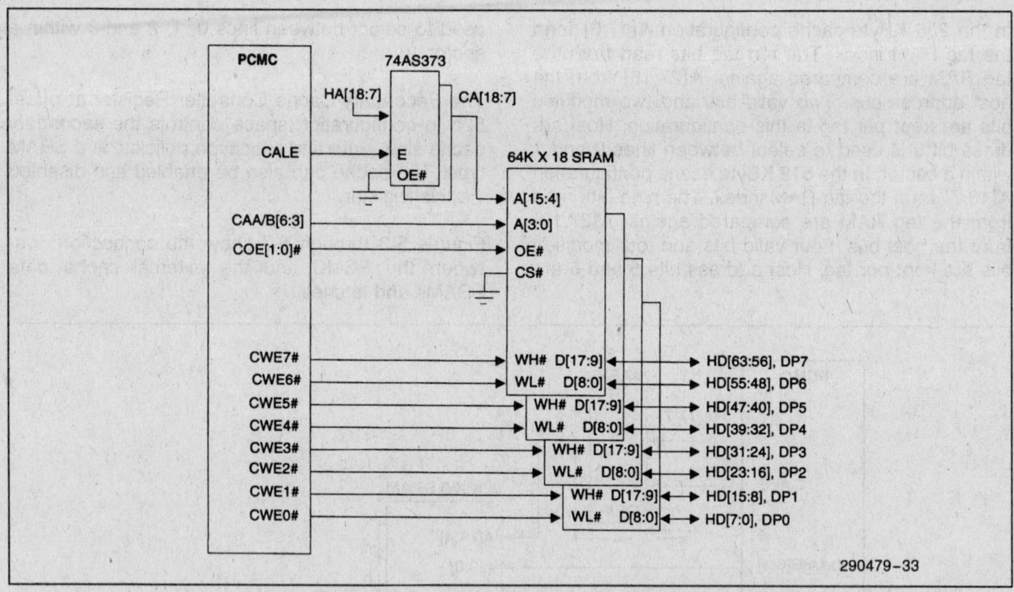

Figure 5-4. PCMC Connections to 512 KByte Cache with Dual-Write Enable Standard SRAMs

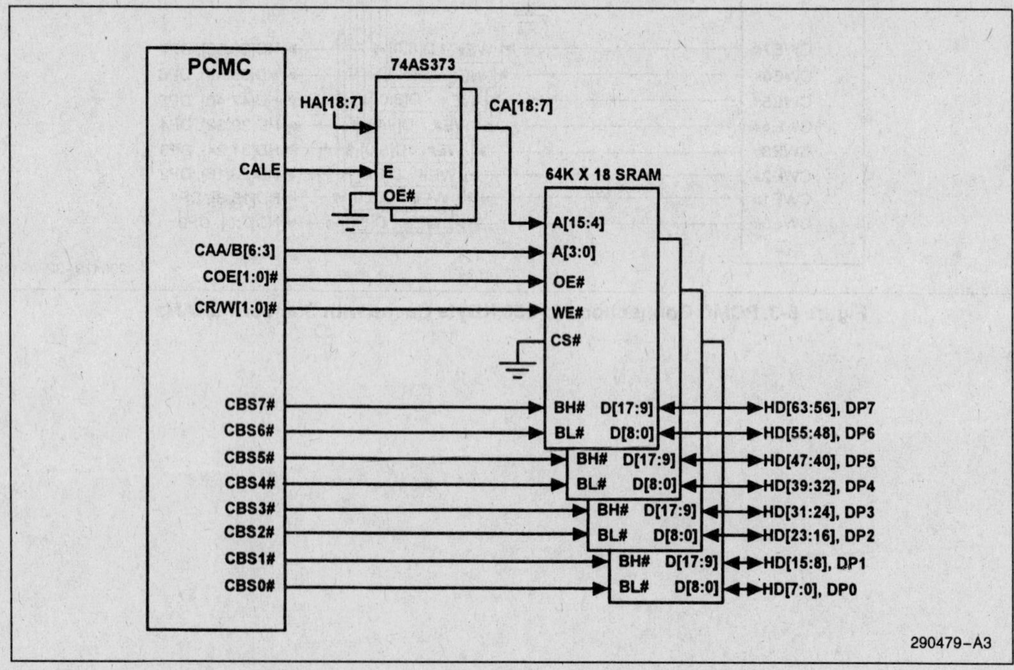

Figure 5-5. PCMC Connections to 512 KByte Cache with Dual-Byte Select SRAMs

PCMC
74AS373
HA[17:7]
CA[17:7]
CALE
E
OE#
HCLK[C-F]
32K X 9 SRAM
CLK
A[14:4]
CAA/B[6:3]
A[3:0]
CADS[1:0]#
ADSC#
CADV[1:0]#
ADV#
COE[1:0]#
OE#
VDD
ADSP#
CS0
CS1#
CWE7#
CWE6#
CWE5#
CWE4#
CWE3#
CWE2#
CWE1#
CWE0#
WE# D[8:0]
HD[63:56], DP7
HD[55:48], DP6
HD[47:40], DP5
HD[39:32], DP4
HD[31:24], DP3
HD[23:16], DP2
HD[15:8], DP1
HD[7:0], DP0
290479-34

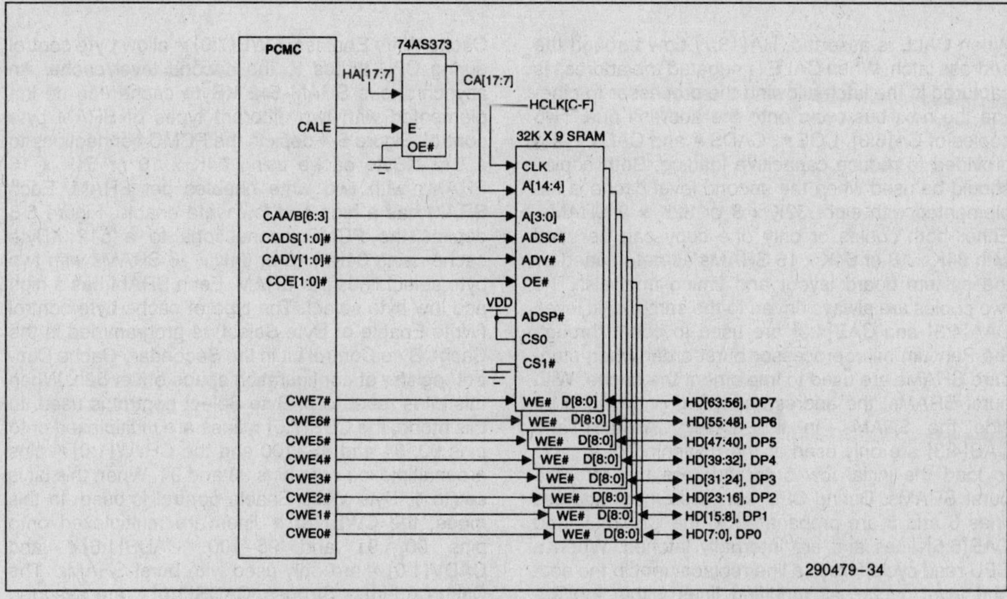

Figure 5-6. PCMC Connections to 256 KByte Cache with Burst SRAMs

PCMC
74AS373
HA[18:7]
CA[18:7]
CALE
E
OE#
HCLK[C-D]
64K X 18 SRAM
CLK
A[15:4]
CAA/B[6:3]
A[3:0]
CADS[1:0]#
ADSC#
CADV[1:0]#
ADV#
COE[1:0]#
OE#
VDD
ADSP#
CS#
CWE7#
CWE6#
CWE5#
CWE4#
CWE3#
CWE2#
CWE1#
CWE0#
WH# D[17:9]
WL# D[8:0]
HD[63:56], DP7
HD[55:48], DP6
HD[47:40], DP5
HD[39:32], DP4
HD[31:24], DP3
HD[23:16], DP2
HD[15:8], DP1
HD[7:0], DP0
290479-35

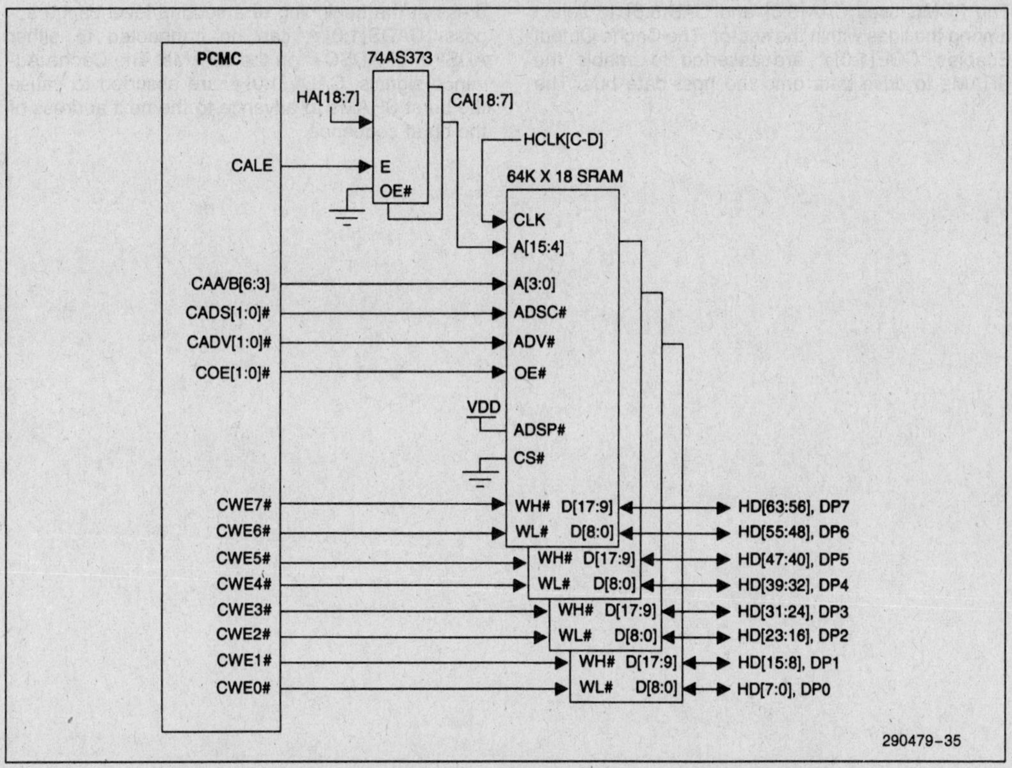

Figure 5-7. PCMC Connections for 512 KByte Cache with Burst SRAMs

When CALE is asserted, HA[18:7] flow through the address latch. When CALE is negated the address is captured in the latch allowing the processor to pipeline the next bus cycle onto the address bus. Two copies of CA[6:3], COE#, CADS# and CADV# are provided to reduce capacitive loading. Both copies should be used when the second level cache is implemented with eight 32K x 8 or 32K x 9 SRAMs. Either both copies or only one copy can be used with 64K x 18 or 64K x 16 SRAMs as determined by the system board layout and timing analysis. The two copies are always driven to the same logic level. CAA[4:3] and CAB[4:3] are used to count through the Pentium microprocessor burst order when standard SRAMs are used to implement the cache. With burst SRAMs, the address counting is provided inside the SRAMs. In this case, CAA[4:3] and CAB[4:3] are only used at the beginning of a cycle to load the initial low order address bits into the burst SRAMs. During CPU accesses, host address lines 6 and 5 are propagated to the CAA[6:5] and CAB[6:5] lines and are internally latched. When a CPU read cycle forces a line replacement in the second level cache, all modified lines within the addressed sector are written back to main memory. The PCMC uses CAA[6:5] and CAB[6:5] to select among the lines within the sector. The Cache Output Enables, COE[1:0]# are asserted to enable the SRAMs to drive data onto the host data bus. The Cache Write Enables, CWE[7:0]# allow byte control during CPU writes to the second level cache. An asynchronous SRAM 512 KByte cache can be implemented with two different types of SRAM byte control. Figure 5-4 depicts the PCMC connections to a 512 KByte cache using 64K x 18 or 64K x 16 SRAMs with two write enables per SRAM. Each SRAM has a high and low write enable. Figure 5-5 depicts the PCMC connections to a 512 KByte cache using 64K x 18 or 64K x 16 SRAMs with two byte select lines per SRAM. Each SRAM has a high and low byte select. The type of cache byte control (Write Enable or Byte Select) is programmed in the Cache Byte Control bit in the Secondary Cache Control register at configuration space offset 52h. When this bit is reset to 0, Byte Select control is used. In this mode, the CBS[7:0]# lines are multiplexed onto pins 90, 91 and 95–100 and the CR/W[1:0]# pins are multiplexed onto pins 93 and 94. When this bit is set to 1, Byte Write Enable control is used. In this mode, the CWE[7:0]# lines are multiplexed onto pins 90, 91 and 95–100. CADS[1:0]# and CADV[1:0]# are only used with burst SRAMs. The Cache Address Strobes, CADS[1:0]# are asserted to cause the burst SRAMs to latch the cache address at the beginning of a second level cache access. CADS[1:0]# can be connected to either ADSP# or ADSC# on the SRAMs. The Cache Advance signals, CADV[1:0]# are asserted to cause the burst SRAMs to advance to the next address of the burst sequence.

5.2 Clock Latencies

Tables 5-1 and 5-2 list the latencies for various CPU transfers to or from the second level cache for standard SRAMs and burst SRAMs. Standard SRAM access times of 12 and 15 ns are recommended for 66 and 60 MHz operation, respectively. Burst SRAM clock access times of 8 and 9 ns are recommended for 66 and 60 MHz operation respectively. Precise SRAM timing requirements should be determined by system board electrical simulation with SRAM I/O buffer models.

Table 5-1. Second Level Cache Latencies with Standard SRAM

Cycle Type	HCLK Count
Burst Read	3-2-2-2
Burst Write	4-2-2-2
Single Read	3
Single Write	4
Pipelined Back-to-Back Burst Reads	3-2-2-2/3-2-2-2
Burst Read followed by Pipelined Write	3-2-2-2/4

Table 5-2. Second Level Cache Latencies with Burst SRAM

Cycle Type	HCLK Count
Burst Read	3-1-1-1
Burst Write	3-1-1-1
Single Read	3
Single Write	3
Pipelined Back-to-Back Burst Reads	3-1-1-1/1-1-1-1
Read Followed by Pipelined Write	3-1-1-1/2

5.3 Standard SRAM Cache Cycles

The following sections describe the activity of the second level cache interface when standard asynchronous SRAMs are used to implement the cache.

5.3.1 BURST READ

Figure 5-8 depicts a burst read from the second level cache with standard SRAMs. The CPU initiates the read cycle by driving address and status onto the bus and asserting ADS#. Initially, the CA[6:3] are a propagation delay from the host address lines A[6:3]. Upon sampling W/R# active and M/IO# inactive, while ADS# is asserted, the PCMC asserts COE# to begin a read cycle from the SRAMs. CALE is negated, latching the address lines on the SRAM address inputs, allowing the CPU to pipeline a new address onto the bus. CA[4:3] cycle through the Pentium microprocessor burst order, completing the cycle. PEN# is asserted with the first BRDY# and negated with the last BRDY# if parity is implemented on the second level cache data SRAMs and the MCHK DRAM/Second Level Cache Data Parity bit in the Error Command Register (offset 70h) is set. Figure 5-9 depicts a burst read from the second level cache with standard 16- or 18-bit wide Dual-Byte Select SRAMs. A single read cycle from the second level cache is very similar to the first transfer of a burst read cycle. CALE is not negated throughout the cycle. COE# is asserted as shown above, but is negated with BRDY#.

When the Secondary Cache Allocation (SCA) bit in the Secondary Cache Control register is set, the PCMC will perform a line fill in the secondary cache even if the CACHE# signal from the CPU is inactive. In this case, AHOLD is asserted to prevent the CPU from beginning a new cycle while the second level cache line fill is completing.

Back-to-back pipelined burst reads from the second level cache are shown in the Figure 5-10.

1

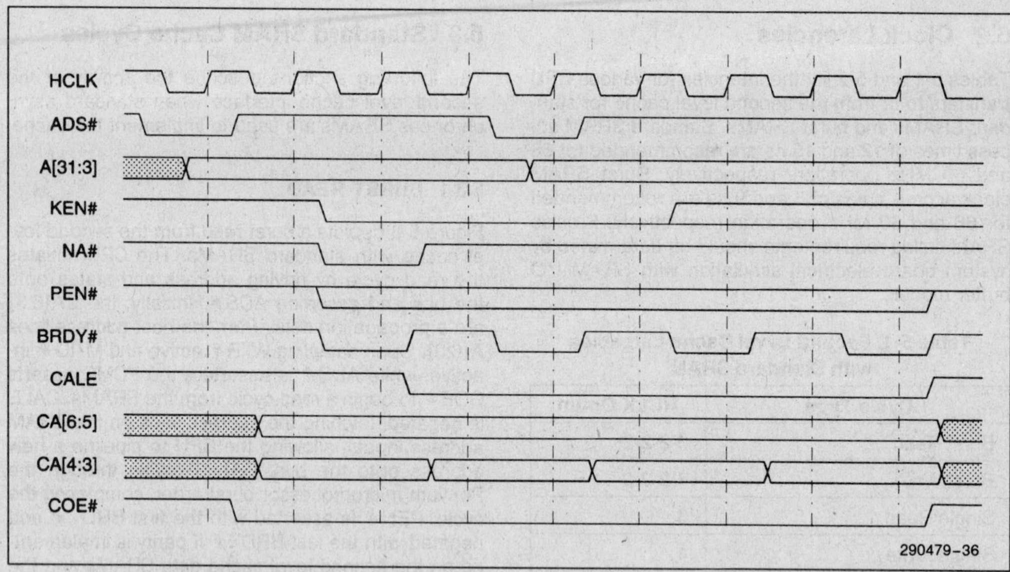

Figure 5-8. CPU Burst Read from Second Level Cache with Standard SRAM

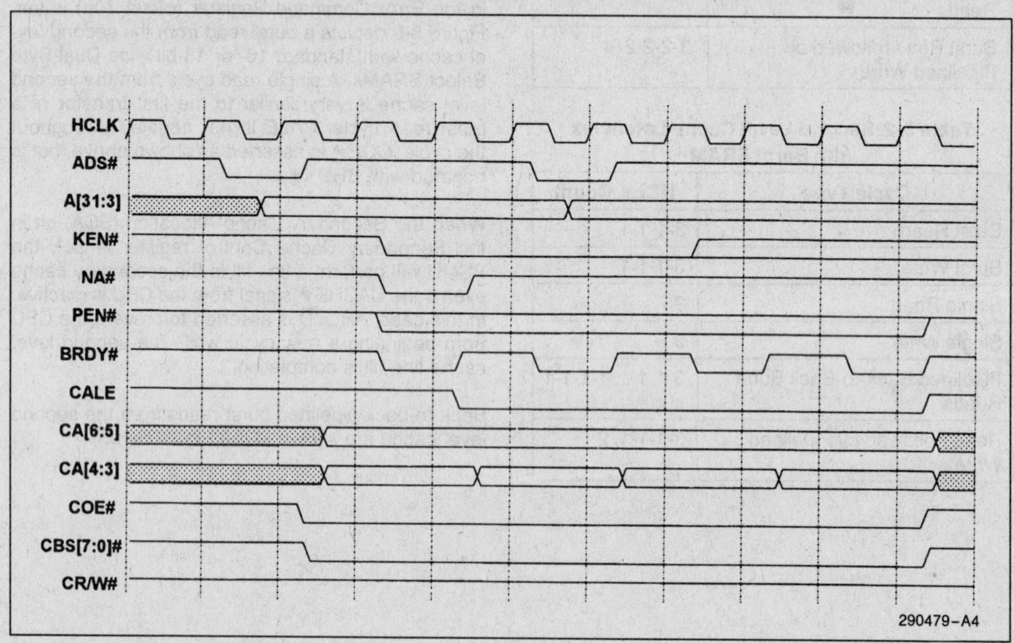

Figure 5-9. Burst Read from Second Level Cache with Dual-Byte Select SRAMs

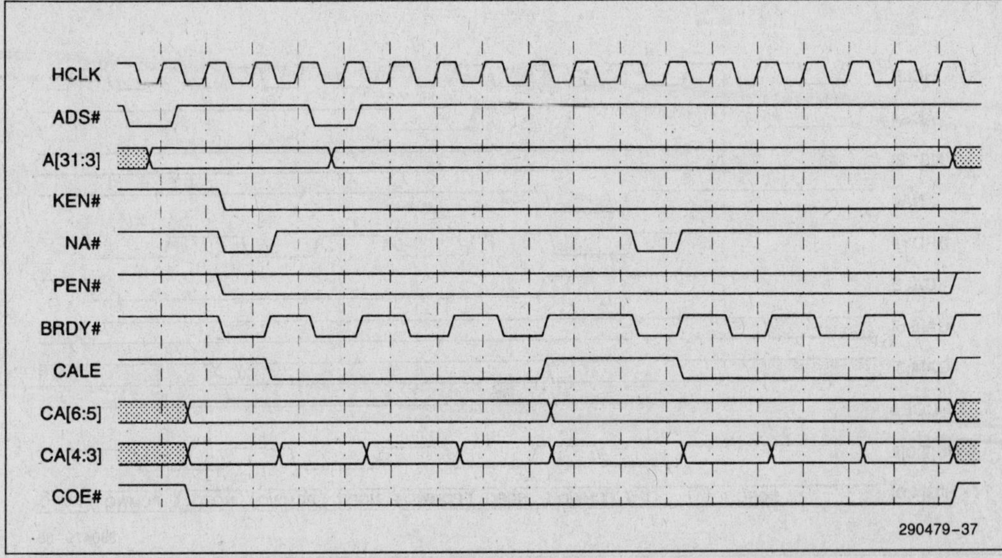

Figure 5-10. Pipelined Back-to-Back Burst Reads from Second Level Cache with Standard SRAM

Due to assertion of NA#, the CPU drives a new address onto the bus before the first cycle is complete. In this case, the second cycle is a hit in the second level cache. Immediately upon completion of the first read cycle, the PCMC begins the second cycle. When the first cycle completes, the PCMC drives the new address to the SRAMs on CA[6:3] and asserts CALE. The second cycle is very similar to the first, completing at a rate of 3-2-2-2. The cache address lines must be held at the SRAM address inputs until the first cycle completes. Only after the last BRDY# is returned, can CALE be asserted and CA[6:3] be changed. Thus, the pipelined cycle completes at the same rate as a non-pipelined cycle.

5.3.2 BURST WRITE

A burst write cycle is used to write back a cache line from the first level cache to either the second level cache or DRAM. Figure 5-11 depicts a burst write cycle to the second level cache with standard SRAMs.

The CPU initiates the write cycle by driving address and status onto the bus and asserting ADS#. Initially, the CA[6:3] propagate from the host address lines A[6:3]. CALE is negated, latching the address lines on the SRAM address inputs, allowing the CPU to pipeline a new address onto the bus. Burst write cycles from the Pentium microprocessor always begin with the low order Qword and advances to the high order Qword. CWE[7:0]# are generated from an internally delayed version of HCLK, providing address setup time to CWE[7:0]# falling and data setup time to CWE[7:0]# rising edges. HIG[4:0] are driven to PCMWQ (Post CPU to Memory Write Buffer Qword) only when the PCMC is programmed for a write-through write policy. When programmed for write-back mode, the modified bit associated with the line is set within the PCMC. The single write cycle is very similar to the first write of a burst write cycle. A burst read cycle followed by a pipelined write cycle with standard SRAMs is depicted in Figure 5-3.

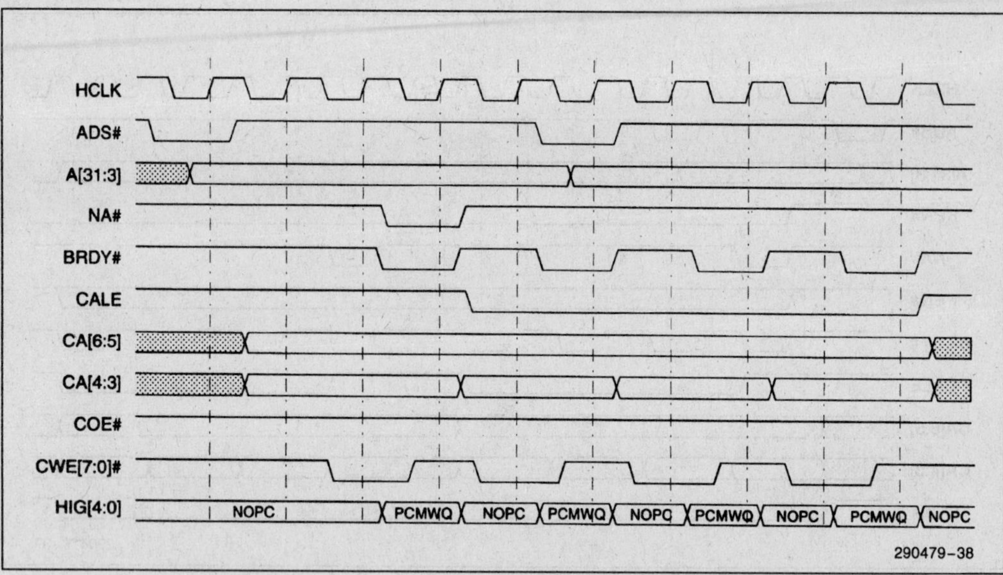

Figure 5-11. Burst Write to Second Level Cache with Standard SRAM

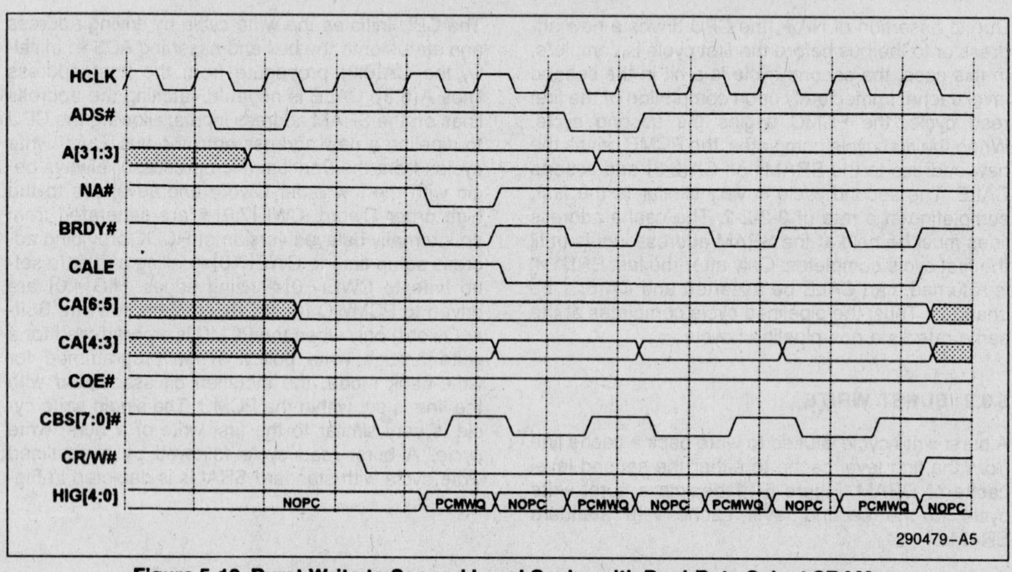

Figure 5-12. Burst Write to Second Level Cache with Dual-Byte Select SRAMs

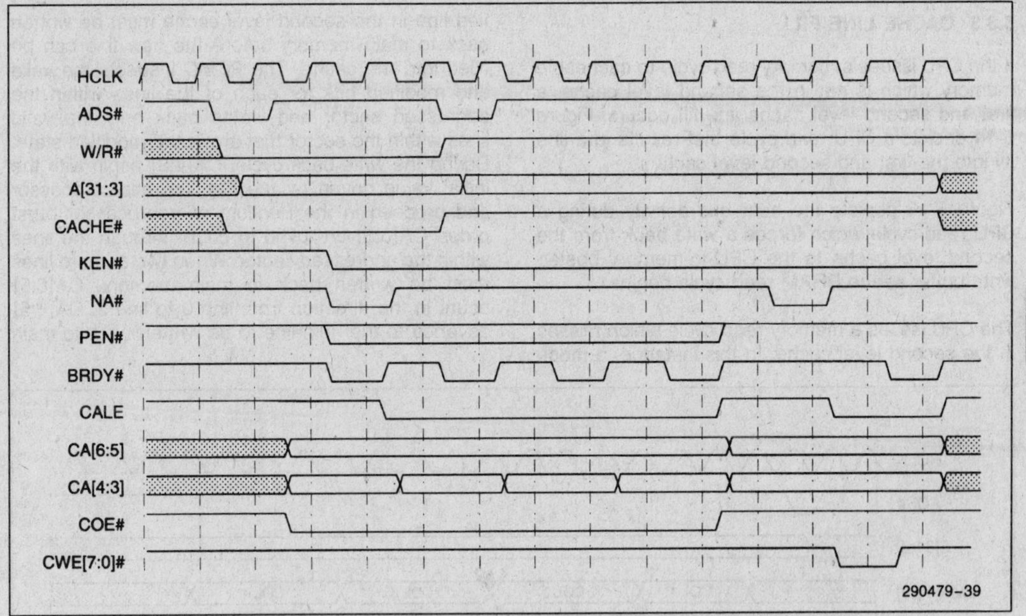

Figure 5-13. Burst Read followed by Pipelined Write with Standard SRAM

1

5.3.3 CACHE LINE FILL

If the CPU issues a memory read cycle to cacheable memory which is not in the second level cache, a first and second level cache line fill occurs. Figure 5-14 depicts a CPU read cycle that results in a line fill into the first and second level caches.

Figure 5-16 depicts the host bus activity during a CPU read cycle which forces a write-back from the second level cache to the CPU-to-memory posted write buffer as the DRAM read cycle begins.

The CPU issues a memory read cycle which misses in the second level cache. In this instance, a modified line in the second level cache must be written back to main memory before the new line can be filled into the cache. The PCMC inspects the valid and modified bits for each of the lines within the addressed sector and writes back only the valid lines within the sector that are in the modified state. During the write-back cycle, CA[4:3] begin with the initial value driven by the Pentium microprocessor and proceed in the Pentium microprocessor burst order. CA[6:5] are used to count through the lines within the addressed sector. When two or more lines must be written back to main memory, CA[6:5] count in the direction from line 0 to line 3. CA[6:5] advance to the next line to be written back to main

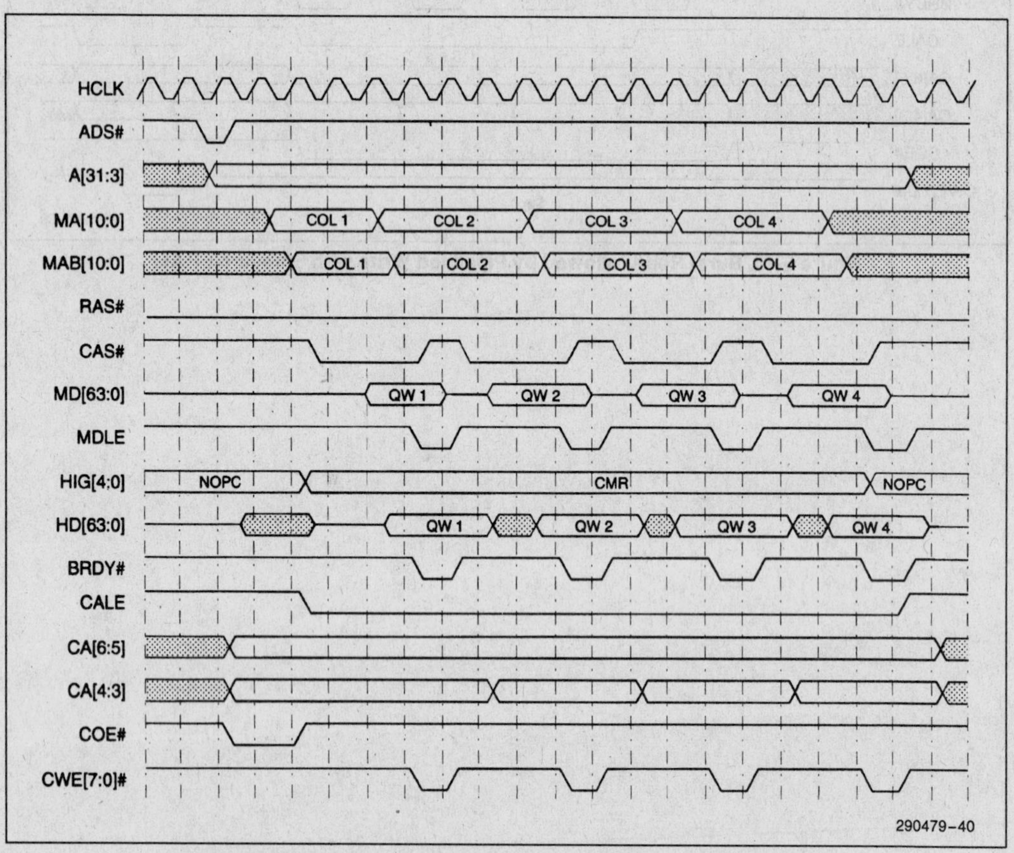

HCLK
ADS#
A[31:3]
MA[10:0] COL 1 COL 2 COL 3 COL 4
MAB[10:0] COL 1 COL 2 COL 3 COL 4
RAS#
CAS#
MD[63:0] QW 1 QW 2 QW 3 QW 4
MDLE
HIG[4:0] NOPC CMR NOPC
HD[63:0] QW 1 QW 2 QW 3 QW 4
BRDY#
CALE
CA[6:5]
CA[4:3]
COE#
CWE[7:0]#

290479-40

Figure 5-14. Cache Line Fill with Standard SRAM, DRAM Page Hit

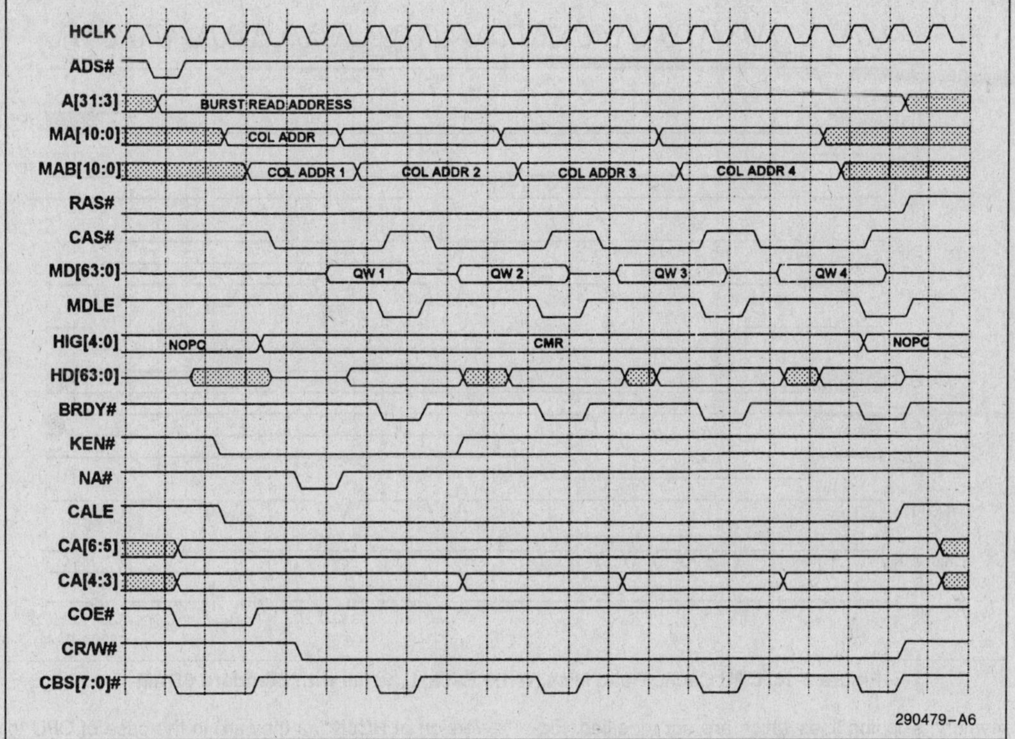

290479–A6

Figure 5-15. Cache Line Fill with Dual-Byte Select Standard SRAM, DRAM Page Hit

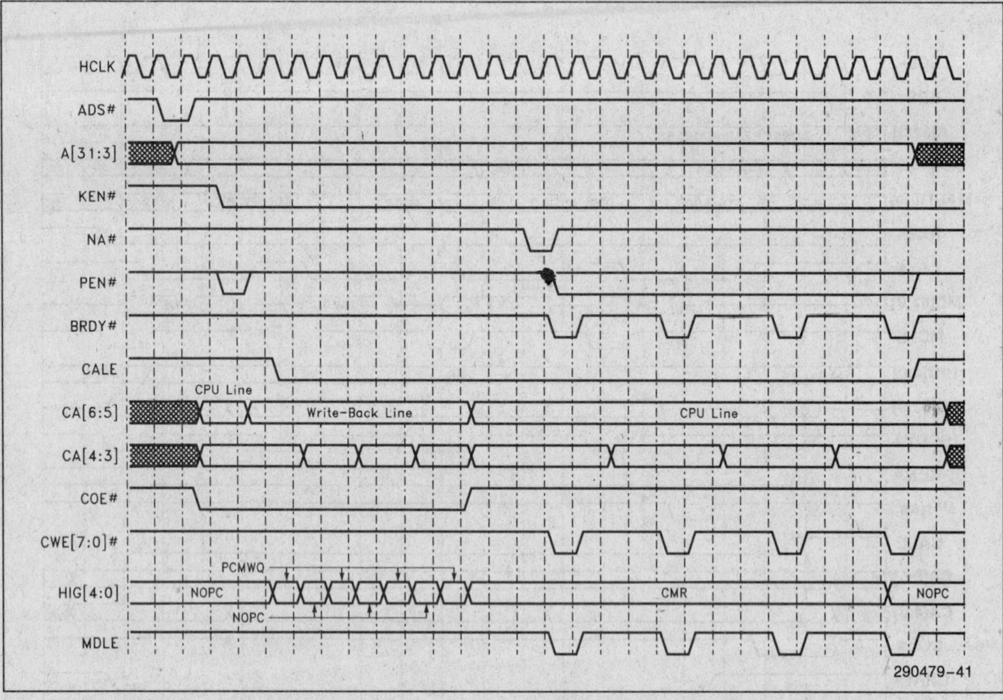

Figure 5-16. CPU Cache Read Miss, Write Back, Line Fill with Standard SRAM

memory, skipping lines which are not modified. Figure 5-16 depicts the case of just one of the lines in a sector being written back to main memory. In this case, the entire line can be posted in the CPU-to-Main Memory posted write buffer by driving the HIG[4:0] lines to the PCMWQ command as each Qword is read from the cache. At the same time, the required DRAM read cycle is beginning. As soon as the de-allocated line is written into the posted write buffer, the HIG[4:0] lines are driven to CMR (CPU Memory Read) to allow data to propagate from the DRAM data lines to the CPU data lines. The CWE[7:0]# lines are not generated from a delayed version of HCLK (as they are in the case of CPU to second level cache burst write), but from ordinary HCLK rising edges. CMR is driven on the HIG[4:0] lines throughout the DRAM read portion of the cycle. With the fourth assertion of BRDY# the HIG[4:0] lines change to NOPC. The LBXs however, do not tri-state the host data lines until MDLE rises. CWE[7:0]# and MDLE track such that MDLE will not rise before CWE[7:0]#. Thus, the LBXs continue to drive the host data lines until CWE[7:0]# are negated. CA[6:3] remain at the valid values until the clock after the last BRDY#, providing address hold time to CWE[7:0]# rising.

PEN# is asserted as shown if the MCHK DRAM/L2 Cache Data Parity Error bit in the Error Command Register (offset 70h) is set. If the second level cache supports parity, PEN# is always asserted during CPU read cycles in the third clock in case the cycle hits in the cache.

If more than one line must be written back to main memory, the PCMC fills the CPU-to-Main Memory Posted Write Buffer and loads another Qword into the buffer as each Qword write completes into main memory. The writes into DRAM proceed as page hit write cycles from one line to the next, completing at a rate of X-4-4-4-5-4-4-4-5-4-4-4 for a three line write-back. All modifed lines except for the last one to be written back are posted and written to memory before the DRAM read cycle begins. The last line to be written back is posted as the DRAM read cycle begins. Thus, the read data is returned to the CPU before the last line is retired to memory.

The line which was written into the second level cache is marked valid and unmodified by the PCMC. All the other lines in the sector are marked invalid. A subsequent CPU read cycle which hits in the same sector (but a different line) in the second level cache would then simply result in a line fill without any write back.

5.4 Burst SRAM Cache Cycles

The following sections show the activity of the second level cache interface when burst SRAMs are used for the second level cache.

5.4.1 BURST READ

Figure 5-17 depicts a burst read from the second level cache with burst SRAMs.

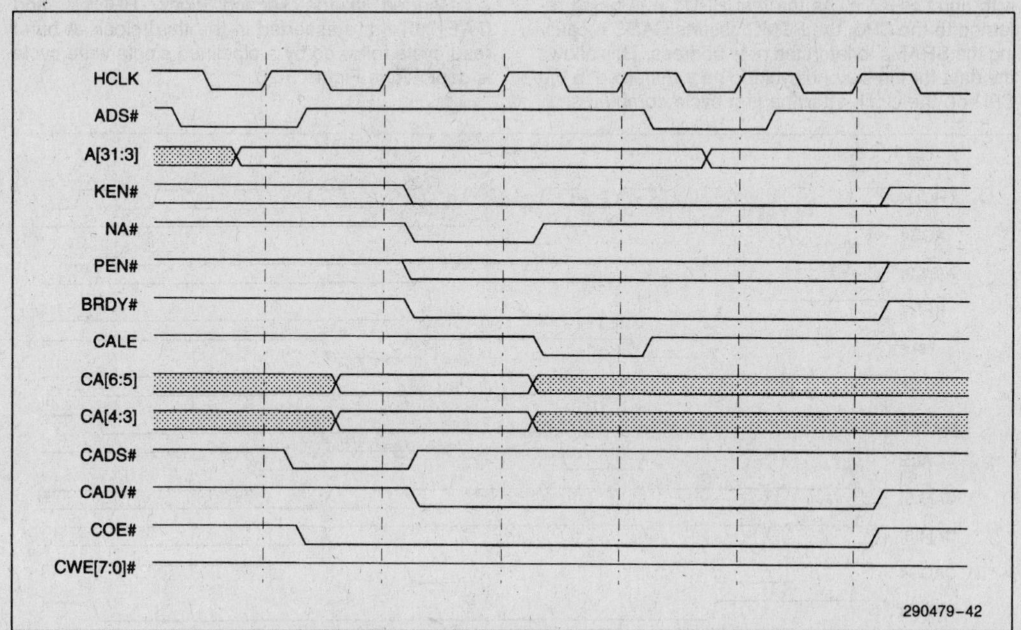

Figure 5-17. CPU Burst Read From Second Level Cache with Burst SRAM

The cycle begins with the CPU driving address and status onto Host Bus and asserting ADS#. The PCMC asserts CADS# and COE# in the second clock. After the address is latched by the burst SRAMs and the PCMC determines that no write back cycles are required from the second level cache, CALE is negated. Back-to-back burst reads from the second level cache are shown in Figure 5-18.

When the Secondary Cache Allocation (SCA) bit in the Secondary Cache Control register is set, the PCMC will perform a line fill in the secondary cache even if the CACHE# signal from the CPU is inactive. In this case, AHOLD is asserted to prevent the CPU from beginning a new cycle while the second level cache line fill is completing.

Back-to-back burst reads which hit in the second level cache complete at a rate of 3-1-1-1/1-1-1-1 with burst SRAMs. As the last BRDY# is being returned to the CPU, the PCMC asserts CADS# causing the SRAMs to latch the new address. This allows the data for the second cycle to be transferred to the CPU on the clock after the first cycle completes.

5.4.2 BURST WRITE

A burst write cycle is used to write back a line from the first level cache to either the the second level cache or DRAM. A burst write cycle from the first level cache to the second level cache is shown in Figure 5-19.

The Pentium microprocessor always writes back lines starting with the low order Qword advancing to the high order Qword. CADS# is asserted in the second clock. CWE[7:0]# and BRDY# are asserted in the third clock. CADV# assertion is delayed by one clock relative to the burst read cycle. HIG[4:0] are driven to PCMWQ (Post CPU-to-Memory Write Buffer Qword) only when the PCMC is programmed for a write-through write policy. When programmed for write-back mode, the modified bit associated with the line is set within the PCMC. The single write is very similar to the first write in a burst write. CADS# is asserted in the second clock. BRDY# and CWE[7:0]# are asserted in the third clock. A burst read cycle followed by a pipelined single write cycle is depicted in Figure 5-20.

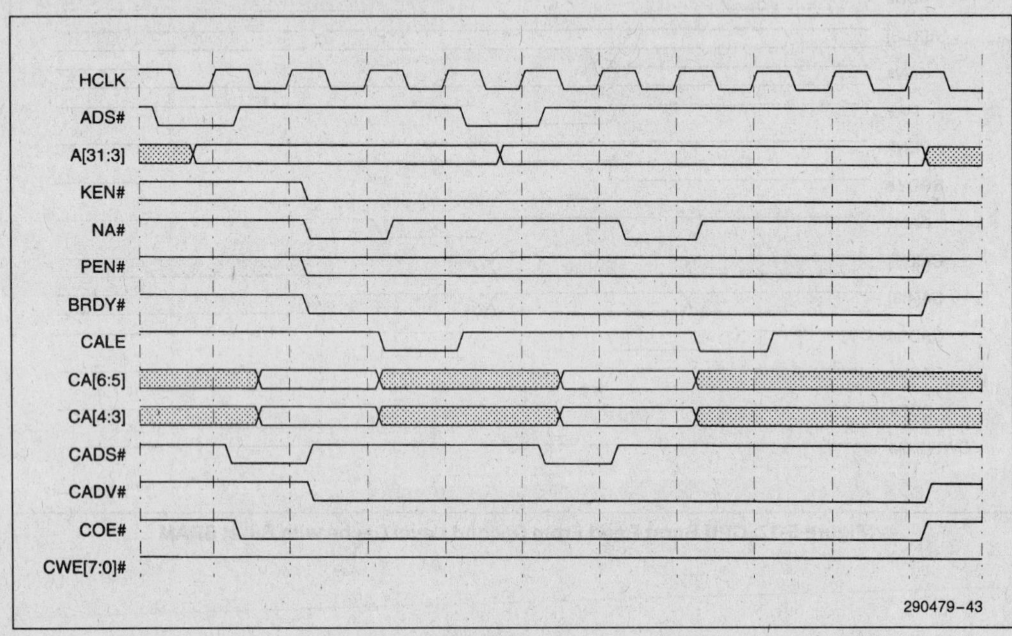

Figure 5-18. Pipelined Back-to-Back Burst Reads from Second Level Cache

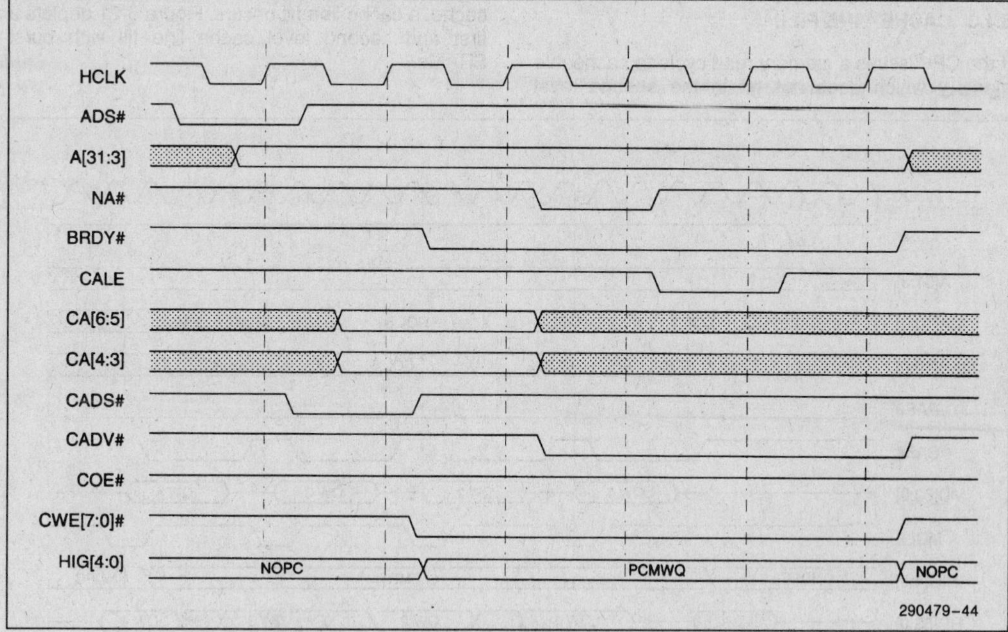

Figure 5-19. Burst Write to Second Level Cache with Burst SRAM

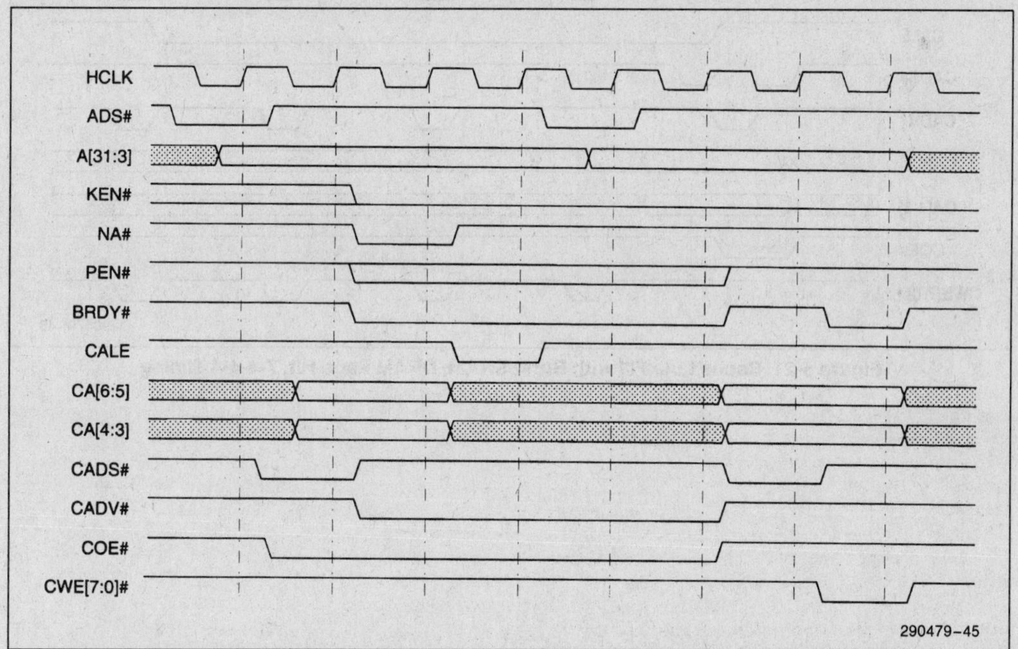

Figure 5-20. Burst Read followed by Pipelined Single Write Cycle with Burst SRAM

5.4.3 CACHE LINE FILL

If the CPU issues a memory read cycle to cacheable memory which does not hit in the second level cache, a cache line fill occurs. Figure 5-21 depicts a first and second level cache line fill with burst SRAMs.

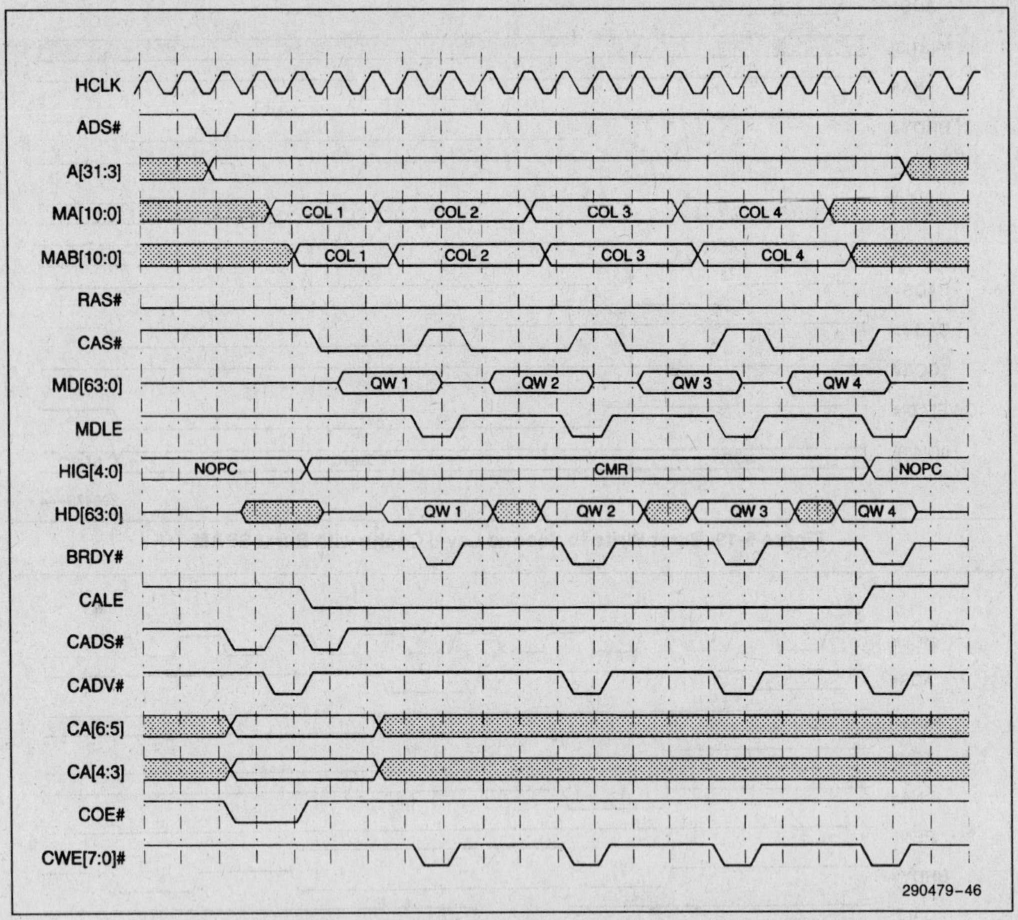

Figure 5-21. Cache Line Fill with Burst SRAM, DRAM Page Hit, 7-4-4-4 Timing

Figure 5-22 depicts a CPU read cycle which forces a write-back in the second level cache.

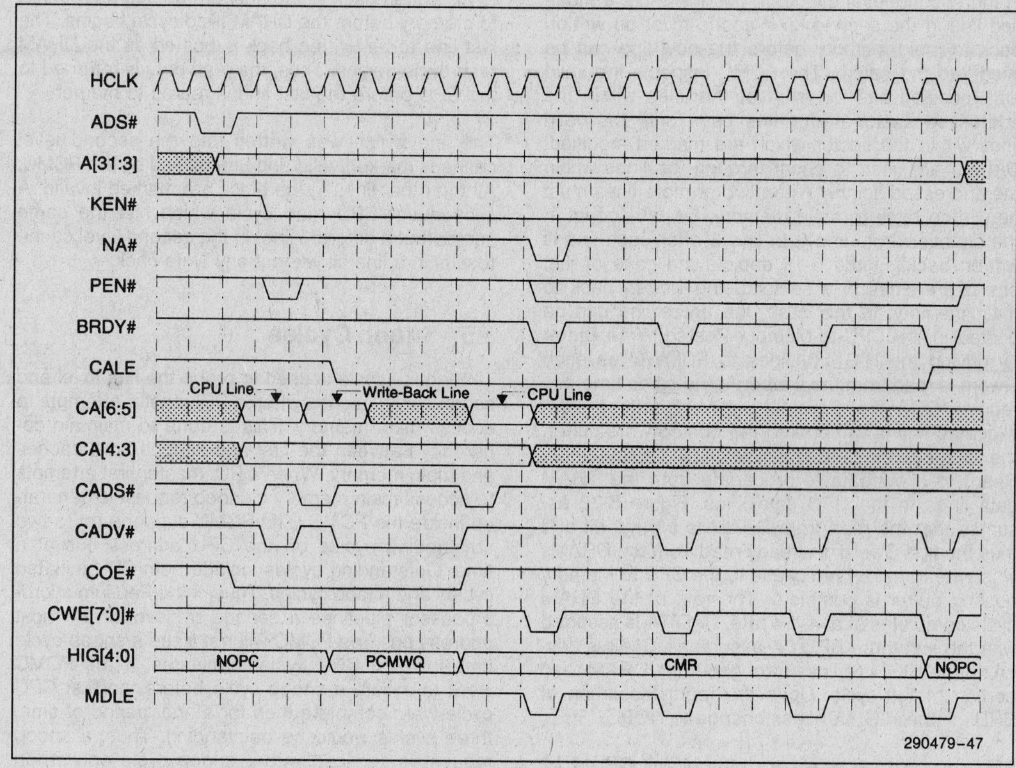

Figure 5-22. CPU Cache Read Miss, Write-Back, Line Fill with Burst SRAM

The CPU issues a memory read cycle which misses in the second level cache. In this instance, a modified line in the second level cache must be written back to main memory before the new line can be filled into the cache. The PCMC inspects the valid and modified bits for each of the lines within the addressed sector and writes back only the valid lines within the sector which are marked modified. CA[6:5] are used to count through the lines within the addressed sector. When two or more lines must be written back to main memory, CA[6:5] count in the direction from line 0 to line 3 after each line is written back. Figure 5-18 depicts the case of just one of the lines in a sector being written back to main memory. In this case, the entire line can be posted in the CPU-to-Memory Posted Write Buffer by driving the HIG[4:0] lines to PCMWQ as each Qword is read from the cache. At the same time, the required DRAM read cycle is beginning. After the deallocated line is written into the posted write buffer, the HIG[4:0] lines are driven to CMR (CPU Memory Read) to allow data to propagate from the DRAM data lines to the CPU data lines. Figure 5-22 assumes that the read from DRAM is a page hit and thus the first Qword is already read from the DRAMs when the transfer from cache to the CPU to Memory posting buffer is complete. The rest of the DRAM cycle completes at a -4-4-4 rate. CADV# is asserted with the last three BRDY# assertions. CMR is driven on the HIG[4:0] lines throughout the DRAM read portion of the cycle. Upon the fourth assertion of BRDY# the HIG[4:0] lines change to NOPC.

PEN# is asserted as shown if the MCHK DRAM/L2 Cache Data Parity Error bit in the Error Command Register (offset 70h) is set. If the second level cache supports parity, PEN# is always asserted during CPU read cycles in clock 3 in case the cycle hits in the cache.

If more than one line must be written back to main memory, the PCMC fills the CPU-to-Main Memory Posted Write Buffer and loads another Qword into the buffer as each Qword write completes into main memory. The writes into DRAM proceed as page hit write cycles from one line to the next, completing at a rate of X-4-4-4-5-4-4-4-5-4-4-4 for a three line write-back. All modifed lines except for the last one to be written back to memory are posted and retired to memory before the DRAM read cycle begins. The last line to be written back is posted as the DRAM read cycle begins. Thus, the read data is returned to the CPU before the last line is retired to memory.

The line which was written into the second level cache is marked valid and unmodified by the PCMC. All the other lines in the block are marked invalid. A subsequent CPU read cycle which hits the same sector (but a different line) in the second level cache results in a line fill without any write-back.

5.5 Snoop Cycles

The inquire cycle is used to probe the first level and second level caches when a PCI master attempts to access main memory. This is done to maintain coherency between the first and second level caches and main memory. When a PCI master first attempts to access main memory a snoop request is generated inside the PCMC. The PCMC supports up to two outstanding cycles on the CPU address bus at a time. Outstanding cycles include both CPU initiated cycles and snoop cycles. Thus, if the Pentium microprocessor pipelines a second cycle onto the host address bus, the PCMC will not issue a snoop cycle until the first CPU cycle terminates. If the PCMC were to initiate a snoop cycle before the first CPU cycle were complete then for a brief period of time, three cycles would be outstanding. Thus, a snoop request is serviced with a snoop cycle only when either no cycle is outstanding on the CPU bus or one cycle is outstanding.

Snoop cycles are performed by driving the PCI master address onto the CPU address bus and asserting EADS#. The Pentium microprocessor then performs a tag lookup to determine if the addressed memory is in the first level cache. At the same time the PCMC performs an internal tag lookup to determine if the addressed memory is in the second level cache. Table 5-3 describes how a PCI master read from main memory is serviced by the PCMC.

Table 5-3. Data Transfers for PCI Master Reads from Main Memory

Snoop Result		Action
First Level Cache	**Second Level Cache**	
Miss	Miss	Data is transferred from DRAM to PCI.
Miss	Hit Unmodified Line	Data is transferred directly from second level cache to PCI. The line remains valid and unmodified in the second level cache.
Miss	Hit Modified Line	Data is transferred directly from second level cache to PCI. Line remains valid and modified in the second level cache. The line is not written to DRAM.
Hit Unmodified Line	Miss	Data is transferred from DRAM to PCI.
Hit Unmodified Line	Hit Unmodified Line	Data is transferred directly from second level cache to PCI. The line remains valid and unmodified in the second level cache.
Hit Unmodified Line	Hit Modified Line	Data is transferred directly from second level cache to PCI. Line remains valid and modified in the second level cache. The line is not written to DRAM.
Hit Modified Line	Miss	A write-back from first level cache occurs. The data is sent to both PCI and the CPU-to-Memory Posted Write Buffer. The CPU-to-Memory Posted Write Buffer is then written to memory.
Hit Modified Line	Hit Unmodified Line	A write-back from first level cache occurs. The data is posted to PCI and written into the second level cache. When the second level cache is in write-back mode, the line is marked modified and is not written to DRAM. When the second level cache is in write-through mode, the line is posted and then written to DRAM.
Hit Modified Line	Hit Modified Line	A write-back from first level cache occurs. The data is posted to PCI and written into the second level cache. The line is not written to DRAM. This scenario can only occur when the second level cache is in write-back mode.

1

PCI master write cycles never result in a write directly into the second level cache. A snoop hit to a modified line in either the first level or second level cache results in a write-back of the line to main memory. The line is invalidated and the PCI write to main memory occurs after the write-back completes. The other lines in the sector are not written back to main memory or invalidated. A PCI master write snoop hit to an unmodified line in either the first level or second level cache results in the line being invalidated. Table 5-4 describes the actions taken by the PCMC when a PCI master writes to main memory.

Table 5-4. Data Transfer for PCI Master Writes to Main Memory

Snoop Result		Action
First Level Cache	**Second Level Cache**	
Miss	Miss	The PCI master write data is transferred from PCI to DRAM.
Miss	Hit Unmodified Line	The PCI master write data is transferred from PCI to DRAM. The line is invalidated in the second level cache.
Miss	Hit Modified Line	A write-back from second level cache to DRAM occurs. The PCI master write data is then written to DRAM. The line is invalidated in the second level cache.
Hit Unmodified Line	Miss	The first level cache line is invalidated. The PCI master write data is written to DRAM.
Hit Unmodified Line	Hit Unmodified Line	The line is invalidated in both the first level and second level caches. The PCI master write data is written to DRAM.
Hit Unmodified Line	Hit Modified Line	The first level cache line is invalidated. The second level cache line is written back to main memory and invalidated. The PCI master write data is then written to DRAM.
Hit Modified Line	Miss	The first level cache line is written back to DRAM and invalidated. The PCI master write data is then written to DRAM.
Hit Modified Line	Hit Unmodified Line	The first level cache line is written back to DRAM and invalidated. The second level cache line is invalidated. The PCI master write data is then written to DRAM.
Hit Modified Line	Hit Modified Line	The first level cache line is written back to DRAM and invalidated. The second level cache line is invalidated. The PCI master write data is then written to DRAM.

A snoop hit results in one of three transfers, a write-back from the first level cache posted to the LBXs, a write-back from the second level cache posted to the LBXs or a write-back from the first level cache posted to the LBXs and written to the second level cache. A snoop cycle which does not result in a write-back is depicted in Figure 5-23.

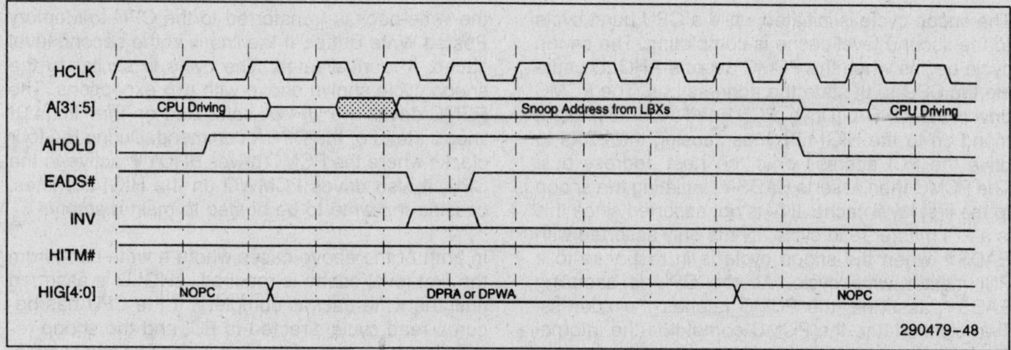

Figure 5-23. Snoop Hit to Unmodified Line in First Level Cache or Snoop Miss

The PCMC begins to service the snoop request by asserting AHOLD, causing the Pentium microprocessor to tri-state the address bus in the clock after assertion. In the case of a PCI master read cycle, the PCMC drives the DPRA (Drive PCI Read Address) command onto the HIG[4:0] lines causing the LBXs to drive the PCI address onto the host address bus. For a write cycle, the PCMC drives the DPWA (Drive PCI Write Address to CPU Address Bus) command on the HIG[4:0] lines, also causing the LBXs to begin driving the host address bus. The PCMC then asserts EADS#, initiating the snoop cycle to the CPU. The INV signal is asserted by the PCMC only during snoops due to PCI master writes. INV remains negated during snoops due to PCI master reads. If the snoop results in a hit to a modified line in the first level cache, the Pentium microprocessor asserts HITM#. The PCMC samples the HITM# signal two clocks after the CPU samples EADS# asserted to determine if the snoop hit in the first level cache. By this time the PCMC has completed an internal tag lookup to determine if the line is in the second level cache. Since this snoop does not result in a write back, the NOPC command is driven on the HIG[4:0] lines, causing the LBXs to tri-state the address bus. The sequence ends with AHOLD negation.

If the Pentium microprocessor asserts ADS# in the same clock as the PCMC asserts AHOLD, the PCMC will assert BOFF# in two cases. First, if the snoop cycle hits a modified line in the first level cache, the PCMC will assert BOFF# for 1 HCLK to re-order the write-back around the currently sending cycle. Second, if the snoop requires a write-back from the second level cache, the PCMC will assert BOFF# to enable the write-back from the secondary cache SRAMS.

Figure 5-24 depicts a snoop hit to a modified line in the first level cache due to a PCI master memory read cycle.

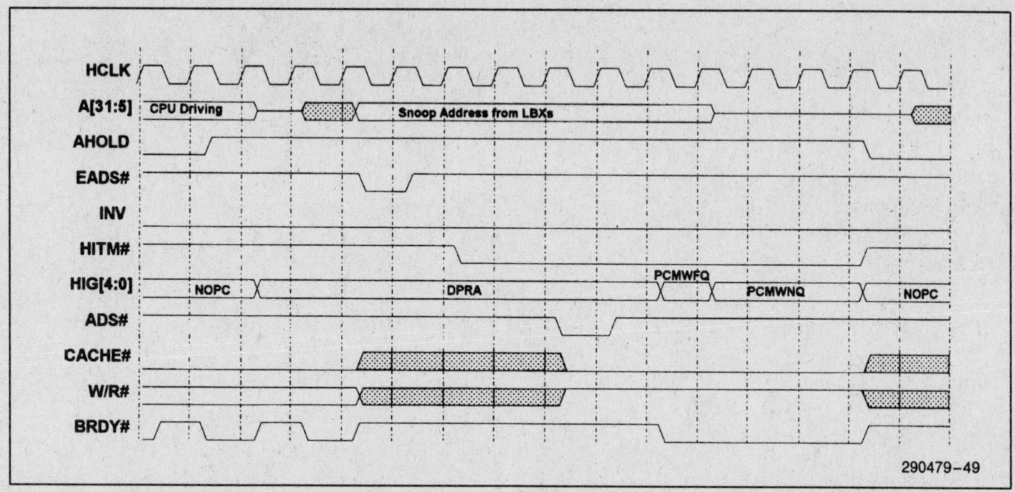

Figure 5-24. Snoop Hit to Modified Line in First Level Cache, Post Memory and PCI

The snoop cycle is initiated while a CPU burst cycle to the second level cache is completing. The snoop cycle begins when the PCMC asserts AHOLD causing the CPU to tri-state the address bus. The PCMC drives the DPRA (Drive PCI Read Address) command on to the HIG[4:0] lines causing the LBXs to drive the PCI address onto the host address bus. The PCMC then asserts EADS#, initiating the snoop to the first level cache. INV is not asserted since this is a PCI master read cycle. INV is only asserted with EADS# when the snoop cycle is in response to a PCI master write cycle. As the CPU is sampling EADS# asserted, the PCMC latches the address. Two clocks later, the PCMC completes the internal tag lookup to determine if the line is in the second level cache. In this instance, the snoop hits a modified line in the first level cache and misses in the second level cache. Thus, the second level cache is not involved in the write-back cycle. The PCMC allows the LBXs to stop driving the address lines by driving NOPC command on the HIG[4:0] lines. The CPU then drives the write-back cycle onto the bus by asserting ADS# and driving the write-back data on the data lines even though AHOLD is still asserted. The write-back into the LBX buffers occurs at a rate of 3-1-1-1. The PCMC drives PCMWFQ on the HIG[4:0] lines for one clock causing the write data to be posted to both PCI and main memory. For the next three clocks, the HIG[4:0] lines are driven to PCMWNQ, posting the final three Qwords to both PCI and main memory.

A similar transfer from first level cache to the LBXs occurs when a snoop due to a PCI master write hits a modified line in the first level cache. In this case, the write-back is transferred to the CPU-to-Memory Posted Write Buffer. If the line is in the second level cache, it is invalidated. The cycle is similar to the snoop cycle shown above with two exceptions. The PCMC drives the DPWA command on the HIG[4:0] lines instead of the DPRA command. During the four clocks where the PCMC drives BRDY# active to the CPU, it also drives PCMWQ on the HIG[4:0] lines, causing the write to be posted to main memory.

In both of the above cases where a write-back from the first level cache is required, AHOLD is asserted until the write-back is complete. If the CPU has begun a read cycle directed to PCI and the snoop results in a hit to a modified line in the first level cache, BOFF# is asserted for one clock to abort the CPU read cycle and re-order the write-back cycle before the read cycle.

When a PCI master read or write cycle hits a modified line in the second level cache and either misses in the first level cache or hits an unmodified line in the first level cache, a write-back from the second level cache to the LBXs occurs. When a PCI master write snoop hits an unmodified line in the second level cache and either misses in the first level cache or hits an unmodified line in the first level cache, no data transfer from the second level cache occurs. The line is simply invalidated. In the case of a PCI master write cycle, the line is invalidated in both the first level and second level caches. In the case of a PCI master memory read cycle, neither cache is invalidated. A PCI master read from main memory which hits either a modified or unmodified line in the second level cache is shown in Figure 5-25.

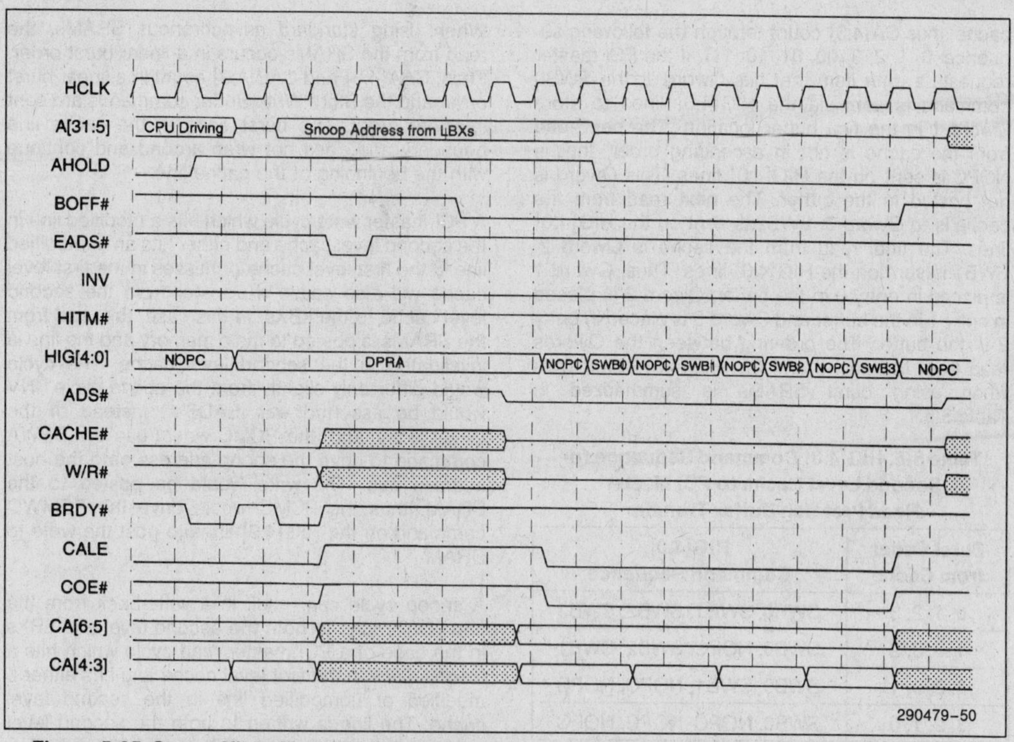

Figure 5-25. Snoop Hit to Modified Line in Second Level Cache, Store in PCI Read Prefetch Buffer

The snoop request is received as a CPU burst access to the second level cache is in progress. The snoop cycle begins with the PCMC asserting AHOLD, causing the CPU to tri-state the Host address bus. The PCMC drives the DPRA command enabling the LBXs to drive the snoop address onto the Host address bus. The PCMC asserts EADS#. INV is not asserted in this case since the snoop cycle is in response to a PCI master read cycle. If the snoop were in response to a PCI master write cycle then INV would be asserted with EADS#. Two clocks after the CPU samples EADS# active, the PCMC completes the internal tag lookup. In this case the snoop hit either an unmodified line or a modified line in the second level cache. Since HITM# is inactive, the snoop did not hit in the first level cache. The PCMC then schedules a read from the second level cache to be written to the LBXs. When the CPU burst cycle completes the PCMC negates the control signals to the second level cache and asserts CALE opening the cache address latch and allowing the snoop address to flow through to the SRAMs. The second level cache executes a read sequence which completes at 3-2-2-2 in the case of standard SRAMs and 3-1-1-1 in the case of burst SRAMs. During all snoop cycles where a write-back from the second level cache is required, BOFF# is asserted throughout the write-back cycle. This prevents the deadlock that would occur if the CPU is in the middle of a non-postable write and the data bus is required for the second level cache write-back.

When using burst SRAMs, the read from the SRAMs follows the Pentium processor burst order. However, the memory to PCI read prefetch buffer in the LBXs is organized as a FIFO and cannot accept data out of order. The SWB0, SWB1, SWB2 and SWB3 commands are used to write data into the buffer in ascending order. In the above example, the PCI master requests a data item which hits Qword 0 in the

cache, thus CA[4:3] count through the following sequence: 0, 1, 2, 3 (00, 01, 10, 11). If the PCI master requests a data item that hits Qword 1, the SWB0 command is sent via the HIG[4:0] lines to store Qword 1 in the first buffer location. The next read from the cache is not in ascending order, thus a NOPC is sent on the HIG[4:0] lines. This Qword is not posted in the buffer. The next read from the cache is to Qword 3. SWB2 is sent on the HIG[4:0] lines. The final read from the cache is Qword 2. SWB1 is sent on the HIG[4:0] lines. Thus, Qword 1 is placed in entry 0 in the buffer, Qword 2 is placed in entry 1 in the buffer and Qword 3 is placed in entry 2 in the buffer. The ordering between the Qwords read from the cache and the HIG[4:0] commands when using burst SRAMs is summarized in Table 5-5.

Table 5-5. HIG[4:0] Command Sequence for Second Level Cache to PCI Master Read Prefetch Buffer Transfer

Burst Order from Cache	HIG[4:0] Command Sequence
0, 1, 2, 3	SWB0, SWB1, SWB2, SWB3
1, 0, 3, 2	SWB0, NOPC, SWB2, SWB1
2, 3, 0, 1	SWB0, SWB1, NOPC, NOPC
3, 2, 1, 0	SWB0, NOPC, NOPC, NOPC

When using standard asynchronous SRAMs, the read from the SRAMs occurs in a linear burst order. Thus, CAA[4:3] and CAB[4:3] count in a linear burst order and the Store Write Buffer commands are sent in linear order. The burst ends at the cache line boundary and does not wrap around and continue with the beginning of the cache line.

A PCI master write cycle which hits a modified line in the second level cache and either hits an unmodified line in the first level cache or misses in the first level cache will also cause a transfer from the second level cache to the LBXs. In this case, the read from the SRAMs is posted to main memory and the line is invalidated in the second level cache. The cycle would differ only slightly from the above cycle. INV would be asserted with EADS#. Instead of the DPRA command, the PCMC would use the DPWA command to drive the snoop address onto the host address bus. The write would be posted to the DRAM, thus the PCMC would drive the PCMWQ command on the HIG[4:0] lines to post the write to DRAM.

A snoop cycle can result in a write-back from the first level cache to both the second level and LBXs in the case of a PCI master read cycle which hits a modified line in the first level cache and hits either a modified or unmodified line in the second level cache. The line is written to both the second level cache and the memory to PCI read prefetch buffer. The cycle is shown in Figure 5-26.

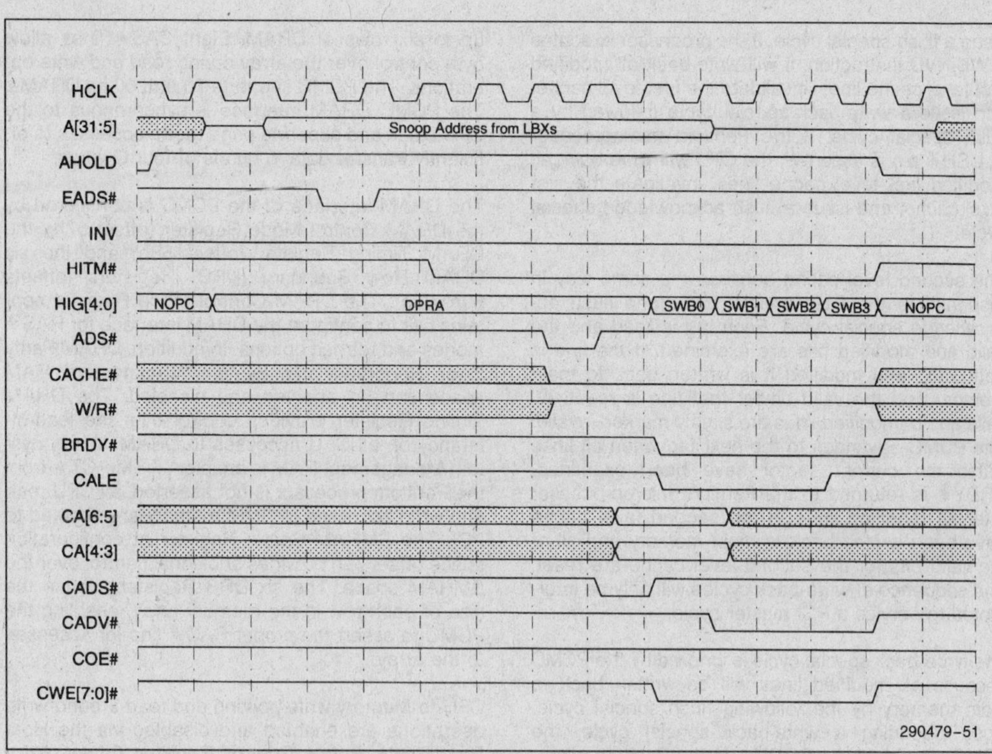

290479-51

Figure 5-26. Snoop Hit to Modified Line in First Level Cache, Write-Back from First Level Cache to Second Level Cache and Send to PCI

This cycle is shown for the case of a second level cache with burst SRAMs. In this case, as it completes the second level cache tag lookup, the PCMC samples HITM# active. The write-back is written to the second level cache and simultaneously stored in the memory to PCI prefetch buffer. In the case shown in Figure 5-22, the PCI master requests a data item which is contained in Qword 0 of the cache line. Note that a write-back from the first level cache always starts with Qword 0 and finishes with Qword 3. Thus the HIG[4:0] lines are sequenced through the following order: SWB0, SWB1, SWB2, SWB3. If the PCI master requests a data item which is contained in Qword 1, the HIG[4:0] lines sequence through the following order: NOPC, SWB0, SWB1, SWB2. If the PCI master requests a data item which is contained in Qword 2, the HIG[4:0] lines would sequence through the following order: NOPC, NOPC, SWB0, SWB1. If the PCI master requests a data item which is contained in Qword 3, the HIG[4:0] lines sequence through the following order: NOPC, NOPC, NOPC, SWB0. AHOLD is negated after the write-back cycle is complete.

If the CPU has begun a read cycle directed to PCI and the snoop results in a hit to a modified line in the first level cache, BOFF# is asserted for one clock to abort the CPU read cycle and re-order the write-back cycle before the pending read cycle.

5.6 Flush, Flush Acknowledge and Write-Back Special Cycles

There are three special cycles that affect the second level cache, flush, flush acknowledge, and write-back.

If the processor executes an INVD instruction, it will invalidate all unmodified first level cache lines and

issue a flush special cycle. If the processor executes a WBINVD instruction, it will write-back all modified first level cache lines, invalidate the first level cache, and issue a write-back special cycle followed by a flush special cycle. If the Pentium microprocesor FLUSH# pin is asserted, the CPU will write-back all modified first level cache lines, invalidate the first level cache, and issue a flush acknowledge special cycle.

The second level cache behaves the same way in response to the flush special cycle and flush acknowledge special cycle. Each tag is read and the valid and modified bits are examined. If the line is both valid and modified it is written back to main memory and the valid bit for that line is reset. All valid and unmodified lines are simply marked invalid. The PCMC advances to the next tag when all lines within the current sector have been examined. BRDY# is returned to the Pentium microprocessor after all modified lines in the second level cache have been written back to main memory and all of the valid bits for the second level cache are reset. The sequence of write-back cycles will only be interrupted to service a PCI master cycle.

The write-back special cycle is ignored by the PCMC because all modified lines will be written back to main memory by the following flush special cycle. Upon decoding a write-back special cycle, the PCMC simply returns BRDY# to the Pentium microprocessor.

6.0 DRAM INTERFACE

6.1 DRAM Interface Overview

The PCMC integrates a high performance DRAM controller supporting from 2 to 192 MBytes of main memory. The PCMC generates the RAS#, CAS#, WE# and multiplexed addresses for the DRAM array, while the data path to DRAM is provided by two 82433LX LBXs. The DRAM controller interface is fully configurable through a set of control registers. Complete descriptions of these registers are given in Section 3.0, Register Description. A brief overview of the registers which configure the DRAM interface is provided in this section.

The PCMC controls a 64-bit memory array (72-bit including parity) ranging in size from 2 MBytes up to 192 MBytes using industry standard 36-bit wide memory modules with fast page-mode DRAMs. Both single- and double-sided SIMMs are supported. The eleven multiplexed address lines, MA[10:0] allow the PCMC to support 256Kx36, 1Mx36, and 4Mx36 SIMMs. The PCMC has six RAS# lines, supporting up to six rows of DRAM. Eight CAS# lines allow byte control over the array during read and write operations. The PCMC supports 70 and 60 ns DRAMs. The PCMC DRAM interface is synchronous to the CPU clock and supports page mode accesses to efficiently transfer data in bursts of four Qwords.

The DRAM interface of the PCMC is configured by the DRAM Control Mode Register (offset 57h), the DRAM Timing Register (offset 58h) and the six DRAM Row Boundary (DRB) Registers (offsets 60h–65h). The DRAM Control Mode Register contains bits to configure the DRAM interface for RAS# modes and refresh options. In addition, DRAM Parity Error Reporting and System Management RAM space can be enabled and disabled. The DRAM Timing Register provides control over the lead-off latency on all CPU accesses to DRAM. When System Management RAM is enabled, if SMIACT# from the Pentium processor is not asserted, all CPU read and write accesses to SMM memory are directed to PCI. The SMRAM Space Register at configuration space offset 72h provides additional control over the SMRAM space. The six DRB Registers define the size of each row in the memory array, enabling the PCMC to assert the proper RAS# line for accesses to the array.

CPU-to-Memory write posting and read-around-write operations are enabled and disabled via the Host Read/Write Buffer Control Register (offset 53h). PCI-to-Memory write posting is enabled and disabled via the PCI Read/Write Buffer Control Register (offset 54h). PCI master reads from main memory always result in the PCMC and LBXs reading the requested data and prefetching the next seven Dwords.

Seven Programmable Attribute Map (PAM) Registers (offsets 59h–5Fh) are used to specify the cacheability and read/write status of the memory space between 512 KBytes and 1 MByte. Each PAM Register defines a specific address area enabling the system to selectively mark specific memory ranges as cacheable, read-only, write-only, read/write or disabled. When a memory range is disabled, all CPU accesses to that range are directed to PCI.

Two other registers also affect the DRAM interface, the Memory Space Gap Register (offsets 78h–79h) and the Frame Buffer Range Register (offsets 7Ch–7Fh). The Memory Space Gap Register is used to place a logical hole in the memory space between 1 MByte to 16 MBytes to accommodate memory mapped ISA boards. The Frame Buffer Range Register, is used to map a linear frame buffer into the Memory Space Gap or above main memory. When enabled, accesses to these ranges are never directed to the DRAM interface, but are always directed to PCI.

6.2 DRAM Configurations

Figure 6-1 illustrates a 12-SIMM configuration which supports single-sided SIMMs.

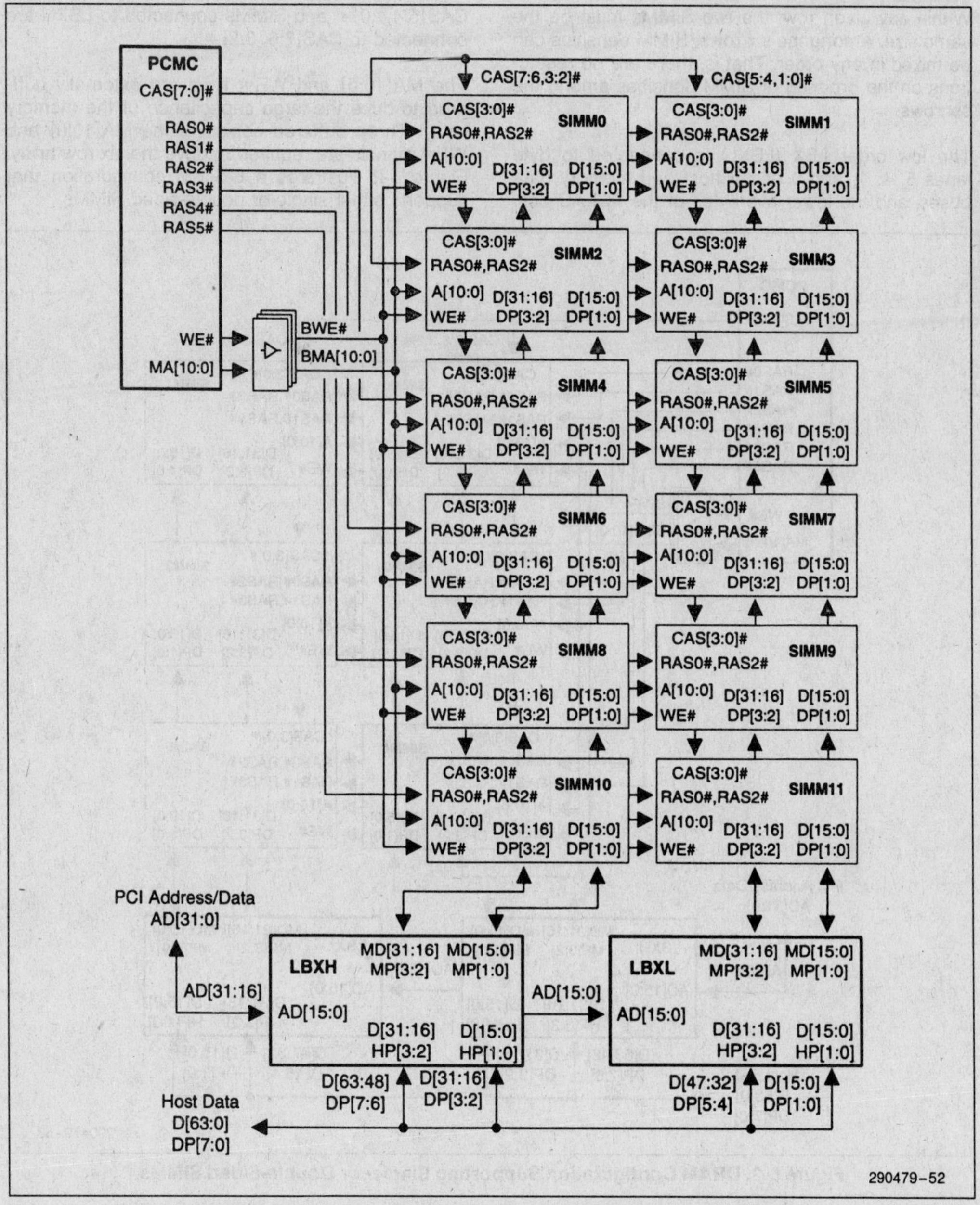

Figure 6-1. DRAM Configuration Supporting Single-Sided SIMMs

A row in the DRAM array is made up of two SIMMs which share a common RAS# line. SIMM0 and SIMM1 are connected to RAS0# and therefore, comprise row 0. SIMM10 and SIMM11 form row 5. Within any given row, the two SIMMs must be the same size. Among the six rows, SIMM densities can be mixed in any order. That is, there are no restrictions on the ordering of SIMM densities among the six rows.

The low order LBX (LBXL) is connected to byte lanes 5, 4, 1, and 0 of the host and memory data buses, and the lower two bytes of the PCI AD bus.

The high order LBX (LBXH) is connected to byte lanes 7, 6, 3, and 2 of the host and memory data buses, and the upper two bytes of the PCI AD bus. Thus, SIMMs connected to LBXL are connected to CAS[5:4,1:0]# and SIMMs connected to LBXH are connected to CAS[7:6, 3:2]#.

The MA[10:0] and WE# lines are externally buffered to drive the large capacitance of the memory array. Three buffered copies of the MA[10:0] and WE# signals are required to drive the six row array. Figure 6-2 illustrates a 6-SIMM configuration that supports either single-or double-sided SIMMs.

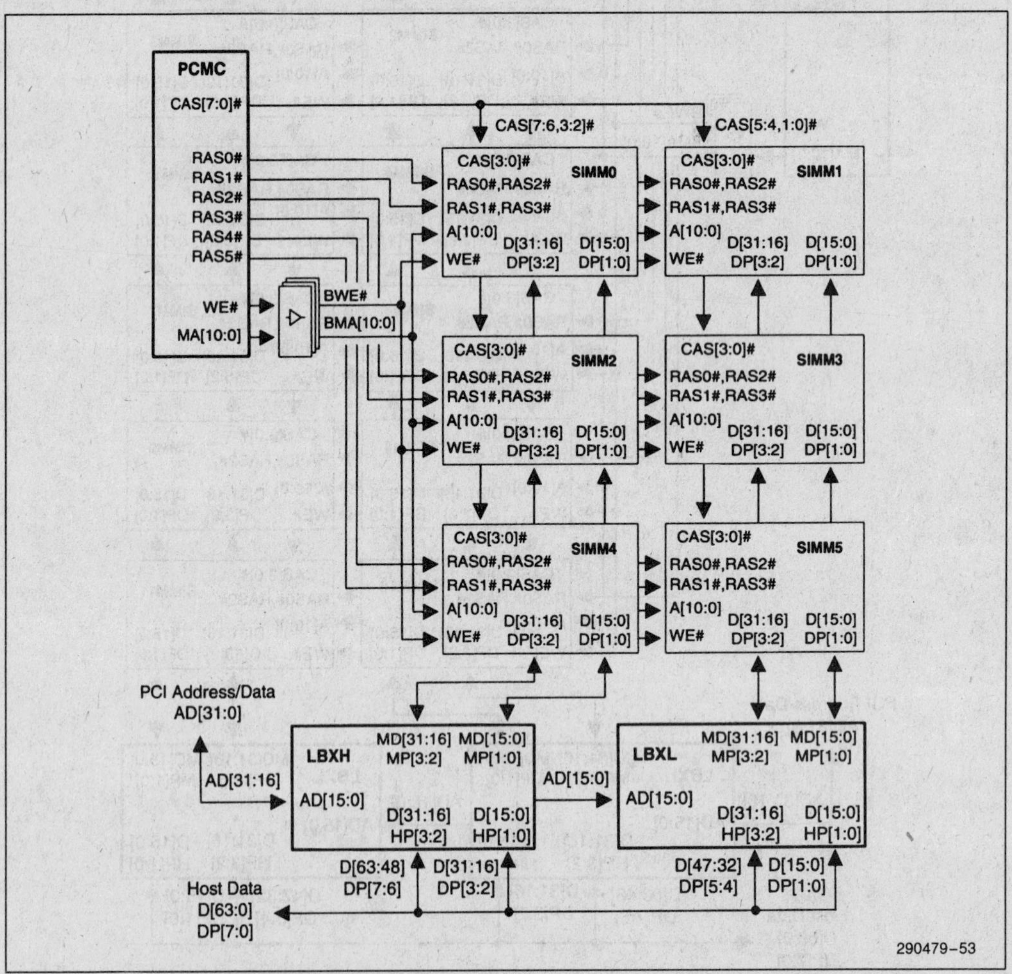

Figure 6-2. DRAM Configuration Supporting Single- or Double-Sided SIMMs

In this configuration, single- and double-sided SIMMs can be mixed. For example, if single-sided SIMMs are installed into the sockets marked SIMM0 and SIMM1, then RAS0# is connected to the SIMMs and RAS1# is not connected. Row 0 is then populated and row 1 is empty. Two double-sided SIMMs could then be installed in the sockets marked SIMM2 and SIMM3, populating rows 2 and 3.

6.3 DRAM Address Translation

The multiplexed row/column address to the DRAM memory array is provided by the MA[10:0] signals. The MA[10:0] bits are derived from the host address bus as defined by Table 6-1.

Table 6-1 DRAM Address Translation

Memory Address, MA[10:0]	10	9	8	7	6	5	4	3	2	1	0
Row Address	A24	A22	A20	A19	A18	A17	A16	A15	A14	A13	A12
Column Address	A23	A21	A11	A10	A9	A8	A7	A6	A5	A4	A3

The MA[10:0] lines are translated from the host address lines A[24:3] for all memory accesses, except those targeted to memory that has been remapped as a result of the creation of a memory space gap in the lower extended memory area. In the case of a cycle targeting remapped memory, the least significant bits come directly from the host address, while the more significant bits depend on the memory space gap start address, gap size, and the size of main memory.

6.4 Cycle Timing Summary

The PCMC DRAM performance is summarized in Table 6-2 for all CPU read and write cycles.

Table 6-2. CPU to DRAM Performance Summary

Cycle Type	Burst Timing	Single Cycle Timing
Read Page Hit	7-4-4-4	7
Read Row Miss	11-4-4-4	11
Read Page Miss	14-4-4-4	14
Posted Write, WT L2	3-1-1-1	3
Posted Write, WB L2	4-1-1-1	4
Write Page Hit	10-4-4-4	10
Write Row Miss	11-4-4-4	11
Write Page Miss	14-4-4-4	14
0-Active RAS# Mode Read	10-4-4-4	10
0-Active RAS# Mode Write	10-4-4-4	10

CPU writes to the CPU-to-Memory Posted Write Buffer are completed at 3-1-1-1 when the second level cache is configured for write-through mode and 4-1-1-1 when the cache is configured for write-back mode. All CPU write lead-off cycles are one clock longer than shown in Table 6-2 when the Secondary Cache is in write-back mode. When the DRAM lead-off wait state bit in the DRAM Timing Register is set to 1, all CPU-to-DRAM lead-off cycles increase by one clock. Table 6-3 shows the refresh performance in CPU clocks.

Table 6-3. Refresh Cycle Performance

Refresh Type	Hidden Refresh	RAS# only Refresh	CAS# before RAS#
Single	12	13	14
Burst of Four	48	52	56

6.5 CPU to DRAM Bus Cycles

6.5.1 READ PAGE HIT

Figure 6-3 depicts a CPU burst read page hit from DRAM. The PCMC decodes the CPU address as a page hit and drives the column address onto the MA[10:0] lines. CAS[7:0]# are then asserted to cause the DRAMs to latch the column address and begin the read cycle. CMR (CPU Memory Read) is driven on the HIG[4:0] lines to enable the memory data to host data path through the LBXs. The PCMC advances the MA[1:0] lines through the Pentium processor burst order, negating and asserting CAS[7:0]# to read each Qword. The host data is latched on the falling edge of MDLE, when CAS[7:0]# are negated. The latch is opened again when MDLE is sampled asserted by the LBXs. The LBXs tri-state the host data bus when HIG[4:0] change to NOPC and MDLE rises. A single read page hit from DRAM is similar to the first read of this sequence. The HIG[4:0] lines are driven to NOPC when BRDY# is asserted.

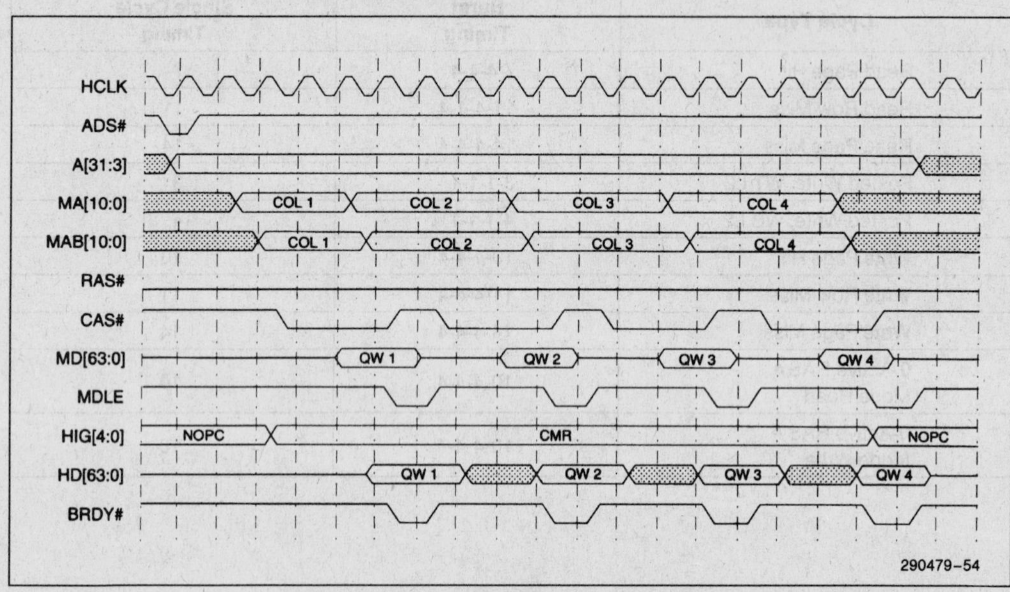

Figure 6-3. Burst DRAM Read Cycle-Page Hit

6.5.2 READ PAGE MISS

Figure 6-4 depicts a CPU burst read page miss from DRAM. The PCMC decodes the CPU address as a page miss and switches from initially driving the column address to driving the row address on the MA[10:0] lines. RAS# is then negated to precharge the DRAMs and then asserted to cause the DRAMs to latch the new row address. The PCMC then switches the MA[10:0] lines to drive the column address and asserts CAS[7:0]#. CMR (CPU Memory Read) is driven on the HIG[4:0] lines to enable the memory data to host data path through the LBXs.

The PCMC advances the MA[1:0] lines through the Pentium microprocessor burst order, negating and asserting CAS[7:0]# to read each Qword. The host data is latched on the falling edge of MDLE, when CAS[7:0]# are negated. The latch is opened again when MDLE is sampled asserted by the LBXs. The LBXs tri-state the host data bus when HIG[4:0] change to NOPC and MDLE rises. A single read page miss from DRAM is similar to the first read of this sequence. The HIG[4:0] lines are driven to NOPC when BRDY# is asserted.

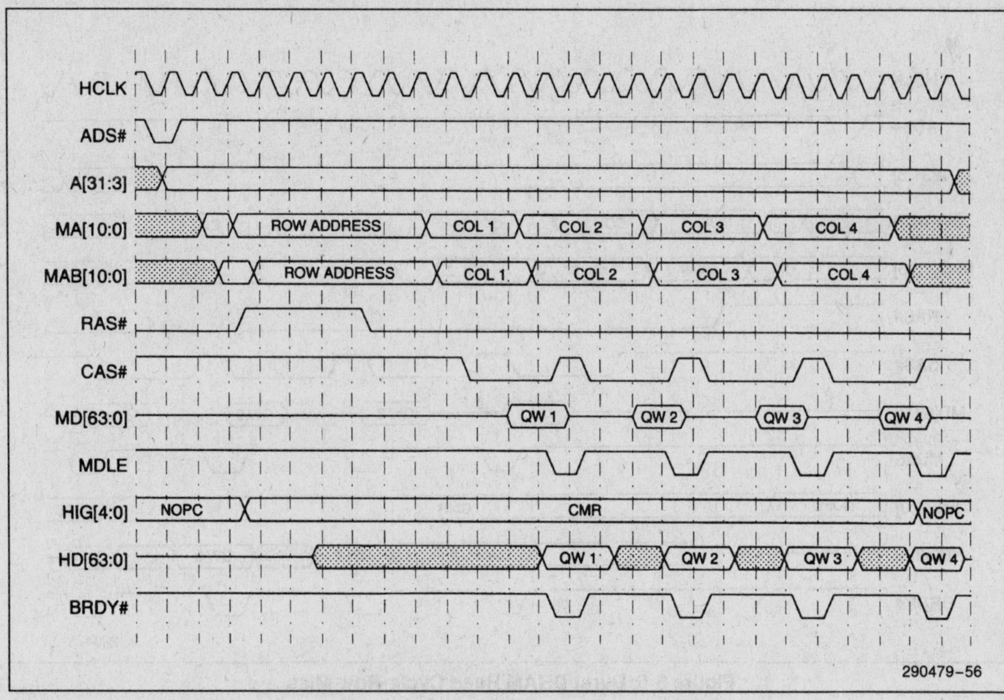

Figure 6-4. DRAM Read Cycle-Page Miss

6.5.3 READ ROW MISS

Figure 6-5 depicts a CPU burst read row miss from DRAM. The PCMC decodes the CPU address as a row miss and switches from initially driving the column address to driving the row address on the MA[10:0] lines. The RAS# signal that was asserted is negated and the RAS# for the currently accessed row is asserted. The PCMC then switches the MA[10:0] lines to drive the column address and asserts CAS[7:0]#. CMR (CPU Memory Read) is driven on the HIG[4:0] lines to enable the memory data to host data path through the LBXs. The PCMC advances the MA[1:0] lines through the Pentium microprocessor burst order, negating and asserting CAS[7:0]# to read each Qword. The host data is latched on the falling edge of MDLE, when CAS[7:0]# are negated. The latch is opened again when MDLE is sampled asserted by the LBXs. The LBXs tri-state the host data bus when HIG[4:0] change to NOPC and MDLE rises. A single read row miss from DRAM is similar to the first read of this sequence. The HIG[4:0] lines are driven to NOPC when BRDY# is asserted.

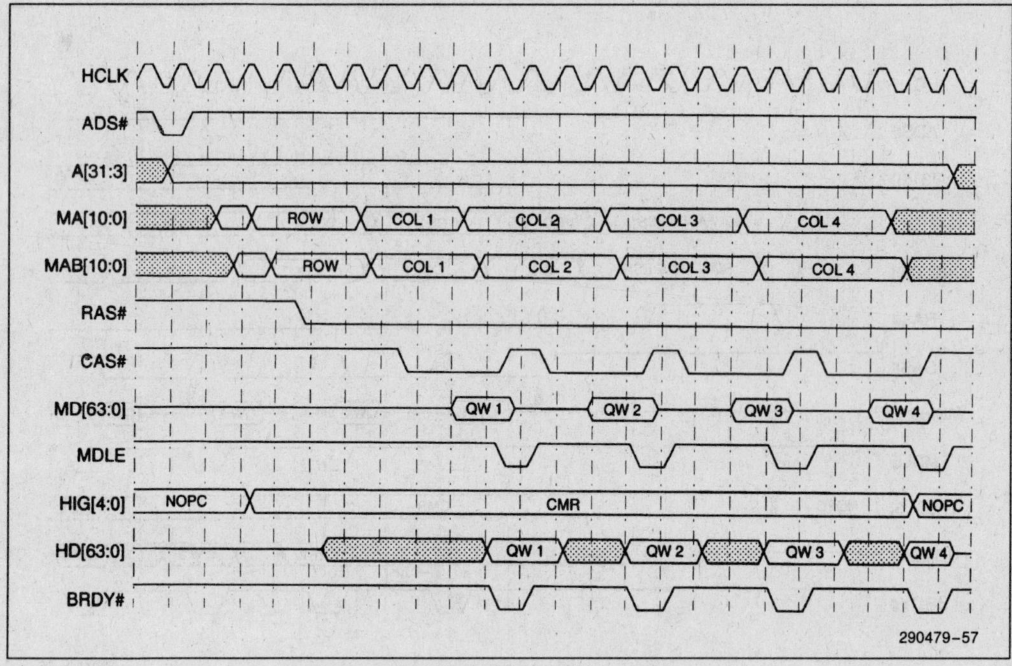

Figure 6-5. Burst DRAM Read Cycle-Row Miss

6.5.4 WRITE PAGE HIT

Figure 6-6 depicts a CPU burst write page hit from DRAM. The PCMC decodes the CPU write cycle as a DRAM page hit. The HIG[4:0] lines are driven to PCMWQ to post the write to the LBXs. In the figure, the write cycle is posted to the CPU-to-Memory Posted Write Buffer at 4-1-1-1. The write is posted at 4-1-1-1 when the second level cache is configured for a write-back policy. The write is posted to DRAM at 3-1-1-1 when the second level cache is configured for a write-through policy. When the cycle is decoded as a page hit, the PCMC asserts WE# and drives the RCMWQ command on MIG[2:0] to enable the LBXs to drive the first Qword of the write onto the memory data lines. MEMDRV is then driven to cause the LBXs to continue to drive the first Qword for three more clocks. CAS[7:0]# are then negated and asserted to perform the writes to the DRAMs as the MA[1:0] lines advance through the Pentium microprocessor burst order. A single write is similar to the first write of the burst sequence. MIG[2:0] are driven to NOPM in the clock after CAS[7:0]# are asserted.

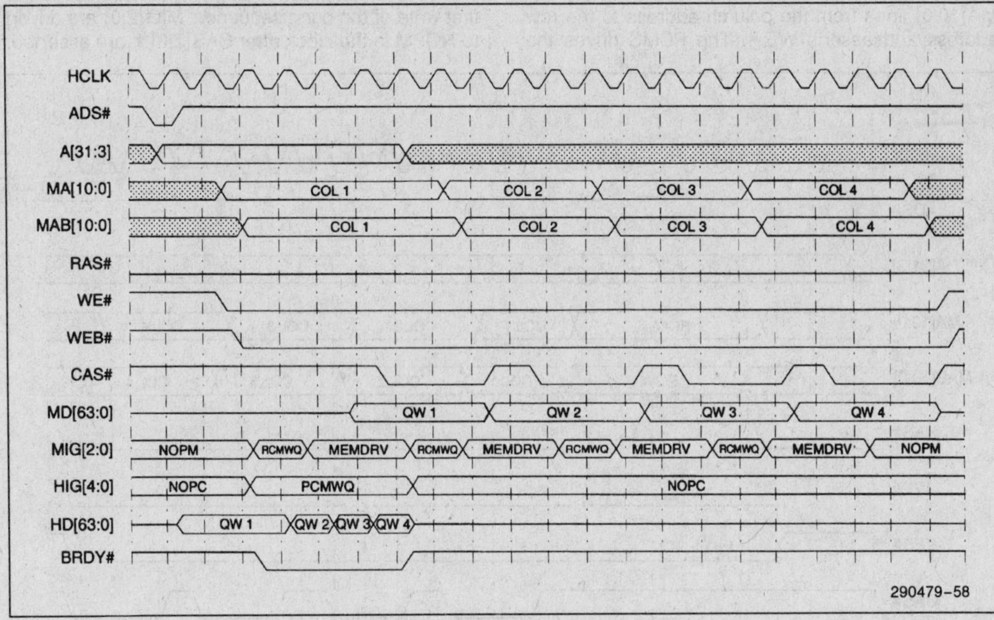

Figure 6-6. Burst DRAM Write Cycle-Page Hit

6.5.5 WRITE PAGE MISS

Figure 6-7 depicts a CPU burst write page miss to DRAM. The PCMC decodes the CPU write cycle as a DRAM page miss. The HIG[4:0] lines are driven to PCMWQ to post the write to the LBXs. In the figure, the write cycle is posted to the CPU-to-Memory Posted Write Buffer at 4-1-1-1. The write is posted at 4-1-1-1 when the second level cache is configured for a write-back policy. The write is posted to DRAM at 3-1-1-1 when the second level cache is configured for a write-through policy. When the cycle is decoded as a page miss, the PCMC switches the MA[10:0] lines from the column address to the row address and asserts WE#. The PCMC drives the RCMWQ command on MIG[2:0] to enable the LBXs to drive the first Qword of the write onto the memory data lines. MEMDRV is then driven to cause the LBXs to continue to drive the first Qword. The RAS# signal for the currently decoded row is negated to precharge the DRAMs. RAS# is then asserted to cause the DRAMs to latch the row address. The PCMC then switches the MA[10:0] lines to the column address and asserts CAS[7:0]# to initiate the first write. CAS[7:0]# are then negated and asserted to perform the writes to the DRAMs as the MA[1:0] lines advance through the Pentium microprocessor burst order. A single write is similar to the first write of the burst sequence. MIG[2:0] are driven to NOPM in the clock after CAS[7:0]# are asserted.

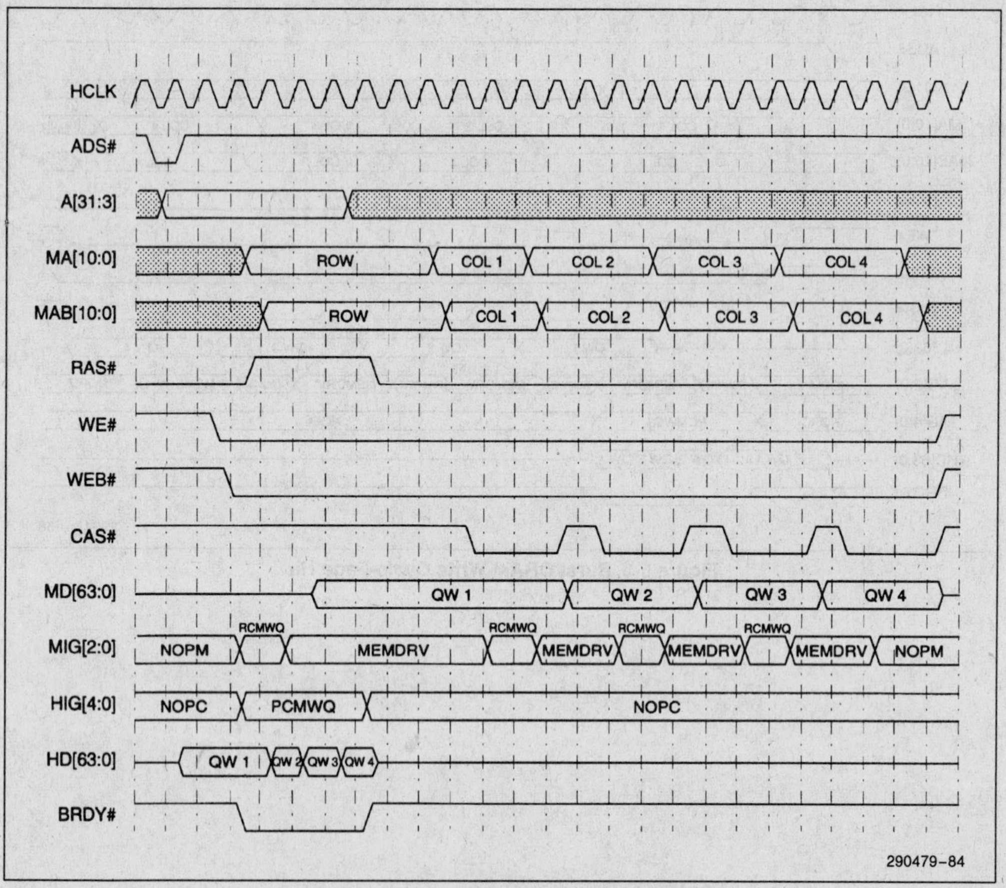

290479-84

Figure 6-7. Burst DRAM Write Cycle-Page Miss

6.5.6 WRITE ROW MISS

Figure 6-8 depicts a CPU burst write row miss to DRAM. The PCMC decodes the CPU write cycle as a DRAM row miss. The HIG[4:0] lines are driven to PCMWQ to post the write to the LBXs. In the figure, the write cycle is posted to the CPU-to-Memory Posted Write Buffer at 4-1-1-1. The write is posted at 4-1-1-1 when the second level cache is configured for a write-back policy. The write is posted to DRAM at 3-1-1-1 when the second level cache is configured for a write-through policy. When the cycle is decoded as a row miss, the PCMC negates the already active RAS# signal, switches the MA[10:0] lines from the column address to the row address and asserts the RAS# signal for the currently decoded row. The PCMC asserts WE# and drives the RCMWQ command on MIG[2:0] to enable the LBXs to drive the first Qword of the write onto the memory data lines. MEMDRV is then driven to cause the LBXs to continue to drive the first Qword. The PCMC then switches the MA[10:0] lines to the column address and asserts CAS[7:0]# to initiate the first write. CAS[7:0]# are then negated and asserted to perform the writes to the DRAMs as the MA[1:0] lines advance through the Pentium microprocessor burst order. A single write is similar to the first write of the burst sequence. MIG[2:0] are driven to NOPM in the clock after CAS[7:0]# are asserted.

290479-85

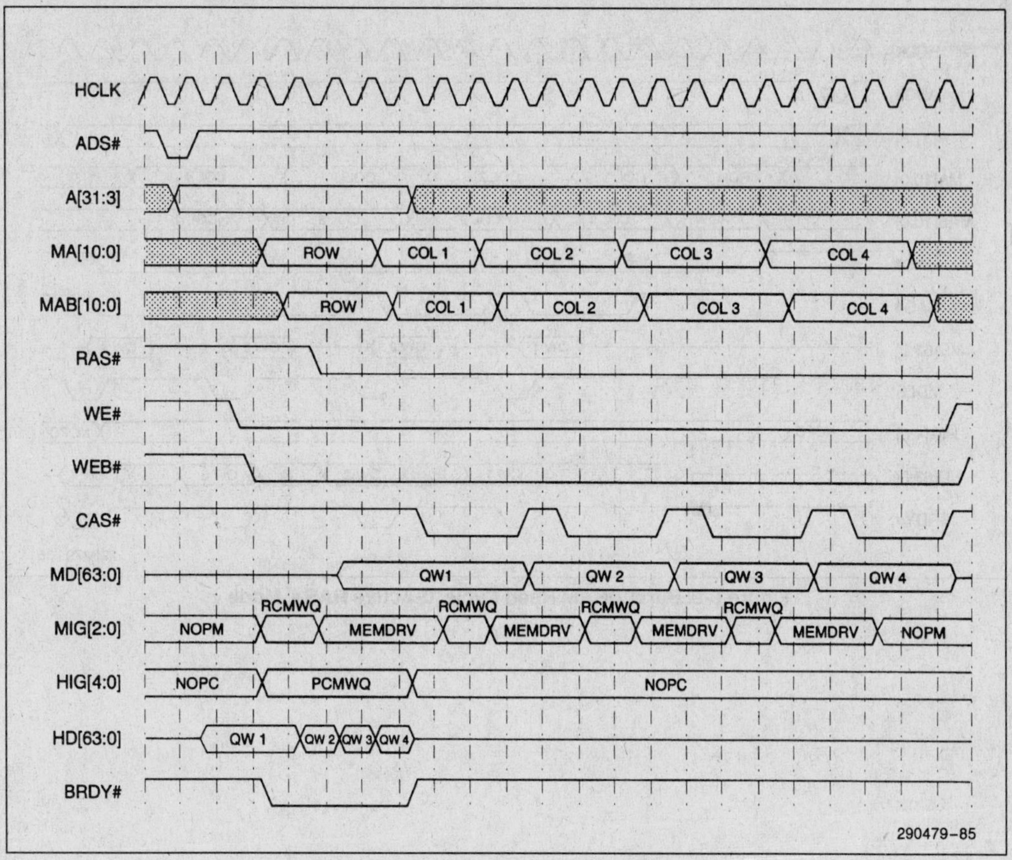

Figure 6-8. Burst DRAM Write Cycle-Row Miss

6.5.7 READ CYCLE, 0-ACTIVE RAS# MODE

When in 0-active RAS# mode, every CPU cycle to DRAM results in a RAS# and CAS# sequence. RAS# is always negated after a cycle completes. Figure 6-9 depicts a CPU burst read cycle from DRAM where the PCMC is configured for 0-active RAS# mode. When in 0-active RAS# mode, the PCMC defaults to driving the row address on the MA[10:0] lines. The PCMC asserts the RAS# signal for the currently decoded row causing the DRAMs to latch the row address. The PCMC then switches the MA[10:0] lines to drive the column address and asserts CAS[7:0]#. CMR (CPU Memory Read) is driven on the HIG[4:0] lines to enable the memory data to host data path through the LBXs. The PCMC advances the MA[1:0] lines through the Pentium microprocessor burst order, negating and asserting CAS[7:0]# to read each Qword. The host data is latched on the falling edge of MDLE, when CAS[7:0]# are negated. The latch is opened again when MDLE is sampled asserted by the LBXs. The LBXs tri-state the host data bus when HIG[4:0] change to NOPC and MDLE rises. A single read row miss from DRAM is similar to the first read of this sequence. The HIG[4:0] lines are driven to NOPC when BRDY# is asserted. RAS# is negated with CAS[7:0]#.

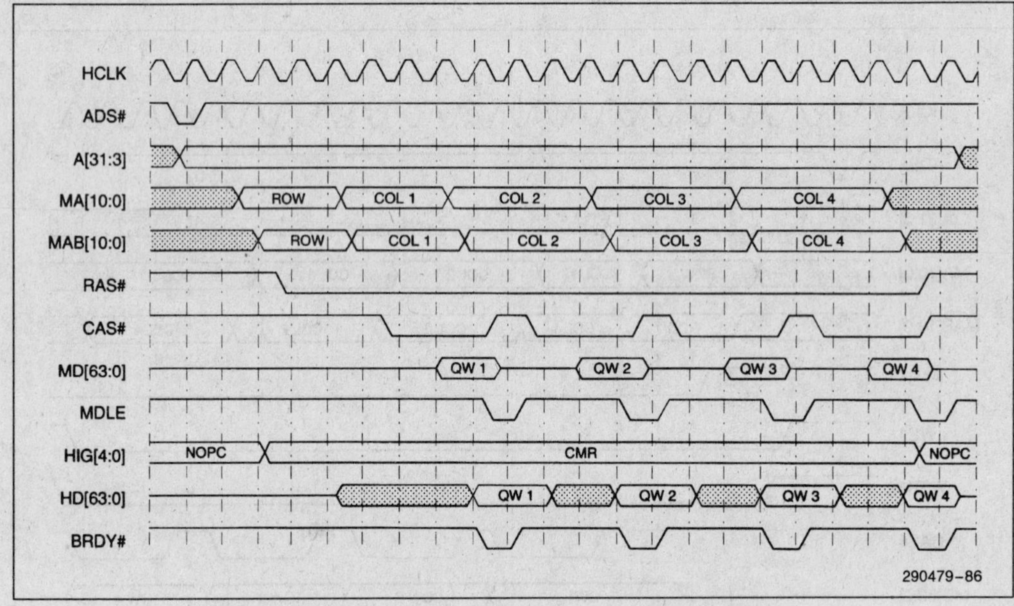

Figure 6-9. Burst DRAM Read Cycle, 0-Active RAS# Mode

6.5.8 WRITE CYCLE, 0-ACTIVE RAS# MODE

When in 0-active RAS# mode, every CPU cycle to DRAM results in a RAS# and CAS# sequence. RAS# is always negated after a cycle completes. Figure 6-10 depicts a CPU Burst Write Cycle to DRAM where the PCMC is configured for 0-active RAS# mode. The HIG[4:0] lines are driven to PCMWQ to post the write to the LBXs. In the figure, the write cycle is posted to the CPU-to-Memory Posted Write Buffer at 4-1-1-1. The write is posted at 4-1-1-1 when the second level cache is configured for a write-back policy. The write is posted to DRAM at 3-1-1-1 when the second level cache is configured for a write-through policy. When in 0-active RAS# mode, the PCMC defaults to driving the row address on the MA[10:0] lines. The PCMC asserts the RAS# signal for the currently decoded row causing the DRAMs to latch the row address. The PCMC asserts WE# and drives the RCMWQ command on MIG[2:0] to enable the LBXs to drive the first Qword of the write onto the memory data lines. MEMDRV is then driven to cause the LBXs to continue to drive the first Qword. The PCMC then switches the MA[10:0] lines to the column address and asserts CAS[7:0]# to initiate the first write. CAS[7:0]# are then negated and asserted to perform the writes to the DRAMs as the MA[1:0] lines advance through the Pentium microprocessor burst order. A single write is similar to the first write of the burst sequence. MIG[2:0] are driven to NOPM in the clock after CAS[7:0]# are asserted.

290479-87

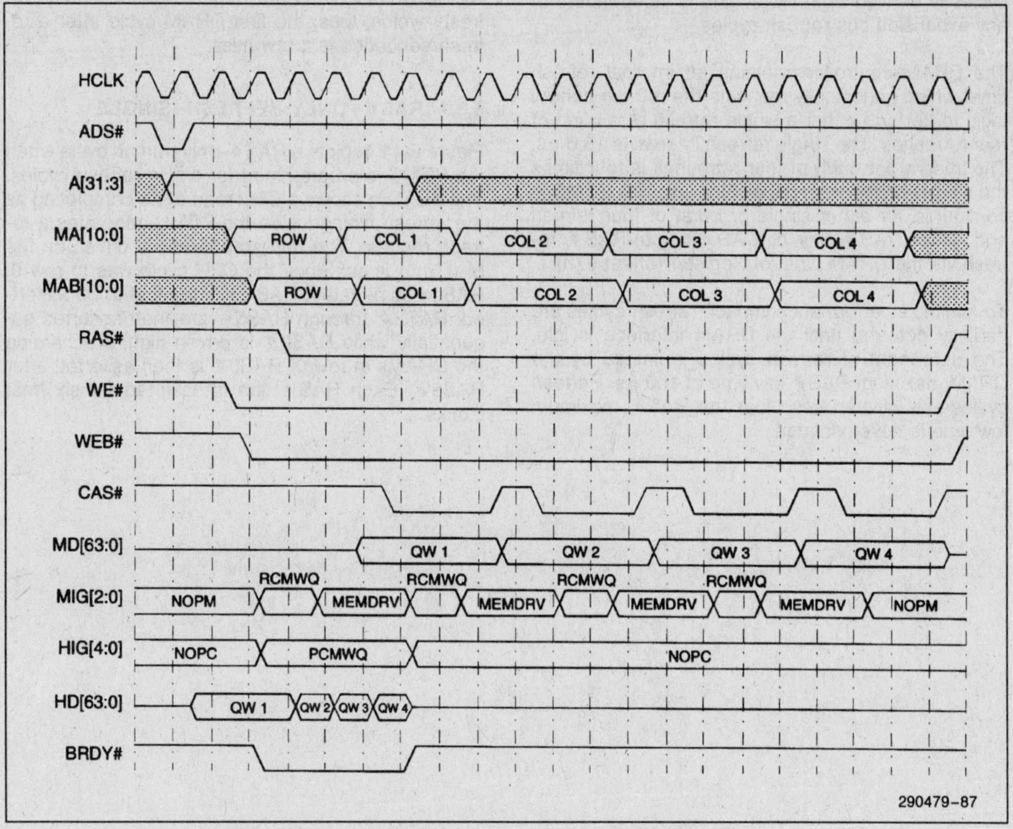

Figure 6-10. Burst DRAM Write Cycle, 0-Active RAS# Mode

6.6 Refresh

The refresh of the DRAM array can be performed by either using RAS#-only or CAS#-before-RAS# refresh cycles. When programmed for CAS#-before-RAS# refresh, hidden refresh cycles are initiated when possible. RAS# only refresh can be used with any type of second level cache configuration (i.e., no second level cache is present, or either a burst SRAM or standard SRAM second level cache is implemented). CAS#-before-RAS# refresh can be enabled when either no second level cache is present or a burst SRAM second level cache is implemented. CAS#-before-RAS# refresh should not be used when a standard SRAM second level cache is implemented. The timing of internally generated refresh cycles is derived from HCLK and is independent of any expansion bus refresh cycles.

The DRAM controller contains an internal refresh timer which periodically requests the refresh control logic to perform either a single refresh or a burst of four refreshes. The single refresh interval is 15.6 µs. The interval for burst of four refreshes is four times the single refresh interval, or 62.4 µs. The PCMC is configured for either single or burst of four refresh and either RAS#-only or CAS#-before-RAS# refresh via the DRAM Control Register (offset 57h).

To minimize performance impact, refresh cycles are partially deferred until the DRAM interface is idle. The deferment of refresh cycles is limited by the DRAM maximum RAS# low time of 100 µs. Refresh cycles are initiated such that the RAS# maximum low time is never violated.

Hidden refresh cycles are run whenever all eight CAS# lines are active when the refresh cycle is internally requested. Normal CAS#-before-RAS# refresh cycles are run whenever the DRAM interface is idle when the refresh is requested, or when any subset of the CAS# lines is inactive as the refresh is internally requested.

To minimize the power surge associated with refreshing a large DRAM array the DRAM interface staggers the assertion of the RAS# signals during both CAS#-before-RAS# and RAS#-only refresh cycles. The order of RAS# edges is dependent on which RAS# was most recently asserted prior to the refresh sequence. The RAS# that was active will be the last to be activated during the refresh sequence. All RAS[5:0]# lines are negated at the end of refresh cycles, thus, the first DRAM cycle after a refresh sequence is a row miss.

6.6.1 RAS#-ONLY REFRESH-SINGLE

Figure 6-11 depicts a RAS#-only refresh cycle when the PCMC is programmed for single refresh cycles. The diagram shows a CPU read cycle completing as the refresh timing inside the PCMC generates a refresh request. The refresh address is driven on the MA[10:0] lines. Since the CPU cycle was to row 0, RAS0# is negated. RAS1# is the first to be asserted. RAS2# through RAS5# are then asserted sequentially while RAS0# is driven high, precharging the DRAMs in row 0. RAS0# is then asserted after RAS5#. Each RAS# line is asserted for six host clocks.

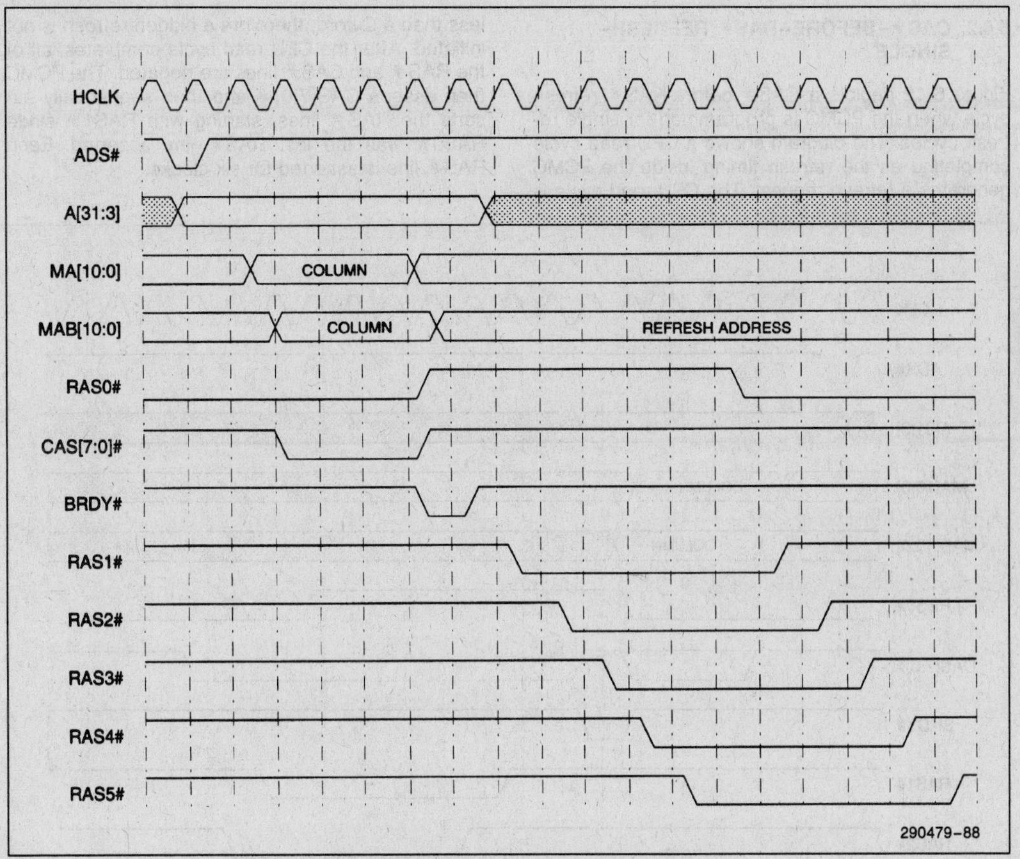

HCLK
ADS#
A[31:3]
MA[10:0] COLUMN
MAB[10:0] COLUMN REFRESH ADDRESS
RAS0#
CAS[7:0]#
BRDY#
RAS1#
RAS2#
RAS3#
RAS4#
RAS5#

290479-88

Figure 6-11. RAS#-Only Refresh-Single

6.6.2 CAS#-BEFORE-RAS# REFRESH-SINGLE

Figure 6-12 depicts a CAS#-before-RAS# refresh cycle when the PCMC is programmed for single refresh cycles. The diagram shows a CPU read cycle completing as the refresh timing inside the PCMC generates a refresh request. The CPU read cycle is less than a Qword, therefore a hidden refresh is not initiated. After the CPU read cycle completes, all of the RAS# and CAS# lines are negated. The PCMC then asserts CAS[7:0]# and then sequentially asserts the RAS# lines, starting with RAS1# since RAS0# was the last RAS# line asserted. Each RAS# line is asserted for six clocks.

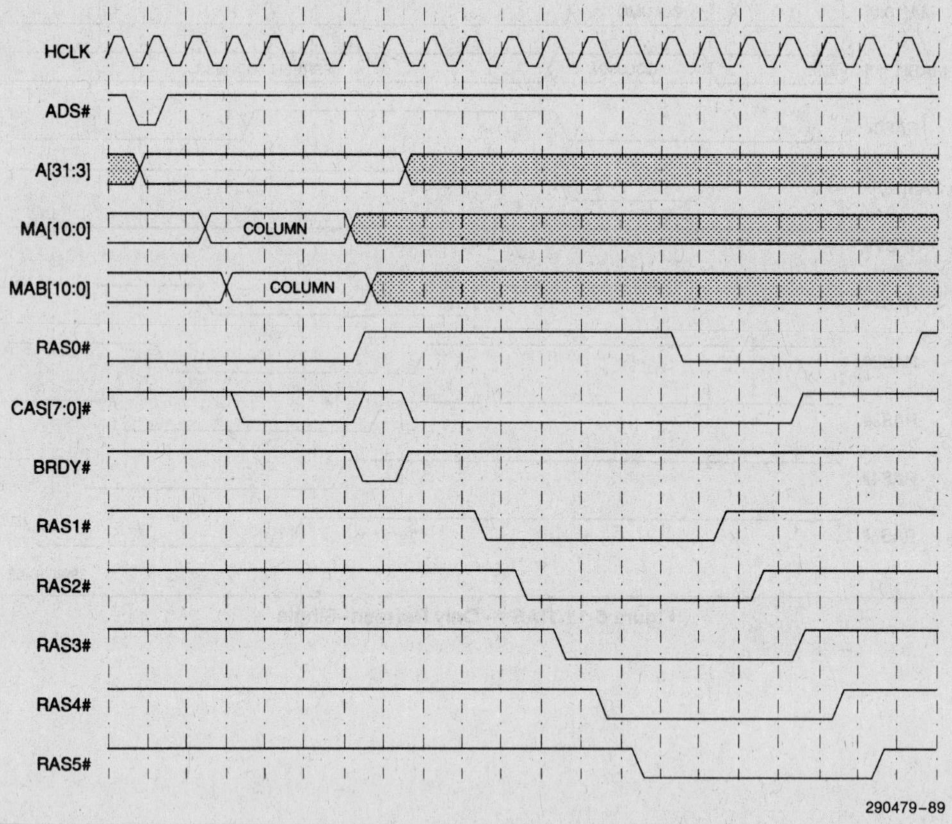

290479-89

Figure 6-12. CAS#-before-RAS# Refresh-Single

6.6.3 HIDDEN REFRESH-SINGLE

Figure 6-13 depicts a hidden refresh cycle which takes place after a DRAM read page hit cycle. The diagram shows a CPU read cycle completing as the refresh timing inside the PCMC generates a refresh request. The CPU read cycle is an entire Qword, therefore a hidden refresh is initiated. After the CPU read cycle completes, RAS# is negated, but all eight CAS# lines remain asserted. The PCMC then sequentially asserts the RAS# lines, starting with RAS1# since RAS0# was the last active RAS# line. Each RAS# line is asserted for six clocks.

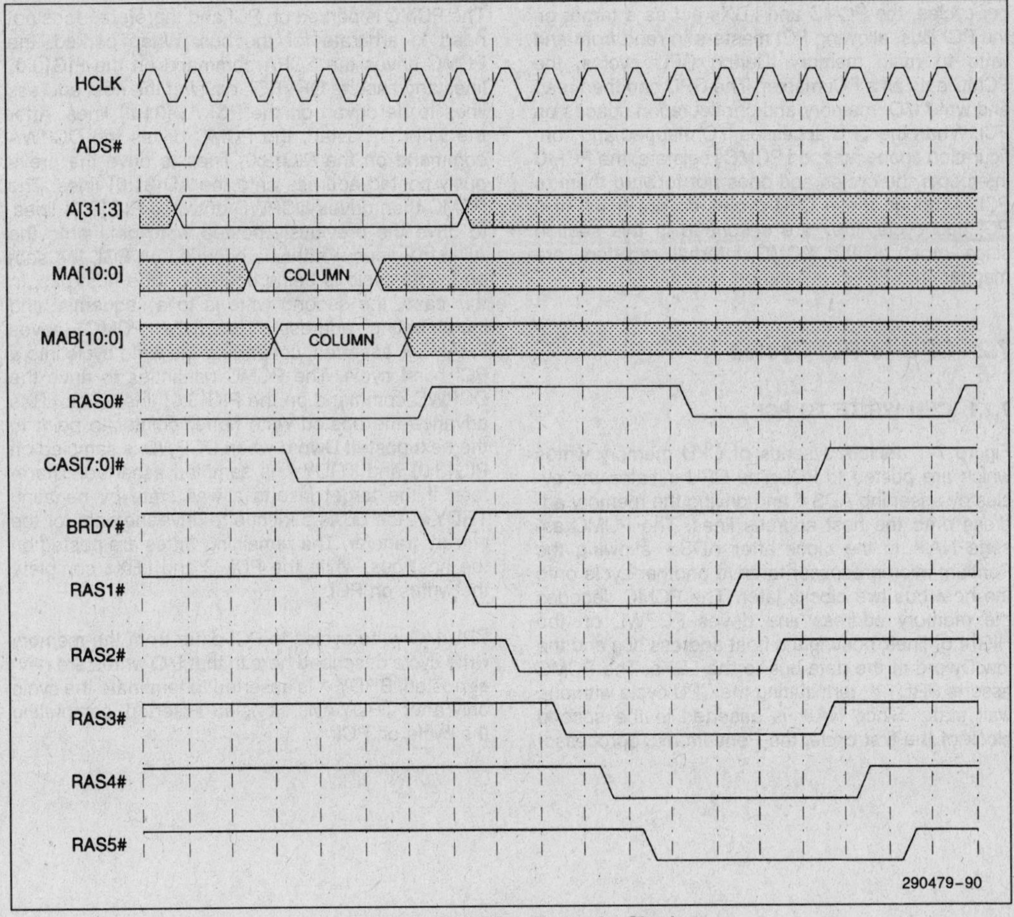

290479-90

Figure 6-13. Hidden Refresh-Single

7.0 PCI INTERFACE

7.1 PCI Interface Overview

The PCMC and LBXs form a high performance bridge from the Pentium microprocessor to PCI and from PCI to main memory. During PCI-to-main memory cycles, the PCMC and LBXs act as a target on the PCI Bus, allowing PCI masters to read from and write to main memory. During CPU cycles, the PCMC acts as a PCI master. The CPU can then read and write I/O, memory and configuration spaces on PCI. When the CPU accesses I/O mapped and configuration space mapped PCMC registers, the PCMC intercepts the cycles and does not forward them to PCI. Although these CPU cycles do not result in a PCI bus cycle, they are described in this section since most of the PCMC internal registers are mapped into PCI configuration space.

7.2 CPU-to-PCI Cycles

7.2.1 CPU WRITE TO PCI

Figure 7-1 depicts a series of CPU memory writes which are posted to PCI. The CPU initiates the cycles by asserting ADS# and driving the memory address onto the host address lines. The PCMC asserts NA# in the clock after ADS# allowing the Pentium microprocessor to drive another cycle onto the host bus two clocks later. The PCMC decodes the memory address and drives PCPWL on the HIG[4:0] lines, posting the host address bus and the low Dword of the data bus to the LBXs. The PCMC asserts BRDY#, terminating the CPU cycle with one wait state. Since NA# is asserted in the second clock of the first cycle, the Pentium microprocessor does not insert an idle cycle after this cycle completes, but immediately drives the next cycle onto the bus. Thus, the Pentium microprocessor maximum Dword write bandwidth of 89 MBytes/second is achieved during back-to-back Dword writes cycles. Each of the following write cycles is posted to the LBXs in three clocks.

The PCMC is parked on PCI and therefore, does not need to arbitrate for the bus. When parked, the PCMC drives the SCPA command on the PIG[3:0] lines and asserts DRVPCI, causing the host address lines to be driven on the PCI AD[31:0] lines. After the write is posted, the PCMC drives the DCPWA command on the PIG[3:0] lines to drive the previously posted address onto the AD[31:0] lines. The PCMC then drives DCPWD onto the PIG[3:0] lines, to drive the previously posted write data onto the AD[31:0] lines. As this is occuring on PCI, the second write cycle is being posted on the host bus. In this case, the second write is to a sequential and incrementing address. Thus, the PCMC leaves FRAME# asserted, converting the write cycle into a PCI burst cycle. The PCMC continues to drive the DCPWD command on the PIG[3:0] lines. The LBXs advance the posted write buffer pointer to point to the next posted Dword when DCPWD is sampled on PIG[3:0] and TRDY# is sampled asserted. Therefore, if the target inserts a wait state by negating TRDY#, the LBXs continue to drive the data for the current transfer. The remaining writes are posted on the host bus, while the PCMC and LBXs complete the writes on PCI.

CPU I/O write cycles to PCI differ from the memory write cycle described here in that I/O writes are never posted. BRDY# is asserted to terminate the cycle only after TRDY# is sampled asserted, completing the cycle on PCI.

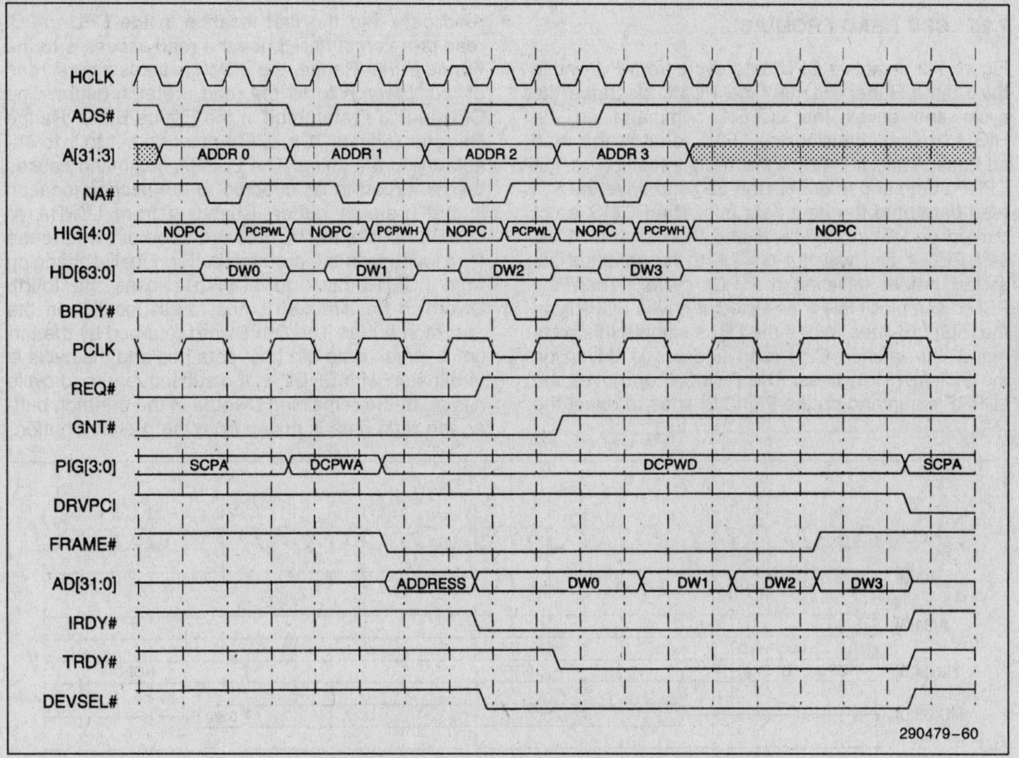

Figure 7-1. CPU Memory Writes to PCI

1

7.2.2 CPU READ FROM PCI

Figure 7-2 depicts a CPU read cycle from PCI within the Frame Buffer Range. The PCMC decodes the cycle and drives the LCPRA command on the HIG[4:0] lines, causing the LBXs to latch the read address. The HIG[4:0] lines then transition to the CPRF command to enable the LBXs to drive the PCI read data onto the host data bus. The PCMC is not parked on PCI in this case, and therefore must assert REQ# and wait for GNT# to be sampled asserted before initiating the PCI cycle. When the PCMC samples GNT# asserted, it drives SCPRA on the PIG[3:0] lines. When the LBXs sample this command, the latched CPU read address is driven on the PCI AD[31:0] lines. The PCMC then drives the LCPRF command on the PIG[3:0] lines to direct the read data into the first location in the CPU-to-PCI read prefetch buffer. Since the read access is to the Frame Buffer Range, the PCMC initiates a burst read of four Dwords to fill the read prefetch buffer. The CPU-to-PCI Prefetch bit in the Frame Buffer Range Register (offsets 7Ch - 7Fh) must be set to 1 to enable the prefetching. The LCPRA command causes the next read to be directed to the second location in the prefetch buffer. Changing from LCPRA to LCPRB causes the third Dword to be directed to the third location in the prefetch buffer. Finally, changing from LCPRB back to LCPRA causes the fourth Dword to be directed to the fourth location in the prefretch buffer. The first Dword returned by the target is dirven onto the host data bus and the cycle is terminated with BRDY#. If a subsequent read cycle hits on of the remaining Dwords in the prefetch buffer, the read data is driven from the prefetch buffer.

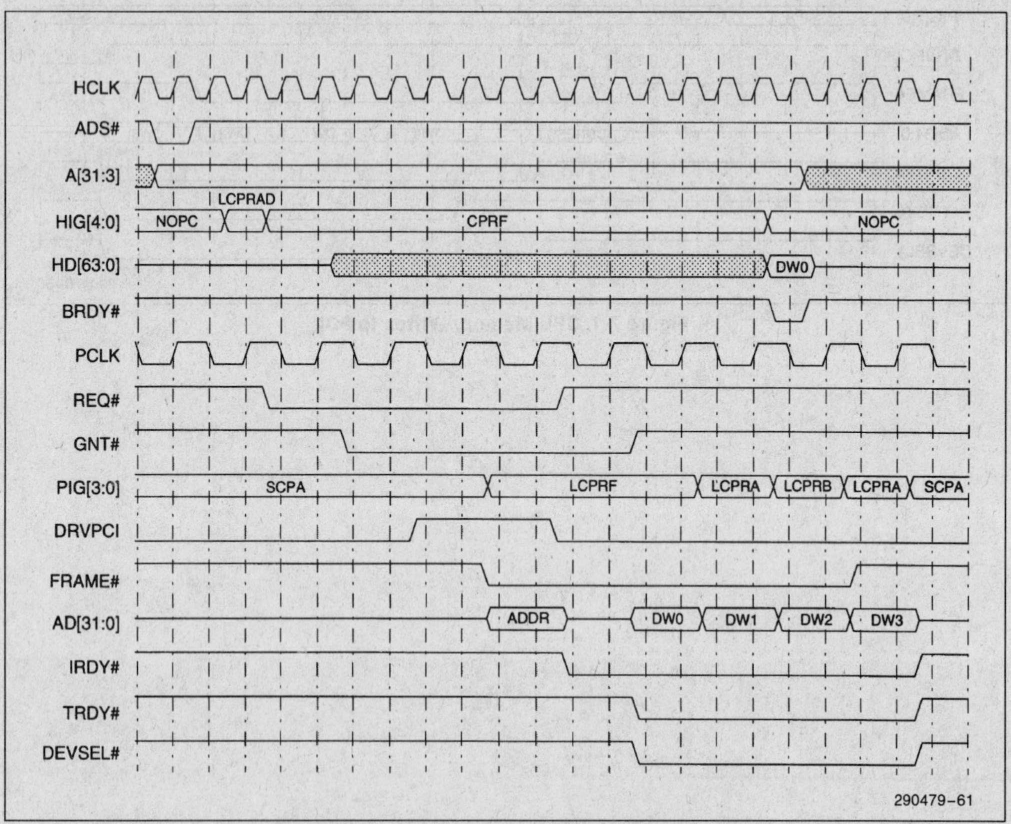

290479-61

Figure 7-2. CPU Read from PCI Frame Buffer Range

7.3 Register Access Cycles

The PCMC contains two registers which are mapped into I/O space, the Configuration Space Enable Register (I/O port CF8h) and the Turbo-Reset Control Register (I/O port CF9h). All other internal PCMC configuration registers are mapped into PCI configuration space. Configuration space must be enabled by writing a non-zero value to the Key field in the CSE Register before accesses to these registers can occur. These registers are mapped to locations C000h through C0FFh in PCI configuration space. If the Key field is programmed with 0h, CPU I/O cycles to locations C000h through CFFFh are forwarded to PCI as ordinary I/O cycles. Externally, accesses to the I/O mapped registers and the configuration space mapped registers use the same bus transfer protocol. Only the PCMC internal decode of the cycle differs. NA# is never asserted during PCMC configuration register or PCI configuration register access cycles. See Section 3.2, PCI Configuration Space Mapped Registers for details on the PCMC configuration space mapping mechanism.

7.3.1 CPU WRITE CYCLE TO PCMC INTERNAL REGISTER

A write to an internal PCMC register (either CSE Register, TRC Register or a configuration space-mapped register) is shown in Figure 7-3. The cycle begins with the address, byte enables and status signals (W/R#, D/C# and M/IO#) being driven to a valid state indicating an I/O write to either CF8h to access the CSE register, CF9h to access the TRC Register or C0XXh when configuration space is enabled to access a PCMC internal configuration register. The PCMC decodes the cycle and asserts AHOLD to tri-state the CPU address lines. The PCMC signals the LBXs to copy either the upper Dword or the lower Dword of the data bus onto the address lines. The PCMC makes the decision on which Dword to copy based on the BE[7:0]# lines. The HIG[4:0] lines are driven to DACPYH or DACPYL depending on whether the lower Dword of the data bus or the upper Dword of the data bus needs to be copied onto the address bus. The LBXs sample the HIG[4:0] command, and drive the data onto the address lines. The PCMC samples the A[31:0] lines on the second rising edge of HCLK after the LBXs begin driving the data. Finally, the PCMC negates AHOLD and asserts BRDY#, terminating the cycle.

If the write is to the CSE Register and the Key field is programmed to 0000b then configuration space is disabled. If the Key field is programmed to a non-zero value then configuration space is enabled.

1

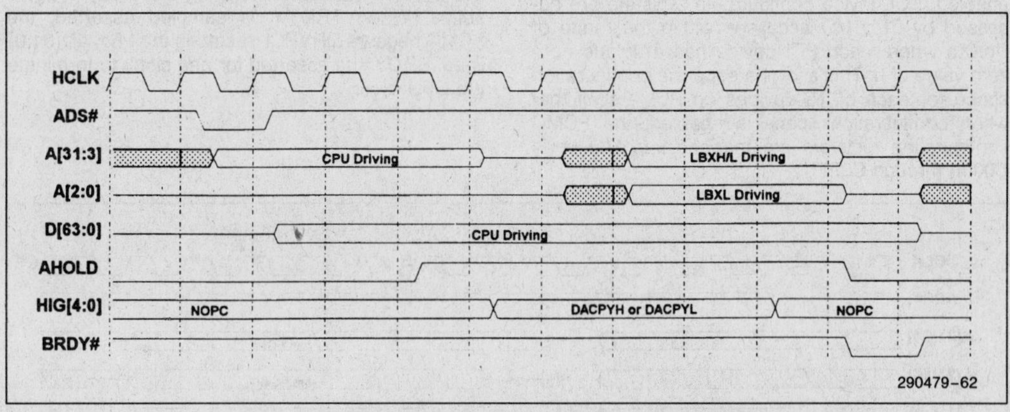

Figure 7-3. CPU Write to a PCMC Configuration Register

7.3.2 CPU READ CYCLE FROM PCMC INTERNAL REGISTER

A read from an internal PCMC register (either CSE Register, TRC Register or a configuration space-mapped register) is shown in Figure 7-4. The I/O read cycle is from either CF8h to access the CSE register, CF9h to access the TRC Register or C0XXh when configuration space is enabled to access a configuration space-mapped register. The PCMC decodes the cycle and asserts AHOLD to tri-state the CPU address lines. The PCMC then drives the contents of the addressed register onto the A[31:0] lines. One byte is enabled on each rising HCLK edge for four consecutive clocks. The PCMC signals the LBXs that the current cycle is a read from an internal PCMC register by issuing the ADCPY command to the LBXs over the HIG[4:0] lines. The LBXs sample the HIG[4:0] command and copy the address lines onto the data lines. Finally, the PCMC negates AHOLD, and asserts BRDY# terminating the cycle.

7.3.3 CPU WRITE TO PCI DEVICE CONFIGURATION REGISTER

In order to write to or read from a PCI device configuration register the Key field in the CSE register must be programmed to a non-zero value, enabling configuration space. When configuration space is enabled, PCI device configuration registers are accessed by CPU I/O accesses within the range of CnXXh where each PCI device has a unique non-zero value of n. This allows a separate configuration space for each of 15 devices on PCI. Recall that when configuration space is enabled, the PCMC configuration registers are mapped into I/O ports C000h through C0FFh.

A write to a PCI device configuration register is shown in Figure 7-5. The PCMC internally latches the host address lines and byte enables. The PCMC asserts AHOLD to tri-state the CPU address bus and drives the address lines with the translated address for the PCI configuration cycle. The translation is described in Section 3.2, PCI Configuration Space Mapped Registers. On the HIG[4:0] lines, the PCMC signals the LBXs to latch either the upper Dword of the host data bus or the lower Dword of the host data bus to be driven onto PCI during the data phase of the PCI cycle. On the PIG[3:0] lines, the PCMC signals the LBXs to drive the latched host address lines on the PCI AD[31:0] lines. The upper two bytes of the address lines are used during configuration as IDSEL signals for the PCI devices. The IDSEL pin on each PCI device is connected to one of the AD[31:17] lines.

The PCMC drives the command for a configuration write (1011) onto the C/BE[3:0]# lines and asserts FRAME# for one PCI clock. The PCMC drives the PIG[3:0] lines signaling the LBXs to drive the contents of the PCI write buffer onto the PCI AD[31:0] lines. This command is driven for only one PCI clock before returning to the SCPA command on the PIG[3:0] lines. The LBXs continue to drive the AD[31:0] lines with the valid write data as long as DRVPCI is asserted. The PCMC then asserts IRDY# and waits until sampling the TRDY# signal active. When TRDY# is sampled asserted, the PCMC negates DRVPCI tri-stating the LBX AD[31:0] lines. BRDY# is asserted for one clock to terminate the CPU cycle.

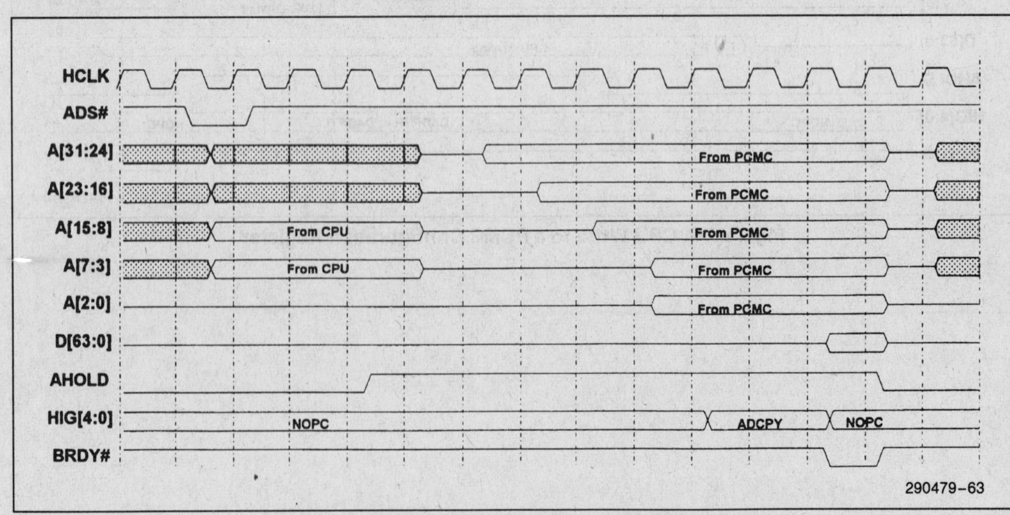

Figure 7-4. CPU Read from PCMC Configuration Register

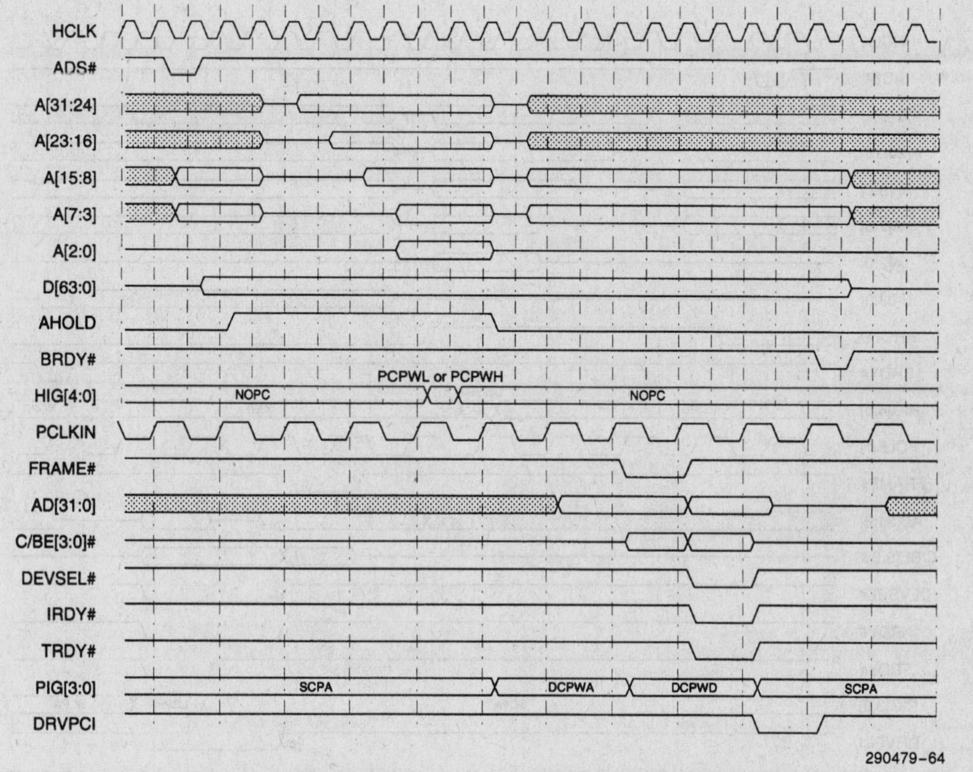

Figure 7-5. CPU Write to PCI Device Configuration Register

7.3.4 CPU READ FROM PCI DEVICE CONFIGURATION REGISTER

In order to write to or read from a PCI device configuration register the Key field in the CSE register must be programmed to a non-zero value, enabling configuration space. When configuration space is enabled, PCI device configuration registers are accessed by CPU I/O accesses within the range of CnXXh where each PCI device has a unique non-zero value of n. This allows a separate configuration space for each of 15 devices on PCI. Recall that when configuration space is enabled, the PCMC configuration registers occupy I/O addresses C0XXH.

A CPU read from a PCI device configuration register is shown in Figure 7- 6. The PCMC internally latches the host address lines and byte enables. The PCMC asserts AHOLD to tri-state the CPU address bus. The PCMC drives the address lines with the translated address for the PCI configuration cycle. The translation is described in Section 3.2, PCI Configuration Space Mapped Registers. On the PIG[3:0] lines, the PCMC signals the LBXs to drive the latched host address lines on the PCI AD[31:0] lines. The upper two bytes of the address lines are used during configuration as IDSEL signals for the PCI devices. The IDSEL pin on each PCI device is connected to one of the AD[31:17] lines.

The PCMC drives the command for a configuration read (1010) onto the C/BE[3:0]# lines and asserts FRAME# for one PCI clock. The PCMC drives the PIG[3:0] lines signaling the LBXs to latch the data on the PCI AD[31:0] lines into the CPU-to-PCI first read prefetch buffer. The PCMC then drives the HIG[4:0] lines signaling the LBXs to drive the data from the buffer onto the host data lines. The PCMC asserts IRDY# and waits until sampling TRDY# active. After TRDY# is sampled active, BRDY# is asserted for one clock to terminate the CPU cycle.

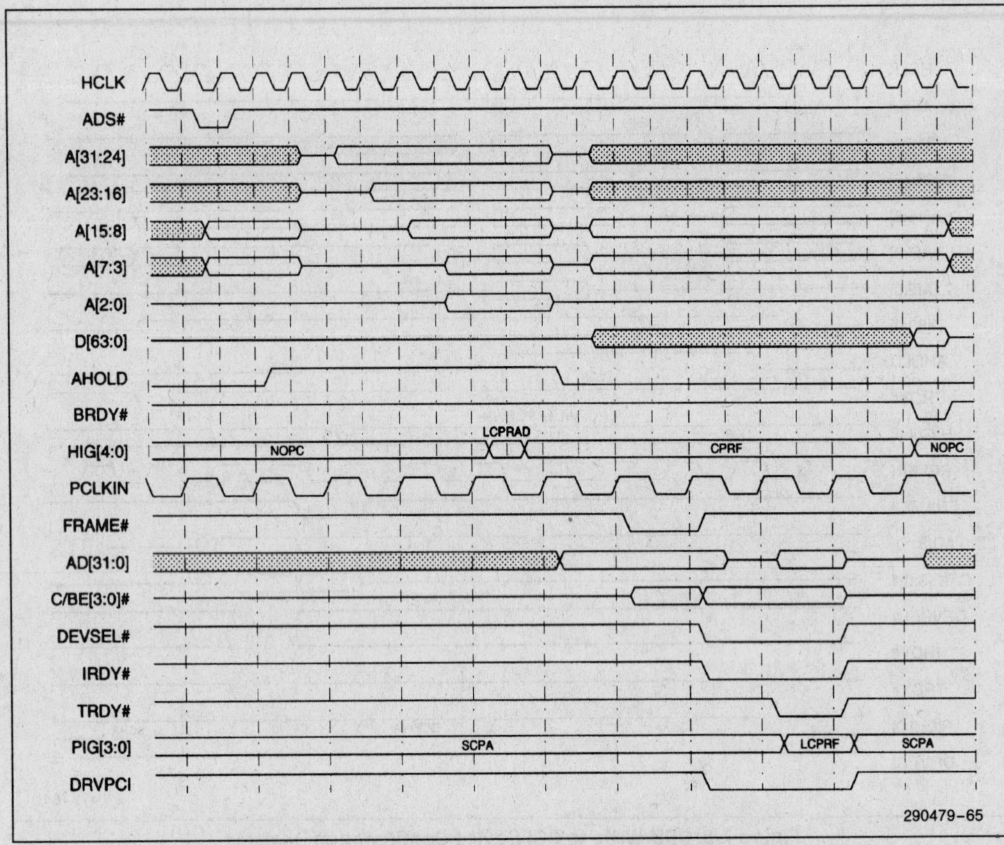

Figure 7-6. CPU Read from PCI Device Configuration Register

During system initialization, the CPU typically attempts to read from the configuration space of all 15 possible PCI devices to detect the presence of the devices. If no device is present, DEVSEL# is not asserted and the cycle is terminated, returning FF...FFh to the CPU. Figure 7-7 depicts an attempted read from a configuration register of a non-existent device. If no device responds then the PCMC aborts the cycle and sends the DRVFF command over the HIG[4:0] lines causing the LBXs to drive FF...FFh onto the host data lines.

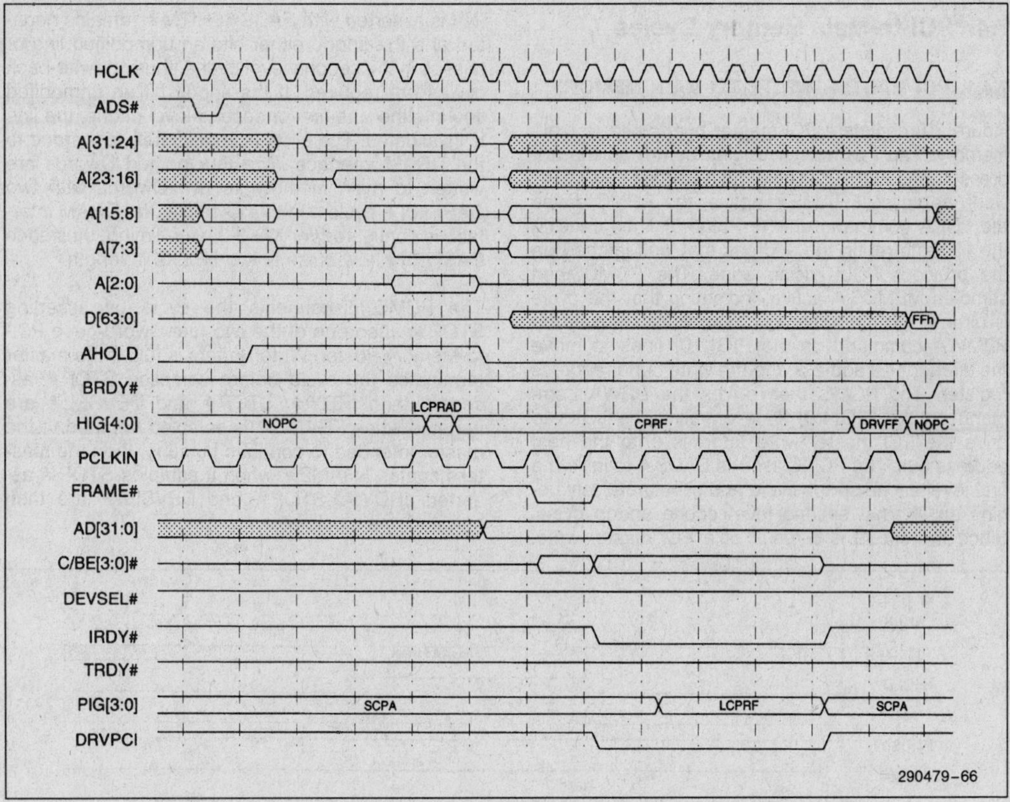

290479-66

Figure 7-7. CPU Attempted Configuration Read from Non-existent PCI Device

7.4 PCI-to-Main Memory Cycles

7.4.1 PCI MASTER WRITE TO MAIN MEMORY

Figure 7-8 depicts a PCI master burst write to main memory. The PCI master begins by driving the address on the AD[31:0] lines and asserting FRAME#. Upon sampling FRAME# active, the PCMC drives the LCPA command on the PIG[3:0] lines causing the LBXs to retain the address that was latched on the previous PCLK rising edge. The PCMC then samples MEMCS# active, indicating that the cycle is directed to main memory. The PCMC drives the PPMWA command on the PIG[3:0] lines to move the latched PCI address into the write buffer address register. The PCMC then drives the DPWA command on the HIG[4:0] lines enabling the LBXs to drive the PCI master write address onto the host address bus. The PCMC asserts EADS# to initiate a first level cache snoop cycle and simultaneously begins an internal second level cache snoop cycle. Since the snoop is a result of a PCI master write, INV is asserted with EADS#. HITM# remains negated and the snoop either hits an unmodified line or misses in the second level cache, thus no write-back cycles are required. If the snoop hit an unmodifed line in either the first or second level cache, the line is invalidated. The cycle is immediately forwarded to the DRAM interface. The four posted Dwords are written to main memory as two Qwords with two CAS[7:0]# cycles. In this example, the DRAM interface is configured for X-3-3-3 write timing, thus each CAS[7:0]# low pulse is two HCLKs in length.

The PCMC disconnects the cycle by asserting STOP# when one of the two four-Dword-deep PCI-to-Memory Posted Write Buffers is full. If the master terminates the cycle before sampling STOP# asserted, then IRDY#, STOP# and DEVSEL# are negated when FRAME# is sampled negated. If the master intended to continue bursting, then the master negates FRAME# when it samples STOP# asserted. IRDY#, STOP# and DEVSEL# are then negated one clock later.

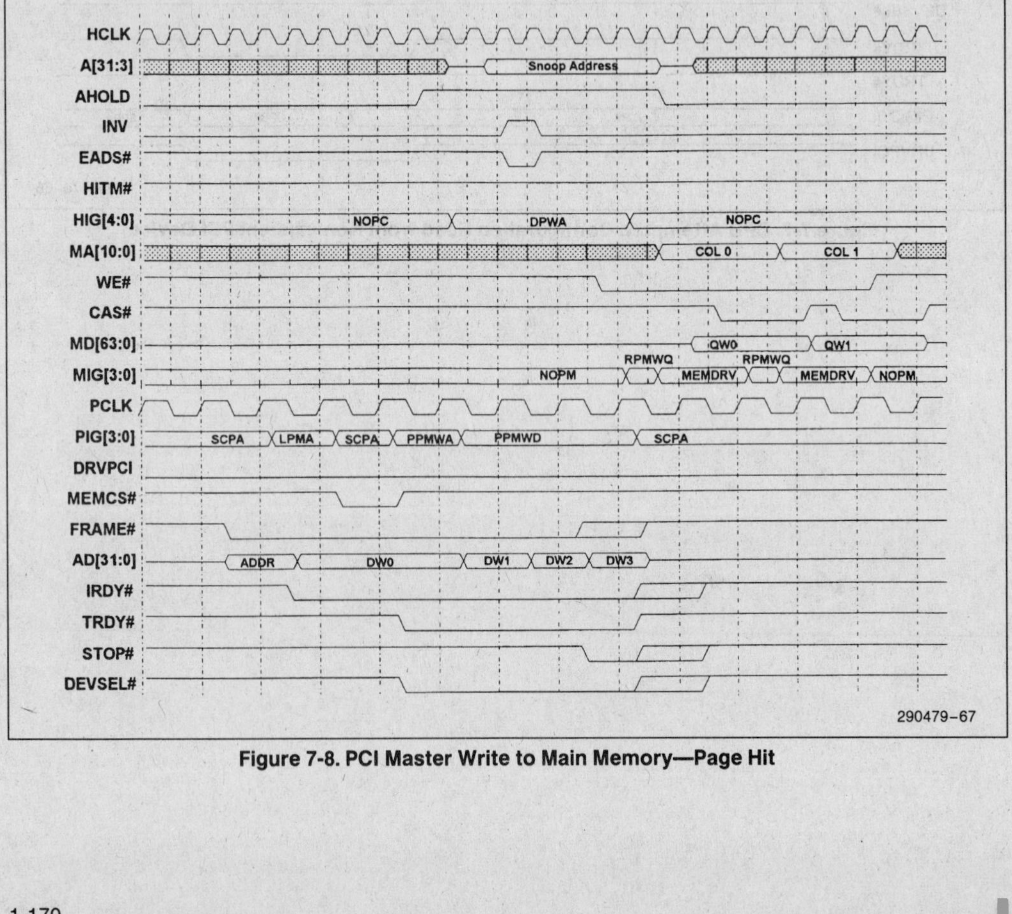

HCLK
A[31:3] Snoop Address
AHOLD
INV
EADS#
HITM#
HIG[4:0] NOPC DPWA NOPC
MA[10:0] COL 0 COL 1
WE#
CAS#
MD[63:0] QW0 QW1
MIG[3:0] NOPM RPMWQ MEMDRV RPMWQ MEMDRV NOPM
PCLK
PIG[3:0] SCPA LPMA SCPA PPMWA PPMWD SCPA
DRVPCI
MEMCS#
FRAME#
AD[31:0] ADDR DW0 DW1 DW2 DW3
IRDY#
TRDY#
STOP#
DEVSEL#

290479–67

Figure 7-8. PCI Master Write to Main Memory—Page Hit

7.4.2 PCI MASTER READ FROM MAIN MEMORY

Figure 7-9 depicts a PCI master read from main memory. The PCI master initiates the cycle by driving the read address on the AD[31:0] lines and asserting FRAME#. The PCMC drives the LPMA command on the PIG[3:0] lines causing the LBXs to retain the address latched on the previous PCLK rising edge. The PCMC drives the DPRA command on the HIG[4:0] lines enabling the LBXs to drive the read address onto the host address lines. The snoop cycle misses in the second level cache and either hits an unmodifed line or misses in the first level cache.

The cycle is then forwarded to the DRAM interface. A read of four Qwords is performed. Each Qword is posted in the PCI-Memory Read Prefetch Buffer. The data is then driven onto PCI in an eight Dword burst cycle. If the master terminates the cycle before sampling STOP#, then IRDY#, STOP# and DEVSEL# are all negated after FRAME# is sampled inactive. If the master intended to continue bursting, then the master negates FRAME# when it samples STOP# asserted and IRDY#, STOP# and DEVSEL# are negated one clock later.

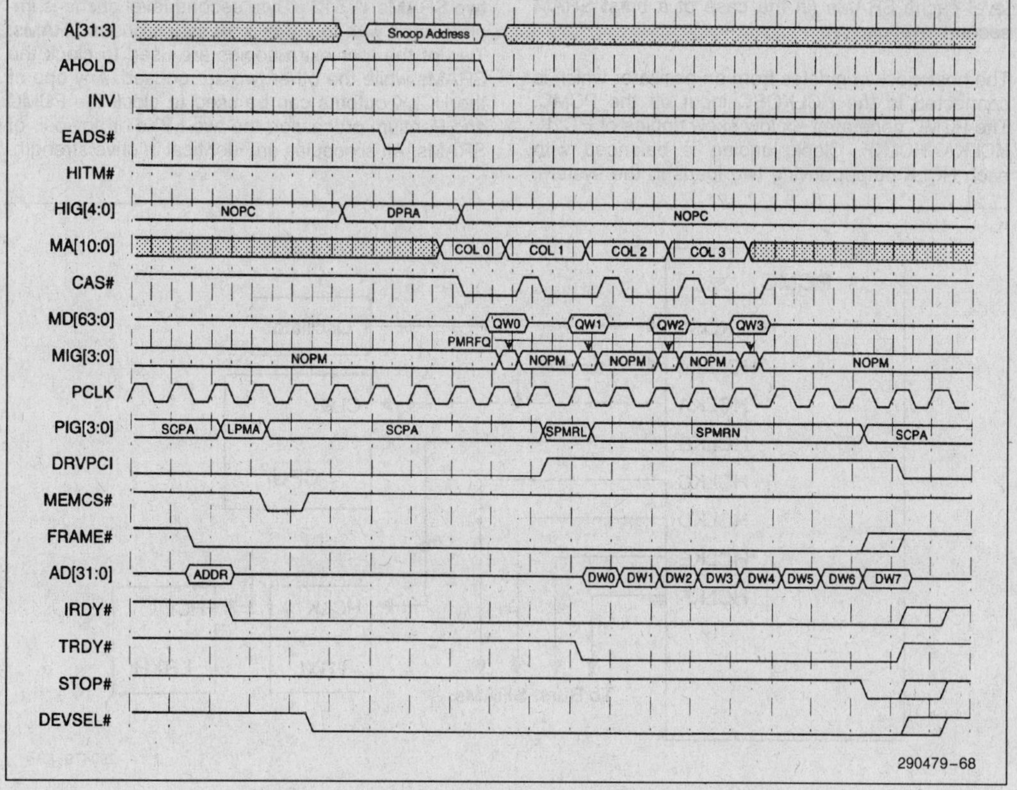

Figure 7-9. PCI Master Read from Main Memory—Page Hit

8.0 SYSTEM CLOCKING AND RESET

8.1 Clock Domains

The PCMC and LBXs operate based on two clocks, HCLK and PCLK. The CPU, second level cache, and the DRAM interfaces operate based on HCLK. The PCI interface timing is based on PCLK.

8.2 Clock Generation and Distribution

Figure 8-1 shows the host clock distribution in the CPU, cache and memory subsystem. HCLK is distributed to the CPU, PCMC, LBXs and the second level cache SRAMs (in the case of a burst SRAM second level cache).

The host clock originates from an oscillator which is connected to the HCLKOSC input on the PCMC. The PCMC generates six low skew copies of HCLK, HCLKA–HCLKF. Clock loading is balanced with each HCLK output driving two loads in the system. Each clock output should drive a trace of length *k* with stubs at the end of the trace of length *l* connecting to the two loads. The *l* and *k* parameters should be matched for each of the six clock outputs to minimize overall system clock skew. One of the HCLK outputs is used to clock the PCMC and the Pentium processor. Because the clock driven to the PCMC HCLKIN input and the Pentium processor CLK input originates with the same HCLK output, clock skew between the PCMC and the CPU can be kept lower than between the PCMC and other system components. Another copy of HCLK is used to clock the LBXs. A 256 KByte burst SRAM second level cache can be implemented with eight 32K x 9 synchronous SRAMs. The four remaining copies of HCLK are used to clock the SRAMs. Each HCLK output drives two SRAMs. A 512 KByte second level cache is implemented with four 64K x 18 synchronous SRAMs. Two of the four extra copies are used to clock the SRAMs while the other two are unused. Any one of the HCLK outputs can be used to clock the PCMC and Pentium processor, the two LBXs or any pair of SRAMs. All six copies are identical in drive strength.

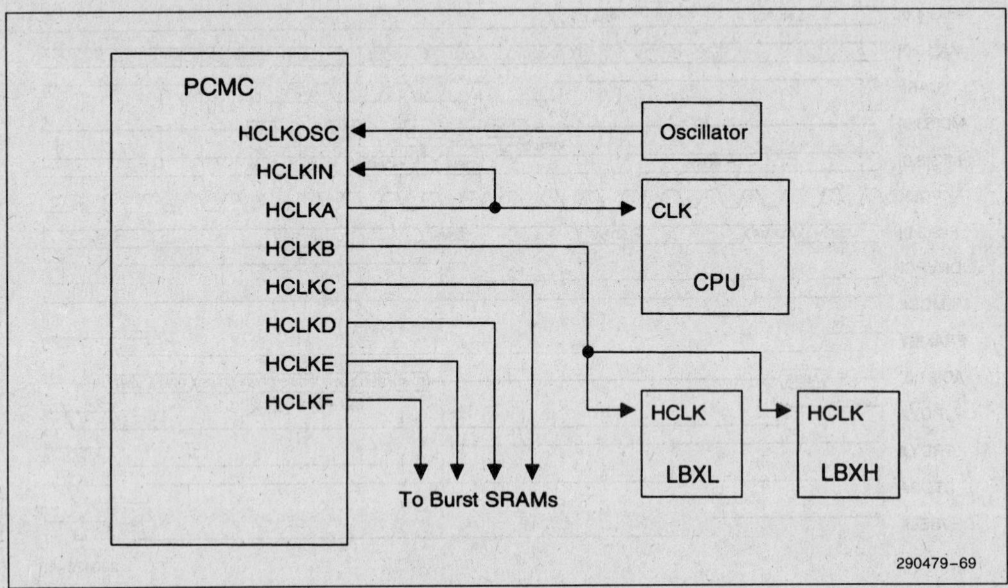

Figure 8-1. HCLK Distribution

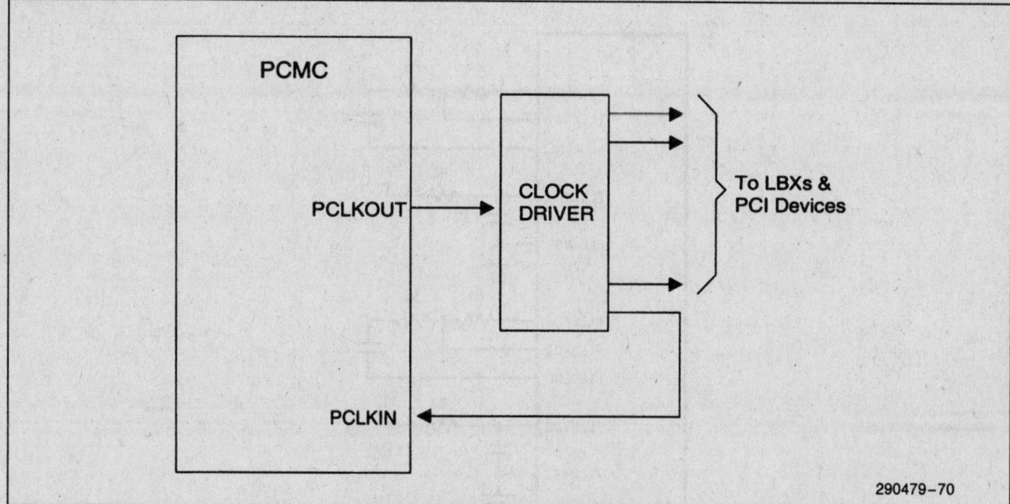

Figure 8-2. PCI Clock Distribution

Figure 8-2 depicts the PCI clock distribution.

The PCMC generates PCLKOUT with an internal Phase Locked Loop (PLL). The PCLKOUT signal is buffered using a single component to produce several low skew copies of PCLK to drive the LBXs and other devices on PCI. One of the outputs of the clock driver is directed back to the PCLKIN input on the PCMC. The PLL locks the rising edges of PCLKIN in phase with the rising edges of HCLKIN. The PLL effectively compensates for the delay of the external clock driver. The resulting PCI clock is one half the frequency of HCLK. Timing for all of the PCI interface signals is based on PCLKIN. All PCI interface inputs are sampled on PCLKIN rising edges and all outputs transition as valid delays from PCLKIN rising edges. Clock skew between the PCLKIN pin on the PCMC and the PCLK pins on the LBXs must be kept within 1.25 ns to guarantee proper operation of the LBXs.

8.3 Phase Locked Loop Circuitry

The PCMC contains two internal Phase Locked Loops (PLLs). Loop filters and power supply decoupling circuitry must be provided externally. Figure 8-3 shows the PCMC connections to the external PLL circuitry.

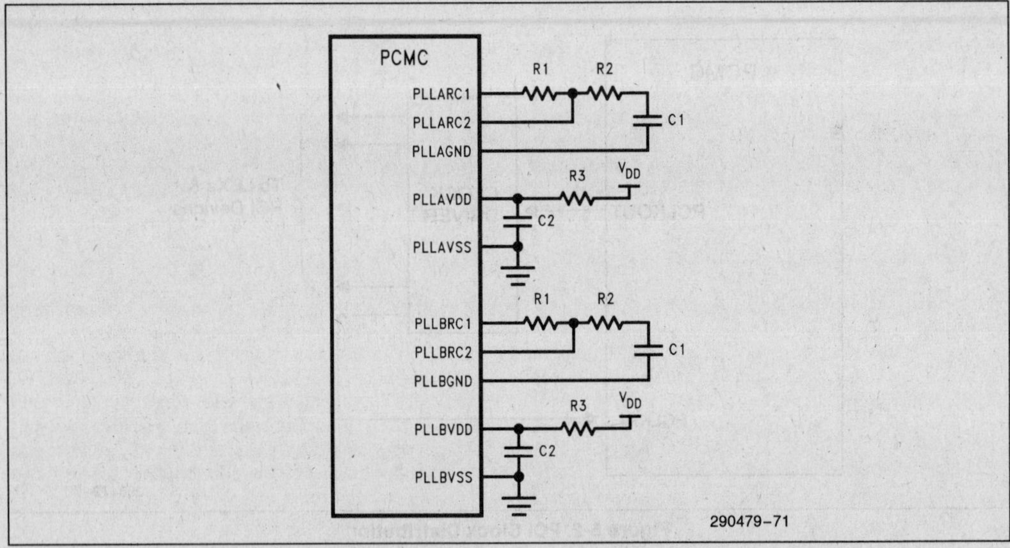

Figure 8-3. PCMC PLL Circuitry Connections

One of the PCMC internal Phase Locked Loops (PLL) locks onto the HCLKIN input. The PLL is used by the PCMC in generating and sampling timing critical signals. An external loop filter is required. The PLLARC1 and PLLARC2 pins connect to the external HCLK loop filter. Two resistors and a capacitor form the loop filter. The loop filter circuitry should be placed as close as possible to the PCMC loop filter pins. The PLL also has dedicated power and ground pins, PLLAVDD, PLLAVSS and PLLAGND. These power pins require a low noise supply. PLLAVDD, PLLAVSS and PLLAGND must be connected to the RC network shown in Figure 8-3.

The second PCMC internal Phase Locked Loop (PLL) locks the PCLKIN input in phase with the HCLKIN input. The PLL is used by the PCMC to keep the PCI clock in phase with the host clock. An external loop filter is required. The PLLBRC1 and PLLBRC2 pins connect to the external PCLK loop filter. Two resistors and a capacitor form the loop filter. The loop filter circuitry should be placed as close as possible to the PCMC loop filter pins. The PLL also has dedicated power and ground pins, PLLBVDD, PLLBVSS and PLLBGND. These power pins require a low noise supply. PLLBVDD, PLLBVSS and PLLBGND must be connected to the RC network shown in Figure 8-3.

The resistance and capacitance values for the external PLL circuitry are listed below.

R1 = 15 KΩ ±5%
R2 = 100Ω ±5%
R3 = 33Ω ±5%
C1 = 0.047 μF ±10%
C2 = 1.0 μF ±10%

8.4 System Reset

Figure 8-4 shows the PCMC system reset connections. The PCMC reset logic monitors PWROK and generates CPURST, PCIRST# and INIT.

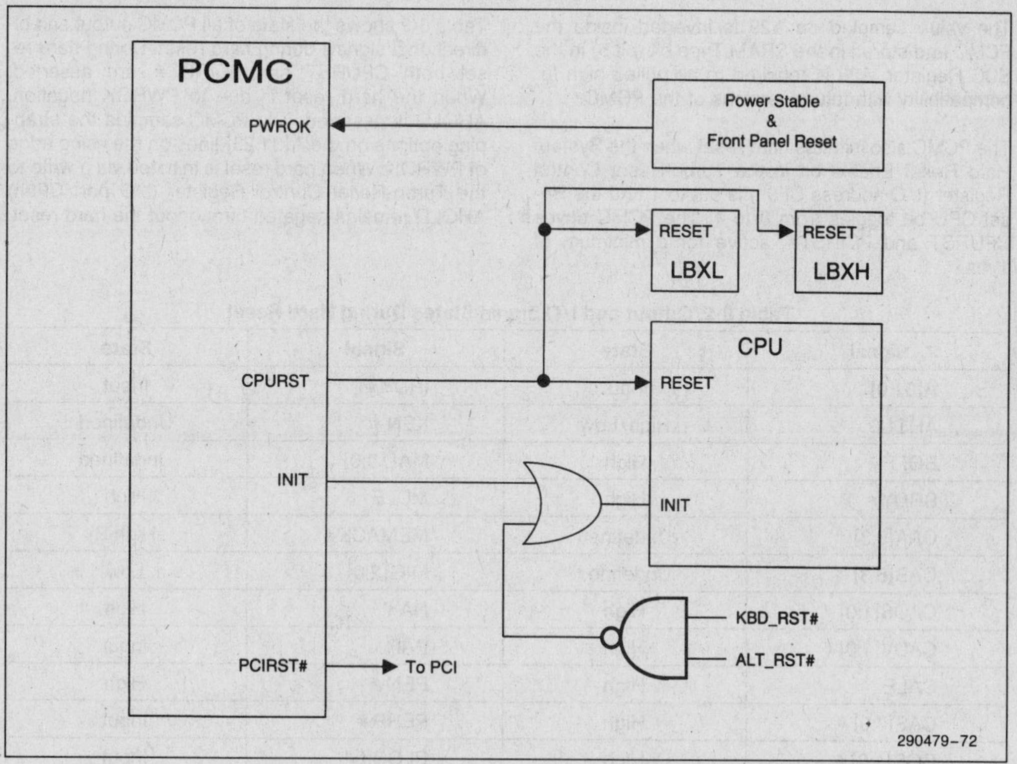

1

Figure 8-4. PCMC System Reset Logic

When asserted, PWROK is an indicator to the PCMC that VDD and HCLK have stabilized long enough for proper system operation. CPURST is asserted to initiate hard reset. INIT is asserted to initiate soft reset. PCIRST# is asserted to reset devices on PCI.

Hard reset is initiated by the PCMC in response to one of two conditions. First, hard reset is initiated when power is first applied to the system. PWROK must be driven inactive and must not be asserted until 1 ms after VDD and HCLK have stabilized at their A.C. and D.C. specifications. While PWROK is negated, the PCMC will assert CPURST and PCIRST#. PWROK can be asserted asynchronously. When PWROK is asserted, the PCMC first ensures that it has been completely initialized before negating CPURST and PCIRST#. CPURST is negated synchronously to the rising edge of HCLK. PCIRST# is negated asynchronously.

When PWROK is negated, the PCMC asserts AHOLD causing the CPU to tri-state the host address lines. Address lines A[31:28] are sampled by the PCMC on the rising edge of PWROK. A[31:30] are inverted and stored in configuration register 52h bits 7 and 6. The A[31:30] strapping options are depicted in Table 8-1.

Table 8-1. A[31:30] Strapping Options

A[31:30]	Configuration Register 52h, Bits [7:6]	Secondary Cache Size
11	00	Cache Not Populated
10	01	Reserved
01	10	256 KB Cache Installed
00	11	512 KB Cache Installed

The value sampled on A29 is inverted inside the PCMC and stored in the SRAM Type bit (bit 5) in the SCC Register. A28 is required to be pulled high for compatibility with future versions of the PCMC.

The PCMC also initiates hard reset when the System Hard Reset Enable bit in the Turbo-Reset Control Register (I/O address CF9h) is set to 1 and the Reset CPU bit toggles from 0 to 1. The PCMC drives CPURST and PCIRST# active for a minimum of 1 ms.

Table 8-2 shows the state of all PCMC output and bidirectional signals during hard reset. During hard reset both CPURST and PCIRST# are asserted. When the hard reset is due to PWROK negation, AHOLD is asserted. The PCMC samples the strapping options on the A[31:28] lines on the rising edge of PWROK. When hard reset is initiated via a write to the Turbo-Reset Control Register (I/O port CF9h) AHOLD remains negated throughout the hard reset.

Table 8-2. Output and I/O Signal States During Hard Reset

Signal	State	Signal	State
A[31:0]	Input	IRDY#	Input
AHOLD	High/Low	KEN#	Undefined
BOFF#	High	MA[10:0]	Undefined
BRDY#	High	MDLE	High
CAA[6:3]	Undefined	MEMACK#	High-Z
CAB[6:3]	Undefined	MIG[2:0]	Low
CADS[1:0]#	High	NA#	High
CADV[1:0]#	High	PAR	Input
CALE	High	PEN#	High
CAS[7:0]#	High	PERR#	Input
COE[1:0]#	High	PLOCK#	Input
CWE[7:0]#	High	PIG3	Low
C/BE[3:0]#	Input	PIG[2:0]	High
DEVSEL#	Input	RAS[5:0]#	High
DRVPCI	Low	REQ#	High-Z
EADS#	High	SERR#	Input
FRAME#	Input	STOP#	Input
HIG[4:0]	Low	TRDY#	Input
INIT	Low	WE#	High
INV	Low		

Soft reset is initiated by the PCMC in response to one of two conditions. First, when the System Hard Reset Enable bit in the TRC Register is reset to 0, and the Reset CPU bit toggles from 0 to 1, the PCMC initiates soft reset by asserting INIT for a minimum of 16 HCLKs. Second, the PCMC initiates soft reset upon detecting a shutdown cycle from the CPU. In this case, the PCMC first broadcasts a shutdown special cycle on PCI and then asserts INIT for a minimum of 16 HCLKs.

9.0 ELECTRICAL CHARACTERISTICS

NOTICE: This is a production data sheet. The specifications are subject to change without notice.

9.1 Absolute Maximum Ratings

Case Temperature under Bias ....0°C to +85°C

Storage Temperature ....−55°C to +150°C

Voltage on Any Pin with Respect to Ground ...−-0.3V to V_{CC} +0.3V

Supply Voltage with Respect to V_{SS} ....−0.3V to +6.5V

Maximum Power Dissipation 2.0W

**WARNING: Stressing the device beyond the "Absolute Maximum Ratings" may cause permanent damage. These are stress ratings only. Operation beyond the "Operating Conditions" is not recommended and extended exposure beyond the "Operating Conditions" may affect device reliability.*

9.2 Thermal Characteristics

The PCMC is designed for operation at case temperatures between 0°C and 85°C. The thermal resistances of the package are given in Table 9-1.

Table 9-1. PCMC Package Thermal Resistance

Parameter	Air Flow Meters/Second (Linear Feet per Minute)				
	0 (0)	0.5 (98.4)	1.0 (196.9)	2.0 (393.7)	5.0 (984.3)
θ_{JA} (°C/W)	31	27	24.5	23	19

θ_{JC} (°C/W)	8.6

1

9.3 D.C. Characteristics

Table 9-2. Functional Operating Range (V_{CC} = 5V ±5%; T_{CASE} = 0°C to +85°C)

Symbol	Parameter	Min	Max	Unit	Notes
V_{IL1}	Input Low Voltage	−0.3	0.8	V	Note 1, V_{CC} = 4.75V
V_{IH1}	Input High Voltage	2.2	V_{CC} + 0.3	V	Note 1, V_{CC} = 5.25V
V_{IL2}	Input Low Voltage	−0.3	1.35	V	Note 2, V_{CC} = 4.75V
V_{IH2}	Input High Voltage	3.85	V_{CC} + 0.3	V	Note 2, V_{CC} = 5.25V
V_{T1-}	Schmitt Trigger Threshold Voltage, Falling Edge	0.7	1.35	V	Note 3, V_{CC} = 5.0V
V_{T1+}	Schmitt Trigger Threshold Voltage, Rising Edge	1.4	2.2	V	Note 3, V_{CC} = 5.0V
V_{H1}	Hysteresis Voltage	0.3	1.2	V	Note 3, V_{CC} = 5.0V
V_{T2-}	Schmitt Trigger Threshold Voltage, Falling Edge	1.25	2.3	V	Note 3, V_{CC} = 5.0V
V_{T2+}	Schmitt Trigger Threshold Voltage, Rising Edge	2.3	3.7	V	Note 3, V_{CC} = 5.0V
V_{H2}	Hysteresis Voltage	0.3	1.2	V	Note 3, V_{CC} = 5.0V
V_{OL1}	Output Low Voltage		0.5	V	Note 4
V_{OH1}	Output High Voltage	V_{CC} − 0.5		V	Note 4
V_{OL2}	Output Low Voltage		0.4	V	Note 5
V_{OH2}	Output High Voltage	2.4		V	Note 5
I_{OL1}	Output Low Current		1	mA	Note 6
I_{OH1}	Output High Current	−1		mA	Note 6
I_{OL2}	Output Low Current		3	mA	Note 7
I_{OH2}	Output High Current	−2		mA	Note 7
I_{OL3}	Output Low Current		6	mA	Note 8
I_{OH3}	Output High Current	−2		mA	Note 8
I_{OL4}	Output Low Current		3	mA	Note 9
I_{OH4}	Output High Current	−1		mA	Note 9
I_{IH}	Input Leakage Current		+10	µA	
I_{IL}	Input Leakage Current		−10	µA	
C_{IN}	Input Capacitance		12	pF	F_C = 1 MHz
C_{OUT}	Output Capacitance		12	pF	F_C = 1 MHz
$C_{I/O}$	I/O Capacitance		12	pF	F_C = 1 MHz

NOTES:

1. V_{IL1} and V_{IH1} apply to the following signals: A[31:0], BE[7:0]#, D/C#, W/R#, M/IO#, HLOCK#, ADS#, PCHK#, HITM#, CACHE#, SMIACT#, PCLKIN, HCLKIN, HCLKOSC, FLSHBUF#, MEMCS#, SERR#, PERR#, MEMREQ#, GNT#, PLOCK#, STOP#, IRDY#, TRDY#, FRAME#, C/BE[3:0]#.
2. V_{IL2} and V_{IH2} apply to the following signals: PPOUT[1:0], EOL.
3. V_{T1-}, V_{T1+} and V_{H1} apply to PWROK. V_{T2-}, V_{T2+} and V_{H2} apply to TESTEN.
4. V_{OL1} and V_{OH1} apply to the following signals: HIG[4:0], MIG[2:0], PIG[3:0], DRVPCI, MDLE.

5. V_{OL2} and V_{OH2} apply to the following signals: REQ#, MEMACK#, FRAME#, C/BE[3:0]#, TRDY#, IRDY#, STOP#, PLOCK#, DEVSEL#, PAR, PERR#, SERR#, BOFF#, AHOLD, BRDY#, NA#, EADS#, KEN#, INV, A[31:0], PCLKOUT, HCLKA - HCLKF, CALE, COE[1:0]#, CWE[7:0]#, CADV[1:0]#, CADS[1:0]#, CAA[6:3], CAB[6:3], RAS[5:0]#, CAS[7:0]#, MA[10:0], WE#.
6. I_{OL1} and I_{OH1} apply to the following signals: HIG[4:0], MIG[2:0], PIG[3:0], DRVPCI, MDLE.
7. I_{OL2} and I_{OH2} apply to the following signals: C/BE[3:0]#, REQ#, MEMACK#, PCIRST#, MA[10:0], WE#.
8. I_{OL3} and I_{OH3} apply to the following signals: FRAME#, TRDY#, IRDY#, STOP#, PLOCK#, DEVSEL#, PAR, PERR#, SERR#.
9. I_{OL4} and I_{OH4} apply to the following signals: BOFF#, AHOLD, BRDY#, NA#, EADS#, KEN#, INV, CPURST, INIT, A[31:0], PCLKOUT, CALE, COE[1:0]#, CADS[1:0]#, CADV[1:0]#, CWE[7:0]#, CAA[6:3], CAB[6:3], RAS[5:0]#, CAS[7:0]#.

9.4 A.C. Characteristics

The A.C. characteristics given in this section consist of propagation delays, valid delays, input setup requirments, input hold requirements, output float delays, output enable delays, output-to-output delays, pulse widths, clock high and low times and clock period specifications. Figures 9-1 through 9-9 define these specifications. Sections 9.4.1 through 9.4.8 list the A.C. Characteristics. Output test loads are listed in the right column.

1

In Figures 9-1 through 9-9, V_T = 1.5V for the following signals:

A[31:0], BE[7:0]#, PEN#, D/C#, W/R#, M/IO#, HLOCK#, ADS#, PCHK#, HITM#, EADS#, BRDY#, BOFF#, AHOLD, NA#, KEN#, INV, CACHE#, SMIACT#, INIT, CPURST, CALE, CADV[1:0]#, COE[1:0]#, CWE[7:0]#, CADS[1:0]#, CAA[6:3], CAB[6:3], WE#, RAS[5:0]#, CAS[7:0]#, MA[10:0], C/BE[3:0]#, FRAME#, TRDY#, IRDY#, STOP#, PLOCK#, GNT#, DEVSEL#, MEMREQ#, PAR, PERR#, SERR#, REQ#, MEMCS#, FLSHBUF#, MEMACK#, PWROK, PCIRST#, HCLKIN, HCLKA-HCLKF, PCLKIN, PCLKOUT.

V_T = 2.5V for the following signals:

PPOUT[1:0], EOL, HIG[4:0], PIG[3:0], MIG[2:0], DRVPCI, MDLE.

9.4.1 HOST CLOCK TIMING, 66 MHz

Table 9-3. Functional Operating Range (V_{CC} = 4.9V to 5.25V, T_{CASE} = 0°C to +70°C)

Symbol	Parameter	Min	Max	Figure	Notes
t1a	HCLKOSC High Time	6.0		9-6	
t1b	HCLKOSC Low Time	5.0		9-6	
t2a	HCLKIN Period	15	20	9-6	
t2b	HCLKIN Period Stability		±100		ps(1)
t2c	HCLKIN High Time	4		9-6	
t2d	HCLKIN Low Time	4		9-6	
t2e	HCLKIN Rise Time		1.5	9-7	
t2f	HCLKIN Fall Time		1.5	9-7	
t3a	HCLKA–HCLKF Output-to-Output Skew		0.5	9-9	0 pF
t3b	HCLKA–HCLKF High Time	5.0		9-6	0 pF
t3c	HCLKA–HCLKF Low Time	5.0		9-6	0 pF

NOTE:
1. Measured on rising edge of adjacent clocks at 1.5V.

9.4.2 CPU INTERFACE TIMING, 66 MHz

Table 9-4. Functional Operating Range (V_{CC} = 4.9V to 5.25V; T_{CASE} = 0°C to +70°C)

Symbol	Parameter	Min	Max	Figure	Notes
t10a	ADS#, HITM#, W/R#, M/IO#, D/C#, HLOCK#, CACHE#, BE[7:0]#, SMIACT# Setup Time to HCLKIN Rising	4.6		9-3	
t10b	ADS#, HITM#, W/R#, M/IO#, D/C#, HLOCK#, CACHE#, BE[7:0]#, SMIACT# Hold Time from HCLKIN Rising	0.8		9-3	
t11a	PCHK# Setup Time to HCLKIN Rising	4.3		9-3	
t11b	PCHK# Hold Time from HCLKIN Rising	1.1		9-3	
t12a	A[18:3] Rising Edge Setup Time to HCLKIN Rising	4.5		9-3	Setup to HCLKIN Rising when ADS# is Sampled Active by PCMC.
t12aa	A[18:3] Falling Edge Setup Time to HCLKIN Rising	3.2		9-3	Setup to HCLKIN Rising when ADS# is Sampled Active by PCMC.
t12ab	A[31:19] Rising Edge Setup Time to HCLKIN Rising	4.7		9-3	Setup to HCLKIN Rising when ADS# is Sampled Active by PCMC.
t12ac	A[31:19] Falling Edge Setup Time to HCLKIN Rising	4.1		9-3	Setup to HCLKIN Rising when ADS# is Sampled Active by PCMC.
t12b	A[31:0] Hold Time from HCLKIN Rising	0.5		9-3	Hold from HCLKIN Rising Two Clocks after ADS# is Sampled Active by PCMC.
t12c	A[31:0] Setup Time to HCLKIN Rising	6.5		9-3	Setup to HCLKIN Rising when EADS# is Sampled Active by the CPU.
t12d	A[31:0] Hold Time from HCLKIN Rising	1.5		9-3	Hold from HCLKIN Rising when EADS# is Sampled Active by the CPU.
t12e	A[31:0] Output Enable from HCLKIN Rising	0	13	9-5	
t12f	A[31:0] Valid Delay from HCLKIN Rising	1.3	13	9-2	0 pF
t12g	A[31:0] Float Delay from HCLKIN Rising	0	13	9-4	
t12h	A[2:0] Propagation Delay from BE[7:0]#	1	16	9-1	0 pF
t13a	BRDY# Rising Edge Valid Delay from HCLKIN Rising	1.7	7.8	9-2	0 pF
t13b	BRDY# Falling Edge Valid Delay from HCLKIN Rising	1.7	7.6	9-2	0 pF
t14	NA# Valid Delay from HCLKIN Rising	1.3	7.8	9-2	0 pF

Table 9-4. Functional Operating Range (V_{CC} = 4.9V to 5.25V; T_{CASE} = 0°C to +70°C) (Continued)

Symbol	Parameter	Min	Max	Figure	Notes
t15a	AHOLD Valid Delay from HCLKIN Rising	1.3	7.1	9-2	0 pF
t15b	BOFF# Valid Delay from HCLKIN Rising	1.8	7.1	9-2	
t16a	EADS#, INV, PEN#, Valid Delay from HCLKIN Rising	1.3	7.4	9-2	0 pF
t16b	CPURST Rising Edge Valid Delay from HCLKIN Rising	0.9	7.5	9-2	
t16c	CPURST Falling Edge Valid Delay from HCLKIN Rising	0.9	7.0	9-2	
t16d	KEN# Valid Delay from HCLKIN Rising	1.3	7.6	9-2	
t17	INIT High Pulse Width	16 HCLKs −5		9-8	Soft Reset via TRC Register or CPU Shutdown Special Cycle, 0 pF
t18	CPURST High Pulse Width	1 ms		9-8	Hard Reset via TRC Register, 0 pF

1

9.4.3 SECOND LEVEL CACHE STANDARD SRAM TIMING, 66 MHz

Table 9-5. Functional Operating Range (V_{CC} = 4.9V to 5.25V; T_{CASE} = 0°C to +70°C)

Symbol	Parameter	Min	Max	Figure	Notes
t20a	CAA[6:3]/CAB[6:3] Propagation Delay from A[6:3]	0	8.5	9-1	0 pF
t20b	CAA[6:3]/CAB[6:3] Valid Delay from HCLKIN Rising	0	7.2	9-2	0 pF
t21a	COE[1:0]# Falling Edge Valid Delay from HCLKIN Rising	0	9	9-2	0 pF
t21b	COE[1:0]# Rising Edge Valid Delay from HCLKIN Rising	0	5.5	9-2	0 pF
t22a	CWE[7:0]#/CBS[7:0]# Falling Edge Valid Delay from HCLKIN Rising	2	14	9-2	CPU Burst or Single Write to Second Level Cache, 0 pF
t22b	CWE[7:0]#/CBS[7:0]# Rising Edge Valid Delay from HCLKIN Rising	3	14	9-2	CPU Burst or Single Write to Write to Second Level Cache, 0 pF
t22c	CWE[7:0]#/CBS[7:0]# Valid Delay from HCLKIN Rising	1.4	7.7	9-2	Cache Line Fill, 0 pF
t22d	CWE[7:0]#/CBS[7:0]# Low Pulse Width	1 HCLK		9-8	0 pF
t22e	CWE[7:0]#/CBS[7:0]# Driven High before CALE Driven High	−1		9-9	Last Write to Second Level Cache during Cache Line Fill, 0 pF
t22f	CAA[4:3]/CAB[4:3] Valid before CWE[7:0]# Falling	1.5		9-9	CPU Burst Write to Second Level Cache, 0 pF
t23	CALE Valid Delay from HCLKIN Rising	0	7.5	9-2	0 pF
t24	CR/W[1:0]# Valid Delay from HCLKIN Rising	1.5	7.6	9-2	0 pF
t25	CBS[7:0]# Valid Delay from HCLKIN Rising, Reads from Cache SRAMs	1.0	12.0	9-2	0 pF

9.4.4 SECOND LEVEL CACHE BURST SRAM TIMING, 66 MHz

Table 9-6. Functional Operating Range (V_{CC} = 4.9V to 5.25V; T_{CASE} = 0°C to +70°C)

Symbol	Parameter	Min	Max	Figure	Notes
t30a	CAA[6:3]/CAB[6:3] Propagation Delay from A[6:3]	0	8.5	9-1	0 pF
t30b	CAA[6:3]/CAB[6:3] Valid Delay from HCLKIN Rising	0	7.0	9-2	0 pF
t31	CADS[1:0]# Valid Delay from HCLKIN Rising	1.5	7.7	9-2	0 pF
t32	CADV[1:0]# Valid Delay from HCLKIN Rising	1.5	7.1	9-2	0 pF
t33	CWE[7:0]# Valid Delay from HCLKIN Rising	1.0	9.0	9-2	0 pF
t34a	COE[1:0]# Falling Edge Valid Delay from HCLKIN Rising	0	9.0	9-2	0 pF
t34b	COE[1:0]# Rising Edge Valid Delay from HCLKIN Rising	0	5.5	9-2	0 pF
t35	CALE Valid Delay from HCLKIN Rising	0	7.5	9-2	0 pF

9.4.5 DRAM INTERFACE TIMING, 66 MHz

Table 9-7. Functional Operating Range (V_{CC} = 4.9V to 5.25V; T_{CASE} = 0°C to +70°C)

Symbol	Parameter	Min	Max	Figure	Notes
t40a	RAS[5:0]# Valid Delay from HCLKIN Rising	0	7.5	9-2	50 pF
t40b	RAS[5:0]# Pulse Width High	4 HCLKs − 5			RAS# Precharge at Beginning of Page Miss Cycle, 50 pF
t41a	CAS[7:0]# Valid Delay from HCLKIN Rising	0	7.5	9-2	50 pF
t41b	CAS[7:0]# Pulse Width High	1 HCLK−5			CAS# Precharge during Burst Cycles, 50 pF
t42	WE# Valid Delay from HCLKIN Rising	0	21	9-2	50 pF
t43a	MA[10:0] Propagation Delay from A[23:3]	0	23	9-1	50 pF
t43b	MA[10:0] Valid Delay from HCLKIN Rising	0	10.1	9-2	50 pF

9.4.6 PCI CLOCK TIMING, 66 MHz

Table 9-8. Functional Operating Range (V_{CC} = 4.9V to 5.25V; T_{CASE} = 0°C to +70°C)

Symbol	Parameter	Min	Max	Figure	Notes
t50a	PCLKOUT High Time	13		9-6	20 pF
t50b	PCLKOUT Low Time	13		9-6	20 pF
t51a	PCLKIN High Time	12		9-6	
t51b	PCLKIN Low Time	12		9-6	
t51c	PCLKIN Rise Time		3	9-7	
t51d	PCLKIN Fall Time		3	9-7	

9.4.7 PCI INTERFACE TIMING, 66 MHz

Table 9-9. Functional Operating Range (V_{CC} = 4.9V to 5.25V; T_{CASE} = 0°C to +70°C)

Symbol	Parameter	Min	Max	Figure	Notes
t60a	C/BE[3:0]#, FRAME#, TRDY#, IRDY#, STOP#, PLOCK#, PAR, PERR#, SERR#, DEVSEL# Valid Delay from PCLKIN Rising	2	11	9-2	Min: 0 pF Max: 50 pF
t60b	C/BE[3:0]#, FRAME#, TRDY#, IRDY#, STOP#, PLOCK#, PAR, PERR#, SERR#, DEVSEL# Output Enable Delay from PCLKIN Rising	2		9-5	
t60c	C/BE[3:0]#, FRAME#, TRDY#, IRDY#, STOP#, PLOCK#, PAR, PERR#, SERR#, DEVSEL# Float Delay from PCLKIN Rising	2	28	9-4	
t60d	C/BE[3:0]#, FRAME#, TRDY#, IRDY#, STOP#, PLOCK#, PAR, PERR#, SERR#, DEVSEL# Setup Time to PCLKIN Rising	7		9-3	
t60e	C/BE[3:0]#, FRAME#, TRDY#, IRDY#, STOP#, PLOCK#, PAR, PERR#, SERR#, DEVSEL# Hold Time from PCLKIN Rising	0		9-3	
t61a	REQ#, MEMACK# Valid Delay from PCLKIN Rising	2	12	9-2	Min: 0 pF Max: 50 pF
t61b	REQ#, MEMACK# Output Enable Delay from PCLKIN Rising	2		9-5	
t61c	REQ#, MEMACK# Float Delay from PCLKIN Rising	2	28	9-4	
t62a	FLSHREQ#, MEMREQ# Setup Time to PCLKIN Rising	12		9-3	
t62b	FLSHREQ#, MEMREQ# Hold Time from PCLKIN Rising	0		9-3	
t63a	GNT# Setup Time to PCLKIN Rising	10		9-3	
t63b	GNT# Hold Time from PCLKIN Rising	0		9-3	
t64a	MEMCS# Setup Time to PCLKIN Rising	7		9-3	
t64b	MEMCS# Hold Time from PCLKIN Rising	0		9-3	
t65	PCIRST# Low Pulse Width	1 ms		9-8	Hard Reset via TRC Register, 0 pF

9.4.8 LBX INTERFACE TIMING, 66 MHz

Table 9-10. Functional Operating Range (V_{CC} = 4.9V to 5.25V; T_{CASE} = 0°C to +70°C)

Symbol	Parameter	Min	Max	Figure	Notes
t70	HIG[4:0] Valid Delay from HCLKIN Rising	0.8	6.5	9-2	0 pF
t71	MIG[2:0] Valid Delay from HCLKIN Rising	0.9	6.5	9-2	0 pF
t72	PIG[3:0] Valid Delay from PCLKIN Rising	0.7	10.9	9-2	0 pF
t73	PCIDRV Valid Delay from PCLKIN Rising	1	13.5	9-2	0 pF
t74a	MDLE Falling Edge Valid Delay from HCLKIN Rising	0.6	5.6	9-2	0 pF
t74b	MDLE Rising Edge Valid Delay from HCLKIN Rising	0.6	6.8	9-2	0 pF
t75a	EOL, PPOUT[1:0] Setup Time to PCLKIN Rising	7.7		9-3	
t75b	EOL, PPOUT[1:0] Hold Time from PCLKIN Rising	1.0		9-3	

1

9.4.9 HOST CLOCK TIMING, 60 MHz

Table 9-11. Functional Operating Range (V_{CC} = 5V ±5%; T_{CASE} = 0°C to +85°C)

Symbol	Parameter	Min	Max	Figure	Notes
t1a	HCLKOSC High Time	6.0		9-6	
t1b	HCLKOSC Low Time	5.0		9-6	
t2a	HCLKIN Period	16.66	20	9-6	
t2b	HCLKIN Period Stability		±100		ps(1)
t2c	HCLKIN High Time	4		9-6	
t2d	HCLKIN Low Time	4		9-6	
t2e	HCLKIN Rise Time		1.5	9-7	
t2f	HCLKIN Fall Time		1.5	9-7	
t3a	HCLKA–HCLKF Output-to-Output Skew		0.5	9-9	0 pF
t3b	HCLKA–HCLKF High Time	5.0		9-6	0 pF
t3c	HCLKA–HCLKF Low Time	5.0		9-6	0 pF

NOTE:
1. Measured on rising edge of adjacent clocks at 1.5V.

9.4.10 CPU INTERFACE TIMING, 60 MHz

Table 9-12. Functional Operating Range (V_{CC} = 5V ±5%; T_{CASE} = 0°C to +85°C)

Symbol	Parameter	Min	Max	Figure	Notes
t10a	ADS#, HITM#, W/R#, M/IO#, D/C#, HLOCK#, CACHE#, BE[7:0]#, SMIACT# Setup Time to HCLKIN Rising	4.6		9-3	
t10b	ADS#, HITM#, W/R#, M/IO#, D/C#, HLOCK#, CACHE#, BE[7:0]#, SMIACT# Hold Time from HCLKIN Rising	0.8		9-3	
t11a	PCHK# Setup Time to HCLKIN Rising	4.3		9-3	
t11b	PCHK# Hold Time from HCLKIN Rising	1.1		9-3	
t12a	A[18:3] Rising Edge Setup Time to HCLKIN Rising	4.5		9-3	Setup to HCLKIN Rising when ADS# is Sampled Active by PCMC.
t12aa	A[18:3] Falling Edge Setup Time to HCLKIN Rising	3.2		9-3	Setup to HCLKIN Rising when ADS# is Sampled Active by PCMC.
t12ab	A[31:19] Rising Edge Setup Time to HCLKIN Rising	4.7		9-3	Setup to HCLKIN Rising when ADS# is Sampled Active by PCMC.
t12ac	A[31:19] Falling Edge Setup Time to HCLKIN Rising	4.1		9-3	Setup to HCLKIN Rising when ADS# is Sampled Active by PCMC.
t12b	A[31:0] Hold Time from HCLKIN Rising	0.5		9-3	Hold from HCLKIN Rising Two Clocks after ADS# is Sampled Active by PCMC.
t12c	A[31:0] Setup Time to HCLKIN Rising	6.5		9-3	Setup to HCLKIN Rising when EADS# is Sampled Active by the CPU.
t12d	A[31:0] Hold Time from HCLKIN Rising	1.5		9-3	Hold from HCLKIN Rising when EADS# is Sampled Active by the CPU.
t12e	A[31:0] Output Enable from HCLKIN Rising	0	13	9-5	
t12f	A[31:0] Valid Delay from HCLKIN Rising	1.3	13	9-2	0 pF
t12g	A[31:0] Float Delay from HCLKIN Rising	0	13	9-4	
t12h	A[2:0] Propagation Delay from BE[7:0]#	1	16	9-1	0 pF
t13a	BRDY# Rising Edge Valid Delay from HCLKIN Rising	2.1	7.9	9-2	0 pF
t13b	BRDY# Falling Edge Valid Delay from HCLKIN Rising	2.1	7.9	9-2	0 pF
t14	NA# Valid Delay from HCLKIN Rising	1.4	8.4	9-2	0 pF

Table 9-12. Functional Operating Range (V_{CC} = 5V ±5%; T_{CASE} = 0°C to +85°C) (Continued)

Symbol	Parameter	Min	Max	Figure	Notes
t15a	AHOLD Valid Delay from HCLKIN Rising	2.0	7.6	9-2	0 pF
t15b	BOFF# Valid Delay from HCLKIN Rising	2.0	7.6	9-2	
t16a	EADS#, INV, PEN#, Valid Delay from HCLKIN Rising	2.0	8.0	9-2	0 pF
t16b	CPURST Rising Edge Valid Delay from HCLKIN Rising	1.2	7.5	9-2	
t16c	CPURST Falling Edge Valid Delay from HCLKIN Rising	1.2	7.5	9-2	
t16d	KEN# Valid Delay from HCLKIN Rising	1.7	8.2	9-2	
t17	INIT High Pulse Width	16 HCLKs −5		9-8	Soft Reset via TRC Register or CPU Shutdown Special Cycle, 0 pF
t18	CPURST High Pulse Width	1 ms		9-8	Hard Reset via TRC Register, 0 pF

1

9.4.11 SECOND LEVEL CACHE STANDARD SRAM TIMING, 60 MHz

Table 9-13. Functional Operating Range (V_{CC} = 5V ±5%; T_{CASE} = 0°C to +85°C)

Symbol	Parameter	Min	Max	Figure	Notes
t20a	CAA[6:3]/CAB[6:3] Propagation Delay from A[6:3]	0	8.5	9-1	0 pF
t20b	CAA[6:3]/CAB[6:3] Valid Delay from HCLKIN Rising	0	7.2	9-2	0 pF
t21a	COE[1:0]# Falling Edge Valid Delay from HCLKIN Rising	0	9.0	9-2	0 pF
t21b	COE[1:0]# Rising Edge Valid Delay from HCLKIN Rising	0	5.5	9-2	0 pF
t22a	CWE[7:0]#/CBS[7:0]# Falling Edge Valid Delay from HCLKIN Rising	2	14	9-2	CPU Burst or Single Write to Second Level Cache, 0 pF
t22b	CWE[7:0]#/CBS[7:0]# Rising Edge Valid Delay from HCLKIN Rising	3	15	9-2	CPU Burst or Single Write to Write to Second Level Cache, 0 pF
t22c	CWE[7:0]#/CBS[7:0]# Valid Delay from HCLKIN Rising	1.4	7.7	9-2	Cache Line Fill, 0 pF
t22d	CWE[7:0]#/CBS[7:0]# Low Pulse Width	1 HCLK		9-8	0 pF
t22e	CWE[7:0]#/CBS[7:0]# Driven High before CALE Driven High	−1		9-9	Last Write to Second Level Cache during Cache Line Fill, 0 pF
t22f	CAA[4:3]/CAB[4:3] Valid before CWE[7:0]#/CBS[7:0]# Falling	1.5		9-9	CPU Burst Write to Second Level Cache, 0 pF
t23	CALE Valid Delay from HCLKIN Rising	0	8	9-2	0 pF
t24	CR/W[1:0]# Valid Delay from HCLKIN Rising	1.5	8.2	9-2	0 pF
t25	CBS[7:0]# Valid Delay from HCLKIN Rising, Reads from Cache SRAMs	1.0	12.0	9-2	0 pF

9.4.12 SECOND LEVEL CACHE BURST SRAM TIMING, 60 MHz

Table 9-14. Functional Operating Range (V_{CC} = 5V ±5%; T_{CASE} = 0°C to +85°C)

Symbol	Parameter	Min	Max	Figure	Notes
t30a	CAA[6:3]/CAB[6:3] Propagation Delay from A[6:3]	0	8.5	9-1	0 pF
t30b	CAA[6:3]/CAB[6:3] Valid Delay from HCLKIN Rising	0	8.2	9-2	0 pF
t31	CADS[1:0]# Valid Delay from HCLKIN Rising	1.5	8.2	9-2	0 pF
t32	CADV[1:0]# Valid Delay from HCLKIN Rising	1.5	8.2	9-2	0 pF
t33	CWE[7:0]# Valid Delay from HCLKIN Rising	1.0	10.5	9-2	0 pF
t34a	COE[1:0]# Falling Edge Valid Delay from HCLKIN Rising	0	9.5	9-2	0 pF
t34b	COE[1:0]# Rising Edge Valid Delay from HCLKIN Rising	0	6.0	9-2	0 pF
t35	CALE Valid Delay from HCLKIN Rising	0	8.5	9-2	0 pF

1

9.4.13 DRAM INTERFACE TIMING, 60 MHz

Table 9-15. Functional Operating Range (V_{CC} = 5V ±5%; T_{CASE} = 0°C to +85°C)

Symbol	Parameter	Min	Max	Figure	Notes
t40a	RAS[5:0]# Valid Delay from HCLKIN Rising	0	8.0	9-2	50 pF
t40b	RAS[5:0]# Pulse Width High	4 HCLKs − 5			RAS# Precharge at Beginning of Page Miss Cycle, 50 pF
t41a	CAS[7:0]# Valid Delay from HCLKIN Rising	0	8.0	9-2	50 pF
t41b	CAS[7:0]# Pulse Width High	1 HCLK−5			CAS# Precharge during Burst Cycles, 50 pF
t42	WE# Valid Delay from HCLKIN Rising	0	21	9-2	50 pF
t43a	MA[10:0] Propagation Delay from A[23:3]	0	23	9-1	50 pF
t43b	MA[10:0] Valid Delay from HCLKIN Rising	0	10.7	9-2	50 pF

9.4.14 PCI CLOCK TIMING, 60 MHz

Table 9-16. Functional Operating Range (V_{CC} = 5V to ±5%; T_{CASE} = 0°C to +85°C)

Symbol	Parameter	Min	Max	Figure	Notes
t50a	PCLKOUT High Time	13		9-6	20 pF
t50b	PCLKOUT Low Time	13		9-6	20 pF
t51a	PCLKIN High Time	12		9-6	
t51b	PCLKIN Low Time	12		9-6	
t51c	PCLKIN Rise Time		3	9-7	
t51d	PCLKIN Fall Time		3	9-7	

9.4.15 PCI INTERFACE TIMING, 60 MHz

Table 9-17. Functional Operating Range (V_{CC} = 5V ±5%; T_{CASE} = 0°C to +85°C)

Symbol	Parameter	Min	Max	Figure	Notes
t60a	C/BE[3:0]#, FRAME#, TRDY#, IRDY#, STOP#, PLOCK#, PAR, PERR#, SERR#, DEVSEL# Valid Delay from PCLKIN Rising	2	11	9-2	Min: 0 pF Max: 50 pF
t60b	C/BE[3:0]#, FRAME#, TRDY#, IRDY#, STOP#, PLOCK#, PAR, PERR#, SERR#, DEVSEL# Output Enable Delay from PCLKIN Rising	2		9-5	
t60c	C/BE[3:0]#, FRAME#, TRDY#, IRDY#, STOP#, PLOCK#, PAR, PERR#, SERR#, DEVSEL# Float Delay from PCLKIN Rising	2	28	9-4	
t60d	C/BE[3:0]#, FRAME#, TRDY#, IRDY#, STOP#, PLOCK#, PAR, PERR#, SERR#, DEVSEL# Setup Time to PCLKIN Rising	9		9-3	
t60e	C/BE[3:0]#, FRAME#, TRDY#, IRDY#, STOP#, PLOCK#, PAR, PERR#, SERR#, DEVSEL# Hold Time from PCLKIN Rising	0		9-3	
t61a	REQ#, MEMACK# Valid Delay from PCLKIN Rising	2	12	9-2	Min: 0 pF Max: 50 pF
t61b	REQ#, MEMACK# Output Enable Delay from PCLKIN Rising	2		9-5	
t61c	REQ#, MEMACK# Float Delay from PCLKIN Rising	2	28	9-4	
t62a	FLSHREQ#, MEMREQ# Setup Time to PCLKIN Rising	12		9-3	
t62b	FLSHREQ#, MEMREQ# Hold Time from PCLKIN Rising	0		9-3	
t63a	GNT# Setup Time to PCLKIN Rising	10		9-3	
t63b	GNT# Hold Time from PCLKIN Rising	0		9-3	
t64a	MEMCS# Setup Time to PCLKIN Rising	7		9-3	
t64b	MEMCS# Hold Time from PCLKIN Rising	0		9-3	
t65	PCIRST# Low Pulse Width	1 ms		9-8	Hard Reset via TRC Register, 0 pF

9.4.16 LBX INTERFACE TIMING, 60 MHz

Table 9-18. Functional Operating Range (V_{CC} = 5V ±5%; T_{CASE} = 0°C to +85°C)

Symbol	Parameter	Min	Max	Figure	Notes
t70	HIG[4:0] Valid Delay from HCLKIN Rising	0.8	6.7	9-2	0 pF
t71	MIG[2:0] Valid Delay from HCLKIN Rising	0.9	6.5	9-2	0 pF
t72	PIG[3:0] Valid Delay from PCLKIN Rising	1.5	12	9-2	0 pF
t73	PCIDRV Valid Delay from PCLKIN Rising	1	13	9-2	0 pF
t74a	MDLE Falling Edge Valid Delay from HCLKIN Rising	0.6	6.8	9-2	0 pF
t74b	MDLE Rising Edge Valid from HCLKIN Rising	0.6	6.8	9-2	0 pF
t75a	EOL, PPOUT[1:0] Setup Time to PCLKIN Rising	7.7		9-3	
t75b	EOL, PPOUT[1:0] Hold Time from PCLKIN Rising	1		9-3	

9.4.17 TIMING DIAGRAMS

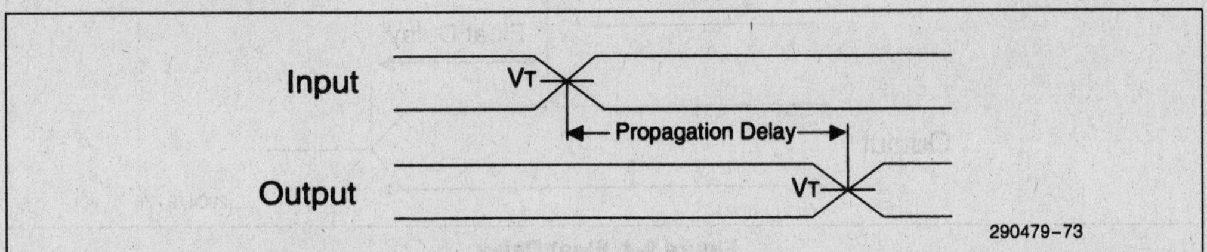

Figure 9-1. Propagation Delay

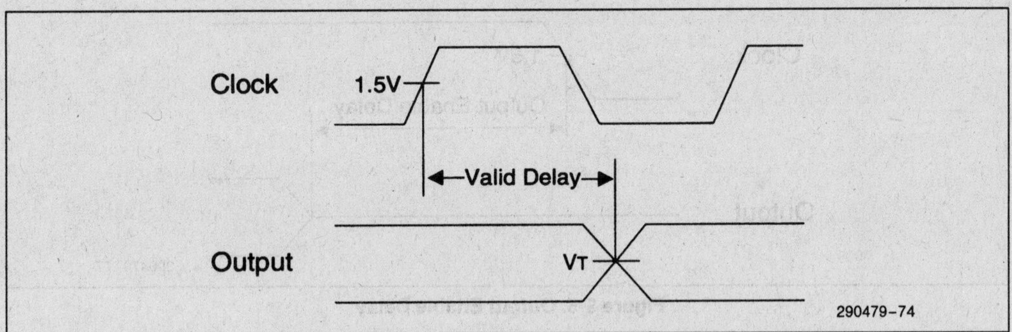

Figure 9-2. Valid Delay from Rising Clock Edge

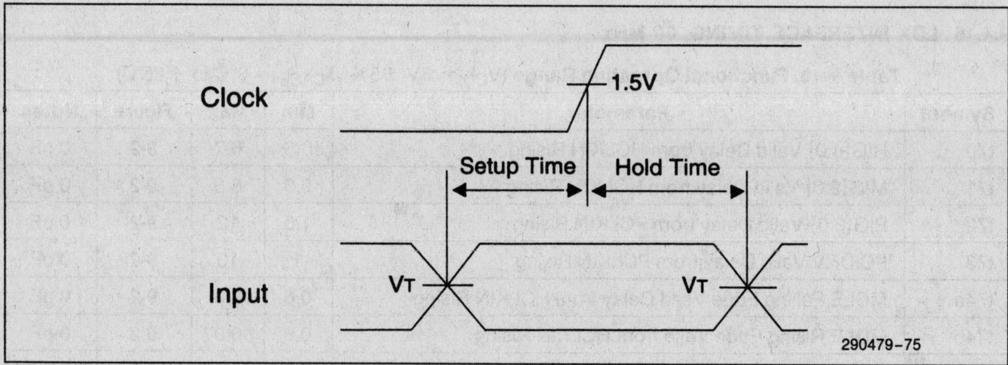

Figure 9-3. Setup and Hold Times

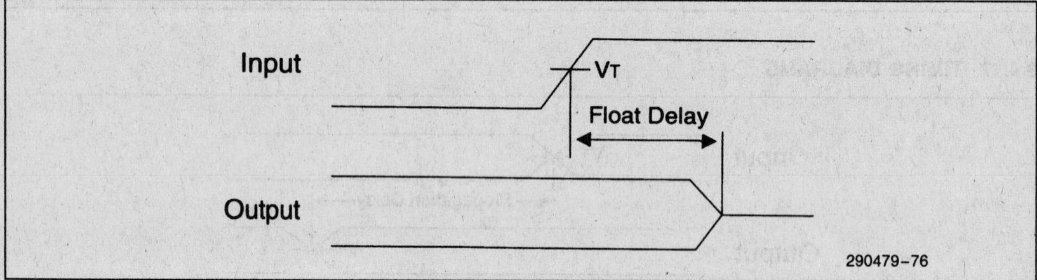

Figure 9-4. Float Delay

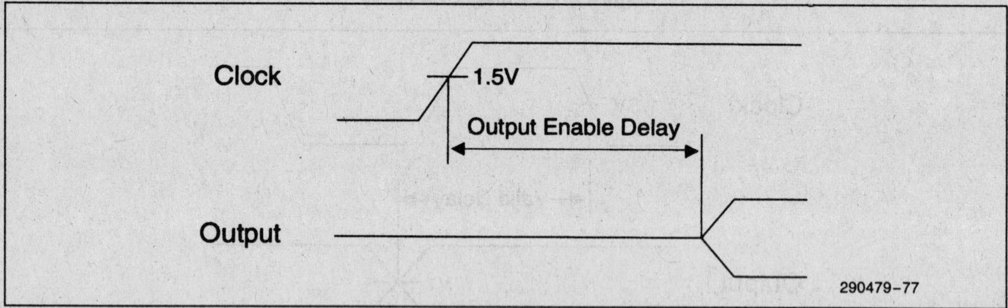

Figure 9-5. Output Enable Delay

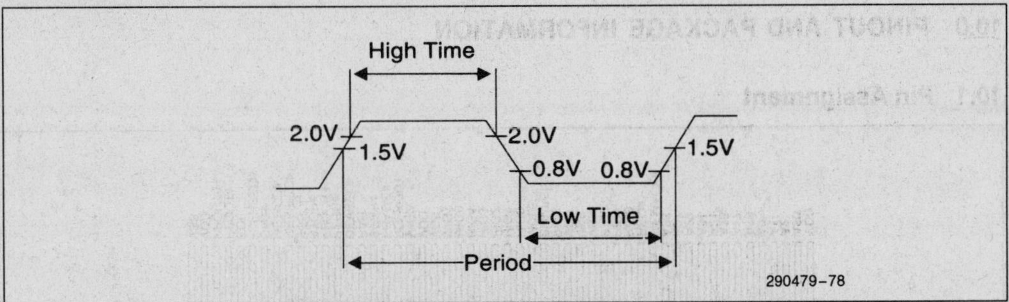

Figure 9-6. Clock High and Low Times and Period

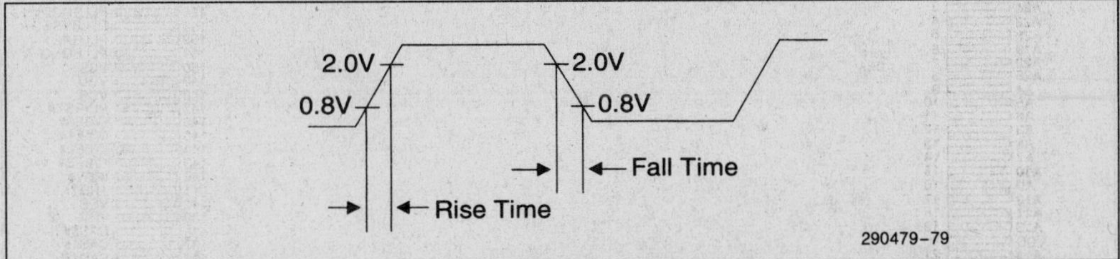

Figure 9-7. Clock Rise and Fall Times

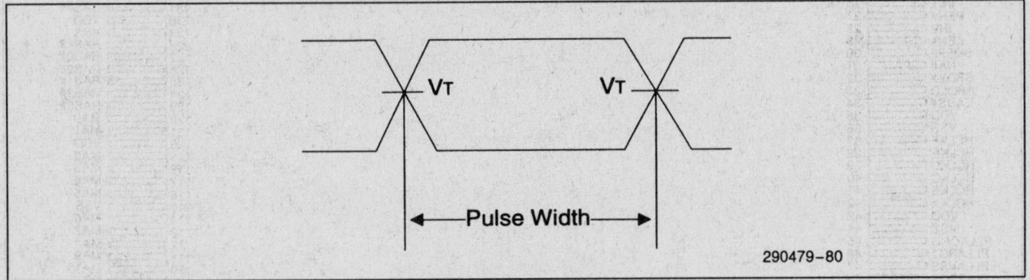

Figure 9-8. Pulse Width

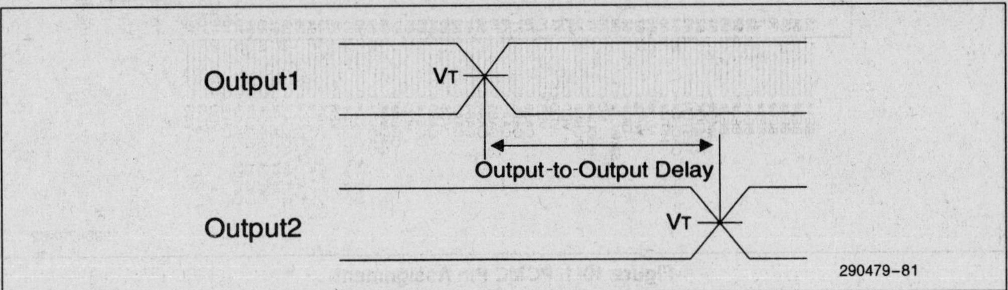

Figure 9-9. Output-to-Output Delay

10.0 PINOUT AND PACKAGE INFORMATION

10.1 Pin Assignment

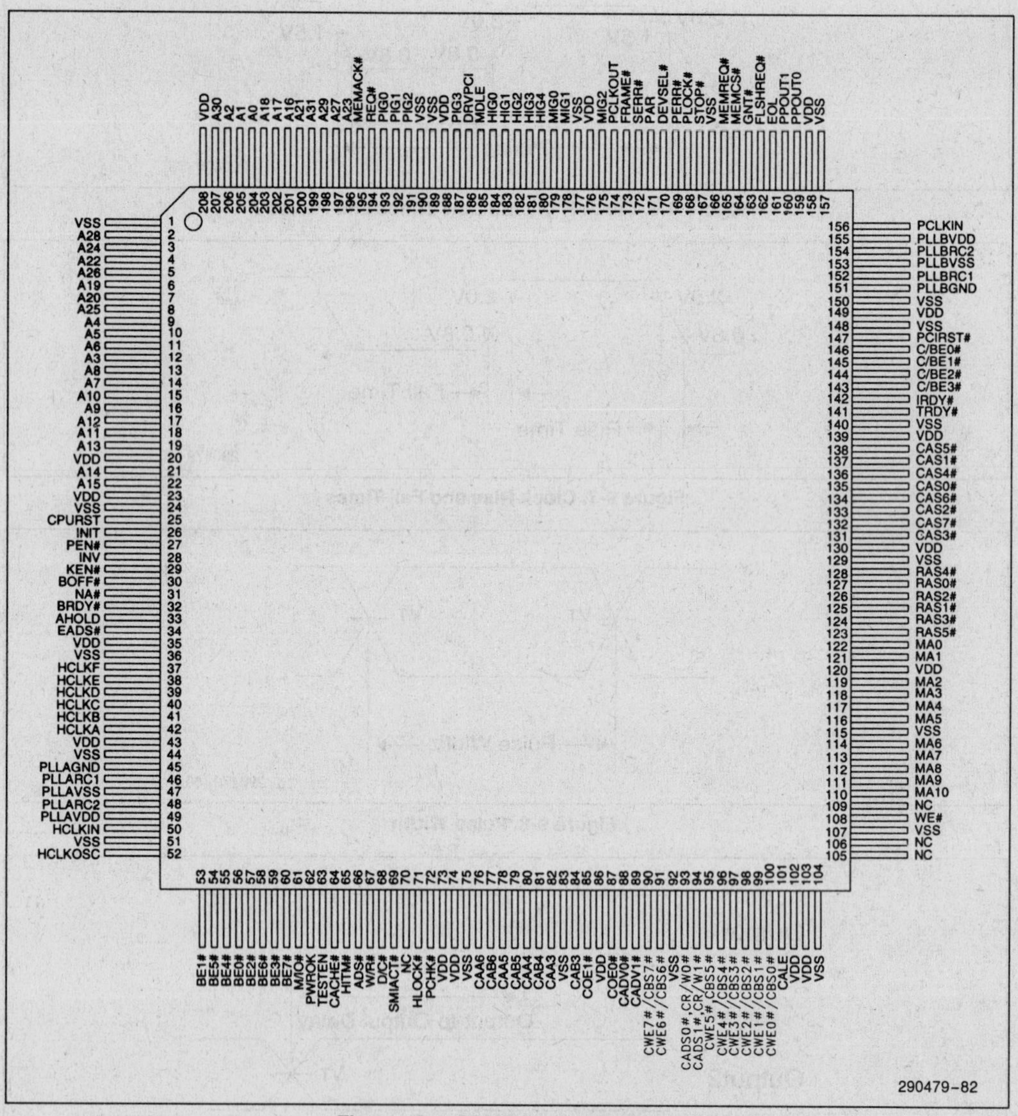

Pin	Signal	Pin	Signal	Pin	Signal	Pin	Signal
1	VSS	53	BE1#	105	NC	157	VSS
2	A28	54	BE5#	106	NC	158	VDD
3	A24	55	BE4#	107	VSS	159	PPOUT0
4	A22	56	BE0#	108	WE#	160	PPOUT1
5	A26	57	BE2#	109	NC	161	EOL
6	A19	58	BE6#	110	MA10	162	FLSHREQ#
7	A20	59	BE3#	111	MA9	163	GNT#
8	A25	60	BE7#	112	MA8	164	MEMCS#
9	A4	61	M/IO#	113	MA7	165	MEMREQ#
10	A5	62	PWROK	114	MA6	166	VSS
11	A6	63	TESTEN	115	VSS	167	STOP#
12	A3	64	CACHE#	116	MA5	168	PLOCK#
13	A8	65	HITM#	117	MA4	169	PERR#
14	A7	66	ADS#	118	MA3	170	DEVSEL#
15	A10	67	W/R#	119	MA2	171	PAR
16	A9	68	D/C#	120	VDD	172	SERR#
17	A12	69	SMIACT#	121	MA1	173	FRAME#
18	A11	70	NC	122	MA0	174	PCLKOUT
19	A13	71	HLOCK#	123	RAS5#	175	MIG2
20	VDD	72	PCHK#	124	RAS3#	176	VDD
21	A14	73	VDD	125	RAS1#	177	VSS
22	A15	74	VDD	126	RAS2#	178	MIG1
23	VDD	75	VSS	127	RAS0#	179	MIG0
24	VSS	76	CAA6	128	RAS4#	180	HIG4
25	CPURST	77	CAB6	129	VSS	181	HIG3
26	INIT	78	CAA5	130	VDD	182	HIG2
27	PEN#	79	CAB5	131	CAS3#	183	HIG1
28	INV	80	CAA4	132	CAS7#	184	HIG0
29	KEN#	81	CAB4	133	CAS2#	185	MDLE
30	BOFF#	82	CAA3	134	CAS6#	186	DRVPCI
31	NA#	83	VSS	135	CAS0#	187	PIG3
32	BRDY#	84	CAB3	136	CAS4#	188	VDD
33	AHOLD	85	COE1#	137	CAS1#	189	VSS
34	EADS#	86	VDD	138	CAS5#	190	VSS
35	VDD	87	COE0#	139	VDD	191	PIG2
36	VSS	88	CADV0#	140	VSS	192	PIG1
37	HCLKF	89	CADV1#	141	TRDY#	193	PIG0
38	HCLKE	90	CWE7#/CBS7#	142	IRDY#	194	REQ#
39	HCLKD	91	CWE6#/CBS6#	143	C/BE3#	195	MEMACK#
40	HCLKC	92	VSS	144	C/BE2#	196	A23
41	HCLKB	93	CADS0#,CR/W0#	145	C/BE1#	197	A27
42	HCLKA	94	CADS1#,CR/W1#	146	C/BE0#	198	A29
43	VDD	95	CWE5#/CBS5#	147	PCIRST#	199	A31
44	VSS	96	CWE4#/CBS4#	148	VSS	200	A21
45	PLLAGND	97	CWE3#/CBS3#	149	VDD	201	A16
46	PLLARC1	98	CWE2#/CBS2#	150	VSS	202	A17
47	PLLAVSS	99	CWE1#/CBS1#	151	PLLBGND	203	A18
48	PLLARC2	100	CWE0#/CBS0#	152	PLLBRC1	204	A0
49	PLLAVDD	101	CALE	153	PLLBVSS	205	A1
50	HCLKIN	102	VDD	154	PLLBRC2	206	A2
51	VSS	103	VDD	155	PLLBVDD	207	A30
52	HCLKOSC	104	VSS	156	PCLKIN	208	VDD

290479–82

Figure 10-1. PCMC Pin Assignment

Table 10-1. Alphabetical Pin Assignment

Signal	Pin #	Type
A0	204	t/s
A1	205	t/s
A2	206	t/s
A3	12	t/s
A4	9	t/s
A5	10	t/s
A6	11	t/s
A7	14	t/s
A8	13	t/s
A9	16	t/s
A10	15	t/s
A11	18	t/s
A12	17	t/s
A13	19	t/s
A14	21	t/s
A15	22	t/s
A16	201	t/s
A17	202	t/s
A18	203	t/s
A19	6	t/s
A20	7	t/s
A21	200	t/s
A22	4	t/s
A23	196	t/s
A24	3	t/s
A25	8	t/s
A26	5	t/s
A27	197	t/s
A28	2	t/s
A29	198	t/s
A30	207	t/s
A31	199	t/s
ADS#	66	in
AHOLD	33	out
BE0#	56	in
BE1#	53	in

Signal	Pin #	Type
BE2#	57	in
BE3#	59	in
BE4#	55	in
BE5#	54	in
BE6#	58	in
BE7#	60	in
BOFF#	30	out
BRDY#	32	out
CAA3	82	out
CAA4	80	out
CAA5	78	out
CAA6	76	out
CAB3	84	out
CAB4	81	out
CAB5	79	out
CAB6	77	out
CACHE#	64	in
CADS0#, CR/W0#	93	out
CADS1#, CR/W1#	94	out
CADV0#	88	out
CADV1#	89	out
CALE	101	out
CAS0#	135	out
CAS1#	137	out
CAS2#	133	out
CAS3#	131	out
CAS4#	136	out
CAS5#	138	out
CAS6#	134	out
CAS7#	132	out
CBE0#	146	t/s
CBE1#	145	t/s
CBE2#	144	t/s
CBE3#	143	t/s
COE0#	87	out
COE1#	85	out
CPURST	25	out

Signal	Pin #	Type
CWE0#/CBS0#	100	out
CWE1#/CBS1#	99	out
CWE2#/CBS2#	98	out
CWE3#/CBS3#	97	out
CWE4#/CBS4#	96	out
CWE5#/CBS5#	95	out
CWE6#/CBS6#	91	out
CWE7#/CBS7#	90	out
D/C#	68	in
DEVSEL#	170	s/t/s
DRVPCI	186	out
EADS#	34	out
EOL	161	in
FLSHREQ#	162	in
FRAME#	173	s/t/s
GNT#	163	in
HCLKA	42	out
HCLKB	41	out
HCLKC	40	out
HCLKD	39	out
HCLKE	38	out
HCLKF	37	out
HCLKIN	50	in
HCLKOSC	52	in
HIG0	184	out
HIG1	183	out
HIG2	182	out
HIG3	181	out
HIG4	180	out
HITM#	65	in
HLOCK#	71	in
INIT	26	out
INV	28	out
IRDY#	142	s/t/s
KEN#	29	out
M/IO#	61	in

Table 10-1. Alphabetical Pin Assignment (Continued)

Signal	Pin #	Type
MA0	122	out
MA1	121	out
MA10	110	out
MA2	119	out
MA3	118	out
MA4	117	out
MA5	116	out
MA6	114	out
MA7	113	out
MA8	112	out
MA9	111	out
MDLE	185	out
MEMACK#	195	out
MEMCS#	164	in
MEMREQ#	165	in
MIG0	179	out
MIG1	178	out
MIG2	175	out
NA#	31	out
NC	70	NC
NC	105	NC
NC	106	NC
NC	109	NC
PAR	171	t/s
PCHK#	72	in
PCIRST#	147	out
PCLKIN	156	in
PCLKOUT	174	out
PEN#	27	out
PERR#	169	s/o/d
PIG0	193	out
PIG1	192	out
PIG2	191	out
PIG3	187	out
PLLAGND	45	V
PLLARC1	46	in
PLLARC2	48	in
PLLAVDD	49	V
PLLAVSS	47	V
PLLBGND	151	V
PLLBRC1	152	in
PLLBRC2	154	in
PLLBVDD	155	V
PLLBVSS	153	V
PLOCK#	168	s/t/s
PPOUT0	159	in
PPOUT1	160	in
PWROK	62	in
RAS0#	127	out
RAS1#	125	out
RAS2#	126	out
RAS3#	124	out
RAS4#	128	out
RAS5#	123	out
REQ#	194	out
SERR#	172	s/o/d
SMIACT#	69	in
STOP#	167	s/t/s
TESTEN	63	in
TRDY#	141	s/t/s
V_{DD}	20	V
V_{DD}	23	V
V_{DD}	35	V
V_{DD}	43	V
V_{DD}	73	V
V_{DD}	74	V
V_{DD}	86	V
V_{DD}	102	V
V_{DD}	103	V
V_{DD}	120	V
V_{DD}	130	V
V_{DD}	139	V
V_{DD}	149	V
V_{DD}	158	V
V_{DD}	176	V
V_{DD}	188	V
V_{DD}	208	V
V_{SS}	1	V
V_{SS}	24	V
V_{SS}	36	V
V_{SS}	44	V
V_{SS}	51	V
V_{SS}	75	V
V_{SS}	83	V
V_{SS}	92	V
V_{SS}	104	V
V_{SS}	107	V
V_{SS}	115	V
V_{SS}	129	V
V_{SS}	140	V
V_{SS}	148	V
V_{SS}	150	V
V_{SS}	157	V
V_{SS}	166	V
V_{SS}	177	V
V_{SS}	189	V
V_{SS}	190	V
W/R#	67	in
WE#	108	out

Table 10-2. Numerical Pin Assignment

Pin #	Signal	Type	Pin #	Signal	Type	Pin #	Signal	Type
1	V_{SS}	V	37	HCLKF	out	73	V_{DD}	V
2	A28	t/s	38	HCLKE	out	74	V_{DD}	V
3	A24	t/s	39	HCLKD	out	75	V_{SS}	V
4	A22	t/s	40	HCLKC	out	76	CAA6	out
5	A26	t/s	41	HCLKB	out	77	CAB6	out
6	A19	t/s	42	HCLKA	out	78	CAA5	out
7	A20	t/s	43	V_{DD}	V	79	CAB5	out
8	A25	t/s	44	V_{SS}	V	80	CAA4	out
9	A4	t/s	45	PLLAGND	V	81	CAB4	out
10	A5	t/s	46	PLLARC1	in	82	CAA3	out
11	A6	t/s	47	PLLAVSS	V	83	V_{SS}	V
12	A3	t/s	48	PLLARC2	in	84	CAB3	out
13	A8	t/s	49	$PLLAV_{DD}$	V	85	COE1#	out
14	A7	t/s	50	HCLKIN	in	86	V_{DD}	V
15	A10	t/s	51	V_{SS}	V	87	COE0#	out
16	A9	t/s	52	HCLKOSC	in	88	CADV0#	out
17	A12	t/s	53	BE1#	in	89	CADV1#	out
18	A11	t/s	54	BE5#	in	90	CWE7#/CBS7#	out
19	A13	t/s	55	BE4#	in	91	CWE6#/CBS6#	out
20	V_{DD}	V	56	BE0#	in	92	V_{SS}	V
21	A14	t/s	57	BE2#	in	93	CADS0#, CR/W0#	out
22	A15	t/s	58	BE6#	in	94	CADS1#, CR/W1#	out
23	V_{DD}	V	59	BE3#	in	95	CWE5#/CBS5#	out
24	V_{SS}	V	60	BE7#	in	96	CWE4#/CBS4#	out
25	CPURST	out	61	M/IO#	in	97	CWE3#/CBS3#	out
26	INIT	out	62	PWROK	in	98	CWE2#/CBS2#	out
27	PEN#	out	63	TESTEN	in	99	CWE1#/CBS1#	out
28	INV	out	64	CACHE#	in	100	CWE0#/CBS0#	out
29	KEN#	out	65	HITM#	in	101	CALE	out
30	BOFF#	out	66	ADS#	in	102	V_{DD}	V
31	NA#	out	67	W/R#	in	103	V_{DD}	V
32	BRDY#	out	68	D/C#	in	104	V_{SS}	V
33	AHOLD	out	69	SMIACT#	in	105	NC	NC
34	EADS#	out	70	NC	NC	106	NC	NC
35	V_{DD}	V	71	HLOCK#	in	107	V_{SS}	V
36	V_{SS}	V	72	PCHK#	in	108	WE#	out

Table 10-2. Numerical Pin Assignment (Continued)

Pin #	Signal	Type	Pin #	Signal	Type	Pin #	Signal	Type
109	NC	NC	142	IRDY#	s/t/s	175	MIG2	out
110	MA10	out	143	CBE3#	t/s	176	V_{DD}	V
111	MA9	out	144	CBE2#	t/s	177	V_{SS}	V
112	MA8	out	145	CBE1#	t/s	178	MIG1	out
113	MA7	out	146	CBE0#	t/s	179	MIG0	out
114	MA6	out	147	PCIRST#	out	180	HIG4	out
115	V_{SS}	V	148	V_{SS}	V	181	HIG3	out
116	MA5	out	149	V_{DD}	V	182	HIG2	out
117	MA4	out	150	V_{SS}	V	183	HIG1	out
118	MA3	out	151	PLLBGND	V	184	HIG0	out
119	MA2	out	152	PLLBRC1	in	185	MDLE	out
120	V_{DD}	V	153	PLLBVSS	V	186	DRVPCI	out
121	MA1	out	154	PLLBRC2	in	187	PIG3	out
122	MA0	out	155	PLLBVDD	V	188	V_{DD}	V
123	RAS5#	out	156	PCLKIN	in	189	V_{SS}	V
124	RAS3#	out	157	V_{SS}	V	190	V_{SS}	V
125	RAS1#	out	158	V_{DD}	V	191	PIG2	out
126	RAS2#	out	159	PPOUT0	in	192	PIG1	out
127	RAS0#	out	160	PPOUT1	in	193	PIG0	out
128	RAS4#	out	161	EOL	in	194	REQ#	out
129	V_{SS}	V	162	FLSHREQ#	in	195	MEMACK#	out
130	V_{DD}	V	163	GNT#	in	196	A23	t/s
131	CAS3#	out	164	MEMCS#	in	197	A27	t/s
132	CAS7#	out	165	MEMREQ#	in	198	A29	t/s
133	CAS2#	out	166	V_{SS}	V	199	A31	t/s
134	CAS6#	out	167	STOP#	s/t/s	200	A21	t/s
135	CAS0#	out	168	PLOCK#	s/t/s	201	A16	t/s
136	CAS4#	out	169	PERR#	s/o/d	202	A17	t/s
137	CAS1#	out	170	DEVSEL#	s/t/s	203	A18	t/s
138	CAS5#	out	171	PAR	t/s	204	A0	t/s
139	V_{DD}	V	172	SERR#	s/o/d	205	A1	t/s
140	V_{SS}	V	173	FRAME#	s/t/s	206	A2	t/s
141	TRDY#	s/t/s	174	PCLKOUT	out	207	A30	t/s
						208	V_{DD}	V

10.2 Package Characteristics

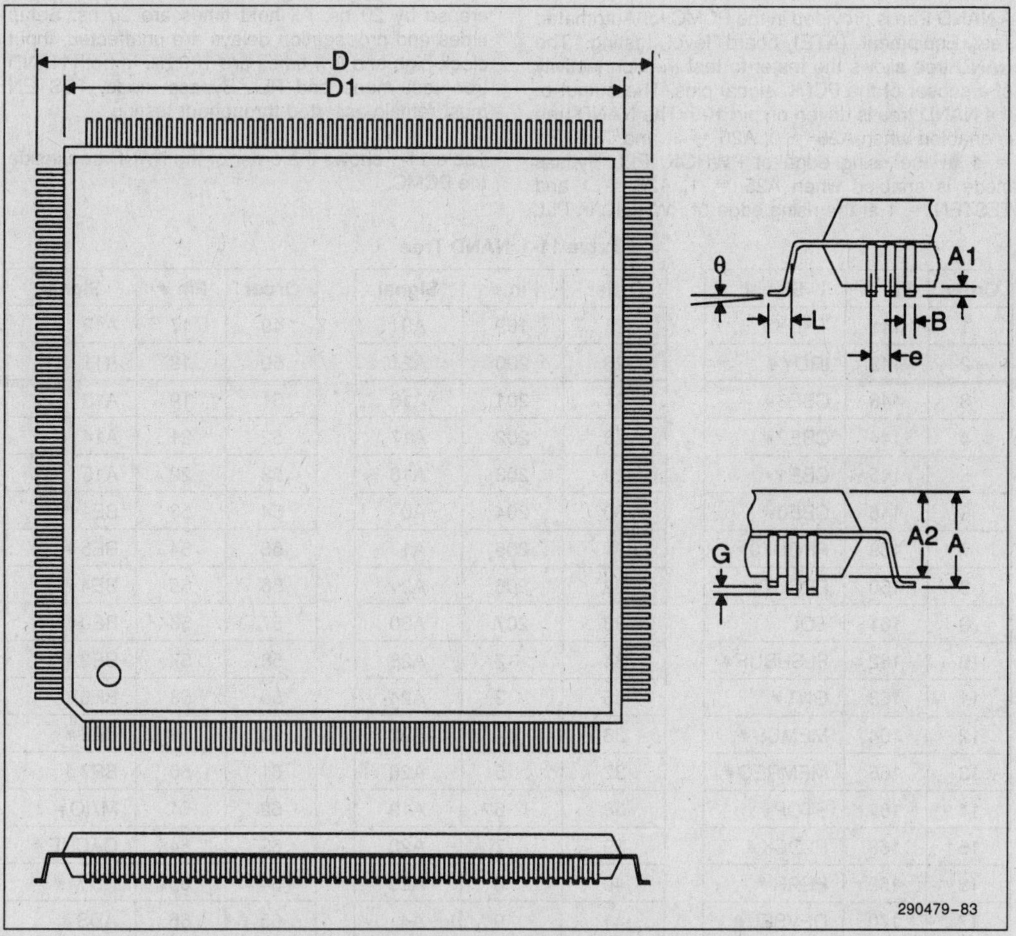

Figure 10-2. 208 Pin Quad Flat Pack (QFP) Dimensions

Symbol	Description	Value (mm)
A	Seating Height	3.5 (max)
A1	Stand-off Height	0.35 ±0.1
A2	Package Height	3.0 (nominal)
B	Lead Width	0.18 +0.1/−0.05
D	Package Length and Width, including pins	30.6 ±0.3
D1	Package Length and Width, excluding pins	28 ±0.1
e	Linear Lead Pitch	0.5 ±0.1
G	Lead Coplanarity	0.1
L	Lead Length	0.5 ±0.2
θ	Lead Angle	0°–10°

11.0 TESTABILITY

A NAND tree is provided in the PCMC for Automated Test Equipment (ATE) board level testing. The NAND tree allows the tester to test the connectivity of a subset of the PCMC signal pins. The output of the NAND tree is driven on pin 109. The NAND tree is enabled when A25 = 0, A26 = 1, and TESTEN = 1 at the rising edge of PWROK. PLL Bypass mode is enabled when A25 = 1, A26 = 1 and TESTEN = 1 at the rising edge of PWROK. In PLL Bypass mode, the PCMC A.C. specifications are affected in the following ways. Output valid delays increase by 20 ns. All hold times are 20 ns. Setup times and propagation delays are unaffected. Input clock high and low times are 100 ns. In both NAND tree test mode and PLL Bypass mode, TESTEN must remain asserted throughout testing.

Table 11-1 shows the order of the NAND tree inside the PCMC.

Table 11-1. NAND Tree

Order	Pin #	Signal	Order	Pin #	Signal	Order	Pin #	Signal
1	141	TRDY#	25	199	A31	49	17	A12
2	142	IRDY#	26	200	A21	50	18	A11
3	143	CBE3#	27	201	A16	51	19	A13
4	144	CBE2#	28	202	A17	52	21	A14
5	145	CBE1#	29	203	A18	53	22	A15
6	146	CBE0#	30	204	A0	54	53	BE1#
7	159	PPOUT0	31	205	A1	55	54	BE5#
8	160	PPOUT1	32	206	A2	56	55	BE4#
9	161	EOL	33	207	A30	57	56	BE0#
10	162	FLSHBUF#	34	2	A28	58	57	BE2#
11	163	GNT#	35	3	A24	59	58	BE6#
12	164	MEMCS#	36	4	A22	60	59	BE3#
13	165	MEMREQ#	37	5	A26	61	60	BE7#
14	167	STOP#	38	6	A19	62	61	M/IO#
15	168	PLOCK#	39	7	A20	63	64	CACHE#
16	169	PERR#	40	8	A25	64	65	HITM#
17	170	DEVSEL#	41	9	A4	65	66	ADS#
18	171	PAR	42	10	A5	66	67	W/R#
19	172	SERR#	43	11	A6	67	68	D/C#
20	173	FRAME#	44	12	A3	68	69	SMIACT#
21	194	REQ#	45	13	A8	69	71	HLOCK#
22	196	A23	46	14	A7	70	72	PCHK#
23	197	A27	47	15	A10	71	63	TESTEN
24	198	A29	48	16	A9			

Additional Testing Notes:
1. HCLKOUT[6:1] can be toggled via HCLKIN.
2. CAx[6:3] are flow through outputs via A[6:3] after PWROK transitions high.
3. MA[10:0] are flow through outputs via A[13:3] after PWROK transitions high.
4. CAS[7:0]# outputs can be tested by performing a DRAM read cycle.
5. PCLKOUT can be tested in PLL bypass mode, frequency is HCLK/2.
6. PCIRST is the NAND Tree output of Tree Cell 6.
7. INIT is the NAND Tree output of Tree Cell 53.

REVISION HISTORY

The following list represents the key differences between version 001 and version 002 of the 82434LX PCI, Cache and Memory Controller (PCMC) Data Sheet.

Section 2.1	Note added that the SMIACT# signal is qualified with values stored in the SMRAM Space Register.
Section 2.3	CR/W[1:0]# and CBS[7:0]# are multiplexed onto the CADS[1:0]# and CWE[7:0]# lines respectively. The new signals enable support of 64K x 16/18 asynchronous cache SRAMs with dual byte select lines.
Section 3.1	Changes made to reflect the Function Number field in the CSE Register. The BIST Enable bit in the TRC Register is now reserved.
Section 3.2	Section rewritten to describe Type 0 and Type 1 Configuration Cycles.
Section 3.2.3	Notes added to bits 6 and 8 in the PCI Command Register Description.
Section 3.2.4	The description of the DEVSEL# Timing bit in the PCI Status Register has been extended.
Section 3.2.5	In the PCI Status Register, bit 15 is changed to a reserved bit and bit 8 is the Data Parity Detected bit.
Section 3.2.6	The revision ID is now 03h.
Section 3.2.8	The Special Cycle Address Register has been removed from the PCMC, hence this section has been removed and replaced with the SCCD Register description.
Sections 3.2.7 through 3.2.9	These sections have been added to indicate the RPLI, SCCD and BCCD registers.
Section 3.2.10	The MLT Register has been truncated to a 4 bit register.
Section 3.2.12	The Host Operating Frequency field has been shortened from two bits to one bit.
Section 3.2.11	All bits of this register are Read Only.
Section 3.2.13	Bits 5 through 0 of the Deturbo Frequency Control Register are now reserved.
Section 3.2.14	Two new bits are defined in the Secondary Cache Control Register. Bit 4 controls Secondary Cache Allocation and bit 3 determines the Cache Byte Control. The description for bits 7 and 6 has been modified. Bit descriptions for bits 4 and 3 have been added. A clarification has been added to the bit 0 description. When bit 0 is reset to 0, the CWE[7:0]# lines will remain inactive, however COE[1:0]# may toggle.
Section 3.2.16	Bit 2 description has been extended. If the PCI TRDY# signal is connected to the LBXs TRDY# pin, this bit must be set before the CPU writes to PCI.
Section 3.2.17	Bits 7 and 6 of the DRAM Control Register have been changed to reserved bits. X-3-3-3 burst timing is no longer supported. SMRAM Enable bit description has been extended.
Section 3.2.18	This section covers the new DRAM Timing Register which provides additional control over the leadoff cycle on reads from DRAM.
Section 3.2.20	Several bits in the DRB Registers are now reserved.
Section 3.2.21	Note added to indicate that bit 6 and 8 of the PCI Command Register are the master enables for bits 7, 6, 5, 4, and 1 of the Error Command Register. Bit 6 of the PCI Command Register is the master enable for bit 3 of the Error Command Register.
Section 3.2.22	Bits 5 and 4 of the Error Status Register are now reserved.
Section 3.2.23	SMRAM Space Register has been added.
Section 3.2.24	Notes added to indicate that the Memory Space Gap starting address must be a multiple of the Memory Space Gap size.
Section 3.2.25	Bit 10 of the Frame Buffer Range Register is now reseved. The Read-around-Write feature is no longer supported. The Buffer Offset field description has been extended.

Section 4.2	Modified to include the features of the SMRAM Space Register.
Section 5.1	Additions made to describe the new Secondary Cache Allocation register bit and the new dual-byte-select SRAM support. Figure 5-5 shows the PCMC connections to dual-byte-select SRAMs.
Section 5.3.1	Description added for CPU read cycles when the SCA bit in the Secondary Cache Control Register is set and CACHE# is inactive. A new figure has been added to depict a CPU read cycle with dual-byte-select SRAMs.
Section 5.3.2	A new figure has been added to depict a CPU write cycle with dual-byte-select SRAMs.
Section 5.3.3	A new figure has been added to depict a cache line fill with dual-byte-select SRAMs.
Section 5.4.1	Description added for CPU read cycles when the SCA bit in the Secondary Cache Control Register is set and CACHE# is inactive.
Section 6.0	All references to X-3-3-3 burst timing have been removed throughout the DRAM interface section.
Section 6.4	Paragraph modified for clarification.
Section 6.6	Description added on when CAS#-before-RAS# refresh can be used.
Section 7.3.1	The figure which depicts a write cycle to a PCMC internal configuration register has been modified.
Section 7.3.2	The figure which depicts a read cycle from a PCMC internal configuration register has been modified.
Section 7.4.1	The figure which depicts a PCI master write to main memory has been modified.
Section 8.3	Modifications made to the Phase Locked Loop circuitry.
Section 8.4	The strapping options on A[31:29] have been changed. The values sampled on these lines are inverted and then stored in the Secondary Cache Control Register. References to the BIST Enable bit and the invoking of BIST in the CPU have been removed. Table 8-2 now indicates that INIT is always driven low during hard reset.
Section 9.4	The A.C. Specifications have been separated for 60 and 66 MHz operation. Several changes have been made to the A.C. Specifications. The 66 MHz A.C. Specifications have a different Functional Operating Range than the 60 MHz A.C. Specifications. For 66 MHz operation, V_{CC} ranges between 4.9 and 5.25 Volts and the maximum case temperature is 70°C.
Section 11.0	This section has been added to document the testability features of the PCMC. This section includes the details of PLL Bypass mode and the NAND Tree inside the PCMC. The effect of PLL Bypass mode on A.C. Specifications is detailed.

82420 PCIset

Intel's 82420 PCIset enables workstation level of performance for Intel486™ CPU desktop systems. The Peripheral Component Interconnect Bus (PCI) is driving a new architecture for PC's—eliminating the I/O bottleneck of standard expansion busses. PCI provides a glueless interface for high performance peripherals such as graphics, SCSI, LAN and video to be placed onto a fast local bus. By utilizing this technology and incorporating read/write bursts along with write buffers into the 82420 PCIset, a new level of performance is now possible for today's Intel486 CPU desktop systems.

The Intel 82420 PCIset is comprised of three components: the 82424 Cache DRAM Controller (CDC), the 82423 Data Path Unit (DPU), and the 82378 System I/O (SIO). The CDC and DPU provide the core system architecture while the SIO is a PCI master/slave agent which bridges the core architecture to the ISA standard expansion bus. Intel also offers two components, the 82374EB (ESC) and 82375EB (PCEB), that work in conjunction to bridge the PCI bus to the EISA expansion bus. Refer to the ESC and PCEB data sheets for information regarding the EISA bridge components.

The chip set supports the Intel486 CPU family as well as the write-back caching capability of Intel's future OverDrive™ processor for the Intel486 DX2 CPU. The high performance memory subsystem supports concurrent operation between PCI bus masters while the CPU accesses memory. An integrated second level cache can be programmed for write-through or write-back operation.

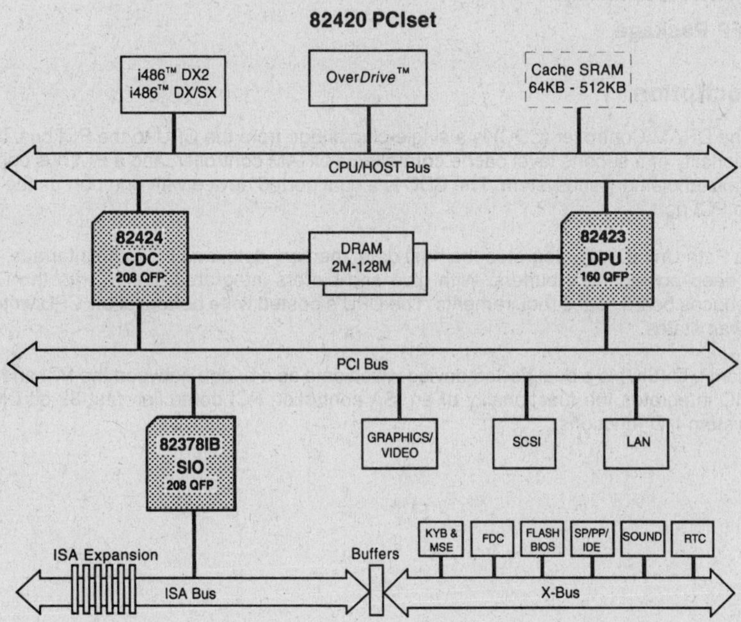

Intel486 and OverDrive are trademarks of Intel Corporation.

October 1993
Order Number: 290467-003

Product Highlights

82424—Cache DRAM Controller (CDC)

- Concurrent Linefill during Copyback Cycles
- Supports Intel486 CPU Family and OverDrive Processors
- Supports Future OverDrive Upgrade Processor in Write-Back Cache Mode
- 64K–512K Level 2 Cache Support
- Level 2 Cache Configurable as Write-Back or Write-Through
- 208-Pin QFP Package

82423—Data Path Unit (DPU)

- Highly Integrated
- Four Dword Write Buffers
- Zero Wait States for CPU Write Cycles
- PCI Burst Write Capability
- 160-Pin QFP Package

82378—System I/O Component (SIO)

- Supports Fast DMA Type A, B, or F Cycles
- Supports DMA Scatter/Gather
- Arbitration Logic for Four PCI Masters
- Reusable across Multiple Platforms
- Directly Drives Six External ISA Slots
- Integrates Many of Today's Common I/O Functions
- 208-Pin QFP Package

Product Description

The 82424 Cache DRAM Controller (CDC) is a single-chip bridge from the CPU to the PCI bus. It provides the integrated functionality of a second level cache controller, a DRAM controller, and a PCI bus controller. It also features an optimized memory subsystem. The CDC is a dual ported device with one port as the host port and the other as the PCI port.

The 82423 Data Path Unit (DPU) integrates the host data, memory data, and PCI data interface, DPU control/parity and four deep posted write buffers. With glue and buffers integrated directly into the DPU, the Intel 82420 PCIset reduces board space requirements. The DPU's posted write buffers allow CPU write cycles to be executed as 0 wait states.

The 82378 System I/O (SIO) is a dual ported device which acts as a bridge between the PCI and standard ISA I/O bus. The SIO integrates the functionality of an ISA controller, PCI controller, fast 32-bit DMA controller, and standard system I/O functions.

82423 DATA PATH UNIT (DPU)

- A 32-bit High Performance Host/PCI/ Memory Data Path
- Operates Synchronous to the CPU and PCI Clocks
- Dual-Port Architecture Allows Concurrent Operations on the Host and PCI Buses
- Burst Read of Memory from the Host and PCI Buses
- Host-to-Memory and Host-to-PCI Post Buffers Permit Zero Wait State Write Performance
- Byte Parity Support for the Host and Memory Buses
  - Optional Parity Generation for Host-to-Memory Transfers
  - Optional Parity Checking for the Secondary Cache Residing on the Host Data Bus
  - Parity Checking for Host and PCI Memory Reads
  - Parity Generation for PCI-to-Memory Writes
- Force Bad Parity to Memory Capability for Diagnostic Purposes

The 82423 Data Path Unit (DPU) provides the 32-bit data path connections between the Host (CPU/cache), main memory, and the Peripheral Component Interconnect (PCI) Bus. The dual-port architecture allows concurrent operations on the Host and PCI Buses. Two 4-Dword deep Post buffers permit Host posting of data to main memory and the PCI Bus. The DPU supports byte parity for the Host and main memory buses. The DPU is intended to be used with the 82424 Cache DRAM Controller (CDC). During bus operations between the Host, main memory, and PCI, the CDC provides the address paths and bus controls. The CDC also controls the data flow through the DPU. Together, these two chips provide a full function dual-port data path connection to main memory and forms a Host/PCI bridge.

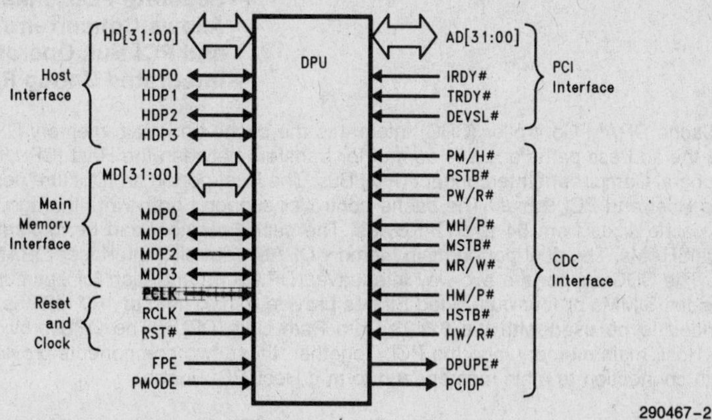

290467-2

IMPORTANT—READ THIS SECTION BEFORE READING THE REST OF THE DATA SHEET.

This data sheet describes the 82423TX and 82423ZX components. All normal text describes the functionality for both components. All features that exist on the 82423ZX are shaded as shown below.

This is an example of what the shaded sections that apply only to the 82423ZX component look like.

82424 CACHE AND DRAM CONTROLLER (CDC)

- **Supports 25/33/*50* MHz Intel486™ SX, Intel487™ SX, Intel486 DX, Intel486 DX2, OverDrive™ for Intel486 and OverDrive for DX2 Processors**
- **Fully Synchronous, 25/33 MHz PCI Bus Capable of Supporting Bus Masters**
- **Supports OverDrive Upgrade Socket, Including OverDrive for DX2 in Write-Back Mode**
- **Programmable Attribute Map for First 1 MByte of Main Memory**
- **Posted Write Buffers for Improved Performance**
- **Integrated DRAM Controller**
  - **2 to 160 MByte Main Memory using 70 ns Fast Page Mode SIMM Memory**
  - **Decoupled Refresh Cycles to Reduce DRAM Access Latency**
  - **Burst Mode PCI Accesses to DRAM Supported at the Rate of x-3-3-3-3-3**
- **Integrated Cache Controller**
  - **Write-Through and Write-Back Cache Options**
  - **64 KB, 128 KB, 256 KB and 512 KB Cache Sizes using Standards SRAMs**
  - **Burst Line Fill of 2-1-1-1 from Secondary Cache at 25 and 33 MHz *and 3-1-1-1 at 50 MHz***
  - **Zero Wait State Write to L2 Cache for a Cacche Write Hit**
  - **Main Memory Posting at Zero Wait States, Enabling Optimum Write-Through Cache Performance**
  - **Concurrent Cache Line Replacement from Secondary Cache in Write-Back Mode**
- **PCI Bridge**
  - **Translates CPU Cycles into PCI Bus Cycles**
  - **Translates Back-to-Back Sequential Memory Write Cycles into PCI Burst Cycles**
  - **Separate PCI-to-Main Memory Port Allows Concurrent/Independent CPU and PCI Bus Operations**
  - **Integrated Snoop Filter**

The 82424 Cache DRAM Controller (CDC) integrates the cache and main memory DRAM control functions and provides the address paths and bus control for transfers between the Host (CPU/cache), main memory, and the Peripheral Component Interconnect (PCI) Bus. The Dual-ported architecture permits concurrent operations on the Host and PCI Buses. The cache controller supports both write-through and write-back cache policies and cache sizes from 64 to 512 KBytes. The cache memory can be implemented using standard asynchronous SRAMs. The dual-ported main memory DRAM controller interfaces DRAM to the Host Bus and the PCI Bus. The CDC supports a two-way interleaved DRAM organization for optimum performance. Up to eight single sides SIMMs or four dual sided SIMMs provide a maximum of 160 MBytes of main memory. The CDC is intended to be used with the 82423 Data Path Unit (DPU). The DPU provides 32-bit data paths between the Host, main memory, and the PCI. Together, these two components provide a full function dual-port data path connection to main memory and form a Host/PCI Bridge.

This data sheet describes the 82424TX, 82424ZX and 82424ZX-50 components. All normal text describes the functionality for all three components. All features that exist on the 82424ZX and 82424ZX-50 are shaded as shown below.

This is an example of what the shaded sections that apply only to the 82424ZX and 82424ZX-50 components look like.

All features that exist only on the 82424ZX-50 are shaded as shown below.

This is an example of what the shaded sections that apply only to the 82424ZX-50 component look like.

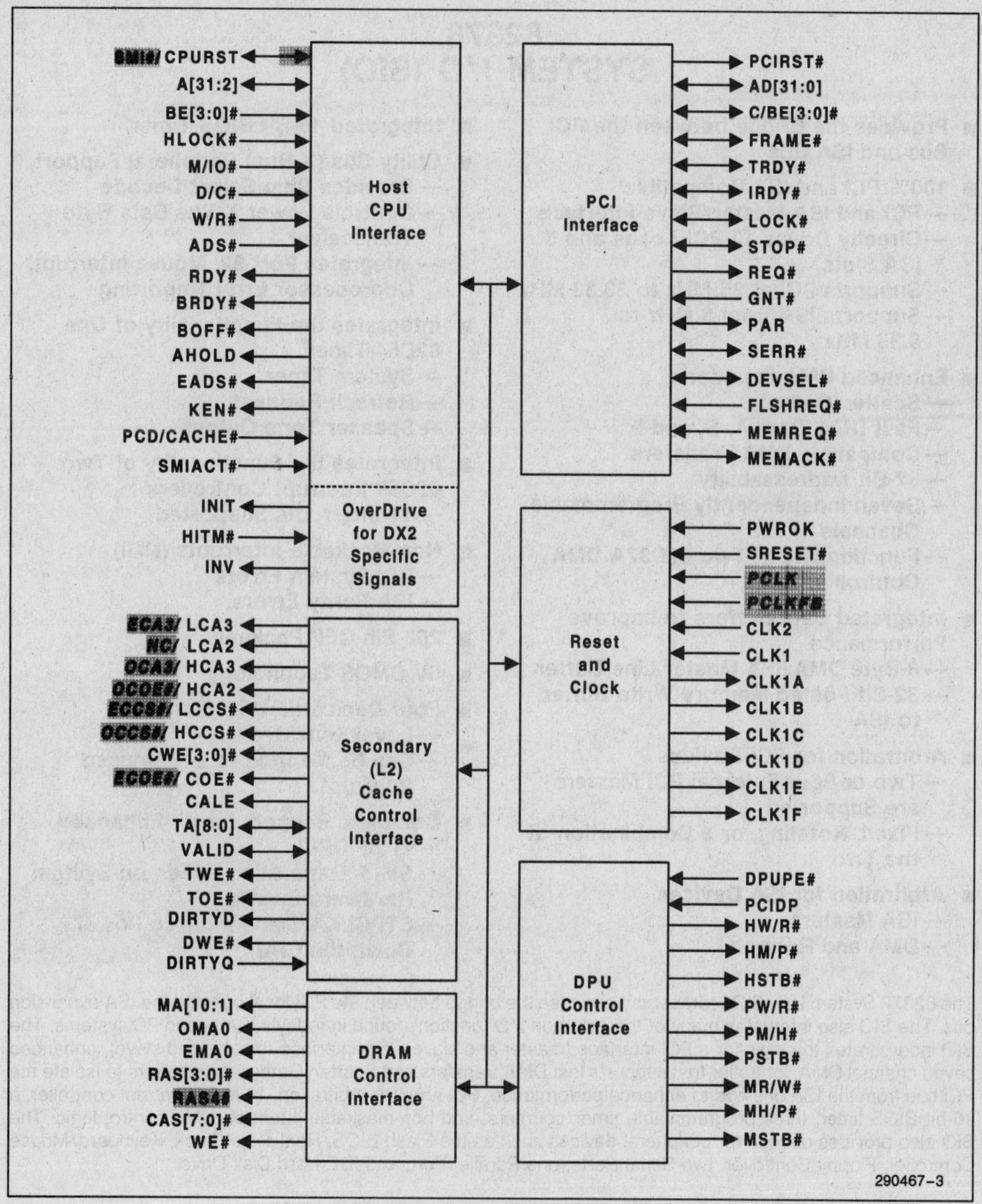

Simplified CDC Block Diagram

1

82378
SYSTEM I/O (SIO)

- Provides the Bridge between the PCI Bus and ISA Bus
- 100% PCI and ISA Compatible
  - — PCI and ISA Master/Slave Interface
  - — Directly Drives 10 PCI Loads and 6 ISA Slots
  - — Supports PCI at 25 MHz to 33.33 MHz
  - — Supports ISA from 6 MHz to 8.33 MHz
- Enhanced DMA Functions
  - — Scatter/Gather
  - — Fast DMA Type A, B, and F
  - — Compatible DMA Transfers
  - — 32-Bit Addressability
  - — Seven Independently Programmable Channels
  - — Functionality of Two 82C37A DMA Controllers
- Integrated Data Buffers to Improve Performance
  - — 8-Byte DMA/ISA Master Line Buffer
  - — 32-Bit Posted Memory Write Buffer to ISA
- Arbitration for PCI Devices
  - — Two or Four External PCI Masters are Supported
  - — Fixed, Rotating, or a Combination of the Two
- Arbitration for ISA Devices
  - — ISA Masters
  - — DMA and Refresh
- Integrated 16-Bit BIOS Timer
- Utility Bus (X-Bus) Peripheral Support
  - — Provides Chip Select Decode
  - — Controls Lower X-Bus Data Byte Transceiver
  - — Integrates Port 92, Mouse Interrupt, Coprocessor Error Reporting
- Integrates the Functionality of One 82C54 Timer
  - — System Timer
  - — Refresh Request
  - — Speaker Tone Output
- Integrates the Functionality of Two 82C59 Interrupt Controllers
  - — 14 Interrupts Supported
- Non-Maskable Interrupts (NMI)
  - — PCI System Errors
  - — ISA Parity Errors
- 208-Pin QFP Package
- 5V CMOS Technology
- Four Dedicated PCI Interrupts
  - — Level Sensitive
  - — Can be Mapped to any Unused Interrupt
- Complete Support for SL Enhanced Intel486 CPU's
  - — SMI# Generation Based on System Hardware Events
  - — STPCLK# Generation to Power Down the CPU

The 82378 System I/O (SIO) component provides the bridge between the PCI local bus and the ISA expansion bus. The SIO also integrates many of the common I/O functions found in today's ISA based PC systems. The SIO incorporates the logic for a PCI interface (master and slave), ISA interface (master and slave), enhanced seven channel DMA controller that supports fast DMA transfers and Scatter/Gather, data buffers to isolate the PCI bus from the ISA bus and to enhance performance, PCI and ISA arbitration, 14 level interrupt controller, a 16-bit BIOS timer, three programmable timer/counters, and non-maskable-interrupt (NMI) control logic. The SIO also provides decode for peripheral devices such as the Flash BIOS, Real Time Clock, Keyboard/Mouse Controller, Floppy Controller, two Serial Ports, one Parallel Port, and IDE Hard Disk Drive.

This data sheet describes the 82378IB and 82338ZB components. All normal text describes the functionality for both components. All features that exist on the 82378ZB are shaded as shown below.

This is an example of what the shaded sections that apply only to the 82378ZB component look like.

SIO Block Diagram

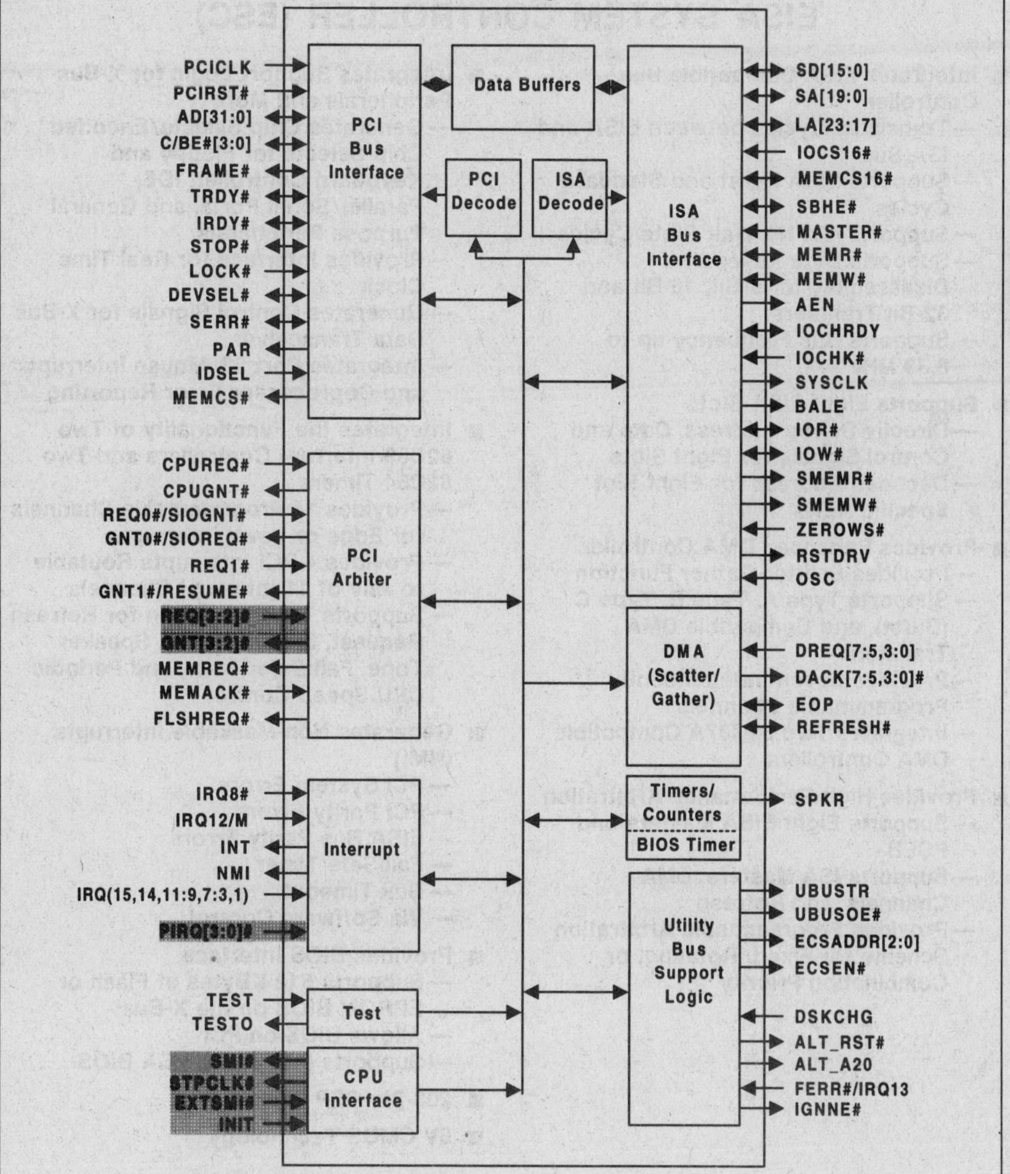

82374EB
EISA SYSTEM CONTROLLER (ESC)

- Integrates EISA Compatible Bus Controller
  - Translates Cycles between EISA and ISA Bus
  - Supports EISA Burst and Standard Cycles
  - Supports ISA No Wait State Cycles
  - Supports Byte Assembly/ Disassembly for 8-Bit, 16-Bit and 32-Bit Transfers
  - Supports Bus Frequency up to 8.33 MHz
- Supports Eight EISA Slots
  - Directly Drives Address, Data and Control Signals for Eight Slots
  - Decodes Address for Eight Slot Specific AENs
- Provides Enhanced DMA Controller
  - Provides Scatter-Gather Function
  - Supports Type A, Type B, Type C (Burst), and Compatible DMA Transfers
  - Provides Seven Independently Programmable Channels
  - Integrates Two 82C37A Compatible DMA Controllers
- Provides High Performance Arbitration
  - Supports Eight EISA Masters and PCEB
  - Supports ISA Masters, DMA Channels, and Refresh
  - Provides Programmable Arbitration Scheme for Fixed, Rotating, or Combination Priority
- Integrates Support Logic for X-Bus Peripherals and More
  - Generates Chip Selects/Encoded Chip Selects for Floppy and Keyboard Controller, IDE, Parallel/Serial Ports, and General Purpose Peripherals
  - Provides Interface for Real Time Clock
  - Generates Control Signals for X-Bus Data Transceiver
  - Integrates Port 92, Mouse Interrupt, and Coprocessor Error Reporting
- Integrates the Functionality of Two 82C59 Interrupt Controllers and Two 82C54 Timers
  - Provides 14 Programmable Channels for Edge or Level Interrupts
  - Provides 4 PCI Interrupts Routable to Any of 11 Interrupt Channels
  - Supports Timer Function for Refresh Request, System Timer, Speaker Tone, Fail Safe Timer, and Periodic CPU Speed Control
- Generates Non-Maskable Interrupts (NMI)
  - PCI System Errors
  - PCI Parity Errors
  - EISA Bus Parity Errors
  - Fail Safe Timer
  - Bus Timeout
  - Via Software Control
- Provides BIOS Interface
  - Supports 512 KBytes of Flash or EPROM BIOS on the X-Bus
  - Allows BIOS on PCI
  - Supports Integrated VGA BIOS
- 208-Pin QFP Package
- 5V CMOS Technology

The 82374EB EISA System Component (ESC) provides all the EISA system compatible functions. The ESC, with the PCEB, provides all the functions to implement an EISA to PCI bridge and EISA I/O subsystem. The ESC integrates the common I/O functions found in today's EISA based PC systems. The ESC incorporates the logic for an EISA (master and slave) interface, EISA Bus Controller, enhanced seven channel DMA controller with Scatter-Gather support, EISA arbitration, 14 channel interrupt controller, five programmable timer/counters, and non-maskable interrupt (NMI) control logic. The ESC also integrates support logic to decode peripheral devices such as the Flash BIOS, Real Time Clock, Keyboard/Mouse Controller, Floppy Controller, two Serial Ports, one Parallel Port, and IDE Hard Disk Drive.

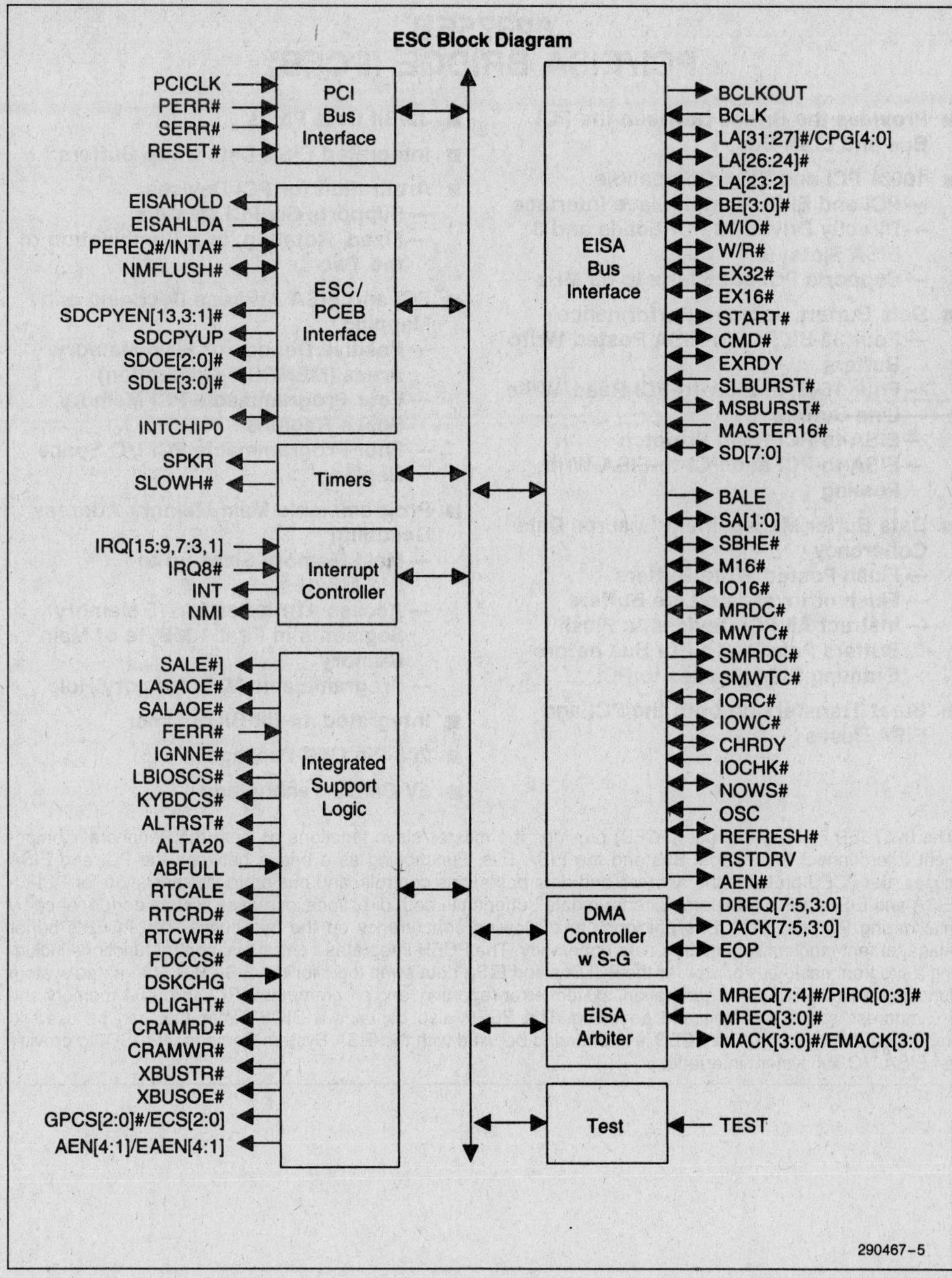
ESC Block Diagram
PCICLK
PERR#
SERR#
RESET#
PCI Bus Interface
EISAHOLD
EISAHLDA
PEREQ#/INTA#
NMFLUSH#
SDCPYEN[13,3:1]#
SDCPYUP
SDOE[2:0]#
SDLE[3:0]#
INTCHIP0
ESC/ PCEB Interface
SPKR
SLOWH#
Timers
IRQ[15:9,7:3,1]
IRQ8#
INT
NMI
Interrupt Controller
SALE#]
LASAOE#
SALAOE#
FERR#
IGNNE#
LBIOSCS#
KYBDCS#
ALTRST#
ALTA20
ABFULL
RTCALE
RTCRD#
RTCWR#
FDCCS#
DSKCHG
DLIGHT#
CRAMRD#
CRAMWR#
XBUSTR#
XBUSOE#
GPCS[2:0]#/ECS[2:0]
AEN[4:1]/EAEN[4:1]
Integrated Support Logic
EISA Bus Interface
BCLKOUT
BCLK
LA[31:27]#/CPG[4:0]
LA[26:24]#
LA[23:2]
BE[3:0]#
M/IO#
W/R#
EX32#
EX16#
START#
CMD#
EXRDY
SLBURST#
MSBURST#
MASTER16#
SD[7:0]
BALE
SA[1:0]
SBHE#
M16#
IO16#
MRDC#
MWTC#
SMRDC#
SMWTC#
IORC#
IOWC#
CHRDY
IOCHK#
NOWS#
OSC
REFRESH#
RSTDRV
AEN#
DMA Controller w S-G
DREQ[7:5,3:0]
DACK[7:5,3:0]
EOP
EISA Arbiter
MREQ[7:4]#/PIRQ[0:3]#
MREQ[3:0]#
MACK[3:0]#/EMACK[3:0]
Test
TEST
290467-5

82375EB
PCI/EISA BRIDGE (PCEB)

- Provides the Bridge between the PCI Bus and EISA Bus
- 100% PCI and EISA Compatible
  - PCI and EISA Master/Slave Interface
  - Directly Drives 10 PCI Loads and 8 EISA Slots
  - Supports PCI at 25 MHz to 33 MHz
- Data Buffers Improve Performance
  - Four 32-Bit PCI-to-EISA Posted Write Buffers
  - Four 16-Byte EISA-to-PCI Read/Write Line Buffers
  - EISA-to-PCI Read Prefetch
  - EISA-to-PCI and PCI-to-EISA Write Posting
- Data Buffer Management Ensures Data Coherency
  - Flush Posted Write Buffers
  - Flush or Invalidate Line Buffers
  - Instruct All PCI Devices to Flush Buffers Pointing to PCI Bus before Granting EISA Access to PCI
- Burst Transfers on both the PCI and EISA Buses
- 32-Bit Data Paths
- Integrated EISA Data Swap Buffers
- Arbitration for PCI Devices
  - Supports Six PCI Masters
  - Fixed, Rotating, or a Combination of the Two
- PCI and EISA Address Decoding and Mapping
  - Positive Decode of Main Memory Areas (MEMCS# Generation)
  - Four Programmable PCI Memory Space Regions
  - Four Programmable PCI I/O Space Regions
- Programmable Main Memory Address Decoding
  - Main Memory Sizes up to 512 MBytes
  - Access Attributes for 15 Memory Segments in First 1 MByte of Main Memory
  - Programmable Main Memory Hole
- Integrated 16-Bit BIOS Timer
- 208-Pin QFP Package
- 5V CMOS Technology

The 82375EB PCI-EISA Bridge (PCEB) provides the master/slave functions on both the Peripheral Component Interconnect (PCI) Local Bus and the EISA Bus. Functioning as a bridge between the PCI and EISA buses, the PCEB provides the address and data paths, bus controls, and bus protocol translation for PCI-to-EISA and EISA-to-PCI transfers. Extensive data buffering in both directions increases system performance by maximizing PCI and EISA Bus efficiency and allowing concurrency on the two buses. The PCEB's buffer management mechanism ensures data coherency. The PCEB integrates central bus control functions including a programmable bus arbiter for the PCI Bus and EISA data swap logic for the EISA Bus. Integrated system functions include PCI parity generation, system error reporting, and programmable PCI and EISA memory and I/O address space mapping and decoding. The PCEB also contains a BIOS Timer that can be used to implement timing loops. The PCEB is intended to be used with the EISA System Component (ESC) to provide an EISA I/O subsystem interface.

PCEB Block Diagram

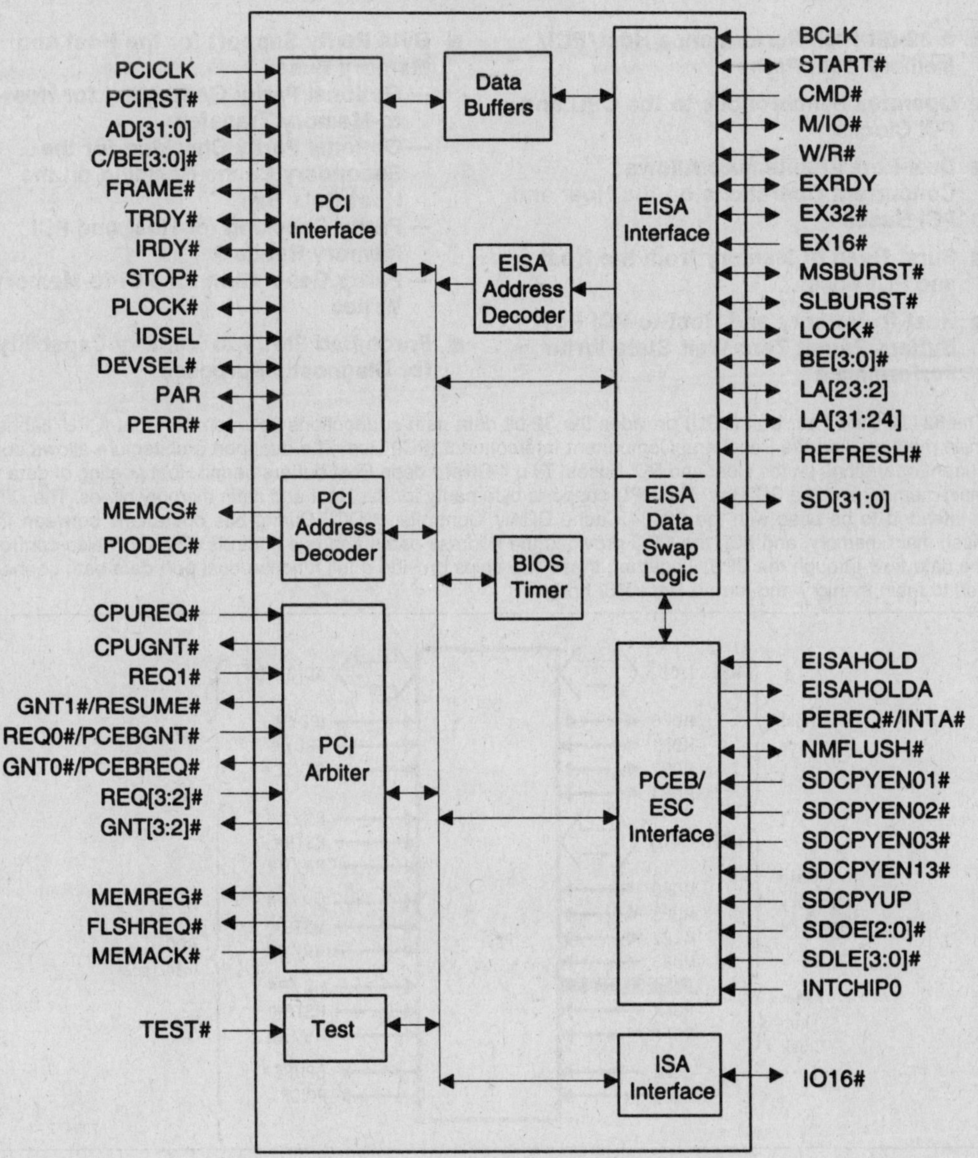

1

intel®

82423 DATA PATH UNIT (DPU)

- **A 32-Bit High Performance Host/PCI/ Memory Data Path**
- **Operates Synchronous to the CPU and PCI Clocks**
- **Dual-Port Architecture Allows Concurrent Operations on the Host and PCI Buses**
- **Burst Read of Memory from the Host and PCI Buses**
- **Host-to-Memory and Host-to-PCI Post Buffers Permit Zero Wait State Write Performance**
- **Byte Parity Support for the Host and Memory Buses**
  - **—Optional Parity Generation for Host-to-Memory Transfers**
  - **—Optional Parity Checking for the Secondary Cache Residing on the Host Data Bus**
  - **—Parity Checking for Host and PCI Memory Reads**
  - **—Parity Generation for PCI-to-Memory Writes**
- **Force Bad Parity to Memory Capability for Diagnostic Purposes**

The 82423 Data Path Unit (DPU) provides the 32-bit data path connections between the Host (CPU/cache), main memory, and the Peripheral Component Interconnect (PCI) Bus. The dual-port architecture allows concurrent operations on the Host and PCI Buses. Two 4-Dword deep Post buffers permit Host posting of data to main memory and the PCI Bus. The DPU supports byte parity for the Host and main memory buses. The DPU is intended to be used with the 82424 Cache DRAM Controller (CDC). During bus operations between the Host, main memory, and PCI, the CDC provides the address paths and bus controls. The CDC also controls the data flow through the DPU. Together, these two chips provide a full function dual-port data path connection to main memory and form a Host/PCI bridge.

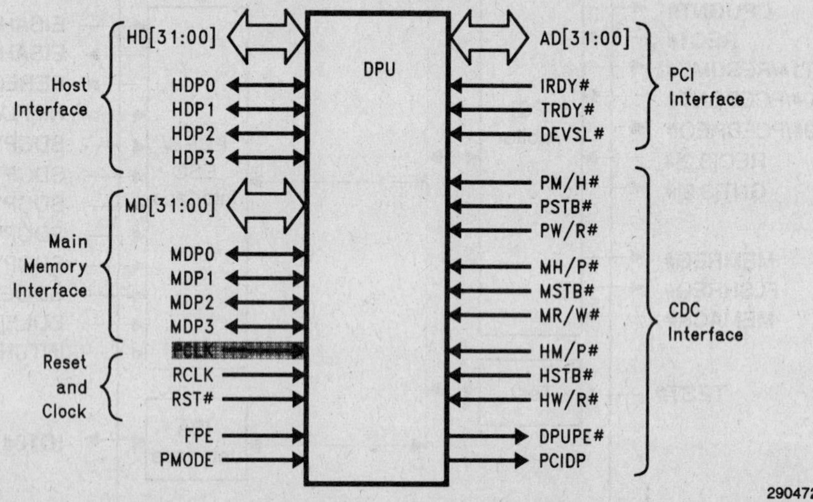

290472–1

This data sheet describes the 82423TX and 82423ZX components. All normal text describes the functionality for both components. All features that exist on the 82423ZX are shaded as shown below.

This is an example of what the shaded sections that apply only to the 82423ZX component look like.

October 1993
Order Number: 290472-003

82424
CACHE AND DRAM CONTROLLER (CDC)

- **Supports 25 MHz/33 MHz/50 MHz Intel486™ SX, Intel487™ SX, Intel486 DX, Intel486 DX2, OverDrive™ for Intel486 and OverDrive for DX2 Processors**
- **Fully Synchronous, 25 MHz/33 MHz PCI Bus Capable of Supporting Bus Masters**
- **Supports OverDrive Upgrade Socket, Including OverDrive for DX2 in Write-Back Mode**
- **Programmable Attribute Map for First 1-Mbyte of Main Memory**
- **Posted Write Buffers for Improved Performance**
- **Integrated DRAM Controller**
  - **— 2-Mbyte to 160-Mbyte Main Memory using 70 ns Fast Page Mode SIMM Memory**
  - **— Decoupled Refresh Cycles to Reduce DRAM Access Latency**
  - **— Burst Mode PCI Accesses to DRAM Supported at the Rate of x-3-3-3-3-3**
- **Integrated Cache Controller**
  - **— Write-Through and Write-Back Cache Options**
  - **— 64 KB, 128 KB, 256 KB and 512 KB Cache Sizes using Standard SRAMs**
  - **— Burst Line Fill of 2-1-1-1 from Secondary Cache at 25 MHz and 33 MHz *and 3-1-1-1 at 50 MHz***
  - **— Zero Wait State Write to L2 Cache for a Cache Write Hit**
  - **— Main Memory Posting at Zero Wait States, Enabling Optimum Write-Through Cache Performance**
  - **— Concurrent Cache Line Replacement from Secondary Cache in Write-Back Mode**
- **PCI Bridge**
  - **— Translates CPU Cycles into PCI Bus Cycles**
  - **— Translates Back-to-Back Sequential Memory Write Cycles Into PCI Burst Cycles**
  - **— Separate PCI-to-Main Memory Port Allows Concurrent/Independent CPU and PCI Bus Operations**
  - **— Integrated Snoop Filter**

The 82424 Cache DRAM Controller (CDC) integrates the cache and main memory DRAM control functions and provides the address paths and bus control for transfers between the Host (CPU/cache), main memory, and the Peripheral Component Interconnect (PCI) Bus. The Dual-ported architecture permits concurrent operations on the Host and PCI Buses. The cache controller supports both write-through and write-back cache policies and cache sizes from 64 Kbytes to 512 Kbytes. The cache memory can be implemented using standard asynchronous SRAMs. The dual-ported main memory DRAM controller interfaces DRAM to the Host Bus and the PCI Bus. The CDC supports a two-way interleaved DRAM organization for optimum performance. Up to eight single sided SIMMs or four dual sided SIMMs provide a maximum of 160 Mbytes of main memory. The CDC is intended to be used with the 82423 Data Path Unit (DPU). The DPU provides 32-bit data paths between the Host, main memory, and the PCI. Together, these two components provide a full function dual-port data path connection to main memory and form a Host/PCI Bridge.

This data sheet describes the 82424TX, 82424ZX and 82424ZX-50 components. All normal text describes the functionality for all three components. All features that exist on the 82424ZX and 82424ZX-50 are shaded as shown below.

This is an example of what the shaded sections that apply only to 82424ZX and 82424ZX-50 components look like.

All features that exist only on the 82424ZX-50 are shaded as shown below.

This is an example of what the shaded sections that apply only to the 82424ZX-50 component look like.

October 1993
Order Number: 290471-003

Simplified CDC Block Diagram

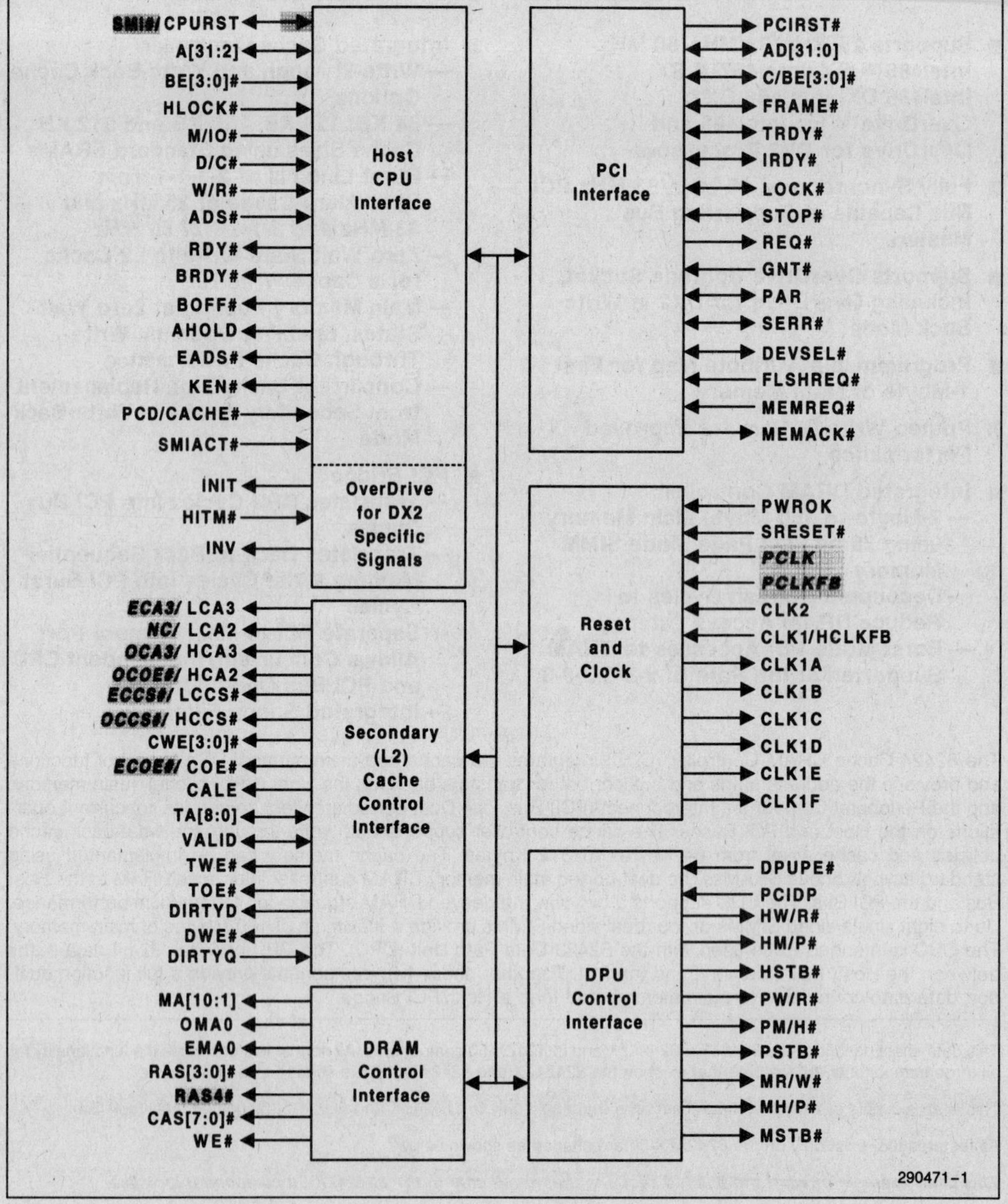

intel®

82420/82430 PCIset BRIDGE COMPONENT

82378 FOR ISA BUSES

- Provides the Bridge between the PCI Bus and ISA Bus
- 100% PCI and ISA Compatible
- Enhanced DMA Functions
- Integrated Data Buffers to Improve Performance
- Integrated 16-bit BIOS Timer
- Arbitration for PCI Devices
- Arbitration for ISA Devices
- Integrates the Functionality of One 82C54 Timer
- Integrates the Functionality of Two 82C59 Interrupt Controllers
- Non-Maskable Interrupts (NMI)

82374EB (ESC) Component/82375EB (PCEB) Component

- Provides the Bridge between the PCI Bus and EISA Bus
- 100% PCI and EISA Compatible
- Data Buffers Improve Performance
- Data Buffer Management Ensures Data Coherency
- Burst Transfers on both the PCI and EISA Buses
- 32-Bit Data Paths
- PCI and EISA Address Decoding and Mapping
- Programmable Main Memory Address Decoding
- Integrated EISA Compatible Bus Controller
- Supports Eight EISA Slots
- Provides Enhanced DMA Controller
- Provides High Performance Arbitration
- Integrates Support Logic for X-Bus Peripheral and more
- Integrates the Functionality of Two 82C59 Interrupt Controllers and Two 82C54 Timers
- Generates Non-Maskable Interrupts
- Provides BIOS Interface

1

The 82420/82430 PCIset Bridge components provide a bridge between the PCI to either EISA or ISA buses. The 82378 provides the bridge between PCI bus and the ISA bus while the 82374EB and 82375EB together provide the bridge between the PCI bus and the EISA bus.

The SIO integrates many of the common I/O functions found in todays ISA based PC systems. The SIO incorporates the logic for a PCI interface master and slave), ISA interface (master and slave), enhanced seven channel DMA controller and support for other decode logic.

The 82374EB EISA System Component (ESC) and 82375EB PCI-EISA Bridge (PCEB) together provide the EISA system compatible master/slave functions on both the PCI Local Bus and the EISA Bus and the common I/O functions found in today's EISA systems. The ESC incorporates the logic for an EISA (master and slave) interface, EISA bus controller, enhanced seven channel DMA controller with Scatter-Gather support, EISA arbitration, 14 channel interrupt controller, five programmable timer/counters and non-maskable control logic. The ESC also integrates support logic to decode peripheral devices such as the Flash BIOS, Real Time Clock, Keyboard/Mouse Controller, Floppy Controller, two Serial Ports, one Parallel Port, and IDE Hard Disk Drive. The PCEB provides the address and data paths, bus controls, and bus protocol translation for PCI-to-EISA and EISA-to-PCI transfers. Extensive data buffering in both directions increases system performance by maximizing PCI and EISA Bus efficiency and allowing concurrency on the two buses. The PCEB integrates central bus control functions, PCI parity generation, system error reporting, and programmable PCI and EISA memory and I/O address space mapping and decoding.

October 1993
Order Number: 290509-001

82378 SYSTEM I/O (SIO)

- Provides the Bridge between the PCI Bus and ISA Bus
- 100% PCI and ISA Compatible
  - PCI and ISA Master/Slave Interface
  - Directly Drives 10 PCI Loads and 6 ISA Slots
  - Supports PCI at 25 MHz and 33.33 MHz
  - Supports ISA from 6 MHz to 8.33 MHz
- Enhanced DMA Functions
  - Scatter/Gather
  - Fast DMA Type A, B, and F
  - Compatible DMA Transfers
  - 32-Bit Addressability
  - Seven Independently Programmable Channels
  - Functionality of Two 82C37A DMA Controllers
- Integrated Data Buffers to Improve Performance
  - 8-Byte DMA/ISA Master Line Buffer
  - 32-Bit Posted Memory Write Buffer to ISA
- Integrated 16-Bit BIOS Timer
- Arbitration for PCI Devices
  - Two or Four External PCI Masters Are Supported
  - Fixed, Rotating, or a Combination of the Two
- Arbitration for ISA Devices
  - ISA Masters
  - DMA and Refresh
- Utility Bus (X-Bus) Peripheral Support
  - Provides Chip Select Decode
  - Controls Lower X-Bus Data Byte Transceiver
  - Integrates Port 92, Mouse Interrupt, Coprocessor Error Reporting
- Integrates the Functionality of One 82C54 Timer
  - System Timer
  - Refresh Request
  - Speaker Tone Output
- Integrates the Functionality of Two 82C59 Interrupt Controllers
  - 14 Interrupts Supported
- Non-Maskable Interrupts (NMI)
  - PCI System Errors
  - ISA Parity Errors
- 208-Pin QFP Package
- 5V CMOS Technology
- Four Dedicated PCI Interrupts
  - Level Sensitive
  - Can be Mapped to Any Unused Interrupt
- Complete Support for SL Enhanced Intel486 CPU's
  - SMI# Generation Based on System Hardware Events
  - STPCLK# Generation to Power Down the CPU

The 82378 System I/O (SIO) component provides the bridge between the PCI local bus and the ISA expansion bus. The SIO also integrates many of the common I/O functions found in today's ISA based PC systems. The SIO incorporates the logic for a PCI interface (master and slave), ISA interface (master and slave), enhanced seven channel DMA controller that supports fast DMA transfers and Scatter/Gather, data buffers to isolate the PCI bus from the ISA bus and to enhance performance, PCI and ISA arbitration, 14 level interrupt controller, a 16-bit BIOS timer, three programmable timer/counters, and non-maskable-interrupt (NMI) control logic. The SIO also provides decode for peripheral devices such as the Flash BIOS, Real Time Clock, Keyboard/Mouse Controller, Floppy Controller, two Serial Ports, one Parallel Port, and IDE Hard Disk Drive.

IMPORTANT—READ THIS SECTION BEFORE READING THE REST OF THE DATA SHEET.

This data sheet describes the 82378IB and 82378ZB components. All normal text describes the functionality for both components. All features that exist on the 82378ZB are shaded as shown below.

This is an example of what the shaded sections that apply only to the 82378ZB component look like.

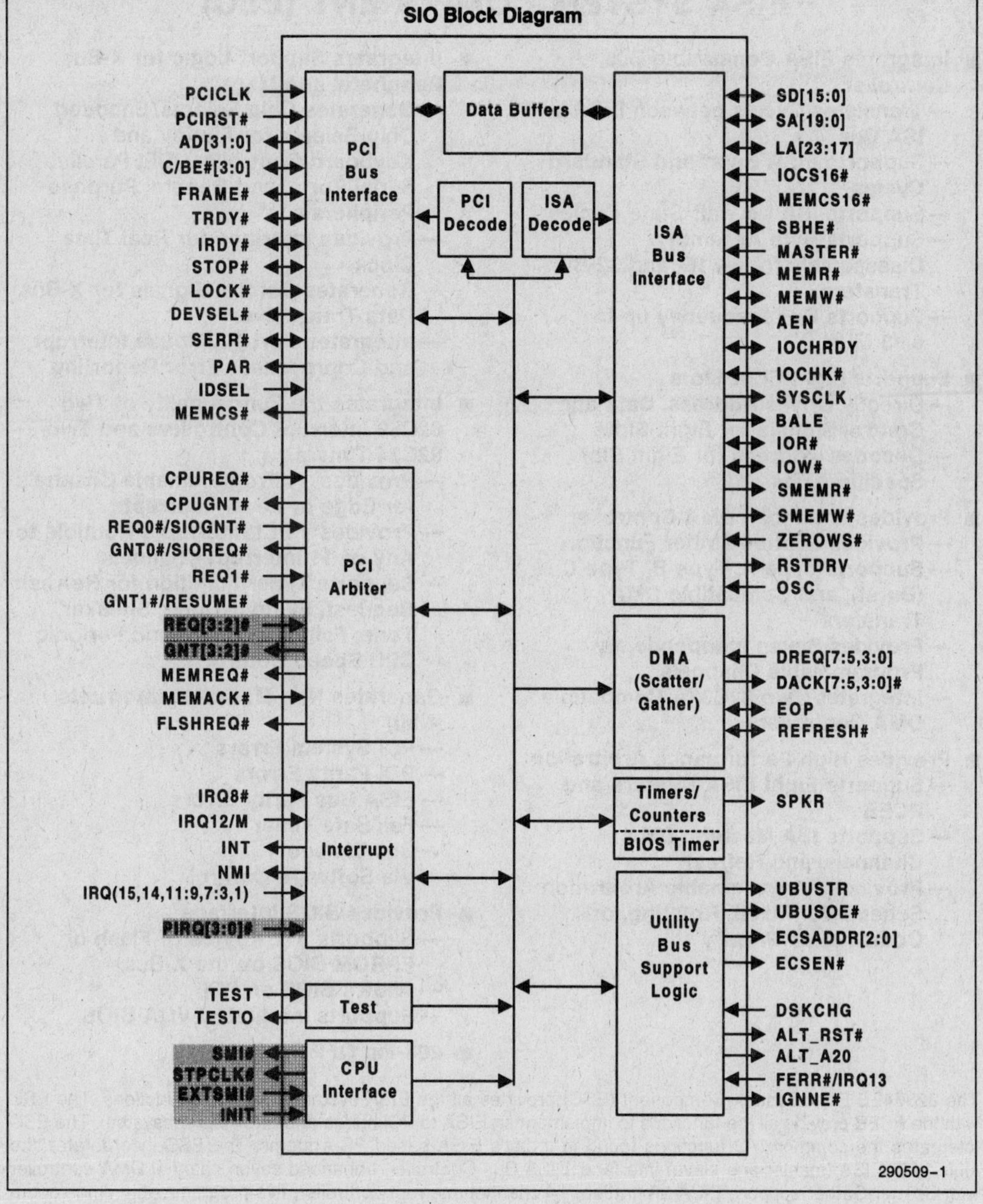

SIO Block Diagram

intel®

82374EB
EISA SYSTEM COMPONENT (ESC)

- **Integrates EISA Compatible Bus Controller**
  - Translates Cycles between EISA and ISA Bus
  - Supports EISA Burst and Standard Cycles
  - Supports ISA No wait State Cycles
  - Supports Byte Assembly/ Disassembly for 8-, 16- and 32-Bit Transfers
  - Supports Bus Frequency up to 8.33 MHz
- **Supports Eight EISA Slots**
  - Directly Drives Address, Data and Control Signals for Eight Slots
  - Decodes Address for Eight Slot Specific AENs
- **Provides Enhanced DMA Controller**
  - Provides Scatter-Gather Function
  - Supports Type A, Type B, Type C (Burst), and Compatible DMA Transfers
  - Provides Seven Independently Programmable Channels
  - Integrates Two 82C37A Compatible DMA Controllers
- **Provides High Performance Arbitration**
  - Supports Eight EISA Masters and PCEB
  - Supports ISA Masters, DMA Channels, and Refresh
  - Provides Programmable Arbitration Scheme for Fixed, Rotating, or Combination Priority
- **Integrates Support Logic for X-Bus Peripheral and More**
  - Generates Chip Selects/Encoded Chip Selects for Floppy and Keyboard Controller, IDE, Parallel/ Serial Ports, and General Purpose Peripherals
  - Provides Interface for Real Time Clock
  - Generates Control Signals for X-Bus Data Transceiver
  - Integrates Port 92, Mouse Interrupt, and Coprocessor Error Reporting
- **Integrates the Functionality of Two 82C59 Interrupt Controllers and Two 82C54 Timers**
  - Provides 14 Programmable Channels for Edge or Level Interrupts
  - Provides 4 PCI Interrupts Routible to Any of 11 Interrupt Channels
  - Supports Timer Function for Refresh Request, System Timer, Speaker Tone, Fail Safe Timer, and Periodic CPU Speed Control
- **Generates Non-Maskable Interrupts (NMI)**
  - PCI System Errors
  - PCI Parity Errors
  - EISA Bus Parity Errors
  - Fail Safe Timer
  - Bus Timeout
  - Via Software Control
- **Provides BIOS Interface**
  - Supports 512 Kbytes of Flash or EPROM BIOS on the X-Bus
  - Allows BIOS on PCI
  - Supports integrated VGA BIOS
- **208-Pin QFP Package**

The 82374EB EISA System Component (ESC) provides all the EISA system compatible functions. The ESC with the PCEB provide all the functions to implement an EISA to PCI bridge and EISA I/O subsystem. The ESC integrates the common I/O functions found in today's EISA based PC systems. The ESC incorporates the logic for a EISA (master and slave) interface, EISA Bus Controller, enhanced seven channel DMA controller with Scatter-Gather support, EISA arbitration, 14 channel interrupt controller, five programmable timer/counters, and Non-Maskable Interrupt (NMI) control logic. The ESC also integrates support logic to decode peripheral devices such as the Flash BIOS, Real Time Clock, Keyboard/Mouse Controller, Floppy Controller, two Serial Ports, one Parallel Port, and IDE Hard Disk Drive.

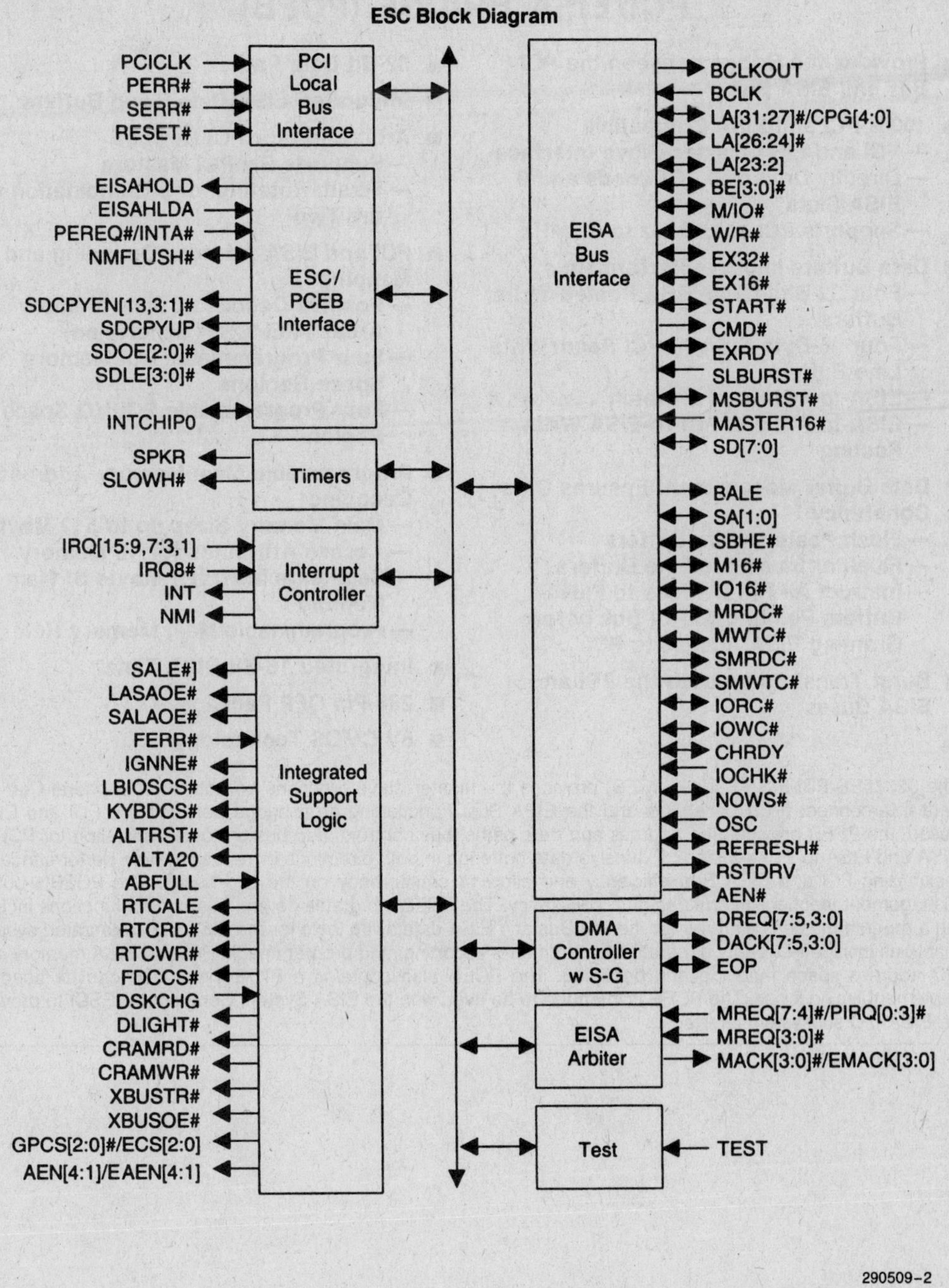

1

ESC Block Diagram

PCICLK
PERR#
SERR#
RESET#
PCI Local Bus Interface

EISAHOLD
EISAHLDA
PEREQ#/INTA#
NMFLUSH#
SDCPYEN[13,3:1]#
SDCPYUP
SDOE[2:0]#
SDLE[3:0]#
INTCHIP0
ESC/ PCEB Interface

SPKR
SLOWH#
Timers

IRQ[15:9,7:3,1]
IRQ8#
INT
NMI
Interrupt Controller

SALE#]
LASAOE#
SALAOE#
FERR#
IGNNE#
LBIOSCS#
KYBDCS#
ALTRST#
ALTA20
ABFULL
RTCALE
RTCRD#
RTCWR#
FDCCS#
DSKCHG
DLIGHT#
CRAMRD#
CRAMWR#
XBUSTR#
XBUSOE#
GPCS[2:0]#/ECS[2:0]
AEN[4:1]/EAEN[4:1]
Integrated Support Logic

EISA Bus Interface
BCLKOUT
BCLK
LA[31:27]#/CPG[4:0]
LA[26:24]#
LA[23:2]
BE[3:0]#
M/IO#
W/R#
EX32#
EX16#
START#
CMD#
EXRDY
SLBURST#
MSBURST#
MASTER16#
SD[7:0]
BALE
SA[1:0]
SBHE#
M16#
IO16#
MRDC#
MWTC#
SMRDC#
SMWTC#
IORC#
IOWC#
CHRDY
IOCHK#
NOWS#
OSC
REFRESH#
RSTDRV
AEN#

DMA Controller w S-G
DREQ[7:5,3:0]
DACK[7:5,3:0]
EOP

EISA Arbiter
MREQ[7:4]#/PIRQ[0:3]#
MREQ[3:0]#
MACK[3:0]#/EMACK[3:0]

Test
TEST

290509-2

82375EB PCI/EISA BRIDGE (PCEB)

- Provides the Bridge between the PCI Bus and EISA Bus
- 100% PCI and EISA Compatible
  - PCI and EISA Master/Slave Interface
  - Directly Drives 10 PCI Loads and 8 EISA Slots
  - Supports PCI at 25 MHz to 33 MHz
- Data Buffers Improve Performance
  - Four 32-Bit PCI-to-EISA Posted Write Buffers
  - Four 16-Byte EISA-to-PCI Read/Write Line Buffers
  - EISA-to-PCI Read Prefetch
  - EISA-to-PCI and PCI-to-EISA Write Posting
- Data Buffer Management Ensures Data Coherency
  - Flush Posted Write Buffers
  - Flush or Invalidate Line Buffers
  - Instruct All PCI Devices to Flush Buffers Pointing to PCI Bus before Granting EISA Access to PCI
- Burst Transfers on both the PCI and EISA Buses
- 32-Bit Data Paths
- Integrated EISA Data Swap Buffers
- Arbitration for PCI Devices
  - Supports Six PCI Masters
  - Fixed, Rotating, or a Combination of the Two
- PCI and EISA Address Decoding and Mapping
  - Positive Decode of Main Memory Areas (MEMCS# Generation)
  - Four Programmable PCI Memory Space Regions
  - Four Programmable PCI I/O Space Regions
- Programmable Main Memory Address Decoding
  - Main Memory Sizes up to 512 Mbytes
  - Access Attributes for 15 Memory Segments in First 1 Mbyte of Main Memory
  - Programmable Main Memory Hole
- Integrated 16-Bit BIOS Timer
- 208-Pin OFP Package
- 5V CMOS Technology

The 82375EB PCI-EISA Bridge (PCEB) provides the master/slave functions on both the Peripheral Component Interconnect (PCI) Local Bus and the EISA Bus. Functioning as a bridge between the PCI and EISA buses, the PCEB provides the address and data paths, bus controls, and bus protocol translation for PCI-to-EISA and EISA-to-PCI transfers. Extensive data buffering in both directions increases system performance by maximizing PCI and EISA Bus efficiency and allowing concurrency on the two buses. The PCEB's buffer management mechanism ensures data coherency. The PCEB integrates central bus control functions including a programmable bus arbiter for the PCI Bus and EISA data swap logic for the EISA Bus. Integrated system functions include PCI parity generation, system error reporting, and programmable PCI and EISA memory and I/O address space mapping and decoding. The PCEB also contains a BIOS Timer that can be used to implement timing loops. The PCEB is intended to be used with the EISA System Component (ESC) to provide an EISA I/O subsystem interface.

PCEB Block Diagram

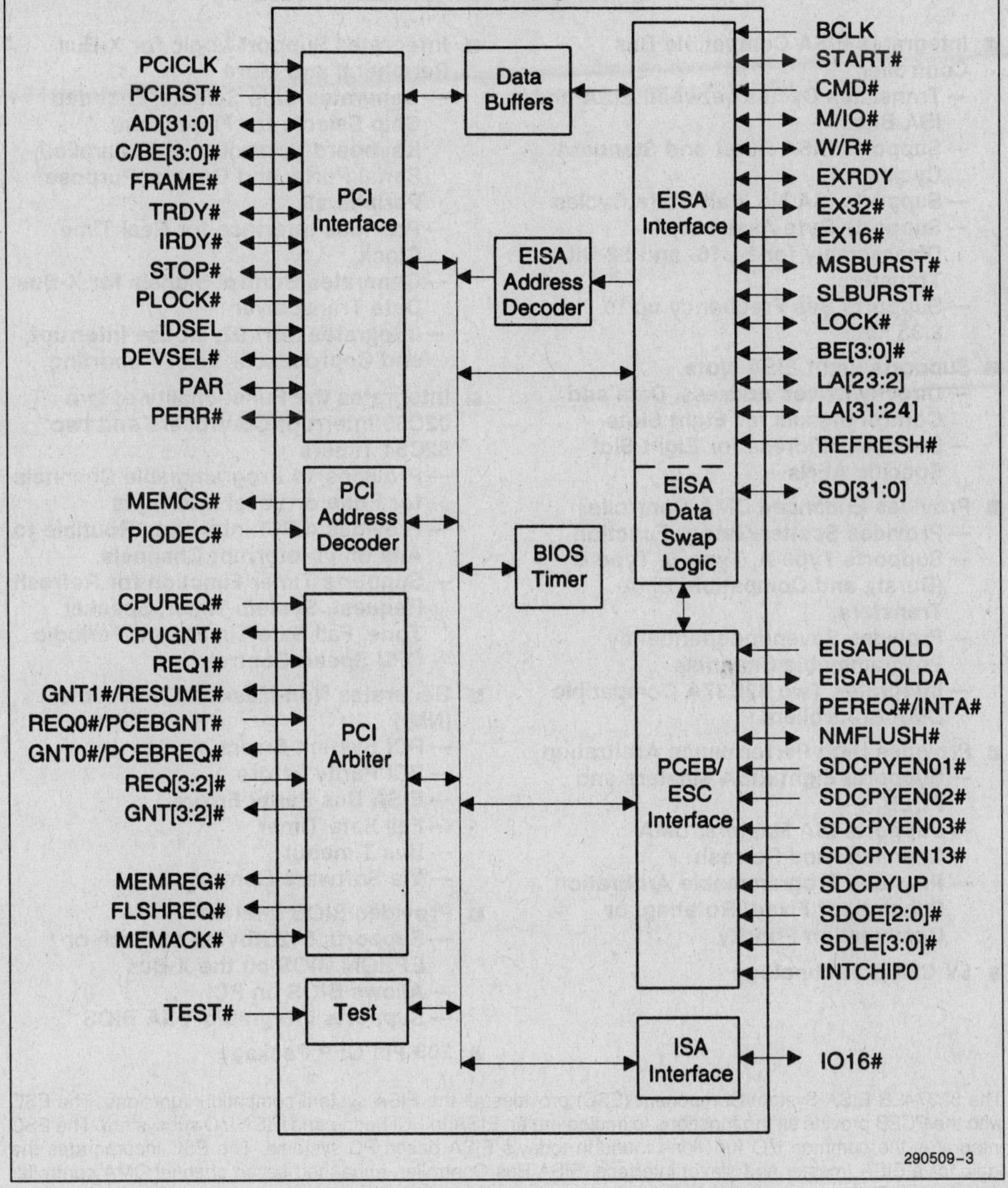

290509-3

intel®

82374EB
EISA SYSTEM COMPONENT (ESC)

- Integrates EISA Compatible Bus Controller
  - Translates Cycles between EISA and ISA Bus
  - Supports EISA Burst and Standard Cycles
  - Supports ISA No Wait State Cycles
  - Supports Byte Assembly/Disassembly for 8-, 16- and 32-Bit Transfers
  - Supports Bus Frequency up to 8.33 MHz
- Supports Eight EISA slots
  - Directly Drives Address, Data and Control Signals for Eight Slots
  - Decodes Address for Eight Slot Specific AENs
- Provides Enhanced DMA Controller
  - Provides Scatter-Gather Function
  - Supports Type A, Type B, Type C (Burst), and Compatible DMA Transfers
  - Provides Seven Independently Programmable Channels
  - Integrates Two 82C37A Compatible DMA Controllers
- Provides High Performance Arbitration
  - Supports Eight EISA Masters and PCEB
  - Supports ISA Masters, DMA Channels, and Refresh
  - Provides Programmable Arbitration Scheme for Fixed, Rotating, or Combination Priority
- 5V CMOS Technology
- Integrates Support Logic for X-Bus Peripheral and More
  - Generates Chip Selects/Encoded Chip Selects for Floppy and Keyboard Controller, IDE, Parallel/Serial Ports, and General Purpose Peripherals
  - Provides Interface for Real Time Clock
  - Generates Control Signals for X-Bus Data Transceiver
  - Integrates Port 92, Mouse Interrupt, and Coprocessor Error Reporting
- Integrates the Functionality of two 82C59 Interrupt Controllers and two 82C54 Timers
  - Provides 14 Programmable Channels for Edge or Level Interrupts
  - Provides 4 PCI Interrupts Routible to Any of 11 Interrupt Channels
  - Supports Timer Function for Refresh Request, System Timer, Speaker Tone, Fail Safe Timer, and Periodic CPU Speed Control
- Generates Non-Maskable Interrupts (NMI)
  - PCI System Errors
  - PCI Parity Errors
  - EISA Bus Parity Errors
  - Fail Safe Timer
  - Bus Timeout
  - Via Software Control
- Provides BIOS Interface
  - Supports 512 Kbytes of Flash or EPROM BIOS on the X-Bus
  - Allows BIOS on PCI
  - Supports Integrated VGA BIOS
- 208-Pin QFP Package

The 82374EB EISA System Component (ESC) provides all the EISA system compatible functions. The ESC with the PCEB provide all the functions to implement an EISA to PCI bridge and EISA I/O subsystem. The ESC integrates the common I/O functions found in today's EISA based PC systems. The ESC incorporates the logic for a EISA (master and slave) interface, EISA Bus Controller, enhanced seven channel DMA controller with Scatter-Gather support, EISA arbitration, 14 channel interrupt controller, five programmable timer/counters, and non-maskable-interrupt (NMI) control logic. The ESC also integrates support logic to decode peripheral devices such as the Flash BIOS, Real Time Clock, Keyboard/Mouse Controller, Floppy Controller, two Serial Ports, one Parallel Port, and IDE Hard Disk Drive.

November 1993
Order Number: 290476-002

82374EB EISA System Component

CONTENTS PAGE

CONTENTS PAGE

CONTENTS PAGE

CONTENTS PAGE

CONTENTS

PAGE

CONTENTS

PAGE

CONTENTS PAGE

CONTENTS PAGE

ESC Block Diagram

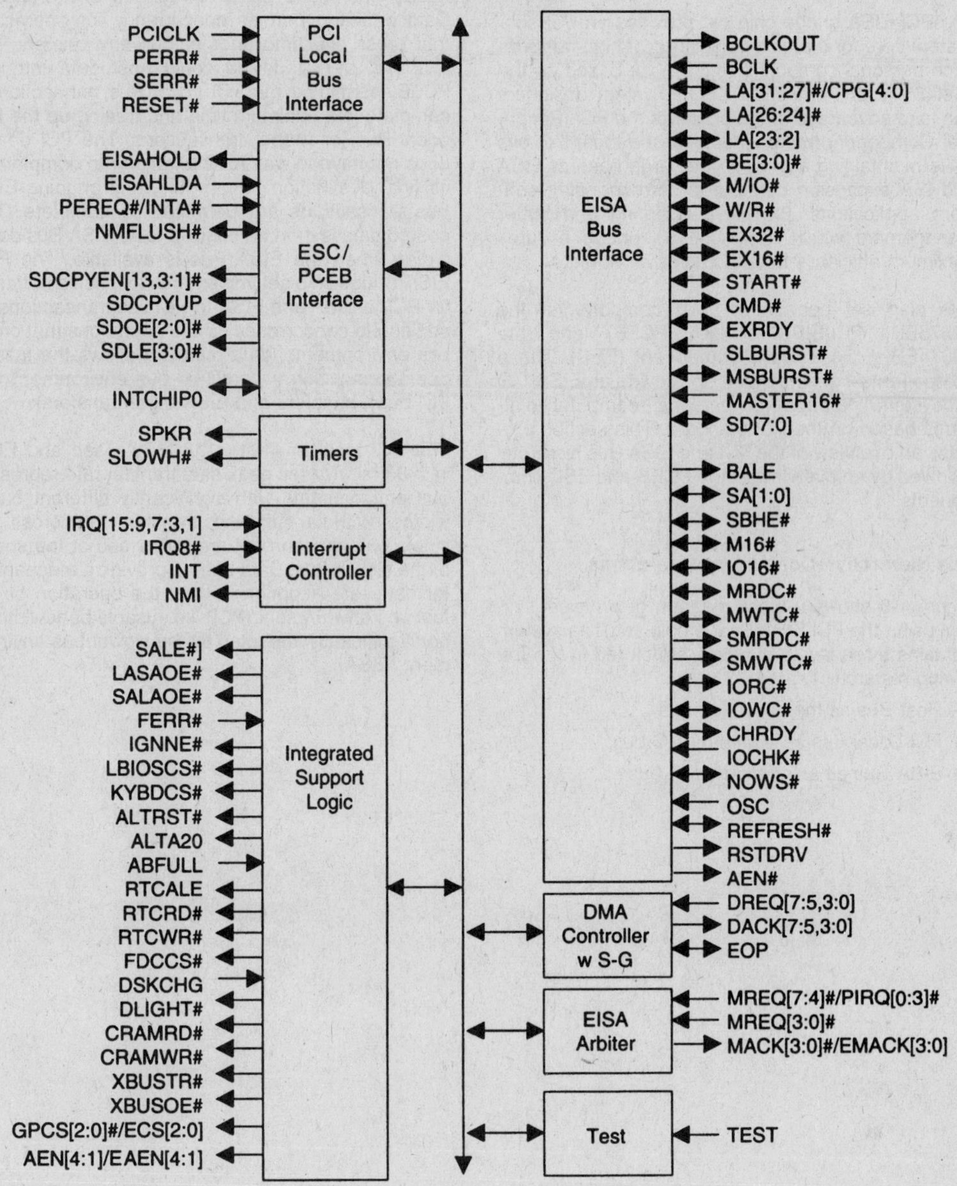

PCI Local Bus Interface
PCICLK
PERR#
SERR#
RESET#

ESC/ PCEB Interface
EISAHOLD
EISAHLDA
PEREQ#/INTA#
NMFLUSH#
SDCPYEN[13,3:1]#
SDCPYUP
SDOE[2:0]#
SDLE[3:0]#
INTCHIP0

Timers
SPKR
SLOWH#

Interrupt Controller
IRQ[15:9,7:3,1]
IRQ8#
INT
NMI

Integrated Support Logic
SALE#]
LASAOE#
SALAOE#
FERR#
IGNNE#
LBIOSCS#
KYBDCS#
ALTRST#
ALTA20
ABFULL
RTCALE
RTCRD#
RTCWR#
FDCCS#
DSKCHG
DLIGHT#
CRAMRD#
CRAMWR#
XBUSTR#
XBUSOE#
GPCS[2:0]#/ECS[2:0]
AEN[4:1]/EAEN[4:1]

EISA Bus Interface
BCLKOUT
BCLK
LA[31:27]#/CPG[4:0]
LA[26:24]#
LA[23:2]
BE[3:0]#
M/IO#
W/R#
EX32#
EX16#
START#
CMD#
EXRDY
SLBURST#
MSBURST#
MASTER16#
SD[7:0]
BALE
SA[1:0]
SBHE#
M16#
IO16#
MRDC#
MWTC#
SMRDC#
SMWTC#
IORC#
IOWC#
CHRDY
IOCHK#
NOWS#
OSC
REFRESH#
RSTDRV
AEN#

DMA Controller w S-G
DREQ[7:5,3:0]
DACK[7:5,3:0]
EOP

EISA Arbiter
MREQ[7:4]#/PIRQ[0:3]#
MREQ[3:0]#
MACK[3:0]#/EMACK[3:0]

Test
TEST

290476–1

1

1.0 ARCHITECTURAL OVERVIEW

The PCI-EISA bridge chip set provides an I/O subsystem core for the next generation of high-performance personal computers (e.g., those based on the Intel486™ or Pentium™ CPU). System designers can take advantage of the power of the PCI (Peripheral Component Interconnect) for the local I/O bus while maintaining access to the large base of EISA and ISA expansion cards, and corresponding software applications. Extensive buffering and buffer management within the PCI-EISA bridge ensures maximum efficiency in both bus environments.

The chip set consists of two components—the 82375EB, PCI-EISA Bridge (PCEB) and the 82374EB, EISA System Component (ESC). These components work in tandem to provide an EISA I/O subsystem interface for personal computer platforms based on the PCI standard. This section provides an overview of the PCI and EISA Bus hierarchy followed by an overview of the PCEB and ESC components.

Bus Hierarchy—Concurrent Operations

Figure 1-0 shows a block diagram of a typical system using the PCI-EISA Bridge chip set. The system contains three levels of buses structured in the following hierarchy:

- Host Bus as the execution bus
- PCI Local Bus as a primary I/O bus
- EISA Bus as a secondary I/O bus

This bus hierarchy allows concurrency for simultaneous operations on all three bus environments. Data buffering permits concurrency for operations that cross over into another bus environment. For example, a PCI device could post data into the PCEB, permitting the PCI Local Bus transaction to complete in a minimum time and freeing up the PCI Local Bus for further transactions. The PCI device does not have to wait for the transfer to complete to its final destination. Meanwhile, any ongoing EISA Bus transactions are permitted to complete. The posted data is then transferred to its EISA Bus destination when the EISA Bus is available. The PCI-EISA Bridge chip set implements extensive buffering for PCI-to-EISA and EISA-to-PCI bus transactions. In addition to concurrency for the operations that cross bus environments, data buffering allows the fastest operations within a particular bus environment (via PCI burst transfers and EISA burst transfers).

The PCI local bus with 132 MByte/sec and EISA with 33 MByte/sec peak data transfer rate represent bus environments with significantly different bandwidths. Without buffering, transfers that cross the single bus environment are performed at the speed of the slower bus. Data buffers provide a mechanism for data rate adoption so that the operation of the fast bus environment (PCI), i.e., usable bandwidth, is not significantly impacted by the slower bus environment (EISA).

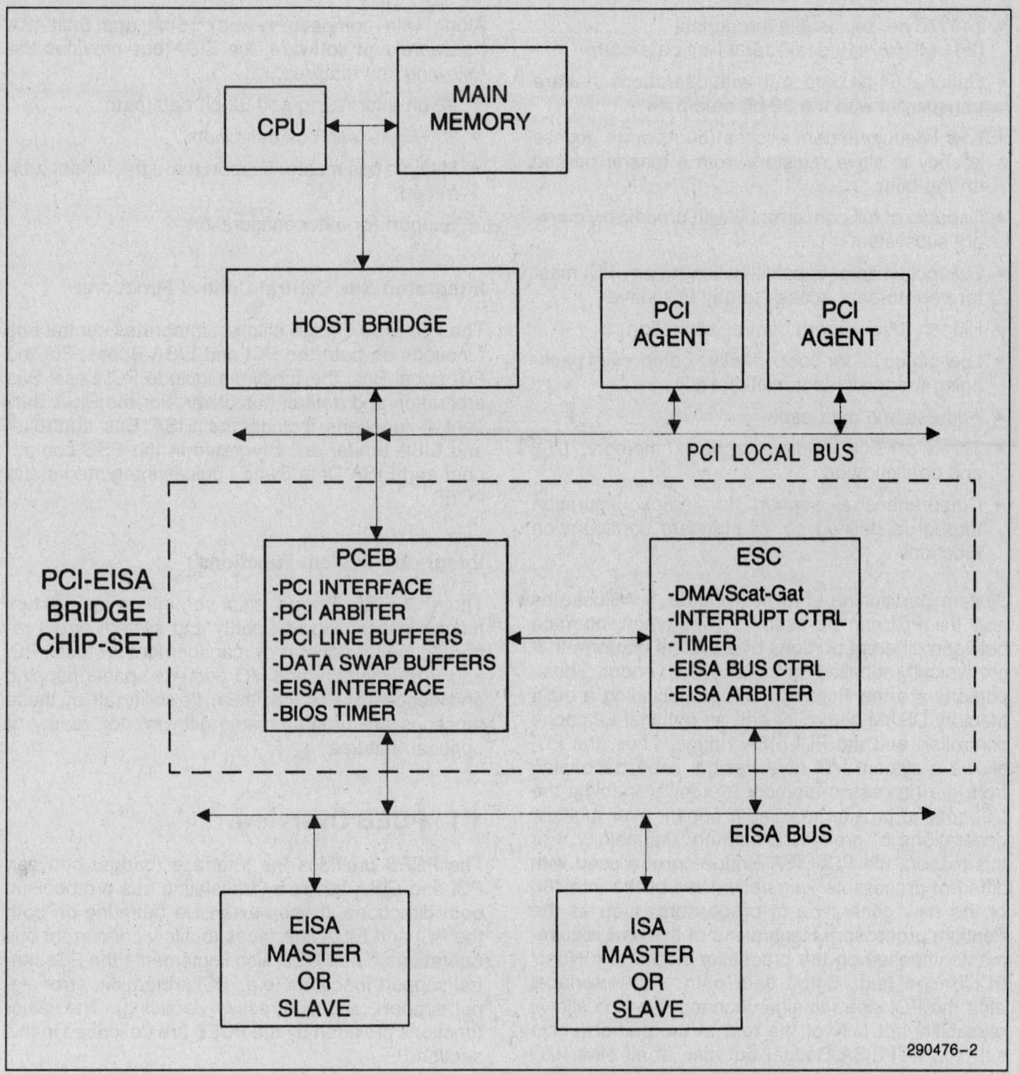

Figure 1-1. PCI-EISA Chip Set System Block Diagram

PCI Local Bus

The PCI Local Bus has been defined to address the growing industry needs for a standardized *local bus* that is not directly dependent on the speed and the size of the processor bus. New generations of personal computer system software such as Windows and Win-NT with sophisticated graphical interfaces, multi-tasking and multi-threading bring new requirements that traditional PC I/O architectures can not satisfy. In addition to the higher bandwidth, reliability and robustness of the I/O subsystem is becoming increasingly important. The PCI environment addresses these needs and provides an upgrade path for the future. PCI features include:

- Processor independent
- Multiplexed, burst mode operation
- Synchronous at frequencies from 20 MHz–33 MHz
- 120 MByte/sec usable throughput (132 MByte/sec peak) for 32-bit data path

- 240 MByte/sec usable throughput (264 MByte/sec peak) for 64-bit data path
- Optional 64-bit data path with operations that are transparent with the 32-bit data path
- Low latency random access (60 ns write access latency to slave registers from a master parked on the bus)
- Capable of full concurrency with processor/memory subsystem
- Full multi-master capability allowing any PCI master peer-to-peer access to any PCI slave
- Hidden (overlapped) central arbitration
- Low pin count for cost effective component packaging (address/data multiplexed)
- Address and data parity
- Three physical address spaces: memory, I/O, and configuration
- Comprehensive support for autoconfiguration through a defined set of standard configuration functions

System partitioning shown in Figure 1-0 illustrates how the PCI can be used as a common interface between different portions of a system platform that are typically supplied by the chip set vendor. These portions are the Host/PCI Bridge (including a main memory DRAM controller and an optional L2 cache controller) and the PCI-EISA Bridge. Thus, the PCI allows a system I/O core design to be decoupled from the processor/memory treadmill, enabling the I/O core to provide maximum benefit over multiple generations of processor/memory technology. For this reason, the PCI-EISA Bridge can be used with different processors (i.e., derivatives of the Intel486 or the new generation of processors, such as the Pentium processor). Regardless of the new requirements imposed on the processor side of the Host/PCI Bridge (e.g., 64-bit data path, 3.3V interface, etc.) the PCI side remains unchanged which allows reusability not only of the rest of the platform chip set (i.e., PCI-EISA Bridge) but also of all other I/O functions interfaced at the PCI level. These functions typically include graphics, SCSI, and LAN.

EISA Bus

The EISA bus in the system shown in the Figure 1-0 represents a second level I/O bus. It allows personal computer platforms built around the PCI as a primary I/O bus to leverage the large EISA/ISA product base. Combinations of PCI and EISA buses, both of which can be used to provide expansion functions, will satisfy even the most demanding applications.

Along with compatibility with 16-bit and 8-bit ISA hardware and software, the EISA bus provides the following key features:

- 32-bit addressing and 32-bit data path
- 33 MByte/sec bus bandwidth
- Multiple bus master support through efficient arbitration
- Support for autoconfiguration

Integrated Bus Central Control Functions

The PCI-EISA Bridge chip set integrates central bus functions on both the PCI and EISA Buses. For the PCI Local Bus, the functions include PCI Local Bus arbitration and default bus driver. For the EISA Bus, central functions include the EISA Bus controller and EISA arbiter are integrated in the ESC component and EISA Data Swap Logic is integrated in the PCEB.

Integrated System Functions

The PCI-EISA Bridge chip set integrates system functions including PCI parity and system errors reporting, buffer coherency management protocol, PCI and EISA memory and I/O address space mapping and decoding. For maximum flexibility all of these functions are programmable allowing for variety of optional features.

1.1 PCEB Overview

The PCEB provides the interface (bridge) between PCI and EISA buses by translating bus protocols in both directions. It uses extensive buffering on both the PCI and EISA interfaces to allow concurrent bus operations. The PCEB also implements the PCI central support functions (e.g., PCI arbitration, error signal support, and subtractive decoding). The major functions provided by the PCEB are described in this section.

PCI Local Bus Interface

The PCEB can be either a master or slave on the PCI Local Bus and supports bus frequencies from 25 MHz to 33 MHz. For PCI-initiated transfers, the PCEB can only be a slave. The PCEB becomes a slave when it positively decodes the cycle. The PCEB also becomes a slave for unclaimed cycles on the PCI Local Bus. These unclaimed cycles are either negatively or subtractively decoded by the PCEB and forwarded to the EISA Bus.

As a slave, the PCEB supports single cycle transfers for memory, I/O, and configuration operations and burst cycles for memory operations. Note that, burst transfers cannot be performed to the PCEB's internal registers. Burst memory write cycles to the EISA Bus can transfer up to four Dwords, depending on available space in the PCEB's Posted Write Buffers. When space is no longer available in the buffers, the PCEB terminates the transaction. This supports the Incremental Latency Mechanism as defined in the Peripheral Component Interconnect (PCI) Specification. Note that, if the Posted Write Buffers are disabled, PCI burst operations are not performed and all transfers are single cycle.

For EISA-inititated transfers to the PCI Local Bus, the PCEB is a PCI master. The PCEB permits EISA devices to access either PCI memory or I/O. While all PCI I/O transfers are single cycle, PCI memory cycles can be either single cycle or burst, depending on the status of the PCEB's Line Buffers. During EISA reads of PCI memory, the PCEB uses a burst read cycle of four Dwords to prefetch data into a Line Buffer. During EISA-to-PCI memory writes, the PCEB uses PCI burst cycles to flush the Line Buffers. The PCEB contains a programmable Master Latency Timer that provides the PCEB with a guaranteed time slice on the PCI Local Bus, after which it surrenders the bus.

As a master on the PCI Local Bus, the PCEB generates address and command signal (C/BE#) parity for read and write cycles, and data parity for write cycles. As a slave, the PCEB generates data parity for read cycles. Parity checking is not supported.

The PCEB, as a resource, can be locked by any PCI master. In the context of locked cycles, the entire PCEB subsystem (including the EISA Bus) is considered a single resource.

PCI Local Bus Arbitration

The PCI arbiter supports six PCI masters—the Host/PCI bridge, PCEB, and four other PCI masters. The arbiter can be programmed for twelve fixed priority schemes, a rotating scheme, or a combination of the fixed and rotating schemes. The arbiter can be programmed for bus parking that permits the Host/PCI Bridge default access to the PCI Local Bus when no other device is requesting service. The arbiter also contains an efficient PCI retry mechanism to minimize PCI Local Bus thrashing when the PCEB generates a retry. The arbiter can be disabled, if an external arbiter is used.

EISA Bus Interface

The PCEB contains a fully EISA-compatible master and slave interface. The PCEB directly drives eight EISA slots without external data or address buffering. The PCEB is only a master or slave on the EISA Bus for transfers between the EISA Bus and PCI Local Bus. For transfers contained to the EISA Bus, the PCEB is never a master or slave. However, the data swap logic contained in the PCEB is involved in these transfers, if data size translation is needed. The PCEB also provide support for I/O recovery.

EISA/ISA masters and DMA can access PCI memory or I/O. The PCEB only forwards EISA cycles to the PCI Local Bus if the address of the transfer matches one of the address ranges programmed into the PCEB for EISA-to-PCI positive decode. This includes the main memory segments used for generating MEMCS# from the EISA Bus, one of the four programmable memory regions, or one of the four programmable I/O regions. For EISA-initiated accesses to the PCI Local Bus, the PCEB is a slave on the EISA Bus. I/O accesses are always non-buffered and memory accesses can be either non-buffered or buffered via the Line Buffers. For buffered accesses, burst cycles are supported.

During PCI-initiated cycles to the EISA Bus, the PCEB is an EISA master. For memory write operations through the Posted Write Buffers, the PCEB uses EISA burst transfers, if supported by the slave, to flush the buffers. Otherwise, single cycle transfers are used. Single cycle transfers are used for all I/O cycles and memory reads.

PCI/EISA Address Decoding

The PCEB contains two address decoders—one to decode PCI-initiated cycles and the other to decode EISA-initiated cycles. The two decoders permit the PCI and EISA Buses to operate concurrently.

The PCEB can also be programmed to provide main memory address decoding on behalf of the Host/PCI bridge. When programmed, the PCEB monitors the PCI and EISA bus cycle addresses, and generates a memory chip select signal (MEMCS#) indicating that the current cycle is targeted to main memory residing behind the Host/PCI bridge. Programmable features include, read/write attributes for specific memory segments and the enabling/disabling of a memory hole. If MEMCS# is not used, this feature can be disabled.

In addition to the main memory address decoding, there are four programmable memory regions and four programmable I/O regions for EISA-initiated cycles. EISA/ISA master or DMA accesses to one of these regions are forwarded to the PCI Local Bus.

Data Buffering

To isolate the slower EISA Bus from the PCI Local Bus, the PCEB provides two types of data buffers. Buffer management control guarantees data coherency.

Four Dword wide Posted Write Buffers permit posting of PCI-initiated memory write cycles to the EISA Bus. For EISA-initiated cycles to the PCI Bus, there are four 16-byte wide Line Buffers. These buffers permit prefetching of PCI memory read data and posting of PCI memory write data.

By using burst transactions to fill or flush these buffers, if appropriate, the PCEB maximizes bus efficiency. For example, an EISA device could fill a Line Buffer with byte, word, or Dword transfers and the PCEB would use a PCI burst cycle to flush the filled line to PCI memory.

BIOS Timer

The PCEB has a 16-bit BIOS Timer. The timer can be used by BIOS software to implement timing loops. The timer count rate is derived from the EISA clock (BCLK) and has an accuracy of ± 1 μs.

1.2 ESC Overview

The ESC implements system functions (e.g., timer/counter, DMA, and interrupt controller) and EISA subsystem control functions (e.g., EISA bus controller and EISA bus arbiter). The major functions provided by the ESC are described in this section.

EISA Controller

The ESC incorporates a 32-bit master and an 8-bit slave. The ESC directly drives eight EISA slots without external data or address buffering. EISA system clock (BCLK) generation is integrated by dividing the PCI clock (divide by 3 or divide by 4) and wait state generation is provided. The AENx and MACKx signals provide a direct interface to four EISA slots and supports eight EISA slots with encoded AENx and MACKx signals.

The ESC contains an 8-bit data bus (lower 8 bits of the EISA data bus) that is used to program the ESC's internal registers. Note that for transfers between the PCI and EISA Buses, the PCEB provides the data path. Thus, the ESC does not require a full 32-bit data bus. A full 32-bit address bus is provided and is used during refresh cycles and for DMA operations.

The ESC performs cycle translation between the EISA Bus and ISA Bus. For mis-matched master/slave combinations, the ESC controls the data swap logic that is located in the PCEB. This control is provided through the PCEB/ESC interface.

DMA Controller

The ESC incorporates the functionality of two 82C37 DMA controllers with seven independently programmable channels. Each channel can be programmed for 8-bit or 16-bit DMA device size, and ISA-compatible, type "A", type "B", or type "C" timings. Full 32-bit addressing is provided. The DMA controller is also responsible for generating refresh cycles.

The DMA controller supports an enhanced feature called scatter/gather. This feature provides the capability of transferring multiple buffers between memory and I/O without CPU intervention. In scatter/gather mode, the DMA can read the memory address and word count from an array of buffer descriptors, located in main memory, called the scatter/gather descriptor (SGD) table. This allows the DMA controller to sustain DMA transfers until all of the buffers in the SGD table are handled.

Interrupt Controller

The ESC contains an EISA compatible interrupt controller that incorporates the functionality of two 82C59 Interrupt Controllers. The two interrupt controllers are cascaded providing 14 external and two internal interrupts.

Timer/Counter

The ESC provides two 82C54 compatible timers (Timer 1 and Timer 2). The counters in Timer 1 support the system timer interrupt (IRQ0#), refresh request, and a speaker tone output (SPKR). The counters in Timer 2 support fail-safe timeout functions and the CPU speed control.

Integrated Support Logic

To minimize the chip count for board designs, the ESC incorporates a number of extended features. The ESC provides support for ALTA20 (Fast A20GATE) and ALTRST with I/O Port 92h. The ESC generates the control signals for SA address buffers and X-Bus buffer. The ESC also provides chip selects for BIOS, the keyboard controller, the floppy disk controller, and three general purpose devices. Support for generating chip selects with an external decoder is provided for IDE, a parallel port, and a serial port. The ESC provides support for a PC/AT compatible coprocessor interface and IRQ13 generation.

2.0 SIGNAL DESCRIPTION

This section provides a detailed description of each signal. The signals (Figure 2-1) are arranged in functional group according to their associated interface.

The "#" symbol at the end of a signal indicates that the active, or asserted state occurs when the signal is at a low voltage level. When "#" is not presented after the signal name, the signal is asserted when at the high voltage level.

The terms assertion and negation are used extensively. This is done to avoid confusion when working with a mixture of "active-low" and "active-high" signals. The term **assert**, or **assertion** indicates that a signal is active, independent of whether that level is represented by a high or low voltage. The term **negate**, or **negation** indicates that a signal is inactive.

The following notations are used to describe the signal type.

in Input is a standard input-only signal.

out Totem Pole Output is a standard active driver.

o/d Open Drain Input/Output.

t/s Tri-State is a bi-directional, tri-state input/output pin.

s/t/s Sustained Tri-State is an active low tri-state signal owned and driven by one and only one agent at a time. The agent that drives a s/t/s pin low must drive it high for at least one clock before letting it float. A new agent can not start driving a s/t/s signal any sooner than one clock after the previous owner tri-states it. A pull-up sustains the inactive state until another agent drives it and is provided by the central resource.

2.1 PCI Local Bus Interface Signals

Pin Name	Type	Description
PCICLK	in	**PCI CLOCK:** PCICLK provides timing for all transactions on the PCI Local Bus. The ESC uses the PCI Clock (PCICLK) to generate EISA Bus Clock (BCLK). The PCICLK is divided by 3 or 4 to generate the BCLK. The EISA Bridge supports PCI Clock frequencies of 25 MHz through 33 MHz.
PERR#	in	**PARITY ERROR:** PERR# indicates a data parity error. PERR# may be pulsed active by any agent that detects an error condition. Upon sampling PERR# active, the ESC generates an NMI interrupt to the CPU.
SERR#	in	**SYSTEM ERROR:** SERR# may be pulsed active by any agent that detects an error condition. Upon sampling SERR# active, the ESC generates an NMI interrupt to the CPU.
RESET#	in	**SYSTEM RESET:** RESET# forces the entire ESC chip into a known state. All internal ESC state machines are reset and all registers are set to their default values. RESET# may be asynchronous to PCICLK when asserted or negated. Although asynchronous, negation must be a clean, bounce-free edge. The ESC uses RESET to generate RSTDRV signal.

2.2 EISA Bus Interface Signals

Pin Name	Type	Description
BCLKOUT	out	**EISA BUS CLOCK OUTPUT:** BCLKOUT is typically buffered to create EISA Bus Clock (BCLK). The BCLK is the system clock used to synchronize events on the EISA/ISA bus. The BCLKOUT is generated by dividing the PCICLK. The ESC uses a divide by 3 or divide by 4 to generate the BCLKOUT.
BCLK	in	**EISA BUS CLOCK:** BCLK is an input to the ESC device. This ESC uses the BCLK to synchronize events on the EISA bus. The ESC generates or samples all the EISA/ISA bus signals on either the rising or the falling edge of BCLK.
LA[31:27]#/ CPG[4:0]	t/s	**EISA ADDRESS BUS/CONFIGURATION RAM PAGE ADDRESS:** These are multiplexed signals. These signals behave as the EISA address bus under all conditions except during access cycle to the Configuration RAM. **EISA ADDRESS BUS:** LA[31:27]# are directly connected to the EISA address bus. The ESC uses the address bus in conjunction with the BE[3:0]# signals as inputs to decode accesses to its internal resources except in DMA and Refresh modes. During DMA and Refresh modes, these are outputs, and the ESC uses these signals in conjunction with BE[3:0]# to drive Memory address. **CONFIGURATION RAM PAGE ADDRESS:** CPG[4:0] are connected to Configuration SRAM address lines. During I/O access to 0800h–08FFh, the ESC drives these signals with the configuration page address (the value contained in register 0C00h). The Configuration RAM Page Address function can be disabled by setting Mode Select register bit 5 = 0.
LA[26:24]# and LA[23:2]	t/s	**EISA ADDRESS BUS:** These signals are directly connected to the EISA address bus. The ESC uses the address bus in conjunction with the BE[3:0]# signals as inputs to decode accesses to its internal resources except in DMA and Refresh modes. During DMA and Refresh modes, these are outputs, and the ESC uses these signals in conjunction with BE[3:0]# to drive Memory address.
BE[3:0]#	t/s	**BYTE ENABLES:** BE[3:0]# signals are directly connected to the EISA address bus. These signals indicate which byte on the 32-bit EISA data bus are involved in the current cycle. BE[3:0]# are inputs during EISA master cycles which do not require assembly/disassembly operation. For EISA master assembly/ disassembly cycles, ISA master cycles, DMA, and Refresh cycles BE[3:0]# are outputs. BE0#: Corresponds to byte lane 0-SD[7:0] BE1#: Corresponds to byte lane 0-SD[15:8] BE2#: Corresponds to byte lane 0-SD[23:16] BE3#: Corresponds to byte lane 0-SD[31:24]
M/IO#	t/s	**MEMORY OR I/O CYCLE:** M/IO# signal is used to differentiate between memory cycles and I/O cycles on the EISA bus. A High value on this signal indicates a memory cycle, and a Low value indicates an I/O cycle. M/IO# is an input to the ESC during EISA master cycles, and M/IO# is an output during ISA, DMA, and ESC initiated Refresh cycles. M/IO# is floated during ISA master initiated Refresh cycles.
W/R#	t/s	**WRITE OR READ CYCLE:** W/R# signal is used to differentiate between write and read cycles on the EISA bus. A High value on this signal indicates a Write cycle, and a Low value indicates a Read cycle. W/R# is an input to the ESC during EISA master cycles, and W/R# is an output during ISA, DMA, and Refresh cycles.

2.2 EISA Bus Interface Signals (Continued)

Pin Name	Type	Description
EX32#	o/d	**EISA 32-BIT DEVICE DECODE:** EX32# signal is asserted by a 32-bit EISA slave device. EX32# assertion indicates that an EISA device has been selected as a slave, and the device has a 32-bit data bus size. The ESC uses this signal as an input as part of its slave decode to determine if data size translation and/or cycle translation is required. EX32# is an output of the ESC during the last portion of the mis-matched cycle. This is an indication to the backed-off EISA master that the data translation has been completed. The backed-off EISA master uses this signal to start driving the EISA bus again.
EX16#	o/d	**EISA 16-BIT DEVICE DECODE:** EX16# signal is asserted by a 16-bit EISA slave device. EX16# assertion indicates that an EISA device has been selected as a slave, and the device has a 16-bit data bus size. The ESC uses this signal as an input as part of its slave decode to determine if data size translation and/or cycle translation is required. EX16# is an output of the ESC during the last portion of the mis-matched cycle. This is an indication to the backed-off EISA master that the data translation has been completed. The backed-off EISA master uses this signal to start driving the EISA bus again.
START#	t/s	**START CYCLE:** START# signal provides timing control at the start of an EISA cycle. START# is asserted for one BCLK. START# is an input to the ESC during EISA master cycles except portions of the EISA master to mis-matched slave cycles where it becomes an output. During ISA, DMA, and Refresh cycles START# is an output.
CMD#	out	**COMMAND:** CMD# signal provides timing control within an EISA cycle. The ESC is a central resource of the CMD# signal, and the ESC generates CMD# during all EISA cycles. CMD# is asserted from the rising edge of BCLK simultaneously with the negation of START#, and remains asserted until the end of the cycle.
EXRDY	o/d	**EISA READY:** EXRDY signal is deasserted by EISA slave devices to add wait states to a cycle. EXRDY is an input to the ESC for EISA master cycles, ISA master cycles, and DMA cycles where an EISA slave has responded with EX32# or EX16# asserted. The ESC samples EXRDY on the falling edge of BCLK after CMD# is asserted (except during DMA compatible cycles). During DMA compatible cycles, EXRDY is sampled on the second falling edge of BCLK after CMD# is driven active. For all types of cycles if EXRDY is sampled inactive, the ESC keeps sampling it on every falling edge of BCLK#. EXRDY is an output for EISA master cycles decoded as accesses to the ESC internal registers. ESC forces EXRDY low for one BCLK at the start of a potential DMA burst write cycle to insure that the initial write data is held long enough to be sampled by the memory slave.
SLBURST#	in	**SLAVE BURST:** SLBURST# signal is asserted by an EISA slave to indicate that the device is capable of accepting EISA burst cycles. The ESC samples SLBURST# on the rising edge of BCLK at the end of START# for all EISA cycles. During DMA cycles, the ESC samples SLBURST# twice; once on the rising edge of BCLK at the beginning of START# and again on the rising edge of BCLK at the end of START#.
MSBURST#	t/s	**MASTER BURST:** MSBURST# signal is asserted by an EISA master to indicate EISA burst cycles. MSBURST# is asserted by an EISA master in response to an asserted SLBURST# signal. The ESC samples SLBURST# on the rising edge of BCLK that CMD# is asserted. If asserted, the ESC samples SLBURST# on all subsequent rising edges of BCLK until sampled negated. The ESC keeps CMD# asserted during Burst cycles. MSBURST# is an output during DMA burst cycles. The ESC drives MSBURST# active on the falling edge of BCLK, one half BCLK after SLBURST# is sampled active at the end of START#.

2.2 EISA Bus Interface Signals (Continued)

Pin Name	Type	Description
MASTER16#	in	**MASTER 16-BIT:** MASTER16# is asserted by a 16-bit EISA Bus master or an ISA Bus master device to indicate that it has control of the EISA Bus or ISA Bus. The ESC samples MASTER16# on the rising edge of BCLK that START# is asserted. If MASTER16# is sampled asserted, the ESC determines that a 16-bit EISA Bus master or an ISA Bus master owns the Bus. If MASTER16# is sampled negated at the first sampling point, the ESC will sample MASTER16# a second time on the rising edge of BCLK at the end of START#. If MASTER16# is sampled asserted here, the ESC determines that a 32-bit EISA Bus master has downshifted to a 16-bit Bus master, and thus, the ESC will disable the data size translation function.
SD[7:0]	t/s	**SYSTEM DATA:** SD[7:0] signals are directly connected to the System Data bus. The SD[7:0] pins are outputs during I/O reads when the ESC internal registers are being accessed and during interrupt acknowledge cycles. The SD[7:0] pins are input during I/O write cycles when the ESC internal registers are being accessed.

2.3 ISA Bus Signals

Pin Name	Type	Description
BALE	out	**BUS ADDRESS LATCH ENABLE:** BALE signal is asserted by the ESC to indicate that an address (SA[19:0], LA[23:17]), AEN and SBHE# signal lines are valid. The LA[23:17] address lines are latched on the trailing edge of BALE. BALE remains active throughout DMA and ISA Master cycles and Refresh cycles.
SA[1:0]	t/s	**ISA ADDRESS BITS 0 AND 1:** SA[1:0] are the least significant bits of the ISA address bus. SA[1:0] are inputs to the ESC during ISA master cycles except during ISA master initiated Refresh cycles. The ESC uses the SA[1:0] in conjunction with SBHE# to generate BE[3:0]# on the EISA bus. The SA[1:0] are outputs of the ESC during EISA master cycles and DMA cycles. The ESC generates these from BE[3:0]#.
SBHE#	t/s	**ISA BYTE HIGH ENABLE:** SBHE# signal indicates that the high byte on the ISA data bus (SD[15:8]) is valid. SBHE# is an input to the ESC during ISA master cycles, except during ISA master initiated Refresh cycles. The ESC uses the SBHE# in conjunction with SA[1:0] to generate BE[3:0]# on the EISA bus. SBHE# is an output during EISA master and DMA cycles.
M16#	o/d	**MEMORY CHIP SELECT 16:** M16# is an input when the ESC component owns the ISA bus. M16# is an output when an external ISA bus Master owns the ISA bus. The ISA slave memory drives this signal Low if it is a 16-bit memory device. For ISA to EISA translation cycles, the ESC combinatorially asserts M16# if either EX32# or EX16# are asserted. This signal has an external pull-up resistor.
IO16#	o/d	**16-BIT I/O CHIP SELECT:** IO16# signal is used to indicate a 16-bit I/O bus cycle. This signal is asserted by the I/O devices to indicate that they support 16-bit I/O bus cycles. All I/O accesses to the ESC registers are run as 8-bit I/O bus cycles. This signal has an external pull-up resistor.
MRDC#	t/s	**MEMORY READ:** MRDC# signal indicates a read cycle to the ISA memory devices. MRDC# is the command to a memory slave that it may drive data onto the ISA data bus. MRDC# is an output when the ESC owns the ISA bus. MRDC# is an input when an external ISA Bus master owns the ISA Bus. This signal is driven by the ESC during refresh cycles.

2.3 ISA Bus Signals (Continued)

Pin Name	Type	Description
MWTC#	t/s	**MEMORY WRITE:** MWTC# signal indicates a write cycle to the ISA memory devices. MWTC# is the command to a memory slave that it may latch data from the ISA data bus. MWTC# is an output when the ESC owns the ISA bus. MWTC# is an input when an ISA Bus master owns the ISA Bus.
SMRDC#	out	**SYSTEM MEMORY READ:** SMRDC# signal is asserted by the ESC to request a memory slave to drive data onto the data lines. SMRDC# indicates that the memory read cycle is for an address below the 1 Mbyte range on the ISA bus. This signal is also asserted during refresh cycles.
SMWTC#	out	**SYSTEM MEMORY WRITE:** SMWTC# signal is asserted by the ESC to request a memory slave to accept data from the data lines. SMWTC# indicates that the memory write cycle is for an address below the 1 Mbyte range.
IORC#	t/s	**I/O READ:** IORC# is the command to an ISA I/O slave device that it may drive data on to the data bus (SD[15:0]). The device must hold the data valid until after IORC# is negated. IORC# is an output when the ESC component owns the ISA bus. IORC# is an input when an ISA Bus master owns the ISA Bus.
IOWC#	t/s	**I/O WRITE:** IOWC# is the command to an ISA I/O slave device that it may latch data from the ISA data bus (SD[15:0]). IOWC# is an output when the ESC component owns the ISA Bus. IOWC# is an input when an ISA Bus master owns the ISA Bus.
CHRDY	o/d	**I/O CHANNEL READY:** CHRDY when asserted allows ISA Bus resources request additional time (wait states) to complete the cycle. CHRDY is an input when the ESC owns the ISA Bus. CHRDY is an input to the ESC during compatible DMA cycles. CHRDY is an output during ISA Bus master cycles to PCI slave or ESC internal register. The ESC will ignore CHRDY for ISA-Bus master accessing an ISA-Bus slave.
IOCHK#	in	**I/O CHANNEL CHECK:** IOCHK# can be asserted by any resource on the ISA Bus. When asserted, it indicates that a parity or an uncorrectable error has occurred for a device or memory on the ISA Bus. A NMI will be generated to the CPU if enabled.
NOWS#	o/d	**ZERO WAIT STATES:** NOWS# indicates that a peripheral device wishes to execute a zero wait state bus cycle (the normal default 16-bit ISA bus memory or I/O cycle is 3 BCLKS). When NOWS# is asserted, a 16-bit memory cycle will occur in two BCLKs and a 16-bit I/O cycle will occur in three BCLKs. When NOWS# is asserted by an 8-bit device the default 6 BCLKs cycle is shortened to 4 or 5 BCLKs. NOWS# is an input when the ESC is performing bus translation cycles. NOWS# is an output when the ESC internal registers are accessed. If CHRDY and NOWS# are both asserted during the same clock then NOWS# will be ignored and wait states will be added as a function of CHRDY (CHRDY has precedence over NOWS#).
OSC	in	**OSCILLIATOR:** OSC is the 14.31818 MHz signal with 50% duty cycle. OSC is used by the ESC timers.
RSTDRV	out	**RESET DRIVE:** RSTDRV is asserted by the ESC. An asserted RSTDRV causes a hardware reset of the devices on the ISA Bus. RSTDRV is asserted whenever the RESET# input to the ESC is asserted.

2.3 ISA Bus Signals (Continued)

Pin Name	Type	Description
REFRESH#	t/s	**REFRESH:** REFRESH# is used by the ESC as an output to indicate when a refresh cycle is in progress. It should be used to enable the SA[15:0] address to the row address inputs of all banks of dynamic memory on the ISA bus so that when MRDC# goes active, the entire expansion bus dynamic memory is refreshed. Memory slaves must not drive any data onto the bus during refresh and should not add wait states since this will affect the entire system throughput. As an output, this signal is driven directly onto the ISA bus. This signal is an output only when the ESC DMA Refresh is a master on the bus responding to an internally generated request for Refresh. Upon RESET this pin will tri-state. Note that address lines [15:8] are driven during refresh, but the value is meaningless and is not used to refresh ISA bus memory. REFRESH# may be asserted by an expansion bus adapter acting as a 16-bit ISA bus master.
AEN#	out	**ADDRESS ENABLE:** AEN# is driven high for Bus master cycles. AEN# is driven low for DMA cycles and Refresh cycles. AEN# is used to disable I/O devices from responding to DMA and Refresh cycles. System designs which do not use the slots specific AENs (AEN[4:1]/EAEN[4:1]) provided by the ESC can use the AEN# signal to generate their own slot specific AENs.
AEN[4:1]/ EAEN[4:1]	out	These pins have a slightly different function depending on the ESC configuration (Mode Select register bit 1 and bit 0). **SLOT SPECIFIC ADDRESS ENABLE:** If the ESC is programmed to support 4 EISA slots, these signals function as Slot Specific Address Enables (AEN[4:1]). **ENCODED SLOT SPECIFIC ADDRESS ENABLE:** If the ESC has been programmed to support more than 4 EISA slots, then these signals behave as Encoded Address Enables (EAEN[4:1]). A discrete decoder is required to generate slot specific AENs. Refer to Section 5.8.1 AEN GENERATION for a detailed description of these signals.

2.4 DMA Signal Description

Pin Name	Type	Description
DREQ[7:5,3:0]	in	**DMA REQUEST:** DREQ signals are either used to request DMA service from the ESC or used to gain control of the ISA Bus by a ISA Bus master. The active level (high or low) is programmed in the Command registers. When the Command register Bit 6 is programmed to 0, DREQ are asserted high, otherwise the DREQ are asserted low. All inactive to active edges of DREQ are assumed to be asynchronous. The request must remain asserted until the appropriate DACK is negated. At power-up and after RESET, these lines should be low (negated).
DACK#[7:5,3:0]	out	**DMA ACKNOWLEDGE:** DACK# indicates that a request for DMA service from the DMA subsystem has been recognized or that an ISA Bus master has been granted the bus. The level of the DACK lines when asserted may be programmed to be either high or low. This is accomplished by programming the DMA Command register. These lines should be used to decode the DMA slave device with the IORC# or IOWC# line to indicate selection. If used to signal acceptance of a bus master request, this signal indicates when it is legal to assert MASTER16#. If the DMA controller has been programmed for a timing mode other than compatible mode, and another device has requested the bus, and a 4 μs time has elapsed, DACK# will be negated and the transfer stopped before the transfer is complete. In this case, the transfer will be restarted at the next arbitration period in which the channel wins the bus. Upon reset these lines are negated.
EOP	t/s	**END OF PROCESS:** EOP pin acts in one of two modes, and it is directly connected to the TC line of the ISA Bus. In the first mode, EOP-In, the pin is an input and can be used by a DMA slave to stop a DMA transfer. In the second mode, TC-Out, it is used as a terminal count output by DMA slaves. An active pulse is generated when the byte counter reaches its last value. **EOP-IN MODE:** During DMA, for all transfer types, the EOP pin is sampled by the ESC. If it is sampled asserted, the address bus is tri-stated and the transfer is terminated. **TC-OUT MODE:** The EOP output will be asserted after a new address has been output if the byte count expires with that transfer. The EOP (TC) will stay asserted until AEN# is negated unless AEN is negated during an autoinitialization. EOP (TC) will be negated before AEN is negated during an autoinitialization. **INTOUT MODE:** In this mode the EOP signal has the same behavior as the Chaining Interrupt or the Scatter-Gather interrupt to the host processor (IRQ13). If a scatter-gather or chaining buffer is expired, EOP will go active on the falling edge of BCLK. Only the currently active channel's interrupt will be reflected on this pin. Other channel's with active interrupts pending will not affect the EOP pin. Whenever all the DMA channels are not in use, the EOP pin is kept in output mode and negated. After reset, the EOP pin is kept in output mode and negated.

2.5 EISA Arbitration Signals

<table>
<tr><th>Pin Name</th><th>Type</th><th>Description</th></tr>
<tr><td>MREQ[3:0]#</td><td>in</td><td>MASTER REQUEST: MREQ[3:0]# are slot specific signals used by EISA bus masters to request bus access. MREQ# once asserted, must remain asserted until the corresponding MACK# is asserted. The MREQ# is negated on the falling edge of BCLK slightly before the end of a master transfer. The LA[ ], BE[ ]#, M/IO#, and W/R# lines should be floated on or before the rising edge of BCLK after MREQ# is negated. The end of the last bus cycle is derived from CMD# in this case. The MREQ# signals are asserted on the falling edge of BCLK. MREQ# is always sampled on the rising edge of BCLK. MREQ# is synchronous with respect to BCLK. After asserting MREQ#, the corresponding master must not assert MREQ# until 1.5 BCLKs after CMD# is negated.</td></tr>
<tr><td>MREQ[7:4]#/
PIRQ[0:3]#</td><td>in</td><td>These pins behave in one of two modes depending on the state of the Mode Select register bit 1 and bit 0.

MASTER REQUEST: MREQ# lines are slot specific signals used by EISA bus masters to request bus access. This signal behaves in the same manner as MREQ[3:0]# signals.

PCI INTERRUPT REQUEST: PIRQ# are used to generate asynchronous interrupts to the CPU via the Programmable Interrupt Controller (82C59) integrated in the ESC. These signals are defined as level sensitive and are asserted low. The PIRQx# can be shared with PC compatible interrupts IRQ3:IRQ7, IRQ9:IRQ15. The PIRQx# Route Control Register determines which PCI interrupt is shared with which PC compatible interrupt.
<table>
<tr><th rowspan="2">Register Bit[1:0]</th><th colspan="4">Pins</th></tr>
<tr><th>MREQ7#/ PIRQ0#</th><th>MREQ6#/ PIRQ1#</th><th>MREQ5#/ PIRQ2#</th><th>MREQ4#/ PIRQ3#</th></tr>
<tr><td>00</td><td>PIRQ0#</td><td>PIRQ1#</td><td>PIRQ2#</td><td>PIRQ3#</td></tr>
<tr><td>01</td><td>PIRQ0#</td><td>PIRQ1#</td><td>MREQ5#</td><td>MREQ4#</td></tr>
<tr><td>10</td><td>PIRQ0#</td><td>MREQ6#</td><td>MREQ5#</td><td>MREQ4#</td></tr>
<tr><td>11</td><td>MREQ7#</td><td>MREQ6#</td><td>MREQ5#</td><td>MREQ4#</td></tr>
</table></td></tr>
<tr><td>MACK[3:0]#/
EMACK[3:0]</td><td>out</td><td>These pins behave in one of two modes depending on the state of the Mode Select register bit 1 and bit 0. If the ESC is programmed to support 4 EISA slots, then these pins are used as MACK#. If the ESC is programmed to support more than 4 EISA slots, then these pins are used as EMACK#

MASTER ACKNOWLEDGE: The MACK[3:0]# signals are asserted from the rising edge of BCLK at which time the bus master may begin driving the LA[ ], BE[ ]#, M/IO#, and W/R# lines on the next falling edge of BCLK. MACK# will stay asserted until the rising edge of BCLK when MREQ# is sampled negated. MACK# is sampled by EISA Bus masters on the falling edge of BCLK. If another device has requested the bus, MACK# will be negated before MREQ# is negated. When MACK# is negated, the granted device has a maximum of 8 μs to negate MREQ# and begin a final bus cycle. The ESC may negate the MACK# signal a minimum of one BCLK after asserting it if another device (or refresh) is requesting the bus. Upon reset MACK# is negated.

ENCODED MASTER ACKNOWLEDGE: EMACK# behaves like MACK#. The difference is that a discrete decoder is required to generate MACK# for the EISA Bus masters.

Refer to Section 5.8.2 MACK Generation for details.</td></tr>
</table>

2.6 Timer Unit Signal

Pin Name	Type	Description
SPKR	out	**SPEAKER DRIVE:** SPKR is the output of Timer 1, Counter 2 and is "ANDed" with Port 061h Bit 1 to provide Speaker Data Enable. This signal drives an external speaker driver device, which in turn drives the ISA system speaker. SPKR has a 24 mA drive capability. Upon reset, its output state is 0.
SLOWH#	out	**SLOW DOWN CPU:** SLOWH# is the output of Timer 2, Counter 2. This counter is used to slow down the main CPU of its execution via the CPU's HOLD pin by pulse width modulation. The first read of I/O register in the 048h-04Bh range will enable SLOWH# signal to follow the output of the Timer 2, Counter 2. Upon reset, SLOWH# is negated. This signal requires an external pull-up resistor (8 KΩ–10 KΩ).

2.7 Interrupt Controller Signals

Pin Name	Type	Description
IRQ[15:9], IRQ8#, IRQ[7:3,1]	in	**INTERRUPT REQUEST:** IRQ These signals provide both system board components and EISA bus I/O devices with a mechanism for asynchronously interrupting the CPU. The assertion mode of each interrupt can be programmed to be edge or level triggered. An asserted IRQ input must remain asserted until after the falling edge of INTA#. If the input is negated before this time, a DEFAULT IRQ7 will occur when the CPU acknowledges the interrupt. (Refer to Section 9.12.7.)
INT	out	**CPU INTERRUPT:** INT is driven by the ESC to signal the CPU that an Interrupt request is pending and needs to be serviced. It is asynchronous with respect to BCLK or PCICLK and it is always an output. The interrupt controllers must be programmed following a reset to ensure that this pin takes on a known state. Upon reset the state of this pin is undefined.
NMI	out	**NON-MASKABLE INTERRUPT:** NMI is used to force a non-maskable interrupt to the CPU. The CPU registers an NMI when it detects a rising edge on NMI. NMI will remain active until a read from the CPU to the NMI register at port 061h is detected by the ESC. This signal is set to low upon reset.

2.8 ESC/PCEB Interface Signals

2.8.1 ARBITRATION AND INTERRUPT ACKNOWLEDGE CONTROL

Pin Name	Type	Description
EISAHOLD	out	**EISA HOLD:** EISAHOLD is used to request control of the EISA bus from its default owner, PCEB. This signal is synchronous to PCICLK and is asserted when RESET# is asserted.
EISAHLDA	in	**EISA HOLD ACKNOWLEDGE:** EISAHLDA is used by the PCEB to inform the ESC that it has been granted ownership of EISA bus. This signal is synchronous to PCICLK.
PEREQ#/ INTA#	in	**PCI TO EISA REQUEST OR INTERRUPT ACKNOWLEDGE:** PEREQ#/INTA# is a dual function signal. The context of the signal pin is determined by the state of EISAHLDA signal. When EISAHLDA is deasserted (0) this signal has the context of Interrupt Acknowledge i.e., if PEREQ#/INTA# is asserted it indicates to the ESC that current cycle on the EISA is an interrupt acknowledge. When EISAHLDA is asserted (1) this signal has the context of PCI-to-EISA Request i.e., if PEREQ#/INTA# is asserted it indicates to the ESC that PCEB needs to obtain the ownership of the EISA bus on behalf of a PCI agent. This signal is synchronous to the PCICLK and it is driven inactive when PCIRST is asserted.

2.8.2 PCEB BUFFER COHERENCY CONTROL

Pin Name	Type	Description
NMFLUSH#	t/s	**NEW MASTER FLUSH:** NMFLUSH# is a bi-directional signal which is used to provide handshake between PCEB and ESC to control flushing of system buffers on behalf of EISA masters. During an EISA bus ownership change, before ESC can grant the bus to the EISA master (or DMA) it must ensure that system buffers are flushed and buffers pointing (potentially) towards EISA subsystem are disabled. The ESC asserts NMFLUSH# signal for one PCI clock indicating the request for system buffer flushing. (After driving NMFLUSH# asserted for 1 PCI clock the ESC tri-states NMFLUSH# signal.) When PCEB samples NMFLUSH# asserted it starts immediately to drive NMFLUSH# asserted and initiates internal and external requests for buffer flushing. After all buffers have been flushed (indicated by the proper handshake signals) the PCEB negates NMFLUSH# for 1 PCI clock and stops driving it. When ESC samples signal deasserted that indicates that all system buffers are flushed, it grants EISA bus to an EISA master (or DMA). The ESC resumes responsibility of default NMFLUSH# driver and starts driving NMFLUSH# deasserted until the next time a new EISA master (or DMA) wins arbitration. This signal is synchronous with PCICLK and will be driven negated by the ESC at reset.
INTCHIP0	t/s	**INTER CHIP 0:** INTCHIP0 is a reserved signal. The INTCHIP0 output of the ESC should be connected to the INTCHIP0 input of the PCEB for proper device operation.

2.8.3 DATA SWAP BUFFER CONTROL

Pin Name	Type	Description
SDCPYEN01# SDCPYEN02# SDCPYEN03# SDCPYEN13#	out	**COPY ENABLE:** These active low signals perform byte copy operation on the EISA data bus (SD). These signal are active during mis-matched cycle, and they are used by the PCEB to enable byte copy operation between SD data byte lanes 0, 1, 2, and 3 as follows: SDCPYEN01# Copy between Byte Lane 0(SD[7:0]) and Byte Lane 1(SD[15:8]) SDCPYEN02# Copy between Byte Lane 0(SD[7:0]) and Byte Lane 2(SD[23:16]) SDCPYEN03# Copy between Byte Lane 0(SD[7:0]) and Byte Lane 3(SD[31:24]) SDCPYEN13# Copy between Byte Lane 1(SD[15:8]) and Byte Lane 3(SD[31:24])
SDCPYUP	out	**SYSTEM (DATA) COPY UP:** SDCPYUP is used to control the direction of the byte copy operation. A High on the signal indicates a COPY UP operation where the lower byte lower word of the SD data bus is copied on to the higher byte or higher word of the bus. A Low on the signal indicates a COPY DOWN operation where the higher byte(s) of the data bus are copied on to the lower byte(s) of the bus. The PCEB uses the signal to perform the actual data byte copy operation during mis-matched cycles.
SDOE[2:0]#	out	**SYSTEM DATA OUTPUT ENABLES:** SDOE# enables the SD data output of the PCEB Data Swap Buffers on to EISA bus. The ESC activates these signals only during mis-matched cycles. The PCEB uses these signals to enable the SD data buffers as follows: SDOE0# Enables byte lane 0 SD[7:0] SDOE1# Enables byte lane 1 SD[15:8] SDOE2# Enables byte lane 2 SD[23:16] and byte lane 3 SD[31:24]
SDLE[3:0]#	out	**SYSTEM DATA LATCH ENABLES:** SDLE[3:0]# enable the latching of EISA data bus. These signals are activated only during mis-matched cycles except PCEB initiated write cycle. The PCEB uses these signals to latch the SD data bus as follows: SDLE0# Latch byte lane 0 SD[7:0] SDLE1# Latch byte lane 0 SD[15:8] SDLE2# Latch byte lane 0 SD[23:16] SDLE3# Latch byte lane 0 SD[31:24]

1

2.9 Integrated Logic Signals

2.9.1 EISA ADDRESS BUFFER CONTROL

Pin Name	Type	Description
SALE#	out	**SA LATCH ENABLE:** SALE# is directly connected to F543s which buffer the LA addresses from the SA addresses. The rising edge of SALE# latches the LA address Bit LA[19:2] to the SA address Bit SA[19:2].
LASAOE#	out	**LA TO SA ADDRESS OUTPUT ENABLE:** LASAOE# is directly connected to the SA output buffer enables of the F543s. The ESC asserts LASAOE# during EISA master cycles. When LASAOE# is asserted, the LA to SA output buffers of the F543s are enabled.
SALAOE#	out	**SA TO LA ADDRESS OUTPUT ENABLE:** SALAOE# is connected to the LA output buffer enables of the F543s. This signal functionally is the exact opposite of LASAOE# signals. The ESC asserts SALAOE# during ISA master cycles. When LASAOE# is asserted, the SA to LA output buffers of the F543s are enabled.

2.9.2 COPROCESSOR INTERFACE

Pin Name	Type	Description
FERR#	in	**NUMERIC CO-PROCESSOR ERROR:** FERR# signal is tied to the Co-processor error signal of the CPU. If FERR# is asserted (Co-processor error detected by the CPU), an internal IRQ13 is be generated and the INT from the ESC will be asserted.
IGNNE#	out	**IGNORE ERROR:** IGNNE# is tied to the ignore numeric error pin of the CPU. IGNNE# is asserted and internal IRQ13 is negated from the falling edge of IOWC# during an I/O write to location 00F0h. IGNNE# will remain asserted until FERR# is negated. Upon reset, this signal is driven negated (high).

2.9.3 BIOS INTERFACE

Pin Name	Type	Description
LBIOSCS#	out	**LATCHED BIOS CHIP-SELECT:** LBIOSCS# indicates that the current address is for the system BIOS. The ESC generates this signal by decoding the EISA LA addresses. The ESC uses a transparent latch to latch the decoded signal. The LBIOSCS# is latched on the falling edge of BALE and qualified with REFRESH#.

2.9.4 KEYBOARD CONTROLLER INTERFACE

Pin Name	Type	Description
KYBDCS#	out	**KEYBOARD CHIP SELECT:** KYBDCS# is connected to the chip select of the 82C42. KYBDCS# is active for I/O addresses 0060h–0064h.
ALTRST#	out	**ALTERNATE RESET:** ALTRST# is used to reset the CPU under program control. This signal is AND'ed together externally with the reset signal (RSTAR#) from the keyboard controller to provide a software means of resetting the CPU. This provides a faster means of reset than is provided by the Keyboard controller. Writing a 1 to Bit 0 in the Port 92 register will cause this signal to pulse active (low) for approximately 4 BCLK's. Before another ALTRST# pulse can be generated, Bit 0 must be written back to a 0. Upon RESET, this signal is driven high (Bit 2 in the Port 92 register is reset low).
ALTA20	out	**ALTERNATE A20:** ALTA20 is used to force A20M# to the CPU low for support of real mode compatible software. This signal is externally OR'ed with the ALTA20 signal from the Keyboard controller and CPURST to control the A20M# input of the CPU. Writing a "0" to Bit 1 of Port 92h register will force ALTA20 inactive (low). This in turn will drive A20M# to the CPU low, if A20GATE from the keyboard controller is also low. Writing a "1" to Bit 1 of the Port 92h register will force ALTA20 active (high), which in turn will drive A20M# to the CPU high, regardless of the state of ALTA20 from the keyboard controller. Upon reset, this signal is driven low.
ABFULL	in	**AUXILIARY BUFFER FULL:** ABFULL is tied directly to the ABFULL signal on the keyboard controller on the system board. This signal indicates that the keyboard controller auxiliary buffer for the mouse interface is full. If the Mouse Interrupt Function bit (offset 4Dh bit 4) is enabled, then the ABFULL signal is connected to the internal IRQ12 (IRQ12 is also available for external use). On a low to high transition on ABFULL the internal IRQ12 is asserted (the internal IRQ12 transitions from low to high if the IRQ12 in the Interrupt controller is programmed for edge triggered mode, the internal IRQ12 is asserted low if the IRQ12 in the interrupt controller is programmed for level triggered mode. A low to high transition on ABFULL will be latched by the ESC. This high level will remain latched internally until an I/O read to port 60h (falling edge of IORC#) or reset (RESET#) has been detected. If this function is not used, ABFULL should be tied low through a 1k resistor.

2.9.5 REAL TIME CLOCK INTERFACE

Pin Name	Type	Description
RTCALE	out	**REAL TIME CLOCK ADDRESS LATCH ENABLE:** RTCALE is directly connected to the system Real Time Clock. The RTC uses this signal to latch the appropriate memory address. A write to port 070h with the appropriate Real Time Clock memory address that will be written to or read from will cause RTCALE to go active.
RTCRD# /PIRQ3#	t/s	**REAL TIME CLOCK READ COMMAND/PCI INTERRUPT REQUEST 3:** When functioning as RTCRD#, this signal is asserted for I/O reads from address 0071h. If the Power On Password protection is enabled (I/O Port 92h bit 3 = 1), then for accesses to RTC addresses 36h-3Fh (Port 70h) RTCRD# will not be asserted. See Section 3.1.3, Mode Select Register Description, for details on alternative function of this signal. **NOTE:** External pull-up resistor (10 KΩ–20 KΩ) must be added to this signal to support alternative function i.e., PIRQ3#.
RTCWR# /PIRQ2#	t/s	**REAL TIME CLOCK WRITE COMMAND/PCI INTERRUPT REQUEST 2:** When functioning as RTCWR#, this signal is also asserted for I/O writes to address 0071h. If the Power On Password protection is enabled (I/O Port 92h bit 3 = 1), then for accesses to RTC addresses 36h–3Fh (Port 70h), RTCWR# will not be generated. See Section 3.1.3, Mode Select Register Description, for details on alternative function of this signal. **NOTE:** External pull-up resistor (10 KΩ–20 KΩ) must be added to this signal to support alternative function, i.e., PIRQ2#.

2.9.6 FLOPPY DISK CONTROLLER INTERFACE

<table>
<tr><th>Pin Name</th><th>Type</th><th>Description</th></tr>
<tr><td>FDCCS#
/PIRQ1#</td><td>t/s</td><td>FLOPPY DISK CONTROLLER CHIP SELECT/PCI INTERRUPT REQUEST 1: This signal pin has a dual function. As FDCCS#, it is an active low output signal asserted for I/O decode of the floppy disk I/O register space. When functioning as FDCCS#, this signal is also asserted whenever IDECS1# is decoded.

See Section 3.1.3, Mode Select Register Description, for details on alternative function of this signal.

NOTE:
External pull-up resistor (10 KΩ–20 KΩ) must be added to this signal to support alternative function i.e., PIRQ1#.</td></tr>
<tr><td>DSKCHG</td><td>in</td><td>DISK CHANGE: DSKCHG signal is tied directly to the DSKCHG signal of the floppy controller. This signal is inverted and driven onto system data line 7 (SD7) during I/O read cycles to floppy address locations 3F7h (primary) or 377h (secondary) as indicated by the table below.

NOTE:
The primary and secondary locations are programmed in the X-Bus Address Decode Enable/Disable Register "A".

<table>
<tr><th>FDCCS#</th><th>IDECSx#</th><th>State of SD7 (output)</th><th>State of XBUSOE#</th></tr>
<tr><td>Decode</td><td>Decode</td><td></td><td></td></tr>
<tr><td>Enabled</td><td>Enabled</td><td>Tri-stated</td><td>Enabled</td></tr>
<tr><td>Enabled</td><td>Disabled</td><td>Driven via DSKCHG</td><td>Disabled</td></tr>
<tr><td>Disabled</td><td>Enabled</td><td>Tri-stated</td><td>Disabled (note)</td></tr>
<tr><td>Disabled</td><td>Disabled</td><td>Tri-stated</td><td>Disabled</td></tr>
</table>

NOTE:
This mode is not supported because of potential contention between the X-Bus buffer and a floppy on the ISA bus driving the system bus at the same time during shared I/O accesses.

This signal is also used to determine if the floppy controller is present on the X-Bus. It is sampled on the trailing edge of RESET, and if high, the floppy is present. For systems that do not support a floppy via the ESC, this pin should strapped low. If sampled low, the SD7 function, and XBUSOE# will not be enabled for accesses to the floppy disk controller.</td></tr>
<tr><td>DLIGHT#
/PIRQ0#</td><td>t/s</td><td>FIXED DISK ACTIVITY LIGHT/PCI INTERRUPT REQUEST 0: This signal pin has a dual function. As DLIGHT#, it is used to control the fixed disk X light. When low, the light is on. When high, the light is off. If either Bit 6 or Bit 7 of the Port 92 register is set to a 1 (Bit 6 and 7 are internally NOR'ed together), DLIGHT# is driven active (low). Setting both Bits 6 and 7 low will cause DLIGHT# to be driven high.

See Section 3.1.3., Mode Select Register Description, for details on alternative function of this signal.

NOTE:
An external pull-up resistor (10 KΩ–20 KΩ) must be added to this signal to support alternative function, i.e., PIRQ0#.</td></tr>
</table>

2.9.7 CONFIGURATION RAM INTERFACE

Pin Name	Type	Description
CRAMRD#	out	**CONFIGURATION RAM READ COMMAND:** CRAMRD# is connected directly to the system Configuration RAM. The ESC asserts CRAMRD# for I/O reads from the address range programmed into the low and high bytes of the configuration RAM command registers.
CRAMWR#	out	**CONFIGURATION RAM WRITE COMMAND:** This is an active Low output. CRAMWR# is connected directly to the system Configuration RAM. The ESC activates CRAMWR# for I/O writes to the address range programmed into the low and high bytes of the configuration RAM command registers.

2.9.8 X-BUS CONTROL AND GENERAL PURPOSE DECODE

Pin Name	Type	Description
XBUSTR#	out	**X-BUS DATA TRANSMIT/RECEIVE:** This signal is tied directly to the direction control of a 74F245 that buffers the X-Bus data, XD[7:0], from the system data bus, SD[7:0]. XBUST/R# is driven high (transmit) during I/O and memory read cycles for EISA and ISA masters. For DMA cycles (channel 2 only), XBUST/R# is driven high for the following cases: 1. Memory Read, I/O Write cycles where LBIOSCS# is asserted. 2. I/O Read, Memory Write cycles where Digital Output Register bit 3 is set to "1". XBUST/R# is driven low (receive) under all other conditions.
XBUSOE#	out	**X-BUS DATA OUTPUT ENABLE:** This signal is tied directly to the output enable of a 74F245 that buffers the X-Bus data, XD[7:0], from the system data bus, SD[7:0]. For EISA and ISA master memory read or write cycles, XBUSOE# is asserted when LBIOSCS# is asserted. Otherwise, XBUSOE# is not asserted. For EISA and ISA master I/O read or write cycles, XBUSOE# is asserted if an ESC supported X-Bus device has been decoded, and the decoding for that device has been enabled via the proper configuration registers. An exception to this is during an I/O read access to floppy location 3F7h (primary) or 377h (secondary) if the IDE decode space is disabled (i.e., IDE is not present on the X-Bus). In this case, XBUSOE# will not be asserted. XBUSOE# will also not be asserted during an I/O access to the floppy controller if DSKCHG is sampled low at reset. XBUSOE# is not asserted during DMA cycles, except for channel 2 DMA. For channel 2 DMA, XBUSOE# is asserted unless the Digital Output Register bit 3 is cleared (set to "0") and LBIOSCS# is not asserted.
GPCS[2:0]# / ECS[2:0]	out	These are dual function signals. The function of these pins is selected through the Mode Select Register bit 4. **GENERAL PURPOSE CHIP SELECT:** GPCS[2:0]# are Chip Selects for peripheral devices. The peripheral devices can be mapped in the I/O range by programming the General Purpose Chip Select Base Address registers and General Purpose Mask registers (offset 64h–6Eh). **ENCODED CHIP SELECT:** ECS[2:0] provide encoded chip select decoding for serial ports, parallel port, IDE and general purpose devices. The device chip selects for the peripheral devices are generated by using a F138 with ECS[2:0] as inputs. Refer to Section 11.9 for details.

2.10 Testing

Pin Name	Type	Description
TEST#	in	**TEST:** TEST# is used to tristate all of the outputs. During normal operation this pin should be tied to ground.

NOTE:
All pins designated as NC (No Connect) require individual pull-up resistors (8K–10 KΩ).

3.0 ESC REGISTER DESCRIPTION

The ESC contains ESC configuration registers, DMA registers, Timer Unit registers, Interrupt Unit registers, and EISA configuration registers. All of the registers are accessable from the EISA bus. During a reset the ESC sets its internal registers to predetermined default states. The default values are indicated in the individual register descriptions.

3.1 ESC Configuration Registers

ESC configuration registers are accessed through an indexing scheme. The index address register is located at I/O address 0022h, and the index data register is located at I/O address 0023h. The offset (data) written into the index address register selects the desired configuration register. Data for the selected configuration register can be read from or written to by performing a read or a write to the index data register. See Table 4-3 for a summary of configuration register index addresses.

3.1.1 ESCID—ESC ID REGISTER

Register Name: ESC ID
Register Location: 02h
Default Value: 00h
Attribute: Read/Write
Size: 8 bits

Since the ESC configuration registers are accessed by the index addressing mechanism using I/O Ports 22h, and 23h, it is possible that another device in the system might use the same approach for configuration. In order to avoid contention with similar index register devices, the ID register must be written with 0Fh. The ESC will not respond to accesses to any other configuration register until the ID byte has been written in the ESC ID Register.

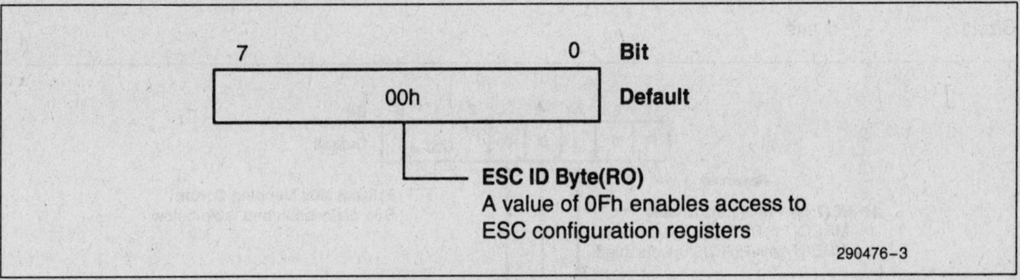

Figure 3-1. ESC ID Register

Table 3-1. ESC ID Register

Bit #	Description
7:0	**ESC ID BYTE:** These bits must be written to a value of 0Fh before the ESC will respond to any other configuration register access. After a reset has occurred all of the configuration registers, except this register, are disabled.

3.1.2 RID—REVISION ID REGISTER

Register Name: Revision ID
Register Offset: 08h
Default Value: Revision Identification Number
Attribute: Read only
Size: 8 bits

This 8-bit register contains device stepping information. Writes to this register have no effect.

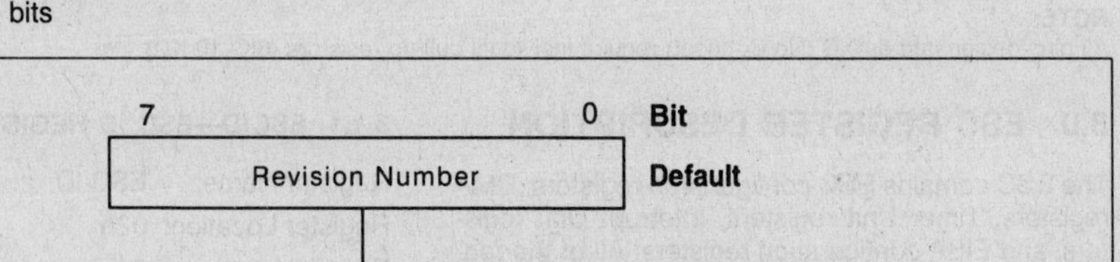

Figure 3-2. Revision ID Register

Table 3-2. Revision ID Register

Bit #	Description
7:0	**REVISION ID BYTE:** These bits contain the stepping information about the device. The register is hardwired during manufacturing. The register is read only. Writes have no affect on the register value.

3.1.3 MS—MODE SELECT REGISTER

Register Name: Mode Select
Register Location: 40h
Default Value: 20h
Attribute: Read/Write
Size: 8 bits

This register selects the various functional modes of the ESC.

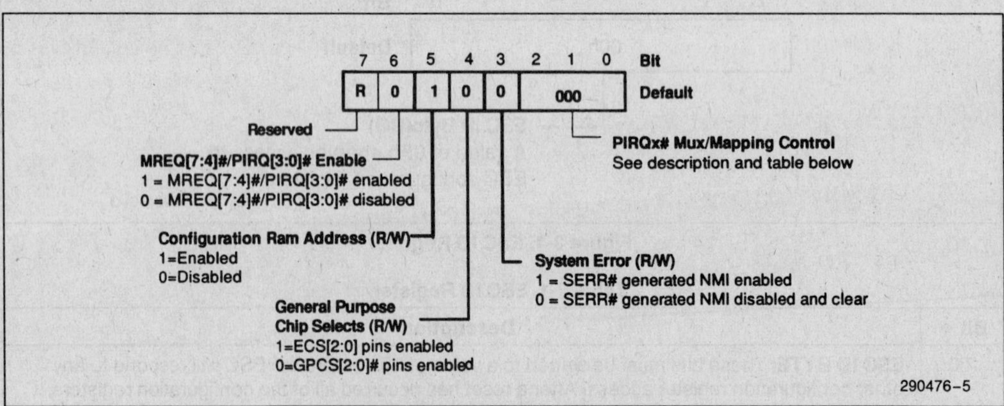

Figure 3-3. Mode Select Register

Table 3-3. Mode Select Register

Bit #	Description
7	**RESERVED.**
6	**MREQ[7:4]#/PIRQ[3:0]# ENABLE:** This bit is used to enable the selected MREQ[7:4]#/PIRQ[3:0]# functionality. The default value for this bit is 0.
5	**CONFIGURATION RAM ADDRESS:** This bit is used to enable or disable the Configuration RAM Page Address (CPG[4:0]) generation. If this bit is set to 1, accesses to the Configuration RAM space will generate the RAM page address on the LA[31:27]# pins. If this bit is set to 0, the CPG[4:0] signals will not be activated. The default for this bit is "1".
4	**GENERAL PURPOSE CHIP SELECTS:** This bit is used to select the functionality of the GPCS[2:0]#/ECS[2:0] pins. If the bit is set to 0, the GPCS[2:0]# functionality is selected. If the bit is set to 1, the ESC[2:0] functionality is selected.
3	**SYSTEM ERROR:** This bit is used to disable or enable the generation of NMI based on SERR# signal pulsing active.
2:0	**PIRQx# MUX/MAPPING CONTROL:** These bits select muxing/mapping of PIRQ[3:0]# with MREQ[7:4]# and group of X-Bus signals (DLIGHT#, FDCCS#, RTCWR#, RTCRD#). Different bit combinations select the number of EISA slots or group of X-Bus signals which can be supported with the certain number of PIRQx# signals by determining the functionality of pins: AEN[4:1]/EAEN[4:1] MACK[3:0]#/EMACK[3:0] MREQ[7:4]#/PIRQ[3:0]# DLIGHT#/PIRQ0# FDCCS#/PIRQ1# RTCWR#/PIRQ2# RTCRD#/PIRQ3# For details see Table 3-4. Default = 000b

Table 3-4. PIRQx# Mux/Mapping Control

Configuration	Signal Function						
Bits [2:0]	AEN[4:1]/ EAEN[4:1]#	MACK[3:0]#/ EMACK[3:0]	MREQ[7:4]/# PIRQ[0:3]#	DLIGHT#/ PIRQ0#	FDDCS#/ PIRQ1#	RTCWR#/ PIRQ2#	RTCRD#/ PIRQ3#
000	EAEN[4:1]#	EMACK[3:0]#	MREQ[7:4]#	PIRQ0#	PIRQ1#	PIRQ2#	PIRQ3#
001	EAEN[4:1]#	EMACK[3:0]#	MREQ[7:4]#	PIRQ0#	PIRQ1#	RTCWR#	RTCRD#
010	EAEN[4:1]#	EMACK[3:0]#	MREQ[7:4]#	PIRQ0#	FDDCS#	RTCWR#	RTCRD#
011	EAEN[4:1]#	EMACK[3:0]#	MREQ[7:4]#	DLIGHT#	FDDCS#	RTCWR#	RTCRD#
100	AEN[4:1]	MACK[3:0]#	PIRQ[0:3]#	DLIGHT#	FDDCS#	RTCWR#	RTCRD#
101	EAEN[4:1]#	EMACK[3:0]#	PIRQ0#, PIRQ1#, MREQ5#, MREQ4#	DLIGHT#	FDDCS#	RTCWR#	RTCRD#
110	EAEN[4:1]#	EMACK[3:0]#	PIRQ0#, MREQ6#, MREQ5#, MREQ4#	DLIGHT#	FDDCS#	RTCWR#	RTCRD#
111	EAEN[4:1]#	EMACK[3:0]#	MREQ[7:4]#	DLIGHT#	FDDCS#	RTCWR#	RTCRD#

3.1.4 BIOSCSA—BIOS CHIP SELECT REGISTER

Register Name: BIOS Chip Select A

Register Location: 42h, 43h

Default Value: 10h, 00h

Attribute: Read/Write

Size: 8 bits

The LBIOSCS# signal is used to decode access to the motherboard BIOS. The ESC decodes memory access to the following address ranges, and if the range has been enabled the LBIOSCS# signal is always asserted for memory reads in the enabled BIOS range. If the BIOS Write Enable bit is set in the configuration register BIOSCSB, the LBIOSCS# is also asserted for memory write cycles.

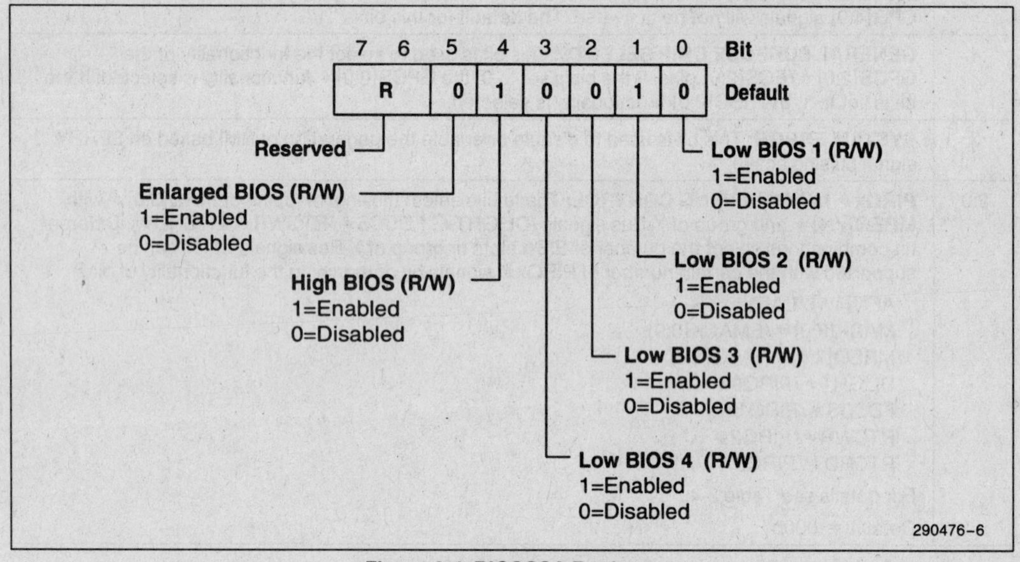

Figure 3-4. BIOSCSA Register

Table 3-5. BIOSCSA Register

Bit #	Description
7:6	**RESERVED.**
5	**ENLARGED BIOS:** During Memory access to locations FFF80000h–FFFDFFFFh with this bit set, LBIOSCS# will be asserted for memory read cycles. If bit 3 of BIOSCSB is set, then LBIOSCS# will be asserted for write cycles as well.
4	**HIGH BIOS:** During Memory access to locations 0F0000h–0FFFFFh, FF0000h–FFFFFFh, FFFF0000h–FFFFFFFFh with this bit set, LBIOSCS# will be asserted for memory read cycles. If bit 3 of BIOSCSB is set, then LBIOSCS# will be asserted for write cycles as well.
3	**LOW BIOS 4:** During Memory access to locations 0EC000h–0EFFFFh, FFEEC000h–FFEEFFFFh, FFFEC000h–FFFEFFFFh with this bit set, LBIOSCS# will be asserted for memory read cycles. If bit 3 of BIOSCSB is set, then LBIOSCS# will be asserted for write cycles as well.
2	**LOW BIOS 3:** During Memory access to locations 0E8000h–0EBFFFh, FFEE8000h–FFEEBFFFh, FFFE8000h–FFFEBFFFh with this bit set, LBIOSCS# will be asserted for memory read cycles. If bit 3 of BIOSCSB is set, then LBIOSCS# will be asserted for write cycles as well.

Table 3-5. BIOSCSA Register (Continued)

Bit #	Description
1	**LOW BIOS 2:** During Memory access to locations 0E4000h–0E7FFFh, FFEE4000h–FFEE7FFFh, FFFE4000h–FFFE7FFFh with this bit set, LBIOSCS# will be asserted for memory read cycles. If bit 3 of BIOSCSB is set, then LBIOSCS# will be asserted for write cycles as well.
0	**LOW BIOS 1:** During Memory access to locations 0E0000h–0E3FFFh, FFEE0000h–FFEE3FFFh, FFFE0000h–FFFE3FFFh with this bit set, LBIOSCS# will be asserted for memory read cycles. If bit 3 of BIOSCSB is set, then LBIOSCS# will be asserted for write cycles as well.

3.1.5 BIOSCSB—BIOS CHIP SELECT REGISTER

Register Name: BIOS Chip Select B
Register Location: 42h, 43h
Default Value: 10h, 00h
Attribute: Read/Write
Size: 8 bits

The LBIOSCS# signal is used to decode access to the motherboard BIOS. The ESC decodes memory access to the following address ranges, and if the range has been enabled the LBIOSCS# signal is always asserted for memory reads in the enabled BIOS range. If the BIOS Write Enable bit is set in the configuration register BIOSCSB, the LBIOSCS# is also asserted for memory write cycles.

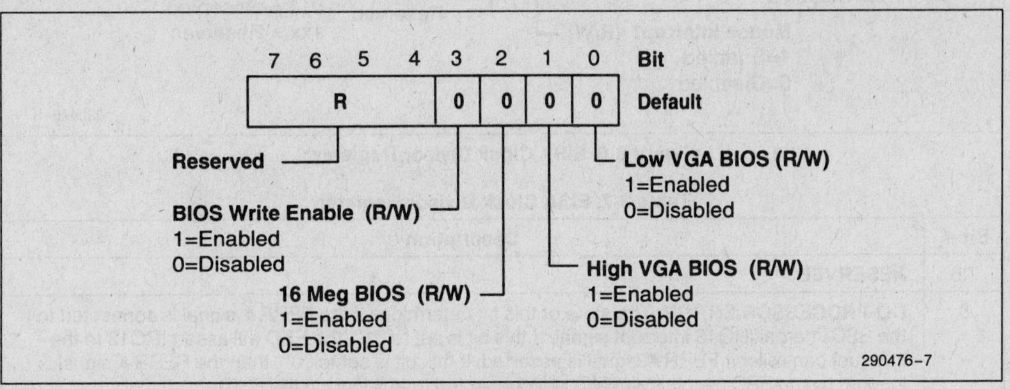

Figure 3-6. BIOSCSB Register

Table 3-6. BIOSCSB Register

Bit #	Description
7:4	**RESERVED.**
3	**BIOS WRITE ENABLE:** When enabled LBIOSCS# is asserted for memory read AND write cycles for addresses in the decoded and enabled BIOS range, otherwise LBIOSCS# is asserted for memory read cycles ONLY.
2	**16 MEG BIOS:** During Memory access to locations FF0000h–FFFFFFh with this bit set, LBIOSCS# will be asserted for memory read cycles. If bit 3 of BIOSCSB is set, then LBIOSCS# will be asserted for write cycles as well.
1	**HIGH VGA BIOS:** During Memory access to locations 0C4000h–0C7FFFh with this bit set, LBIOSCS# will be asserted for memory read cycles. If bit 3 of BIOSCSB is set, then LBIOSCS# will be asserted for write cycles as well.
0	**LOW VGA BIOS:** During Memory access to locations 0C0000h–0C3FFFh with this bit set, LBIOSCS# will be asserted for memory read cycles. If bit 3 of BIOSCSB is set, then LBIOSCS# will be asserted for write cycles as well.

3.1.6 CLKDIV—EISA CLOCK DIVISOR REGISTER

Register Name: EISA Clock Divisor
Register Location: 4Dh
Default Value: xx00x000b
Attribute: Read/Write
Size: 8 bits

This register is used to select the integer value used to divide the PCI clock (PCICLK) to generate the EISA Bus Clock (BCLK). In addition, the register provides a bit to enable/disable the ABFULL function, and a bit to enable/disable the co-processor error support.

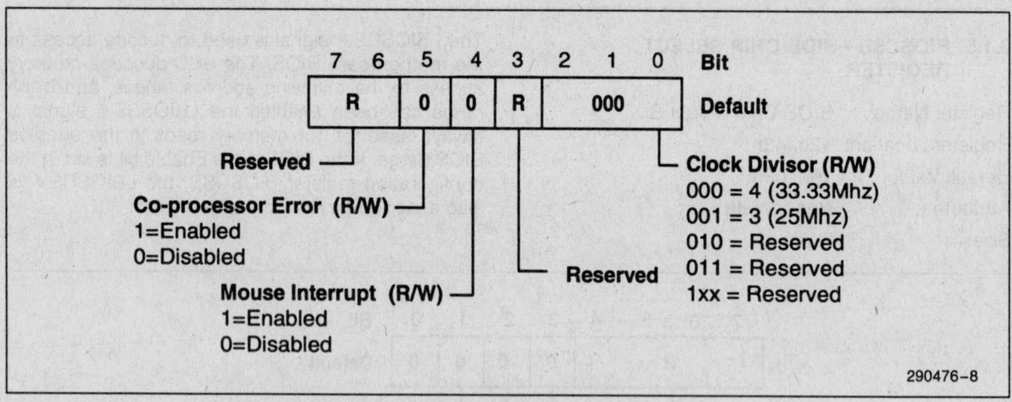

Figure 3-6. EISA Clock Divisor Register

Table 3-7. EISA Clock Divisor Register

Bit #	Description
7:6	**RESERVED.**
5	**CO-PROCESSOR ERROR:** The state of this bit determines if the FERR# signal is connected to the ESC internal IRQ13 interrupt signal. If this bit is set to "1", the ESC will assert IRQ13 to the interrupt controller if FERR# signal is asserted. If this bit is set to "0", then the FERR# signal is ignored by the ESC (i.e., this signal is not connected to any logic in the ESC).
4	**MOUSE INTERRUPT:** The state of this bit determines if the ABFULL signal is connected to the ESC internal IRQ12 interrupt signal. If this bit is set to "1", a low to high transition on the ABFULL signal will generate interrupt on the IRQ12 signal. If this bit is set to "0", then the ABFULL signal is ignored by the ESC (i.e., this signal is not connected to any logic in the ESC).
3	**RESERVED.**
2:0	**CLOCK DIVISOR:** These bits are used to select the integer that is used to divide the PCICLK down to generate the BCLK. Upon reset, these bits are set to 000b (divisor or 4).

Bit 2	Bit 1	Bit 0	Divisor	BCLK
0	0	0	4 (33.33 MHz)	8.33 MHz
0	0	1	3 (25 MHz)	8.33 MHz
0	1	0	Reserved	
0	1	1	Reserved	
1	x	x	Reserved	

3.1.7 PCSA—PERIPHERAL CHIP SELECT A REGISTER

Register Name:	Peripheral Chip Select A
Register Location:	4Eh
Default Value:	xx000111b
Attribute:	Read/Write
Size:	8 bits

This register is used to enable or disable accesses to the RTC, Keyboard Controller, Floppy Disk controller, and IDE. Disabling any of these bits will prevent the chip select and X-Bus transceiver control signal (XBUSOE#) for that device from being generated. This register is also used to select which address range (primary or secondary) will be decoded for the resident floppy controller and IDE. **It also allows control of where keyboard controller is physically located (X-Bus or elsewhere).** This insures that there is no contention with the X-Bus transceiver driving the system data bus during read accesses to these devices.

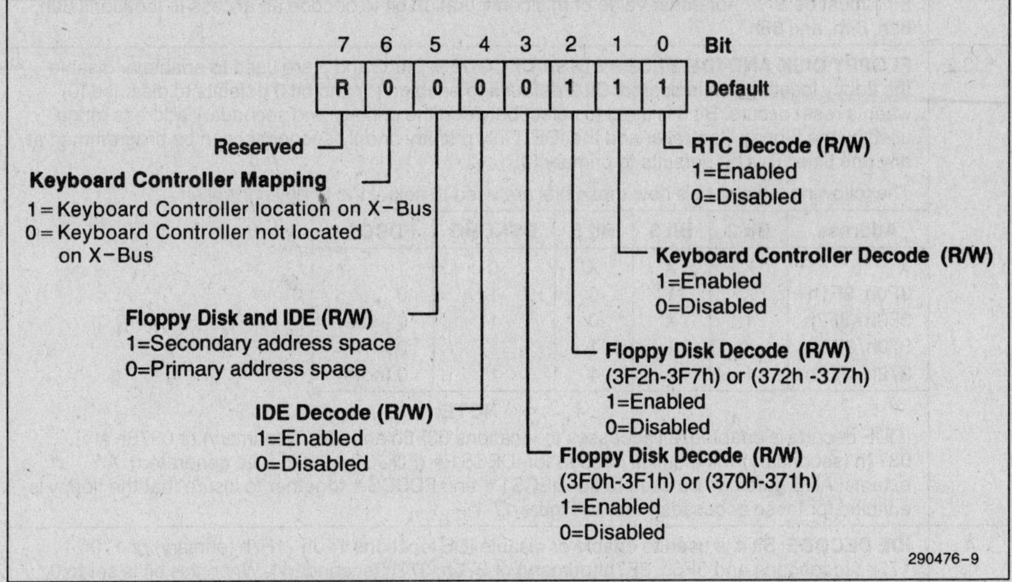

Figure 3-7. PCSA Register

Table 3-8. PCSA Register

<table>
<tr><th>Bit #</th><th>Description</th></tr>
<tr><td>7</td><td>RESERVED.</td></tr>
<tr><td>6</td><td>KEYBOARD CONTROLLER MAPPING:
0 = keyboard controller mapped to the X-Bus
1 = keyboard controller not mapped to the X-bus
DEFAULT = 0
When bit is "0", the Keyboard Controller encoded chip-select signal and the X-Bus transceiver enable (XBUSOE#) will be generated for accesses to address locations 60h, 62h, 64h and 66h. When bit is a "1", the Keyboard Controller chip-select signals will be generated for accesses to address locations 60h, 62h, 64h and 66h, but the X-Bus transceiver (XBUSOE#) will be disabled. Bit 1 must be a "1" for either value of this configuration bit to decode an access to locations 60h, 62h, 64h, and 66h.</td></tr>
<tr><td>5, 3:2</td><td>FLOPPY DISK AND IDE, FLOPPY DISK DECODES: Bits 2 and 3 are used to enable or disable the floppy locations as indicated. Bit 2 defaults to enabled (1) and bit 3 defaults to disabled (0) when a reset occurs. Bit 5 is used to select between the primary and secondary address range used by the Floppy Controller and the IDE. Only primary or only secondary can be programmed at any one time. This bit defaults to primary (0).
The following table shows how these bits are used to select the floppy controller:
<table>
<tr><th>Address</th><th>Bit 2</th><th>Bit 3</th><th>Bit 5</th><th>DSKCHG</th><th>FDCCS#</th></tr>
<tr><td>X</td><td>X</td><td>X</td><td>X</td><td>0</td><td>1</td></tr>
<tr><td>3F0h, 3F1h</td><td>X</td><td>1</td><td>0</td><td>1</td><td>0</td></tr>
<tr><td>3F2h–3F7h</td><td>1</td><td>X</td><td>0</td><td>1</td><td>0 (note)</td></tr>
<tr><td>370h, 371h</td><td>X</td><td>1</td><td>1</td><td>1</td><td>0</td></tr>
<tr><td>372h–37Fh</td><td>1</td><td>X</td><td>1</td><td>1</td><td>0 (note)</td></tr>
</table>
NOTE:
If IDE decode is enabled, all accesses to locations 03F6h and 03F7h (primary) or 0376h and 0377h (secondary) will result in decode for IDECS1# (FDCCS# will not be generated). An external AND gate can be used to tie IDECS1# and FDCCS# together to insure that the floppy is enabled for these accesses (refer to Figure 17-1).</td></tr>
<tr><td>4</td><td>IDE DECODE: Bit 4 is used to enable or disable IDE locations 1F0h–1F7h (primary) or 170h–177h (secondary) and 3F6h, 3F7h (primary) or 376h, 377h (secondary). When this bit is set to 0, the IDE encoded chip select signals and the X-Bus transceiver signal (XBUSOE#) are not generated for these addresses.</td></tr>
<tr><td>1</td><td>KEYBOARD CONTROLLER DECODE: Enables (1) or disables (0) the Keyboard Controller address locations 60h, 62h, 64h, and 66h. When this bit is set to 0, the Keyboard Controller encoded chip select signals and the X-Bus transceiver signal (XBUSOE#) are not generated for these locations.
NOTE:
The value of this bit will affect control function (keyboard controlling mapping) provided by bit 6 of the same register.</td></tr>
<tr><td>0</td><td>REAL TIME CLOCK DECODE: Enables (1) or disables (0) the RTC address locations 70h–77h. When this bit is set to 0, the RTC encoded chip select signals RTCALE, RTCRD, RTCWR#, and XBUSOE# signals are not generated for these addresses.</td></tr>
</table>

3.1.8 PCSB—PERIPHERAL CHIP SELECT B REGISTER

Register Name:	Peripheral Chip Select B
Register Location:	4Fh
Default Value:	CFh
Attribute:	Read/Write
Size:	8 bits

This register is used to enable or disable generation of the X-Bus transceiver signal (XBUSOE#) for accesses to the serial ports and parallel port locations. When disabled, the XBUSOE# signal for that device will not be generated.

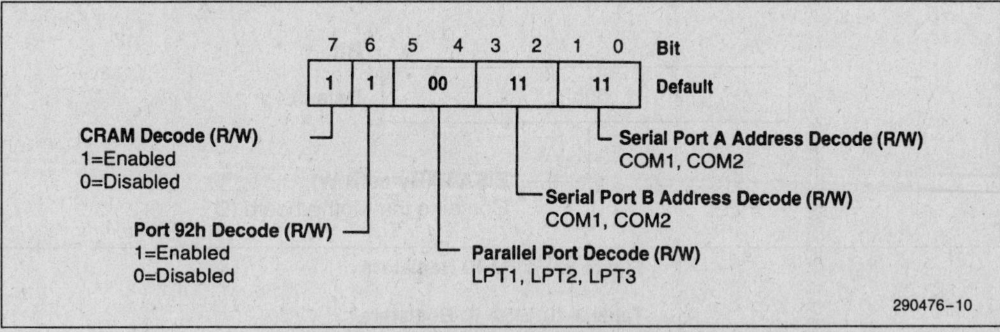

Figure 3-8. Peripheral Chip Select B Register

Table 3-9. Peripheral Chip Select B Register

Bit #	Description
7	**CRAM DECODE:** This bit is used to enable (1) or disable (0) I/O write accesses to location 0C00h and I/O read/write accesses to locations 0800h-08FFh. The configuration RAM read and write (CRAMRD#, CRAMWR#) strobes are valid for accesses to 0800h-08FFh.
6	**Port 92 DECODE:** This bit is used to disable (0) access to Port 92. This bit defaults to enable (1) at PCIRST.
5:4	**PARALLEL PORT DECODE:** These bits are used to select which Parallel Port address range (LPT1, 2, or 3) is decoded. **Bit 5 Bit 4** 0 0 LPT1 (3BCh–3BFh) 0 1 LPT2 (378h–37Fh) 1 0 LPT3 (278h–27Fh) 1 1 Disabled
3:2	**SERIAL PORT B ADDRESS DECODE:** If either COM1 or COM2 address ranges are selected, these bits default to disabled upon PCIRST. **Bit 3 Bit 2** 0 0 3F8h–3FFh (COM1) 0 1 2F8h–2FFh (COM2) 1 0 Reserved 1 1 Port A disabled
1:0	**SERIAL PORT A ADDRESS DECODE:** If either COM1 or COM2 address ranges are selected, these bits default to disabled upon PCIRST. **Bit 1 Bit 0** 0 0 3F8h–3FFh (COM1) 0 1 2F8h–2FFh (COM2) 1 0 Reserved 1 1 Port A disabled

3.1.9 EISAID[4:1]—EISA ID REGISTERS

Register Name: EISA ID Register (Byte 1, Byte 2, Byte 3, Byte 4)

Register Offset: 50h, 51h, 52h, 53h

Default Value: 00h, 00h, 00h, 00h

Attribute: Read/Write only

Size: 8 bits

These 8-bit registers contain the EISA motherboard ID. The data in the register is reflected on the data bus for I/O cycles addressed to 0C80h–0C83h respectively.

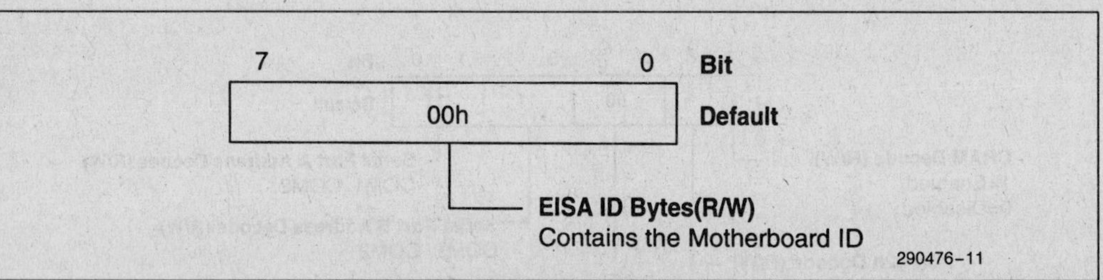

Figure 3-9. EISA ID Registers

Table 3-10. EISA ID Registers

Bit #	Description
7:0	**EISA ID BYTE:** These bits contain the EISA Motherboard ID information. On power-up these bits default to 00h. These bits are written with the ID value during configuration. The value of these bits are reflected in I/O registers 0C80h–0C83h.

3.1.10 SGRBA—SCATTER-GATHER RELOCATE BASE ADDRESS REGISTER

Register Name: S-G Relocate Base Address
Register Location: 57h
Default Value: 04h
Attribute: Read/Write
Size: 8 bits

The value programmed in this register determines the high order I/O address of the S-G registers. The default value is 04h.

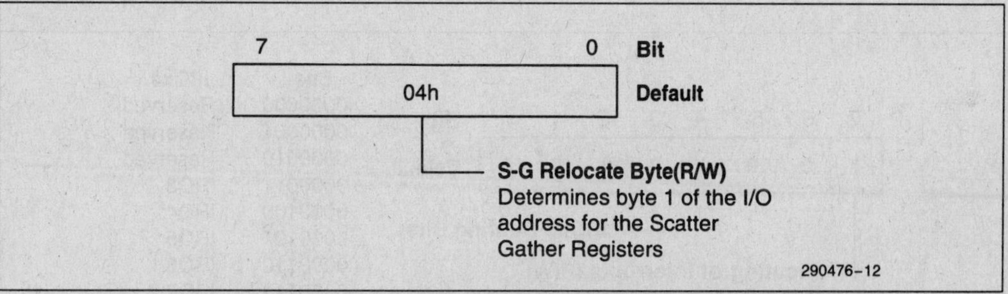

Figure 3-10. S-G Relocate Base Address Register

Table 3-11. S-G Relocate Base Address Register

Bit #	Description
7:0	**S-G RELOCATE BYTE:** These bits determine the I/O location of the Scatter-Gather Registers. The Scatter-Gather register relocation range is xx10h–xx3Fh (default 0410h - 043Fh). These bits determine the Byte 1 of the I/O address. Address signals LA[15:8] are compared against the contents of this register (Bit[7:0]) to determine I/O accesses to the Scatter-Gather registers. The default on power-up is 04h.

3.1.11 PIRQ[0:3]#—PIRQ ROUTE CONTROL REGISTERS

Register Name: PIRQ0#, PIRQ1#, PIRQ2#, PIRQ3# Route Control

Register Location: 60h, 61h, 62h, 63h

Default Value: 80h

Attribute: Read/Write

Size: 8 bits

These registers control the routing of PCI Interrupts (PIRQ[0:3]#) to the PC compatible interrupts. Each PCI interrupt can be independently routed to 1 of 11 compatible interrupts.

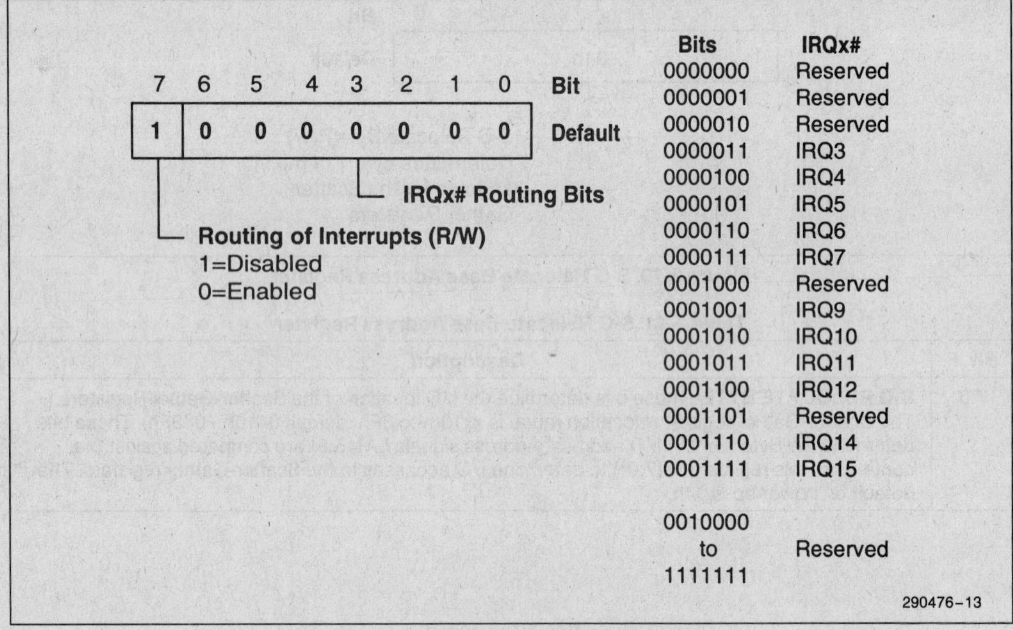

Figure 3-11. PIRQ Route Control Registers

Table 3-12. PIRQ Route Control Register

Bit #	Description
7	**ROUTING OF INTERRUPTS:** When enabled this bit routes the PCI Interrupt signal to the PC compatible interrupt signal specified in bits[6:0]. After a reset or a power-on this bit is disabled (set to 1).
6:0	**IRQx# ROUTING BITS:** These bits specify which IRQ signal to generate when the PCI Interrupt for this register has been triggered.

3.1.12 GPCSLA[2:0]—GENERAL PURPOSE CHIP SELECT LOW ADDRESS REGISTER

Register Name: General Purpose Chip Select Low Address
Register Location: 64h, 68h, 6Ch
Default Value: 00h
Attribute: Read/Write
Size: 8 bits

This register contains the low byte of the General Purpose Peripheral mapping address. The contents of this register are compared with the LA[7:0] address lines. The contents of this register, the GPCSHA Register and the GPCSM Register control the generation the GPCS[2:0]# signal or the ESC[2:0] signal (101, 110 combination). If Mode Select Register (offset 40h) bit 4 = 1, offset register 6Ch is ignored.

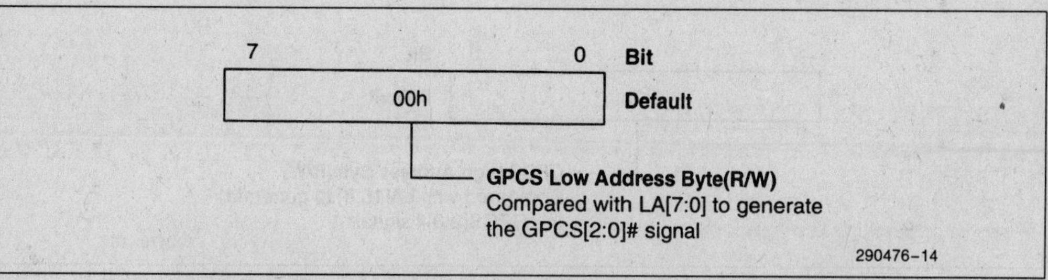

Figure 3-12. General Purpose Chip Select Low Address Byte Register

Table 3-13. General Purpose Chip Select Low Address Byte Register

Bit #	Description
7:0	**GPCS LOW ADDRESS BYTE:** The contents of these bits are compared with the address lines LA[7:0] to generate the GPCS[2:0] # signal or the ECS[2:0] combination for this register. The mask register (GPCSM[2:0]) determines which bits to use during the comparison.

3.1.13 GPCSHA[2:0]—GENERAL PURPOSE CHIP SELECT HIGH ADDRESS REGISTER

Register Name: General Purpose Chip Select High Address
Register Location: 65h, 69h, 6Dh
Default Value: C0h
Attribute: Read/Write
Size: 8 bits

This register contains the high byte of the General Purpose Peripheral mapping address. The contents of this register are compared with the LA[15:8] address lines. The contents of this register, the GPCSLA Register and the GPCSM Register control the generation the GPCS[2:0]# signal or the ESC[2:0] signal (101, 110 combination). If Mode Select Register (offset 40h) bit 4 = 1, offset register 6Dh is ignored.

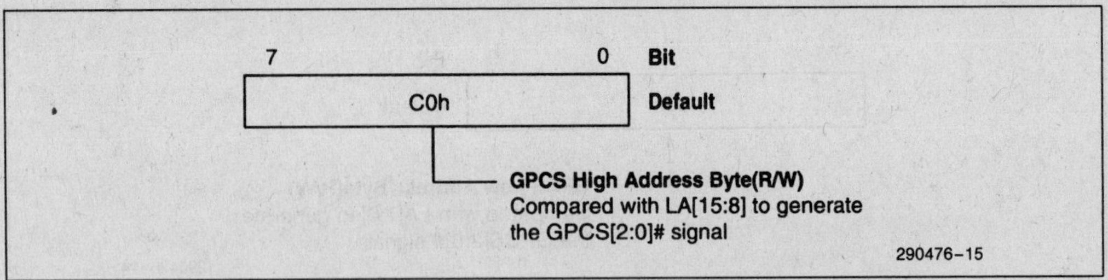

Figure 3-13. General Purpose Chip Select High Address Byte Register

Table 3-14. General Purpose Chip Select High Address Byte Register

Bit #	Description
7:0	**GPCS HIGH ADDRESS BYTE:** The contents of these bits are compared with the address lines LA[15:8] to generate the GPCS[2:0] # signal or the ECS[2:0] combination for this register.

3.1.14 GPCSM[2:0]—GENERAL PURPOSE CHIP SELECT MASK REGISTER

Register Name: General Purpose Chip Select Mask Register

Register Location: 66h, 6Ah, 6Eh

Default Value: 00h

Attribute: Read/Write

Size: 8 bits

This register contains the mask bits for determining the address range for which the GPCSx# signals are generated. If a register bit is set to a 1 then the corresponding bit in the GPCSL register is not compared with the address signal in the generation of the GPCSx# signals. If Mode Select Register (offset 40h) bit 4 = 1, offset register 6Eh is ignored.

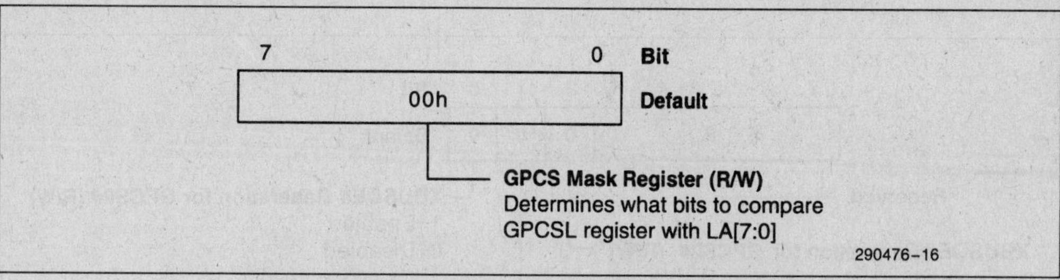

Figure 3-14. General Purpose Chip Select Mask Register

Table 3-15. General Purpose Chip Select Mask Register

Bit #	Description
7:0	**GPCS MASK REGISTER:** The contents of these bits are used to determine which bits to compare GPCSLA[2:0] with the address lines LA[7:0]. A "1" bit means the bit should not be compared.

3.1.15 GPXBC—GENERAL PURPOSE PERIPHERAL X-BUS CONTROL REGISTER

Register Name: General Purpose Peripheral X-Bus Control
Register Location: 6Fh
Default Value: xxxx x000b
Attribute: Read/Write
Size: 8 bits

The register controls the generation of the X-Bus buffer output enable (XBUSOE#) signal for I/O accesses to the peripherals mapped in the General Purpose Chip Select address decode range. This register determines if the General Purpose Peripheral is placed on the X-Bus or not. If the General Purpose Peripheral is on the X-Bus, then the corresponding bit is set to "1". Otherwise the bit is set to "0".

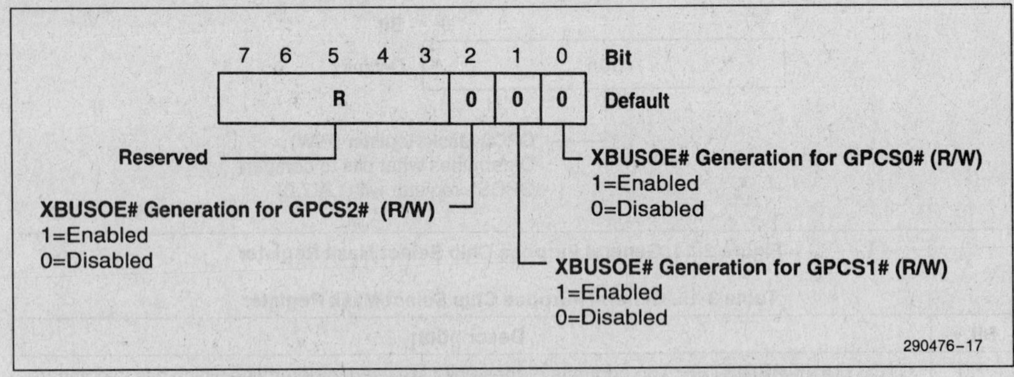

Figure 3-15. General Purpose Peripheral X-Bus Control Register

Table 3-16. General Purpose Peripheral X-Bus Control Register

Bit #	Description
7:3	**RESERVED.**
2	**XBUSOE# GENERATION FOR GPCS2#:** When this bit is enabled XBUSOE# will be generated when GPCS2# is generated.
1	**XBUSOE# GENERATION FOR GPCS1#:** When this bit is enabled XBUSOE# will be generated when GPCS1# is generated.
0	**XBUSOE# GENERATION FOR GPCS0#:** When this bit is enabled XBUSOE# will be generated when GPCS0# is generated.

3.1.16 TEST CONTROL REGISTER

Register Name: Test Control Register
Register Location: 88h
Default Value: 00h
Attribute: Read/Write
Size: 8 bits

This register provides control for ESC manufacturing test modes. The functionality of this register is reserved.

3.2 DMA Register Description

The ESC contains DMA circuitry that incorporates the functionality of two 82C37 DMA controllers (DMA1 and DMA2). The DMA registers control the operation of the DMA controllers and are all accessible from the EISA Bus. This section describes the DMA registers. Unless otherwise stated, a reset sets each register to its default value. The operation of the DMA is further described in Chapter 6.0, DMA Controller.

3.2.1 DCOM—COMMAND REGISTER

Register Name: DMA Command
Register Location: 08h—Channels 0–3
0D0h—Channels 4–7
Default Value: 00000000b
Attribute: Write Only
Size: 8 bits

This 8-bit register controls the configuration of the DMA. It is programmed by the microprocessor in the Program Condition and is cleared by reset or a Master Clear instruction. Note that disabling Channels 4–7 will also disable Channels 0–3, since Channels 0–3 are cascaded onto Channel 4. The DREQ and DACK# channel assertion sensitivity is assigned by channel group, not per individual Channel. For priority resolution the DMA consists of two logical channel groups—Channels 0–3 (Controller 1–DMA1) and Channels 4–7 (Controller 2–DMA2). Both groups may be assigned fixed priority, one group can be assigned fixed priority and the second rotating priority, or both groups may be assigned rotating priority. A detailed description of the channel priority scheme is found in the DMA functional description, Section 6.5. Following a reset or DMA Master Clear, both DMA-1 and DMA-2 are enabled in fixed priority, the DREQ sense level is active high, and the DACK# assertion level is active low.

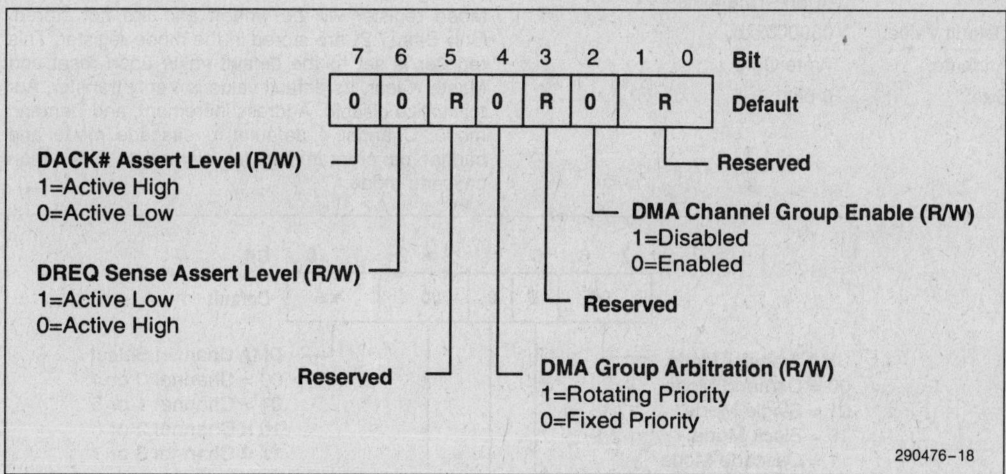

Figure 3-16. DMA Command Register

Table 3-17. DMA Command Register

Bit #	Description
7	**DACK# ASSERT LEVEL:** Bit 7 controls the DMA channel request acknowledge (DACK#) assertion level. Following reset, the DACK# assertion level is active low. The low level indicates recognition and acknowledgement of the DMA request to the DMA slave requesting service. Writing a 0 to Bit 7 assigns active low as the assertion level. When a 1 is written to this bit, a high level on the DACK# line indicates acknowledgement of the request for DMA service to the DMA slave.
6	**DREQ SENSE ASSERT LEVEL:** Bit 6 controls the DMA channel request (DREQ) assertion detect level. Following reset, the DREQ sense assert level is active high. In this condition, an active high level sampled on DREQ is decoded as an active DMA channel request. Writing a 0 to Bit 6 assigns active high as the sense assert level. When a 1 is written to this bit, a low level on the DREQ line is decoded as an active DMA channel request.
5, 3, 1:0	**RESERVED:** Must be 0.
4	**DMA GROUP ARBITRATION:** Each channel group is individually assigned either fixed or rotating arbitration priority. At reset, each group is initialized in fixed priority. Writing a 0 to Bit 4 assigns fixed priority to the channel group, while writing a 1 assigns rotating priority to the group.
2	**DMA GROUP ENABLE:** Writing a 1 to this bit disables the DMA channel group, while writing a 0 to this bit enables the DMA channel group. Both channel groups are enabled following reset. Disabling Channel group 4–7 also disables Channel group 0–3, which is cascaded through Channel 4.

3.2.2 DCM—DMA CHANNEL MODE REGISTER

Register Name: DMA Channel Mode

Register Location: 0Bh—Channels 0–3
0D6h—Channels 4–7

Default Value: 000000xxb

Attribute: Write Only

Size: 6 bits

Each channel has a 6-bit Mode register associated with it. The Mode registers provide control over DMA Transfer type, transfer mode, address increment/decrement, and autoinitialization. When writing to the register, Bits [1:0] determine which channel's Mode register will be written and are not stored. Only Bits [7:2] are stored in the mode register. This register is set to the default value upon reset and Master Clear. Its default value is Verify transfer, Autoinitialize disable, Address increment, and Demand mode. Channel 4 defaults to cascade mode and cannot be programmed for any mode other than cascade mode.

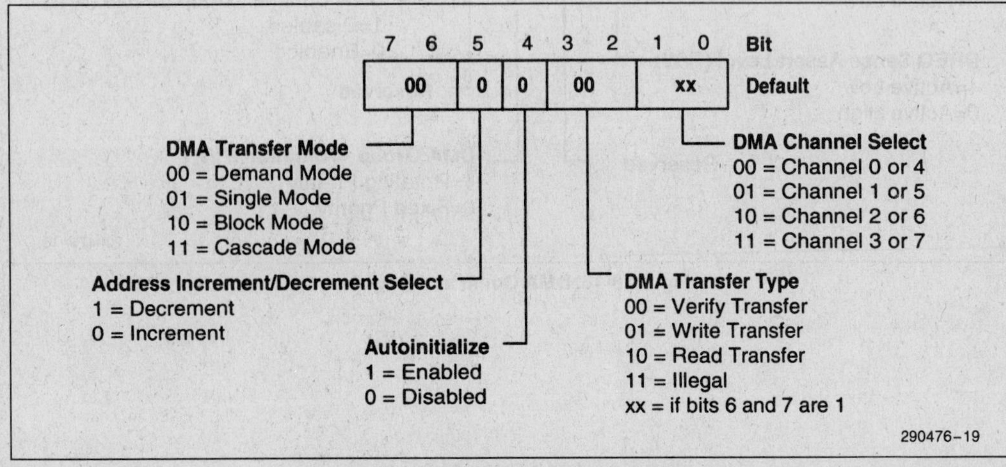

Figure 3-17. DMA Channel Mode Register

Table 3-18. DMA Channel Mode Register

Bit #	Description
7:6	**DMA TRANSFER MODE:** Each DMA channel can be programmed in one of four different modes: single transfer, block transfer, demand transfer and cascade. **Bit 7 Bit 6 Transfer Mode** 0 0 Demand mode 0 1 Single mode 1 0 Block mode 1 1 Cascade mode
5	**ADDRESS INCREMENT/DECREMENT SELECT:** Bit 5 controls address increment/decrement during multi-byte DMA transfers. When bit 5 = 0, address increment is selected. When bit 5 = 1, address decrement is selected. Address increment is the default after a PCIRST# cycle or Master Clear command.
4	**AUTOINITIALIZE ENABLE:** When bit 4 = 1, the DMA restores the Base Page, Address, and Word count information to their respective current registers following a terminal count (TC). When bit 4 = 0, the autoinitialize feature is disabled and the DMA does not restore the above mentioned registers. A PCIRST# or Master Clear disables autoinitialization (sets bit 4 to 0).
3:2	**DMA TRANSFER TYPE:** Verify, write and read transfer types are available. Verify transfer is the default transfer type upon PCIRST# or Master Clear. Write transfers move data from an I/O device to memory. Read transfers move data from memory to an I/O device. Verify transfers are pseudo transfers; addresses are generated as in a normal read or write transfer and the device responds to EOP etc. However, with Verify transfers, the ISA memory and I/O cycle lines are not driven. Bit combination 11 is illegal. When the channel is programmed for cascade ([7:6] = 11) the transfer type bits are irrelevant. **Bit 3 Bit 2 Transfer Type** 0 0 Verify transfer 0 1 Write transfer 1 0 Read transfer 1 1 Illegal
1:0	**DMA CHANNEL SELECT:** Bits [1:0] select the DMA Channel Mode Register that will be written by bits [7:2]. **Bit 1 Bit 0 Channel** 0 0 Channel 0 (4) 0 1 Channel 1 (5) 1 0 Channel 2 (6) 1 1 Channel 3 (7)

3.2.3 DCEM—DMA CHANNEL EXTENDED MODE REGISTER

Register Name: DMA Channel Extended Mode
Register Location: 040Bh—Channels 0–3
04D6h—Channels 4–7
Default Value: 000000xxb
Attribute: Write Only
Size: 6 bits

Each channel has a 6-bit Extended Mode register associated with it. The register is used to program the DMA device data size, timing mode, EOP input/output selection, and Stop register selection. When writing to the register, Bits [1:0] determine which channel's Extended Mode register will be written and are not stored. Only Bits [7:2] are stored in the extended mode register. Four timing modes are available: ISA-compatible, A, B, and Burst.

The default bit values for each DMA group are selected upon reset. A Master Clear or any other programming sequence will not set the default register settings. The default programmed values for DMA1 Channels 0–3 are 8-bit I/O Count by Bytes, Compatible timing, and EOP output. The default values for DMA2 Channels 4–7 are 16-bit I/O Count by Words with shifted address, Compatible timing, and EOP output. These default settings provide a rigorous ISA-compatible DMA implementation.

NOTE:
DMA1/DMA2 refer to the original PC-AT implementation which used two discrete 8237 DMA controllers. In this context, DMA1 refers to DMA Channels 0–3 and DMA2 refers to DMA Channels 4–7. The PC-AT used Channel 4 (Channel 0 of DMA2) as a cascade channel for DMA1. Consequently, Channel 4 is not used in compatible DMA controllers although the compatible DMA registers are kept to maintain compatibility with the original PC-AT. Because Channel 4 is not used, the DMA controller does not support extended registers for Channel 4.

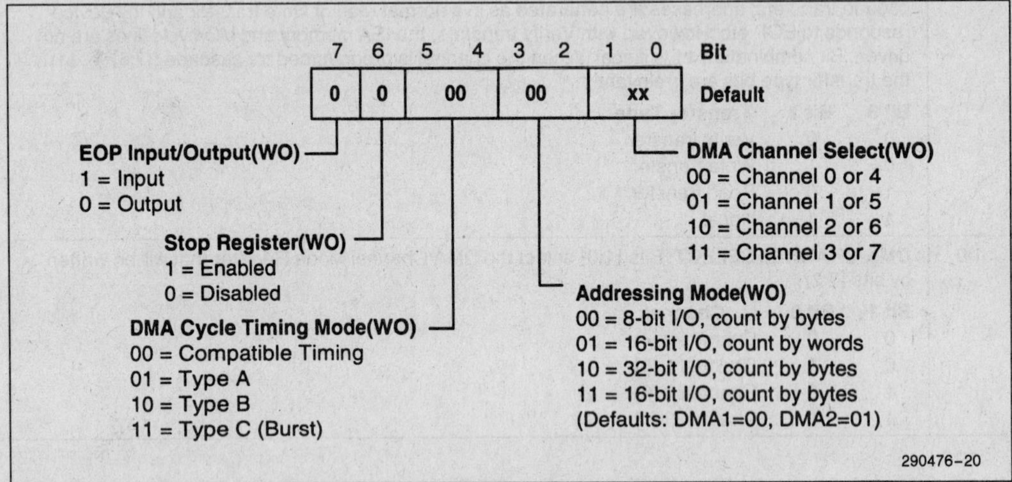

Figure 3-18. DMA Channel Extended Mode Register

Table 3-19. DMA Channel Extended Mode Register

Bit #	Description
7	**EOP INPUT/OUTPUT:** Bit 7 of this register selects whether or not the Stop registers associated with this channel are to be used. Normally the Stop Registers will not be used. This function was added to help support data communication or other devices that work from a ring buffer in memory. Upon reset, the Bit 7 is set to "0"-Stop register disabled. The detailed Stop register functional description discusses the use of the Stop registers.
6	**STOP REGISTER:** Bit 6 of the Extended Mode register selects whether the EOP signal is to be used as an output during DMA on this channel or an input. EOP will generally be used as an output, as was available on the PCAT. The input function was added to support Data Communication and other devices that would like to trigger an autoinitialize when a collision or some other event occurs. The direction of EOP is switched when DACK is changed (when a different channel wins the arbitration and is granted the bus). There may be some overlap of the ESC driving the EOP signal along with the DMA slave. However, during this overlap both devices will be driving the signal to a low level (negated). For example, assume Channel 2 is about to go inactive (DACK negated) and channel 1 is about to go active. If Channel 2 is programmed for "EOP OUT" and Channel 1 is programmed for "EOP IN", when Channel 2's DACK is negated and Channel 1's DACK is asserted, the ESC may be driving EOP to a low value on behalf of Channel 2 at the same time the device connected to Channel 1 is driving EOP in to the ESC, also at an inactive level. This overlap will only last until the ESC EOP output buffer is tri-stated, and will not effect the DMA operation. Upon reset, the value of Bit 6 is 0 (EOP output selected).
5:4	**DMA CYCLE TIMING MODE:** The ESC supports four DMA transfer timings: ISA-compatible, Type A, Type B, and Burst. Each timing and its corresponding code are described below. Upon reset, compatible timing is selected and the value of these bits is "00". The cycle timings noted below are for a BCLK (8.33 MHz, maximum BCLK frequency). DMA cycles to ISA expansion bus memory will default to compatible timing if the channel is programmed in one of the performance timing modes (Type A, B, or Burst). 00 Compatible Timing DMA slaves on the ISA bus may run compatible DMA cycles. Bits [5:4] must be programmed to "00". Compatible timing is provided for DMA slave devices, which, due to some design limitation, cannot support one of the faster timings. Compatible timing runs at 9 BCLKs (1080 ns/single cycle) and 8 BCLKs (960 ns/cycle) during the repeated portion of a BLOCK or DEMAND mode transfers. 01 Type "A" Timing Type "A" timing is provided to allow shorter cycles to EISA memory. If ISA memory is decoded, the system automaticallly reverts to ISA DMA type compatible timing on a cycle-by-cycle basis. Type "A" timing runs at 7 BCLKs (840 ns/single cycle) and 6 BCLKs (720 ns/cycle) during the repeated portion of a BLOCK or DEMAND mode transfer. Type "A" timing varies from compatible timing primarily in shortening the memory operation to the minimum allowed by system memory. The I/O portion of the cycle (data setup on write, I/O read access time) is the same as with compatible cycles. The actual active command time is shorter, but it is expected that the DMA devices which provide the data access time or write data setup time should not require excess IOR# or IOW# command active time. Because of this, most ISA DMA devices should be able to use type "A" timing. 10 Type "B" Timing Type "B" timing is provided for 8-bit and 16-bit ISA or EISA DMA devices which can accept faster I/O timing. Type "B" only works with EISA memory. Type "B" timing runs at 6 BCLKs (720 ns/single cycle) and 4 BCLKs (480 ns/cycle) during the repeated portion of a BLOCK or DEMAND mode transfer. Type "B" timing requires faster DMA slave devices than compatible timing in that the cycles are shortened so that the data setup time on I/O write cycles is shortened and the I/O read access time is required to be faster. Some of the current ISA devices should be able to support type "B" timing, but these will probably be more recent designs using relatively fast technology.

Table 3-19. DMA Channel Extended Mode Register (Continued)

Bit #	Description
5:4	**DMA CYCLE TIMING MODE:** (Continued) 11 Type "C" Timing (Burst) Burst timing is provided for high performance EISA DMA devices. The DMA slave device needs to monitor the EXRDY and IORC# or IOWC# signals to determine when to change the data (on writes) or sample the data (on reads). This timing will allow up to 33 MBytes per second transfer rate with a 32-bit DMA device and 32-bit memory. Note that 8-bit or 16-bit DMA devices are supported (through the programmable Address size) and that they use the "byte lanes" natural to their size for the data transfer. As with all bursts, the system will revert to two BCLK cycles if the memory does not support burst. When a DMA burst cycle accesses non-burst memory and the DMA cycle crosses a page boundary into burstable memory, the ESC will continue performing non-burst cycles. This will not cause a problem since the data is still transferred correctly.
3:2	**ADDRESSING MODE:** The ESC supports 8-, 16-, and 32-bit DMA device data sizes. The four data size options are programmable with Bits [3:2]. Both the 8-bit I/O, "Count By Bytes" Mode and the 16-bit I/O, "Count By Words" (Address Shifted) Mode are ISA compatible. The 16-bit and 32-bit I/O, "Count By Bytes" Modes are EISA extensions. Byte assembly/disassembly is performed by the EISA Bus Controller. Each of the data transfer size modes is discussed below. 00 8-bit I/O, "Count By Bytes" Mode In 8-bit I/O, "count by bytes" mode, the address counter can be programmed to any address. The count register is programmed with the "number of bytes minus 1" to transfer. 01 16-bit I/O, "Count By Words" (Address Shifted) Mode In "count by words" mode (address shifted), the address counter can be programmed to any even address, but must be programmed with the address value shifted right by one bit. The Page registers are not shifted during DMA transfers. Thus, the least significant bit of the Low Page register is ignored when the address is driven out onto the bus. The Word Count register is programmed with the number of words minus 1 to be transferred. 10 32-Bit I/O, "Count By Bytes" Mode In 32-bit "count by bytes" mode, the address counter can be programmed to any byte address. For most DMA devices, however, it should only be programmed to a Dword aligned address. If the starting address is not Dword aligned then the DMA controller will do a partial Dword transfer during the first and last transfers if necessary. The bus controller logic will do the byte/word assembly necessary to read or write any size memory device and both the DMA and bus controllers support burst for this mode. In this mode, the Address register is usually incremented or decremented by four and the byte count is usually decremented by four. The Count register should be programmed with the number of bytes to be transferred minus 1. 11 16-Bit I/O, "Count By Bytes" Mode In 16-bit "count by bytes" mode, the address counter can be programmed to any byte address. For most DMA devices, however, it should be programmed only to even addresses. If the address is programmed to an odd address, then the DMA controller will do a partial word transfer during the first and last transfer if necessary. The bus controller will do the byte/word assembly necessary to write any size memory device. In this mode, the Address register is incremented or decremented by two and the byte count is decremented by the number of bytes transferred during each bus cycle. The Word Count register is programmed with the "number of bytes minus 1" to be transferred. This mode is offered as an extension of the two ISA compatible modes discussed above. This mode should only be programmed for 16-bit ISA DMA slaves.
1:0	**DMA CHANNEL SELECT:** Bits [1:0] selects the particular channel that will have its DMA Channel Extend Mode Register programmed with bits [7:2]. **Bit 1 Bit 0 Channel** 0 0 Channel 0 (4) 0 1 Channel 1 (5) 1 0 Channel 2 (6) 1 1 Channel 3 (7)

3.2.4 DR—DMA REQUEST REGISTER

Register Name: DMA Request

Register Location: 09h—Channels 0–3
0D2h—Channels 4–7

Default Value: 000000xxb

Attribute: Write Only

Size: 4 bits

Each channel has a Request bit associated with it in one of the two 4-bit Request registers. The Request register is used by software to initiate a DMA request. The DMA responds to the software request as though DREQ[x] is asserted. These requests are non-maskable and subject to prioritization by the Priority Encoder network (refer to the Channel Priority Functional Description). Each register bit is set or reset separately under software control or is cleared upon generation of a TC. The entire register is cleared upon reset or a Master Clear. It is not cleared upon a RSTDRV output. To set or reset a bit, the software loads the proper form of the data word. Bits [1:0] determine which channel Request register will be written. In order to make a software request, the channel must be in Block Mode. The Request register status for DMA1 and DMA2 is output on Bits [7:4] of a Status register read to the appropriate port.

1

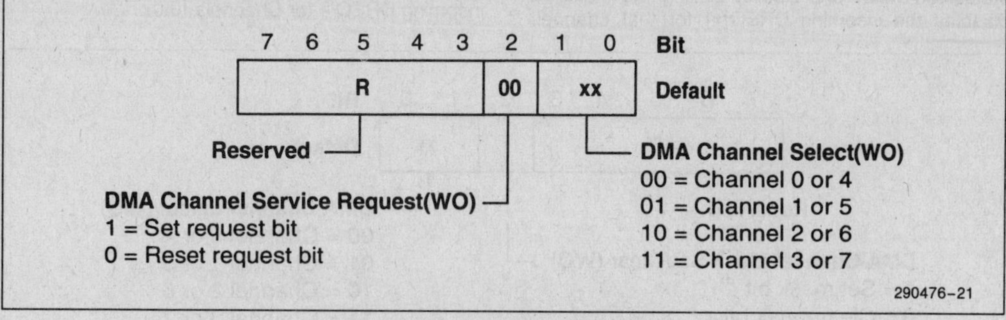

Figure 3-19. DMA Request Register

Table 3-20. DMA Request Register

Bit #	Description
7:3	**RESERVED:** (must be 0)
2	**DMA CHANNEL SERVICE REQUEST:** Writing a 0 to Bit 2 resets the individual software DMA channel request bit. Writing a 1 to Bit 2 will set the request bit. The request bit for each DMA channel is reset to 0 upon a reset or a Master Clear.
1:0	**DMA CHANNEL SELECT:** Bits [1:0] select the DMA channel mode register to program with bit 2. **Bit 1 / Bit 0 / Channel** 0 / 0 / Channel 0 0 / 1 / Channel 1 (5) 1 / 0 / Channel 2 (6) 1 / 1 / Channel 3 (7)

3.2.5 MASK REGISTER—WRITE SINGLE MASK BIT

Register Name: Mask Register—Write Single Mask Bit

Register Location: 0Ah—Channels 0–3
0D4h—Channels 4–7

Default Value: 000001xxb

Attribute: Write Only

Size: 1 bit/channel

Each DMA channel has a mask bit that can disable an incoming DMA channel service request DREQ[x] assertion. Two 4-bit registers store the current mask status for DMA1 and DMA2. Setting the mask bit disables the incoming DREQ[x] for that channel. Clearing the mask bit enables the incoming DREQ[x]. A channel's mask bit is automatically set when the Current Word Count register reaches terminal count (unless the channel is programmed for autoinitialization). Each mask bit may also be set or cleared under software control. The entire register is also set by a reset or a Master Clear. Setting the entire register disables all DMA requests until a clear Mask register instruction allows them to occur. This instruction format is similar to the format used with the Request register.

Individually masking DMA Channel 4 (DMA controller 2, Channel 0) will automatically mask DMA Channels [3:0], as this Channel group is logically cascaded onto Channel 4. Setting this mask bit disables the incoming DREQ's for Channels [3:0].

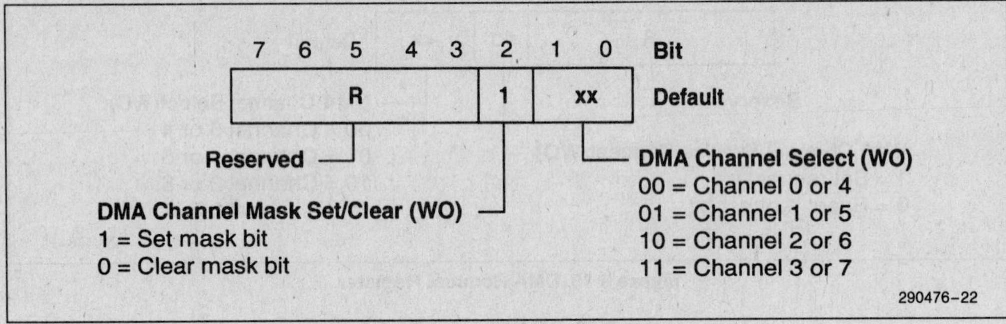

Figure 3-20. Mask Register Single Bit

Table 3-21. Mask Register Single Bit

Bit #	Description
7:3	**RESERVED:** (must be 0)
2	**DMA CHANNEL MASK SET/CLEAR:** Writing a 1 to Bit 2 sets the mask bit and disables the incoming DREQ for the selected channel. Writing a 0 to Bit 2 clears the mask bit and enables the incoming DREQ for the elected channel.
1:0	**DMA CHANNEL SELECT:** Bits [1:0] select the DMA Channel Mode Register to program with bit 2. **Bit 1 / Bit 0 / Channel** 0 / 0 / Channel 0 (4) 0 / 1 / Channel 1 (5) 1 / 0 / Channel 2 (6) 1 / 1 / Channel 3 (7)

3.2.6 MASK REGISTER—WRITE ALL MASK REGISTER BITS

Register Name: Mask Register-Write All Mask Register Bits

Register Location: 0Fh—Channels 0–3
0DEh—Channels 4–7

Default Value: 00001111b

Attribute: Read/Write

Size: 4 bits

This command allows enabling and disabling of incoming DREQ assertions by writing the mask bits for each controller, DMA1 or DMA2, simultaneously rather than by individual channel as is done with the "Write Single Mask Bit" command. Two 4-bit registers store the current mask status for DMA1 and DMA2. Setting the mask bit disables the incoming DREQ[x] for that channel. Clearing the mask bit enables the incoming DREQ[x]. Unlike the "Write Single Mask Bit" command, this command includes a status read to check the current mask status of the selected DMA channel group. When read, the mask register current status appears on Bits [3:0]. A channel's mask bit is automatically set when the Current Word Count register reaches terminal count (unless the channel is programmed for autoinitialization). The entire register is also set by a reset or a Master Clear. Setting the entire register disables all DMA requests until a clear Mask register instruction allows them to occur.

Two important points should be taken into consideration when programming the mask registers. First, individually masking DMA Channel 4 (DMA controller 2, Channel 0) will automatically mask DMA Channels [3:0], as this channel group is logically cascaded onto Channel 4. Second, masking off DMA controller 2 with a write to port 0DEh will also mask off DREQ assertions from DMA controller 1 for the same reason: when DMA Channel 4 is masked, so are DMA Channels 0–3.

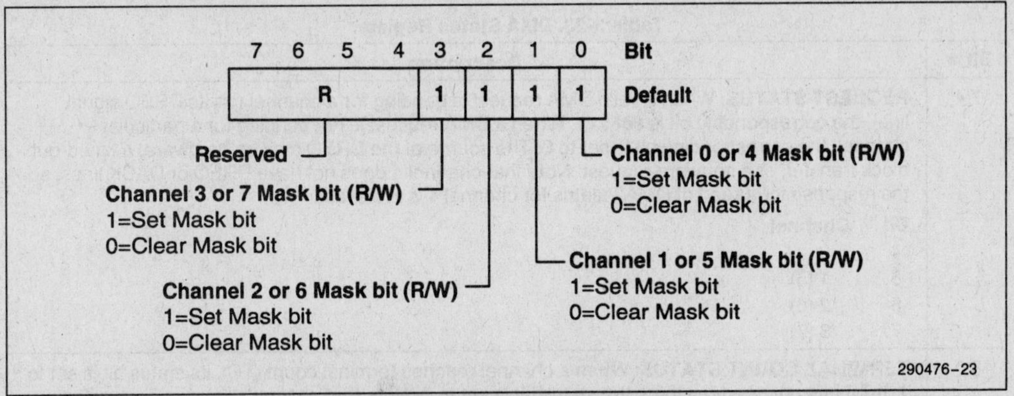

Figure 3-21. Mask Register All Bits

Table 3-22. Mask Register All Bits

Bit #	Description
7:4	**RESERVED:** Must be 0
3:0	**CHANNEL MASK BITS:** Setting the bit(s) to a 1 disables the corresponding DREQ(s). Setting the bit(s) to a 0 enables the corresponding DREQ(s). Bits [3:0] are set to 1 upon PCIRST# or Master Clear. When read, bits [3:0] indicate the DMA channel [3:0] ([7:4]) mask status. **Bit Channel** 0 0 (4) 1 1 (5) 2 2 (6) 3 3 (7) **NOTE:** Disabling channel 4 also disables channels 0–3 due to the cascade of DMA1 through channel 4 of DMA2.

3.2.7 DS—DMA STATUS REGISTER

Register Name: Status

Register Location: 08h—Channels 0–3
0D0h—Channels 4–7

Default Value: 00h

Attribute: Read Only

Size: 8 bits

Each DMA controller has a read-only Status register. A Status register read is used when determining which channels have reached terminal count and which channels have a pending DMA request. Bits [3:0] are set every time a TC is reached by that channel. These bits are cleared upon reset and on each Status Read. Bits [7:4] are set whenever their corresponding channel is requesting service.

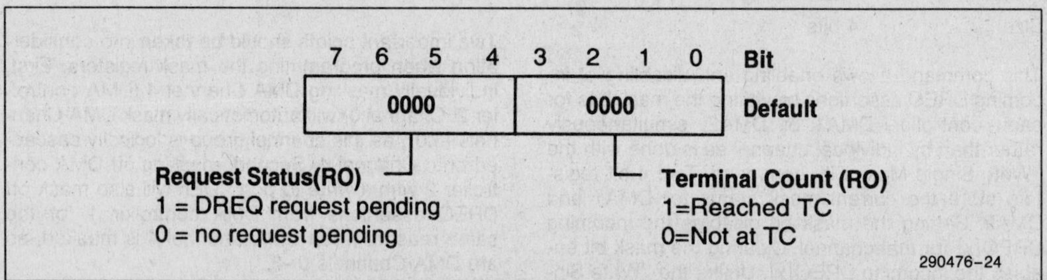

Figure 3-22. DMA Status Register

Table 3-23. DMA Status Register

Bit #	Description
7:4	**REQUEST STATUS:** When a valid DMA request is pending for a channel (on its DREQ signal line), the corresponding bit is set to 1. When a DMA request is not pending for a particular channel, the corresponding bit is set to 0. The source of the DREQ may be hardware, a timed-out block transfer, or a software request. Note that channel 4 does not have DREQ or DACK lines, so the response for a read of DMA2 status for channel 4 is irrelevant. **Bit Channel** 4 0 5 1 (5) 6 2 (6) 7 3 (7)
3:0	**TERMINAL COUNT STATUS:** When a channel reaches terminal count (TC), its status bit is set to 1. If TC has not been reached, the status bit is set to 0. Note that channel 4 is programmed for cascade, and is not used for a DMA transfer. Therefore, the TC bit response for a status read on DMA2 for channel 4 is irrelevant. **Bit Channel** 0 0 1 1 (5) 2 2 (6) 3 3 (7)

3.2.8 DMA BASE AND CURRENT ADDRESS REGISTER (8237 COMPATIBLE SEGMENT)

Register Name: DMA Base and Current Address Register (8237 Compatible Segment)

Register Location: 000h—DMA Channel 0
002h—DMA Channel 1
004h—DMA Channel 2
006h—DMA Channel 3
0C0h—DMA Channel 4
0C4h—DMA Channel 5
0C8h—DMA Channel 6
0CCh—DMA Channel 7

Default Value: 0000h

Attribute: Read/Write

Size: 16 bits per channel

Each channel has a 16-bit Current Address register. This register holds the value of the 16 least significant bits of the full 32-bit address used during DMA transfers. The address is automatically incremented or decremented after each transfer and the intermediate values of the address are stored in the Current Address register during the transfer. This register is written to or read from by the microprocessor or bus master in successive 8-bit bytes. The programmer must issue the "Clear Byte Pointer Flip-Flop" command to reset the internal byte pointer and correctly align the write prior to programming the Current address register. After clearing the Byte Pointer Flip-flop, the first write to the Current Address port programs the low byte, Bits [7:0], and the second write programs the high byte, Bits [15:8]. This procedure applies for read cycles also. It may also be re-initialized by an autoinitialize back to its original value. Autoinitialize takes place only after a TC or EOP.

Each channel has a Base Address register located at the same port address as the corresponding Current Address register. These registers store the original value of their associated Current registers. During autoinitialize these values are used to restore the Current registers to their original values. The Base registers are written simultaneously with their corresponding Current register in successive 8-bit bytes by the microprocessor. The Base registers cannot be read by any external agents.

In Scatter-Gather Mode these registers store the lowest 16 bits of the current memory address. During a Scatter-Gather transfer the DMA will load a reserve buffer into the base memory address register.

In Chaining Mode, these registers store the lowest 16 bits of the current memory address. The CPU will program the base register set with a reserve buffer.

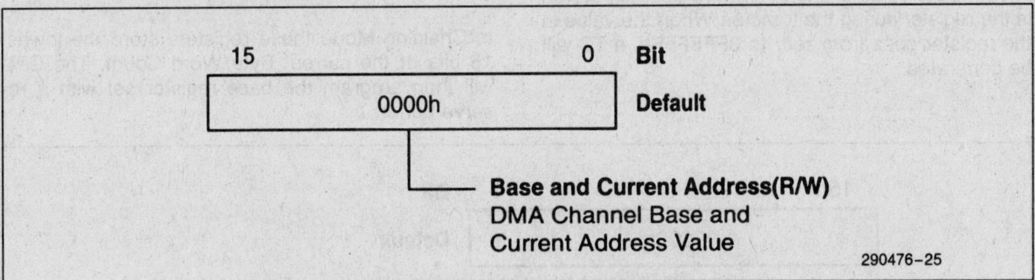

Figure 3-23. DMA Base and Current Address Register

Table 3-24. DMA Base and Current Address Register

Bit #	Description
15:0	**BASE AND CURRENT ADDRESS:** These bits represent the 16 least significant address bits used during DMA transfers. Together with the DMA Low Page register, they help form the ISA-compatible 24-bit DMA address. As an extension of the ISA compatible functionality, the DMA High Page register completes the 32-bit address needed when implementing ESC extensions such as DMA to the PCI bus slaves that can take advantage of full 32-bit addressability. Upon reset or Master Clear, the value of these bits is 0000h.

3.2.9 DMA BASE AND CURRENT BYTE/WORD COUNT REGISTER (8237 COMPATIBLE SEGMENT)

Register Name: DMA Base and Current Byte/Word Count Register (8237 Compatible Segment)

Register Location: 001h—DMA Channel 0
003h—DMA Channel 1
005h—DMA Channel 2
007h—DMA Channel 3
0C2h—DMA Channel 4
0C6h—DMA Channel 5
0CAh—DMA Channel 6
0CEh—DMA Channel 7

Default Value: 0000h

Attribute: Read/Write

Size: 16 bits per channel

Each channel has a 16-bit Current Byte/Word Count register. This register determines the lower 16 bits for the number of transfers to be performed. There is a total of 24 bits in the Byte/Word Count registers. The uppermost 8 bits are in the High Byte/Word Count register. The actual number of transfers will be one more than the number programmed in the Current Byte/Word Count register (i.e., programming a count of 100 will result in 101 transfers). The byte/word count is decremented after each transfer. The intermediate value of the byte/word count is stored in the register during the transfer. When the value in the register goes from zero to 0FFFFFFh, a TC will be generated.

Following the end of a DMA service it may also be re-initialized by an autoinitialization back to its original value. Autoinitialize can occur only when a TC occurs. If it is not autoinitialized, this register will have a count of FFFFh after TC.

When the Extended Mode register is programmed for "count by word" transfers to/from a 16-bit I/O, with shifted address, the Byte/Word count will indicate the number of 16-bit words to be transferred.

When the Extended Mode register is programmed for "count by byte" transfers, the Byte/Word Count will indicate the number of bytes to be transferred. The number of bytes does not need to be a multiple of the transfer size in this case.

Each channel has a Base Byte/Word Count register located at the same port address as the corresponding Current Byte/Word Count register. These registers store the original value of their associated Current registers. During Autoinitialize these values are used to restore the Current registers to their original values. The Base registers cannot be read by any external agents.

In Scatter-Gather mode these registers store the lowest 16 bits of the current Byte/Word Count. During a Scatter-Gather transfer the DMA will load a reserve buffer into the base Byte/Word Count register.

In Chaining Mode these registers store the lowest 16 bits of the current Byte/Word Count. The CPU will then program the base register set with a reserve buffer.

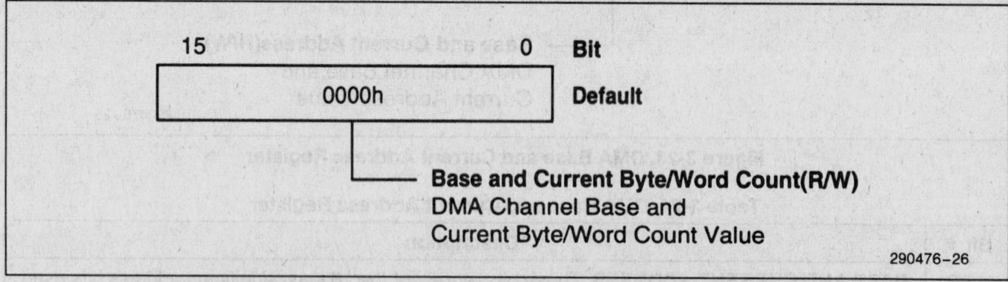

Figure 3-24. DMA Base and Current Byte/Word Count Register

Table 3-25. DMA Base and Current Byte/Word Count Register

Bit #	Description
15:0	**BASE AND CURRENT BYTE/WORD COUNT:** These bits represent the lower 16 byte/word count bits used when counting down a DMA transfer. Upon reset or Master Clear, the value of these bits is 0000h.

3.2.10 DMA BASE AND CURRENT HIGH BYTE/WORD COUNT REGISTER DMA BASE HIGH BYTE/WORD COUNT REGISTER

Register Name: DMA Base and Current High Byte/Word Count (Read/Write)
DMA Base High Byte/Word Count (Write Only)

Register Location: 401h—DMA Channel 0
403h—DMA Channel 1
405h—DMA Channel 2
407h—DMA Channel 3
4C6h—DMA Channel 5
4CAh—DMA Channel 6
4CEh—DMA Channel 7

Default Value: 00h

Attribute: Read/Write

Size: 8 bits per channel

Each channel has a 8-bit Current High Byte/Word Count register. This register provides the uppermost 8 bits for the number of transfers to be performed. The byte/word count is decremented after each transfer. The intermediate value of the byte/word count is stored in the register during the transfer. When the value in the register goes from zero to FFFFh, a TC may be generated.

Following the end of a DMA service it may also be re-initialized by an Autoinitialization back to its original value. Autoinitialize can occur only when a TC occurs. If it is not Autoinitialized, this register will have a count of FFFFh after TC.

The High Byte/Word Count register must be the last Byte/Word Count register programmed. Writing to the 8237 Compatible Byte/Word Count registers will clear the High Byte/Word Count register to 00h.

When the Extended Mode register is programmed for "count by word" transfers to/from a 16-bit I/O, with shifted address, the Byte/Word count will indicate the number of 16-bit words to be transferred.

When the Extended Mode register is programmed for "count by byte" transfers, the Byte/Word Count will indicate the number of bytes to be transferred. The number of bytes does not need to be a multiple of the transfer size in this case.

Each channel has a Base High Byte/Word Count register located at the same port address as the corresponding Current High Byte/Word Count register. These registers store the original value of their associated Current registers. During autoinitialize these values are used to restore the Current registers to their original values. Normally, the Base registers are written simultaneously with their corresponding Current register in successive 8-bit bytes by the microprocessor. However, in Chaining Mode only the Base register set is programmed and the Current register is not affected. The Base registers cannot be read by any external agents.

In Scatter-Gather mode these registers store the lowest 8 bits of the current High Byte/Word Count. During a Scatter-Gather transfer the DMA will load a reserve buffer into the base High Byte/Word Count register.

In Chaining Mode these registers store the lowest 8 bits of the current High Byte/Word Count. The CPU will then program the base register set with a reserve buffer.

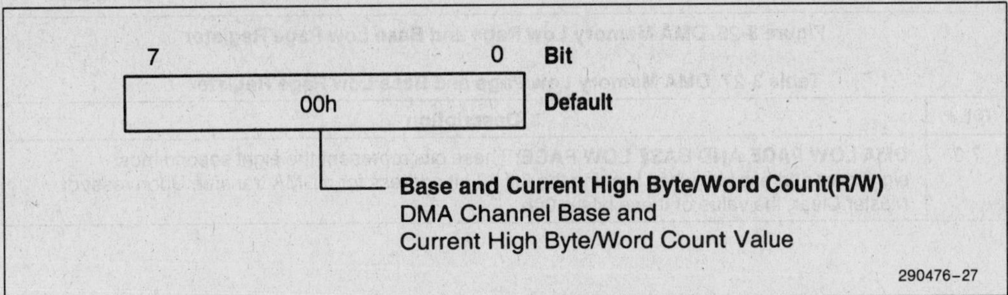

Figure 3-25. DMA Base and Current High Byte/Word Count Register

Table 3-26. DMA Base and Current High Byte/Word Count Register

Bit #	Description
7:0	**BASE AND CURRENT HIGH BYTE/WORD COUNT:** These bits represent the 8 high order byte/word count bits used when counting down a DMA transfer. Upon reset or Master Clear, the value of these bits is 00h.

3.2.11 DMA MEMORY LOW PAGE REGISTER DMA MEMORY BASE LOW PAGE REGISTER

Register Name:	DMA Memory Low Page (Read/Write) DMA Memory Base Low Page (Write Only)
Register Location:	087h—DMA Channel 0 083h—DMA Channel 1 081h—DMA Channel 2 082h—DMA Channel 3 08Bh—DMA Channel 5 089h—DMA Channel 6 08Ah—DMA Channel 7
Default Value:	00h
Size:	8 bits per channel

Each channel has an 8-bit Low Page register associated with it. The DMA memory Low Page register contains the eight second most-significant bits of the 32-bit address. It works in conjunction with the DMA controller's High Page register and Current Address register to define the complete (32-bit) address for the DMA channel. This 8-bit register is read or written directly by the processor or bus master. It may also be re-initialized by an Autoinitialize back to its original value. Autoinitialize takes place only after a TC or EOP.

Each channel has a Base Low Page Address register located at the same port address as the corresponding Current Low Page register. These registers store the original value of their associated Current Low Page registers. During autoinitialize these values are used to restore the Current Low Page registers to their original values. The 8-bit Base Low Page registers are written simultaneously with their corresponding Current Low Page register by the microprocessor. The Base Low Page registers cannot be read by any external agents.

During Scatter-Gather these registers store the 8 bits from the third byte of the current memory address. During a Scatter-Gather transfer the DMA will load a reserve buffer into the base memory address register.

In Chaining Mode these registers store the 8 bits from the third byte of the current memory address. The CPU will program the base register set with a reserve buffer.

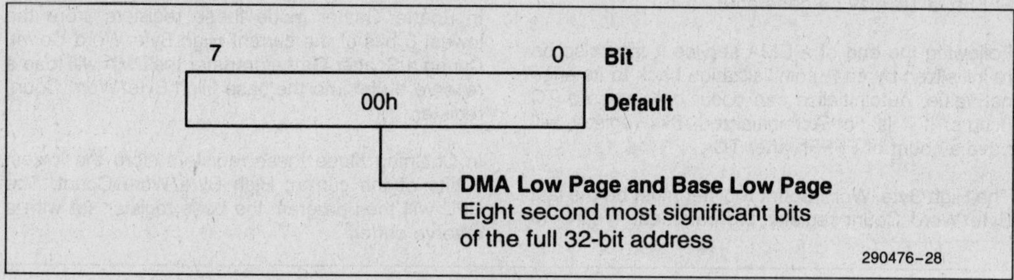

Figure 3-26. DMA Memory Low Page and Base Low Page Register

Table 3-27. DMA Memory Low Page and Base Low Page Register

Bit #	Description
7:0	**DMA LOW PAGE AND BASE LOW PAGE:** These bits represent the eight second most-significant address bits when forming the full 32-bit address for a DMA transfer. Upon reset or Master Clear, the value of these bits is 00h.

3.2.12 DMA PAGE REGISTER

Register Name: DMA Page (Read/Write)
Register Location: 080h, 84h, 85h, 86h, 88h, 8Ch, 8Dh, 8Eh
Default Value: xxh
Attribute: Read/Write
Size: 8 bits

These registers have no effect on the DMA operation. These registers provide extra storage space in the I/O space for DMA routines.

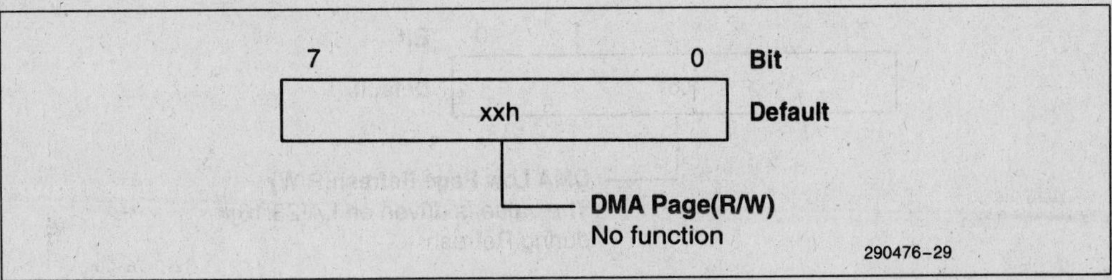

Figure 3-27. DMA Page Register

Table 3-28. DMA Page Register

Bit #	Description
7:0	**DMA PAGE:** These bits have no effect on the DMA operation. These bits only provide storage space in the I/O map.

3.2.13 DMA LOW PAGE REFRESH REGISTER

Register Name: DMA Low Page Refresh
Register Location: 08Fh
Default Value: xxh
Attribute: Read/Write
Size: 8 bits

The contents of this register are driven on the address byte 2 (LA[23:16]#) during Refresh cycles.

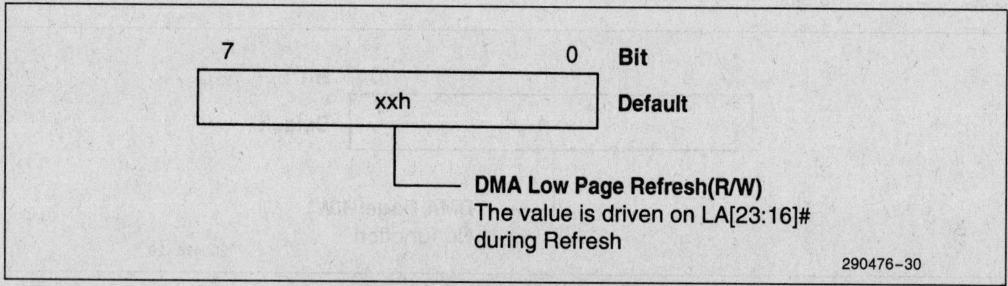

Figure 3-28. DMA Low Page Refresh Register

Table 3-29. DMA Low Page Refresh Register

Bit #	Description
7:0	**DMA LOW PAGE REFRESH:** The contents of the bits are driven on to the address bus during refresh.

3.2.14 DMA MEMORY HIGH PAGE REGISTER DMA MEMORY BASE HIGH PAGE REGISTER

Register Name: DMA Memory High Page (Read/Write)
DMA Memory Base High Page (Write Only)

Register Location: 0487h—DMA Channel 0
0483h—DMA Channel 1
0481h—DMA Channel 2
0482h—DMA Channel 3
048Bh—DMA Channel 5
0489h—DMA Channel 6
048Ah—DMA Channel 7

Default Value: 00h

Size: 8 bits per channel

Each channel has an 8-bit High Page register. The DMA memory High Page register contains the eight most-significant bits of the 32-bit address. It works in conjunction with the DMA controller's Low Page register and Current Address register to define the complete (32-bit) address for the DMA channels and corresponds to the "Current Address" register for each channel. This 8-bit register is read or written directly by the processor or bus master. It may also be re-initialized by an Autoinitialize back to its original value. Autoinitialize takes place only after a TC or EOP.

This register is reset to 00h during the programming of both the low page register and the Current Address register. Thus, if this register is not programmed after the other address and Low Page registers are programmed, then its value will be zero. In this case, the DMA channel will operate the same as an 82C37 (from an addressing standpoint). This is the address compatibility mode.

If the high 8 bits of the address are programmed after the other addresses, then the channel will modify its operation to increment (or decrement) the entire 32-bit address. This is unlike the 82C37 "Page" register in the original PCs which could only increment to a 64k boundary (for 8-bit channels) or 128k (for 16-bit channels). This is extended address mode. In this mode, the ISA bus controller will generate the signals MEMR# and MEMW# only for addresses below 16 Mbytes.

Each channel has a Base High Page Address register located at the same port address as the corresponding Current High Page Address register. These registers store the original value of their associated Current registers. During Autoinitialize these values are used to restore the Current registers to their original values. The 8-bit Base High Page registers are written simultaneously with their corresponding Current register by the microprocessor. The Base registers cannot be read by any external agents.

During Scatter-Gather these registers store the 8 bits from the highest byte of the current memory address. During a Scatter-Gather transfer the DMA will load a reserve buffer into the base memory address register.

In Chaining Mode these registers store the 8 bits from the highest byte of the current memory address. The CPU will program the base register set with a reserve buffer.

1

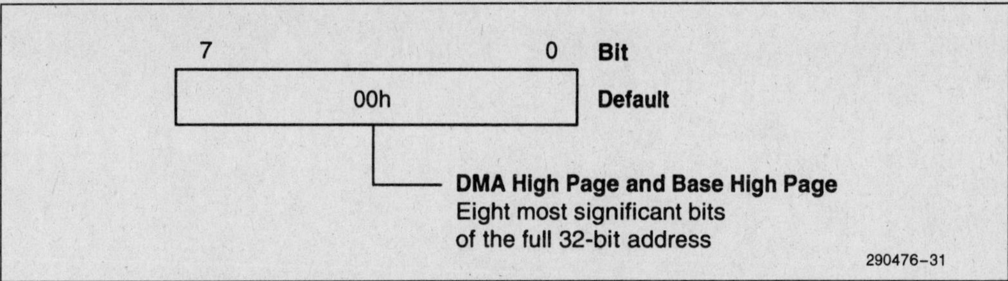

Figure 3-29. DMA Memory High Page and Base High Page Register

Table 3-30. DMA Memory High Page and Base High Page Register

Bit #	Description
7:0	**DMA HIGH PAGE AND BASE HIGH PAGE:** These bits represent the eight most-significant address bits when forming the full 32-bit address for a DMA transfer. Upon reset or Master Clear, the value of these bits is 00h.

3.2.15 DMA HIGH PAGE REGISTER REFRESH

Register Name:	DMA High Page Register Refresh (Read/Write)
Register Location:	048Fh
Default Value:	xxh
Attribute:	Read/Write
Size:	8 bits per channel

The contents of this register are driven on the address byte 3 (LA[31:24]#) during Refresh cycles.

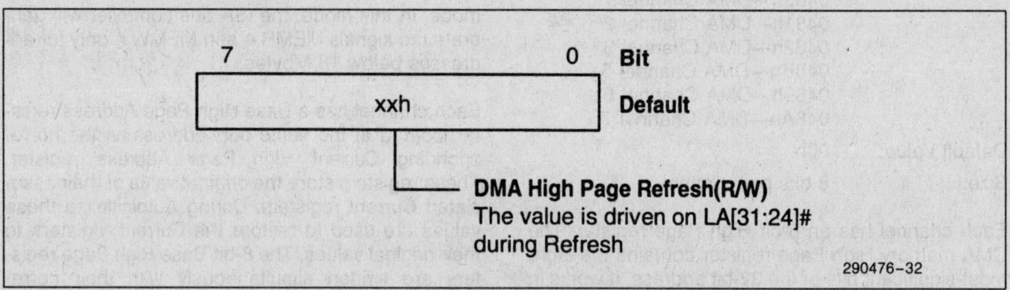

Figure 3-30. DMA High Page Refresh Register

Table 3-31. DMA High Page Refresh Register

Bit #	Description
7:0	**DMA HIGH PAGE REFRESH:** The contents of the bits are driven on to the address bus during refresh.

3.2.16 STOP REGISTERS

Register Name: Stop Registers

Register Location:

04E0h—CH0 Stop Reg Bits [7:2]
04E1h—CH0 Stop Reg Bits [15:8]
04E2h—CH0 Stop Reg Bits [23:16]
04E4h—CH1 Stop Reg Bits [7:2]
04E5h—CH1 Stop Reg Bits [15:8]
04E6h—CH1 Stop Reg Bits [23:16]
04E8h—CH2 Stop Reg Bits [7:2]
04E9h—CH2 Stop Reg Bits [15:8]
04EAh—CH2 Stop Reg Bits [23:16]
04ECh—CH3 Stop Reg Bits [7:2]
04EDh—CH3 Stop Reg Bits [15:8]
04EEh—CH3 Stop Reg Bits [23:16]
04F4h—CH5 Stop Reg Bits [7:2]
04F5h—CH5 Stop Reg Bits [15:8]
04F6h—CH5 Stop Reg Bits [23:16]
04F8h—CH6 Stop Reg Bits [7:2]
04F9h—CH6 Stop Reg Bits [15:8]
04FAh—CH6 Stop Reg Bits [23:16]
04FCh—CH7 Stop Reg Bits [7:2]
04FDh—CH7 Stop Reg Bits [15:8]
04FEh—CH7 Stop Reg Bits [23:16]

Default Value: See Below
Attribute: Read/Write
Size: See Below

The Stop registers are used to support a common data communication structure, the ring buffer. The ring buffer data structure and Stop register operation are described in Section 6.7.4. The Stop registers, in conjunction with a channel's Base and Current address and byte count registers, are used to define a fixed portion of memory for use by the ring buffer data structure. Following a reset, these registers are all reset to "0".

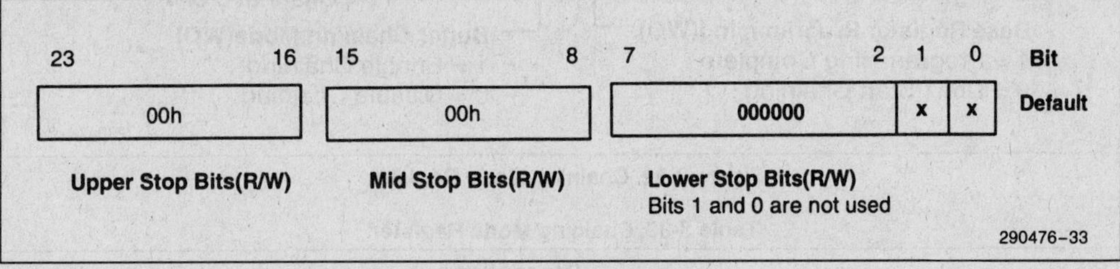

Figure 3-31. Stop Registers

Table 3-32. Stop Registers

Bit #	Description
23:2	**UPPER, MID, LOWER STOP BITS:** These 22 bits provide the Stop Address. If the Stop function is enabled then the channel will Stop whenever its Memory Address matches the Stop Address.

3.2.17 CHAINING MODE REGISTER

Register Name: Chaining Mode Register
Register Location: 040Ah—Channels 0–3
04D4h—Channels 4–7
Default Value: 000000xxb
Attribute: Write Only
Size: 8 bits

Each channel has a Chaining Mode register. The Chaining Mode register enables or disables DMA buffer chaining and indicates when the DMA Base registers are being programmed. When writing to the register, Bits [1:0] determine which channel's Chaining Mode register to program. The chaining status and interrupt status for all channels can be determined by reading the Chaining Mode Status, Channel Interrupt Status, and Chain Buffer Expiration Control registers. The Chaining Mode register is reset to zero upon reset, access (read or write) of a channel's Mode register or Extended Mode register, or a Master Clear. The values upon reset are disable chaining mode and generate IRQ13.

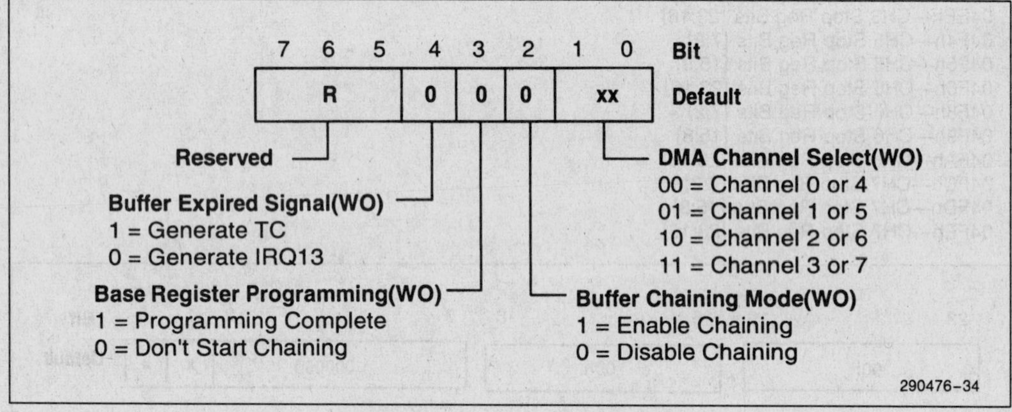

Figure 3-32. Chaining Mode Register

Table 3-33. Chaining Mode Register

Bit #	Description
7:5	**RESERVED:** (must be 0)
4	**BUFFER EXPIRED SIGNAL:** After one of the two buffers in the DMA expires then the DMA will inform the CPU that the next buffer should be loaded into the base register set. This bit determines whether IRQ13 or EOP should be used to inform the CPU that the buffer is complete.
3	**BASE REGISTER PROGRAMMING:** After the reserve buffer's address and word count are written to the base register set, this bit should be set to 1 to inform the DMA that the second buffer is ready for transfer.
2	**BUFFER CHAINING MODE:** Bit 2 enables the chaining mode logic. If the bit is set to 1 after the initial DMA address and word count are programmed, then the Base address and word count are available for programming the next buffer in the chain.
1:0	**DMA CHANNEL SELECT:** Bits [1:0] select the DMA channel mode register to program with Bits [4:2].

3.2.18 CHAINING MODE STATUS REGISTER

Register Name: Chaining Mode Status Register
Register Location: 04D4h
Default Value: 00h
Attribute: Read Only
Size: 8 bits

This register is read only and is used to determine if chaining mode for a particular channel is enabled or disabled. A "1" read in this register indicates that the channel's chaining mode is enabled. A "0" indicates that the chaining mode is disabled. All Chaining mode bits are disabled after a reset with reset. After the DMA is used in Chaining mode the CPU will need to clear the Chaining mode enable bit if non-Chaining mode is desired.

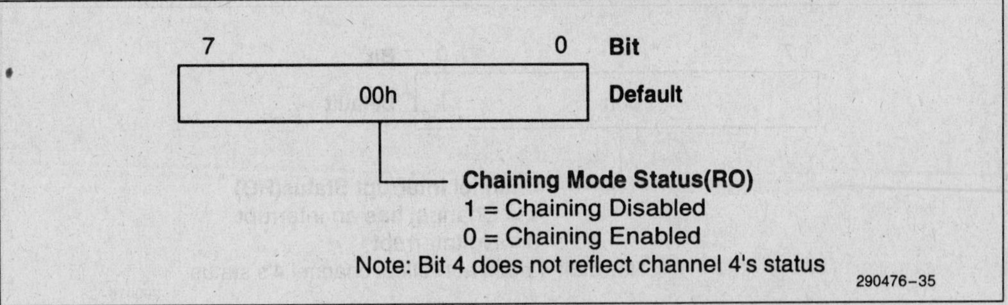

Figure 3-33. Chaining Mode Status Register

Table 3-34. Chaining Mode Status Register

Bit #	Description
7:5, 3:0	**CHAINING MODE STATUS:** If this bit is set to 1 then this channel has chaining enabled by writing 1 to Bit 2 of the Chaining Mode Register. This bit can be reset to 0 by either writing a 0 to Bit 2 of the Chaining Mode Register or reset being asserted or by a Master Clear Command.

3.2.19 CHANNEL INTERRUPT STATUS REGISTER

Register Name: Channel Interrupt Status
Register Location: 040Ah
Default Value: 00h
Attribute: Read Only
Size: 8 bits

Channel Interrupt Status is a read only register and is used to indicate the source (channel) of a DMA chaining interrupt on IRQ13. The DMA controller asserts IRQ13 after reaching terminal count, with chaining mode enabled. It does not assert IRQ13 during the initial programming sequence that loads the Base registers. After a reset, a read of this register will produce 00h.

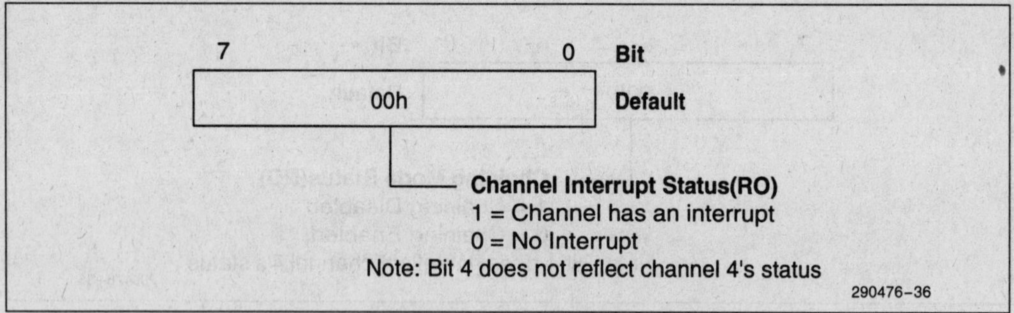

Figure 3-34. Channel Interrupt Status Register

Table 3-35. Channel Interrupt Status Register

Bit #	Description
7:5, 3:0	**CHAINING INTERRUPT STATUS:** When a channel interrupt status read returns a "0", Bit [7:5, 3:0] indicates that channel did not assert IRQ13. When a channel interrupt status read returns a "1", then that channel asserted IRQ13 after reaching a Terminal Count.

3.2.20 CHAIN BUFFER EXPIRATION CONTROL REGISTER

Register Name: Chain Buffer Expiration Control
Register Location: 040Ch
Default Value: 00h
Attribute: Read Only
Size: 8 bits

This register is read only and reflects the outcome of the expiration of a chain buffer. A Chain Buffer Expiration Control register bit with 0 indicates the DMA controller asserts IRQ13 when the DMA controller reaches terminal count. A "1" indicates the DMA controller asserts TC when the DMA controller reaches terminal count. This bit is programmed in Bit 4 of the Chaining Mode register.

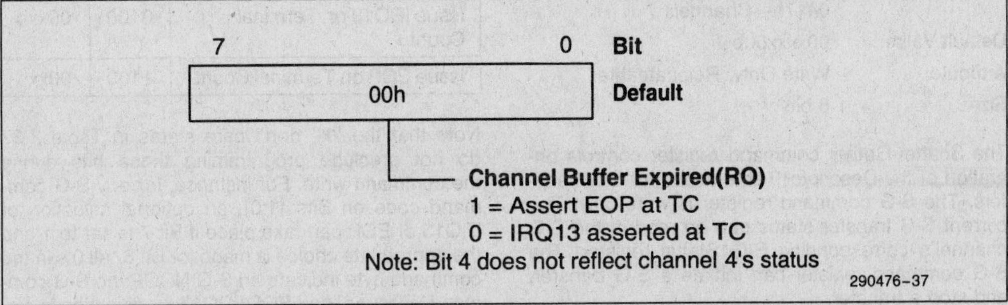

Figure 3-35. Chain Buffer Expiration Control Register

Table 3-36. Chain Buffer Expiration Control Register

Bit #	Description
7:5, 3:0	**CHAINING BUFFER EXPIRED:** When a chain buffer expiration control read returns "0", Bit [7:5, 3:0] indicates that Channel [7:5, 3:0] will assert IRQ13 when the DMA channel reaches terminal count. When a chain buffer expiration control read returns "1", Bit [7:5, 3:0] indicates that Channel [7:5, 3:0] will assert TC when the DMA controller reaches terminal count. This bit will reset to 0 following a reset.

1

3.2.21 SCATTER-GATHER COMMAND REGISTER

Register Name: Scatter-Gather Command
Register Location: 0410h—Channels 0
0411h—Channels 1
0412h—Channels 2
0413h—Channels 3
0415h—Channels 5
0416h—Channels 6
0417h—Channels 7
Default Value: 00xxxx00b
Attribute: Write Only, Relocateable
Size: 8 bits

The Scatter-Gather command register controls operation of the Descriptor Table aspect of S-G transfers. The S-G command register is write only. The current S-G transfer status can be read in the S-G channel's corresponding S-G Status register. The S-G command register can initiate a S-G transfer, and stop a transfer.

Scatter-Gather commands are issued with command codes. Bits [1:0] are used to implement the code mechanism. The S-G codes are described in the table below. Bit 7 is used to control the IRQ13/EOP assertion that follows a terminal count. Bit 6 controls the effect of Bit 7. Common Scatter-Gather command writes are listed in Table 3-37.

Table 3-37. Scatter-Gather Command Bits

Command	Bits	
	7654	3210
No S-G Operation (S-G NOOP)	0000	0000b
Start S-G	xx00	0001b
Stop S-G	xx00	0010b
Issue IRQ13 on Terminal Count	0100	00xxb
Issue EOP on Terminal Count	1100	00xxb

Note that the "x" don't care states in Table 3-37 do not preclude programming those bits during the command write. For instance, for any S-G command code on Bits [1:0], an optional selection of IRQ13 or EOP can take place if Bit 7 is set to 1 and the appropriate choice is made for Bit 6. All 0's in the command byte indicate an S-G NOOP: no S-G command is issued, and EOP/IRQ13 modification is disabled. Note that an EOP/IRQ13 modification can be made while disabling the S-G command bits (Bits[1:0] = 00b); conversely, an S-G command may be issued while EOP/IRQ13 modification is disabled (Bit 6 = 0b). After a reset, or Master Clear, IRQ13 is disabled and EOP is enabled.

The Start command assumes the Base and Current registers are both empty and will request a prefetch automatically. It also sets the status register to S-G Active, Base Empty, Current Empty, not Terminated, and Next Null Indicator to 0. The EOP/IRQ13 bit will still reflect the last value programmed.

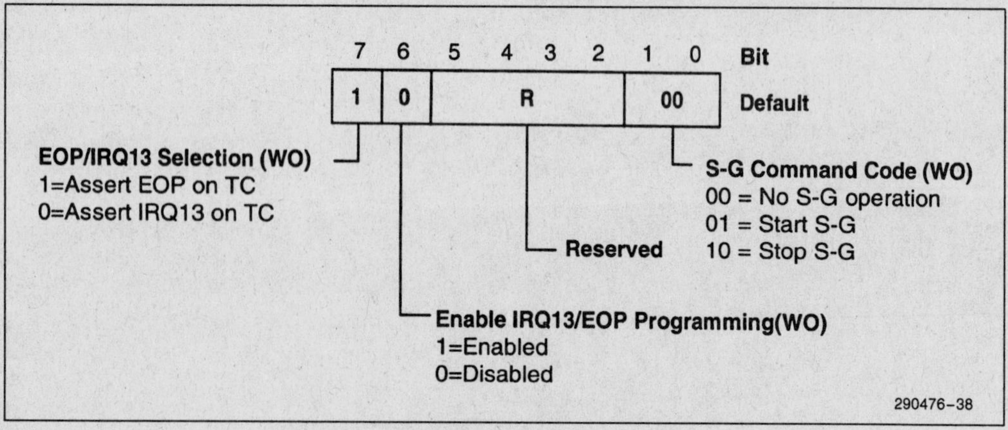

Figure 3-36. Scatter-Gather Command Register

Table 3-38. Scatter-Gather Command Register

Bit #	Description
7	**EOP/IRQ13 SELECTION:** Bit 7 is used to select whether EOP or IRQ will be asserted at termination caused by the last buffer expiring. The last buffer can be either the last buffer in the list or the last buffer loaded in the DMA while it is suspended. If this bit is set to 1 then EOP will be asserted whenever the last buffer is completed. If this bit is set to 0 then IRQ13 will be asserted whenever the last buffer is completed. EOP can be used to alert an expansion bus I/O device that a scatter-gather termination condition was reached; the I/O device in turn can assert its own interrupt request line, and invoke a dedicated interrupt handling routine. IRQ13 should be used whenever the CPU needs to be notified directly. Following reset, or Master Clear, the value stored for this bit is 0, and IRQ13 is selected. Bit 6 must be set to a 1 to enable this bit during an S-G Command register write. When Bit 6 is a 0 during the write, Bit 7 will not have any effect on the current EOP/IRQ13 selection.
6	**ENABLE IRQ13/EOP PROGRAMMING:** Enabling IRQ13/EOP programming allows initialization or modification of the S-G termination handling bits. If Bit 5 is reset to "0", Bit 7 will not have any affect on the state of IRQ13 or EOP assertion. When Bit 5 is set to a "1", Bit 7 determines the termination handling following a terminal count.
5:2	**RESERVED.**
1:0	**S-G COMMAND CODE:** 00 = No S-G command operation is performed. Bits[7:5] may still be used to program EOP/IRQ13 selection. 01 = The Start command initiates the scatter-gather process. Immediately after the Start command is issued a request is issued to fetch the initial buffer to fill the Base Register set in preparation for performing a transfer. The Buffer Prefetch request has the same priority with respect to other channels as the DREQ it is associated with. Within the channel, DREQ is higher in priority than a prefetch request. 10 = The Stop command halts a Scatter-Gather transfer immediately. When a Stop command is given, the Terminate bit in the S-G Status register and the DMA channel mask bit are both set. 11 = Reserved

The S-G Status register contains information on the S-G transfer status. This register maintains dynamic status information on S-G Transfer Activity, the Current and Base Buffer state, S-G Transfer Termination, and the End of the List indicator.

3.2.22 SCATTER-GATHER STATUS REGISTER

Register Name: Scatter-Gather Status

Register Location: Channels 0
0419h—Channels 1
041Ah—Channels 2
041Bh—Channels 3
041Dh—Channels 5
041Eh—Channels 6
041Fh—Channels 7

Default Value: 08h

Attribute: Read Only, Relocatable

Size: 8 bits

The Scatter-Gather Status register provides Scatter-Gather process status information to the CPU or Master. An Active bit is set to 1 after the S-G Start command is issued. The Active bit will be 0 before the initial Start command, following a terminal count, and after an S-G Stop command is issued. The Current Buffer and Base Buffer State bits indicate whether the corresponding register has a buffer loaded. It is possible for the Base Buffer State to be set while the Current Buffer State is cleared. When the Current Buffer transfer is complete, the Base Buffer will not be moved into the Current Buffer until the start of the next data transfer. Thus, the Current Buffer State is empty (cleared), while the Base Buffer State is full (set). The Terminate bit is set active after a Stop command, after TC for the last buffer in the list and both Base and Current buffers have expired. The EOP and IRQ13 bits indicate which end of process indicator will be used to alert the system of an S-G process termination. The EOL status bit is set if DMA controller has loaded the last buffer of the Link List.

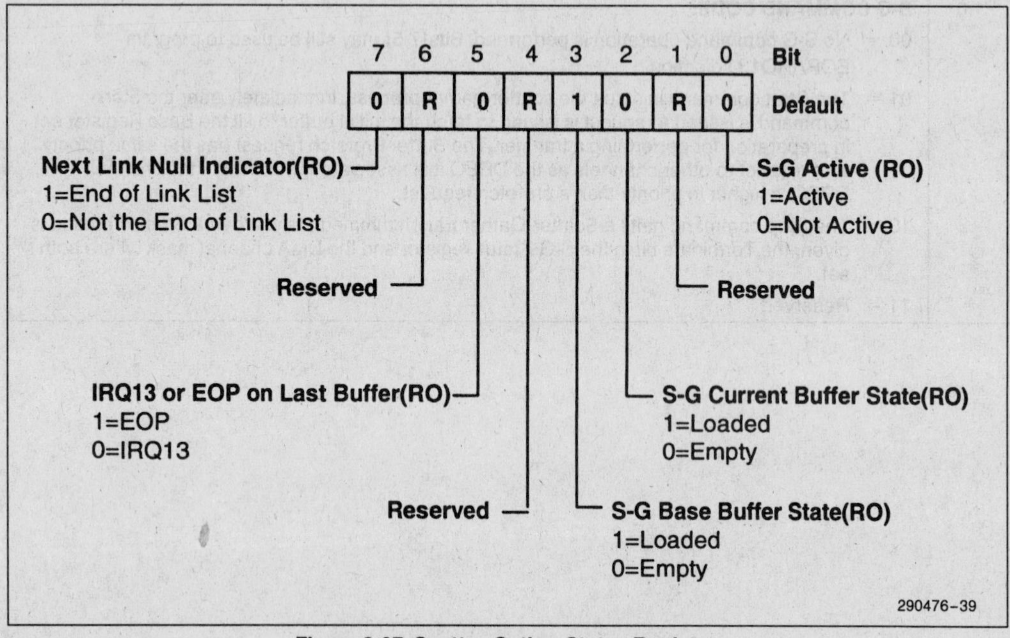

Figure 3-37. Scatter-Gather Status Register

Table 3-39. Scatter-Gather Status Register

Bit #	Description
7	**NEXT LINK NULL INDICATOR:** If the Next SGD fetched from memory during a fetch operation has the EOL value (1), the current value of the Next Link register is not overwritten. Instead, Bit 7 of the channel's S-G Status register, the Next Link Null indicator, is set to a "1". If the fetch returns a EOL value not equal to (1), this bit is reset to "0". This status bit is written after every fetch operation. Following reset, or Master Clear, this bit is reset to "0". This bit is also cleared by an S-G Start Command Write.
6	**RESERVED.**
5	**IRQ13 OR EOP ON LAST BUFFER:** When the IRQ13/EOP status bit contains a "1", EOP was either defaulted to at reset or selected through the S-G Command register as the S-G process termination indicator. EOP will be issued to alert the system when a terminal count occurs or following the Stop Command. When this bit is returned as a "0", an IRQ13 will be issued to alert the CPU of this same status.
4	**RESERVED.**
3	**S-G BASE BUFFER STATE:** When the Base Buffer status bit contains a "0", the Base Buffer is empty. When the Base Buffer Status bit is set to "1", the Base buffer has a buffer link loaded. Note that the Base Buffer State may be set while the Current buffer state is cleared. This condition occurs when the Current Buffer expires following a transfer; the Base Buffer will not be moved into the Current Register until the start of the next DMA transfer.
2	**S-G CURRENT BUFFER STATE:** When the Current Buffer status bit contains a "0", the Current Buffer is empty. When the Current Buffer status bit is set to "1", the Current Buffer has a buffer link loaded and is considered full. Following reset, Bit 2 is reset to "0".
1	**RESERVED.**
0	**S-G ACTIVE:** The Scatter-Gather Active bit indicates the current S-G transfer status. Bit 0 will be a 1 after a S-G Start Command is issued. Bit 0 will be a 0 before the Start command is issued. Bit 0 will be a 0 after terminal count on the last buffer on the channel is reached. Bit 0 will also be a 0 after a S-G Stop command has been issued. Following reset, or Master Clear, this bit is reset to "0".

1

3.2.23 SCATTER-GATHER DESCRIPTOR TABLE POINTER REGISTER

Register Name: Scatter-Gather Descriptor Table Pointer

Register Location: 0420h–0423h—Channels 0
0424h–0424h—Channels 1
0428h–042Bh—Channels 2
042Ch–042Ch—Channels 3
0434h–0437h—Channels 5
0438h–043Bh—Channels 6
043Ch–043Fh—Channels 7

Default Value: See below

Attribute: Read/Write, Relocatable

Size: 32 bits

The SGD Table Pointer register contains the 32-bit pointer to the first SGD entry in the SGD table in memory. Before the start of a S-G transfer, this register should have been programmed to point to the first SGD in the SGD table. Following a "Start" command, it initiates reading the first SGD entry by pointing to the first SGD entry to be fetched from the memory. Subsequently, at the end of the each buffer block transfer, the contents of the SGD table pointer registers are incremented by 8 until the end of the SGD table is reached.

When programmed by the CPU, the SGD Table Pointer Registers can be programmed with a single 32-bit PCI write.

NOTE:
The PCEB and EISA Bus Controller will split the 32-bit write into four 8-bit writes.

Following a prefetch to the address pointed to by the channel's SGD table pointer register, the new Memory Address is loaded into the Base Address register, the new Byte Count is loaded into the Base Byte Count register, and the newly fetched Next SGD replaces the current Next SGD value.

The end of the SGD table is indicated by a End of Table field having a MSB equal to 1. When this value is read during a SGD fetch, the current SGD value is not replaced. Instead, Bit 7 of the channel's status register is set to a 1 when the EOL is read from memory.

Table 3-40. Scatter-Gather Table Pointer Register

Bit #	Description
31:0	**SGD TABLE POINTER:** The SGD table pointer register contains a 32-bit pointer to the main memory location where the software maintains the Scatter-Gather Descriptors for the linked-list buffers. These bits are translated into A[31:0] signals for accessing memory on the PCI.

3.2.24 CLEAR BYTE POINTER FLIP-FLOP REGISTER

Register Name: Clear Byte Pointer Flip-Flop
Register Location: 00Ch—Channels 0-3
0D8h—Channels 4-7
Default Value: xxh
Attribute: Write Only
Size: n/a

This command is executed prior to writing or reading new address or word count information to the DMA. This initializes the flip-flop to a known state so that subsequent accesses to register contents by the microprocessor will address upper and lower bytes in the correct sequence.

The Clear Byte Pointer command clears the internal latch used to address the upper or lower byte of the 16-bit address and Word Count registers. The latch is also cleared at power on by reset and by the Master Clear command. The Host CPU may read or write a 16-bit DMA controller register by performing two consecutive accesses to the I/O port. The Clear Byte Pointer command precedes the first access. The first I/O write to a register port loads the least significant byte, and the second access automatically accesses the most significant byte.

When the Host CPU is reading or writing DMA registers, two Byte Pointer Flip-Flops are used; one for Channels 0-3 and one for Channels 4-7. Both of these act independently. There are separate software commands for clearing each of them (0Ch for Channels 0-3, 0D8h for Channels 4-7).

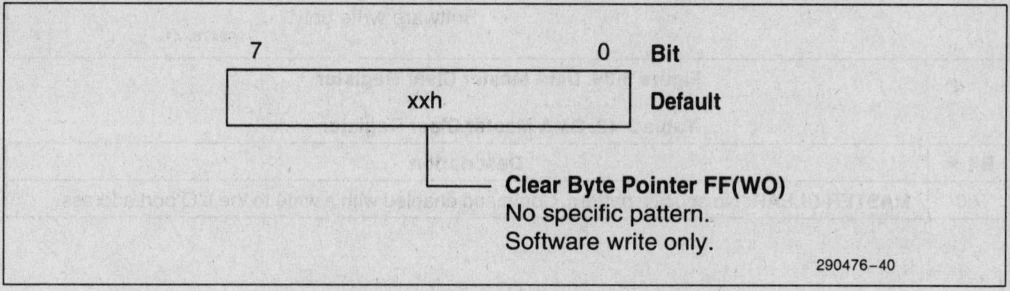

Figure 3-38. Clear Byte Pointer Flip-Flop Register

Table 3-41. Clear Byte Pointer Flip-Flop Register

Bit #	Description
7:0	**CLEAR BYTE POINTER FF:** No specific pattern. Command enabled with a write to the I/O port address.

3.2.25 DMC—DMA MASTER CLEAR REGISTER

Register Name: Master Clear

Register Location: 00Dh—Channels 0–3
0DAh—Channels 4–7

Default Value: xxh

Attribute: Write Only

Size: n/a

This software instruction has the same effect as the hardware Reset. The Command, Status, Request, and Internal First/Last Flip-Flop registers are cleared and the Mask register is set. The DMA controller will enter the idle cycle.

There are two independent Master Clear Commands, 0Dh which acts on Channels 0–3, and 0DAh which acts on Channels 4–7.

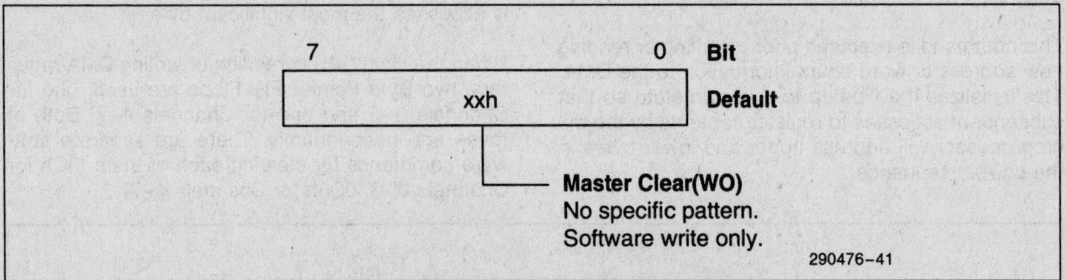

Figure 3-39. DMA Master Clear Register

Table 3-42. DMA Master Clear Register

Bit #	Description
7:0	**MASTER CLEAR:** No specific pattern. Command enabled with a write to the I/O port address.

3.2.26 DCM—DMA CLEAR MASK REGISTER

Register Name: Clear Mask

Register Location: Port Address:
00Eh—Channels 0–3
0DCh—Channels 4–7

Default Value: xxh

Attribute: Write Only

Size: n/a

This command clears the mask bits of all four channels, enabling them to accept DMA requests. I/O port 0Eh is used for Channels 0–3 and I/O port 0DCh is used for Channels 4–7.

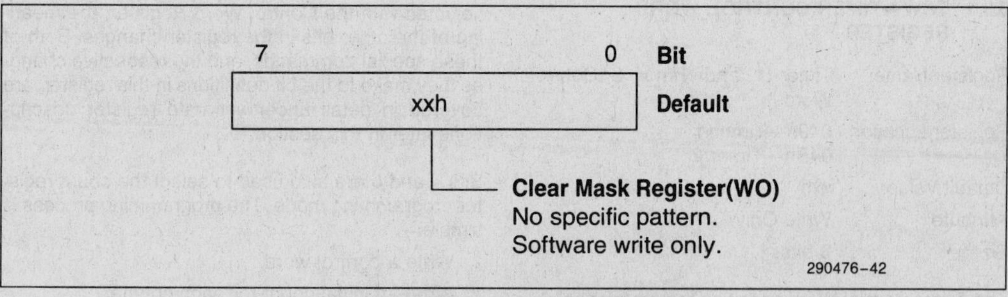

Figure 3-40. DMA Clear Mask Register

Table 3-43. DMA Clear Mask Register

Bit #	Description
7:0	**CLEAR MASK:** No specific pattern. Command enabled with a write to the I/O port address.

3.3 Timer Unit Registers

The ESC contains five counters that are equivalent to those found in the 82C54 Programmable Interval Timer. The Timer registers control these counters and can be accessed from the EISA Bus via I/O space. This section describes the counter/timer registers on the ESC. The counter/timer operations are further described in Chapter 8.0, Interval Timers.

3.3.1 TCW—TIMER CONTROL WORD REGISTER

Register Name:	Timer 1 and Timer 2 Control Word
Register Location:	043h—Timer 1 04Bh—Timer 2
Default Value:	xxh
Attribute:	Write Only
Size:	8 bits

The Timer Control Word specifies the counter selection, the operating mode, the counter byte programming order and size of the COUNT value, and whether it counts down in a 16-bit or binary-coded decimal (BCD) format. After writing the control word, a new count may be written at any time. The new value will take effect according to the programmed mode.

There are six programmable counting modes. Typically, the ESC Timer Unit Counters 0 and 2 are programmed for Mode 3, the Square Wave Mode, while Counter 1 is programmed in Mode 2, the Rate Generator Mode.

Two special commands are selected through the Control Word Register. The Counter Latch Command is selected when Bits[5:4] are both "0". The Read-Back Command is selected when Bits[7:6] are both "1". When either of these two commands are selected with the Control Word Register, the meaning of the other bits in the register changes. Both of these special commands, and the respective changes they make to the bit definitions in this register, are covered in detail under separate register descriptions later in this section.

Bits 4 and 5 are also used to select the count register programming mode. The programming process is simple:

1. Write a control word.
2. Write an initial count for each counter.
3. Load the LSB, MSB, or LSB then MSB.

The read/write selection chosen with the control word dictates the programming sequence that must follow when initializing the specified counter.

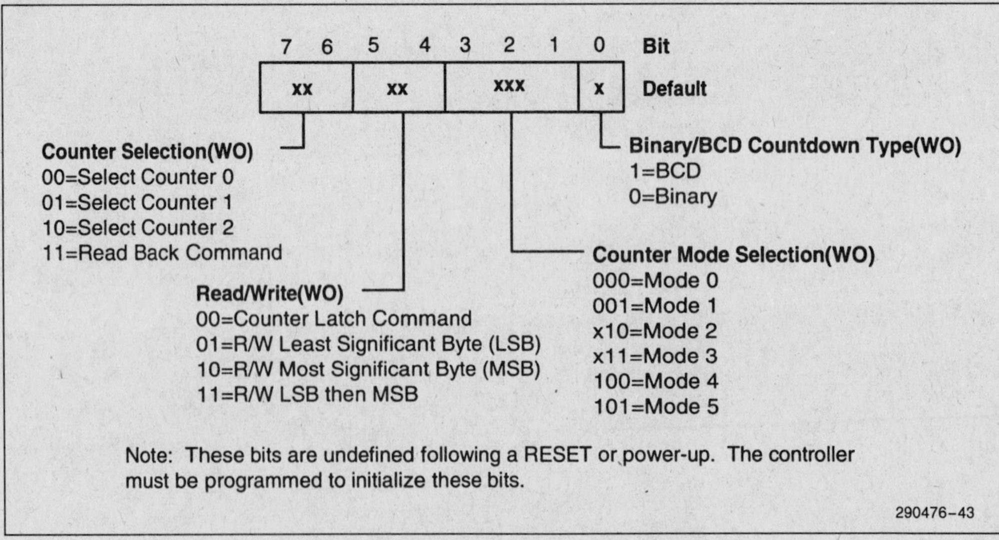

Figure 3-41. Timer Control Word Register

If a counter is programmed to read/write two-byte counts, the following precaution applies: A program must not transfer control between writing the first and second byte to another routine which also writes into that same counter. Otherwise, the counter will be loaded with an incorrect count. The count must always be completely loaded with both bytes.

Bits 6 and 7 are also used to select the counter for the control word you are writing.

Following reset, the control words for each register are undefined. You must program each timer to bring it into a known state. However, each counter OUT signal is reset to 0 following reset. The SPKR output, interrupt controller input IRQ0 (internal), Bit 5 of port 061h, and the internally generated Refresh request are each reset to 0 following reset.

Table 3-44. Timer Control Word Register

<table>
<tr><th>Bit #</th><th>Description</th></tr>
<tr><td>7:6</td><td>COUNTER SELECT: The Counter Selection bits select the counter the control word acts upon as shown below. The Read Back Command is selected when bits[7:6] are both 1.
Bit 7 | Bit 6 | Function
0 | 0 | Counter 0 select
0 | 1 | Counter 1 select
1 | 0 | Counter 2 select
1 | 1 | Read Back Command (see Section 3.3.2)</td></tr>
<tr><td>5:4</td><td>READ/WRITE SELECT: Bits [5:4] are the read/write control bits. The Counter Latch Command is selected when bits[5:4] are both 0. The read/write options include read/write least significant byte, read/write most significant byte, or read/write the LSB and then the MSB. The actual counter programming is done through the counter I/O port (040h, 041h, and 042h for counters 0, 1, and 2, respectively).
Bit 5 | Bit 4 | Function
0 | 0 | Counter Latch Command (see Section 3.3.3)
0 | 1 | R/W Least Significant Byte (LSB)
1 | 0 | R/W Most Significant Byte (MSB)
1 | 1 | R/W LSB then MSB</td></tr>
<tr><td>3:1</td><td>COUNTER MODE SELECTION: Bits [3:1] select one of six possible modes of operation for the counter as shown below.
Bit 3 | Bit 2 | Bit 1 | Mode | Function
0 | 0 | 0 | 0 | Out signal on end of count (= 0)
0 | 0 | 1 | 1 | Hardware retriggerable one-shot
X | 1 | 0 | 2 | Rate generator (divide by n counter)
X | 1 | 1 | 3 | Square wave output
1 | 0 | 0 | 4 | Software triggered strobe
1 | 0 | 1 | 5 | Hardware triggered strobe</td></tr>
<tr><td>0</td><td>BINARY/BCD COUNTDOWN SELECT: When bit 0 = 0, a binary countdown is used. The largest possible binary count is 2^{16}. When bit 0 = 1, a binary coded decimal (BCD) count is used. The largest BCD count allowed is 10^4.</td></tr>
</table>

3.3.2 TIMER READ BACK COMMAND REGISTER

Register Name: Timer Read Back Command

Register Location: 043h—Timer 1
04Bh—Timer 2

Default Value: xxh

Attribute: Write Only

Size: 8 bits

The Read-Back command is used to determine the count value, programmed mode, and current states of the OUT pin and Null Count flag of the selected counter or counters. The Read-Back command is written to the Control Word register, which latches the current states of the above mentioned variables. The value of the counter and its status may then be read by I/O access to the counter address.

Status and/or count may be latched on one, two, or all three of the counters by selecting the counter during the write. The Count latched will stay latched until read, regardless of further latch commands. The count must be read before newer latch commands latch a new count. The Status latched by the read-back command will also remain latched until after a read to the counter's I/O port. To reiterate, the Status and Count are unlatched only after a counter read of the Status register, the Count register, or the Status and Count register in succession.

Both count and status of the selected counter(s) may be latched simultaneously by setting both the COUNT# and STATUS# Bits [5:4] = 00b. This is functionally the same as issuing two consecutive, separate read-back commands. As stated above, if multiple count and/or status read-back commands are issued to the same counter(s) without any intervening reads, all but the first are ignored.

If both count and status of a counter are latched, the first read operation from that counter will return the latched status, regardless of which was latched first. The next one or two reads (depending on whether the counter is programmed for one or two byte counts) return the latched count. Subsequent reads return an unlatched count.

A register description of the Status Byte read follows later in this Section. Note that bit definitions for a write to this port changed when the read-back command was selected, when compared to a normal control word write to this same port.

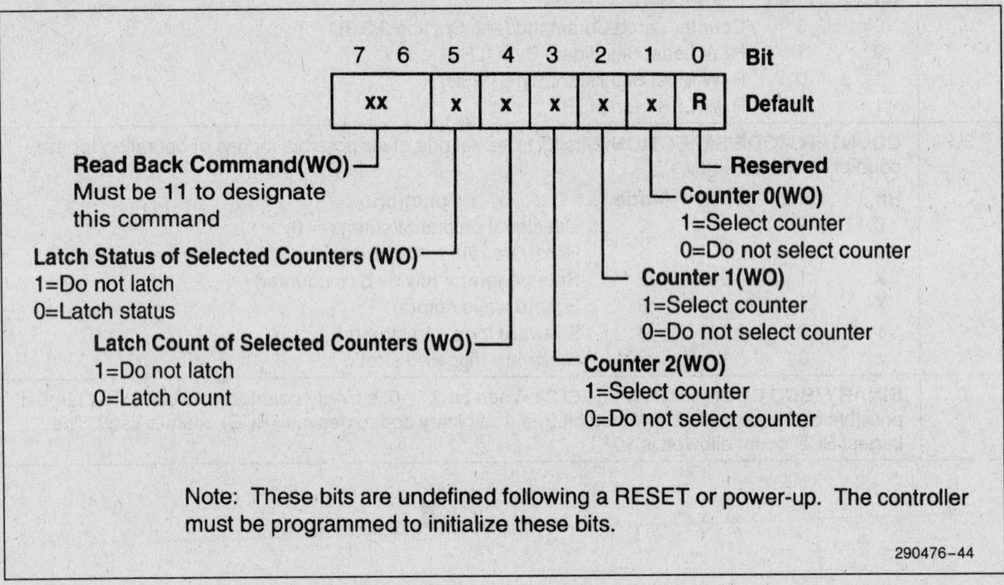

Figure 3-42. Timer Read Back Command Register

Table 3-45. Timer Read Back Command Register

Bit #	Description
7:6	**READ BACK COMMAND:** When Bits[7:6] are both "1", the read-back command is selected during a write to the control word. The normal meanings (mode, countdown, r/w select) of the bits in the control register at I/O address 043h change when the read-back command is selected. Following the read-back command, I/O reads from the selected counter's I/O addresses produce the current latch status, the current latched count, or both if Bits 4 and 5 are both "0".
5	**LATCH STATUS OF SELECTED COUNTERS:** When Bit 5 is a "1", the Current Count value of the selected counters will be latched. When Bit 4 is a "0", the Status will not be latched.
4	**LATCH COUNT OF SELECTED COUNTERS:** When Bit 4 is a "1", the Status of the selected counters will be latched. When Bit 4 is a "0", the Status will not be latched. The Status byte format is described in the next register description.
3	**COUNTER 2:** Counter 2 is selected for the latch command selected with Bits 4 and 5 if Bit 3 is a "1". If Bit 3 is a "0", Status and/or Count will not be latched.
2	**COUNTER 1:** Counter 1 is selected for the latch command selected with Bits 4 and 5 if Bit 2 is a "1". If Bit 2 is a "0", Status and/or Count will not be latched.
1	**COUNTER 0:** Counter 0 is selected for the latch command selected with Bits 4 and 5 if Bit 1 is a "1". If Bit 1 is a "0", Status and/or Count will not be latched.
0	**RESERVED:** Must be 0.

3.3.3 COUNTER LATCH COMMAND REGISTER

Register Name: Counter Latch Command
Register Location: 043h—Timer 1
04Bh—Timer 2
Default Value: xxh
Attribute: Write Only
Size: 8 bits

The Counter Latch command latches the current count value at the time the command is received. This command is used to insure that the count read from the counter is accurate (particularly when reading a two-byte count). The count value is then read from each counter's Count register. One, two or all three counters may be latched with one counter latch command.

If a Counter is latched once and then, some time later, latched again before the count is read, the second Counter Latch Command is ignored. The count read will be the count at the time the first Counter Latch Command was issued.

The count must be read according to the programmed format. Specifically, if the Counter is programmed for two byte counts, two bytes must be read. The two bytes do not have to be read one right after the other; read, write, or programming operations for other Counters may be inserted between them.

One precaution is worth noting. If a Counter is programmed to read/write two-byte counts, a program must not transfer control between reading the first and second byte to another routine which also reads from that same Counter. Otherwise, an incorrect count will be read. Finish reading the latched two-byte count before transferring control to another routine.

Note that bit definitions for a write to this port have changed when the read-back command was selected, when compared to a normal control word write to this same port.

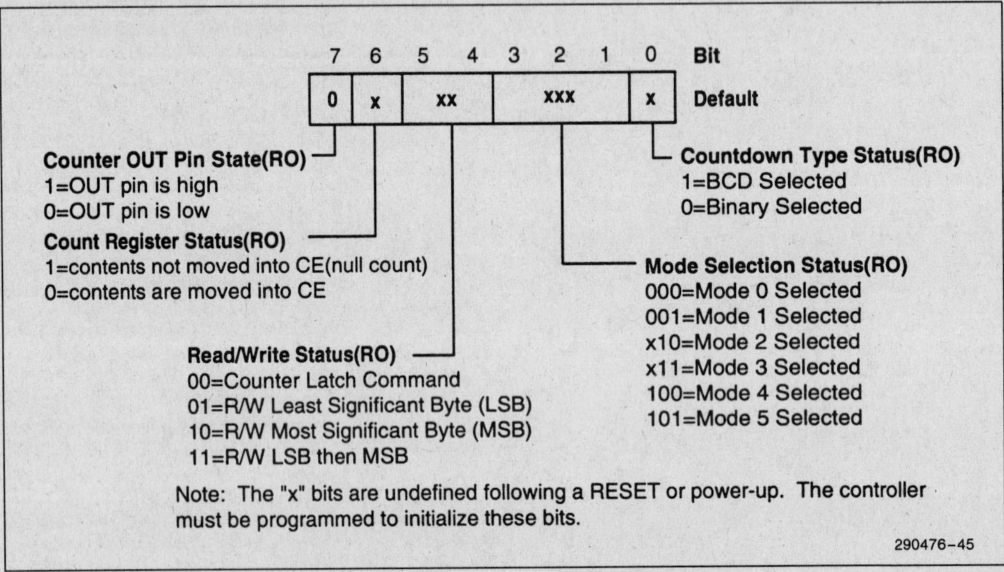

Figure 3-43. Counter Latch Command Register

Table 3-46. Counter Latch Command Register

Bit #	Description
7:6	**COUNTER SELECTION:** Bits 6 and 7 are used to select the counter for latching. **Bit 7 Bit 6 Function** 0 0 Latch counter 0 select 0 1 Latch counter 1 select 1 0 Latch counter 2 select 1 1 Read Back Command select
5:4	**SPECIFIES COUNTER LATCH COMMAND:** When Bits[5:4] are both "0", the Counter Latch command is selected during a write to the control word. The normal meanings (mode, countdown, r/w select) of the bits in the control register at I/O address 043h change when the Counter Latch command is selected. Following the Counter Latch command, I/O reads from the selected counter's I/O addresses produce the current latched count.
3:0	**RESERVED:** Must be 0.

3.3.4 TIMER STATUS BYTE FORMAT REGISTER

Register Name: Timer Status Byte Format
Register Location: 040h—Timer 1, Counter 0
041h—Timer 1, Counter 1
042h—Timer 1, Counter 2
048h—Timer 2, Counter 0
04Ah—Timer 2, Counter 2
Default Value: 0xxxxxxxb
Attribute: Read Only
Size: 8 bits per counter

Each Counter's Status Byte may be read following a Timer Read-Back Command. The Read-Back command is programmed through the counter control register. If "Latch Status" is chosen as a Read-Back option for a given counter, the next read from the counter's I/O port address returns the Status byte.

The Status byte returns the countdown type, either BCD or binary; the Counter Operational Mode; the Read/Write Selection status; the Null count, also referred to as the Count Register Status; and the current State of the counter OUT pin.

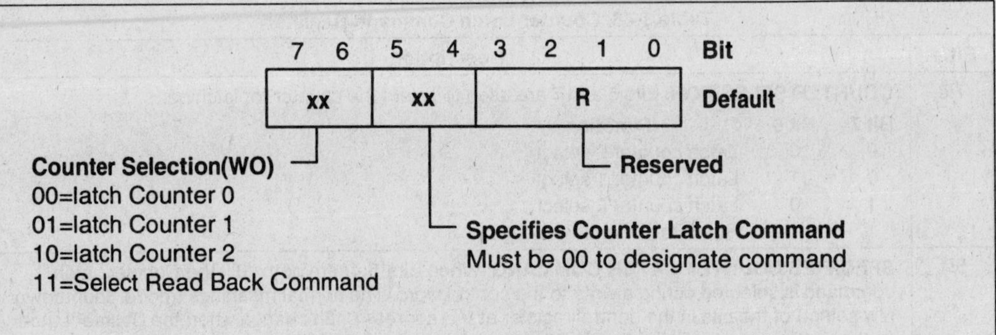

Figure 3-44. Timer Status Byte Format Register

Table 3-47. Timer Status Byte Format Register

Bit #	Description
7	**COUNTER OUT PIN STATE:** When this bit is a "1", the OUT pin of the counter is also a "1". When this bit is a "0", the OUT pin of the counter is also a "0".
6	**COUNT REGISTER STATUS:** Also referred to as Null Count, indicates when the last count written to the Count Register (CR) has been loaded into the counting element (CE). The exact time this happens depends on the counter Mode and is described in the Mode definitions, but until the count is loaded into the counting element (CE), it can't be read from the counter. If the count is latched or read before the load time, the count value returned will not reflect the new count written to the register. When Bit 6 is a "0", the count has been transferred from CR to CE and is available for reading. When Bit 6 is a "1", the Null count condition exists. The count has not been transferred from CR to CE and is not yet available for reading.
5:4	**READ/WRITE STATUS:** Bits[5:4] reflect the read/write selection made through Bits[5:4] of the control register. The binary codes returned during the status read match the codes used to program the counter read/write selection.
3:1	**MODE SELECTION STATUS:** Bits[3:1] return the counter mode programming. The binary code returned matches the code used to program the counter mode, as listed under the bit function above.
0	**COUNTDOWN TYPE STATUS:** Bit 0 reflects the current countdown type, either 0 for binary countdown or a 1 for binary coded decimal (BCD) countdown.

3.3.5 COUNTER ACCESS PORTS

Register Name: Counter Access Ports
Register Location: 040h—Timer 1, Counter 0
041h—Timer 1, Counter 1
042h—Timer 1, Counter 2
048h—Timer 2, Counter 0
04Ah—Timer 2, Counter 2
Default Value: xxh
Attribute: Read/Write
Size: 8 bits per counter

Each of these I/O ports is used for writing count values to the count registers; reading the current count value from the counter by either an I/O read, after a counter-latch command, or after a read-back command; and reading the Status byte following a read-back command.

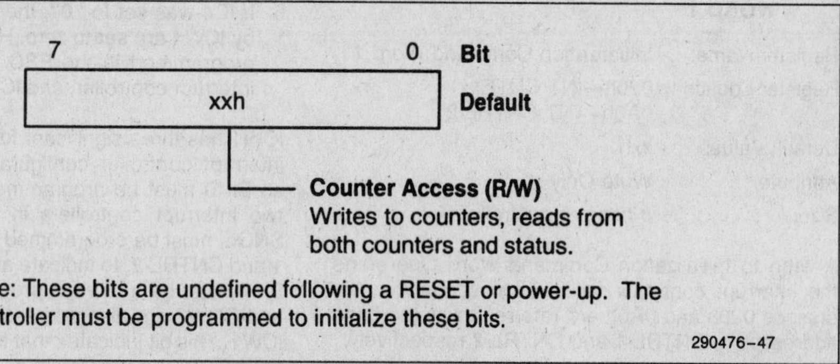

Figure 3-45. Counter Access Ports Register

Table 3-48. Counter Access Ports Register

Bit #	Description
7:0	**COUNTER ACCESS:** Each counter I/O port address is used to program the 16-bit count register. The order of programming, either LSB only, MSB only, or LSB then MSB, is defined with the Counter Control register at I/O port address 043h. The counter I/O port is also used to read the current count from the count register, and return the status of the counter programming following a read-back command.

3.4 Interrupt Controller Registers

The ESC contains an EISA compatible interrupt controller that incorporates the functionality of two 82C59 interrupt controllers. The interrupt registers control the operation of the interrupt controller and can be accessed from the EISA Bus via I/O space. This section describes the Interrupt registers. The operation of the Interrupt Controller is described in Chapter 9.0.

3.4.1 ICW1—INITIALIZATION COMMAND WORD 1

Register Name: Initialization Command Word 1

Register Location: 020h—INT CNTRL-1
0A0h—INT CNTRL-2

Default Value: xxh

Attribute: Write Only

Size: 8 bits per controller

A write to Initialization Command Word One starts the interrupt controller initialization sequence. Addresses 020h and 0A0h are referred to as the base addresses of CNTRL-1 and CNTRL-2 respectively.

An I/O write to the CNTRL-1 or CNTRL-2 base address with Bit 4 equal to 1 is interpreted as ICW1. For ESC-based EISA systems, three I/O writes to "base address + 1" must follow the ICW1. The first write to "base address + 1" performs ICW2, the second write performs ICW3, and the third write performs ICW4.

ICW1 starts the initialization sequence during which the following automatically occur:

1. The edge sense circuit is reset, which means that following initialization, an interrupt request (IRQ) input must make a low-to-high transition to generate an interrupt.
2. The Interrupt Mask register is cleared.
3. IRQ7 input is assigned priority 7.
4. The slave mode address is set to 7.
5. Special Mask Mode is cleared and Status Read is set to IRR.
6. If IC4 was set to "0", then all functions selected by ICW4 are set to zero. However, ICW4 must be programmed in the ESC implementation of this interrupt controller, and IC4 must be set to a "1".

ICW1 has three significant functions within the ESC interrupt controller configuration. ICW4 is needed, so Bit 0 must be programmed to a "1". There are two interrupt controllers in the system, so Bit 1, SNGL, must be programmed to a 0 on both CNTRL-1 and CNTRL-2, to indicate a cascade configuration. Bit 4 must be a 1 when programming ICW1. OCW2 and OCW3 are also addressed at the same port as ICW1. This bit indicates that ICW1, and not OCW2 or OCW3, will be programmed during the write to this port.

Bit 2, ADI, and Bits [7:5], A7–A5, are specific to an MSC-85 implementation. These bits are not used by the ESC interrupt controllers. Bits [7:5,2] should each be initialized to "0".

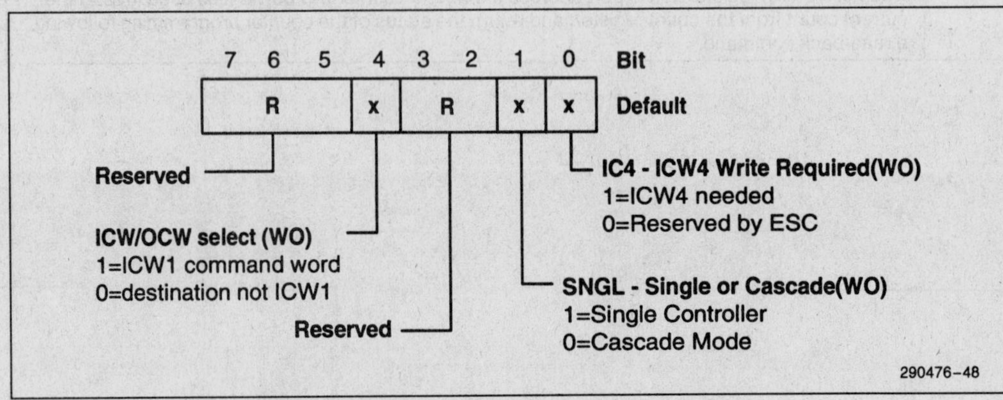

Figure 3-46. Initialization Command Word 1 Register

Table 3-49. Initialization Command Word 1 Register

Bit #	Description
7:5	**RESERVED:** A7–A5 are MCS-85 implementation specific bits. They are not needed by the ESC. These bits should be 000b when programming the ESC.
4	**ICW/OCW SELECT:** Bit 4 must be a 1 to select ICW1. After the fixed initialization sequence to ICW1, ICW2, ICW3, and ICW4, the controller base address is used to write to OCW2 and OCW3. Bit 4 is a 0 on writes to these registers. A 1 on this bit at any time will force the interrupt controller to interpret the write as an ICW1. The controller will then expect to see ICW2, ICW3, and ICW4.
3	**RESERVED:** This bit is not used in the ESC.
2	**RESERVED:** ADI: Ignored for the ESC.
1	**SNGL:** This bit must be programmed to a 0 to indicate that two interrupt controllers are operating in cascade mode on the ESC.
0	**IC4:** This bit must be set to a "1". IC4 indicates that ICW4 needs to be programmed. The ESC requires that ICW4 be programmed to indicate that the controllers are operating in an 80x86 type system.

3.4.2 ICW2—INITIALIZATION COMMAND WORD 2

Register Name: Initialization Command Word 2

Register Location: 021h—INT CNTRL-1
0A1h—INT CNTRL-2I

Default Value: xxh

Attribute: Write Only

Size: 8 bits per controller

ICW2 is used to initialize the interrupt controller with the five most significant bits of the interrupt vector address. The value programmed for Bits[7:3] is used by the CPU to define the base address in the interrupt vector table for the interrupt routines associated with each IRQ on the controller. Typical ISA ICW2 values are 04h for CNTRL-1 and 70h for CNTRL-2. Section 9.8.1 of the Interrupt Unit Functional Description contains a table detailing the interrupt vectors for each interrupt request level, as they would appear when the vector is driven onto the data bus.

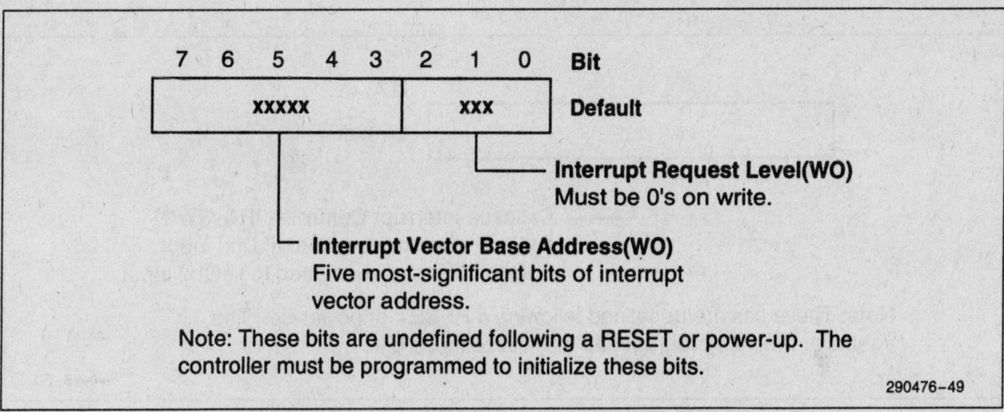

Figure 3-47. Initialization Command Word 2 Register

Table 3-50. Initialization Command Word 2 Register

Bit #	Description
7:3	**INTERRUPT VECTOR BASE ADDRESS:** Bits [7:3] define the base address in the interrupt vector table for the interrupt routines associated with each interrupt request level input. For CNTRL-1, a typical value is 00001b, and for CNTRL-2, 10000b. The interrupt controller combines a binary code representing the interrupt level to receive service with this base address to form the interrupt vector that is driven out onto the bus. For example, the complete interrupt vector for IRQ[0] (CNTRL-1), would be 0000 1000b (CNTRL-1 [7:3] = 00001b and 000b representing IRQ[0]). This vector is used by the CPU to point to the address information that defines the start of the interrupt routine.
2:0	**INTERRUPT REQUEST LEVEL:** When writing ICW2, these bits should all be "0". During an interrupt acknowledge cycle, these bits will be programmed by the interrupt controller with the interrupt code representing the interrupt level to be serviced. This interrupt code is combined with Bits [7:3] to form the complete interrupt vector driven onto the data bus during the second INTA# cycle. The table in Section 9.8.1 outlines each of these codes. The code is a simple three bit binary code: 000b represents IRQ0 (IRQ8), 001b IRQ1 (IRQ9), 010b IRQ2 (IRQ10), and so on until 111b IRQ7 (IRQ15).

3.4.3 ICW3—INITIALIZATION COMMAND WORD 3 (MASTER)

Register Name: Initialization Command Word 3—Controller 1—Master Unit
Register Location: 021h—INT CNTRL-1
Default Value: xxh
Attribute: Write Only
Size: 8 bits

The meaning of ICW3 differs between CNTRL-1 and CNTRL-2. On CNTRL-1, the master controller, ICW3 indicates which CNTRL-1 IRQ line physically connects the INT output of CNTRL-2 to CNTRL-1. ICW3 must be programmed to 04h, indicating the cascade of the CNTRL-2 INT output to the IRQ[2] input of CNTRL-1.

An interrupt request on IRQ2 causes CNTRL-1 to enable CNTRL-2 to present the interrupt vector address during the second interrupt acknowledge cycle.

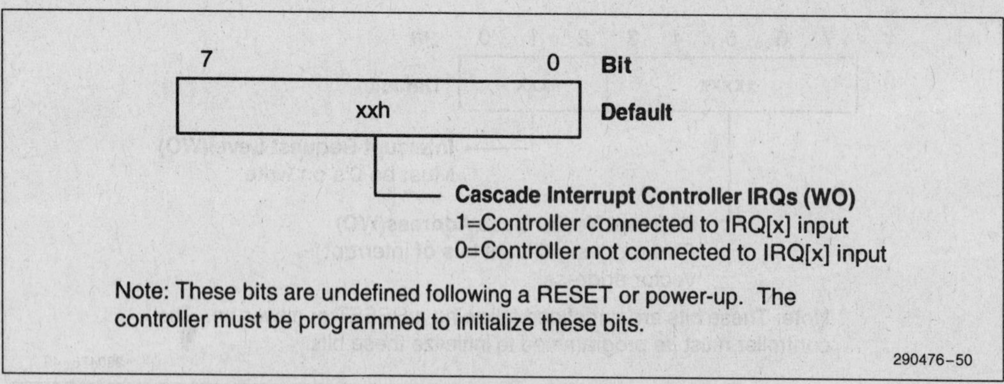

Figure 3-48. Initialization Command Word 3 Register (Master)

Table 3-51. Initialization Command Word 3 Register (Master)

Bit #	Description
7:3, 1:0	**CASCADE INTERRUPT CONTROLLER IRQs:** Bits [7:3] and Bits [1:0] must be programmed to "0".
2	**CASCADE INTERRUPT CONTROLLER IRQs:** Bit 2 must always be programmed to a "1". This bit indicates that CNTRL-2, the slave controller, is cascaded on interrupt request line two (IRQ[2]). When an interrupt request is asserted to CNTRL-2, the IRQ goes through the priority resolver. After the slave controller priority resolution is finished, the INT output of CNTRL-2 is asserted. However, this INT assertion does not go directly to the CPU. Instead, the INT assertion cascades into IRQ[2] on CNTRL-1. IRQ[2] must go through the priority resolution process on CNTRL-1. If it wins the priority resolution on CNTRL-1 and the CNTRL-1 INT signal is asserted to the CPU, the returning interrupt acknowledge cycle is really destined for CNTRL-2. The interrupt was originally requested at CNTRL-2, so the interrupt acknowledge is destined for CNTRL-2, and not a response for IRQ[2] on CNTRL-1. When an interrupt request from IRQ[2] wins the priority arbitration, in reality an interrupt from CNTRL-2 has won the arbitration. Because Bit 2 of ICW3 on the master is set to "1", the master knows which identification code to broadcast on the internal cascade lines, alerting the slave controller that it is responsible for driving the interrupt vector during the second INTA# pulse.

3.4.4 ICW3—INITIALIZATION COMMAND WORD 3 (SLAVE)

Register Name: Initialization Command Word 3—Controller 2—Slave Unit
Register Location: INT CNTRL-2 Port Address—0A1h
Default Value: xxh
Attribute: Write Only
Size: 8 bits

On CNTRL-2 (the slave controller), ICW3 is the slave identification code broadcast by CNTRL-1 from the trailing edge of the first INTA# pulse to the trailing edge of the second INTA# pulse. CNTRL-2 compares the value programmed in ICW3 with the incoming identification code. The code is broadcast over three ESC internal cascade lines. ICW3 must be programmed to 02h for CNTRL-2. When 010b is broadcast by CNTRL-1 during the INTA# sequence, CNTRL-2 assumes responsibility for broadcasting the interrupt vector during the second interrupt acknowledge cycle.

As an illustration, consider an interrupt request on IRQ[2] of CNTRL-1. By definition, a request on IRQ[2] must have been asserted by CNTRL-2. If IRQ[2] wins the priority resolution on CNTRL-1, the interrupt acknowledge cycle returned by the CPU following the interrupt is destined for CNTRL-2, not CNTRL-1. CNTRL-1 will see the INTA# signal, and knowing that the actual destination is CNTRL-2, will broadcast a slave identification code across the internal cascade lines. CNTRL-2 will compare this incoming value with the 010b stored in ICW3. Following a positive decode of the incoming message from CNTRL-1, CNTRL-2 will drive the appropriate interrupt vector onto the data bus during the second interrupt acknowledge cycle.

Figure 3-49. Initialization Command Word 3 Register (Slave)

Table 3-52. Initialization Command Word 3 Register (Slave)

Bit #	Description
7:3	**RESERVED:** Must be 0.
2:0	**SLAVE IDENTIFICATION CODE:** The Slave Identification code must be programmed to 010b during the initialization sequence. The code stored in ICW3 is compared to the incoming slave identification code broadcast by the master controller during interrupt acknowledge cycles.

3.4.5 ICW4—INITIALIZATION COMMAND WORD 4

Register Name: Initialization Command Word 4

Register Location: 021h—INT CNTRL-1
0A1h—INT CNTRL-2

Default Value: xxh

Attribute: Write Only

Size: 8 bits

Both ESC interrupt controllers must have ICW4 programmed as part of their initialization sequence. Minimally, the microprocessor mode bit, Bit 0, must be set to a 1 to indicate to the controller that it is operating in an 80x86 based system. Failure to program this bit will result in improper controller operation during interrupt acknowledge cycles. Additionally, the Automatic End of Interrupt (AEOI) may be selected, as well as the Special Fully Nested Mode (SFNM) of operation.

The default programming for ICW4 is 01h, which selects 80x86 mode, normal EOI, buffered mode, and special fully nested mode disabled.

Bits 2 and 3 must be programmed to 0 for the ESC interrupt unit to function correctly.

Both Bit 1, AEOI, and Bit 4, SFNM, can be programmed if the system developer chooses to invoke either mode.

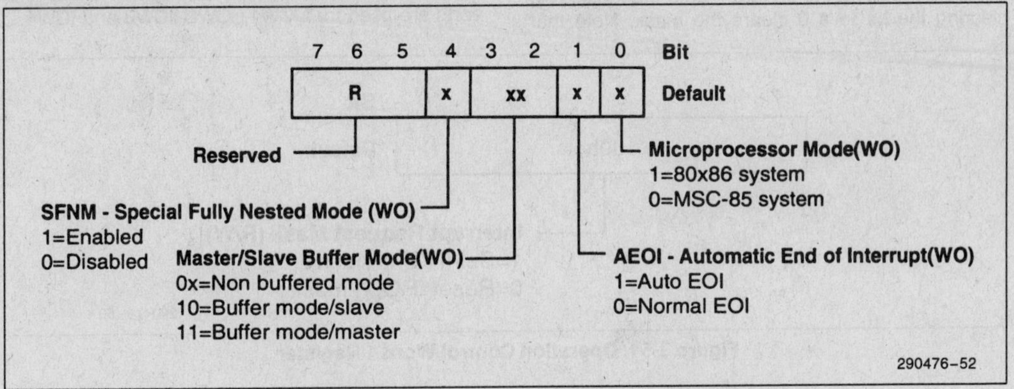

Figure 3-50. Operation Control Word 1 Register

Table 3-53. Operation Command Word 1 Register

Bit #	Description
7:5	**RESERVED:** Must be 0.
4	**SFNM:** Bit 4, SFNM, should normally be disabled by writing a 0 to this bit. If SFNM = 1, the special fully nested mode is programmed.
3:2	**MASTER/SLAVE BUFFER MODE—BUF:** Bit 3, BUF, must be programmed to 0 for the ESC. This is non-buffered mode. As illustrated in Figure 3-50, different programming options are offered for Bits 2 and 3. However, within the ESC interrupt unit, Bits 2 and 3 must always be programmed to 00b.
1	**AEOI:** Bit 1, AEOI, should normally be programmed to "0". This is the normal end of interrupt. If AEOI = 1, the automatic end of interrupt mode is programmed.
0	**MICROPROCESSOR MODE:** The Microprocessor Mode bit must be programmed to 1 to indicate that the interrupt controller is operating in an 80x86 based system. Never program this bit to "0".

3.4.6 OCW1—OPERATION CONTROL WORD 1

Register Name: Operation Control Word 1

Register Location: 021h—INT CNTRL-1
0A1h—INT CNTRL-2

Default Value: xxh

Attribute: Read/Write

Size: 8 bits

OCW1 sets and clears the mask bits in the interrupt Mask register (IMR). Each interrupt request line may be selectively masked or unmasked any time after initialization. A single byte is written to this register. Each bit position in the byte represents the same-numbered channel: Bit 0 = IRQ[0], Bit 1 = IRQ[1] and so on. Setting the bit to a 1 sets the mask, and clearing the bit to a 0 clears the mask. Note that masking IRQ[2] on CNTRL-1 will also mask all of controller 2's interrupt requests (IRQ8–IRQ15). Reading OCW1 returns the controller's mask register status.

The IMR stores the bits which mask the interrupt lines to be masked. The IMR operates on the IRR. Masking of a higher priority input will not affect the interrupt request lines of lower priority.

Unlike status reads of the ISR and IRR, for reading the IMR, no OCW3 is needed. The output data bus will contain the IMR whenever I/O read is active and the I/O port address is 021h or 0A1h (OCW1).

All writes to OCW1 must occur following the ICW1–ICW4 initialization sequence, since the same I/O ports are used for OCW1, ICW2, ICW3 and ICW4.

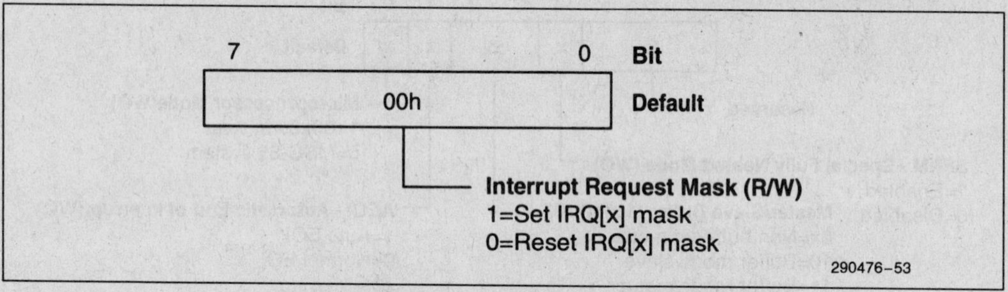

Figure 3-51. Operation Control Word 1 Register

Table 3-54. Operation Control Word 1 Register

Bit #	Description
7:0	**INTERRUPT REQUEST MASK:** When a 1 is written to any bit in this register, the corresponding IRQ[x] line is masked. For example, if Bit 4 is set to a "1", then IRQ[4] will be masked. Interrupt requests on IRQ[4] will not set Channel 4's interrupt request register (IRR) bit as long as the channel is masked. When a 0 is written to any bit in this register, the corresponding IRQ[x] mask bit is cleared, and interrupt requests will again be accepted by the controller. Note that masking IRQ[2] on CNTRL-1 will also mask the interrupt requests from CNTRL-2, which is physically cascaded to IRQ[2].

3.4.7 OCW2—OPERATION CONTROL WORD 2

Register Name: Operation Control Word 2
Register Location: 020h—INT CNTRL-1
0A0h—INT CNTRL-2
Default Value: xxh
Attribute: Write Only
Size: 8 bits

OCW2 controls both the Rotate Mode and the End of Interrupt Mode, and combinations of the two. The three high order bits in an OCW2 write represent the encoded command. The three low order bits are used to select individual interrupt channels during three of the seven commands. The three low order bits (labeled L2, L1 and L0) are used when Bit 6, the SL bit, is set to a 1 during the command.

Following a reset and ICW initialization, the controller enters the fully nested mode of operation. Non-specific EOI without rotation is the default. Both rotation mode and specific EOI mode are disabled following initialization.

1

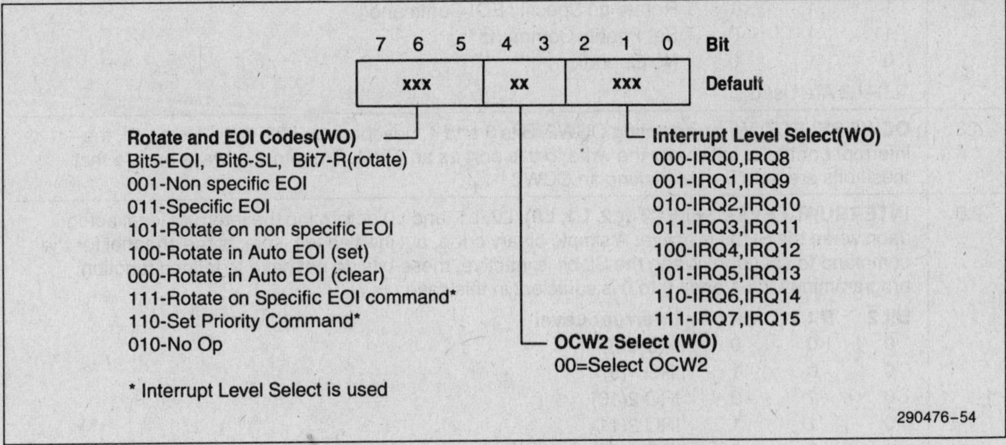

Figure 3-52. Operation Control Word 2 Register

Table 3-55. Operation Control Word 2 Register

<table>
<tr><th>Bit #</th><th>Description</th></tr>
<tr><td>7:5</td><td>ROTATE AND EOI CODES: R, SL, EOI—These three bits control the Rotate and End of Interrupt modes and combinations of the two. A chart of these combinations is listed above under the bit definition.
Bit 7 / Bit 6 / Bit 5 — Function
0 0 1 Non-specific EOI command
0 1 1 Specific EOI Command
1 0 1 Rotate on Non-Specific EOI Command
1 0 0 Rotate in Auto EOI Mode (Set)
0 0 0 Rotate in Auto EOI Mode (Clear)
1 1 1 Rotate on Specific EOI Command*
1 1 0 Set Priority Command*
0 1 0 No Operation
*L0–L2 Are Used</td></tr>
<tr><td>4:3</td><td>OCW2 SELECT: When selecting OCW2, Bits 3 and 4 must both be "0". If Bit 4 is a "1", the interrupt controller interprets the write to this port as an ICW1. Therefore, always ensure that these bits are both 0 when writing an OCW2.</td></tr>
<tr><td>2:0</td><td>INTERRUPT LEVEL SELECT (L2, L1, L0): L2, L1, and L0 determine the interrupt level acted upon when the SL bit is active. A simple binary code, outlined above, selects the channel for the command to act upon. When the SL bit is inactive, these bits do not have a defined function; programming L2, L1 and L0 to 0 is sufficient in this case.
Bit 2 / Bit 1 / Bit 0 — Interrupt Level
0 0 0 IRQ 0(8)
0 0 1 IRQ 1(9)
0 1 0 IRQ 2(10)
0 1 1 IRQ 3(11)
1 0 0 IRQ 4(12)
1 0 1 IRQ 5(13)
1 1 0 IRQ 6(14)
1 1 1 IRQ 7(15)</td></tr>
</table>

3.4.8 OCW3—OPERATION CONTROL WORD 3

Register Name: Operation Control Word 3

Register Location: 020h—INT CNTRL-1
0A0h—INT CNTRL-2

Default Value: x01xxx10b

Attribute: Read/Write

Size: 8 bits

OCW3 serves three important functions; Enable Special Mask Mode, Poll Mode control, and IRR/ISR register read control.

First, OCW3 is used to set or reset the Special Mask Mode (SMM). The Special Mask Mode can be used by an interrupt service routine to dynamically alter the system priority structure while the routine is executing, through selective enabling/disabling of the other channel's mask bits.

Second, the Poll Mode is enabled when a write to OCW3 is issued with Bit 2 equal to "1". The next I/O read to the interrupt controller is treated like an interrupt acknowledge; a binary code representing the highest priority level interrupt request is released onto the bus.

Third, OCW3 provides control for reading the In-Service Register (ISR) and the Interrupt Request Register (IRR). Either the ISR or IRR is selected for reading with a write to OCW3. Bits 0 and 1 carry the encoded command to select either register. The next I/O read to the OCW3 port address will return the register status specified during the previous write. The register specified for a status read is retained by the interrupt controller. Therefore, a write to OCW3 prior to every status read command is unnecessary, provided the status read desired is from the register selected with the last OCW3 write.

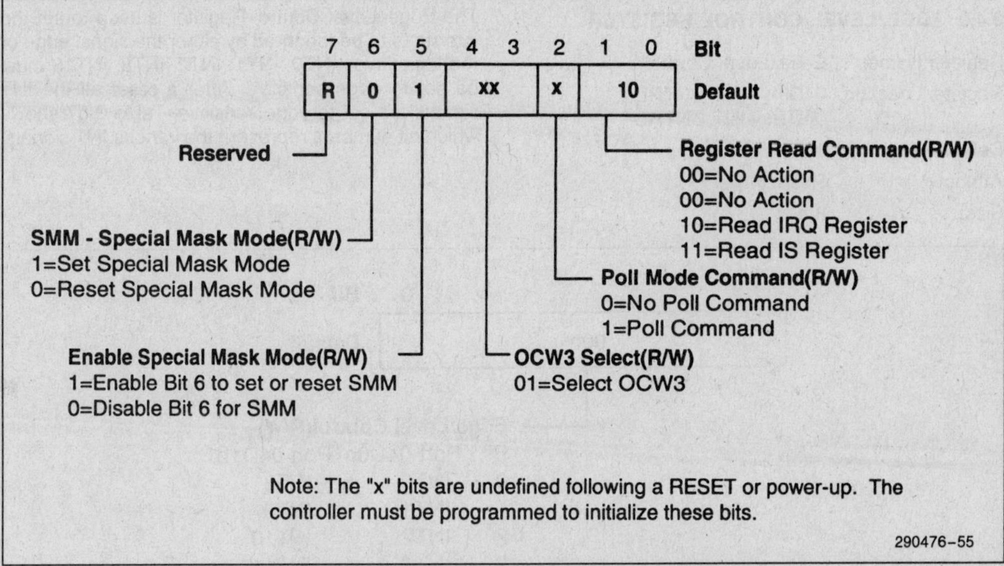

Figure 3-53. Operation Control Word 3 Register

Table 3-56. Operation Control Word 3 Register

Bit #	Description
7	**RESERVED:** Must be 0.
6	**SMM:** If ESMM = 1 and SMM = 1 the Interrupt Controller will enter Special Mask Mode. If ESMM = 1 and SMM = 0 the Interrupt Controller will revert to normal mask mode. When ESMM = 0, SMM has no effect.
5	**ENABLE SPECIAL MASK MODE:** When this bit is set to 1 it enables the SMM bit to set or reset the Special Mask Mode. When ESMM = 0 the SMM bit becomes a "don't care".
4:3	**OCW3 SELECT:** When selecting OCW3, Bit 3 must be a 1 and Bit 4 must be "0". If Bit 4 is a "1", the Interrupt Controller interprets the write to this port as an ICW1. Therefore, always ensure that Bits[4:3] are "01b" when writing an OCW3.
2	**POLL MODE COMMAND:** When Bit 2 is a "0", the Poll command is not issued. When Bit 2 is a "1", the next I/O read to the Interrupt Controller is treated as an Interrupt Acknowledge cycle. An encoded byte is driven onto the data bus, representing the highest priority level requesting service.
1:0	**REGISTER READ COMMAND:** Bits [1:0] provide control for reading the In-Service Register (ISR) and the Interrupt Request Register (IRR). When bit 1 = 0, bit 0 will not affect the register read selection. When bit 1 = 1, bit 0 selects the register status returned following an OCW3 read. If bit 0 = 0, the IRR will be read. If bit 0 = 1, the ISR will be read. Following ICW initialization, the default OCW3 port address read will be "read IRR". To retain the current selection (read ISR or read IRR), always write a 0 to bit 1 when programming this register. The selected register can be read repeatedly without reprogramming OCW3. To select a new status register, OCW3 must be reprogrammed prior to attempting the read. **Bit 1** **Bit 0** **Function** 0 0 No Action 0 1 No Action 1 0 Read IRQ Register 1 1 Read IS Register

3.4.9 EDGE/LEVEL CONTROL REGISTER

Register Name: Edge/Level Control
Register Location: 04D0h—INT CNTRL-1
04D1h—INT CNTRL-1
Default Value: 00h
Attribute: Read/Write
Size: 8 bits

The Edge/Level Control Register is used to set the interrupts to be triggered by either the signal edge or the logic level. INT0, INT1, INT2, INT8, INT13 must be set to edge sensitive. After a reset all the INT signals are set to edge sensitive. Table 3-57 shows which bit numbers represent the various INT signals.

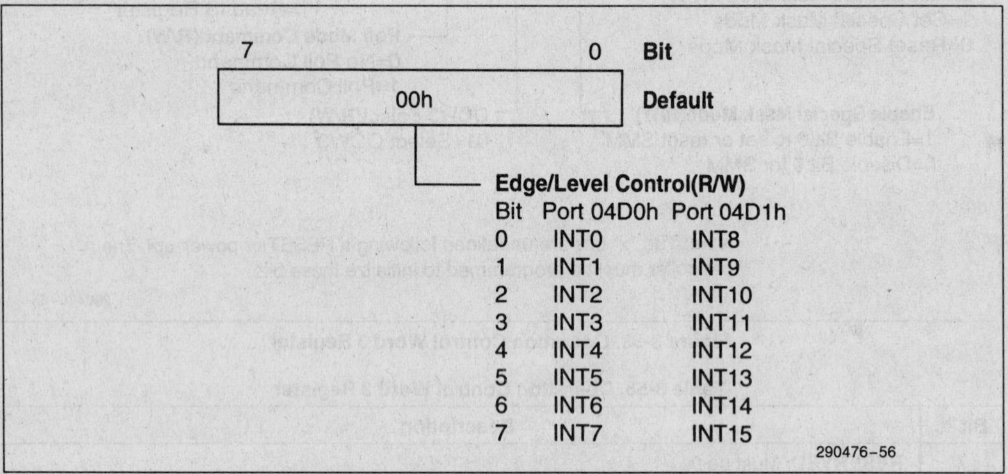

Figure 3-54. Edge/Level Select Register

Table 3-57. Edge/Level Select Register

Bit #	Description
7:0	**EDGE/LEVEL SELECT:** The bits select if the interrupts are triggered by either the signal edge or the logic level. A 0 bit represents an edge sensitive interrupt, and a 1 is for level sensitive. Bit[2:0] and bit 13 are must always be set to 0. After a reset or power-on these registers are set to 00h.

3.4.10 NMI STATUS AND CONTROL REGISTER

Register Name: NMI Status and Control
Register Location: 061h
Default Value: 00h
Attribute: Read/Write
Size: 8 bits

This register is used to check the status of different system components, control the output of the Speaker Counter (Timer 1, Counter 2), and gate the counter output that drives the SPKR signal.

Bits 4, 5, 6, and 7 are read-only. When writing to this port, these bits must be written as 0's. Bit 6 returns the IOCHK# NMI status. This input signal comes from the EISA bus. It is used for parity errors on memory cards plugged into the bus, and for other high priority interrupts. The current status of Bit 3 enables or disables this IOCHK# NMI source. Bit 5 is the current state of the OUT pin of Timer 1, Counter 2. Bit 4 toggles from 1–0 or from 0–1 after every Refresh cycle. Following reset, Bits 4 and 6 are both "0". Bit 5 is undetermined until Counter 2 is properly programmed. Bit 7 returns the PCI System Board Parity Error status (PERR#). If "0", Bit 7 indicates that PERR# was not pulsed active by a PCI agent. If "1", Bit 7 indicates that PERR# was pulsed active by a PCI agent and that an NMI will be issued to the CPU. This NMI can be disabled with Bit 2 of this register.

Bits 0–3 are both read and write. Bit 0 is the GATE input signal for Timer 1, Counter 2. The GATE input is used to disable counting in Counter 2. The Counter 2 output is ANDed with Bit 1 to form the SPKR output signal. Bit 1 gates the Counter 2 OUT value. When Bit 1 is disabled, the SPKR signal is disabled; when Bit 1 is enabled, the SPKR output follows the value at the OUT pin of Counter 2. The Counter 2 OUT pin status can be checked by reading port 061h and checking Bit 5. Bit 2 is used to enable the system board error (ERR#) signal. Bit 3 enables or disables the incoming IOCHK# NMI signal from the expansion bus. Each of these Bits is reset to 0 following reset.

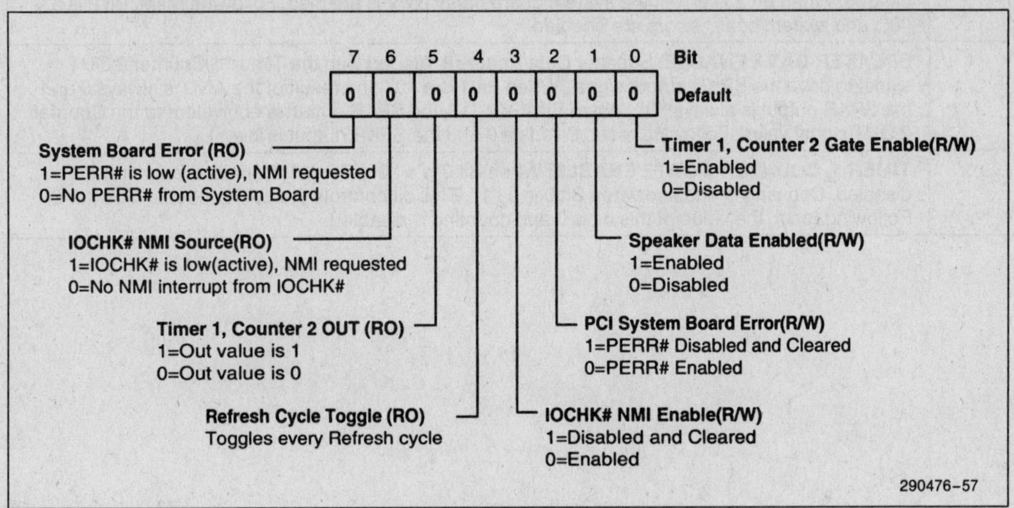

Figure 3-55. NMI Status and Control Register

Table 3-58. NMI Status and Control Register

Bit #	Description
7	**SYSTEM BOARD ERROR:** Bit 7 is set if a system board agent (PCI devices or main memory) detects a system board error and pulses the PCI ERR# line. This interrupt is enabled by setting Bit 2 to "0". To reset the interrupt, set Bit 2 to 0 and then set it to "1". This bit is read-only. When writing to port 061h, Bit 6 must be a "0".
6	**IOCHK# NMI SOURCE:** Bit 6 is set if an expansion board asserts IOCHK# on the ISA/ESC bus. This interrupt is enabled by setting Bit 3 to "0". To reset the interrupt, set Bit 3 to 0 and then set it to "1". This bit is read-only. When writing to port 061h, Bit 6 must be a "0".
5	**TIMER 1, COUNTER 2:** The Timer 1, Counter 2 OUT signal state is reflected in Bit 5. The value on this bit following a read is the current state of the Counter 2 OUT signal. Counter 2 must be programmed following a reset for this bit to have a determinate value. Bit 5 is read-only. When writing to port 061h, Bit 5 must be a "0".
4	**REFRESH CYCLE TOGGLE:** The Refresh Cycle Toggle signal toggles from either 0 to 1 or 1 to 0 following every refresh cycle. This bit is a 0 following reset. This bit is read-only. When writing to port 061h, Bit 4 must be a "0".
3	**IOCHK# NMI ENABLE:** When Bit 3 is a "1", IOCHK# NMI's are disabled and cleared, and when Bit 3 is a "0", IOCHK# NMI's are enabled. Following reset, Bit 3 is reset to 0 and IOCHK# NMI's are enabled.
2	**PCI SYSTEM BOARD ERROR:** When Bit 2 is a "1", the system board error is disabled and cleared. When Bit 2 is a "0", the system board parity error is enabled. Following reset, Bit 2 is a "0", and system board errors are enabled.
1	**SPEAKER DATA ENABLE:** Speaker Data Enable is ANDed with the Timer 1, Counter 2 OUT signal to drive the SPKR output signal. When Bit 1 is a "0", the result of the AND is always 0 and the SPKR output is always "0". When Bit 1 is a "1", the SPKR output is equivalent to the Counter 2 OUT signal value. Following reset, Bit 1 is a 0 and the SPKR output is low.
0	**TIMER 1, COUNTER 2 GATE ENABLE:** When Bit 0 is a "0", Timer 1, Counter 2 counting is disabled. Counting is enabled when Bit 0 is a "1". This bit controls the GATE input to Counter 2. Following reset, the value of this bit is 0 and counting is disabled.

3.4.11 NMI CONTROL AND REAL-TIME CLOCK ADDRESS

Register Name: NMI Enable/Disable and Real-Time Clock Address
Register Location: 070h
Default Value: See below
Attribute: Write Only
Size: 8 bits

The Mask register for the NMI interrupt is at I/O address 070h. The most-significant bit enables or disables all NMI sources including PERR#, SERR#, IOCHK#, Fail-Safe Timer, Bus Timeout, and the NMI Port. Write an 80h to port 70h to mask the NMI signal. This port is shared with the real-time clock. The real-time clock uses the lower six bits of this port to address memory locations. Writing to port 70h sets both the enable/disable bit and the memory address pointer. Do not modify the contents of this register without considering the effects on the state of the other bits.

1

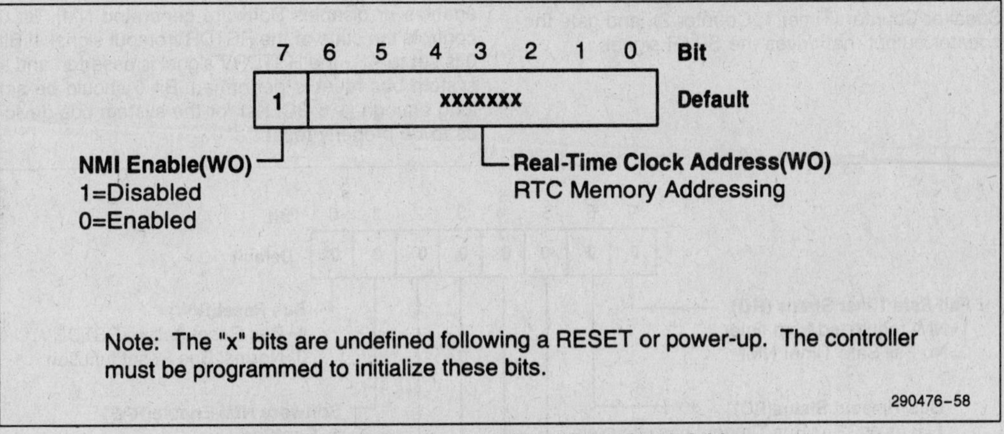

Figure 3-56. NMI Control and Real-Time Clock Address

Table 3-59. NMI Control and Real-Time Clock Address Register

Bit #	Description
7	**NMI ENABLE:** Setting Bit 7 to a 1 will disable all NMI sources. Resetting the bit to a 0 enables the NMI interrupt.
6:0	**REAL-TIME CLOCK ADDRESS:** Used by the Real-Time Clock on the Base I/O component to address memory locations. Not used for NMI enabling/disabling.

3.4.12 NMI EXTENDED STATUS AND CONTROL REGISTER

Register Name:	NMI Extended Status and Control
Register Location:	Port address-0461h
Default Value:	See below
Attribute:	Read/Write
Size:	8 bits

This register is used to check the status of different system components, control the output of the Speaker Counter (Timer 1, Counter 2), and gate the counter output that drives the SPKR signal.

Bits 4, 5, 6, and 7 are read-only. Bits 0–3 are both read and write. When writing to this port, these bits must be written as 0's. Bit 7 returns the Fail-Safe Timer Status. This input comes from Timer 2, Counter 0. The current status of Bit 2 enables or disables this Fail-Safe Timer NMI source. Bit 6 returns the Bus Timeout Status. Bit 6 is set if either a 64 BCLK or a 256 BCLK occurs. The current status of Bit 3 enables or disables this Fail-Safe Timer NMI source. If NMI is caused by a Bus Timeout, Bit 4 distinguished between the 8 μs (64 BCLK) and 32 μs (256 BCLK) timeout. Bit 5 is the current state of an I/O write to port 0462h. The current status of Bit 1 enables or disables Software generated NMI. Bit 0 controls the state of the RSTDRV output signal. If Bit 0 is set to "1", the RSTDRV signal is asserted and a system bus reset is performed. Bit 0 should be set long enough (>8 BCLKs) for the system bus devices to be properly reset.

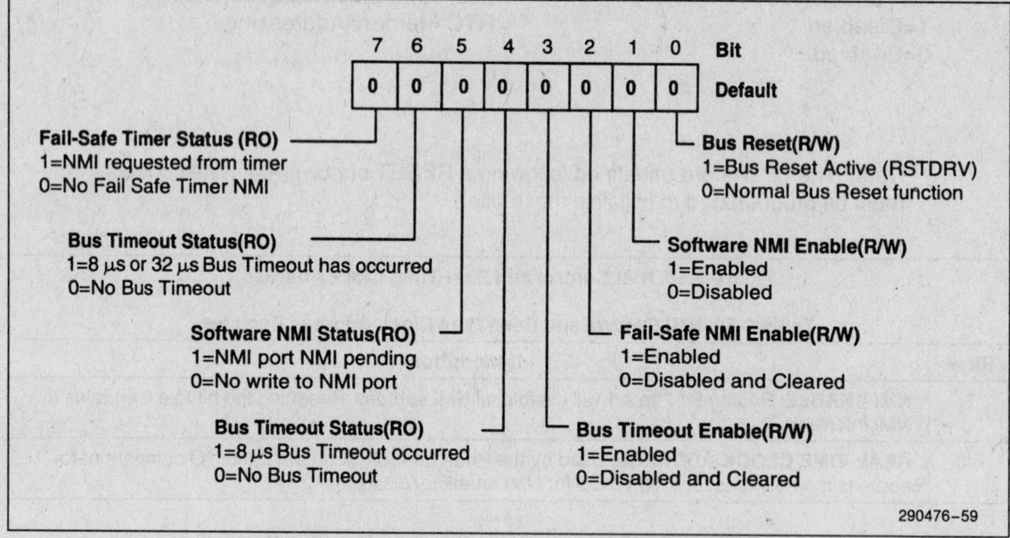

Figure 3-57. NMI Extended Status and Control Register

Table 3-60. NMI Extended Status and Control Register

Bit #	Description
7	**FAIL-SAFE TIMER STATUS:** This bit indicates the status of the Fail-Safe Timer. When Timer 2, Counter 0 count expires, this bit is set to a 1 if Bit 2 has previously been set to "1". A value of 0 indicates that the current NMI was not caused by the Fail-Safe Timer. A value of 1 indicates that the Fail-Safe timer has timed out.
6	**BUS TIMEOUT STATUS:** This bit indicates the status of Bus master timeout logic. If this bit is "0", the Bus Master timeout logic has not detected a bus timeout. If this bit is "1", the bus master timeout logic has detected a bus timeout.
5	**SOFTWARE NMI STATUS:** This bit indicates the status of the Software NMI port writes. A write to I/O port 0462 of any value will set this bit to 1 if Bit 1 is set to "1". If this bit is "0", the current NMI was not caused by a write to the NMI Port. If this bit is "1", the current NMI was caused by a write to the NMI Port.
4	**BUS TIMEOUT STATUS:** This bit indicates the status of the 8 μs EISA Bus master timeout event. If the bit is "0", the current NMI was not caused by the 8 μs EISA bus master timeout. If this bit is "1", the current NMI was caused by this bus timeout.
3	**BUS TIMEOUT ENABLE:** This bit enables/disables NMI EISA bus timeout. If this bit is "0", an NMI will not be generated for bus timeout. Also the NMI condition caused by the Bus timeout will be cleared. If this bit is 1 an NMI will be generated when Timer 2 Counter 0 count expires.
2	**FAIL-SAFE NMI ENABLE:** This bit enables/disables NMI when the Fail-Safe Timer times out. If this bit is "0", an NMI will not be generated when the Timer 2 Counter 0 count expires. Also the NMI condition caused by the Fail-Safe Timer will be cleared. If this bit is 1 an NMI will be generated when Timer 2 Counter 0 count expires.
1	**SOFTWARE NMI ENABLE:** This bit enables/disables software generated NMI. If this Bit is "0", a write to I/O port 0462h will not generate an NMI. If this bit is 1, NMI will be generated for a write to I/O port 0462h.
0	**BUS RESET:** When Bit 0 is a "0", RSTDRV signal functions as a normal reset drive signal. When Bit 0 is "1", the RSTDRV signal is asserted. Following reset, Bit 0 is a "0" and the RSTDRV output is low.

1

3.4.13 SOFTWARE NMI GENERATION

Register Name: Software NMI Generation
Register Location: 462h
Default Value: xxh
Attribute: Write Only
Size: 8 bits

A write to this port with any data will cause an NMI. This port provides a software mechanism to cause an NMI if interrupts are enabled.

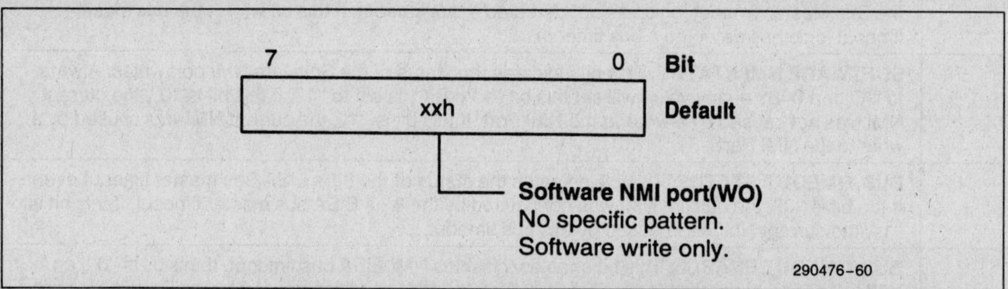

Figure 3-58. Software NMI Generation Register

Table 3-61. Configuration RAM Page Register

Bit #	Description
7:0	**SOFTWARE NMI PORT:** The bit pattern is not specific. A write to this port will generate a Software NMI if enabled.

3.5 EISA Configuration, Floppy Support, and Port 92h

3.5.1 CONFIGURATION RAM PAGE REGISTER

Register Name: Configuration RAM Page
Register Location: 0C00h
Default Value: xxx00000b
Attribute: Read/Write
Size: 8 bits

This register contains the Configuration RAM Page address. During accesses to the Configuration RAM (0800h–08FFh), the ESC drives the CPG[4:0] signals with the value of Bits[4:0] of this register. The CPG[4:0] signals are connected to address pins ADDR[12:8] of the Configuration RAM.

1

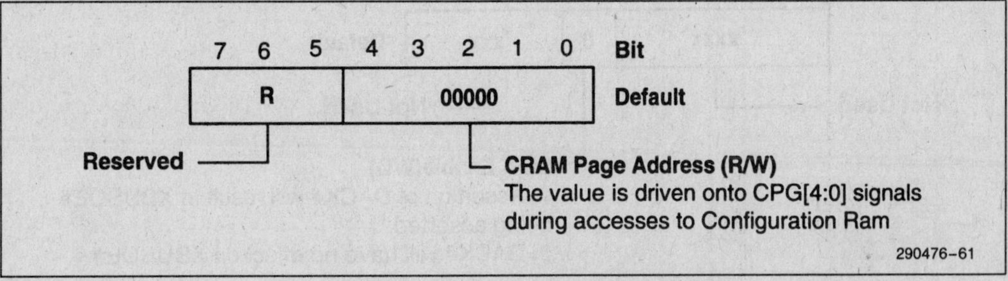

Figure 3-59. Configuration RAM Page Register

Table 3-62. Configuration RAM Page Register

Bit #	Description
7:5	**RESERVED.**
4:0	**CRAM PAGE ADDRESS:** The value of these bits selects a specific page from the Configuration RAM space. The SA[7:0] addresses select the location within this page during I/O accesses to the Configuration RAM.

3.5.2 DIGITAL OUTPUT REGISTER

Register Name: Digital Output
Register Location: 03F2h (Primary), 0372h (Secondary)
Default Value: xxxx0xxxb
Attribute: Write only
Size: 8 bits

This register is used to prevent XBUSOE# from responding to DACK2# during a DMA read access to a floppy controller on the ISA bus. If a second floppy (residing on the ISA bus) is using DACK2# in conjunction with a floppy on the X-Bus, this prevents the floppy on the X-Bus and the X-Bus transceiver from responding to an access targeted for the floppy on the ISA bus. This register is also located in the floppy controller device.

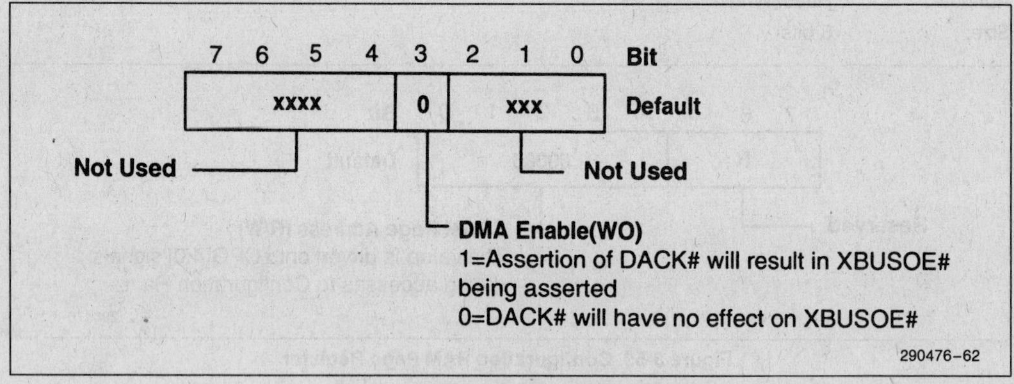

Figure 3-60. Digital Output Register

Table 3-63. Digital Output Register

Bit #	Description
7:4	**NOT USED:** These bits exist in the 82077 FDC. Refer to the 82077 data sheet for further details.
3	**DMA ENABLE:** When this bit is a 1, the assertion of DACK# will result in XBUSOE# being asserted. If this bit is 0, DACK2# has no effect on XBUSOE#. This port bit also exists on the 82077 FDC. This bit defaults to disable (0).
2:0	**NOT USED:** These bits exist in the 82077 FDC. Refer to the 82077 data sheet for further details.

3.5.3 PORT 92 REGISTER

Register Name: Port 92
Register Location: 92h
Default Value: 00100100b
Attribute: Read/Write
Size: 8 bits

This register is used to support the alternate reset (ALTRST#), alternate A20 (ALTA20), power-on password protection, and fixed disk light function (DLIGHT#). This register is only accessible if Bit 6 in the Peripheral Chip Select Enable B Register is set to "1".

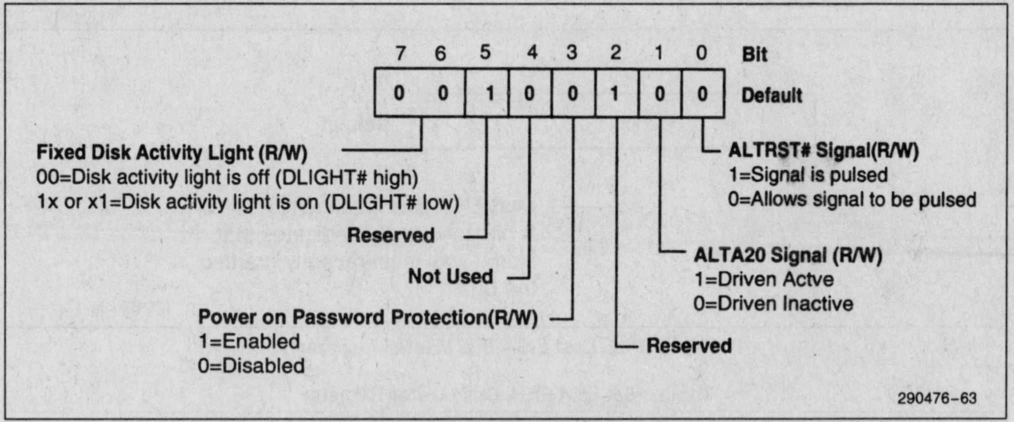

Figure 3-61. Port 92 Register

Table 3-64. Port 92 Register

Bit #	Description
7:6	**FIXED DISK ACTIVITY LIGHT:** These bits are used to turn the Fixed Disk Activity Light on and off. When either of these bits are set to a 1, the light is turned on (DLIGHT# driven active). To turn the light off, both of these bits must be 0.
5	**RESERVED:** This bit is reserved and will always return a 1 when read.
4	**NOT USED:** This bit is not used and will always return a 0 when read.
3	**POWER ON PASSWORD PROTECTION:** A 1 on this bit enables power-on password protection by inhibiting accesses to the RTC memory for RTC addresses (port 70h) from 36h to 3Fh. This is accomplished by not generating RTCRD# and RTCWR# signals for these accesses.
2	**RESERVED:** This bit is reserved and will always return a 1 when read.
1	**ALTA20 SIGNAL:** Writing a 0 to this bit causes the ALTA20 signal to be driven low. Writing a 1 to this bit causes the ALTA20 signal to be driven high.
0	**ALTRST# SIGNAL:** This read/write bit provides an alternate system reset function. This function provides an alternate means to reset the system CPU to effect a mode switch from Protected Virtual Address Mode to the Real Address Mode. This provides a faster means of reset than is provided by the Keyboard controller. This bit is set to a 0 by a system reset. Writing a 1 to this bit will cause the ALTRST# signal to pulse active (low) for approximately 4 SYSCLK's. Before another ALTRST# pulse can be generated, this bit must be written back to a 0.

3.5.4 LAST EISA BUS MASTER GRANTED REGISTER

Register Name: Last EISA Bus Master Granted
Register Location: 0464h
Default Value: xxh
Attribute: Read Only
Size: 8 bits

This register contains information about which EISA bus master most recently had control of the EISA bus. A bit read of 0 indicates that the corresponding slot most recently was granted the bus.

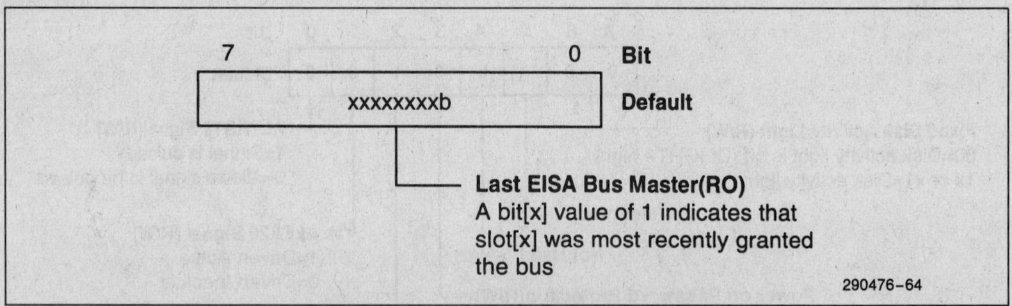

Figure 3-62. Last EISA Bus Master Register

Table 3-65. Last EISA Bus Master Register

Bit #	Description
7:0	**LAST EISA BUS MASTER:** A value of 1 is placed in the bit position of the most recently granted EISA Bus Master.

4.0 ADDRESS DECODING

The ESC contains an address decoder to decode EISA/ISA master cycles. The ESC address decoder uses the address line LA[31:2], and byte enable BE[3:0]# to decode EISA master cycles. For ISA master cycles, the ESC uses address line LA[31:2], SA[1:0], and high byte enable SHBE# for address decode.

The ESC decodes the following set of addresses.

1. BIOS memory space.
2. I/O addresses contained within the ESC.
3. Configuration registers.
4. X-Bus Peripherals

4.1 BIOS Memory Space

The ESC supports a total of 512 Kbytes of BIOS. The ESC will assert the LBIOSCS# signal for memory cycles decoded to be in the BIOS space. The 512 Kbytes of BIOS includes the conventional 128 Kbytes of BIOS and 384 Kbytes of enlarged BIOS.

The 128 Kbytes conventional BIOS memory space is mapped at 1 MB boundary between memory address 000E0000h–000FFFFFh. The 128K conventional BIOS memory space is split into one 64K region, and four 16K regions. These regions are Low BIOS region 1 (000E0000h–000E3FFFh), Low BIOS region 2 (000E4000h–000E7FFFh), Low BIOS region 3 (000E8000h–000EBFFFh), and Low BIOS region 4 (000EC000h–000EFFFFh) and High BIOS region (000F0000h–000FFFFFh). The ESC will assert the LBIOSCS# signal for memory cycles to these regions if the corresponding configuration bits in the BIOS Chip Select A register are set to enable (see Table 4-1).

The conventional BIOS is aliased at multiple memory regions. The aliased memory regions are at 16 MB boundary (High BIOS only), 4 GB minus 1M boundary, and 4 GB boundary. The ESC will assert LBIOSCS# for memory cycles to these aliased regions if the corresponding configuration bits in the BIOS Chip Select B register are also set to enable (see Table 4-1).

1

The ESC supported VGA BIOS on the motherboard by aliasing the VGA BIOS region to the conventional BIOS region. The VGA BIOS is accessed at memory region 0000C0000h–0000C7FFF. The VGA BIOS region is divided into a Low VGA region (000C0000h–000C3FFFh) and a High VGA region (000C4000h–000C7FFFh). If the BIOS Chip Select B register bit 0 (Low VGA BIOS Enable) and bit 1 (High VGA BIOS Enable) are set to enable, memory accesses to Low VGA BIOS region and High VGA BIOS region will be aliased to conventional Low BIOS region 1 and Low BIOS region 2 respectively and the ESC will assert LBIOSCS#

The ESC supports the 384 Kbytes of enlarged BIOS as specified by the PCI specification. This 384 Kbyte region is mapped in memory space below the 4G aliased conventional BIOS. The enlarged BIOS is accessed between FFF80000h–FFFDFFFFh memory space. If the enlarged BIOS is enabled in the BIOS Enable Chip Select 1 register bit 5 (Enlarged BIOS Enable), the ESC will assert LBIOSCS# signal for accesses to this region.

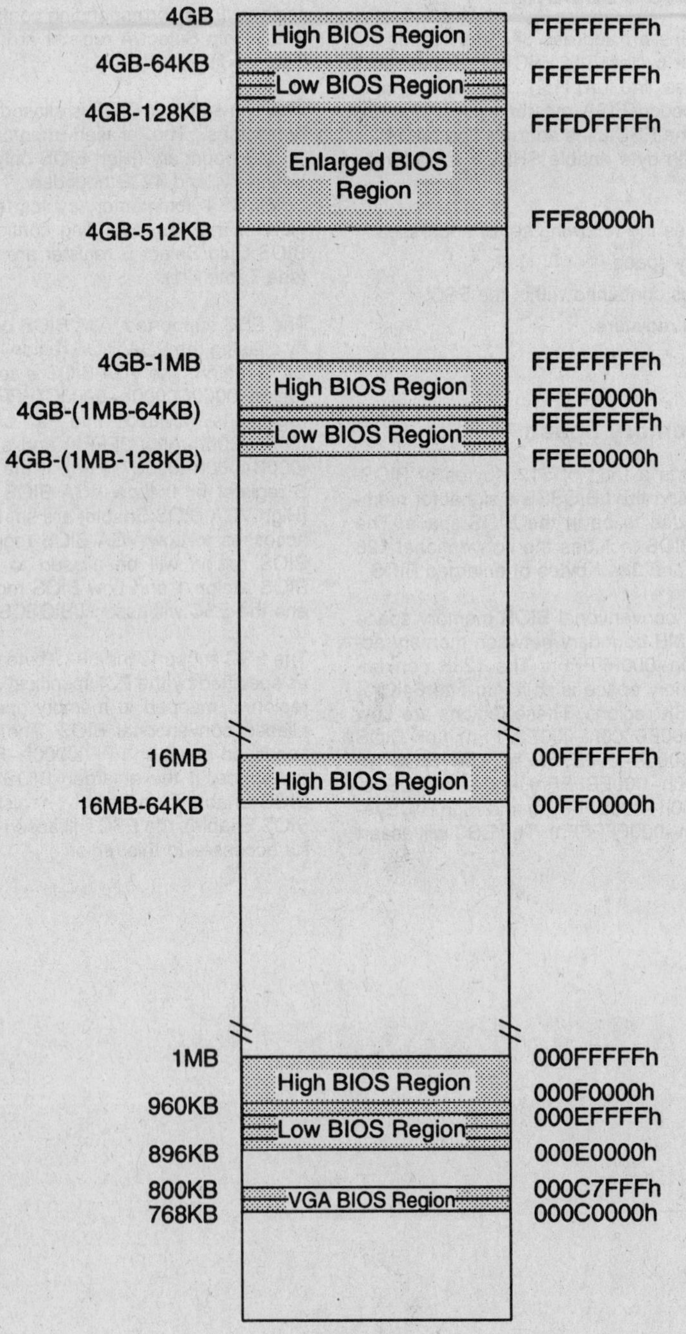

Figure 4-1. BIOS Memory Map

Table 4-1. BIOS Chip Select Enable Table

Memory Address Range	Low BIOS En 1	Low BIOS En 2	Low BIOS En 3	Low BIOS En 4	High BIOS En	ENL BIOS En	Low VGA BIOS En	High VGA BIOS En	16M BIOS En	LBIOSCS# Asserted
000C0000h to 000C3FFFh	x	x	x	x	x	x	0	x	x	No
	x	x	x	x	x	x	1	x	x	Yes
000C4000h to 000C7FFFh	x	x	x	x	x	x	x	0	x	No
	x	x	x	x	x	x	x	1	x	Yes
000E0000h to 000E3FFFh	0	x	x	x	x	x	x	x	x	No
	1	x	x	x	x	x	x	x	x	Yes
000E4000h to 000E7FFFh	x	0	x	x	x	x	x	x	x	No
	x	1	x	x	x	x	x	x	x	Yes
000E8000h to 000EBFFFh	x	x	0	x	x	x	x	x	x	No
	x	x	1	x	x	x	x	x	x	Yes
000EC000h to 000EFFFFh	x	x	x	0	x	x	x	x	x	No
	x	x	x	1	x	x	x	x	x	Yes
000F0000h to 000FFFFFh	x	x	x	x	0	x	x	x	x	No
(960 KB to 1 MB)	x	x	x	x	1	x	x	x	x	Yes
00FF0000h to 00FFFFFFh	x	x	x	x	x	x	x	x	0	No
(16 MB–64 KB to 16 MB)	x	x	x	x	0	x	x	x	1	No
	x	x	x	x	1	x	x	x	1	Yes
FFEE0000h to FFEE3FFFh	0	x	x	x	x	x	x	x	x	No
	1	x	x	x	x	x	x	x	x	Yes
FFEE4000h to FFEE7FFFh	x	0	x	x	x	x	x	x	x	No
	x	1	x	x	x	x	x	x	x	Yes
FFEE8000h to FFEEBFFFh	x	x	0	x	x	x	x	x	x	No
	x	x	1	x	x	x	x	x	x	Yes
FFEEC000h to FFEEFFFFh	x	x	x	0	x	x	x	x	x	No
	x	x	x	1	x	x	x	x	x	Yes
FFEF0000h to FFEFFFFFh	x	x	x	x	0	x	x	x	x	No
	x	x	x	x	1	x	x	x	x	Yes
FFF80000h to FFFDFFFFh	x	x	x	x	x	0	x	x	x	No
(4 GB–512 KB to 4G–128 KB)	x	x	x	x	x	1	x	x	x	Yes
FFFE0000h to FFFE3FFFh	0	x	x	x	x	x	x	x	x	No
	1	x	x	x	x	x	x	x	x	Yes
FFFE4000h to FFFE7FFFh	x	0	x	x	x	x	x	x	x	No
	x	1	x	x	x	x	x	x	x	Yes
FFFE8000h to FFFEBFFFh	x	x	0	x	x	x	x	x	x	No
	x	x	1	x	x	x	x	x	x	Yes
FFFEC000h to FFFEFFFFh	x	x	x	0	x	x	x	x	x	No
	x	x	x	1	x	x	x	x	x	Yes
FFFF0000h to FFFFFFFFh	x	x	x	x	0	x	x	x	x	No
	x	x	x	x	1	x	x	x	x	Yes

NOTES:

1. "x" in the above table represents a don't care condition.
2. All the region control bits for the BIOS space are in the BIOS Chip Select A register and BIOS Chip Select 2 register at configuration offsets 42h and 43h respectively.

4.2 I/O Addresses Contained within the ESC

The ESC integrates functions like DMA, Programmable Interrupt Controller, and Timers. All the compatibility registers associated with these functions are also integrated into the ESC. The ESC also integrates some additional registers like EISA System ID register in order to reduce the overall chip count in the system.

All the registers integrated in the ESC are located in the I/O range. These are 8-bit registers and are accessed through the ESC EISA interface. The ESC internal registers are at fixed I/O locations with the exception of DMA Scatter-Gather registers. The DMA Scatter-Gather registers default to the I/O addresses 0410h to 043Fh upon reset. These registers can be relocated by programming the Scatter-Gather Relocate Base Address register. The DMA Scatter-Gather registers can be relocated to I/O addresses range xx10h–xx3Fh.

Registers at I/O addresses 70h, 372h, and 3F2h are shared registers between ESC and external logic. Port 70h is duplicated in the Real Time Clock logic. Bit 3 of ports 372h and 3F2h reside in the ESC and the other bits reside in the Floppy Disk Controller.

Table 4-2 documents the I/O address to the ESC internal registers.

Table 4-2. ESC I/O Register Address Map

Port	Address				Type	Name	Block
	FEDC	BA98	7654	3210			
0000h	0000	0000	000x	0000	R/W	DMA1 CH0 Base and Current Address	DMA
0001h	0000	0000	000x	0001	R/W	DMA1 CH0 Base and Current Count	DMA
0002h	0000	0000	000x	0010	R/W	DMA1 CH1 Base and Current Address	DMA
0003h	0000	0000	000x	0011	R/W	DMA1 CH1 Base and Current Count	DMA
0004h	0000	0000	000x	0100	R/W	DMA1 CH2 Base and Current Address	DMA
0005h	0000	0000	000x	0101	R/W	DMA1 CH2 Base and Current Count	DMA
0006h	0000	0000	000x	0110	R/W	DMA1 CH3 Base and Current Address	DMA
0007h	0000	0000	000x	0111	R/W	DMA1 CH3 Base and Current Count	DMA
0008h	0000	0000	000x	1000	R/W	DMA1 Status(r) Command(w) Register	DMA
0009h	0000	0000	000x	1001	WO	DMA1 Write Request Register	DMA
000Ah	0000	0000	000x	1010	WO	DMA1 Write Single Mask Bit	DMA
000Bh	0000	0000	000x	1011	WO	DMA1 Write Mode Register	DMA
000Ch	0000	0000	000x	1100	WO	DMA1 Clear Byte Pointer	DMA
000Dh	0000	0000	000x	1101	WO	DMA1 Master Clear	DMA
000Eh	0000	0000	000x	1110	WO	DMA1 Clear Mask Register	DMA
000Fh	0000	0000	000x	1111	R/W	DMA1 Read/Write All Mask Register Bits	DMA
0020h	0000	0000	001x	xx00	R/W	INT 1 Control Register	PIC
0021h	0000	0000	001x	xx01	R/W	INT 1 Mask Register	PIC
0022h	0000	0000	0010	0010	R/W	Configuration Address Index Register	CONF
0023h	0000	0000	0010	0011	R/W	Configuration Data Index Register	CONF
0040h	0000	0000	010x	0000	R/W	Timer 1—Counter 0 System Clock	TC
0041h	0000	0000	010x	0001	R/W	Timer 1—Counter 1 Refresh Request	TC
0042h	0000	0000	010x	0010	R/W	Timer 1 Counter 2 Speaker Tone	TC
0043h	0000	0000	010x	0011	WO	Timer 1 Command Mode Register	TC
0048h	0000	0000	010x	1000	R/W	Timer 2—Counter 0 Fail-Safe Timer	TC

Table 4-2. ESC I/O Register Address Map (Continued)

Port	Address				Type	Name	Block
	FEDC	BA98	7654	3210			
0049h	0000	0000	010x	1001	R/W	Timer 2 Counter 1—Reserved	TC
004Ah	0000	0000	010x	1010	R/W	Timer 2 Counter 2 CPU Speed Control	TC
004Bh	0000	0000	010x	1011	WO	Timer 2 Command Mode Register	TC
0061h	0000	0000	0110	00x1	R/W	NMI Status and Control	Control
0070h*	0000	0000	0111	0xx0	WO	NMI Mask Register	Control
0080h	0000	0000	100x	0000	R/W	DMA Page Register— Reserved	DMA
0081h	0000	0000	100x	0001	R/W	DMA Channel 2 Page Register	DMA
0082h	0000	0000	1000	0010	R/W	DMA Channel 3 Page Register	DMA
0083h	0000	0000	100x	0011	R/W	DMA Channel 1 Page Register	DMA
0084h	0000	0000	100x	0100	R/W	DMA Page Register— Reserved	DMA
0085h	0000	0000	100x	0101	R/W	DMA Page Register— Reserved	DMA
0086h	0000	0000	100x	0110	R/W	DMA Page Register— Reserved	DMA
0087h	0000	0000	100x	0111	R/W	DMA Channel 0 Page Register	DMA
0088h	0000	0000	100x	1000	R/W	DMA Page Register— Reserved	DMA
0089h	0000	0000	100x	1001	R/W	DMA Channel 6 Page Register	DMA
008Ah	0000	0000	100x	1010	R/W	DMA Channel 7 Page Register	DMA
008Bh	0000	0000	100x	1011	R/W	DMA Channel 5 Page Register	DMA
008Ch	0000	0000	100x	1100	R/W	DMA Page Register— Reserved	DMA
008Dh	0000	0000	100x	1101	R/W	DMA Page Register— Reserved	DMA
008Eh	0000	0000	100x	1110	R/W	DMA Page Register— Reserved	DMA
008Fh	0000	0000	100x	1111	R/W	DMA Refresh Page Register	DMA
0092h	0000	0000	1001	0010	R/W	System Control Port	Control
00A0h	0000	0000	101x	xx00	R/W	INT 2 Control Register	PIC
00A1h	0000	0000	101x	xx01	R/W	INT 2 Mask Register	PIC
00C0h	0000	0000	1100	000x	R/W	DMA2 CH0 Base and Current Address	DMA
00C2h	0000	0000	1100	001x	R/W	DMA2 CH0 Base and Current Count	DMA
00C4h	0000	0000	1100	010x	R/W	DMA2 CH1 Base and Current Address	DMA
00C6h	0000	0000	1100	011x	R/W	DMA2 CH1 Base and Current Count	DMA
00C8h	0000	0000	1100	100x	R/W	DMA2 CH2 Base and Current Address	DMA
00CAh	0000	0000	1100	101x	R/W	DMA2 CH2 Base and Current Count	DMA
00CCh	0000	0000	1100	110x	R/W	DMA2 CH3 Base and Current Address	DMA
00CEh	0000	0000	1100	111x	R/W	DMA2 CH3 Base and Current Count	DMA
00D0h	0000	0000	1101	000x	R/W	DMA2 Status(r) Command(w) Register	DMA
00D2h	0000	0000	1101	001x	WO	DMA2 Write Request Register	DMA
00D4h	0000	0000	1101	010x	WO	DMA2 Write Single Mask Bit	DMA
00D6h	0000	0000	1101	011x	WO	DMA2 Write Mode Register	DMA

Table 4-2. ESC I/O Register Address Map (Continued)

Port	Address				Type	Name	Block
	FEDC	BA98	7654	3210			
00D8h	0000	0000	1101	100x	WO	DMA2 Clear Byte Pointer	DMA
00DAh	0000	0000	1101	101x	WO	DMA2 Master Clear	DMA
00DCh	0000	0000	1101	110x	WO	DMA2 Clear Mask Register	DMA
00DEh	0000	0000	1101	111x	R/W	DMA2 Read/Write All Mask Register Bits	DMA
00F0h	0000	0000	1111	0000	WO	Reset IRQ13	IRQ13
0372h &	0000	0011	0111	0010	WO	Secondary Floppy Disk Digital Output Register	FDCCS#
03F2h &	0000	0011	1111	0001	WO	Primary Floppy Disk Digital Output Register	FDCCS#
0400h	0000	0100	0000	0000	R/W	Reserved	DMA
0401h	0000	0100	0000	0001	R/W	DMA1 CH0 Base/Current Count	DMA
0402h	0000	0100	0000	0010	R/W	Reserved	DMA
0403h	0000	0100	0000	0011	R/W	DMA1 CH1 Base/Current Count	DMA
0404h	0000	0100	0000	0100	R/W	Reserved	DMA
0405h	0000	0100	0000	0101	R/W	DMA1 CH2 Base/Current Count	DMA
0406h	0000	0100	0000	0110	R/W	Reserved	DMA
0407h	0000	0100	0000	0111	R/W	DMA1 CH3 Base/Current Count	DMA
0408h	0000	0100	0000	1000	R/W	Reserved	DMA
0409h	0000	0100	0000	1001	R/W	Reserved	DMA
040Ah	0000	0100	0000	1010	R/W	DMA Chaining Mode Status/Interrupt Pending	DMA
040Bh	0000	0100	0000	1011	WO	DMA1 Extended Mode Register	DMA
040Ch	0000	0100	0000	1100	WO	Chaining Buffer Control Register	DMA
040Dh	0000	0100	0000	1101	R/W	Reserved	DMA
040Eh	0000	0100	0000	1110	R/W	Reserved	DMA
040Fh	0000	0100	0000	1111	R/W	Reserved	DMA
0410h	0000	0100	0010	0000	WO	DMA CH0 S-G Command Register	DMA
0411h	0000	0100	0010	0001	WO	DMA CH1 S-G Command Register	DMA
0412h	0000	0100	0010	0010	WO	DMA CH2 S-G Command Regsiter	DMA
0413h	0000	0100	0010	0011	WO	DMA CH3 S-G Command Register	DMA
0415h	0000	0100	0010	0101	WO	DMA CH5 S-G Command Register	DMA
0416h	0000	0100	0010	0110	WO	DMA CH6 S-G Command Register	DMA
0417h	0000	0100	0010	0111	WO	DMA CH7 S-G Command Register	DMA
0418h	0000	0100	0010	1000	WO	DMA CH0 S-G Status Register	DMA
0419h	0000	0100	0010	1001	WO	DMA CH1 S-G Status Register	DMA
041Ah	0000	0100	0010	1010	WO	DMA CH2 S-G Status Register	DMA
041Bh	0000	0100	0010	1011	WO	DMA CH3 S-G Status Register	DMA
041Dh	0000	0100	0010	1101	WO	DMA CH5 S-G Status Register	DMA
041Eh	0000	0100	0010	1110	WO	DMA CH6 S-G Status Register	DMA

Table 4-2. ESC I/O Register Address Map (Continued)

Port	Address				Type	Name	Block
	FEDC	BA98	7654	3210			
041Fh	0000	0100	0010	1111	WO	DMA CH7 S-G Status Register	DMA
0420h	0000	0100	0010	0000	RO	DMA CH0 S-G Descriptor Pointer Register	DMA
0421h	0000	0100	0010	0001	RO	DMA CH0 S-G Descriptor Pointer Register	DMA
0422h	0000	0100	0010	0010	RO	DMA CH0 S-G Descriptor Pointer Register	DMA
0423h	0000	0100	0010	0011	RO	DMA CH0 S-G Descriptor Pointer Register	DMA
0424h	0000	0100	0010	0100	RO	DMA CH1 S-G Descriptor Pointer Register	DMA
0425h	0000	0100	0010	0101	RO	DMA CH1 S-G Descriptor Pointer Register	DMA
0426h	0000	0100	0010	0110	RO	DMA CH1 S-G Descriptor Pointer Register	DMA
0427h	0000	0100	0010	0111	RO	DMA CH1 S-G Descriptor Pointer Register	DMA
0428h	0000	0100	0010	1000	RO	DMA CH2 S-G Descriptor Pointer Register	DMA
0429h	0000	0100	0010	1001	RO	DMA CH2 S-G Descriptor Pointer Register	DMA
042Ah	0000	0100	0010	1010	RO	DMA CH2 S-G Descriptor Pointer Register	DMA
042Bh	0000	0100	0010	1011	RO	DMA CH2 S-G Descriptor Pointer Register	DMA
042Ch	0000	0100	0010	1100	RO	DMA CH3 S-G Descriptor Pointer Register	DMA
042Dh	0000	0100	0010	1101	RO	DMA CH3 S-G Descriptor Pointer Register	DMA
042Eh	0000	0100	0010	1110	RO	DMA CH3 S-G Descriptor Pointer Register	DMA
042Fh	0000	0100	0010	1111	RO	DMA CH3 S-G Descriptor Pointer Register	DMA
0434h	0000	0100	0011	0100	RO	DMA CH5 S-G Descriptor Pointer Register	DMA
0435h	0000	0100	0011	0101	RO	DMA CH5 S-G Descriptor Pointer Register	DMA
0436h	0000	0100	0011	0110	RO	DMA CH5 S-G Descriptor Pointer Register	DMA
0437h	0000	0100	0011	0111	RO	DMA CH5 S-G Descriptor Pointer Register	DMA
0438h	0000	0100	0011	1000	RO	DMA CH6 S-G Descriptor Pointer Register	DMA
0439h	0000	0100	0011	1001	RO	DMA CH6 S-G Descriptor Pointer Register	DMA
043Ah	0000	0100	0011	1010	RO	DMA CH6 S-G Descriptor Pointer Register	DMA
043Bh	0000	0100	0011	1011	RO	DMA CH6 S-G Descriptor Pointer Register	DMA
043Ch	0000	0100	0011	1100	RO	DMA CH7 S-G Descriptor Pointer Register	DMA
043Dh	0000	0100	0011	1101	RO	DMA CH7 S-G Descriptor Pointer Register	DMA
043Eh	0000	0100	0011	1110	RO	DMA CH7 S-G Descriptor Pointer Register	DMA
043Fh	0000	0100	0011	1111	RO	DMA CH7 S-G Descriptor Pointer Register	DMA
0461h	0000	0100	0110	0001	R/W	Extended NMI and Reset Control	Control
0462h	0000	0100	0110	0010	R/W	NMI I/O Interrupt Port	Control
0464h	0000	0100	0110	0100	RO	Last EISA Bus Master Granted (L)	Control
0480h	0000	0100	1000	0000	R/W	Reserved	DMA
0481h	0000	0100	1000	0001	R/W	DMA CH2 High Page Register	DMA
0482h	0000	0100	1000	0010	R/W	DMA CH3 High Page Register	DMA
0483h	0000	0100	1000	0011	R/W	DMA CH1 High Page Register	DMA

1

Table 4-2. ESC I/O Register Address Map (Continued)

Port	Address				Type	Name	Block
	FEDC	BA98	7654	3210			
0484h	0000	0100	1000	0100	R/W	Reserved	DMA
0485h	0000	0100	1000	0101	R/W	Reserved	DMA
0486h	0000	0100	1000	0110	R/W	Reserved	DMA
0487h	0000	0100	1000	0111	R/W	DMA CH0 High Page Register	DMA
0488h	0000	0100	1000	1000	R/W	Reserved	DMA
0489h	0000	0100	1000	1001	R/W	DMA CH6 High Page Register	DMA
048Ah	0000	0100	1000	1010	R/W	DMA CH7 High Page Register	DMA
048Bh	0000	0100	1000	1011	R/W	DMA CH5 High Page Register	DMA
048Ch	0000	0100	1000	1110	R/W	Reserved	DMA
048Dh	0000	0100	1000	1101	R/W	Reserved	DMA
048Eh	0000	0100	1000	1110	R/W	Reserved	DMA
048Fh	0000	0100	100x	1111	R/W	DMA Refresh High Page Register	DMA
04C2h	0000	0100	1100	0010	R/W	Reserved	DMA
04C6h	0000	0100	1100	0110	R/W	DMA CH5 High Base and Current Count Register	DMA
04CAh	0000	0100	1100	1010	R/W	DMA CH6 High Base and Current Count Register	DMA
04CEh	0000	0100	1100	1110	R/W	DMA CH7 High Base and Current Count Register	DMA
04D0h	0000	0100	1101	0000	R/W	INT-1 Edge/Level Control Register	PIC
04D1h	0000	0100	1101	0001	R/W	INT-2 Edge/Level Control Register	PIC
04D2h	0000	0100	1101	0010	R/W	Reserved	DMA
04D3h	0000	0100	1101	0011	R/W	Reserved	DMA
04D4h	0000	0100	1101	0100	R/W	DMA2 Chaining Mode	DMA
04D5h	0000	0100	1101	1001	R/W	Reserved	DMA
04D6h	0000	0100	1101	0010	WO	DMA2 Extended Mode Register	DMA
04D7h	0000	0100	1101	0111	R/W	Reserved	DMA
04D8h	0000	0100	1101	1000	R/W	Reserved	DMA
04D9h	0000	0100	1101	1001	R/W	Reserved	DMA
04DAh	0000	0100	1101	1010	R/W	Reserved	DMA
04DBh	0000	0100	1101	1011	R/W	Reserved	DMA
04DCh	0000	0100	1101	1100	R/W	Reserved	DMA
04DDh	0000	0100	1101	1101	R/W	Reserved	DMA
04DEh	0000	0100	1101	1110	R/W	Reserved	DMA
04DFh	0000	0100	1101	1111	R/W	Reserved	DMA
04E0h	0000	0100	1110	0000	R/W	DMA CH0 Stop Register Bits [7:2]	DMA
04E1h	0000	0100	1110	0001	R/W	DMA CH0 Stop Register Bits [15:8]	DMA
04E2h	0000	0100	1110	0010	R/W	DMA CH0 Stop Register Bits [23:16]	DMA
04E3h	0000	0100	1110	0011	R/W	Reserved	DMA

Table 4-2. ESC I/O Register Address Map (Continued)

Port	Address				Type	Name	Block
	FEDC	BA98	7654	3210			
04E4h	0000	0100	1110	0100	R/W	DMA CH1 Stop Register Bits [7:2]	DMA
04E5h	0000	0100	1110	0101	R/W	DMA CH1 Stop Register Bits [15:8]	DMA
04E6h	0000	0100	1110	0110	R/W	DMA CH1 Stop Register Bits [23:16]	DMA
04E7h	0000	0100	1110	0111	R/W	Reserved	DMA
04E8h	0000	0100	1110	1000	R/W	DMA CH2 Stop Register Bits [7:2]	DMA
04E9h	0000	0100	1110	1001	R/W	DMA CH2 Stop Register Bits [15:8]	DMA
04EAh	0000	0100	1110	1010	R/W	DMA CH2 Stop Register Bits [23:16]	DMA
04EBh	0000	0100	1110	1011	R/W	Reserved	DMA
04ECh	0000	0100	1110	1100	R/W	DMA CH3 Stop Register Bits [7:2]	DMA
04EDh	0000	0100	1110	1101	R/W	DMA CH3 Stop Register Bits [15:8]	DMA
04EEh	0000	0100	1110	1110	R/W	DMA CH3 Stop Register Bits [23:16]	DMA
04EFh	0000	0100	1110	1111	R/W	Reserved	DMA
04F0h	0000	0100	1111	0000	R/W	Reserved	DMA
04F1h	0000	0100	1111	0001	R/W	Reserved	DMA
04F2h	0000	0100	1111	0010	R/W	Reserved	DMA
04F3h	0000	0100	1111	0011	R/W	Reserved	DMA
04F4h	0000	0100	1111	0100	R/W	DMA CH5 Stop Register Bits [7:2]	DMA
04F5h	0000	0100	1111	0101	R/W	DMA CH5 Stop Register Bits [15:8]	DMA
04F6h	0000	0100	1111	0110	R/W	DMA CH5 Stop Register Bits [23:16]	DMA
04F7h	0000	0100	1111	0111	R/W	Reserved	DMA
04F8h	0000	0100	1111	1000	R/W	DMA CH6 Stop Register Bits [7:2]	DMA
04F9h	0000	0100	1111	1001	R/W	DMA CH6 Stop Register Bits [15:8]	DMA
04FAh	0000	0100	1111	1010	R/W	DMA CH6 Stop Register Bits [23:16]	DMA
04FBh	0000	0100	1111	1011	R/W	Reserved	DMA
04FC	0000	0100	1111	1100	R/W	DMA CH7 Stop Register Bits [7:2]	DMA
04FDh	0000	0100	1111	1101	R/W	DMA CH7 Stop Register Bits [15:8]	DMA
04FEh	0000	0100	1111	0111	R/W	DMA CH7 Stop Register Bits [23:16]	DMA
04FFh	0000	0100	1111	1111	R/W	Reserved	DMA
0C00h	0000	1100	0000	0000	R/W	Configuration RAM Page Register	Conf
0C80h	0000	1100	100	0000	RO	System Board ID Byte Lane 1 Bits [7:0]	Board ID
0C81h	0000	1100	100	0001	RO	System Board ID Byte Lane 2 Bits [15:8]	Board ID
0C82h	0000	1100	100	0010	RO	System Board ID Byte Lane 3 Bits [23:16]	Board ID
0C83h	0000	1100	1000	0011	RO	System Board ID Byte Lane 4 Bits [31:24]	Board ID

NOTES:
*Port 70h resides in the ESC, in addition the lower 7 bits of Port 70h reside in Real Time Clock.
& Bit 3 of ports 372h and 3F2h reside in the ESC while the other bits reside on the ISA bus.

4.3 Configuration Addresses

ESC configuration registers are accessed through I/O registers 22h and 23h. These I/O registers are used as index address register (22h) and index data register (23h). The index address register is used to write the configuration register address. The data (configuration register address) in register 22h is used to decode a configuration register. The selected configuration register can be read or written to by performing a read or a write operation to the index data register at I/O address 23h.

Table 4-3. Configuration Register Index Address

Configuration Offset	Abbreviation	Register Name
00h–01h		Reserved
02h	ESCID	ESC ID
03h–07h		Reserved
08h	RID	Revision ID
09h–3Fh		Reserved
40h	MS	Mode Select
41h		Reserved
42h	BIOSCSA	BIOS Chip Select A
43h	BIOSCSB	BIOS Chip Select B
44h–4Ch		Reserved
4Dh	CLKDIV	BCLK Clock Divisor
4Eh	PCSA	Peripheral Chip Select A
4Fh	PCSB	Peripheral Chip Select B
50h	EISAID1	EISA ID Byte 1
51h	EISAID2	EISA ID Byte 2
52h	EISAID3	EISA ID Byte 3
53h	EISAID4	EISA ID Byte 4
54h–56h		Reserved
57h	SGRBA	Scatter-Gather Relocate Base Address
58h–59h		Reserved
60h	PIRQRC0	PIRQ0# Route Control
61h	PIRQRC1	PIRQ1# Route Control

Table 4-3. Configuration Register Index Address (Continued)

Configuration Offset	Abbreviation	Register Name
62h	PIRQRC2	PIRQ2# Route Control
63h	PIRQRC3	PIRQ3# Route Control
64h	GPCSLA0	General Purpose Chip Select 0 Base Low Address
65h	GPCSHA0	General Purpose Chip Select 0 Base High Address
66h	GPCSM0	General Purpose Chip Select 0 Mask
67h		Reserved
68h	GPCSLA1	General Purpose Chip Select 1 Base Low Address
69h	GPCSHA1	General Purpose Chip Select 1 Base High Address
6Ah	GPCSM1	General Purpose Chip Select 1 Mask
6Bh		Reserved
6Ch	GPCSLA2	General Purpose Chip Select 2 Base Low Address
6Dh	GPCSHA2	General Purpose Chip Select 2 Base High Address
6Eh	GPCSM2	General Purpose Chip Select 2 Mask
6Fh	GPXBC	General Purpose Peripheral X-Bus Control
70h–87h		Reserved
88h	TSTC	Test Control
89h–9Fh		Reserved

4.4 X-Bus Peripherals

The ESC generates chip selects for certain functions that typically reside on the X-Bus. The ESC asserts the chip selects combinatorially from the LA addresses. The ESC generates chip select signals for the Keyboard Controller, Floppy Disk Controller, IDE, Parallel Port, Serial Port, and General Purpose peripherals. The ESC also generates read and write strobes for Real Time Clock and Configuration RAM. The read and write strobes are a function of LA addresses, the ISA read and write strobes (IORC# and IOWC#), and BCLK. All of the peripherals supported by the ESC are at fixed I/O addresses with the exception of the general purpose peripherals. The ESC support for these peripherals can be enabled or disabled through configuration registers Peripheral Chip Select A and Peripheral Chip Select B. The general purpose peripherals are mapped to I/O addresses by programming a set of configuration registers: General Purpose Chip Select x Base Low Address register, General Purpose Chip Select x Base High Address register, and General Purpose Chip Select x Mask register.

Table 4-4. X-Bus Chip Selects Decode

Port	FEDC	BA98	7654	3210	R/W	Name	Chip Select
0060h	0000	0000	0110	00x0	R/W	Keyboard Controller	KYBDCS#
0064h	0000	0000	0110	01x0	R/W	Keyboard Controller	KYBDCS#
0070h	0000	0000	0111	0xx0	W	Real Time Clock	RTCALE
0071h	0000	0000	0111	0xx1	R/W	Real Time Clock	RTCWR#/RTCRD#
0170h to 0177h	0000	0001	0111	0xxx	R/W	IDE Controller 0-Secondary	ECS[2:0] = 011 (IDECS0#)
01F0h to 01F7h	0000	0001	1111	0xxx	R/W	IDE Controller 0-Primary	ECS[2:0] = 011 (IDECS0#)
0278h to 027Bh	0000	0010	0111	1000 to 1011	R/W	Parallel Port LPT3	ECS[2:0] = 010 (LPTCS#)
02F8h to 02FFh	0000	0010	1111	xxxx	R/W	Serial Port COM2	ECS[2:0] = 00x (COMxCS#)
0370h to 0357h	0000	0011	0111	0000 to 0101	R/W	Floppy Disk Controller-Secondary	FDCCS#
0376h	0000	0011	0111	0111	R/W	IDE Controller 1-Secondary	ECS[2:0] = 100 (IDECS1#)
0377h	0000	0011	0111	0110	R/W	IDE Controller 1-Secondary	ECS[2:0] = 100 (IDECS1#)
0377h	0000	0011	0111	0111	R/W	Floppy Disk Controller-Secondary	FDCCS#
0378h to 037Bh	0000	0011	0111	1000 to 1011	R/W	Parallel Port LPT2	ECS[2:0] = 010 (LPTCS#)
03BCh to 03BFh	0000	0011	1011	11xx	R/W	Parallel Port LPT1	ECS[2:0] = 010 (LPTCS#)
03F0h to 0375h	0000	0011	1111	0000 to 0101	R/W	Floppy Disk Controller-Primary	FDCCS#
03F6h	0000	0011	0111	0110	R/W	IDE Controller 1-Primary	ECS[2:0] = 100 (IDECS1#)
03F7h	0000	0011	0111	0111	R/W	IDE Controller 1-Primary	ECS[2:0] = 100 (IDECS1#)
03F7h	0000	0011	0111	0111	R/W	Floppy Disk Controller-Secondary	FDCCS#
03F8h to 03FFh	0000	0011	1111	1000	R/W	Serial Port COM 1	ECS[2:0] = 00x (COMxCS#)
0800h to 08FFh	0000	1000	xxxx	xxxx	W/R	Configuration RAM	CRAMWR#/CRAMRD#

5.0 EISA CONTROLLER FUNCTIONAL DESCRIPTION

5.1 Overview

The EISA controller in the ESC provides Master/Slave EISA interface function for the ESC internal resources. In addition, the ESC acts as an EISA central resource for the system. As a system central resource, the EISA controller is responsible for generating the translation control signals necessary for bus-to-bus transfers. This translation includes transfer between devices on EISA Bus and ISA Bus and transfers between different size master device and slave device. The EISA controller generates the control signals for EISA Data Swap Buffers integrated in the PCEB. The ESC EISA interface generates cycles for DMA transfers, and refresh. The ESC internal registers are accessed through the EISA slave interface. The ESC is responsible for supporting the following:

Service EISA Master cycles to:

- EISA slaves devices.
- ISA slave devices.
- ESC internal registers.

Service ISA Master cycles to:

- EISA slave devices.
- ISA (mis-matched) slave devices.
- ESC internal registers.

Service DMA cycles :

- From/to DMA slave on the EISA bus to/from memory on the EISA/ISA bus.
- From/to DMA slave on the ISA bus to/from memory on the EISA/ISA bus.
- From/to DMA slave on the EISA/ISA bus to/from memory on the PCI bus.

Service REFRESH cycles :

The EISA controller will service the refresh cycle by generating the appropriate address and command signals. These cycles are initiated by either the ESC internal refresh logic or by an external ISA Bus Master.

Generates DATA SWAP BUFFER control:

The EISA controller generates the control signals for the data bus swap control (assembly/disassembly) and swapping process to support data size mismatches of the devices on the EISA and ISA buses. The actual data steering and swapping is performed by the PCEB.

Generate WAIT STATES:

The wait state generator is responsible for generating the wait states based on the sampling of the EXRDY, CHRDY, NOWS# and the default wait states. The default wait state depends on the cycle type.

5.2 Clock Generation

The ESC generates the EISA Bus clock. The ESC uses a divider circuit to generate the EISA Bus clock. The ESC supports PCI bus frequencies between 25 MHz and 33 MHz. The PCI clock is divided by 3 or 4 by the clock generation logic in the ESC. The EISA Clock Divisor register bits [2:0] select the divide value.

The ESC provides the EISA Bus clock as the BCLKOUT output. Although the ESC is capable of driving 240 pF load on the BCLKOUT pin, it is recommended that this signal be buffered to produce the EISA BCLK signal.

The ESC EISA control logic and EISA interface is synchronous to the BCLK input. A maximum delay of 15 ns is allowed between the BCLKOUT output and the BCLK input for proper device functionality.

Table 5-1. PCICLK and BCLK Frequency Relationship

PCICLK (MHz)	DIVISOR (Programmable)	BCLK (MHz)
25	3	8.33
30	4*	7.5
33.3	4*	8.33

NOTE:
*The ESC wakes up after reset with a default divisor value of 4.

5.2.1 CLOCK STRETCHING

The ESC is capable of stretching EISA Bus clock (BCLKOUT) for PCEB generated EISA cycles. The ESC stretches the EISA Bus clock (BCLKOUT) in order to minimize the synchronization penalty between PCI clock and EISA clock for accesses to EISA Bus by PCI agents. The PCEB initiates an EISA cycle by asserting START# synchronous to PCICLK. The ESC ensures the START# minimum pulse width is met by stretching the EISA Bus clock low time.

The ESC samples START# on every PCICLK when the PCEB has the EISA Bus. After sampling START# asserted, the ESC delays the rising edge of BCLKOUT until the START# has met the 115 ns minimum pulse width specification.

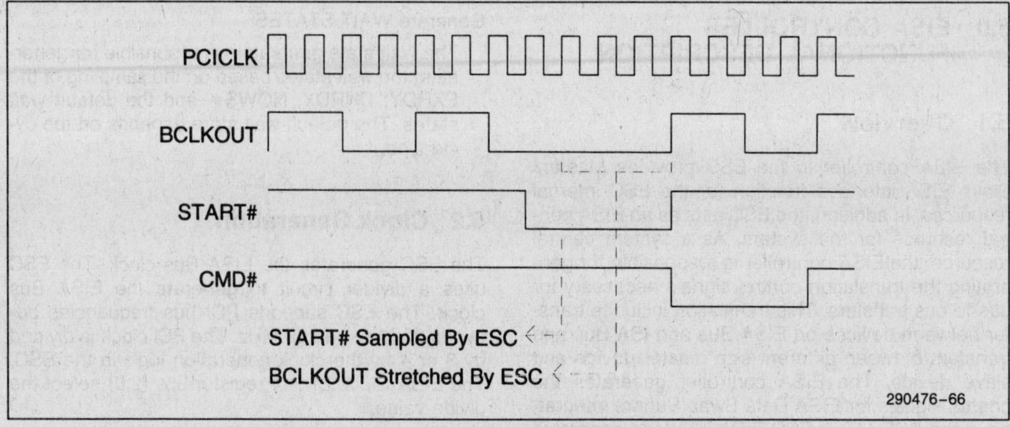

Figure 5-1. BCLK Stretching

5.3 EISA Master Cycles

EISA Master cycles are initiated on the EISA bus by an EISA Master (including PCEB for PCI agents). These cycles are accesses to the following resources:

— EISA slaves devices (including PCEB for PCI agents)

— ISA slave devices

— ESC internal registers (8-bit EISA Slave)

An EISA master gains control of the bus by asserting MREQx# (PEREQ# in case of PCEB) to the ESC. The ESC, after performing the necessary arbitration, asserts the corresponding MACKn# (negates EISAHOLD in case of the PCEB). Refer to Chapter 7.0 for arbitration protocol.

In response to receiving the acknowledge signal, the EISA Master starts the cycle by driving the bus with LA[31:02], BE[3:0], W/R, and M/IO. The EISA Master then asserts START# to indicate the beginning of the current cycle. A 16-bit EISA Master will also assert MASTER16# at this time. The ESC generates SBEH#, S1, and S0 signals from the BE[3:0]# signals.

5.3.1 EISA MASTER TO 32-BIT EISA SLAVE

An EISA slave after decoding its address asserts EX32# or EX16#. The EISA master and the ESC use these signals to determine the EISA slave data size. The 32-bit or 16-bit EISA master continues with the cycles if EX32# or EX16# is asserted respectively. The ESC acts as a central resources for the EISA master and generates CMD# for the cycles. The ESC asserts CMD# on the same BCLK edge that START# is negated. The ESC monitors the EXRDY signal on the EISA bus to determine when to negate the CMD#. An EISA Slave can extend the cycle by negating EXRDY. EISA specifications require that EXRDY not be held negated for more than 2.5 µs. A burstable EISA slave asserts SLBURST# signal the same time the slave decodes its address. The EISA master will sample SLBURST# and assert MSBURST# if it is capable of bursting. The ESC keeps the CMD# asserted during a burst EISA transfer. The ESC deasserts CMD# to indicate the end of the burst transfer after the EISA master deasserts MSBURST#.

If EX16# is asserted, a 32-bit EISA master backs-off the bus by floating BE[3:0]# and START# (see Section 5.3.4). The ESC acts as a central resource for the EISA master in this case and takes over the mastership of the EISA bus by deriving START#, CMD#, and the appropriate byte enables. The ESC generates the necessary translation cycles for the EISA master and returns the bus ownership to the master by asserting EX32# and EX16#. The ESC monitors the EXRDY signal on the EISA bus to determine when to negate the CMD#. An EISA Slave can extend the cycle by negating EXRDY. EISA specification require that EXRDY not be held negated for more than 2.5 µs. A burstable EISA slave will assert SLBURST# signal the same time when its address is decoded. The EISA master will sample SLBURST# and assert MSBURST# if it is capable of bursting. The ESC keeps the CMD# asserted during a burst EISA transfer. The ESC deasserts CMD# to indicate the end of the burst transfer after the EISA master deasserts MSBURST#.

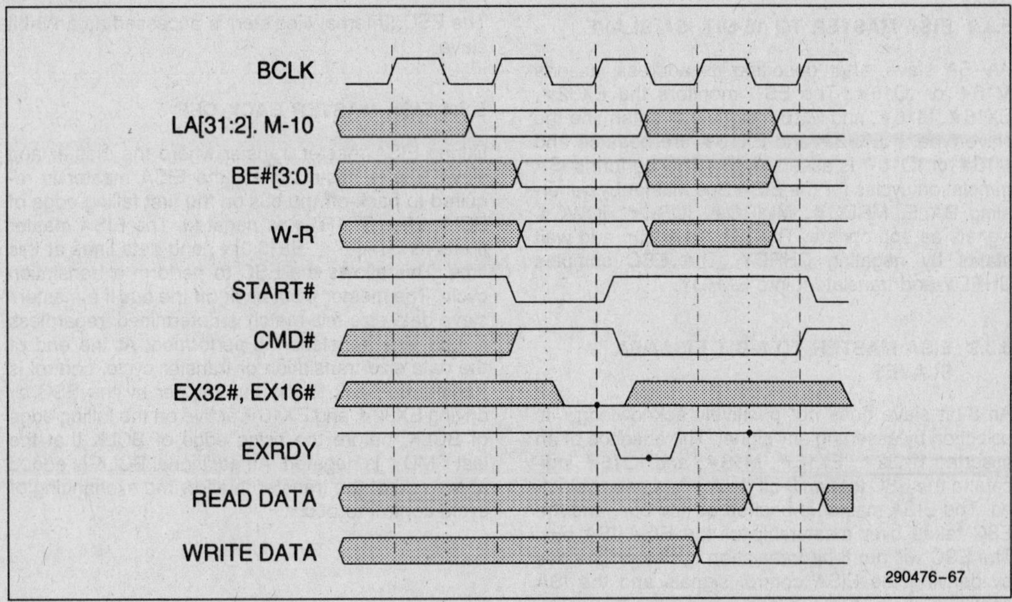

Figure 5-2. Standard EISA Master to EISA Slave Cycle

BCLK
LA[31:2] M-10 1 2 3
BE[3:0]# 1 2 3
W/R#
START#
CMD# 1 2 3
EX 32#, EX16#
EXRDY
MSBURST#
SLBURST#
READ DATA 1 2 3
WRITE DATA 1 2 3
290476-68

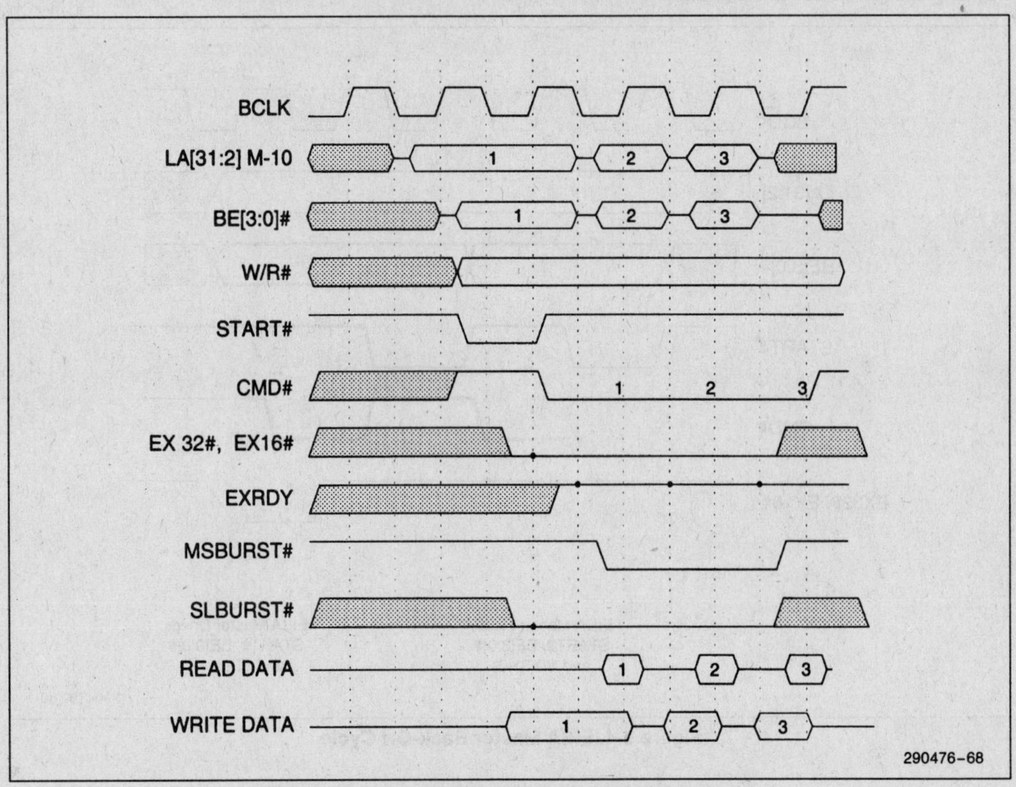

Figure 5-3. Burst EISA Master to EISA Slave Cycle

5.3.2 EISA MASTER TO 16-BIT ISA SLAVE

An ISA slave, after decoding its address, asserts M16# or IO16#. The ESC monitors the EX32#, EX16#, M16#, and IO16# signals to determine the slave type. If EX32# and EX16# are negated and M16# or IO16# is asserted, the ESC performs ISA translation cycles for the EISA Bus master by generating BALE, MRDC#, MWRC#, IORC#, IOWC# signals as appropriate. The ISA slave can add wait states by negating CHRDY. The ESC samples CHRDY and translate it into EXRDY.

5.3.3 EISA MASTER TO 8-BIT EISA/ISA SLAVES

An 8-bit slave does not positively acknowledge its selection by asserting any signal. The absence of an asserted EX32#, EX16#, M16#, and IO16# indicate to the ESC that an 8-bit device has been selected. The EISA master is backed-off the bus, and the ESC takes over mastership of the EISA/ISA bus. The ESC will run 8-bit translation cycles on the bus by deriving the EISA control signals and the ISA control signals. A slave can extend the cycles by negating EXRDY or CHRDY signals.

The ESC (Internal Register) is accessed as an 8-bit slave.

5.3.4 EISA MASTER BACK-OFF

During EISA master transfer where the master and slave size is mis-matched, the EISA master is required to back-off the bus on the first falling edge of BCLK after START# is negated. The EISA master floats its START#, BE[3:0]#, and data lines at this time. This allows the ESC to perform a translation cycle. The master must back-off the bus if a master/slave data size mis-match is determined, regardless if data size translation is performed. At the end of the data size translation or transfer cycle, control is transferred back to the bus master by the ESC by driving EX32# and EX16# active on the falling edge of BCLK, before the rising edge of BCLK that the last CMD# is negated. An additional BCLK is added at the end of the transfer to allow the exchanging of cycle control to occur.

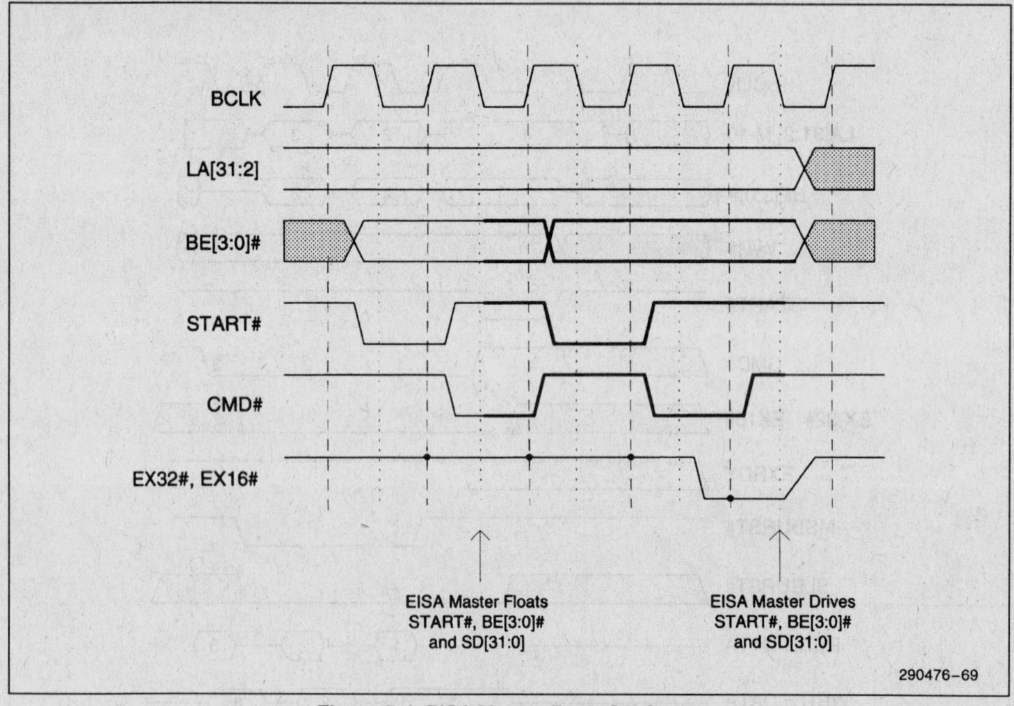

Figure 5-4. EISA Master Back-Off Cycle

5.4 ISA Master Cycles

ISA cycles are initiated on the ISA bus by an ISA master. These cycles are accesses to the following system resources:

— EISA slaves devices (including PCEB for PCI agents).

— ISA slave devices.

— ESC internal registers (8-bit EISA Slave).

The ISA Master initiates such a cycle by asserting the DREQx# line to the ESC. The ESC, after performing the necessary arbitration, asserts the corresponding DACKx# line. Upon receiving an acknowledge from the ESC, the ISA master asserts the MASTER16# signal line to indicate that it has control of the ISA bus and a cycle on the ISA bus will take place.

The ESC translates the ISA address signals SBHE#, SA1, and SA0 to EISA byte enables BE[3:0]#.

5.4.1 ISA MASTER TO 32-BIT/16-BIT EISA SLAVE

An EISA slave will decode the address to determine if it has been selected. In response to a positive decode, the EISA slave will assert EX32# or EX16#. The ESC samples these signals to determine if an EISA Slave has been selected. If these signals are asserted, the ESC will perform ISA to EISA cycle translation by driving the EISA control signals.

The ISA Master asserts one of the ISA command signals MRDC#, MWTC#, IORC# or IOWC# depending on whether or not the access is to a memory, an I/O device or an I/O register. The ISA command signals will remain active until the end of the cycle. The ESC will generate the EISA translation by generating the EISA control signals; START#, CMD#, M/IO#, and W/R#.

The EISA slave can add wait states by negating EXRDY. The ESC samples EXRDY and translates it into CHRDY. The ESC will also generate the control signals to steer the data to the appropriate byte lanes for mis-matched cycles.

5.4.2 ISA MASTER TO 16-BIT ISA SLAVE

An ISA Master initiates cycles to ISA slave devices. These cycles are either memory read/write or I/O read/write. The ISA bus Master is assumed to be 16-bit device, and it can access either 8-bit or 16-bit slave devices that reside on the ISA-bus. A 16-bit ISA slave device will respond to a valid address by asserting M16# for memory cycles and IO16# for I/O cycles.

The ESC is inactive during ISA Master cycles where either M16# or IO16# is sampled asserted.

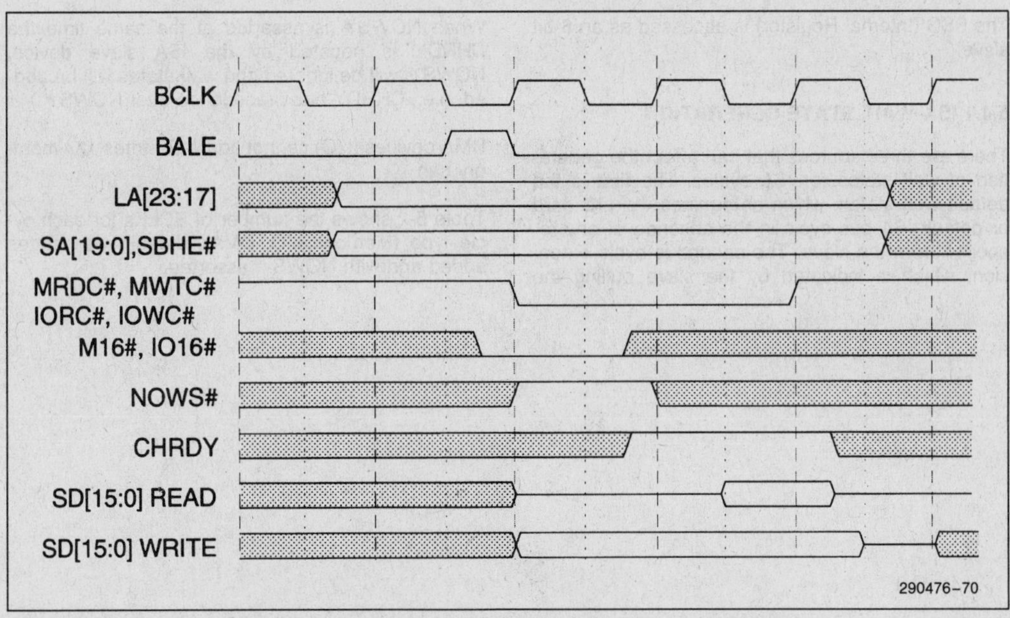

Figure 5-5. ISA Master to 16-Bit ISA Slave Cycles (3 BCLKs)

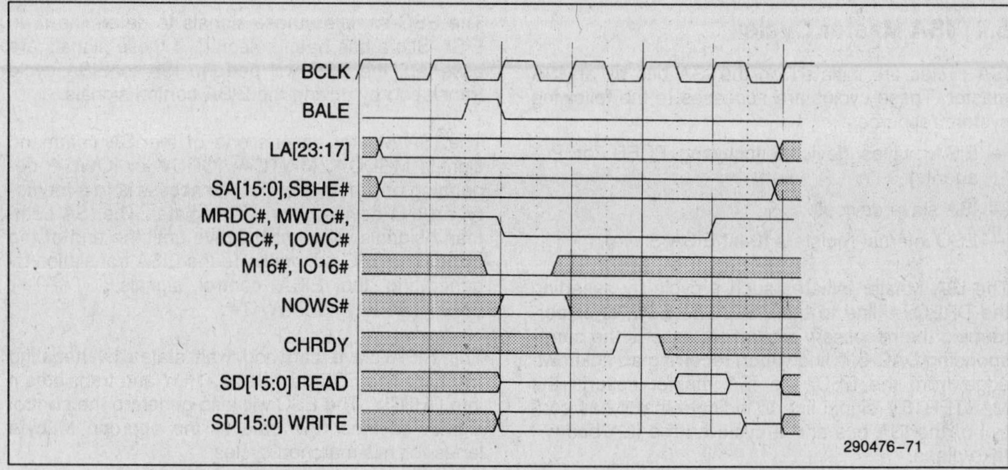

Figure 5-6. ISA Master to 16-Bit ISA Slave Extended Cycle (4 BCLKs)

5.4.3 ISA MASTER TO 8-BIT EISA/ISA SLAVE

An 8-bit slave does not positively acknowledge its selection by asserting any signal. The absence of an asserted EX32#, EX16#, M16#, and IO16# indicate to the ESC that an 8-bit device has been selected. The EISA master is backed-off the bus, and the ESC takes over mastership of the EISA/ISA bus. The ESC will run 8-bit translation cycles on the bus by deriving the EISA control signals and the ISA control signals. A slave can extend the cycles by negating EXRDY or CHRDY signals.

The ESC (Internal Register) is accessed as an 8-bit slave.

5.4.4 ISA WAIT STATE GENERATION

There are three sources that can affect the generation of wait states for ISA cycles. The first is the default wait states, which determines the standard or default ISA bus cycle in the absence of any response from the slave. The second is cycle extension, which is indicated by the slave pulling the CHRDY signal line inactive (low). The CHRDY is high by default due to a pull-up resistor. Thus, the cycle will be extended until the CHRDY is returned to its active high value. The third way to change the number of wait states is when the slave asserts the NOWS# signal which makes the cycle shorter than the default or standard cycle.

ISA Memory slaves (8 bits and 16 bits) and ISA I/O slaves (only 8 bits) can shorten their default cycles by asserting the NOWS# signal lines. A 16-bit I/O slave cannot shorten its default cycles.

When NOWS# is asserted at the same time the CHRDY is negated by the ISA slave device, NOWS# will be ignored and wait states will be added. (i.e.; CHRDY has precedence over NOWS#.)

DMA devices (I/O) cannot add wait states, but memory can.

Table 5-2 shows the number of BCLKs for each cycle type (Memory, I/O, DMA), default, wait states added and with NOWS# asserted.

Table 5-2. Number of BCLKs for ISA Master Cycles

Cycle Type	Bus Size	No Wait State NOWS# = 0	Standard CHRDY = 1 NOWS# = 1	One Wait State CHRDY = 0
		Number of BCLKs		
Memory Read/Write	16	2	3	4
Memory Read/Write	8	4, 5	6	7
I/O Read/Write	16	3	3	4
I/O Read/Write	8	4, 5	6	7
DMA Compatible	8/16	8	8	10
DMA Type A*	8/16	NA	6	7
DMA Type B*	8/16	NA	4	5
DMA Type C†	8/16	NA	2	3

NOTES:
* If ISA memory responds, the ESC will extend the cycle by 1 BCLK.
† If ISA memory responds, the ESC will use DMA Type B read cycle timing.

5.5 Mis-Match Cycles

Data size translation is performed by the ESC for all mis-matched cycles. A mis-matched cycle is defined as a cycle in which the bus master and bus slave do not have equal data bus sizes (e.g., a 32-bit EISA master accessing a 16-bit ISA slave). The data size translation is performed in conjunction with the PCEB. The ESC generates the appropriate cycles and data steering control signals for mis-matched cycles. The PCEB uses the data steering control signals from the ESC to latch and redirect the data to the appropriate byte lanes. The ESC will perform one or more of the following operations depending on the master and slave type, transfer direction, and the number of byte enables active.

Table 5-3. Mis-Match Master Slave Combinations

Master Type		Slave Type: 32-Bit EISA	16-Bit EISA	16-Bit ISA	8-Bit EISA/ISA
32-Bit EISA with 16-Bit Downshift	Standard	Match	Mis-Match	Mis-Match	Mis-Match
	Burst	Match	Match	NA	NA
32-Bit EISA	Standard	Match	Mis-Match	Mis-Match	Mis-Match
	Burst	Match	NA	NA	NA
16-Bit EISA	Standard	Mis-Match	Match	Mis-Match	Mis-Match
	Burst	Mis-Match	Match	NA	NA

NOTE:
NA: Not Applicable. The cycle will never occur.

5.6 Data Swap Buffer Control Logic

For all mis-matched cycles, the ESC is responsible for performing data size translations. The ESC performs these data size translations by either becoming the master of the EISA/ISA Bus (see Section 5.3.4) or by directing the flow of data to the appropriate byte lanes. In both cases, the ESC generates Data Swap Buffer control signals to perform data size translation.

— SDCPYEN[13, 3:1]

— SDCPYUP

— SDOE[2:0]#

— SDLE[3:0]#

The Data Swap Buffers are integrated in the PCEB (see PCEB data sheet Chapter 8.0 for Data Swap Buffer function description).

The data size translation cycles consist of one or combinations of Assembly, Disassembly, Copy Up/Down, and Redrive.

Assembly

This occurs during reads when an EISA master data size is greater than the slave data size. ISA masters are required to perform assemble when accessing 8-bit slaves. Assembly consists of two, three, or four cycles depending on the master data size, slave data size, and number of active byte enables. During the assembly process, the data is latched into the PCEB data latch/buffers. This data is driven or redriven on to the EISA bus during the last cycle. The master after initiating the cycle backs-off the bus (see the EISA master back-off section for details) when a mis-matched is detected. The ESC becomes the bus master and runs the appropriate number of cycles. At the end of the last cycle, the ESC transfers the control of bus back to the original master.

Disassembly

This occurs during writes when the EISA master data size is greater than the slave data size. ISA masters are required to perform disassemble when accessing 8-bit slaves. Disassembly consists of two, three, or four cycles depending on the master data size, slave data size, and number of active byte enables. During the disassembly process, the data is latched in the PCEB latch/buffers on the first cycle. This data is driven or redriven on to the EISA bus on subsequent cycles. The master after initiating the cycle backs-off the bus (see the EISA master back-off section for details) when a mis-matched is detected. The ESC becomes the bus master and runs the appropriate number of cycles. At the end of the last cycle, the ESC transfers the control of bus back to the original master.

Copy-Up

This occurs during reads when the master data size is greater than the slave data size and during writes when the master data size is smaller than the slave data size. The copy-up function is used for cycles with and without assembly/disassembly.

Copy-Down

This occurs during writes when the master data size is greater than the slave data size and during reads when the master data size is smaller than the slave data size. The copy-down function is used for cycles with and without assembly/disassembly.

Re-Drive

This occurs during reads and writes when both the master and slave are on the EISA/ISA bus and the PCEB is neither a master nor a slave. The re-drive function is always performed in conjunction with assembly/disassembly. During the assembly process, the last cycle is a re-drive cycle. During disassembly, all the cycles except the first cycle are re-drive cycles.

5.7 Servicing DMA Cycles

The ESC is responsible for performing DMA transfers. If the memory is determined (EX32# or EX16# asserted) to be on the EISA bus, the DMA cycle can be "A", "B", or "C" type. If the memory is determined to be on the ISA bus, then the DMA cycle will run as a compatible cycle. The DMA transfers are described in detail in Section 8.0.

5.8 Refresh Cycles

The ESC support refresh cycles on the EISA/ISA bus. The ESC asserts the REFRESH# signal to indicate when a refresh cycle is in progress. Refresh cycles are generated by two sources: the refresh unit inside the ESC or an external ISA bus masters. The EISA bus controller will enable the address lines LA[15:2] and the BE[3:0]#. The High and Low Page register contents will also be placed on the LA[31:16] bus during refresh. Memory slaves on the EISA/ISA bus must not drive any data onto the data bus during the refresh cycle. Slow memory slaves on the EISA/ISA may extend the refresh cycle by negating the EXRDY or CHRDY signal respectively. The refresh cycles are also described in Section 6.11.

5.9 EISA Slot Support

The ESC support up of 8 EISA slots. The ESC provides support for the 8 slots as follows:

— The ESC address and data output buffers directly drive 240 pF capacitive load on the Bus.

— The ESC generates slot specific AENx signals.

— The ESC supports EISA masters in all 8 slots.

The ESC generates encoded AENs and encoded Master Acknowledge signals for 8 slots and 8 masters. These signals must be decoded on the system board to generate the slot specific AENx signals and MACKx# signals. The ESC can be programmed through Mode Select register bit[1:0] to directly generate these signals for 4 slots and 4 masters.

5.9.1 AEN GENERATION

The ESC directly generates the slot specific AEN signals if the ESC is configured to support 4 AENx.

Table 5-4. AEN Generation

CYCLE	A15:A12	A11:A8	A7:A4	A3:A0	AEN4	AEN3	AEN2	AEN1
DMA	xxxx	xxxx	xxxx	xxxx	1	1	1	1
I/O	0000	xx00	xxxx	xxxx	1	1	1	1
I/O	0001	xx00	xxxx	xxxx	1	1	1	0
I/O	0010	xx00	xxxx	xxxx	1	1	0	1
I/O	0011	xx00	xxxx	xxxx	1	0	1	1
I/O	0100	xx00	xxxx	xxxx	0	1	1	1
I/O	0101 to 1111	xx00	xxxx	xxxx	1	1	1	1
I/O	xxxx	xx01	xxxx	xxxx	0	0	0	0
I/O	xxxx	xx10	xxxx	xxxx	0	0	0	0
I/O	xxxx	xx11	xxxx	xxxx	0	0	0	0
MEM	xxxx	xxxx	xxxx	xxxx	0	0	0	0

If the ESC is programmed to support more than 4 EISA AENx, the ESC will generate Encoded AEN signals. Discrete logic like a F138 is required to generate the slot specific AENs.

Table 5-5. Encoded AEN (AEN) Generation

CYCLE	A15:A12	A11:A8	A7:A4	A3:A0	EAEN4	EAEN3	EAEN2	EAEN1
DMA	xxxx	xxxx	xxxx	xxxx	1	1	1	1
I/O	0000	xx00	xxxx	xxxx	1	1	1	1
I/O	0001	xx00	xxxx	xxxx	0	0	0	1
I/O	0010	xx00	xxxx	xxxx	0	0	1	0
I/O	0011	xx00	xxxx	xxxx	0	0	1	1
I/O	0100	xx00	xxxx	xxxx	0	1	0	0
I/O	0101	xx00	xxxx	xxxx	0	1	0	1
I/O	0110	xx00	xxxx	xxxx	0	1	1	0
I/O	0111	xx00	xxxx	xxxx	0	1	1	1
I/O	1000	xx00	xxxx	xxxx	1	0	0	0
I/O	1001 to 1111	xx00	xxxx	xxxx	1	1	1	1
I/O	xxxx	xx01	xxxx	xxxx	0	0	0	0
I/O	xxxx	xx10	xxxx	xxxx	0	0	0	0
I/O	xxxx	xx11	xxxx	xxxx	0	0	0	0
MEM	xxxx	xxxx	xxxx	xxxx	0	0	0	0

NOTE:
EAEN[4:1] combinations not specified in the table are Reserved.

5.9.2 MACKx# GENERATION

The ESC generates the EISA Master Acknowledge signals if the ESC is configured to directly support 4 masters through the Mode Select Register bit[1:0]. In this case the ESC generates MACKx#s for Master 0–3.

If the ESC is programmed to support more than 4 EISA slots, the ESC will generate Encoded (E)MACKx#s. Discrete logic like a F138 is required to generate the MACKx#s for the Masters.

Table 5-6. Encoded MACK# (EMACKx#) Generation

EMACK[4:1]	MACK7#	MACK6#	MACK5#	MACK4#	MACK3#	MACK2#	MACK1#	MACK0#
0000	1	1	1	1	1	1	1	0
0001	1	1	1	1	1	1	0	1
0010	1	1	1	1	1	0	1	1
0011	1	1	1	1	0	1	1	1
0100	1	1	1	0	1	1	1	1
0101	1	1	0	1	1	1	1	1
0110	1	0	1	1	1	1	1	1
0111	0	1	1	1	1	1	1	1
1111	1	1	1	1	1	1	1	1

NOTE:
EMACK[4:1] combinations 1000–1110 are Reserved.

6.0 DMA CONTROLLER

6.1 DMA Controller Overview

The DMA circuitry incorporates the functionality of two 82C37 DMA controllers with seven independently programmable channels, (Channels 0–3 and Channels 5–7). DMA Channel 4 is used to cascade the two controllers together and will default to cascade mode in the Mode register. In addition to accepting requests from DMA slaves, the DMA also responds to requests that are initiated by software. Software may initiate a DMA service request by setting any DMA Channel Request register bit to a 1. The DMA controller for Channels 0–3 is referred to as "DMA-1" and the controller for Channels 4–7 is "DMA-2".

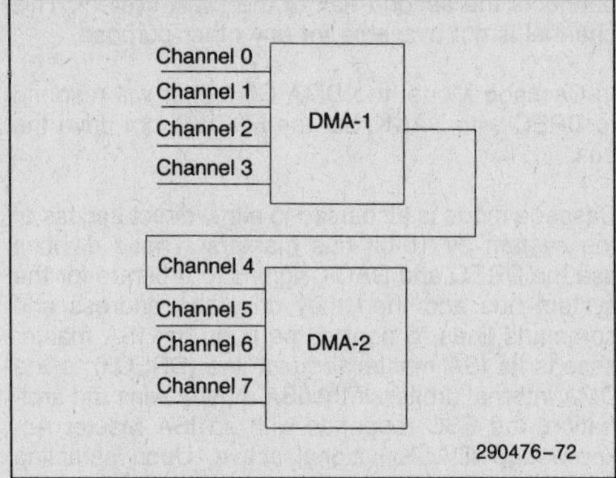

Figure 6-1. Internal DMA Controller

Each DMA channel can be programmed for 8-bit or 16-bit DMA device size. Each channel can also be programmed for compatibility, Type "A", Type "B", or Type "C" (burst transfer) timings. Each DMA channel defaults to the PC-AT compatible settings for DMA device size: channels [3:0] default to 8-bit, count-by-bytes transfers, while channels [7:5] default to 16-bit, count-by-words (address shifted) transfers. The ESC provides the timing control and data size translation necessary for DMA transfers between EISA/ISA agents of mismatched bus sizes.

The DMA Controller supports full 32-bit addressing. Each channel includes a 16-bit ISA compatible Current register which holds the 16 least-significant bits of the 32-bit address, and an ISA compatible Low Page register which contains the eight second most significant bits. An additional High Page register contains the eight most significant bits of the 32-bit address. The address counter can be programmed as either 16-bit compatible address counter or a full 32-bit address counter.

The channels can also be programmed for any of four transfer modes. The transfer modes include single, block, demand, or cascade. Each of the three active transfer modes (single, block, and demand), can perform three different types of transfers (read, write, or verify).

The DMA Controller also features refresh address generation, and auto-initialization following a DMA termination. EISA compatible buffer chaining is included as well as Stop registers to support ring buffer structures.

Scatter-Gather reduces CPU overhead by eliminating reprogramming of the DMA and I/O between buffers as well as reducing the number of interrupts.

The DMA Controller includes the EISA Bus arbiter which works with the PCEB's PCI bus arbiter. The arbiter determines which requester from among the requesting DMA slaves, EISA bus masters, the PCI bus, or Refresh should have the bus.

The DMA Controller is at any time either in master mode or slave mode. In master mode, the DMA controller is either servicing a DMA slave's request for DMA cycles, allowing an ISA master to use the bus via a cascaded DREQ signal, or granting the bus to an EISA master via MREQ#/MACK#. In slave mode, the ESC monitors both the EISA bus decoding and responding to I/O read and write commands that address its registers.

When the DMA is in master mode and servicing a DMA slave, it works in conjunction with the ESC EISA bus controller to create bus cycles on the EISA bus. The DMA places addresses onto the internal address bus and the bus controller informs the DMA when to place a new address on the internal bus.

6.2 DMA Transfer Modes

The channels can be programmed for any of four transfer modes. The transfer modes include single, block, demand, or cascade. Each of the three active transfer modes (single, block, and demand), can perform three different types of transfers (read, write, or verify). The ESC does not support memory to memory transfers.

6.2.1 SINGLE TRANSFER MODE

In Single Transfer mode the DMA is programmed to make one transfer only. The byte/word count will be decremented and the address decremented or incremented following each transfer. When the byte/word count "rolls over" from zero to FFFFFFh, or an external EOP is encountered, a Terminal Count (TC) will load a new buffer via Scatter-Gather, buffer chaining or autoinitialize if it is programmed to do so.

DREQ must be held active until DACK becomes active in order to be recognized. If DREQ is held active throughout the single transfer, the bus will be released to the CPU after a single transfer. With the DREQ asserted high, the DMA I/O device will rearbitrate for the bus. Upon winning the bus, another single transfer will be performed. This allows other bus masters a chance to arbitrate for, win, and execute cycles on the EISA Bus.

6.2.2 BLOCK TRANSFER MODE

In Block Transfer mode the DMA is activated by DREQ to continue making transfers during the service until a TC, caused by either a byte/word count going to FFFFFFh or an external EOP, is encountered. DREQ need only be held active until DACK becomes active. If the channel has been programmed for it, a new buffer will be loaded by Scatter-Gather, buffer chaining or Auto-initialization at the end of the service. In this mode, it is possible to lock out other devices for a period of time (including refresh) if the transfer count is programmed to a large number and Compatible timing is selected. Block mode can effectively be used with Type "A", Type "B", or Burst timing since the channel can be interrupted through the 4 μs timeout mechanism, and other devices (or Refresh) can arbitrate for and win the bus. See Chapter 7.0 on the EISA Bus Arbitration for a detailed description of the 4 μs timeout mechanism.

6.2.3 DEMAND TRANSFER MODE

In Demand Transfer mode the DMA channel is programmed to continue making transfers until a TC (Terminal Count) is encountered or an external EOP is encountered, or until the DMA I/O device pulls DREQ inactive. Thus, transfers may continue until the I/O device has exhausted its data capacity. After the I/O device catches up, the DMA service is re-established when the DMA I/O device reasserts the channel's DREQ. During the time between services when the system is allowed to operate, the intermediate values of address and byte/word count are stored in the DMA controller Current Address and Current Byte/Word Count registers. A TC can cause a new buffer to be loaded via Scatter-Gather, buffer chaining or Autoinitialize at the end of the service if the channel has been programmed for it.

6.2.4 CASCADE MODE

This mode is used to cascade more than one DMA controller together for simple system DMA requests for the additional device propagate through the priority network circuitry of the preceding device. The priority chain is preserved and the new device must wait for its turn to acknowledge requests. Within the ESC architecture, Channel 0 of DMA Controller two (DMA-2, Ch 4) is used to cascade DMA Controller one (DMA-1) to provide a total of seven DMA channels. Channel 0 on DMA-2 (labeled Ch 4 overall) connects the second half of the DMA system. This channel is not available for any other purpose.

In Cascade Mode, the DMA Controller will respond to DREQ with DACK, but the ESC will not drive the bus.

Cascade mode is also used to allow direct access of the system by 16-bit bus masters. These devices use the DREQ and DACK signals to arbitrate for the system bus and then they drive the address and command lines to control the bus. The ISA master asserts its ISA master request line (DREQx) to the DMA internal arbiter. If the ISA master wins the arbitration, the ESC responds with an ISA Master Acknowledge (DACKx) signal active. Upon sampling the DACKx line active, the ISA Master asserts MASTER16# signal and takes control of the EISA bus. The ISA Master has control of the EISA Bus, and the ISA Master may run cycles until it negates the MASTER16# signal.

6.3 DMA Transfer Types

Each of the three active transfer modes (Single, Block, or Demand) can perform three different types of transfers. These transfers are Read, Write and Verify.

Write Transfer

Write transfers move data from an EISA/ISA I/O device to memory located on EISA/ISA Bus or PCI Local Bus. The DMA indicates the transfer type to the EISA bus controller. The bus controller will activate IORC# and the appropriate EISA control signals (M/IO# and W/R#) to indicate a memory write.

Read Transfer

Read transfers move data from EISA/ISA or PCI memory to an EISA/ISA I/O device. The DMA indicates the transfer type to the EISA bus controller. The bus controller will activate IOWC# and the appropriate EISA control signals (M/IO# and W/R#) to indicate a memory read.

Verify Transfer

Verify transfers are pseudo transfers. The DMA controller operates as in Read or Write transfers, generating addresses and producing TC, etc. However, the ESC does not assert the memory and I/O control signals. Only the DACK signals are asserted. Internally the DMA controller will count BCLKs so that the DACK signals have a defined pulse width. This pulse width is nine BCLKs long. If Verify transfers are repeated during Block or Demand DMA requests, each additional pseudo transfer will add eight BCLKs. The DACK signals will not be toggled for repeated transfers.

6.4 DMA Timing

The ESC DMA provides four transfer timings. In addition to the compatible timings, the ESC DMA provides Type "A", Type "B", and Type "C" (Burst) timings for I/O slave devices capable of running at faster speeds.

1

6.4.1 COMPATIBLE TIMINGS

Compatible timing is provided for DMA slave devices. Compatible timing runs at 9 BCLKs (1080 ns/single cycle) and 8 BCLKs (960 ns/cycle) during the repeated portion of a Block or Demand mode transfers.

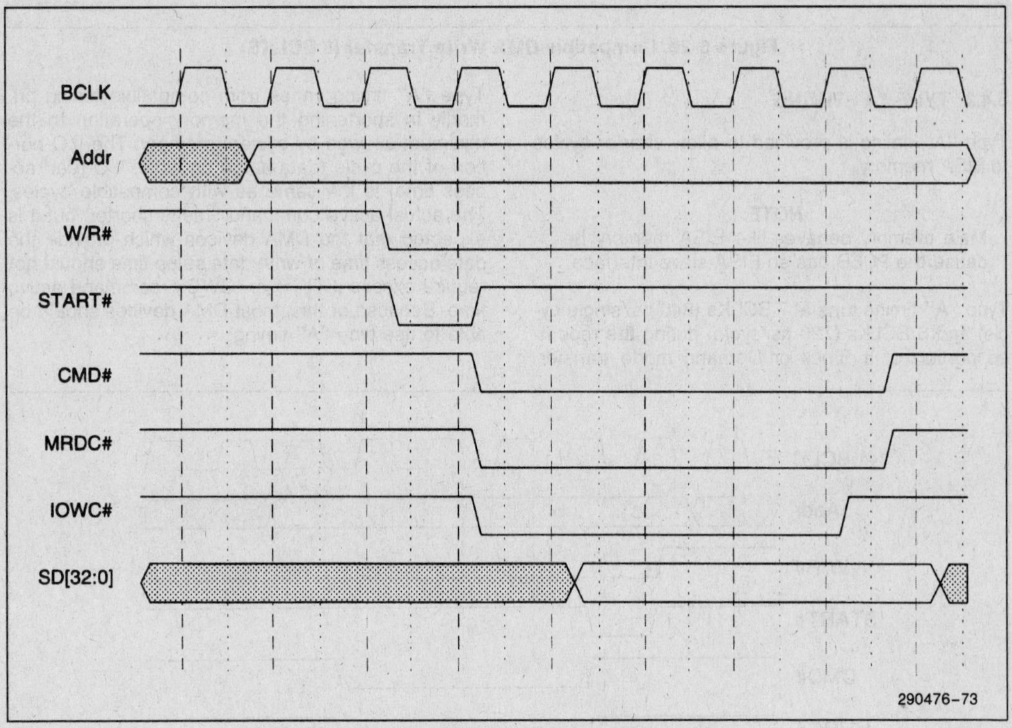

BCLK
Addr
W/R#
START#
CMD#
MRDC#
IOWC#
SD[32:0]
290476-73

Figure 6-2a. Compatible DMA Read Transfer (8 BCLKs)

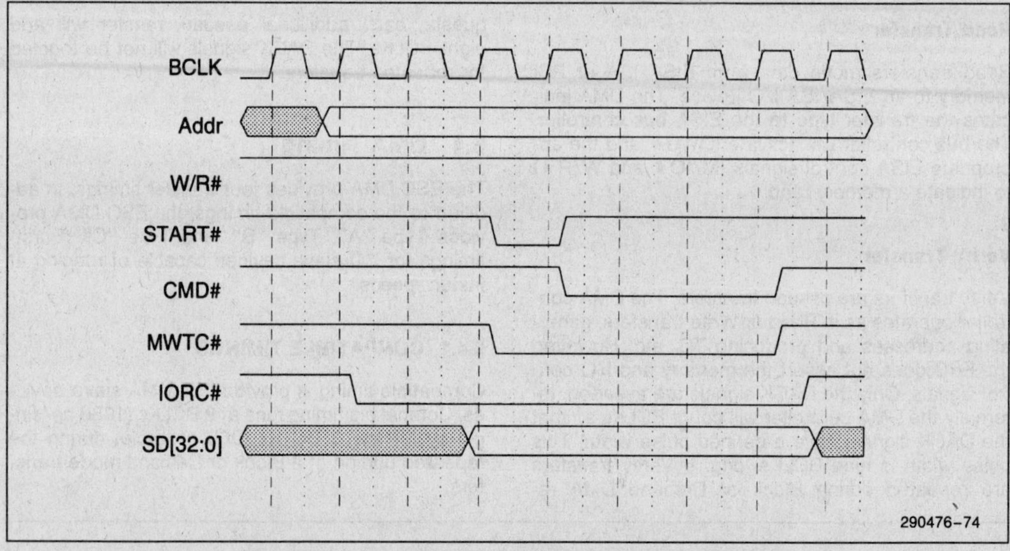

Figure 6-2b. Compatible DMA Write Transfer (8 BCLKS)

6.4.2 TYPE "A" TIMING

Type "A" timing is provided to allow shorter cycles to EISA memory.

NOTE:
Main memory behaves like EISA memory because the PCEB has an EISA slave interface.

Type "A" timing runs at 7 BCLKs (840 ns/single cycle) and 6 BCLKs (720 ns/cycle) during the repeated portion of a Block or Demand mode transfer. Type "A" timing varies from compatible timing primarily in shortening the memory operation to the minimum allowed by system memory. The I/O portion of the cycle (data setup on write, I/O read access time) is the same as with compatible cycles. The actual active command time is shorter, but it is expected that the DMA devices which provide the data access time or write data setup time should not require excess IORC# or IOWC# command active time. Because of this, most DMA devices should be able to use type "A" timing.

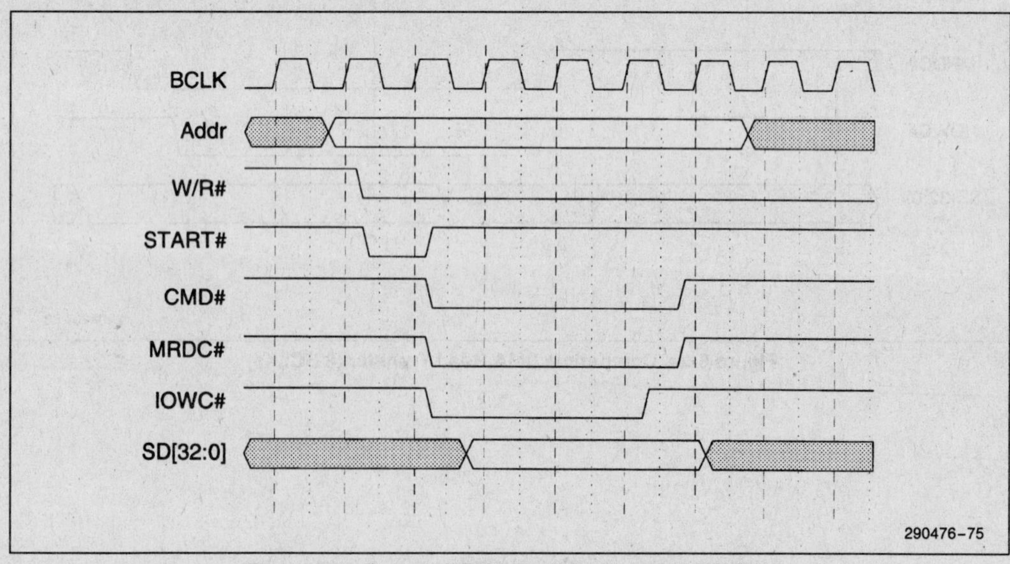

Figure 6-3a. Type "A" DMA Read Transfers (6 BCLKS)

6.4.3 TYPE "B" TIMING

Type "B" timing is provided for 8-bit/16-bit DMA devices which can accept faster I/O timing. Type "B" only works with fast system memory. Type "B" timing runs at 6 BCLKs (720 ns/single cycle) and 4 BCLKs (480 ns/cycle) during the repeated portion of a Block or Demand mode transfer. Type "B" timing requires faster DMA slave devices than compatible timing in that the cycles are shortened so that the data setup time on I/O write cycles is shortened and the I/O read access time is required to be faster. Some of the current ISA devices should be able to support type "B" timing, but these will probably be more recent designs using relatively fast technology.

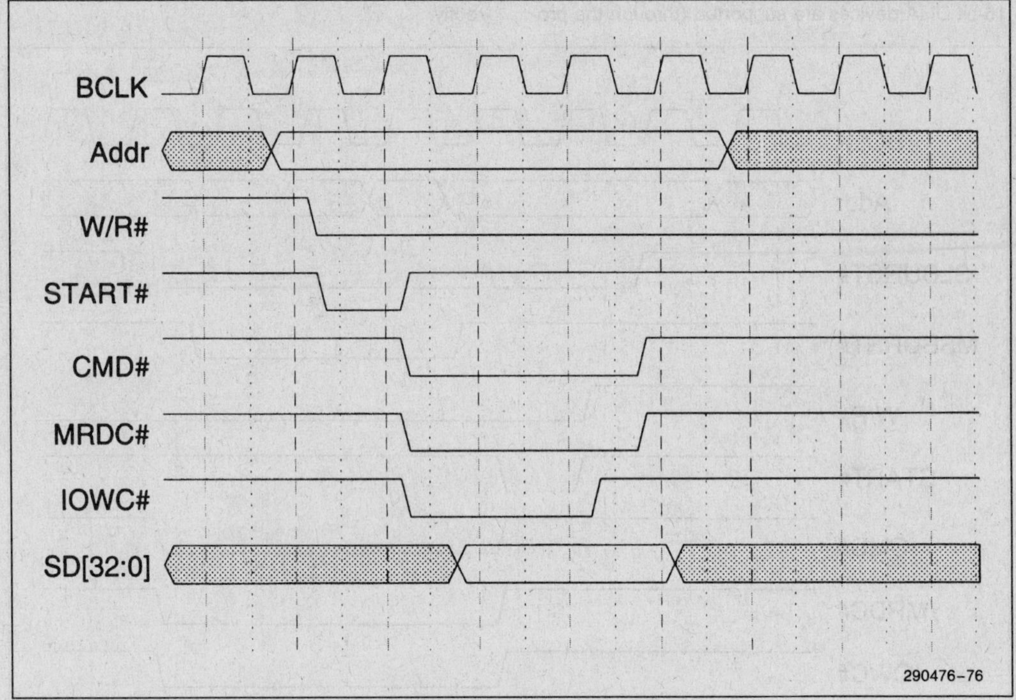

Figure 6-4a. Type "B" DMA Read Transfer (4 BCLKS)

1

6.4.4 TYPE "C" (BURST) TIMING

Type "C" (burst) timing is provided for EISA DMA devices. The DMA slave device needs to monitor EXRDY and IORC# or IOWC# signals to determine when to change the data (on writes) or sample the data (on reads). This timing will allow up to 33 MBytes per second transfer rate with a 32-bit DMA device and 32-bit memory. Note that 8-bit or 16-bit DMA devices are supported (through the programmable DMA address increment) and that they use the "byte lanes" natural to their size for the data transfer. As with all bursts, the system will revert to two BCLK cycles if the memory does not support burst. When a DMA burst cycle accesses non-burst memory and the DMA cycle crosses a page boundary into burstable memory, the ESC will continue performing standard (non-burst) cycles. This will not cause a problem since the data is transferred correctly.

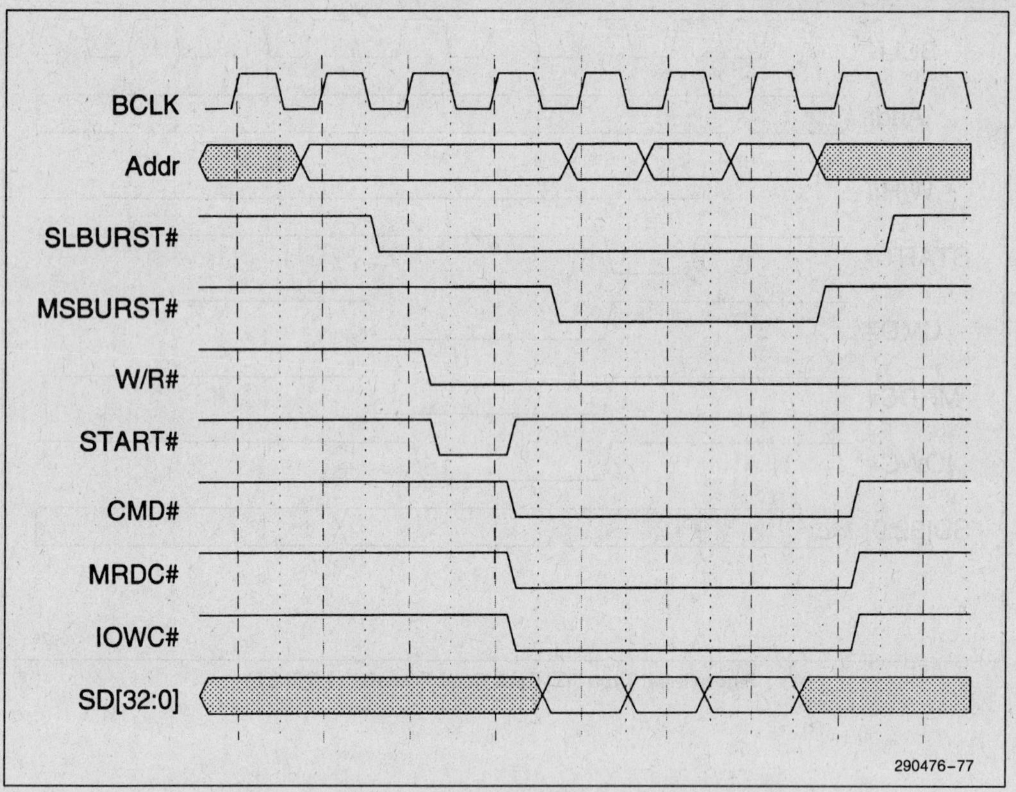

BCLK
Addr
SLBURST#
MSBURST#
W/R#
START#
CMD#
MRDC#
IOWC#
SD[32:0]
290476-77

Figure 6-5a. Type "C" (Burst) DMA Read Transfers (1 BCLK)

6.5 Channel Priority

For priority resolution the DMA consists of two logical channel groups-channels 0–3 and channels 4–6. Each group may be in either Fixed or Rotate mode, as determined by the Command register.

For arbitration purposes, the source of the DMA request is transparent. DMA I/O slaves normally assert their DREQ line to arbitrate for DMA service. However, a software request for DMA service can be presented through each channel's DMA Request register. A software request is subject to the same prioritization as any hardware request. Please see the detailed register description in Section 3.2 for Request Register programming information.

Fixed Priority

The initial fixed priority structure is as follows:

Table 6-1. Initial Fixed Priority Structure

High Priority	Low Priority
(0, 1, 2, 3) 5, 6, 7	

The fixed priority ordering is 0, 1, 2, 3, 5, 6, and 7. In this scheme, Channel 0 has the highest priority, and Channel 7 has the lowest priority. Channels [3:0] of DMA-1 assume the priority position of Channel 4 in DMA-2, thus taking priority over Channels 5, 6, and 7.

Rotating Priority

Rotation allows for "fairness" in priority resolution. The priority chain rotates so that the last channel serviced is assigned the lowest priority in the Channel group (0–3, 5–7).

Channels 0–3 rotate as a group of 4. They are always placed between Channel 5 and Channel 7 in the priority list.

Channel 5–7 rotate as part of a group of 4. That is, Channels (5–7) form the first three partners in the rotation, while Channel group (0–3) comprises the fourth position in the arbitration.

Table 6-2 demonstrates rotation priority:

Table 6-2. Rotating Priority Example

Programmed Mode	Action	Priority
		High . . . Low
Group (0–3) is in rotation mode.	1. Initial Setting	(0, 1, 2, 3), 5, 6, 7
Group (4–7) is in fixed mode.	2. After servicing channel 2	(3, 0, 1, 2), 5, 6, 7
	3. After servicing channel 3	(0, 1, 2, 3), 5, 6, 7
Group (0–3) in rotation mode.	1. Initial Setting	(0, 1, 2, 3), 5, 6, 7
Group (4–7) is in rotation mode.	2. After servicing channel 0	5, 6, 7, (1, 2, 3, 0)
	3. After servicing channel 5	6, 7, (1, 2, 3, 0), 5
(note that the first servicing of channel 0 caused double rotation).	4. After servicing channel 6	7, (1, 2, 3, 0), 5, 6
	5. After servicing channel 7	(1, 2, 3, 0), 5, 6, 7

6.6 Scatter-Gather Functional Description

Scatter-Gather provides the capability of transferring multiple buffers between memory and I/O without CPU intervention. In Scatter-Gather, the DMA can read the memory address and word count from an array of buffer descriptors called the Scatter-Gather Descriptor (SGD) Table. This allows the DMA to sustain DMA transfers until all buffers in the Scatter-Gather Descriptior Table are transferred.

The Scatter-Gather Command register and Scatter-Gather Status register are used to control the operational aspect of Scatter-Gather transfers (see Section 3.2 for details of these registers). The Scatter-Gather Descriptior Next Link register holds the address of the next buffer descriptor in the Scatter-Gather Descriptor Table.

The next buffer descriptor is fetched from the Scatter-Gather Descriptor Table by a DMA read transfer. DACK# will not be asserted for this transfer because the I/O device is the DMA itself and the DACK is internal to the ESC. The ESC will assert IOWC# for these bus cycles like any other DMA

transfer. The ESC will behave as an 8-bit I/O slave and will run type "B" timings for a Scatter-Gather buffer descriptor transfer. EOP will be asserted at the end of the transfer.

To initiate a typical Scatter-Gather transfer between memory and I/O device following steps involved:

Software prepares a Scatter-Gather Descriptor (SGD) Table in system memory. Each Scatter-Gather descriptor is 8 bytes long and consists of an address pointer to the starting address and the transfer count of the memory buffer to be transferred. In any given SGD Table, two consecutive SGDs are offset by 8 bytes and are aligned on a 4-byte boundary.

Each Scatter-Gather Descriptor for the linked list must contain the following information:

a) Memory Address (buffer start) 4 bytes
b) Byte Count (buffer size) 3 bytes
c) End of Link List 1 bit (MSB)

Initialize DMA Mode and Extended Mode registers with transfer specific information like 8-bit/16-bit I/O device, Transfer Mode, Transfer Type, etc.

Software provides the starting address of the Scatter-Gather Descriptor Table by loading the Scatter-Gather Descriptor Table Pointer register.

Engage the Scatter-Gather machine by writing a Start command to the Scatter-Gather Command register.

The Mask register should be cleared as the last step of programming the DMA register set. This is to prevent DMA from starting a transfer with a partially loaded command description.

Once the register set is loaded and the channel is unmasked, the DMA will generate an internal request to fetch the first buffer from the Scatter-Gather Descriptor Table.

The DMA will then respond to DREQ or software requests. The first transfer from the first buffer will move the memory address and word count from the Base register set to the Current register set. As long as Scatter-Gather is active and the Base register set is not loaded and the last buffer has not been fetched, the channel will generate a request to fetch a reserve buffer into the Base register set. The reserve buffer is loaded to minimize latency problems going from one buffer to another. Fetching a reserve buffer has a lower priority than completing DMA for the channel.

The DMA controller will terminate a Scatter-Gather cycle by detecting an End of List (EOL) bit in the SGD. After the EOL bit is detected, the channel will transfer the buffers in the Base and Current register sets if they are loaded. At Terminal Count the channel will assert EOP or IRQ13 depending on its programming and set the Terminate bit in the Scatter-Gather Status register. The Active bit in the Scatter-Gather Status register will be reset and the channel's Mask bit will be set.

The above discussion describes how to accomplish a Scatter-Gather transfer in Demand Mode. For Block Mode transfers, a slighty different method is required. The following describes a Block Mode transfer:

— Program Scatter-Gather information
— Enable Scatter-Gather via Command Register
— Kick-off DMA device
— Poll DMA status register for active DREQ
— Set software request bit
— Remove channel mask

	byte 3	byte 2	byte 1	byte 0	Address
Dword 0	Memory Address				XXX0h XXX3h
Dword 1	EOL	RESERVED	Byte Count		XXX4h XXX7h

290478-78

Figure 6-6. Scatter-Gather Descriptor Format

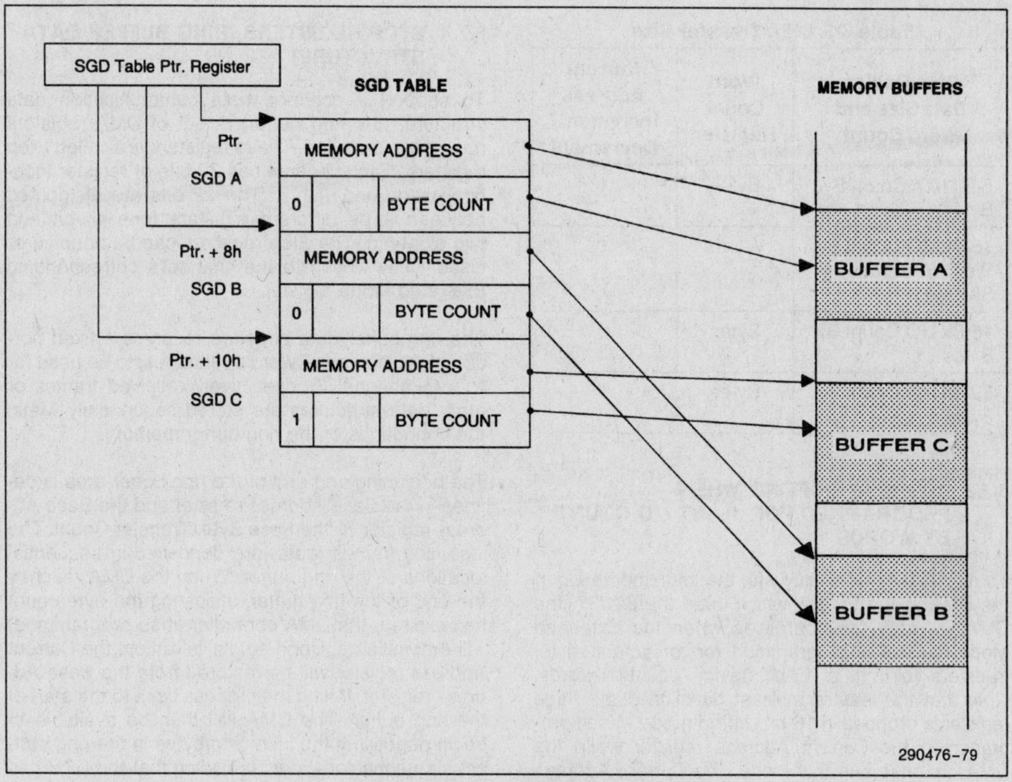

Figure 6-7. Link List Example

6.7 Register Functionality

Please see Section 3.2 for detailed information on register programming, bit definitions, and default values/functions after a reset.

DMA Channel 4 is used to cascade the two DMA controllers together and should not be programmed for any mode other than cascade. The Mode register for Channel 4 will default to cascade mode. Special attention should also be taken when programming the Command and Mask registers as related to Channel 4 (refer to the Command and Mask register descriptions, Section 3.2).

6.7.1 ADDRESS COMPATIBILITY MODE

Whenever the DMA is operating in Address Compatibility mode, the addresses do not increment or decrement through the High and Low Page registers, and the high page register is set to 00h. This is compatible with the 82C37 and Low Page register implementation used in the PC AT. This mode is set when any of the lower three address bytes of a channel are programmed. If the upper byte of a channel's address is programmed last, the channel will go into Extended Address Mode. In this mode, the high byte may be any value and the address will increment or decrement through the entire 32-bit address.

After reset is negated all channels will be set to Address Compatibility Mode. The DMA Master Clear command will also reset the proper channels to Address Compatibility Mode. The Address Compatibility Mode bits are stored on a per channel basis.

6.7.2 SUMMARY OF THE DMA TRANSFER SIZES

Table 6-3 lists each of the DMA device transfer sizes. The column labeled "Word Count Register" indicates that the register contents represent either the number of bytes to transfer or the number of 16-bit words to transfer. The column labeled "Current Address Register Increment/Decrement" indicates the number added to or taken from the Current Address register after each DMA transfer cycle. The Mode Register determines if the Current Address register will be incremented or decremented.

Table 6-3. DMA Transfer Size

DMA Device Date Size and Word Count	Word Count Register	Current Address Increment/ Decrement
8-Bit I/O, Count By Bytes	Bytes	1
16-Bit I/O,Count By Words (Address Shifted)	Words	1
16-Bit I/O,Count By Bytes	Bytes	2
32-Bit I/O,Count By Bytes	Bytes	4

6.7.3 ADDRESS SHIFTING WHEN PROGRAMMED FOR 16-BIT I/O COUNT BY WORDS

To maintain compatibility with the implementation of the DMA in the PC/AT which used the 82C37, the DMA will shift the addresses when the Extended Mode register is programmed for, or defaulted to, transfers to/from a 16-bit device count-by-words. Note that the least significant bit of the Low Page register is dropped in 16-bit shifted mode. When programming the Current Address register while the DMA channel is in this mode, the Current Address must be programmed to an even address with the address value shifted right by one bit. The address shifting is shown in Table 6-4.

6.7.4 STOP REGISTERS (RING BUFFER DATA STRUCTURE)

To support a common data communication data structure, (the ring buffer), a set of DMA registers have been provided. These registers are called Stop registers. Each channel has 22 bits of register location associated with it. The 22 bits are distributed between three different registers (one six-bit and two eight-bit). The Stop registers can be enabled or disabled by writing to the channel's corresponding Extended Mode register.

The ring buffer data structure reserves a fixed portion of memory, on Dword boundaries, to be used for a DMA channel. Consecutively received frames or other data structures are stored sequentially within the boundaries of the ring buffer memory.

The beginning and end of the ring buffer area is defined in the Base Address register and the Base Address register + the Base Byte/Transfer Count. The incoming frames (data) are deposited in sequential locations of the ring buffer. When the DMA reaches the end of the ring buffer, indicating the byte count has expired, the DMA controller (if so programmed) will Autoinitialize. Upon autoinitialization, the Current Address register will be restored from the Base Address register, taking the process back to the start of the ring buffer. The DMA will then be available to begin depositing the incoming bytes in the ring buffers sequential locations, providing that the CPU has read the data that was previously placed in those locations. The DMA determines that the CPU has read certain data by the value that the CPU writes into the Stop register.

Table 6-4. Address Shifting in 16-Bit I/O DMA Transfers

Output Address	8-Bit I/O Programmed Address	16-Bit I/O Programmed Address (Shifted)	16-Bit I/O Programmed Address (No Shift)	32-Bit I/O Programmed Address (No Shift)
A0 A[16:1] A[31:17]	A0 A[16:1] A[31:17]	"0" A[15:0] A[31:17]	A0 A[16:01] A[31:17]	A0 A[16:01] A[31:17]

NOTE:
The least significant bit of the Low Register is dropped in 16-bit shifted mode.

Once the data of a frame is read by the CPU, the memory location it occupies becomes available for other incoming frames. The Stop register prevents the DMA from over writing data that has not yet been read by the CPU. After the CPU has read a frame from memory it will update the Stop register to point to the location that was last read. The DMA will not deposit data into any location beyond that pointed to by the stop register. The last address transferred before the channel is masked is the first address that matches the Stop register.

For example:

If the stop register = 00001Ch, the last three transfers will be:

Table 6-5. Stop Register Functionality Example

	By Bytes	By Words	By Words
Increment	XX00001Ah XX00001Bh XX00001Ch	XX000018h XX00001Ah XX00001Ch	XX000018h XX00001Ah XX00001Ch
Decrement	XX000021h XX000020h XX00001Fh	XX000023h XX000021h XX00001Fh	XX000023h XX000021h XX00001Fh

The Stop registers store values to compare against LA[23:2] only, so the size of the ring buffer is limited to 16 MBytes.

6.7.5 BUFFER CHAINING MODE AND STATUS REGISTERS

The Chaining Mode registers are used to implement the buffer chaining mode of a channel. The buffer chaining mode is useful when transferring data from a peripheral to several different areas of memory with one continuous transfer operation. Four registers are used to implement this function: the Chaining Mode register, the Chaining Mode Status Register, the Channel Interrupt Status register, and the Chain Buffer Expiration Control register.

The Chaining Mode register controls the buffer chaining initialization. Buffer chaining mode can be enabled or disabled. A Chaining Mode bit is used to indicate if Base register programming is complete and chaining can begin, or to hold off chaining because the Base registers still need programming. Another bit dictates the buffer expiration response by indicating whether an IRQ13 or EOP should be issued when the buffer needs reprogramming.

The Chaining Mode Status Register indicates whether each channel's chaining mode is enabled or disabled.

The Channel Interrupt Status Register indicates the channel source of a DMA chaining interrupt on IRQ13. The CPU can read this register to determine which channel asserted IRQ13 following a buffer expiration.

The Chain Buffer Expiration Control Register is a read only register that reflects the outcome after the expiration of a chain buffer. If a channel bit is set to 0, IRQ13 will be activated following the buffer expiration. If a channel bit is set to 1, EOP will be asserted following the buffer expiration.

6.7.6 AUTOINITIALIZE

By programming a bit in the Mode register, a channel may be set up as an Autoinitialize channel. During Autoinitialize initialization, the original values of the Current page, Current address and Current Byte/Word Count registers are automatically restored from the Base Address, and Word count registers of that channel following TC. The Base registers are loaded simultaneously with the Current registers by the microprocessor and remain unchanged throughout the DMA service. The mask bit is not set when the channel is in Autoinitialize. Following Autoinitialize the channel is ready to perform another DMA service, without CPU intervention, as soon as a valid DREQ is detected.

NOTE:

Autoinitialize will not function if the channel is also programmed for Scatter-Gather or buffer chaining. Only one of these features should be enabled at a time.

6.8 Software Commands

These are additional special software commands which can be executed in the Program Condition. They do not depend on any specific bit pattern on the data bus. The three software commands are:

1. Byte Pointer Flip-Flop
2. Master Clear, and
3. Clear Mask Register.

6.8.1 CLEAR BYTE POINTER FLIP-FLOP

This command is executed prior to writing or reading new address or word count information to the DMA. This initializes the flip-flop to a known state so that subsequent accesses to register contents by the microprocessor will address upper and lower bytes in the correct sequence.

1

When the CPU is reading or writing DMA registers, two Byte Pointer Flip-Flops are used; one for Channels 0–3 and one for Channels 4–6. Both of these act independently. There are separate software commands for clearing each of them (0Ch for Channels 0–3, 0D8h for Channels 4–7).

An additional Byte Pointer Flip-Flop has been added for use when EISA masters are reading and writing DMA registers. (The arbiter state will be used to determine the current master of the bus.) This Flip-Flop is cleared when an EISA Master performs a write to either 00Ch or 0D8h. There is one Byte Pointer Flip-Flop per eight DMA channels. This Byte Pointer was added to eliminate the problem of the CPU's byte pointer getting out of synchronization if an EISA Master takes the bus during the CPU's DMA programming.

6.8.2 DMA MASTER CLEAR

This software instruction has the same effect as the hardware Reset. The Command, Status, Request, and Internal First/Last Flip-Flop registers are cleared and the Mask register is set. The DMA Controller will enter the idle cycle.

There are two independent Master Clear Commands, 0Dh which acts on Channels 0–3, and 0DAh which acts on Channels 4–6.

6.8.3 CLEAR MASK REGISTER

This command clears the mask bits of all four channels, enabling them to accept DMA requests. I/O port 00Eh is used for Channels 0–3 and I/O port 0DCh is used for Channels 4–6.

6.9 Terminal Count/EOP Summary

This is a summary of the events that will happen as a result of a terminal count or external EOP when running DMA in various modes.

Table 6-6. Terminal Count/EOP Summary Table

Conditions				
AUTOINIT	No		Yes	
Event				
Word Counter Expired	Yes	X	Yes	X
EOP Input	X	Asserted	X	Asserted
Result				
Status TC	set	set	set	set
Mask	set	set	—	—
SW Request	clr	clr	clr	clr
Current Register	—	—	load	load

NOTES:
load = Load Current From Base
"—" = No Change
X = Don't Care
clr = Clear

6.10 Buffer Chaining

The buffer chaining mode of a channel is useful for transferring data from a peripheral to several different areas of memory within one transfer operation (from the DMA device's viewpoint). This is accomplished by causing the DMA to interrupt the CPU for more programming information while the previously programmed transfer is still in progress. Upon completion of the previous transfer, the DMA controller will then load the new transfer information automatically. In this way, the entire transfer can be completed without interrupting the operation of the DMA device. This mode is most useful for DMA single-cycle or demand modes where the transfer process allows time for the CPU to execute the interrupt routine.

The buffer chaining mode of a channel may be entered by programming the address and count of a transfer as usual. After the initial address and count is programmed, the Base registers are selected via the Chaining Mode register Chaining Mode Enabled bit. The address and count for the second transfer and both the Chaining Mode Enabled and the Program Complete bit of the Chaining Mode register should be programmed at this point, before starting the DMA process. When, during the DMA process, the Current Buffer is expired, the Base address, Page, and Count registers will be transferred to the Current registers and a signal that the buffer has been expired is sent to the programming master.

This signal will be an IRQ13 if the master is the CPU, or a TC if the programming master is an EISA Master device. The type of programming master is indicated in the DMA's Chaining Mode Register, Bit 4. If the CPU is the programming master for the Channel, TC will be generated only if the Current buffer expires and there is no Next Buffer stored in the Base registers.

Upon the expiration of a Current Buffer, the new Base register contents should be programmed and both the Chaining Mode Enabled and Program complete bits of the Chaining Mode register should be set. This resets the interrupt, if the CPU was the programming master, and allows for the next Base register to Current register transfer. If the Program Complete bit is not set before the current transfer reaches TC, then the DMA controller will set the Mask Bit and the TC bit in the Status register and stop transferring data. In this case, an over-run is likely to occur. To determine if this has, a read of either Status register or the Mask register can be done (the Mask register has been made readable). If the channel is masked or has registered a TC, the DMA channel has been stopped and the full address, count, and chaining mode must be programmed to return to normal operation.

Note that if the CPU is the programming master, an interrupt will only be generated if a Current Buffer expires and chaining mode is enabled. It will not occur during initial programming. The Channel Interrupt Status register will indicate pending interrupts only. That is, it will indicate an empty Base register with Chaining Mode enabled. When Chaining mode is enabled, only the Base registers are written by the processor, and only the Current registers can be read. The Current registers are only updated on a TC.

6.11 Refresh Unit

The ESC provides an EISA Bus compatible refresh unit that provides 14 bits of refresh address for EISA/ISA bus DRAMS that do not have their own local refresh units. The refresh system uses the combined functions of the Interval Timers, the DMA Arbiter, DMA address counter, and EISA Bus Controller. Functionally, the Refresh unit is a sub-section of the ESC DMA unit. The DMA Address Counter is used to increment the Refresh Address register following each refresh cycle. Interval Counter 1, Timer 1 generates an internal refresh request. The DMA Arbiter detects a Refresh signal from either the Counter/Timer or the REFRESH# input and determines when the refresh will be done. The DMA drives the refresh address out onto the LA address bus. The cycle is decoded and driven onto the EISA address bus by the EISA Bus Controller. The ESC EISA Bus Controller is responsible for generating the EISA cycle control signals. Timer 1 Counter 1 should be programmed to provide a refresh request about every 15 μs.

Requests for refresh cycles are generated by two sources: the ESC (Timer 1 Counter 1), and 16-bit masters that activate REFRESH# when they own the EISA bus.

If a 16-bit ISA bus master holds the bus longer than 15 μs, it must initiate memory refresh cycles. If the ISA Master initiates a Refresh cycle while it owns the bus, it floats the address lines and cycle control signals and asserts REFRESH# to the ESC. The ESC EISA Bus Controller generates the cycle control signals and the ESC DMA Refresh unit supplies the refresh address. The ISA Master must then wait one BCLK after MRDC# is negated before floating REFRESH# and driving the address lines and control signals.

Typically, the refresh cycle length is five BCLK's. The I/O slave can insert one wait state to extend the cycle to six BCLK's by asserting CHRDY. The ESC EISA Bus Controller, upon seeing REFRESH#, knows to run refresh cycles instead of DMA cycles.

7.0 EISA BUS ARBITRATION

The ESC receives requests for EISA Bus ownership from several different sources; from DMA devices, from the Refresh counter, from EISA masters and from PCI agents. PCI agents requesting the EISA Bus request the EISA Bus through the PCEB. Additionally, 16-bit ISA Masters may request the bus through a cascaded DMA channel (see the Cascade mode description in Section 6.2.4).

7.1 Arbitration Priority

At the top level of the arbiter, the ESC uses a three way rotating priority arbitration method. On a fully loaded bus, the order in which the devices are granted bus access is independent of the order in which they assert a bus request, since devices are serviced based on their position in the rotation. The arbitration scheme assures that DMA channels and EISA masters are able to access the bus with minimal latency.

The PCEB and EISA Masters share one of the slots in the three way rotating priority scheme. This sharing is a two way rotation between the CPU and EISA Masters as a group. In this arbitration scheme, the PCEB acts on behalf of the CPU and all other PCI masters.

1

EISA Masters have a rotating priority structure which can handle up to eight master requests.

The next position in the top level arbiter is occupied by the DMA. The DMA's DREQ lines can be placed in either fixed or rotating priority. The default mode is fixed and by programming the DMA Command registers, the priority can be modified to rotating priority mode.

7.2 Preemption

An EISA compatible arbiter ensures that minimum latencies are observed for both EISA DMA devices, and EISA Masters.

7.2.1 PCEB EISA BUS ACQUISITION AND PCEB PREEMPTION

EISA Bus arbitration is intended to be optimized for CPU access to the EISA bus. Since the CPU accesses the EISA Bus through the PCEB, the PCEB is assumed to be the default owner of the EISA bus. The arbitration interface between the PCEB and the ESC is implemented as a HOLD/HLDA (EISAHOLD/EISAHLDA) pair.

If a PCI cycle requires access to the EISA Bus while EISAHLDA signal is asserted (EISA Bus busy) the PCI cycle is retried, and the PCEB requests the EISA bus by asserting PEREQ#. The ESC, after sampling PEREQ# asserted, preempts the current owner of the EISA Bus. The ESC grants the EISA Bus by negating EISAHOLD signal.

The ESC asserts EISAHOLD to the PCEB when the ESC needs to acquire the ownership of the EISA bus. While EISAHOLD is asserted, the arbitration process is dynamic and may change, i.e., the ESC is still accepting EISA Bus requests. When the PCEB returns EISAHLDA, the arbiter freezes the arbitration process and determines the winner. If the new winner is an EISA Master or DMA channel, the ESC will assert NMFLUSH#. The ESC tri-states the NMFLUSH# output driver on the following clock. The PCEB holds NMFLUSH# asserted until all buffers are flushed. After all buffers are flushed, the PCEB negates NMFLUSH# and then tri-state the output buffer. After sampling NMFLUSH# negated, the ESC resumes driving NMFLUSH# on the next PCI clock. This way the ESC does not assert MACK# or DACK# until the PCEB acknowledges that all line buffers have been flushed.

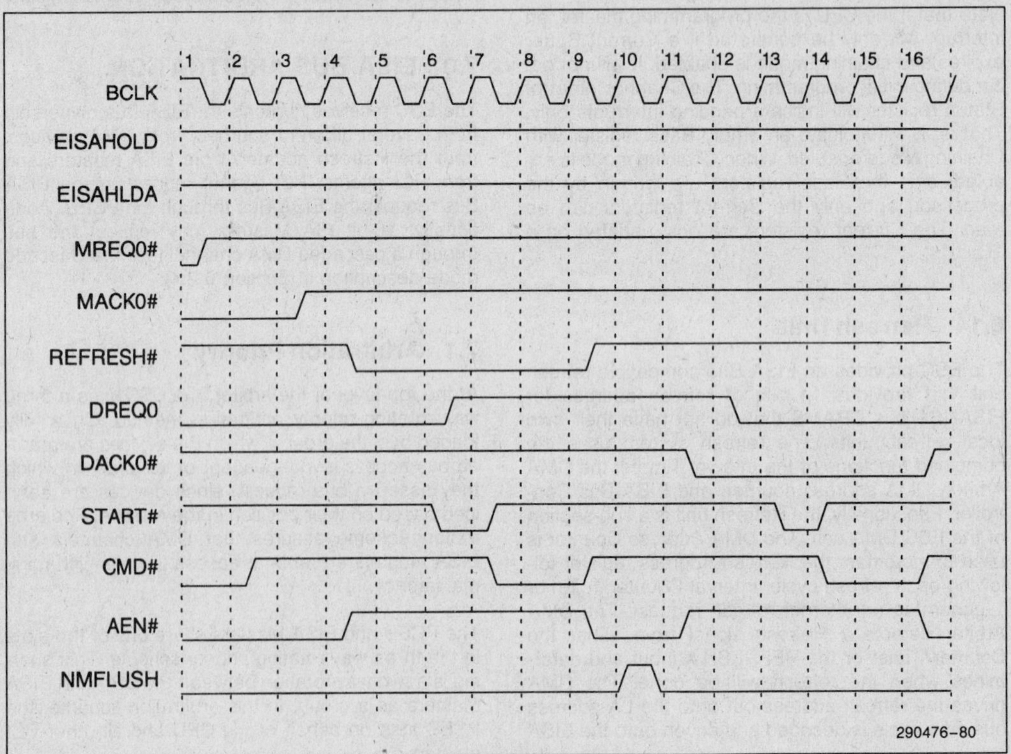

290476-80

Figure 7-1. EISA Arbitration

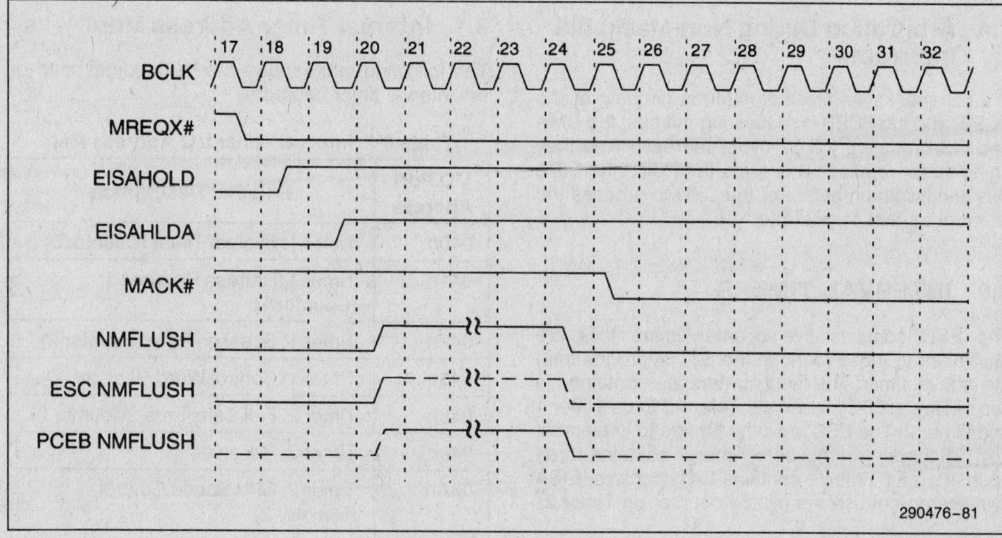

Figure 7-2. PCEB Preemption

7.2.2 EISA MASTER PREEMPTION

EISA specification requires that EISA Masters must release the bus within 64 BCLKs (8 μs) after the ESC negates MACKx#. If the bus master attempts to start a new bus cycle after this timeout period, a bus timeout (NMI) is generated and the RSTDRV is asserted to reset the offending bus master.

7.2.3 DMA PREEMPTION

A DMA slave device that is not programmed for compatible timing is preempted from the EISA Bus by another device that requests use of the bus. This will occur regardless of the priority of the pending request. For DMA devices not using compatible timing mode, the DMA controller stops the DMA transfer and releases the bus within 32 BCLK (4 μs) of a preemption request. Upon the expiration of the 4 μs timer, the DACK is negated after the current DMA cycle has completed. The EISA Bus then arbitrated for and granted to the highest priority requester. This feature allows flexibility in programming the DMA for long transfer sequences in a performance timing mode while guaranteeing that vital system services such as Refresh are allowed access to the expansion bus.

The 4 μs timer is not used in compatible timing mode. It is only used for DMA channels programmed for Type "A", Type "B", or Type "C" (Burst) timing. The 4 μs timer is also not used for 16-bit ISA masters cascaded through the DMA DREQ lines.

If the DMA channel that was preempted by the 4 μs timer is operating in Block mode, an internal bit will be set so that the channel will be arbitrated for again, independent of the state of DREQ.

7.3 Slave Timeouts

A slave which does not release EXRDY or CHRDY can cause the CMD# active time to exceed 256 BCLKs (32 μs). The ESC does not monitor EXRDY or CHRDY for this timeout. Typically this function is provided in a system through a third party add-in card. The add-in cards which monitor EXRDY or CHRDY assert IOCHK signal when the 256 BCLK count expires. The ESC in response asserts NMI.

The only way that a 16-bit ISA Master can be preempted from the EISA bus is if it exceeds the 256 BCLK (32 μs) limit on CMD# active.

7.4 Arbitration During Non-Maskable Interrupts

If a non-maskable interrupt (NMI) is pending at the PCEB, and the PCEB is requesting the bus, the DMA and EISA Masters will be bypassed each time they come up for rotation. This gives the PCEB the EISA Bus bandwidth on behalf of the CPU to process the interrupt as fast as possible.

8.0 INTERVAL TIMERS

The ESC contains five counter/timers that are equivalent to those found in the 82C54 programmable interval timer. The five counters arc contained in two separate ESC timer units, referred to as Timer 1 and Timer 2. The ESC uses the Timers to implement key EISA system functions. Timer 1 contains three counters, and Timer 2 contains two counters. EISA systems do not use the middle counter on Timer 2.

Interval Timer 1, Counter 0 is connected to the interrupt controller IRQ0 and provides a system timer interrupt for a time-of-day, diskette time-out, or other system timing functions. Counter 1 generates a refresh-request signal and Counter 2 generates the tone for the speaker.

Interval Timer 2, Counter 0 implements a fail safe timer. Counter 0 generates NMI at regular intervals, thus preventing the system from locking up. Counter 1 is not used. Counter 2 is used to slow down the CPU by means of pulse-width modulation. The output of Timer-2 Counter 2 is tied to the SLOWH# signal.

Table 8-1. Interval Timer Functions

Interval Timer Functions		
Function	**Counter 0 System Timer**	**Counter 0 Fail-Safe Timer**
Gate	Always On	Always On
Clock In	1.193 MHz (OSC/12)	0.298 MHz (OSC/48)
Out	INT-1 IRQ0	NMI Interrupt
	Counter 1 Refresh Request	
Gate	Always On	
Clock In	1.193 MHz (0SC/12)	
Out	Refresh Request	
	Counter 2	**Counter 2**
Gate	Programmable Port 61h	Refresh Request
Clock In	1.193 MHz (OSC/12)	8 MHz (BCLK)
Out	Speaker	CPU Speed Control (SLOWH#)

8.1 Interval Timer Address Map

The following table shows the I/O address map of the interval timer counters:

Table 8-2. Interval Timer I/O Address Map

I/O Port Address	Register Description
040h	Timer 1, System Timer (Counter 0)
041h	Timer 1, Refresh Request (Counter 1)
042h	Timer 1, Speaker Tone (Counter 2)
043h	Timer 1, Control Word Register
048h	Timer 2, Fail-Safe Timer (Counter 0)
049h	Timer 2, Reserved
04Ah	Timer 2, CPU Speed Control (Counter 2)
04Bh	Timer 2, Control Word Register

Timer 1—Counter 0, System Timer

This counter functions as the system timer by controlling the state of IRQ[0] and is typically programmed for Mode 3 operation. The counter produces a square wave with a period equal to the product of the counter period (838 ns) and the initial count value. The counter loads the initial count value one counter period after software writes the count value to the counter I/O address. The counter initially asserts IRQ[0] and decrements the count value by two each counter period. The counter negates IRQ[0] when the count value reaches 0. It then reloads the initial count value and again decrements the initial count value by two each counter period. The counter then asserts IRQ[0] when the count value reaches "0", reloads the initial count value, and repeats the cycle, alternately asserting and negating IRQ[0].

Timer 1—Counter 1, Refresh Request Signal

This counter provides the Refresh Request signal and is typically programmed for Mode 2 operation. The counter negates Refresh Request for one counter period (833 ns) during each count cycle. The initial count value is loaded one counter period after being written to the counter I/O address. The counter initially asserts Refresh Request, and negates it for 1 counter period when the count value reaches 1. The counter then asserts Refresh Request and continues counting from the initial count value.

Timer 1—Counter 2, Speaker Tone

This counter provides the speaker tone and is typically programmed for Mode 3 operation. The counter provides a speaker frequency equal to the counter clock frequency (1.193 MHz) divided by the initial count value. The speaker must be enabled by a write to port 061h (see Section 3.7 on the NMI Status and Control ports).

Timer 2—Counter 0, Fail-Safe Timer

This counter functions as a fail-safe timer by preventing the system from locking up. This counter generates an interrupt on the NMI line as the count expires by setting bit 7 on Port 0461. Software routines can avoid the Fail-Safe NMI by resetting the counter before the timer count expires.

Timer 2—Counter 2, CPU Speed Control

This counter generates the SLOWH# to the CPU and is typically programmed for Mode 1 operation. The counter is triggered by the refresh request signal generated by Timer 1—Counter 1 only. If the counter is programmed, the counters SLOWH# output will stop the CPU for the programmed period of the one-shot every time a refresh request occurs. This counter is not configured or programmed until a speed reduction in the system is required.

8.2 Programming the Interval Timer

The counter/timers are programmed by I/O accesses and are addressed as though they are contained in two separate 82C54 interval timers. Timer 1 contains three counters and Timer 2 contains two counters. Each Timer is controlled by a separate Control Word register.

The interval timer is an I/O-mapped device. Several commands are available:

- The Control Word Command specifies:
  —which counter to read or write
  —the operating mode
  —the count format (binary or BCD)
- The Counter Latch Command latches the current count so that it can be read by the system. The countdown process continues.
- The Read Back Command reads the count value, programmed mode, the current state of the OUT pins, and the state of the Null Count Flag of the selected counter.

The Read/Write Logic selects the Control Word register during an I/O write when address lines A1, A0 = 11. This condition occurs during an I/O write to port addresses 043h and 04Bh, the addresses for the Control Word Register on Timer 1 and Control Word Register on Timer 2 respectively. If the CPU writes to port 043h or port 04Bh, the data is stored in the respective Control Word Register and is interpreted as a Control Word used to define the operation of the Counters.

The Control Word Register is write-only. Counter Status information is available with the Read-Back Command.

Table 8-3 lists the six operating modes for the interval counters. Section 8.4 describes each mode's function in detail.

Table 8-3. Counter Operating Modes

Mode	Function
0	Out signal on end of count (=0)
1	Hardware retriggerable one-shot
2	Rate generator (divide by n counter)
3	Square wave output
4	Software triggered strobe
5	Hardware triggered strobe

Because the timer counters wake up in an unknown state after power-up, multiple refresh requests may be queued up. To avoid possible multiple refresh cycles after power-up, program the timer counter immediately after power-up.

Write Operations

Programming the interval timer is a simple process:

1. Write a control word.
2. Write an initial count for each counter.
3. Load the least and/or most significant bytes (as required by Control Word Bits 5, 4) of the 16-bit counter.

The programming procedure for the ESC timer units is very flexible. Only two conventions need to be observed. First, for each Counter, the Control Word must be written before the initial count is written. Second, the initial count must follow the count format specified in the Control Word (least significant byte only, most significant byte only, or least significant byte and then most significant byte).

Since the Control Word Register and the three Counters have separate addresses (selected by the A1, A0 inputs), and each Control Word specifies the Counter it applies to (SC0, SC1 bits), no special instruction sequence is required. Any programming sequence that follows the conventions above is acceptable.

A new initial count may be written to a Counter at any time without affecting the Counter's programmed Mode in any way. Counting will be affected as described in the Mode definitions. The new count must follow the programmed count format.

If a Counter is programmed to read/write two-byte counts, the following precaution applies: A program must not transfer control between writing the first and second byte to another routine which also writes into that same Counter. Otherwise, the Counter will be loaded with an incorrect count.

Interval Timer Control Word Format

The Control Word specifies the counter, the operating mode, the order and size of the COUNT value, and whether it counts down in a 16-bit or binary-coded decimal (BCD) format. After writing the control word, a new count may be written at any time. The new value will take effect according to the programmed mode.

If a counter is programmed to read/write two-byte counts, the following precaution applies: A program must not transfer control between writing the first and second byte to another routine which also writes into that same counter. Otherwise, the counter will be loaded with an incorrect count. The count must always be completely loaded with both bytes.

Read Operations

It is often desirable to read the value of a Counter without disturbing the count in progress. This is easily done in the ESC timer units.

There are three possible methods for reading the counters: a simple read operation, the Counter Latch Command, and the Read-Back Command.

Counter I/O Port Read

The first method is to perform a simple read operation. To read the Counter the CLK input of the selected Counter must be inhibited by using either the GATE input or external logic. Otherwise, the count may be in the process of changing when it is read, giving an undefined result. When reading the count value directly, follow the format programmed in the control register: read LSB, read MSB, or read LSB then MSB. Within the ESC timer unit, the GATE input on Timer 1 Counter 0, Counter 1 and Timer 2 Counter 0 are tied high. Therefore, the direct register read should not be used on these two counters. The GATE input of Timer 1 Counter 2 is controlled through I/O port 061h. If the GATE is disabled through this register, direct I/O reads of port 042h will return the current count value.

Counter Latch Command

The Counter Latch command latches the count at the time the command is received. This command is used to insure that the count read from the counter is accurate (particularly when reading a two-byte count). The count value is then read from each counter's Count register as was programmed by the Control register.

The selected Counter's output latch (OL) latches the count at the time the Counter Latch Command is received. This count is held in the latch until it is read by the CPU (or until the Counter is reprogrammed). The count is then unlatched automatically and the OL returns to "following" the counting element (CE). This allows reading the contents of the Counters "on the fly" without affecting counting in progress. Multiple Counter Latch Commands may be used to latch more than one Counter. Each latched Counter's OL holds its count until it is read. Counter Latch Commands do not affect the programmed Mode of the Counter in any way. The Counter Latch Command can be used for each counter in the ESC timer unit.

If a Counter is latched and then, some time later, latched again before the count is read, the second Counter Latch Command is ignored. The count read will be the count at the time the first Counter Latch Command was issued.

With either method, the count must be read according to the programmed format; specifically, if the Counter is programmed for two byte counts, two bytes must be read. The two bytes do not have to be read one right after the other; read, write, or programming operations for other Counters may be inserted between them.

Another feature of the ESC timer unit is that reads and writes of the same Counter may be interleaved. For example, if the Counter is programmed for two byte counts, the following sequence is valid:

1. Read least significant byte.
2. Write new least significant byte.
3. Read most significant byte.
4. Write new most significant byte.

One precaution is worth noting. If a Counter is programmed to read/write two-byte counts, a program must not transfer control between reading the first and second byte to another routine which also reads from that same Counter. Otherwise, an incorrect count will be read.

Read Back Command

The third method uses the Read-Back command. The Read-Back command is used to determine the count value, programmed mode, and current states of the OUT pin and Null Count flag of the selected counter or counters. The Read-Back command is written to the Control Word register, which causes the current states of the above mentioned variables to be latched. The value of the counter and its status may then be read by I/O access to the counter address.

The read-back command may be used to latch multiple counter output latches (OL) by setting the COUNT# bit D5 = 0 and selecting the desired counter(s). This single command is functionally equivalent to several counter latch commands, one for each counter latched. Each counter's latched count is held until it is read (or the counter is reprogrammed). Once read, a counter is automatically unlatched. The other counters remain latched until they are read. If multiple count read-back commands are issued to the same counter without reading the count, all but the first are ignored; i.e., the count which will be read is the count at the time the first read-back command was issued.

The read-back command may also be used to latch status information of selected counter(s) by setting STATUS# bit D4 = 0. Status must be latched to be read. The status of a counter is accessed by a read from that counter's I/O port address.

If multiple counter status latch operations are performed without reading the status, all but the first are ignored. The status returned from the read is the counter status at the time the first status read-back command was issued.

Both count and status of the selected counter(s) may be latched simultaneously by setting both the COUNT# and STATUS# bits [5:4] = 00b. This is functionally the same as issuing two consecutive, separate read-back commands. The above discussions apply here also. Specifically, if multiple count and/or status read-back commands are issued to the same counter(s) without any intervening reads, all but the first are ignored.

If both count and status of a counter are latched, the first read operation from that counter will return the latched status, regardless of which was latched first. The next one or two reads (depending on whether the counter is programmed for one or two type counts) return the latched count. Subsequent reads return unlatched count.

9.0 INTERRUPT CONTROLLER

The ESC provides an EISA compatible interrupt controller which incorporates the functionality of two 82C59 interrupt controllers. The two controllers are cascaded so that 14 external and two internal interrupts are possible. The master interrupt controller provides IRQ [7:0] and the slave interrupt controller provides IRQ [15:8] (see Figure 9-1). The two internal interrupts are used for internal functions only and are not available at the chip periphery. IRQ2 is used to cascade the two controllers together and IRQ0 is used as a system timer interrupt and is tied to Interval Timer 1, Counter 0. The remaining 14 interrupt lines (IRQ1, IRQ3–IRQ15) are available for external system interrupts. Edge or level sense selection is programmable on a by-controller basis.

The Interrupt Controller consists of two separate 82C59 cores. Interrupt Controller 1 (CNTRL-1) and Interrupt Controller 2 (CNTRL-2) are initialized separately, and can be programmed to operate in different modes. The default settings are: 80x86 Mode, Edge Sensitive (IRQ0-15) Detection, Normal EOI, Non-Buffered Mode, Special Fully Nested Mode disabled, and Cascade Mode. CNTRL-1 is connected as the Master Interrupt Controller and CNTRL-2 is connected as the Slave Interrupt Controller.

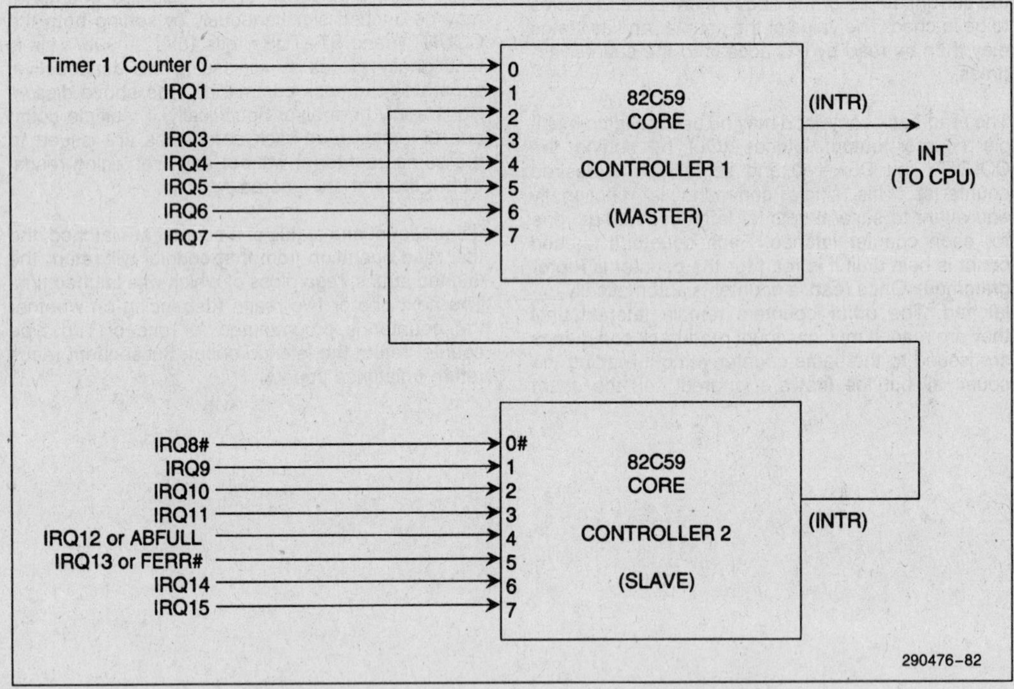

Figure 9-1. Block Diagram of The Interrupt Controller

Table 9-1 lists the I/O port address map for the interrupt registers:

Table 9-1. I/O Address Map

Interrupts	I/O Address	# of Bits	Register
IRQ[7:0]	0020h	8	CNTRL-1 Control Register
IRQ[7:0]	0021h	8	CNTRL-1 Mask Register
IRQ[7:0]	04D0h	8	CNTRL-1 Edge/Level Control Register
IRQ[15:8]	00A0h	8	CNTRL-2 Control Register
IRQ[15:8]	00A1h	8	CNTRL-2 Mask Register
IRQ[15:8]	04D1h	8	CNTRL-2 Edge/Level Control Register

IRQ0, and IRQ2 are connected to the interrupt controllers internally. The other interrupts are always generated externally. IRQ12 and IRQ13 may be generated internally through the ABFULL and FERR# signals respectively.

Table 9-2. Typical Interrupt Functions

Priority	Label	Controller	Typical Interrupt Source
1	IRQ0	1	Interval Timer 1, Counter 0 OUT
2	IRQ1	1	Keyboard
3–10	IRQ2	1	Interrupt from Controller 2
3	IRQ8#	2	Real Time Clock
4	IRQ9	2	Expansion Bus Pin B04
5	IRQ10	2	Expansion Bus Pin D03
6	IRQ11	2	Expansion Bus Pin D04
7	IRQ12	2	Expansion Bus Pin D05
8	IRQ13	2	Coprocessor Error, Chaining
9	IRQ14	2	Fixed Disk Drive Controller Expansion Bus Pin D07
10	IRQ15	2	Expansion Bus Pin D06
11	IRQ3	1	Serial Port 2, Expansion Bus B25
12	IRQ4	1	Serial Port 1, Expansion Bus B24
13	IRQ5	1	Parallel Port 2, Expansion Bus B23
14	IRQ6	1	Diskette Controller, Expansion Bus B22
15	IRQ7	1	Parallel Port 1, Expansion Bus B21

9.1 Interrupt Controller Internal Registers

Several registers are contained internally within each 82C59. The interrupts at the IRQ input lines are handled by two registers in cascade, the Interrupt Request Register (IRR) and the In-Service Register (ISR). The IRR is used to store all the interrupt levels which are requesting service and the ISR is used to store all the interrupt levels which are being serviced.

Internal circuitry determines the priorities of the bits set in the IRR. The highest priority is selected and strobed into the corresponding bit of the ISR during Interrupt Acknowledge Cycles.

The Interrupt Mask Register (IMR) stores the bits which mask the incoming interrupt lines. The IMR operates on the IRR. Masking of a higher priority input will not affect the interrupt request lines of lower priority inputs.

9.2 Interrupt Sequence

The powerful features of the Interrupt Controller in a microcomputer system are its programmability and the interrupt routine addressing capability. The latter allows direct or indirect jumping to the specific interrupt routine requested without any polling of the interrupting devices. The following shows the interrupt sequence for an x86 type system (the 8080 mode of the interrupt controller must never be selected when programming the ESC).

Note that externally, the interrupt acknowledge cycle sequence appears different than in a traditional discrete 82C59 implementation. However, the traditional interrupt acknowledge sequence is generated within the ESC and it is an EISA compatible implementation.

1. One or more of the Interrupt Request (IRQ[x]) lines are raised high, setting the corresponding IRR bit(s).
2. The Interrupt Controller evaluates these requests, and sends an INT to the CPU, if appropriate.
3. The CPU acknowledges the INT and responds with an interrupt acknowledge cycle. This cycle is translated into a PCI bus command. This PCI command is broadcast over the PCI bus as a single cycle as opposed to the two cycle method typically used.
4. Upon receiving an interrupt acknowledge cycle from the CPU over the PCI, the PCEB converts the single cycle into an INTA# pulse to the ESC. The ESC uses the INTA# pulse to generate the two cycles that the internal 8259 pair can respond to with the expected interrupt vector. The cycle conversion is performed by a functional block in the ESC Interrupt Controller Unit. The internally generated interrupt acknowledge cycle is completed as soon as possible as the PCI bus is held in wait states until the interrupt vector data is returned. Each cycle appears as an interrupt acknowledge pulse on the INTA# pin of the cascaded interrupt controllers. These two pulses are not observable at the ESC periphery.
5. Upon receiving the first internally generated interrupt acknowledge, the highest priority ISR bit is set and the corresponding IRR bit is reset. The Interrupt Controller does not drive the Data Bus during this cycle. On the trailing edge of the first cycle pulse, a slave identification code is broadcast by the master to the slave on a private, internal three bit wide bus. The slave controller uses these bits to determine if it must respond with an interrupt vector during the second INTA# cycle.
6. Upon receiving the second internally generated interrupt acknowledge, the Interrupt Controller releases an 8-bit pointer (the interrupt vector) onto the Data Bus where it is read by the CPU.
7. This completes the interrupt cycle. In the AEOI mode the ISR bit is reset at the end of the second interrupt acknowledge cycle pulse. Otherwise, the ISR bit remains set until an appropriate EOI command is issued at the end of the interrupt subroutine.

If no interrupt request is present at step four of either sequence (i.e., the request was too short in duration) the Interrupt Controller will issue an interrupt level 7.

9.3 80x86 Mode

When initializing the control registers of the 82C59, an option exists in Initialization Control Word Four (ICW4) to select either an 80x86 or an MSC-85 microprocessor based system. The interrupt acknowledge cycle is different in an MSC-85 based system than in the 80x86 based system: the interrupt acknowledge takes three INTA# pulses with the MSC-85, rather than the two pulses with the 80x86. The ESC is used only in an 80x86 based system. You must program each interrupt controller's ICW4 bit-0 to a "1" to indicate that the interrupt controller is operating in an 80x86 based system. This setting ensures proper operation during an interrupt acknowledge.

9.4 ESC Interrupt Acknowledge Cycle

As discussed, the CPU generates an interrupt acknowledge cycle that is translated into a single PCI command and broadcast across the PCI bus to the PCEB. The PCEB pulses the INTA# signal to the ESC. The ESC Interrupt Unit translates the INTA# signal into the two INTA# pulses expected by the interrupt controller subsystem. The Interrupt Controller uses the first interrupt acknowledge cycle to internally freeze the state of the interrupts for priority resolution. The first controller (CNTRL-1), as a master, issues a three bit interrupt code on the cascade lines to CNTRL-2 (internal to the ESC) at the end of the INTA# pulse. On this first cycle the interrupt controller block does not issue any data to the processor and leaves its data bus buffers disabled. CNTRL-2 decodes the information on the cascade lines, compares the code to the byte stored in Initialization Command Word Three (ICW3), and determines if it will have to broadcast the interrupt vector during the second interrupt acknowledge cycle. On the second interrupt acknowledge cycle, the master (CNTRL-1) or slave (CNTRL-2), will send a byte of data to the processor with the acknowledged interrupt code composed as follows:

Table 9-3. Content of Interrupt Vector Byte for 80x86 System Mode

	D7	D6	D5	D4	D3	D2	D1	D0
IRQ7, 15	T7	T6	T5	T4	T3	1	1	1
IRQ6, 14	T7	T6	T5	T4	T3	1	1	0
IRQ5, 13	T7	T6	T5	T4	T3	1	0	1
IRQ4, 12	T7	T6	T5	T4	T3	1	0	0
IRQ3, 11	T7	T6	T5	T4	T3	0	1	1
IRQ2, 10	T7	T6	T5	T4	T3	0	1	0
IRQ1, 9	T7	T6	T5	T4	T3	0	0	1
IRQ0, 8	T7	T6	T5	T4	T3	0	0	0

NOTE:
T7–T3 represent the interrupt vector address (refer to Section 3.7, ICW2 register description).

The byte of data released by the interrupt unit onto the data bus is referred to as the "interrupt vector". The format for this data is illustrated on a per-interrupt basis in Table 9-3.

9.5 Programming the Interrupt Controller

The Interrupt Controller accepts two types of command words generated by the CPU or bus master:

1. Initialization Command Words (ICWs): Before normal operation can begin, each Interrupt Controller in the system must be initialized. In the 82C59, this is a two to four byte sequence. However, for the ESC, each controller must be initialized with a four byte sequence. This four byte sequence is required to configure the interrupt controller correctly for the ESC implementation. This implementation is EISA-compatible.

The four initialization command words are referred to by their acronyms: ICW1, ICW2, ICW3, and ICW4.

The base address for each interrupt controller is a fixed location in the I/O memory space, at 0020h for CNTRL-1 and at 00A0h for CNTRL-2.

An I/O write to the CNTRL-1 or CNTRL-2 base address with data bit 4 equal to 1 is interpreted as ICW1. For ESC-based EISA systems, three I/O writes to "base address + 1" (021h for CNTRL-1 and 0A0h for CNTRL-2) must follow the ICW1. The first write to "base address + 1" (021h/0A0h) performs ICW2, the second write performs ICW3, and the third write performs ICW4.

ICW1 starts the initialization sequence during which the following automatically occur:

1. Following initialization, an interrupt request (IRQ) input must make a low-to-high transition to generate an interrupt.
2. The Interrupt Mask Register is cleared.
3. IRQ7 input is assigned priority 7.
4. The slave mode address is set to 7.
5. Special Mask Mode is cleared and Status Read is set to IRR.

ICW2 is programmed to provide bits [7:3] of the interrupt vector that will be released onto the data bus by the interrupt controller during an interrupt acknowledge. A different base [7:3] is selected for each interrupt controller. Suggested values for a typical EISA system are listed in Table 9-4.

ICW3 is programmed differently for CNTRL-1 and CNTRL-2, and has a different meaning for each controller.

For CNTRL-1, the master controller, ICW3 is used to indicate which IRQx input line is used to cascade CNTRL-2, the slave controller. Within the ESC interrupt unit, IRQ2 on CNTRL-1 is used to cascade the INT output of CNTRL-2. Consequently, bit-2 of ICW3 on CNTRL-1 is set to a 1, and the other bits are set to 0's.

For CNTRL-2, ICW3 is the slave identification code used during an interrupt acknowledge cycle. CNTRL-1 broadcasts a code to CNTRL-2 over three internal cascade lines if an IRQ[x] line from CNTRL-2 won the priority arbitration on the master controller and was granted an interrupt acknowledge by the CPU. CNTRL-2 compares this identification code to the value stored in ICW3, and if the code is equal to bits [2:0] of ICW3, CNTRL-2 assumes responsibility for broadcasting the interrupt vector during the second interrupt acknowledge cycle pulse.

ICW4 must be programmed on both controllers. At the very least, bit 0 must be set to a 1 to indicate that the controllers are operating in an 80x86 system.

2. Operation Command Words (OCWs): These are the command words which dynamically reprogram the Interrupt Controller to operate in various interrupt modes.

Any interrupt lines can be masked by writing an OCW1. A 1 written in any bit of this command word will mask incoming interrupt requests on the corresponding IRQx line.

OCW2 is used to control the rotation of interrupt priorities when operating in the rotating priority mode and to control the End of Interrupt (EOI) function of the controller.

OCW3 is used to set up reads of the ISR and IRR, to enable or disable the Special Mask Mode (SMM), and to set up the interrupt controller in polled interrupt mode.

The OCWs can be written into the Interrupt Controller any time after initialization. Table 9-4 shows an example of typical values programmed by the BIOS at power-up for the ESC interrupt controller.

Table 9-4. Suggested Default Values for Interrupt Controller Registers

Port	Value	Description of Contents
020h	11h	CNTLR-1, ICW1
021h	08h	CNTLR-1, ICW2 Vector Address for 000020h
021h	04h	CNTLR-1, ICW3 Indicates Slave Connection
021h	01h	CNTLR-1, ICW3 ICW4 8086 Mode
021h	B8h	CNTLR-1, Interrupt Mask (may vary)
4D0h	00h	CNTLR-1, Edge/Level Control Register
0A0h	11h	CNTLR-2, ICW1
0A1h	70h	CNTLR-2, ICW2 Vector Address for 0001C0h
0A1h	02h	CNTLR-2, ICW3 Indicates Slave ID
0A1h	01h	CNTL4-2, ICW4 8086 Mode
4D1h	00h	CNTLR-2, Edge/Level Control Register
0A1h	BDh	CNTLR-2, Interrupt Mask (may vary)

The following flow chart illustrates the sequence software must follow to load the interrupt controller Initialization Command Words (ICWs). The sequence must be executed for CNTRL-1 and CNTRL-2. After writing ICW1, ICW2, ICW3, and ICW4 must be written in order. Any divergence from this sequence, such as an attempt to program an OCW, will result in improper initialization of the interrupt controller and unexpected, erratic system behavior. It is suggested that CNTRL-2 be initialized first, followed by CNTRL-1.

In the ESC, it is required that all four Initialization Command Words (ICWs) be initialized. Also, as shown in Figure 9-3, all ICWs must be programmed prior to programming the OCWs.

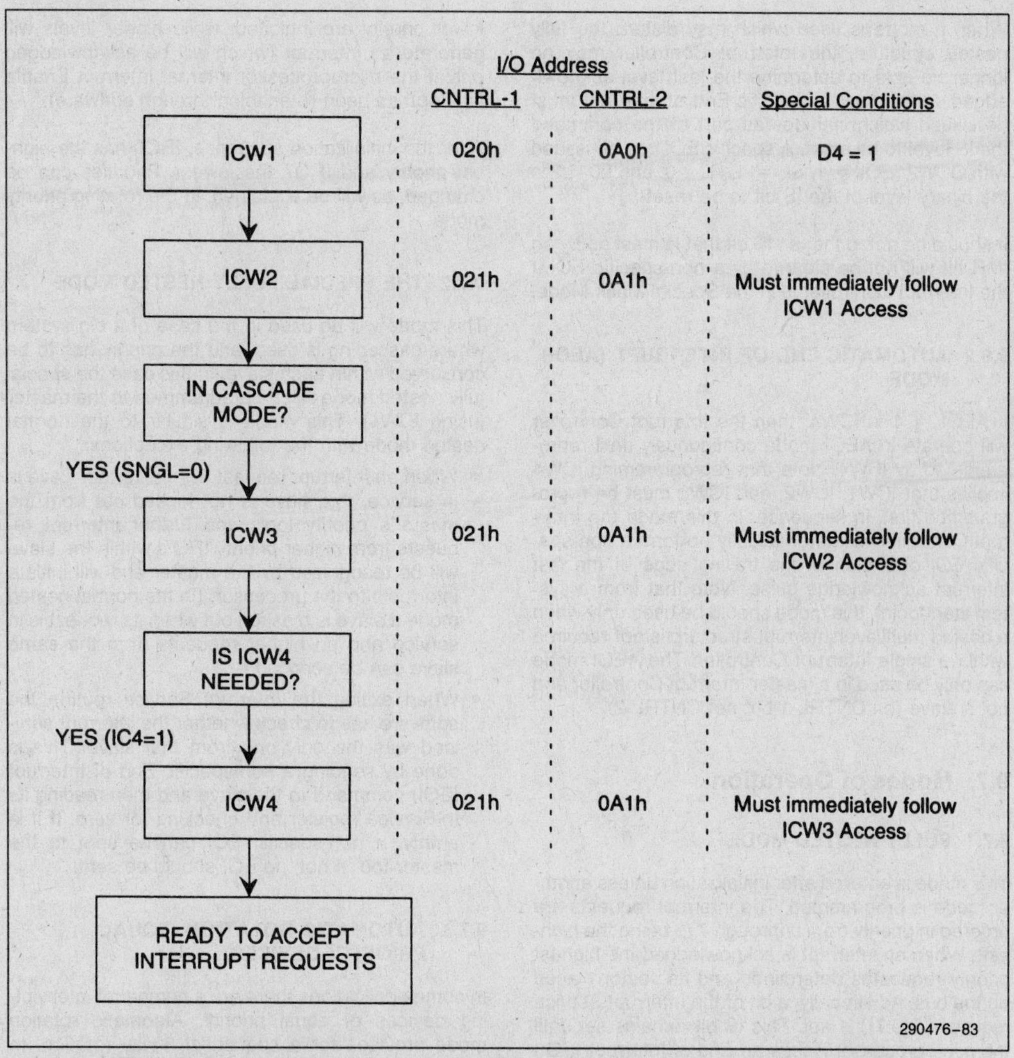

	I/O Address CNTRL-1	CNTRL-2	Special Conditions
ICW1	020h	0A0h	D4 = 1
ICW2	021h	0A1h	Must immediately follow ICW1 Access
IN CASCADE MODE? YES (SNGL=0)			
ICW3	021h	0A1h	Must immediately follow ICW2 Access
IS ICW4 NEEDED? YES (IC4=1)			
ICW4	021h	0A1h	Must immediately follow ICW3 Access
READY TO ACCEPT INTERRUPT REQUESTS			

290476–83

Figure 9-2. Initialization Sequence for ESC Initialization Command Words (ICWs)

9.6 End-of-Interrupt Operation

9.6.1 END OF INTERRUPT (EOI)

The In Service (IS) bit can be reset either automatically following the trailing edge of the second internal INTA# pulse (when AEOI bit in ICW1 is set) or by a command word that must be issued to the Interrupt Controller before returning from a service routine (EOI command). An EOI command must be issued twice with this cascaded interrupt controller configuration, once for the master and once for the slave.

There are two forms of EOI commands: Specific and Non-Specific. When the Interrupt Controller is operated in modes which preserve the fully nested structure, it can determine which IS bit to reset on EOI. When a Non-Specific EOI command is issued, the Interrupt Controller will automatically reset the highest IS bit of those that are set, since in the fully nested mode the highest IS level was necessarily the last level acknowledged and serviced. A non-specific EOI can be issued with OCW2 (EOI = 1, SL = 0, R = 0).

When a mode is used which may disturb the fully nested structure, the Interrupt Controller may no longer be able to determine the last level acknowledged. In this case a Specific End of Interrupt must be issued which includes as part of the command the IS level to be reset. A specific EOI can be issued with OCW2 (EOI = 1, SL = 1, R = 0, and L0–L2 is the binary level of the IS bit to be reset).

It should be noted that an IS bit that is masked by an IMR bit will not be cleared by a non-specific EOI if the Interrupt Controller is in the Special Mask Mode.

9.6.2 AUTOMATIC END OF INTERRUPT (AEOI) MODE

If AEOI = 1 in ICW4, then the Interrupt Controller will operate in AEOI mode continuously until reprogrammed by ICW4. Note that reprogramming ICW4 implies that ICW1, ICW2, and ICW3 must be reprogrammed first, in sequence. In this mode the Interrupt Controller will automatically perform a non-specific EOI operation at the trailing edge of the last interrupt acknowledge pulse. Note that from a system standpoint, this mode should be used only when a nested multilevel interrupt structure is not required within a single Interrupt Controller. The AEOI mode can only be used in a master Interrupt Controller and not a slave (on CNTRL-1 but not CNTRL-2).

9.7 Modes of Operation

9.7.1 FULLY NESTED MODE

This mode is entered after initialization unless another mode is programmed. The interrupt requests are ordered in priority from 0 through 7 (0 being the highest). When an interrupt is acknowledged the highest priority request is determined and its vector placed on the bus. Additionally, a bit of the Interrupt Service register (IS[0:7]) is set. This IS bit remains set until the microprocessor issues an End of Interrupt (EOI) command immediately before returning from the service routine. Or, if the AEOI (Automatic End of Interrupt) bit is set, this IS bit remains set until the trailing edge of the second internal INTA#. While the IS bit is set, all further interrupts of the same or lower priority are inhibited, while higher levels will generate an interrupt (which will be acknowledged only if the microprocessor internal Interrupt Enable flip-flop has been re-enabled through software).

After the initialization sequence, IRQ0 has the highest priority and IRQ7 the lowest. Priorities can be changed, as will be explained, in the rotating priority mode.

9.7.2 THE SPECIAL FULLY NESTED MODE

This mode will be used in the case of a big system where cascading is used, and the priority has to be conserved within each slave. In this case the special fully nested mode will be programmed to the master (using ICW4). This mode is similar to the normal nested mode with the following exceptions:

- When an interrupt request from a certain slave is in service, this slave is not locked out from the master's priority logic and further interrupt requests from higher priority IRQ's within the slave will be recognized by the master and will initiate interrupts to the processor. (In the normal nested mode a slave is masked out when its request is in service and no higher requests from the same slave can be serviced.)
- When exiting the Interrupt Service routine the software has to check whether the interrupt serviced was the only one from that slave. This is done by sending a non-specific End of Interrupt (EOI) command to the slave and then reading its In-Service register and checking for zero. If it is empty, a non-specific EOI can be sent to the master too. If not, no EOI should be sent.

9.7.3 AUTOMATIC ROTATION (EQUAL PRIORITY DEVICES)

In some applications there are a number of interrupting devices of equal priority. Automatic rotation mode provides for a sequential 8-way rotation. In this mode a device receives the lowest priority after being serviced. In the worst case, a device requesting an interrupt will have to wait until each of seven other devices are serviced at most once. Figure 9-3 shows an example of automatic rotation.

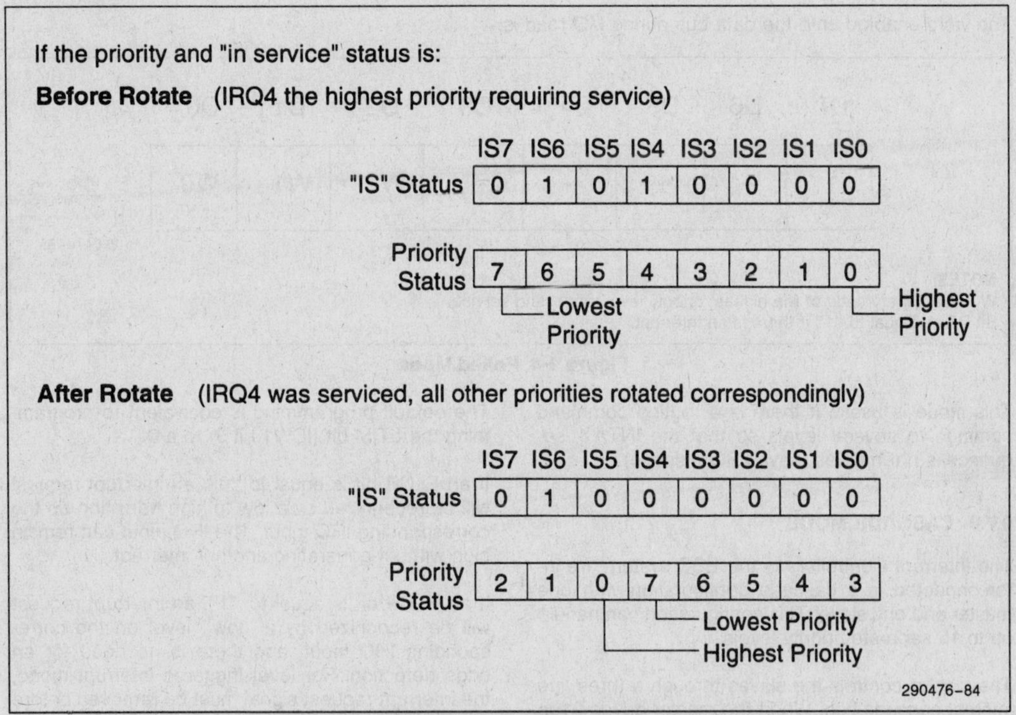

If the priority and "in service" status is:

Before Rotate (IRQ4 the highest priority requiring service)

	IS7	IS6	IS5	IS4	IS3	IS2	IS1	IS0
"IS" Status	0	1	0	1	0	0	0	0
Priority Status	7	6	5	4	3	2	1	0

Lowest Priority (IS6) — Highest Priority (IS0)

After Rotate (IRQ4 was serviced, all other priorities rotated correspondingly)

	IS7	IS6	IS5	IS4	IS3	IS2	IS1	IS0
"IS" Status	0	1	0	0	0	0	0	0
Priority Status	2	1	0	7	6	5	4	3

Lowest Priority (IS4) — Highest Priority (IS5)

290476-84

Figure 9-3. Automatic Rotation Mode Example

There are two ways to accomplish Automatic Rotation using OCW2, the Rotation on Non-Specific EOI Command (R = 1, SL = 0, EOI = 1) and the Rotate in Automatic EOI Mode which is set by (R = 1, SL = 0, EOI = 0) and cleared by (R = 0, SL = 0, EOI = 0).

9.7.4 SPECIFIC ROTATION (SPECIFIC PRIORITY)

The programmer can change priorities by programming the bottom priority and thus fixing all other priorities. For example, if IRQ5 is programmed as the bottom priority device, then IRQ6 will be the highest priority device.

The Set Priority command is issued in OCW2 where: R = 1, SL = 1; L0–L2 is the binary priority level code of the bottom priority device. See the register description for the bit definitions.

Note that in this mode internal status is updated by software control during OCW2. However, it is independent of the End of Interrupt (EOI) command (also executed by OCW2). Priority changes can be executed during an EOI command by using the Rotate on Specific EOI command in OCW2 (R = 1, SL = 1, EOI = 1 and L0–L2 = IRQ level to receive bottom priority).

9.7.5 POLL COMMAND

The Polled Mode can be used to conserve space in the interrupt vector table. Multiple interrupts that can be serviced by one interrupt service routine do not need separate vectors if the service routine uses the poll command.

The Polled Mode can also be used to expand the number of interrupts. The polling interrupt service routine can call the appropriate service routine, instead of providing the interrupt vectors in the vector table.

In this mode the INT output is not used and the microprocessor internal Interrupt Enable flip-flop is reset, disabling its interrupt input. Service to devices is achieved by software using a Poll command.

The Poll command is issued by setting P = 1 in OCW3. The Interrupt Controller treats the next I/O read pulse to the Interrupt Controller as an interrupt acknowledge, sets the appropriate IS bit if there is a request, and reads the priority level. Interrupts are frozen from the I/O write to the I/O read.

1

The word enabled onto the data bus during I/O read is:

D7	D6	D5	D4	D3	D2	D1	D0
1	--	--	--	--	W2	W1	W0

290476-85

NOTES:
W0–W2: Binary code of the highest priority level requesting service.
Bit D7–1: Equal to "1" if there is an interrupt.

Figure 9-4. Polled Mode

This mode is useful if there is a routine command common to several levels so that the INTA# sequence is not needed (saves ROM space).

9.7.6 CASCADE MODE

The Interrupt Controllers in the ESC system are interconnected in a cascade configuration with one master and one slave. This configuration can handle up to 15 separate priority levels.

The master controls the slaves through a three line internal cascade bus. When the master drives 010b on the cascade bus, this bus acts like a chip select to the slave controller.

In a cascade configuration, the slave interrupt outputs are connected to the master interrupt request inputs. When a slave request line is activated and afterwards acknowledged, the master will enable the corresponding slave to release the interrupt vector address during the second INTA# cycle of the interrupt acknowledge sequence.

Each Interrupt Controller in the cascaded system must follow a separate initialization sequence and can be programmed to work in a different mode. An EOI command must be issued twice: once for the master and once for the slave.

9.7.7 EDGE AND LEVEL TRIGGERED MODES

There are two ELCR registers, one for each 82C59 bank. They are located at I/O ports 04D0h (for the Master Bank, IRQ[0:1,3:7]) and 04D1h (for the Slave Bank, IRQ[8#:15]). They allow the edge and level sense selection to be made on an interrupt by interrupt basis instead of on a complete bank. Only the interrupts that connect to the EISA bus may be programmed for level sensitivity. That is IRQ (0,1,2,8#,13) must be programmed for edge sensitive operation. The LTIM bit is disabled in the ESC. The default programming is equivalent to programming the LTIM bit (ICW1 bit 3) to a 0.

If an ELCR bit is equal to "0", an interrupt request will be recognized by a low to high transition on the corresponding IRQ input. The IRQ input can remain high without generating another interrupt.

If an ELCR bit is equal to "1", an interrupt request will be recognized by a "low" level on the corresponding IRQ input, and there is no need for an edge detection. For level triggered interrupt mode, the interrupt request signal must be removed before the EOI command is issued or the CPU interrupt must be disabled. This is necessary to prevent a second interrupt from occurring.

In both the edge and level triggered modes the IRQ inputs must remain active until after the falling edge of the first INTA#. If the IRQ input goes inactive before this time a DEFAULT IRQ7 will occur when the CPU acknowledges the interrupt. This can be a useful safeguard for detecting interrupts caused by spurious noise glitches on the IRQ inputs. To implement this feature the IRQ7 routine is used for "clean up" simply executing a return instruction, thus ignoring the interrupt. If IRQ7 is needed for other purposes a default IRQ7 can still be detected by reading the ISR. A normal IRQ7 interrupt will set the corresponding ISR bit, a default IRQ7 won't. If a default IRQ7 routine occurs during a normal IRQ7 routine, however, the ISR will remain set. In this case it is necessary to keep track of whether or not the IRQ7 routine was previously entered. If another IRQ7 occurs it is a default.

IRQ13 still appears externally to be an edge sensitive interrupt even though it is shared internally with the Chaining interrupt. The Chaining interrupt is ORed after the edge sense logic.

9.8 Register Functionality

For a detailed description of the Interrupt Controller register set, please see Section 3.4, Interrupt Unit Register description.

9.8.1 INITIALIZATION COMMAND WORDS

Four initialization command words (ICWs) are used to initialize each interrupt controller. Each controller is initialized separately. Following this initialization sequence, the interrupt controller is ready to accept interrupts.

9.8.2 OPERATION CONTROL WORDS (OCWS)

After the Initialization Command Words (ICWs) are programmed into the Interrupt Controller, the chip is ready to accept interrupt requests at its input lines. However, Interrupt Controller operation can be dynamically modified to fit specific software/hardware expectations. Different modes of operation are dynamically selected following initialization through the use of Operation Command Words (OCWs).

9.9 Interrupt Masks

9.9.1 MASKING ON AN INDIVIDUAL INTERRUPT REQUEST BASIS

Each Interrupt Request input can be masked individually by the Interrupt Mask register (IMR). This register is programmed through OCW1. Each bit in the IMR masks one interrupt channel if it is set to a "1". Bit 0 masks IRQ0, Bit 1 masks IRQ1 and so forth. Masking an IRQ channel does not affect the other channel's operation, with one notable exception. Masking IRQ[2] on CNTRL-1 will mask off all requests for service from CNTRL-2. The CNTRL-2 INT output is physically connected to the CNTRL-1 IRQ[2] input.

9.9.2 SPECIAL MASK MODE

Some applications may require an interrupt service routine to dynamically alter the system priority structure during its execution under software control. For example, the routine may wish to inhibit lower priority requests for a portion of its execution but enable some of them for another portion.

The difficulty here is that if an Interrupt Request is acknowledged and an End of Interrupt command did not reset its IS bit (i.e., while executing a service routine), the Interrupt Controller would have inhibited all lower priority requests with no easy way for the routine to enable them.

The Special Mask Mode enables all interrupts not masked by a bit set in the Mask Register. Interrupt service routines that require dynamic alteration of interrupt priorities can take advantage of the Special Mask Mode. For example, a service routine can inhibit lower priority requests during a part of the interrupt service, then enable some of them during another part.

In the Special Mask Mode, when a mask bit is set in OCW1, it inhibits further interrupts at that level and enables interrupts from all other levels (lower as well as higher) that are not masked.

Thus, any interrupts may be selectively enabled by loading the Mask register with the appropriate pattern.

Without Special Mask Mode, if an interrupt service routine acknowledges an interrupt without issuing an EOI to clear the IS bit, the interrupt controller inhibits all lower priority requests. The Special Mask Mode provides an easy way for the interrupt service routine to selectively enable only the interrupts needed by loading the Mask register.

The special Mask Mode is set by OCW3 where: SSMM = 1, SMM = 1, and cleared where SSMM = 1, SMM = 0.

9.10 Reading the Interrupt Controller Status

The input status of several internal registers can be read to update the user information on the system. The Interrupt Request Register (IRR) and In-Service Register (ISR) can be read via OCW3, as discussed in Section 3.7. The Interrupt Mask Register (IMR) is read via a read of OCW1, as discussed in Section 3.7. Here are brief descriptions of the ISR, the IRR, and the IMR.

Interrupt Request Register (IRR): 8-bit register which contains the status of each interrupt request line. Bits that are clear indicate interrupts that have not requested service. The Interrupt Controller clears the IRR's highest priority bit during an interrupt acknowledge cycle. (Not affected by IMR).

In-Service Register (ISR): 8-bit register indicating the priority levels currently receiving service. Bits that are set indicate interrupts that have been acknowledged and their interrupt service routine started. Bits that are cleared indicate interrupt requests that have not been acknowledged, or interrupt request lines that have not been asserted. Only the highest priority interrupt service routine executes at any time. The lower priority interrupt services are suspended while higher priority interrupts are serviced. The ISR is updated when an End of Interrupt Command is issued.

Interrupt Mask Register (IMR): 8-bit register indicating which interrupt request lines are masked.

The IRR can be read when, prior to the I/O read cycle, a Read Register Command is issued with OCW3 (RR = 1, RIS = 0).

The ISR can be read when, prior to the I/O read cycle, a Read Register Command is issued with OCW3 (RR = 1, RIS = 1).

The interrupt controller retains the ISR/IRR status read selection following each write to OCW3. Therefore, there is no need to write an OCW3 before every status read operation, as long as the current status read corresponds to the previously selected register. For example, if the ISR is selected for status read by an OCW3 write, the ISR can be read over and over again without writing to OCW3 again. However, to read the IRR, OCW3 will have to be reprogrammed for this status read prior to the OCW3 read to check the IRR. This is not true when poll mode is used. Polling Mode overrides status read when P = 1, RR = 1 in OCW3.

After initialization, the Interrupt Controller is set to read the IRR.

As stated, OCW1 is used for reading the IMR. The output data bus will contain the IMR status whenever I/O read is active. The address is 021h or 061h (OCW1).

9.11 Non-Maskable Interrupt (NMI)

An NMI is an interrupt requiring immediate attention and has priority over the normal interrupt lines (IRQx). The ESC indicates error conditions by generating a non-maskable interrupt.

The ESC generates NMI interrupts based on the following Hardware and Software events.

Hardware Events:

1. Motherboard Parity Errors.

   Memory parity errors for the motherboard memory. These errors are reported to the ESC through the PERR# signal line.

2. System Errors.

   System error on the motherboard. The system board uses the SERR# signal to indicate system errors to the ESC.

3. Add-In Board Parity Errors.

   Parity errors on the add-in memory boards on the EISA expansion bus. IOCHK# signal on the EISA bus is driven low by the add-in board logic when this error occurs.

4. Fail-Safe Timer Timeout.

   Fail-Safe Timer (Timer 2, Counter 0) count expires. If this counter has been set and enabled, and the count expires before a software routine can reset the counter.

5. Bus Timeout.

   An EISA bus Master or Slave exceeds the allocated time on the bus. A bus timeout occurs if an EISA Master does not relinquish the bus (MREQ# negated) within 64 BCLKS after it has been preempted (MACK# negated). A bus timeout also occurs if a memory slave extends the cycle (CHRDY negated) long enough to keep CMD# asserted for more than 256 BCLKS. The DMA controller does not cause a bus timeout. The ESC asserts RESDRV when a bus timeout occurs.

Software Events:

1. Software Generated NMI.

   If an I/O Write access to Port 0462h occurs. The data value for this write is a don't care.

The NMI logic incorporates four different 8-bit registers. These registers are used by the CPU to determine the source of the interrupt and to enable or disable/clear the interrupts. Please see Section 3.4, Interrupt Unit Register description, for the register details.

Table 9-5. NMI Register I/O Address Map

I/O Port Address	Register Description
0061h	NMI Status Register
0070h	NMI Enable Register
0461h	Extended NMI Register
0462h	Software NMI Register

Table 9-6. NMI Source Enable/Disable and Status Port Bits

NMI Source	I/O Port Bit for Status Reads	I/O Port Bit for Enable/Disable
PERR#	Port 0061h, Bit 7	Port 0061h, Bit 2
IOCHK#	Port 0061h, Bit 6	Port 0061h, Bit 3
Fail-Safe	Port 0461h, Bit 7	Port 0461h, Bit 2
Bus Timeout	Port 0461h, Bit 6	Port 0461h, Bit 3
Write to Port 0462h	Port 0461h, Bit 5	Port 0461h, Bit 1

The individual enable/disable bits clear the NMI detect flip-flops when disabled.

All NMI sources can be enabled or disabled by setting Port 070h bit [7]. This disable function does not clear the NMI detect Flip-Flops. This means, if NMI is disabled then enabled via Port 070h, then an NMI will occur when Port 070h is re-enabled if one of the NMI detect Flip-Flops had been previously set.

To ensure that all NMI requests are serviced, the NMI service routine software needs to incorporate a few very specific requirements. These requirements are due to the edge detect circuitry of the host microprocessor, 80386 or 80486. The software flow would need to be the following:

1. NMI is detected by the processor on the rising edge of the NMI input.
2. The processor will read the status stored in port 061h and 0461h to determine what sources caused the NMI. The processor may then reset the register bits controlling the sources that it has determined to be active. Between the time the processor reads the NMI sources and resets them, an NMI may have been generated by another source. The level of NMI will then remain active. This new NMI source will not be recognized by the processor because there was no edge on NMI.
3. The processor must then disable all NMI's by writing bit [7] of port 070H high and then enable all NMI's by writing bit [7] of port 070H low. This will cause the NMI output to transition low then high if there are any pending NMI sources. The CPU's NMI input logic will then register a new NMI.

1

10.0 PCEB/ESC INTERFACE

The PCEB/ESC interface (Figure 10-1) provides the inter-chip communications between the PCEB and ESC. The interface provides control information between the two components for PCI/EISA arbitration, data size translations (controlling the PCEB's EISA data swap buffer), and interrupt acknowledge cycles.

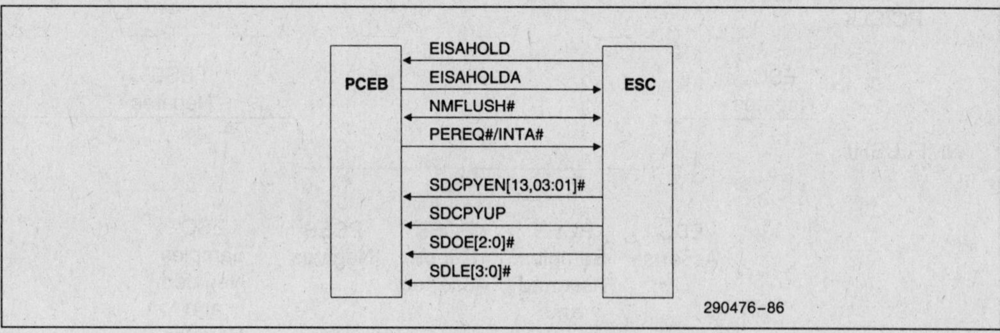

Figure 10-1. PCEB/ESC Interface Signals

10.1 Arbitration Control Signals

The PCEB contains the arbitration circuitry for the PCI Local Bus and the ESC contains the arbitration circuitry for the EISA Bus. The PCEB/ESC Interface contains a set of arbitration control signals (EISAHOLD, EISAHOLDA, NMFLUSH#, and PEREQ#/INTA#) that synchronize bus arbitration and ownership changes between the two bus environments. The signals also force PCI device data buffer flushing, if needed, to maintain data coherency during EISA Bus ownership changes.

The PCEB is the default owner of the EISA Bus. If another EISA/ISA master or DMA wants to use the bus, the ESC asserts EISAHOLD to instruct the PCEB to relinquish EISA Bus ownership. The PCEB completes any current EISA Bus transaction, tri-states its EISA Bus signals, and asserts EISAHOLDA to inform the ESC that the PCEB is off the bus.

For ownership changes, other than for a refresh cycle, the ESC asserts the NMFLUSH# signal to the PCEB (for one PCICLK) to instruct the PCEB to flush its Line Buffers pointing to the PCI Local Bus. The assertion of NMFLUSH# also instructs the PCEB to initiate flushing and to temporarily disable system buffers on the PCI Local Bus (via MEMREQ#, MEMACK, and FLSHREQ#). The buffer flushing maintains data coherency, in the event that the new EISA Bus master wants to access the PCI Local Bus. Buffer flushing also prevents dead-lock conditions between the PCI Local Bus and EISA Bus. Since the ESC/PCEB does not know ahead of time, whether the new master is going to access the PCI Local Bus or a device on the EISA Bus, buffers pointing to the PCI Local Bus are always flushed when there is a change of EISA Bus ownership, except for refresh cycles. For refresh cycles, the ESC controls the cycle and, thus, knows that the cycle is not an access to the PCI Local Bus and does not initiate a flush request to the PCEB. After a refresh cycle, the ESC always surrenders control of the EISA Bus back to the PCEB.

NMFLUSH# is a bi-directional signal that is negated by the ESC when buffer flushing is not being requested. The ESC asserts NMFLUSH# to request buffer flushing. When the PCEB samples NMFLUSH# asserted, it starts driving the signal in the asserted state and begins the buffer flushing process. (The ESC tri-states NMFLUSH# after asserting it for the initial 1 PCICLK period.) The PCEB keeps NMFLUSH# asserted until all buffers are flushed and then it negates the signal for 1 PCICLK. When the ESC samples NMFLUSH# negated, it starts driving the signal in the negated state, completing the handshake. When the ESC samples NMFLUSH# negated, it grants ownership to the winner of the EISA Bus arbitration (at the time NMFLUSH# was negated). Note that for a refresh cycle, NMFLUSH# is not asserted by the ESC.

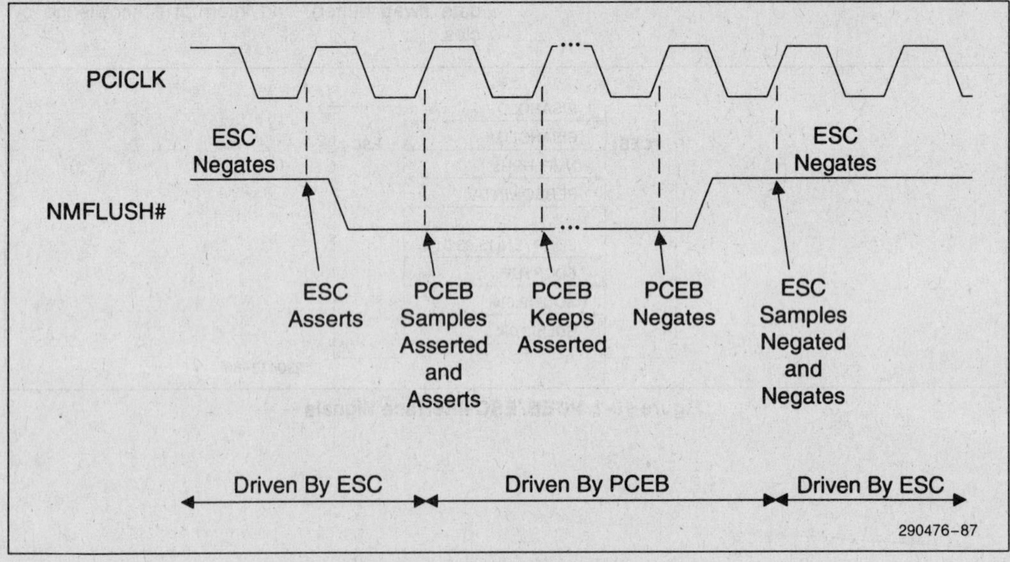

Figure 10-2. NMFLUSH# Protocol

When the EISA master completes its transfer and gets off the bus (i.e., removes its request to the ESC), the ESC negates EISAHOLD and the PCEB, in turn, negates EISAHOLDA. At this point, the PCEB resumes its default ownership of the EISA Bus.

If a PCI master requests access to the EISA Bus while the bus is owned by a master other than the PCEB, the PCEB retries the PCI cycle and requests ownership of the EISA Bus by asserting PEREQ#/INTA# to the ESC. PEREQ#/INTA# is a dual function signal that is a PCEB request for the EISA Bus (PEREQ# function) when EISAHOLDA is asserted. In response to the PCEB request for EISA Bus ownership, the ESC removes the grant to the EISA master. When the EISA master completes its current transactions and relinquishes the bus (removes its bus request), the ESC negates EISAHOLD and the PCEB, in turn, negates EISAHOLDA. At this point, a grant can be given to the PCI device for a transfer to the EISA Bus. Note that the INTA# function of the PEREQ#/INTA# signal is described in Section 10.3, Interrupt Acknowledge Control.

10.2 EISA Data Swap Buffer Control Signals

The cycles in the EISA environment may require data size translations before the data can be transferred to its intermediate or final destination. As an example, a 32-bit EISA master write cycle to a 16-bit EISA slave requires a disassembly of a 32-bit Dword into 16-bit Words. Similarly, a 32-bit EISA master read cycle to a 16-bit slave requires an assembly of two 16-bit Words into a 32-bit Dword. The PCEB contains EISA data swap buffers to support data size translations on the EISA Bus. The operation of the data swap buffers is described in the PCEB data sheet. The ESC controls the operation of the PCEB's data swap buffers with the following PCEB/ESC interface signals. These signals are outputs from the ESC and are inputs to the PCEB.

- SDCPYEN[13,3:1]#
- SDCPYUP
- SDOE[2:0]#
- SDLE[3:0]#

Copy Enable Outputs (SDCPYEN[13,3:1]#)

These signals enable the byte copy operations between data byte lanes 0, 1, 2 and 3 as shown in the Table 10-1. ISA master cycles do not perform assembly/disassembly operations. Thus, these cycles use SDCPYEN[13,3:1]# to perform the byte routing and byte copying between lanes. EISA master cycles however, can have assembly/disassembly operations. These cycles use SDCPYEN[13,3:1]# in conjunction with SDCPYUP and SDLE[3:0]#.

Table 10-1. Byte Copy Operations

Signal	Copy between Byte Lanes
SDCPYEN01#	Byte 0 (bits [7:0]) and Byte 1 (bits [15:8])
SDCPYEN02#	Byte 0 (bits [7:0]) and Byte 2 (bits [23:16])
SDCPYEN03#	Byte 0 (bits [7:0]) and Byte 3 (bits [31:24])
SDCPYEN13#	Byte 1 (bits [15:8]) and Byte 3 (bits [31:24])

System Data Copy Up (SDCPYUP)

SDCPYUP controls the direction of the byte copy operations. When SDCPYUP is asserted (high), active lower bytes are copied onto the higher bytes. The direction is reversed when SDCPYUP is negated (low).

System Data Output Enable (SDOE[2:0]#)

These signals enable the output of the data swap buffers onto the EISA Bus (Table 10-2). SDOE[2:0] are re-drive signals in case of mis-matched cycles between EISA to EISA, EISA to ISA, ISA to ISA and the DMA cycles between the devices on EISA.

Table 10-2. Output Enable Operations

Signal	Byte Lane
SDOE0#	Applies to Byte 0 (bits [7:0])
SDOE1#	Applies to Byte 1 (bits [15:8])
SDOE2#	Applies to Byte 2 and Byte 3 (bits [31:16])

System Data to Internal (PCEB) Data Latch Enables (SDLE[3:0]#)

These signals latch the data from the EISA Bus into the data swap latches. The data is then either sent to the PCI Local Bus via the PCEB or re-driven onto the EISA Bus. SDLE[3:0]# latch the data from the corresponding EISA Bus byte lanes during PCI reads from EISA, EISA writes to PCI, DMA cycles between an EISA device and the PCEB. These signals also latch data during mismatched cycles between EISA to EISA, EISA to ISA, ISA to ISA, the DMA cycles between the devices on EISA, and any cycles that require copying of bytes, as opposed to copying and assembly/disassembly.

1

10.3 Interrupt Acknowledge Control

PEREQ#/INTA# (PCI to EISA Request or Interrupt Acknowledge) is a dual function signal and the selected function depends on the status of EISAHLDA. When EISAHLDA is negated, this signal is an interrupt acknowledge (INTA#) and supports interrupt processing. If interrupt acknowledge is enabled via the PCEB's PCICON Register and EISAHOLDA is negated, the PCEB asserts PEREQ#/INTA# when a PCI interrupt acknowledge cycle is being serviced. This informs the ESC that the forwarded EISA I/O read from location 04h is an interrupt acknowledge cycle. Thus, the ESC uses this signal to distinguish between a request for the interrupt vector and a read of the ESC's DMA register located at 04h. The ESC responds to the read request by placing the interrupt vector on SD[7:0].

11.0 INTEGRATED SUPPORT LOGIC

The ESC integrates support logic for assorted functions for a typical EISA system board. The following functions are directly supported by the ESC.

— EISA Address Buffer Control

— Coprocessor Interface

— BIOS Interface

— Keyboard Controller Interface

— Real Time Clock Interface

— Floppy Disk Controller Interface

— Configuration RAM Interface

— X-Bus and IDE Decode

11.1 EISA Address Buffer Control

The EISA Bus consists of unlatched addresses (LA[31:2]) and latched addresses (SA[19:2]). EISA devices generate or monitor LA addresses, and ISA devices generate or monitor SA addresses. Three Discrete F543s are used to generate the SA address from LA and LA addresses from SA addresses (see Figure 11-1). The ESC generates the control signals SALE#, LASAOE#, and SALAOE# for the F543s. These signals control the direction of the address flow. For EISA master, DMA, and Refresh cycles, the LA addresses are generated by the master device, and the SA addresses are driven by the F543s. For ISA master devices, the SA addresses are generated by the master device, and the LA addresses are driven by the F543s.

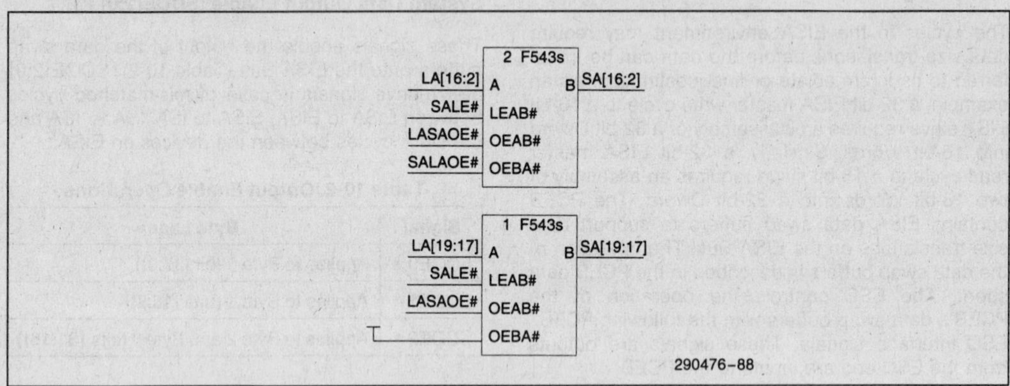

Figure 11-1. EISA Address Buffers

Table 11-1. EISA Address Buffer Control Function

Signal	Cycle Type			
	EISA Master	ISA Master	DMA	Refresh
SALE#	Pulses	Low	Pulses	Pulses
LASAOE#	Low	High	Low	Low
SALAOE#	High	Low	High	High

11.2 Coprocessor Interface

The numeric coprocessor interface is designed to support PC/AT compatible numeric coprocessor exception handling. The EISA Clock Divisor configuration register bit 5 needs to be set to a 1 in order to enable the coprocessor error support in the ESC. The coprocessor interface consists of FERR# signal and IGNNE# signal. The FERR# signal and IGNNE# signals are connected directly to the Floating Point Error pin and Ignore Floating Point Error pin of the CPU respectively.

Whenever an error during computation is detected, the CPU asserts the FERR# signal to the ESC. The ESC internally generates an interrupt on the IRQ13 line of the integrated Interrupt Controller. The result is a asserted INT signal to the CPU.

When the ESC detects an I/O write to the internal port 00F0h, the ESC deasserts the internal IRQ13 line to the integrated Interrupt Controller. At the same time the ESC asserts the IGNNE# signal. The ESC keeps the IGNNE# signal asserted until the FERR# signal is negated by the CPU.

If the coprocessor error support is enabled in the EISA Clock Divisor configuration register then the ESC IRQ13 pins cannot be used, and this pin should be tied to ground.

11.3 BIOS Interface

The ESC supports a total of 512 Kbytes of BIOS memory. The ESC asserts the LBIOSCS# signal for EISA or ISA memory cycles decoded to be in the BIOS space. The 512 Kbytes of BIOS includes the conventional 128 Kbytes of BIOS and 384 Kbytes of enlarged BIOS. The 128 Kbytes of conventional BIOS is divided into multiple regions. Each region can be independently enabled or disabled by setting the appropriate bits in the BIOS Chip Select A register and BIOS Chip Select B register. The 128 Kbytes of conventional BIOS is also aliased at different locations within the memory space. Refer to Section 4.1, BIOS Memory Space, for details.

The ESC generates the LBIOSCS# signal by internally latching the output of the BIOS address decode with BALE signal. The ESC asserts the LBIOSCS# for all read cycles in the enabled BIOS memory space. The ESC will assert LBIOSCS# signal for write cycles in the enabled BIOS memory space only if the BIOS Chip Select B register bit 3 is set to 1 (BIOS write enable).

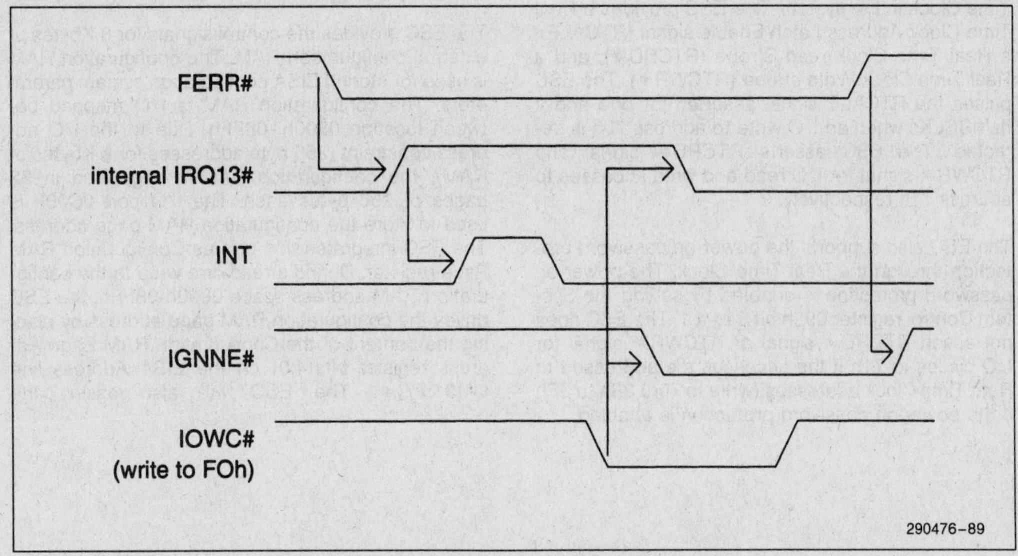

Figure 11-2. Coprocessor Interface Waveform

11.4 Keyboard Controller Interface

The ESC provides a complete inferface to a glueless interface to a 8x42 Keyboard Controller. The ESC Keyboard Controller interface consists of Keyboard Controller Chip Select (KYBDCS#) signal, Mouse interrupt (ABFULL) signal. The ESC also supports the fast Keyboard commands for CPU reset (ALTRST#) and address A20 enable (ALTA20) by integrating Port 92h.

The ESC asserts the KYBDCS# signal for I/O cycles to addresses 60h and 64h if the Peripheral Chip Select A register bit 1 is set to 1. The ESC uses the ABFULL signal to internally generate an interrupt request to the integrated Interrupt Controller on the IRQ12 line if EISA Clock Divisor register bit 4 is set to 1 (Mouse Interrupt Enable). A low to high transition on the ABFULL signal is internally latched by the ESC. The high level on this latch remains until a write to I/O port 60h is detected or the ESC is reset.

The ALTRST# is used to reset the CPU under software control. The ESC ALTRST# signal needs to be AND'ed externally with the reset signal from the keyboard controller. A write to the System Control register (092h) bit 0 to set the bit to a 1 from a 0 causes the ESC to pulse the ALTRST# signal. The ALTRST# signal is asserted for approximately 4 BCLKs. The ESC will not pulse the ALTRST# signal if bit 0 has previously been set to a 1.

11.5 Real Time Clock

The ESC provides a glueless interface for the Real Time Clock in the system. The ESC provides a Real Time Clock Address Latch Enable signal (RTCALE), a Real Time Clock read Strobe (RTCRD#), and a Real Time Clock Write strobe (RTCWR#). The ESC pulses the RTCALE signal asserted for one and a half BCLKs when an I/O write to address 70h is detected. The ESC asserts RTCRD# signal and RTCWR# signal for I/O read and write accesses to address 71h respectively.

The ESC also supports the power-on password protection through the Real Time Clock. The power-on password protection is enabled by setting the System Control register 092h bit 3 to a 1. The ESC does not assert RTCRD# signal or RTCWR# signal for I/O cycles to 71h if the accesses are addressed to Real Time Clock addresses (write to 70h) 36h to 3Fh if the power-on password protection is enabled.

11.6 Floppy Disk Control Interface

The ESC supports interface to the 82077(SL) Floppy Disk Controller chip. The ESC provides a Floppy Disk Controller Chip Select signal (FDCCS#). The ESC also provides a buffered Drive Interface (DSKCHG#) signal. In addition, the ESC generates the control for the disk light.

The ESC supports both the primary address range (03F0h-03F7h) and secondary address range (0370h-0377h) of the Floppy Disk Controller. The state of Peripheral Chip Select A register bit 5 determines which address range is decoded by the ESC as access to Floppy Disk Controller. If bit 5 is set to 0, the ESC will decode the primary Floppy Disk Controller address range. If bit 5 is set to 1, the ESC will decode the secondary Floppy Disk Controller address range.

The ESC supports the Drive Interface signal. During I/O accesses to address 03F7h (primary) or 0377h (secondary), the ESC drives the inverted state of the DSKCHG# signal on to the SD7 data line. The ESC uses the DSKCHG# signal to determine if the Floppy Disk Controller is present on the X-Bus. If the DSKCHG# signal is sampled low during reset, the ESC will disable Floppy Disk Controller support.

The ESC also supports the Disk Light function by generating the DLIGHT# signal. If System Control 092h register bit 6 or bit 7 is set to a 1, the ESC will assert the DLIGHT# signal.

11.7 Configuration RAM Interface

The ESC provides the control signals for 8 Kbytes of external configuration RAM. The configuration RAM is used for storing EISA configuration system parameters. The configuration RAM is I/O mapped between location 0800h–08FFh. Due to the I/O address constraint (256 byte addresses for 8 Kbytes of RAM), the configuration RAM is organized in 32 pages of 256 bytes each. The I/O port 0C00h is used to store the configuration RAM page address. The ESC integrates this port as Configuration RAM Page register. During a read or a write to the configuration RAM address space 0800h-08FFh, the ESC drives the configuration RAM page address by placing the content of the Configuration RAM Page Address register bits[4:0] on the EISA Address line LA[31:27]#. The ESC will also assert the

CRAMRD# signal or the CRAMWR# signal for I/O read and write accesses to I/O address 0800h-08FFh. The ESC will only generate the configuration RAM page address and assert the CRAMRD# signal and CRAMWR# signal if the Peripheral Chip Select B register bit 7 is set to 1.

11.8 General Purpose Peripherals, IDE, Parallel Port, and Serial Port Interface

The ESC provides three dual function pins (GPCS[2:0]#, ECS[2:0]). The functionality of these pins is selected through the configuration Mode Select register bit 4. If Mode Select register bit 4 is set to 0 the general purpose chip select functionality is selected. If Mode Select register bit 4 is set to 1, the encoded chip select functionality is selected.

In general purpose chip select mode, the ESC generates three general purpose chip selects (GPCS[2:0]#). The decode for each general purpose chip selects is programmed through a set of three configuration registers; General Purpose Chip Select x Base Low Address register, General Purpose Chip Select x Base High Address register, and General Purpose Chip Select x Mask register. Each General Purpose Peripheral can be mapped anywhere in the 64 Kbytes of I/O address. The general purpose peripheral address range is programmable from 1 byte to 256 bytes with 2^n granuality.

In encoded chip select mode (ESC[2:0]), in addition to decoding the general purpose chip select 0 address and general purpose chip select 1 address, the ESC also decodes IDE, Parallel Ports, and Serial Ports addresses. The encoded chip select mode requires an external decoder like a F138 to generate the device chip selects from the ESC[2:0] signals.

The ESC generates encoded chip selects for two Serial Ports, COMACS# (ECS[2:0]=000) and COMBCS# (ESC[2:0]=001). The ESC supports Serial Port COM1 and Serial Port COM2. Accesses to Serial Port COM1 or Serial Port COM2 are individually programmed through Peripheral Chip Select B register bits [0:3] to generate an encoded chip select for COMACS# or COMBCS#.

1

Table 11-2. Encoded Chip Select Decode

ESC2	ESC1	ESC0	PERIPHERAL CS
0	0	0	COMACS#
0	0	1	COMBCS#
0	1	0	LPTCS#
0	1	1	IDECS0#
1	0	0	IDECS1#
1	0	1	GPCS0#
1	1	0	GPCS1#
1	1	1	Idle State

Refer to Section 4.5 for the address decode of the peripheral chip selects.

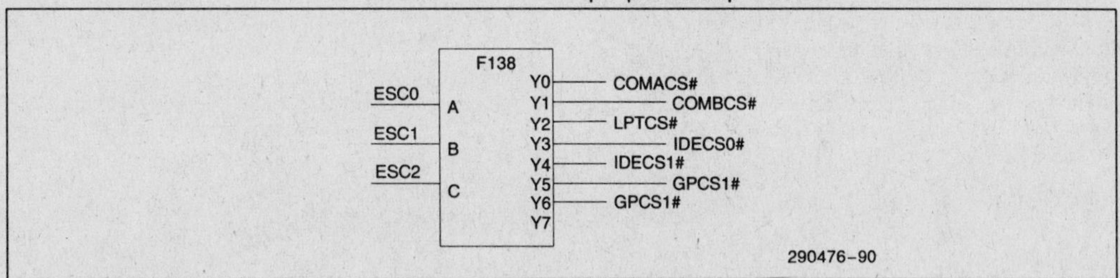

Figure 11-3. Encoded Chip Select Decoder Logic

11.9 X-Bus Control and General Purpose Decode

The X-Bus is a secondary data bus buffered from the EISA Bus. The X-Bus is used to interface with peripheral devices that do not require a high speed interface. Typically a discrete buffer device like a F245 is used to buffer the EISA Bus from the X-Bus. The ESC provides two control signals, XBUSTR# and XBUSOE#, for the discrete F245 buffer.

The XBUSTR# signal controls the direction of the data flow of the F245. When the XBUSTR# signal is high, the data direction of the F245 buffer is from the XD[7:0] bus to the SD[7:0] bus. The ESC drives the XBUSTR# signal high during EISA master I/O read cycles, ISA master I/O read cycles, DMA write cycles (write to memory), and memory read cycles decoded to be in the X-Bus BIOS address space. The ESC also drives the XBUSTR# signal high for DMA reads (reads from memory/writes to I/O) from the X-Bus BIOS address space. The X-Bus BIOS address space is defined as the enabled regions and enabled aliases of the BIOS memory space. See Section 4.1, BIOS Memory Space, for detailed description of the BIOS memory map and the configuration bits.

The XBUSOE# signal controls outputs of the F245. When the XBUSOE# signal is asserted, the F245 drives its A buffers or B buffers depending on the state of the XBUSTR# signal. The ESC asserts the XBUSOE# signal for I/O cycles decoded to be in the address range of the peripherals supported by the ESC if these peripherals are enabled in the Peripheral Chip Select A register and Peripheral Chip Select B register.

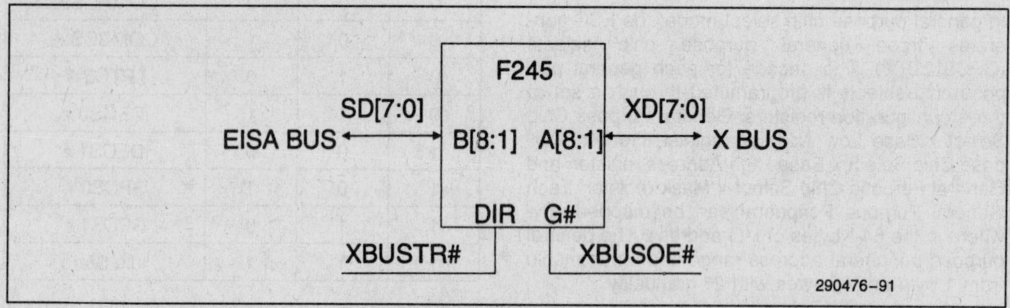

Figure 11-4. X-Bus Data Buffer

12.0 ELECTRICAL CHARACTERISTICS

12.1 Maximum Ratings

Case Temperature Under Bias . . . −65°C to +110°C

Storage Temperature . . . . −65°C to +150°C

Supply Voltages
with Respect to Ground . . . −0.5V to V_{CC} + 0.5V

Voltage On Any Pin . . . . −0.5V to V_{CC} + 0.5V

Power Dissipation . . . . .0.70W Fully Loaded
. . . . .0.55W with Four Slots

NOTICE: This is a production data sheet. The specifications are subject to change without notice.

**WARNING: Stressing the device beyond the "Absolute Maximum Ratings" may cause permanent damage. These are stress ratings only. Operation beyond the "Operating Conditions" is not recommended and extended exposure beyond the "Operating Conditions" may affect device reliability.*

12.2 D.C. Characteristics

12.2.1 JUNCTION TEMPERATURE SPECIFICATIONS

The junction temperature for the ESC is +93°C with a case temperature of 85°C. To guarantee device operation at +85°C case temperature the ambient temperature allowable is shown in Table 12-1.

Table 12-1. ESC Maximum Allowable Ambient Temperature/Air Flow Rates

EISA Loading	Still	100 lfpm	200 lfpm	400 lfpm
4 Slots	63°C	66°C	69°C	72°C
8 Slots	56°C	60°C	63°C	67°C

12.2.2 EISA BUS D.C. SPECIFICATIONS

EISA Signals

BCLKOUT(out), BCLK(in), LA[31:27]#/CPG[4:0](t/s), LA[26:2](t/s), BE[3:0]#(t/s), M/IO#(t/s), W/R#(t/s), EX32#(o/d), EX16#(o/d), START#(t/s), CMD#(out), EXRDY(o/d), SLBURST#(in), MSBURST#(t/s), MASTER16#(in), SD[7:0](t/s)

ISA Signals

BALE(out), SA[1:0](t/s), SBHE#(t/s), M16#(o/d), IO16#(o/d), MRDC#(t/s), MWTC#(t/s), SMRDC#(out), SMWTC#(out), IORC#(t/s), IOWC#(t/s), CHRDY(o/d), IOCHK#(in), NOWS#(o/d), OSC(in), RSTDRV(out), REFRESH#(t/s), AEN#(out), AEN[4:1]/EAEN[4:1](out)

DMA and Arbitration Signals

DREQ[3:0,7:5](in), DACK[3:0,7:5]#(out), EOP(t/s), MREQ[3:0]#(in), MREQ[7:4]#/PIRQ[0:3]#(in), MACK[3:0]#/EMACK[3:0](out)

X-Bus and Integrated Logic Signals

SPKR(out), SLOWH#(out), IRQ[15:1](in), INT(out), NMI(out), SALE#(out), LASAOE#(out), SALAOE#(out), FERR#(in), IGNNE#(out), LBIOSCS#(out), KYBDCS#(out), ALTRST#(out), ALTA20(out), ABFULL(in), RTCALE(out), RTCRD#(out), RTCWR#(out), FDCCS#(out), DSKCHG(in), DLIGHT#(out), CRAMRD#(out), CRAMWR#(out), XBUSTR#(out), XBUSOE#(out), GPCS[2:0]#/ECS[2:0](out)

Interchip Signals

EISAHOLD(out), EISAHLDA(in), PEREQ#/INTA#(in), NMFLUSH#(t/s), SDCPYEN[13:01]#(out), SDCPYUP(out), SDOE[2:0]#(out), SDLE[3:0]#(out)

Table 12-2. EISA Bus D.C. Specifications (V_{DD} = 5V ±5%, T_{case} = 0°C to +85°C)

Symbol	Parameter	Min	Max	Test Conditions	Notes
V_{IL1}	Input Low Voltage		0.8V		
V_{IH1}	Input High Voltage	2.0V			
V_{IL2}	Input Low Voltage		0.8V		1
V_{IH2}	Input High Voltage	V_{CC} − 0.8V			1
V_{OL1}	Output Low Voltage		0.45V	I_{OL} = 24 mA	2
V_{OH1}	Output High Voltage	2.4V		I_{OH} = −5.0 mA	2
V_{OL2}	Output Low Voltage		0.45V	I_{OL} = 1 mA	3
V_{OH2}	Output High Voltage	V_{CC} − 0.45V		I_{OH} = −1 mA	3
V_{OL3}	Output Low Voltage		0.45V	I_{OL} = 8.0 mA	4
V_{OH3}	Output High Voltage	2.4V		I_{OH} = −2.0 mA	4
I_{LI}	Input Leakage Current		±15 μA	0V < V_{IN} < V_{CC}	
I_{LO}	Output Leakage Current		±15 μA	0.45V < V_{IN} < V_{CC}	
C_{IN}	Capacitance Input		8 pF		
C_{OUT}	Capacitance Output		15 pF	@1 MHz	
I_{CC}	V_{CC} Supply Current		TBD	TBD	

NOTES:

1. All EISA Bus signals use V_{IL1}, V_{IH1} for input levels except for the Interchip signals: SDCPYEN#, SDCPYUP, SDOE#, SDLE#, EISAHOLD, EISAHLDA, PEREQ#/INTA#, INTCHIP0, NMFLUSH#.
2. BALE, BCLKOUT, BE[3:0]#, CHRDY, CMD#, EOP, EX16#, EX32#, EXRDY, IO16#, IORC#, IOWC#, LA[31:2], M16#, M/IO#, MRDC#, MSBURST#, MWTC#, REFRESH#, RSTDRV, SA[1:0], SBHE#, SD[7:0], SMRDC#, SMWTC#, START#, W/R#, SPKR#.
3. ALTA20, AEN[4:1], ALTRST#, CRAMRD#, CRAMWT#, INT, DLIGHT, EISAHOLD, FDCCS#, IDECS#, IGNNE#, KEYBDCS#, LASAOE#, LBIOSCS#, NMFLUSH#, RTCALE, RTCRD#, RTCWR#, SALAOE#, SALE#, SDCPYEN[13:01]#, SDCPYUP, SDLE[3:0]#, SDOE[2:0]#, SLOWH#, XBUSOE#, XBUSTR#.
4. DACK[7:5,3:0], MACK[7:0]#.

12.2.3 PCI LOCAL BUS D.C. SPECIFICATIONS

PCI System Signals

PCICLK(in), RESET(in)

PCI Shared Signals

PERR#(in), SERR#(in)

Table 12-3. PCI Local Bus D.C. Specifications (V_{DD} = 5V ±5%, T_{case} = 0°C to +85°C)

Symbol	Parameter	Min	Max	Test Conditions
V_{IL}	Input Low Voltage		0.8V	
V_{IH}	Input High Voltage	2.0V	5.5V	
I_{IL}	Low-Level Input Current		−70 μA	V_{IN} = 0.5V
I_{IH}	High-Level Input Current		−70 μA	V_{IN} = 2.7V
$C_{I/O}$	Input/Output Capacitance		10 pF	@ 1 MHz
C_{CLK}	PCICLK Signal Input Capacitance		17 pF	@ 1 MHz
I_{CC}	V_{CC} Supply Current		TBD	TBD

1

12.3 A.C. Characteristics

In Tables 12-5 through 12-10, the Symbol column shows the timing variable used in the A.C. timing waveforms. The parameter column contains the description of the timing and its reference signal. If the timing is for a particular bus cycle, the cycles will be listed in parenthesis. Burst cycles include standard timings for their requirements. The Min column lists either the minimum delay time, setup time, or hold time requirement in nano-seconds unless stated otherwise. The Max column lists the maximum delay time also in nano-seconds. The Figure column shows what A.C. timing waveforms the parameter can be found. The Note column may contain a number to refer to a specific note found at the end of the table.

The A.C. specifications are based upon the specified capacitive loading values in Table 12-4. The minimum capacitive loading value is 50 pF for all signals.

Table 12-4. Capacitive Loading Table

Signals	Loading
BALE, BCLKOUT, BE[3:0]#, CHRDY, CMD#, EOP, EX16#, EX32#, EXRDY, IO16#, IORC#, IOWC#, LA[31:2], M16#, M/IO#, MRDC#, MSBURST#, MWTC#, REFRESH#, RSTDRV, SA[1:0], SBHE#, SD[7:0], SMRDC#, SMWTC#, START#, W/R#	240 pF
ALTA20, AEN[4:1], ALTRST#, CRAMRD#, CRAMWT#, INT, DLIGHT, FDCCS#, IDECS#, IGNNE#, KEYBDCS#, LASAOE#, LBIOSCS#, NMFLUSH#, RTCALE, RTCRD#, RTCWR#, SALAOE#, SALE#, SLOWH#, SPKR, XBUSOE#, XBUSTR#, PCICLK, RESET, PERR#, SERR#	50 pF
DACK[7:5,3:0], MACK[7:0]#	120 pF
EISAHOLD, SDCPYEN[13:1]#, SDCPYUP, SDLE[3:0]#, SDOE[2:0]#	30 pF

12.3.1 CLOCK SIGNALS A.C. SPECIFICATIONS

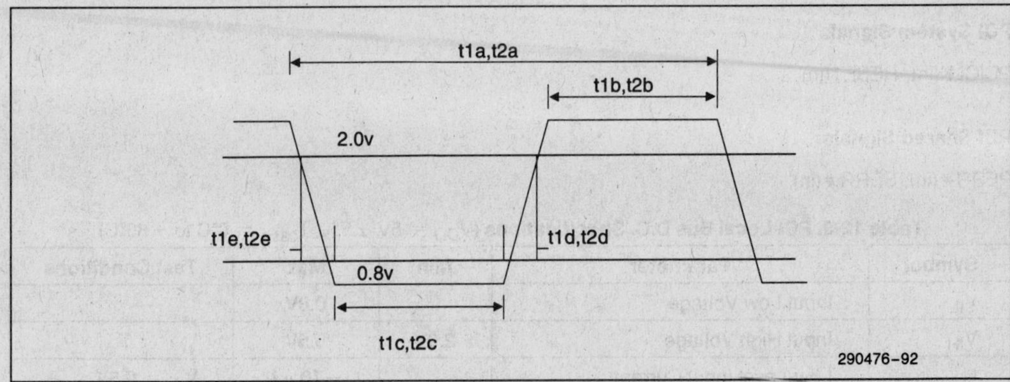

Figure 12-1. Clock Timings

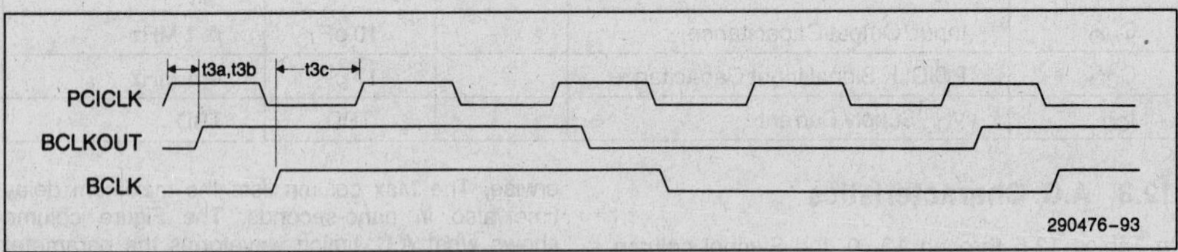

Figure 12-2. BCLKOUT and BCLK

Table 12-5. Clock Signals A.C. Specifications (V_{DD} = 5V ±5%, T_{case} = 0°C to +85°C)

Symbol	Parameter	Min	Max	Figures	Notes
PCICLK(1)					
t1a	Cycle Time	30		12-1	
t1b	High Time (at 2.0V)	40% * Tcyc		12-1	
t1c	Low Time (at 0.8V)	40% * Tcyc		12-1	
t1d	Rise Time (0.8V to 2.0V)	3		12-1	
t1e	Fall Time (2.0V to 0.8V)	3		12-1	
BCLK, BCLKOUT					
t2a	Clock Period (0.8V to 0.8V)	120		12-1	
t2b	Low Time (at 0.8V)	55		12-1	
t2c	High Time (at 2.0V)	56		12-1	
t2d	Rise Time (0.8V to 2.0V)		7	12-1	
t2e	Fall Time (2.0V to 0.8V)		6	12-1	
t3a	BCLKOUT Delay from PCICLK Rising (240 pF)	5	17	12-2	
t3b	BCLKOUT Delay from PCICLK Rising (30 pF)	2	9	12-2	
t3c	BCLK Setup to PCICLK Rising	4		12-2	
t3d	BCLK Hold from PCICLK Rising	4		12-2	
OSC					
t2a	Clock Period (0.8V to 0.8V)	65	70	12-1	
t2b	Low Time (0.8V)	20		12-1	
t2c	High Time (2.0V)	20		12-1	

12.3.2 A.C. SPECIFICATIONS

Table 12-6. EISA Interface A.C. Specifications (V_{DD} = 5V ±5%, T_{case} = 0°C to +85°C)

Symbol	Parameter	Min	Max	Figures	Notes
EISA MASTER					
BE[3:0]#					
t4a	Delay from BCLK Rising/Falling (Assembly, Disassembly)	1	30	12-6,7,8	
t4b	Setup to BCLK Rising	80		12-3	
t4c	Setup to BCLK Falling (Burst)	30		12-9	
t4d	Hold from BCLK Rising	20		12-3	
t4e	Hold from BCLK Falling (Burst)	2		12-9	
SA0, SA1, SBHE#					
t5	Valid Delay from BCLK Falling		30	12-3	
M/IO#					
t6a	Setup to BCLK Rising	80		12-3	
t6b	Hold from BCLK Rising	20		12-3	
W/R#					
t7a	Setup to BCLK Falling	25		12-3	
t7b	Hold from BCLK Rising	20		12-3	
MASTER16#					
t8a	Setup to BCLK Rising	17		12-10	
t8b	Hold from BCLK Rising	0		12-10	
MRDC#, MWTC#, IORC#, IOWC#, SMRDC#, SMWTC#					
t9a	Delay from BCLK Rising/Falling	2	30	12-11	
t9b	IOWC# Delay from BCLK Rising/Falling	3.5	25	12-11	
START#					
t10a	Delay from BCLK Rising	1	25	12-4,6,7	
t10b	Setup to BCLK Rising	23		12-3	
t10c	Hold from BCLK Rising	0		12-3	
t10d	Pulsewidth	Tper-5		12-4,6,7	
t10e	START# Setup to PCICLK Rising	9			
CMD#					
t11	Delay from BCLK Rising	1	30	12-3	
BALE					
t12	Delay from BCLK Rising/Falling	1	20	12-3	
MSBURST#					
t13a	Setup to BCLK Falling	12		12-12	
t13b	Hold from BCLK Falling	20		12-12	

Table 12-6. EISA Interface A.C. Specifications (V_{DD} = 5V ±5%, T_{case} = 0°C to +85°C) (Continued)

Symbol	Parameter	Min	Max	Figures	Notes
EISA MASTER (continued)					
EX32#, EX16#					
t14a	Valid Delay from BCLK Falling (End of Backoff)	3	32	12-6	
t14b	Setup to BCLK Rising	25		12-3	
t14c	Hold from BCLK Rising	55		12-3	
t14d	Float Delay from BCLK Falling (End of Backoff)	2	19	12-6	
IO16#					
t15a	Setup to BCLK Falling	20		12-13	
t15b	Hold from BCLK Falling	20		12-13	
M16#					
t16a	Setup to BCLK Rising	18		12-14	
t16b	Hold from BCLK Falling	0		12-14	
NOWS#					
t17a	Setup to BCLK Falling	10		12-15	5
t17b	Hold from BCLK Falling	20		12-15	5
CHRDY					
t18a	Negate Setup to BCLK Falling	7		12-18	
t18b	Assert Setup to BCLK Rising	10		12-18	
t18c	Negated Pulsewidth	10		12-18	
EXRDY#					
t19a	Setup to BCLK Falling	13		12-19	
t19b	Hold from BCLK Falling	0		12-19	
ISA MASTER					
BE[3:0]#					
t20	Valid Delay from SA[1:0], SBHE# Valid		60	12-4	
M/IO, W/R					
t21	Delay from IORC#, IOWC#, MRDC# Asserted		40	12-4	
SMRDC#, SMWTC#					
t22	Delay from MRDC#, MWTC# Asserted	0	25	12-4	
START#					
t23a	Delay from BCLK Rising	1	25	12-4	
t23b	Pulsewidth	Tper-5		12-4	

1

Table 12-6. EISA Interface A.C. Specifications (V_{DD} = 5V ±5%, T_{case} = 0°C to +85°C) (Continued)

Symbol	Parameter	Min	Max	Figures	Notes
ISA MASTER (Continued)					
CMD#					
t24a	Delay from BCLK Rising	1	30	12-4	
t24b	Delay from MRDC#, IORC# Rising (Read)	0	30	12-4	
IO16#, M16#					
t25	Delay from EX32#, EX16# Asserted		50	12-4	
CHRDY					
t26a	Negate Delay from MRDC#, MWTC#, IORC#, IOWC#		60	12-4	
t26b	Float Delay from BCLK Falling		15	12-4	
DMA CYCLES					
LA[31:2]					
t27a	Delay from BCLK Falling (DMA "C")	2	30	12-19	
t27b	Delay from BCLK Falling (DMA "A, B", Refresh)		50	12-18	
BE[3:0]#					
t28a	Delay from BCLK Falling (DMA "C")	2	30	12-19	
t28b	Delay from BCLK Falling (DMA "A, B", Refresh)		50	12-18	
SA0, SA1, SBHE#					
t29	Delay from BCLK Falling (DMA "A, B", Refresh)		50	12-18	
REFRESH#					
t30a	Delay from BCLK Rising		50	12-25	
t30b	Setup to BCLK Rising	18		12-25	
t30c	Hold from BCLK Rising	3		12-25	

Table 12-6. EISA Interface A.C. Specifications (V_{DD} = 5V ±5%, T_{case} = 0°C to +85°C) (Continued)

Symbol	Parameter	Min	Max	Figures	Notes
DMA CYCLES (Continued)					
AEN#, AEN[4:1]/EAEN[4:1]					
t31	Delay from BCLK Falling		50	12-18	
M/IO, W/R					
t32	Delay from BCLK Falling (DMA "A, B", Refresh)	1	50	12-18	
MRDC#, MWTC#, IORC#, IOWC#, SMRDC#, SMWTC#					
t33a	Delay from BCLK Rising/Falling	2	30	12-11	
t33b	IOWC# Delay from BCLK Rising	3	25	12-11	
START#					
t34a	Delay from BCLK Rising	1	25	12-18	
t34b	Pulsewidth	Tper-5		12-18	
CMD#					
t35	Delay from BCLK Rising/Falling	1	30	12-18	
SLBURST#					
t36a	Setup to BCLK Rising (DMA "C")	15		12-19	
t36b	Hold from BCLK Rising (DMA "C")	25		12-19	
MSBURST#					
t37	Delay from BCLK Falling (DMA "C")	1	30	12-19	
EXRDY#					
t38a	Valid Delay from BCLK Rising	1	32	12-20	
t38b	Setup to BCLK Falling	13		12-17	
t38c	Hold from BCLK Falling	0		12-17	
t38d	Float Delay from BCLK Falling	2	30	12-20	
EOP					
t39a	Delay from BCLK (DMA "A, B")		40	12-21	
t39b	Setup to BCLK Rising (EOPIN Mode)	15		12-21	
t39c	Hold from BCLK Rising (EOPIN Mode)	15		12-21	
t39d	Float Delay from DACK# Rising (DMA "A, B")		30	12-21	
SLAVE ACCESS					
SD[7:0]					
t40a	Valid Data Delay from BCLK Rising (Read)		60	12-22	
t40b	Setup to BCLK Rising (Write)	15		12-22	
t40c	Hold from BCLK Rising (Write)	5		12-22	
t40d	Float Delay from CMD# Negated (Read)		30	12-22	
NOWS#					
t41	Asserted from LA Valid		60	12-23	
CPG[4:0]#					
t42	Valid Delay from LA Valid		60	12-23	4

Table 12-7. Data Swap Logic A.C. Specifications (V_{DD} = 5V ±5%, T_{case} = 0°C to +85°C)

Symbol	Parameter	Min	Max	Figures	Notes
SDCPYEN[13:1]#					
t43a	Delay from BCLK Rising/Falling (Standard Mismatch, Assembly)	5	25	12-5,6	
t43b	Negate Delay from BCLK Rising (Disassembly)		25	12-7	
t43c	Assert Delay from BCLK Falling (Disassembly)		19	12-7	
t43d	Delay from BCLK Rising/Falling (Burst Mismatch)	5	15	12-9	
t43e	Valid Delay from IO16# Asserted (ISA 16-Bit Slave)		20	12-24	
t43f	SDCPYUP Setup to SDCPYEN[13:1]# Valid	0		12-26	
t43g	Delay from MRDC#, MWTC#, IORC#, IOWC# Asserted/Negated (ISA Mismatch)	2	20	12-25	
SDCPYUP					
t44a	Delay from BCLK Rising/Falling (Standard Mismatch, Assembly, Disassembly)	2	25	12-5, 6	
t44b	Delay from MWTC#, IOWC# Asserted/Negated (ISA Mismatch)	2	20	12-26	
SDLE[3:0]#					
t45a	Assert Delay from BCLK Rising (Assembly)	1	25	12-6	
t45b	Deassert Setup to CMD# Negated (Assembly)	2		12-6	
t45c	Deassert Setup to SDCPYEN[13:01]# Negated (Assembly)	2		12-6	
t45d	Delay from BCLK Falling (Disassembly)		25	12-8	
SDOE[2:0]#					
t46a	Delay from BCLK Rising/Falling (Redrive)	1	12.5	12-6	3
t46b	Delay from BCLK Rising/Falling (Disassembly)	1	25	12-8	
t46c	Assert Delay from BCLK Falling (Disassembly)	1	21	12-8	

Table 12-8. Arbitration, Timer, Interrupt A.C. Specifications (V_{DD} = 5V ±5%, T_{case} = 0°C to +85°C)

Symbol	Parameter	Min	Max	Figures	Notes
MREQ[7:0]#					
t47a	Setup to BCLK Rising	17		12-27	
t47b	Hold from BCLK Rising	15		12-27	
MACK[3:0]#/EMACK[3:0]					
t48a	Delay from BCLK Rising		40	12-27	
t48c	Delay from MREQx# Rising	240		12-27	
DREQ[7:5,3:0]					
t49a	Setup to BCLK Rising	15		12-4,27	
t49b	Hold from BCLK Rising	15		12-4,27	
DACK[7:5,3:0]#					
t50a	Delay from BCLK Rising		50	12-4,27	
t50b	Delay from DREQ Falling	240		12-4,27	

Table 12-8. Arbitration, Timer, Interrupt A.C. Specifications
(V_{DD} = 5V ±5%, T_{case} = 0°C to +85°C) (Continued)

Symbol	Parameter	Min	Max	Figures	Notes
INT					
t51a	Delay from PIRQ[0:3], IRQ[15:1], OSC, BCLK, FERR#		200	12-28	
t51b	Delay from ABFULL Asserted		100	12-28	
NMI					
t52	Delay from IOCHK, SERR# Asserted		200	12-29	
RSTDRV					
t53	Delay from RESET# Asserted/Negated		100	12-29	
SLOWH#					
t54	Delay from BCLK Falling		200	12-28	
SPKR					
t55a	Delay from BCLK Falling		100	12-28	
t55b	Delay from OSC Rising		200	12-28	

Table 12-9. Interchip Signals A.C. Specifications (V_{DD} = 5V ±5%, T_{case} = 0°C to +85°C)

Symbol	Parameter	Min	Max	Figures	Notes
EISAHOLD					
t56	Delay from PCICLK Rising	4	15	12-30	
EISAHOLDA					
t57a	Setup to PCICLK Rising	9		12-30	
t57b	Hold from PCICLK Rising	2		12-30	
PEREQ#/INTA#					
t58a	Setup to PCICLK Rising	9		12-30	
t58b	Hold from PCICLK Rising	2		12-30	
NMFLUSH#					
t59a	Delay from PCICLK Rising (Request from ESC)	4	15	12-31	
t59b	Setup from PCICLK Rising (Acknowledge from PCEB)	9		12-31	
t59c	Hold from PCICLK Rising (Acknowledge from PCEB)	2		12-31	

Table 12-10. Integrated Logic Support Signals
A.C. Specifications (V_{DD} = 5V ±5%, T_{case} = 0°C to +85°C)

Symbol	Parameter	Min	Max	Figures	Notes
EISA ADDRESS BUFFER CONTROL (SALE#, LASAOE#, SALAOE#)					
t60a	SALE# Negate Delay from BCLK Rising (DMA Master)	1	38	12-32	2
t60b	SALE# Assert Delay from BCLK Rising (DMA Master)	1	38	12-32	
t60c	SALE# Delay from BCLK Falling/Rising (EISA Master, DMA Assembly/Disassembly)	1	14	12-3	
t60d	SALE# Delay from BCLK Rising (ISA Master)	1	38	12-4	
t61a	LASAOE# Delay from BCLK Rising		30	12-4	
t61b	SALAOE# Delay from BCLK Rising		35	12-4	
t61c	SALAOE# Negate Delay from REFRESH# Asserted		35	12-25	

1

Table 12-10. Integrated Logic Support Signals
A.C. Specifications (V_{DD} = 5V ±5%, T_{case} = 0°C to +85°C) (Continued)

Symbol	Parameter	Min	Max	Figures	Notes
COPROCESSOR INTERFACE (FERR#, IGNNE#)					
t62a	Asserted Delay from IOWC# Asserted		100	12-33	
t62b	Deassert Delay from FERR# Negated		100	12-33	
CHIP SELECTS (LBIOSCS#, KYBDCS#, FDCCS#, GPCS[2:0]#/ECS[2:0]#)					
t63	Delay from LA Valid and BALE Asserted		60	12-34	
KEYBOARD CONTROLLER (ALTRST#, ALTA20, ABFULL)					
t64a	ALTRST# Asserted Pulsewidth	480		12-35	
t64b	ALTA20 Delay from BCLK Rising		50	12-35	
REAL TIME CLOCK (RTCRD#, RTCWR#, RTCALE)					
t65a	RTCALE Delay from BCLK Rising		40	12-36	
t65b	RTCRD# Assert Delay from XBUSTR# Negated		50	12-36	
t65c	RTCRD# Deassert Delay from IORC# Negated		30	12-36	
t65d	RTCWR# Assert Delay from IOWC# Asserted		50	12-36	
t65e	RTCWR# Deassert Delay from BCLK Rising		50	12-36	
CONFIGURATION RAM (CRAMRD#, CRAMWR#)					
t66a	CRAMRD# Assert Delay from XBUSTR# Negated		50	12-36	
t66b	CRAMRD# Deassert Delay from IORC# Negated		30	12-36	
t66c	CRAMWR# Assert Delay from IOWC# Asserted		50	12-36	
t66d	CRAMWR# Deassert Delay from BCLK Rising		50	12-36	
X-BUS CONTROL (XBUST/R#, XBUSOE#)					
EISA, ISA MASTER					
t67a	XBUST/R# Delay from IORC#, IOWC#, MRDC#, MWTC#		20	12-36,37	
t67b	XBUSOE# Delay from IORC#, IOWC#, MRDC#, MWTC#		35	12-37	
t67c	XBUST/R# Hold from IORC#, IOWC#, MRDC#, MWTC# Inactive	25	110	12-37	
t67d	XBUSOE# Inactive Delay from IORC#, IOWC#, MRDC#, MWTC# Inactive	29	115	12-37	
t67e	XBUSOE# Active Delay from XBUST/R# Active	3	12	12-37	
t67f	XBUST/R# Inactive Delay from XBUSOE# Inactive	10	40	12-37	

1

Table 12-10. Integrated Logic Support Signals
A.C. Specifications (V_{DD} = 5V ±5%, T_{case} = 0°C to +85°C) (Continued)

Symbol	Parameter	Min	Max	Figures	Notes
DMA					
t67g	XBUST/R# Active Delay from DACK2 Active		25	12-38	
t67h	XBUSOE# Active Delay from DACK2 Active		37	12-38	
t67i	XBUST/R# Inactive Delay from DACK2 Inactive		25	12-38	
t67j	XBUSOE# Inactive Delay from DACK2 Inactive	10	65	12-38	
t67k	XBUSOE# Active Delay from XBUST/R # Active	3	16	12-38	
t67l	XBUST/R# Inactive Delay from XBUSOE# Inactive	9	40	12-38	
FLOPPY DISK CONTROLLER (DSKCHG)					
t68a	DSKCHG Valid to SD7 Valid		25	12-39	
t68b	IORC# Asserted to SD7 Driven		35	12-39	
t68c	IORC# Negated to SD7 Floated		25	12-39	

NOTES:
1. PCICLK input must meet PCI Specification requirements for clock skew.
2. For DMA type "A, B" read cycles SALE# is asserted for one BCLK. For DMA compatible read, type "B" write, type "C" read and write SALE# is asserted for two BCLKs. For DMA compatible write, and type "A" write SALE# is asserted for three BCLKs.
3. For EISA redrive cycles SDOE is negated on the first rising edge of BCLK. For DMA type "B" redrive cycles SDOE is negated on the second falling edge of BCLK. For DMA type "C" redrive cycles SDOE is negated on the third falling edge of BCLK.
4. The CPG[4:0] signals are shared with LA[31:27]# and are outputs only during I/O access to 0800h-08FFh.
5. For an 8-bit ISA slave, NOWS# is sampled starting on the second falling edge of BCLK after CMD# is asserted. 16-bit ISA slaves are sampled starting on the first falling edge of BCLK after CMD# is asserted.

12.3.3 A.C. TIMING WAVEFORMS

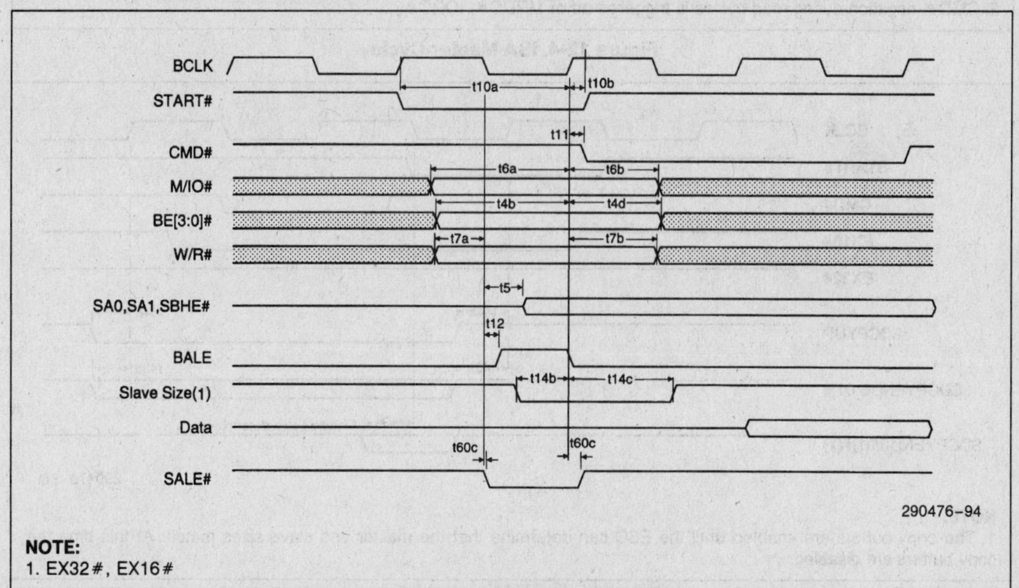

Figure 12-3. EISA Master Cycle

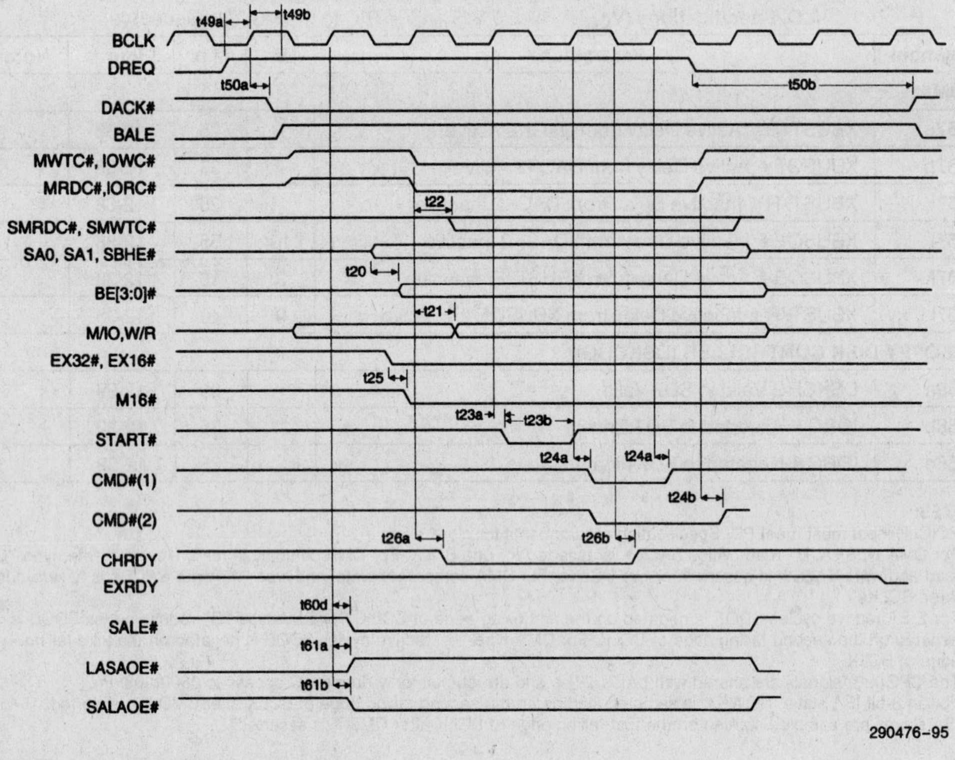

t49a t49b
BCLK
DREQ
t50a t50b
DACK#
BALE
MWTC#, IOWC#
MRDC#,IORC#
t22
SMRDC#, SMWTC#
SA0, SA1, SBHE#
t20
BE[3:0]#
t21
M/IO,W/R
EX32#, EX16#
t25
M16#
t23a t23b
START#
t24a t24a
CMD#(1)
t24b
CMD#(2)
t26a t26b
CHRDY
EXRDY
t60d
SALE#
t61a
LASAOE#
t61b
SALAOE#

290476-95

NOTES:
1. CMD# negation during write cycles is triggered off of BCLK rising.
2. CMD# negation during read cycles is triggered off of MRDC#, IORC#.

Figure 12-4. ISA Master Cycle

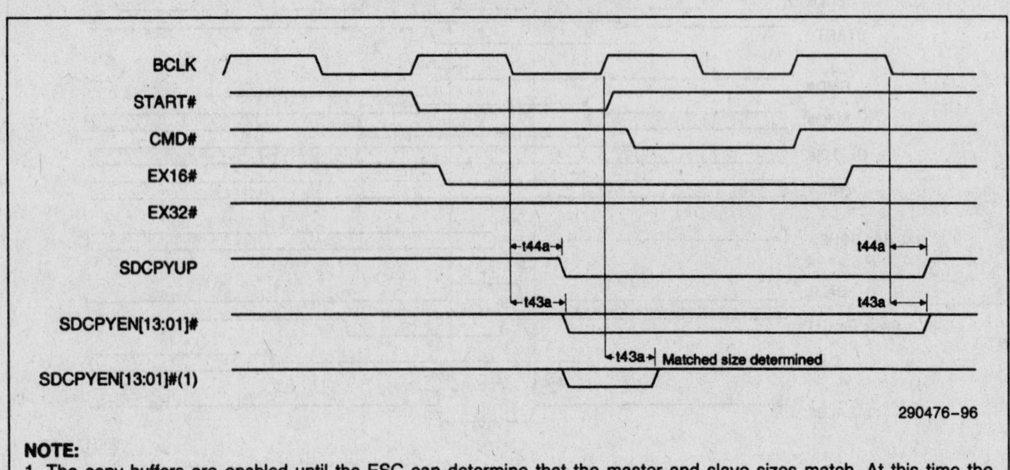

NOTE:
1. The copy buffers are enabled until the ESC can determine that the master and slave sizes match. At this time the copy buffers are disabled.

Figure 12-5. Mismatch

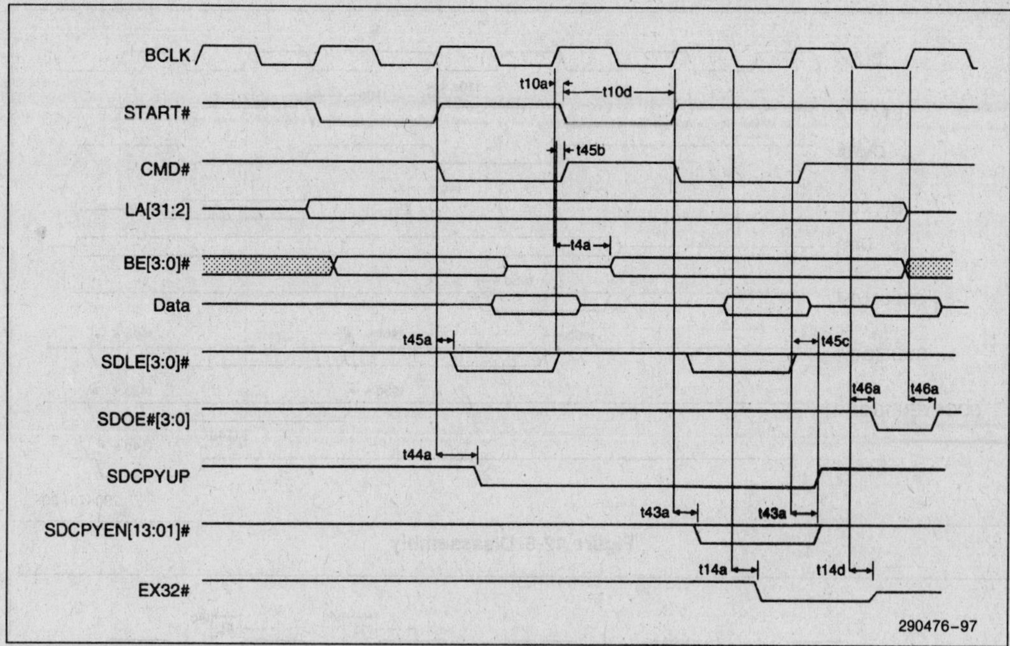

Figure 12-6. Assembly with Redrive

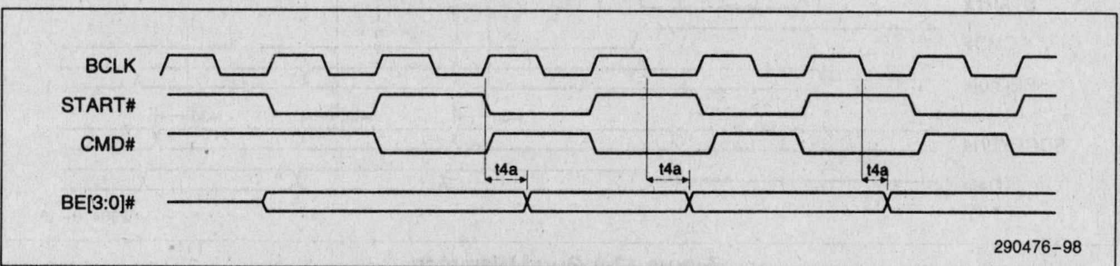

Figure 12-7. DMA Assembly, Disassembly

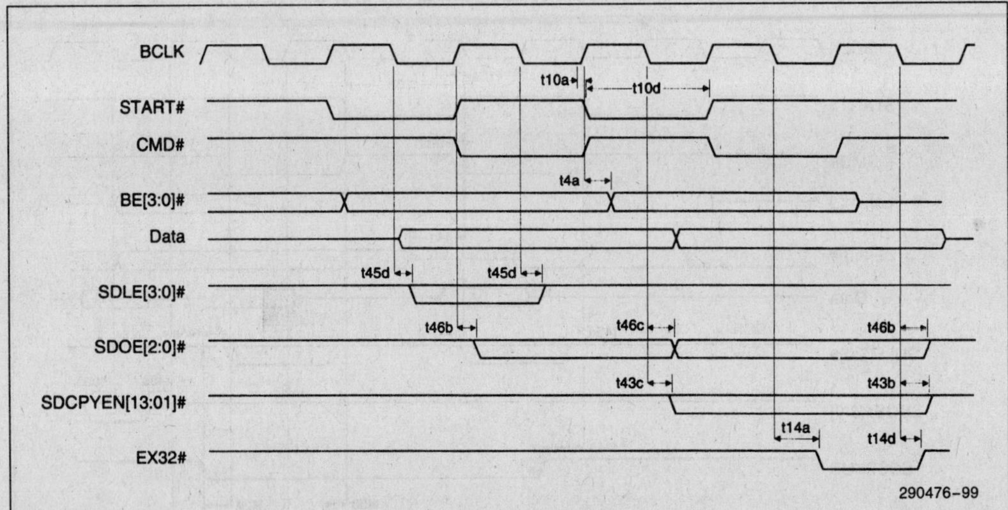

Figure 12-8. Disassembly

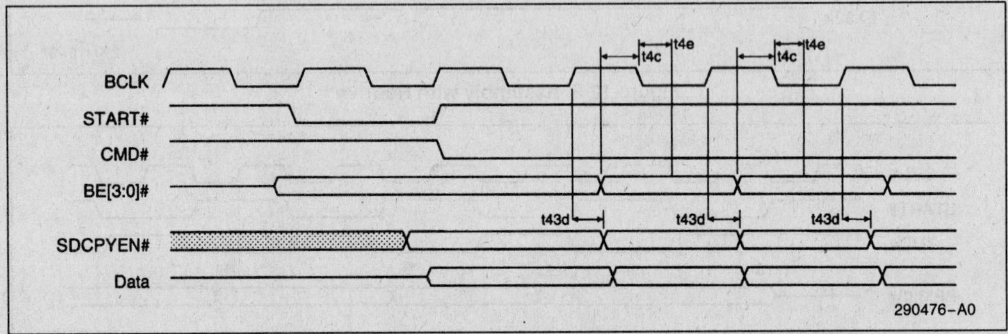

Figure 12-9. Burst Mismatch

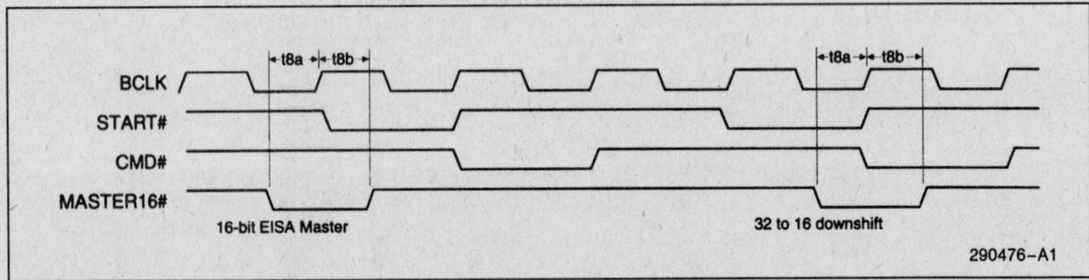

Figure 12-10. MASTER16# Signal

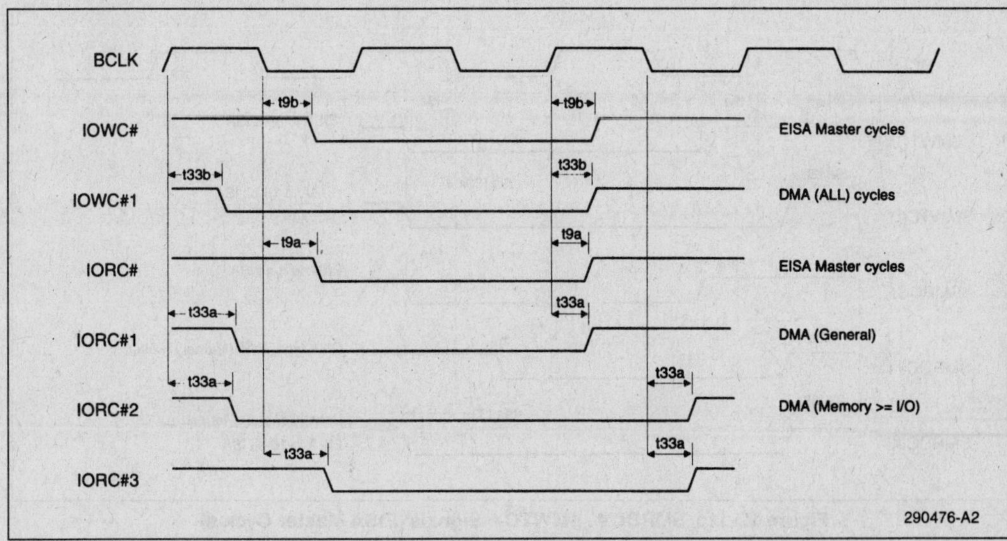

Figure 12-11a. IORC#, IOWC# Signals

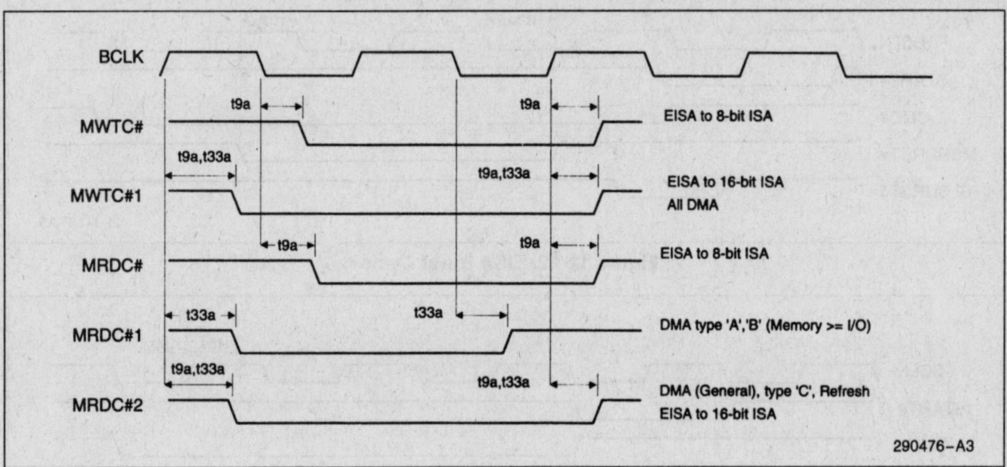

Figure 12-11b. MRDC#, MWTC# Signals

1

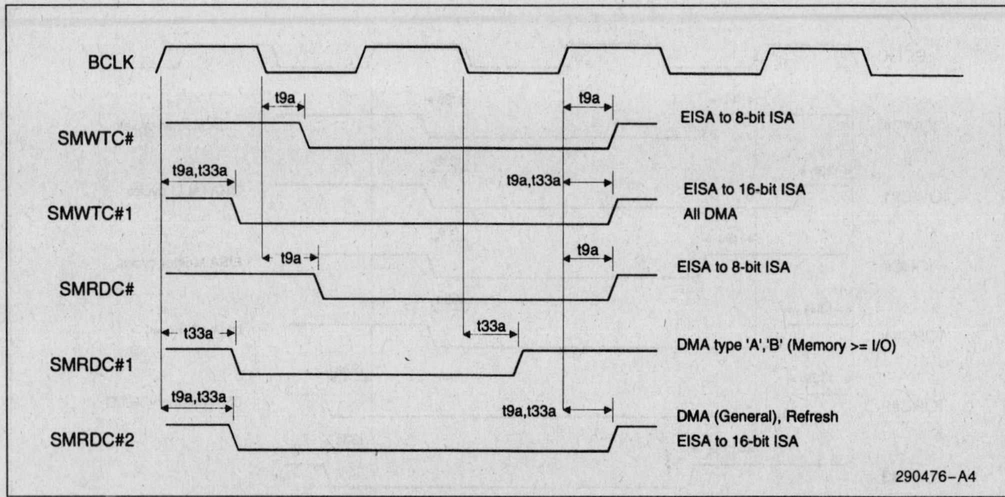

Figure 12-11c. SMRDC#, SMWTC# Signals (EISA Master Cycles)

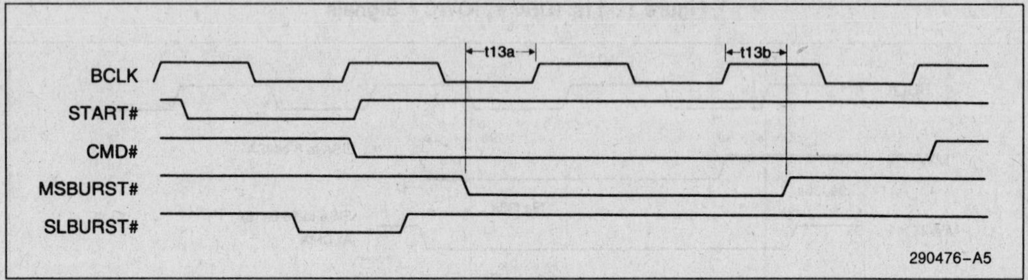

Figure 12-12. EISA Burst Cycle

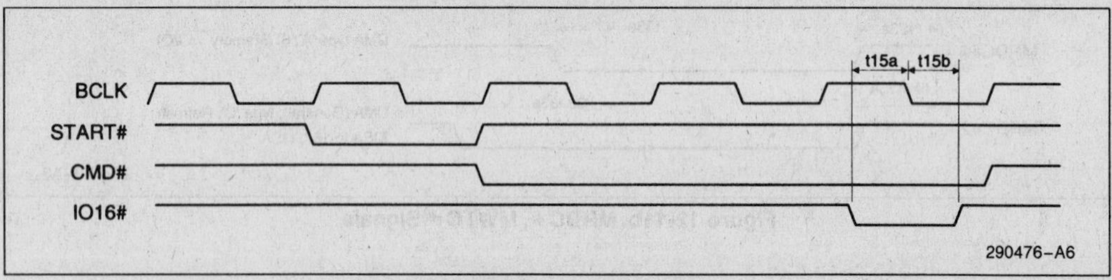

Figure 12-13. IO16# Signal

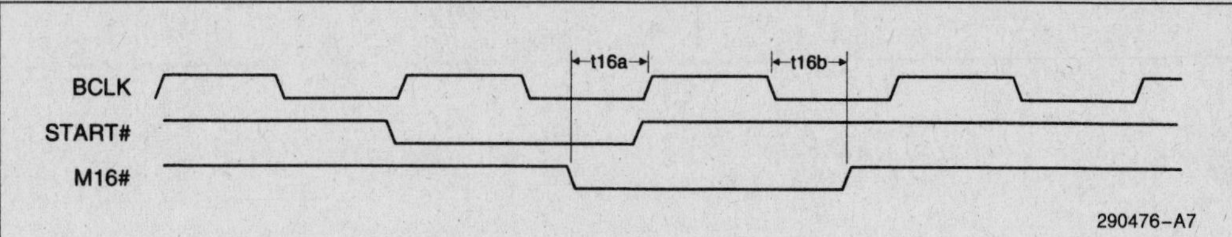

Figure 12-14. M16# Signal

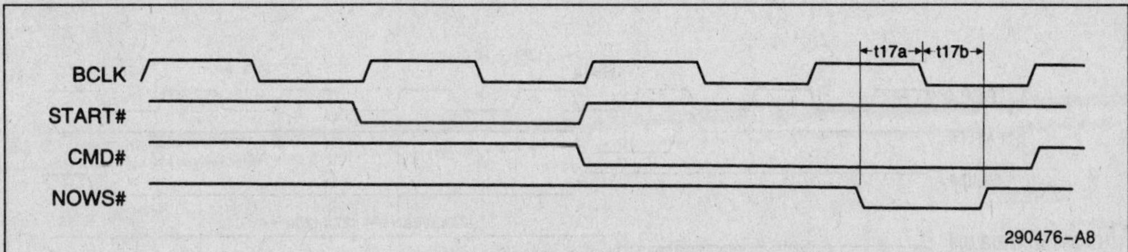

Figure 12-15. NOWS# Signal

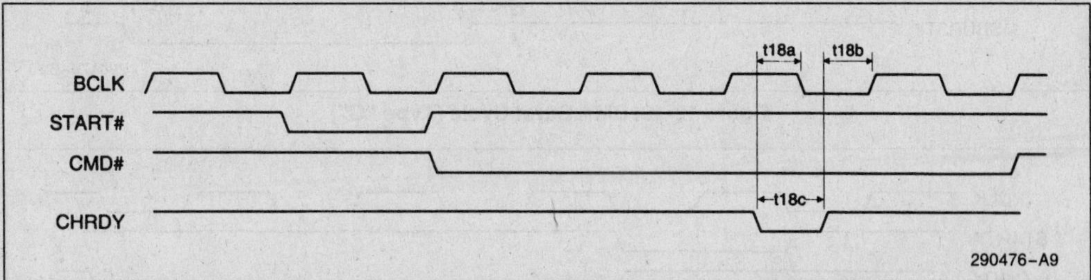

Figure 12-16. EISA Master to ISA Slave (CHRDY)

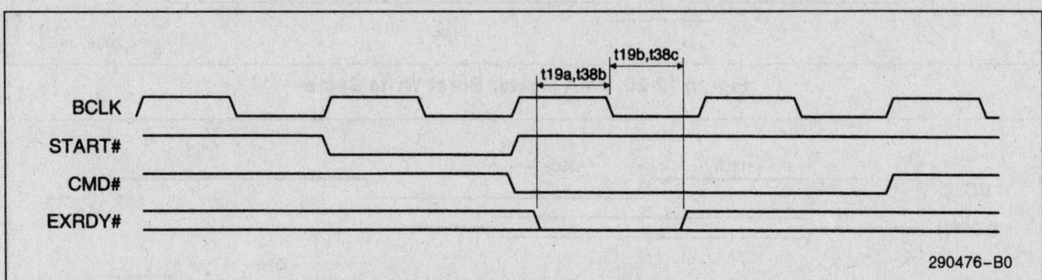

Figure 12-17. EISA Slave (EXRDY)

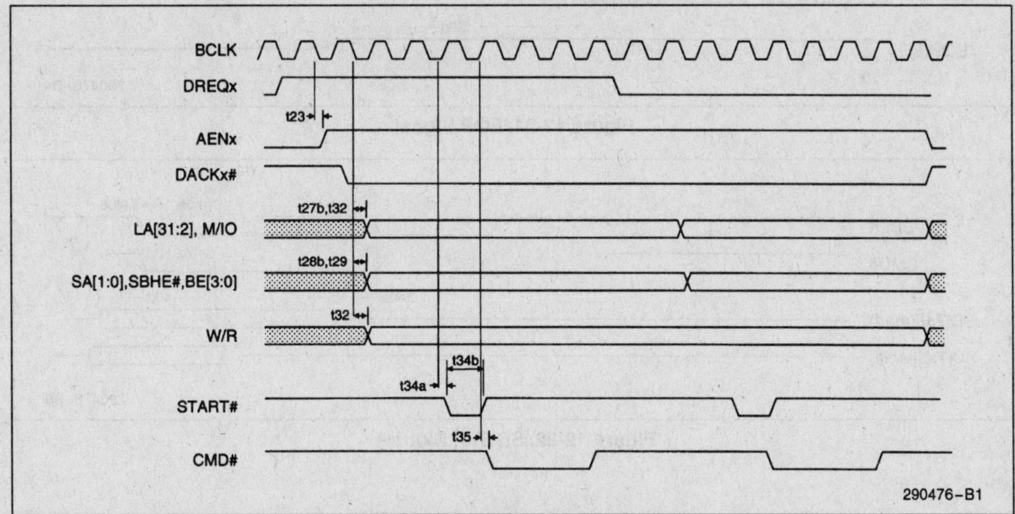

Figure 12-18. DMA Cycle (General)

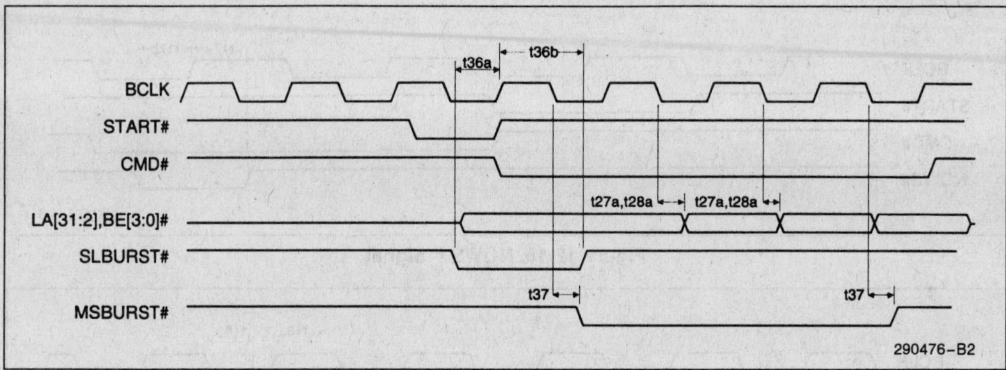

Figure 12-19. DMA Burst Cycle (Type "C")

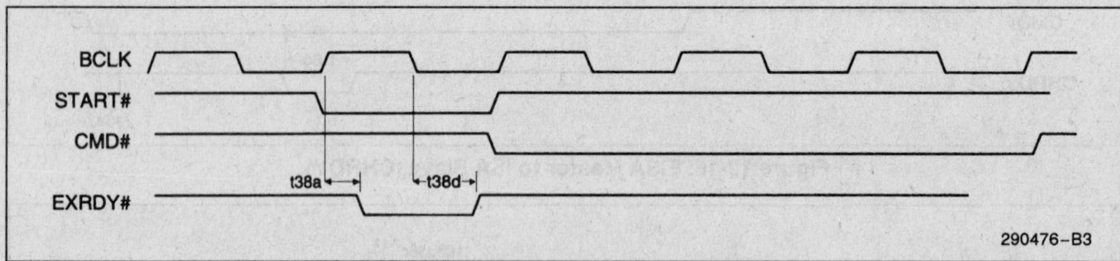

Figure 12-20. DMA Master Burst Write Cycle

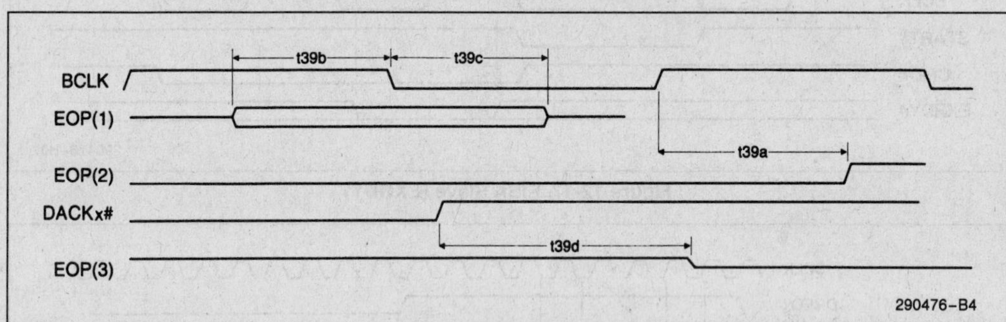

Figure 12-21. EOP Signal

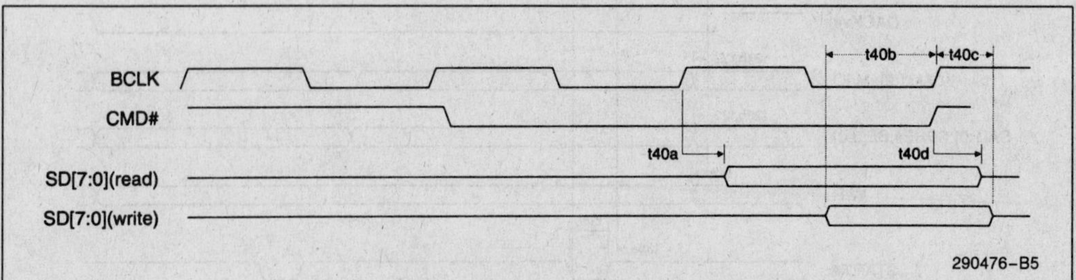

Figure 12-22. SD[7:0] Signals

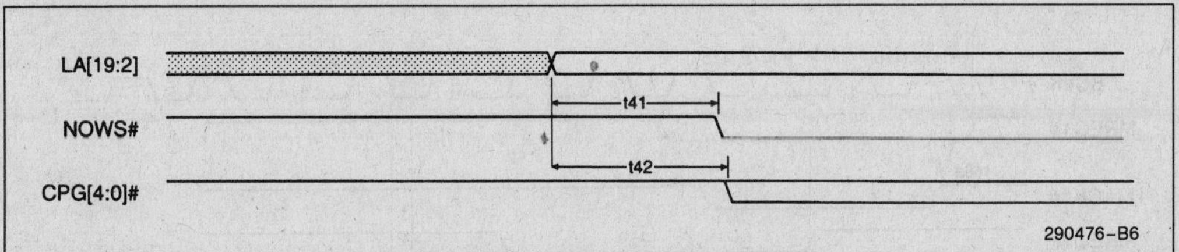

Figure 12-23. NOWS#, CPG[4:0]# Signals

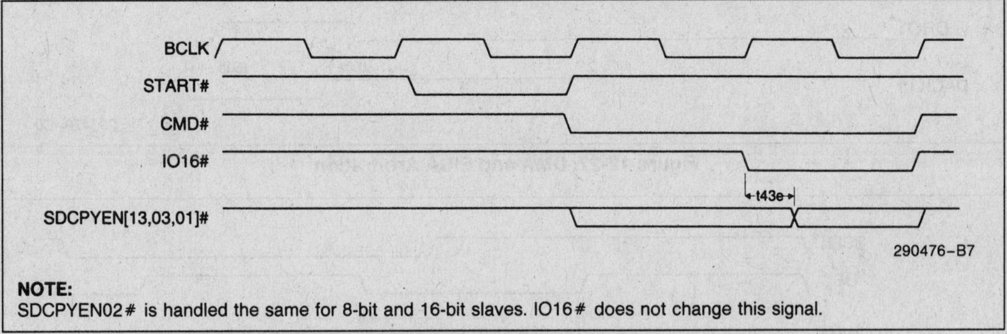

Figure 12-24. EISA or DMA Master Read from 16-Bit ISA I/O

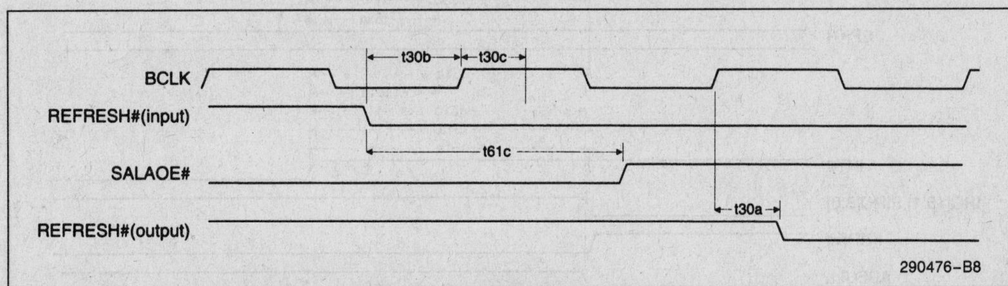

Figure 12-25. REFRESH# Signal

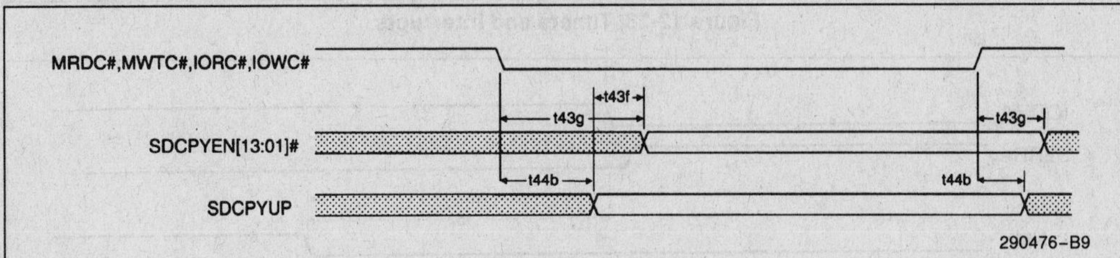

Figure 12-26. ISA Mismatch

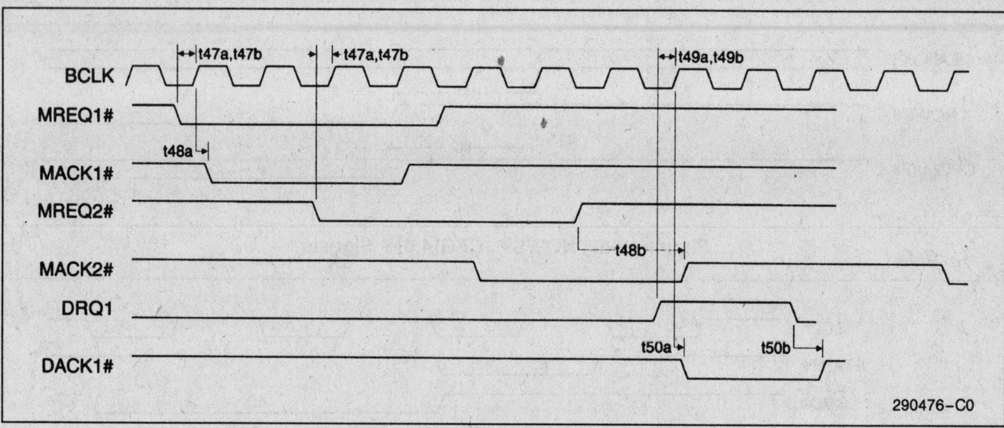

Figure 12-27. DMA and EISA Arbitration

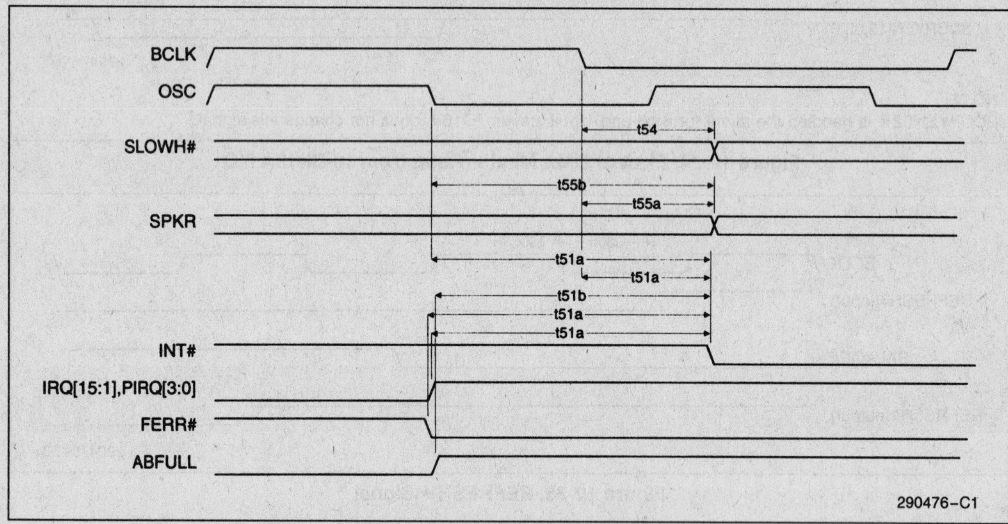

Figure 12-28. Timers and Interrupts

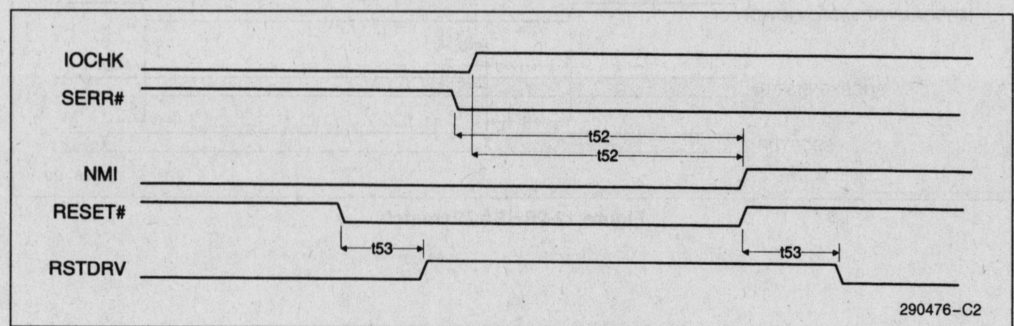

Figure 12-29. NMI and RSTDRV

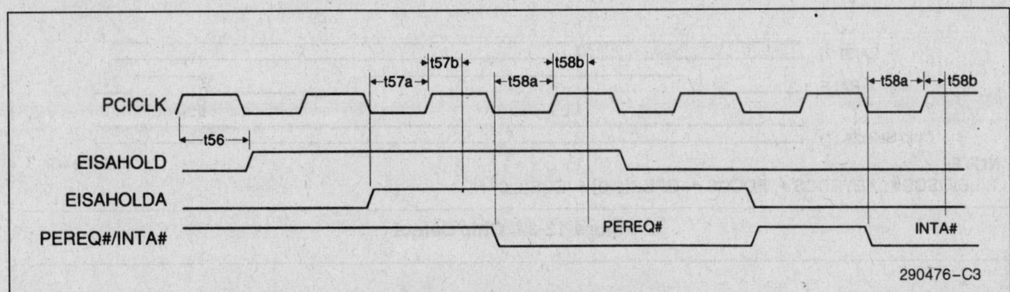

Figure 12-30. EISAHOLD Signals

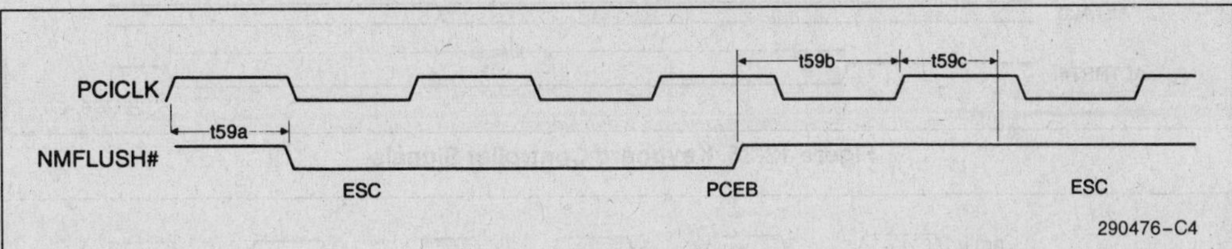

Figure 12-31. Flush Request

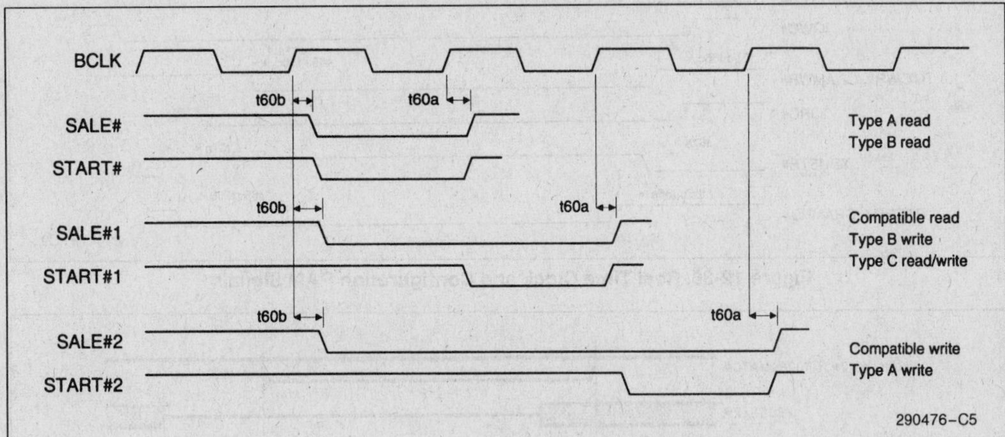

Figure 12-32. SALE for DMA Cycles

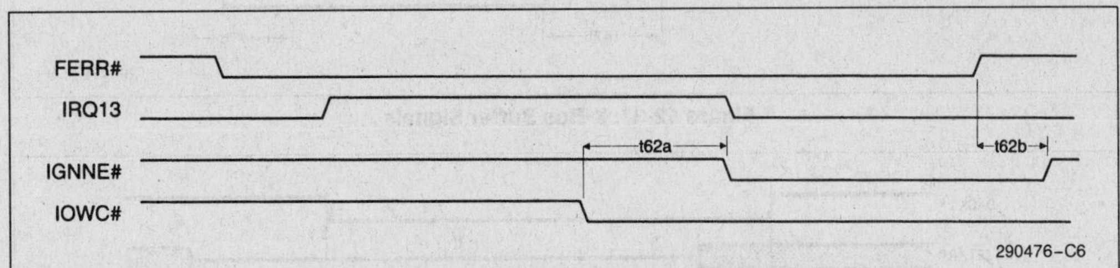

Figure 12-33. IGNNE# Signal

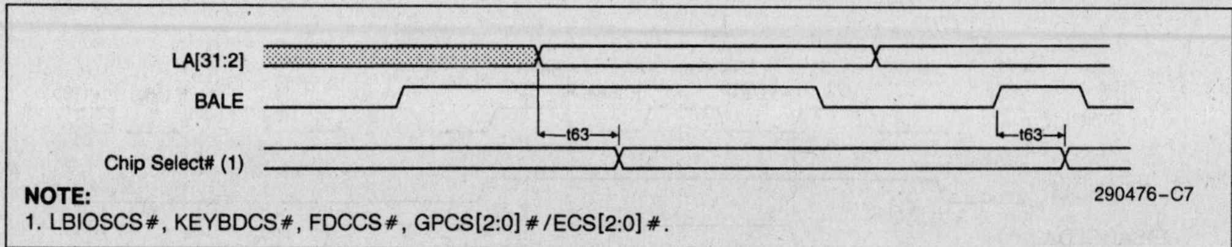

Figure 12-34. Chip Select

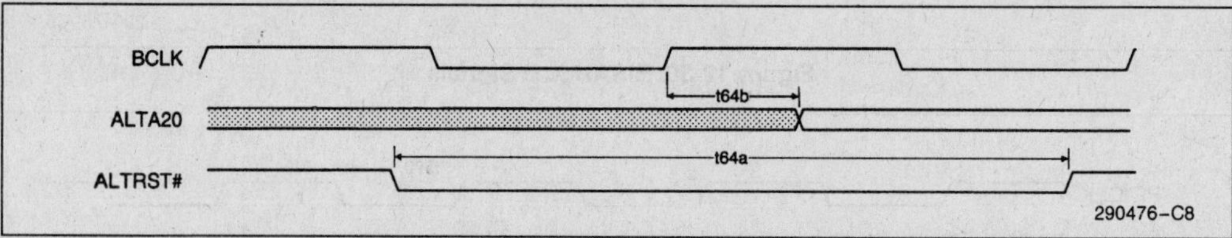

Figure 12-35. Keyboard Controller Signals

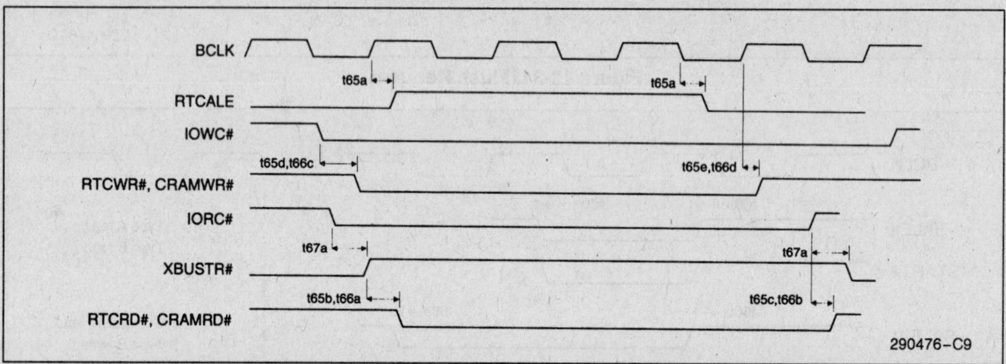

Figure 12-36. Real Time Clock and Configuration RAM Signals

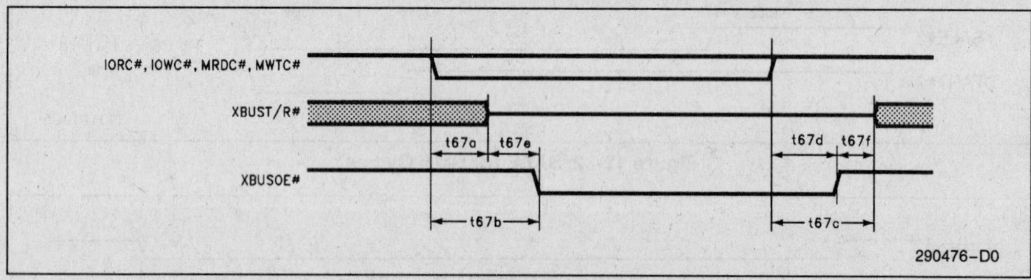

Figure 12-37. X-Bus Buffer Signals

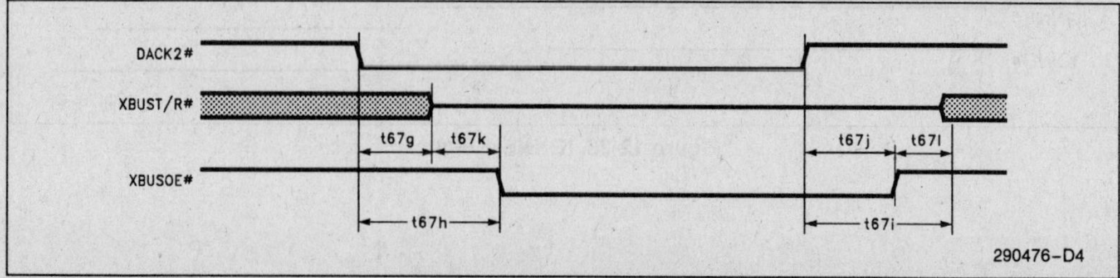

Figure 12-38. X-Bus Buffer Signals

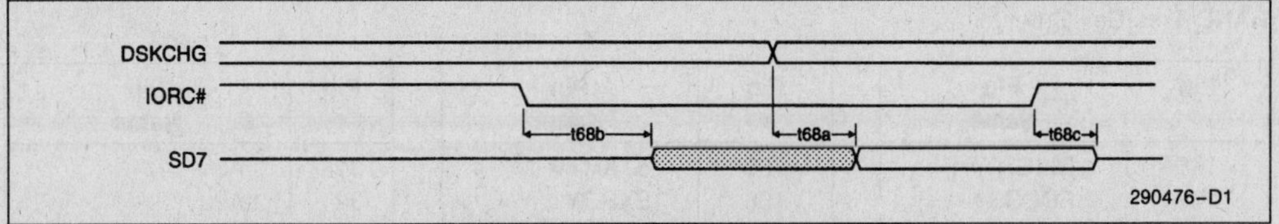

Figure 12-39. DSKCHG Signal

12.4 NAND Tree

A NAND Tree is provided primarily for V_{IL}/V_{IH} testing. The NAND Tree is also useful for Automated Test Equipment (ATE) at board level testing. The NAND Tree allows the tester to test the solder connections for each individual signal pin.

The TEST# pin, along with IRQ5 and IRQ3, activates the NAND Tree. Asserting TEST# causes the output pulse train to appear on the EISAHOLD pin. IRQ5 must be driven high in order to enable the NAND Tree. The assertion of IRQ3 causes the ESC to disable its buffers.

The sequence of the ATE test is as follows:

1. Drive TEST# low, IRQ3 high, and IRQ5 high.
2. Drive each pin that is a part of the NAND Tree high. Please note that not every pin is included in the tree. See the table below for details.
3. Starting at pin 165 (DLIGHT#) and continuing with pins 167, 168, etc., individually drive each pin low. Expect EISAHOLD to toggle after each corresponding input pin is toggled. The final pin in the tree is pin 100 (EISAHLDA). Not every pin is toggled in sequential order. Please refer to the table for tree ordering. When IRQ3 is driven low, the test mode is exited, and the ESC's buffers will be enabled.
4. Before enabling the ESC's buffers (via IRQ3), turn off tester drivers.
5. Reset the ESC prior to proceeding with further testing.

1

NAND Tree Cell Order:

Pin #	Pin Name
165	DLIGHT#[1]
167	FDCCS#
168	RTCWR#
169	RTCRD#
102	INTCHIP0
106	REFRESH#
107	NC
108	NC
109	NC
110	IOCHK#
111	RSTDRV
112	IRQ9
113	DREQ2
114	NOWS#
115	CHRDY
116	SMWTC#
121	SMRDC#
122	IOWC#
123	IORC#
125	DREQ3
127	DREQ1
135	IRQ7
136	IRQ6
141	BALE
142	OSC
143	SA1
144	SA0
145	M16#
146	SBHE#
147	IO16#
148	IRQ10
149	IRQ11
150	IRQ12
151	IRQ15
152	IRQ14
164	CRAMRD#
166	DSKCHG
171	ABFULL
179	CMD#

Pin #	Pin Name
180	START#
186	EXRDY
187	EX32#
188	EX16#
189	SLBURST#
190	EOP
191	SPKR
193	IRQ8#
194	IRQ13
195	IRQ1
197	DREQ0
198	MRDC#
200	MWTC#
201	DREQ5
203	DREQ6
205	DREQ7
206	MASTER16#
3	LA31#/CPG4
4	LA30#/CPG3
5	LA29#/CPG2
6	LA28#/CPG1
7	LA27#/CPG0
8	LA26#
10	LA25#
11	LA24#
12	LA16
13	LA15
15	LA14
16	LA13
17	LA12
19	LA11
20	LA10
21	LA9
22	LA8
23	LA7
24	LA6
28	LA5
29	LA4
30	LA23

Pin #	Pin Name
31	LA3
32	LA22
33	LA2
34	LA21
36	LA20
40	LA19
42	MREQ7#/PIRQ0#
43	LA18
44	MREQ6#/PIRQ1#
45	LA17
46	MREQ5#/PIRQ2#
47	MREQ4#/PIRQ3#
48	MREQ3#
49	MREQ2#
50	MREQ1#
50	MREQ0#
55	BE0#
56	BE1#
57	BE2#
58	BE3#
59	SD0
60	SD1
61	SD2
63	SD3
64	SD4
65	SD5
66	SD6
67	SD7
70	W/R#
71	M/IO#
72	MSBURST#
91	FERR#
95	RESET#
96	PERR#
97	SERR#
98	NMFLUSH#
99	PEREQ#/INTA#
138	IRQ4
139	IRQ3[2]
100	EISAHLDA[3]

NOTES:
1. First Pin in NAND Tree
2. Enables ESC's Buffers When "0"
3. Last Pin in NAND Tree

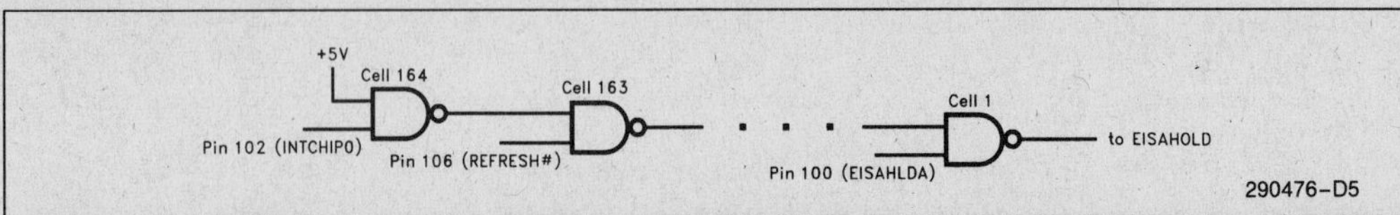

Figure 12-40. NAND Tree

13.0 PINOUT AND PACKAGE INFORMATION

The ESC package is a 208-pin plastic Quad flat pack (PQFP). The package signals are shown in Figure 13-1 and listed in Tables 13-1 and 13-2.

13.1 Pinout and Pin Assignment

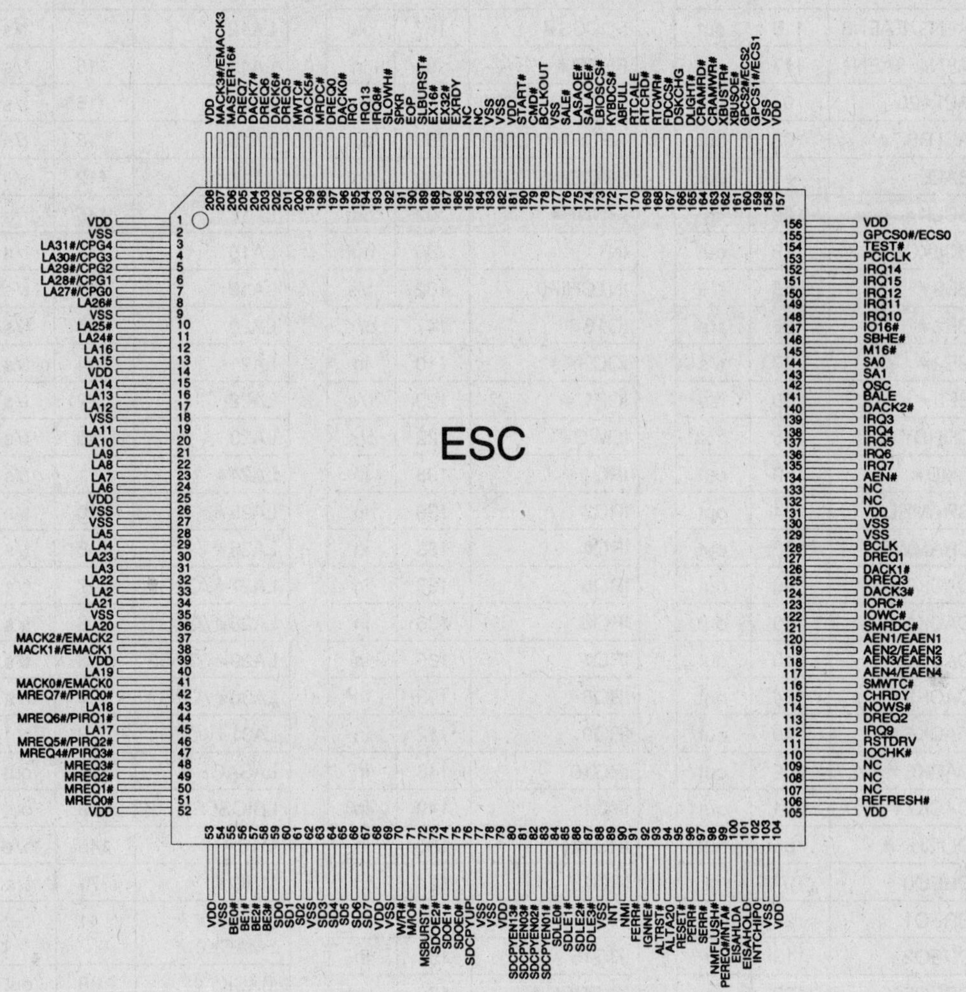

Figure 13-1. ESC Package Pinout

Table 13-1. ESC Alphabetical Pin Assignment

Name	Pin #	Type
ABFULL	171	in
AEN#	134	out
AEN1/EAEN1	120	out
AEN2/EAEN2	119	out
AEN3/EAEN3	118	out
AEN4/EAEN4	117	out
ALTA20	94	out
ALTRST#	93	out
BALE	141	out
BCLK	128	in
BCLKOUT	178	out
BE0#	55	t/s
BE1#	56	t/s
BE2#	57	t/s
BE3#	58	t/s
CHRDY	115	o/d
CMD#	179	out
CRAMRD#	164	out
CRAMWR#	163	out
DACK0#	196	out
DACK1#	126	out
DACK2#	140	out
DACK3#	124	out
DACK5#	199	out
DACK6#	202	out
DACK7#	204	out
DLIGHT#	165	out
DREQ0	197	in
DREQ1	127	in
DREQ2	113	in
DREQ3	125	in
DREQ5	201	in
DREQ6	203	in
DREQ7	205	in
DSKCHG	166	in
EISAHLDA	100	in
EISAHOLD	101	out
EOP	190	t/s
EX16#	188	o/d
EX32#	187	o/d
EXRDY	186	o/d
FDCCS#	167	out
FERR#	91	in
GPCS0#/ECS0	155	out
GPCS1#/ECS1	159	out
GPCS2#/ECS2	160	out
IGNNE#	92	out
INT	89	out
INTCHIP0	102	t/s
IO16#	147	o/d
IOCHK#	110	in
IORC#	123	t/s
IOWC#	122	t/s
IRQ1	195	in
IRQ3	139	in
IRQ4	138	in
IRQ5	137	in
IRQ6	136	in
IRQ7	135	in
IRQ8#	193	in
IRQ9	112	in
IRQ10	148	in
IRQ11	149	in
IRQ12	150	in
IRQ13	194	in
IRQ14	152	in
IRQ15	151	in
KYBDCS#	172	out
LA2	33	t/s
LA3	31	t/s
LA4	29	t/s
LA5	28	t/s
LA6	24	t/s
LA7	23	t/s
LA8	22	t/s
LA9	21	t/s
LA10	20	t/s
LA11	19	t/s
LA12	17	t/s
LA13	16	t/s
LA14	15	t/s
LA15	13	t/s
LA16	12	t/s
LA17	45	t/s
LA18	43	t/s
LA19	40	t/s
LA20	36	t/s
LA21	34	t/s
LA22	32	t/s
LA23	30	t/s
LA24#	11	t/s
LA25#	10	t/s
LA26#	8	t/s
LA27#/CPG0	7	t/s
LA28#/CPG1	6	t/s
LA29#/CPG2	5	t/s
LA30#/CPG3	4	t/s
LA31#/CPG4	3	t/s
LASAOE#	175	out
LBIOSCS#	173	out
M16#	145	o/d
M/IO#	71	t/s
MACK0#/ EMACK0	41	out
MACK1#/ EMACK1	38	out
MACK2#/ EMACK2	37	out
MACK3#/ EMACK3	207	out
MASTER16#	206	in

Table 13-1. ESC Alphabetical Pin Assignment (Continued)

Name	Pin #	Type
MRDC#	198	t/s
MREQ0#	51	in
MREQ1#	50	in
MREQ2#	49	in
MREQ3#	48	in
MREQ4#/ PIRQ3#	47	in
MREQ5#/ PIRQ2#	46	in
MREQ6#/ PIRQ1#	44	in
MREQ7#/ PIRQ0#	42	in
MSBURST#	72	t/s
MWTC#	200	t/s
NC	107	NC
NC	108	NC
NC	109	NC
NC	132	NC
NC	133	NC
NC	184	NC
NC	185	NC
NMFLUSH#	98	t/s
NMI	90	out
NOWS#	114	o/d
OSC	142	in
PCICLK	153	in
PEREQ#/INTA#	99	in
PERR#	96	in
REFRESH#	106	t/s
RESET#	95	in
RSTDRV	111	out
RTCALE	170	out
RTCRD#	169	out
RTCWR#	168	out
SA0	144	t/s

Name	Pin #	Type
SA1	143	t/s
SALAOE#	174	out
SALE#	176	out
SBHE#	146	t/s
SD0	59	t/s
SD1	60	t/s
SD2	61	t/s
SD3	63	t/s
SD4	64	t/s
SD5	65	t/s
SD6	66	t/s
SD7	67	t/s
SDCPYEN01#	83	out
SDCPYEN02#	82	out
SDCPYEN03#	81	out
SDCPYEN13#	80	out
SDCPYUP	76	out
SDLE0#	84	out
SDLE1#	85	out
SDLE2#	86	out
SDLE3#	87	out
SDOE0#	75	out
SDOE1#	74	out
SDOE2#	73	out
SERR#	97	in
SLBURST#	189	in
SLOWH#	192	out
SMRDC#	121	out
SMWTC#	116	out
SPKR	191	out
START#	180	t/s
TEST#	154	in
V_{DD}	1	V
V_{DD}	14	V
V_{DD}	25	V

Name	Pin #	Type
V_{DD}	39	V
V_{DD}	52	V
V_{DD}	53	V
V_{DD}	68	V
V_{DD}	79	V
V_{DD}	104	V
V_{DD}	105	V
V_{DD}	131	V
V_{DD}	156	V
V_{DD}	157	V
V_{DD}	181	V
V_{DD}	208	V
V_{SS}	2	V
V_{SS}	9	V
V_{SS}	18	V
V_{SS}	26	V
V_{SS}	27	V
V_{SS}	35	V
V_{SS}	54	V
V_{SS}	62	V
V_{SS}	69	V
V_{SS}	77	V
V_{SS}	78	V
V_{SS}	88	V
V_{SS}	103	V
V_{SS}	129	V
V_{SS}	130	V
V_{SS}	158	V
V_{SS}	177	V
V_{SS}	182	V
V_{SS}	183	V
W/R#	70	t/s
XBUSOE#	161	out
XBUSTR#	162	out

NOTE:
NC pins require individual pull-up resistors of 8K–10K.

1

Table 13-2. ESC Numerical Pin Assignment

Pin #	Name	Type
1	V_{DD}	V
2	V_{SS}	V
3	LA31#/CPG4	t/s
4	LA30#/CPG3	t/s
5	LA29#/CPG2	t/s
6	LA28#/CPG1	t/s
7	LA27#/CPG0	t/s
8	LA26#	t/s
9	V_{SS}	V
10	LA25#	t/s
11	LA24#	t/s
12	LA16	t/s
13	LA15	t/s
14	V_{DD}	V
15	LA14	t/s
16	LA13	t/s
17	LA12	t/s
18	V_{SS}	V
19	LA11	t/s
20	LA10	t/s
21	LA9	t/s
22	LA8	t/s
23	LA7	t/s
24	LA6	t/s
25	V_{DD}	V
26	V_{SS}	V
27	V_{SS}	V
28	LA5	t/s
29	LA4	t/s
30	LA23	t/s
31	LA3	t/s
32	LA22	t/s
33	LA2	t/s
34	LA21	t/s
35	V_{SS}	V
36	LA20	t/s

Pin #	Name	Type
37	MACK2#/ EMACK2	out
38	MACK1#/ EMACK1	out
39	V_{DD}	V
40	LA19	t/s
41	MACK0#/ EMACK0	out
42	MREQ7#/ PIRQ0#	in
43	LA18	t/s
44	MREQ6#/ PIRQ1#	in
45	LA17	t/s
46	MREQ5#/ PIRQ2#	in
47	MREQ4#/ PIRQ3#	in
48	MREQ3#	in
49	MREQ2#	in
50	MREQ1#	in
51	MREQ0#	in
52	V_{DD}	V
53	V_{DD}	V
54	V_{SS}	V
55	BE0#	t/s
56	BE1#	t/s
57	BE2#	t/s
58	BE3#	t/s
59	SD0	t/s
60	SD1	t/s
61	SD2	t/s
62	V_{SS}	V
63	SD3	t/s
64	SD4	t/s
65	SD5	t/s
66	SD6	t/s
67	SD7	t/s

Pin #	Name	Type
68	V_{DD}	V
69	V_{SS}	V
70	W/R#	t/s
71	M/IO#	t/s
72	MSBURST#	t/s
73	SDOE2#	out
74	SDOE1#	out
75	SDOE0#	out
76	SDCPYUP	out
77	V_{SS}	V
78	V_{SS}	V
79	V_{DD}	V
80	SDCPYEN13#	out
81	SDCPYEN03#	out
82	SDCPYEN02#	out
83	SDCPYEN01#	out
84	SDLE0#	out
85	SDLE1#	out
86	SDLE2#	out
87	SDLE3#	out
88	V_{SS}	V
89	INT	out
90	NMI	out
91	FERR#	in
92	IGNNE#	out
93	ALTRST#	out
94	ALTA20	out
95	RESET#	in
96	PERR#	in
97	SERR#	in
98	NMFLUSH#	t/s
99	PEREQ#/ INTA#	in
100	EISAHLDA	in
101	EISAHOLD	out
102	INTCHIP0	t/s

NOTE:
NC pins require individual pull-up resistors of 8K–10K.

Table 13-2. ESC Numerical Pin Assignment (Continued)

Pin #	Name	Type
103	V_{SS}	V
104	V_{DD}	V
105	V_{DD}	V
106	REERESH#	t/s
107	NC	NC
108	NC	NC
109	NC	NC
110	IOCHK#	in
111	RSTDRV	out
112	IRQ9	in
113	DREQ2	in
114	NOWS#	o/d
115	CHRDY	o/d
116	SMWTC#	out
117	AEN4/EAEN4	out
118	AEN3/EAEN3	out
119	AEN2/EAEN2	out
120	AEN1/EAEN1	out
121	SMRDC#	out
122	IOWC#	t/s
123	IORC#	t/s
124	DACK3#	out
125	DREQ3	in
126	DACK1#	out
127	DREQ1	in
128	BCLK	in
129	V_{SS}	V
130	V_{SS}	V
131	V_{DD}	V
132	NC	NC
133	NC	NC
134	AEN#	out
135	IRQ7	in
136	IRQ6	in
137	IRQ5	in
138	IRQ4	in
139	IRQ3	in
140	DACK2#	out
141	BALE	out
142	OSC	in
143	SA1	t/s
144	SA0	t/s
145	M16#	o/d
146	SBHE#	t/s
147	IO16#	o/d
148	IRQ10	in
149	IRQ11	in
150	IRQ12	in
151	IRQ15	in
152	IRQ14	in
153	PCICLK	in
154	TEST#	in
155	GPCS0#/ECS0	out
156	V_{DD}	V
157	V_{DD}	V
158	V_{SS}	V
159	GPCS1#/ECS1	out
160	GPCS2#/ECS2	out
161	XBUSOE#	out
162	XBUSTR#	out
163	CRAMWR#	out
164	CRAMRD#	out
165	DLIGHT#	out
166	DSKCHG	in
167	FDCCS#	out
168	RTCWR#	out
169	RTCRD#	out
170	RTCALE	out
171	ABFULL	in
172	KYBDCS#	out
173	LBIOSCS#	out
174	SALAOE#	out
175	LASAOE#	out
176	SALE#	out
177	V_{SS}	V
178	BCLKOUT	out
179	CMD#	out
180	START#	t/s
181	V_{DD}	V
182	V_{SS}	V
183	V_{SS}	V
184	NC	NC
185	NC	NC
186	EXRDY	o/d
187	EX32#	o/d
188	EX16#	o/d
189	SLBURST#	in
190	EOP	t/s
191	SPKR	out
192	SLOWH#	out
193	IRQ8#	in
194	IRQ13	in
195	IRQ1	in
196	DACK0#	out
197	DREQ0	in
198	MRDC#	t/s
199	DACK5#	out
200	MWTC#	t/s
201	DREQ5	in
202	DACK6#	out
203	DREQ6	in
204	DACK7#	out
205	DREQ7	in
206	MASTER16#	in
207	MACK3#/ EMACK3	out
208	V_{DD}	V

13.2 Package Characteristics

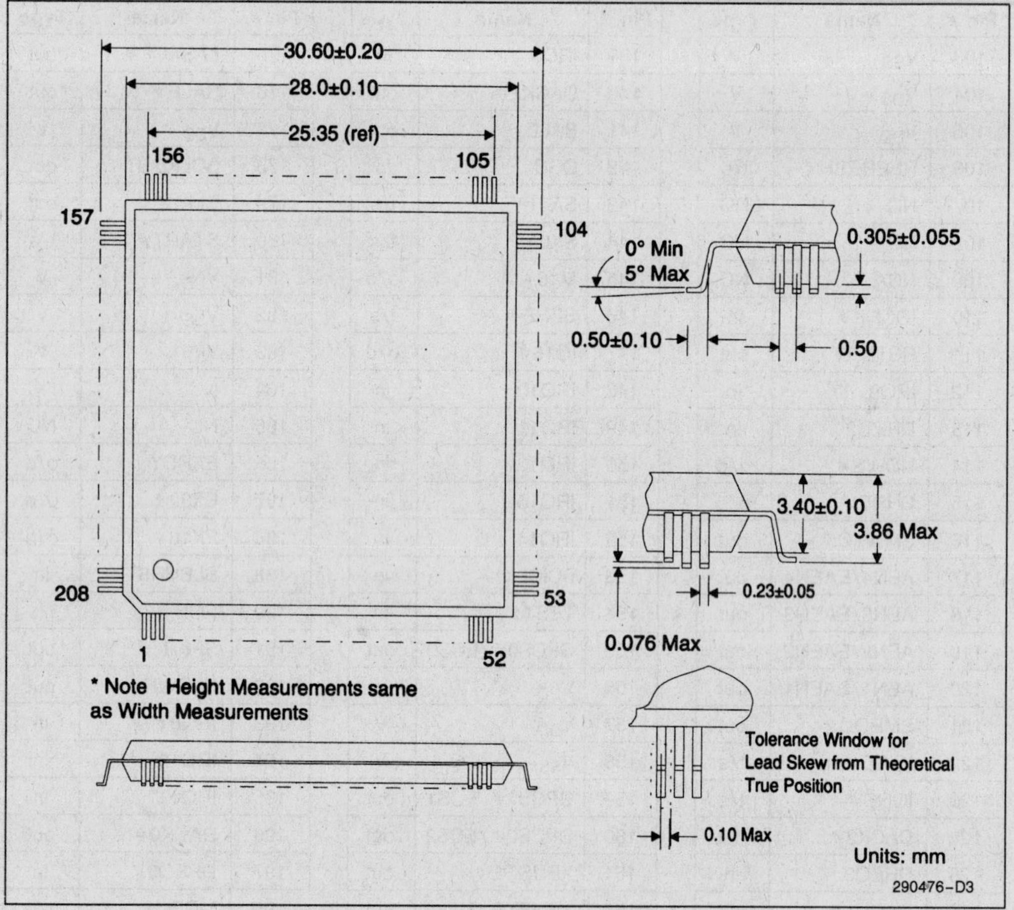

30.60±0.20
28.0±0.10
25.35 (ref)
156
105
157
104
208
53
1
52
* Note Height Measurements same as Width Measurements
0° Min
5° Max
0.305±0.055
0.50±0.10
0.50
3.40±0.10
3.86 Max
0.23±0.05
0.076 Max
Tolerance Window for Lead Skew from Theoretical True Position
0.10 Max
Units: mm
290476–D3

Figure 13-2. Packaging Dimension Information

14.0 REVISION HISTORY

The following list represents the key differences between version -001 and -002 of the 82374EB EISA System Component (ESC) data sheet.

Section 2.6 The external pull-up resistor requirement was added to SLOWH# signal description.

Section 2.9.5 The RTCRD#, RTCWR# signal descriptions were modified.

Section 2.9.6 The FDCCS#, DLIGHT# signal descriptions were modified.

Section 2.9.8 The XBUST/R#, XBUSOE# signal descriptions were modified.

Section 2.10 The external pull-up resistor requirement was added for all pins designated as NC (no-connect).

Section 3.1.3 The Mode Select Register was redefined. Option for routing PIRQ[3:0]# to unused X-Bus signals added.

Section 3.1.7 The Peripheral Chip Select A register description was modified. Previously reserved bit 6 defined as Keyboard Controller Mapping.

Section 6.6 The method for accomplishing block mode Scatter-Gather transfers was added.

Section 12.3.2 The AC Specifications were modified and added.

Section 12.4 NAND Tree information added.

82375EB
PCI-EISA Bridge (PCEB)

- **Provides the Bridge Between the PCI Bus and EISA Bus**
- **100% PCI and EISA Compatible**
  - **PCI and EISA Master/Slave Interface**
  - **Directly Drives 10 PCI Loads and 8 EISA Slots**
  - **Supports PCI at 25 MHz to 33 MHz**
- **Data Buffers Improve Performance**
  - **Four 32-bit PCI-to-EISA Posted Write Buffers**
  - **Four 16-byte EISA-to-PCI Read/Write Line Buffers**
  - **EISA-to-PCI Read Prefetch**
  - **EISA-to-PCI and PCI-to-EISA Write Posting**
- **Data Buffer Management Ensures Data Coherency**
  - **Flush Posted Write Buffers**
  - **Flush or Invalidate Line Buffers**
  - **System-Wide Data Buffer Coherency Control**
- **Burst Transfers on both the PCI and EISA Busses**
- **32-Bit Data Paths**
- **Integrated EISA Data Swap Buffers**
- **Arbitration for PCI Devices**
  - **Supports Six PCI Masters**
  - **Fixed, Rotating, or a Combination of the Two**
- **PCI and EISA Address Decoding and Mapping**
  - **Positive Decode of Main Memory Areas (MEMCS# Generation)**
  - **Four Programmable PCI Memory Space Regions**
  - **Four Programmable PCI I/O Space Regions**
- **Programmable Main Memory Address Decoding**
  - **Main Memory Sizes Up To 512 MBytes**
  - **Access Attributes for 15 Memory Segments in First 1 MByte of Main Memory**
  - **Programmable Main Memory Hole**
- **Integrated 16-bit BIOS Timer**

1

The 82375EB PCI-EISA Bridge (PCEB) provides the master/slave functions on both the Peripheral Component Interconnect (PCI) Bus and the EISA Bus. Functioning as a bridge between the PCI and EISA buses, the PCEB provides the address and data paths, bus controls, and bus protocol translation for PCI-to-EISA and EISA-to-PCI transfers. Extensive data buffering in both directions increases system performance by maximizing PCI and EISA Bus efficiency and allowing concurrency on the two buses. The PCEB's buffer management mechanism ensures data coherency. The PCEB integrates central bus control functions including a programmable bus arbiter for the PCI Bus and EISA data swap buffers for the EISA Bus. Integrated system functions include PCI parity generation, system error reporting, and programmable PCI and EISA memory and I/O address space mapping and decoding. The PCEB also contains a BIOS Timer that can be used to implement timing loops. The PCEB is intended to be used with the EISA System Component (ESC) to provide an EISA I/O subsystem interface.

October 1993
Order Number: 290477-002

82375EB PCI-EISA BRIDGE (PCEB)

CONTENTS PAGE

CONTENTS PAGE

CONTENTS PAGE

CONTENTS PAGE

1

CONTENTS

CONTENTS

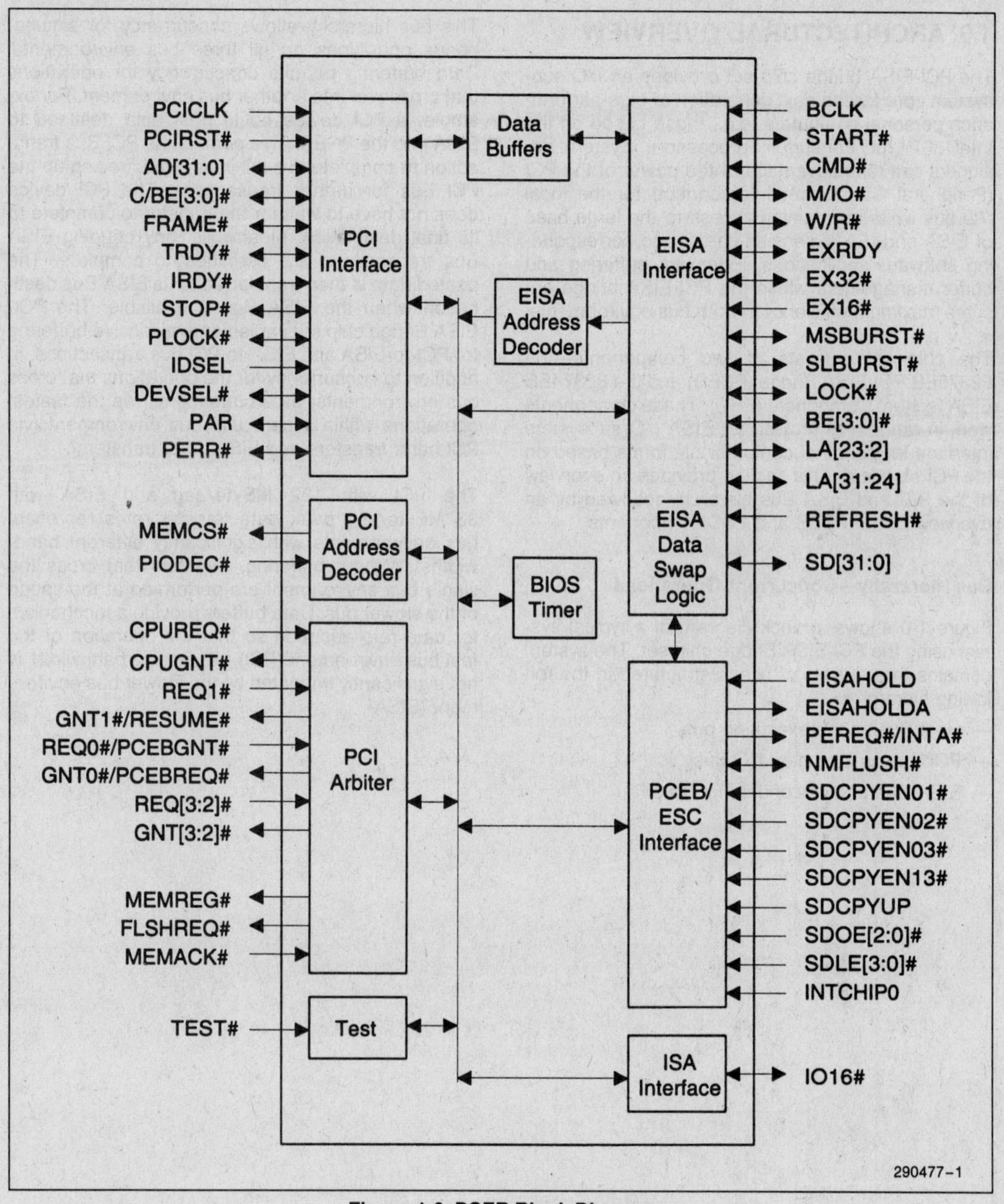

Figure 1-0. PCEB Block Diagram

1

1.0 ARCHITECTURAL OVERVIEW

The PCI-EISA bridge chip set provides an I/O subsystem core for the next generation of high-performance personal computers (e.g., those based on the Intel486™ or Pentium™ processor). System designers can take advantage of the power of the PCI (Peripheral Component Interconnect) for the local I/O bus while maintaining access to the large base of EISA and ISA expansion cards, and corresponding software applications. Extensive buffering and buffer management within the PCI-EISA bridge ensures maximum efficiency in both bus environments.

The chip set consists of two components—the 82375EB PCI-EISA Bridge (PCEB) and the 82374EB EISA System Component (ESC). These components work in tandem to provide an EISA I/O subsystem interface for personal computer platforms based on the PCI standard. This section provides an overview of the PCI and EISA Bus hierarchy followed by an overview of the PCEB and ESC components.

Bus Hierarchy—Concurrent Operations

Figure 1-0 shows a block diagram of a typical system using the PCI-EISA Bridge chip set. The system contains three levels of buses structured in the following hierarchy:

— Host Bus as the execution bus

— PCI Bus as a primary I/O bus

— EISA Bus as a secondary I/O bus

This bus hierarchy allows concurrency for simultaneous operations on all three bus environments. Data buffering permits concurrency for operations that crossover into another bus environment. For example, a PCI device could post data destined to EISA into the PCEB. This permits the PCI Bus transaction to complete in a minimum time, freeing up the PCI Bus for further transactions. The PCI device does not have to wait for the transfer to complete to its final destination. Meanwhile, any ongoing EISA Bus transactions are permitted to complete. The posted data is then transferred to its EISA Bus destination when the EISA Bus is available. The PCI-EISA Bridge chip set implements extensive buffering for PCI-to-EISA and EISA-to-PCI bus transactions. In addition to concurrency for the operations that cross bus environments, data buffering allows the fastest operations within a particular bus environment (via PCI burst transfers and EISA burst transfers).

The PCI with 132 MByte/sec and EISA with 33 MByte/sec peak data transfer rates represent bus environments with significantly different bandwidths. Without buffering, transfers that cross the single bus environment are performed at the speed of the slower bus. Data buffers provide a mechanism for data rate adoption so that the operation of the fast bus environment (PCI), i.e., usable bandwidth, is not significantly impacted by the slower bus environment (EISA).

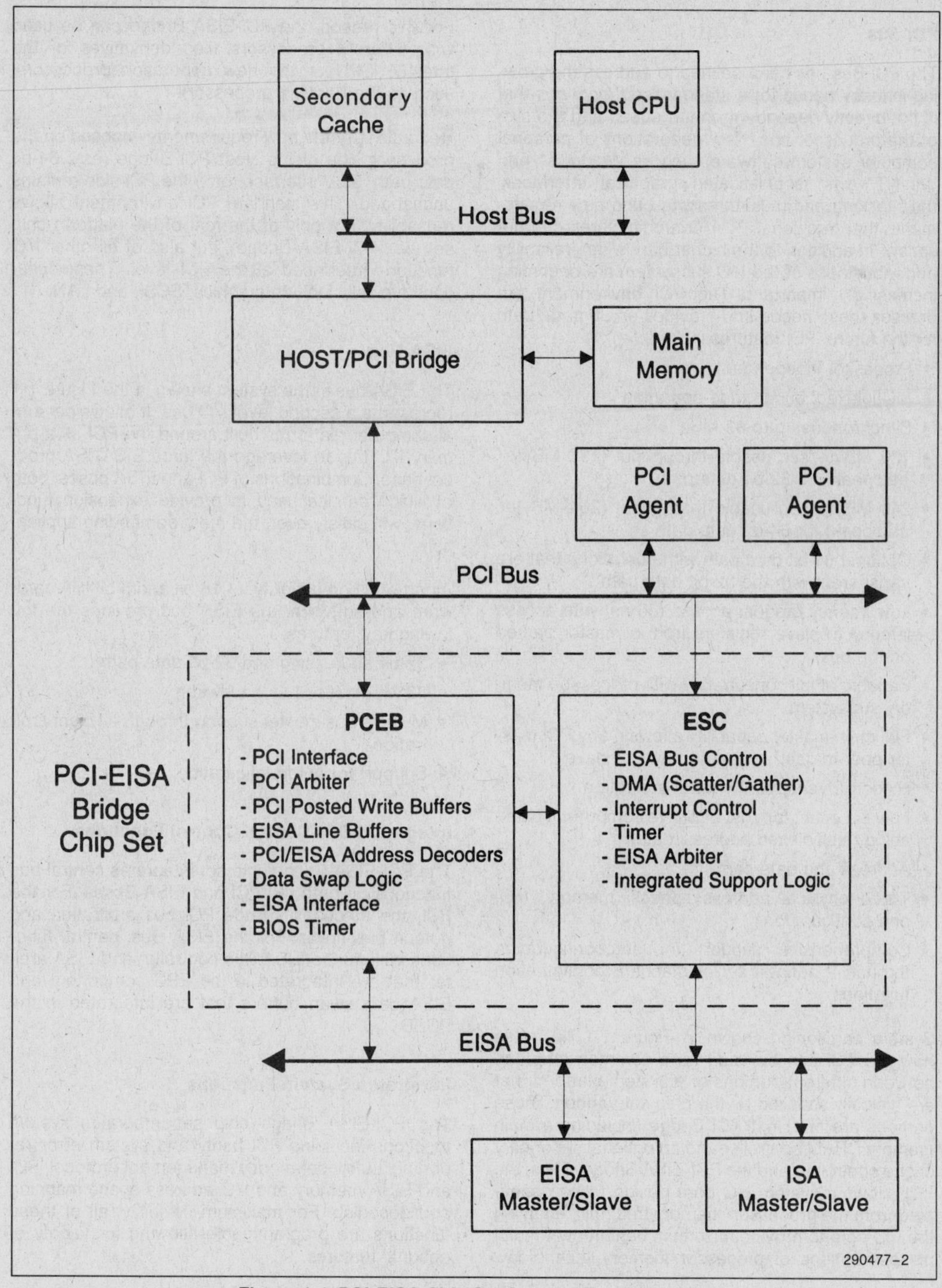

1

Secondary Cache

Host CPU

Host Bus

HOST/PCI Bridge

Main Memory

PCI Agent

PCI Agent

PCI Bus

PCI-EISA Bridge Chip Set

PCEB
- PCI Interface
- PCI Arbiter
- PCI Posted Write Buffers
- EISA Line Buffers
- PCI/EISA Address Decoders
- Data Swap Logic
- EISA Interface
- BIOS Timer

ESC
- EISA Bus Control
- DMA (Scatter/Gather)
- Interrupt Control
- Timer
- EISA Arbiter
- Integrated Support Logic

EISA Bus

EISA Master/Slave

ISA Master/Slave

290477–2

Figure 1-1. PCI-EISA Chip Set System Block Diagram

PCI Bus

The PCI Bus has been defined to address the growing industry needs for a standardized *local bus* that is not directly dependent on the speed and the size of the processor bus. New generations of personal computer system software such as Windows* and Win-NT* with sophisticated graphical interfaces, multi-tasking and multi-threading bring new requirements that traditional PC I/O architectures can not satisfy. In addition to the higher bandwidth, reliability and robustness of the I/O subsystem are becoming increasingly important. The PCI environment addresses these needs and provides an upgrade path for the future. PCI features include:

- Processor independent
- Multiplexed, burst mode operation
- Synchronous up to 33 MHz
- 120 MByte/sec usable throughput (132 MByte/sec peak) for 32-bit data path
- 240 MByte/sec usable throughput (264 MByte/sec peak) for 64-bit data path
- Optional 64-bit data path with operations that are transparent with the 32-bit data path
- Low latency random access (60 ns write access latency to slave registers from a master parked on the bus)
- Capable of full concurrency with processor/memory subsystem
- Full multi-master capability allowing any PCI master peer-to-peer access to any PCI slave
- Hidden (overlapped) central arbitration
- Low pin count for cost effective component packaging (multiplexed address/data)
- Address and data parity
- Three physical address spaces: memory, I/O, and configuration
- Comprehensive support for autoconfiguration through a defined set of standard configuration functions

System partitioning shown in Figure 1-1 illustrates how the PCI can be used as a common interface between different portions of a system platform that are typically supplied by the chip set vendor. These portions are the Host/PCI Bridge (including a main memory DRAM controller and an optional secondary cache controller) and the PCI-EISA Bridge. Thus, the PCI allows a system I/O core design to be decoupled from the processor/memory treadmill, enabling the I/O core to provide maximum benefit over multiple generations of processor/memory technology. For this reason, the PCI-EISA Bridge can be used with different processors (i.e., derivatives of the Intel486 CPU or the new generation processors, such as the Pentium processor).

Regardless of the new requirements imposed on the processor side of the Host/PCI Bridge (e.g., 64-bit data path, 3.3V interface, etc.) the PCI side remains unchanged. This standard PCI environment allows reusability, not only of the rest of the platform chip set (i.e., PCI-EISA Bridge), but also of all other I/O functions interfaced at the PCI level. These functions typically include graphics, SCSI, and LAN.

EISA Bus

The EISA bus in the system shown in the Figure 1-1 represents a second level I/O bus. It allows personal computer platforms built around the PCI as a primary I/O bus to leverage the large EISA/ISA product base. Combinations of PCI and EISA buses, both of which can be used to provide expansion functions, will satisfy even the most demanding applications.

Along with compatibility for 16-bit and 8-bit ISA hardware and software, the EISA bus provides the following key features:

- 32-bit addressing and 32-bit data path
- 33 MByte/sec bus bandwidth
- Multiple bus master support through efficient arbitration
- Support for autoconfiguration

Integrated Bus Central Control Functions

The PCI-EISA Bridge chip set integrates central bus functions on both the PCI and EISA Buses. For the PCI, the functions include PCI bus arbitration and default bus driver. For the EISA Bus, central functions include the EISA Bus controller and EISA arbiter that are integrated in the ESC component and EISA data swap buffers that are integrated in the PCEB.

Integrated System Functions

The PCI-EISA Bridge chip set integrates system functions including PCI parity and system error reporting, buffer coherency management protocol, PCI and EISA memory and I/O address space mapping and decoding. For maximum flexibility, all of these functions are programmable allowing for variety of optional features.

1.1 PCEB Overview

The PCEB and ESC form a PCI-EISA Bridge chip set. The PCEB/ESC interface provides the inter-chip communications between these two devices. The major functions provided by the PCEB are described in this section.

PCI Bus Interface

The PCEB can be either a master or slave on the PCI Bus and supports bus frequencies from 25 MHz to 33 MHz. For PCI-initiated transfers, the PCEB can only be a slave. The PCEB becomes a slave when it positively decodes the cycle. The PCEB also becomes a slave for unclaimed cycles on the PCI Bus. These unclaimed cycles are either negatively or subtractively decoded by the PCEB and forwarded to the EISA Bus.

As a slave, the PCEB supports single cycle transfers for memory, I/O, and configuration operations and burst cycles for memory operations. Note that burst transfers cannot be performed to the PCEB's internal registers. Burst memory write cycles to the EISA Bus can transfer up to four Dwords, depending on available space in the PCEB's Posted Write Buffers. When space is no longer available in the buffers, the PCEB terminates the transaction. This supports the Incremental Latency Mechanism as defined in the PCI Specification. Note that, if the Posted Write Buffers are disabled, PCI burst operations are not performed and all transfers are single cycle.

For EISA-initiated transfers to the PCI Bus, the PCEB is a PCI master. The PCEB permits EISA devices to access either PCI memory or I/O. While all PCI I/O transfers are single cycle, PCI memory cycles can be either single cycle or burst, depending on the status of the PCEB's Line Buffers. During EISA reads of PCI memory, the PCEB uses a burst read cycle of four Dwords to prefetch data into a Line Buffer. During EISA-to-PCI memory writes, the PCEB uses PCI burst cycles to flush the Line Buffers. The PCEB contains a programmable Master Latency Timer that provides the PCEB with a guaranteed time slice on the PCI Bus, after which it surrenders the bus.

As a master on the PCI Bus, the PCEB generates address and command signal (C/BE#) parity for read and write cycles, and data parity for write cycles. As a slave, the PCEB generates data parity for read cycles. Parity checking is not supported.

The PCEB, as a resource, can be locked by any PCI master. In the context of locked cycles, the entire PCEB subsystem (including the EISA Bus) is considered a single resource.

PCI Bus Arbitration

The PCI arbiter supports six PCI masters—The Host/PCI bridge, PCEB, and four other PCI masters. The arbiter can be programmed for twenty-four fixed priority schemes, a rotating scheme, or a combination of the fixed and rotating schemes. The arbiter can be programmed for bus parking that permits the Host/PCI Bridge default access to the PCI Bus when no other device is requesting service. The arbiter also contains an efficient PCI retry mechanism to minimize PCI Bus thrashing when the PCEB generates a retry. The arbiter can be disabled, if an external arbiter is used.

EISA Bus Interface

The PCEB contains a fully EISA-compatible master and slave interface. The PCEB directly drives eight EISA slots without external data or address buffering. The PCEB is only a master or slave on the EISA Bus for transfers between the EISA Bus and PCI Bus. For transfers contained to the EISA Bus, the PCEB is never a master or slave. However, the data swap buffers contained in the PCEB is involved in these transfers, if data size translation is needed. The PCEB also provides support for I/O recovery.

EISA/ISA masters and DMA can access PCI memory or I/O. The PCEB only forwards EISA cycles to the PCI Bus if the address of the transfer matches one of the address ranges programmed into the PCEB for EISA-to-PCI positive decode. This includes the main memory segments used for generating MEMCS# from the EISA Bus, one of the four programmable memory regions, or one of the four programmable I/O regions. For EISA-initiated accesses to the PCI Bus, the PCEB is a slave on the EISA Bus. I/O accesses are always non-buffered and memory accesses can be either non-buffered or buffered via the Line Buffers. For buffered accesses, burst cycles are supported.

During PCI-initiated cycles to the EISA Bus, the PCEB is an EISA master. For memory write operations through the Posted Write Buffers, the PCEB uses EISA burst transfers, if supported by the slave, to flush the buffers. Otherwise, single cycle transfers are used. Single cycle transfers are used for all I/O cycles and memory reads.

PCI/EISA Address Decoding

The PCEB contains two address decoders—one to decode PCI-initiated cycles and the other to decode EISA-initiated cycles. The two decoders permit the PCI and EISA Buses to operate concurrently.

The PCEB can also be programmed to provide main memory address decoding on behalf of the Host/PCI bridge. When programmed, the PCEB monitors the PCI and EISA bus cycle addresses, and generates a memory chip select signal (MEMCS#) indicating that the current cycle is targeted to main memory residing behind the Host/PCI bridge. Programmable features include, read/write attributes for specific memory segments and the enabling/disabling of a memory hole. If not used, the MEMCS# feature can be disabled.

In addition to the main memory address decoding, there are four programmable memory regions and four programmable I/O regions for EISA-initiated cycles. EISA/ISA master or DMA accesses to one of these regions are forwarded to the PCI Bus.

Data Buffering

To isolate the slower EISA Bus from the PCI Bus, the PCEB provides two types of data buffers. Buffer management control guarantees data coherency.

Four Dword wide Posted Write Buffers permit posting of PCI-initiated memory write cycles to the EISA Bus. For EISA-initiated cycles to the PCI Bus, there are four 16-byte wide Line Buffers. The Line Buffers permit prefetching of read data from PCI memory and posting of data being written to PCI memory.

By using burst transactions to fill or flush these buffers, when appropriate, the PCEB maximizes bus efficiency. For example, an EISA device could fill a Line Buffer with byte, word, or Dword transfers and the PCEB would use a PCI burst cycle to flush the filled line to PCI memory.

BIOS Timer

The PCEB has a 16-bit BIOS Timer. The timer can be used by BIOS software to implement timing loops. The timer count rate is derived from the EISA clock (BCLK) and has an accuracy of ±1 μs.

1.2 ESC Overview

The PCEB and ESC form a PCI-EISA bridge. The PCEB/ESC interface provides the inter-chip communications between these two devices. The major functions provided by the ESC are described in this section.

EISA Controller

The ESC incorporates a 32-bit master and an 8-bit slave. The ESC directly drives eight EISA slots without external data or address buffering. EISA system clock (BCLK) generation is integrated by dividing the PCI clock (divide by 3 or divide by 4) and wait state generation is provided. The AENx and MACKx signals provide a direct interface to four EISA slots and supports eight EISA slots with encoded AENx and MACKx signals.

The ESC contains an 8-bit data bus (lower 8 bits of the EISA data bus) that is used to program the ESC's internal registers. Note that for transfers between the PCI and EISA Buses, the PCEB provides the data path. Thus, the ESC does not require a full 32-bit data bus. A full 32-bit address bus is provided and is used during refresh cycles and for DMA operations.

The ESC performs cycle translation between the EISA Bus and ISA Bus. For mis-matched master/slave combinations, the ESC controls the data swap buffers that are located in the PCEB. This control is provided through the PCEB/ESC interface.

DMA Controller

The ESC incorporates the functionality of two 82C37 DMA controllers with eight independently programmable channels. Each channel can be programmed for 8-bit, 16-bit, or 32-bit DMA device size, and ISA-compatible, type "A", type "B", or type "C" timings. Full 32-bit addressing is provided. The DMA controller is also responsible for generating refresh cycles.

The DMA controller supports an enhanced feature called scatter/gather. This feature provides the capability of transferring multiple buffers between memory and I/O without CPU intervention. In scatter/gather mode, the DMA can read the memory address and word count from an array of buffer descriptors, located in main memory, called the scatter/gather descriptor (SGD) table. This allows the DMA controller to sustain DMA transfers until all of the buffers in the SGD table are handled.

Interrupt Controller

The ESC contains an EISA compatible interrupt controller that incorporates the functionality of two 82C59 Interrupt Controllers. The two interrupt controllers are cascaded providing 14 external and two internal interrupts.

Timer/Counter

The ESC provides two 82C54 compatible timers (Timer 1 and Timer 2). The counters in Timer 1 support the system timer interrupt (IRQ0#), refresh request, and a speaker tone output (SPKR). The counters in Timer 2 support fail-safe time-out functions and the CPU speed control.

Integrated Support Logic

To minimize the chip count for board designs, the ESC incorporates a number of extended features. The ESC provides support for ALTA20 (Fast A20GATE) and ALTRST with I/O Port 92h. The ESC generates the control signals for SA address buffers and X-Bus buffer. The ESC also provides chip selects for BIOS, the keyboard controller, the floppy disk controller, and three general purpose devices. Support for generating chip selects with an external decoder is provided for IDE, a parallel port, and a serial port. The ESC provides support for a PC/AT compatible coprocessor interface and IRQ13 generation.

2.0 SIGNAL DESCRIPTION

This section provides a detailed description of each signal. The signals are arranged in functional groups according to their associated interface.

The "#" symbol at the end of a signal name indicates that the active, or asserted state occurs when the signal is at a low voltage level. When "#" is not present after the signal name, the signal is asserted when at the high voltage level.

The terms assertion and negation are used extensively. This is done to avoid confusion when working with a mixture of "active-low" and "active-high" signals. The term **assert**, or **assertion** indicates that a signal is active, independent of whether that level is represented by a high or low voltage. The term **negate,** or **negation** indicates that a signal is inactive.

The following notations are used to describe the signal type.

in Input is a standard input-only signal.

out Totem Pole output is a standard active driver.

s/o/d Sustained Open Drain input/output

t/s Tri-State is a bi-directional, tri-state input/output pin.

s/t/s Sustained Tri-State is an active low tri-state signal owned and driven by one and only one agent at a time. The agent that drives a s/t/s pin low must drive it high for at least one clock before letting it float. A new agent can not start driving a s/t/s signal any sooner than one clock after the previous owner tri-states it. An external pull-up is required to sustain the inactive state until another agent drives it and must be provided by the central resource.

2.1 PCI Bus Interface Signals

Pin Name	Type	Description
PCICLK	in	**PCI CLOCK:** PCICLK provides timing for all transactions on the PCI Bus. All other PCI signals are sampled on the rising edge of PCICLK and all timing parameters are defined with respect to this edge. Frequencies supported by the PCEB range from 25 MHz to 33 MHz.
PCIRST#	in	**PCI RESET:** PCIRST# forces the PCEB into a known state. All t/s and s/t/s signals are forced to a high impedance state, and the s/o/d signals are allowed to float high. The PCEB negates all GNT# lines to the PCI Bus and the PCEB negates its internal request. The PCEB drives AD[31:0], C/BE[3:0]#, and PAR during reset to keep these signals from floating (depending on the state of CPUREQ# and REQ1#—as described in the following paragraph). As long as PCIRST# is asserted and CPUREQ# is high, the PCEB drives the AD[31:0] signals to keep them from floating. If CPUREQ# is low and REQ1# is low, the PCEB does not drive AD[31:0] while PCIRST# is asserted. If CPUREQ# is low and REQ1# is high, the PCEB drives AD[31:0] while PCIRST# is asserted. All PCEB registers are set to their default values. PCIRST# may be asynchronous to PCICLK when asserted or negated. Although asynchronous, the negation of PCIRST# must be a clean, bounce-free edge. PCIRST# must be asserted for a minimum 1 ms, and PCICLK must be active during the last 100 μs of the PCIRST# pulse.
AD[31:0]	t/s	**ADDRESS AND DATA:** AD[31:0] is a multiplexed address and data bus. During the first clock of a transaction, AD[31:0] contain a physical address. During subsequent clocks, AD[31:0] contain data. A PCEB bus transaction consists of an address phase followed by one or more data phases. Little-endian byte ordering is used. AD[7:0] define the least significant byte (LSB) and AD[31:24] the most significant byte (MSB). The information contained in the two low order address bits varies by address space. In the I/O address space, AD[1:0] are used to provide full byte address. In the memory and configuration address space, AD[1:0] are driven "00" during the address phase. The other three encodings are reserved. See Section 5.0, PCI Interface for more details. When the PCEB is a target, AD[31:0] are inputs during the address phase of a transaction. During the following data phase(s), the PCEB may be asked to supply data on AD[31:0] as for a PCI read, or accept data as for a PCI write. As an Initiator, the PCEB drives a valid address on AD[31:0] (with exceptions related to AD[1:0]) during the address phase, and drives write or latches read data on AD[31:0] during the data phase. As long as PCIRST# is asserted and CPUREQ# is high, the PCEB drives the AD[31:0] signals to keep them from floating. If CPUREQ# is low and REQ1# is low, the PCEB does not drive AD[31:0] while PCIRST# is asserted. If CPUREQ# is low and REQ1# is high, the PCEB drives AD[31:0] while PCIRST# is asserted. When the internal arbiter is enabled (CPUREQ# sampled high at the time when PCIRST# is negated), the PCEB acts as the central resource responsible for driving the AD[31:0] signals when no one is granted the PCI Bus and the bus is idle. When the internal arbiter is disabled, the PCEB does not drive AD[31:0] as the central resource. The PCEB is always responsible for driving AD[31:0] when it is granted the bus (PCEBGNT# and idle bus) and as appropriate when it participates in bus transactions. During reset, these signals are tri-stated.

2.1 PCI Bus Interface Signals (Continued)

Pin Name	Type	Description
C/BE[3:0]#	t/s	**BUS COMMAND AND BYTE ENABLES:** The command and byte enable signals are multiplexed on the same PCI pins. During the address phase of a transaction, C/BE[3:0]# define the bus command for bus command definitions. During the data phase, C/BE[3:0]# are used as Byte Enables. The Byte Enables determine which byte lanes carry meaningful data. C/BE[0]# applies to byte 0 and C/BE[3]# to byte 3. C/BE[3:0]# are not used for address decoding. The PCEB drives C/BE[3:0]# as an initiator of a PCI Bus cycle and monitors C/BE[3:0]# as a target. As long as PCIRST# is asserted and CPUREQ# is high, the PCEB drives C/BE[3:0]# to keep them from floating. If CPUREQ# is low and REQ1# is low, the PCEB does not drive C/BE[3:0]# while PCIRST# is asserted. If CPUREQ# is low and REQ1# is high, the PCEB drives C/BE[3:0]# while PCIRST# is asserted. When the internal arbiter is enabled (CPUREQ# sampled high at the time when PCIRST# is negated), the PCEB acts as the central resource responsible for driving the C/BE[3:0]# signals when no device is granted the PCI Bus and the bus is idle. When the internal arbiter is disabled, the PCEB does not drive C/BE[3:0]# as the central resource. The PCEB is always responsible for driving C/BE[3:0]# when it is granted the bus (PCEBGNT# and idle bus) and as appropriate when it is the master of a transaction. During reset, these signals are tri-stated.
FRAME#	s/t/s	**FRAME:** FRAME# is driven by the current initiator to indicate the beginning and duration of an access. FRAME# is asserted to indicate that a bus transaction is beginning. During a transaction, data transfers continue while FRAME# is asserted. When FRAME# is negated, the transaction is in the final data phase. FRAME# is an input when the PCEB is the target. FRAME# is an output when the PCEB is the initiator. During reset, these signals are tri-stated.
TRDY#	s/t/s	**TARGET READY:** TRDY#, as an output, indicates the PCEB target's ability to complete the current data phase of the transaction. TRDY# is used in conjunction with IRDY#. A data phase is completed on any clock that both TRDY# and IRDY# are sampled asserted. When PCEB is the target during a read cycle, TRDY# indicates that the PCEB has valid data present on AD[31:0]. During a write, it indicates that the PCEB, as a target, is prepared to latch data. TRDY# is an input to the PCEB when the PCEB is the initiator. During reset, these signals are tri-stated.
IRDY#	s/t/s	**INITIATOR READY:** IRDY#, as an output, indicates the PCEB initiator's ability to complete the current data phase of the transaction. IRDY# is used in conjunction with TRDY#. A data phase is completed on any clock that both IRDY# and TRDY# are sampled asserted. When PCEB is the initiator of a write cycle, IRDY# indicates that the PCEB has valid data present on AD[31:0]. During a read, it indicates the PCEB is prepared to latch data. IRDY# is an input to the PCEB when the PCEB is the target. During reset, these signals are tri-stated.
STOP#	s/t/s	**STOP:** As a target, the PCEB asserts STOP# to request that the master stop the current transaction. When the PCEB is an initiator, STOP# is an input. As an initiator, the PCEB stops the current transaction when STOP# is asserted. Different semantics of the STOP# signal are defined in the context of other handshake signals (TRDY# and DEVSEL#). During reset, these signals are tri-stated.

2.1 PCI Bus Interface Signals (Continued)

Pin Name	Type	Description
PLOCK#	s/t/s	**PCI LOCK:** PLOCK# indicates an atomic operation that may require multiple transactions to complete. PLOCK# is an input when PCEB is the target and output when PCEB is the initiator. When PLOCK# is sampled negated during the address phase of a transaction, a PCI agent acting as a target will consider itself a locked resource until it samples PLOCK# and FRAME# negated. When other masters attempt accesses to the PCEB (practically to the EISA subsystem) while the PCEB is locked, the PCEB responds with a retry termination. During reset, this signal is tri-stated.
IDSEL	in	**INITIALIZATION DEVICE SELECT:** IDSEL is used as a chip select during configuration read and write transactions. The PCEB samples IDSEL during the address phase of a transaction. If the PCEB samples IDSEL asserted during a configuration read or write, the PCEB responds by asserting DEVSEL# on the next cycle.
DEVSEL#	s/t/s	**DEVICE SELECT:** The PCEB asserts DEVSEL# to claim a PCI transaction as a result of positive, negative, or subtractive decode. As an output, the PCEB asserts DEVSEL# when it samples IDSEL asserted during configuration cycles to PCEB configuration registers. As an input, DEVSEL# indicates the response to a PCEB-initiated transaction. The PCEB, when not a master, samples this signal for all PCI transactions to decide whether or not to negatively or subtractively decode the cycle (except for configuration and special cycles). During reset, this signal is tri-stated.
PAR	t/s	**PARITY:** PAR is even parity across AD[31:0] and C/BE[3:0]#. When acting as a master, the PCEB drives PAR during the address and write data phases. As a target, the PCEB drives PAR during read data phases. As long as PCIRST# is asserted and CPUREQ# is high, the PCEB drives the PAR signal to keep it from floating. If CPUREQ# is low and REQ1# is low, the PCEB does not drive PAR while PCIRST# is asserted. If CPUREQ# is low and REQ1# is high, the PCEB drives PAR while PCIRST# is asserted. When the internal arbiter is enabled (CPUREQ# sampled high at the time when PCIRST# is negated), the PCEB acts as the central resource responsible for driving the PAR signal when no other device is granted the PCI Bus and the bus is idle. When the internal arbiter is disabled, the PCEB does not drive PAR as the central resource. The PCEB is always responsible for driving PAR when it is granted the bus (PCEBGNT# and idle bus) and as appropriate when it is the master of a transaction. Note that the driving and tri-stating of the PAR signal is always one clock delayed from the corresponding driving and tri-stating of the AD[31:0] and C/BE[3:0]# signals. During reset, this signal is tri-stated.
PERR#	s/o/d	**PARITY ERROR:** PERR# reports data parity errors on all transactions, except special cycles. This signal can only be asserted (by the agent receiving data) two clocks following the data (which is one clock following the PAR signal that covered the data). The duration of PERR# is one clock for each data phase that a data parity error is detected. (If multiple data errors occur during a single transaction the PERR# signal is asserted for more than a single clock.) PERR# must be driven high for one clock before being tri-stated. During reset, this signal is tri-stated.

2.2 PCI Arbiter Signals

Pin Name	Type	Description
CPUREQ#	in	**CPU REQUEST:** CPUREQ# has the following functions: 1. CPUREQ# is used to determine if the PCEB needs to drive the AD, C/BE#, and PAR signals while PCIRST# is asserted. As long as PCIRST# is asserted and CPUREQ# is high, the PCEB drives the AD, C/BE#, and PAR signals to keep them from floating. If CPUREQ# is low and REQ1# is low, the PCEB does not drive these signals while PCIRST# is asserted. If CPUREQ# is low and REQ1# is high, the PCEB drives these signals while PCIRST# is asserted. 2. If CPUREQ# is sampled high when PCIRST# makes a low-to-high transition, the internal arbiter is enabled. If it is sampled low, the internal arbiter is disabled. This requires system logic to drive the CPUREQ# during PCIRST# to determine the PCI arbiter configuration. 3. When the PCEB's internal PCI arbiter is enabled, this signal, if asserted, indicates that the Host CPU requests use of the PCI Bus. If the internal arbiter is disabled, this signal is meaningless after reset.
REQ1#	in	**REQUEST-1:** REQ1# provides the following two functions: 1. REQ1# is used, along with CPUREQ#, to determine if the PCEB will drive AD, C/BE#, and PAR during reset. If CPUREQ# is low and REQ1# is low, the PCEB does not drive AD, C/BE#, and PAR while PCIRST# is asserted. If CPUREQ# is low and REQ1# is high while PCIRST# is asserted, the PCEB drives the AD, C/BE#, and PAR signals during reset. 2. If the PCEB's internal arbiter is enabled, this signal is configured as REQ1#. An active low assertion indicates that master-1 requests the PCI Bus. If the internal arbiter is disabled, this pin is meaningless after reset.
REQ0#/ PCEBGNT#	in	**REQUEST-0 OR PCEB GRANT:** REQ0#/PCEBGNT# is a dual function pin. If the PCEB's internal arbiter is enabled, this pin is configured as REQ0#. An active low assertion indicates that master-0 requests the PCI Bus. If the internal arbiter is disabled, this pin is configured as PCEBGNT# which, when asserted, indicates the external PCI arbiter has granted use of the bus to the PCEB.
REQ[2:3]#	in	**REQUEST:** If the PCEB's internal arbiter is enabled, these signals are configured as REQ2# and REQ3#. A bus master asserts the corresponding request signal to request the PCI Bus. If the internal arbiter is disabled, these signals are meaningless after reset.
CPUGNT#	out	**CPU GRANT:** If the PCEB's internal arbiter is enabled, this signal is configured as CPUGNT#. The PCEB's internal arbiter asserts CPUGNT# to indicate that the CPU master (Host Bridge) has been granted the PCI Bus. If the internal arbiter is disabled, this pin is meaningless. During PCI reset, CPUGNT# is tri-stated. This signal requires an external pull-up resistor.
GNT0#/ PCEBREQ#	out	**GRANT-0 OR PCEB REQUEST:** GNT0#/PCEBREQ# is a dual function pin. If the PCEB's internal arbiter is enabled, this pin is configured as GNT0#. The PCEB's internal arbiter asserts GNT0# to indicate that master-0 (REQ0#) has been granted the PCI Bus. If the internal arbiter is disabled, this pin is configured as PCEBREQ#. The PCEB asserts PCEBREQ# to request the PCI Bus. During PCI reset, this signal is tri-stated. This signal requires an external pull-up resistor.

2.2 PCI Arbiter Signals (Continued)

<table>
<tr><th>Pin Name</th><th>Type</th><th>Description</th></tr>
<tr><td>GNT1#/
RESUME#</td><td>out</td><td>GRANT-1 OR RESUME: GNT1#/ RESUME# is dual function pin. If the PCEB's internal arbiter is enabled, this pin is configured as GNT1#. The PCEB's internal arbiter asserts GNT1# to indicate that master-1 has been granted the PCI Bus. If the internal arbiter is disabled, this pin is configured as RESUME#. The PCEB asserts RESUME# to indicate that the conditions causing the PCEB to retry the cycle have passed. During PCI reset, this signal is tri-stated. This signal requires an external pull-up resistor.</td></tr>
<tr><td>GNT[2:3]#</td><td>out</td><td>GRANT: If the PCEB's internal arbiter is enabled, these pins are configured as GNT2# and GNT3#. The PCEB's internal arbiter drives these pins low to indicate that the corresponding initiator (REQ2# or REQ3#) has been granted the PCI Bus. During PCI reset, these signals are tri-stated. This signal requires an external pull-up resistor.</td></tr>
<tr><td>MEMREQ#</td><td>out</td><td>MEMORY REQUEST: If the PCEB is configured in Guaranteed Access Time (GAT) Mode, MEMREQ# is asserted when an EISA device or DMA requests the EISA Bus. The PCEB asserts this signal (along with FLSHREQ#) to indicate that the PCEB requires ownership of main memory. The PCEB asserts FLSHREQ# concurrently with asserting MEMREQ#. MEMREQ# is high upon reset.
<table>
<tr><th>FLSHREQ#</th><th>MEMREQ#</th><th>Meaning</th></tr>
<tr><td>1</td><td>1</td><td>Idle</td></tr>
<tr><td>0</td><td>1</td><td>Flush buffers pointing towards PCI to avoid ISA deadlock</td></tr>
<tr><td>1</td><td>0</td><td>Reserved</td></tr>
<tr><td>0</td><td>0</td><td>GAT mode. Guarantee PCI Bus immediate access to main memory (this may or may not require the PCI-to-main memory buffers to be flushed first depending on the number of buffers).</td></tr>
</table>
This signal is synchronous to the PCI clock. During reset, this signal is high.</td></tr>
<tr><td>FLSHREQ#</td><td>out</td><td>FLUSH REQUEST: FLSHREQ# is asserted by the PCEB to command all of the system's posted write buffers pointing towards PCI to be flushed. This is required before granting the EISA Bus to an EISA master or the DMA. This signal is synchronous to the PCI clock. During reset, this signal is high.</td></tr>
<tr><td>MEMACK#</td><td>in</td><td>MEMORY ACKNOWLEDGE: MEMACK# is the response handshake that indicates to the PCEB that the function requested over the MEMREQ# and/or FLSHREQ# signals has been completed.

If the PCEB is configured for Guaranteed Access Time Mode through the Arbiter Control Register, and both MEMREQ# and FLSHREQ# are asserted, the assertion of MEMACK# indicates to the PCEB that ownership of main memory has been granted and that all system buffers have been flushed and temporarily disabled.

If FLSHREQ# is asserted and MEMREQ# is not asserted (with GAT mode being either enabled or disabled), the assertion of MEMACK# indicates that the system's posted write buffers pointing towards PCI are flushed and temporarily disabled, and the EISA Bus can be granted to an EISA master or DMA.

This signal is synchronous to the PCI clock.</td></tr>
</table>

2.3 Address Decoder Signals

Pin Name	Type	Description
MEMCS#	out	**MEMORY CHIP SELECT:** MEMCS# is a programmable address decode signal provided to a Host CPU bridge. A Host bridge can use MEMCS# to forward a PCI cycle to the main memory behind the bridge. MEMCS# is asserted one PCI clock after FRAME# is sampled asserted (address phase) and is valid for one clock cycle before being negated. MEMCS# is high upon reset.
PIODEC#	in	**PCI I/O SPACE DECODER:** PIODEC# can be used to provide arbitrarily complex EISA-to-PCI I/O address space mapping. This signal can be connected to the decode select output of an external I/O address decoder. When PIODEC# is asserted during an EISA I/O cycle, that cycle is forwarded to the PCI Bus. Note that an external pull-up resistor is required if this input signal is not used (i.e., not driven by the external logic).

2.4 EISA Interface Signals

Pin Name	Type	Description
BCLK	in	**BUS CLOCK:** BCLK is the system clock used to synchronize events on the EISA Bus. The ESC device generates BCLK (BCLKOUT), which is a divided down clock from a PCICLK. BCLK runs at a frequency that is dependent on PCICLK and a selected division factor (within the ESC). For example, a 25 MHz PCICLK and a division factor of 3 results in an 8.33 MHz BCLK.
START#	t/s	**START:** START# provides timing control at the start of the cycle and remains asserted for one BCLK period. When the PCEB is an EISA master, START# is an output signal. START# is asserted after LA[31:24]#, LA[23:2] and M/IO# become valid. START# is negated on the rising edge of the BCLK, one BCLK after it was asserted. The trailing edge of START# is always delayed from the rising edge of BCLK. When the PCEB is an EISA master, for cycles to a mismatched slave (see note at the end of this section), START# becomes an input signal at the end of the first START# phase and remains an input until the negation of the last CMD#. The ESC gains the control of the transfer and generates START#. When the PCEB is an EISA slave, START# is an input signal. It is sampled on the rising edge of BCLK. Upon PCIRST#, this signal is tri-stated and placed in output mode.

2.4 EISA Interface Signals (Continued)

Pin Name	Type	Description
CMD#	in	**COMMAND:** CMD# provides timing control within the cycle. In all cases, CMD# is an input to the PCEB from the ESC. CMD# is asserted from the rising edge of BCLK, simultaneously with the negation of START#, and remains asserted until the end of the cycle.
M/IO#	t/s	**MEMORY OR I/O:** M/IO# identifies the current cycle as a memory or an I/O cycle. M/IO# is pipelined from one cycle to the next and must be latched by the slave. M/IO# = 1 indicates a memory cycle and M/IO# = 0 indicates an I/O cycle. When the PCEB is an EISA master, the M/IO# is an output signal. When the PCEB is an EISA slave, M/IO# is an input signal. The PCEB responds as an EISA slave for both memory and I/O cycles. Upon PCIRST#, this signal is tri-stated and is placed in output mode.
W/R#	t/s	**WRITE OR READ:** W/R# identifies the cycle as a write or a read cycle. The W/R# signal is pipelined from one cycle to the next and must be latched by the slave. W/R# = 1 indicates a write cycle and W/R# = 0 indicates a read cycle. When the PCEB is an EISA master, W/R# is an output signal. When the PCEB is an EISA slave, W/R# is an input signal. Upon PCIRST#, this signal is tri-stated and placed in output mode.
EXRDY	od	**EISA READY:** EXRDY is used by EISA I/O and memory slaves to request wait states during a cycle. Each wait state is a BCLK period. The PCEB, as an EISA master or slave, samples EXRDY. As an input, the EXRDY is sampled on the falling edge of BCLK after CMD# has been asserted, and if inactive, each falling edge thereafter. When PCEB is an EISA slave, it may drive EXRDY low to introduce wait states. During reset, this signal is not driven.
EX32#	od	**EISA 32-BIT:** EX32# is used by the EISA slaves to indicate support of 32-bit transfers. When the PCEB is an EISA master, it samples EX32# on the same rising edge of BCLK that START# is negated. During mismatched cycles (see note at the end of this section), EX32# (and EX16#) is used to transfer the control back to the PCEB. EX32# (along with EX16#) is asserted by the ESC on the falling edge of BCLK before the rising edge of the BCLK when the last CMD# is negated. This indicates that the cycle control is transferred back to the PCEB. As an EISA slave, the PCEB always drives EX32# to indicate 32-bit support for EISA cycles. During reset, this signal is not driven.
EX16#	in	**EISA 16-BIT:** EX16# is used by the EISA slaves to indicate their support of 16-bit transfers. As an EISA master, the PCEB samples EX16# on the same rising edge of BCLK that START# is negated. During mismatched cycles (see note at the end of this section), EX16# (and EX32#) is used to transfer the control back to the PCEB. EX16# (along with EX32#) is asserted by the ESC on the falling edge of the BCLK before the rising edge of the BCLK when the last CMD# is negated. This indicates that the cycle control is transferred back to the PCEB. As an EISA slave, the PCEB never asserts EX16#.

2.4 EISA Interface Signals (Continued)

Pin Name	Type	Description
MSBURST#	t/s	**MASTER BURST:** MSBURST# is an output when the PCEB is an EISA master and an input when the PCEB is a slave. As a master, the PCEB asserts MSBURST# to indicate to the slave that the next cycle is a burst cycle. If the PCEB samples SLBURST# asserted on the rising edge of BCLK after START# is asserted, the PCEB asserts MSBURST# on the next BCLK edge and proceeds with the burst cycle. As a slave, the PCEB monitors this signal in response to the PCEB asserting SLBURST#. The EISA master asserts MSBURST# to the PCEB to indicate that the next cycle is a burst cycle. As a slave, the PCEB samples MSBURST# on the rising edge of BCLK after the rising edge of BCLK that CMD# is asserted by the ESC. MSBURST# is sampled on all subsequent rising edges of BCLK until the signal is sampled negated. The burst cycle is terminated on the rising edge of BCLK when MSBURST# is sampled negated, unless EXRDY is sampled negated on the previous falling edge of BCLK. During reset, this signal is tri-stated.
SLBURST#	t/s	**SLAVE BURST:** SLBURST# is an input when the PCEB is an EISA master and an output when the PCEB is a slave. When the PCEB is a master, the slave indicates that it supports burst cycles by asserting SLBURST# to the PCEB. The PCEB samples SLBURST# on the rising edge of BCLK at the end of START# for EISA master cycles. When the PCEB is an EISA slave, this signal is an output. As a slave, the PCEB asserts this signal to the master indicating that the PCEB supports EISA burst cycles. During reset, this signal is tri-stated.
LOCK#	t/s	**LOCK:** When asserted, LOCK# guarantees exclusive memory access. This signal is asserted by the PCEB when the PCI master is running locked cycles to EISA slaves. When asserted, this signal locks the EISA subsystem. LOCK# can also be activated by a device on the EISA Bus. This condition is propagated to the PCI Bus via the PLOCK# signal. During reset, this signal is tri-stated.
BE[3:0]#	t/s	**BYTE ENABLES:** BE[3:0]# identify the specific bytes that are valid during the current EISA Bus cycles. When the PCEB is an EISA master and the cycles are directed to a matched slave (slave supports 32-bit transfers), the BE[3:0]# are outputs from the PCEB. When the cycles are directed to a mis-matched slave (slave does not support 32-bit transfers—see note at the end of this section), the BE[3:0]# are floated one and half BCLKs after START# is asserted. These signals become inputs (driven by the ESC) for the rest of the cycle. BE[3:0]# are pipelined signals and must be latched by the addressed slave. When the PCEB is an EISA/ISA/DMA slave, BE[3:0]# are inputs to the PCEB. Upon PCIRST#, these signals are tri-stated and placed in output mode.

2.4 EISA Interface Signals (Continued)

Pin Name	Type	Description
LA[31:24]#, LA[23:2]	t/s	**LATCHABLE ADDRESS:** LA[31:24]# and LA[23:2] are the EISA address signals. When the PCEB is an EISA master, these signals are outputs from the PCEB. These addresses are pipelined and must be latched by the EISA slave. LA[31:24]# and LA[23:2] are valid on the falling edge of START#. Note that the upper address bits are inverted before being driven on LA[31:24]#. The timing for LA[31:24]# and LA[23:2] are the same. When the PCEB is an EISA slave, these signals are inputs and are latched by the PCEB. For I/O cycles, the PCEB, as an EISA master, floats LA[31:24]# to allow for ESC's address multiplexing (during I/O cycle to configuration RAM). LA[23:2] are actively driven by the PCEB. For memory cycles, the PCEB as an EISA master, drives the LA address lines. During reset, these signals are tri-stated.
SD[31:0]	t/s	**SYSTEM DATA:** SD[31:0] are bi-directional data lines that transfer data between the PCEB and other EISA devices. Data transfer between EISA and PCI devices use these signals. The data swapping logic in the PCEB ensures that the data is available on the correct byte lanes for any given transfer. During reset, these signals are tri-stated.
REFRESH#	in	**REFRESH:** When asserted, REFRESH# indicates to the PCEB that the current cycle on the EISA Bus is a refresh cycle. It is used by the PCEB decoder to distinguish between EISA memory read cycles and refresh cycles.

NOTE:

Mis-matched Cycles. When the PCEB is an EISA master, cycles to the slaves, other than 32 bits transfers, are considered a mis-matched cycle. For mis-matched cycles, the PCEB backs off the EISA Bus one and half BCLKs after it asserted START# by releasing (floating) START#, BE[3:0]# and the SD[31:0] lines. The ESC device then takes control of the transfer. The ESC controls the transfer until the last transfer. At the end of the last transfer, control is transferred back to the PCEB. The ESC transfers control back to the PCEB by asserting EX32# and EX16# on the falling edge of BCLK before the rising edge of BCLK when the last CMD# is negated.

2.5 ISA Interface Signals

An ISA interface signal is included to improve the PCEB's handling of I/O cycles on the EISA side of the bridge. This signal permits ISA masters to address PCI I/O slaves using the full 16-bit bus size. The signal also allows the PCEB to identify 8-bit I/O slaves for purposes of generating the correct amount of I/O recovery.

Pin Name	Type	Description
IO16#	o/d	**16-BIT I/O CHIP SELECT:** As an EISA slave, the PCEB asserts IO16# when PIODEC# is asserted or an I/O cycle to PCI is detected. As an EISA master, the PCEB uses IO16# as an input to determine the correct amount of I/O recovery time from the I/O Recovery Time (IORT) Register. This register contains bit-fields that are used to program recovery times for 8-bit and 16-bit I/O. When IO16# is asserted, the recovery time programmed into the 16-bit I/O field (bits [1:0]), if enabled, is used. When IO16# is negated, the recovery time programmed into the 8-bit I/O field (bits [5:3]), if enabled, is used. This signal must have an external pull-up resistor. During reset, this signal is not driven.

2.6 PCEB/ESC Interface Signals

Pin Name	Type	Description
ARBITRATION AND INTERRUPT ACKNOWLEDGE CONTROL		
EISAHOLD	in	**EISA HOLD:** EISAHOLD is used by the ESC to request control of the EISA Bus from the PCEB. This signal is synchronous to PCICLK and is driven inactive when PCIRST# is asserted.
EISAHLDA	out	**EISA HOLD ACKNOWLEDGE:** The PCEB asserts EISAHLDA to inform the ESC that it has been granted ownership of the EISA Bus. This signal is synchronous to the PCICLK. During PCIRST#, this signal is low.
PEREQ#/ INTA#	out	**PCI-TO-EISA REQUEST OR INTERRUPT ACKNOWLEDGE:** PEREQ#/INTA# is a dual-function signal. The signal function is determined by the state of EISAHLDA signal. When EISAHLDA is negated, this signal is an interrupt acknowledge (i.e., PEREQ#/INTA# asserted indicates to the ESC that the current cycle on the EISA is an interrupt acknowledge). When EISAHLDA is asserted, this signal is a PCI-to-EISA request (i.e., PEREQ#/INTA# asserted indicates to the ESC that the PCEB needs to obtain the ownership of the EISA Bus on behalf of a PCI agent). This signal is synchronous to the PCICLK and it is driven inactive when PCIRST# is asserted.
PCEB BUFFER COHERENCY CONTROL		
NMFLUSH#	t/s	**NEW MASTER FLUSH:** The bi-directional NMFLUSH# signal provides handshake between the PCEB and ESC to control flushing of PCI system buffers on behalf of EISA masters. During an EISA Bus ownership change, before the ESC can grant the bus to the EISA master (or DMA), the ESC must ensure that system buffers are flushed and the buffers pointing towards the EISA subsystem are disabled. The ESC asserts NMFLUSH# for one PCI clock to request system buffer flushing. (After asserting NMFLUSH# for 1 PCI clock, the ESC tri-states NMFLUSH#.) When the PCEB samples NMFLUSH# asserted, it starts immediately to assert NMFLUSH# and begins flushing its internal buffers, if necessary. The PCEB also requests PCI system buffer flushing via the MEMREQ#, FLSHREQ#, and MEMACK# signals. When the PCEB completes its internal buffer flushing and MEMACK# is asserted (indicating that the PCI system buffer flushing is complete), the PCEB negates NMFLUSH# for 1 PCI clock and stops driving it. When the ESC samples NMFLUSH# negated, it grants the EISA Bus to an EISA master (or DMA). The ESC resumes responsibility of the default NMFLUSH# driver and starts driving NMFLUSH# negated until the next time a new EISA master (or DMA) wins arbitration. This signal is synchronous with PCICLK and is negated by the ESC at reset.
INTCHIP0	t/s	**INTER CHIP 0:** INTCHIP0 is a reserved signal. The INTCHIP0 signal on the PCEB must be connected to the INTCHIP0 signal pin on the ESC for proper device operation. This signal requires an external pull-up resistor.

1

2.6 PCEB/ESC Interface Signals (Continued)

Pin Name	Type	Description
DATA SWAP BUFFER CONTROL		
SDCPYEN01# SDCPYEN02# SDCPYEN03# SDCPYEN13#	in	**COPY ENABLE:** These active Low signals perform byte copy operation on the EISA data bus (SD[31:0]). The Copy Enable signals are asserted during mis-matched cycles and are used by the PCEB to enable byte copy operations between the SD data byte lanes 0, 1, 2, and 3 as follows: SDCPYEN01#: Copy between Byte Lane 0 (SD[7:0]) and Byte Lane 1 (SD[15:8]) SDCPYEN02#: Copy between Byte Lane 0 (SD[7:0]) and Byte Lane 2 (SD[23:16]) SDCPYEN03#: Copy between Byte Lane 0 (SD[7:0]) and Byte Lane 3 (SD[31:24]) SDCPYEN13#: Copy between Byte Lane 1 (SD[15:8]) and Byte Lane 3 (SD[31:24]) Note that the direction of the copy is controlled by SDCPYUP.
SDCPYUP	in	**SYSTEM (DATA) COPY UP:** SDCPYUP controls the direction of the byte copy operation. A high on SDCPYUP indicates a COPY UP operation where the lower byte(s) of the SD data bus are copied onto the higher byte(s) of the bus. A low on the signal indicates a COPY DOWN operation where the higher byte(s) of the data bus are copied on to the lower byte(s) of the bus. The PCEB uses this signal to perform the actual data byte copy operation during mis-matched cycles.
SDOE[2:0]#	in	**SYSTEM DATA OUTPUT ENABLE:** These active Low signals enable the SD data output onto the EISA Bus. The ESC only activates these signals during mis-matched cycles. The PCEB uses these signals to enable the SD data buffers as follows: SDOE0#: Enables Byte Lane 0 SD[7:0] SDOE1#: Enables Byte Lane 1 SD[15:8] SDOE2#: Enables Byte Lane 3 SD[31:24] and Byte Lane 2 SD[23:16]
SDLE[3:0]#	in	**SYSTEM DATA LATCH ENABLE:** SDLE[3:0]# enable the latching of data on the EISA Bus. These signals are activated only during mis-matched cycles, except PCEB-initiated write cycles. The PCEB uses these signals to latch the SD data bus as follows: SDLE0#: Latch Byte Lane 0 SD[7:0] SDLE1#: Latch Byte Lane 0 SD[15:8] SDLE2#: Latch Byte Lane 0 SD[23:16] SDLE3#: Latch Byte Lane 0 SD[31:24]

2.7 Test Signal

Pin Name	Type	Description
TEST#	in	**TEST:** This pin is used to tri-state all PCEB outputs. During normal operations, this pin must be tied high.

NOTE:
All pins designated as NC (no-connect) require individual pull-up resistors (8 KΩ–10 KΩ).

3.0 REGISTER DESCRIPTION

The PCEB contains both PCI configuration registers and I/O registers. The configuration registers (Table 3-1) are located in PCI configuration space and are only accessible from the PCI Bus. The addresses shown in Table 3-1 for each register are offset values that appear on AD[7:2] and C/BE[3:0]#. The configuration registers can be accessed as byte, word (16-bit), or Dword (32-bit) quantities. All multi-byte numeric fields use "little-endian" ordering (i.e., lower addresses contain the least significant parts of the fields).

The BIOS Timer is the only non-configuration register (Section 3.2, I/O Registers). This register, like the configuration registers, is only accessible from the PCI Bus. The BIOS Timer Register can be accessed as byte, word, or Dword quantities.

Some of the PCEB registers contain reserved bits. These bits are labeled "Reserved". Software must take care to deal correctly with bit-encoded fields that are reserved. On reads, software must use appropriate masks to extract the defined bits and not rely on reserved bits being any particular value. On writes, software must ensure that the values of reserved bits are preserved. That is, the values of reserved bit positions must first be read, merged with the new values for other bit positions and the data then written back.

In addition to reserved bits within a register, the PCEB contains address locations in the PCI configuration space that are marked "Reserved" (Table 3-1).The PCEB responds to accesses to these address locations by completing the PCI cycle. When a reserved register location is read, 0000h is returned. Writes have no affect on the PCEB.

During a hard reset (PCIRST# asserted), the PCEB registers are set to pre-determined **default** states. The default values are indicated in the individual register descriptions.

3.1 Configuration Registers

Table 3-1 summarizes the PCEB configuration space registers. Following the table, is a detailed description of each register and register bit. The register descriptions are arranged in the order that they appear in Table 3-1. The following nomenclature is used for access attributes.

RO **Read Only.** If a register is read only, writes to this register have no effect.

R/W **Read/Write.** A register with this attribute can be read and written.

R/WC **Read/Write Clear.** A register bit with this attribute can be read and written. However, a write of a 1 clears (sets to 0) the corresponding bit and a write of a 0 has no effect.

NOTE:

Some register fields are used to program address ranges for various PCEB functions. The register contents represent the address bit value and not the signal level on the bus. For example, the upper address lines on the EISA Bus have inverted signals (LA[31:24]#). However, this inversion is automatically handled by the PCEB hardware and is transparent to the programmer.

Table 3-1. Configuration Registers

Configuration Address Offset	Abbreviation	Register Name	Access
00h-01h	VID	Vendor Identification	RO
02h-03h	DID	Device Identification	RO
04h-05h	PCICMD	Command Register	R/W
06h-07h	PCISTS	Status Register	RO, R/WC
08h	RID	Revision Identification	RO
09h-0Ch	—	Reserved	—
0Dh	MLTIM	Master Latency Timer	R/W
0Eh-3Fh	—	Reserved	—
40h	PCICON	PCI Control	R/W
41h	ARBCON	PCI Arbiter Control	R/W
42h	ARBPRI	PCI Arbiter Priority Control	R/W
43h	ARBPRIX	PCI Arbiter Priority Control Extension	R/W
44h	MCSCON	MEMCS# Control	R/W
45h	MCSBOH	MEMCS# Bottom of Hole	R/W
46h	MCSTOH	MEMCS# Top of Hole	R/W
47h	MCSTOM	MEMCS# Top of Memory	R/W
48h-49h	EADC1	EISA Address Decode Control 1	R/W
4Ah-4Bh	—	Reserved	—
4Ch	IORTC	ISA I/O Recovery Time Control	R/W
4Dh-53h	—	Reserved	—
54h	MAR1	MEMCS# Attribute Register #1	R/W
55h	MAR2	MEMCS# Attribute Register #2	R/W
56h	MAR3	MEMCS# Attribute Register #3	R/W
57h	—	Reserved	—
58h	PDCON	PCI Decode Control	R/W
59h	—	Reserved	—
5Ah	EADC2	EISA Address Decode Control 2	R/W
5Bh	—	Reserved	—
5Ch	EPMRA	EISA-to-PCI Memory Region Attributes	R/W
5Dh-5Fh	—	Reserved	—
60h-6Fh	MEMREGN[4:1]	EISA-to-PCI Memory Region Address (4 registers)	R/W
70h-77Fh	IOREGN[4:1]	EISA-to-PCI I/O Region Address (4 registers)	R/W
80h-81h	BTMR	BIOS Timer Base Address	R/W
84h	ELTCR	EISA Latency Timer Control Register	R/W
85h-87h	—	Reserved	—
88h-8Bh	PTCR	PCEB Test Control Register—***DO NOT WRITE!***	—
8Ch-FFh	—	Reserved	—

3.1.1 VID—VENDOR IDENTIFICATION REGISTER

Register Name: Vendor Identification
Address Offset: 00h-01h
Default Value: 8086h
Attribute: Read Only
Size: 16 bits

The VID Register contains the vendor identification number. This register, along with the Device Identification Register, uniquely identify any PCI device. Writes to this register have no effect.

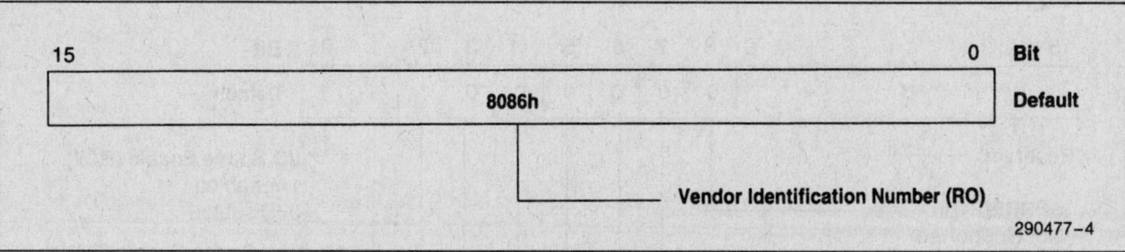

Figure 3-1. Vendor Identification Register

Table 3-2. Vendor Identification Register

Bit	Description
15:0	**VENDOR IDENTIFICATION NUMBER:** This is a 16-bit value assigned to Intel.

3.1.2 DID—DEVICE IDENTIFICATION REGISTER

Register Name: Device Identification
Address Offset: 02h-03h
Default Value: 0482h
Attribute: Read Only
Size: 16 bits

The DID Register contains the device identification number. This register, along with the VID Register, define the PCEB. Writes to this register have no effect.

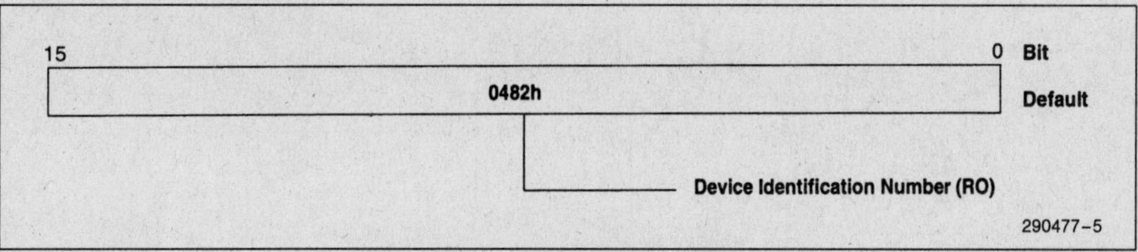

Figure 3-2. Device Identification Register

Table 3-3. Device Identification Register

Bit	Description
15:0	**DEVICE IDENTIFICATION NUMBER:** This is a 16-bit value assigned to the PCEB.

3.1.3 PCICMD—PCI COMMAND REGISTER

Register Name: PCI Command
Address Offset: 04h-05h
Default Value: 0007h
Attribute: Read/Write
Size: 16 bits

This 16-bit register contains PCI interface control information. This register enables/disables PCI parity error checking, enables/disables PCEB bus master capability, and enables/disables the PCEB to respond to PCI-originated memory and I/O cycles. Note that, for certain PCI functions that are not implemented within the PCEB, the control bits are still shown (labeled "not supported").

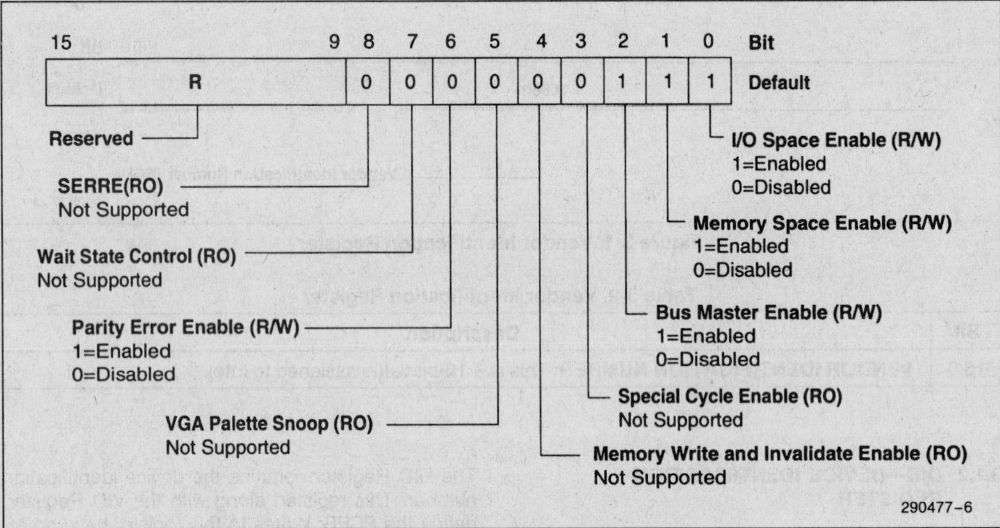

Figure 3-3. PCI Command Register

Table 3-4. PCI Command Register

Bit	Description
15:9	**RESERVED.**
8	**SERR# ENABLE (SERRE)—NOT SUPPORTED:** Function of this bit is to control the SERR# signal. Since the PCEB does not implement the SERR# signal, this bit always reads as 0 (disabled).
7	**WAIT STATE CONTROL (WSC)—NOT SUPPORTED:** This bit controls insertion of wait-states for devices that do not meet the 33-10 PCI specification. Since PCEB meets the 33-10 specification, this control function is not implemented. WSC is always read as 0.
6	**PARITY ERROR ENABLE (PERRE):** PERRE controls the PCEB's response to PCI parity errors. When PERRE = 1, the PCEB asserts the PERR# signal when a parity error is detected. When PERRE = 0, the PCEB ignores any parity errors that it detects. After PCIRST#, PERRE = 0 (parity checking disabled).
5	**VGA PALETTE SNOOP (VGPS)—NOT SUPPORTED:** This bit is intended only for specific control of PCI-based VGA devices and it is not applicable to the PCEB. This bit is not implemented and always reads as 0.
4	**MEMORY WRITE AND INVALIDATE ENABLE (MWIE)—NOT SUPPORTED:** This is an enable bit for using the Memory Write and Invalidate command. The PCEB doesn't support this command as a master. As a slave, the PCEB aliases this command to a memory write. This bit always reads as 0 (disabled).
3	**SPECIAL CYCLE ENABLE (SCE)—NOT SUPPORTED:** Since this capability is not implemented, the PCEB does not respond to any type of special cycle. This bit always reads as 0.
2	**BUS MASTER ENABLE (BME):** BME enables/disables the PCEB's PCI Bus master capability. When BME = 0, the PCEB bus master capability is disabled. This prevents the PCEB from requesting the PCI Bus on behalf of EISA/ISA masters, the DMA, or the Line Buffers. When BME = 1, the bus master capability is enabled. This bit is set to 1 after PCIRST#.
1	**MEMORY SPACE ENABLE (MSE):** This bit enables the PCEB to accept PCI-originated memory cycles. When MSE = 1, the PCEB responds to PCI-originated memory cycles to the EISA Bus. When MSE = 0, the PCEB does not respond to PCI-originated memory cycles to the EISA Bus (DEVSEL# is inhibited). This bit is set to 1 (enabled for BIOS access) after PCIRST#.
0	**I/O SPACE ENABLE (IOSE):** This bit enables the PCEB to accept PCI-originated I/O cycles. When IOSE = 1, the PCEB responds to PCI-originated I/O cycles. When IOSE = 0, the PCEB does not respond to a PCI I/O cycle (DEVSEL# is inhibited), including I/O cycles bound for the EISA Bus. This bit is set to 1 (I/O space enabled) after PCIRST#.

3.1.4 PCISTS—PCI STATUS REGISTER

Register Name: PCI Status
Address Offset: 06h-07h
Default Value: 0200h
Attribute: Read Only, Read/Write Clear
Size: 16 bits

This 16-bit register provides status information for PCI Bus-related events. Some bits are read/write clear. These bits are set to 0 whenever the register is written, and the data in the corresponding bit location is 1 (R/WC). For example, to clear bit 12 and not affect any other bits, write the value 0001_0000_0000_0000b to this register. Note that for certain PCI functions that are not implemented in the PCEB, the control bits are still shown (labeled "not supported").

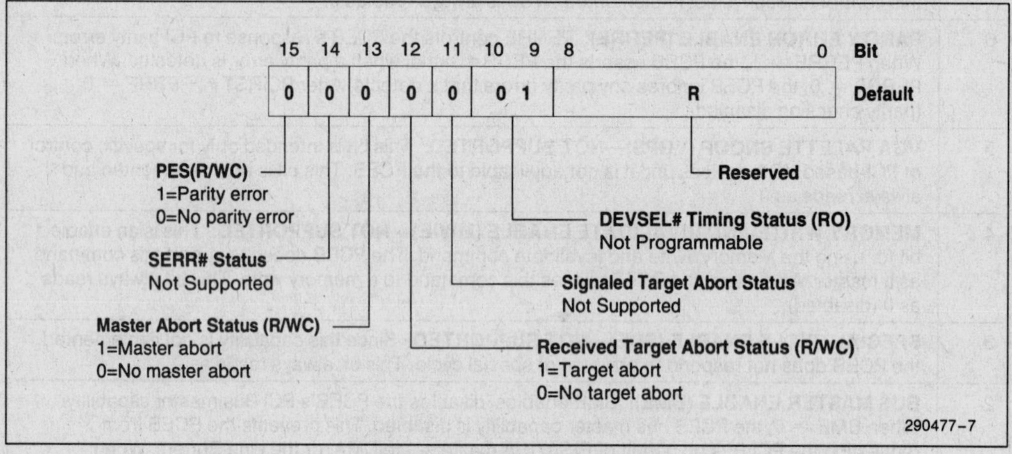

Figure 3-4. PCI Status Register

Table 3-5. PCI Status Register

Bit	Description
15	**PARITY ERROR STATUS (PERRS):** This bit is set to 1 whenever the PCEB detects a parity error, even if parity error handling is disabled (as controlled by bit 6 in the PCI Command Register). Software sets PERRS to 0 by writing a 1 to this bit location.
14	**SERR# STATUS (SERRS)—NOT IMPLEMENTED:** This bit is used to indicate that a PCI device asserted the SERR# signal. The PCEB does not implement this signal. SERRS is always read as 0.
13	**MASTER ABORT STATUS (MA):** When the PCEB, as a master, generates a master abort, this bit is set to 1. Software sets MA to 0 by writing a 1 to this bit location.
12	**RECEIVED TARGET ABORT STATUS (RTAS):** When the PCEB, as a master, receives a target abort condition, this bit is set to 1. Software sets RTAS to 0 by writing a 1 to this bit location.
11	**SIGNALED TARGET ABORT STATUS (STAS)—NOT IMPLEMENTED:** This bit is set to 1 by a PCI target device when they generate a Target Abort. Since the PCEB never generates a target abort, this bit is not implemented and will always be read as a 0.
10:9	**DEVSEL TIMING STATUS (DEVT):** This read only field indicates the timing of the DEVSEL# signal when PCEB responds as a target. The PCI Specification defines three allowable timings for assertion of DEVSEL#: 00b = fast, 01b = medium, and 10b = slow (11b is reserved). DEVT indicates the slowest time that a device asserts DEVSEL# for any bus command, except configuration read and configuration write cycles. The PCEB implements medium speed DEVSEL# timing and, therefore, DEVT[10:9] = 01 when read.
8:0	**RESERVED.**

3.1.5 RID—REVISION IDENTIFICATION REGISTER

Register Name: Revision Identification
Address Offset: 08h
Default Value: Revision Identification number
Attribute: Read Only
Size: 8 bits

This 8-bit register contains the device revision number of the PCEB. Writes to this register have no effect.

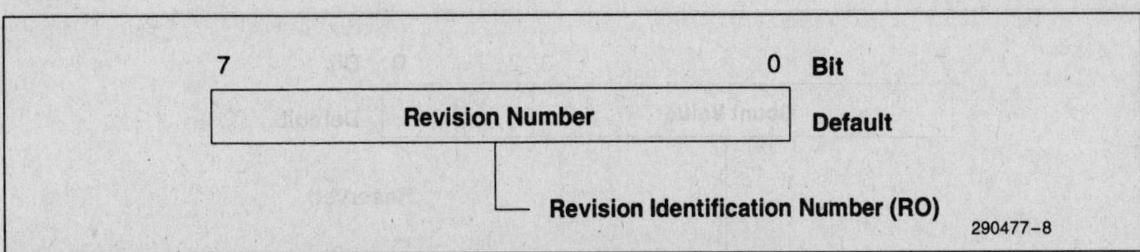

Figure 3-5. Revision Identification Register

Table 3-6. Revision Identification Register

Bit	Description
7:0	**REVISION IDENTIFICATION NUMBER:** This 8-bit value is the revision number of the PCEB.

3.1.6 MLT—MASTER LATENCY TIMER REGISTER

Register Name: Master Latency Timer
Address Offset: 0Dh
Default Value: 00h
Attribute: Read/Write
Size: 8 bits

This 8-bit register contains the programmable value of the Master Latency Timer for use when the PCEB is a master on the PCI Bus. The granularity of the timer is 8 PCI clocks. Thus, bits [2:0] are not used and always read as 0s.

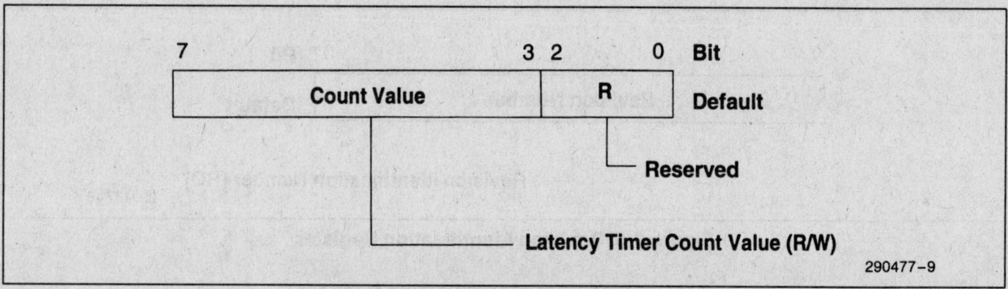

Figure 3-6. Master Latency Timer Register

Table 3-7. Master Latency Timer Register

Bit #	Bit Function
7:3	**COUNT VALUE:** This 5-bit field contains the count value of the Master Latency Timer, with a granularity of 8 PCI clocks. For example, value 00101b provides a time-out period of 5x8 = 40 PCI clocks. Maximum count value is 11111b, which corresponds to 248 PCI clocks. After PCIRST#, the default value of these bits is 00000b.
2:0	**RESERVED.**

3.1.7 PCICON—PCI CONTROL REGISTER

Register Name: PCI Control
Address Offset: 40h
Default Value: 00h
Attribute: Read/Write
Size: 8 bits

This 8-bit register enables/disables the PCEB's data buffers, defines the subtractive decoding sample point, and enables/disables response to the PCI interrupt acknowledge cycle.

NOTE:
The Line Buffers and Posted Write Buffers are typically enabled or disabled during system initialization. These buffers should not be dynamically enabled/disabled during runtime. Otherwise, data coherency can be affected, if a buffer containing valid write data is disabled and then, later, re-enabled.

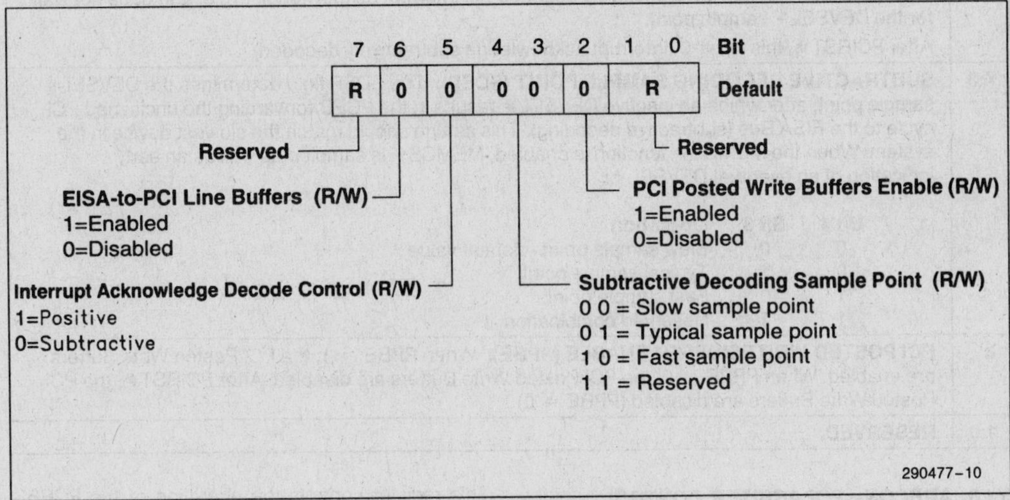

Figure 3-7. PCI Control Register

Table 3-8. PCI Control Register

Bit	Description
7	**RESERVED.**
6	**EISA-TO-PCI LINE BUFFER ENABLE (ELBE):** When ELBE = 0, the EISA-to-PCI Line Buffers are disabled and when ELBE = 1, the EISA-to-PCI Line Buffers are enabled. After PCIRST#, the Line Buffers are disabled (ELBE = 0).
5	**INTERRUPT ACKNOWLEDGE DECODE CONTROL:** When this bit = 0, interrupt acknowledge cycles are handled in a subtractive decode manner. That is, the PCEB will wait until the DEVSEL# sample point after which, if DEVSEL# is sampled inactive, the interrupt acknowledge cycle is handled in the normal fashion (i.e., uses the PEREQ#/INTA# signal to fetch the vector from the ESC). When this bit = 1, the PCEB positively decodes the interrupt acknowledge cycle, and does not wait for the DEVSEL# sample point. After PCIRST#, this bit = 0 (interrupt acknowledge subtractively decoded).
4:3	**SUBTRACTIVE DECODING SAMPLE POINT (SDSP):** The SDSP field determines the DEVSEL# sample point, after which an inactive DEVSEL# results in the PCEB forwarding the unclaimed PCI cycle to the EISA Bus (subtractive decoding). This setting should match the slowest device in the system. When the MEMCS# function is enabled, MEMCS# is sampled as well as an early indication of an eventual DEVSEL#. **Bit 4 Bit 3 Operation** 0 0 Slow sample point - default value 0 1 Typical sample point 1 0 Fast sample point 1 1 Reserved combination
2	**PCI POSTED WRITE BUFFER ENABLE (PPBE):** When PPBE = 1, the PCI Posted Write Buffers are enabled. When PPBE = 0, the PCI Posted Write Buffers are disabled. After PCIRST#, the PCI Posted Write Buffers are disabled (PPBE = 0).
1:0	**RESERVED.**

3.1.8 ARBCON—PCI ARBITER CONTROL REGISTER

Register Name: PCI Arbiter Control
Address Offset: 41h
Default Value: 80h
Attribute: Read/Write
Size: 8 bits

This register controls the operation of the PCEB's internal PCI arbiter. The register enables/disables auto-PEREQ#, controls the master retry timer, enables/disables CPU bus parking, controls bus lock, and enables/disables the guaranteed access time (GAT) mode for EISA/ISA accesses.

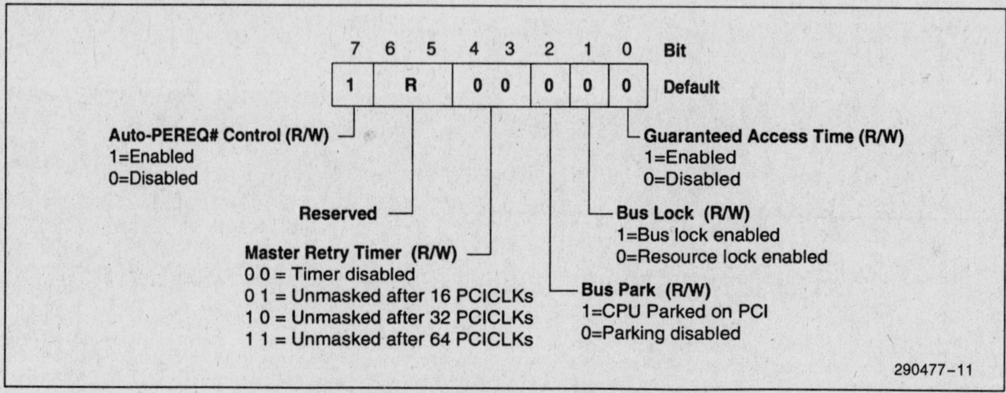

Figure 3-8. PCI Arbiter Control Register

Table 3-9. PCI Arbiter Control Register

Bit	Description
7	**AUTO-PEREQ# CONTROL (APC):** APC enables/disables control of the auto-PEREQ# function when GAT mode is enabled via bit 0 (GAT = 1). When APC = 1 (and GAT = 1), the PEREQ# signal is asserted whenever the EISAHLDA signal is asserted. When APC = 0, the PEREQ# signal is not automatically asserted but it will be activated upon PCI Bus request from any PCI agent. After PCIRST#, APC = 1 (enabled). See note below.
6:5	**RESERVED.**
4:3	**MASTER RETRY TIMER (MRT):** This 2-bit field determines the number of PCICLKs after the first retry that a PCI initiator's bus request will be masked. **Bit 4 / Bit 3 / Operation** 0 / 0 / Timer disabled, Retries never masked—Default 0 / 1 / Retries unmasked after 16 PCICLK's 1 / 0 / Retries unmasked after 32 PCICLK's 1 / 1 / Retries unmasked after 64 PCICLK's
2	**BUS PARK (BP):** When BP = 1, the PCEB parks CPUREQ# on the PCI Bus when it detects the PCI Bus idle. If BP = 0, the PCEB takes responsibility for driving AD, C/BE# and PAR signals upon detection of bus idle state, if the internal arbiter is enabled. After PCIRST#, BP = 0 (disabled).
1	**BUS LOCK (BL):** When BL = 1, Bus Lock is enabled. The arbiter considers the entire PCI Bus locked upon initiation of any LOCKed transaction. When BL = 0, Resource Lock is enabled. A LOCKed agent is considered a locked resource and other agents may continue normal PCI transactions. After PCIRST#, BL = 0 (disabled).
0	**GUARANTEED ACCESS TIME (GAT):** When GAT = 1, the PCEB is configured for Guaranteed Access Time mode. This mode guarantees the 2.1 μs CHRDY time-out specification for the EISA/ISA Bus. When the PCEB is a PCI initiator on behalf of an EISA/ISA master, the PCI and main memory bus (host) are arbitrated for in serial and must be owned before the EISA/ISA master is given ownership of the EISA Bus. If the PCEB is not programmed for Guaranteed Access Time (GAT = 0), the EISA/ISA master is first granted the EISA Bus, before the PCI Bus is arbitrated. After a PCIRST#, GAT = 0 (disabled).

NOTE:
The PCMC Host bridge device requires that bit 7 be set to 1 (default). However, other chip sets might need to have this function disabled to provide more optimum performance for EISA subsystems. This functionality is built-in to prevent starvation of PCI agents (in particular, the host bridge, i.e., CPU) when EISA masters are performing transactions in the GAT mode. If this function is disabled, the host bridge must be capable of generating the PCI Bus request, even when the Host Bus is not controlled by the CPU (CPU tri-stated all Host Bus signals, or even only address bus, in response to HOLD/AHOLD). The CPU pin that provides an indication of a request for the external bus (e.g., after cache miss) can be used by the host bridge to generate the request for the PCI Bus during GAT mode operations, even when no address lines are driven by the CPU.

1

3.1.9 ARBPRIX—PCI ARBITER PRIORITY CONTROL EXTENSION REGISTER

Register Name: PCI Arbiter Priority Control Extension
Address Offset: 43h
Default Value: 00h
Attribute: Read/Write
Size: 8 bits

This register controls the Fixed Priority Mode for Bank 3 of the PCEB's Internal arbiter. This register is used in conjunction with the PCI Arbiter Priority Control Register (ARBPRI, offset 42h).

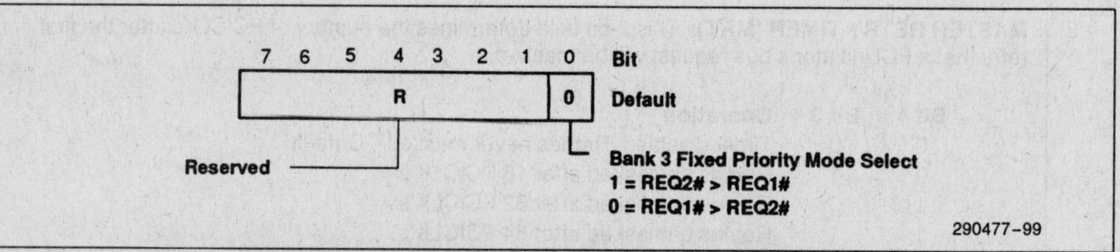

Figure 3-9. PCI Arbiter Priority Control Extension Register

Table 3-10. PCI Arbiter Priority Control Register

Bit	Description
7:1	**RESERVED.**
0	**BANK 3 FIXED PRIORITY MODE SELECT:** 0 = REQ1# higher priority; 1 = REQ2# higher priority.

3.1.10 ARBPRI—PCI ARBITER PRIORITY CONTROL REGISTER

Register Name: PCI Arbiter Priority Control
Address Offset: 42h
Default Value: 04h
Attribute: Read/Write
Size: 8 bits

This register controls the operating modes of the PCEB's internal PCI arbiter. The arbiter consists of four arbitration banks that support up to six masters and three arbitration priority modes—fixed priority, rotating priority and mixed priority modes. See Section 5.4, PCI Bus Arbitration for details on programming and using different arbitration modes.

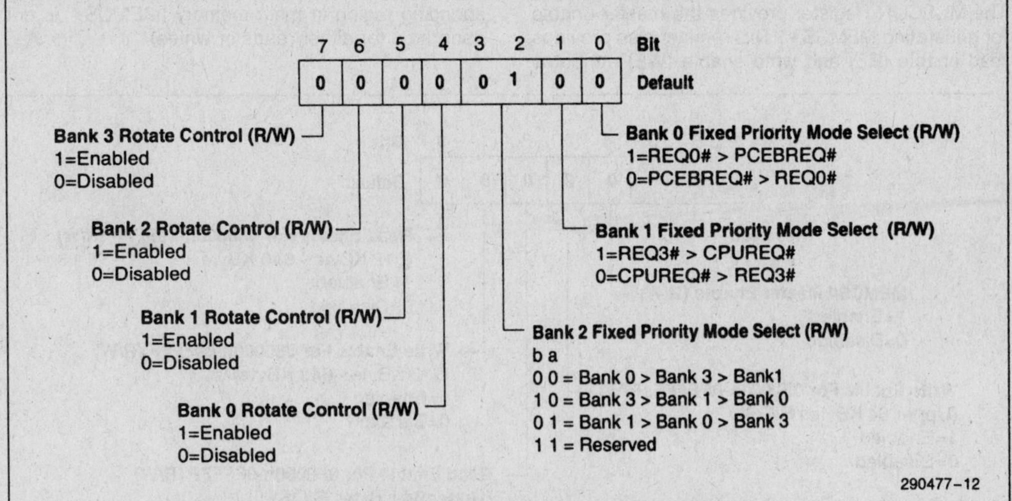

Figure 3-10. PCI Arbiter Priority Control Register

Table 3-11. PCI Arbiter Priority Control Register

Bit	Description
7	Bank 3 Rotate Control
6	Bank 2 Rotate Control
5	Bank 1 Rotate Control
4	Bank 0 Rotate Control
3:2	Bank 2 Fixed Priority Mode Select−b,a
1	Bank 1 Fixed Priority Mode Select
0	Bank 0 Fixed Priority Mode Select

3.1.11 MCSCON—MEMCS# CONTROL REGISTER

Register Name: MEMCS# Control
Address Offset: 44h
Default Value: 00h
Attribute: Read/Write
Size: 8 bits

The MCSCON Register provides the master enable for generating MEMCS#. This register also provides read enable (RE) and write enable (WE) attributes for two main memory regions (the 512 KByte–640 KByte region and an upper BIOS region). PCI accesses within the enabled regions result in the generation of MEMCS#. Note that the 0–512 KByte region does not have RE and WE attribute bits. The 0–512 KByte region can only be disabled with the MEMCS# Master Enable bit (bit 4). Note also, that when the RE and WE bits are both 0 for a particular region, the PCI master can not access the corresponding region in main memory (MEMCS# is not generated for either reads or writes).

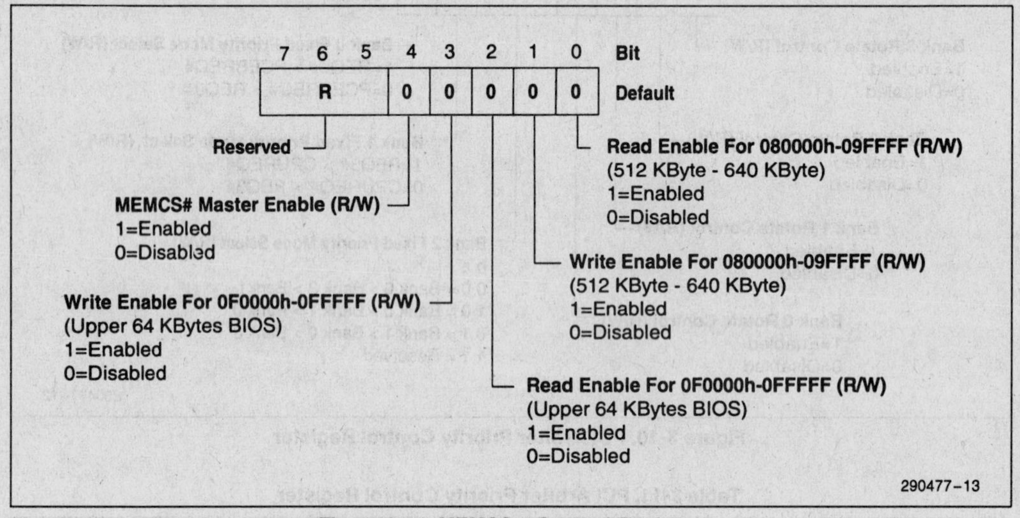

Figure 3-11. MEMCS# Control Register

Table 3-12. MEMCS# Control Register

Bit	Description
7:5	**RESERVED.**
4	**MEMCS# MASTER ENABLE:** When bit 4 = 1, the PCEB asserts MEMCS# for all accesses to the defined MEMCS# region (as defined by the MCSTOM Register and excluding the memory hole defined by the MCSBOH and MCSTOH Registers), if the accessed location is in a region enabled by bits [3:0] of this register or in the regions defined by the MAR1, MAR2, and MAR3 registers. When bit 4 = 0, the entire MEMCS# function is disabled and MEMCS# is never asserted.
3	**WRITE ENABLE FOR 0F0000h–0FFFFFh (UPPER 64 KBYTE BIOS):** When bit 3 = 1, the PCEB generates MEMCS# for PCI master memory write accesses to the address range 0F0000h–0FFFFFh. When bit 3 = 0, the PCEB does not generate MEMCS# for PCI master memory write accesses to the address range 0F0000h–0FFFFFh.
2	**READ ENABLE FOR 0F0000h–0FFFFFh (UPPER 64 KBYTE BIOS):** When bit 2 = 1, the PCEB generates MEMCS# for PCI master memory read accesses to the address range 0F0000h–0FFFFFh. When bit 2 = 0, the PCEB does not generate MEMCS# for PCI master memory read accesses to the address range 0F0000h–0FFFFFh.
1	**WRITE ENABLE FOR 080000h–09FFFFh (512 KBYTE–640 KBYTE):** When bit 1 = 1, the PCEB generates MEMCS# for PCI master memory write accesses to the address range 080000h–009FFFFh. When bit 1 = 0, the PCEB does not generate MEMCS# for PCI master memory write accesses to the address range 080000h–09FFFFh.
0	**READ ENABLE FOR 080000h–09FFFFh (512 KBYTE–640 KBYTE):** When bit 0 = 1, the PCEB generates MEMCS# for PCI master memory read accesses to the address range 080000h–09FFFFh. When bit 0 = 0, the PCEB does not generate MEMCS# for PCI master memory read accesses to the address range 080000h–09FFFFh.

3.1.12 MCSBOH—MEMCS# BOTTOM OF HOLE REGISTER

Register Name: MEMCS# Bottom of Hole
Address Offset: 45h
Default Value: 10h
Attribute: Read/Write
Size: 8 bits

This register defines the bottom of the MEMCS# hole. MEMCS# is not generated for accesses to addresses within the hole defined by this register and the MCSTOH Register. The hole is defined by the following equation: TOH ≥ address ≥ BOH. TOH is the top of the MEMCS# hole defined by the MCSTOH Register and BOH is the bottom of the MEMCS# hole defined by this register.

For example, to program the BOH at 1 MByte, the value of 10h should be written to this register. To program the BOH at 2 MByte + 64 KByte this register should be programmed to 21h. To program the BOH at 8 MByte this register should be programmed to 80h.

When the TOH < BOH the hole is disabled. If TOH = BOH, the hole size is 64 KBytes. It is the responsibility of the programmer to guarantee that the BOH is at or above 1 MB. AD[31:24] must be 0's for the hole, meaning the hole is restricted to be under the 16 MByte boundary. The default value for the BOH and TOH disables the hole.

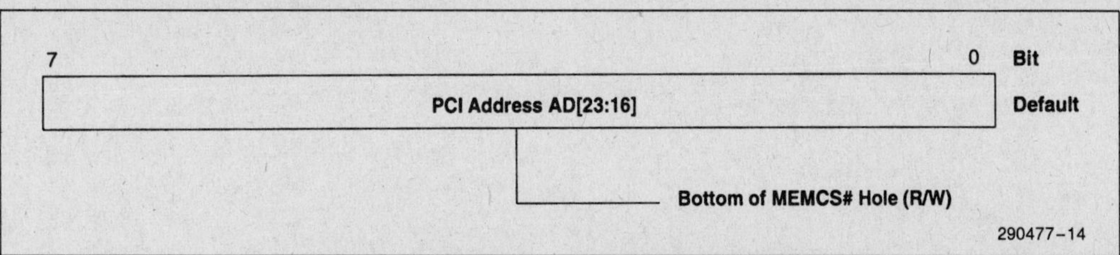

Figure 3-12. MEMCS# Bottom of Hole Register

Table 3-13. MEMCS# Bottom of Hole Register

Bit	Description
7:0	**BOTTOM OF MEMCS# HOLE:** Bits [7:0] correspond to address lines AD[23:16], respectively.

3.1.13 MCSTOH—MEMCS# TOP OF HOLE REGISTER

Register Name: MEMCS# Top of Hole
Address Offset: 46h
Default Value: 0Fh
Attribute: Read/Write
Size: 8 bits

This register defines the top of the MEMCS# hole. MEMCS# is not generated for accesses to addresses within the hole defined by this register and the MCSBOH Register. The hole is defined by the following equation: TOH ≥ address ≥ BOH. TOH is the top of the MEMCS# hole defined by this register and BOH is the bottom of the MEMCS# hole defined by the MCSBOH Register.

For example, to program the TOH at 1 MByte + 64 KByte, this register should be programmed to 10h. To program the TOH at 2 MByte + 128 KByte this register should be programmed to 21h. To program the TOH at 12 MByte this register should be programmed to BFh.

When the TOH < BOH the hole is disabled. If TOH = BOH, the hole size is 64 KBytes. It is the responsibility of the programmer to guarantee that the TOH is above 1 MByte. AD[31:24] must be 0's for the hole, meaning the hole is restricted to be under the 16 MByte boundary. The default value for the BOH and TOH disables the hole.

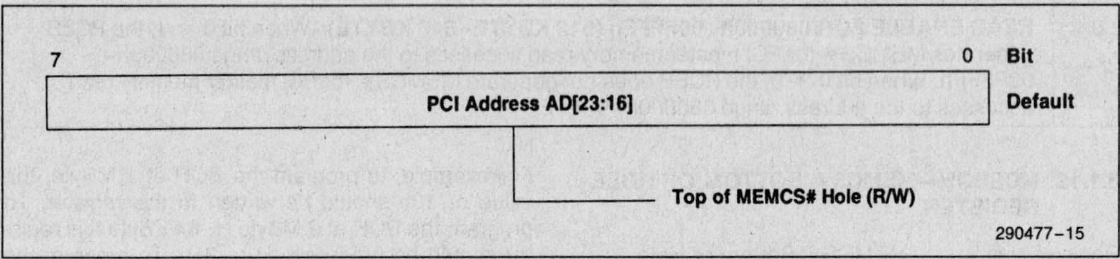

Figure 3-13. MEMCS# Top of Hole Register

Table 3-14. MEMCS# Top of Hole Register

Bit	Description
7:0	**TOP OF MEMCS# HOLE:** Bits [7:0] correspond to address lines AD[23:16], respectively.

3.1.14 MCSTOM—MEMCS# TOP OF MEMORY REGISTER

Register Name: MEMCS# Top of Memory
Address Offset: 47h
Default Value: 00h
Attribute: Read/Write
Size: 8 bits

This register determines MEMCS# top of memory boundary. The top of memory boundary ranges from 2 MBytes-1 to 512 MBytes-1, in 2 MByte increments. This register is typically set to the top of main memory. Accesses ≥ 1 MByte and ≤ top of memory boundary results in the assertion of the MEMCS# signal (unless the address resides in the hole programmed via the MCSBOH and MCSTOH Registers). A value of 00h sets top of memory at 2 MBytes-1 (including the 2 MByte-1 address). A value of FFh sets the top of memory at 512 MByte-1 (including the 512 MByte-1 address).

1

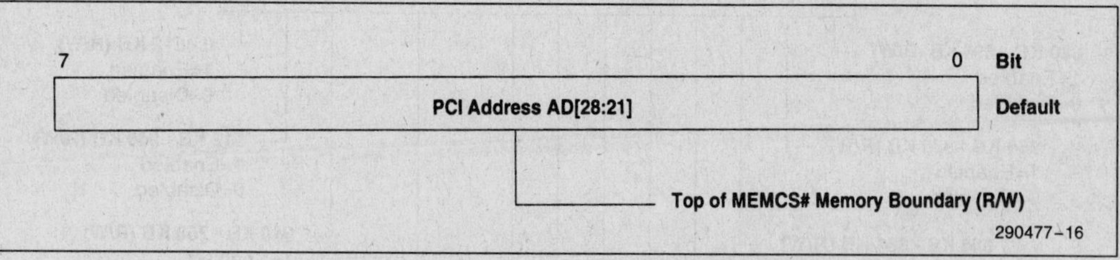

Figure 3-14. MEMCS# Top of Memory Register

Table 3-15. MEMCS# Top of Memory Register

Bit	Description
7:0	**TOP OF MEMCS# MEMORY BOUNDARY:** Bits [7:0] correspond to address lines AD[28:21], respectively.

3.1.15 EADC1—EISA ADDRESS DECODE CONTROL 1 REGISTER

Register Name: EISA Address Decode Control 1
Address Offset: 48h-49h
Default Value: 0001h
Attribute: Read/Write
Size: 16 bits

This 16-bit register specifies EISA-to-PCI mapping of the 0-1 MByte memory address range. For each bit position, the memory block is enabled if the corresponding bit = 1 and is disabled if the bit = 0. EISA or DMA memory cycles to the enabled blocks result in the EISA cycle being forwarded to the PCI Bus. For disabled memory blocks, the EISA memory cycle is not forwarded to the PCI Bus.

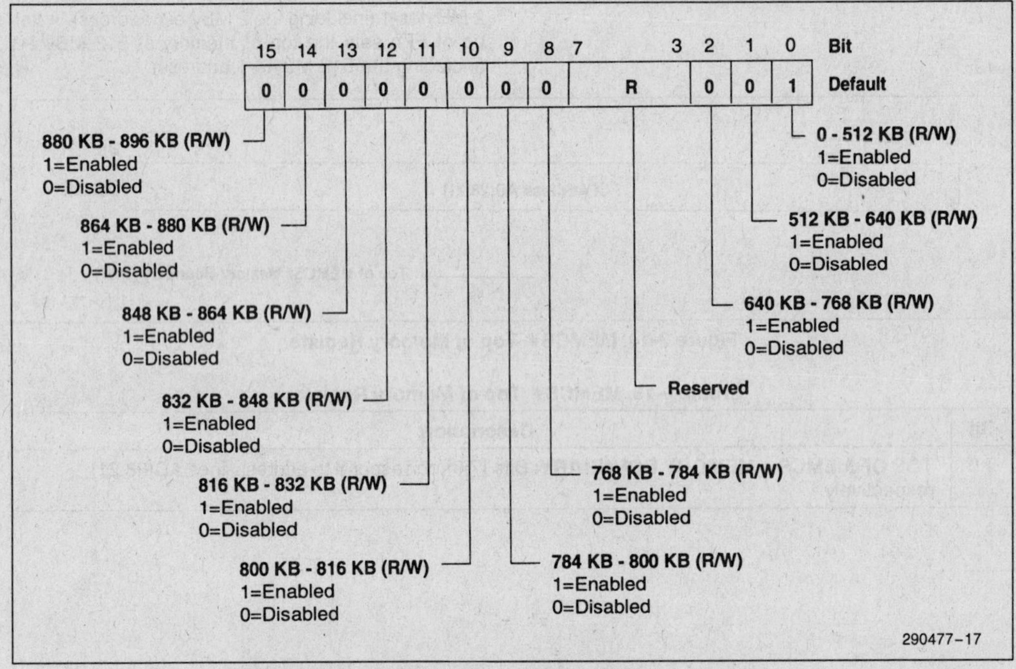

Figure 3-15. EISA Address Decode Control 1 Register

Table 3-16. EISA Address Decode Control 1 Register

Bit	Description
15	**880 KBYTES–896 KBYTES MEMORY ENABLE:** EISA-to-PCI mapping for this memory space is enabled when this bit is 1 and disabled when this bit is 0.
14	**864 KBYTES–880 KBYTES MEMORY ENABLE:** EISA-to-PCI mapping for this memory space is enabled when this bit is 1 and disabled when this bit is 0.
13	**848 KBTES–864 KBYTES MEMORY ENABLE:** EISA-to-PCI mapping for this memory space is enabled when this bit is 1 and disabled when this bit is 0.
12	**832 KBTES–848 KBYTES MEMORY ENABLE:** EISA-to-PCI mapping for this memory space is enabled when this bit is 1 and disabled when this bit is 0.
11	**816 KBTES–832 KBYTES MEMORY ENABLE:** EISA-to-PCI mapping for this memory space is enabled when this bit is 1 and disabled when this bit is 0.
10	**800 KBTES–816 KBYTES MEMORY ENABLE:** EISA-to-PCI mapping for this memory space is enabled when this bit is 1 and disabled when this bit is 0.
9	**784 KBTES–800 KBYTES MEMORY ENABLE:** EISA-to-PCI mapping for this memory space is enabled when this bit is 1 and disabled when this bit is 0.
8	**768 KBTES–784 KBYTES MEMORY ENABLE:** EISA-to-PCI mapping for this memory space is enabled when this bit is 1 and disabled when this bit is 0.
7:3	**RESERVED.**
2	**640 KBTES–768 KBYTES VGA MEMORY ENABLE:** EISA-to-PCI mapping for this memory space is enabled when this bit is 1 and disabled when this bit is 0.
1	**512 KBTES–640 KBYTES MEMORY ENABLE:** EISA-to-PCI mapping for this memory space is enabled when this bit is 1 and disabled when this bit is 0.
0	**0–512 KBYTES MEMORY ENABLE:** EISA-to-PCI mapping for this memory space is enabled when this bit is 1 and disabled when this bit is 0.

3.1.16 IORT—ISA I/O RECOVERY TIMER REGISTER

Register Name: ISA I/O Recovery Time
Address Offset: 4Ch
Default Value: 56h
Attribute: Read/Write
Size: 8 bits

The I/O recovery logic is used to guarantee a minimum amount of time between back-to-back 8-bit and 16-bit PCI-to-ISA I/O slave accesses. These minimum times are programmable.

The I/O recovery mechanism in the PCEB is used to add recovery delay between PCI-originated 8-bit and 16-bit I/O cycles to ISA devices. The delay is measured from the rising edge of the EISA command signal (CMD#) to the falling edge of the next EISA command. The delay is equal to the number of EISA Bus clocks (BCLKs) that correspond to the value contained in bits [1:0] for 16-bit I/O devices and in bits [5:3] for 8-bit I/O devices. Note that no additional delay is inserted for back-to-back I/O "sub-cycles" generated as a result of byte assembly or disassembly. This register defaults to 8-bit and 16-bit recovery enabled with two clocks of I/O recovery.

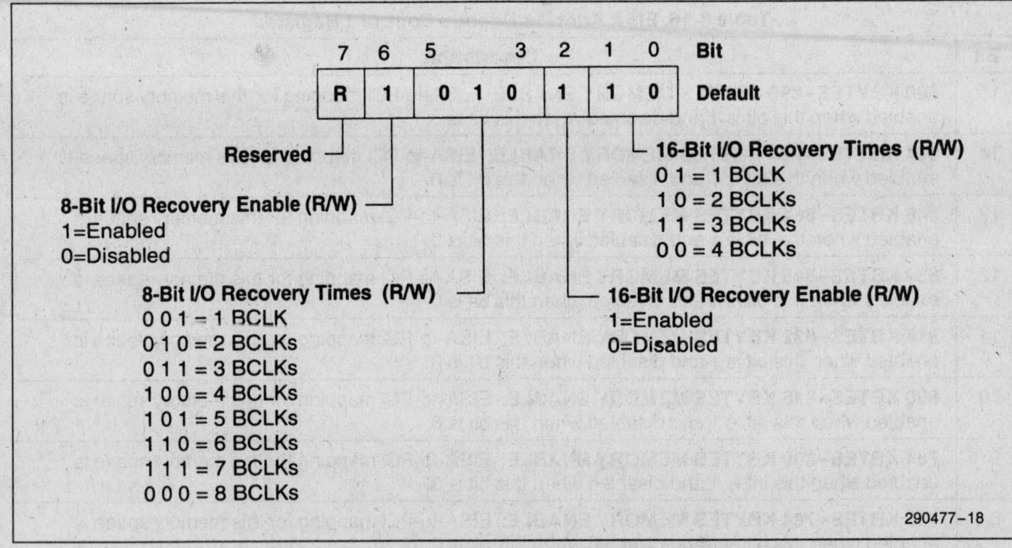

Figure 3-16. ISA Controller Recovery Timer Register

Table 3-17. ISA Controller Recovery Timer Register

Bit	Description
7	**RESERVED.**
6	**8-BIT I/O RECOVERY ENABLE:** This bit enables the recovery times programmed into bits 0 and 1 of this register. When this bit is set to 1, the recovery times shown for bits 5-3 are enabled. When this bit is set to 0, recovery times are disabled.
5:3	**8-BIT I/O RECOVERY TIMES:** This 3-bit field defines the recovery times for 8-bit I/O. Programmable delays between back-to-back 8-bit PCI cycles to ISA I/O slaves is shown in terms of EISA clock cycles (BCLK). The selected delay programmed into this field is enabled/disabled via bit 6 of this register. **Bit 5 / Bit 4 / Bit 3 / BCLK** 0 0 1 1 0 1 0 2 0 1 1 3 1 0 0 4 1 0 1 5 1 1 0 6 1 1 1 7 0 0 0 8
2	**16-BIT I/O RECOVERY ENABLE:** This bit enables the recovery times programmed into bits 0 and 1 of this register. When this bit is set to 1, the recovery times shown for bits 0 and 1 are enabled. When this bit is set to 0, recovery times are disabled.
1:0	**16-BIT I/O RECOVERY TIMES:** This 2-bit field defines the Recovery time for 16-bit I/O. Programmable delays between back-to-back 16-bit PCI cycles to ISA I/O slaves is shown in terms of EISA clock cycles (BCLK). The selected delay programmed into this field is enabled/disabled via bit 2 of this register. **Bit 1 / Bit 0 / BCLK** 0 1 1 1 0 2 1 1 3 0 0 4

3.1.17 MAR1—MEMCS# ATTRIBUTE REGISTER #1

Register Name: MEMCS# Attribute Register #1
Address Offset: 54h
Default Value: 00h
Attribute: Read/Write
Size: 8 bits

RE—Read Enable. When the RE bit (bit 6, 4, 2, 0) is set to a 1, the PCEB generates MEMCS# for PCI master, DMA, or EISA master memory read accesses to the corresponding segment in main memory. When the RE bit is set to a 0, the PCEB does not generate MEMCS# for PCI master, DMA, or EISA master memory read accesses to the corresponding segment. When the RE and WE bits are both 0 (or bit 4 in the MEMCS# Control Register is set to a 0 - disabled), the PCI master, DMA, or EISA master can not access the corresponding segment in main memory.

WE—Write Enable. When the WE bit (bit 7, 5, 3, 1) is set to a 1, the PCEB generates MEMCS# for PCI master, DMA, or EISA master memory write accesses to the corresponding segment in main memory. When this bit is set to a 0, the PCEB does not generate MEMCS# for PCI master, DMA, or EISA master memory write accesses to the corresponding segment. When the RE and WE bits are both 0 (or bit 4 in the MEMCS# Control Register is set to a 0 - disabled), the PCI master, DMA, or EISA master can not access the corresponding segment in main memory.

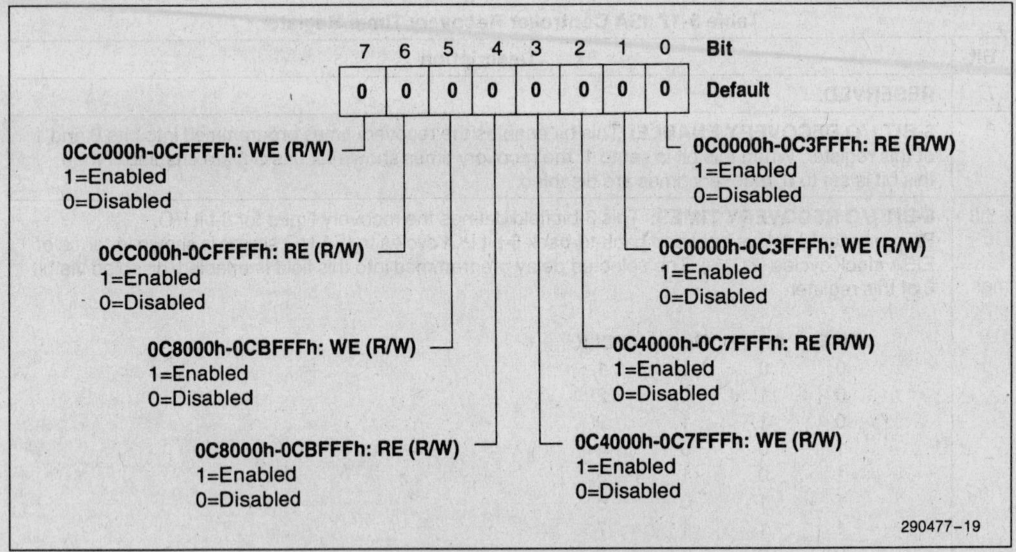

Figure 3-17. MEMCS# Attribute Register #1

Table 3-18. MEMCS# Attribute Register #1

Bit	Description
7	0CC000h–0CFFFFh Add-on BIOS: WE
6	0CC000h–0CFFFFh Add-on BIOS: RE
5	0C8000h–0CBFFFh Add-on BIOS: WE
4	0C8000h–0CBFFFh Add-on BIOS: RE
3	0C4000h–0C7FFFh Add-on BIOS: WE
2	0C4000h–0C7FFFh Add-on BIOS: RE
1	0C0000h–0C3FFFh Add-on BIOS: WE
0	0C0000h–0C3FFFh Add-on BIOS: RE

3.1.18 MAR2—MEMCS# ATTRIBUTE REGISTER #2

Register Name: MEMCS# Attribute Register #2
Address Offset: 55h
Default Value: 00h
Attribute: Read/Write
Size: 8 bits

RE—Read Enable. When the RE bit (bit 6, 4, 2, 0) is set to a 1, the PCEB generates MEMCS# for PCI master, DMA, or EISA master memory read accesses to the corresponding segment in main memory. When this bit is set to a 0, the PCEB does not generate MEMCS# for PCI master, DMA, or EISA master memory read accesses to the corresponding segment. When the RE and WE bits are both 0 (or bit 4 in the MEMCS# Control Register is set to a 0 - disabled), the PCI master, DMA, or EISA master can not access the corresponding segment in main memory.

WE—Write Enable. When the WE bit (bit 7, 5, 3, 1) is set to a 1, the PCEB generates MEMCS# for PCI master, DMA, or EISA master memory write accesses to the corresponding segment in main memory. When this bit is set to a 0, the PCEB does not generate MEMCS# for PCI master, DMA, or EISA master memory write accesses to the corresponding segment. When the RE and WE bits are both 0 (or bit 4 in the MEMCS# Control Register is set to a 0 - disabled), the PCI master, DMA, or EISA master can not access the corresponding segment in main memory.

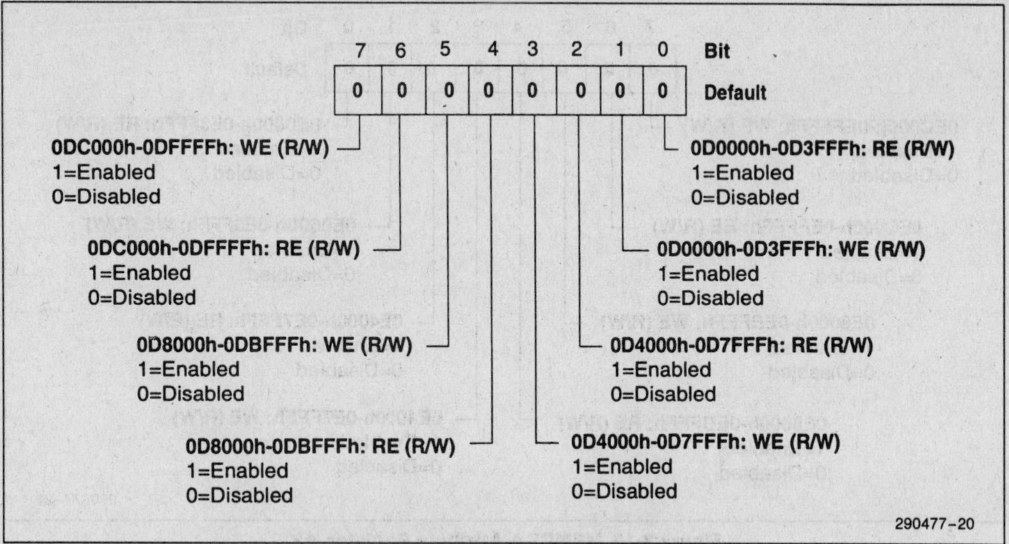

Figure 3-18. MEMCS# Attribute Register #2

Table 3-19. MEMCS# Attribute Register #2

Bit	Description
7	0DC000h–0DFFFFh Add-on BIOS: WE
6	0DC000h–0DFFFFh Add-on BIOS: RE
5	0D8000h–0DBFFFh Add-on BIOS: WE
4	0D8000h–0DBFFFh Add-on BIOS: RE
3	0D4000h–0D7FFFh Add-on BIOS: WE
2	0D4000h–0D7FFFh Add-on BIOS: RE
1	0D0000h–0D3FFFh Add-on BIOS: WE
0	0D0000h–0D3FFFh Add-on BIOS: RE

3.1.19 MAR3—MEMCS# ATTRIBUTE REGISTER #3

Register Name: MEMCS# Attribute Register #3
Address Offset: 56h
Default Value: 00h
Attribute: Read/Write
Size: 8 bits

RE—Read Enable. When the RE bit (bit 6, 4, 2, 0) is set to a 1, the PCEB generates MEMCS# for PCI master, DMA, EISA master memory read accesses to the corresponding segment in main memory. When this bit is set to a 0, the PCEB does not generate MEMCS# for PCI master, DMA, or EISA master memory read accesses to the corresponding segment. When the RE and WE bits are both 0 (or bit 4 in the MEMCS# Control Register is set to a 0 - disabled), the PCI master can not access the corresponding segment in main memory.

WE—Write Enable. When the WE bit (bit 7, 5, 3, 1) is set to a 1, the PCEB generates MEMCS# for PCI master, DMA, EISA master memory write accesses to the corresponding segment in main memory. When this bit is set to a 0, the PCEB does not generate MEMCS# for PCI master, DMA, or EISA master memory write accesses to the corresponding segment. When the RE and WE bits are both 0 (or bit 4 in the MEMCS# Control Register is set to a 0 - disabled), the PCI master can not access the corresponding segment in main memory.

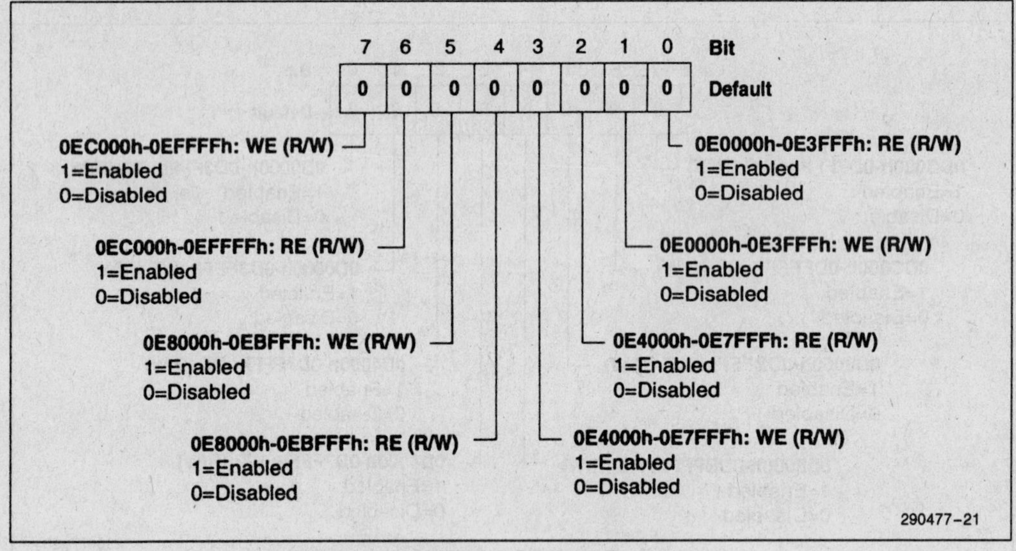

Figure 3-19. MEMCS# Attribute Register #3

Table 3-20. MEMCS# Attribute Register #3

Bit	Description
7	0EC000h–0EFFFFh BIOS Extension: WE
6	0EC000h–0EFFFFh BIOS Extension: RE
5	0E8000h–0EBFFFh BIOS Extension: WE
4	0E8000h–0EBFFFh BIOS Extension: RE
3	0E4000h–0E7FFFh BIOS Extension: WE
2	0E4000h–0E7FFFh BIOS Extension: RE
1	0E0000h–0E3FFFh BIOS Extension: WE
0	0E0000h–0E3FFFh BIOS Extension: RE

3.1.20 PDCON—PCI DECODE CONTROL REGISTER

Register Name: PCI Decode Control
Address Offset: 58h
Default Value: 00h
Attribute: Read/Write
Size: 8 bits

This register controls the mode of address decode (subtractive or negative) for memory cycles on the PCI Bus. This register is used to enable/disable positive decode of PCI accesses to the IDE and 8259 locations residing in the expansion bus subsystem.

Subtractive Decoding

PCI memory cycles that are not claimed on the PCI Bus (i.e., DEVSEL# inactive) are forwarded to the EISA Bus. This is the default on power up.

Negative Decoding

PCI memory cycles that are not mapped to one of the regions defined by A, B, or C below, are immediately forwarded to the EISA Bus (i.e., without waiting for DEVSEL# time-out). PCI memory cycles that are decoded to one of the four programmable PCI memory regions, but are not claimed (DEVSEL# negated), are forwarded to the EISA Bus by subtractive decode.

A. Main memory locations defined by the MEMCS# mapping (MCSCON, MCSBOH, MCSTOH, MCSTOM, MAR1, MAR2, and MAR3 Registers).

B. The enabled Video Frame Buffer region, 0A0000h–0BFFFFh (as indicated by bit 2 of the EADC1 Register).

C. The four programmable PCI memory regions (defind by the MEMREGN[4:1] registers.

NOTE:

If there are devices on the PCI that are not mapped into any of the regions defined by A, B, or C, then negative decoding can not be used.

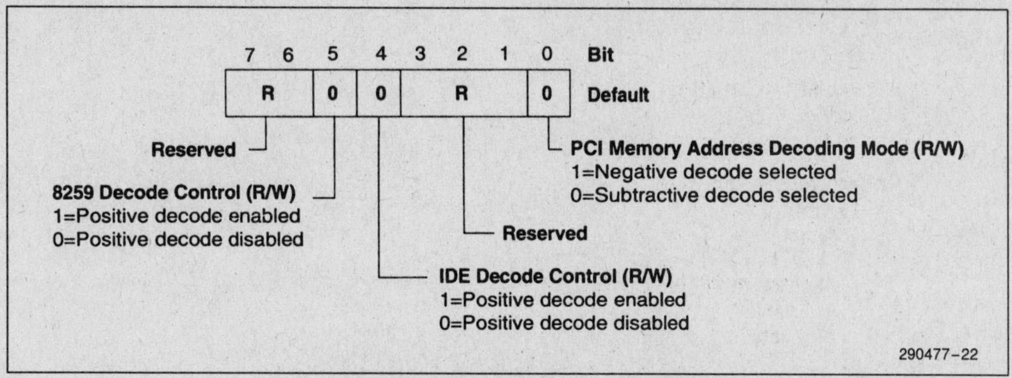

Figure 3-20. PCI Decode Control Register

Table 3-21. PCI Decode Control Register

Bit	Description
7:6	**RESERVED.**
5	**8259 DECODE CONTROL (8259DC):** This bit enables/disables positive decode of 8259 locations 0020h, 0021h, 00A0h and 00A1h. When this bit is 1, positive decode for these locations are enabled. When this bit is 0, positive decode for these locations is disabled. After reset, this bit is 0. Note that if positive decode is disabled, these 8259 locations can still be accessed via subtractive decode.
4	**IDE DECODE CONTROL (IDEDC):** This bit enables/disables positive decode of IDE locations 1F0h–1F7h (primary) or 170h–177h (secondary) and 3F6h, 3F7h (primary) or 376h, 377h (secondary). When IDEDC = 0, positive decode is disabled. When IDECD = 1, positive decode is enabled. After reset, this bit is 0. Note that if positive decode is disabled, these IDE locations can still be accessed via subtractive decode.
3:1	**RESERVED.**
0	**PCI MEMORY ADDRESS DECODING MODE (PMAD):** This bit selects between subtractive and negative decoding. When PMAD = 1, negative decoding is selected. When PMAD = 0, subtractive decoding is selected. After reset, this bit is 0.

3.1.21 EADC2—EISA ADDRESS DECODER CONTROL EXTENSION REGISTER

Register Name: EISA Address Decoder Control Extension
Address Offset: 5Ah
Default Value: 00h
Attribute: Read/Write
Size: 8 bits

This register specifies EISA-to-PCI mapping for the 896 KByte to 1 MByte memory address range (BIOS). If this memory block is enabled, EISA memory accesses in this range will result in the EISA cycles being forwarded to the PCI Bus. (Note that enabling this block is necessary if BIOS resides within the PCI and not within the EISA subsystem.)

This register also defines mapping for the 16 MByte minus 64 KByte to 16 MByte memory address range. This mapping is important if the BIOS is aliased at the top 64 KBytes of 16 MBytes. If the region is enabled and this address range is within the hole defined by the MCSBOH and MCSTOH Registers or above the top of main memory defined by the MCSTOM Register, the EISA cycle is forwarded to the PCI.

1

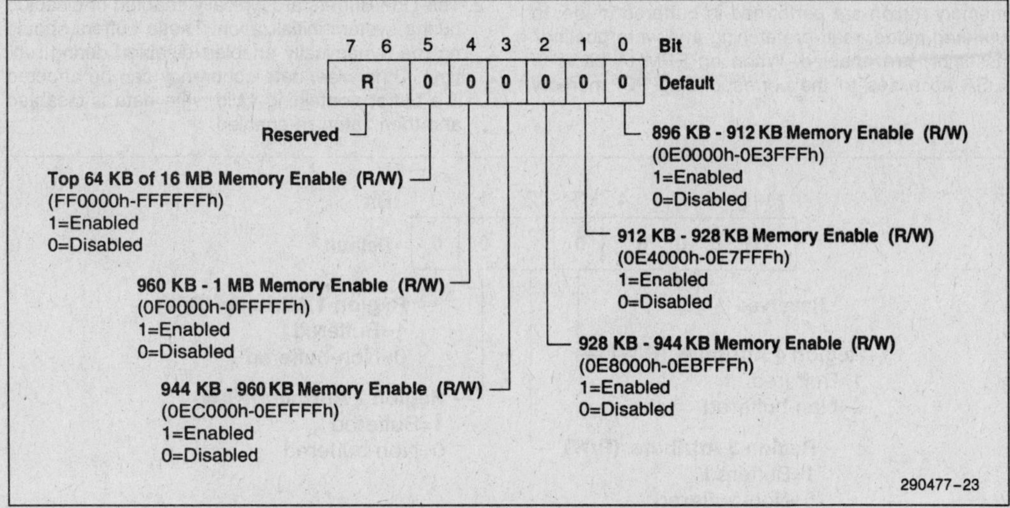

Figure 3-21. EISA Address Decoder Control Extension Register

Table 3-22. EISA Address Decoder Control Extension Register

Bit	Description
7:6	**RESERVED.**
5	**TOP 64 KBYTE OF 16 MBYTE MEMORY SPACE ENABLE (FF0000h–FFFFFFh):** This memory block is enabled when this bit is 1 and disabled when this bit is 0.
4	**960 KBYTES–1 MBYTE MEMORY SPACE ENABLE (0F0000h–0FFFFFh):** This memory block is enabled when this bit is 1 and disabled when this bit is 0.
3	**944 KBYTES–960 KBYTE MEMORY SPACE ENABLE (0EC000h–0EFFFFh):** This memory block is enabled when this bit is 1 and disabled when this bit is 0.
2	**928 KBYTES–944 KBYTE MEMORY SPACE ENABLE (0E8000h–0EBFFFh):** This memory block is enabled when this bit is 1 and disabled when this bit is 0.
1	**912 KBYTES–928 KBYTE MEMORY SPACE ENABLE (0E4000h–0E7FFFh):** This memory block is enabled when this bit is 1 and disabled when this bit is 0.
0	**896 KBYTES–912 KBYTE MEMORY SPACE ENABLE (0E0000h–0E3FFFh):** This memory block is enabled when this bit is 1 and disabled when this bit is 0.

3.1.22 EPMRA—EISA-TO-PCI MEMORY REGION ATTRIBUTES REGISTER

Register Name: EISA-to-PCI Memory Region Attributes
Address Offset: 5Ch
Default Value: 00h
Attribute: Read/Write
Size: 8 bits

This register defines buffering attributes for EISA accesses to PCI memory regions specified by MEMREGN[4:1] Registers. When an EPMRA bit is 1 (and the Line Buffers are enabled via the PCICON Register), EISA accesses to the corresponding PCI memory region are performed in buffered mode. In buffered mode, read prefetching and write posting/assembly are enabled. When an EPMRA bit is 0, EISA accesses to the corresponding PCI memory region are performed in non-buffered mode. In non-buffered mode, a buffer bypass path is used to complete the transaction.

NOTE:

1. Using buffered mode for EISA accesses to PCI memory regions that contain memory-mapped I/O devices can cause unintended side effects. In buffered mode, strong ordering is not preserved within a Dword. If the order of the writes to an I/O device is important, non-buffered mode should be used. Also, read-prefetch can cause unintended changes of status registers in the memory-mapped I/O device.
2. The Line Buffers are typically enabled or disabled during system initialization. These buffers should not be dynamically enabled/disabled during run-time. Otherwise, data coherency can be affected if a buffer containing valid write data is disabled and then, later, re-enabled.

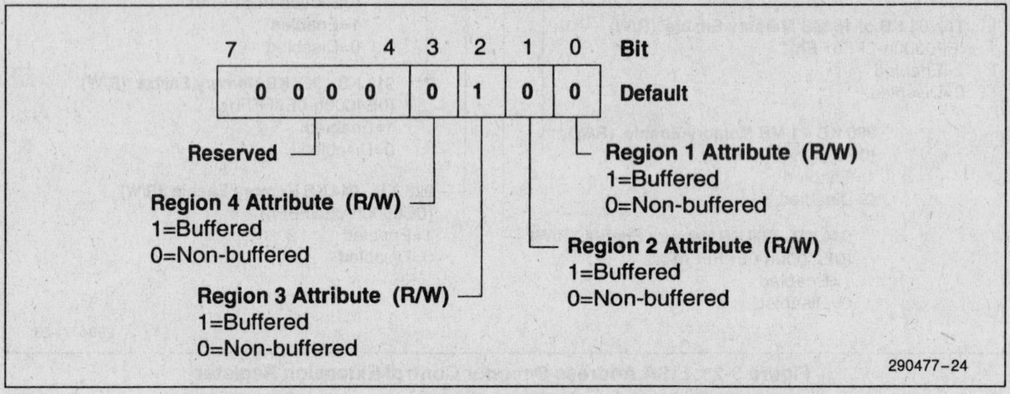

Figure 3-22. EISA-to-PCI Memory Region Attributes Register

Table 3-23. EISA-to-PCI Memory Region Attributes Register

Bit	Description
7:4	**RESERVED.**
3	**REGION 4 ATTRIBUTE (REG-4):** EISA accesses to this PCI memory region are buffered when this bit is 1 and non-buffered when this bit is 0. If the Line Buffers are disabled via the PCICON Register (bit 6), buffering is disabled, regardless of the value of this bit.
2	**REGION 3 ATTRIBUTE (REG-3):** EISA accesses to this PCI memory region are buffered when this bit is 1 and non-buffered when this bit is 0. If the Line Buffers are disabled via the PCICON Register (bit 6), buffering is disabled, regardless of the value of this bit.
1	**REGION 2 ATTRIBUTE (REG-2):** EISA accesses to this PCI memory region are buffered when this bit is 1 and non-buffered when this bit is 0. If the Line Buffers are disabled via the PCICON Register (bit 6), buffering is disabled, regardless of the value of this bit.
0	**REGION 1 ATTRIBUTE (REG-1):** EISA accesses to this PCI memory region are buffered when this bit is 1 and non-buffered when this bit is 0. If the Line Buffers are disabled via the PCICON Register (bit 6), buffering is disabled, regardless of the value of this bit.

3.1.23 MEMREGN[4:1]—EISA-TO-PCI MEMORY REGION ADDRESS REGISTERS

Register Name: EISA-to-PCI Memory Region Address
Address Offset: 60h-6Fh
Default Value: 0000FFFFh
Attribute: Read/Write
Size: 32 bits

These 32-bit registers provide four windows for EISA-to-PCI memory accesses. Each window defines a positively decoded programmable address region for mapping EISA memory space to the corresponding PCI memory space. This base and limit address fields define the size and location of the region within the 4 GByte PCI memory space. The base and limit addresses can be aligned on any 64 KByte boundary and each region can be sized in 64 KByte increments, up to the theoretical maximum size of 4 GBytes. The default values of this register ensure that the regions are initially disabled.

A region is selected based on the following formula: Base Address ≤ address ≤ Limit Address.

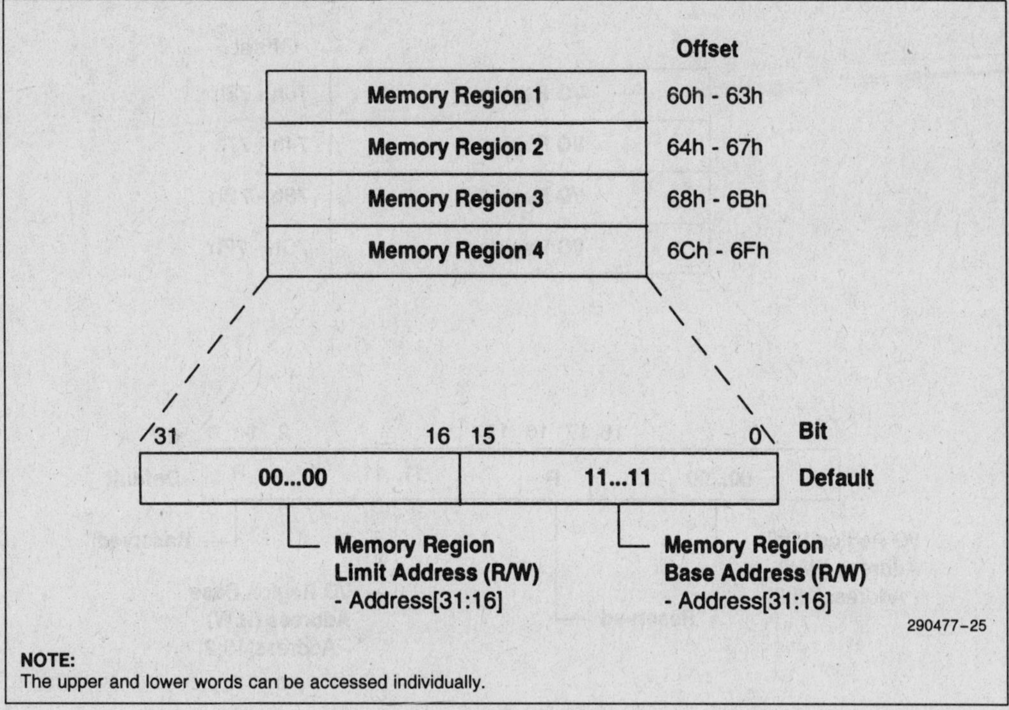

NOTE:
The upper and lower words can be accessed individually.

Figure 3-23. EISA-to-PCI Memory Region Address Register

Table 3-24. EISA-to-PCI Memory Region Address Register

Bit	Description
31:16	**MEMORY REGION LIMIT ADDRESS:** For EISA-to-PCI accesses, bits [31:16] correspond to address lines LA[31:16] on the EISA Bus and AD[31:16] on the PCI Bus. This field determines the limit address of the memory region within the 4 GByte PCI memory space.
15:0	**MEMORY REGION BASE ADDRESS:** For EISA-to-PCI accesses, bits [15:0] correspond to address lines LA[31:16] on the EISA Bus and AD[31:16] on the PCI Bus. This field determines the starting address of the memory region within the 4 GByte PCI memory space.

3.1.24 IOREGN[4:1]—EISA-TO-PCI I/O REGION ADDRESS REGISTERS

Register Name: EISA-to-PCI I/O Region Address
Address Offset: 70h-7Fh
Default Value: 0000FFFCh
Attribute: Read/Write
Size: 32 bits

These 32-bit registers provide four windows for EISA-to-PCI I/O accesses. The windows define positively decoded programmable address regions for mapping EISA I/O space to the corresponding PCI I/O space. Each register determines the starting and limit addresses of the particular region within the 64 KByte PCI I/O space. The base and limit addresses can be aligned on any Dword boundary and each region can be sized in Dword increments (32 bits) up to the theoretical maximum size of 64 KByte. Default values for the base and limit fields ensure that the regions are initially disabled.

The I/O regions are selected based on the following formula: Base Address ≤ address ≤ Limit Address.

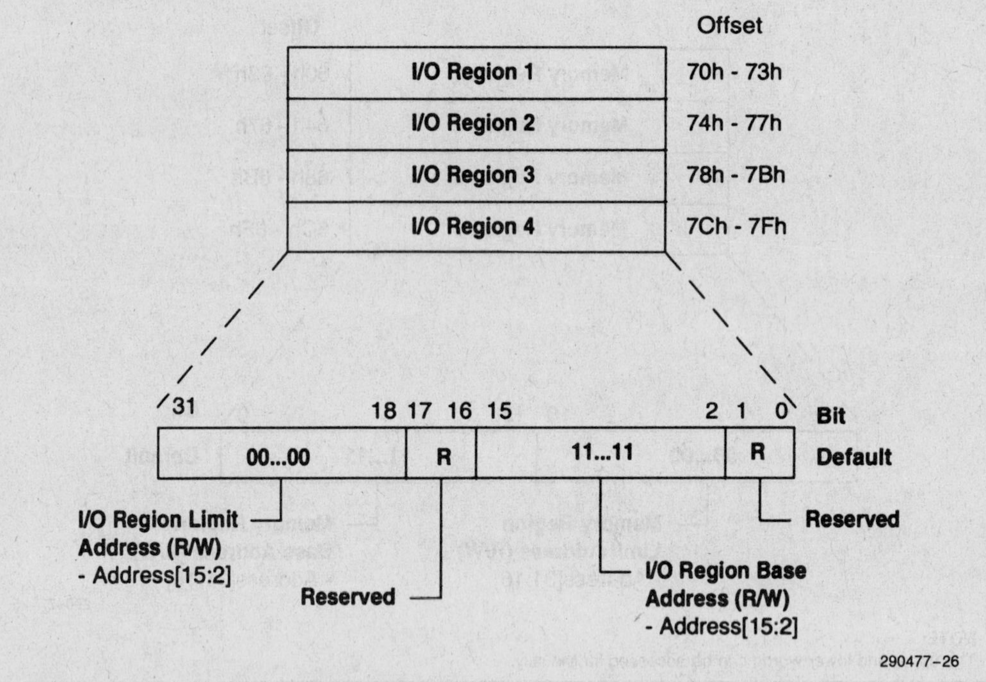

NOTE:
The upper and lower words can be accessed individually.

Figure 3-24. EISA-to-PCI I/O Memory Region Address Register

Table 3-25. EISA-to-PCI I/O Region Address Register

Bit	Description
31:18	**I/O REGION LIMIT ADDRESS:** For EISA-to-PCI I/O accesses, bits [31:18] correspond to address lines LA[15:2] on the EISA Bus and AD[15:2] on the PCI Bus. This field determines the limit address of the region within the 64 KByte PCI I/O space.
17:16	**RESERVED.**
15:2	**I/O REGION BASE ADDRESS.** For EISA-to-PCI I/O accesses, bits [15:2] correspond to address lines LA[15:2] on the EISA Bus and AD[15:2] on the PCI Bus. This field determines the starting address of the region within the 64 KByte PCI I/O space.
1:0	**RESERVED.**

3.1.25 BTMR BIOS TIMER BASE ADDRESS REGISTER

Register Name: BIOS Timer Base Address
Address Offset: 80h-81h
Default Value: 0078h
Attribute: Read/Write
Size: 16 bits

This 16-bit register determines the base address for the BIOS Timer Register located in PCI I/O space. The BIOS Timer resides in the PCEB and is the only internal resource mapped to PCI I/O space. The base address can be set at Dword boundaries anywhere in the 64 KByte PCI I/O space. This register also provides the BIOS Timer access enable/disable control bit.

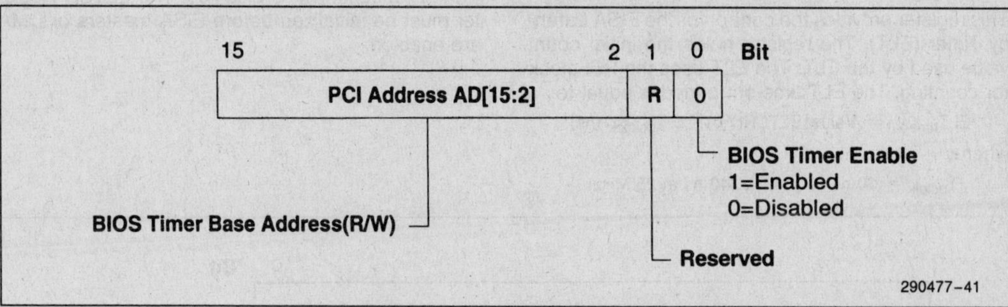

Figure 3-25. BIOS Timer Base Address Register

Table 3-26. BIOS Timer Base Address Register

Bit	Description
15:2	**BIOS TIMER BASE ADDRESS:** Bits [15:2] correspond to PCI address lines AD[15:2].
1	**RESERVED.**
0	**BTE (BIOS TIMER ENABLE):** When BTE = 1, the BIOS Timer is enabled. When BTE = 0, the BIOS Timer is disabled. The default is 0 (disabled).

3.1.26 ELTCR—EISA LATENCY TIMER CONTROL REGISTER

Register Name: EISA Latency Timer Control
Address Offset: 84h
Default Value: 7Fh
Attribute: Read/Write
Size: 8 bits

This register provides the control for the EISA Latency Timer (ELT). The register holds the initial count value used by the ELT. The ELT uses the PCI clock for counting. The ELT time-out period is equal to:

$$ELT_{timeout} = Value\{ELTCR(7:0)\} \times T_{pciclck}\ [ns]$$

where:

T_{pciclk} = 30 ns at 33 MHz (40 ns at 25 MHz).

Therefore, a maximum ELT time-out period at 33 MHz is 256 x 30 ns = 7.68 ms. The value written into this register is system dependent. It should be based on PCI latency characteristics controlled by the PCI Master Latency Timer mechanism and on EISA Bus arbitration/latency parametrics. A typical value corresponds to the ELT time-out period of 1-3 ms. When the value in the ELTCR Register is 0, the ELT mechanism is disabled. The ELTCR Register must be initialized before EISA masters or DMA are enabled.

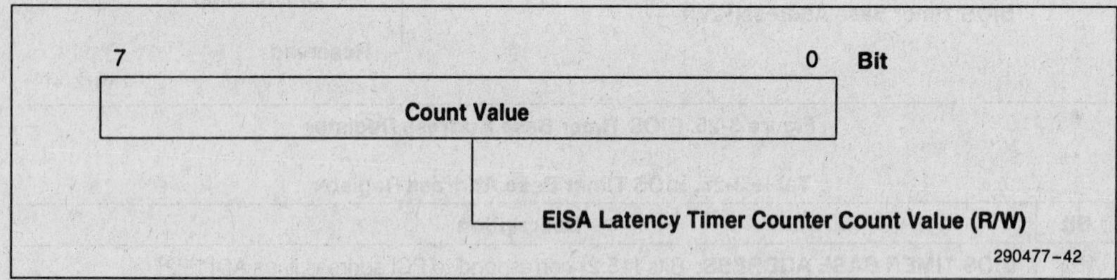

Figure 3-26. EISA Latency Timer Control Register

Table 3-27. EISA Latency Timer Control Register

Bit	Description
7:0	**EISA LATENCY TIMER COUNT VALUE:** Bits[7:0] contain the initial count value for the EISA Latency Timer. When this field contains 00h, the EISA Latency Timer is disabled.

3.2 I/O Registers

The only PCEB internal resource mapped to the PCI I/O space is the BIOS Timer Register.

3.2.1 BIOS TIMER REGISTER

Register Name: BIOS Timer
Register Location: Programmable I/O Address Location (Dword aligned)
Default Value: 00 00 xx xxh
Attribute: Read/Write
Size: 32 bits

This 32-bit register is mapped to the PCI I/O space location determined by the value in the BTMR Register. Bit 0 of BTMR must be 1 to enable access to the BIOS Timer. The BIOS timer clock is derived from the EISA Bus clock (BCLK); either 8.25 MHz or 8.33 MHz depending on the PCI clock. BCLK is divided by 8 to obtain the timer clock of 1.03 MHz or 1.04 MHz. If a frequency other than 33 MHz or 25 MHz is used for PCI clock, the BIOS Timer clock will be affected. (It will always keep the same relation to the BCLK, i.e., 1:4 or 1:3, depending on the clock divisor.) The BIOS Timer is only accessible from the PCI Bus and is not accessible from the EISA Bus.

After data is written into BIOS Timer Register (BE1# and/or BE0# must be asserted), the BIOS timer starts decrementing until it reaches zero. It "freezes" at zero until the new count value is written.

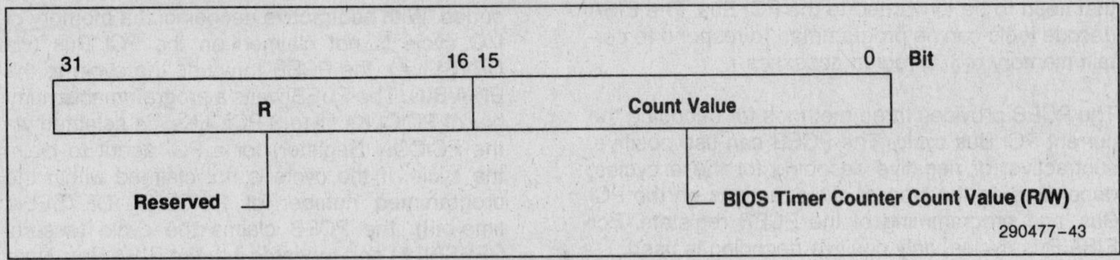

Figure 3-27. BIOS Timer Register

Table 3-28. BIOS Timer Register

Bit	Description
31:16	**RESERVED.**
15:0	**BIOS TIMER COUNT VALUE:** The initial count value is written to bits [15:0] to start the timer. The value read is the current value of the BIOS Timer.

4.0 ADDRESS DECODING

Conceptually, the PCEB contains two programmable address decoders: one to decode PCI Bus cycles that need to be forwarded to the EISA Bus or serviced internally and the other to decode EISA Bus cycles that need to be forwarded to the PCI Bus. Two decoders permit the PCI and EISA Buses to operate concurrently. The PCEB can be programmed to respond to certain PCI memory or I/O region accesses as well as configuration space accesses to the PCEB's internal configuration registers. PCEB address decoding is discussed in Section 4.1.

The EISA address decoder decodes EISA Bus cycles generated by the bus master (DMA controller, ISA compatible master, or EISA compatible master) that need to be forwarded to the PCI Bus. The EISA decode logic can be programmed to respond to certain memory or I/O region accesses.

The PCEB provides three methods for decoding the current PCI Bus cycle. The PCEB can use positive, subtractive, or negative decoding for these cycles, depending on the type of cycle, actions on the PCI Bus, and programming of the PCEB registers. For EISA Bus cycles, only positive decoding is used.

1. **Positive decoding.** With positive decoding, the PCI/EISA Bus cycle address is compared to the corresponding address ranges set up in the PCEB for positive decode. A match causes the PCEB decode logic to immediately service the cycle. The PCEB can be programmed (via the configuration registers) to positively decode selected memory or I/O accesses on both the PCI Bus and EISA Bus. Depending on the programming of the internal registers, the PCEB provides positive decoding for PCI accesses to selected address ranges in memory and I/O spaces and for EISA accesses to selected address ranges in memory and I/O spaces. Note that the decoding method for PCI accesses to the PCEB internal registers (configuration and I/O space registers) is not programmable and these accesses are always positively decoded.
2. **Subtractive decoding.** For PCI memory or I/O cycles, the PCEB uses subtractive decoding (or negative decoding, described in #3 of this list) to respond to addresses that are not positively decoded. With subtractive decoding, if a memory or I/O cycle is not claimed on the PCI Bus (via DEVSEL#), the PCEB forwards the cycle to the EISA Bus. The PCEB waits a programmable number of PCICLKs (1 to 3 PCICLKs, as selected via the PCICON Register) for a PCI agent to claim the cycle. If the cycle is not claimed within the programmed number of PCICLKs (DEVSEL# time-out), the PCEB claims the cycle (asserts DEVSEL#) and forwards it to the EISA Bus. Note that the number of PCICLKs for a DEVSEL# time-out should be programmed to accommodate the slowest PCI Bus device.

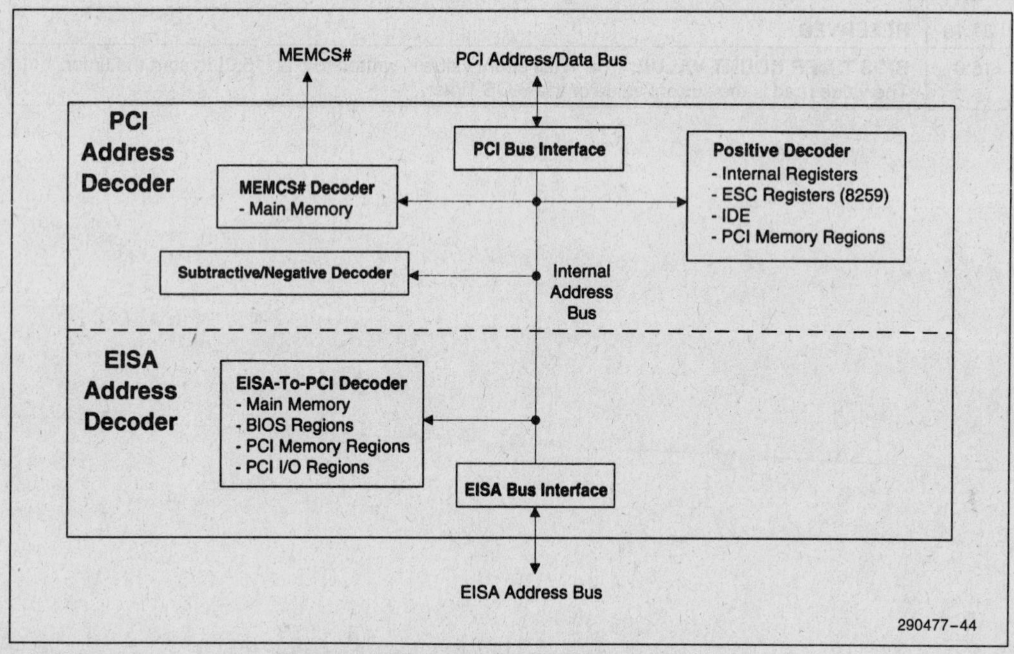

Figure 4-1. Block Diagram Of Address Decoder

3. **Negative decoding.** Negative decoding is a programmable option (via the PDCON Register) that is only used for PCI memory cycles. With negative decoding, a PCI memory cycle that is not positively decoded by the PCEB as a main memory area (one of the MEMCS# generation areas) and is not in one of the four programmable EISA-to-PCI memory regions (defined by MEMREGN[4:1] is immediately forwarded to the EISA Bus. This occurs without waiting for a DEVSEL# time-out to see if the cycle is going to be claimed on the PCI Bus. Thus, negative decoding can reduce the latency incurred by waiting for a DEVSEL# time-out that is associated with subtractive decoding. This increases throughput to the EISA Bus for unclaimed PCI memory cycles. If the DEVSEL# time-out is set to 1 PCICLK, negative decoding does not provide a latency improvement over subtractive decoding. However, for a 2 PCICLK time-out, the latency is reduced by 1 PCICLK and for a 3 PCICLK time-out, the latency is reduced by 2 PCICLKs. For more information on negative (and subtractive) decoding, see Section 4.1.1.3, Subtractively and Negatively Decoded Cycles to EISA.

NOTE:
Negative decoding imposes a restriction on the PCI system memory address map. PCI memory-mapped devices are restricted to one of the four programmable EISA-to-PCI regions (MEMREGN[4:1]). These regions always use subtractive decoding to forward an unclaimed cycle to the EISA Bus, even if negative decoding is enabled. Locating devices in these regions ensures that the PCI device has the allotted number of programmed PCICLKs (DEVSEL# time-out) to respond with DEVSEL#. Further, since the PCEB does not negatively decode I/O space addresses, enabling this feature does not impose restrictions on devices that are mapped to PCI I/O space.

4.1 PCI Cycle Address Decoding

The PCEB decodes addresses presented on the multiplexed PCI address/data bus during the address bus phase. AD[31:0] and the byte enables (C/BE[3:0]# during the data phase) are used for address decoding. C/BE[3:0]# are used during the data phase to indicate which byte lanes contain valid data. For memory cycles, the PCI address decoding is always a function of AD[31:2]. In the case of I/O cycles, all 32 address bits (AD[31:0]) are used to provide addressing with byte granularity. For configuration cycles, only a subset of the address lines carry address information.

The PCEB decodes the following PCI cycle addresses based on the contents of the relevant programmable registers:

1. Positively decodes PCEB configuration registers.
2. Positively decodes I/O addresses contained within the PCEB (BIOS Timer).
3. Positively decodes the following compatibility I/O registers to improve performance:
    - Interrupt controller (8259) I/O registers contained within the ESC to optimize interrupt processing, if enabled through the PDCON Register.
    - IDE registers, if enabled through the PDCON Register.
4. Positively decodes four programmable memory address regions contained within the PCI memory space.
5. Positively decodes memory addresses for selected regions of main memory (located behind the Host/PCI Bridge). When a main memory address is positively decoded, the PCEB asserts the MEMCS# signal to the Host/PCI Bridge. The PCEB does not assert DEVSEL#.
6. Subtractively or negatively decodes cycles to the EISA Bus (see Section 4.1.1, Memory Space Address Decoding).

NOTE:
A PCI requirement is that, upon power-up, PCI agents do not respond to any address. Typically, the only access to a PCI agent is through the IDSEL configuration mechanism until the agent is enabled during initialization. The PCEB/ESC subsystem is an exception to this since it controls access to the BIOS boot code. The PCEB subtractively decodes BIOS accesses and passes the accesses to the EISA Bus where the ESC generates BIOS chip select. This allows BIOS memory to be located in the PCI memory space.

4.1.1 MEMORY SPACE ADDRESS DECODING

The MCSCON, MCSTOP, MCSBOH, MCSTOM, and PDCON Registers are used to program the decoding for PCI Bus memory cycles.

4.1.1.1 Main Memory Decoding (MEMCS#)

The PCEB supports positive decode of main memory areas by generating a memory chip select signal (MEMCS#) to the Host/PCI Bridge that contains the main memory interface control. The PCEB supports memory sizes up to 512 MBytes (i.e., the PCEB can be programmed to generate MEMCS# for this memory range). For PCI memory accesses above 512 MByte (512 MBytes to 4 GBytes), the PCEB does not generate MEMCS# and unclaimed cycles are forwarded to the EISA Bus using either subtractive or negative decoding.

If a memory region is enabled, accesses to that region are positively decoded and result in the PCEB asserting MEMCS#. If a memory region is disabled, accesses do not generate MEMCS# and the cycle is either subtractively or negatively decoded and forwarded to the EISA Bus.

Within the 512 MByte main memory range, the PCEB supports the enabling/disabling of sixteen individual memory ranges (Figure 4-2). Fourteen of the ranges are within the 640 KByte–1 MByte area and have Read Enable (RE) and Write Enable (WE) attributes. These attributes permit positive address decoding for reads and writes to be independently enabled/disabled. This permits, for example, an address range to be positively decoded for a memory read and subtractively (or negatively) decoded to the EISA Bus for a memory write.

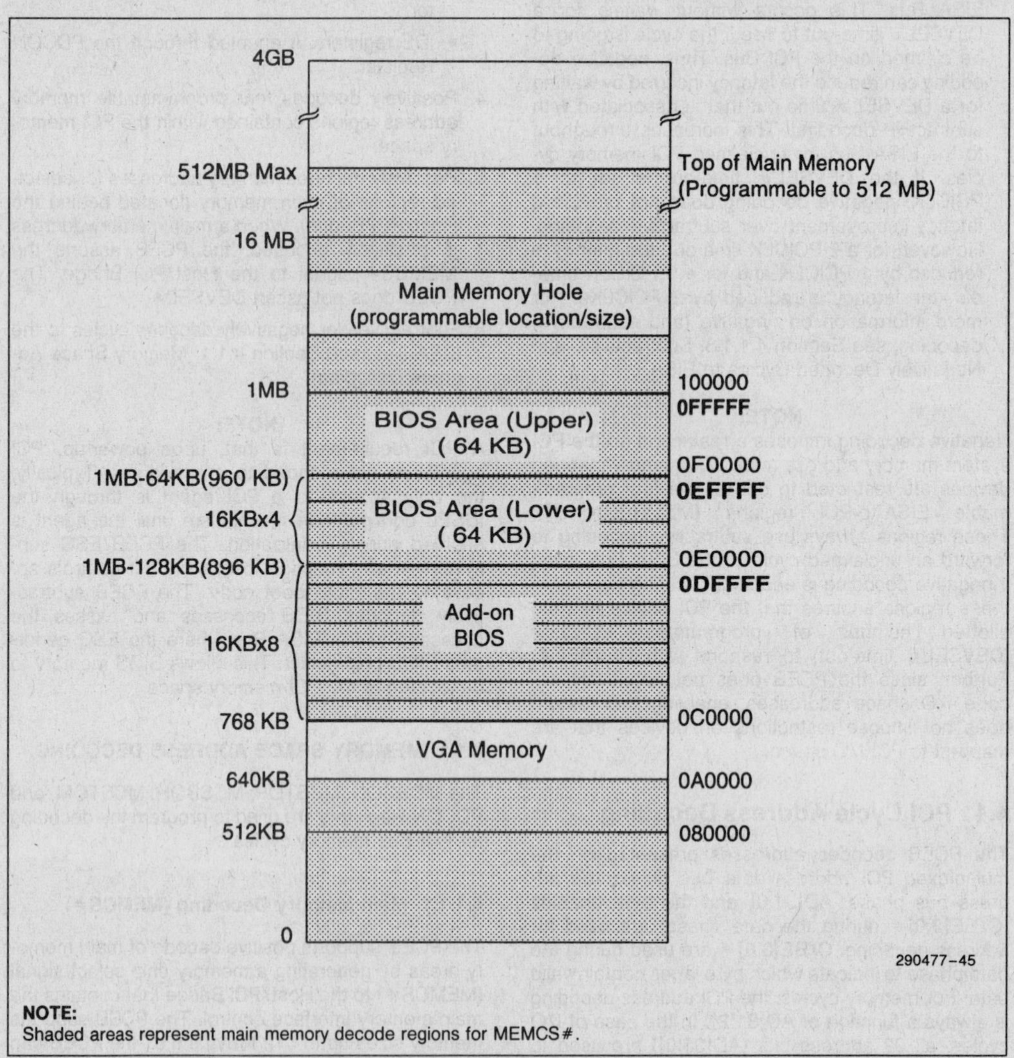

NOTE:
Shaded areas represent main memory decode regions for MEMCS#.

Figure 4-2. MEMCS# Decode Areas

The fifteenth range (0 KByte–512 KByte) and sixteenth range (programmable limit address from 2 MByte up to 512 MByte on 2 MByte increments) can be enabled or disabled but do not have RE/WE attributes. A seventeenth range is available that identifies a memory hole. Addresses within this hole will not generate a MEMCS#. These memory address ranges are:

- 0 KByte to 512 KByte
- 512 KByte to 640 KByte
- 640 KBytes to 768 KBytes (VGA memory page)
- 960 KByte to 1 MByte (BIOS Area)
- 768 KByte to 896 KByte in 16 KByte segments (total of 8 segments)
- 896 KByte to 960 KByte in 16 KByte segments (total of 4 segments)
- 960 KByte to 1 MByte (Upper BIOS area)
- 1 MByte to 512 MByte in 2 MByte increments.
- Programmable memory hole in 64 KByte increments between 1 MByte and 16 MByte.

Table 4-1 summarizes the attribute registers used in MEMCS# decoding. The MCSCON, MAR1, MAR2, and MAR3 Registers are used to assign RE/WE attributes to a particular memory range. The MEMCS# hole is programmed using the MCSTOH and MCSBOH Registers. The region above 1 MByte is programmed using the MCSTOM Register. The region from 0 KByte–512 KByte is enabled/disabled using bit 4 of the MCSCON Register. MCSCON bit 4 is also used to enable and disable the entire MEMCS# function.

Table 4-1. Read Enable/Write Enable Attributes For MEMCS# Decoding

Memory Attribute Registers (Register bits are shown in brackets)	Attribute		Memory Segments	Comments
MCSCON[1:0]	WE	RE	080000h–09FFFFh	512K to 640K
MCSCON[3:2]	WE	RE	0F0000h–0FFFFFh	BIOS Area
MAR1[1:0]	WE	RE	0C0000h–0C3FFFh	Add-on BIOS
MAR1[3:2]	WE	RE	0C4000h–0C7FFFh	Add-on BIOS
MAR1[5:4]	WE	RE	0C8000h–0CBFFFh	Add-on BIOS
MAR1[7:6]	WE	RE	0CC000h–0CFFFFh	Add-on BIOS
MAR2[1:0]	WE	RE	0D0000h–0D3FFFh	Add-on BIOS
MAR2[3:2]	WE	RE	0D4000h–0D7FFFh	Add-on BIOS
MAR2[5:4]	WE	RE	0D8000h–0DBFFFh	Add-on BIOS
MAR2[7:6]	WE	RE	0DC000h–0DFFFFh	Add-on BIOS
MAR3[1:0]	WE	RE	0E0000h–0E3FFFh	BIOS Extension
MAR3[3:2]	WE	RE	0E4000h–0E7FFFh	BIOS Extension
MAR3[5:4]	WE	RE	0E8000h–0EBFFFh	BIOS Extension
MAR3[7:6]	WE	RE	0EC000h–0EFFFFh	BIOS Extension

The PCEB generates MEMCS# from the decode of the PCI address. MEMCS# is asserted during the first data phase as indicated in the Figure 4-3. MEMCS# is only asserted for one PCI clock period. The PCEB does not take any other action as a result of this decode, except to generate MEMCS#. It is the responsibility of the device using the MEMCS# signal to generate DEVSEL#, TRDY# and any other cycle response. The device using the MEMCS# will always generate DEVSEL# on the next clock. This fact can be used to avoid an extra clock delay in the subtractive decoder described in the next section.

4.1.1.2 BIOS Memory Space

The BIOS memory space is subtractively decoded. BIOS is typically "shadowed" after configuration and initialization is complete. Thus, negative decoding is not implemented for accesses to the BIOS EPROM residing on the expansion bus.

The ESC decoder supports BIOS space up to 512 KBytes. The standard 128 KByte BIOS memory space is 000E 0000h to 000F FFFFh (top of 1 MByte), and aliased at FFFE 0000h to FFFF FFFFh (top of 4 GByte) and FFEE 0000h to FFEF FFFFh

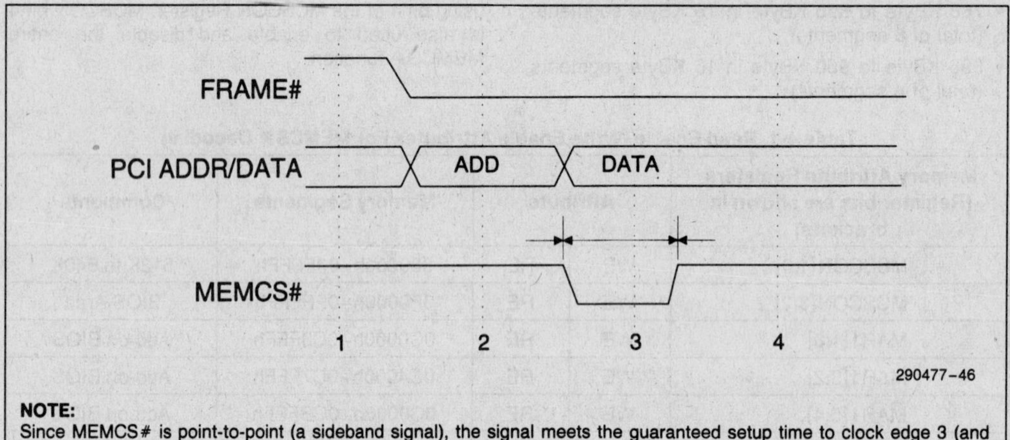

NOTE:
Since MEMCS# is point-to-point (a sideband signal), the signal meets the guaranteed setup time to clock edge 3 (and clock edge 4). This fast generation of MEMCS# prevents the penalty caused by the decoding delay.

Figure 4-3. MEMCS# Generation

(top of 4 GByte−1 MByte). These aliased regions account for the CPU reset vector and the uncertainty of the state of the A20Gate when a software reset occurs.

Note that the ESC component contains the BIOS space decoder that provides address aliasing for BIOS at 4 GByte or 4 GByte−1 MByte by ignoring the LA20 address line.

The additional 384 KByte BIOS memory space at FFF8 0000h to FFFD FFFFh is known as the enlarged BIOS memory space. Note that EISA memory (other than BIOS) must not reside within the address range from 4 GByte−1.5 MByte to 4 GByte−1 MByte and from 4 GByte−512 KByte to 4 GByte to avoid conflict with BIOS space.

Since the BIOS device is 8 bits or 16 bits wide and typically has very long access times, PCI burst reads from BIOS space invoke a disconnect target termination (using the STOP# signal) after the first data transaction in order to meet the PCI incremental latency guidelines.

4.1.1.3 Subtractively and Negatively Decoded Cycles to EISA

The PCEB uses subtractive and negative decoding to forward PCI Bus cycles to the EISA Bus. These modes are defined at the beginning of Section 4.0. Bit 0 of the PDCON Register selects between negative and subtractive decoding.

For subtractive decoding, the DEVSEL# sample point can be configured to three different settings by programming the PCICON Register. If the "fast" point is selected, the cycle is forwarded to EISA when DEVSEL# is inactive at the F sample point. If the "typical" point is selected, DEVSEL# is sampled on both F and T, and, if inactive, the cycle is forwarded to EISA. If the "slow" point is selected, DEVSEL# is sampled at F, T, and S. The sample point should be configured to match the slowest PCI device in the system. This programmable capability permits systems to optimize the DEVSEL# time-out latency to the response capabilities of the PCI devices in the system. The sample point selected must accommodate the slowest device on the PCI Bus. Note that when these unclaimed cycles are forwarded to the EISA Bus, the PCEB drives the DEVSEL# active.

An active MEMCS# always results in an active DEVSEL# on the "Typical" sample point.

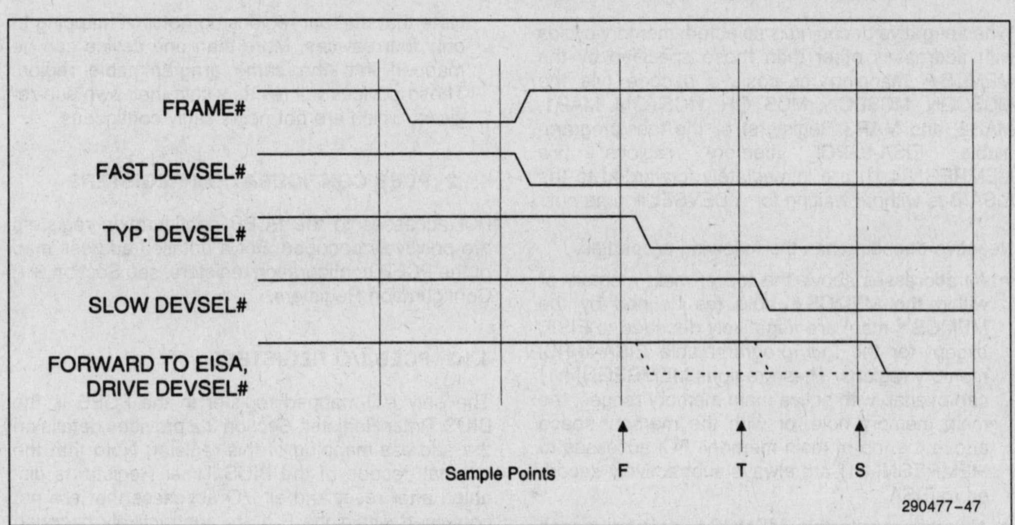

Figure 4-4. DEVSEL# Sample Points

Only unclaimed PCI cycles within the memory address range from 0 GByte to 4 GByte and I/O address range from 0 KByte to 64 KByte are forwarded to EISA. Unclaimed PCI I/O cycles to address locations above 64 KBytes are not forwarded to the EISA Bus and the PCEB does not respond with DEVSEL#. In this case, these unclaimed cycles cause the master to terminate the PCI cycle with a master abort.

If negative decoding is used, the PCEB begins the PCI-to-EISA cycle forwarding process at the "fast" sample point. Compared to the system that uses subtractive decode at the "slow" sample point, negative decoding reduces the decoding overhead by 2 PCI clock cycles. In the case of subtractive decode at the "typical" sampling point, negative decoding reduces the overhead by 1 PCI clock.

The PCEB contains programmable configuration registers that define address ranges for PCI resident devices. There is a set of registers associated with MEMCS# decoding of main memory areas and a set of registers for defining address mapping of up to four EISA memory regions that are mapped to the PCI. Note that there is no equivalent mechanism for mapping the PCI memory regions to EISA and, therefore, all PCI memory cycles that need to be forwarded to the EISA Bus use either subtractive or negative decoding.

When negative decoding is selected, memory cycles with addresses other than those specified by the MEMCS# mapping for positive decode (via the MCSCON, MCSBOH, MCSTOH, MCSTOM, MAR1, MAR2, and MAR3 Registers) or the four programmable EISA-to-PCI memory regions (via MEMREGN[4:1]) are immediately forwarded to the EISA Bus without waiting for a DEVSEL# time-out.

Negative decoding has the following properties.

- All addresses above the top of main memory or within the MEMCS# hole (as defined by the MEMCS# map) are negatively decoded to EISA, except for the four programmable EISA-to-PCI memory regions. These regions MEMREGN[4:1] can overlap with active main memory ranges, the main memory hole, or with the memory space above the top of main memory. PCI accesses to MEMREGN[4:1] are always subtractively decoded to EISA.
- All addresses within MEMCS# defined ranges 640 KByte to 1 MByte can be either mapped to PCI or EISA using positive decoding. Some of these regions allow more detailed mapping based on programmable access attributes (read enable and write enable). This permits a region to be positively decoded for the enabled attribute and negatively decoded, if enabled, to the EISA Bus for the disabled attribute. For example, if a region is enabled for reads and disabled for writes, accesses to the region are positively decoded to the PCI for reads and negatively decoded, if enabled, to EISA for writes. If negative decoding is disabled (i.e., subtractive decoding enabled), the write is subtractively decoded to EISA.
- When negative decoding is enabled, Region [4:1] can still be set up for subtractive decoding. A PCI device that requires subtractive decoding must reside within Region [4:1]. As a result, the subtractive decoding penalty is only associated with some address ranges (i.e., some devices) and not with all non-PCI ranges. This feature can be used with PCI devices that dynamically change response on PCI cycles based on cycle type or an internal device state (e.g., intervention cycle).

  If a PCI device can not be located in one of the regions (Region [4:1]), then negative decoding can not be used. This could occur for systems with very specific address mapping requirements or systems where the device addresses that reside on the PCI Bus are highly fragmented and could not be accommodated with four regions.

  Note that the four regions do not limit mapping to only four devices. More than one device can be mapped into the same programmable region. These devices will reside within their own sub-regions, which are not necessarily contiguous.

4.1.2 PCEB CONFIGURATION REGISTERS

PCI accesses to the PCEB configuration registers are positively decoded. For a detailed address map of the PCEB configuration registers, see Section 3.1, Configuration Registers.

4.1.3 PCEB I/O REGISTERS

The only I/O-mapped register in the PCEB is the BIOS Timer Register. Section 3.2 provides details on the address mapping of this register. Note that the internal decode of the BIOS Timer Register is disabled after reset and all I/O accesses that are not contained within the PCI are subtractively decoded and passed to EISA Bus. To enable I/O access to the PCEB's BIOS Timer Register, The BTMR Register must be programmed.

4.1.4 POSITIVELY DECODED COMPATIBILITY I/O REGISTERS

The 8259 interrupt controller and IDE register locations are positively decoded. Access to the corresponding I/O address ranges must first be enabled through the PDCON Register.

PCI accesses to these registers are broadcast to the EISA Bus. These PCI accesses require the ownership of the EISA Bus, and will be retried if the EISA Bus is owned by an EISA/ISA master or the DMA.

ESC Resident PIC Registers

Access to the 8259 registers are positively decoded, if enabled through PDCON Register, to minimize access time to the system interrupt controller during interrupt processing (in particular during the EOI command sequence). Table 4-2 shows the 8259 I/O address map. After PCIRST#, positively decoded access to these address ranges is disabled.

EISA Resident IDE Registers

The PCI address decoder positively decodes IDE I/O addresses (Primary and Secondary IDE) that exist within the EISA subsystem (typically on the X-Bus or as an ISA slave). This feature is implemented to minimize the decoding penalty for the systems that use IDE as a mass-storage controller. Table 4-3 shows IDE's I/O address map. Note that the PDCON Register controls the enable/disable function for IDE decoding. After PCIRST#, positive decode of the IDE address range is disabled.

1

Table 4-2. ESC Resident Programmable Interrupt Controller (PIC) Registers

Address (hex)	Address Bits				Access Type	Register Name
	FEDC	BA98	7654	3210		
0020h	0000	0000	001x	xx00	R/W	INT 1 Control Register
0021h	0000	0000	001x	xx01	R/W	INT 1 Mask Register
00A0h	0000	0000	101x	xx00	R/W	INT 2 Control Register
00A1h	0000	0000	101x	xx01	R/W	INT 2 Mask Register

Table 4-3. EISA Resident IDE Registers

Address (hex)	Address Bits				Access Type	Register Name
	FEDC	BA98	7654	3210		
0170h	0000	0001	0111	0000	R/W	Secondary Data Register
0171h	0000	0001	0111	0001	R/W	Secondary Error Register
0172h	0000	0001	0111	0010	R/W	Secondary Sector Count Register
0173h	0000	0001	0111	0011	R/W	Secondary Sector Number Register
0174h	0000	0001	0111	0100	R/W	Secondary Cylinder Low Register
0175h	0000	0001	0111	0101	R/W	Secondary Cylinder High Register
0176h	0000	0001	0111	0110	R/W	Secondary Drive/Head Register
0177h	0000	0001	0111	0111	R/W	Secondary Status Register
01F1h	0000	0001	1111	0001	R/W	Primary Error Register
01F2h	0000	0001	1111	0010	R/W	Primary Sector Count Register
01F3h	0000	0001	1111	0011	R/W	Primary Sector Number Register
01F4h	0000	0001	1111	0100	R/W	Primary Cylinder Low Register
01F5h	0000	0001	1111	0101	R/W	Primary Cylinder High Register
01F6h	0000	0001	1111	0110	R/W	Primary Drive/Head Register
01F7h	0000	0001	1111	0111	R/W	Primary Status Register
0376h	0000	0011	0111	0110	R/W	Secondary Alternate Status Register
0377h	0000	0011	0111	0111	R	Secondary Drive Address Register
03F6h	0000	0011	1111	0110	R/W	Primary Alternate Status Register
03F7h	0000	0011	1111	0111	R	Primary Drive Address Register

4.2 EISA Cycle Address Decoding

For EISA Bus cycles, the PCEB address decoder determines the destination of EISA/ISA master and DMA cycles. This decoder provides the following functions:

- Positively decodes memory and I/O addresses that have been programmed into the PCEB for forwarding to the PCI Bus. This includes accesses to devices that reside directly on the PCI (memory Regions [4:1] and I/O Regions [4:1]) and segments of main memory that resides behind the Host/PCI Bridge.
- Provides access attributes for memory Regions [4:1]. These attributes are used to select the most optimum access mode (buffered or non-buffered).
- All cycles that are not positively decoded to be forwarded to PCI are contained within EISA.

NOTE:
The registers that reside in the PCEB (configuration registers and BIOS Timer) are not accessible from the EISA Bus.

4.2.1 POSITIVELY DECODED MEMORY CYCLES TO MAIN MEMORY

The EISA/ISA master or DMA addresses that are positively decoded by the PCEB are forwarded to the PCI Bus. If the address is not positively decoded by the PCEB, the cycle is not forwarded to the PCI Bus. Subtractive and negative decoding are not used on the EISA Bus.

The PCEB permits several EISA memory address ranges (items a-i, below) to be positively decoded. EISA Bus cycles to these regions are forwarded to the PCI Bus. Regions described by a-f and h are fixed and can be enabled or disabled independently. These regions are controlled by the EADC1 and EADC2 Registers.

The region described by g defines a space starting at 1 MByte with a programmable upper boundary of 4 GByte–2 MByte. Within this region a hole can be opened. Its size and location are programmable to allow a hole to be opened in memory space (for a frame buffer on the EISA Bus, for example). The size of this region and the hole are controlled by the MCSTOM, MCSBOH and MCSTOH Registers. If a hole in main memory is defined, then accesses to that address range are contained within EISA, unless defined by the EISA-to-PCI memory regions as a PCI destined access. (See next section.)

a. 0 KByte to 512 KByte
b. 512 KByte to 640 KByte
c. 640 KByte to 768 KByte (VGA memory)
d. 768 KByte to 896 KByte in eight 16 KByte sections (Expansion ROM)
e. 896 KByte to 960 KByte in four 16 KByte sections (lower BIOS area)
f. 960 KByte to 1 MByte (upper BIOS area)
g. 1 MByte to the top of memory (up to 4 GByte–2 MByte) within which a hole can be opened. Accesses to the hole are not forwarded to PCI. The top of the region can be programmed on 2 MByte boundaries up to 4 GByte–2 MByte. The hole can be between 64 KByte and 4 GByte–2 MByte in 64 KByte increments and located on any 64 KByte boundary.
h. 16 MByte–64 KByte to 16 MByte (FF0000h–FFFFFFh). EISA memory cycles in this range are always forwarded to the PCI Bus, if this range exists in main memory as defined by the MEMCS# registers. In this case, the enable/disable control bit in EADC2 Register is a don't care. If this range is not defined in main memory (i.e., above the top of memory or defined as a hole in the main memory), EISA cycles to this address range are forwarded to the PCI Bus, based on the enable/disable bit in the EADC2 Register. (This capability is used to support access of BIOS at 16 MBytes.)
i. 4 GByte–2 MByte to 4 GByte. The address map must be programmed in a such way that this address range is always contained within EISA. This is to avoid conflict with local BIOS memory response in this address range. If this region must be mapped to PCI, then programming of the BIOS decoder Registers contained within the ESC must ensure that there is no conflict. To map this region to PCI, one of the four programmable EISA-to-PCI memory regions must be used. Mapping of this region to the PCI might be required in the case when BIOS resides on the PCI and the PCI/EISA system must have consistent address maps for both PCI and EISA.

For detailed information on the PCEB registers used to control these address regions, refer to Section 3.1, PCEB Configuration Registers.

EISA memory cycles positively decoded for forwarding to PCI are allowed to be handled by the PCEB's Line Buffer management logic, if the line buffering is enabled through the PCICON Register.

For EISA-to-PCI transactions there are 2 modes of Line Buffer Operation:

- Buffered: Read-prefetch, write posting with data assembly.
- Non-buffered: Bypass path used.

Accesses within the main memory address range are normally performed in buffered mode. If there are programmable memory regions defined within

1

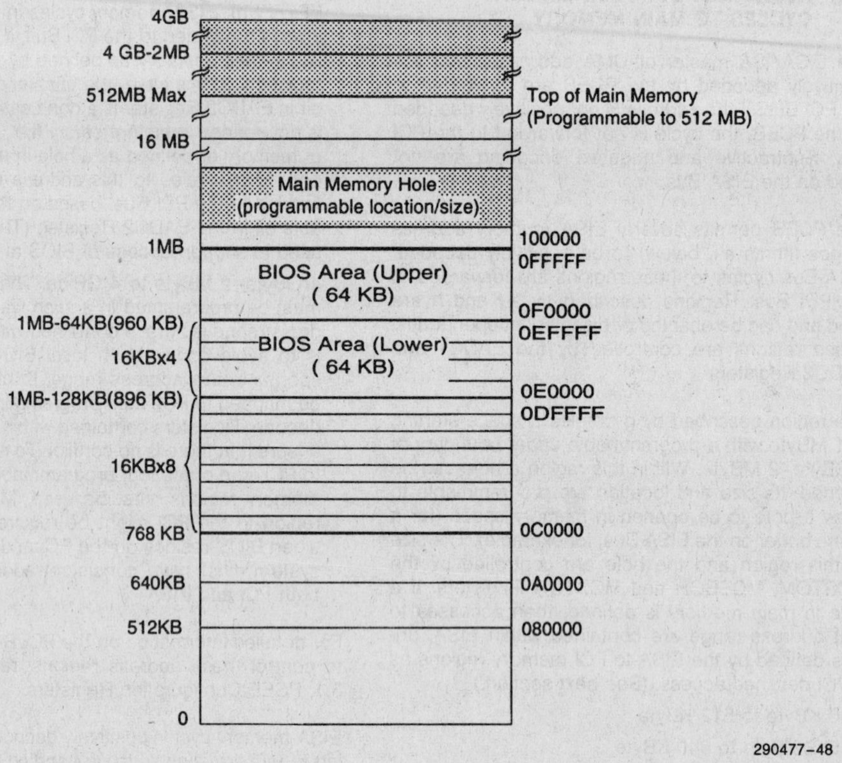

NOTES:

1. The four programmable EISA-to-PCI regions (Regions [4:1]) are not shown. These regions can be located anywhere within the 4 GByte memory space. Accesses to these regions are forwarded to the PCI Bus.
2. EISA cycles that access shaded regions are contained to the EISA Bus, unless the access hits one of the four programmable EISA-to-PCI regions described in Note 1.
3. Memory accesses to non-shaded areas are forwarded to the PCI Bus, if the region is enabled. If the region is disabled, the access is contained to the EISA Bus, unless the access hits one of the four programmable EISA-to-PCI regions described in note 1.

Figure 4-5. EISA Address Decoder Map

the main memory hole or above the top of the main memory MEMREGN[4:1], then the mode of access depends on configuration bits of the EPMRA Register. Access attribute bits associated with these regions override the default buffered mode for a particular address range in the case of programmable regions overlapping with active main memory regions.

Access to the 64 KByte area at the top of 16 MBytes (FF0000h–FFFFFFh) on the PCI, if this region is within main memory or within the main memory hole and enabled via the EADC2 Register, are always forwarded in a non-buffered mode, unless overlapped with a programmable region that defines buffered access mode.

4.2.2 PROGRAMMABLE EISA-TO-PCI MEMORY ADDRESS REGIONS

The PCEB supports four programmable memory regions for EISA-to-PCI transfers. The PCEB positively decodes EISA memory accesses to these regions and forwards the cycle to the PCI Bus. This feature permits EISA master accesses to PCI devices that reside within these address ranges.

Regions can be enabled or disabled. After reset, all regions are disabled. Each region has an associated Base and Limit Address fields MEMREGN[4:1] that determine the size and location of each region. These registers are programmed with the starting

address of the region (Base) and ending address of the region (Limit). The address range for a particular region is defined by the following equation:

Base_Address ≤ Address ≤ Limit_Address

These regions can be defined anywhere in the 4 GByte address space at 64 KByte boundaries and with 64 KByte granularity. In practical applications, the regions will be mapped within the main memory hole or above the top of the memory defined by the MEMCS# map.

Access to the memory locations within a region can be performed in one of two modes:

- **Non-Buffered Mode:** PCEB's EISA-to-PCI Line Buffers can be disabled for all EISA-to-PCI memory read/write accesses through the PCICON Register or for selected accesses through EPMRA Register.
- **Buffered Mode:** Line Buffers enabled. Read-prefetch and write-assembly/posting allowed (without strong ordering).

Since buffered mode provides maximum performance (and concurrency in non-GAT mode), it should be selected, unless the particular region is used for memory-mapped I/O devices. I/O devices can not be accessed in read-prefetch or write-assembly/posted fashion because of potential side-effects (see Section 6.0, Data Buffering).

4.2.3 PROGRAMMABLE EISA-TO-PCI I/O ADDRESS REGIONS

The PCEB provides four programmable I/O address regions. These regions are defined by Base and Limit address fields contained in the associated IOREGN[4:1] Registers. These regions can be defined anywhere within the 64 KByte I/O space on Dword boundaries (and with Dword granularity). See Section 4.1, PCEB Configuration Registers.

4.2.4 EXTERNAL EISA-TO-PCI I/O ADDRESS DECODER

Since the I/O address map may be highly fragmented, it is impractical to provide enough programmable regions to completely define mapping of registers for I/O devices on the PCI. The PCEB's input signal pin PIODEC# can be used, if a more complex I/O decode scheme is needed. PIODEC# complements the functions of the four PCEB programmable I/O regions with external decode logic. If PIODEC# is asserted during an EISA I/O cycle, the cycle is forwarded to the PCI Bus.

If the PIODEC# signal is not used, a pull-up resistor is required to provide an inactive signal level.

4.3 Palette DAC Snoop Mechanism

Some advanced graphics EISA/ISA expansion boards use the pre-DAC VGA pixel data from the VGA Special Feature Connector and merge it with advanced graphics data (multi-media for example). The merged data is then run through a replicated palette DAC on the advanced graphics expansion board to create the video monitor signal. The replicated palette DAC is kept coherent by snooping VGA palette DAC writes. Snooping becomes an issue in a system where the VGA controller is placed on the PCI Bus and the snooping graphics board is on the EISA expansion bus. Normally, the PCI VGA controller will respond to the palette DAC writes with DEVSEL#, so the PCEB will not propagate the cycle to the EISA Bus using subtractive decoding.

The burden for solving this problem is placed on the VGA subsystem residing on the PCI. The VGA subsystem on PCI must have an enable/disable bit associated with palette DAC accesses. When this bit is enabled the PCI VGA device responds in handshake fashion (generates DEVSEL#, TRDY#, etc.) to I/O reads and writes to the palette DAC space.

When this bit is disabled, the PCI VGA device responds in handshake fashion only to I/O reads to palette DAC space. I/O writes to the palette DAC space will be snooped (data latched) by the PCI VGA device, but the PCI VGA subsystem will not generate a DEVSEL#. In this case, the I/O write will be forwarded to the EISA Bus by the PCEB as a result of subtractive decode. The PCI VGA device must be able to snoop these cycles in the minimum EISA cycle time.

The state of palette-DAC snooping control bit does not affect I/O reads from the palette DAC space. Regardless of whether this bit is enabled or disabled, the PCI VGA device will service the I/O reads from the palette DAC space.

5.0 PCI INTERFACE

The PCEB provides the PCI Interface for the PCI-EISA Bridge. The PCEB can be an initiator (master) or target (slave) on the PCI Bus and supports the basic PCI Bus commands as described in Section 5.1.1, PCI Command Set. For EISA-to-PCI transfers, the PCEB is a master on the PCI Bus on behalf of the requesting EISA device. An EISA device can read and write either PCI memory or I/O space.

The PCEB forwards unclaimed PCI Bus cycles to EISA. For PCI Bus cycles that are not claimed, the PCEB becomes a slave on the PCI Bus (claiming the cycle via subtractive or negative decoding) and forwards the cycle to the EISA Bus.

This section describes the PCI Bus transactions supported by the PCEB. The section also covers the PCI Bus latency mechanisms in the PCEB that limit a master's time on the bus and the PCEB support of parity. In addition, the PCEB contains PCI Bus arbitration circuitry that supports up to six masters. PCI Bus arbitration is described in Section 5.4.

NOTES:

1. All signals are sampled on the rising edge of the PCI clock. Each signal has a setup and hold window with respect to the rising clock edge, in which transitions are not allowed. Outside of this range, signal values or transitions have no significance.
2. The terms initiator and master are synonymous. Likewise, the terms target and slave are synonymous.
3. Readers should be familiar with the PCI Bus specification.

5.1 PCI Bus Transactions

This section presents the PCI Bus transactions supported by the PCEB.

5.1.1 PCI COMMAND SET

PCI Bus commands indicate to the target the type of transaction requested by the master. These commands are encoded on the C/BE[3:0]# lines during the address phase of a transfer. Table 5-1 summarizes the PCEB's support of the PCI Bus commands.

Table 5-1. PCEB-Supported PCI Bus Commands

C/BE[3:0]#	Command Type	Supported As Target	Supported As Initiator
0000	Interrupt Acknowledge	Yes	No
0001	Special Cycle	No	No
0010	I/O Read	Yes	Yes
0011	I/O Write	Yes	Yes
0100	Reserved	N/A[3]	N/A[3]
0101	Reserved	N/A[3]	N/A[3]
0110	Memory Read	Yes	Yes
0111	Memory Write	Yes	Yes
1000	Reserved	N/A[3]	N/A[3]
1001	Reserved	N/A[3]	N/A[3]
1010	Configuration Read	Yes	No
1011	Configuration Write	Yes	No
1100	Memory Read Multiple	No[2]	No
1101	Reserved	N/A[3]	N/A[3]
1110	Memory Read Line	No[2]	No
1111	Memory Write and Invalidate	No[1]	No

NOTES:

1. As a target, the PCEB treats this command as a memory write command.
2. As a target, the PCEB treats this command as a memory read command.
3. The PCEB considers a reserved command invalid and, as a target, completely ignores the transaction. All internal address decoding is ignored and the PCEB never asserts DEVSEL#. As a PCI master, the PCEB never generates a bus cycle with a reserved command type.

5.1.2 PCI CYCLE DESCRIPTIONS

Each PCI Command is listed below with the following format of information:

Command Type
PCEB target support
—Decode method
—Data path
—PCEB response
—Result of no response on EISA
PCEB initiator support
—Data path
—Conditions for generating command
—Result of no response on PCI

Interrupt Acknowledge

Target support:
Decode: Positive and Subtractive
Data Path: Flow through
Response:
The interrupt acknowledge cycle is subject to retry. If the PCEB is locked, or if the interrupt acknowledge cycle triggers buffer management activity, or if the EISA Bus is occupied by an EISA/ISA master or the DMA, the interrupt acknowledge cycle is retried.

The interrupt acknowledge command is a single byte read that is implicitly addressed to the interrupt controller in the ESC component. The address bits are logical "don't cares" during the address phase and the byte enables indicate to the PCEB that an 8-bit interrupt vector is to be returned on byte 0. After performing the necessary buffer management operations and obtaining ownership of the EISA Bus, the PCEB generates a single pulse on the PEREQ#/INTA# inter-chip signal and performs an I/O read cycle (on the EISA Bus) to the ESC internal registers residing at I/O address 04h. The ESC decode logic uses the PEREQ#/INTA# signal to distinguish between standard accesses to I/O address 04h (DMA controller) and special accesses that result in a vector being read by the PCEB. The PCEB holds the PCI Bus, in wait states, until the interrupt vector is returned. PEREQ#/INTA# remains asserted until the end of the read cycle.

Result of no response on EISA:
The PCEB runs a standard length EISA I/O read cycle and terminates normally. The value of the data returned as an interrupt vector is meaningless.

Initiator support: None.

Special Cycle

Target support: None.

Initiator support: None.

I/O Read

Target support:
Decode: Positive (PCEB and some ESC registers) and Subtractive
Data Path: Flow through
PCEB Response:
The PCEB claims I/O read cycles via positive or subtractive decoding and generates DEVSEL#. The internal PCEB registers (BIOS Timer) and the IDE and the 8259 registers are positively decoded. Any unclaimed cycle below 64 KByte is subtractively decoded and forwarded to the EISA Bus. The I/O read cycle is subject to retry. If the PCEB is locked, if the cycle triggers buffer management activity, or if the EISA Bus is occupied by an EISA/ISA master or the DMA, the I/O read cycle is retried. If the cycle gets retried due to an occupied EISA Bus, the EISA Bus is requested.

Once an I/O read cycle is accepted (not retried) by the PCEB, the PCI Bus is held in wait states using TRDY# until the cycle is completed internally or on the EISA Bus.

Burst I/O reads to the EISA Bus or to the PCEB are not supported. Therefore, any burst I/O read cycles decoded by the PCEB are target terminated after the first data transaction using the disconnect semantics of the STOP# signal (Figure 5-12, Disconnect A).

Result of no response on EISA:
The PCEB runs a standard length EISA I/O cycle and terminates normally.

Initiator support:
The PCEB generates PCI Bus I/O read cycles on behalf of an EISA master. EISA cycles are forwarded to the PCI Bus if the I/O address is within one of four programmable I/O address regions as defined in Section 4.0, Address Decoding.

Result of no response on PCI:
Master abort due to DEVSEL# time-out. PCEB returns data value FFFFFFFFh.

I/O Write

Target support:
Decode: Positive (PCEB/ESC registers) and Subtractive
Data Path: Flow through
PCEB Response:
I/O write cycles can be claimed by the PCEB via positive or subtractive decoding. In either case, the PCEB generates DEVSEL#. The internal PCEB registers (BIOS Timer), IDE registers and 8259 registers are positively decoded, if enabled. Any unclaimed cycle below 64 KByte is subtractively decoded and forwarded to the EISA Bus. The I/O write cycle is subject to retry. If the PCEB is locked, if the cycle triggers buffer management activity, or if the EISA Bus is occupied by an EISA/ISA master or the DMA, the I/O write cycle is retried. If the cycle is retried due to an occupied EISA Bus, the EISA Bus is requested.

Once an I/O write cycle is accepted (not retried) by the PCEB, the PCI Bus is held in wait states using TRDY# until the cycle is completed within the PCEB or on the EISA Bus.

Burst I/O writes to the EISA Bus or to the PCEB are not supported. Therefore, any burst I/O write cycles decoded by the PCEB are target terminated after the first data transaction using the disconnect semantics of the STOP# signal (Figure 5-12, Disconnect A).

Result of no response on EISA:
The PCEB runs a standard length EISA I/O cycle and terminates normally.

Initiator support:
The PCEB generates PCI I/O write cycles on behalf of an EISA master. EISA cycles are forwarded to the PCI Bus if the I/O address is within one of the four programmable I/O address regions defined in Section 4.0, Address Decoding.

Result of no response on PCI:
Master abort due to DEVSEL# time-out.

Memory Read

Target support:
Decode: Negative and Subtractive
Data Path: Flow through
PCEB Response:
Memory read cycles may be claimed by the PCEB via negative or subtractive decoding. The PCEB claims the cycle by asserting DEVSEL#. Unclaimed PCI cycles (DEVSEL# time-out) are claimed by the PCEB via subtractively decoding and forwarded to the EISA Bus. The memory read cycle is subject to retry. If the PCEB is locked, if the cycle triggers buffer management activity, or if the EISA Bus is occupied by an EISA/ISA master or the DMA, the memory read cycle is retried. If the cycle is retried due to an occupied EISA Bus, the EISA Bus is requested.

Once a memory read cycle is accepted (not retried) by the PCEB, the PCI Bus is held in wait states, using TRDY#, until the cycle is completed to the EISA Bus.

Incremental burst memory reads destined for the EISA Bus take longer than the allowed 8 PCICLKs. Therefore, any burst memory read cycle decoded by the PCEB causes the PCEB to target terminate the cycle after the first data transaction using the disconnect semantics of the STOP# signal (Figure 5-8, Disconnect A).

Result of no response on EISA:
The PCEB runs a standard length EISA memory read cycle and terminates normally.

Initiator support:
Data Path: Line Buffer when enabled. Flow through when Line Buffer is disabled or it is a bypass cycle.
Cycle Generation Conditions:
As an initiator, the PCEB generates a PCI memory read cycle when it decodes an EISA memory read cycle destined to the PCI that can not be serviced by the Line Buffer. This condition occurs for EISA/ISA master and DMA cycles that can not be serviced by the Line Buffer because the Line Buffer is empty, there is a Line Buffer miss, or Line Buffering is disabled.

As an initiator, the PCEB only generates linear incrementing burst ordering that is signaled by AD[1:0] = 00 during the address phase. Other types of burst transfers (i.e., cache line toggle mode) are never initiated by the PCEB.

The PCEB generates a burst memory read when it is fetching 16 bytes into one of the four Line Buffers.

Result of no response on PCI:
Master abort due to DEVSEL# time-out. PCEB returns data value FFFFFFFFh.

Memory Write

Target support:
Decode: Negative and Subtractive
Data Path: Posted Write Buffer or flow through
PCEB Response:
Memory write cycles may be claimed by the PCEB via negative or subtractive decoding. The PCEB asserts DEVSEL# to claim the cycle. Unclaimed PCI cycles (DEVSEL# time-out) within the 4 GByte memory space are claimed by the PCEB via subtrac-

tively decoding and forwarded to the EISA Bus. The memory write cycle is subject to retry. If the PCEB is locked, if the cycle triggers buffer management activity, if the PCI Posted Write Buffer (PWB) is full, or if posting is disabled because the EISA Bus is occupied by an EISA/ISA master or the DMA, the memory write cycle is retried. If the cycle is retried due to a disabled buffer because the EISA Bus is occupied, the EISA Bus is requested.

Once a memory write cycle is accepted (not retried) by the PCEB, the cycle is posted, if the PCI Posted Write buffer is enabled, and the PCI cycle is terminated in zero wait states. If the PCI Posted Write Buffer is disabled, the PCEB holds the PCI Bus, in wait states, using TRDY# until the cycle is completed on the EISA Bus.

As a target, the PCEB only supports linear incrementing burst ordering that is signaled by the master with AD[1:0] = 00 during the address phase. Burst with any other type of ordering (AD[1:0] ≠ 00) is split into single data phase transfers using target disconnect.

Incremental burst memory writes destined for the EISA Bus are posted at 0 wait states until the PWB is full (4 Dwords). When the PWB is full, burst memory writes are target terminated using the disconnect semantics of the STOP# signal (Figure 5-12, Disconnect A/B).

Result of no response on EISA:
The PCEB initiates a standard length EISA memory write cycle and terminates normally.

Initiator support:
Data Path: Line Buffer when enabled, flow through when Line Buffer is disabled.
Cycle Generation Conditions:
As an initiator, the PCEB generates a PCI memory write cycle when it decodes an EISA memory write cycle destined to PCI, that can not be serviced by the Line Buffer because it is disabled. This occurs for EISA/ISA masters and DMA cycles when the Line Buffer is disabled. The PCEB also generates a memory write cycle when the Line Buffer needs to be flushed. The Line Buffer is flushed under several conditions, including when the 16 byte line is full, when there is a "miss" to the current 16 byte line, or when it is required by the buffer management logic. (See Section 6.0, Data Buffering).

As an initiator, the PCEB generates only linear incrementing burst ordering that is signaled by AD[1:0] = "00" during address phase. Other types of burst transfers (i.e., cache line toggle mode) are never initiated by the PCEB.

Result of no response on PCI: Master abort due to DEVSEL# time-out.

Configuration Read, Configuration Write

Target support:
Decode: via IDSEL pin
Data Path: Flow through
PCEB Response:
The PCEB responds to configuration cycles by generating DEVSEL# when its IDSEL signal is asserted, regardless of the address. During configuration cycles, AD[7:2] are used to address the PCEB's configuration space. AD[31:8] are not used and are logical "don't cares". AD[1:0] must be zero.

Result of no response on EISA: N/A

Initiator support:
Configuration cycles are never generated by the PCEB.

Memory Read Multiple

Target support:
The PCEB aliases this command to a normal memory read cycle. See the Memory Read command description.

Initiator support:
Memory read multiple cycles are never generated by the PCEB.

Memory Read Line

Target support:
The PCEB aliases this command to a normal memory read. See the Memory Read command description.

Initiator support:
Memory read line cycles are never generated by the PCEB.

1

Memory Write and Invalidate

Target support:
PCEB Response:
The PCEB treats this command like a memory write. See the Memory Write command description.

Initiator support:
Cycle Generation Conditions: The PCEB does not generate this command cycle.

5.1.3 PCI TRANSFER BASICS

The basic bus transfer mechanism on the PCI Bus is a burst. A burst is comprised of an address phase and one or more data phases. The PCI protocol specifies the following types of burst ordering (signaled via AD[1:0] during the address phase):

AD[1:0]	Burst Order
0 0	Linear Incrementing
0 1	Cache line toggle mode
1 X	Reserved

The PCEB only supports linear incrementing burst ordering, both as a target and as an initiator. Data transfers for ordering other than linear incrementing are disconnected by the PCEB (burst split into multiple single data transfers).

The fundamentals of all PCI data transfers are controlled with the following three signals:

- FRAME# is driven by the PCI master to indicate the beginning and end of a transaction.
- IRDY# is driven by the PCI master, allowing it to force wait states.
- TRDY# is driven by the PCI target, allowing it to force wait states.

The PCI Bus is idle when both FRAME# and IRDY# are negated. The first clock edge that FRAME# is sampled asserted is the address phase, and the address and bus command code are transferred on that clock edge. The next clock edge begins the first of one or more data phases. During the data phases, data is transferred between master and slave on each clock edge that both IRDY# and TRDY# are sampled asserted. Wait states may be inserted by either the master (by negating IRDY#) or the target (by negating TRDY#). When a PCI master has one more data transfer to complete the cycle (which could be immediately after the address phase), it negates FRAME#. IRDY# must be asserted at this time, indicating that the master is ready for the final data transfer. After the target indicates the final data transfer (TRDY# asserted), the master negates IRDY#, causing the target's PCI interface to return to the idle state (FRAME# and IRDY# negated), on the next clock edge.

For I/O cycles, PCI addressing is on byte boundaries and all 32 AD lines are decoded to provide the byte address. For memory cycles, AD[1:0] are used to define the type of burst ordering. For configuration cycles, DEVSEL# is strictly a function of IDSEL#. Configuration registers are selected as Dwords using AD[7:2]. The AD[1:0] must be 00 for the target to directly respond to the configuration cycle. The byte enables determine which byte lanes contain valid data.

Each PCI agent is responsible for its own positive address decode. Only one agent (the PCEB) on the PCI Bus may use subtractive decoding. The little endian addressing model is used.

The byte enables are used to determine which bytes carry meaningful data. These signals are permitted to change between data phases. The byte enables must be driven valid from the edge of the clock that starts each data phase and must stay valid for the entire data phase. In Figure 5-1, the data phases begin on clocks 3 and 4. (Changing byte enables during a read burst transaction is generally not useful, but is supported on the bus.) The master is permitted to change the byte enables on each new data phase, although the read diagram does not show this. The timing for changing byte enables is the same for read and write transactions. If byte enables are important for the target on a read transaction, the target must wait for the byte enables to be driven on each data phase before completing the transfer.

5.1.3.1 Turn-Around-Cycle Definition

A turn-around-cycle is required on all signals that may be driven by more than one agent. The turn-around-cycle is required to avoid contention when one agent stops driving a signal and another agent begins, and must last at least one clock. The symbol that represents a turn-around-cycle in the timing relationship figures is a circular set of two lines, each with an arrow that points to the other's tail. This turn-around-cycle occurs at different times for different signals. For example, the turn-around-cycle for IRDY#, TRDY# and DEVSEL# occurs during the address phase and for FRAME#, C/BE# and AD, it occurs during the idle cycle.

5.1.3.2 Idle Cycle Definition

The cycle between clocks 7 and 8 in Figure 5-2 is called an idle cycle. Idle cycles appear on the PCI Bus between the end of one transaction and the beginning of the next. An idle cycle occurs when both FRAME# and IRDY# are negated.

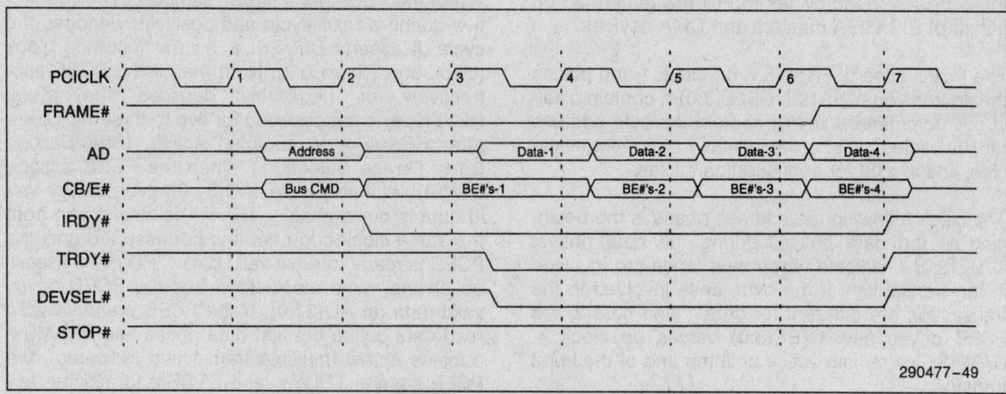

Figure 5-1. PCEB Burst Read From PCI Memory

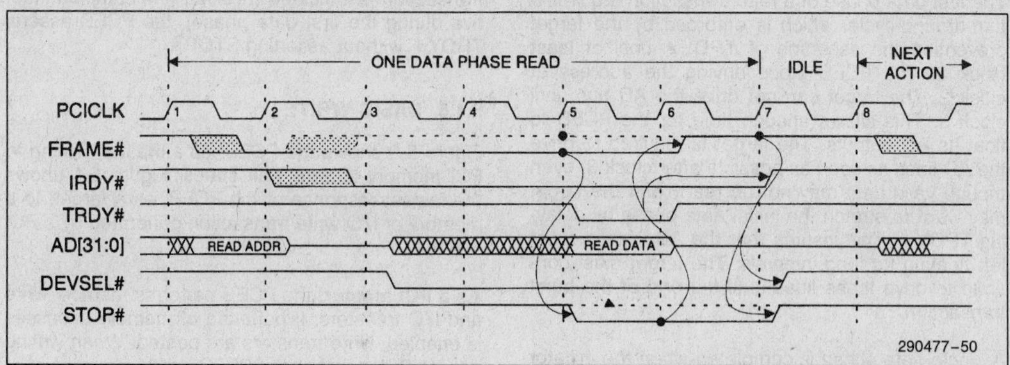

Figure 5-2. PCI Master Read from the PCEB (Burst with Target Termination)

5.1.4 BASIC READ

As a PCI master, the PCEB performs memory and I/O read transfers. Figure 5-1 shows a PCEB zero wait state burst read from PCI memory (PCEB is a master). If buffering of memory accesses is enabled, read transfers use prefetching. When reading data from PCI memory, the PCEB requests a minimum of 16 bytes (one data line of the Line Buffer), via a four data phase burst read cycle, to fill one of its internal Line Buffers. The PCEB does not buffer PCI I/O reads and only required data is transferred during these cycles. Read cycles to PCI are generated on behalf of EISA/ISA masters and DMA devices.

The PCEB asserts FRAME# on clock 1 and places the address on AD[31:2]. CB/E[3:0]# contain a valid bus command. AD[1:0] contain the byte address for I/O cycles, burst order indication for memory cycles, and are 00 for configuration cycles.

The clock following the address phase is the beginning of the data phase. During the data phase, C/BE[3:0]# indicate which byte lanes are involved in the transaction. If the byte lanes involved in the transaction are different for data 1 and data 2, the PCEB drives new C/BE[3:0] values on clock 4. C/BE[3:0]# remain active until the end of the burst transfer.

The first data phase of a read transaction requires a turn-around-cycle, which is enforced by the target preventing the assertion of TRDY# until at least clock 3. The PCEB stops driving the address at clock 2. The target can not drive the AD bus until clock 3. This allows enough time for the PCEB to float its AD outputs. The target is required to drive the AD lines as soon as possible after clock 3, even though valid data may not be ready and the target may want to stretch the initial data phase by delaying TRDY#. This insures that the AD lines are not left floating for long intervals. The target must continue to drive these lines until the end of the burst transaction.

A single data phase is completed when the initiator of the cycle samples TRDY# asserted on the same clock that IRDY# is asserted. To add wait states, the target must negate TRDY# for one or more clock cycles. As a master, the PCEB does not add wait states. In Figure 5-1, data is transferred on clocks 4 and 5. The PCEB knows, at clock 6, that the next data phase is the last and negates FRAME#. As noted before, the PCEB can burst a maximum of four data cycles when reading from PCI memory.

As a PCI target, the PCEB responds to both I/O and memory read transfers. Figure 5-2 shows the PCEB, as a target, responding to a PCI master read cycle. For multiple read transactions, the PCEB always target terminates after the first data read transaction by asserting STOP# and TRDY#. These signals are asserted at the end of the first data phase. For single read transactions, the PCEB completes the cycle in a normal fashion (by asserting TRDY# without asserting STOP#). Figure 5-2 shows the fastest PCEB response to an access of an internal configuration register. During EISA Bus read accesses, the PCEB always adds wait states by negating TRDY# until the transfer on the EISA Bus is completed.

When the PCEB, as a target, samples FRAME# active during a read cycle and positively decodes the cycle, it asserts DEVSEL# on the following clock (clock 3 in Figure 5-2). Note that, if the PCEB subtractively or negatively decodes the cycle, DEVSEL# is not asserted for two to three PCICLK's after FRAME# is sampled active. (See Section 5.1.9, Device Selection.) When the PCEB asserts DEVSEL#, it also drives AD[31:0], even though valid data is not available. TRDY# is also driven from the same clock edge but it is not asserted until the PCEB is ready to drive valid data. TRDY# is asserted on the same clock edge that the PCEB drives valid data on AD[31:0]. If the PCEB presents valid read data during the first data phase and FRAME# remains active (multiple transaction indicated), the PCEB asserts TRDY# and STOP# to indicate target termination of the transfer (Figure 5-2). If a single transaction is indicated (FRAME# is sampled inactive during the first data phase), the PCEB asserts TRDY# without asserting STOP#.

5.1.5 BASIC WRITE

Figure 5-3 shows the PCEB, as a master, writing to PCI memory in zero wait states. Figure 5-4 shows the fastest response of the PCEB, as a target, to a memory or I/O write transaction generated by a PCI master.

As a PCI master, the PCEB performs memory write and I/O transfers. If buffering of memory accesses is enabled, write transfers are posted. When writing data to PCI memory, the PCEB writes a maximum of 16 bytes (one line of the Line Buffer) using a burst write cycle. I/O writes are always non-buffered transactions.

The PCEB generates PCI write cycles on behalf of EISA masters and DMA devices, and when the PCEB flushes its internal Line Buffer.

As a PCI target, the PCEB responds to both I/O and memory write transfers. If the EISA Bus is occupied, the PCI write is retried by the PCEB. When the PCEB owns the EISA Bus, the transaction proceeds. For burst I/O writes, the PCEB always target terminates after the first data transaction by asserting

STOP# and TRDY# at the end of the first data phase. If the internal Posted Write Buffer (PWB) is disabled during a burst memory write, the PCEB always target terminates after the first data phase. When the PWB is enabled, there is a space in the buffer, and the EISA Bus is owned by the PCEB, the write is posted until the PWB is filled. Additional data phases, when the PWB is full, causes the PCEB to terminate the transaction with a retry. For single write transactions that are not terminated with retry, the PCEB finishes the cycle in a normal fashion by asserting TRDY# without asserting STOP#.

Figure 5-4 shows the fastest PCEB response to a write cycle targeted to an internal PCI configuration register. During I/O write accesses to the EISA Bus or during memory writes to the EISA Bus when the PWB is disabled, the PCEB always adds wait states. The PCEB adds wait states by holding TRDY# high until the transfer on the EISA Bus is completed.

During a single memory write access to EISA memory when the PWB is enabled, the PCEB performs the access in a one wait state cycle. (Note: This is due to timing constraints for address decoding that the PCI specification places on devices that can support 0 wait write operations for the first data phase.) During postable burst memory writes, only the first data phase has a wait state. The rest of the data phases (up to 4) are transferred in 0 wait states.

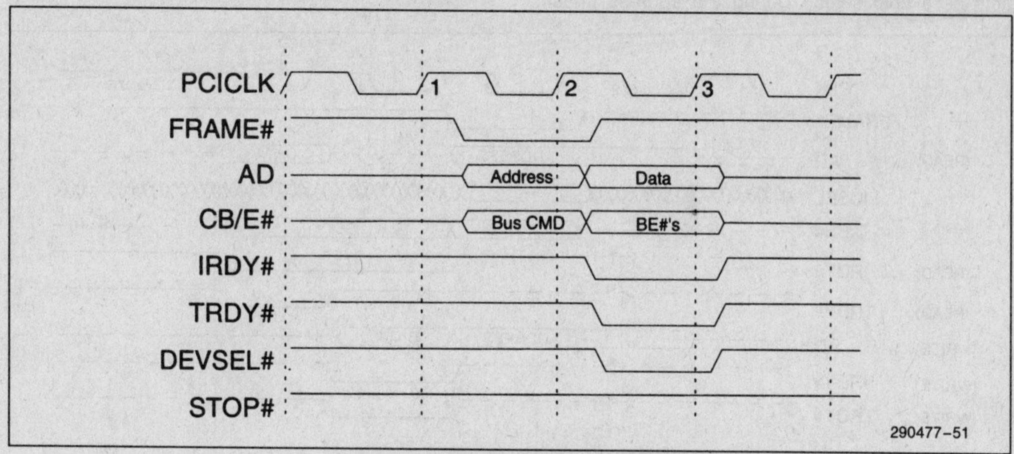

Figure 5-3. PCEB Write to PCI Memory

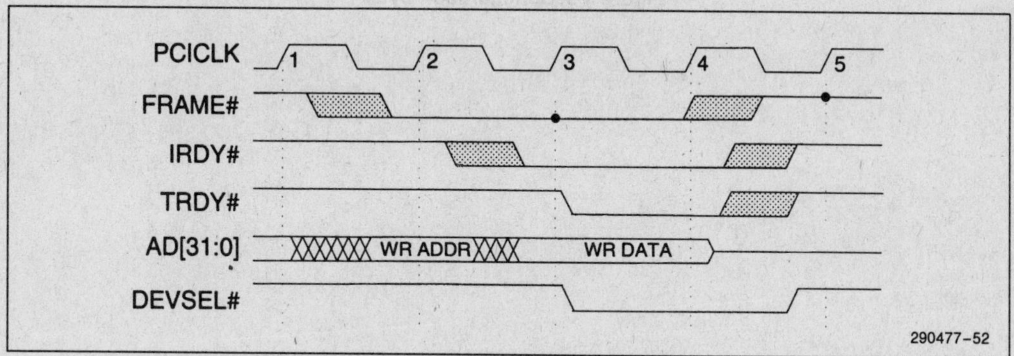

Figure 5-4. Fastest PCI Write to PCEB

5.1.6 CONFIGURATION CYCLES

One of the requirements of the PCI specification is that upon power-up, PCI agents do not respond to any address. The only access allowed is through the IDSEL configuration mechanism. The PCEB is an exception to this since it controls access to the BIOS boot code. All PCEB/ESC subsystem addresses that are enabled after reset are accessible immediately after power up.

The configuration read or write command is used to configure the PCEB. During the address phase of the configuration read or write cycle, the PCEB samples its IDSEL (ID select) signal (not the address lines) to generate DEVSEL#. In this way, IDSEL acts as a chip select. During the address phase, AD[7:2] are used to select a particular configuration register and BE[3:0] to select a particular byte(s). The PCEB only responds to configuration cycles if AD[1:0] = 00. Reference Figure 5-5 for configuration reads and writes. Note that IDSEL is normally a "don't care", except during the address phase of a transaction. Upon decode of a configuration cycle and sampling IDSEL active, the PCEB responds by asserting DEVSEL# and TRDY#. An unclaimed configuration cycle is never forwarded to the EISA Bus.

Configuration cycles are not normally run in burst mode. If this happens, the PCEB splits the transfer into single cycles using the slave termination mechanism.

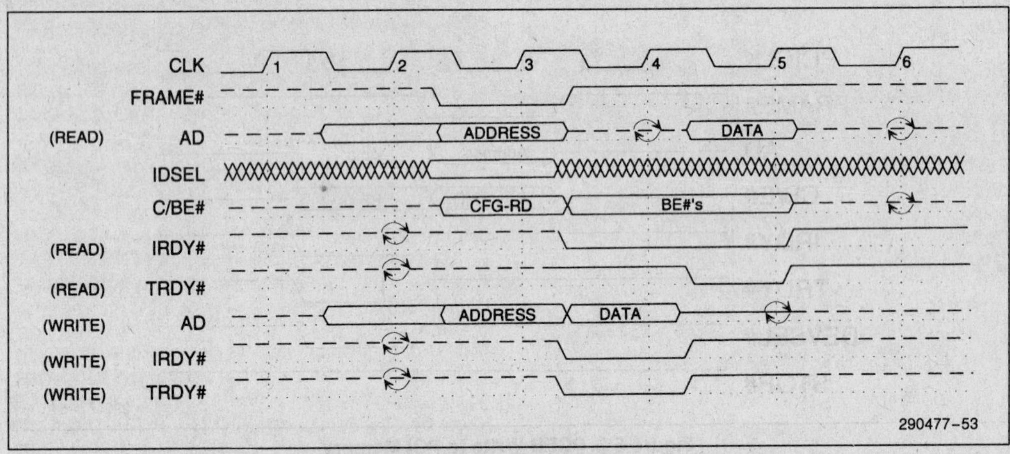

Figure 5-5. Configuration Cycle

5.1.7 INTERRUPT ACKNOWLEDGE CYCLE

The PCEB responds to an interrupt acknowledge cycle as decoded from the command during a valid address cycle (FRAME# asserted). The AD bus itself is a "don't care" to the PCEB during the address phase and, therefore, status of the internal PCI address decoder is not used for forwarding the cycle to the EISA Bus where the system interrupt controller resides.

The PCEB converts the PCI interrupt acknowledge cycle into an EISA I/O read access to the address 04h, with special semantics indicated to the ESC via the inter-chip signaling. Before the PCI interrupt acknowledge cycle can be converted into an EISA I/O read cycle, the EISA Bus must be owned. If the EISA Bus is not owned by the PCEB (EISAHLDA asserted), the PEREQ#/INTA# signal is asserted with PEREQ# semantics (PCI-to-EISA request). After the EISA Bus is acquired by the PCEB, the interrupt acknowledge sequence can proceed. The PCEB starts an I/O read cycle to address 04h and asserts PEREQ#/INTA# with INTA# semantics. The PEREQ#/INTA# remains asserted for the duration of the EISA I/O read cycle. Therefore, only a single pulse is generated on the PEREQ#/INTA# signal. Conversion of the single PCI interrupt acknowledge cycle into two interrupt acknowledge pulses (that is required for 8259 compatibility) occurs inside the ESC where the 8259-based interrupt controller resides. The ESC's EISA decoder uses the PEREQ#/INTA# signal (with INTA# semantics) to distinguish between normal I/O reads to the register located at address 04h (DMA1 Ch2 Base and Current Address) and the interrupt acknowledge sequence. The ESC holds the EISA Bus in wait states until the interrupt vector is returned to the PCEB (via SD[7:0]). The PCEB passes the vector to the PCI via AD[7:0] and then terminates the cycles both on EISA and PCI. Note that for compatibility reasons, only the ESC (containing the DMA controller) can respond to the EISA I/O read from 04h.

1

Figure 5-6 shows the PCI portion of a positively decoded interrupt acknowledge sequence. The EISA portion of the sequence matches normal EISA I/O read timing, except that the PEREQ#/INTA# inter-chip signal is asserted during the bus cycle with INTA# semantics and, during the PCEB/ESC EISA Bus ownership exchange handshake, with PEREQ# semantics. Note that in order for the PCEB to positively decode interrupt acknowledge cycles, bit 5 in the PCI Control register (PCICON) must be set to 1. Otherwise, interrupt acknowledge cycles will be subtractively decoded.

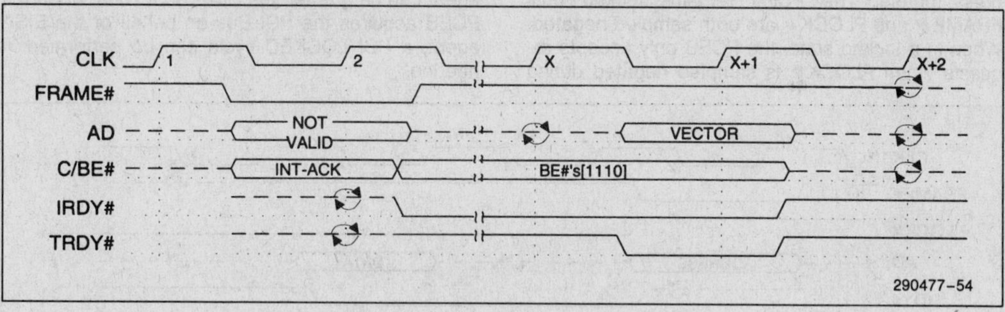

Figure 5-6. PCI Interrupt Acknowledge Cycle

5.1.8 EXCLUSIVE ACCESS

Refer to Figures 5-7, 5-8, and 5-9 for exclusive access timing relationships.

Target support:

PCI provides an exclusive access mechanism that allows non-exclusive accesses to proceed in the face of exclusive accesses. This is referred to as a Resource Lock. (Note that the exclusive access mechanism that locks the entire bus is Bus Lock.) The PCEB, as a resource, can be locked by any PCI initiator. In the context of locked cycles, the PCEB and entire EISA subsystem are considered a single resource. (EISA subsystem is indirectly locked during an exclusive access to the PCEB.) A locked access to any address contained within the EISA subsystem locks the entire subsystem from the PCI side. The PLOCK# signal is propagated to the EISA LOCK# signal. Note that write posting (PCI-to-EISA) is disabled for PCI locked cycles propagated to the EISA subsystem. The EISA Bus is not released to the ESC until the locked sequence is complete. A subsequent PCI initiator access to the EISA subsystem, while it is locked, results in a retry. The PCEB becomes locked when it is the target of the access and PLOCK# is sampled negated during the address phase. The PCEB remains locked until FRAME# and PLOCK# are both sampled negated. When in a locked state, the PCEB only accepts requests when PLOCK# is sampled negated during the address phase. If PLOCK# is asserted during the address phase, the PCEB responds by asserting STOP# with TRDY# negated (RETRY).

As an unlocked target, the PCEB ignores PLOCK# when deciding if it should respond to a PCI address decoder hit. Also, if PLOCK# is sampled asserted during an address phase, the PCEB does not go into a locked state.

As a locked target, the PCEB responds to an initiator when it samples PLOCK# negated during the address phase of the cycle in which the PCEB is the target of the access. The locking master may negate PLOCK# at the end of the last data phase. When FRAME# and PLOCK# are both sampled negated, the PCEB goes to the unlocked state.

Note that the PCEB does not release the EISA Bus when it is in the locked state.

Initiator support:

When an EISA locked access to the PCI is encountered (EISA LOCK# asserted), the cycle is propagated to the PCI Bus as a PCI locked cycle. Line Buffers in the PCEB are bypassed. The PLOCK# signal must be negated (released) before an EISA agent can be granted the EISA Bus. Thus, when the PCEB acquires the PCI Bus on behalf of the EISA agent, a PCI LOCKED cycle can be performed, if needed.

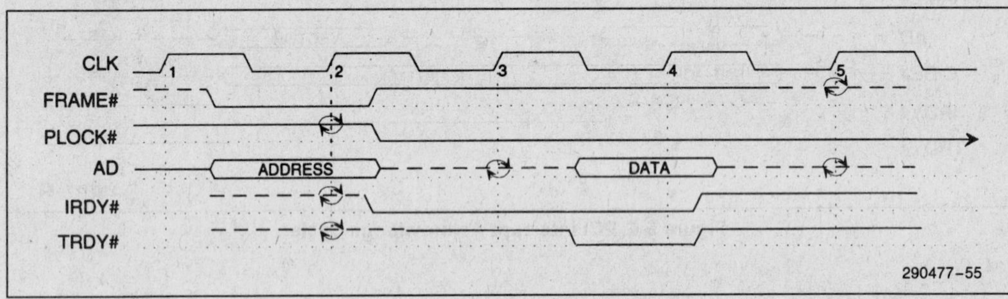

Figure 5-7. Beginning a Locked Cycle

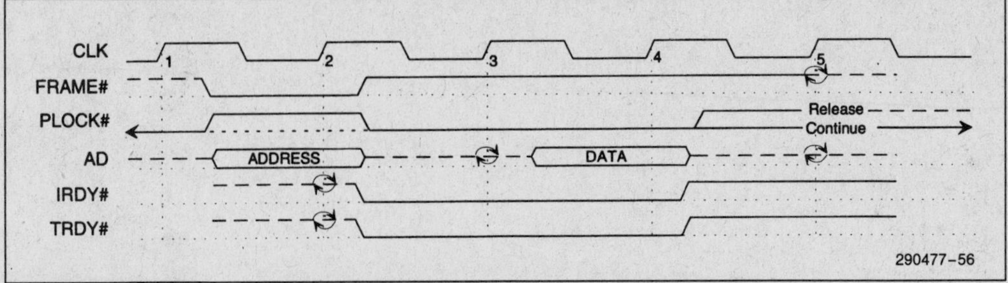

Figure 5-8. Continuing Locked Cycle

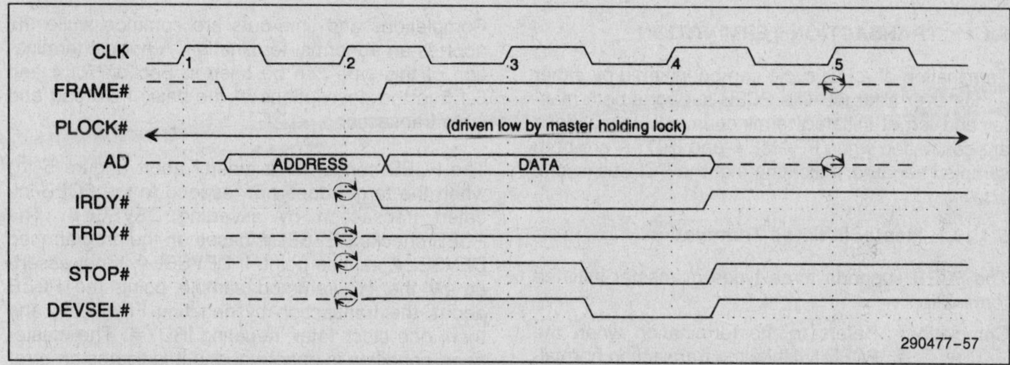

Figure 5-9. Access to Locked Target with PLOCK# Asserted During Address Phase

5.1.9 DEVICE SELECTION

The PCEB asserts DEVSEL# to indicate that it is the target of the PCI transaction. DEVSEL# is asserted when the PCEB, as a target, positively, subtractively, or negatively decodes the PCI transaction. In all cases except one, once the PCEB asserts DEVSEL#, the signal remains asserted until FRAME# is negated (IRDY# is asserted) and either STOP# or TRDY# is asserted. The exception is a target abort, described in Section 5.1.10, Transaction Termination.

For most systems, PCI target devices are able to complete a decode and assert DEVSEL# within 2 or 3 clocks of FRAME# (medium and slow in Figure 5-10). Accordingly, since the PCEB subtractively or negatively decodes all unclaimed PCI cycles (except configuration cycles), it provides a configuration option to reduce by 1 or 2 clocks the edge at which it samples DEVSEL#, allowing faster access to the expansion bus. Use of this option is limited by the slowest positive decode agent on the bus. This is described in more detail in Section 4.0, Address Decoding.

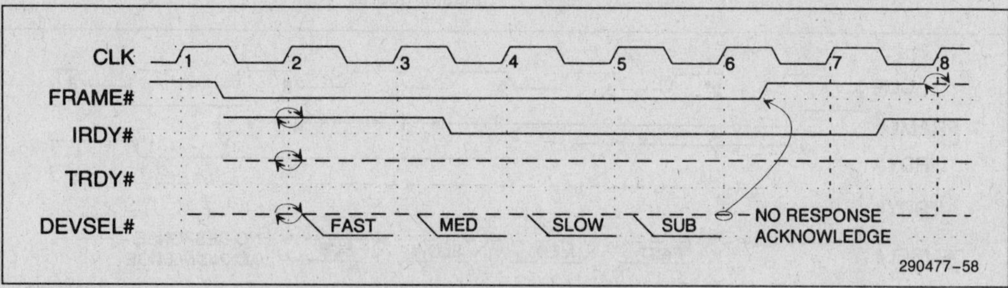

Figure 5-10. Device Selection (DEVSEL#)

5.1.10 TRANSACTION TERMINATION

Termination of a PCI cycle can be initiated by either a master or a target. The PCEB supports both master and target initiated termination. All transactions are concluded when FRAME# and IRDY# are both sampled negated, indicating that the PCI Bus is idle.

5.1.10.1 Master Initiated Termination

The PCEB supports three types of master initiated termination:

Completion: Refers to the termination when the PCEB finishes the transaction normally. This is the most common type of termination.

Time-out: Refers to termination when the PCEB's GNT# line is negated and its internal Master Latency Timer has expired. The intended transaction is not necessarily concluded. The timer may have expired because of a target-induced access latency, or because the intended operation was very long.

Abort: Refers to termination when there is no target response (no DEVSEL# asserted) to a transaction within the programmed DEVSEL# response time.

Completions and time-outs are common while the abort is an abnormal termination. A normal termination of this type can be seen in Section 5.1.4 and 5.1.5 in the descriptions of the basic PCI read and write transaction.

The PCEB sends out a master abort (Figure 5-11) when the target does not respond to the PCEB-initiated transaction by asserting DEVSEL#. The PCEB checks DEVSEL# based on the programmed DEVSEL# sample point. If DEVSEL# is not asserted by the programmed sample point, the PCEB aborts the transaction by negating FRAME#, and then, one clock later, negating IRDY#. The master abort condition is abnormal and it indicates an error condition. The PCEB does not retry the cycle.

If the transaction is an EISA-to-PCI memory or I/O write, the PCEB terminates the EISA cycle with EXRDY. If the transaction is an EISA-to-PCI memory or I/O read, the PCEB returns FFFFFFFFh on the EISA Bus. This is identical to the way an unclaimed cycle is handled on the "normally ready" EISA Bus. If the Line Buffer is the requester of the PCI transaction, the master abort mechanism ends the PCI cycle, but no data is transferred into or out of the Line Buffer. The Line Buffer does not retry the cycle. The Received Master Abort Status bit in the PCI Status Register is set to 1 indicating that the PCEB issued a master abort.

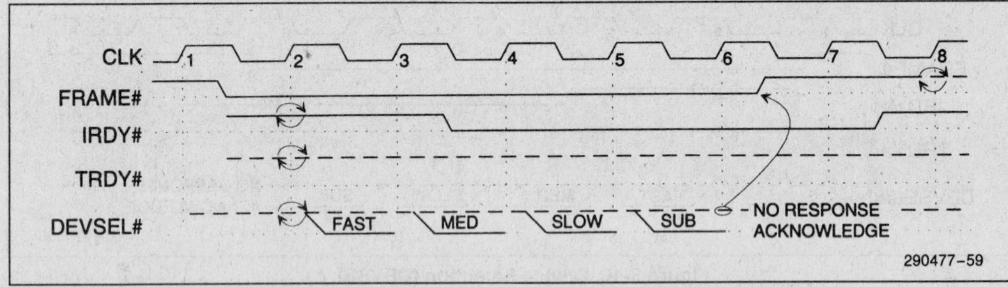

Figure 5-11. Master Initiated Termination (Master Abort)

5.1.10.2 Target Initiated Termination

The PCEB supports two forms of target-initiated termination:

Disconnect: A disconnect termination occurs when the target is unable to respond within the latency guidelines of the PCI specifications. Note that this is not usually done on the first data phase.

Retry: Retry refers to a termination requested because the PCEB is currently in a state that makes it unable to process the transaction.

Figures 5-12 and 5-13 show four types of target-initiated terminations. In general, the PCEB initiates a disconnect for PCI cycles destined to EISA after the first data phase due to incremental latency requirements. The exception is the case of a PCI memory write cycle destined to the EISA subsystem when Posted Write Buffers (PWB) are enabled and there is a space available in the PWB. When the PWBs are completely full, the PCEB generates a disconnect during burst access. If the first data phase can not be posted, the PCEB generates a retry.

The difference between disconnect and retry is that the PCEB does not assert TRDY# for the retry case. This instructs the initiator to retry the transfer at a later time. No data is transferred in a retry termination since TRDY# and IRDY# are never both asserted. The PCEB retries a PCI initiator when:

- the PCEB buffers require management activity.
- the PCEB is locked and another PCI device attempts to select the PCEB without negating PLOCK# during the address phase.
- the EISA Bus is occupied by an EISA/ISA master or DMA.
- the cycle is a memory write and the Posted Write Buffer is full.

Target abort is another form of target-initiated termination. Target abort resembles a retry, though the target must also negate DEVSEL#, along with assertion of STOP#. As a target, the PCEB never generates a target abort.

As a master, if the PCEB receives a target abort, it relinquishes the PCI Bus and sets the Received Target Abort Status bit in the PCI Status Register to a 1.

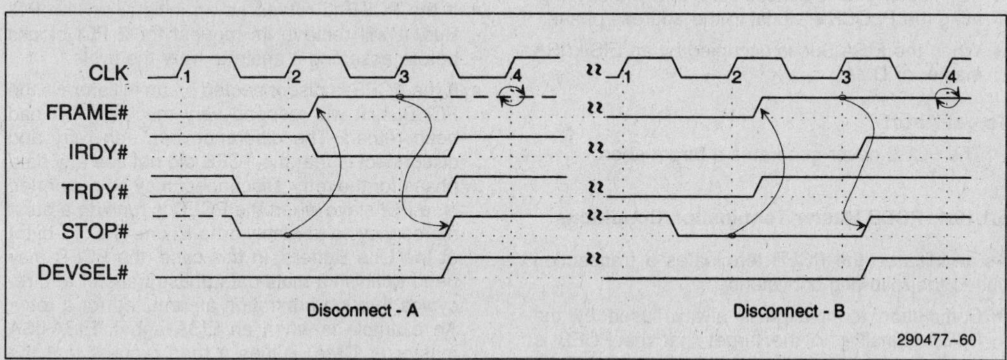

Figure 5-12. Target Initiated Termination

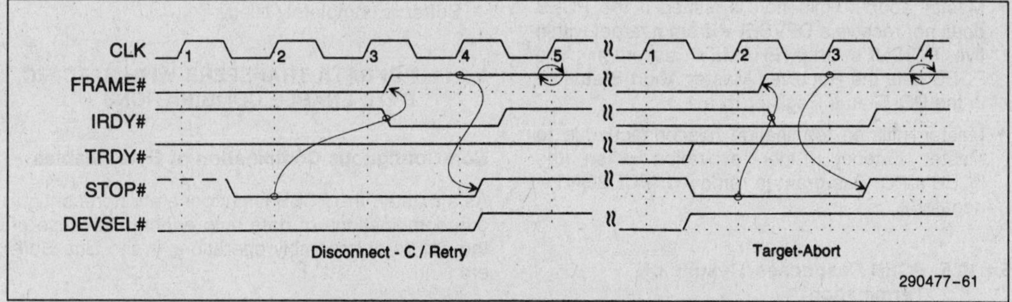

Figure 5-13. Target Initiated Termination

5.1.10.3 PCEB Target Termination Conditions

As a target, the PCEB terminates a transaction due to the following conditions:

Disconnect

- When a target, the PCEB always responds with a disconnect to a multiple data phase transaction (see the Incremental Latency Timer section), except in the case of memory write transactions, which can be posted. During posting, as soon as all PWBs are occupied the PCEB terminates the cycle using disconnect semantics. This is because the next data phases would exceed the 8 PCI clock incremental latency limit and the PCI would be kept in wait states for more than 2 BCLKs (= 8 PCICLKs), until one of the PWBs is emptied to its destination on the EISA Bus.

Retry

- For memory write cycles when all posted write buffers are full. (See Section 6.0, Data Buffering.)
- When the pending PCI cycle initiates buffer management activity.
- When the PCEB is locked, as a resource, and a PCI master tries to access the PCEB without negating the PLOCK# signal in the address phase.
- When the EISA Bus is occupied by an EISA/ISA master or DMA.

Target Abort

- The PCEB never generates a target abort.

5.1.10.4 PCEB Master Termination Conditions

As an initiator, the PCEB terminates a transaction due to the following conditions:

- Completion termination is always used by the PCEB signaling to the target that the PCEB is ready to complete the final data phase of the transaction.
- Master abort termination is issued if the PCEB does not receive a DEVSEL# from a target within five PCICLK's after FRAME# assertion. The PCEB sets the Received Master Abort Status bit in the PCI Status Register to a 1.
- Master initiated termination (disconnect) due to Master Latency Timer expiration when the PCEB's PCI Bus grant is removed (PCEBGNT# negated).

5.1.10.5 PCEB Responses/Results of Termination

PCEB's response, as a target, to a master termination:

- Completion termination is the normal way of terminating a transaction.
- If a PCI initiator times out due to LT time-out and ends the current transaction, the PCEB cannot detect a difference between normal completion termination and time-out forced termination.

PCEB's response as a master to target termination:

- If the PCEB receives a target abort, it means that the target device is not capable of handling the transaction. The PCEB does not try the cycle again. If an EISA/ISA master or the DMA is waiting for the PCI cycle to terminate (EXRDY negated), the target abort condition causes the PCEB to assert EXRDY to terminate the EISA cycle. Note that write data is lost and the read data is meaningless. This is identical to the way an unclaimed cycle is handled on the "normally ready" EISA Bus. If the Line Buffer is the requester of the PCI transaction, the target abort mechanism ends the PCI cycle, but no valid data transfers are performed into or out of the Line Buffer. The Line Buffer does not try the cycle again. The Received Target Abort Status bit in the PCI Status Register is set to 1 indicating that the PCEB experienced a target abort condition.
- If the PCEB is retried as an initiator on the PCI Bus, it will remove its request for 2 PCI clocks before asserting it again to retry the cycle.
- If the PCEB is disconnected as an initiator on the PCI Bus, it will respond very much as if it had been retried. The difference between retry and disconnect is that the PCEB did not see any data phase for the retry. Disconnect may be generated by a PCI slave when the PCEB is running a burst memory cycle to empty or to fill one line (16-byte) of the Line Buffers. In this case, the PCEB may need to finish a multi-data phase transfer and recycles through arbitration as required for a retry. An example is when an EISA agent (EISA/ISA master or DMA) issues a read request that the PCEB translates into a 16-byte prefetch (one line) and the PCEB is disconnected before the Line Buffer is completely filled.

5.1.11 PCI DATA TRANSFERS WITH SPECIFIC BYTE ENABLE COMBINATIONS

Non-Contiguous Combination of Byte Enables

As a master, the PCEB might generate non-contiguous combinations of data byte enables because of the nature of assembly operations in the Line Buffers.

As a target, the PCEB might need to respond to a non-contiguous combination of data byte enables. These cycles can not be passed directly to the EISA Bus; the EISA Bus specification does not allow non-contiguous combinations of byte enables. If this situation occurs, the PCEB splits the 32-bit transactions into two 16-bit transactions by first performing the lower word transfer (indicated by BE1# and BE0#) and then the upper word transfer (indicated by BE3# and BE2#).

BE[3:0]# = 1111

As a master, the PCEB might generate this combination of data byte enables during Line Buffer flush operations (burst write) to optimize the usage of the PCI Bus. Correct parity is driven during this transaction on the PCI Bus.

As a target, the PCEB might need to respond to this combination of data byte enables. If BE[3:0]# = 1111, the PCEB completes the transfer by asserting TRDY# and providing parity for read cycles. The PCEB does not forward the cycle to the EISA Bus and data is not posted in the Posted Write Buffers.

5.2 PCI Bus Latency

The PCI specification provides two mechanisms that limit a master's time on the bus. They ensure predictable bus acquisitions when other masters are requesting bus access. These mechanisms are master-initiated termination supported by a Master Latency Timer (MLT) and a target-initiated termination (specifically, disconnect) supported by a target's incremental latency mechanism.

5.2.1 MASTER LATENCY TIMER (MLT)

The PCEB has a programmable Master Latency Timer (MLT). The MLT is cleared and suspended whenever the PCEB is not asserting FRAME#. The MLT is controlled via the MLT Register (see Section 4.1, PCEB Configuration Registers). When the PCEB, as a master, asserts FRAME#, it enables its MLT to count. If the PCEB completes its transaction (negates FRAME#) before the count expires, the MLT is ignored. If the count expires before the transaction completes (count = number clocks programmed into the MLT Register), the PCEB initiates a transaction termination as soon as its GNT# is removed. The number of clocks programmed into the MLT Register represents the guaranteed time slice (measured in PCICLKs) allotted to the PCEB; after which it surrenders the bus as soon as its GNT# is removed. (Actual termination does not occur until the target is ready.)

5.2.2 INCREMENTAL LATENCY MECHANISM

As a target, the PCEB supports the Incremental Latency Mechanism for PCI-to-EISA cycles. The PCI specification states that for multi-data phase PCI cycles, if the incremental latency from current data phase (N) to the next data phase (N+1) is greater than eight PCICLKs, the target must manipulate TRDY# and STOP# to stop the transaction after the current data phase (N). If the PCEB's internal PWBs are enabled, the EISA Bus is owned by the PCEB, and there is a space available in the PWBs, then the PCI memory cycles destined to EISA are posted until all PWBs are occupied. When the PWBs are occupied, the following cycle is disconnected (in the case of burst) or retried (in the case of single cycles). All other PCI-to-EISA cycles (memory read and I/O read or write) are automatically terminated (during a burst) after the first data phase because they require more than eight PCICLKs to complete on the EISA Bus.

Therefore, the PCEB does not need to specifically implement an 8 PCICLK timer and the PCEB handles a disconnect in a pre-determined fashion, based on the type of current transaction.

5.3 PCI Bus Parity Support and Error Reporting

PCI provides for parity and asynchronous system errors to be detected and reported separately. The PCEB/ESC chip set implements both mechanisms. The PCEB implements only parity generation and checking and it does not interface to the SERR# signal. Reporting of both PERR# and SERR# indicated errors is implemented in the ESC.

5.3.1 PARITY GENERATION AND CHECKING

The PCEB supports parity generation and checking on the PCI Bus. During the address and data phases, parity covers AD[31:0] and the C/BE[3:0]# lines, regardless of whether or not all lines carry meaningful information. Byte lanes that are not actually transferring data are still required to be driven with stable (albeit meaningless) data and are included in the parity calculation. Parity is calculated such that the number of 1s on AD[31:0], C/BE[3:0]#, and the PAR signals is an even number.

The role of the PCEB in parity generation/checking depends on the phase of the cycle (address or data), the type of bus cycle (read or write), and whether the PCEB is a master or target. The following paragraphs and Figure 5-14 summarize behavior of the PCEB during the address and data phase of a PCI Bus cycle.

1

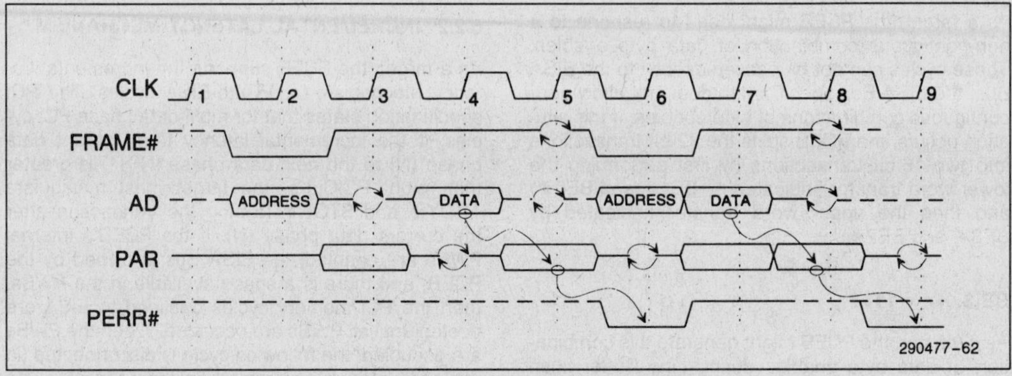

Figure 5-14. Parity Operation

5.3.1.1 Address Phase

As a master, the PCEB drives AD[31:0] and C/BE[3:0]# and calculates the corresponding parity value and drives it on the PAR signal, 1 clock later. As a target, the PCEB does not check parity during the address phase of a bus cycle.

5.3.1.2 Data Phase

As a master during a write cycle, the PCEB drives AD[31:0] and C/BE[3:0]# and calculates the corresponding parity value and drives it on the PAR signal, 1 clock later.

As a master during a read cycle, the PCEB only drives C/BE[31:0]#. The responding target drives AD[31:0] lines (data) and calculates parity based on the received C/BE[3:0]# and outgoing AD[31:0] signals. The target drives PAR during the following clock. The PCEB calculates parity based on the outgoing C/BE[3:0]# and the incoming AD[31:0] signals at the end of the data phase. It compares it with the incoming value of the PAR signal and asserts PERR# if there is no match.

As a target during a write cycle, the PCEB calculates parity on the incoming AD[31:0] and C/BE[3:0]# signals, and compares the result on the next clock with the incoming value on the PAR signal. If the value does not match, the PCEB asserts PERR#.

As a target during a read cycle, the PCEB calculates parity on the incoming C/BE[3:0]# and outgoing AD[31:0] signals. The PCEB drives the calculated parity value during the next clock. The master of the transaction receives the data, calculates parity on its outgoing C/BE[3:0]# and incoming AD[31:0] signals and compares its calculated value, on the next clock, with the parity value on the PAR signal (supplied by the PCEB). If the values do not match, the master asserts PERR#.

5.3.2 PARITY ERROR—PERR# SIGNAL

When the PCEB is involved in a bus transaction (master or target), it asserts the PERR# signal, if enabled via the PCICMD Register, to indicate a parity error for the bus cycle. PERR# is a sustained tri-state (s/t/s) type of signal (see Section 2.0, Signal Description). Note that PCI parity errors signaled by PERR#, are reported to the host processor via the ESC's system interrupt control logic. When the PCEB detects a parity error during one of its bus transactions, it sets the parity error status bit in the PCI Status Register, regardless of whether the PERR# signal is enabled via the PCICMD Register.

5.3.3 SYSTEM ERRORS

The PCEB does not generate system errors (SERR#). Thus, the PCEB does not have the capability of indicating parity errors during the address phase in which it is a potential target (i.e., not a master). Note that system errors are reported via the ESC (companion chip).

5.4 PCI Bus Arbitration

The PCEB contains a PCI Bus arbiter that supports six PCI Bus masters—The Host/PCI Bridge, PCEB, and four other masters. The PCEB's REQ#/GNT# signals are internal. If an external arbiter is used, the internal arbiter can be disabled. When disabled, the PCEB's internal REQ#, GNT#, and RESUME# signals become visible for an external arbiter (via the GNT0#/PCEBREQ#, REQ0#/PCEBGNT#, and GNT1#/RESUME# dual-function signal pins, respectively). During power-up, the internal arbiter is enabled if CPUREQ# is sampled high when PCIRST# makes a low-to-high transition.

The internal arbiter contains several features that contribute to system efficiency:

- Use of the internal RESUME# signal to re-enable a backed-off initiator in order to minimize PCI Bus thrashing when the PCEB generates a retry.
- A programmable timer to re-enable retried initiators after a number of PCICLK's.
- A programmable PCI Bus lock or PCI resource lock function.
- The CPU (Host/PCI) can be optionally parked on the PCI Bus.

In addition, the PCEB has three PCI sideband signals (FLUSHREQ#, MEMREQ#, and MEMACK#) that are used to control system buffer coherency and control operations for the Guaranteed Access Time (GAT) mode.

5.4.1 PCI ARBITER CONFIGURATION

The PCI arbitration priority scheme is programmable through the configuration registers. The arbiter consists of four (4) banks that can be configured so that the six (6) masters can be arranged in a purely rotating priority scheme, one of 24 fixed priority schemes, or a hybrid combination.

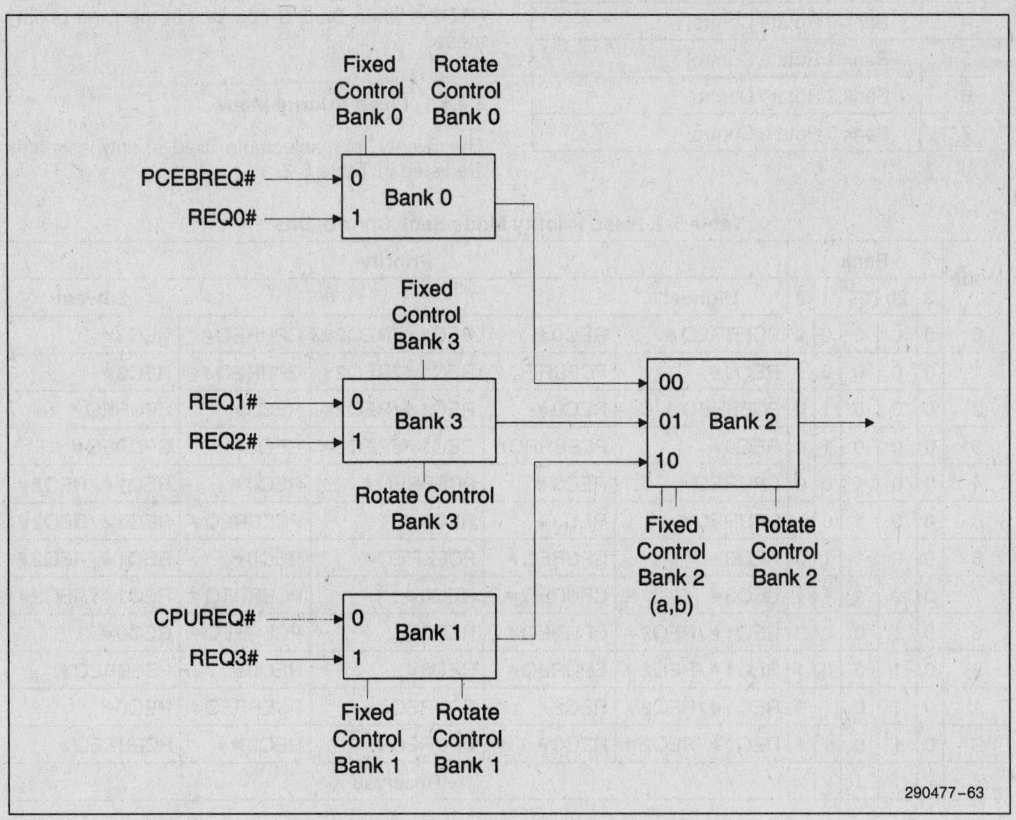

Figure 5-15. Arbiter Conceptual Block Diagram

NOTE:

PCEBREQ#/PCEBGNT# are PCEB internal signals.

The PCEB implements PCI arbiter priority configuration registers ARBPRI and ARBPRIX mapped in the PCI's configuration space. Definition of the registers is as follows:

ARBPRI

Bit	Description
0	Bank 0 Fixed Priority Mode Select
1	Bank 1 Fixed Priority Mode Select
2	Bank 2 Fixed Priority Mode Select A
3	Bank 2 Fixed Priority Mode Select B
4	Bank 0 Rotate Control
5	Bank 1 Rotate Control
6	Bank 2 Rotate Control
7	Bank 3 Rotate Control

This register defaults to 04h at reset. This selects fixed mode #4 with the CPU the highest priority device guaranteeing that BIOS accesses can take place.

ARBPRIX

Bit	Description
0	Bank 3 Fixed Priority Mode select
1–7	Reserved

This register defaults to 00h at reset. Default value selects REQ1# as a higher priority request than REQ2# when Bank 3 operates in the fixed priority mode.

5.4.1.1 Fixed Priority Mode

The twenty four selectable fixed priority schemes are listed in Table 5-2.

Table 5-2. Fixed Priority Mode Bank Control Bits

Mode	Bank					Priority				
	3	2b	2a	1	0	Highest				Lowest
0	0	0	0	0	0	PCEBREQ#	REQ0#	REQ1#/REQ2#	CPUREQ#	REQ3#
1	0	0	0	0	1	REQ0#	PCEBREQ#	REQ1#/REQ2#	CPUREQ#	REQ3#
2	0	0	0	1	0	PCEBREQ#	REQ0#	REQ1#/REQ2#	REQ3#	CPUREQ#
3	0	0	0	1	1	REQ0#	PCEBREQ#	REQ1#/REQ2#	REQ3#	CPUREQ#
4	0	0	1	0	0	CPUREQ#	REQ3#	PCEBREQ#	REQ0#	REQ1#/REQ2#
5	0	0	1	0	1	CPUREQ#	REQ3#	REQ0#	PCEBREQ#	REQ1#/REQ2#
6	0	0	1	1	0	REQ3#	CPUREQ#	PCEBREQ#	REQ0#	REQ1#/REQ2#
7	0	0	1	1	1	REQ3#	CPUREQ#	REQ0#	PCEBREQ#	REQ1#/REQ2#
8	0	1	0	0	0	REQ1#/REQ2#	CPUREQ#	REQ3#	PCEBREQ#	REQ0#
9	0	1	0	0	1	REQ1#/REQ2#	CPUREQ#	REQ3#	REQ0#	PCEBREQ#
A	0	1	0	1	0	REQ1#/REQ2#	REQ3#	CPUREQ#	PCEBREQ#	REQ0#
B	0	1	0	1	1	REQ1#/REQ2#	REQ3#	CPUREQ#	REQ0#	PCEBREQ#
	x	1	1	x	x	Reserved				

Table 5-2. Fixed Priority Mode Bank Control Bits (Continued)

Mode	Bank					Priority				
	3	2b	2a	1	0	Highest				Lowest
10	1	0	0	0	0	PCEBREQ#	REQ0#	REQ2#/REQ1#	CPUREQ#	REQ3#
11	1	0	0	0	1	REQ0#	PCEBREQ#	REQ1#/REQ1#	CPUREQ#	REQ3#
12	1	0	0	1	0	PCEBREQ#	REQ0#	REQ2#/REQ1#	REQ3#	CPUREQ#
13	1	0	0	1	1	REQ0#	PCEBREQ#	REQ2#/REQ1#	REQ3#	CPUREQ#
14	1	0	1	0	0	CPUREQ#	REQ3#	PCEBREQ#	REQ0#	REQ2#/REQ1#
15	1	0	1	0	1	CPUREQ#	REQ3#	REQ0#	PCEBREQ#	REQ2#/REQ1#
16	1	0	1	1	0	REQ3#	CPUREQ#	PCEBREQ#	REQ0#	REQ2#/REQ1#
17	1	0	1	1	1	REQ3#	CPUREQ#	REQ0#	PCEBREQ#	REQ2#/REQ1#
18	1	1	0	0	0	REQ2#/REQ1#	CPUREQ#	REQ3#	PCEBREQ#	REQ0#
19	1	1	0	0	1	REQ2#/REQ1#	CPUREQ#	REQ3#	REQ0#	PCEBREQ#
1A	1	1	0	1	0	REQ2#/REQ1#	REQ3#	CPUREQ#	PCEBREQ#	REQ0#
1B	1	1	0	1	1	REQ2#/REQ1#	REQ3#	CPUREQ#	REQ0#	PCEBREQ#
	x	1	1	x	x	Reserved				

Note that these two tables are permutations of the same table with different value of the Bank 3 fixed priority control bit.

The fixed bank control bit(s) selects which requester is the highest priority device within that particular bank. Bits 4–7 must all be programmed to 0's (rotate mode disabled) to get these combinations.

The selectable fixed schemes provide 24 of the 128 possible fixed mode permutations possible for the six masters.

5.4.1.2 Rotating Priority Mode

When any bank rotate control bit is set to a one, that particular bank rotates between the requesting inputs. Any or all banks can be set in rotate mode. If all four banks are set in rotate mode, the six supported masters are all rotated and the arbiter is in a pure rotating priority mode. If, within a rotating bank, the highest priority device (a) does not have an active request, the lower priority device (b or c) will be granted the bus. However, this does not change the rotation scheme. When the bank toggles, device b is the highest priority. Because of this, the maximum latency a device can encounter is two complete rotations.

5.4.1.3 Mixed Priority Mode

Any combination of fixed priority and rotate priority modes can be used in different arbitration banks to achieve a specific arbitration scheme.

5.4.1.4 Locking Masters

When a master acquires the PLOCK# signal, the arbiter gives that master highest priority until PLOCK# is negated and FRAME# is negated. This insures that a master that locked a resource will eventually be able to unlock that same resource.

5.4.2 POWER-UP CONFIGURATION

The PCEB's internal arbiter is enabled if CPUREQ# is sampled high on the low-to-high edge of PCIRST#. After PCIRST#, the internal arbiter, if enabled, is set to fixed priority mode number 4 with CPU parking turned off. Fixed mode number 4 guarantees that the CPU is capable of accessing BIOS to configure the system, regardless of the state of the other REQ#'s. Note that the Host/PCI Bridge should drive CPUREQ# high during the rising edge of PCIRST#. When the internal arbiter is enabled, the PCEB acts as the central resource and drives AD[31:0], C/BE[3:0]#, and PAR when no device is granted the PCI Bus and the bus is idle. The PCEB always drives these signals when it is granted the bus (PCEBGNT# and PCI Bus idle) and as appropriate when it is the master of a transaction. After reset, if the internal arbiter is enabled, CPUGNT#, GNT[3:0]#, and the internal PCEBGNT# are driven, based on the arbitration scheme and the asserted REQ#'s.

If an external arbiter is present in the system, the CPUREQ# signal should be tied low. When CPUREQ# is sampled low on the rising edge of the PCIRST#, the internal arbiter is disabled. When the internal arbiter is disabled, the PCEB does not drive AD[31:0], C/BE[3:0]#, and PAR as the central resource. The PCEB only drives these signals when it is granted the bus (PCEBGNT# and idle bus) and as appropriate when it is the master of a transaction. If the internal arbiter is disabled, GNT0# becomes PCEBREQ# (output signal), GNT1# becomes RESUME# (output signal), and REQ0# becomes PCEBGNT# (input signal). This exposes the normally embedded PCEB arbitration signals. Since these signals retain their input/output character there is no contention issue.

5.4.3 ARBITRATION SIGNALING PROTOCOL

An agent requests the PCI Bus by asserting its REQ#. When the arbiter determines that an agent may use the PCI Bus, it asserts the agent's GNT#. Figure 5-16 shows an example of the basic arbitration cycle. Two agents (A and B) are used to illustrate how the arbiter alternates bus accesses. Note in Figure 5-16 that the current owner of the bus may keep its REQ# (REQ#-A) asserted when it requires additional transactions.

REQ#-A is asserted prior to or at clock 1 to request use of the PCI Bus. Agent A is granted access to the bus (GNT#-A is asserted) at clock 2. Agent A may start a transaction at clock 2 because FRAME# and IRDY# are negated and GNT#-A is asserted. Agent A's transaction starts when FRAME# is asserted (clock 3). Agent A requests another transaction by keeping REQ#-A asserted.

When FRAME# is asserted on clock 3, the arbiter determines that agent B has priority and asserts GNT#-B and negates GNT#-A on clock 4. When agent A completes its transaction on clock 4, it relinquishes the bus. All PCI agents can determine the end of the current transaction when both FRAME# and IRDY# are negated. Agent B becomes the PCI Bus owner on clock 5 (FRAME# and IRDY# are negated) and completes its transaction on clock 7. Note that REQ#-B is negated and FRAME# is asserted on clock 6, indicating that agent B requires only a single transaction. The arbiter grants the next transaction to agent A because its REQ# is still asserted.

5.4.3.1 REQ# and GNT# Rules

Figure 5-16 illustrates basic arbitration. Once asserted, GNT# may be negated according to the following rules:

1. If GNT# is negated at the same time that FRAME# is asserted, the bus transaction is valid and will continue.
2. One GNT# can be negated coincident with another being asserted, if the bus is not in the idle state. Otherwise, a one clock delay is incurred between the negation of the current master's GNT# and assertion of the next master's GNT#, to comply with the PCI specification.
3. While FRAME# is negated, GNT# may be negated, at any time, in order to service a higher priority master, or in response to the associated REQ# being negated.
4. If the MEMREQ# and MEMACK# are asserted, once the PCEB is granted the PCI Bus, the arbiter will not remove the internal grant until the PCEB removes its request.

5.4.3.2 Back-to-Back Transactions

Figure 5-17 illustrates arbitration for a back-to-back access. There are two types of back-to-back transactions by the same initiator; those that do not require a turn-around-cycle (see Section 5.1.3.1, Turn-Around-Cycle Definition) and those that do. A turn-around-cycle is not required when the initiator's second transaction is to the same target as the first transaction (to insure no TRDY# contention), and the first transaction is a write. This is a fast back-to-back. Under all other conditions, the initiator must insert a minimum of one turn-around-cycle.

During a fast back-to-back transaction, the initiator starts the next transaction immediately, without a turn-around-cycle. The last data phase completes when FRAME# is negated, and IRDY# and TRDY# are asserted. The current initiator starts another transaction on the same PCICLK that the last data is transferred for the previous transaction.

As a master, the PCEB does not know if it is accessing the same target, and, thus, does not generate fast back-to-back accesses. As a slave, the PCEB is capable of decoding fast back-to-back cycles.

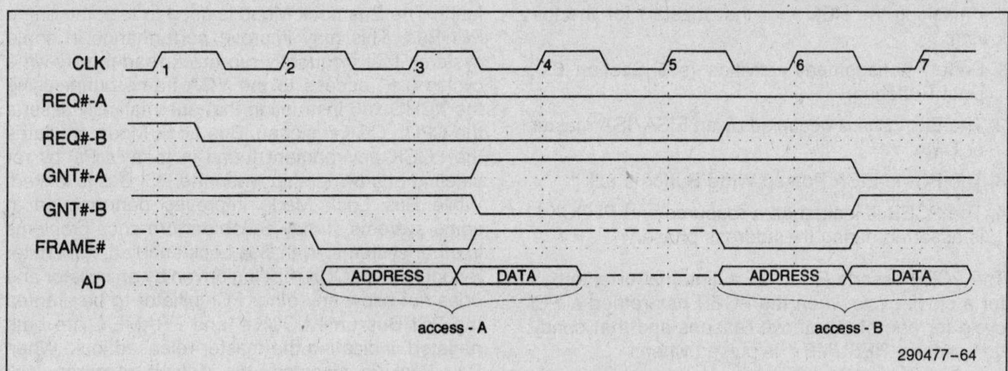

Figure 5-16. Basic Arbitration

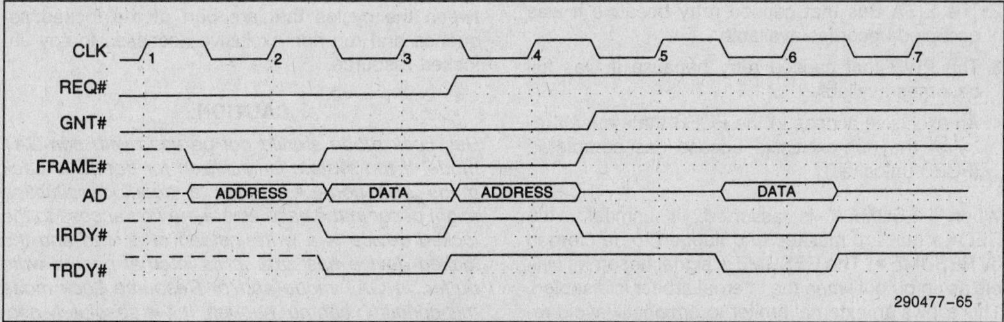

Figure 5-17. Arbitration for Back-to-Back Access

5.4.4 RETRY THRASHING RESOLVE

When a PCI initiator's access is retried, the initiator releases the PCI Bus for a minimum of two PCI clocks and then normally requests the PCI Bus again. To avoid thrashing of the bus with retry after retry, the PCI arbiter's state tracer provides REQ# masking. Tracking retried masters requires latching GNT# during FRAME# so that the correct retried master can be masked. The state tracer masks a REQ# after that particular agent is retried on the PCI Bus. The state tracer differentiates between two retry events. The two events include:

1. PCEB target retries
2. All other retries

For initiators that were retried by the PCEB as a target, the masked REQ# is flagged to be cleared upon RESUME# active. All other retries trigger the Master Retry Timer (described in Section 5.4.4.2, Master Retry Timer). When this timer expires, the mask is cleared.

5.4.4.1 Resume Function (RESUME#)

The PCEB forces a retry to a PCI master (resulting in the masking the REQ# of that master) for the following:

1. Buffer management activities (see Section 6.0, Data Buffering)
2. The EISA Bus is occupied by an EISA/ISA master or DMA
3. The PCI-to-EISA Posted Write Buffer is full
4. The PCEB is locked as a resource and PLOCK# is asserted during the address phase.

The PCEB asserts RESUME# (internal or external) for a clock cycle when the PCEB has retried a PCI cycle for one of the above reasons and that condition passes. RESUME# is pulsed when:

1. The buffer management triggered by the retried cycle is complete.
2. The EISA Bus that caused retry because it was occupied becomes available.
3. The PWB that caused retry because it was full becomes available.
4. An exclusive access to the PCEB that caused retry of the non-exclusive access has completed (PCEB unlocked).

When RESUME# is asserted, it unmasks the REQ#s that are masked and flagged to be cleared by RESUME#. The RESUME# signal becomes visible as an output when the internal arbiter is disabled. This allows an external arbiter to optionally avoid retry thrashing associated with the PCEB (i.e., EISA Bus) as a target. When asserted, RESUME# is asserted for one PCICLK.

5.4.4.2 Master Retry Timer

For any other retried PCI cycle, the arbiter masks the REQ# and flags it to be cleared by the expiration of a programmable timer. The first retry in this category triggers the programmable timer. Subsequent retries in this category are masked but do not reset the timer. Expiration of this programmable timer unmasks all REQ#s that are masked for this reason. The Retry Timer is programmable to 0 (disabled), 16, 32, or 64 PCICLKs.

If no other PCI masters are requesting the PCI Bus, all of the REQ#s masked for the timer are cleared and the timer is set to 0. Note that when there is a pending request that is internally masked, the PCEB does not park the CPU on the PCI Bus (i.e., PCI agent that uses CPUREQ#/CPUGNT# signal pair). This is necessary to assist the Host/PCI bridge in determining when to re-enable its disabled posted write buffers.

5.4.5 BUS LOCK MODE

As an option, the PCEB arbiter can be configured to run in Bus Lock Mode or Resource Lock Mode (default). The Bus Lock Mode is used to lock the entire PCI Bus. This may improve performance in some systems that frequently run quick read-modify-write cycles (i.e., access to the VGA frame buffer using the XCHG x86 instruction that automatically asserts the CPU LOCK# signal). Bus Lock Mode emulates the LOCK environment found in today's PC by restricting bus ownership when the PCI Bus is locked. While Bus Lock Mode improves performance in some systems, it may cause performance problems in other systems. With Bus Lock enabled, the arbiter recognizes a LOCK# being driven by an initiator and does not allow any other PCI initiator to be granted the PCI Bus until LOCK# and FRAME# are both negated, indicating the master released lock. When Bus Lock is disabled, the default resource lock mechanism is implemented (normal resource lock) and a higher priority PCI initiator could intervene between the cycles that are part of the locked sequence and run non-exclusive accesses to any unlocked resource.

CAUTION:

Bus Lock mode should not be used with non-GAT mode. If the system is initialized for both Bus Lock mode and non-GAT mode a deadlock situation might occur in the case where the first access to the locked device is a write instead of a read and the locked device has data in its internal posted write buffer. In GAT mode and/or Resource Lock mode this condition can not happen. If it is absolutely necessary to operate the system in the above mentioned combination of modes, then the posted write buffers of the device that might be involved in locked operations (typically semaphore in main memory) must be disabled.

5.4.6 MEMREQ#, FLSHREQ#, AND MEMACK# PROTOCOL

Before an EISA master or DMA can be granted the PCI Bus, it is necessary that all PCI system posted write buffers be flushed (including the PCEB Posted Write Buffer). Also, since the EISA-originated cycle could access memory on the Host/PCI Bridge, it is possible that the EISA master or DMA could be held in wait states (via EXRDY) waiting for the Host/PCI Bridge arbitration for longer than the 2.1 μs EISA/ISA specification. The PCEB has an optional mode called Guaranteed Access Time mode (GAT) that ensures that this timing specification is not violated. This is accomplished by delaying the EISA grant signal to the requesting master or DMA until the EISA Bus, PCI Bus, and the system memory bus are arbitrated for and owned.

The three sideband signals, MEMREQ#, FLSHREQ#, and MEMACK# are used to support the system Posted Write Buffer flushing and Guaranteed Access Time mechanism. The MEMACK# signal is the common acknowledge signal for both mechanisms. Note that, when MEMREQ# is asserted, FLSHREQ# is also asserted. Table 5-3 shows the relationship between MEMREQ# and FLSHREQ#.

Table 5-3. FLSHREQ# and MEMREQ#

FLSHREQ#	MEMREQ#	Meaning
1	1	Idle.
0	1	Flush buffers pointing towards the PCI Bus to avoid EISA deadlock.
1	0	Reserved.
0	0	GAT mode. Guarantees PCI Bus immediate access to main memory.

5.4.6.1. Flushing System Posted Write Buffers

Once an EISA Bus owner (EISA/ISA master or the DMA) begins a cycle on the EISA Bus, the cycle can not be backed-off. It can only be held in wait states via EXRDY. In order to know the destination of EISA master cycles, the cycle needs to begin. After the cycle is started, no other device can intervene and gain ownership of the EISA Bus until the cycle is completed and arbitration is performed. A potential deadlock condition exists when an EISA-originated cycle to the PCI Bus forces a mandatory transaction to EISA, or when the PCI target is inaccessible due to an interacting event that also requires the EISA Bus. To avoid this potential deadlock, all PCI posted write buffers in the system must be disabled and flushed, before an EISA/ISA master or DMA can be granted the EISA Bus. The buffers must remain disabled while the EISA Bus is occupied. The following steps indicate the PCEB (and ESC) handshake for flushing the system posted write buffers.

1. When an EISA/ISA master, DMA or refresh logic requests the EISA Bus, the ESC component asserts EISAHOLD to the PCEB.

2. The PCEB completes the present cycle (and does not accept any new cycle), flushes its PCI-to-EISA Posted Write Buffers and gives the EISA Bus to the ESC by floating its EISA interface and asserting EISAHLDA. Before giving the bus to the ESC, the PCEB checks to see if it itself is locked as a PCI resource. It can not grant the EISA Bus as long as the PCEB is locked.

   At this point the PCEB's EISA-to-PCI Line Buffers and other system buffers (Host/PCI Bridge buffers) that are pointing to PCI are not yet flushed. The reason for this is that the ESC might request the bus in order to run a refresh cycle that does not require buffer flushing. That is not known until the EISA arbitration is frozen (after EISAHLDA is asserted).

   a. If the ESC needs to perform a refresh cycle, then it negates NMFLUSH# (an ESC-to-PCEB flush control signal). ESC drives the EISA Bus until it completes the refresh cycle and then gives the bus to the PCEB by negating EISAHOLD.

   b. If the ESC requested the EISA Bus on behalf of the EISA master, DMA or ISA master, then it asserts NMFLUSH# and tri-states the EISA Bus. The PCEB asserts the FLSHREQ# signal to the Host/PCI Bridge (and other bridges) to disable and flush posted write buffers. The PCEB flushes its internal EISA-to-PCI Posted Write Buffers, if they contain valid write data.

4. When the Host/PCI Bridge completes its buffer disabling and flushing, it asserts MEMACK# to the PCEB. Other bridges in the system may also need to disable and flush their posted write buffers pointing towards PCI. This means that other devices may also generate MEMACK#. All of the MEMACK#s need to be "wire-OR'd". When the PCEB receives MEMACK# indicating that all posted write buffers have been flushed, it asserts NMFLUSH# to the ESC and the ESC gives the bus grant to the EISA device.

5. The PCEB continues to assert FLSHREQ# while the EISA/ISA master or DMA owns the EISA Bus. While FLSHREQ# is asserted the Host/PCI Bridge must keep its posted write buffers flushed.
6. MEMACK# should be driven inactive as soon as possible by the Host/PCI Bridge and other bridges after FLSHREQ# is negated. The PCEB waits until it detects MEMACK# negated before it can generate another FLSHREQ#.

5.4.6.2 Guaranteed Access Time Mode

When the PCEB's Guaranteed Access Time Mode is enabled (via the ARBCON Register), MEMREQ# and MEMACK# are used to guarantee that the ISA 2.1 μs CHRDY specification is not violated. Note that EISA's 2.5 μs maximum negation time of the EXRDY signal is a subset of the ISA requirement. Thus, 2.1 μs satisfies both bus requirements.

When an **EISA/ISA master or DMA slave** requests the EISA Bus (MREQ# or DREQ# active), the EISA Bus, the PCI Bus, and the memory bus must be arbitrated for and all three must be owned before the EISA/ISA master or DMA is granted the EISA Bus. The following lists the sequence of events:

1. An EISA/ISA master, DMA, or refresh logic requests the EISA Bus. The ESC asserts EISAHOLD signal to the PCEB.
2. The PCEB completes the present cycle (i.e., does not accept any new cycle), flushes its PCI-to-EISA posted write buffers and gives the bus to the ESC by floating its EISA interface and asserting EISAHLDA. Before giving the bus to the ESC, the PCEB checks to see if it is locked as a PCI resource. It can not grant the EISA Bus as long as the PCEB is locked.

At this point, the PCEB's EISA-to-PCI Line Buffers and other system buffers (e.g., Host/PCI Bridge buffers) that are pointing to the PCI Bus are not flushed. The reason is that the ESC might request the bus to run a refresh cycle that does not require buffer flushing. This is not known until the EISA arbitration is frozen (after EISAHLDA is asserted).

3a. If the ESC needs to perform a refresh cycle, then it asserts NMFLUSH# (an ESC-to-PCEB flush control signal). The ESC drives the EISA Bus until it completes the refresh cycle and then gives the bus to the PCEB by negating EISAHOLD.

3b. If the ESC requested the EISA Bus on behalf of the EISA master, DMA or ISA master, then it asserts NMFLUSH# and tri-states the EISA Bus. If the PCEB is programmed in GAT (Guaranteed Access Time mode), the MEMREQ# and FLSHREQ# signals are asserted simultaneously to indicate request for direct access to main memory and a request to flush the system's posted write buffers pointing towards the PCI (including the PCEB's internal buffers). These requirements are necessary to insure that once the PCI and EISA Buses are dedicated to the PCEB, the cycle generated by the PCEB will not require the PCI or EISA Buses, thus creating a deadlock. MEMREQ# and FLSHREQ# are asserted as long as the EISA/ISA master or DMA owns the EISA Bus.

4. Once the Host/PCI Bridge has disabled and flushed its posted write buffers, and the memory bus is dedicated to the PCI interface, it asserts MEMACK#. Other bridges in the system may also need to disable and flush their posted write buffers pointing towards PCI due to the FLSHREQ# signal. This means that other devices may also generate a MEMACK#. All of the MEMACK#s need to be "wire-OR'd". When the PCEB receives MEMACK#, it assumes that all of the critical posted write buffers in the system have been flushed and that the PCEB has direct access to main memory, located behind the Host/PCI Bridge.
5. When MEMACK# is asserted by the PCEB, it will request the PCI Bus (internal or external PCEBREQ# signal). Before requesting the PCI Bus, the PCEB checks to see that the PCI Bus does not have an active lock. The PCI Bus is granted to the PCEB when it wins the bus through the normal arbitration mechanism. Once the PCEB is granted the PCI Bus (internal or external PCEBGNT#), the PCEB checks to see if PLOCK# is negated before it grants the EISA Bus. If the PCI Bus is locked when the PCEB is granted the PCI Bus, the PCEB releases the REQ# signal and waits until the PLOCK# is negated before asserting REQ# again. Once the PCEB owns the PCI Bus (internal or external PCEBGNT#), and the MEMACK# and MEMREQ# signals are asserted, the PCI arbiter will not grant the PCI Bus to any other PCI master except the PCEB until the PCEB releases its PCI REQ# line.
6. When the PCEB is granted the PCI Bus (internal or external PCEBGNT#) and LOCK# is inactive, it asserts NMFLUSH# to the ESC and the ESC gives the bus grant to the EISA device.
7. When the EISA Bus is no longer owned by an EISA master or DMA, the PCEB negates MEMREQ# and FLSHREQ# and the PCI request signal (internal or external PCEBREQ#). The negation of MEMREQ# and FLSHREQ# indicates that direct access to the resource behind the bridge is no longer needed and that the posted write buffers may be enabled. Note that MEMACK# should be driven inactive as soon as possible by the Host/PCI Bridge and other

bridges after MEMREQ# is negated. The PCEB waits until it detects MEMACK# negated before it can generate another MEMREQ# or FLSHREQ#.

The use of MEMREQ#, FLSHREQ#, and MEMACK# does not guarantee GAT mode functionality with ISA masters that don't acknowledge CHRDY. These signals just guarantee the CHRDY inactive specification.

5.4.6.3 Interrupt Synchronization—Buffer Flushing

The ESC contains the system interrupt controller. Therefore, the PCEB/ESC chip set is the default destination of the PCI interrupt acknowledge cycles. Interrupts in the system are commonly used as a synchronization mechanism. If interrupts are used by the EISA agents to notify the Host CPU that data has been written to main memory, then posted data buffers must be flushed before the vector is returned during the interrupt acknowledge sequence. The PCEB handles this transparently to the rest of the system hardware/software. It retries the PCI interrupt acknowledge cycles and flushes the PCEB Line Buffers, if necessary.

5.4.6.4 System Buffer Flushing Protocol-State Machine

Figure 5-18 illustrates the functionality of the state machine contained within PCEB that implements the system buffer flushing protocol.

Definition of States

Normal: State where normal buffering is enabled.

WaitForGAT: Waiting for acknowledgment that the system has all buffers flushed and disabled and the EISA Bus master will have ownership of the entire system.

GAT: State where the system is ready for an EISA master to take over and have complete access to the system. The EISA Bus may be granted.

FlushEISA: Request for all devices in the system to flush all buffered writes that could end up going to the EISA Bus.

EISAbusy: State where an EISA Bus master owns the standard bus and no write data that might go to the EISA Bus may be posted.

Definition of Signals

GAT: GAT mode status bit.

REQ: EISA master request for PCI.

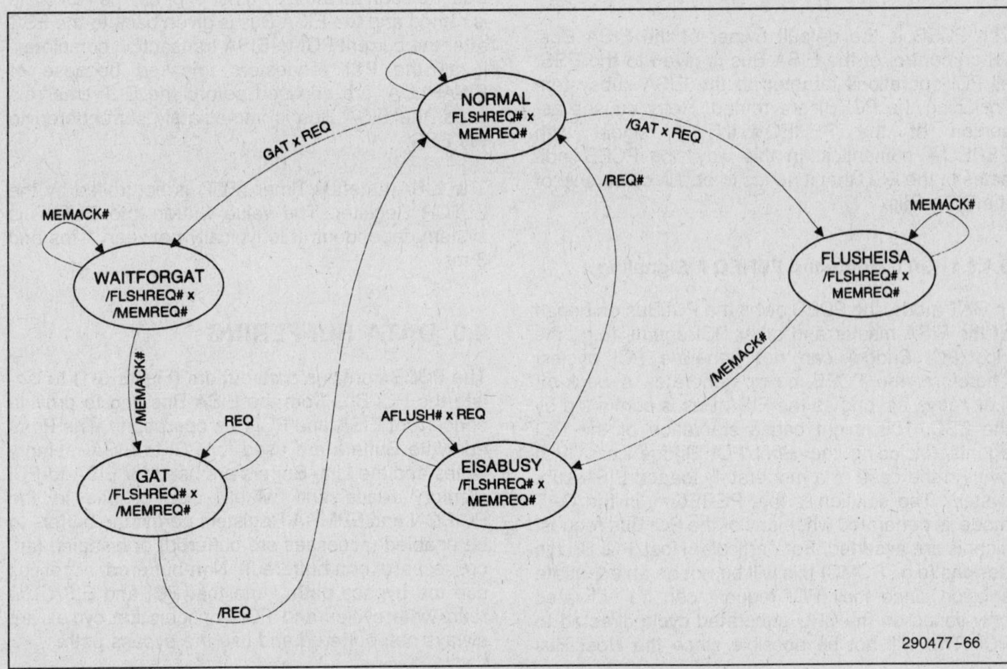

Figure 5-18. Buffer Flush Protocol-State Machine

5.4.7 BUS PARKING

PCI Bus parking can be enabled/disabled via the ARBCON Register. Parking is only allowed for the device that is connected to CPUREQ# (i.e., the Host/PCI Bridge). REQ[3:0]#, and the internal PCEBREQ# are not allowed to park on the PCI Bus. When bus parking is enabled, CPUGNT# is asserted when no other agent is currently using or requesting the bus. This achieves the minimum PCI arbitration latency possible.

Arbitration Latency

Parked: 0 PCICLKs for parked agent, 2 PCICLKs for all other.

Not Parked: 1 PCICLK for all agents.

Upon assertion of CPUGNT# due to bus parking enabled and the PCI Bus idle, the CPU (i.e., parked agent) must ensure AD[31:0], C/BE[3:0]#, and (one PCICLK later) PAR are driven. If bus parking is disabled, then the PCEB drives these signals when the bus is idle.

5.4.8 PCI ARBITRATION AND PCEB/ESC EISA OWNERSHIP EXCHANGE

There are two aspects of PCEB/ESC EISA Bus ownership exchange that are explained in this section. They are related to GAT mode and RESUME/RETRY operations.

The PCEB is the default owner of the EISA Bus. When control of the EISA Bus is given to the ESC, all PCI operations targeted to the EISA subsystem (including the PCEB) are retried. Retry causes assertion of the PEREQ#/INTA# signal with PEREQ# semantics. In this way, the PCEB indicates to the ESC that it needs to obtain ownership of the EISA Bus.

5.4.8.1 GAT Mode and PEREQ# Signaling

In GAT mode, the PCEB owns the PCI Bus on behalf of the EISA master and other PCI agents (e.g., the Host/PCI Bridge) can not generate PCI cycles. Therefore, the PCEB never generates a back-off (i.e., retry), as long as the EISA Bus is controlled by the ESC. This might cause starvation of the PCI agents (including the Host/PCI Bridge i.e., CPU) even in the case of a moderately loaded EISA subsystem. The solution is that PEREQ#, in the GAT mode, is generated when any of the PCI Bus request signals are asserted. For particular Host/PCI Bridge designs (e.g., PCMC) this will be not be an adequate solution since their PCI request can be activated only based on the CPU generated cycle directed to PCI. This will not be possible since the Host Bus (CPU bus) in the GAT mode is controlled by the Host/PCI Bridge and not by the CPU. The solution to this type of design is to generate PEREQ# immediately after entering the GAT mode. This feature is controlled via ARBCON Register (bit 7).

5.4.8.2 PCI Retry and EISA Latency Timer (ELT) Mechanism

When a PCI cycle is retried by the PCEB (in non-GAT mode) because the EISA Bus is controlled by the ESC (EISAHLDA asserted), an internal flag is set for the corresponding PCI master. This flag masks the request of a particular master until the PCEB acquires the ownership of EISA and RESUME condition clears the flag. If the PCI master, which is now unmasked, does not acquire the ownership of the PCI Bus within the time period before ESC asserts EISAHOLD again, the EISA Bus can be surrendered to the ESC. Unmasked masters will eventually gain the access to the PCI Bus, but the EISA Bus will not be available and the master will be retried again. This scenario can be repeated multiple times with one or more PCI masters and starvation will occur.

To solve this situation, the PCEB arbitration logic incorporates an EISA Latency Timer mechanism. This mechanism is based on the programmable timer that is started each time that the ESC requires the bus (EISAHOLD asserted) and there is a PCI agent that has been previously retried because of the EISA Bus. As soon as the ELT timer expires, the PCI cycle is retried and the EISA Bus is given back to the ESC after the current PCI-to-EISA transaction completes. If all the PCI requesters, masked because of EISAHLDA, are serviced before the ELT timer expires, the EISA Bus is immediately surrendered to the ESC.

The EISA Latency Timer (ELT) is controlled by the ELTCR Register. The value written into ELTCR is system dependent. It is typically between 1 ms and 3 ms.

6.0 DATA BUFFERING

The PCEB contains data buffers (Figure 6-1) to isolate the PCI Bus from the EISA Bus and to provide concurrent EISA and PCI Bus operations. The Posted Write Buffers are used for PCI-to-EISA memory writes and the Line Buffers are used for EISA-to-PCI memory reads and writes. Control bits in the PCICON and EPMRA Registers permit the buffers to be enabled (accesses are buffered) or disabled (accesses are non-buffered). Non-buffered accesses use the bypass path. Note that PCI and EISA I/O read/write cycles and PCI configuration cycles are always non-buffered and use the bypass path.

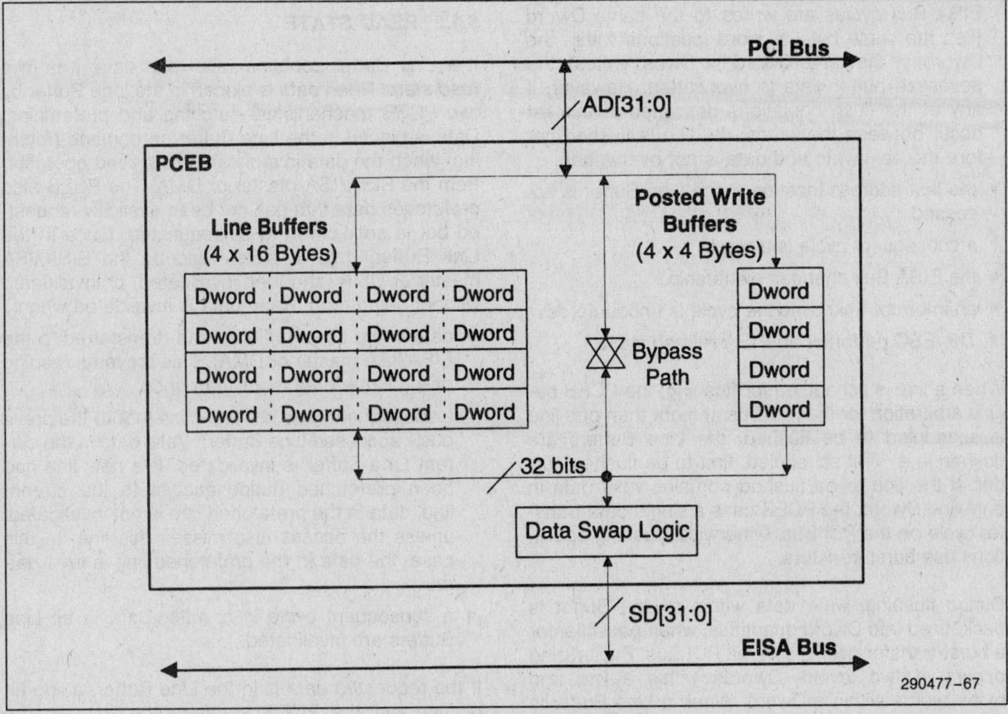

Figure 6-1. PCEB Data Buffers

When data is temporarily stored in the buffers between the EISA Bus and PCI Bus, there are potential data coherency issues. The PCEB guarantees data coherency by intervening when data coherency could be lost and either flushing or invalidating the buffered data, as appropriate.

6.1 Line Buffers

The PCEB contains four Line Buffers that are each four Dwords wide (16 bytes). The Line Buffers are bidirectional and are used by the EISA/ISA master and DMA to assemble/disassemble data. The data in each Line Buffer is aligned on 16-byte boundaries. When data is placed in one of the Line Buffers, the PCEB maintains the corresponding 16-byte boundary address until the data in the line is transferred to its destination or invalidated.

The Line Buffers can be enabled/disabled by writing to the PCICON Register. In addition, when the Line Buffers are enabled via the PCICON Register, buffering for accesses to the four programmable EISA-to-PCI memory regions (Region [4:1]) can be selectively disabled via the EPMRA Register.

During buffer operations, the four Line Buffers, collectively, are either in a write state or in a read state. These states are described in the following sections.

6.1.1 WRITE STATE

If a Line Buffer contains valid write data, it is in a *write state*. In the write state, data from the EISA/ISA master or DMA is posted in the Line Buffers. Posting means that the write operation on the EISA Bus completes when the data is latched in the buffer. The EISA master does not have to wait for the write to complete to its destination (memory on the PCI Bus). Posting permits the EISA Bus cycle to complete in a minimum time and permits concurrent EISA and PCI Bus operations. During posting, data accumulates in the Line Buffer until it is flushed (written to PCI memory) over the PCI Bus. A Line Buffer is scheduled for flushing by the PCEB when:

- the line becomes full.
- a subsequent write is a line miss (not within the current line boundary address range).
- the write is to an address of a lower Dword than the previous write. Note that writes to lower addresses within the same Dword do not cause a flush. Note also, that if two (or more) consecutive

EISA Bus cycles are writes to the same Dword (i.e., the same byte or word locations within the Dword, or the same Dword for Dword writes), the accessed buffer data is overwritten. However, if any of the flush conditions described in this list occur between the writes, the line is flushed before the next write and data is not overwritten.

- the last address location in the Line Buffer is accessed.
- a subsequent cycle is a read.
- the EISA Bus changes ownership.
- an interrupt acknowledge cycle is encountered.
- The ESC performs an EISA refresh cycle.

When a line is scheduled for flushing, the PCEB begins arbitration for the PCI Bus. If more than one line is scheduled to be flushed, the Line Buffers are flushed in a "first scheduled, first to be flushed" order. If the line to be flushed contains valid data in only one Dword, the PCEB uses a single data transfer cycle on the PCI Bus. Otherwise, flushing operations use burst transfers.

During flushing, write data within a Line Buffer is packetized into Dword quantities, when possible, for a burst transfer over the 32-bit PCI Bus. Packetizing occurs at two levels—Dwords within a line and bytes/words within a Dword. When a Line Buffer is flushed, all of the valid Dwords within the line are packetized into a single PCI burst write cycle. In addition, all valid data bytes within a Dword boundary are packetized into a single data phase of the burst cycle. Packetizing reduces the PCI arbitration latency and increases the effective PCI Bus bandwidth. When multiple Line Buffers are scheduled for flushing, each Line Buffer is packetized separately. Packetizing across Line Buffer boundaries is not permitted.

During flushing, strong ordering is preserved at the Dword level (i.e., the Dwords are flushed to PCI memory in the same order that they were written into the Line Buffer). Note, however, that strong ordering is not preserved at the byte or word levels (i.e., even if byte or word transfers were used by the EISA/ISA master or DMA to sequentially write to a Dword within a Line Buffer, all of the bytes in the resulting Dword boundary are simultaneously flushed to PCI memory).

Because strong ordering is not preserved within a Dword boundary, care should be used when accessing memory-mapped I/O devices. If the order of byte or word writes to a memory-mapped I/O device needs to be preserved, buffered accesses should not be used. By locating memory-mapped I/O devices in the four programmable EISA-to-PCI memory regions, buffering to these devices can be selectively disabled.

6.1.2 READ STATE

If a Line Buffer contains valid read data, it is in a *read state*. Read data is placed in the Line Buffer by two PCEB mechanisms—fetching and prefetching. Data is placed in the Line Buffer on demand (fetching) when the data is requested by a read operation from the EISA/ISA master or DMA. The PCEB also prefetches data that has not been explicitly requested but is anticipated to be requested. Once in the Line Buffer, data is either read by the EISA/ISA master or DMA (and then invalidated) or invalidated without being read. Read data is invalidated when:

- data in the Line Buffer is read (transferred to the EISA/ISA master or DMA). This prevents reading of the same data more than once.
- a subsequent read is a line miss (not to the previously accessed Line Buffer). Valid data in the current Line Buffer is invalidated. If a new line had been prefetched during access to the current line, data in the prefetched line is not invalidated, unless the access also misses this line. In this case, the data in the prefetched line is invalidated.
- a subsequent cycle is a write. Data in all Line Buffers are invalidated.

If the requested data is in the Line Buffer, a line hit occurs and the PCEB transfers the data to the EISA/ISA master or DMA (and invalidates the hit data in the buffer). If EISA Bus reads hit two consecutive line addresses, the PCEB prefetches the next sequential line of data from PCI memory (using a PCI Bus burst transfer). This prefetch occurs concurrently with EISA Bus reads of data in the already fetched Line Buffer. If consecutive addresses are not accessed, the PCEB does not prefetch the next line.

A line miss occurs if the requested data is not in the Line Buffer. If a line miss occurs, the PCEB invalidates data in the missed Line Buffer. If the requested data is in a prefetched line, the read is serviced. If a line was not prefetched or the read missed the prefetched line, the PCEB invalidates any prefetched data and fetches the Dword containing the requested data. During this fetch, the PCEB holds off the EISA/ISA master or DMA with wait states (by negating EXRDY). When the requested data is in the Line Buffer, it is transferred to the EISA Bus. Simultaneously with the EISA Bus transfer, the PCEB prefetches the rest of the line data (Dwords whose addresses are within the line and above the Dword address of the requested data). The Dword containing the requested data and the rest of the Dwords in the line (located at higher addresses) are fetched from PCI memory using a burst transfer, unless the requested data is in the last Dword of a line. In this case, a single cycle read occurs on the PCI Bus.

For the purposes of data read operations, all four 4-Dword buffers are used to form two 8-Dword lines (32 bytes each). There are only two address pointers, one for each line. Fetching fractions of a line is accomplished as described above, that is starting from the first requested Dword.

The MSBURST# input signal is used to supplement control of the prefetch sequence. The MSBURST# signal is activated only when an EISA master desires to do burst transfers to access sequential data (although this is not an absolute EISA rule, i.e., theoretically the data can be non-sequential) after an EISA slave indicates its ability via SLBURST#. This will occur during the first data transfer.

The Line Buffer Control Logic dynamically switches between two prefetch modes:

— Half Line Prefetch (16 bytes fetch)

— Full Line Prefetch (32 bytes fetch)

The prefetch control logic has implemented a Sequential Access Flag which is cleared before the initial prefetch. Initial prefetch (first data fetch) starts in the Half Line Prefetch mode and is extended to Full Line Prefetch mode immediately after MSBURST# is sampled asserted at which time the Sequential Access Flag is automatically set (this is done on-the-fly during the first line fetch). If after the initial prefetch the Sequential Access Flag has not been set (MSBURST# remained not asserted) and the control logic recognizes two consecutive hits (in incrementally sequential Dwords including the first one which is originally requested), the Sequential Access Flag is set and the prefetch control logic switches to Full Line Prefetch mode. An additional 32-byte line (or fraction depending on alignment) will be fetched.

When the Sequential Access Flag is set, prefetching is accomplished using the Full Line Prefetch mode. Each time a line buffer (32 bytes) is available, an additional line will be fetched as long as the Sequential Access Flag remains set.

Whenever out-of-order access is recognized within the prefetched data or a miss occurs when there is valid fetched data, the Sequential Access Flag is cleared and the prefetch mode changes to Half Line Prefetch. Also, the Sequential Access Flag is cleared whenever MSBURST# transitions from actived to inactive.

When the Sequential Access Flag is not asserted, the prefetch control logic operates in Half Line Prefetch mode during which only 16 bytes of data is fetched at a time. The same test for sequential access is repeated, and if sequential access is recognized, the Sequential Access Flag is set and the control logic switches to Full Line Prefetch mode.

6.2 Posted Write Buffers

The PCEB contains four Posted Write Buffers (PWB). The buffers are each one Dword wide (4 bytes). The PWBs are uni-directional and are used by PCI devices (including the CPU via the Host/PCI Bridge) to transfer data from a PCI master to EISA memory. If the PWBs are enabled, PCI-to-EISA memory writes are posted in the PWBs. If these buffers are disabled, PCI-to-EISA memory writes are not posted and use the bypass path. Posting means that the PCI Bus operation completes when the data is placed in the PWBs. The PCI operation does not have to wait for the transfer to complete to its destination on the EISA Bus, as is the case of a non-posted write. (Non-posted writes occur when the PWBs are disabled or a PCI I/O or configuration write occurs.) Posting permits the PCI Bus operation to complete in a minimum time.

To maintain strong ordering, data assembly within a Dword is not allowed. Thus, during each data phase of a PCI Bus write operation to the PWBs, each data transfer (byte, word, or Dword) is placed in separate PWBs. The corresponding address is stored for each PWB, until the data is written to the EISA/ISA device.

Posting is only permitted when the PCEB owns the EISA Bus. If the PCEB does not own the EISA Bus, the PCI master is retried and the PCEB requests the EISA Bus. The PCEB masks retried PCI masters until the EISA Bus is acquired, at which time the PCI masters are unmasked. If the PWBs are full and a new PCI-to-EISA memory write cycle occurs, the PCI master is retried and the PWBs flushed. After the first PWB is flushed, the PCI masters are unmasked and posting is permitted. If a PCI burst write fills the PWBs, the PCEB issues a disconnect to the PCI master and flushes the PWBs.

If an EISA/ISA master or DMA requests the EISA Bus during posting, the EISA latency timer is started. Posting and flushing of the PWBs can continue until the timer expires. If the timer expires, the PCEB allows the PCI master to complete the current bus cycle and retries further PCI requests. If the current PCI Bus cycle requires posting of more than four data transfers (or the PWBs become full), the PCEB issues a PCI target disconnect. When the PWBs are flushed, the PCEB grants ownership to the requesting EISA/ISA master or DMA.

NOTES:

1. If posting is disabled via the PCICON Register, a PCI master requesting a PCI-to-EISA transfer is retried until the PCEB owns the EISA Bus. Each PCI-to-EISA Bus transfer must complete all the way to the EISA destination before the next

transfer can begin. The PCEB, on behalf of the EISA/ISA master or DMA, introduces wait states to the PCI master, if necessary.

2. If the ESC requests the EISA Bus to do a refresh cycle, the PCEB temporarily gives the bus to the ESC and does not flush the PWBs.

6.3 Buffer Management Summary

Table 6-1 shows Line Buffer and Posted Write Buffer actions for different cycles. Note that the first three columns together define the cycles that may trigger buffer activity.

7.0 EISA INTERFACE

The PCEB provides a fully EISA Bus compatible master and slave interface. This interface provides address and data signal drive capability for eight EISA slots and supports the following types of cycles:

- PCI-initiated memory and I/O read/write accesses to an EISA/ISA device.
- EISA/ISA/DMA-initiated memory and I/O read/write accesses to a PCI device (i.e., via the Line Buffers, if necessary).
- Accesses contained within the EISA Bus (only data swap buffers involved).

For transfers between the EISA Bus and PCI Bus, the PCEB translates the bus protocols. For PCI master-initiated cycles to the EISA Bus, the PCEB is a slave on the PCI Bus and a master on the EISA Bus. For EISA master-initiated cycles to the PCI Bus, the PCEB is a slave on the EISA Bus and a master on the PCI Bus.

NOTES:

1. The PCEB is not involved in refresh cycles on the EISA Bus. When the REFRESH# signal is asserted, the PCEB disables EISA Bus address decoding.
2. Wait state generation on the EISA Bus is performed by the ESC. ISA memory slaves (8 bits or 16 bits) and ISA I/O slaves can shorten their default or standard cycles by asserting the NOWS# signal line. It is the responsibility of the ESC to shorten these cycles when NOWS# is asserted. Note that ISA I/O 16-bit devices can shorten their cycles by asserting NOWS#. If CHRDY and NOWS# are driven low during the same cycle, NOWS# will not be used and wait states are added as a function of CHRDY. For more details

Table 6-1. Buffer Management Summary

Master (Origin)	Cycle Type	Slave (Destination)	Line Buffer Data in Write State	Line Buffer Data in Read State	Posted Write Buffers
PCI	Memory Read	EISA	Flush	No Action	Flush
PCI	Memory Write	EISA	No Action	Invalidate	Flush if full post if not full
PCI	I/O Read	EISA	Flush	No Action	Flush
PCI	I/O Write	EISA	No Action	Invalidate	Flush
PCI	Interrupt Acknowledge	PCEB/ESC	Flush	No Action	Flush
PCI	Configuration Cycle	PCEB Registers	No Action	No Action	No Action
PCI	Memory Read/Write	PCI	No Action	No Action	No Action
PCI	I/O Read/Write	PCI	No Action	No Action	No Action
EISA	Bus Ownership Change	—	Flush	No Action	Flush
EISA	Memory Read/Write	EISA	No Action	No Action	No Action(2)
EISA	Memory Read/Write	PCI	(Note 1)	(Note 1)	No Action(2)
EISA	I/O Read/Write	EISA	No Action	No Action	No Action(2)
EISA	I/O Read/Write	PCI	Flush	Invalidate	No Action(2)

NOTES:
1. Change from write to read operation or from read to write causes the Line Buffers to be flush or invalidate, respectively.
2. Buffers are already flushed.
3. LOCKed cycles (both from PCI and EISA) are not buffered within the PCEB. They are processed using the bypass path.

on the wait state generation and the NOWS# signal, refer to the ESC data sheet.

3. All locked PCI cycles (PLOCK# asserted) destined to the EISA Bus are converted to EISA locked cycles using the LOCK# signal protocol. The PCEB is a locked resource during these cycles and maintains control of the EISA Bus until the locked PCI sequence is complete.
4. All locked EISA cycles (LOCK# asserted) destined to PCI are converted to PCI locked cycles using the PLOCK# signal protocol. The PLOCK# signal remains active as long as the EISA LOCK# signal is asserted.
5. The PCEB contains EISA data swap buffers for data size translations between mismatched PCI Bus and EISA Bus transfers and between mismatched devices contained on the EISA Bus. Thus, if data size translation is needed, the PCEB is involved in cycles contained to the EISA Bus, even if the PCEB is neither the master or slave. For data size translation operations, see Section 8.0, EISA Data Swap Buffers.
6. For ISA master cycles to PCI memory or I/O, the ESC translates the ISA signals to EISA signals. The PCEB, as an EISA slave, forwards the cycle to the PCI Bus.
7. For ISA master cycles to ISA/EISA slaves, the PCEB is not involved, except when the cycle requires data size translations. See the ESC data sheet for cycles that are contained within the EISA Bus (i.e., EISA-to-EISA, EISA-to-ISA, ISA-to-ISA, and ISA-to-EISA device cycles).
8. In this section, LA[31:24]# and LA[23:2] are collectively referred to as LA[31:2].

7.1 PCEB as an EISA Master

The PCEB is an EISA master for PCI-initiated cycles targeted to the EISA Bus. When the PCEB decodes the PCI cycle as a cycle destined to the EISA Bus (via subtractive or negative decoding, as described in Section 4.0, Address Decoding), the PCEB becomes a slave on the PCI Bus. If the PCEB owns the EISA Bus, the cycle is forwarded to the EISA/ISA device. If the PCEB does not own the EISA Bus (EISAHOLDA is asserted to the ESC), the PCI master is retried and the PCEB issues an EISA Bus request to the ESC.

For PCI-to-EISA I/O read/write accesses, memory reads, and non-posted memory writes (Posted Write Buffers are disabled), the PCEB runs standard EISA Bus cycles. When the Posted Write Buffers are enabled, the PCEB posts PCI write data in the buffers. The data is transferred to the EISA Bus when the buffers are flushed. If just one buffer needs to be flushed, the PCEB runs a standard EISA cycle. For more than one buffer, the PCEB runs a burst cycle, if bursts are supported by the slave. If the slave does not support bursts, consecutive standard cycles are run.

When cycles are forwarded to a matched EISA/ISA slave, the PCEB is the EISA master and controls the transfer until the cycle is terminated. For mismatched cycles to an EISA/ISA slave, the PCEB backs off the EISA Bus as described in Section 7.1.3, Back-Off Cycle.

7.1.1 STANDARD EISA MEMORY AND I/O READ/WRITE CYCLES

The standard EISA cycle completes one transfer each two BCLK periods (zero wait states). The standard EISA memory or I/O cycle begins when the PCEB presents a valid address on LA[31:2] and drives M/IO# high for a memory cycle and low for an I/O cycle. The address can become valid at the end of the previous cycle to allow address pipelining. The EISA slave decodes the address and asserts the appropriate signals to indicate the type of slave and whether it can perform any special timings. The slave asserts EX32# or EX16# to indicate support of EISA cycles.

For extended cycles, the EISA slave introduces wait states using the EXRDY signal. Wait states allow a slower slave to get ready to complete the transfer. The slave negates EXRDY after it decodes a valid address and samples START# asserted. The slave may hold EXRDY negated for a maximum of 2.5 μs to complete a transfer, and must release EXRDY synchronous to the falling edge of BCLK to allow a cycle to complete. Note that the PCEB, as an EISA master, never introduces wait states.

Figure 7-1 shows three data transfer cycles between an EISA master and an EISA slave. The first transfer is an extended transfer (EXRDY negated), followed by two standard cycles. For PCI cycles that are forwarded to the EISA Bus, the PCEB is the EISA master. The PCEB asserts START# to indicate the start of a cycle. The PCEB also drives W/R# to indicate a read or write cycle and BE[3:0]# to indicate the active bytes. The LA[31:2] and the BE[3:0] remain valid until after the negation of START#. A slave that needs to latch the address does so on the trailing edge of START#.

The ESC asserts CMD# simultaneously with the negation of START# to control data transfer to or from the slave. If a read cycle is being performed, the slave presents the requested data when CMD# is asserted and holds it valid until CMD# is negated by the ESC. For a write cycle, the PCEB presents the data prior to the assertion of CMD# and the slave latches it on or before the trailing edge of CMD#.

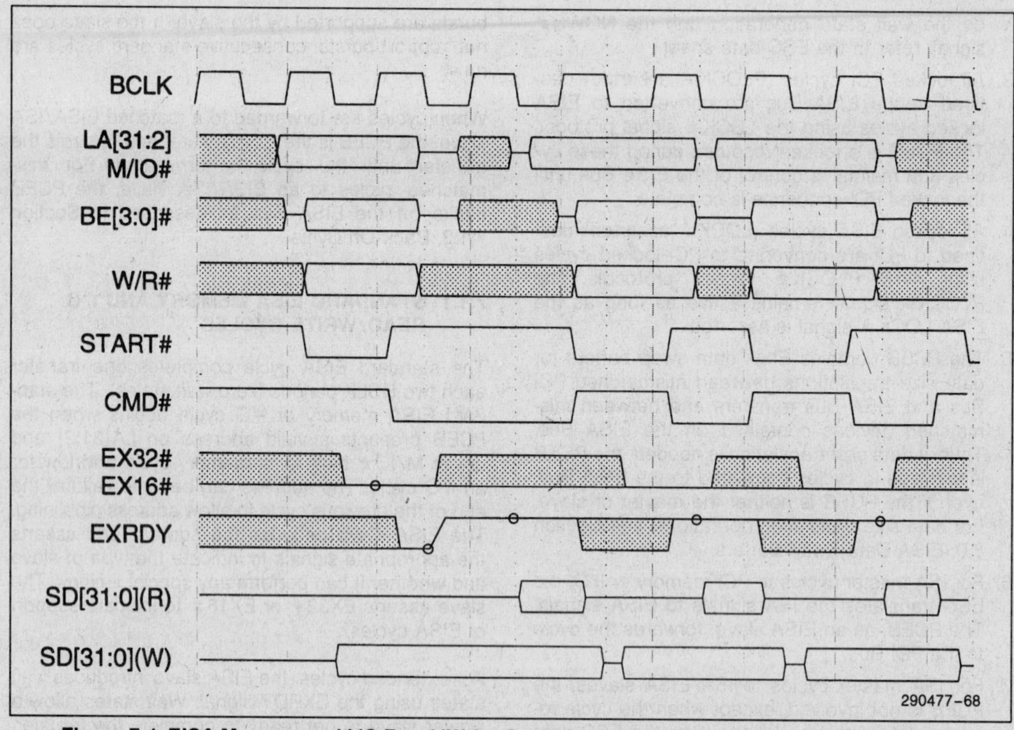

Figure 7-1. EISA Memory and I/O Read/Write Cycle (one extended and two standard cycles)

7.1.2 EISA MEMORY BURST CYCLES

The EISA burst cycle permits a continuous sequence of read or write cycles in zero wait-states (1 BCLK per transfer). As an EISA master, the PCEB can generate burst memory writes during PCI-to-EISA Posted Write Buffer flushing. However, the PCEB does not generate burst memory reads. Figure 7-2 shows a burst write on the EISA Bus. During the burst, five data transfers occur with a wait state added on the third data transfer.

The first transfer in a burst transfer begins like a standard cycle. The PCEB, as a bus master, presents a valid address on LA[31:2]. The memory slave, after decoding the address and M/IO#, responds by asserting SLBURST#. The PCEB samples SLBURST# on the rising edge of BCLK at the trailing edge of START#. The PCEB asserts MSBURST# on the falling edge of BCLK and presents a second address to the slave. The ESC holds CMD# asserted while the burst is being performed. If SLBURST# is not asserted by the slave, the PCEB does not assert MSBURST# and runs a standard cycle.

The PCEB presents the write data on the rising edge of BCLK, a half cycle after presenting the address. An EISA memory slave that asserts SLBURST# must sample memory write data on a rising BCLK edge when CMD# is asserted (regardless of the state of MSBURST#). The PCEB terminates the burst cycles by negating MSBURST# and completing the last transfer.

Although a burst transfer normally performs zero wait state cycles, a slave can add wait states during a burst sequence by negating EXRDY before the falling edge of BCLK (with CMD# asserted). The PCEB, as a master, samples EXRDY on the falling edge of BCLK and extends the cycle until EXRDY is asserted. The PCEB can still change the next address even though EXRDY is negated.

Addresses asserted during a burst sequence to a memory must be within a 1024 byte memory page (address lines LA[31:10] can not change during the burst). To cross a page boundary, the burst sequence is terminated by the PCEB by negating the MSBURST# on the last cycle in the page. If the burst cycle crosses a page boundary, the PCEB terminates the cycle at the page boundary and the burst cycle is restarted on the new page.

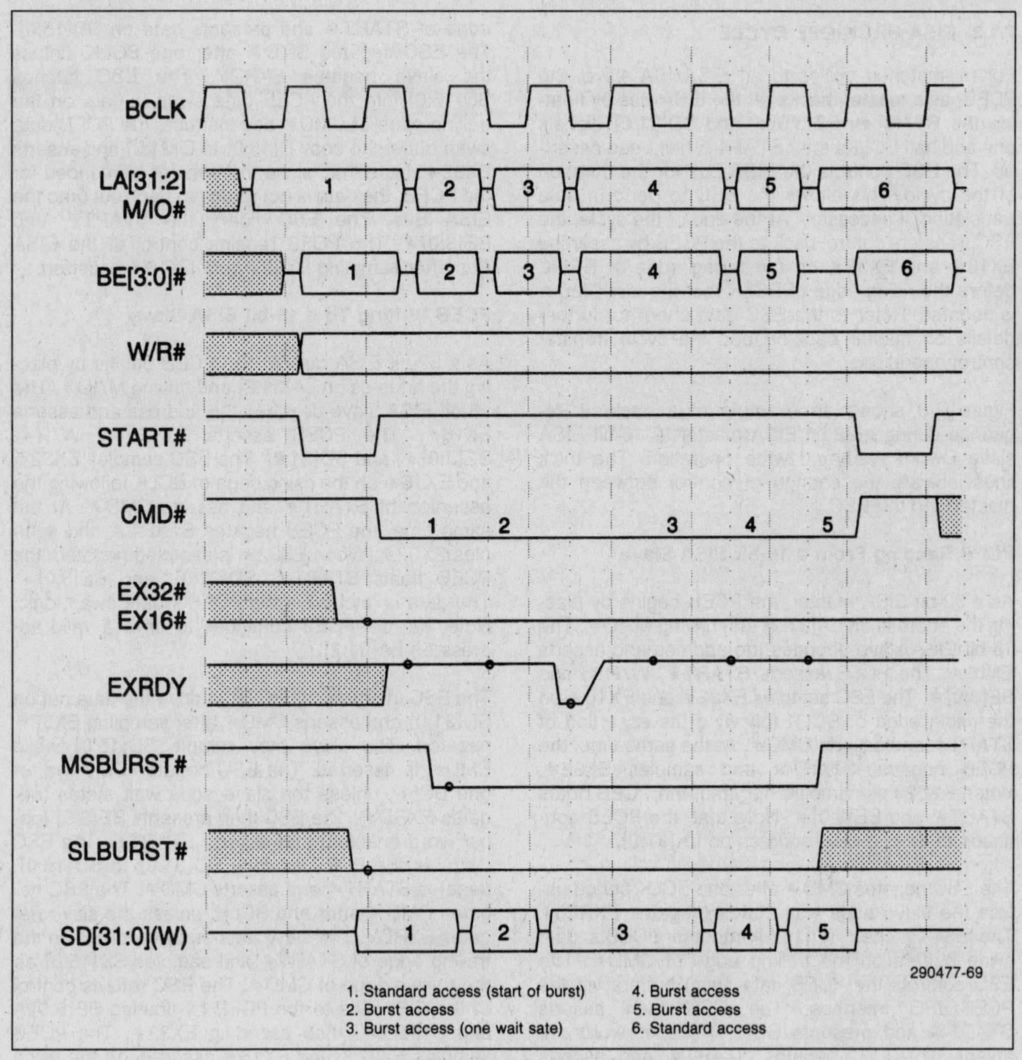

1

BCLK

LA[31:2] M/IO# — 1 2 3 4 5 6

BE[3:0]# — 1 2 3 4 5 6

W/R#

START#

CMD# — 1 2 3 4 5

EX32# EX16#

EXRDY

MSBURST#

SLBURST#

SD[31:0](W) — 1 2 3 4 5

290477-69

1. Standard access (start of burst)
2. Burst access
3. Burst access (one wait sate)
4. Burst access
5. Burst access
6. Standard access

Figure 7-2. EISA Memory Write Burst Cycle

7.1.3 EISA BACK-OFF CYCLE

For mismatched cycles to an EISA/ISA slave, the PCEB, as a master, backs off the EISA Bus by floating the START#, BE[3:0]# and SD[31:0] signals one and half BCLKs after START# has been asserted. The ESC controls the EISA Bus for the duration of the cycle. This allows the ESC to perform data translation, if necessary. At the end of the cycle, the ESC transfers control back to the PCEB by asserting EX16# and EX32# on the falling edge of BCLK, before the rising edge of BCLK that the last CMD# is negated. Refer to the ESC data sheet for further details on master back-off and the cycle transfer control operations.

Figure 7-3 shows an example of a back-off sequence during a 32-bit EISA master to 16-bit EISA slave Dword read and write operation. The thick lines indicate the change of control between the master and the ESC.

PCEB Reading From a 16-bit EISA Slave

As a 32-bit EISA master, the PCEB begins by placing the address on LA[31:2] and driving M/IO#. The 16-bit EISA slave decodes the address and asserts EX16#. The PCEB asserts START#, W/R#, and BE[3:0]#. The ESC samples EX32# and EX16# on the rising edge of BCLK following the assertion of START# and asserts CMD#. At the same time, the PCEB negates START# and samples EX32#. When EX32# is sampled negated, the PCEB floats START# and BE[3:0]#. Note that, the PCEB continues to drive a valid address on LA[31:2].

The ESC negates CMD# after one BCLK period unless the slave adds wait states (negates EXRDY). The ESC latches SD[15:0] into the PCEB's data swap buffers on the trailing edge of CMD#. The ESC controls the PCEB data swap buffers via the PCEB/ESC Interface. The ESC then asserts START# and presents BE[3:0] (upper word enabled). The ESC negates START# and asserts CMD#. The slave latches the address on the trailing edge of START# and presents data on SD[15:0]. The ESC negates CMD# after one BCLK, unless the slave negates EXRDY. The ESC latches SD[15:0] into the PCEB data swap buffers on the trailing edge of CMD# and instructs the PCEB data swap buffers to copy D[15:0] to D[31:0] and asserts EX32#. Note that, since the transfer is intended for the PCEB, the data is not re-driven back out onto the EISA Bus. The ESC floats the START# and BE[3:0]#. The PCEB regains control of the EISA Bus after sampling EX32# and EX16# asserted.

PCEB Writing To a 16-bit EISA Slave

As a 32-bit EISA master, the PCEB begins by placing the address on LA[31:2] and driving M/IO#. The 16-bit EISA slave decodes the address and asserts EX16#. The PCEB asserts START#, W/R#, BE[3:0]#, and SD[31:0]. The ESC samples EX32# and EX16# on the rising edge of BCLK following the assertion of START# and asserts CMD#. At the same time, the PCEB negates START# and samples EX32#. When EX32# is sampled negated, the PCEB floats START#, SD[31:0], and BE[3:0]#. The data is latched in the PCEB's data swap logic. Note that the PCEB continues to drive a valid address on LA[31:2].

The ESC instructs the PCEB to drive the data out on SD[31:0] and asserts CMD# after sampling EX32# negated. The slave may sample SD[15:0] while CMD# is asserted. The ESC negates CMD# after one BCLK, unless the slave adds wait states (negates EXRDY). The ESC then presents BE[3:0] (upper word enabled) and asserts START#. The ESC instructs the PCEB to copy SD[31:0] to SD[15:0], negates START# and asserts CMD#. The ESC negates CMD# after one BCLK, unless the slave negates EXRDY. The slave latches the address on the trailing edge of START# and samples SD[15:0] on the trailing edge of CMD#. The ESC returns control of the EISA Bus to the PCEB by floating BE[3:0]# and START#, then asserting EX32#. The PCEB samples EX32# and EX16# asserted on the rising edge of BCLK.

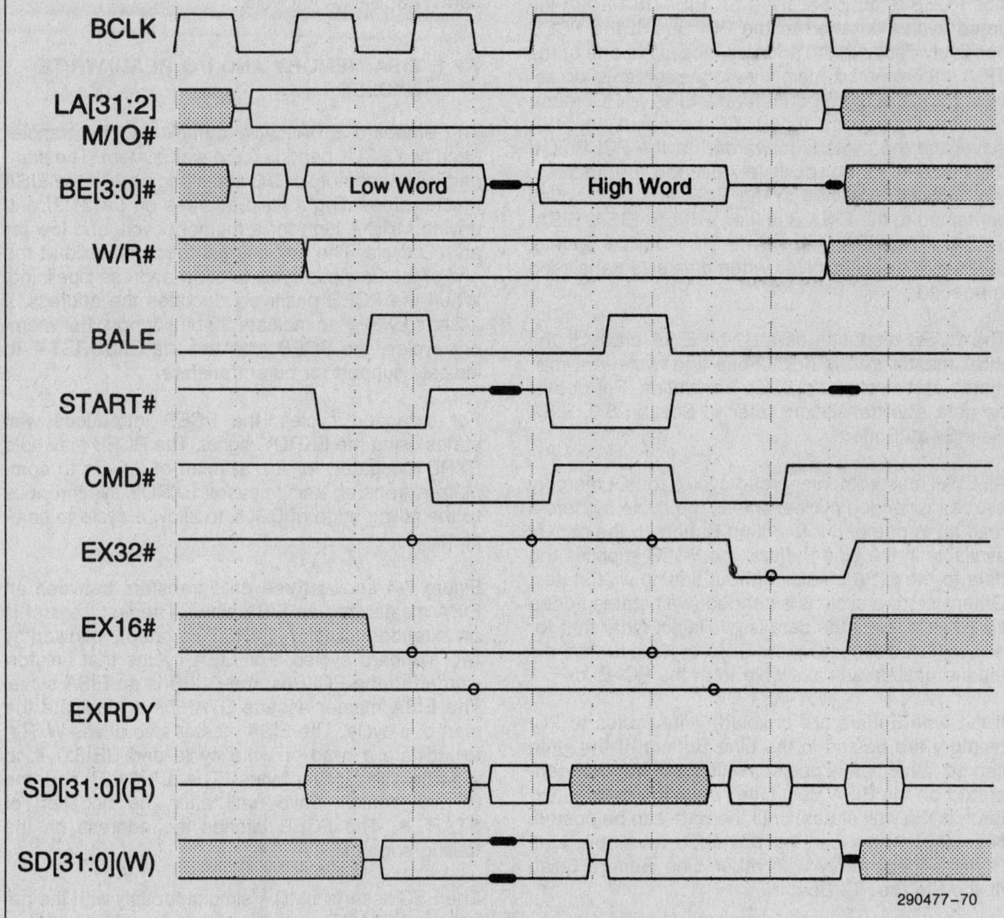

Figure 7-3. EISA Back-Off Cycle

7.2 PCEB as an EISA Slave

The PCEB is an EISA slave for EISA/ISA/DMA-initiated cycles targeted to the PCI Bus. If the PCEB positively decodes the address (access to one of the EISA programmed main memory segments or access to one of the programmable EISA-to-PCI memory or I/O regions), the PCEB becomes an EISA slave and the cycle is forwarded to the PCI Bus. If the PCEB does not positively decode the address, the cycle is contained to the EISA Bus. For cycles contained to the EISA Bus (i.e., EISA-to-EISA, EISA-to-ISA, ISA-to-ISA, and ISA-to-EISA device cycles), the PCEB is only involved when data size translation is needed.

The PCEB responds as a 32-bit EISA slave. If the EISA master size is not 32-bits, the cycle is a mismatch and invokes data size translation. For details on data size translation, refer to Section 8.0, EISA Data Swap Buffers.

All EISA master memory read cycles to PCI memory start as extended cycles, unless the cycle triggers a read hit to one of the four Line Buffers. If the data is available in the Line Buffers, the PCEB supplies the data to the EISA master without adding wait states. Otherwise, the cycle is extended (wait states added via EXRDY) until the data is available. Note that for non-buffered accesses, the EISA cycle is always extended until data is available from the PCI Bus.

If the Line Buffers are enabled, write cycles to PCI memory are posted in the Line Buffers. If the write can be immediately posted, wait states are not generated on the EISA Bus. Otherwise, the cycle is extended (via wait states) until the data can be posted. Note that writes can be posted to available Line Buffers concurrently with other Line Buffers being flushed to the PCI Bus.

All EISA master I/O read/write accesses to PCI I/O space are non-buffered and always start as extended cycles. Data transfer on the EISA Bus occurs when the requested data is available from the PCI Bus.

For mismatched cycles to the PCEB, the EISA/ISA master backs off the EISA Bus as described in Section 7.1.3, Back-Off Cycle.

7.2.1 EISA MEMORY AND I/O READ/WRITE CYCLES

The standard EISA cycle completes one transfer each two BCLK periods (zero wait states). The standard EISA memory or I/O cycle begins with the EISA master presenting a valid address on LA[31:2] and driving M/IO# high for a memory cycle and low for an I/O cycle. The address can become valid at the end of the previous cycle to allow address pipelining. When the PCEB positively decodes the address, it asserts EX32# to indicate 32-bit support. For memory cycles, the PCEB also asserts SLBURST# to indicate support for burst transfers.

For extended cycles, the PCEB introduces wait states using the EXRDY signal. The PCEB may hold EXRDY negated for a maximum of 2.5 μs to complete a transfer, and releases EXRDY synchronous to the falling edge of BCLK to allow a cycle to complete.

Figure 7-4 shows three data transfers between an EISA master and an EISA slave. The first transfer is an extended transfer (EXRDY negated), followed by two standard cycles. For EISA cycles that are forwarded to the PCI Bus, the PCEB is an EISA slave. The EISA master asserts START# to indicate the start of a cycle. The EISA master also drives W/R# to indicate a read or write cycle and BE[3:0]# to indicate the active bytes. The LA[31:2] and the BE[3:0] remain valid until after the negation of START#. The PCEB latches the address on the trailing edge of START#.

The ESC asserts CMD# simultaneously with the negation of START# to control data transfer to or from the PCEB. If a read cycle is being performed, the PCEB presents the requested data when CMD# is asserted and holds it valid until CMD# is negated by the ESC. For a write cycle, the EISA master must present the data prior to the assertion of CMD# and the PCEB latches it on the trailing edge of CMD#.

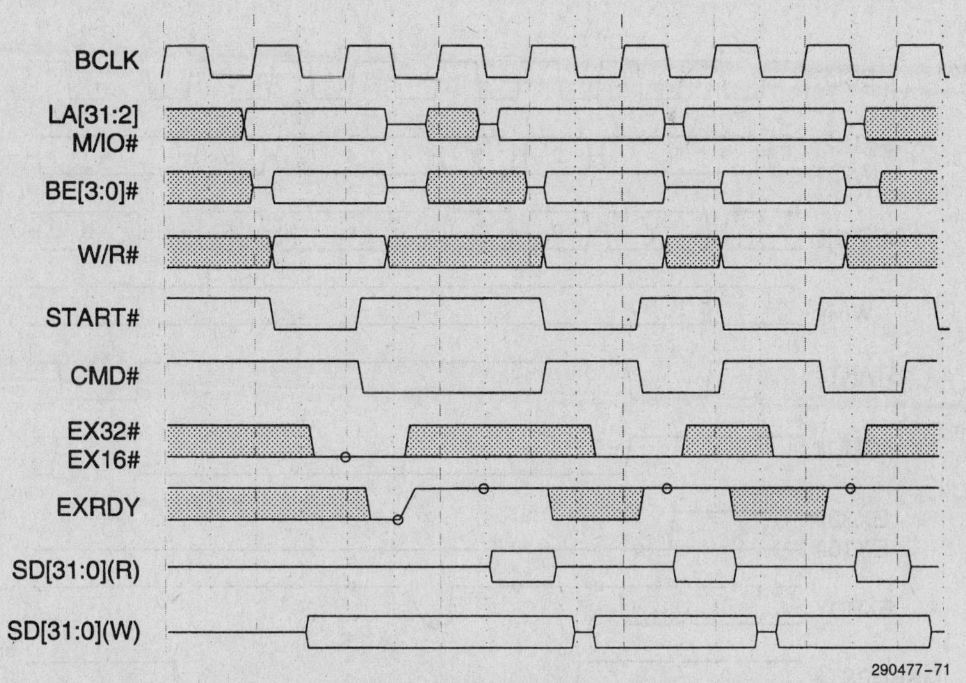

290477-71

Figure 7-4. EISA Memory and I/O Read/Write Cycles (one extended and two standard cycles)

7.2.2 EISA MEMORY BURST CYCLES

The EISA burst cycles permit a continuous sequence of read or write cycles in zero wait-states (1 BCLK per transfer). A burst transfer is either all reads or all writes. Mixed cycles are not allowed. As an EISA slave, the PCEB supports burst memory reads and burst memory writes from/to its Line Buffers. Figure 7-5 shows an example of a burst sequence for both memory reads and writes on the EISA Bus. During the particular burst sequence, five data transfers occur with a wait state added on the third data transfer.

The first transfer in a burst transfer begins like the standard cycle described above. The EISA master presents a valid address on LA[31:2]. The PCEB, after decoding the address and M/IO#, responds by asserting SLBURST#. The EISA master must sample SLBURST# on the rising edge of BCLK at the trailing edge of START#. The EISA master asserts MSBURST# on the falling edge of BCLK and presents a second address to the PCEB. The ESC holds CMD# asserted while the burst is being performed. If MSBURST# is not asserted by the master, the cycle is run as a standard cycle.

If the cycle is a burst read, the EISA master presents burst addresses on the falling edge of every BCLK. The PCEB presents the data for that address, which is sampled one and half BCLKs later. If the cycle is a burst write, the EISA master presents the data on the rising edge of BCLK, a half cycle after presenting the address. The PCEB samples memory write data on the rising BCLK edge when CMD# is asserted (regardless of the state of MSBURST#). The EISA master terminates the burst cycles by negating MSBURST# and completing the last transfer.

To add wait states during a burst sequence, the PCEB negates EXRDY before the falling edge of BCLK (with CMD# asserted). The EISA master samples EXRDY on the falling edge of BCLK and extends the cycle until EXRDY is asserted. The EISA master can still change the next address even though EXRDY is negated.

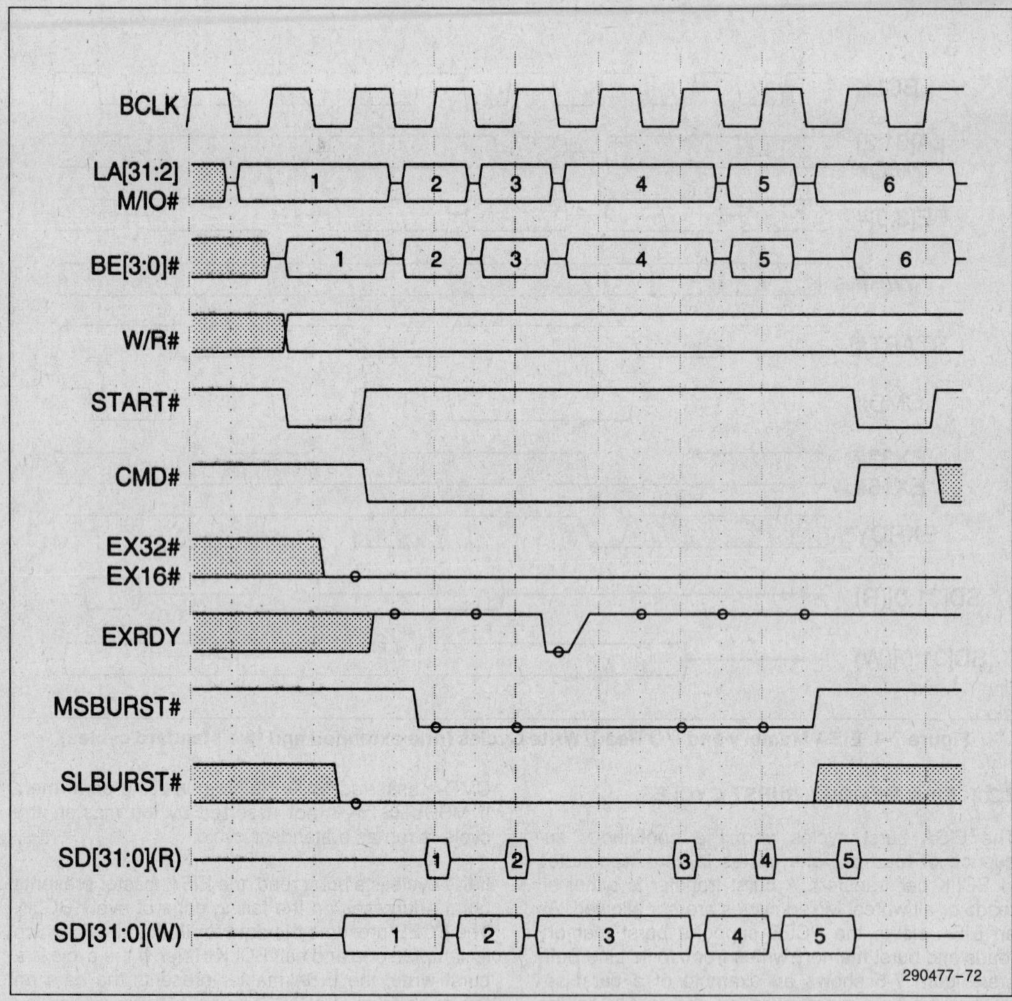

Figure 7-5. EISA Burst Cycle

7.3 I/O Recovery

The I/O recovery mechanism in the PCEB guarantees a minimum amount of time between back-to-back 8-bit and 16-bit PCI cycles to ISA I/O slaves. Delay times (in BCLKs) for 8-bit and 16-bit cycles are individually programmed via the IORT Register. Accesses to an 8-bit device followed by an access to a 16-bit device use the 8-bit recovery time. Similarly, accesses to a 16-bit device followed by an access to an 8-bit device use the 16-bit recovery time. The PCEB cycles to EISA I/O, DMA cycles, and EISA/ISA bus masters to I/O slaves do not require any delay between back-to-back I/O accesses.

Note that I/O recovery is only required for ISA I/O devices. However, since the PCEB does not distinguish between 8-bit ISA and 8-bit EISA, the delay is also applied to 8-bit EISA I/O accesses (i.e., the ESC).

8.0 EISA DATA SWAP BUFFERS

The PCEB contains a set of buffers/latches that perform data swapping and data size translations on the EISA Bus when the master and slave data bus sizes do not match (e.g., 32-bit EISA master accessing a 16-bit EISA slave). During a data size translation, the PCEB performs one or more of the following operations, depending on the master/slave type (PCI/EISA/ISA), transfer direction (read/write), and the number of byte enables active (BE[3:0]#):

- Data assembly or disassembly
- Data copying (up or down)
- Data re-drive

These operations are described in this section. An example is provided in Section 8.3, The Re-drive Operation, that shows a cycle where all three functions are used.

The PCEB performs data size translations on the EISA Bus using the data swap buffer control signals generated by the ESC. These signals are described in Section 10.0, PCEB/ESC Interface.

8.1 Data Assembly and Disassembly

The data assembly/disassembly process occurs during PCI, EISA/ISA, and DMA cycles when the master data size is greater than the slave data size. For example, if a 32-bit PCI master is performing a 32-bit read cycle to an 8-bit ISA slave, the ESC intervenes and performs four 8-bit reads. The data is assembled in the PCEB (Figure 8-1). Once assembled, the PCEB transfers the data as a single Dword to the 32-bit PCI master during the fourth cycle. For a 32-bit write cycle, the PCEB disassembles the Dword by performing four write cycles to the slave. The actual number of cycles required to perform an assembly/disassembly process and make a transfer is a function of the number of bytes (BE[3:0]#) requested and the master/slave size combination.

During EISA master assembly/disassembly transfers, cycle control is transferred from the master to the ESC. The master relinquishes control by backing off the bus (i.e., by floating its START#, BE[3:0], and SD[31:0] signals on the first falling edge of BCLK after START# is negated). The ESC controls the assembly/disassembly process in the PCEB via the data swap buffer control signals on the PCEB/ESC interface. At the end of the assembly/disassembly process, cycle control is transferred back to the bus master (by the ESC asserting EX16# and EX32#). An additional BCLK is added at the end of the transfer to allow the exchanging of cycle control to occur. During DMA transfers, cycle control is maintained by the ESC for the entire cycle.

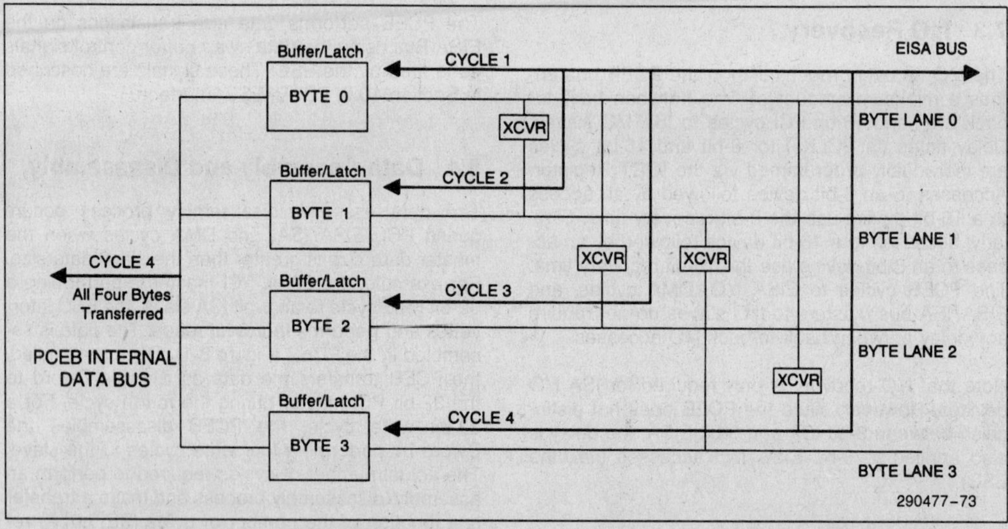

Figure 8-1. Assembly Function: PCI 32-bit Read from an 8-bit EISA or ISA Slave-BE[3:0]# = 0000

8.2 The Copy Operation (Up or Down)

The copy operation is invoked during data transfers between byte lanes. This operation allows the assembly/disassembly of the data pieces during the cycles between mismatched master/slave combinations. For example, Section 8.1, Data Assembly and Disassembly, describes a 32-bit master read from an 8-bit slave where the data is copied up during the assembly process. Copy-up is used for data assembly and copy-down is used for data disassembly.

The copy-up and copy-down operations are also used during transfers where assembly or disassembly are not required. These transfers are:

- When the master size is smaller than the slave size (e.g., 16-bit EISA master cycle to a 32-bit EISA slave).
- Between a mis-matched master/slave combination when only a byte or a word needs to be transferred (e.g., 32-bit EISA master cycle to an 8-bit ISA slave and only a byte needs to be transferred).

The number of bytes copied up or down is a function of the number of bytes requested (BE[3:0]#) and the master/slave size combinations. During EISA master cycles where the data copying is performed, cycle control is transferred from the bus master to the ESC, except during transfers where the master's data size is smaller than the slave's data size. During DMA transfers, bus control is maintained by the ESC throughout the transfer.

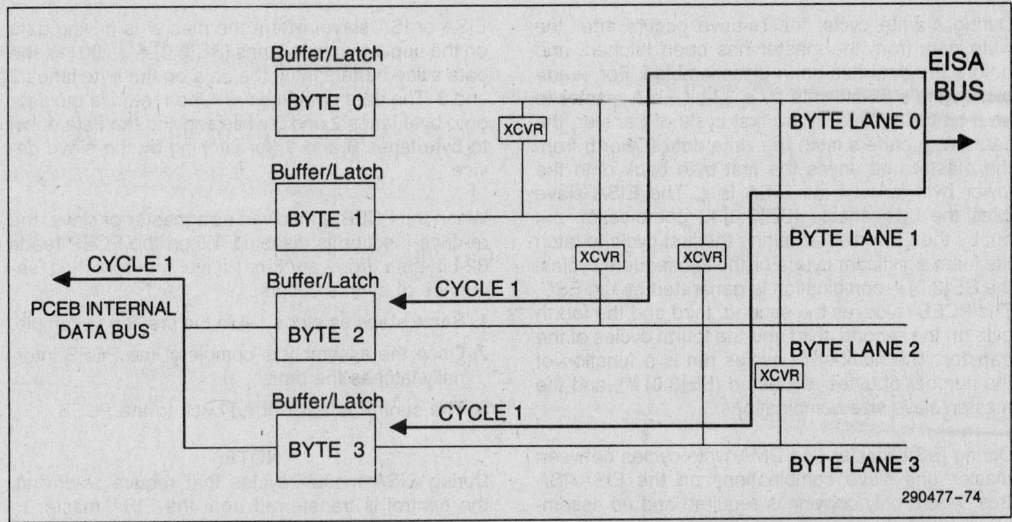

Figure 8-2. Copy Function: PCI 16-bit Read from a 16-bit EISA or ISA Slave-BE[3:0]# = 0011

8.3 The Re-drive Operation

The re-drive operation is used when both the master and the slave, other than PCEB, are on the EISA Bus and the master/slave size combination is mismatched. Specifically, re-drive occurs:

- during EISA master and DMA cycles (excluding DMA compatible cycles) where the master's data size is greater than the slave's data size.
- during EISA master cycles to ISA slaves where the master/slave match in the size.
- during DMA burst write cycles to a non-burst memory slave.

During a re-drive cycle, the data is latched from the EISA Bus, and then driven back onto the appropriate EISA byte lanes. During a read cycle, the re-drive occurs after the necessary sub-cycles have been completed and the read data has been assembled. For example, when a 32-bit EISA master (other than PCEB) performs 32-bit read from an 8-bit EISA slave, the following sequence of events occurs:

1. The 32-bit EISA master initiates the read cycle. Since the master/slave combination is a mismatch, the master backs off the bus. The EISA master floats its START#, BE[3:0]# and SD[31: 0] lines. The cycle control is then transferred to the ESC.
2. The ESC brings in the first 8-bit data (byte 0) in the first cycle. The ESC asserts SDLE0# to the PCEB.
3. When SDLE0# is asserted, the PCEB latches byte 0 into the least significant byte lane.
4. In the second cycle, the ESC reads the next 8-bit data (byte 1). The PCEB uses SDLE1#, SDCPYUP and SDCPYEN0-1# to latch byte 1 and copy it to the second least significant byte lane (copy-up). This process continues for byte 2 and byte 3. On the fourth cycle, the Dword assembly is complete. During each of the 4 cycles, the ESC generates BE[3:0]# combinations.
5. The ESC instructs the PCEB to re-drive the assembled word to the master by asserting SDOE[2:0]#. In this case, all three SDOE[2:0]# signals are asserted.
6. When SDOE[2:0]# are asserted, the PCEB drives the 32-bit assembled data on SD[31:0] to be latched by the master. The ESC generates the byte enables (BE[3:0]#).
7. The ESC completes the transfer.
8. At the end of the cycle, the ESC transfers control of the EISA Bus back to the EISA master.

During a write cycle, the re-drive occurs after the write data from the master has been latched, and before the data has been disassembled. For example, during a 32-bit write by a 32-bit EISA master to an 8-bit EISA slave, in the first cycle of transfer, the data swap buffers latch the write data (Dword) from the master and drives the first byte back onto the lower byte lane of the EISA Bus. The EISA slave uses the byte enable (BE[3:0]#) combination put out by the EISA master during the first cycle to latch the least significant byte. For the subsequent cycles, the BE[3:0]# combination is generated by the ESC. The PCEB re-drives the second, third and the fourth byte on the second, third and the fourth cycles of the transfer. The number of cycles run is a function of the number of bytes requested (BE[3:0]#), and the master/slave size combinations.

During EISA master and DMA write cycles between master and slave combinations on the EISA/ISA Bus, where only copying is required and no assembly/disassembly is required, the swap logic treats this as a re-drive cycle. For example, during a write transfer between a 32-bit EISA master and a 16-bit EISA or ISA slave, where the master is driving data on the upper two byte lanes (BE[3:0]# = 0011), the data swap buffers latch the data on the byte lanes 2 and 3. The data swap logic will then re-drive the data onto byte lanes 2 and 3 while copying the data down to byte lanes 0 and 1, for latching by the slave device.

When the PCEB is involved as a master or slave, the re-drive function is disabled. When the PCEB reads 32-bit data from an 8-bit slave the following sequence of events occurs:

1. Same steps as steps 1-4 in the previous example.
2. Once the assembly is complete, the PCEB internally latches the data.
3. The control is transferred back to the PCEB.

NOTE:

During EISA master cycles that require re-driving, the control is transferred from the EISA master to the ESC before the data is re-driven on the data bus. However; during the DMA cycles, the cycle control is maintained by the ESC throughout the entire cycle.

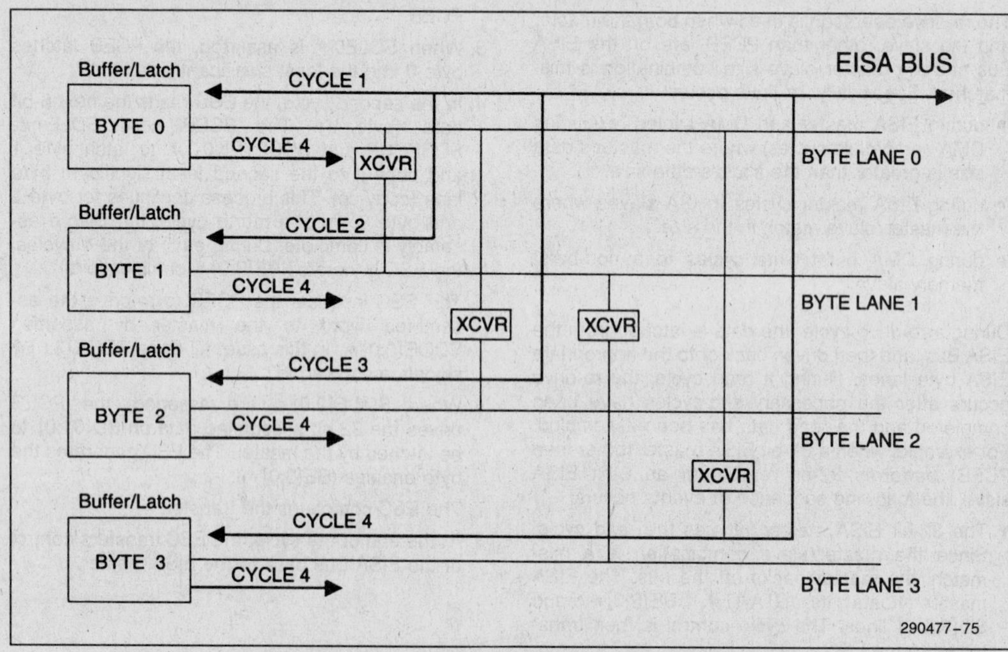

Figure 8-3. Re-Drive Function: 32-bit EISA Master Accessing an 8-bit EISA or ISA Slave—32-bit Read/BE[3:0]# = 0000

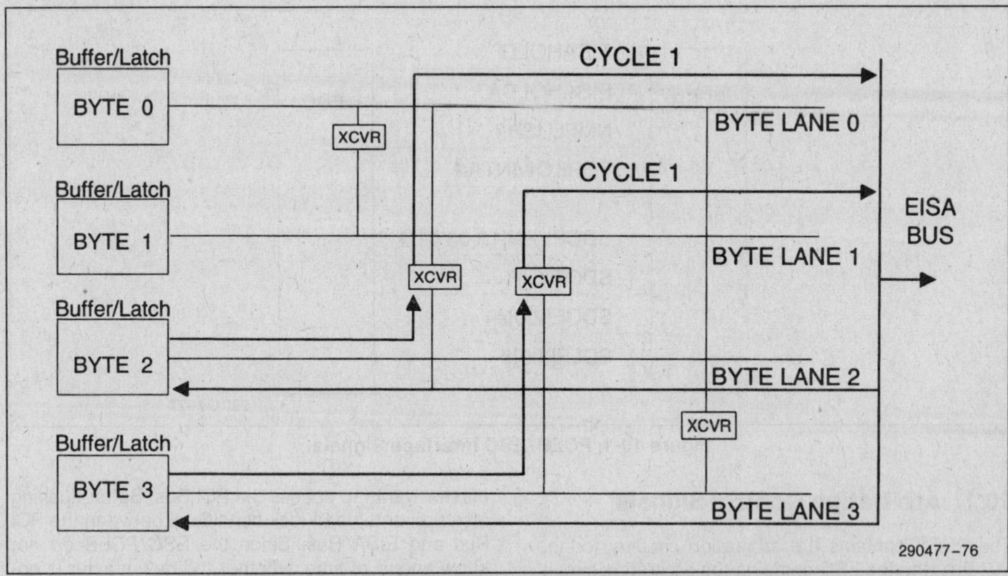

Figure 8-4. Copy with Re-Drive: 32-bit EISA Master Accessing a 16-bit EISA or ISA Slave—One Word Write/BE[3:0]# = 0011

9.0 BIOS TIMER

The PCEB provides a system BIOS Timer that decrements at each edge of its 1.03 MHz/1.04 MHz clock (derived from the 8.25 MHz/8.33 MHz BCLK). Since the state of the counter is undefined at power-up, the BIOS Timer Register must be programmed before it can be used. The timer can be enabled/disabled by writing to the BIOS Timer Address Register.

The BIOS Timer Register can be accessed as a single 16-bit quantity or as 32-bit quantity. For 32-bit accesses, the upper 16 bits are don't care (reserved). The BIOS Timer I/O address location is software programmable. The address is determined by the value programmed into the BTMR Register and can be located on Dword boundaries anywhere in the 64 KByte PCI I/O space.

The BIOS Timer clock has a frequency of 1.03 MHz or 1.04 MHz, depending on the value of BCLK (derived either from 25 MHz or 33 MHz PCICLK). This allows time intervals to be counted from 0 to approximately 65 milliseconds. The accuracy of the counter is ±1 μs.

9.1 BIOS Timer Operations

A write operation (either 16-bit or 32-bit) to the BIOS Timer Register initiates the counting sequence. After initialization, the BIOS timer starts decrementing until it reaches zero. When the value in the timer reaches zero, the timer stops decrementing and register value remains at zero until the timer is re-initialized.

After the timer is initialized, the current value can be read at any time. The timer can be re-programmed (new initial value written to the BIOS Timer Register) before the register value reaches zero. All write and read operations to the BIOS Timer Register should include all 16 counter bits. Separate accesses to the individual bytes of the counter must be avoided since this can cause unexpected results (incorrect count intervals).

10.0 PCEB/ESC INTERFACE

The PCEB/ESC interface (Figure 10-1) provides the inter-chip communications between the PCEB and ESC. The interface provides control information between the two components for PCI/EISA arbitration, data size translations (controlling the PCEB's EISA data swap buffers), and interrupt acknowledge cycles.

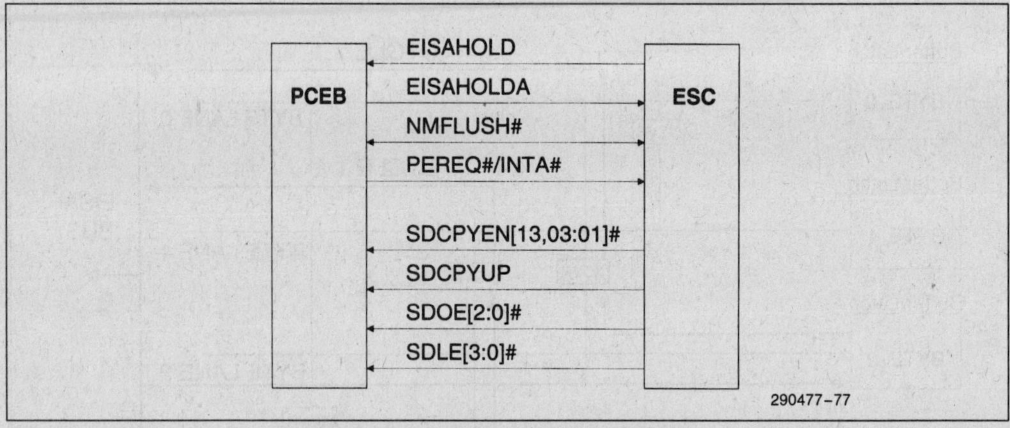

Figure 10-1. PCEB/ESC Interface Signals

10.1 Arbitration Control Signals

The PCEB contains the arbitration circuitry for the PCI Bus and the ESC contains the arbitration circuitry for the EISA Bus. The PCEB/ESC Interface contains a set of arbitration control signals (EISAHOLD, EISAHOLDA, NMFLUSH#, and PEREQ#/INTA#) that synchronize bus arbitration and ownership changes between the two bus environments. The signals also force PCI device data buffer flushing, if needed, to maintain data coherency during EISA Bus ownership changes.

The PCEB is the default owner of the EISA Bus. If another EISA/ISA master or DMA wants to use the bus, the ESC asserts EISAHOLD to instruct the PCEB to relinquish EISA Bus ownership. The PCEB completes any current EISA Bus transaction, tri-states its EISA Bus signals, and asserts EISAHOLDA to inform the ESC that the PCEB is off the bus.

For ownership changes, other than for a refresh cycle, the ESC asserts the NMFLUSH# signal to the PCEB (for one PCICLK) to instruct the PCEB to flush its Line Buffers pointing to the PCI Bus. The assertion of NMFLUSH# also instructs the PCEB to initiate flushing and to temporarily disable system buffers on the PCI Bus (via MEMREQ#, MEMACK#, and FLSHREQ#). The buffer flushing maintains data coherency, in the event that the new EISA Bus master wants to access the PCI Bus. Buffer flushing also prevents dead-lock conditions between the PCI Bus and EISA Bus. Since the ESC/PCEB do not know ahead of time, whether the new master is going to access the PCI Bus or a device on the EISA Bus, buffers pointing to the PCI Bus are always flushed when there is a change of EISA Bus ownership, except for refresh cycles. For refresh cycles, the ESC controls the cycle and, thus, knows that the cycle is not an access to the PCI Bus and does not initiate a flush request to the PCEB. After a refresh cycle, the ESC always surrenders control of the EISA Bus back to the PCEB.

NMFLUSH# is a bi-directional signal that is negated by the ESC when buffer flushing is not being requested. The ESC asserts NMFLUSH# to request buffer flushing. When the PCEB samples NMFLUSH# asserted, it starts driving the signal in the asserted state and begins the buffer flushing process. (The ESC tri-states NMFLUSH# after asserting it for the initial 1 PCICLK period.) The PCEB keeps NMFLUSH# asserted until all buffers are flushed and then it negates the signal for 1 PCICLK. When the ESC samples NMFLUSH# negated, it starts driving the signal in the negated state, completing the handshake. When the ESC samples NMFLUSH# negated, it grants ownership to the winner of the EISA Bus arbitration (at the time NMFLUSH# was negated). Note that for a refresh cycle, NMFLUSH# is not asserted by the ESC.

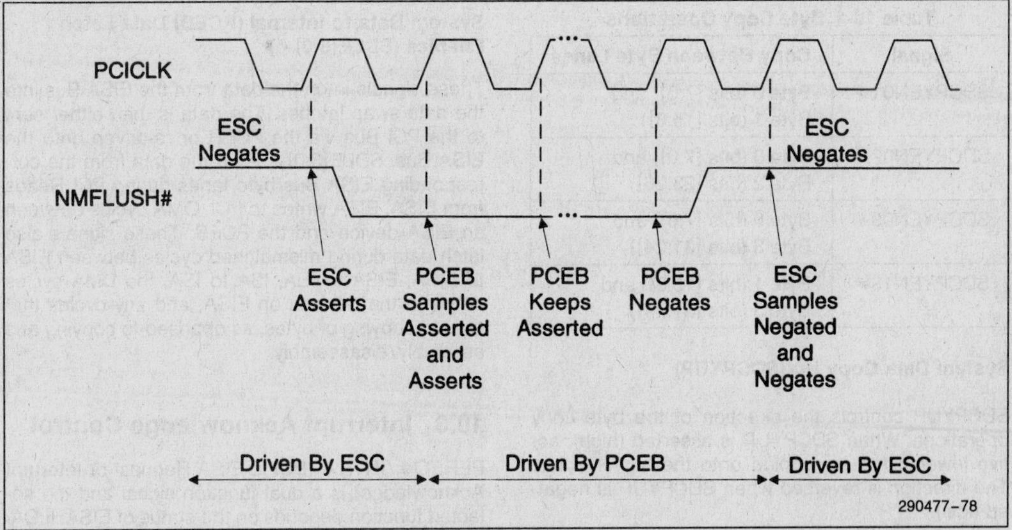

Figure 10-2. NMFLUSH# Protocol

When the EISA master completes its transfer and gets off the bus (i.e., removes its request to the ESC), the ESC negates EISAHOLD and the PCEB, in turn, negates EISAHOLDA. At this point, the PCEB resumes its default ownership of the EISA Bus.

If a PCI master requests access to the EISA Bus while the bus is owned by a master other than the PCEB, the PCEB retries the PCI cycle and requests ownership of the EISA Bus by asserting PEREQ#/INTA# to the ESC. PEREQ#/INTA# is a dual function signal that is a PCEB request for the EISA Bus (PEREQ# function) when EISAHOLDA is asserted. In response to the PCEB request for EISA Bus ownership, the ESC removes the grant to the EISA master. When the EISA master completes its current transactions and relinquishes the bus (removes its bus request), the ESC negates EISAHOLD and the PCEB, in turn, negates EISAHOLDA. At this point, a grant can be given to the PCI device for a transfer to the EISA Bus. Note that the INTA# function of the PEREQ#/INTA# signal is described in Section 10.3, Interrupt Acknowledge Control.

10.2 EISA Data Swap Buffer Control Signals

The cycles in the EISA environment may require data size translations before the data can be transferred to its intermediate or final destination. As an example, a 32-bit EISA master write cycle to a 16-bit EISA slave requires a disassembly of a 32-bit Dword into 16-bit words. Similarly, a 32-bit EISA master read cycle to a 16-bit slave requires an assembly of two 16-bit words into a 32-bit Dword. The PCEB contains EISA data swap buffers to support data size translations on the EISA Bus. The operation of the data swap buffers is described in Section 8.0, EISA Data Swap Buffers. The ESC controls the operation of the PCEB's data swap buffers with the following PCEB/ESC interface signals. These signals are outputs from the ESC and inputs to the PCEB.

- SDCPYEN[13,03:01]#
- SDCPYUP
- SDOE[2:0]#
- SDLE[3:0]#

Copy Enable Outputs (SDCPYEN[13,03:01]#)

These signals enable the byte copy operations between data byte lanes 0, 1, 2 and 3 as shown in Table 10-1. ISA master cycles do not perform assembly/disassembly operations. Thus, these cycles use SDCPYEN[13,03:01]# to perform the byte routing and byte copying between lanes. EISA master cycles however, can have assembly/disassembly operations. These cycles use SDCPYEN[13,03:01]# in conjunction with SDCPYUP and SDLE[3:0]#.

Table 10-1. Byte Copy Operations

Signal	Copy Between Byte Lanes
SDCPYEN01#	Byte 0 (bits [7:0]) and Byte 1 (bits [15:8])
SDCPYEN02#	Byte 0 (bits [7:0]) and Byte 2 (bits [23:26])
SDCPYEN03#	Byte 0 (bits [7:0]) and Byte 3 (bits [31:24])
SDCPYEN13#	Byte 1 (bits [15:8]) and Byte 3 (bits [31:24])

System Data Copy Up (SDCPYUP)

SDCPYUP controls the direction of the byte copy operations. When SDCPYUP is asserted (high), active lower bytes are copied onto the higher bytes. The direction is reversed when SDCPYUP is negated (low).

System Data Output Enable (SDOE[2:0]#)

These signals enable the output of the data swap buffers onto the EISA Bus (Table 10-2). SDOE[2:0] are re-drive signals in case of mis-matched cycles between EISA to EISA, EISA to ISA, ISA to ISA and the DMA cycles between the devices on EISA.

Table 10-2. Output Enable Operations

Signal	Byte Lane
SDOE0#	Applies to Byte 0 (bits [7:0])
SDOE1#	Applies to Byte 1 (bits [15:8])
SDOE2#	Applies to Byte 2 and Byte 3 (bits [31:16])

System Data to Internal (PCEB) Data Latch Enables (SDLE[3:0]#)

These signals latch the data from the EISA Bus into the data swap latches. The data is then either sent to the PCI Bus via the PCEB or re-driven onto the EISA Bus. SDLE[3:0]# latch the data from the corresponding EISA Bus byte lanes during PCI Reads from EISA, EISA writes to PCI, DMA cycles between an EISA device and the PCEB. These signals also latch data during mismatched cycles between EISA to EISA, EISA to ISA, ISA to ISA, the DMA cycles between the devices on EISA, and any cycles that require copying of bytes, as opposed to copying and assembly/disassembly.

10.3 Interrupt Acknowledge Control

PEREQ#/INTA# (PCI to EISA Request or Interrupt Acknowledge) is a dual function signal and the selected function depends on the status of EISAHLDA. When EISAHLDA is negated, this signal is an interrupt acknowledge (INTA#) and supports interrupt processing. If interrupt acknowledge is enabled via the PCEB's PCICON Register and EISAHOLDA is negated, the PCEB asserts PEREQ#/INTA# when a PCI interrupt acknowledge cycle is being serviced. This informs the ESC that the forwarded EISA I/O read from location 04h is an interrupt acknowledge cycle. Thus, the ESC uses this signal to distinguish between a request for the interrupt vector and a read of the ESC's DMA register located at 04h. The ESC responds to the read request by placing the interrupt vector on SD[7:0].

11.0 ELECTRICAL CHARACTERISTICS

11.1 Absolute Maximum Ratings

Case Temperature Under Bias . . . −65°C to +110°C

Storage Temperature . . . . −65°C to +150°C

Supply Voltages with Respect to Ground . . . . −0.5V to V_{CC} + 0.5V

Voltage On Any Pin . . . . −0.5V to V_{CC} + 0.5V

Power Dissipation . . . . 0.95 watts fully loaded
0.75 watts with four slots

NOTICE: This is a production data sheet. The specifications are subject to change without notice.

**WARNING: Stressing the device beyond the "Absolute Maximum Ratings" may cause permanent damage. These are stress ratings only. Operation beyond the "Operating Conditions" is not recommended and extended exposure beyond the "Operating Conditions" may affect device reliability.*

11.2 D.C. Characteristics

11.2.1 JUNCTION TEMPERATURE SPECIFICATIONS

The junction temperature for the PCEB is 95°C with a case temperature of 85°C. To guarantee device operation at 85°C case temperature the ambient temperature allowable is shown in Table 11-1.

Table 11-1. PCEB Maximum Allowable Ambient Temperature/Air Flow Rates

EISA Loading	Still	100 lfpm	200 lfpm	400 lfpm
4 Slots	53°C	58°C	61°C	66°C
8 Slots	44°C	49°C	54°C	59°C

11.2.2 EISA BUS D.C. SPECIFICATIONS

EISA Signals
BCLK(in), START#(t/s), CMD#(in), M/IO#(t/s), W/R#(t/s), EXRDY(o/d), EX32#(o/d), EX16#(in), MSBURST#(t/s), SLBURST#(t/s), LOCK#(t/s), BE[3:0]#(t/s), LA[31:2](t/s), SD[31:0](t/s), REFRESH#(in)

ISA Signals
IO16(out)

Interchip Signals
SDCPYEN[13,03:01]#(in), SDCPYUP(in), SDOE[2:0]#(in), SDLE[3:0]#(in), EISAHOLD(in), EISAHOLDA(out), PEREQ#/INTA#(out), INTCHIP0(t/s), NMFLUSH#(t/s)

Table 11-2. EISA/ISA Bus D.C. Specifications (V_{DD} = 5V ±5%, T_{case} = 0°C to +85°C)

Symbol	Parameter	Min	Max	Test Conditions	Notes
V_{IL1}	Input Low Voltage		0.8V		
V_{IH1}	Input High Voltage	2.0V			
V_{IL2}	Input Low Voltage		0.8V		1
V_{IH2}	Input High Voltage	V_{CC} − 0.8V			1
V_{OL1}	Output Low Voltage		0.45V	I_{OL} = 24 mA	2
V_{OH1}	Output High Voltage	2.4V		I_{OH} = −5.0 mA	2
V_{OL2}	Output Low Voltage		0.45V	I_{OL} = 1 mA	3
V_{OH2}	Output High Voltage	V_{CC} − 0.45V		I_{OH} = −1 mA	3
I_{LI}	Input Leakage Current		±15 μA	0V < V_{IN} < V_{CC}	
I_{LO}	Output Leakage Current		±15 μA	0.45V < V_{IN} < V_{CC}	
C_{IN}	Capacitance Input		8 pF		
C_{OUT}	Capacitance Output		15 pF	at 1 MHz	
I_{CC}	V_{CC} Supply Current		TBD	TBD	

NOTES:
1. All EISA Bus signals use V_{IL1}, V_{IH1} for input levels except for the Interchip signals: SDCPYEN#, SDCPYUP, SDOE#, SDLE#, EISAHOLD, EISAHLDA, PEREQ#/INTA#, INTCHIP0, NMFLUSH#.
2. BE[3:0]#, EX16#, EX32#, EXRDY, LA[31:2], LOCK#, M/IO#, MSBURST#, SD[31:0], SLBURST#, START#, W/R#.
3. SDCPYEN#, SDCPYUP, SDOE#, SDLE#, EISAHOLD, EISAHLDA, PEREQ#/INTA#, INTCHIP0, NMFLUSH#.

11.2.3 PCI BUS D.C. SPECIFICATIONS

PCI System Signals
PCICLK(in), PCIRST(in)

PCI Shared Signals
AD[31:0](t/s), C/BE[3:0]#(t/s), FRAME#(s/t/s), TRDY(s/t/s), IRDY(s/t/s), TOP#(s/t/s), PCILOCK#(s/t/s), IDSEL(in), DEVSEL#(s/t/s), PAR(t/s), PERR#(s/t/s)

PCI Sideband Signals
CPUREQ#(in), REQ1#(in), REQ0#/PCEBGNT#(in), REQ[2:3]#(in), CPUGNT#(out), GNT0#/PCEBREQ# (out), GNT1#/RESUME#(out), GNT[2:3]#(out), MEMREQ#(out), FLSHREQ#(out), MEMACK#(in), MEMCS#(out), PIODEC#(in)

1

Table 11-3. PCI Bus D.C. Specifications (V_{DD} = 5V ±5%, T_{case} = 0°C to +85°C)

Symbol	Parameter	Min	Max	Test Conditions	Notes
V_{IL}	Input Low Voltage		0.8V		
V_{IH}	Input High Voltage	2.0V	5.5 V		
V_{OL}	Output Low Voltage		0.55V	I_{OL1} = 3 mA, $I_{OL}2$ = 6 mA	1
V_{OH}	Output High Voltage	2.4 V		I_{OH} = −2.0 mA	
I_{IL}	Low-level Input Current		−70 μA	V_{IN} = 0.5V	
I_{IH}	High-level Input Current		70 μA	V_{IN} = 2.7V	
$C_{I/O}$	Input/Output Capacitance		10 pF	at 1 MHz	
C_{CLK}	PCICLK Signal Input Capacitance		17 pF	at 1 MHz	
I_{CC}	V_{CC} Supply Current		TBD	TBD	

NOTE:
1. I_{OL2} applies to those signals requiring external pull-ups: FRAME#, TRD#, IRDY#, STOP#, LOCK#, DEVSEL#.

11.3 A.C. Characteristics

In Tables 11-5 through 11-13, the Symbol column shows the timing variable used in the A.C. timing waveforms. The parameter column contains the description of the timing and its reference signal. If the timing is for a particular bus cycle, the cycles are listed in parenthesis. Burst cycles include standard timings for their requirements. The Min column lists either the minimum delay time, setup time, or hold time requirement in nano-seconds, unless stated otherwise. The Max column lists the maximum delay time, also in nano-seconds. The Figure column shows what A.C. timing waveforms the parameter can be found. The Note column may contain a number to refer to a specific note found at the end of the table.

The A.C. specifications are based upon the specified capacitive loading values in the table below. The minimum capacitive loading value is 50 pF for all signals.

Table 11-4. Capacitive Loading Table

Signals	Loading
BE[3:0]#, EX16#, EX32#, EXRDY, LA[31:2], LOCK#, M/IO#, MSBURST#, SD[31:0], SLBURST#, START#, W/R#	240 pF
SDCPYEN#, SDCPYUP, SDOE#, SDLE#, EISAHOLD, EISAHLDA, PEREQ#/INTA#, INTCHIP0, NMFLUSH#, PCICLK, PCIRST, AD[31:0], C/BE[3:0]#, FRAME#, TRDY, IRDY, STOP#, PCILOCK#, IDSEL, DEVSEL#, PAR, PERR#, CPUREQ#, REQ1#, REQ0#/PCEBGNT#, REQ[2:3]#, CPUGNT#, GNT0#/PCEBREQ#, GNT1#/RESUME#, GNT[2:3]#, MEMREQ#, FLSHREQ#, MEMACK#, MEMCS#, PIODEC#	50 pF

11.3.1 CLOCK SIGNALS A.C. SPECIFICATIONS

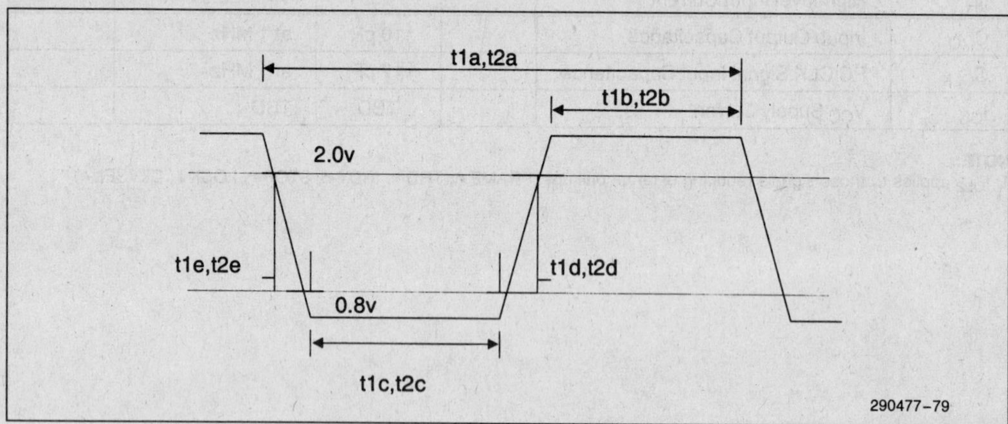

Figure 11-1. PCICLK, BCLK Timing

Table 11-5. Clock Signals A.C. Specifications (V_{DD} = 5V ±5%, T_{case} = 0° to +85°C)

Symbol	Parameter	Min	Max	Figures	Notes
PCICLK					
t1a	Cycle Time	30		11-1	
t1b	High Time (at 2.0V)	40% * T_{cyc}		11-1	
t1c	Low Time (at 0.8V)	40% * T_{cyc}		11-1	
t1d	Rise Time (0.8V to 2.0V)	3		11-1	
t1e	Fall Time (2.0V to 0.8V)	3		10-0	
BCLK					
t2a	Clock Period (0.8V to 0.8V)	120		10-1	
t2b	Low Time (at 0.8V)	55		10-1	
t2c	High Time (at 2.0V)	56		10-1	
t2d	Rise Time (0.8V to 2.0V)		7	10-1	
t2e	Fall Time (2.0V to 0.8V)		6	10-1	

1

11.3.2 PCI A.C. SPECIFICATIONS

Table 11-6. PCI A.C. Specifications (V_{DD} = 5V ±5%, T_{case} = 0° to +85°C)

Symbol	Parameter	Min	Max	Figures	Notes
PCIRST#					
t3a	Pulsewidth	1 ms		11-11	
t3b	PCICLK Active Setup to PCIRST# Deasserted	100 µs		11-11	
AD[31:0], C/BE[3:0]#, FRAME#, IRDY#,PAR, PERR#, TRDY#, DEVSEL#, STOP#, PCILOCK#, IDSEL					
t4a	Delay from PCICLK Rising	2	11	11-10	
t4b	Setup to PCICLK Rising	7		11-10	
t4c	Hold from PCICLK Rising	0		11-10	
REQ[3:0]#/GNT[3:0]#, PCEBREQ#, RESUME#, CPUREQ#, CPUGNT#					
t5a	GNT Delay from PCICLK Rising	2	12	11-9	
t5b	REQ Setup to PCICLK Rising	12		11-9	
t5c	REQ Hold from PCICLK Rising	0		11-9	
MEMREQ#, FLSHREQ#, MEMACK#					
t36a	MEMREQ#, FLSHREQ# Delay from PCICLK Rising	2	12	11-12	
t36b	MEMACK# Setup to PCICLK Rising	12		11-12	
t36c	MEMACK# Hold from PCICLK Rising	12		11-12	

11.3.3 EISA INTERFACE A.C. SPECIFICATIONS

Table 11-7. EISA Master Interface A.C. Specifications (V_{DD} = 5V ±5%, T_{case} = 0°C to +85°C)

Symbol	Parameter	Min	Max	Figures	Notes
EISA MASTER					
LA[31:2]					
t6a	Delay from BCLK Falling	2	30	11-2	
t6b	Float Delay from BCLK Falling (End of Master Mode)	0	40	11-13	
BE[3:0]#					
t7a	Delay from BCLK Rising	0	25	11-2	
t7b	Float Delay from BCLK Falling (End of Master Mode)	0	40	11-13	
t7c	Float Delay from BCLK Falling (Backoff Cycle)	0	40	11-6	
M/IO					
t8a	Delay from BCLK Falling	2	30	11-2	
t8b	Float Delay from BCLK Falling (End of Master Mode)	0	40	11-13	
W/R					
t9a	Delay from BCLK Rising	0	25	11-2	
t9b	Float Delay from BCLK Falling (End of Master Mode)	0	40	11-13	
START#					
t10a	Delay from BCLK Rising	2	25	11-2	
t10b	Float Delay from BCLK Falling (Backoff Cycle)	0	40	11-6	
t10c	Float Delay from BCLK Falling (End of Master Mode)	0	40	11-13	
EX32#, EX16#					
t11a	Setup to BCLK Rising	25		11-2	
t11b	Setup to BCLK Rising (End of Backoff Cycle)	15		11-6	
t11c	Hold from BCLK Rising	55		11-2	
t11d	Hold from BCLK Rising (End of Backoff Cycle)	50		11-6	
EXRDY					
t12a	Setup to BCLK Falling	15		11-2	
t12b	Hold from BCLK Falling	5		11-2	
LOCK					
t13a	Delay from BCLK Rising	2	60	11-2	
t13b	Float Delay from BCLK Falling (End of Master Mode)	0	40	11-13	
SD[31:0]					
t14a	Delay from BCLK Falling (Write)	5	40	11-2	
t14b	Setup Time to BCLK Rising (Read)	12		11-2, 4	
t14c	Hold Time from BCLK Rising (Read)	4		11-2, 4	
t14d	Float Delay from BCLK Falling (Backoff Write Cycles)	0	50	11-6	
t14e	Float Delay from BCLK Falling (End of Master Mode)			11-13	

Table 11-7. EISA Master Interface A.C. Specifications
(V_{DD} = 5V ±5%, T_{case} = 0°C to +85°C) (Continued)

Symbol	Parameter	Min	Max	Figures	Notes
EISA MASTER BURST CYCLES					
LA[31:2]					
t15	Delay from BCLK Falling	2	30	11-4	
BE[3:0]#					
t16	Delay from BCLK Falling	2	30	11-4	
MSBURST#					
t17a	Delay from BCLK Falling	2	35	11-4	
t17b	Float Delay from BCLK Falling (End of Master Mode)	0	40	11-13	
SLBURST#					
t18a	Setup to BCLK Rising	15		11-4	
t18b	Hold from BCLK Rising	55		11-4	
SD[31:0]					
t19a	Delay from BCLK Rising (Write)	5	40	11-4	
t19b	Setup to BCLK Rising (Read)	15		11-4	
t19c	Hold from BCLK Rising (Read)	5		11-4	

Table 11-8. EISA Slave Interface A.C. Specifications (V_{DD} = 5V ±5%, T_{case} = 0° to +85°C)

Symbol	Parameter	Min	Max	Figures	Notes
EISA SLAVE					
LA[31:2]					
t20a	Setup to BCLK Rising	10		11-3	
t20b	Hold from BCLK Rising	20		11-3	
BE[3:0]#					
t21a	Setup to BCLK Rising at CMD# Time	80		11-3	
t21b	Hold from BCLK Rising	20		11-3	
M/IO					
t22a	Setup to BCLK Rising	10		11-3	
t22b	Hold from BCLK Rising	20		11-3	
W/R					
t23a	Setup to BCLK Rising at CMD# Time	80		11-3	
t23b	Hold from BCLK Rising	20		11-3	
START#					
t24a	Setup to BCLK Rising	88		11-3	
t24b	Asserted Pulsewidth	115		11-3	
EX32#, EX16#					
t25a	Delay from LA Valid	2	54	11-3	
t25b	Delay from PIODEC# Asserted		15	11-14	1

Table 11-8. EISA Slave Interface A.C. Specifications (V_{DD} = 5V ±5%, T_{case} = 0° to +85°C) (Continued)

Symbol	Parameter	Min	Max	Figures	Notes
EXRDY					
t26a	Negate Delay from BCLK Rising		35	11-3	
t26b	Float Delay from BCLK Rising	3	34	11-3	
LOCK					
t27a	Setup to BCLK Rising	54		11-3	
t27b	Hold from BCLK Rising	2		11-3	
SD[31:0]					
t28a	Delay from BCLK Rising (Read)	0	50	11-3	
t28b	Setup to BCLK Rising (Write)	110		11-3, 5	
t28c	Hold from BCLK Rising (Write)	25		11-3, 5	
EISA SLAVE BURST CYCLES					
LA[31:2]					
t29a	Setup to BCLK Rising	5		11-5	
t29b	Hold from BCLK Rising	2		11-5	
BE[3:0]#					
t30a	Setup to BCLK Rising	5		11-5	
t30b	Hold from BCLK Rising	2		11-5	
MSBURST#					
t31a	Setup to BCLK Rising	14		11-5	
t31b	Hold from BCLK Rising	45		11-5	
SLBURST#					
t32	Delay from LA Valid	2	55	11-5	
SD[31:0]					
t33a	Delay from BCLK Rising (Read)	35	80	11-5	
t33b	Setup to BCLK Rising (Write)	55		11-5	
t33c	Hold from BCLK Rising (Write)	5		11-5	

11.3.4 ISA INTERFACE A.C. SPECIFICATIONS

Table 11-9. ISA Interface A.C. Specifications (V_{DD} = 5V ±5%, T_{case} = 0° to +85°C)

Symbol	Parameter	Min	Max	Figures	Notes
REFRESH#					
t34	Setup to START# Asserted	5		11-15	
IO16#					
t35a	Assert Delay from BCLK Rising		70	11-15	
t35b	Assert Delay from PIODEC Asserted		15	11-15	2
t35c	Setup to CMD# Asserted	10		11-18	
t35d	Hold from CMD# Negated	0		11-18	

11.3.5 DATA SWAP BUFFERS A.C. SPECIFICATIONS

Table 11-10. Data Swap A.C. Specifications (V_{DD} = 5V ±5%, T_{case} = 0° to +85°C)

Symbol	Parameter	Min	Max	Figures	Notes
SDCPYEN[13,03:01]#, SDCPYUP#					
t37a	Asserted to Valid Data Delay	2	21	11-16	
t37b	SDCPYUP# Setup to SDCPYEN# Asserted	0		11-16	
SD[x] to SD[x]					
t37c	Copy Buffer Propogation Delay		16.5	11-16	
SDLE[3:0]#					
t38a	Data Setup Time to SDLE# Rising	3.5		11-16	
t38b	Data Hold Time from SDLE# Rising	3.5		11-16	
SDOE[2:0]#					
t39	Asserted to Valid Data Delay		17.5	11-16	

1

11.3.6 ARBITRATION AND INTERRUPT ACKNOWLEDGE A.C. SPECIFICATIONS

Table 11-11. Arbitration and Interrupt Acknowledge A.C. Specifications (V_{DD} = 5V ±5%, T_{case} = 0° to +85°C)

Symbol	Parameter	Min	Max	Figures	Notes
EISAHOLD					
t40a	Setup to PCICLK Rising	9		11-7	
t40b	Hold from PCICLK Rising	2		11-7	
EISAHOLDA					
t41	Delay from PCICLK Rising	4	15	11-7	
PEREQ#/INTA#					
t42	Delay from PCICLK Rising	4	15	11-7	

11.3.7 BUFFER COHERENCY A.C. SPECIFICATIONS

Table 11-12. Buffer Coherency A.C. Specifications (V_{DD} = 5V ±5%, T_{case} = 0° to +85°C)

Symbol	Parameter	Min	Max	Figures	Notes
INTCHIP0, NMFLUSH#					
t43a	Delay from PCICLK Rising (Acknowledge from PCEB)	4	15	11-8	
t43b	Setup to PCICLK Rising (Request from ESC)	9		11-8	
t43c	Hold from PCICLK Rising	2		11-8	

11.3.8 ADDRESS DECODER A.C. SPECIFICATIONS

Table 11-13. Address Decoder A.C. Specifications (V_{DD} = 5V ±5%, T_{case} = 0° to +85°C)

Symbol	Parameter	Min	Max	Figures	Notes
MEMCS#					
t44	Delay from PCICLK Rising (Acknowledge from PECB	2	17	11-17	

NOTES:
1. EX32# must still meet the propogation requirement from LA valid.
2. PIODEC must be provided in time to meet the EISA specification.

11.3.9 A.C. TIMING WAVEFORMS

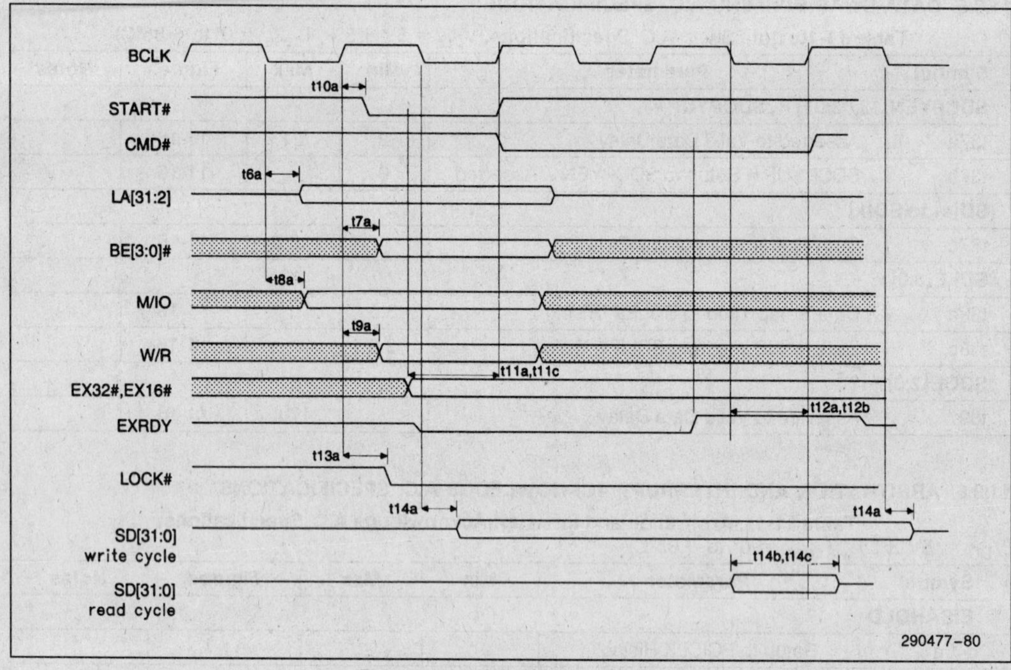

Figure 11-2. EISA Master Cycle

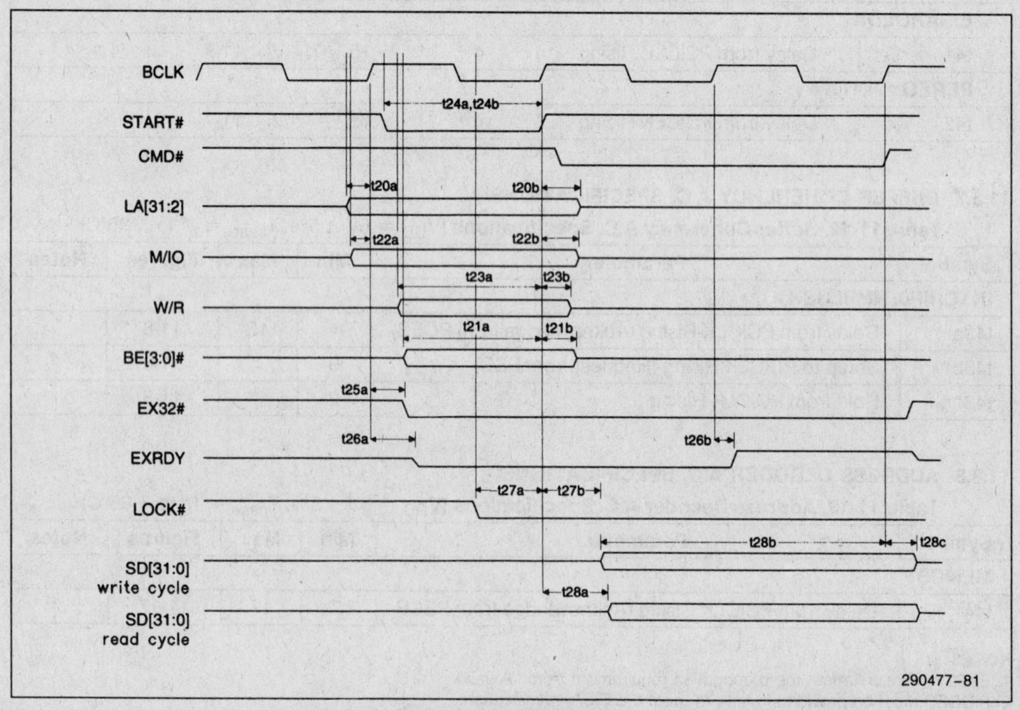

Figure 11-3. EISA Slave

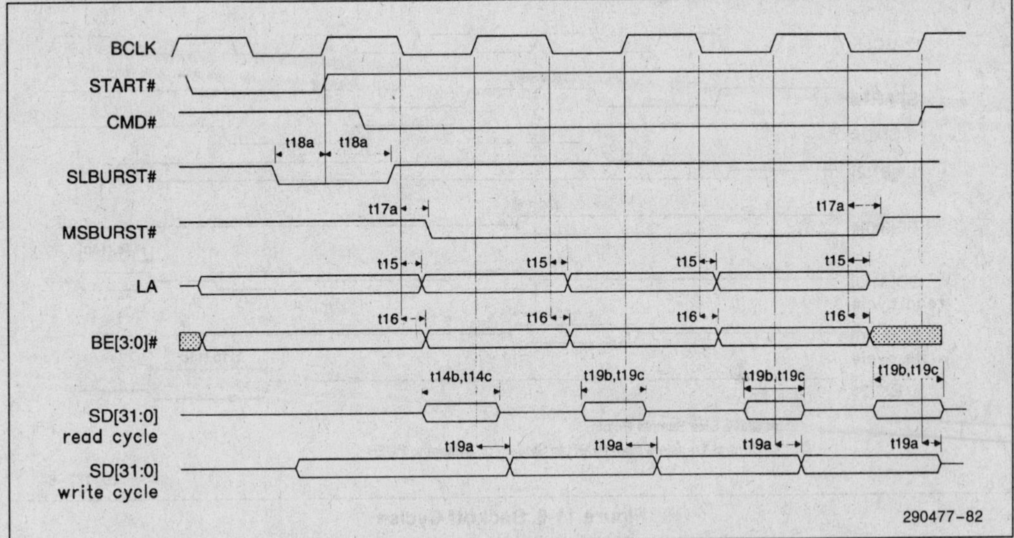

Figure 11-4. EISA Master Burst

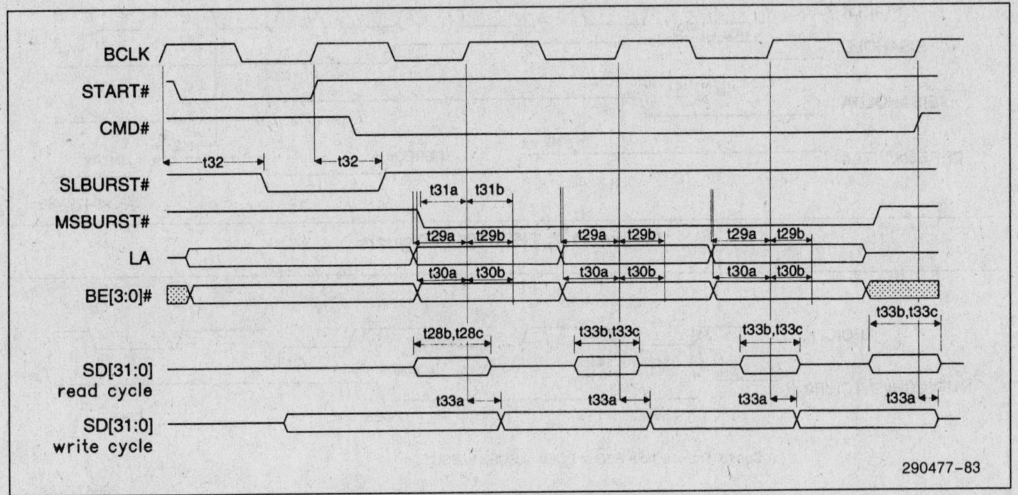

Figure 11-5. EISA Slave Burst

1

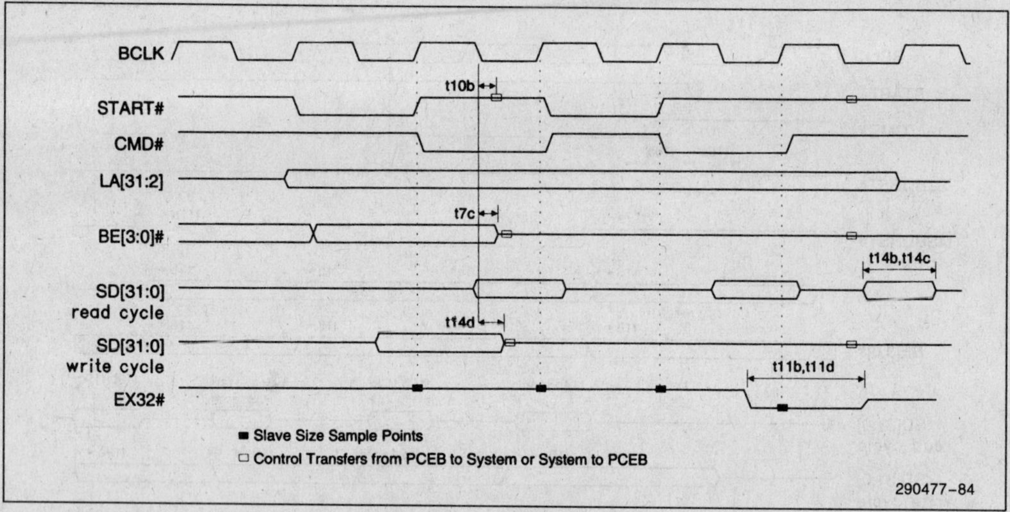

Figure 11-6. Backoff Cycles

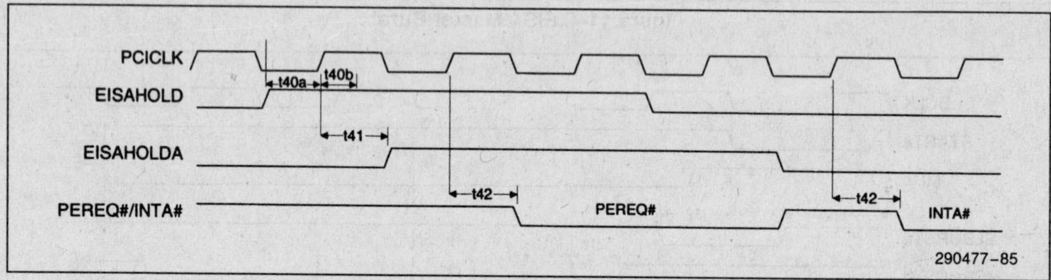

Figure 11-7. EISAHOLD Signals

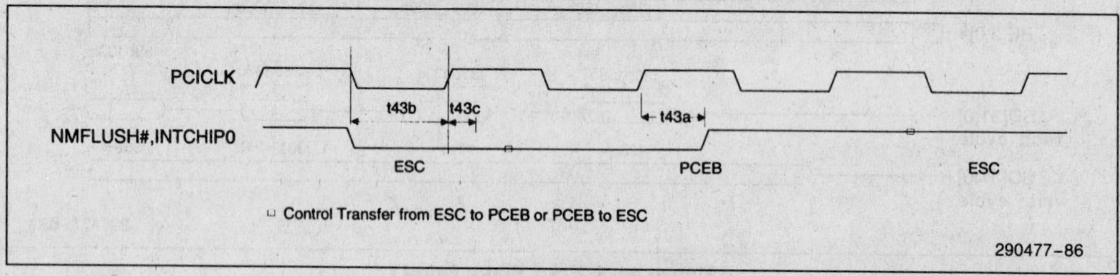

Figure 11-8. Flush Requests

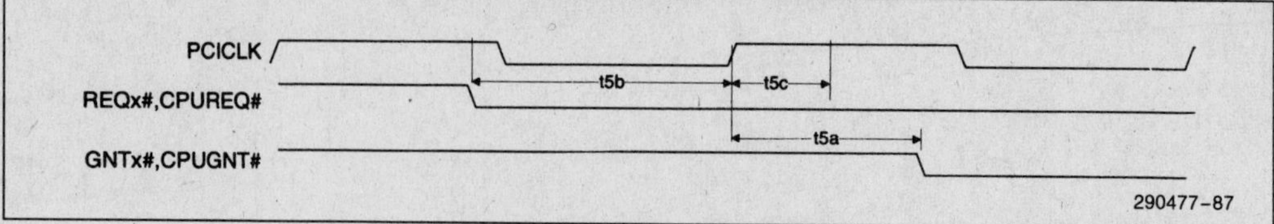

Figure 11-9. PCI Bus Arbitration

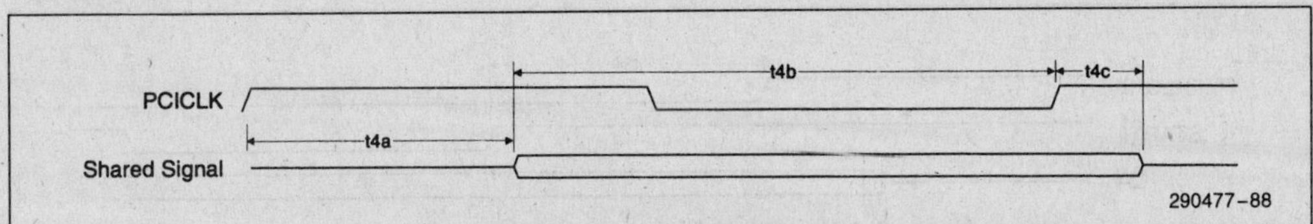

Figure 11-10. PCI Shared Signals

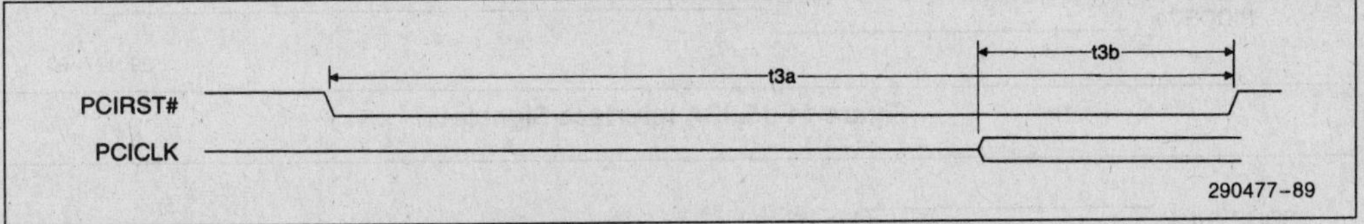

Figure 11-11. PCIRST# Signal

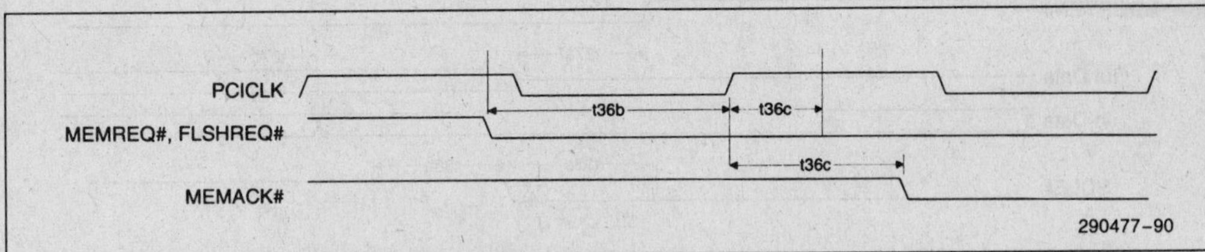

Figure 11-12. MEMREQ#, FLSHREQ#, MEMACK# Signals

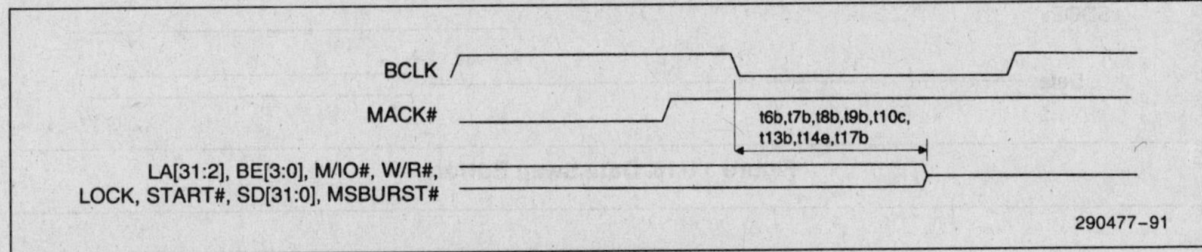

Figure 11-13. End of Master Mode

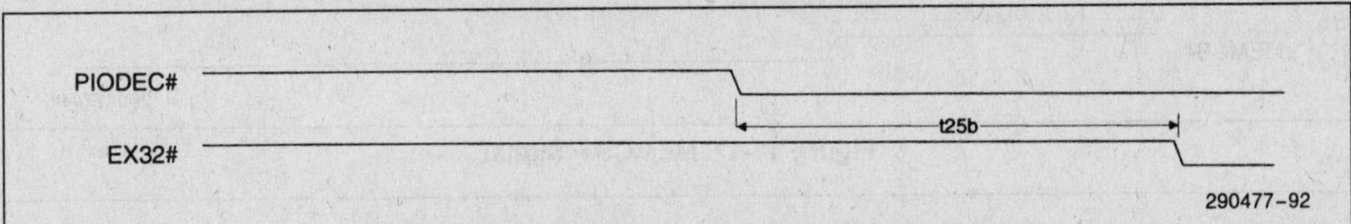

Figure 11-14. PIODEC# to EX32# Propogation

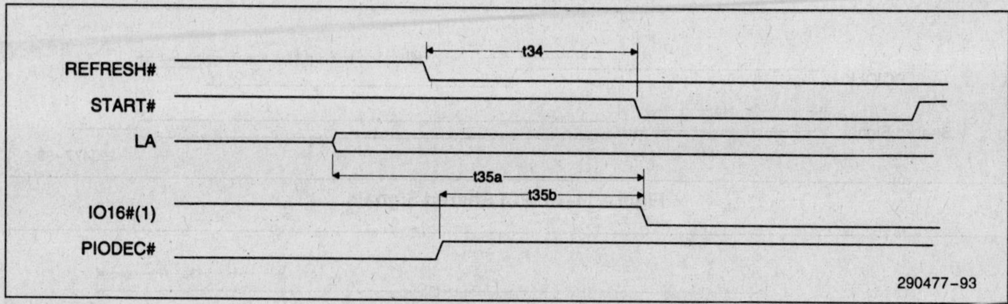

Figure 11-15. ISA Interface Signals

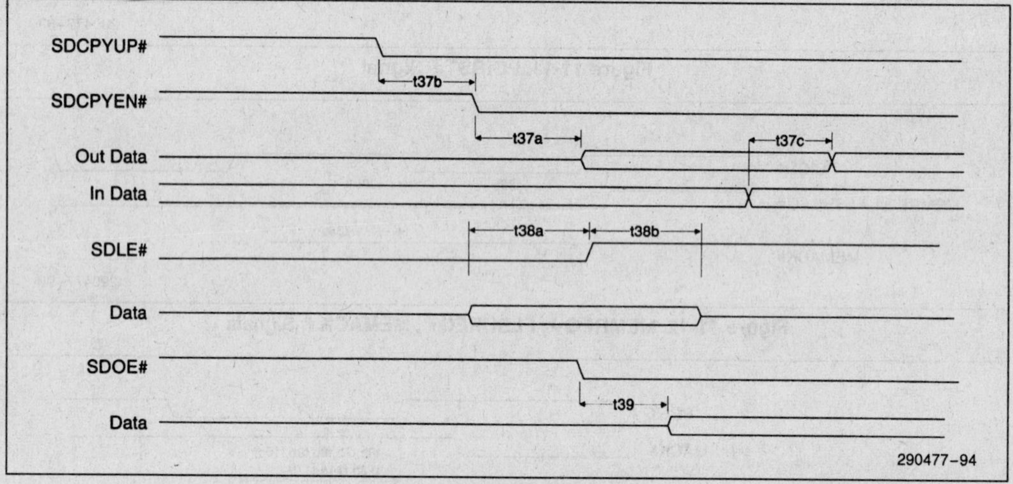

Figure 11-16. Data Swap Buffers

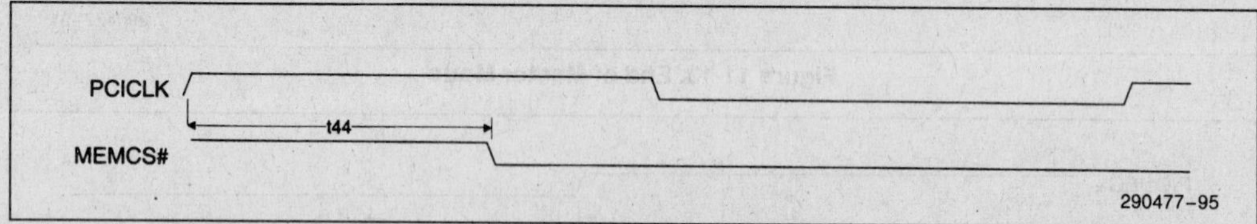

Figure 11-17. MEMCS# Signal

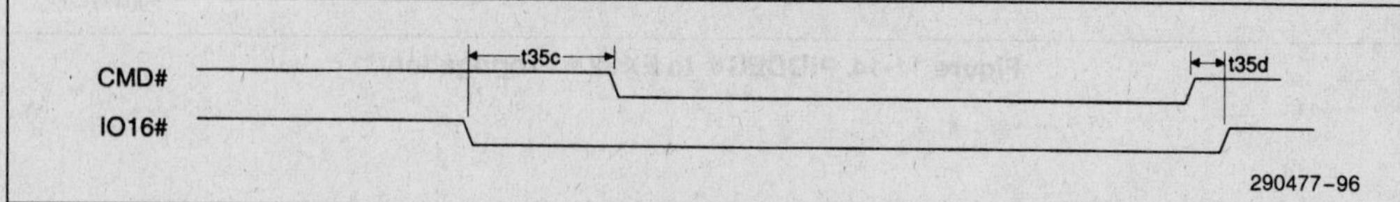

Figure 11-18. IO16# Signal

11.4 NAND Tree

A NAND Tree is provided primarily for V_{IL}/V_{IH} testing. The NAND Tree is also useful for Automated Test Equipment (ATE) at board level testing. The NAND Tree allows the tester to test the solder connections for each individual signal pin.

The TEST# pin, along with BCLK, PIODEC# and EX16#, activates the NAND Tree. The following combinations of PIODEC#, EX16#, and TEST# will cause each buffer to be tri-stated:

PIODEC# = "1" and EX16# = "0" and
TEST# = "0"

or

PIODEC# = "0" and EX16# = "1"

Care must be taken as the test is in progress to ensure that one of the preceding combinations is valid. Otherwise, the test mode will be exited.

Asserting TEST# causes the output pulse train to appear on the EISAHLDA pin. BCLK must be driven low in order to enable the NAND Tree.

The sequence of the ATE test is as follows:

1. Drive TEST# low, EX16# high, PIODEC# low, and BCLK low.
2. Drive each pin high, except for the pins mentioned in the discussion above (TEST#, PIODEC#, and BCLK).
3. Starting at pin 168 (IO16#) and continuing with pins 169, 170, etc., individually drive each pin low, remembering to toggle PIODEC# from low to high when EX16# is toggled from high to low. Also, when PIODEC# is driven low, EX16# must be driven high. Expect EISAHLDA to toggle after each corresponding input pin is toggled. The final pin in the tree is pin 166 (LOCK#). BCLK is not part of the tree, and EISAHLDA is operated only as an output. Also, please note that no-connect (NC), V_{CC}, and V_{SS} pins are not a part of the NAND Tree.
4. Turn off tester drivers before enabling the PCEB's buffers (via PIODEC#, TEST#, and EX16#).
5. Reset the PCEB prior to proceeding with further testing.

1

NAND Tree Cell Order:

Pin #	Pin Name	Pin #	Pin Name	Pin #	Pin Name
168	IO16#[(1)]	3	LA31#	44	SD20
169	CMD#	4	LA30#	45	LA17
170	START	5	LA29#	47	SD21
171	EXRDY	6	LA28#	48	SD22
172	EX32#	7	LA27#	49	SD23
173	EX16#[(2)]	8	LA26#	50	SD24
174	SLBURST#	10	LA25#	51	SD25
175	SDLE3#	11	LA24#	55	SD8
176	SDLE2#	12	LA16	56	SD26
177	SDLE1#	13	LA15	57	SD9
178	SDLE0#	15	LA14	58	SD27
179	SDCPYEN01#	16	LA13	59	SD28
180	SDCPYEN02#	17	LA12	60	SD10
184	SDCPYEN03#	18	V_{SS}	61	SD11
185	SDCPYEN13#	19	LA11	64	SD29
186	SDCPYUP	20	LA10	65	SD12
187	SDOE0#	21	LA9	66	SD30
188	SDOE1#	22	LA8	67	SD13
189	SDOE2#	23	LA7	68	SD31
190	MSBURST#	24	LA6	69	SD14
191	M/IO#	28	LA5	70	SD15
192	W/R#	29	LA4	71	REQ0#
195	SD7	30	LA23	72	REQ1#
196	SD6	31	LA3	73	REQ2#
197	SD5	32	LA22	74	REQ3#
198	SD4	33	LA2	75	CPUREQ#
199	SD3	34	LA21	76	CPUGNT#
201	SD2	36	LA20	80	GNT3#
202	SD1	37	SD16	81	GNT2#
203	SD0	38	SD17	82	GNT1#
204	BE3#	40	LA19	83	GNT0#
205	BE2#	41	SD18	85	FLSHREQ#
206	BE1#	42	SD19	86	MEMACK#
207	BE0#	43	LA18	87	MEMREQ#

NOTES:
1. Start of NAND Tree.
2. Must be "1" when PIODEC# is "0" and must be "0" when PIODEC# is "1".
3. Must be "0" when EX16# is "1" and must be "1" when EX16# is "0".

Pin #	Pin Name
88	MEMCS#
89	PIODEC#(3)
91	PCICLK
92	IDSEL
93	PCIRST#
97	AD31
98	AD30
99	AD29
100	AD28
101	AD27
102	AD26
107	AD25
108	AD24
109	C/BE3#
110	AD23
111	AD22
112	AD21
114	AD20
115	AD19

Pin #	Pin Name
117	AD18
118	AD17
119	AD16
120	C/BE2#
122	FRAME#
123	IRDY#
124	TRDY#
125	DEVSEL#
126	STOP#
127	PLOCK#
128	PERR#
134	PAR
135	C/BE1#
136	AD15
137	AD14
138	AD13
139	AD12
141	AD11

Pin #	Pin Name
142	AD10
143	AD9
144	C/BE0#
146	AD6
147	AD7
148	AD6
150	AD5
151	AD4
152	AD3
153	AD2
154	AD1
155	AD0
160	REFRESH#
161	INTCHIP0
162	EISAHOLD
164	PEREQ#/INTA#
165	NMFLUSH#
166	LOCK#

1

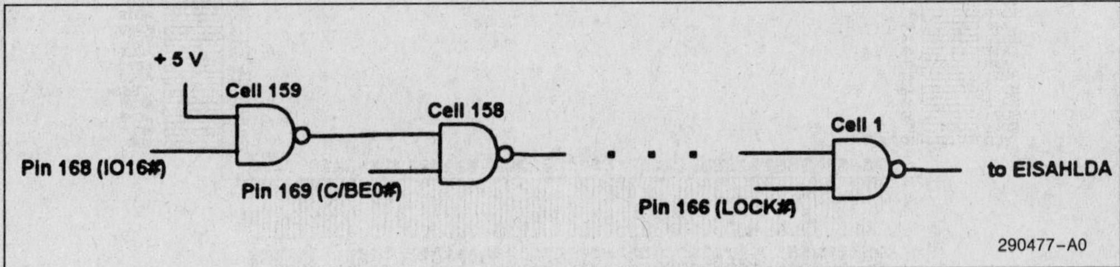

Figure 11-19. NAND Tree

12.0 PINOUT AND PACKAGE INFORMATION

12.1 Pin Assignment

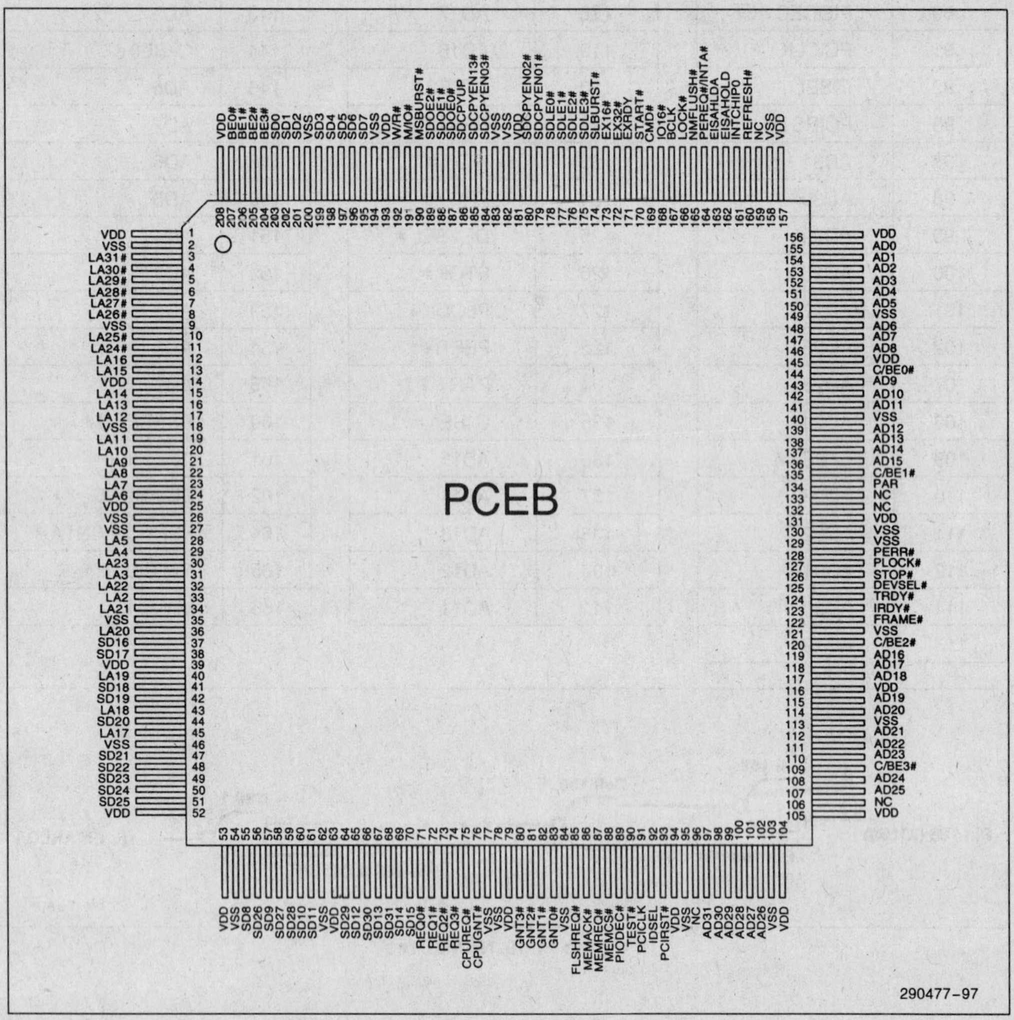

PCEB

Pin	Name	Pin	Name	Pin	Name	Pin	Name
1	VDD	53	VDD	105	VDD	157	VDD
2	VSS	54	VSS	106	NC	158	VSS
3	LA31#	55	SD8	107	AD25	159	NC
4	LA30#	56	SD26	108	AD24	160	REFRESH#
5	LA29#	57	SD9	109	C/BE3#	161	INTCHIP0
6	LA28#	58	SD27	110	AD23	162	EISAHOLD
7	LA27#	59	SD28	111	AD22	163	EISAHLDA
8	LA26#	60	SD10	112	AD21	164	PEREQ#/INTA#
9	VSS	61	SD11	113	VSS	165	NMFLUSH#
10	LA25#	62	VSS	114	AD20	166	LOCK#
11	LA24#	63	VDD	115	AD19	167	BCLK
12	LA16	64	SD29	116	VDD	168	IO16#
13	LA15	65	SD12	117	AD18	169	CMD#
14	VDD	66	SD30	118	AD17	170	START#
15	LA14	67	SD13	119	AD16	171	EXRDY
16	LA13	68	SD31	120	C/BE2#	172	EX32#
17	LA12	69	SD14	121	VSS	173	EX16#
18	VSS	70	SD15	122	FRAME#	174	SLBURST#
19	LA11	71	REQ0#	123	IRDY#	175	SDLE3#
20	LA10	72	REQ1#	124	TRDY#	176	SDLE2#
21	LA9	73	REQ2#	125	DEVSEL#	177	SDLE1#
22	LA8	74	REQ3#	126	STOP#	178	SDLE0#
23	LA7	75	CPUREQ#	127	PLOCK#	179	SDCPYEN01#
24	LA6	76	CPUGNT#	128	PERR#	180	SDCPYEN02#
25	VDD	77	VSS	129	VSS	181	VDD
26	VSS	78	VSS	130	VSS	182	VSS
27	VSS	79	VDD	131	VDD	183	VSS
28	LA5	80	GNT3#	132	NC	184	SDCPYEN03#
29	LA4	81	GNT2#	133	NC	185	SDCPYEN13#
30	LA23	82	GNT1#	134	PAR	186	SDCPYUP
31	LA3	83	GNT0#	135	C/BE1#	187	SDOE0#
32	LA22	84	VSS	136	AD15	188	SDOE1#
33	LA2	85	FLSHREQ#	137	AD14	189	SDOE2#
34	LA21	86	MEMACK#	138	AD13	190	MSBURST#
35	VSS	87	MEMREQ#	139	AD12	191	M/IO#
36	LA20	88	MEMCS#	140	VSS	192	W/R#
37	SD16	89	PIODEC#	141	AD11	193	VDD
38	SD17	90	TEST#	142	AD10	194	VSS
39	VDD	91	PCICLK	143	AD9	195	SD7
40	LA19	92	IDSEL	144	C/BE0#	196	SD6
41	SD18	93	PCIRST#	145	VDD	197	SD5
42	SD19	94	VDD	146	AD8	198	SD4
43	LA18	95	VSS	147	AD7	199	SD3
44	SD20	96	NC	148	AD6	200	VSS
45	LA17	97	AD31	149	VSS	201	SD2
46	VSS	98	AD30	150	AD5	202	SD1
47	SD21	99	AD29	151	AD4	203	SD0
48	SD22	100	AD28	152	AD3	204	BE3#
49	SD23	101	AD27	153	AD2	205	BE2#
50	SD24	102	AD26	154	AD1	206	BE1#
51	SD25	103	VSS	155	AD0	207	BE0#
52	VDD	104	VDD	156	VDD	208	VDD

290477-97

Figure 12-1. Pinout

Table 12-1. Alphabetical PCEB Pin Assignment

Name	Pin#	Type
AD0	155	t/s
AD1	154	t/s
AD2	153	t/s
AD3	152	t/s
AD4	151	t/s
AD5	150	t/s
AD6	148	t/s
AD7	147	t/s
AD8	146	t/s
AD9	143	t/s
AD10	142	t/s
AD11	141	t/s
AD12	139	t/s
AD13	138	t/s
AD14	137	t/s
AD15	136	t/s
AD16	119	t/s
AD17	118	t/s
AD18	117	t/s
AD19	115	t/s
AD20	114	t/s
AD21	112	t/s
AD22	111	t/s
AD23	110	t/s
AD24	108	t/s
AD25	107	t/s
AD26	102	t/s
AD27	101	t/s
AD28	100	t/s
AD29	99	t/s
AD30	98	t/s
AD31	97	t/s
BCLK	167	in
BE0#	207	t/s
BE1#	206	t/s
BE2#	205	t/s
BE3#	204	t/s
C/BE0#	144	t/s
C/BE1#	135	t/s
C/BE2#	120	t/s
C/BE3#	109	t/s
CMD#	169	in
CPUGNT#	76	out
CPUREQ#	75	in
DEVSEL#	125	s/t/s
EISAHLDA	163	out
EISAHOLD	162	in
EX16#	173	in
EX32#	172	o/d
EXRDY	171	o/d
FLSHREQ#	85	out
FRAME#	122	s/t/s
GNT0#	83	out
GNT1#	82	out
GNT2#	81	out
GNT3#	80	out
IDSEL	92	in
INTCHIP0	161	t/s
IO16#	168	o/d
IRDY#	123	s/t/s
LA2	33	t/s
LA3	31	t/s
LA4	29	t/s
LA5	28	t/s
LA6	24	t/s
LA7	23	t/s
LA8	22	t/s
LA9	21	t/s
LA10	20	t/s
LA11	19	t/s
LA12	17	t/s
LA13	16	t/s
LA14	15	t/s
LA15	13	t/s
LA16	12	t/s
LA17	45	t/s
LA18	43	t/s
LA19	40	t/s
LA20	36	t/s
LA21	34	t/s
LA22	32	t/s
LA23	30	t/s
LA24#	11	t/s
LA25#	10	t/s
LA26#	8	t/s
LA27#	7	t/s
LA28#	6	t/s
LA29#	5	t/s
LA30#	4	t/s
LA31#	3	t/s
LOCK#	166	t/s
M/IO#	191	t/s
MEMACK#	86	in
MEMCS#	88	out
MEMREQ#	87	out
MSBURST#	190	t/s
NC	96	NC
NC	106	NC
NC	132	NC
NC	133	NC
NC	159	NC
NMFLUSH#	165	t/s
PAR	134	t/s
PCICLK	91	in
PCIRST#	93	in
PEREQ#/ INTA#	164	out
PERR#	128	s/o/d
PIODEC#	89	in
PLOCK#	127	s/t/s
REFRESH#	160	in
REQ0#	71	in
REQ1#	72	in
REQ2#	73	in
REQ3#	74	in
SD0	203	t/s
SD1	202	t/s
SD2	201	t/s
SD3	199	t/s
SD4	198	t/s
SD5	197	t/s
SD6	196	t/s
SD7	195	t/s
SD8	55	t/s
SD9	57	t/s
SD10	60	t/s
SD11	61	t/s
SD12	65	t/s
SD13	67	t/s

Table 12-1. Alphabetical PCEB Pin Assignment (Continued)

Name	Pin#	Type
SD14	69	t/s
SD15	70	t/s
SD16	37	t/s
SD17	38	t/s
SD18	41	t/s
SD19	42	t/s
SD20	44	t/s
SD21	47	t/s
SD22	48	t/s
SD23	49	t/s
SD24	50	t/s
SD25	51	t/s
SD26	56	t/s
SD27	58	t/s
SD28	59	t/s
SD29	64	t/s
SD30	66	t/s
SD31	68	t/s
SDCPYEN01#	179	in
SDCPYEN02#	180	in
SDCPYEN03#	184	in
SDCPYEN13#	185	in
SDCPYUP	186	in
SDLE0#	178	in
SDLE1#	177	in
SDLE2#	176	in
SDLE3#	175	in

Name	Pin#	Type
SDOE0#	187	in
SDOE1#	188	in
SDOE2#	189	in
SLBURST#	174	t/s
START#	170	t/s
STOP#	126	s/t/s
TEST#	90	in
TRDY#	124	s/t/s
V_{DD}	1	V
V_{DD}	14	V
V_{DD}	25	V
V_{DD}	39	V
V_{DD}	52	V
V_{DD}	53	V
V_{DD}	63	V
V_{DD}	79	V
V_{DD}	94	V
V_{DD}	104	V
V_{DD}	105	V
V_{DD}	116	V
V_{DD}	131	V
V_{DD}	145	V
V_{DD}	156	V
V_{DD}	157	V
V_{DD}	181	V
V_{DD}	193	V
V_{DD}	208	V

Name	Pin#	Type
V_{SS}	2	V
V_{SS}	9	V
V_{SS}	18	V
V_{SS}	26	V
V_{SS}	27	V
V_{SS}	35	V
V_{SS}	46	V
V_{SS}	54	V
V_{SS}	62	V
V_{SS}	77	V
V_{SS}	78	V
V_{SS}	84	V
V_{SS}	95	V
V_{SS}	103	V
V_{SS}	113	V
V_{SS}	121	V
V_{SS}	129	V
V_{SS}	130	V
V_{SS}	140	V
V_{SS}	149	V
V_{SS}	158	V
V_{SS}	182	V
V_{SS}	183	V
V_{SS}	194	V
V_{SS}	200	V
W/R#	192	t/s

Table 12-2. Numerical PCEB Pin Assignment

Pin #	Name	Type	Pin #	Name	Type	Pin #	Name	Type
1	V_{DD}	V	46	V_{SS}	V	91	PCICLK	in
2	V_{SS}	V	47	SD21	t/s	92	IDSEL	in
3	LA31#	t/s	48	SD22	t/S	93	PCIRST#	in
4	LA30#	t/s	49	SD23	t/s	94	V_{DD}	V
5	LA29#	t/s	50	SD24	t/s	95	V_{SS}	V
6	LA28#	t/s	51	SD25	t/s	96	NC	NC
7	LA27#	t/s	52	V_{DD}	V	97	AD31	t/s
8	LA26#	t/s	53	V_{DD}	V	98	AD30	t/s
9	V_{SS}	V	54	V_{SS}	V	99	AD29	t/s
10	LA25#	t/s	55	SD8	t/s	100	AD28	t/s
11	LA24#	t/s	56	SD26	t/s	101	AD27	t/s
12	LA16	t/s	57	SD9	t/s	102	AD26	t/s
13	LA15	t/s	58	SD27	t/s	103	V_{SS}	V
14	V_{DD}	V	59	SD28	t/s	104	V_{DD}	V
15	LA14	t/s	60	SD10	t/s	105	V_{DD}	V
16	LA13	t/s	61	SD11	t/s	106	NC	NC
17	LA12	t/s	62	V_{SS}	V	107	AD25	t/s
18	V_{SS}	V	63	V_{DD}	V	108	AD24	t/s
19	LA11	t/s	64	SD29	t/s	109	C/BE3#	t/s
20	LA10	t/s	65	SD12	t/s	110	AD23	t/s
21	LA9	t/s	66	SD30	t/s	111	AD22	t/s
22	LA8	t/s	67	SD13	t/s	112	AD21	t/s
23	LA7	t/s	68	SD31	t/s	113	V_{SS}	V
24	LA6	t/s	69	SD14	t/s	114	AD20	t/s
25	V_{DD}	V	70	SD15	t/s	115	AD19	t/s
26	V_{SS}	V	71	REQ0#	in	116	V_{DD}	V
27	V_{SS}	V	72	REQ1#	in	117	AD18	t/s
28	LA5	t/s	73	REQ2#	in	118	AD17	t/s
29	LA4	t/s	74	REQ3#	in	119	AD16	t/s
30	LA23	t/s	75	CPUREQ#	in	120	C/BE2#	t/s
31	LA3	t/s	76	CPUGNT#	out	121	V_{SS}	V
32	LA22	t/s	77	V_{SS}	V	122	FRAME#	s/t/s
33	LA2	t/s	78	V_{SS}	V	123	IRDY#	s/t/s
34	LA21	t/s	79	V_{DD}	V	124	TRDY#	s/t/s
35	V_{SS}	V	80	GNT3#	out	125	DEVSEL#	s/t/s
36	LA20	t/s	81	GNT2#	out	126	STOP#	s/t/s
37	SD16	t/s	82	GNT1#	out	127	PLOCK#	s/t/s
38	SD17	t/s	83	GNT0#	out	128	PERR#	s/o/d
39	V_{DD}	V	84	V_{SS}	V	129	V_{SS}	V
40	LA19	t/s	85	FLSHREQ#	out	130	V_{SS}	V
41	SD18	t/s	86	MEMACK#	in	131	V_{DD}	V
42	SD19	t/s	87	MEMREQ#	out	132	NC	NC
43	LA18	t/s	88	MEMCS#	out	133	NC	NC
44	SD20	t/s	89	PIODEC#	in	134	PAR	t/s
45	LA17	t/s	90	TEST#	in	135	C/BE1#	t/s

Table 12-2. Numerical PCEB Pin Assignment (Continued)

Pin #	Name	Type
136	AD15	t/s
137	AD14	t/s
138	AD13	t/s
139	AD12	t/s
140	V_{SS}	Vv
141	AD11	t/s
142	AD10	t/s
143	AD9	t/s
144	C/BE0#	t/s
145	V_{DD}	V
146	AD8	t/s
147	AD7	t/s
148	AD6	t/s
149	V_{SS}	V
150	AD5	t/s
151	AD4	t/s
152	AD3	t/s
153	AD2	t/s
154	AD1	t/s
155	AD0	t/s
156	V_{DD}	V
157	V_{DD}	V
158	V_{SS}	V
159	NC	NC
160	REFRESH#	in
161	INTCHIP0	t/s
162	EISAHOLD	in
163	EISAHLDA	out
164	PEREQ#/ INTA#	out
165	NMFLUSH#	t/s
166	LOCK#	t/s
167	BCLK	in
168	IO16#	o/d
169	CMD#	in
170	START#	t/s
171	EXRDY	o/d
172	EX32#	o/d
173	EX16#	in
174	SLBURST#	t/s
175	SDLE3#	in
176	SDLE2#	in
177	SDLE1#	in
178	SDLE0#	in
179	SDCPYEN01#	in
180	SDCPYEN02#	in
181	V_{DD}	V
182	V_{SS}	V
183	V_{SS}	V
184	SDCPYEN03#	in
185	SDCPYEN13#	in
186	SDCPYUP	in
187	SDOE0#	in
188	SDOE1#	in
189	SDOE2#	in
190	MSBURST#	t/s
191	M/IO#	t/s
192	W/R#	t/s
193	V_{DD}	V
194	V_{SS}	V
195	SD7	t/s
196	SD6	t/s
197	SD5	t/s
198	SD4	t/s
199	SD3	t/s
200	V_{SS}	V
201	SD2	t/s
202	SD1	t/s
203	SD0	t/s
204	BE3#	t/s
205	BE2#	t/s
206	BE1#	t/s
207	BE0#	t/s
208	V_{DD}	V

12.2 Package Characteristics

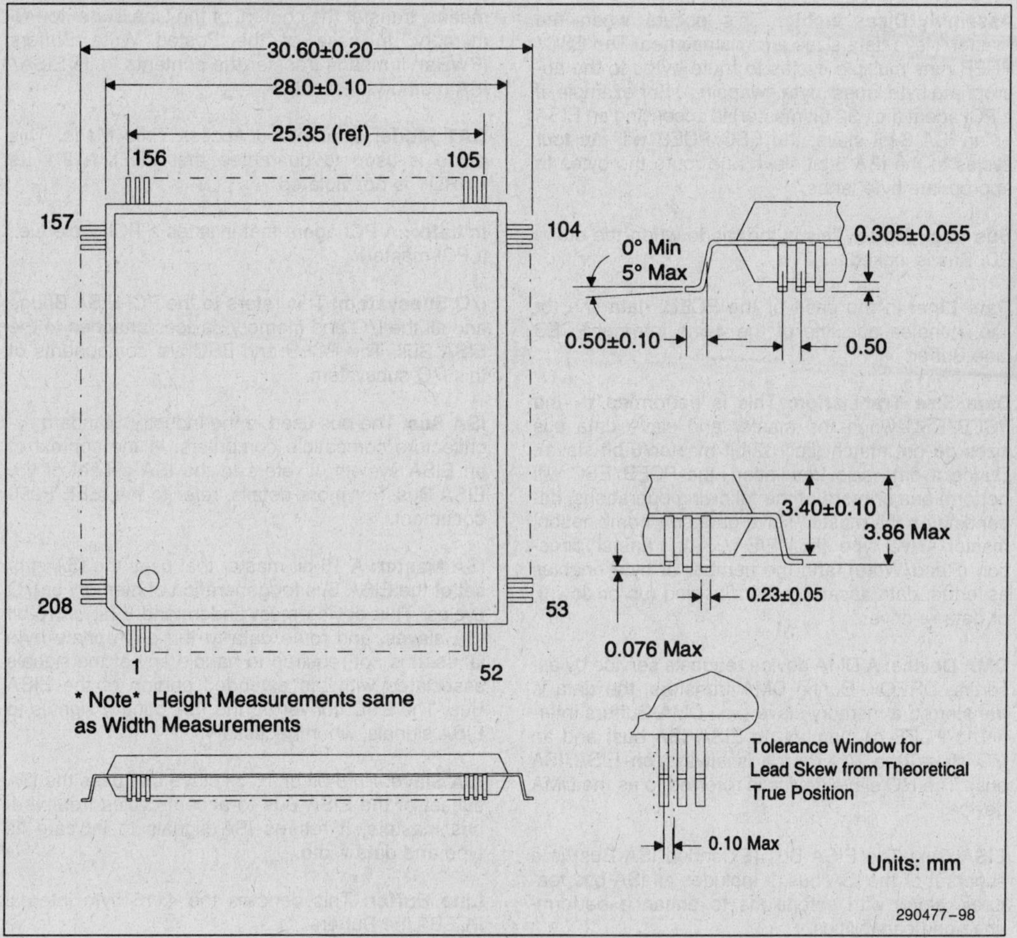

Figure 12-2. 208-Pin Quad Flat Pack (QFP) Dimensions

13.0 TERMINOLOGY

Assembly/Disassembly: This occurs when the master/slave data sizes are mismatched. The ESC/PCEB runs multiple cycles to route bytes to the appropriate byte lanes (byte swapping). For example, if a PCI agent (i.e., 32-bit master) is accessing an EISA or an ISA 8-bit slave, the ESC/PCEB will run four cycles to the ISA 8-bit slave and route the bytes to appropriate byte lanes.

Bus Lock Mode: This is the mode when the entire PCI Bus is locked.

Data Line: In the case of the PCEB, data line (or line) denotes one line of the 4-line internal PCEB Line Buffer.

Data Size Translation: This is performed by the PCEB/ESC when the master and slave data bus sizes do not match (i.e., 32-bit master/8-bit slave). During a data size translation, the PCEB/ESC will perform one or more of the following operations, depending on the master/slave data size combination, master/slave type (PCI/EISA/ISA), transfer direction (Read/Write), and the number of byte enables asserted: data assembly, data coping (up or down), or data re-drive.

DMA Device: A DMA device requests service by asserting DREQx. During DMA transfers, the data is transferred a memory slave (i.e., DMA Buffers internal to PCEB or memory on EISA/ISA bus) and an I/O slave (the I/O device is always on EISA/ISA bus). The I/O slave device is referred to as the DMA device.

EISA Bus: The EISA Bus (Extended ISA Bus) is a superset of the ISA bus. It includes all ISA bus features, along with extensions to enhance performance and capabilities.

EISA Master: A 16-bit or 32-bit bus master that uses the EISA signal set to generate memory or I/O cycles. The ESC component converts the EISA control signals to ISA signals, when necessary.

EISA Slave: An 8-bit, 16-bit, or 32-bit memory I/O slave device that uses the extended signals set of the EISA Bus to accept cycles from various masters. An EISA slave returns information about its type and data width using extended and ISA signals.

ESC: Integrated EISA Peripherals. This component is connected to the EISA/ISA bus and to the PCEB component. The ESC works in tandem with the PCEB component to translate bus protocols between the PCI and EISA/ISA buses.

Flush: Transfer the contents of the buffer to its destination. In the case of the Line Buffers, this term means, transfer the content of the Line Buffer to PCI memory. In case of the Posted Write Buffers (PWBs), it means transfer the contents to its EISA/ISA memory destination.

GAT Mode: Guaranteed Access Time Mode. This mode is used to guarantee that the ISA 2.1 μs CHRDY is not violated.

Initiator: A PCI agent that initiates a PCI cycle (i.e., a PCI master).

I/O Subsystem: This refers to the PCI-EISA Bridge and all the I/O and memory devices attached to the EISA Bus. The PCEB and ESC are components of this I/O subsystem.

ISA Bus: The bus used in the Industry Standard Architecture compatible computers. In the context of an EISA system, it refers to the ISA subset of the EISA Bus. For more details, refer to the IEEE P996 document.

ISA Master: A 16-bit master that uses the ISA subset of the EISA Bus for generation of memory or I/O cycles. This device must understand 8-bit or 16-bit ISA slaves, and route data to the appropriate byte lanes. It is not required to handle any of the signals associated with the extended portion of the EISA Bus. The ESC converted the ISA control signals to EISA signals, when necessary.

ISA Slave: An 8-bit or 16-bit slave that uses the ISA subset of the EISA Bus to accept cycles from various masters. It returns ISA signals to indicate its type and data width.

Line Buffer: This denotes the 4x16 byte internal PCEB Line Buffers.

Memory Subsystem: This consists of the second level (L2) Cache (Cache Controller and SRAMs), the memory (DRAMs, DRAM Controller, Data Buffers), and PCI Bridge.

Mis-matched Data Size: A master and slave that do not have equal data sizes (i.e., PCI agent accessing an 8-bit ISA slave, or a 16-bit DMA device accessing a 32-bit EISA memory slave).

PCEB: PCI-EISA Bridge. This component is connected to the PCI and EISA Buses. The PCEB works in tandem with the ESC component to translate bus protocols between the PCI and the EISA/ISA bus.

PCI: Peripheral Component Interconnect. This is the physical interconnect mechanism intended for use between highly integrated peripheral controller components and processor/memory systems. PCI is a multiplexed version of the Intel 486 bus, with control mechanism modified and extended for optimal I/O support. Refer to PCI Specification Revision 1.0 for more details.

PCI Agent: A 32-bit master that resides on the PCI Bus.

Posted Write Buffers: These are 4-byte wide unidirectional buffers used in the PCEB for PCI master access to EISA/ISA slaves.

Re-drive: This occurs when both the master and slave are on the EISA/ISA bus, and the master/slave data size combination is mismatched (i.e., 32-bit EISA master accessing an 8-bit ISA slave).

During a re-drive cycle, the data is latched from the EISA/ISA bus and then driven back onto the appropriate EISA/ISA byte lane.

Read State: Data residing in the Line Buffers has been READ from the PCI memory.

Target: The destination of the PCI cycle (i.e., a PCI slave).

Target Abort: This resembles the RETRY, though the Target must deassert DEVSEL# along with the assertion of STOP#.

Turn-Around Cycle: This is a required PCI cycle when one or more signals are driven by more than one agent. This cycle is required to avoid contention when one agent stops driving a signal and another agent begins. A turn-around cycle must last at least one clock.

14.0 REVISION HISTORY

The following list represents the key differences between version -001 and version -002 of the 82375EB PCI-EISA Bridge (PCEB) data sheet.

Section 2.2 External pull-up resistor requirements added to CPUGNT#, GNT0#/PCEBREQ#, GNT1#/RESUME#, and GNT[3:2]# signal descriptions.

Section 2.6 External pull-up resistor requirement added to INTCHIP0 signal description.

Section 2.7 External pull-up requirement added for all signals designated as NC (no-connect).

Section 3.1.6 Master Latency Timer Register default value changed from 08h to 00h.

Section 3.1.7 PCI Control Register redefined to allow subtractive decoding of PCI Interrupt Acknowledge cycles.

Section 3.1.9 Previously reserved PCEB configuration register located at offset 43h defined as PCI Arbiter Priority Control Extension. This was done in order to allow programmability for bank 3.

Section 3.1.26 EISA Latency Timer Register default value changed from 00h to 7Fh.

Section 5.1.7 Discussion of PCI Interrupt Acknowledge cycles modified to reflect the subtractive decode option.

Section 5.4.1 Arbiter discussion modified to reflect the programmability of bank 3.

Section 5.4.1.1 Arbiter discussion modified to reflect the programmability of bank 3.

Section 6.1.2 EISA PCI Line Buffer discussion appended to include enhanced read prefetch algorithm.

Section 11.3.6 Changes to A.C. Specifications made.

Section 11.3.7 Changes to A.C. Specifications made.

Section 11.4 NAND Tree information added.

82378
SYSTEM I/O (SIO)

- Provides the Bridge between the PCI Bus and ISA Bus
- 100% PCI and ISA Compatible
  - PCI and ISA Master/Slave Interface
  - Directly Drives 10 PCI Loads and 6 ISA Slots
  - Supports PCI at 25 MHz and 33.33 MHz
  - Supports ISA from 6 MHz to 8.33 MHz
- Enhanced DMA Functions
  - Scatter/Gather
  - Fast DMA Type A, B, and F
  - Compatible DMA Transfers
  - 32-Bit Addressability
  - Seven Independently Programmable Channels
  - Functionality of Two 82C37A DMA Controllers
- Integrated Data Buffers to Improve Performance
  - 8-Byte DMA/ISA Master Line Buffer
  - 32-Bit Posted Memory Write Buffer to ISA
- Arbitration for PCI Devices
  - Two or Four External PCI Masters Are Supported
  - Fixed, Rotating, or a Combination of the Two
- Integrated 16-Bit BIOS Timer
- Arbitration for ISA Devices
  - ISA Masters
  - DMA and Refresh
- Utility Bus (X-Bus) Peripheral Support
  - Provides Chip Select Decode
  - Controls Lower X-Bus Data Byte Transceiver
  - Integrates Port 92, Mouse Interrupt, Coprocessor Error Reporting
- Integrates the Functionality of One 82C54 Timer
  - System Timer
  - Refresh Request
  - Speaker Tone Output
- Integrates the Functionality of Two 82C59 Interrupt Controllers
  - 14 Interrupts Supported
- Non-Maskable Interrupts (NMI)
  - PCI System Errors
  - ISA Parity Errors
- 208-Pin QFP Package
- 5V CMOS Technology
- Four Dedicated PCI Interrupts
  - Level Sensitive
  - Can be Mapped to Any Unused Interrupt
- Complete Support for SL Enhanced Intel486 CPU's
  - SMI# Generation Based on System Hardware Events
  - STPCLK# Generation to Power Down the CPU

The 82378 System I/O (SIO) component provides the bridge between the PCI local bus and the ISA expansion bus. The SIO also integrates many of the common I/O functions found in today's ISA based PC systems. The SIO incorporates the logic for a PCI interface (master and slave), ISA interface (master and slave), enhanced seven channel DMA controller that supports fast DMA transfers and Scatter/Gather, data buffers to isolate the PCI bus from the ISA bus and to enhance performance. PCI and ISA arbitration, 14 level interrupt controller, a 16-bit BIOS timer, three programmable timer/counters, and non-maskable-interrupt (NMI) control logic. The SIO also provides decode for peripheral devices such as the Flash BIOS, Real Time Clock, Keyboard/Mouse Controller, Floppy Controller, two Serial Ports, one Parallel Port, and IDE Hard Disk Drive.

This data sheet describes the 82378IB and 82378ZB components. All normal text describes the functionality for both components. All features that exist on the 82378ZB are shaded as shown below.

This is an example of what the shaded sections that apply only to the 82378ZB component look like.

October 1993
Order Number: 290473-003

SIO Block Diagram

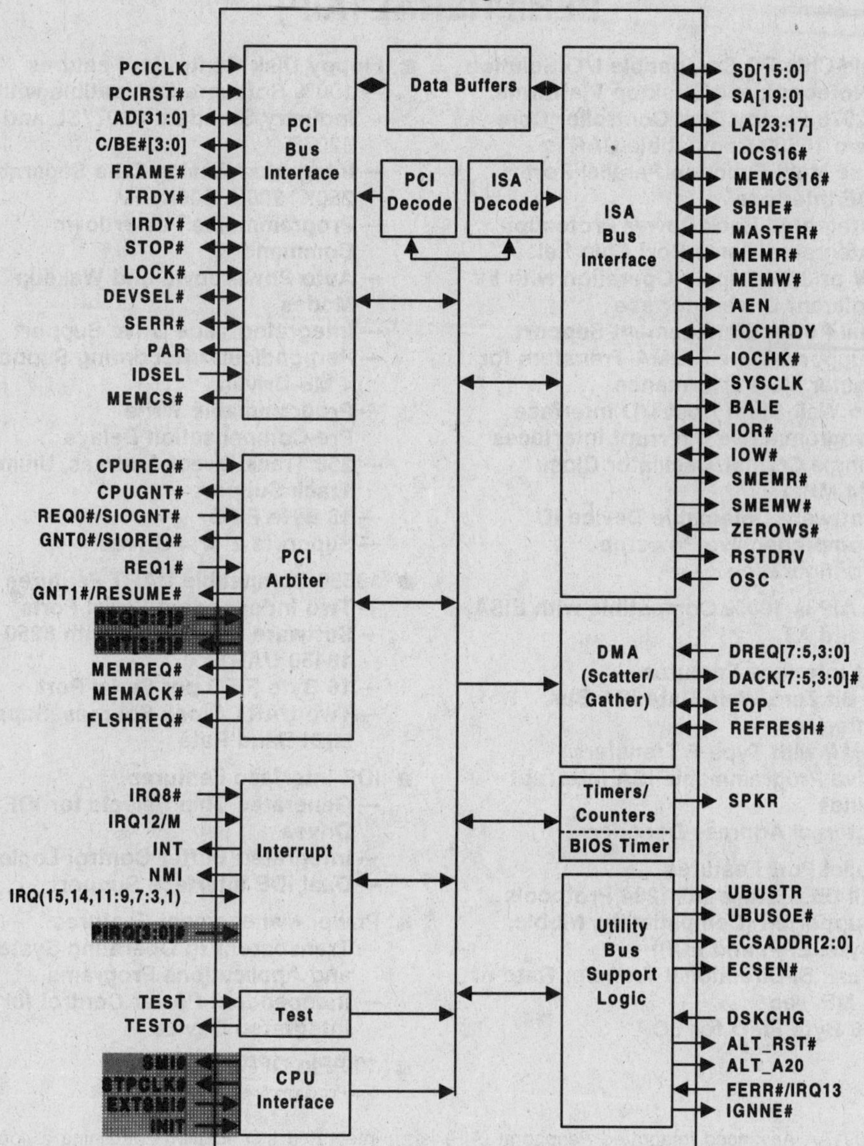

82091AA ADVANCED INTEGRATED PERIPHERAL (AIP)

- Single-Chip PC Compatible I/O Solution for Notebook and Desktop Platforms:
  - 82078 Floppy Disk Controller Core
  - Two 16550 Compatible UARTs
  - One Multi-Function Parallel Port
  - IDE Interface
  - Integrated Back Power Protection
  - Integrated Game Port Chip Select
  - 5V or 3.3V Supply Operation with 5V Tolerant Drive Interface
  - Full Power Management Support
  - Supports Type F DMA Transfers for Faster I/O Performance
  - No Wait-State Host I/O Interface
  - Programmable Interrupt Interfaces
  - Single Crystal/Oscillator Clock (24 MHz)
  - Software Detectable Device ID
  - Comprehensive Powerup Configuration
- The AIP is 100% Compatible with EISA, ISA and AT
- Host Interface Features
  - 8-Bit Zero Wait-State ISA Bus Interface
  - DMA with Type F Transfers
  - Five Programmable ISA Interrupt Lines
  - Internal Address Decoder
- Parallel Port Features
  - All IEEE Standard 1284 Protocols Supported (Compatibility, Nibble, Byte, EPP, and ECP)
  - Peak Bi-Directional Transfer Rate of 2 MB/sec
  - 16 Byte FIFO for ECP
- Floppy Disk Controller Features
  - 100% Software Compatible with Industry Standard 82077SL and 82078
  - Integrated Analog Data Separator 250K, 300K, 500K, 1M
  - Programmable Powerdown Command
  - Auto Powerdown and Wakeup Modes
  - Integrated Tape Drive Support
  - Perpendicular Recording Support for 4 MB Drives
  - Programmable Write Pre-Compensation Delays
  - 256 Track Direct Address, Unlimited Track Support
  - 16 Byte FIFO
  - Supports 2 or 4 Drives
- 16550 Compatible UART Features
  - Two Independent Serial Ports
  - Software Compatible with 8250 and 16450 UARTs
  - 16 Byte FIFO per Serial Port
  - Two UART Clock Sources, Supports MIDI Baud Rate
- IDE Interface Features
  - Generates Chip Selects for IDE Drives
  - Integrated Buffer Control Logic
  - Dual IDE Interface Support
- Power Management Features
  - Transparent to Operating Systems and Applications Programs
  - Independent Power Control for Each Integrated Device
- 100-Pin QFP Package

  See Packaging Spec. 240800

The 82091AA Advanced Integrated Peripheral (AIP) is an integrated I/O solution containing a floppy disk controller, 2 serial ports, a multi-function parallel port, an IDE interface, and a game port on a single chip. The integration of these I/O devices results in a minimization of form factor, cost and power consumption. The floppy disk controller is the 82078 core with a data rate up to 2 Mbs. The serial ports are 16550 compatible. The parallel port supports all of the IEEE Standard 1284 protocols (ECP, EPP, Byte, Compatibility, and Nibble). The IDE interface supports 8-bit or 16-bit programmed I/O and 16-bit DMA. The Host Interface is an 8-bit ISA

October 1993
Order Number: 290486-001

interface optimized for type "F" DMA and no wait-state I/O accesses. Improved throughput and performance, the AIP contains six 16-byte FIFOstwo for each serial port, one for the parallel port, and one for the floppy disk controller. The AIP also includes power management and 3.3V capability for power sensitive applications such as notebooks. The AIP supports both motherboard and add-in card configurations.

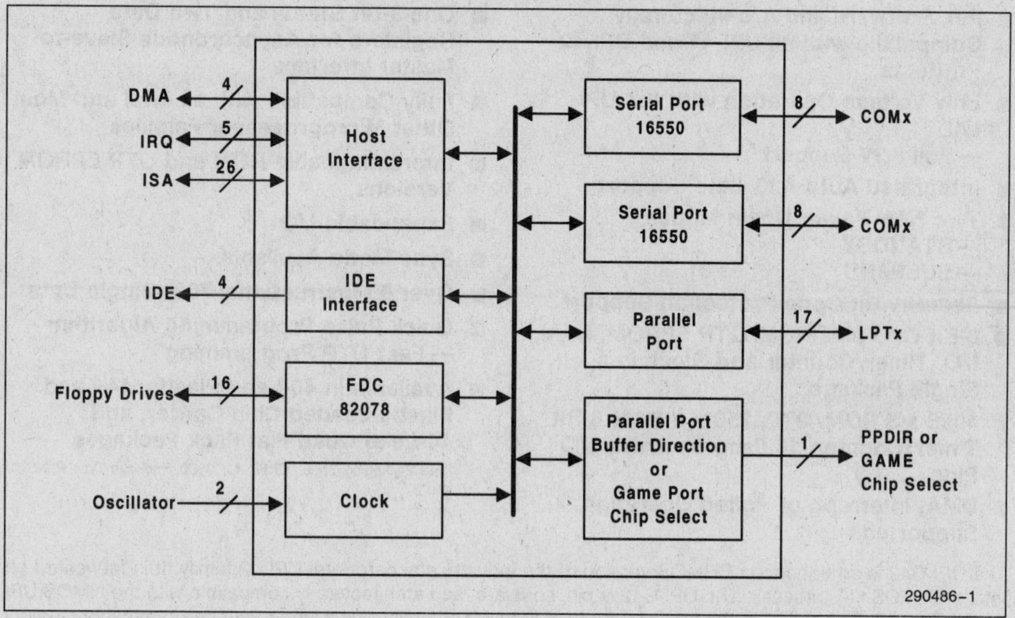

Figure 1. 82091AA Advanced Integrated Peripheral Block Diagram

PRELIMINARY

UPI-C42/UPI-L42 UNIVERSAL PERIPHERAL INTERFACE CHMOS 8-BIT SLAVE MICROCONTROLLER

- Pin, Software and Architecturally Compatible with all UPI-41 and UPI-42 Products
- Low Voltage Operation with the UPI-L42
  - — Full 3.3V Support
- Integrated Auto A20 Gate Support
- Two New Power Down Modes
  - — STANDBY
  - — SUSPEND
- Security Bit Code Protection Support
- 8-Bit CPU plus ROM/OTP EPROM, RAM, I/O, Timer/Counter and Clock in a Single Package
- 4096 x 8 ROM/OTP, 256 x 8 RAM 8-Bit Timer/Counter, 18 Programmable I/O Pins
- DMA, Interrupt, or Polled Operation Supported
- One 8-Bit Status and Two Data Registers for Asynchronous Slave-to-Master Interface
- Fully Compatible with all Intel and Most Other Microprocessor Families
- Interchangeable ROM and OTP EPROM Versions
- Expandable I/O
- Sync Mode Available
- Over 90 Instructions: 70% Single Byte
- Quick Pulse Programming Algorithm
  - — Fast OTP Programming
- Available in 40-Lead Plastic, 44-Lead Plastic Leaded Chip Carrier, and 44-Lead Quad Flat Pack Packages

(See Packaging Spec., Order #240800, Package Type P, N, and S)

The UPI-C42 is an enhanced CHMOS version of the industry standard Intel UPI-42 family. It is fabricated on Intel's CHMOS III-E process. The UPI-C42 is pin, software, and architecturally compatible with the NMOS UPI family. The UPI-C42 has all of the same features of the NMOS family plus a larger user programmable memory array (4K), integrated auto A20 gate support, and lower power consumption inherent to a CHMOS product.

The UPI-L42 offers the same functionality and socket compatibility as the UPI-C42 as well as providing low voltage 3.3V operation.

The UPI-C42 is essentially a "slave" microcontroller, or a microcontroller with a slave interface included on the chip. Interface registers are included to enable the UPI device to function as a slave peripheral controller in the MCS Modules and iAPX family, as well as other 8-, 16-, and 32-bit systems.

To allow full user flexibility, the program memory is available in ROM and One-Time Programmable EPROM (OTP).

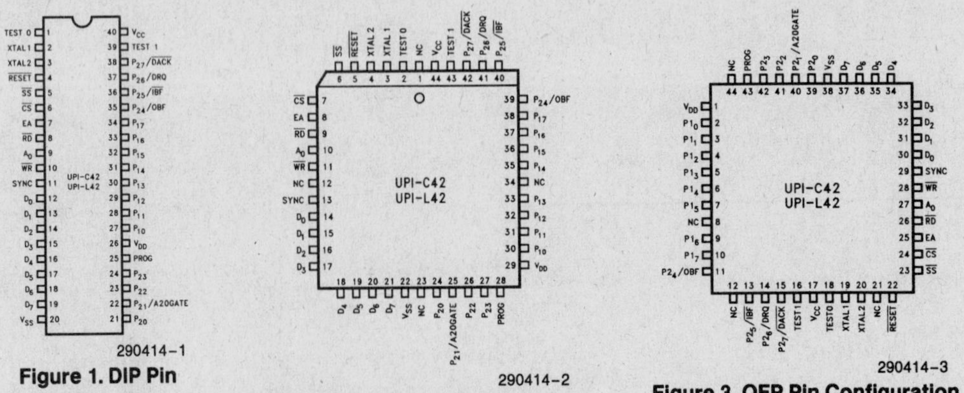

Figure 1. DIP Pin Configuration

Figure 2. PLCC Pin Configuration

Figure 3. QFP Pin Configuration

Refer to Chapter 4 for the complete data sheet on this device.

October 1993
Order Number: 290414-003

1

82350 EISA Chip Set

September 1992

Order Number: 290220-004

82350 EISA CHIP SET

CONTENTS

PAGE

EISA TERMINOLOGY

ISA BUS— The bus used in Industry Standard Architecture compatible computers. In the context of an EISA system, it refers to the ISA subset of the EISA bus.

EISA BUS— Extended ISA bus, a superset of the ISA bus. It includes all ISA bus features, along with extensions to enhance performance and capabilities.

HOST CPU— The main system processor, located on a separate Host Bus. This uses the EBC and other system board facilities to interface to the EISA bus.

CPU CYCLE— 386 CPU and/or the 82385 subsystem, or 80486 CPU is the master running the cycle.

EISA MASTER— A 16-bit or 32-bit bus master that uses the EISA signal set to generate memory or I/O cycles. The bus controller will convert the EISA control signals to ISA signals, when necessary.

ISA MASTER—A 16-bit bus master that uses the ISA subset of the EISA bus for generation of memory or I/O cycles. This device must understand 8-bit or 16-bit ISA slaves, and route data to the appropriate byte lanes. It is not required to handle any of the signals associated with the extended portion of the EISA bus.

EISA SLAVE— An 8-bit, 16-bit or 32-bit memory or I/O slave device that uses the extended signal set of the EISA bus to accept cycles from various masters. It returns information about its type and width using extended and ISA signals.

ISA SLAVE— A 16-bit or 8-bit slave that uses the ISA subset of the EISA bus to accept cycles from various masters. !t returns ISA signals to indicate its type and width.

DMA SLAVE— An I/O device that uses the DMA signals (DREQ, DACK#) of the system board ISP to perform a direct memory access.

ISACMD— The ISA command signals (IORC#, IOWC#, MRDC#, MWTC#)

ASSEMBLY/DISASSEMBLY— This occurs when the master/slave data bus size are mismatched. The EBC runs multiple cycles to route bytes to the appropriate byte lanes (byte swapping). For example, if the 32-bit CPU is accessing an 8-bit slave, the EBC will need to run four cycles to the 8-bit slave and route the bytes to appropriate byte lanes.

CYCLE TRANSLATION— This is performed by the EBC when the master and slave are on different busses (Host/EISA/ISA). The EBC will translate the master protocol to the slave protocol (Host master accessing EISA slave).

EISA System Introduction

Extended Industry Standard Architecture (EISA) is a high performance 32-bit architecture based upon the Industry Standard Architecture (ISA) (PC AT*). The wide acceptance of the 32-bit 386 microprocessor family has led to this interest in extending ISA to 32-bits. EISA's advanced capabilities and 32-bit architecture can unleash the full potential of the 386 and i486™ CPUs.

The EISA consortium has defined the EISA bus in response to the demand for a 32-bit high performance ISA compatible system. The open industry standard allows for industry wide participation, compatibility, and differentiation.

EISA brings advances in performance and convenience to the user. It provides 32-bit memory addressing and data transfers for CPU, DMA and bus masters allowing 33 Mbyte/second transfer rate for DMA and bus masters on the EISA bus. EISA provides a specification for auto-configuration of add-in cards that will eliminate the need for jumpers and switches on EISA cards. Interrupts are shareable and programmable. Figure 1 and 2 show the types of busses in an EISA system. A new bus-arbitration makes possible a new generation of intelligent bus master add-in cards that bring advanced applications to PCs.

Since the EISA system is 100% compatible with the ISA 8-bit and 16-bit expansion boards and software, ISA cards can be plugged into the EISA connector slots. The EISA slots can be defined as ISA or EISA for ease of compatibility during configuration. The EISA connector is a superset of the ISA connector maintaining full compatibility with ISA expansion cards and software. Simultaneous use of EISA and ISA add-in boards is available with automatic system and expansion board configuration.

82350 EISA Chip Set Highlights

The Intel 82350 EISA chip set is the industry's first 100% EISA/ISA compatible chip set. The 82350

EISA chip set supports the 33 MHz and 25 MHz 386 CPU or i486 CPU, 82385 Cache Controller, and optional 80387 numerics coprocessor. The EISA chip set includes three chips:

82352DT	EISA Bus Buffers (EBB) (Optional)
82357	Integrated System Peripheral (ISP)
82358	EISA Bus Controller (EBC)

Information on the 82352DT EBB device is located in a separate data sheet.

The ISP performs the DMA functions of the system and is fully compatible with ISA functions. It integrates seven 32-bit DMA channels, five 16-bit timer/counters, two eight channel interrupt controllers, and provides for multiple NMI control and generation. It provides refresh address generation and keeps track of pending refresh requests when the bus is unavailable. The ISP supports multiple EISA bus masters while offering intelligent system arbiter services which grant the bus on a rotational basis.

The EBC is the EISA "engine". It is an intelligent bus controller that controls 8, 16 and 32-bit bus masters and slaves. It provides the state machine interface to Host, ISA and EISA busses and other IC's in the chip set. It offers a simple interface to the 386/i486 CPU and EISA bus. The EBC services as a bridge between the EISA and ISA devices. Data bus size mismatches are handled automatically by the EBC (including byte assembly and disassembly). It also guarantees cache operation on the Host, EISA, and ISA busses.

More information on EBC and ISP devices can be found in the data sheets in this document.

The 82355 Bus Master Interface Chip (BMIC) is a new device for add-in cards that takes advantage of the EISA bus master capabilities. Information on the 82355 BMIC is located in a separate data sheet.

290220-1

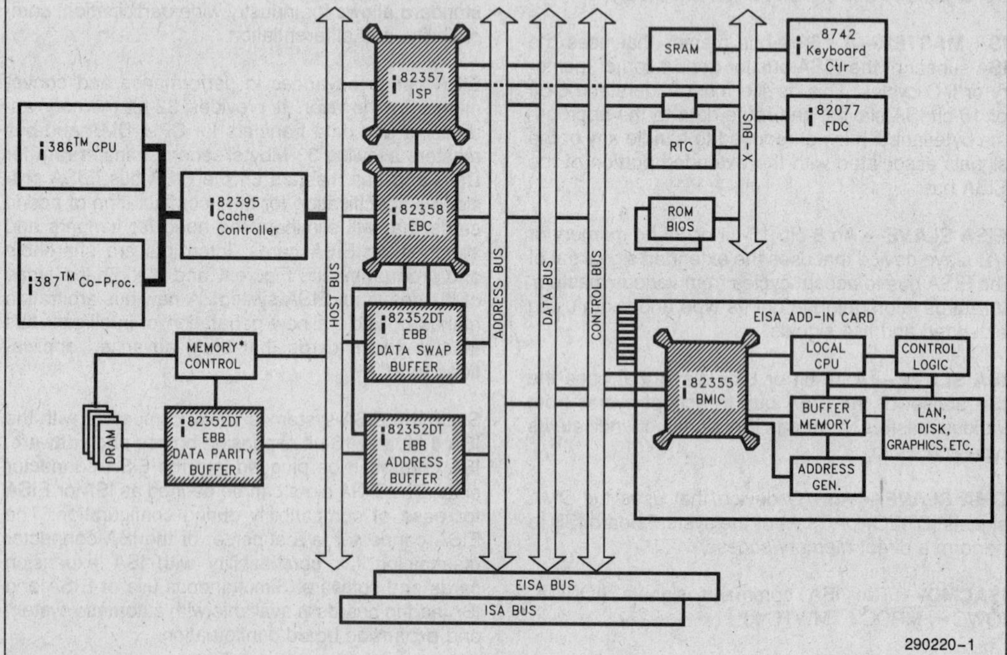

NOTE:
*Memory Controller can be implemented as:
1) Discrete
2) ASIC (Custom)
3) ASIC (Standard)

Figure 1. Intel's 386 CPU System with 82350 EISA Chip Set

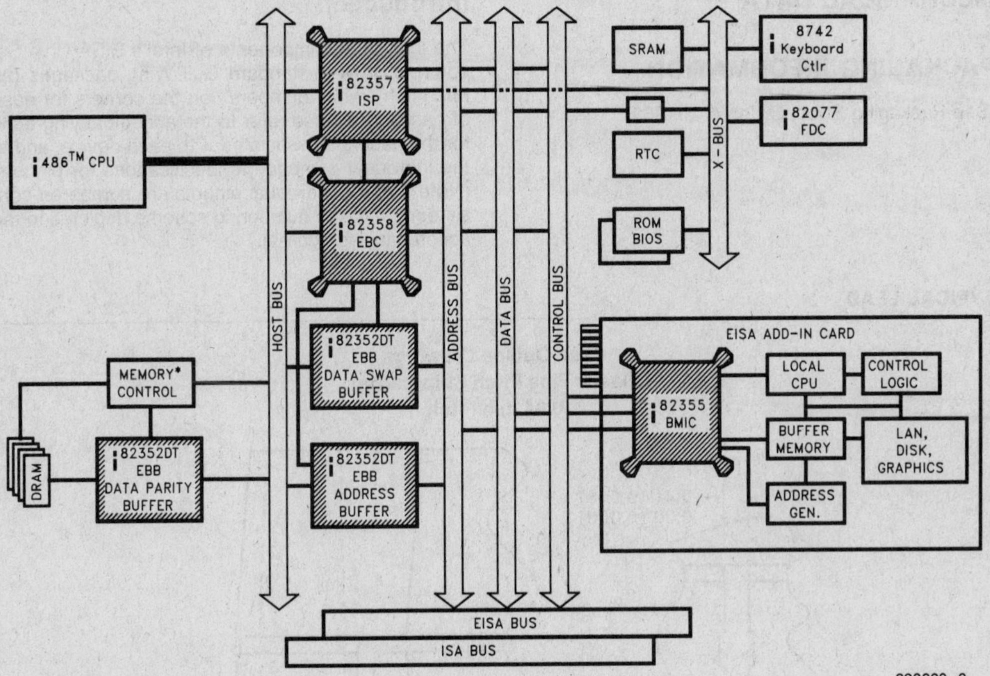

NOTE:
*Memory Controller can be implemented as:
1) Discrete
2) ASIC (Custom)
3) ASIC (Standard)

Figure 2. Intel's i486™ CPU System with 82350 EISA Chip Set

1

MECHANICAL DATA

PACKAGING INFORMATION

(See Packaging Spec. Order # 231369)

Introduction

The individual components of Intel's EISA Chip Set come in JEDEC standard Gull Wing packages (25 MIL pitch), with "bumpers" on the corners for ease of handling. Please refer to the accompanying table for the package associated with each device, and to the individual component specifications for pinouts. (Note that the individual pinouts are numbered consistently with the numbering scheme depicted in the accompanying figures).

TYPICAL LEAD

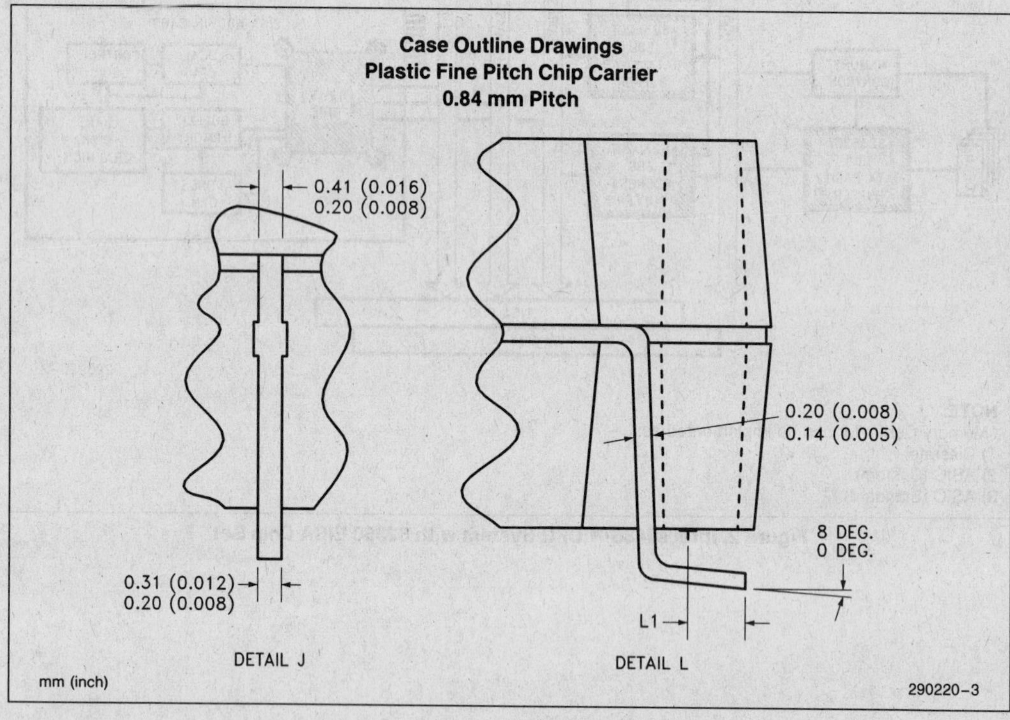

Symbol	Description	Inch		mm	
		Min	Max	Min	Max
N	Lead Count	132		132	
A	Package Height	0.160	0.170	4.06	4.32
A1	Standoff	0.020	0.030	0.51	0.76
D, E	Terminal Dimension	1.075	1.085	27.31	27.56
D1, E1	Package Body	0.947	0.953	24.05	24.21
D2, E2	Bumper Distance	1.097	1.103	27.86	28.02
D3, E3	Lead Dimension	0.800 Ref		20.32 Ref	
L1	Foot Length	0.020	0.030	0.51	0.76

PRINCIPAL DIMENSIONS & DATUMS

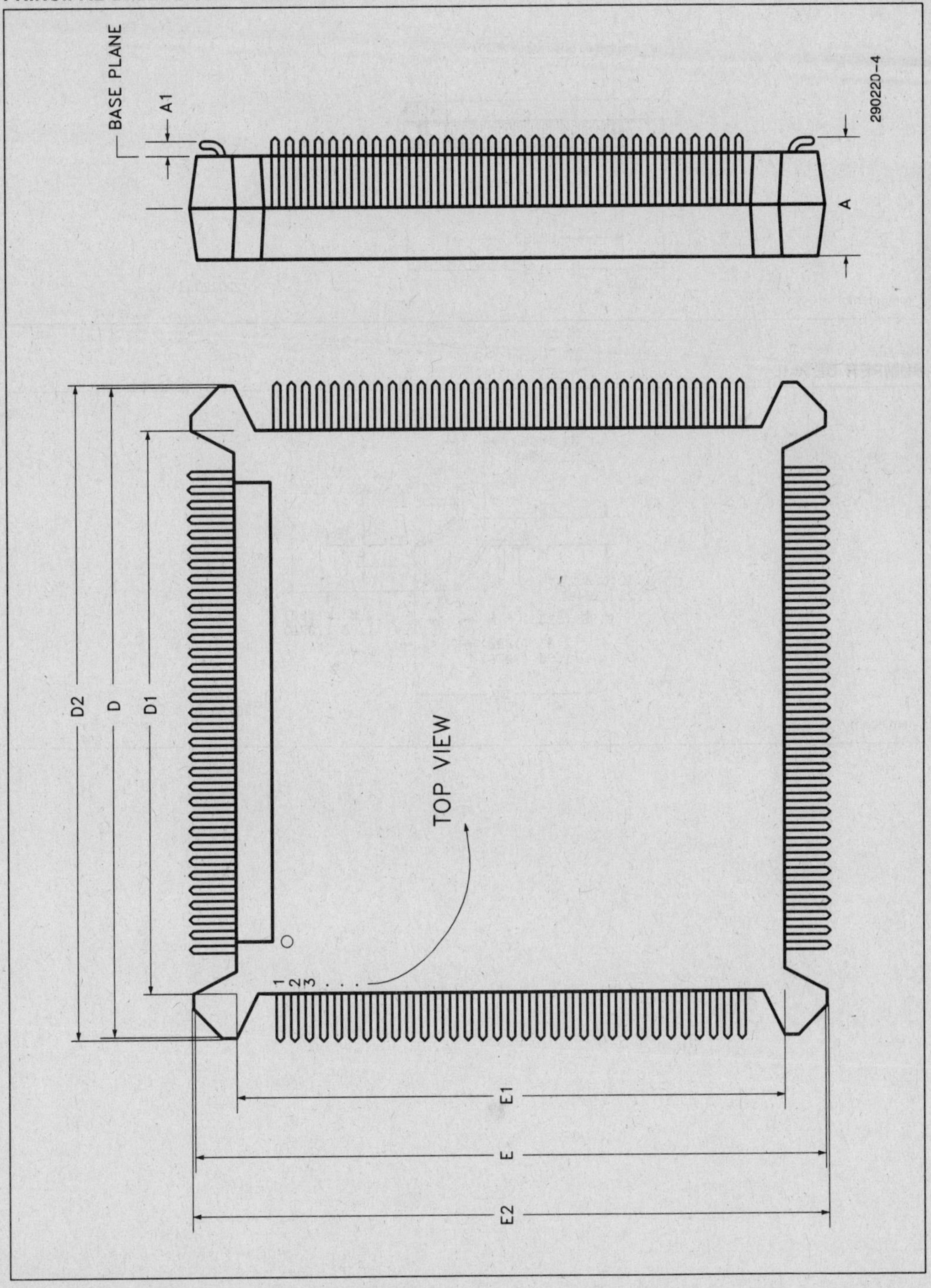

TERMINAL DETAILS

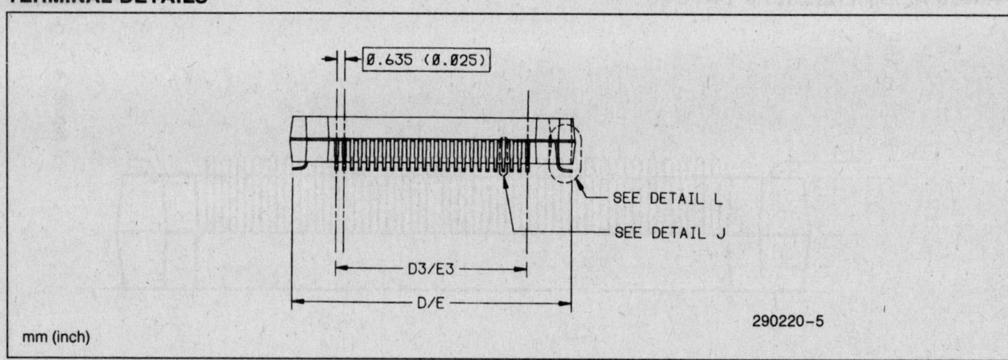

BUMPER DETAIL

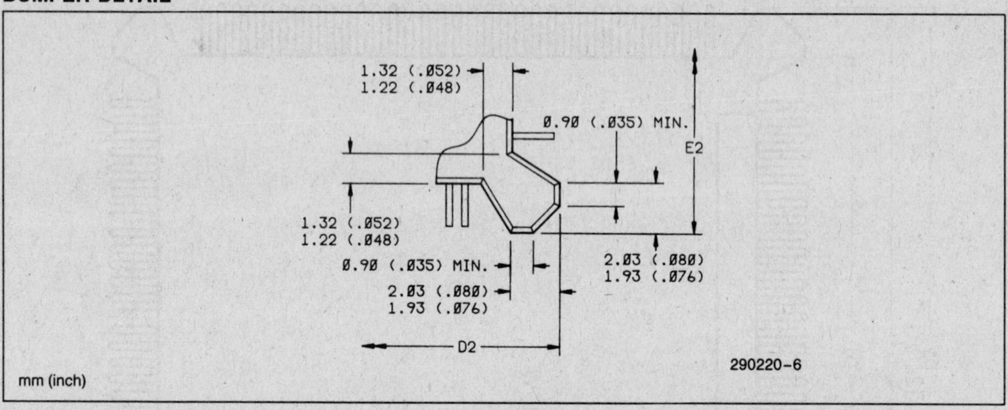

1

Package Thermal Specification

The 82357 ISP and 82358 EBC are specified for operation when the case temperature is within the range of 0°C to 85°C. The case temperature may be measured in any environment, to determine whether the device is within the specified operating range.

The PQFP case temperature should be measured at the center of the top surface opposite the pins, as shown in the figure below.

PLASTIC QUAD FLAT PACK (PQFP)

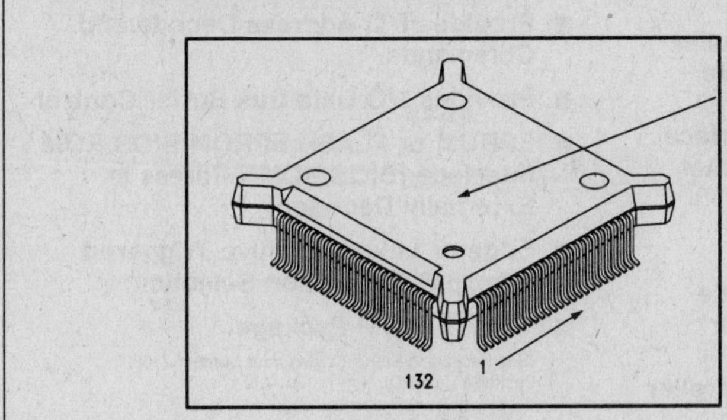

290220–7

Table 2. 82357 ISP and 82358 DT EBC PQFP Package Thermal Characteristics

Parameter	Thermal Resistance— °C/Watt						
	Air Flow Rate (ft/min)						
	0	50	100	200	400	600	800
θ Junction—Case	7	7	7	7	7	7	7
θ Case to Ambient	22	21	19.5	17.5	14.5	12	10

NOTES:
1. Table 2 applies to the PQFP device plugged into a socket or soldered directly into the board.
2. $\theta_{JA} = \theta_{JC} + \theta_{CA}$.

PROCESS NAME:
1.2μ CHMOS III P-well

I_{CC} AT HOT WITH NO RESISTIVE LOADS:
150 mA Max at 85°C.

82351 LOCAL I/O EISA SUPPORT PERIPHERAL (LIO.E)

- **EISA and PC/AT System Fully Compatible Local I/O Controller**
- **Integrates:**
  - **—Local I/O Address Decoder**
  - **—EISA System Configuration Registers**
  - **—Fast CPU Reset and A20 Gate Port (92h)**
  - **—Two External Serial I/O Controller Interfaces with Four Assignable Interrupts Generation**
  - **—External Real Time Clock Interface**
  - **—External EISA Configuration RAM Interface**
  - **—Parallel Port Interface**
  - **—i486 and 386 CPU Compatible Numeric Co-Processor Interface**
  - **—External Floppy Disk Controller Interface**
  - **—External Keyboard (8x42) Controller Interface including Interrupt Generation**
  - **—EISA System ID Register**
- **Fast A20GATE, CPU RESET, and FLUSH# Generation by Snooping Keyboard Controller Commands**
- **Four Programmable General Purpose Chip Selects for Additional Local I/O Devices**
- **Provides I/O Address Decode and Commands**
- **Provides I/O Data Bus Buffer Control**
- **EPROM or FLASH EPROM BIOS ROM Interface (BIOS ROM Address is Externally Decoded)**
- **Edge or Level Sensitive Triggered Interrupt Generation Selection**
- **132 Pin PQFP Package**

  (See Packaging Specification Order Number 240800, Package Type KD)

Standard Configuration

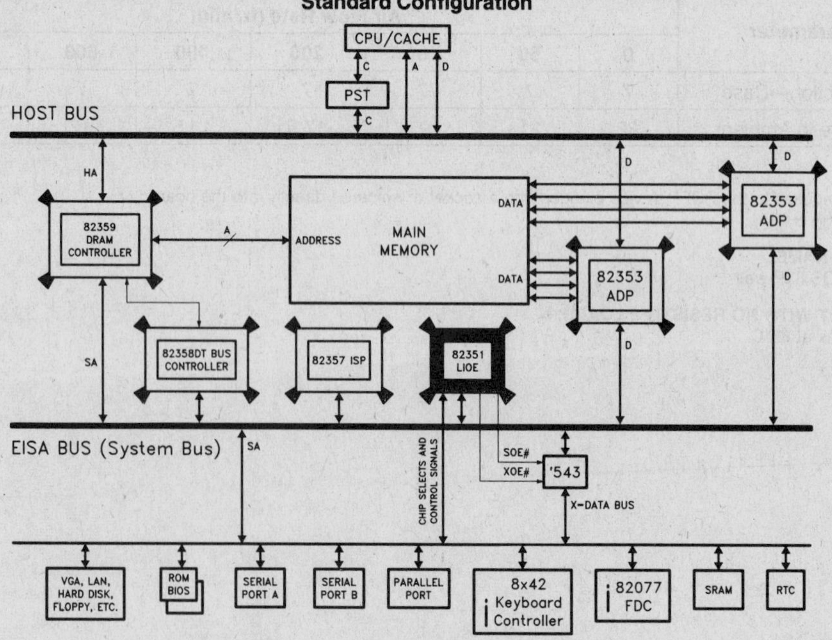

Figure 1-1. System Block Diagram

The complete document for this product is available on Intel's "Data-on-Demand" CD-ROM system. To obtain a copy, contact your local Intel field sales office, Intel technical distributor or call 1-800-548-4725.

October 1992
Order Number: 290386-005

82352DT EISA BUS BUFFER (EBB)

- **Designed Specifically for EISA Bus Requirements**
- **Provides Three Modes of Operation**
  - **— Data Latch and Swap Functions Allow Swapping and Assembly of Data between the Host and EISA/ISA Buses on a Byte by Byte Basis (Mode 0)**
  - **— Provides a Buffered Path with Parity Generation/Check between the Host Data Bus and DRAM (Mode 1)**
  - **— Address Latch Functions Provide Latching between the Host and EISA/ISA Buses (LA and SA Addresses) (Mode 3)**
- **120-Pin Quad Flat Pack (QFP)**
- **Similar in Function to Discrete Implementation Using 74F543s/544, 74180s, and 74ALS245s**
- **Replaces 19 Discrete Components**
  - **— Three 82352DTs are Used Per 82350 EISA System**
- **The 82352DT Interfaces Easily to the System**
  - **— Buffer Control for the 32-Bit Mode W/O Parity and the EISA Address Mode is Provided by the 82358 (EISA Bus Controller)**

(See Packaging Specification Order Number 240800, Package Type S)

1

The 82352DT design allows it to replace the multiple address and data latch-buffer/driver ICs used in EISA applications. The EBB provides three modes of operation: a 32-bit mode without parity to replace the EISA data swap buffers, a 32-bit mode with parity to replace the EISA DRAM data parity buffers, and an EISA address mode to replace the host to EISA/ISA address buffers. Mode 2 on the EBB is reserved. The same chip is strapped in three different ways to obtain the three configurations.

82352DT is manufactured and tested for Intel by LSI Logic in accordance with their internal standards.

The complete document for this product is available on Intel's "Data-on-Demand" CD-ROM system. To obtain a copy, contact your local Intel field sales office, Intel technical distributor or call 1-800-548-4725.

October 1993
Order Number: 290254-007

PRELIMINARY

82357
INTEGRATED SYSTEM PERIPHERAL (ISP)

- **Provides Enhanced DMA Functions**
  - **ISA/EISA DMA Compatible Cycles**
  - **All Transfers are Fly-By Transfers**
  - **32-Bit Addressability**
  - **Seven Independently Programmable Channels**
  - **Provides Timing Control for 8-, 16-, and 32-Bit DMA Data Transfers**
  - **Provides Timing Control for Compatible, Type "A", Type "B", and Type "C" (Burst) Cycle Types**
  - **33 Mbytes/sec Maximum Data Transfer Rate**
  - **Provides Refresh Address Generation**
  - **Supports Data Communication Devices and Other Devices That Work from a Ring Buffer in Memory**
  - **Incorporates the Functionality of Two 82C37A DMA Controllers**
- **Provides High Performance Arbitration**
  - **For CPU, EISA/ISA Bus Masters, DMA Channels, and Refresh**
- **Incorporates the Functionality of Two 82C59A Interrupt Controllers**
  - **14 Independently Programmable Channels for Level-or-Edge Triggered Interrupts**
- **Five Programmable 16-Bit Counter/Timers**
  - **Generates Refresh Request Signal**
  - **System Timer Interrupt**
  - **Speaker Tone Output**
  - **Fail-Safe Timer**
  - **Periodic CPU Speed Control**
  - **82C54 Programmable Interval Timer Compatible**
- **Provides Logic for Generation/Control of Non-Maskable Interrupts**
  - **Parity Errors for System and Expansion Board Memory**
  - **8 μs and 32 μs Bus Timeout**
  - **Immediate NMI Interrupt via Software Control**
  - **Fail-Safe Timer**
- **132-Pin PQFP Package**
  (See Packaging Specifications: Order Number 240800, Package Type NG)

82357 Internal Block Diagram

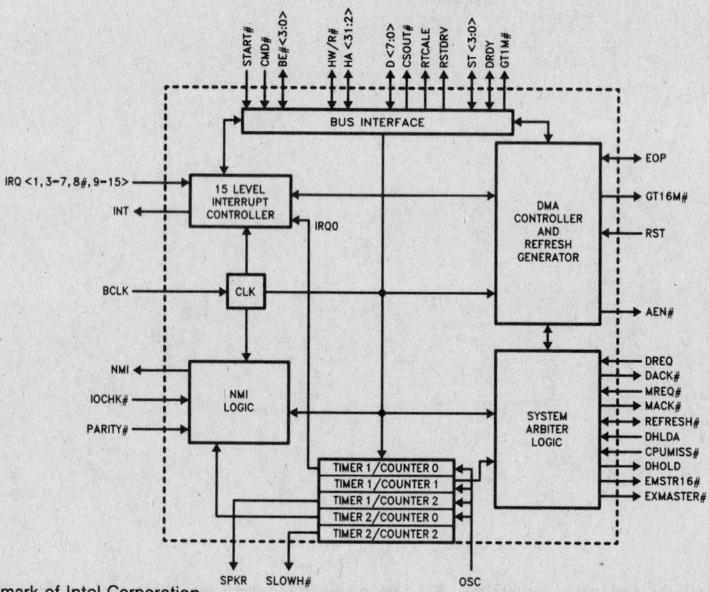

290253-78

Intel486 is a trademark of Intel Corporation.

The complete document for this product is available on Intel's "Data-on-Demand" CD-ROM system. To obtain a copy, contact your local Intel field sales office, Intel technical distributor or call 1-800-548-4725.

October 1992
Order Number: 290253-006

82358DT EISA BUS CONTROLLER

- **Supports 82350 and 82350DT Chip Set Based Systems**
  - **Mode Selectable for Either 82350 or 82350DT Based Systems**
  - **Mode Defaults to 82350 Based Systems**
- **Socket Compatible with the 82358 (EISA Bus Controller)**
- **Provides EISA/ISA Bus Cycle Compatibility**
  - **EISA/ISA Standard Memory or I/O Cycles**
  - **EISA/ISA Wait State Cycles**
  - **ISA No Wait State Cycles**
  - **EISA Burst Cycles**
- **Supports Intel386™ & Intel486™ Microprocessors**
- **Translates Host (CPU) and 82359 (DRAM Controller) Cycles to EISA/ISA Bus Cycles**
- **Generates ISA Signals for EISA Masters**
- **Generates EISA Signals for ISA Masters**
- **Supports 8-, 16-, or 32-bit DMA Cycles**
  - **Type A, B, or C (Burst) Cycles**
  - **Compatible Cycles**
- **Supports Host and EISA/ISA Refresh Cycles**
- **Generates Control Signals for Address and Data Buffers**
  - **82353 (ADP) and 82352 (EBB)**
- **Supports Byte Assembly/Disassembly for 8-, 16-, or 32-Bit Transfers**
- **Selectable Host (CPU) Posted Memory Write Support to EISA/ISA Bus**
- **Cache Controller (82385, 82395) Interface to Maximize Performance for 386 Based Systems**
- **Supports I/O Recovery Mechanism**
- **Generates CPU, 82385, and System Software Resets**
- **132-Pin PQFP Package**
- **Low Power CHMOS Technology**

(See Packaging Specification Order #240800, Package Type NG)

The 82358DT EISA Bus Controller is part of Intel's 82350 and 82350DT chip sets. There are five mode or function select pins which allow the 82358DT to be programmed for use in either 82350 or 82350DT based systems. The mode pins also provide support for posted memory write cycles to the EISA/ISA bus and Intel486™ burst support. The 82358DT defaults to 82350 mode and is 100% socket compatible with the 82358 (EBC).

The 82358DT interfaces the 386 and Intel486 microprocessors to the Extended Industry Standard Architecture (EISA) bus. It is used to facilitate bus cycles between the Host (CPU) bus and the EISA/ISA bus. In an 82350 system, the 82358DT interfaces to the cycle address and control signals of the Host bus. In an 82350DT system, the 82358DT interfaces to the cycle address and control signals of the 82359 DRAM controller. The 82358DT generates the appropriate data conversion and alignment control signals to implement an external byte assembly/disassembly mechanism for transferring data of different widths between the Host, EISA, and Industry Standard Architecture (ISA) buses. It also provides the cycle translation between the Host, EISA, and ISA buses.

The 82358DT is tightly coupled with the 82357 DMA controller (ISP) to run 8-. 16-, or 32-Bit EISA/ISA DMA transfers.

The 82358DT features hardware enforced I/O recovery logic to provide I/O recovery time between back- to-back I/O cycles.

The 82358DT provides special cache hardware interface signals to implement a high performance 386 based system with an 82385 or 82395 cache controller.

The 82358DT also provides resets to the Intel486, 80386, 82385, and other devices in the system to provide an integrated synchronous system reset.

The complete document for this product is available on Intel's "Data-on-Demand" CD-ROM system. To obtain a copy, contact your local Intel field sales office, Intel technical distributor or call 1-800-548-4725.

October 1992
Order Number: 290380-004

82355 BUS MASTER INTERFACE CONTROLLER (BMIC)

- **Designed for use in 32-Bit EISA Bus Master Expansion Board Designs**
  - **—Integrates Three Interfaces (EISA, Local CPU, and Transfer Buffer)**
- **Supports 16- and 32-Bit Burst Transfers**
  - **—33 Mbytes/Sec Maximum Data Transfers**
- **Supports 32-Bit Non-Burst and Mismatched Data Size Transfers**
- **Supports 32-Bit EISA Addressability (4 Gigabyte)**
- **Two independent Data Transfer Channels with 24-Byte FIFOs**
  - **—Expansion Board Timing and EISA Timing Operate Asynchronously**
- **Supports Peek/Poke Operation with the Ability to Access Individual Locations in EISA Memory or I/O space**
- **Automatically Handles Misaligned Doubleword Data Transfers with No Performance Penalty**
- **Supports Automatic Handling of Complete EISA Bus Master Protocol**
  - **—EISA Arbitration/Preemption**
  - **—Cycle Timing and Execution**
  - **—Byte Alignment**
  - **—1K Boundary Detection**
- **Supports Local Data Transfer Protocol Similar to Traditional DMA**
- **Supports a General Purpose Command and Status Interface**
  - **—Local and EISA System Interrupt Support**
  - **—General Purpose Information Transfers**
  - **—Set-and-Test-Functions in I/O Space (Semaphore Function)**
  - **—Supports the EISA Expansion Board ID Function**
- **Supports Decode of Slot Specific and General I/O Addresses**
- **132-Pin JEDEC PQFP Package**
  (See Packaging Specification Order #240800, Package Type NG)

82355 Internal Block Diagram

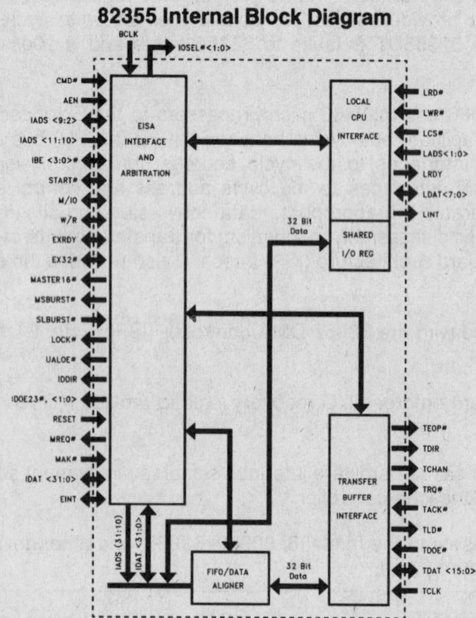

290255–1

September 1993
Order Number: 290255-007

82355 Bus Master Interface Controller (BMIC)

CONTENTS

PAGE

1

CONTENTS

PAGE

CONTENTS

PAGE

1.0 INTRODUCTION

The 82355 Bus Master Interface Controller (BMIC) is a highly integrated Bus Master designed for use in 32-Bit EISA Bus Master expansion board designs and supports all of the enhancements defined in the EISA specifications required for EISA bus master applications. The BMIC provides a simple, yet, powerful and flexible interface between the functions on the expansion board and the EISA bus. With the help of external buffer devices, the BMIC provides all EISA control, address, and data signals necessary to interface to the EISA bus.

The primary function of the 82355 is to support 16- and 32-bit burst data transfers between functions on the EISA expansion board and the EISA bus. Data transfer rates of up to 33 Mbytes/sec are supported (the fastest transfer rate available on an EISA bus). The following logic on the BMIC supports efficient burst transfers:

- Arbitration logic, for gaining control of the EISA bus
- Two transfer-address and byte counters
- Two data FIFOs, which allow expansion board and EISA bus timing to operate asynchronously
- Data shifters, which align data to specific byte boundaries
- A transfer buffer interface, for the data transfers on the expansion board
- General-purpose command and status interface logic
- Local processor interface, to allow programming by an on-board processor
- EISA slave interface, to allow communication with the EISA system

The BMIC greatly simplifies the design of EISA expansion boards. With the 82355, a board can be implemented with simple logic similar to that used in traditional ISA DMA designs. The EISA standard allows designs with 32-bit data and address buses, burst transfers, and automatic handling of the full EISA bus master protocol.

To maximize system throughput, the 82355 BMIC incorporates three fully concurrent interfaces: EISA interface, Transfer Buffer interface, and Local Processor interface. The EISA interface incorporates two 24-byte FIFOs, and implements the full EISA protocol. The Transfer Buffer interface is optimized for high speed static RAM buffers, and can operate at a maximum frequency of 20 MHz. The Local Processor interface supports a generic slave interface, and allows the local processor to fully program the BMIC for operation. Local processors are supported with the ability to access individual locations in system memory or I/O space; this peek-and-poke feature allows the expansion board to communicate easily with other devices in the system. All three interfaces can operate simultaneously, thus maximizing overall system performance.

Address-generation support for the data transfer buffer logic on the expansion board is provided on-chip. The transfer logic on the expansion board can use a high-speed asynchronous transfer clock. The BMIC handles all synchronization with the EISA bus. A FIFO within the BMIC eliminates performance degradation on burst transfers caused by synchronization delays. The BMIC also provides a set of programmable address comparators that drive external chip selects on the expansion board to assist local devices in decoding I/O address ranges.

1.1 BMIC Terminology/Definitions

EISA BUS MASTER—A 32- or 16-bit device that uses the extended part of the EISA bus to generate memory or I/O cycles.

Downshifting Bus Master—A "downshifting" master is a 32-bit master which can convert to a 16-bit master "on the fly". The BMIC will only downshift from a 32-bit master to a 16-bit master if programmed for burst mode (refer to Section 4.2.1).

EISA READ—A data transfer (burst, non-burst (two BCLK), or mismatched) from system to the expansion board across transfer channel 1.

EISA WRITE—A data transfer (burst, non-burst (two BCLK), or mismatched) from the expansion board to system memory across one of the two transfer channels.

I/O ADDRESS DECODE SUPPORT—Refers to slot specific or general I/O address decoding.

Slot Specific Address Decoding—Refers to the decoding of unique addresses allocated to EISA slot specific expansion boards. These addresses are: X000h–X0FFh, X400h–X4FFh, X800h–X8FFh, and XC00h–XCFFh, where X represents the EISA slot number. EISA slot number "0" is reserved for the EISA system board.

General I/O Address Decoding—Refers to the decoding of addresses allocated to ISA expansion boards. These addresses are: 0100h–03FFh.

LOCAL PROCESSOR—A processor located on the expansion board.

SYSTEM CPU—Processor located on the motherboard.

SYSTEM MEMORY—Memory located on the EISA bus or motherboard.

TRANSFER INTERRUPTION—A transfer interruption is defined as an occurrence resulting in a break in a transfer caused by one of the following conditions: A FIFO pause, a FIFO stall, a channel preemption, a channel clear or suspension, a 1K page break, or a transfer complete (EOP).

FIFO Pause—This is a condition where the EISA bus does not provide or take data at a rate fast enough to keep up with the expansion board transfer buffer logic. During an EISA read, this condition is defined as an empty FIFO. During an EISA write, this condition is defined as a full FIFO. A FIFO pause is considered a preferred condition and under normal operations should occur frequently. A FIFO pause will result in the BMIC negating TRQ# until the FIFO becomes not full during an EISA write or not empty during an EISA read.

FIFO Stall—This is a condition where the transfer buffer logic on the expansion board does not provide or take data at a rate fast enough to keep up with the EISA bus. During an EISA read, this condition is defined as a full FIFO. During an EISA write, this condition is defined as an empty FIFO. Under normal operations, a FIFO stall is expected to be a rare and exceptional event. For additional information regarding a FIFO stall, refer to Section 6.2.

Channel Clear—A channel clear results in the immediate termination of the current transfer and the flushing of the channel's corresponding FIFO. A channel clear is initiated by setting the CFGCL bit in the corresponding channel's Configuration register to a 1. For additional information regarding channel clear, refer to Section 8.2.4.2.

Channel Suspension—This temporarily prevents a channel from proceeding with a transfer. A transfer can be temporarily suspended by setting the CFGSU bit in the corresponding channel's Configuration register to a 1.

Channel Preemption—The BMIC can be preempted from the EISA bus by the 82357 (ISP). The 82357 negates MAK# indicating to the BMIC that it must finish the current bus cycle and relinquish control of the EISA bus by negating MREQ# within 64 BCLK periods. The BMIC is programmable to relinquish the bus within 0, 32, or 64 BCLKs from the negation of MAK# (refer to Section 4.4.2).

1K Page Break—The temporary termination of a burst, non-burst (two BCLK), or mismatched data transfer due to a 1K page address boundary crossing (refer to Section 4.2.2).

Transfer Complete (EOP)—End of process due to the transfer byte count being exhausted or a channel being cleared (channel clear). A transfer complete (EOP) will result in the BMIC asserting TEOP# with the last cycle (refer to Section 5.4).

TRANSFER BUFFER LOGIC—Logic located on the expansion board used to support the transfer and storage of data during BMIC EISA master mode transfers between the expansion board and system memory.

The transfer buffer logic interfaces to the Transfer Buffer Interface of the BMIC. Refer to Section 5.2 for additional information regarding transfer buffer logic.

2.0 BMIC INTERFACE ILLUSTRATION

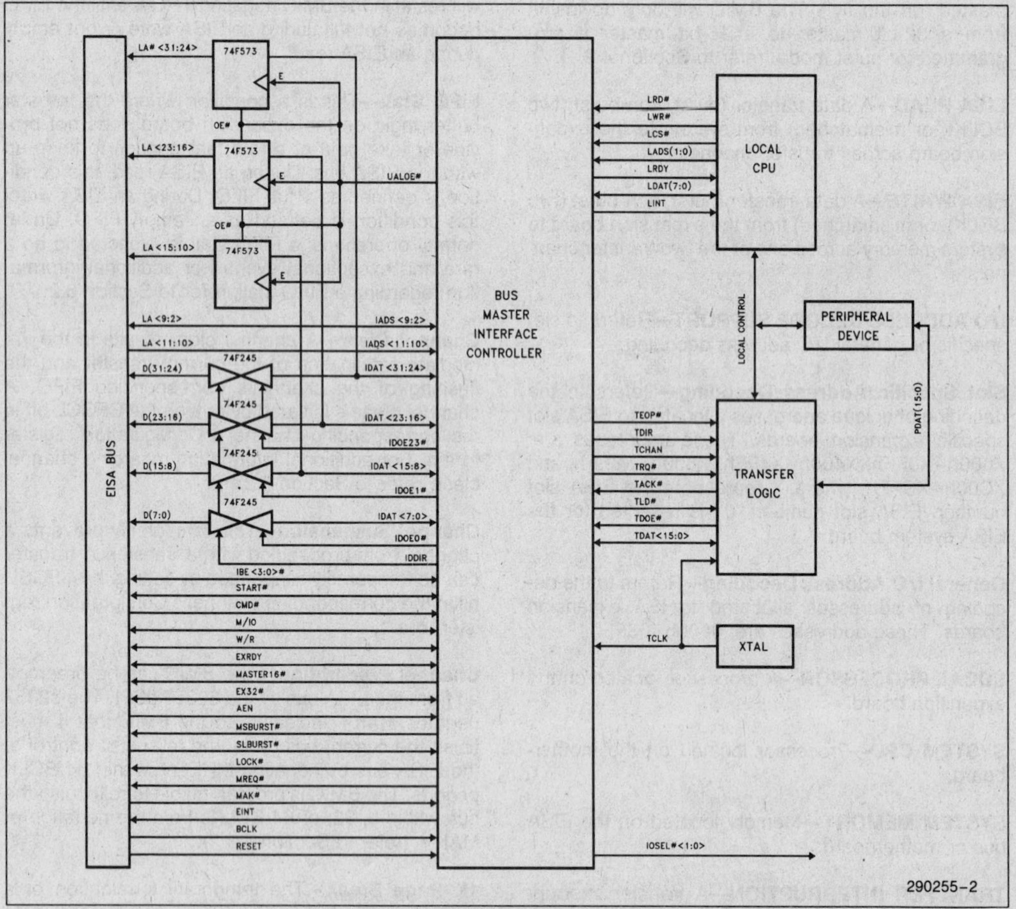

Figure 2-1. BMIC System Interface

3.0 FUNCTIONAL OVERVIEW

The following is a brief discussion of the functional blocks and features of the 82355. The EISA interface, Transfer Buffer interface, FIFO/Data Aligner, and Local interface each have a corresponding detailed section later in this data sheet.

3.1 EISA Master and EISA Slave Operations

In EISA slave mode, the 82355 monitors the EISA address lines <11:2> for general I/O address decoding, slot-specific address decoding, and Shared register accessing. During slave mode operations, all internal registers are accessible through the Local Processor interface, and all Shared registers are accessible through either the Local Processor interface or the EISA interface of the BMIC.

In EISA master mode, the 82355 becomes the master of the EISA bus. It may perform burst, non-burst (two BCLK), mismatched, or Peek/Poke data transfers at this time. During master mode operations, all internal registers are accessible through the Local Processor interface of the BMIC.

The arbiter portion of the BMIC determines which mode the device is in, performs the EISA arbitration, and provides the control signals necessary to regulate the slave and master activities internal to the chip. In slave mode, the arbiter also mediates between the EISA side and the local side during Shared register accesses.

The following is a table of the functions that can be performed during master and slave operations:

	Shared Reg. Accessing	Local CPU Only Reg. Accessing	EISA I/O Address Decoding	Data Transfers
EISA Slave Mode	YES (1, 2)	YES	YES	NO
EISA Master Mode	YES (2)	YES	NO	YES

NOTE:
Shared Reg. Accessing refers to the registers that are accessible through either the EISA interface or Local Processor interface.
Local Processor Only Reg. Accessing refers to the registers that are accessible through the Local Processor interface only.
EISA I/O Address Decoding refers to either general or slot specific I/O decoding support for the expansion board.
Data Transfers refer to either burst, non-burst (two BCLK), mismatched, or peek/poke data transfers.
YES = Can Be Performed
NO = Can Not Be Performed
1 = EISA interface
2 = Local interface

3.2 82355 Internal Architecture Description

The 82355 contains four blocks of control logic. The EISA interface block, Transfer Buffer interface block, FIFO/Data Aligner block, and the Local Processor interface block.

3.2.1 EISA INTERFACE BLOCK

The EISA interface block provides the following functions:

- generates the 32-bit EISA address for burst, non-burst (two BCLK), and peek/poke data transfers
- generates the EISA control signals necessary to implement an EISA 16-bit or 32-bit bus master, and a 32-bit EISA slave
- generates the control signals necessary to enable and disable the external buffer devices
- performs the EISA arbitration and provides the internal control signals required to regulate the slave and master activities of the BMIC
- integrates the registers necessary for the above operations as well as the registers required to provide the configuration and status of the data transfers between the EISA bus and the memory buffer on the expansion board

The EISA memory address range of the 82355 covers the 4 Gigabytes and supports the detection of 1K page address boundaries during burst, non-burst (two BCLK), and mismatched data cycles to and from system memory.

During slave mode, the EISA interface also supports slot specific and general I/O address decode necessary for Shared Register accesses and general decode as required by the expansion board. The shared register addresses are mapped into the slot specific I/O range (C80h-C9Fh).

The EISA interface block contains 43 registers necessary to execute the above functions. A detailed description of the registers and their functions can be found under Register Description (Sections 8.1 and 8.2).

3.2.2 TRANSFER BUFFER INTERFACE BLOCK

The Transfer Buffer interface block provides the group of signals that are required to perform 16-bit data transfers to and from the memory buffer on the expansion board. The protocol used is similar to that found in standard DMA designs. The interface includes a 16-bit data bus (TDAT), seven control signals and a transfer clock (TCLK). The transfer clock can run completely asynchronous to the EISA BCLK signal.

The Transfer Buffer interface block also provides a 16-bit transfer start address which is generated at the beginning of all new data transfers to and from the memory buffer on the expansion board. The 16 TDAT data lines are used to transfer the address.

The Transfer Buffer interface block contains eight registers. A detailed description of the registers and their functions can be found under Register Description (Section 8.2).

3.2.3 FIFO/DATA ALIGNER BLOCK

The FIFO/Data Aligner block is used to isolate and simplify the timing relationships between the EISA bus and the bus master expansion board. This allows the transfer buffer logic and EISA bus timing to operate asynchronously. The FIFO provides the data channel between the EISA bus and the expansion board during BMIC master data transfers and the Data Aligner provides the byte alignment and assembly necessary for the EISA bus.

There are two dual-port, six doubleword wide (24 byte) FIFOs on-board, one per transfer channel. The data is written into the FIFO from either the EISA bus side or the expansion board side, depending on the direction of the transfer. The transfer direction is controlled by a bit in the Transfer Base Count register set.

3.2.4 LOCAL PROCESSOR INTERFACE BLOCK

The Local Processor interface block provides the interface between the BMIC and the local processor. If a local processor is not present, the processor interface can be connected to the ISA bus. The Local Processor interface block is based on an 8086 style slave mode and provides an 8-bit data path for BMIC programming. All of the BMICs internal registers are accessible through this interface.

The Local Processor interface block contains a group of Shared registers used to support general-purpose command and status interactions between the system CPU or EISA bus master and the local processor. In addition to the command/status registers, the CPU interface includes a set of ID registers for EISA expansion board ID support, and a set of Peek/Poke data registers used to hold the data during peek/poke operations.

The local interface portion of the BMIC also contains three 8-bit registers which are used by the local processor to access all of the BMICs internal registers. These registers are mapped into the local processor interface and include a local status register, local data register, and a local index register (refer to Section 3.2.6.1).

The Local Processor block contains 31 registers. A detailed description of the registers and their functions can be found under Register Description (Sections 8.1 and 8.2).

3.2.5 DATA TRANSFER TYPES

The BMIC supports four types of data transfers on the EISA bus: Burst, non-burst (two BCLK), peek/poke or locked exchange, and mismatched. For all of the above transfer types, the addressed slave device can negate EXRDY if wait state timing is required (each wait state is one BCLK).

The primary function of the BMIC is to support 16- and 32-bit burst data transfers between functions on the expansion board and the EISA memory. If the addressed memory is not capable of supporting burst transfers, the BMIC will run either 32-bit non-burst (two BCLK) cycles or, with the support of the 82358 EISA Bus Controller, run mismatched data cycles.

The burst cycle type provides a continuous sequence of one BCLK read or write cycles to and from 16- or 32-bit EISA memory. Burst cycles can not be used with I/O devices or ISA devices (slaves or masters).

The non-burst cycle type provides a continuous sequence of two BCLK read or write transfers to and from 32-bit EISA memory. The BMIC will only respond as a 32-bit master when configured for two BCLK transfers (refer to Section 4.2.1).

The peek/poke and locked exchange feature allows local processor accesses to and from individual I/O space or system memory locations on the EISA bus. The BMIC responds as a 32-bit master and generates two BCLK cycles when configured for peek/poke transfers (refer to Section 4.3). A locked exchange transfer consists of six BCLKs (peek followed by a poke). A peek/poke data transfer has the same timings as a non-burst (two BCLK) data transfer.

The mismatched cycle type provides a means of communicating with 8- or 16-bit EISA or ISA devices. In the event the I/O or memory slave device that has been addressed requires a data size translation, the BMIC will back-off the bus and allow the 82358 EISA Bus Controller to perform the necessary data size translations (refer to Section 4.2.1). The BMIC will generate mismatched cycles as required for all data transfers (burst, non-burst, peek, poke, or locked-exchange).

The following table identifies the BMIC cycle types, master sizes, slave types accessible (memory-I/O), and BCLKs per cycle.

Transfer Type	BMIC Master Size		Slave Type Accessible		BCLKs per Cycle
	16-Bit	32-Bit	I/O	Memory	
Burst	X	X		X	1
Mismatched		X		X	*
Non-Burst		X		X	2
Mismatched		X		X	*
Peek/Poke		X	X	X	2
Mismatched		X	X	X	*
Locked Exchange		X	X	X	6
Mismatched		X	X	X	*

*Depends on slave type/size (EISA/ISA, I/O/Memory, 8-bit/16-bit)

For all of the above transfer types, the addressed slave device can negate EXRDY if wait-state timing is required (each wait-state is one BCLK).

3.2.6 REGISTER ACCESSING

The BMIC provides three distinct groups of registers; the Shared register set, the Local Processor Only register set, and the Index register set. The Shared register set is used by the system CPU or EISA bus master and the local processor for general-purpose command and status interactions and expansion board ID support. The Local Processor only registers are used by the local processor to program the BMIC and provide status for data transfers across the EISA bus and Transfer Buffer interface. The Local Processor Only register set also provides address range decode support for slot specific and general I/O address ranges of interest to the expansion board. The Index register set is used by the local processor as a means of accessing all of the above registers through an indexing scheme.

The Shared register set is accessible through either the EISA interface or the Local Processor interface, the remaining two register sets are accessible through the Local Processor interface only. In the case of contention between the EISA bus and the local processor accessing a Shared register simultaneously, the local processor on the expansion board will have initial priority. Consecutive multiple accesses to the BMIC's shared registers result in a rotational arbitration between the EISA bus and the local processor.

3.2.6.1 Register Accessing through the Local Processor Interface

Register accessing on the local side of the BMIC is accomplished using an indexing procedure. The local interface portion of the BMIC contains two 8-bit registers which are used by the local processor to access all of the BMIC's internal registers. These registers are mapped into the Local Processor interface and include a local data register and a local index register. The registers are selected using the two local address lines (LADS<1:0>). The BMIC's internal register set is read by writing the address of the register to be accessed into the local index register. The register contents are then read through the Local Data register. To write to one of the BMIC's internal registers, the local processor must first write the address of the register to be accessed into the local index register, same as a read, then write the new data value to the Local Data register.

An optional auto-increment mode is supported by the BMIC, which automatically increments the index register after each register read or write. This allows for efficient programming of the register set by using byte string moves. If the Local Index register is given a local index address with bit (7) set high, the local index address will automatically increment each time the Local Data register is read or written.

The Local Status/Control register is directly mapped into the Local Processor interface and is also accessible using the two address lines (LADS<1:0>).

3.2.6.2 Register Accessing through the EISA Interface

The shared registers are mapped directly into the EISA slot-specific I/O space XC80–XC9F. The EISA address lines <11:2> and the byte enables <3:0> are used for decode during shared register accesses.

A standard slave read or write access to the BMIC consists of two BCLKs + one wait-state (one wait-state = one BCLK period). During a slave cycle where the EISA access loses the internal register access through arbitration to the local processor, the cycle will consist of two BCLKs + two wait-states. The BMIC will negate EXRDY for one BCLK for each wait-state required.

3.2.7 INTERRUPTS

The BMIC provides two interrupt request lines, one for the EISA side (EINT), and one for the local side (LINT). The EISA interrupt (EINT) can be programmed for either edge or level-triggered operations. During edge-triggered operations the EINT signal will transition from a low level to a high level. In level-triggered mode, the EISA interrupt signal is an active low open collector output. The local interrupt signal (LINT) can be programmed for either active low or active high level operations and will default to active low operation upon reset. The LINT signal is not an open collector output during active low operations and will require external logic if interrupts need to be tied together on the local side. The EINT and LINT modes of operation are programmed through the Global Configuration register.

3.2.7.1 Interrupt Sources

Several events can trigger each of the two interrupt request signals, and the events can be enabled or disabled on an individual or global basis (refer to Sections 8.1.1.3 and 8.2.2). The system CPU or EISA bus master can only be interrupted by an I/O write from the local processor to the BMIC EISA System Doorbell register. However, the local processor can be interrupted by several sources which are listed below:

— An I/O write from the system CPU or EISA bus master to the BMIC Local Doorbell register.

— The completion of a data transfer on one of the transfer channels.

3.2.7.2 Interrupt Handling

To prevent the BMIC from allowing undetected interrupts from occurring, when servicing an interrupt initiated by the BMIC, all additional interrupts must be disabled prior to reading the Local or EISA System Doorbell Status registers. The interrupts are disabled by writing to the Local or EISA System Doorbell Enable registers, depending on the source of the interrupt.

This is required due to the nature of the interrupt mechanism of the BMIC. All interrupt sources have an edge triggered nature internal to the BMIC, with each event being 'OR'ed together. Additional interrupt sources occurring after the first interrupt will set their appropriate bit in the Status register, but they will not generate an external interrupt until the initial event has been cleared. Thus if the Status register was read first, and another interrupt occurred after this read, the second interrupt would remain undetected in the status register until another event occurred. Disabling of the interrupts prior to reading the status register will prevent this from occurring.

4.0 EISA INTERFACE

4.1 EISA Interface Signals

The BMIC provides a complete interface to the EISA bus and supplies all of the control signals, data lines, and address lines necessary to implement a 16- or 32-bit EISA bus master and a 32-bit EISA slave. This includes a 32-bit data path, a 32-bit address path, and 20 EISA control signals. The BMIC also provides five control signals used to enable and disable the external data buffers and address latches, as shown in Figure 2-1.

The BMIC uses four 74F245 external bidirectional buffers to drive and receive the 32 EISA data and three 74F573 external latches to latch and drive the upper 22 EISA address lines. The external data buffers and address latches should be comprised of "F" or "AS" type logic to meet EISA speed requirements.

The upper 22 EISA addresses are multiplexed through the 22 upper EISA data lines of the BMIC. They are latched externally by the 74F573's. EISA address lines <11:2> and byte enable lines <3:0> are tied directly to the EISA bus. Address lines 10 and 11 are input directly to the BMIC for slave mode address decode. During EISA master operation, lines 10 and 11 are driven indirectly through the external latches.

As a slave, the BMIC receives address lines IADS<11:2> and byte enable lines IBE<3:0># for I/O address decode. Address lines <11:2> are used for slot specific decode and address lines <9:2> are used for general I/O address decode. Address lines <11:2> along with IBE<3:0># are used by the BMIC during Shared register accesses. Address lines <31:12> are not used by the BMIC in slave mode.

The following address lines are used during I/O decoding as shown:
Slot specific I/O address decoding (expansion board)—IADS<11:2>
Slot specific I/O address decoding (shared registers)—IADS<11:2>/IBE<3:0>#
General I/O address decoding (expansion board)—IADS<9:2>

All of the BMIC EISA control signals function as defined in the EISA bus specification. The signals are used to support the following cycles:

BMIC as a Master

(Cycle Type Performed)				
Master Type	**Burst**	**Non-Burst**	**Mismatched**	**Peek/Poke/Locked Exchange**
32-Bit	X	X	X	X
16-Bit	X			

BMIC as a Slave

1. Responds to EISA shared register accesses as 32-bit slave.
2. Responds to slot specific and general I/O accesses (refer to Section 4.8).

4.2 Transfer Channels

The BMIC contains two identical independent transfer channels which are configurable to run either burst or non-burst (two BCLK) cycles to and from system memory. The BMIC will automatically run non-burst (two BCLK) or mismatched cycles if the memory the BMIC has addressed cannot run burst cycles. Mismatched cycles will be run if data size translation is required.

Channel 0 must be used for EISA READ operation only. Channel 1 can be used for both EISA READ and EISA WRITE operations.

Each channel has three sets of registers to regulate data transfers. These are the Base register group, the Current register group, and the Data Status/Control register group. This implementation of a triple register set allows a processor to begin programming the next transfer on the channel while the current transfer is being executed.

The Base register set contains seven 8-bit registers. These registers are programmed by the local processor when a transfer is required across one of the channels. Four Transfer Channel Base Address registers are combined to form the starting 32-bit EISA address to be used during the transfer. The remaining three registers are the Transfer Channel Base Count Registers. The Base Count registers are combined to determine the number of transfers (in bytes) to be performed. The number of bytes which can be transferred ranges from 1 byte to 4 Mbytes. The most significant bit of the Transfer Channel Base Count register group is used to control the start of the transfer and the second most significant bit is used to control the direction of the transfer (refer to Section 8.2.3.3).

The Current register set contains seven registers each of which corresponds to a Base register. These registers are loaded from the Base registers. The Transfer Channel Current Address registers contain the 32-bit real-time EISA memory address. The Transfer Channel Current Count registers contain the number of bytes remaining to be transferred on the channel. The current register set is readable by the local processor. However, there are possible coherency problems involved with reading multiple bytes while the current registers are being updated during a transfer. To avoid these problems, a channel's transfer should be temporarily suspended (using the channel's Configuration Register) before trying to read the channel's current register set.

The Status/Control register set contains three registers: the Transfer Channel Strobe register, Transfer Channel Configuration register, and the Transfer Channel Status register. The Transfer Channel Strobe register is used to initiate the transfer of data from the Base register set to the associated Current register set. A transfer request for that channel will be generated following the Current register load. The Transfer Channel Configuration register is used to program the mode of the transfer. The Transfer Channel Status register provides current FIFO and transfer channel status.

To initialize a transfer over either of the two transfer channels, the following steps must be completed:

1. Verify that the Base registers for the desired transfer channel are available.

   The Transfer Channel Base Address and Base Count registers must be available before they can be programmed. This is determined by the status of bits 0 and 1 in the Local Status/Control register. A "1" in either of the two bits indicates that the corresponding channel is currently running a transfer and the Base registers are busy. A "0" indicates that the Base registers are free and available for programming. In the event that the Base registers are not available, the local processor must wait until the data transfer executing on the requested channel has completed, at which time bits "0" or "1" (depending on which channel was programmed) in the Local Status/Control registers will be reset to 0. Programming the Base registers during a Base register Busy state, is illegal and will corrupt the Base register data of the pending transfer. Programming the Transfer Configuration register during a cycle in progress may cause the termination of the transfer, depending on which bit in the register was changed.

2. Program the transfer channel's associated Transfer Base register set with the desired transfer information (Base registers must be available).

3. Initiate the Base register to Current register load and schedule a transfer request by writing to the channel's Transfer Strobe register.

   If a transfer is in progress on the requested channel and a write to the associated channel's Strobe register is done, the Base to Current register load will take place immediately after the data transfer on the requested channel has completed.

4.2.1 BURST AND NON-BURST MODES OF OPERATION

The BMIC can be programmed for burst or non-burst (two BCLK) data transfers to and from EISA memory. This is determined by a write to the Channel Configuration Register.

If burst mode is enabled, the BMIC will look for the SLBURST# signal at the beginning of the transfer to determine if the slave device that was addressed is

1

capable of running burst cycles. If the slave device does not respond with an active SLBURST# signal, the BMIC will not activate the MSBURST# signal and will proceed with either non-burst (two BCLK) bus cycles or mismatched cycles.

In burst mode, the BMIC can respond as a 16- or 32-bit master. The BMIC informs the system of this capability by driving MASTER16# low from the same BCLK rising edge that START# is asserted. MASTER16# will remain low for one BCLK. The BMIC will automatically "downshift" from a 32- to a 16-bit master if the EX32# signal is sampled inactive and the SLBURST# signal is sampled active at the beginning of a transfer. If EX32# and SLBURST# are sampled active at the beginning of the transfer, the BMIC will proceed with a 32-bit burst transfer.

In non-burst mode, the BMIC will respond as a 32-bit master. The BMIC will look for the EX32# signal at the beginning of the transfer to determine if the system memory it has addressed has the same bus width. If the EX32# signal is not returned (mismatched cycle indicated), the BMIC will "back-off" the bus by floating START#, IBE#<3:0>, and IDAT<31:0> to allow the 82358 EISA Bus Controller to take control of the transfer. The EISA Bus Controller will then proceed to assemble or disassemble the data as needed. The EISA Bus Controller will return the EX32# signal after the mismatched cycle is complete, indicating to the BMIC that a new address can be placed on the bus. If the EX32# signal is sampled active at the beginning of the transfer, the BMIC will proceed with a 32-bit non-burst (two BCLK) transfer.

4.2.2 1K PAGE ADDRESS BOUNDARY DETECTION

During burst, non-burst (two BCLK), and mismatched data cycles, the BMIC provides the support to detect 1K page address boundary crossings. If the BMIC detects that the current cycle is about to cross a 1K page boundary, the transfer will be temporarily terminated on the next cycle. The BMIC will then arbitrate between restarting the transfer on the current channel, selecting the second channel, doing a peek/poke cycle, or preempting the channel (refer to Section 4.4 for information regarding BMIC arbitration).

Example: Transfer = 32-bit transfer and page address boundary is at location 400h = 1024

1. The BMIC detects that the current cycle is about to cross a 1K page address boundary—current address (3FCh = 1020).
2. Address after BMIC has executed the current cycle (400h = 1024).
3. Transfer is temporarily terminated (interrupted).
4. BMIC will now arbitrate between restarting the transfer on a new page, selecting the second channel, doing a peek/poke cycle, or preempting the channel.

4.3 Peek/Poke, Locked Exchange Transfers

To allow the local processor to communicate with other devices in the main system, the BMIC allows the local processor to execute individual I/O or memory cycles over the EISA bus. These cycles can be thought of as being similar to "peek" and "poke" statements in the Basic programming language. These cycles may be reads, writes, or locked exchanges in 8-, 16-, 24-, or 32-bit values. All cycles must be contained within a single doubleword.

The Peek/Poke operation requires the following set of registers: Four 8-bit Peek/Poke Address registers which are combined to provide the 32-bit Peek/Poke address; One 8-bit Peek/Poke Control register which contains the bits defining whether the cycle is I/O or memory, peek (read)/poke (write) or locked exchange, and which byte enables are to be active during the cycle; and four 8-bit Peek/Poke Data registers which are used to hold the data for the Peek/Poke cycle. During all peek/poke or locked exchange cycles, byte enables IBE<3:0># are derived from bits 0–3 in the Peek/Poke Control register set. The lower two bits of the Peek/Poke Address register are ignored. Peek, poke, or locked exchange cycles will not be generated for illegal combinations of byte enables (i.e., 1111, 1010, 0110, 0101, 0100, 0010).

To do an individual write cycle (poke), the local processor must first write to the Peek/Poke Address register set to specify the 32-bit memory address or the 16-bit I/O address. It must then write the data to be transferred into the Peek/Poke Data register set. The data must be placed in the appropriate byte positions in the Data register set so that it goes out on the correct byte lanes during a 32-bit bus master transfer.

Once the appropriate data and address have been programmed, the local processor must write to the Peek/Poke Control register to specify the cycle type and initiate the cycle. After this write to the Peek/Poke Control register, bit 2 in the Local Status/Control register will be set to a 1 by the BMIC to indicate that a peek/poke request is pending and that the peek/poke registers are busy. When the poke cycle has finished executing on the EISA bus, the Peek/Poke status bit 2 in the Local Status/Control register will return to normal (0).

To do an individual read cycle (peek), the local processor must write to the Peek/Poke Address registers, then to the Peek/Poke control register to initiate the read cycle. The Peek/Poke status bit 2 in the Local Status/Control register will be set high by the BMIC and remain active until the peek cycle finishes on the EISA bus. The local processor can then read the data from the Peek/Poke data registers.

NOTE:
When running consecutive peek transfers, the data must be read from the Peek/Poke data registers before each new peek transfer is generated. The BMIC will read the data off the EISA bus from all four byte lanes regardless of which Byte enables (IBE<3:0>#) are active. (Although all bytes are read, the value of the byte enables are important to the system and must be programmed for the peek transfer).

When a locked exchange cycle is requested by the local processor, a peek cycle is scheduled first and then immediately followed by a poke cycle. The LOCK# signal is active during the locked exchange cycle to indicate to the system that no other accesses to the addressed location can be made.

Whenever the BMIC is commanded to do an EISA POKE cycle, the BMIC will assert the MREQ# signal low normally, transfer up to four bytes of data, and release the bus by de-asserting MREQ# high. A potential problem exists, however, when the slave device extends the cycle by de-asserting EXRDY low. If the slave holds this signal low past the time that the BMIC is forced to release MREQ# high (it has been preempted while waiting for the slave to assert EXRDY high), then the BMIC will drive MREQ# back low again immediately after this cycle ends if there is another transfer pending (TBI, PEEK, POKE or LOCKED-EXCHANGE). Note that according to the EISA spec, MREQ* signal description "A bus master must wait at least two BCLKs after releasing the bus before reasserting its MREQx*". To adhere to EISA specifications, it is required that LOCKED-EXCHANGE cycles be used in lieu of POKE cycles.

Any consecutive Peek/Poke or Locked exchange transfers must be initiated only after the previous Peek/Poke or Locked exchange has been completed. This can be accomplished by making sure that bit 2 of the local status/control register is set to a zero before initiating the transfer.

4.4 Arbitration

4.4.1 EISA/BMIC ARBITRATION

The BMIC will begin master mode operation any time a transfer request is pending. If more than one transfer request is pending, the BMIC will service them in the following order. Peek/Poke cycles have the highest priority access to the EISA bus followed by the two data channels. Once the BMIC has gained control of the EISA bus, the BMIC will first perform any peek, poke, or locked exchange transfers that may be pending. If there are no peek, poke, or locked exchange transfers pending, the BMIC will run data transfers initiated by either of the two transfer channels. The two transfer channels have equal priority with respect to each other and are serviced in an alternating fashion. The priorities and assignments are as follows:

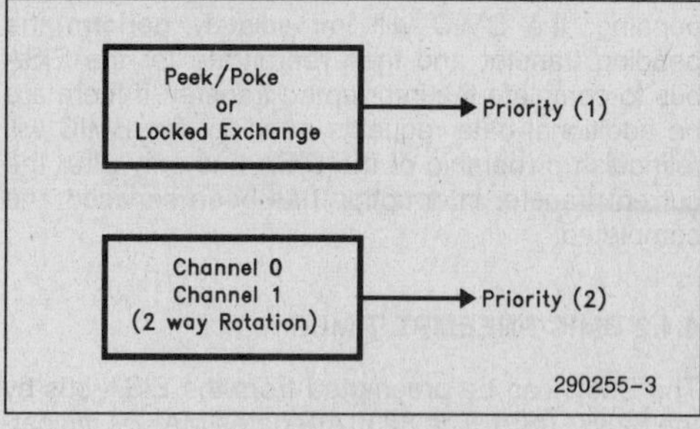

290255-3

The BMIC will maintain ownership of the EISA bus until it has serviced all outstanding data transfer requests or it is preempted from the bus by the removal of the MAK# signal. The BMIC can be configured to relinquish the EISA bus immediately, 4 μs, or 8 μs after a preempt is received. If the BMIC has completed all outstanding data transfer requests prior to the time-out of the preempt timer, it will give up the bus. If the BMIC finishes one task prior to the time-out of the preempt timer, it will start on the next pending transfer request unless the request is a peek, poke, or locked exchange cycle. The BMIC will not start a set of peek, poke, or locked exchange cycles after the MAK# signal has been removed. If a transfer is cut-off due to a preempt timer time-out, the BMIC, upon regaining access to the EISA bus and following its internal arbitration priority scheme, will continue the transfer that was preempted at the point the transfer was cut-off.

When a channel is interrupted for any reason, 1K page break, FIFO stall, channel clear, channel suspend, or transfer complete, the BMIC may immediately relinquish the EISA bus depending on the state of the CFGFF bit in the Channel Configuration register set.

NOTE:
During a FIFO pause, the CFGFF bit in the associated Channel's Configuration register is ignored. The function of the CFGFF bit, as related to the above channel interruptions, is as follows:

If the CFGFF bit = 1, the BMIC will immediately relinquish control of the EISA bus upon the detection of any of the above interruptions. This will occur

regardless if there are additional data transfer requests pending. If there are additional data transfer requests pending, the BMIC will reassert MREQ# a minimum of two BCLKs later to reacquire the EISA bus. The BMIC will follow the arbitration priority scheme outlined above when servicing a data transfer request after a transfer interruption has occurred.

If the CFGFF bit = 0, the BMIC retains ownership of the EISA bus upon detection of a FIFO stall or 1K page break as long as a preempt timer timeout has not occurred. If there are additional data requests pending, the BMIC will immediately perform the pending transfer and then rearbitrate for the EISA bus to complete the interrupted transfer. If there are no additional data requests pending, the BMIC will relinquish ownership of the EISA bus only after the current transfer interruption has been serviced and completed.

4.4.2 BMIC PREEMPT TIMER

The BMIC can be preempted from the EISA bus by the 82357 (ISP). The 82357 negates MAK#, indicating to the BMIC that it must finish the current bus cycle and relinquish control of the EISA bus by negating MREQ# within 64 BCLK periods (8 μs).

The BMIC provides a programmable preempt timer which can be programmed to relinquish the bus within 3, 32, or 64 BCLKs. The preempt timer is programmable through the Global Configuration register.

The following diagrams illustrate the latest the BMIC will start a new transfer after MAK# has been negated.

Depending on the type of transfer started, the BMIC will respond as follows:

Assumptions:

1. The 82357 has negated the MAK# signal at BCLK zero.
2. The preempt timer is programmed to relinquish the EISA bus within 64 BCLKs after the negation of MAK#.
3. Let X = programmed value of preempt delay (in BCLKs).

BMIC Response:

For all transfers, the BMIC will negate MREQ# within (X-2.5) BCLK periods following the MAK# transition to an inactive state (BCLK 61.5).

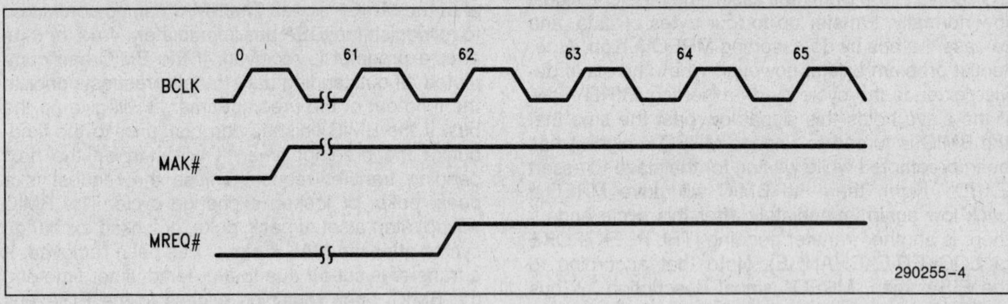

For all transfers, the BMIC may assert START# on any of the first X-3 rising edges of BCLK following the MAK# transition to an inactive state (BCLK 61).

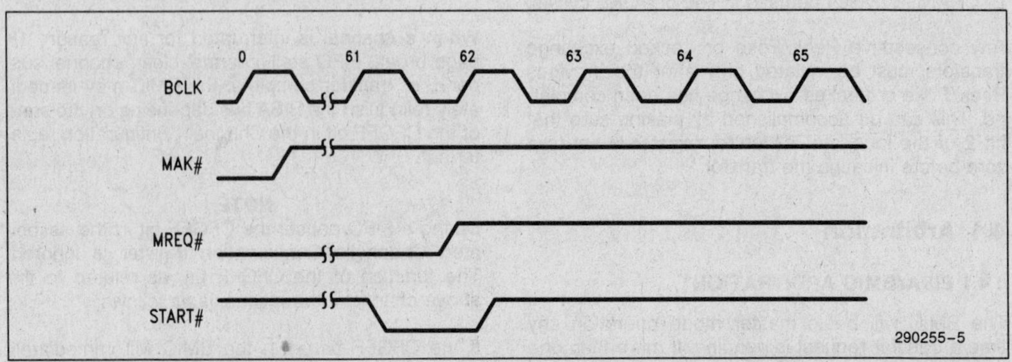

If the last cycle is a non-burst two BCLK cycle, CMD# will become inactive within (X-1) BCLK periods from the inactive transition of MAK# (BCLK 63), this is assuming that EXRDY is active.

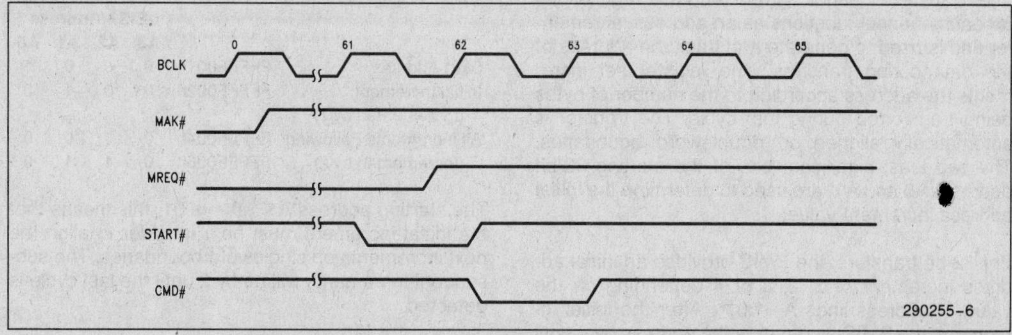

290255-6

If the last cycle is a burst EISA cycle, the BMIC will negate MSBURST# within (X-0.5) BCLK periods from the inactive transition of MAK# (BCLK 63.5). The last CMD# will go inactive within X BCLK periods from the deassertion of MAK# (BCLK 64). This is assuming EXRDY is active.

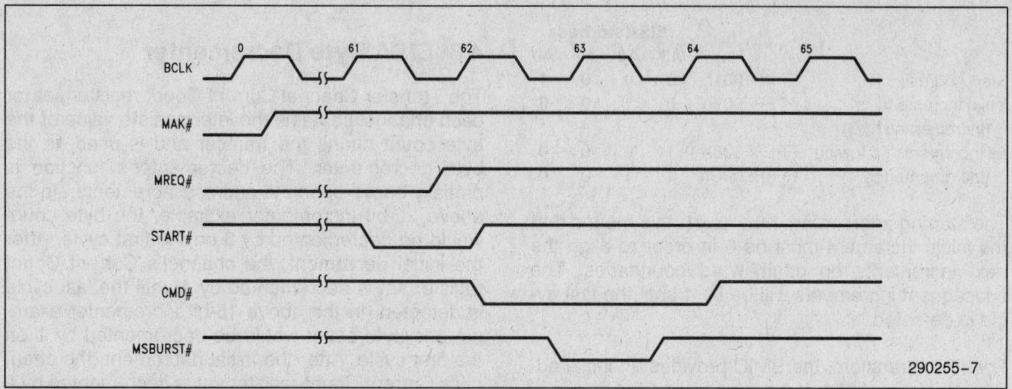

290255-7

If the last cycle is mismatched, cycle completion will be controlled by the system. The BMIC will drive the LA address, M/IO, and W/R signals until the falling edge of BCLK after the last CMD# inactive transition.

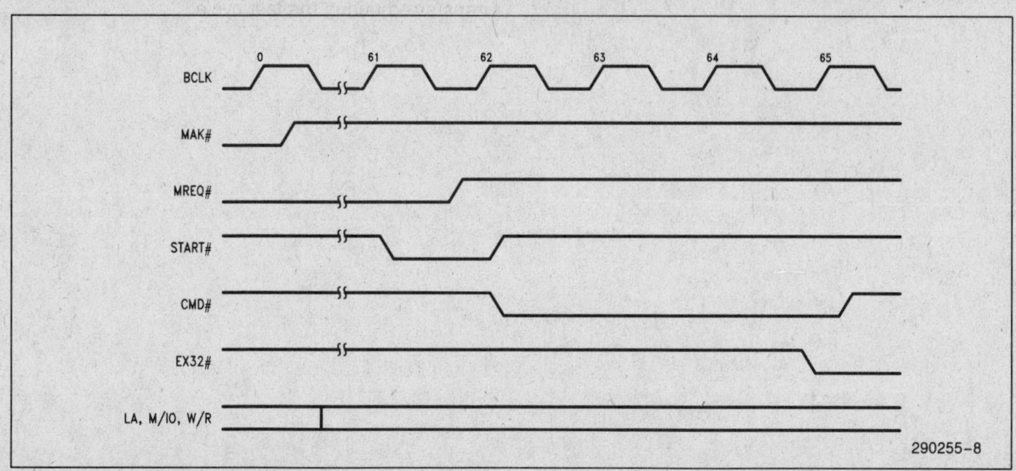

290255-8

4.5 EISA Address Incrementer

The Transfer Channel Current Address register set for each channel functions as an address incrementer and is used to generate and track the address of the data during transfers. The register set increments the address according to the number of bytes being transferred during that cycle. The transfer is automatically aligned on doubleword boundaries. The two least significant bits of the starting 32-bit address (A0 and A1) are used to determine the initial address increment value.

For 32-bit transfers, the BMIC provides an initial address increment of 1, 2, 3 or 4 depending on the value of address lines A<1:0>. After the initial increment, the BMIC increments the address by 4 until the last cycle is detected.

The following example illustrates the BMIC address incrementer during a 32-bit master mode transfer.

		EISA Address			
		A3	**A2**	**A1**	**A0**
Start Address	FFFFF001h	0	0	0	1
Initial Increment (Incremented by 3)	FFFFF004h	0	1	0	0
All Increments Following (Incremented by 4)	FFFFF008h	1	0	0	0
	FFFFF00Ch	1	1	0	0

The starting address A<1:0> is 01, this means that the initial increment must be 3 in order to align the next increments on doubleword boundaries. The subsequent increments will be by 4 until the last cycle is detected.

For 16-bit transfers, the BMIC provides an initial address increment of 1 or 2 depending on the status of address lines A<1:0>. After the initial increment, the BMIC increments the address by two until the last cycle is detected.

The following example illustrates the BMIC address incrementer during a 16-bit master mode transfer.

		EISA Address			
		A3	**A2**	**A1**	**A0**
Start Address	FFFFF001h	0	0	0	1
Initial Increment (Incremented by 1)	FFFFF002h	0	0	1	0
All Increments Following (Incremented by 2)	FFFFF004h	0	1	0	0
	FFFFF006h	0	1	1	0

The starting address A<1:0> is 01, this means that the initial increment must be 1 in order to align the next increments on singleword boundaries. The subsequent increments will be by 2 until the last cycle is detected.

NOTE:

The BMIC internally assembles 32-bit dwords. When a 16-bit burst transfer is preempted, the transfer will stop on a doubleword boundary.

4.6 EISA Byte Decrementer

The Transfer Channel Current Count register set for each channel contains the intermediate value of the byte count during the transfer and is used as the byte decrementer. The decrementer's function is partially based upon the address incrementer. In the above 32-bit incrementer example, the byte count would be decremented by 3 on the first cycle. After the initial decrement, the channel's Current Count register set is decremented by 4 until the last cycle is detected. In the above 16-bit incrementer example, the byte count would be decremented by 1 on the first cycle. After the initial decrement, the channel's Current Count register set is decremented by 2 until the last cycle is detected. Note that the Current Count register does not decrement entirely to zero. Instead, it retains the value of the number of bytes transferred during the last cycle.

4.7 EISA Address Incrementer/Byte Decrementer Illustration

The following table illustrates the various states of (A0, A1) vs the transfer byte-count and the initial address during a 32-bit transfer.

Byte Count	Starting Address	Next Address	Initial Increment	Number of Bytes Left	Last Cycle	Number of Cycles Left
1	XXX 0000	NA	NA	0	Yes	0
	XXX 0001	NA	NA	0	Yes	0
	XXX 0010	NA	NA	0	Yes	0
	XXX 0011	NA	NA	0	Yes	0
2	XXX 0000	NA	NA	0	Yes	0
	XXX 0001	NA	NA	0	Yes	0
	XXX 0010	NA	NA	0	Yes	0
	XXX 0011	XXX 0100	1	1	No	1
3	XXX 0000	NA	NA	0	Yes	0
	XXX 0001	NA	NA	0	Yes	0
	XXX 0010	XXX 0100	2	1	No	1
	XXX 0011	XXX 0100	1	2	No	1
4	XXX 0000	NA	NA	0	Yes	0
	XXX 0001	XXX 0100	3	1	No	1
	XXX 0010	XXX 0100	2	2	No	1
	XXX 0011	XXX 0100	1	3	No	1
5	XXX 0000	XXX 0100	4	1	No	1
	XXX 0001	XXX 0100	3	2	No	1
	XXX 0010	XXX 0100	2	3	No	1
	XXX 0011	XXX 0100	1	4	No	1
6	XXX 0000	XXX 0100	4	2	No	1
	XXX 0001	XXX 0100	3	3	No	1
	XXX 0010	XXX 0100	2	4	No	1
	XXX 0011	XXX 0100	1	5	No	2
7	XXX 0000	XXX 0100	4	3	No	1
	XXX 0001	XXX 0100	3	4	No	1
	XXX 0010	XXX 0100	2	5	No	2
	XXX 0011	XXX 0100	1	6	No	2
8	XXX 0000	XXX 0100	4	4	No	1
	XXX 0001	XXX 0100	3	5	No	2
	XXX 0010	XXX 0100	2	6	No	2
	XXX 0011	XXX 0100	1	7	No	2
9	XXX 0000	XXX 0100	4	5	No	2
	XXX 0001	XXX 0100	3	6	No	2
	XXX 0010	XXX 0100	2	7	No	2
	XXX 0011	XXX 0100	1	8	No	2
10	XXX 0000	XXX 0100	4	6	No	2
	XXX 0001	XXX 0100	3	7	No	2
	XXX 0010	XXX 0100	2	8	No	2
	XXX 0011	XXX 0100	1	9	No	3

NOTES:
1. "X" = Don't Care
2. If the "byte count" is less than or equal to the "initial increment", then the current cycle = the first cycle = the last cycle.
3. If the number of bytes left is less than or equal to 4, then the next cycle = the last cycle.
4. For information regarding byte alignment, refer to Section 6.3.1.

4.8 I/O Address Range Decode Support

The BMIC provides on-board decoder logic, two I/O select pins (IOSEL<1:0>#), and a set of 8-bit I/O Decode Range registers to support both general I/O decode and expansion board slot specific I/O decode. The BMIC also uses the AEN signal when decoding I/O locations.

The set of I/O Decode registers include two I/O Decode Range Base Address registers and two I/O Decode Range Control registers (refer to Section 8.2.6). The I/O Decode registers are used to define the address ranges of interest to the bus master expansion board. Each IOSEL#<1:0> pin has an associated Control and Base register along with an associated address range as defined by the I/O Decode register set.

Through the I/O Decode Range Control register set, the BMIC can be programmed to respond to a select I/O address range as either an 8-bit or 32-bit EISA device. The only control signal provided by the BMIC to the EISA bus during an I/O decode is the EX32# signal. The output state of the EX32# pin on the BMIC will indicate the elected response (low = 32-bit EISA, high = 8-bit EISA). The Control register set controls the size of the I/O decode range, the I/O decode type (slot specific or general I/O), and the I/O decode address latching. The I/O address can be latched by the CMD# signal (de-pipelined) or merely decoded. By latching the I/O address, the associated IOSEL# line will remain active a minimum of 5 ns from the rising edge of CMD#.

The IDOEs do not go active during an IOSEL cycle outside the shared register access space.

The I/O decode range size depends on the value of bits <4:0> in the Control register. Each of these bits masks a corresponding address comparison bit in the Base register. If no bits are masked in the Control register, the BMIC will decode a doubleword address. The bits are masked as follows:

I/O Control Register	I/O Base Register Bit Masked	EISA Address Bit Masked
Bit 0	Bit 0	IADS2
Bit 1	Bit 1	IADS3
Bit 2	Bit 2	IADS4
Bit 3	Bit 3	IADS5
Bit 4	Bit 4, 5	IADS<7:6>

The I/O Decode Range Base Address register contains the address range that is used during the I/O decode address comparison. The following table gives the bits in the I/O Base Address Register and the EISA Address that are used during the comparison:

I/O Base Address Register	(EISA Address Bits)	
	Slot Specific	General I/O
Bit 0	IADS2	IADS2
Bit 1	IADS3	IADS3
Bit 2	IADS4	IADS4
Bit 3	IADS5	IADS5
Bit 4	IADS6	IADS6
Bit 5	IADS7	IADS7
Bit 6	IADS10	IADS8
Bit 7	IADS11	IADS9

If bit 6 in the I/O Decode Range Control register is programmed for General I/O decode, and the two most significant bits in the I/O Decode Range Base Address register are programmed to 0 (IADS<9:8>), I/O decoding for that range will be disabled. This is done to ensure that the I/O address does not conflict with the slot specific address range or the EISA system board address range. The following table summarizes the EISA system I/O address mapping:

I/O Address Range (HEX)	I/O Range Reserved for
0000–00FF	EISA/ISA System Board
0100–03FF	General I/O (ISA Expansion Board)
0400–04FF	ISP (82357)
0500–07FF	General I/O (Alias of 0100h–03FFh)
0800–08FF	EISA System Board
0900–0BFF	General I/O (Alias of 0100h–03FFh)
0C00–0CFF	EISA System Board
0D00–0FFF	General I/O (Alias of 0100h–03FFh)
Slot Specific Range where X = Slot Number	
X000–X0FF	Slot (X)
X100–X3FF	General I/O (Alias of 0100h–03FFh)
X400–X4FF	Slot (X)
X500–X7FF	General I/O (Alias of 0100h–03FFh)
X800–X8FF	Slot (X)
X900–XBFF	General I/O (Alias of 0100h–03FFh)
XC00–XCFF	Slot (X) (BMIC Registers 0C80h–0CAFh)
XD00–XFFF	General I/O (Alias of 0100h–03FFh)

The following is an example of the BMIC programmed for slot specific decode:

I/O Decode Range 0 Control register programmed for (EFh)

	Bit 7	Bit 6	Bit 5	Bit 4	Bit 3	Bit 2	Bit 1	Bit 0
(EFh)	1	1	1	0	1	1	1	1

— Bit 7—Respond as a 32-bit EISA slave
— Bit 6—Slot specific decode enabled
— Bit 5—Slot specific address latched by CMD#
— Bit 4—Compare I/O Decode Range 0 Base Address Bits (5) and (4) with EISA address signals IADS7 and IADS6 respectively
— Bit 3—Mask I/O Decode Range 0 Base Address Bit (3)
— Bit 2—Mask I/O Decode Range 0 Base Address Bit (2)
— Bit 1—Mask I/O Decode Range 0 Base Address Bit (1)
— Bit 0—Mask I/O Decode Range 0 Base Address Bit (0)

I/O Decode Range 0 Base Address register programmed for (2-h)

	IADS11	IADS10	IADS7	IADS6	IADS5	IADS4	IADS3	IADS2
	Bit 7	Bit 6	Bit 5	Bit 4	Bit 3	Bit 2	Bit 1	Bit 0
(2-h)	0	0	1	0	—	—	—	—

EISA slot specific address range decoded—X080h through X0BFh where X represents the expansion board slot number

```
        (X080h)                     (X0BFh)
xxxx000010(00) (00)00throughxxxx000010(11) (11)11
              ↑    ↑                     ↑    ↑
                  EISA Address
                  Bits Masked
                  (IADS<5:2>)
```

Byte enables IBE<3:0># and EISA address lines IADS<1:0> are not used during either slot specific or general I/O decode. During slot specific I/O decode, EISA address lines IADS<9:8> must be 0 to ensure that the I/O address does not conflict with the ISA general I/O address range (0100h–03FFh).

IOSEL0# and EX32# will be driven low by the BMIC if addresses X080h through X0BFh are present on the EISA bus.

AEN is used as part of the decode and must be negated low when a response from the BMIC is required.

5.0 TRANSFER BUFFER INTERFACE

5.1 Transfer Buffer Interface Signals

The Transfer Buffer Interface portion of the BMIC provides the signals essential for interfacing to the expansion board as required for EISA-to-expansion board and expansion board-to-EISA burst data transfers. The Transfer Buffer Interface is designed to interface to a high speed transfer buffer and simple logic similar to that used in traditional DMA designs. This interface includes a 16-bit data bus, one clock input, and seven control signals.

The 16-bit data lines TDAT<15:0> are used by the BMIC to transfer the data to and from the transfer buffer logic on the expansion board during transfers. The data is word aligned. The BMIC automatically assembles the words received from the expansion board into 32-bit dwords for 32-bit transfers over the EISA bus. The data lines are also used by the BMIC to transport internally generated transfer start and real-time addresses to the external logic for use during data transfers (refer to Section 5.3).

The clock input (TCLK) controls the transfer rate between the BMIC and the external transfer buffer logic. The TCLK can be asynchronous to the BCLK.

The seven control signals include:

— Transfer Request (TRQ#): an output to request data transfers over the Transfer Buffer interface.
— Transfer Acknowledge (TACK#): An input to acknowledge data transfers. The TACK# signal may be used by the transfer buffer logic to add wait states to the data cycle.
— Data Transfer Direction (TDIR): An output to inform the external transfer buffer logic as to the direction of the current transfer (EISA read or EISA write).
— Transfer Channel Select (TCHAN): An output to indicate which of the two channels is currently active.
— Transfer Address Counter Load (TLD#): An output to load the current transfer start address to an external address counter, depending on the expansion board application.
— Transfer Data Output Enable (TDOE#): An input that unconditionally disables the BMIC from driving the TDAT<15:0> lines. With this signal, the BMIC can be prevented from driving the TDAT<15:0> lines while the local processor accesses the transfer buffer logic on the expansion board. No handshaking is required, so throughput is increased.
— Transfer End-of-Process (TEOP#): TEOP# is a status output pin that signals the end of a data transfer to the external transfer buffer logic.

NOTE:
Refer to Section 9.4 for additional information regarding the above signals.

5.2 External Transfer Buffer Logic

The Transfer Buffer interface is designed for high speed devices, such as SRAM based designs, or FIFOs. The Transfer Buffer interface data path is 16 bits wide. This requires the transfer clock (TCLK) to run at a speed of 16 MHz to 20 MHz to maintain the EISA maximum data rate of 33 Mbytes/sec. The fast cycle times required on the data Transfer Buffer interface can be implemented in the controlled environment found locally on the expansion board. If two BCLK transfers are used on the EISA side (16 Mbytes/sec), the timing requirements for the transfer buffer can be relaxed, and lower cost implementations can be utilized.

If the transfer buffer controller does dynamic arbitration for the transfer buffer between the BMIC and the peripheral device(s) on the expansion board, the peripheral device accesses should be short enough so that the BMIC's data FIFO can handle the interruption to its data flow without stalling the EISA transfer.

Examples of transfer buffer architecture implementations that could be interfaced to the BMIC include:

— A FIFO implementation which is large enough to buffer the difference in throughput rates between the peripheral device on the expansion board and the EISA Bus. See Section 5.2.1.

— A small high-speed DMA like device that generates addressing for a SRAM based transfer buffer.

— A controller implementation for dual-ported SRAM for high transfer buffer bandwidth.

— A page or nibble-mode dynamic-RAM controller implementation for large, low cost transfer buffers.

— For graphics systems, the frame buffer itself can be used for the transfer buffer with a non-linear address generator for transferring windows in the screen image.

5.2.1 FIFO IMPLEMENTATION

During EISA writes, the BMIC will overread the transfer buffer (read data beyond the number of bytes to be transferred) by a maximum of 28 bytes. These overread bytes may contain valid data (back to back transfers) which will be lost. The data loss can be avoided through software or hardware. The software solution avoids back to back transfers. This implies that there is data for only one transfer in the FIFO at any given time.

The hardware solution requires an external 22-bit Byte Counter and a Flip-Flop. The terminal count of the Byte Counter is used to SET the Flip-Flop which disables BMIC reads to the FIFO. The BMIC will continue to read (overread) "stale" data. The BMIC TEOP# output signal is used to RESET the Flip-Flop enabling BMIC reads to the external FIFO.

5.3 Transfer Interface Start Address Generation

The BMIC provides four 8-bit Transfer Buffer Interface (TBI) registers, two Base and two Current registers, which can be programmed with 16-bit transfer start addresses. Each transfer channel has an associated Base and Current register pair. The Base registers contain the start address and the Current registers provide the real-time address used to track the current transfer. The Current registers will increment by one each time a 16-bit word is transferred across the Transfer Buffer interface.

The 16-bit start address is transferred across the TDAT<15:0> lines to the transfer buffer logic at the beginning of all new data transfers (i.e., each time the TBI Base register set contents are transferred to the TBI Current register set). The contents of the TBI Base registers are transferred to the TBI Current registers after a write to the associated channel's Transfer Strobe register is completed (refer to Section 4.2). The BMIC provides a load signal (TLD#) which can be used to latch the start address into an external address counter for use by the transfer buffer logic.

The BMIC can also be programmed to generate the transfer address each time the associated channel regains the bus, in which case, the address will be the real-time address. By programming the CFGEA bit in the Channel Configuration register to a "1", the start address will be transferred to the transfer buffer logic at the beginning of all new transfers and the real-time address will be transferred each time the associated channel regains the bus. If the CFGEA bit is set to a "0", the transfer start address will be transferred at the beginning of all new transfers and the real-time address will not be transferred.

NOTE:

The TBI Current register set is readable by the local processor. However, there are possible coherency problems involved with reading multiple bytes while the current registers are being updated during a transfer. To avoid these problems, the channel's transfer should be temporarily suspended (using the channel's Configuration Register) before trying to read the channel's TBI Current register set.

5.4 Transfer Buffer Interface Timing Example

Figures 5-1 and 5-2 illustrate the start up and conclusion of a transfer cycle across the Transfer Buffer interface and should be used as a reference when reading the following text.

1. At the start of a data transfer TCHAN and TDIR change to their new values prior to the falling edge of TLD# to set up the cycle. TCHAN and TDIR will not change states as long as TRQ# is asserted.
2. TLD# is asserted until acknowledged by TACK#. The transfer address is transferred to the external logic each time the TBI Base register contents are transferred to the TBI Current register set (new transfer) and, if programmed, each time the current channel regains the bus.
3. The new address is loaded using the TDAT bus during TLD# at point (A). The TDAT bus should be turned on by asserting TDOE# during TLD# if the internal start address is required. Once the external channel address and direction are set up, the data transfer can begin.
4. Data transfer requests are signaled by TRQ# being asserted (low). TRQ# will remain active until the data transfer is completed or a transfer interruption occurs (refer to Section 1.0) followed by TACK# active. During an EISA write, there will be a one TCLK delay between TLD# deasserting and TRQ# asserting as denoted by point (D) in Figure 5-2. This is to allow time for the external buffers to change direction after the TLD# has been completed.
5. Each word transfer to or from the BMIC is acknowledged by the TACK# signal. If TACK# is active at the rising edge of TCLK, one word will be transferred. If TACK# is not active at the rising edge of TCLK, the word that is currently being transferred will be inhibited and a wait state will

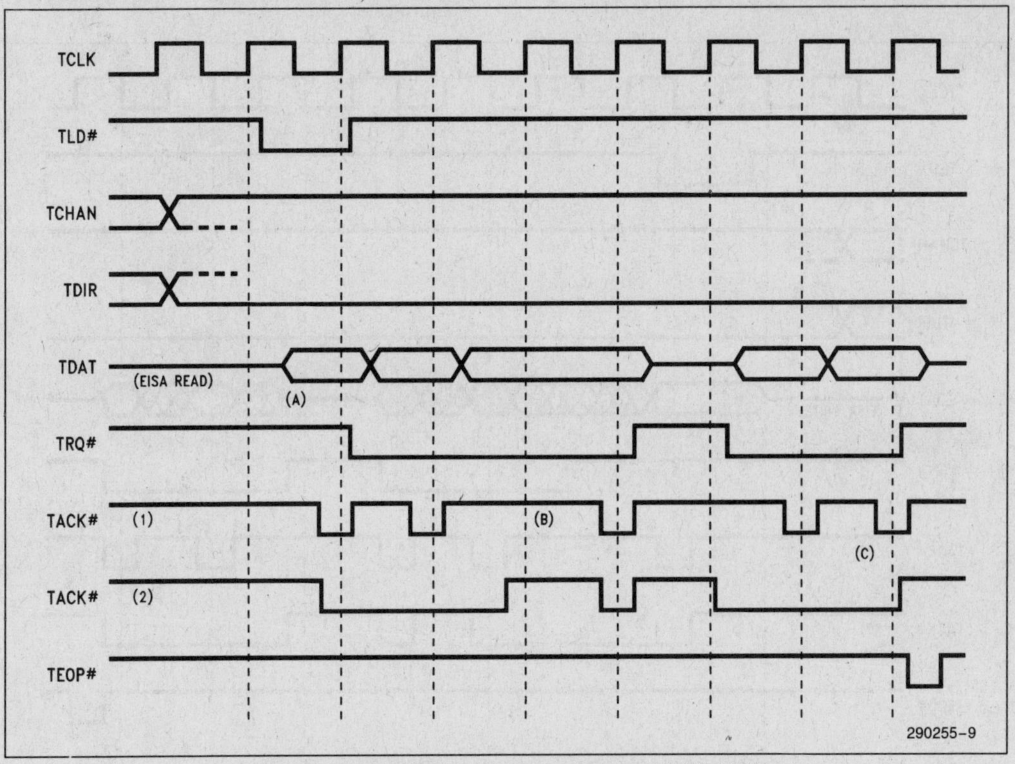

290255-9

Figure 5-1. Transfer Buffer Interface Timing (EISA READ)

be inserted. This is shown at point (B) in Figure 5-1. Such a wait may be needed when the external transfer buffer logic is arbitrating between the BMIC and the I/O subsystem on the expansion board. Wait states may also be inserted by stretching TCLK at point (C) in both of the figures. Clock stretching is possible as long as the one to one ratio of TCLK to BCLK is not violated.

NOTE:
A long TCLK stretch time will hang the Transfer Buffer interface. Also, TCLK must be running during the time TRQ# is inactive in order for the Transfer Buffer interface to function properly.

As indicated above, TACK# must be stable at the rising edge of TCLK. However, TACK# can assume any convenient pattern at other times. As shown by the first pattern, TACK# (1) pulses low at the TCLK edge that data is transferred. This pattern is particularly useful when TCLK wait-states are desired as indicated at point (B) in Figure 5-1. The alternate pattern (TACK#2) is useful during TCLK stretching since TACK# is always low during TRQ# as shown at point (C). This is effective since the transfer clock edge timing is controlled by the amount TCLK is stretched.

6. TEOP# is asserted at the end of a transfer by the BMIC.

   The BMIC will indicate end-of-process by asserting TEOP# shortly after the negation of the last CMD# in the transfer. During an EISA write transfer, the BMIC will assert TEOP# a maximum of two TCLKs after CMD# is negated. During an EISA read transfer, the BMIC will assert TEOP# typically eight TCLKs after the negation of CMD#. In either case (EISA read or EISA write), the TEOP# signal is delayed from the rising edge of TCLK.

NOTE:
The BMIC will assert the expansion board interrupt signal (LINT) at the end of a transfer, if so programmed in the Transfer Channel Configuration register.

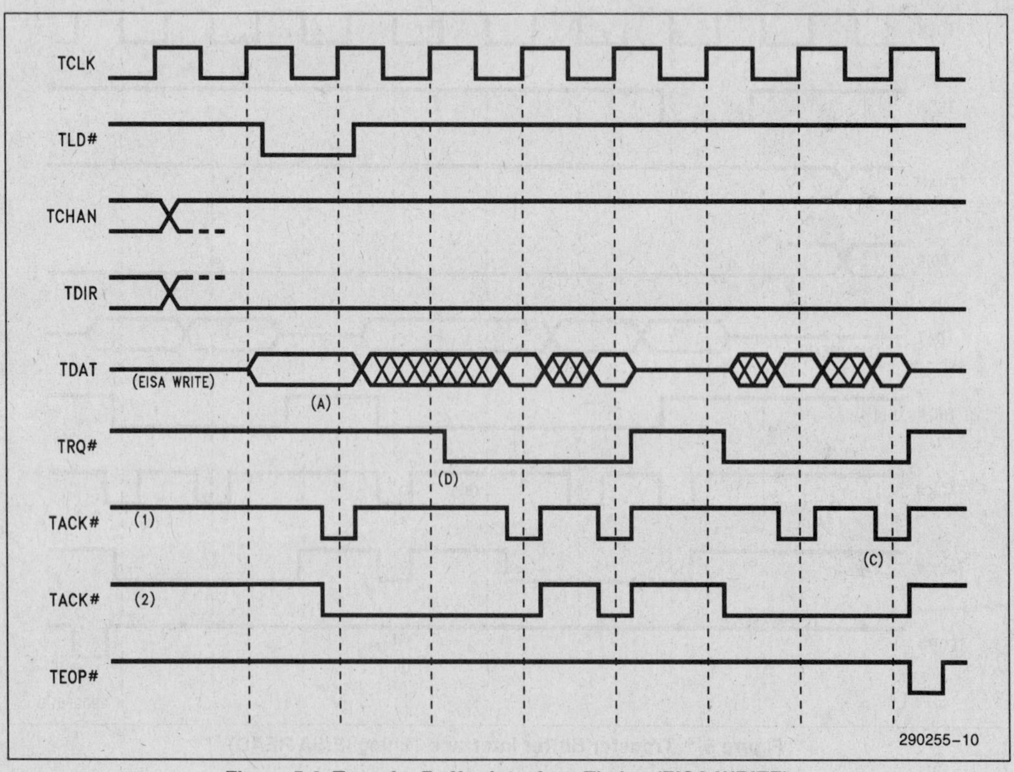

Figure 5-2. Transfer Buffer Interface Timing (EISA WRITE)

6.0 FIFO/DATA ALIGNER

6.1 FIFO/Data Aligner

The BMIC uses two identical FIFOs, one per transfer channel, and a common data aligner for data transfers between system memory and the bus master expansion board. The primary function of the FIFO/Data Aligner Unit is to help isolate and simplify the timing relationships between the EISA bus and the devices on the expansion board.

The FIFO allows the timing on the expansion Board side of the BMIC to be based on a locally generated clock signal. This transfer clock (TCLK) can be independent of the EISA BCLK signal that governs EISA bus timing. The FIFO also provides latency protection for wait states generated on either the EISA bus or expansion board.

The Data Aligner arranges the 16-bit data from the external transfer buffer to any arbitrary byte alignment in system memory. The data aligner also performs the assembly and disassembly of the EISA data during the transfer. The TDAT data assembly and disassembly is done by the Transfer Buffer interface portion of the BMIC.

6.2 FIFOs

Each FIFO on-board the BMIC is 24 bytes in size. The transfer data is written into the FIFOs from either the expansion board or the EISA bus side, depending on the direction of transfer. The data is written into the FIFO as doublewords during the transfer. However, if the data is not doubleword aligned, partial FIFO loads will be done at the beginning or end of a transfer depending on the byte count, address programmed and the direction of the transfer.

The condition of the FIFOs can be determined by a read to the Transfer Channel Status register set. A read to this register will indicate whether the FIFOs are stalled or active. A FIFO stall is defined as a FIFO that is full during an EISA read or empty during an EISA write. In either case, the transfer buffer logic is unable to keep up with the EISA device. If a FIFO stall occurs, the transfer will be stopped and the BMIC will either service the transfer request with the highest priority or relinquish the EISA bus to the system. The BMIC will relinquish the bus to the system if the CFGFF bit in the channel's corresponding Configuration register is set to a 1.

6.3 Data Aligner

6.3.1 EISA BYTE ALIGNMENT

The BMIC automatically handles the byte alignment for the EISA bus in the case of misaligned doubleword boundaries and assumes no performance penalty. The BMIC will do any partial doubleword transfers as required at the beginning and the end of all transfers. The two least significant bits of the 32-bit transfer start address (A1 and A0) are used to provide the byte alignment for both EISA read and EISA write transfers. The following tables illustate the BMIC's byte alignment approach during 32- and 16-bit transfers:

In the following tables "—" represents no data transferred and the digits represent the data items being transferred. The byte alignment for an EISA read is identical to that of an EISA write.

EISA Write (32-bit/12-byte Transfer) and (16-bit/6-byte Transfer)

		(32-Bit)				(16-Bit)			
A1	**A0**	**Output Data to EISA Bus**				**Output Data to EISA Bus**			
Byte Lane	**→**	**3**	**2**	**1**	**0**	**3**	**2**	**1**	**0**
0	0	03	02	01	00	—	—	01	00
		07	06	05	04	—	—	03	02
		11	10	09	08	—	—	05	04
0	1	02	01	00	—	—	—	00	—
		06	05	04	03	—	—	02	01
		10	09	08	07	—	—	04	03
		—	—	—	11	—	—	—	05
1	0	01	00	—	—	—	—	01	00
		05	04	03	02	—	—	03	02
		09	08	07	06	—	—	05	04
		—	—	11	10	—	—	—	—
1	1	00	—	—	—	—	—	00	—
		04	03	02	01	—	—	02	01
		08	07	06	05	—	—	04	03
		—	11	10	09	—	—	—	05

6.3.2 DATA ASSEMBLY/DISASSEMBLY

Before being placed on either the TDAT or IDAT data buses during an EISA read or EISA write, the data will be assembled or disassembled as required. The IDAT data is assembled and disassembled by the FIFO/data aligner portion of the BMIC and the TDAT data is assembled and disassembled by the Transfer Buffer interface portion of the BMIC. The following paragraphs illustrate the BMIC's assembly and disassembly approach during 32- and 16-bit transfers. The illustration assumes that byte alignment is not required.

During 32-bit EISA read transfers, the 32-bit doublewords are removed from the EISA bus and placed into the FIFO. After flowing through the FIFO, the 32-bit doublewords are copied-down to 16-bit words and then placed on the TDAT bus.

During 32-bit EISA write transfers, the 16-bit words are removed from the TDAT lines, assembled into 32-bit doublewords, and then placed into the FIFO. After flowing through the FIFO, the 32-bit data is placed on the EISA bus. No further assembly or disassembly is required after the FIFO as the data is already in 32-bit doubleword form.

During 16-bit EISA read burst transfers, the 16-bit words are removed from the EISA bus, assembled into 32-bit doublewords, and then placed into the FIFO. After flowing through the FIFO, the 32-bit data is copied-down to 16-bit words and then placed on the TDAT bus.

During 16-bit EISA write burst transfers, the 16-bit words are removed from the TDAT bus, assembled into 32-bit doublewords, and then placed into the FIFO. After flowing through the FIFO, the 32-bit data is copied-down to 16-bit words and then placed on the EISA bus.

7.0 LOCAL PROCESSOR INTERFACE

The BMIC's Local Processor interface is based on an asynchronous, 8-bit interface. All of the slave signals required for a local processor to program the BMIC are provided through this interface. These signals include (LCS#, LRD#, LWR#); two address lines (LADS0 and LADS1) for addressing internal registers; an 8-bit data path (LDAT); an interrupt signal (LINT); and a ready signal (LRDY). LINT allows the BMIC to interrupt the local processor and the ready signal (LRDY) indicates when valid data is available on the LDAT lines (shared register accesses only, see below). If a local processor is not used, the Local Processor interface can be connected to the 8-bit ISA bus (refer to Section 7.3). The choice of the local microprocessor or microcontroller used depends upon the specific application and the degree of performance and data processing needed (refer to Section 7.2).

The Local Processor interface portion of the BMIC contains two 8-bit registers which are used by the local processor to access all of the BMIC's internal registers. These registers are mapped into the Local Processor interface and include a Local Data register and a Local Index register. These registers are selected using the Local Processor interface's two address lines. The Local Status/Control register is also directly mapped into the Local Processor interface and is used to provide the local processor with the interrupt, peek/poke, and Base register status.

The BMIC allows the local processor and the EISA bus to communicate with each other through a set of Command/Status registers. The Command/Status registers are referred to as shared registers and include a set of Mailbox registers, Semaphore ports, and doorbell registers. The mailbox registers are used to pass messages to and from the local processor and the EISA bus and are controlled by the Semaphore ports. The Doorbell register set is used to inform the respective processor of new messages. Also part of the shared register set are the ID registers, which are used to support the EISA expansion board ID function.

The BMIC allows the local processor access to individual locations in system memory or I/O space using the Peek/Poke feature. The local processor can also initiate BMIC burst and non-burst (two BCLK) data transfers to and from system memory.

7.1 Shared Registers—Status/Command Support

As data transfer rates increase, it is critical that an efficient command and status passing mechanism be implemented so that command and status exchange does not become a new bottleneck to system performance. The BMIC utilizes a high-performance command/status interface between the main system and the local processor to minimize command/status overhead.

The Shared registers are a group of registers accessable by the system CPU or EISA bus master and the local processor for general-purpose command and status interactions and EISA expansion board ID function support. The features of the BMIC command/status support include a pair of semaphore ports, a set of interrupt ports ("doorbell registers"), and a set of mailbox registers. With these functions, many different types of high-performance communication protocols can be defined between the system and the expansion board. The Global

Configuration register, the System Interrupt Enable/Control register, and the ID registers are also part of the shared register set.

7.1.1 SEMAPHORE PORTS

The two semaphore ports are specifically designed to allow set-and-test functions in I/O space. Specifically, the ports are used to lock access to the mailbox registers and to lock access to links in main memory. Each of the semaphore ports consists of two parts: the semaphore flag bit and the semaphore test bit.

When a write occurs to the semaphore flag bit through either the EISA interface or the Local Processor interface, the old value of the semaphore flag bit is copied to the appropriate semaphore test bit. The old value of the semaphore flag bit is then available in the test bit to be read back by the processor. If the value read back from the semaphore test bit is a "1", the requested resource is unavailable for use. If the value read back is a "0", the requested resource is available for use and is now locked by the requesting processor or bus master. In this manner, set-and-test algorithms can be implemented without using the EISA bus lock function. The processor or EISA bus master unlocks the semaphore by simply writing a "0" to the associated semaphore flag bit.

NOTE:
The Semaphore ports and resources are locking only in a software sense, as in any semaphore in main memory. The Semaphore ports are identical and are not associated with either interface (EISA or Local). The protocol for the semaphores and the effect they have on other shared registers, like the Mailbox registers, is strictly a matter of how the system software chooses to use them.

Implementing the semaphore in the BMIC instead of main memory eliminates the need for the BMIC to arbitrate for the EISA bus every time it wishes to update or test the semaphore. Note that the semaphore scheme described here is functional only when a single device on the EISA is communicating with the BMIC; the semaphore coordinates "locks" between the single device and the local processor. In the case that multiple masters attempt to lock access to the BMIC, the masters must first agree amongst themselves which one has the privilege to use the BMIC semaphore port(s).

7.1.2 MAILBOX REGISTERS

A set of 16 8-bit general-purpose mailbox registers are used to pass information between the bus master expansion board and the EISA system. The 16 registers are mapped contiguously in EISA slot-specific I/O space, so they can be accessed as bytes, words, or doublewords. These registers can be used to directly pass command and status information, or they can be used as pointers to larger command blocks in memory.

The mailbox registers can be read or written at any time from either the EISA bus or the Local Processor interface. An internal arbitration is implemented in such a way that if there is a simultaneous read and write from both sides of a mailbox register, then the read operation will not contain indeterminate bits. In other words, when a read operation is done on a mailbox register at the same time as a write operation to that register, the bit pattern that is read will be either the old bit pattern in the mailbox, or the new bit pattern being written, but never some transitory, invalid bit pattern.

7.1.3 DOORBELL REGISTERS

There are two 8-bit doorbell Interrupt/Status registers in the BMIC, one assigned to the EISA side and one assigned to the expansion board side. The EISA System Doorbell register is used by the local processor to request service from the EISA side and the Local Doorbell register is used by the device on the EISA side to send an interrupt request to the local processor on the bus master expansion board. The doorbell Interrupt/Status registers are implemented with "sticky" bits, so that individual bits in the register can be set by the interrupting device or reset by the servicing device without knowledge of the states of the other bits in the register. The eight bits in each doorbell register allow up to eight separate devices or events in each direction to have interrupt requests pending simultaneously. The interrupt requests pending in either of the two Doorbell registers are ORed with the other interrupt sources from within the BMIC, and the result is sent out over one of the two interrupt pins: LINT or EINT.

Each doorbell register has an associated 8-bit Interrupt Enable register used to enable or disable the interrupts on an individual basis. The BMIC also includes a System Interrupt Enable/Control register and a Local Status/Control register used to disable the system (EINT) and local (LINT) interrupts and to verify the status of the system and local interrupts on a global basis (refer to Sections 8.1.1.3.3 and 8.2.2).

The following paragraphs describe the operation of the Local Doorbell Interrupt/Status register. The EISA System Doorbell Interrupt/Status register is similar, but operates in the opposite direction.

Each device or event that can interrupt the bus master expansion board can be assigned a bit position within the BMIC's Local Interrupt/Status Doorbell

register. When the device on the EISA bus wants to send an interrupt request to the bus master expansion board, it writes to the Local Interrupt/Status Doorbell register (from the EISA side) with that device's assigned bit position set active. This will set that bit in the Local Interrupt/Status Doorbell register, but leave the other bits in the register unaffected. If that bit position is not disabled, then the interrupt signal to the local processor will be asserted.

When the local processor services the interrupt, it checks the Local Status/Control Register to determine the source of the interrupt. If the control register indicates that the Local Doorbell register is one of the active interrupt sources, then the local processor can read the Local Doorbell register to determine which bits are active and requesting interrupts. If the local processor decides to service one of the requests from the Local Doorbell register, it can write to the Local Doorbell register with that bit's position set. This action will cause that bit in the Local Doorbell register to reset, but the other bits will remain unaffected. Thus, each bit in the Local Doorbell register is like a set-reset flip-flop, with the EISA bus controlling the "set" input, and the Local Processor interface controlling the "reset" input.

7.2 Local Processor Recommendations

The Local Processor interface to the BMIC will support numerous processors, from the 8088 microprocessor to the 376 embedded processor.

The 80186, 80C186, 80188, and 80C188 family of processors provides a clean interface to the BMIC's Local Processor interface and eliminates the need for additional logic. An on-board programmable wait-state generator eliminates the need for external wait-state generation logic between the processor and the BMIC during non-shared register accesses.

7.3 Requirements for No Local Processor

The BMIC allows for expansion board designs that do not require a local processor. To support the programming of the BMIC in a no local processor board design, the Local Processor interface must be connected to the ISA bus. However, when the ISA bus is used, the BMIC must be informed that there is no local processor and that it must change its function slightly (refer to next section). To inform the BMIC that no local processor is present, LRDY must be driven low during RESET and remain low a minimum of two BCLKs after RESET is negated.

The following circuit can be used to establish the proper LRDY/RESET timing as required for a no local processor design (see Figure 7-1).

7.4 EISA ID Function Support/ Registers

The BMIC provides support for the EISA expansion board ID function. The primary ID implementation takes advantage of the local processor. Upon reset, the local processor executes a routine from its ROM that writes the product identifier for the expansion board to the four 8-bit ID registers in the BMIC. The registers are accessed through the Local Processor interface and are located at local index addresses 00h–03h. On the EISA side, these registers are mapped into the EISA slot specific ID address range XC80h–XC83h.

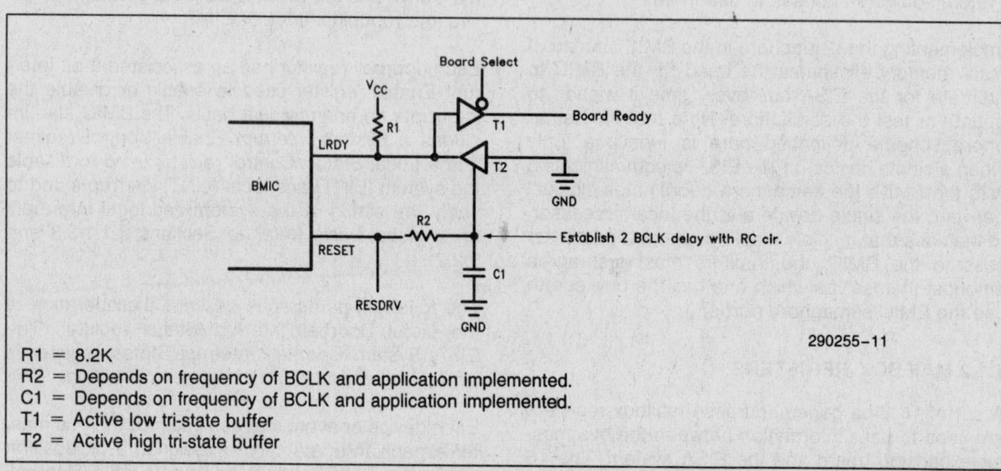

Figure 7-1. LRDY/RESET Circuit with No Local Processor

If the host CPU accesses the ID registers in the BMIC before the local processor has programmed them, the BMIC will return the setup delay ID code 0111XXXXh in the byte 0 ID register located at EISA slot specific I/O address XC80h. The byte 0 ID register should be programmed last by the local processor.

If a local processor is not used, external registers will have to be implemented on the expansion board to hold the expansion board ID value. The BMIC will automatically set its I/O Decode Range 0 Control register to decode 8-bit EISA ID addresses. The IOSEL0# output signal can then be used to trigger external logic on the expansion board to enable ID data onto the IDAT<7:0> data lines. The ID register must be connected as shown in Figure 7-2. The external logic should monitor SA1 and SA0 on the ISA bus to determine which data byte to drive.

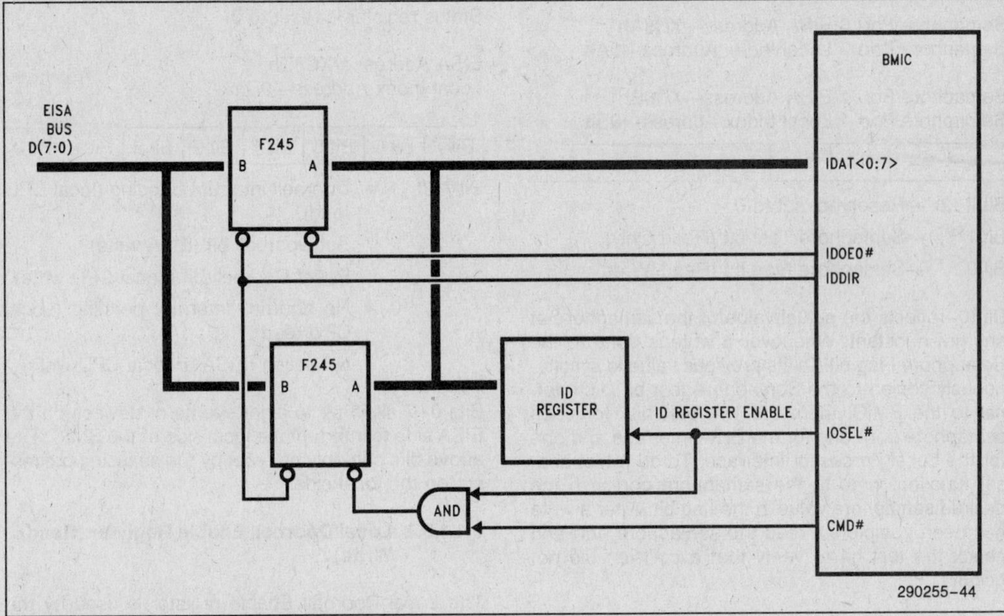

Figure 7-2. IDOE0# Connection during ID Register Access

8.0 REGISTER DESCRIPTION

8.1 Shared Register Description

The following is a table of the Shared register group listing the number of registers, register type (read/write) as related to the local and EISA side, register name, and register size:

Number	EISA	Local Type	Register Name Type	Active Bits per Register
2	R/W	R/W	Semaphore Register	2 Bits
16	R/W	R/W	Mailbox Register	8 Bits
1	R/W	R/W	Local Doorbell Interrupt/Status Register	8 Bits
1	R	R/W	Local Doorbell Enable Register	8 Bits
1	R/W	R/W	EISA System Doorbell Interrupt/Status Register	8 Bits
1	R/W	R	EISA System Doorbell Enable Register	8 Bits
1	R/W	R	System Interrupt Enable/Control Register	8 Bits
1	R	R/W	Global Configuration Register	8 Bits
4	R	R/W	ID Register	8 Bits

8.1.1 COMMAND/STATUS SUPPORT REGISTERS

8.1.1.1 Semaphore Ports (Read/Write)

The BMIC contains two Semaphore ports which can be used to software lock resources between the EISA bus and the local processor. Each semaphore port controls a 1-bit semaphore flag. Upon reset, the Semaphore ports are reset to 0.

Semaphore Port 0 EISA Address—XC8Ah
Semaphore Port 0 Local Index Address—0Ah

Semaphore Port 1 EISA Address—XC8Bh
Semaphore Port 1 Local Index Address—0Bh

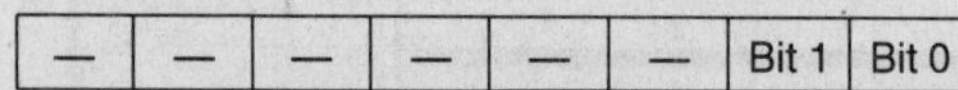

—	—	—	—	—	—	Bit 1	Bit 0

Bit 7–2 —Reserved, set to 0

Bit 1 —Semaphore Test bit (Read Only)

Bit 0 —Semaphore Flag bit (Read/Write)

Bit (0) reflects the actual value of the semaphore at any given instant. Whenever a write is done to the Semaphore Flag bit (0), its previous value is simultaneously copied to the Semaphore test bit (1). Internal to the BMIC, there are two test bits for each semaphore port: one for the EISA interface and one for the Local Processor interface. To do a test-and-set function, write to the semaphore port with the desired semaphore value in the flag bit. After a write has been completed, read the semaphore port and check the test bit to verify that a collision did not occur.

8.1.1.2 Mailbox Registers (Read/Write)

The mailbox registers are sixteen 8-bit, general purpose registers. The format of the contents of the mailbox registers is user-defined. The Mailbox register set is not initialized to a fixed value upon reset.

EISA Address—XC90h through XC9Fh
Local Index Address—10h through 1Fh

Bit 7	Bit 6	Bit 5	Bit 4	Bit 3	Bit 2	Bit 1	Bit 0

8.1.1.3 Doorbell Registers

8.1.1.3.1 Local Doorbell Interrupt/Status Register (Read/Write)

This register is implemented with "sticky" bits (refer to Section 7.1.3). The Local Doorbell Interrupt/Status register is used by the EISA bus to send an interrupt request to the expansion board. When read from, this register indicates the status of pending interrupt events. Upon reset, the Doorbell Interrupt/Status register is reset to 0.

EISA Address—XC8Dh
Local Index Address—0Dh

Bit 7	Bit 6	Bit 5	Bit 4	Bit 3	Bit 2	Bit 1	Bit 0

Bit 7–0 1 = Doorbell interrupt pending (local CPU read)
Set Doorbell bit (EISA write)
Reset Doorbell bit (Local CPU write)

0 = No doorbell interrupt pending (Local CPU read)
No action (EISA or local CPU write)

Bits 0–7 allow up to eight events or devices on the EISA side to interrupt the local side of the BMIC. The above bits can only be reset by the servicing processor on the local side.

8.1.1.3.2 Local Doorbell Enable Register (Read/Write)

The Local Doorbell Enable register is used by the local processor to enable or disable interrupt requests to the local expansion board. This register is read only from the EISA side. Upon reset, the Doorbell Enable register is set to 0.

EISA Address—XC8Ch
Local Index Address—0Ch

Bit 7	Bit 6	Bit 5	Bit 4	Bit 3	Bit 2	Bit 1	Bit 0

Bit 7–0 1 = Enable doorbell interrupt for corresponding bit position

0 = Disable doorbell interrupt for corresponding bit position
No action (local CPU write)

Bits 0 through 7 act as interrupt enables for bits 0 through 7 in the Local Doorbell Interrupt/Status register respectively.

8.1.1.3.3 EISA System Doorbell Interrupt/Status Register (Read/Write)

This register is implemented with "sticky" bits (refer to Section 7.1.3). The EISA System Doorbell Interrupt/Status register is used by the expansion board to send an interrupt request to the EISA bus. When read from, this register indicates the status of pending interrupt events. Upon reset, the EISA System Doorbell Interrupt/Status register is reset to 0.

EISA Address—XC8Fh
Local Index Address—0Fh

Bit 7	Bit 6	Bit 5	Bit 4	Bit 3	Bit 2	Bit 1	Bit 0

Bit 7–0 1 = Doorbell interrupt pending (EISA read)
Set Doorbell bit (Local CPU write)
Reset Doorbell bit (EISA write)
0 = No doorbell interrupt pending

Bits 7–0 allow up to eight events or devices on the expansion board to send interrupts to the EISA bus. The above bits can only be reset by the servicing processor on the EISA side.

8.1.1.3.4 EISA System Doorbell Enable Register (Read/Write)

The EISA System Doorbell Enable register is used by the EISA processor to enable or disable interrupt requests to the EISA side. This register is read only from the local side. Upon reset, the EISA System Doorbell Enable register is reset to 0.

EISA Address—XC8Eh
Local Index Address—0Eh

Bit 7	Bit 6	Bit 5	Bit 4	Bit 3	Bit 2	Bit 1	Bit 0

Bit 7–0 1 = Enable doorbell interrupt for corresponding bit position
0 = Disable doorbell interrupt for corresponding bit position

Bits 0 through 7 act as interrupt enables for bits 0 through 7 in the EISA System Doorbell Interrupt/Status register respectively.

8.1.1.3.5 System Interrupt Enable/Control Register (Read/Write)

This register is used by the processor on the EISA side to disable the EINT signal. The EISA processor also can read this register to determine whether there are any pending interrupt requests in the EISA System Doorbell Interrupt/Status register. This register is read only from the local side. Upon reset, this register is reset to 0.

EISA Address—XC89h
Local Index Address—09h

—	—	—	—	—	—	Bit 1	Bit 0

Bit 7–2 — Reserved, set to 0

Bit 1 — (read-only bit)
1 = Enabled interrupts are pending in EISA System Doorbell Interrupt/Status register
0 = No enabled interrupts are pending in EISA System Doorbell Interrupt/Status register

Bit 0 —
1 = Enable interrupts from System Doorbell register (EISA write)
0 = Disable interrupts from System Doorbell register (EISA write)

8.1.2 GLOBAL CONFIGURATION REGISTER (READ/WRITE)

This register is used to program the type of protocol, edge or level-triggered, that will be used with the EINT and LINT interrupt signals. The Global Configuration register is also used to program the preempt timer and provide four bits for a BMIC hardware revision number. This register is read only from the EISA side. Upon reset, bits 0–3 are reset to 0.

EISA Address—XC88h
Local Index Address—08h

Bit 7	Bit 6	Bit 5	Bit 4	Bit 3	Bit 2	Bit 1	Bit 0

Bits 7–4 (read-only)

Hardware revision number of the BMIC

Bit 3 1 = System interrupt pin (EINT) uses edge-triggered protocol (Active high)

0 = System interrupt pin (EINT) uses level-triggered protocol (Active low open collector)

Bit 2 1 = Local interrupt pin (LINT) is set for active high operation

0 = Local interrupt pin (LINT) is set for active low operation

Bits 1, 0 Delay to give up bus after preempt

00 = 3 BCLKs

01 = 32 BCLKs

10 = 64 BCLKs

11 = reserved

EISA Address—XC80h through XC83h (bytes 0–3)
Local Index Address—0h through 3h (bytes 0–3)

ID Register Bytes 0–3:

	7	6	5	4	3	2	1	0
Byte 0	—	MCC14	MCC13	MCC12	MCC11	MCC10	MCC24	MCC23
Byte 1	MCC22	MCC21	MCC20	MCC34	MCC33	MCC32	MCC31	MCC30
Byte 2	MCC43	MCC42	MCC41	MCC40	MCC53	MCC52	MCC51	MCC50
Byte 3	MCC63	MCC62	MCC61	MCC60	MCC73	MCC72	MCC71	MCC70

ID Register Byte 0:

Bit 7	—	Reserved
Bits 6–2	MCC1<4:0>	First character of manufacturer's code
Bits 1, 0	MCC2<4:3>	First portion of second character of manufacturer's code

ID Register Byte 1:

Bits 7–5	MCC2<2:0>	Second portion of second character of manufacturer's code
Bits 4–0	MCC3<4:0>	Third character of manufacturer's code

ID Register Byte 2:

Bits 7–4	MCC4<3:0>	First hex digit of product number
Bits 3–0	MCC5<3:0>	Second hex digit of product number

ID Register Byte 3:

Bits 7–4	MCC6<3:0>	Third hex digit of product number
Bits 4–0	MCC7<3:0>	Hexadecimal digit of product revision

8.1.3 ID REGISTERS

The ID register set consists of four 8-bit registers. These registers are programmed at initialization time with the product identifier for the expansion board which contains the BMIC. The registers are mapped as read-only into the EISA ID I/O address range. Upon reset, the ID byte 0 register will contain the value 0111XXXX, which is the EISA ID delay value. The local processor should program byte 0 last. If the external ID support scheme is selected, then these registers are disabled. The bit definitions defined below have significance for the EISA ID protocol but not for any BMIC hardware functionality. Upon reset, ID bytes 1–3 are not initialized to a fixed value.

8.2 Local Processor Only Registers

The following is a table of the Local Processor Only register group listing the number of registers, register type (read/write) as related to the local side, register name, and register size:

Number	Local Type	Register Name	Active Bits per Register
INDEX REGISTERS			
1	R/W	Local Index Register	8 Bits
1	R/W	Local Data Register	8 Bits
1	R/W	Local Status/Control Register	8 Bits
DATA CHANNEL TRANSFER REGISTERS			
4	R/W	Data Transfer Channel 0 Base Address Register	8 Bits
4	R/W	Data Transfer Channel 1 Base Address Register	8 Bits
4	R	Data Transfer Channel 0 Current Address Register	8 Bits
4	R	Data Transfer Channel 1 Current Address Register	8 Bits
3	R/W	Data Transfer Channel 0 Base Count Register	8 Bits
3	R/W	Data Transfer Channel 1 Base Count Register	8 Bits
3	R	Data Transfer Channel 0 Current Count Register	8 Bits
3	R	Data Transfer Channel 1 Current Count Register	8 Bits
DATA TRANSFER CONTROL/STATUS REGISTERS			
1	W	Channel 0 Transfer Strobe Register	0
1	W	Channel 1 Transfer Strobe Register	0
1	R/W	Channel 0 Configuration Register	8 Bits
1	R/W	Channel 1 Configuration Register	8 Bits
1	R/W	Channel 0 Status Register	6 Bits
1	R/W	Channel 1 Status Register	6 Bits
PEEK/POKE REGISTER			
4	R/W	Peek/Poke Address Register	8 Bits
4	R/W	Peek/Poke Data Register	8 Bits
1	R/W	Peek/Poke Control Register	8 Bits
I/O DECODE REGISTERS			
1	R/W	I/O Decode Range 0 Base Address Register	8 Bits
1	R/W	I/O Decode Range 1 Base Address Register	8 Bits
1	R/W	I/O Decode Range 0 Control Register	8 Bits
1	R/W	I/O Decode Range 1 Control Register	8 Bits
TRANSFER BUFFER INTERFACE (TBI) REGISTERS			
2	R/W	TBI Channel 0 Base Address Register	8 Bits
2	R/W	TBI Channel 1 Base Address Register	8 Bits
2	R	TBI Channel 0 Current Address Register	8 Bits
2	R	TBI Channel 1 Current Address Register	8 Bits

1

8.2.1 INDEX REGISTERS

The BMIC's register set is accessed using the local Index and Local Data register set (refer to Section 3.2.6.1). The Local Index and Local Data registers are mapped directly into the Local Processor interface of the BMIC.

8.2.1.1 Local Index Register (Read/Write)

The Local Index register contains the address of the BMIC register that is currently being accessed. An optional auto-increment mode is supported through this register, which automatically increments the index register after each Local Data register read or write. Upon reset, the Local Index register is set to 0.

Local Address—1h

Bit 7	Bit 6	Bit 5	Bit 4	Bit 3	Bit 2	Bit 1	Bit 0

Bit 7 — 1 = Autoincrement local index register after access to local data register

0 = Do not autoincrement

Bits 6–0 — Local index address

8.2.1.2 Local Data Register (Read/Write)

During a BMIC local register access, the value of the register being accessed is passed through this register.

Local Address—0h

Bit 7	Bit 6	Bit 5	Bit 4	Bit 3	Bit 2	Bit 1	Bit 0

8.2.2 LOCAL STATUS/CONTROL REGISTER (READ/WRITE)

The Local Status/Control register is directly mapped into the Local Processor interface and is accessible using the two address lines (LADS<1:0>). This register provides current local doorbell interrupt status, current Channel 0 and Channel 1 interrupt and Base register status, and current peek/poke cycle status. This register is also used by the local processor on the expansion board to disable and provide the current status of the LINT signal (active or inactive). Bit 4 in this register is read/write and the remaining bits are read only. Upon reset, the Local Status/Control register is reset to 0.

Local Address—2h

Bit 7	Bit 6	Bit 5	Bit 4	Bit 3	Bit 2	Bit 1	Bit 0

Bit 7 — R 1 = Enabled interrupts are pending in Local Doorbell register

0 = No enabled interrupts are pending in Local Doorbell register

Bit 6 — R 1 = Enabled interrupts are pending from channel 1 events

0 = No enabled interrupts are pending from channel 1 events

Bit 5 — R 1 = Enabled interrupts are pending from channel 0 events

0 = No enabled interrupts are pending from channel 0 events

Bit 4 — R/W 1 = Local interrupts enabled

0 = All local interrupts disabled

Bit 3 — R 1 = Local interrupt signal (LINT) is currently active

0 = LINT signal is currently inactive

Bit 2 — R 1 = Most recent peek/poke command is still pending

0 = Most recent peek/poke command is complete

Bit 1 — R 1 = Base register set for channel 1 is busy

0 = Base register set channel 1 is available

Bit 0 — R 1 = Base register set for channel 0 is busy

0 = Base register set for channel 0 is available

8.2.3 DATA CHANNEL TRANSFER REGISTERS

The Data Channel Transfer register set is used to control burst and standard EISA data transfers. Each transfer channel has a set of Base and Current registers, and also a Transfer Strobe, Configuration, and Status register.

NOTE:

The Base register set and the Transfer Strobe register must be initialized before a transfer can take place. They are not initialized to a fixed value upon reset.

8.2.3.1 Channel 0 and 1 Transfer Base Address Registers (Read/Write)

Each Channel has an associated Base Address register set. The Transfer Base Address registers are programmed with the 32-bit starting address to be used during the data transfer. After the Base registers have been programmed, they should not be programmed again until the contents of the Base registers have been transferred to the Current registers. The Base Address registers are not initialized to a fixed value upon reset.

Channel 0 Local Index Address—43h through 46h (bytes 0 through 3)
Channel 1 Local Index Address—63h through 66h (bytes 0 through 3)

BYTE 3	BYTE 2	BYTE 1	BYTE 0

8.2.3.2 Channel 0 and 1 Transfer Current Address Registers (Read Only)

Each Channel has an associated Current Address register set. The Transfer Current Address registers contain the real-time status of the 32-bit transfer address. The Current Address registers are not initialized to a fixed value upon reset.

NOTE:
The current register set is readable by the local processor. However, there are possible coherency problems involved with reading multiple bytes while the current registers are being updated during a transfer. To avoid these problems, a channel's transfer should be temporarily suspended (using the channel's Configuration Register) before trying to read the channel's current register set.

Channel 0 Local Index Address—53h through 56h (bytes 0 through 3)
Channel 1 Local Index Address—73h through 76h (bytes 0 through 3)

BYTE 3	BYTE 2	BYTE 1	BYTE 0

8.2.3.3 Channel 0 and 1 Transfer Base Count Registers (Read/Write)

Each Channel has an associated Base Count register set. The Transfer Base Count registers are programmed with the number of bytes to be transferred. Each Channel has 22 bits of counter space for a maximum transfer block size of 4 Mbytes. Bits 22 and 23 are used for channel control. The Base Count registers are not initialized to a fixed value upon reset.

Channel 0 Local Address—40h through 42h (bytes 0 through 2)
Channel 1 Local Address—60h through 62h (bytes 0 through 2)

BYTE 2			BYTE 1	BYTE 0
Bit 23	Bit 22	Bit 16–21	Bits 8–15	Bits 0–7

Bit 23 — R/W 1 = Start transfer as soon as base register set is copied to current register set

0 = Hold transfer after current register set is loaded. Wait for transfer suspend bit 0 to be reset

Bit 22 — W 1 = Transfer from bus master expansion board to EISA bus (EISA write)

0 = Transfer from EISA bus to bus master expansion board (EISA read). This is applicable only to channel 1 and not for channel 0, as channel 0 can perform EISA WRITE transfers only.

Bits 0–21 — R/W Transfer byte count

If bit 23 in the Base Count register is not set to a 1, the channel suspend bit (CFGSU) in that channel's corresponding configuration register is automatically set to a 1. The bit will be set during the Base register to Current register transfer. This ensures that a channel request for that channel is not generated. When the local processor resets the channel suspend bit to 0 in the corresponding Configuration register, a transfer request will be generated.

NOTE:
If the initial byte count is programmed to be "0", no transfer request will be generated and no transfer will occur.

8.2.3.4 Channel 0 and 1 Transfer Current Count Registers (Read Only)

Each Channel has an associated Current Count register set. The Transfer Current Count registers contain the 22-bit value representing the number of bytes remaining to be transferred on the channel. This value can be from one byte to four Mbytes. Bit 23 is reserved. Bit 22 is used to indicate the direction of the transfer. Upon reset, the Current Count registers are not initialized. At the end of a transfer, this register contains the value of the number of bytes transferred during the last cycle.

Channel 0 Local Index Address—50h through 52h (bytes 0 through 2)
Channel 1 Local Index Address—70h through 72h (bytes 0 through 2)

BYTE 2			BYTE 1	BYTE 0
Bit 23	Bit 22	Bit 16–21	Bits 8–15	Bits 0–7

Bit 23 — Reserved

Bit 22 — 1 = Current transfer is from bus master expansion board to EISA bus

0 = Current transfer is from EISA bus to bus master expansion board

Bits 0–21 — Current transfer byte count

8.2.4 DATA TRANSFER STATUS/CONTROL REGISTERS

8.2.4.1 Channel 0 and 1 Transfer Strobe Registers (Write Only)

Each channel has an associated Transfer Channel Strobe register. The Strobe register is used to initiate the transfer of information from the Base register set to the Current register set. The act of writing to this register will initiate the Base to Current transfer. There are no bits to this register, the data written to this register is ignored and the register cannot be read.

If bit 23 in the Transfer Base Count Register is set to a 1, the data transfer will be requested immediately. Otherwise, the transfer will wait until the transfer suspend bit CFGSU for the corresponding channel is reset. The transfer suspend bit is located in the Configuration register.

Channel 0 Local Index Address—49h
Channel 1 Local Index Address—69h

8.2.4.2 Channel 0 and 1 Transfer Channel Configuration Registers (Read/Write)

Each channel has an associated Transfer Configuration register. Upon reset, the Configuration registers are reset to 0. The Configuration register set is used to configure the channels as follows:

Channel 0 Local Index Address—48h
Channel 1 Local Index Address—68h

Bit 7	Bit 6	Bit 5	Bit 4	Bit 3	Bit 2	Bit 1	Bit 0
CFGEA	CFGIE	CFGIT	CFGFF	CFGBR	CFGCL	CFGEI	CFGSU

Bit 7 — CFGEA 1 = Enable real-time address transfer to transfer buffer logic

0 = Disable real-time address transfer to transfer buffer logic

Bit 6 — CFGIE Reserved. This bit must always be written with 0.

Bit 5 — CFGIT 1 = Enable interrupt on transfer complete

0 = Disable interrupt on transfer complete

Bit 4 — CFGFF 1 = Give up ownership of EISA bus if a transfer interruption occurs on this channel

0 = Retain ownership of EISA bus if a transfer interruption occurs on this channel

Bit 3 — CFGBR 1 = Enable EISA burst transfer

0 = Disable burst transfers (channel uses non-burst (2 BCLK) cycle transfers)

Bit 2 — CFGCL 1 = Clear channel

Stop any transfers and flush the data FIFO

0 = No operation

Always returns a 0 when read

Bit 1 — CFGEI Reserved. This bit must always be written with 0.

Bit 0 — CFGSU 1 = Temporarily suspend transfer

0 = Allow transfer to proceed

The CFGEA Bit enables the real-time address transfer to the transfer buffer logic. If the CFGEA bit is set to a 1, the transfer buffer real-time address for the active channel is transferred to the transfer buffer logic each time that channel regains the bus and the start address is transferred each time the Base register contents are loaded into the corresponding Current registers. If the CFGEA bit is set to 0, the address load signal (TLD#) is activated only when the Base is loaded into the Current register (refer to Section 5.3).

The CFGIE Bit is a reserved bit. Zero (0) must always be written at this bit location. This bit can be ignored during register reads.

The CFGIT Bit enables an interrupt on transfer complete (EOP).

The CFGFF Bit controls whether EISA bus ownership is relinquished or maintained after a transfer interruption. When a channel is interrupted for any reason, (1K page break, FIFO stall, channel clear, transfer suspend, or transfer complete), the BMIC may relinquish the EISA bus depending on the state of the CFGFF bit in the above register. The function of the CFGFF bit, as related to the above channel interruptions, is as follows:

If the CFGFF bit = 1, the BMIC will relinquish control of the EISA bus upon the detection of any of the above interruptions. This will occur regardless if there are additional data transfer requests pending. If there are additional data transfer requests pending, the BMIC will reassert MREQ# a minimum of two BCLK's later to reacquire the EISA bus.

If the CFGFF bit = 0, the BMIC retains ownership of the EISA bus upon detection of a FIFO stall or 1K page break as long as a preempt timer timeout has not occurred. If there are additional data requests pending, the BMIC will immediately perform the pending transfer and then rearbitrate for the EISA bus to complete the interrupted transfer. If there are no additional data requests pending, the BMIC will relinquish ownership of the EISA bus only after the current transfer interruption has been serviced and completed.

NOTE:
During a FIFO pause, CFGFF is ignored.

The CFGBR Bit defines the type of transfer cycles (burst or non-burst) that can be requested on the transfer channel. If burst cycles have been selected and system memory is unable to run burst cycles, the BMIC will default to non-burst (two BCLK) or mismatched cycles.

The CFGCL Bit is used to generate a channel clear. A channel clear terminates the current transfer and flushes the associated FIFO. The FIFO is reset during the next Base to Current register copy.

Before a channel is issued a clear command, the channel must first be suspended by writing a "1" into Bit 0 (CFGSU) of the Transfer Channel Configuration Register. Next the Transfer Channel Status Register must be read. If the TSTTC (Bit 0) is set to a "1", then the channel has already completed the transfer. The channel is then unsuspended (write a "0" into Bit 0 [CFGSU] of the Transfer Channel Configuration Register), and the TSTTC bit is then cleared.

If the TSTTC bit is a "0", then the TSTEN bit is checked. If this bit is a "1", then the channel has not returned to idle yet, and the Transfer Channel Status Register is re-polled. If the TSTEN bit is a "0", then the channel has successfully returned to idle and can now be cleared with no errors. This is done by setting Bit 2 (CFGCL bit) to a "1" in the Transfer Channel Configuration Register. A flowchart for this operation is shown in the following figure.

1

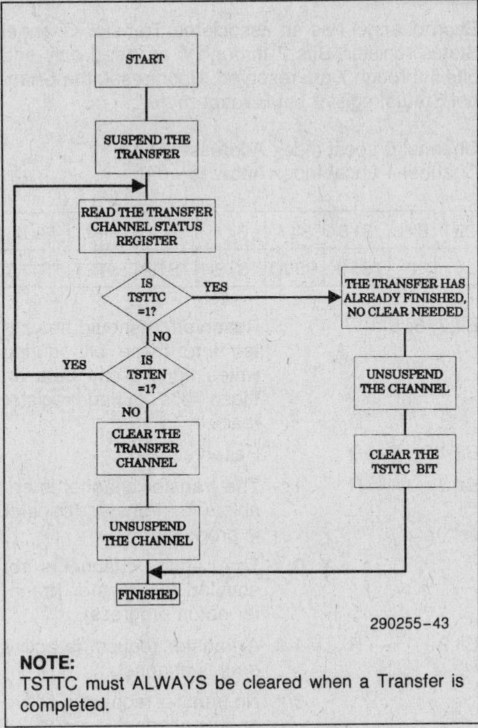

NOTE:
TSTTC must ALWAYS be cleared when a Transfer is completed.

Figure 8-1. Channel Clear Flowchart

If a channel is enabled for a transfer during a Channel clear, the BMIC will generate an end of process by asserting TEOP#. If the channel is not enabled for a transfer or the channel clear is preceded by a channel suspend, a TEOP# will not be generated. The channel clear will be active for at least two complete BCLK cycles.

The CFGEI Bit is a reserved bit. Zero (0) must always be written at this bit location. This bit can be ignored during register reads.

The CFGSU Bit is used to temporarily suspend the data transfer.

8.2.4.3 Channel 0 and 1 Transfer Channel Status Registers (Read/Write)

Each channel has an associated Transfer Channel Status register. Bits 2 through 4 are read only and bits 5 through 7 are reserved. Upon reset, the Channel Status register set is reset to "0".

Channel 0 Local Index Address—4Ah
Channel 1 Local Index Address—6Ah

Bit 7	Bit 6	Bit 5	Bit 4	Bit 3	Bit 2	Bit 1	Bit 0
0	0	TST1K	RSVD	TSTEN	TSTIP	TSTET	TSTTC

Bit 7, 6, 5 —W Reserved. 0 should be written into these bits during writes. Ignore any data on these bits during register reads

Bit 4 — R Reserved

Bit 3 — R 1 = The transfer channel is enabled for transfer (transfer in progress)

0 = The transfer channel is not enabled for transfer (transfer not in progress)

Bit 2 — R 1 = A transfer request is active on this channel.

0 = No transfer request is active on this channel.

Bit 1 — Reserved. Ignore data at this bit location.

Bit 0 — R/W 1 = Transfer completed on this channel (read)

Reset this bit (write)

0 = No transfer completion on this channel (read)

No action (write)

Bits (7), (6), TST1K, and (4) are reserved. Any data read from these bits should be ignored.

The TSTIP and TSTEN Bits are read only and indicate whether the corresponding channel is requesting a transfer or whether the channel's transfer is currently in progress.

The TSTET Bit is a reserved bit and should be ignored during all register reads. Zero (0) should always be written at this bit location.

The TSTTC Bit is read/write and is used to indicate the current end-of-process status of the transfer. If an EOP occurs, the BMIC will set bit (0) to a "1" and generate an interrupt to the local processor. The BMIC will not generate the interrupt if the CFGIT bit in the channel's corresponding Transfer Configuration register is set to a "0".

NOTE:
The TSTTC bit is implemented as a sticky bit. This bit can be reset by the local processor without affecting the status of the other bits in the register.

8.2.5 PEEK/POKE REGISTERS

The Peek/Poke register set consists of four 8-bit Address registers, four 8-bit Data registers and one Peek/Poke control register. The Address and Data registers are used to define the 32-bit address and data that will be used during the peek/poke cycles, and the Control register is used to request and define the type of cycle that will be generated (peek, poke, or locked exchange). The peek/poke or locked exchange cycle is initiated by writing to the Peek/Poke control register. During Reset, the Peek/Poke Address registers and the Control register are reset to "0".

8.2.5.1 Peek/Poke Address Registers (Read/Write)

The four 8-bit Peek/Poke Address registers contain the 32-bit peek/poke address. Only the lower 16 bits are used for I/O cycles. Address bits 0 and 1 are ignored. Upon reset, this register is reset to "0".

Local Index Address—34h through 37h (bytes 0 through 3)

BYTE 3	BYTE 2	BYTE 1	BYTE 0
Bits 24–31	Bits 16–23	Bits 8–15	Bits 2–7

8.2.5.2 Peek/Poke Data Registers (Read/Write)

The four 8-bit peek/poke data registers hold the data for the peek/poke cycle. Each peek/poke data register is associated with one byte lane. During peek transfers, only those peek/poke data registers whose corresponding byte enable bit is set in the peek/poke control register contain valid data. During poke transfers, the data must be placed in the appropriate register as determined by the corresponding byte enable bit.

Local Index Address—30h through 33h (bytes 0 through 3)

BYTE 3	BYTE 2	BYTE 1	BYTE 0
Bits 24–31	Bits 16–23	Bits 8–15	Bits 0–7

The Shared register timings (t85, t93, t96–t98) are used when accessing the Peek/Poke Data registers.

8.2.5.3 Peek/Poke Control Register (Read/Write)

The Peek/Poke Control register is written to by the local processor when a peek/poke transfer is desired over the EISA bus. Upon reset, this register is reset to "0".

Local Index Address—38h

Bit 7	Bit 6	Bit 5	Bit 4	Bit 3	Bit 2	Bit 1	Bit 0

Bit 7 — Reserved. Set to 0

Bits 6, 5 — 10 = Do read cycle (peek)
01 = Do write cycle (poke)
11 = Do locked exchange cycle (peek/poke)
00 = Do Nothing (Nop)

Bit 4 — 1 = Do memory cycle
0 = Do I/O cycle

Bit 3, Bit 2, Bit 1, Bit 0 — 1 = Byte enable for given byte lane
0 = Byte disable for given byte lane

Bits (6) and (5) are used to define the type of cycle requested (peek, poke or locked exchange).

Bit (4) defines whether the cycle is memory or I/O.

Bits (3–0) are used to define the byte enables for the doubleword data written to or read from the Peek/Poke data register. Peek/Poke cycles will not be generated for illegal combinations of byte enables.

ILLEGAL COMBINATIONS OF BYTE ENABLES:

Bits 3–0	IBE# <3:0>
0000	1111
0101	1010
1001	0110
1010	0101
1011	0100
1101	0010

NOTE:
Bits 3–0 in the above register are active high whereas the EISA byte enables (IBE# <3:0>) are active low.

8.2.6 I/O RANGE DECODE REGISTERS

The I/O Decode Range register set consists of two I/O Decode Range Base Address registers and two I/O Decode Range Control Registers. The Address registers are used to define the address range of interest to the expansion board and the Control registers are used to define the decode range size, type of decode (slot specific or general), and the response of the local I/O (32-bit EISA or 8-bit EISA). The I/O decode register set controls the two IOSEL# pins on the BMIC. Each pin has an associated Address and Control register.

Upon reset, the I/O Decode Range registers are initialized according to the following table:

Local Processor	*Local Processor Not Present		*Local Processor Present	
Range	**Rng 0**	**Rng 1**	**Rng 0**	**Rng 1**
Control Registers	60h	60h	20h	20h
Address Registers	E0h	00h	00h	00h

*Refer to Section 7.3 for information regarding "local processor present" or "local processor not present".

8.2.6.1 Range 0 and 1 I/O Decode Base Address Registers (Read/Write)

Each Decode range and IOSEL# pin has an associated I/O Decode Range Base Address register.

Range 0 Local Index Address—39h
Range 1 Local Index Address—3Bh

Bit 7	Bit 6	Bit 5	Bit 4	Bit 3	Bit 2	Bit 1	Bit 0

During general I/O decode, bits 7–0 are used to compare against EISA address lines LA<9:2>. During slot specific decode, bits 7 and 6 are compared against EISA address lines LA<11:10> and bits 5–0 are compared against EISA address lines LA<7:2> (refer to Section 4.8).

8.2.6.2 Range 0 and 1 I/O Decode Control Registers (Read/Write)

Each Decode range and IOSEL# pin has an associated I/O Decode Range Control register.

Range 0 Local Index Address—3Ah
Range 1 Local Index Address—3Ch

Bit 7	Bit 6	Bit 5	Bit 4	Bit 3	Bit 2	Bit 1	Bit 0

Bit 7 — 1 = Respond as a 32-bit EISA I/O device
0 = Respond as an 8-bit EISA I/O device

Bit 6 — 1 = Slot Specific I/O Decode
0 = General I/O Decode

Bit 5 — 1 = IOSEL# held during CMD# active
0 = IOSEL# follows I/O address changes

Bit 4, Bit 3, Bit 2, Bit 1, Bit 0:
1 = Do not compare I/O Range Base Address Register and corresponding EISA address bit (Mask)
0 = Compare I/O Range Base Address Register with corresponding EISA address bit

Refer to Section 4.8 for a complete description of the I/O Decode Range Control registers and the BMIC decode function in general.

8.2.7 TRANSFER BUFFER INTERFACE (TBI) REGISTERS (READ/WRITE)

The TBI registers are programmed to provide the 16-bit start address of the data transfer for use by the transfer buffer logic (refer to Section 5.3). Each transfer channel has a corresponding TBI Base and Current Address register set. The contents of the TBI Base Address registers are transferred to the TBI Current Address registers during a write to the channel's corresponding Transfer Channel Strobe Register.

8.2.7.1 Channel 0 and 1 TBI Base Address Registers (Read/Write)

The BMIC provides two 8-bit TBI Base Address registers per channel. The registers are programmed with the 16-bit start address of the data in the Transfer Buffer memory space. The TBI Base Address register set is not initialized to a fixed value upon reset.

Channel 0 Local Index Address—4Bh and 4Ch (byte 0 and 1)
Channel 1 Local Index Address—6Bh and 6Ch (byte 0 and 1)

Byte 1	Byte 0

8.2.7.2 Channel 0 and 1 TBI Current Address Registers (Read Only)

The BMIC provides two 8-bit TBI Current Address registers per channel. The TBI Current Address registers contain the 16-bit real-time address of the data transfer. The contents of the Current register set are transferred to the external buffer logic at the beginning of every new data block transfer. The BMIC may also be programmed to transfer the contents of the Current Address register each time the corresponding channel regains control of the bus (refer to Section 5.3). The TBI Current Address register set is reset to "0" upon device reset.

Channel 0 Local Index Address—58h and 59h (byte 0 and 1)
Channel 1 Local Index Address—78h and 79h (byte 0 and 1)

Byte 1	Byte 0

NOTE:
The TBI current registers contain real-time status and may change at anytime. If a stable value is needed while reading a set of these registers, the channel should be temporarily suspended by setting the CFGSU bit in the Channel Configuration register to a "1" before these registers are read.

9.0 DETAILED PIN DESCRIPTION

9.1 EISA Interface Signals

Pin Name	Description
START#	I/O TRI-STATED (EISA CYCLE START STROBE) The START# signal provides timing control at the start of a cycle. During EISA master mode, the BMIC drives this signal low after LA<31:2> and M/IO become valid and negates START# on the rising edge of BCLK after one BCLK cycle time. During EISA slave mode, the BMIC uses this signal to indicate the start of a slave bus cycle. It is sampled on the rising edge of BCLK. Upon reset, this pin is tri-stated and placed in input mode.
CMD#	INPUT (EISA COMMAND STROBE) The CMD# provides timing control within the cycle. The 82358 Bus Controller asserts CMD# on the rising edge of BCLK, simultaneously with the negation of START#. CMD# is held low until the end of the cycle. The BMIC uses CMD# in EISA slave mode for timing control during internal Shared register read/write accesses.
M/IO	I/O TRI-STATED (EISA MEMORY/IO CYCLE STATUS PIN) M/IO is used to indicate that the type of cycle in progress is a memory cycle (high) or I/O cycle (low). M/IO is pipelined from one cycle to the next and must be latched by the addressed memory slave if needed for the whole cycle. During EISA master mode, the BMIC drives this signal. The BMIC will drive this pin high during burst and non-burst (two BCLK) cycles. The value of M/IO in a Peek/Poke or locked exchange cycle depends on the programmed value of bit 4 in the Peek/Poke Control register. During EISA slave mode, the M/IO pin is an input. As a slave, the BMIC will respond only as an I/O device. Upon reset, this pin is tri-stated and placed in input mode.
W/R	I/O TRI-STATED (EISA WRITE/READ CYCLE STATUS PIN) The W/R status signal identifies the cycle as a write (high) or read (low). W/R is pipelined from one cycle to the next and must be latched by the addressed memory slave if needed for the whole cycle. During EISA master mode, the BMIC drives this signal. During EISA slave mode, this pin is an input. Upon reset, W/R is tri-stated and placed in input mode.
EXRDY	I/O OPEN COLLECTOR (EISA READY SIGNAL) EXRDY is used by EISA I/O and memory slaves to request wait states during a cycle. Each wait state is one BCLK period. During EISA master mode, the BMIC first samples this signal on the falling edge of BCLK after CMD# is asserted. If it is low, the BMIC will insert a wait state, and continue inserting wait states as long as EXRDY is low at each successive falling edge of BCLK. During EISA slave mode, the BMIC drives EXRDY inactive until it is ready to complete cycles addressed to it. The EXRDY pin is an open collector output.
EX32#	I/O OPEN COLLECTOR (EISA 32-BIT SLAVE RESPONSE PIN) EX32# is an open collector and is used by memory or I/O slaves to indicate their support of 32-bit transfers. During EISA master mode, the BMIC samples EX32# on the same rising edge of BCLK that START# is deasserted. The BMIC uses this pin to determine if the addressed slave is capable of 32-bit transfers. During peek/poke and non-burst EISA data transfers, the BMIC is a 32-bit master only and will allow the 82358 Bus Controller to do all necessary bus conversions. During EISA slave mode, the BMIC drives EX32# low if it has 32-bit data to send to the EISA bus, otherwise this signal is inactive.

9.1 EISA Interface Signals (Continued)

Pin Name	Description
MASTER16#	OUTPUT OPEN COLLECTOR (EISA 16-BIT MASTER CONTROL) In master mode, the BMIC will assert MASTER16# (at the same time as START#) for one BCLK period when it is capable of downshifting from a 32-bit master to a 16-bit master. The BMIC will downshift if necessary during memory burst transfers only. The BMIC will automatically downshift from a 32- to 16-bit master if the EX32# signal is sampled inactive and the SLBURST# signal is sampled active. MASTER16# has no function in slave mode.
AEN	INPUT (EISA ADDRESS ENABLE SIGNAL) The BMIC uses AEN when in EISA slave mode to qualify I/O addresses. When negated (low), the BMIC uses AEN to decode possible accesses to its general and slot specific I/O space. When asserted (high), the address on the EISA bus will be ignored by the BMIC. AEN is sampled on the falling edge of CMD#. This signal is not used in master mode.
MSBURST#	OUTPUT TRI-STATED (EISA MASTER BURST SIGNAL) The BMIC asserts MSBURST# to indicate to the addressed memory slave that the BMIC will provide burst cycles. If the BMIC samples SLBURST# active on the rising edge of BCLK after START# is asserted, the BMIC will activate MSBURST# on the next BCLK falling edge and will proceed with burst cycles. If the BMIC samples SLBURST negated, MSBURST# will not be activated and the BMIC will proceed with either non-burst (two BCLK) or mismatched cycles, depending on the size of the slave device addressed. This signal is not used in slave mode. Upon reset, this pin is tri-stated.
SLBURST#	INPUT (EISA SLAVE BURST SIGNAL) The BMIC uses this signal in master mode to determine if the addresed slave memory is capable of supporting burst transfers. If the BMIC samples SLBURST# active on the rising edge of BCLK after START# is asserted, the BMIC will proceed with burst cycles. If the BMIC samples SLBURST# negated, either non-burst (two BCLK) or mismatched cycles will be generated.
LOCK#	OUTPUT TRI-STATED (EISA RESOURCE LOCK SIGNAL) The BMIC asserts this signal to guarantee exclusive memory and I/O access during locked peek/poke exchange. Upon reset, this pin is tri-stated.
MREQ#	OUTPUT (EISA MASTER BUS REQUEST SIGNAL) MREQ# is asserted by the BMIC to request EISA bus access. The BMIC will begin driving the bus with the address and control signals on the falling edge of BCLK, two BCLKs after MAK# is sampled active. During an EISA write transfer, MREQ# will not be asserted until the FIFO on the selected channel is full. During an EISA read transfer, MREQ# will be asserted immediately after receiving a transfer request, assuming that a slave cycle is not currently in progress. Upon reset, this pin is driven inactive high.
MAK#	INPUT (EISA MASTER BUS ACKNOWLEDGE SIGNAL) The MAK# signal is asserted by the 82357 (ISP) to grant EISA bus access to the BMIC. The BMIC samples MAK# on the falling edge of BCLK and will begin driving the bus with the address and control signals on the falling edge of BCLK, two BCLKs after MAK# is sampled active. The MAK# signal may be negated by the ISP to indicate to the BMIC that another device requires EISA bus access. The BMIC will negate MREQ# to release the bus within 64 BCLKs (8 μs) of sampling MAK# negated.
EINT	OUTPUT OPEN COLLECTOR (EISA INTERRUPT REQUEST SIGNAL) The EINT line is used by the BMIC to interrupt the system CPU or EISA bus master to request service. EINT can be programmed for either edge or level-triggered operations and is an open collector output in level-triggered mode. Upon reset, EINT is placed in level-triggered mode and floating.
BCLK	INPUT (EISA BUS CLOCK) This clock signal is used by the BMIC to synchronize the EISA control signals and data transfers to the system clock. BCLK typically runs at a frequency of 8.33 MHz with a normal duty cycle of 50%. The BCLK period is sometimes extended by the 82358 (EBC) by up to one BCLK period for synchronization purposes.

9.1 EISA Interface Signals (Continued)

Pin Name	Description
RESET	INPUT (EISA RESET SIGNAL) This signal is used by the BMIC to initialize all of its internal registers and state machines to a known state. This signal is asynchronous with respect to BCLK. To reset the BMIC properly, the RESET signal must be active for eight BCLK periods.
IDAT<31:0>	I/O TRI-STATED (EISA DATA LINES/UPPER 22 ADDRESS LINES) These data signals interface to the EISA bus through external, 74F245 bi-directional TTL buffers. The upper 22 data lines are also multiplexed to function as the upper 22 EISA address lines. The 22 upper address signals are latched into external 74F573 TTL latches during transfers as necessary by the BMIC. Both the external data buffers and the address latches are controlled by the BMIC during all slave and master mode data transfers. Upon reset, these pins are tri-stated.
IADS<11:10>	(INPUT) (EISA ADDRESS INPUT LINES) These two address lines are input only and are only used during slave mode. They are used along with IADS<9:2> and EISA byte enables IBE<3:0> # for I/O address decoding. The corresponding EISA output address lines LA<11:10> are part of the upper 22 address lines that are multiplexed and sent out through the upper 22 data lines.
IADS<9:2>	I/O TRI-STATED (EISA LOWER ADDRESS LINES) These eight address lines are part of the lower EISA address lines and are connected directly to the EISA bus. When the BMIC is a master, it drives these lines directly to the EISA bus. The upper 22 addresses are latched from the data bus. IADS<9:2> are pipelined from one cycle to the next and should be latched by the addressed slave if required for the whole cycle. When the BMIC is a slave, it monitors these lines along with EISA address lines IADS<11:10> and EISA byte enables IBE<3:0> # for I/O address decoding. Upon reset, these pins are tri-stated and placed in input mode. The following address lines are used during I/O decoding as shown: Slot specific I/O address decoding (expansion board)—IADS<11:2> Slot specific I/O address decoding (shared registers)—IADS<11:2>/IBE<3:0> # General I/O address decoding (expansion board)—IADS<9:2>
IBE<3:0> #	I/O TRI-STATED (EISA BYTE ENABLES) IBE# <3:0> are the byte enables of the EISA bus and identify the specific bytes that are active during the current EISA bus cycle. During EISA master mode, the BMIC drives these signals. IBE# <3:0> are pipelined from one cycle to the next and should be latched by the addressed slave if required for the whole cycle. During EISA slave mode, the byte enables are inputs and are used along with EISA address lines IADS<11:2> for internal shared register decoding. Upon reset, these pins are tri-stated and placed in input mode.

9.2 EISA Buffer Control Signals

Pin Name	Description
UALOE#	OUTPUT (EISA UPPER ADDRESS LATCH STROBE AND OUTPUT ENABLE) The UALOE# signal is used by the BMIC to control the external latching of the upper 22 address lines LA<31:10>. UALOE# is designed to be connected to the latch enables and output enables of the 74F573 external address latches. The BMIC updates the external address latches at the beginning of all master mode transfers. The desired address value is placed on the IDAT<31:10> lines and latched by the external latches on the falling edge of UALOE# at the beginning of the transfer. During EISA master mode to enable the EISA address lines <31:10>, the BMIC drives UALOE# low on the rising edge of BCLK, one BCLK prior to the falling edge of START#. UALOE# will remain active until the end of the cycle. During slave mode, the BMIC holds UALOE# high to disable the latches. For additional information with regards to the timing for this signal, refer to the A.C. timing and Basic Function timing sections. Upon reset, this pin is driven inactive high.
IDDIR	OUTPUT (EISA DATA DIRECTION SIGNAL) The IDDIR signal is used by the BMIC to control the direction of the external 74F245 data buffers. During data transfers from the BMIC to the EISA bus, this signal will be driven low. During data transfers from the EISA bus to the BMIC, this signal will be driven high. For additional information regarding the timing for this signal, refer to the A.C. timing and Basic Function timing sections (master and slave). Upon reset, this pin is driven high.
IDOE23# IDOE1# IDOE0#	OUTPUT (EISA DATA BYTE LANE BUFFER ENABLES) The IDOE# signals are used by the BMIC to control the output enables on the external 74F245 data buffers. The IDOE# signals will be driven so that the data buffers are enabled at the appropriate times during master and slave transfers. For additional information with regards to the timing for these signals, refer to the A.C. timing and Basic Function timing sections. Upon reset, these signals are driven inactive high.

9.3 Address Decode Signals

Pin Name	Description
IOSEL#<1:0>	OUTPUT (ADDRESS RANGE DECODE OUTPUTS) The IOSEL# signals are used by the BMIC to enable external logic on the expansion board during slot specific and general purpose I/O decode. These pins become active when the LA<11:2> address lines on the EISA bus contain a value mapped into one of the two possible I/O address decode ranges provided by the BMIC (refer to Section 4.8). Upon reset, these pins are driven inactive high.

9.4 Transfer Buffer Interface Signals

Pin Name	Description
TRQ#	OUTPUT (LOCAL DATA TRANSFER REQUEST SIGNAL) When a data transfer is desired over the Transfer Buffer interface, TRQ# is driven low, indicating to the transfer buffer logic that a transfer is following. TRQ# will remain active until the data transfer is completed or a transfer interruption occurs. Upon reset, this pin is driven inactive high.
TACK#	INPUT (LOCAL DATA TRANSFER ACKNOWLEDGE SIGNAL) External logic uses this signal to acknowledge the transfer of a data item (16-bit word) over the Transfer Buffer interface.
TLD#	OUTPUT (LOCAL ADDRESS COUNTER LOAD SIGNAL) This signal when asserted (low) is used to load the transfer start address and the transfer real-time address into an external address counter as required for data transfers (refer to Section 5.3). TLD# is asserted at the beginning of all new channel accesses to the transfer buffer logic and will remain asserted until acknowledged by TACK#. Upon reset, this pin is driven inactive high.
TDIR	OUTPUT (DATA TRANSFER DIRECTION SIGNAL) This signal is used to inform the transfer buffer logic as to the direction of the current data transfer. When driven (high) data will be transferred from the EISA bus to the expansion board. When driven (low) data will be transferred from the expansion board to the EISA bus. TDIR will be held valid whenever TLD# and TRQ# are active. TDIR will not change states when TRQ# is active. Upon reset, this pin is driven high.
TCHAN	OUTPUT (TRANSFER CHANNEL SELECT SIGNAL) This signal is used by the BMIC to inform the transfer buffer logic as to which channel will be active during the transfer. When driven (low) transfer channel 0 is active and when driven (high) transfer channel 1 is active. TCHAN has the same timings as TDIR and will not change states when TLD# or TRQ# are active. Upon reset, this pin is driven low.
TDAT<15:0>	I/O TRI-STATED (TRANSFER DATA LINES) This bidirectional bus is the BMIC's Transfer Buffer interface data bus. It is used during data transfers between the external transfer buffer logic and the BMIC. The data transferred across the TDAT bus is word aligned. The data lines are also used to transport the transfer address to the transfer buffer logic on the expansion board (refer to Section 5.3). The TDAT bus can be unconditionally disabled by driving the TDOE# signal high. **NOTE:** During EISA write data transfers, the TDAT lines are inputs and operate independent of the value of TDOE#. Upon reset, the TDAT bus is tri-stated.
TDOE#	INPUT (TRANSFER INTERFACE DATA OUTPUT ENABLE) When driven high, this pin can be used by external logic to unconditionally disable the BMIC from driving the TDAT<15:0> lines. This feature eliminates the need for the BMIC to gain prior permission to drive the TDAT bus and also allows external logic the ability to time-share the TDAT bus.
TEOP#	OUTPUT OPEN COLLECTOR (TRANSFER END-OF-PROCESS SIGNAL) This signal is an open collector signal that indicates the end of a transfer to the external transfer buffer logic. TEOP# is driven low by the BMIC to indicate the end of transfer. The TEOP# pin requires an external 2.5K to 3.2K pullup resistor for proper operation.
TCLK	INPUT (TRANSFER CLOCK) All transfer control signals are synchronous to this clock. The frequency should be in the range of 16 MHz to 20 MHz to maintain a 33 Mbyte/sec burst transfer rate over the EISA bus. This clock may be completely asynchronous to the EISA BCLK signal.

9.5 Local Processor Interface Signals

Pin Name	Description
LDAT<7:0>	I/O TRI-STATED (LOCAL PROCESSOR INTERFACE DATA BUS) This bidirectional bus is used to transfer commands and status between the BMIC and the local processor on the expansion board. If a local Processor is not present, this bus will need to be connected to the ISA bus (refer to Section 7.3). Upon reset these pins are tri-stated.
LRD#	INPUT (LOCAL PROCESSOR INTERFACE READ STROBE) The local processor asserts LRD# to indicate to the BMIC that it should drive its data onto the LDAT bus. LRD# is asserted for register access to the BMIC's Local Processor interface. The LADS lines and the LCS# signal must be valid 10 ns before the falling edge of LRD# and remain valid until LRD# is deasserted.
LWR#	INPUT (LOCAL PROCESSOR INTERFACE STROBE) The local processor asserts LWR# to indicate to the BMIC that it may latch data from the LDAT bus. LWR# is asserted for write accesses to the BMIC's Local Processor interface. The LADS lines and the LCS signal must be valid 10 ns before the falling edge of LWR# and remain valid until LWR# is deasserted.
LCS#	INPUT (LOCAL PROCESSOR INTERFACE CHIP) A (low) on this pin enables LWR# and LRD# communication between the BMIC and the local processor on the expansion board. The LRD# and LWR# signals are ignored unless the LCS# signal is active. LCS# must be asserted 10 ns before LRD# and LWR# and remain active until the inactive edge of LRD# and LWR#.
LADS<1:0>	INPUT (LOCAL PROCESSOR ADDRESS SELECT) These address lines are used by the local processor to select the Local Data, Local Index, and Local Status/Control registers. The BMIC uses these registers as part of an indexing scheme to access all of its internal registers (refer to Sections 3.2.6.1 and 8.2.1). **LADS1 LADS0** 0 0 = Local Data register 0 1 = Local Index register 1 0 = Local Status/Control register 1 1 = Reserved
LINT	OUTPUT (LOCAL PROCESSOR INTERRUPT SIGNAL) This signal informs the local processor that an event has occurred which requires the local processor's attention. This pin can be programmed for either active high or active low level operations. After being asserted, LINT will not return to an inactive state until the interrupt has been serviced. The LINT signal is not an open collector output during active low operations and will require external logic if interrupts need to be tied together on the local side. Upon reset, this pin is driven high and placed in active low level mode.
LRDY	I/O (LOCAL PROCESSOR READY) This signal is the acknowledgement from the BMIC to the local processor that it is finished with the current Shared register access cycle. The LRDY pin is also used by external logic to indicate to the BMIC that a local processor is not present. If a local processor is not present, the LRDY signal must be driven low during reset (refer to Section 7.3). If a local processor is present, a weak pullup resistor must be connected to the LRDY output to insure that LRDY is high during the time reset is active.

9.6 Power Supplies

V_{CC} — 11 Power pins

V_{SS} — 13 Ground pins

Total number of power supply pins: 24

10.0 BASIC FUNCTION TIMING DIAGRAMS

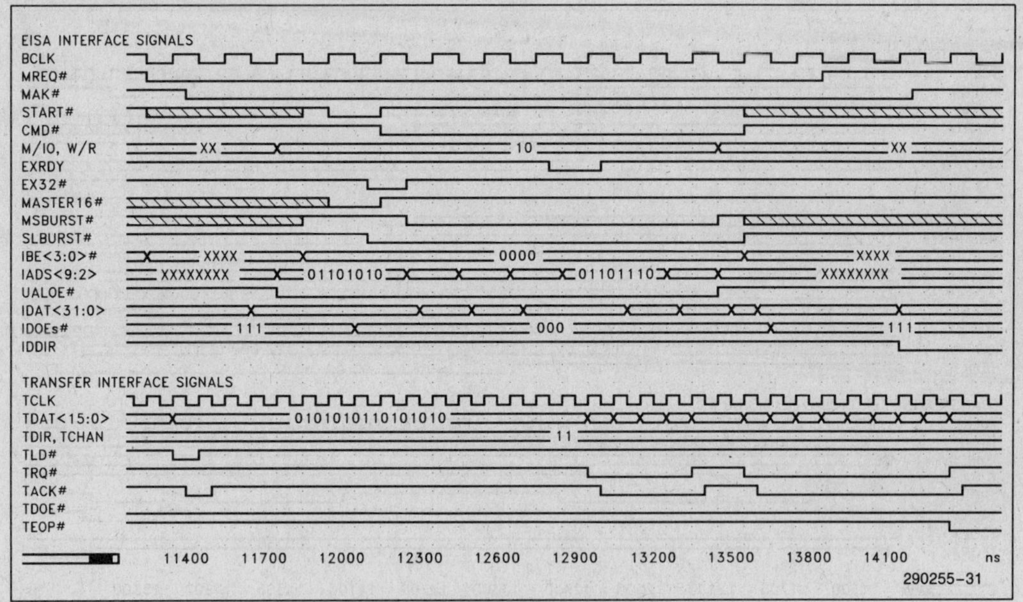

Figure 10-1. 32-Bit Burst Cycle (EISA Read)

1

10.0 BASIC FUNCTION TIMING DIAGRAMS (Continued)

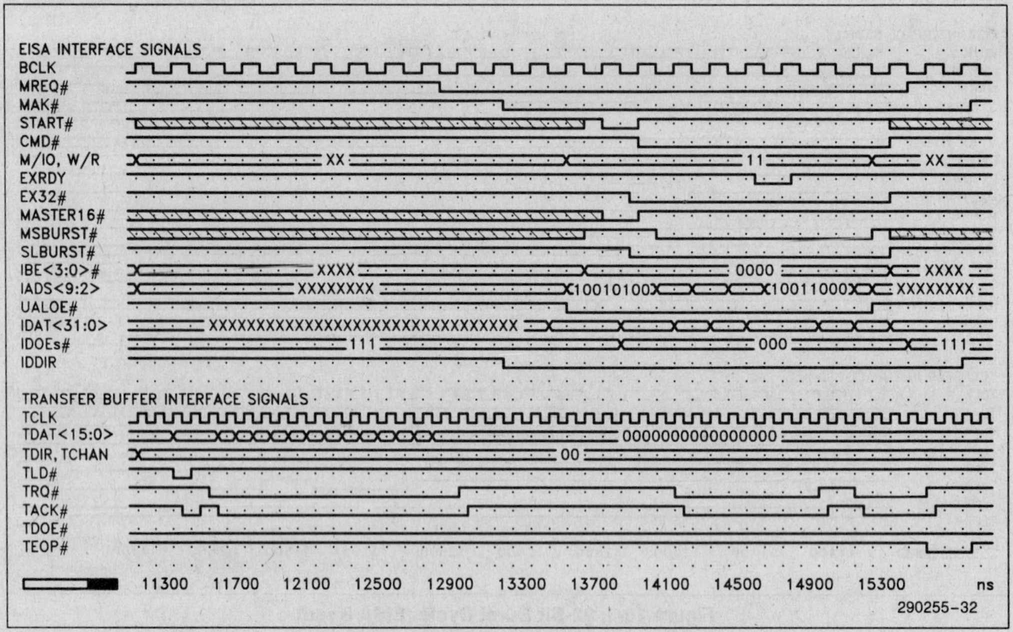

Figure 10-2. 32-Bit Burst Cycle (EISA Write)

10.0 BASIC FUNCTION TIMING DIAGRAMS (Continued)

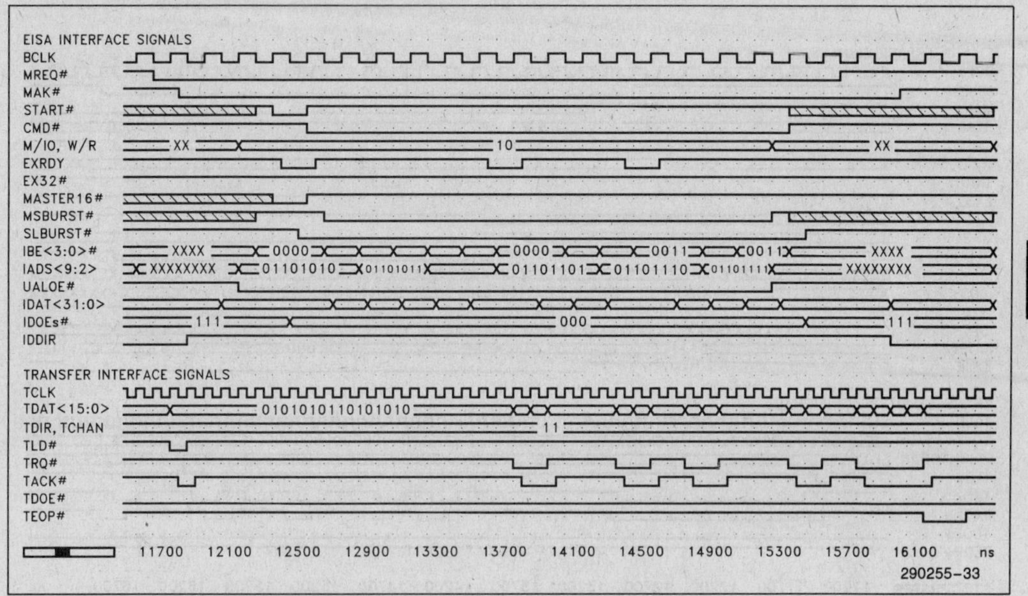

Figure 10-3. 16-Bit Burst Cycle (EISA Read)

10.0 BASIC FUNCTION TIMING DIAGRAMS (Continued)

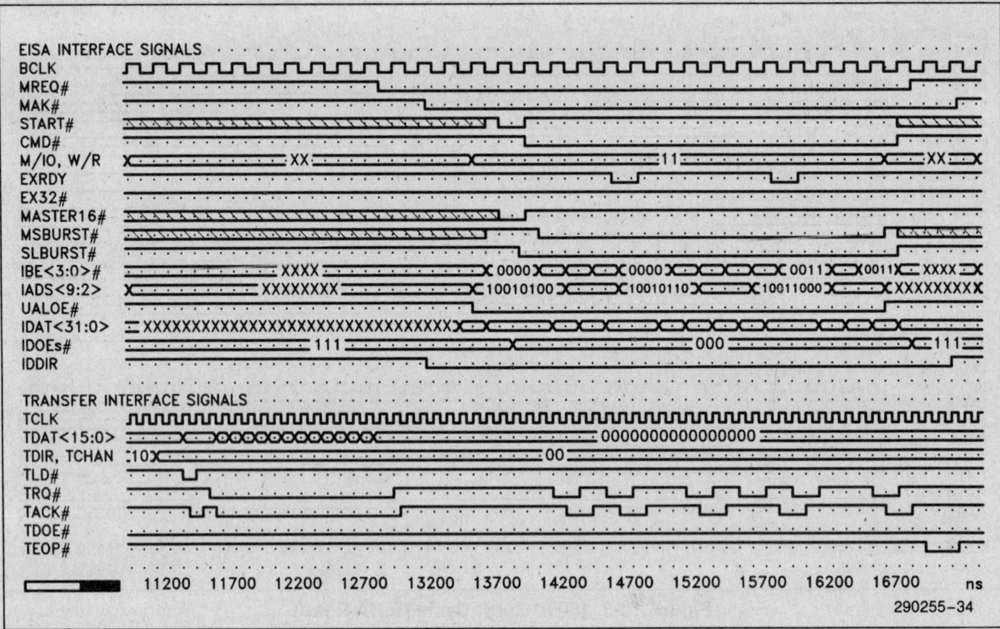

Figure 10-4. 16-Bit Burst Cycle (EISA Write)

10.0 BASIC FUNCTION TIMING DIAGRAMS (Continued)

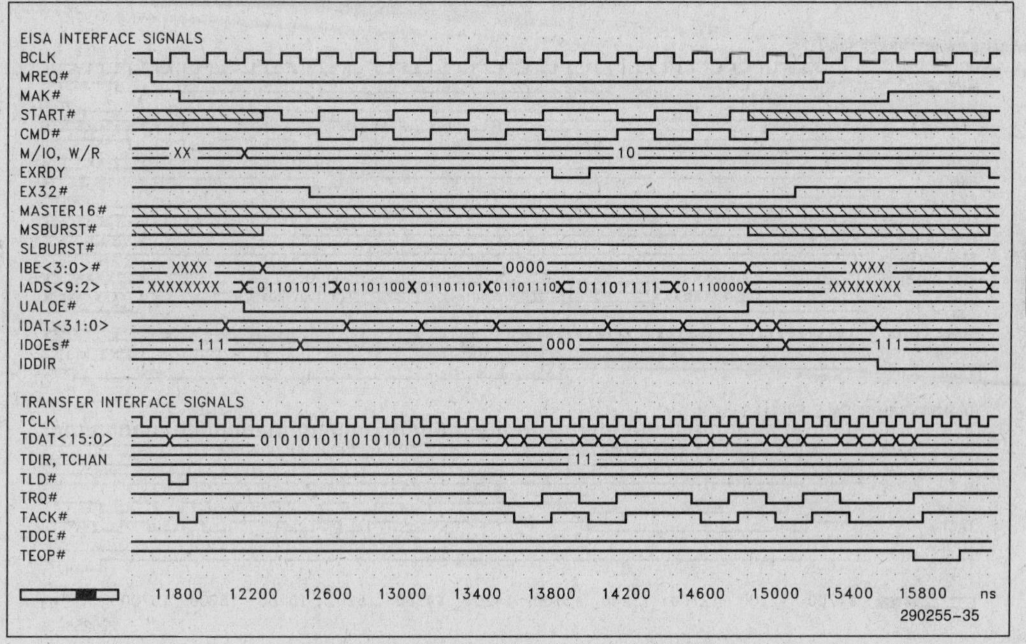

Figure 10-5. 32-Bit Non-Burst Cycle (EISA Read)

10.0 BASIC FUNCTION TIMING DIAGRAMS (Continued)

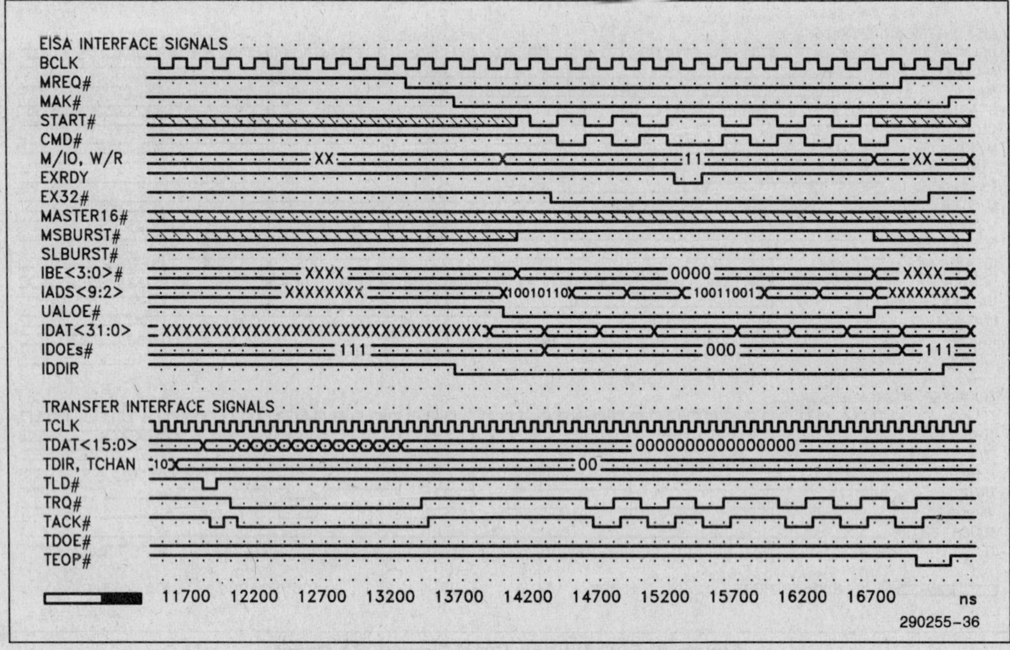

Figure 10-6. 32-Bit Non-Burst Cycle (EISA Write)

10.0 BASIC FUNCTION TIMING DIAGRAMS (Continued)

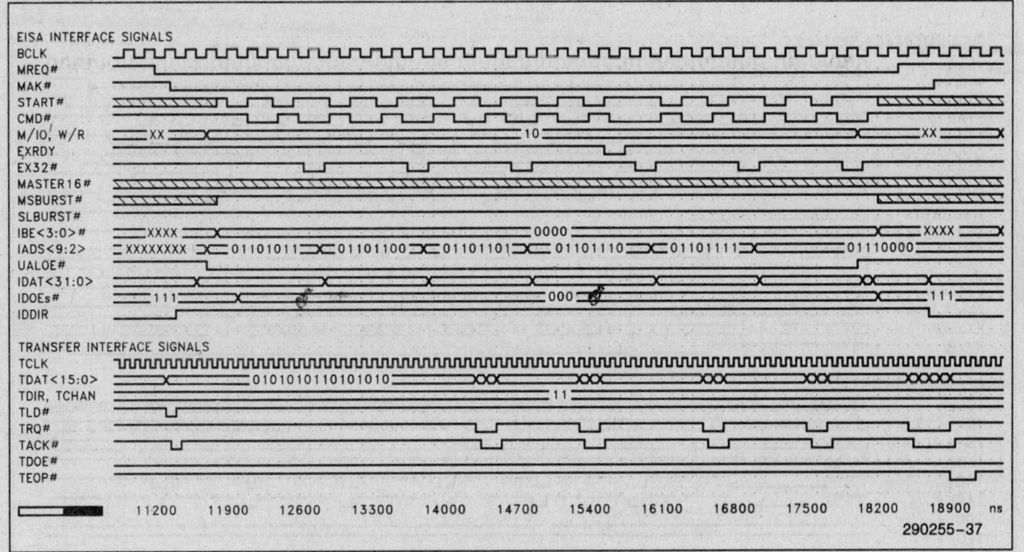

Figure 10-7. Mismatched Cycle (EISA Read)

10.0 BASIC FUNCTION TIMING DIAGRAMS (Continued)

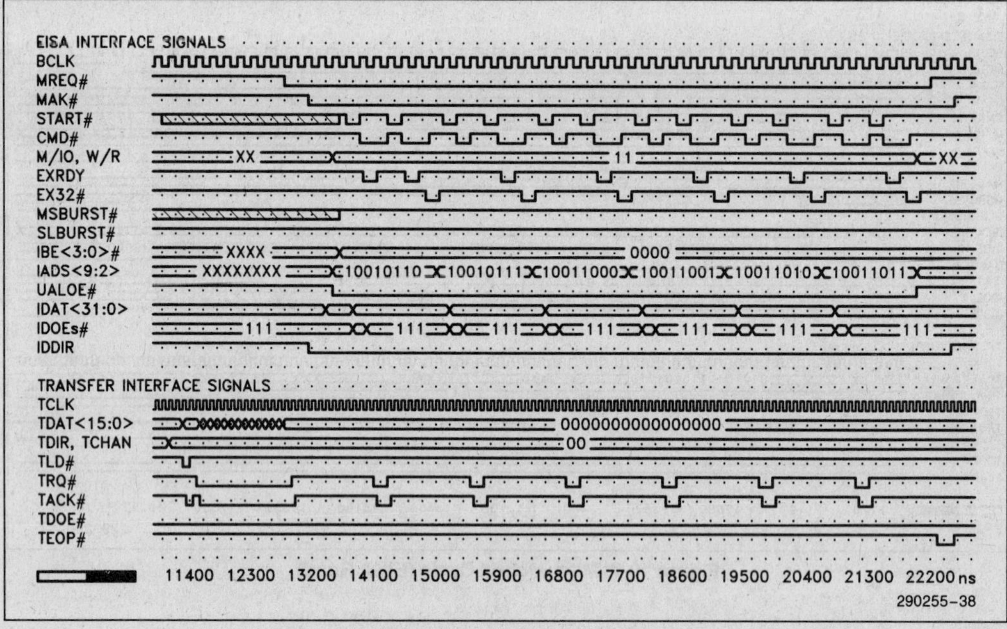

Figure 10-8. Mismatched Cycle (EISA Write)

10.0 BASIC FUNCTION TIMING DIAGRAMS (Continued)

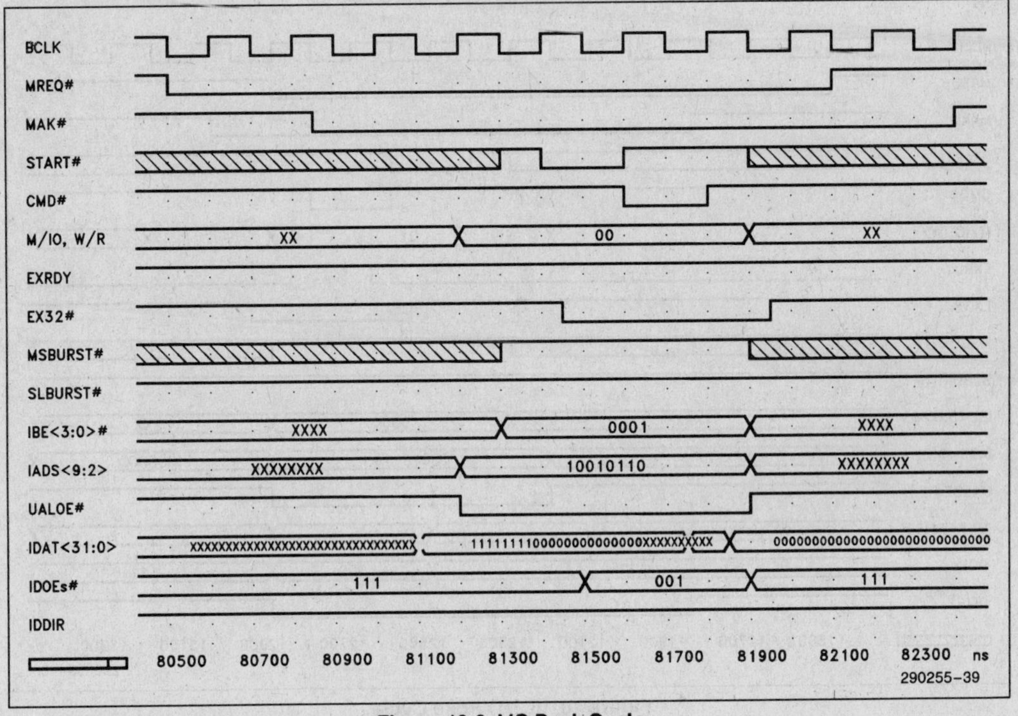

Figure 10-9. I/O Peek Cycle

10.0 BASIC FUNCTION TIMING DIAGRAMS (Continued)

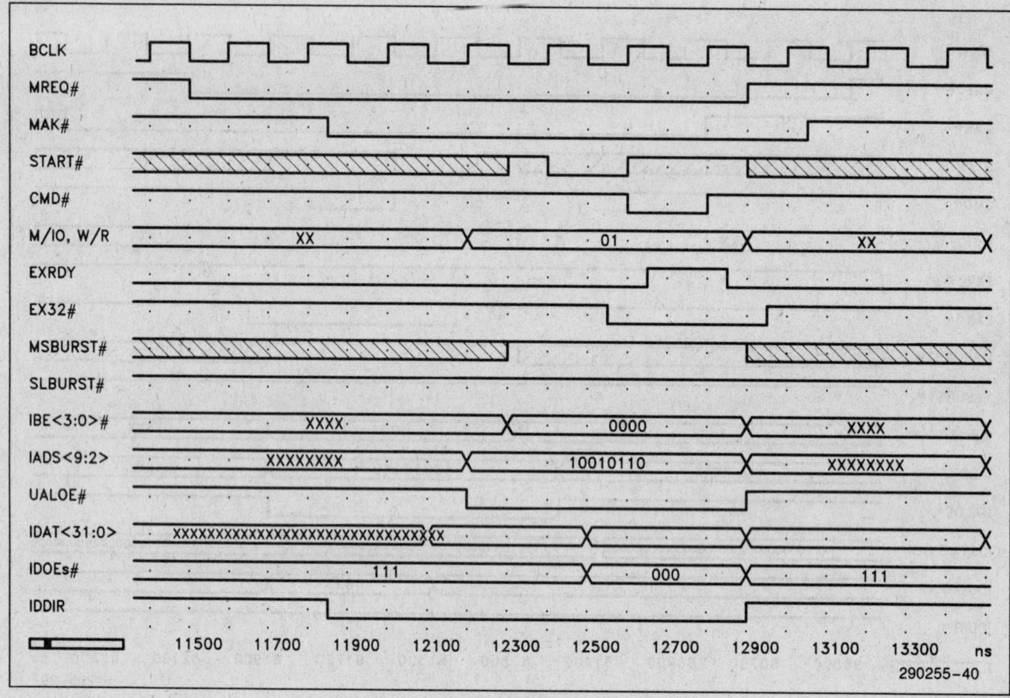

Figure 10-10. I/O Poke Cycle

10.0 BASIC FUNCTION TIMING DIAGRAMS (Continued)

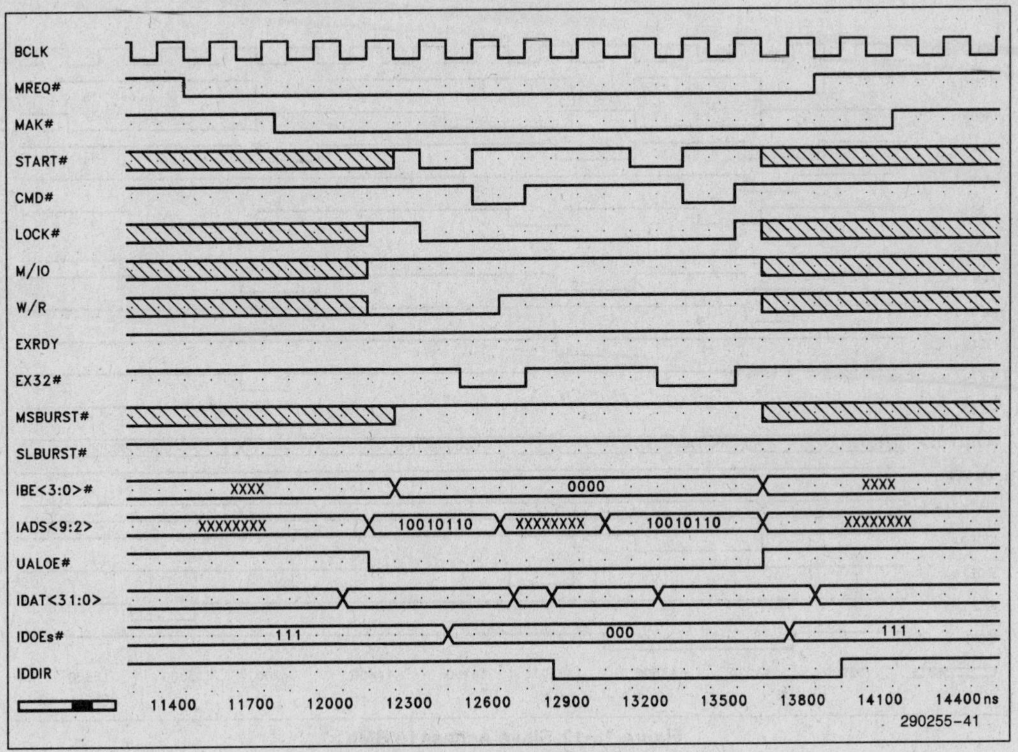

BCLK
MREQ#
MAK#
START#
CMD#
LOCK#
M/IO
W/R
EXRDY
EX32#
MSBURST#
SLBURST#
IBE<3:0># XXXX 0000 XXXX
IADS<9:2> XXXXXXXX 10010110 XXXXXXXX 10010110 XXXXXXXX
UALOE#
IDAT<31:0>
IDOEs# 111 000 111
IDDIR
11400 11700 12000 12300 12600 12900 13200 13500 13800 14100 14400 ns

290255-41

Figure 10-11. Locked Exchange Cycle

10.0 BASIC FUNCTION TIMING DIAGRAMS (Continued)

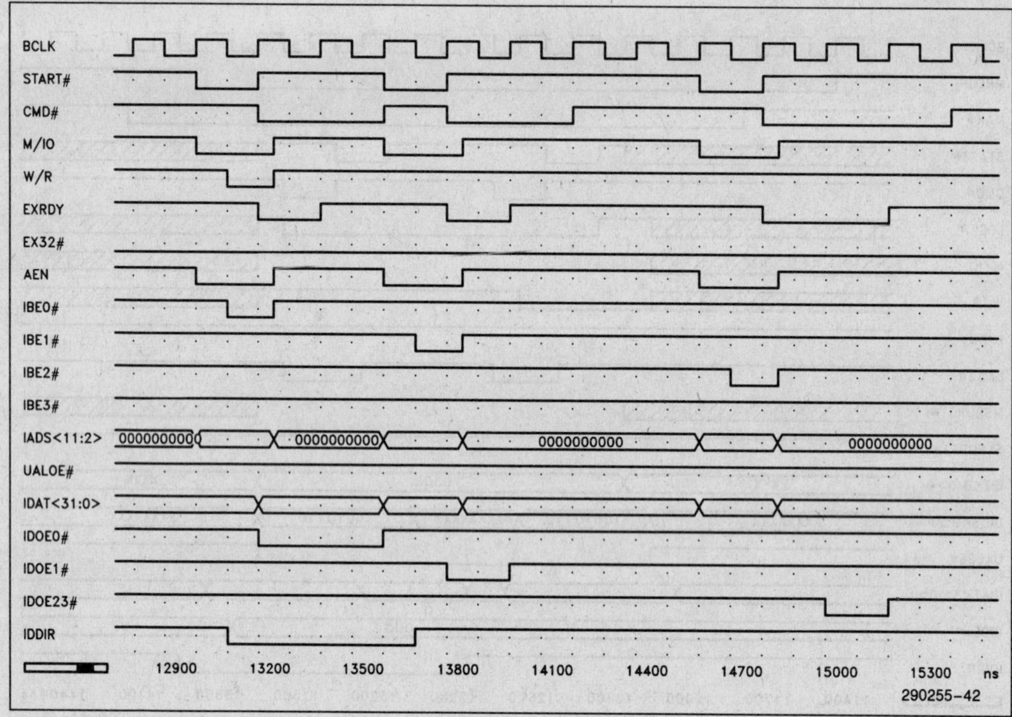

Figure 10-12. Slave Access to BMIC

11.0 D.C. SPECIFICATIONS

NOTICE: This is a production data sheet. The specifications are subject to change without notice.

11.1 Maximum Ratings*

Case Temperature under Bias . . . −65°C to +110°C

Storage Temperature . . . . −65°C to +150°C

Supply Voltages with Respect to Ground . . . . −0.5V to +6.5V

Voltage on Any Pin . . . . −0.5V to V_{CC} + 0.5V

**WARNING: Stressing the device beyond the "Absolute Maximum Ratings" may cause permanent damage. These are stress ratings only. Operation beyond the "Operating Conditions" is not recommended and extended exposure beyond the "Operating Conditions" may affect device reliability.*

11.2 D.C. Characteristics Table

T_{CASE} = 0°C to 70°C, V_{CC} = 5V ±5%, $T_{AMBIENT}$ = 0°C to 55°C

Symbol	Parameter	Limits		Units	Test Conditions
		Min	Max		
V_{IL}	Input Low Voltage	−0.5	0.8	V	
V_{IH}	Input High Voltage	2.0	V_{CC}+0.5	V	
V_{ILC}	CLOCK Input Low	−0.5	0.8	V	
V_{IHC}	CLOCK Input High	2.0	V_{CC}+0.5	V	
V_{OL1}	Output Low Voltage		0.45	V	I_{OL} = 2.5 mA
V_{OH1}	Output High Voltage	2.4		V	I_{OH} = −2.5 mA
V_{OL2}	Output Low Voltage		0.45	V	I_{OL} = 6 mA
V_{OH2}	Output High Voltage	2.4		V	I_{OH} = −4 mA
V_{OL3}	Output Low Voltage		0.45	V	I_{OL} = 24 mA
V_{OH3}	Output High Voltage	V_{CC}−0.4		V	I_{OH} = −100 μA
V_{OL4}	Output Low Voltage		0.45	V	I_{OL} = 4.0 mA
V_{OH4}	Output High Voltage	2.4		V	I_{OH} = −2.5 mA
ILI	Input Leakage		±10	μA	
ILO	Output Leakage		±10	μA	
C_{IN}	Capacitance Input		10	pF	@ 1 MHz(2)
C_{OUT}	Capacitance Output or I/O		12	pF	@ 1 MHz(2)
C_{CLK}	BCLK or TCLK		15	pF	@ 1 MHz(2)
I_{CC}	V_{CC} Supply Current		190	mA	(3)

NOTES:

1. V_{OL1} = IDOE23#, IDOE1#, IDOE0#, LRDY, LDAT<7:0>, IDAT<31:0>, TEOP#, TDIR, TCHAN, IOSEL0#, IOSEL1#, TRQ#, TLD#, and TDAT<15:0>
   V_{OL2} = MREQ#, EINT, and LINT
   V_{OL3} = IADS<9:2>, START#, M/IO, W/R, EXRDY, MASTER16#, EX32#, IBE#<3:0>, MSBURST#, and LOCK#
   V_{OL4} = UALOE#, IDDIR
   V_{OH1} = IDOE23#, IDOE1#, IDOE0#, LRDY, LDAT<7:0>, IDAT<31:0>, TDIR, TCHAN, TRQ#, TLD#, IOSEL0#, IOSEL1#, TDAT<15:0>, MREQ#, EINT, LINT, and TEOP#
   V_{OH2} = IADS<9:2>, START#, M/IO, W/R, IBE#<3:0>, MSBURST#, LOCK#, EXRDY, EX32#, and MASTER16#
   V_{OH3} = UALOE#, IDDIR, IDOE23#, IDOE1#, IDOE0#, IADS<9:2>, LRDY, LDAT<7:0>, IDAT<31:0>, TDIR, TCHAN, EINT, IOSEL0#, IOSEL1#, TRQ#, TLD#, TDAT<15:0>, MREQ#, LINT, IADS<9:2>, START#, M/IO, W/R, IBE#<3:0>, MSBURST#, LOCK#, and TEOP#
   V_{OH4} = UALOE#, IDDIR
   The following outputs are open collector: EXRDY, EX32#, MASTER16#, and TEOP#; EINT is an open collector output when programmed for active low operation.
2. Sampled only
3. Tested at V_{CC} = 5.30V and Frequency = BCLK (8.33 MHz) and TCLK (20 MHz)

12.0 A.C. SPECIFICATIONS

12.1 A.C. Characteristics Tables

The A.C. specifications given in the following tables consist of output delays/float times and input setup and hold times.

T_{CASE} = 0°C to 70°C, V_{CC} = 5V ±5%, $T_{AMBIENT}$ = 0°C to 55°C

BCLK Timing

Symbol	Parameter	Min	Max	Units	Notes
t1	Period	120	2500	ns	Typical = 125 ns
t2	High Time	50		ns	Measured @ 2.0V
t3	Low Time	50		ns	Measured @ 0.8V
t4	Rise Time		10	ns	(13)
t5	Fall Time		10	ns	(13)

Reset Timing

Symbol	Parameter	Min	Max	Units	Notes
t6	Pulse Width	8 (t1)		ns	

Master Timing

Symbol	Parameter	Min	Max	Units	Notes
	MREQ#				
t7	Delay ACT/Inact		33	ns	From BCLK Falling
	MAK#				
t8	Setup Time	10		ns	To BCLK Falling
t9	Hold Time	25		ns	From BCLK Falling
	IADS<9:2>, M/IO, W/R				
t10	Delay Valid	2	45	ns	From BCLK Falling(17)
	IADS<9:2>, M/IO, W/R				
t10a	Delay Valid		75	ns	From BCLK Rising(18)
t11	Delay Float		40	ns	From BCLK Falling(7)
	IBE# <3:0>				
t12	Delay Valid	2	45	ns	From BCLK Falling
t13	Delay Float		40	ns	From BCLK Falling(7, 8)
	START#				
t14	Delay Act/Inact		25	ns	From BCLK Rising
t15	Delay Float		40	ns	From BCLK Falling(7, 8)
	EX32#				
t16	Setup Time	15		ns	To BCLK Rising(9)
t17	Hold Time	50		ns	From BCLK Rising(9)
	EXRDY				
t18	Setup Time	15		ns	To BCLK Falling
t19	Hold Time	2		ns	From BCLK Falling
	IDAT<31:0>				
t20	Delay Valid	3	27	ns	From BCLK Falling(1)
t21	Delay Float		25	ns	From BCLK Falling(7, 8)
t22	Setup Time	4		ns	To BCLK Rising(2)
t23	Hold Time	6		ns	From BCLK Rising(2)
	IDAT<31:10>				
t24	Delay Valid		45	ns	From BCLK Falling(10)
	LOCK#				
t25	Delay Act/Inact	2	60	ns	From BCLK Rising
t26	Delay Float		40	ns	From BCLK Falling(7)
	IDOE#				
t27	Delay Act/Inact		25	ns	From BCLK Falling
	UALOE#				
t28a	Delay Active		60	ns	From BCLK Rising
t28b	Delay Inactive		35	ns	From BCLK Falling
	IDDIR				
t29	Delay Act/Inact		40	ns	From BCLK Falling

Master Timing (Burst)

Symbol	Parameter	Min	Max	Units	Notes
	MSBURST#				
t30	Delay ACT/INACT		35	ns	From BCLK Falling
t31	Delay Float		40	ns	From BCLK Rising(8)
	START#, IBE# <3:0>				
t31a	Delay Float		40	ns	From BCLK Rising(19)
	SLBURST#				
t32	Setup Time	15		ns	To BCLK Rising
t33	Hold Time	50		ns	From BCLK Rising
	IDOE#				
t34	Delay Act/Inact		25	ns	From BCLK Rising
	IDAT<31:0>				
t35	Setup Time (Read)	5		ns	To BCLK Rising(2)
t36	Hold Time (Read)	6		ns	From BCLK Rising(2)
t37	Delay Valid	3	27	ns	From BCLK Rising(1)
t38	Delay Invalid	0		ns	From BCLK Rising(1)
	MASTER16#				
t39	Delay Act		50	ns	From BCLK Rising
t40	Delay Float	1	40	ns	From BCLK Rising(7,8)

Slave Timing

Symbol	Parameter	Min	Max	Units	Notes
	IADS<11:12>, M/IO				
t41	Setup Time	120		ns	To CMD# Falling
t42	Hold Time	25		ns	From CMD# Falling
	EX32#				
t43	Delay Act/Float		54	ns	From IADS<11:2>, M/IO
t44	Delay Act/Float		34	ns	From AEN
	AEN				
t45	Setup Time	95		ns	To CMD# Falling
t46	Hold Time	25		ns	From CMD# Falling
	START#				
t47	Pulse Width	110		ns	
	IBE#<3:0>, W/R				
t48	Setup Time	80		ns	To CMD# Falling
t49	Hold Time	25		ns	From CMD# Falling
	EXRDY				
t50	Delay Negated		124	ns	From START# Falling(3)
t51	Delay Float	1	40	ns	From BCLK Falling
	CMD#				
t52	Pulse Width	110		ns	
	IDAT<31:0>				
t53	Setup Time	−35		ns	To CMD# Falling(2)
t54	Hold Time	0		ns	From CMD# Rising(2)
t55	Delay Valid		100	ns	From BCLK Rising(1)
t56	Delay Invalid	0		ns	From CMD# Rising(1)
t57	Delay Float		50	ns	From CMD# Rising
	IDDIR				
t58	Delay Valid		50	ns	From W/R Valid
t59	Delay Invalid	2		ns	From CMD# Rising
	IDOE#				
t60	Delay Act (Read)		25	ns	From CMD# Falling
t61	Delay Inact (Read)		20	ns	From CMD# Rising
t62	Delay Act/Inact (Write)		45	ns	From BCLK Rising
	IOSEL#				
t63	Delay Active		60	ns	From IADS<11:2>
t64	Delay Inactive	5		ns	From CMD# Rising If Latched

Transfer Buffer Interface Timing

Symbol	Parameter	Min	Max	Units	Notes
	TCLK				
t65	Period	50	250	ns	
t66	High Time	18		ns	Measured @ 2.0V
t67	Low Time	20		ns	Measured @ 0.8V
	TRQ#				
t68	Delay Act/Inact		15	ns	From TCLK Rising
	TLD#				
t69	Delay Act/Inact		25	ns	From TCLK Rising
	TEOP#				
t70	Delay Act/Float		25	ns	From TCLK Rising
	TCHAN, TDIR				
t73	Setup Time	25		ns	To TLD# or TRQ# Active(11)
	TACK#				
t74	Setup Time	15		ns	To TCLK Rising
t75	Hold Time	1		ns	To TCLK Rising
	TDAT<15:0>				
t76	Delay Valid	4	25	ns	From TCLK Rising/TDOE# Falling
t77	Delay Float		25	ns	From TCLK/TDOE# Rising
t78	Setup Time	10		ns	To TCLK Rising
t79	Hold Time	1		ns	From TCLK Rising
t80	Ratio of TCLK to BCLK	1.1			

Local Processor Interface Timing (Read Cycle)

Symbol	Parameter	Min	Max	Units	Notes
	LADS<1:0>, LCS#				
t81	Setup Time	10		ns	To LRD# Falling
t82	Hold Time	0		ns	From LRD# Rising
	LRD#				
t83	Pulse Width	150		ns	
	LDAT<7:0>				
t84	Delay Valid		130	ns	From LRD# Falling(4)
t85	Max Delay Valid		2.5 (t1) + 120	ns	From LRD# Falling(5)
t86	Delay Float		40	ns	From LRD# Rising
	LRD# (Inact) to LRD# (Act) or LWR# (Act)				
t87	Recovery Time	60		ns	

Local Processor Interface (Write Cycle)

Symbol	Parameter	Min	Max	Units	Notes
	LADS<1:0>, LCS#				
t88	Setup Time	10		ns	To LWR# Falling
t89	Hold Time	0		ns	From LWR# Rising
	LWR#				
t90	Pulse Width	100		ns	(4)
	LDAT<7:0>				
t91	Setup Time	60		ns	To LWR# Rising(4)
t92	Hold Time	10		ns	From LWR# Rising
t93	Data Valid		70	ns	From LWR# Falling(5)
	LWR# (Inact) to LWR# (Act) or LRD# (Act)				
t94	Recovery Time	60		ns	

Local Processor Ready Timing

Symbol	Parameter	Min	Max	Units	Notes
	LRDY				
t95	Delay Inactive		50	ns	From LADS and LCS# Valid(5)
	Delay Active				From LRD# or LWR# Active
t96	Max Delay		3.5 (t1) + 60	ns	(5, 6)
t97	Max Delay		2.5 (t1) + 60	ns	(5, 6)
t98	Min Delay	1.5 (t1)		ns	(5, 6)
	LDAT<7:0>				
t99	Delay Valid		0	ns	From LRDY Rising(5, 12)

NOTES FOR A.C TIMINGS:

1. Specification does not include allowance for 13 ns max. and 2 ns min. into 240 pF for external buffer delay to EISA bus.
2. Specification does not include allowance for 8 ns max. and 1 ns min. into 25 pF for external input delay from EISA bus.
3. Delay includes 40 ns for pull-up rise time (300Ω into 240 pF, 2V rise).
4. Applies to all non-shared registers excluding the Peek/Poke Data registers. LRDY will remain active.
5. Applies to the Peek/Poke Data and Shared Registers. LRDY will be taken inactive as soon as LA<1:0> and LCS# are valid, and remain inactive until valid data is available, or has been written. The deassertion of the local read strobe (LRD#) or local write strobe (LWR#) indicates the end of the current shared register or peek/poke data register access. If the local chip select (LCS#) input remains asserted and the local address selects remain low (LADS<1:0>) after LRD# or LWR# deasserts, a new shared register or peek/poke data register cycle begins. Under these conditions, the LRDY output will become inactive again (driven low) within the time specified by t95.
6. The maximum LRDY delay, 3.5 (t1) + 60 ns from LRD# or LWR#, only occurs if the local processor access loses the internal register access arbitration to an EISA access and if the following BCLK cycle is stretched. Without BCLK stretching, the maximum delay is 2.5 (t1) +60 ns. The minimum LRDY delay is 1.5 (t1). **NOTE:** The maximum BCLK stretch that will be seen by the BMIC is one BCLK period; this is assuming that the bus controller is the 82358 (EBC). If the 82358 is not used as the bus controller, the LRDY and data delay max. specs (t96/t85) will not necessarily be valid.
7. Exiting master mode, the address lines <31:2>, M/IO, LOCK# START#, IBE#<3:0>, MSBURST#, IDAT<31:0>, and W/R will float no later than the falling edge of BCLK after CMD# is deasserted.
8. During a mismatched cycle START#, IBE#<3:0>, and IDAT<31:0> will float from the first falling edge of BCLK after START# is negated.
9. Includes mismatched cycles.
10. Refers to the upper 22 EISA address lines which are multiplexed into the upper 22 data lines IDAT<31:10>. The address will be available for latching into the external address latches 45 ns from the falling edge of BCLK.
11. The TDIR and TCHAN signals are referenced to the falling edge of TRQ# during the cycles that TLD# is not requested.
12. LRDY going active will always be delayed from data valid. The maximum delay seen will be no greater than one (t1) period.
13. Characterized, not tested.
14. Under non-preempt, MREQ# will deassert a minimum of 0.5 BCLKs after the negating edge of the last CMD# of the transfer, depending on the cycle type (refer to the Basic Function Timings, Section 10.0).
15. During an EISA read transfer, the BMIC will assert TEOP# typically eight TCLKs after CMD# is deasserted from the last EISA cycle, indicating end of transfer (refer to the Basic Function Timings, Section 10.0).
16. During an EISA write transfer, the BMIC will assert TEOP# two TCLKs after CMD# is deasserted, indicating end of transfer (refer to the Basic Function Timings, Section 10.0).
17. For address changes while CMD# is active.
18. During an upper address load cycle, at the beginning of a transfer sequence, CMD# is inactive.
19. For "Downshifting Cases" where the transfer is misaligned.

12.2 A.C. Characteristics Waveforms

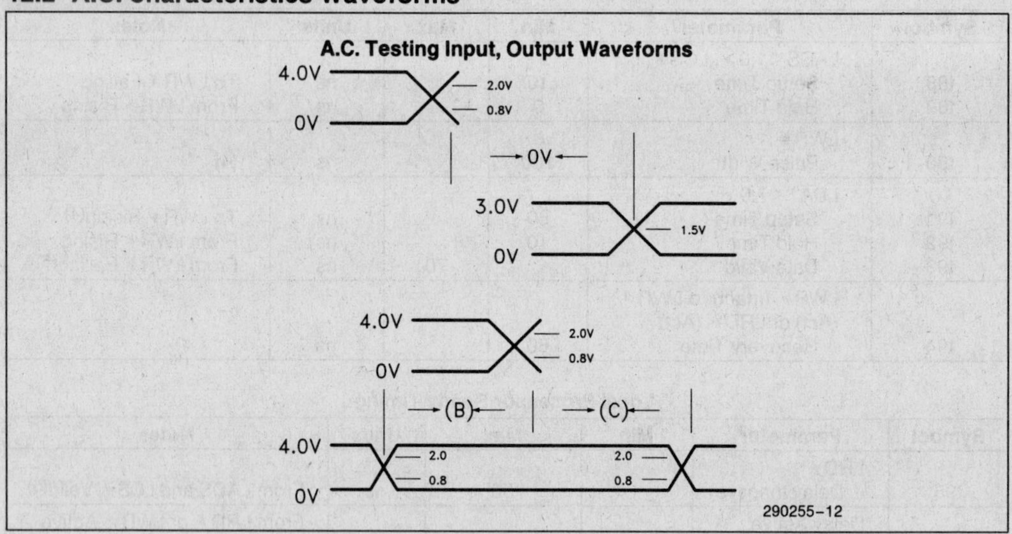

290255–12

NOTE:
The input waveforms have tr < 2.0 ns from 0.8V to 2.0V

A. Output delay specification referenced from one of the following signals: BCLK, TCLK, CMD#, START#, AEN, IADS<11:2>, W/R, TDOE#, LRD#, LWR#, LADS<1:0>, LCS#, LRD#, or LWR#.

B. Minimum input setup specification referenced to one of the following signals: BCLK, TCLK, CMD#, LWR#, LRD#, TLD#, or TRQ#.

C. Minimum input hold specification referenced to one of the following signals: BCLK, TCLK, CMD#, LWR#, LRD#, TLD#, or TRQ#.

A.C. Testing: All inputs are driven at 4V for a logic "1" and 0V for a logic "0". A.C. Timings are measured from the 0.8V and 2.0V levels on the source signal to either the 0.8V and 2V or 1.5V level on the signal under test; except as noted by the following:

1. BCLK and TCLK high time measurements are made at 2.0V
2. BCLK and TCLK low time measurements are made at 0.8V
3. START#, CMD#, LRD#, and LWR# pulse width measurements are made at 0.8V

A.C. TEST LOADS

CL = 25 pF on IDAT<31:0>, IDOE#, IOSEL#<1:0>, TRQ#, TLD#, TEOP#, TDAT<15:0>, TCHAN, TDIR, LRDY, and LDAT<7:0>
CL = 35 pF on IDDIR
CL = 50 pF on UALOE# and LINT
CL = 120 pF on MREQ# and EINT
CL = 240 pF on IADS<9:2>, BE#<3:0>, W/R, START#, EX32#, LOCK, MSBURST#, MASTER16#, EXRDY, and M/IO

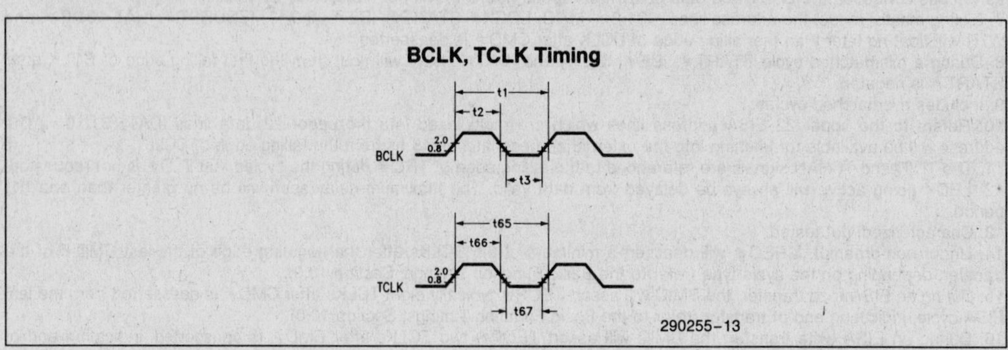

290255–13

Master Timing
(Includes: all Cycle Types—Initial Burst, Non-Burst, Peek/Poke, and Mismatched)

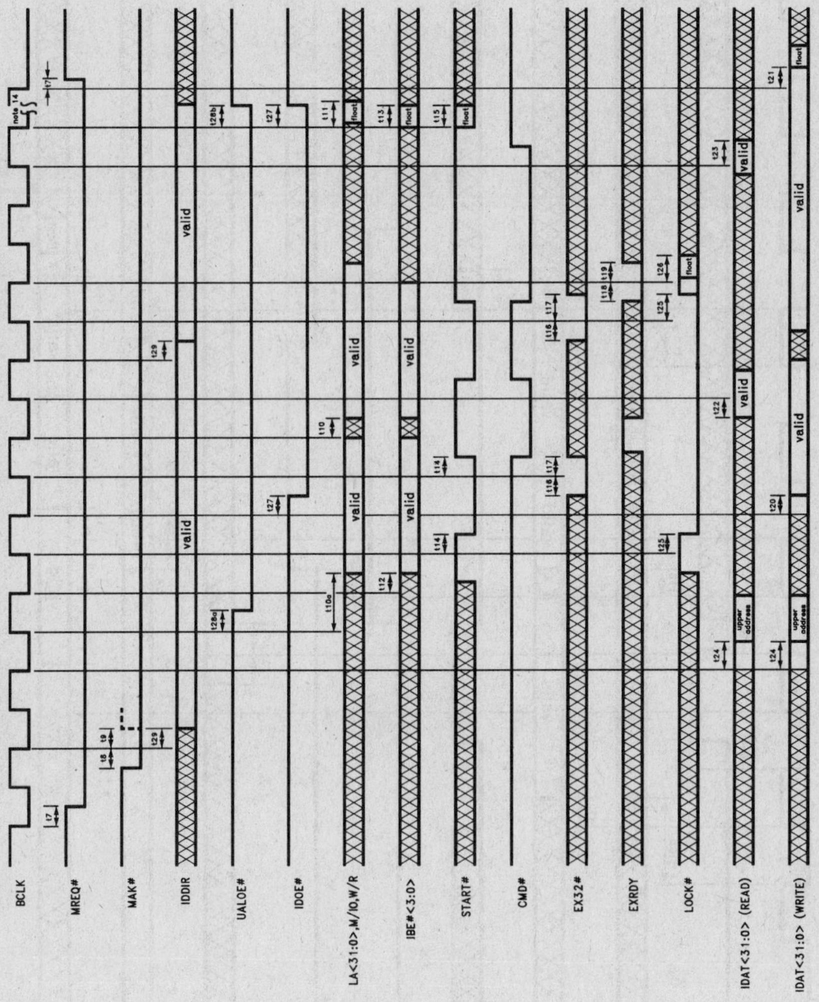
BCLK
MREQ#
MAK#
IDDIR
UALOE#
IDOE#
LA<31:0>,M/IO,W/R
IBE#<3:0>
START#
CMD#
EX32#
EXRDY
LOCK#
IDAT<31:0> (READ)
IDAT<31:0> (WRITE)
valid
float
upper address
note 14

290255-14

Master Timing (Burst)

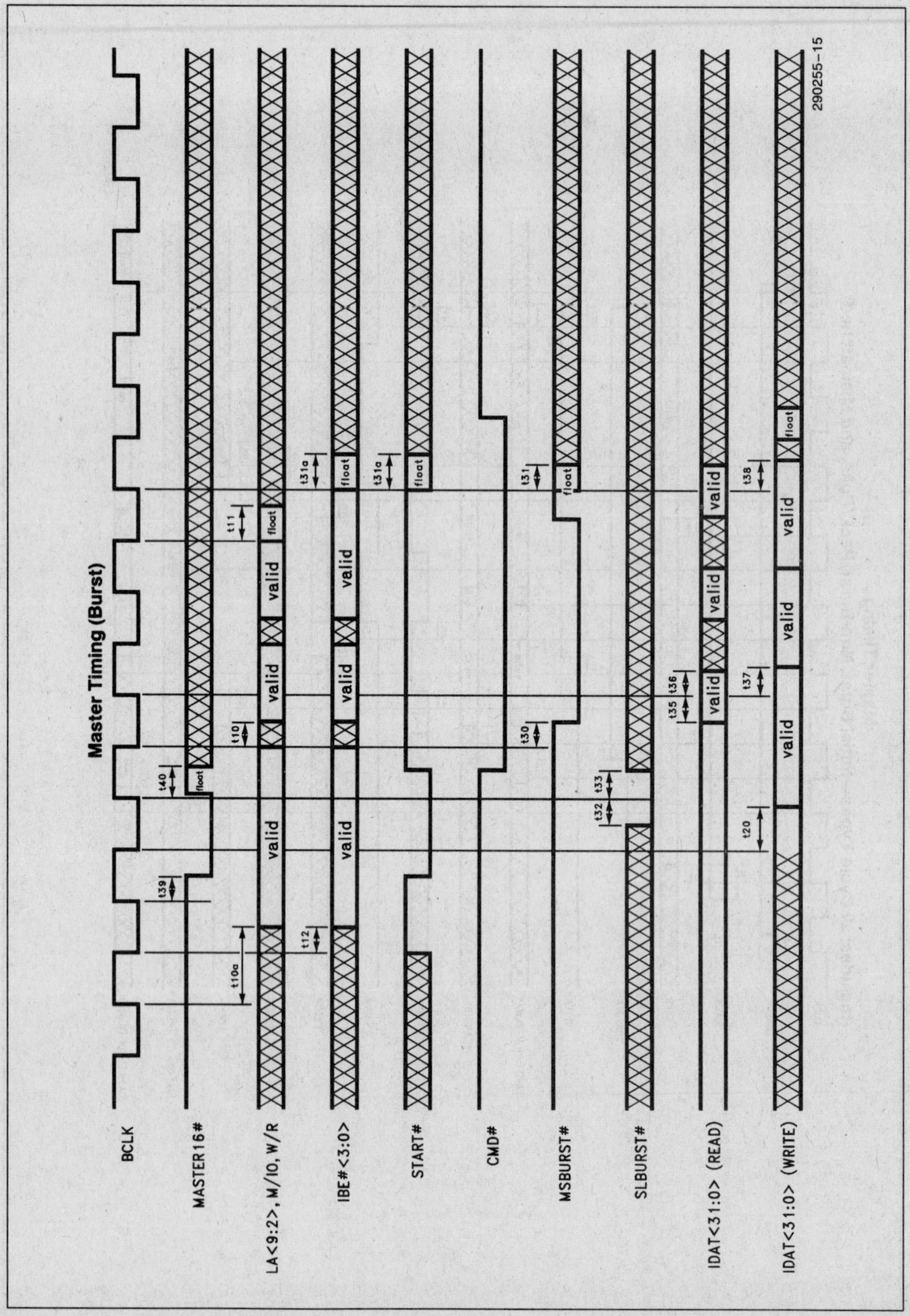

BCLK
MASTER16#
LA<9:2>, M/IO, W/R
IBE#<3:0>
START#
CMD#
MSBURST#
SLBURST#
IDAT<31:0> (READ)
IDAT<31:0> (WRITE)

t39 t40 t10a t10 t11 t12 t31a t31a t30 t31 t32 t33 t35 t36 t20 t37 t38

valid float

290255-15

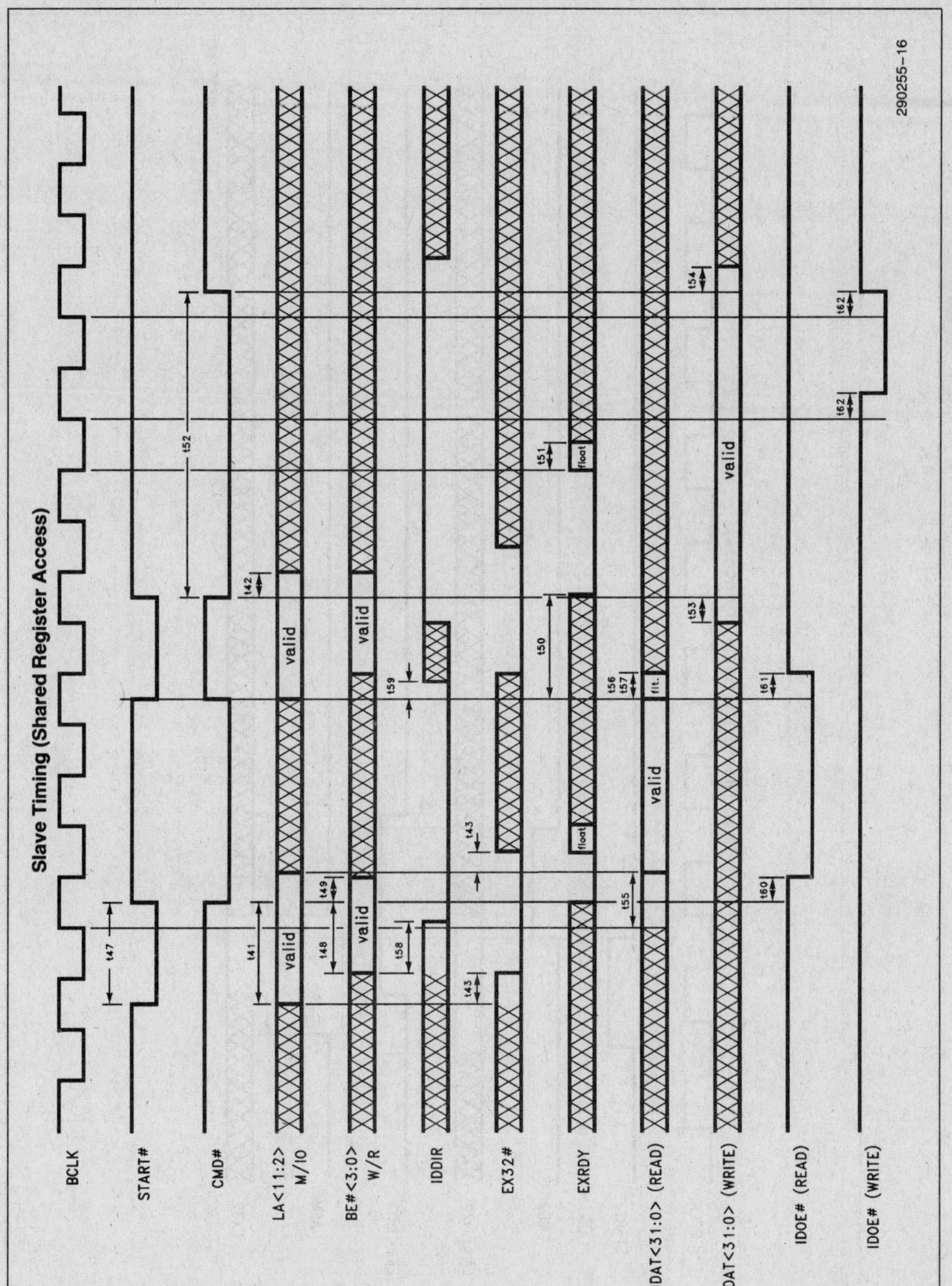

Slave Timing (Shared Register Access)
BCLK
START#
CMD#
LA<11:2> M/IO
BE#<3:0> W/R
IDDIR
EX32#
EXRDY
IDAT<31:0> (READ)
IDAT<31:0> (WRITE)
IDOE# (READ)
IDOE# (WRITE)
valid
float
flt.
t41
t42
t43
t47
t48
t49
t50
t51
t52
t53
t54
t55
t56
t57
t58
t59
t60
t61
t62
290255-16

Slave Timing (I/O Register Access)

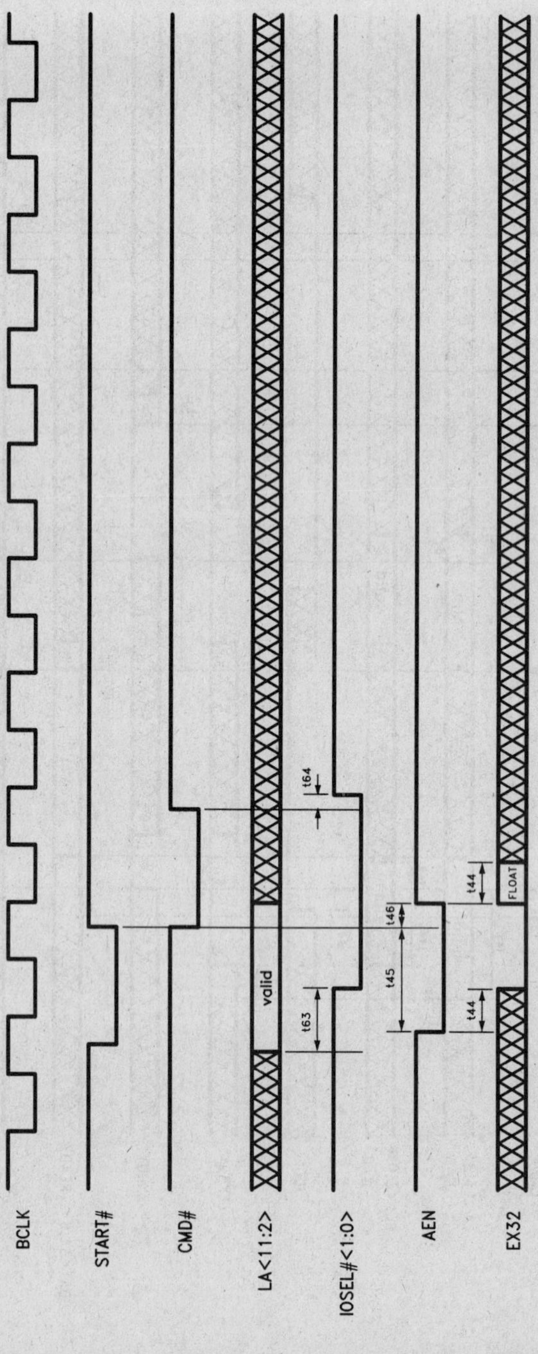

BCLK

START#

CMD#

LA<11:2>

IOSEL#<1:0>

AEN

EX32

valid

FLOAT

t63 t64 t45 t46 t44 t44

290255–17

Transfer Buffer Interface Timing (EISA Read)

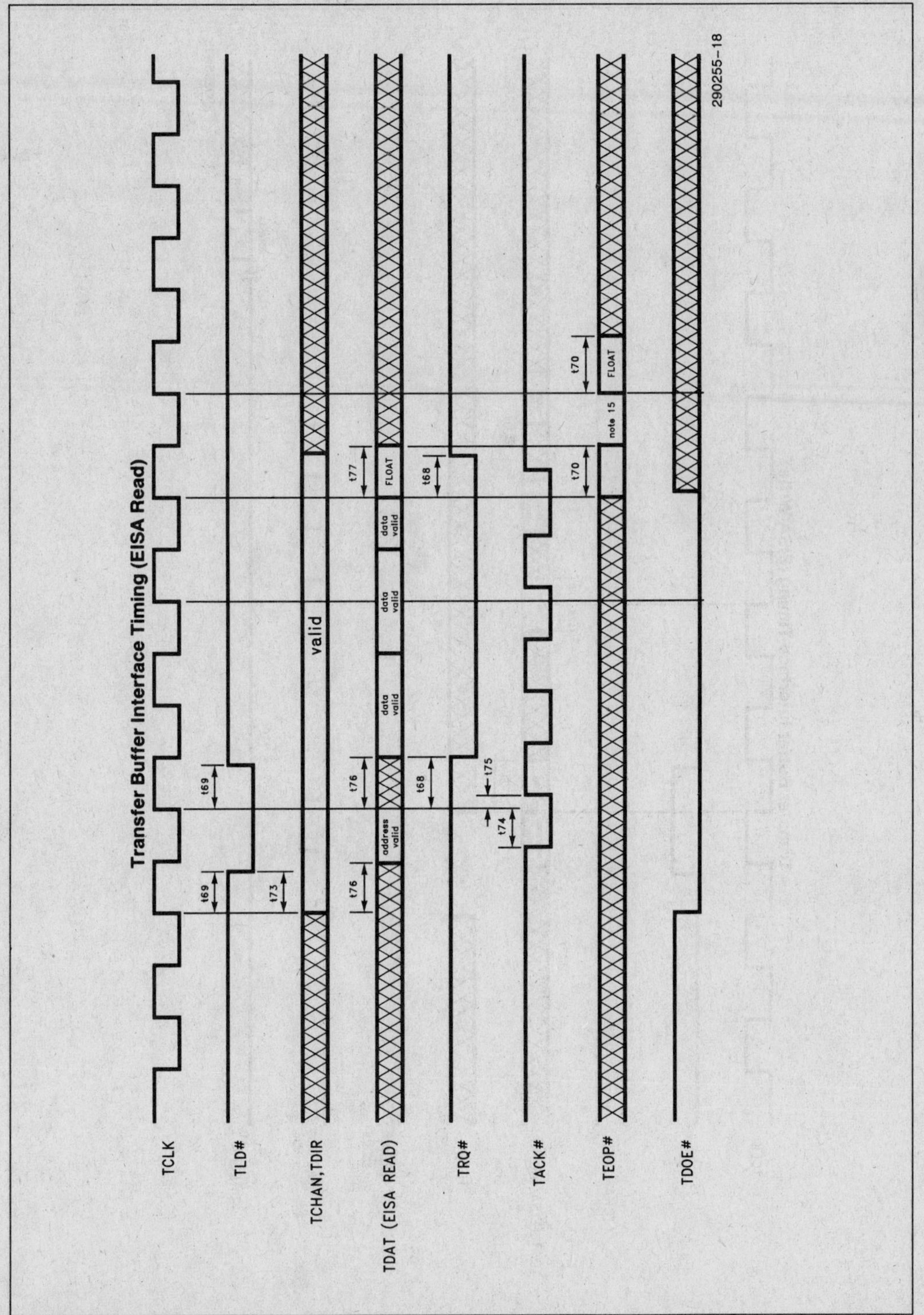

TCLK

TLD#

TCHAN, TDIR

TDAT (EISA READ)

TRQ#

TACK#

TEOP#

TDOE#

valid

address valid

data valid

data valid

data valid

data valid

FLOAT

note 15

FLOAT

t69 t69 t73 t76 t76 t77 t68 t68 t74 t75 t70 t70

290255-18

Transfer Buffer Interface Timing (EISA Write)

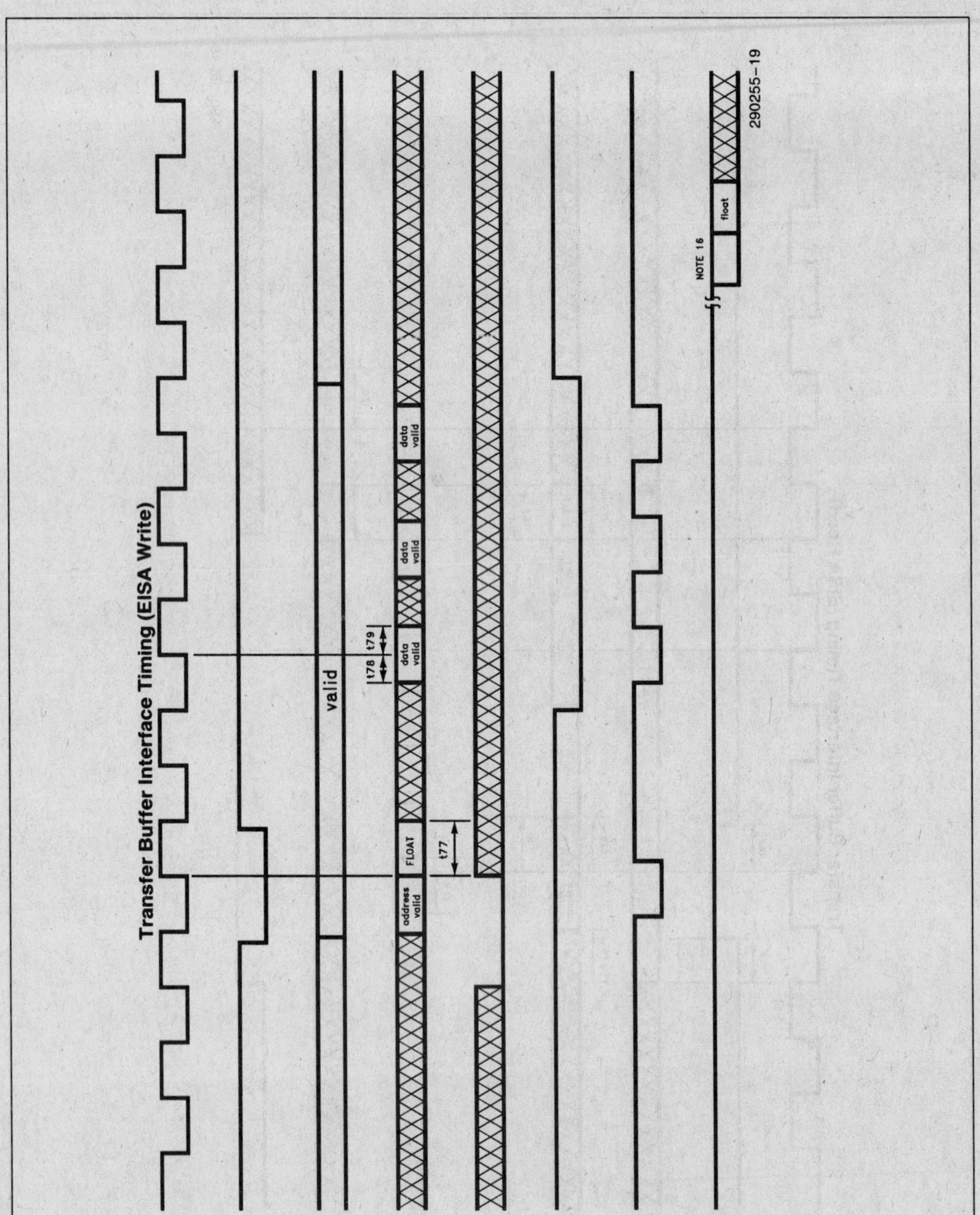

TCLK

TLD#

TCHAN, TDIR

valid

TDAT (EISA WRITE)

address valid

FLOAT

data valid

data valid

data valid

t78

t79

t77

TDOE#

TRQ#

TACK#

TEOP#

NOTE 16

float

290255–19

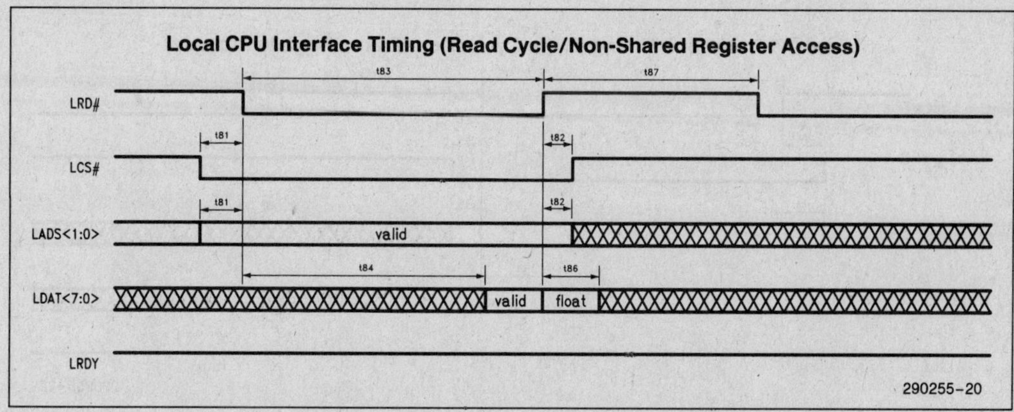

290255-20

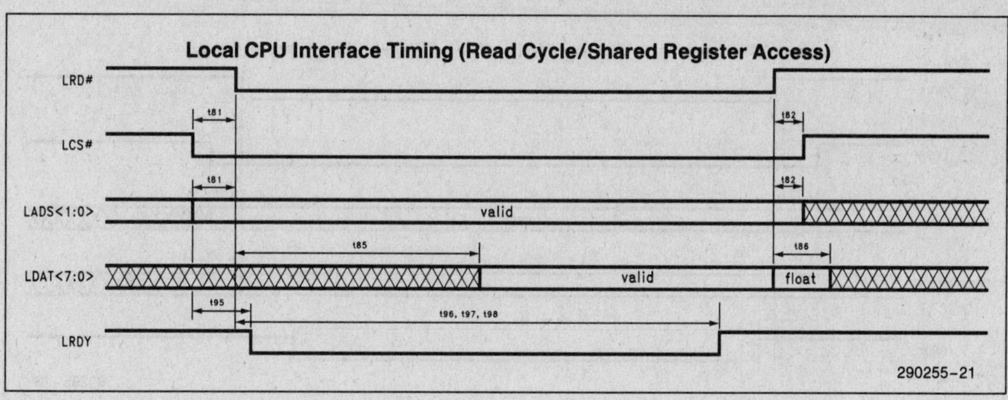

290255-21

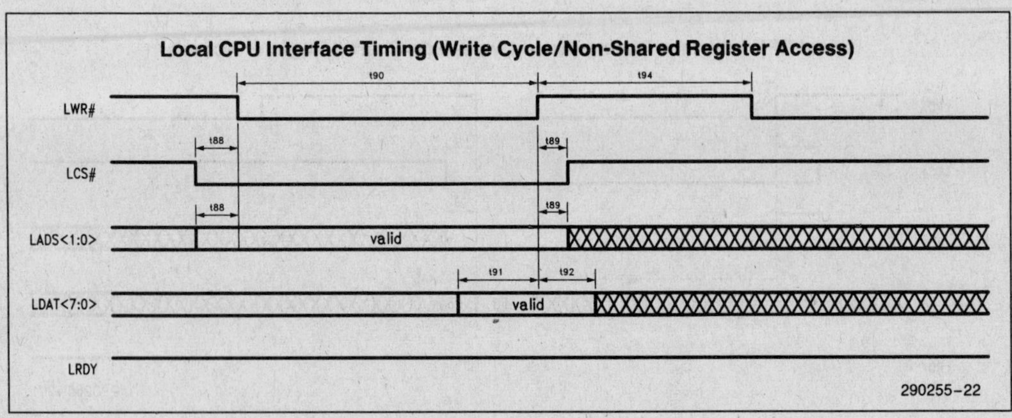
Local CPU Interface Timing (Write Cycle/Non-Shared Register Access)
t90
t94
LWR#
t88
t89
LCS#
t88
t89
LADS<1:0>
valid
t91
t92
LDAT<7:0>
valid
LRDY
290255-22

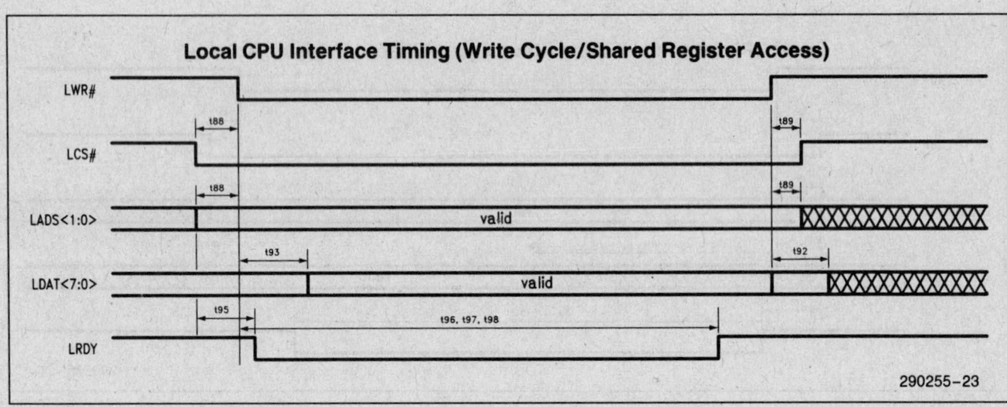
Local CPU Interface Timing (Write Cycle/Shared Register Access)
LWR#
t88
t89
LCS#
t88
t89
LADS<1:0>
valid
t93
t92
LDAT<7:0>
valid
t95
t96, t97, t98
LRDY
290255-23

13.0 BMIC PN AND PACKAGE INFORMATION

13.1 Signal Overview

Name = Pin Name, Type = I—Input, O—Output, OC—Open Collector, B—Both Input and Output, BC—Both and Open Collector, Pin = Pin Location

Name	Type	Pin	Description
EISA BUS INTERFACE SIGNALS			
START#	B	84	EISA Start of Cycle
CMD#	I	102	EISA Command Strobe
M/IO	B	81	EISA Memory/IO Cycle Status Signal
W/R	B	80	EISA Write/Read Status Signal
EXRDY	I, OC	103	EISA Ready Signal
EX32#	I, OC	104	EISA 32-Bit Slave Response Signal
MASTER16#	OC	82	EISA 16-Bit Master Control Signal
IBE#<3:0>	B	64, 61, 60 59	EISA Byte Enable Lines
AEN	I	107	EISA Address Enable Signal
MSBURST#	O	96	EISA Master Burst Signal
SLBURST#	I	97	EISA Slave Burst Signal
LOCK#	O	98	EISA Resource Lock Signal
MREQ#	O	99	EISA Bus Master Request Signal
MAK#	I	100	EISA Master Bus Acknowledge Signal
EINT	OC	109	EISA Interrupt Request Signal
BCLK	I	101	EISA Bus Clock
RESET	I	125	EISA Reset Signal
IDAT<31:0>	B	Section	EISA Data Lines
IADS<11:10>	I	105, 106	EISA Address Input Lines
IADS<9:2>	B	57–55, 53, 44, 40–38	EISA Lower Address Lines
EISA BUFFER CONTROL SIGNALS			
UALOE#	O	78	EISA Upper Address Latch and Output Enable
IDDIR	O	79	EISA Data Buffer Direction Signal
IDOE23#	O	75	EISA Data Byte Line Buffer Enable (Bytes 3, 2)
IDOE#<1:0>	O	76, 77	EISA Data Byte Line Buffer Enables (Bytes 1, 0)
TRANSFER BUFFER INTERFACE SIGNALS			
TCLK	I	32	Transfer Clock
TRQ#	O	7	Transfer Data Request Signal
TACK#	I	6	Transfer Data Acknowledge Signal
TDIR	O	3	Transfer Data Direction Signal
TCHAN	O	4	Transfer Data Channel Select Signal
TLD#	O	5	Transfer Address Counter Load Signal
TDOE#	I	2	Transfer Data Bus Output Enable
TEOP#	I, OC	1	Transfer End-of-Process
TDAT<15:0>	B	Section	Transfer Data Bus Lines

13.1 Signal Overview (Continued)

Name = Pin Name, Type = I—Input, O—Output, OC—Open Collector, B—Both Input and Output, BC—Both and Open Collector, Pin = Pin Location

Name	Type	Pin	Description
LOCAL PROCESSOR INTERFACE SIGNALS			
LRD#	I	130	Local Read Signal
LWR#	I	129	Local Write Signal
LCS#	I	128	Local Chip Select Signal
LDAT<7:0>	B	121–118 115–112	Local Data Bus Lines
LADS<1:0>	I	127, 126	Local Address Register Select Signals
LRDY#	B	122	Local Ready Signal
LINT#	O	123	Local Processor Interrupt Signal
MISCELLANEOUS SIGNALS			
IOSEL#<1:0>	O	111, 110	Expansion Board Address Range Decode Signals
POWER PINS			
V_{CC}		108, 124	Power Pins for the Internal Logic
V_{SS}		42, 58	Ground Pins for the Internal Logic
V_{CCB}		12, 23, 41, 63, 74, 83, 94, 117, 132	Power Pins for the Output Buffers
V_{SSB}		13, 22, 33, 43, 54, 62, 73, 85, 95, 116, 131	Ground Pins for the Output Buffers

13.2 Device Pinout

I = Input, O = Output, OC = Open Collector, B – Both Input and Output, BC = Both and Open Collector

Device Pinout—132 Lead PQFP

A Row			B Row			C Row			D Row		
Pin	Label	Type	Pin	Label	Type	Pin	Label	Type	Pin	Label	Type
1	TEOP#	I, OC	34	IDAT2	B	67	IDAT9	B	100	MAK#	I
2	TDOE#	I	35	IDAT18	B	68	IDAT25	B	101	BCLK	I
3	TDIR	O	36	IDAT3	B	69	IDAT10	B	102	CMD#	I
4	TCHAN	O	37	IDAT19	B	70	IDAT26	B	103	EXRDY	I, OC
5	TLD#	O	38	IADS2	B	71	IDAT11	B	104	EX32#	I, OC
6	TACK#	I	39	IADS3	B	72	IDAT27	B	105	IADS11	I
7	TRQ#	O	40	IADS4	B	73	V_{SSB}		106	IADS10	I
8	TDAT0	B	41	V_{CCB}		74	V_{CCB}		107	AEN	I
9	TDAT1	B	42	V_{SS}		75	IDOE23#	O	108	V_{CC}	
10	TDAT2	B	43	V_{SSB}		76	IDOE1#	O	109	EINT	OC
11	TDAT3	B	44	IADS5	B	77	IDOE0#	O	110	IOSEL0#	O
12	V_{CCB}		45	IDAT4	B	78	UALOE#	O	111	IOSEL1#	O
13	V_{SSB}		46	IDAT20	B	79	IDDIR	O	112	LDAT0	B
14	TDAT4	B	47	IDAT5	B	80	W/R	B	113	LDAT1	B
15	TDAT5	B	48	IDAT21	B	81	M/IO	B	114	LDAT2	B
16	TDAT6	B	49	IDAT6	B	82	MASTER16#	OC	115	LDAT3	B
17	TDAT7	B	50	IDAT22	B	83	V_{CCB}		116	V_{SSB}	
18	TDAT8	B	51	IDAT7	B	84	START#	B	117	V_{CCB}	
19	TDAT9	B	52	IDAT23	B	85	V_{SSB}		118	LDAT4	B
20	TDAT10	B	53	IADS6	B	86	IDAT12	B	119	LDAT5	B
21	TDAT11	B	54	V_{SSB}		87	IDAT28	B	120	LDAT6	B
22	V_{SSB}		55	IADS7	B	88	IDAT13	B	121	LDAT7	B
23	V_{CCB}		56	IADS8	B	89	IDAT29	B	122	LRDY	B
24	TDAT12	B	57	IADS9	B	90	IDAT14	B	123	LINT	O
25	TDAT13	B	58	V_{SS}		91	IDAT30	B	124	V_{CC}	
26	TDAT14	B	59	IBE0#	B	92	IDAT15	B	125	RESET	I
27	TDAT15	B	60	IBE1#	B	93	IDAT31	B	126	LADS0	I
28	IDAT0	B	61	IBE2#	B	94	V_{CCB}		127	LADS1	I
29	IDAT16	B	62	V_{SSB}		95	V_{SSB}		128	LCS#	I
30	IDAT1	B	63	V_{CCB}		96	MSBURST#	O	129	LWR#	I
31	IDAT17	B	64	IBE3#	B	97	SLBURST#	I	130	LRD#	I
32	TCLK	I	65	IDAT8	B	98	LOCK#	O	131	V_{SSB}	
33	V_{SSB}		66	IDAT24	B	99	MREQ#	O	132	V_{CCB}	

13.3 132-Pin PQFP Package Pinout

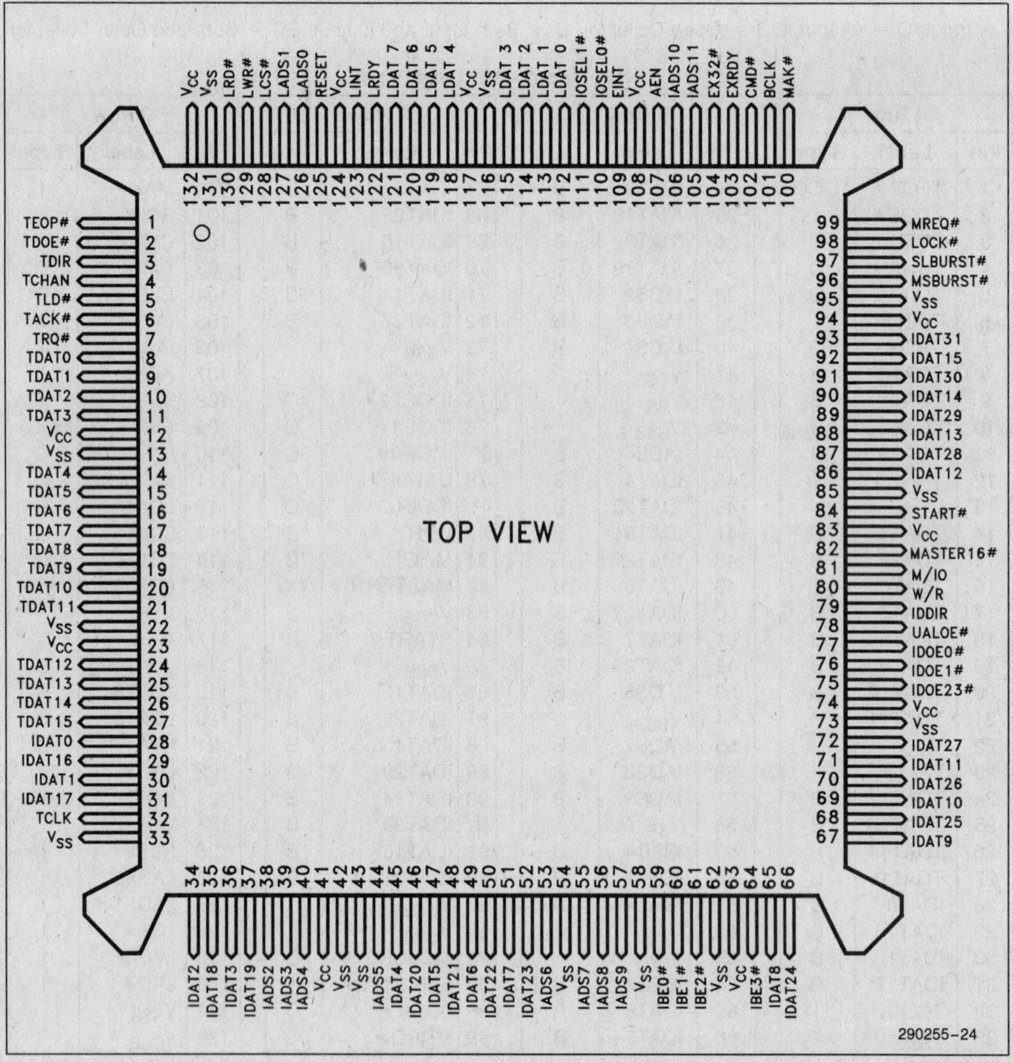

TOP VIEW

Pin	Signal	Pin	Signal	Pin	Signal	Pin	Signal
1	TEOP#	34	IDAT2	67	IDAT9	100	MAK#
2	TDOE#	35	IDAT18	68	IDAT25	101	BCLK
3	TDIR	36	IDAT3	69	IDAT10	102	CMD#
4	TCHAN	37	IDAT19	70	IDAT26	103	EXRDY
5	TLD#	38	IADS2	71	IDAT11	104	EX32#
6	TACK#	39	IADS3	72	IDAT27	105	IADS11
7	TRQ#	40	IADS4	73	V_{SS}	106	IADS10
8	TDAT0	41	V_{CC}	74	V_{CC}	107	AEN
9	TDAT1	42	V_{SS}	75	IDOE23#	108	V_{CC}
10	TDAT2	43	V_{SS}	76	IDOE1#	109	EINT
11	TDAT3	44	IADS5	77	IDOE0#	110	IOSEL0#
12	V_{CC}	45	IDAT4	78	UALOE#	111	IOSEL1#
13	V_{SS}	46	IDAT20	79	IDDIR	112	LDAT 0
14	TDAT4	47	IDAT5	80	W/R	113	LDAT 1
15	TDAT5	48	IDAT21	81	M/IO	114	LDAT 2
16	TDAT6	49	IDAT6	82	MASTER16#	115	LDAT 3
17	TDAT7	50	IDAT22	83	V_{CC}	116	V_{SS}
18	TDAT8	51	IDAT7	84	START#	117	V_{CC}
19	TDAT9	52	IDAT23	85	V_{SS}	118	LDAT 4
20	TDAT10	53	IADS6	86	IDAT12	119	LDAT 5
21	TDAT11	54	V_{SS}	87	IDAT28	120	LDAT 6
22	V_{SS}	55	IADS7	88	IDAT13	121	LDAT 7
23	V_{CC}	56	IADS8	89	IDAT29	122	LRDY
24	TDAT12	57	IADS9	90	IDAT14	123	LINT
25	TDAT13	58	V_{SS}	91	IDAT30	124	V_{CC}
26	TDAT14	59	IBE0#	92	IDAT15	125	RESET
27	TDAT15	60	IBE1#	93	IDAT31	126	LADS0
28	IDAT0	61	IBE2#	94	V_{CC}	127	LADS1
29	IDAT16	62	V_{SS}	95	V_{SS}	128	LCS#
30	IDAT1	63	V_{CC}	96	MSBURST#	129	LWR#
31	IDAT17	64	IBE3#	97	SLBURST#	130	LRD#
32	TCLK	65	IDAT8	98	LOCK#	131	V_{SS}
33	V_{SS}	66	IDAT24	99	MREQ#	132	V_{CC}

290255-24

PACKAGING INFORMATION

(See Packaging Specification Order # 240800, Package Type NG)

Introduction

The individual components of Intel's EISA Chip Set come in JEDEC standard Gull Wing packages (25 MIL pitch), with "bumpers" on the corners for ease of handling. Please refer to the accompanying table for the package associated with each device, and to the individual component specifications for pinouts. (Note that the individual pinouts are numbered consistently with the numbering scheme depicted in the accompanying figures.)

PLASTIC QUAD FLAT PACK (PQFP)

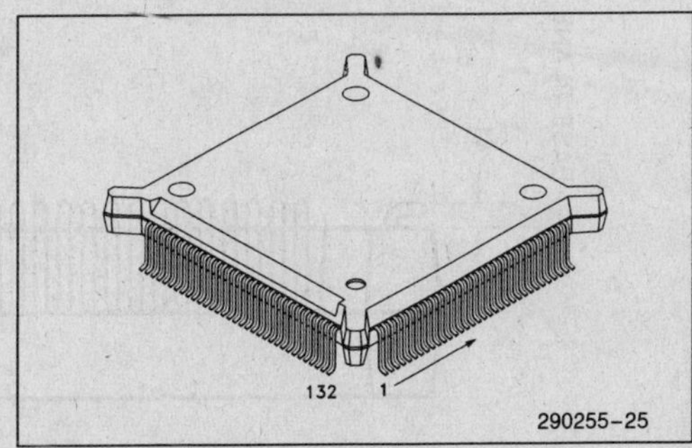

1

TYPICAL LEAD

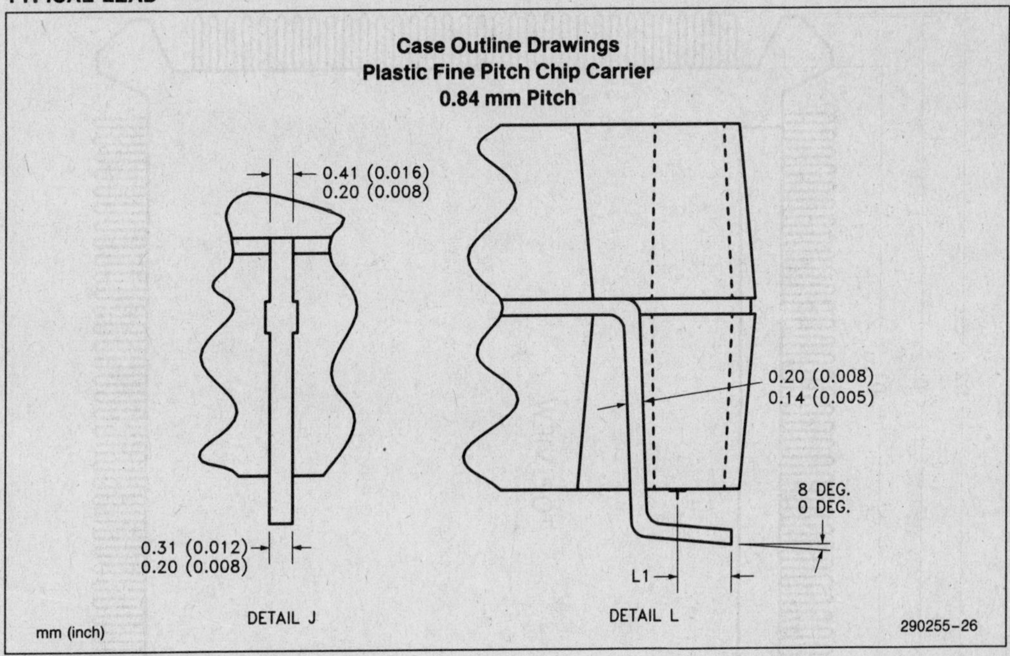

Symbol	Description	Inch		mm	
		Min	Max	Min	Max
N	Lead Count	132		132	
A	Package Height	0.160	0.170	4.06	4.32
A1	Standoff	0.020	0.030	0.51	0.76
D, E	Terminal Dimension	1.075	1.085	27.31	27.56
D1, E1	Package Body	0.947	0.953	24.05	24.21
D2, E2	Bumper Distance	1.097	1.103	27.86	28.02
D3, E3	Lead Dimension	0.800 Ref		20.32 Ref	
L1	Foot Length	0.020	0.030	0.51	0.76

13.4 PRINCIPAL DIMENSIONS & DATUMS

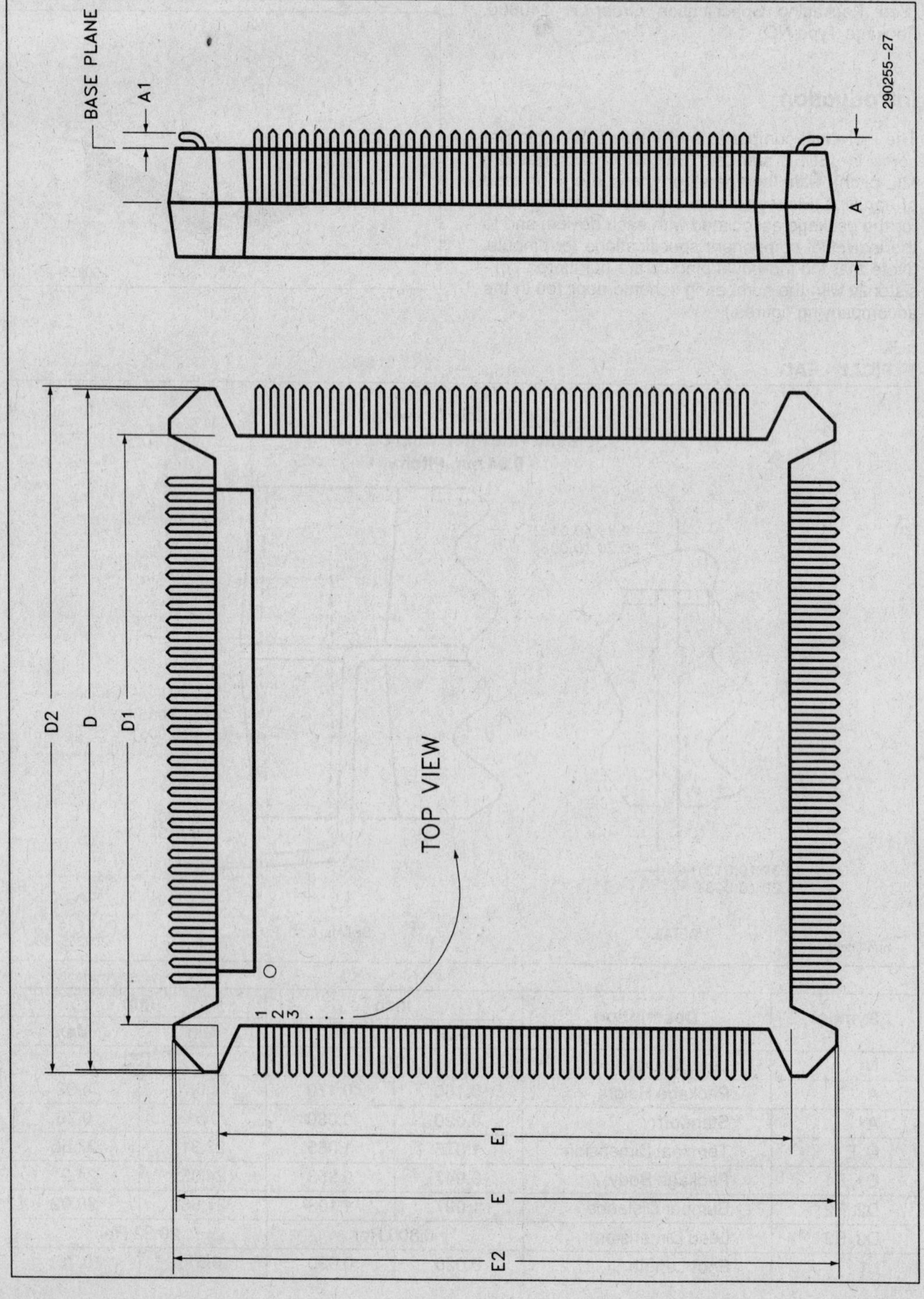

BASE PLANE
A1
A
D2
D
D1
TOP VIEW
1 2 3 . . .
E1
E
E2

290255-27

TERMINAL DETAILS

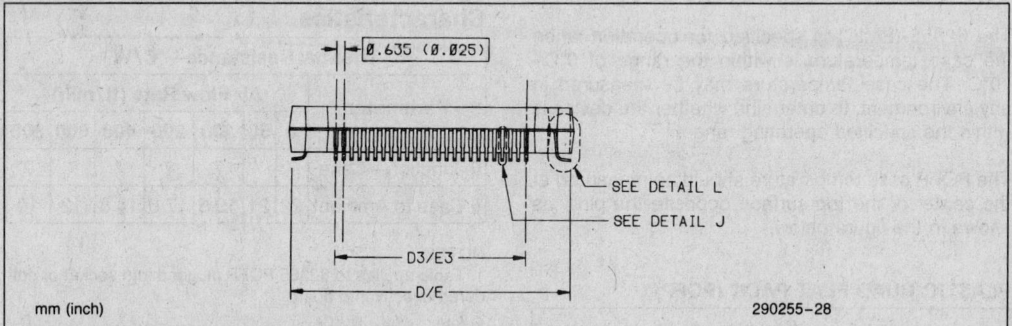

BUMPER DETAIL

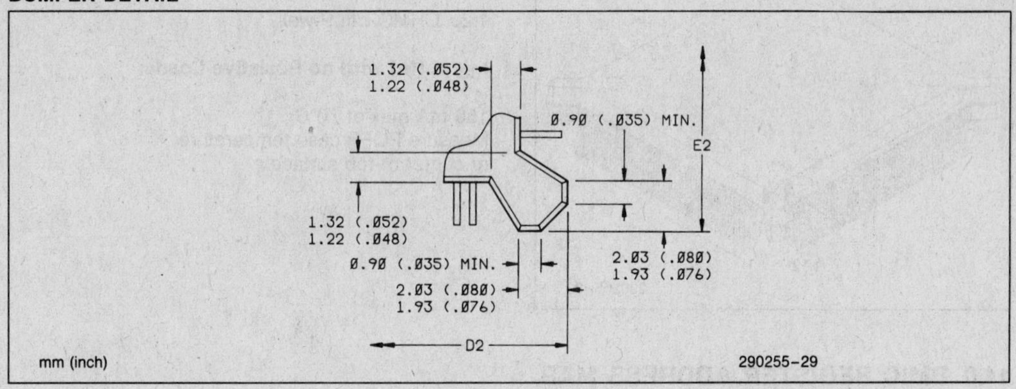

13.5 Package Thermal Specification

The 82355 (BMIC) is specified for operation when the case temperature is within the range of 0°C–70°C. The case temperature may be measured in any environment, to determine whether the device is within the specified operating range.

The PQFP case temperature should be measured at the center of the top surface opposite the pins, as shown in the figure below.

PLASTIC QUAD FLAT PACK (PQFP)

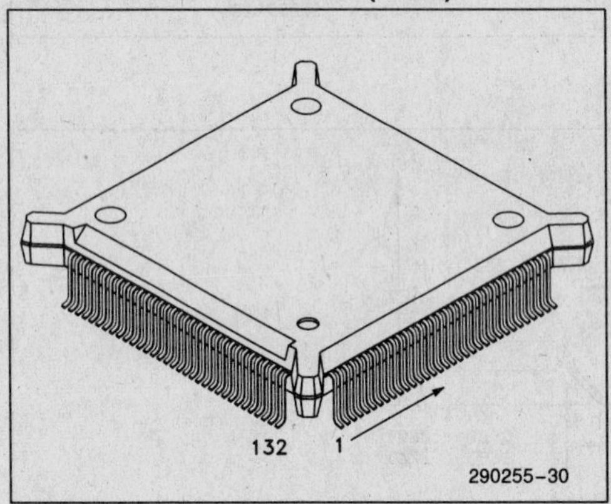

82355 PQFP Package Thermal Characteristics

Thermal Resistance—°C/W							
Parameter	Air Flow Rate (ft/min)						
	0	50	100	200	400	600	800
θ Junction—Case	7	7	7	7	7	7	7
θ Case to Ambient	22	21	19.5	17.5	14.5	12	10

NOTES:
1. Table applies to 82355 PQFP plugged into socket or soldered directly into board.
2. $\theta_{JA} = \theta_{JC} + \theta_{CA}$.

Process Name:

1.2μ CHMOS III P-well

I_{CC} at Hot with no Resistive Loads:

150 mA max at 70°C
Measure PQFP case temperature
at center of top surface

14.0 BMIC REGISTER ADDRESS MAP

14.1 Index Register Set

The following registers are mapped directly into the local processor interface:

Local Address	Type	Register Description
0	R/W	Local Data Register
1	R/W	Local Index Register
2	R/W	Local Status/Control Register
3	—	Reserved

14.2 Shared Register Set

EISA Address	Type	Index Address	Type	Register Description
XC80	R	00	R/W	ID Byte 0
XC81	R	01	R/W	ID Byte 1
XC82	R	02	R/W	ID Byte 2
XC83	R	03	R/W	ID Byte 3
XC84	—	04	—	Non BMIC Register (For Expansion Board Use)
XC85	—	05	—	Non BMIC Register (For Expansion Board Use)
XC86	—	06	—	Non BMIC Register (For Expansion Board Use)
XC87	—	07	—	Non BMIC Register (For Expansion Board Use)
XC88	R	08	R/W	Global Configuration Register
XC89	R/W	09	R	System Interrupt Enable/Control Register
XC8A	R/W	0A	R/W	Semaphore Port 0
XC8B	R/W	0B	R/W	Semaphore Port 1
XC8C	R	0C	R/W	Local Doorbell Enable Register
XC8D	R/W	0D	R/W	Local Doorbell Interrupt/Status Register
XC8E	R/W	0E	R	EISA System Doorbell Enable Register
XC8F	R/W	0F	R/W	EISA System Doorbell Interrupt/Status Register
XC90	R/W	10	R/W	Mailbox Register (1)
XC91	R/W	11	R/W	Mailbox Register (2)
XC92	R/W	12	R/W	Mailbox Register (3)
XC93	R/W	13	R/W	Mailbox Register (4)
XC94	R/W	14	R/W	Mailbox Register (5)
XC95	R/W	15	R/W	Mailbox Register (6)
XC96	R/W	16	R/W	Mailbox Register (7)
XC97	R/W	17	R/W	Mailbox Register (8)
XC98	R/W	18	R/W	Mailbox Register (9)
XC99	R/W	19	R/W	Mailbox Register (10)
XC9A	R/W	1A	R/W	Mailbox Register (11)
XC9B	R/W	1B	R/W	Mailbox Register (12)
XC9C	R/W	1C	R/W	Mailbox Register (13)
XC9D	R/W	1D	R/W	Mailbox Register (14)
XC9E	R/W	1E	R/W	Mailbox Register (15)
XC9F	R/W	1F	R/W	Mailbox Register (16)
XCA0–XCAF	R/W	20–2F	—	Reserved

1

14.3 Processor Only Register Set

Index Address	Type	Register Description
30	R/W	Peek/Poke Data Register Byte 0
31	R/W	Peek/Poke Data Register Byte 1
32	R/W	Peek/Poke Data Register Byte 2
33	R/W	Peek/Poke Data Register Byte 3
34	R/W	Peek/Poke Address Register Byte 0
35	R/W	Peek/Poke Address Register Byte 1
36	R/W	Peek/Poke Address Registor Byte 2
37	R/W	Peek/Poke Address Register Byte 3
38	R/W	Peek/Poke Control Register
39	R/W	I/O Decode Range 0 Base Address Register
3A	R/W	I/O Decode Range 0 Control Register
3B	R/W	I/O Decode Range 1 Base Address Register
3C	R/W	I/O Decode Range 1 Control Register
3D	—	Reserved
3E	—	Reserved
3F	—	Reserved
40	R/W	Channel 0 Base Count Register Byte 0
41	R/W	Channel 0 Base Count Register Byte 1
42	R/W	Channel 0 Base Count Register Byte 2
43	R/W	Channel 0 Base Address Register Byte 0
44	R/W	Channel 0 Base Address Register Byte 1
45	R/W	Channel 0 Base Address Register Byte 2
46	R/W	Channel 0 Base Address Register Byte 3
47	—	Reserved
48	R/W	Channel 0 Configuration Register
49	W	Channel 0 Transfer Strobe Register
4A	R/W	Channel 0 Status Register
4B	R/W	Channel 0 TBI Base Address Register Byte 0
4C	R/W	Channel 0 TBI Base Address Register Byte 1
4D	—	Reserved
4E	—	Reserved
4F	—	Reserved
50	R	Channel 0 Current Count Register Byte 0
51	R	Channel 0 Current Count Register Byte 1
52	R	Channel 0 Current Count Register Byte 2
53	R	Channel 0 Current Address Register Byte 0
54	R	Channel 0 Current Address Register Byte 1
55	R	Channel 0 Current Address Register Byte 2
56	R	Channel 0 Current Address Register Byte 3
57	—	Reserved
58	R	Channel 0 TBI Current Address Register Byte 0
59	R	Channel 0 TBI Current Address Register Byte 1
5A	—	Reserved
5B	—	Reserved
5C	—	Reserved
5D	—	Reserved
5E	—	Reserved
5F	—	Reserved

14.3 Processor Only Register Set (Continued)

Index Address	Type	Register Description
60	R/W	Channel 1 Base Count Register Byte 0
61	R/W	Channel 1 Base Count Register Byte 1
62	R/W	Channel 1 Base Count Register Byte 2
63	R/W	Channel 1 Base Address Register Byte 0
64	R/W	Channel 1 Base Address Register Byte 1
65	R/W	Channel 1 Base Address Register Byte 2
66	R/W	Channel 1 Base Address Register Byte 3
67	—	Reserved
68	R/W	Channel 1 Configuration Register
69	W	Channel 1 Transfer Strobe Register
6A	R/W	Channel 1 Status Register
6B	R/W	Channel 1 TBI Base Address Register Byte 0
6C	R/W	Channel 1 TBI Base Address Register Byte 1
6D	—	Reserved
6E	—	Reserved
6F	—	Reserved
70	R	Channel 1 Current Count Register Byte 0
71	R	Channel 1 Current Count Register Byte 1
72	R	Channel 1 Current Count Register Byte 2
73	R	Channel 1 Current Address Register Byte 0
74	R	Channel 1 Current Address Register Byte 1
75	R	Channel 1 Current Address Register Byte 2
76	R	Channel 1 Current Address Register Byte 3
77	—	Reserved
78	R	Channel 1 TBI Current Address Register Byte 0
79	R	Channel 1 TBI Current Address Register Byte 1
7A	—	Reserved
7B	—	Reserved
7C	—	Reserved
7D	—	Reserved
7E	—	Reserved
7F	—	Reserved

NOTES:
1. TBI = Transfer Buffer Interface
2. X = Slot number
3. All the reserved locations, when read, will return a value of no practical use to the user.
4. The "non BMIC" register locations (XC84h–XC87h & 04h–07h) are locations to be used by registers implemented externally on the expansion board. The BMIC will not respond to these locations (XC84h–CC87h) when accessed from the EISA side. However, the BMIC can be programmed to support the decode of the EISA addresses (XC84h–XC87h) through its I/O decode register set (refer to Section 4.8). All "non BMIC" register locations (04h–07h) when read from the local side, will return a value of no practical use to the user.

82355 Revision Summary

The following changes have been made since revision 006:

Section 1.1 EISA READ definitions has been changed from "A data transfer (burst, non-burst (two BCLK), or mismatched) from system to the expansion board across one of the two transfer channels" to "A data transfer (burst, non-burst (two BCLK), or mismatched) from system to the expansion board across Channel 1 transfer channel 1."

Section 4.2 New paragraph added after the first paragraph:

Channel 0 can be used for EISA READ operation only. Channel 1 can be used for both EISA READ and EISA WRITE operations.

Section 8.1.2 Bits 7–4 has been changed to Third hex digit of product number

Bits 4–0 has been changed to Hexadecimal digit of product revision

Section 8.2.3.3 Sentence added to Bit 22:

This is applicable only to channel 1 and not for channel 0, as channel 0 can perform EISA WRITE transfers only.

Section 10.0 Figure 10-1 TDIR, TCHAN timing diagram has changed from 10 to 11.

Figure 10-3 TDIR, TCHAN timing diagram has changed from 10 to 11.

Figure 10-7 TDIR, TCHAN timing diagram has changed from 10 to 11.

The following changes have been made since revision 005:

Section 4.3 New paragraph added at the end. This paragraph reads:

Any consecutive Peek/Poke or Locked exchanged transfers must be initiated only after the previous Peek/Poke or Locked exchange has been completed. This can be accomplished by making sure that bit 2 of the local status/control register is set to a zero before initiating the transfer.

Section 4.8 New paragraph added after the third paragraph. This paragraph reads:

The IDOEs do not go active during an IOSEL cycle outside the shared register access space.

Section 7.4 The third paragraph had two sentences deleted that is replaced with Figure 7-2, IDOEO# Connection during ID Register Access. The sentences that were deleted read as follows:

The external lines connected to the IDAT <7:0> lines should be connected to the bus between the BMIC and the external F245 data buffers. The BMIC will enable the external data buffers to drive byte lane 0 of the EISA bus upon detection of the ID address.

The following changes have been made since revision 004:

Section 4.3 New paragraph added at the end. This paragraph reads:

Whenever the BMIC is commanded to do an EISA POKE cycle, the BMIC will assert the MREQ# signal low normally, transfer up to four bytes of data, and release the bus by de-asserting MREQ# high. A potential problem exists, however, when the slave device extends the cycle by de-asserting EXRDY low. If the slave holds this signal low past the time that the BMIC is forced to release MREQ# high (it has been preempted while waiting for the slave to assert EXRDY high), then the BMIC will drive MREQ# back low again immediately after this cycle ends if there is another transfer pending (TBI, PEEK, POKE or LOCKED-EXCHANGE). Note that according to the EISA spec, "A bus master must wait at least two BCLKs after releasing the bus before re-asserting its MREQx*"(EISA spec, MREQ* signal description). To adhere to EISA specifications, it is required that LOCKED-EXCHANGE cycles be used in lieu of POKE cycles.

Section 8.2.3.4 New sentence added at the end of paragraph one:

At the end of a transfer, this register contains the value of the number of bytes transferred during the last cycle.

Section 8.2.4.2 Two paragraphs added for the CFGCL bit:

Before a channel is issued a clear command, the channel must first be suspended by writing a "1" into Bit 0 (CFGSU) of the Transfer Channel Configuration Register. Next the Transfer Channel Status Register must be read. If the TSTTC (Bit 0) is set to a "1", then the channel has already completed the transfer. The channel is then unsuspended (write a "0" into Bit 0 [CFGSU] of the Transfer Channel Configuration Register), and the TSTTC bit is then cleared.

If the TSTTC bit is a "0", then the TSTEN bit is checked. If this bit is a "1", then the channel has not returned to idle yet, and the Transfer Channel Status Register is repolled. If the TSTEN bit is a "0", then the channel has successfully returned to idle and can now be cleared with no errors. This is done by setting Bit 2 (CFGCL bit) to a 1 in the Transfer Channel Configuration Register. A flowchart for this operation is shown in the following figure.

Figure 8-1 was added to the data sheet.

Section 8.2.4.3 Bit 4 has been changed to reserved.

First paragraph under bit description has been changed to read, "Bits (7), (6), TST1K, and (4) are reserved. Any data read from these bits should be ignored".

The paragraph following this one has been deleted.

Section 11.2 Max Limits on symbols C_{OUT} and C_{CLK} have been changed.

Note 1 has been corrected.

Section 12.1 Symbol t1 has been corrected to read 2500 instead of 250 for max.

Symbol t20 has been corrected to read 3 for min.

Symbol t22 has been corrected to 4 from 7 for min.

Symbol t35 has been corrected to 5 from 7 for min.

Symbol t37 has been corrected to 3 for min.

Symbol t40 has been corrected to 1 for min.

Symbol t50 has been corrected to 124 from 125 for max.

Symbol t51 has been corrected to 1 for min.

Section 12.2 The Local CPU Interface Timing (Read Cycle/Shared Register Access) table has been corrected. The signal LDAT<7:0> has changed one portion from valid to float.

PC I/O Peripherals

2

2

82091AA ADVANCED INTEGRATED PERIPHERAL (AIP)

- Single-Chip PC Compatible I/O Solution for Notebook and Desktop Platforms:
  - 82078 Floppy Disk Controller Core
  - Two 16550 Compatible UARTs
  - One Multi-Function Parallel Port
  - IDE Interface
  - Integrated Back Power Protection
  - Integrated Game Port Chip Select
  - 5V or 3.3V Supply Operation with 5V Tolerant Drive Interface
  - Full Power Management Support
  - Supports Type F DMA Transfers for Faster I/O Performance
  - No Wait-State Host I/O Interface
  - Programmable Interrupt Interfaces
  - Single Crystal/Oscillator Clock (24 MHz)
  - Software Detectable Device ID
  - Comprehensive Powerup Configuration
- The AIP is 100% Compatible with EISA, ISA and AT
- Host Interface Features
  - 8-Bit Zero Wait-State ISA Bus Interface
  - DMA with Type F Transfers
  - Five Programmable ISA Interrupt Lines
  - Internal Address Decoder
- Parallel Port Features
  - All IEEE Standard 1284 Protocols Supported (Compatibility, Nibble, Byte, EPP, and ECP)
  - Peak Bi-Directional Transfer Rate of 2 MB/sec
  - 16 Byte FIFO for ECP
- Floppy Disk Controller Features
  - 100% Software Compatible with Industry Standard 82077SL and 82078
  - Integrated Analog Data Separator 250K, 300K, 500K, 1M
  - Programmable Powerdown Command
  - Auto Powerdown and Wakeup Modes
  - Integrated Tape Drive Support
  - Perpendicular Recording Support for 4 MB Drives
  - Programmable Write Pre-Compensation Delays
  - 256 Track Direct Address, Unlimited Track Support
  - 16 Byte FIFO
  - Supports 2 or 4 Drives
- 16550 Compatible UART Features
  - Two Independent Serial Ports
  - Software Compatible with 8250 and 16450 UARTs
  - 16 Byte FIFO per Serial Port
  - Two UART Clock Sources, Supports MIDI Baud Rate
- IDE Interface Features
  - Generates Chip Selects for IDE Drives
  - Integrated Buffer Control Logic
  - Dual IDE Interface Support
- Power Management Features
  - Transparent to Operating Systems and Applications Programs
  - Independent Power Control for Each Integrated Device
- 100-Pin QFP Package

  See Packaging Spec. 240800

The 82091AA Advanced Integrated Peripheral (AIP) is an integrated I/O solution containing a floppy disk controller, 2 serial ports, a multi-function parallel port, an IDE interface, and a game port on a single chip. The integration of these I/O devices results in a minimization of form factor, cost and power consumption. The floppy disk controller is the 82078 core with a data rate up to 2 Mbs. The serial ports are 16550 compatible. The parallel port supports all of the IEEE Standard 1284 protocols (ECP, EPP, Byte, Compatibility, and Nibble). The IDE interface supports 8-bit or 16-bit programmed I/O and 16-bit DMA. The Host Interface is an 8-bit ISA

October 1993
Order Number: 290486-001

interface optimized for type "F" DMA and no wait-state I/O accesses. Improved throughput and performance, the AIP contains six 16-byte FIFOstwo for each serial port, one for the parallel port, and one for the floppy disk controller. The AIP also includes power management and 3.3V capability for power sensitive applications such as notebooks. The AIP supports both motherboard and add-in card configurations.

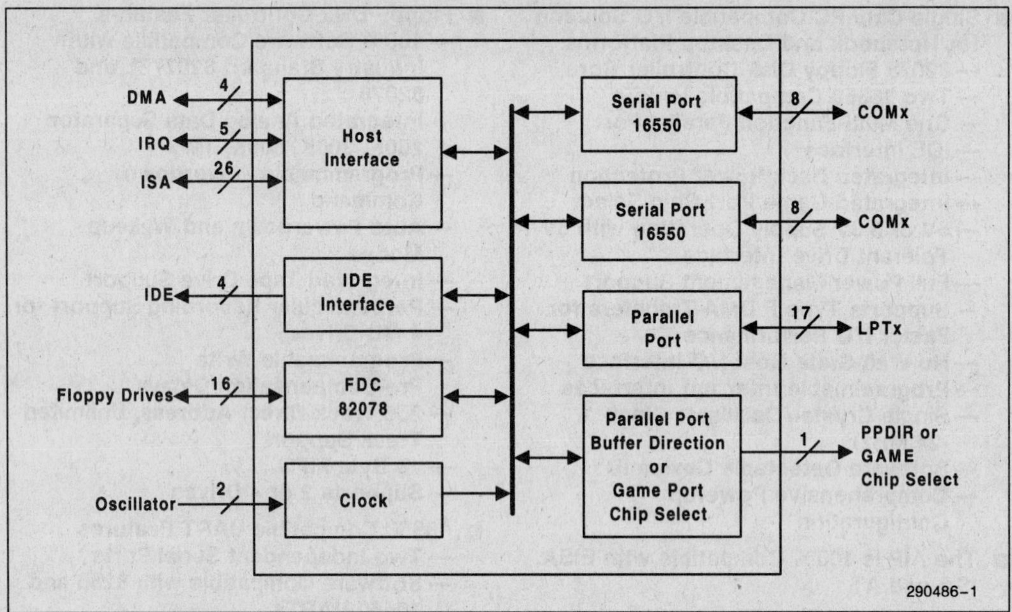

Figure 1. 82091AA Advanced Integrated Peripheral Block Diagram

82092AA
PCI TO PCMCIA/ENHANCED IDE CONTROLLER (PPEC)

- **Provides the Ultimate Plug and Play Solution for High Performance PCI Desktop Systems**
  - **—Supports Combination of PCMCIA and Enhanced IDE Interfaces**
  - **—Contains a 32-Bit PCI Local Bus Slave Interface Running at 25 MHz/33 MHz**
  - **—Supports Motherboard and Add-in Card Implementations**
- **Compliant with PCMCIA 2.01/JEIDA 4.1 Interface Standard**
  - **—Supports up to Four 68-Pin Standard PC Card Sockets, Cascadable for Additional Sockets**
  - **—Each Socket Interchangeably Supports Either Memory or I/O PC Cards**
  - **—Software Compatible with the Industry Standard 82365SL PCIC**
  - **—Supports PCMCIA-ATA Disk Drive Devices**
- **Interfaces Four Enhanced IDE Devices**
  - **—Provides Write Posting and Read Prefetching to Support High Performance IDE Devices**
  - **—Primary and Secondary IDE Devices can be Independently Programmed for Various Speed Selections**
- **Dual Voltage Operation**
  - **—Each PCMCIA Socket Automatically Configures to Support Either 3.3V or 5.0V PC Cards**
- **Power Management**
  - **—Individual Socket Power Control**
  - **—Hot Insertion/Removal Capability**
- **Flexible System Configuration Options**
  - **—Two-Socket Configuration With On-Chip Buffering**
  - **—Four-Socket Configuration with Partial External Buffering**
- **System Bus Timings Compatible with Intel Pentium™ and Intel486™ Microprocessor Families**
  - **—Supports All Intel PCIsets**
  - **—Programmable PCMCIA and IDE Interface Timing**
  - **—Easily Configured to Support Other Standard Architectures**
- **Eliminates Need for System Configuration Jumpers**
  - **—Address Mapping for PCMCIA 2.01/JEIDA 4.1 PC Card Memory**
  - **—Address Windowing for I/O Space**
  - **—Full 4 GBytes PCI Address Range**
  - **—Selectable Interrupt Steering from PC Card to System Interrupt Lines or PCI Interrupts**
- **208-Pin QFP Package**

(See Packaging Spec. Order No. 240800, Package Type S)

The 82092AA is a high-bandwidth, software-configurable bridge that interfaces as many as four PCMCIA (PC Memory Card International Association) PC Cards and four enhanced IDE devices to the Peripheral Component Interconnect (PCI) Bus. It is software compatible with the Intel 82365SL PC Card Interface Controller, but features a 32-bit PCI interface for maximum system performance. The PPEC simplifies system design by reducing component count between the PCI Bus, PC Cards and IDE devices, and maximizes system flexibility by providing such benefits as PC Card select decoding, multiple memory address translation maps, power management, and I/O interrupt steering. In addition, the PPEC supports auto-configuration allowing dynamic system setup upon insertion or removal of PC Cards. The enhanced IDE interface has programmable transfer rates that can support today's fastest IDE devices, including Mode 3 (I/O Channel Ready) operation, as well as any future IDE modes. The four IDE devices supported by PPEC may include Hard Disk Drives, CD-ROMs, Tape Drives and any future IDE-based peripherals.

October 1993
Order Number: 290511-001

82077AA
CHMOS SINGLE-CHIP FLOPPY DISK CONTROLLER

- **Single-Chip Floppy Disk Solution**
  - **100% PC AT* Compatible**
  - **100% PS/2* Compatible**
  - **100% PS/2 Model 30 Compatible**
  - **Integrated Drive and Data Bus Buffers**
- **Integrated Analog Data Separator**
  - **250 Kbits/sec**
  - **300 Kbits/sec**
  - **500 Kbits/sec**
  - **1 Mbits/sec**
- **High Speed Processor Interface**
- **Perpendicular Recording Support**
- **Integrated Tape Drive Support**
- **12 mA Host Interface Drivers, 40 mA Disk Drivers**
- **Four Fully Decoded Drive Select and Motor Signals**
- **Programmable Write Precompensation Delays**
- **Addresses 256 Tracks Directly, Supports Unlimited Tracks**
- **16 Byte FIFO**
- **68-Pin PLCC**
  (See Packaging Spec., Order #240800, Package Type N)

The 82077AA floppy disk controller has completely integrated all of the logic required for floppy disk control. The 82077AA, a 24 MHz crystal, a resistor package and a device chip select implements a PC AT or PS/2 solution. All programmable options default to compatible values. The dual PLL data separator has better performance than most board level/discrete PLL implementations. The FIFO allows better system performance in multi-master systems (e.g. PS/2, EISA). The 82077AA is available in three versions—82077AA-5, 82077AA and 82077AA-1. 82077AA-1 has all features listed in this data sheet. It supports both tape drives and 4 Mb floppy drives. The 82077AA supports 4 Mb floppy drives and is capable of operation at all data rates through 1 Mbps. The 82077AA-5 supports 500/300/250 Kbps data rates for high and low density floppy drives.

The 82077AA is fabricated with Intel's CHMOS III technology and is available in a 68-lead PLCC (plastic) package.

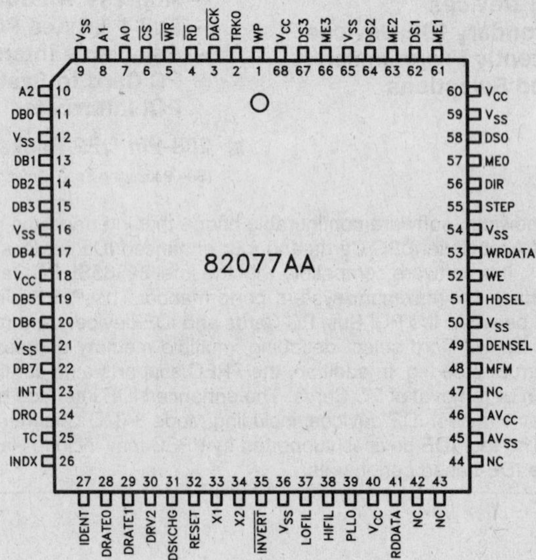

Figure 1. 82077AA Pinout

*PS/2 and PC AT are trademarks of IBM.

The complete document for this product is available on Intel's "Data-on-Demand" CD-ROM system. To obtain a copy, contact your local Intel field sales office, Intel technical distributor or call 1-800-548-4725.

October 1993
Order Number: 290166-007

82077SL
CHMOS SINGLE-CHIP FLOPPY DISK CONTROLLER

- **Completely Compatible with Industry Standard 82077AA**
- **Single-Chip Laptop Desktop Floppy Disk Controller Solution**
  - **— 100% PC AT* Compatible**
  - **— 100% PS/2* Compatible**
  - **— 100% PS/2 Model 30 Compatible**
  - **— Fully Compatible with Intel's 386SL Microprocessor SuperSet**
  - **— Integrated Drive and Data Bus Buffers**
- **Power Management Features**
  - **— Application Software Transparency**
  - **— Programmable Powerdown Command**
  - **— Auto Powerdown and Wakeup Modes**
  - **— Two External Power Management Pins**
  - **— Typical Power Consumption in Power Down: 10 μA**
- **High Speed Processor Interface**
- **Integrated Analog Data Separator**
  - **— 250 Kbits/sec**
  - **— 300 Kbits/sec**
  - **— 500 Kbits/sec**
  - **— 1 Mbits/sec**
- **Programmable Crystal Oscillator for On or Off**
- **Integrated Tape Drive Support**
- **Perpendicular Recording Support**
- **12 mA Host Interface Drivers, 40 mA Disk Drivers**
- **Four Fully Decoded Drive Select and Motor Signals**
- **Programmable Write Precompensation Delays**
- **Addresses 256 Tracks Directly, Supports Unlimited Tracks**
- **16 Byte FIFO**
- **68-Pin PLCC**
  (See Packaging Handbook Order Number #240800, Package Type N)

The 82077SL, a 24 MHz crystal, a resistor package, and a device chip select implements a complete laptop solution. All programmable options default to 82077AA compatible values. The dual PLL data separator has better performance than most board level/discrete PLL implementations. The FIFO allows better system performance in multi-master systems (e.g., Microchannel, EISA).

The 82077SL is a superset of 82077AA. The 82077SL incorporates power management features while maintaining complete compatibility with the 82077AA/8272A floppy disk controllers. It contains programmable power management features while integrating all of the logic required for floppy disk control. The power management features are transparent to any application software. The 82077SL is available in three versions—82077SL-5, 82077SL and 82077SL-1. 82077SL-1 has all features listed in this data sheet. It supports both tape drives and 4 MB floppy drives. The 82077SL supports 4 MB floppy drives and is capable of operation at all data rates through 1 Mbps. The 82077SL-5 supports 500/300/250 Kbps data rates for high and low density floppy drives.

The 82077SL is fabricated with Intel's advanced CHMOS III technology and is available in a 68-lead PLCC (plastic) package.

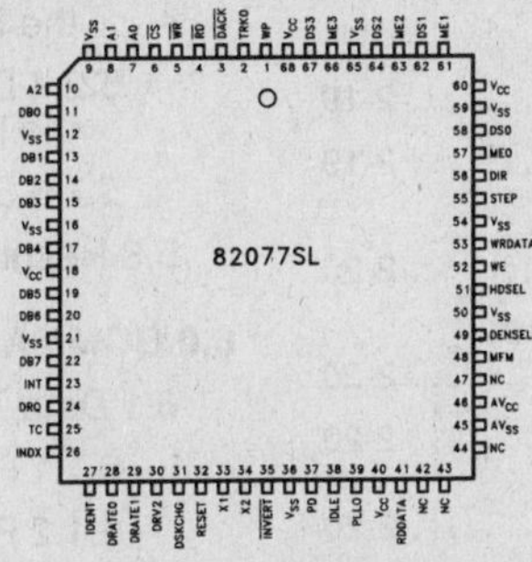

Figure 1. 82077SL Pinout

*PS/2 and PC AT are trademarks of IBM.

October 1993
Order Number: 290410-004

82077SL CHMOS Single-Chip Floppy Disk Controller

CONTENTS

PAGE

CONTENTS

PAGE

CONTENTS PAGE

CONTENTS PAGE

Table 1. 82077SL Pin Description

<table>
<tr><th>Symbol</th><th>Pin #</th><th>I/O</th><th>Description</th></tr>
<tr><td colspan="4">HOST INTERFACE</td></tr>
<tr><td>RESET</td><td>32</td><td>I</td><td>RESET: A high level places the 82077SL in a known idle state. All registers are cleared except those set by the Specify command.</td></tr>
<tr><td>$\overline{CS}$</td><td>6</td><td>I</td><td>CHIP SELECT: Decodes base address range and qualifies $\overline{RD}$ and $\overline{WR}$ inputs.</td></tr>
<tr><td>A0
A1
A2</td><td>7
8
10</td><td>I</td><td>ADDRESS: Selects one of the host interface registers:
<table>
<tr><th>A2</th><th>A1</th><th>A0</th><th>Access Type</th><th>Register</th><th></th></tr>
<tr><td>0</td><td>0</td><td>0</td><td>R</td><td>Status Register A</td><td>SRA</td></tr>
<tr><td>0</td><td>0</td><td>1</td><td>R</td><td>Status Register B</td><td>SRB</td></tr>
<tr><td>0</td><td>1</td><td>0</td><td>R/W</td><td>Digital Output Register</td><td>DOR</td></tr>
<tr><td>0</td><td>1</td><td>1</td><td>R/W</td><td>Tape Drive Register</td><td>TDR</td></tr>
<tr><td>1</td><td>0</td><td>0</td><td>R</td><td>Main Status Register</td><td>MSR</td></tr>
<tr><td>1</td><td>0</td><td>0</td><td>W</td><td>Data Rate Select Register</td><td>DSR</td></tr>
<tr><td>1</td><td>0</td><td>1</td><td>R/W</td><td>Data (First In First Out)</td><td>FIFO</td></tr>
<tr><td>1</td><td>1</td><td>0</td><td></td><td>Reserved</td><td></td></tr>
<tr><td>1</td><td>1</td><td>1</td><td>R</td><td>Digital Input Register</td><td>DIR</td></tr>
<tr><td>1</td><td>1</td><td>1</td><td>W</td><td>Configuration Control Register</td><td>CCR</td></tr>
</table></td></tr>
<tr><td>DB0
DB1
DB2
DB3
DB4
DB5
DB6
DB7</td><td>11
13
14
15
17
19
20
22</td><td>I/O</td><td>DATA BUS: Data bus with 12 mA drive</td></tr>
<tr><td>$\overline{RD}$</td><td>4</td><td>I</td><td>READ: Control signal</td></tr>
<tr><td>$\overline{WR}$</td><td>5</td><td>I</td><td>WRITE: Control signal</td></tr>
<tr><td>DRQ</td><td>24</td><td>O</td><td>DMA REQUEST: Requests service from a DMA controller. Normally active high, but goes to high impedance in AT and Model 30 modes when the appropriate bit is set in the DOR.</td></tr>
<tr><td>$\overline{DACK}$</td><td>3</td><td>I</td><td>DMA ACKNOWLEDGE: Control input that qualifies the $\overline{RD}$, $\overline{WR}$ inputs in DMA cycles. Normally active low, but is disabled in AT and Model 30 modes when the appropriate bit is set in the DOR.</td></tr>
<tr><td>TC</td><td>25</td><td>I</td><td>TERMINAL COUNT: Control line from a DMA controller that terminates the current disk transfer. TC is accepted only while $\overline{DACK}$ is active. This input is active high in the AT, and Model 30 modes and active low in the PS/2 mode.</td></tr>
<tr><td>INT</td><td>23</td><td>O</td><td>INTERRUPT: Signals a data transfer in non-DMA mode and when status is valid. Normally active high, but goes to high impedance in AT, and Model 30 modes when the appropriate bit is set in the DOR.</td></tr>
<tr><td>X1
X2</td><td>33
34</td><td></td><td>CRYSTAL 1,2: Connection for a 24 MHz fundamental mode parallel resonant crystal. X1 may be driven with a MOS level clock and X2 would be left unconnected.</td></tr>
</table>

Table 1. 82077SL Pin Description (Continued)

Symbol	Pin #	I/O	Description
HOST INTERFACE (Continued)			
IDENT	27	I	**IDENTITY:** Upon Hardware RESET, this input (along with MFM pin) selects between the three interface modes. After RESET, this input selects the type of drive being accessed and alters the level on DENSEL. The MFM pin is also sampled at Hardware RESET, and then becomes an output again. Internal pull-ups on MFM permit a no connect. **IDENT / MFM / INTERFACE** 1 / 1 or NC / AT Mode 1 / 0 / ILLEGAL 0 / 1 or NC / PS/2 Mode 0 / 0 / Model 30 Mode **AT MODE:** Major options are: enables DMA Gate logic, TC is active high, Status Registers A & B not available. **PS/2 MODE:** Major options are: No DMA Gate logic, TC is active low, Status Registers A & B are available. **MODEL 30 MODE:** Major options are: enable DMA Gate logic, TC is active high, Status Registers A & B available. After Hardware reset this pin determines the polarity of the DENSEL pin. IDENT at a logic level of "1", DENSEL will be active high for high (500 Kbps/1 Mbps) data rates (typically used for 5.25" drives). IDENT at a logic level of "0", DENSEL will be active low for high data rates (typically used for 3.5" drives). This assumes the $\overline{\text{INVERT}}$ pin to be tied to ground.
DISK CONTROL (All outputs have 40 mA drive capability)			
$\overline{\text{INVERT}}$	35	I	**INVERT:** Strapping option. Determines the polartity of **all** signals in this section. Should be strapped to ground when using the internal buffers and these signals become active LOW. When strapped to VCC, these signals become active high and external inverting drivers and receivers are required.
ME0 ME1 ME2 ME3	57 61 63 66	O	**ME0–3:** Decoded Motor enables for drives 0–3. The motor enable pins are directly controlled via the Digital Output Register.
DS0 DS1 DS2 DS3	58 62 64 67	O	**DRIVE SELECT 0–3:** Decoded drive selects for drives 0–3. These outputs are decoded from the select bits in the Digital Output Register and gated by ME0–3.
HDSEL	51	O	**HEAD SELECT:** Selects which side of a disk is to be used. An active level selects side 1.
STEP	55	O	**STEP:** Supplies step pulses to the drive.
DIR	56	O	**DIRECTION:** Controls the direction the head moves when a step signal is present. The head moves toward the center if active.
WRDATA	53	O	**WRITE DATA:** FM or MFM serial data to the drive. Precompensation value is selectable through software.
WE	52	O	**WRITE ENABLE:** Drive control signal that enables the head to write onto the disk.
DENSEL	49	O	**DENSITY SELECT:** Indicates whether a low (250/300 Kbps) or high (500 Kbps/1 Mbps) data rate has been selected.
DSKCHG	31	I	**DISK CHANGE:** This input is reflected in the Digital Input Register.

2

Table 1. 82077SL Pin Description (Continued)

Symbol	Pin #	I/O	Description
DISK CONTROL (All outputs have 40 mA drive capability) (Continued)			
DRV2	30	I	**DRIVE2:** This indicates whether a second drive is installed and is reflected in Status Register A.
TRK0	2	I	**TRACK0:** Control line that indicates that the head is on track 0.
WP	1	I	**WRITE PROTECT:** Indicates whether the disk drive is write protected.
INDX	26	I	**INDEX:** Indicates the beginning of the track.
PLL SECTION			
RDDATA	41	I	**READ DATA:** Serial data from the disk. INVERT also affects the polarity of this signal.
MFM	48	I/O	**MFM:** At Hardware RESET, aids in configuring the 82077SL. Internal pull-up allows a no connect if a "1" is required. After reset this pin becomes an output and indicates the current data encoding/decoding mode (Note: If the pin is held at logic level "0" during hardware RESET it must be pulled to "1" after reset to enable the output. The pin can be released on the falling edge of hardware RESET to enable the output). MFM is active high (MFM). MFM may be left tied low after hardware reset, in this case the MFM function will be disabled.
DRATE0 DRATE1	28 29	O	**DATARATE0–1:** Reflects the contents of bits 0,1 of the Data Rate Register. (Drive capability of +6.0 mA @ 0.4V and −4.0 mA @ 2.4V)
PLL0	39	I	**PLL0:** This input optimizes the data separator for either floppy disks or tape drives. A "1" (or V_{CC}) selects the floppy mode, a "0" (or GND) selects tape mode.
POWERDOWN STATUS			
IDLE	38	O	**IDLE:** This pin indicates that the part is in the IDLE state and can be powered down. IDLE state is defined as MSR = 80H, INT = 0, and the head being "unloaded" (as defined in Section 6.2.6). Whenever the part is in this state, IDLE pin is active high. If the part is powered down by the Auto Mode, IDLE pin is set high and if the part is powered down by setting the DSR POWERDOWN bit, IDLE pin is set low.
PD	37	O	**POWERDOWN:** This pin is active high whenever the part is in powerdown state, either via DSR POWERDOWN bit or via the Auto Mode. This pin can be used to disable external oscillator's output.
MISCELLANEOUS			
VCC	18 40 60 68		**Voltage:** +5V
GND	9 12 16 21 36 50 54 59 65		**Ground**
AVCC	46		**Analog Supply**
AVSS	45		**Analog Ground**
NC	42 43 44 47		**No Connection:** These pins **MUST** be left unconnected.

1.0 INTRODUCTION

The 82077SL is a single-chip floppy disk controller for portable PC designs, PC-AT, Microchannel and EISA systems. The 82077SL includes all the power management features necessary to implement a powerful laptop and notebook solution. The 82077SL is fully compatible with the 82077AA. The pin out remains the same with the exception of two new powerdown status pins, PD and IDLE. These pins will replace the LOFIL and HIFIL pins on the 82077AA that are used to connect an external capacitor.

The 82077SL, a 24 MHz crystal, a resistor package and a chip select implement a complete design. The power management features of the 82077SL are designed to be transparent to all application software. The 82077SL will seem awake to the software even when it is in powerdown mode. All drive control signals are fully decoded and have 40 mA drive buffers with selectable polarity. Signals returned from the drive are sent through on-chip input buffers with hysteresis for noise immunity. The integrated analog data separator needs no external compensation of components, yet allows for wide motor variation with exceptionally low soft error rates. The microprocessor interface has 12 mA drive buffers on the data bus plus 100% hardware register compatibility for PC-AT and Microchannel systems. The 16-byte FIFO with programmable thresholds is extremely useful in multi-master systems (Microchannel, EISA) or systems with large bus latency.

Upon hardware reset, (Pin 32) the 82077SL defaults to 8272A functionality. Figure 1-1 is a block diagram of the 82077SL.

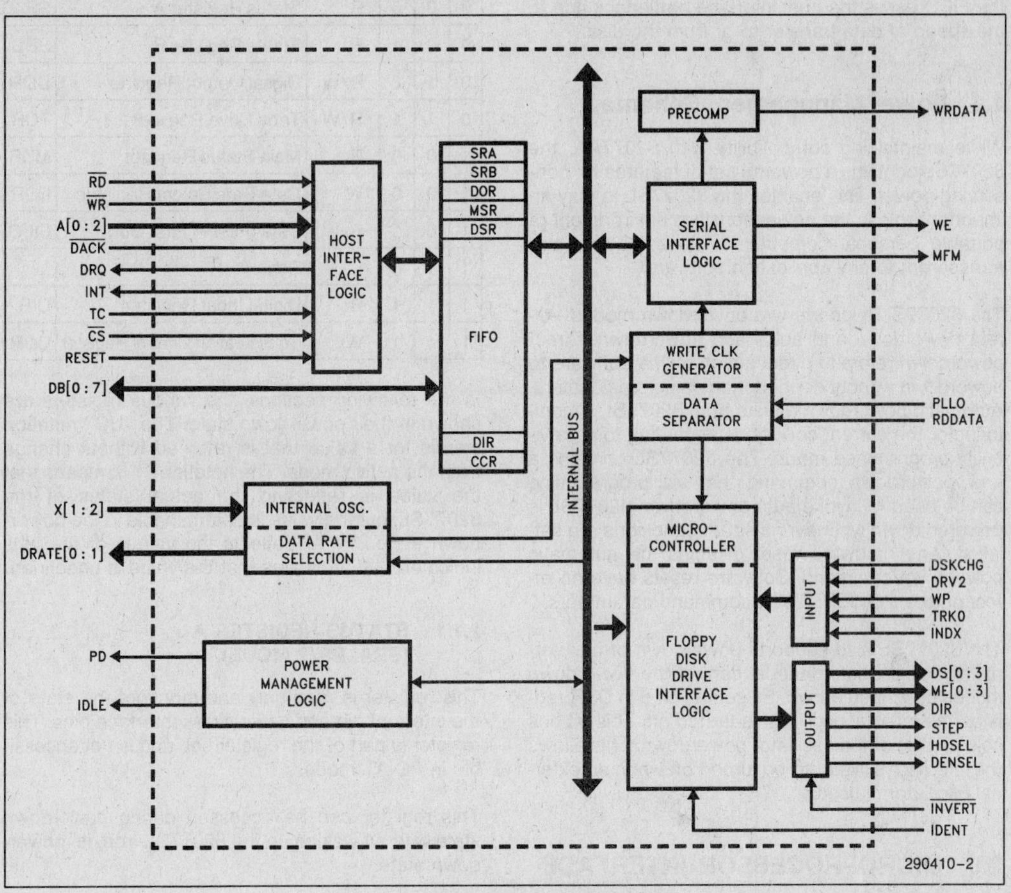

2

Figure 1-1. 82077SL Block Diagram

1.1 Perpendicular Recording Mode

An added capability of the 82077SL is the ability to interface directly to perpendicular recording floppy drives. Perpendicular recording differs from the traditional longitudinal method by orienting the magnetic bits vertically. This scheme packs in more data bits for the same area.

The 82077SL with perpendicular recording drives can read standard 3.5″ floppies as well as read and write perpendicular media. Some manufacturers offer drives that can read and write standard and perpendicular media in a perpendicular media drive.

A single command puts the 82077SL into perpendicular mode. All other commands operate as they normally do. The perpendicular mode requires the 1 Mbps data rate of the 82077SL. At this data rate, the FIFO eases the host interface bottleneck due to the speed of data transfer to or from the disk.

1.2 Power Management Scheme

While maintaining compatibility with 82077AA, the 82077SL contains a powerful set of features for conserving power. This enables the 82077SL to play an important role in the power sensitive environment of portable personal computers. These features are transparent to any application software.

The 82077SL supports two powerdown modes—direct powerdown and automatic powerdown. Direct powerdown refers to direct action by the software to powerdown without dependence on external factors. Automatic powerdown results from 82077SL's monitoring of the current conditions according to a previously programmed mode. The 82077SL contains a new powerdown command that via programming can be used to invoke auto powerdown. 82077SL is powered down whenever a set of conditions are satisfied. Any hardware reset disables the automatic powerdown command. Software resets have no effect on the POWERDOWN command parameters.

The 82077SL also supports powerdown of its internal crystal oscillator independent of the powerdown modes described above. By setting bit 5 in DSR register, the internal oscillator is turned off. This bit has sole control of the oscillator powerdown. This allows the internal oscillator to be turned off when an external oscillator is used.

2.0 MICROPROCESSOR INTERFACE

The interface consists of the standard asynchronous signals: $\overline{RD}$, $\overline{WR}$, $\overline{CS}$, A0–A2, INT, DMA control and a data bus. The address lines select between configuration registers, the FIFO and control/status registers. This interface can be switched between PC AT, Model 30, or PS/2 normal modes. The PS/2 register sets are a superset of the registers found in a PC-AT.

2.1 Status, Data and Control Registers

As shown below, the base address range is supplied via the $\overline{CS}$ pin. For PC-AT or PS/2 designs, the primary and secondary address ranges are 3F0 Hex to 37F Hex and 370 Hex to 377 Hex respectively.

A2	A1	A0	Access Type	Register	
0	0	0	R	Status Register A	SRA
0	0	1	R	Status Register B	SRB
0	1	0	R/W	Digital Output Register	DOR
0	1	1	R/W	Tape Drive Register	TDR
1	0	0	R	Main Status Register	MSR
1	0	0	W	Data Rate Select Register	DSR
1	0	1	R/W	Data (First In First Out)	FIFO
1	1	0		Reserved	
1	1	1	R	Digital Input Register	DIR
1	1	1	W	Configuration Control Register	CCR

In the following sections, the various registers are shown in their powerdown state. The "UC" notation stands for a value that is returned without change from the active mode. The notation " * " means that the value is reflecting the actual status of the 82077SL, but the value is determinable in the powerdown state. "N/A" reflects the values of the pins indicated. "X" indicates that the value is undefined.

2.1.1a STATUS REGISTER A (SRA, PS/2 MODE)

This register is read-only and monitors the state of the interrupt pin and several disk interface pins. This register is part of the register set, and is not accessible in PC-AT mode.

This register can be accessed during powerdown state without waking up the 82077SL from its powerdown state.

Bits	7	6°	5	4°	3	2°	1°C	0
Function	INT PENDING	$\overline{\text{DRV2}}$	STEP	$\overline{\text{TRK0}}$	HDSEL	$\overline{\text{INDX}}$	$\overline{\text{WP}}$	DIR
H/W Reset State	0	N/A	0	N/A	0	N/A	N/A	0
Auto PD State	0*	UC	0*	1	0*	1	1	0*

The INT PENDING bit is used by software to monitor the state of the 82077SL INTERRUPT pin. The bits marked with a " ° " reflect the state of drive signals on the cable and are independent of the state of the $\overline{\text{INVERT}}$ pin.

The INT PENDING bit is low by definition for 82077SL to be in powerdown. The bits reflecting the floppy disk drive input pins (TRK0, INDEX and WP) are forced to an inactive state. The floppy disk drive outputs (HDSEL, STEP, and DIR) also go to their inactive, default state.

As a read-only register, there is no default value associated with a reset other than some drive bits will change with a reset. The INT PENDING, STEP, HDSEL, and DIR bits will be low after reset.

2.1.1b STATUS REGISTER A (SRA, MODEL 30 MODE)

Bits	7	6	5	4	3	2	1	0
Function	INT PENDING	DRQ	STEP F/F	TRK0	$\overline{\text{HDSEL}}$	INDX	WP	$\overline{\text{DIR}}$
H/W Reset State	0	0	0	N/A	1	N/A	N/A	1
Auto PD State	0*	0*	0	0	1*	0	0	1*

This register has the following changes in PS/2 Model 30 Mode. Disk interface pins (Bits 0, 1, 2, 3, & 4) are inverted from PS/2 Mode. The DRQ bit monitors the status of the DMA Request pin. The STEP bit is latched with the Step output going active and is cleared with a read to the DIR register, Hardware or Software RESET.

The DRQ bit is low by definition for 82077SL to be in powerdown. The bits reflecting the floppy disk drive input pins (TRK0, INDEX and WP) are forced to reflect an inactive state. The floppy disk drive outputs (HDSEL, STEP, and DIR) also go to their inactive, default state.

2.1.2a STATUS REGISTER B (SRB, PS/2 MODE)

This register is read-only and monitors the state of several disk interface pins. This register is part of the PS/2 register set, and is not accessible in PC-AT mode.

Bits	7	6	5	4	3*	2	1	0
Function	1	1	DRIVE SEL 0	WRDATA TOGGLE	RDDATA TOGGLE	WE	MOT EN1	MOT EN0
H/W Reset State	1	1	0	0	0	0	0	0
Auto PD State	1	1	UC	0	0	0*	0	0

As the only drive input, RDDATA TOGGLE's activity is independent of the $\overline{\text{INVERT}}$ pin level and reflects the level as seen on the cable.

The two TOGGLE bits do not read back the state of their respective pins directly. Instead, the pins drive a Flip/Flop which produces a wider and more reliably read pulse. Bits 6 and 7 are undefined and always return a 1.

After any reset, the activity on the TOGGLE pins are cleared. Drive select and Motor bits cleared by the RESET pin and not software resets.

2.1.2b STATUS REGISTER B (SRB, MODEL 30 MODE)

Bits	7	6	5	4	3	2	1	0
Function	$\overline{\text{DRV2}}$	$\overline{\text{DS1}}$	$\overline{\text{DS0}}$	WRDATA F/F	RDDATA F/F	WE F/F	$\overline{\text{DS3}}$	$\overline{\text{DS2}}$
H/W Reset State	N/A	1	1	0	0	0	1	1
Auto PD State	UC	UC	UC	0	0	0	UC	UC

This register has the following changes in Model 30 Mode. Bits 0, 1, 5, and 6 return the decoded value of the Drive Select bits in the DOR register. Bits 2, 3, and 4 are set by their respective active going edges and are cleared by reading the DIR register. The WRDATA bit is triggered by raw WRDATA signals and is not gated by WE. Bits 2, 3, and 4 are cleared to a low level by either Hardware or Software RESET.

2.1.3 DIGITAL OUTPUT REGISTER (DOR)

The Digital Output Register contains the drive select and motor enable bits, a reset bit and a $\overline{\text{DMA GATE}}$ bit.

Bits	7	6	5	4	3	2	1	0
Function	MOT EN3	MOT EN2	MOT EN1	MOT EN0	DMA $\overline{\text{GATE}}$	$\overline{\text{RESET}}$	DRIVE SEL1	DRIVE SEL2
H/W Reset State	0	0	0	0	0	0	0	0
Auto PD State	0*	0*	0*	0*	UC	1*	UC	UC

The MOT ENx bits directly control their respective motor enable pins (ME0–3). A one means the pin is active, the $\overline{\text{INVERT}}$ pin determines the active level. The DRIVE SELx bits are decoded to provide four drive select lines and only one may be active at a time. A one is active and the $\overline{\text{INVERT}}$ pin determines the level on the cable. Standard programming practice is to set both MOT ENx and DRIVE SELx bits at the same time.

Table 2-1 lists a set of DOR values to activate the drive select and motor enable for each drive.

Table 2-1. Drive Activation Values

Drive	DOR Value
0	1CH
1	2DH
2	4EH
3	8FH

The $\overline{\text{DMAGATE}}$ bit is enabled only in PC-AT and Model 30 Modes. If $\overline{\text{DMAGATE}}$ is set low, the INT and DRQ outputs are tristated and the $\overline{\text{DACK}}$ and TC inputs are disabled. $\overline{\text{DMAGATE}}$ set high will enable INT, DRQ, TC, and $\overline{\text{DACK}}$ to the system. In PS/2 Mode $\overline{\text{DMAGATE}}$ has no effect upon INT, DRQ, TC or $\overline{\text{DACK}}$ pins and they are always active.

The DOR reset bit and the Motor Enable bits have to be inactive when the 82077SL is in powerdown. The $\overline{\text{DMAGATE}}$ and DRIVE SEL bits are unchanged. During powerdown, writing to the DOR does not awaken the 82077SL with the exception of activating any of the motor enable bits. Setting the motor enable bits active (high) will wake up the part.

This $\overline{\text{RESET}}$ bit clears the basic core of the 82077SL and the FIFO circuits when the LOCK bit is set to "0" (see Section 5.3.2 for LOCK bit definition). Once set, it remains set until the user clears this bit. This bit is set by a chip reset and the 82077SL is held in a reset state until the user clears this bit. The $\overline{\text{RESET}}$ bit has no effect upon this register.

2.1.4 TAPE DRIVE REGISTER (TDR)

Bits	7	6	5	4	3	2	1	0
Function	—	—	—	—	—	—	TAPE SEL1	TAPE SEL0
H/W Reset State	—	—	—	—	—	—	0	0
Auto PD State	—	—	—	—	—	—	UC	UC

This register allows the user to assign tape support to a particular drive during initialization. Any future references to that drive number automatically invokes tape support. Hardware reset clears this register; software resets have not effect. TDR[2:7] are not writable and remain tristated if read. The tape select bits are hardware RESET to zeros, making Drive 0 not available for tape support. Drive 0 is reserved for the floppy boot drive. The tuning of the PLL for tape characteristics can also be done in hardware. If a 0 (GND) is applied to pin 39 (PLL0) the PLL is optimized for tape drives, a 1 (V_{CC}) optimizes the PLL for floppies. This hardware selection mechanism overrides the software selection scheme. A typical hardware application would route the Drive Select pin used for tape drive support to pin 39 (PLL0). For further explanation on optimizing 82077 for tape drives please refer to Section 10.2.4.

2

2.1.5 DATARATE SELECT REGISTER (DSR)

Bits	7	6	5	4	3	2	1	0
Function	S/W RESET	POWER DOWN	PDOSC	PRE-COMP2	PRE-COMP1	PRE-COMP0	DRATE SEL1	DRATE SEL0
H/W Reset State	0	0	0	0	0	0	1	0
Auto PD State	0	0	UC	UC	UC	UC	UC	UC

This register ensures backward compatibility with the 82072 floppy controller and is write-only. Changing the data rate changes the timings of the drive control signals. To ensure that drive timings are not violated when changing data rates, choose a drive timing such that the fastest data rate will not violate the timing.

This register is identical to the one used in 82077AA with the exception of bit 5. This bit in the 82077SL denoted by PDOSC is used to implement crystal oscillator power management. The internal oscillator in the 82077SL can be programmed to be either powered on or off via the PDOSC bit. This capability is independent of the chip's powerdown state. In other words, auto powerdown mode and powerdown via activating POWERDOWN bit has no effect over the power state of the oscillator.

In the default state the PDOSC bit is low and the oscillator is powered up. When this bit is programmed to a one, the oscillator is shut off. Hardware reset clears this bit to a zero. Neither of the software resets (via DOR or DSR) have any effect on this bit. When an external oscillator is used, this bit can be set to reduce power consumption. When an internal oscillator is used, this bit can be set to turn off the oscillator to conserve power. However, PDOSC must go high only when the part is in the powerdown state, otherwise the part will not function correctly and must be hardware reset once the oscillator has turned back on and stabilized. Setting the PDOSC bit has no effect on the clock input to the 82077SL (the X1 pin). The clock input is separately disabled when the part is powered down.

S/W RESET behaves the same as DOR RESET except that this reset is self clearing.

POWERDOWN bit implements direct powerdown. Setting this bit high will put the 82077SL into the powerdown state regardless of the state of the part. The part is internally reset and then put into powerdown. No status is saved and any operation in progress is aborted. Unlike the 82077AA this mode of powerdown does not turn off the internal oscillator. Any hardware or software reset will exit the 82077SL from this powerdown state. When 82077SL enters powerdown via this state it affects the floppy disk drive interface as suggested in Section 4.2.2. The state of the floppy disk drive pins during powerdown via the DSR register behaves similarly to that during auto powerdown.

PRECOMP 0–2 adjusts the WRDATA output to the disk to compensate for magnetic media phenomena known as bit shifting. The data patterns that are susceptible to bit shifting are well understood and the 82077SL compensates the data pattern as it is written to the disk. The amount of precompensation is dependent upon the drive and media but in most cases the default value is acceptable.

The 82077SL starts precompensating the data pattern starting on Track 0. The CONFIGURE command can change the track that precompensating starts on. Table 2-2 lists the precompensation values that can be selected and Table 2-3 lists the default precompensation values. The default value is selected if the three bits are zeros.

DRATE 0–1 select one of the four data rates as listed in Table 2-4. The default value is 250 Kbps upon a chip ("Hardware") reset. Other ("Software") Resets do not affect the DRATE or PRECOMP bits.

Table 2-2. Precompensation Delays

PRECOMP 432	Precompensation Delay
111	0.00 ns—DISABLED
001	41.67 ns
010	83.34 ns
011	125.00 ns
100	166.67 ns
101	208.33 ns
110	250.00 ns
000	DEFAULT

Table 2-3. Default Precompensation Delays

Data Rate	Precompensation Delays
1 Mbps	41.67 ns
500 Kbps	125 ns
300 Kbps	125 ns
250 Kbps	125 ns

Table 2-4. Data Rates

DRATESEL		DATA RATE	
1	0	MFM	FM
1	1	1 Mbps	Illegal
0	0	500 Kbps	250 Kbps
0	1	300 Kbps	150 Kbps
1	0	250 Kbps	125 Kbps

2.1.6 MAIN STATUS REGISTER (MSR)

Bits	7	6	5	4	3*	2	1	0
Function	RQM	DIO	NON DMA	CMD BSY	DRV3 BUSY	DRV2 BUSY	DRV1 BUSY	DRV0 BUSY
H/W Reset State	0	X	X	X	X	X	X	X
Auto PD State	1	0	0	0	0	0	0	0

The Main Status Register is a read-only register and is used for controlling command input and result output for all commands.

RQM—Indicates that the host can transfer data if set to a 1. No access is permitted if set to a 0.

DIO—Indicates the direction of a data transfer once RQM is set. A 1 indicates a read and a 0 indicates a write is required.

NON-DMA—This mode is selected in the SPECIFY command and will be set to a 1 during the execution phase of a command. This is for polled data transfers and helps differentiate between the data transfer phase and the reading of result bytes.

COMMAND BUSY—This bit is set to a one when a command is in progress. This bit will go active after the command byte has been accepted and goes inactive at the end of the results phase. If there is no result phase (SEEK, RECALIBRATE commands), this bit is returned to a 0 after the last command byte.

DRV x BUSY—These bits are set to ones when a drive is in the seek portion of a command, including seeks, and recalibrates.

2.1.7 FIFO (DATA)

All command parameter information and disk data transfers go through the FIFO. The FIFO is 16 bytes in size and has programmable threshold values. Data transfers are governed by the RQM and DIO bits in the Main Status Register.

The FIFO defaults to an 8272A compatible mode after a "Hardware" reset (Reset via pin 32). "Software" Resets (Reset via DOR or DSR register) can also place the 82077SL into 8272A compatible mode if the LOCK bit is set to "0" (See section 5.3.2 for the definition of the LOCK bit). This maintains PC-AT hardware compatibility. The default values can be changed through the CONFIGURE command (enable full FIFO operation with threshold control). The advantage of the FIFO is that it allows the system a larger DMA latency without causing a disk error. Table 2.5 gives several examples of the delays with a FIFO. The data is based upon the following formula:

$$\text{Threshold\#} \times \left| \frac{1}{\text{DATA RATE}} \times 8 \right| - 1.5\ \mu s = \text{DELAY}$$

Table 2-5. FIFO Service Delay

FIFO Threshold Examples	Maximum Delay to Servicing at 1 Mbps Data Rate
1 byte	1 × 8 μs − 1.5 μs = 6.5 μs
2 bytes	2 × 8 μs − 1.5 μs = 14.5 μs
8 bytes	8 × 8 μs − 1.5 μs = 62.5 μs
15 bytes	15 × 8 μs − 1.5 μs = 118.5 μs

FIFO Threshold Examples	Maximum Delay to Servicing at 500 Kbps Data Rate
1 byte	1 × 16 μs − 1.5 μs = 14.5 μs
2 bytes	2 × 16 μs − 1.5 μs = 30.5 μs
8 bytes	8 × 16 μs − 1.5 μs = 126.5 μs
15 bytes	15 × 16 μs − 1.5 μs = 238.5 μs

At the start of a command, the FIFO action is always disabled and command parameters must be sent based upon the RQM and DIO bit settings. As the 82077SL enters the command execution phase, it clears the FIFO of any data to ensure that invalid data is not transferred.

An overrun or underrun will terminate the current command and the transfer of data. Disk writes will complete the current sector by generating a 00 pattern and valid CRC.

2.1.8a DIGITAL INPUT REGISTER (DIR, PC-AT MODE)

This register is read only in all modes. In PC-AT mode only bit 7 is driven, all other bits remain tristated.

Bits	7	6	5	4	3*	2	1	0
Function	DSKCHG	—	—	—	—	—	—	—
H/W Reset State	N/A	—	—	—	—	—	—	—
Auto PD State	0	—	—	—	—	—	—	—

DSKCHG monitors the pin of the same name and reflects the opposite value seen on the disk cable, regardless of the value of $\overline{\text{INVERT}}$. The DSKCHG bit is forced inactive along with all the inputs from the floppy disk drive. All the other bits remain tristated.

2.1.8b DIGITAL INPUT REGISTER (DIR, PS/2 MODE)

Bits	7	6	5	4	3	2	1	0
Function	DSK CHG	1	1	1	1	DRATE SEL1	DRATE SEL0	HIGH $\overline{\text{DENS}}$
H/W Reset State	N/A	1	1	1	1	1	0	1
Auto PD State	0	1	1	1	1	UC	UC	UC

The following is changed in PS/2 Mode: Bits 6, 5, 4, and 3 return a value of "1", and the DRATE SEL1-0 return the value of the current data rate selected (see Table 2-4 for values).

$\overline{\text{HIGH DENS}}$ is low whenever the 500 Kbps or 1 Mbps data rates are selected. This bit is independent of the effects of the IDENT and $\overline{\text{INVERT}}$ pins.

The DSKCHG bit is forced inactive along with all the inputs from the floppy disk drive. All the other bits (as applicable) remain unchanged.

Table 2-6 shows the state of the DENSEL pin when $\overline{\text{INVERT}}$ is low.

This pin is set high after a pin RESET and is unaffected by DOR and DSR resets.

Table 2-6. DENSEL Encoding

Data Rate	IDENT*	DENSEL
1 Mbps	0	0
	1	1
500 Kbps	0	0
	1	1
300 Kbps	0	1
	1	0
250 Kbps	0	1
	1	0

*After ("Hardware") Chip Reset

2.1.8c DIGITAL INPUT REGISTER (DIR, MODEL 30 MODE)

Bits	7	6	5	4	3	2	1	0
Function	$\overline{\text{DSK CHG}}$	0	0	0	$\overline{\text{DMA GATE}}$	NOPREC	DRATE SEL1	DRATE SEL0
H/W Reset State	N/A	0	0	0	0	0	1	0
Auto PD State	1	0	0	0	UC	UC	UC	UC

The following is changed in Model 30 Mode: Bits 6, 5, and 4 return a value of "0", and Bit 7 ($\overline{\text{DSKCHG}}$) is inverted in Model 30 Mode.

The DSKCHG bit is forced inactive along with all the inputs from the floppy disk drive. All the other bits (as applicable) remain unchanged.

Bit 3 reflects the value of $\overline{\text{DMAGATE}}$ bit set in the DOR register.

Bit 2 reflects the value of NOPREC bit set in the CCR register.

2.1.9a CONFIGURATION CONTROL REGISTER (CCR, PC AT and PS/2 MODES)

This register sets the datarate and is write only. In the PC-AT it is named the DSR.

Bits	7	6	5	4	3	2	1	0
Function	—	—	—	—	—	—	DRATE SEL1	DRATE SEL0
H/W Reset State	—	—	—	—	—	—	1	0
Auto PD State	—	—	—	—	—	—	UC	UC

Refer to the table in the Data Rate Select Register for values. Unused bits should be set to 0.

2.1.9b CONFIGURATION CONTROL REGISTER (CCR, MODEL 30 MODE)

Bits	7	6	5	4	3	2	1	0
Function	—	—	—	—	—	NOPREC	DRATE SEL1	DRATE SEL0
H/W Reset State	—	—	—	—	—	0	1	0
Auto PD State	—	—	—	—	—	UC	UC	UC

NOPREC has no function, and is reset to "0" with a Hardware RESET only.

2.2 RESET

There are three sources of reset on the 82077SL; the RESET pin, a reset generated via a bit in the DOR and a reset generated via a bit in the DSR. All resets take the 82077SL out of the power down state.

On entering the reset state, all operations are terminated and the 82077SL enters an idle state. Activating reset while a disk write activity is in progress will corrupt the data and CRC.

On exiting the reset state, various internal registers are cleared, and the 82077SL waits for a new command. Drive polling will start unless disabled by a new CONFIGURE command.

2.2.1 RESET PIN ("HARDWARE") RESET

The RESET pin is a global reset and clears all registers except those programmed by the SPECIFY command. The DOR Reset bit is enabled and must be cleared by the host to exit the reset state.

2.2.2 DOR RESET vs DSR RESET ("SOFTWARE" RESET)

These two resets are functionally the same. The DSR Reset is included to maintain 82072 compatibility. Both will reset the 8272 core which affects drive status information. The FIFO circuits will also be reset if the LOCK bit is a "0" (See Section 5.3.2 for the definition of the LOCK bit). The DSR Reset clears itself automatically while the DOR Reset requires the host to manually clear it. DOR Reset has precedence over the DSR Reset. The DOR Reset is set automatically upon a pin RESET. The user must manually clear this reset bit in the DOR to exit the reset state.

The t30a specification in the A.C. Specifications gives the minimum amount of time that the DOR reset must be held active. This amount of time that the DOR reset must be held active is dependent upon the data rate. 82077SL requires that the DOR reset bit must be held active for at least 0.5 μs at 250 Kbps. This is less than a typical ISA I/O cycle time.

2.3 DMA Transfers

DMA transfers are enabled with the SPECIFY command and are initiated by the 82077SL by activating the DRQ pin during a data transfer command. The FIFO is enabled directly by asserting $\overline{\text{DACK}}$ and addresses need not be valid. $\overline{\text{CS}}$ can be held inactive during DMA transfers.

3.0 DRIVE INTERFACE

The 82077SL has integrated all of the logic needed to interface to a floppy disk or a tape drive which use floppy interface. All drive outputs have 40 mA drive capability and all inputs use a receive buffer with hysteresis. The internal analog data separator requires no external components, yet allows for an extremely wide capture range with high levels of read-data jitter, and ISV. The designer needs only to run the 82077SL disk drive signals to the disk or tape drive connector.

3.1 Cable Interface

The $\overline{\text{INVERT}}$ pin selects between using the internal buffers on the 82077SL or user supplied inverting buffers. $\overline{\text{INVERT}}$ pulled to V_{CC} disables the internal buffers; pulled to ground will enable them. There is no need to use external buffers with the 82077SL in typical PC applications.

The polarity of the DENSEL pin is controlled through the IDENT pin, after hardware reset. For 5.25″ drives a high on DENSEL tells the drive that either the 500 Kbps or 1 Mbps data rate is selected. For some 3.5″ drives the polarity of DENSEL changes to a low for high data rates. See **Table 2-6 DENSEL Encoding** for $\overline{\text{IDENT}}$ pin settings.

Additionally, the two types of drives have different electrical interfaces. Generally, the 5.25″ drive uses open collector drivers and the 3.5″ drives (as used on PS/2) use totem-pole drivers. The output buffers on the 82077SL do not change between open collector or totem-pole, they are always totem-pole. For design information on interfacing 5.25″ and 3.5″ drives to a single 82077SL, refer to Section 9.

3.2 Data Separator

The function of the data separator is to lock onto the incoming serial read data. When lock is achieved the serial front end logic of the chip is provided with a clock which is synchronized to the read data. The synchronized clock, called Data Window, is used to internally sample the serial data. One state of Data Window is used to sample the data portion of the bit cell, and the alternate state samples the clock portion. Serial to parallel conversion logic separates the read data into clock and data bytes.

To support reliable disk reads the data separator must track fluctuations in the read data frequency. Frequency errors primarily arise from two sources: motor rotation speed variation and instantaneous speed variation (ISV). A second condition, and one that opposes the ability to track frequency shifts is the response to bit jitter.

The internal data separator consists of two analog phase lock loops (PLLs) as shown in Figure 3-1. The two PLLs are referred to as the reference PLL and the data PLL. The reference PLL (the master PLL) is used to bias the data PLL (the slave PLL). The reference PLL adjusts the data PLL's operating point as a function of process, junction temperature and supply voltage. Using this architecture it was possible to eliminate the need for external trim components.

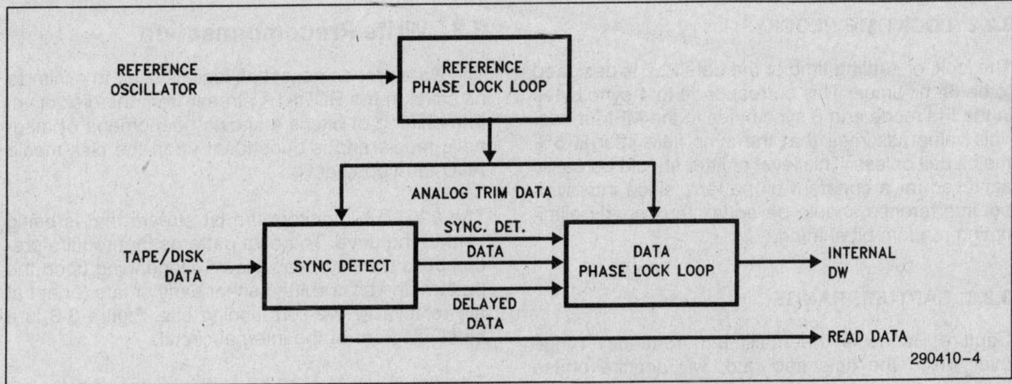

Figure 3-1. Data Separator Block Diagram

PHASE LOCK LOOP OVERVIEW

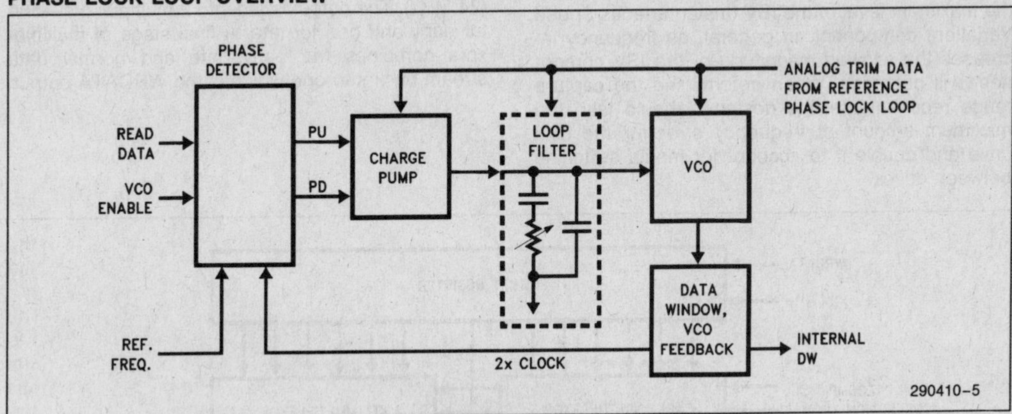

Figure 3-2. Data PLL

Figure 3-2 shows the data PLL. The reference PLL has control over the loop gain by its influence on the charge pump and the VCO. In addition the reference PLL controls the loop filter time constant. As a result the closed loop transfer function of the data PLL is controlled, and immune to the first order, to environmental factors and process variation.

Systems with analog PLLs are often very sensitive to noise. In the design of this data separator many steps were taken to avoid noise sensitivity problems. The analog section of the chip has a separate VSS pin (AVSS) which should be connected externally to a noise free ground. This provides a clean basis for VSS referenced signals. In addition many analog circuit features were employed to make the overall system as insensitive to noise as possible.

3.2.1 JITTER TOLERANCE

The jitter immunity of the system is dominated by the data PLL's response to phase impulses. This is measured as a percentage of the theoretical data window by dividing the maximum readable bit shift by a ¼ bitcell distance. For instance, if the maximum allowable bit shift is 300 ns for a 500 Kbps data stream, the jitter tolerance is 60%. The graph in Figures 13-1 thru 13-4 of the Data Separator Characteristics sections illustrate the jitter tolerance of the 82077SL across each frequency range.

3.2.2 LOCKTIME (tLOCK)

The lock, or settling time of the data PLL is designed to be 64 bit times. This corresponds to 4 sync bytes in the FM mode and 8 sync bytes in the MFM mode. This value assumes that the sync field jitter is 5% the bit cell or less. This level of jitter should be easily achieved for a constant bit pattern, since intersymbol interference should be equal, thus nearly eliminating random bit shifting.

3.2.3 CAPTURE RANGE

Capture Range is the maximum frequency range over which the data separator will acquire phase lock with the incoming RDDATA signal. In a floppy disk environment, this frequency variation is composed of two components: drive motor speed error and ISV. Frequency is a factor which may determine the maximum level of the ISV (Instantaneous Speed Variation) component. In general, as frequency increases the allowed magnitude of the ISV component will decrease. When determining the capture range requirements, the designer should take the maximum amount of frequency error for the disk drive and double it to account for media switching between drives.

3.3 Write Precompensation

The write precompensation logic is used to minimize bit shifts in the RDDATA stream from the disk drive. The shifting of bits is a known phenomena of magnetic media and is dependent upon the disk media AND the floppy drive.

The 82077SL monitors the bit stream that is being sent to the drive. The data patterns that require precompensation are well known. Depending upon the pattern, the bit is shifted either early or late (or not at all) relative to the surrounding bits. Figure 3-3 is a block diagram of the internal circuit.

The top block is a 13-bit shift register with the no delay tap being in the center. This allows 6 levels of early and late shifting with respect to nominal. The shift register is clocked at the main clock rate (24 MHz). The output is fed into 2 multiplexors—one for early and one for late. A final stage of multiplexors combines the early, late and normal data stream back into one which is the WRDATA output.

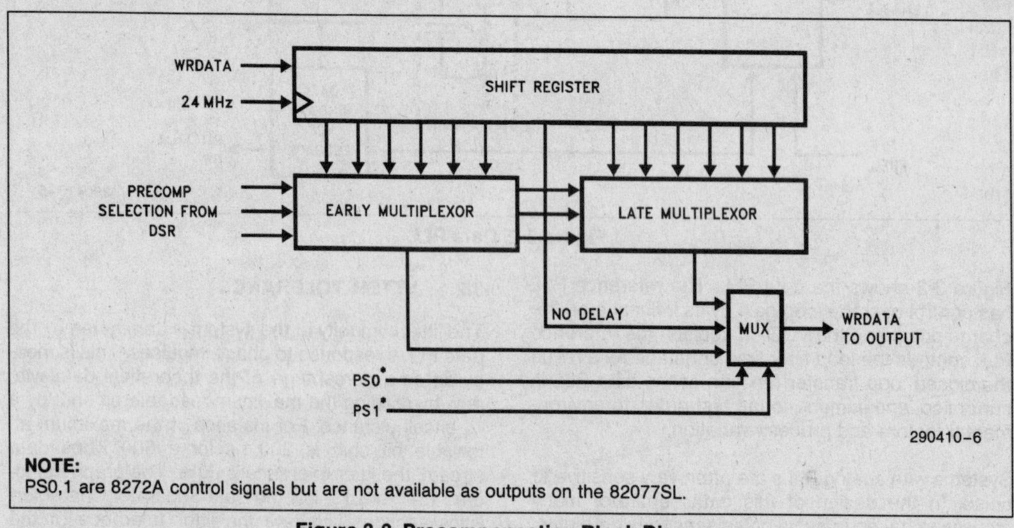

NOTE:
PS0,1 are 8272A control signals but are not available as outputs on the 82077SL.

Figure 3-3. Precompensation Block Diagram

4.0 POWER MANAGEMENT FEATURES

The 82077SL contains power management features that makes it ideal for design of portable personal computers. These features can be classified into power management of the part and that of the internal oscillator. The powerdown of the part is done independently of the internal oscillator in the 82077SL.

4.1 Oscillator Power Management

The 82077SL supports a built-in crystal oscillator that can be programmed to be either powered down or active, independent of the power state of the chip. This capability is implemented by the PDOSC bit in the DSR. When PDOSC is set low, the internal oscillator is on and when it is set high the internal oscillator is off. DSR powerdown does not turn off the oscillator.

When the external oscillator is used, power can be saved by turning off the internal oscillator. If the internal oscillator is used, the oscillator may be powered up (even when the rest of the chip is powered off) allowing the chip to wake up quickly and in a stable state. It is recommended to keep the internal oscillator on even when in the powerdown state. The main reason for this is that the recovery time of the oscillator during wake up may take tens of milliseconds under the worst case, which may create problems with any sensitive application software. In a typical application the internal oscillator should be on unless the system goes into a power saving or standby mode (such a mode request would be made by a system time out or by a user). In this case, the system software would take over and must turn on the oscillator sufficiently ahead of awakening the part.

In the case of the external oscillators, the power up characteristics are similar. If the external source remains active during the time the 82077SL is powered down, then the recovery time effect is minimized. The PD pin can be used to turn off the external source. While the PD pin is active 82077SL does not require a clock source. However, when the PD pin is inactive, the clocking source, once it starts oscillating, must be completely stable to ensure that the 82077SL operates properly.

4.2 Part Power Management

This section deals with the power management of the rest of the chip excluding the oscillator. This shows how powerdown modes and wake up modes are activated.

4.2.1 POWERDOWN MODES

The rest of the chip is powered down in two ways—direct powerdown and automatic powerdown. Direct powerdown results in immediate powerdown of the part without regard to the current state of the part. Automatic powerdown results when certain conditions become true within the part.

4.2.1.a Direct Powerdown

Direct powerdown is conducted via the POWERDOWN bit in the DSR register (bit 6). This mode is compatible to the 82077AA. Programming this bit high will powerdown 82077SL after the part is internally reset. All current status is lost if this type of powerdown mode is used. The part can exit powerdown from this mode via any hardware or software reset. This type of powerdown will override the automatic powerdown. If the part is in automatic powerdown when the DSR powerdown is issued then all the previous status of the part will be lost and the 82077SL will be reset to its default values.

4.2.1.b Auto Powerdown

Automatic powerdown is conducted via a "Set Powerdown Mode" command. There are four conditions required before the part will enter powerdown. All these conditions must be true for the part to initiate the powerdown sequence. These conditions are listed as follows:

1. The motor enable pins ME[0:3] must be inactive,
2. The part must be idle; this is indicated by MSR = 80H and INT = 0 (INT may be high even if MSR = 80H due to polling interrupt),
3. The head unload timer (HUT—explained in Section 6.2.6) must have expired, and
4. The auto powerdown timer must have timed out.

The command can be used to enable powerdown by setting the AUTO PD bit in the command to high. The command also provides a capability of programming a minimum power up time via the MIN DLY bit in the command. The minimum power up time refers to a minimum amount of time the part will remain powered up after being awakened or reset. An internal timer is initiated as soon as the auto powerdown command is enabled. The part is then powered down provided all the remaining conditions are met. Any software reset will reinitialize the timer. Changing of data rate extends the auto powerdown timer by up to 10 ms, but only if the data rate is changed during the countdown.

Disabling the auto powerdown mode cancels the timers and holds the 82077SL out of auto powerdown.

4.2.2 WAKE UP MODES

This section describes the conditions for awakening the part from both direct and automatic powerdown. Power conservation or extension of battery life is the main reason power management is required. This means that the 82077SL must be kept in powerdown state as long as possible and should be powered up as late as possible without compromising software transparency.

To keep the part in powerdown mode as late as possible implies that the part should wake up as fast as possible. However, some amount of time is required for the part to exit powerdown state and prepare the internal microcontroller to accept commands. Application software is very sensitive to such a delay and in order to maintain software transparency, the recovery time of the wake up process must be carefully controlled by the system software.

4.2.2.a Wake Up from DSR Powerdown

If the 82077SL enters the powerdown through the DSR powerdown bit, it must be reset to exit. Any form of software or hardware reset will serve, although DSR is recommended. No other register access will awaken the part, including writing to the DOR's motor enable (ME[0:3]) bits.

If DSR powerdown is used when the part is in auto powerdown, the DSR powerdown will override the auto powerdown. However, when the part is awakened by a software reset, the auto powerdown command (including the minimum delay timer) will once again become effective as previously programmed. If the part is awakened via a hardware reset, the auto powerdown is disabled.

After reset, the part will go through a normal sequence. The drive status will be initialized. The FIFO mode will be set to default mode on a hardware reset or on a software reset if the LOCK command has not blocked it. Finally, after a delay, the polling interrupt will be issued.

4.2.2.b Wake Up from Auto Powerdown

If the part enters the powerdown state through the auto powerdown mode, then the part can be awakened by reset or by appropriate access to certain registers.

If a hardware or software reset is used then the part will go through the normal reset sequence. If the access is through the selected registers, then the 82077SL resumes operation as though it was never in powerdown. Besides activating the RESET pin or one of the software reset bits in the DOR or DSR, the following register accesses will wake up the part:

1. Enabling any one of the motor enable bits in the DOR register (reading the DOR does not awaken the part)
2. A read from the MSR register
3. A read or write to the FIFO register

Any of these actions will wake up the part. Once awake, 82077SL will reinitiate the auto powerdown timer for 10 ms or 0.5 sec. (depending on the MIN DLY bit the auto powerdown command). The part will powerdown again when all the powerdown conditions stated in Section 4.2.1b are satisfied.

4.3 Register Behavior

The register descriptions and their values in the powerdown state were given in Section 2.1. Table 4.1 reiterates the AT and PS/2 (including model 30) configuration registers available. It also shows the type of access permitted. In order to maintain software transparency, access to all the registers must be maintained. As Table 4.1 shows, two sets of registers are distinguished based on whether their access results in the part remaining in powerdown state or exiting it.

Access to all other registers is possible without awakening the part. These registers can be accessed during powerdown without changing the status of the part. A read from these registers will reflect the true status as shown in the register description in Section 2.1. A write to the part will result in the part retaining the data and subsequently reflecting it when the part awakens. Accessing the part during powerdown may cause an increase in the power consumption by the part. The part will revert back to its low power mode when the access has been completed.

4.4 Pin Behavior

The 82077SL is specifically designed for the portable PC systems in which the power conservation is a primary concern. This makes the behavior of the pins during powerdown very important.

The pins of 82077SL can be divided into two major categories—system interface and floppy disk drive interface. The floppy disk drive pins are disabled such that no power will be drawn through the 82077SL as a result of any voltage applied to the pin within the 82077SL's power supply range. The floppy disk drive interface pins are configurable by the FDI TRI bit in the auto powerdown command. When the bit is set the output pins of the floppy disk drive retain their original state. All other pins are either disabled or unchanged as depicted in Table 4-4. Most of the system interface pins are left active to monitor system accesses that may wake up the part.

4.4.1 SYSTEM INTERFACE PINS

Table 4.2 gives the state of the system interface pins in the powerdown state. Pins unaffected by powerdown are labeled "UC". Input pins are "DISABLED" to prevent them from causing currents internal to the 82077SL when they have indeterminate input values.

Table 4-1. 82077SL Register Behavior

Address	Available Registers		Access Permitted
	PC-AT	PS/2 (Model 30)	
Access to these registers DOES NOT wake up the part			
000	—	SRA	R
001	—	SRB	R
010	DOR*	DOR*	R/W
011	TDR	TDR	R/W
100	DSR*	DSR*	W
110	—	—	—
111	DIR	DIR	R
111	CCR	CCR	W
Access to these registers wakes up the part			
100	MSR	MSR	R
101	FIFO	FIFO	R/W

NOTE:
*Writing to the DOR or DSR does not wake up the part, however, writing any of the motor enable bits or doing a software reset (either via DOR or DSR reset bits) will wake up the part.

Table 4-2. 82077SL System Interface Pins

System Pins	State in Power Down	System Pins	State in Power Down
Input Pins		**Output Pins**	
$\overline{CS}$	UC	DRQ	UC (Low)
$\overline{RD}$	UC	INT	UC (Low)
$\overline{WR}$	UC	PD	HIGH
A[0:2]	UC	IDLE	High (Auto PD) Low (DSR PD)
DB[0:7]	UC	DB[0:7]	UC
RESET	UC		
IDENT	UC		
$\overline{DACK}$	Disabled		
TC	Disabled		
X[1:2]	Programmable		

Two pins which can be used to indicate the status of the part are IDLE and PD. These pins have replaced the HIFIL and LOFIL pins in the 82077AA. The capacitor required on the 82077AA has been integrated on the chip. Table 4-3 shows how these pins reflect the 82077SL status.

Table 4-3. 82077SL Status Pins

PD	IDLE	MSR	Part Status
1	1	80H	Auto Powerdown
1	0	RQM = 1; MSR[6:0] = X	DSR Powerdown
0	1	80H	Idle
0	0	—	Busy

The IDLE pin indicates when the part is idle state and can be powered down. It is a combination of MSR equalling 80H, the head being unloaded and the INT pin being low. As shown in the table the IDLE pin will be low when the part is in DSR powerdown state. The PD pin is active whenever the part is in the powerdown state. It is active for either mode of powerdown. The PD pin can be used to turn off an external oscillator of other floppy disk drive interface hardware.

2

4.4.2 FDD INTERFACE PINS

The FDD interface "input" pins during powerdown are disabled or unchanged as shown in Table 4-4. The floppy disk drive "output" pins are programmable by the FDI TRI bit in the auto powerdown command. Setting of the FDI TRI bit in the auto power down command results in the interface retaining its normal state. When this bit is low (default state) all output pins in the FDD interface to the floppy disk drive itself are TRISTATED. Pins used for local logic control or part programming are unaffected. Table 4-4 depicts the state of the floppy disk interface pins in the powerdown state (FDI TRI is low).

Table 4-4. 82077SL FDD Interface Pins

FDD Pins	State in Powerdown	System Pins	State in Powerdown
Input Pins		**Output Pins (FDI TRI = 0)**	
RDDATA	Disabled	ME[0:3]	Tristated
WP	Disabled	DS[0:3]	Tristated
TRK0	Disabled	DIR	Tristated
INDX	Disabled	STEP	Tristated
DRV2	Disabled	WRDATA	Tristated
DSKCHG	Disabled	WE	Tristated
$\overline{INVERT}$	UC	HDSEL	Tristated
MFM	UC	DENSEL	Tristated
		DRATE[0:1]	Tristated

5.0 CONTROLLER PHASES

For simplicity, command handling in the 82077SL can be divided into three phases: Command, Execution and Result. Each phase is described in the following secions.

When there is no command in progress, the 82077SL can be in idle, drive polling or powerdown state.

5.1 Command Phase

After a reset, the 82077SL enters the command phase and is ready to accept a command from the host. For each of the commands, a defined set of command code bytes and parameter bytes has to be written to the 82077SL before the command phase is complete (Please refer to Section 6.0 for the command descriptions). These bytes of data must be transferred in the order prescribed.

Before writing to the 82077SL, the host must examine the RQM and DIO bits of the Main Status Register. RQM, DIO must be equal to "1" and "0" respectively before command bytes may be written. RQM is set false by the 82077SL after each write cycle until the received byte is processed. The 82077SL asserts RQM again to request each parameter byte of the command, unless an illegal command condition is detected. After the last parameter byte is received, RQM remains "0", and the 82077SL automatically enters the next phase as defined by the command definition.

The FIFO is disabled during the command phase to retain compatibility with the 8272A, and to provide for the proper handling of the "Invalid Command" condition.

5.2 Execution Phase

All data transfers to or from the 82077SL occur during the execution phase, which can proceed in DMA or non-DMA mode as indicated in the SPECIFY command.

Each data byte is transferred by an INT or DRQ depending on the DMA mode. The CONFIGURE command can enable the FIFO and set the FIFO threshold value.

The following paragraphs detail the operation of the FIFO flow control. In these descriptions, <threshold> is defined as the number of bytes available to the 82077SL when service is requested from the host, and ranges from 1 to 16. The parameter FIFOTHR which the user programs is one less, and ranges from 0 to 15.

A low threshold value (i.e. 2) results in longer periods of time between service requests, but requires faster servicing of the request, for both read and write cases. The host reads (writes) from (to) the FIFO until empty (full), then the transfer request goes inactive. The host must be very responsive to the service request. This is the desired case for use with a "fast" system.

A high value of threshold (l.e. 12) is used with a "sluggish" system by affording a long latency period after a service request, but results in more frequent service requests.

5.2.1 NON-DMA MODE, TRANSFERS FROM THE FIFO TO THE HOST

The INT pin and RQM bits in the Main Status Register are activated when the FIFO contains (16−<threshold>) bytes, or the last bytes of a full sector transfer have been placed in the FIFO. The INT pin can be used for interrupt driven systems and RQM can be used for polled sytems. The host must respond to the request by reading data from the FIFO. This process is repeated until the last byte is transferred out of the FIFO. The 82077SL will deactivate the INT pin and RQM bit when the FIFO becomes empty.

5.2.2 NON-DMA MODE, TRANSFERS FROM THE HOST TO THE FIFO

The INT pin and RQM bit in the Main Status Register are activated upon entering the execution phase of data transfer commands. The host must respond to the request by writing data into the FIFO. The INT pin and RQM bit remain true until the FIFO becomes full. They are set true again when the FIFO has <threshold> bytes remaining in the FIFO. The INT pin will also be deactivated if TC and DACK# both go inactive. The 82077SL enters the result phase after the last byte is taken by the 82077SL from the FIFO (i.e. FIFO empty condition).

5.2.3 DMA MODE, TRANSFERS FROM THE FIFO TO THE HOST

The 82077SL activates the DRQ pin when the FIFO contains (16−<threshold>) bytes, or the last byte of a full sector transfer has been placed in the FIFO. The DMA controller must respond to the request by reading data from the FIFO. The 82077SL will deactivate the DRQ pin when the FIFO becomes empty. DRQ goes inactive after DACK# goes active for the last byte of a data transfer (or on the active edge of RD#, on the last byte, if no edge is present on DACK#). A data underrun may occur if DRQ is not removed in time to prevent an unwanted cycle.

5.2.4 DMA MODE, TRANSFERS FROM THE HOST TO THE FIFO

The 82077SL activates the DRQ pin when entering the execution phase of the data transfer commands. The DMA controller must respond by activating the DACK# and WR# pins and placing data in the FIFO. DRQ remains active until the FIFO becomes full. DRQ is again set true when the FIFO has <threshold> bytes remaining in the FIFO. The 82077SL will also deactivate the DRQ pin when TC becomes true (qualified by DACK#), indicating that no more data is required. DRQ goes inactive after DACK# goes active for the last byte of a data transfer (or on the active edge of WR# of the last byte, if no edge is present on DACK#). A data overrun may occur if DRQ is not removed in time to prevent an unwanted cycle.

5.2.5 DATA TRANSFER TERMINATION

The 82077SL supports terminal count explicitly through the TC pin and implicitly through the underrun/overrun and end-of-track (EOT) functions. For full sector transfers, the EOT parameter can define the last sector to be transferred in a single or multisector transfer. If the last sector to be transferred is a partial sector, the host can stop transferring the data in mid-sector, and the 82077SL will continue to complete the sector as if a hardware TC was received. The only difference between these implicit functions and TC is that they return "abnormal termination" result status. Such status indications can be ignored if they were expected.

Note that when the host is sending data to the FIFO of the 82077SL, the internal sector count will be complete when 82077SL reads the last byte from its side of the FIFO. There may be a delay in the removal of the transfer request signal of up to the time taken for the 82077SL to read the last 16 bytes from the FIFO. The host must tolerate this delay.

5.3 Result Phase

The generation of INT determines the beginning of the result phase. For each of the commands, a defined set of result bytes has to be read from the 82077SL before the result phase is complete. (Refer to Section 6.0 on command descriptions.) These bytes of data must be read out for another command to start.

RQM and DIO must both equal "1" before the result bytes may be read from the FIFO. After all the result bytes have been read, the RQM and DIO bits switch to "1" and "0" respectively, and the CB bit is cleared. This indicates that the 82077SL is ready to accept the next command.

6.0 COMMAND SET/DESCRIPTIONS

Commands can be written whenever the 82077SL is in the command phase. Each command has a unique set of needed parameters and status results. The 82077SL checks to see that the first byte is a valid command and, if valid, proceeds with the command. If it was invalid, the next time the RQM bit in the MSR register is a "1" the DIO and CB bits will also be "1", indicating the FIFO must be read. A result byte of 80H will be read out of the FIFO, indicating an invalid command was issued. After reading the result byte from the FIFO the 82077SL will return to the command phase. Table 6-1 is a summary of the Command set.

Table 6-1. 82077SL Command Set

Phase	R/W	DATA BUS D_7	D_6	D_5	D_4	D_3	D_2	D_1	D_0	Remarks
						READ DATA				
Command	W	MT	MFM	SK	0	0	1	1	0	Command Codes
	W	0	0	0	0	0	HDS	DS1	DS0	
	W					C				Sector ID information prior to Command execution
	W					H				
	W					R				
	W					N				
	W					EOT				
	W					GPL				
	W					DTL				
Execution										Data transfer between the FDD and system
Result	R					ST 0				Status information after Command execution
	R					ST 1				
	R					ST 2				
	R					C				Sector ID information after Command execution
	R					H				
	R					R				
	R					N				
						READ DELETED DATA				
Command	W	MT	MFM	SK	0	1	1	0	0	Command Codes
	W	0	0	0	0	0	HDS	DS1	DS0	
	W					C				Sector ID information prior to Command execution
	W					H				
	W					R				
	W					N				
	W					EOT				
	W					GPL				
	W					DTL				
Execution										Data transfer between the FDD and system
Result	R					ST 0				Status information after Command execution
	R					ST 1				
	R					ST 2				
	R					C				Sector ID information after Command execution
	R					H				
	R					R				
	R					N				
						WRITE DATA				
Command	W	MT	MFM	0	0	0	1	0	1	Command Codes
	W	0	0	0	0	0	HDS	DS1	DS0	
	W					C				Sector ID information prior to Command execution
	W					H				
	W					R				
	W					N				
	W					EOT				
	W					GPL				
	W					DTL				
Execution										Data transfer between the system and FDD
Result	R					ST 0				Status information after Command execution
	R					ST 1				
	R					ST 2				
	R					C				Sector ID information after Command execution
	R					H				
	R					R				
	R					N				

Table 6-1. 82077SL Command Set (Continued)

Phase	R/W	D7	D6	D5	D4	D3	D2	D1	D0	Remarks
		DATA BUS								
WRITE DELETED DATA										
Command	W	MT	MFM	0	0	1	0	0	1	Command Codes
	W	0	0	0	0	0	HDS	DS1	DS0	
	W					C				Sector ID information prior to Command execution
	W					H				
	W					R				
	W					N				
	W					EOT				
	W					GPL				
	W					DTL				
Execution										Data transfer between the FDD and system
Result	R					ST 0				Status information after Command execution
	R					ST 1				
	R					ST 2				
	R					C				Sector ID information after Command execution
	R					H				
	R					R				
	R					N				
READ TRACK										
Command	W	0	MFM	0	0	0	0	1	0	Command Codes
	W	0	0	0	0	0	HDS	DS1	DS0	
	W					C				Sector ID information prior to Command execution
	W					H				
	W					R				
	W					N				
	W					EOT				
	W					GPL				
	W					DTL				
Execution										Data transfer between the FDD and system. FDC reads all of cylinders contents from index hole to EOT
Result	R					ST 0				Status information after Command execution
	R					ST 1				
	R					ST 2				
	R					C				Sector ID information after Command execution
	R					H				
	R					R				
	R					N				
VERIFY										
Command	W	MT	MFM	SK	1	0	1	1	0	Command Codes
	W	EC	0	0	0	0	HDS	DS1	DS0	
	W					C				Sector ID information prior to Command execution
	W					H				
	W					R				
	W					N				
	W					EOT				
	W					GPL				
	W					DTL/SC				
Execution										No data transfer takes place
Result	R					ST 0				Status information after Command execution
	R					ST 1				
	R					ST 2				
	R					C				Sector ID information after Command execution
	R					H				
	R					R				
	R					N				
VERSION										
Command	W	0	0	0	1	0	0	0	0	Command Code
Result	R	1	0	0	1	0	0	0	0	Enhanced Controller

Table 6-1. 82077SL Command Set (Continued)

Phase	R/W	DATA BUS								Remarks
		D_7	D_6	D_5	D_4	D_3	D_2	D_1	D_0	
FORMAT TRACK										
Command	W	0	MFM	0	0	1	1	0	1	Command Codes
	W	0	0	0	0	0	HDS	DS1	DS0	
	W	N								Bytes/Sector
	W	SC								Sectors/Cylinder
	W	GPL								Gap 3
	W	D								Filler Byte
Execution For Each Sector Repeat:	W	C								
	W	H								Input Sector Parameters
	W	R								
	W	N								
										82077SL formats an entire cylinder
Result	R	ST 0								Status information after Command execution
	R	ST 1								
	R	ST 2								
	R	Undefined								
	R	Undefined								
	R	Undefined								
	R	Undefined								
SCAN EQUAL										
Command	W	MT	MFM	SK	1	0	0	0	0	Command Codes
	W	0	0	0	0	0	HDS	DS1	DS0	
	W	C								Sector ID Information Prior to Command Execution
	W	H								
	W	R								
	W	N								
	W	EOT								
	W	GPL								
	W	STP								
Execution										Data Compared Between the FDO and Main-System
Result	R	ST 0								Status Information After Command Execution
	R	ST 1								
	R	ST 2								
	R	C								Sector ID Information After Command Execution
	R	H								
	R	R								
	R	N								

Table 6-1. 82077SL Command Set (Continued)

Phase	R/W	DATA BUS								Remarks
		D_7	D_6	D_5	D_4	D_3	D_2	D_1	D_0	
SCAN LOW OR EQUAL										
Command	W	MT	MFM	SK	1	1	0	0	1	Command Codes
	W	0	0	0	0	0	HDS	DS1	DS0	
	W	C								Sector ID Information Prior to Command Execution
	W	H								
	W	R								
	W	N								
	W	EOT								
	W	GPL								
	W	STP								
Execution										Data Compared Between the FDO and Main-System
Result	R	ST 0								Status Information After Command Execution
	R	ST 1								
	R	ST 2								
	R	C								Sector ID Information After Command Execution
	R	H								
	R	R								
	R	N								
SCAN HIGH OR EQUAL										
Command	W	MT	MFM	SK	1	1	1	0	1	Command Codes
	W	0	0	0	0	0	HDS	DS1	DS0	
	W	C								Sector ID Information Prior to Command Execution
	W	H								
	W	R								
	W	N								
	W	EOT								
	W	GPL								
	W	STP								
Execution										Data Compared Between the FDO and Main-System
Result	R	ST 0								Status Information After Command Execution
	R	ST 1								
	R	ST 2								
	R	C								Sector ID Information After Command Execution
	R	H								
	R	R								
	R	N								

Table 6-1. 82077SL Command Set (Continued)

Phase	R/W	DATA BUS								Remarks
		D_7	D_6	D_5	D_4	D_3	D_2	D_1	D_0	
RECALIBRATE										
Command	W	0	0	0	0	0	1	1	1	Command Codes
	W	0	0	0	0	0	0	DS1	DS0	
Execution										Head retracted to Track 0 Interrupt
SENSE INTERRUPT STATUS										
Command	W	0	0	0	0	1	0	0	0	Command Codes
Result	R	ST 0								Status information at the end of each seek operation
	R	PCN								
SPECIFY										
Command	W	0	0	0	0	0	0	1	1	Command Codes
	W	SRT				HUT				
	W	HLT							ND	
SENSE DRIVE STATUS										
Command	W	0	0	0	0	0	1	0	0	Command Codes
	W	0	0	0	0	0	HDS	DS1	DS0	
Result	R	ST 3								Status information about FDD
SEEK										
Command	W	0	0	0	0	1	1	1	1	Command Codes
	W	0	0	0	0	0	HDS	DS1	DS0	
	W	NCN								
Execution										Head is positioned over proper Cylinder on Diskette
CONFIGURE										
Command	W	0	0	0	1	0	0	1	1	Configure Information
	W	0	0	0	0	0	0	0	0	
	W	0	EIS	EFIFO	POLL	FIFOTHR				
	W	PRETRK								
RELATIVE SEEK										
Command	W	1	DIR	0	0	1	1	1	1	
	W	0	0	0	0	0	HDS	DS1	DS0	
	W	RCN								

Table 6-1. 82077SL Command Set (Continued)

Phase	R/W	D7	D6	D5	D4	D3	D2	D1	D0	Remarks
						DUMPREG				
Command	W	0	0	0	0	1	1	1	0	*Note
Execution										Registers placed in FIFO
Result	R				PCN-Drive 0					
	R				PCN-Drive 1					
	R				PCN-Drive 2					
	R				PCN-Drive 3					
	R		SRT					HUT		
	R				HLT				ND	
	R				SC/EOT					
	R	LOCK	0	D_3	D_2	D_1	D_0	GAP	WGATE	
	R	0	EIS	EFIFO	POLL			FIFOTHR		
	R				PRETRK					
						READ ID				
Command	W	0	MFM	0	0	1	0	1	0	Commands
	W	0	0	0	0	0	HDS	DS1	DS0	
Execution										The first correct ID information on the Cylinder is stored in Data Register
Result	R				ST 0					Status information after Command execution
	R				ST 1					
	R				ST 2					
	R				C					
	R				H					Disk status after the Command has completed.
	R				R					
	R				N					
						PERPENDICULAR MODE				
Command	W	0	0	0	1	0	0	1	0	Command Codes
	W	OW	0	D_3	D_2	D_1	D0	GAP	WGATE	
						LOCK				
Command	W	LOCK	0	0	1	0	1	0	0	Command Code
Result	R	0	0	0	LOCK	0	0	0	0	
						POWERDOWN MODE				
Command	W	0	0	0	1	0	1	1	1	Command Codes
	W	0	0	0	0	0	FDI TRI	MIN DLY	AUTO PD	
Result	R	0	0	0	0	0	FDI TRI	MIN DLY	AUTO PD	
						INVALID				
Command	W				Invalid Codes					Invalid Command Codes (NoOp — 82077SL goes into Standby State)
Result	R				ST 0					ST 0 = 80H

SC is returned if the last command that was issued was the FORMAT command. EOT is returned if the last command was a READ or WRITE.

NOTE:
These bits are used internally only. They are not reflected in the Drive Select pins. It is the users responsibility to maintain correspondence between these bits and the Drive Select pins (DOR).

PARAMETER ABBREVIATIONS

Symbol	Description
AUTO PD	Auto powerdown control. If this bit is 0, then the automatic powerdown is disabled. If it is set to 1, then the automatic powerdown is enabled.
C	Cylinder address. The currently selected cylinder address, 0 to 255.
D_0, D_1 D_2, D_3	Drive Select 0-3. Designates which drives are Perpendicular drives, a "1" indicating Perpendicular drive.
D	Data pattern. The pattern to be written in each sector data field during formatting.
DIR	Direction control. If this bit is 0, then the head will step out from the spindle during a relative seek. If set to a 1, the head will step in toward the spindle.
DS0, DS1	Disk Drive Select.

DS1	DS0	
0	0	drive 0
0	1	drive 1
1	0	drive 2
1	1	drive 3

Symbol	Description
DTL	Special sector size. By setting N to zero (00), DTL may be used to control the number of bytes transferred in disk read/write commands. The sector size (N = 0) is set to 128. If the actual sector (on the diskette) is larger than DTL, the remainder of the actual sector is read but is not passed to the host during read commands; during write commands, the remainder of the actual sector is written with all zero bytes. The CRC check code is calculated with the actual sector. When N is not zero, DTL has no meaning and should be set to FF HEX.
EC	Enable Count. When this bit is "1" the "DTL" parameter of the Verify Command becomes SC (Number of sectors per track).
EFIFO	Enable FIFO. When this bit is 0, the FIFO is enabled. A "1" puts the 82077SL in the 8272A compatible mode where the FIFO is disabled.
EIS	Enable implied seek. When set, a seek operation will be performed before executing any read or write command that requires the C parameter in the command phase. A "0" disables the implied seek.
EOT	End of track. The final sector number of the current track.
FDI TRI	Floppy Drive Interface Tristate: If this bit is 0, then the output pins of the floppy disk drive interface are tristated. This is also the default state. If it is set to 1, then the floppy disk drive interface remains unchanged.
GAP	Alters Gap 2 length when using Perpendicular Mode.
GPL	Gap length. The gap 3 size. (Gap 3 is the space between sectors excluding the VCO synchronization field).
H/HDS	Head address. Selected head: 0 or 1 (disk side 0 or 1) as encoded in the sector ID field.
HLT	Head load time. The time interval that 82077SL waits after loading the head and before initiating a read or write operation. Refer to the SPECIFY command for actual delays.
HUT	Head unload time. The time interval from the end of the execution phase (of a read or write command) until the head is unloaded. Refer to the SPECIFY command for actual delays.
Lock	Lock defines whether EFIFO, FIFOTHR, and PRETRK parameters of the CONFIGURE command can be reset to their default values by a "Software Reset" (Reset made by setting the proper bit in the DSR or DOR registers).
MFM	MFM/FM mode selector. A one selects the double density (MFM) mode.
MIN DLY	Minimum power up time control. This bit is active only if AUTO PD bit is enabled. Setting this bit to a 0, assigns a 10 ms minimum power up time and setting this bit to a 1, assigns a 0.5 sec. minimum power up time.
MT	Multi-track selector. When set, this flag selects the multi-track operating mode. In this mode, the 82077SL treats a complete cylinder, under head 0 and 1, as a single track. The 82077SL operates as if this expanded track started at the first sector under head 0 and ended at the last sector under head 1. With this flag set, a multitrack read or write operation will automatically continue to the first sector under head 1 when the 82077SL finishes operating on the last sector under head 0.

Symbol	Description
N	Sector size code. This specifies the number of bytes in a sector. If this parameter is "00", then the sector size is 128 bytes. The number of bytes transferred is determined by the DTL parameter. Otherwise the sector size is (2 raised to the "N'th" power) times 128. All values up to "07" hex are allowable. "07"h would equal a sector size of 16k. It is the users responsibility to not select combinations that are not possible with the drive.

N	Sector Size
00	128 bytes
01	256 bytes
02	512 bytes
03	1024 bytes
..	...
07	16 Kbytes

Symbol	Description
NCN	New cylinder number. The desired cylinder number.
ND	Non-DMA mode flag. When set to 1, indicates that the 82077SL is to operate in the non-DMA mode. In this mode, the host is interrupted for each data transfer. When set to 0, the 82077SL operates in DMA mode, interfacing to a DMA controller by means of the DRQ and DACK# signals.
OW	The bits denoted D_0, D_1, D_2, and D_3 of the **PERPENDICULAR MODE** command can only be overwritten when the OW bit is set to "1"
PCN	Present cylinder number. The current position of the head at the completion of SENSE INTERRUPT STATUS command.
POLL	Polling disable. When set, the internal polling routine is disabled. When clear, polling is enabled.
PRETRK	Precompensation start track number. Programmable from track 00 to FFH.
R	Sector address. The sector number to be read or written. In multi-sector transfers, this parameter specifies the sector number of the first sector to be read or written.
RCN	Relative cylinder number. Relative cylinder offset from present cylinder as used by the RELATIVE SEEK command.
SC	Number of sectors. The number of sectors to be initialized by the FORMAT command. The number of sectors to be verified during a Verify Command, when EC is set.
SK	Skip flag. When set to 1, sectors containing a deleted data address mark will automatically be skipped during the execution of READ DATA. If READ DELETED is executed, only sectors with a deleted address mark will be accessed. When set to "0", the sector is read or written the same as the read and write commands.
SRT	Step rate interval. The time interval between step pulses issued by the 82077SL. Programmable from 0.5 to 8 milliseconds, in increments of 0.5 ms at the 1 Mbit data rate. Refer to the SPECIFY command for actual delays.
ST0 ST1 ST2 ST3	Status register 0–3. Registers within the 82077SL that store status information after a command has been executed. This status information is available to the host during the result phase after command execution.
WGATE	Write gate alters timing of WE, to allow for pre-erase loads in perpendicular drives.

6.1 Data Transfer Commands

All of the READ DATA, WRITE DATA and VERIFY type commands use the same parameter bytes and return the same results information. The only difference being the coding of bits 0–4 in the first byte.

An implied seek will be executed if the feature was enabled by the CONFIGURE command. This seek is completely transparent to the user. The Drive Busy bit for the drive will go active in the Main Status Register during the seek portion of the command. If the seek portion fails, it will be reflected in the results status normally returned for a READ/WRITE DATA command. Status Register 0 (ST0) would contain the error code and C would contain the cylinder on which the seek failed.

6.1.1 READ DATA

A set of nine (9) bytes is required to place the 82077SL into the Read Data Mode. After the READ DATA command has been issued, the 82077SL loads the head (if it is in the unloaded state), waits the specified head settling time (defined in the SPECIFY command), and begins reading ID Address Marks and ID fields. When the sector address read off the diskette matches with the sector address specified in the command, the 82077SL reads the sector's data field and transfers the data to the FIFO.

After completion of the read operation from the current sector, the sector address is incremented by one, and the data from the next logical sector is read and output via the FIFO. This continuous read function is called "Multi-Sector Read Operation". Upon receipt of TC, or an implied TC (FIFO overrun/underrun), the 82077SL stops sending data, but will continue to read data from the current sector, check the CRC bytes, and at the end of the sector terminate the READ DATA Command.

N determines the number of bytes per sector (see Table 6-2 below). If N is set to zero, the sector size is set to 128. The DTL value determines the number of bytes to be transferred. If DTL is less than 128, the 82077SL transfers the specified number of bytes to the host. For reads, it continues to read the entire 128 byte sector and checks for CRC errors. For writes it completes the 128 byte sector by filling in zeroes. If N is not set to 00 Hex, DTL should be set to FF Hex, and has no impact on the number of bytes transferred.

Table 6-2. Sector Sizes

N	Sector Size
00	128 bytes
01	256 bytes
02	512 bytes
03	1024 bytes
..	...
07	16 Kbytes

The amount of data which can be handled with a single command to the 82077SL depends upon MT (multi-track) and N (Number of bytes/sector).

Table 6-3. Effects of MT and N Bits

MT	N	Max. Transfer Capacity	Final Sector Read from Disk
0	1	256 × 26 = 6,656	26 at side 0 or 1
1	1	256 × 52 = 13,312	26 at side 1
0	2	512 × 15 = 7,680	15 at side 0 or 1
1	2	512 × 30 = 15,360	15 at side 1
0	3	1024 × 8 = 8,192	8 at side 0 or 1
1	3	1024 × 16 = 16,384	16 at side 1

The Multi-Track function (MT) allows the 82077SL to read data from both sides of the diskette. For a particular cylinder, data will be transferred starting at Sector 1, Side 0 and completing at the last sector of the same track at Side 1.

If the host terminates a read or write operation in the 82077SL, then the ID information in the result phase is dependent upon the state of the MT bit and EOT byte. Refer to Table 6-6. The termination must be normal.

At the completion of the READ DATA Command, the head is not unloaded until after the Head Unload Time Interval (specified in the SPECIFY command) has elapsed. If the host issues another command before the head unloads then the head settling time may be saved between subsequent reads.

If the 82077SL detects a pulse on the IDX pin twice without finding the specified sector (meaning that the diskette's index hole passes through index detect logic in the drive twice), the 82077SL sets the IC code in Status Register 0 to "01" (Abnormal termination), and sets the ND bit in Status Register 1 to "1" indicating a sector not found, and terminates the READ DATA Command.

After reading the ID and Data Fields in each sector, the 82077SL checks the CRC bytes. If a CRC error occurs in the ID or data field, the 82077SL sets the IC code in Status Register 0 to "01" (Abnormal termination), sets the DE bit flag in Status Register 1 to "1", sets the DD bit in Status Register 2 to "1" if CRC is incorrect in the ID field, and terminates the READ DATA Command.

Table 6-4 below describes the affect of the SK bit on the READ DATA command execution and results.

Table 6-4. Skip Bit vs READ DATA Command

SK Bit Value	Data Address Mark Type Encountered	Results		
		Sector Read?	CM Bit of ST2 Set?	Description of Results
0	Normal Data	Yes	No	Normal Termination.
0	Deleted Data	Yes	Yes	Address Not Incremented. Next Sector Not Searched For.
1	Normal Data	Yes	No	Normal Termination.
1	Deleted Data	No	Yes	Normal Termination Sector Not Read ("Skipped").

Except where noted in Table 6-4, the C or R value of the sector address is automatically incremented (see Table 6-6).

6.1.2 READ DELETED DATA

This command is the same as the READ DATA command, only it operates on sectors that contain a Deleted Data Address Mark at the beginning of a Data Field.

Table 6-5 describes the affect of the SK bit on the READ DELETED DATA command execution and results.

Table 6-5. Skip Bit vs READ DELETED DATA Command

SK Bit Value	Data Address Mark Type Encountered	Results		
		Sector Read?	CM Bit of ST2 Set?	Description of Results
0	Normal Data	Yes	Yes	Address Not Incremented. Next Sector Not Searched For.
0	Deleted Data	Yes	No	Normal Termination.
1	Normal Data	No	Yes	Normal Termination Sector Not Read ("Skipped").
1	Deleted Data	Yes	No	Normal Termination.

Except where noted in Table 6-5 above, the C or R value of the sector address is automatically incremented (See Table 6-6).

6.1.3 READ TRACK

This command is similar to the READ DATA command except that the entire data field is read continuously from each of the sectors of a track. Immediately after encountering a pulse on the IDX pin, the 82077SL starts to read all data fields on the track as continuous blocks of data without regard to logical sector numbers. If the 82077SL finds an error in the ID or DATA CRC check bytes, it continues to read data from the track and sets the appropriate error bits at the end of the command. The 82077SL compares the ID information read from each sector with the specified value in the command, and sets the ND flag of Status Register 1 to a "1" if there is no comparison. Multi-track or skip operations are not allowed with this command. The MT and SK bits (Bits D7 and D5 of the first command byte respectively) should always be set to "0".

This command terminates when the EOT specified number of sectors have been read. If the 82077SL does not find an ID Address Mark on the diskette after the second occurrence of a pulse on the IDX pin, then it sets the IC code in Status Register 0 to "01" (Abnormal termination), sets the MA bit in Status Register 1 to "1", and terminates the command.

2

Table 6-6. Result Phase Table

MT	Head	Final Sector Transferred to Host	ID Information at Result Phase			
			C	H	R	N
0	0	Less than EOT	NC	NC	R+1	NC
		Equal to EOT	C+1	NC	01	NC
	1	Less than EOT	NC	NC	R+1	NC
		Equal to EOT	C+1	NC	01	NC
1	0	Less than EOT	NC	NC	R+1	NC
		Equal to EOT	NC	LSB	01	NC
	1	Less than EOT	NC	NC	R+1	NC
		Equal to EOT	C+1	LSB	01	NC

NC: no change, the same value as the one at the beginning of command execution.
LSB: least significant bit, the LSB of H is complemented.

6.1.4 WRITE DATA

After the WRITE DATA command has been issued, the 82077SL loads the head (if it is in the unloaded state), waits the specified head load time if unloaded (defined in the SPECIFY command), and begins reading ID Fields. When the sector address read from the diskette matches the sector address specified in the command, the 82077SL reads the data from the host via the FIFO, and writes it to the sector's data field.

After writing data into the current sector, the 82077SL computes the CRC value and writes it into the CRC field at the end of the sector transfer. The Sector Number stored in "R" is incremented by one, and the 82077SL continues writing to the next data field. The 82077SL continues this "Multi-Sector Write Operation". Upon receipt of a terminal count signal or if a FIFO over/under run occurs while a data field is being written, then the remainder of the data field is filled with zeros.

The 82077SL reads the ID field of each sector and checks the CRC bytes. If it detects a CRC error in one of the ID Fields, it sets the IC code in Status Register 0 to "01" (Abnormal termination), sets the DE bit of Status Register 1 to "1", and terminates the WRITE DATA command.

The WRITE DATA command operates in much the same manner as the READ DATA command. The following items are the same. Please refer to the READ DATA Command for details:

- Transfer Capacity
- EN (End of Cylinder) bit
- ND (No Data) bit
- Head Load, Unload Time Interval
- ID information when the host terminates the command.
- Definition of DTL when N = 0 and when N does not = 0.

6.1.5 WRITE DELETED DATA

This command is almost the same as the WRITE DATA command except that a Deleted Data Address Mark is written at the beginning of the Data Field instead of the normal Data Address Mark. This command is typically used to mark a bad sector containing an error on the floppy disk.

6.1.6 VERIFY

The VERIFY command is used to verify the data stored on a disk. This command acts exactly like a READ DATA command except that no data is transferred to the host. Data is read from the disk, CRC computed and checked against the previously stored value.

Because no data is transferred to the host, TC (pin 25) cannot be used to terminate this command. By setting the EC bit to "1" an implicit TC will be issued to the 82077SL. This implicit TC will occur when the SC value has decrement to 0 (an SC value of 0 will verify 256 sectors). This command can also be terminated by setting the EC bit to "0" and the EOT value equal to the final sector to be checked. If EC is set to "0" DTL/SC should be programmed to 0FFH. Refer to Table 6-6 and Table 6-7 for information concerning the values of MT and EC versus SC and EOT value.

Definitions:

Sectors Per Side = Number of formatted sectors per each side of the disk.

Sectors Remaining = Number of formatted sectors left which can be read, including side 1 of the disk if MT is set to "1".

Table 6-7. Verify Command Result Phase Table

MT	EC	SC/EOT Value	Termination Result
0	0	SC = DTL EOT ≤ # Sectors Per Side	Successful Termination Result Phase Valid
0	0	SC = DTL EOT > # Sectors Per Side	Unsuccessful Termination Result Phase Invalid
0	1	SC ≤ # Sectors Remaining AND EOT ≤ # Sectors Per Side	Successful Termination Result Phase Valid
0	1	SC > # Sectors Remaining OR EOT > # Sectors Per Side	Unsuccessful Termination Result Phase Invalid
1	0	SC = DTL EOT ≤ # Sectors Per Side	Successful Termination Result Phase Valid
1	0	SC = DTL EOT > # Sectors Per Side	Unsuccessful Termination Result Phase Invalid
1	1	SC ≤ # Sectors Remaining AND EOT ≤ # Sectors Per Side	Successful Termination Result Phase Valid
1	1	SC > # Sectors Remaining OR EOT > # Sectors Per Side	Unsuccessful Termination Result Phase Invalid

NOTE:
If MT is set to "1" and the SC value is greater than the number of remaining formatted sectors on Side 0, verifying will continue on Side 1 of the disk.

6.1.7 FORMAT TRACK

The FORMAT command allows an entire track to be formatted. After a pulse from the IDX pin is detected, the 82077SL starts writing data on the disk including Gaps, Address Marks, ID Fields and Data Fields, per the IBM System 34 (MFM). The particular values that will be written to the gap and data field are controlled by the values programmed into N, SC, GPL, and D which are specified by the host during the command phase. The data field of the sector is filled with the data byte specified by D. The ID Field for each sector is supplied by the host; that is, four data bytes per sector are needed by the 82077SL for C, H, R, and N (cylinder, head, sector number and sector size respectively).

After formatting each sector, the host must send new values for C, H, R and N to the 82077SL for the next sector on the track. The R value (sector number) is the only value that must be changed by the host after each sector is formatted. This allows the disk to be formatted with nonsequential sector addresses (interleaving). This incrementing and formatting continues for the whole track until the 82077SL encounters a pulse on the IDX pin again and it terminates the command.

Table 6-8 contains typical values for gap fields which are dependent upon the size of the sector and the number of sectors on each track. Actual values can vary due to drive electronics.

Table 6-8. Typical Values for Formatting

		Sector Size	N	SC	GPL1	GPL2
5.25″ Drives	FM	128	00	12	07	09
		128	00	10	10	19
		512	02	08	18	30
		1024	03	04	46	87
		2048	04	02	C8	FF
		4096	05	01	C8	FF
		...	...			
	MFM	256	01	12	0A	0C
		256	01	10	20	32
		512*	02	09	2A	50
		1024	03	04	80	F0
		2048	04	02	C8	FF
		4096	05	01	C8	FF
		...	...			
3.5″ Drives	FM	128	0	0F	07	1B
		256	1	09	0F	2A
		512	2	05	1B	3A
	MFM	256	1	0F	0E	36
		512**	2	09	1B	54
		1024	3	05	35	74

GPL1 = suggested GPL values in read and write commands to avoid splice point between data field and ID field of contiguous sections.
GPL2 = suggested GPL value in FORMAT TRACK command.
*PC-AT values (typical)
**PS/2 values (typical). Applies with 1.0 MB and 2.0 MB drives.

NOTE:
All values except Sector Size are in Hex.

6.1.7.1 Format Fields

GAP 4a	SYNC	IAM		GAP 1	SYNC	IDAM		C Y L	H D	S E C	N O	C R C	GAP 2	SYNC	DATA AM		DATA	C R C	GAP 3	GAP 4b
80x 4E	12x 00	3x C2	FC	50x 4E	12x 00	3x A1	FE						22x 4E	12x 00	3x A1	FB F8				

Figure 6-1. System 34 Format Double Density

GAP 4a	SYNC	IAM	GAP 1	SYNC	IDAM	C Y L	H D	S E C	N O	C R C	GAP 2	SYNC	DATA AM	DATA	C R C	GAP 3	GAP 4b
40x FF	6x 00	FC	26x FF	6x 00	FE						11x FF	6x 00	FB or F8				

Figure 6-2. System 3740 Format Single Density

GAP 4a	SYNC	IAM		GAP 1	SYNC	IDAM		C Y L	H D	S E C	N O	C R C	GAP 2	SYNC	DATA AM		DATA	C R C	GAP 3	GAP 4b
80x 4E	12x 00	3x C2	FC	50x 4E	12x 00	3x A1	FE						41x 4E	12x 00	3x A1	FB F8				

Figure 6-3. Perpendicular Format

6.1.8 SCAN COMMANDS

The SCAN Commands allow data which is being read from the diskette to be compared against data which is being supplied from the main system (Processor in NON-DMA mode, and DMA Controller in DMA mode). The FDC compares the data on a byte-by-byte basis, and looks for a sector of data which meets the conditions of $D_{FDO} = D_{Processor}$, $D_{FDO} \le D_{Processor}$, or $D_{FDO} \ge D_{Processor}$. Ones complement arithmetic is used for comparison (FF = largest number, 00 = smallest number). After a whole sector of data is compared, if the conditions are not met, the sector number is incremented (R + STP → R), and the scan operation is continued. The scan operation continues until one of the following conditions occurs; the conditions for scan are met (equal, low, or high), the last sector on the track is reached (EOT), or the terminal count signal is received.

If the conditions for scan are met then the FDC sets the SH (Scan Hit) flag of Status Register 2 to a 1 (high), and terminates the Scan Command. If the conditions for scan are not met between the starting sector (as specified by R) and the last sector on the cylinder (EOT), then the FDC sets the SN (Scan Not Satisfied) flag of Status Register 2 to a 1 (high), and terminates the Scan Command. The receipt of a TERMINAL COUNT signal from the Processor or DMA Controller during the scan operation will cause the FDC to complete the comparison of the particular byte which is in process, and then to terminate the command. Table 6-9 shows the status of bits SH and SN under various conditions of SCAN.

If the FDC encounters a Deleted Data Address Mark on one of the sectors (and SK = 0), then it regards the sector as the last sector on the cylinder, sets CM (Control Mark) flag of Status Register 2 to a 1 (high) and terminates the command. If SK = 1, the FDC skips the sector with the Deleted Address Mark, and reads the next sector. In the second case (SK = 1), the FDC sets the CM (Control Mark) flag of Status Register 2 to a 1 (high) in order to show that a Deleted Sector has been encountered.

When either the STP (contiguous sectors STP = 01, or alternate sectors STP = 02) sectors are read or the MT (Multi-Track) is programmed, it is necessary to remember that the last sector on the track must be read. For example, if STP = 02, MT = 0, the sectors are numbered sequentially 1 through 26, and we start the Scan Command at sector 21; the following will happen. Sectors 21, 23, andf 25 will be read, then the next sector (26) will be skipped and the Index Hole will be encountered before the EOT value of 26 can be read. This will result in an abnormal termination of the command. If the EOT had been set at 25 or the scanning started at sector 20, then the Scan Command would be completed in a normal manner.

During the Scan Command data is supplied by either the processor or DMA Controller for comparison against the data read from the diskette. In order to avoid having the OR (Over Run) flag set in Status Register 1, it is necessary to ahve the data available in less than 27 µs (FM Mode) or 13 µs (MFM Mode). If an Overrun occurs the FDC terminates the command.

Table 6-9. Scan Status Codes

Command	Status Register 2		Comments
	Bit 2 = SN	**Bit 3 = SH**	
Scan Equal	0	1	$D_{FDO} = D_{Processor}$
	1	0	$D_{FDO} \neq D_{Processor}$
Scan Low or Equal	0	1	$D_{FDO} = D_{Processor}$
	0	0	$D_{FDO} < D_{Processor}$
	1	0	$D_{FDO} \not> D_{Processor}$
Scan High or Equal	0	1	$D_{FDO} = D_{Processor}$
	0	0	$D_{FDO} > D_{Processor}$
	1	0	$D_{FDO} \not< D_{Processor}$

6.2 Control Commands

Control commands differ from the other commands in that no data transfer takes place. Three commands generate an interrupt when complete; READ ID, RECALIBRATE and SEEK. The other control commands do not generate an interrupt.

6.2.1 READ ID

The READ ID command is used to find the present position of the recording heads. The 82077SL stores the values from the first ID Field it is able to read into its registers. If the 82077SL does not find an ID Address Mark on the diskette after the second occurrence of a pulse on the IDX pin, it then sets the IC code in Status Register 0 to "01" (Abnormal termination), sets the MA bit in Status Register 1 to "1", and terminates the command.

The following commands will generate an interrupt upon completion. They do not return any result bytes. It is highly recommended that control commands be followed by the SENSE INTERRUPT STATUS command. Otherwise, valuable interrupt status information will be lost.

6.2.2 RECALIBRATE

This command causes the read/write head within the 82077SL to retract to the track 0 position. The 82077SL clears the contents of the PCN counter, and checks the status of the TRK0 pin from the FDD. As long as the TRK0 pin is low, the DIR pin remains 0 and step pulses are issued. When the TRK0 pin goes high, the SE bit in Status Register 0 is set to "1", and the command is terminated. If the TRK0 pin is still low after 79 step pulses have been issued, the 82077SL sets the SE and the EC bits of Status Register 0 to "1", and terminates the command. Disks capable of handling more than 80 tracks per side may require more than one RECALIBRATE command to return the head back to physical Track 0.

The RECALIBRATE command does not have a result phase. SENSE INTERRUPT STATUS command must be issued after the RECALIBRATE command to effectively terminate it and to provide verification of the head position (PCN). During the command phase of the recalibrate operation, the 82077SL is in the BUSY state, but during the execution phase it is in a NON BUSY state. At this time another RECALIBRATE command may be issued, and in this manner, parallel RECALIBRATE operations may be done on up to 4 drives at once.

Upon power up, the software must issue a RECALIBRATE command to properly initialize all drives and the controller.

6.2.3 SEEK

The read/write head within the drive is moved from track to track under the control of the SEEK Command. The 82077SL compares the PCN which is the current head position with the NCN and performs the following operation if there is a difference:

—PCN < NCN: Direction signal to drive set to "1" (step in), and issues step pulses.

—PCN > NCN: Direction signal to drive set to "0" (step out), and issues step pulses.

The rate at which step pulses are issued is controlled by SRT (Stepping Rate Time) in the SPECIFY command. After each step pulse is issued, NCN is compared against PCN, and when NCN = PCN, then the SE bit in Status Register 0 is set to "1", and the command is terminated.

During the command phase of the seek or recalibrate operation, the 82077SL is in the BUSY state, but during the execution phase it is in the NON BUSY state.

Note that if implied seek is not enabled, the read and write commands should be preceded by:

1) SEEK command;	Step to the proper track
2) SENSE INTERRUPT STATUS command;	Terminate the Seek command
3) READ ID.	Verify head is on proper track
4) Issue READ/WRITE command.	

The SEEK command does not have a result phase. Therefore, it is highly recommended that the SENSE INTERRUPT STATUS Command be issued after the SEEK command to terminate it and to provide verification of the head position (PCN). The H bit (Head Address) in ST0 will always return a "0". When exiting DSR POWERDOWN mode, the 82077SL clears the PCN value and the status information to zero. Prior to issuing the DSR POWERDOWN command, it is highly recommended that the user service all pending interrupts through the SENSE INTERRUPT STATUS command.

6.2.4 SENSE INTERRUPT STATUS

An interrupt signal on INT pin is generated by the 82077SL for one of the following reasons:

1. Upon entering the Result Phase of:
   a. READ DATA Command
   b. READ TRACK Command
   c. READ ID Command
   d. READ DELETED DATA Command
   e. WRITE DATA Command
   f. FORMAT TRACK Command
   g. WRITE DELETED DATA Command
   h. VERIFY Command
2. End of SEEK, RELATIVE SEEK or RECALIBRATE Command
3. 82077SL requires a data transfer during the execution phase in the non-DMA Mode

The SENSE INTERRUPT STATUS command resets the interrupt signal and via the IC code and SE bit of Status Register 0, identifies the cause of the interrupt. If a SENSE INTERRUPT STATUS command is issued when no active interrupt condition is present, the status register ST0 will return a value of 80H (invalid command).

Table 6-9. Interrupt Identification

SE	IC	Interrupt Due To
0	11	Polling
1	00	Normal Termination of SEEK or RECALIBRATE command
1	01	Abnormal Termination of SEEK or RECALIBRATE command

The SEEK, RELATIVE SEEK and the RECALIBRATE commands have no result phase. SENSE INTERRUPT STATUS command must be issued immediately after these commands to terminate them and to provide verification of the head position (PCN). The H (Head Address) bit in ST0 will always return a "0". If a SENSE INTERRUPT STATUS is not issued, the drive, will continue to be BUSY and may effect the operation of the next command.

6.2.5 SENSE DRIVE STATUS

SENSE DRIVE STATUS obtains drive status information. It has no execution phase and goes directly to the result phase from the command phase. STATUS REGISTER 3 contains the drive status information.

6.2.6 SPECIFY

The SPECIFY command sets the initial values for each of the three internal timers. The HUT (Head Unload Time) defines the time from the end of the execution phase of one of the read/write commands to the head unload state. The SRT (Step Rate Time) defines the time interval between adjacent step pulses. Note that the spacing between the first and second step pulses may be shorter than the remaining step pulses. The HLT (Head Load Time) defines the time between the Head Load signal goes high and the read, write operation starts. The values change with the data rate speed selection and are documented in Table 6-10. The values are the same for MFM and FM.

Table 6-10. Drive Control Delays (ms)

	HUT				SRT			
	1M	500K	300K	250K	1M	500K	300K	250K
0	128	256	426	512	8.0	16	26.7	32
1	8	16	26.7	32	7.5	15	25	30
..	..	..	..	..	..	..	..	..
E	112	224	373	448	1.0	2	3.33	4
F	120	240	400	480	0.5	1	1.67	2

	HLT			
	1M	500K	300K	250K
00	128	256	426	512
01	1	2	3.3	4
02	2	4	6.7	8
..	..	..	..	.
7F	126	252	420	504
7F	127	254	423	508

The choice of DMA or NON-DMA operations is made by the ND bit. When this bit is "1", the NON-DMA mode is selected, and when ND is "0", the DMA mode is selected. In DMA mode, data transfers are signalled by the DRQ pin. Non-DMA mode uses the RQM bit and the INT pin to signal data transfers.

6.2.7 CONFIGURE

Issued to select the special features of the 82077SL. A CONFIGURE command need not be issued if the default values of the 82077SL meet the system requirements.

CONFIGURE DEFAULT VALUES:

EIS — No Implied Seeks
EFIFO — FIFO Disabled
POLL — Polling Enabled
FIFOTHR — FIFO Threshold Set to 1 Byte
PRETRK — Pre-Compensation Set to Track 0

EIS—Enable implied seek. When set to "1", the 82077SL will perform a SEEK operation before executing a read or write command. Defaults to no implied seek.

EFIFO—A "1" puts the FIFO into the 8272A compatible mode where the FIFO is disabled. This means data transfers are asked for on a byte by byte basis. Defaults to "1", FIFO disabled. The threshold defaults to one.

POLL—Disable polling of the drives. Defaults to "0", polling enabled. When enabled, a single interrupt is generated after a RESET. No polling is performed while the drive head is loaded and the head unload delay has not expired.

FIFOTHR—The FIFO threshold in the execution phase of read or write commands. This is programmable from 1 to 16 bytes. Defaults to one byte. A "00" selects one byte "0F" selects 16 bytes.

PRETRK—Pre-compensation start track number. Programmable from track 0 to 255. Defaults to track 0. A "00" selects track 0, "FF" selects 255.

6.2.8 VERSION

The VERSION command checks to see if the controller is an enhanced type or the older type (8272A/765A). A value of 90 H is returned as the result byte, defining an enhanced FDD controller is in use. No interrupts are generated.

6.2.9 RELATIVE SEEK

The command is coded the same as for SEEK, except for the MSB of the first byte and the DIR bit.

DIR Head Step Direction Control.

DIR	Action
0	Step Head Out
1	Step Head In

RCN Relative Cylinder Number that determines how many tracks to step the head in or out from the current track number.

The RELATIVE SEEK command differs from the SEEK command in that it steps the head the absolute number of tracks specified in the command instead of making a comparison against an internal register. The SEEK command is good for drives that support a maximum of 256 tracks. RELATIVE SEEKs cannot be overlapped with other RELATIVE SEEKs. Only one RELATIVE SEEK can be active at a time. Bit 4 of Status Register 0 (EC) will be set if RELATIVE SEEK attempts to step outward beyond Track 0.

As an example, assume that a floppy drive has 300 useable tracks and that the host needs to read track 300 and the head is on any track (0–255). If a SEEK command was issued, the head would stop at track 255. If a RELATIVE SEEK command was issued, the 82077SL would move the head the specified number of tracks, regardless of the internal cylinder position register (but would increment the register). If the head had been on track 40 (D), the maximum track that the 82077SL could position the head on using RELATIVE SEEK, would be 296 (D), the initial track, +256 (D). The maximum count that the head can be moved with a single RELATIVE SEEK command is 256 (D).

The internal register, PCN, would overflow as the cylinder number crossed track 255 and would contain 40 (D). The resulting PCN value is thus (NCN + PCN) mod 256. Functionally, the 82077SL starts counting from 0 again as the track number goes above 255(D). It is the users responsibility to compensate 82077SL functions (precompensation track number) when accessing tracks greater than 255. The 82077SL does not keep track that it is working in an "extended track area" (greater than 255). Any command issued would use the current PCN value except for the RECALIBRATE command which only looks for the TRACK0 signal. RECALIBRATE would return an error if the head was farther than 79 due to its limitation of issuing a maximum 80 step pulses. The user simply needs to issue a second RECALIBRATE command. The SEEK command and implied seeks will function correctly within the 44 (D) track (299–255) area of the "extended track area". It is the users responsibility not to issue a new track position that would exceed the maximum track that is present in the extended area.

To return to the standard floppy range (0–255) of tracks, a RELATIVE SEEK would be issued to cross the track 255 boundary.

A RELATIVE SEEK can be used instead of the normal SEEK but the host is required to calculate the difference between the current head location and the new (target) head location. This may require the host to issue a READ ID command to ensure that the head is physically on the track that software assumes it to be. Different 82077SL commands will return different cylinder results which may be difficult to keep track of with software without the READ ID command.

6.2.10 DUMPREG

The DUMPREG command is designed to support system run-time diagnostics and application software development and debug.

6.2.11 PERPENDICULAR MODE COMMAND

The PERPENDICULAR MODE command should be issued prior to executing READ/WRITE/FORMAT commands that access a disk drive with perpendicular recording capability. With this command, the length of the Gap2 field and VCO enable timing can be altered to accommodate the unique requirements of these drives. Table 6-11 describes the effects of the WGATE and GAP bits for the PERPENDICULAR MODE command. Upon a reset, the 82077SL will default to the conventional mode (WGATE = 0, GAP = 0).

Selection of the 500 Kbps and 1 Mbps perpendicular modes is independent of the actual data rate selected in the Data rate Select Register. The user must ensure that the two data rates remain consistent.

The Gap2 and VCO timing requirements for perpendicular recording type drives are dictated by the design of the read/write head. In the design of this head, a pre-erase head precedes the normal read/write head by a distance of 200 micrometers. This works out to about 38 bytes at a 1 Mbps recording density. Whenever the write head is enabled by the Write Gate signal the pre-erase head is also activated at the same time. Thus, when the write head is initially turned on, flux transitions recorded on the media for the first 38 bytes will not be preconditioned with the pre-erase head since it has not yet been activated. To accommodate this head activation and deactivation time, the Gap2 field is expanded to a length of 41 bytes. The format field shown in Figure 5-3 illustrates the change in the Gap2 field size for the perpendicular format.

On the read back by the 82077SL, the controller must begin synchronization at the beginning of the Sync field. For the conventional mode, the internal PLL VCO is enabled (VCOEN) approximately 24 bytes from the start of the Gap2 field. But when the controller operates in the 1 Mbps perpendicular mode (WGATE = 1, GAP = 1), VCOEN goes active after 43 bytes to accommodate the increased Gap2 field size. For both cases, an approximate 2 byte cushion is maintained from the beginning of the sync field for the purposes of avoiding write splices in the presence of motor speed variation.

For the WRITE DATA case, the 82077SL activates Write Gate at the beginning of the sync field under the conventional mode. The controller then writes a new sync field, data address mark, data field, and CRC as shown in Figure 6-1. With the pre-erase head of the perpendicular drive, the write head must be activated in the Gap2 field to insure a proper write of the new sync field. For the 1 Mbps perpendicular mode (WGATE = 1, GAP = 1), 38 bytes will be written in the Gap2 space. Since the bit density is proportional to the data rate, 19 bytes will be written in the Gap2 field for the 500 Kbps perpendicular mode (WGATE = 1, GAP = 0).

It should be noted that none of the alterations in Gap2 size, VCO timing, or Write Gate timing affect normal program flow. The information provided here is just for background purposes and is not needed for normal operation. Once the PERPENDICULAR MODE command is invoked, 82077SL software behavior from the user standpoint is unchanged.

2

Table 6-11. Effects of WGATE and GAP Bits

GAP	WGATE	MODE	VCO Low Time after Index Pulse	Length of Gap2 Format Field	Portion of Gap2 Written by Write Data Operation	Gap2 VCO Low Time for Read Operations
0	0	Conventional Mode	33 Bytes	22 Bytes	0 Bytes	24 Bytes
0	1	Perpendicular Mode (500 Kbps Data Rate)	33 Bytes	22 Bytes	19 Bytes	24 Bytes
1	0	Reserved (Conventional)	33 Bytes	22 Bytes	0 Bytes	24 Bytes
1	1	Perpendicular Mode (1 Mbps Data Rate)	18 Bytes	41 Bytes	38 Bytes	43 Bytes

NOTE:
When either GAP or WGATE bit is set, the current value of precompensation in the DSR is used.

6.2.12 POWERDOWN MODE COMMAND

The POWERDOWN MODE command allows the automatic power management of the 82077SL. This especially allows the extension of battery life in portable PC systems. This command should be issued during the BIOS power on self test (POST) to enable auto powerdown.

As soon as the command is enabled, a 10 ms or a 0.5 sec minimum power up timer is initiated depending on whether the MIN DLY bit is set to 0 or 1. This timer is one of the required conditions that has to be satisfied before the part will enter auto powerdown. Any software reset will reinitialize the timer. The timer countdown is also extended by up to 10 ms if the data rate is changed during the timer's countdown. Without this timer 82077SL would have been put to sleep immediately after 82077SL is idle. The minimum delay gives software a chance to interact with 82077SL without incurring an additional overhead due to recovery time.

The command also allows the output pins of floppy disk drive interface to be tristated or left unaltered during auto powerdown. This is done by the FDI TRI bit. In the default condition (FDI TRI = 0) the output pins of the floppy disk drive are tristated. Setting this bit leaves the interface unchanged from the normal state.

The results phase returns the values programmed for MIN DLY, FDI TRI and AUTO PD. The results phase of the auto powerdown mode command has its two most significant bits set to zero to distinguish it from the 82077AA's command of the same value which returns an "Illegal Command" status of 80H. The auto powerdown mode is disabled by a hardware reset. Software results have no effect on the POWERDOWN MODE command parameters.

6.3 Command Set Enhancements

The PERPENDICULAR MODE and DUMPREG commands were enhanced along with the addition of a new LOCK command in the 82077AA. These enhancements also hold for the 82077SL and are explained in this section of the data sheet. The commands were enhanced/added in order to provide protection against older software application package which could inadvertently cause system compatibility problems. The modifications/additions are fully backward compatible with the 82077AA which do not support the enhancements.

6.3.1 PERPENDICULAR MODE

The PERPENDICULAR MODE Command is enhanced to allow the system designers to designate specific drives as Perpendicular recording drives. This enhancement is made so that the system designer does not have to worry about older application software packages which bypass their system's FDC (Floppy Disk Controller) routines. The enhancement will also allow data transfers between Conventional and Perpendicular drives without having to issue PERPENDICULAR MODE commands between the accesses of the two different drives, nor having to change write pre-compensation values. The following is an explanation of how this enhancement is implemented:

With the old implementation, the user must properly program both the PERPENDICULAR MODE command and write pre-compensation value before accessing either a Conventional or Perpendicular drive. These programmed values apply to all drives (D0–D3) which the 82077SL may access. It should also be noted that any form of RESET "Hardware" or "Software" will configure the PERPENDICULAR MODE command for Conventional mode (GAP and WGATE = "0").

With the enhanced implementation, both the GAP and WGATE bits have the same affects as the old implementation except for when they are both programmed for value of "0" (Conventional mode). For the case when both GAP and WGATE equal "0" the PERPENDICULAR MODE command will have the following effect on the 82077SL: 1) If any of the new bits D0, D1, D2, and D3 are programmed to "1" the corresponding drive will automatically be programmed for Perpendicular mode (ie: GAP2 being

Old PERPENDICULAR MODE command:

Phase	R/W	Data Bus								Remarks
		D7	D6	D5	D4	D3	D2	D1	D0	
PERPENDICULAR MODE										
Command	W	0	0	0	1	0	0	1	0	Command Code
	W	0	0	0	0	0	0	GAP	WGATE	

NOTE:
For the definition of GAP and WGATE bits see Table 6-11 and Section 6.2.11 of the data sheet.
For the Enhanced PERPENDICULAR MODE command definition see Table 6-1.

written during a write operation, the programmed Data Rate will determine the length of GAP2.), and data will be written with 0 ns write pre-compensation. 2) any of the new bits (D0–D3) that are programmed for "0" the designated drive will be programmed for Conventional Mode and data will be written with the currently programmed write pre-compensation value. 3) Bits D0, D1, D2, and D3 can only be over written when the OW bit is written as a "1". The status of these bits can be determined by interpreting the eighth result byte of the enhanced DUMPREG Command (See Section 6.3.3). (Note: if either the GAP or WGATE bit is a "1", then bits D0–D3 are ignored.)

"Software" and "Hardware" RESET will have the following effects on the enhanced PERPENDICULAR MODE command:

1) "Software" RESETs (Reset via DOR or DSR registers) will only clear GAP and WGATE bits to "0", D3, D2, D1, and D0 will retain their previously programmed values.
2) "Hardware" RESETs (Reset via pin 32) will clear all bits (GAP, Wgate, D0, D1, D2, and D3) to "0" (All Drives Conventional Mode).

6.3.2 LOCK

In order to protect a system with long DMA latencies against older application software packages that can disable the 82077SL's FIFO the following LOCK Command has been has been retained in the 82077SL's command set: [Note: This command should only be used by the system's FDC routines, and ISVs (Independent Software Vendors) should refrain from using it. If an ISV's application calls for having the 82077SL FIFO disabled a CONFIGURE Command should be used to toggle the EFIFO (Enable FIFO) bit. ISV can determine the value of the LOCK bit by interpreting the eighth result byte of an DUMPREG Command (See Section 6.3.3).]

The LOCK command defines whether EFIFO, FIFOTHR, and PRETRK parameters of the CONFIGURE command can be RESET by the DOR and DSR registers. When the LOCK bit is set to a "1" all subsequent "software" RESETs by the DOR and DSR registers will not change the previously set parameter values in the CONFIGURE command. When the LOCK bit is set to a "0" "software" RESETs by the DOR or DSR registers will return these parameters to their default values (See Section 6.2.7). All "hardware" Resets by pin 32 will set the LOCK bit to a "0" value, and will return EFIFO, FIFOTHR, and PRETRK to their default values. A Status byte is returned immediately after issuing the command byte. This Status byte reflects the value of the Lock bit set by the command byte. (Note: No interrupts are generated at the end of this command.)

6.3.3 ENHANCED DUMPREG COMMAND

To accommodate the new LOCK command and enhanced PERPENDICULAR MODE command the eighth result byte of DUMPREG command has been modified in the following manner:

Phase	R/W	Data Bus								Remarks
		D7	D6	D5	D4	D3	D2	D1	D0	
DUMPREG										
Result	R	**Eighth Result Byte** — Undefined —								Old
	R	LOCK	0	D3	D2	D1	D0	GAP	WGATE	Enhanced

NOTES:
1. Data bit 7 reflects the status of the new LOCK bit set by the LOCK Command.
2. Data Bits D0–D5 reflect the status for bits D3, D2, D1, D0, GAP and WGATE set by the PERPENDICULAR MODE Command.

7.0 STATUS REGISTER ENCODING

The contents of these registers are available only through a command sequence.

7.1 Status Register 0

Bit No.	Symbol	Name	Description
7, 6	IC	Interrupt Code	00-Normal termination of command. The specified command was properly executed and completed without error. 01-Abnormal termination of command. Command execution was started, but was not successfully completed. 10-Invalid command. The requested command could not be executed. 11-Abnormal termination caused by Polling.
5	SE	Seek End	The 82077SL completed a SEEK or RECALIBRATE command, or a READ or WRITE with implied seek command.
4	EC	Equipment Check	The TRK0 pin failed to become a "1" after: 1. 80 step pulses in the RECALIBRATE command. 2. The RELATIVE SEEK command causes the 82077SL to step outward beyond Track 0.
3	—	—	Unused. This bit is always "0".
2	H	Head Address	The current head address.
1, 0	DS1, 0	Drive Select	The current selected drive.

7.2 Status Register 1

Bit No.	Symbol	Name	Description
7	EN	End of Cylinder	The 82077SL tried to access a sector beyond the final sector of the track (255D). Will be set if TC is not issued after Read or Write Data Command.
6	—	—	Unused. This bit is always "0".
5	DE	Data Error	The 82077SL detected a CRC error in either the ID field or the data field of a sector.
4	OR	Overrun/ Underrun	Becomes set if the 82077SL does not receive CPU or DMA service within the required time interval, resulting in data overrun or underrun.
3	—	—	Unused. This bit is always "0".
2	ND	No Data	Any one of the following: 1. READ DATA, READ DELETED DATA command, the 82077SL did not find the specified sector. 2. READ ID command, the 82077SL cannot read the ID field without an error. 3. READ TRACK command, the 82077SL cannot find the proper sector sequence.
1	NW	Not Writable	WP pin became a "1" while the 82077SL is executing a WRITE DATA, WRITE DELETED DATA, or FORMAT TRACK command.
0	MA	Missing Address Mark	Any one of the following: 1. The 82077SL did not detect an ID address mark at the specified track after encountering the index pulse from the IDX pin twice. 2. The 82077SL cannot detect a data address mark or a deleted data address mark on the specified track.

7.3 Status Register 2

Bit No.	Symbol	Name	Description
7	—	—	Unused. This bit is always "0".
6	CM	Control Mark	Any one of the following: 1. READ DATA command, the 82077SL encounters a deleted data address mark. 2. READ DELETED DATA command, the 82077SL encounters a data address mark.
5	DD	Data Error in Data Field.	The 82077SL detected a CRC error in the data field.
4	WC	Wrong Cylinder	The track address from the sector ID field is different from the track address maintained inside the 82077SL.
3	—	—	Unused. This bit is always "0".
2	—	—	Unused. This bit is always "0".
1	BC	Bad Cylinder	The track address from the sector ID field is different from the track address maintained inside the 82077SL and is equal to FF hex which indicates a bad track with a hard error according to the IBM soft-sectored format.
0	MD	Missing Data Address Mark	The 82077SL cannot detect a data address mark or a deleted data address mark.

7.4 Status Register 3

Bit No.	Symbol	Name	Description
7	—	—	Unused. This bit is always "0".
6	WP	Write Protected	Indicates the status of the WP pin.
5	—	—	Unused. This bit is always "1".
4	T0	TRACK 0	Indicates the status of the TRK0 pin.
3	—	—	Unused. This bit is always "1".
2	HD	Head Address	Indicates the status of the HDSEL pin.
1, 0	DS1, 0	Drive Select	Indicates the status of the DS1, DS0 pins.

8.0 COMPATIBILITY

The 82077SL was designed with software compatibility in mind. It is a fully backwards compatible solution with the older generation 8272A and NEC765A/B disk controllers. The 82077SL also implements on-board registers for compatibility with the Personal System/2s as well as PC/AT and PC/XT floppy disk controller subsystems. The 82077SL is fully compatible with Intel's 386SL Microprocessor Superset. The 82077SL represents a superset of features that are available on 82077AA. Upon a hardware reset of the 82077SL, all registers, functions and enhancements default to a PS/2, PC/AT, or PS/2 Model 30 compatible operating mode depending on how the IDENT and MFM pins are sampled during Hardware Reset.

8.1 Register Set Compatibility

The register set contained within the 82077SL is a culmination of hardware registers based on the architectural growth of the IBM personal computer line. Table 8-1 indicates the registers required for compatibility based on the type of computer.

Table 8-1. 82077SL Register Support

82077SL Register	8272A	82072	PC/XT	PC/AT	PS/2	Mod 30
SRA					X	X
SRB					X	X
DOR			X	X	X	X
MSR	X	X	X	X	X	X
DSR		X				
Data (FIFO)	X	X	X	X	X	X
DIR				X	X	X
CCR		X*		X	X	X

*CCR is emulated by DSR in an 82072 PC/AT design.

8.2 PS/2 vs. AT vs. Model 30 Mode

To maintain compatibility between PS/2, PC/AT, and Model 30 environments the IDENT and MFM pins are provided. The 82077SL is placed into the proper mode of operations upon Hardware RESET with the appropriate settings of the IDENT and MFM pins. The proper settings of the IDENT and MFM pins are described in IDENT's pin description. Differences between the three modes are described in the following sections.

8.2.1 PS/2 MODE

IDENT strapped low causes the polarity of DENSEL to be active low for high (500 Kbps/1 Mbps) data rates (typically used for 3.5″ drives). This polalrity of DENSEL assumes INVERT# to be low. A comprehensive description of DENSEL behavior is given in Table 2-6.

The $\overline{\text{DMAGATE}}$ bit in the Digital Output Register (DOR) will not cause the DRQ or INT output signals to tristate. This maintains consistency with the operation of the floppy disk controller subsystem in the PS/2 architecture.

TC is an active low input signal that is internally qualified by $\overline{\text{DACK}}$ being active low.

8.2.2 PC/AT MODE

IDENT strapped high causes the polarity of DENSEL to be active high for high (500 Kbps/1 Mbps) data rates (typically used for 5.25″ drives). This polarity of DENSEL assumes INVERT# to be low. A comprehensive description of DENSEL behavior is given in Table 2-6.

If the $\overline{\text{DMAGATE}}$ bit is written to a "0" in the Digital Output Register (DOR), DRQ and INT will tristate. If $\overline{\text{DMAGATE}}$ is written to a "1", then DRQ and INT will be driven appropriately by the 82077SL.

TC is an active high input signal that is internally qualified by DACK# being active low.

8.2.3 MODEL 30 MODE

IDENT strapped low causes the polarity of DENSEL to be active low for high (500 Kbps/1 Mbps) data rates (typically used for 3.5″ drives). This polarity of DENSEL assumes INVERT# to be low. A comprehensive description of DENSEL behavior is given in Table 2-6.

$\overline{\text{DMAGATE}}$ and TC function the same as in PC/AT Mode.

8.3 Compatibility with the FIFO

The FIFO of the 82077SL is designed to be transparent to non-FIFO disk controller software developed on the older generation 8272A standard. Operation of the 82077SL FIFO can be broken down into two tiers of compatibility. For first tier compatibility, the FIFO is left in the default disabled condition upon a "Hardware" reset (via pin 32). In this mode the FIFO operates in a byte mode and provides complete compability with non-FIFO based software. For second tier compatibility, the FIFO is enabled via the CONFIGURE command. When the FIFO is enabled, it will temporarily enter a byte mode during the command and result phase of disk controller operation. This allows for compatible operation when interrogating the Main Status Register (MSR) for the purpose of transferring a byte at a time to or from the disk controller. For normal disk controller applications, the system designer can still take advantage of the FIFO for time critical data transfers during the execution phase and not create any conflicts with non-FIFO software during the command or result phase.

In some instances, use of the FIFO in any form has conflicted with certain specialized software. An example of a compatibility conflict using the FIFO is with software that monitors the progress of a data transfer during the execution phase. If the software assumed the disk controller was operating in a single byte mode and counted the number of bytes transferred to or from the disk controller to trigger some time dependent event on the disk media (i.e. head position over a specific data field), the same software will not have an identical time relationship if the FIFO is enabled. This is because the FIFO allows data to be queued up, and then burst transferred across the host bus. To accommodate software of this type, it is recommended that the FIFO be disabled.

8.4 Drive Polling

The 82077SL supports the polling mode of the older generation 8272A. This mode is enabled upon a reset and can be disabled via the CONFIGURE command. This mode is supported for the sole purpose of providing backwards compatibility with software that expects it's presence.

The intended purpose of drive polling dates back to 8″ drives as a means to monitor any change in status for each disk drive present in the system. Each of the drives is selected for a period of time and its READY signal sampled. After a delay, the next drive is selected. Since the 82077SL does not support READY in this capacity (internally tied true), the polling sequence is only simulated and does not affect the drive select lines (DS0–DS3) when it is active. If enabled, it occurs whenever the 82077SL is waiting for a command or during SEEKs and RECALIBRATEs (but not IMPLIED SEEKs). Each drive is assumed to be not ready after a reset and a "ready" value for each drive is saved in an internal register as the simulated drive is polled. An interrupt will be generated on the first polling loop because of the initial "not ready" status. This interrupt must be followed with a SENSE INTERRUPT STATUS command from the host to clear the interrupt condition for each of the four logical drives.

9.0 PROGRAMMING GUIDELINES

Programming the 82077SL is identical to any other 8272A compatible disk controller with the exception of some additional commands. For the new designer it is useful to provide some guidelines on how to program the 82077SL. A typical disk operation involves more than issuing a command and waiting for the results. The control of the floppy disk drive is a low level operation that requires software intervention at different stages. New commands and features have been added to the 82077SL to reduce the complexity of this software interface.

9.1 Command and Result Phase Handshaking

Before a command or parameter byte can be issued to the 82077SL, the Main Status Register (MSR) must be interrogated for a ready status and proper FIFO direction. A typical floppy controller device driver should contain a subroutine for sending command or parameter bytes. For this discussion, the routine will be called "Send_byte" with the flowchart shown in Figure 9-1.

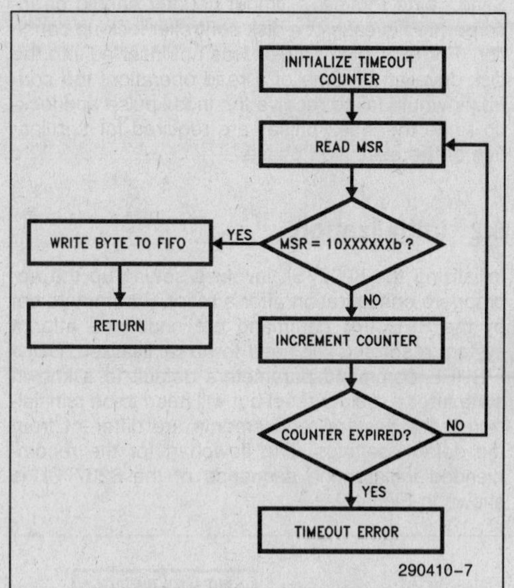

Figure 9-1. Send_Byte Routine

The routine loops until RQM is 1 and DIO is 0 indicating a ready status and FIFO direction is inward. If this condition is true, the 82077SL is ready to accept a command or parameter byte. A timeout counter is used to insure software response within a reasonable amount of time in case of no response by the 82077SL. As a note, the programmer must be careful how the maximum delay is chosen to avoid unnecessary timeouts. For example, if a new command is issued when the 82077SL is in the middle of a polling routine, the MSR will not indicate a ready status for the next parameter byte until the polling sequence completes the loop. This could cause a delay between the first and second bytes of up to 250 μs (@ 250 Kbps). If polling is disabled, this maximum delay is 175 μs. There should also be enough timeout margin to accommodate a shift of the software to a higher speed system. A timeout value that results in satisfactory operation on a 16 MHz CPU might fail when the software is moved to a system with a 25 MHz CPU. A recommended solution is to derive the timeout counter from a system hardware counter that is fixed in frequency from CPU clock to CPU clock.

For reading result bytes from the 82077SL, a similar routine is used. Figure 9-2 illustrates the flowchart for the routine "Get_byte". The MSR is polled until

RQM is 1 and DIO is 1, which indicates a ready status and outward FIFO direction. At this point, the host can read a byte from the FIFO. As in the Send_byte routine, a timout counter should be incorporated in case of a disk controller lock-up condition. For example, if a disk was not inserted into the disk drive at the time of a read operation, the controller would fail to receive the index pulse and lock-up since the index pulses are required for termination of the execution phase.

9.2 Initialization

Initializing the 82077SL involves setting up the appropriate configuration after a reset. Parameters set by the SPECIFY command are undefined after a system reset and will need to be reinitialized. CONFIGURE command parameters default to a known state after a system reset but will need to be reinitialized if the system requirements are different from the default settings. The flowchart for the recommended initialization sequence of the 82077SL is shown in Figure 9-3.

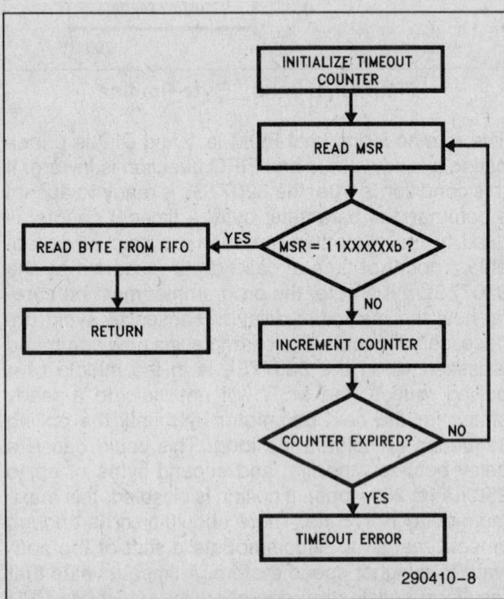

Figure 9-2. Get_Byte Routine

Following a reset of the 82077SL, the Configuration Control Register (CCR) should be reinitialized for the appropriate data rate. An external reset via the RESET pin will cause the data rate and write precompensation values to default to 250 Kbps (10b) and 125 ns (000b) respectively. Since the 125 ns write precompensation value is optimal for the 5¼″ and 3½″ disk drive environment, most applications will not require the value to be changed in the initialization sequence. As a note, a software reset issued via the DOR or DSR will not affect the data rate or write precompensation values. But it is recommended as a safe programming practice to always program the data rate after a reset, regardless of the type.

Since polling is enabled after a reset of the 82077SL, four SENSE INTERRUPT STATUS commands need to be issued afterwards to clear the status flags for each drive. The flowchart in Figure 9-3 illustrates how the software clears each of the four interrupt status flags internally queued by the 82077SL. It should be noted that although four SENSE INTERRUPT STATUS commands are issued, the INT pin is only active until the first SENSE INTERRUPT STATUS command is executed.

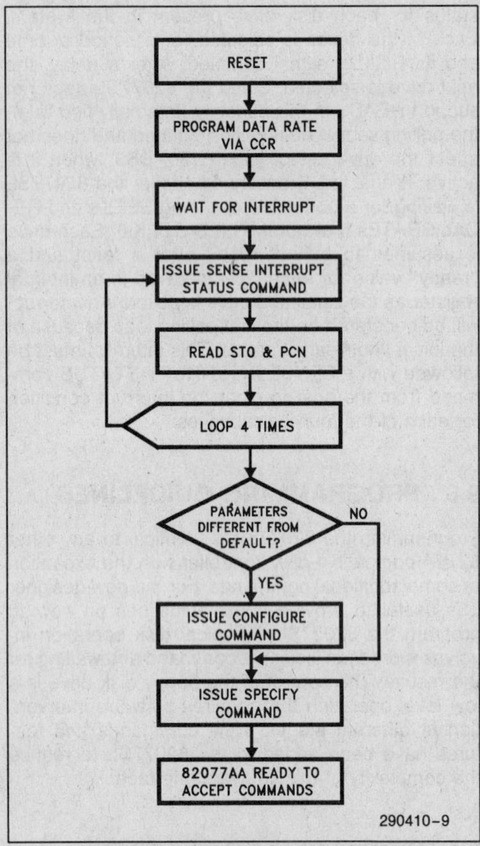

Figure 9-3. Initialization Flowchart

As a note, if the CONFIGURE command is issued within 250 μs of the trailing edge of reset (@ 1 Mbps), the polling mode of the 82077SL can be disabled before the polling initiated interrupt occurs. Since polling stops when the 82077SL enters the command phase, it is only time critical up to the first byte of the CONFIGURE command. If disabled in time, the system software no longer needs to issue the four SENSE INTERRUPT STATUS commands to clear the internal interrupt flags normally caused by polling.

The CONFIGURE command should also be issued if the system requirements are different from the default settings (as described in Section 6.2.7). For example, the CONFIGURE command can be used to enable the FIFO, set the threshold, and enable Implied Seeks.

The non-DMA mode flag, step rate (SRT), head load (HLT), and head unload times (HUT) programmed by the SPECIFY command do not default to a known state after a reset. This behavior is consistent with the 8272A and has been preserved here for compatibility. Thus, it is necessary to always issue a SPECIFY command in the initialization routine.

9.3 Recalibrates and Seeks

Commands that position the disk head are different from the typical READ/WRITE/FORMAT command in the sense that there is no result phase. Once a RECALIBRATE, SEEK, or RELATIVE SEEK command has been issued, the 82077SL will return a ready status in the Main Status Register (MSR) and perform the head positioning operation as a background task. When the seek is complete, the 82077SL will assert the INT signal to request service. A SENSE INTERRUPT STATUS command should then be asserted to clear the interrupt and read the status of the operation. Since the drive and motor enable signals are directly controlled through the Digital Output Register (DOR) on the 82077SL, a write to the DOR will need to precede the RECALIBRATE or SEEK command if the drive and motor is not already enabled. Figure 9-4 shows the flow chart for this operation.

9.4 Read/Write Data Operations

A read or write data operation requires several steps to complete successfully. The motor needs to be turned on, the head positioned to the correct cylinder, the DMA controller initialized, the read or write command initiated, and an error recovery scheme implemented. The flowchart in Figure 9-5 highlights a recommended algorithm for performing a read or write data operation.

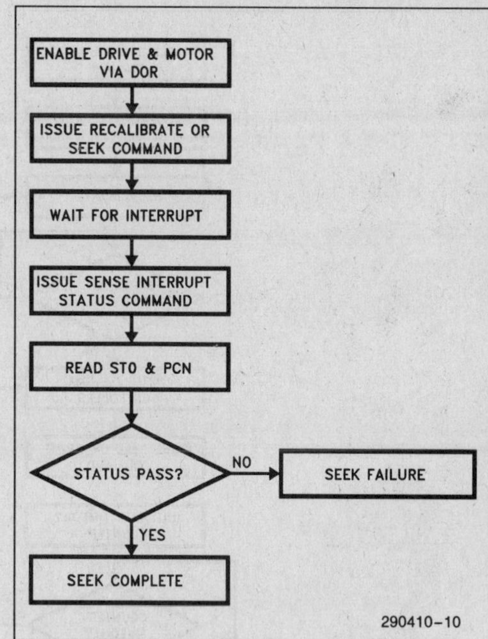

Figure 9-4. Recalibrate and Seek Operations

Before data can be transferred to or from the diskette, the disk drive motor must be brought up to speed. For most 3½″ disk drives, the spin-up time is 300 ms, while the 5¼″ drive usually requires about 500 ms due to the increased moment of inertia associated with the larger diameter diskette.

One technique for minimizing the motor spin-up delay in the read data case is to begin the read operation immediately after the motor is turned on. When the motor is not initially up to speed, the internal data separator will fail to lock onto the incoming data stream and report a failure in the status registers. The read operation is then repeated until successful status is obtained. There is no risk of a data integrity problem since the data field is CRC validated. But, it is not recommended to use this technique for the write data operation even though it requires successful reading of the ID field before the write takes place. The data separator performance of the 82077SL is such that locking to the data stream could take place while the motor speed variation is still significant. This could result in errors when an attempt is made to read the disk media by other disk controllers that have a narrower incoming data stream frequency bandwidth.

After the motor has been turned on, the matching data rate for the media inserted into the disk drive should then be programmed to the 82077SL via the Configuration Control Register (CCR). The 82077SL

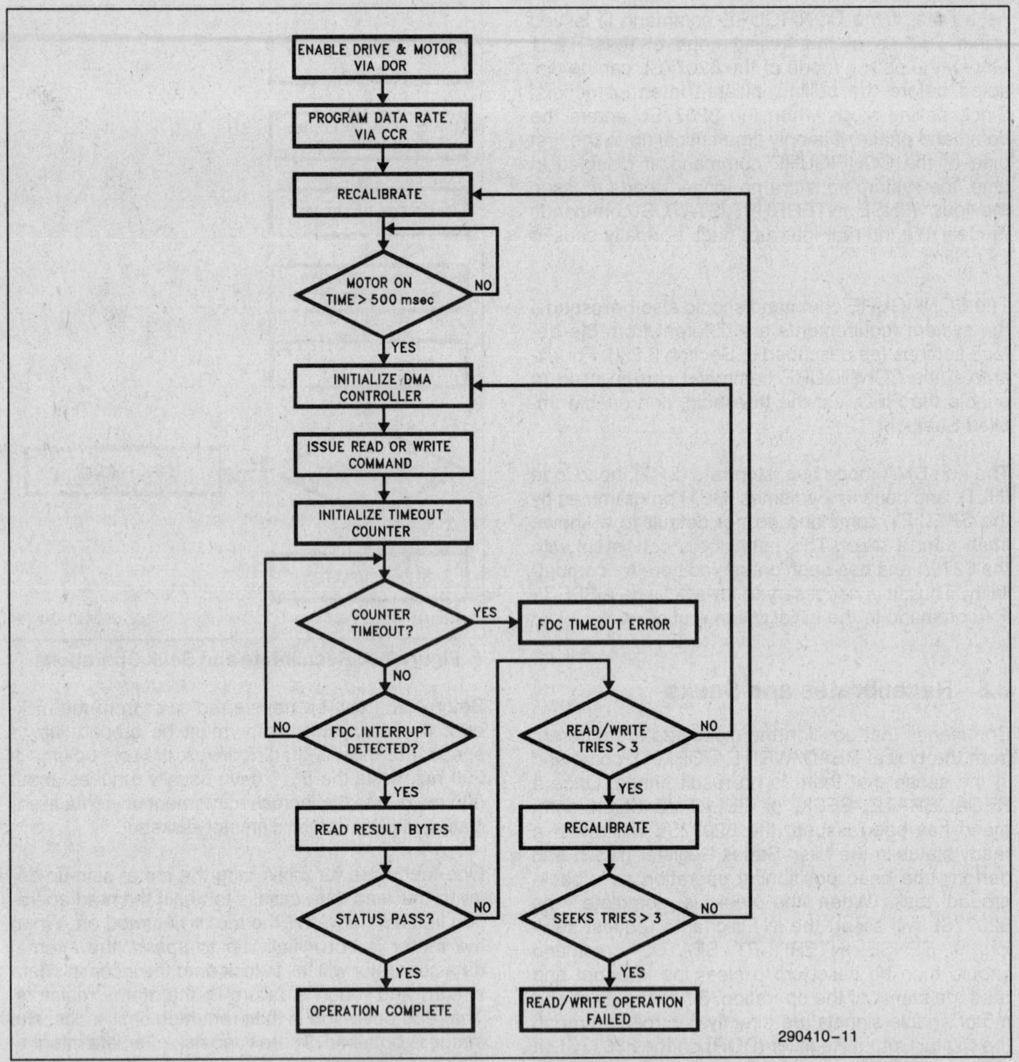

Figure 9-5. Read/Write Operation

is designed to allow a different data rate to be programmed arbitrarily without disrupting the integrity of the device. In some applications, it is required to automatically determine the recorded data rate of the inserted media. One technique for doing this is to perform a READ ID operation at each available data rate until a successful status is returned in the result phase.

If implied seeks are not enabled, the disk drive head must be positioned over the correct cylinder by executing a SEEK command. After the seek is complete, a head settling time needs to be asserted before the read or write operation begins. For most drives, this delay should be a minimum of 15 ms. When using implied seeks, the minimum head settling time can be enforced by the head load time (HLT) parameter designated in the SPECIFY command. For example, a HLT value of 8 will yield an effective head settling time of 16 ms for a programmed data rate of 500 Kbps. Of course if the head is already positioned over the correct cylinder, the head settling time does not need to be enforced.

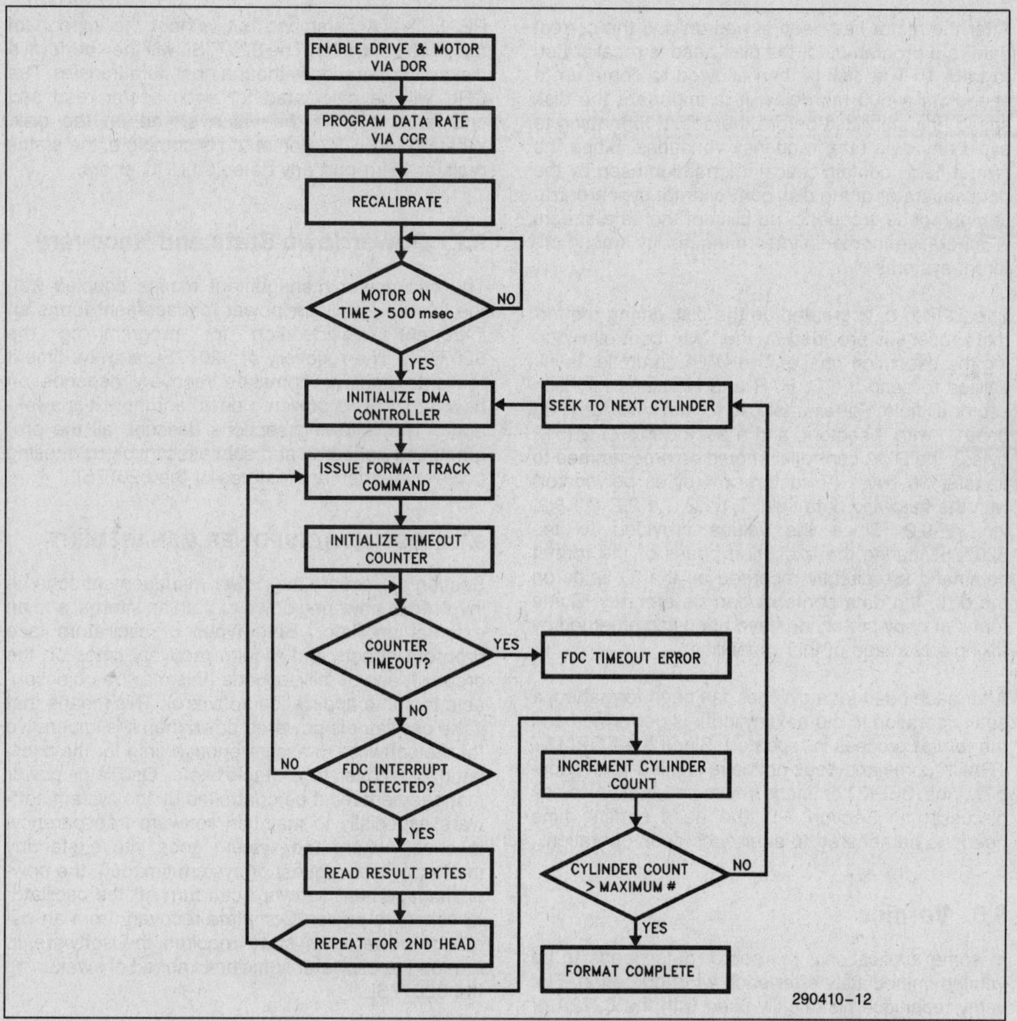

ENABLE DRIVE & MOTOR VIA DOR

PROGRAM DATA RATE VIA CCR

RECALIBRATE

MOTOR ON TIME > 500 msec

NO

YES

INITIALIZE DMA CONTROLLER

SEEK TO NEXT CYLINDER

ISSUE FORMAT TRACK COMMAND

INITIALIZE TIMEOUT COUNTER

COUNTER TIMEOUT?

YES

FDC TIMEOUT ERROR

NO

FDC INTERRUPT DETECTED?

NO

YES

INCREMENT CYLINDER COUNT

CYLINDER COUNT > MAXIMUM #

NO

YES

READ RESULT BYTES

REPEAT FOR 2ND HEAD

FORMAT COMPLETE

290410-12

Figure 9-6 Formatting

The DMA controller is then initialized for the data transfer and the read or write command is executed. Typically the DMA controller will assert Terminal Count (TC) when the data transfer is complete. The 82077SL will then complete the current data transfer and assert the INT signal signifying it has entered the result phase. The result phase can also be entered by the 82077SL if an error is encountered or the last sector number equals the End of Track (EOT) parameter.

Based on the algorithm in Figure 9-5, if an error is encountered after reading the result bytes, two more retries are performed by reinitializing the DMA controller and re-issuing the read or write data command. A persisting failure could indicate the seek operation did not achieve proper alignment between the head and the track. The disk head should then be recalibrated and the seek repeated for a maximum of two more tries. Unsuccessful operation after this point should be reported as a disk failure to the operating system.

9.5 Formatting

The disk formatting procedure involves positioning the head on each track and creating a fixed format field used for organizing the data fields. The flowchart in Figure 9-6 highlights the typical format procedure.

After the motor has been turned on and the correct data rate programmed, the disk head is recalibrated to track 0. The disk is then allowed to come up to speed via a 500 ms delay. It is important the disk speed has stabilized before the actual formatting to avoid any data rate frequency variations. Since the format fields contain critical information used by the data separator of the disk controller for synchronization purposes, frequency stability of the data stream is imperative for media interchangeability among different systems.

The ID field data created on the disk during the format process is provided by the DMA controller during the execution phase. The DMA controller is initialized to send the C, H, R and N values for each sector ID field. For example, to format cylinder 7, on head 1, with 9 sectors, and a sector size of 2 (512 bytes), the DMA controller should be programmed to transfer 36 bytes (9 sectors x 4 bytes per sector) with the following data field: 7,1,1,2, 7,1,2,2, 7,1,3,2, ... 7,1,9,2. Since the values provided to the 82077SL during the execution phase of the format command are directly recorded as the ID fields on the disk, the data contents can be arbitrary. Some forms of copy protection have been implemented by taking advantage of this capability.

After each head for a cylinder has been formatted, a seek operation to the next cylinder is performed and the format process is repeated. Since the FORMAT TRACK command does not have implied seek capability, the SEEK command must be used. Also, as discussed in Section 9-2, the head settling time needs to be adhered to after each seek operation.

9.6 Verifies

In some applications, the sector data needs to be verified immediately after each write operation. The verify technique historically used with the 8272A or 82072 disk controller involved reinitializing the DMA controller to perform a read transfer or verify transfer (DACK# is asserted but not RD#) immediately after each write operation. A read command is then to be issued to the disk controller and the resulting status indicates if the CRC validated the previously written data. This technique has the drawback of requiring additional software intervention by having to reprogram the DMA controller between each sector write operation. The 82077SL supports this older verify technique but also provides a new VERIFY command that does not require the use of the DMA controller. This is also available in 82077AA.

To verify a write data transfer or format track operation using the VERIFY command, the software simply issues the command with the same format as a READ DATA command but without the support of the DMA controller. The 82077SL will then perform a disk read operation without a host data transfer. The CRC will be calculated for each sector read and compared against the value stored on the disk. When the VERIFY command is complete, the status register will report any detected CRC errors.

9.7 Powerdown State and Recovery

The two power management modes coupled with the internal oscillator power management forms an important consideration for programming the 82077SL. The recovery of 82077SL and the time it takes to achieve complete recovery depends on how 82077SL is powered down and how it is awakened. The following sections describe all the programming concerns and subtleties involved in using power management features of the 82077SL.

9.7.1 OSCILLATOR POWER MANAGEMENT

Section 4.1 covers the power management scheme involved in powering down of both an internal and an external oscillator. Both types of oscillators face drop out effects and require recovery times on the order of tens of milliseconds (this may be objectionable to some application software). This means that if the oscillator is powered down then it is imperative for the software to assure enough time for the oscillator to recover to a stable state. Oscillator power management must be controlled by the system software especially to maintain software transparency. In cases where the system goes into a standby mode (by user request or system timeout), the power management software can turn off the oscillator to conserve power. Complete recovery from an oscillator powerdown state requires the software to turn on the oscillator sufficiently ahead of awakening the 82077SL.

9.7.2 PART POWER MANAGEMENT

The part powerdown and wake up modes are covered in Section 4.2 in detail. This section is meant to address the programming concerns for the part (excluding the oscillator) during these modes.

9.7.2.a Powerdown Modes

For both types of powerdown modes—DSR powerdown and auto powerdown, if reset is used to exit the part from powerdown then the internal microcontroller will go through a standard sequence: register initialization followed after some delay by an interrupt.

Software transparency in auto powerdown mode is preserved by MSR retaining the value of 80H which indicates that the part is ready to receive a command. This feature allows the part to powerdown while maintaining its responsiveness to any application software.

9.7.2.b Wake Up Modes

Wake up from DSR powerdown results in the part being internally reset and all present status being lost. During DSR powerdown the RQM bit in the MSR is set. A software or hardware reset will wake up the part.

The case for wake up from auto powerdown is different. The BIOS and application software are very sensitive to delays involved in writing the first command bytes to the 82077SL. Most programs have short error timeouts in these cases. Such programs would not tolerate any floppy disk controller that was unable to receive the first byte of a command at any time. The following describes how 82077SL uniquely sustains its software transparency during wake up sequences.

Prior to writing a command to 82077SL, it is first necessary to read the MSR to ensure that the 82077SL is ready (RQM bit must be set) to receive the command. When the part detects a MSR read, it assumes that another command will follow and begins the wake up process. While the part is waking up it does not change the state of the MSR (MSR = 80H) and is able to receive the command in the FIFO. At this point one of the two following scenarios can occur.

- No other command is sent subsequent to the MSR read. The part wakes up and initializes the minimum power up timer. Upon the expiration of this timer the part is once again put in powerdown state.
- Another command follows the MSR read. If the command is send during the part's recovery from powerdown, the part remembers the command, clears the RQM bit (to prevent further bytes being written) and acts on the command once it is fully awake.

If the MSR was not checked prior to writing of a command, the part will proceed as stated above with the RQM bit cleared and the command byte held until the internal microcontroller is ready. Writing the motor enable bits in DOR active will initiate the wake up sequence with RQM set high, ready to receive any command.

As it is clear from the above discussion, the immediate access to the floppy disk controller for the first command byte is vital to software transparency. The recovery of the part from powerdown may involve a delay after the first command byte has been issued. However, all programs have tolerance for the delay after the first command byte is issued. In a powered up chip, it is possible for the microcontroller to be in its "polling loop". As a result the tolerance for this delay provides an excellent window for recovery of the part.

10.0 DESIGN APPLICATIONS

10.1 PC/AT Floppy Disk Controller

This section presents a design application of a PC/AT compatible floppy disk controller. With an 82077SL, a 24 MHz crystal, a resistor package, and a device chip select, a complete floppy disk controller can be built. The 82077SL integrates all the necessary building blocks for a reliable and low cost solution. But before we discuss the design application using the 82077SL, it is helpful to describe the architecture of the original IBM PC/AT floppy disk controller design that uses the 8272A.

10.1.1 PC/AT FLOPPY DISK CONTROLLER ARCHITECTURE

The standard IBM PC/AT floppy disk controller using the 8272A requires 34 devices for a complete solution. The block diagram in Figure 10-1 illustrates the complexity of the disk controller. A major portion of this logic involves the design of the data separator. The reliability of the disk controller is primarily dictated by the performance and stability of the data separator. Discrete board level analog phase lock loops generally offer good bit jitter margins but suffer from instability and tuning problems in the manufacturing stage if not carefully designed. While digital data separator designs offer stability and generally a lower chip count, they suffer from poor performance in the recovery of data.

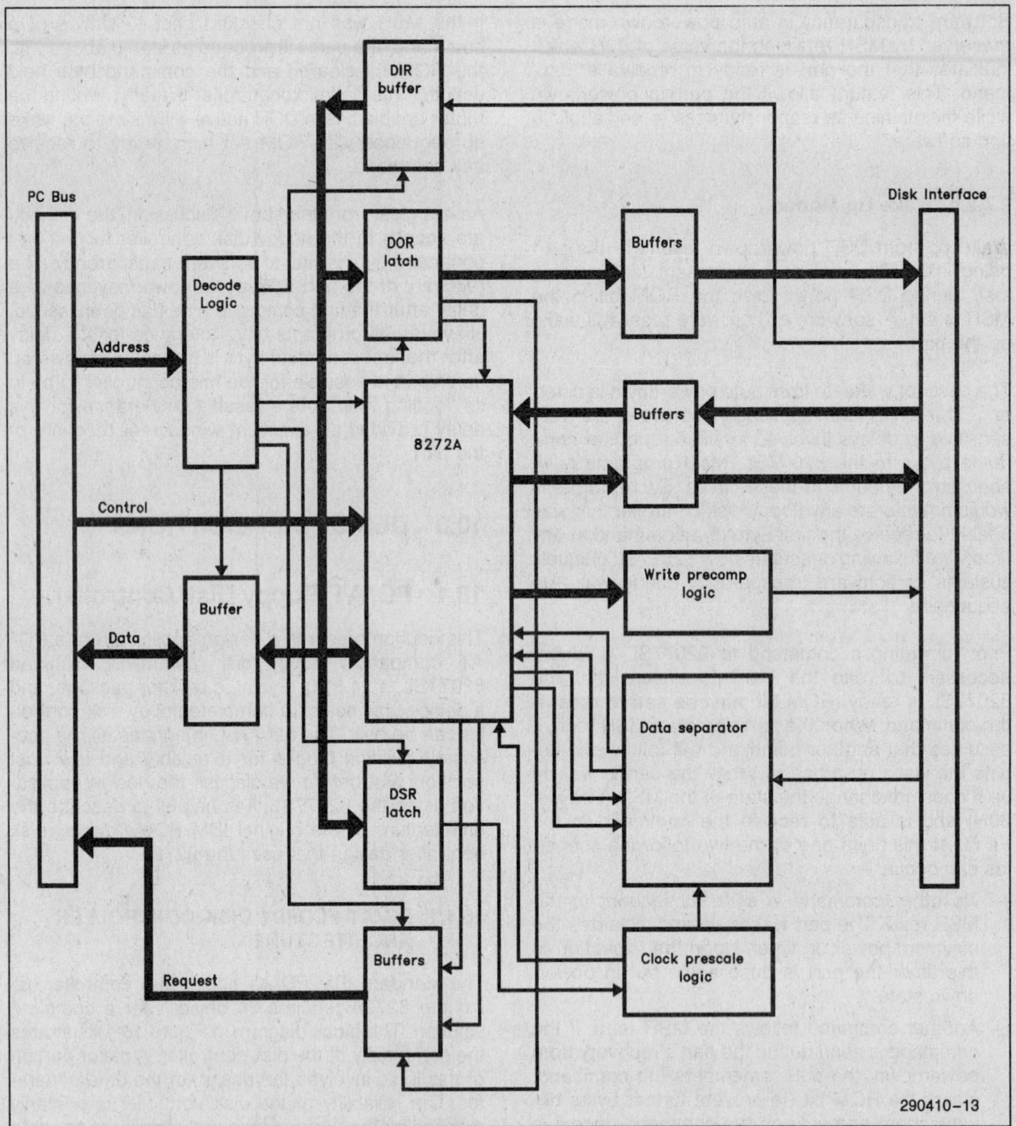

Figure 10-1. Standard IBM PC/AT Floppy Disk Controller

Table 10-1 indicates the drive and media types the IBM PC/AT disk controller can support. This requires the data separator to operate at three different data rates: 250 Kbps, 300 Kbps and 500 Kbps. Clocks to the data separator and disk controller need to be prescaled correspondingly to accommodate each of these data rates. The clock prescaling is controlled by the Data rate Select Register (DSR). Supporting all three data rates can compromise the performance of the phase lock loop (PLL) if steps are not taken in the design to adjust the performance parameters of the PLL with the data rate.

Table 10-1. Standard PC/AT Drives and Media Formats

Capacity	Drive Speed	Data Rate	Sectors	Cylinders
360 Kbyte	300 RPM	250 Kbps	9	40
*360 Kbyte	360 RPM	300 Kbps	9	40
1.2 Mbyte	360 RPM	500 Kbps	15	80

*360 Kbyte diskette in a 1.2 Mbyte drive.

The PC/AT disk controller provides direct control of the drive selects and motors via the Digital Output Register (DOR). As a result, drive selects on the 8272A are not utilized. This places drive selection and motor speed-up control responsibility with the software. The DOR is also used to perform a software reset of the disk controller and tristate the DRQ2 and IRQ6 output signals on the PC bus.

The design of the disk controller also requires address decode logic for the disk controller and register set, buffering for both the disk interface and PC bus, support for write precompensation and monitoring of the disk change signal via a separate read only register (DIR). An I/O address map of the complete register set for the PC/AT floppy disk controller is shown in Table 10-2.

Table 10-2. I/O Address Map for the PC/AT

I/O Address	Access Type	Description
3F0H	—	Unused
3F1H	—	Unused
3F2H	Write	Digital Output Register
3F3H	—	Unused
3F4H	Read	Main Status Register
3F5H	Read/Write	Data Register
3F6H	—	Unused
3F7H	Write	Data Rate Select Register
3F7H	Read	Digital Input Register

10.1.2 82077SL PC/AT SOLUTION

The 82077SL integrates the entire PC/AT controller design with the exception of the address decode on a single chip. The schematic for this solution is shown in Figure 10-2. The chip select for the 82077SL is generated by a 16L8 PAL that is programmed to decode addresses 03F0H thru 03F7H when AEN (Address Enable) is low. The programming equation for the PAL is shown in a ABEL file format in Figure 10-3. An alternative address decode solution could be provided by using a 74LS133 13 input NAND gate and 74LS04 inverter to decode A3–A14 and AEN. Although the PC/AT allows for a 64K I/O address space, decoding down to a 32K I/O address space is sufficient with the existing base of add-in cards.

A direct connection between the disk interface and the 82077SL is provided by on-chip output buffers with a 40 mA sink capability. Open collector outputs from the disk drive are terminated at the disk controller with a 150Ω resistor pack. The 82077SL disk interface inputs contain a schmitt trigger input structure for higher noise immunity. The host interface is a similar direct connection with 12 mA sink capabilities on DB0–DB7, INT and DRQ.

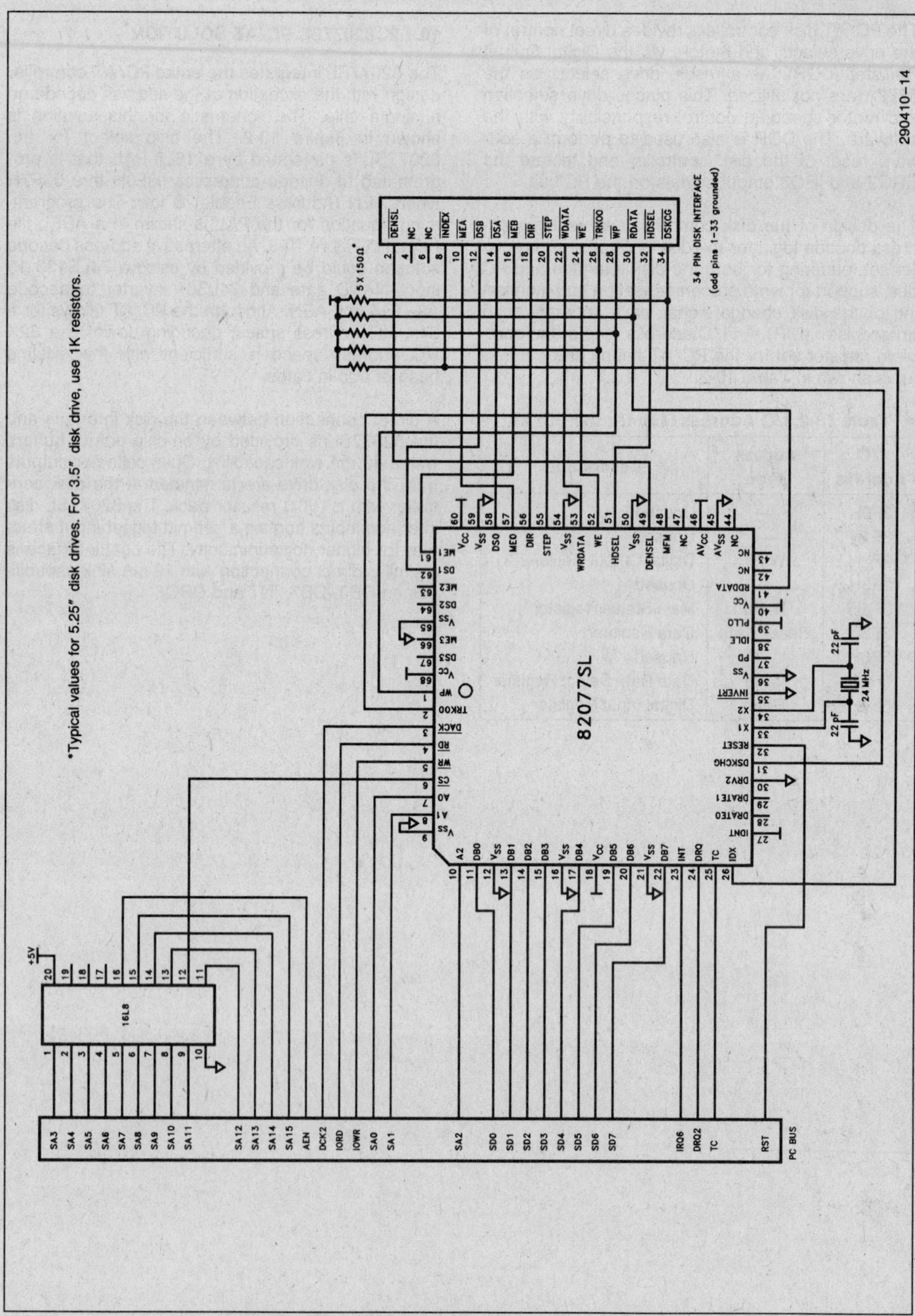

Figure 10-2. 82077SL PC/AT Floppy Disk Controller

```
MODULE PCAT077_LOGIC;

TITLE "82077SL PC/AT FLOPPY DISK CONTROLLER';
PCAT077 DEVICE "P16L8';

GND,VCC                                 PIN 10,20;
SA3,SA4,SA5,SA6,SA7,SA8,SA9,SA10        PIN 1,2,3,4,5,6,7,8;
SA11,SA12,SA13,SA14,SA15,AEN            PIN 9,11,13,14,15,16;
CS077_                                  PIN 12;

EQUATIONS

"" CHIP SELECT FOR THE 82077SL (3F0H -- 3F7H)

CS077_ = !(!SA15 & !SA14 & !SA13 & !SA12 & !SA11 & !SA10 &
           SA9 & SA8 & SA7 & SA6 & SA5 & SA4 & !SA3 & !AEN);

END PCAT077_LOGIC
```

Figure 10-3. PAL Equation File for a PC/AT Compatible FDC Board

10.2 3.5″ Drive Interfacing

The 82077SL is designed to interface to both 3.5″ and 5.25″ disk drives. This is facilitated by the 82077SL by orienting IDENT to get the proper polarity of DENSEL for the disk drive being used. Typically DENSEL is active high for high (500 Kbps/1 Mbps) data rates on 5.25″ drives. And DENSEL is typically active low for high data rates on 3.5″ drives. A complete description of how to orient IDENT to get the proper polarity for DENSEL is given in Table 2-6.

10.2.1 3.5″ DRIVES UNDER THE AT MODE

When interfacing the 82077SL floppy disk controller with a 3.5″ disk drive in a PC/AT application, it is possible that two design changes will need to be implemented for the design discussed in Section 10.1. Most 3.5″ disk drives incorporate a totem pole interface structure as opposed to open collector. Outputs of the disk drive will drive both high or low voltage levels when the drive is selected, and float only when the drive has been deselected. These totem pole outputs generally can only sink or source 4 mA of current. As a result, it is recommended to replace the 150Ω termination resistor pack with a 4.7 KΩ package to pull floating signals inactive. Some other 3.5″ drives do have an open collector interface, but have limited sink capability. In these cases, the drive manufacturer manuals usually suggest a 1 KΩ termination.

A second possible change required under "AT mode" operation involves high capacity 3.5″ disk drives that utilize a density select signal to switch between media recorded at a 250 Kbps and 500 Kbps data rate. The polarity of this signal is typically inverted for 3.5″ drives versus 5.25″ drives. Thus, an inverter can be added between the DENSEL output of the 82077SL and the disk drive interface connector when using 3.5″ drives.

But drives that do not support both data rates or drives with an automatic density detection feature via an optical sensor do not require the use of the DENSEL signal.

Another method is to change the polarity of IDENT with a drive select signal. ORing RESET with the drive select signal (DS0–3) used for the 3.5″ disk drive will produce the proper polarity for DENSEL (assuming INVERT# is low).

10.2.2 3.5″ DRIVES UNDER THE PS/2 MODES

If IDENT is strapped to ground, the DENSEL output signal polarity will reflect a typical 3.5″ drive mode of operation. That is, DENSEL will be high for 250 Kbps or 300 Kbps and low for 500 Kbps or 1 Mbps (assuming INVERT# is low). Thus the only change from the disk interface shown in Figure 10-2 is to replace the 150Ω termination resistor pack with a value of about 10 KΩ. This will prevent excessive current consumption on the CMOS inputs of the 82077SL by pulling them inactive when the drive(s) are deselected.

10.2.3 COMBINING 5.25″ AND 3.5″ DRIVES

If 5.25″ and 3.5″ drives are to be combined in a design, then steps need to be taken to avoid contention problems on the disk interface. Since 3.5″ drives do not have a large sink capability, the 150Ω termination resistor pack required by 5.25″ drives cannot be used with the 3.5″ drive. To accommodate both drives with the same disk controller, the outputs of the 3.5″ drive should be buffered before connecting to the 82077SL disk interface inputs. The 82077SL inputs are then connected to the necessary resistive termination load for the 5.25″ interface.

The block diagram in Figure 10-4 highlights how a combined interface could be designed. In this example, the 5.25″ drive is connected to drive select 0 (DS0) and the 3.5″ drive is connected to drive select 1 (DS1). DS1 is also used to enable a 74LS244 buffer on the output signals of the 3.5″ drive. The drive select logic of the 82077SL is mutually exclusive and prevents the activation of the buffer and 5.25″ drive at the same time. Since the 74LS244 has an I_{OL} of 24 mA, the termination resistor should be increased to 220Ω. This could impact the reliability of the 5.25″ drive interface if the cable lengths are greater than 5 feet.

To accommodate the polarity reversal of the DENSEL signal for 3.5″ drives, it is routed through an inverter for the 3.5″ drive interface. A 1 KΩ pull-up should be placed on the output of the inverter to satisfy the I_{OH} requirements for the 3.5″ drive when using a 74LS04.

10.2.4 OPTIMIZING 82077SL-1 FOR TAPE DRIVE MODE

The floppy disk controller can be configured for the tape drive mode by both hardware and software. Configuring the 82077SL-1 for the tape drive mode refers to optimization of the internal data separator in order to deal with the effect of ISV which is more pronounced on a tape drive than on a floppy disk controller. Hardware selection is done by setting the PLL0 (pin 39) to 0 or GND. This optimizes the data separator for tape drives by changing the loop filter component values and loop gain. TDR selection is disabled under this mode. Software selection of the tape drive mode for the FDC is implemented via setting of the appropriate bits in the tape drive register (TDR). This selection is enabled only while PLL0 is set high. This aids the user in configuring the particular drives as tape drive even when in floppy mode.

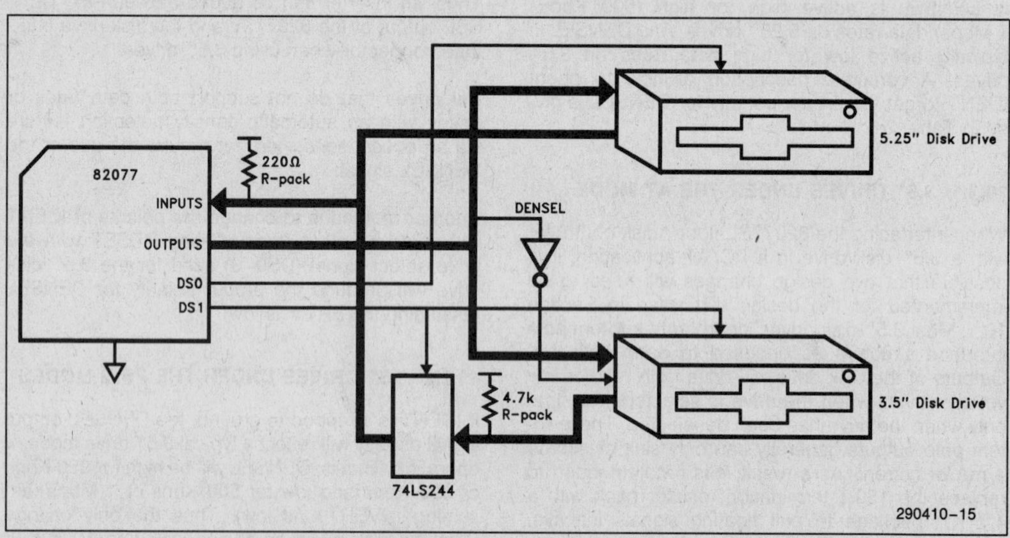

Figure 10-4. Combined 3.5″ and 5.25″ Drive Interface

As shown below the TDR contains two bits which can be utilized to assign tape support to a particular drive during initialization.

7	6	5	4	3	2	1	0
*	*	*	*	*	*	TAPE SEL1	TAPE SEL1

Hardware resets clears this register but it remains unaffected by any software reset. TDR[2:7] remain in a tristated condition and are not readable. Drive 0 is reserved for the floppy boot drive and cannot be configured for tape drives using the TDR (software mechanism). Hardware selection overrides any selection made by the software, i.e., by setting PLL0 to GND, tape drive mode will be selected regardless of the changes made to the TDR. Although the software mechanism does not allow to select drive 0 for tape drive, when PLL0 = 0 any drive can be supported for tape drive.

82077SL-1 has the capability to support up to a total of four drives. Most PC systems today have at least one floppy disk drive. This leaves the possibility of installing up to three tape drives. The following describes a way to configure the floppy disk controller in a multiple tape drive environment. This also depends on whether the system manufacturer wishes to leave certain drive slots fixed for tape drives or variable by the user.

All Tape Drives Are Variable—If the drives chosen as tape drives are variable then the configuration mechanism used is strictly software. After strapping PLL0 high, the bits TDR[0:1] can be programmed during initialization for various drives that can be selected as tape drives. It should be noted that in this case drive 0 cannot be selected as one of the tape drives.

Combination of Fixed/Variable Tape Drives—If any drive can be determined to be fixed then either the motor enable pin or the drive select pin of that particular drive can be used to drive PLL0 to GND when selected. Figure 10-5A and Figure 10-5B show two scenarios where drives that are fixed for tape drive use their motor enable or drive select signals to drive PLL0 to GND.

Figure 10-5C shows by using jumpers flexibility can be incorporated in the system and the drive/s to be fixed for tape drives can be left to the user.

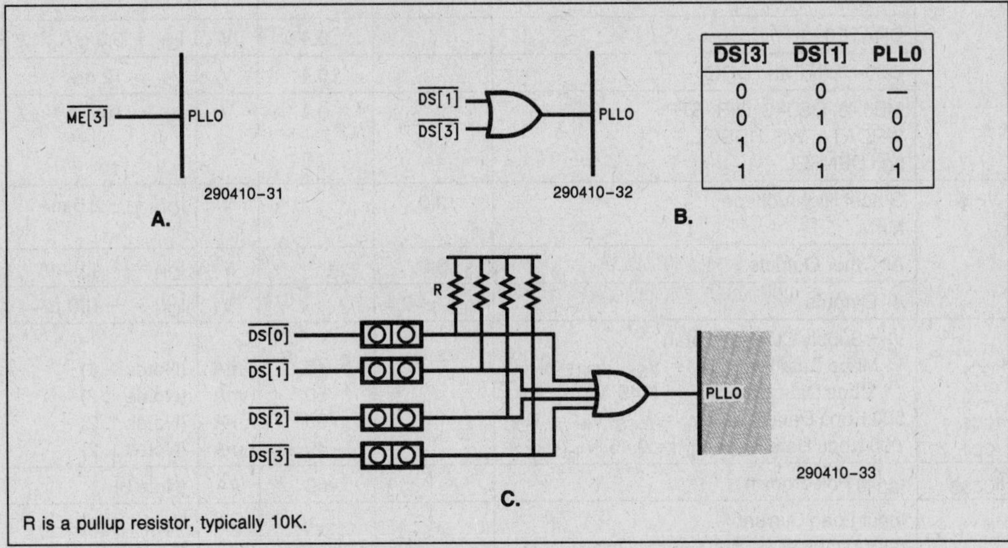

Figure 10-5. Optimizing 82077SL-1 for Tape Drive Mode

11.0 D.C. SPECIFICATIONS

11.1 Absolute Maximum Ratings

Storage Temperature .... −65°C to +150°C

Supply Voltage .... −0.5 to +8.0V

Voltage on Any Input .... GND − 2V to 6.5V

Voltage on Any Output . . GND − 0.5V to VCC + 0.5V

Power Dissipation .... 1 Watt

NOTICE: This is a production data sheet. The specifications are subject to change without notice.

******WARNING: Stressing the device beyond the "Absolute Maximum Ratings" may cause permanent damage. These are stress ratings only. Operation beyond the "Operating Conditions" is not recommended and extended exposure beyond the "Operating Conditions" may affect device reliability.*

11.2 D.C. Characteristics

T_A = 0°C to = 70°C, V_{CC} = +5V ±10%, V_{SS} = AV_{SS} = 0V

Symbol	Parameter	Min	Max	Unit	Test Conditions
V_{ILC}	Input Low Voltage, X1	−0.5	0.8	V	
V_{IHC}	Input High Voltage, X1	3.9	V_{CC} +0.5	V	
V_{IL}	Input Low Voltage (all pins except X1)	−0.5	0.8	V	
V_{IH}	Input High Voltage (all pins except X1)	2.0	V_{CC} +0.5	V	
V_{OL}	Output Low Voltage MFM		0.4	V	I_{OL} = 2.5 mA
	DRATE0–1		0.4	V	I_{OL} = 6.0 mA
	DB0–7, INT and DRQ		0.4	V	I_{OL} = 12 mA
	ME0–3, DS0–3, DIR, STP WRDATA, WE, HDSEL and DENSEL		0.4	V	I_{OL} = 40 mA
V_{OH}	Output High Voltage MFM	3.0		V	I_{OH} = −2.5 mA
	All Other Outputs	3.0		V	I_{OH} = −4.0 mA
	All Outputs	V_{CC} − 0.4		V	I_{OH} = −100 μA
	V_{CC} Supply Current (Total)				
I_{CC1}	1 Mbps Data Rate, V_{IL} = V_{SS}, V_{IH} = V_{CC}		45	mA	(Notes 1, 2)
I_{CC2}	1 Mbps Data Rate, V_{IL} = 0.45, V_{IH} = 2.4		50	mA	(Notes 1, 2)
I_{CC3}	500 Kbps Data Rate, V_{IL} = V_{SS}, V_{IH} = V_{CC}		35	mA	(Notes 1, 2)
I_{CC4}	500 Kbps Data Rate, V_{IL} = 0.45, V_{IH} = 2.4		40	mA	(Notes 1, 2)
I_{CCSB}	I_{CC} in Powerdown		60	μA	(Note 3)
I_{IL}	Input Load Current (all input pins)		10	μA	V_{IN} = V_{CC}
			−10	μA	V_{IN} = 0V
I_{OFL}	Data Bus Output Float Leakage		±10	μA	0.45 < V_{OUT} < V_{CC}

NOTES:
1. The data bus are the only inputs that may be floated.
2. Tested while reading a sync field of "00". Outputs not connected to D.C. Loads.
3. V_{IL} = V_{SS}, V_{IH} = V_{CC}; Outputs not connected to D.C. loads.

Capacitance

C_{IN}	Input Capacitance	10	pF	F = 1 MHz, T_A = 25°C
C_{IN1}	Clock Input Capacitance	20	pF	Sampled, not 100% Tested
$C_{I/O}$	Input/Output Capacitance	20	pF	

NOTE:
All pins except pins under test are tied to AC ground.

LOAD CIRCUIT

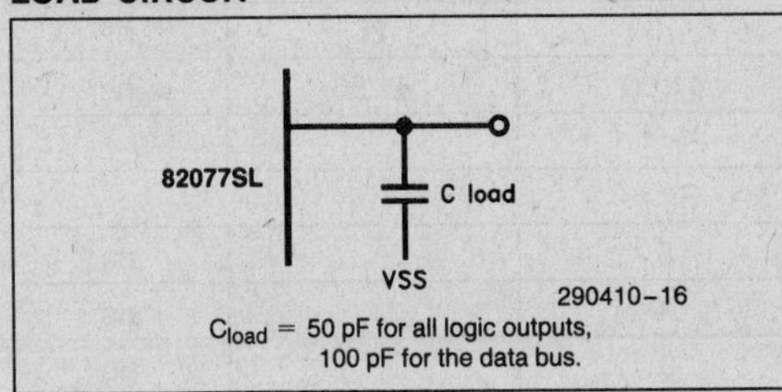

A. C. TESTING INPUT, OUTPUT WAVEFORM

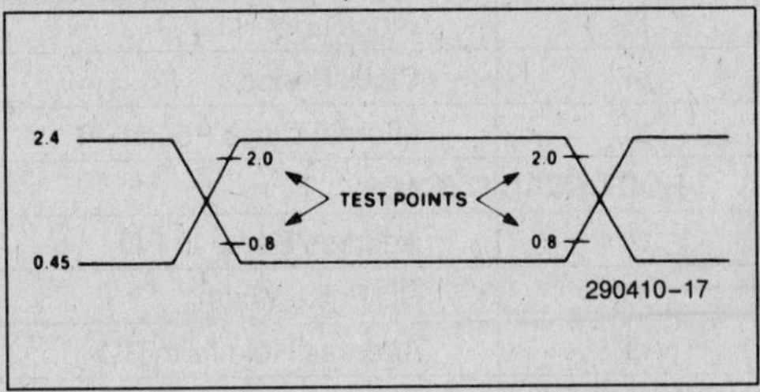

11.3 Oscillator

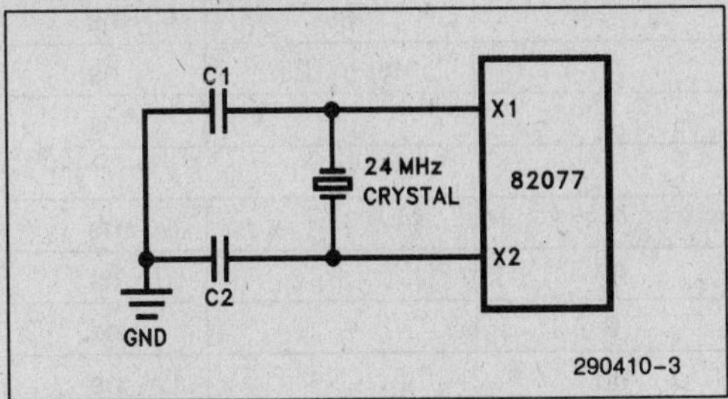

Figure 11-2. Crystal Oscillator Circuit

The 24 MHz clock can be supplied either by a crystal or a MOS level square wave. All internal timings are referenced to this clock or a scaled count which is data rate dependent.

The crystal oscillator must be allowed to run for 10 ms after VCC has reached 4.5V or exiting the POWERDOWN mode to guarantee that it is stable.

Crystal Specifications

Frequency:	24 MHz ±0.1%
Mode:	Parallel Resonant Fundamental Mode
Series Resistance:	Less than 40Ω
Shunt Capacitance:	Less than 5 pF

12.0 A.C. SPECIFICATIONS

T_A = 0°C to 70°C, V_{CC} = +5V ±10%, V_{SS} = AV_{SS} = 0V

Symbol	Parameter	Min	Max	Unit
CLOCK TIMINGS				
t1	Clock Rise Time		10	ns
	Clock Fall Time		10	ns
t2	Clock High Time(7)	16	26	ns
t3	Clock Low Time(7)	16	26	ns
t4	Clock Period	41.66	41.66	ns
t5	Internal Clock Period(3)			
HOST READ CYCLES				
t7	Address Setup to $\overline{RD}$	5		ns
t8	$\overline{RD}$ Pulse Width	90		ns
t9	Address Hold from RD	0		ns
t10	Data Valid from $\overline{RD}$(12)		80	ns
t11	Command Inactive	60		ns
t12	Output Float Delay		35	ns
t13	INT Delay from RD(16)		t5 + 125	ns
t14	Data Hold from $\overline{RD}$	5		ns
HOST WRITE CYCLES				
t15	Address Setup to $\overline{WR}$	5		ns
t16	$\overline{WR}$ Pulse Width	90		ns
t17	Address Hold from WR	0		ns
t18	Command Inactive	60		ns
t19	Data Setup to WR	70		ns
t20	Data Hold from WR	0		ns
t21	INT Delay from WR(16)		t5 + 125	ns
DMA CYCLES				
t22	DRQ Cycle Period(1)	6.5		μs
t23	DACK to DRQ Inactive		75	ns
t23a	DRQ to DACK Inactive	(Note 15)		ns
t24	RD to DRQ Inactive(4)		100	ns
t25	DACK Setup to $\overline{RD}$, $\overline{WR}$	5		ns
t26	DACK Hold from RD, WR	0		ns
t27	DRQ to $\overline{RD}$, $\overline{WR}$ Active(1)	0	6	μs
t28	Terminal Count Width(10)	50		ns
t29	TC to DRQ Inactive		150	ns
RESET				
t30	"Hardware" Reset Width(5)	170		t4
t30a	"Software" Reset Width(5)	(Note 11)		ns
t31	Reset to Control Inactive		2	μs

A.C. SPECIFICATIONS (Continued)

T_A = 0°C to 70°C, V_{CC} = +5V ±10%, V_{SS} = AV_{SS} = 0V

Symbol	Parameter	Min	Max	Unit
WRITE DATA TIMING				
t32	Write Data Width(6)			ns
DRIVE CONTROL				
t35	DIR Setup to STEP(14)	1.0		μs
t36	DIR Hold from STEP	10		μs
t37	STEP Active Time (High)	2.5		μs
t38	STEP Cycle Time(2)			μs
t39	INDEX Pulse Width	5		t5
t41	WE to HDSEL Change	(Note 13)		ms
READ DATA TIMING				
t40	Read Data Pulse Width	50		ns
f44	PLL Data Rate			
	82077SL-1		1M	bits/sec
	82077SL		1M	bits/sec
	82077SL-5		500K	bits/sec
t44	Data Rate Period = 1/f44			
tLOCK	Lockup Time		64	t44

NOTES:

1. This timing is for FIFO threshold = 1. When FIFO threshold is N bytes, the value should be multiplied by N and subtract 1.5 μs. The value shown is for 1 Mbps, scales linearly with data rate.
2. This value can range from 0.5 ms to 8.0 ms and is dependent upon data rate and the Specify command value.
3. Many timings are a function of the selected data rate. The nominal values for the internal clock period (t5) for the various data rates are:

1 Mbps	3 x oscillator period = 125 ns
500 Kbps	6 x oscillator period = 250 ns
300 Kbps	10 x oscillator period = 420 ns
250 Kbps	12 x oscillator period = 500 ns

4. If $\overline{DACK}$ transitions before $\overline{RD}$, then this specification is ignored. If there is no transition on $\overline{DACK}$, then this becomes the DRQ inactive delay.
5. Reset requires a stable oscillator to meet the minimum active period.
6. Based on the internal clock period (t5). For various data rates, the Write Data Width minimum values are:

1 Mbps	5 x oscillator period −50 ns = 150 ns
500 Kbps	10 x oscillator period −50 ns = 360 ns
300 Kbps	16 x oscillator period −50 ns = 615 ns
250 Kbps	19 x oscillator period −50 ns = 740 ns

7. Test points for clock high time are 3.5V. Due to transitional times, clock high time max and clock low time max cannot be met simultaneously. Clock high time min and clock low time max cannot be met simultaneously.
8. Based on internal clock period (t5).
9. Jitter tolerance is defined as: $\frac{\text{Maximum bit shift from nominal position}}{\text{1/4 period of nominal data rate}} \times 100\%$

It is a measure of the allowable bit jitter that may be present and still be correctly detected. The data separator jitter tolerance is measured under dynamic conditions that jitters the bit stream according to a reverse precompensation algorithm.

10. TC width is defined as the time that both TC and DACK are active.

A.C. SPECIFICATIONS (Continued)

NOTES: (Continued)

11. The minimum reset active period for a software reset is dependent on the data rate, after the 82077SL has been properly reset using the t30 spec. The minimum software reset period then becomes:

1 Mbps	3 x t4 =	125 ns
500 Kbps	6 x t4 =	250 ns
300 Kbps	10 x t4 =	420 ns
250 Kbps	12 x t4 =	500 ns

12. Status Register's status bits which are not latched may be updated during a Host read operation.
13. The minimum MFM values for WE to HDSEL change (t41) for the various data rates are:

1 Mbps	0.5 ms + [8 x GPL]
500 Kbps	1.0 ms + [16 x GPL]
300 Kbps	1.6 ms + [26.66 x GPL]
250 Kbps	2.0 ms + [32 x GPL]

GPL is the size of gap 3 defined in the sixth byte of a Write Command.

14. This timing is a function of the selected data rate as follows:

1 Mbps	1.0 μs Min
500 Kbps	2.0 μs Min
300 Kbps	3.3 μs Min
250 Kbps	4.0 μs Min

15. This timing is a function of the internal clock period (t5) and is given as (2/3) t5. The values of t5 are shown in Note 3.
16. The timings t13 and t21 are specified for INT signal in the polling mode only. These timings in case of the result phase of the read and write commands are microcode dependent.
17.

Part Specification	Supported Feature	
	Tape Drive Mode	Perpendicular Mode
82077SL-1	Yes	Yes
82077SL		Yes
82077SL-5		

CLOCK TIMINGS

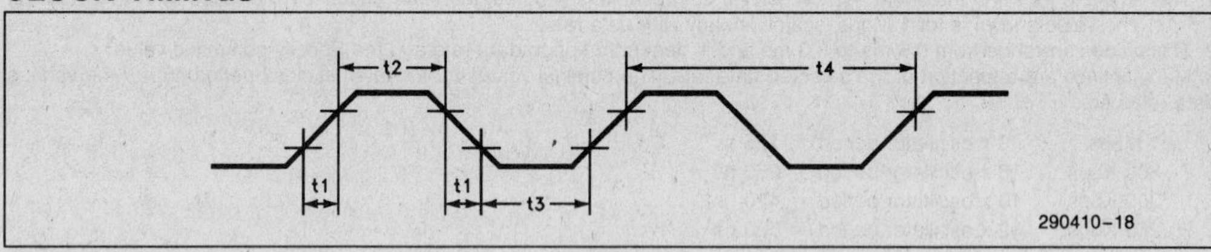

HOST READ CYCLES

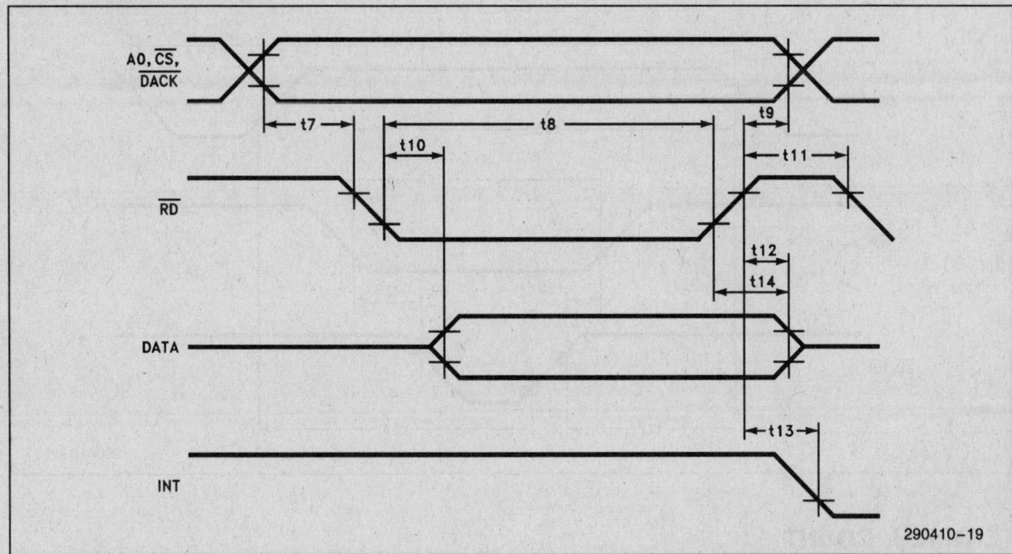

HOST WRITE CYCLES

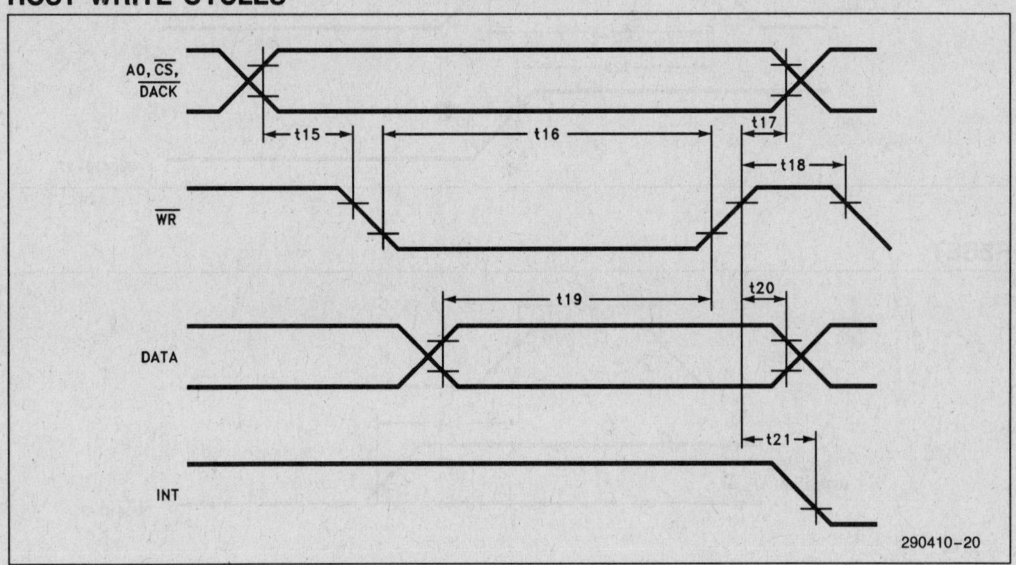

2

DMA CYCLES

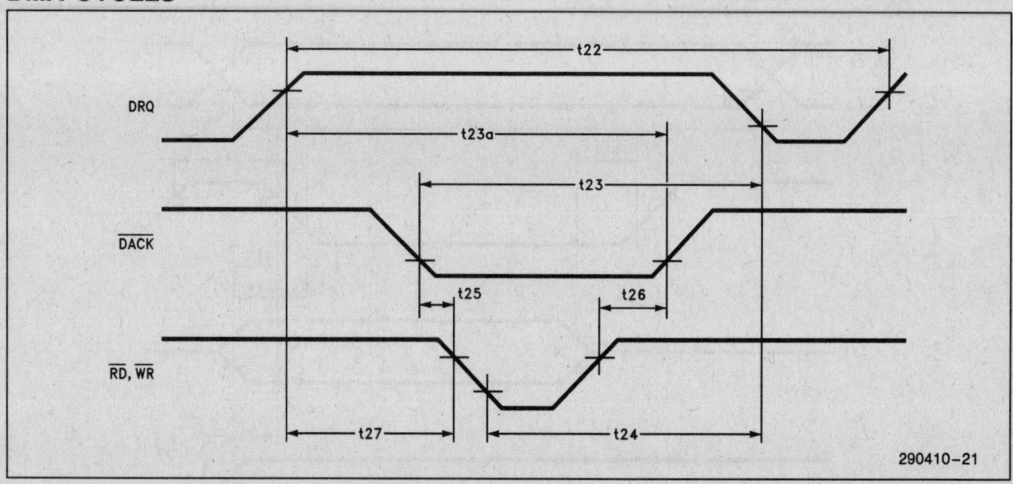

290410-21

TERMINAL COUNT

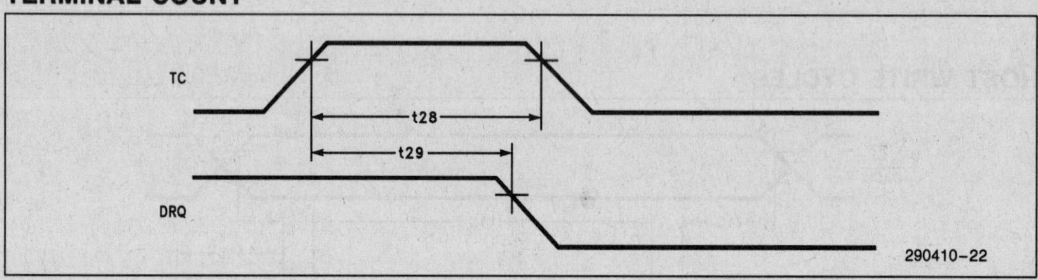

290410-22

RESET

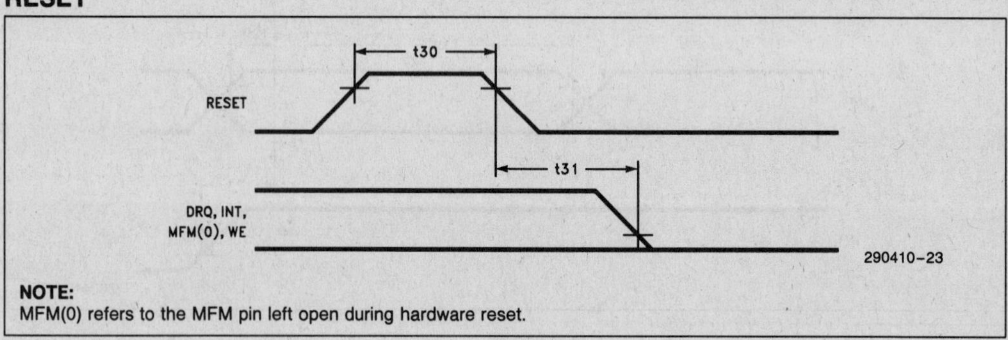

290410-23

NOTE:
MFM(0) refers to the MFM pin left open during hardware reset.

WRITE DATA TIMING

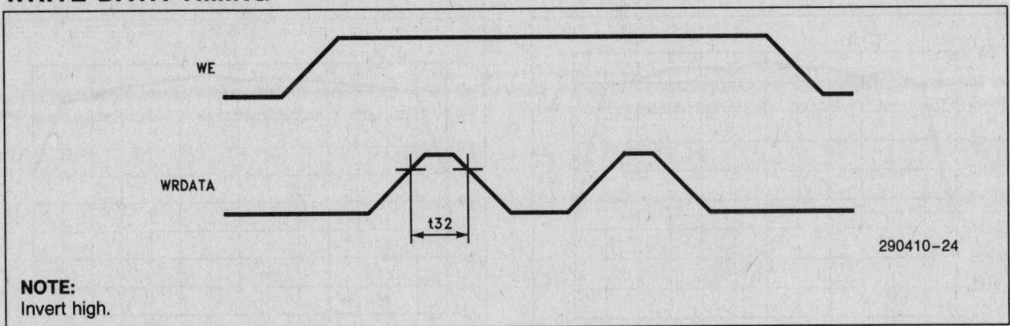

NOTE:
Invert high.

DRIVE CONTROL

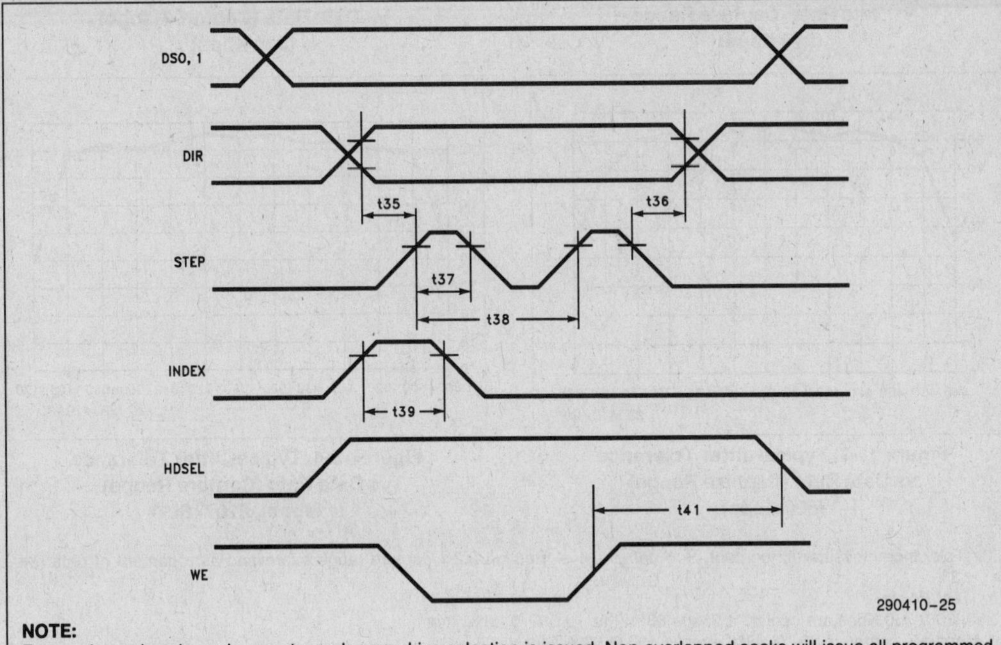

NOTE:
For overlapped seeks, only one step pulse per drive selection is issued. Non-overlapped seeks will issue all programmed step pulses. Invert high.

INTERNAL PLL

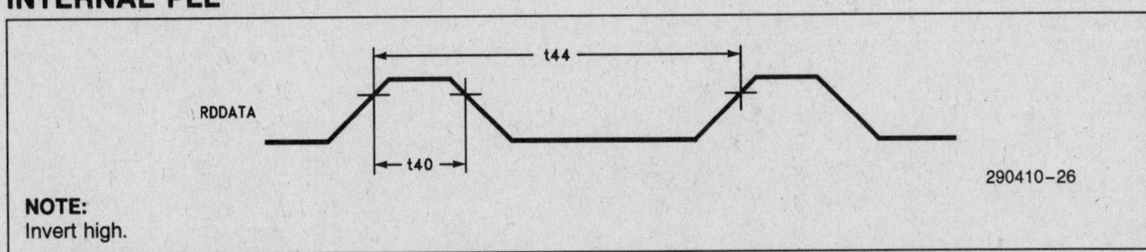

NOTE:
Invert high.

13.0 DATA SEPARATOR CHARACTERISTICS FOR FLOPPY DISK MODE

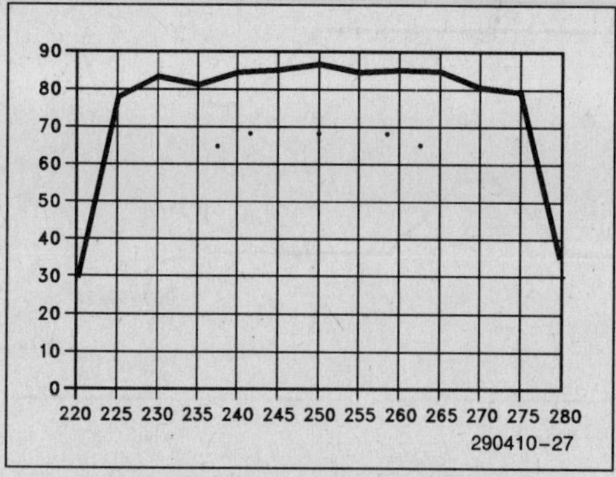

Figure 13-1. Typical Jitter Tolerance vs Data Rate (Capture Range) (250 Kbps)

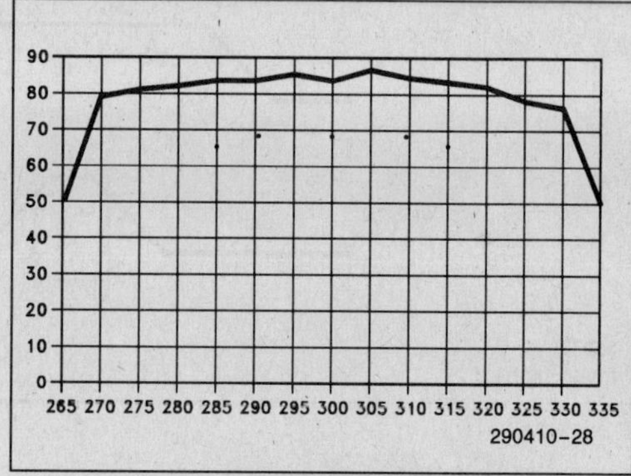

Figure 13-2. Typical Jitter Tolerance vs Data Rate (Capture Range) (300 Kbps)

Figure 13-3. Typical Jitter Tolerance vs Data Rate (Capture Range) (500 Kbps)

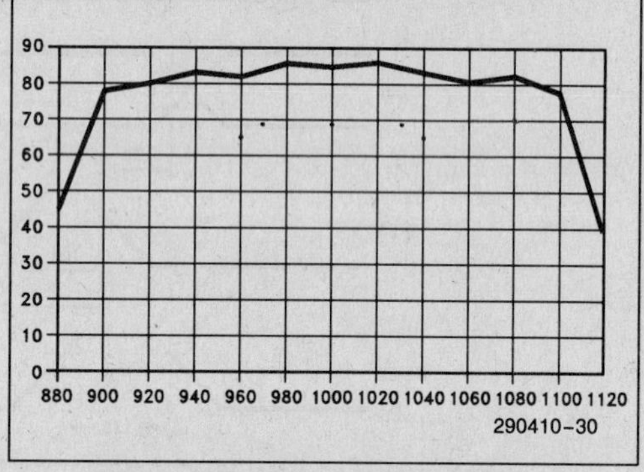

Figure 13-4. Typical Jitter Tolerance vs Data Rate (Capture Range) (1 Mbps), 82077SL-1

Jitter Tolerance measured in percent. See datasheet — Section 3.2.1 capture range expressed as a percent of data rate, i.e., ±3%.

• = Test Points:

250, 300, 500 Kbps are center, ±3% @ 68% jitter, ±5% @ 65% jitter

1 Mbps are center, ±3% @ 68% jitter, ±4% @ 63% jitter

Test points are tested at temperature and V_{CC} limits. Refer to the datasheet. Typical conditions are: room temperature, nominal V_{CC}.

14.0 DATA SEPARATOR CHARACTERISTICS FOR TAPE DRIVE MODE

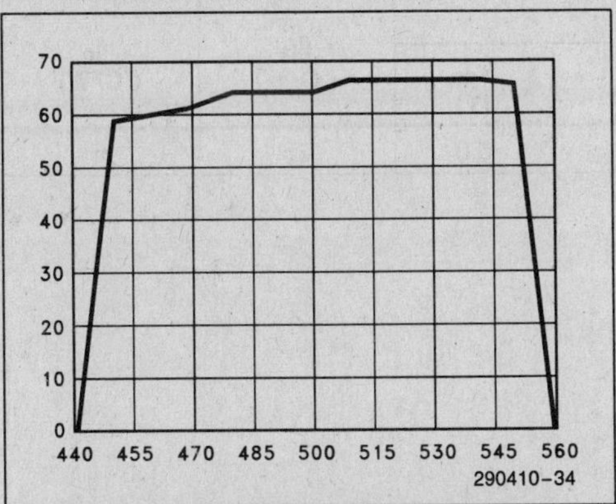

Figure 14-1. Typical Jitter Tolerance vs Data Rate (Capture Range) (±0% ISV, 500 Kbps)

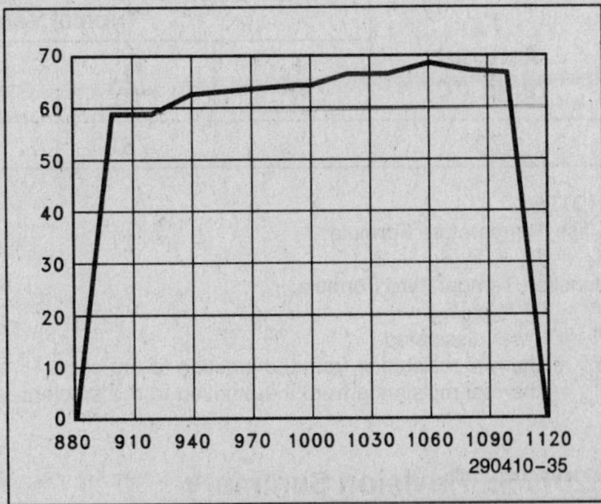

Figure 14-2. Typical Jitter Tolerance vs Data Rate (Capture Range) (±0% ISV, 1 Mbps)

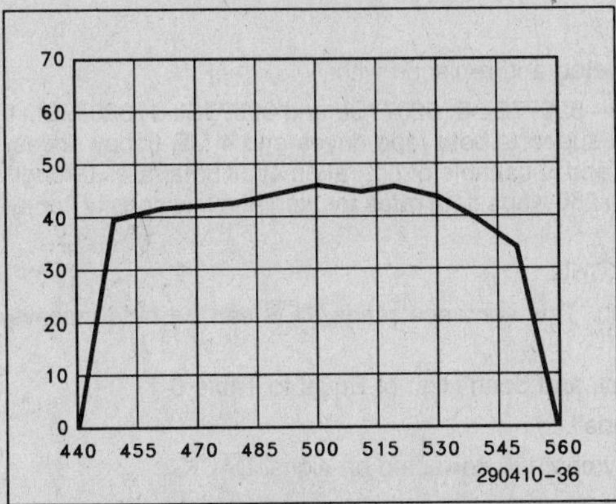

Figure 14-3. Typical Jitter Tolerance vs Data Rate (Capture Range) (±3% ISV, 500 Kbps)

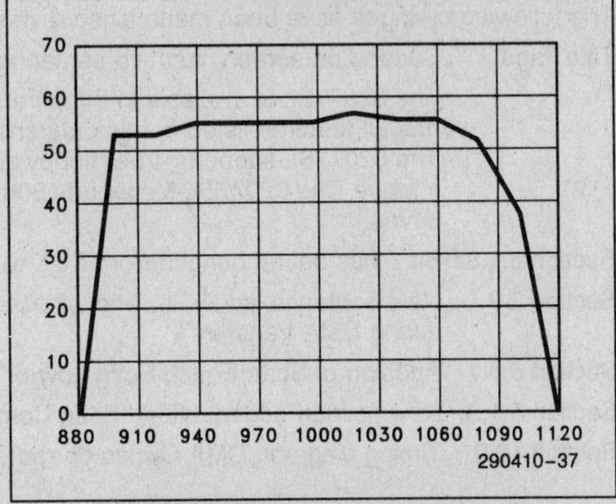

Figure 14-4. Typical Jitter Tolerance vs Data Rate (Capture Range) (±3% ISV, 1 Mbps)

NOTES:
1. Jitter Tolerance measured in percent. See datasheet — Section 3.2.1 capture range expressed as a percent of data rate, i.e., ±5%.
2. Typical conditions are: room temperature, nominal V_{CC}.

15.0 82077SL 68-LEAD PLCC PACKAGE THERMAL CHARACTERISTICS

T_A Ambient Temp. (°C)	Typical Values				θ_{ja} (°C/W)	θ_{jc} (°C/W)
	T_c (°C)	T_j (°C)	I_{cc} (mA)	V_{cc} (V)		
70	75	75	30	5.0	36	5

NOTES:
Case Temperature Formula:
$T_c = T_a + P [\theta_{ja} - \theta_{jc}]$
Junction Temperature Formula:
$T_j = T_c + p [\theta_{jc}]$
P = Power dissipated
θ_{jc} = thermal resistance from the junction to the case.
θ_{ja} = thermal resistance from the junction to the ambient.

82077SL Revision Summary

The following changes have been made since revision 003:

1. The 82077SL does not support the FM Mode.

The following changes have been made since revision 002:

Title Page	Second paragraph, last two sentences deleted and replaced with: The 82077SL is available in three versions—82077SL-5, 82077SL and 82077SL-1. 82077SL-1 has all features listed in this data sheet. It supports both tape drives and 4 MB floppy drives. The 82077SL supports 4 MB floppy drives and is capable of operation at all data rates through 1 Mbps. The 82077SL-5 supports 500/300/250 Kbps data rates for high and low density floppy drives.
Section 2.1.8a	Bit 7 has been changed from DSK to DSKCHG.
Section 2.3	New sentence added to end of paragraph. This sentence reads, "$\overline{\text{CS}}$ can be held inactive during DMA transfers".
Section 6.0	Addition of Scan Equal, Scan Low or Equal, and Scan High or Equal to Table 6-1.
Section 6.1.8	New section added, titled "Scan Commands".
Section 12.0	Timing diagram, DMA Cycles corrected. Symbol t26 corrected on signal $\overline{\text{DACK}}$.

82078 CHMOS SINGLE-CHIP FLOPPY DISK CONTROLLER

- Small Footprint and Low Height Packages
- Supports Standard 5.0V as Well as Low Voltage 3.3V Platforms
  - Selectable 3.3V and 5.0V Configuration
  - 5.0V Tolerant Drive Interface
- Enhanced Power Management
  - Application Software Transparency
  - Programmable Powerdown Command
  - Save and Restore Commands for 0V Powerdown
  - Auto Powerdown and Wakeup Modes
  - Two External Power Management Pins
  - Consumes No Power While in Powerdown
- Programmable Internal Oscillator
- Floppy Drive Support Features
  - Drive Specification Command
  - Media ID Capability Provides Media Recognition
  - Drive ID Capability Allows the User to Recognize the Type of Drive
  - Selectable Boot Drive
  - Standard IBM and ISO Format Features
  - Format with Write Command for High Performance in Mass Floppy Duplication
- Integrated Host/Disk Interface Drivers
- Integrated Analog Data Separator
  - 250 Kbits/sec
  - 300 Kbits/ sec
  - 500 Kbits/ sec
  - 1 Mbits/sec
  - 2 Mbits/sec
- Integrated Tape Drive Support
  - Standard 1 Mbps/500 Kbps/ 250 Kbps Tape Drives
  - New 2 Mbps Tape Drive Mode
- Perpendicular Recording Support for 4 MB Drives
- Fully Decoded Drive Select and Motor Signals
- Programmable Write Precompensation Delays
- Addresses 256 Tracks Directly, Supports Unlimited Tracks
- 16 Byte FIFO
- Single-Chip Floppy Disk Controller Solution for Portables and Desktops
  - 100% PC-AT* Compatible
  - 100% PS/2* Compatible
  - 100% PS/2 Model 30 Compatible
  - Fully Compatible with Intel's 386SL Microprocessor SuperSet
  - Integrated Drive and Data Bus Buffers
- Available in 64 Pin QFP and 44 Pin QFP Package
  (See Package Specification Order Number 240800, Package Type S)

2

The 82078 Product Family brings a set of enhanced floppy disk controllers. These include several features that allow for easy implementation in both the portable and desktop market. The current family includes a 64 pin and a 44 pin part in the smaller form factor QFP package. The 3.3V version of the 64 pin part provides an ideal solution for the rapidly emerging 3.3V platforms. It also allows for a 5.0V tolerant floppy drive interface that lets the users retain their normal 5.0V drives. Another version of the 64 pin part provides support for 2 Mbps data rate tape drives.

September 1993
Order Number: 290468-003

Table 1-0. 64 Pin Part Versions

	3.3V	5.0V	2 Mbps Data Rate
82078SL	X	X	
82078-1		X	X

The 44 pin is targeted for platforms that are operated at 3.3V or 5.0V and do not require more than two drive support. The 82078-5 is designed for price sensitive 5.0V designs which do not include 4 MB drive support.

Table 2-0. 44 Pin Part Versions

	3.3V	5.0V	1 Mbps Data Rate
82078		X	X
82078-5		X	
82078-3	X		X

Both parts can be operated at 1 Mbps/500 Kbps/300 Kbps/250 Kbps. Additionally, one version of the 64 pin part provides 2 Mbps data rate operation specific for the new tape drives.

The 82078 is fabricated with Intel's advanced CHMOS III technology.

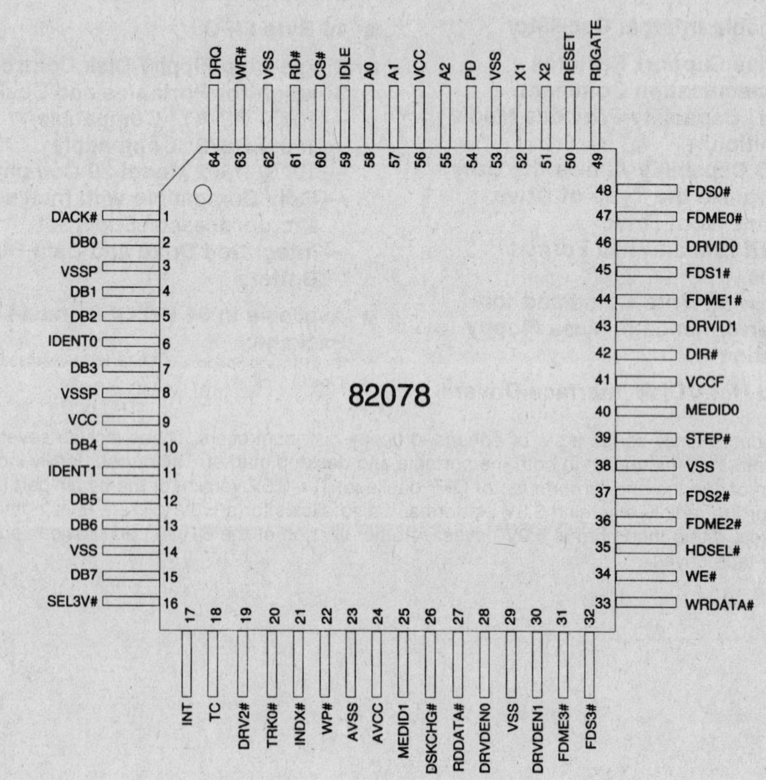

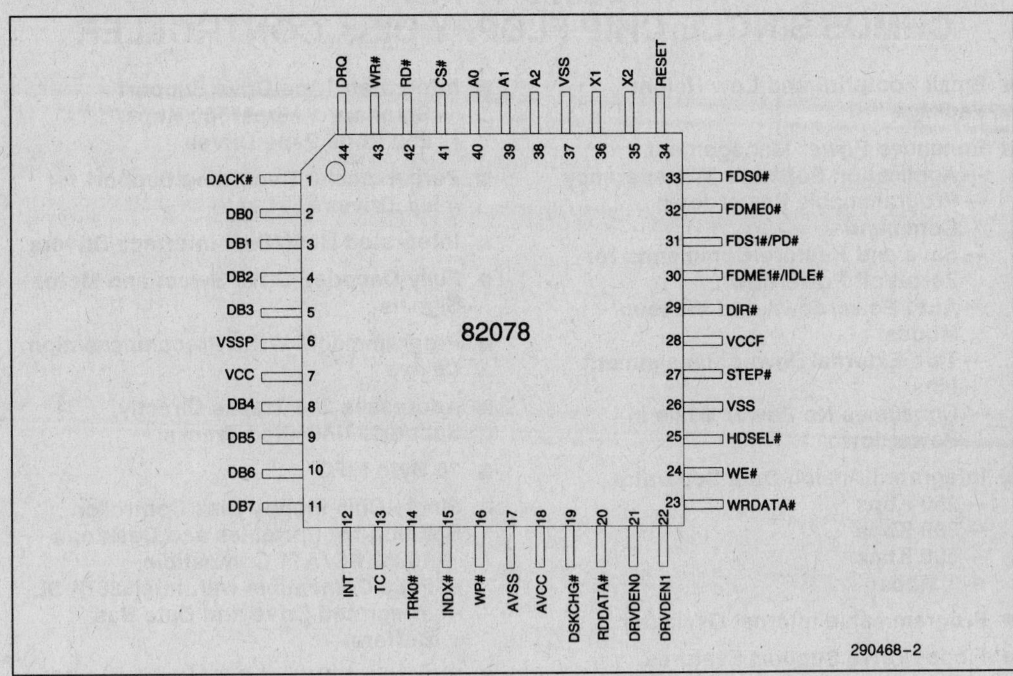
DRQ
WR#
RD#
CS#
A0
A1
A2
VSS
X1
X2
RESET
44 43 42 41 40 39 38 37 36 35 34
DACK# 1
DB0 2
DB1 3
DB2 4
DB3 5
VSSP 6
VCC 7
DB4 8
DB5 9
DB6 10
DB7 11
82078
33 FDS0#
32 FDME0#
31 FDS1#/PD#
30 FDME1#/IDLE#
29 DIR#
28 VCCF
27 STEP#
26 VSS
25 HDSEL#
24 WE#
23 WRDATA#
12 13 14 15 16 17 18 19 20 21 22
INT
TC
TRK0#
INDX#
WP#
AVSS
AVCC
DSKCHG#
RDDATA#
DRVDEN0
DRVDEN1

290468-2

82078 44 PIN CHMOS SINGLE-CHIP FLOPPY DISK CONTROLLER

- Small Footprint and Low Height Package
- Enhanced Power Management
  - Application Software Transparency
  - Programmable Powerdown Command
  - Save and Restore Commands for Zero-Volt Powerdown
  - Auto Powerdown and Wakeup Modes
  - Two External Power Management Pins
  - Consumes No Power While in Powerdown
- Integrated Analog Data Separator
  - 250 Kbps
  - 300 Kbps
  - 500 Kbps
  - 1 Mbps
- Programmable Internal Oscillator
- Floppy Drive Support Features
  - Drive Specification Command
  - Selectable Boot Drive
  - Standard IBM and ISO Format Features
  - Format with Write Command for High Performance in Mass Floppy Duplication
- Integrated Tape Drive Support
  - Standard 1 Mbps/500 Kbps/ 250 Kbps Tape Drives
- Perpendicular Recording Support for 4 MB Drives
- Integrated Host/Disk Interface Drivers
- Fully Decoded Drive Select and Motor Signals
- Programmable Write Precompensation Delays
- Addresses 256 Tracks Directly, Supports Unlimited Tracks
- 16 Byte FIFO
- Single-Chip Floppy Disk Controller Solution for Portables and Desktops
  - 100% PC/AT* Compatible
  - Fully Compatible with Intel386™ SL
  - Integrated Drive and Data Bus Buffers
- Separate 5.0V and 3.3V Versions of the 44 Pin part are Available
- Available in a 44 Pin QFP Package

The 82078, a 24 MHz crystal, a resistor package, and a device chip select implements a complete solution. All programmable options default to 82078 compatible values. The dual PLL data separator has better performance than most board level/discrete PLL implementations. The FIFO allows better system performance in multi-master (e.g., Microchannel, EISA).

The 82078 maintains complete software compatibility with the 82077SL/82077AA/8272A floppy disk controllers. It contains programmable power management features while integrating all of the logic required for floppy disk control. The power management features are transparent to any application software.

The 82078 is fabricated with Intel's advanced CHMOS III technology and is also available in a 64-lead QFP package.

October 1993
Order Number: 290474-003

82078 44 Pin CHMOS Single-Chip Floppy Disk Controller

CONTENTS PAGE

CONTENTS PAGE

2

CONTENTS PAGE

CONTENTS PAGE

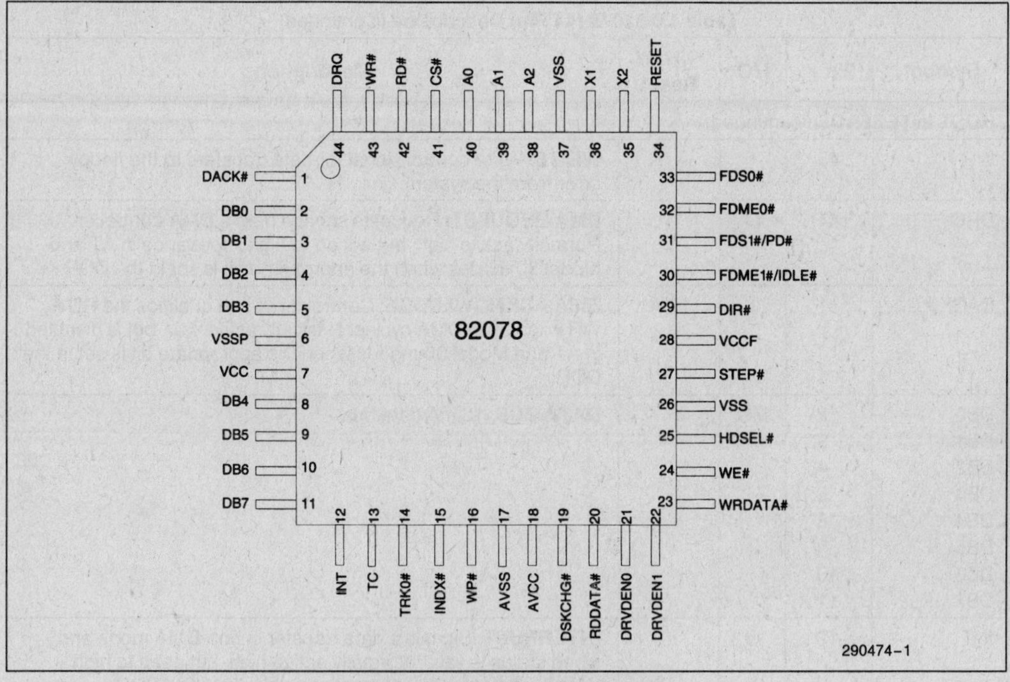

Figure 1-0. 82078 44 Pin Pinout

Table 1.0. 82078 (44 Pin) Description

Symbol	Pin #	I/O	@ H/W Reset	Description
HOST INTERFACE				
RESET	34	I	N/A	**RESET:** A high level places the 82078 in a known idle state. All registers are cleared except those set by the Specify command.
A0 A1 A2	40 39 38	I	N/A	**ADDRESS:** Selects one of the host interface registers: **A2 A1 A0 Access Register** 0 0 0 R Reserved 0 0 1 R/W Status Register B SRB 0 1 0 R/W Digital Output Register DOR 0 1 1 R/W Tape Drive Register TDR 1 0 0 R Main Status Register MSR 1 0 0 W Data Rate Select Register DSR 1 0 1 R/W Data Register (FIFO) FIFO 1 1 0 Reserved 1 1 1 R Digital Input Register DIR 1 1 1 W Configuration Control Register CCR
CS#	41	I	N/A	**CHIP SELECT:** Decodes the base address range and qualifies RD# and WR#.
RD#	42	I	N/A	**READ:** Read control signal for data transfers from the floppy drive to the system.

Table 1.0 82078 (44 Pin) Description (Continued)

Symbol	Pin #	I/O	@ H/W Reset	Description
HOST INTERFACE (Continued)				
WR#	43	I	N/A	**WRITE:** Write control signal for data transfers to the floppy drive from the system.
DRQ	44	O		**DMA REQUEST:** Requests service from a DMA controller. Normally active high, but will go to high impedance in AT and Model 30 modes when the appropriate bit is set in the DOR.
DACK#	1	I	N/A	**DMA ACKNOWLEDGE:** Control input that qualifies the RD#, WR# inputs in DMA cycles. Normally active low, but is disabled in AT and Model 30 modes when the appropriate bit is set in the DOR.
DB0 DB1 DB2 DB3 DB4 DB5 DB6 DB7	2 3 4 5 8 9 10 11	I/O		**DATA BUS:** 12 mA data bus.
INT	12	O		**INTERRUPT:** Signals a data transfer in non-DMA mode and when status is valid. Normally active high, but goes to high impedance when the appropriate bit is set in the DOR.
TC	13	I	N/A	**TERMINAL COUNT:** Control line from a DMA controller that terminates the current disk transfer. TC is effective only when qualified by DACK#. This input is active high.
X1 X2	36 35		N/A	**EXTERNAL CLOCK OR CRYSTAL:** Connection for a 24 MHz fundamental mode parallel resonant crystal. X1 can also be driven by an external clock (external oscillator) which can be either at 48 MHz or 24 MHz. If external oscillator is used then the PDOSC bit can be set to turn off the internal oscillator. Also, if a 48 MHz external oscillator is used then the CLK48 bit must be set in the enhanced CONFIGURE command.
PLL SECTION				
RDDATA#	20	I	N/A	**READ DATA:** Serial data from the floppy disk.
DISK CONTROL				
TRK0#	14	I	N/A	**TRACK0:** This is an active low signal that indicates that the head on track 0.
INDX#	15	I	N/A	**INDEX:** This is an active low signal that indicates the beginning of the track.
WP#	16	I	N/A	**WRITE PROTECT:** This is an active low signal that indicates whether the floppy disk in the drive is write protected.
DSKCHG#	19	I	N/A	**DISK CHANGE:** This is an input from the floppy drive reflected in the DIR.
DRVDEN0, DRVDEN1	21 22	O		**DRIVE DENSITY:** These signals are used by the floppy drive to configure the drive for the appropriate media.
WRDATA#	23	O		**WRITE DATA:** MFM serial data to the drive. Precompensation value is selectable through software.

Table 1.0 82078 (44 Pin) Description (Continued)

Symbol	Pin #	I/O	@ H/W Reset	Description
DISK CONTROL (Continued)				
WE#	24	O		**WRITE ENABLE:** Floppy drive control signal that enables the head to write onto the floppy disk.
STEP#	27	O		**STEP:** Supplies step pulses to the floppy drive to move the head between tracks.
DIR#	29	O		**DIRECTION:** It is an active low signal which controls the direction the head moves when a step signal is present. The head moves inwards towards the center if this signal is active.
HDSEL#	25	O		**HEAD SELECT:** Selects which side of the floppy disk is to be used for the corresponding data transfer. It is active low and an active level selects head 1, otherwise it defaults to head 0.
FDME0#	32	O		**FLOPPY DRIVE MOTOR ENABLE 0:** Decoded motor enable for drive 0. The motor enable pins are directly controlled via the DOR and are a function of the mapping based on BOOTSEL bits in the TDR.
FDME1#/IDLE#	30	O		**FLOPPY DRIVE MOTOR ENABLE** or **IDLE:** One of these is selected based on the level of the 44PDEN bit in the auto powerdown command. **FLOPPY DRIVE MOTOR ENABLE 1:** Decoded motor enable for drive 1. The motor enable pins are directly controlled via the DOR and are a function of the mapping based on BOOTSEL bits in the TDR. **IDLE:** This pin indicates that the part is in the IDLE state and can be powered down. IDLE state is defined as MSR = 80H, INT = 0, and the head being "unloaded" (as defined in the section describing powerdown). Whenever the part is in this state, IDLE pin is active low. If the part is powered down by the Auto Powerdown Mode, IDLE pin is set low. If the part is powered down by setting the DSR POWERDOWN bit, IDLE pin is set high.
FDS0#	33	O		**FLOPPY DRIVE SELECT 0:** Decoded floppy drive select for drive 0. These outputs are decoded from the select bits in the DOR and are a function of the mapping based on BOOTSEL bits in the TDR.
FDS1#/PD#	31	O		**FLOPPY DRIVE MOTOR ENABLE** or **PD:** One of these is selected based on the level of the 44PDEN bit in the auto powerdown command. **FLOPPY DRIVE SELECT 1:** Decoded floppy drive select for drive 1. These outputs are decoded from the select bits in the DOR and are a function of the mapping based on BOOTSEL bits in the TDR. **POWERDOWN:** This pin is active low whenever the part is in powerdown state, either via DSR POWERDOWN bit or via the Auto Powerdown Mode. This pin can be used to disable an external oscillator's output.

2

Table 1.0. 82078 (44 Pin) Description (Continued)

Symbol	Pin #	I/O	@ H/W Reset	Description
POWER AND GROUND SIGNALS				
V_{CC}	7		N/A	**Power Supply***
V_{SSP}	6		N/A	**GROUND:** 0V
V_{SS}	26 37		N/A	**GROUND:** 0V
AV_{CC}	18		N/A	**ANALOG VOLTAGE**
V_{CCF}	28		N/A	**VOLTAGE:** +5V for a 5V floppy drive, +3.3V for a 3.3V drive.
AV_{SS}	17		N/A	**ANALOG GROUND**

NOTE:
*The digital power supply V_{CC} and the analog power supply AV_{CC} should either be the same or regulated to be within 0.1V of either.

1.0 INTRODUCTION

The 82078 (44 pin) enhanced floppy disk controller incorporates several new features allowing for easy implementation in both the portable and desktop markets. It provides a low cost, small form factor solution targeted for 5.0V and 3.3V platforms that do not require more than two drive support.

The 82078 (44 pin) implements these new features while remaining functionally compatible with 82077SL/82077AA/8272A floppy disk controllers.

Together with a 24 MHz crystal, a resistor package and a device chip select, these devices allow for the most integrated solution available. The integrated analog PLL data separator has better performance than most board level discrete PLL implementations and can be operated at 1 Mbps/500 Kbps/ 300 Kbps/250 Kbps. A 16-byte FIFO substantially improves system performance especially in multi-master systems (e.g. Microchannel, EISA).

Figure 1-1 is a block diagram of the 82078.

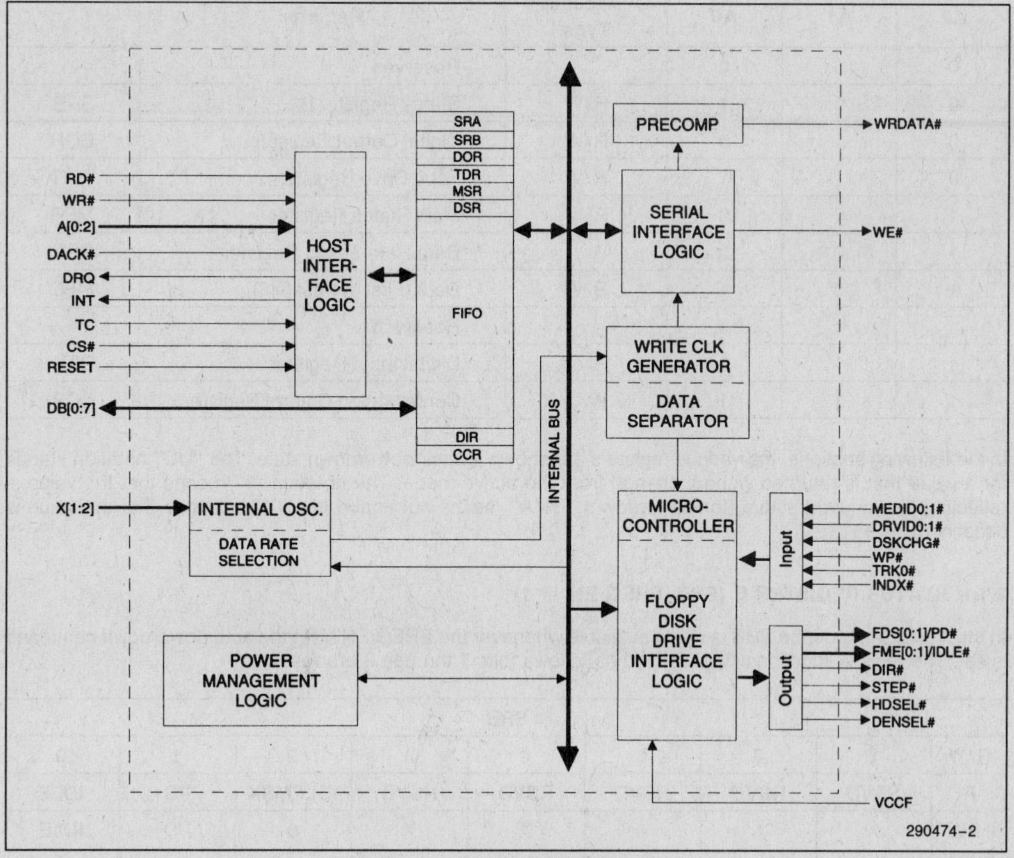

Figure 1-1. 82078 Block Diagram

2.0 MICROPROCESSOR INTERFACE

The interface consists of the standard asynchronous signals: RD#, WR#, CS#, A0–A2, INT, DMA control and a data bus. The address lines select between configuration registers, the FIFO and control/status registers.

2.1 Status, Data, and Control Registers

As shown below, the base address range is supplied via the CS# pin. For PC-AT or PS/2 designs, the primary and secondary address ranges are 3F0 Hex to 3F7 Hex and 370 Hex to 377 Hex respectively.

A2	A1	A0	Access Type	Register	
0	0	0		Reserved	
0	0	1	R/W	Status Register B	SRB
0	1	0	R/W	Digital Output Register	DOR
0	1	1	R/W	Tape Drive Register	TDR
1	0	0	R	Main Status Register	MSR
1	0	0	W	Data Rate Select Register	DSR
1	0	1	R/W	Data (First In First Out)	FIFO
1	1	0		Reserved	
1	1	1	R	Digital Input Register	DIR
1	1	1	W	Configuration Control Register	CCR

In the following sections, the various registers are shown in their powerdown state. The "UC" notation stands for a value that is returned without change from the active mode. The notation "*" means that the value is reflecting the required status (for powerdown). "N/A" means not applicable. "X" indicates that the value is undefined.

2.1.1 STATUS REGISTER B (SRB, EREG EN = 1)

In the AT/EISA mode the SRB is made available whenever the EREG EN bit in the auto powerdown command is set. The register functionality is defined as follows (bits 7 through 3 are reserved):

SRB								
R/W	**7**	**6**	**5**	**4**	**3**	**2**	**1**	**0**
R	**RSVD**	**RSVD**	**RSVD**	**RSVD**	**RSVD**	**IDLEMSK**	**PD**	**IDLE**
H/W Reset	X	X	X	X	X	0	PD	IDLE
Auto PD	X	X	X	X	X	UC	UC	UC
W	0	0	0	0	0	IDLEMSK	RSVD	RSVD
H/W Reset	N/A	N/A	N/A	N/A	N/A	0	N/A	N/A
Auto PD	N/A	N/A	N/A	N/A	N/A	UC	N/A	N/A

PD and IDLE reflect the inverted values on the corresponding pins when 44PD EN = 1 (these pins are muxed with FDS1 and FDME1). The signal on the IDLE# pin can be masked by setting IDLEMSK bit high in this register. The IDLE bit will remain unaffected. Since some systems will use the IDLE# pin to provide interrupt to the SMM power management, its disabling allows less external interrupt logic and reduction in board space. Only hardware reset will clear the IDLEMSK bit to zero. When the IDLEMSK bit is set, there is no way to distinguish between autopowerdown and DSR powerdown.

NOTE:
The 44 pin versions of the 82078 are designed to support *either* PD# and IDLE# or FDME1# and FDS1#, but not both simultaneously.

IDLEMSK	IDLE# (pin)
0	unmasked
1	masked

2.1.2 DIGITAL OUTPUT REGISTER (DOR)

The Digital Output Register contains the drive select and motor enable bits, a reset bit and a DMAGATE# bit.

Bits	7	6	5	4	3	2	1	0
Function	RSVD	RSVD	MOT EN1	MOT EN0	DMA GATE#	RESET#	RSVD	DRIVE SEL
H/W Reset State	0	0	0	0	0	0	0	0
Auto PD State	0	0	0*	0*	UC	1*	UC	UC

The MOT ENx bits directly control their respective motor enable pins (FDME0–1). The DRIVE SEL bit is decoded to provide four drive select lines and only one may be active at a time. Standard programming practice is to set both MOT ENx and DRIVE SELx bits at the same time.

NOTE:
The 44 pin versions of the 82078 are designed to support *either* PD# and IDLE# or FDME1# and FDS1#, but not both simultaneously.

Table 2-1 lists a set of DOR values to activate the drive select and motor enable for each drive.

Table 2-1. Drive Activation Value

Drive	DOR Value
0	1CH
1	2DH

The DMAGATE# bit is enabled only in PC-AT. If DMAGATE# is set low, the INT and DRQ outputs are tri-stated and the DACK# and TC inputs are disabled. DMAGATE# set high will enable INT, DRQ, TC, and DACK# to the system.

The DOR reset bit and the Motor Enable bits have to be inactive when the 82078 is in powerdown. The DMAGATE# and DRIVE SEL bits are unchanged. During powerdown, writing to the DOR does not awaken the 82078 with the exception of activating any of the motor enable bits. Setting the motor enable bits active (high) will wake up the part.

This RESET# bit clears the basic core of the 82078 and the FIFO circuits when the LOCK bit is set to "0" (see Section 5.3.2 for LOCK bit definitions). Once set, it remains set until the user clears this bit. This bit is set by a chip reset and the 82078 is held in a reset state until the user clears this bit. The RESET# bit has no effect upon the register.

2.1.3 ENHANCED TAPE DRIVE REGISTER (TDR)

TDR								
R/W	**7***	**6***	**5***	**4***	**3***	**2***	**1**	**0**
R	**RSVD**	**RSVD**	**RSVD**	**RSVD**	**RSVD**	**BOOTSEL**	**TAPESEL1**	**TAPESEL0**
H/W Reset	N/A	N/A	N/A	N/A	N/A	0	0	0
Auto PD	N/A	N/A	N/A	N/A	N/A	UC	UC	UC
W	0	0	0	0	0	BOOTSEL	TAPESEL1	TAPESEL0
H/W Reset	N/A	N/A	N/A	N/A	N/A	0	0	0
Auto PD	N/A	N/A	N/A	N/A	N/A	UC	UC	UC

NOTE:
*These bits are only available when EREG EN = 1, otherwise the bits are tri-stated.

This register allows the user to assign tape support to a particular drive during initialization. Any future references to that drive number automatically invokes tape support. Hardware reset clears this register; software resets have no effect. The tape select bits are hardware RESET to zeros, making Drive 0 **not** available for tape support. Drive 0 is reserved for the floppy boot drive.

The BOOTSEL bit in the 44 pin part is used to remap the drive selects and motor enables. The functionality is as described below:

44PD EN	BOOTSEL(TDR)	Mapping
0	0	Default → DS0 → FDS0, ME0 → FDME0 DS1 → FDS1, ME1 → FDME1
0	1	DS0 → FDS1, ME0 → FDME1 DS1 → FDS0, ME1 → FDME0
1	X	DS0 → FDS0, ME0 → FDME0 DS1 → PD, ME1 → IDLE

The 44PD EN bit in the Auto Powerdown command has precedence over the BOOTSEL bit mapping as shown above.

2.1.4 DATARATE SELECT REGISTER (DSR)

Bits	7	6	5	4	3	2	1	0
Function	S/W RESET	POWER DOWN	PDOSC	PRE-COMP2	PRE COMP1	PRE COMP0	DRATE SEL1	DRATE SEL0
H/W Reset State	0	0	0	0	0	0	1	0
Auto PD State	S/W RESET	POWER DOWN	PDOSC	PRE-COMP2	PRE-COMP1	PRE-COMP0	DRATE SEL1	DRATE SEL0

This register ensures backward compatibility with the 82072 floppy controller and is write-only. Changing the data rate changes the timings of the drive control signals. To ensure that drive timings are not violated when changing data rates, choose a drive timing such that the fastest data rate will not violate the timing.

The PDOSC bit is used to implement crystal oscillator power management. The internal oscillator in the 82078 can be programmed to be either powered on or off via PDOSC. This capability is independent of the chip's powerdown state. Auto powerdown mode and powerdown via the POWERDOWN bit have no effect over the power state of the oscillator.

In the default state the PDOSC bit is low and the oscillator is powered up. When this bit is programmed to a one, the oscillator is shut off. Hardware reset clears this bit to a zero. Neither of the software resets (via DOR or DSR) have any effect on this bit. Note, PDOSC should only be set high when the part is in the powerdown state, otherwise the part will not function correctly and must be hardware reset once the oscillator has turned back on and stabilized. Setting the PDOSC bit has no effect on the clock input to the 82078 (the X1 pin). The clock input is separately disabled when the part is powered down. The SAVE command checks the status of PDOSC, however the RESTORE command will not restore the bit high.

S/W RESET behaves the same as DOR RESET except that this reset is self cleaning.

POWERDOWN bit implements direct powerdown. Setting this bit high will put the 82078 into the powerdown state regardless of the state of the part. The part is internally reset and then put into powerdown. No status is saved and any operation in progress is aborted. A hardware or software reset will exit the 82078 from this powerdown state.

PRECOMP 0–2 adjusts the WRDATA output to the disk to compensate for magnetic media phenomena known as bit shifting. The data patterns that are susceptible to bit shifting are well understood and the 82078 compensates the data pattern as it is written to the disk. The amount of pre-compensation is dependent upon the drive and media but in most cases the default value is acceptable.

Table 2-2. Precompensation Delays

PRECOMP	Precompensation Delays
DSR[4,3,2]	x1 @ 24 MHz
111	0.00 ns – Disabled
001	41.67
010	83.34
011	125.00
100	166.67
101	208.33
110	250.00
000	DEFAULT

Table 2-3. Default Precompensation Delays

Data Rate	Precompensation Delays (ns)
1 Mbps	41.67
0.5 Mbps	125
0.3 Mbps	125
0.25 Mbps	125

The 82078 starts pre-compensating the data pattern starting on Track 0. The CONFIGURE command can change the track that pre-compensating starts on. Table 2-2 lists the pre-compensation values that can be selected and Table 2-3 lists the default pre-compensation values. The default value is selected if the three bits are zeroes.

DRATE 0–1 select one of the four data rates as listed in Table 2-4. The default value is 250 Kbps upon after a "Hardware" reset. Other "Software" Resets do not affect the DRATE or PRECOMP bits.

Table 2-4. Data Rates

DRATESEL0	DRATESEL1	DATA RATE
1	1	1 Mbps
0	0	500 Kbps
0	1	300 Kbps
1	0	250 Kbps

2.1.5 MAIN STATUS REGISTER (MSR)

Bits	7	6	5	4	3	2	1	0
Function	RQM	DIO	NON DMA	CMD BSY	RSVD	RSVD	DRV1 BUSY	DRV0 BUSY
H/W Reset State	0	X	X	X	X	X	X	X
Auto PD State	1	0	0	0	0	0	0	0

The Main Status Register is a read-only register and is used for controlling command input and result output for all commands.

RQM—Indicates that the host can transfer data if set to 1. No access is permitted if set to a 0.

DIO—Indicates the direction of a data transfer once RQM is set. A 1 indicates a read and a 0 indicates a write is required.

NON-DMA—This mode is selected in the SPECIFY command and will be set to a 1 during the execution phase of a command. This is for polled data transfers and helps differentiate between the data transfer phase and the reading of result bytes.

COMMAND BUSY—This bit is set to a one when a command is in progress. It goes active after the command byte has been accepted and goes inactive at the end of the results phase. If there is no result phase (SEEK, RECALIBRATE commands), the bit returns to a 0 after the last command byte.

DRV x BUSY—These bits are set to ones when a drive is in the seek portion of a command, including seeks and recalibrates.

Some example values of the MSR are:

- MSR = 80H; The controller is ready to receive a command.
- MSR = 90H; executing a command or waiting for the host to read status bytes (assume DMA mode).
- MSR = D0H; waiting for the host to write status bytes.

2.1.6 FIFO (DATA)

All command parameter information and disk data transfers go through the FIFO. The FIFO is 16 bytes in size and has programmable threshold values. Data transfers are governed by the RQM and DIO bits in the Main Status Register.

The FIFO defaults to an 8272A compatible mode after a "Hardware" reset (Reset via pin 32). "Software" Resets (Reset via DOR or DSR register) can also place the 82078 into 8272A compatible mode if the LOCK bit is set to "0" (See the definition of the LOCK bit), maintaining PC-AT hardware compatibility. The default values can be changed through the CONFIGURE command (enable full FIFO operation with threshold control). The advantage of the FIFO is that it allows the system a larger DMA latency without causing a disk error. Table 2-5 gives several examples of the delays with a FIFO. The data is based upon the following formula:

$$\text{Threshold\#} \times 1/\text{DATA RATE} \times 8 - 1.5\ \mu s = \text{DELAY}$$

Table 2-5. Delay Servicing Time

FIFO Threshold Examples	Maximum Delay to Servicing at 1 Mbps Data Rate*
1 byte	1 × 8 μs − 1.5 μs = 6.5 μs
2 bytes	2 × 8 μs − 1.5 μs = 14.5 μs
8 bytes	8 × 8 μs − 1.5 μs = 62.5 μs
15 bytes	15 × 8 μs − 1.5 μs = 118.5 μs

NOTE:
*Not available on the 82078-5.

FIFO Threshold Examples	Maximum Delay to Servicing at 500 Kbps Data Rate*
1 byte	1 × 16 μs − 1.5 μs = 14.5 μs
2 bytes	2 × 16 μs − 1.5 μs = 30.5 μs
8 bytes	8 × 16 μs − 1.5 μs = 126.5 μs
15 bytes	15 × 16 μs − 1.5 μs = 238.5 μs

At the start of a command, the FIFO action is always disabled and command parameters must be sent based upon the RQM and DIO bit settings. As the 82078 enters the command execution phase, it clears the FIFO of any data to ensure that invalid data is not transferred. An overrun or underrun will terminate the current command and the transfer of data. Disk writes will complete the current sector by generating a 00 pattern and valid CRC.

2.1.7 DIGITAL INPUT REGISTER (DIR)

Only bit 7 is driven, all other bits remain tri-stated.

Bits	7	6	5	4	3	2	1	0
Function	DSK CHG#	—	—	—	—	—	—	—
H/W Reset State	DSK CHG#	—	—	—	—	—	—	—
Auto PD State	0	—	—	—	—	—	—	—

NOTE:
(—) means these bits are tri-stated.

DSKCHG# monitors the pin of the same name and reflects the opposite value seen on the disk cable. The DSKCHG# bit is forced inactive along with all the inputs from the floppy disk drive. All the other bits remain tri-stated.

2.2 Reset

There are three sources of reset on the 82078; the RESET pin, a reset generated via a bit in the DOR and a reset generated via a bit in the DSR. All resets take the 82078 out of the powerdown state.

In entering the reset state, all operations are terminated and the 82078 enters an idle state. Activating reset while a disk write activity is in progress will corrupt the data and CRC.

On exiting the reset state, various internal registers are cleared, and the 82078 waits for a new command. Drive polling will start unless disabled by a new CONFIGURE command.

2.2.1 RESET PIN ("HARDWARE") RESET

The RESET pin is a global reset and clears all registers except those programmed by the SPECIFY command. The DOR Reset bit is enabled and must be cleared by the host to exit the reset state.

2.2.2 DOR RESET vs DSR RESET ("SOFTWARE" RESET)

These two resets are functionally the same. The DSR Reset is included to maintain 82072 compatibility. Both will reset the 8272 core which affects drive status information. The FIFO circuits will also be reset if the LOCK bit is a "0" (see definition of the LOCK bit). The DSR Reset clears itself automatically while the DOR Reset requires the host to manually clear it. DOR Reset has precedence over the DSR Reset. The DOR Reset is set automatically upon a pin RESET. The user must manually clear this reset bit in the DOR to exit the reset state.

The t30a specification in the A.C. Specifications gives the minimum amount of time that the DOR reset must be held active. This amount of time that the DOR reset must be held active is dependent upon the data rate. 82078 requires that the DOR reset bit must be held active for at least 0.5 μs at 250 Kbps. This is less than a typical ISA I/O cycle time.

2

2.3 DMA Transfers

DMA transfers are enabled with the SPECIFY command and are initiated by the 82078 by activating the DRQ pin during a data transfer command. The FIFO is enabled directly by asserting DACK# and addresses need not be valid (CS# can be held inactive during DMA transfers).

3.0 DRIVE INTERFACE

The 82078 has integrated all of the logic needed to interface to a floppy disk or a tape drive which use floppy interface. All drive outputs have 12 mA drive capability and all inputs use a receive buffer with hysteresis. The internal analog data separator requires no external components, yet allows for an extremely wide capture range with high levels of read-data jitter, and ISV. The designer needs only to run the 82078 disk drive signals to the disk or tape drive connector.

3.1 Cable Interface

Generally, 5.25" drive uses open collector drivers and 3.5" drives use totem-pole drivers. The output buffers on the 82078 do not change between open collector or totem-pole, they are always totem-pole.

DRVDEN0 and DRVDEN1 connect to pins 2 and 6 or 33 (on most disk drives) to select the data rate sent from the drive to the 82078. The polarity of DRVDEN0 and DRVDEN1 can be programmed through the Drive Specification command (see the command description for more information).

3.2 Host and FDD Interface Drivers

The chart below shows the drive capabilities of the 82078.

Drive Requirement	3.3V (I_{OL}/I_{OH})	5.0V (I_{OL}/I_{OH})
82078 Drivers	FDD = 6 mA/−2 mA SYS = 6 mA/−2 mA	FDD = 12 mA/−4 mA SYS = 12 mA/−4 mA

Today's floppy disk drives have reduced the output buffer's drive requirements on the floppy drive interface to 6 mA per drive at 5.0V. To support 2 drives, the drive output buffer drive capability needs to be 12 mA (at 5.0V). This is a reduction from 40 mA needed on the 82077SL. At 3.3V the 82078 halves the drive capability to 6 mA (3 mA per drive).

The slew rate control on the output buffers of the 82078 has been changed to reduce noise. The di/dt of the output drivers has been controlled such that the noise on the signal is minimized. The transition times are illustrated in the table below:

Signal Edge	Transition Time (ns)
t_{HL}	>5 ns
t_{LH}	>5 ns

NOTE:
*At 5.6V, 0°C, 50 pF load, 10% V_{CC} to 90% V_{CC}.

3.3 Data Separator

The function of the data separator is to lock onto the incoming serial read data. When lock is achieved the serial front end logic of the chip is provided with a clock which is synchronized to the read data. The synchronized clock, called Data Window, is used to internally sample the serial data. One state of Data Window is used to sample the data portion of the bit cell, and the alternate state samples the clock portion. Serial to parallel conversion logic separates the read data into clock and data bytes.

To support reliable disk reads the data separator must track fluctuations in the read data frequency. Frequency errors primarily arise from two sources: motor rotation speed variation and instantaneous speed variation (ISV). A second condition, and one that opposes the ability to track frequency shifts is the response to bit jitter.

The internal data separator consists of two analog phase lock loops (PLLs) as shown in Figure 3-1. The two PLLs are referred to as the reference PLL and the data PLL. The reference PLL (the master PLL) is used to bias the data PLL (the slave PLL). The reference PLL adjusts the data PLL's operating point as a function of process, junction temperature and supply voltage. Using this architecture it was possible to eliminate the need for external trim components.

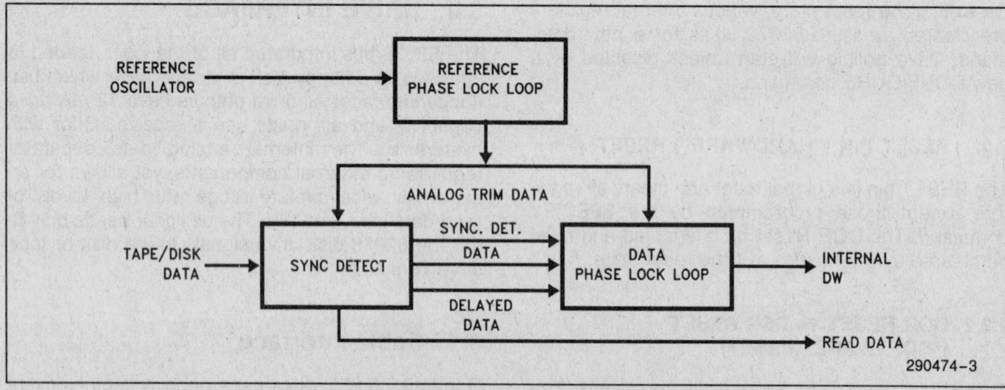

Figure 3-1. Data Separator Block Diagram

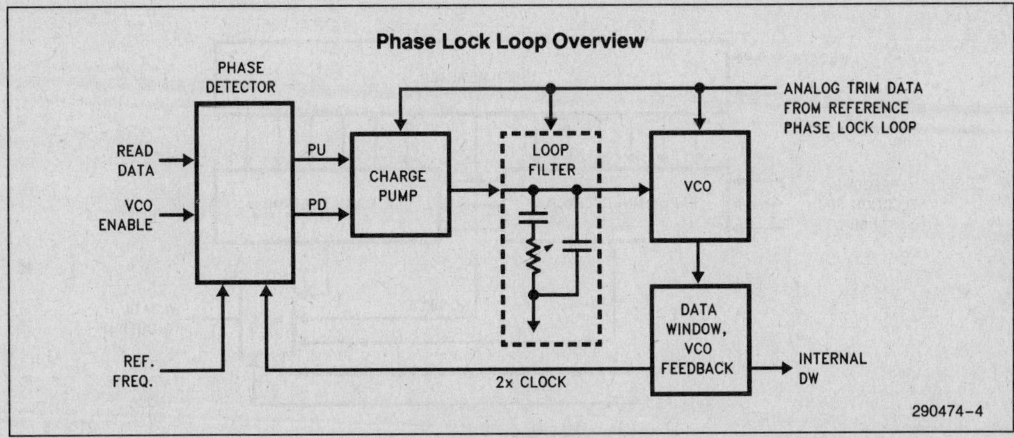

Figure 3-2. Data PLL

Figure 3-2 shows the data PLL. The reference PLL has control over the loop gain by its influence on the charge pump and the VCO. In addition, the reference PLL controls the loop filter time constant. As a result, the closed loop transfer function of the data PLL is controlled, and immune to the first order, to environmental factors and process variation.

Systems with analog PLLs are often very sensitive to noise. In the design of this data separator, many steps were taken to avoid noise sensitivity problems. The analog section of the chip has a separate V_{SS} pin (AV_{SS}) which should be connected externally to a noise free ground. This provides a clean basis for V_{SS} referenced signals. In addition, many analog circuit features were employed to make the overall system as insensitive to noise as possible.

3.3.1 JITTER TOLERANCE

The jitter immunity of the system is dominated by the data PLL's response to phase impulses. This is measured as a percentage of the theoretical data window by dividing the maximum readable bit shift by a ¼ bitcell distance. For instance, if the maximum allowable bit shift is 300 ns for a 500 Kbps data stream, the jitter tolerance is 60%.

3.3.2 LOCKTIME (t_{LOCK})

The lock, or settling time of the data PLL is designed to be 64-bit times (8 sync bytes). The value assumes that the sync field jitter is 5% the bit cell or less. This level of jitter is realistic for a constant bit pattern. Intersymbol interference should be equal, thus nearly eliminating random bit shifting.

3.3.3 CAPTURE RANGE

Capture Range is the maximum frequency range over which the data separator will acquire phase lock with the incoming RDDATA signal. In a floppy disk environment, this frequency variation is composed of two components: drive motor speed error and ISV. Frequency is a factor which may determine the maximum level of the ISV (Instantaneous Speed Variation) component. In general, as frequency increases the allowed magnitude of the ISV component will decrease. When determining the capture range requirements, the designer should take the maximum amount of frequency error for the disk drive and double it to account for media switching between drives.

3.4 Write Precompensation

The write precompensation logic is used to minimize bit shifts in the RDDATA stream from the disk drive. The shifting of bits is a known phenomena of magnetic media and is dependent upon the disk media AND the floppy drive.

The 82078 monitors the bit stream that is being sent to the drive. The data patterns that require precompensation are well known. Depending upon the pattern, the bit is shifted either early or late (or not at all) relative to the surrounding bits. Figure 3-3 is a block diagram of the internal circuit.

The top block is a 13-bit shift register with the no delay tap being in the center. This allows 6 levels of early and late shifting with respect to nominal. The shift register is clocked at the main clock rate (24 MHz). The output is fed into 2 multiplexors, one for early and one for late. A final stage of multiplexors combines the early, late and normal data stream back into one which is the WRDATA output.

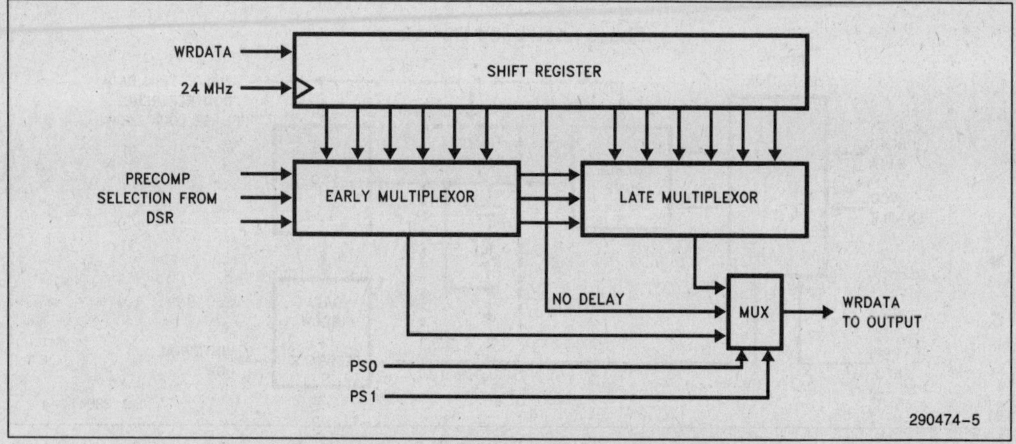

Figure 3-3. Precompensation Block Diagram

4.0 POWER MANAGEMENT FEATURES

The 82078 contains power management features that makes it ideal for design of portable personal computers. These features can be classified into power management of the part and that of the internal oscillator. The powerdown of the part is done independently of the internal oscillator in the 82078.

4.1 Power Management Scheme

The portable market share of the personal computing market has increased significantly. To improve power conservation on portable platforms, designs are migrating from 5.0V to 3.3V. Intel's 82078-3 allows designers to incorporate 3.3V floppy disk controller support in their systems.

The 82078 supports two powerdown modes, direct powerdown and automatic powerdown. Direct powerdown refers to direct action by the software to powerdown without dependence on external factors. Automatic powerdown results from 82078's monitoring of the current conditions according to a previously programmed mode. Any hardware reset disables the automatic POWERDOWN command, however software resets have no effect on the command. The 82078 also supports powerdown of its internal crystal oscillator independent of the powerdown modes described above. By setting bit 5 (PDOSC) in the DSR register, the internal oscillator is turned off. This bit has sole control of the oscillator powerdown, allowing the internal clock to be turned off when an external oscillator is used.

4.2 Oscillator Power Management

The 82078 supports a built-in crystal oscillator that can be programmed to be either powered down or active, independent of the power state of the chip. This capability is implemented by the PDOSC bit in the DSR. When PDOSC is set low, the internal oscillator is on. When PDOSC is set high, the internal oscillator is off. Note, a DSR powerdown does not turn off the oscillator.

When the external oscillator is used, power can be saved by turning off the internal oscillator. If the internal oscillator is used, the oscillator may be powered up (even when the rest of the chip is powered off) allowing the chip to wake up quickly and in a stable state. It is recommended to keep the internal oscillator on even when in the powerdown state. The main reason for this is that the recovery time of the oscillator during wake up may take tens of milliseconds under the worst case, which may create problems with any sensitive application software. In a typical application the internal oscillator should be on unless the system goes into a power saving or standby mode (such a mode request would be made by a system time out or by a user). In this case, the system software would take over and must turn on the oscillator sufficiently ahead of awakening the part.

In the case of the external oscillators, the power up characteristics are similar. If the external source remains active during the time the 82078 is powered down, then the recovery time effect is minimized. The PD# pin can be used to turn off the external source. While the PD# pin is active 82078 does not require a clock source. However, when the PD# pin is inactive, the clocking source, once it starts oscillating, must be completely stable to ensure that the 82078 operates properly.

4.3 Part Power Management

This section deals with the power management of the rest of the chip excluding the oscillator. This section explains powerdown modes and wake up modes.

4.3.1 DIRECT POWERDOWN

Direct powerdown is conducted via the POWERDOWN bit in the DSR register (bit 6). Programming this bit high will powerdown 82078. All status is lost if this type of powerdown mode is used. The part can exit powerdown from this mode via any hardware or software reset. This type of powerdown overrides the automatic powerdown. When the part is in automatic powerdown and the DSR powerdown is issued, the previous status of the part is lost and the 82078 resets to software default values.

4.3.2 AUTO POWERDOWN

Automatic powerdown is conducted via a "Powerdown Mode" command. There are four conditions required before the part will enter powerdown. All of these conditions must be true for the part to initiate the powerdown sequence. These conditions follow:

1. The motor enable pins FDME[0:1] must be inactive.
2. The part must be idle; this is indicated by MSR = 80H and INT = 0 (INT may be high even if MSR = 80H due to polling interrupt).
3. The Head Unload Timer (HUT, explained in the SPECIFY command) must have expired.
4. The auto powerdown timer must have timed out.

The command can be used to enable powerdown by setting the AUTO PD bit in the command to high. The command also provides a capability of programming a minimum power up time via the MIN DLY bit in the command. The minimum power up time refers to a minimum amount of time the part will remain powered up after being awakened or reset. An internal timer is initiated as soon as the auto powerdown command is enabled. The part is then powered down provided all the remaining conditions are met. Any software reset will reinitialize the timer. Changing of data rate extends the auto powerdown timer by up to 10 ms, but only if the data rate is changed during the countdown.

Disabling the auto powerdown mode cancels the timers and holds the 82078 out of auto powerdown.

The IDLE# pin can be masked via the IDLEMSK bit in Status Register B (EREG EN = 1).

4.3.3 WAKE UP MODES

This section describes the conditions for awakening the part from both direct and automatic powerdown. Power conservation or extension of battery life is the main reason power management is required. This means that the 82078 must be kept in powerdown state as long as possible and should be powered up as late as possible without compromising software transparency.

To keep the part in powerdown mode as late as possible implies that the part should wake up as fast as possible. However, some amount of time is required for the part to exit powerdown state and prepare the internal microcontroller to accept commands. Application software is very sensitive to such a delay and in order to maintain software transparency, the recovery time of the wake up process must be carefully controlled by the system software.

4.3.3.1 Wake Up from DSR Powerdown

If the 82078 enters the powerdown through the DSR powerdown bit, it must be reset to exit. Any form of software or hardware reset will serve, although DSR is recommended. No other register access will awaken the part, including writing to the DOR's motor enable (FDME[0:1]) bits.

If DSR powerdown is used when the part is in auto powerdown, the DSR powerdown will override the auto powerdown. However, when the part is awakened by a software reset, the auto powerdown command (including the minimum delay timer) will once again become effective as previously programmed. If the part is awakened via a hardware reset, the auto powerdown is disabled.

After reset, the part will go through a normal sequence. The drive status will be initialized. The FIFO mode will be set to default mode on a hardware reset or on a software reset if the LOCK command has not blocked it. Finally, after a delay, the polling interrupt will be issued.

4.3.3.2 Wake Up from Auto Powerdown

If the part enters the powerdown state through the auto powerdown mode, then the part can be awakened by reset or by appropriate access to certain registers.

If a hardware or software reset is used then the part will go through the normal reset sequence. If the access is through the selected registers, then the 82078 resumes operation as though it was never in powerdown. Besides activating the RESET pin or

one of the software reset bits in the DOR or DSR, the following register accesses will wake up the part:

1. Enabling any one of the motor enable bits in the DOR register (reading the DOR does not awaken the part)
2. A read from the MSR register
3. A read or write to the FIFO register

Any of these actions will wake up the part. Once awake, 82078 will reinitiate the auto powerdown timer for 10 ms or 0.5s (depending on the MIN DLY bit the auto powerdown command). The part will powerdown again when all the auto powerdown conditions are satisfied.

4.4 Register Behavior

The register descriptions and their values in the powerdown state are listed in the Microprocessor Interface section. Table 4-1 reiterates the configuration registers available. It also shows the type of access permitted. In order to maintain software transparency, access to all the registers must be maintained. As Table 4-1 shows, two sets of registers are distinguished based on whether their access results in the part remaining in powerdown state or exiting it.

Table 4-1. 82078 Register Behavior

Address	Available Registers	Access
Access to these registers DOES NOT wake up the part		
000	—	
001	SRB (EREG EN = 1)	R/W
010	DOR*	R/W
011	TDR	R/W
100	DSR*	W
110	—	—
111	DIR	R
111	CCR	W
Access to these registers wakes up the part		
100	MSR	R
101	FIFO	R/W

NOTE:
*Writing to the DOR or DSR does not wake up the part, however, writing any of the motor enable bits or doing a software reset (either via DOR or DSR reset bits) will wake up the part.

Access to all other registers is possible without awakening the part. These registers can be accessed during powerdown without changing the status of the part. A read from these registers will reflect the true status as shown in the register description in Section 2.1. A write to the part will result in the part retaining the data and subsequently reflecting it when the part awakens. Accessing the part during powerdown may cause an increase in the power consumption by the part. The part will revert back to its low power mode when the access has been completed. None of the extended registers effect the behavior of the powerdown mode.

4.5 Pin Behavior

The 82078 is specifically designed for the portable PC systems in which the power conservation is a primary concern. This makes the behavior of the pins during powerdown very important.

The pins of 82078 can be divided into two major categories; system interface and floppy disk drive interface. The floppy disk drive pins are disabled such that no power will be drawn through the 82078 as a result of any voltage applied to the pin within the 82078's power supply range. The floppy disk drive interface pins are configurable by the FDI TRI bit in the auto powerdown command. When the bit is set the output pins of the floppy disk drive retain their original state. All other pins are either disabled or unchanged as depicted in Table 4-4. Most of the system interface pins are left active to monitor system accesses that may wake up the part.

4.5.1 System Interface Pins

Table 4-2 gives the state of the system interface pins in the powerdown state. Pins unaffected by powerdown are labeled "UC". Input pins are "DISABLED" to prevent them from causing currents internal to the 82078 when they have indeterminate input values.

Table 4-2. System Interface Pins

System Pins	State In Power Down	System Pins	State In Power Down
Input Pins		Output Pins	
CS#	UC	DRQ	UC (Low)
RD#	UC	INT	UC (Low)
WR#	UC	PD#*	HIGH
A[0:2]	UC	IDLE#*	High (Auto PD) Low (DSR PD)
DB[0:7]	UC	DB[0:7]	UC
RESET	UC		
DACK#	Disabled		
TC	Disabled		
X[1:2]	Programmable		

NOTE:
*These pins are muxed with FDS1 and FDME1 and are only available when 44PD EN = 1.

Two pins which can be used to indicate the status of the part are IDLE# and PD#. Table 4-3 shows how these pins reflect the 82078 status. Note that these pins are only enabled when 44PD EN = 1.

Table 4-3. 82078 Status Pins

PD	IDLE	MSR	Part Status
1	1	80H	Auto Powerdown
1	0	RQM = 1; MSR[6:0] = X	DSR Powerdown
0	1	80H	Idle
0	0	—	Busy

The IDLE# pin indicates when the part is in idle state and can be powered down. It is a combination of MSR equaling 80H, the head being unloaded and the INT pin being low. As shown in the table, the IDLE# pin will be low when the part is in DSR powerdown state. The PD# pin is active whenever the part is in the powerdown state. It is active for either mode of powerdown. The PD# pin can be used to turn off an external oscillator of other floppy disk drive interface hardware.

4.5.2 FDD INTERFACE PINS

The FDD interface "input" pins during powerdown are disabled or unchanged as shown in Table 4-4. The floppy disk drive "output" pins are programmable by the FDI TRI bit in the auto powerdown command. Setting of the FDI TRI bit in the auto power down command results in the interface retaining its normal state. When this bit is low (default state) all output pins in the FDD interface to the floppy disk drive itself are tri-stated. Pins used for local logic control or part programming are unaffected. Table 4-4 depicts the state of the floppy disk interface pins in the powerdown state (FDI TRI is low).

Table 4-4. 82078 FDD Interface Pins

FDD Pins	State In Powerdown	FDD Pins	State In Powerdown
Input Pins		Output Pins (FDI TRI = 0)	
RDDATA#	Disabled	FDME[0:1]#	Tristated
WP#	Disabled	FDS[0:1]#	Tristated
TRK0#	Disabled	DIR#	Tristated
INDX#	Disabled	STEP#	Tristated
DSKCHG#	Disabled	WRDATA#	Tristated
		WE#	Tristated
		HDSEL#	Tristated
		DRVDEN[0:1]	Tristated

5.0 CONTROLLER PHASES

For simplicity, command handling in the 82078 can be divided into three phases: Command, Execution and Result. Each phase is described in the following sections.

When there is no command in progress, the 82078 can be in idle, drive polling or powerdown state.

5.1 Command Phase

After a reset, the 82078 enters the command phase and is ready to accept a command from the host. For each of the commands, a defined set of command code bytes and parameter bytes has to be written to the 82078 before the command phase is complete (Please refer to Section 6.0 for the command descriptions). These bytes of data must be transferred in the order prescribed.

Before writing to the 82078, the host must examine the RQM and DIO bits of the Main Status Register. RQM, DIO must be equal to "1" and "0" respectively before command bytes may be written. RQM is set false by the 82078 after each write cycle until the received byte is processed. The 82078 asserts RQM again to request each parameter byte of the command, unless an illegal command condition is detected. After the last parameter byte is received, RQM remains "0", and the 82078 automatically enters the next phase as defined by the command definition.

The FIFO is disabled during the command phase to retain compatibility with the 8272A, and to provide for the proper handling of the "Invalid Command" condition.

5.2 Execution Phase

All data transfers to or from the 82078 occur during the execution phase, which can proceed in DMA or non-DMA mode as indicated in the SPECIFY command.

Each data byte is transferred by an INT or DRQ depending on the DMA mode. The CONFIGURE command can enable the FIFO and set the FIFO threshold value.

The following paragraphs detail the operation of the FIFO flow control. In these descriptions, (threshold) is defined as the number of bytes available to the 82078 when service is requested from the host, and ranges from 1 to 16. The parameter FIFOTHR which the user programs is one less, and ranges from 0 to 15.

A low threshold value (i.e. 2) results in longer periods of time between service requests, but requires faster servicing of the request, for both read and write cases. The host reads (writes) from (to) the FIFO until empty (full), then the transfer request goes inactive. The host must be very responsive to the service request. This is the desired case for use with a "fast" system.

A high value of threshold (i.e. 12) is used with a "sluggish" system by affording a long latency period after a service request, but results in more frequent service requests.

5.2.1 NON-DMA MODE, TRANSFERS FROM THE FIFO TO THE HOST

The INT pin and RQM bits in the Main Status Register are activated when the FIFO contains 16 (or set threshold) bytes, or the last bytes of a full sector transfer have been placed in the FIFO. The INT pin can be used for interrupt driven systems and RQM can be used for polled sytems. The host must respond to the request by reading data from the FIFO. This process is repeated until the last byte is transferred out of the FIFO, then 82078 deactivates the INT pin and RQM bit.

5.2.2 NON-DMA MODE, TRANSFERS FROM THE HOST TO THE FIFO

The INT pin and RQM bit in the Main Status Register are activated upon entering the execution phase of data transfer commands. The host must respond to the request by writing data into the FIFO. The INT pin and RQM bit remain true until the FIFO becomes full. They are set true again when the FIFO has (threshold) bytes remaining in the FIFO. The INT pin will also be deactivated if TC and DACK# both go inactive. The 82078 enters the result phase after the last byte is taken by the 82078 from the FIFO (i.e. FIFO empty condition).

5.2.3 DMA MODE, TRANSFERS FROM THE FIFO TO THE HOST

The 82078 activates the DRQ pin when the FIFO contains 16 (or set threshold) bytes, or the last byte of a full sector transfer has been placed in the FIFO. The DMA controller must respond to the request by reading data from the FIFO. The 82078 will deactivate the DRQ pin when the FIFO becomes empty. DRQ goes inactive after DACK# goes active for the last byte of a data transfer (or on the active edge of RD#, on the last byte, if no edge is present on DACK#) Note that DACK# and TC must overlap for at least 50 ns for proper functionality.

5.2.4 DMA MODE, TRANSFERS FROM THE HOST TO THE FIFO

The 82078 activates the DRQ pin when entering the execution phase of the data transfer commands. The DMA controller must respond by activating the DACK# and WR# pins and placing data in the FIFO. DRQ remains active until the FIFO becomes full. DRQ is again set true when the FIFO has (threshold) bytes remaining in the FIFO. The 82078 will also deactivate the DRQ pin when TC becomes true (qualified by DACK# by overlapping by 50 ns), indicating that no more data is required. DRQ goes inactive after DACK# goes active for the last byte of a data transfer (or on the active edge of WR# of the last byte, if no edge is present on DACK#).

5.2.5 DATA TRANSFER TERMINATION

The 82078 supports terminal count explicitly through the TC pin and implicitly through the underrun/overrun and end-of-track (EOT) functions. For full sector transfers, the EOT parameter can define the last sector to be transferred in a single or multisector transfer. If the last sector to be transferred is a partial sector, the host can stop transferring the data in mid-sector, and the 82078 will continue to complete the sector as if a hardware TC was received. The only difference between these implicit functions and TC is that they return "abnormal termination" result status. Such status indications can be ignored if they were expected.

Note that when the host is sending data to the FIFO of the 82078, the internal sector count will be complete when 82078 reads the last byte from its side of the FIFO. There may be a delay in the removal of the transfer request signal of up to the time taken for the 82078 to read the last 16 bytes from the FIFO. The host must tolerate this delay.

5.3 Result Phase

The generation of INT determines the beginning of the result phase. For each of the commands, a defined set of result bytes has to be read from the 82078 before the result phase is complete. (Refer to Section 6.0 on command descriptions.) These bytes of data must be read out for another command to start.

RQM and DIO must both equal "1" before the result bytes may be read from the FIFO. After all the result bytes have been read, the RQM and DIO bits switch to "1" and "0" respectively, and the CB bit is cleared. This indicates that the 82078 is ready to accept the next command.

6.0 COMMAND SET/DESCRIPTIONS

Commands can be written whenever the 82078 is in the command phase. Each command has a unique set of needed parameters and status results. The 82078 checks to see that the first byte is a valid command and, if valid, proceeds with the command. If it was invalid, the next time the RQM bit in the MSR register is a "1" the DIO and CB bits will also be "1", indicating the FIFO must be read. A result byte of 80H will be read out of the FIFO, indicating an invalid command was issued. After reading the result byte from the FIFO the 82078 will return to the command phase. Table 6-1 is a summary of the Command set.

Table 6-1. 82078 Command Set

Phase	R/W	DATA BUS								Remarks
		D_7	D_6	D_5	D_4	D_3	D_2	D_1	D_0	
READ DATA										
Command	W	MT	MFM	SK	0	0	1	1	0	Command Codes
	W	0	0	0	0	0	HDS	DS1	DS0	
	W					C				Sector ID Information Prior to Command Execution
	W					H				
	W					R				
	W					N				
	W					EOT				
	W					GPL				
	W					DTL				
Execution										Data Transfer Between the FDD and System
Result	R					ST 0				Status Information After Command Execution
	R					ST 1				
	R					ST 2				
	R					C				
	R					H				Sector ID Information After Command Execution
	R					R				
	R					N				
READ DELETED DATA										
Command	W	MT	MFM	SK	0	1	1	0	0	Command Codes
	W	0	0	0	0	0	HDS	DS1	DS0	
	W					C				Sector ID Information Prior to Command Execution
	W					H				
	W					R				
	W					N				
	W					EOT				
	W					GPL				
	W					DTL				
Execution										Data Transfer Between the FDD and System
Result	R					ST 0				Status Information After Command Execution
	R					ST 1				
	R					ST 2				
	R					C				
	R					H				Sector ID Information After Command Execution
	R					R				
	R					N				
WRITE DATA										
Command	W	MT	MFM	0	0	0	1	0	1	Command Codes
	W	0	0	0	0	0	HDS	DS1	DS0	
	W					C				Sector ID Information Prior to Command Execution
	W					H				
	W					R				
	W					N				
	W					EOT				
	W					GPL				
	W					DTL				
Execution										Data Transfer Between the FDD and System
Result	R					ST 0				Status Information After Command Execution
	R					ST 1				
	R					ST 2				
	R					C				
	R					H				Sector ID Information After Command Execution
	R					R				
	R					N				

Table 6-1. 82078 Command Set (Continued)

Phase	R/W	DATA BUS								Remarks
		D_7	D_6	D_5	D_4	D_3	D_2	D_1	D_0	
					WRITE DELETED DATA					
Command	W	MT	MFM	0	0	1	0	0	1	Command Codes
	W	0	0	0	0	0	HDS	DS1	DS0	
	W				C					Sector ID Information Prior to Command Execution
	W				H					
	W				R					
	W				N					
	W				EOT					
	W				GPL					
	W				DTL					
Execution										Data Transfer Between the FDD and System
Result	R				ST 0					Status Information After Command Execution
	R				ST 1					
	R				ST 2					
	R				C					Sector ID Information After Command Execution
	R				H					
	R				R					
	R				N					
					READ TRACK					
Command	W	0	MFM	0	0	0	0	1	0	Command Codes
	W	0	0	0	0	0	HDS	DS1	DS0	
	W				C					Sector ID Information Prior to Command Execution
	W				H					
	W				R					
	W				N					
	W				EOT					
	W				GPL					
	W				DTL					
Execution										Data Transfer Between the FDD and System. FDC Reads All Sectors from Index Hole to EOT
Result	R				ST 0					Status Information After Command Execution
	R				ST 1					
	R				ST 2					
	R				C					Sector ID Information After Command Execution
	R				H					
	R				R					
	R				N					
					VERIFY					
Command	W	MT	MFM	SK	1	0	1	1	0	Command Codes
	W	EC	0	0	0	0	HDS	DS1	DS0	
	W				C					Sector ID Information Prior to Command Execution
	W				H					
	W				R					
	W				N					
	W				EOT					
	W				GPL					
	W				DTL/SC					
Execution										No Data Transfer Takes Place
Result	R				ST 0					Status Information After Command Execution
	R				ST 1					
	R				ST 2					
	R				C					Sector ID Information After Command Execution
	R				H					
	R				R					
	R				N					
					VERSION					
Command	W	0	0	0	1	0	0	0	0	Command Code
Result	R	1	0	0	1	0	0	0	0	Enhanced Controller

Table 6-1. 82078 Command Set (Continued)

Phase	R/W	DATA BUS D_7	D_6	D_5	D_4	D_3	D_2	D_1	D_0	Remarks
FORMAT TRACK										
Command	W	0	MFM	0	0	1	1	0	1	Command Codes
	W	0	0	0	0	0	HDS	DS1	DS0	
	W				N					Bytes/Sector
	W				SC					Sectors/Cylinder
	W				GPL					Gap3
	W				D					Filler Byte
Execution For Each Sector Repeat:	W				C					Input Sector Parameters
	W				H					
	W				R					
	W				N					
										82078 Formats an Entire Cylinder
Result	R				ST 0					Status Information After Command Execution
	R				ST 1					
	R				ST 2					
	R				Undefined					
	R				Undefined					
	R				Undefined					
	R				Undefined					
SCAN EQUAL										
Command	W	MT	MFM	SK	1	0	0	0	0	Command Codes
	W	0	0	0	0	0	HDS	DS1	DS0	
	W				C					Sector ID Information Prior to Command Execution
	W				H					
	W				R					
	W				N					
	W				EOT					
	W				GPL					
	W				STP					
Execution										Data Compared Between the FDO and Main-System
Result	R				ST 0					Status Information After Command Execution
	R				ST 1					
	R				ST 2					
	R				C					Sector ID Information After Command Execution
	R				H					
	R				R					
	R				N					

Table 6-1. 82078 Command Set (Continued)

Phase	R/W	DATA BUS								Remarks
		D_7	D_6	D_5	D_4	D_3	D_2	D_1	D_0	
SCAN LOW OR EQUAL										
Command	W	MT	MFM	SK	1	1	0	0	1	Command Codes
	W	0	0	0	0	0	HDS	DS1	DS0	
	W				C					Sector ID Information Prior to Command Execution
	W				H					
	W				R					
	W				N					
	W				EOT					
	W				GPL					
	W				STP					
Execution										Data Compared Between the FDO and Main-System
Result	R				ST 0					Status Information After Command Execution
	R				ST 1					
	R				ST 2					
	R				C					Sector ID Information After Command Execution
	R				H					
	R				R					
	R				N					
SCAN HIGH OR EQUAL										
Command	W	MT	MFM	SK	1	1	1	0	1	Command Codes
	W	0	0	0	0	0	HDS	DS1	DS0	
	W				C					Sector ID Information Prior to Command Execution
	W				H					
	W				R					
	W				N					
	W				EOT					
	W				GPL					
	W				STP					
Execution										Data Compared Between the FDO and Main-System
Result	R				ST 0					Status Information After Command Execution
	R				ST 1					
	R				ST 2					
	R				C					Sector ID Information After Command Execution
	R				H					
	R				R					
	R				N					

Table 6-1. 82078 Command Set (Continued)

Phase	R/W	DATA BUS								Remarks
		D_7	D_6	D_5	D_4	D_3	D_2	D_1	D_0	
RECALIBRATE										
Command	W	0	0	0	0	0	1	1	1	Command Codes
	W	0	0	0	0	0	0	DS0	DS1	Enhanced Controller
Execution										Head Retracted to Track 0 Interrupt
SENSE INTERRUPT STATUS										
Command	W	0	0	0	0	1	0	0	0	Command Codes
Result	R	ST 0								Status Information at the End of Each Seek Operation
	R	PCN								
SPECIFY										
Command	W	0	0	0	0	0	0	1	1	Command Codes
	W	SRT				HUT				
	W	HLT							ND	
SENSE DRIVE STATUS										
Command	W	0	0	0	0	0	1	0	0	Command Codes
	W	0	0	0	0	0	HDS	DS1	DS0	
Result	R	ST 3								Status Information About FDD
DRIVE SPECIFICATION COMMAND										
Command Phase	W	1	0	0	0	1	1	1	0	Command Codes
	W	0	FD1	FD0	PTS	DRT1	DRT0	DT1	DT0	
	:	:	:	:	:	:	:	:	:	0–46 Bytes Issued
	W	DN	NRP	0	0	0	0	0	0	
Result Phase	R	0	0	0	PTS	DRT1	DRT0	DT1	DT0	Drive 0
	R	0	0	0	PTS	DRT1	DRT0	DT1	DT0	Drive 1
	R	0	0	0	0	0	0	0	0	RSVD
	R	0	0	0	0	0	0	0	0	RSVD
SEEK										
Command	W	0	0	0	0	1	1	1	1	Command Codes
	W	0	0	0	0	0	HDS	DS1	DS0	
	W	NCN								
Execution										Head is Positioned Over Proper Cylinder on Diskette
CONFIGURE										
Command	W	0	0	0	1	0	0	1	1	Command Code
	W	0	0	0	0	0	0	0	0	
	W	0	EIS	EFIFO	POLL	FIFOTHR				
	W	PRETRK								
RELATIVE SEEK										
Command	W	1	DIR	0	0	1	1	1	1	
	W	0	0	0	0	0	HDS	DS1	DS0	
	W	RCN								

Table 6-1. 82078 Command Set (Continued)

Phase	R/W	D7	D6	D5	D4	D3	D2	D1	D0	Remarks
		DUMPREG								
Command	W	0	0	0	0	1	1	1	0	*Note
Execution										Registers Placed in FIFO
Result	R	PCN-Drive 0								
	R	PCN-Drive 1								
	R	RSVD								
	R	RSVD								
	R	SRT				HUT				
	R	HLT							ND	
	R	SC/EOT								
	R	LOCK	0	0	0	D_1	D_0	GAP	WGATE	
	R	0	EIS	EFIFO	POLL	FIFOTHR				
	R	PRETRK								
		READ ID								
Command	W	0	MFM	0	0	1	0	1	0	Commands
	W	0	0	0	0	0	HDS	DS1	DS0	
Execution										The First Correct ID Information on the Cylinder is Stored in Data Register
Result	R	ST 0								Status Information After Command Execution
	R	ST 1								
	R	ST 2								
	R	C								Disk Status After the Command has Completed
	R	H								
	R	R								
	R	N								
		PERPENDICULAR MODE								
Command	W	0	0	0	1	0	0	1	0	Command Codes
	W	OW	0	0	0	D_1	D0	GAP	WGATE	
		LOCK								
Command	W	LOCK	0	0	1	0	1	0	0	Command Codes
Result	R	0	0	0	LOCK	0	0	0	0	
		PART ID								
Command	W	0	0	0	1	1	0	0	0	Command Code
Result	R	0	1	0	—STEPPING—				1	Part ID Number
		POWERDOWN MODE								
Command	W	0	0	0	1	0	1	1	1	Command Code
	W	0	0	EREG EN	44PD EN	0 0	FDI TRI	MIN DLY	AUTO PD	
Result	R	0	0	EREG EN	44PD EN	0	FDI TRI	MIN DLY	AUTO PD	
		OPTION								
Command	W	0	0	1	1	0	0	1	1	Command Code
	W	——RSVD——							ISO	

Table 6-1. 82078 Command Set (Continued)

Phase	R/W	DATA BUS								Remarks
		D_7	D_6	D_5	D_4	D_3	D_2	D_1	D_0	
SAVE										
Command Phase	W	0	0	1	0	1	1	1	0	Command Code
Result Phase	R	RSVD	SEL 3V#*	PD OSC	PC2	PC1	PC0	DRATE1	DRATE0	Save Info to Reprogram the FDC
	R	0	0	0	0	0	0	0	ISO	
	R	PCN-Drive 0								
	R	PCN-Drive 1								
	R	RSVD								
	R	RSVD								
	R	SRT				HUT				
	R	HLT							ND	
	R	SC/EOT								
	R	LOCK	0	0	0	D_1	D_0	GAP	WGATE	
	R	0	EIS	EFIFO	POLL	FIFOTHR				
	R	PRETRK								
	R	0	0	EREG EN	44PD EN	RSVD	FDI TRI	MIN DLY	AUTO PD	
	R	DISK/STATUS								
	R	RSVD								
RESTORE										
Command Phase	W	0	1	0	0	1	1	1	0	Command Code
	W	0	SEL 3V#*	0	PC2	PC1	PC0	DRATE1	DRATE0	Restore Original
	W	0	0	0	0	0	0	0	ISO	Register Status
	W	PCN-Drive 0								
	W	PCN-Drive 1								
	W	RSVD								
	W	RSVD								
	W	SRT				HUT				
	W	HLT							ND	
	W	SC/EOT								
	W	LOCK	0	0	0	D_1	D_0	GAP	WGATE	
	W	0	EIS	EFIFO	POLL	FIFOTHR				
	W	PRETRK								
	W	0	0	EREG EN	44PD EN	RSVD	FDI TRI	MIN DLY	AUTO PD	
	W	DISK/STATUS								
	W	RSVD								
	W	RSVD								

NOTE:
*For the 82078, 82078-5, SEL3V# = 1. For the 82078-3, SEL3V# = 0.

Table 6-1. 82078 Command Set (Continued)

Phase	R/W	DATA BUS								Remarks
		D_7	D_6	D_5	D_4	D_3	D_2	D_1	D_0	
FORMAT AND WRITE										
Command	W	1	MFM	1	0	1	1	0	1	Command Code
	W	0	0	0	0	0	HDS	DS1	DS0	
	W	N								
	W	SC								
	W	GPL								
	W	D								
Execution Repeated for each Sector	W	C								Input Sector Parameters
	W	H								
	W	R								
	W	N								
	W	Data Transfer of N Bytes								82078 Formats and Writes Entire Track
Result Phase	R	ST 0								
	R	ST 1								
	R	ST 2								
	R	Undefined								
	R	Undefined								
	R	Undefined								
	R	Undefined								
INVALID										
Command	W	Invalid Codes								Invalid Command Codes (NoOp — 82078 Goes into Standby State)
Result	R	ST 0								ST 0 = 80H

Parameter Abbreviations

Symbol **Description**

44PD EN Powerdown pin status. This bit allows the PD and IDLE pins to be available at FDS1 and FDME1 instead of the DS1 and ME1 pins. The BOOTSEL bit in the 44 pin part remaps the drive selects and motor enables when this bit is low. See the table below for functionality:

44PD EN	BOOTSEL(TDR)	Mapping		
0	0	Default	→	DS0 → FDS0, ME0 → FDME0 DS1 → FDS1, ME1 → FDME1
0	1			DS0 → FDS1, ME0 → FDME1 DS1 → FDS0, ME1 → FDME0
1	X			DS0 → FDS0, ME0 → FDME0 DS1 → PD, ME1 → IDLE

AUTO PD Auto powerdown control. If this bit is 0, then the automatic powerdown is disabled. If it is set to 1, then the automatic powerdown is enabled.

C Cylinder address. The currently selected cylinder address, 0 to 255.

D0, D1 Drive Select 0–3. Designates which drives are Perpendicular drives, a "1" indicating Perpendicular drive.

D Data pattern. The pattern to be written in each sector data field during formatting.

DN Done. This bit indicates that this is the last byte of the drive specification command. The 82078 checks to see if this bit is high or low. If it is low, it expects more bytes.

DN = 0 82078 expects more subsequent bytes.

DN = 1 Terminates the command phase and jumps to the results phase. An additional benefit is that by setting this bit high, a direct check of the current drive specifications can be done.

DIR Direction control. If this bit is 0, then the head will step out from the spindle during a relative seek. If set to a 1, the head will step in toward the spindle.

DS0, DS1 Disk Drive Select.

DS1	DS0	
0	0	drive 0
0	1	drive 1
1	0	RSVD
1	1	RSVD

DTL Special sector size. By setting N to zero (00), DTL may be used to control the number of bytes transferred in disk read/write commands. The sector size (N = 0) is set to 128. If the actual sector (on the diskette) is larger than DTL, the remainder of the actual sector is read but is not passed to the host during read commands; during write commands, the remainder of the actual sector is written with all zero bytes. The CRC check code is calculated with the actual sector. When N is not zero, DTL has no meaning and should be set to FF HEX.

DRATE[0:1] Data rate values from the DSR register.

DRT0, DRT1 Data rate table select. These two bits select between the different data rate tables. The default is the conventional table. These also provide mapping of the data rates selected in the DSR and CCR. The table below shows this.

Bits in DSR/CCR					
DRT0	**DRT1**	**DRATE1**	**DRATE0**	**Data Rate**	**Operation**
0	0	1	1	1 Mbps	Default
		0	0	500 Kbps	
		0	1	300 Kbps	
		1	0	250 Kbps	
0	1	RSVD	RSVD	RSVD	RSVD
1	0	RSVD	RSVD	RSVD	RSVD
1	1	1	1	1 Mbps	Perpendicular mode FDDs
		0	0	500 Kbps	
		0	1	RSVD	
		1	0	250 Kbps	

DT0, DT1 Drive density select type. These bits select the outputs on DRVDEN0 and DRVDEN1 based on mode of operation that was selected via the IDENT1 and IDENT0 pins. More information is available in the Design Applications section.

EC Enable Count. When this bit is "1" the "DTL" parameter of the Verify Command becomes SC (Number of sectors per track).

EFIFO Enable FIFO. When this bit is 0, the FIFO is enabled. A "1" puts the 82078 in the 8272A compatible mode where the FIFO is disabled.

EIS Enable implied seek. When set, a seek operation will be performed before executing any read or write command that requires the C parameter in the command phase. A "0" disables the implied seek.

EOT End of track. The final sector number of the current track.

EREG EN Enhanced Register Enable.

EREG EN = 1 The TDR register is extended and SRB is made visible to the user.

EREG EN = 0 Standard registers are used.

FDI TRI Floppy Drive Interface Tristate: If this bit is 0, then the output pins of the floppy disk drive interface are tri-stated. This is also the default state. If it is set to 1, then the floppy disk drive interface remains unchanged.

FD0, FD1 Floppy drive select. These two bits select which physical drive is being specified. The FDn corresponds to FDSn and FDMEn on the floppy drive interface. The drive is selected independent of the BOOTSELn bits. Please refer to Section 2.1.1 which explains the distinction between physical drives and their virtual mapping as defined by the BOOTSEL1 and BOOTSEL0 bits.

FD1	**FD0**	**Drive Slot**
0	0	drive 0
0	1	drive 1
1	0	RSVD
1	1	RSVD

GAP Alters Gap2 length when using Perpendicular Mode.

GPL Gap length. The Gap3 size. (Gap3 is the space between sectors excluding the VCO synchronization field).

HDS Head address. Selected head: 0 or 1 (disk side 0 or 1) as encoded in the sector ID field.

HLT Head load time. The time interval that 82078 waits after loading the head and before initiating a read or write operation. Refer to the SPECIFY command for actual delays.

HUT Head unload time. The time interval from the end of the execution phase (of a read or write command) until the head is unloaded. Refer to the SPECIFY command for actual delays.

ISO ISO Format: If this bit is set high the ISO format is used for all data transfer commands. When this bit is set low the normal IBM system 34 and perpendicular is used. The default is ISO = 0.

Lock	Lock defines whether EFIFO, FIFOTHR, and PRETRK parameters of the CONFIGURE command can be reset to their default values by a "Software Reset" (Reset made by setting the proper bit in the DSR or DOR registers).
MFM	MFM mode. A one selects the double density (MFM) mode. A zero is reserved.
MIN DLY	Minimum power up time control. This bit is active only if AUTO PD bit is enabled. Setting this bit to a 0, assigns a 10 ms minimum power up time and setting this bit to a 1, assigns a 0.5s minimum power up time.
MT	Multi-track selector. When set, this flag selects the multi-track operating mode. In this mode, the 82078 treats a complete cylinder, under head 0 and 1, as a single track. The 82078 operates as if this expanded track started at the first sector under head 0 and ended at the last sector under head 1. With this flag set, a multitrack read or write operation will automatically continue to the first sector under head 1 when the 82078 finishes operating on the last sector under head 0.
N	Sector size code. This specifies the number of bytes in a sector. If this parameter is "00", then the sector size is 128 bytes. The number of bytes transferred is determined by the DTL parameter. Otherwise the sector size is (2 raised to the "N'th" power) times 128. All values up to "07" hex are allowable. "07"h would equal a sector size of 16K. It is the users responsibility to not select combinations that are not possible with the drive.

N	Sector Size
00	128 bytes
01	256 bytes
02	512 bytes
03	1024
..	...
07	16 Kbytes

NCN	New cylinder number. The desired cylinder number.
ND	Non-DMA mode flag. When set to 1, indicates that the 82078 is to operate in the non-DMA mode. In this mode, the host is interrupted for each data transfer. When set to 0, the 82078 operates in DMA mode, interfacing to a DMA controller by means of the DRQ and DACK# signals.
NRP	No Results phase. When this bit is set high the result phase is skipped. When this bit is low the result phase will be generated.
OW	The bits denoted D0, D1, D2, and D3 of the PERPENDICULAR MODE command can only be overwritten when the OW bit is set to "1".
PCN	Present cylinder number. The current position of the head at the completion of SENSE INTERRUPT STATUS command.
PC2, PC1, PC0	Precompensation values from the DSR register.
PDOSC	When this bit is set, the internal oscillator is turned off.
PTS	Precompensation table select. This bit selects whether to enable the precompensation value programmed in the DSR or not. In the default state, the value programmed in DSR will be used. PTS = 0 DSR programmed precompensation delays PTS = 1 No precompensation delay is selected for the corresponding drive.
POLL	Polling disable. When set, the internal polling routine is disabled. When clear, polling is enabled.
PRETRK	Precompensation start track number. Programmable from track 00 to FFH.
R	Sector address. The sector number to be read or written. In multi-sector transfers, this parameter specifies the sector number of the first sector to be read or written.
RCN	Relative cylinder number. Relative cylinder offset from present cylinder as used by the RELATIVE SEEK command.
SC	Number of sectors. The number of sectors to be initialized by the FORMAT command. The number of sectors to be verified during a Verify Command, when EC is set.

SK	Skip flag. When set to 1, sectors containing a deleted data address mark will automatically be skipped during the execution of READ DATA. If READ DELETED is executed, only sectors with a deleted address mark will be accessed. When set to "0", the sector is read or written the same as the read and write commands.
SRT	Step rate interval. The time interval between step pulses issued by the 82078. Programmable from 0.5 ms to 8 ms, in increments of 0.5 ms at the 1 Mbit data rate. Refer to the SPECIFY command for actual delays.
ST0–3	Status registers 0–3. Registers within the 82078 that store status information after a command has been executed. This status information is available to the host during the result phase after command execution.
STEPPING	These bits identify the stepping of the 82078.
WGATE	Write gate alters timing of WE, to allow for pre-erase loads in perpendicular drives.

6.1 Data Transfer Commands

All of the READ DATA, WRITE DATA and VERIFY type commands use the same parameter bytes and return the same results information. The only difference being the coding of bits 0–4 in the first byte.

An implied seek will be executed if the feature was enabled by the CONFIGURE command. This seek is completely transparent to the user. The Drive Busy bit for the drive will go active in the Main Status Register during the seek portion of the command. If the seek portion fails, it will be reflected in the results status normally returned for a READ/WRITE DATA command. Status Register 0 (ST0) would contain the error code and C would contain the cylinder on which the seek failed.

6.1.1 READ DATA

A set of nine (9) bytes is required to place the 82078 into the Read Data Mode. After the READ DATA command has been issued, the 82078 loads the head (if it is in the unloaded state), waits the specified head settling time (defined in the SPECIFY command), and begins reading ID Address Marks and ID fields. When the sector address read off the diskette matches with the sector address specified in the command, the 82078 reads the sector's data field and transfers the data to the FIFO.

After completion of the read operation from the current sector, the sector address is incremented by one, and the data from the next logical sector is read and output via the FIFO. This continuous read function is called "Multi-Sector Read Operation". Upon receipt of TC, or an implied TC (FIFO overrun/underrun), the 82078 stops sending data, but will continue to read data from the current sector, check the CRC bytes, and at the end of the sector terminate the READ DATA Command.

N determines the number of bytes per sector (see Table 6-2). If N is set to zero, the sector size is set to 128. The DTL value determines the number of bytes to be transferred. If DTL is less than 128, the 82078 transfers the specified number of bytes to the host. For reads, it continues to read the entire 128 byte sector and checks for CRC errors. For writes it completes the 128 byte sector by filling in zeroes. If N is not set to 00 Hex, DTL should be set to FF Hex, and has no impact on the number of bytes transferred.

Table 6-2. Sector Sizes

N	Sector Size
00	128 bytes
01	256 bytes
02	512 bytes
03	1024 bytes
—	—
07	16 Kbytes

The amount of data which can be handled with a single command to the 82078 depends upon MT (multi-track) and N (Number of bytes/sector).

Table 6-3. Effects of MT and N Bits

MT	N	Max. Transfer Capacity	Final Sector Read from Disk
0	1	256 × 26 = 6656	26 at side 0 or 1
1	1	256 × 52 = 13312	26 at side 1
0	2	512 × 15 = 7680	15 at side 0 or 1
1	2	512 × 30 = 15360	15 at side 1
0	3	1024 × 8 = 8192	8 at side 0 or 1
1	3	1024 × 16 = 16384	16 at side 1

The Multi-Track function (MT) allows the 82078 to read data from both sides of the diskette. For a particular cylinder, data will be transferred starting at Sector 1, Side 0 and completing at the last sector of the same track at Side 1.

If the host terminates a read or write operation in the 82078, then the ID information in the result phase is dependent upon the state of the MT bit and EOT byte. Refer to Table 6-6. The termination must be normal.

At the completion of the READ DATA Command, the head is not unloaded until after the Head Unload Time Interval (specified in the SPECIFY command) has elapsed. If the host issues another command before the head unloads then the head settling time may be saved between subsequent reads.

If the 82078 detects a pulse on the INDX# pin twice without finding the specified sector (meaning that the diskette's index hole passes through index detect logic in the drive twice), the 82078 sets the IC code in Status Register 0 to "01" (Abnormal termination), and sets the ND bit in Status Register 1 to "1" indicating a sector not found, and terminates the READ DATA Command.

After reading the ID and Data Fields in each sector, the 82078 checks the CRC bytes. If a CRC error occurs in the ID or data field, the 82078 sets the IC code in Status Register 0 to "01" (Abnormal termination), sets the DE bit flag in Status Register 1 to "1", sets the DD bit in Status Register 2 to "1" if CRC is incorrect in the ID field, and terminates the READ DATA Command.

Table 6-4 below describes the affect of the SK bit on the READ DATA command execution and results.

Table 6-4. Skip Bit vs READ DATA Command

SK Bit Value	Data Address Mark Type Encountered	Results		
		Sector Read?	CM Bit of ST2 Set?	Description of Results
0	Normal Data	Yes	No	Normal Termination.
0	Deleted Data	Yes	Yes	Address Not Incremented. Next Sector Not Searched For.
1	Normal Data	Yes	No	Normal Termination.
1	Deleted Data	No	Yes	Normal Termination Sector Not Read ("Skipped").

Except where noted in Table 6-4, the C or R value of the sector address is automatically incremented (see Table 6-6).

6.1.2 READ DELETED DATA

This command is the same as the READ DATA command, only it operates on sectors that contain a Deleted Data Address Mark at the beginning of a Data Field.

Table 6-5 describes the affect of the SK bit on the READ DELETED DATA command execution and results.

Table 6-5. Skip Bit vs READ DELETED DATA Command

SK Bit Value	Data Address Mark Type Encountered	Results		
		Sector Read?	CM Bit of ST2 Set?	Description of Results
0	Normal Data	Yes	Yes	Normal Termination.
0	Deleted Data	Yes	No	Address Not Incremented. Next Sector Not Searched For.
1	Normal Data	No	Yes	Normal Termination Sector Not Read ("Skipped").
1	Deleted Data	Yes	No	Normal Termination.

Except where noted in Table 6-5 above, the C or R value of the sector address is automatically incremented (see Table 6-6).

6.1.3 READ TRACK

This command is similar to the READ DATA command except that the entire data field is read continuously from each of the sectors of a track. Immediately after encountering a pulse on the INDX# pin, the 82078 starts to read all data fields on the track as continuous blocks of data without regard to logical sector numbers. If the 82078 finds an error in the ID or DATA CRC check bytes, it continues to read data from the track and sets the appropriate error bits at the end of the command. The 82078 compares the ID information read from each sector with the specified value in the command, and sets the ND flag of Status Register 1 to a "1" if there is no comparison.

Multi-track or skip operations are not allowed with this command. The MT and SK bits (Bits D7 and D5 of the first command byte respectively) should always be set to "0".

This command terminates when the EOT specified number of sectors have been read. If the 82078 does not find an ID Address Mark on the diskette after the second occurrence of a pulse on the INDX# pin, then it sets the IC code in Status Register 0 to "01" (Abnormal termination), sets the MA bit in Status Register 1 to "1", and terminates the command.

Table 6-6. Result Phase Table

MT	Head	Final Sector Transferred to Host	ID Information at Result Phase			
			C	H	R	N
0	0	Less than EOT	NC	NC	R+1	NC
		Equal to EOT	C+1	NC	01	NC
	1	Less than EOT	NC	NC	R+1	NC
		Equal to EOT	C+1	NC	01	NC
1	0	Less than EOT	NC	NC	R+1	NC
		Equal to EOT	NC	LSB	01	NC
	1	Less than EOT	NC	NC	R+1	NC
		Equal to EOT	C+1	LSB	01	NC

NOTES:
NC: No Change, the same value as the one at the beginning of command execution.
LSB: Least Significant Bit, the LSB of H is complemented.

6.1.4 WRITE DATA

After the WRITE DATA command has been issued, the 82078 loads the head (if it is in the unloaded state), waits the specified head load time if unloaded (defined in the SPECIFY command), and begins reading ID Fields. When the sector address read from the diskette matches the sector address specified in the command, the 82078 reads the data from the host via the FIFO, and writes it to the sector's data field.

After writing data into the current sector, the 82078 computes the CRC value and writes it into the CRC field at the end of the sector transfer. The Sector Number stored in "R" is incremented by one, and the 82078 continues writing to the next data field. The 82078 continues this "Multi-Sector Write Operation". Upon receipt of a terminal count signal or if a FIFO over/under run occurs while a data field is being written, then the remainder of the data field is filled with zeros.

The 82078 reads the ID field of each sector and checks the CRC bytes. If it detects a CRC error in one of the ID Fields, it sets the IC code in Status Register 0 to "01" (Abnormal termination), sets the DE bit of Status Register 1 to "1", and terminates the WRITE DATA command.

The WRITE DATA command operates in much the same manner as the READ DATA command. The following items are the same. Please refer to the READ DATA Command for details:

- Transfer Capacity
- EN (End of Cylinder) bit
- ND (No Data) bit
- Head Load, Unload Time Interval
- ID information when the host terminates the command.
- Definition of DTL when N = 0 and when N does not = 0.

6.1.5 WRITE DELETED DATA

This command is almost the same as the WRITE DATA command except that a Deleted Data Address Mark is written at the beginning of the Data Field instead of the normal Data Address Mark. This command is typically used to mark a bad sector containing an error on the floppy disk.

6.1.6 VERIFY

The VERIFY command is used to verify the data stored on a disk. This command acts exactly like a READ DATA command except that no data is transferred to the host. Data is read from the disk, CRC computed and checked against the previously stored value.

Because no data is transferred to the host, TC (pin-25) cannot be used to terminate this command. By setting the EC bit to "1" an implicit TC will be issued to the 82078. This implicit TC will occur when the SC value has decrement to 0 (an SC value of 0 will verify 256 sectors). This command can also be terminated by setting the EC bit to "0" and the EOT value equal to the final sector to be checked. If EC is set to "0" DTL/SC should be programmed to 0FFH. Refer to Table 6-6 and Table 6-7 for information concerning the values of MT and EC versus SC and EOT value.

Definitions:

Sectors Per Side = Number of formatted sectors per each side of the disk.

Sectors Remaining = Number of formatted sectors left which can be read, including side 1 of the disk if MT is set to "1".

2

Table 6-7. Verify Command Result Phase Table

MT	EC	SC/EOT Value	Termination Result
0	0	SC = DTL EOT ≤ # Sectors Per Side	Successful Termination Result Phase Valid
0	0	SC = DTL EOT > # Sectors Per Side	Unsuccessful Termination Result Phase Invalid
0	1	SC ≤ # Sectors Remaining AND EOT ≤ # Sectors Per Side	Successful Termination Result Phase Valid
0	1	SC > # Sectors Remaining OR EOT > # Sectors Per Side	Unsuccessful Termination Result Phase Invalid
1	0	SC = DTL EOT ≤ # Sectors Per Side	Successful Termination Result Phase Valid
1	0	SC = DTL EOT > # Sectors Per Side	Unsuccessful Termination Result Phase Invalid
1	1	SC ≤ # Sectors Remaining AND EOT ≤ # Sectors Per Side	Successful Termination Result Phase Valid
1	1	SC > # Sectors Remaining OR EOT > # Sectors Per Side	Unsuccessful Termination Result Phase Invalid

NOTE:
If MT is set to "1" and the SC value is greater than the number of remaining formatted sectors on Side 0, verifying will continue on Side 1 of the disk.

6.1.7 FORMAT TRACK

The FORMAT command allows an entire track to be formatted. After a pulse from the INDX# pin is detected, the 82078 starts writing data on the disk including Gaps, Address Marks, ID Fields and Data Fields, per the IBM System 34 (MFM). The particular values that will be written to the gap and data field are controlled by the values programmed into N, SC, GPL, and D which are specified by the host during the command phase. The data field of the sector is filled with the data byte specified by D. The ID Field for each sector is supplied by the host; that is, four data bytes per sector are needed by the 82078 for C, H, R, and N (cylinder, head, sector number and sector size respectively).

After formatting each sector, the host must send new values for C, H, R and N to the 82078 for the next sector on the track. The R value (sector number) is the only value that must be changed by the host after each sector is formatted. This allows the disk to be formatted with nonsequential sector addresses (interleaving). This incrementing and formatting continues for the whole track until the 82078 encounters a pulse on the INDX# pin again and it terminates the command.

Table 6-8 contains typical values for gap fields which are dependent upon the size of the sector and the number of sectors on each track. Actual values can vary due to drive electronics.

Table 6-8. Typical PC-AT Values for Formatting

Drive Form	MEDIA	Sector Size	N	SC	GPL1	GPL2
5.25″	1.2M	512	02	0F	2A	50
	360K	512	02	09	2A	50
3.5″	2.88M	512	02	24	38	53
	1.44M	512	02	18	1B	54
	720K	512	02	09	1B	54

NOTE:
All values except Sector Size are in Hex.

Gap3 is programmable during reads, writes, and formats.

GPL1 = suggested Gap3 values in read and write commands to avoid splice point between data field and ID field of contiguous sections.

GPL2 = suggested Gap3 value in FORMAT TRACK command.

6.1.7.1 Format Fields

Table 6-9. System 34 Format Double Density

GAP 4a 80x 4E	SYNC 12x 00	IAM		GAP1 50x 4E	SYNC 12x 00	IDAM		CYL	HD	SEC	NO	CRC	GAP2 22x 4E	SYNC 12x 00	DATA AM		DATA	CRC	GAP3	GAP 4b
		3x C2	FC			3x A1	FE								3x A1	FB F8				

Table 6-10. ISO Format

GAP1 32x 4E	SYNC 12x 00	IDAM		CYL	HD	SEC	NO	CRC	GAP2 22x 4E	SYNC 12x 00	DATA AM		DATA	CRC	GAP3	GAP 4b
		3x A1	FE								3x A1	FB F8				

Table 6-11. Perpendicular Format

GAP 4a 80x 4E	SYNC 12x 00	IAM		GAP1 50x 4E	SYNC 12x 00	IDAM		CYL	HD	SEC	NO	CRC	GAP2 41x 4E	SYNC 12x 00	DATA AM		DATA	CRC	GAP3	GAP 4b
		3x C2	FC			3x A1	FE								3x A1	FB F8				

6.2 Scan Commands

The SCAN Commands allow data which is being read from the diskette to be compared against data which is being supplied from the main system (Processor in NON-DMA mode, and DMA Controller in DMA mode). The FDC compares the data on a byte-by-byte basis, and looks for a sector of data which meets the conditions of $D_{FDD} = D_{Processor}$, $D_{FDD} \leq D_{Processor}$, or $D_{FDD} \geq D_{Processor}$. Ones complement arithmetic is used for comparison (FF = largest number, 00 = smallest number). After a whole sector of data is compared, if the conditions are not met, the sector number is incremented (R + STP → R), and the scan operation is continued. The scan operation continues until one of the following conditions occur, the conditions for scan are met (equal, low, or high), the last sector on the track is reached (EOT), or the terminal count signal is received.

Table 6-12. Scan Status Codes

Command	Status Register 2		Comments
	Bit 2 = SN	Bit 3 = SH	
Scan Equal	0 1	1 0	$D_{FDD} = D_{Processor}$ $D_{FDD} \neq D_{Processor}$
Scan Low or Equal	0 0 1	1 0 0	$D_{FDD} = D_{Processor}$ $D_{FDD} < D_{Processor}$ $D_{FDD} \ngtr D_{Processor}$
Scan High or Equal	0 0 1	1 0 0	$D_{FDD} = D_{Processor}$ $D_{FDD} > D_{Processor}$ $D_{FDD} \nless D_{Proceeeor}$

If the conditions for scan are met then the FDC sets the SH (Scan Hit) flag of Status Register 2 to a 1 (high), and terminates the Scan Command, If the conditions for scan are not met between the starting sector (as specified by R) and the last sector on the cylinder (EOT), then the FDC sets the SN (Scan Not Satisfied) flag of Status Register 2 to a 1 (high), and terminates the Scan Command. The receipt of a TERMINAL COUNT signal from the Processor or DMA Controller during the scan operation will cause the FDC to complete the comparison of the particular byte which is in process, and then to terminate the command. Table 6-12 shows the status of bits SH and SN under various conditions of SCAN.

If the FDC encounters a Deleted Data Address Mark on one of the sectors (and SK = 0), then it regards the sector as the last sector on the cylinder, sets CM (Control Mark) flag of Status Register 2 to a 1 (high) and terminates the command. If SK = 1, the FDC skips the sector with the Deleted Address Mark, and reads the next sector. In the second case (SK = 1), the FDC sets the CM (Control Mark) flag of Status Register 2 to a 1 (high) in order to show that a Deleted Sector had been encountered.

When either the STP (contiguous sectors STP = 01, or alternate sectors STP = 02 sectors are read) or the MT (Multi-Track) are programmed, it is necessary to remember that the last sector on the track must be read. For example, if STP = 02, MT = 0, the sectors are numbered sequentially 1 through 26, and we start the Scan Command at sector 21; the following will happen. Sectors 21, 23, and 25 will be read, then the next sector (26) will be skipped and the index Hole will be encountered before the EOT value of 26 can be read. This will result in an abnormal termination of the command. If the EOT had been set at 25 or the scanning started at sector 20, then the Scan Command would be completed in a normal manner.

During the Scan Command data is supplied by either the processor or DMA Controller for comparison against the data read from the diskette. In order to avoid having the OR (Over Run) flag set in Status Register 1, it is necessary to have the data available in less than 13 μs. If an Overrun occurs the FDC terminates the command.

6.3 Control Commands

Control commands differ from the other commands in that no data transfer takes place. Three commands generate an interrupt when complete; READ ID, RECALIBRATE and SEEK. The other control commands do not generate an interrupt.

6.3.1 READ ID

The READ ID command is used to find the present position of the recording heads. The 82078 stores the values from the first ID Field it is able to read into its registers. If the 82078 does not find an ID Address Mark on the diskette after the second occurrence of a pulse on the INDX# pin, it then sets the IC code in Status Register 0 to "01" (Abnormal termination), sets the MA bit in Status Register 1 to "1", and terminates the command.

The following commands will generate an interrupt upon completion. They do not return any result bytes. It is highly recommended that control commands be followed by the SENSE INTERRUPT STATUS command. Otherwise, valuable interrupt status information will be lost.

6.3.2 RECALIBRATE

This command causes the read/write head within the 82078 to retract to the track 0 position. The 82078 clears the contents of the PCN counter, and checks the status of the TRK0 pin from the FDD. As long as the TRK0 pin is low, the DIR pin remains 0 and step pulses are issued. When the TRK0 pin goes high, the SE bit in Status Register 0 is set to "1", and the command is terminated. If the TRK0 pin is still low after 79 step pulses the command is terminated. Disks capable of handling more than 80 tracks per side may require more than one RECALIBRATE command to return the head back to physical Track 0.

The RECALIBRATE command does not have a result phase. SENSE INTERRUPT STATUS command must be issued after the RECALIBRATE command to effectively terminate it and to provide verification of the head position (PCN). During the command phase of the recalibrate operation, the 82078 is in the BUSY state, but during the execution phase it is in a NON BUSY state. At this time another RECALIBRATE command may be issued, and in this manner, parallel RECALIBRATE operations may be done on up to 2 drives at once.

Upon power up, the software must issue a RECALIBRATE command to properly initialize all drives and the controller.

6.3.3 DRIVE SPECIFICATION COMMAND

The 82078 uses two pins, DRVDEN0 and DRVDEN1 to select the density for modern drives. These signals inform the drive of the type of diskette in the drive. The Drive Specification command specifies the polarity of the DRVDEN0 and DRVDEN1 pins. It also enables or disables DSR programmed precompensation.

This command removes the need for a hardware workaround to accommodate differing specifications among drives. By programming this command during BIOS's POST routine, the floppy disk controller will internally configure the correct values for DRVDEN0 and DRVDEN1 with corresponding precompensation value and data rate table enabled for the particular type of drive.

This command is protected from software resets. After executing the DRIVE SPEC command, subsequent software resets will not clear the programmed parameters. Only another DRIVE SPEC command or H/W reset can reset it to default values. The 6 LSBs of the last byte of this command are reserved for future use.

The DRATE0 and DRATE1 are values as programmed in the DSR register. The DENSEL is high for high data rates (1 Mbps and 500 Kbps) and low for low data rates (300 Kbps and 250 Kbps).

The following table describes the drives that are supported with the DT0, DT1 bits of the Drive Specification command:

DRVDENn Polarities

DT0	DT1	Data Rate	DRVDEN0	DRVDEN1
0*	0*	1 Mbps	1	1
		500 Kbps	1	0
		300 Kbps	0	1
		250 Kbps	0	0
0	1	1 Mbps	1	1
		500 Kbps	0	0
		300 Kbps	0	1
		250 Kbps	1	0
1	0	1 Mbps	0	1
		500 Kbps	0	0
		300 Kbps	1	1
		250 Kbps	1	0
1	1	1 Mbps	1	1
		500 Kbps	0	0
		300 Kbps	1	0
		250 Kbps	0	1

NOTE:
(*) Denotes the default setting.

6.3.4 SEEK

The read/write head within the drive is moved from track to track under the control of the SEEK command. The 82078 compares the PCN which is the current head position with the NCN and performs the following operation if there is a difference:

PCN < NCN: Direction signal to drive set to "1" (step in), and issues step pulses.

PCN > NCN: Direction signal to drive set to "0" (step out), and issues step pulses.

The rate at which step pulses are issued is controlled by SRT (Stepping Rate Time) in the SPECIFY command. After each step pulse is issued, NCN is compared against PCN, and when NCN = PCN, then the SE bit in Status Register 0 is set to "1", and the command is terminated.

2

During the command phase of the seek or recalibrate operation, the 82078 is in the BUSY state, but during the execution phase it is in the NON BUSY state.

Note that if implied seek is not enabled, the read and write commands should be preceded by:

1. SEEK command; Step to the proper track
2. SENSE INTERRUPT STATUS command; Terminate the Seek command
3. READ ID. Verify head is on proper track
4. Issue READ/WRITE command.

The SEEK command does not have a result phase. Therefore, it is highly recommended that the SENSE INTERRUPT STATUS command be issued after the SEEK command to terminate it and to provide verification of the head position (PCN). The H bit (Head Address) in ST0 will always return a "0". When exiting DSR POWERDOWN mode, the 82078 clears the PCN value and the status information to zero. Prior to issuing the DSR POWERDOWN command, it is highly recommended that the user service all pending interrupts through the SENSE INTERRUPT STATUS command.

6.3.5 SENSE INTERRUPT STATUS

An interrupt signal on INT pin is generated by the 82078 for one of the following reasons:

1. Upon entering the Result Phase of:
    a. READ DATA Command
    b. READ TRACK Command
    c. READ ID Command
    d. READ DELETED DATA Command
    e. WRITE DATA Command

f. FORMAT TRACK Command

g. WRITE DELETED DATA Command

h. VERIFY Command

2. End of SEEK, RELATIVE SEEK or RECALIBRATE Command
3. 82078 requires a data transfer during the execution phase in the non-DMA Mode

The SENSE INTERRUPT STATUS command resets the interrupt signal and via the IC code and SE bit of Status Register 0, identifies the cause of the interrupt. If a SENSE INTERRUPT STATUS command is issued when no active interrupt condition is present, the status register ST0 will return a value of 80H (invalid command).

Table 6-13. Interrupt Indentification

SE	IC	Interrupt Due To
0	11	Polling
1	00	Normal Termination of SEEK or RECALIBRATE command
1	01	Abnormal Termination of SEEK or RECALIBRATE command

The SEEK, RELATIVE SEEK and the RECALIBRATE commands have no result phase. SENSE INTERRUPT STATUS command must be issued immediately after these commands to terminate them and to provide verification of the head position (PCN). The H (Head Address) bit in ST0 will always return a "0". If a SENSE INTERRUPT STATUS is not issued, the drive, will continue to be BUSY and may effect the operation of the next command.

6.3.6 SENSE DRIVE STATUS

SENSE DRIVE STATUS obtains drive status information. It has no execution phase and goes directly to the result phase from the command phase. STATUS REGISTER 3 contains the drive status information.

6.3.7 SPECIFY

The SPECIFY command sets the initial values for each of the three internal timers. The HUT (Head Unload Time) defines the time from the end of the execution phase of one of the read/write commands to the head unload state. The SRT (Step Rate Time) defines the time interval between adjacent step pulses. Note that the spacing between the first and second step pulses may be shorter than the remaining step pulses. The HLT (Head Load Time) defines the time between the command phase to the execution phase of a read/write data command. The Head Unload Time (HUT) timer starts at the end of the execution phase to the beginning of the result phase of a read/write command. The values change with the data rate speed selection and are documented in Table 6-14.

Table 6-14. Drive Control Delays (ms)

	HUT				SRT			
	1M	500K	300K	250K	1M	500K	300K	250K
0	128	256	426	512	8.0	16	26.7	32
1	8	16	26.7	32	7.5	15	25	30
—	—	—	—	—	—	—	—	—
A	80	160	267	320	3.0	6.0	10.2	12
B	88	176	294	352	2.5	5.0	8.35	10
C	96	192	320	384	2.0	4.0	6.68	8
D	104	208	346	416	1.5	3.0	5.01	6
E	112	224	373	448	1.0	2.0	3.33	4
F	120	240	400	480	0.5	1.0	1.67	2

Table 6-15. Head Load Time (ms)

	HLT			
	1M	500K	300K	250K
00	128	256	426	512
01	1	2	3.3	4
02	2	4	6.7	8
—	—	—	—	—
7E	126	252	420	504
7F	127	254	423	508

The choice of DMA or NON-DMA operations is made by the ND bit. When this bit is "1", the NON-DMA mode is selected, and when ND is "0", the DMA mode is selected. In DMA mode, data transfers are signalled by the DRQ pin. Non-DMA mode uses the RQM bit and the INT pin to signal data transfers.

6.3.8 CONFIGURE

Issue the configure command to enable features like the programmable FIFO and set the beginning track for pre-compensation. A CONFIGURE command need not be issued if the default values of the 82078 meet the system requirements.

CONFIGURE DEFAULT VALUES:

EIS	No Implied Seeks
EFIFO	FIFO Disabled
POLL	Polling Enabled
FIFOTHR	FIFO Threshold Set to 1 Byte
PRETRK	Pre-Compensation Set to Track 0

EIS—Enable Implied Seek. When set to "1", the 82078 will perform a SEEK operation before executing a read or write command. Defaults to no implied seek.

EFIFO—A "1" puts the FIFO into the 8272A compatible mode where the FIFO is disabled. This means data transfers are asked for on a byte by byte basis. Defaults to "1", FIFO disabled. The threshold defaults to one.

POLL—Disable polling of the drives. Defaults to "0", polling enabled. When enabled, a single interrupt is generated after a RESET. No polling is performed while the drive head is loaded and the head unload delay has not expired.

FIFOTHR—The FIFO threshold in the execution phase of read or write commands. This is programmable from 1 to 16 bytes. Defaults to one byte. A "00" selects one byte, "0F" selects 16 bytes.

PRETRK—Pre-compensation start track number. Programmable from track 0 to 255. Defaults to track 0. A "00" selects track 0, "FF" selects 255.

6.3.9 VERSION

The VERSION command checks to see if the controller is an enhanced type (82077, 82077AA, 82077SL) or the older type (8272A/765A). A value of 90H is returned as the result byte, defining an enhanced FDD controller is in use. No interrupts are generated. Refer to the Part ID command for more identification information on the 82078.

6.3.10 RELATIVE SEEK

The command is coded the same as for SEEK, except for the MSB of the first byte and the DIR bit.

DIR Head Step Direction Control

DIR	Action
0	Step Head Out
1	Step Head In

RCN Relative Cylinder Number that determines how many tracks to step the head in or out from the current track number.

The RELATIVE SEEK command differs from the SEEK command in that it steps the head the absolute number of tracks specified in the command instead of making a comparison against an internal register. The SEEK command is good for drives that support a maximum of 256 tracks. RELATIVE SEEKs cannot be overlapped with other RELATIVE SEEKs. Only one RELATIVE SEEK can be active at a time. Bit 4 of Status Register 0 (EC) will be set if RELATIVE SEEK attempts to step outward beyond Track 0.

As an example, assume that a floppy drive has 300 useable tracks and that the host needs to read track 300 and the head is on any track (0—255). If a SEEK command was issued, the head would stop at track 255. If a RELATIVE SEEK command was issued, the 82078 would move the head the specified number of tracks, regardless of the internal cylinder position register (but would increment the register). If the head had been on track 40 (D), the maximum track that the 82078 could position the head on using RELATIVE SEEK, would be 296 (D), the initial track, +256 (D). The maximum count that the head can be moved with a single RELATIVE SEEK command is 256 (D).

The internal register, PCN, would overflow as the cylinder number crossed track 255 and would contain 40 (D). The resulting PCN value is thus (NCN + PCN) mod 256. Functionally, the 82078 starts counting from 0 again as the track number goes above 255(D). It is the users responsibility to compensate 82078 functions (precompensation track number) when accessing tracks greater than 255. The 82078 does not keep track that it is working in an "extended track area" (greater than 255). Any command issued would use the current PCN value except for the RECALIBRATE command which only looks for the TRACK0 signal. RECALIBRATE would return an error if the head was farther than 79 due to its limitation of issuing a maximum 80 step pulses. The user simply needs to issue a second RECALIBRATE command. The SEEK command and implied seeks will function correctly within the 44 (D) track (299–255) area of the "extended track area". It is the users responsibility not to issue a new track position that would exceed the maximum track that is present in the extended area.

To return to the standard floppy range (0-255) of tracks, a RELATIVE SEEK would be issued to cross the track 255 boundary.

A RELATIVE SEEK can be used instead of the normal SEEK but the host is required to calculate the difference between the current head location and the new (target) head location. This may require the host to issue a READ ID command to ensure that the head is physically on the track that software assumes it to be. Different 82078 commands will return different cylinder results which may be difficult to keep track of with software without the READ ID command.

6.3.11 DUMPREG

The DUMPREG command is designed to support system run-time diagnostics and application software development and debug. The command returns pertinent information regarding the internal status of the 82078. This can be used to verify the values initialized in the 82078.

6.3.12 PERPENDICULAR MODE COMMAND

Note, perpendicular mode functionality is not available on the 82078-5.

6.3.12.1 About Perpendicular Recording Mode

An added capability of the 82078 is the ability to interface directly to perpendicular recording floppy drives. Perpendicular recording differs from the traditional longitudinal method by orienting the magnetic bits vertically. This scheme packs in more data bits for the same area.

6.3.12.2 The Perpendicular Mode Command

The PERPENDICULAR MODE command allows the system designers to designate specific drives as Perpendicular recording drives. Data transfers between Conventional and Perpendicular drives are allowed without having to issue PERPENDICULAR MODE commands between the accesses of the two different drives, nor having to change write pre-compensation values.

With this command, the length of the Gap2 field and VCO enable timing can be altered to accommodate the unique requirements of these drives. Table 6-16 describes the effects of the WGATE and GAP bits for the PERPENDICULAR MODE command.

When both GAP and WGATE equal "0" the PERPENDICULAR MODE command will have the following effect on the 82078-1) if any of the new bits D0, D1, D2, and D3 are programmed to "1" the corresponding drive will automatically be programmed for Perpendicular mode (ie: GAP2 being written during a write operation, the programmed Data Rate will determine the length of GAP2.), and data will be written with 0 ns write pre-compensation. 2) Any of the new bits (D0–D1) that are programmed for "0", the designated drive, will be programmed for Conventional Mode and data will be written with the currently programmed write pre-compensation value. 3) Bits D0 and D1 can only be over written when the OW bit is written as a "1". The status of these bits can be determined by interpreting the eighth result byte of the DUMPREG command.

NOTE:
If either the GAP or WGATE bit is a "1", then bits D0–D1 are ignored.

"Software" and "Hardware" RESET will have the following effects on the enhanced PERPENDICULAR MODE command:

1. "Software" RESETs (Reset via DOR or DSR registers) will only clear GAP and WGATE bits to "0", D1 and D0 will retain their previously programmed values.
2. "Hardware" RESETs (Reset via pin-32) will clear all bits (GAP, WGATE, D0 and D1) to "0" (All Drives Conventional Mode).

Table 6-16. Effects of WGATE and GAP Bits

GAP	WGATE	MODE	VCO Low Time after Index Pulse	Length of Gap2 Format Field	Portion of Gap2 Written by Write Data Operation	Gap2 VCO Low Time for Read Operations
0	0	Conventional Mode	33 Bytes	22 Bytes	0 Bytes	24 Bytes
0	1	Perpendicular Mode (500 Kbps Data Rate)	33 Bytes	22 Bytes	19 Bytes	24 Bytes
1	0	Reserved (Conventional)	33 Bytes	22 Bytes	0 Bytes	24 Bytes
1	1	Perpendicular Mode (1 Mbps Data Rate)	18 Bytes	41 Bytes	38 Bytes	43 Bytes

NOTE:
When either GAP or WGATE bit is set, the current value of precompensation in the DSR is used.

6.3.13 POWERDOWN MODE COMMAND

The POWERDOWN MODE command allows the automatic power management and enables the enhanced registers (EREG EN) of the 82078. The use of the command can extend the battery life in portable PC applications. To enable auto powerdown the command may be issued during the BIOS power on self test (POST).

This command includes the ability to configure the 82078 into the enhanced mode extending the SRB and TDR registers. These extended registers accommodate bits that give more information about floppy drive interface, allow for boot drive selection, and identify the values of the PD and IDLE status.

As soon as the command is enabled, a 10 ms or a 0.5s minimum power up timer is initiated depending on whether the MIN DLY bit is set to 0 or 1. This timer is one of the required conditions that has to be satisfied before the part will enter auto powerdown. Any software reset will reinitialize the timer. The timer countdown is also extended by up to 10 ms if the data rate is changed during the timer's countdown. Without this timer 82078 would have been put to sleep immediately after 82078 is idle. The minimum delay gives software a chance to interact with 82078 without incurring an additional overhead due to recovery time.

The command also allows the output pins of floppy disk drive interface to be tri-stated or left unaltered during auto powerdown. This is done by the FDI TRI bit. In the default condition (FDI TRI = 0) the output pins of the floppy disk drive are tri-stated. Setting this bit leaves the interface unchanged from the normal state.

The results phase returns the values programmed for MIN DLY, FDI TRI and AUTO PD. The auto powerdown mode is disabled by a hardware reset. Software results have no effect on the POWERDOWN MODE command parameters.

6.3.14 PART ID COMMAND

This command can be used to identify the floppy disk controller as an enhanced controller. The first stepping of the 82078 (all 44 pin versions) will yield 0x41 in the result phase of this command. Any future enhancements on these parts will be denoted by the 5 LSBs (0x01 to 0x1F).

6.3.15 OPTION COMMAND

The standard IBM format includes an index address field consisting of 80 bytes of GAP4a, 12 bytes of the sync field, four bytes identifying the IAM and 50 bytes of GAP1. Under the ISO format, most of this preamble is not used. The ISO format allows only 32 bytes of GAP1 after the index mark. The ISO bit in this command allows the 82078 to configure the data transfer commands to recognize this format. The MSBs in this command are reserved for any other enhancements made available to the user in the future.

6.3.16 SAVE COMMAND

The first byte corresponds to the values programmed in the DSR with the exception of CLK48. The DRATE1, DRATE0 used here are unmapped. The second byte is used for configuring the bits from the OPTION command. All future enhancements to the OPTION command will be reflected in this byte as well. The next nine result bytes are explained in the Parameter Abbreviations section after the command summary. The 13th byte is the value associated with the auto powerdown command. The disk status is used internally by 82078. There are two reserved bytes at the end of this command for future use.

This command is similar to the Dumpreg command but it additionally allows the user to read back the precompensation values as well as the programmed data rate. It also allows the user to read the values programmed in the auto power down command. The precompensation values will be returned as programmed in the DSR register. This command is used in conjunction with the Restore command should prove very useful for SMM power management. This command reserves the last two bytes for future enhancements.

6.3.17 RESTORE COMMAND

Using Restore with the Save command, allows the SMM power management to restore the 82078 to its original state after a system powerdown. It also serves as a succinct way to provide most of the initialization requirements normally handled by the system. The sequence of initializing the 82078 after a reset occurred and assuming a Save command was issued follows:

- Issue the Drive Spec command (if the design utilizes this command)
- Issue the Restore command (pass the 16 bytes retrieved previously during SAVE)

The Restore command will program the data rate and precompensation value via the DSR. It then restores the values normally programmed through the Configure, Specify, and Perpendicular commands. It also enables the previously selected values for the AUTO Powerdown command. The PCN values are set restored to their previous values and the user is responsible for issuing the seek and recalibrate commands to restore the head to the proper location. There are some drives that do not recalibrate in which case the Restore command will restore the previous state completely. The PDOSC bit is retrievable using the Save command, however, the system designer must set it correctly. The software must allow at least 20μs to execute the Restore command. When using the BOOTSEL bits in the TDR, the user must restore or reinitialize these bits to their proper values.

6.3.18 FORMAT AND WRITE COMMAND

The format and write command is capable of simultaneously formatting and writing data to the diskette. It is essentially the same as the normal format command. With the exception that included in the execution for each sector is not only the C, H, R, and N but also the data transfer of N bytes. The D value is ignored. This command formats the entire track. High speed floppy diskette duplication can be done fast and efficiently with this command. The user can format the diskette and put data on it in a single pass. This is very useful for software duplication applications by reducing the time required to format and copy diskettes.

6.3.19 LOCK

The LOCK command is included to protect a system with long DMA latencies against older application software packages that can disable the 82078's FIFO. [Note: This command should only be used by the system's FDC routines, and ISVs (Independent Software Vendors) should refrain from using it. If an ISV's application calls for having the 82078 FIFO disabled, a CONFIGURE command should be used to toggle the EFIFO (Enable FIFO) bit. ISV can determine the value of the LOCK bit by interpreting the eighth result byte of an DUMPREG command.]

The LOCK command defines whether EFIFO, FIFOTHR, and PRETRK parameters of the CONFIGURE command can be RESET by the DOR and DSR registers. When the LOCK bit is set to a "1" all subsequent "software" RESETs by the DOR and DSR registers will not change the previously set parameter values in the CONFIGURE command. When the LOCK bit is set to a "0", "software" RESETs the DOR or DSR registers will return these parameters to their default values. All "hardware" Resets will set the LOCK bit to a "0" value, and will return EFIFO, FIFOTHR, and PRETRK to their default values. A Status byte is returned immediately after issuing the command byte. This Status byte reflects the value of the Lock bit set by the command byte.

NOTE:

No interrupts are generated at the end of this command.

7.0 STATUS REGISTER ENCODING

The contents of these registers are available only through a command sequence.

7.1 Status Register 0

Bit #	Symbol	Name	Description
7, 6	IC	Interrupt Code	00— Normal termination of command. The specified command was properly executed and completed without error. 01— Abnormal termination of command. Command execution was started, but was not successfully completed. 10— Invalid command. The requested command could not be executed. 11— Abnormal termination caused by Polling.
5	SE	Seek End	The 82078 completed a SEEK or RECALIBRATE command, or a READ or WRITE with implied seek command.
4	EC	Equipment Check	The TRK0 pin failed to become a "1" after: 1. 80 step pulses in the RECALIBRATE command. 2. The RELATIVE SEEK command causes the 82078 to step outward beyond Track 0.
3	—	—	Unused. This bit is always "0".
2	H	Head Address	The current head address.
1, 0	DS1, 0	Drive Select	The current selected drive.

7.2 Status Register 1

Bit #	Symbol	Name	Description
7	EN	End of Cylinder	The 82078 tried to access a sector beyond the final sector of the track (255D). Will be set if TC is not issued after Read or Write.
6	—	—	Unused. This bit is always "0".
5	DE	Data Error	The 82078 detected a CRC error in either the ID field or the data field of a sector.
4	OR	Overrun/ Underrun	Becomes set if the 82078 does not receive CPU or DMA service within the required time interval, resulting in data overrun or underrun.
3	—	—	Unused. This bit is always "0".
2	ND	No Data	Any one of the following: 1. READ DATA, READ DELETED DATA command, the 82078 did not find the specified sector. 2. READ ID command, the 82078 cannot read the ID field without an error. 3. READ TRACK command, the 82078 cannot find the proper sector sequence.
1	NW	Not Writable	WP pin became a "1" while the 82078 is executing a WRITE DATA, WRITE DELETED DATA, or FORMAT TRACK command.
0	MA	Missing Address Mark	Any one of the following: 1. The 82078 did not detect an ID address mark at the specified track after encountering the index pulse from the INDX# pin twice. 2. The 82078 cannot detect a data address mark or a deleted data address mark on the specified track.

2

7.3 Status Register 2

Bit #	Symbol	Name	Description
7	—	—	Unused. This bit is always "0".
6	CM	Control Mark	Any of the following: 1. READ DATA command, the 82078 encounters a deleted data address mark. 2. READ DELETED DATA command, the 82078 encountered a data address mark.
5	DD	Data Error in Data Field	The 82078 detected a CRC error in the date field.
4	WC	Wrong Cylinder	The track address from the sector ID field is different from the track address maintained inside the 82078.
3	—	—	Unused. This bit is always "0".
2	—	—	Unused. This bit is always "0".
1	BC	Bad Cylinder	The track address from the sector ID field is different from the track address maintained inside the 82078 and is equal to FF hex which indicates a bad track with a hard error according to the IBM soft-sectored format.
0	MD	Missing Data Address Mark	The 82078 cannot detect a data address mark or a deleted data address mark.

7.4 Status Register 3

Bit #	Symbol	Name	Description
7	—	—	Unused. This bit is always "0".
6	WP	Write Protected	Indicates the status of the WP pin.
5	—	—	Unused. This bit is always "1".
4	T0	TRACK 0	Indicates the status of TRK0 pin.
3	—	—	Unused. This bit is always "1".
2	HD	Head Address	Indicates the status of the HDSEL pin.
1, 0	DS1, 0	Drive Select	Indicates the status of the DS1, DS0 pins.

8.0 COMPATIBILITY

The 82078 was designed with software compatibility in mind. It is a fully backwards compatible solution with the older generation 8272A and NEC765A/B disk controllers. It is fully compatible with Intel's 386/486SL Microprocessor Superset.

8.1 Compatibility with the FIFO

The FIFO of the 82078 is designed to be transparent to non-FIFO disk controller software developed on the older generation 8272A standard. Operation of the 82078 FIFO can be broken down into two tiers of compatibility. For first tier compatibility, the FIFO is left in the default disabled condition upon a "Hardware" reset. In this mode the FIFO operates in a byte mode and provides complete compability with non-FIFO based software. For second tier compatibility, the FIFO is enabled via the CONFIGURE command. When the FIFO is enabled, it will temporarily enter a byte mode during the command and result phase of disk controller operation. This allows for compatible operation when interrogating the Main Status Register (MSR) for the purpose of transferring a byte at a time to or from the disk controller. For normal disk controller applications, the system designer can still take advantage of the FIFO for time critical data transfers during the execution phase and not create any conflicts with non-FIFO software during the command or result phase.

In some instances, use of the FIFO in any form has conflicted with certain specialized software. An example of a compatibility conflict using the FIFO is with software that monitors the progress of a data transfer during the execution phase. If the software assumed the disk controller was operating in a single byte mode and counted the number of bytes transferred to or from the disk controller to trigger some time dependent event on the disk media (i.e. head position over a specific data field), the same software will not have an identical time relationship if the FIFO is enabled. This is because the FIFO allows data to be queued up, and then burst transferred across the host bus. To accommodate software of this type, it is recommended that the FIFO be disabled.

8.2 Drive Polling

The 82078 supports the polling mode of the older generation 8272A. This mode is enabled upon a reset and can be disabled via the CONFIGURE command. This mode is supported for the sole purpose of providing backward compatibility with software that expects it's presence.

The intended purpose of drive polling dates back to 8″ drives as a means to monitor any change in status for each disk drive present in the system. Each of the drives is selected for a period of time and its READY signal sampled. After a delay, the next drive is selected. Since the 82078 does not support READY in this capacity (internally tied true), the polling sequence is only simulated and does not affect the drive select lines (DS0–DS3) when it is active. If enabled, it occurs whenever the 82078 is waiting for a command or during SEEKs and RECALIBRATEs (but not IMPLIED SEEKs). Each drive is assumed to be not ready after a reset and a "ready" value for each drive is saved in an internal register as the simulated drive is polled. An interrupt will be generated on the first polling loop because of the initial "not ready" status. This interrupt must be followed with a SENSE INTERRUPT STATUS command from the host to clear the interrupt condition for each of the four logical drives.

9.0 PROGRAMMING GUIDELINES

Programming the 82078 is identical to any other 8272A compatible disk controller with the exception of some additional commands. For the new designer it is useful to provide some guidelines on how to program the 82078. A typical disk operation involves more than issuing a command and waiting for the results. The control of the floppy disk drive is a low level operation that requires software intervention at different stages. New commands and features have been added to the 82078 to reduce the complexity of this software interface.

9.1 Command and Result Phase Handshaking

Before a command or parameter byte can be issued to the 82078, the Main Status Register (MSR) must be interrogated for a ready status and proper FIFO direction. A typical floppy controller device driver should contain a subroutine for sending command or parameter bytes. For this discussion, the routine will be called "Send_byte" with the flowchart shown in Figure 9-1.

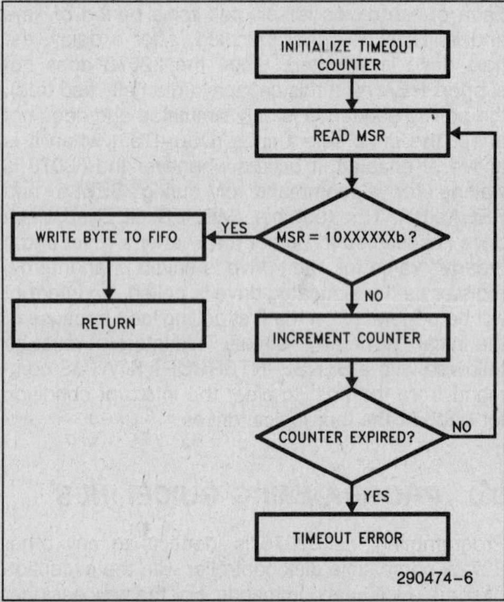

Figure 9-1. Send_Byte Routine

The routine loops until RQM is 1 and DIO is 0 indicating a ready status and FIFO direction is inward. If this condition is true, the 82078 is ready to accept a command or parameter byte. A timeout counter is used to insure software response within a reasonable amount of time in case of no response by the 82078. As a note, the programmer must be careful how the maximum delay is chosen to avoid unnecessary timeouts. For example, if a new command is issued when the 82078 is in the middle of a polling routine, the MSR will not indicate a ready status for the next parameter byte until the polling sequence completes the loop. This could cause a delay between the first and second bytes of up to 250 μs (@ 250 Kbps). If polling is disabled, this maximum delay is 175 μs. There should also be enough timeout margin to accommodate a shift of the software to a higher speed system. A timeout value that results in satisfactory operation on a 16 MHz CPU might fail when the software is moved to a system with a 25 MHz CPU. A recommended solution is to derive the timeout counter from a system hardware counter that is fixed in frequency from CPU clock to CPU clock.

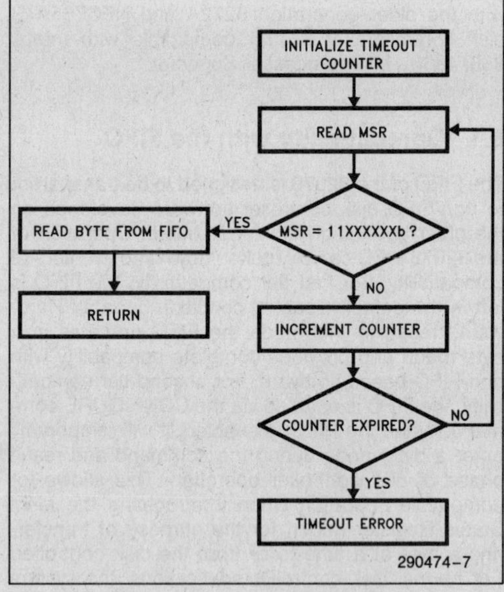

Figure 9-2. Get_Byte Routine

For reading result bytes from the 82078, a similar routine is used. Figure 9-2 illustrates the flowchart for the routine "Get_byte". The MSR is polled until RQM is 1 and DIO is 1, which indicates a ready status and outward FIFO direction. At this point, the host can read a byte from the FIFO. As in the Send_byte routine, a timout counter should be incorporated in case of a disk controller lock-up condition. For example, if a disk was not inserted into the disk drive at the time of a read operation, the controller would fail to receive the index pulse and lockup since the index pulses are required for termination of the execution phase.

9.2 Initialization

Initializing the 82078 involves setting up the appropriate configuration after a reset. Parameters set by the SPECIFY command are undefined after a system reset and will need to be reinitialized. CONFIGURE command parameters default to a known state after a system reset but will need to be reinitialized if the system requirements are different from the default settings. This can be accomplished in two ways; either issue the individual commands, or issue the Restore command (assuming the Save command was issued). The Restore command is a succinct way to initialize the 82078, this is the preferable method if the system power management powers the 82078 on and off frequently. The flowchart for the recommended initialization sequence of the 82078 is shown in Figure 9-3.

Following a reset of the 82078, the Configuration Control Register (CCR) should be reinitialized for the appropriate data rate. An external reset via the RESET pin will cause the data rate and write precompensation values to default to 250 Kbps (10b) and 125 ns (000b) respectively. Since the 125 ns write precompensation value is optimal for the 5¼″ and 3½″ disk drive environment, most applications will not require the value to be changed in the initialization sequence. As a note, a software reset issued via the DOR or DSR will not affect the data rate or write precompensation values. But it is recommended as a safe programming practice to always program the data rate after a reset, regardless of the type.

Since polling is enabled after a reset of the 82078, four SENSE INTERRUPT STATUS commands need to be issued afterwards to clear the status flags for each drive. The flowchart in Figure 9-3 illustrates how the software clears each of the four interrupt status flags internally queued by the 82078. It should be noted that although four SENSE INTERRUPT STATUS commands are issued, the INT pin is only active until the first SENSE INTERRUPT STATUS command is executed.

As a note, if the CONFIGURE command is issued within 250 μs of the trailing edge of reset (@1 Mbps), the polling mode of the 82078 can be disabled before the polling initiated interrupt occurs. Since polling stops when the 82078 enters the command phase, it is only time critical up to the first byte of the CONFIGURE command. If disabled in time, the system software no longer needs to issue the four SENSE INTERRUPT STATUS commands to clear the internal interrupt flags normally caused by polling.

The CONFIGURE command should also be issued if the system requirements are different from the default settings. For example, the CONFIGURE command can be used to enable the FIFO, set the threshold, and enable Implied Seeks.

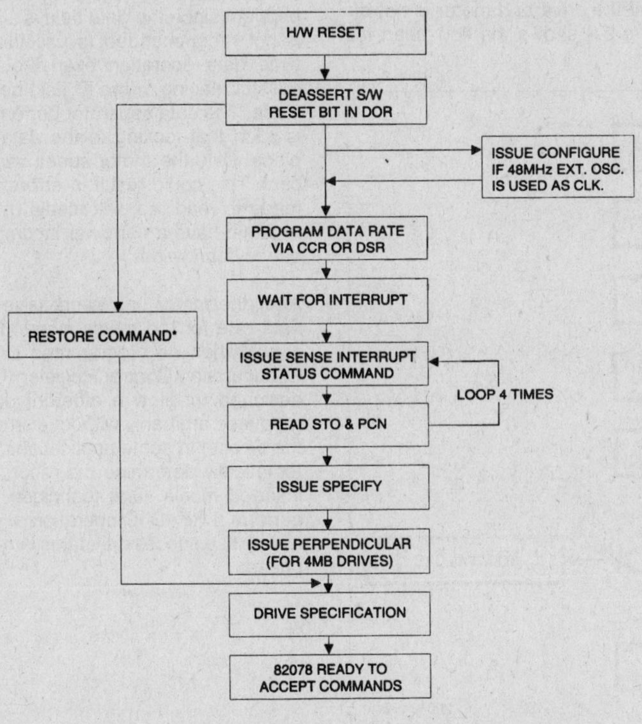

H/W RESET
DEASSERT S/W RESET BIT IN DOR
ISSUE CONFIGURE IF 48MHz EXT. OSC. IS USED AS CLK.
PROGRAM DATA RATE VIA CCR OR DSR
WAIT FOR INTERRUPT
RESTORE COMMAND*
ISSUE SENSE INTERRUPT STATUS COMMAND
LOOP 4 TIMES
READ ST0 & PCN
ISSUE SPECIFY
ISSUE PERPENDICULAR (FOR 4MB DRIVES)
DRIVE SPECIFICATION
82078 READY TO ACCEPT COMMANDS

290474–26

NOTE:
(*) A sense interrupt status may be required if the Restore command is not issued within 250 μs of the trailing edge of a H/W reset (@1 Mbps).

Figure 9-3. Initialization Flowchart

The non-DMA mode flag, step rate (SRT), head load (HLT), and head unload times (HUT) programmed by the SPECIFY command do not default to a known state after a reset. This behavior is consistent with the 8272A and has been preserved here for compatibility. Thus, it is necessary to always issue a SPECIFY command in the initialization routine.

9.3 Recalibrates and Seeks

Commands that position the disk head are different from the typical READ/WRITE/FORMAT command in the sense that there is no result phase. Once a RECALIBRATE, SEEK, or RELATIVE SEEK command has been issued, the 82078 will return a ready status in the Main Status Register (MSR) and perform the head positioning operation as a background task. When the seek is complete, the 82078 will assert the INT signal to request service. A SENSE INTERRUPT STATUS command should then be asserted to clear the interrupt and read the status of the operation. Since the drive and motor enable signals are directly controlled through the Digital Output Register (DOR) on the 82078, a write to the DOR will need to precede the RECALIBRATE or SEEK command if the drive and motor is not already enabled. Figure 9-4 shows the flow chart for this operation.

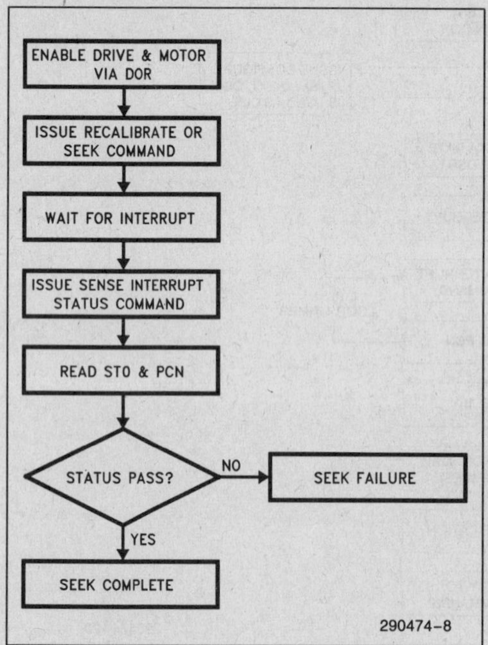

Figure 9-4. Recalibrate and Seek Operations

9.4 Read/Write Data Operations

A read or write data operation requires several steps to complete successfully. The motor needs to be turned on, the head positioned to the correct cylinder, the DMA controller initialized, the read or write command initiated, and an error recovery scheme implemented. The flowchart in Figure 9-5 highlights a recommended algorithm for performing a read or write data operation.

Before data can be transferred to or from the diskette, the disk drive motor must be brought up to speed. For most 3½″ disk drives, the spin-up time is 300 ms, while the 5¼″ drive usually requires about 500 ms due to the increased moment of inertia associated with the larger diameter diskette.

One technique for minimizing the motor spin-up delay in the read data case is to begin the read operation immediately after the motor is turned on. When the motor is not initially up to speed, the internal data separator will fail to lock onto the incoming data stream and report a failure in the status registers. The read operation is then repeated until successful status is obtained. There is no risk of a data integrity problem since the data field is CRC validated. But, it is not recommended to use this technique for the write data operation even though it requires successful reading of the ID field before the write takes place. The data separator performance of the 82078 is such that locking to the data stream could take place while the motor speed variation is still significant. This could result in errors when an attempt is made to read the disk media by other disk controllers that have a narrower incoming data stream frequency bandwidth.

After the motor has been turned on, the matching data rate for the media inserted into the disk drive should then be programmed to the 82078 via the Configuration Control Register (CCR). The 82078 is designed to allow a different data rate to be programmed arbitrarily without disrupting the integrity of the device. In some applications, it is required to automatically determine the recorded data rate of the inserted media. One technique for doing this is to perform a READ ID operation at each available data rate until a successful status is returned in the result phase.

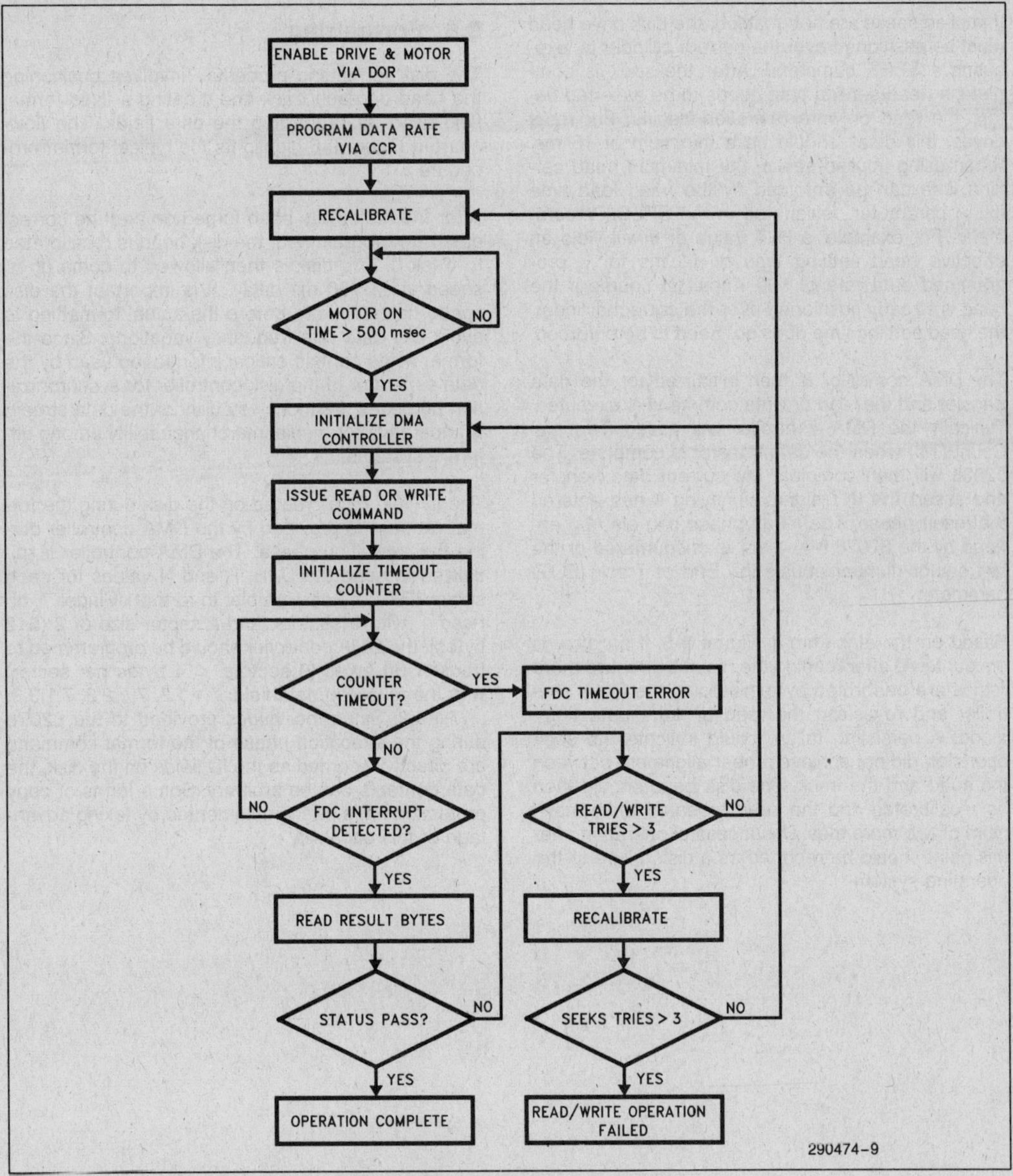

ENABLE DRIVE & MOTOR VIA DOR
PROGRAM DATA RATE VIA CCR
RECALIBRATE
MOTOR ON TIME > 500 msec
NO
YES
INITIALIZE DMA CONTROLLER
ISSUE READ OR WRITE COMMAND
INITIALIZE TIMEOUT COUNTER
COUNTER TIMEOUT?
YES
FDC TIMEOUT ERROR
NO
FDC INTERRUPT DETECTED?
NO
YES
READ RESULT BYTES
STATUS PASS?
NO
YES
OPERATION COMPLETE
READ/WRITE TRIES > 3
NO
YES
RECALIBRATE
SEEKS TRIES > 3
NO
YES
READ/WRITE OPERATION FAILED

290474-9

Figure 9-5. Read/Write Operation

2

If implied seeks are not enabled, the disk drive head must be positioned over the correct cylinder by executing a SEEK command. After the seek is complete, a head settling time needs to be asserted before the read or write operation begins. For most drives, this delay should be a minimum of 15 ms. When using implied seeks, the minimum head settling time can be enforced by the head load time (HLT) parameter designated in the SPECIFY command. For example, a HLT value of 8 will yield an effective head settling time of 16 ms for a programmed data rate of 500 Kbps. Of course if the head is already positioned over the correct cylinder, the head settling time does not need to be enforced.

The DMA controller is then initialized for the data transfer and the read or write command is executed. Typically the DMA controller will assert Terminal Count (TC) when the data transfer is complete. The 82078 will then complete the current data transfer and assert the INT signal signifying it has entered the result phase. The result phase can also be entered by the 82078 if an error is encountered or the last sector number equals the End of Track (EOT) parameter.

Based on the algorithm in Figure 9-5, if an error is encountered after reading the result bytes, two more retries are performed by reinitializing the DMA controller and re-issuing the read or write data command. A persisting failure could indicate the seek operation did not achieve proper alignment between the head and the track. The disk head should then be recalibrated and the seek repeated for a maximum of two more tries. Unsuccessful operation after this point should be reported as a disk failure to the operating system.

9.5 Formatting

The disk formatting procedure involves positioning the head on each track and creating a fixed format field used for organizing the data fields. The flowchart in Figure 9-6 highlights the typical format procedure.

After the motor has been turned on and the correct data rate programmed, the disk head is recalibrated to track 0. The disk is then allowed to come up to speed via a 500 ms delay. It is important the disk speed has stabilized before the actual formatting to avoid any data rate frequency variations. Since the format fields contain critical information used by the data separator of the disk controller for synchronization purposes, frequency stability of the data stream is imperative for media interchangeability among different systems.

The ID field data created on the disk during the format process is provided by the DMA controller during the execution phase. The DMA controller is initialized to send the C, H, R and N values for each sector ID field. For example, to format cylinder 7, on head 1, with 9 sectors, and a sector size of 2 (512 bytes), the DMA controller should be programmed to transfer 36 bytes (9 sectors × 4 bytes per sector) with the following data field: 7,1,1,2, 7,1,2,2, 7,1,3,2, ... 7,1,9,2. Since the values provided to the 82078 during the execution phase of the format command are directly recorded as the ID fields on the disk, the data contents can be arbitrary. Some forms of copy protection have been implemented by taking advantage of this capability.

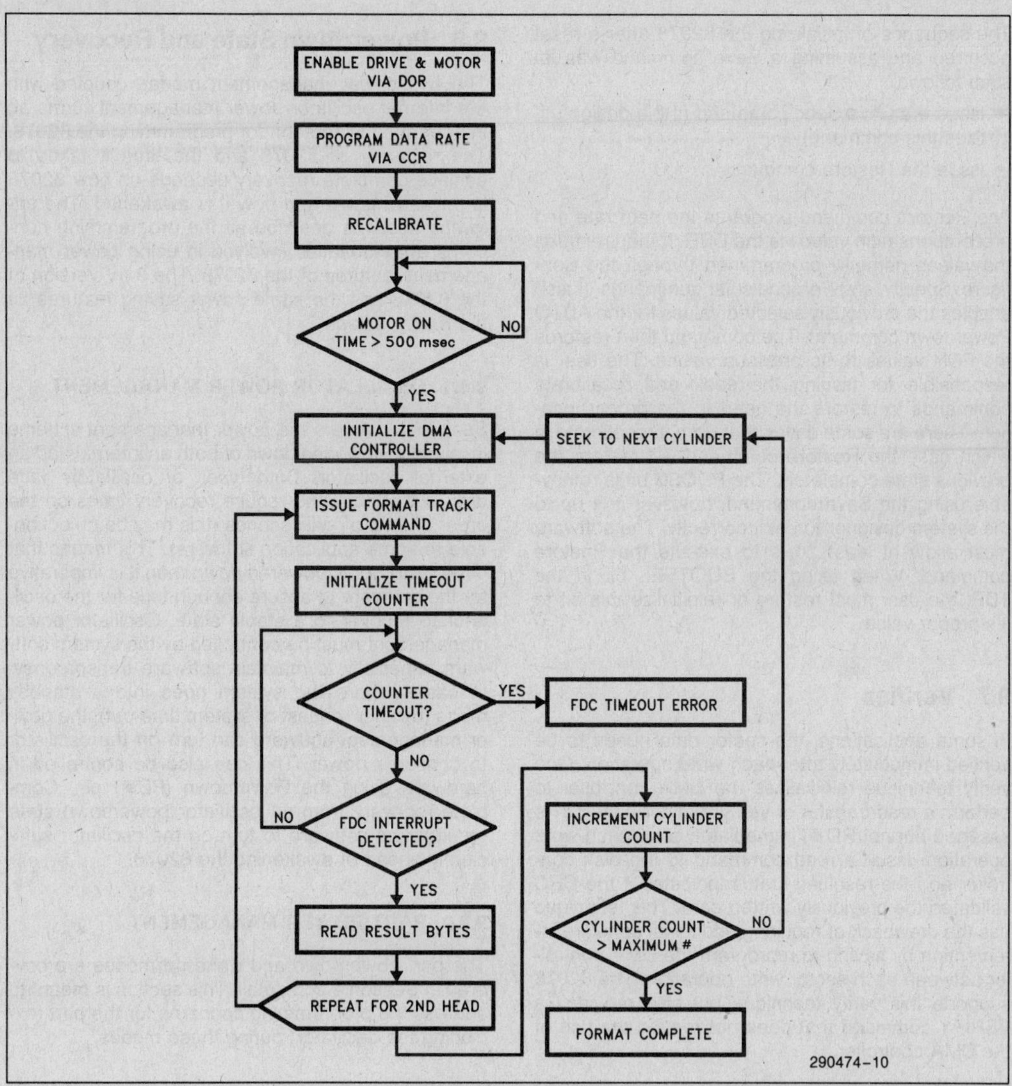

ENABLE DRIVE & MOTOR VIA DOR
PROGRAM DATA RATE VIA CCR
RECALIBRATE
MOTOR ON TIME > 500 msec
NO
YES
INITIALIZE DMA CONTROLLER
SEEK TO NEXT CYLINDER
ISSUE FORMAT TRACK COMMAND
INITIALIZE TIMEOUT COUNTER
COUNTER TIMEOUT?
YES
FDC TIMEOUT ERROR
NO
NO
FDC INTERRUPT DETECTED?
YES
INCREMENT CYLINDER COUNT
CYLINDER COUNT > MAXIMUM #
NO
READ RESULT BYTES
YES
REPEAT FOR 2ND HEAD
FORMAT COMPLETE
290474–10

Figure 9-6. Formatting

After each head for a cylinder has been formatted, a seek operation to the next cylinder is performed and the format process is repeated. Since the FORMAT TRACK command does not have implied seek capability, the SEEK command must be used. Also, as discussed in Section 9-2, the head settling time needs to be adhered to after each seek operation.

9.6 Save and Restore

The Save and Restore commands were developed for portable systems that use zero-volt powerdown to conserve power. These systems turn off the V_{CC} to most of the system and retain the system status in a specific location. In older floppy controller designs, in order for system designers to retrieve the floppy controller status, a lot of separate commands and register reads were required. The Save command stores the key status information in a single command, the Restore command restores this information with a single command. These commands can be integrated into the SMM module that is responsible for zero-volt powerdown.

The sequence of initializing the 82078 after a reset occurred and assuming a Save command was issued follows:

- Issue the Drive Spec command (if the design utilizes this command)
- Issue the Restore command

The Restore command programs the data rate and precompensation value via the DSR. It then restores the values normally programmed through the Configure, Specify, and Perpendicular commands. It also enables the previously selected values for the AUTO Powerdown command. The command then restores the PCN values to its previous values. The user is responsible for issuing the seek and recalibrate commands to restore the head to the proper location. There are some drives that do not recalibrate in which case the Restore command will restore the previous state completely. The PDOSC bit is retrievable using the Save command, however it is up to the system designer to set it correctly. The software must allow at least 20μs to execute the Restore command. When using the BOOTSEL bit in the TDR, the user must restore or reinitialize this bit to it's proper value.

9.7 Verifies

In some applications, the sector data needs to be verified immediately after each write operation. One verify technique reinitializes the DMA controller to perform a read transfer or verify transfer (DACK# is asserted but not RD#) immediately after each write operation. Issue a read command to the disk controller and the resulting status indicates if the CRC validated the previously written data. This technique has the drawback of requiring additional software intervention by having to reprogram the DMA controller between each sector write operation. The 82078 supports this verify technique but also provides a VERIFY command that does not require the use of the DMA controller.

To verify a write data transfer or format track operation using the VERIFY command, the software simply issues the command with the same format as a READ DATA command but without the support of the DMA controller. The 82078 will then perform a disk read operation without a host data transfer. The CRC will be calculated for each sector read and compared against the value stored on the disk. When the VERIFY command is complete, the status register reports detected CRC errors.

9.8 Powerdown State and Recovery

The two power management modes coupled with the internal oscillator power management forms an important consideration for programming the 82078. The recovery of 82078 and the time it takes to achieve complete recovery depends on how 82078 is powered down and how it is awakened. The following sections describe all the programming concerns and subtleties involved in using power management features of the 82078. The 3.3V version of the 82078 has the same power saving features as the 5.0V versions.

9.8.1 OSCILLATOR POWER MANAGEMENT

Section 4.1 covers the power management scheme involved in powering down of both an internal and an external oscillator. Both types of oscillators face drop out effects and require recovery times on the order of tens of milliseconds (this may be objectionable to some application software). This means that if the oscillator is powered down then it is imperative for the software to assure enough time for the oscillator to recover to a stable state. Oscillator power management must be controlled by the system software especially to maintain software transparency. In cases where the system goes into a standby mode (by user request or system time-out), the power management software can turn off the oscillator to conserve power. This can also be controlled in hardware using the Powerdown (PD#) pin. Complete recovery from an oscillator powerdown state requires the software to turn on the oscillator sufficiently ahead of awakening the 82078.

9.8.2 PART POWER MANAGEMENT

The part powerdown and wake up modes are covered in Section 4.2 in detail. This section is meant to address the programming concerns for the part (excluding the oscillator) during these modes.

9.8.2.1 Powerdown Modes

For both types of powerdown modes—DSR powerdown and auto powerdown, if reset is used to exit the part from powerdown then the internal microcontroller will go through a standard sequence: register initialization followed after some delay by an interrupt.

Software transparency in auto powerdown mode is preserved by MSR retaining the value of 80H which indicates that the part is ready to receive a command. This feature allows the part to powerdown while maintaining its responsiveness to any application software.

The PD and IDLE status bits can be monitored via the Status Register B (SRB, EREG EN = 1). Since the IDLE# pin stays high when the 82078 is in idle state, the IDLEMSK bit can be used to set the pin low again (as part of a power management routine).

NOTE:
The IDLEMSK prevents the user from knowing if the part has entered auto powerdown or DSR powerdown.

9.8.2.2 Wake Up Modes

Wake up from DSR powerdown results in the part being internally reset and all present status being lost. During DSR powerdown the RQM bit in the MSR is set. A software or hardware reset will wake up the part.

The case for wake up from auto powerdown is different. The BIOS and application software are very sensitive to delays involved in writing the first command bytes to the 82078. Most programs have short error time-outs in these cases. Such programs would not tolerate any floppy disk controller that was unable to receive the first byte of a command at any time. The following describes how 82078 uniquely sustains its software transparency during wake up sequences.

Prior to writing a command to 82078, it is first necessary to read the MSR to ensure that the 82078 is ready (RQM bit must be set) to receive the command. When the part detects a MSR read, it assumes that another command will follow and begins the wake up process. While the part is waking up it does not change the state of the MSR (MSR = 80H) and is able to receive the command in the FIFO. At this point one of the two following scenarios can occur.

No other command is sent subsequent to the MSR read. The part wakes up and initializes the minimum power up timer. Upon the expiration of this timer the part is once again put in powerdown state.

Another command follows the MSR read. If the command is sent during the part's recovery from powerdown, the part remembers the command, clears the RQM bit (to prevent further bytes being written) and acts on the command once it is fully awake.

If the MSR was not checked prior to writing of a command, the part will proceed as stated above with the RQM bit cleared and the command byte held until the internal microcontroller is ready. Writing the motor enable bits in DOR active will initiate the wake up sequence with RQM set high, ready to receive any command.

As it is clear from the above discussion, the immediate access to the floppy disk controller for the first command byte is vital to software transparency. The recovery of the part from powerdown may involve a delay after the first command byte has been issued. However, all programs have tolerance for the delay after the first command byte is issued. In a powered up chip, it is possible for the microcontroller to be in its "polling loop". As a result, the tolerance for this delay provides an excellent window for recovery of the part.

2

10.0 DESIGN APPLICATIONS

10.1 Operating the 82078-3 in a 3.3V Design

The design for 3.3V is the same as it is for 5.0V, however the floppy drive interface signals can be at either 3.3V or 5.0V levels depending on the voltage on the V_{CCF} pin. The V_{CCF} pin allows the FDD interface to be operated in mixed (3.3V/5.0V) mode. For example, if the system operates at 3.3V and the floppy disk drive operates at 5.0V, the 82078 can be configured to operate at 3.3V with 5.0V available to the drive interface. See Figure 10-1 for a schematic.

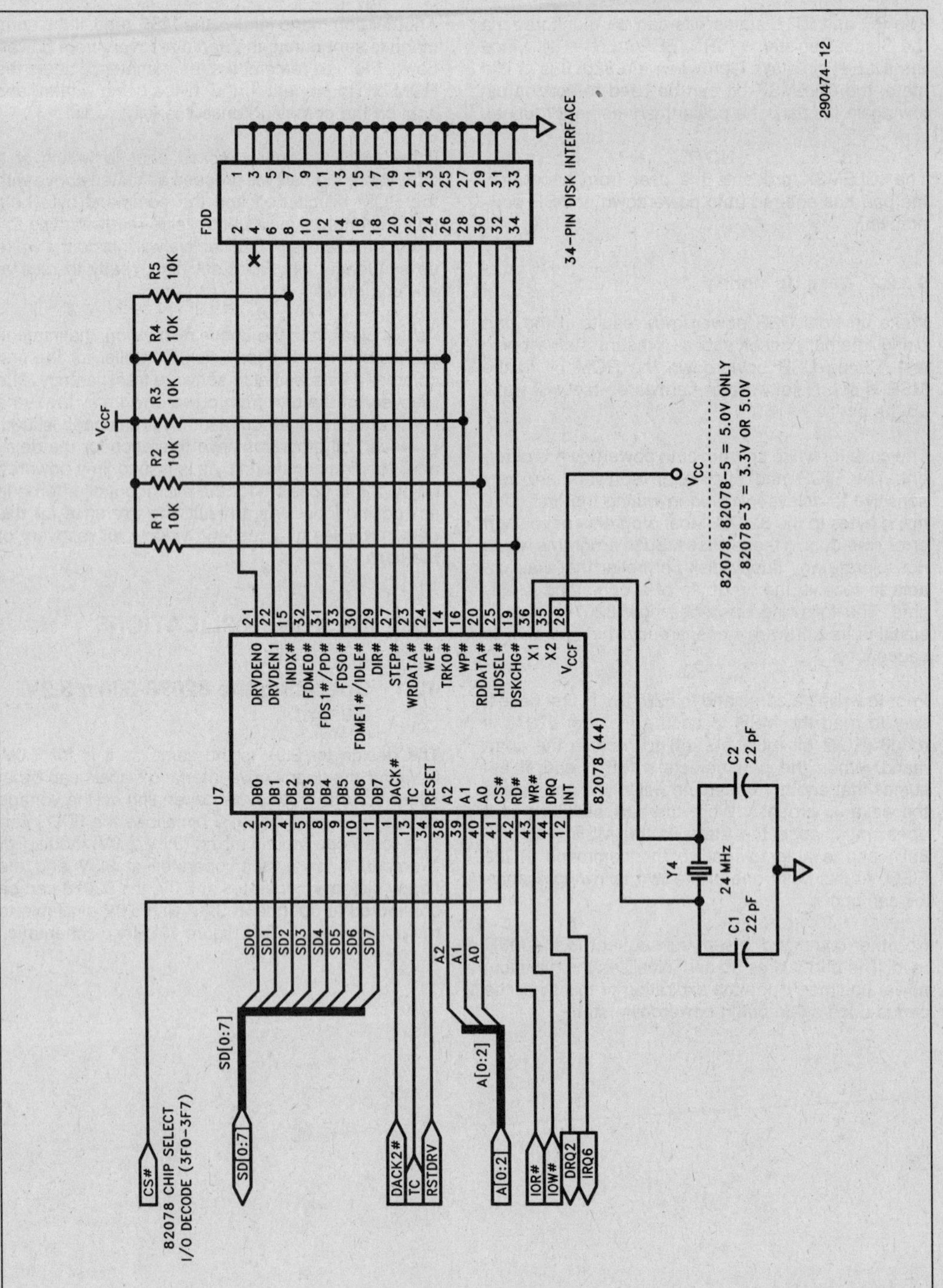

290474-12

Figure 10-1. 82078 PC/AT Design

10.2 Selectable Boot Drive

Generally a standard personal computer is configured with a 1.2 MB 5.25″ disk drive and a 1.44 MB or 2.88 MB 3.5″ disk drive. Usually the drive that connects as "A:" is the boot drive. At times the user may want to configure "B:" as the boot drive. Currently some BIOS' use a special implementation in software to accomplish this. The 82078 now offers this capability more efficiently by configuring the boot drives.

The 82078 allows for virtual drive designations. This is a result of multiplexing the boot drive select and motor enable lines, as shown in Figure 10-2.

The DRIVE SEL1 and the DRIVE SEL2 bits in the DOR register decode internally to generate the signals DSn. The MEn signals generate directly from the DOR register. The DSn and MEn signals get mapped to actual FDSn and FDMEn pins based on the BOOTSELn bits (selected in the TDR register). The exact mapping of BOOTSEL vs the FDSn and FDMEn pins is shown in the following table.

44PD EN	BOOTSEL (TDR)	Mapping
0	0	Default → DS0 → FDS0, ME0 → FDME0 DS1 → FDS1, ME1 → FDME1
0	1	DS0 → FDS1, ME0 → FDME1 DS1 → FDS0, ME1 → FDME0
1	X	DS0 → FDS0, ME0 → FDME0 DS1 → PD, ME1 → IDLE

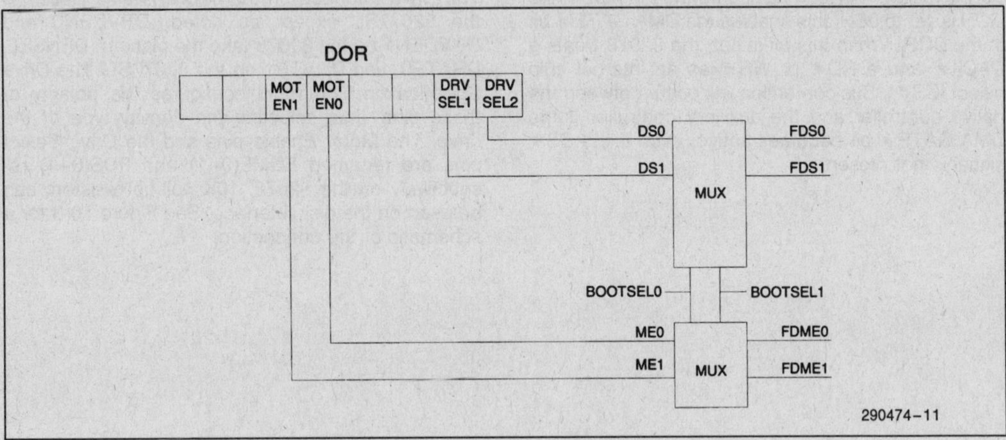

Figure 10-2. Virtual Drive Configuration

The BOOTSEL bit allows users to multiplex the output drive signals allowing different drives to be the boot drive. The DSn and MEn bits are considered virtual designations since the DSn and MEn signals get remapped to different corresponding physical FDSn and FDMEn pins. In other words, once the BOOTSEL bit is configured for a non-default selection, all future references made to the controller will be assumed as virtual designations. Note, due to the virtual designations TAPESEL[1:0] = 00 would never enable tape mode due to boot drive restrictions.

10.3 How to Disable the Native Floppy Contoller on the Motherboard

There are occasions when the floppy controller designed onto the motherboard of a system needs to be disabled in order to operate another floppy controller on the expansion bus. This can be done without changing the BIOS or remapping the address of the floppy controller (provided there is a jumper, or another way to disable the chip select on the native controller).

Upon reset, the DOR register in the 82078 is set to 00H. If the CS# is left enabled during the POST, the DOR is set to 0CH, this enables the DMA GATE# bit in the DOR. When this bit is set, the 82078 treats a DACK# and a RD# or WR# as an internal chip select (CS#). Bus contention will occur between the native controller and the auxiliary controller if the DMA GATE# bit becomes active, even if the CS# signal is not present.

The proper way to disable the native floppy controller is to disable the CS# before the system is turned on. This will prevent the native controller from getting initialized. Another option is to map the native controller to a secondary address space, then disable the DMA GATE# via the DOR disabling the DMA GATE#. This assumes that the native controller is switched to a secondary address space.

10.4 Replacing the 82077SL with a 82078 in a 5.0V Design

The 82078 easily replaces the 5.0V 82077SL with minimum design changes. With a few exceptions, most of the signals are named as they were in the 82077SL. Some pins were eliminated and others renamed to accommodate a reduced pin count and smaller package.

The connections to the AT bus are the same as the 82077SL with the following exceptions: MFM and IDENT have been removed. The PLL0 pin was removed. Tape drive mode on the 82078 must be configured via the Tape Drive Register (TDR).

The Drive Interface on the 82078 is also similar to the 82077SL except as noted: DRVDEN0 and DRVDEN1 on the 82078 take the place of DENSEL, DRATE0, and DRATE1 on the 82077SL. The Drive Specification Command configures the polarity of these pins, thus selecting the density type of the drive. The Motor Enable pins and the Drive Select pins are renamed FDME(0–1) and FDS(0–1) respectively on the 82078. 10K pull-up resistors can be used on the disk interface. See Figure 10-3 for a schematic of the connection.

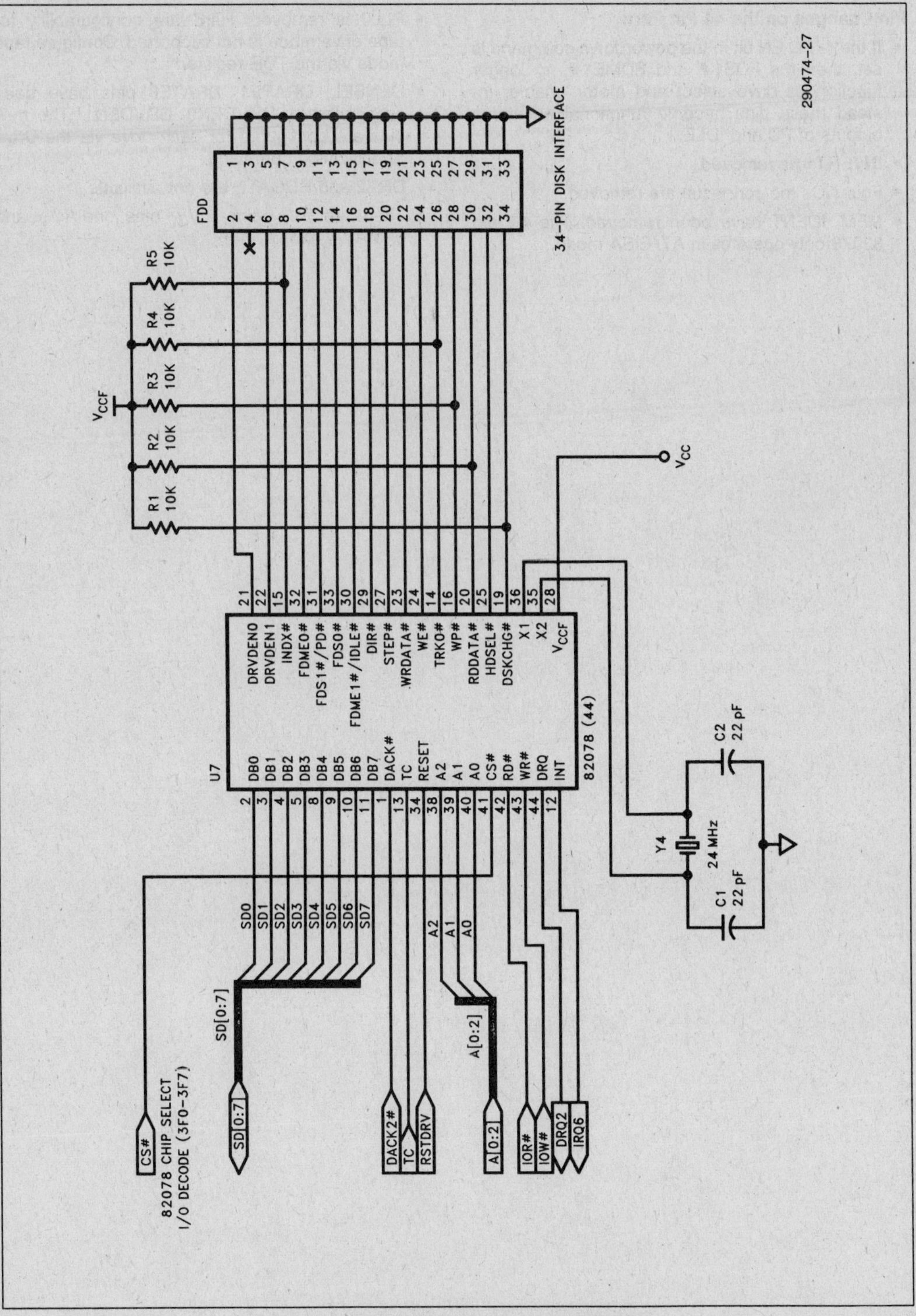

290474-27

Figure 10-3. 82077SL Conversion to 82078

Pin Changes on the 44 Pin Part:

- If the 44PD EN bit in the powerdown command is set, then the FDS1# and FDME1# no longer function as drive select and motor enable. Instead these pins become functional as status outputs of PD and IDLE.
- INVERT# is removed.
- Four NCs (no connects) are removed.
- MFM, IDENT have been removed. The 44 pin 82078 only operates in AT/EISA mode.
- PLL0 is removed. Hardware configurability for tape drive mode is not supported. Configure tape mode via the TDR register.
- DENSEL, DRATE1, DRATE0 pins have been substituted by DRVDEN0, DRVDEN1. The new pins are configured for each drive via the Drive Specification command.
- DRV2 and RDGATE are not available.
- There are 3 V_{SS} pins, 2 V_{CC} pins, one AV_{SS} and one AV_{CC} pin.

11.0 D.C. SPECIFICATIONS

NOTICE: This is a production data sheet. The specifications are subject to change without notice.

11.1 Absolute Maximum Ratings

Storage Temperature .... −65°C to +150°C
Supply Voltage .... −0.5 to +8.0V
Voltage on Any Input .... GND − 2V to 6.5V
Voltage on Any Output . GND − 0.5V to V_{CC} + 0.5V
Power Dissipation 1W

***WARNING:** *Stressing the device beyond the "Absolute Maximum Ratings" may cause permanent damage. These are stress ratings only. Operation beyond the "Operating Conditions" is not recommended and extended exposure beyond the "Operating Conditions" may affect device reliability.*

11.2 D.C. Characteristics T_A = 0°C to +70°C, V_{SS} = AV_{SS} = 0V

44 PIN D.C. CHARACTERISTICS

Symbol	Parameter	V_{CC} = +5V ±10%			V_{CC} = 3.3V ±0.3V		
		Min (V)	Max (V)	Test Conditions	Min (V)	Max (V)	Test Conditions
V_{ILC}	Input Low Voltage, X1	−0.5	0.8		−0.3	0.8	
V_{IHC}	Input High Voltage, X1	3.9	V_{CC} + 0.5		2.4	V_{CC} + 0.3	
V_{IL}	Input Low Voltage (All Pins except X1)	−0.5	0.8		−0.3	0.8	
V_{IH}	Input High Voltage (All Pins except X1)	2.0	V_{CC} + 0.5		2.0	V_{CC} + 0.3	
V_{OL}	System Interface		0.4	I_{OL} = 12 mA		0.4	I_{OL} = 6 mA
	FDD Interface Outptus		0.4	I_{OL} = 12 mA		0.4	I_{OL} = 6 mA
V_{OH}	All Outputs	3.0		I_{OH} = −4.0 mA	2.4		I_{OH} = −2.0 mA
	All Outputs	V_{CC} − 0.4		I_{OH} = −100 μA	V_{CC} − 0.2		I_{OH} = −100 μA

44 PIN D.C. CHARACTERISTICS I_{CC}

Symbol	Parameter	V_{CC} = +5V ±10%			V_{CC} = +3.3V ±0.3V		
		Typical	Max	Test Condition	Typical	Max	Test Condition
I_{CC1}	1 Mbps Data Rate V_{IL} = V_{SS}, V_{IH} = V_{CC}	15.4 mA	25 mA	(Notes 1, 2)	8.4 mA	16 mA	(Notes 1, 2)
I_{CC2}	1 Mbps Data Rate V_{IL} = 0.45, V_{IH} = 2.4	20.8 mA	30 mA	(Notes 1, 2)	8.6 mA	16 mA	(Notes 1, 2)
I_{CC3}	500 Kbps Data Rate V_{IL} = V_{SS}, V_{IH} = V_{CC}	11.8 mA	20 mA	(Notes 1, 2)	6.2 mA	14 mA	(Notes 1, 2)
I_{CC4}	500 Kbps Data Rate V_{IL} = 0.45, V_{IH} = 2.4	17.6 mA	25 mA	(Notes 1, 2)	6.2 mA	14 mA	(Notes 1, 2)
I_{CCSB}	I_{CC} in Powerdown	0 μA	60 μA	(Notes 3, 4)	0 μA	60 μA	(Notes 3, 4)
I_{IL}	Input Load Current (All Input Pins)		10 μA −10 μA	V_{IN} = V_{CC} V_{IN} = 0V		10 μA −10 μA	V_{IN} = V_{CC} V_{IN} = 0V

44 PIN D.C. CHARACTERISTICS I_{CC} (Continued)

Symbol	Parameter	$V_{CC} = +5V \pm 10\%$			$V_{CC} = +3.3V \pm 0.3V$		
		Typical	Max	Test Condition	Typical	Max	Test Condition
I_{OFL}	Data Bus Output Float Leakage		±10 μA	$0.45 < V_{OUT} < V_{CC}$		±10 μA	$0.45 < V_{OUT} < V_{CC}$

NOTES:
1. Only the data bus inputs may float.
2. Tested while reading a sync field of "00". Outputs not connected to D.C. loads.
3. $V_{IL} = V_{SS}$, $V_{IH} = V_{CC}$; Outputs not connected to D.C. loads.
4. Typical value with the oscillator off.

CAPACITANCE

C_{IN}	Input Capacitance	10	pF	f = 1 MHz, T_A = 25°C
C_{IN1}	Clock Input Capacitance	20	pF	Sampled, Not 100% Tested
$C_{I/O}$	Input/Output Capacitance	20	pF	

NOTE:
All pins except pins under test are tied to A.C. ground.

LOAD CIRCUIT

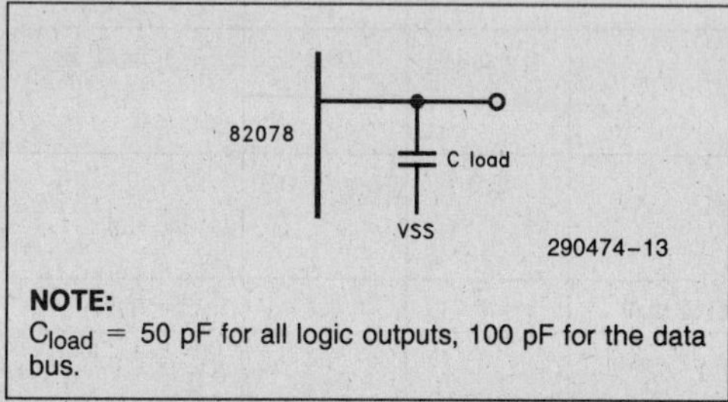

290474–13

NOTE:
C_{load} = 50 pF for all logic outputs, 100 pF for the data bus.

A.C. TESTING INPUT, OUTPUT WAVEFORM

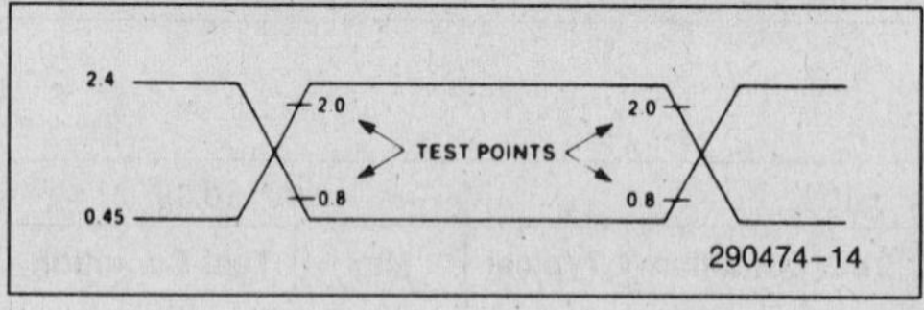

290474–14

11.3 Oscillator

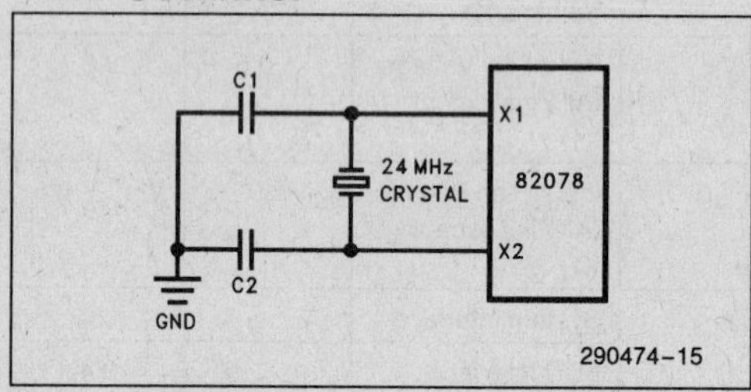

290474–15

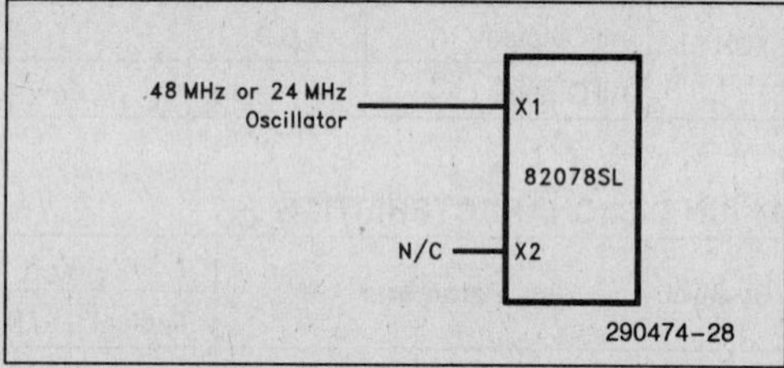

290474–28

The 24 MHz clock can be supplied either by a crystal or a MOS level square wave. All internal timings are referenced to this clock or a scaled count which is data rate dependent.

The crystal oscillator must be allowed to run for 10 ms after V_{CC} has reached 4.5V or exiting the POWERDOWN mode to guarantee that it is stable.

Frequency:	24 MHz ±0.1%
Mode:	Parallel Resonant Fundamental Mode
Series Resistance:	Less than 40Ω
Shunt Capacitance:	Less than 5 pF

12.0 A.C. SPECIFICATIONS

T_A = 0°C to +70°C, V_{CC} = +5V ±10%, +3.3V ±0.3V, V_{SS} = AV_{SS} = 0V

Symbol	Parameter	Min	Max	Unit
CLOCK TIMINGS				
t1	Clock Rise Time		10	ns
	Clock Fall Time		10	ns
t2	Clock High Time(7)	16	26	ns
t3	Clock Low Time(7)	16	26	ns
t4	Clock Period	41.66	41.66	ns
t5	Internal Clock Period (3)			
HOST READ CYCLES				
t7	Address Setup to RD#	5		ns
t8	RD# Pulse Width	90		ns
t9	Address Hold from RD#	0		ns
t10	Data Valid from RD#(12)		80	ns
t11	Command Inactive	60		ns
t12	Output Float Delay		35	ns
t13	INT Delay from RD#(16)		t5 + 125	ns
t14	Data Hold from RD#	5		ns
HOST WRITE CYCLES				
t15	Address Setup to WR#	5		ns
t16	WR# Pulse Width	90		ns
t17	Address Hold from WR#	0		ns
t18	Command Inactive	60		ns
t19	Data Setup to WR#	70		ns
t20	Data Hold from WR#	0		ns
t21	INT Delay from WR#(16)		t5 + 125	ns
DMA CYCLES				
t22	DRQ Cycle Period(1)	6.5		μs
t23	DACK# to DRQ Inactive		75	ns
t23a	DRQ to DACK# Inactive	(Note 15)		ns
t24	RD# to DRQ Inactive(4)		100	ns
t25	DACK# Setup to RD#, WR#	5		ns
t26	DACK# Hold from RD#, WR#	0		ns
t27	DRQ to RD#, WR# Active(1)	0	6	μs
t28	Terminal Count Width(10)	50		ns
t29	TC to DRQ Inactive		150	ns

12.0 A.C. SPECIFICATIONS

T_A = 0°C to +70°C, V_{CC} = +5V ±10%, +3.3V ±0.3V, V_{SS} = AV_{SS} = 0V (Continued)

Symbol	Parameter	Min	Max	Unit
RESET				
t30	"Hardware" Reset Width(5)	1.13		μs
t30a	"Software" Reset Width(5)	(Note 11)		ns
t31	Reset to Control Inactive		2	μs
WRITE DATA TIMING				
t32	Data Width(6)			ns
DRIVE CONTROL				
t35	DIR# Setup to STEP#(14)	1.0		μs
t36	DIR# Hold from STEP#	10		μs
t37	STEP# Active Time (High)	2.5		μs
t38	STEP# Cycle Time(2)			μs
t39	INDEX# Pulse Width	5		t5
t41	WE# to HDSEL# Change	(Note 13)		ms
READ DATA TIMING				
t40	Read Data Pulse Width	50		ns
t44	PLL Data Rate	90		ns
	82078		1M	bits/sec
t44	Data Rate Period = 1/f44			
tLOCK	Lockup Time		64	t44

NOTES:

1. This timing is for FIFO threshold = 1. When FIFO threshold is N bytes, the value should be multiplied by N and subtract 1.5 μs. The value shown is for 1 Mbps, scales linearly with data rate.
2. This value can range from 0.5 ms to 8.0 ms and is dependent upon data rate and the Specify command value.
3. Many timings are a function of the selected data rate. The nominal values for the internal clock period (t5) for the various data rates are:

1 Mbps	3 × oscillator period = 125 ns
500 Kbps	6 × oscillator period = 250 ns
300 Kbps	10 × oscillator period = 420 ns
250 Kbps	12 × oscillator period = 500 ns

4. If DACK# transitions before RD#, then this specification is ignored. If there is no transition on DACK#, then this becomes the DRQ inactive delay.

5. Reset requires a stable oscillator to meet the minimum active period.
6. Based on the internal clock period (t5). For various data rates, the Write Data Width minimum values are:

1 Mbps	5 × oscillator period − 50 ns = 150 ns
500 Kbps	10 × oscillator period − 50 ns = 360 ns
300 Kbps	16 × oscillator period − 50 ns = 615 ns
250 Kbps	19 × oscillator period − 50 ns = 740 ns

7. Test points for clock high time are 3.5V. Due to transitional times, clock high time max and clock low time max cannot be met simultaneously. Clock high time min and clock low time max can not be met simultaneously.
8. Based on internal clock period (t5).
9. Jitter tolerance is defined as:

   (Maximum bit shift from nominal position ÷ ¼ period of nominal data rate) × 100%

   is a measure of the allowable bit jitter that may be present and still be correctly detected. The data separator jitter tolerance is measured under dynamic conditions that jitters the bit stream according to a reverse precompensation algorithm.
10. TC width is defined as the time that both TC and DACK# are active. Note that TC and DACK# must overlap at least 50 ns.
11. The minimum reset active period for a software reset is dependent on the data rate, after the 82078 has been properly reset using the t30 spec. The minimum software reset period then becomes:

1 Mbps	3 × t4 = 125 ns
500 Kbps	6 × t4 = 250 ns
300 Kbps	10 × t4 = 420 ns
250 Kbps	12 × t4 = 500 ns

12. Status Register's status bits which are not latched may be updated during a Host read operation.
13. The minimum MFM values for WE to HDSEL change (t41) for the various data rates are:

1 Mbps	0.5 ms + [8 × GPL]
500 Kbps	1.0 ms + [16 × GPL]
300 Kbps	1.6 ms + [26.66 × GPL]
250 Kbps	2.0 ms + [32 × GPL]

   GPL is the size of gap3 defined in the sixth byte of a Write Command.
14. This timing is a function of the selected data rate as follows:

1 Mbps	1.0 μs min
500 Kbps	2.0 μs min
300 Kbps	3.3 μs min
250 Kbps	4.0 μs min

15. This timing is a function of the internal clock period (t5) and is given as (⅔) t5. The values of t5 are shown in Note 3.
16. The timings t13 and t21 are specified for INT signal in the polling mode only. These timings in case of the result phase of the read and write commands are microcode dependent.

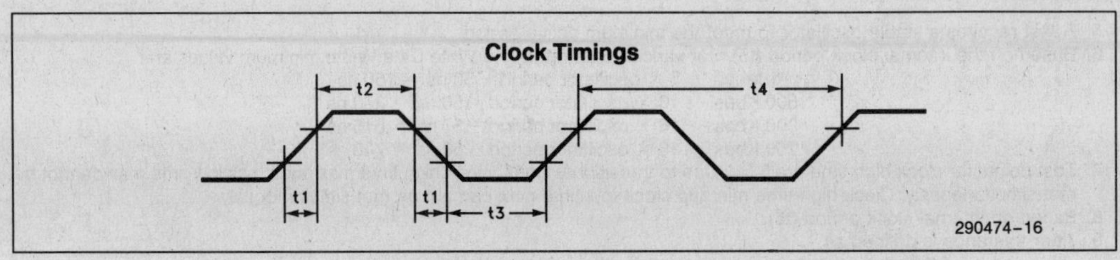
Clock Timings
t2
t4
t1
t1
t3
290474-16

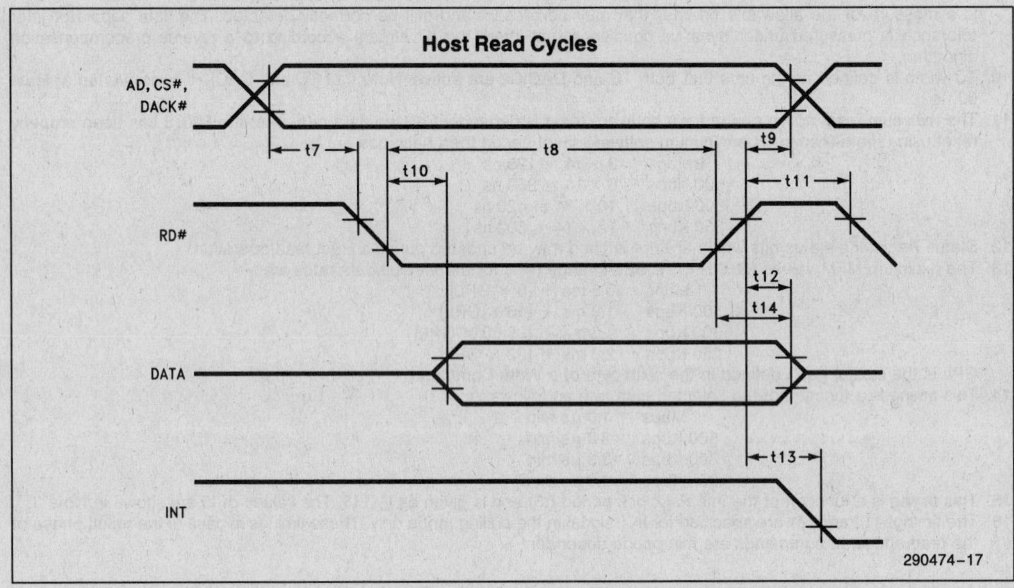
Host Read Cycles
AD, CS#, DACK#
t7
t8
t9
t10
t11
RD#
t12
t14
DATA
t13
INT
290474-17

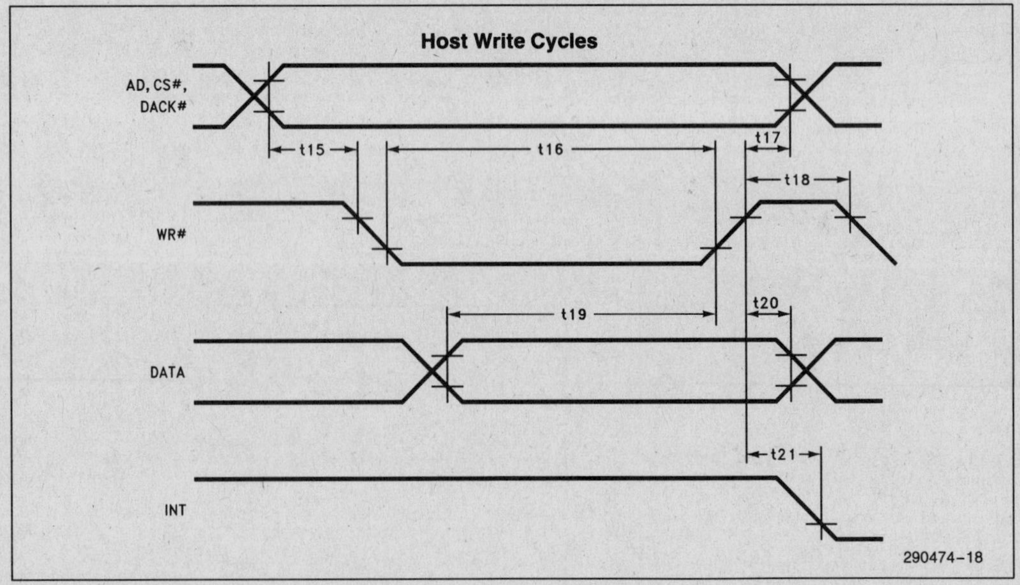
Host Write Cycles
AD, CS#, DACK#
t15
t16
t17
t18
WR#
t19
t20
DATA
t21
INT
290474-18

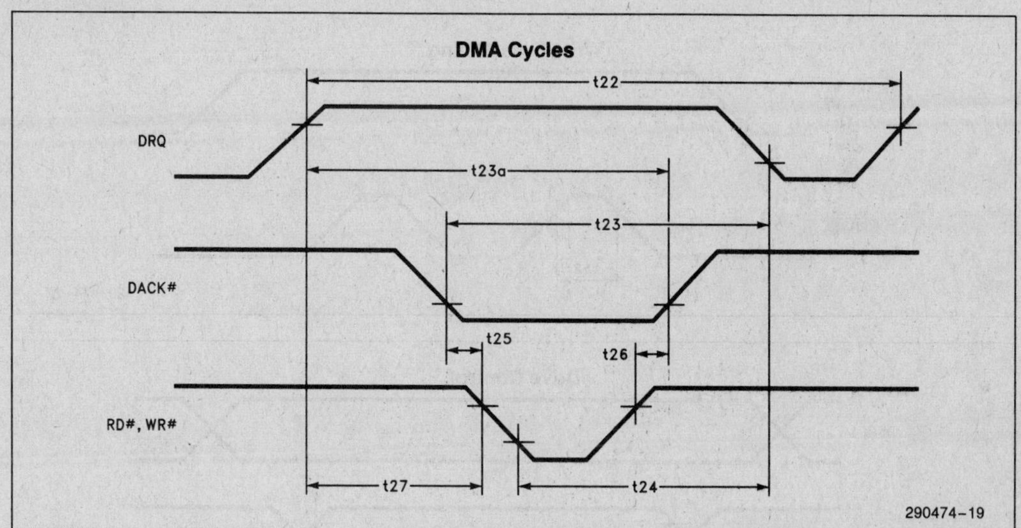

290474-19

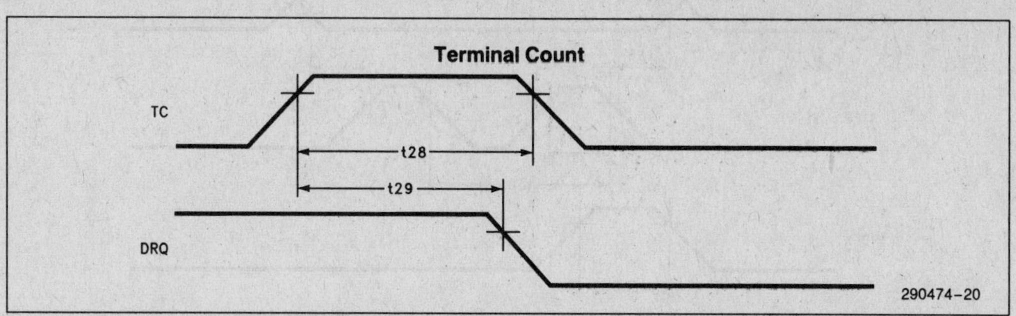

290474-20

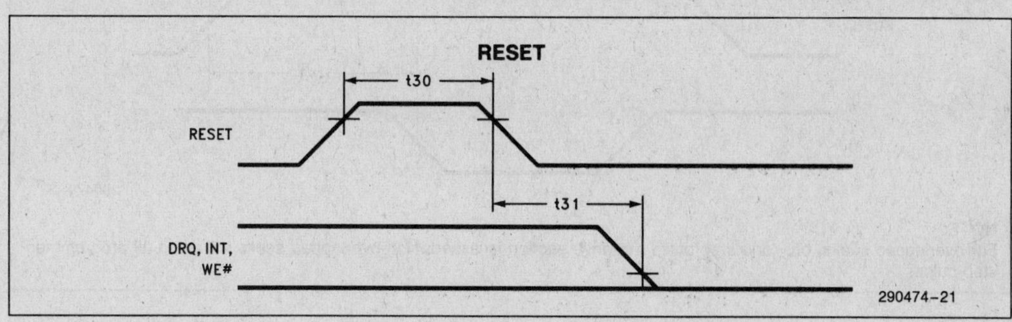

290474-21

2

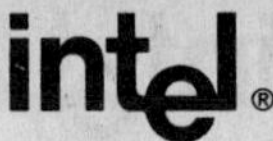

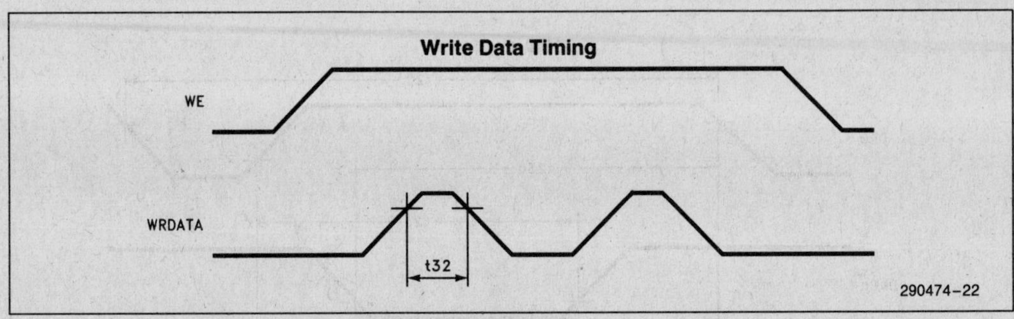

Write Data Timing

WE
WRDATA
t32

290474-22

Drive Control

DSO, 1
DIR
t35
t36
STEP
t37
t38
INDEX
t39
HDSEL
t41
WE

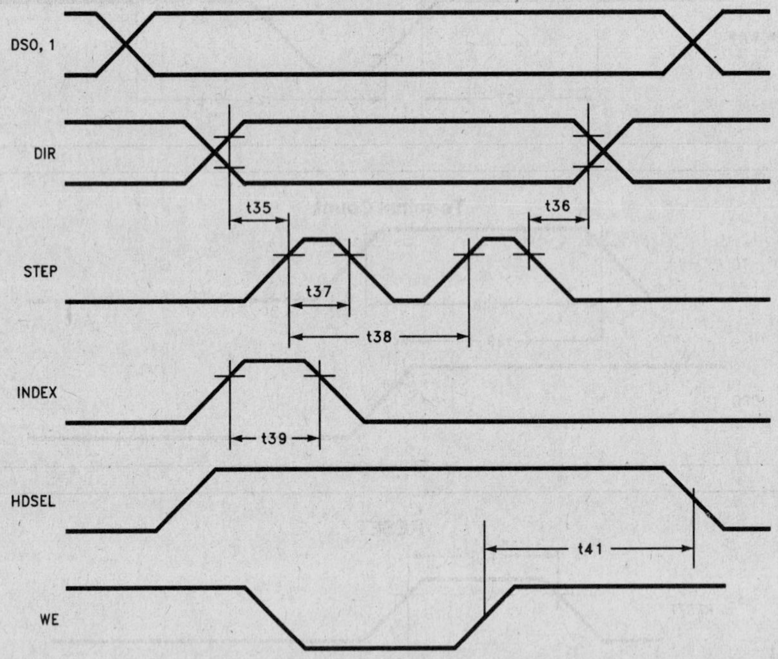

290474-23

NOTE:
For overlapped seeks, only one step pulse per drive section is issued. Non-overlapped seeks will issue all programmed step pulses.

Internal PLL

t44
RDDATA
t40

290474-24

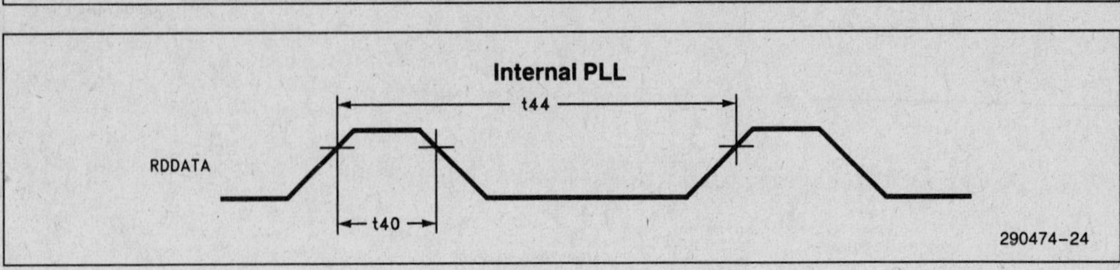

12.1 Package Outline for the 44 Pin QFP Part

82078 addresses the current need of the smaller and thinner packages, for the current market. The size of the part is becoming increasingly important in the portable computer market. The QFP part considerably reduces the real estate consumed. The package outline with the appropriate dimensions are given below:

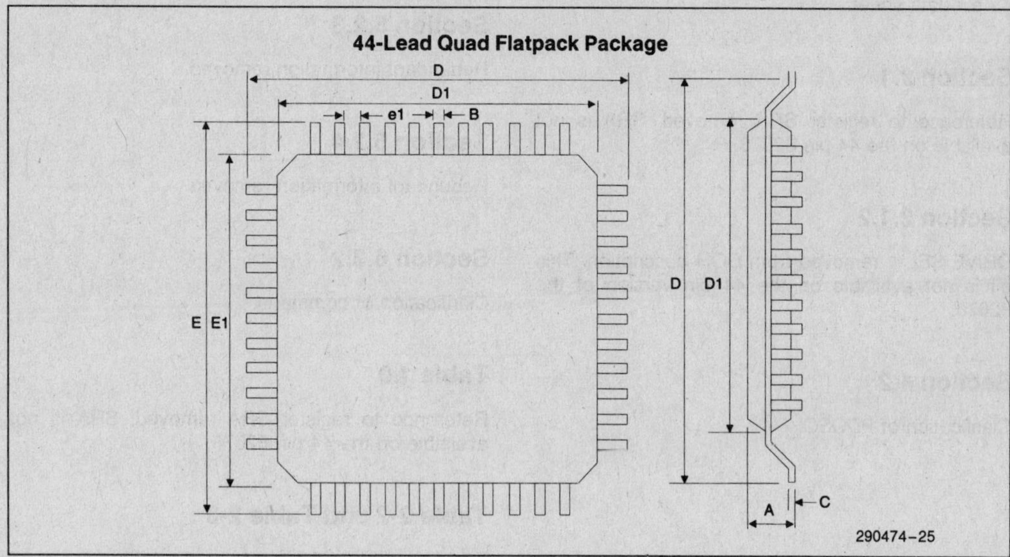

290474-25

Description	Symbol	44 Pin QFP Package	
		Nominal (mm)	Tolerance (mm)
Overall Height	A	2.10	±0.25
Stand Off	A1	0.35	±0.15
Lead Width	B	0.30	±0.10
Lead Thickness	C	0.15	±0.05
Terminal	D	12.4	±0.40
Long Side	D1	10.0	±0.10
Terminal	E	12.4	±0.40
Short Side	E1	10.0	±0.10
Lead Spacing	e1	0.80	±0.15
Lead Count	N	44	

13.0 REVISION HISTORY FOR THE 82078 44 PIN

The following list represents the key differences between version 002 and version 003 of the 82078 44 pin data sheet.

Section 2.1

Reference to register SRA removed. SRA is not available on the 44 pin 82078.

Section 2.1.2

DRIVE SEL 1 removed from DOR description. This bit is not available on the 44 pin version of the 82078.

Section 4.2

Clarification of PDOSC.

Section 4.4

Reference to register SRA removed. SRA is not available on the 44 pin 82078.

Section 5.2.3

Redundant information removed.

Section 5.2.4

Redundant information removed.

Section 6.3.2

Clarification of command.

Table 1.0

Reference to register SRA removed. SRA is not available on the 44 pin 82078.

Table 2-2 and Table 2-3

Table headings swapped to proper tables.

intel®

82078 64 PIN
CHMOS SINGLE-CHIP FLOPPY DISK CONTROLLER

- Small Footprint and Low Height Packages
- Supports Standard 5.0V as well as Low Voltage 3.3V Platforms
  - Selectable 3.3V and 5.0V Configuration
  - 5.0V Tolerant Drive Interface
- Enhanced Power Management
  - Application Software Transparency
  - Programmable Powerdown Command
  - Save and Restore Commands for Zero-Volt Powerdown
  - Auto Powerdown and Wakeup Modes
  - Two External Power Management Pins
  - Consumes no Power when in Powerdown
- Integrated Analog Data Separator
  - 250 Kbps
  - 300 Kbps
  - 500 Kbps
  - 1 Mbps
  - 2 Mbps
- Programmable Internal Oscillator
- Floppy Drive Support Features
  - Drive Specification Command
  - Media ID Capability Provides Media Recognition
  - Drive ID Capability Allows the User to Recognize the Type of Drive
  - Selectable Boot Drive
  - Standard IBM and ISO Format Features
  - Format with Write Command for High Performance in Mass Floppy Duplication
- Integrated Tape Drive Support
  - Standard 1 Mbps/500 Kbps/250 Kbps Tape Drives
  - New 2 Mbps Tape Drive Mode
- Perpendicular Recording Support for 4 MB Drives
- Integrated Host/Disk Interface Drivers
- Fully Decoded Drive Select and Motor Signals
- Programmable Write Precompensation Delays
- Addresses 256 Tracks Directly, Supports Unlimited Tracks
- 16 Byte FIFO
- Single-Chip Floppy Disk Controller Solution for Portables and Desktops
  - 100% PC AT* Compatible
  - 100% PS/2* Compatible
  - 100% PS/2 Model 30 Compatible
  - Fully Compatible with Intel386™ SL Microprocessor SuperSet
- Integrated Drive and Data Bus Buffers
- Available in 64 Pin QFP Package

The 82078, a 24 MHz crystal, a resistor package, and a device chip select implements a complete solution. All programmable options default to 82078 compatible values. The dual PLL data separator has better performance than most board level/discrete PLL implementations. The FIFO allows better system performance in multi-master (e.g., Microchannel, EISA).

The 82078 maintains complete software compatibility with the 82077SL/82077AA/8272A floppy disk controllers. It contains programmable power management features while integrating all of the logic required for floppy disk control. The power management features are transparent to any application software. There are two versions of 82078 floppy disk controllers, the 82078SL and 82078-1.

The 82078 is fabricated with Intel's advanced CHMOS III technology and is also available in a 44-lead QFP package.

*Other brands and names are the property of their respective owner.

October 1993
Order Number: 290475-003

82078 64 Pin CHMOS Single-Chip Floppy Disk Controller

CONTENTS PAGE

CONTENTS PAGE

CONTENTS PAGE

CONTENTS PAGE

2

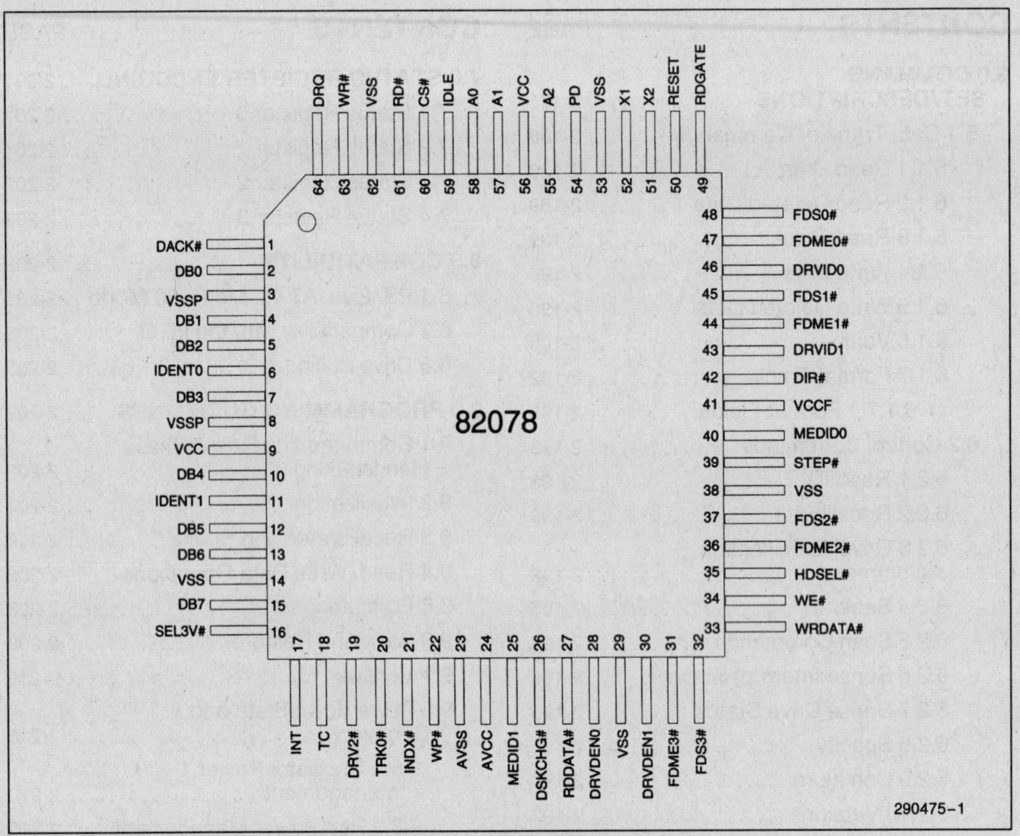

64 DRQ, 63 WR#, 62 VSS, 61 RD#, 60 CS#, 59 IDLE, 58 A0, 57 A1, 56 VCC, 55 A2, 54 PD, 53 VSS, 52 X1, 51 X2, 50 RESET, 49 RDGATE

DACK# 1, DB0 2, VSSP 3, DB1 4, DB2 5, IDENT0 6, DB3 7, VSSP 8, VCC 9, DB4 10, IDENT1 11, DB5 12, DB6 13, VSS 14, DB7 15, SEL3V# 16

82078

48 FDS0#, 47 FDME0#, 46 DRVID0, 45 FDS1#, 44 FDME1#, 43 DRVID1, 42 DIR#, 41 VCCF, 40 MEDID0, 39 STEP#, 38 VSS, 37 FDS2#, 36 FDME2#, 35 HDSEL#, 34 WE#, 33 WRDATA#

17 INT, 18 TC, 19 DRV2#, 20 TRK0#, 21 INDX#, 22 WP#, 23 AVSS, 24 AVCC, 25 MEDID1, 26 DSKCHG#, 27 RDDATA#, 28 DRVDEN0, 29 VSS, 30 DRVDEN1, 31 FDME3#, 32 FDS3#

290475–1

Figure 1-0. 82078 Pinout

Table 1-0. 82078 (64 Pin) Description

Symbol	Pin #	I/O	@ H/W Reset	Description
HOST INTERFACE				
RESET	50	I	N/A	**RESET:** A high level places the 82078 in a known idle state. All registers are cleared except those set by the Specify command.
A0 A1 A2	58 57 55	I	N/A	**ADDRESS:** Selects one of the host interface registers: **A2 A1 A0 Access Register** 0 0 0 R Status Register A SRA 0 0 1 R/W Status Register B SRB 0 1 0 R/W Digital Output Register DOR 0 1 1 R/W Tape Drive Register TDR 1 0 0 R Main Status Register MSR 1 0 0 W Data Rate Select Register DSR 1 0 1 R/W Data Register (FIFO) FIFO 1 1 0 Reserved 1 1 1 R Digital Input Register DIR 1 1 1 W Configuration Control Register CCR
CS#	60	I	N/A	**CHIP SELECT:** Decodes the base address range and qualifies RD# and WR#.

Table 1-0. 82078 (64 Pin) Description (Continued)

Symbol	Pin #	I/O	@ H/W Reset	Description
HOST INTERFACE (Continued)				
RD#	61	I	N/A	**READ:** Read control signal for data transfers from the floppy drive to the system.
WR#	63	I	N/A	**WRITE:** Write control signal for data transfers to the floppy drive from the system.
DRQ	64	O		**DMA REQUEST:** Requests service from a DMA controller. Normally active high, but will go to high impedance in AT and Model 30 modes when the appropriate bit is set in the DOR.
DACK#	1	I	N/A	**DMA ACKNOWLEDGE:** Control input that qualifies the RD#, WR# inputs in DMA cycles. Normally active low, but is disabled in AT and Model 30 modes when the appropriate bit is set in the DOR.
DB0 DB1 DB2 DB3 DB4 DB5 DB6 DB7	2 4 5 7 10 12 13 15	I/O		**DATA BUS:** 12 mA data bus.
IDENT0 IDENT1	6 11	I	N/A	**IDENTITY:** These inputs decode between the several operation modes available to the user. These pins have no effect on the DRVDEN pins. **IDENT0 IDENT1 INTERFACE** 1 1 AT mode 1 0 ILLEGAL 0 1 PS/2 mode 0 0 Model 30 **AT MODE:** Major options are: enables DMA gate logic, TC is active high, Status Register B is available based on a bit the powerdown command. **PS/2 MODE:** Major options are: no DMA gate logic, TC is active low, Status Registers A & B are available. **MODEL 30 MODE:** Major options are: enable DMA gate logic, TC is active high, Status Registers A & B are available.
INT	17	O		**INTERRUPT:** Signals a data transfer in non-DMA mode and when status is valid. Normally active high, but goes to high impedance when the appropriate bit is set in the DOR.
TC	18	I	N/A	**TERMINAL COUNT:** Control line from a DMA controller that terminates the current disk transfer. TC is effective only when qualified by DACK#. This input is active high in the AT, and Model 30 modes when the appropriate bit is set in the DOR.
X1 X2	52 51		N/A	**EXTERNAL CLOCK OR CRYSTAL:** Connection for a 24 MHz fundamental mode parallel resonant crystal. X1 can also be driven by an external clock (external oscillator) which can be either at 48 MHz or 24 MHz. If external oscillator is used then the PDOSC bit can be set to turn off the internal oscillator. Also, if a 48 MHz exernal oscillator is used then the CLK48 bit must be set in the enhanced CONFIGURE command.

Table 1-0. 82078 (64 Pin) Description (Continued)

Symbol	Pin #	I/O	@ H/W Reset	Description
POWER MANAGEMENT				
SEL3V#	16	I	N/A	**SELECT 3.3V:** This is a control pin that is used to select between 3.3V operation and 5.0V operation. This is an active low signal and selects 3.3V mode of operation when tied to ground.
PD	54	O		**POWERDOWN:** This pin is active high whenever the part is in powerdown state, either via DSR POWERDOWN bit or via the Auto Powerdown Mode. This pin can be used to disable an external oscillator's output.
IDLE	59	O		**IDLE:** This pin indicates that the part is in the IDLE state and can be powered down. IDLE state is defined as MSR = 80H, INT = 0, and the head being "unloaded" (as defined in Section 4.0, Power Management Features). Whenever the part is in this state, IDLE pin is active high. If the part is powered down by the Auto Powerdown Mode, IDLE pin is set high and if the part is powered down by setting the DSR POWERDOWN bit, IDLE pin is set low.
PLL SECTION				
RDDATA#	27	I	N/A	**READ DATA:** Serial data from the floppy disk.
RDGATE	49	O		**READ GATE:** This signal is basically used for diagnostic purposes.
DISK CONTROL				
DRV2#	19	I	N/A	**DRIVE2:** This is an active low signal that indicates whether a second drive is installed and is reflected in SRA.
TRK0#	20	I	N/A	**TRACK0:** This is an active low signal that indicates that the head is on track 0.
INDX#	21	I	N/A	**INDEX:** This is an active low signal that indicates the beginning of the track.
WP#	22	I	N/A	**WRITE PROTECT:** This is an active low signal that indicates whether the floppy disk in the drive is write protected.
MEDID1 MEDID0	25 40	I	N/A	**MEDIA ID:** These are active high signals that are output from the drive to indicate the density type of the media installed in the floppy drive. These should be tied low if not being used.
DSKCHG#	26	I	N/A	**DISK CHANGE:** This is an input from the floppy drive reflected in the DIR.
DRVDEN0 DRVDEN1	28 30	O		**DRIVE DENSITY:** These signals are used by the floppy drive to configure the drive for the appropriate media.
FDME3# FDME2# FDME1# FDME0#	31 36 44 47	O		**FLOPPY DRIVE MOTOR ENABLE:** Decoded motor enables for drives 0 to 3. The motor enable pins are directly controlled via the DOR and are a function of the mapping based on BOOTSEL bits in the TDR.
FDS3# FDS2# FDS1# FDS0#	32 37 45 48	O		**FLOPPY DRIVE SELECT:** Decoded floppy drive selects for drives 0 to 3. These outputs are decoded from the select bits in the DOR and are a function of the mapping based on BOOTSEL bits in the TDR.
WRDATA#	33	O		**WRITE DATA:** MFM serial data to the drive. Precompensation value is selectable through software.

Table 1-0. 82078 (64 Pin) Description (Continued)

Symbol	Pin #	I/O	@ H/W Reset	Description
DISK CONTROL (Continued)				
WE#	34	O		**WRITE ENABLE:** Floppy drive control signal that enables the head to write onto the floppy disk.
HDSEL#	35	O		**HEAD SELECT:** Selects which side of the floppy disk is to be used for the corresponding data transfer. It is active low and an active level selects head 1, otherwise it defaults to head 0.
STEP#	39	O		**STEP:** Supplies step pulses to the floppy drive to move the head between tracks.
DIR#	42	O		**DIRECTION:** It is an active low signal which controls the direction the head moves when a step signal is present. The head moves inwards towards the center if this signal is active.
DRVID0 DRVID1	46 43	I	N/A	**DRIVE ID:** These signals are input from the floppy drive and indicate the type of drive being used. These should be tied low if not being used.
POWER AND GROUND SIGNALS				
V_{CCF}	41		N/A	**VOLTAGE:** +5V for 5V floppy drive and 3.3V for 3.3V floppy drive.*
V_{CC}	9 56		N/A	**VOLTAGE:** +5V or 3.3V
V_{SSP}	3 8		N/A	**GROUND:** 0V
V_{SS}	14 29 38 53 62		N/A	**GROUND:** 0V
AV_{CC}	24		N/A	**ANALOG VOLTAGE**
AV_{SS}	23		N/A	**ANALOG GROUND**

***NOTE:**
The digital power supply V_{CC} and the analog power supply AV_{CC} should either be the same or regulated to be within 0.1V of either.

1.0 INTRODUCTION

The 82078, a 24 MHz (or 48 MHz) oscillator, a resistor package and a chip select implement a complete design. The power management features of the 82078 are transparent to application software, the 82078 seems awake to the software even in power-down mode. All drive control signals are fully decoded and have 24 mA (12 mA @ 3.3V) drive buffers. Signals returned from the drive are sent through on-chip input buffers with hysteresis for noise immunity. The integrated analog data separator needs no external compensation of components, yet allows for wide motor variation with exceptionally low soft error rates. The microprocessor interface has 12 mA drive buffers on the data bus plus 100% hardware register compatibility for PC-AT and Microchannel systems. The 16-byte FIFO with programmable thresholds is extremely useful in multi-master systems (Micro-Channel, EISA) or systems with large bus latency.

The 82078 features:

- 3.3V operation
- Small QFP package
- 2 Mbps data rate for tape drives
- Register enhancements from the 82077SL

Several pin changes accommodate the reduced pin count (from the 68 pin 82077SL) and the added features. Functional compatibility refers to software transparency between 82077SL/AA and the 82078. The 64 pin part will implement a superset of the features required to support all platforms, but is not pin to pin compatible to the 82077SL.

The 82078SL is capable of operating at both 3.3V and 5.0V. The 82078-1 only operates at 5.0V but has an available 2 Mbps tape drive data rate. All other features are available on both parts.

Part Specification	3.3V	5.0V	2 Mbps Data Rate
82078SL	X	X	
82078-1		X	X

Figure 1-1 is a block diagram of the 82078.

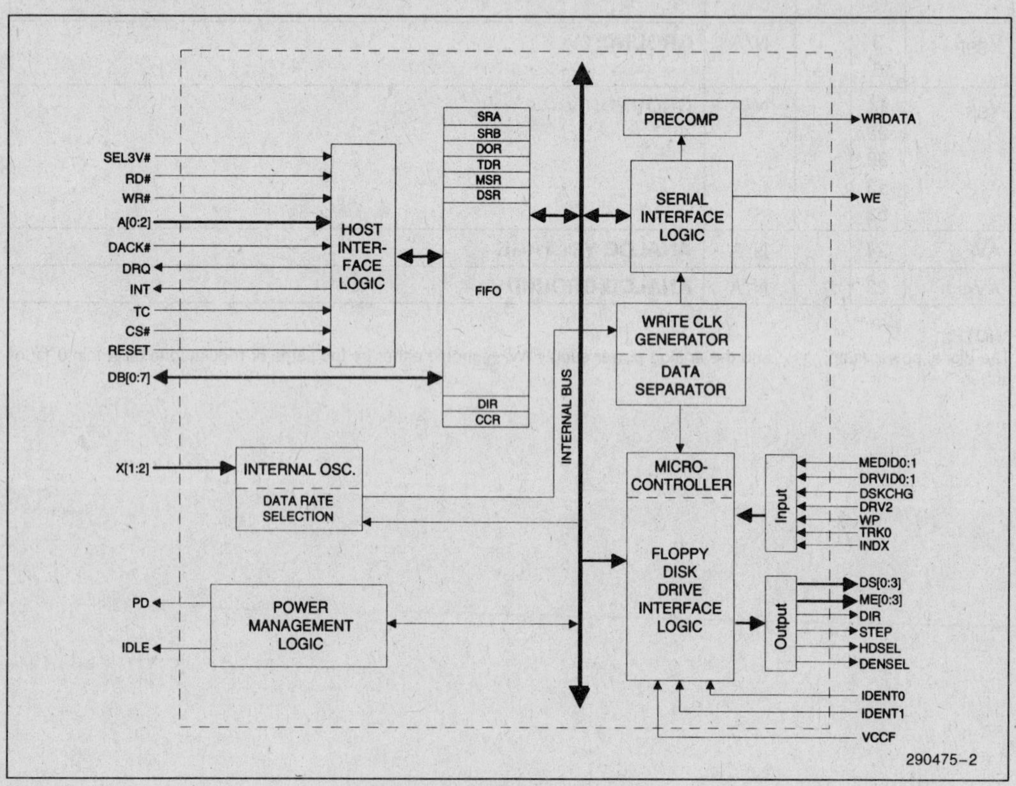

290475–2

Figure 1-1. 82078 Block Diagram

2.0 MICROPROCESSOR INTERFACE

The interface consists of the standard asynchronous signals: RD#, WR#, CS#, A0–A2, INT, DMA control and a data bus. The address lines select between configuration registers, the FIFO and control/status registers. This interface can be switched between PC AT, Model 30, or PS/2 normal modes. The PS/2 register sets are a superset of the registers found in a PC-AT.

2.1 Status, Data and Control Registers

As shown below, the base address range is supplied via the CS# pin. For PC-AT or PS/2 designs, the primary and secondary address ranges are 3F0 Hex to 3F7 Hex and 370 Hex to 377 Hex respectively.

A2	A1	A0	Access Type	Register	
0	0	0	R	Status Register A	SRA
0	0	1	R/W	Status Register B	SRB
0	1	0	R/W	Digital Output Register	DOR
0	1	1	R/W	Tape Drive Register	TDR
1	0	0	R	Main Status Register	MSR
1	0	0	W	Data Rate Select Register	DSR
1	0	1	R/W	Data (First In First Out)	FIFO
1	1	0		Reserved	
1	1	1	R	Digital Input Register	DIR
1	1	1	W	Configuration Control Register	CCR

In the following sections, the various registers are shown in their powerdown state. The "UC" notation stands for a value that is returned without change from the active mode. The notation "*" means that the value is reflecting the required status (for powerdown). "n/a" means not applicable. "X" indicates that the value is undefined.

2.1.1 STATUS REGISTER A (SRA, PS/2 MODE)

This register is read-only and monitors the state of the interrupt pin and several disk interface pins. This register is part of the register set, and is not accessible in PC-AT mode.

This register can be accessed during powerdown state without waking up the 82078 from its powerdown state.

Bits	7	6	5	4	3	2	1	0
Function	INT PENDING	DRV2#	STEP	TRK0#	HDSEL	INDX#	WP#	DIR
H/W Reset State	0	DRV2#	0	TRK0#	0	INDX#	WP#	0
Auto PD State	0*	UC	0*	1	0*	1	1	0*

The INT PENDING bit is used by software to monitor the state of the 82078 INTERRUPT pin. By definition, the INT PENDING bit is low in powerdown state. The bits reflecting the floppy disk drive input pins (TRK0, INDEX, and WP) are forced inactive. Floppy disk drive outputs (HDSEL, STEP, and DIR) also go to their inactive, default state.

As a read-only register, there is no default value associated with a reset other than some drive bits will change with a reset. The INT PENDING, STEP, HDSEL, and DIR bits will be low after reset.

2.1.2 STATUS REGISTER A (SRA, MODEL 30 MODE)

Bits	7	6	5	4	3	2	1	0
Function	INT PENDING	DRQ	STEP F/F	TRK0	HDSEL#	INDX#	WP	DIR#
H/W Reset State	0	0	0	TRK0	1	INDX#	WP	1
Auto PD State	0*	0*	0	0	1*	0	0	1*

This register has the following changes in PS/2 Model 30 Mode. Disk interface pins (Bits 0, 1, 2, 3, and 4) are inverted from PS/2 Mode. The DRQ bit monitors the status of the DMA Request pin. The STEP bit is latched with the Step output going active and is cleared with a read to the DIR register, Hardware or Software RESET.

The DRQ bit is low by definition for 82078 to be in powerdown. The bits reflecting the floppy disk drive input pins (TRK0, INDEX, and WP) are forced to reflect an inactive state. The floppy disk drive outputs (HDSEL, STEP, and DIR) also go to their inactive, default state.

2.1.3 STATUS REGISTER B (SRB, ENHANCED AT/EISA)

In the AT/EISA mode the SRB is made available whenever the EREG EN bit in the auto powerdown command is set. The register functionality is defined as follows (bits 7 through 3 are reserved):

PD and IDLE reflect the values on the corresponding pins. The signal on the IDLE pin can be masked by setting IDLEMSK bit high in this register. The IDLE bit will remain unaffected. Since some systems will use the IDLE pin to provide interrupt to the SMM power management, its disabling allows less external interrupt logic and reduction in board space. Only hardware reset will clear the IDLEMSK bit to zero.

When the IDLEMSK bit is set, the user cannot distinguish between auto powerdown and DSR powerdown (i.e., by using the IDLE pin).

IDLEMSK	IDLE (pin)
0	unmasked
1	masked

SRB								
Bits	**7**	**6**	**5**	**4**	**3**	**2**	**1**	**0**
R	RSVD	RSVD	RSVD	RSVD	RSVD	IDLEMSK	PD	IDLE
H/W Reset	X	X	X	X	X	0	PD	IDLE
Auto PD	X	X	X	X	X	UC	UC	UC
W	0	0	0	0	0	IDLEMSK	RSVD	RSVD
H/W Reset	n/a	n/a	n/a	n/a	n/a	0	n/a	n/a
Auto PD	n/a	n/a	n/a	n/a	n/a	UC	n/a	n/a

2.1.4 STATUS REGISTER B (SRB, PS/2 MODE)

Bits	7	6	5	4	3	2	1	0
Function	1	1	DRIVE SEL 0	WRDATA TOGGLE	RDDATA TOGGLE	WE	MOT EN1	MOT EN2
H/W Reset State	1	1	0	0	0	0	0	0
Auto PD State	1	1	UC	0	0	0*	0	0

As the only drive input, RDATA TOGGLE's activity reflects the level as seen on the cable.

The two TOGGLE bits do not read back the state of their respective pins directly. Instead, the pins drive a Flip/Flop which produces a wider and more reliable read pulse. Bits 6 and 7 are undefined and always return to a 1.

After any reset, the activity on the TOGGLE pin is cleared. Drive select and Motor bits cleared by the RESET pin and not software resets.

2

2.1.5 STATUS REGISTER B (SRB, MODEL 30 MODE)

Bits	7	6	5	4	3	2	1	0
Function	DRV2#	DS1#	DS0#	WRDATA F/F	RDDATA F/F	WE F/F	DS3#	DS2#
H/W Reset State	DRV2#	1	1	0	0	0	1	1
Auto PD State	UC	UC	UC	0	0	0*	UC	UC

This register has the following changes in Model 30 Mode. Bits 0, 1, 5, and 6 return the decoded value of the Drive Select bits in the DOR register. Bits 2, 3, and 4 are set by their respective active going edges and are cleared by reading the DIR register. The WRDATA bit is triggered by raw WRDATA signals and is not gated by WE. Bits 2, 3, and 4 are cleared to low level by either Hardware or Software RESET.

2.1.6 DIGITAL OUTPUT REGISTER (DOR)

The Digital Output Register contains the drive select and motor enable bits, a reset bit and a DMA GATE# bit.

Bits	7	6	5	4	3	2	1	0
Function	MOT EN3	MOT EN2	MOT EN1	MOT EN0	DMA GATE#	RESET#	DRIVE SEL1	DRIVE SEL2
H/W Reset State	0	0	0	0	0	0	0	0
Auto PD State	0*	0*	0*	0*	UC	1*	UC	UC

The MOT ENx bits directly control their respective motor enable pins (FDME0–3). The DRIVE SELx bits are decoded to provide four drive select lines and only one may be active at a time. Standard programming practice is to set both MOT ENx and DRIVE SELx bits at the same time.

Table 2-1 lists a set of DOR values to activate the drive select and motor enable for each drive.

Table 2-1. Drive Activation Value

Drive	DOR Value
0	1CH
1	2DH
2	4EH
3	8FH

The DMAGATE# bit is enabled only in PC-AT and Model 30 Modes. If DMAGATE# is set low, the INT and DRQ outputs are tri-stated and the DACK# and TC inputs are disabled. DMAGATE# set high will enable INT, DRQ, TC, and DACK# to the system. In PS/2 Mode DMAGATE# has no effect upon INT, DRQ, TC, or DACK# pins, they are always active.

The DOR reset bit and the Motor Enable bits have to be inactive when the 82078 is in powerdown. The DMAGATE# and DRIVE SEL bits are unchanged. During powerdown, writing to the DOR does not awaken the 82078 with the exception of activating any of the motor enable bits. Setting the motor enable bits active (high) will wake up the part.

This RESET# bit clears the basic core of the 82078 and the FIFO circuits when the LOCK bit is set to "0" (see Section 5.3.2 for LOCK bit definitions). Once set, it remains set until the user clears this bit. This bit is set by a chip reset and the 82078 is held in a reset state until the user clears this bit. The RESET# bit has no effect upon the register.

2.1.7 TAPE DRIVE REGISTER (TDR AT/EISA, PS/2, MODEL 30)

Bits	7	6	5	4	3	2	1	0
Function	—	—	—	—	—	—	TAPE SEL1	TAPE SEL0
H/W Reset State	—	—	—	—	—	—	0	0
Auto PD State	—	—	—	—	—	—	UC	UC

(—) means these bits are not writable and remain tri-stated if read.

This register allows the user to assign tape support to a particular drive during initialization. Any future references to that drive number automatically invokes tape support. Hardware reset clears this register; software resets have no effect. By default, the tape select bits are hardware RESET to zeros, making Drive 0 not available for tape support.

2.1.8 ENHANCED TAPE DRIVE REGISTER (TDR, AT, PS/2, MODEL 30, EREG EN = 1)

In the PS/2 and Model 30 mode and AT/EISA mode the extended TDR is made available only when the EREG EN bit is set, otherwise the bits are tri-stated. The register functionality is defined as follows:

TDR								
Bits	**7**	**6**	**5**	**4**	**3**	**2**	**1**	**0**
R	MEDID1	MEDID0	DRVID1	DRVID0	BOOTSEL1	BOOTSEL0	TAPESEL1	TAPESEL0
H/W Reset	MEDID1	MEDID0	DRVID1	DRVID0	0	0	0	0
Auto PD	UC	UC	UC	UC	UC	UC	UC	UC
W	0	0	0	0	BOOTSEL1	BOOTSEL0	TAPESEL1	TAPESEL0
H/W Reset	n/a	n/a	n/a	n/a	0	0	0	0
Auto PD	n/a	n/a	n/a	n/a	BOOTSEL1	BOOTSEL0	TAPESEL1	TAPESEL0

MEDID1, MEDID0 reflect the values on the respective pins. Similarly, the DRVID0, DRVID1 reflect the values on the DRVID1 and DRVID0 pins.

The TAPESEL1, TAPESEL0 functionality is retained as defined in the non-enhanced TDR, except that the application of boot drive restriction (boot drive cannot be a tape drive) depends on what drive selected is by the BOOTSEL1, BOOTSEL0 bits.

The BOOTSEL1, BOOTSEL0 are not reset by software resets and are decoded as shown below. These bits allow for reconfiguring the boot up drive and only reset by hardware reset. A drive can be enabled by remapping the internal DS0 and ME0 to one of the other drive select and motor enable lines (Refer to "Selectable Boot Drives" in the Design applications chapter). Once a non-default value for BOOTSEL1 and BOOTSEL0 is selected, all programmable bits are virtual designations of drives, i.e., it is the user's responsibility to know the mapping scheme detailed in the following table.

BOOTSEL1	BOOTSEL0	Mapping:
0	0	DS0 → FDS0, ME0 → FDME0 DS1 → FDS1, ME1 → FDME1 DS2 → FDS2, ME2 → FDME2
0	1	DS0 → FDS1, ME0 → FDME1 DS1 → FDS0, ME1 → FDME0 DS2 → FDS2, ME2 → FDME2
1	0	DS0 → FDS2, ME0 → FDME2 DS1 → FDS1, ME1 → FDME1 DS2 → FDS0, ME2 → FDME0
1	1	Reserved

2.1.9 DATARATE SELECT REGISTER (DSR)

Bits	7	6	5	4	3	2	1	0
Function	S/W RESET	POWER DOWN	PDOSC	PRE COMP2	PRE COMP1	PRE COMP0	DRATE SEL1	DRATE SEL0
H/W Reset State	0	0	0	0	0	0	1	0
Auto PD State	S/W RESET	POWER DOWN	PDOSC	PRE COMP2	PRE COMP1	PRE COMP0	DRATE SEL1	DRATE SEL0

This register ensures backward compatibility with the 82072 floppy controller and is write-only. Changing the data rate changes the timings of the drive control signals. To ensure that drive timings are not violated when changing data rates, choose a drive timing such that the fastest data rate will not violate the timing.

The PDOSC bit is used to implement crystal oscillator power management. The internal oscillator in the 82078 can be programmed to be either powered on or off via PDOSC. This capability is independent of the chip's powerdown state. Auto powerdown mode and powerdown via POWERDOWN bit has no effect over the power state of the oscillator.

In the default state the PDOSC bit is low and the oscillator is powered up. When this bit is programmed to a one, the oscillator is shut off. Hardware reset clears this bit to a zero. Neither of the software resets (via DOR or DSR) have any effect on this bit. Note, PDOSC should only be set high when the part is in the powerdown state, otherwise the part will not function correctly and must be hardware reset once the oscillator has turned back on and stabilized. Setting the PDOSC bit has no effect on the clock input to the 82078 (the X1 pin). The clock input is separately disabled when the part is powered down. The SAVE command checks the status of PDOSC, however, the RESTORE command will not restore the bit high.

S/W RESET behaves the same as DOR RESET except that this reset is self cleaning.

POWERDOWN bit implements direct powerdown. Setting this bit high will put the 82078 into the powerdown state regardless of the state of the part. The part is internally reset and then put into powerdown. No status is saved and any operation in progress is aborted. A hardware or software reset will exit the 82078 from this powerdown state.

2

PRECOMP 0-2 adjusts the WRDATA output to the disk to compensate for magnetic media phenomena known as bit shifting. The data patterns that are susceptible to bit shifting are well understood and the 82078 compensates the data pattern as it is written to the disk. The amount of pre-compensation is dependent upon the drive and media, but in most cases the default value is acceptable.

Table 2-2. Precompensation Delays

PRECOMP	Precompensation Delays	
DSR[432]	x1 @ 24 MHz	x1 @ 48 MHz if CLK48 = 1, enabled only @ 2 Mbps if CLK48 = 0, enabled at all data rates
111	0.00 ns-disabled	
001	41.67	20.84
010	83.34	41.67
011	125.00	62.5
100	166.67	83.34
101	208.33	104.17
110	250.00	125
000	DEFAULT	

Table 2-3. Default Precompensation Delays

Data Rate	Precompensation Delays (ns)
2 Mbps	20.84
1 Mbps	41.67
0.5 Mbps	125
0.3 Mbps	125
0.25 Mbps	125

The 82078 starts pre-compensating the data pattern starting on Track 0. The CONFIGURE command can change the track that pre-compensating starts on. Table 2-2 lists the pre-compensation values that can be selected and Table 2-3 lists the default pre-compensation values. The default value is selected if the three bits are zeroes.

DRATE 0-1 select one of the four data rates as listed in Table 2-4. The default value is 250 Kbps after a "Hardware" reset. Other "Software" Resets do not affect the DRATE or PRECOMP bits.

Table 2-4. Data Rates

DRATESEL1	DRATESEL0	DATA RATE
1	1	1 Mbps
0	0	500 Kbps
0	1	300 Kbps
1	0	250 Kbps

2.1.10 MAIN STATUS REGISTER (MSR)

Bits	7	6	5	4	3*	2	1	0
Function	RQM	DIO	NON DMA	CMD BSY	DRV3 BUSY	DRV2 BUSY	DRV1 BUSY	DRV0 BUSY
H/W Reset State	0	X	X	X	X	X	X	X
Auto PD State	1	0	0	0	0	0	0	0

The Main Status Register is a read-only register and is used for controlling command input and result output for all commands.

RQM—Indicates that the host can transfer data if set to 1. No access is permitted if set to a 0.

DIO—Indicates the direction of a data transfer once RQM is set. A 1 indicates a read and a 0 indicates a write is required.

NON-DMA—This mode is selected in the SPECIFY command and will be set to a 1 during the execution phase of a command. This is for polled data transfers and helps differentiate between the data transfers and the reading of result bytes.

COMMAND BUSY—This bit is set to a one when a command is in progress. This bit goes active after the command byte has been accepted and goes inactive at the end of the results phase. If there is no result phase (SEEK, RECALIBRATE commands), this bit returns to a 0.

DRV x BUSY—These bits are set to ones when a drive is in the seek portion of a command, including seeks and recalibrates.

Some example values of the MSR are:

- MSR = 80H; The controller is ready to receive a command.
- MSR = 90H; executing a command or waiting for the host to read status bytes (assume DMA mode).
- MSR = D0H; waiting for the host to write status bytes.

2.1.11 FIFO (DATA)

All command parameter information and disk data transfers go through the FIFO. The FIFO is 16 bytes in size and has programmable threshold values. Data transfers are governed by the RQM and DIO bits in the Main Status Register.

The FIFO defaults to an 8272A compatible mode after a "Hardware" reset (Reset via pin 32). "Software" Resets (Reset via DOR or DSR register) can also place the 82078 into 8272A compatible mode if the LOCK bit is set to "0" (See the definition of the LOCK bit), maintaining PC-AT hardware compatibility. The default values can be changed through the CONFIGURE command (enable full FIFO operation with threshold control). The advantage of the FIFO is that it allows the system a larger DMA latency without causing a disk error. Table 2-5 gives several examples of the delays with a FIFO. The data is based upon the following formula:

$$\text{Threshold\#} \times 1/\text{DATA RATE} \times 8 - 1.5\ \mu s = \text{DELAY}$$

Table 2-5. FIFO Threshold Examples

FIFO Threshold Examples	Maximum Delay to Servicing at 1 Mbps Data Rate
1 byte	$1 \times 8\ \mu s - 1.5\ \mu s = 6.5\ \mu s$
2 bytes	$2 \times 8\ \mu s - 1.5\ \mu s = 14.5\ \mu s$
8 bytes	$8 \times 8\ \mu s - 1.5\ \mu s = 62.5\ \mu s$
15 bytes	$15 \times 8\ \mu s - 1.5\ \mu s = 118.5\ \mu s$

FIFO Threshold Examples	Maximum Delay to Servicing at 500 Kbps Data Rate
1 byte	$1 \times 16\ \mu s - 1.5\ \mu s = 14.5\ \mu s$
2 bytes	$2 \times 16\ \mu s - 1.5\ \mu s = 30.5\ \mu s$
8 bytes	$8 \times 16\ \mu s - 1.5\ \mu s = 126.5\ \mu s$
15 bytes	$15 \times 16\ \mu s - 1.5\ \mu s = 238.5\ \mu s$

At the start of a command, the FIFO action is always disabled and command parameters must be sent based upon the RQM and DIO bit settings. As the 82078 enters the command execution phase, it clears the FIFO of any data to ensure that invalid data is not transferred. An overrun or underrun will terminate the current command and the transfer of data. Disk writes will complete the current sector by generating a 00 pattern and valid CRC.

2.1.12 DIGITAL INPUT REGISTER (DIR, PC-AT MODE)

This register is read only in all modes. In PC-AT mode only bit 7 is driven, all other bits remain tri-stated.

Bits	7	6	5	4	3	2	1	0
Function	DSK CHG	—	—	—	—	—	—	—
H/2 Reset State	DSK CHG	—	—	—	—	—	—	—
Auto PD State	0	—	—	—	—	—	—	—

(—) means these bits are tri-stated when read.

DSKCHG monitors the pin of the same name and reflects the opposite value seen on the disk cable. The DSKCHG bit is forced inactive along with all the inputs from the floppy disk drive. All the other bits remain tri-stated.

2.1.13 DIGITAL INPUT REGISTER (DIR, PS/2 MODE)

DIR								
R/W	7	6*	5*	4*	3	2	1	0
R	DSK CHG	IDLE	PD	IDLEMSK	1	DRATE SEL1	DRATE SEL0	HIGH DENS#
H/W Reset	DSK CHG	1	1	1	1	1	0	1
Auto PD	0	1	1	UC	1	UC	UC	UC

(*) These bits are only available when PS2 STAT = 1: Bits 5 and 6 show the status of PD (powerdown) and IDLE respectively. Bit 4 shows the status of IDLEMSK, this bit disables the IDLE pin when active.

Bit 3 returns a value of "1", and the DRATE SEL1-0 return the value of the current data rate selected (see Table 2-4 for values).

HIGHDENS# is low whenever the 500 Kbps or 1 Mbps data rates are selected. It is high when either 250 Kbps, 300 Kbps, or 2 Mbps is selected.

The DSKCHG bit is forced inactive along with all the inputs from the floppy disk drive. All the other bits (as applicable) remain unchanged.

The Drive Specification Command modifies the DRATE SEL bits. Refer to Table 6-2 for a description.

2.1.14 DIGITAL INPUT REGISTER (DIR, MODEL 30 MODE)

Bits	7	6*	5*	4*	3	2	1	0
Function	DSK CHG#	IDLE	PD	IDLEMSK	DMA GATE#	NOPREC	DRATE SEL1	DRATE SEL0
H/W Reset State	N/A	0	0	0	0	0	1	0
Auto PD State	1	1	1	UC	UC	UC	UC	UC

(*) These bits are only available when PS2 STAT = 1: Bits 5 and 6 show the status of PD (powerdown) and IDLE respectively. Bit 4 shows the status of IDLEMSK, this bit disables the IDLE pin when active. Bit 7 (DSKCHG) is inverted in Model 30 Mode.

The DSKCHG# bit is forced inactive along with all the inputs from the floppy disk drive. All the other bits (as applicable) remain unchanged.

The Drive Specification Command modifies the DRATE SEL bits. Refer to Table 6-2 for information regarding the mapping of these bits.

Bit 3 reflects the value of DMAGATE# bit set in the DOR register.

Bit 2 reflects the value of NOPREC bit set in the CCR register.

2.1.15 CONFIGURATION CONTROL REGISTER (CCR, PC AT and PS/2 MODES)

This register sets the datarate and is write only.

Bits	7	6	5	4*	3	2	1	0
Function	—	—	—	IDLEMSK	—	—	DRATE SEL1	DRATE SEL0
H/W Restate State	—	—	—		—	—	1	0
Auto PD State	—	—	—	IDLEMSK	—	—	DRATE SEL1	DRATE SEL0

(*) This bit is enabled only when PS2 STAT = 1 (Powerdown Mode). Refer to the table in the Data Rate Select Register for values. Unused bits should be set to 0. IDLEMSK is not available in the CCR for PC AT mode. In PC AT, IDLEMSK is available in the SRB.

2.1.16 CONFIGURATION CONTROL REGISTER (CCR, MODEL 30 MODE)

Bits	7	6	5	4*	3	2	1	0
Function	—	—	—	IDLEMSK	—	NOPREC	DRATE SEL1	DRATE SEL0
H/W Reset State	—	—	—	0	—	0	1	0
Auto PD State	—	—	—	UC	—	UC	UC	UC

(*) This bit is enabled only when PS2 STAT = 1 (Powerdown Mode). NOPREC has no function, and is reset to "0" with a Hardware RESET only.

2.2 Reset

There are three sources of reset on the 82078; the RESET pin, a reset generated via a bit in the DOR and a reset generated via a bit in the DSR. All resets take the 82078 out of the powerdown state.

In entering the reset state, all operations are terminated and the 82078 enters an idle state. Activating reset while a disk write activity is in progress will corrupt the data and CRC.

On exiting the reset state, various internal registers are cleared, and the 82078 waits for a new command. Drive polling will start unless disabled by a new CONFIGURE command.

2.2.1 RESET PIN ("HARDWARE") RESET

The RESET pin is a global reset and clears all registers except those programmed by the SPECIFY command. The DOR Reset bit is enabled and must be cleared by the host to exit the reset state.

2.2.2 DOR RESET vs DSR RESET ("SOFTWARE" RESET)

These two resets are functionally the same. The DSR Reset is included to maintain 82072 compatibility. Both will reset the 82072 core which affects drive status information. The FIFO circuits will also be reset if the LOCK bit is a "0" (see definition of the LOCK bit). The DSR Reset clears itself automatically while the DOR Reset requires the host to manually clear it. DOR Reset has precedence over the DSR Reset. The DOR Reset is set automatically upon a pin RESET. The user must manually clear this reset bit in the DOR to exit the reset state.

The t30a specification in the A.C. Specifications gives the minimum amount of time that the DOR reset must be held active. This amount of time that the DOR reset must be held active is dependent upon the data rate. The 82078 requires that the DOR reset bit must be held active for at least 0.5 μs at 250 Kbps. This is less than a typical ISA I/O cycle time.

2.3 DMA Transfers

DMA transfers are enabled with the SPECIFY command and are initiated by the 82078 by activating the DRQ pin during a data transfer command. The FIFO is enabled directly by asserting DACK# and addresses need not be valid (CS# can be held inactive during DMA transfers).

3.0 DRIVE INTERFACE

The 82078 has integrated all of the logic needed to interface to a floppy disk or a tape drive which use floppy interface. All drive outputs have 24 mA drive capability and all inputs use a receive buffer with hysteresis. The internal analog data separator requires no external components, yet allows for an extremely wide capture range with high levels of read-data jitter, and ISV. The designer needs only to run the 82078 disk drive signals to the disk or tape drive connector.

3.1 Cable Interface

Generally, 5.25" drive uses open collector drivers and 3.5" drives (as used on PS/2) use totem-pole drivers. The output buffers on the 82078 do not change between open collector or totem-pole, they are always totem-pole.

DRVDEN0 and DRVDEN1 connect to pins 2 and 6 or 33 (on most disk drives) to select the data rate sent from the drive to the 82078. The polarity of DRVDEN0 and DRVDEN1 can be programmed through the Drive Specification command (see the command description for more information).

When the 82078SL is operating at 3.3V, the floppy drive interface can be configured to either 5.0V or 3.3V, via the V_{CCF} (pin 41). The drive interface follows the voltage level on V_{CCF}. A selectable drive interface allows the system designer the greatest flexibility when designing a low voltage system.

4.4.3.2 Wake Up from Auto Powerdown

If the part enters the powerdown state through the auto powerdown mode, then the part can be awakened by reset or by appropriate access to certain registers.

If a hardware or software reset is used then the part will go through the normal reset sequence. If the access is through the selected registers, then the 82078 resumes operation as though it was never in powerdown. Besides activating the RESET pin or one of the software reset bits in the DOR or DSR, the following register accesses will wake up the part:

1. Enabling any one of the motor enable bits in the DOR register (reading the DOR does not awaken the part).
2. A read from the MSR register.
3. A read or write to the FIFO register.

Any of these actions will wake up the part. Once awake, 82078 will reinitiate the auto powerdown timer for 10 ms or 0.5 sec. (depending on the MIN DLY bit the auto powerdown command). When operating at 2 Mbps, the time is halved to 5 ms or 0.25 sec. depending on the MIN DLY bit. The part will powerdown again when all the auto powerdown conditions are satisfied.

4.5 Register Behavior

The register descriptions and their values in the powerdown state are listed in the Microprocessor Interface section. Table 4-1 reiterates the AT and PS/2 (including model 30) configuration registers available. It also shows the type of access permitted. In order to maintain software transparency, access to all the registers must be maintained. As Table 4-1 shows, two sets of registers are distinguished based on whether their access results in the part remaining in powerdown state or exiting it.

2

Table 4-1. 82078 Register Behavior

Address	Available Registers		Access
	PC-AT	PS/2 (Model 30)	Permitted
Access to these registers DOES NOT wake up the part			
000	—	SRA	R
001	SRB (EREG EN = 1)	SRB	R/W
010	DOR*	DOR*	R/W
011	TDR	TDR	R/W
100	DSR*	DSR*	W
110	—	—	—
111	DIR	DIR	R
111	CCR	CCR	W
Access to these registers wake up the part			
100	MSR	MSR	R
101	FIFO	FIFO	R/W

*Writing to the DOR or DSR does not wake up the part, however, writing any of the motor enable bits or doing a software reset (either via DOR or DSR reset bits) will wake up the part.

Access to all other registers is possible without awakening the part. These registers can be accessed during powerdown without changing the status of the part. A read from these registers will reflect the true status as shown in the register description in Section 2.1. A write to the part will result in the part retaining the data and subsequently reflecting it when the part awakens. Accessing the part during powerdown may cause an increase in the power consumption by the part. The part will revert back to its low power mode when the access has been completed. None of the extended registers effect the behavior of the powerdown mode.

4.6 Pin Behavior

The 82078 is specifically designed for the portable PC systems in which the power conservation is a primary concern. This makes the behavior of the pins during powerdown very important.

The pins of 82078 can be divided into two major categories; system interface and floppy disk drive interface. The floppy disk drive pins are disabled such that no power will be drawn through the 82078 as a result of any voltage applied to the pin within the 82078's power supply range. The floppy disk drive interface pins are configurable by the FDI TRI bit in the auto powerdown command. When the bit is set the output pins of the floppy disk drive retain their original state. All other pins are either disabled or unchanged as depicted in Table 4-4. Most of the system interface pins are left active to monitor system accesses that may wake up the part.

4.6.1 SYSTEM INTERFACE PINS

Table 4-2 gives the state of the system interface pins in the powerdown state. Pins unaffected by powerdown are labeled "UC". Input pins are "DISABLED" to prevent them from causing currents internal to the 82078 when they have indeterminate input values.

Table 4-2. System Interface Pins

System Pins	State In Powerdown	System Pins	State In Powerdown
Input Pins		**Output Pins**	
CS#	UC	DRQ	UC (Low)
RD#	UC	INT	UC (Low)
WR#	UC	PD	HIGH
A[0:2]	UC	IDLE	High (Auto PD) Low (DSR PD)
DB[0:7]	UC	DB[0:7]	UC
RESET	UC		
IDENTn	UC		
DACK#	Disabled		
TC	Disabled		
X[1:2]	Programmable		

Two pins which can be used to indicate the status of the part are IDLE and PD. Table 4-3 shows how these pins reflect the 82078 status.

Table 4-3. 82078 Status Pins

PD	IDLE	MSR	Part Status
1	1	80H	Auto Powerdown
1	0	RQM = 1; MSR[6:0] = X	DSR Powerdown
0	1	80H	Idle
0	0	—	Busy

The IDLE pin indicates when the part is idle state and can be powered down. It is a combination of MSR equalling 80H, the head being unloaded and the INT pin being low. As shown in the table the IDLE pin will be low when the part is in DSR powerdown state. The PD pin is active whenever the part is in the powerdown state. It is active for either mode of powerdown. The PD pin can be used to turn off an external oscillator of other floppy disk drive interface hardware.

4.6.2 FDD INTERFACE PINS

The FDD interface "input" pins during powerdown are disabled or unchanged as shown in Table 4-4. The floppy disk drive "output" pins are programmable by the FDI TRI bit in the auto powerdown command. Setting of the FDI TRI bit in the auto powerdown command results in the interface retaining its normal state. When this bit is low (default state) all output pins in the FDD interface to the floppy disk drive itself are tri-stated. Pins used for local logic control or part programming are unaffected. Table 4-4 depicts the state of the floppy disk interface pins in the powerdown state (FDI TRI is low).

Table 4-4. 82078 FDD Interface Pins

FDD Pins	State In Powerdown	FDD Pins	State in Powerdown
Input Pins		Output Pins (FDI TRI = 0)	
RDDATA	Disabled	FDME[0:3]#	Tristated
WP	Disabled	FDS[0:3]#	Tristated
TRK0	Disabled	DIR#	Tristated
INDX#	Disabled	STEP#	Tristated
DRV2#	Disabled	WRDATA#	Tristated
DSKCHG#	Disabled	WE#	Tristated
		HDSEL#	Tristated
		DRVDEN[0:1]#	Tristated

5.0 CONTROLLER PHASES

For simplicity, command handling in the 82078 can be divided into three phases: Command, Execution and Result. Each phase is described in the following sections.

When there is no command in progress, the 82078 can be in idle, drive polling or powerdown state.

5.1 Command Phase

After a reset, the 82078 enters the command phase and is ready to accept a command from the host. For each of the commands, a defined set of command code bytes and parameter bytes has to be written to the 82078 before the command phase is complete (Please refer to Section 6.0 for the command descriptions). These bytes of data must be transferred in the order prescribed.

Before writing to the 82078, the host must examine the RQM and DIO bits of the Main Status Register. RQM, DIO must be equal to "1" and "0" respectively before command bytes may be written. RQM is set false by the 82078 after each write cycle until the received byte is processed. The 82078 asserts RQM again to request each parameter byte of the command, unless an illegal command condition is detected. After the last parameter byte is received, RQM remains "0", and the 82078 automatically enters the next phase as defined by the command definition.

The FIFO is disabled during the command phase to retain compatibility with the 8272A, and to provide for the proper handling of the "Invalid Command" condition.

5.2 Execution Phase

All data transfers to or from the 82078 occur during the execution phase, which can proceed in DMA or non-DMA mode as indicated in the SPECIFY command.

Each data byte is transferred by an INT or DRQ depending on the DMA mode. The CONFIGURE command can enable the FIFO and set the FIFO threshold value.

The following paragraphs detail the operation of the FIFO flow control. In these descriptions, (threshold) is defined as the number of bytes available to the 82078 when service is requested from the host, and ranges from 1 to 16. The parameter FIFOTHR which the user programs is one less, and ranges from 0 to 15.

A low threshold value (i.e., 2) results in longer periods of time between service requests, but requires faster servicing of the request, for both read and write cases. The host reads (writes) from (to) the FIFO until empty (full), then the transfer request goes inactive. The host must be very responsive to the service request. This is the desired case for use with a "fast" system.

A high value of threshold (i.e., 12) is used with a "sluggish" system by affording a long latency period after a service request, but results in more frequent service requests.

5.2.1 NON-DMA MODE, TRANSFERS FROM THE FIFO TO THE HOST

The INT pin and RQM bits in the Main Status Register are activated when the FIFO contains 16 (or set threshold) bytes, or the last bytes of a full sector transfer have been placed in the FIFO. The INT pin can be used for interrupt driven systems and RQM can be used for polled sytems. The host must respond to the request by reading data from the FIFO. This process is repeated until the last byte is transferred out of the FIFO, then 82078 deactivates the INT pin and RQM bit.

5.2.2 NON-DMA MODE, TRANSFERS FROM THE HOST TO THE FIFO

The INT pin and RQM bit in the Main Status Register are activated upon entering the execution phase of data transfer commands. The host must respond to the request by writing data into the FIFO. The INT pin and RQM bit remain true until the FIFO becomes full. They are set true again when the FIFO has (threshold) bytes remaining in the FIFO. The INT pin will also be deactivated if TC and DACK# both go inactive. The 82078 enters the result phase after the last byte is taken by the 82078 from the FIFO (i.e., FIFO empty condition).

5.2.3 DMA MODE, TRANSFERS FROM THE FIFO TO THE HOST

The 82078 activates the DRQ pin when the FIFO contains 16 (or set threshold) bytes, or the last byte of a full sector transfer has been placed in the FIFO. The DMA controller must respond to the request by reading data from the FIFO. The 82078 will deactivate the DRQ pin when the FIFO becomes empty. DRQ goes inactive after DACK# goes active for the last byte of a data transfer (or on the active edge of RD#, on the last byte, if no edge is present on DACK#). Note that DACK# and TC must overlap for at least 50 ns for proper functionality.

5.2.4 DMA MODE, TRANSFERS FROM THE HOST TO THE FIFO

The 82078 activates the DRQ pin when entering the execution phase of the data transfer commands. The DMA controller must respond by activating the DACK# and WR# pins and placing data in the FIFO. DRQ remains active until the FIFO becomes full. DRQ is again set true when the FIFO has (threshold) bytes remaining in the FIFO. The 82078 will also deactivate the DRQ pin when TC becomes true (qualified by DACK# by overlapping by 50 ns), indicating that no more data is required. DRQ goes inactive after DACK# goes active for the last byte of a data transfer (or on the active edge of WR# of the last byte, if no edge is present on DACK#).

5.2.5 DATA TRANSFER TERMINATION

The 82078 supports terminal count explicitly through the TC pin and implicitly through the underrun/overrun and end-of-track (EOT) functions. For full sector transfers, the EOT parameter can define the last sector to be transferred in a single or multisector transfer. If the last sector to be transferred is a partial sector, the host can stop transferring the data in mid-sector, and the 82078 will continue to complete the sector as if a hardware TC was received. The only difference between these implicit functions and TC is that they return "abnormal termination" result status. Such status indications can be ignored if they were expected.

Note that when the host is sending data to the FIFO of the 82078, the internal sector count will be complete when 82078 reads the last byte from its side of the FIFO. There may be a delay in the removal of the transfer request signal of up to the time taken for the 82078 to read the last 16 bytes from the FIFO. The host must tolerate this delay.

5.3 Result Phase

The generation of INT determines the beginning of the result phase. For each of the commands, a defined set of result bytes has to be read from the 82078 before the result phase is complete. (Refer to Section 6.0 on command descriptions.) These bytes of data must be read out for another command to start.

RQM and DIO must both equal "1" before the result bytes may be read from the FIFO. After all the result bytes have been read, the RQM and DIO bits switch to "1" and "0" respectively, and the CB bit is cleared. This indicates that the 82078 is ready to accept the next command.

6.0 COMMAND SET/DESCRIPTIONS

Commands can be written whenever the 82078 is in the command phase. Each command has a unique set of needed parameters and status results. The 82078 checks to see that the first byte is a valid command and, if valid, proceeds with the command. If it was invalid, the next time the RQM bit in the MSR register is a "1" the DIO and CB bits will also be "1", indicating the FIFO must be read. A result byte of 80H will be read out of the FIFO, indicating an invalid command was issued. After reading the result byte from the FIFO the 82078 will return to the command phase. Table 6-1 is a summary of the Command set.

Table 6-1. 82078 Command Set

Phase	R/W	DATA BUS D7	D6	D5	D4	D3	D2	D1	D0	Remarks
						READ DATA				
Command	W	MT	MFM	SK	0	0	1	1	0	Command Codes
	W	0	0	0	0	0	HDS	DS1	DS0	
	W					C				Sector ID Information prior to Command Execution
	W					H				
	W					R				
	W					N				
	W					EOT				
	W					GPL				
	W					DTL				
Execution										Data Transfer between the FDD and System
Result	R					ST 0				Status Information after Command Execution
	R					ST 1				
	R					ST 2				
	R					C				Sector ID Information after Command Execution
	R					H				
	R					R				
	R					N				
						READ DELETED DATA				
Command	W	MT	MFM	SK	0	1	1	0	0	Command Codes
	W	0	0	0	0	0	HDS	DS1	DS0	
	W					C				Sector ID Information prior to Command Execution
	W					H				
	W					R				
	W					N				
	W					EOT				
	W					GPL				
	W					DTL				
Execution										Data Transfer between the FDD and System
Result	R					ST 0				Status Information after Command Execution
	R					ST 1				
	R					ST 2				
	R					C				Sector ID Information after Command Execution
	R					H				
	R					R				
	R					N				
						WRITE DATA				
Command	W	MT	MFM	0	0	0	1	0	1	Command Codes
	W	0	0	0	0	0	HDS	DS1	DS0	
	W					C				Sector ID Information prior to Command Execution
	W					H				
	W					R				
	W					N				
	W					EOT				
	W					GPL				
	W					DTL				
Execution										Data Transfer between the FDD and System
Result	R					ST 0				Status Information after Command Execution
	R					ST 1				
	R					ST 2				
	R					C				Sector ID Information after Command Execution
	R					H				
	R					R				
	R					N				

Table 6-1. 82078 Command Set (Continued)

Phase	R/W	D_7	D_6	D_5	D_4	D_3	D_2	D_1	D_0	Remarks
		WRITE DELETED DATA								
Command	W	MT	MFM	0	0	1	0	0	1	Command Codes
	W	0	0	0	0	0	HDS	DS1	DS0	
	W	C								Sector ID Information prior to Command Execution
	W	H								
	W	R								
	W	N								
	W	EOT								
	W	GPL								
	W	DTL								
Execution										Data Transfer between the FDD and System
Result	R	ST 0								Status Information after Command Execution
	R	ST 1								
	R	ST 2								
	R	C								Sector ID Information after Command Execution
	R	H								
	R	R								
	R	N								
		READ TRACK								
Command	W	0	MFM	0	0	0	0	1	0	Command Codes
	W	0	0	0	0	0	HDS	DS1	DS0	
	W	C								Sector ID Information prior to Command Execution
	W	H								
	W	R								
	W	N								
	W	EOT								
	W	GPL								
	W	DTL								
Execution										Data Transfer between the FDD and System. FDC Reads All Sectors from Index Hole to EOT
Result	R	ST 0								Status Information after Command Execution
	R	ST 1								
	R	ST 2								
	R	C								Sector ID Information after Command Execution
	R	H								
	R	R								
	R	N								
		VERIFY								
Command	W	MT	MFM	SK	1	0	1	1	0	Command Codes
	W	EC	0	0	0	0	HDS	DS1	DS0	
	W	C								Sector ID Information prior to Command Execution
	W	H								
	W	R								
	W	N								
	W	EOT								
	W	GPL								
	W	DTL/SC								
Execution										Data Transfer between the FDD and System
Result	R	ST 0								Status Information after Command Execution
	R	ST 1								
	R	ST 2								
	R	C								Sector ID Information after Command Execution
	R	H								
	R	R								
	R	N								
		VERSION								
Command	W	0	0	0	1	0	0	0	0	Command Code
Result	R	1	0	0	1	0	0	0	0	Enhanced Controller

2

Table 6-1. 82078 Command Set (Continued)

Phase	R/W	D7	D6	D5	D4	D3	D2	D1	D0	Remarks
		DATA BUS								
FORMAT TRACK										
Command	W	0	MFM	0	0	1	1	0	1	Command Codes
	W	0	0	0	0	0	HDS	DS1	DS0	
	W	N								Bytes/Sector
	W	SC								Sectors/Cylinder
	W	GPL								Gap3
	W	D								Filler Byte
Execution For Each Sector Repeat:	W	C								
	W	H								Input Sector Parameters
	W	R								
	W	N								
										82078 Formats an Entire Cylinder
Result	R	ST 0								Status Information after Command Execution
	R	ST 1								
	R	ST 2								
	R	Undefined								
	R	Undefined								
	R	Undefined								
	R	Undefined								
SCAN EQUAL										
Command	W	MT	MFM	SK	1	0	0	0	1	Command Codes
	W	0	0	0	0	0	HDS	DS1	DS0	
	W	C								Sector ID Information prior to Command Execution
	W	H								
	W	R								
	W	N								
	W	EOT								
	W	GPL								
	W	STP								
Execution										Data Compared between the FDD and Main-System
Result	R	ST 0								Status Information after Command Execution
	R	ST 1								
	R	ST 2								
	R	C								Sector ID Information after Command Execution
	R	H								
	R	R								
	R	N								

Table 6-1. 82078 Command Set (Continued)

Phase	R/W	DATA BUS								Remarks
		D_7	D_6	D_5	D_4	D_3	D_2	D_1	D_0	
SCAN LOW OR EQUAL										
Command	W	MT	MFM	SK	1	1	0	0	1	Command Codes
	W	0	0	0	0	0	HDS	DS1	DS0	
	W				C					Sector ID Information Prior to Command Execution
	W				H					
	W				R					
	W				N					
	W				EOT					
	W				GPL					
	W				STP					
Execution										Data Compared Between the FDD and Main-System
Result	R				ST 0					Status Information After Command Execution
	R				ST 1					
	R				ST 2					
	R				C					
	R				H					Sector ID Information After Command Execution
	R				R					
	R				N					
SCAN HIGH OR EQUAL										
Command	W	MT	MFM	SK	1	1	1	0	1	Command Codes
	W	0	0	0	0	0	HDS	DS1	DS0	
	W				C					Sector ID Information Prior to Command Execution
	W				H					
	W				R					
	W				N					
	W				EOT					
	W				GPL					
	W				STP					
Execution										Data Compared Between the FDD and Main-System
Result	R				ST 0					Status Information After Command Execution
	R				ST 1					
	R				ST 2					
	R				C					
	R				H					Sector ID Information After Command Execution
	R				R					
	R				N					

2

Table 6-1. 82078 Command Set (Continued)

Phase	R/W	D_7	D_6	D_5	D_4	D_3	D_2	D_1	D_0	Remarks
					RECALIBRATE					
Command	W	0	0	0	0	0	1	1	1	Command Codes
	W	0	0	0	0	0	0	DS1	DS0	Enhanced Controller
Execution										Head Retracted to Track 0 Interrupt
					SENSE INTERRUPT STATUS					
Command	W	0	0	0	1	0	0	0	0	Command Codes
Result	R				ST 0					Status Information at the End of each Seek Operation
	R				PVN					
					SPECIFY					
Command	W	0	0	0	0	0	0	1	1	Command Codes
	W		SRT				HUT			
	W				HLT				ND	
					SENSE DRIVE STATUS					
Command	W	0	0	0	0	0	1	0	0	Command Codes
	W	0	0	0	0	0	HDS	DS1	DS0	
Result	R				ST 3					Status Information about FDD
					DRIVE SPECIFICATION COMMAND					
Command	W	1	0	0	0	1	1	1	0	Command Codes
Phase	W	0	FD1	FD0	PTS	DRT1	DRT0	DT1	DT0	
	:	:	:	:	:	:	:	:	:	0–46 bytes issued
	W	DN	NRP	0	0	0	0	0	0	
Result	R	0	0	0	PTS	DRT1	DRT0	DT1	DT0	Drive 0
Phase	R	0	0	0	PTS	DRT1	DRT0	DT1	DT0	Drive 1
	R	0	0	0	PTS	DRT1	DRT0	DT1	DT0	Drive 2
	R	0	0	0	PTS	DRT1	DRT0	DT1	DT0	Drive 3
					SEEK					
Command	W	0	0	0	0	1	1	1	1	Command Codes
	W	0	0	0	0	0	HDS	DS1	DS0	
	W				NCN					
Execution										Head is Positioned over Proper Cylinder on Diskette
					CONFIGURE					
Command	W	CLK48	0	0	1	0	0	1	1	Command Code
	W	0	0	0	0	0	0	0	0	
	W	0	EIS	EFIFO	POLL		FIFOTHR			
	W				PRETRK					
					RELATIVE SEEK					
Command	W	1	DIR	0	0	1	1	1	1	
	W	0	0	0	0	0	HDS	DS1	DS0	
	W				RCN					

Table 6-1. 82078 Command Set (Continued)

Phase	R/W	D7	D6	D5	D4	D3	D2	D1	D0	Remarks
					DUMPREG					
Command	W	0	0	0	0	1	1	1	0	*Note Registers Placed in FIFO
Execution										
Result	R				PCN-Drive 0 [D7–D0]					
	R				PCN-Drive 1 [D7–D0]					
	R				PCN-Drive 2 [D7–D0]					
	R				PCN-Drive 3 [D7–D0]					
	R			SRT [D7–D4]				HUT [D3–D0]		
	R				HLT [D7–D1]				ND	
	R				SC/EOT [D7–D0]					
	R	LOCK	0	D_3	D_2	D_1	D_0	GAP	WGATE	
	R	0	EIS	EFIFO	POLL		FIFOTHR [D3–D0]			
	R				PRETRK [D7–D0]					
					READ ID					
Command	W	0	MFM	0	0	1	0	1	0	Commands
	W	0	0	0	0	0	HDS	DS1	DS0	
Execution										The First Correct ID Information on the Cylinder is Stored in Data Register
Result	R					ST 0 [D7–D0]				Status Information after Command Execution
	R					ST 1 [D7–D0]				
	R					ST 2 [D7–D0]				
	R					C [D7–D0]				Disk Status after the Command has Completed
	R					H [D7–D0]				
	R					R [D7–D0]				
	R					N [D7–D0]				
					PERPENDICULAR MODE					
Command	W	0	0	0	1	0	0	1	0	Command Codes
	W	OW	0	D_3	D_2	D_1	D0	GAP	WGATE	
					LOCK					
Command	W	LOCK	0	0	1	0	1	0	0	Command Codes
Result	R	0	0	0	LOCK	0	0	0	0	
					PART ID					
Command	W	0	0	0	1	1	0	0	0	Command Code
Result	R	0	0	0		STEPPING [D4–D1]			1	Part ID Number
					POWERDOWN MODE					
Command	W	0	0	0	1	0	1	1	1	Command Code
	W	0	0	EREG EN	X	PS2 STAT	FDI TRI	MIN DLY	AUTO PD	
Result	R	0	0	EREG EN	X	PS2 STAT	FDI TRI	MIN DLY	AUTO PD	
					OPTION					
Command	W	0	0	1	1	0	0	1	1	Command Code
	W				RSVD [D7–D1]				ISO	

Table 6-1. 82078 Command Set (Continued)

Phase	R/W	D7	D6	D5	D4	D3	D2	D1	D0	Remarks
SAVE										
Command Phase	W	0	0	1	0	1	1	1	0	Command Code
Result Phase	R	CLK 48	SEL 3V#	PD OSC	PC2	PC1	PC0	DRATE1	DRATE0	Save Info to Reprogram the FDC
	R	0	0	0	0	0	0	0	ISO	
	R	PCN-Drive 0								
	R	PCN-Drive 1								
	R	PCN-Drive 2								
	R	PCN-Drive 3								
	R	SRT				HUT				
	R	HLT							ND	
	R	SC/EOT								
	R	LOCK	0	D_3	D_2	D_1	D_0	GAP	WGATE	
	R	0	EIS	EFIFO	POLL	FIFOTHR				
	R	PRETRK								
	R	0	0	EREG EN	RSVD	PS2 STAT	FDI TRI	MIN DLY	AUTO PD	
	R	DISK/STATUS								
	R	RSVD								
	R	RSVD								
RESTORE										
Command Phase	W	0	1	0	0	1	1	1	0	Command Code
Result	W	CLK48	SEL 3V#	0	PC2	PC1	PC0	DRATE1	DRATE0	Restore Original Register Status
	W	0	0	0	0	0	0	0	ISO	
	W	PCN-Drive 0								
	W	PCN-Drive 1								
	W	PCN-Drive 2								
	W	PCN-Drive 3								
	W	SRT				HUT				
	W	HLT							ND	
	W	SC/EOT								
	W	LOCK	0	D_3	D_2	D_1	D_0	GAP	WGATE	
	W	0	EIS	EFIFO	POLL	FIFOTHR				
	W	PRETRK								
	W	0	0	EREG EN	RSVD	PS2 STAT	FDI TRI	MIN DLY	AUTO PD	
	W	DISK/STATUS								
	W	RSVD								
	W	RSVD								

Table 6-1. 82078 Command Set (Continued)

Phase	R/W	D_7	D_6	D_5	D_4	D_3	D_2	D_1	D_0	Remarks
					FORMAT AND WRITE					
Command	W	1	MFM	1	0	1	1	0	1	Command Code
	W	0	0	0	0	0	HDS	DS1	DS0	
	W				N					
	W				SC					
	W				GPL					
	W				D					
Execution Repeated for each Sector	W				C					Input Sector Parameters
	W				H					
	W				R					
	W				N					
	W				Data Transfer of N Bytes					
										82078 Formats and Writes Entire Track
Result Phase	R				ST 0					
	R				ST 1					
	R				ST 2					
	R				Undefined					
	R				Undefined					
	R				Undefined					
	R				Undefined					
					INVALID					
Command	W				Invalid Codes					Invalid Command Codes (NoOp — 82078 goes into Standby State)
Result	R				ST 0					ST 0 = 80H

2

PARAMETER ABBREVIATIONS

Symbol	Description
AUTO PD	Auto powerdown control. If this bit is 0, then the automatic powerdown is disabled. If it is set to 1, then the automatic powerdown is enabled.
C	Cylinder address. The currently selected cylinder address, 0 to 255.
CLK48	CLK48 = 1 indicates an external 48 MHz oscillator is being used. CLK48 = 0 indicates a 24 MHz clock.
D0, D1, D2, D3	Drive Select 0-3. Designates which drives are Perpendicular drives, a "1" indicating Perpendicular drive.
D	Data pattern. The pattern to be written in each sector data field during formatting.
DN	Done. This bit indicates that this is the last byte of the drive specification command. The 82078 checks to see if this bit is high or low. If it is low, it expects more bytes. DN = 0 82078 expects more subsequent bytes. DN = 1 Terminates the command phase and jumps to the results phase. An additional benefit is that by setting this bit high, a direct check of the current drive specifications can be done.
DIR	Direction control. If this bit is 0, then the head will step out from the spindle during a relative seek. If set to a 1, the head will step in toward the spindle.
DS0, DS1	Disk Drive Select.

DS1	DS0	
0	0	Drive 0
0	1	Drive 1
1	0	Drive 2
1	1	Drive 3

Symbol	Description
DTL	Special sector size. By setting N to zero (00), DTL may be used to control the number of bytes transferred in disk read/write commands. The sector size (N = 0) is set to 128. If the actual sector (on the diskette) is larger than DTL, the remainder of the actual sector is read but is not passed to the host during read commands; during write commands, the remainder of the actual sector is written with all zero bytes. The CRC check code is calculated with the actual sector. When N is not zero, DTL has no meaning and should be set to FF HEX.
DRATE1, DRATE0	Data rate values from the DSR register.
DRT0, DRT1	Data rate table select. These two bits select between the different data rate tables. The default is the conventional table. These also provide mapping of the data rates selected in the DSR and CCR. The mapped values are provided for read back by the system software are as shown in the DIR (in PS/2 Mode only). Table 6-2 shows this.
DT0, DT1	Drive density select type. These bits select the outputs on DRVDEN0 and DRVDEN1 based on mode of operation that was selected via the IDENT1 and IDENT0 pins. More information is available in the Design Applications section.

Table 6-2. Data Rate Select Table

		Bits in DSR/CCR			Bits returned via DIR (Only available in PS/2)		
DRT0	**DRT1**	**DRATE0**	**DRATE1**	**Data Rate**	**DRATE0**	**DRATE1**	**Operation**
0	0	1	1	1 Mbps	1	1	Default
		0	0	500 Kbps	0	0	
		1	0	300 Kbps	1	0	
		0	1	250 Kbps	0	1	
0	1	1	1	1 Mbps	1	1	2 Mbps Tape Drive
		0	0	500 Kbps	0	0	
		1	0	2 Mbps	1	1	
		0	1	250 Kbps	0	1	
1	0	—RSVD—					RSVD
1	1	1	1	1 Mbps	1	1	Perpendicular mode FDDs
		0	0	500 Kbps	0	0	
		1	0	RSVD			
		0	1	250 Kbps	0	1	

EC — Enable Count. When this bit is "1" the "DTL" parameter of the Verify Command becomes SC (Number of sectors per track).

EFIFO — Enable FIFO. When this bit is 0, the FIFO is enabled. A "1" puts the 82078 in the 8272A compatible mode where the FIFO is disabled.

EIS — Enable implied seek. When set, a seek operation will be performed before executing any read or write command that requires the C parameter in the command phase. A "0" disables the implied seek.

EOT — End of track. The final sector number of the current track.

EREG EN — Enhanced Register Enable.

- EREG EN = 1 — In PS/2 mode the TDR register is extended. In AT/EISA mode, the TDR register is extended and SRB is made visible to the user.
- EREG EN = 0 — Standard AT/EISA and PS/2 registers are used.

FDI TRI — Floppy Drive Interface Tri-state: If this bit is 0, then the output pins of the floppy disk drive interface are tri-stated. This is also the default state. If it is set to 1, then the floppy disk drive interface remains unchanged.

FD0, FD1 — Floppy drive select. These two bits select which physical drive is being specified. The FDn corresponds to FDSn and FDMEn on the floppy drive interface. The drive is selected independent of the BOOTSELn bits. Please refer to Section 2.1.1 which explains the distinction between physical drives and their virtual mapping as defined by the BOOTSEL1 and BOOTSEL0 bits.

FD0	FD1	Drive Slot
0	0	Drive 0
0	1	Drive 1
1	0	Drive 2
1	1	Drive 3

GAP — Alters Gap 2 length when using Perpendicular Mode.

GPL — Gap length. The gap 3 size. (Gap 3 is the space between sectors excluding the VCO synchronization field).

HDS — Head address. Selected head: 0 or 1 (disk side 0 or 1) as encoded in the sector ID field.

HLT — Head load time. The time interval that 82078 waits after loading the head and before initiating a read or write operation. Refer to the SPECIFY command for actual delays.

HUT — Head unload time. The time interval from the end of the execution phase (of a read or write command) until the head is unloaded. Refer to the SPECIFY command for actual delays.

ISO — ISO Format: If this bit is set high the ISO format is used for all data transfer commands. When this bit is set low the normal IBM system 34 and perpendicular is used. The default is ISO = 0.

Lock — Lock defines whether EFIFO, FIFOTHR, and PRETRK parameters of the CONFIGURE command can be reset to their default values by a "Software Reset" (Reset made by setting the proper bit in the DSR or DOR registers).

MFM — MFM mode. A one selects the double density (MFM) mode. A zero is reserved.

MIN DLY — Minimum power up time control. This bit is active only if AUTO PD bit is enabled. Setting this bit to a 0, assigns a 10 ms minimum power up time and setting this bit to a 1, assigns a 0.5 sec. minimum power up time (unless 2 Mbps, then 5 ms to 0.25 sec.).

MT — Multi-track selector. When set, this flag selects the multi-track operating mode. In this mode, the 82078 treats a complete cylinder, under head 0 and 1, as a single track. The 82078 operates as if this expanded track started at the first sector under head 0 and ended at the last sector under head 1. With this flag set, a multitrack read or write operation will automatically continue to the first sector under head 1 when the 82078 finishes operating on the last sector under head 0.

N — Sector size code. This specifies the number of bytes in a sector. If this parameter is "00", then the sector size is 128 bytes. The number of bytes transferred is determined by the DTL parameter. Otherwise the sector size is (2 raised to the "N'th" power) times 128. All values up to "07" hex are allowable. "07"h would equal a sector size of 16k. It is the users responsibility to not select combinations that are not possible with the drive.

N	Sector Size
00	128 bytes
01	256 bytes
02	512 bytes
03	1024 bytes
—	—
07	16 Kbytes

NCN — New cylinder number. The desired cylinder number.

ND — Non-DMA mode flag. When set to 1, indicates that the 82078 is to operate in the non-DMA mode. In this mode, the host is interrupted for each data transfer. When set to 0, the 82078 operates in DMA mode, interfacing to a DMA controller by means of the DRQ and DACK# signals.

NRP — No Results phase. When this bit is set high the result phase is skipped. When this bit is low the result phase will be generated.

OW — The bits denoted D0, D1, D2, and D3 of the PERPENDICULAR MODE command can only be overwritten when the OW bit is set to "1".

PCN — Present cylinder number. The current position of the head at the completion of SENSE INTERRUPT STATUS command.

PC2, PC1, PC0 — Precompensation values from the DSR register.

PDOSC — When this bit is set, the internal oscillator is turned off.

This may be done if using the external 48 MHz oscillator.

PS/2 STAT — PS/2 status. This bit is functional only in the PS/2 mode. In all other modes this bit will not have any effect. When set high this bit enables two bits (bits 5 and 6) in the DIR register to reflect the values of PD and IDLE respectively except when IDLEMSK (bit 4) is set. Default value is 0.

PTS — Precompensation table select. This bit selects whether to enable the precompensation value programmed in the DSR or not. In the default state, the value programmed in DSR will be used.

PTS = 0 DSR programmed precompensation delays.

PTS = 1 No precompensation delay is selected for the corresponding drive.

POLL	Polling disable. When set, the internal polling routine is disabled. When clear, polling is enabled.
PRETRK	Precompensation start track number. Programmable from track 00 to FFH.
R	Sector address. The sector number to be read or written. In multi-sector transfers, this parameter specifies the sector number of the first sector to be read or written.
RCN	Relative cylinder number. Relative cylinder offset from present cylinder as used by the RELATIVE SEEK command.
SC	Number of sectors. The number of sectors to be initialized by the FORMAT command. The number of sectors to be verified during a Verify Command, when EC is set.
SEL3V#	SEL3V# = 1 indicates that the part is operating at 5.0V. SEL3V# = 0 indicates that the part is operating at 3.3V.
SK	Skip flag. When set to 1, sectors containing a deleted data address mark will automatically be skipped during the execution of READ DATA. If READ DELETED is executed, only sectors with a deleted address mark will be accessed. When set to "0", the sector is read or written the same as the read and write commands.
SRT	Step rate interval. The time interval between step pulses issued by the 82078. Programmable from 0.5 ms to 8 ms, in increments of 0.5 ms at the 1 Mbit data rate. Refer to the SPECIFY command for actual delays.
ST0-3	Status registers 0–3. Registers within the 82078 that store status information after a command has been executed. This status information is available to the host during the result phase after command execution.
STEPPING	These bits identify the stepping of the 82078.
WGATE	Write gate alters timing of WE, to allow for pre-erase loads in perpendicular drives.

2

6.1 Data Transfer Commands

All of the READ DATA, WRITE DATA and VERIFY type commands use the same parameter bytes and return the same results information. The only difference being the coding of bits 0–4 in the first byte.

An implied seek will be executed if the feature was enabled by the CONFIGURE command. This seek is completely transparent to the user. The Drive Busy bit for the drive will go active in the Main Status Register during the seek portion of the command. If the seek portion fails, it will be reflected in the results status normally returned for a READ/WRITE DATA command. Status Register 0 (ST0) would contain the error code and C would contain the cylinder on which the seek failed.

6.1.1 READ DATA

A set of nine (9) bytes is required to place the 82078 into the Read Data Mode. After the READ DATA command has been issued, the 82078 loads the head (if it is in the unloaded state), waits the specified head settling time (defined in the SPECIFY command), and begins reading ID Address Marks and ID fields. When the sector address read off the diskette matches with the sector address specified in the command, the 82078 reads the sector's data field and transfers the data to the FIFO.

After completion of the read operation from the current sector, the sector address is incremented by one, and the data from the next logical sector is read and output via the FIFO. This continuous read function is called "Multi-Sector Read Operation". Upon receipt of TC, or an implied TC (FIFO overrun/underrun), the 82078 stops sending data, but will continue to read data from the current sector, check the CRC bytes, and at the end of the sector terminate the READ DATA Command.

N determines the number of bytes per sector (see Table 6-3). If N is set to zero, the sector size is set to 128. The DTL value determines the number of bytes to be transferred. If DTL is less than 128, the 82078 transfers the specified number of bytes to the host. For reads, it continues to read the entire 128 byte sector and checks for CRC errors. For writes it completes the 128 byte sector by filling in zeroes. If N is not set to 00 Hex, DTL should be set to FF Hex, and has no impact on the number of bytes transferred.

Table 6-3. Sector Sizes

N	Sector Size
00	128 bytes
01	256 bytes
02	512 bytes
03	1024 bytes
—	—
07	16 Kbytes

The amount of data which can be handled with a single command to the 82078 depends upon MT (multi-track) and N (Number of bytes/sector).

Table 6-4. Effects of MT and N Bits

MT	N	Max. Transfer Capacity	Final Sector Read from Disk
0	1	256 × 26 = 656	26 at side 0 or 1
1	1	256 × 52 = 13312	26 at side 1
0	2	512 × 15 = 7680	15 at side 0 or 1
1	2	512 × 30 = 15360	15 at side 1
0	3	1024 × 8 = 8192	8 at side 0 or 1
1	3	1024 × 16 = 16384	16 at side 1

The Multi-Track function (MT) allows the 82078 to read data from both sides of the diskette. For a particular cylinder, data will be transferred starting at Sector 1, Side 0 and completing at the last sector of the same track at Side 1.

If the host terminates a read or write operation in the 82078, then the ID information in the result phase is dependent upon the state of the MT bit and EOT byte. Refer to Table 6-7. The termination must be normal.

At the completion of the READ DATA Command, the head is not unloaded until after the Head Unload Time Interval (specified in the SPECIFY command) has elapsed. If the host issues another command before the head unloads then the head settling time may be saved between subsequent reads.

If the 82078 detects a pulse on the INDX# pin twice without finding the specified sector (meaning that the diskette's index hole passes through index detect logic in the drive twice), the 82078 sets the IC code in Status Register 0 to "01" (Abnormal termination), and sets the ND bit in Status Register 1 to "1" indicating a sector not found, and terminates the READ DATA Command.

After reading the ID and Data Fields in each sector, the 82078 checks the CRC bytes. If a CRC error occurs in the ID or data field, the 82078 sets the IC code in Status Register 0 to "01" (Abnormal termination), sets the DE bit flag in Status Register 1 to "1", sets the DD bit in Status Register 2 to "1" if CRC is incorrect in the ID field, and terminates the READ DATA Command.

Table 6-5 describes the affect of the SK bit on the READ DATA command execution and results.

Table 6-5. Skip Bit vs READ DATA Command

SK Bit Value	Data Address Mark Type Encountered	Results		
		Sector Read?	CM Bit of ST2 Set?	Description of Results
0	Normal Data	Yes	No	Normal Termination.
0	Deleted Data	Yes	Yes	Address Not Incremented. Next Sector Not Searched For.
1	Normal Data	Yes	No	Normal Termination.
1	Deleted Data	No	Yes	Normal Termination Sector Not Read ("Skipped").

Except where noted in Table 6-5, the C or R value of the sector address is automatically incremented (see Table 6-7).

6.1.2 READ DELETED DATA

This command is the same as the READ DATA command, only it operates on sectors that contain a Deleted Data Address Mark at the beginning of a Data Field.

Table 6-6 describes the affect of the SK bit on the READ DELETED DATA command execution and results.

Table 6-6. Skip Bit vs READ DELETED DATA Command

SK Bit Value	Data Address Mark Type Encountered	Results		
		Sector Read?	CM Bit of ST2 Set?	Description of Results
0	Normal Data	Yes	Yes	Normal Termination.
0	Deleted Data	Yes	No	Address Not Incremented. Next Sector Not Searched For.
1	Normal Data	No	Yes	Normal Termination Sector Not Read ("Skipped").
1	Deleted Data	Yes	No	Normal Termination.

Except where noted in Table 6-6 above, the C or R value of the sector address is automatically incremented (see Table 6-7).

6.1.3 READ TRACK

This command is similar to the READ DATA command except that the entire data field is read continuously from each of the sectors of a track. Immediately after encountering a pulse on the INDX# pin, the 82078 starts to read all data fields on the track as continuous blocks of data without regard to logical sector numbers. If the 82078 finds an error in the ID or DATA CRC check bytes, it continues to read data from the track and sets the appropriate error bits at the end of the command. The 82078 compares the ID information read from each sector with the specified value in the command, and sets the ND flag of Status Register 1 to a "1" if there is no comparison.

Multi-track or skip operations are not allowed with this command. The MT and SK bits (Bits D7 and D5 of the first command byte respectively) should always be set to "0".

2

Table 6-7. Result Phase Table

MT	Head	Final Sector Transferred to Host	ID Information at Result Phase			
			C	H	R	N
0	0	Less than EOT	NC	NC	R+1	NC
		Equal to EOT	C+1	NC	01	NC
	1	Less than EOT	NC	NC	R+1	NC
		Equal to EOT	C+1	NC	01	NC
1	0	Less than EOT	NC	NC	R+1	NC
		Equal to EOT	NC	LSB	01	NC
	1	Less than EOT	NC	NC	R+1	NC
		Equal to EOT	C+1	LSB	01	NC

NC: No Change, the same value as the one at the beginning of command execution.
LSB: Least Significant Bit, the LSB of H is complemented.

This command terminates when the EOT specified number of sectors have been read. If the 82078 does not find an ID Address Mark on the diskette after the second occurrence of a pulse on the INDX# pin, then it sets the IC code in Status Register 0 to "01" (Abnormal termination), sets the MA bit in Status Register 1 to "1", and terminates the command.

6.1.4 WRITE DATA

After the WRITE DATA command has been issued, the 82078 loads the head (if it is in the unloaded state), waits the specified head load time if unloaded (defined in the SPECIFY command), and begins reading ID Fields. When the sector address read from the diskette matches the sector address specified in the command, the 82078 reads the data from the host via the FIFO, and writes it to the sector's data field.

After writing data into the current sector, the 82078 computes the CRC value and writes it into the CRC field at the end of the sector transfer. The Sector Number stored in "R" is incremented by one, and the 82078 continues writing to the next data field. The 82078 continues this "Multi-Sector Write Operation". Upon receipt of a terminal count signal or if a FIFO over/under run occurs while a data field is being written, then the remainder of the data field is filled with zeroes.

The 82078 reads the ID field of each sector and checks the CRC bytes. If it detects a CRC error in one of the ID Fields, it sets the IC code in Status Register 0 to "01" (Abnormal termination), sets the DE bit of Status Register 1 to "1", and terminates the WRITE DATA command.

The WRITE DATA command operates in much the same manner as the READ DATA command. The following items are the same. Please refer to the READ DATA Command for details:

- Transfer Capacity
- (End of Cylinder) bit
- ND (No Data) bit
- Head Load, Unload Time Interval
- ID information when the host terminates the command.
- Definition of DTL when N = 0 and when N does not = 0.

6.1.5 WRITE DELETED DATA

This command is almost the same as the WRITE DATA command except that a Deleted Data Address Mark is written at the beginning of the Data Field instead of the normal Data Address Mark. This command is typically used to mark a bad sector containing an error on the floppy disk.

6.1.6 VERIFY

The VERIFY command is used to verify the data stored on a disk. This command acts exactly like a READ DATA command except that no data is transferred to the host. Data is read from the disk, CRC computed and checked against the previously stored value.

Because no data is transferred to the host, TC (pin 25) cannot be used to terminate this command. By setting the EC bit to "1" an implicit TC will be issued to the 82078. This implicit TC will occur when the SC value has decrement to 0 (an SC value of 0 will verify 256 sectors). This command can also be terminated by setting the EC bit to "0" and the EOT value equal to the final sector to be checked. If EC is set to "0" DTL/SC should be programmed to 0FFH. Refer to Table 6-6 and Table 6-7 for information concerning the values of MT and EC versus SC and EOT value.

Definitions:

Sectors Per Side = Number of formatted sectors per each side of the disk.

Sectors Remaining = Number of formatted sectors left which can be read, including side 1 of the disk if MT is set to "1".

Table 6-8. Verify Command Result Phase Table

MT	EC	SC/EOT Value	Termination Result
0	0	SC = DTL EOT ≤ # Sectors Per Side	Successful Termination Result Phase Valid
0	0	SC = DTL EOT > # Sectors Per Side	Unsuccessful Termination Result Phase Invalid
0	1	SC ≤ # Sectors Remaining AND EOT ≤ # Sectors Per Side	Successful Termination Result Phase Valid
0	1	SC > # Sectors Remaining OR EOT > # Sectors Per Side	Unsuccessful Termination Result Phase Invalid
1	0	SC = DTL EOT ≤ # Sectors Per Side	Successful Termination Result Phase Valid
1	0	SC = DTL EOT > # Sectors Per Side	Unsuccessful Termination Result Phase Invalid
1	1	SC ≤ # Sectors Remaining AND EOT ≤ # Sectors Per Side	Successful Termination Result Phase Valid
1	1	SC > # Sectors Remaining OR EOT > # Sectors Per Side	Unsuccessful Termination Result Phase Invalid

NOTE:
If MT is set to "1" and the SC value is greater than the number of remaining formatted sectors on Side 0, verifying will continue on Side 1 of the disk.

2

6.1.7 FORMAT TRACK

The FORMAT command allows an entire track to be formatted. After a pulse from the INDX# pin is detected, the 82078 starts writing data on the disk including Gaps, Address Marks, ID Fields and Data Fields, per the IBM System 34 (MFM). The particular values that will be written to the gap and data field are controlled by the values programmed into N, SC, GPL, and D which are specified by the host during the command phase. The data field of the sector is filled with the data byte specified by D. The ID Field for each sector is supplied by the host; that is, four data bytes per sector are needed by the 82078 for C, H, R, and N (cylinder, head, sector number and sector size respectively).

After formatting each sector, the host must send new values for C, H, R and N to the 82078 for the next sector on the track. The R value (sector number) is the only value that must be changed by the host after each sector is formatted. This allows the disk to be formatted with nonsequential sector addresses (interleaving). This incrementing and formatting continues for the whole track until the 82078 encounters a pulse on the INDX# pin again and it terminates the command.

Table 6-9 contains typical values for gap fields which are dependent upon the size of the sector and the number of sectors on each track. Actual values can vary due to drive electronics.

Table 6-9. Typical PC-AT Values for Formatting

Drive Form	MEDIA	Sector Size	N	SC	GPL1	GPL2
5.25″	1.2M	512	02	0F	2A	50
	360K	512	02	09	2A	50
3.5″	2.88M	512	02	24	38	53
	1.44M	512	02	18	1B	54
	720K	512	02	09	1B	54

NOTE:
All values except Sector Size are in Hex.

Gap3 is programmable during reads, writes, and formats.

GPL1 = suggested Gap3 values in read and write commands to avoid splice point between data field and ID field of contiguous sections.

GPL2 = suggested Gap3 value in FORMAT TRACK command.

6.1.7.1 Format Fields

Table 6-10. System 34 Format Double Density

GAP 4a	SYNC	IAM		GAP 1	SYNC	IDAM		CYL	HD	SEC	NO	CRC	GAP 2	SYNC	DATA AM		DATA	CRC	GAP 3	GAP 4b
80x 4E	12x 00	3x C2	FC	50x 4E	12x 00	3x A1	FE						22x 4E	12x 00	3x A1	FB F8				

Table 6-11. ISO Format

GAP 1	SYNC	IDAM		CYL	HD	SEC	NO	CRC	GAP 2	SYNC	DATA AM		DATA	CRC	GAP 3	GAP 4b
32x 4E	12x 00	3x A1	FE						22x 4E	12x 00	3x A1	FB F8				

Table 6-12. Perpendicular Format

GAP 4a	SYNC	IAM		GAP 1	SYNC	IDAM		CYL	HD	SEC	NO	CRC	GAP 2	SYNC	DATA AM		DATA	CRC	GAP 3	GAP 4b
80x 4E	12x 00	3x C2	FC	50x 4E	12x 00	3x A1	FE						41x 4E	12x 00	3x A1	FB F8				

6.2 Control Commands

Control commands differ from the other commands in that no data transfer takes place. Three commands generate an interrupt when complete; READ ID, RECALIBRATE and SEEK. The other control commands do not generate an interrupt.

6.2.1 READ ID

The READ ID command is used to find the present position of the recording heads. The 82078 stores the values from the first ID Field it is able to read into its registers. If the 82078 does not find an ID Address Mark on the diskette after the second occurrence of a pulse on the INDX# pin, it then sets the IC code in Status Register 0 to "01" (Abnormal termination), sets the MA bit in Status Register 1 to "1", and terminates the command.

The following commands will generate an interrupt upon completion. They do not return any result bytes. It is highly recommended that control commands be followed by the SENSE INTERRUPT STATUS command. Otherwise, valuable interrupt status information will be lost.

6.2.2 RECALIBRATE

This command causes the read/write head within the 82078 to retract to the track 0 position. The 82078 clears the contents of the PCN counter, and checks the status of the TRK0 pin from the FDD. As long as the TRK0 pin is low, the DIR pin remains 0 and step pulses are issued. When the TRK0 pin goes high, the SE bit in Status Register 0 is set to "1", and the command is terminated. If the TRK0 pin is still low after 79 step pulses have been issued, the 82078 sets the SE and the EC bits of Status Register 0 to "1", and terminates the command. Disks capable of handling more than 80 tracks per side may require more than one RECALIBRATE command to return the head back to physical Track 0.

The RECALIBRATE command does not have a result phase. SENSE INTERRUPT STATUS command must be issued after the RECALIBRATE command to effectively terminate it and to provide verification of the head position (PCN). During the command phase of the recalibrate operation, the 82078 is in the BUSY state, but during the execution phase it is in a NON BUSY state. At this time another RECALIBRATE command may be issued, and in this manner, parallel RECALIBRATE operations may be done on up to 4 drives at once.

Upon power up, the software must issue a RECALIBRATE command to properly initialize all drives and the controller.

6.2.3 DRIVE SPECIFICATION COMMAND

The 82078 uses two pins, DRVDEN0 and DRVDEN1 to select the density for modern drives. These signals inform the drive of the type of diskette in the drive. The Drive Specification command specifies the polarity of the DRVDEN0 and DRVDEN1 pins. It also enables or disables DSR programmed precompensation.

This command removes the need for a hardware workaround to accommodate differing specifications among drives. By programming this command during BIOS's POST routine, the floppy disk controller will internally configure the correct values for DRVDEN0 and DRVDEN1 with corresponding precompensation value and data rate table enabled for the particular type of drive.

This command is protected from software resets. After executing the DRIVE SPEC command, subsequent software resets will not clear the programmed parameters. Only another DRIVE SPEC command or H/W reset can reset it to default values. The 6 LSBs of the last byte of this command are reserved for future use.

The DRATE0 and DRATE1 are values as programmed in the DSR register. The DENSEL is high for high data rates (1 Mbps and 500 Kbps) and low for low data rates (300 Kbps and 250 Kbps).

Table 6-13 describes the drives that are supported with the DT0, DT1 bits of the Drive Specification command:

2

Table 6-13. Drive Support via the Drive Specification Command

DRVDENn Polarities for AT/EISA Mode (IDENT0, IDENT1 = 11)

DT0	DT1	Data Rate	DRVDEN0	DRVDEN1
0*	0*	1 Mbps	1	1
		500 Kbps	1	0
		300 Kbps	0	1
		250 Kbps	0	0
0	1	1 Mbps	1	1
		500 Kbps	0	0
		300 Kbps	0	1
		250 Kbps	1	0
1	0	1 Mbps	0	1
		500 Kbps	0	0
		300 Kbps	1	1
		250 Kbps	1	0
1	1	1 Mbps	1	1
		500 Kbps	0	0
		300 Kbps	1	0
		250 Kbps	0	1

(*) Denotes the default setting

DRVDEN Polarities for PS/2, Model 30 Mode (IDENT0, IDENT1 = 0X)

DT0	DT1	Data Rate	DRVDEN0	DRVDEN1
0*	0*	1 Mbps	1	1
		500 Kbps	0	0
		300 Kbps	1	0
		250 Kbps	0	1
0	1	1 Mbps	1	1
		500 Kbps	1	0
		300 Kbps	0	1
		250 Kbps	0	0
1	0	1 Mbps	0	1
		500 Kbps	0	0
		300 Kbps	1	1
		250 Kbps	1	0
1	1	1 Mbps	1	1
		500 Kbps	0	0
		300 Kbps	0	1
		250 Kbps	1	0

(*) Denotes the default setting

6.2.4 SEEK

The read/write head within the drive is moved from track to track under the control of the SEEK Command. The 82078 compares the PCN which is the current head position with the NCN and performs the following operation if there is a difference:

PCN < NCN: Direction signal to drive set to "1" (step in), and issues step pulses.

PCN > NCN: Direction signal to drive set to "0" (step out), and issues step pulses.

The rate at which step pulses are issued is controlled by SRT (Stepping Rate Time) in the SPECIFY command. After each step pulse is issued, NCN is compared against PCN, and when NCN = PCN, then the SE bit in Status Register 0 is set to "1", and the command is terminated.

During the command phase of the seek or recalibrate operation, the 82078 is in the BUSY state, but during the execution phase it is in the NON BUSY state.

Note that if implied seek is not enabled, the read and write commands should be preceded by:

1. SEEK command; Step to the proper track
2. SENSE INTERRUPT STATUS command; Terminate the Seek command
3. READ ID. Verify head is on proper track
4. Issue READ/WRITE command.

The SEEK command does not have a result phase. Therefore, it is highly recommended that the SENSE INTERRUPT STATUS Command be issued after the SEEK command to terminate it and to provide verification of the head position (PCN). The H bit (Head Address) in ST0 will always return a "0". When exiting DSR POWERDOWN mode, the 82078 clears the PCN value and the status information to zero. Prior to issuing the DSR POWERDOWN command, it is highly recommended that the user service all pending interrupts through the SENSE INTERRUPT STATUS command.

6.2.5 SCAN COMMANDS

The SCAN Commands allow data which is being read from the diskette to be compared against data which is being supplied from the main system (Processor in NON-DMA mode, and DMA Controller in DMA mode). The FDC compares the data on a byte-by-byte basis, and looks for a sector of data which meets the conditions of $D_{FDD} = D_{Processor}$, $D_{FDD} \leq D_{Processor}$, or $D_{FDD} \geq D_{Processor}$. Ones complement arithmetic is used for comparison (FF = largest number, 00 = smallest number). After a whole sector of data is compared, if the conditions are not met, the sector number is incremented (R + STP → R), and the scan operation is continued. The scan operation continues until one of the following conditions occur; the conditions for scan are met (equal, low, or high), the last sector on the track is reached (EOT), or the terminal count signal is received.

If the conditions for scan are met then the FDC sets the SH (Scan Hit) flag of Status Register 2 to a 1 (high), and terminates the Scan Command. If the conditions for scan are not met between the starting sector (as specified by R) and the last sector on the cylinder (EOT), then the FDC sets the SN (Scan Not Satisfied) flag of Status Register 2 to a 1 (high), and terminates the Scan Command. The receipt of a TERMINAL COUNT signal from the Processor or DMA Controller during the scan operation will cause the FDC to complete the comparison of the particular byte which is in process, and then to terminate the command. Table 6-9 shows the status of bits SH and SN under various conditions of SCAN.

If the FDC encounters a Deleted Data Address Mark on one of the sectors (and SK = 0), then it regards the sector as the last sector on the cylinder, sets CM (Control Mark) flag of Status Register 2 to a 1 (high) and terminates the command. If SK = 1, the FDC skips the sector with the Deleted Address Mark, and reads the next sector. In the second case (SK = 1), the FDC sets the CM (Control Mark) flag of Status Register 2 to a 1 (high) in order to show that a Deleted Sector has been encountered.

When either the STP (contiguous sectors STP = 01, or alternate sectors STP = 02 sectors are read) or the MT (Multi-Track) are programmed, it is necessary to remember that the last sector on the track must be read. For example, if STP = 02, MT = 0, the sectors are numbered sequentially 1 through 26, and we start the Scan Command at sector 21; the following will happen. Sectors 21, 23, and 25 will be read, then the next sector (26) will be skipped and the Index Hole will be encountered before the EOT value of 26 can be read. This will result in an abnormal termination of the command. If the EOT had been set at 25 or the scanning started at sector 20, then the Scan Command would be completed in a normal manner.

During the Scan Command data is supplied by either the processor or DMA Controller for comparison against the data read from the diskette. In order to avoid having the OR (Over Run) flag set in Status Register 1, it is necessary to have the data available in less than 13 μs. If an Overrun occurs the FDC terminates the command.

2

Table 6-13. Scan Status Codes

Command	Status Register 2		Comments
	Bit 2 = SN	Bit 3 = SH	
Scan Equal	0 1	1 0	$D_{FDD} = D_{Processor}$ $D_{FDD} \neq D_{Processor}$
Scan Low or Equal	0 0 1	1 0 0	$D_{FDD} = D_{Processor}$ $D_{FDD} < D_{Processor}$ $D_{FDD} \not> D_{Processor}$
Scan High or Equal	0 0 1	1 0 0	$D_{FDD} = D_{Processor}$ $D_{FDD} > D_{Processor}$ $D_{FDD} \not< D_{Processor}$

6.2.6 SENSE INTERRUPT STATUS

An interrupt signal on INT pin is generated by the 82078 for one of the following reasons:

1. Upon entering the Result Phase of:
   a. READ DATA Command
   b. READ TRACK Command
   c. READ ID Command
   d. READ DELETED DATA Command
   e. WRITE DATA Command
   f. FORMAT TRACK Command
   g. WRITE DELETED DATA Command
   h. VERIFY Command
2. End of SEEK, RELATIVE SEEK or RECALIBRATE Command
3. 82078 requires a data transfer during the execution phase in the non-DMA Mode

The SENSE INTERRUPT STATUS command resets the interrupt signal and via the IC code and SE bit of Status Register 0, identifies the cause of the interrupt. If a SENSE INTERRUPT STATUS command is issued when no active interrupt condition is present, the status register ST0 will return a value of 80H (invalid command).

Table 6-14. Interrupt Identification

SE	IC	Interrupt Due To
0	11	Polling
1	00	Normal Termination of SEEK or RECALIBRATE command
1	01	Abnormal Termination of SEEK or RECALIBRATE command

The SEEK, RELATIVE SEEK and the RECALIBRATE commands have no result phase. SENSE INTERRUPT STATUS command must be issued immediately after these commands to terminate them and to provide verification of the head position (PCN). The H (Head Address) bit in ST0 will always return a "0". If a SENSE INTERRUPT STATUS is not issued, the drive will continue to be BUSY and may effect the operation of the next command.

6.2.7 SENSE DRIVE STATUS

SENSE DRIVE STATUS obtains drive status information. It has no execution phase and goes directly to the result phase from the command phase. STATUS REGISTER 3 contains the drive status information.

6.2.8 SPECIFY

The SPECIFY command sets the initial values for each of the three internal timers. The HUT (Head Unload Time) defines the time from the end of the execution phase of one of the read/write commands to the head unload state. The SRT (Step Rate Time) defines the time interval between adjacent step pulses. Note that the spacing between the first and second step pulses may be shorter than the remaining step pulses. The HLT (Head Load Time) defines the time between the command phase to the execution phase of a read/write data command. The Head Unload Time (HUT) timer starts at the end of the execution phase to the beginning of the result phase of a read/write command. The values change with the data rate speed selection and are documented in Table 6-15.

Table 6-15. Drive Control Delays (ms)

	HUT				SRT			
	1M	500K	300K	250K	1M	500K	300K	250K
0	128	256	426	512	8.0	16	26.7	32
1	8	16	26.7	32	7.5	15	25	30
—	—	—	—	—	—	—	—	—
A	80	160	267	320	3.0	6.0	10.2	12
B	88	176	294	352	2.5	5.0	8.35	10
C	96	192	320	384	2.0	4.0	6.68	8
D	104	208	346	416	1.5	3.0	5.01	6
E	112	224	373	448	1.0	2.0	3.33	4
F	120	240	400	480	0.5	1.0	1.67	2

	HLT			
	1M	**500K**	**300K**	**250K**
00	128	256	426	512
01	1	2	3.3	4
02	2	4	6.7	8
—	—	—	—	—
7E	126	252	420	504
7F	127	254	423	508

The choice of DMA or NON-DMA operations is made by the ND bit. When this bit is "1", the NON-DMA mode is selected, and when ND is "0", the DMA mode is selected. In DMA mode, data transfers are signalled by the DRQ pin. Non-DMA mode uses the RQM bit and the INT pin to signal data transfers.

6.2.9 CONFIGURE

Issue the configure command to enable features like the programmable FIFO and set the beginning track for pre-compensation. A CONFIGURE command need not be issued if the default values of the 82078 meet the system requirements. The CLK48 bit allows the 82078 to connect to a 48 MHz oscillator, this can reduce board space if there is a 48 MHz signal already available on the system.

CONFIGURE DEFAULT VALUES:

EIS — No Implied Seeks
EFIFO — FIFO Disabled
POLL — Polling Enabled
FIFOTHR — FIFO Threshold Set to 1 Byte
PRETRK — Pre-Compensation Set to Track 0

EIS—Enable implied seek. When set to "1", the 82078 will perform a SEEK operation before executing a read or write command. Defaults to no implied seek.

EFIFO—A "1" puts the FIFO into the 8272A compatible mode where the FIFO is disabled. This means data transfers are asked for on a byte by byte basis. Defaults to "1", FIFO disabled. The threshold defaults to one.

POLL—Disable polling of the drives. Defaults to "0", polling enabled. When enabled, a single interrupt is generated after a RESET. No polling is performed while the drive head is loaded and the head unload delay has not expired.

FIFOTHR—The FIFO threshold in the execution phase of read or write commands. This is programmable from 1 byte to 16 bytes. Defaults to one byte. A "00" selects one byte, "0F" selects 16 bytes.

PRETRK—Pre-compensation start track number. Programmable from track 0 to 255. Defaults to track 0. A "00" selects track 0, "FF" selects 255.

CLK48—Default is "0", external clock is assumed to be 24 MHz. If a 48 MHz external oscillator is used the bit must be set high. Note that the 82078 does not support a 48 MHz crystal, only an external oscillator. For more information refer to the section about the 2 Mbps data rate. Note, this must be enabled first during the initialization routine of the POST if a 48 MHz oscillator is used.

2

6.2.10 VERSION

The VERSION command checks to see if the controller is an enhanced type (82077, 82077AA, 82077SL) or the older type (8272A/765A). A value of 90H is returned as the result byte, defining an enhanced FDD controller is in use. No interrupts are generated.

6.2.11 RELATIVE SEEK

The command is coded the same as for SEEK, except for the MSB of the first byte and the DIR bit.

DIR Head Step Direction Control.

DIR	Action
0	Step Head Out
1	Step Head In

RCN Relative Cylinder Number that determines how many tracks to step the head in or out from the current track number.

The RELATIVE SEEK command differs from the SEEK command in that it steps the head the absolute number of tracks specified in the command instead of making a comparison against an internal register. The SEEK command is good for drives that support a maximum of 256 tracks. RELATIVE SEEKs cannot be overlapped with other RELATIVE SEEKs. Only one RELATIVE SEEK can be active at a time. Bit 4 of Status Register 0 (EC) will be set if RELATIVE SEEK attempts to step outward beyond Track 0.

As an example, assume that a floppy drive has 300 useable tracks and that the host needs to read track 300 and the head is on any track (0–255). If a SEEK

command was issued, the head would stop at track 255. If a RELATIVE SEEK command was issued, the 82078 would move the head the specified number of tracks, regardless of the internal cylinder position register (but would increment the register). If the head had been on track 40 (D), the maximum track that the 82078 could position the head on using RELATIVE SEEK, would be 296 (D), the initial track, +256 (D). The maximum count that the head can be moved with a single RELATIVE SEEK command is 256 (D).

The internal register, PCN, would overflow as the cylinder number crossed track 255 and would contain 40 (D). The resulting PCN value is thus (NCN + PCN) mod 256. Functionally, the 82078 starts counting from 0 again as the track number goes above 255(D). It is the users responsibility to compensate 82078 functions (precompensation track number) when accessing tracks greater than 255. The 82078 does not keep track that it is working in an "extended track area" (greater than 255). Any command issued would use the current PCN value except for the RECALIBRATE command which only looks for the TRACK0 signal. RECALIBRATE would return an error if the head was farther than 79 due to its limitation of issuing a maximum 80 step pulses. The user simply needs to issue a second RECALIBRATE command. The SEEK command and implied seeks will function correctly within the 44 (D) track (299–255) area of the "extended track area". It is the users responsibility not to issue a new track position that would exceed the maximum track that is present in the extended area.

To return to the standard floppy range (0–255) of tracks, a RELATIVE SEEK would be issued to cross the track 255 boundary.

A RELATIVE SEEK can be used instead of the normal SEEK but the host is required to calculate the difference between the current head location and the new (target) head location. This may require the host to issue a READ ID command to ensure that the head is physically on the track that software assumes it to be. Different 82078 commands will return different cylinder results which may be difficult to keep track of with software without the READ ID command.

6.2.12 DUMPREG

The DUMPREG command is designed to support system run-time diagnostics and application software development and debug. The command returns pertinent information regarding the internal status of the 82078. This can be used to verify the values initialized in the 82078.

6.2.13 PERPENDICULAR MODE COMMAND

6.2.13.1 About Perpendicular Recording Mode

An added capability of the 82078 is the ability to interface directly to perpendicular recording floppy drives. Perpendicular recording differs from the traditional longitudinal method by orienting the magnetic bits vertically. This scheme packs in more data bits for the same area.

6.2.13.2 The Perpendicular Mode Command

The PERPENDICULAR MODE Command allows the system designers to designate specific drives as

Table 6-16. Effects of WGATE and GAP Bits

GAP	WGATE	MODE	VCO Low Time after Index Pulse	Length of Gap2 Format Field	Portion of Gap2 Written by Write Data Operation	Gap2 VCO Low Time for Read Operations
0	0	Conventional Mode	33 Bytes	22 Bytes	0 Bytes	24 Bytes
0	1	Perpendicular Mode (500 Kbps Data Rate)	33 Bytes	22 Bytes	19 Bytes	24 Bytes
1	0	Reserved (Conventional)	33 Bytes	22 Bytes	0 Bytes	24 Bytes
1	1	Perpendicular Mode (1 Mbps Data Rate)	18 Bytes	41 Bytes	38 Bytes	43 Bytes

NOTE:
When either GAP or WGATE bit is set, the current value of precompensation in the DSR is used.

Perpendicular recording drives. Data transfers between Conventional and Perpendicular drives are allowed without having to issue PERPENDICULAR MODE commands between the accesses of the two different drives, nor having to change write pre-compensation values.

With this command, the length of the Gap2 field and VCO enable timing can be altered to accommodate the unique requirements of these drives. Table 6-16 describes the effects of the WGATE and GAP bits for the PERPENDICULAR MODE command.

When both GAP and WGATE equal "0" the PERPENDICULAR MODE command will have the following effect on the 82078: 1) If any of the new bits D0, D1, D2, and D3 are programmed to "1" the corresponding drive will automatically be programmed for Perpendicular mode (i.e.: GAP2 being written during a write operation, the programmed Data Rate will determine the length of GAP2), and data will be written with 0 ns write pre-compensation. 2) any of the new bits (D0–D3) that are programmed for "0" the designated drive will be programmed for Conventional Mode and data will be written with the currently programmed write pre-compensation value. 3) Bits D0, D1, D2, and D3 can only be over written when the OW bit is written as a "1". The status of these bits can be determined by interpreting the eighth result byte of the DUMPREG Command. (Note: if either the GAP or WGATE bit is a "1", then bits D0–D3 are ignored.)

"Software" and "Hardware" RESET will have the following effects on the enhanced PERPENDICULAR MODE command:

1. "Software" RESETs (Reset via DOR or DSR registers) will only clear GAP and WGATE bits to "0", D3, D2, D1, and D0 will retain their previously programmed values.
2. "Hardware" RESETs (Reset via pin 32) will clear all bits (GAP, WGATE, D0, D1, D2, and D3) to "0" (All Drives Conventional Mode).

6.2.14 POWERDOWN MODE COMMAND

The POWERDOWN MODE command allows the automatic power management and enables the enhanced registers (EREG EN) of the 82078. The use of the command can extend the battery life in portable PC applications. To enable auto powerdown the command may be issued during the BIOS power on self test (POST).

This command includes the ability to configure the 82078 into the enhanced AT/EISA and PS/2 mode. In the enhanced PS/2 and Model 30 modes, this makes the PD and IDLE pin status visible in the DIR register. In the enhanced AT/EISA modes, this command extends the SRB and TDR register. These extended registers accommodate bits that give more information about floppy drive interface, allow for boot drive selection, and identify the values of the PD and IDLE status.

As soon as the command is enabled, a 10 ms or a 0.5 sec. (5 ms or 0.25 with 2Mbps tape mode) minimum powerup timer is initiated depending on whether the MIN DLY bit is set to 0 or 1. This timer is one of the required conditions that has to be satisfied before the part will enter auto powerdown. Any software reset will reinitialize the timer. The timer countdown is also extended by up to 10 ms if the data rate is changed during the timer's countdown. Without this timer 82078 would have been put to sleep immediately after 82078 is idle. The minimum delay gives software a chance to interact with 82078 without incurring an additional overhead due to recovery time.

The command also allows the output pins of floppy disk drive interface to be tri-stated or left unaltered during auto powerdown. This is done by the FDI TRI bit. In the default condition (FDI TRI = 0) the output pins of the floppy disk drive are tri-stated. Setting this bit leaves the interface unchanged from the normal state.

The results phase returns the values programmed for MIN DLY, FDI TRI and AUTO PD. The auto powerdown mode is disabled by a hardware reset. Software results have no effect on the POWERDOWN MODE command parameters.

6.2.15 PART ID COMMAND

This command can be used to identify the floppy disk controller as an enhanced controller. The first stepping of both versions of the 64 pin 82078 will yield 0x01 in the result phase of this command. Any future enhancements on these parts will be denoted by the 5 LSBs (0x01 to 0x1F).

6.2.16 OPTION COMMAND

The standard IBM format includes an index address field consisting of 80 bytes of GAP 4a, 12 bytes of the sync field, four bytes identifying the IAM and 50 bytes of GAP 1. Under the ISO format most of this preamble is not used. The ISO format allows only 32 bytes of GAP 1 after the index mark. The ISO bit in this command allows the 82078 to configure the data transfer commands to recognize this format. The MSBs in this command are reserved for any other enhancements made available to the user in the future.

6.2.17 SAVE COMMAND

The first byte corresponds to the values programmed in the DSR with the exception of CLK48. The DRATE1, DRATE0 used here are unmapped. The second byte is used for configuring the bits from the OPTION command. All future enhancements to the OPTION command will be reflected in this byte as well. The next nine result bytes are explained in the Parameter Abbreviations section after the command summary. The 13th byte is the value associated with the auto powerdown command. The disk status is used internally by 82078. There are two reserved bytes at the end of this command for future use.

This command is similar to the DUMPREG command but it additionally allows the user to read back the precompensation values as well as the programmed data rate. It also allows the user to read the values programmed in the auto powerdown command. The precompensation values will be returned as programmed in the DSR register. This command is used in conjunction with the Restore command should prove very useful for SMM power management. This command reserves the last two bytes for future enhancements.

6.2.18 RESTORE COMMAND

Using Restore with the Save command, allows the SMM power management to restore the 82078 to its original state after a system powerdown. It also serves as a succinct way to provide most of the initialization requirements normally handled by the system. The sequence of initializing the 82078 after a reset occurred and assuming a Save command was issued follows:

- Issue the Drive Spec command (if the design utilizes this command)
- Issue the Restore command (pass the 16 bytes retrieved previously during SAVE)

The Restore command will program the data rate and precompensation value via the DSR. It then restores the values normally programmed through the Configure, Specify, and Perpendicular commands. It also enables the previously selected values for the AUTO Powerdown command. The PCN values are set restored to their previous values and the user is responsible for issuing the seek and recalibrate commands to restore the head to the proper location. There are some drives that do not recalibrate in which case the Restore command will restore the previous state completely. The PDOSC bit is retrievable using the Save command, however, the system designer must set it correctly. The software must allow at least 20 μs to execute the Restore command. When using the BOOTSEL bits in the TDR, the user must restore or reinitialize these bits to their proper values.

6.2.19 FORMAT AND WRITE COMMAND

The format and write command is capable of simultaneously formatting and writing data to the diskette. It is essentially the same as the normal format command. With the exception that included in the execution for each sector is not only the C, H, R, and N but also the data transfer of N bytes. The D value is ignored. This command formats the entire track. High speed floppy diskette duplication can be done fast and efficiently with this command. The user can format the diskette and put data on it in a single pass. This is very useful for software duplication applications by reducing the time required to format and copy diskettes.

6.2.20 LOCK

The LOCK command is included to protect a system with long DMA latencies against older application software packages that can disable the 82078's FIFO.

NOTE:
This command should only be used by the system's FDC routines, and ISVs (Independent Software Vendors) should refrain from using it. If an ISV's application calls for having the 82078 FIFO disabled a CONFIGURE Command should be used to toggle the EFIFO (Enable FIFO) bit. ISV can determine the value of the LOCK bit by interpreting the eighth result byte of an DUMPREG Command.

The LOCK command defines whether EFIFO, FIFOTHR, and PRETRK parameters of the CONFIGURE command can be RESET by the DOR and DSR registers. When the LOCK bit is set to a "1" all subsequent "software" RESETs by the DOR and DSR registers will not change the previously set parameter values in the CONFIGURE command. When the LOCK bit is set to a "0" 'software" RESETs by the DOR or DSR registers will return these parameters to their default values. All "hardware" Resets will set the LOCK bit to a "0" value, and will return EFIFO, FIFOTHR, and PRETRK to their default values. A Status byte is returned immediately after issuing the command byte. This Status byte reflects the value of the Lock bit set by the command byte.

NOTE:
No interrupts are generated at the end of this command.

7.0 STATUS REGISTER ENCODING

The contents of these registers are available only through a command sequence.

7.1 Status Register 0

Bit No.	Symbol	Name	Description
7, 6	IC	Interrupt Code	00—Normal termination of command. The specified command was properly executed and completed without error. 01—Abnormal termination of command. Command execution was started, but was not successfully completed. 10—Invalid command. The requested command could not be executed. 11—Abnormal termination caused by Polling.
5	SE	Seek End	The 82078 completed a SEEK or RECALIBRATE command, or a READ or WRITE with implied seek command.
4	EC	Equipment Check	The TRK0 pin failed to become a "1" after: 1. 80 step pulses in the RECALIBRATE command. 2. The RELATIVE SEEK command causes the 82078 to step outward beyond Track 0.
3	—	—	Unused. This bit is always "0".
2	H	Head Address	The current head address.
1, 0	DS1, 0	Drive Select	The current selected drive.

7.2 Status Register 1

Bit No.	Symbol	Name	Description
7	EN	End of Cylinder	The 82078 tried to access a sector beyond the final sector of the track (255D). Will be set if TC is not issued after Read or Write Data Command.
6	—	—	Unused. This bit is always "0".
5	DE	Data Error	The 82078 detected a CRC error in either the ID field or the data field of a sector.
4	OR	Overrun/ Underrun	Becomes set if the 82078 does not receive CPU or DMA service within the required time interval, resulting in data overrun or underrun.
3	—	—	Unused. This bit is always "0".
2	ND	No Data	Any one of the following: 1. READ DATA, READ DELETED DATA command, the 82078 did not find the specified sector. 2. READ ID command, the 82078 cannot read the ID field without an error. 3. READ TRACK command, the 82078 cannot find the proper sector sequence.
1	NW	Not Writable	WP pin became a "1" while the 82078 is executing a WRITE DATA, WRITE DELETED DATA, or FORMAT TRACK command.
0	MA	Missing Address Mark	Any one of the following: 1. The 82078 did not detect an ID address mark at the specified track after encountering the index pulse from the INDX# pin twice. 2. The 82078 cannot detect a data address mark or a deleted data address mark on the specified track.

7.3 Status Register 2

Bit No.	Symbol	Name	Description
7	—	—	Unused. This bit is always "0".
6	CM	Control Mark	Any one of the following: 1. READ DATA command, the 82078 encounters a deleted data address mark. 2. READ DELETED DATA command, the 82078 encountered a data address mark.
5	DD	Data Error in Data Field	The 82078 detected a CRC error in the data field.
4	WC	Wrong Cylinder	The track address from the sector ID field is different from the track address maintained inside the 82078.
3	—	—	Unused. This bit is always "0".
2	—	—	Unused. This bit is always "0".
1	BC	Bad Cylinder	The track address from the sector ID field is different from the track address maintained inside the 82078 and is equal to FF hex which indicates a bad track with a hard error according to the IBM soft-sectored format.
0	MD	Missing Data Address Mark	The 82078 cannot detect a data address mark or a deleted data address mark.

7.4 Status Register 3

Bit No.	Symbol	Name	Description
7	—	—	Unused. This bit is always "0".
6	WP	Write Protected	Indicates the status of the WP pin.
5	—	—	Unused. This bit is always "1".
4	T0	TRACK 0	Indicates the status of the TRK0 pin.
3	—	—	Unused. This bit is always "1".
2	HD	Head Address	Indicates the status of the HDSEL pin.
1, 0	DS1, 0	Drive Select	Indicates the status of the DS1, DS0 pins.

8.0 COMPATIBILITY

The 82078 was designed with software compatibility in mind. It is a fully backwards compatible solution with the older generation 8272A and NEC765A/B disk controllers. The 82078 also implements on-board registers for compatibility with the Personal System/2s as well as PC/AT and PC/XT floppy disk controller subsystems. The 82078 is fully compatible with Intel's 386/486SL Microprocessor Superset. Upon reset, the 82078 samples IDENT0 and IDENT1 to determine PS/2, PC/AT or PS/2 Model 30 mode.

8.1 PS/2 vs AT vs Model 30 Mode

The 82078 operates in three different modes: PS/2, PC/AT, and Model 30. The 82078 is placed into the proper mode of operations upon Hardware RESET with the appropriate settings of the IDENT0 and IDENT1 pins.

8.2 Compatibility with the FIFO

The FIFO of the 82078 is designed to be transparent to non-FIFO disk controller software developed on the older generation 8272A standard. Operation of the 82078 FIFO can be broken down into two tiers of compatibility. For first tier compatibility, the FIFO is left in the default disabled condition upon a "Hardware" reset. In this mode the FIFO operates in a byte mode and provides complete compability with non-FIFO based software. For second tier compatibility, the FIFO is enabled via the CONFIGURE command. When the FIFO is enabled, it will temporarily enter a byte mode during the command and result phase of disk controller operation. This allows for compatible operation when interrogating the Main Status Register (MSR) for the purpose of transferring a byte at a time to or from the disk controller. For normal disk controller applications, the system designer can still take advantage of the FIFO for time critical data transfers during the execution phase and not create any conflicts with non-FIFO software during the command or result phase.

In some instances, use of the FIFO in any form has conflicted with certain specialized software. An example of a compatibility conflict using the FIFO is with software that monitors the progress of a data transfer during the execution phase. If the software assumed the disk controller was operating in a single byte mode and counted the number of bytes transferred to or from the disk controller to trigger some time dependent event on the disk media (i.e., head position over a specific data field), the same software will not have an identical time relationship if the FIFO is enabled. This is because the FIFO allows data to be queued up, and then burst transferred across the host bus. To accommodate software of this type, it is recommended that the FIFO be disabled.

8.3 Drive Polling

The 82078 supports the polling mode of the older generation 8272A. This mode is enabled upon a reset and can be disabled via the CONFIGURE command. This mode is supported for the sole purpose of providing backward compatibility with software that expects its presence.

The intended purpose of drive polling dates back to 8″ drives as a means to monitor any change in status for each disk drive present in the system. Each of the drives is selected for a period of time and its READY signal sampled. After a delay, the next drive is selected. Since the 82078 does not support READY in this capacity (internally tied true), the polling sequence is only simulated and does not affect the drive select lines (DS0–DS3) when it is active. If enabled, it occurs whenever the 82078 is waiting for a command or during SEEKs and RECALIBRATEs (but not IMPLIED SEEKs). Each drive is assumed to be not ready after a reset and a "ready" value for each drive is saved in an internal register as the simulated drive is polled. An interrupt will be generated on the first polling loop because of the initial "not ready" status. This interrupt must be followed with a SENSE INTERRUPT STATUS command from the host to clear the interrupt condition for each of the four logical drives.

9.0 Programming Guidelines

Programming the 82078 is identical to any other 8272A compatible disk controller with the exception of some additional commands. For the new designer, it is useful to provide some guidelines on how to program the 82078. A typical disk operation involves more than issuing a command and waiting for the results. The control of the floppy disk drive is a low level operation that requires software intervention at different stages. New commands and features have been added to the 82078 to reduce the complexity of this software interface.

9.1 Command and Result Phase Handshaking

Before a command or parameter byte can be issued to the 82078, the Main Status Register (MSR) must be interrogated for a ready status and proper FIFO direction. A typical floppy controller device driver should contain a subroutine for sending command or

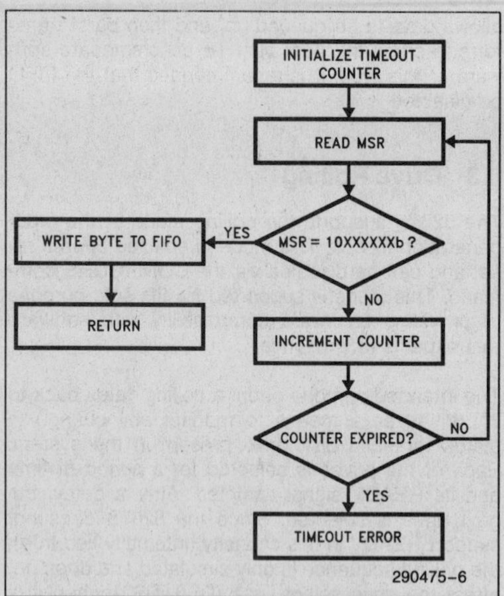

Figure 9-1. Send_Byte Routine

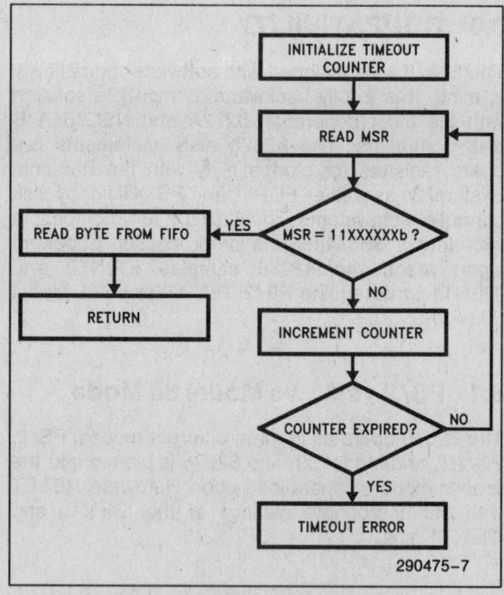

Figure 9-2. Get_Byte Routine

parameter bytes. For this discussion, the routine will be called "Send_byte" with the flowchart shown in Figure 9-1.

The routine loops until RQM is 1 and DIO is 0 indicating a ready status and FIFO direction is inward. If this condition is true, the 82078 is ready to accept a command or parameter byte. A timeout counter is used to insure software response within a reasonable amount of time in case of no response by the 82078. As a note, the programmer must be careful how the maximum delay is chosen to avoid unnecessary timeouts. For example, if a new command is issued when the 82078 is in the middle of a polling routine, the MSR will not indicate a ready status for the next parameter byte until the polling sequence completes the loop. This could cause a delay between the first and second bytes of up to 250 μs (@ 250 Kbps). If polling is disabled, this maximum delay is 175 μs. There should also be enough timeout margin to accommodate a shift of the software to a higher speed system. A timeout value that results in satisfactory operation on a 16 MHz CPU might fail when the software is moved to a system with a 25 MHz CPU. A recommended solution is to derive the timeout counter from a system hardware counter that is fixed in frequency from CPU clock to CPU clock.

For reading result bytes from the 82078, a similar routine is used. Figure 9-2 illustrates the flowchart for the routine "Get_byte". The MSR is polled until RQM is 1 and DIO is 1, which indicates a ready status and outward FIFO direction. At this point, the host can read a byte from the FIFO. As in the Send_byte routine, a timeout counter should be incorporated in case of a disk controller lock-up condition. For example, if a disk was not inserted into the disk drive at the time of a read operation, the controller would fail to receive the index pulse and lock-up since the index pulses are required for termination of the execution phase.

9.2 Initialization

Initializing the 82078 involves setting up the appropriate configuration after a reset. Parameters set by the SPECIFY command are undefined after a system reset and will need to be reinitialized. CONFIGURE command parameters default to a known state after a system reset but will need to be reinitialized if the system requirements are different from the default settings. This can be accomplished in two ways, either issue the individual commands, or issue the Restore command (assuming the Save command was issued). The Restore command is a succinct way to initialize the 82078, this is the preferable method if the system power management powers the 82078 on and off frequently. The flowchart for the recommended initialization sequence of the 82078 is shown in Figure 9-3.

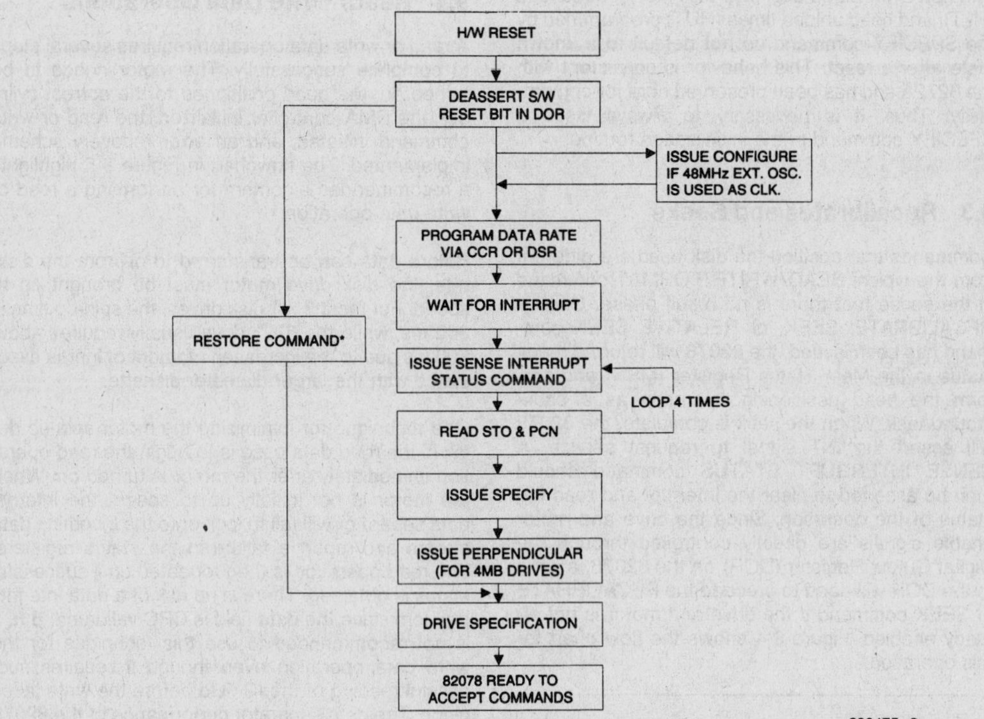

*Sense Interrupt Status may be required if Restore CMD is not issued within 250 μs of trailing edge of H/W reset (@1 Mbps).

Figure 9-3. Initialization Flowchart

Following a reset of the 82078, the Configuration Control Register (CCR) should be reinitialized for the appropriate data rate. An external reset via the RESET pin will cause the data rate and write precompensation values to default to 250 Kbps (10b) and 125 ns (000b) respectively. Since the 125 ns write precompensation value is optimal for the 5 ¼″ and 3 ½″ disk drive environment, most applications will not require the value to be changed in the initialization sequence. As a note, a software reset issued via the DOR or DSR will not affect the data rate or write precompensation values. But it is recommended as a safe programming practice to always program the data rate after a reset, regardless of the type.

Since polling is enabled after a reset of the 82078, four SENSE INTERRUPT STATUS commands need to be issued afterwards to clear the status flags for each drive. The flowchart in Figure 9-3 illustrates how the software clears each of the four interrupt status flags internally queued by the 82078. It should be noted that although four SENSE INTERRUPT STATUS commands are issued, the INT pin is only active until the first SENSE INTERRUPT STATUS command is executed.

As a note, if the CONFIGURE command is issued within 250 μs of the trailing edge of reset (@1 Mbps), the polling mode of the 82078 can be disabled before the polling initiated interrupt occurs. Since polling stops when the 82078 enters the command phase, it is only time critical up to the first byte of the CONFIGURE command. If disabled in time, the system software no longer needs to issue the four SENSE INTERRUPT STATUS commands to clear the internal interrupt flags normally caused by polling.

The CONFIGURE command should also be issued if the system requirements are different from the default settings. For example, the CONFIGURE command can be used to enable the FIFO, set the threshold, and enable Implied Seeks.

The non-DMA mode flag, step rate (SRT), head load (HLT), and head unload times (HUT) programmed by the SPECIFY command do not default to a known state after a reset. This behavior is consistent with the 8272A and has been preserved here for compatibility. Thus, it is necessary to always issue a SPECIFY command in the initialization routine.

9.3 Recalibrates and Seeks

Commands that position the disk head are different from the typical READ/WRITE/FORMAT command in the sense that there is no result phase. Once a RECALIBRATE, SEEK, or RELATIVE SEEK command has been issued, the 82078 will return a ready status in the Main Status Register (MSR) and perform the head positioning operation as a background task. When the seek is complete, the 82078 will assert the INT signal to request service. A SENSE INTERRUPT STATUS command should then be asserted to clear the interrupt and read the status of the operation. Since the drive and motor enable signals are directly controlled through the Digital Output Register (DOR) on the 82078, a write to the DOR will need to precede the RECALIBRATE or SEEK command if the drive and motor is not already enabled. Figure 9-4 shows the flow chart for this operation.

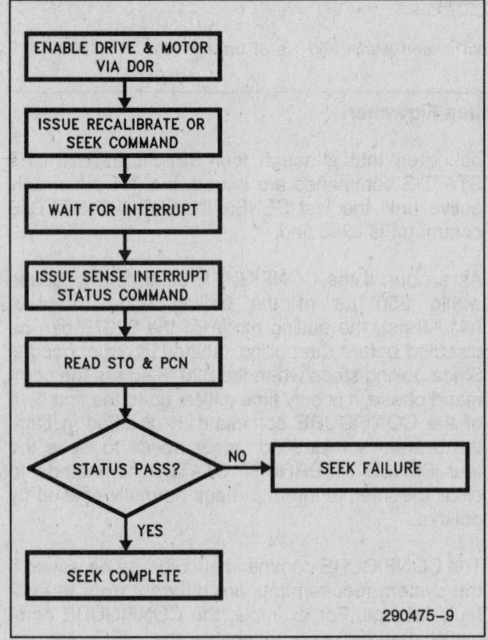

Figure 9-4. Recalibrate and Seek Operations

9.4 Read/Write Data Operations

A read or write data operation requires several steps to complete successfully. The motor needs to be turned on, the head positioned to the correct cylinder, the DMA controller initialized, the read or write command initiated, and an error recovery scheme implemented. The flowchart in Figure 9-5 highlights a recommended algorithm for performing a read or write data operation.

Before data can be transferred to or from the diskette, the disk drive motor must be brought up to speed. For most 3½″ disk drives, the spin-up time is 300 ms, while the 5¼″ drive usually requires about 500 ms due to the increased moment of inertia associated with the larger diameter diskette.

One technique for minimizing the motor spin-up delay in the read data case is to begin the read operation immediately after the motor is turned on. When the motor is not initially up to speed, the internal data separator will fail to lock onto the incoming data stream and report a failure in the status registers. The read operation is then repeated until successful status is obtained. There is no risk of a data integrity problem since the data field is CRC validated. But, it is not recommended to use this technique for the write data operation even though it requires successful reading of the ID field before the write takes place. The data separator performance of the 82078 is such that locking to the data stream could take place while the motor speed variation is still significant. This could result in errors when an attempt is made to read the disk media by other disk controllers that have a narrower incoming data stream frequency bandwidth.

After the motor has been turned on, the matching data rate for the media inserted into the disk drive should then be programmed to the 82078 via the Configuration Control Register (CCR). The 82078 is designed to allow a different data rate to be programmed arbitrarily without disrupting the integrity of the device. In some applications, it is required to automatically determine the recorded data rate of the inserted media. One technique for doing this is to perform a READ ID operation at each available data rate until a successful status is returned in the result phase.

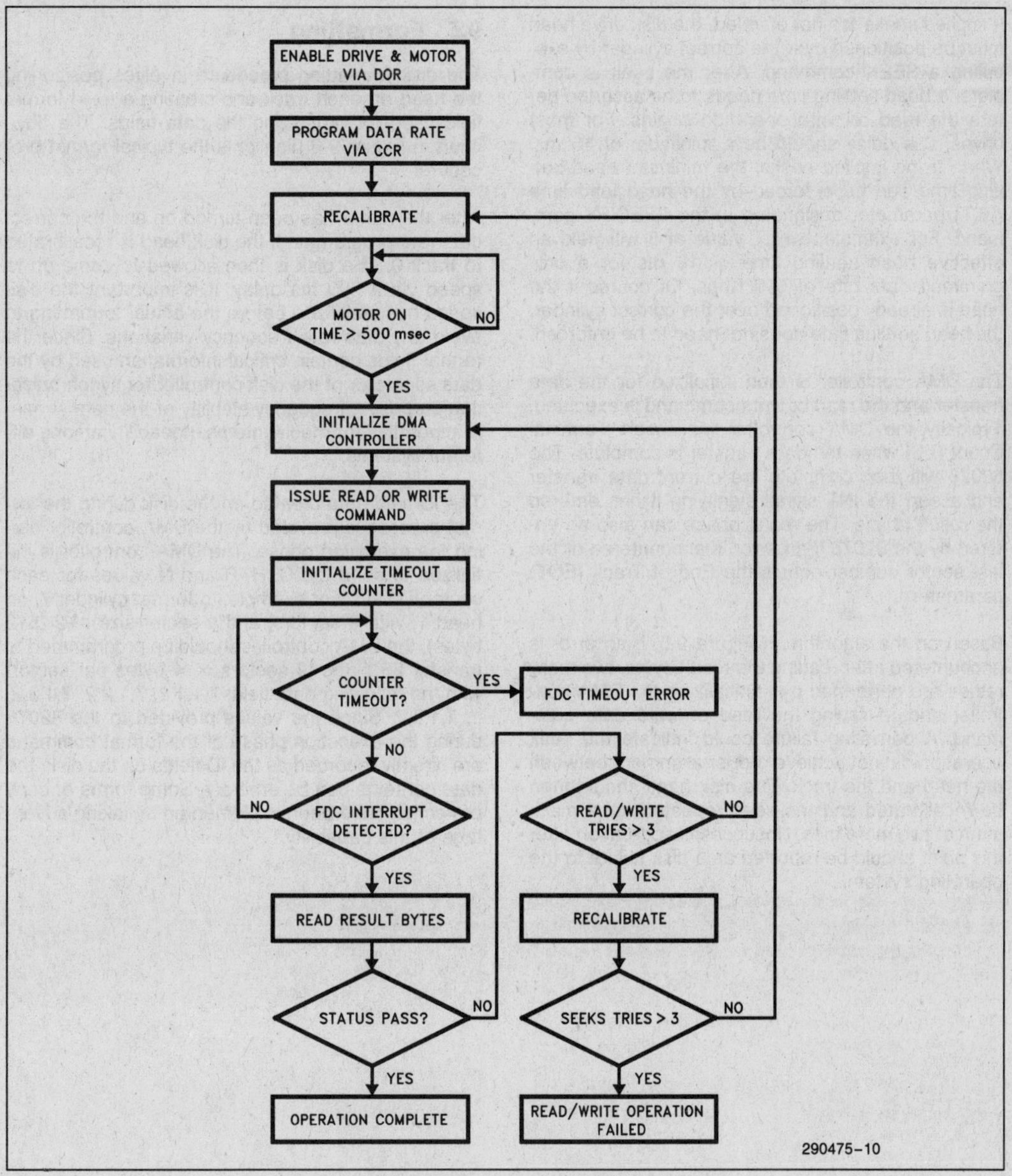

ENABLE DRIVE & MOTOR VIA DOR

PROGRAM DATA RATE VIA CCR

RECALIBRATE

MOTOR ON TIME > 500 msec — NO / YES

INITIALIZE DMA CONTROLLER

ISSUE READ OR WRITE COMMAND

INITIALIZE TIMEOUT COUNTER

COUNTER TIMEOUT? — YES: FDC TIMEOUT ERROR / NO

FDC INTERRUPT DETECTED? — NO / YES

READ RESULT BYTES

STATUS PASS? — NO / YES

OPERATION COMPLETE

READ/WRITE TRIES > 3 — NO / YES

RECALIBRATE

SEEKS TRIES > 3 — NO / YES

READ/WRITE OPERATION FAILED

290475-10

Figure 9-5. Read/Write Operation

2

If implied seeks are not enabled, the disk drive head must be positioned over the correct cylinder by executing a SEEK command. After the seek is complete, a head settling time needs to be asserted before the read or write operation begins. For most drives, this delay should be a minimum of 15 ms. When using implied seeks, the minimum head settling time can be enforced by the head load time (HLT) parameter designated in the SPECIFY command. For example, a HLT value of 8 will yield an effective head settling time of 16 ms for a programmed data rate of 500 Kbps. Of course if the head is already positioned over the correct cylinder, the head settling time does not need to be enforced.

The DMA controller is then initialized for the data transfer and the read or write command is executed. Typically the DMA controller will assert Terminal Count (TC) when the data transfer is complete. The 82078 will then complete the current data transfer and assert the INT signal signifying it has entered the result phase. The result phase can also be entered by the 82078 if an error is encountered or the last sector number equals the End of Track (EOT) parameter.

Based on the algorithm in Figure 9-5, if an error is encountered after reading the result bytes, two more retries are performed by reinitializing the DMA controller and re-issuing the read or write data command. A persisting failure could indicate the seek operation did not achieve proper alignment between the head and the track. The disk head should then be recalibrated and the seek repeated for a maximum of two more tries. Unsuccessful operation after this point should be reported as a disk failure to the operating system.

9.5 Formatting

The disk formatting procedure involves positioning the head on each track and creating a fixed format field used for organizing the data fields. The flowchart in Figure 9-6 highlights the typical format procedure.

After the motor has been turned on and the correct data rate programmed, the disk head is recalibrated to track 0. The disk is then allowed to come up to speed via a 500 ms delay. It is important the disk speed has stabilized before the actual formatting to avoid any data rate frequency variations. Since the format fields contain critical information used by the data separator of the disk controller for synchronization purposes, frequency stability of the data stream is imperative for media interchangeability among different systems.

The ID field data created on the disk during the format process is provided by the DMA controller during the execution phase. The DMA controller is initialized to send the C, H, R and N values for each sector ID field. For example, to format cylinder 7, on head 1, with 9 sectors, and a sector size of 2 (512 bytes), the DMA controller should be programmed to transfer 36 bytes (9 sectors × 4 bytes per sector) with the following data field: 7,1,1,2, 7,1,2,2, 7,1,3,2, ... 7,1,9,2. Since the values provided to the 82078 during the execution phase of the format command are directly recorded as the ID fields on the disk, the data contents can be arbitrary. Some forms of copy protection have been implemented by taking advantage of this capability.

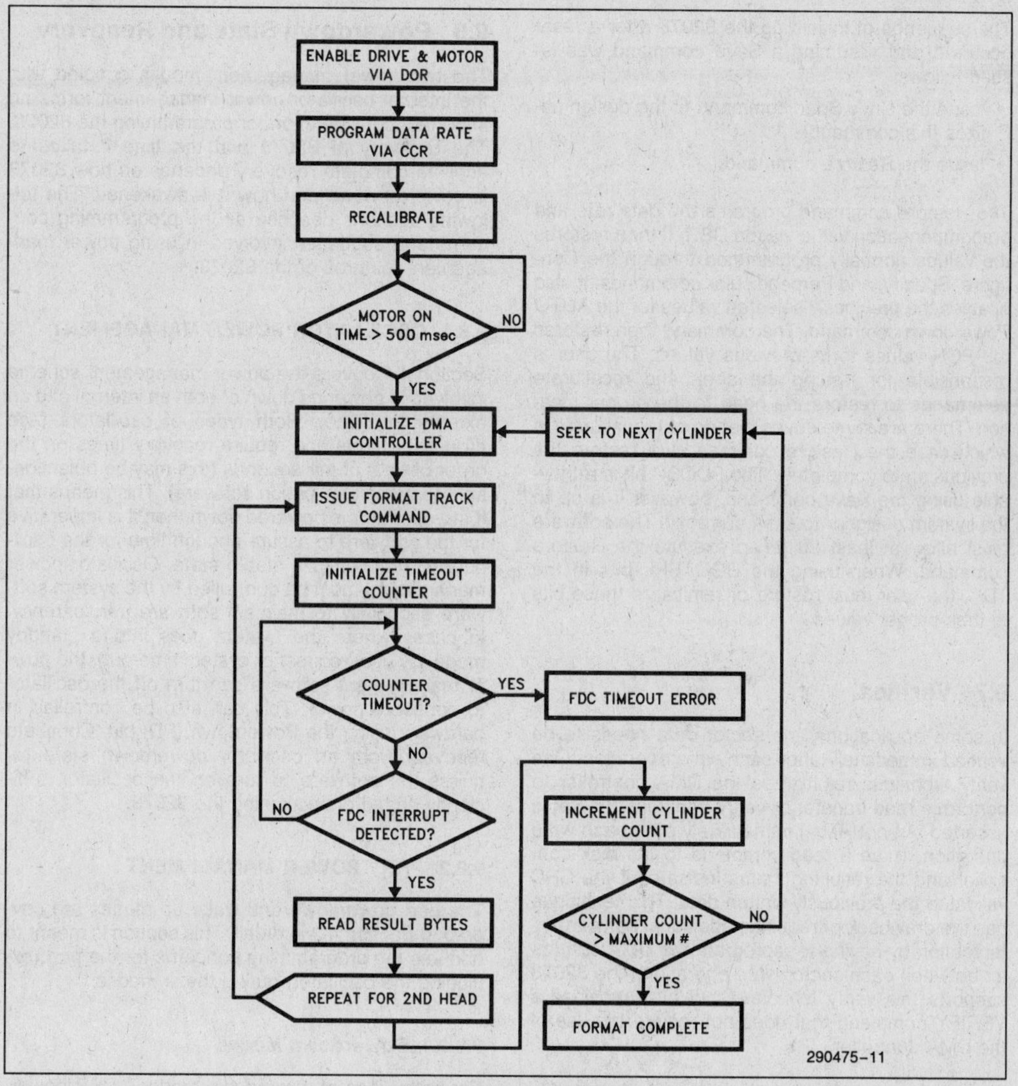

Figure 9-6. Formatting

After each head for a cylinder has been formatted, a seek operation to the next cylinder is performed and the format process is repeated. Since the FORMAT TRACK command does not have implied seek capability, the SEEK command must be used. Also, as discussed in Section 9.2, the head settling time needs to be adhered to after each seek operation.

9.6 Save and Restore

The Save and Restore commands were developed for portable systems that use zero-volt powerdown to conserve power. These systems turn off the V_{CC} to most of the system and retain the system status in a specific location. In older floppy controller designs, in order for system designers to retrieve the floppy controller status, a lot of separate commands and register reads were required. The Save command stores the key status information in a single command, the Restore command restores this information with a single command. These commands can be integrated into the SMM module that is responsible for zero-volt powerdown.

The sequence of initializing the 82078 after a reset occurred and assuming a Save command was issued follows:

- Issue the Drive Spec command (if the design utilizes this command)
- Issue the Restore command

The Restore command programs the data rate and precompensation value via the DSR. It then restores the values normally programmed through the Configure, Specify, and Perpendicular commands. It also enables the previously selected values for the AUTO Powerdown command. The command then restores the PCN values to its previous values. The user is responsible for issuing the seek and recalibrate commands to restore the head to the proper location. There are some drives that do not recalibrate in which case the Restore command will restore the previous state completely. The PDOSC bit is retrievable using the Save command, however it is up to the system designer to set it correctly. The software must allow at least 20 μs to execute the Restore command. When using the BOOTSEL bits in the TDR, the user must restore or reinitialize these bits to their proper values.

9.7 Verifies

In some applications, the sector data needs to be verified immediately after each write operation. One verify technique reinitializes the DMA controller to perform a read transfer or verify transfer (DACK# is asserted but not RD#) immediately after each write operation. Issue a read command to the disk controller and the resulting status indicates if the CRC validated the previously written data. This technique has the drawback of requiring additional software intervention by having to reprogram the DMA controller between each sector write operation. The 82078 supports this verify technique but also provides a VERIFY command that does not require the use of the DMA controller.

To verify a write data transfer or format track operation using the VERIFY command, the software simply issues the command with the same format as a READ DATA command but without the support of the DMA controller. The 82078 will then perform a disk read operation without a host data transfer. The CRC will be calculated for each sector read and compared against the value stored on the disk. When the VERIFY command is complete, the status register reports detected CRC errors.

9.8 Powerdown State and Recovery

The two power management modes coupled with the internal oscillator power management forms an important consideration for programming the 82078. The recovery of 82078 and the time it takes to achieve complete recovery depends on how 82078 is powered down and how it is awakened. The following sections describe all the programming concerns and subtleties involved in using power management features of the 82078.

9.8.1 OSCILLATOR POWER MANAGEMENT

Section 4.1 covers the power management scheme involved in powering down of both an internal and an external oscillator. Both types of oscillators face drop out effects and require recovery times on the order of tens of milliseconds (this may be objectionable to some application software). This means that if the oscillator is powered down then it is imperative for the software to assure enough time for the oscillator to recover to a stable state. Oscillator power management must be controlled by the system software especially to maintain software transparency. In cases where the system goes into a standby mode (by user request or system time-out), the power management software can turn off the oscillator to conserve power. This can also be controlled in hardware using the Powerdown (PD) pin. Complete recovery from an oscillator powerdown state requires the software to turn on the oscillator sufficiently ahead of awakening the 82078.

9.8.2 PART POWER MANAGEMENT

The part powerdown and wake up modes are covered in Section 4.2 in detail. This section is meant to address the programming concerns for the part (excluding the oscillator) during these modes.

9.8.2.1 Powerdown Modes

For both types of powerdown modes—DSR powerdown and auto powerdown, if reset is used to exit the part from powerdown then the internal microcontroller will go through a standard sequence: register initialization followed after some delay by an interrupt.

Software transparency in auto powerdown mode is preserved by MSR retaining the value of 80H which indicates that the part is ready to receive a command. This feature allows the part to powerdown while maintaining its responsiveness to any application software.

The PD and IDLE status bits can be monitored via the Status Register B (SRB, enhanced AT/EISA mode) and in the Digital Input Register (DIR, PS/2 and Model 30). Since the IDLE pin stays high when the 82078 is in idle state, the IDLEMSK bit can be used to set the pin low again (as part of a power management routine).

9.8.2.2 Wake Up Modes

Wake up from DSR powerdown results in the part being internally reset and all present status being lost. During DSR powerdown the RQM bit in the MSR is set. A software or hardware reset will wake up the part.

The case for wake up from auto powerdown is different. The BIOS and application software are very sensitive to delays involved in writing the first command bytes to the 82078. Most programs have short error time-outs in these cases. Such programs would not tolerate any floppy disk controller that was unable to receive the first byte of a command at any time. The following describes how 82078 uniquely sustains its software transparency during wake up sequences.

Prior to writing a command to 82078, it is first necessary to read the MSR to ensure that the 82078 is ready (RQM bit must be set) to receive the command. When the part detects a MSR read, it assumes that another command will follow and begins the wake up process. While the part is waking up it does not change the state of the MSR (MSR = 80H) and is able to receive the command in the FIFO. At this point one of the two following scenarios can occur.

No other command is sent subsequent to the MSR read. The part wakes up and initializes the minimum power up timer. Upon the expiration of this timer the part is once again put in powerdown state.

Another command follows the MSR read. If the command is sent during the part's recovery from powerdown, the part remembers the command, clears the RQM bit (to prevent further bytes being written) and acts on the command once it is fully awake.

If the MSR was not checked prior to writing of a command, the part will proceed as stated above with the RQM bit cleared and the command byte held until the internal microcontroller is ready. Writing the motor enable bits in DOR active will initiate the wake up sequence with RQM set high, ready to receive any command.

As it is clear from the above discussion, the immediate access to the floppy disk controller for the first command byte is vital to software transparency. The recovery of the part from powerdown may involve a delay after the first command byte has been issued. However, all programs have tolerance for the delay after the first command byte is issued. In a powered up chip, it is possible for the microcontroller to be in its "polling loop". As a result the tolerance for this delay provides an excellent window for recovery of the part.

10.0 DESIGN APPLICATIONS

10.1 Operating the 82078SL in a 3.3V Design

The design for 3.3V is the same as for 5.0V with two exceptions: The SEL3V# pin must be held low to select 3.3V operation, and the VCCF pin can be either 3.3V or 5.0V (VCCF can only be 5.0V when SEL3V# is high). The VCCF pin allows the controller to be operated in mixed (3.3V/5.0V) mode. For example, if the system operates at 3.3V and the floppy disk drive operates at 5.0V, the 82078 can be configured to operate at 3.3V with 5.0V available to the drive interface. See Figure 10-1 for a schematic.

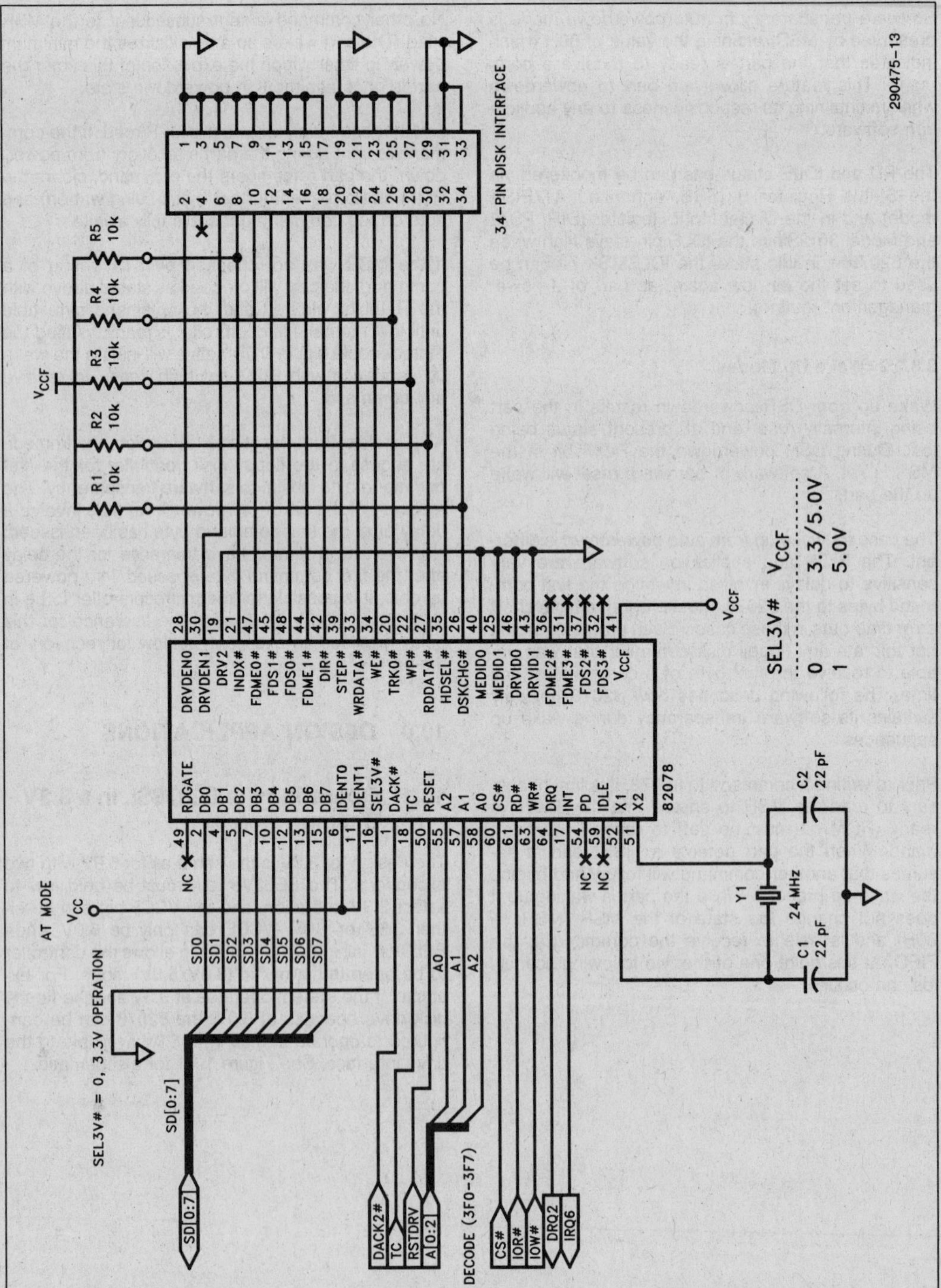

Figure 10-1. 82078SL 3.3V Design

10.2 Selectable Boot Drive

Generally a standard personal computer is configured with a 1.2 Mb 5.25″ disk drive and a 1.44 or 2.88 Mb 3.5″ disk drive. Usually the drive connects as "A:" and is the boot drive. At times the user may want to configure "B:" as the boot drive. Currently some BIOS' use a special implementation in software to accomplish this. The 82078 now offers this capability more efficiently by configuring the boot drives.

The 82078 allows for virtual drive designations. This is a result of allowing multiplexing the boot drive select and motor enable lines. This is shown in the Figure 10-2.

The DRIVE SEL1 and the DRIVE SEL2 bits in the DOR register decode internally to generate the signals DSn. The MEn signals generate directly from the DOR register. The DSn and MEn signals get mapped to actual FDSn and FDMEn pins based on the BOOTSELn bits (selected in the TDR register). The exact mapping of BOOTSEL vs. the FDSn and FDMEn pins is shown in the following table.

BOOTSEL1	BOOTSEL0	Mapping:
0	0	DS0 → FDS0, ME0 → FDME0 DS1 → FDS1, ME1 → FDME1 DS2 → FDS2, ME2 → FDME2
0	1	DS0 → FDS1, ME0 → FDME1 DS1 → FDS0, ME1 → FDME0 DS2 → FDS2, ME2 → FDME2
1	0	DS0 → FDS2, ME0 → FDME2 DS1 → FDS1, ME1 → FDME1 DS2 → FDS0, ME2 → FDME0
1	1	Reserved

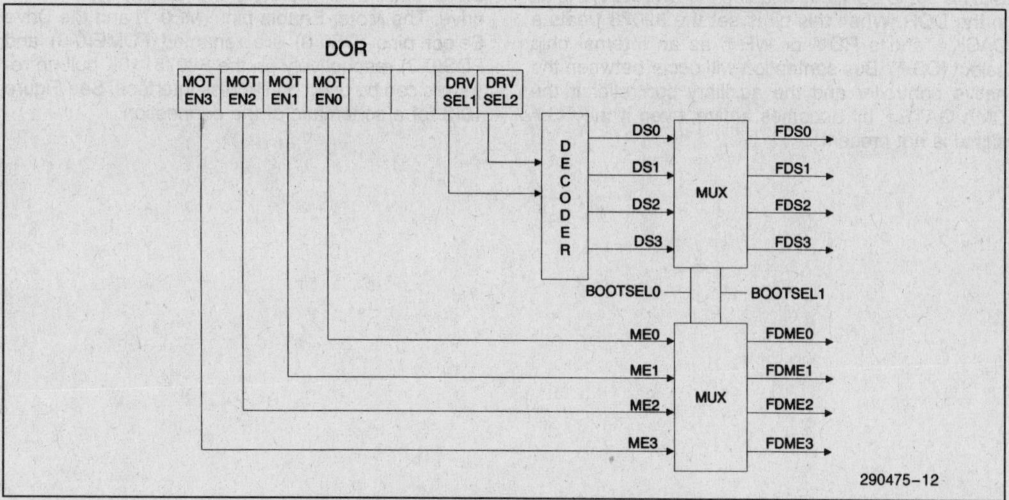

Figure 10-2. Virtual Drive Configuration

The BOOTSELn bits allow users to multiplex the output drive signals allowing different drives to be the boot drive. The DSn and MEn bits are considered virtual designations since the DSn and MEn signals get remapped to different corresponding physical FDSn and FDMEn pins. In other words, once the BOOTSELn bits are configured for a non-default selection, all future references made to the controller will be assumed as virtual designations. For example, if BOOTSEL1, BOOTSEL0 = 10 then DOR[1:0] = 00 refers to drive 2 and FDS2, FDME2 lines will be activated. Also, if TAPESEL[1:0] = 10, then tape mode is selected whenever FDS0, FDME0 are selected. Note, due to the virtual designations TAPESEL[1:0] = 00 would never enable tape mode due to boot drive restrictions.

10.3 How to Disable the Native Floppy Controller on the Motherboard

There are occasions when the floppy controller designed onto the motherboard of a system needs to be disabled in order to operate another floppy controller on the expansion bus. This can be done without changing the BIOS or remapping the address of the floppy controller (provided there is a jumper, or another way to disable the chip select on the native controller).

Upon reset, the DOR register in the 82078 is set to 00H. If the CS# is left enabled during the POST, the DOR is set to 0CH, this enables the DMA GATE# bit in the DOR. When this bit is set the 82078 treats a DACK# and a RD# or WR# as an internal chip select (CS#). Bus contention will occur between the native controller and the auxiliary controller if the DMA GATE# bit becomes active, even if the CS# signal is not present.

The proper way to disable the native floppy controller is to disable the CS# before the system is turned on. This will prevent the native controller from getting initialized. Another option is to map the native controller to a secondary address space, then disable the DMA GATE# via the DOR disabling the DMA GATE#. This assumes that the native controller is switchable to a secondary address space.

10.4 Replacing the 82077SL with a 82078 in a 5.0V Design

The 82078 easily replaces the 5.0V 82077SL with minimum design changes. With a few exceptions, most of the signals are named as they were in the 82077SL. Some pins were eliminated and other renamed to accommodate a reduced pin count and smaller package.

The connections to the AT bus are the same as the 82077SL with the following exceptions: MFM and IDENT have been replaced by IDENT1 and IDENT0. The PLL0 pin was removed. Configure the tape drive mode on the 82078 via the Tape Drive Register (TDR).

The Drive Interface on the 82078 is also similar to the 82077SL except as noted: DRVDEN0 and DRVDEN1 on the 82078 take the place of DENSEL, DRATE0, and DRATE1 on the 82077SL. The Drive Specification Command configures the polarity of these pins, thus selecting the density type of the drive. The Motor Enable pins (ME0-3) and the Drive Select pins (DS0-3) are renamed FDME(0-3) and FDS(0-3) respectively on the 82078. 10K pull-up resistors can be used on the disk interface. See Figure 10-3 for a schematic of the connection.

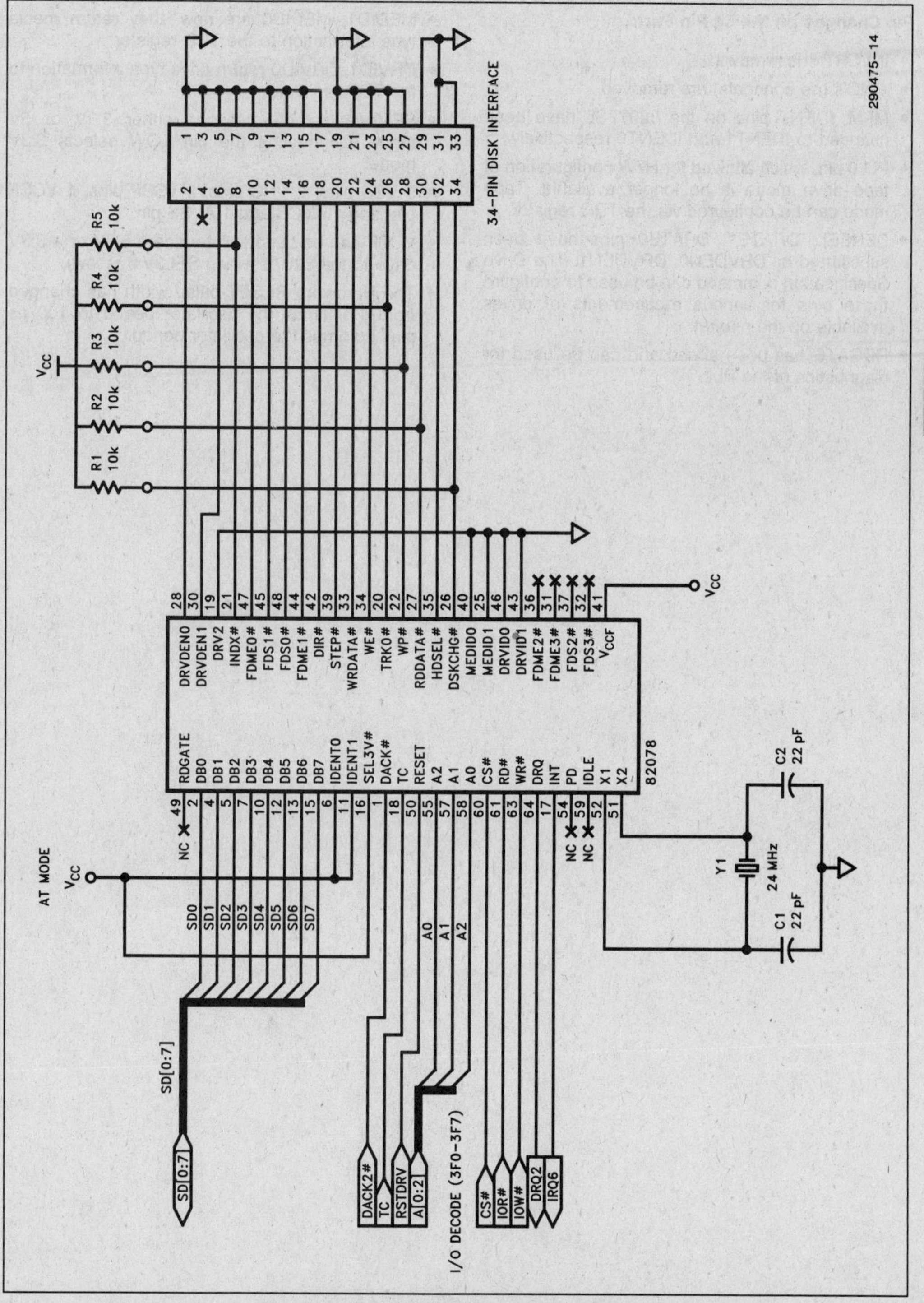

290475-14

Figure 10-3. 82077SL Conversion to 82078-1

2

Pin Changes on the 64 Pin Part:

- INVERT# is removed
- 4 NC's (no connects) are removed
- MFM, IDENT pins on the 82077SL have been changed to IDENT1 and IDENT0 respectively.
- PLL0 pin, which allowed for H/W configuration of tape drive mode is no longer available. Tape mode can be configured via the TDR register.
- DENSEL, DRATE1, DRATE0 pins have been substituted by DRVDEN0, DRVDEN1. The Drive Specification command can be used to configure these pins for various requirements of drives available on the market.
- RDGATE has been added and can be used for diagnostics of the PLL.
- MEDID1, MEDID0 are new, they return media type information to the TDR register.
- DRVID1, DRVID0 return drive type information to the TDR register.
- SEL3V# selects between either 3.3V or 5V mode. Connecting the pin LOW selects 3.3V mode.
- 5 VSS pins, 2 VCC pins, 2 VSSP pins, 1 VCCF pin, and 1 AVCC and 1 AVSS pin.
- VCCF can be used to interface a 5.0V or a 3.3V drive to the 82078 (when SEL3V# is low).
- The Hardware RESET pulse width has changed from 170 times the oscillator period to 100 ns plus 25 times the oscillator period.

11.0 D.C. SPECIFICATIONS

11.1 Absolute Maximum Ratings

Storage Temperature	−65°C to +150°C
Supply Voltage	−0.5V to +8.0V
Voltage on Any Input	GND −2V to 6.5V
Voltage on Any Output	GND −0.5V to V_{CC} +0.5V
Power Dissipation	1W

11.2 D.C. Characteristics $T_A = 0°C$ to 70°C, $V_{SS} = AV_{SS} = 0V$

64 PIN D.C. CHARACTERISTICS

Symbol	Parameter	$V_{CC} = +5V \pm 10\%$			$V_{CC} = 3.3V \pm 0.3V$		
		Min(V)	Max(V)	Test Conditions	Min(V)	Max(V)	Test Conditions
V_{ILC}	Input Low Voltage, X1	−0.5	0.8		−0.3	0.8	
V_{IHC}	Input High Voltage, X1	3.9	V_{CC} + 0.5		2.4	V_{CC} + 0.3	
V_{IL}	Input Low Voltage (all pins except X1)	−0.5	0.8		−0.3	0.8	
V_{IH}	Input High Voltage (all pins except X1)	2.0	V_{CC} + 0.5		2.0	V_{CC} + 0.3	
V_{OL}	System Interface		0.4	I_{OL} = 12 mA		0.4	I_{OL} = 6 mA
	FDD Interface outputs		0.4	I_{OL} = 24 mA		0.4	I_{OL} = 12 mA
	Status Outputs (Note 6)		0.4	I_{OL} = 4 mA		0.4	I_{OL} = 4 mA
V_{OH}	All outputs	3.0		I_{OH} = −4.0 mA	2.4		I_{OH} = −2.0 mA
	All outputs	V_{CC} − 0.4		I_{OH} = −100 μA	V_{CC} − 0.2		I_{OH} = −100 μA

64 PIN D.C. CHARACTERISTICS (I_{CC})

Symbol	Parameter	$V_{CC} = +5V \pm 10\%$			$V_{CC} = 3.3V \pm 0.3V$		
		Typ	Max(A)	Test Conditions	Typ	Max(A)	Test Conditions
I_{CC1}	1 Mbps Data Rate $V_{IL} = V_{SS}$, $V_{IH} = V_{CC}$	15.4 mA	25 mA	(Notes 1, 2, 5)	8.4 mA	16 mA	(Notes 1, 2)
I_{CC2}	1 Mbps Data Rate V_{IL} = 0.45V, V_{IH} = 2.4V	20.8 mA	30 mA	(Notes 1, 2, 5)	8.6 mA	16 mA	(Notes 1, 2)
I_{CC3}	500 Kbps Data Rate $V_{IL} = V_{SS}$, $V_{IH} = V_{CC}$	11.8 mA	20 mA	(Notes 1, 2)	6.2 mA	14 mA	(Notes 1, 2)
I_{CC4}	500 Kbps Data Rate V_{IL} = 0.45V, V_{IH} = 2.4V	17.6 mA	25 mA	(Notes 1, 2)	6.2 mA	14 mA	(Notes 1, 2)
I_{CCSB}	I_{CC} in Powerdown	0 μA	60 μA	(Notes 3, 4)	0 μA	60 μA	(Notes 3, 4)

64 PIN D.C. CHARACTERISTICS (I_{CC}) (Continued)

Symbol	Parameter	V_{CC} = +5V ±10%			V_{CC} = 3.3V ± 0.3V		
		Typ	Max(A)	Test Conditions	Typ	Max(A)	Test Conditions
I_{IL}	Input Load Current (all input pins)		10 μA −10 μA	$V_{IN} = V_{CC}$ V_{IN} = 0V		10 μA −10 μA	$V_{IN} = V_{CC}$ V_{IN} = 0V
I_{OFL}	Data Bus Output Float Leakage		±10 μA	0.45 < $V_{OUT} < V_{CC}$		±10 μA ±10 μA	$0.45 < V_{OUT} < V_{CC}$

NOTES:
1. Only the data bus inputs may float.
2. Tested while reading a sync field of "00". Outputs not connected to D.C. loads.
3. $V_{IL} = V_{SS}$, $V_{IH} = V_{CC}$; Outputs not connected to D.C. loads.
4. Typical value with the oscillator off.
5. I_{CC} for 2 Mbps Data Rate: Max 40 mA (TTL), 35 mA (CMOS) at 5.5V, typical 29.2 mA (TTL) and 24.4 (CMOS).
6. Status outputs are PD, IDLE, and RDGATE.

64 PIN MIXED MODE D.C. CHARACTERISTICS

Symbol	Parameter	V_{CC} = 3.3V ±0.3V, V_{CCF} = +5V ±10%		
		Min(V)	Max(V)	Test Conditions
V_{ILC}	Input Low Voltage, X1	−0.3	0.8	
V_{IHC}	Input High Voltage, X1	2.4	V_{CC} + 0.3	
V_{IL}	Input Low Voltage (system pins except X1) (floppy drive interface pins)	−0.3 −0.5	0.8 0.8	
V_{IH}	Input High Voltage (system interface pins except X1) (floppy drive interface pins)	2.0 2.0	V_{CC} + 0.3 V_{CC} + 0.5	
V_{OL}	System Interface		0.4	I_{OL} = 6 mA
	FDD Interface outputs		0.4	I_{OL} = 24 mA
V_{OH}	All system outputs	2.4		I_{OH} = −2.0 mA
	All FDD interface outputs	3.0		I_{OH} = −4.0 mA
	All system outputs	V_{CC} − 0.2		I_{OH} = −100 μA
	All FDD interface outputs	V_{CC} − 0.4		I_{OH} = −100 μA

CAPACITANCE

C_{IN}	Input Capacitance	10	pF	F = 1 MHz, T_A = 25°C
C_{IN1}	Clock Input Capacitance	20	pF	Sampled, not 100% Tested
$C_{I/O}$	Input/Output Capacitance	20	pF	

NOTE:
All pins except pins under test are tied to AC ground.

LOAD CIRCUIT

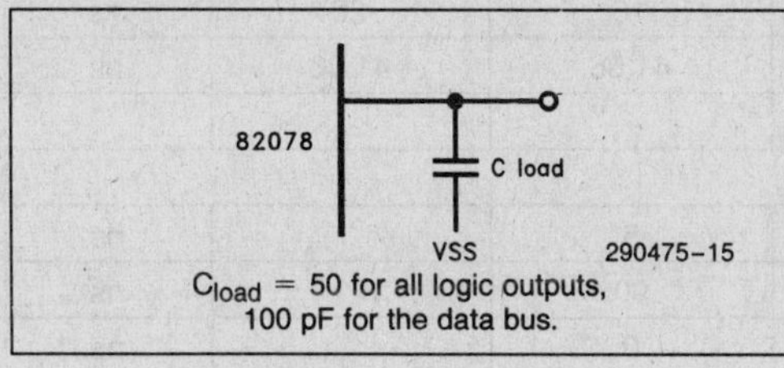

A.C. TESTING INPUT, OUTPUT WAVEFORM

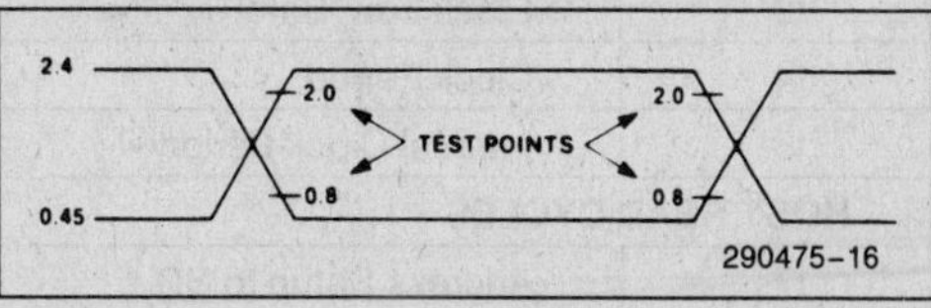

11.3 Oscillator

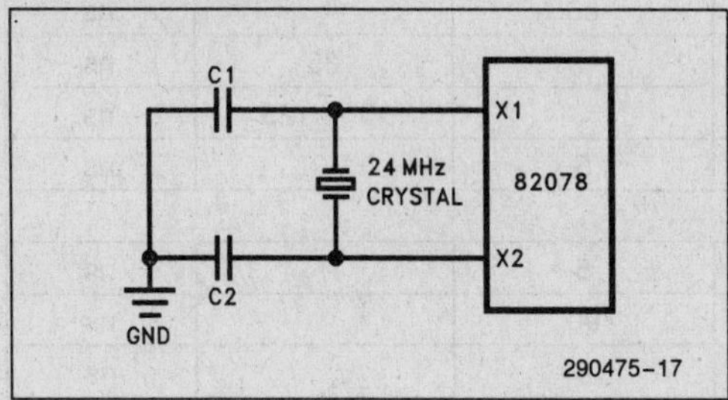

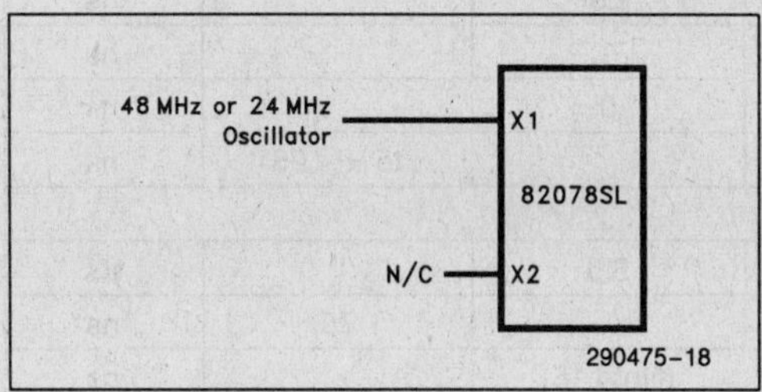

The 24 MHz clock can be supplied either by a crystal or a MOS level square wave. All internal timings are referenced to this clock or a scaled count which is data rate dependent.

The crystal oscillator must be allowed to run for 10 ms after V_{CC} has reached 4.5V or exiting the POWERDOWN mode to guarantee that it is stable.

Frequency:	24 MHz ±0.1%
Mode:	Parallel Resonant
	Fundamental Mode
Series Resistance:	Less than 40Ω
Shunt Capacitance:	Less than 5 pF

12.0 A.C. SPECIFICATIONS

T_A = 0°C to 70°C, V_{CC} = +5V ±10%, +3.3V ±0.3V, V_{SS} = AV_{SS} = 0V

Symbol	Parameter	Min	Max	Unit
CLOCK TIMINGS				
t1	Clock Rise Time		10	ns
	Clock Fall Time		10	ns
t2	Clock High Time(7)	16	26	ns
t3	Clock Low Time(7)	16	26	ns
t4	Clock Period	41.66	41.66	ns
t5	Internal Clock Period(3)			
HOST READ CYCLES				
t7	Address Setup to RD#	5		ns
t8	RD# Pulse Width	90		ns
t9	Address Hold from RD#	0		ns
t10	Data Valid from RD#(12)		80	ns
t11	Command Inactive	60		ns
t12	Output Float Delay		35	ns
t13	INT Delay from RD#(16)		t5 + 125	ns
t14	Data Hold from RD#	5		ns
HOST WRITE CYCLES				
t15	Address Setup to WR#	5		ns
t16	WR# Pulse Width	90		ns
t17	Address Hold from WR#	0		ns
t18	Command Inactive	60		ns
t19	Data Setup to WR#	70		ns
t20	Data Hold from WR#	0		ns
t21	INT Delay from WR#(16)		t5 + 125	ns
DMA CYCLES				
t22	DRQ Cycle Period(1)	6.5		μs
t23	DACK# to DRQ Inactive		75	ns
t23a	DRQ to DACK# Inactive	(Note 15)		ns
t24	RD# to DRQ Inactive(4)		100	ns
t25	DACK# Setup to RD#, WR#	5		ns
t26	DACK# Hold from RD#, WR#	0		ns
t27	DRQ to RD#, WR# Active(1)	0	6	μs
t28	Terminal Count Width(10)	50		ns
t29	TC to DRQ Inactive		150	ns
RESET				
t30	"Hardware" Reset Width(5)	1.13		μs
t30a	"Software" Reset Width(5)	(Note 11)		ns
t31	Reset to Control Inactive		2	μs

A.C. SPECIFICATIONS

T_A = 0°C to 70°C, V_{CC} = +5V ±10%, +3.3V ±0.3V, V_{SS} = AV_{SS} = 0V (Continued)

Symbol	Parameter	Min	Max	Unit
WRITE DATA TIMING				
t32	Write Data Width(6)			ns
DRIVE CONTROL				
t35	DIR# Setup to STEP#(14)	1.0		μs
t36	DIR# Hold from STEP#	10		μs
t37	STEP# Active Time (High)	2.5		μs
t38	STEP# Cycle Time(2)			μs
t39	INDEX# Pulse Width	5		t5
t41	WE# to HDSEL# Change	(Note 13)		ms
READ DATA TIMING				
t40	Read Data Pulse Width	50		ns
t44	82078-1		2M	bits/sec
	82078SL		1M	bits/sec
t44	Data Rate Period = 1/f44			
tLOCK	Lockup Time		64	t44

NOTES:

1. This timing is for FIFO threshold = 1. When FIFO threshold is N bytes, the value should be multiplied by N and subtract 1.5 μs. The value shown is for 1 Mbps, scales linearly with data rate.
2. This value can range from 0.5 ms to 8.0 ms and is dependent upon data rate and the Specify command value.
3. Many timings are a function of the selected data rate. The nominal values for the internal clock period (t5) for the various data rates are:

2 Mbps	1.5x oscillator period = 62.5 ns
1 Mbps	3x oscillator period = 125 ns
500 Kbps	6x oscillator period = 250 ns
300 Kbps	10x oscillator period = 420 ns
250 Kbps	12x oscillator period = 500 ns

4. If DACK# transitions before RD#, then this specification is ignored. If there is no transition on DACK#, then this becomes the DRQ inactive delay.
5. Reset requires a stable oscillator to meet the minimum active period.

6. Based on the internal clock period (t5). For various data rates, the Write Data Width minimum values are:
   - 2 Mbps 2.5x oscillator period −50 ns = 75 ns
   - 1 Mbps 5x oscillator period −50 ns = 150 ns
   - 500 Kbps 10x oscillator period −50 ns = 360 ns
   - 300 Kbps 16x oscillator period −50 ns = 615 ns
   - 250 Kbps 19x oscillator period −50 ns = 740 ns
7. Test points for clock high time are 3.5V. Due to transitional times, clock high time max and clock low time max cannot be met simultaneously. Clock high time min and clock low time max can not be met simultaneously.
8. Based on internal clock period (t5).
9. Jitter tolerance is defined as:
   (Maximum bit shift from nominal position ÷ ¼ period of nominal data rate) × 100% is a measure of the allowable bit jitter that may be present and still be correctly detected. The data separator jitter tolerance is measured under dynamic conditions that jitters the bit stream according to a reverse precompensation algorithm.
10. TC width is defined as the time that both TC and DACK# are active. Note that TC and DACK# must overlap at least 50 ns.
11. The minimum reset active period for a software reset is dependent on the data rate, after the 82078 has been properly reset using the t30 spec. The minimum software reset period then becomes:
    - 2 Mbps 1.5 x t4 = 62.5 ns
    - 1 Mbps 3 x t4 = 125 ns
    - 500 Kbps 6 x t4 = 250 ns
    - 300 Kbps 10 x t4 = 420 ns
    - 250 Kbps 12 x t4 = 500 ns
12. Status Register's status bits which are not latched may be updated during a Host read operation.
13. The minimum MFM values for WE to HDSEL change (t41) for the various data rates are:
    - 2 Mbps 0.5 ms + [4 x GPL]
    - 1 Mbps 0.5 ms + [8 x GPL]
    - 500 Kbps 1.0 ms + [16 x GPL]
    - 300 Kbps 1.6 ms + [26.66 x GPL]
    - 250 Kbps 2.0 ms + [32 x GPL]

    GPL is the size of gap 3 defined in the sixth byte of a Write Command.
14. This timing is a function of the selected data rate as follows:
    - 2 Mbps 0.5 μs Min
    - 1 Mbps 1.0 μs Min
    - 500 Kbps 2.0 μs Min
    - 300 Kbps 3.3 μs Min
    - 250 Kbps 4.0 μs Min
15. This timing is a function of the internal clock period (t5) and is given as (⅔) t5. The values of t5 are shown in Note 3.
16. The timings t13 and t21 are specified for INT signal in the polling mode only. These timings in case of the result phase of the read and write commands are microcode dependent.

Part Specification	3.3V	5.0V	2 Mbps Data Rate
82078SL	X	X	
82078-1		X	X

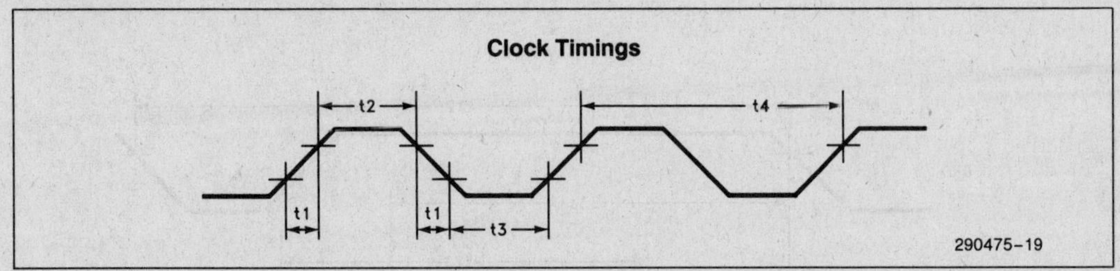

290475-19

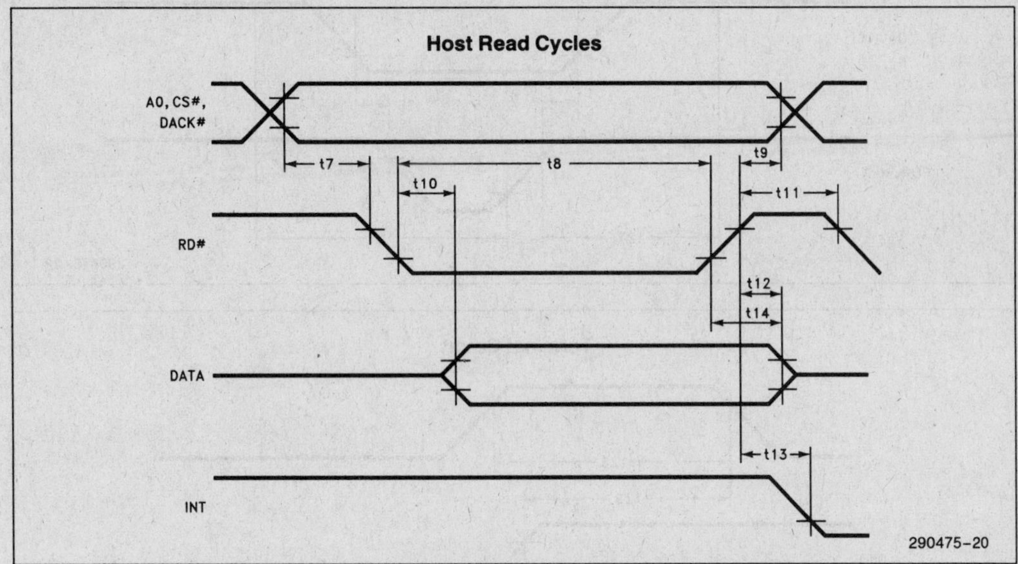

290475-20

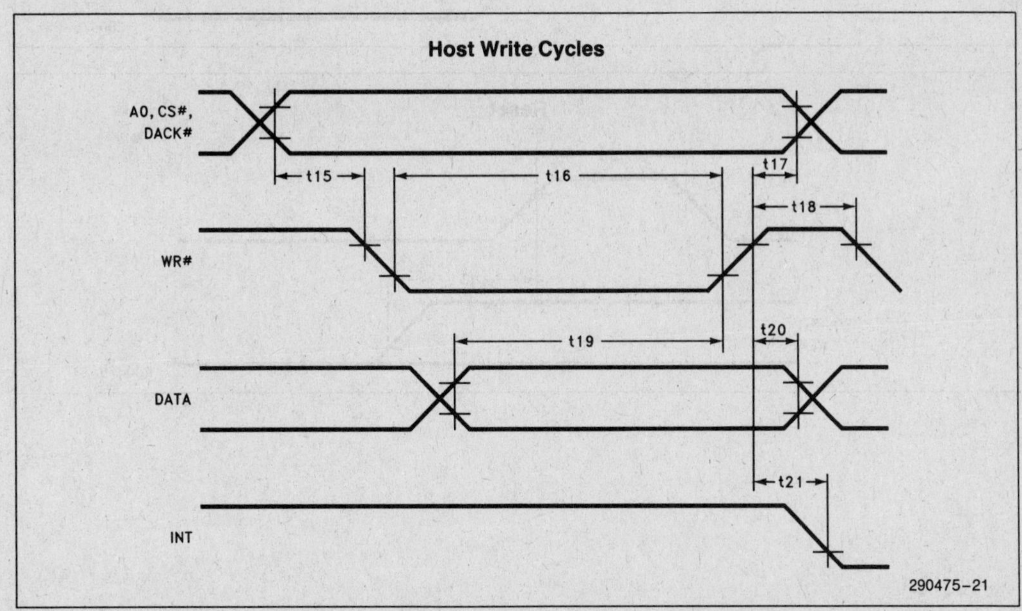

290475-21

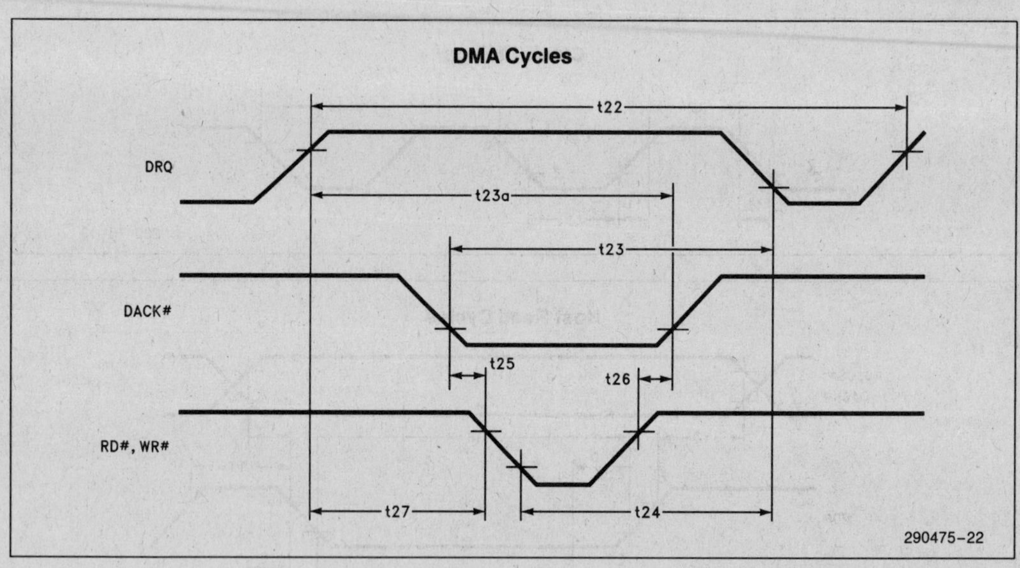
DMA Cycles
t22
DRQ
t23a
t23
DACK#
t25
t26
RD#, WR#
t27
t24
290475-22

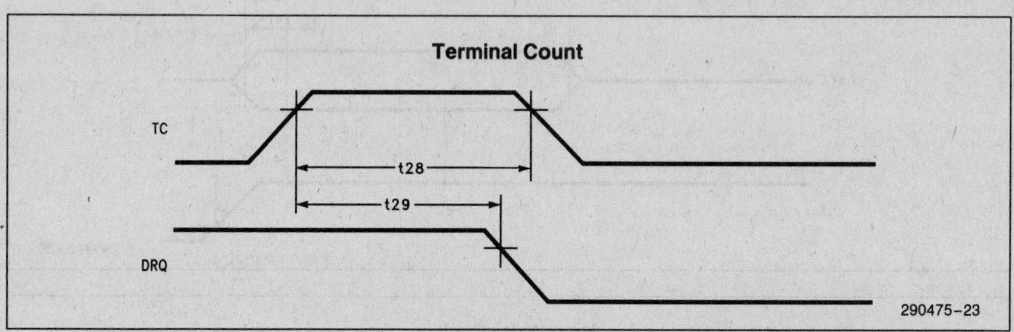
Terminal Count
TC
t28
t29
DRQ
290475-23

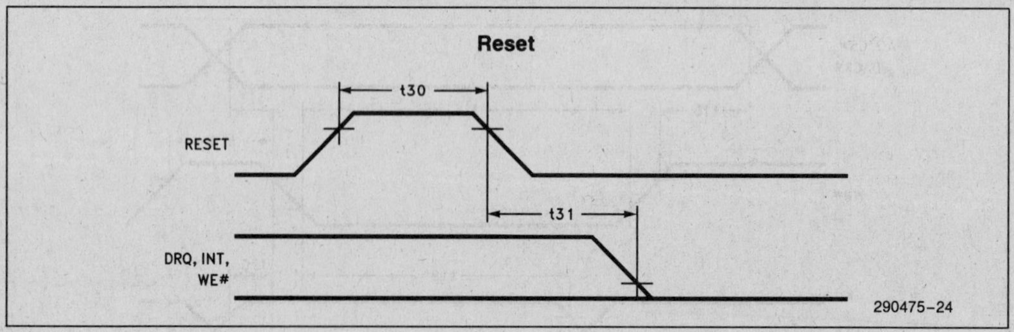
Reset
t30
RESET
t31
DRQ, INT,
WE#
290475-24

290475-25

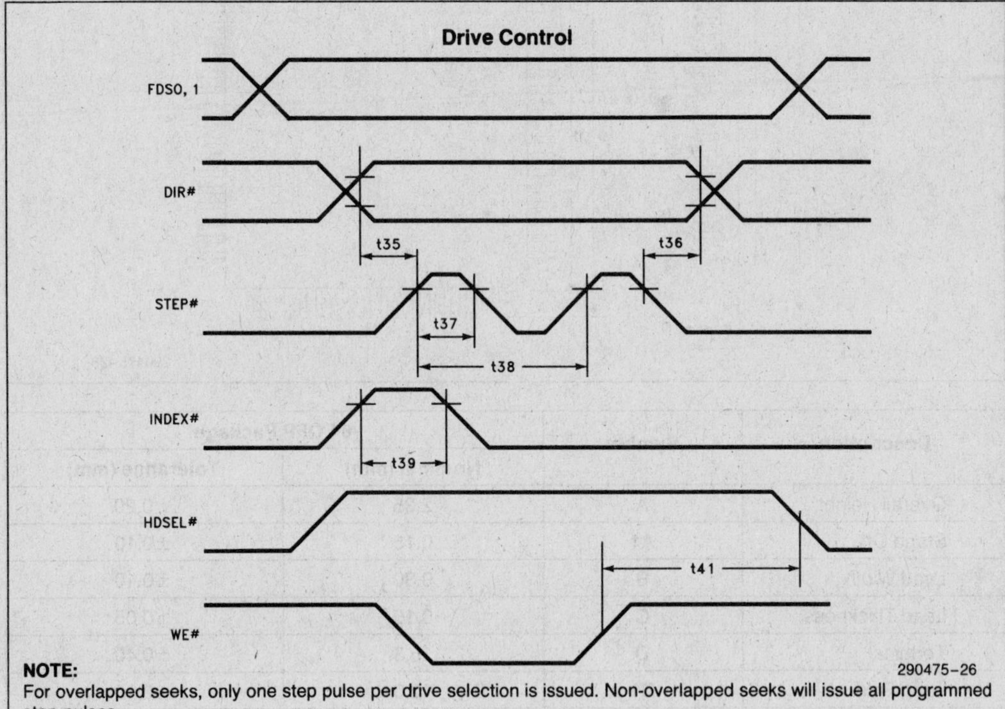

290475-26

NOTE:
For overlapped seeks, only one step pulse per drive selection is issued. Non-overlapped seeks will issue all programmed step pulses.

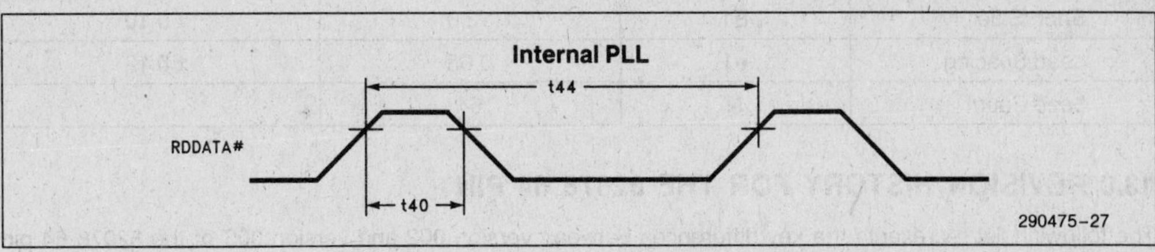

290475-27

12.1 Package Outline for the 64 QFP Part

The 82078 addresses the current need of the smaller and thinner packages, for the current market. The size of the part is becoming increasingly important in the portable computer market. The QFP part considerably reduces the real estate consumed. The package outline, with the appropriate dimensions is given below:

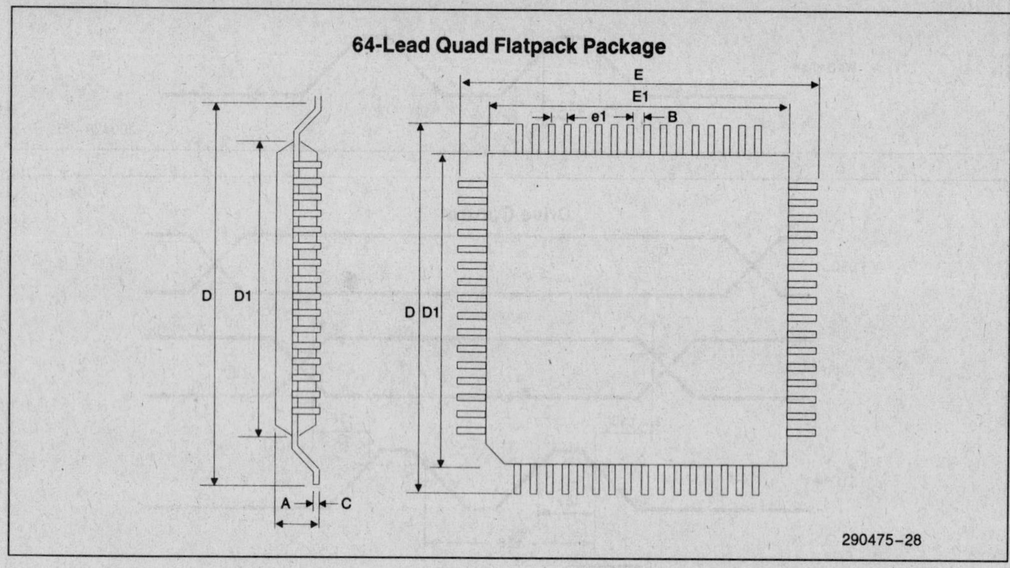

Description	Symbol	64 QFP Package	
		Nominal (mm)	Tolerance (mm)
Overall Height	A	2.35	±0.20
Stand Off	A1	0.15	±0.10
Lead Width	B	0.30	±0.10
Lead Thickness	C	0.15	±0.05
Terminal	D	15.3	±0.40
Long Side	D1	12.0	±0.10
Terminal	E	15.3	±0.40
Short Side	E1	12.0	±0.10
Lead Spacing	e1	0.65	±0.12
Lead Count	N	64	

13.0 REVISION HISTORY FOR THE 82078 64 PIN

The following list represents the key differences between version 002 and version 003 of the 82078 64 pin data sheet.

Section 5.2.3	Redundant information removed.
Section 5.2.4	Redundant information removed.
Section 8.0	Description of IDENT0 and IDENT1 changed to clarify their function.
Section 11.2	New Vol specification added for status pins.
Table 6-2	Data in table reordered to be consistent.

AP-358

APPLICATION NOTE

Intel 82077SL for Super Dense Floppies

292093-1

September 1992

Intel 82077SL for Super Dense Floppies

CONTENTS PAGE

INTRODUCTION

The evolution of the floppy has been marked in little over a decade by a significant increase in capacity accompanied by a noticeable decrease in the form factor from the early 8 inch floppy disks to the present day 3.5 inch floppy disks. This decade will also be remarkable as OEMs adopt "Super" dense floppies.

The most commonly seen floppies today are invariably one of the form factors – the 5.25″ or the 3.5″. Each form factor has several associated capacity ranges. The 5.25″ floppies available are: 180 KB (single density), 360 KB (double density) and 1.2 MB (high density). The 3.5″ floppies available are: 720 KB (double density) and 1.44 MB (high density). The emerging super dense floppies will evolve on the installed base of 3.5″ floppies. The latest member of this set is the 2.88 MB (extra density) floppy, pioneered by Toshiba. The cornerstone of market acceptance of newer drives is compatibility to the older family. The 2.88 MB (formatted) floppy drive allows the user to format, read from and write to the lower density diskettes.

As programs and data files get bigger, the demand for higher capacity floppies becomes obvious. There are several 3.5″ higher density drives available from various vendors with capacities well into the 20 MB range. NEC has introduced a 13 MB drive and companies such as Insite have introduced 20 MB drives. Both drives require servo-mechanisms to accurately position the head over the right track. NEC's drive has the standard floppy drive interface whereas Insite's interface is SCSI based. The market for these floppy drives will remain a niche unless they receive more OEM support.

Initiated by Toshiba's research and innovation of the higher density 4 MB floppy disk media, the market is headed towards the super dense floppy drive. After IBM's endorsement of the 4 MB (unformatted) floppy disk drives on their PS/2 model 57 and PS/2 model 90, several OEMs have shown a growing interest in "super" dense floppy disk drives. The latest DOS 5.0 supports the new 4 MB floppy media and BIOS vendors like Pheonix, AMI, Award, Quadtel, System Soft, and Microid all support the newer 4 MB floppy media.

PURPOSE

An important consideration to implement the 4 MB floppy drive is the floppy disk controller. Intel's highly integrated floppy disk controller, 82077AA/SL, has led the market in supporting the 4 MB floppy drive. Two ingredients are necessary to fully support these drives: 1 Mbps transfer rate and the perpendicular recording mode. This paper deals with a discussion of what the perpendicular mode is and how can a 4 MB floppy disk drive be implemented in a system using the 82077AA/SL.

PERPENDICULAR RECORDING MODE

Toshiba has taken the 2 MB floppy and doubled the storage capacity by doubling the number of bits per track. Toshiba achieved this by an innovative magnetic recording mode, called the vertical or the perpendicular recording mode. This mode utilizes magnetization perpendicular to the recording medium plane. This is in contrast to the current mode of longitudinal recording which uses the magnetization parallel to the recording plane. By making the bits stand vertical as opposed to on their side, recording density is effectively doubled, Figure 1. The new perpendicular mode of recording not only produces sharp magnetization transitions necessary at higher recording densities, but is also more stable.

The 4 MB disks utilize barium ferrite coated substrates to achieve perpendicular mode of magnetization. Current disks use cobalt iron oxide (Co-g-Fe_2O_3) coating for longitudinal recording. The barium ferrite ensures good head to medium contact, stable output and durability in terms of long use. High coercivity is required to attain high recording density for a longitudinal recording medium (coercivity specification of a disk refers to the magnetic field strength required to make an accurate record on the disk). A conventional head could not be used in this case; however, the barium ferrite disk has low coercivity and the conventional ferrite head can be used. The new combination heads include a pre-erase mechanism, i.e., the ferrite ring heads containing erase elements followed by the read/write head. These erase elements have deep overwrite penetration and ensure complete erasure for writing new data. The distance between the erase elements and the read/write head is about 200mm. This distance is important from the floppy disk controller point of view and will be discussed in later sections.

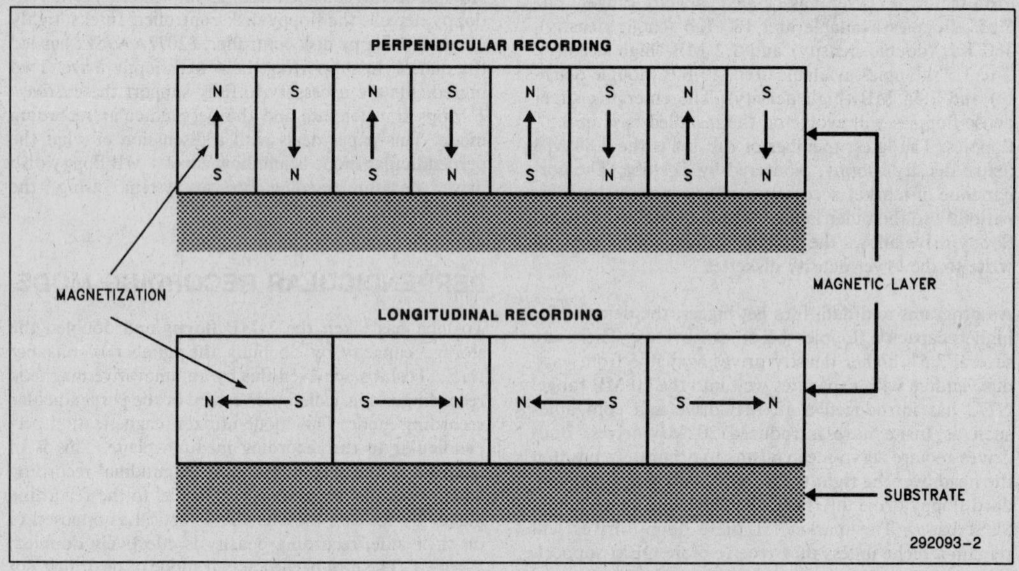

Figure 1. Perpendicular vs Longitudinal Recording

PERPENDICULAR DRIVE FORMAT AND SPECIFICATION

Figures 2a and 2b show the IBM drive format for both double density and perpendicular modes of recording. The main difference in recording format is the length of Gap2 between the ID field and the Data field. The main reason for the increased Gap2 length is the pre-erase head preceding the read/write head on the newer 4 MB floppy drives. The size of the data field is maintained at 512 KBytes standard. The increase in the capacity is implemented by increasing the number of sectors from 18 to 36. Table 1 shows the specifications of the various capacity 3.5″ drives.

PERPENDICULAR MODE COMMAND

The current 82077AA/SL parts contain the "enhanced" perpendicular mode command as shown in Figure 3. This is a two byte command with the first byte being the command code (0x12H). The 2nd byte contains the parameters required to enable perpendicular mode recording. The former command (in the older 82077 parts) included only the WGATE and GAP bits. This command is compatible to the older mode where only the two LSBs are written. The enhanced mode allows system designers to designate specific drives as perpendicular recording drives. The second byte will be referenced as the PR[0:7] byte for ease of discussion. The following discusses the use of the enhanced perpendicular recording mode.

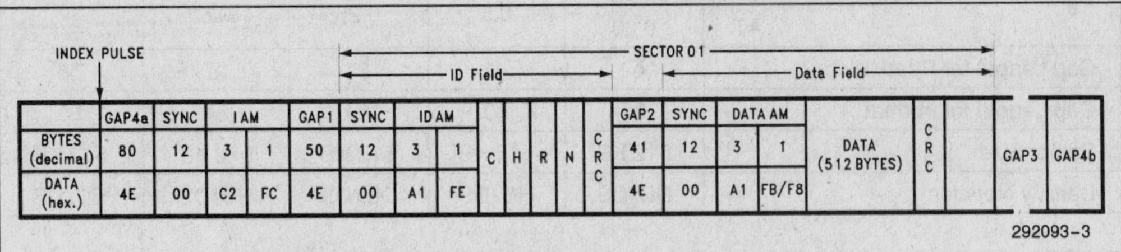

Figure 2a. Conventional IBM 1 MB and 2 MB Format (MFM)

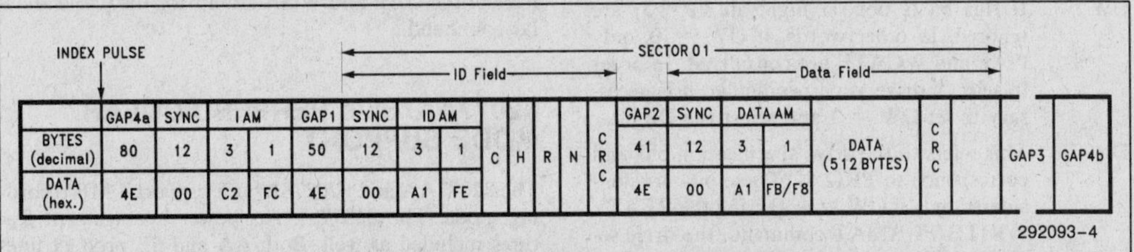

Figure 2b. Perpendicular 4 MB Format (MFM)

Phase	R/W	Data Bus								Remarks
		D7	D6	D5	D4	D3	D2	D1	D0	
PERPENDICULAR MODE COMMAND										
Command	W	0	0	0	1	0	0	1	0	Command Code
	W	OW	0	D3	D2	D1	D0	GAP	WGATE	PR

Figure 3. Perpendicular Mode Command

Table 1. Specifications of FDDs

Various Parameters Used in the Different Kinds of FDDs.		5.25″ 360 KB	5.25″ 1.2 MB	3.5″ 720 KB	3.5″ 1.44 MB	3.5″ 2.88 MB
Number of Cylinders		40	80	80	80	80
Sectors/Track		9	15	9	18	36
Formatted Capacity		354 KB	1.2 MB	720 KB	1.44 MB	2.88MB
Unformatted Capacity		360 KB	1.6 MB	1 MB	2 MB	4 MB
Rotation Speed (rpm)	XT AT	300 360	360	300	300	300
Track Density (tpi)		48	96	135	135	135
Recording Density (bpi)		5876	9870	8717	17432	34868
Data Transfer Rate (Mbps)	XT AT	0.25 0.30	0.5	0.25	0.5	1
Gap Length for Read/Write		42	42	27	27	56
Gap Length for Format		80	80	84	84	83
Sector Size		512 KB	512 KB	512 KB	512 KB	512 KB
Density Notation		DD/DS	HD/DS	DD/DS	HD/DS	ED/DS

The following describes the various functions of the programmed bits in the PR:

OW — If this bit is not set high, all PR[2:5] are ignored. In other words, if OW = 0, only GAP and WGATE are considered. In order to select a drive as perpendicular, it is necessary to set OW = 1 and select the Dn bit.

Dn — This refers to the drive specification bits and corresponds to PR[2:5]. These bits are considered only if OW = 1. During the READ/WRITE/FORMAT command, the drive selected in these commands is compared to Dn. If the bits match then perpendicular mode will be enabled for that drive. For example, if D0 is set then drive 0 will be configured for perpendicular mode.

GAP — This alters the Gap2 length as required by the perpendicular mode format.

WGATE — Write gate alters timing of WE to allow for pre-erase loads in perpendicular drives.

The VCOEN timing and the length of the Gap2 field (explained above) can be altered to accommodate the unique requirements of the 4 MB floppy drives by GAP and WGATE bits of the PR. Table 2 describes the effects of the GAP and WGATE bits for the perpendicular command.

82077AA/SL's PERPENDICULAR MODE SUPPORT

The 82077AA and 82077SL both support 4 MB recording mode. The 82077SL has power management features included as well. Both AA and SL product lines have three versions each out of which two of the versions support the 4 MB floppy drives. The 82077AA-1, 82077AA, 82077SL, and 82077SL-1 all support the 4 MB floppy drives. A single command puts the 82077AA/SL into the perpendicular mode. This mode also requires the data rate to be set at 1 Mbps. The FIFO that is unique to Intel's 82077AA/SL parts may become necessary to remove the host interface bottleneck due to the higher data rate. The 4 MB floppy disk drives are downward compatible to 1 MB and 2 MB floppy diskettes. The following discussion explains the implications of the new 4 MB combination head and the functionality of the perpendicular mode command.

Table 2. Effects of GAP and WGATE Bits

GAP	WGATE	Mode	VCO Low Time after Index Pulse	Length of Gap2 Format Field	Portion of Gap2 Written by Write Data Operation	Gap2 VCO Low Time for Read Operations
0	0	Conventional	33 Bytes	22 Bytes	0 Bytes	24 Bytes
0	1	Perpendicular (Data Rate = 500 kbps)	33 Bytes	22 Bytes	19 Bytes	24 Bytes
1	0	Conventional	33 Bytes	22 Bytes	0 Bytes	24 Bytes
1	1	Perpendicular	33 Bytes	41 Bytes	38 Bytes	43 Bytes

The implementation of 4 MB drives requires understanding the Gap2 (see Figures 2a and 2b) and VCO timing requirements unique to these drives. These new requirements are dictated by the design of the "combination head" in these drives. Rewriting of disks in the 4 MB drives requires a pre-erase gap to erase the magnetic flux on the disk preceding the writing by the read/write gap. The read/write gap in the 4 MB drive does not have sufficient penetration (as shown in Figure 4a) to overwrite the existing data. In the conventional drives, the read/write gap had sufficient depth and could effectively overwrite the older data as depicted in Figure 4b. It must be noted that it is necessary to write the conventional 2 MB media in the 4 MB drive at 500 Kbps perpendicular mode. This ensures proper erasure of existing data and reliable write of the new data. The pre-erase gap in the 4 MB floppy drives is activated only during format and write commands. Both the pre-erase gap and read/write gap are activated at the same time.

As shown in Figure 4a, the pre-erase gap precedes the read/write gap by 200mm. This distance translated to bytes is about 38 bytes at a data rate of 1 Mbps and 19 bytes at 500 Kbps. Whenever the read/write gap is enabled by the Write Gate signal the pre-erase gap is activated at the same time.

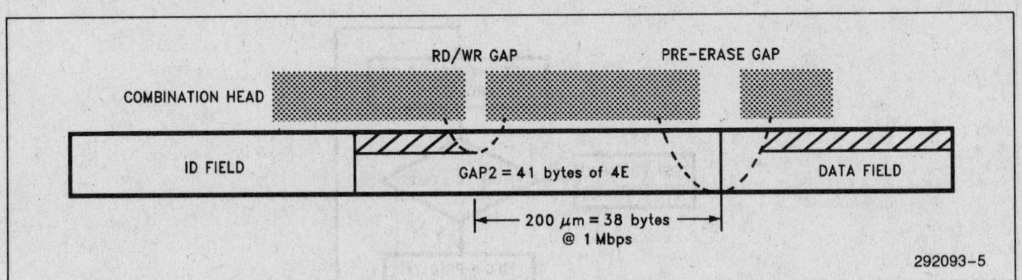

Figure 4a. Head Design for the 4 MB Perpendicular Mode

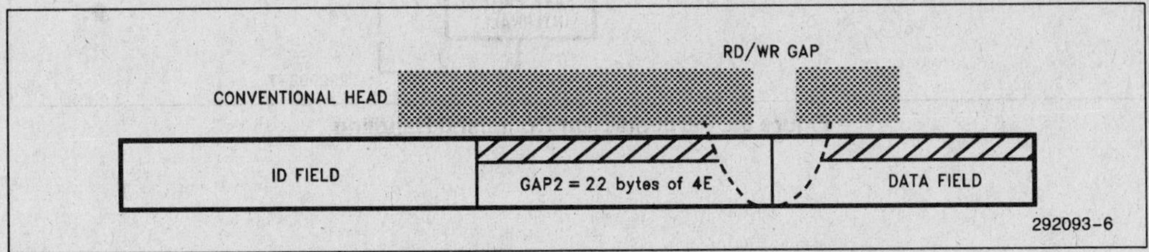

Figure 4b. Head Design for the Conventional 2 MB Mode

In conventional drives, the Write Gate is asserted at the beginning of the sync field, i.e., when the read/write is at the beginning of the data field. The controller then writes the new sync field, data address mark, data field and CRC (see Figure 2a). With the combination head, the read/write gap must be activated in the Gap2 field to ensure proper write of the new sync field. To accommodate both the distance between the pre-erase gap and read/write gap and the head activation and deactivation time, the Gap2 field is expanded to a length of 41 bytes at 1 Mbps (see Figure 2b). Since the bit density is proportional to the data rate, 19 bytes will be written in the Gap2 field at 500 Kbps data rate in the perpendicular mode.

On the read back by the 82077AA/SL, the controller must begin the synchronization at the beginning of the sync field. For conventional mode, the internal PLL VCO is enabled (VCOEN) approximately 24 bytes from the start of the Gap2 field. However, at 1 Mbps perpendicular mode the VCOEN goes active after 43 bytes to accomodate the increased Gap2 field size. For each case, a 2 byte cushion is maintained from the beginning of the sync field to avoid write splices caused by motor speed variation.

It should be noted that none of the alterations in Gap2 size, VCO timing or Write Gate timing affect the normal program flow. Once the perpendicular command is invoked, 82077AA/SL behaviour from the user standpoint is unchanged.

PROGRAMMING PERPENDICULAR MODE

Figures 5a and 5b show a flowchart on how the perpendicular recording mode is implemented on the 82077AA/SL. The perpendicular mode command can be issued during initialization. As shown in Figure 5a the perpendicular command stores the PR value internally. This value is used during the data transfer commands for configuration in order to deal with the perpendicular drives. Table 2 shows how the Gap2 length, VCOEN timing or Write Gate timing is affected. The OW bit is also tested for in this part of the loop. The enhanced perpendicular mode is enabled by setting the OW = 1, setting the Dn bits corresponding to the installed perpendicular drive high and leaving PR[0:1] = '00'.

As shown in Figure 5b, the Gap2 length is initially set to the conventional length of 22 bytes. Next the PR[0:1] bits (GAP, WGATE) are checked if they are set to '00'. If the PR[0:1] bits are set to '10' then, perpendicular mode is disabled and conventional mode is retained. If the PR[0:1] = '01' or '11' the VCOEN is

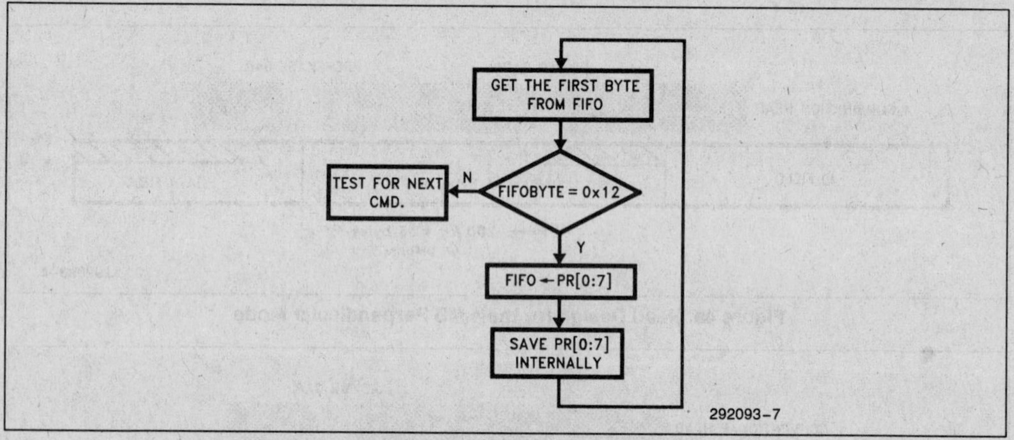

Figure 5a. Perpendicular Command Handling

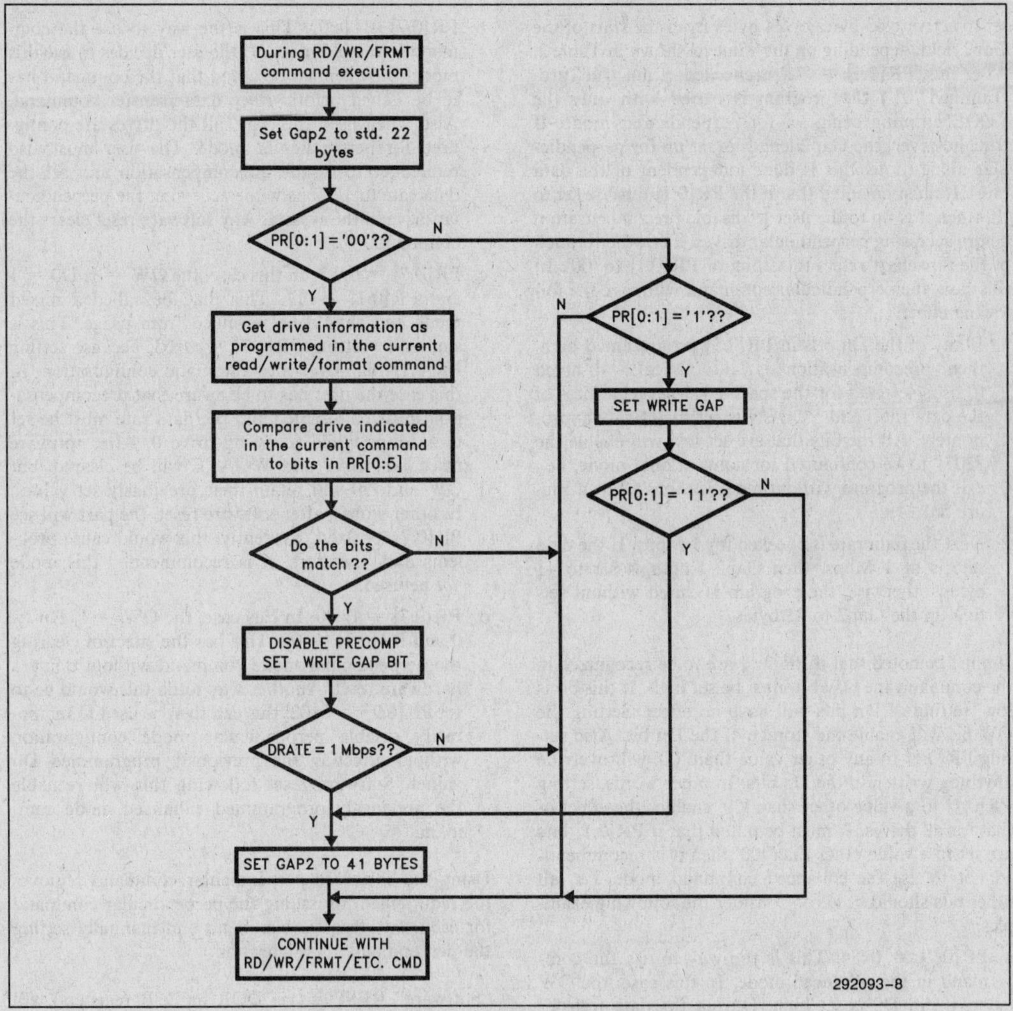

During RD/WR/FRMT command execution

Set Gap2 to std. 22 bytes

PR[0:1] = '00'??

N

Y

Get drive information as programmed in the current read/write/format command

Compare drive indicated in the current command to bits in PR[0:5]

Do the bits match ??

N

Y

DISABLE PRECOMP SET WRITE GAP BIT

DRATE = 1 Mbps??

N

Y

SET GAP2 TO 41 BYTES

PR[0:1] = '1'??

N

Y

SET WRITE GAP

PR[0:1] = '11'??

N

Y

CONTINUE WITH RD/WR/FRMT/ETC. CMD

292093–8

Figure 5b. During Data Transfer Commands

set to activate 43 bytes or 24 bytes from the start of the Gap2 field, depending on the value as shown in Table 2. After this, PR[0:1] = '11' is checked; if not true (programmed '01') the program is exited with only the VCOEN timing being set for perpendicular mode. If true, however, the Gap2 length is set up for perpendicular mode (note: this is done independent of the data rate). It must be noted that if the PR[0:1] bits are set to '11' then it is up to the user to disable precompensation before accessing perpendicular drives. The other branch of the flowchart refers to setting of PR[0:1] to '00'. In this case, the perpendicular command will have the following effect:

1. If any of the Dn bits in PR[2:5] programmed high, then precompensation is automatically disabled (0 ns is selected for the specified drive regardless of the data rate) and VCOEN is set to activate appropriately. All the bits that are set low will enable the 82077 to be configured for conventional mode, i.e., exit the program without modifications (shown Figure 5b).
2. Next the data rate is checked for 1 Mbps. If the data rate is at 1 Mbps, then Gap2 length is set to 41 bytes, otherwise, the program is exited without setting up the Gap2 to 41 bytes.

It must be noted that if PR[2:5] are to be recognized in the command the OW bit must be set high. If this bit is low, setting of Dn bits will have no effect. Setting the OW bit will enable the storage of the Dn bit. Also setting PR[0:1] to any other value than '00' will override anything written in the Dn bits. In other words, setting PR[0:1] to a value other than '00' enables the effect of that for all drives. It must be noted that if PR[0:1] bits are set to a value other than '00' then it is recommended not to use the enhanced command mode, i.e., all other bits should be zero. Consider the following examples:

a. PR[0:7] = 0x84; This is the way to use the command in the enhanced mode. In this case, the OW = 1 and D0 is set high. During the data transfer command, if D0 is selected it will be automatically configured for perpendicular mode. If D1 is accessed, however, it will be configured for conventional mode. Similarly, if PR[0:7] = 0x88 then D1 is configured for perpendicular mode and D0 is configured for conventional mode. Software resets do not clear this mode.

b. PR[0:7] = 0x03; This is the way to use the command in the old mode. If the user decides to use this mode, then it must be noted that the command has to be issued before every data transfer command. Also when used this way, all the drives are configured for perpendicular mode. The user must also remember to disable precompensation and set the data rate to 1 Mbps while accessing the perpendicular drive in the system. Any software reset clears the command.

c. PR[0:7] = 0x87; In this case, the OW = 1, D0 = 1 and PR[0:1] = 11. This may be called a mixed mode and should be refrained from usage. This is similar to setting PR[0:7] = 0x03, because setting PR[0:1] high overrides automatic configuration. In this case the user has to be aware that precompensation must be disabled and the data rate must be set to 1 Mbps while accessing drive 0. After software reset, bits GAP and WGATE will be cleared, but OW and D0 will retain their previously set values. In other words, after software reset, the part will see PR[0:7] = 0x84. Evidently, this would cause problems and, therefore, it is recommended this mode *not* be used.

d. PR[0:7] = 0x80; In this case, the OW = 1, Dn = 0 and PR[0:1] = 00. This has the effect of clearing the perpendicular mode command without doing a hardware reset. Another way to do this would be to set PR[0:7] = 0x02; this can then be used to temporarily disable perpendicular mode configuration without affecting the previously programmed Dn values. Software reset following this will reenable the previously programmed enhanced mode command.

Using the enhanced perpendicular command removes the requirement of issuing the perpendicular command for each data transfer command and manually setting the perpendicular configuration.

"Software" RESETs (via DOR or DSR registers) will only clear the PR[0:1] values to '0'. Dn bits will retain their previously programmed values. "Hardware" RESETs will clear all the programmed bits including OW and Dn bits to '0'. The status of these bits can be determined by issuing the dumpreg command and checking the 8th result byte. This byte will contain the programmed values of the Dn and PR[0:1] bits as shown in Figure 6. The OW bit is *not* returned in this result byte.

Phase	R/W	Data Bus								Remarks
		D7	D6	D5	D4	D3	D2	D1	D0	
DUMPREG COMMAND										
Command		Eighth Result Byte								
	R	LOCK	0	D3	D2	D1	D0	GAP	WGATE	

Figure 6. Dumpreg Command

INTERFACE BETWEEN 82077AA/SL AND THE DRIVE

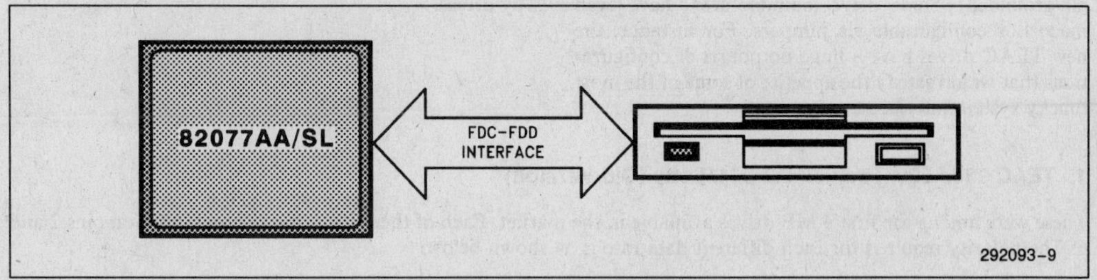

There is currently no industry-wide standard for the FDC to FDD interface. There are numerous floppy drive vendors, each with their own modes and interface pins to enable 4 MB perpendicular mode. The drive interface not only varies from manufacturer to manufacturer but also within a manufacturer's product line. The differences on the interface mainly originate from configuring the floppy drive into the 4 MB mode. Depending on the drive, the differences can create problems of daisy-chaining a 4 MB drive with the standard 1 MB and 2 MB drives. Of course, for laptops this is not a problem since most of them use a single floppy drive. Lack of an industry standard makes it necessary to look at each drive and build a interface for that particular drive.

The following is a brief discussion about some of the floppy drives available in the market and how these can be interfaced with the 82077AA/SL. It is important to note that although a manufacturer's name may be given in connection with the interface described, Intel does not guarantee that the interface discussed will apply to all the drives from that manufacturer. The main goal is introduce to the reader how to interface the 82077AA/SL with a 4 MB floppy drive.

Previously, for the conventional 1 MB and 2 MB AT mode drives, a single Density Select input was used by floppy drives to select between high density and low density drives. A high on this input enabled high density operation (500 Kbps) whereas a low enabled low density operation (300 Kbps/250 Kbps). This signal was asserted high or low by the floppy disk controller depending on the data rate programmed. For the 4 MB operation, there are two inputs defined by the floppy drive manufacturers. The polarity of these inputs enables the selected density operation. Implementing this requires at least 1 new pin to be defined on the FDC-FDD interface. Most floppy vendors have elected to take pin 2 (originally density select) and redefine the polarity to conform to one of these new density select inputs and another pin to be the other density select input. However, the new density select on pin 2 is not compatible to the old density select input in many of the floppy drives. This precludes the user from daisy chaining 4 MB drives with conventional drives. Another problem is that the second density select pin varies on its location on the FDC-FDD interface from drive to drive.

The way that the BIOS determines what type of diskette is in what type of drive is by trial and error. The system tries to read the diskette at 250 Kbps; if it fails then it will set the data rate to higher value and retry. The BIOS does this until the right data rate is selected. This method will still be implemented for the 4 MB drives by some BIOS vendors. However, the 4 MB drives available today also have two media sense ID pins that relate to the user what type of media is present in the floppy drive. This information will also require two pins on the FDC-FDD interface. The location of these pins is once again variable from drive to drive.

Some manufacturers have circumvented the entire standardization problem by including an auto configuration in the drive. In these cases, the type of floppy put into the drive is sensed by the hole (each 4/2/1 MB diskette has a hole in different locations identifying it) on the diskette. Then the drive automatically sets itself up for this mode. The BIOS must obviously set up the floppy disk controller for the correct data rate which could be done if the media sense ID was read and decoded as to the data rate. Due to lack of extra pins on the even side of the floppy connector the newer locations of some of the functions are migrating to the odd pins (previously all grounded). Some drive manufacturers have even made this configurable via jumpers. For instance, the new TEAC drives have a huge potpourri of configurations that would satisfy the appetite of some of the most finicky system interfaces.

The 82077AA/SL currently has two output pins DRATE0 and DRATE1 (pins 28 and 29 respectively) which directly reflect the data rate programmed in the DSR and CCR registers. These two pins can be used to select the correct density on the drive. These two can also be used with the combination of DENSEL to select the correct data rate. At the present time the 82077AA/SL does not support media sense ID. However, the user could easily make it readable directly by BIOS. The following is a discussion on what combination of DRATE0, DRATE1, and DENSEL could be used to interface to some of the currently available floppy drives.

1. TEAC 235J-600/Toshiba PD-211/Sony (Old Version)

These were among the first 4 MB drives available in the market. Each of them has a mode select input on pins 2 and 6. The polarity required for each different data rate is as shown below:

Data Rate	Capacity	DRATE1	DRATE0	MODSEL0 pin 2	MODSEL1 pin 6
1 Mbps	4 MB	1	1	1	0
500 Kbps	2 MB	0	0	0	1
300 Kbps/ 1 Mbps	4 MB	0	1	1	1
250 Kbps	1 MB	1	0	0	0

It is clear from the above that DRATE0 = MODSEL0 and MODSEL1 = DRATE1#. This would mean taking the drate signals onto pins 2 and 6 of the FDC-FDD interface. Unfortunately this solution requires an inverting gate. TEAC has recently, however, come out with a new version called TEAC 235J-3653. On this drive there are a number of possible configurations into which the drive can be put into, however, only the best way to interface to the 82077AA/SL will be discussed. The requirements are as shown below. This shows that HDIN = DENSEL (original signal for conventional drives) and EDIN = DRATE0. As suggested in the TEAC spec for method 1, the straps connected are MSC, HI2 (sets HDIN on pin 2), DC34 and EI6 (sets EDIN on pin 6). Pins 4, 29, and 33 are left open. Since pin 2 has the same polarity as the conventional drive requirement and the secondary input is connected via pin 6 (no connect on the conventional drives) daisy chaining this TEAC drive with a conventional drive does not cause any incompatibility. Figure 7 shows how the TEAC can be connected to the 82077AA/SL. It also shows daisy chaining of the TEAC drive with a conventional drive.

Data Rate	Capacity	DENSEL	DRATE1	DRATE0	HDIN pin 2	EDIN pin 6
1 Mbps	4 MB	1	1	1	X	1
500 Kbps	2 MB	1	0	0	1	0
300 Kbps/ 1 Mbps	4 MB	0	0	1	X	1
250 Kbps	1 MB	0	1	0	0	0

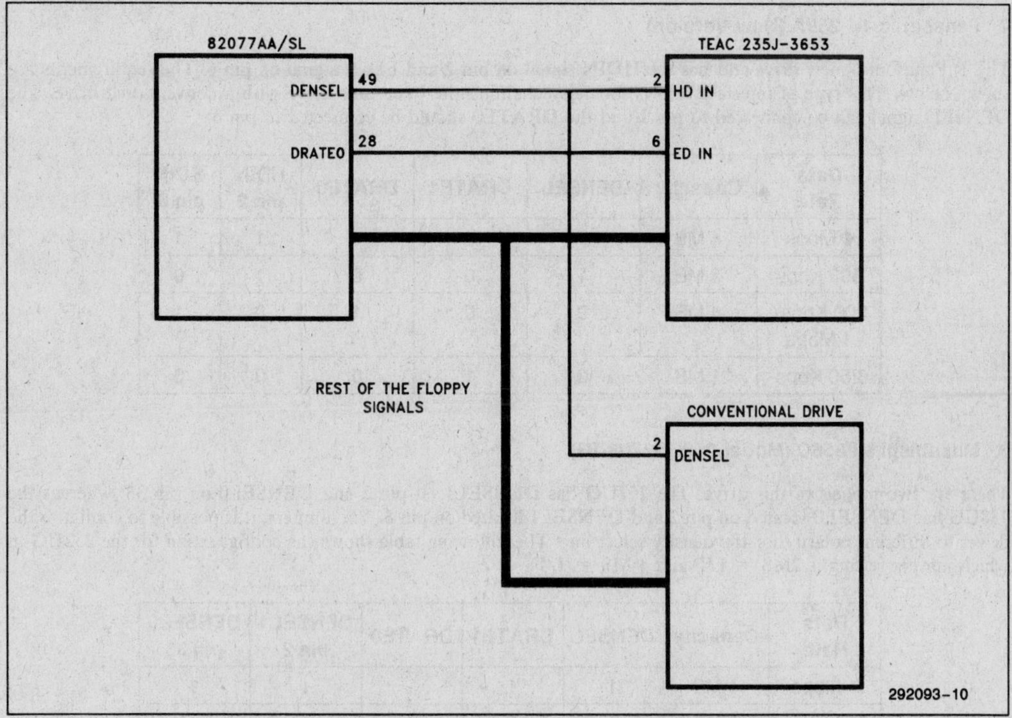

Figure 7. Interfacing 82077AA/SL to TEAC 235J-3653

2

2. Panasonic JU-259A (New Version)

This is Panasonic's new drive and has the HDIN signal on pin 2 and EDIN signal on pin 6. The requirements are shown below. This type of interface allows for daisy chaining the Panasonic drive with a conventional drive. The DENSEL signal can be connected to pin 2 and the DRATE0 should be connected to pin 6.

Data Rate	Capacity	DENSEL	DRATE1	DRATE0	HDIN pin 2	EDIN pin 6
1 Mbps	4 MB	1	1	1	1	1
500 Kbps	2 MB	1	0	0	1	0
300 Kbps/ 1 Mbps	4 MB	0	0	1	0	1
250 Kbps	1 MB	0	1	0	0	0

3. Mitsubishi MF356C (Model 252UG/788UG)

There are two models of this drive. The 252UG has DENSEL1 on pin 2 and DENSEL0 on pin 33, whereas the 788UG has DENSEL0 located on pin 2 and DENSEL1 located on pin 6. Via jumpers, it is possible to configure the drives to different polarity for the density select line. The following table shows the configuration for the 252UG in which jumper setting is 2MS = I/F and 4 MS = I/F.

Data Rate	Capacity	DENSEL	DRATE1	DRATE0	DENSEL1 pin 2	DENSEL0 pin 33
1 Mbps	4 MB	1	1	1	1	1
500 Kbps	2 MB	1	0	0	1	0
300 Kbps/ 1 Mbps	4 MB	0	0	1	0	1
250 Kbps	1 MB	0	1	0	0	0

The correct connection requirement is: DENSEL (from 82077AA/SL) = DENSEL1 and DRATE0 = DENSEL0. Although there are other configurations, this provides the best one, since daisy chaining is possible without any problem.

4. Epson SMD-1060

This drive has 3 different modes of operation. Mode B is the best and is similar to Mitsubishi's drives as described above. In this mode, HDI signal is connected to pin 2 and EDI is connected to pin 33. Mode B is enabled by inserting jumpers across 3-4 and 7-8 (SS01 B block) and 1-2 and 3-4 (SS03 block) for the drive with the power separated type (i.e., a connector for the floppy signals and another one for power supply) of 34-pin connector.

Data Rate	Capacity	DENSEL	DRATE1	DRATE0	HDI pin 2	EDI pin 33
1 Mbps	4 MB	1	1	1	1	1
500 Kbps	2 MB	1	0	0	1	0
300 Kbps/ 1 Mbps	4 MB	0	0	1	0	1
250 Kbps	1 MB	0	1	0	0	0

As demonstrated by the table, HDI = DENSEL and EDI = DRATE0. These connections would ensure daisy chaining capability without any problems.

5. Sony MP-F40W-14/15

The dash 14 and 15 are two drives from Sony that handle 4 MB requirements. The MP-F40W-14 has the DENSITY SELECT 1, DENSITY SELECT 0 on pins 2 and 33 respectively, whereas the MP-F40W-15 has the DENSITY SELECT 1, DENSITY SELECT 0 on pins 2 and 6 respectively. As it is obvious from the table below, daisy chaining is easily done if the 82077AA/SL is connected in the PS/2 mode (by tying IDENT low) with either type of drive, the only difference being the location of DENSITY SELECT 0.

Data Rate	Capacity	DENSEL PS/2 mode (IDENT = 0)	DRATE1	DRATE0	DENSITY SELECT1 pin 2	DENSITY SELECT0 pin 6/33
1 Mbps	4 MB	0	1	1	0	1
500 Kbps	2 MB	0	0	0	0	0
300 Kbps/ 1 Mbps	4 MB	1	0	1	1	1
250 Kbps	1 MB	1	1	0	1	0

If the drive is used in the PS/2 mode, then DENSITY SELECT1 = DENSEL and DENSITY SELECT0 = DRATE0. To use the drive in AT mode, DENSITY SELECT1 = DRATE1 and DENSITY SELECT0 = DRATE0, as shown below. However, daisy chaining is not possible.

Data Rate	Capacity	DENSEL PS/2 mode (IDENT = 0)	DRATE1	DRATE0	DENSITY SELECT1 pin 2	DENSITY SELECT0 pin 6/33
1 Mbps	4 MB	0	1	1	1	1
500 Kbps	2 MB	0	0	0	0	0
300 Kbps/ 1 Mbps	4 MB	1	0	1	0	1
250 Kbps	1 MB	1	1	0	1	0

6. Toshiba ND3571

Toshiba MB drive has the HD mode selection on pin 6 and ED mode selection on pin 2. This causes daisy chaining problems with conventional drives as shown in the figure below:

Data Rate	Capacity	DENSEL	DRATE1	DRATE0	ED Mode pin 2	HD Mode pin 6
1 Mbps	4 MB	1	1	1	1	1
500 Kbps	2 MB	1	0	0	0	1
300 Kbps/ 1 Mbps	4 MB	0	0	1	1	0
250 Kbps	1 MB	0	1	0	0	0

The DENSEL from the 82077 is connected to pin 6 and DRATE0 is connected to pin 2.

82077SL 4 MB DESIGN

This section presents a design application of a PC/AT compatible floppy disk controller. The 82077SL integrates the entire PC/AT controller design with the exception of the address decode on a single chip. The schematic for this solution is shown in Figure 8. The chip select for the 82077SL is generated by a 85C220 μPLD that is programmed to decode addresses 03F0H through 03F7H when AEN is low. The programming equations for the μPLD is in the Intel's .ADF format and can be processed using the IPLSII compiler (available from Intel).

A floppy disk interface is provided by on-chip output buffers with a 40 mA sink capability. The outputs from the disk drive are terminated at the floppy disk controller with a 1 KΩ resistor pack. The 82077SL disk interface inputs contain a Schmitt trigger input structure for higher noise immunity. The host interface is a similar direct connection with on-chip 12 mA sink capable buffers on DB0–7, INT and DRQ.

The schematic shows eleven jumpers numbered J1 through J11. The table below describes the functions of these jumpers as well as their normal connections. The normal connections allow the BIOS to work without modification. In the normal mode, the 82077SL responds to DRQ2 and DACK2# as well as IRQ6. Depending on the type of drive interfaced to this board, the DENOUT0 and DENOUT1 signals can be tied. With the setting to 2–3 on J8 and J9, the default setting is DENSEL on DRVDEN0 and DRATE0 on DRVDEN1. PIN6/33 SELECT is used to set for pin 6 as the EDIN input. The J11 should always be closed. It can be used to measure the current consumption of 82077SL. J7 selects between the primary and secondary address spaces. There are two resistor packs used for pullups on input signals from the floppy drive interface. These resistors are rated at 1K. Please note that if using older 5.25″ drives, the pullup on some of them is 150Ω. Most modem 5.25″ drives use a 1K value. In order to ensure the correct value please refer to the floppy drive specification manual.

For further information, please contact your local Intel sales office.

Jumper	Description	Normal Connection
J1	DRQ1: DMA request 1 used with DACK1# to allow for DMA transfers	Open
J2	DRQ2: DMA request 2 used with DACK2# to allow for DMA transfers	Closed
J3	DACK1: DMA acknowledge 1 used with DRQ1 to allow for DMA transfers	Open
J4	DACK2: DMA acknowledge 2 used with DRQ2 to allow for DMA transfers	Closed
J5	IRQ5: Interrupt line 5 used to generate floppy interrupts	Open
J6	IRQ6: Interrupt line 6 used to generate floppy interrupts	Closed
J7	DRV2: Address selection (between 3FX and 37X address ranges)	Open
J8	DENOUT0: Used with DENOUT1 to select the values of DRVDEN1,0	2–3
J9	DENOUT1: Used with DENOUT0 to select the values of DRVDEN1,0	2–3
J10	PIN6/33 SELECT: Used to select between pin 6 and pin 33 for EDIN input	1–2 or 2–3
J11	V_{BB}/V_{CC}: Connection between two power layers	Closed

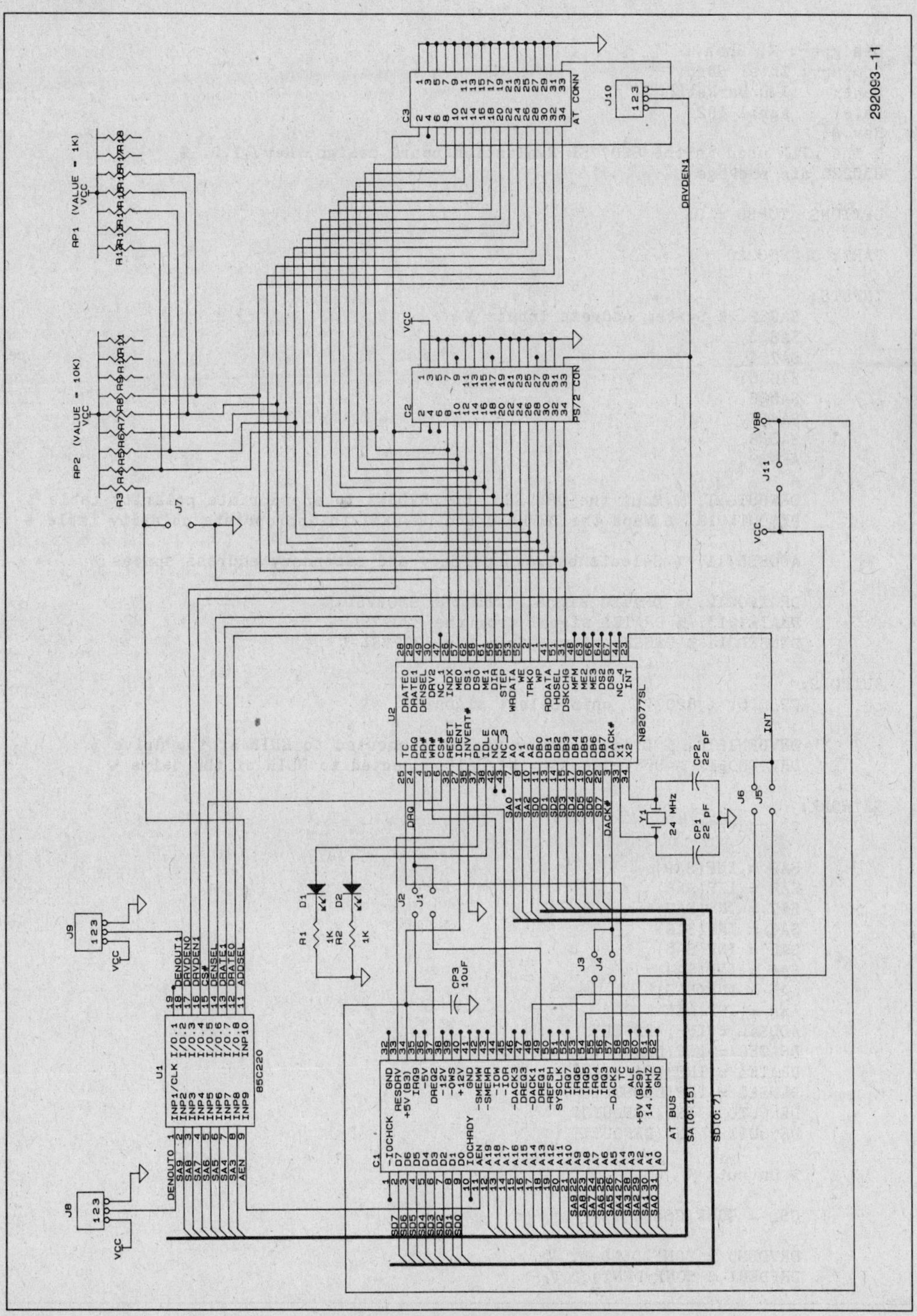

Figure 8. 82077SL Evaluation Board

```
Designer: K. Shah
Company: Intel Corp.
Dept:    IMD Marketing
Date:    April '92
Rev.#:
% The µPLD used in the 82077SL Evaluation board design, Rev.#1.0. %
85C220 dip package

OPTIONS: TURBO = ON

PART:    85C220

INPUTS:
        SA9@2, % System Address Inputs %
        SA8@3,
        SA7@4,
        SA6@5,
        SA5@6,
        SA4@7,
        SA3@8,
        AEN@9,

        DENOUT0@1, % Maps the DRVDEN0 and DRVDEN1 to appropriate polarity table %
        DENOUT1@18, % Maps the DRVDEN0 and DRVDEN1 to appropriate polarity table %

        ADDSEL@11, % Selects between primary and secondary address spaces %

        DRATE0@12, % DRATE0 signal from the 82077SL %
        DRATE1@13, % DRATE1 signal from the 82077SL %
        DENSEL@14 % DENSEL signal from the 82077SL %

OUTPUTS:
        CS_@15, % 82077SL chip select signal %

        DRVDEN1@16, % Drive density signal connected to EDIN of the drive %
        DRVDEN0@17 % Drive density signal connected to HDIN of the drive %

NETWORK:
        % Inputs %

        SA9 = INP(SA9)
        SA8 = INP(SA8)
        SA7 = INP(SA7)
        SA6 = INP(SA6)
        SA5 = INP(SA5)
        SA4 = INP(SA4)
        SA3 = INP(SA3)
        AEN = INP(AEN)
        ADDSEL = INP(ADDSEL)
        DRATE0 = INP(DRATE0)
        DRATE1 = INP(DRATE1)
        DENSEL = INP(DENSEL)
        DENOUT0 = INP(DENOUT0)
        DENOUT1 = INP(DENOUT1)

        % Outputs %

        CS_ = CONF(CSeq, VCC)

        DRVDEN0 = CONF(DEN0eq, VCC)
        DRVDEN1 = CONF(DEN1eq, VCC)
```

```
EQUATIONS:

        % CS_is activated for 3F0-3F7 and 370-377 address spaces %
        CSeq = (AEN' * SA9 * SA8 * SA7' * SA6 * SA5 * SA4 * SA3' * ADDSEL'
              + AEN' * SA9 * SA8 * SA7 * SA6 * SA5 * SA4 * SA3' * ADDSEL)';

        % These are the signals generated on DRVDEN0 and DRVDEN1 for the FDC-FDD
          interface
        DENOUT1  DENOUT0  DRVDEN0  DRVDEN1
             0    0        DENSEL   DRATE0
             0    1        DENSEL'  DRATE0
             1    0        DRATE1   DRATE0
             1    1        DRATE0   DRATE1
        %

        DEN0eq = DENSEL * (DENOUT0' * DENOUT1') + DENSEL' * (DENOUT0 * DENOUT1')
                + DRATE1 * (DENOUT0' * DENOUT1) + DRATE0 * (DENOUT0 * DENOUT1);
        DEN1eq = DRATE1 * (DENOUT0 * DENOUT1) + DRATE0 * (DENOUT0' + DENOUT1');

END$
```

2

82077SL Application Note Revision Summary

The following changes have been made since revision 001:

Table 2 kBps was corrected to kbps.

Page 12 3. Mitsubishi MF356C description modified to read: "There are two models of this drive. The 252UG has DENSEL1 on pin 2 and DENSEL0 on pin 33, whereas the 788UG has DENSEL0 located on pin 2 and DENSEL1 located on pin 6. Via jumpers, it is possible to configure the drives to different polarity for the density select lines. The following table shows the configuration for the 252UG in which jumper setting is 2 MS = I/F and 4 MS = I/F."

Figure 8 Arrow added to diagram.

Page 17 Columns corrected to line up properly.

Memory Controllers 3

3

8206 ERROR DETECTION AND CORRECTION UNIT

- Detects All Single Bit, and Double Bit and Most Multiple Bit Errors
- Corrects All Single Bit Errors

3 Selections	8206-1	8206
Detection	35 ns	42 ns
Correction	55 ns	67 ns

- Syndrome Outputs for Error Logging
- Automatic Error Scrubbing with 8207
- Expandable to Handle 80 Bit Memories
- Separate Input and Output Busses—No Timing Strobes Required
- Supports Read With and Without Correction, Writes, Partial (Byte) Writes, and Read-Modify-Writes
- HMOS III Technology for Low Power
- 68 Pin Leadless JEDEC Package
- 68 Pin Grid Array Package

The HMOS 8206 Error Detection and Correction Unit is a high-speed device that provides error detection and correction for memory systems (static and dynamic) requiring high reliability and performance. Each 8206 handles 8 or 16 data bits and up to 8 check bits. 8206's can be cascaded to provide correction and detection for up to 80 bits of data. Other 8206 features include the ability to handle byte writes, memory initialization, and error logging.

3

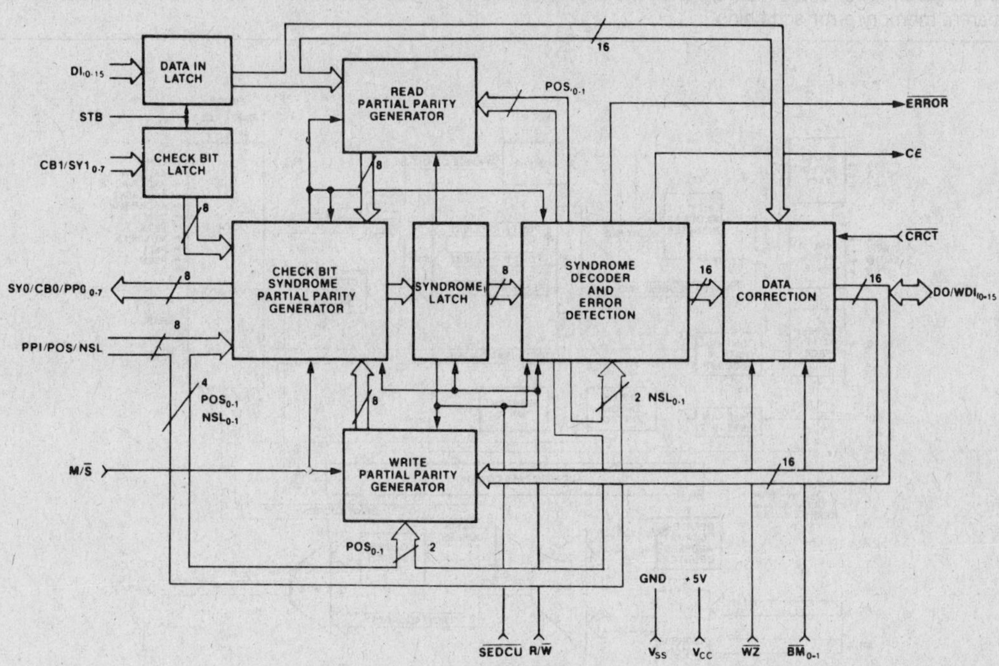

Figure 1. 8206 Block Diagram

The complete document for this product is available on Intel's "Data-on-Demand" CD-ROM system. To obtain a copy, contact your local Intel field sales office, Intel technical distributor or call 1-800-548-4725.

September 1987
Order Number: 205220-008

8207
DUAL-PORT DYNAMIC RAM CONTROLLER

- Provides All Signals Necessary to Control 16K, 64K and 256K Dynamic RAMs
- Directly Addresses and Drives up to 2 Megabytes without External Drivers
- Supports Single and Dual-Port Configurations
- Automatic RAM Initialization in All Modes
- Four Programmable Refresh Modes
- Transparent Memory Scrubbing in ECC Mode
- Fast Cycle Support for 8 MHz 80286 with 8207-16
- Slow Cycle Support for 8 MHz, 10 MHz 8086/88, 80186/188 with 8207-8, 8207-10
- Provides Signals to Directly Control the 8206 Error Detection and Correction Unit
- Supports Synchronous or Asynchronous Operation on Either Port
- 68 Lead JEDEC Type A Leadless Chip Carrier (LCC) and Pin Grid Array (PGA), Both in Ceramic.

The Intel 8207 Dual-Port Dynamic RAM Controller is a high-performance, systems-oriented, Dynamic RAM controller that is designed to easily interface 16K, 64K and 256K Dynamic RAMs to Intel and other microprocessor systems. A dual-port interface allows two different busses to independently access memory. When configured with an 8206 Error Detection and Correction Unit the 8207 supplies the necessary logic for designing large error-corrected memory arrays. This combination provides automatic memory initialization and transparent memory error scrubbing.

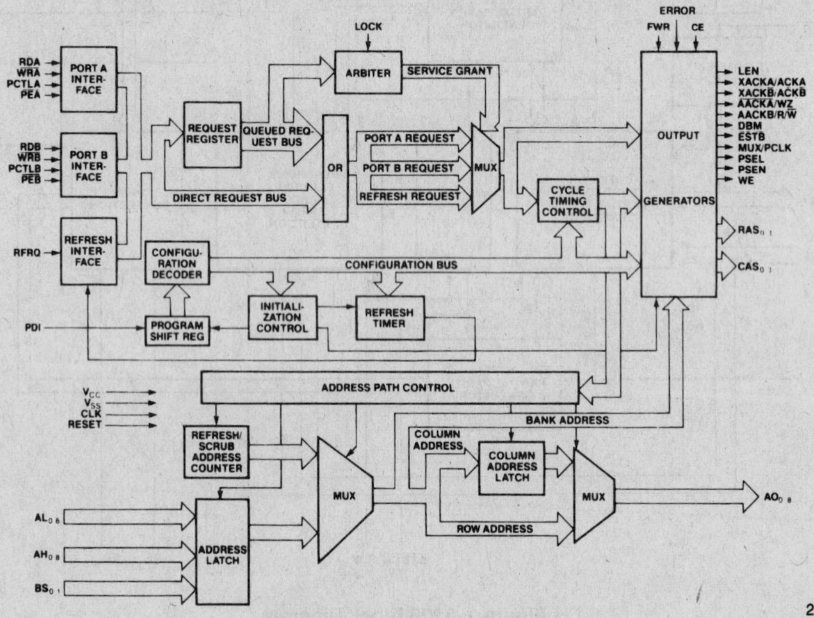

Figure 1. 8207 Block Diagram

The complete document for this product is available on Intel's "Data-on-Demand" CD-ROM system. To obtain a copy, contact your local Intel field sales office, Intel technical distributor or call 1-800-548-4725.

September 1987
Order Number: 210463-007

82C08
CHMOS DYNAMIC RAM CONTROLLER

- **0 Wait State with INTEL μProcessors**
- **iAPX 286 (10, 8 MHz) } 82C08-20 20 MHz, 82C08-16 16 MHz**
  iAPX 186/88, 86/88 } 82C08-10 10 MHz, 82C08-8 8 MHz
- **Supports 64K and 256K DRAMs (256K x 1 and 256K x 4 Organizations)**
- **Power Down Mode with Programmable Memory Refresh using Battery Backup**
- **Directly Addresses and Drives up to 1 Megabyte without External Drivers**
- **Microprocessor Data Transfer and Advance Acknowledge Signals**
- **Five Programmable Refresh Modes**
- **Automatic RAM Warm-up**
- **Pin-Compatible with 8208**
- **48 Lead Plastic DIP; 68 Lead PLCC**
  (See Intel Packaging; Order Number: 231369-001)
- **Compatible with Normal Modes of Static Column and Ripplemode DRAMs**

The Intel 82C08 Dynamic RAM Controller is a CMOS, high performance, systems oriented, Dynamic RAM controller that is designed to easily interface 64K and 256K Dynamic RAMs to Intel and other microprocessors. The 82C08 also has a power down mode where only the refresh logic is activated using battery backup.

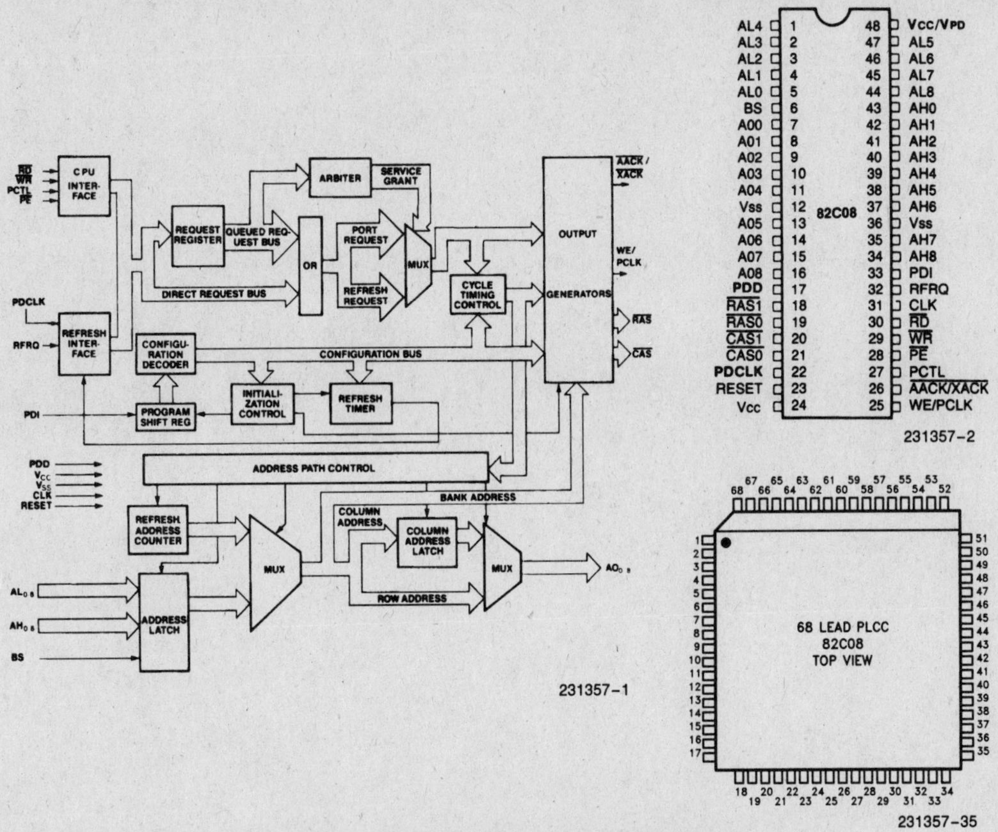

3

231357-1

Pin	Signal	Pin	Signal
1	AL4	48	Vcc/VPD
2	AL3	47	AL5
3	AL2	46	AL6
4	AL1	45	AL7
5	AL0	44	AL8
6	BS	43	AH0
7	A00	42	AH1
8	A01	41	AH2
9	A02	40	AH3
10	A03	39	AH4
11	A04	38	AH5
12	Vss	37	AH6
13	A05	36	Vss
14	A06	35	AH7
15	A07	34	AH8
16	A08	33	PDI
17	PDD	32	RFRQ
18	$\overline{RAS1}$	31	CLK
19	$\overline{RAS0}$	30	$\overline{RD}$
20	$\overline{CAS1}$	29	$\overline{WR}$
21	$\overline{CAS0}$	28	$\overline{PE}$
22	PDCLK	27	PCTL
23	RESET	26	$\overline{AACK}/\overline{XACK}$
24	Vcc	25	WE/PCLK

231357-2

68 LEAD PLCC
82C08
TOP VIEW

231357-35

Figure 1. Block Diagram and Pinout Diagrams

The complete document for this product is available on Intel's "Data-on-Demand" CD-ROM system. To obtain a copy, contact your local Intel field sales office, Intel technical distributor or call 1-800-548-4725.

September 1990
Order Number: 231357-008

UPI Keyboard Controllers 4

Microprocessor Peripherals UPI-41A/41AH/42/42AH User's Manual

October 1993

Order Number: 231318-006

Microprocessor Peripherals
UPI-41A/41AH/42/42AH User's Manual

CONTENTS

CONTENTS

CHAPTER 1 INTRODUCTION

Accompanying the introduction of microprocessors such as the 8088, 8086, 80186 and 80286 there has been a rapid proliferation of intelligent peripheral devices. These special purpose peripherals extend CPU performance and flexibility in a number of important ways.

Table 1-1. Intelligent Peripheral Devices

8255 (GPIO)	Programmable Peripheral Interface
8251A(USART)	Programmable Communication Interface
8253 (TIMER)	Programmable Interval Timer
8257 (DMA)	Programmable DMA Controller
8259	Programmable Interrupt Controller
82077AA	Programmable Floppy Disk Controller
8273 (SDLC)	Programmable Synchronous Data Link Controller
8274	Programmable Multiprotocol-Serial Communications Controller
8275/8276 (CRT)	Programmable CRT Controllers
8279 (PKD)	Programmable Keyboard/Display Controller
8291A, 8292, 8293	Programmable GPIB System Talker, Listener, Controller

Intelligent devices like the 82077AA floppy disk controller and 8273 synchronous data link controller (see Table 1-1) can preprocess serial data and perform control tasks which off-load the main system processor. Higher overall system throughput is achieved and software complexity is greatly reduced. The intelligent peripheral chips simplify master processor control tasks by performing many functions externally in peripheral hardware rather than internally in main processor software.

Intelligent peripherals also provide system flexibility. They contain on-chip mode registers which are programmed by the master processor during system initialization. These control registers allow the peripheral to be configured into many different operation modes. The user-defined program for the peripheral is stored in main system memory and is transferred to the peripheral's registers whenever a mode change is required. Of course, this type of flexibility requires software overhead in the master system which tends to limit the benefit derived from the peripheral chip.

In the past, intelligent peripherals were designed to handle very specialized tasks. Separate chips were designed for communication disciplines, parallel I/O, keyboard encoding, interval timing, CRT control, etc. Yet, in spite of the large number of devices available and the increased flexibility built into these chips, there is still a large number of microcomputer peripheral control tasks which are not satisfied.

With the introduction of the Universal Peripheral Interface (UPI) microcomputer, Intel has taken the intelligent peripheral concept a step further by providing an intelligent controller that is fully user programmable. It is a complete single-chip microcomputer which can connect directly to a master processor data bus. It has the same advantages of intelligence and flexibility which previous peripheral chips offered. In addition, UPIs are user-programmable: it has 1K/2K bytes of ROM or EPROM memory for program storage plus 64/128/256 bytes of RAM memory UPI-41A, 41AH/42, 42AH respectively for data storage or initialization from the master processor. The UPI device allows a designer to fully specify his control algorithm in the peripheral chip without relying on the master processor. Devices like printer controllers and keyboard scanners can be completely self-contained, relying on the master processor only for data transfer.

The UPI family currently consists of seven components:

- 8741A microcomputer with 1K EPROM memory
- 8741AH microcomputer with 1K OTP EPROM memory
- 8041AH microcomputer with 1K ROM memory
- 8742 microcomputer with 2K EPROM memory
- 8742AH microcomputer with 2K "OTP" EPROM memory
- 8042AH microcomputer with 2K ROM memory
- 8243 I/O expander device

The UPI-41A/41AH/42/42AH family of microcomputers are functionally equivalent except for the type and amount of program memory available with each. In addition, the UPI-41AH/42AH family has a Signature Row outside the EPROM Array. The UPI-41AH/42AH family also has a Security Feature which renders the EPROM Array unreadable when set.

All UPI's have the following main features:

- 8-bit CPU
- 8-bit data bus interface registers
- Interval timer/event counter
- Two 8-bit TTL compatible I/O ports
- Resident clock oscillator circuits

The UPI family has the following differences:

Table 1-2

<table>
<tr><th>UPI-41A</th><th>UPI-42</th><th>UPI-41AH</th><th>UPI-42AH</th></tr>
<tr><td>1K x 8 EPROM

64 x 8 RAM</td><td>2K x 8 EPROM

128 x 8 RAM</td><td>1K x 8 ROM
or 1K x 8 OTP
128 x 8 RAM</td><td>2K x 8 ROM
or 2K x 8 OTP
256 x 8 RAM</td></tr>
<tr><td></td><td></td><td colspan="2">*Set Security Feature
**Signature Row Feature
32 Bytes with:
1. Test Code/Checksum
2. Intel Signature
3. Security Byte
4. User Signature</td></tr>
<tr><td colspan="4">PROGRAMMING</td></tr>
<tr><td>UPI-41A</td><td>UPI-42</td><td colspan="2">UPI-41AH/UPI-42AH</td></tr>
<tr><td>V_{DD} = 25V
I_{DD} = 50 ms
EA = 21.5V–24.5V
V_{PH} = 21.5V–24.5V
TPW = 50 ms</td><td>21V
50 mA
18V
18V
50 ms</td><td colspan="2">12.5V
30 mA
12.5V
20.V–5.5V
1 ms</td></tr>
<tr><td colspan="4">PIN DESCRIPTION</td></tr>
<tr><td colspan="2">UPI-41A/UPI-42</td><td colspan="2">UPI-41AH/UPI-42AH</td></tr>
<tr><td colspan="2">(T1) T1 functions as a test input which can be directly tested using conditional branching instructions. It functions as the event timer input under software control.</td><td colspan="2">T1 functions as a test input that can be directly tested using conditional branching instructions. It works as the event timer input under software control. It is used during sync mode to reset the instruction state to S1 and synchronize the internal clock to phase 1.</td></tr>
<tr><td colspan="2">(SS) Single step input used with the sync output to step the program through each instruction.</td><td colspan="2">Single step input used with the sync output to step the program through each instruction.
This pin is used to put the device in sync mode by applying +12.5V to it.</td></tr>
<tr><td colspan="2">Port 1 (P10–P17): 8-bit, Quasi-Bidirectional I/O Lines.</td><td colspan="2">Port 1 (P10–P17): 8-bit, Quasi-Bidirectional I/O Lines. P10–P17 access the Signature Row and Security Bit.</td></tr>
</table>

NOTES:

*For a complete description of the Security Feature, refer to the UPI-41AH/42AH Datasheet.

**For a complete description of the Signature Row, refer to the UPI-41AH/42AH Datasheet.

HMOS processing has been applied to the UPI family to allow for additional performance and memory capability while reducing costs. The UPI-41A/41AH/42/42AH are all pin and software compatible. This allows growth in present designs to incorporate new features and add additional performance. For new designs, the additional memory and performance of the UPI-41A/41AH/42/42AH extends the UPI 'grow your own solution' concept to more complex motor control tasks, 80-column printers and process control applications as examples.

The 8243 device is an I/O multiplexer which allows expansion of I/O to over 100 lines (if seven devices are used). All three parts are fabricated with N-channel MOS technology and require a single, 5V supply for operation.

INTERFACE REGISTERS FOR MULTI-PROCESSOR CONFIGURATIONS

In the normal configuration, the UPI-41A/41AH/42/42AH interfaces to the system bus, just like any intelligent peripheral device (see Figure 1-1). The host processor and the UPI-41A/41AH/42/42AH form a loosely coupled multi-processor system, that is, communications between the two processors are direct. Common resources are three addressable registers located physically on the UPI-41A/41AH/42/42AH. These registers are the Data Bus Buffer Input (DBBIN), Data Bus Buffer Output (DBBOUT), and Status (STATUS) registers. The host processor may read data from DBBOUT or write commands and data into DBBIN. The status of DBBOUT and DBBIN plus user-defined status is supplied in STATUS. The host may read STATUS at any time. An interrupt to the UPI processor is automatically generated (if enabled) when DBBIN is loaded.

Because the UPI contains a complete microcomputer with program memory, data memory, and CPU it can function as a "Universal" controller. A designer can program the UPI to control printers, tape transports, or multiple serial communication channels. The UPI can also handle off-line arithmetic processing, or any number of other low speed control tasks.

POWERFUL 8-BIT PROCESSOR

The UPI contains a powerful, 8-bit CPU with as fast as 1.2 μsec cycle time and two single-level interrupts. Its instruction set includes over 90 instructions for easy software development. Most instructions are single byte and single cycle and none are more than two bytes long. The instruction set is optimized for bit manipulation and I/O operations. Special instructions are included to allow binary or BCD arithmetic operations, table look-up routines, loop counters, and N-way branch routines.

4

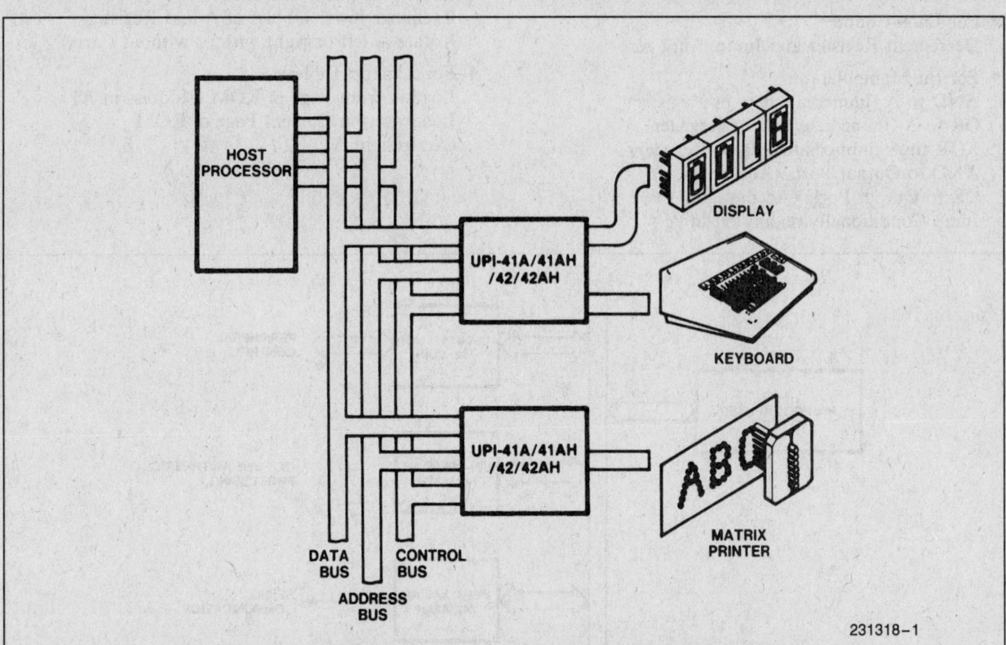

Figure 1-1. Interfacing Peripherals To Microcomputer Systems

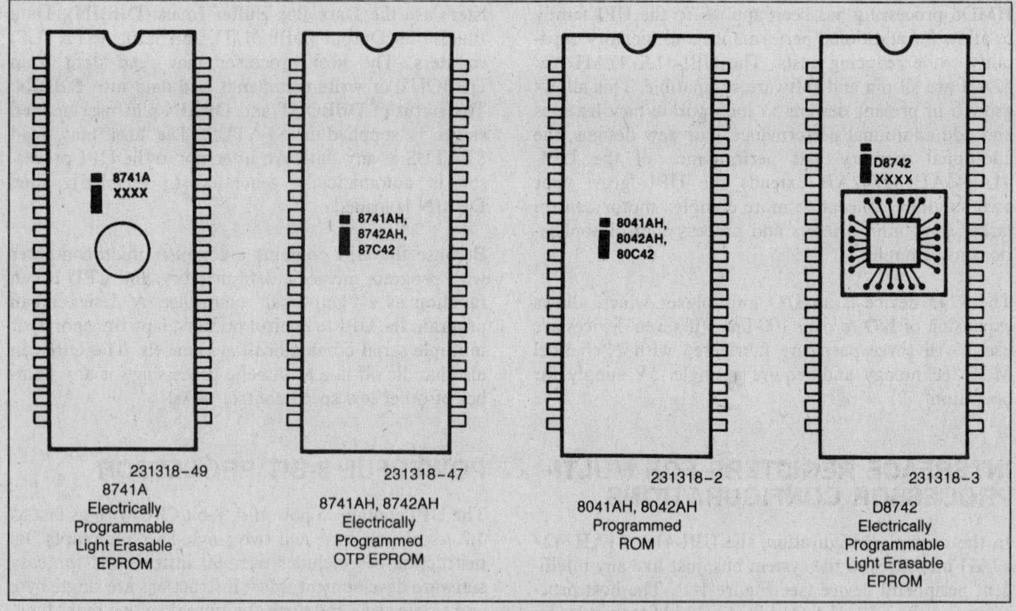

Figure 1-2. Pin Compatible ROM/EPROM Versions

SPECIAL INSTRUCTION SET FEATURES

- For Loop Counters:
  Decrement Register and Jump if not zero.
- For Bit Manipulation:
  AND to A (immediate data or Register)
  OR to A (immediate data or Register)
  XOR to A (immediate data or Register)
  AND to Output Ports (Accumulator)
  OR to Output Ports (Accumulator)
  Jump Conditionally on any bit in A
- For BDC Arithmetic:
  Decimal Adjust A
  Swap 4-bit Nibbles of A
  Exchange lower nibbles of A and Register
  Rotate A left or right with or without Carry
- For Lookup Tables:
  Load A from Page of ROM (Address in A)
  Load A from Current Page of ROM
  (Address in A)

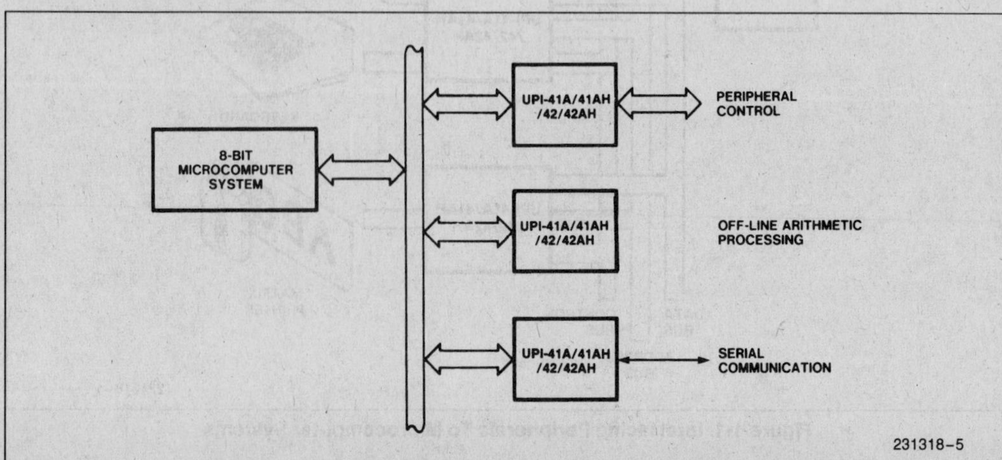

Figure 1-3. Interfaces and Protocols for Multiprocessor Systems

Features for Peripheral Control

The UPI 8-bit interval timer/event counter can be used to generate complex timing sequences for control applications or it can count external events such as switch closures and position encoder pulses. Software timing loops can be simplified or eliminated by the interval timer. If enabled, an interrupt to the CPU will occur when the timer overflows.

The UPI I/O complement contains two TTL-compatible 8-bit bidirectional I/O ports and two general-purpose test inputs. Each of the 16 port lines can individually function as either input or output under software control. Four of the port lines can also function as an interface for the 8243 I/O expander which provides four additional 4-bit ports that are directly addressable by UPI software. The 8243 expander allows low cost I/O expansion for large control applications while maintaining easy and efficient software port addressing.

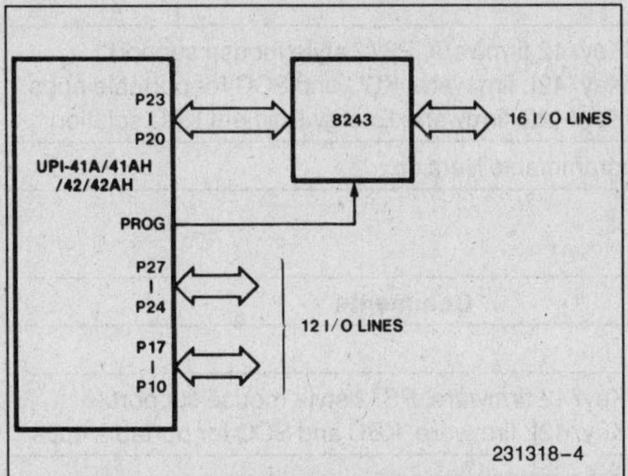

Figure 1-4. 8243 I/O Expander Interface

On-Chip Memory

The UPI's 64/128/256 bytes data memory include dual working register banks and an 8-level program counter stack. Switching between the register banks allows fast response to interrupts. The stack is used to store return addresses and processor status upon entering a subroutine.

The UPI program memory is available in three types to allow flexibility in moving from design to prototype to production with the same PC layout. The 8741A/8742 device with EPROM memory is very economical for initial system design and development. Its program memory can be electrically programmed using the Intel Universal PROM Programmer. When changes are needed, the entire program can be erased using UV lamp and reprogrammed in about 20 minutes. This means the 8741A/8742 can be used as a single chip "breadboard" for very complex interface and control problems. After the 8741A/8742 is programmed it can be tested in the actual production level PC board and the actual functional environment. Changes required during system debugging can be made in the 8741A/8742 program much more easily than they could be made in a random logic design. The system configuration and PC layout can remain fixed during the development process and the turn around time between changes can be reduced to a minimum.

At any point during the development cycle, the 8741A/8742 EPROM part can be replaced with the low cost UPI-41AH/42AH respectively with factory mask programmed memory or OTP EPROM. The transition from system development to mass production is made smoothly because the 8741A/8742, 8741AH and 8041AH, 8742AH and 8042AH parts are completely pin compatible. This feature allows extensive testing with the EPROM part, even into initial shipments to customers. Yet, the transition to low-cost ROMs or OTP EPROM is simplified to the point of being merely a package substitution.

PREPROGRAMMED UPI's

The 8242AH, 8292, and 8294 are 8042AH's that are programmed by Intel and sold as standard peripherals. Intel offers a complete line of factory programmed keyboard controllers. These devices contain firmware developed by Phoenix Technologies Ltd. and Award Software Inc. See Table 1-3 for a complete listing of Intels' entire keyboard controller product line. The 8292 is a GPIB controller, part of a three chip GPIB system. The 8294 is a Data Encryption Unit that implements the National Bureau of Standards data encryption algorithm. These parts illustrate the great flexibility offered by the UPI family.

Table 1-3. Keyboard Controller Family Product Selection Guide

UPI-42: The industry standard for desktop Keyboard Control.

Device	Package	ROM	OTP	Comments
8042	N, P	2K		ROM Device
8242 8242PC 8242WA 8242WB	N, P N, P N, P N, P			Phoenix firmware version 2.5 Phoenix MultiKey/42 firmware, PS/2 style mouse support Award firmware version 3.57 Award firmware version 4.14, PS/2 style mouse support
8742	N, P, D		2K	Available as OTP (N, P) or EPROM (D)

UPI-C42: A low power CHMOS version of the UPI-42. The UPI-C42 doubles the user programmable memory size, adds Auto A20 Gate support, includes Standby (**) and Suspend power down modes, and is available in a space saving 44-lead QFP pkg.

Device	Package	ROM	OTP	Comments
80C42	N, P, S	4K		ROM Device
82C42PC 82C42PD 82C42PE	N, P, S N, P, S N, P, S			Phoenix MultiKey/42 firmware, PS/2 style mouse support Phoenix MultiKey/42L firmware, KBC and SCC for portable apps. Phoenix MultiKey/42G firmware, Energy Efficient KBC solution
87C42	N, P, S		4K	One Time Programmable Version

UPI-L42: The low voltage 3.3V version of the UPI-C42.

Device	Package	ROM	OTP	Comments
80L42	N, P, S	4K		ROM Device
82L42PC 82L42PD	N, P, S N, P, S			Phoenix MultiKey/42 firmware, PS/2 style mouse support Phoenix MultiKey/42L firmware, KBC and SCC for portable apps.
87L42	N, P, S		4K	One Time Programmable Version

NOTES:
N = 44 lead PLCC, P = 40 lead PDIP, S = 44 lead QFP, D = 40 lead CERDIP
KBC = Key Board Control, SCC = Scan Code Control
(**) Standby feature not supported on current (B-1) stepping

DEVELOPMENT SUPPORT

The UPI microcomputer is fully supported by Intel with development tools like the UPP PROM programmer already mentioned. The combination of device features and Intel development support make the UPI an ideal component for low-speed peripheral control applications.

UPI DEVELOPMENT SUPPORT

- 8048/UPI-41A/41AH/42/42AH Assembler
- Universal PROM Programmer UPP Series
- Application Engineers
- Training Courses

CHAPTER 2
FUNCTIONAL DESCRIPTION

The UPI microcomputer is an intelligent peripheral controller designed to operate in iAPX-86, 88, MCS-85, MCS-80, MCS-51 and MCS-48 systems. The UPI's architecture, illustrated in Figure 2-1, is based on a low cost, single-chip microcomputer with program memory, data memory, CPU, I/O, event timer and clock oscillator in a single 40-pin package. Special interface registers are included which enable the UPI to function as a peripheral to an 8-bit master processor.

This chapter provides a basic description of the UPI microcomputer and its system interface registers. Unless otherwise noted the descriptions in this section apply to the 8741AH, 8742AH with OTP EPROM memory, the 8741A/8742 (with UV erasable program memory) and the 8041AH, 8042AH. These devices are so similar that they can be considered identical under most circumstances. All functions described in this chapter apply to the UPI-41A/41AH/42/42AH.

PIN DESCRIPTION

The UPI-41A/41AH/42/42AH are packaged in 40-pin Dual In-Line (DIP) packages. The pin configuration for both devices is shown in Figure 2-2. Figure 2-3 illustrates the UPI Logic Symbol.

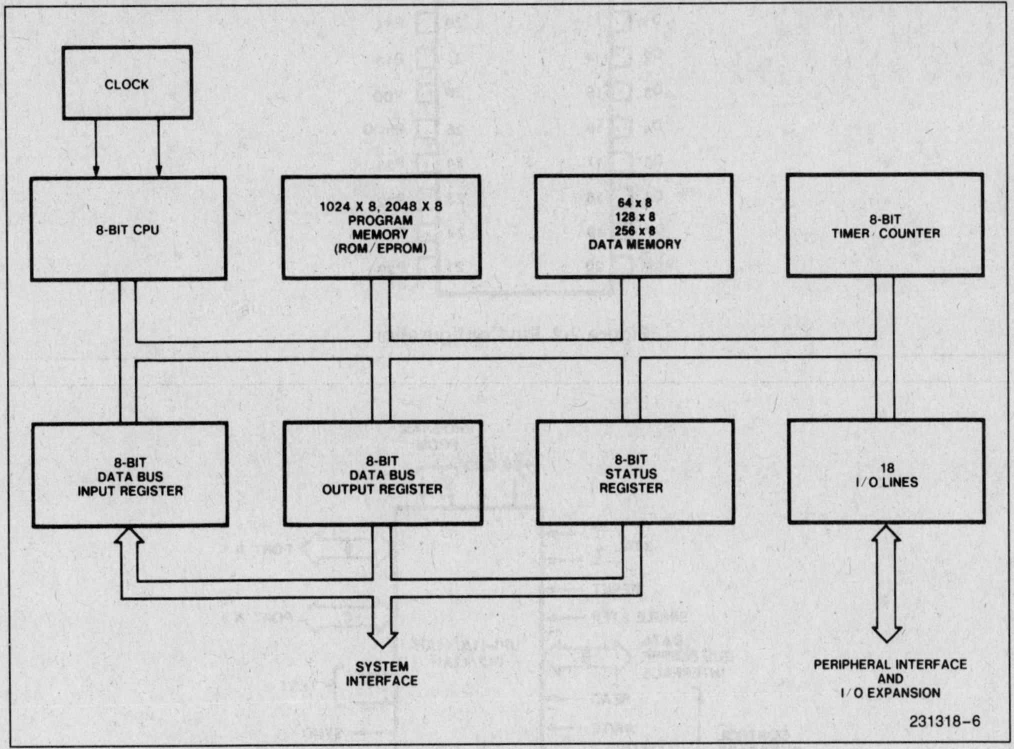

Figure 2-1. UPI-41A/41AH/42/42AH Single Chip Microcomputer

4

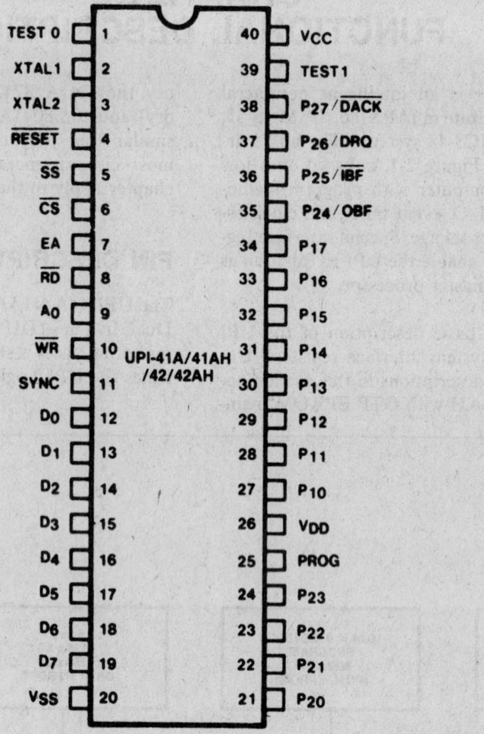

Pin	Name	Pin	Name
1	TEST 0	40	V_{CC}
2	XTAL 1	39	TEST 1
3	XTAL 2	38	P_{27}/$\overline{DACK}$
4	$\overline{RESET}$	37	P_{26}/DRQ
5	$\overline{SS}$	36	P_{25}/$\overline{IBF}$
6	$\overline{CS}$	35	P_{24}/OBF
7	EA	34	P_{17}
8	$\overline{RD}$	33	P_{16}
9	A_0	32	P_{15}
10	$\overline{WR}$	31	P_{14}
11	SYNC	30	P_{13}
12	D_0	29	P_{12}
13	D_1	28	P_{11}
14	D_2	27	P_{10}
15	D_3	26	V_{DD}
16	D_4	25	PROG
17	D_5	24	P_{23}
18	D_6	23	P_{22}
19	D_7	22	P_{21}
20	V_{SS}	21	P_{20}

UPI-41A/41AH/42/42AH

231318-7

Figure 2-2. Pin Configuration

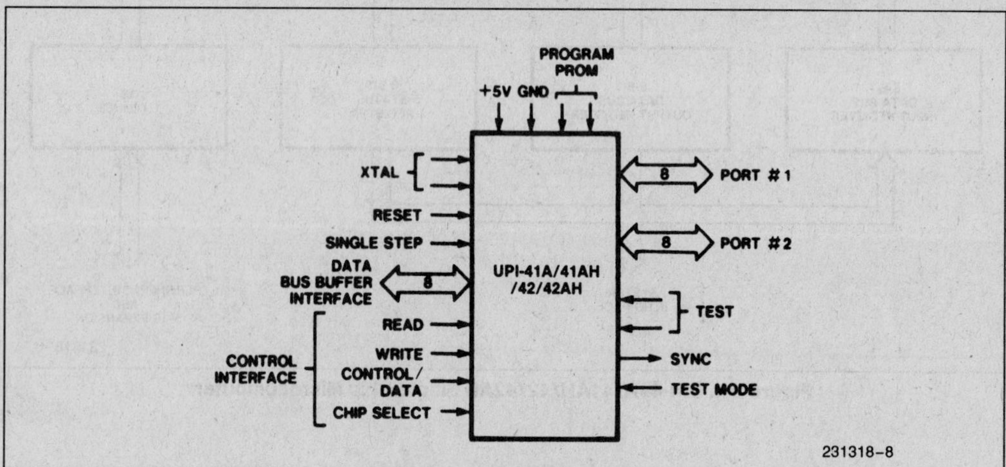

Figure 2-3. Logic Symbol

The following section summarizes the functions of each UPI pin. NOTE that several pins have two or more functions which are described in separate paragraphs.

Table 2-1. Pin Description

Symbol	Pin No.	Type	Name and Function
D_0–D_7 (BUS)	12–19	I/O	**DATA BUS:** Three-state, bidirectional DATA BUS BUFFER lines used to interface the UPI-41A/41AH/42/42AH microcomputer to an 8-bit master system data bus.
P_{10}–P_{17}	27-34	I/O	**PORT 1:** 8-bit, PORT 1 quasi-bidirectional I/O lines.
P_{20}–P_{27}	21-24 35–38	I/O	**PORT 2:** 8-bit, PORT 2 quasi-bidirectional I/O lines. The lower 4 bits (P_{20}–P_{23}) interface directly to the 8243 I/O expander device and contain address and data information during PORT 4–7 access. The upper 4 bits (P_{24}–P_{27}) can be programmed to provide interrupt Request and DMA Handshake capability. Software control can configure P_{24} as Output Buffer Full (OBF) interrupt, P_{25} as Input Buffer Full ($\overline{IBF}$) interrupt, P_{26} as DMA Request (DRQ), and P_{27} as DMA ACKnowledge ($\overline{DACK}$).
$\overline{WR}$	10	I	**WRITE:** I/O write input which enables the master CPU to write data and command words to the UPI INPUT DATA BUS BUFFER.
$\overline{RD}$	8	I	**READ:** I/O read input which enables the master CPU to read data and status words from the OUTPUT DATA BUS BUFFER or status register.
$\overline{CS}$	6	I	**CHIP SELECT:** Chip select input used to select one UPI-41A/41AH/42/42AH microcomputer out of several connected to a common data bus.
A_0	9	I	**COMMAND/DATA SELECT:** Address input used by the master processor to indicate whether byte transfer is data ($A_0 = 0$) or command ($A_0 = 1$).
TEST 0, TEST 1	1 39	I	**TEST INPUTS:** Input pins can be directly tested using conditional branch instructions. **FREQUENCY REFERENCE:** TEST 1 (T_1) also functions as the event timer input (under software control). TEST0 (T_0) is used during PROM programming and verification in the UPI-41A/41AH/42/42AH.
XTAL 1, XTAL 2	2 3	I	**INPUTS:** Inputs for a crystal, LC or an external timing signal to determine the internal oscillator frequency.
SYNC	11	O	**OUTPUT CLOCK:** Output signal which occurs once per UPI instruction cycle. SYNC can be used as a strobe for external circuitry; it is also used to synchronize single step operation.
EA	7	I	**EXTERNAL ACCESS:** External access input which allows emulation, testing and PROM/ROM verification.
PROG	25	I/O	**PROGRAM:** Multifunction pin used as the program pulse input during PROM programming. During I/O expander access the PROG pin acts as an address/data strobe to the 8243.
$\overline{RESET}$	4	I	**RESET:** Input used to reset status flip-flops and to set the program counter to zero. $\overline{RESET}$ is also used during PROM programming and verification.
$\overline{SS}$	5	I	**SINGLE STEP:** Single step input used in conjunction with the SYNC output to step the program through each instruction.
V_{CC}	40		**POWER:** +5V main power supply pin.
V_{DD}	26		**POWER:** +5V during normal operation. +25V for UPI-41A, 21V for UPI-42 programming operation, +12V for programming, UPI-41AH/42AH. Low power standby pin in ROM version.
V_{SS}	20		**GROUND:** Circuit ground potential.

4

The following sections provide a detailed functional description of the UPI microcomputer. Figure 2-4 illustrates the functional blocks within the UPI device.

CPU SECTION

The CPU section of the UPI-41A/41AH/42/42AH microcomputer performs basic data manipulations and controls data flow throughout the single chip computer via the internal 8-bit data bus. The CPU section includes the following functional blocks shown in Figure 2-4:

- Arithmetic Logic Unit (ALU)
- Instruction Decoder
- Accumulator
- Flags

Arithmetic Logic Units (ALU)

The ALU is capable of performing the following operations:

- ADD with or without carry
- AND, OR, and EXCLUSIVE OR
- Increment, Decrement
- Bit complement
- Rotate left or right
- Swap
- BCD decimal adjust

In a typical operation data from the accumulator is combined in the ALU with data from some other source on the UPI-41A/41AH/42/42AH internal bus (such as a register or an I/O port). The result of an ALU operation can be transferred to the internal bus or back to the accumulator.

If an operation such as an ADD or ROTATE requires more than 8 bits, the CARRY flag is used as an indicator. Likewise, during decimal adjust and other BCD operations the AUXILIARY CARRY flag can be set and acted upon. These flags are part of the Program Status Word (PSW).

Instruction Decoder

During an instruction fetch, the operation code (opcode) portion of each program instruction is stored and decoded by the instruction decoder. The decoder generates outputs used along with various timing signals to control the functions performed in the ALU. Also, the instruction decoder controls the source and destination of ALU data.

Accumulator

The accumulator is the single most important register in the processor. It is the primary source of data to the ALU and is often the destination for results as well. Data to and from the I/O ports and memory normally passes through the accumulator.

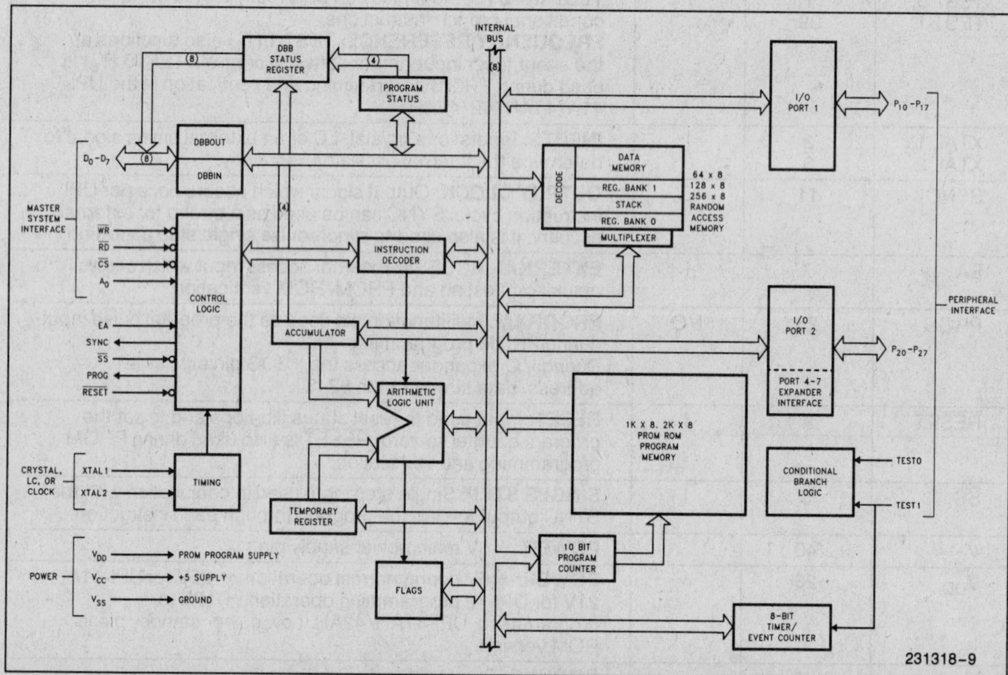

Figure 2-4. UPI-41A/41AH/42/42AH Block Diagram

PROGRAM MEMORY

The UPI-41A/41AH/42/42AH microcomputer has 1024, 2048 8-bit words of resident, read-only memory for program storage. Each of these memory locations is directly addressable by a 10-bit program counter. Depending on the type of application and the number of program changes anticipated, three types of program memory are available:

- 8041AH, 8042AH with mask programmed ROM Memory
- 8741AH, 8742AH with electrically programmable OTP EPROM Memory
- 8741A and 8742 with electrically programmable EPROM Memory

A program memory map is illustrated in Figure 2-5. Memory is divided into 256 location 'pages' and three locations are reserved for special use:

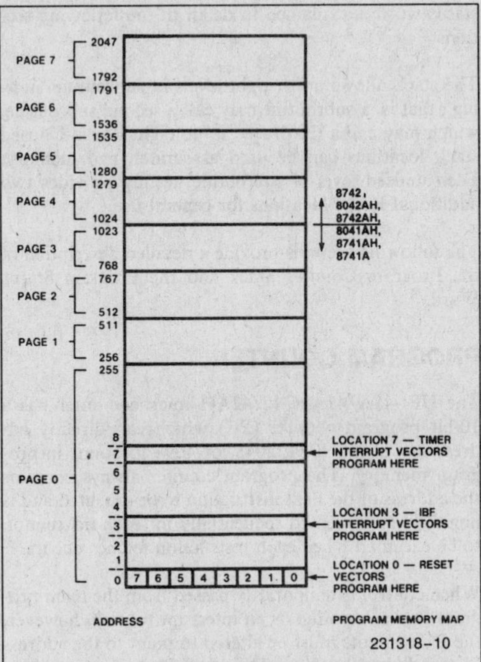

Figure 2-5. Program Memory Map

INTERRUPT VECTORS

1) **Location 0**
   Following a $\overline{\text{RESET}}$ input to the processor, the next instruction is automatically fetched from location 0.

2) **Location 3**
   An interrupt generated by an Input Buffer Full (IBF) condition (when the IBF interrupt is enabled) causes the next instruction to be fetched from location 3.

3) **Location 7**
   A timer overflow interrupt (when enabled) will cause the next instruction to be fetched from location 7.

Following a system $\overline{\text{RESET}}$, program execution begins at location 0. Instructions in program memory are normally executed sequentially. Program control can be transferred out of the main line of code by an input buffer full (IBF) interrupt or a timer interrupt, or when a jump or call instruction is encountered. An IBF interrupt (if enabled) will automatically transfer control to location 3 while a timer interrupt will transfer control to location 7.

All conditional JUMP instructions and the indirect JUMP instruction are limited in range to the current 256-location page (that is, they alter PC bits 0–7 only). If a conditional JUMP or indirect JUMP begins in location 255 of a page, it must reference a destination on the following page.

Program memory can be used to store constants as well as program instructions. The UPI-41AH, 42AH instruction set contains an instruction (MOVP3) designed specifically for efficient transfer of look-up table information from page 3 of memory.

DATA MEMORY

The UPI-41A has 64 8-bit words of Random Access Memory, the UPI-41AH has 128 8-bit words of Random Access Memory; the UPI-42 has 128 8-bit words of RAM; and the UPI-42AH has 256 8-bit words of RAM. This memory contains two working register banks, an 8-level program counter stack and a scratch pad memory, as shown in Figure 2-6. The amount of scratch pad memory available is variable depending on the number of addresses nested in the stack and the number of working registers being used.

Addressing Data Memory

The first eight locations in RAM are designated as working registers R_0–R_7. These locations (or registers) can be addressed directly by specifying a register number in the instruction. Since these locations are easily addressed, they are generally used to store frequently

accessed intermediate results. Other locations in data memory are addressed indirectly by using R_0 or R_1 to specify the desired address.

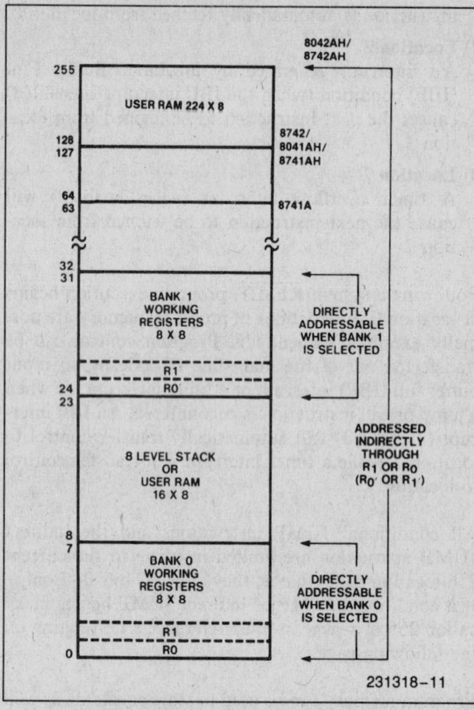

Figure 2-6. Data Memory Map

Working Registers

Dual banks of eight working registers are included in the UPI-41A/41AH/42/42AH data memory. Locations 0–7 make up register bank 0 and locations 24–13 form register bank 1. A $\overline{\text{RESET}}$ signal automatically selects register bank 0. When bank 0 is selected, references to R_0–R_7 in UPI-41A/41AH/42/42AH instructions operate on locations 0–7 in data memory. A "select register bank" instruction is used to selected between the banks during program execution. If the instruction SEL RB1 (Select Register Bank 1) is executed, then program references to R_0–R_7 will operate on locations 24–31. As stated previously, registers 0 and 1 in the active register bank are used as indirect address registers for all locations in data memory.

Register bank 1 is normally reserved for handling interrupt service routines, thereby preserving the contents of the main program registers. The SEL RB1 instruction can be issued at the beginning of an interrupt service routine. Then, upon return to the main program, an RETR (return & restore status) instruction will automatically restore the previously selected bank. During interrupt processing, registers in bank 0 can be accessed indirectly using $R_{0'}$ and $R_{1'}$.

If register bank 1 is not used, registers 24–31 can still serve as additional scratch pad memory.

Program Counter Stack

RAM locations 8–23 are used as an 8-level program counter stack. When program control is temporarily passed from the main program to a subroutine or interrupt service routine, the 10-bit program counter and bits 4–7 of the program status word (PSW) are stored in two stack locations. When control is returned to the main program via an RETR instruction, the program counter and PSW bits 4–7 are restored. Returning via an RET instruction does not restore the PSW bits, however. The program counter stack is addressed by three stack pointer bits in the PSW (bits 0–2). Operation of the program counter stack and the program status word is explained in detail in the following sections.

The stack allows up to eight levels of subroutine 'nesting'; that is, a subroutine may call a second subroutine, which may call a third, etc., up to eight levels. Unused stack locations can be used as scratch pad memory. Each unused level of subroutine nesting provides two additional RAM locations for general use.

The following sections provide a detailed description of the Program Counter Stack and the Program Status Word.

PROGRAM COUNTER

The UPI-41A/41AH/42/42AH microcomputer has a 10-bit program counter (PC) which can directly address any of the 1024, 2048, or 4096 locations in program memory. The program counter always contains the address of the next instruction to be executed and is normally incremented sequentially for each instruction to be executed when each instruction fetches occurs.

When control is temporarily passed from the main program to a subroutine or an interrupt routine, however, the PC contents must be altered to point to the address of the desired routine. The stack is used to save the current PC contents so that, at the end of the routine, main program execution can continue. The program counter is initialized to zero by a $\overline{\text{RESET}}$ signal.

PROGRAM COUNTER STACK

The Program Counter Stack is composed of 16 locations in Data Memory as illustrated in Figure 2-7. These RAM locations (8 through 23) are used to store the 10-bit program counter and 4 bits of the program status word.

An interrupt or Call to a subroutine causes the contents of the program counter to be stored in one of the 8 register pairs of the program counter stack.

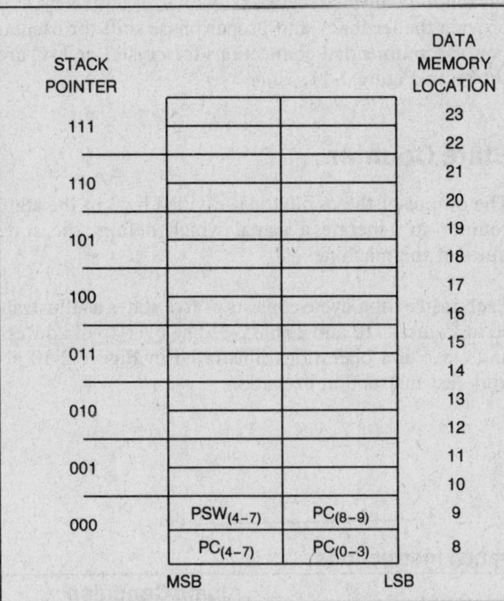

Figure 2-7. Program Counter Stack

A 3-bit Stack Pointer which is part of the Program Status Word (PSW) determines the stack pair to be used at a given time. The stack pointer is initialized by a $\overline{\text{RESET}}$ signal to 00H which corresponds to RAM locations 8 and 9.

The first call or interrupt results in the program counter and PSW contents being transferred to RAM locations 8 and 9 in the format shown in Figure 2-7. The stack pointer is automatically incremented by 1 to point to location is 10 and 11 in anticipation of another CALL.

Nesting of subroutines within subroutines can continue up to 8 levels without overflowing the stack. If overflow does occur the deepest address stored (locations 8 and 9) will be overwritten and lost since the stack pointer overflows from 07H to 00H. Likewise, the stack pointer will underflow from 00H to 07H.

The end of a subroutine is signaled by a return instruction, either RET or RETR. Each instruction will automatically decrement the Stack Pointer and transfer the contents of the proper RAM register pair to the Program Counter.

PROGRAM STATUS WORD

The 8-bit program status word illustrated in Figure 2-8 is used to store general information about program execution. In addition to the 3-bit Stack Pointer discussed previously, the PSW includes the following flags:

- CY — Carry
- AC — Auxiliary Carry
- F_0 — Flag 0
- BS — Register Bank Select

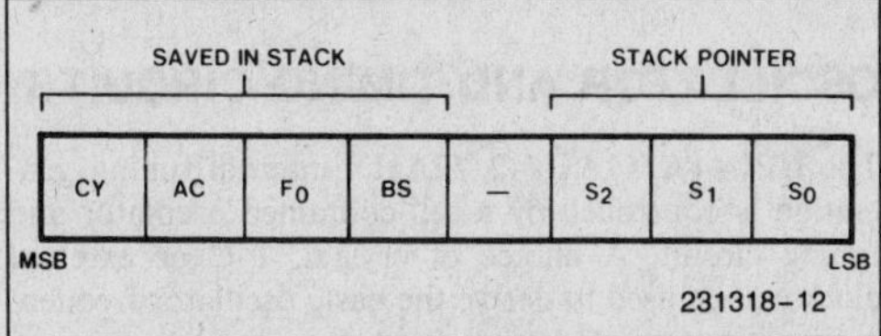

Figure 2-8. Program Status Word

The Program Status Word (PSW) is actually a collection of flip-flops located throughout the machine which are read or written as a whole. The PSW can be loaded to or from the accumulator by the MOV A, PSW or MOV PSW, A instructions. The ability to write directly to the PSW allows easy restoration of machine status after a power-down sequence.

The upper 4 bits of the PSW (bits 4, 5, 6, and 7) are stored in the PC Stack with every subroutine CALL or interrupt vector. Restoring the bits on a return is optional. The bits are restored if an RETR instruction is executed, but not if an RET is executed.

PSW bit definitions are as follows:

- Bits 0–2 Stack Pointer Bits S_0, S_1, S_2
- Bit 3 Not Used
- Bit 4 Working Register Bank
  0 = Bank 0
  1 = Bank 1
- Bit 5 Flag 0 bit (F_0)
  This is a general purpose flag which can be cleared or complemented and tested with conditional jump instructions. It may be used during data transfer to an external processor.
- Bit 6 Auxiliary Carry (AC)
  The flag status is determined by an ADD instruction and is used by the Decimal Adjustment instruction DAA
- Bit 7 Carry (CY)
  The flag indicates that a previous operation resulted in overflow of the accumulator.

CONDITIONAL BRANCH LOGIC

Conditional Branch Logic in the UPI-41AH, 42AH allows the status of various processor flags, inputs, and other hardware functions to directly affect program execution. The status is sampled in state 3 of the first cycle.

Table 2-2 lists the internal conditions which are testable and indicates the condition which will cause a jump. In all cases, the destination address must be within the page of program memory (256 locations) in which the jump instruction occurs.

OSCILLATOR AND TIMING CIRCUITS

The UPI-41A/41AH/42/42AH's internal timing generation is controlled by a self-contained oscillator and timing circuit. A choice of crystal, L-C or external clock can be used to derive the basic oscillator frequency.

The resident timing circuit consists of an oscillator, a state counter and a cycle counter as illustrated in Figure 2-9. Figure 2-10 shows instruction cycle timing.

Oscillator

The on-board oscillator is a series resonant circuit with a frequency range of 1 to 12.5 MHz depending on which UPI is used. Refer to Table 1.1. Pins XTAL 1 and XTAL 2 are input and output (respectively) of a high gain amplifier stage. A crystal or inductor and capacitor connected between XTAL 1 and XTAL 2 provide the feedback and proper phase shift for oscillation. Recommended connections for crystal or L-C are shown in Figure 2-11.

State Counter

The output of the oscillator is divided by 3 in the state counter to generate a signal which defines the state times of the machine.

Each instruction cycle consists of five states as illustrated in Figure 2-10 and Table 2-3. The overlap of address and execution operations illustrated in Figure 2-10 allows fast instruction execution.

Table 2-2. Conditional Branch Instructions

Device	Instruction Mnemonic		Jump Condition Jump if:
Accumulator	JZ	addr	All bits zero
	JNZ	addr	Any bit not zero
Accumulator bit	JBb	addr	Bit "b" = 1
Carry flag	JC	addr	Carry flag = 1
	JNC	addr	Carry flag = 0
User flag	JFO	addr	F_0 flag = 1
	JF1	addr	F_1 flag = 1
Timer flag	JTF	addr	Timer flag = 1
Test Input 0	JT0	addr	T_0 = 1
	JNT0	addr	T_0 = 0
Test Input 1	JT1	addr	T_1 = 1
	JNT1	addr	T_1 = 0
Input Buffer flag	JNIBF	addr	IBF flag = 0
Output Buffer flag	JOBF	addr	OBF flag = 1

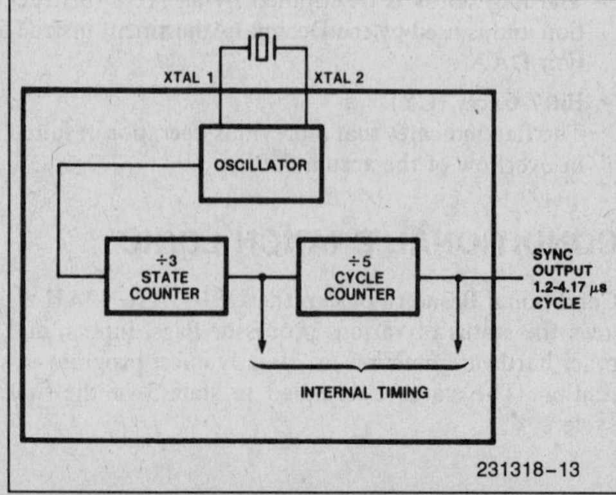

Figure 2-9. Oscillator Configuration

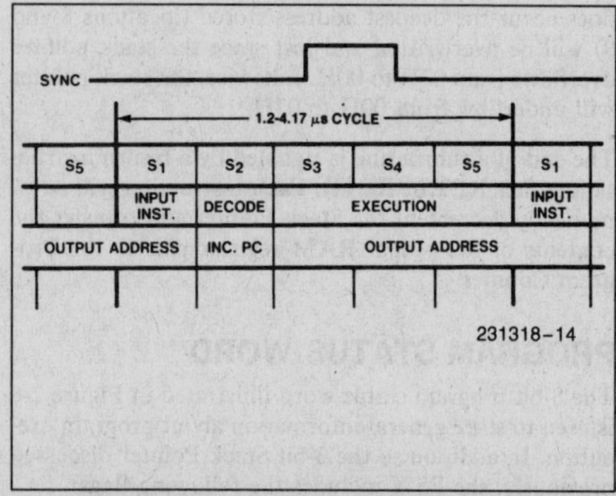

Figure 2-10. Instruction Cycle Timing

Table 2-3. Instruction Timing Diagram

Instruction	CYCLE 1					CYCLE 2				
	S1	S2	S3	S4	S5	S1	S2	S3	S4	S5
IN A,Pp	Fetch Instruction	Increment Program Counter	—	Increment Timer	—	—	Read Port	—	—	—
OUTL Pp,A	Fetch Instruction	Increment Program Counter	—	Increment Timer	Output To Port	—	—	—	—	—
ANL Pp, DATA	Fetch Instruction	Increment Program Counter	—	Increment Timer	Read Port	Fetch Immediate Data	—	Increment Program Counter	Output To Port	—
ORL Pp, DATA	Fetch Instruction	Increment Program Counter	—	Increment Timer	Read Port	Fetch Immediate Data	—	Increment Program Counter	Output To Port	—
MOVD A,Pp	Fetch Instruction	Increment Program Counter	Output Opcode/Address	Increment Timer	—	—	Read P2 Lower	—	—	—
MOVD Pp, A	Fetch Instruction	Increment Program Counter	Output Opcode/Address	Increment Timer	Output Data To P2 Lower	—	—	—	—	—
D Pp, A	Fetch Instruction	Increment Program Counter	Output Opcode/Address	Increment Timer	Output Data	—	—	—	—	—
ORLD Pp, A	Fetch Instruction	Increment Program Counter	Output Opcode/Address	Increment Timer	Output Data	—	—	—	—	—
J (Conditional)	Fetch Instruction	Increment Program Counter	Sample Condition	Increment Timer	—	Fetch Immediate Data	—	Update Program Counter	—	—
MOV STS, A	Fetch Instruction	Increment Program Counter	—	Increment Timer	Update Status Register					
IN A, DBB	Fetch Instruction	Increment Program Counter	—	Increment Timer	—					
OUT DBB, A	Fetch Instruction	Increment Program Counter	—	Increment Timer	Output To Port					
STRT T STRT CNT	Fetch Instruction	Increment Program Counter	—	—	Start Counter					
STOP TCNT	Fetch Instruction	Increment Program Counter	—	—	Stop Counter					
EN I	Fetch Instruction	Increment Program Counter	—	Enable Interrupt	—					
DIS I	Fetch Instruction	Increment Program Counter	—	Disable Interrupt	—					
EN DMA	Fetch Instruction	Increment Program Counter	—	DMA Enabled DRQ Cleared	—					
EN FLAGS	Fetch Instruction	Increment Program Counter	—	OBF, $\overline{IBF}$ Output Enabled	—					

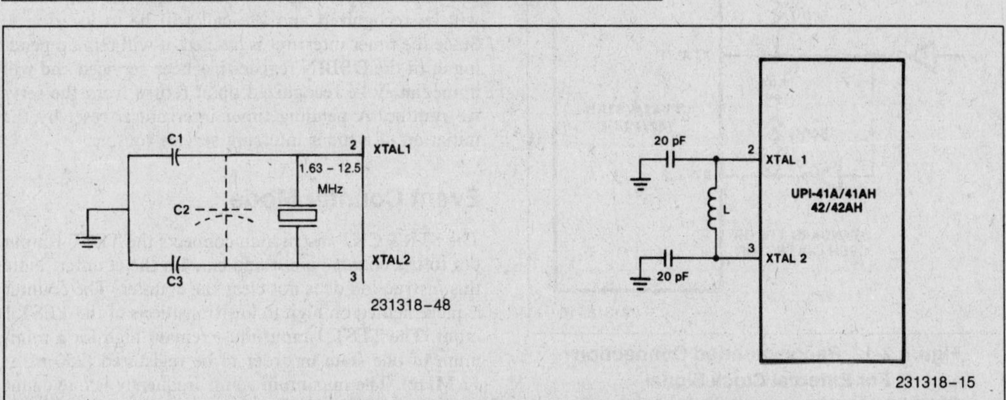

Figure 2-11. Recommended Crystal and L-C Connections

Cycle Counter

The output of the state counter is divided by 5 in the cycle counter to generate a signal which defines a machine cycle. This signal is call SYNC and is available continuously on the SYNC output pin. It can be used to synchronize external circuitry or as a general purpose clock output. It is also used for synchronizing single-step.

Frequency Reference

The external crystal provides high speed and accurate timing generation. A crystal frequency of 5.9904 MHz is useful for generation of standard communication frequencies by the UPI-41A/41AH/42/42AH. However, if an accurate frequency reference and maximum processor speed are not required, an inductor and capacitor may be used in place of the crystal as shown in Figure 2-11.

A recommended range of inductance and capacitance combinations is given below:

- L = 130 μH corresponds to 3 MHz
- L = 45 μH corresponds to 5 MHz

An external clock signal can also be used as a frequency reference to the UPI-41A/41AH/42/42AH; however, the levels are *not* TTL compatible. The signal must be in the 1–12.5 MHz frequency range depending on which UPI is used. Refer to Table 1-2. The signal must be connected to pins XTAL 1 and XTAL 2 by buffers with a suitable pull-up resistor to guarantee that a logic "1" is above 3.8 volts. The recommended connection is shown in Figure 2-12.

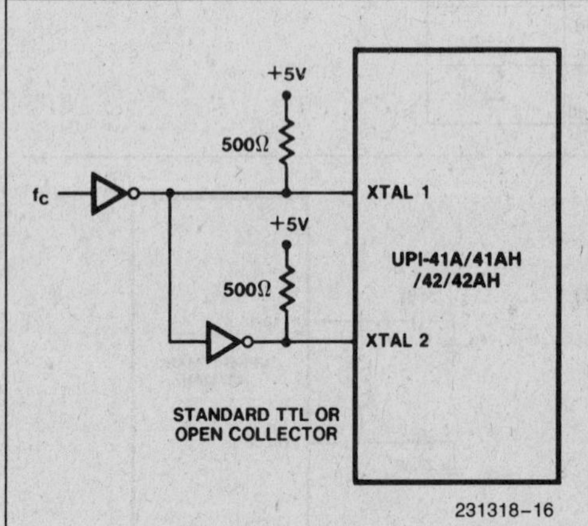

Figure 2-12. Recommended Connection For External Clock Signal

INTERVAL TIMER/EVENT COUNTER

The UPI-41A/41AH/42/42AH has a resident 8-bit timer/counter which has several software selectable modes of operation. As an interval timer, it can generate accurate delays from 80 microseconds to 20.48 milliseconds without placing undue burden on the processor. In the counter mode, external events such as switch closures or tachometer pulses can be counted and used to direct program flow.

Timer Configuration

Figure 2-13 illustrates the basic timer/counter configuration. An 8-bit register is used to count pulses from either the internal clock and prescaler or from an external source. The counter is presettable and readable with two MOV instructions which transfer the contents of the accumulator to the counter and vice-versa (i.e. MOV T, A and MOV A, T). The counter is stopped by a $\overline{\text{RESET}}$ or STOP TCNT instruction and remains stopped until restarted either as a timer (START T instruction) or as a counter (START CNT instruction). Once started, the counter will increment to its maximum count (FFH) and overflow to zero continuing its count until stopped by a STOP TCNT instruction or $\overline{\text{RESET}}$.

The increment from maximum count to zero (overflow) results in setting the Timer Flag (TF) and generating an interrupt request. The state of the overflow flag is testable with the conditional jump instruction, JTF. The flag is reset by executing a JTF or by a $\overline{\text{RESET}}$ signal.

The timer interrupt request is stored in a latch and ORed with the input buffer full interrupt request. The timer interrupt can be enabled or disabled independent of the IBF interrupt by the EN TCNTI and DIS TCTNI instructions. If enabled, the counter overflow will cause a subroutine call to location 7 where the timer service routine is stored. If the timer and Input Buffer Full interrupts occur simultaneously, the IBF source will be recognized and the call will be to location 3. Since the timer interrupt is latched, it will remain pending until the DBBIN register has been serviced and will immediately be recognized upon return from the service routine. A pending timer interrupt is reset by the initiation of a timer interrupt service routine.

Event Counter Mode

The STRT CNT instruction connects the TEST 1 input pin to the counter input and enables the counter. Note this instruction does not clear the counter. The counter is incremented on high to low transitions of the TEST 1 input. The TEST 1 input must remain high for a minimum of one state in order to be registered (250 ns at 12 MHz). The maximum count frequency is one count per three instruction cycles (267 kHz at 12 MHz). There is no minimum frequency limit.

Timer Mode

The STRT T instruction connects the internal clock to the counter input and enables the counter. The input clock is derived from the SYNC signal of the internal oscillator and the divide-by-32 prescaler. The configuration is illustrated in Figure 2-13. Note this instruction does not clear the timer register. Various delays and timing sequences between 40 μsec and 10.24 msec can easily be generated with a minimum of software timing loops (at 12 MHz).

Times longer than 10.24 msec can be accurately measured by accumulating multiple overflows in a register under software control. For time resolution less than 40 μsec, an external clock can be applied to the TEST 1 counter input (see Event Counter Mode). The minimum time resolution with an external clock is 3.75 μsec (267 kHz at 12 MHz).

TEST 1 Event Counter Input

The TEST 1 pin is multifunctional. It is automatically initialized as a test input by a $\overline{\text{RESET}}$ signal and can be tested using UPI-41A conditional branch instructions.

In the second mode of operation, illustrated in Figure 2-13, the TEST 1 pin is used as an input to the internal 8-bit event counter. The Start Counter (STRT CNT) instruction controls an internal switch which connects TEST 1 through an edge detector to the 8-bit internal counter. Note that this instruction does not inhibit the testing of TEST 1 via conditional Jump instructions.

In the counter mode the TEST 1 input is sampled once per instruction cycle. After a high level is detected, the next occurrence of a low level at TEST 1 will cause the counter to increment by one.

The event counter functions can be stopped by the Stop Timer/Counter (STOP TCNT) instruction. When this instruction is executed the TEST 1 pin becomes a test input and functions as previously described.

TEST INPUTS

There are two multifunction pins designated as Test Inputs, TEST 0 and TEST 1. In the normal mode of operation, status of each of these lines can be directly tested using the following conditional Jump instructions:

- JT0 Jump if TEST 0 = 1
- JNT0 Jump if TEST 0 = 0
- JT1 Jump if TEST 1 = 1
- JNT1 Jump if TEST 1 = 0

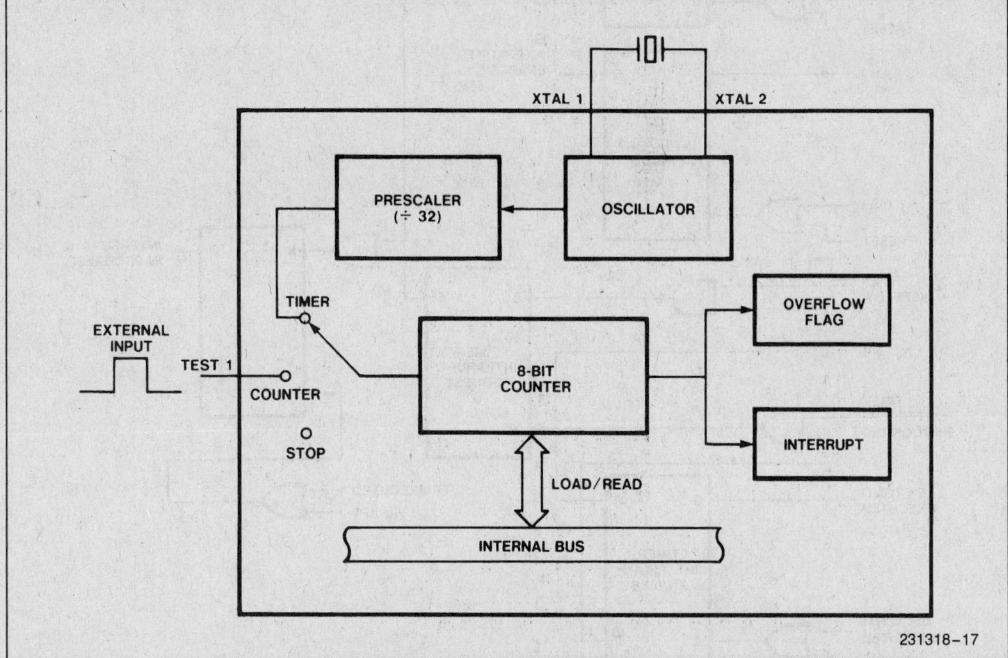

Figure 2-13. Timer Counter

The test imputs are TTL compatible. An external logic signal connected to one of the test inputs will be sampled at the time the appropriate conditional jump instruction is executed. The path of program execution will be altered depending on the state of the external signal when sampled.

INTERRUPTS

The UPI-41A/41AH/42/42AH has the following internal interrupts:

- Input Buffer Full (IBF) interrupt
- Timer Overflow interrupt

The IBF interrupt forces a CALL to location 3 in program memory; a timer-overflow interrupts forces a CALL to location 7. The IBF interrupt is enabled by the EN I instruction and disabled by the DIS I instruction. The timer-overflow interrupt is enabled and disabled by the EN TNCTI and DIS TCNTI instructions, respectively.

Figure 2-14 illustrates the internal interrupt logic. An IBF interrupt request is generated whenever $\overline{WR}$ and $\overline{CS}$ are both low, regardless of whether interrupts are enabled. The interrupt request is cleared upon entering the IBF service routine only. That is, the DIS I instruction does not clear a pending IBF interrupt.

Interrupt Timing Latency

When the IBF interrupt is enabled and an IBF interrupt request occurs, an interrupt sequence is intiated as soon as the currently executing instruction is completed. The following sequence occurs:

- A CALL to location 3 is forced.
- The program counter and bits 4–7 of the Program Status Word are stored in the stack.
- The stack pointer is incremented.

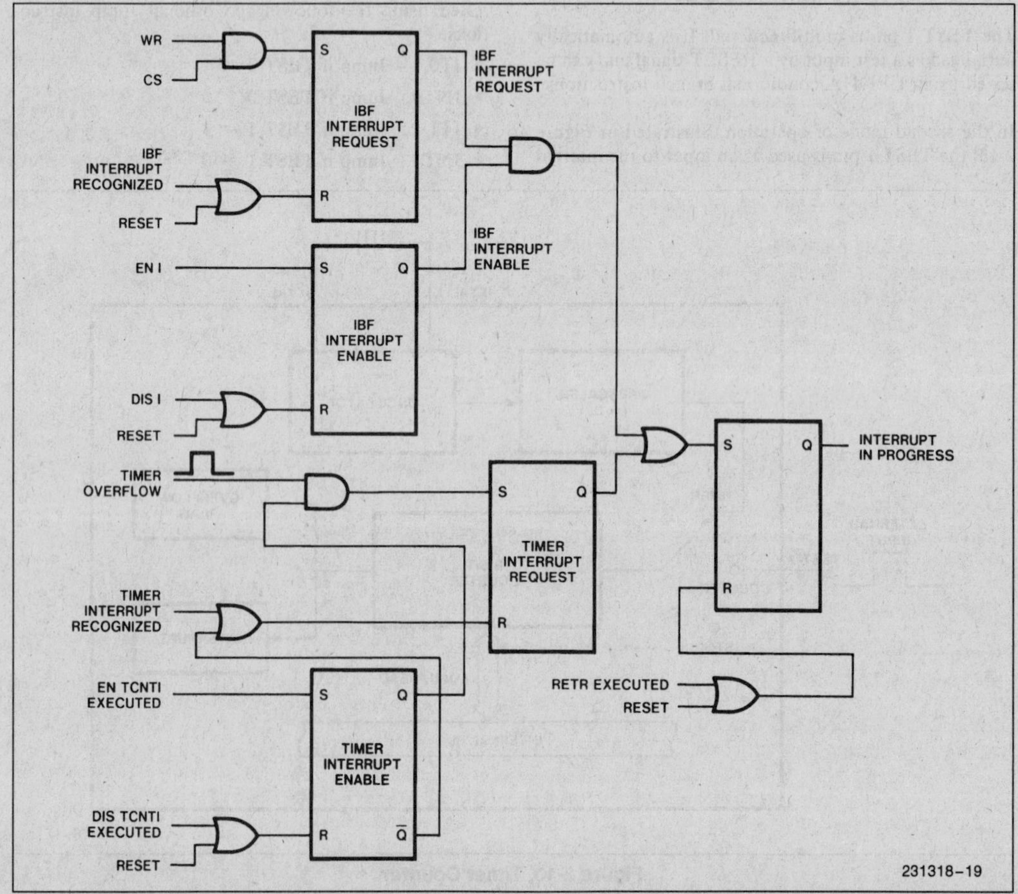

WR
CS
S Q
IBF INTERRUPT REQUEST
IBF INTERRUPT REQUEST
IBF INTERRUPT RECOGNIZED
RESET
R
EN I
S Q
IBF INTERRUPT ENABLE
IBF INTERRUPT ENABLE
DIS I
RESET
R
TIMER OVERFLOW
S Q
TIMER INTERRUPT REQUEST
R
S Q
INTERRUPT IN PROGRESS
R
TIMER INTERRUPT RECOGNIZED
EN TCNTI EXECUTED
S Q
TIMER INTERRUPT ENABLE
DIS TCNTI EXECUTED
RESET
R $\overline{Q}$
RETR EXECUTED
RESET
231318–19

Figure 2-14. Interrupt Logic

Location 3 in program memory should contain an unconditional jump to the beginning of the IBF interrupt service routine elsewhere in program memory. At the end of the service routine, an RETR (Return and Restore Status) instruction is used to return control to the main program. This instruction will restore the program counter and PSW bits 4–7, providing automatic restoration of the previously active register bank as well. RETR also re-enables interrupts.

A timer-overflow interrupt is enabled by the EN TCNTI instruction and disabled by the DIS TCNTI instruction. If enabled, this interrupt occurs when the timer/counter register overflows. A CALL to location 7 is forced and the interrupt routine proceeds as described above.

The interrupt service latency is the sum of current instruction time, interrupt recognition time, and the internal call to the interrupt vector address. The worst case latency time for servicing an interrupt is 7 clock cycles. Best case latency is 4 clock cycles.

Interrupt Timing

Interrupt inputs may be enabled or disabled under program control using EN I, DIS I, EN TCNTI and DIS TCNTI instructions. Also, a $\overline{\text{RESET}}$ input will disable interrupts. An interrupt request must be removed before the RETR instruction is executed to return from the service routine, otherwise the processor will re-enter the service routine immediately. Thus, the $\overline{\text{WR}}$ and $\overline{\text{CS}}$ inputs should not be held low longer than the duration of the interrupt service routine.

The interrupt system is single level. Once an interrupt is detected, all further interrupt requests are latched but are not acted upon until execution of an RETR instruction re-enables the interrupt input logic. This occurs at the beginning of the second cycle of the RETR instruction. If an IBF interrupt and a timer-overflow interrupt occur simultaneously, the IBF interrupt will be recognized first and the timer-overflow interrupt will remain pending until the end of the interrupt service routine.

External Interrupts

An external interrupt can be created using the UPI-41A/41AH/42/42AH timer/counter in the event counter mode. The counter is first preset to FFH and the EN TCNTI instruction is executed. A timer-overflow interrupt is generated by the first high to low transition of the TEST 1 input pin. Also, if an IBF interrupt occurs during servicing of the timer/counter interrupt, it will remain pending until the end of the servicc routine.

Host Interrupts And DMA

If needed, two external interrupts to the host system can be created using the EN FLAGS instruction. This instruction allocates two I/O lines on PORT 2 (P_{24} and P_{25}). P_{24} is the Output Buffer Full interrupt request line to the host system; P_{25} is the Input Buffer empty interrupt request line. These interrupt outputs reflect the internal status of the OBF flag and the IBF inverted flag. Note, these outputs may be inhibited by writing a "0" to these pins. Reenabling interrupts is done by writing a "1" to these port pins. Interrupts are typically enabled after power on since the I/O ports are set in a "1" condition. The EN FLAG's effect is only cancelled by a device RESET.

DMA handshaking controls are available from two pins on PORT 2 of the UPI-41A/41AH/42/42AH microcomputer. These lines (P_{26} and P_{27}) are enabled by the EN DMA instruction. P_{26} becomes DMA request (DRQ) and P_{27} becomes DMA acknowledge ($\overline{\text{DACK}}$). The UPI program initiates a DMA request by writing a "1" to P_{26}. The DMA controller transfers the data into the DBBIN data register using DACK which acts as a chip select. The EN DMA instruction can only be cancelled by a chip RESET.

RESET

The $\overline{\text{RESET}}$ input provides a means for internal initialization of the processor. An automatic initialization pulse can be generated at power-on by simply connecting a 1 μfd capacitor between the $\overline{\text{RESET}}$ input and ground as shown in Figure 2-15. It has an internal pull-up resistor to charge the capacitor and a Schmitt-trigger circuit to generate a clean transition. A 2-stage synchronizer has been added to support reliable operation up to 12.5 MHz.

If automatic initialization is used, $\overline{\text{RESET}}$ should be held low for at least 10 milliseconds to allow the power supply to stabilize. If an external $\overline{\text{RESET}}$ signal is used, $\overline{\text{RESET}}$ may be held low for a minimum of 8 instruction cycles. Figure 2-15 illustrates a configuration using an external TTL gate to generate the $\overline{\text{RESET}}$ input. This configuration can be used to derive the $\overline{\text{RESET}}$ signal from the 8224 clock generator in an 8080 system.

4

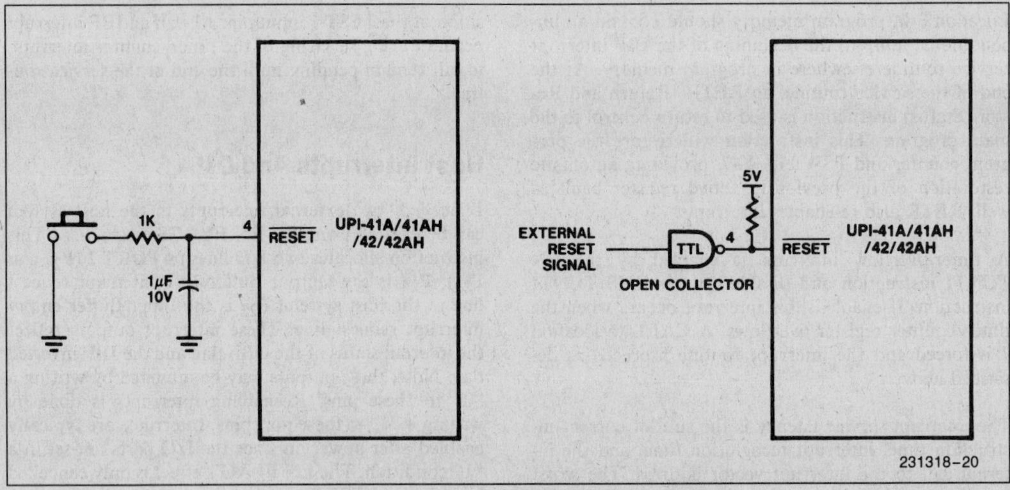

Figure 2-15. External Reset Configuration

The $\overline{\text{RESET}}$ input performs the following functions:

- Disables Interrupts
- Clears Program Counter to Zero
- Clears Stack Pointer
- Clears Status Register and Flags
- Clears Timer and Timer Flag
- Stops Timer
- Selects Register Bank 0
- Sets PORTS 1 and 2 to Input Mode

DATA BUS BUFFER

Two 8-bit data bus buffer registers, DBBIN and DBBOUT, serve as temporary buffers for commands and data flowing between it and the master processor. Externally, data is transmitted or received by the DBB registers upon execution of an INput or OUTput instruction by the master processor. Four control signals are used:

- A_0 Address input signifying control or data
- $\overline{\text{CS}}$ Chip Select
- $\overline{\text{RD}}$ Read Strobe
- $\overline{\text{WR}}$ Write Strobe

Transfer can be implemented with or without UPI program interference by enabling or disabling an internal UPI interrupt. Internally, data transfer between the DBB and the UPI accumulator is under software control and is completely asynchronous to the external processor timing. This allows the UPI software to handle peripheral control tasks independent of the main processor while still maintaining a data interface with the master system.

Configuration

Figure 2-16 illustrates the internal configuration of the DBB registers. Data is stored in two 8-bit buffer registers, DBBIN and DBBOUT. DBBIN and DBBOUT may be accessed by the external processor using the $\overline{\text{WR}}$ line and the $\overline{\text{RD}}$ line, respectively. The data bus is a bidirectional, three-state bus which can be connected directly to an 8-bit microprocessor system. Four control lines ($\overline{\text{WR}}$, $\overline{\text{RD}}$, $\overline{\text{CS}}$, A_0) are used by the external processor to transfer data to and from the DBBIN and DBBOUT registers.

An 8-bit register containing status flags is used to indicate the status of the DBB registers. The eight status flags are defined as follows:

- **OBF Output Buffer Full**
  This flag is automatically set when the UPI-Microcomputer loads the DBBOUT register and is cleared when the master processor reads the data register.
- **IBF Input Buffer Full**
  This flag is set when the master processor writes a character to the DBBIN register and is cleared when the UPI INputs the data register contents to its accumulator.

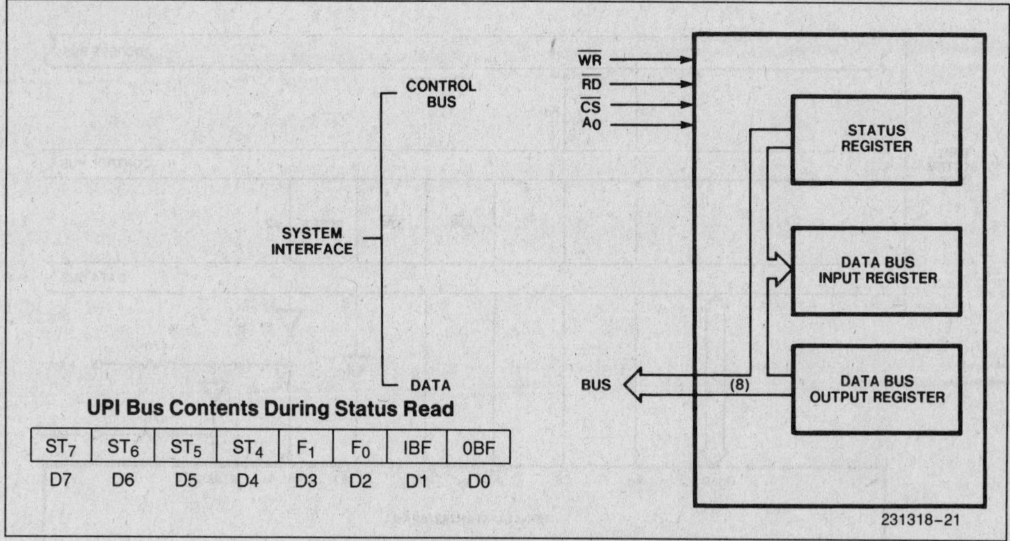

Figure 2-16. Data Bus Buffer Configuration

- **F_0**
  This is a general purpose flag which can be cleared or toggled under UPI software control. The flag is used to transfer UPI status information to the master processor.
- **F_1 Command/Data**
  This flag is set to the condition of the A_0 input line when the master processor writes a character to the data register. The F_1 flag can also be cleared or toggled under UPI-Microcomputer program control.
- **ST4 through ST7**
  These bits are user defined status bits. They are defined by the MOV STS,A instruction.

SYSTEM INTERFACE

Figure 2-17 illustrates how a UPI-Microcomputer can be connected to a standard 8080-type bus system. Data lines D_0–D_7 form a three-state, bidirectional port which can be connected directly to the system data bus. The UPI bus interface has sufficient drive capability (400 μA) for small systems, however, a larger system may require buffers.

Four control signals are required to handle the data and status information transfer:

- $\overline{WR}$
  I/O WRITE signal used to transfer data from the system bus to the UPI DBBIN register and set the F_1 flag in the status register.
- $\overline{RD}$
  I/O READ signal used to transfer data from the DBBOUT register or status register to the system data bus.
- $\overline{CS}$
  CHIP SELECT signal used to enable one 8041AH out of several connected to a common bus.
- A_0
  Address input used to select either the 8-bit status register or DBBOUT register during an I/O READ. Also, the signal is used to set the F_1 flag in the status register during an I/O WRITE.

The $\overline{WR}$ and $\overline{RD}$ signals are active low and are standard MCS-80 peripheral control signals used to synchronize data transfer between the system bus and peripheral devices.

The $\overline{CS}$ and A_0 signals are decoded from the address bus of the master system. In a system with few I/O devices a linear addressing configuration can be used where A_0 and A_1 lines are connected directly to A_0 and $\overline{CS}$ inputs (see Figure 2-17).

Data Read

Table 2-4 illustrates the relative timing of a DBBOUT Read. When $\overline{CS}$, A_0, and $\overline{RD}$ are low, the contents of the DBBOUT register is placed on the three-state Data lines D_0–D_7 and the OBF flag is cleared.

The master processor uses $\overline{CS}$, A_0, $\overline{WR}$, and $\overline{RD}$ to control data transfer between the DBBOUT register and the master system. The following operations are under master processor control:

4

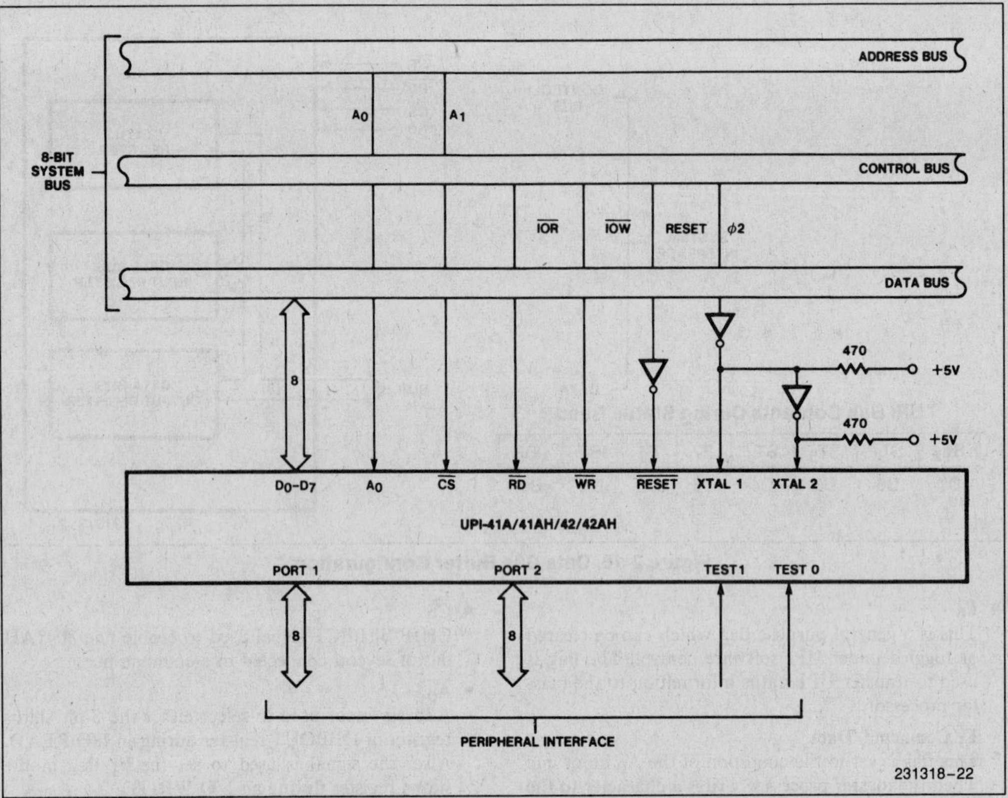

Figure 2-17. Interface to 8080 System Bus

Table 2-4. Data Transfer Controls

$\overline{CS}$	$\overline{RD}$	$\overline{WR}$	A_0	
0	0	1	0	Read DBBOUT register
0	0	1	1	Read STATUS register
0	1	0	0	Write DBBIN data register
0	1	0	1	Write DBBIN command register
1	x	x	x	Disable DBB

Status Read

Table 2-4 shows the logic sequence required for a STATUS register read. When $\overline{CS}$ and $\overline{RD}$ are low with A_0 high, the contents of the 8-bit status register appears on Data lines D_0–D_7.

Data Write

Table 2-4 shows the sequence for writing information to the DBBIN register. When $\overline{CS}$ and $\overline{WR}$ are low, the contents of the system data bus is latched into DBBIN. Also, the IBF flag is set and an interrupt is generated, if enabled.

Command Write

During any write (Table 2-4), the state of the A_0 input is latched into the status register in the F_1 (command/data) flag location. This additional bit is used to signal whether DBBIN contents are command ($A_0 = 1$) or data ($A_0 = 0$) information.

INPUT/OUTPUT INTERFACE

The UPI-41A/41AH/42/42AH has 16 lines for input and output functions. These I/O lines are grouped as two 8-bit TTL compatible ports: PORTS 1 and 2. The port lines can individually function as either inputs or outputs under software control. In addition, the lower 4 lines of PORT 2 can be used to interface to an 8243 I/O expander device to increase I/O capacity to 28 or more lines. The additional lines are grouped as 4-bit ports: PORTS 4, 5, 6, and 7.

PORTS 1 and 2

PORTS 1 and 2 are each 8 bits wide and have the same I/O characteristics. Data written to these ports by an

OUTL Pp,A instruction is latched and remains unchanged until it is rewritten. Input data is sampled at the time the IN, A, Pp instruction is executed. Therefore, input data must be present at the PORT until read by an INput instruction. PORT 1 and 2 inputs are fully TTL compatible and outputs will drive one standard TTL load.

Circuit Configuration

The PORT 1 and 2 lines have a special output structure (shown in Figure 2-18) that allows each line to serve as an input, an output, or both, even though outputs are statically latched.

Each line has a permanent high impedance pull-up (50 KΩ) which is sufficient to provide source current for a TTL high level, yet can be pulled low by a standard TTL gate drive. Whenever a "1" is written to a line, a low impedance pull-up (250Ω) is switched in momentarily (500 ns) to provide a fast transition from 0 to 1. When a "0" is written to the line, a low impedance pull-down (300Ω) is active to provide TTL current sinking capability.

To use a particular PORT pin as an input, a logic "1" must first be written to that pin.

NOTE:
A $\overline{\text{RESET}}$ initializes all PORT pins to the high impedance logic "1" state.

An external TTL device connected to the pin has sufficient current sinking capability to pull-down the pin to the low state. An IN A, Pp instruction will sample the status of PORT pin and will input the proper logic level. With no external input connected, the IN A,Pp instruction inputs the previous output status.

This structure allows input and output information on the same pin and also allows any mix of input and output lines on the same port. However, when inputs and outputs are mixed on one PORT, a PORT write will cause the strong internal pull-ups to turn on at all inputs. If a switch or other low impedance device is connected to an input, a PORT write ("1" to an input) could cause current limits on internal lines to be exceeded. Figure 2-19 illustrates the recommended connection when inputs and outputs are mixed on one PORT.

The bidirectional port structure in combination with the UPI-41A/41AH/42/42AH logical AND and OR instructions provide an efficient means for handling single line inputs and outputs within an 8-bit processor.

PORTS 4, 5, 6, and 7

By using an 8243 I/O expander, 16 additional I/O lines can be connected to the UPI-41AH, 42AH and directly addressed as 4-bit I/O ports using UPI-41AH, 42AH

4

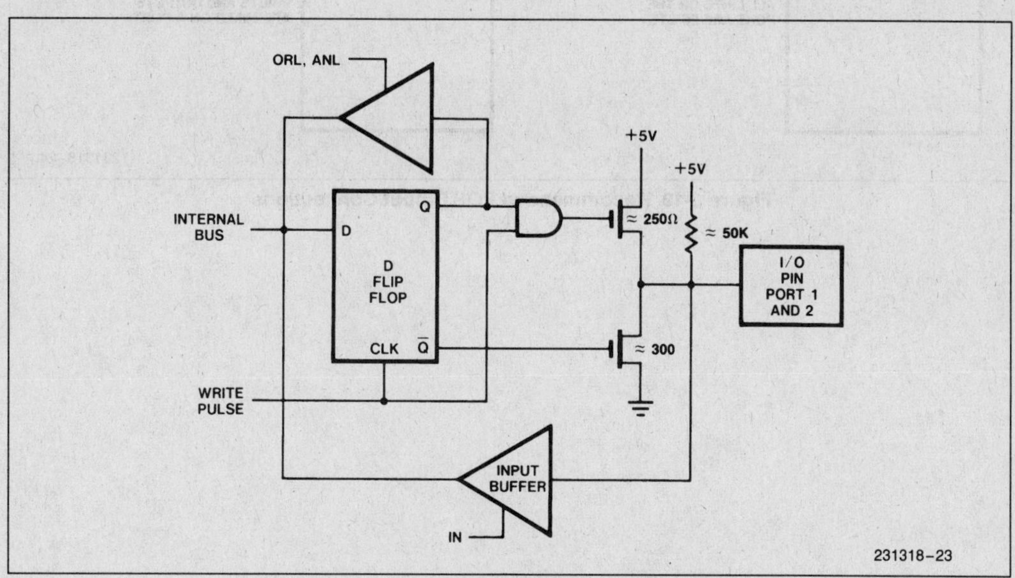

Figure 2-18. Quasi-Bidirectional Port Structure

instructions. This feature saves program space and design time, and improves the bit handling capability of the UPI-41A/41AH/42/42AH.

The lower half of PORT 2 provides an interface to the 8243 as illustrated in Figure 2-20. The PROG pin is used as a strobe to clock address and data information via the PORT 2 interface. The extra 16 I/O lines are referred to in UPI software as PORTS 4, 5, 6, and 7. Each PORT can be directly addressed and can be ANDed and ORed with an immediate data mask. Data can be moved directly to the accumulator from the expander PORTS (or vice-versa).

The 8243 I/O ports, PORTS 4, 5, 6, and 7, provide more drive capability than the UPI-41A/41AH/42/42AH bidirectional ports. The 8243 output is capable of driving about 5 standard TTL loads.

Multiple 8243's can be connected to the PORT 2 interface. In normal operation, only one of the 8243's would be active at the time an Input or Output command is executed. The upper half of PORT 2 is used to provide chip select signals to the 8043's. Figure 2-21 shows how four 8243's could be connected. Software is needed to select and set the proper PORT 2 pin before an INPUT or OUTPUT command to PORTS 4–7 is executed. In general, the software overhead required is very minor compared to the added flexibility of having a large number of I/O pins available.

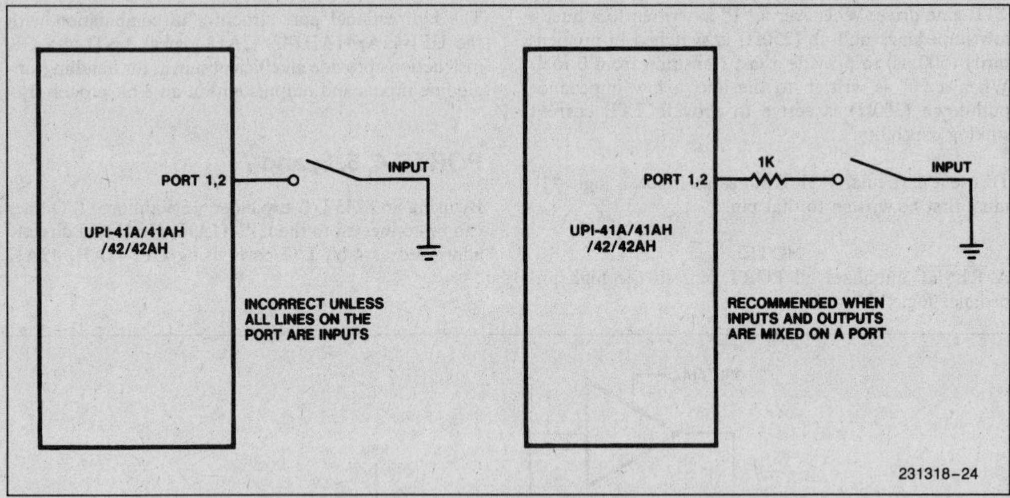

Figure 2-19. Recommended PORT Input Connections

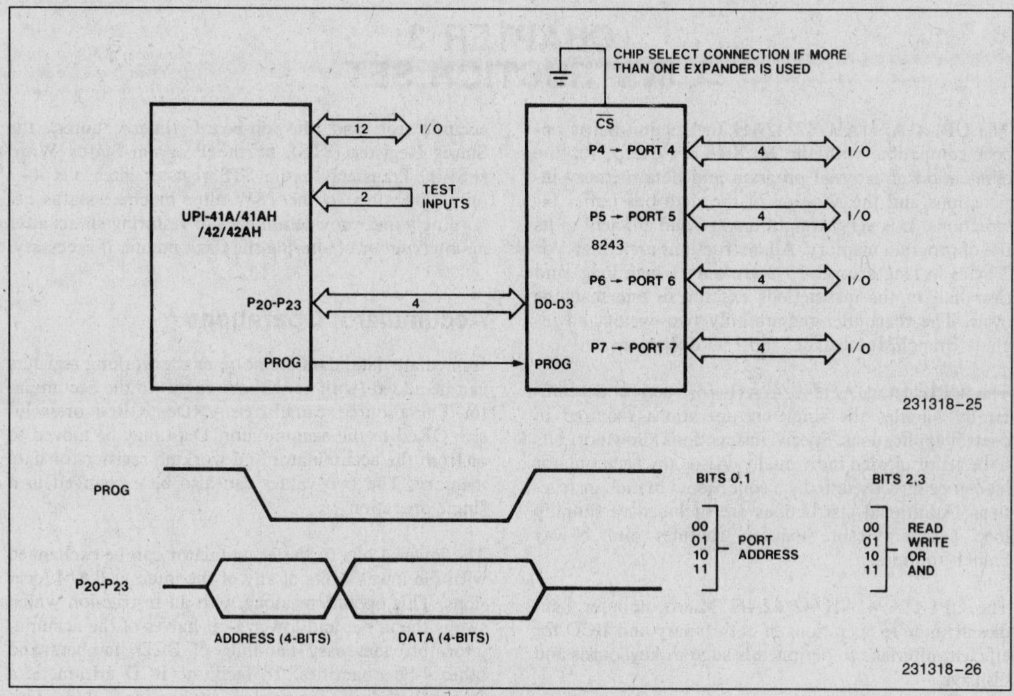

Figure 2-20. 8243 Expander Interface

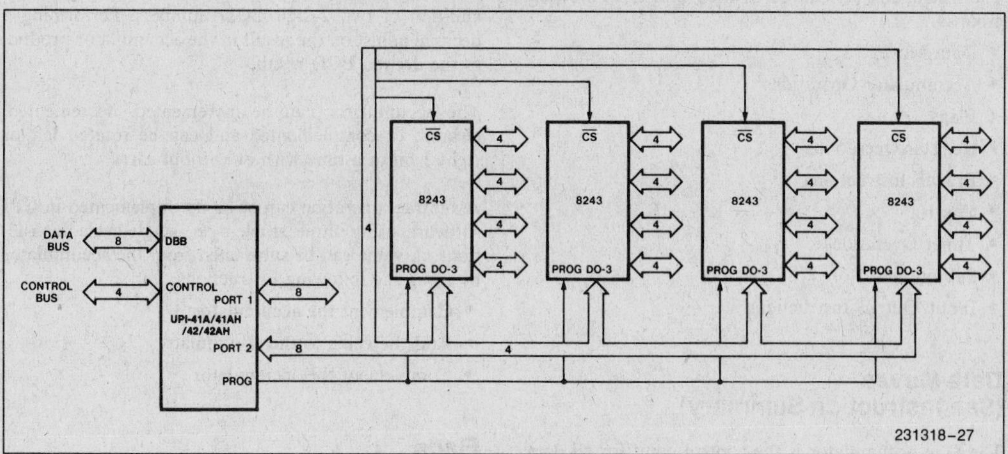

Figure 2-21. Multiple 8243 Expansion

4

CHAPTER 3
INSTRUCTION SET

The UPI-41A/41AH/42/42AH Instruction Set is opcode-compatible with the MCS-48 set except for the elimination of external program and data memory instructions and the addition of the data bus buffer instructions. It is very straightforward and efficient in its use of program memory. All instructions are either 1 or 2 bytes in length (over 70% are only 1 byte long) and over half of the instructions execute in one machine cycle. The remainder require only two cycles and include Branch, Immediate, and I/O operations.

The UPI-41A/41AH/42/42AH Instruction Set efficiently handles the single-bit operations required in control applications. Special instructions allow port bits to be set or cleared individually. Also, any accumulator bit can be directly tested via conditional branch instructions. Additional instructions are included to simplify loop counters, table look-up routines and N-way branch routines.

The UPI-41A/41AH/42/42AH Microcomputer handles arithmetic operations in both binary and BCD for efficient interface to peripherals such as keyboards and displays.

The instruction set can be divided into the following groups:

- Data Moves
- Accumulator Operations
- Flags
- Register Operations
- Branch Instructions
- Control
- Timer Operations
- Subroutines
- Input/Output Instructions

Data Moves (See Instruction Summary)

The 8-bit accumulator is the control point for all data transfers within the UPI-41A/41AH/42/42AH. Data can be transferred between the 8 registers of each working register bank and the accumulator directly (i.e., with a source or destination register specified by 3 bits in the instruction). The remaining locations in the RAM array are addressed either by R_0 or R_1 of the active register bank. Transfers to and from RAM require one cycle.

Constants stored in Program Memory can be loaded directly into the accumulator or the eight working registers. Data can also be transferred directly between the accumulator and the on-board timer/counter, the Status Register (STS), or the Program Status Word (PSW). Transfers to the STS register alter bits 4–7 only. Transfers to the PSW alter machine status accordingly and provide a means of restoring status after an interrupt or of altering the stack pointer if necessary.

Accumulator Operations

Immediate data, data memory, or the working registers can be added (with or without carry) to the accumulator. These sources can also be ANDed, ORed, or exclusive ORed to the accumulator. Data may be moved to or from the accumulator and working registers or data memory. The two values can also be exchanged in a single operation.

The lower 4 bits of the accumulator can be exchanged with the lower 4 bits of any of the internal RAM locations. This operation, along with an instruction which swaps the upper and lower 4-bit halves of the accumulator, provides easy handling of BCD numbers and other 4-bit quantities. To facilitate BCD arithmetic a Decimal Adjust instruction is also included. This instruction is used to correct the result of the binary addition of two 2-digit BCD numbers. Performing a decimal adjust on the result in the accumulator produces the desired BCD result.

The accumulator can be incremented, decremented, cleared, or complemented and can be rotated left or right 1 bit at a time with or without carry.

A subtract operation can be easily implemented in UPI software using three single-byte, single-cycle instructions. A value can be subtracted from the accumulator by using the following instructions:

- Complement the accumulator
- Add the value to the accumulator
- Complement the accumulator

Flags

There are four user accessible flags:

- Carry
- Auxiliary Carry
- F_0
- F_1

The Carry flag indicates overflow of the accumulator, while the Auxiliary Carry flag indicates overflow between BCD digits and is used during decimal adjust

operations. Both Carry and Auxiliary Carry are part of the Program Status Word (PSW) and are stored in the stack during subroutine calls. The F_0 and F_1 flags are general-purpose flags which can be cleared or complemented by UPI instructions. F_0 is accessible via the Program Status Word and is stored in the stack with the Carry flags. F_1 reflects the condition of the A_0 line, and caution must be used when setting or clearing it.

Register Operations

The working registers can be accessed via the accumulator as explained above, or they can be loaded with immediate data constants from program memory. In addition, they can be incremented or decremented directly, or they can be used as loop counters as explained in the section on branch instructions.

Additional Data Memory locations can be accessed with indirect instructions via R_0 and R_1.

Branch Instructions

The UPI-41A/41AH/42/42AH Instruction Set includes 17 jump instructions. The unconditional allows jumps anywhere in the 1K words of program memory. All other jump instructions are limited to the current page (256 words) of program memory.

Conditional jump instructions can test the following inputs and maching flags:

- TEST 0 input pin
- TEST 1 input pin
- Input Buffer Full flag
- Output Buffer Full flag
- Timer flag
- Accumulator zero
- Accumulator bit
- Carry flag
- F_0 flag
- F_1 flag

The conditions tested by these instructions are the instantaneous values at the time the conditional jump instruction is executed. For instance, the jump on accumulator zero instruction tests the accumulator itself, not an intermediate flag.

The decrement register and jump if not zero (DJNZ) instruction combines decrement and branch operations in a single instruction which is useful in implementing a loop counter. This instruction can designate any of the 8 working registers as a counter and can effect a branch to any address within the current page of execution.

A special indirect jump instruction (JMPP @A) allows the program to be vectored to any one of several different locations based on the contents of the accumulator. The contents of the accumulator point to a location in program memory which contains the jump address. As an example, this instruction could be used to vector to any one of several routines based on an ASCII character which has been loaded into the accumulator. In this way, ASCII inputs can be used to initiate various routines.

Control

The UPI-41A/41AH/42/42AH Instruction Set has six instructions for control of the DMA, interrupts, and selection of working registers banks.

The UPI-41A/41AH/42/42AH provides two instructions for control of the external microcomputer system. IBF and OBF flags can be routed to PORT 2 allowing interrupts of the external processor. DMA handshaking signals can also be enabled using lines from PORT 2.

The IBF interrupt can be enabled and disabled using two instructions. Also, the interrupt is automatically disabled following a RESET input or during an interrupt service routine.

The working register bank switch instructions allow the programmer to immediately substitute a second 8 register bank for the one in use. This effectively provides either 16 working registers or the means for quickly saving the contents of the first 8 registers in response to an interrupt. The user has the option of switching register banks when an interrupt occurs. However, if the banks are switched, the original bank will automatically be restored upon execution of a return and restore status (RETR) instruction at the end of the interrupt service routine.

Timer

The 8-bit on-board timer/counter can be loaded or read via the accumulator while the counter is stopped or while counting.

The counter can be started as a timer with an internal clock source or as an event counter or timer with an

external clock applied to the TEST 1 pin. The instruction executed determines which clock source is used. A single instruction stops the counter whether it is operating with an internal or an external clock source. In addition, two instructions allow the timer interrupt to be enabled or disabled.

Subroutines

Subroutines are entered by executing a call instruction. Calls can be made to any address in the 1K word program memory. Two separate return instructions determine whether or not status (i.e., the upper 4 bits of the PSW) is restored upon return from a subroutine.

Input/Output Instructions

Two 8-bit data bus buffer registers (DBBIN and DBBOUT) and an 8-bit status register (STS) enable the UPI-41A universal peripheral interface to communicate with the external microcomputer system. Data can be INputted from the DBBIN register to the accumulator. Data can be OUTputted from the accumulator to the DBBOUT register.

The STS register contains four user-definable bits (ST_4–ST_7) plus four reserved status bits (IBF, OBF, F_0 and F_1). The user-definable bits are set from the accumulator.

The UPI-41A/41AH/42/42AH peripheral interface has two 8-bit static I/O ports which can be loaded to and from the accumulator. Outputs are statically latched but inputs to the ports are sampled at the time an IN instruction is executed. In addition, immediate data from program memory can be ANDed and ORed directly to PORTS 1 and 2 with the result remaining on the port. This allows "masks" stored in program memory to be used to set or reset individual bits on the I/O ports. PORTS 1 and 2 are configured to allow input on a given pin by first writing a "1" to the pin.

Four additional 4-bit ports are available through the 8243 I/O expander device. The 8243 interfaces to the UPI-41A/41AH/42/42AH peripheral interface via four PORT 2 lines which form an expander bus. The 8243 ports have their own AND and OR instructions like the on-board ports, as well as move instructions to transfer data in or out. The expander AND or OR instructions, however, combine the contents of the accumulator with the selected port rather than with immediate data as is done with the on-board ports.

INSTRUCTION SET DESCRIPTION

The following section provides a detailed description of each UPI instruction and illustrates how the instructions are used.

For further information about programming the UPI, consult the *8048/8041AH Assembly Language Manual.*

Table 3-1. Symbols and Abbreviations Used

Symbol	Definition
A	Accumulator
C	Carry
DBBIN	Data Bus Buffer Input
DBBOUT	Data Bus Buffer Output
F_0, F_1	FLAG 0, FLAG 1 (C/D flag)
I	Interrupt
P	Mnemonic for "in-page" operation
PC	Program Counter
Pp	Port designator (p = 1, 2, or 4–7)
PSW	Program Status Word
Rr	Register designator (r = 0–7)
SP	Stack Pointer
STS	Status register
T	Timer
TF	Timer Flag
T_0, T_1	TEST 0, TEST 1
#	Immediate data prefix
@	Indirect address prefix
(( ))	Double parentheses show the effect of @, that is @RO is shown as ((RO)).
( )	Contents of

Table 3-2. Instruction Set Summary

Mnemonic	Description	Bytes	Cycle
ACCUMULATOR			
ADD A, Rr	Add register to A	1	1
ADD A, @Rr	Add data memory to A	1	1
ADD A, #data	Add immediate to A	2	2
ADDC A, Rr	Add register to A with carry	1	1
ADDC A, @Rr	Add data memory to A with carry	1	1
ADDC A, #data	Add immediate to A with carry	2	2
ANL A, Rr	And register to A	1	1
ANL A, @Rr	And data memory to A	1	1
ANL A, #data	And immediate to A	2	2
ORL A, Rr	Or register to A	1	1
ORL A, @Rr	Or data memory to A	1	1
ORL A, #data	Or immediate to A	2	2
XRL A, Rr	Exclusive Or register to A	1	1
XRL A, @Rr	Exclusive Or data memory to A	1	1
XRL A, #data	Exclusive Or immediate to A	2	2
INC A	Increment A	1	1
DEC A	Decrement A	1	1
CLR A	Clear A	1	1
CPL A	Complement A	1	1
DA A	Decimal Adjust A	1	1
SWAP A	Swap nibbles of A	1	1
RL A	Rotate A left	1	1
RLC A	Rotate A left through carry	1	1
RR A	Rotate A right	1	1
RRC A	Rotate A right through carry	1	1
INPUT/OUTPUT			
IN A, Pp	Input port to A	1	2
OUTL Pp, A	Output A to port	1	2
ANL Pp, #data	And immediate to port	2	2
ORL Pp, #data	Or immediate to port	2	2
IN A,DBB	Input DDB to A, clear IBF	1	1
OUT DBB, A	Output A to DBB, Set OBF	1	1
MOV STS,A	A_4-A_7 to bits 4–7 of status	1	1
MOVD A,Pp	Input Expander port to A	1	2
MOVD Pp,A	Output A to Expander port	1	2
ANLD Pp,A	And A to Expander port	1	2
ORLD Pp,A	Or A to Expander port	1	2
DATA MOVES			
MOV A, Rr	Move register to A	1	1
MOV A, @Rr	Move data memory to A	1	1
MOV A, #data	Move immediate to A	2	2
MOV Rr, A	Move A to register	1	1
MOV @Rr, A	Move A to data memory	1	1
MOV Rr, #data	Move immediate to register	2	2
MOV @Rr, #data	Move immediate to data memory	2	2
MOV A, PSW	Move PSW to A	1	1
MOV PSW, A	Move A to PSW	1	1
XCH A, Rr	Exchange A and registers	1	1
XCH A, @Rr	Exchange A and data memory	1	1
XCHD A, @Rr	Exchange digit of A and register	1	1
DATA MOVES (Continued)			
MOVP A, @A	Move to A from current page	1	2
MOVP3 A, @A	Move to A from page 3	1	2
TIMER/COUNTER			
MOV A,T	Read Timer/Counter	1	1
MOV T,A	Load Timer/Counter	1	1
STRT T	Start Timer	1	1
STRT CNT	Start Counter	1	1
STOP TCNT	Stop Timer/Counter	1	1
EN TCNTI	Enable Timer/Counter	1	1
DIS TCNTI	Disable Timer/Counter Interrupt	1	1
CONTROL			
EN DMA	Enable DMA Handshake Lines	1	1
EN I	Enable IBF interrupt	1	1
DIS I	Disable IBF interrupt	1	1
EN FLAGS	Enable Master Interrupts	1	1
SEL RB0	Select register bank 0	1	1
SEL RB1	Select register bank 1	1	1
NOP	No Operation	1	1
REGISTERS			
INC Rr	Increment register	1	1
INC @Rr	Increment data memory	1	1
DEC Rr	Decrement register	1	1
SUBROUTINE			
CALL addr	Jump to subroutine	2	2
RET	Return	1	2
RETR	Return and restore status	1	2
FLAGS			
CLR C	Clear Carry	1	1
CPL C	Complement Carry	1	1
CLR F0	Clear Flag 0	1	1
CPL F0	Complement Flag 0	1	1
CLR F1	Clear F_1 Flag	1	1
CPL F1	Complement F_1 Flag	1	1
BRANCH			
JMP addr	Jump unconditional	2	2
JMPP @A	Jump indirect	1	2
DJNZ Rr, addr	Decrement register and jump on non-zero	2	2
JC addr	Jump on Carry = 1	2	2
JNC addr	Jump on Carry = 0	2	2
JZ addr	Jump on A zero	2	2
JNZ addr	Jump on A not zero	2	2
JT0 addr	Jump on T_0 = 1	2	2
JNT0 addr	Jump on T_0 = 0	2	2
JT1 addr	Jump on T_1 = 1	2	2
JNT1 addr	Jump on T_1 = 0	2	2
JF0 addr	Jump on F_0 Flag = 1	2	2
JF1 addr	Jump on F_1 Flag = 1	2	2
JTF addr	Jump on Timer Flag = 1	2	2
JNIBF addr	Jump on IBF Flag = 0	2	2
JOBF addr	Jump on OBF Flag = 1	2	2
JBb addr	Jump on Accumulator Bit	2	2

ALPHABETIC LISTING

ADD A,Rr Add Register Contents to Accumulator

Opcode: | 0 1 1 0 | 1 r_2 r_1 r_0 |

The contents of register 'r' are added to the accumulator. Carry is affected.

(A) ← (A) + (Rr)   r = 0–7

Example:

```
ADDREG: ADD A,R6          ;ADD REG 6 CONTENTS
                          ;TO ACC
```

ADD A,@Rr Add Data Memory Contents to Accumulator

Opcode: | 0 1 1 0 | 0 0 0 r |

The contents of the standard data memory location address by register 'r' bits 0–7 are added to the accumulator. Carry is affected.

(A) ← (A) + ((Rr))   r = 0–1

Example:

```
ADDM: MOV RO,#47          ;MOVE 47 DECIMAL TO REG 0
      ADD A,@RO           ;ADD VALUE OF LOCATION
                          ;47 TO ACC
```

ADD A,#data Add Immediate Data to Accumulator

Opcode: | 0 0 0 0 | 0 0 1 1 | • | d_7 d_6 d_5 d_4 | d_3 d_2 d_1 d_0 |

This is a 2-cycle instruction. The specified data is added to the accumulator. Carry is affected.

(A) ← (A) + data

Example:

```
ADDID: ADD A,#ADDER       ;ADD VALUE OF SYMBOL
                          ;ADDER' TO ACC
```

ADDC A,Rr Add Carry and Register Contents to Accumulator

Opcode: | 0 1 1 1 | 1 r_2 r_1 r_0 |

The content of the carry bit is added to accumulator location 0. The contents of register 'r' are then added to the accumulator. Carry is affected.

(A) ← (A) + (Rr) + (C)   r = 0–7

Example:

```
ADDRGC: ADDC A,R4         ;ADD CARRY AND REG 4
                          ;CONTENTS TO ACC
```

ADDC A,@Rr Add Carry and Data Memory Contents to Accumulator

Opcode: | 0 1 1 1 | 0 0 0 r |

The content of the carry bit is added to accumulator location 0. Then the contents of the standard data memory location addressed by register 'r' bits 0–7 are added to the accumulator. Carry is affected.

(A) ← (A) + ((Rr)) + (C)   r = 0–1

Example:

```
ADDMC: MOV R1,#40        ;MOV '40' DEC TO REG 1
       ADDC A,@R1        ;ADD CARRY AND LOCATION 40
                         ;CONTENTS TO ACC
```

ADDC A,#data Add Carry and Immediate Data to Accumulator

Opcode: | 0 0 0 1 | 0 0 1 1 | • | d_7 d_6 d_5 d_4 | d_3 d_2 d_1 d_0 |

This is a 2-cycle instruction. The content of the carry bit is added to accumulator location 0. Then the specified data is added to the accumulator. Carry is affected.

(A) ← (A) + data + (C)

Example:

```
ADDC A,#255              ;ADD CARRY AND '225' DEC
                         ;TO ACC
```

4

ANL A,Rr Logical AND Accumulator With Register Mask

Opcode: | 0 1 0 1 | 1 r_2 r_1 r_0 |

Data in the accumulator is logically ANDed with the mask contained in working register 'r'.

(A) ← (A) AND (Rr)   r = 0–7

Example:

```
ANDREG: ANL A,R3         ;'AND' ACC CONTENTS WITH MASK
                         ;MASK IN REG 3
```

ANL A,@Rr Logical AND Accumulator With Memory Mask

Opcode: | 0 1 0 1 | 0 0 0 r |

Data in the accumulator is logically ANDed with the mask contained in the data memory location referenced by register 'r', bits 0–7.

(A) ← (A) AND ((Rr))   r = 0–1

Example:

```
ANDDM: MOV R0,#0FFH      MOV 'FF' HEX TO REG 0
       ANL A,#0AFH       ;'AND' ACC CONTENTS WITH
                         ;MASK IN LOCATION 63
```

ANL A,#data Logical AND Accumulator With Immediate Mask

Opcode: | 0101 | 0011 | • | d_7 d_6 d_5 d_4 | d_3 d_2 d_1 d_0 |

This is a 2-cycle instruction. Data in the accumulator is logically ANDed with an immediately-specified mask.
(A) ← (A) AND data

Example:

```
ANDID: ANL A,#0AFH        ;'AND' ACC CONTENTS
                          ;WITH MASK 10101111
       ANL A,#3+X/Y       ;'AND' ACC CONTENTS
                          ;WITH VALUE OF EXP
                          '3+X/Y'
```

ANL PP,#data Logical AND PORT 1-2 With Immediate Mask

Opcode: | 1001 | 1 0 p_1 p_0 | • | d_7 d_6 d_5 d_4 | d_3 d_2 d_1 d_0 |

This is a 2-cycle instruction. Data on the port 'p' is logically ANDed with an immediately-specified mask.
(Pp) ← (Pp) AND data   p = 1-2

Note: Bits 0-1 of the opcode are used to represent PORT 1 and PORT 2. If you are coding in binary rather than assembly language, the mapping is as follows:

Bits	p1	p0	Port
	0	0	X
	0	1	1
	1	0	2
	1	1	X

Example:

```
ANDP2: ANL P2,#OF0H       ;'AND' PORT 2 CONTENTS
                          ;WITH MASK'F0' HEX
                          ;(CLEAR P20-23)
```

ANLD Pp,A Logical AND Port 4-7 With Accumulator Mask

Opcode: | 1001 | 1 1 p_1 p_0 |

This is a 2-cycle instruction. Data on port 'p' on the 8243 expander is logically ANDed with the digit mask contained in accumulator bits 0-3.
(Pp) ← (Pp) AND (A0-3)   p = 4-7

Note: The mapping of Port 'p' to opcode bits p_1, p_0 is as follows:

P1	P0	Port
0	0	4
0	1	5
1	0	6
1	1	7

Example:

```
ANDP4: ANLD P4,A          ;'AND' PORT 4 CONTENTS
                          ;WITH ACC BITS 0-3
```

CALL address Subroutine Call

Opcode: | a_{10} a_9 a_8 1 | 0 1 0 0 | • | a_7 a_6 a_5 a_4 | a_3 a_2 a_1 a_0 |

This is a 2-cycle instruction. The program counter and PSW bits 4–7 are saved in the stack. The stack pointer (PSW bits 0–2) is updated. Program control is then passed to the location specified by 'address'.

Execution continues at the instruction following the CALL upon return from the subroutine.
$((SP)) \leftarrow (PC), (PSW_{4-7})$
$(SP) \leftarrow (SP) + 1$
$(PC_{8-9}) \leftarrow (addr_{8-9})$
$(PC_{0-7}) \leftarrow (addr_{0-7})$

Example: Add three groups of two numbers. Put subtotals in locations 50, 51 and total in location 52.

```
        MOV R0,#50      ;MOVE '50' DEC TO ADDRESS
                        ;REG 0
BEGADD: MOV A,R1        ;MOVE CONTENTS OF REG 1
                        ;TO ACC
        ADD A,R2        ;ADD REG 2 TO ACC
        CALL SUBTOT     ;CALL SUBROUTINE 'SUBTOT'
        ADD A,R3        ;ADD REG 3 TO ACC
        ADD A,R4        ;ADD REG 4 TO ACC
        CALL SUBTOT     ;CALL SUBROUTINE 'SUBTOT'
        ADD A,R5        ;ADD REG 5 TO ACC
        ADD A,R6        ;ADD REG 6 TO ACC
        CALL SUBTOT     ;CALL SUBROUTINE 'SUBTOT'
          •
          •
          •
SUBTOT: MOV @R0,A       ;MOVE CONTENTS OF ACC TO
                        ;LOCATION ADDRESSED BY
                        ;REG 0
        INC R0          ;INCREMENT REG 0
        RET             ;RETURN TO MAIN PROGRAM
```

CLR A Clear Accumulator

Opcode: | 0 0 1 0 | 0 1 1 1 |

The contents of the accumulator are cleared to zero.
$(A) \leftarrow 00H$

CLR C Clear Carry Bit

Opcode: | 1 0 0 1 | 0 1 1 1 |

During normal program execution, the carry bit can be set to one by the ADD, ADDC, RLC, CPLC, RRC, and DAA instructions. This instruction resets the carry bit to zero.
$(C) \leftarrow 0$

CLR F1 Clear Flag 1

Opcode: | 1 0 1 0 | 0 1 0 1 |

The F_1 flag is cleared to zero.
$(F_1) \leftarrow 0$

4

CLR F0 Clear Flag 0

Opcode: | 1 0 0 0 | 0 1 0 1 |

F_0 flag is cleared to zero.
$(F_0) \leftarrow 0$

CPL A Complement Accumulator

Opcode: | 0 0 1 1 | 0 1 1 1 |

The contents of the accumulator are complemented. This is strictly a one's complement. Each one is changed to zero and vice-versa.
$(A) \leftarrow$ NOT (A)

Example: Assume accumulator contains 01101010.

```
CPLA: CPL A                    ;ACC CONTENTS ARE COMPLE-
                               ;MENTED TO 10010101
```

CPL C Complement Carry Bit

Opcode: | 1 0 1 0 | 0 1 1 1 |

The setting of the carry bit is complemented; one is changed to zero, and zero is changed to one.
$(C) \leftarrow$ NOT (C)

Example: Set C to one; current setting is unknown.

```
CT01: CLR C                    ;C IS CLEARED TO ZERO
      CPL C                    ;C IS SET TO ONE
```

CPL F0 COMPLEMENT FLAG 0

Opcode: | 1 0 0 1 | 0 1 0 1 |

The setting of Flag 0 is complemented; one is changed to zero, and zero is changed to one.
$F_0 \leftarrow$ NOT (F0)

CPL F1 Complement Flag 1

Opcode: | 1 0 1 1 | 0 1 0 1 |

The setting of the F_1 Flag is complemented; one is changed to zero, and zero is changed to one.
$(F_1) \leftarrow$ NOT (F_1)

DA A Decimal Adjust Accumulator

Opcode: | 0 1 0 1 | 0 1 1 1 |

The 8-bit accumulator value is adjusted to form two 4-bit Binary Coded Decimal (BCD) digits following the binary addition of BCD numbers. The carry bit C is affected. If the contents of bits 0–3 are greater than nine, or if AC is one, the accumulator is incremented by six.

The four high-order bits are then checked. If bits 4–7 exceed nine, or if C is one, these bits are increased by six. If an overflow occurs, C is set to one; otherwise, it is cleared to zero.

Example: Assume accumulator contains 9AH.

```
DA A          ;ACC ADJUSTED TO 01H with C set
C   AC        ACC
0   0         9AH   INITIAL CONTENTS
              06H   ADD SIX TO LOW DIGIT
0   0         A1H
              60H   ADD SIX TO HIGH DIGIT

1   0         01H   RESULT
```

DEC A Decrement Accumulator

Opcode: | 0 0 0 0 | 0 1 1 1 |

The contents of the accumulator are decremented by one.
(A) ← (A) − 1

Example: Decrement contents of data memory location 63.

```
MOV R0,#3FH       ;MOVE '3F' HEX TO REG 0
MOV A,@R0         ;MOVE CONTENTS OF LOCATION 63
                  ;TO ACC
DEC A             ;DECREMENT ACC
MOV @R0,A         ;MOVE CONTENTS OF ACC TO
                  ;LOCATION 63
```

DEC Rr Decrement Register

Opcode: | 1 1 0 0 | 1 r_2 r_1 r_0 |

The contents of working register 'r' are decremented by one.
(Rr) ← (Rr) − 1   r = 0–7

Example: DECR1: DEC R1   ;DECREMENT ADDRESS REG 1

DIS I Disable IBF Interrupt

Opcode: | 0 0 0 1 | 0 1 0 1 |

The input Buffer Full interrupt is disabled. The interrupt sequence is not initiated by $\overline{WR}$ and $\overline{CS}$, however, an IBF interrupt request is latched and remains pending until an EN I (enable IBF interrupt) instruction is executed.

Note: The IBF flag is set and cleared independent of the IBF interrupt request so that handshaking protocol can continue normally.

DIS TCNTI Disable Timer/Counter Interrupt

Opcode: | 0 0 1 1 | 0 1 0 1 |

The timer/counter interrupt is disabled. Any pending timer interrupt request is cleared. The interrupt sequence is not initiated by an overflow, but the timer flag is set and time accumulation continues.

DJNZ Rr, address Decrement Register and Test

Opcode: | 1 1 1 0 | 1 r_2 r_1 r_0 | • | a_7 a_6 a_5 a_4 | a_3 a_2 a_1 a_0 |

This is a 2-cycle instruction. Register 'r' is decremented and tested for zero. If the register contains all zeros, program control falls through to the next instruction. If the register contents are not zero, control jumps to the specified address within the current page.
(Rr) ← (Rr) − 1
If R ≠ 0, then;
(PC_{0-7}) ← addr

Note: A 10-bit address specification does not cause an error if the DJNZ instruction and the jump target are on the same page. If the DJNZ instruction begins in location 255 of a page, it will jump to a target address on the following page. Otherwise, it is limited to a jump within the current page.

Example: Increment values in data memory locations 50–54.

```
       MOV R0,#50              ;MOVE '50' DEC TO ADDRESS
                               ;REG 0
       MOV R3,#05              ;MOVE '5' DEC TO COUNTER
                               ;REG 3
INCRT: INC @R0                 ;INCREMENT CONTENTS OF
                               ;LOCATION ADDRESSED BY
                               ;REG 0
       INC R0                  ;INCREMENT ADDRESS IN REG 0
       DJNZ R3,INCRT           ;DECREMENT REG 3——JUMP TO
                               ;'INCRT' IF REG 3 NONZERO
       NEXT——                  ;'NEXT' ROUTINE EXECUTED
                               ;IF R3 IS ZERO
```

EN DMA Enable DMA Handshake Lines

Opcode: | 1 1 1 0 | 0 1 0 1 |

DMA handshaking is enabled using P_{26} as DMA request (DRQ) and P_{27} as DMA acknowledge ($\overline{DACK}$). The $\overline{DACK}$ lines forces $\overline{CS}$ and A_0 low internally and clears DRQ.

EN FLAGS Enable Master Interrupts

Opcode: | 1 1 1 1 | 0 1 0 1 |

The Output Buffer Full (OBF) and the Input Buffer Full (IBF) flags (IBF is inverted) are routed to P_{24} and P_{25}. For proper operation, a "1" should be written to P_{25} and P_{24} before the EN FLAGS instruction. A "0" written to P_{24} or P_{25} disables the pin.

EN I Enable IBF Interrupt

Opcode: | 0000 | 0101 |

The Input Buffer Full interrupt is enabled. A low signal on $\overline{WR}$ and $\overline{CS}$ initiates the interrupt sequence.

EN TCNTI Enable Timer/Counter Interrupt

Opcode: | 0010 | 0101 |

The timer/counter interrupt is enabled. An overflow of this register initiates the interrupt sequence.

IN A,DBB Input Data Bus Buffer Contents to Accumulator

Opcode: | 0010 | 0010 |

Data in the DBBIN register is transferred to the accumulator and the Input Buffer Full (IBF) flag is set to zero.
(A) ← (DBB)
(IBF) ← 0

Example:

```
INDBB: IN A,DBB          ;INPUT DBBIN CONTENTS TO
                         ;ACCUMULATOR
```

4

IN A,Pp Input Port 1–2 Data to Accumulator

Opcode: | 0000 | 1 0 p_1 p_0 |

This is a 2-cycle instruction. Data present on port 'p' is transferred (read) to the accumulator.
(A) ← (Pp) p = 1–2 (see ANL instruction)

Example:

```
INP 12: IN A,P1          ;INPUT PORT 1 CONTENTS
                         ;TO ACC
        MOV R6,A         ;MOVE ACC CONTENTS TO
                         ;REG 6
        IN A,P2          ;INPUT PORT 2 CONTENTS
                         ;TO ACC
        MOV R7,A         ;MOVE ACC CONTENTS TO REG 7
```

INC A Increment Accumulator

Opcode: | 0001 | 0111 |

The contents of the accumulator are incremented by one.
(A) ← (A) + 1

Example: Increment contents of location 10 in data memory.

```
INCA: MOV R0,#10         ;MOV '10' DEC TO ADDRESS
                         ;REG 0
      MOV A,@R0          ;MOVE CONTENTS OF LOCATION
                         ;10 TO ACC
      INC A              ;INCREMENT ACC
      MOV @R0,A          ;MOVE ACC CONTENTS TO
                         ;LOCATION 10
```

INC Rr Increment Register

Opcode: | 0 0 0 1 | 1 r_2 r_1 r_0 |

The contents of working register 'r' are incremented by one.
(Rr) ← (Rr) + 1 r = 0–7

Example: INCR0: INC R0 ;INCREMENT ADDRESS REG 0

INC @Rr Increment Data Memory Location

Opcode: | 0 0 0 1 | 0 0 0 r |

The contents of the resident data memory location addressed by register 'r' bits 0–7 are incremented by one.
((Rr)) ← ((Rr)) + 1 r = 0–1

Example:

```
INCDM: MOV R1,#OFFH          ;MOVE ONES TO REG 1
       INC @R1               ;INCREMENT LOCATION 63
```

JBb address Jump If Accumulator Bit is Set

Opcode: | b_2 b_1 b_0 1 | 0 0 1 0 | • | a_7 a_6 a_5 a_4 | a_3 a_2 a_1 a_0 |

This is a 2-cycle instruction. Control passes to the specified address if accumulator bit 'b' is set to one.
(PC_{0-7}) addr if b = 1
(PC) ← (PC) + 2 if b = 0

Example:

```
JB4IS1: JB4 NEXT             ;JUMP TO 'NEXT' ROUTINE
                             ;IF ACC BIT 4 = 1
```

JC address Jump If Carry Is Set

Opcode: | 1 1 1 1 | 0 1 1 0 | • | a_7 a_6 a_5 a_4 | a_3 a_2 a_1 a_0 |

This is a 2-cycle instruction. Control passes to the specified address if the carry bit is set to one.
(PC_{0-7}) ← addr if C = 1
(PC) ← (PC) + 2 if C = 0

Example:

```
JC1: JC OVERFLOW             ;JUMP TO 'OVFLOW' ROUTINE
                             ;IF C = 1
```

JF0 address Jump If Flag 0 is Set

Opcode: | 1 0 1 1 | 0 1 1 0 | • | a_7 a_6 a_5 a_4 | a_3 a_2 a_1 a_0 |

This is a 2-cycle instruction. Control passes to the specified address if flag 0 is set to one.
(PC_{0-7}) ← addr if F_0 = 1

Example:

```
JF0IS1: JF0 TOTAL            ;JUMP TO 'TOTAL' ROUTINE
                             ;IF F0 = 1
```

JF1 address Jump If C/D Flag (F1) Is Set

Opcode: | 0 1 1 1 | 0 1 1 0 | • | a_7 a_6 a_5 a_4 | a_3 a_2 a_1 a_0 |

This is a 2-cycle instruction. Control passes to the specified address if the C/D flag (F_1) is set to one.

$(PC_{0-7}) \leftarrow$ addr   if $F_1 = 1$

Example: JF 1IS1: JF1 FILBUF   ;JUMP TO 'FILBUF'
;ROUTINE IF $F_1 = 1$

JMP address Direct Jump Within 1K Block

Opcode: | a_{10} a_9 a_8 0 | 0 1 0 0 | • | a_7 a_6 a_5 a_4 | a_3 a_2 a_1 a_0 |

This is a 2-cycle instruction. Bits 0–10 of the program counter are replaced with the directly-specified address.

$(PC_{8-10}) \leftarrow$ addr 8–10
$(PC_{0-7}) \leftarrow$ addr 0–7

Example:
JMP SUBTOT   ;JUMP TO SUBROUTINE 'SUBTOT'
JMP $-6   ;JUMP TO INSTRUCTION SIX LOCATIONS
;BEFORE CURRENT LOCATION
JMP 2FH   ;JUMP TO ADDRESS '2F' HEX

4

JMPP @A Indirect Jump Within Page

Opcode: | 1 0 1 1 | 0 0 1 1 |

This is a 2-cycle instruction. The contents of the program memory location pointed to by the accumulator are substituted for the 'page' portion of the program counter (PC 0–7).

$(PC_{0-7}) \leftarrow ((A))$

Example: Assume accumulator contains OFH
JMPPAG: JMPP @A   ;JMP TO ADDRESS STORED IN
;LOCATION 15 IN CURRENT PAGE

JNC address Jump If Carry Is Not Set

Opcode: | 1 1 1 0 | 0 1 1 0 | • | a_7 a_6 a_5 a_4 | a_3 a_2 a_1 a_0 |

This is a 2-cycle instruction. Control passes to the specified address if the carry bit is not set, that is, equals zero.

$(PC_{0-7}) \leftarrow$ addr   if $C = 0$

Example: JC0: JNC NOVFLO   ;JUMP TO 'NOVFLO' ROUTINE
;IF $C = 0$

JNIBF address Jump If Input Buffer Full Flag Is Low

Opcode: | 1 1 0 1 | 0 1 1 0 | • | a_7 a_6 a_5 a_4 | a_3 a_2 a_1 a_0 |

This is a 2-cycle instruction. Control passes to the specified address if the Input Buffer Full flag is low (IBF = 0).

$(PC_{0-7}) \leftarrow$ addr   if IBF = 0

Example: LOC 3:JNIBF LOC 3   ;JUMP TO SELF IF IBF = 0
;OTHERWISE CONTINUE

JNTO address Jump if TEST 0 is Low

Opcode: | 0 0 1 0 | 0 1 1 0 | • | a_7 a_6 a_5 a_4 | a_3 a_2 a_1 a_0 |

This is a 2-cycle instruction. Control passes to the specified address, if the TEST 0 signal is low. Pin is sampled during SYNC.

$(PC_{0-7}) \leftarrow$ addr   if $T_0 = 0$

Example: JT0LOW: JNT0 60   ;JUMP TO LOCATION 60 DEC
;IF $T_0 = 0$

JNT1 address Jump If TEST 1 is Low

Opcode: | 0 1 0 0 | 0 1 1 0 | • | a_7 a_6 a_5 a_4 | a_3 a_2 a_1 a_0 |

This is a 2-cycle instruction. Control passes to the specified address if the TEST 1 signal is low. Pin is sampled during SYNC.

$(PC_{0-7}) \leftarrow$ addr   if $T_1 = 0$

Example: JT1LOW: JNT1 OBBH   ;JUMP TO LOCATION 'BB' HEX
;IF $T_1 = 0$

JNZ address Jump If Accumulator Is Not Zero

Opcode: | 1 0 0 1 | 0 1 1 0 | • | a_7 a_6 a_5 a_4 | a_3 a_2 a_1 a_0 |

This is a 2-cycle instruction. Control passes to the specified address if the accumulator contents are nonzero at the time this instruction is executed.

$(PC_{0-7}) \leftarrow$ addr   if $A \neq 0$

Example: JACCNO: JNZ OABH   ;JUMP TO LOCATION 'AB' HEX
;IF ACC VALUE IS NONZERO

JOBF Address Jump If Output Buffer Full Flag Is Set

Opcode: | 1 0 0 0 | 0 1 1 0 | • | a_7 a_6 a_5 a_4 | a_3 a_2 a_1 a_0 |

This is a 2-cycle instruction. Control passes to the specified address if the Output Buffer Full (OBF) flag is set (= 1) at the time this instruction is executed.

$(PC_{0-7}) \leftarrow$ addr   if OBF = 1

Example: JOBFHI: JOBF OAAH   ;JUMP TO LOCATION 'AA' HEX
;IF OBF = 1

JTF address Jump If Timer Flag is Set

Opcode: | 0 0 0 1 | 0 1 1 0 | • | a_7 a_6 a_5 a_4 | a_3 a_2 a_1 a_0 |

This is a 2-cycle instruction. Control passes to the specified address if the timer flag is set to one, that is, the timer/counter register overflows to zero. The timer flag is cleared upon execution of this instruction. (This overflow initiates an interrupt service sequence if the timer-overflow interrupt is enabled.)

$(PC_{0-7}) \leftarrow$ addr   if TF = 1

Example: JTF1: JTF TIMER   ;JUMP TO 'TIMER' ROUTINE
;IF TF = 1

JTO address Jump If TEST 0 Is High

Opcode:

0 0 1 1	0 1 1 0	•	a_7 a_6 a_5 a_4	a_3 a_2 a_1 a_0

This is a 2-cycle instruction. Control passes to the specified address if the TEST 0 signal is high (= 1). Pin is sampled during SYNC.

$(PC_{0-7}) \leftarrow$ addr   if $T_0 = 1$

Example: JTOHI: JTO 53   ;JUMP TO LOCATION 53 DEC ;IF $T_0 = 1$

JT1 address Jump If TEST 1 Is High

Opcode:

0 1 0 1	0 1 1 0	•	a_7 a_6 a_5 a_4	a_3 a_2 a_1 a_0

This is a 2-cycle instruction. Control passes to the specified address if the TEST 1 signal is high (= 1). Pin is sampled during SYNC.

$(PC_{0-7}) \leftarrow$ addr   if $T_1 = 1$

Example: JT1HI: JT1 COUNT   ;JUMP TO 'COUNT' ROUTINE ;IF $T_1 = 1$

JZ address Jump If Accumulator Is Zero

Opcode:

1 1 0 0	0 1 1 0	•	a_7 a_6 a_5 a_4	a_3 a_2 a_1 a_0

This is a 2-cycle instruction. Control passes to the specified address if the accumulator contains all zeros at the time this instruction is executed.

$(PC_{0-7}) \leftarrow$ addr   if $A = 0$

Example: JACCO: JZ OA3H   ;JUMP TO LOCATION 'A3' HEX ;IF ACC VALUE IS ZERO

MOV A,#data Move Immediate Data to Accumulator

Opcode:

0 0 1 0	0 0 1 1	•	d_7 d_6 d_5 d_4	d_3 d_2 d_1 d_0

This is a 2-cycle instruction. The 8-bit value spedified by 'data' is loaded in the accumulator.

$(A) \leftarrow$ data

Example: MOV A,#OA3H   ;MOV 'A3' HEX TO ACC

MOV A,PSW Move PSW Contents to Accumulator

Opcode:

1 1 0 0	0 1 1 1

The contents of the program status word are moved to the accumulator.

$(A) \leftarrow (PSW)$

Example: Jump to 'RB1SET' routine if bank switch, PSW bit 4, is set.

```
BSCHK: MOV A,PSW          ;MOV PSW CONTENTS TO ACC
       JB4 RB1 SET        ;JUMP TO 'RB1SET' IF ACC
                          ;BIT 4 = 1
```

MOV A,Rr Move Register Contents to Accumulator

Opcode: | 1 1 1 1 | 1 r_2 r_1 r_0 |

Eight bits of data are moved from working register 'r' into the accumulator.
(A) ← (Rr) r = 0–7

Example:

```
MAR: MOV A,R3                ;MOVE CONTENTS OF REG 3
                             ;TO ACC
```

MOV A,@Rr Move Data Memory Contents to Accumulator

Opcode: | 1 1 1 1 | 0 0 0 r |

The contents of the data memory location addressed by bits 0–7 of register 'r' are moved to the accumulator. Register 'r' contents are unaffected.
(A) ← ((Rr)) r = 0–1

Example: Assume R1 contains 00110110.

```
MADM: MOV A,@R1              ;MOVE CONTENTS OF DATA MEM
                             ;LOCATION 54 TO ACC
```

MOV A,T Move Timer/Counter Contents to Accumulator

Opcode: | 0 1 0 0 | 0 0 1 0 |

The contents of the timer/event-counter register are moved to the accumulator. The timer/event-counter is not stopped.
(A) ← (T)

Example: Jump to "Exit" routine when timer reaches '64', that is, when bit 6 is set—assuming initialization to zero.

```
TIMCHK: MOV A,T              ;MOVE TIMER CONTENTS TO
                             ;ACC
        JB6 EXIT             ;JUMP TO 'EXIT' IF ACC BIT
                             ;6 = 1
```

MOV PSW,A Move Accumulator Contents to PSW

Opcode: | 1 1 0 1 | 0 1 1 1 |

The contents of the accumulator are moved into the program status word. All condition bits and the stack pointer are affected by this move.
(PSW) ← (A)

Example: Move up stack pointer by two memory locations, that is, increment the pointer by one.

```
INCPTR: MOV A,PSW            ;MOVE PSW CONTENTS TO ACC
        INC A                ;INCREMENT ACC BY ONE
        MOV PSW,A            ;MOVE ACC CONTENTS TO PSW
```

MOV Rr,A Move Accumulator Contents to Register

Opcode: | 1 0 1 0 | 1 r_2 r_1 r_0 |

The contents of the accumulator are moved to register 'r'

(Rr) ← (A) r = 0–7

Example:

```
MRA MOV R0,A                    ;MOVE CONTENTS OF ACC TO
                                ;REG 0
```

MOV Rr,#data Move Immediate Data to Register

Opcode: | 1 0 1 1 | 1 r_2 r_1 r_0 | • | d_7 d_6 d_5 d_4 | d_3 d_2 d_1 d_0 |

This is a 2-cycle instruction. The 8-bit value specified by 'data' is moved to register 'r'.

(Rr) ← data r = 0–7

Example:

```
MIR4: MOV R4,#HEXTEN            ;THE VALUE OF THE SYMBOL
                                ;'HEXTEN' IS MOVED INTO
                                ;REG 4
MIR5: MOV R5,#PI*(R*R)          ;THE VAUE OF THE
                                ;EXPRESSION 'PI*(R*R)'
                                ;IS MOVED INTO REG 5
MIR6: MOV R6,#OADH              ;'AD' HEX IS MOVED INTO
                                REG 6
```

4

MOV @Rr,A Move Accumulator Contents to Data Memory

Opcode: | 1 0 1 0 | 0 0 0 r |

The contents of the accumulator are moved to the data memory location whose address is specified by bits 0–7 of register 'r'. Register 'r' contents are unaffected.

((Rr)) ← (A) r = 0–1

Example: Assume R0 contains 11000111.

```
MDMA: MOV @R,A                  ;MOVE CONTENTS OF ACC TO
                                ;LOCATION 7 (REG)
```

MOV @Rr,#data Move Immediate Data to Data Memory

Opcode: | 1 0 1 1 | 0 0 0 r | • | d_7 d_6 d_5 d_4 | d_3 d_2 d_1 d_0 |

This is a 2-cycle instruction. The 8-bit value specified by 'data' is moved to the standard data memory location addressed by register 'r', bit 0–7.

Example: Move the hexadecimal value AC3F to locations 62–63.

```
MIDM: MOV R0,#62                ;MOVE '62' DEC TO ADDR REG0
      MOV @RO,#OACH             ;MOVE 'AC' HEX TO LOCATION 62
      INC R0                    ;INCREMENT REG 0 TO '63'
      MOV @RO,#3FH              ;MOVE '3F' HEX TO LOCATION 63
```

MOV STS,A Move Accumulator Contents to STS Register

Opcode: | 1 0 0 1 | 0 0 0 0 |

The contents of the accumulator are moved into the status register. Only bits 4–7 are affected.
$(STS_{4-7}) \leftarrow (A_{4-7})$

Example: Set ST_4–ST_7 to "1".

```
MSTS: MOV A,#0F0H          ;SET ACC
      MOV STS,A            ;MOVE TO STS
```

MOV T,A Move Accumulator Contents to Timer/Counter

Opcode: | 0 1 1 0 | 0 0 1 0 |

The contents of the accumulator are moved to the timer/event-counter register.
$(T) \leftarrow (A)$

Example: Initialize and start event counter.

```
INITEC: CLR A              ;CLEAR ACC TO ZEROS
        MOV T,A            ;MOVE ZEROS TO EVENT COUNTER
        STRT CNT           ;START COUNTER
```

MOVD A,Pp Move Port 4–7 Data to Accumulator

Opcode: | 0 0 0 0 | 1 1 p_1 p_0 |

This is a 2-cycle instruction. Data on 8243 port 'p' is moved (read) to accumulator bits 0–3. Accumulator bits 4–7 are zeroed.
$(A_{0-3}) \leftarrow Pp$ $p = 4–7$
$(A_{4-7}) \leftarrow 0$

Note: Bits 0–1 of the opcode are used to represent PORTS 4–7. If you are coding in binary rather than assembly language, the mapping is as follows:

Bits		Port
p_1	p_0	
0	0	4
0	1	5
1	0	6
1	1	7

Example:

```
INPPT5: MOVD A,P5          ;MOVE PORT 5 DATA TO ACC
                           ;BITS 0-3, ZERO ACC BITS 4-7
```

MOVD Pp,A Move Accumulator Data to Port 4, 5, 6 and 7

Opcode: | 0 0 1 1 | 1 1 p_1 p_0 |

This is a 2-cycle instruction. Data in accumulator bits 0–3 is moved (written) to 8243 port 'p'. Accumulator bits 4–7 are unaffected. (See NOTE above regarding port mapping.)

Example: Move data in accumulator to ports 4 and 5.

```
OUTP45: MOVD P4,A          ;MOVE ACC BITS 0-3 TO PORT 4
        SWAP A             ;EXCHANGE ACC BITS 0-3 AND 4-7
        MOVD P5,A          ;MOVE ACC BITS 0-3 TO PORT 5
```

MOVP A,@A Move Current Page Data to Accumulator

Opcode: | 1010 | 0011 |

This is a 2-cycle instruction. The contents of the program memory location addressed by the accumulator are moved to the accumulator. Only bits 0–7 of the program counter are affected, limiting the program memory reference to the current page. The program counter is restored following this operation.

(A) ← ((A))

Note: This a 1-byte, 2-cycle instruction. If it appears in location 255 of a program memory page, @A addresses a location in the following page.

Example:

```
MOV128: MOV A,#128          ;MOVE '128' DEC TO ACC
        MOVP A,@A           ;CONTENTS OF 129TH LOCATION
                            ;IN CURRENT PAGE ARE MOVED TO
                            ;ACC
```

MOVP3 A,@A Move Page 3 Data to Accumulator

Opcode: | 1110 | 0011 |

This is a 2-cycle instruction. The contents of the program memory location within page 3, addressed by the accumulator, are moved to the accumulator. The program counter is restored following this operation.

(A) ← ((A)) within page 3

Example: Look up ASCII equivalent of hexadecimal code in table contained at the beginning of page 3. Note that ASCII characters are designated by a 7-bit code; the eighth bit is always reset.

```
TABSCH: MOV A,#OB8H         ;MOVE 'B8' HEX TO ACC (10111000)
        ANL A,#7FH          ;LOGICAL AND ACC TO MASK BIT
                            ;7 (00111000)
MOVP3, A,@A                 ;MOVE CONTENTS OF LOCATION
                            ;'38' HEX IN PAGE 3 TO ACC
                            ;(ASCII '8')
```

Access contents of location in page 3 labelled TAB1. Assume current program location is not in page 3.

```
TABSCH: MOV A,#TAB1         ;ISOLATE BITS 0-7
                            ;OF LABEL
                            ;ADDRESS VALUE
        MOVP3 A,@A          ;MOVE CONTENT OF PAGE 3
                            ;LOCATION LABELED 'TAB1'
                            ;TO ACC
```

NOP The NOP Instruction

Opcode: | 0000 | 0000 |

No operation is performed. Execution continues with the following instruction.

ORL A,Rr Logical OR Accumulator With Register Mask

Opcode: | 0100 | 1 r_2 r_1 r_0 |

Data in the accumulator is logically ORed with the mask contained in working register 'r'.

(A) ← (A) OR (Rr)   r = 0–7

Example:

```
ORREG: ORL A,R4             ;'OR' ACC CONTENTS WITH
                            ;MASK IN REG 4
```

4

ORL A,@Rr Logical OR Accumulator With Memory Mask

Opcode: | 0100 | 000r |

Data in the accumulator is logically ORed with the mask contained in the data memory location referenced by register 'r', bits 0-7.

(A) ← (A) OR ((Rr)) r = 0-1

Example:

```
ORDM: MOVE R0,#3FH          ;MOVE '3F' HEX TO REG 0
      ORL A, @R0            ;'OR' ACC CONTENTS WITH MASK
                            ;IN LOCATION 63
```

ORL A,#Data Logical OR Accumulator With Immediate Mask

Opcode: | 0100 | 0011 | • | d_7 d_6 d_5 d_4 | d_3 d_2 d_1 d_0 |

This is a 2-cycle instruction. Data in the accumulator is logically ORed with an immediately-specified mask.

(A) ← (A) OR data

Example:

```
ORID: ORL A,#'X'            ;'OR' ACC CONTENTS WITH MASK
                            ;01011000 (ASCII VALUE OF 'X')
```

ORL Pp,#data Logical OR Port 1-2 With Immediate Mask

Opcode: | 1000 | 1 0 p_1 p_0 | • | d_7 d_6 d_5 d_4 | d_3 d_2 d_1 d_0 |

This is a 2-cycle instruction. Data on port 'p' is logically ORed with an immediately-specified mask.

(Pp) ← (Pp) OR data p = 1-2 (see OUTL instruction)

Example:

```
ORP1: ORL P1,#OFH           ;'OR' PORT 1 CONTENTS WITH
                            ;MASK 'FF' HEX (SET PORT 1
                            'TO ALL ONES)
```

ORLD Pp,A Logical OR Port 4-7 With Accumulator Mask

Opcode: | 1000 | 1 1 p_1 p_0 |

This is a 2-cycle instruction. Data on 8243 port 'p' is logically ORed with the digit mask contained in accumulator bits 0-3,

(Pp) (Pp) OR (A_{0-3}) p = 4-7 (See MOVD instruction)

Example:

```
ORP7; ORLD P7,A             ;'OR' PORT 7 CONTENTS
                            ;WITH ACC BITS 0-3
```

OUT DBB,A Output Accumulator Contents to Data Bus Buffer

Opcode: | 0000 | 0010 |

Contents of the accumulator are transferred to the Data Bus Buffer Output register and the Output Buffer Full (OBF) flag is set to one.

(DBB) ← (A)
OBF ← 1

Example:

```
OUTDBB: OUT DBB,A           ;OUTPUT THE CONTENTS OF
                            ;THE ACC TO DBBOUT
```

OUTL Pp,A Output Accumulator Data to Port 1 and 2

Opcode:

0 0 1 1	1 0 p_1 p_0

This is a 2-cycle instruction. Data residing in the accumulator is transferred (written) to port 'p' and latched.
(Pp) ← (A) P = 1–2

Note: Bits 0–1 of the opcode are used to represent PORT 1 and PORT 2. If you are coding in binary rather than assembly language, the mapping is as follows:

Bits		Port
p_1	p_0	
0	0	X
0	1	1
1	0	2
1	1	X

Example:

```
OUTLP; MOV A,R7      ;MOVE REG 7 CONTENTS TO ACC
       OUTL P2,A     ;OUTPUT ACC CONTENTS TO PORT2
       MOV A,R6      ;MOVE REG 6 CONTENTS TO ACC
       OUTL P1,A     ;OUTPUT ACC CONTENTS TO PORT 1
```

RET Return Without PSW Restore

Opcode:

1 0 0 0	0 0 1 1

This is a 2-cycle instruction. The stack pointer (PSW bits 0–2 is decremented. The program counter is then restored from the stack. PSW bits 4–7 are not restored.
(SP) ← (SP) − 1
(PC) ← ((SP))

RETR Return With PSW Restore

Opcode:

1 0 0 1	0 0 1 1

This is a 2-cycle instruction. The stack pointer is decremented. The program counter and bits 4–7 of the PSW are then restored from the stack. Note that RETR should be used to return from an interrupt, but should not be used within the interrupt service routine as it signals the end of an interrupt routine.
(SP) ← (SP) − 1
(PC) ← ((SP))
(PSW_{4-7}) ← ((SP))

RL A Rotate Left Without Carry

Opcode:

1 1 1 0	0 1 1 1

The contents of the accumulator are rotated left one bit. Bit 7 is rotated into the bit 0 position.
(A_{n+1}) ← (A_n) n = 0–6
(A_0) ← (A_7)

Example: Assume accumulator contains 10110001.

```
RLNC: RL A       ;NEW ACC CONTENTS ARE 01100011
```

RLC A Rotate Left Through Carry

Opcode:

1111	0111

The contents of the accumulator are rotated left one bit. Bit 7 replaces the carry bit; the carry bit is rotated into the bit 0 position.

$(A_{n+1}) \leftarrow (A_n)$ $n = 0\text{–}6$
$(A_0) \leftarrow (C)$
$(C) \leftarrow (A7)$

Example: Assume accumulator contains a 'signed' number; isolate sign without changing value.

```
RLTC: CLR C              ;CLEAR CARRY TO ZERO
      RLC A              ;ROTATE ACC LEFT, SIGN
                         ;BIT (7) IS PLACED IN CARRY
      RR A               ;ROTATE ACC RIGHT—VALUE
                         ;(BITS 0-6) IS RESTORED,
                         ;CARRY UNCHANGED, BIT 7
                         ;IS ZERO
```

RR A Rotate Right Without Carry

Opcode:

0111	0111

The contents of the accumulator are rotated right one bit. Bit 0 is rotated into the bit 7 position.

$(A) \leftarrow (A_{n+1})$ $n = 0\text{–}6$
$(A_7) \leftarrow (A_0)$

Example Assume accumulator contains 10110001.

```
RRNC: RRA                ;NEW ACC CONTENTS ARE 11011000
```

RRC A Rotate Right Through Carry

Opcode:

0110	0111

The contents of the accumulator are rotated one bit. Bit 0 replaces the carry bit; the carry bit is rotated into the bit 7 position.

$(A_n) \leftarrow (A_n + 1)$ $n = 0\text{–}6$
$(A_7) \leftarrow (C)$
$(C) \leftarrow (A_0)$

Example Assume carry is not set and accumulator contains 10110001.

```
RRTC: RRCA               ;CARRY IS SET AND ACC
                         ;CONTAINS 01011000
```

SEL RB0 Select Register Bank 0

Opcode: | 1 1 0 0 | 0 1 0 1 |

PSW BIT 4 is set to zero. References to working registers 0–7 address data memory locations 0–7. This is the recommended setting for normal program execution.
(BS) ← 0

SEL RB1 Select Register Bank 1

Opcode: | 1 1 0 1 | 0 1 0 1 |

PSW bit 4 is set to one. References to working registers 0–7 address data memory locations 24–31. This is the recommended setting for interrupt service routines, since locations 0–7 are left intact. The setting of PSW bit 4 in effect at the time of an interrupt is restored by the RETR instruction when the interrupt service routine is completed.

Example: Assume an IBF interrupt has occurred, control has passed to program memory location 3, and PSW bit 4 was zero before the interrupt.

```
LOC3: JMP INIT               ;JUMP TO ROUTINE 'INIT'
      .
      .
      .
INIT: MOV R7,A               ;MOV ACC CONTENTS TO
                             ;LOCATION 7
      SEL RB1                ;SELECT REG BANK 1
      MOV R7,#OFAH           ;MOVE 'FA' HEX TO LOCATION 31
      .
      .
      .
      SEL RB0                ;SELECT REG BANK 0
      MOV A,R7               ;RESTORE ACC FROM LOCATION 7
      RETR                   ;RETURN——RESTORE PC AND PSW
```

4

STOP TCNT Stop Timer/Event Counter

Opcode: 0110 0101

This instruction is used to stop both time accumulation and event counting.

Example: Disable interrupt, but jump to interrupt routine after eight overflows and stop timer. Count overflows in register 7.

```
START: DIS TCNTI          ;DISABLE TIMER INTERRUPT
       CLR A              ;CLEAR ACC TO ZERO
       MOV T,A            ;MOV ZERO TO TIMER
       MOV R7,A           ;MOVE ZERO TO REG 7
       STRT T             ;START TIMER
MAIN:  JTF COUNT          ;JUMP TO ROUTINE 'COUNT'
                          ;IF TF = 1 AND CLEAR TIMER FLAG
       JMP MAIN           ;CLOSE LOOP
COUNT: INC R7             ;INCREMENT REG 7
       MOV A,R7           ;MOVE REG 7 CONTENTS TO ACC
       JB3 INT            ;JUMP TO ROUTINE 'INT' IF ACC
                          ;BIT 3 IS SET (REG 7 = 8)
       JMP MAIN           ;OTHERWISE RETURN TO ROUTINE
                          ;MAIN
       .
       .
       .
INT: STOP TCNT            ;STOP TIMER
       JMP 7H             ;JUMP TO LOCATION 7 (TIMER
                          ;INTERRUPT ROUTINE)
```

STRT CNT Start Event Counter

Opcode: 0100 0101

The TEST 1 (T_1) pin is enabled as the event-counter input and the counter is started. The event-counter register is incremented with each high to low transition on the T_1 pin.

Example: Initialize and start event counter. Assume overflow is desired with first T_1 input.

```
STARTC: EN TCNTI          ;ENABLE COUNTER INTERRUPT
        MOV A,#OFFH       ;MOVE 'FF' HEX (ONES) TO
                          ;ACC
        MOV T,A           ;MOVE ONES TO COUNTER
        STRT CNT          ;INPUT AND START
```

STRT T Start Timer

Opcode: 0101 0101

Timer accumulation is initiated in the timer register. The register is incremented every 32 instruction cycles. The prescaler which counts the 32 cycles is cleared but the timer register is not.

Example: Initialize and start timer.

```
STARTT: EN TCNTI          ;ENABLE TIMER INTERRUPT
        CLR A             :CLEAR ACC TO ZEROS
        MOV T,A           ;MOVE ZEROS TO TIMER
        STRT T            ;START TIMER
```

SWAP A Swap Nibbles Within Accumulator

Opcode: | 0 1 0 0 | 0 1 1 1 |

Bits 0–3 of the accumulator are swapped with bits 4-7 of the accumulator.
$(A_{4-7}) \longleftrightarrow (A_{0-3})$

Example: Pack bits 0–3 of locations 50-51 into location 50.

```
PCKDIG: MOV R0,#50          ;MOVE '50' DEC TO REG 0
        MOV R1,#51          ;MOVE '51' DEC TO REG 1
        XCHD A,@R0          ;EXCHANGE BIT 0-3 OF ACC
                            ;AND LOCATION 50
        SWAP A              ;SWAP BITS 0-3 AND 4-7 OF ACC
        XCHD A,@ R1         ;EXCHANGE BITS 0-3 OF ACC AND
                            ;LOCATION 51
        MOV @R0,A           ;MOVE CONTENTS OF ACC TO
                            ;LOCATION 51
```

XCH ARr Exchange Accumulator-Register Contents

Opcode: | 0 0 1 0 | 1 r_2 r_1 r_0 |

The contents of the accumulator and the contents of working register 'r' are exchanged.
$(A) \longleftrightarrow (Rr)$ $r = 0–7$

Example: Move PSW contents to Reg 7 without losing accumulator contents.

```
XCHAR7: XCH A,R7            ;EXCHANGE CONTENTS OF REG 7
                            ;AND ACC
        MOV A,PSW           ;MOVE PSW CONTENTS TO ACC
        XCH, A,R7           ;EXCHANGE CONTENTS OF REG 7
                            ;AND ACC AGAIN
```

XCH A,@Rr Exchange Accumulator and Data Memory Contents

Opcode: | 0 0 1 0 | 0 0 0 r |

The contents of the accumulator and the contents of the data memory location addressed by bits 0–7 of register 'r' are exchanged. Register 'r' contents are unaffected.
$(A) \longleftrightarrow ((Rr))$ $r = 0–1$

Example: Decrement contents of location 52.

```
DEC 52: MOV R0,#52          ;MOVE '52' DEC TO ADDRESS
                            ;REG 0
        XCH A,@R0           ;EXCHANGE CONTENTS OF ACC
                            ;AND LOCATION 52
        DEC A               ;DECREMENT ACC CONTENTS
        XCH A,@R0           ;EXCHANGE CONTENTS OF ACC
                            ;AND LOCATION 52 AGAIN
```

XCHD A,@Rr Exchange Accumulator and Data Memory 4-bit Data

Opcode:

0 0 1 1	0 0 0 r

This instruction exchanges bits 0–3 of the accumulator with bits 0–3 of the data memory location addressed by bits 0–7 of register 'r'. Bits 4–7 of the accumulator, bits 4–7 of the data memory location, and the contents of register 'r' are unaffected.

$(A_{0-3}) \longleftrightarrow ((Rr_{0-3}))$ r = 0–1

Example: Assume program counter contents have been stacked in locations 22-23.

```
XCHNIB: MOV R0,#23        ;MOVE '23' DEC TO REG 0
        CLR A             ;CLEAR ACC TO ZEROS
        XCHD A,@R0        ;EXCHANGE BITS 0-3 OF ACC
                          ;AND LOCATION 23 (BITS 8-11
                          ;OF PC ARE ZEROED, ADDRESS
                          ;REFERS TO PAGE 0)
```

XRL A,Rr Logical XOR Accumulator With Register Mask

Opcode:

1 1 0 1	1 r_2 r_1 r_0

Data in the accumulator is EXCLUSIVE ORed with the mask contained in working register 'r'.

(A) ⟷ (A) XOR (Rr) r = 0–7

Example:

```
XORREG: XRL A,R5          ;'XOR' ACC CONTENTS WITH
                          ;MASK IN REG 5
```

XRL A,@Rr Logical XOR Accumulator With Memory Mask

Opcode:

1 1 0 1	0 0 0 r

Data in the accumulator is EXCLUSIVE ORed with the mask contained in the data memory location address by register 'r', bits 0–7.

(A) ← (A) XOR ((Rr)) r = 0–1

Example:

```
XORDM: MOV R1,#20H        ;MOVE '20' HEX TO REG 1
       XRL A,@R1          ;'XOR' ACC CONTENTS WITH MASK
                          ;IN LOCATION 32
```

XRL A,#data, Logical XOR Accumulator With Immediate Mask

Opcode:

1 1 0 1	0 0 1 1	•	d_7 d_6 d_5 d_4	d_3 d_2 d_1 d_0

This is a 2-cycle instruction. Data in the accumulator is EXCLUSIVE ORed with an immediately-specified mask.

(A) ← (A) XOR data

Example:

```
XORID: XRL A,#HEXTEN      ;XOR CONTENTS OF ACC WITH
                          ;MASK EQUAL VALUE OF SYMBOL
                          ;'HEXTEN'
```

CHAPTER 4
SINGLE-STEP AND PROGRAMMING POWER-DOWN MODES

SINGLE-STEP

The UPI family has a single-step mode which allows the user to manually step through his program one instruction at a time. While stopped, the address of the next instruction to be fetched is available on PORT 1 and the lower 2 bits of PORT 2. The single-step feature simplifies program debugging by allowing the user to easily follow program execution.

Figure 4-1 illustrates a recommended circuit for single-step operation, while Figure 4-2 shows the timing relationship between the SYNC output and the $\overline{SS}$ input. During single-step operation, PORT 1 and part of PORT 2 are used to output address information. In order to retain the normal I/O functions of PORTS 1 and 2, a separate latch can be used as shown in Figure 4-3.

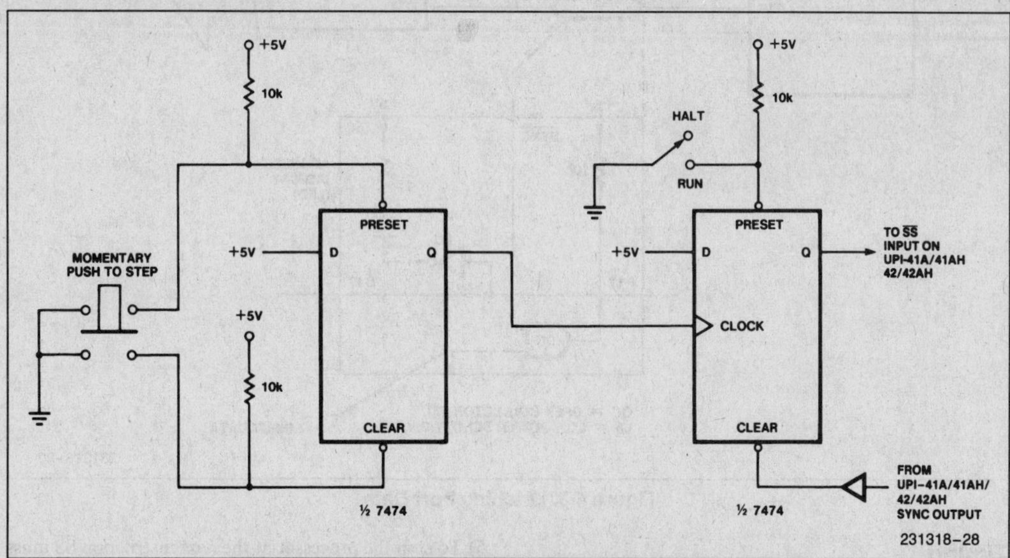

Figure 4-1. Single-Step Circuit

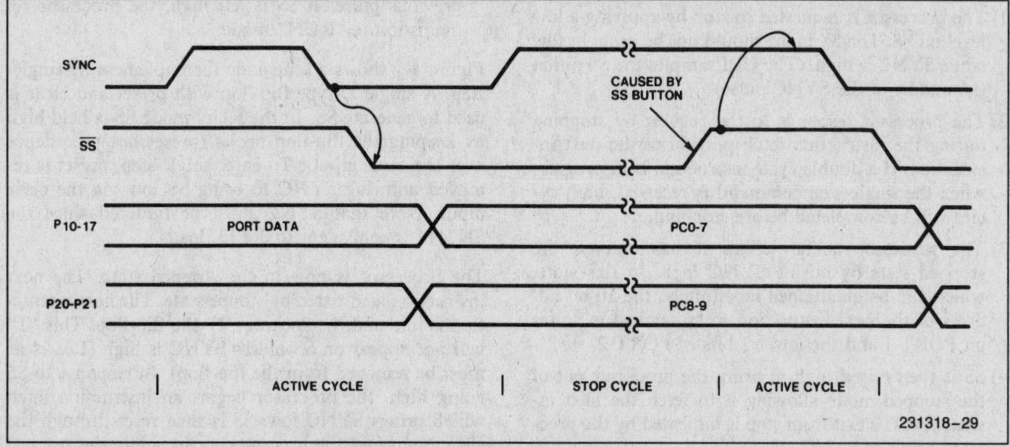

Figure 4-2. Single-Step Timing

4

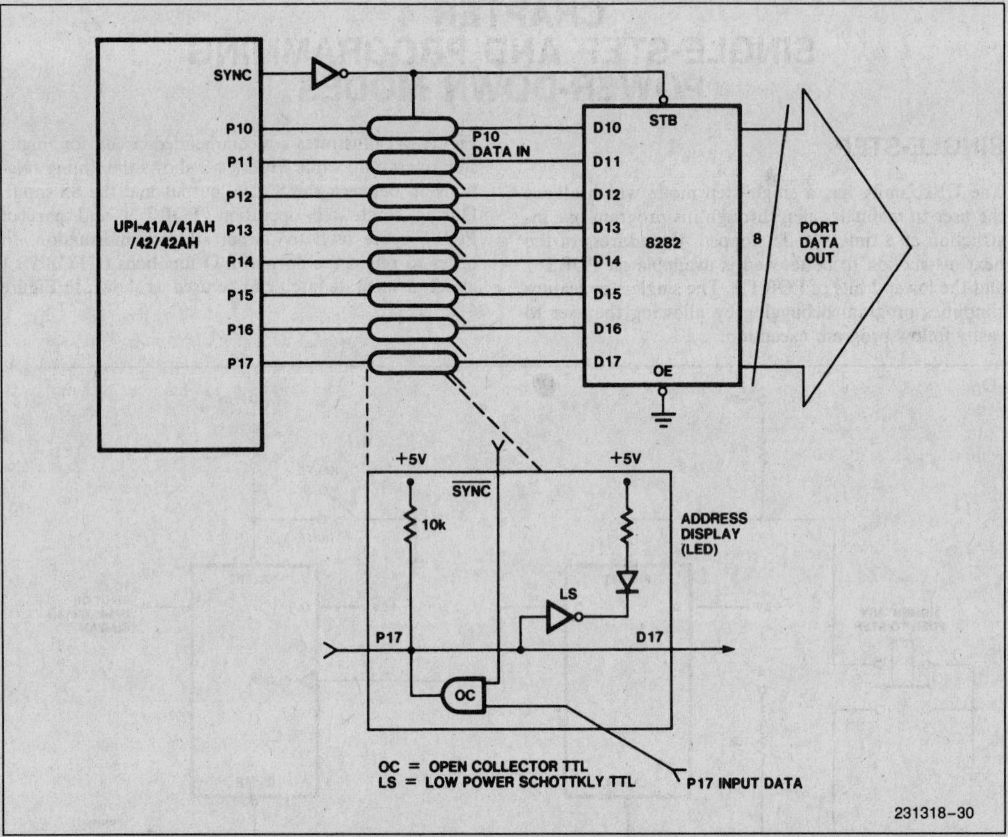

231318-30

Figure 4-3. Latching Port Data

Timing

The sequence of single-step operation is as follows:

1) The processor is requested to stop by applying a low level on $\overline{SS}$. The $\overline{SS}$ input should not be brought low while SYNC is high. (The UPI samples the $\overline{SS}$ pin in the middle of the SYNC pulse).

2) The processor responds to the request by stopping during the instruction fetch portion of the next instruction. If a double cycle instruction is in progress when the single-step command is received, both cycles will be completed before stopping.

3) The processor acknowledges it has entered the stopped state by raising SYNC high. In this state, which can be maintained indefinitely, the 10-bit address of the next instruction to be fetched is preset on PORT 1 and the lower 2 bits of PORT 2.

4) $\overline{SS}$ is then raised high to bring the processor out of the stopped mode allowing it to fetch the next instruction.The exit from stop is indicated by the processor bringing SYNC low.

5) To stop the processor at the next instruction $\overline{SS}$ must be brought low again before the next SYNC pulse—the circuit in Figure 4-1 uses the trailing edge of the previous pulse. If $\overline{SS}$ is left high, the processor remains in the "RUN" mode.

Figure 4-1 shows a schematic for implementing single-step. A single D-type flip-flop with preset and clear is used to generate $\overline{SS}$. In the RUN mode $\overline{SS}$ is held high by keeping the flip-flop preset (preset has precedence over the clear input). To enter single-step, preset is removed allowing SYNC to bring $\overline{SS}$ low via the clear input. Note that SYNC must be buffered since the SN7474 is equivalent to 3 TTL loads.

The processor is now in the stopped state. The next instruction is initiated by stoppe state. The next instruction is initiated by clocking "1" the flip-flop. This "1" will not appear on $\overline{SS}$ unless SYNC is high (I.e., clear must be removed from the flip-flop). In response to $\overline{SS}$ going high, the processor begins an instruction fetch which brings SYNC low. $\overline{SS}$ is then reset through the clear input and the processor again enters the stopped state.

EXTERNAL ACCESS

The UPI family has an External Access mode (EA) which puts the processor into a test mode. This mode allows the user to disable the internal program memory and execute from external memory. External Access mode is useful in testing because it allows the user to test the processor's functions directly. It is only useful for testing since this mode uses D_0-D_7, PORTS 10–17 and PORTS 20–22.

This mode is invoked by connecting the EA pin to 5V. The 11-bit current program counter contents then come out on PORTS 10–17 and PORTS 20–22 after the SYNC output goes high. (PORT 10 is the least significant bit.) The desired instruction opcode is placed on D_0-D_7 before the start of state S_1. During state S_1, the opcode is sampled from D_0-D_7 and subsequently executed in place of the internal program memory contents.

The program counter contents are multiplexed with the I/O port data on PORTS 10–17 and PORTS 20–22. The I/O port data may be demultiplexed using an external latch on the rising edge of SYNC. The program counter contents may be demultiplexed similarly using the trailing edge of SYNC.

Reading and/or writing the Data Bus Buffer registers is still allowed although only when D_0-D_7 are not being sampled for opcode data. In practice, since this sampling time is not known externally, reads or writes on the system bus are done during SYNC high time. Approximately 600 ns are available for each read or write cycle.

POWER DOWN MODE (UPI-41AH/42AH ONLY)

Extra circuitry is included in the UPI-41AH/42AH version to allow low-power, standby operation. Power is removed from all system elements except the internal data RAM in the low-power mode. Thus the contents of RAM can be maintained and the device draws only 10 to 15% of its normal power.

The V_{CC} pin serves as the 5V power supply pin for all of the UPI-41AH/42AH version's circuitry except the data RAM array. The V_{DD} pin supplies only the RAM array. In normal operation, both V_{CC} and V_{DD} are connected to the same 5V power supply.

To enter the Power-Down mode, the $\overline{RESET}$ signal to the UPI is asserted. This ensures the memory will not be inadvertently altered by the UPI during power-down. The V_{CC} pin is then grounded while V_{DD} is maintained at 5V. Figure 4-4 illustrates a recommended Power-Down sequence. The sequence typically occurs as follows:

1) Imminent power supply failure is detected by user defined circuitry. The signal must occur early enough to guarantee the UPI-41AH/42AH can save all necessary data before V_{CC} falls outside normal operating tolerance.
2) A "Power Failure" signal is used to interrupt the processor (via a timer overflow interrupt, for instance) and call a Power Failure service routine.
3) The Power Failure routine saves all important data and machine status in the RAM array. The routine may also initiate transfer of a backup supply to the V_{DD} pin and indicate to external circuitry that the Power Failure routine is complete.
4) A $\overline{RESET}$ signal is applied by external hardware to guarantee data will not be altered as the power supply falls out of limits. $\overline{RESET}$ must be low until V_{CC} reaches ground potential.

Recovery from the Power-Down mode can occur as any other power-on sequence. An external 1 μfd capacitor on the $\overline{RESET}$ input will provide the necessary initialization pulse.

4

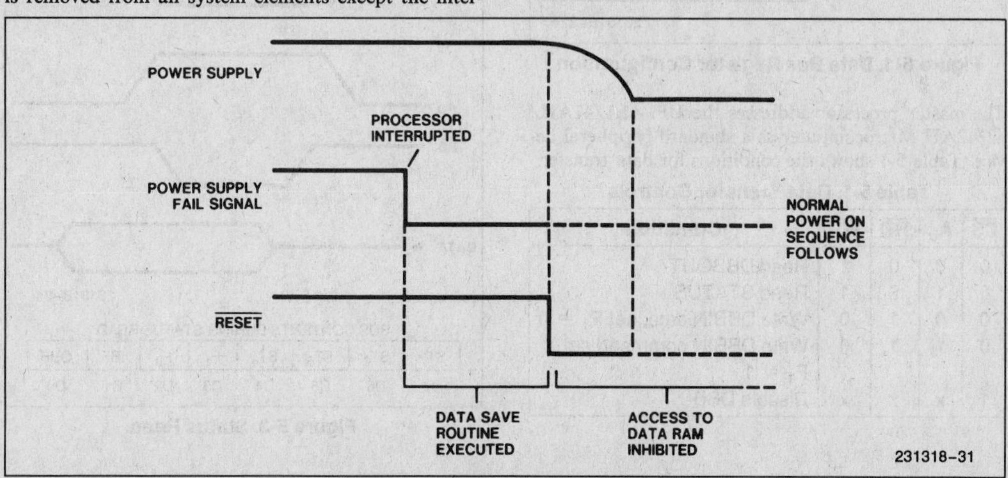

Figure 4-4. Power-Down Sequence

CHAPTER 5 SYSTEM OPERATION

BUS INTERFACE

The UPI-41A/41AH/42/42AH Microcomputer functions as a peripheral to a master processor by using the data bus buffer registers to handle data transfers. The DBB configuration is illustrated in Figure 5-1. The UPI Microcomputer's 8 three-state data lines (D_7-D_0) connect directly to the master processor's data bus. Data transfer to the master is controlled by 4 external inputs to the UPI:

- A_0 Address Input signifying command or data
- $\overline{CS}$ Chip Select
- $\overline{RD}$ Read strobe
- $\overline{WR}$ Write strobe

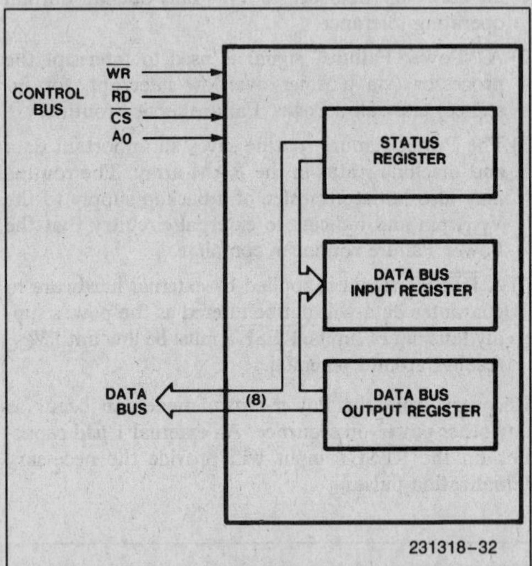

Figure 5-1. Data Bus Register Configuration

The master processor addresses the UPI-41A/41AH/42/42AH Microcomputer as a standard peripheral device. Table 5-1 shows the conditions for data transfer:

Table 5-1. Data Transfer Controls

$\overline{CS}$	A_0	$\overline{RD}$	$\overline{WR}$	Condition
0	0	0	1	Read DBBOUT
0	1	0	1	Read STATUS
0	0	1	0	Write DBBIN data, set $F_1 = 0$
0	1	1	0	Write DBBIN command set $F_1 = 1$
1	x	x	x	Disable DBB

Reading the DBBOUT Register

The sequence for reading the DBBOUT register is shown in Figure 5-2. This operation causes the 8-bit contents of the DBBOUT register to be placed on the system Data Bus. The OBF flag is cleared automatically.

Reading STATUS

The sequence for reading the UPI Microcomputer's 8 STATUS bits is shown in Figure 5-3. This operation causes the 8-bit STATUS register contents to be placed on the system Data Bus as shown.

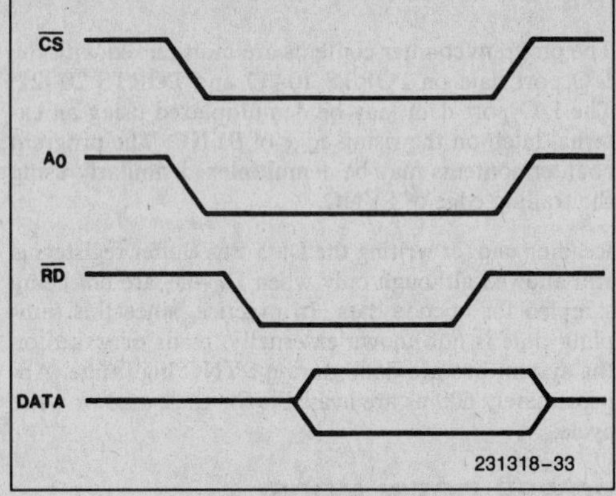

Figure 5-2. DBBOUT Read

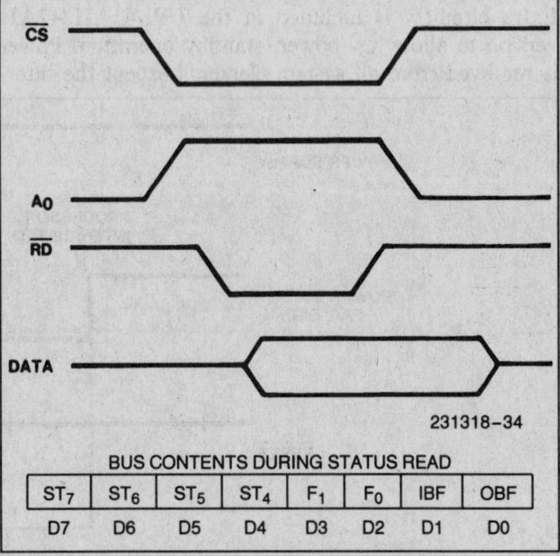

Figure 5-3. Status Read

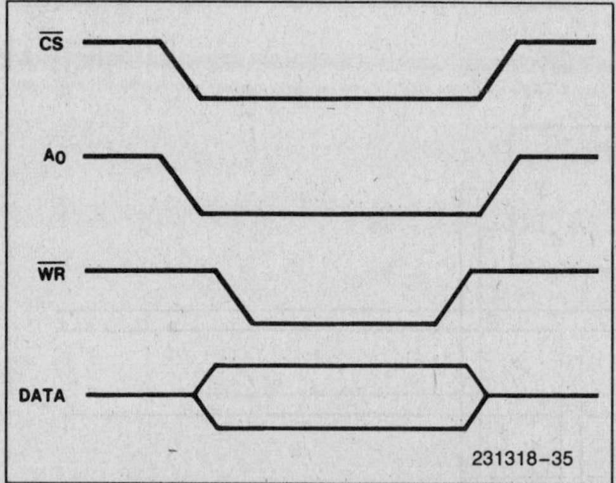

Figure 5-4. Writing Data to DBBIN

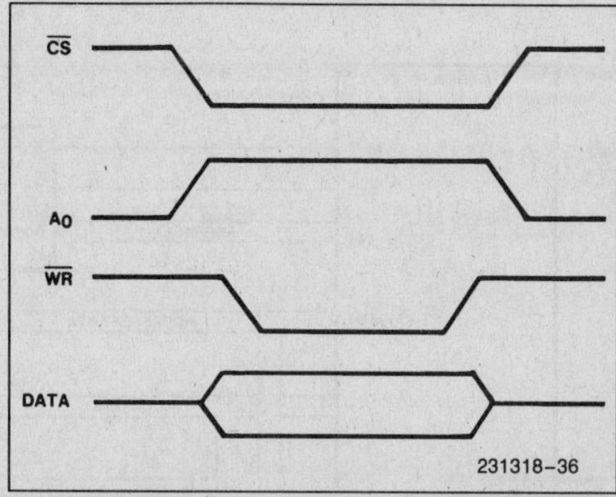

Figure 5-5. Writing Commands to DBBIN

Write Data to DBBIN

The sequence for writing data to the DBBIN register is shown in Figure 5-4. This operation causes the system Data Bus contents to be transferred to the DBBIN register and the IBF flag is set. Also, the F_1 flag is cleared ($F_1 = 0$) and an interrupt request is generated. When the IBF interrupt is enabled, a jump to location 3 will occur. The interrupt request is cleared upon entering the IBF service routine or by a system RESET input.

Writing Commands to DBBIN

The sequence for writing commands to the DBBIN register is shown in Figure 5-5. This sequence is identical to a data write except that the A_0 input is latched in the F_1 flag ($F_1 = 1$). The IBF flag is set and an interrupt request is generated when the master writes a command to DBB.

Operations of Data Bus Registers

The UPI-41A/41AH/42/42AH Microcomputer controls the transfer of DBB data to its accumulator by executing INput and OUTput instructions. An IN A,DBB instruction causes the contents to be transferred to the UPI accumulator and the IBF flag is cleared.

The OUT DBB,A instruction causes the contents of the accumulator to be transferred to the DBBOUT register. The OBF flag is set.

The UPI's data bus buffer interface is applicable to a variety of microprocessors including the 8086, 8088, 8085AH, 8080, and 8048.

A description of the interface to each of these processors follows.

DESIGN EXAMPLES

8085AH Interface

Figure 5-6 illustrates an 8085AH system using a UPI-41A/41AH/42/42AH. The 8085AH system uses a multiplexed address and data bus. During I/O the 8 upper address lines (A_8–A_{15}) contain the same I/O address as the lower 8 address/data lines (A_0–A_7); therefore I/O address decoding is done using only the upper 8 lines to eliminate latching of the address. An 8205 decoder provides address decoding for both the UPI and the 8237. Data is transferred using the two DMA handshaking lines of PORT 2. The 8237 performs the actual bus transfer operation. Using the UPI-41A/41AH/42/42AH's OBF master interrupt, the UPI notifies the 8085AH upon transfer completion using the RST 5.5 interrupt input. The $\overline{\text{IBF}}$ master interrupt is not used in this example.

8088 Interface

Figure 5-7 illustrates a UPI-41A/41AH/42/42AH interface to an 8088 minimum mode system. Two 8-bit latches are used to demultiplex the address and data bus. The address bus is 20-lines wide. For I/O only, the lower 16 address lines are used, providing an addressing range of 64K. UPI address selection is accomplished using an 8205 decoder. The A_0 address line of the bus is connected to the corresponding UPI input for register selection. Since the UPI is polled by the 8088, neither DMA nor master interrupt capabilities of the UPI are used in the figure.

8086 Interface

The UPI-41A/41AH/42/42AH can be used on an 8086 maximum mode system as shown in Figure 5-8. The address and data bus is demultiplexed using three

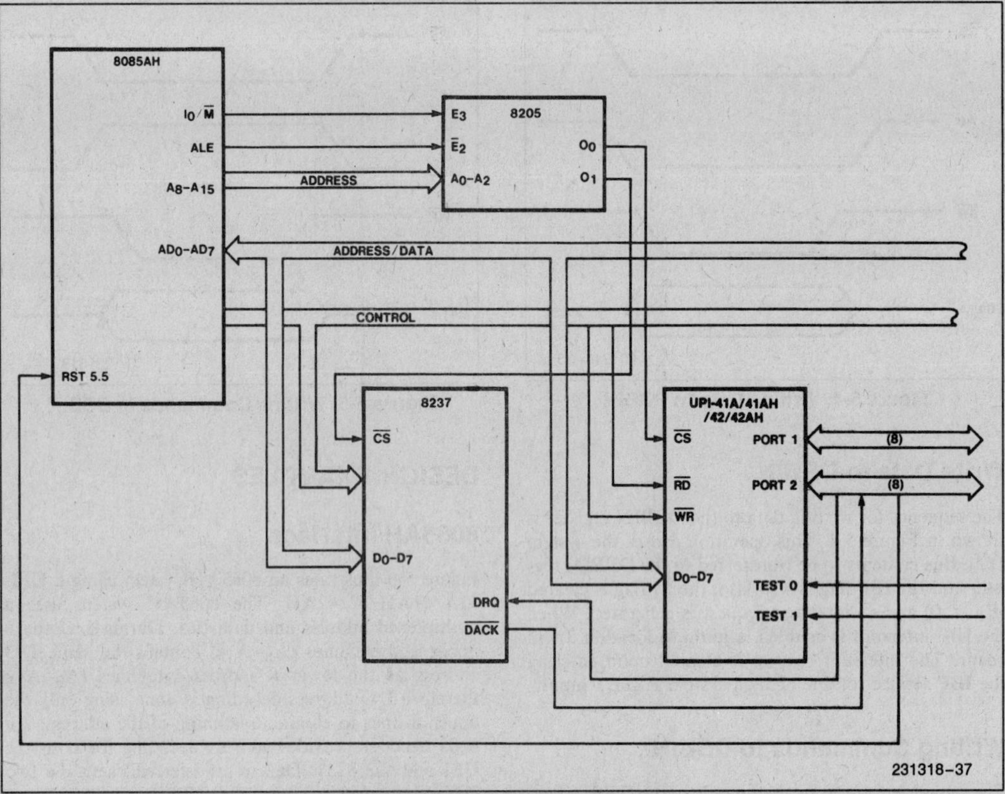

231318-37

Figure 5-6. 8085AH-UPI System

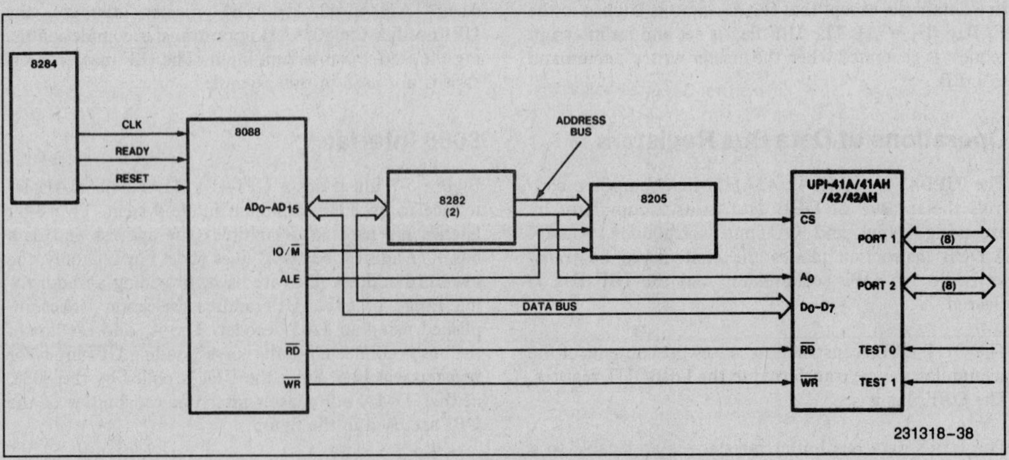

Figure 5-7. 8088-UPI Minimum Mode System

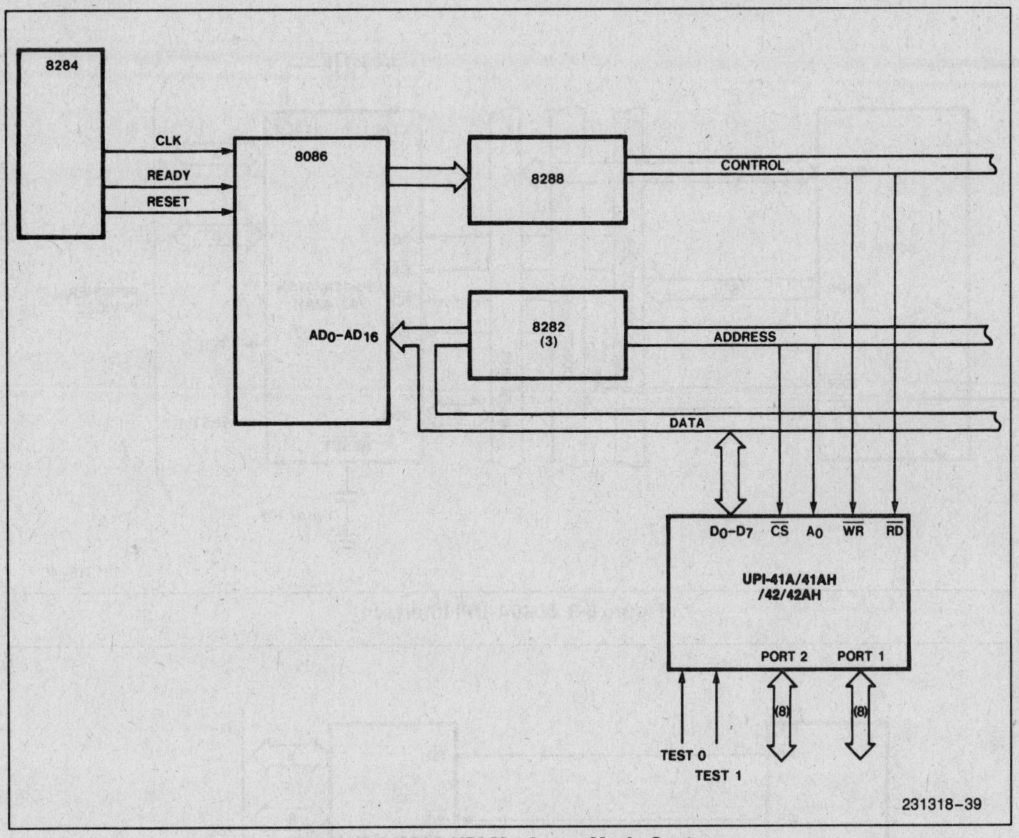

8284
CLK
READY
RESET
8086
8288
CONTROL
AD_0–AD_{16}
8282 (3)
ADDRESS
DATA
D_0–D_7 $\overline{CS}$ A_0 $\overline{WR}$ $\overline{RD}$
UPI-41A/41AH /42/42AH
PORT 2
PORT 1
(8)
(8)
TEST 0
TEST 1
231318–39

Figure 5-8. 8086-UPI Maximum Mode Systems

8282 latches providing separate address and data buses. The address bus is 20-lines wide and the data bus is 16-lines wide. Multiplexed control lines are decoded by the 8288. The UPI's $\overline{CS}$ input is provided by linear selection. Note that the UPI is both I/O mapped and memory mapped as a result of the linear addressing technique. An address decoder may be used to limit the UPI-41A/41AH/42/42AH to a specific I/O mapped address. Address line A_1 is connected to the UPI's A_0 input. This insures that the registers of the UPI will have even I/O addresses. Data will be transferred on D_0–D_7 lines only. This allows the I/O registers to be accessed using byte manipulation instructions.

8080 Interface

Figure 5-9 illustrates the interface to an 8080A system. In this example, a crystal and capacitor are used for UPI-41A/41AH/42/42AH timing reference and power-on RESET. If the 2-MHz 8080A 2-phase clock were used instead of the crystal, the UPI-41A/41AH/42/42AH would run at only 16% full speed.

The A_0 and $\overline{CS}$ inputs are direct connections to the 8080 address bus. In larger systems, however, either of these inputs may be decoded from the 16 address lines.

The $\overline{RD}$ and $\overline{WR}$ inputs to the UPI can be either the $\overline{IOR}$ and $\overline{IOW}$ or the $\overline{MEMR}$ and $\overline{MEMR}$ signals depending on the I/O mapping technique to be used.

The UPI can be addressed as an I/O device using INput and OUTput instructions in 8080 software.

8048 Interface

Figure 5-10 shows the UPI interface to an 8048 master processor.

The 8048 $\overline{RD}$ and $\overline{WR}$ outputs are directly compatible with the UPI. Figure 5-11 shows a distributed processing system with up to seven UPI's connected to a single 8048 master processor.

In this configuration the 8048 uses PORT 0 as a data bus. I/O PORT 2 is used to select one of the seven

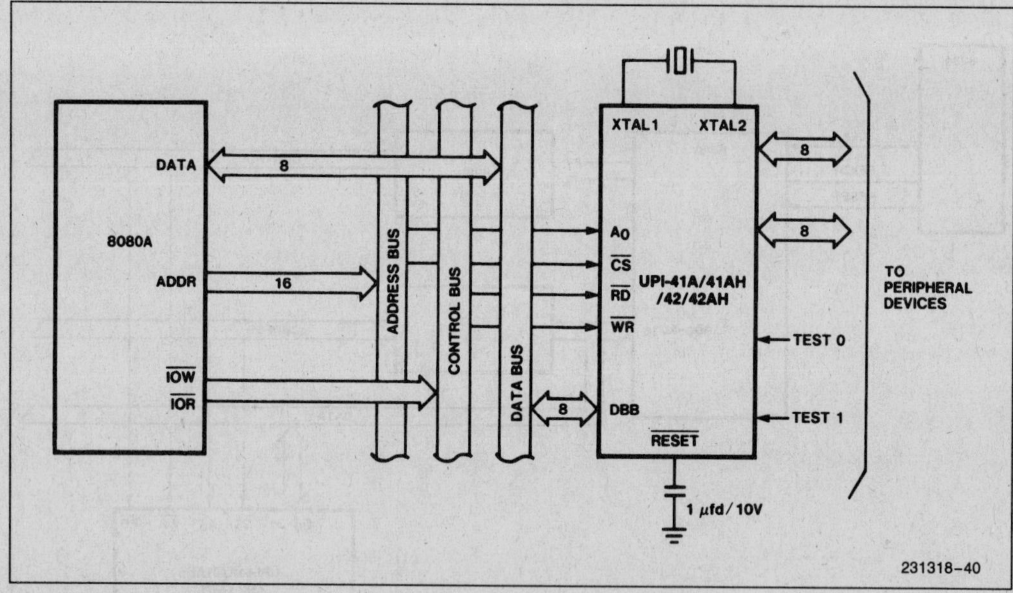

Figure 5-9. 8080A-UPI Interface

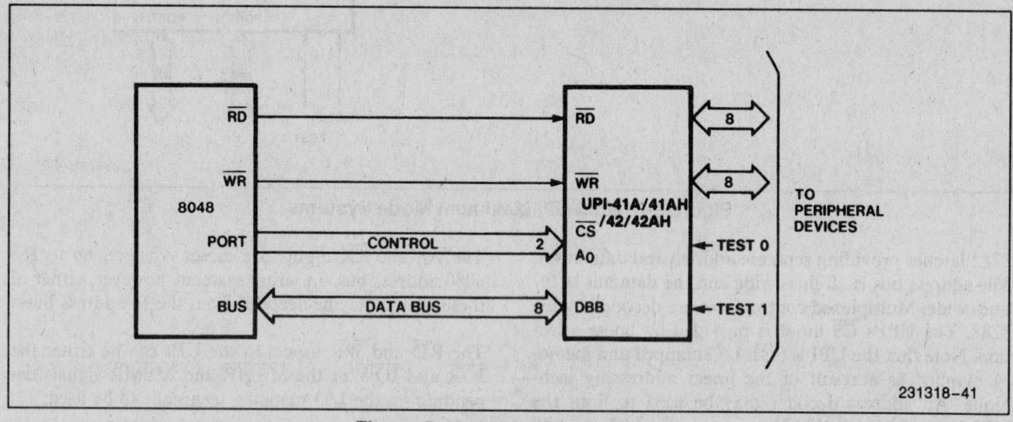

Figure 5-10. 8048-UPI Interface

UPI's when data transfer occurs. The UPI's are programmed to handle isolated tasks and, since they operate in parallel, system throughput is increased.

GENERAL HANDSHAKING PROTOCOL

1) Master reads STATUS register ($\overline{RD}$, $\overline{CS}$, A_0 = (0, 0, 1)) in polling or in response to either an $\overline{IBF}$ or an OBF interrupt.
2) If the UPI DBBIN register is empty (IBF flag = 0), Master writes a word to the DBBIN register ($\overline{WR}$, $\overline{CS}$, A_0 = (0, 0, 1) or (0, 0, 0)). If A_0 = 1, write command word, set F_1. If A_0 = 0, write data word, F_1 = 0.
3) If the UPI DBBOUT register is full (OBF flag = 1), Master reads a word from the DBBOUT register ($\overline{RD}$, $\overline{CS}$, A_0 = (0,0, 0)).
4) UPI recognizes IBF (via IBF interrupt or JNIBF). Input data or command word is processed, depending on F1; IBF is reset. Repeat step 1 above.
5) UPI recognizes OBF flag = 0 (via JOBF). Next word is output to DBBOUT register, OBF is set. Repeat step 1 above.

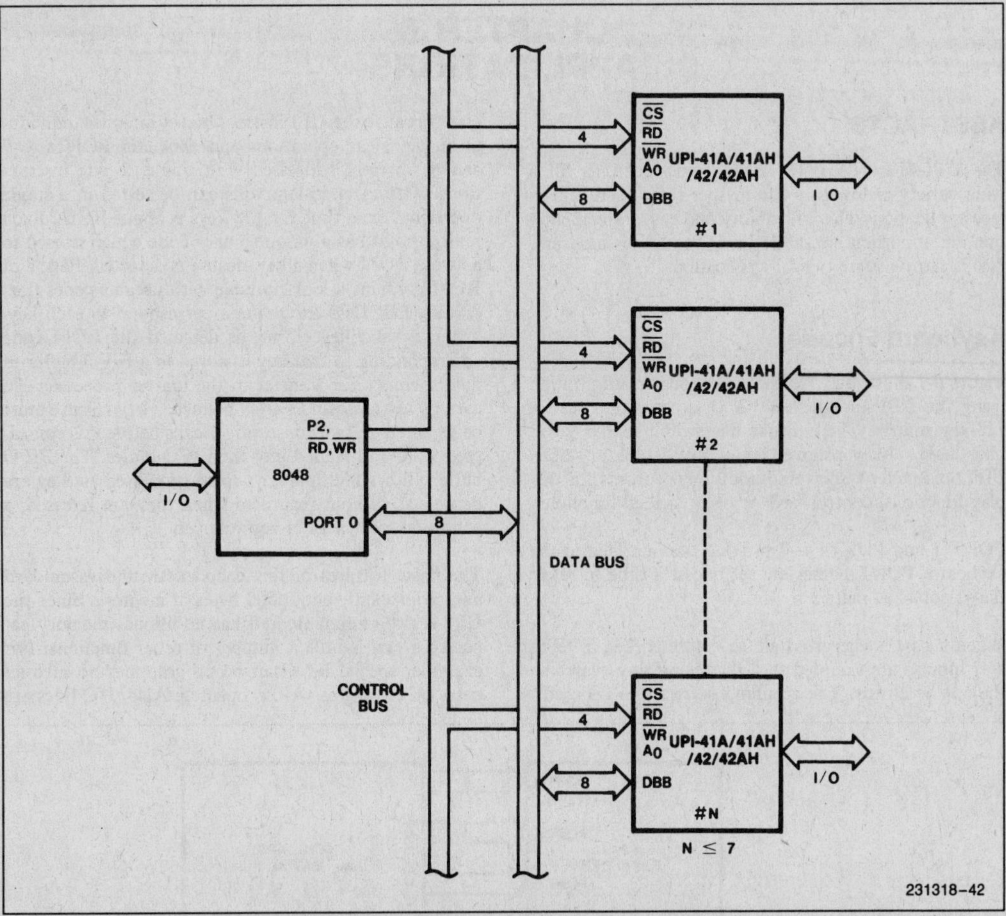

Figure 5-11. Distributed Processor System

4

CHAPTER 6 APPLICATIONS

ABSTRACTS

The UPI-41A/41AH/42/42AH is designed to fill a wide variety of low to medium speed peripheral interface applications where flexibility and easy implementation are important considerations. The following examples illustrate some typical applications.

Keyboard Encoder

Figure 6-1 illustrates a keyboard encoder configuration using the UPI and the 8243 I/O expander to scan a 128-key matrix. The encoder has switch matrix scanning logic, N-key rollover logic, ROM look-up table, FIFO character buffer, and additional outputs for display functions, control keys or other special functions.

PORT 1 and PORTs 4–7 provide the interface to the keyboard. PORT 1 lines are set one at a time to select the various key matrix rows.

When a row is energized all 16 columns (i.e., PORTs 4–7 inputs) are sampled to determine if any switch in the row is closed. The scanning software is code efficient because the UPI instruction set includes individual bit set/clear operations and expander PORTs 4–7 can be directly addressed with single, 2-byte instructions. Also, accumulator bits can be tested in a single operation. Scan time for 128 keys is about 10 ms. Each matrix point has a unique binary code which is used to address ROM when a key closure is detected. Page 3 of ROM contains a look-up table with useable codes (i.e., ASCII, EBCDIC, etc.) which correspond to each key. When a valid key closure is detected the ROM code corresponding to that key is stored in a FIFO buffer in data memory for transfer to the master processor. To avoid stray noise and switch bounce, a key closure must be detected on two consecutive scans before it is considered valid and loaded into the FIFO buffer. The FIFO buffer allows multiple keys to be processed as they are depressed without regard to when they are released, a condition known as N-key rollover.

The basic features of this encoder are fairly standard and require only about 500 bytes of memory. Since the UPI is programmable and has additional memory capacity it can handle a number of other functions. For example, special keys can be programmed to give an entry on closing as well as opening. Also, I/O lines are

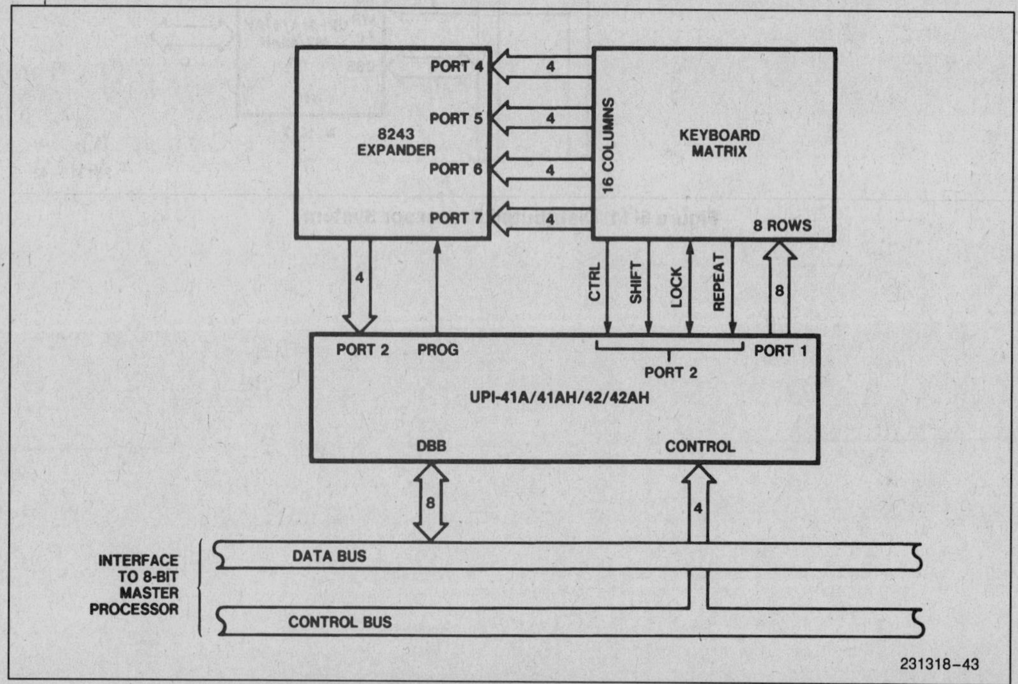

Figure 6-1. Keyboard Encoder Configuration

available to control a 16-digit, 7-segment display. The UPI can also be programmed to recognize special combinations of characters such as commands, then transfer only the decoded information to the master processor.

Matrix Printer Interface

The matrix printer interface illustrated in Figure 6-2 is a typical application for the UPI. The actual printer mechanism could be any of the numerous dot-matrix types and similar configurations can be shown for drum, spherical head, daisy wheel or chain type printers.

The bus structure shown represents a generalized, 8-bit system bus configuration. The UPI's three-state interface port and asynchronous data buffer registers allow it to connect directly to this type of system for efficient, two-way data transfer.

The UPI's two on-board I/O ports provide up to 16 input and output signals to control the printer mechanism. The timer/event counter is used for generating a timing sequence to control print head position, line feed, carriage return, and other sequences. The on-board program memory provides character generation for 5 x 7, 7 x 9, or other dot matrix formats. As an added feature a portion of the data memory can be used as a FIFO buffer so that the master processor can send a block of data at a high rate. The UPI can then output characters from the buffer at a rate the printer can accept while the master processor returns to other tasks.

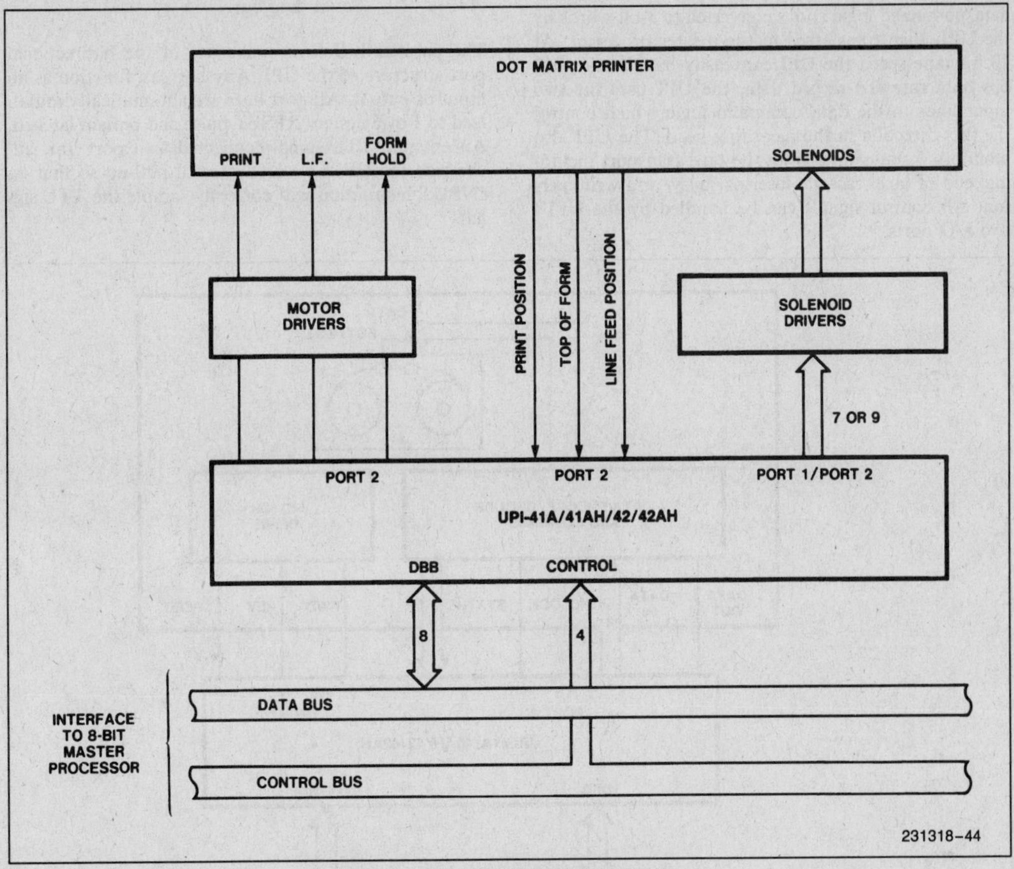

Figure 6-2. Matrix Printer Controller

The 8295 Printer Controller is an example of an UPI preprogrammed as a dot matrix printer interface.

Tape Cassette Controller

Figure 6-3 illustrates a digital cassette interface which can be implemented with the UPI. Two sections of the tape transport are controlled by the UPI: digital data/command logic, and motor servo control.

The motor servo requires a speed reference in the form of a monostable pulse whose width is proportional to the desired speed. The UPI monitors a prerecorded clock from the tape and uses its on-board interval timer to generate the required speed reference pulses at each clock transition.

Recorded data from the tape is supplied serially by the data/command logic and is converted to 8-bit words by the UPI, then transferred to the master processor. At 10 ips tape speed the UPI can easily handle the 8000 bps data rate. To record data, the UPI uses the two input lines to the data/command logic which control the flux direction in the recording head. The UPI also monitors 4 status lines from the tape transport including: end of tape, cassette inserted, busy, and write permit. All control signals can be handled by the UPI's two I/O ports.

Universal I/O Interface

Figure 6-4 shows an I/O interface design based on the UPI. This configuration includes 12 parallel I/O lines and a serial (RS232C) interface for full duplex data transfer up to 1200 baud. This type of design can be used to interface a master processor to a broad spectrum of peripheral devices as well as to a serial communication channel.

PORT 1 is used strictly for I/O in this example while PORT 2 lines provide five functions:

- $P_{23}-P_{20}$ I/O lines (bidirectional)
- P_{24} Request to send (RTS)
- P_{25} Clear to send (CTS)
- P_{26} Interrupt to master
- P_{27} Serial data out

The parallel I/O lines make use of the bidirectional port structure of the UPI. Any line can function as an input or output. All port lines are automatically initialized to 1 by a system $\overline{\text{RESET}}$ pulse and remain latched. An external TTL signal connected to a port line will override the UPI's 50 KΩ internal pull-up so that an INPUT instruction will correctly sample the TTL signal.

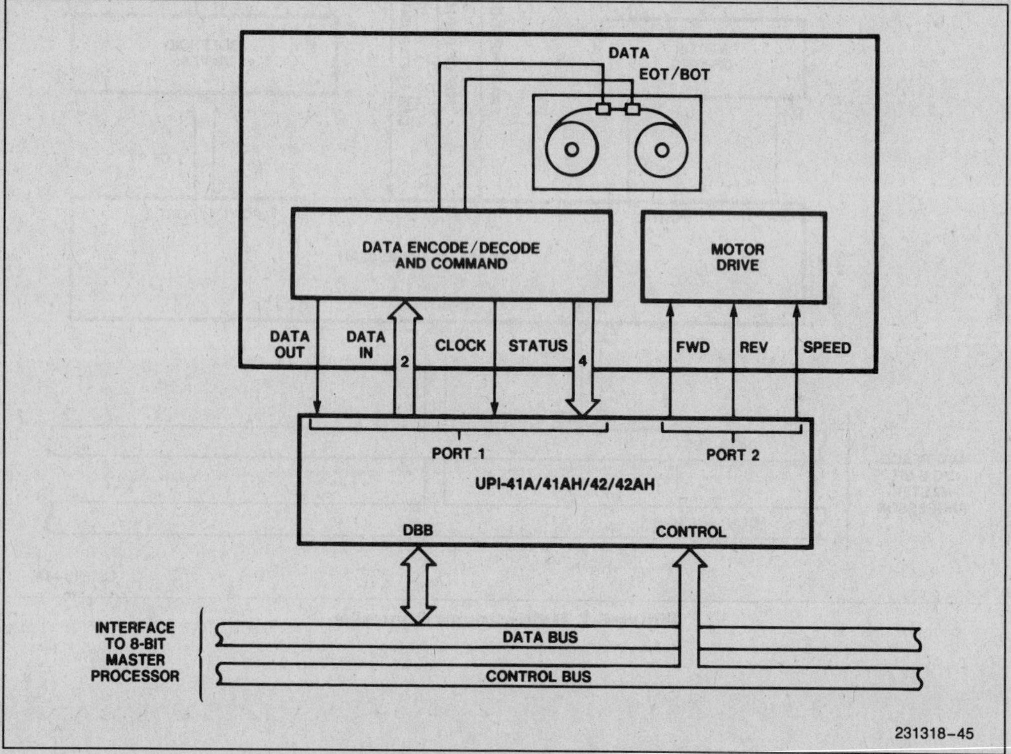

231318–45

Figure 6-3. Tape Transport Controller

Four PORT 2 lines function as general I/O similar to PORT 1. Also, the RTS signal is generated on PORT 2 under software control when the UPI has serial data to send. The CTS signal is monitored via PORT 2 as an enable to the UPI to send serial data. A PORT 2 line is also used as a software generated interrupt to the master processor. The interrupt functions as a service request when the UPI has a byte of data to transfer or when it is ready to receive. Alternatively, the EN FLAGS instruction could be used to create the OBF and $\overline{IBF}$ interrupts on P_{24} and P_{25}.

The RS232C interface is implemented using the TEST 0 pin as a receive input and a PORT 2 pin as a transmit output. External packages (A_0, A_1) are used to provide RS232C drive requirements. The serial receive software is interrupt driven and uses the on-chip timer to perform time critical serial control. After a start bit is detected the interval timer can be preset to generate an interrupt at the proper time for sampling the serial bit stream. This eliminates the need for software timing loops and allows the processor to proceed to other tasks (i.e., parallel I/O operations) between serial bit samples. Software flags are used so the main program can determine when the interrupt driven receive program has a character assembled for it.

This type of configuration allows system designers flexibility in designing custom I/O interfaces for specific serial and parallel I/O applications. For instance, a second or third serial channel could be substituted in place of the parallel I/O if required. The UPI's data memory can buffer data and commands for up to 4 low-speed channels (110 baud teletypewriter, etc.)

Application Notes

The following application notes illustrate the various applications of the UPI family. Other related publications including the *Microcontroller Handbook* are available through the Intel Literature Department.

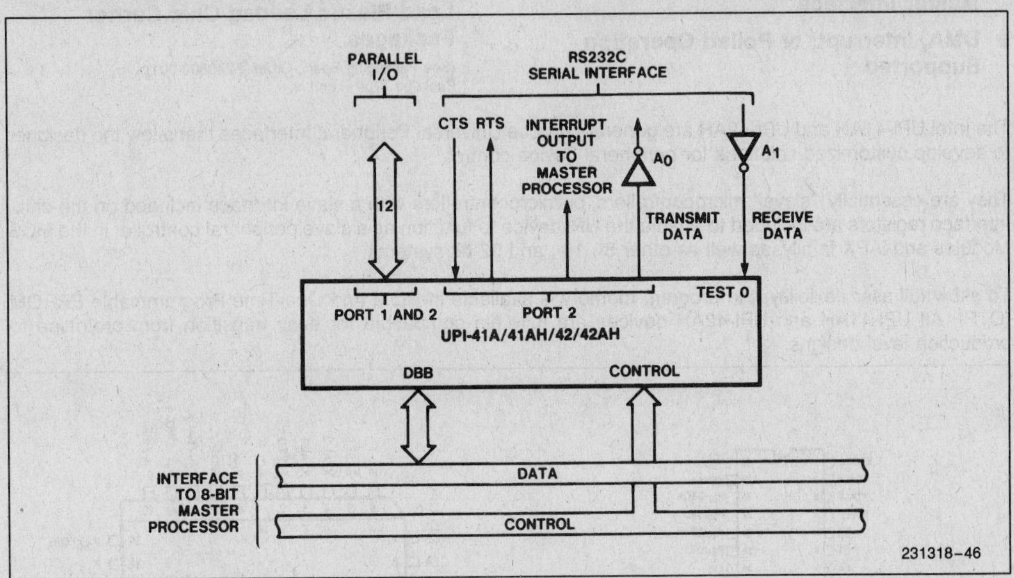

Figure 6-4. Universal I/O Interface

UPI-41AH/42AH UNIVERSAL PERIPHERAL INTERFACE 8-BIT SLAVE MICROCONTROLLER

- **UPI-41: 6 MHz; UPI-42: 12.5 MHz**
- **Pin, Software and Architecturally Compatible with all UPI-41 and UPI-42 Products**
- **8-Bit CPU plus ROM/OTP EPROM, RAM, I/O, Timer/Counter and Clock in a Single Package**
- **2048 x 8 ROM/OTP, 256 x 8 RAM on UPI-42, 1024 x 8 ROM/OTP, 128 x 8 RAM on UPI-41, 8-Bit Timer/Counter, 18 Programmable I/O Pins**
- **One 8-Bit Status and Two Data Registers for Asynchronous Slave-to-Master Interface**
- **DMA, Interrupt, or Polled Operation Supported**
- **Fully Compatible with all Intel and Most Other Microprocessor Families**
- **Interchangeable ROM and OTP EPROM Versions**
- **Expandable I/O**
- **Sync Mode Available**
- **Over 90 Instructions: 70% Single Byte**
- **Available in EXPRESS — Standard Temperature Range**
- **inteligent Programming Algorithm — Fast OTP Programming**
- **Available in 40-Lead Plastic and 44-Lead Plastic Leaded Chip Carrier Packages**
  (See Packaging Spec., Order #240800-001)
  Package Type P and N

The Intel UPI-41AH and UPI-42AH are general-purpose Universal Peripheral Interfaces that allow the designer to develop customized solutions for peripheral device control.

They are essentially "slave" microcontrollers, or microcontrollers with a slave interface included on the chip. Interface registers are included to enable the UPI device to function as a slave peripheral controller in the MCS Modules and iAPX family, as well as other 8-, 16-, and 32-bit systems.

To allow full user flexibility, the program memory is available in ROM and One-Time Programmable EPROM (OTP). All UPI-41AH and UPI-42AH devices are fully pin compatible for easy transition from prototype to production level designs.

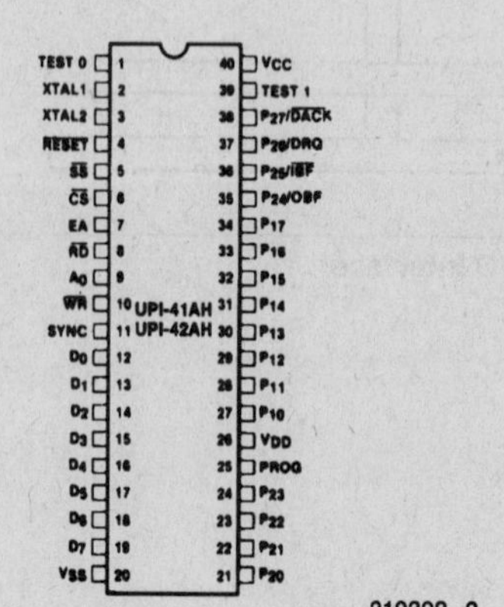

210393-2

Figure 1. DIP Pin Configuration

210393-3

Figure 2. PLCC Pin Configuration

October 1991
Order Number: 210393-007

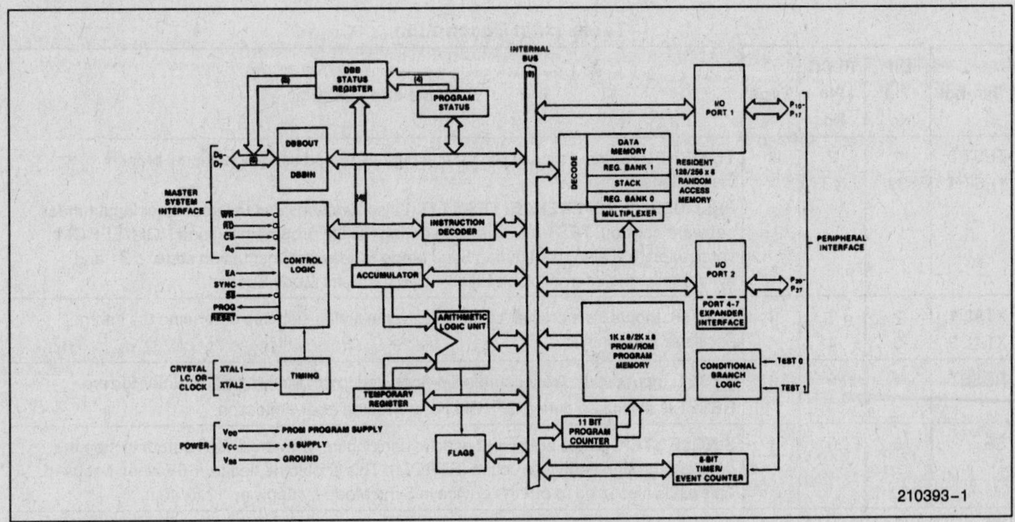

Figure 3. Block Diagram

UPI PRODUCT MATRIX

UPI Device	ROM	OTP EPROM	RAM	Programming Voltage
8042AH	2K	—	256	—
8242AH	2K	—	256	—
8742AH	—	2K	256	12.5V
8041AH	1K	—	128	—
8741AH	—	1K	128	12.5V

THE INTEL 8242

As shown in the UPI-42 product matrix, the UPI-42 will be offered as a pre-programmed 8042 with several software vendors' keyboard controller firmware. The current list of available 8242 versions include keyboard controller firmware from both Phoenix Technologies Ltd. and Award Software Inc. The 8242 is programmed with Phoenix Technologies Ltd. keyboard controller firmware for AT-compatible systems. This keyboard controller is fully compatible with all AT-compatible operating systems and applications. The 8242PC also contains Phoenix Technologies Ltd. firmware. This keyboard controller provides support for AT, PS/2 and most EISA platforms as well as PS/2-style mouse support for either AT or PS/2 platforms.

The 8242WA contains Award Software Inc. firmware. This device provides at AT-compatible keyboard controller for use in IBM PC AT compatible computers. The 8242WB contains a version of Award Software Inc. firmware that provides PS/2 style mouse support in addition to the standard features of the 8242WA.

*Contact factory for current code revision available in the 8242.

Table 1. Pin Description

Symbol	DIP Pin No.	PLCC Pin No.	Type	Name and Function
TEST 0, TEST 1	1 39	2 43	I	**TEST INPUTS:** Input pins which can be directly tested using conditional branch instructions. **FREQUENCY REFERENCE:** TEST 1 (T_1) also functions as the event timer input (under software control). TEST 0 (T_0) is used during PROM programming and ROM/EPROM verification. It is also used during Sync Mode to reset the instruction state to S1 and synchronize the internal clock to PH1. See the Sync Mode Section.
XTAL 1, XTAL 2	2 3	3 4	I	**INPUTS:** Inputs for a crystal, LC or an external timing signal to determine the internal oscillator frequency.
$\overline{\text{RESET}}$	4	5	I	**RESET:** Input used to reset status flip-flops and to set the program counter to zero. $\overline{\text{RESET}}$ is also used during EPROM programming and verification.
$\overline{\text{SS}}$	5	6	I	**SINGLE STEP:** Single step input used in conjunction with the SYNC output to step the program through each instruction (EPROM). This should be tied to +5V when not used. This pin is also used to put the device in Sync Mode by applying 12.5V to it.
$\overline{\text{CS}}$	6	7	I	**CHIP SELECT:** Chip select input used to select one UPI microcomputer out of several connected to a common data bus.
EA	7	8	I	**EXTERNAL ACCESS:** External access input which allows emulation, testing and ROM/EPROM verification. This pin should be tied low if unused.
$\overline{\text{RD}}$	8	9	I	**READ:** I/O read input which enables the master CPU to read data and status words from the OUTPUT DATA BUS BUFFER or status register.
A_0	9	10	I	**COMMAND/DATA SELECT:** Address Input used by the master processor to indicate whether byte transfer is data ($A_0 = 0$, F1 is reset) or command ($A_0 = 1$, F1 is set). $A_0 = 0$ during program and verify operations.
$\overline{\text{WR}}$	10	11	I	**WRITE:** I/O write input which enables the master CPU to write data and command words to the UPI INPUT DATA BUS BUFFER.
SYNC	11	13	O	**OUTPUT CLOCK:** Output signal which occurs once per UPI instruction cycle. SYNC can be used as a strobe for external circuitry; it is also used to synchronize single step operation.
D_0–D_7 (BUS)	12–19	14–21	I/O	**DATA BUS:** Three-state, bidirectional DATA BUS BUFFER lines used to interface the UPI microcomputer to an 8-bit master system data bus.
P_{10}–P_{17}	27–34	30–33 35–38	I/O	**PORT 1:** 8-bit, PORT 1 quasi-bidirectional I/O lines. P_{10}–P_{17} access the signature row and security bit.
P_{20}–P_{27}	21–24 35–38	24–27 39–42	I/O	**PORT 2:** 8-bit, PORT 2 quasi-bidirectional I/O lines. The lower 4 bits (P_{20}–P_{23}) interface directly to the 8243 I/O expander device and contain address and data information during PORT 4–7 access. The upper 4 bits (P_{24}–P_{27}) can be programmed to provide interrupt Request and DMA Handshake capability. Software control can configure P_{24} as Output Buffer Full (OBF) interrupt, P_{25} as Input Buffer Full ($\overline{\text{IBF}}$) interrupt, P_{26} as DMA Request (DRQ), and P_{27} as DMA ACKnowledge ($\overline{\text{DACK}}$).
PROG	25	28	I/O	**PROGRAM:** Multifunction pin used as the program pulse input during PROM programming. During I/O expander access the PROG pin acts as an address/data strobe to the 8243. This pin should be tied high if unused.
V_{CC}	40	44		**POWER:** +5V main power supply pin.
V_{DD}	26	29		**POWER:** +5V during normal operation. +12.5V during programming operation. Low power standby supply pin.
V_{SS}	20	22		**GROUND:** Circuit ground potential.

UPI-41AH and UPI-42AH FEATURES

1. Two Data Bus Buffers, one for input and one for output. This allows a much cleaner Master/Slave protocol.

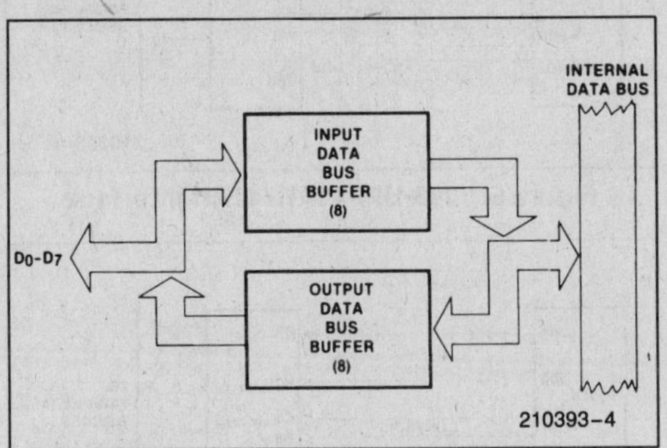

210393-4

2. 8 Bits of Status

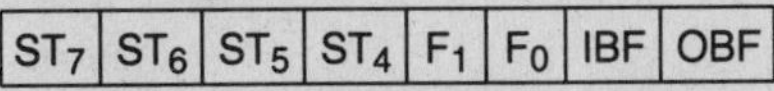

ST_7	ST_6	ST_5	ST_4	F_1	F_0	IBF	OBF
D_7	D_6	D_5	D_4	D_3	D_2	D_1	D_0

ST_4–ST_7 are user definable status bits. These bits are defined by the "MOV STS, A" single byte, single cycle instruction. Bits 4–7 of the acccumulator are moved to bits 4–7 of the status register. Bits 0–3 of the status register are not affected.

MOV STS, A Op Code: 90H

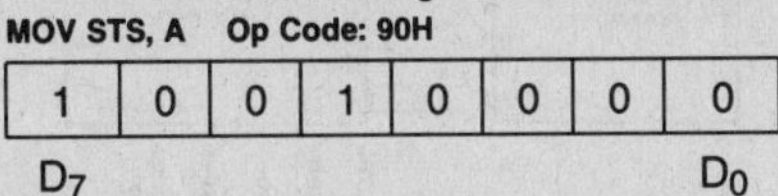

1	0	0	1	0	0	0	0
D_7							D_0

3. $\overline{RD}$ and $\overline{WR}$ are edge triggered. IBF, OBF, F_1 and INT change internally after the trailing edge of $\overline{RD}$ or $\overline{WR}$.

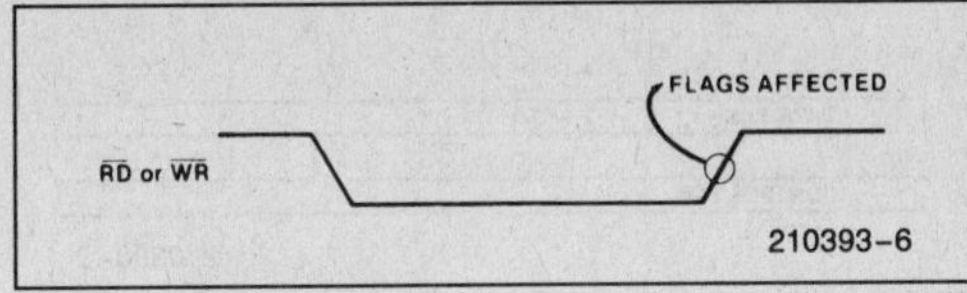

210393-6

During the time that the host CPU is reading the status register, the UPI is prevented from updating this register or is 'locked out.'

4. P_{24} and P_{25} are port pins or Buffer Flag pins which can be used to interrupt a master processor. These pins default to port pins on Reset.

If the "EN FLAGS" instruction has been executed, P_{24} becomes the OBF (Output Buffer Full) pin. A "1" written to P_{24} enables the OBF pin (the pin outputs the OBF Status Bit). A "0" written to P_{24} disables the OBF pin (the pin remains low). This pin can be used to indicate that valid data is available from the UPI (in Output Data Bus Buffer).

If "EN FLAGS" has been executed, P_{25} becomes the $\overline{IBF}$ (Input Buffer Full) pin. A "1" written to P_{25} enables the $\overline{IBF}$ pin (the pin outputs the inverse of the IBF Status Bit. A "0" written to P_{25} disables the $\overline{IBF}$ pin (the pin remains low). This pin can be used to indicate that the UPI is ready for data.

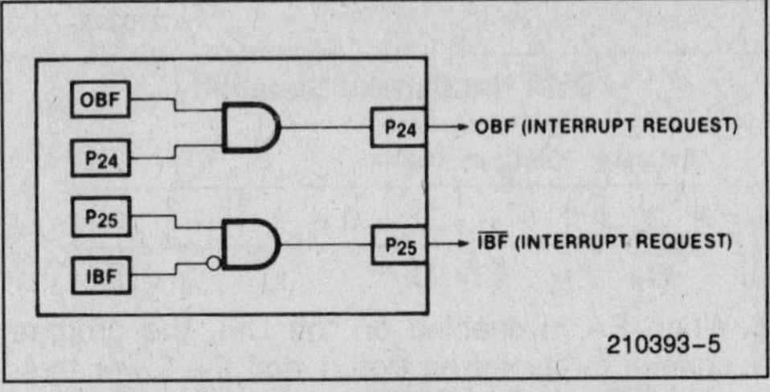

210393-5

Data Bus Buffer Interrupt Capability

EN FLAGS Op Code: 0F5H

1	1	1	1	0	1	0	1
D_7							D_0

5. P_{26} and P_{27} are port pins or DMA handshake pins for use with a DMA controller. These pins default to port pins on Reset.

If the "EN DMA" instruction has been executed, P_{26} becomes the DRQ (DMA Request) pin. A "1" written to P_{26} causes a DMA request (DRQ is activated). DRQ is deactivated by DACK•RD, DACK•WR, or execution of the "EN DMA" instruction.

If "EN DMA" has been executed, P_{27} becomes the $\overline{DACK}$ (DMA ACKnowledge) pin. This pin acts as a chip select input for the Data Bus Buffer registers during DMA transfers.

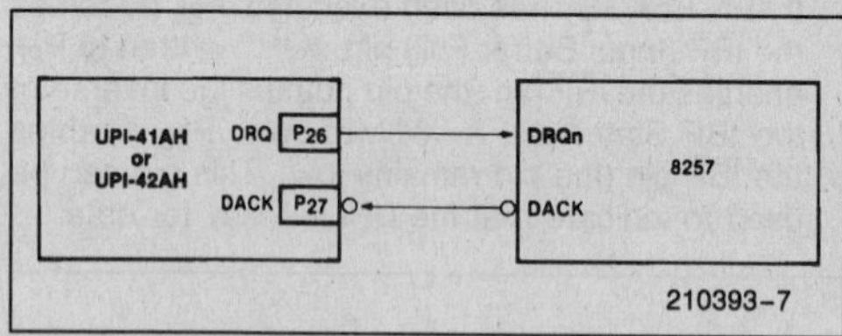

DMA Handshake Capability

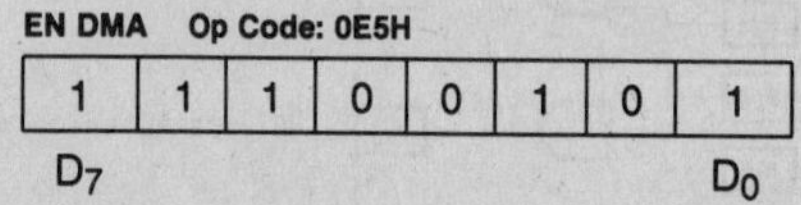

EN DMA Op Code: 0E5H

1	1	1	0	0	1	0	1
D_7							D_0

6. When EA is enabled on the UPI, the program counter is placed on Port 1 and the lower three bits of Port 2 (MSB = P_{22}, LSB = P_{10}). On the UPI this information is multiplexed with PORT DATA (see port timing diagrams at end of this data sheet).

7. The 8741AH and 8742AH support the int$_e$ligent Programming Algorithm. (See the Programming Section.)

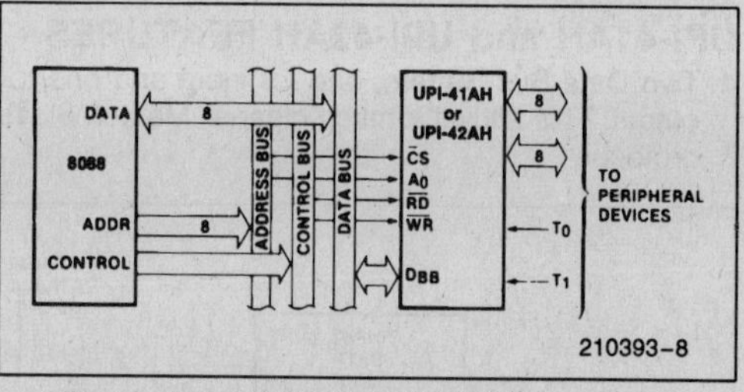

Figure 5. 8088-UPI-41AH/42AH Interface

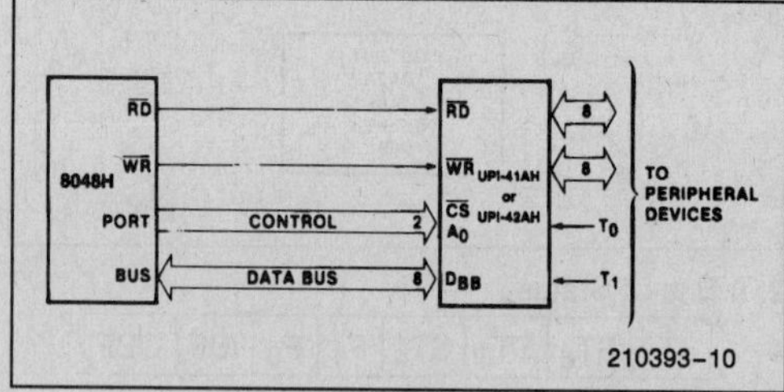

Figure 6. 8048H-UPI-41/42 Interface

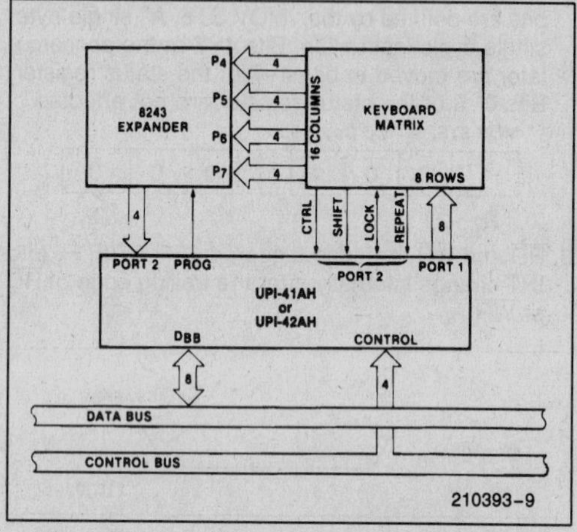

Figure 7. UPI-41/42-8243 Keyboard Scanner

APPLICATIONS

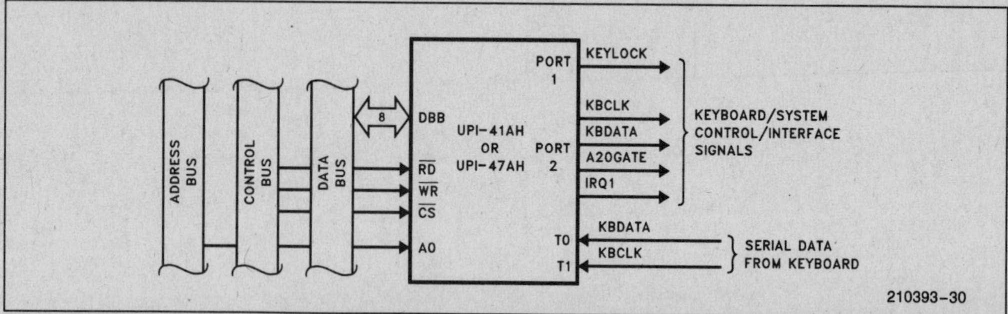

Figure 4. UPI-41AH/42AH Keyboard Controller

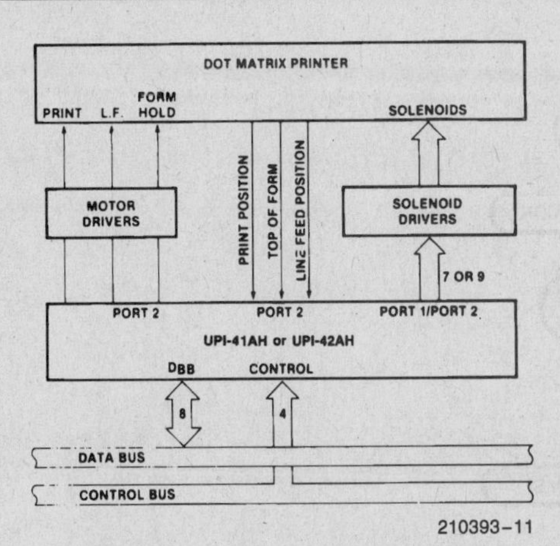

Figure 8. UPI-41AH/42AH 80-Column Matrix Printer Interface

PROGRAMMING AND VERIFYING THE 8741AH AND 8742AH OTP EPROM

Programming Verification

In brief, the programming process consists of: activating the program mode, applying an address, latching the address, applying data, and applying a programming pulse. Each word is programmed completely before moving on to the next and is followed by a verification step. The following is a list of the pins used for programming and a description of their functions:

Pin	Function
XTAL 1	2 Clock Inputs
$\overline{\text{Reset}}$	Initialization and Address Latching
Test 0	Selection of Program or Verify Mode
EA	Activation of Program/Verify Signature Row/Security Bit Modes
BUS	Address and Data Input Data Output During Verify
P_{20-22}	Address Input
V_{DD}	Programming Power Supply
PROG	Program Pulse Input

WARNING
An attempt to program a missocketed 8741AH or 8742AH will result in severe damage to the part. An indication of a properly socketed part is the appearance of the SYNC clock output. The lack of this clock may be used to disable the programmer.

The Program/Verify sequence is:

1. CS = 5V, V_{CC} = 5V, V_{DD} = 5V, RESET = 0V, A_0 = 0V, TEST 0 = 5V, clock applied or internal oscillator operating, BUS floating, PROG = 5V.
2. Insert 8741AH or 8742AH in programming socket
3. TEST 0 = 0V (select program mode)
4. EA = 12.5V (active program mode)
5. V_{CC} = 6V (programming supply)
6. V_{DD} = 12.5V (programming power)
7. Address applied to BUS and P_{20-22}
8. $\overline{\text{RESET}}$ = 5V (latch address)
9. Data applied to BUS
10. PROG = 5V followed by one 1 ms pulse to 0V
11. TEST 0 = 5V (verify mode)
12. Read and verify data on BUS
13. TEST 0 = 0V
14. Apply overprogram pulse
15. $\overline{\text{RESET}}$ = 0V and repeat from step 6
16. Programmer should be at conditions of step 1 when 8741AH or 8742AH is removed from socket

Please follow the int$_e$ligent Programming flow chart for proper programming procedure.

4

int$_e$ligent Programming Algorithm

The int$_e$ligent Programming Algorithm rapidly programs Intel 8741AH/8742AH EPROMs using an efficient and reliable method particularly suited to the production programming environment. Typical programming time for individual devices is on the order of 10 seconds. Programming reliability is also ensured as the incremental program margin of each byte is continually monitored to determine when it has been successfully programmed. A flowchart of the 8741AH/8742AH int$_e$ligent Programming Algorithm is shown in Figure 9.

The int$_e$ligent Programming Algorithm utilizes two different pulse types: initial and overprogram. The duration of the initial PROG pulse(s) is one millisecond, which will then be followed by a longer overprogram pulse of length 3X msec. X is an iteration counter and is equal to the number of the initial one millisecond pulses applied to a particular 8741AH/8742AH location, before a correct verify occurs. Up to 25 one-millisecond pulses per byte are provided for before the overprogram pulse is applied.

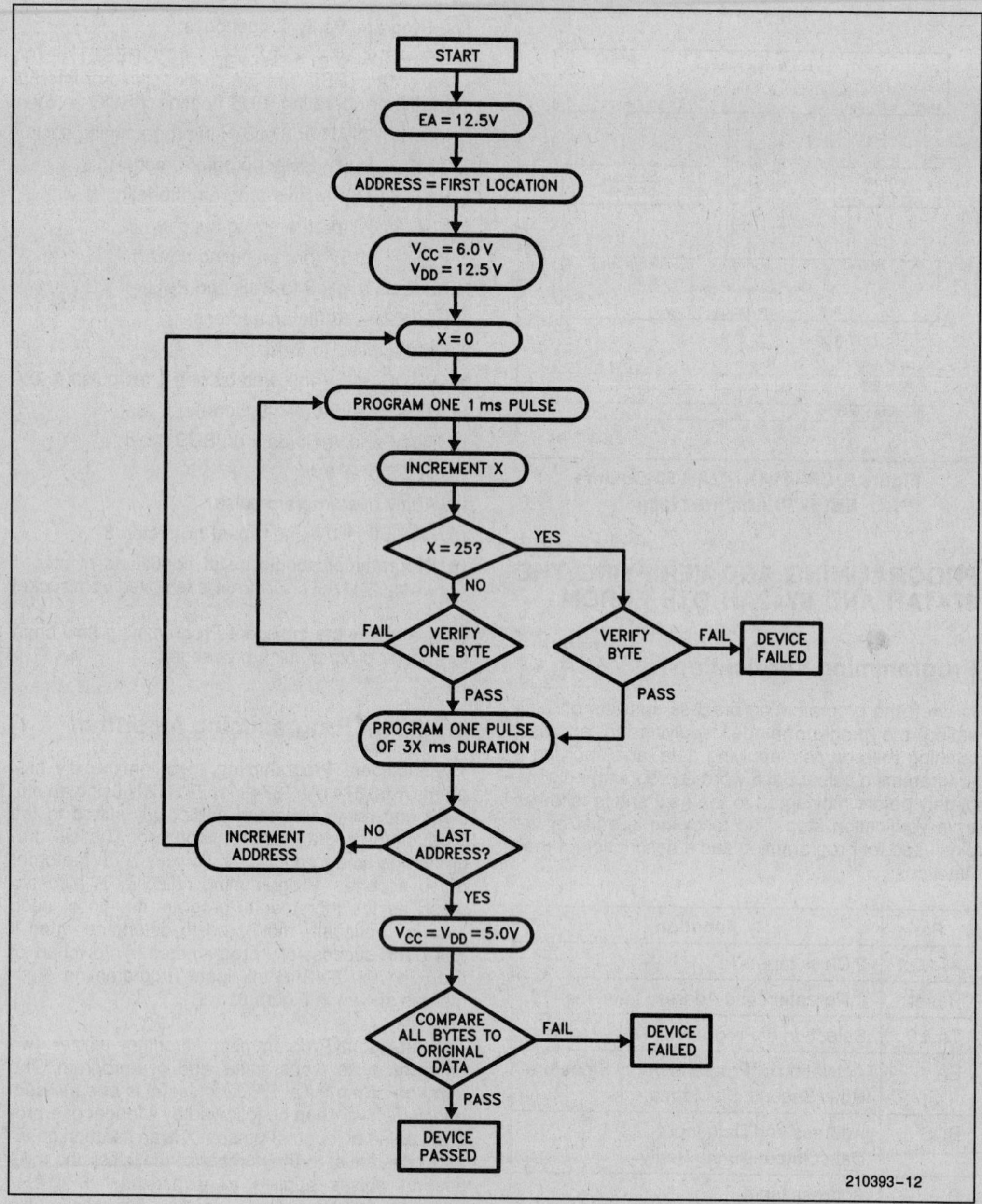

Figure 9. Programming Algorithm

The entire sequence of program pulses and byte verifications is performed at V_{CC} = 6.0V and V_{DD} = 12.5V. When the int_eligent Programming cycle has been completed, all bytes should be compared to the original data with V_{CC} = 5.0, V_{DD} = 5V.

Verify

A verify should be performed on the programmed bits to determine that they have been correctly programmed. The verify is performed with T0 = 5V, V_{DD} = 5V, EA = 12.5V, $\overline{SS}$ = 5V, PROG = 5V, A0 = 0V, and $\overline{CS}$ = 5V.

SECURITY BIT

The security bit is a single EPROM cell outside the EPROM array. The user can program this bit with the appropriate access code and the normal programming procedure, to inhibit any external access to the EPROM contents. Thus the user's resident program is protected. There is no direct external access to this bit. However, the security byte in the signature row has the same address and can be used to check indirectly whether the security bit has been programmed or not. The security bit has no effect on the signature mode, so the security byte can always be examined.

SECURITY BIT PROGRAMMING/ VERIFICATION

Programming

a. Read the security byte of the signature mode. Make sure it is 00H.

b. Apply access code to appropriate inputs to put the device into security mode.

c. Apply high voltage to EA and V_{DD} pins.

d. Follow the programming procedure as per the int$_e$ligent Programming Algorithm with known data on the databus. Not only the security bit, but also the security byte of the signature row is programmed.

e. Verify that the security byte of the signature mode contains the same data as appeared on the data bus. (If DB0–DB7 = high, the security byte will contain FFH.)

f. Read two consecutive known bytes from the EPROM array and verify that the wrong data are retrieved in at least one verification. If the EPROM can still be read, the security bit may have not been fully programmed though the security byte in the signature mode has.

Verification

Since the security bit address overlaps the address of the security byte of the signature mode, it can be used to check indirectly whether the security bit has been programmed or not. Therefore, the security bit verification is a mere read operation of the security byte of the signature row (0FFH = security bit programmed; 00H = security bit unprogrammed). Note that during the security bit programming, the reading of the security byte does not necessarily indicate that the security bit has been successfully programmed. Thus, it is recommended that two consecutive known bytes in the EPROM array be read and the wrong data should be read at least once, because it is highly improbable that random data coincides with the correct ones twice.

4

SIGNATURE MODE

The UPI-41AH/42AH has an additional 32 bytes of EPROM available for Intel and user signatures and miscellaneous purposes. The 32 bytes are partitioned as follows:

A. **Test code/checksum**—This can accommodate up to 25 bytes of code for testing the internal nodes that are not testable by executing from the external memory. The test code/checksum is present on ROMs, and OTPs.

B. **Intel signature**—This allows the programmer to read from the UPI-41AH/42AH the manufacturer of the device and the exact product name. It facilitates automatic device identification and will be present in the ROM and OTP versions. Location 10H contains the manufacturer code. For Intel, it is 89H. Location 11H contains the device code.

The code is 43H and 42H for the 8042AH and OTP 8742AH, and 41H and 40H for the 8041AH and OTP 8741AH, respectively. The code is 44H for any device with the security bit set by Intel.

C. **User signature**—The user signature memory is implemented in the EPROM and consists of 2 bytes for the customer to program his own signature code (for identification purposes and quick sorting of previously programmed materials).

D. **Test signature**—This memory is used to store testing information such as: test data, bin number, etc. (for use in quality and manufacturing control).

E. **Security byte**—This byte is used to check whether the security bit has been programmed (see the security bit section).

The signature mode can be accessed by setting P10 = 0, P11–P17 = 1, and then following the programming and/or verification procedures. The location of the various address partitions are as follows:

	Address		Device Type	No. of Bytes
Test Code/Checksum	0 16H	0FH 1EH	ROM/OTP	25
Intel Signature	10H	11H	ROM/OTP	2
User Signature	12H	13H	OTP	2
Test Signature	14H	15H	ROM/OTP	2
Security Byte	1FH		OTP	1

SYNC MODE

The Sync Mode is provided to ease the design of multiple controller circuits by allowing the designer to force the device into known phase and state time. The Sync Mode may also be utilized by automatic test equipment (ATE) for quick, easy, and efficient synchronizing between the tester and the DUT (device under test).

Sync Mode is enabled when $\overline{SS}$ pin is raised to high voltage level of +12 volts. To begin synchronization, T0 is raised to 5 volts at least four clock cycles after $\overline{SS}$. T0 must be high for at least four X1 clock cycles to fully reset the prescaler and time state generators. T0 may then be brought down during low state of X1. Two clock cycles later, with the rising edge of X1, the device enters into Time State 1, Phase 1. $\overline{SS}$ is then brought down to 5 volts 4 clocks later after T0. RESET is allowed to go high 5 tCY (75 clocks) later for normal execution of code.

SYNC MODE TIMING DIAGRAMS

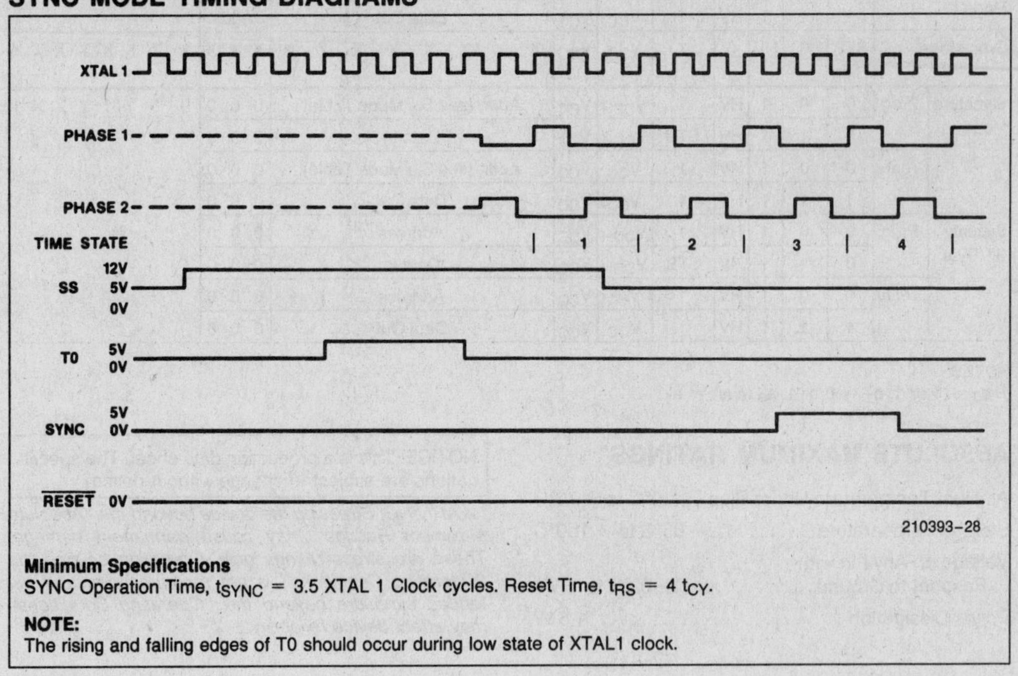

Minimum Specifications
SYNC Operation Time, t_{SYNC} = 3.5 XTAL 1 Clock cycles. Reset Time, t_{RS} = 4 t_{CY}.

NOTE:
The rising and falling edges of T0 should occur during low state of XTAL1 clock.

ACCESS CODE

The following table summarizes the access codes required to invoke the Sync Mode, Signature Mode, and the Security Bit, respectively. Also, the programming and verification modes are included for comparison.

Modes		Control Signals							Data Bus	Access Code	
										Port 2	Port 1
		T0	RST	SS	EA	PROG	V_{DD}	V_{CC}	0 1 2 3 4 5 6 7	0 1 2	0 1 2 3 4 5 6 7
Programming Mode		0	0	1	HV	1	V_{DDH}	V_{CC}	Address	Addr	a_0 a_1 X X X X X X
		0	1	1	HV	STB	V_{DDH}	V_{CC}	Data In	Addr	
Verification Mode		0	0	1	HV	1	V_{CC}	V_{CC}	Address	Addr	a_0 a_1 X X X X X X
		1	1	1	HV	1	V_{CC}	V_{CC}	Data Out	Addr	
Sync Mode		STB High	0	HV	0	X	V_{CC}	V_{CC}	X X X X X X X X	X X X	X X X X X X X X
Signature Mode	Prog	0	0	1	HV	1	V_{DDH}	V_{CC}	Addr. (see Sig Mode Table)	0 0 0	0 1 1 1 1 X X 1
		0	1	1	HV	STB	V_{DDH}	V_{CC}	Data In	0 0 0	
	Verify	0	0	1	HV	1	V_{CC}	V_{CC}	Addr. (see Sig Mode Table)	0 0 0	
		1	1	1	HV	1	V_{CC}	V_{CC}	Data Out	0 0 0	
Security Bit/Byte	Prog	0	0	1	HV	1	V_{DDH}	V_{CC}	Address	0 0 0	
		0	1	1	HV	STB	V_{DDH}	V_{CC}	Data In	0 0 0	
	Verify	0	0	1	HV	1	V_{CC}	V_{CC}	Address	0 0 0	
		1	1	1	HV	1	V_{CC}	V_{CC}	Data Out	0 0 0	

NOTES:
1. a_0 = 0 or 1; a_1 = 0 or 1. a_0 must = a_1.

ABSOLUTE MAXIMUM RATINGS*

Ambient Temperature Under Bias ....0°C to +70°C

Storage Temperature ....−65°C to +150°C

Voltage on Any Pin with Respect to Ground..............−0.5V to +7V

Power Dissipation ....1.5 W

NOTICE: This is a production data sheet. The specifications are subject to change without notice.

**WARNING: Stressing the device beyond the "Absolute Maximum Ratings" may cause permanent damage. These are stress ratings only. Operation beyond the "Operating Conditions" is not recommended and extended exposure beyond the "Operating Conditions" may affect device reliability.*

D.C. CHARACTERISTICS T_A = 0°C to +70°C, V_{CC} = V_{DD} = +5V ±10%

Symbol	Parameter	UPI-41AH/42AH		Units	Notes
		Min	Max		
V_{IL}	Input Low Voltage (Except XTAL1, XTAL2, RESET)	−0.5	0.8	V	
V_{IL1}	Input Low Voltage (XTAL1, XTAL2, RESET)	−0.5	0.6	V	
V_{IH}	Input High Voltage (Except XTAL1, XTAL2, RESET)	2.0	V_{CC}	V	
V_{IH1}	Input High Voltage (XTAL1, RESET)	3.5	V_{CC}	V	
V_{IH2}	Input High Voltage (XTAL2)	2.2	V_{CC}	V	
V_{OL}	Output Low Voltage (D_0–D_7)		0.45	V	I_{OL} = 2.0 mA

D.C. CHARACTERISTICS T_A = 0°C to +70°C, V_{CC} = V_{DD} = +5V ±10% (Continued)

Symbol	Parameter	UPI-41AH/42AH		Units	Notes
		Min	Max		
V_{OL1}	Output Low Voltage ($P_{10}P_{17}$, $P_{20}P_{27}$, Sync)		0.45	V	I_{OL} = 1.6 mA
V_{OL2}	Output Low Voltage (PROG)		0.45	V	I_{OL} = 1.0 mA
V_{OH}	Output High Voltage (D_0–D_7)	2.4		V	I_{OH} = −400 μA
V_{OH1}	Output High Voltage (All Other Outputs)	2.4			I_{OH} = −50 μA
I_{IL}	Input Leakage Current (T_0, T_1, RD, WR, CS, A_0, EA)		±10	μA	$V_{SS} \leq V_{IN} \leq V_{CC}$
I_{OFL}	Output Leakage Current (D_0–D_7, High Z State)		±10	μA	V_{SS} +0.45 $\leq V_{OUT} \leq V_{CC}$
I_{LI}	Low Input Load Current ($P_{10}P_{17}$, $P_{20}P_{27}$)		0.3	mA	V_{IL} = 0.8V
I_{LI1}	Low Input Load Current (RESET, SS)		0.2	mA	V_{IL} = 0.8V
I_{DD}	V_{DD} Supply Current		20	mA	Typical = 8 mA
$I_{CC} + I_{DD}$	Total Supply Current		135	mA	Typical = 80 mA
I_{DD} Standby	Power Down Supply Current		20	mA	Typical = 8 mA
I_{IH}	Input Leakage Current (P_{10}–P_{17}, P_{20}–P_{27})		100	μA	V_{IN} = V_{CC}
C_{IN}	Input Capacitance		10	pF	T_A = 25°C (1)
C_{IO}	I/O Capacitance		20	pF	T_A = 25°C (1)

4

NOTE:
1. Sampled, not 100% tested.

D.C. CHARACTERISTICS—PROGRAMMING

T_A = 25°C ±5°C, V_{CC} = 6V ±0.25V, V_{DD} = 12.5V ±0.5V

Symbol	Parameter	Min	Max	Units
V_{DDH}	V_{DD} Program Voltage High Level	12	13	V(1)
V_{DDL}	V_{DD} Voltage Low Level	4.75	5.25	V
V_{PH}	PROG Program Voltage High Level	2.0	5.5	V
V_{PL}	PROG Voltage Low Level	−0.5	0.8	V
V_{EAH}	Input High Voltage for EA	12.0	13.0	V(2)
V_{EAL}	EA Voltage Low Level	−0.5	5.25	V
I_{DD}	V_{DD} High Voltage Supply Current		50.0	mA
I_{EA}	EA High Voltage Supply Current		1.0	mA

NOTES:
1. Voltages over 13V applied to pin V_{DD} will permanently damage the device.
2. V_{EAH} must be applied to EA before V_{DDH} and removed after V_{DDL}.
3. V_{CC} must be applied simultaneously or before V_{DD} and must be removed simultaneously or after V_{DD}.

A.C. CHARACTERISTICS $T_A = 0°C$ to $+70°C$, $V_{SS} = 0V$, $V_{CC} = V_{DD} = +5V \pm 10\%$

DBB READ

Symbol	Parameter	Min	Max	Units
t_{AR}	CS, A_0 Setup to RD ↓	0		ns
t_{RA}	CS, A_0 Hold After RD ↑	0		ns
t_{RR}	RD Pulse Width	160		ns
t_{AD}	CS, A_0 to Data Out Delay		130	ns
t_{RD}	RD ↓ to Data Out Delay	0	130	ns
t_{DF}	RD ↑ to Data Float Delay		85	ns

DBB WRITE

Symbol	Parameter	Min	Max	Units
t_{AW}	CS, A_0 Setup to WR ↓	0		ns
t_{WA}	CS, A_0 Hold After WR ↑	0		ns
t_{WW}	WR Pulse Width	160		ns
t_{DW}	Data Setup to WR ↑	130		ns
t_{WD}	Data Hold After WR ↑	0		ns

CLOCK

Symbol	Parameter	Min	Max	Units
t_{CY} (UPI-41AH/42AH)	Cycle Time	1.2	9.20	μs(1)
t_{CYC} (UPI-41AH/42AH)	Clock Period	80	613	ns
t_{PWH}	Clock High Time	30		ns
t_{PWL}	Clock Low Time	30		ns
t_R	Clock Rise Time		10	ns
t_F	Clock Fall Time		10	ns

NOTE:
1. $t_{CY} = 15/f(XTAL)$

A.C. CHARACTERISTICS DMA

Symbol	Parameter	Min	Max	Units
t_{ACC}	DACK to WR or RD	0		ns
t_{CAC}	RD or WR to DACK	0		ns
t_{ACD}	DACK to Data Valid	0	130	ns
t_{CRQ}	RD or WR to DRQ Cleared		110	ns(1)

NOTE:
1. $C_L = 150$ pF.

A.C. CHARACTERISTICS—PROGRAMMING

T_A = 25°C ±5°C, V_{CC} = 6V ±0.25V, V_{DDL} = +5V ±0.25V, V_{DDH} = 12.5V ±0.5V
(8741AH/8742AH ONLY)

Symbol	Parameter	Min	Max	Units
t_{AW}	Address Setup Time to RESET ↑	$4t_{CY}$		
t_{WA}	Address Hold Time After RESET ↑	$4t_{CY}$		
t_{DW}	Data in Setup Time to PROG ↓	$4t_{CY}$		
t_{WD}	Data in Hold Time After PROG ↑	$4t_{CY}$		
t_{PW}	Initial Program Pulse Width	0.95	1.05	ms(1)
t_{TW}	Test 0 Setup Time for Program Mode	$4t_{CY}$		
t_{WT}	Test 0 Hold Time After Program Mode	$4t_{CY}$		
t_{DO}	Test 0 to Data Out Delay		$4t_{CY}$	
t_{WW}	RESET Pulse Width to Latch Address	$4t_{CY}$		
t_r, t_f	PROG Rise and Fall Times	0.5	100	μs
t_{CY}	CPU Operation Cycle Time	2.5	3.75	μs
t_{RE}	RESET Setup Time Before EA ↑	$4t_{CY}$		
t_{OPW}	Overprogram Pulse Width	2.85	78.75	ms(2)
t_{DE}	EA High to V_{DD} High	$1t_{CY}$		

NOTES:
1. Typical Initial Program Pulse width tolerance = 1 ms ±5%.
2. This variation is a function of the iteration counter value, X.
3. If TEST 0 is high, t_{DO} can be triggered by RESET ↑.

A.C. CHARACTERISTICS PORT 2 T_A = 0°C to +70°C, V_{CC} = +5V ±10%

Symbol	Parameter	$f(t_{CY})$(3)	Min	Max	Units
t_{CP}	Port Control Setup Before Falling Edge of PROG	$1/15\ t_{CY}-28$	55		ns(1)
t_{PC}	Port Control Hold After Falling Edge of PROG	$1/10\ t_{CY}$	125		ns(2)
t_{PR}	PROG to Time P2 Input Must Be Valid	$8/15\ t_{CY}-16$		650	ns(1)
t_{PF}	Input Data Hold Time		0	150	ns(2)
t_{DP}	Output Data Setup Time	$2/10\ t_{CY}$	250		ns(1)
t_{PD}	Output Data Hold Time	$1/10\ t_{CY}-80$	45		ns(2)
t_{PP}	PROG Pulse Width	$6/10\ t_{CY}$	750		ns

NOTES:
1. C_L = 80 pF.
2. C_L = 20 pF.
3. t_{CY} = 1.25 μs.

A.C. TESTING INPUT/OUTPUT WAVEFORM

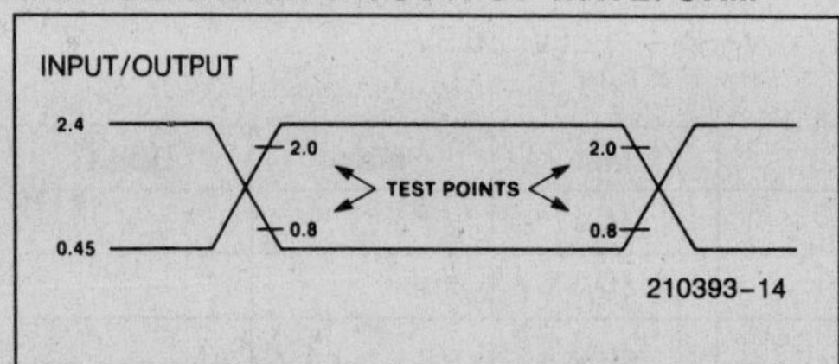

210393-14

A.C. TESTING LOAD CIRCUIT

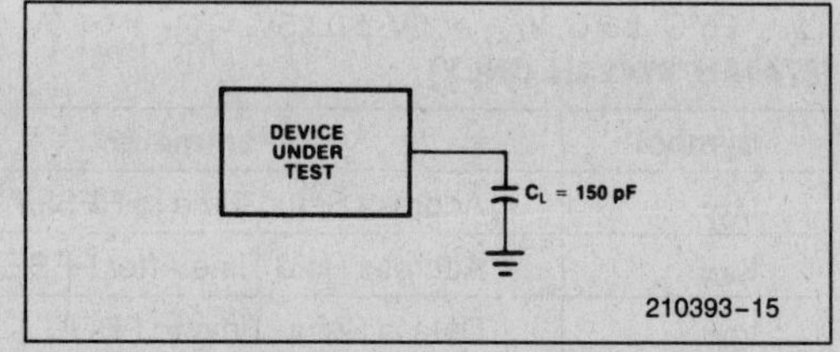

210393-15

DRIVING FROM EXTERNAL SOURCE-TWO OPTIONS

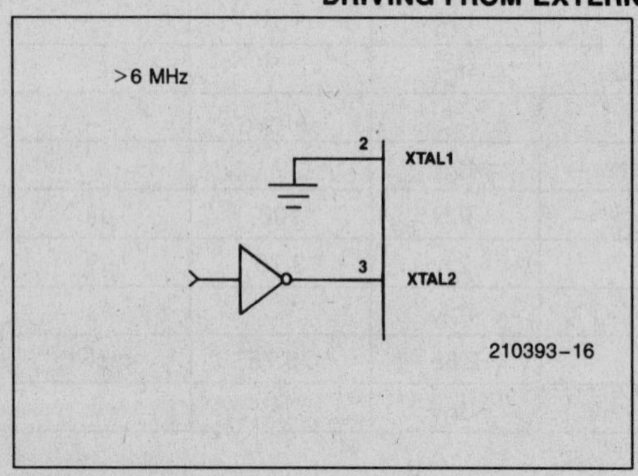

210393-16

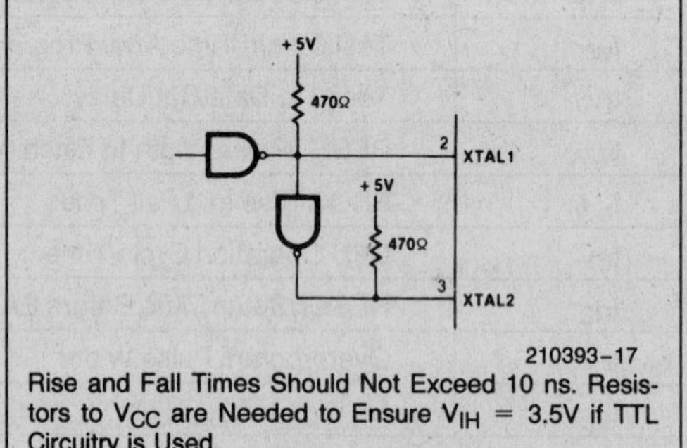

210393-17

Rise and Fall Times Should Not Exceed 10 ns. Resistors to V_{CC} are Needed to Ensure V_{IH} = 3.5V if TTL Circuitry is Used.

LC OSCILLATOR MODE

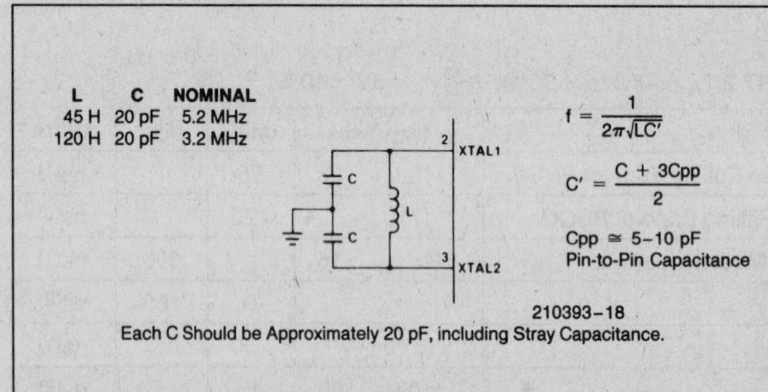

$$f = \frac{1}{2\pi\sqrt{LC'}}$$

$$C' = \frac{C + 3Cpp}{2}$$

Cpp ≅ 5–10 pF
Pin-to-Pin Capacitance

210393-18

Each C Should be Approximately 20 pF, including Stray Capacitance.

CRYSTAL OSCILLATOR MODE

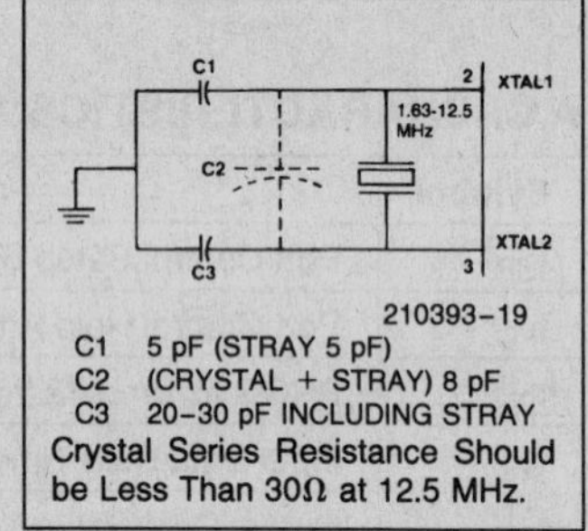

210393-19

C1 5 pF (STRAY 5 pF)
C2 (CRYSTAL + STRAY) 8 pF
C3 20–30 pF INCLUDING STRAY

Crystal Series Resistance Should be Less Than 30Ω at 12.5 MHz.

WAVEFORMS

READ OPERATION—DATA BUS BUFFER REGISTER

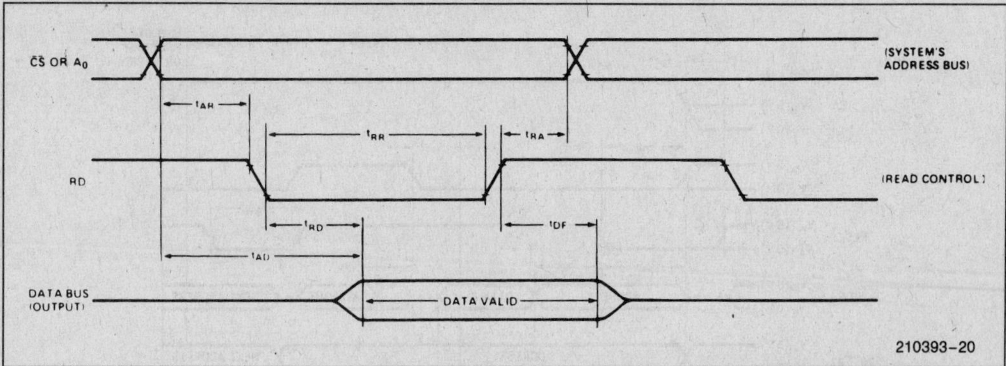

WRITE OPERATION—DATA BUS BUFFER REGISTER

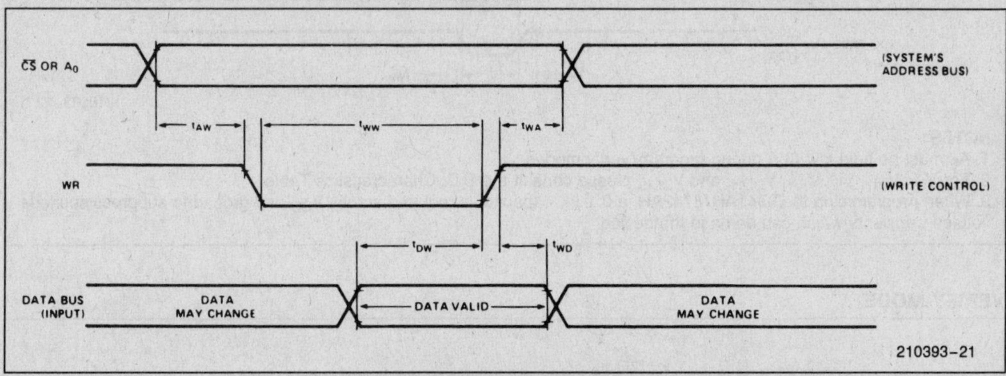

CLOCK TIMING

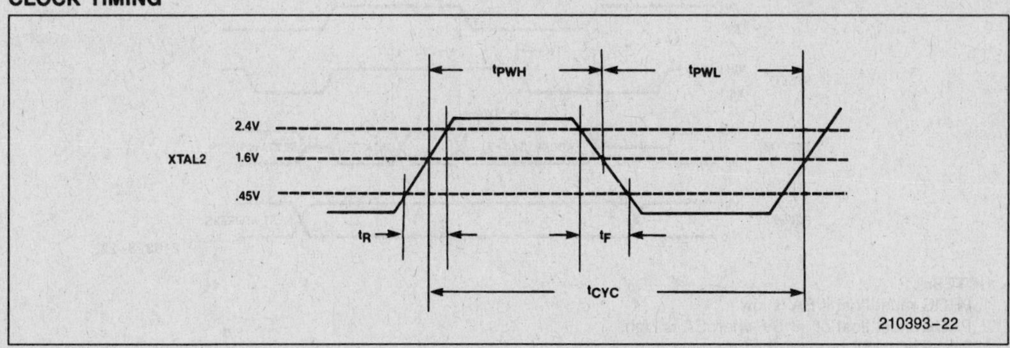

WAVEFORMS (Continued)

COMBINATION PROGRAM/VERIFY MODE

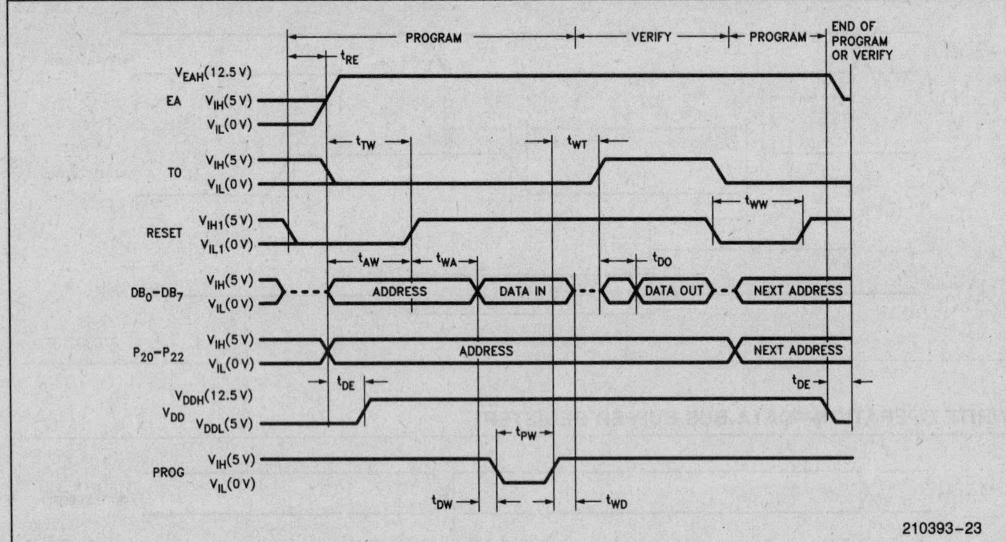

NOTES:
1. A_0 must be held low (0V) during program/verify modes.
2. For V_{IH}, V_{IH1}, V_{IL}, V_{IL1}, V_{DDH}, and V_{DDL}, please consult the D.C. Characteristics Table.
3. When programming the 8741AH/8742AH, a 0.1 μF capacitor is required across V_{DD} and ground to suppress spurious voltage transients which can damage the device.

VERIFY MODE

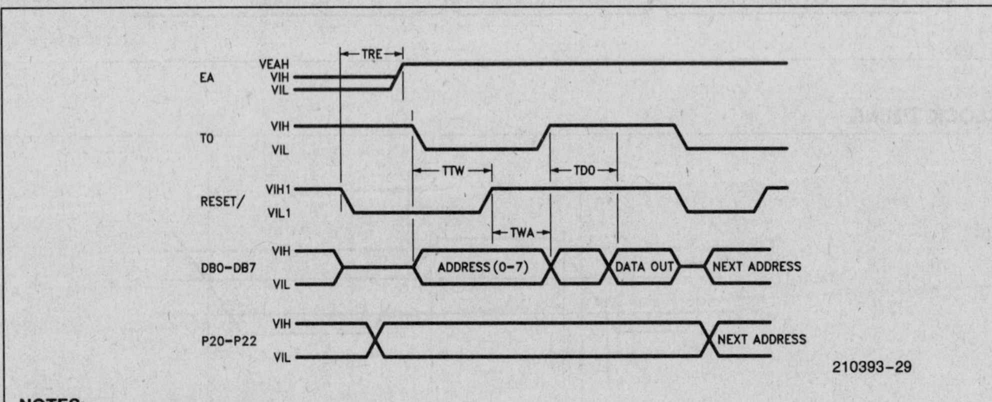

NOTES:
1. PROG must float if EA is low.
2. PROG must float or = 5V when EA is high.
3. $P_{10}-P_{17}$ = 5V or must float.
4. $P_{24}-P_{27}$ = 5V or must float.
5. A_0 must be held low during programming/verify modes.

WAVEFORMS (Continued)

DMA

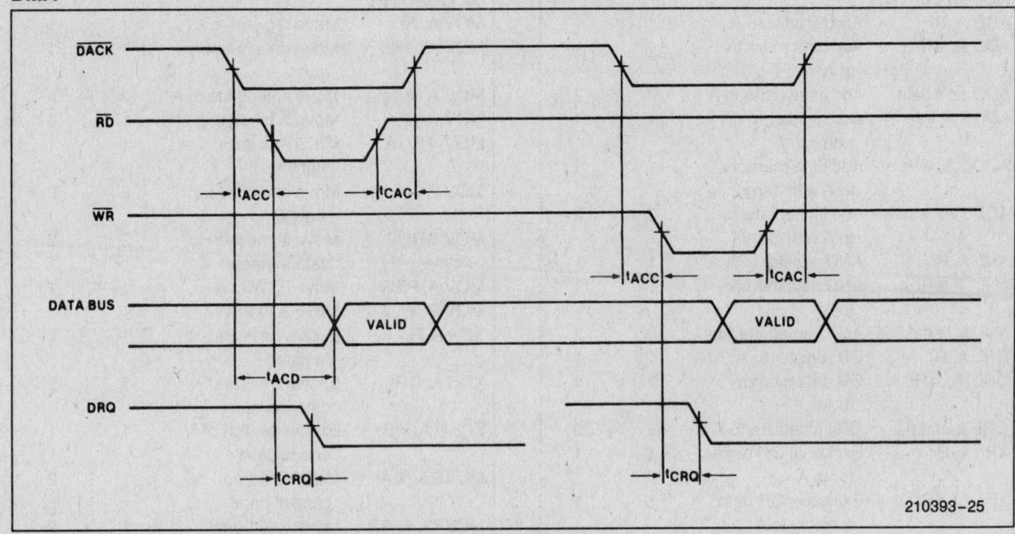

PORT 2

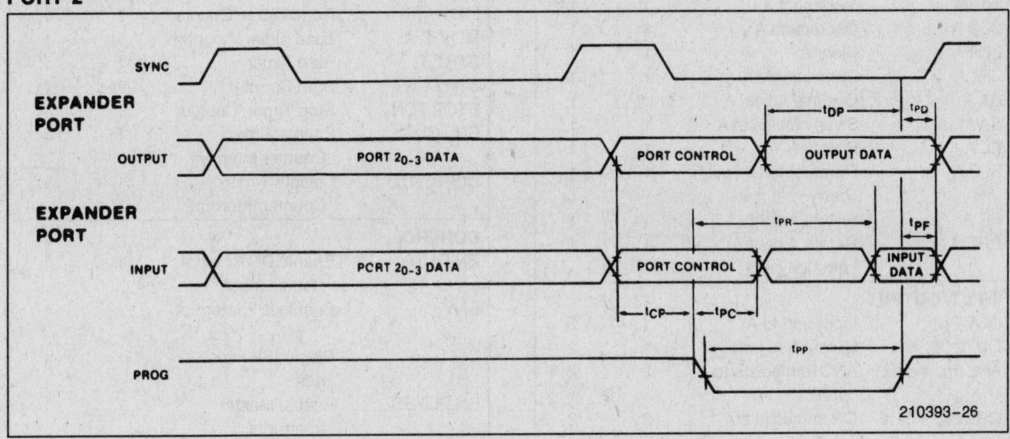

PORT TIMING DURING EXTERNAL ACCESS (EA)

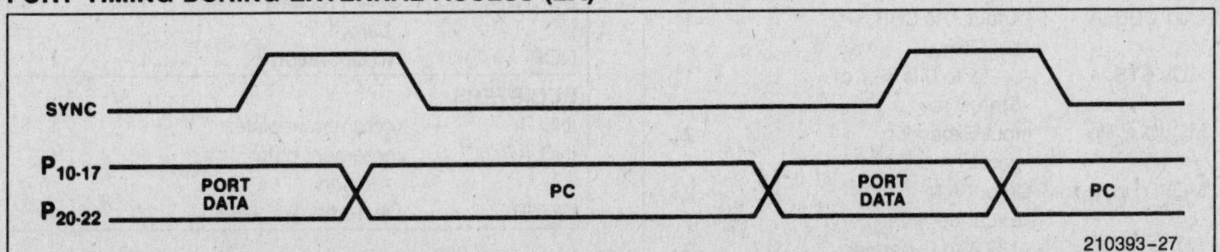

On the Rising Edge of SYNC and EA is Enabled, Port Data is Valid and can be Strobed. On the Trailing Edge of Sync the Program Counter Contents are Available.

Table 2. UPI Instruction Set

Mnemonic	Description	Bytes	Cycles
ACCUMULATOR			
ADD A, Rr	Add register to A	1	1
ADD A, @Rr	Add data memory to A	1	1
ADD A, #data	Add immediate to A	2	2
ADDC A, Rr	Add register to A with carry	1	1
ADDC A, @Rr	Add data memory to A with carry	1	1
ADDC A, #data	Add immediate to A with carry	2	2
ANL A, Rr	AND register to A	1	1
ANL, A @Rr	AND data memory to A	1	1
ANL A, #data	AND immediate to A	2	2
ORL A, Rr	OR register to A	1	1
ORL, A, @Rr	OR data memory to A	1	1
ORL A, #data	OR immediate to A	2	2
XRL A, Rr	Exclusive OR register to A	1	1
XRL A, @Rr	Exclusive OR data memory to A	1	1
XRL A, #data	Exclusive OR immediate to A	2	2
INC A	Increment A	1	1
DEC A	Decrement A	1	1
CLR A	Clear A	1	1
CPL A	Complement A	1	1
DA A	Decimal Adjust A	1	1
SWAP A	Swap nibbles of A	1	1
RL A	Rotate A left	1	1
RLC A	Rotate A left through carry	1	1
RR A	Rotate A right	1	1
RRC A	Rotate A right through carry	1	1
INPUT/OUTPUT			
IN A, Pp	Input port to A	1	2
OUTL Pp, A	Output A to port	1	2
ANL Pp, #data	AND immediate to port	2	2
ORL Pp, #data	OR immediate to port	2	2
IN A, DBB	Input DBB to A, clear IBF	1	1
OUT DBB, A	Output A to DBB, set OBF	1	1
MOV STS, A	A_4–A_7 to Bits 4–7 of Status	1	1
MOVD A, Pp	Input Expander port to A	1	2
MOVD Pp, A	Output A to Expander port	1	2
ANLD Pp, A	AND A to Expander port	1	2
ORLD Pp, A	OR A to Expander port	1	2

Mnemonic	Description	Bytes	Cycles
DATA MOVES			
MOV A, Rr	Move register to A	1	1
MOV A, @Rr	Move data memory to A	1	1
MOV A, #data	Move immediate to A	2	2
MOV Rr, A	Move A to register	1	1
MOV @Rr, A	Move A to data memory	1	1
MOV Rr, #data	Move immediate to register	2	2
MOV @Rr, #data	Move immediate to data memory	2	2
MOV A, PSW	Move PSW to A	1	1
MOV PSW, A	Move A to PSW	1	1
XCH A, Rr	Exchange A and register	1	1
XCH A, @Rr	Exchange A and data memory	1	1
XCHD A, @Rr	Exchange digit of A and register	1	1
MOVP A, @A	Move to A from current page	1	2
MOVP3, A, @A	Move to A from page 3	1	2
TIMER/COUNTER			
MOV A, T	Read Timer/Counter	1	1
MOV T, A	Load Timer/Counter	1	1
STRT T	Start Timer	1	1
STRT CNT	Start Counter	1	1
STOP TCNT	Stop Timer/Counter	1	1
EN TCNTI	Enable Timer/Counter Interrupt	1	1
DIS TCNTI	Disable Timer/Counter Interrupt	1	1
CONTROL			
EN DMA	Enable DMA Handshake Lines	1	1
EN I	Enable IBF Interrupt	1	1
DIS I	Diable IBF Interrupt	1	1
EN FLAGS	Enable Master Interrupts	1	1
SEL RB0	Select register bank 0	1	1
SEL RB1	Select register bank 1	1	1
NOP	No Operation	1	1
REGISTERS			
INC Rr	Increment register	1	1
INC @Rr	Increment data memory	1	1
DEC Rr	Decrement register	1	1

Table 2. UPI Instruction Set (Continued)

Mnemonic	Description	Bytes	Cycles
SUBROUTINE			
CALL addr	Jump to subroutine	2	2
RET	Return	1	2
RETR	Return and restore status	1	2
FLAGS			
CLR C	Clear Carry	1	1
CPL C	Complement Carry	1	1
CLR F0	Clear Flag 0	1	1
CPL F0	Complement Flag 0	1	1
CLR F1	Clear F1 Flag	1	1
CPL F1	Complement F1 Flag	1	1
BRANCH			
JMP addr	Jump unconditional	2	2
JMPP @A	Jump indirect	1	2
DJNZ Rr, addr	Decrement register and jump	2	2
JC addr	Jump on Carry = 1	2	2
JNC addr	Jump on Carry = 0	2	2
JZ addr	Jump on A Zero	2	2
JNZ addr	Jump on A not Zero	2	2
JT0 addr	Jump on T0 = 1	2	2
JNT0 addr	Jump on T0 = 0	2	2
JT1 addr	Jump on T1 = 1	2	2
JNT1 addr	Jump on T1 = 0	2	2
JF0 addr	Jump on F0 Flag = 1	2	2
JF1 addr	Jump on F1 Flag = 1	2	2
JTF addr	Jump on Timer Flag = 1, Clear Flag	2	2
JNIBF addr	Jump on IBF Flag = 0	2	2
JOBF addr	Jump on OBF Flag = 1	2	2
JBb addr	Jump on Accumula-tor Bit	2	2

8741A UNIVERSAL PERIPHERAL INTERFACE 8-BIT MICROCOMPUTER

- 8-Bit CPU plus ROM, RAM, I/O, Timer and Clock in a Single Package
- One 8-Bit Status and Two Data Registers for Asynchronous Slave-to-Master Interface
- DMA, Interrupt, or Polled Operation Supported
- 1024 x 8 EPROM, 64 x 8 RAM, 8-Bit Timer/Counter, 18 Programmable I/O Pins
- Fully Compatible with All Microprocessor Families
- 3.6 MHz 8741A-8 Available
- Expandable I/O
- RAM Power-Down Capability
- Over 90 Instructions: 70% Single Byte
- Available in EXPRESS
  — Standard Temperature Range
  — Extended Temperature Range

The Intel 8741A is a general purpose, programmable interface device designed for use with a variety of 8-bit microprocessor systems. It contains a low cost microcomputer with program memory, data memory, 8-bit CPU, I/O ports, timer/counter, and clock in a single 40-pin package. Interface registers are included to enable the UPI device to function as a peripheral controller in MCS®-48, MCS-80, MCS-85, MCS-86, and other 8-bit systems.

The UPI-41A has 1K words of program memory and 64 words of data memory on-chip.

The device has two 8-bit, TTL compatible I/O ports and two test inputs. Individual port lines can function as either inputs or outputs under software control. I/O can be expanded with the 8243 device which is directly compatible and has 16 I/O lines. An 8-bit programmable timer/counter is included in the UPI device for generating timing sequences or counting external inputs. Additional UPI features include: single 5V supply, single-step mode for debug and dual working register banks.

Because it's a complete microcomputer, the UPI provides more flexibility for the designer than conventional LSI interface devices. It is designed to be an efficient controller as well as an arithmetic processor. Applications include keyboard scanning, printer control, display multiplexing and similar functions which involve interfacing peripheral devices to microprocessor systems.

Pin Configuration

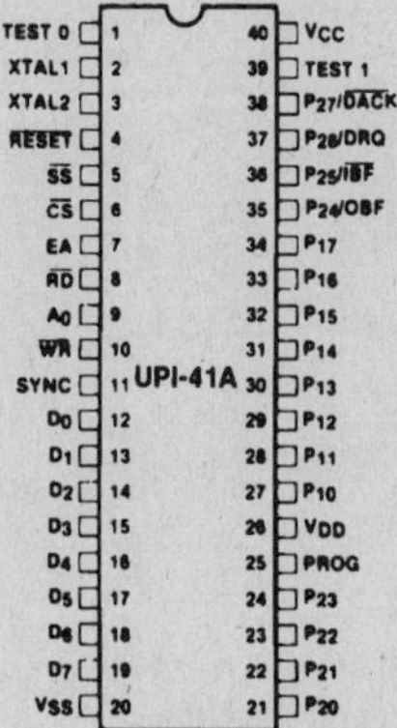

290241–2

October 1989
Order Number: 290241-001

Block Diagram

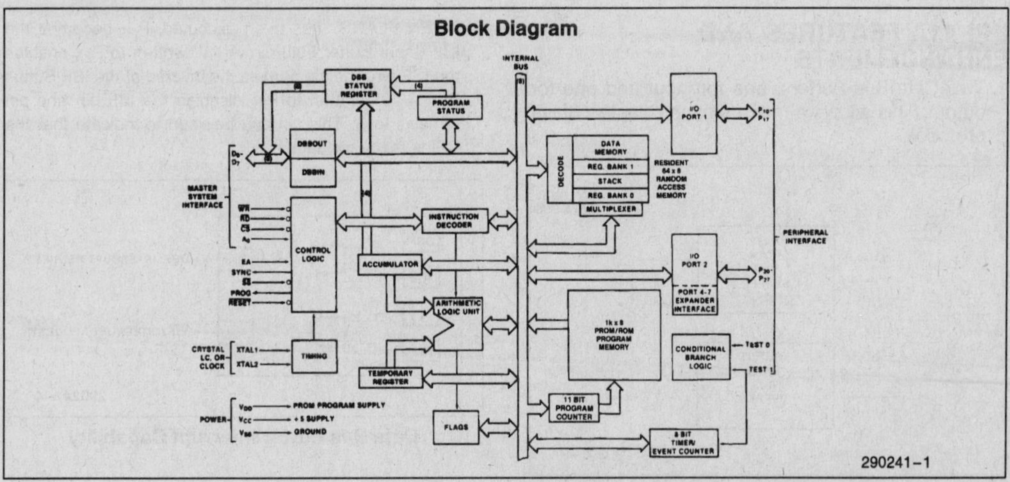

290241–1

Table 1. Pin Description

Signal	Description
D_0–D_7 (BUS)	Three-state, bidirectional DATA BUS BUFFER lines used to interface the UPI-41A to an 8-bit master system data bus.
P_{10}–P_{17}	8-bit, PORT 1 quasi-bidirectional I/O lines.
P_{20}–P_{27}	8-bit, PORT 2 quasi-bidirectional I/O lines. The lower 4 bits (P_{20}–P_{23}) interface directly to the 8243 I/O expander device and contain address and data information during PORT 4–7 access. The upper 4 bits (P_{24}–P_{27}) can be programmed to provide interrupt Request and DMA Handshake capability. Software control can configure P_{24} as OBF (Output Buffer Full), P_{25} as $\overline{\text{IBF}}$ (Input Buffer Full), P_{26} as DRQ (DMA Request), and P_{27} as $\overline{\text{DACK}}$ (DMA ACKnowledge).
$\overline{\text{WR}}$	I/O write input which enables the master CPU to write data and command words to the UPI-41A INPUT DATA BUS BUFFER.
$\overline{\text{RD}}$	I/O read input which enables the master CPU to read data and status words from the OUTPUT DATA BUS BUFFER or status register.
$\overline{\text{CS}}$	Chip select input used to select one UPI-41A out of several connected to a common data bus.
A_0	Address input used by the master processor to indicate whether byte transfer is data or command. During a write operation flag F_1 is set to the status of the A_0 input.
TEST 0, TEST 1	Input pins which can be directly tested using conditional branch instructions. (T_1) also functions as the event timer input (under software control). T_0 is used during PROM programming and verification in the 8741A.
XTAL 1, XTAL 2	Inputs for a crystal, LC or an external timing signal to determine the internal oscillator frequency.
SYNC	Output signal which occurs once per UPI-41A instruction cycle. SYNC can be used as a strobe for external circuitry; it is also used to synchronize single step operation.
EA	External access input which allows emulation, testing and PROM verification.
PROG	Multifunction pin used as the program pulse input during PROM programming. During I/O expander access the PROG pin acts as an address/data strobe to the 8243.
$\overline{\text{RESET}}$	Input used to reset status flip-flops and to set the program counter to zero. $\overline{\text{RESET}}$ is also used during PROM programming and verification. $\overline{\text{RESET}}$ should be held low for a minimum of 8 instruction cycles after power-up.
$\overline{\text{SS}}$	Single step input used in the 8741A in conjunction with the SYNC output to step the program through each instruction.
V_{CC}	+5V main power supply pin.
V_{DD}	+5V during normal operation. +25V during programming operation. Low power standby supply pin in ROM version.
V_{SS}	Circuit ground potential.

4

UPI-41A FEATURES AND ENHANCEMENTS

1. Two Data Bus Buffers, one for input and one for output. This allows a much cleaner Master/Slave protocol.

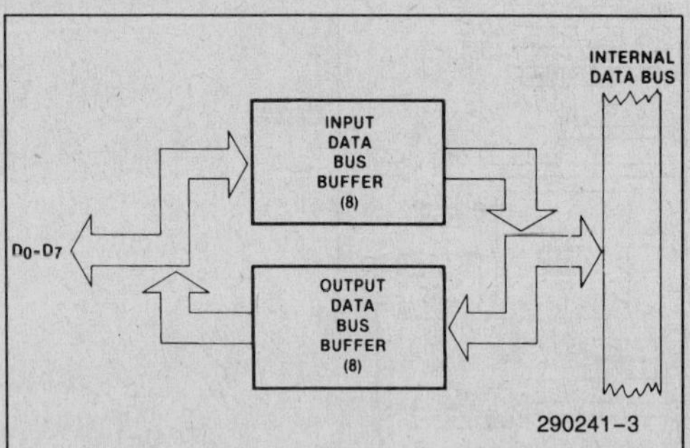

290241-3

2. 8 Bits of Status

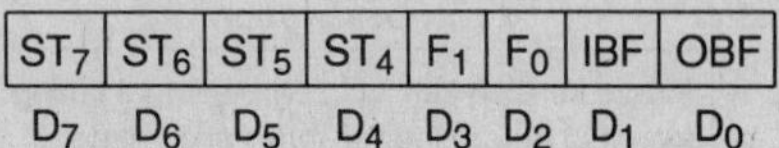

ST_7	ST_6	ST_5	ST_4	F_1	F_0	IBF	OBF
D_7	D_6	D_5	D_4	D_3	D_2	D_1	D_0

ST_4–ST_7 are user definable status bits. These bits are defined by the "MOV STS, A" single byte, single cycle instruction. Bits 4–7 of the accumulator are moved to bits 4–7 of the status register. Bits 0–3 of the status register are not affected.

MOV STS, A Op Code: 90H

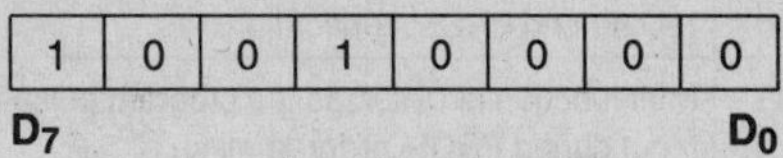

1	0	0	1	0	0	0	0
D_7							D_0

3. $\overline{RD}$ and $\overline{WR}$ are edge triggered. IBF, OBF, F_1 and $\overline{INT}$ change internally after the trailing edge of $\overline{RD}$ or $\overline{WR}$.

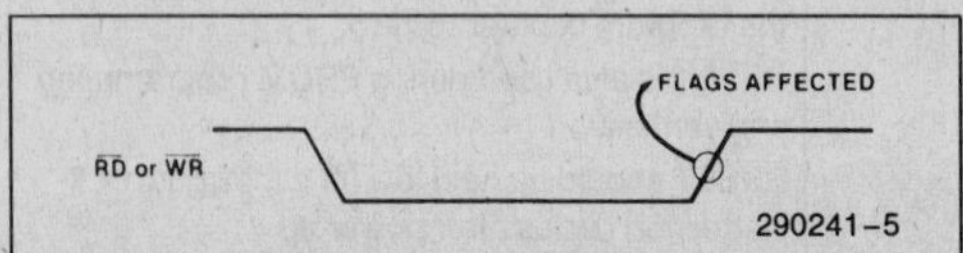

290241-5

4. P_{24} and P_{25} are port pins or Buffer Flag pins which can be used to interrupt a master processor. These pins default to port pins on Reset.

If the "EN FLAGS" instruction has been executed, P_{24} becomes the OBF (Output Buffer Full) pin. A "1" written to P_{24} enables the OBF pin (the pin outputs the OBF Status Bit). A "0" written to P_{24} disables the OBF pin (the pin remains low). This pin can be used to indicate that valid data is available from the UPI41A (in Output Data Bus Buffer).

If "EN FLAGS" has been executed, P_{25} becomes the $\overline{IBF}$ (Input Buffer Full) pin. A "1" written to P_{25} enables the $\overline{IBF}$ pin (the pin outputs the inverse of the IBF Status Bit). A "0" written to P_{25} disables the $\overline{IBF}$ pin (the pin remains low). This pin can be used to indicate that the UPI is ready for data.

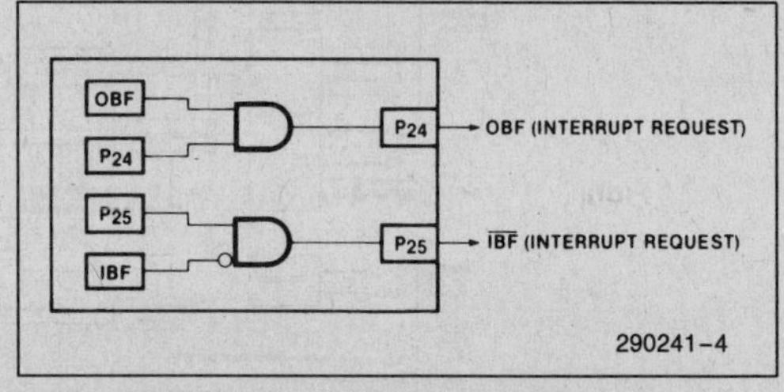

290241-4

Data Bus Buffer Interrupt Capability

EN FLAGS Op Code: 0F5H

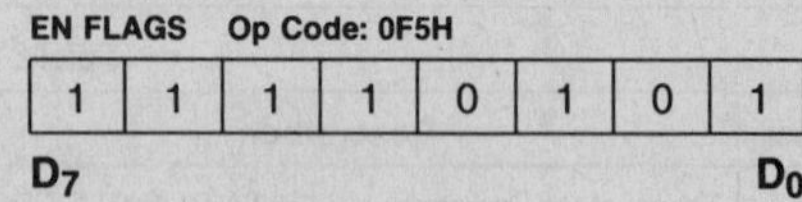

1	1	1	1	0	1	0	1
D_7							D_0

5. P_{26} and P_{27} are port pins or DMA handshake pins for use with a DMA controller. These pins default to port pins on Reset.

If the "EN DMA" instruction has been executed, P_{26} becomes the DRQ (DMA Request) pin. A "1" written to P_{26} causes a DMA request (DRQ is activated). DRQ is deactivated by DACK•RD, DACK•WR, or execution of the "EN DMA" instruction.

If "EN DMA" has been executed, P_{27} becomes the $\overline{DACK}$ (DMA Acknowledge) pin. This pin acts as a chip select input for the Data Bus Buffer registers during DMA transfers.

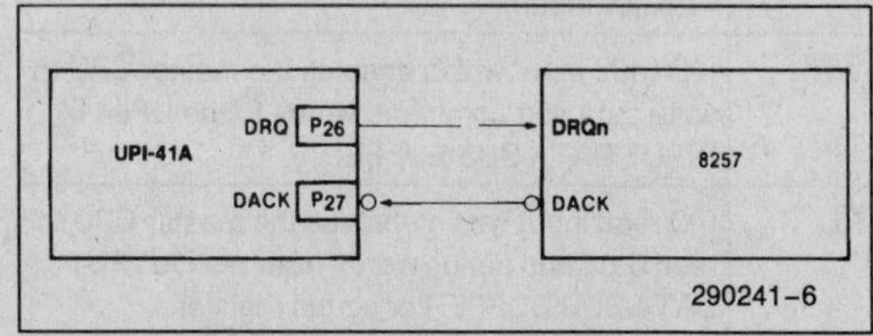

290241-6

DMA Handshake Capability

EN DMA Op Code: 0E5H

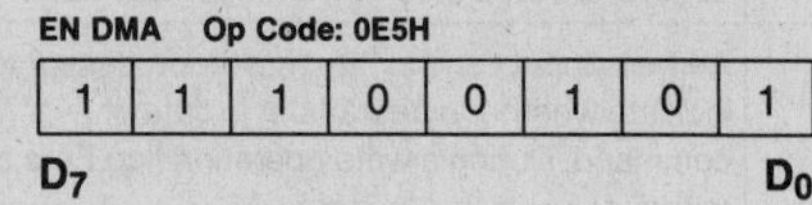

1	1	1	0	0	1	0	1
D_7							D_0

APPLICATIONS

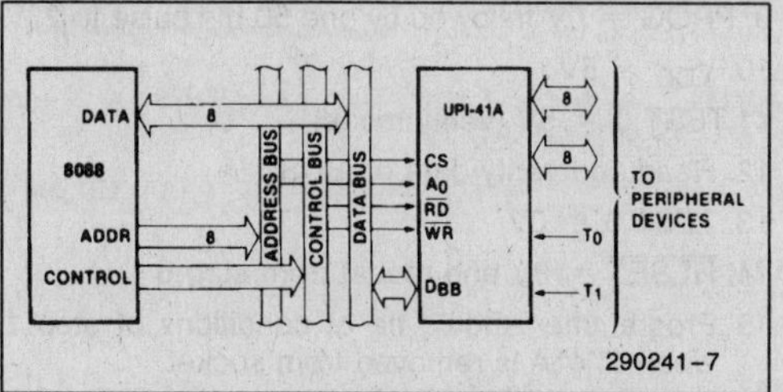

Figure 1. 8085A-8741A Interface

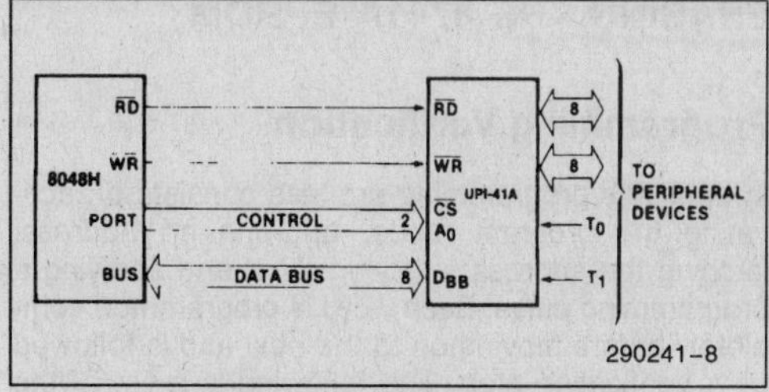

Figure 2. 8048-8741A Interface

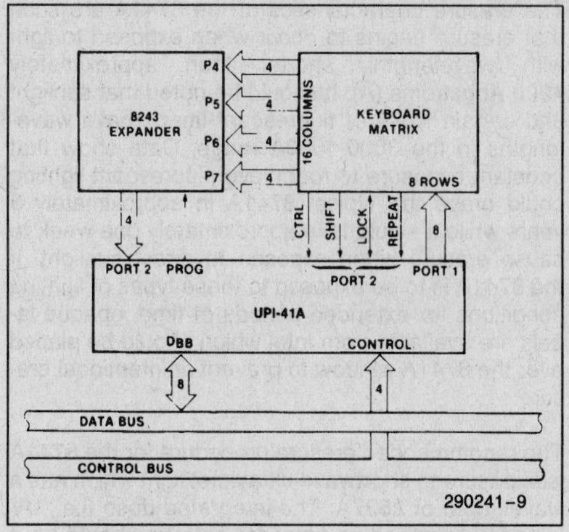

Figure 3. 8741A-8243 Keyboard Scanner

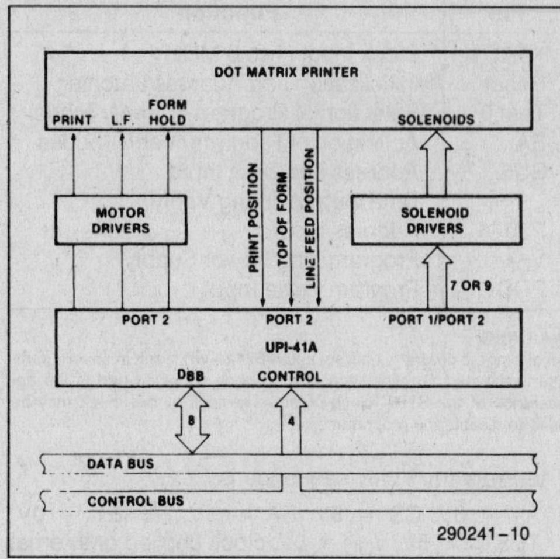

Figure 4. 8741A Matrix Printer Interface

4

PROGRAMMING, VERIFYING, AND ERASING THE 8741A EPROM

Programming Verification

In brief, the programming process consists of: activating the program mode, applying an address, latching the address, applying data, and applying a programming pulse. Each word is programmed completely before moving on to the next and is followed by a verification step. The following is a list of the pins used for programming and a description of their functions:

Pin	Function
XTAL 1	Clock Input (1 to 6 MHz)
$\overline{\text{Reset}}$	Initialization and Address Latching
Test 0	Selection of Program or Verify Mode
EA	Activation of Program/Verify Modes
BUS	Address and Data Input Data Output during Verify
P20–1	Address Input
V_{DD}	Programming Power Supply
PROG	Program Pulse Input

WARNING:
An attempt to program a missocketed 8741A will result in severe damage to the part. An indication of a properly socketed part is the appearance of the SYNC clock output. The lack of this clock may be used to disable the programmer.

The Program/Verify sequence is:

1. A_0 = 0V, CS = 5V, EA = 5V, $\overline{\text{RESET}}$ = 0V, TEST0 = 5V, V_{DD} = 5V, clock applied or internal oscillator operating, BUS and PROG floating
2. Insert 8741A in programming socket
3. TEST 0 = 0V (select program mode)
4. EA = 23V (active program mode)
5. Address applied to BUS and P20–1
6. $\overline{\text{RESET}}$ = 5V (latch address)
7. Data applied to BUS
8. V_{DD} = 25V (programming power)
9. PROG = 0V followed by one 50 ms pulse to 23V
10. V_{DD} = 5V
11. TEST 0 = 5V (verify mode)
12. Read and verify data on BUS
13. TEST 0 = 0V
14. $\overline{\text{RESET}}$ = 0V and repeat from step 6
15. Programmer should be at conditions of step 1 when 8741A is removed from socket

8741A Erasure Characteristics

The erasure characteristics of the 8741A are such that erasure begins to occur when exposed to light with wavelengths shorter than approximately 4000 Angstroms (Å). It should be noted that sunlight and certain types of fluorescent lamps have wavelengths in the 3000-4000Å range. Data show that constant exposure to room level fluorescent lighting could erase the typical 8741A in approximately 3 years while it would take approximately one week to cause erasure when exposed to direct sunlight. If the 8741A is to be exposed to these types of lighting conditions for extended periods of time, opaque labels are available from Intel which should be placed over the 8741A window to prevent unintentional erasure.

The recommended erasure procedure for the 8741A is exposure to shortwave ultraviolet light which has a wavelength of 2537Å. The integrated dose (i.e., UV intensity × exposure time) for erasure should be a minimum of 15 w-sec/cm^2. The erasure time with this dosage is approximately 15 to 20 minutes using an ultraviolet lamp with a 12,000 $\mu W/cm^2$ power rating. The 8741A should be placed within one inch of the lamp tubes during erasure. Some lamps have a filter on their tubes which should be removed before erasure.

ABSOLUTE MAXIMUM RATINGS*

Ambient Temperature under Bias ....0°C to +70°C

Storage Temperature ....−65°C to +150°C

Voltage on Any Pin with
Respect to Ground................0.5V to +7V

Power Dissipation..........................1.5W

NOTICE: This is a production data sheet. The specifications are subject to change without notice.

**WARNING: Stressing the device beyond the "Absolute Maximum Ratings" may cause permanent damage. These are stress ratings only. Operation beyond the "Operating Conditions" is not recommended and extended exposure beyond the "Operating Conditions" may affect device reliability.*

D.C. CHARACTERISTICS

T_A = 0°C to +70°C, V_{SS} 0V, V_{CC} = V_{DD} = +5V ±10%

Symbol	Parameter	Min	Max	Unit	Test Conditions
V_{IL}	Input Low Voltage (except XTAL1, XTAL2, $\overline{RESET}$)	−0.5	0.8	V	
V_{IL1}	Input Low Voltage (XTAL1, XTAL2, $\overline{RESET}$)	−0.5	0.6	V	
V_{IH}	Input High Voltage (except XTAL1, XTAL2, $\overline{RESET}$)	2.2	V_{CC}		
V_{IH1}	Input High Voltage (XTAL1, XTAL2, $\overline{RESET}$)	3.8	V_{CC}	V	
V_{OL}	Output Low Voltage (D_0–D_7)		0.45	V	I_{OL} = 2.0 mA
V_{OL1}	Output Low Voltage ($P_{10}P_{17}$, $P_{20}P_{27}$, Sync)		0.45	V	I_{OL} = 1.6 mA
V_{OL2}	Output Low Voltage (PROG)		0.45	V	I_{OL} = 1.0 mA
V_{OH}	Output High Voltage (D_0–D_7)	2.4		V	I_{OH} = −400 μA
V_{OH1}	Output High Voltage (All Other Outputs)	2.4		V	I_{OH} = −50 μA
I_{IL}	Input Leakage Current (T_0, T_1, $\overline{RD}$,$\overline{WR}$, $\overline{CS}$, A_0, EA)		±10	μA	$V_{SS} \leq V_{IN} \leq V_{CC}$
I_{OZ}	Output Leakage Current (D_0–D_7, High Z State)		±10	μA	V_{SS} +0.45 $\leq V_{IN} \leq V_{CC}$
I_{LI}	Low Input Load Current ($P_{10}P_{17}$, $P_{20}P_{27}$)		0.5	mA	V_{IL} = 0.8V
I_{LI1}	Low Input Load Current ($\overline{RESET}$, $\overline{SS}$)		0.2	mA	V_{IL} = 0.8V
I_{DD}	V_{DD} Supply Current		15	mA	Typical = 5 mA
I_{CC} + I_{DD}	Total Supply Current		125	mA	Typical = 60 mA

A.C. CHARACTERISTICS T_A = 0°C to +70°C, V_{SS} = 0V, V_{CC} = V_{DD} = +5V ±10%

DBB READ

Symbol	Parameter	Min	Max	Unit	Test Conditions
t_{AR}	$\overline{CS}$, A_0 Setup to $\overline{RD}$ ↓	0		ns	
t_{RA}	$\overline{CS}$, A_0 Hold after $\overline{RD}$ ↑	0		ns	
t_{RR}	$\overline{RD}$ Pulse Width	250		ns	
t_{AD}	$\overline{CS}$, A_0 to Data Out Delay		225	ns	C_L = 150 pF
t_{RD}	$\overline{RD}$ ↓ to Data Out Delay		225	ns	C_L = 150 pF
t_{DF}	$\overline{RD}$ ↑ to Data Float Delay		100	ns	
t_{CY}	Cycle Time (except 8741A-8)	2.5	15	μs	6.0 MHz XTAL
t_{CY}	Cycle Time (8741A-8)	4.17	15	μs	3.6 MHz XTAL

DBB WRITE

Symbol	Parameter	Min	Max	Units	Test Conditions
t_{AW}	$\overline{CS}$, A_0 Setup to $\overline{WR}$ ↓	0		ns	
t_{WA}	$\overline{CS}$, A_0 Hold after $\overline{WR}$ ↑	0		ns	
t_{WW}	$\overline{WR}$ Pulse Width	250		ns	
t_{DW}	Data Setup to $\overline{WR}$ ↑	150		ns	
t_{WD}	Data Hold after $\overline{WR}$ ↑	0		ns	

A.C. TIMING SPECIFICATION FOR PROGRAMMING

T_A = 0°C to +70°C, V_{CC} = +5V ±10%

Symbol	Parameter	Min	Max	Units	Test Conditions
t_{AW}	Address Setup Time to $\overline{RESET}$ ↑	$4t_{CY}$			
t_{WA}	Address Hold Time after $\overline{RESET}$ ↑	$4t_{CY}$			
t_{DW}	Data in Setup Time to PROG ↑	$4t_{CY}$			
t_{WD}	Data in Hold Time after PROG ↓	$4t_{CY}$			
t_{PH}	$\overline{RESET}$ Hold Time to Verify	$4t_{CY}$			
t_{VDDW}	V_{DD} Setup Time to PROG ↑	$4t_{CY}$			
t_{VDDH}	V_{DD} Hold Time after PROG ↓	0			
t_{PW}	Program Pulse Width	50	60	ms	
t_{TW}	Test 0 Setup Time for Program Mode	$4t_{CY}$			
t_{WT}	Test 0 Hold Time after Program Mode	$4t_{CY}$			
t_{DO}	Test 0 to Data Out Delay		$4t_{CY}$		
t_{WW}	$\overline{RESET}$ Pulse Width to Latch Address	$4t_{CY}$			
t_r, t_f	V_{DD} and PROG Rise and Fall Times	0.5	2.0	μs	
t_{CY}	CPU Operation Cycle Time	5.0		μs	
t_{RE}	$\overline{RESET}$ Setup Time before EA ↑	$4t_{CY}$			

NOTE:
1. If TEST 0 is high, t_{DO} can be triggered by $\overline{RESET}$ ↑.

D.C. SPECIFICATION FOR PROGRAMMING

T_A = 25°C ±5°C, V_{CC} = 5V ±5%, V_{DD} = 25V ±1V

Symbol	Parameter	Min	Max	Units	Test Conditions
V_{DOH}	V_{DD} Program Voltage High Level	24.0	26.0	V	
V_{DDL}	V_{DD} Voltage Low Level	4.75	5.25	V	
V_{PH}	PROG Program Voltage High Level	21.5	24.5	V	
V_{PL}	PROG Voltage Low Level		0.2	V	
V_{EAH}	EA Program or Verify Voltage High Level	21.5	24.5	V	
V_{EAL}	EA Voltage Low Level		5.25	V	
I_{DD}	V_{DD} High Voltage Supply Current		30.0	mA	
I_{PROG}	PROG High Voltage Supply Current		16.0	mA	
I_{EA}	EA High Voltage Supply Current		1.0	mA	

A.C. CHARACTERISTICS—DMA

Symbol	Parameter	Min	Max	Units	Test Conditions
t_{ACC}	$\overline{DACK}$ to $\overline{WR}$ or $\overline{RD}$	0		ns	
t_{CAC}	$\overline{RD}$ or $\overline{WR}$ to $\overline{DACK}$	0		ns	
t_{ACD}	$\overline{DACK}$ to Data Valid		225	ns	$C_L = 150$ pF
t_{CRQ}	$\overline{RD}$ or $\overline{WR}$ to DRQ Cleared		200	ns	

A.C. CHARACTERISTICS—PORT 2 $T_A = 0°C$ to $+70°C$, $V_{CC} = +5V \pm 10\%$

Symbol	Parameter	Min	Max	Units	Test Conditions
t_{CP}	Port Control Setup before Falling Edge of PROG	10		ns	
t_{PC}	Port Control Hold after Falling Edge of PROG	100		ns	
t_{PR}	PROG to Time P2 Input Must Be Valid		810	ns	
t_{PF}	Input Data Hold Time	0	150	ns	
t_{DP}	Output Data Setup Time	250		ns	
t_{PD}	Output Data Hold Time	65		ns	
t_{PP}	PROG Pulse Width	1200		ns	

A.C. TESTING INPUT/OUTPUT WAVEFORM

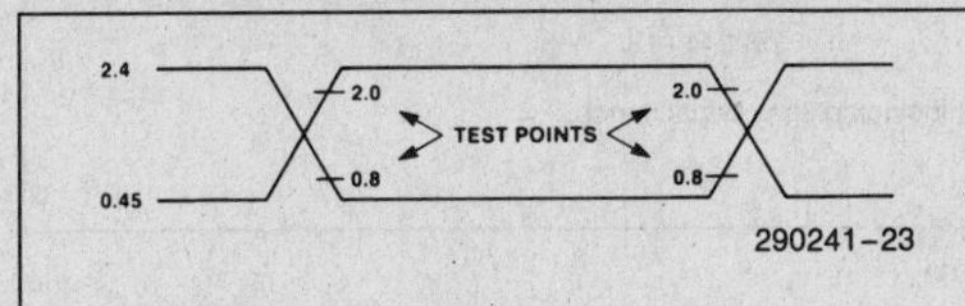

290241-23

A.C. TESTING LOAD CIRCUIT

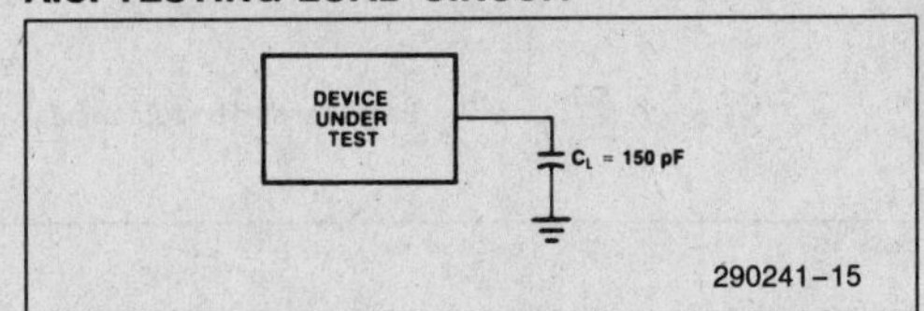

290241-15

TYPICAL 8741A CURRENT

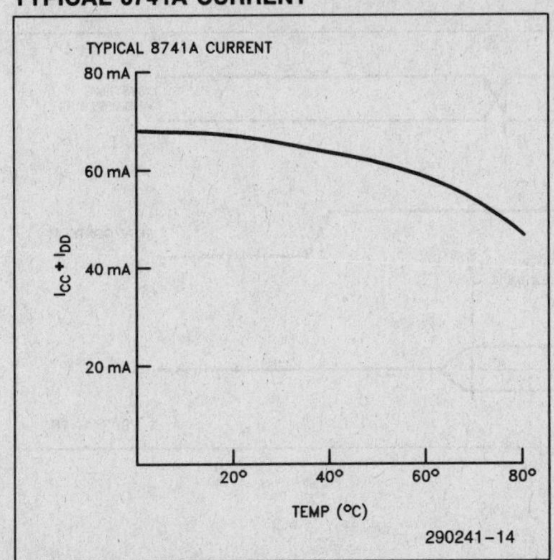

290241-14

CRYSTAL OSCILLATOR MODE

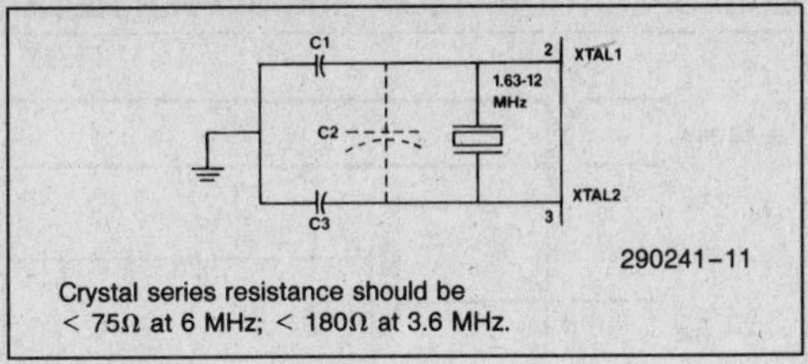

290241-11

Crystal series resistance should be < 75Ω at 6 MHz; < 180Ω at 3.6 MHz.

DRIVING FROM EXTERNAL SOURCE

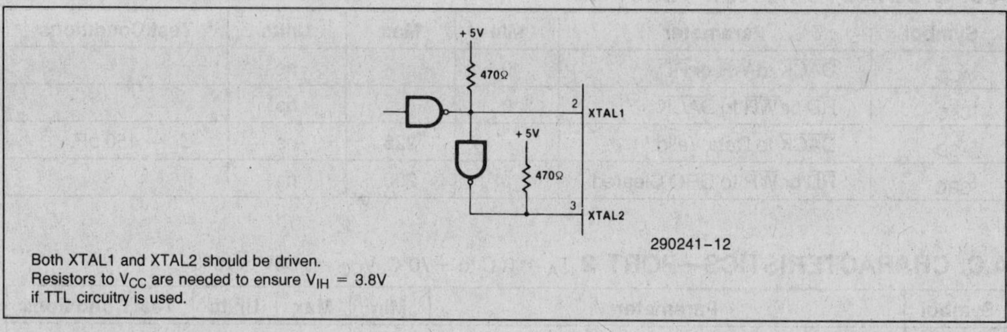

LC OSCILLATOR MODE

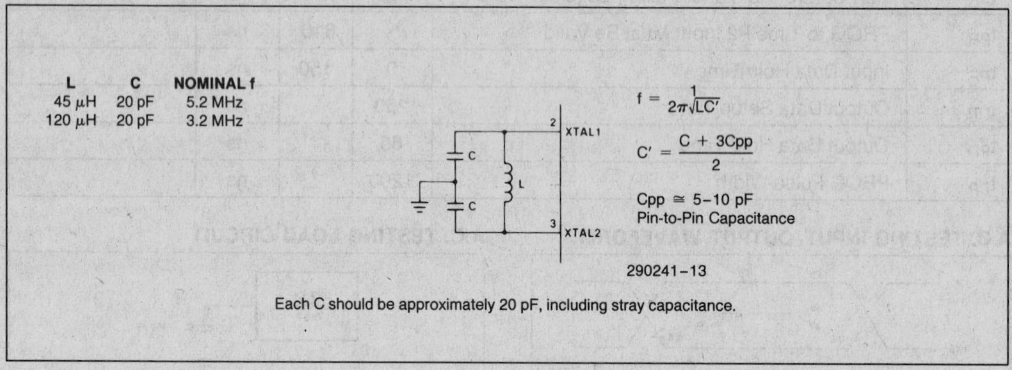

WAVEFORMS

READ OPERATION—DATA BUS BUFFER REGISTER

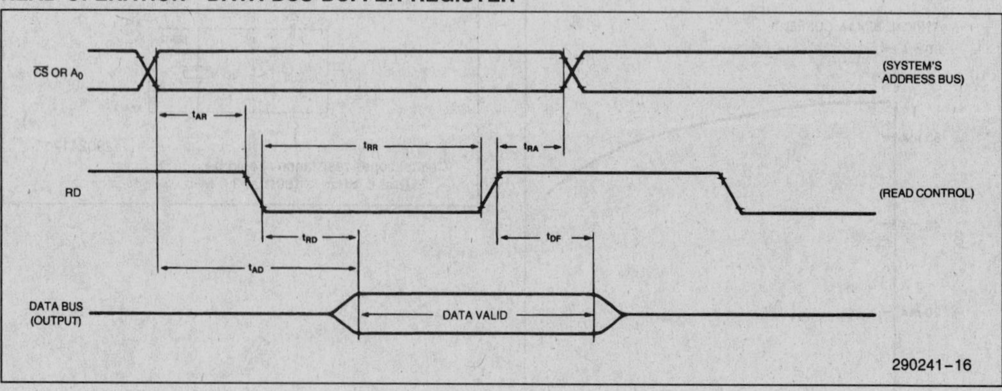

WAVEFORMS

WRITE OPERATION—DATA BUS BUFFER REGISTER

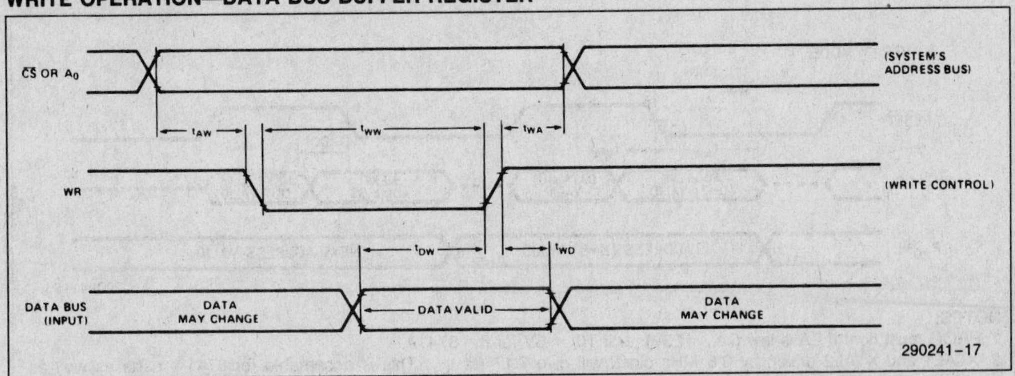

COMBINATION PROGRAM/VERIFY MODE

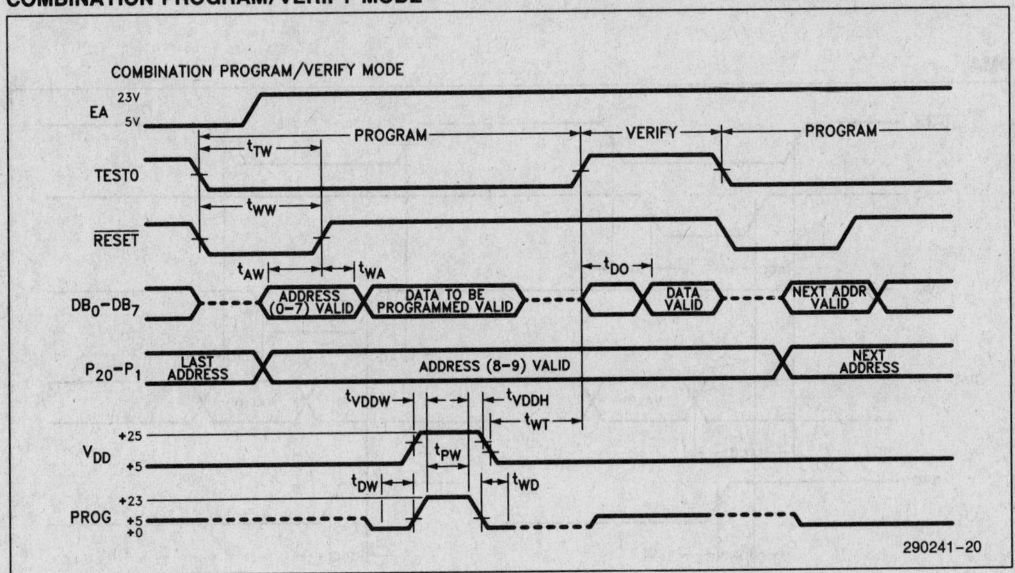

WAVEFORMS

VERIFY MODE

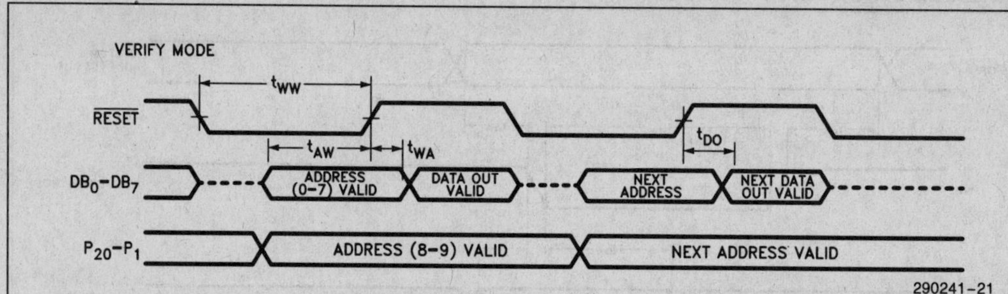

290241-21

NOTES:

1. PROG must float if EA is low (i.e., ≠23V), or if T0 = 5V for the 8741A.
2. XTAL1 and XTAL2 driven by 3.6 MHz clock will give 7.17 μs t_{CY}. This is acceptable for 8741-8 parts as well as standard parts.
PROG must float or = 5V when EA is high.
3. A_0 must be held low (i.e., = 0V) during program/verify modes.

DMA

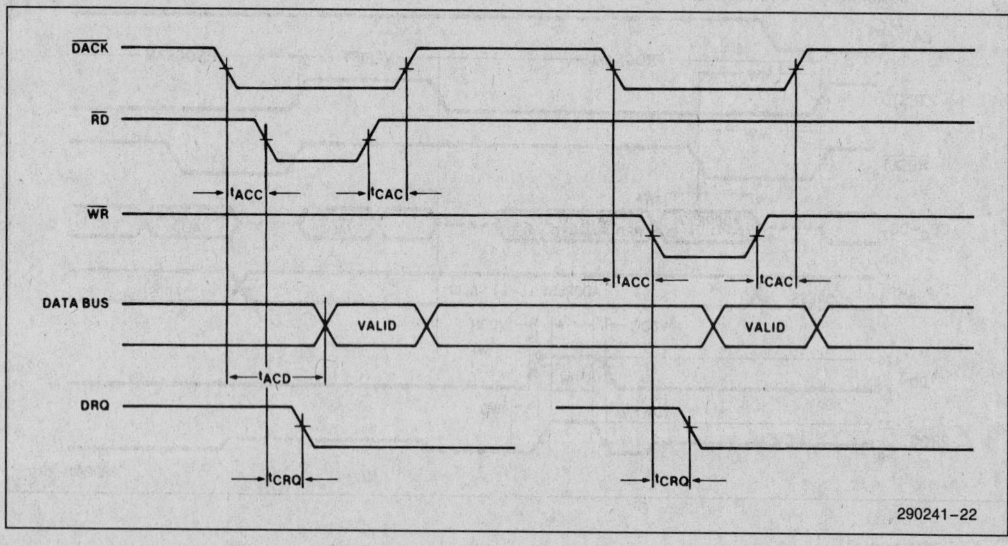

290241-22

PORT 2 TIMING

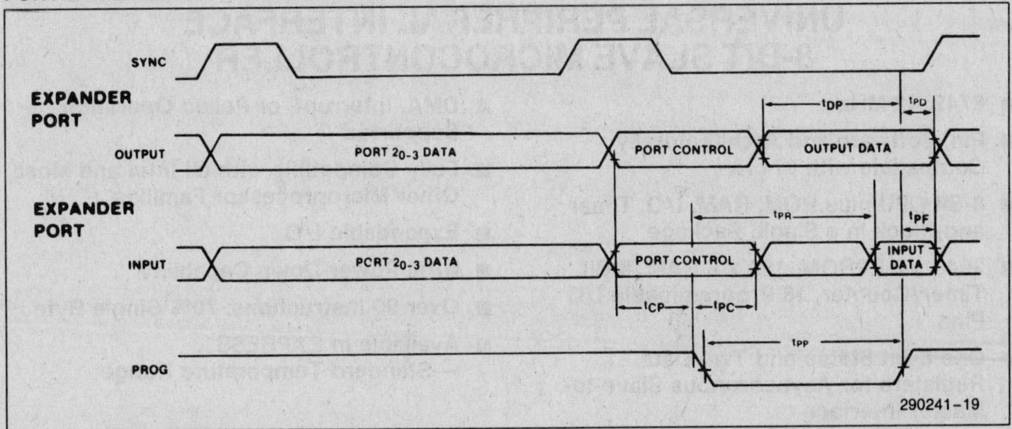

290241-19

PORT TIMING DURING EXTERNAL ACCESS (EA)

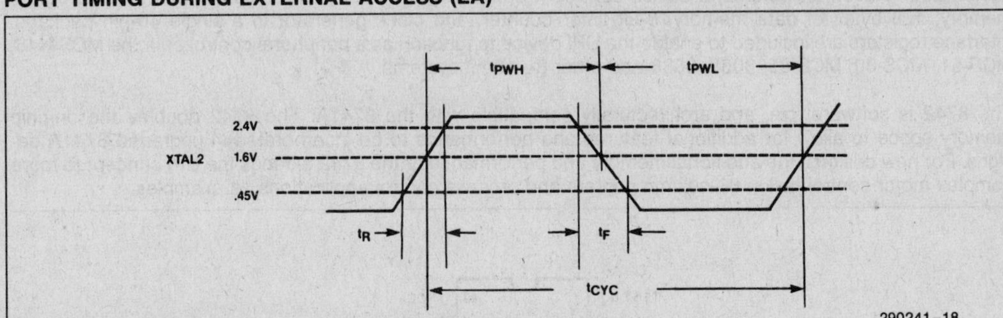

290241-18

On the rising edge of SYNC and EA is enabled, port data is valid and can be strobed. On the trailing edge of sync the program counter contents are available.

8742
UNIVERSAL PERIPHERAL INTERFACE 8-BIT SLAVE MICROCONTROLLER

- **8742: 12 MHz**
- **Pin, Software and Architecturally Compatible with 8741A**
- **8-Bit CPU plus ROM, RAM, I/O, Timer and Clock in a Single Package**
- **2048 x 8 EPROM, 128 x 8 RAM, 8-Bit Timer/Counter, 18 Programmable I/O Pins**
- **One 8-Bit Status and Two Data Registers for Asynchronous Slave-to-Master Interface**
- **DMA, Interrupt, or Polled Operation Supported**
- **Fully Compatible with all Intel and Most Other Microprocessor Families**
- **Expandable I/O**
- **RAM Power-Down Capability**
- **Over 90 Instructions: 70% Single Byte**
- **Available in EXPRESS — Standard Temperature Range**

The Intel 8742 is a general-purpose Universal Peripheral Interface that allows designers to grow their own customized solution for peripheral device control. It contains a low-cost microcomputer with 2K of program memory, 128 bytes of data memory, 8-bit timer/counter, and clock generator in a single 40-pin package. Interface registers are included to enable the UPI device to function as a peripheral controller in the MCS®-48, MCS-51, MCS-80, MCS-85, 8088, 8086 and other 8-, 16-bit systems.

The 8742 is software, pin, and architecturally compatible with the 8741A. The 8742 doubles the on-chip memory space to allow for additional features and performance to be incorporated in upgraded 8741A designs. For new designs, the additional memory and performance of the 8742 extends the UPI concept to more complex motor control tasks, 80-column printers and process control applications as examples.

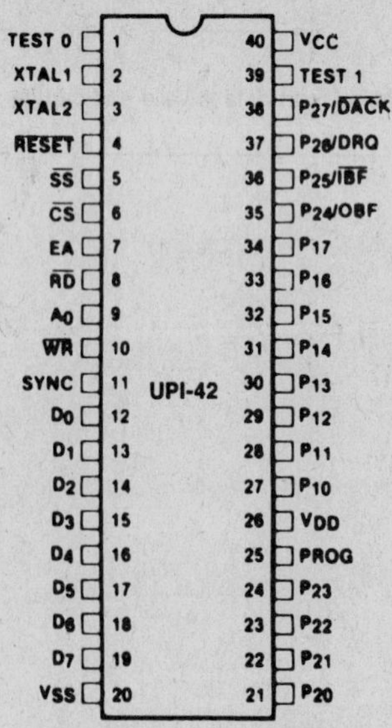

Figure 1. Pin Configuration

November 1991
Order Number: 290256-001

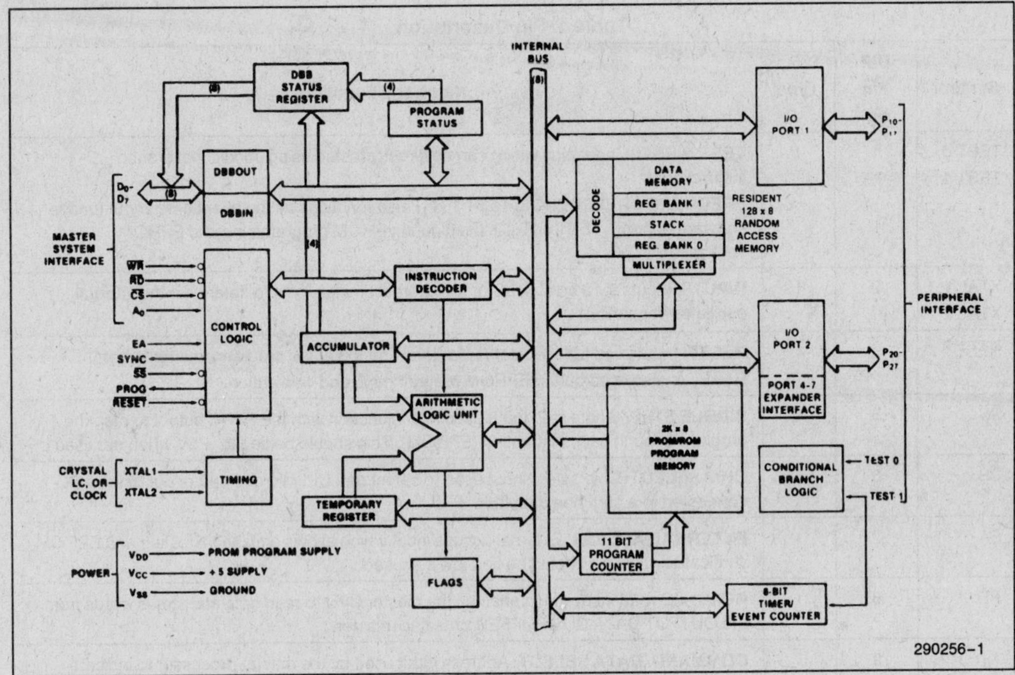

Figure 2. Block Diagram

4

Table 1. Pin Description

Symbol	DIP Pin No.	Type	Name and Function
TEST 0, TEST 1	1 39	I	**TEST INPUTS:** Input pins which can be directly tested using conditional branch instructions. **FREQUENCY REFERENCE:** TEST 1 (T_1) also functions as the event timer input (under software control). TEST 0 (T_0) is used during PROM programming and EPROM verification.
XTAL 1, XTAL 2	2 3	I	**INPUTS:** Inputs for a crystal, LC or an external timing signal to determine the internal oscillator frequency.
$\overline{\text{RESET}}$	4	I	**RESET:** Input used to reset status flip-flops and to set the program counter to zero. $\overline{\text{RESET}}$ is also used during EPROM programming and verification.
$\overline{\text{SS}}$	5	I	**SINGLE STEP:** Single step input used in conjunction with the SYNC output to step the program through each instruction (EPROM). This should be tied to +5V when not used.
$\overline{\text{CS}}$	6	I	**CHIP SELECT:** Chip select input used to select one UPI microcomputer out of several connected to a common data bus.
EA	7	I	**EXTERNAL ACCESS:** External access input which allows emulation, testing and EPROM verification. This pin should be tied low if unused.
$\overline{\text{RD}}$	8	I	**READ:** I/O read input which enables the master CPU to read data and status words from the OUTPUT DATA BUS BUFFER or status register.
A_0	9	I	**COMMAND/DATA SELECT:** Address Input used by the master processor to indicate whether byte transfer is data ($A_0 = 0$, F1 is reset) or command ($A_0 = 1$, F1 is set). $A_0 = 0$ during program and verify operations.
$\overline{\text{WR}}$	10	I	**WRITE:** I/O write input which enables the master CPU to write data and command words to the UPI INPUT DATA BUS BUFFER.
SYNC	11	O	**OUTPUT CLOCK:** Output signal which occurs once per UPI instruction cycle. SYNC can be used as a strobe for external circuitry; it is also used to synchronize single step operation.
D_0–D_7 (BUS)	12–19	I/O	**DATA BUS:** Three-state, bidirectional DATA BUS BUFFER lines used to interface the UPI microcomputer to an 8-bit master system data bus.
P_{10}–P_{17}	27–34	I/O	**PORT 1:** 8-bit, PORT 1 quasi-bidirectional I/O lines.
P_{20}–P_{27}	21–24 35–38	I/O	**PORT 2:** 8-bit, PORT 2 quasi-bidirectional I/O lines. The lower 4 bits (P_{20}–P_{23}) interface directly to the 8243 I/O expander device and contain address and data information during PORT 4–7 access. The upper 4 bits (P_{24}–P_{27}) can be programmed to provide interrupt Request and DMA Handshake capability. Software control can configure P_{24} as Output Buffer Full (OBF) interrupt, P_{25} as Input Buffer Full ($\overline{\text{IBF}}$) interrupt, P_{26} as DMA Request (DRQ), and P_{27} as DMA ACKnowledge ($\overline{\text{DACK}}$).
PROG	25	I/O	**PROGRAM:** Multifunction pin used as the program pulse input during PROM programming. During I/O expander access the PROG pin acts as an address/data strobe to the 8243. This pin should be tied high if unused.
V_{CC}	40		**POWER:** +5V main power supply pin.
V_{DD}	26		**POWER:** +5V during normal operation. +21V during programming operation. Low power standby supply pin.
V_{SS}	20		**GROUND:** Circuit ground potential.

UPI-42 FEATURES

1. Two Data Bus Buffers, one for input and one for output. This allows a much cleaner Master/Slave protocol.

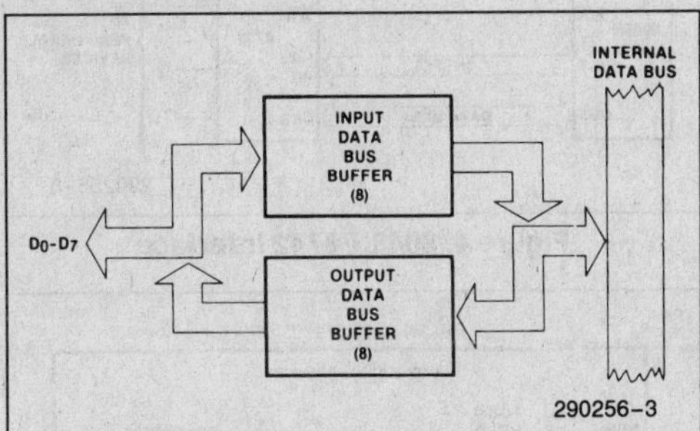

2. 8 Bits of Status

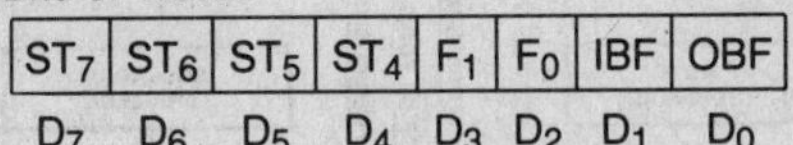

ST_7	ST_6	ST_5	ST_4	F_1	F_0	IBF	OBF
D_7	D_6	D_5	D_4	D_3	D_2	D_1	D_0

ST_4–ST_7 are user definable status bits. These bits are defined by the "MOV STS, A" single byte, single cycle instruction. Bits 4–7 of the acccumulator are moved to bits 4–7 of the status register. Bits 0–3 of the status register are not affected.

MOV STS, A Op Code: 90H

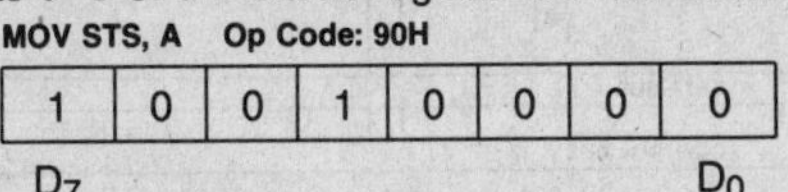

D_7							D_0
1	0	0	1	0	0	0	0

3. $\overline{RD}$ and $\overline{WR}$ are edge triggered. IBF, OBF, F_1 and INT change internally after the trailing edge of $\overline{RD}$ or $\overline{WR}$.

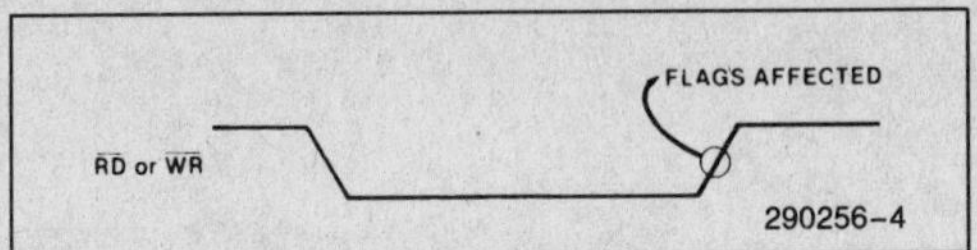

During the time that the host CPU is reading the status register, the 8742 is prevented from updating this register or is "locked out".

4. P_{24} and P_{25} are port pins or Buffer Flag pins which can be used to interrupt a master processor. These pins default to port pins on Reset.

If the "EN FLAGS" instruction has been executed, P_{24} becomes the OBF (Output Buffer Full) pin. A "1" written to P_{24} enables the OBF pin (the pin outputs the OBF Status Bit). A "0" written to P_{24} disables the OBF pin (the pin remains low). This pin can be used to indicate that valid data is available from the UPI-41A (in Output Data Bus Buffer).

If "EN FLAGS" has been executed, P_{25} becomes the $\overline{IBF}$ (Input Buffer Full) pin. A "1" written to P_{25} enables the $\overline{IBF}$ pin (the pin outputs the inverse of the IBF Status Bit. A "0" written to P_{25} disables the $\overline{IBF}$ pin (the pin remains low). This pin can be used to indicate that the UPI is ready for data.

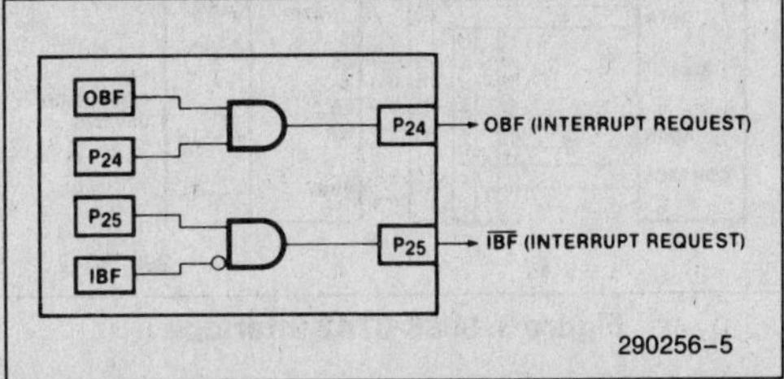

Data Bus Buffer Interrupt Capability

EN FLAGS Op Code: 0F5H

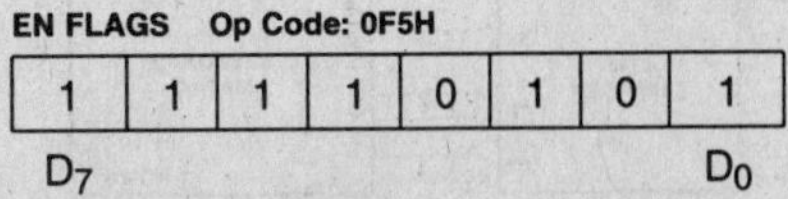

D_7							D_0
1	1	1	1	0	1	0	1

5. P_{26} and P_{27} are port pins or DMA handshake pins for use with a DMA controller. These pins default to port pins on Reset.

If the "EN DMA" instruction has been executed, P_{26} becomes the DRQ (DMA Request) pin. A "1" written to P_{26} causes a DMA request (DRQ is activated). DRQ is deactivated by DACK•RD, DACK•WR, or execution of the "EN DMA" instruction.

If "EN DMA" has been executed, P_{27} becomes the $\overline{DACK}$ (DMA Acknowledge) pin. This pin acts as a chip select input for the Data Bus Buffer registers during DMA transfers.

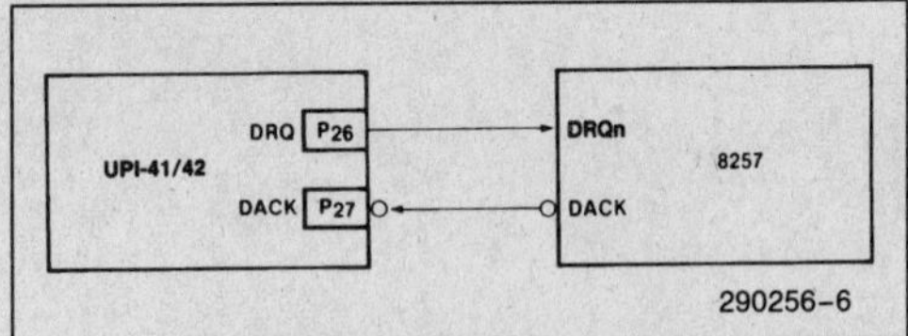

DMA Handshake Capability

EN DMA Op Code: 0E5H

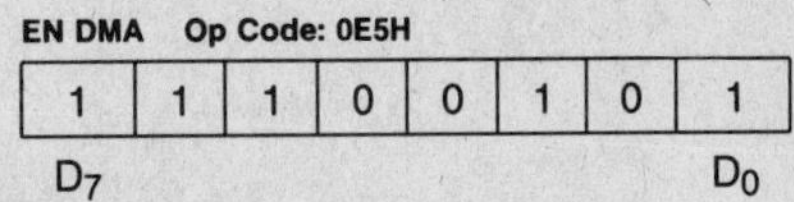

D_7							D_0
1	1	1	0	0	1	0	1

6. The RESET input on the 8742, includes a 2-stage synchronizer to support reliable reset operation for 12 MHz operation.

7. When EA is enabled on the 8742, the program counter is placed on Port 1 and the lower three bits of Port 2 (MSB = P_{22}, LSB = P_{10}). On the 8742 this information is multiplexed with PORT DATA (see port timing diagrams at end of this data sheet).

APPLICATIONS

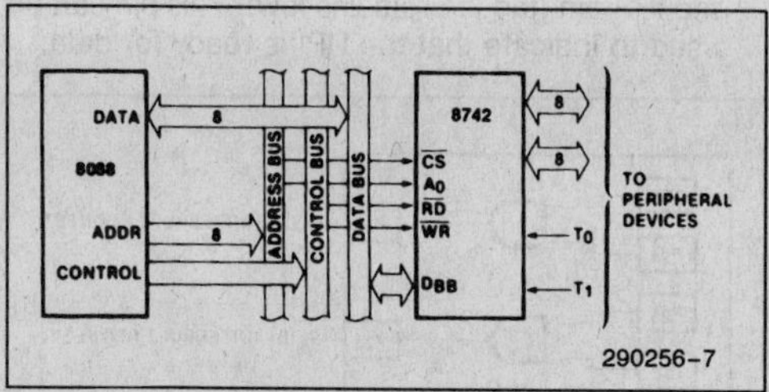

Figure 3. 8088-8742 Interface

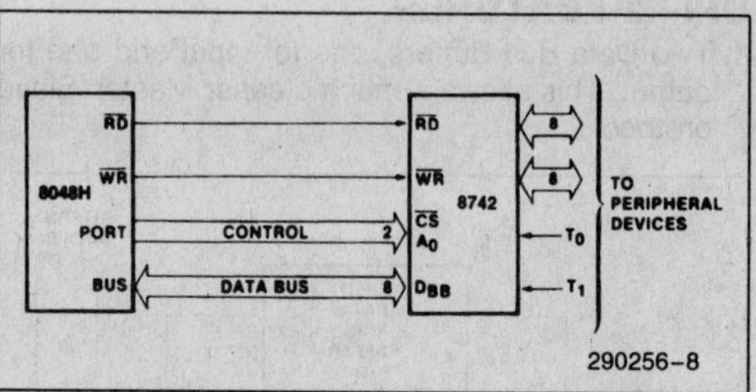

Figure 4. 8048H-8742 Interface

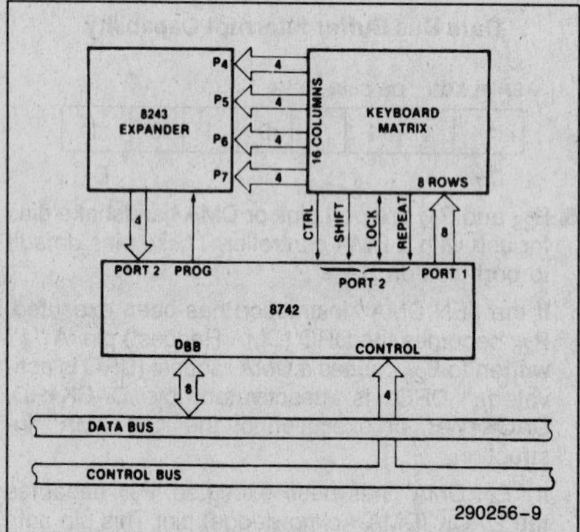

Figure 5. 8742-8243 Keyboard Scanner

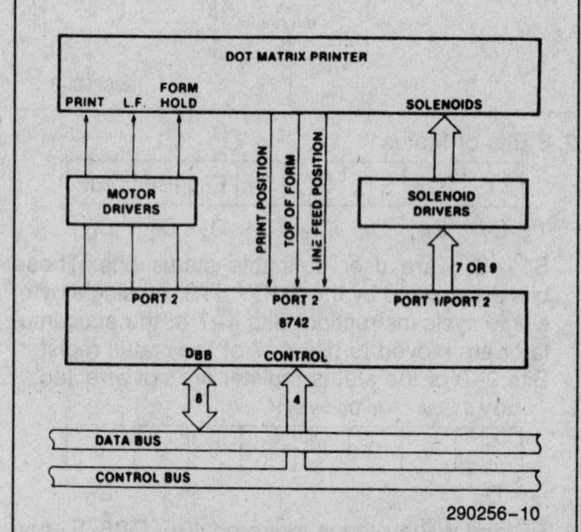

Figure 6. 8742 80-Column Matrix Printer Interface

PROGRAMMING, VERIFYING, AND ERASING THE 8742 EPROM

Programming Verification

In brief, the programming process consists of: activating the program mode, applying an address, latching the address, applying data, and applying a programming pulse. Each word is programmed completely before moving on to the next and is followed by a verification step. The following is a list of the pins used for programming and a description of their functions:

Pin	Function
XTAL 1	Clock-Input
$\overline{\text{Reset}}$	Initialization and Address Latching
Test 0	Selection of Program or Verify Mode
EA	Activation of Program/Verify Modes
BUS	Address and Data Input Data Output During Verify
P_{20-12}	Address Input
V_{DD}	Programming Power Supply
PROG	Program Pulse Input

WARNING
An attempt to program a missocketed 8742 will result in severe damage to the part. An indication of a properly socketed part is the appearance of the SYNC clock output. The lack of this clock may be used to disable the programmer.

The Program/Verify sequence is:

1. A_0 = 0V, CS = 5V, EA = 5V, RESET = 0V, TESTO = 5V, V_{DD} = 5V, clock applied or internal oscillator operating, BUS floating, PROG = 5V.
2. Insert 8742 in programming socket
3. TEST 0 = 0V (select program mode)
4. EA = 18V (active program mode)
5. Address applied to BUS and P_{20-22}
6. $\overline{\text{RESET}}$ = 5V (latch address)
7. Data applied to BUS**
8. V_{DD} = 21V (programming power)
9. PROG = V_{CC} followed by one 50 ms pulse to 18V
10. V_{DD} = 5V
11. TEST 0 = 5V (verify mode)
12. Read and verify data on BUS
13. TEST 0 = 0V
14. $\overline{\text{RESET}}$ = 0V and repeat from step 5
15. Programmer should be at conditions of step 1 when 8742 is removed from socket

8742 Erasure Characteristics

The erasure characteristics of the 8742 are such that erasure begins to occur when exposed to light with wavelengths shorter than approximately 4000 Angstroms (Å). It should be noted that sunlight and certain types of fluorescent lamps have wavelengths in the 3000-4000Å range. Data shows that constant exposure to room level fluorescent lighting could erase the typical 8742 in approximately 3 years while it would take approximately one week to cause erasure when exposed to direct sunlight. If the 8742 is to be exposed to these types of lighting conditions for extended periods of time, opaque labels are available from Intel which should be placed over the 8742 window to prevent unintentional erasure.

The recommended erasure procedure for the 8742 is exposure to shortwave ultraviolet light which has a wavelength of 2537Å. The integrated dose (i.e., UV intensity × exposure time) for erasure should be a minimum of 15 w-sec/cm^2. The erasure time with this dosage is approximately 15 to 20 minutes using an ultraviolet lamp with a 12,000 μW/cm^2 power rating. The 8742 should be placed within one inch of the lamp tubes during erasure. Some lamps have a filter on their tubes which should be removed before erasure.

ABSOLUTE MAXIMUM RATINGS*

Ambient Temperature Under Bias ......0°C to 70°C
Storage Temperature .... −65°C to +150°C
Voltage on Any Pin With Respect to Ground .... −0.5 to +7V
Power Dissipation 1.5W

NOTICE: This is a production data sheet. The specifications are subject to change without notice.

******WARNING: Stressing the device beyond the "Absolute Maximum Ratings" may cause permanent damage. These are stress ratings only. Operation beyond the "Operating Conditions" is not recommended and extended exposure beyond the "Operating Conditions" may affect device reliability.*

D.C. CHARACTERISTICS T_A = 0° to +70°C, $V_{CC} = V_{DD}$ = +5V ±10%

Symbol	Parameter	8742		Units	Test Conditions
		Min	Max		
V_{IL}	Input Low Voltage (Except XTAL1, XTAL2, RESET)	−0.5	0.8	V	
V_{IL1}	Input Low Voltage (XTAL1, XTAL2, RESET)	−0.5	0.6	V	
V_{IH}	Input High Voltage (Except XTAL1, XTAL2, RESET)	2.0	V_{CC}	V	
V_{IH1}	Input High Voltage (XTLA1, XTAL2, RESET)	3.5	V_{CC}	V	
V_{OL}	Output Low Voltage (D_0–D_7)		0.45	V	I_{OL} = 2.0 mA
V_{OL1}	Output Low Voltage (P_{10}–P_{17}, P_{20}–P_{27}, Sync)		0.45	V	I_{OL} = 1.6 mA
V_{OL2}	Output Low Voltage (PROG)		0.45	V	I_{OL} = 1.0 mA
V_{OH}	Output High Voltage (D_0–D_7)	2.4		V	I_{OH} = −400 μA
V_{OH1}	Output High Voltage (All Other Outputs)	2.4			I_{OH} = −50 μA
I_{IL}	Input Leakage Current (T_0, T_1, RD, WR, CS, A_0, EA)		±10	μA	$V_{SS} \leq V_{IN} \leq V_{CC}$
I_{OFL}	Output Leakage Current (D_0–D_7, High Z State)		±10	μA	$V_{SS} + 0.45 \leq V_{OUT} \leq V_{CC}$
I_{LI}	Low Input Load Current (P_{10}–P_{17}, P_{20}–P_{27})		0.3	mA	V_{IL} = 0.8V
I_{LI1}	Low Input Load Current (RESET, SS)		0.2	mA	V_{IL} = 0.8V
I_{DD}	V_{DD} Supply Current		10	mA	Typical = 5 mA
$I_{CC} + I_{DD}$	Total Supply Current		125	mA	Typical = 60 mA
I_{IH}	Input Leakage Current (P_{10}–P_{17}, P_{20}–P_{27})		100	μA	$V_{IN} = V_{CC}$
C_{IN}	Input Capacitance		10	pF	
C_{IO}	I/O Capacitance		20	pF	

D.C. CHARACTERISTICS—PROGRAMMING

T_A = 25°C ±5°C, V_{CC} = 5V ±5%, V_{DD} = 21V ±0.5V

Symbol	Parameter	Min	Max	Units	Test Conditions
V_{DOH}	V_{DD} Program Voltage High Level	20.5	21.5	V	
V_{DDL}	V_{DD} Voltage Low Level	4.75	5.25	V	
V_{PH}	PROG Program Voltage High Level	17.5	18.5	V	
V_{PL}	PROG Voltage Low Level	V_{CC}−0.5	V_{CC}	V	
V_{EAH}	EA Program or Verify Voltage High Level	17.5	18.5	V	
V_{EAL}	EA Voltage Low Level		5.25	V	
I_{DD}	V_{DD} High Voltage Supply Current		30.0	mA	
I_{PROG}	PROG High Voltage Supply Current		1.0	mA	
I_{EA}	EA High Voltage Supply Current		1.0	mA	

A.C. CHARACTERISTICS $T_A = 0°C$ to $+70°C$, $V_{SS} = 0V$, $V_{CC} = V_{DD} = +5V \pm 10\%$

DBB READ

Symbol	Parameter	8742		Units
		Min	Max	
t_{AR}	CS, A_0 Setup to RD ↓	0		ns
t_{RA}	CS, A_0 Hold after RD ↑	0		ns
t_{RR}	RD Pulse Width	160		ns
t_{AD}	CS, A_0 to Data Out Delay		130	ns
t_{RD}	RD ↓ to Data Out Delay		130	ns
t_{DF}	RD ↑ to Data Float Delay		85	ns
t_{CY}	Cycle Time	1.25	15	μs[(1)]

DBB WRITE

Symbol	Parameter	Min	Max	Units
t_{AW}	CS, A_0 Setup to WR ↓	0		ns
t_{WA}	CS, A_0 Hold after WR ↑	0		ns
t_{WW}	WR Pulse Width	160		ns
t_{DW}	Data Setup to WR ↑	130		ns
t_{WD}	Data Hold after WR ↑	0		ns

NOTE:
1. $T_{CY} = 15/f(XTAL)$

4

A.C. CHARACTERISTICS $T_A = 25°C \pm 5°C$, $V_{CC} = 5V \pm 5\%$, $V_{DD} = +21V \pm 0.5$

PROGRAMMING

Symbol	Parameter	Min	Max	Units	Test Conditions
t_{AW}	Address Setup Time to RESET ↑	$4t_{CY}$			
t_{WA}	Address Hold Time after RESET ↑	$4t_{CY}$			
t_{DW}	Data in Setup Time to PROG ↑	$4t_{CY}$			
t_{WD}	Data in Hold Time after PROG ↓	$4t_{CY}$			
t_{PH}	RESET Hold Time to Verify	$4t_{CY}$			
t_{VDDW}	V_{DD} Setup Time to PROG ↑	0	1.0	mS	
t_{VDDH}	V_{DD} Hold Time after PROG ↑	0	1.0	mS	
t_{PW}	Program Pulse Width	50	60	mS	
t_{TW}	Test 0 Setup Time for Program Mode	$4t_{CY}$			
t_{WT}	Test 0 Hold Time after Program Mode	$4t_{CY}$			
t_{DO}	Test 0 to Data Out Delay		$4t_{CY}$		
t_{WW}	RESET Pulse Width to Latch Address	$4t_{CY}$			
t_r, t_f	V_{DD} and PROG Rise and Fall Times	0.5	2.0	μs	
t_{CY}	CPU Operation Cycle Time	4.0		μs	
t_{RE}	RESET Setup Time before EA ↑	$4t_{CY}$			

NOTE:
If TEST 0 is high, t_{DO} can be triggered by RESET ↑.

A.C. CHARACTERISTICS DMA

Symbol	Parameter	8642/8742		Units
		Min	Max	
t_{ACC}	DACK to WR or RD	0		ns
t_{CAC}	RD or WR to DACK	0		ns
t_{ACD}	DACK to Data Valid		130	ns
t_{CRQ}	RD or WR to DRQ Cleared		100	ns(1)

NOTE:
1. C_L = 150 pF.

A.C. CHARACTERISTICS PORT 2 T_A = 0°C to +70°C, V_{CC} = +5V ±10%

Symbol	Parameter	f(t_{CY})	8742/8642(3)		Units
			Min	Max	
t_{CP}	Port Control Setup before Falling Edge of PROG	1/15 t_{CY} − 28	55		ns(1)
t_{PC}	Port Control Hold after Falling Edge of PROG	1/10 t_{CY}	125		ns(2)
t_{PR}	PROG to Time P2 Input Must Be Valid	8/15 t_{CY} − 16		650	ns(1)
t_{PF}	Input Data Hold Time		0	150	ns(2)
t_{DP}	Output Data Setup Time	2/10 t_{CY}	250		ns(1)
t_{PD}	Output Data Hold Time	1/10 t_{CY} − 80	45		ns(2)
t_{PP}	PROG Pulse Width	6/10 t_{CY}	750		ns

NOTES:
1. C_L = 80 pF.
2. C_L = 20 pF.
3. t_{CY} = 1.25 μs.

A.C. TESTING INPUT/OUTPUT WAVEFORM

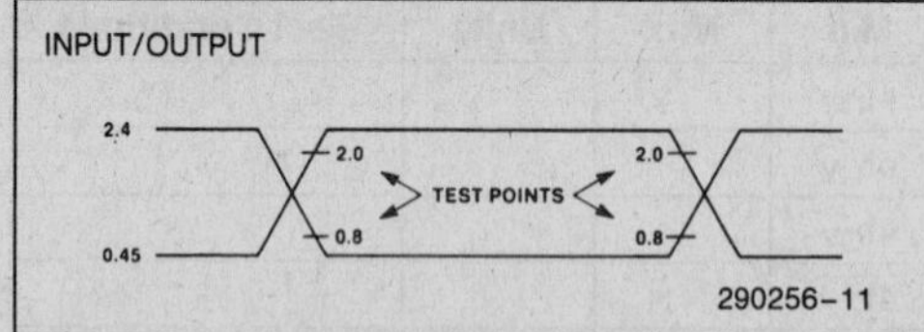

290256–11

A.C. TESTING LOAD CIRCUIT

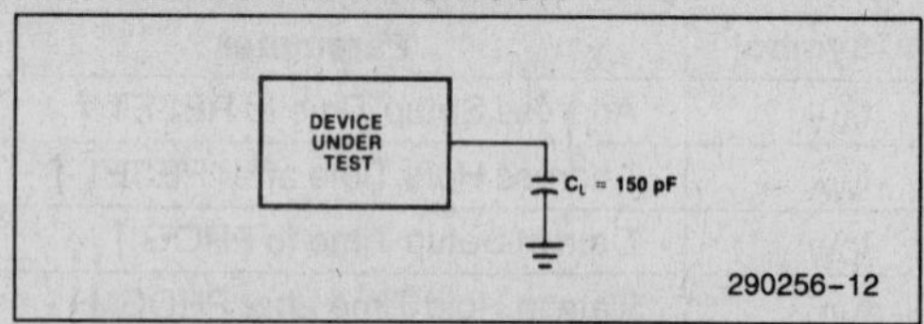

290256–12

CRYSTAL OSCILLATOR MODE

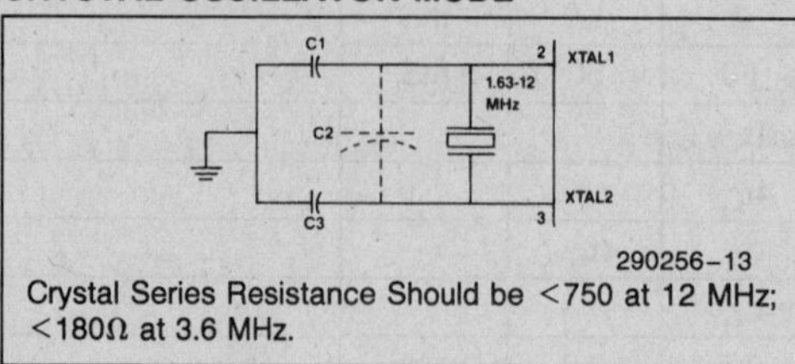

290256–13

Crystal Series Resistance Should be <75Ω at 12 MHz; <180Ω at 3.6 MHz.

DRIVING FROM EXTERNAL SOURCE

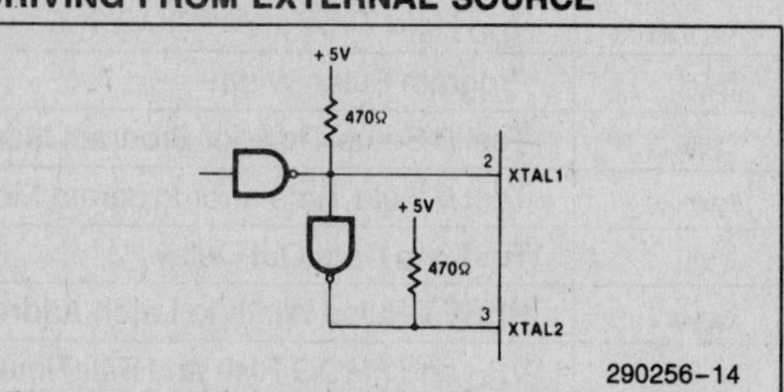

290256–14

Rise and Fall Times Should Not Exceed 20 ns. Resistors to V_{CC} are Needed to Ensure V_{IH} = 3.5V if TTL Circuitry is Used.

LC OSCILLATOR MODE

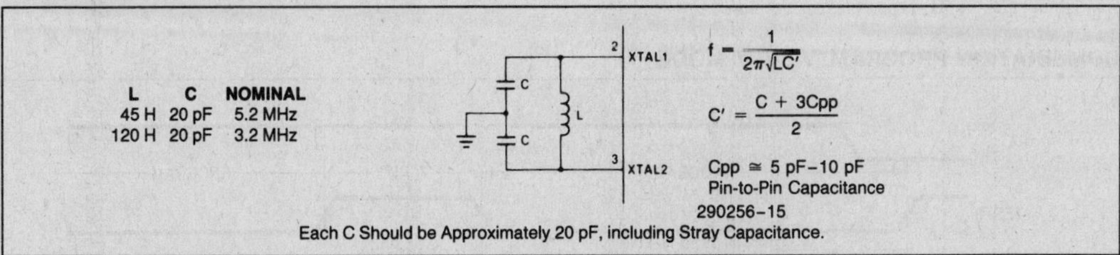

290256-15

Each C Should be Approximately 20 pF, including Stray Capacitance.

WAVEFORMS

READ OPERATION—DATA BUS BUFFER REGISTER

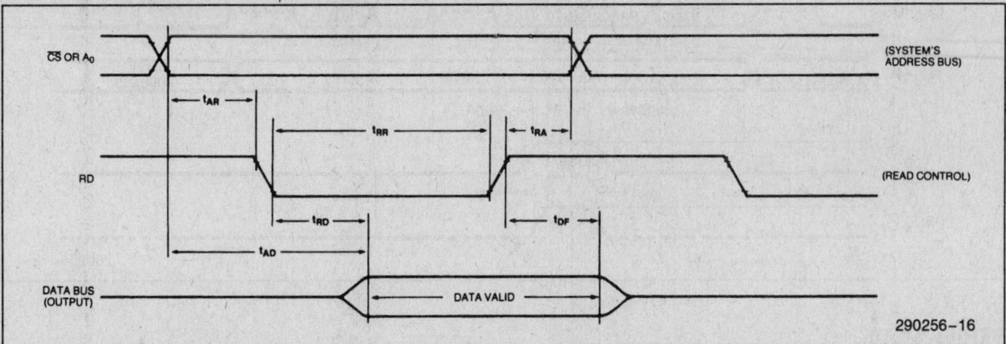

290256-16

WRITE OPERATION—DATA BUS BUFFER REGISTER

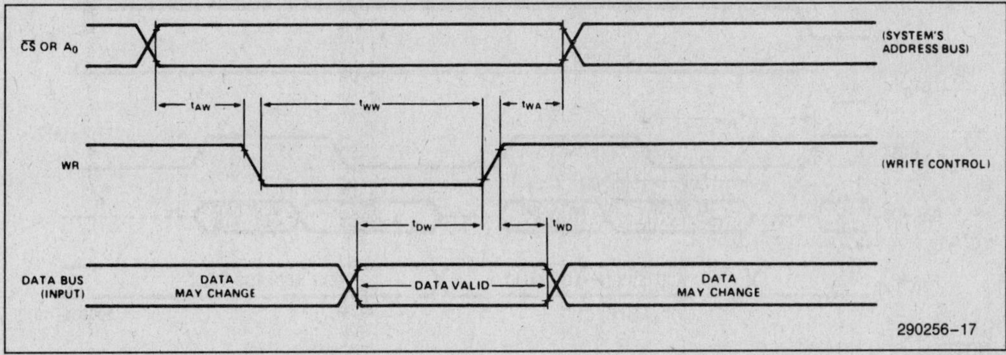

290256-17

CLOCK TIMING

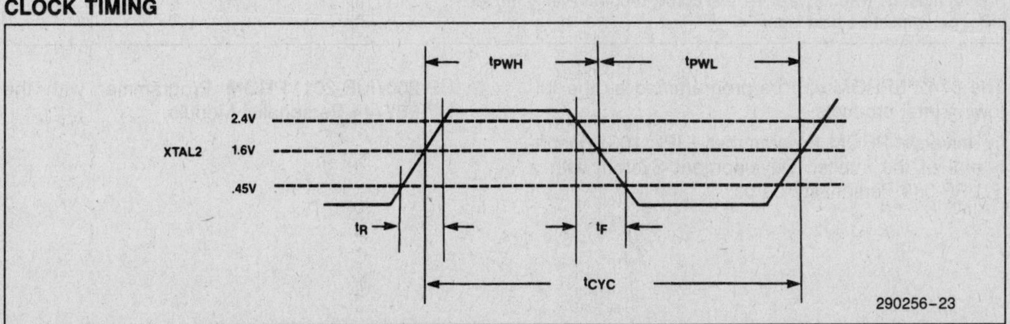

290256-23

WAVEFORMS

COMBINATION PROGRAM/VERIFY MODE

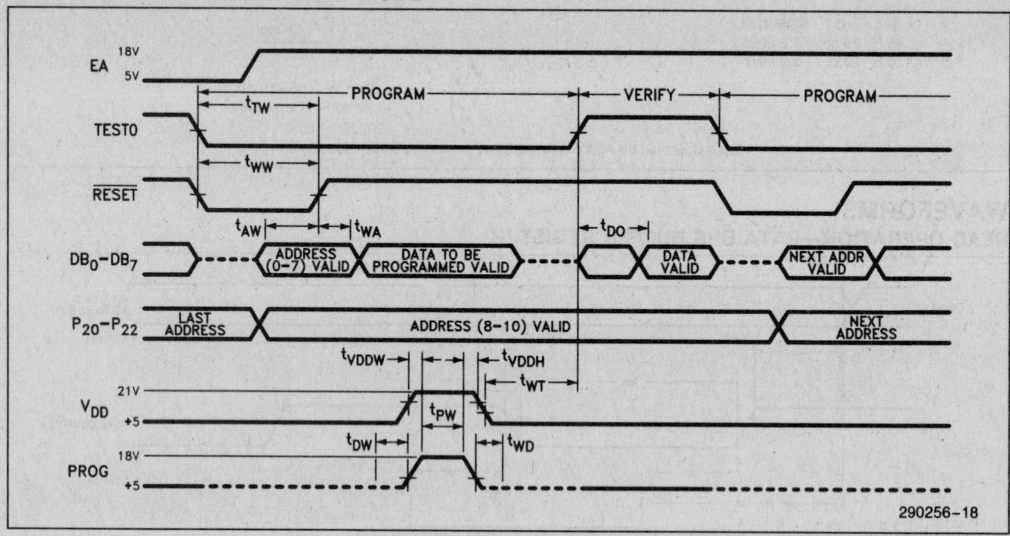

VERIFY MODE

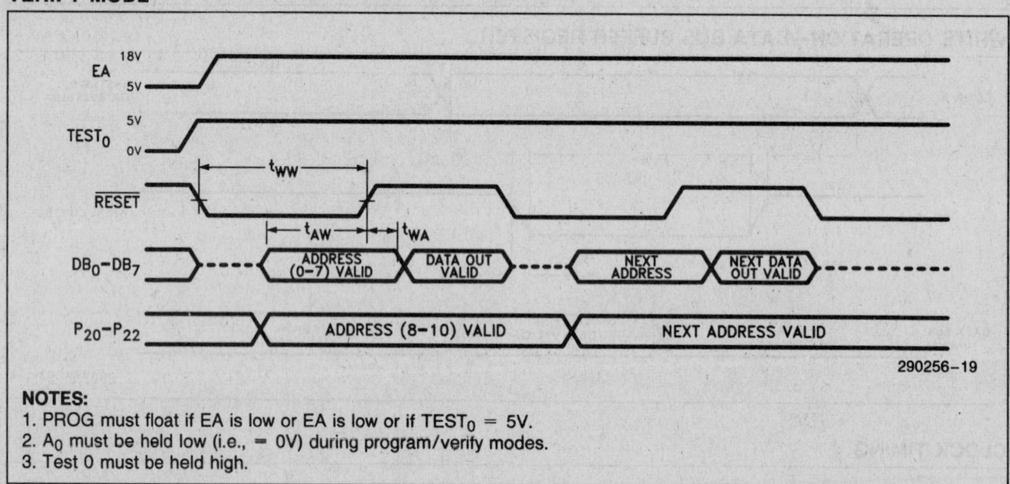

NOTES:
1. PROG must float if EA is low or EA is low or if $TEST_0 = 5V$.
2. A_0 must be held low (i.e., = 0V) during program/verify modes.
3. Test 0 must be held high.

The 8742 EPROM can be programmed by the following Intel products:

1. Universal PROM Programmer (UPP 103) peripheral of the Intellec Development System with a UPP-549 Personality Card.
2. iUP-200/iUP-201 PROM Programmer with the iUP-F87/44 Personality Module.

WAVEFORMS (Continued)

DMA

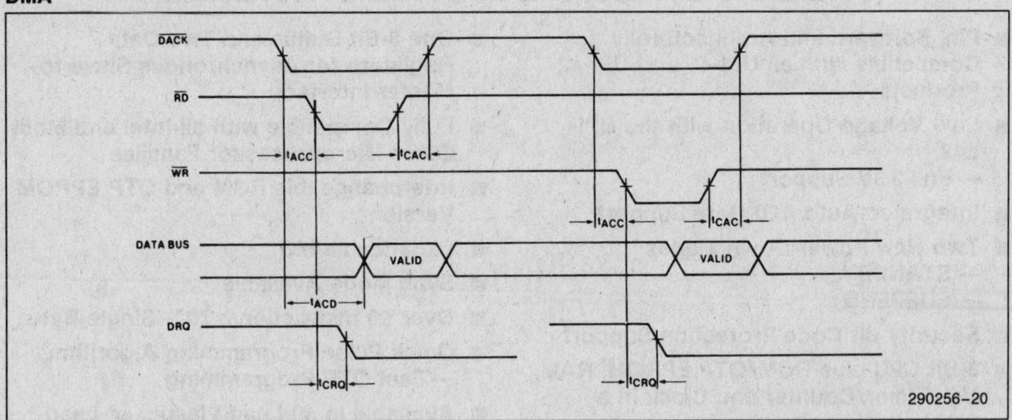

PORT 2

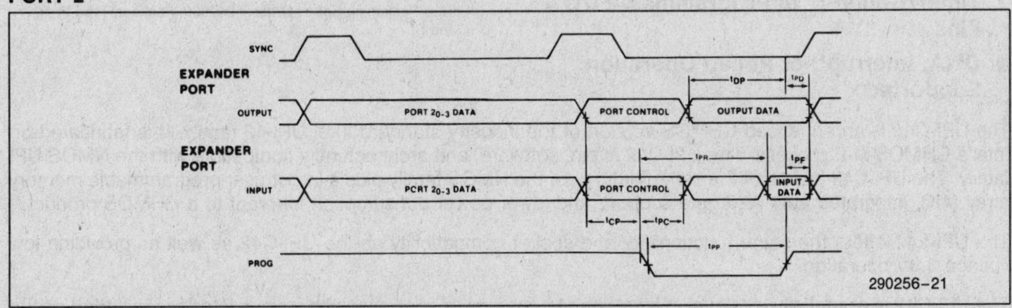

PORT TIMING DURING EXTERNAL ACCESS (EA)

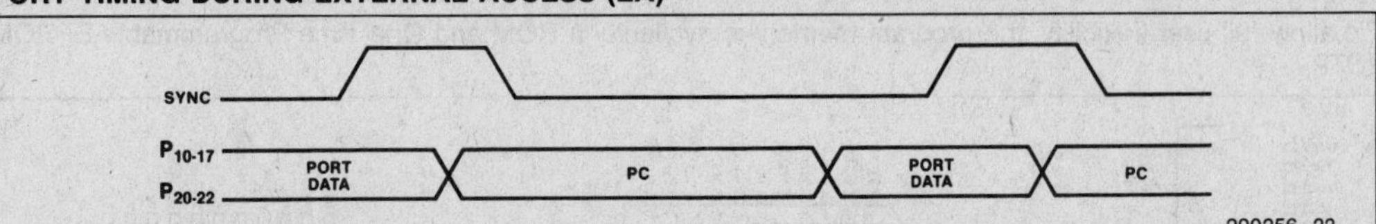

On the Rising Edge of SYNC and EA is Enabled, Port Data is Valid and can be Strobed on the Trailing Edge of Sync the Program Counter Contents are Available.

PRELIMINARY

UPI-C42/UPI-L42 UNIVERSAL PERIPHERAL INTERFACE CHMOS 8-BIT SLAVE MICROCONTROLLER

- **Pin, Software and Architecturally Compatible with all UPI-41 and UPI-42 Products**
- **Low Voltage Operation with the UPI-L42**
  - **— Full 3.3V Support**
- **Integrated Auto A20 Gate Support**
- **Two New Power Down Modes**
  - **— STANDBY**
  - **— SUSPEND**
- **Security Bit Code Protection Support**
- **8-Bit CPU plus ROM/OTP EPROM, RAM, I/O, Timer/Counter and Clock in a Single Package**
- **4096 x 8 ROM/OTP, 256 x 8 RAM 8-Bit Timer/Counter, 18 Programmable I/O Pins**
- **DMA, Interrupt, or Polled Operation Supported**
- **One 8-Bit Status and Two Data Registers for Asynchronous Slave-to-Master Interface**
- **Fully Compatible with all Intel and Most Other Microprocessor Families**
- **Interchangeable ROM and OTP EPROM Versions**
- **Expandable I/O**
- **Sync Mode Available**
- **Over 90 Instructions: 70% Single Byte**
- **Quick Pulse Programming Algorithm**
  - **— Fast OTP Programming**
- **Available in 40-Lead Plastic, 44-Lead Plastic Leaded Chip Carrier, and 44-Lead Quad Flat Pack Packages**
  (See Packaging Spec., Order #240800, Package Type P, N, and S)

The UPI-C42 is an enhanced CHMOS version of the industry standard Intel UPI-42 family. It is fabricated on Intel's CHMOS III-E process. The UPI-C42 is pin, software, and architecturally compatible with the NMOS UPI family. The UPI-C42 has all of the same features of the NMOS family plus a larger user programmable memory array (4K), integrated auto A20 gate support, and lower power consumption inherent to a CHMOS product.

The UPI-L42 offers the same functionality and socket compatibility as the UPI-C42 as well as providing low voltage 3.3V operation.

The UPI-C42 is essentially a "slave" microcontroller, or a microcontroller with a slave interface included on the chip. Interface registers are included to enable the UPI device to function as a slave peripheral controller in the MCS Modules and iAPX family, as well as other 8-, 16-, and 32-bit systems.

To allow full user flexibility, the program memory is available in ROM and One-Time Programmable EPROM (OTP).

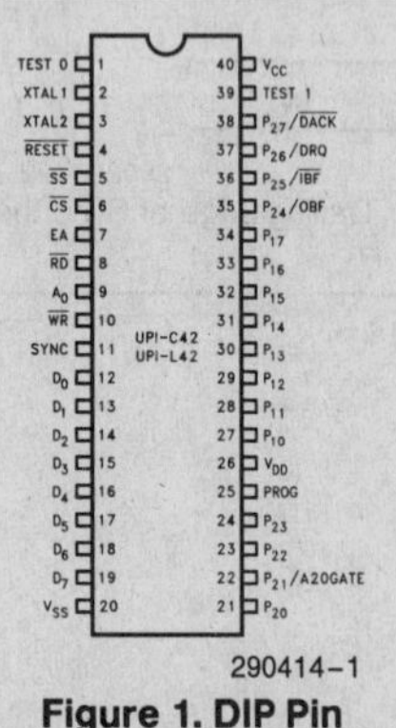

Figure 1. DIP Pin Configuration

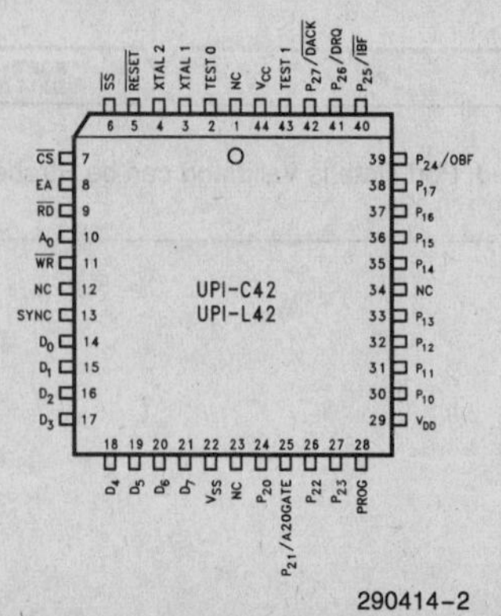

Figure 2. PLCC Pin Configuration

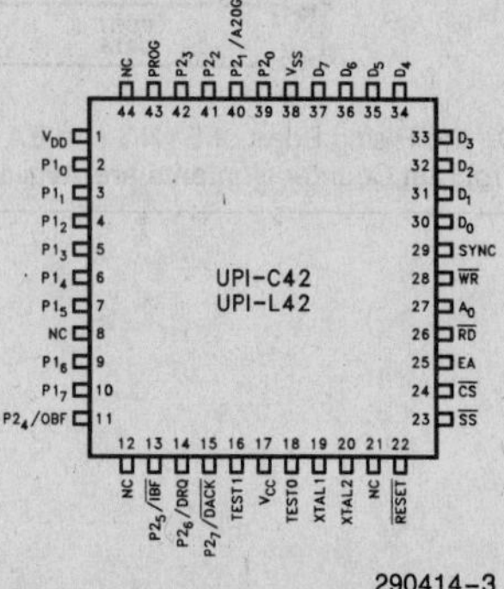

Figure 3. QFP Pin Configuration

October 1993
Order Number: 290414-003

Table 1. Pin Description

Symbol	DIP Pin No.	PLCC Pin No.	QFP Pin No.	Type	Name and Function
TEST 0, TEST 1	1 39	2 43	18 16	I	**TEST INPUTS:** Input pins which can be directly tested using conditional branch instructions. **FREQUENCY REFERENCE:** TEST 1 (T_1) functions as the event timer input (under software control) and during the STANDBY power down mode, as a method of resuming normal operation. TEST 0 (T_0) is a multi-function pin used during PROM programming and ROM/EPROM verification, during Sync Mode to reset the instruction state to S1 and synchronize the internal clock to PH1, and during the STANDBY power down mode, as a method of resuming normal operation (see Powerdown section).
XTAL 1	2	3	19	O	**OUTPUT:** Output from the oscillator amplifier.
XTAL 2	3	4	20	I	**INPUT:** Input to the oscillator amplifier and internal clock generator circuits.
$\overline{\text{RESET}}$	4	5	22	I	**RESET:** Input used to reset status flip-flops and to set the program counter to zero. $\overline{\text{RESET}}$ is also used during EPROM programming and verification.
$\overline{\text{SS}}$	5	6	23	I	**SINGLE STEP:** Single step input used in conjunction with the SYNC output to step the program through each instruction (EPROM). This should be tied to +5V when not used. This pin is also used to put the device in Sync Mode by applying 12.5V to it.
$\overline{\text{CS}}$	6	7	24	I	**CHIP SELECT:** Chip select input used to select one UPI microcomputer out of several connected to a common data bus.
EA	7	8	25	I	**EXTERNAL ACCESS:** External access input which allows emulation, testing and ROM/EPROM verification. This pin should be tied low if unused.
$\overline{\text{RD}}$	8	9	26	I	**READ:** I/O read input which enables the master CPU to read data and status words from the OUTPUT DATA BUS BUFFER or status register.
A_0	9	10	27	I	**COMMAND/DATA SELECT:** Address Input used by the master processor to indicate whether byte transfer is data (A_0 = 0, F1 is reset) or command (A_0 = 1, F1 is set). A_0 = 0 during program and verify operations.
$\overline{\text{WR}}$	10	11	28	I	**WRITE:** I/O write input which enables the master CPU to write data and command words to the UPI INPUT DATA BUS BUFFER.
SYNC	11	13	29	O	**OUTPUT CLOCK:** Output signal which occurs once per UPI instruction cycle. SYNC can be used as a strobe for external circuitry; it is also used to synchronize single step operation.
D_0–D_7 (BUS)	12–19	14–21	30–37	I/O	**DATA BUS:** Three-state, bidirectional DATA BUS BUFFER lines used to interface the UPI microcomputer to an 8-bit master system data bus.
P_{10}–P_{17}	27–34	30–33 35–38	2–10	I/O	**PORT 1:** 8-bit, PORT 1 quasi-bidirectional I/O lines. P_{10}–P_{17} access the signature row and security bit.
P_{20}–P_{27}	21–24 35–38	24–27 39–42	39–42 11, 13–15	I/O	**PORT 2:** 8-bit, PORT 2 quasi-bidirectional I/O lines. The lower 4 bits (P_{20}–P_{23}) interface directly to the 8243 I/O expander device and contain address and data information during PORT 4–7 access. P_{21} can be programmed to provide Auto A20 Gate support. The upper 4 bits (P_{24}–P_{27}) can be programmed to provide interrupt Request and DMA Handshake capability. Software control can configure P_{24} as Output Buffer Full (OBF) interrupt, P_{25} as Input Buffer Full ($\overline{\text{IBF}}$) interrupt, P_{26} as DMA Request (DRQ), and P_{27} as DMA ACKnowledge ($\overline{\text{DACK}}$).

4

Table 1. Pin Description (Continued)

Symbol	DIP Pin No.	PLCC Pin No.	QFP Pin No.	Type	Name and Function
PROG	25	28	43	I/O	**PROGRAM:** Multifunction pin used as the program pulse input during PROM programming. During I/O expander access the PROG pin acts as an address/data strobe to the 8243. This pin should be tied high if unused.
V_{CC}	40	44	17		**POWER:** +5V main power supply pin.
V_{DD}	26	29	1		**POWER:** +5V during normal operation. +12.75V during programming operation. Low power standby supply pin.
V_{SS}	20	22	38		**GROUND:** Circuit ground potential.

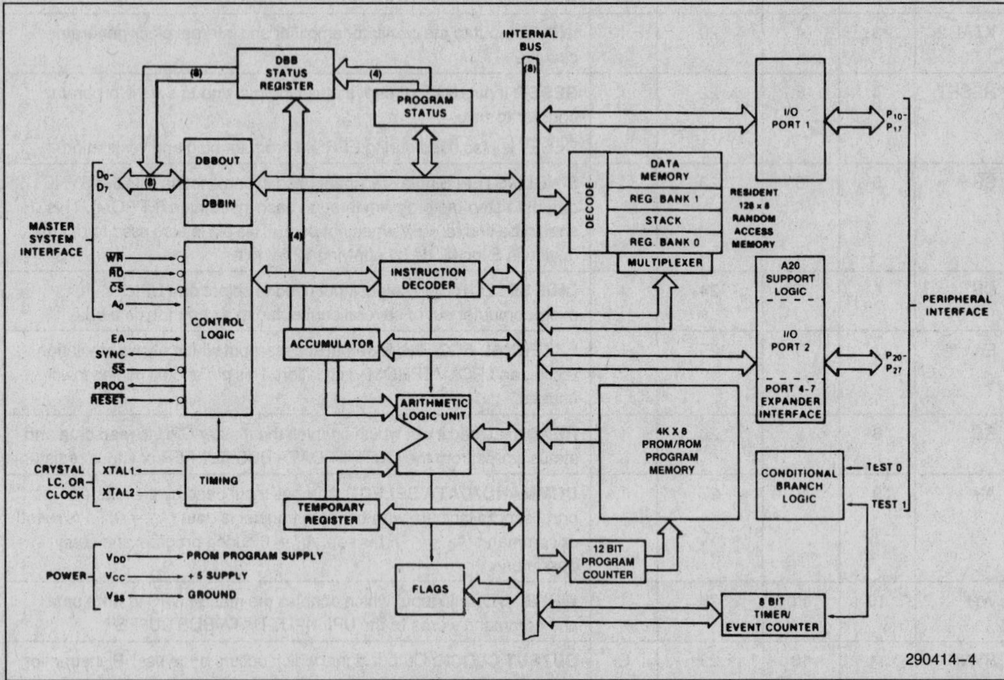

Figure 4. Block Diagram

UPI-C42/L42 PRODUCT SELECTION GUIDE

UPI-C42: Low power CHMOS version of the UPI-42.

Device	Package	ROM	OTP	Comments
80C42	N, P S	4K		ROM Device
82C42PC 82C42PD 82C42PE	N, P, S N, P, S N, P, S			Phoenix MultiKey/42 firmware, PS/2 style mouse support Phoenix MultiKey/42L firmware, KBC and SCC for portable apps. Phoenix MultiKey/42G firmware, Energy Efficient KBC solution
87C42	N, P, S		4K	One Time Programmable Version

UPI-L42: The low voltage 3.3V version of the UPI-C42.

Device	Package	ROM	OTP	Comments
80L42	N, P S	4K		ROM Device
82L42PC 82L42PD	N, P, S N, P, S			Phoenix MultiKey/42 firmware, PS/2 style mouse support Phoenix MultiKey/42L firmware, KBC and SCC for portable apps.
87L42	N, P, S		4K	One Time Programmable Version

N = 44 lead PLCC, P = 40 lead PDIP, S = 44 lead QFP, D = 40 lead CERDIP
KBC = Key Board Control, SCC = Scan Code Control

THE INTEL 82C42

As shown in the UPI-C42 product matrix, the UPI-C42 is offered as a pre-programmed 80C42 with various versions of MultiKey/42 keyboard controller firmware developed by Phoenix Technologies Ltd.

The 82C42PC provides a low powered solution for industry standard keyboard and PS/2 style mouse control. The 82C42PD provides a cost effective means for keyboard and scan code control for notebook platforms. The 82C42PE allows a quick time to market, low cost solution for energy efficient desktop designs.

4

UPI-42 COMPATIBLE FEATURES

1. Two Data Bus Buffers, one for input and one for output. This allows a much cleaner Master/Slave protocol.

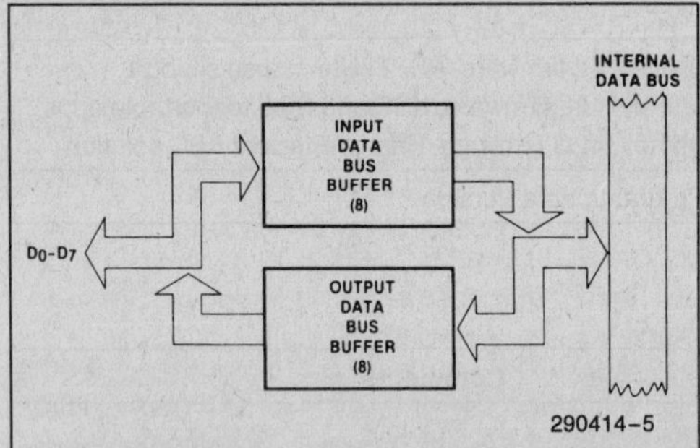

290414-5

2. 8 Bits of Status

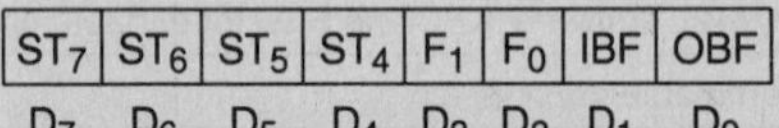

ST_7	ST_6	ST_5	ST_4	F_1	F_0	IBF	OBF
D_7	D_6	D_5	D_4	D_3	D_2	D_1	D_0

ST_4–ST_7 are user definable status bits. These bits are defined by the "MOV STS, A" single byte, single cycle instruction. Bits 4–7 of the acccumulator are moved to bits 4–7 of the status register. Bits 0–3 of the status register are not affected.

MOV STS, A Op Code: 90H

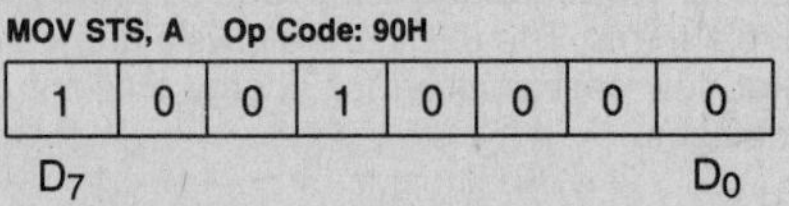

1	0	0	1	0	0	0	0
D_7							D_0

3. $\overline{RD}$ and $\overline{WR}$ are edge triggered. IBF, OBF, F_1 and INT change internally after the trailing edge of $\overline{RD}$ or $\overline{WR}$.

   During the time that the host CPU is reading the status register, the UPI is prevented from updating this register or is 'locked out.'

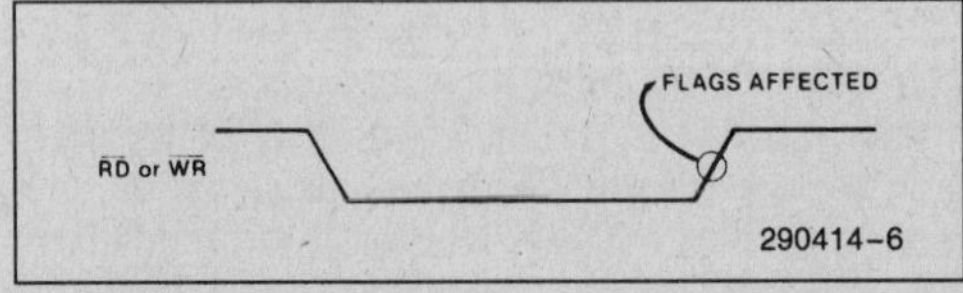

290414-6

4. P_{24} and P_{25} are port pins or Buffer Flag pins which can be used to interrupt a master processor. These pins default to port pins on Reset.

   If the "EN FLAGS" instruction has been executed, P_{24} becomes the OBF (Output Buffer Full) pin. A "1" written to P_{24} enables the OBF pin (the pin outputs the OBF Status Bit). A "0" written to P_{24} disables the OBF pin (the pin remains low). This pin can be used to indicate that valid data is available from the UPI (in Output Data Bus Buffer).

   If "EN FLAGS" has been executed, P_{25} becomes the $\overline{IBF}$ (Input Buffer Full) pin. A "1" written to P_{25} enables the $\overline{IBF}$ pin (the pin outputs the inverse of the IBF Status Bit. A "0" written to P_{25} disables the $\overline{IBF}$ pin (the pin remains low). This pin can be used to indicate that the UPI is ready for data.

Data Bus Buffer Interrupt Capability

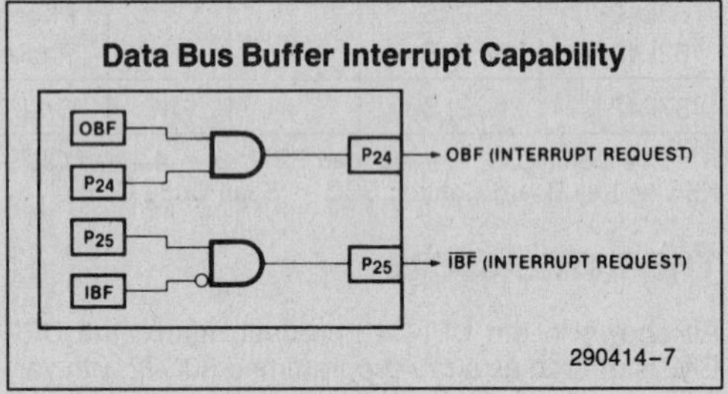

290414-7

EN FLAGS Op Code: 0F5H

1	1	1	1	0	1	0	1
D_7							D_0

5. P_{26} and P_{27} are port pins or DMA handshake pins for use with a DMA controller. These pins default to port pins on Reset.

   If the "EN DMA" instruction has been executed, P_{26} becomes the DRQ (DMA Request) pin. A "1" written to P_{26} causes a DMA request (DRQ is activated). DRQ is deactivated by DACK•RD, DACK•WR, or execution of the "EN DMA" instruction.

DMA Handshake Capability

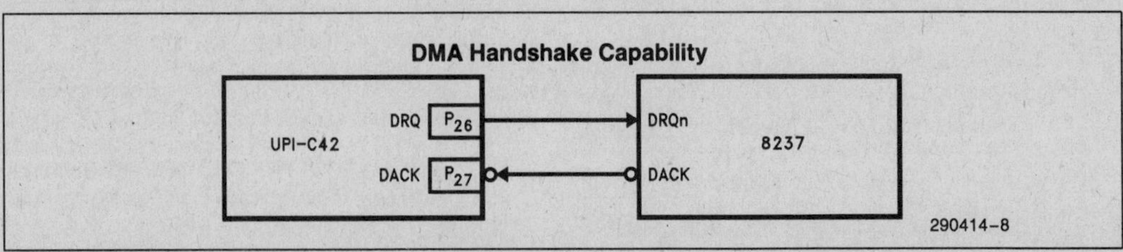

290414-8

If "EN DMA" has been executed, P_{27} becomes the $\overline{DACK}$ (DMA ACKnowledge) pin. This pin acts as a chip select input for the Data Bus Buffer registers during DMA transfers.

EN DMA Op Code: 0E5H

1	1	1	0	0	1	0	1
D_7							D_0

6. When EA is enabled on the UPI, the program counter is placed on Port 1 and the lower four bits of Port 2 (MSB = P_{23}, LSB = P_{10}). On the UPI this information is multiplexed with PORT DATA (see port timing diagrams at end of this data sheet).
7. The UPI-C42 supports the Quick Pulse Programming Algorithm, but can also be programmed with the Intelligent Programming Algorithm. (See the Programming Section.)

UPI-C42 FEATURES

Programmable Memory Size Increase

The user programmable memory on the UPI-C42 will be increased from the 2K available in the NMOS product by 2X to 4K. The larger user programmable memory array will allow the user to develop more complex peripheral control micro-code. P2.3 (port 2 bit 3) has been designated as the extra address pin required to support the programming of the extra 2K of user programmable memory.

The new instruction SEL PMB1 (73h) allows for access to the upper 2K bank (locations 2048–4095). The additional memory is completely transparent to users not wishing to take advantage of the extra memory space. No new commands are required to access the lower 2K bytes. The SEL PMB0 (63h) has also been added to the UPI-C42 instruction set to allow for switching between memory banks.

Extended Memory Program Addressing (Beyond 2K)

For programs of 2K words or less, the UPI-C42 addresses program memory in the conventional manner. Addresses beyond 2047 can be reached by executing a program memory bank switch instruction (SEL PMB0, SEL PMB1) followed by a branch instruction (JMP or CALL). The bank switch feature extends the range of branch instructions beyond their normal 2K range and at the same time prevents the user from inadvertently crossing the 2K boundary.

PROGRAM MEMORY BANK SWITCH

The switching of 2K program memory banks is accomplished by directly setting or resetting the most significant bit of the program counter (bit 11); see Figure 5. Bit 11 is not altered by normal incrementing of the program counter, but is loaded with the contents of a special flip-flop each time a JMP or CALL instruction is executed. This special flip-flop is set by executing an SEL PMB1 instruction and reset by SEL PMB0. Therefore, the SEL PMB instruction may be executed at any time prior to the actual bank switch which occurs during the next branch instruction encountered. Since all twelve bits of the program counter, including bit 11, are stored in the stack, when a Call is executed, the user may jump to subroutines across the 2K boundary and the proper PC will be restored upon return. However, the bank switch flip-flop will not be altered on return.

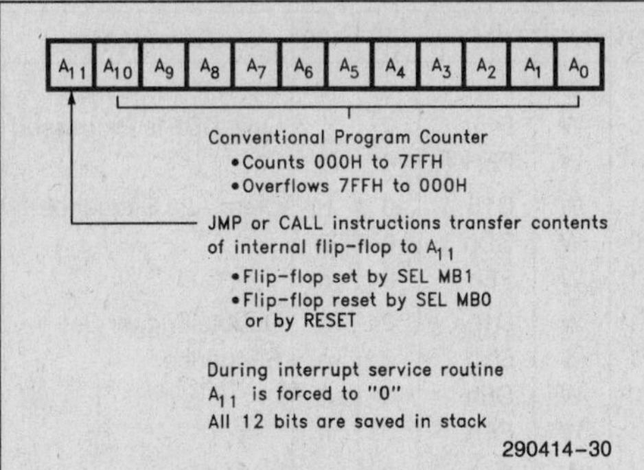

Figure 5. Program Counter

INTERRUPT ROUTINES

Interrupts always vector the program counter to location 3 or 7 in the first 2K bank, and bit 11 of the program counter is held at "0" during the interrupt service routine. The end of the service routine is signaled by the execution of an RETR instruction. Interrupt service routines should therefore be contained entirely in the lower 2K words of program memory. The execution of a SEL PMB0 or SEL PMB1 instruction within an interrupt routine is not recommended since it will not alter PC11 while in the routine, but will change the internal flip-flop.

Automatic A20 Gate Support

This feature has been provided to enhance the performance of the UPI-C42 when being used in a keyboard controller application. The UPI-C42 design has included on chip logic to support a hardware GATEA20 feature. This feature is enabled by the A20EN instruction and remains enabled until the de-

vice is reset. It is important to note that the execution of the A20EN instruction redefines Port 2, bit 1 as a pure output pin with read only characteristics. The state of this pin can be modified only through a valid "D1" command sequence (see Table 1). Once enabled, the A20 logic will process a "D1" command sequence (write to output port) by setting/resetting the A20 bit on port 2, bit 1 (P2.1) without requiring service from the internal CPU. The host can directly control the status of the A20 bit. At no time during this host interface transaction will the IBF flag in the status register be activated. If the A20EN instruction is not issued, the UPI-C42 treats the "D1" command like any other command/data sequence. The on chip GATEA20 logic will ignore all GATEA20 command/data sequences. Table 1 gives several possible GATEA20 command/data sequences and UPI-C42 responses.

Table 1. D1 Command Sequences

A0	R/W	DB Pins	IBF	A20	Comments
1	W	D1h	0	n(1)	Set A20 Sequence
0	W	DFh	0	1	Only DB1 Is Processed
1	W	FFH(2)	0	n	
1	W	D1h	0	n	Clear A20 Sequence
0	W	DDh	0	0	
1	W	FFh	0	n	
1	W	D1h	0	n	Double Trigger Set
1	W	D1h	0	n	Sequence
0	W	DFh	0	1	
1	W	FFh	0	n	
1	W	D1h	0	n	Invalid Sequence
1	W	XXh(3)	1	n	No Change in State
0	W	DDh	1	n	of A20 Bit

NOTES:
1. Indicates that P2.1 remains at the previous logic level.
2. Only FFh commands in a valid A20 sequence have no effect on IBF. An FFh issued at any other time will activate IBF.
3. Any command except D1.

The above sequences assume that the GATEA20 logic has been enabled via the A20EN instruction. As noted, only the value on DB 1 (data bus, bit 1) is processed. This bit will be directly passed through to P2.1 (port 2, bit 1). The A2OEN mode can be used in conjunction with both powerdown modes.

POWERDOWN

The UPI-C42 will support two new power down modes: Standby and Suspend. The Standby mode will allow the UPI-C42 to conserve power during periods of inactivity. In the standby mode, the oscillator will remain running. The port pins will be frozen at their last state and the internal CPU operation will halt. This mode will reduce power to 6 mA. This mode will be exited by writing to the DBBIN (causing the IBF flag to be set), a change in the state of the T0/T1 input, if an ENTX instruction was executed prior to standby, or by RESET. If RESET is used to exit the standby mode CPU operation will begin from PC = 000h. This mode is entered by the execution of the STANDBY instruction. It should be noted that when the A2OEN mode is used in conjunction with the standby powerdown mode, an A20 sequence will not generate an IBF therefore the UPI-C42 will remain in the standby mode.

The Suspend mode differs from standby in that the oscillator is not running and the internal CPU operation is stopped. The suspend mode consumes 40 μA. This mode can only be exited by a RESET. This mode is entered by the execution of the SUSPEND instruction. Both powerdown modes are summarized on the following page.

Standby Mode Summary

- Oscillator Running
- CPU Operation Halted (No Internal Clocks)
- Ports Frozen at Last State
- Low Power Mode (I_{CC} = 6 mA)
- This mode is exited by:
  RESET
  IBF Interrupt
  T0/T1 Toggled (If Enabled)

Suspend Mode Summary

- Oscillator Not Running
- CPU Operation Stopped
- Ports Tristated with Weak (~2–10 μA) Pull-Up
- Micropower Mode ($I_{CC} \leq$ 40 μA)
- This mode is exited by RESET

Table 2 covers all pin states in both the standby and suspend modes. In addition to these two new power down modes, the UPI-C42 will also support the NMOS power down mode as outlined in Chapter 4 of the UPI-42AH users manual.

Table 2. Power Down Mode Pin States

Pins	Standby	Suspend
Ports 1 and 2 Outputs Inputs	 Normal Enabled	 Tristate Weak Pull-Up Disabled
DBB(1) Outputs Inputs	 Normal Normal	 Normal Normal
System Control (RD#, WR#, CS#, A0)	Enabled	Disabled
Reset#	Enabled	Enabled
Crystal Osc. (XTAL1, XTAL2)	Enabled	Disabled
Test 0, Test 1	Enabled	Disabled
Prog	High	High
Sync	High	High
EA	Enabled, Weak Pull-Up	Disabled, No Pull-Up
SS#	Enabled, Weak Pull-Up	Disabled, Weak Pull-Up
I_{CC}	~6 mA	<40 μA

NOTES:
1. DBB outputs are Tristate unless CS# and RD# are active. DBB inputs are disabled unless CS# and WR# are active.
2. A "disabled" input will not cause current to be drawn regardless of input level (within the supply range).
3. Weak pull-ups have current capability of typically 5 μA.

NEW UPI-C42 INSTRUCTIONS

The UPI-C42 will support several new instructions to allow for the use of new C42 features. These instructions are not necessary to the user who does not wish to take advantage of any new C42 functionality. The C42 will be completely compatible with all current NMOS code/applications. In order to use new features, however, some code modifications will be necessary. All new instructions can easily be inserted into existing code by use of the ASM-48 macro facility as shown in the following example:

```
Macname MACRO
        DB  63H
        ENDM
```

New Instructions

The following is a list of additions to the UPI-42 instruction set. These instructions apply only to the UPI-C42. These instructions must be added to existing code in order to use any new functionality.

SEL PMB0 Select Program Memory Bank 0

```
OPCODE  0110 0011 (63h)
```

PC Bit 11 is set to zero on next JMP or CALL instruction. All references to program memory fall within the range of 0–2047 (0–7FFh).

SEL PMB1 Select Program Memory Bank 1

```
OPCODE  0111 0011 (73h)
```

PC Bit 11 is set to one on next JMP or CALL instruction. All references to program memory fall within the range of 2048–4095 (800h–FFFh).

ENA20 Enables Auto A20 hardware

```
OPCODE  0011 0011 (33h)
```

Enables on chip logic to support Auto A20 Gate feature. Will remain enabled until device is reset. This

4

circuitry gives the host direct control of port 2 bit 1 (P2.1) without intervention by the internal CPU. When this opcode is executed, P2.1 becomes a dedicated output pin. The status of this pin is read-able but can only be altered through a valid "D1" command sequence (see Table 1).

ENTX Enable T0/T1 Wake Up Function

```
OPCODE  1100 0011 (C3H)
```

Enables on chip logic to allow the T0 or T1 input pin to "wake" the UPI-C42 from the STANDBY power down mode.

STANDBY Invoke Standby Power Down Mode

```
OPCODE  0000 0001 (01h)
```

Enables deivce to enter low power (mA range) mode. In this mode the external oscillator is running, CPU operation is suspended and the port pins remain frozen at their last state. This mode can be exited via a RESET, a change in state on the T0 or T1 pin, or an IBF interrupt.

SUSPEND Invoke Suspend Power Down Mode

```
OPCODE  1000 0010 (82h) or 1110 0010
(E2h)
```

Enables device to enter micro power mode. In this mode the external oscillator is off, CPU operation is stopped, and the Port pins are tristated. This mode can only be exited via a RESET signal.

PROGRAMMING AND VERIFYING THE UPI-C42

The UPI-C42 programming will differ from the NMOS device in three ways. First, the C42 will have a 4K user programmable array. The UPI-C42 will also be programmed using the Intel Quick-Pulse Programming Algorithm. Finally, port 2 bit three (P2.3) will be used during program as the extra address pin required to program the upper 2K bank of additional memory. None of these differences have any effect on the full CHMOS to NMOS device compatibility. The extra memory is fully transparent to the user who does not need, or want, to use the extra memory space of the UPI-C42.

In brief, the programming process consists of: activating the program mode, applying an address, latching the address, applying data, and applying a programming pulse. Each word is programmed completely before moving on to the next and is followed by a verification step. The following is a list of the pins used for programming and a description of their functions:

Pin	Function
XTAL 2	Clock Input
$\overline{\text{Reset}}$	Initialization and Address Latching
Test 0	Selection of Program or Verify Mode
EA	Activation of Program/Verify Signature Row/Security Bit Modes
BUS	Address and Data Input Data Output During Verify
P_{20-23}	Address Input
V_{DD}	Programming Power Supply
PROG	Program Pulse Input

WARNING
An attempt to program a missocketed UPI-C42 will result in severe damage to the part. An indication of a properly socketed part is the appearance of the SYNC clock output. The lack of this clock may be used to disable the programmer.

The Program/Verify sequence is:

1. Insert 87C42 in programming socket
2. CS = 5V, V_{CC} = 5V, V_{DD} = 5V, RESET = 0V, A_0 = 0V, TEST 0 = 5V, clock applied or internal oscillator operating, BUS floating, PROG = 5V.
3. TEST 0 = 0V (select program mode)
4. EA = 12.75V (active program mode)
5. V_{CC} = 6.25V (programming supply)
6. V_{DD} = 12.75V (programming power)
7. Address applied to BUS and P_{20-23}
8. $\overline{\text{RESET}}$ = 5V (latch address)
9. Data applied to BUS
10. PROG = 5V followed by one 100 μs pulse to 0V
11. TEST 0 = 5V (verify mode)
12. Read and verify data on BUS
13. TEST 0 = 0V
14. $\overline{\text{RESET}}$ = 0V and repeat from step 6
15. Programmer should be at conditions of step 1 when the 87C42 is removed from socket

Please follow the Quick-Pulse Programming flow chart for proper programming procedure shown in Figure 6.

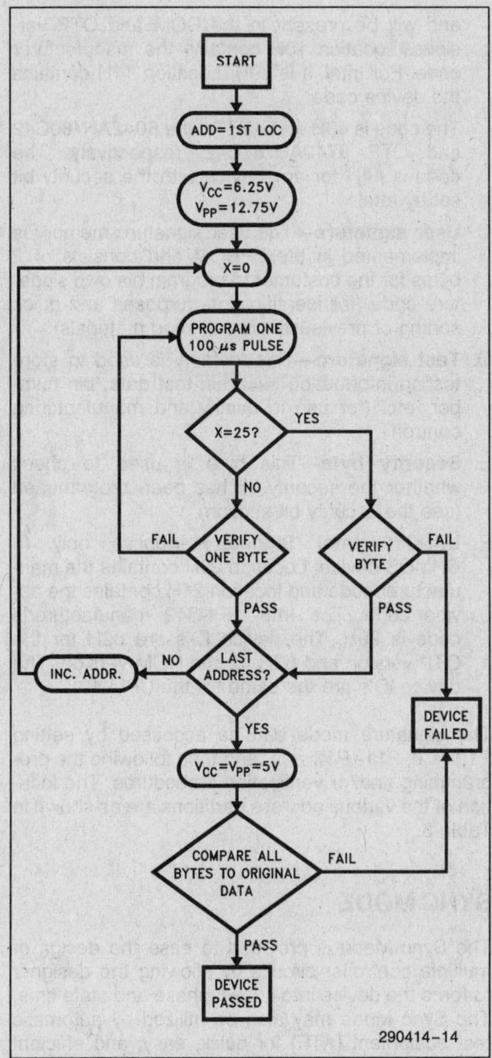

Figure 6. Quick-Pulse Programming Algorithm

Quick-Pulse Programming Algorithm

As previously stated, the UPI-C42 will be programmed using the Quick-Pulse Programming Algorithm, developed by Intel to substantially reduce the thorughput time in production programming.

The Quick-Pulse Programming Algorithm uses initial pulses of 100 µs followed by a byte verification to determine when the address byte has been successfully programmed. Up to 25 100 µs pulses per byte are provided before a failure is recognized. A flow chart of the Quick-Pulse Programming Algorithm is shown in Figure 6.

The entire sequence of program pulses and byte verifications is performed at V_{CC} = 6.25V and V_{DD} = 12.75V. When programming has been completed, all bytes should be compared to the original data with V_{CC} = V_{DD} = 5V.

A verify should be performed on the programmed bits to ensure that they have been correctly programmed. The verify is performed with T0 = 5V, V_{DD} = 5V, EA = 12.75V, SS# = 5V, PROG = 5V, A0 = 0V, and CS# = 5V.

In addition to the Quick-Pulse Programming Algorithm, the UPI-C42 OPT is also compatible with Intel's Int$_e$ligent Programming Algorithm which is used to program the NMOS UPI-42AH OTP devices.

The entire sequence of program pulses and byte verifications is performed at V_{CC} = 6.25V and V_{DD} = 12.75V. When the int$_e$ligent Programming cycle has been completed, all bytes should be compared to the original data with V_{CC} = 5.0, V_{DD} = 5V.

Verify

A verify should be performed on the programmed bits to determine that they have been correctly programmed. The verify is performed with T0 = 5V, V_{DD} = 5V, EA = 12.75V, $\overline{SS}$ = 5V, PROG = 5V, A0 = 0V, and $\overline{CS}$ = 5V.

SECURITY BIT

The security bit is a single EPROM cell outside the EPROM array. The user can program this bit with the appropriate access code and the normal programming procedure, to inhibit any external access to the EPROM contents. Thus the user's resident program is protected. There is no direct external access to this bit. However, the security byte in the signature row has the same address and can be used to check indirectly whether the security bit has been programmed or not. The security bit has no effect on the signature mode, so the security byte can always be examined.

SECURITY BIT PROGRAMMING/ VERIFICATION

Programming

a. Read the security byte of the signature mode. Make sure it is 00H.

4

b. Apply access code to appropriate inputs to put the device into security mode.

c. Apply high voltage to EA and V_{DD} pins.

d. Follow the programming procedure as per the Quick-Pulse Programming Algorithm with known data on the databus. Not only the security bit, but also the security byte of the signature row is programmed.

e. Verify that the security byte of the signature mode contains the same data as appeared on the data bus. (If DB0–DB7 = high, the security byte will contain FFH.)

f. Read two consecutive known bytes from the EPROM array and verify that the wrong data are retrieved in at least one verification. If the EPROM can still be read, the security bit may have not been fully programmed though the security byte in the signature mode has.

Verification

Since the security bit address overlaps the address of the security byte of the signature mode, it can be used to check indirectly whether the security bit has been programmed or not. Therefore, the security bit verification is a mere read operation of the security byte of the signature row (0FFH = security bit programmed; 00H = security bit unprogrammed). Note that during the security bit programming, the reading of the security byte does not necessarily indicate that the security bit has been successfully programmed. Thus, it is recommended that two consecutive known bytes in the EPROM array be read and the wrong data should be read at least once, because it is highly improbable that random data coincides with the correct ones twice.

SIGNATURE MODE

The UPI-C42 has an additional 64 bytes of EPROM available for Intel and user signatures and miscellaneous purposes. The 64 bytes are partitioned as follows:

A. **Test code/checksum—**This can accommodate up to 25 bytes of code for testing the internal nodes that are not testable by executing from the external memory. The test code/checksum is present on ROMs, and OTPs.

B. **Intel signature**—This allows the programmer to read from the UPI-41AH/42AH/C42 the manufacturer of the device and the exact product name. It facilitates automatic device identification and will be present in the ROM and OTP versions. Location 10H contains the manufacturer code. For Intel, it is 89H. Location 11H contains the device code.

   The code is 43H and 42H for the 8042AH/80C42 and OTP 8742AH/87C42, respectively. The code is 44H for any device with the security bit set by Intel.

C. **User signature**—The user signature memory is implemented in the EPROM and consists of 2 bytes for the customer to program his own signature code (for identification purposes and quick sorting of previously programmed materials).

D. **Test signature**—This memory is used to store testing information such as: test data, bin number, etc. (for use in quality and manufacturing control).

E. **Security byte**—This byte is used to check whether the security bit has been programmed (see the security bit section).

F. **UPI-C42 Intel Signature**—Applies only to CHMOS device. Location 20H contains the manufacturer code and location 21H contains the device code. The Intel UPI-C42 manufacturer's code is 99H. The device ID's are 82H for the OTP version and 83H for the ROM version. The device ID's are the same for the UPI-L42.

The signature mode can be accessed by setting P10 = 0, P11–P17 = 1, and then following the programming and/or verification procedures. The location of the various address partitions are as shown in Table 3.

SYNC MODE

The Sync Mode is provided to ease the design of multiple controller circuits by allowing the designer to force the device into known phase and state time. The Sync Mode may also be utilized by automatic test equipment (ATE) for quick, easy, and efficient synchronizing between the tester and the DUT (device under test).

Sync Mode is enabled when $\overline{SS}$ pin is raised to high voltage level of +12 volts. To begin synchronization, T0 is raised to 5 volts at least four clock cycles after $\overline{SS}$. T0 must be high for at least four X2 clock cycles to fully reset the prescaler and time state generators. T0 may then be brought down during low state of X2. Two clock cycles later, with the rising edge of X2, the device enters into Time State 1, Phase 1. $\overline{SS}$ is then brought down to 5 volts 4 clocks later after T0. RESET is allowed to go high 5 tCY (75 clocks) later for normal execution of code.

Table 3. Signature Mode Table

	Address		Device Type	No. of Bytes
Test Code/Checksum	0 16H	0FH 1EH	ROM/OTP	25
Intel Signature	10H	11H	ROM/OTP	2
User Signature	12H	13H	OTP	2
Test Signature	14H	15H	ROM/OTP	2
Security Byte	1FH or	3FH	ROM/OTP	2
UPI-C42 Intel Signature	20H	21H	ROM/OTP	2
User Defined UPI-C42 OTP EPROM Space	22H	3EH	ROM/OTP	30

ACCESS CODE

The following table summarizes the access codes required to invoke the Sync Mode, Signature Mode, and the Security Bit, respectively. Also, the programming and verification modes are included for comparison.

Modes		Control Signals							Data Bus	Access Code	
										Port 2	Port 1
		T0	RST	SS	EA	PROG	V_{DD}	V_{CC}	0 1 2 3 4 5 6 7	0 1 2 3	0 1 2 3 4 5 6 7
Programming Mode		0	0	1	HV	1	V_{DDH}	V_{CC}	Address	Addr	a_0 a_1 X X X X X X
		0	1	1	HV	STB	V_{DDH}	V_{CC}	Data In	Addr	
Verification Mode		0	0	1	HV	1	V_{CC}	V_{CC}	Address	Addr	a_0 a_1 X X X X X X
		1	1	1	HV	1	V_{CC}	V_{CC}	Data Out	Addr	
Sync Mode		STB High	0	HV	0	X	V_{CC}	V_{CC}	X X X X X X X X	X X X	X X X X X X X X
Signature Mode	Prog	0	0	1	HV	1	V_{DDH}	V_{CC}	Addr. (see Sig Mode Table)	0 0 0	0 1 1 1 1 X X 1
		0	1	1	HV	STB	V_{DDH}	V_{CC}	Data In	0 0 0	
	Verify	0	0	1	HV	1	V_{CC}	V_{CC}	Addr. (see Sig Mode Table)	0 0 0	
		1	1	1	HV	1	V_{CC}	V_{CC}	Data Out	0 0 0	
Security Bit/Byte	Prog	0	0	1	HV	1	V_{DDH}	V_{CC}	Address	0 0 0	
		0	1	1	HV	STB	V_{DDH}	V_{CC}	Data In	0 0 0	
	Verify	0	0	1	HV	1	V_{CC}	V_{CC}	Address	0 0 0	
		1	1	1	HV	1	V_{CC}	V_{CC}	Data Out	0 0 0	

NOTE:
1. a_0 = 0 or 1; a_1 = 0 or 1. a_0 must = a_1.

SYNC MODE TIMING DIAGRAMS

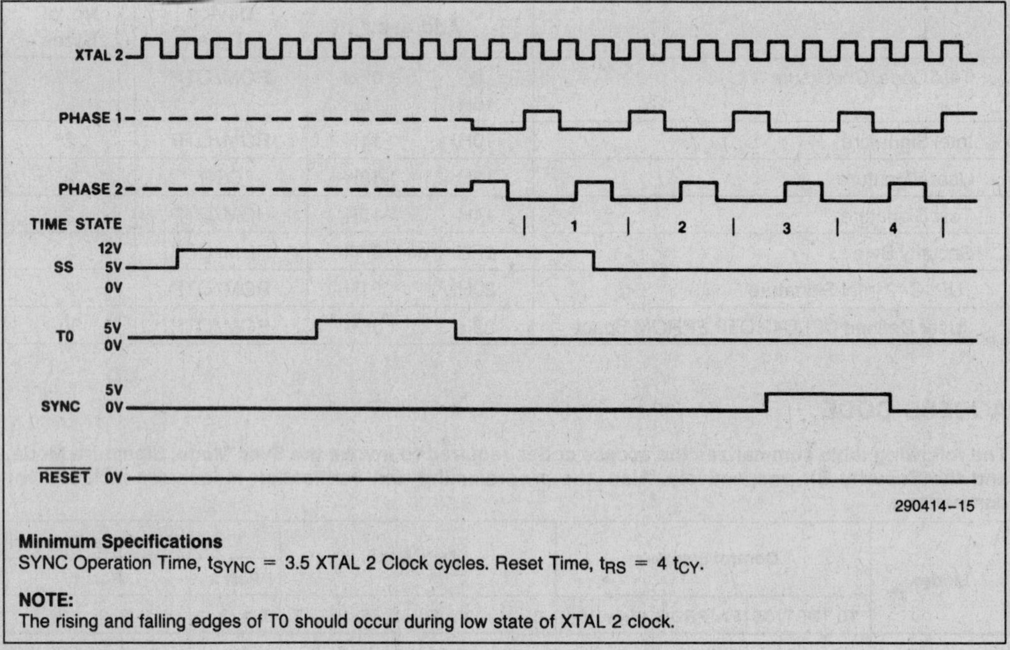

Minimum Specifications
SYNC Operation Time, t_{SYNC} = 3.5 XTAL 2 Clock cycles. Reset Time, t_{RS} = 4 t_{CY}.

NOTE:
The rising and falling edges of T0 should occur during low state of XTAL 2 clock.

APPLICATIONS

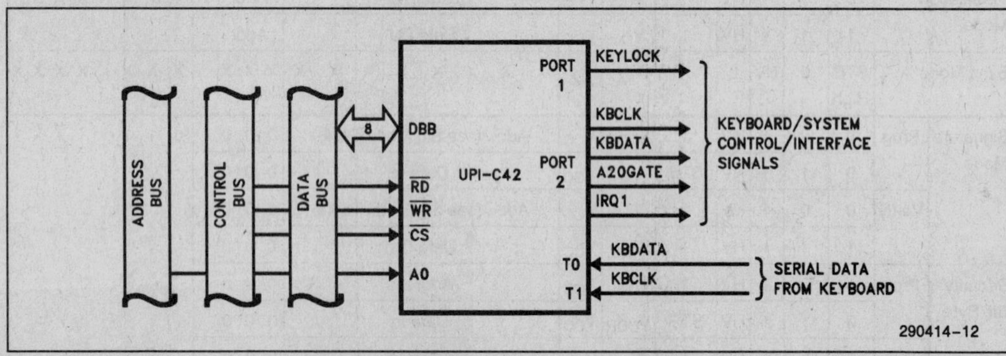

Figure 7. UPI-C42 Keyboard Controller

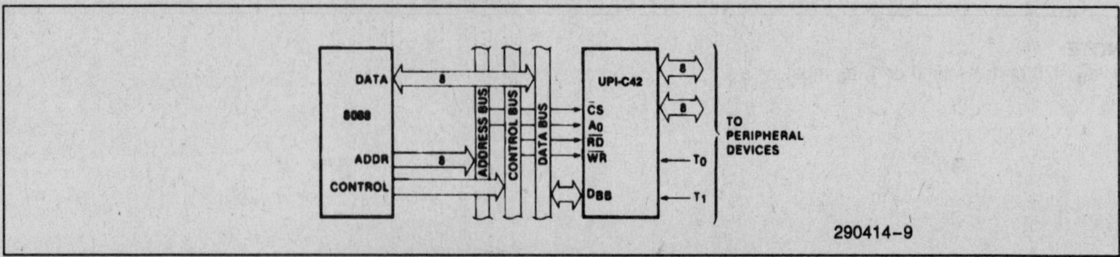

Figure 8. 8088-UPI-C42 Interface

APPLICATIONS (Continued)

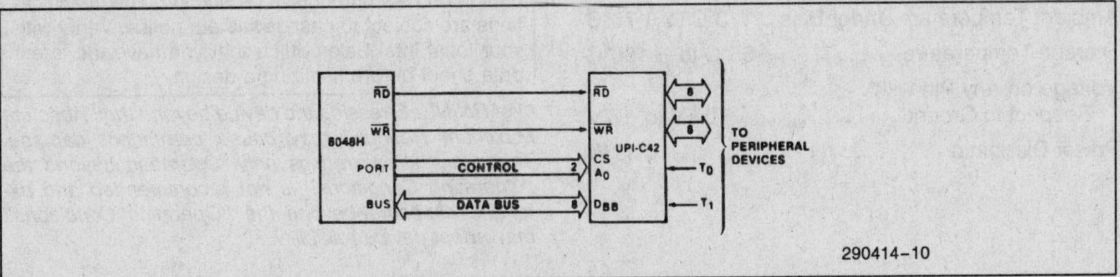

Figure 9. 8048H-UPI-C42 Interface

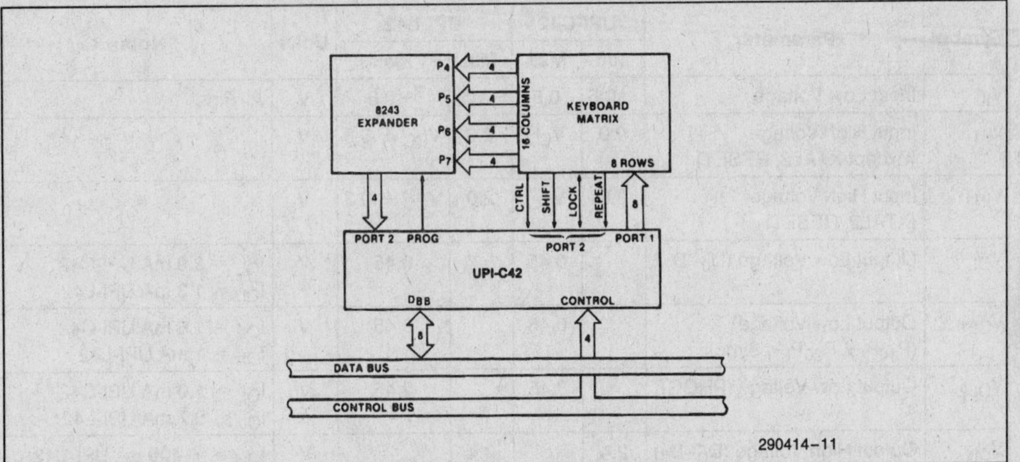

Figure 10. UPI-C42-8243 Keyboard Scanner

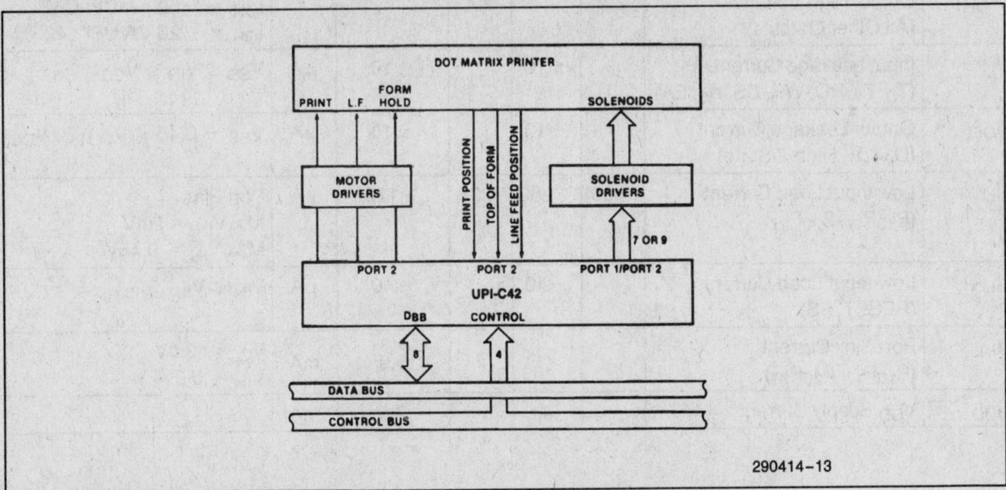

Figure 11. UPI-C42 80-Column Matrix Printer Interface

ABSOLUTE MAXIMUM RATINGS*

Ambient Temperature Under Bias ....0°C to +70°C
Storage Temperature ....−65°C to +150°C
Voltage on Any Pin with
Respect to Ground..............−0.5V to +7V
Power Dissipation ....1.5 W

NOTICE: This data sheet contains preliminary information on new products in production. The specifications are subject to change without notice. Verify with your local Intel Sales office that you have the latest data sheet before finalizing a design.

**WARNING: Stressing the device beyond the "Absolute Maximum Ratings" may cause permanent damage. These are stress ratings only. Operation beyond the "Operating Conditions" is not recommended and extended exposure beyond the "Operating Conditions" may affect device reliability.*

DC CHARACTERISTICS T_A = 0°C to +70°C, V_{CC} = V_{DD} = +5V ±10%; +3.3V ±10% UPI-L42

Symbol	Parameter	UPI-C42		UPI-L42		Units	Notes
		Min	Max	Min	Max		
V_{IL}	Input Low Voltage	−0.5	0.8	−0.3	+0.8	V	All Pins
V_{IH}	Input High Voltage (Except XTAL2, RESET)	2.0	V_{CC}	2.0	V_{CC} + 0.3	V	
V_{IH1}	Input High Voltage (XTAL2, RESET)	3.5	V_{CC}	2.0	V_{CC} + 0.3	V	
V_{OL}	Output Low Voltage (D_0–D_7)		0.45		0.45	V	I_{OL} = 2.0 mA UPI-C42 I_{OL} = 1.3 mA UPI-L42
V_{OL1}	Output Low Voltage ($P_{10}P_{17}$, $P_{20}P_{27}$, Sync)		0.45		0.45	V	I_{OL} = 1.6 mA UPI-C42 I_{OL} = 1 mA UPI-L42
V_{OL2}	Output Low Voltage (PROG)		0.45		0.45	V	I_{OL} = 1.0 mA UPI-C42 I_{OL} = 0.7 mA UPI-L42
V_{OH}	Output High Voltage (D_0–D_7)	2.4		2.4		V	I_{OH} = −400 μA UPI-C42 I_{OH} = −260 μA UPI-L42
V_{OH1}	Output High Voltage (All Other Outputs)	2.4		2.4			I_{OH} = −50 μA UPI-C42 I_{OH} = −25 μA UPI-L42
I_{IL}	Input Leakage Current (T_0, T_1, RD, WR, CS, A_0, EA)		±10		±10	μA	$V_{SS} \le V_{IN} \le V_{CC}$
I_{OFL}	Output Leakage Current (D_0–D_7, High Z State)		±10		±10	μA	$V_{SS} + 0.45 \le V_{OUT} \le V_{CC}$
I_{LI}	Low Input Load Current ($P_{10}P_{17}$, $P_{20}P_{27}$)	−50	−250	−35	−175	μA	Port Pins Min V_{IN} = 2.4V Max V_{IN} = 0.45V
I_{LI1}	Low Input Load Current (RESET, SS)		−40		−40	μA	$V_{IN} \le V_{IL}$
I_{HL}	Port Sink Current ($P_{10}P_{17}$, $P_{20}P_{27}$)				5.0	mA	V_{CC} = 3.0V V_{IH} = 5.0V
I_{DD}	V_{DD} Supply Current		4		2.5	mA	

DC CHARACTERISTICS

T_A = 0°C to +70°C, V_{CC} = V_{DD} = +5V ±10%; +3.3V ±10% UPI-L42 (Continued)

Symbol	Parameter	UPI-C42		UPI-L42		Units	Notes
		Min	Max	Min	Max		
$I_{CC} + I_{DD}$	Total Supply Current: Active Mode @ 12.5 MHz		30		20	mA	Typical 14 mA UPI-C42, 9 mA UPI-L42
	Standby Mode @ 12.5 MHz		6		4	mA	Osc. Running Typical 3 mA UPI-C42, 2 mA UPI-L42
	Suspend Mode		40		26	μA	Osc. Off(1, 4)
I_{DD} Standby	Power Down Supply Current		5		3.5	mA	NMOS Compatible Power Down Mode
I_{IH}	Input Leakage Current (P_{10}–P_{17}, P_{20}–P_{27})		100		100	μA	$V_{IN} = V_{CC}$
C_{IN}	Input Capacitance		10		10	pF	T_A = 25°C (1)
C_{IO}	I/O Capacitance		20		20	pF	T_A = 25°C (1)

NOTE:
1. Sampled, not 100% tested.

DC CHARACTERISTICS—PROGRAMMING (UPI-C42 AND UPI-L42)

T_A = 25°C ±5°C, V_{CC} = 6.25V ±0.25V, V_{DD} = 12.75V ±0.25V

Symbol	Parameter	Min	Max	Units
V_{DDH}	V_{DD} Program Voltage High Level	12.5	13	V(1)
V_{DDL}	V_{DD} Voltage Low Level	4.75	5.25	V
V_{PH}	PROG Program Voltage High Level	2.0	5.5	V
V_{PL}	PROG Voltage Low Level	−0.5	0.8	V
V_{EAH}	Input High Voltage for EA	12.0	13.0	V(2)
V_{EAL}	EA Voltage Low Level	−0.5	5.25	V
I_{DD}	V_{DD} High Voltage Supply Current		50.0	mA
I_{EA}	EA High Voltage Supply Current		1.0	mA(4)

NOTES:
1. Voltages over 13V applied to pin V_{DD} will permanently damage the device.
2. V_{EAH} must be applied to EA before V_{DDH} and removed after V_{DDL}.
3. V_{CC} must be applied simultaneously or before V_{DD} and must be removed simultaneously or after V_{DD}.
4. Sampled, not 100% tested.

AC CHARACTERISTICS

T_A = 0°C to +70°C, V_{SS} = 0V, V_{CC} = V_{DD} = +5V ±10%; +3.3V ±10% for the UPI-L42

NOTE:
All AC Characteristics apply to both the UPI-C42 and UPI-L42

DBB READ

Symbol	Parameter	Min	Max	Units
t_{AR}	CS, A_0 Setup to RD ↓	0		ns
t_{RA}	CS, A_0 Hold After RD ↑	0		ns
t_{RR}	RD Pulse Width	160		ns
t_{AD}	CS, A_0 to Data Out Delay		130	ns
t_{RD}	RD ↓ to Data Out Delay	0	130	ns
t_{DF}	RD ↑ to Data Float Delay		85	ns

DBB WRITE

Symbol	Parameter	Min	Max	Units
t_{AW}	CS, A_0 Setup to WR ↓	0		ns
t_{WA}	CS, A_0 Hold After WR ↑	0		ns
t_{WW}	WR Pulse Width	160		ns
t_{DW}	Data Setup to WR ↑	130		ns
t_{WD}	Data Hold After WR ↑	0		ns

AC CHARACTERISTICS

T_A = 0°C to +70°C, V_{SS} = 0V, V_{CC} = V_{DD} = +5V ±10%; +3.3V ±10% for the UPI-L42 (Continued)

CLOCK

Symbol	Parameter	Min	Max	Units
t_{CY} UPI-C42/UPI-L42	Cycle Time	1.2	9.20	μs(1)
t_{CYC} UPI-C42/UPI-L42	Clock Period	80	613	ns
t_{PWH}	Clock High Time	30		ns
t_{PWL}	Clock Low Time	30		ns
t_R	Clock Rise Time		10	ns
t_F	Clock Fall Time		10	ns

NOTE:
1. t_{CY} = 15/f(XTAL)

AC CHARACTERISTICS DMA

Symbol	Parameter	Min	Max	Units
t_{ACC}	DACK to WR or RD	0		ns
t_{CAC}	RD or WR to DACK	0		ns
t_{ACD}	DACK to Data Valid	0	130	ns
t_{CRQ}	RD or WR to DRQ Cleared		110	ns(1)

NOTE:
1. C_L = 150 pF.

AC CHARACTERISTICS PORT 2

Symbol	Parameter	f(t_{CY})(3)	Min	Max	Units
t_{CP}	Port Control Setup Before Falling Edge of PROG	1/15 t_{CY} − 28	55		ns(1)
t_{PC}	Port Control Hold After Falling Edge of PROG	1/10 t_{CY}	125		ns(2)
t_{PR}	PROG to Time P2 Input Must Be Valid	8/15 t_{CY} − 16		650	ns(1)
t_{PF}	Input Data Hold Time		0	150	ns(2)
t_{DP}	Output Data Setup Time	2/10 t_{CY}	250		ns(1)
t_{PD}	Output Data Hold Time	1/10 t_{CY} − 80	45		ns(2)
t_{PP}	PROG Pulse Width	6/10 t_{CY}	750		ns

NOTES:
1. C_L = 80 pF.
2. C_L = 20 pF.
3. t_{CY} = 1.25 μs.

AC CHARACTERISTICS—PROGRAMMING (UPI-C42 AND UPI-L42)

$T_A = 25°C \pm 5°C$, $V_{CC} = 6.25V \pm 0.25V$, $V_{DDL} = +5V \pm 0.25V$, $V_{DDH} = 12.75V \pm 0.25V$

(87C42/87L42 ONLY)

Symbol	Parameter	Min	Max	Units
t_{AW}	Address Setup Time to RESET ↑	$4t_{CY}$		
t_{WA}	Address Hold Time after RESET ↑	$4t_{CY}$		
t_{DW}	Data in Setup Time to PROG ↓	$4t_{CY}$		
t_{WD}	Data in Hold Time after PROG ↑	$4t_{CY}$		
t_{PW}	Initial Program Pulse Width	95	105	μs
t_{TW}	Test 0 Setup Time for Program Mode	$4t_{CY}$		
t_{WT}	Test 0 Hold Time after Program Mode	$4t_{CY}$		
t_{DO}	Test 0 to Data Out Delay		$4t_{CY}$	
t_{WW}	RESET Pulse Width to Latch Address	$4t_{CY}$		
t_r, t_f	PROG Rise and Fall Times	0.5	100	μs
t_{CY}	CPU Operation Cycle Time	2.5	3.75	μs
t_{RE}	RESET Setup Time before EA ↑	$4t_{CY}$		
t_{OPW}	Overprogram Pulse Width	2.85	78.75	ms(1)
t_{DE}	EA High to V_{DD} High	$1t_{CY}$		

NOTES:
1. This variation is a function of the iteration counter value, X.
2. If TEST 0 is high, t_{DO} can be triggered by RESET ↑.

AC TESTING INPUT/OUTPUT WAVEFORM

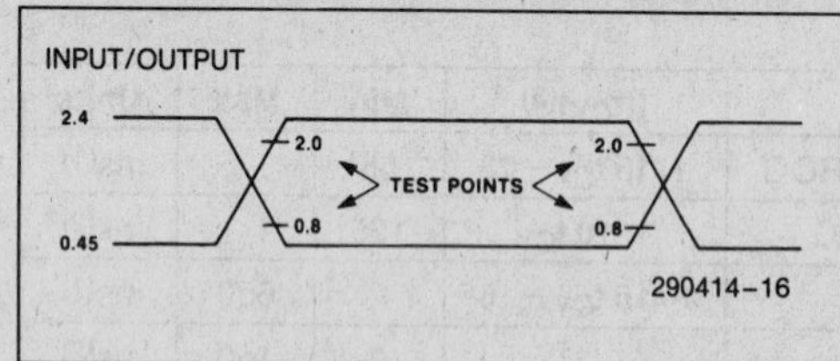

AC TESTING LOAD CIRCUIT

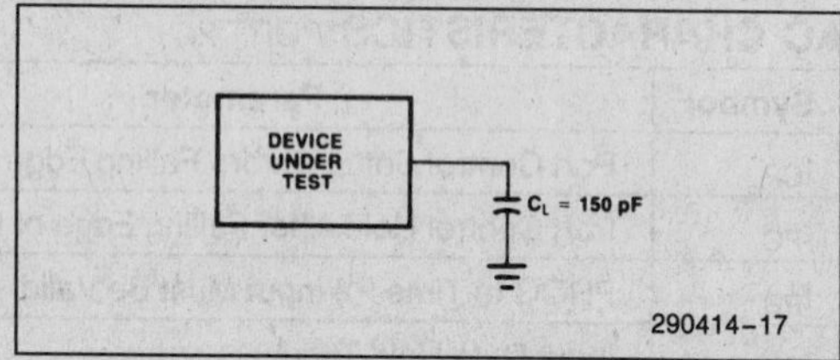

DRIVING FROM AN EXTERNAL SOURCE

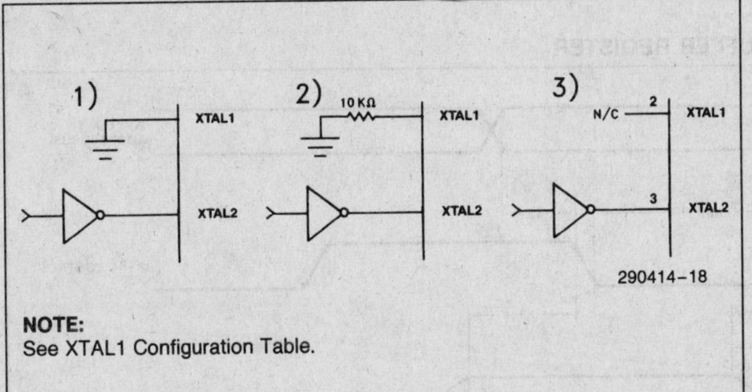

290414-18

NOTE:
See XTAL1 Configuration Table.

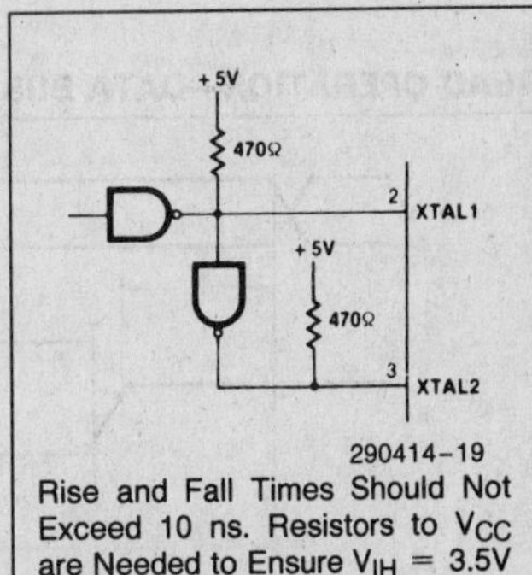

290414-19

Rise and Fall Times Should Not Exceed 10 ns. Resistors to V_{CC} are Needed to Ensure $V_{IH} = 3.5V$ if TTL Circuitry is Used.

LC OSCILLATOR MODE

L	C	NOMINAL
45 H	20 pF	5.2 MHz
120 H	20 pF	3.2 MHz

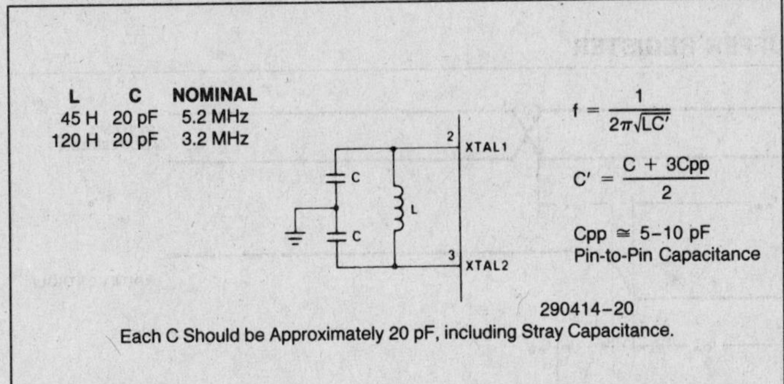

$$f = \frac{1}{2\pi\sqrt{LC'}}$$

$$C' = \frac{C + 3Cpp}{2}$$

$Cpp \cong 5\text{–}10$ pF
Pin-to-Pin Capacitance

290414-20

Each C Should be Approximately 20 pF, including Stray Capacitance.

CRYSTAL OSCILLATOR MODE

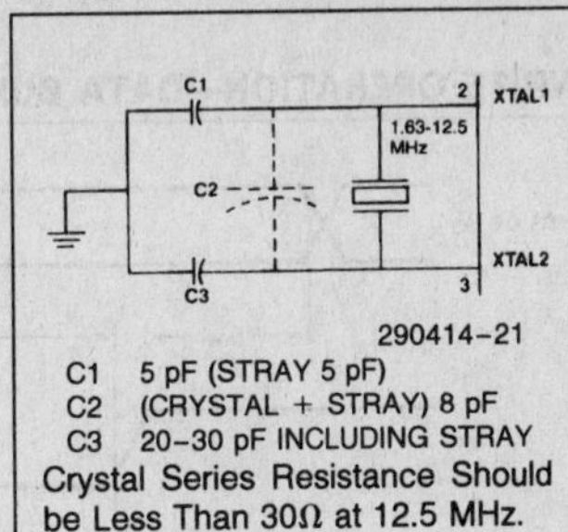

290414-21

C1 5 pF (STRAY 5 pF)
C2 (CRYSTAL + STRAY) 8 pF
C3 20–30 pF INCLUDING STRAY

Crystal Series Resistance Should be Less Than 30Ω at 12.5 MHz.

XTAL1 Configuration Table

XTAL1 Connection		
1) to Ground	**2) 10 KΩ Resistor to Ground**	**3) Not Connected**
Not recommended for CHMOS designs. Causes approximately 16 mA of additional current flow through the XTAL1 pin on UPI-C42 and approximately 11 mA of additional current through XTAL1 on the UPI-L42.	Recommended configuration for designs which will use both NMOS and CHMOS parts. This configuration limits the additional current through the XTAL1 pin to approximately 1 mA, while maintaining compatibility with the NMOS device.	Low power configuration recommended for CHMOS only designs to provide lowest possible power consumption. This configuration will not work with the NMOS device.

WAVEFORMS

READ OPERATION—DATA BUS BUFFER REGISTER

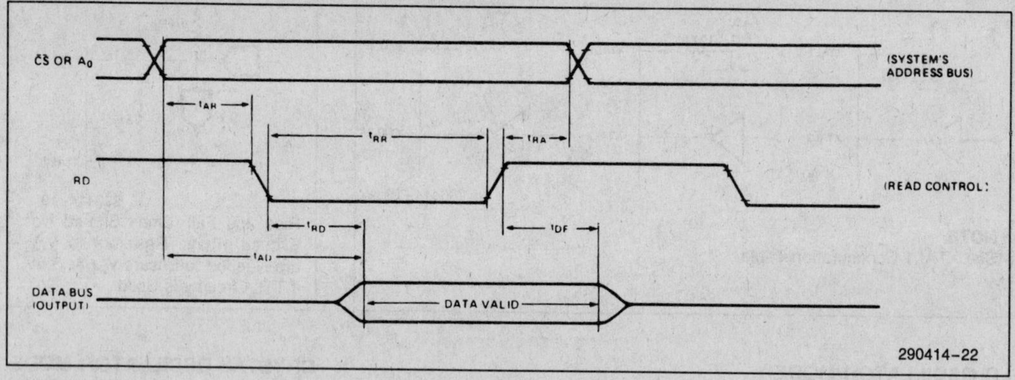

290414-22

WRITE OPERATION—DATA BUS BUFFER REGISTER

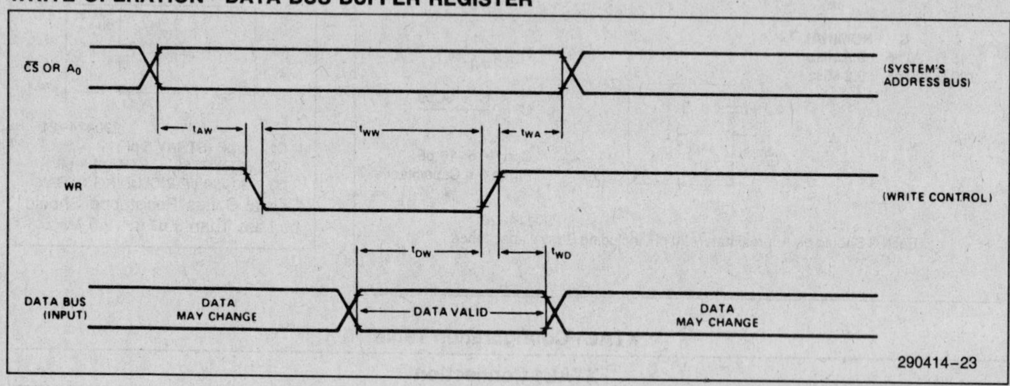

290414-23

CLOCK TIMING

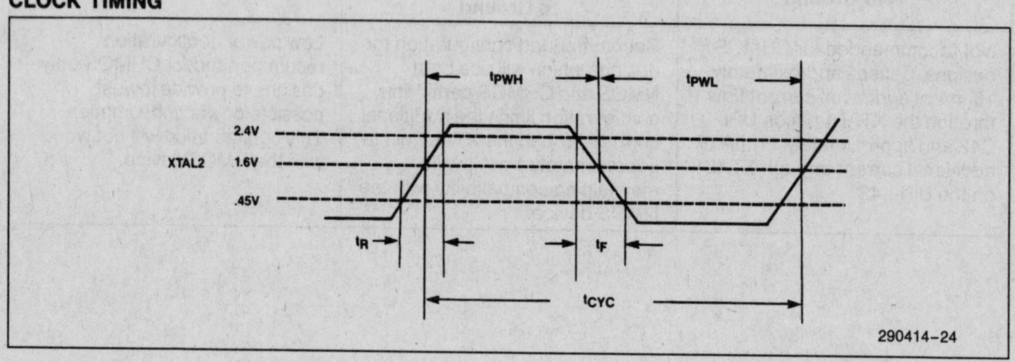

290414-24

WAVEFORMS (Continued)

COMBINATION PROGRAM/VERIFY MODE

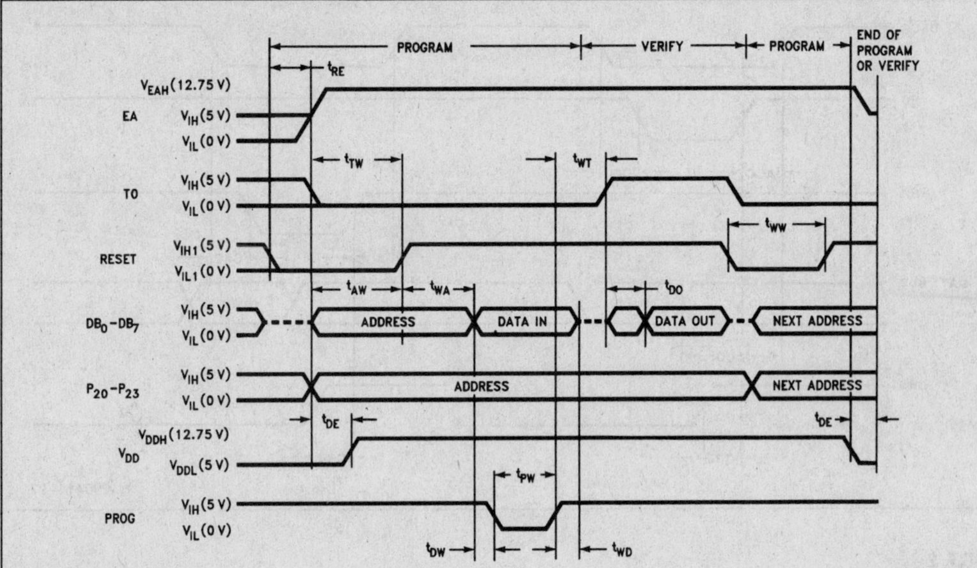

290414-25

NOTES:
1. A_0 must be held low (0V) during program/verify modes.
2. For V_{IH}, V_{IH1}, V_{IL}, V_{IL1}, V_{DDH}, and V_{DDL}, please consult the D.C. Characteristics Table.
3. When programming the 87C42, a 0.1 μF capacitor is required across V_{DD} and ground to suppress spurious voltage transients which can damage the device.

VERIFY MODE

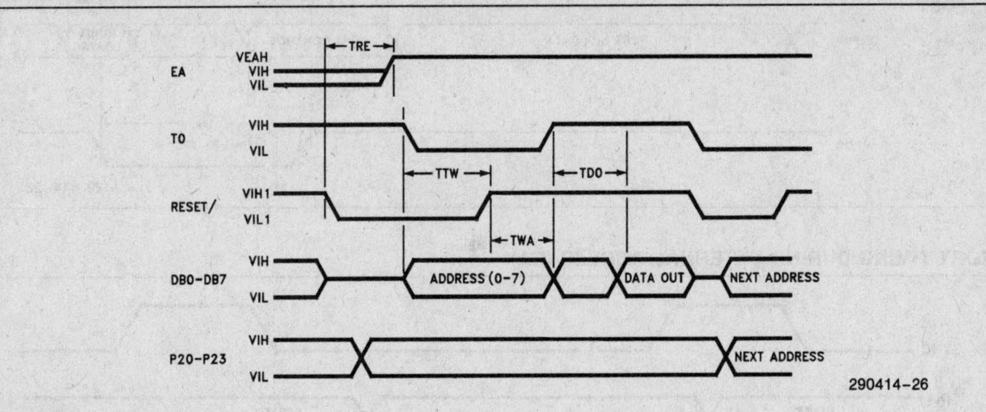

290414-26

NOTES:
1. PROG must float if EA is low.
2. PROG must float or = 5V when EA is high.
3. $P_{10}-P_{17}$ = 5V or must float.
4. $P_{24}-P_{27}$ = 5V or must float.
5. A_0 must be held low during programming/verify modes.

WAVEFORMS (Continued)

DMA

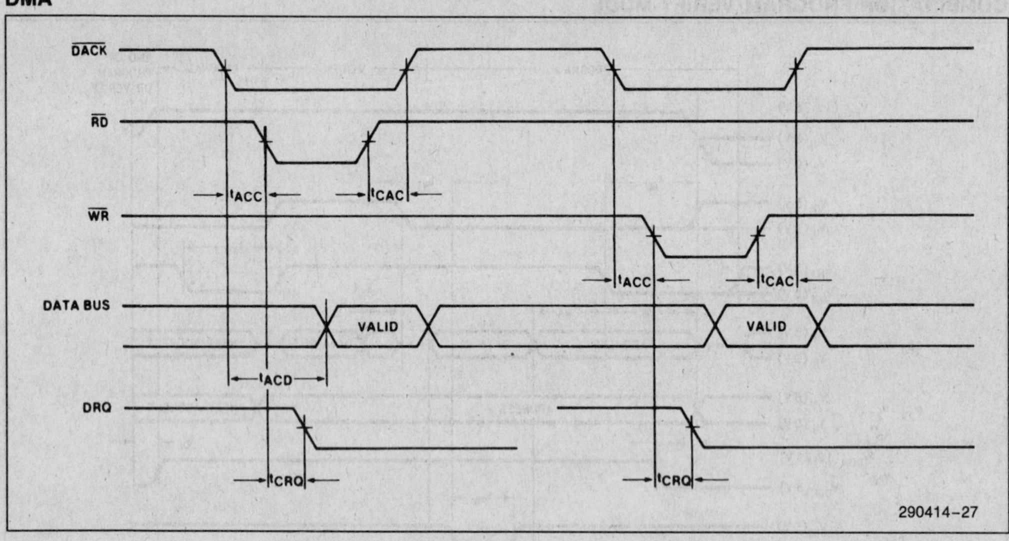

PORT 2

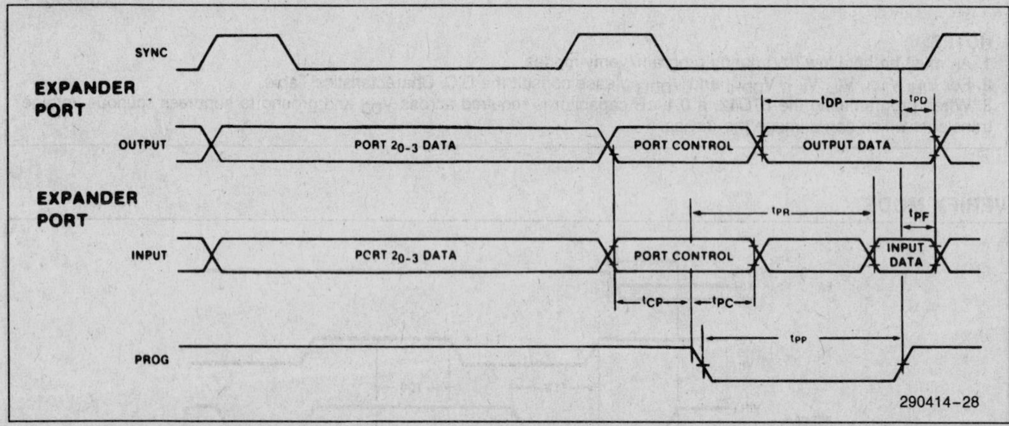

PORT TIMING DURING EXTERNAL ACCESS (EA)

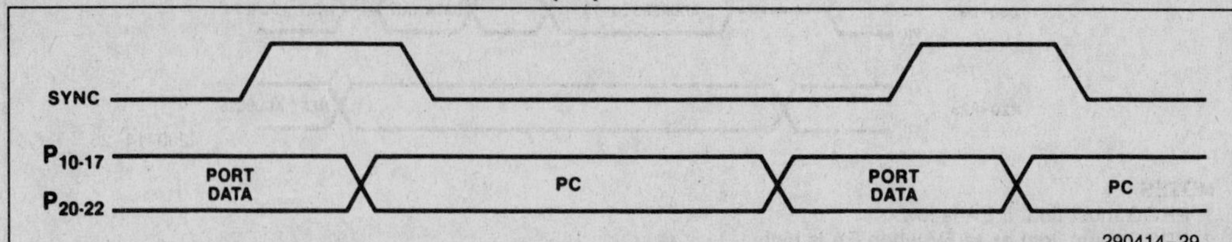

On the Rising Edge of SYNC and EA is Enabled, Port Data is Valid and can be Strobed. On the Trailing Edge of Sync the Program Counter Contents are Available.

Table 4. UPI Instruction Set

Mnemonic	Description	Bytes	Cycles
ACCUMULATOR			
ADD A, Rr	Add register to A	1	1
ADD A, @Rr	Add data memory to A	1	1
ADD A, #data	Add immediate to A	2	2
ADDC A, Rr	Add register to A with carry	1	1
ADDC A, @Rr	Add data memory to A with carry	1	1
ADDC A, #data	Add immediate to A with carry	2	2
ANL A, Rr	AND register to A	1	1
ANL, A @Rr	AND data memory to A	1	1
ANL A, #data	AND immediate to A	2	2
ORL A, Rr	OR register to A	1	1
ORL, A, @Rr	OR data memory to A	1	1
ORL A, #data	OR immediate to A	2	2
XRL A, Rr	Exclusive OR register to A	1	1
XRL A, @Rr	Exclusive OR data memory to A	1	1
XRL A, #data	Exclusive OR immediate to A	2	2
INC A	Increment A	1	1
DEC A	Decrement A	1	1
CLR A	Clear A	1	1
CPL A	Complement A	1	1
DA A	Decimal Adjust A	1	1
SWAP A	Swap nibbles of A	1	1
RL A	Rotate A left	1	1
RLC A	Rotate A left through carry	1	1
RR A	Rotate A right	1	1
RRC A	Rotate A right through carry	1	1
INPUT/OUTPUT			
IN A, Pp	Input port to A	1	2
OUTL Pp, A	Output A to port	1	2
ANL Pp, #data	AND immediate to port	2	2
ORL Pp, #data	OR immediate to port	2	2
IN A, DBB	Input DBB to A, clear IBF	1	1
OUT DBB, A	Output A to DBB, set OBF	1	1
MOV STS, A	A_4–A_7 to Bits 4–7 of Status	1	1
MOVD A, Pp	Input Expander port to A	1	2
MOVD Pp, A	Output A to Expander port	1	2
ANLD Pp, A	AND A to Expander port	1	2
ORLD Pp, A	OR A to Expander port	1	2

Mnemonic	Description	Bytes	Cycles
DATA MOVES			
MOV A, Rr	Move register to A	1	1
MOV A, @Rr	Move data memory to A	1	1
MOV A, #data	Move immediate to A	2	2
MOV Rr, A	Move A to register	1	1
MOV @Rr, A	Move A to data memory	1	1
MOV Rr, #data	Move immediate to register	2	2
MOV @Rr, #data	Move immediate to data memory	2	2
MOV A, PSW	Move PSW to A	1	1
MOV PSW, A	Move A to PSW	1	1
XCH A, Rr	Exchange A and register	1	1
XCH A, @Rr	Exchange A and data memory	1	1
XCHD A, @Rr	Exchange digit of A and register	1	1
MOVP A, @A	Move to A from current page	1	2
MOVP3, A, @A	Move to A from page 3	1	2
TIMER/COUNTER			
MOV A, T	Read Timer/Counter	1	1
MOV T, A	Load Timer/Counter	1	1
STRT T	Start Timer	1	1
STRT CNT	Start Counter	1	1
STOP TCNT	Stop Timer/Counter	1	1
EN TCNTI	Enable Timer/Counter Interrupt	1	1
DIS TCNTI	Disable Timer/Counter Interrupt	1	1
CONTROL			
*EN A20	Enable A20 Logic	1	1
EN DMA	Enable DMA Handshake Lines	1	1
EN I	Enable IBF Interrupt	1	1
*EN Tx	Enable T0/T1 Wake Up Function	1	1
DIS I	Diable IBF Interrupt	1	1
EN FLAGS	Enable Master Interrupts	1	1
*SEL PMB0	Select Program memory bank 0	1	1
*SEL PMB1	Select Program memory bank 1	1	1
SEL RB0	Select register bank 0	1	1
SEL RB1	Select register bank 1	1	1

* UPI-C42/UPI-L42 Only.

Table 4. UPI Instruction Set (Continued)

Mnemonic	Description	Bytes	Cycles
CONTROL (Continued)			
*STANDBY	Invoke Standby Power-down mode	1	2
*SUSPEND	Invoke Suspend Power-down mode	1	2
NOP	No Operation	1	1
REGISTERS			
INC Rr	Increment register	1	1
INC @Rr	Increment data memory	1	1
DEC Rr	Decrement register	1	1
SUBROUTINE			
CALL addr	Jump to subroutine	2	2
RET	Return	1	2
RETR	Return and restore status	1	2
FLAGS			
CLR C	Clear Carry	1	1
CPL C	Complement Carry	1	1
CLR F0	Clear Flag 0	1	1
CPL F0	Complement Flag 0	1	1
CLR F1	Clear F1 Flag	1	1
CPL F1	Complement F1 Flag	1	1

*UPI-C42/UPI-L42 Only.

Mnemonic	Description	Bytes	Cycles
BRANCH			
JMP addr	Jump unconditional	2	2
JMPP @A	Jump indirect	1	2
DJNZ Rr, addr	Decrement register and jump	2	2
JC addr	Jump on Carry = 1	2	2
JNC addr	Jump on Carry = 0	2	2
JZ addr	Jump on A Zero	2	2
JNZ addr	Jump on A not Zero	2	2
JT0 addr	Jump on T0 = 1	2	2
JNT0 addr	Jump on T0 = 0	2	2
JT1 addr	Jump on T1 = 1	2	2
JNT1 addr	Jump on T1 = 0	2	2
JF0 addr	Jump on F0 Flag = 1	2	2
JF1 addr	Jump on F1 Flag = 1	2	2
JTF addr	Jump on Timer Flag = 1, Clear Flag	2	2
JNIBF addr	Jump on IBF Flag = 0	2	2
JOBF addr	Jump on OBF Flag = 1	2	2
JBb addr	Jump on Accumulator Bit	2	2

REVISION SUMMARY

The following has been changed since Revision -002:

1. Added information on keyboard controller product family.
2. Added I_{HI} specification for the UPI-L42.

The following has been changed since Revision -001:

1. Added UPI-L42 references and specification.

Support Peripherals 5

5

UPI-452
CHMOS PROGRAMMABLE I/O PROCESSOR

83C452 - 8K × 8 Mask Programmable Internal ROM

80C452 - External ROM/EPROM

- **83C452/80C452:3.5 to 14 MHz Clock Rate**
- **Software Compatible with the MCS-51 Family**
- **128-Byte Bi-Directional FIFO Slave Interface**
- **Two DMA Channels**
- **256 × 8-Bit Internal RAM**
- **34 Additional Special Function Registers**
- **40 Programmable I/O Lines**
- **Two 16-Bit Timer/Counters**
- **Boolean Processor**
- **Bit Addressable RAM**
- **8 Interrupt Sources**
- **Programmable Full Duplex Serial Channel**
- **64K Program Memory Space**
- **64K Data Memory Space**
- **68-Pin PGA and PLCC**
  (See Packaging Spec., Order: #231369)

The Intel UPI-452 (Universal Peripheral Interface) is a 68 pin CHMOS Slave I/O Processor with a sophisticated bi-directional FIFO buffer interface on the slave bus and a two channel DMA processor on-chip. The UPI-452 is the newest member of Intel's UPI family of products. It is a general-purpose slave I/O Processor that allows the designer to grow a customized interface solution.

The UPI-452 contains a complete 80C51 with twice the on-chip data and program memory. The sophisticated slave FIFO module acts as a buffer between the UPI-452 internal CPU and the external host CPU. To both the external host and the internal CPU, the FIFO module looks like a bi-directional bottomless buffer that can both read and write data. The FIFO manages the transfer of data independent of the UPI-452 core CPU and generates an interrupt or DMA request to either CPU, host or internal, as a FIFO service request.

5

The FIFO consists of two channels:the Input FIFO and the Output FIFO. The division of the FIFO module array, 128 bytes, between Input channel and Output channel is programmable by the user. Each FIFO byte has an additional logical ninth bit to distinguish between a data byte and a Data Stream Command byte. Additionally, Immediate Commands allow direct, interrupt driven, bi-directional communication between the UPI-452 internal CPU and external host CPU, bypassing the FIFO.

The on-chip DMA processor allows high speed data transfers from one writeable memory space to another. As many as 64K bytes can be transferred in a single DMA operation. Three distinct memory spaces may be used in DMA operations; Internal Data Memory, External Data Memory, and the Special Function Registers (including the FIFO IN, FIFO OUT, and Serial Channel Special Functions Registers).

The complete document for this product is available on Intel's "Data-on-Demand" CD-ROM system. To obtain a copy, contact your local Intel field sales office, Intel technical distributor or call 1-800-548-4725.

November 1990
Order Number: 231428-005

8231A ARITHMETIC PROCESSING UNIT

- **Fixed Point Single and Double Precision (16/32 Bit)**
- **Floating Point Single Precision (32 Bit)**
- **Binary Data Formats**
- **Add, Subtract, Multiply and Divide**
- **Trignometric and Inverse Trigonometric Functions**
- **Square Roots, Logarithms, Exponentiation**
- **Float to Fixed and Fixed to Float Conversions**
- **Stack Oriented Operand Storage**
- **Compatible with all Intel and most other Microprocessor Families**
- **Direct Memory Access or Programmed I/O Data Transfers**
- **End of Execution Signal**
- **General Purpose 8-Bit Data Bus Interface**
- **Standard 24 Pin Package**
- **+12V and +5V Power Supplies**
- **Advanced N-Channel Silicon Gate HMOS Technology**

The Intel 8231A Arithmetic Processing Unit (APU) is a monolithic HMOS LSI device that provides high performance fixed and floating point arithmetic and floating point trigonometric operations. It may be used to enhance the mathematical capability of a wide variety of processor-oriented systems. Chebyshev polynomials are used in the implementation of the APU algorithms.

All transfers, including operand, result, status and command information, take place over an 8-bit bidirectional data bus. Operands are pushed onto an internal stack and commands are issued to perform operations on the data and the stack. Results are then available to be retrieved from the stack.

Transfers to and from the APU may be handled by the associated processor using conventional programmed I/O, or may be handled by a direct memory access controller for improved performance. Upon completion of each command, the APU issues an end of execution signal that may be used as an interrupt by the CPU to help coordinate program execution.

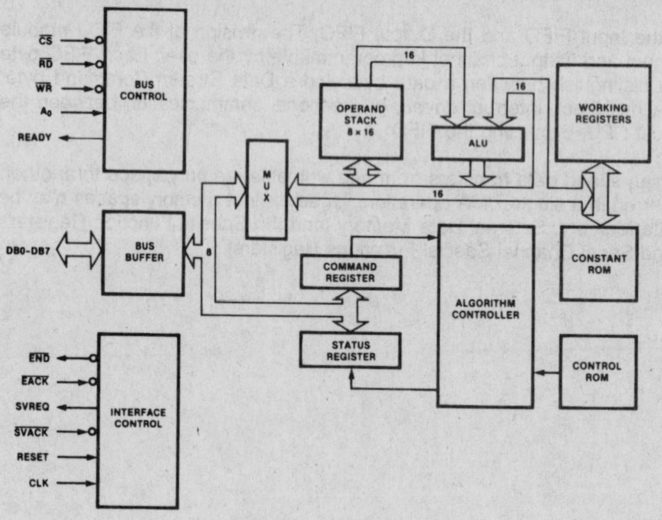

Figure 1. Block Diagram

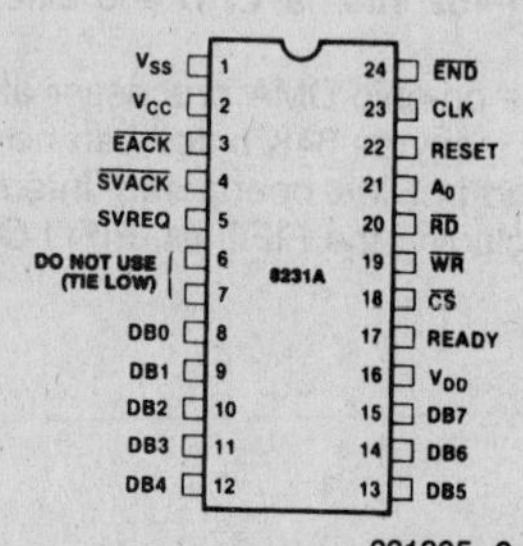

Figure 2. Pin Configuration

The complete document for this product is available on Intel's "Data-on-Demand" CD-ROM system. To obtain a copy, contact your local Intel field sales office, Intel technical distributor or call 1-800-548-4725.

September 1993
Order Number: 231305-003

8237A HIGH PERFORMANCE PROGRAMMABLE DMA CONTROLLER (8237A-5)

- Enable/Disable Control of Individual DMA Requests
- Four Independent DMA Channels
- Independent Autoinitialization of All Channels
- Memory-to-Memory Transfers
- Memory Block Initialization
- Address Increment or Decrement
- High Performance: Transfers up to 1.6M Bytes/Second with 5 MHz 8237A-5
- Directly Expandable to Any Number of Channels
- End of Process Input for Terminating Transfers
- Software DMA Requests
- Independent Polarity Control for DREQ and DACK Signals
- Available in EXPRESS
  — Standard Temperature Range
- Available in 40-Lead Cerdip and Plastic Packages
  (See Packaging Spec, Order #231369)

The 8237A Multimode Direct Memory Access (DMA) Controller is a peripheral interface circuit for microprocessor systems. It is designed to improve system performance by allowing external devices to directly transfer information from the system memory. Memory-to-memory transfer capability is also provided. The 8237A offers a wide variety of programmable control features to enhance data throughput and system optimization and to allow dynamic reconfiguration under program control.

The 8237A is designed to be used in conjunction with an external 8-bit address latch. It contains four independent channels and may be expanded to any number of channels by cascading additional controller chips. The three basic transfer modes allow programmability of the types of DMA service by the user. Each channel can be individually programmed to Autoinitialize to its original condition following an End of Process ($\overline{EOP}$). Each channel has a full 64K address and word count capability.

5

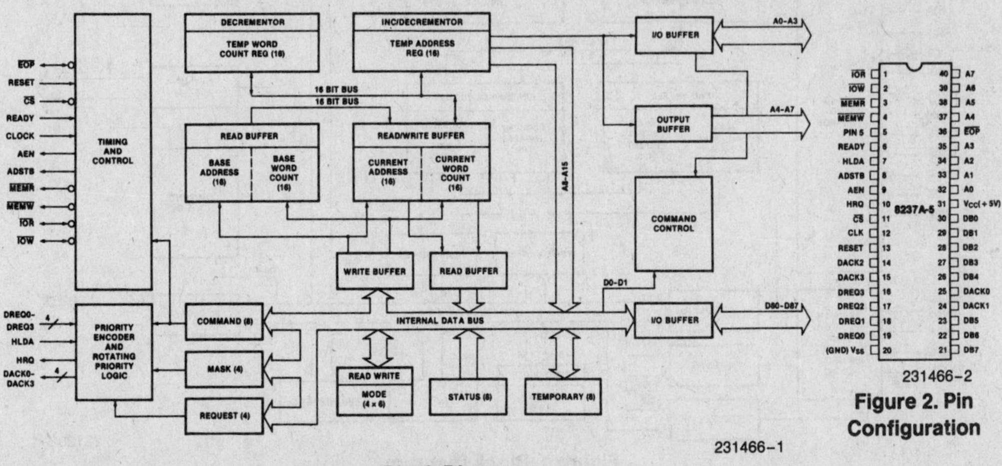

231466–2

Figure 2. Pin Configuration

231466–1

Figure 1. Block Diagram

The complete document for this product is available on Intel's "Data-on-Demand" CD-ROM system. To obtain a copy, contact your local Intel field sales office, Intel technical distributor or call 1-800-548-4725.

September 1993
Order Number: 231466-005

82C37A-5
CHMOS HIGH PERFORMANCE PROGRAMMABLE DMA CONTROLLER

- Pin Compatible with NMOS 8237A-5
- Enable/Disable Control of Individual DMA Requests
- Fully Static Design with Frequency Range from DC to 5 MHz
- Low Power Operation
- Four Independent DMA Channels
- Independent Autoinitialization of all Channels
- Memory-to-Memory Transfers
- Memory Block Initialization
- Address Increment or Decrement
- High performance: 5 MHz Speed Transfers up to 1.6 MBytes/Second
- Directly Expandable to any Number of Channels
- End of Process Input for Terminating Transfers
- Software DMA Requests
- Independent Polarity Control for DREQ and DACK Signals
- Available in 40-Lead Plastic DIP

The Intel 82C37A-5 Multimode Direct Memory Access (DMA) Controller is a CHMOS peripheral interface circuit for microprocessor systems. It is designed to improve system performance by allowing external devices to directly transfer information from the system memory. Memory-to-memory transfer capability is also provided. The 82C37A-5 offers a wide variety of programmable control features to enhance data throughput and system optimization and to allow dynamic reconfiguration under program control.

The 82C37A-5 is designed to be used in conjunction with an external 8-bit address register. It contains four independent channels and may be expanded to any number of channels by cascading additional controller chips.

The three basic transfer modes allow programmability of the types of DMA service by the user. Each channel can be individually programmed to Autoinitialize to its original condition following an End of Process ($\overline{EOP}$).

Each channel has a full 64K address and word count capability.

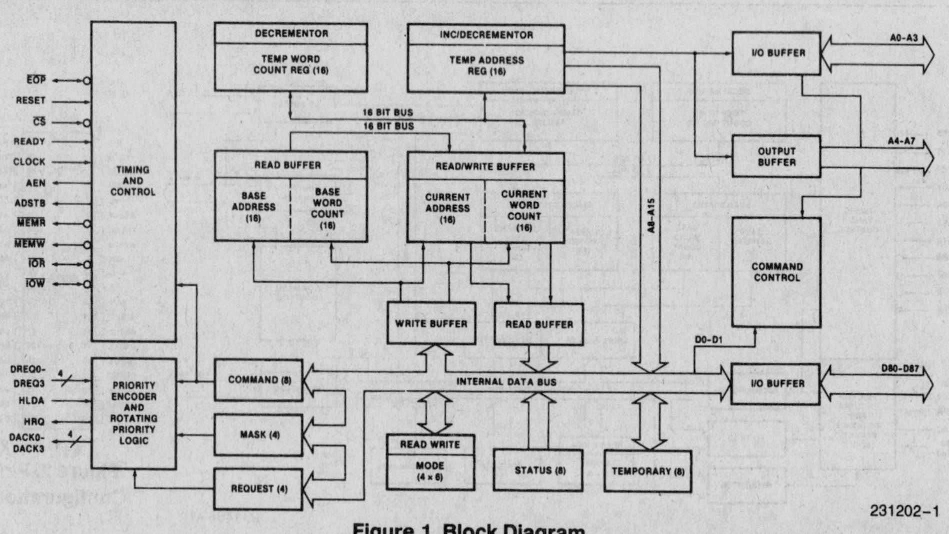

Figure 1. Block Diagram

September 1988
Order Number: 231202-005

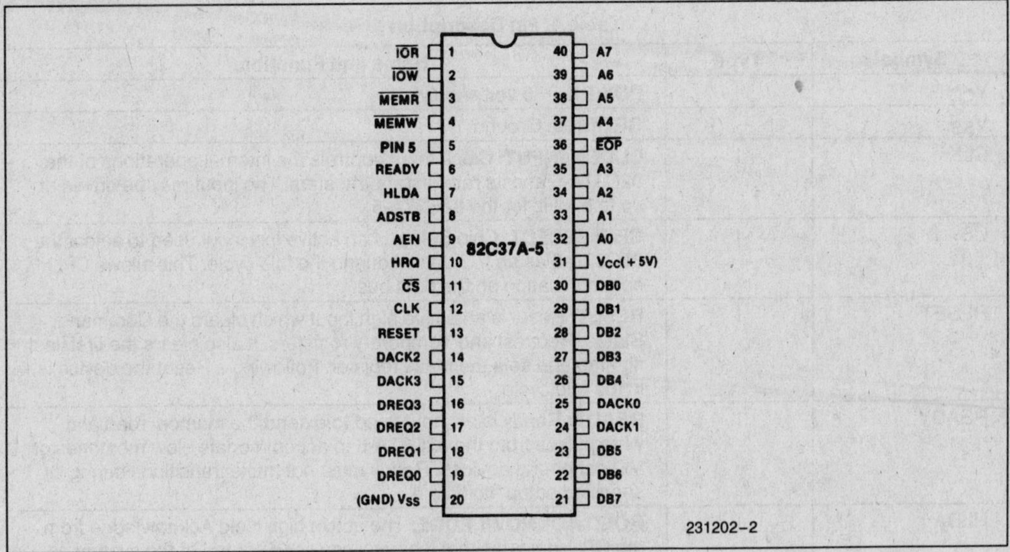

Figure 2. 82C37A-5 40-Lead DIP Configuration

5

Table 1. Pin Description

Symbol	Type	Name and Function
V_{CC}		**POWER:** +5 volt supply.
V_{SS}		**GROUND:** Ground.
CLK	I	**CLOCK INPUT:** Clock Input controls the internal operations of the 82C37A-5 and its rate of data transfers. The input may be driven at up to 5 MHz for the 82C37A-5.
$\overline{CS}$	I	**CHIP SELECT:** Chip Select is an active low input used to select the 82C37A-5 as an I/O device during the Idle cycle. This allows CPU communication on the data bus.
RESET	I	**RESET:** Reset is an active high input which clears the Command, Status, Request and Temporary registers. It also clears the first/last flip-flop and sets the Mask register. Following a Reset the device is in the Idle cycle.
READY	I	**READY:** Ready is an input used to extend the memory read and write pulses from the 82C37A-5 to accommodate slow memories or I/O peripheral devices. Ready must not make transitions during its specified setup/hold time.
HLDA	I	**HOLD ACKNOWLEDGE:** The active high Hold Acknowledge from the CPU indicates that it has relinquished control of the system busses.
DREQ0–DREQ3	I	**DMA REQUEST:** The DMA Request lines are individual asynchronous channel request inputs used by peripheral circuits to obtain DMA service. In fixed Priority, DREQ0 has the highest priority and DREQ3 has the lowest priority. A request is generated by activating the DREQ line of a channel. DACK will acknowledge the recognition of DREQ signal. Polarity of DREQ is programmable. Reset initializes these lines to active high. DREQ must be maintained until the corresponding DACK goes active.
DB0–DB7	I/O	**DATA BUS:** The Data Bus lines are bidirectional three-state signals connected to the system data bus. The outputs are enabled in the Program condition during the I/O Read to output the contents of an Address register, a Status register, the Temporary register or a Word Count register to the CPU. The outputs are disabled and the inputs are read during an I/O Write cycle when the CPU is programming the 82C37A-5 control registers. During DMA cycles the most significant 8 bits of the address are output onto the data bus to be strobed into an external latch by ADSTB. In memory-to-memory operations, data from the memory comes into the 82C37A-5 on the data bus during the read-from-memory transfer. In the write-to-memory transfer, the data bus outputs place the data into the new memory location.
$\overline{IOR}$	I/O	**I/O READ:** I/O Read is a bidirectional active low three-state line. In the Idle cycle, it is an input control signal used by the CPU to read the control registers. In the Active cycle, it is an output control signal used by the 82C37A-5 to access data from a peripheral during a DMA Write transfer.
$\overline{IOW}$	I/O	**I/O WRITE:** I/O Write is a bidirectional active low three-state line. In the Idle cycle, it is an input control signal used by the CPU to load information into the 82C37A-5. In the Active cycle, it is an output control signal used by the 82C37A-5 to load data to the peripheral during a DMA Read transfer.

Table 1. Pin Description (Continued)

Symbol	Type	Name and Function
$\overline{EOP}$	I/O	**END OF PROCESS:** End of Process is an active low bidirectional signal. Information concerning the completion of DMA services is available at the bidirectional $\overline{EOP}$ pin. The 82C37A-5 allows an external signal to terminate an active DMA service. This is accomplished by pulling the $\overline{EOP}$ input low with an external $\overline{EOP}$ signal. The 82C37A-5 also generates a pulse when the terminal count (TC) for any channel is reached. This generates an $\overline{EOP}$ signal which is output through the $\overline{EOP}$ Line. The reception of $\overline{EOP}$, either internal or external, will cause the 82C37A-5 to terminate the service, reset the request, and, if Autoinitialize is enabled, to write the base registers to the current registers of that channel. The mask bit and TC bit in the status word will be set for the currently active channel by $\overline{EOP}$ unless the channel is programmed for Autoinitialize. In that case, the mask bit remains unchanged. During memory-to-memory transfers, $\overline{EOP}$ will be output when the TC for channel 1 occurs. $\overline{EOP}$ should be tied high with a pull-up resistor if it is not used to prevent erroneous end of process inputs.
A0–A3	I/O	**ADDRESS:** The four least significant address lines are bidirectional three-state signals. In the Idle cycle they are inputs and are used by the CPU to address the register to be loaded or read. In the Active cycle they are outputs and provide the lower 4 bits of the output address.
A4–A7	O	**ADDRESS:** The four most significant address lines are three-state outputs and provide 4 bits of address. These lines are enabled only during the DMA service.
HRQ	O	**HOLD REQUEST:** This is the Hold Request to the CPU and is used to request control of the system bus. If the corresponding mask bit is clear, the presence of any valid DREQ causes 82C37A-5 to issue the HRQ. After HRQ goes active at least one clock cycle (TCY) must occur before HLDA goes active.
DACK0–DACK3	O	**DMA ACKNOWLEDGE:** DMA Acknowledge is used to notify the individual peripherals when one has been granted a DMA cycle. The sense of these lines is programmable. Reset initializes them to active low.
AEN	O	**ADDRESS ENABLE:** Address Enable enables the 8-bit latch containing the upper 8 address bits onto the system address bus. AEN can also be used to disable other system bus drivers during DMA transfers. AEN is active HIGH.
ADSTB	O	**ADDRESS STROBE:** The active high, Address Strobe is used to strobe the upper address byte into an external latch.
$\overline{MEMR}$	O	**MEMORY READ:** The Memory Read signal is an active low three-state output used to access data from the selected memory location during a DMA Read or a memory-to-memory transfer.
$\overline{MEMW}$	O	**MEMORY WRITE:** The Memory Write is an active low three-state output used to write data to the selected memory location during a DMA Write or a memory-to-memory transfer.
PIN5	I	**PIN5:** This pin should always be at a logic HIGH level. An internal pull-up resistor will establish a logic HIGH when the pin is left floating. It is recommended, however, that PIN5 be connected to V_{CC}.

5

FUNCTIONAL DESCRIPTION

The 82C37A-5 block diagram includes the major logic blocks and all of the internal registers. The data interconnection paths are also shown. Not shown are the various control signals between the blocks. The 82C37A-5 contains 344 bits of internal memory in the form of registers. Figure 3 lists these registers by name and shows the size of each. A detailed description of the registers and their functions can be found under Register Description.

Name	Size	Number
Base Address Registers	16 bits	4
Base Word Count Registers	16 bits	4
Current Address Registers	16 bits	4
Current Word Count Registers	16 bits	4
Temporary Address Register	16 bits	1
Temporary Word Count Register	16 bits	1
Status Register	8 bits	1
Command Register	8 bits	1
Temporary Register	8 bits	1
Mode Registers	6 bits	4
Mask Register	4 bits	1
Request Register	4 bits	1

Figure 3. 82C37A-5 Internal Registers

The 82C37A-5 contains three basic blocks of control logic. The Timing Control block generates internal timing and external control signals for the 82C37A-5. The Program Command Control block decodes the various commands given to the 82C37A-5 by the microprocessor prior to servicing a DMA Request. It also decodes the Mode Control word used to select the type of DMA during the servicing. The Priority Encoder block resolves priority contention between DMA channels requesting service simultaneously.

DMA Operation

The 82C37A-5 is designed to operate in two major cycles. These are called Idle and Active cycles. Each device cycle is made up of a number of states. The 82C37A-5 can assume seven separate states, each composed of one full clock period. State 1 (S1) is the inactive state. It is entered when the 82C37A-5 has no valid DMA requests pending. While in S1, the DMA controller is inactive but may be in the Program Condition, being programmed by the processor. State 0 (S0) is the first state of a DMA service. The 82C37A-5 has requested a hold but the processor has not yet returned an acknowledge. The 82C37A-5 may still be programmed until it receives HLDA from the CPU. An acknowledge from the CPU will signal that DMA transfers may begin. S1, S2, S3 and S4 are the working states of the DMA service. If more time is needed to complete a transfer than is available with normal timing, wait states (SW) can be inserted between S2 or S3 and S4 by the use of the Ready line on the 82C37A-5. Note that the data is transferred directly from the I/O device to memory (or vice versa) with $\overline{IOR}$ and $\overline{MEMW}$ (or $\overline{MEMR}$ and $\overline{IOW}$) being active at the same time. The data is not read into or driven out of the 82C37A-5 in I/O-to-memory or memory-to-I/O DMA transfers.

Memory-to-memory transfers require a read-from and a write-to-memory to complete each transfer. The states, which resemble the normal working states, use two digit numbers for identification. Eight states are required for a single transfer. The first four states (S11, S12, S13, S14) are used for the read-from-memory half and the last four states (S21, S22, S23, S24) for the write-to-memory half of the transfer.

IDLE CYCLE

When no channel is requesting service, the 82C37A-5 will enter the Idle cycle and perform "S1" states. In this cycle the 82C37A-5 will sample the DREQ lines every clock cycle to determine if any channel is requesting a DMA service. The device will also sample $\overline{CS}$, looking for an attempt by the microprocessor to write or read the internal registers of the 82C37A-5. When $\overline{CS}$ is low and HLDA is low, the 82C37A-5 enters the Program Condition. The CPU can now establish, change or inspect the internal definition of the part by reading from or writing to the internal registers. Address lines A0–A3 are inputs to the device and select which registers will be read or written. The $\overline{IOR}$ and $\overline{IOW}$ lines are used to select and time reads or writes. Due to the number and size of the internal registers, an internal flip-flop is used to generate an additional bit of address. This bit is used to determine the upper or lower byte of the 16-bit Address and Word Count registers. The flip-flop is reset by Master Clear or Reset. A separate software command can also reset this flip-flop.

Special software commands can be executed by the 82C37A-5 in the Program Condition. These commands are decoded as sets of addresses with the $\overline{CS}$ and $\overline{IOW}$. The commands do not make use of the data bus. Instructions include Clear First/Last Flip-Flop and Master Clear.

ACTIVE CYCLE

When the 82C37A-5 is in the Idle cycle and a non-masked channel requests a DMA service, the device will output an HRQ to the microprocessor and enter the Active cycle. It is in this cycle that the DMA service will take place, in one of four modes:

Single Transfer Mode — In Single Transfer mode the device is programmed to make one transfer only. The word count will be decremented and the address decremented or incremented following each transfer. When the word count "rolls over" from zero to FFFFH, a Terminal Count (TC) will cause an Autoinitialize if the channel has been programmed to do so.

DREQ must be held active until DACK becomes active in order to be recognized. If DREQ is held active throughout the single transfer, HRQ will go inactive and release the bus to the system. It will again go active and, upon receipt of a new HLDA, another single transfer will be performed, in 8080A, 8085AH, 80C88, or 80C86 system this will ensure one full machine cycle execution between DMA transfers. Details of timing between the 82C37A-5 and other bus control protocols will depend upon the characteristics of the microprocessor involved.

Block Transfer Mode — In Block Transfer mode the device is activated by DREQ to continue making transfers during the service until a TC, caused by word count going to FFFFH, or an external End of Process (EOP) is encountered. DREQ need only be held active until DACK becomes active. Again, an Autoinitialization will occur at the end of the service if the channel has been programmed for it.

Demand Transfer Mode — In Demand Transfer mode the device is programmed to continue making transfers until a TC or external $\overline{EOP}$ is encountered or until DREQ goes inactive. Thus transfers may continue until the I/O device has exhausted its data capacity. After the I/O device has had a chance to catch up, the DMA service is re-established by means of a DREQ. During the time between services when the microprocessor is allowed to operate, the intermediate values of address and word count are stored in the 82C37A-5 Current Address and Current Word Count registers. Only an $\overline{EOP}$ can cause an Autoinitialize at the end of the service. $\overline{EOP}$ is generated either by TC or by an external signal.

Cascade Mode — This mode is used to cascade more than one 82C37A-5 together for simple system expansion. The HRQ and HLDA signals from the additional 82C37A-5 are connected to the DREQ and DACK signals of a channel of the initial 82C37A-5. This allows the DMA requests of the additional device to propagate through the priority network circuitry of the preceding device. The priority chain is preserved and the new device must wait for its turn to acknowledge requests. Since the cascade channel of the initial 82C37A-5 is used only for prioritizing the additional device, it does not output any address or control signals of its own. These could conflict with the outputs of the active channel in the added device. The 82C37A-5 will respond to DREQ and DACK but all other outputs except HRQ will be disabled. The ready input is ignored.

Figure 4 shows two additional devices cascaded into an initial device using two of the previous channels. This forms a two level DMA system. More 82C37A-5s could be added at the second level by using the remaining channels of the first level. Additional devices can also be added by cascading into the channels of the second level devices, forming a third level.

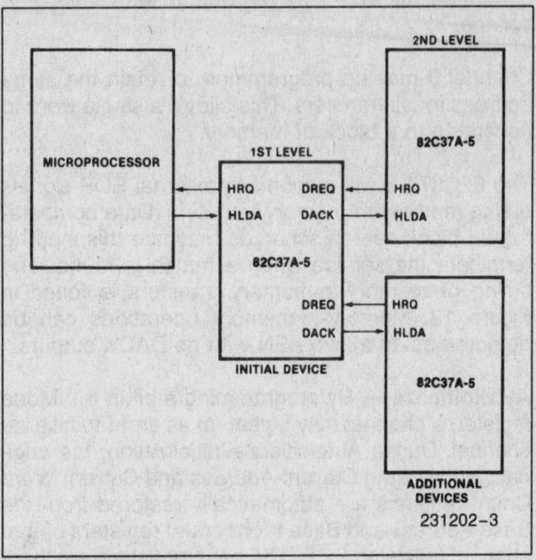

Figure 4. Cascaded 82C37A-5s

TRANSFER TYPES

Each of the three active transfer modes can perform three different types of transfers. These are Read, Write and Verify. Write transfers move data from and I/O device to the memory by activating $\overline{MEMW}$ and $\overline{IOR}$. Read transfers move data from memory to an I/O device by activating $\overline{MEMR}$ and $\overline{IOW}$. Verify transfers are pseudo transfers. The 82C37A-5 operates as in Read or Write transfers generating addresses, and responding to EOP, etc. However, the memory and I/O control lines all remain inactive. The ready input is ignored in verify mode.

Memory-to-Memory — To perform block moves of data from one memory address space to another with a minimum of program effort and time, the 82C37A-5 includes a memory-to-memory transfer feature. Programming a bit in the Command register selects channels 0 to 1 to operate as memory-to-memory transfer channels. The transfer is initiated by setting the software DREQ for channel 0. The

5

82C37A-5 requests a DMA service in the normal manner. After HLDA is true, the device, using four state transfers in Block Transfer mode, reads data from the memory. The channel 0 Current Address register is the source for the address used and is decremented or incremented in the normal manner. The data byte read from the memory is stored in the 82C37A-5 internal Temporary register. Channel 1 then performs a four-state transfer of the data from the Temporary register to memory using the address in its Current Address register and incrementing or decrementing it in the normal manner. The channel 1 current Word Count is decremented. When the word count of channel 1 goes to FFFFH, a TC is generated causing an $\overline{EOP}$ output terminating the service.

Channel 0 may be programmed to retain the same address for all transfers. This allows a single word to be written to a block of memory.

The 82C37A-5 will respond to external $\overline{EOP}$ signals during memory-to-memory transfers. Data comparators in block search schemes may use this input to terminate the service when a match is found. The timing of memory-to-memory transfers is found in Figure 12. Memory-to-memory operations can be detected as an active AEN with no DACK outputs.

Autoinitialize — By programming a bit in the Mode register, a channel may be set up as an Autoinitialize channel. During Autoinitialize initialization, the original values of the Current Address and Current Word Count registers are automatically restored from the Base Address and Base Word count registers of that channel following $\overline{EOP}$. The base registers are loaded simultaneously with the current registers by the microprocessor and remain unchanged throughout the DMA service. The mask bit is not altered when the channel is in Autoinitialize. Following Autoinitialize the channel is ready to perform another DMA service, without CPU intervention, as soon as a valid DREQ is detected. In order to Autoinitialize both channels in a memory-to-memory transfer, both word counts should be programmed identically. If interrupted externally, $\overline{EOP}$ pulses should be applied in both bus cycles.

Priority — The 82C37A-5 has two types of priority encoding available as software selectable options. The first is Fixed Priority which fixes the channels in priority order based upon the descending value of their number. The channel with the lowest priority is 3 followed by 2, 1 and the highest priority channel, 0. After the recognition of any one channel for service, the other channels are prevented from interfering with that service until it is completed.

The second scheme is Rotating Priority. The last channel to get service becomes the lowest priority channel with the others rotating accordingly.

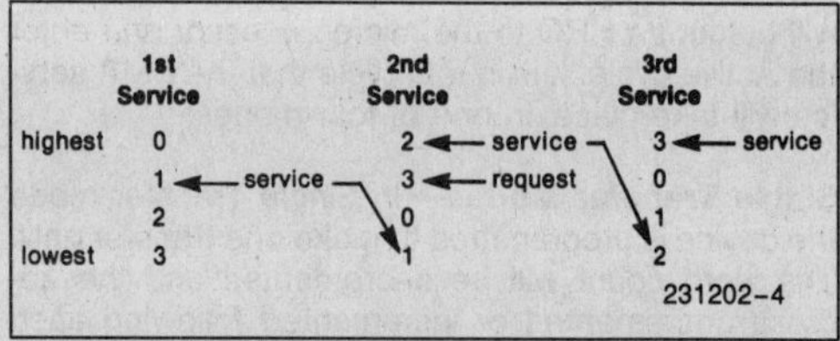

With Rotating Priority in a single chip DMA system, any device requesting service is guaranteed to be recognized after no more than three higher priority services have occurred. This prevents any one channel from monopolizing the system.

Compressed Timing — In order to achieve even greater throughput where system characteristics permit, the 82C37A-5 can compress the transfer time to two clock cycles. From Figure 11 it can be seen that state S3 is used to extend the access time of the read pulse. By removing state S3, the read pulse width is made equal to the write pulse width and a transfer consists only of state S2 to change the address and state S4 to perform the read/write. S1 states will still occur when A8–A15 need updating (see Address Generation). Timing for compressed transfers is found in Figure 14.

Address Generation — In order to reduce pin count, the 82C37A-5 multiplexes the eight higher order address bits on the data lines. State S1 is used to output the higher order address bits to an external latch from which they may be placed on the address bus. The falling edge of Address Strobe (ADSTB) is used to load these bits from the data lines to the latch. Address Enable (AEN) is used to enable the bits onto the address bus through a three-state enable. The lower order address bits are output by the 82C37A-5 directly. Lines A0–A7 should be connected to the address bus. Figure 11 shows the time relationships between CLK, AEN, ADSTB, DB0–DB7 and A0–A7.

During Block and Demand Transfer mode services, which include multiple transfers, the addresses generated will be sequential. For many transfers the data held in the external address latch will remain the same. This data need only change when a carry or borrow from A7 to A8 takes place in the normal sequence of addresses. To save time and speed transfers, the 82C37A-5 executes S1 states only when updating of A8–A15 in the latch is necessary. This means for long services, S1 states and Address Strobes may occur only once every 256 transfers, a savings of 255 clock cycles for each 256 transfers.

REGISTER DESCRIPTION

Current Address Register — Each channel has a 16-bit Current Address register. This register holds the value of the address used during DMA transfers. The address is automatically incremented or decremented after each transfer and the intermediate values of the address are stored in the Current Address register during the transfer. This register is written or read by the microprocessor in successive 8-bit bytes. It may also be reinitialized by an Autoinitialize back to its original value. Autoinitialize takes place only after an $\overline{EOP}$.

Current Word Register — Each channel has a 16-bit Current Word Count register. This register determines the number of transfers to be performed. The actual number of transfers will be one more than the number programmed in the Current Word Count register (i.e., programming a count of 100 will result in 101 transfers). The word count is decremented after each transfer. The intermediate value of the word count is stored in the register during the transfer. When the value in the register goes from zero to FFFFH, a TC will be generated. This register is loaded or read in successive 8-bit bytes by the microprocessor in the Program Condition. Following the end of a DMA service it may also be reinitialized by an Autoinitialization back to its original value. Autoinitialize can occur only when an $\overline{EOP}$ occurs. If it is not Autoinitialized, this register will have a count of FFFFH after TC.

Base Address and Base Word Count Registers — Each channel has a pair of Base Address and Base Word Count registers. These 16-bit registers store the original value of their associated current registers. During Autoinitialize these values are used to restore the current registers to their original values. The base registers are written simultaneously with their corresponding current register in 8-bit bytes in the Program Condition by the microprocessor. These registers cannot be read by the microprocessor.

Command Register — This 8-bit register controls the operation of the 82C37A-5. It is programmed by the microprocessor in the Program Condition and is cleared by Reset or a Master Clear instruction. The following table lists the function of the command bits. See Figure 6 for address coding.

Mode Register — Each channel has a 6-bit Mode register associated with it. When the register is being written to by the microprocessor in the Program Condition, bits 0 and 1 determine which channel Mode register is to be written.

Request Register — The 82C37A-5 can respond to requests for DMA service which are initiated by software as well as by a DREQ. Each channel has a request bit associated with it in the 4-bit Request register. These are non-maskable and subject to prioritization by the Priority Encoder network. Each register bit is set or reset separately under software control or is cleared upon generation of a TC or external $\overline{EOP}$. The entire register is cleared by a Reset. To set or reset a bit, the software loads the proper form of the data word. See Figure 5 for register ad-

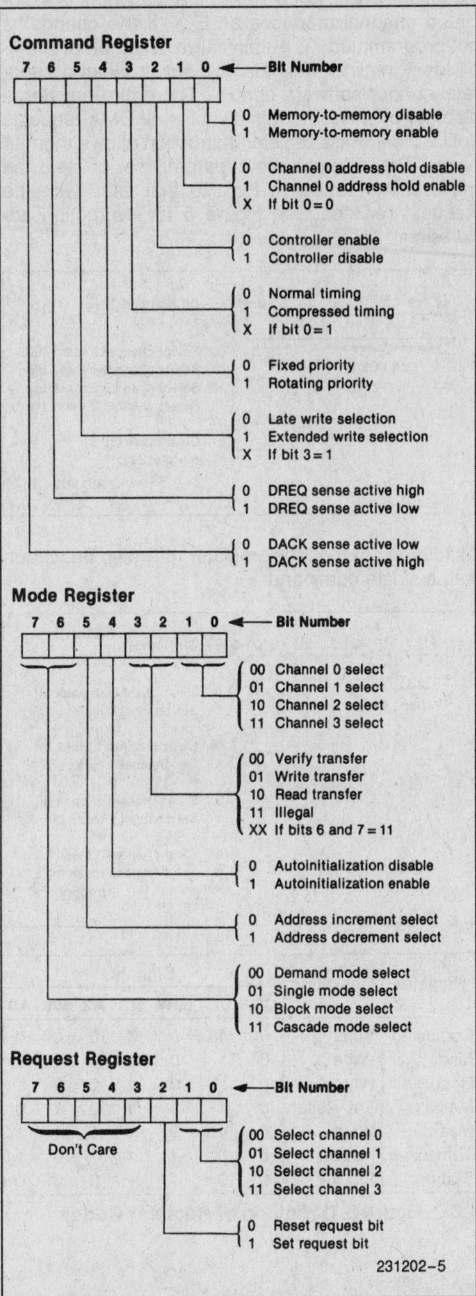

5

dress coding. In order to make a software request, the channel must be in Block Mode.

Mask Register — Each channel has associated with it a mask bit which can be set to disable the incoming DREQ. Each mask bit is set when its associated channel produces an $\overline{EOP}$ if the channel is not programmed for Autoinitialize. Each bit of the 4-bit Mask register may also be set or cleared separately under software control. The entire register is also set by a Reset. This disables all DMA requests until a clear Mask register instruction allows them to occur. The instruction to separately set or clear the mask bits is similar in form to that used with the Request register. See Figure 5 for instruction addressing.

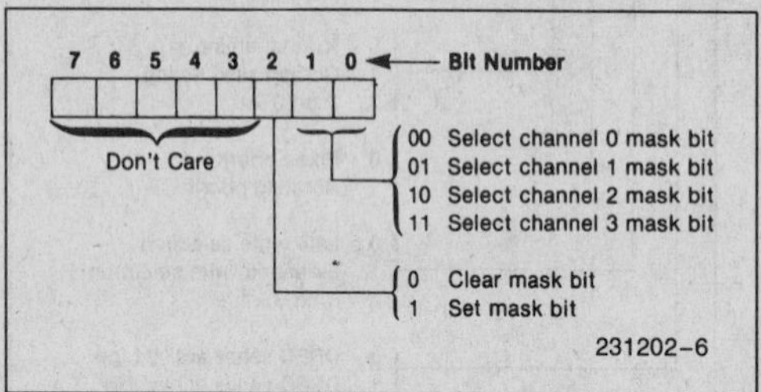

All four bits of the Mask register may also be written with a single command.

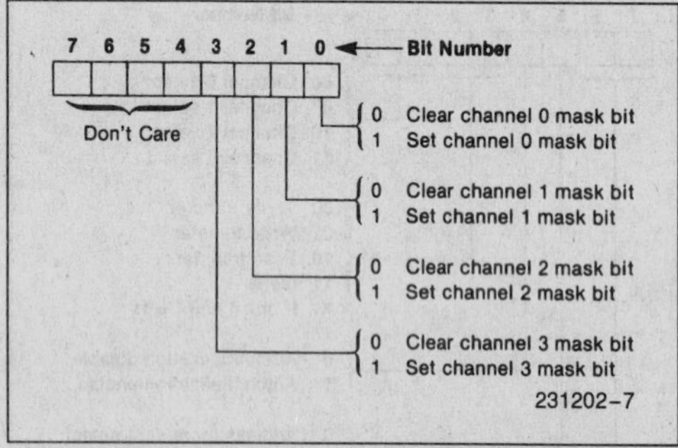

Register	Operation	Signals						
		$\overline{CS}$	$\overline{IOR}$	$\overline{IOW}$	A3	A2	A1	A0
Command	Write	0	1	0	1	0	0	0
Mode	Write	0	1	0	1	0	1	1
Request	Write	0	1	0	1	0	0	1
Mask	Set/Reset	0	1	0	1	0	1	0
Mask	Write	0	1	0	1	1	1	1
Temporary	Read	0	0	1	1	1	0	1
Status	Read	0	0	1	1	0	0	0

Figure 5. Definition of Register Codes

Status Register — The Status register is available to be read out of the 82C37A-5 by the microprocessor. It contains information about the status of the devices at this point. This information includes which channels have reached a terminal count and which channels have pending DMA requests. Bits 0–3 are set every time a TC is reached by that channel or an external $\overline{EOP}$ is applied. These bits are cleared upon Reset and on each Status Read. Bits 4–7 are set whenever their corresponding channel is requesting service.

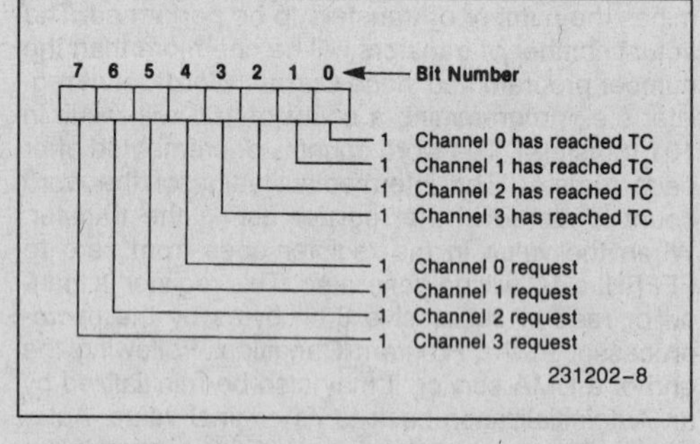

Temporary Register — The Temporary register is used to hold data during memory-to-memory transfers. Following the completion of the transfers, the last word moved can be read by the microprocessor in the Program Condition. The Temporary register always contains the last byte transferred in the previous memory-to-memory operation, unless cleared by a Reset.

Software Commands — These are additional special software commands which can be executed in the Program Condition. They do not depend on any specific bit pattern on the data bus. The three software commands are:

Clear First/Last Flip-Flop: This command is executed prior to writing or reading new address or word count information to the 82C37A-5. This initializes the flip-flop to a known state so that subsequent accesses to register contents by the microprocessor will address upper and lower bytes in the correct sequence.

Master Clear: This software instruction has the same effect as the hardware Reset. The Command, Status, Request, Temporary, and Internal First/Last Flip-Flop registers are cleared and the Mask register is set. The 82C37A-5 will enter the Idle cycle.

Clear Mask Register: This command clears the mask bits of all four channels, enabling them to accept DMA requests.

Figure 6 lists the address codes for the software commands:

Signals						Operation
A3	A2	A1	A0	$\overline{IOR}$	$\overline{IOW}$	
1	0	0	0	0	1	Read Status Register
1	0	0	0	1	0	Write Command Register
1	0	0	1	0	1	Illegal
1	0	0	1	1	0	Write Request Register
1	0	1	0	0	1	Illegal
1	0	1	0	1	0	Write Single Mask Register Bit
1	0	1	1	0	1	Illegal
1	0	1	1	1	0	Write Mode Register
1	1	0	0	0	1	Illegal
1	1	0	0	1	0	Clear Byte Pointer Flip-Flop
1	1	0	1	0	1	Read Temporary Register
1	1	0	1	1	0	Master Clear
1	1	1	0	0	1	Illegal
1	1	1	0	1	0	Clear Mask Register
1	1	1	1	0	1	Illegal
1	1	1	1	1	0	Write All Mask Register Bits

Figure 6. Software Command Codes

PROGRAMMING

The 82C37A-5 will accept programming from the host processor any time that HLDA is inactive; this is true even if HRQ is active. The responsibility of the host is to assure that programming and HLDA are mutually exclusive. Note that a problem can occur if a DMA request occurs, on an unmasked channel while the 82C37A-5 is being programmed. For instance, the CPU may be starting to reprogram the two byte Address register of channel 1 when channel 1 receives a DMA request. If the 82C37A-5 is enabled (bit 2 in the command register is 0) and channel 1 is unmasked, a DMA service will occur after only one byte of the Address register has been reprogrammed. This can be avoided by disabling the controller (setting bit 2 in the command register) or masking the channel before programming any other registers. Once the programming is complete, the controller can be enabled/unmasked.

Channel	Register	Operation	Signals							Internal Flip-Flop	Data Bus DB0–DB7
			$\overline{CS}$	$\overline{IOR}$	$\overline{IOW}$	A3	A2	A1	A0		
0	Base and Current Address	Write	0	1	0	0	0	0	0	0	A0–A7
			0	1	0	0	0	0	0	1	A8–A15
	Current Address	Read	0	0	1	0	0	0	0	0	A0–A7
			0	0	1	0	0	0	0	1	A8–A15
	Base and Current Word Count	Write	0	1	0	0	0	0	1	0	W0–W7
			0	1	0	0	0	0	1	1	W8–W15
	Current Word Count	Read	0	0	1	0	0	0	1	0	W0–W7
			0	0	1	0	0	0	1	1	W8–W15
1	Base and Current Address	Write	0	1	0	0	0	1	0	0	A0–A7
			0	1	0	0	0	1	0	1	A8–A15
	Current Address	Read	0	0	1	0	0	1	0	0	A0–A7
			0	0	1	0	0	1	0	1	A8–A15
	Base and Current Word Count	Write	0	1	0	0	0	1	1	0	W0–W7
			0	1	0	0	0	1	1	1	W8–W15
	Current Word Count	Read	0	0	1	0	0	1	1	0	W0–W7
			0	0	1	0	0	1	1	1	W8–W15
2	Base and Current Address	Write	0	1	0	0	1	0	0	0	A0–A7
			0	1	0	0	1	0	0	1	A8–A15
	Current Address	Read	0	0	1	0	1	0	0	0	A0–A7
			0	0	1	0	1	0	0	1	A8–A15
	Base and Current Word Count	Write	0	1	0	0	1	0	1	0	W0–W7
			0	1	0	0	1	0	1	1	W8–W15
	Current Word Count	Read	0	0	1	0	1	0	1	0	W0–W7
			0	0	1	0	1	0	1	1	W8–W15
3	Base and Current Address	Write	0	1	0	0	1	1	0	0	A0–A7
			0	1	0	0	1	1	0	1	A8–A15
	Current Address	Read	0	0	1	0	1	1	0	0	A0–A7
			0	0	1	0	1	1	0	1	A8–A15
	Base and Current Word Count	Write	0	1	0	0	1	1	1	0	W0–W7
			0	1	0	0	1	1	1	1	W8–W15
	Current Word Count	Read	0	0	1	0	1	1	1	0	W0–W7
			0	0	1	0	1	1	1	1	W8–W15

Figure 7. Word Count and Address Register Command Codes

After power-up it is suggested that all internal locations, especially the Mode registers, be loaded with some valid value. This should be done even if some channels are unused.

APPLICATION INFORMATION

Figure 8 shows a convenient method for configuring a DMA system with the 82C37A-5 controller and an 8080A/8085AH microprocessor system. The multimode DMA controller issues a HRQ to the processor whenever there is at least one valid DMA request from a peripheral device. When the processor replies with a HLDA signal, the 82C37A-5 takes control of the address bus, the data bus and the control bus. The address for the first transfer operation comes out in two bytes — the least significant 8 bits on the eight address outputs and the most significant 8 bits on the data bus. The contents of the data bus are then latched into the 8-bit latch to complete the full 16 bits of the address bus. After the initial transfer takes place, the latch is updated only after a carry or borrow is generated in the least significant address byte. Four DMA channels are provided when one 82C37A-5 is used.

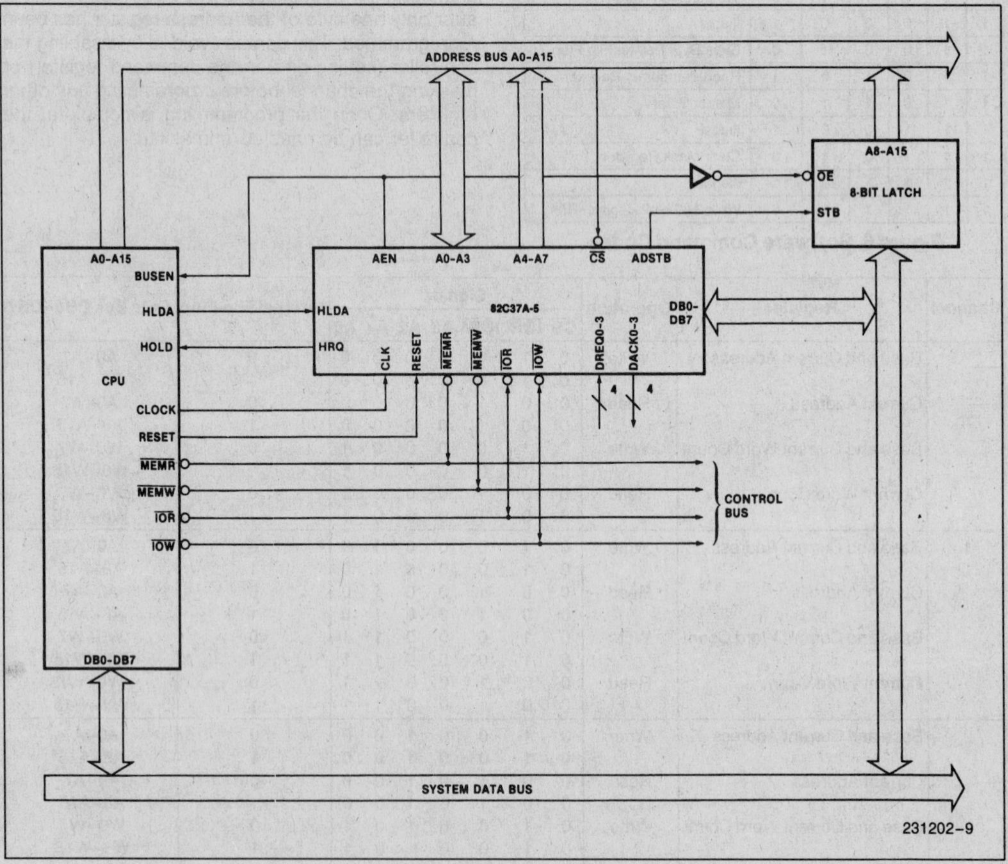

231202-9

Figure 8. 82C37A-5 System Interface

ABSOLUTE MAXIMUM RATINGS*

Ambient Temperature under Bias ......0°C to 70°C
Case Temperature ....0°C to +75°C
Storage Temperature ....−55°C to +150°C
Voltage on Any Pin with
Respect to Ground..............−0.5V to +7V
Power Dissipation.......................1.0 Watt

NOTICE: This is a production data sheet. The specifications are subject to change without notice.

*WARNING: *Stressing the device beyond the "Absolute Maximum Ratings" may cause permanent damage. These are stress ratings only. Operation beyond the "Operating Conditions" is not recommended and extended exposure beyond the "Operating Conditions" may affect device reliability.*

D.C. CHARACTERISTICS

T_A = 0°C to 70°C, T_{CASE} = 0°C to 75°C, V_{CC} = +5.0V ±5%, GND = 0V

Symbol	Parameter	Min	Typ	Max	Unit	Test Conditions
V_{OH}	Output High Voltage	3.7			V	I_{OH} = −1.0 mA
V_{OL}	Output LOW Voltage			0.40	V	I_{OL} = 3.2 mA
V_{IH}	Input HIGH Voltage	2.2		V_{CC} + 0.5	V	
V_{IL}	Input LOW Voltage	−0.5		0.8	V	
I_{LI}	Input Load Current			±10	μA	0V ≤ V_{IN} ≤ V_{CC}
I_{LO}	Output Leakage Current			±10	μA	0V ≤ V_{OUT} ≤ V_{CC}
I_{CC}	V_{CC} Supply Current			10	mA	(Note 1)
I_{CCS}	Standby Supply Current			10	μA	HLDA = 0V, V_{IL} = 0V, V_{IH} = V_{CC}
C_O	Output Capacitance		4	8	pF	fc = 1.0 MHz, Inputs = 0V
C_I	Input Capacitance		8	15	pF	
C_{IO}	I/O Capacitance		10	18	pF	

5

A.C. CHARACTERISTICS—DMA (MASTER) MODE

T_A = 0°C to 70°C, T_{CASE} = 0°C to 75°C, V_{CC} = +5V ±5%, GND = 0V

Symbol	Parameter	Min	Max	Unit
TAEL	AEN HIGH from CLK LOW (S1) Delay Time		200	ns
TAET	AEN LOW from CLK HIGH (SI) Delay Time		130	ns
TAFAB	ADR Active to Float Delay from CLK HIGH		90	ns
TAFC	$\overline{READ}$ or $\overline{WRITE}$ Float from CLK HIGH		120	ns
TAFDB	DB Active to Float Delay from CLK HIGH		170	ns
TAHR	ADR from $\overline{READ}$ HIGH Hold Time	TCY-100		ns
TAHS	DB from ADSTB LOW Hold Time	30		ns
TAHW	ADR from $\overline{WRITE}$ HIGH Hold Time	TCY-50		ns
TAK	DACK Valid from CLK LOW Delay Time (Note 3)		170	ns
	$\overline{EOP}$ HIGH from CLK HIGH Delay Time (Note 4)		170	ns
	$\overline{EOP}$ LOW from CLK HIGH Delay Time		170	ns
TASM	ADR Stable from CLK HIGH		170	ns
TASS	DB to ADSTB LOW Setup Time	100		ns
TCH	Clock High Time (Transitions ≤ 10 ns)	68		ns
TCL	Clock LOW Time (Transitions ≤ 10 ns)	68		ns
TCY	CLK Cycle Time	200		ns
TDCL	CLK HIGH to $\overline{READ}$ or $\overline{WRITE}$ LOW Delay (Note 2)		190	ns
TDCTR	$\overline{READ}$ HIGH from CLK HIGH (S4) Delay Time (Note 2)		190	ns
TDCTW	$\overline{WRITE}$ HIGH from CLK HIGH (S4) Delay Time (Note 2)		130	ns
TDQ1	HRQ Valid from CLK HIGH Delay Time		120	ns
TEPS	$\overline{EOP}$ LOW from CLK LOW Setup Time	40		ns
TEPW	$\overline{EOP}$ Pulse Width	220		ns
TFAAB	ADR Float to Active Delay from CLK HIGH		170	ns
TFAC	$\overline{READ}$ or $\overline{WRITE}$ Active from CLK HIGH		150	ns
TFADB	DB Float to Active Delay from CLK HIGH		200	ns
THS	HLDA Valid to CLK HIGH Setup Time	75		ns
TIDH	Input Data from $\overline{MEMR}$ HIGH Hold Time	0		ns
TIDS	Input Data to $\overline{MEMR}$ HIGH Setup Time	170		ns
TODH	Output Data from $\overline{MEMW}$ HIGH Hold Time	10		ns
TODV	Output Data Valid to $\overline{MEMW}$ HIGH	125		ns
TQS	DREQ to CLK LOW (SI, S4) Setup Time (Note 3)	0		ns
TRH	CLK to READY LOW Hold Time	20		ns
TRS	READY to CLK LOW Setup Time	60		ns
TSTL	ADSTB HIGH from CLK HIGH Delay Time		130	ns
TSTT	ADSTB LOW from CLK HIGH Delay Time		90	ns

A.C. CHARACTERISTICS—PERIPHERAL (SLAVE) MODE

T_A = 0°C to 70°C, T_{CASE} = 0°C to 75°C, V_{CC} = +5V ±5%, GND = 0V

Symbol	Parameter	Min	Max	Unit
TAR	ADR Valid or $\overline{\text{CS}}$ LOW to $\overline{\text{READ}}$ LOW	50		ns
TAW	ADR Valid to $\overline{\text{WRITE}}$ HIGH Setup Time	130		ns
TCW	CS LOW to $\overline{\text{WRITE}}$ HIGH Setup Time	130		ns
TDW	Data Valid to $\overline{\text{WRITE}}$ HIGH Setup Time	130		ns
TRA	ADR or CS Hold from $\overline{\text{READ}}$ HIGH	0		ns
TRDE	Data Access from $\overline{\text{READ}}$ LOW		140	ns
TRDF	DB Float Delay from $\overline{\text{READ}}$ HIGH	0	70	ns
TRSTD	Power Supply HIGH to RESET LOW Setup Time	500		ns
TRSTS	RESET to First $\overline{\text{IOWR}}$	2TCY		ns
TRSTW	RESET Pulse Width	300		ns
TRW	$\overline{\text{READ}}$ Width	200		ns
TWA	ADR from $\overline{\text{WRITE}}$ HIGH Hold Time	20		ns
TWC	CS HIGH from $\overline{\text{WRITE}}$ HIGH Hold Time	20		ns
TWD	Data from $\overline{\text{WRITE}}$ HIGH Hold Time	30		ns
TWWS	Write Width	160		ns

NOTES:
1. Input frequency 5 MHz, when RESET, V_{IN} = 0V/V_{CC}, C_L = 0 pF.
2. The net $\overline{\text{IOW}}$ or $\overline{\text{MEMW}}$ Pulse width for normal write will be TCY-100 ns and for extended write will be 2TCY-100 ns. The net $\overline{\text{IOR}}$ or $\overline{\text{MEMR}}$ pulse width for normal read will be 2TCY-50 ns and for compressed read will be TCY-50 ns.
3. DREQ and DACK signals may be active high or active low. Timing diagrams assume the active high mode for DREQ and active low for DACK.
4. $\overline{\text{EOP}}$ is an open collector output. This parameter assumes the presence of a 2.2K pullup to V_{CC}.

5

A.C. TESTING INPUT/OUTPUT WAVEFORM

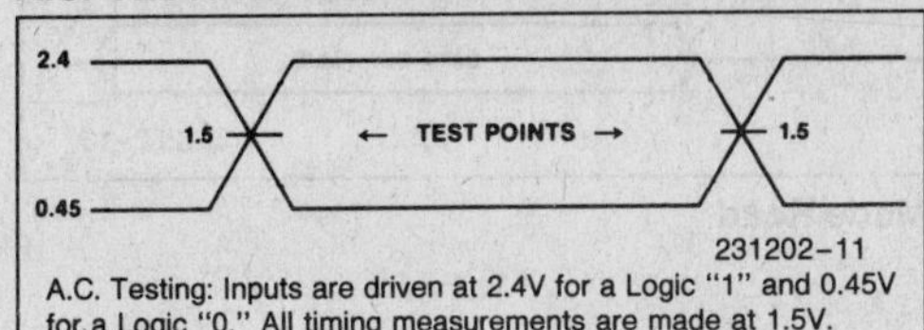

A.C. Testing: Inputs are driven at 2.4V for a Logic "1" and 0.45V for a Logic "0." All timing measurements are made at 1.5V.

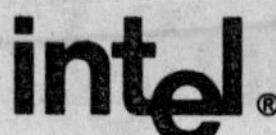

WAVEFORMS

SLAVE MODE WRITE TIMING

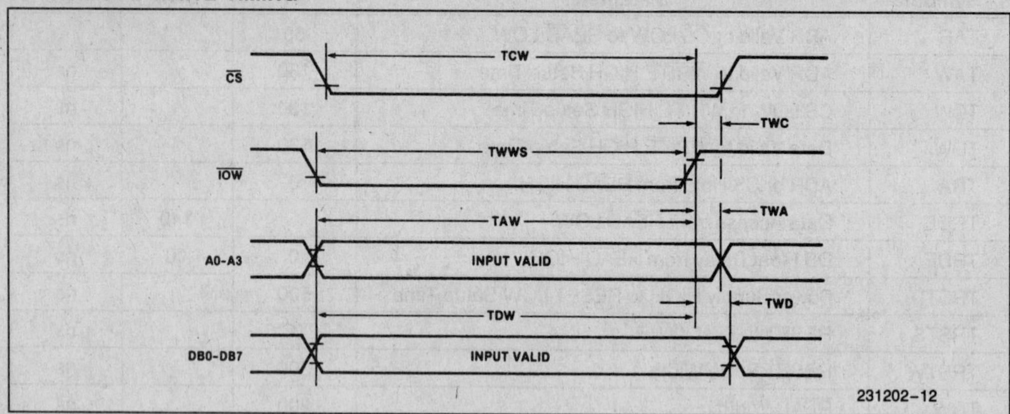

Figure 9. Slave Mode Write

SLAVE MODE READ TIMING

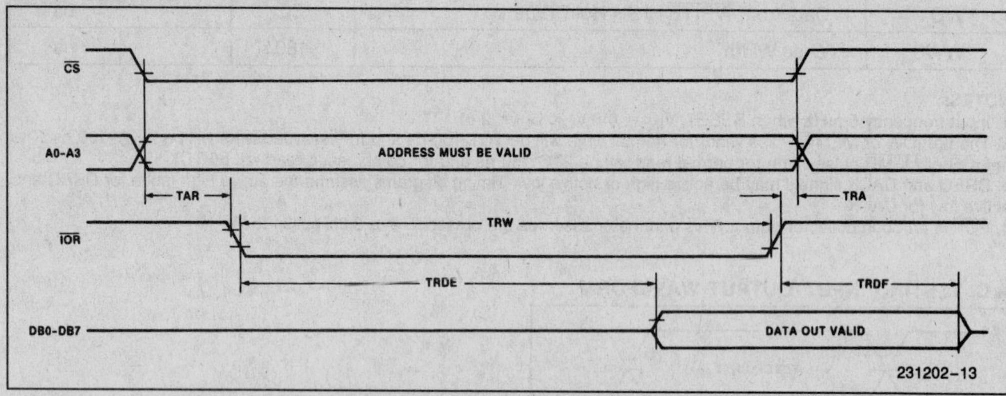

Figure 10. Slave Mode Read

WAVEFORMS (Continued)

DMA TRANSFER TIMING

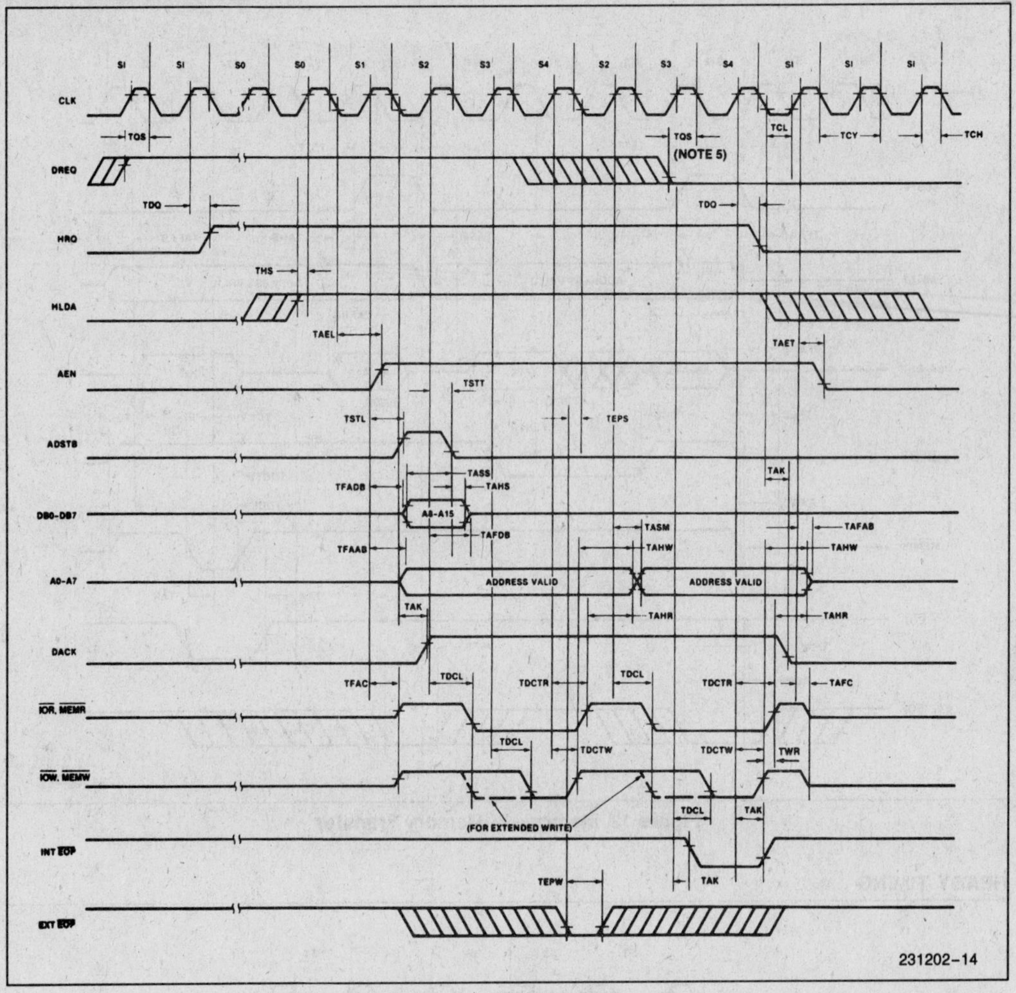

231202-14

Figure 11. DMA Transfer

WAVEFORMS (Continued)

MEMORY-TO-MEMORY TRANSFER TIMING

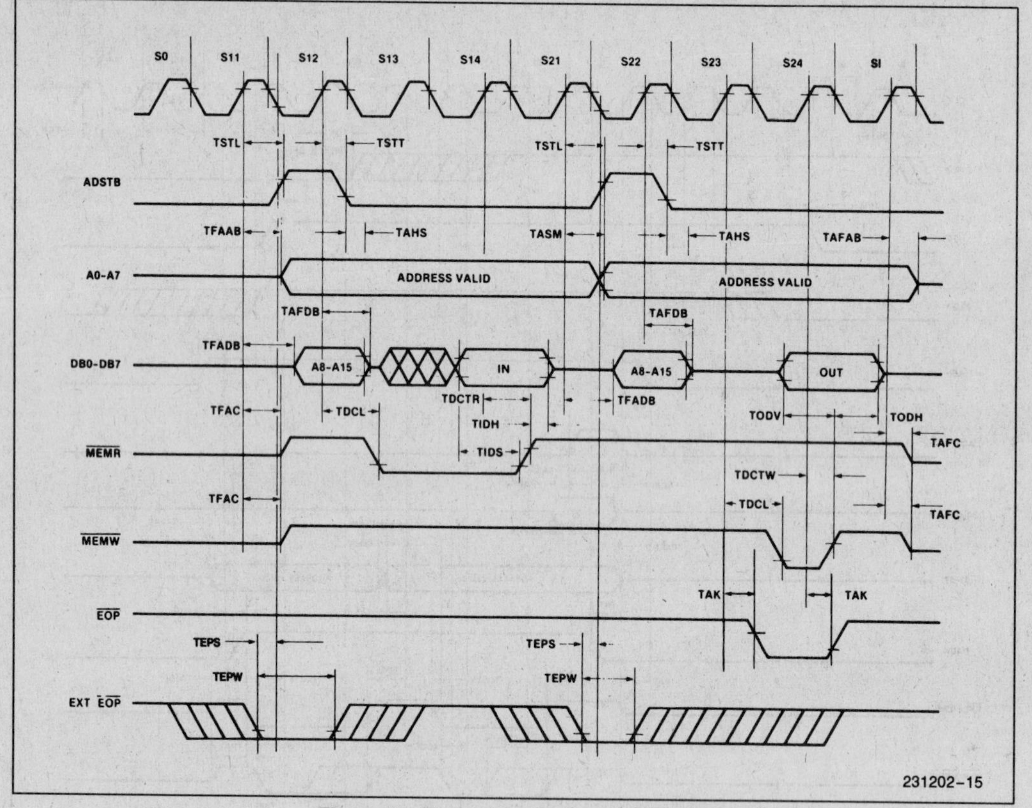

S0 S11 S12 S13 S14 S21 S22 S23 S24 SI
TSTL TSTT TSTL TSTT
ADSTB
TFAAB TAHS TASM TAHS TAFAB
A0-A7
ADDRESS VALID
ADDRESS VALID
TAFDB TAFDB
TFADB
DB0-DB7
A8-A15
IN
A8-A15
OUT
TDCTR TFADB
TFAC TDCL
TIDH
TODV TODH
TIDS
TAFC
MEMR
TDCTW
TFAC TDCL
TAFC
MEMW
TAK TAK
EOP
TEPS TEPS
TEPW TEPW
EXT EOP

231202–15

Figure 12. Memory-to-Memory Transfer

READY TIMING

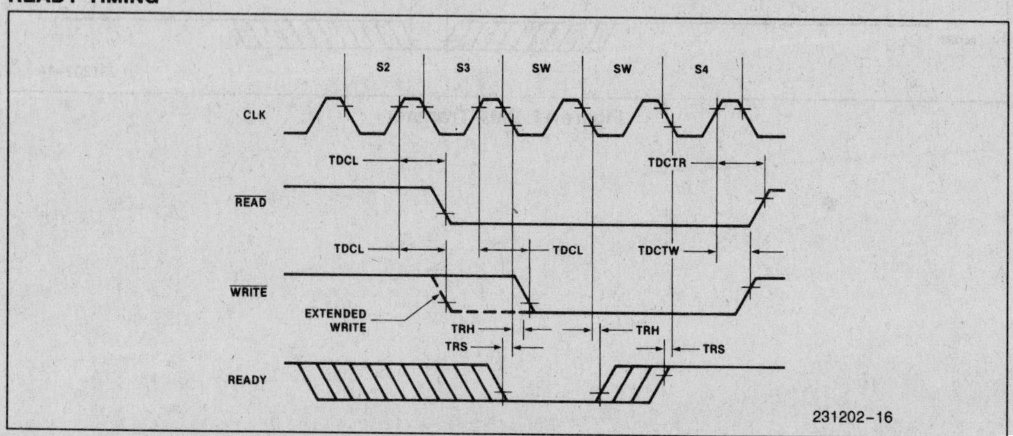

Figure 13. Ready

WAVEFORMS (Continued)

COMPRESSED TRANSFER TIMING

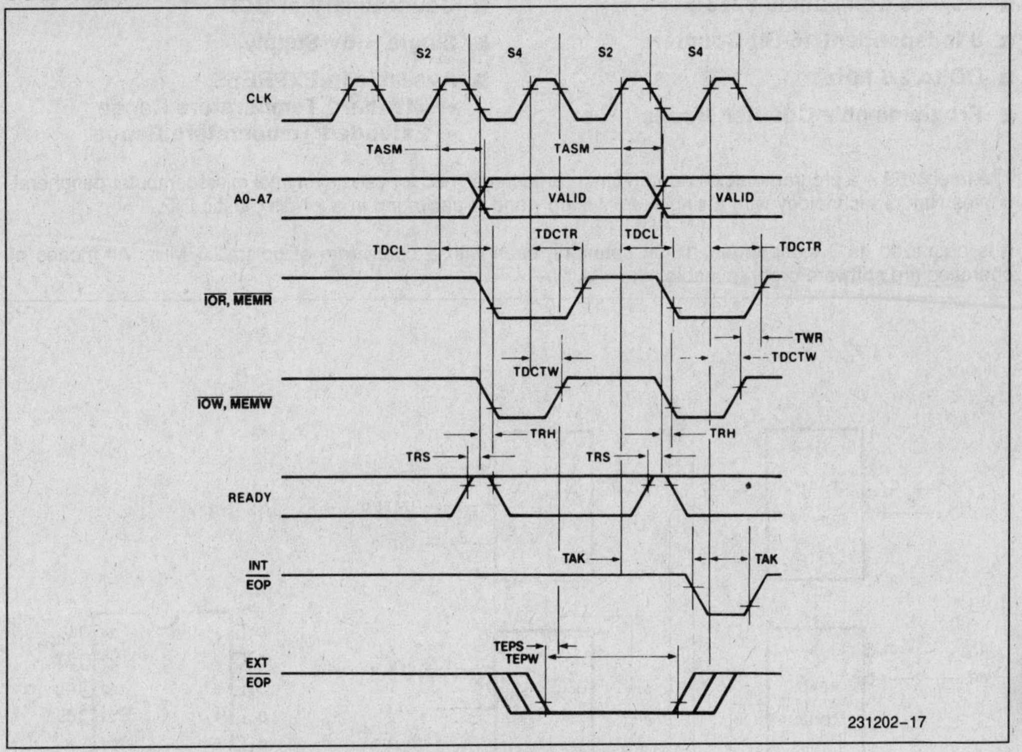

231202-17

Figure 14. Compressed Transfer

RESET TIMING

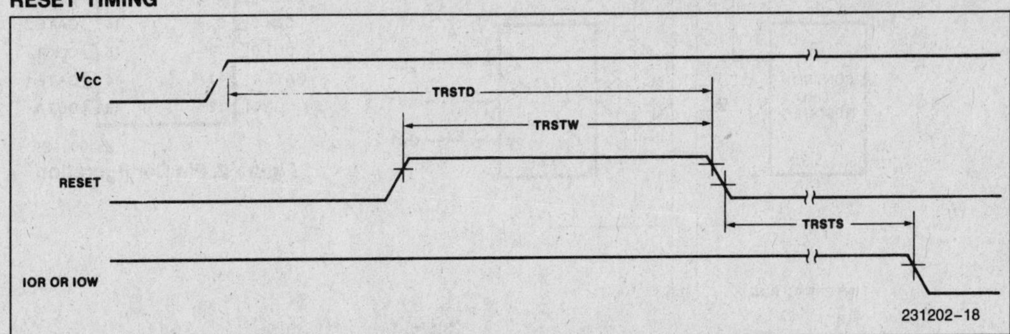

Figure 15. Reset

DATA SHEET REVISION REVIEW

The following list represents key differences between this and the -004 data sheet. Please review this summary carefully.

1. The "PRELIMINARY" markings have been removed from the data sheet. The 82C37A-5 is no longer a preliminary part.
2. A section of the Functional Description describing 82C37A-5 operation with the 8085 CPU has been deleted.

8253/8253-5 PROGRAMMABLE INTERVAL TIMER

- **MCS-85 Compatible 8253-5**
- **3 Independent 16-Bit Counters**
- **DC to 2.6 MHz**
- **Programmable Counter Modes**
- **Count Binary or BCD**
- **Single +5V Supply**
- **Available in EXPRESS**
  - **—Standard Temperature Range**
  - **—Extended Temperature Range**

The Intel 8253 is a programmable counter/timer device designed for use as an Intel microcomputer peripheral. It uses NMOS technology with a single +5V supply and is packaged in a 24-pin plastic DIP.

It is organized as 3 independent 16-bit counters, each with a count rate of up to 2.6 MHz. All modes of operation are software programmable.

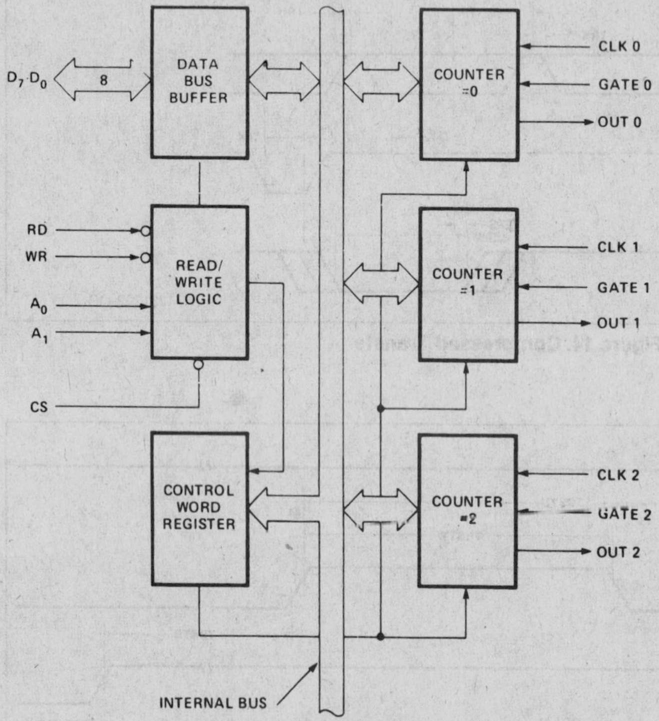

231306-1

Figure 1. Block Diagram

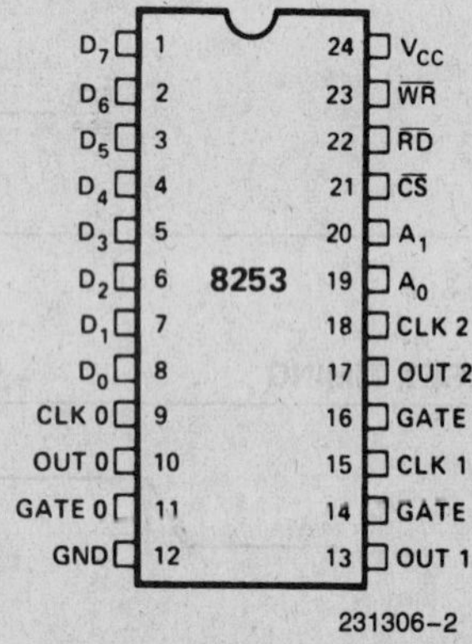

231306-2

Figure 2. Pin Configuration

The complete document for this product is available on Intel's "Data-on-Demand" CD-ROM system. To obtain a copy, contact your local Intel field sales office, Intel technical distributor or call 1-800-548-4725.

November 1986
Order Number: 231306-001

8254
PROGRAMMABLE INTERVAL TIMER

- **Compatible with All Intel and Most Other Microprocessors**
- **Handles Inputs from DC to 10 MHz**
  - **— 8 MHz 8254**
  - **— 10 MHz 8254-2**
- **Status Read-Back Command**
- **Six Programmable Counter Modes**
- **Three Independent 16-Bit Counters**
- **Binary or BCD Counting**
- **Single +5V Supply**
- **Available in EXPRESS**
  - **— Standard Temperature Range**

The Intel 8254 is a counter/timer device designed to solve the common timing control problems in microcomputer system design. It provides three independent 16-bit counters, each capable of handling clock inputs up to 10 MHz. All modes are software programmable. The 8254 is a superset of the 8253.

The 8254 uses HMOS technology and comes in a 24-pin plastic or CERDIP package.

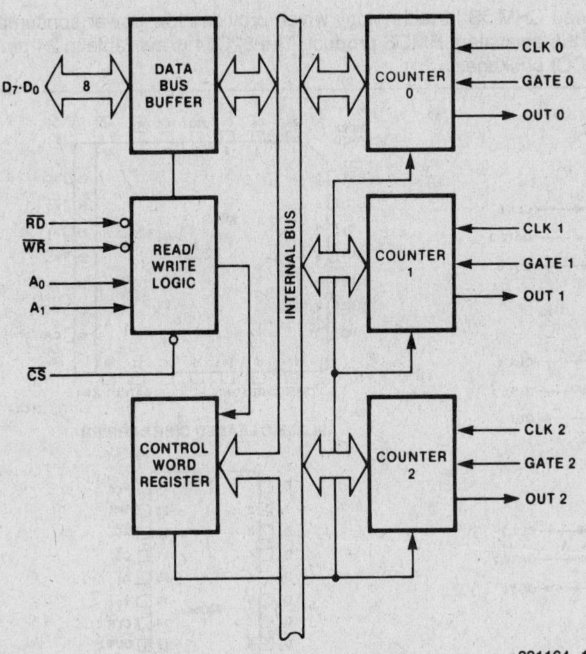

Figure 1. 8254 Block Diagram

Pin	Name	Pin	Name
1	D_7	24	V_{CC}
2	D_6	23	$\overline{WR}$
3	D_5	22	$\overline{RD}$
4	D_4	21	$\overline{CS}$
5	D_3	20	A_1
6	D_2	19	A_0
7	D_1	18	CLK 2
8	D_0	17	OUT 2
9	CLK 0	16	GATE 2
10	OUT 0	15	CLK 1
11	GATE 0	14	GATE 1
12	GND	13	OUT 1

8254

231164–2

Figure 2. Pin Configuration

The complete document for this product is available on Intel's "Data-on-Demand" CD-ROM system. To obtain a copy, contact your local Intel field sales office, Intel technical distributor or call 1-800-548-4725.

September 1993
Order Number: 231164-005

82C54
CHMOS PROGRAMMABLE INTERVAL TIMER

- **Compatible with all Intel and most other microprocessors**
- **High Speed, "Zero Wait State" Operation with 8 MHz 8086/88 and 80186/188**
- **Handles Inputs from DC — 10 MHz for 82C54-2**
- **Available in EXPRESS**
  - **— Standard Temperature Range**
  - **— Extended Temperature Range**
- **Three independent 16-bit counters**
- **Low Power CHMOS**
  - **— I_{CC} = 10 mA @ 8 MHz Count frequency**
- **Completely TTL Compatible**
- **Six Programmable Counter Modes**
- **Binary or BCD counting**
- **Status Read Back Command**
- **Available in 24-Pin DIP and 28-Pin PLCC**

The Intel 82C54 is a high-performance, CHMOS version of the industry standard 8254 counter/timer which is designed to solve the timing control problems common in microcomputer system design. It provides three independent 16-bit counters, each capable of handling clock inputs up to 10 MHz. All modes are software programmable. The 82C54 is pin compatible with the HMOS 8254, and is a superset of the 8253.

Six programmable timer modes allow the 82C54 to be used as an event counter, elapsed time indicator, programmable one-shot, and in many other applications.

The 82C54 is fabricated on Intel's advanced CHMOS III technology which provides low power consumption with performance equal to or greater than the equivalent HMOS product. The 82C54 is available in 24-pin DIP and 28-pin plastic leaded chip carrier (PLCC) packages.

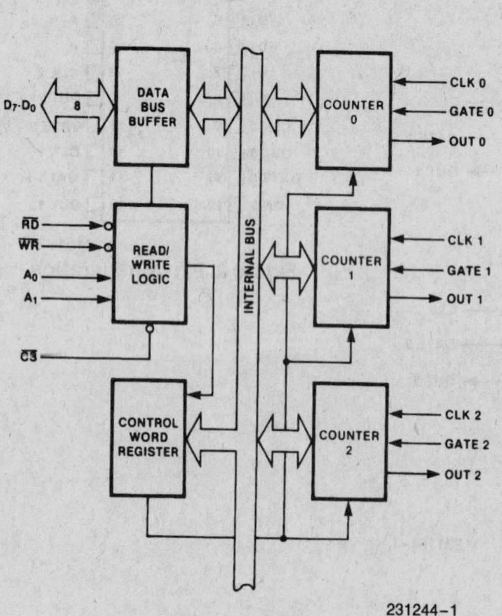

Figure 1. 82C54 Block Diagram

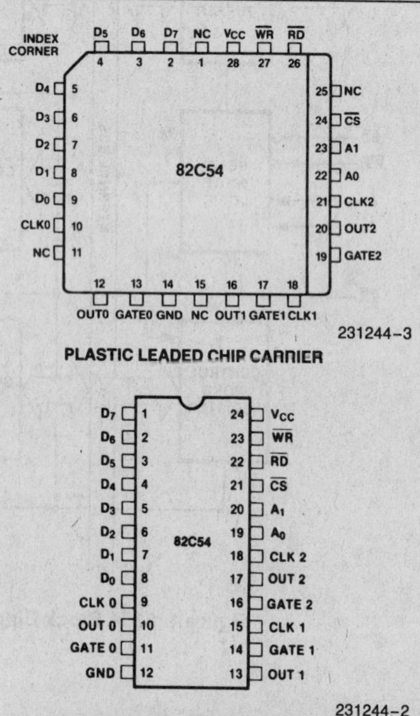

Figure 2. 82C54 Pinout

September 1993
Order Number: 231244-006

Table 1. Pin Description

Symbol	Pin Number		Type	Function
	DIP	PLCC		
D_7-D_0	1-8	2-9	I/O	Data: Bidirectional tri-state data bus lines, connected to system data bus.
CLK 0	9	10	I	Clock 0: Clock input of Counter 0.
OUT 0	10	12	O	Output 0: Output of Counter 0.
GATE 0	11	13	I	Gate 0: Gate input of Counter 0.
GND	12	14		Ground: Power supply connection.
OUT 1	13	16	O	Out 1: Output of Counter 1.
GATE 1	14	17	I	Gate 1: Gate input of Counter 1.
CLK 1	15	18	I	Clock 1: Clock input of Counter 1.
GATE 2	16	19	I	Gate 2: Gate input of Counter 2.
OUT 2	17	20	O	Out 2: Output of Counter 2.
CLK 2	18	21	I	Clock 2: Clock input of Counter 2.
A_1, A_0	20-19	23-22	I	Address: Used to select one of the three Counters or the Control Word Register for read or write operations. Normally connected to the system address bus. A_1 / A_0 / Selects: 0 0 Counter 0 0 1 Counter 1 1 0 Counter 2 1 1 Control Word Register
$\overline{CS}$	21	24	I	Chip Select: A low on this input enables the 82C54 to respond to $\overline{RD}$ and $\overline{WR}$ signals. $\overline{RD}$ and $\overline{WR}$ are ignored otherwise.
$\overline{RD}$	22	26	I	Read Control: This input is low during CPU read operations.
$\overline{WR}$	23	27	I	Write Control: This input is low during CPU write operations.
V_{CC}	24	28		Power: +5V power supply connection.
NC		1, 11, 15, 25		No Connect

FUNCTIONAL DESCRIPTION

General

The 82C54 is a programmable interval timer/counter designed for use with Intel microcomputer systems. It is a general purpose, multi-timing element that can be treated as an array of I/O ports in the system software.

The 82C54 solves one of the most common problems in any microcomputer system, the generation of accurate time delays under software control. Instead of setting up timing loops in software, the programmer configures the 82C54 to match his requirements and programs one of the counters for the desired delay. After the desired delay, the 82C54 will interrupt the CPU. Software overhead is minimal and variable length delays can easily be accommodated.

Some of the other counter/timer functions common to microcomputers which can be implemented with the 82C54 are:

- Real time clock
- Even counter
- Digital one-shot
- Programmable rate generator
- Square wave generator
- Binary rate multiplier
- Complex waveform generator
- Complex motor controller

Block Diagram

DATA BUS BUFFER

This 3-state, bi-directional, 8-bit buffer is used to interface the 82C54 to the system bus (see Figure 3).

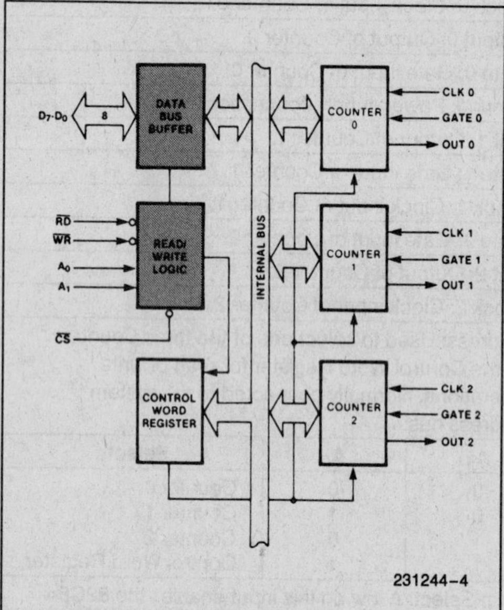

Figure 3. Block Diagram Showing Data Bus Buffer and Read/Write Logic Functions

READ/WRITE LOGIC

The Read/Write Logic accepts inputs from the system bus and generates control signals for the other functional blocks of the 82C54. A_1 and A_0 select one of the three counters or the Control Word Register to be read from/written into. A "low" on the $\overline{RD}$ input tells the 82C54 that the CPU is reading one of the counters. A "low" on the $\overline{WR}$ input tells the 82C54 that the CPU is writing either a Control Word or an initial count. Both $\overline{RD}$ and $\overline{WR}$ are qualified by $\overline{CS}$; $\overline{RD}$ and $\overline{WR}$ are ignored unless the 82C54 has been selected by holding $\overline{CS}$ low.

CONTROL WORD REGISTER

The Control Word Register (see Figure 4) is selected by the Read/Write Logic when $A_1, A_0 = 11$. If the CPU then does a write operation to the 82C54, the data is stored in the Control Word Register and is interpreted as a Control Word used to define the operation of the Counters.

The Control Word Register can only be written to; status information is available with the Read-Back Command.

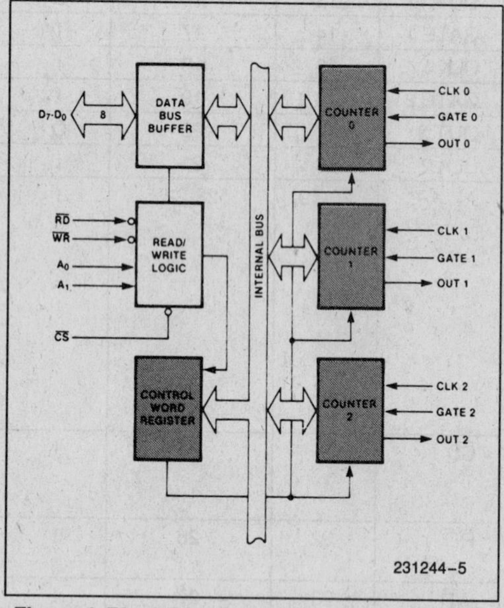

Figure 4. Block Diagram Showing Control Word Register and Counter Functions

COUNTER 0, COUNTER 1, COUNTER 2

These three functional blocks are identical in operation, so only a single Counter will be described. The internal block diagram of a single counter is shown in Figure 5.

The Counters are fully independent. Each Counter may operate in a different Mode.

The Control Word Register is shown in the figure; it is not part of the Counter itself, but its contents determine how the Counter operates.

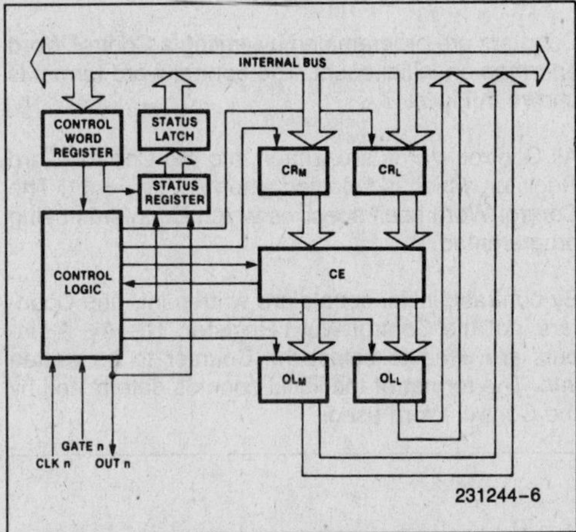

Figure 5. Internal Block Diagram of a Counter

The status register, shown in the Figure, when latched, contains the current contents of the Control Word Register and status of the output and null count flag. (See detailed explanation of the Read-Back command.)

The actual counter is labelled CE (for "Counting Element"). It is a 16-bit presettable synchronous down counter.

OL_M and OL_L are two 8-bit latches. OL stands for "Output Latch"; the subscripts M and L stand for "Most significant byte" and "Least significant byte" respectively. Both are normally referred to as one unit and called just OL. These latches normally "follow" the CE, but if a suitable Counter Latch Command is sent to the 82C54, the latches "latch" the present count until read by the CPU and then return to "following" the CE. One latch at a time is enabled by the counter's Control Logic to drive the internal bus. This is how the 16-bit Counter communicates over the 8-bit internal bus. Note that the CE itself cannot be read; whenever you read the count, it is the OL that is being read.

Similarly, there are two 8-bit registers called CR_M and CR_L (for "Count Register"). Both are normally referred to as one unit and called just CR. When a new count is written to the Counter, the count is stored in the CR and later transferred to the CE. The Control Logic allows one register at a time to be loaded from the internal bus. Both bytes are transferred to the CE simultaneously. CR_M and CR_L are cleared when the Counter is programmed. In this way, if the Counter has been programmed for one byte counts (either most significant byte only or least significant byte only) the other byte will be zero. Note that the CE cannot be written into; whenever a count is written, it is written into the CR.

The Control Logic is also shown in the diagram. CLK n, GATE n, and OUT n are all connected to the outside world through the Control Logic.

82C54 SYSTEM INTERFACE

The 82C54 is treated by the systems software as an array of peripheral I/O ports; three are counters and the fourth is a control register for MODE programming.

Basically, the select inputs A_0, A_1 connect to the A_0, A_1 address bus signals of the CPU. The $\overline{CS}$ can be derived directly from the address bus using a linear select method. Or it can be connected to the output of a decoder, such as an Intel 8205 for larger systems.

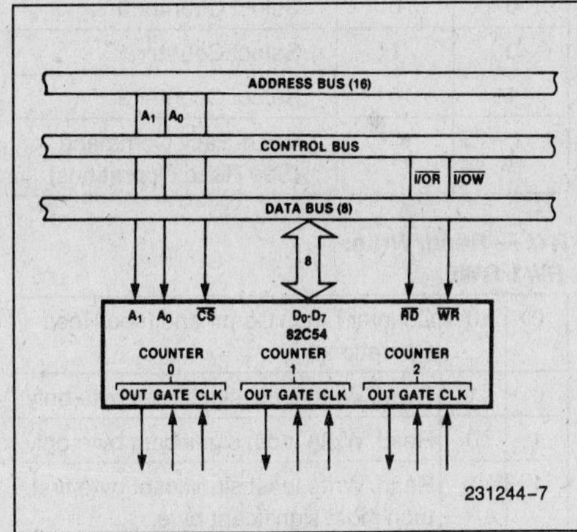

Figure 6. 82C54 System Interface

5

OPERATIONAL DESCRIPTION

General

After power-up, the state of the 82C54 is undefined. The Mode, count value, and output of all Counters are undefined.

How each Counter operates is determined when it is programmed. Each Counter must be programmed before it can be used. Unused counters need not be programmed.

Programming the 82C54

Counters are programmed by writing a Control Word and then an initial count. The control word format is shown in Figure 7.

All Control Words are written into the Control Word Register, which is selected when $A_1, A_0 = 11$. The Control Word itself specifies which Counter is being programmed.

By contrast, initial counts are written into the Counters, not the Control Word Register. The A_1, A_0 inputs are used to select the Counter to be written into. The format of the initial count is determined by the Control Word used.

Control Word Format

$A_1, A_0 = 11$ $\overline{CS} = 0$ $\overline{RD} = 1$ $\overline{WR} = 0$

D_7	D_6	D_5	D_4	D_3	D_2	D_1	D_0
SC1	SC0	RW1	RW0	M2	M1	M0	BCD

SC — Select Counter:

SC1	SC0	
0	0	Select Counter 0
0	1	Select Counter 1
1	0	Select Counter 2
1	1	Read-Back Command (See Read Operations)

RW — Read/Write:

RW1	RW0	
0	0	Counter Latch Command (see Read Operations)
0	1	Read/Write least significant byte only.
1	0	Read/Write most significant byte only.
1	1	Read/Write least significant byte first, then most significant byte.

M — MODE:

M2	M1	M0	
0	0	0	Mode 0
0	0	1	Mode 1
X	1	0	Mode 2
X	1	1	Mode 3
1	0	0	Mode 4
1	0	1	Mode 5

BCD:

0	Binary Counter 16-bits
1	Binary Coded Decimal (BCD) Counter (4 Decades)

NOTE: Don't care bits (X) should be 0 to insure compatibility with future Intel products.

Figure 7. Control Word Format

Write Operations

The programming procedure for the 82C54 is very flexible. Only two conventions need to be remembered:

1) For each Counter, the Control Word must be written before the initial count is written.
2) The initial count must follow the count format specified in the Control Word (least significant byte only, most significant byte only, or least significant byte and then most significant byte).

Since the Control Word Register and the three Counters have separate addresses (selected by the A_1, A_0 inputs), and each Control Word specifies the Counter it applies to (SC0, SC1 bits), no special instruction sequence is required. Any programming sequence that follows the conventions above is acceptable.

A new initial count may be written to a Counter at any time without affecting the Counter's programmed Mode in any way. Counting will be affected as described in the Mode definitions. The new count must follow the programmed count format.

If a Counter is programmed to read/write two-byte counts, the following precaution applies: A program must not transfer control between writing the first and second byte to another routine which also writes into that same Counter. Otherwise, the Counter will be loaded with an incorrect count.

		A_1	A_0
Control Word —	Counter 0	1	1
LSB of count —	Counter 0	0	0
MSB of count —	Counter 0	0	0
Control Word —	Counter 1	1	1
LSB of count —	Counter 1	0	1
MSB of count —	Counter 1	0	1
Control Word —	Counter 2	1	1
LSB of count —	Counter 2	1	0
MSB of count —	Counter 2	1	0

		A_1	A_0
Control Word —	Counter 2	1	1
Control Word —	Counter 1	1	1
Control Word —	Counter 0	1	1
LSB of count —	Counter 2	1	0
MSB of count —	Counter 2	1	0
LSB of count —	Counter 1	0	1
MSB of count —	Counter 1	0	1
LSB of count —	Counter 0	0	0
MSB of count —	Counter 0	0	0

		A_1	A_0
Control Word —	Counter 0	1	1
Counter Word —	Counter 1	1	1
Control Word —	Counter 2	1	1
LSB of count —	Counter 2	1	0
LSB of count —	Counter 1	0	1
LSB of count —	Counter 0	0	0
MSB of count —	Counter 0	0	0
MSB of count —	Counter 1	0	1
MSB of count —	Counter 2	1	0

		A_1	A_0
Control Word —	Counter 1	1	1
Control Word —	Counter 0	1	1
LSB of count —	Counter 1	0	1
Control Word —	Counter 2	1	1
LSB of count —	Counter 0	0	0
MSB of count —	Counter 1	0	1
LSB of count —	Counter 2	1	0
MSB of count —	Counter 0	0	0
MSB of count —	Counter 2	1	0

NOTE:
In all four examples, all counters are programmed to read/write two-byte counts.
These are only four of many possible programming sequences.

Figure 8. A Few Possible Programming Sequences

Read Operations

It is often desirable to read the value of a Counter without disturbing the count in progress. This is easily done in the 82C54.

There are three possible methods for reading the counters: a simple read operation, the Counter Latch Command, and the Read-Back Command. Each is explained below. The first method is to perform a simple read operation. To read the Counter, which is selected with the A1, A0 inputs, the CLK input of the selected Counter must be inhibited by using either the GATE input or external logic. Otherwise, the count may be in the process of changing when it is read, giving an undefined result.

5

COUNTER LATCH COMMAND

The second method uses the "Counter Latch Command". Like a Control Word, this command is written to the Control Word Register, which is selected when A_1, A_0 = 11. Also like a Control Word, the SC0, SC1 bits select one of the three Counters, but two other bits, D5 and D4, distinguish this command from a Control Word.

$A_1, A_0 = 11; \overline{CS} = 0; \overline{RD} = 1; \overline{WR} = 0$

D_7	D_6	D_5	D_4	D_3	D_2	D_1	D_0
SC1	SC0	0	0	X	X	X	X

SC1, SC0 - specify counter to be latched

SC1	SC0	Counter
0	0	0
0	1	1
1	0	2
1	1	Read-Back Command

D5,D4 - 00 designates Counter Latch Command

X - don't care

NOTE:
Don't care bits (X) should be 0 to insure compatibility with future Intel products.

Figure 9. Counter Latching Command Format

The selected Counter's output latch (OL) latches the count at the time the Counter Latch Command is received. This count is held in the latch until it is read by the CPU (or until the Counter is reprogrammed). The count is then unlatched automatically and the OL returns to "following" the counting element (CE). This allows reading the contents of the Counters "on the fly" without affecting counting in progress. Multiple Counter Latch Commands may be used to latch more than one Counter. Each latched Counter's OL holds its count until it is read. Counter Latch Commands do not affect the programmed Mode of the Counter in any way.

If a Counter is latched and then, some time later, latched again before the count is read, the second Counter Latch Command is ignored. The count read will be the count at the time the first Counter Latch Command was issued.

With either method, the count must be read according to the programmed format; specifically, if the Counter is programmed for two byte counts, two bytes must be read. The two bytes do not have to be read one right after the other; read or write or programming operations of other Counters may be inserted between them.

Another feature of the 82C54 is that reads and writes of the same Counter may be interleaved; for example, if the Counter is programmed for two byte counts, the following sequence is valid.

1. Read least significant byte.
2. Write new least significant byte.
3. Read most significant byte.
4. Write new most significant byte.

If a Counter is programmed to read/write two-byte counts, the following precaution applies; A program must not transfer control between reading the first and second byte to another routine which also reads from that same Counter. Otherwise, an incorrect count will be read.

READ-BACK COMMAND

The third method uses the Read-Back command. This command allows the user to check the count value, programmed Mode, and current state of the OUT pin and Null Count flag of the selected counter(s).

The command is written into the Control Word Register and has the format shown in Figure 10. The command applies to the counters selected by setting their corresponding bits D3,D2,D1 = 1.

A0, A1 = 11 $\overline{CS}$ = 0 $\overline{RD}$ = 1 $\overline{WR}$ = 0

D_7	D_6	D_5	D_4	D_3	D_2	D_1	D_0
1	1	$\overline{\text{COUNT}}$	$\overline{\text{STATUS}}$	CNT 2	CNT 1	CNT 0	0

D_5: 0 = Latch count of selected counter(s)
D_4: 0 = Latch status of selected counter(s)
D_3: 1 = Select counter 2
D_2: 1 = Select counter 1
D_1: 1 = Select counter 0
D_0: Reserved for future expansion; must be 0

Figure 10. Read-Back Command Format

The read-back command may be used to latch multiple counter output latches (OL) by setting the $\overline{\text{COUNT}}$ bit D5=0 and selecting the desired counter(s). This single command is functionally equivalent to several counter latch commands, one for each counter latched. Each counter's latched count is held until it is read (or the counter is reprogrammed). That counter is automatically unlatched when read, but other counters remain latched until they are read. If multiple count read-back commands are issued to the same counter without reading the count, all but the first are ignored; i.e., the count which will be read is the count at the time the first read-back command was issued.

The read-back command may also be used to latch status information of selected counter(s) by setting $\overline{\text{STATUS}}$ bit D4=0. Status must be latched to be read; status of a counter is accessed by a read from that counter.

The counter status format is shown in Figure 11. Bits D5 through D0 contain the counter's programmed Mode exactly as written in the last Mode Control Word. OUTPUT bit D7 contains the current state of the OUT pin. This allows the user to monitor the counter's output via software, possibly eliminating some hardware from a system.

D_7	D_6	D_5	D_4	D_3	D_2	D_1	D_0
OUTPUT	NULL COUNT	RW1	RW0	M2	M1	M0	BCD

D_7 1 = Out Pin is 1
0 = Out Pin is 0
D_6 1 = Null count
0 = Count available for reading
D_5-D_0 Counter Programmed Mode (See Figure 7)

Figure 11. Status Byte

NULL COUNT bit D6 indicates when the last count written to the counter register (CR) has been loaded into the counting element (CE). The exact time this happens depends on the Mode of the counter and is described in the Mode Definitions, but until the count is loaded into the counting element (CE), it can't be read from the counter. If the count is latched or read before this time, the count value will not reflect the new count just written. The operation of Null Count is shown in Figure 12.

THIS ACTION:	CAUSES:
A. Write to the control word register:[1]	Null count = 1
B. Write to the count register (CR);[2]	Null count = 1
C. New count is loaded into CE (CR → CE);	Null count = 0

[1] Only the counter specified by the control word will have its null count set to 1. Null count bits of other counters are unaffected.

[2] If the counter is programmed for two-byte counts (least significant byte then most significant byte) null count goes to 1 when the second byte is written.

Figure 12. Null Count Operation

If multiple status latch operations of the counter(s) are performed without reading the status, all but the first are ignored; i.e., the status that will be read is the status of the counter at the time the first status read-back command was issued.

Both count and status of the selected counter(s) may be latched simultaneously by setting both $\overline{\text{COUNT}}$ and $\overline{\text{STATUS}}$ bits D5,D4=0. This is functionally the same as issuing two separate read-back commands at once, and the above discussions apply here also. Specifically, if multiple count and/or status read-back commands are issued to the same counter(s) without any intervening reads, all but the first are ignored. This is illustrated in Figure 13.

If both count and status of a counter are latched, the first read operation of that counter will return latched status, regardless of which was latched first. The next one or two reads (depending on whether the counter is programmed for one or two type counts) return latched count. Subsequent reads return unlatched count.

D_7	D_6	D_5	D_4	D_3	D_2	D_1	D_0	Description	Results
1	1	0	0	0	0	1	0	Read back count and status of Counter 0	Count and status latched for Counter 0
1	1	1	0	0	1	0	0	Read back status of Counter 1	Status latched for Counter 1
1	1	1	0	1	1	0	0	Read back status of Counters 2, 1	Status latched for Counter 2, but not Counter 1
1	1	0	1	1	0	0	0	Read back count of Counter 2	Count latched for Counter 2
1	1	0	0	0	1	0	0	Read back count and status of Counter 1	Count latched for Counter 1, but not status
1	1	1	0	0	0	1	0	Read back status of Counter 1	Command ignored, status already latched for Counter 1

Figure 13. Read-Back Command Example

$\overline{CS}$	$\overline{RD}$	$\overline{WR}$	A_1	A_0	
0	1	0	0	0	Write into Counter 0
0	1	0	0	1	Write into Counter 1
0	1	0	1	0	Write into Counter 2
0	1	0	1	1	Write Control Word
0	0	1	0	0	Read from Counter 0
0	0	1	0	1	Read from Counter 1
0	0	1	1	0	Read from Counter 2
0	0	1	1	1	No-Operation (3-State)
1	X	X	X	X	No-Operation (3-State)
0	1	1	X	X	No-Operation (3-State)

Figure 14. Read/Write Operations Summary

Mode Definitions

The following are defined for use in describing the operation of the 82C54.

CLK PULSE: a rising edge, then a falling edge, in that order, of a Counter's CLK input.

TRIGGER: a rising edge of a Counter's GATE input.

COUNTER LOADING: the transfer of a count from the CR to the CE (refer to the "Functional Description")

MODE 0: INTERRUPT ON TERMINAL COUNT

Mode 0 is typically used for event counting. After the Control Word is written, OUT is initially low, and will remain low until the Counter reaches zero. OUT then goes high and remains high until a new count or a new Mode 0 Control Word is written into the Counter.

GATE = 1 enables counting; GATE = 0 disables counting. GATE has no effect on OUT.

After the Control Word and initial count are written to a Counter, the initial count will be loaded on the next CLK pulse. This CLK pulse does not decrement the count, so for an initial count of N, OUT does not go high until N + 1 CLK pulses after the initial count is written.

If a new count is written to the Counter, it will be loaded on the next CLK pulse and counting will continue from the new count. If a two-byte count is written, the following happens:

1) Writing the first byte does not disable counting. OUT is set low immediately (no clock pulse required).
2) Writing the second byte allows the new count to be loaded on the next CLK pulse.

This allows the counting sequence to be synchronized by software. Again, OUT does not go high until N + 1 CLK pulses after the new count of N is written.

If an initial count is written while GATE = 0, it will still be loaded on the next CLK pulse. When GATE goes high, OUT will go high N CLK pulses later; no CLK pulse is needed to load the Counter as this has already been done.

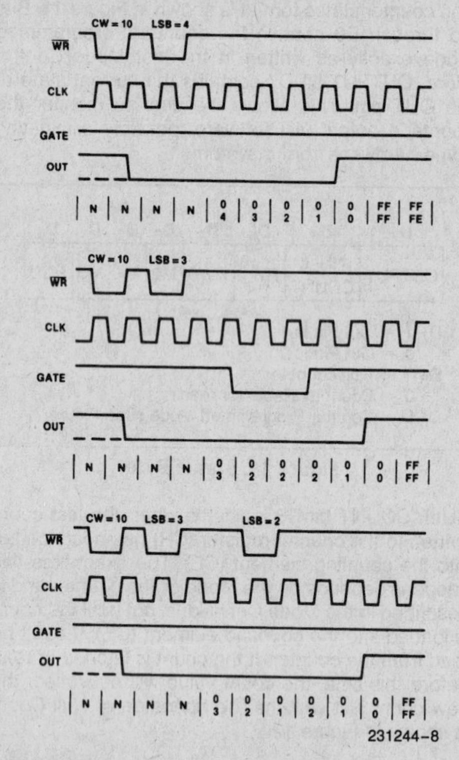

NOTE:
The Following Conventions Apply To All Mode Timing Diagrams:
1. Counters are programmed for binary (not BCD) counting and for Reading/Writing least significant byte (LSB) only.
2. The counter is always selected ($\overline{CS}$ always low).
3. CW stands for "Control Word"; CW = 10 means a control word of 10, hex is written to the counter.
4. LSB stands for "Least Significant Byte" of count.
5. Numbers below diagrams are count values.
The lower number is the least significant byte.
The upper number is the most significant byte. Since the counter is programmed to Read/Write LSB only, the most significant byte cannot be read.
N stands for an undefined count.
Vertical lines show transitions between count values.

Figure 15. Mode 0

MODE 1: HARDWARE RETRIGGERABLE ONE-SHOT

OUT will be initially high. OUT will go low on the CLK pulse following a trigger to begin the one-shot pulse, and will remain low until the Counter reaches zero. OUT will then go high and remain high until the CLK pulse after the next trigger.

After writing the Control Word and initial count, the Counter is armed. A trigger results in loading the Counter and setting OUT low on the next CLK pulse, thus starting the one-shot pulse. An initial count of N will result in a one-shot pulse N CLK cycles in duration. The one-shot is retriggerable, hence OUT will remain low for N CLK pulses after any trigger. The one-shot pulse can be repeated without rewriting the same count into the counter. GATE has no effect on OUT.

If a new count is written to the Counter during a one-shot pulse, the current one-shot is not affected unless the Counter is retriggered. In that case, the Counter is loaded with the new count and the one-shot pulse continues until the new count expires.

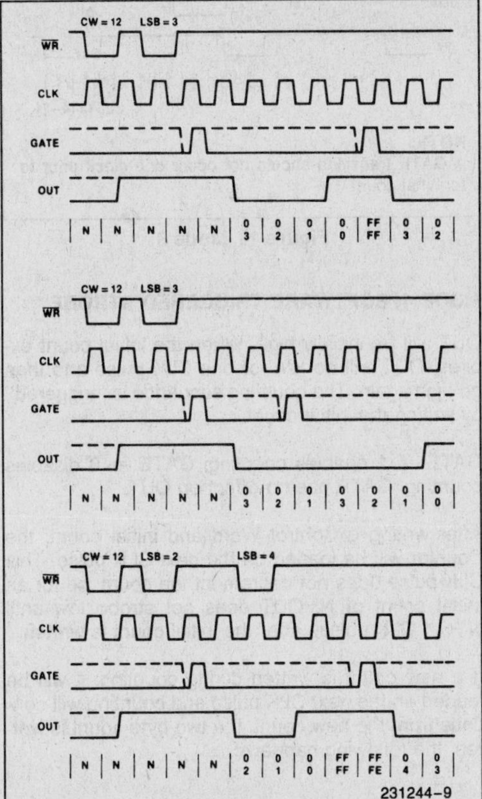

Figure 16. Mode 1

MODE 2: RATE GENERATOR

This Mode functions like a divide-by-N counter. It is typicially used to generate a Real Time Clock interrupt. OUT will initially be high. When the initial count has decremented to 1, OUT goes low for one CLK pulse. OUT then goes high again, the Counter reloads the initial count and the process is repeated. Mode 2 is periodic; the same sequence is repeated indefinitely. For an initial count of N, the sequence repeats every N CLK cycles.

GATE = 1 enables counting; GATE = 0 disables counting. If GATE goes low during an output pulse, OUT is set high immediately. A trigger reloads the Counter with the initial count on the next CLK pulse; OUT goes low N CLK pulses after the trigger. Thus the GATE input can be used to synchronize the Counter.

After writing a Control Word and initial count, the Counter will be loaded on the next CLK pulse. OUT goes low N CLK Pulses after the initial count is written. This allows the Counter to be synchronized by software also.

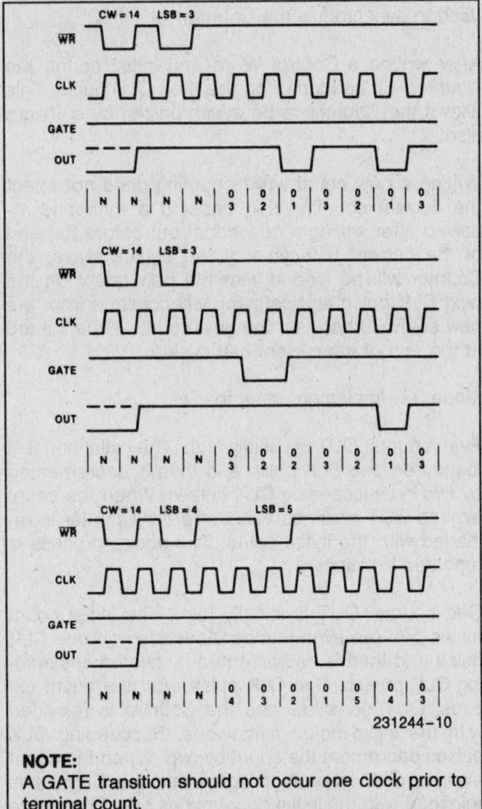

Figure 17. Mode 2

5

Writing a new count while counting does not affect the current counting sequence. If a trigger is received after writing a new count but before the end of the current period, the Counter will be loaded with the new count on the next CLK pulse and counting will continue from the new count. Otherwise, the new count will be loaded at the end of the current counting cycle. In mode 2, a COUNT of 1 is illegal.

MODE 3: SQUARE WAVE MODE

Mode 3 is typically used for Baud rate generation. Mode 3 is similar to Mode 2 except for the duty cycle of OUT. OUT will initially be high. When half the initial count has expired, OUT goes low for the remainder of the count. Mode 3 is periodic; the sequence above is repeated indefinitely. An initial count of N results in a square wave with a period of N CLK cycles.

GATE = 1 enables counting; GATE = 0 disables counting. If GATE goes low while OUT is low, OUT is set high immediately; no CLK pulse is required. A trigger reloads the Counter with the initial count on the next CLK pulse. Thus the GATE input can be used to synchronize the Counter.

After writing a Control Word and initial count, the Counter will be loaded on the next CLK pulse. This allows the Counter to be synchronized by software also.

Writing a new count while counting does not affect the current counting sequence. If a trigger is received after writing a new count but before the end of the current half-cycle of the square wave, the Counter will be loaded with the new count on the next CLK pulse and counting will continue from the new count. Otherwise, the new count will be loaded at the end of the current half-cycle.

Mode 3 is implemented as follows:

Even counts: OUT is initially high. The initial count is loaded on one CLK pulse and then is decremented by two on succeeding CLK pulses. When the count expires OUT changes value and the Counter is reloaded with the initial count. The above process is repeated indefinitely.

Odd counts: OUT is initially high. The initial count minus one (an even number) is loaded on one CLK pulse and then is decremented by two on succeeding CLK pulses. One CLK pulse *after* the count expires, OUT goes low and the Counter is reloaded with the initial count minus one. Succeeding CLK pulses decrement the count by two. When the count expires, OUT goes high again and the Counter is reloaded with the initial count minus one. The above process is repeated indefinitely. So for odd counts, OUT will be high for (N + 1)/2 counts and low for (N − 1)/2 counts.

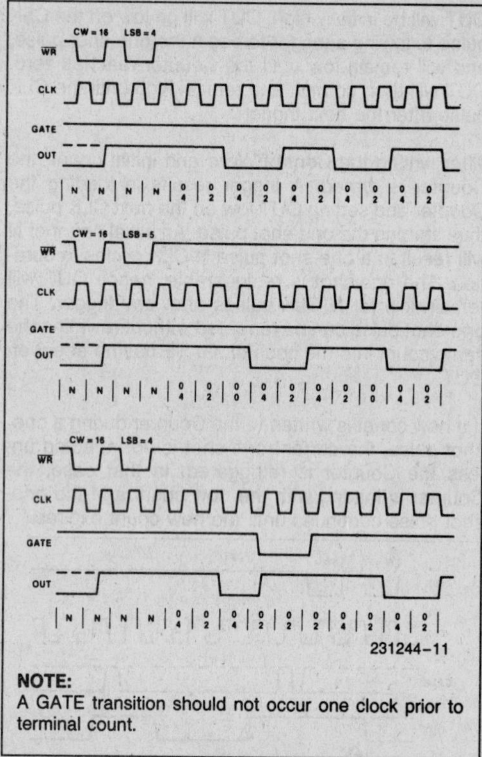

NOTE:
A GATE transition should not occur one clock prior to terminal count.

Figure 18. Mode 3

MODE 4: SOFTWARE TRIGGERED STROBE

OUT will be initially high. When the initial count expires, OUT will go low for one CLK pulse and then go high again. The counting sequence is "triggered" by writing the initial count.

GATE = 1 enables counting; GATE = 0 disables counting. GATE has no effect on OUT.

After writing a Control Word and initial count, the Counter will be loaded on the next CLK pulse. This CLK pulse does not decrement the count, so for an initial count of N, OUT does not strobe low until N + 1 CLK pulses after the initial count is written.

If a new count is written during counting, it will be loaded on the next CLK pulse and counting will continue from the new count. If a two-byte count is written, the following happens:

1) Writing the first byte has no effect on counting.
2) Writing the second byte allows the new count to be loaded on the next CLK pulse.

This allows the sequence to be "retriggered" by software. OUT strobes low N+1 CLK pulses after the new count of N is written.

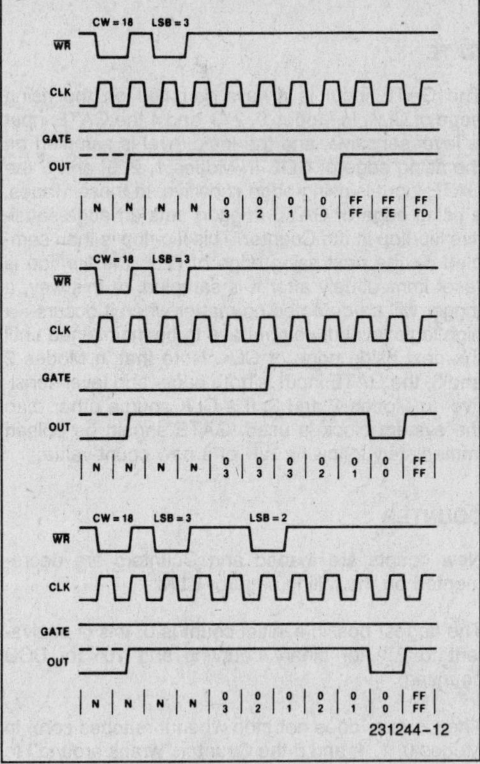

Figure 19. Mode 4

MODE 5: HARDWARE TRIGGERED STROBE (RETRIGGERABLE)

OUT will initially be high. Counting is triggered by a rising edge of GATE. When the initial count has expired, OUT will go low for one CLK pulse and then go high again.

After writing the Control Word and initial count, the counter will not be loaded until the CLK pulse after a trigger. This CLK pulse does not decrement the count, so for an initial count of N, OUT does not strobe low until N+1 CLK pulses after a trigger.

A trigger results in the Counter being loaded with the initial count on the next CLK pulse. The counting sequence is retriggerable. OUT will not strobe low for N + 1 CLK pulses after any trigger. GATE has no effect on OUT.

If a new count is written during counting, the current counting sequence will not be affected. If a trigger occurs after the new count is written but before the current count expires, the Counter will be loaded with the new count on the next CLK pulse and counting will continue from there.

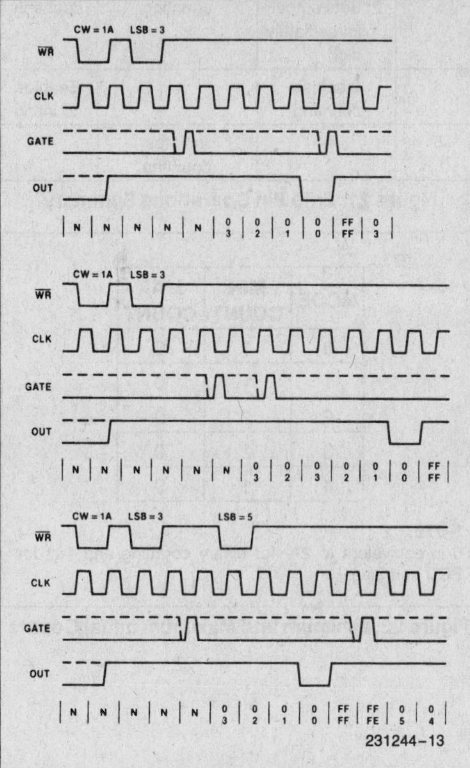

Figure 20. Mode 5

Signal Status Modes	Low Or Going Low	Rising	High
0	Disables counting	—	Enables counting
1	—	1) Initiates counting 2) Resets output after next clock	—
2	1) Disables counting 2) Sets output immediately high	Initiates counting	Enables counting
3	1) Disables counting 2) Sets output immediately high	Initiates counting	Enables counting
4	Disables counting	—	Enables counting
5	—	Initiates counting	—

Figure 21. Gate Pin Operations Summary

MODE	MIN COUNT	MAX COUNT
0	1	0
1	1	0
2	2	0
3	2	0
4	1	0

NOTE:
0 is equivalent to 2^{16} for binary counting and 10^4 for BCD counting

Figure 22. Minimum and Maximum initial Counts

Operation Common to All Modes

Programming

When a Control Word is written to a Counter, all Control Logic is immediately reset and OUT goes to a known initial state; no CLK pulses are required for this.

GATE

The GATE input is always sampled on the rising edge of CLK. In Modes 0, 2, 3, and 4 the GATE input is level sensitive, and the logic level is sampled on the rising edge of CLK. In Modes 1, 2, 3, and 5 the GATE input is rising-edge sensitive. In these Modes, a rising edge of GATE (trigger) sets an edge-sensitive flip-flop in the Counter. This flip-flop is then sampled on the next rising edge of CLK; the flip-flop is reset immediately after it is sampled. In this way, a trigger will be detected no matter when it occurs—a high logic level does not have to be maintained until the next rising edge of CLK. Note that in Modes 2 and 3, the GATE input is both edge- and level-sensitive. In Modes 2 and 3, if a CLK source other than the system clock is used, GATE should be pulsed immediately following $\overline{WR}$ of a new count value.

COUNTER

New counts are loaded and Counters are decremented on the falling edge of CLK.

The largest possible initial count is 0; this is equivalent to 2^{16} for binary counting and 10^4 for BCD counting.

The Counter does not stop when it reaches zero. In Modes 0, 1, 4, and 5 the Counter "wraps around" to the highest count, either FFFF hex for binary counting or 9999 for BCD counting, and continues counting. Modes 2 and 3 are periodic; the Counter reloads itself with the initial count and continues counting from there.

ABSOLUTE MAXIMUM RATINGS*

Ambient Temperature Under Bias....... 0°C to 70°C
Storage Temperature .... −65° to +150°C
Supply Voltage .... −0.5 to +8.0V
Operating Voltage .... +4V to +7V
Voltage on any Input.......... GND −2V to +6.5V
Voltage on any Output .. GND −0.5V to V_{CC} + 0.5V
Power Dissipation .... 1 Watt

NOTICE: This is a production data sheet. The specifications are subject to change without notice.

**WARNING: Stressing the device beyond the "Absolute Maximum Ratings" may cause permanent damage. These are stress ratings only. Operation beyond the "Operating Conditions" is not recommended and extended exposure beyond the "Operating Conditions" may affect device reliability.*

D.C. CHARACTERISTICS

(T_A = 0°C to 70°C, V_{CC} = 5V ± 10%, GND = 0V) (T_A = −40°C to +85°C for Extended Temperature)

Symbol	Parameter	Min	Max	Units	Test Conditions
V_{IL}	Input Low Voltage	−0.5	0.8	V	
V_{IH}	Input High Voltage	2.0	V_{CC} + 0.5	V	
V_{OL}	Output Low Voltage		0.4	V	I_{OL} = 2.5 mA
V_{OH}	Output High Voltage	3.0 V_{CC} − 0.4		V V	I_{OH} = −2.5 mA I_{OH} = −100 μA
I_{IL}	Input Load Current		±2.0	μA	V_{IN} = V_{CC} to 0V
I_{OFL}	Output Float Leakage Current		±10	μA	V_{OUT} = V_{CC} to 0.0V
I_{CC}	V_{CC} Supply Current		20	mA	Clk Freq = 8MHz 82C54 10MHz 82C54-2
I_{CCSB}	V_{CC} Supply Current-Standby		10	μA	CLK Freq = DC $\overline{CS}$ = V_{CC}. All Inputs/Data Bus V_{CC} All Outputs Floating
I_{CCSB1}	V_{CC} Supply Current-Standby		150	μA	CLK Freq = DC $\overline{CS}$ = V_{CC}. All Other Inputs, I/O Pins = V_{GND}, Outputs Open
C_{IN}	Input Capacitance		10	pF	f_c = 1 MHz
$C_{I/O}$	I/O Capacitance		20	pF	Unmeasured pins returned to GND(5)
C_{OUT}	Output Capacitance		20	pF	

5

A.C. CHARACTERISTICS

(T_A = 0°C to 70°C, V_{CC} = 5V ±10%, GND = 0V) (T_A = −40°C to +85°C for Extended Temperature)

BUS PARAMETERS (Note 1)

READ CYCLE

Symbol	Parameter	82C54-2		Units
		Min	Max	
t_{AR}	Address Stable Before $\overline{RD}$ ↓	30		ns
t_{SR}	$\overline{CS}$ Stable Before $\overline{RD}$ ↓	0		ns
t_{RA}	Address Hold Time After $\overline{RD}$ ↑	0		ns
t_{RR}	$\overline{RD}$ Pulse Width	95		ns
t_{RD}	Data Delay from $\overline{RD}$ ↓		85	ns
t_{AD}	Data Delay from Address		185	ns
t_{DF}	$\overline{RD}$ ↑ to Data Floating	5	65	ns
t_{RV}	Command Recovery Time	165		ns

NOTE:
1. AC timings measured at V_{OH} = 2.0V, V_{OL} = 0.8V.

A.C. CHARACTERISTICS (Continued)

WRITE CYCLE

Symbol	Parameter	82C54-2		Units
		Min	Max	
t_{AW}	Address Stable Before $\overline{WR}$ ↓	0		ns
t_{SW}	$\overline{CS}$ Stable Before $\overline{WR}$ ↓	0		ns
t_{WA}	Address Hold Time After $\overline{WR}$ ↑	0		ns
t_{WW}	$\overline{WR}$ Pulse Width	95		ns
t_{DW}	Data Setup Time Before $\overline{WR}$ ↑	95		ns
t_{WD}	Data Hold Time After $\overline{WR}$ ↑	0		ns
t_{RV}	Command Recovery Time	165		ns

CLOCK AND GATE

Symbol	Parameter	82C54-2		Units
		Min	Max	
t_{CLK}	Clock Period	100	DC	ns
t_{PWH}	High Pulse Width	30(3)		ns
t_{PWL}	Low Pulse Width	50(3)		ns
T_R	Clock Rise Time		25	ns
t_F	Clock Fall Time		25	ns
t_{GW}	Gate Width High	50		ns
t_{GL}	Gate Width Low	50		ns
t_{GS}	Gate Setup Time to CLK ↑	40		ns
t_{GH}	Gate Hold Time After CLK ↑	50(2)		ns
T_{OD}	Output Delay from CLK ↓		100	ns
t_{ODG}	Output Delay from Gate ↓		100	ns
t_{WC}	CLK Delay for Loading(4)	0	55	ns
t_{WG}	Gate Delay for Sampling(4)	−5	40	ns
t_{WO}	OUT Delay from Mode Write		240	ns
t_{CL}	CLK Set Up for Count Latch	−40	40	ns

NOTES:

2. In Modes 1 and 5 triggers are sampled on each rising clock edge. A second trigger within 70 ns for the 82C54-2 of the rising clock edge may not be detected.
3. Low-going glitches that violate t_{PWH}, t_{PWL} may cause errors requiring counter reprogramming.
4. Except for Extended Temp., See Extended Temp. A.C. Characteristics below.
5. Sampled not 100% tested. $T_A = 25°C$.
6. If CLK present at T_{WC} min then Count equals N+2 CLK pulses, T_{WC} max equals Count N+1 CLK pulse. T_{WC} min to T_{WC} max, count will be either N+1 or N+2 CLK pulses.
7. In Modes 1 and 5, if GATE is present when writing a new Count value, at T_{WG} min Counter will not be triggered, at T_{WG} max Counter will be triggered.
8. If CLK present when writing a Counter Latch or ReadBack Command, at T_{CL} min CLK will be reflected in count value latched, at T_{CL} max CLK will not be reflected in the count value latched. Writing a Counter Latch or ReadBack Command between T_{CL} min and T_{WL} max will result in a latched count vallue which is ± one least significant bit.

EXTENDED TEMPERATURE (T_A = −40°C to +85°C for Extended Temperature)

Symbol	Parameter	82C54-2		Units
		Min	Max	
t_{WC}	CLK Delay for Loading	−25	25	ns
t_{WG}	Gate Delay for Sampling	−25	25	ns

WAVEFORMS

WRITE

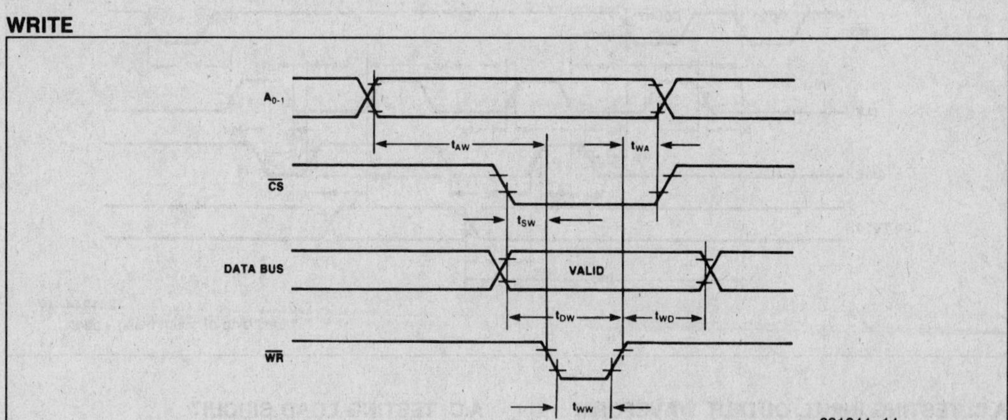

231244-14

READ

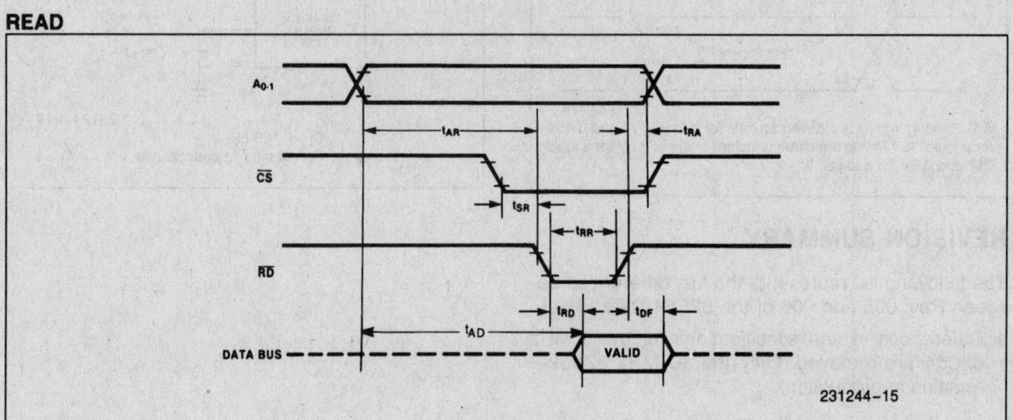

231244-15

RECOVERY

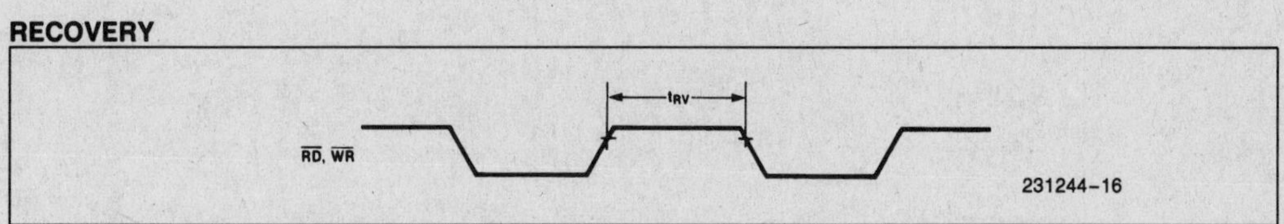

231244-16

5

CLOCK AND GATE

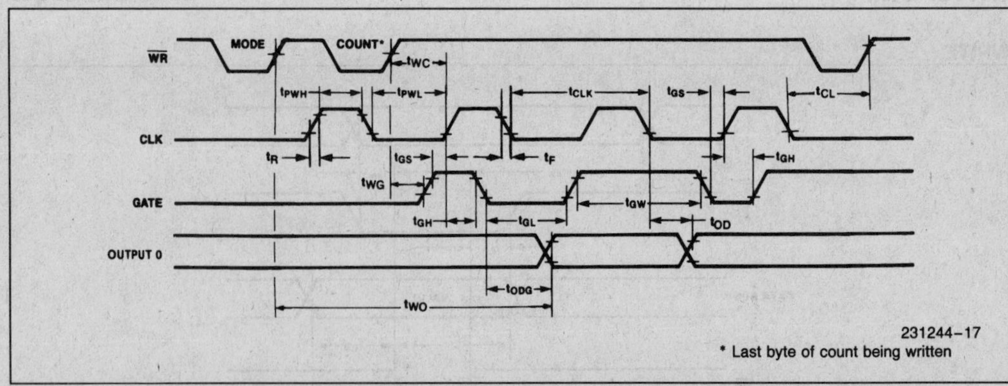

231244–17

* Last byte of count being written

A.C. TESTING INPUT, OUTPUT WAVEFORM

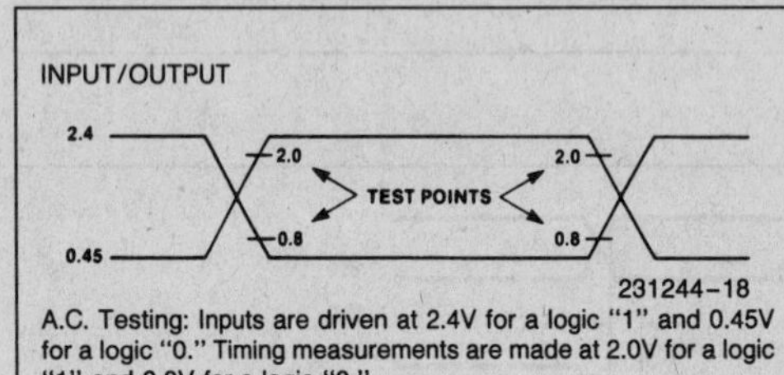

231244–18

A.C. Testing: Inputs are driven at 2.4V for a logic "1" and 0.45V for a logic "0." Timing measurements are made at 2.0V for a logic "1" and 0.8V for a logic "0."

A.C. TESTING LOAD CIRCUIT

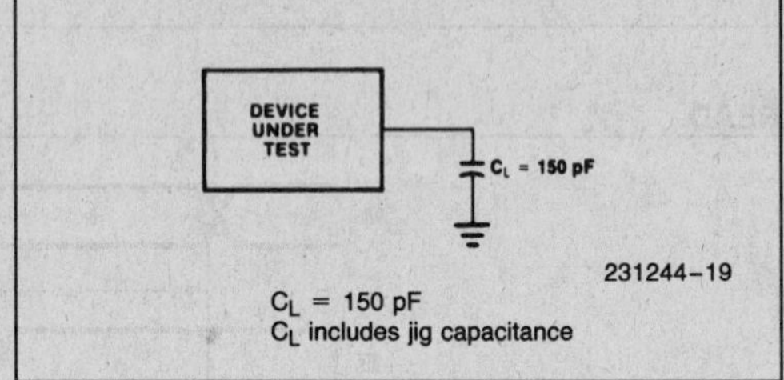

231244–19

C_L = 150 pF
C_L includes jig capacitance

REVISION SUMMARY

The following list represents the key differences between Rev. 005 and 006 of the 82C54 Data Sheet.

1. References to and specifications for the 8 MHz 82C54 are removed. Only the 10 MHz 82C52-2 remains in production.

8255A-5
PROGRAMMABLE PERIPHERAL INTERFACE

- **MCS-85 Compatible 8255A-5**
- **24 Programmable I/O Pins**
- **Completely TTL Compatible**
- **Fully Compatible with Intel Microprocessor Families**
- **Improved Timing Characteristics**
- **Direct Bit Set/Reset Capability Easing Control Application Interface**
- **Reduces System Package Count**
- **Improved DC Driving Capability**
- **Available in EXPRESS**
  - **—Standard Temperature Range**
  - **—Extended Temperature Range**
- **40 Pin DIP Package**
  (See Intel Packaging: Order Number: 240800-001, Package Type P)

The Intel 8255A is a general purpose programmable I/O device designed for use with Intel microprocessors. It has 24 I/O pins which may be individually programmed in 2 groups of 12 and used in 3 major modes of operation. In the first mode (MODE 0), each group of 12 I/O pins may be programmed in sets of 4 to be input or output. In MODE 1, the second mode, each group may be programmed to have 8 lines of input or output. Of the remaining 4 pins, 3 are used for handshaking and interrupt control signals. The third mode of operation (MODE 2) is a bidirectional bus mode which uses 8 lines for a bidirectional bus, and 5 lines, borrowing one from the other group, for handshaking.

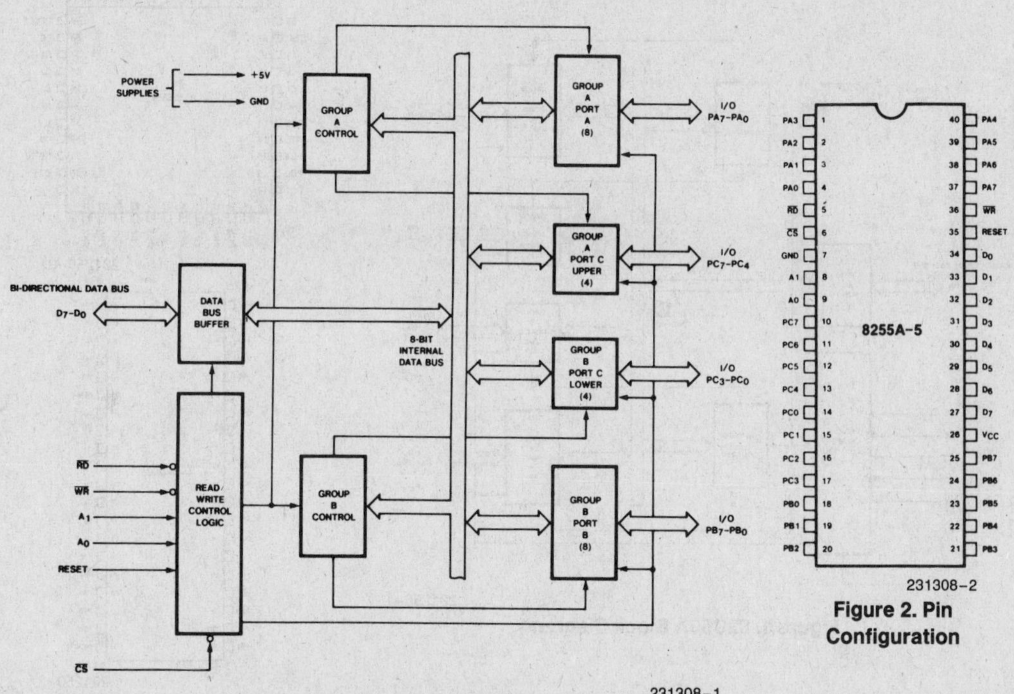

231308–1

Figure 1. 8255A Block Diagram

231308–2

Figure 2. Pin Configuration

The complete document for this product is available on Intel's "Data-on-Demand" CD-ROM system. To obtain a copy, contact your local Intel field sales office, Intel technical distributor or call 1-800-548-4725.

September 1993
Order Number: 231308-004

intel®

82C55A
CHMOS PROGRAMMABLE PERIPHERAL INTERFACE

- **Compatible with all Intel and Most Other Microprocessors**
- **High Speed, "Zero Wait State" Operation with 8 MHz 8086/88 and 80186/188**
- **24 Programmable I/O Pins**
- **Low Power CHMOS**
- **Completely TTL Compatible**
- **Control Word Read-Back Capability**
- **Direct Bit Set/Reset Capability**
- **2.5 mA DC Drive Capability on all I/O Port Outputs**
- **Available in 40-Pin DIP and 44-Pin PLCC**
- **Available in EXPRESS**
  - **—Standard Temperature Range**
  - **—Extended Temperature Range**

The Intel 82C55A is a high-performance, CHMOS version of the industry standard 8255A general purpose programmable I/O device which is designed for use with all Intel and most other microprocessors. It provides 24 I/O pins which may be individually programmed in 2 groups of 12 and used in 3 major modes of operation. The 82C55A is pin compatible with the NMOS 8255A and 8255A-5.

In MODE 0, each group of 12 I/O pins may be programmed in sets of 4 and 8 to be inputs or outputs. In MODE 1, each group may be programmed to have 8 lines of input or output. 3 of the remaining 4 pins are used for handshaking and interrupt control signals. MODE 2 is a strobed bi-directional bus configuration.

The 82C55A is fabricated on Intel's advanced CHMOS III technology which provides low power consumption with performance equal to or greater than the equivalent NMOS product. The 82C55A is available in 40-pin DIP and 44-pin plastic leaded chip carrier (PLCC) packages.

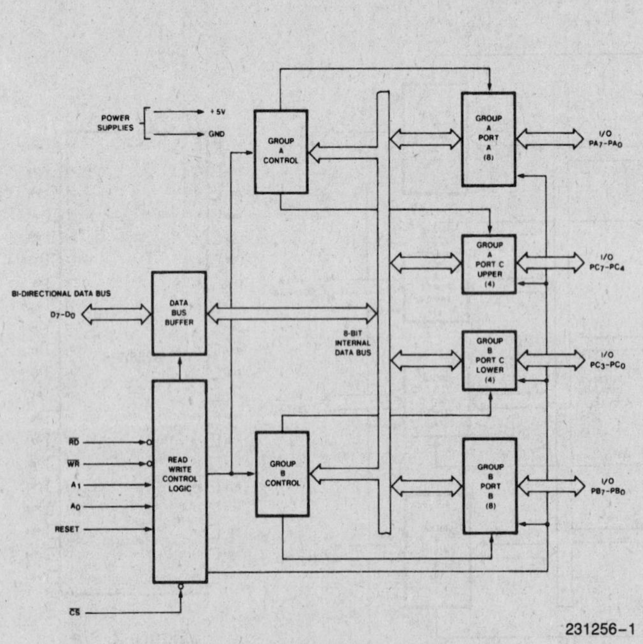

Figure 1. 82C55A Block Diagram

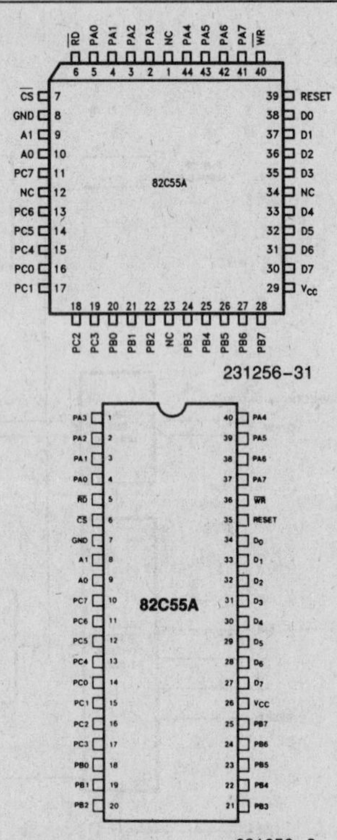

Figure 2. 82C55A Pinout

Diagrams are for pin reference only. Package sizes are not to scale.

The complete document for this product is available on Intel's "Data-on-Demand" CD-ROM system. To obtain a copy, contact your local Intel field sales office, Intel technical distributor or call 1-800-548-4725.

September 1987
Order Number: 231256-004

8256AH
MULTIFUNCTION MICROPROCESSOR SUPPORT CONTROLLER

- **Programmable Serial Asynchronous Communications Interface for 5-, 6-, 7-, or 8-Bit Characters, 1, 1½, or 2 Stop Bits, and Parity Generation**
- **On-Board Baud Rate Generator Programmable for 13 Common Baud Rates up to 19.2 KBits/Second, or an External Baud Clock Maximum of 1M Bit/Second**
- **Five 8-Bit Programmable Timer/Counters; Four Can Be Cascaded to Two 16-Bit Timer/Counters**
- **Two 8-Bit Programmable Parallel I/O Ports; Port 1 Can Be Programmed for Port 2 Handshake Controls and Event Counter Inputs**
- **Eight-Level Priority Interrupt Controller Programmable for 8085 or iAPX 86, iAPX 88 Systems and for Fully Nested Interrupt Capability**
- **Programmable System Clock to 1 ×, 2 ×, 3 ×, or 5 × 1.024 MHz**

The Intel 8256AH Multifunction Universal Asynchronous Receiver-Transmitter (MUART) combines five commonly used functions into a single 40-pin device. It is designed to interface to the 8086/88, iAPX 186/188, and 8051 to perform serial communications, parallel I/O, timing, event counting, and priority interrupt functions. All of these functions are fully programmable through nine internal registers. In addition, the five timer/counters and two parallel I/O ports can be accessed directly by the microprocessor.

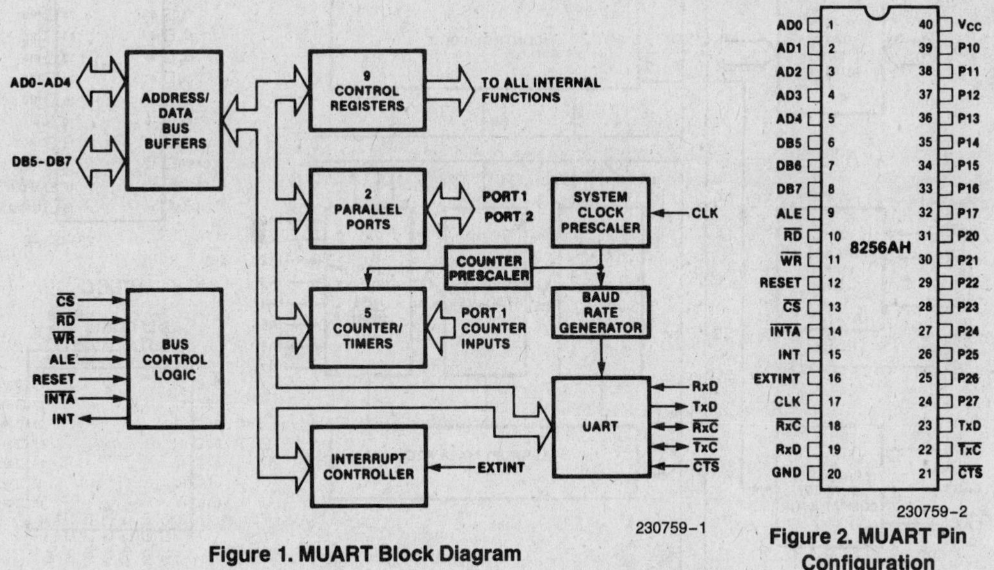

230759-1

Figure 1. MUART Block Diagram

230759-2

Figure 2. MUART Pin Configuration

The complete document for this product is available on Intel's "Data-on-Demand" CD-ROM system. To obtain a copy, contact your local Intel field sales office, Intel technical distributor or call 1-800-548-4725.

September 1990
Order Number: 230759-002

8259A PROGRAMMABLE INTERRUPT CONTROLLER (8259A/8259A-2)

- **8086, 8088 Compatible**
- **MCS-80, MCS-85 Compatible**
- **Eight-Level Priority Controller**
- **Expandable to 64 Levels**
- **Programmable Interrupt Modes**
- **Individual Request Mask Capability**
- **Single +5V Supply (No Clocks)**
- **Available in 28-Pin DIP and 28-Lead PLCC Package**
  (See Packaging Spec., Order #231369)
- **Available in EXPRESS**
  - **Standard Temperature Range**
  - **Extended Temperature Range**

The Intel 8259A Programmable Interrupt Controller handles up to eight vectored priority interrupts for the CPU. It is cascadable for up to 64 vectored priority interrupts without additional circuitry. It is packaged in a 28-pin DIP, uses NMOS technology and requires a single +5V supply. Circuitry is static, requiring no clock input.

The 8259A is designed to minimize the software and real time overhead in handling multi-level priority interrupts. It has several modes, permitting optimization for a variety of system requirements.

The 8259A is fully upward compatible with the Intel 8259. Software originally written for the 8259 will operate the 8259A in all 8259 equivalent modes (MCS-80/85, Non-Buffered, Edge Triggered).

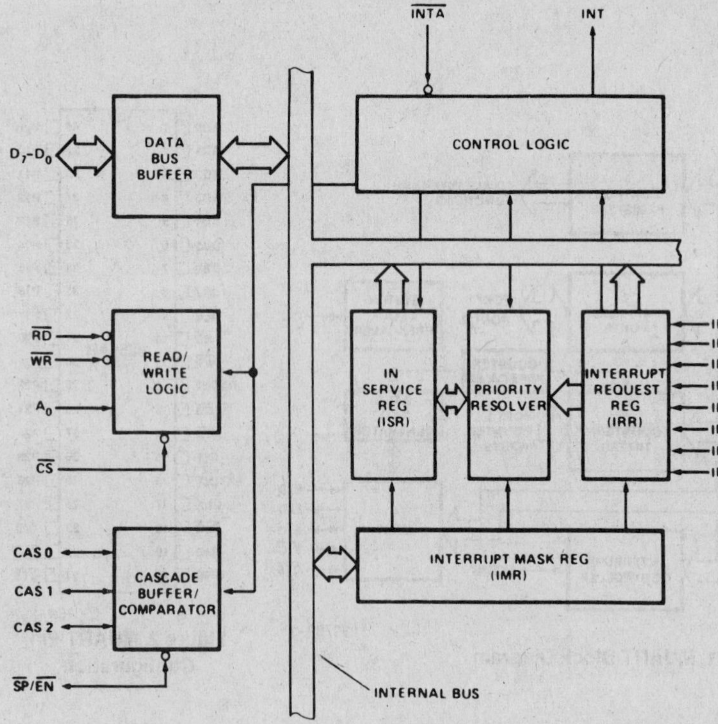

231468–1

Figure 1. Block Diagram

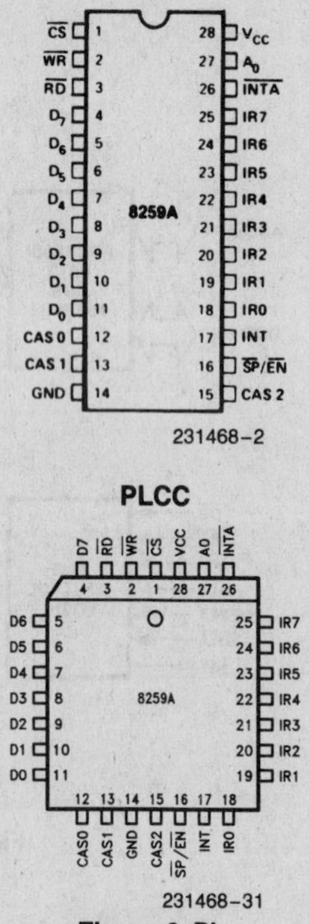

DIP

Pin	Name	Pin	Name
1	$\overline{CS}$	28	V_{CC}
2	$\overline{WR}$	27	A_0
3	$\overline{RD}$	26	$\overline{INTA}$
4	D_7	25	IR7
5	D_6	24	IR6
6	D_5	23	IR5
7	D_4	22	IR4
8	D_3	21	IR3
9	D_2	20	IR2
10	D_1	19	IR1
11	D_0	18	IR0
12	CAS 0	17	INT
13	CAS 1	16	$\overline{SP}/\overline{EN}$
14	GND	15	CAS 2

231468–2

PLCC

231468–31

Figure 2. Pin Configurations

The complete document for this product is available on Intel's "Data-on-Demand" CD-ROM system. To obtain a copy, contact your local Intel field sales office, Intel technical distributor or call 1-800-548-4725.

December 1988
Order Number: 231468-003

82C59A-2
CHMOS Programmable Interrupt Controller

- Pin Compatible with NMOS 8259A-2
- Eight-Level Priority Controller
- Expandable to 64 levels
- Programmable Interrupt Modes
- Low Standby Power—10 μA
- Individual Request Mask Capability
- 80C86/88 and 8080/85/86/88 Compatible
- Fully Static Design
- Single 5V Power Supply
- Available in 28-Pin Plastic DIP (See Packaging Spec., Order #231369)

The Intel 82C59A-2 is a high performance CHMOS version of the NMOS 8259A-2 Priority Interrupt Controller. The 82C59A-2 is designed to relieve the system CPU from the task of polling in a multi-level priority interrupt system. The high speed and industry standard configuration of the 82C59A-2, make it compatible with microprocessors such as the 80C86/88, 8086/88 and 8080/85.

The 82C59A-2 can handle up to 8 vectored priority interrupts for the CPU and is cascadable to 64 without additional circuitry. It is designed to minimize the software and real time overhead in handling multi-level priority interrupts. Two modes of operation make the 82C59A-2 optimal for a variety of system requirements. Static CHMOS circuit design, requiring no clock input, insures low operating power. It is packaged in a 28-pin plastic DIP.

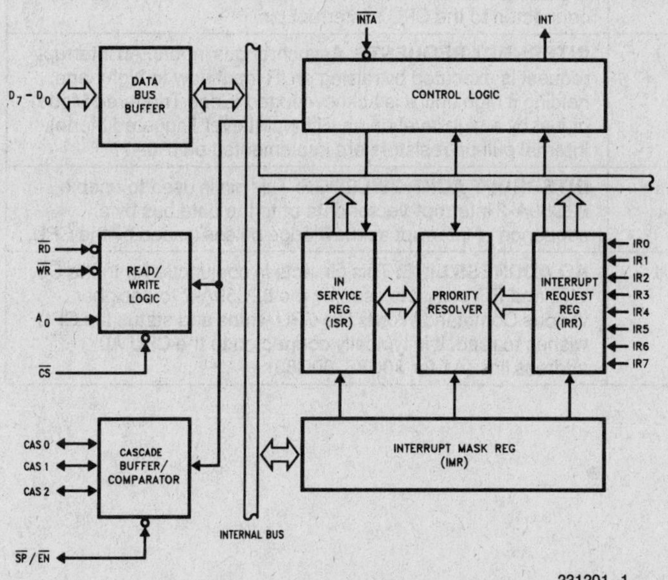

Figure 1. Block Diagram

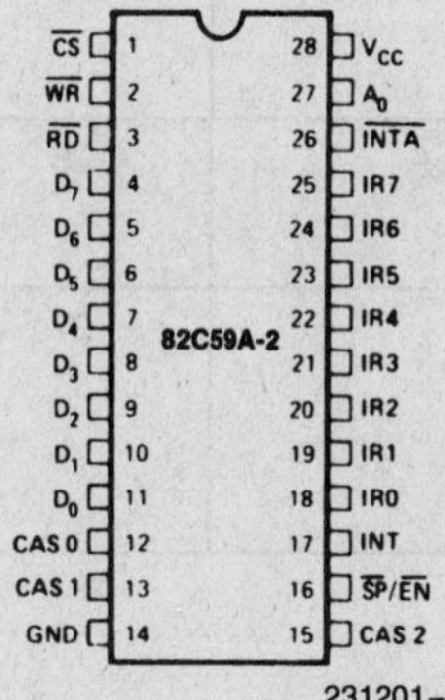

Figure 2. Pin Configuration

5

October 1988
Order Number: 231201-004

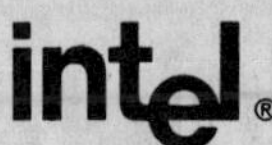

Table 1. Pin Description

Symbol	Pin No.	Type	Name and Function
V_{CC}	28	I	**SUPPLY:** +5V Supply.
GND	14	I	**GROUND.**
$\overline{CS}$	1	I	**CHIP SELECT:** A low on this pin enables $\overline{RD}$ and $\overline{WR}$ communication between the CPU and the 82C59A-2. INTA functions are independent of CS.
$\overline{WR}$	2	I	**WRITE:** A low on this pin when $\overline{CS}$ is low enables the 82C59A-2 to accept command words from the CPU.
$\overline{RD}$	3	I	**READ:** A low on this pin when $\overline{CS}$ is low enables the 82C59A-2 to release status onto the data bus for the CPU.
D_7–D_0	4–11	I/O	**BIDIRECTIONAL DATA BUS:** Control, status and interrupt-vector information is transferred via this bus.
CAS_0–CAS_2	12, 13, 15	I/O	**CASCADE LINES:** The CAS lines form a private 82C59A-2 bus to control a multiple 82C59A-2 structure. These pins are outputs for a master 82C59A-2 and inputs for a slave 82C59A-2.
$\overline{SP}/\overline{EN}$	16	I/O	**SLAVE PROGRAM/ENABLE BUFFER:** This is a dual function pin. When in the Buffered Mode it can be used as an output to control buffer transceivers (EN). When not in the buffered mode it is used as an input to designate a master (SP = 1) or slave (SP = 0).
INT	17	O	**INTERRUPT:** This pin goes high whenever a valid interrupt request is asserted. It is used to interrupt the CPU, thus it is connected to the CPU's interrupt pin.
IR_0–IR_7	18–25	I	**INTERRUPT REQUESTS:** Asynchronous inputs. An interrupt request is executed by raising an IR input (low to high), and holding it high until it is acknowledged (Edge Triggered Mode), or just by a high level on an IR input (Level Triggered Mode). Internal pull-up resistors are implemented on IR0–7.
$\overline{INTA}$	26	I	**INTERRUPT ACKNOWLEDGE:** This pin is used to enable 82C59A-2 interrupt-vector data onto the data bus by a sequence of interrupt acknowledge pulses issued by the CPU.
A_0	27	I	**AO ADDRESS LINE:** This pin acts in conjunction with the $\overline{CS}$, $\overline{WR}$, and $\overline{RD}$ pins. It is used by the 82C59A-2 to decipher various Command Words the CPU writes and status the CPU wishes to read. It is typically connected to the CPU A0 address line (A1 for 80C86, 80C88).

FUNCTIONAL DESCRIPTION

Interrupts in Microcomputer Systems

Microcomputer system design requires that I/O devices such as keyboards, displays, sensors and other components receive servicing in an efficient manner so that large amounts of the total system tasks can be assumed by the microcomputer with little or no effect on throughput.

The most common method of servicing such devices is the *Polled* approach. This is where the processor must test each device in sequence and in effect "ask" each one if it needs servicing. It is easy to see that a large portion of the main program is looping through this continuous polling cycle and that such a method would have a serious, detrimental effect on system throughput, thus limiting the tasks that could be assumed by the microcomputer and reducing the cost effectiveness of using such devices.

A more desirable method would be one that would allow the microprocessor to be executing its main program and only stop to service peripheral devices when it is told to do so by the device itself. In effect, the method would provide an external asynchronous input that would inform the processor that it should complete whatever instruction that is currently being executed and fetch a new routine that will service the requesting device. Once this servicing is complete, however, the processor would resume exactly where it left off.

This method is called *Interrupt*. It is easy to see that system throughput would drastically increase, and thus more tasks could be assumed by the microcomputer to further enhance its cost effectiveness.

The Programmable Interrupt Controller (PIC) functions as an overall manager in an Interrupt-Driven system environment. It accepts requests from the peripheral equipment, determines which of the incoming requests is of the highest importance (priority), ascertains whether the incoming request has a higher priority value than the level currently being serviced, and issues an interrupt to the CPU based on this determination.

Each peripheral device or structure usually has a special program or "routine" that is associated with its specific functional or operational requirements; this is referred to as a "service routine". The PIC, after issuing an Interrupt to the CPU, must somehow input information into the CPU that can "point" the Program Counter to the service routine associated with the requesting device. This "pointer" is an address in a vectoring table and will often be referred to, in this document, as vectoring data.

The 82C59A-2

The 82C59A-2 is a device specifically designed for use in real time, interrupt driven microcomputer sys-

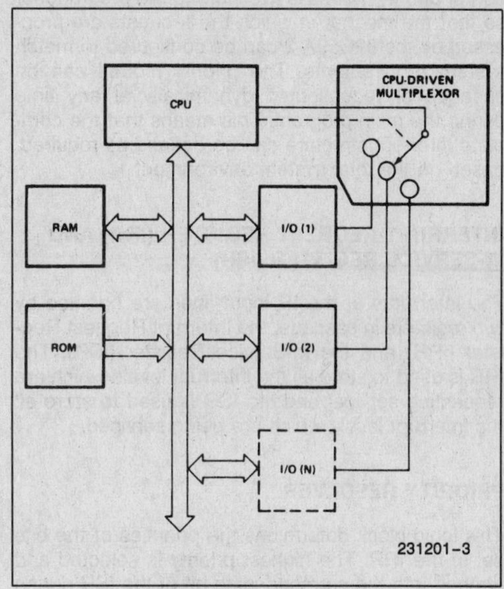

Figure 3a. Polled Method

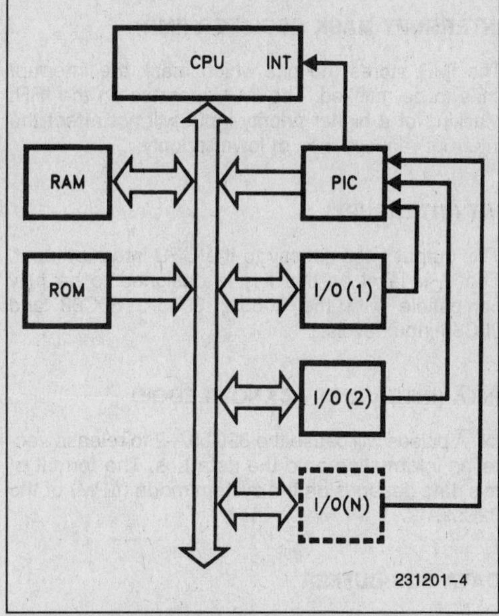

Figure 3b. Interrupt Method

tems. It manages eight levels or requests and has built-in features for expandability to other 82C59A-2's (up to 64 levels). It is programmed by the system's software as an I/O peripheral. A selection of priority modes is available to the programmer so that the manner in which the requests are processed by the 82C59A-2 can be configured to match system requirements. The priority modes can be changed or reconfigured dynamically at any time during the main program. This means that the complete interrupt structure can be defined as required, based on the total system environment.

INTERRUPT REQUEST REGISTER (IRR) AND IN-SERVICE REGISTER (ISR)

The interrupts at the IR input lines are handled by two registers in cascade, the Interrupt Request Register (IRR) and the In-Service Register (ISR). The IRR is used to store all the interrupt levels which are requesting service; and the ISR is used to store all the interrupt levels which are being serviced.

PRIORITY RESOLVER

This logic block determines the priorities of the bits set in the IRR. The highest priority is selected and strobed into the corresponding bit of the ISR during $\overline{\text{INTA}}$ pulse.

INTERRUPT MASK REGISTER (IMR)

The IMR stores the bits which mask the interrupt lines to be masked. The IMR operates on the IRR. Masking of a higher priority input will not affect the interrupt request lines of lower priority.

INT (INTERRUPT)

This output goes directly to the CPU interrupt input. The V_{OH} level on this line is designed to be fully compatible with the 8080A, 8085A, 80C88 and 80C86 input levels.

$\overline{\text{INTA}}$ (INTERRUPT ACKNOWLEDGE)

$\overline{\text{INTA}}$ pulses will cause the 82C59A-2 to release vectoring information onto the data bus. The format of this data depends on the system mode (μPM) of the 82C59A-2.

DATA BUS BUFFER

This 3-state, bidirectional 8-bit buffer is used to interface the 82C59A-2 to the system Data Bus. Control words and status information are transferred through the Data Bus Buffer.

READ/WRITE CONTROL LOGIC

The function of this block is to accept OUTput commands from the CPU. It contains the Initialization Command Word (ICW) registers and Operation Command Word (OCW) registers which store the various control formats for device operation. This function block also allows the status of the 82C59A-2 to be transferred onto the Data Bus.

$\overline{\text{CS}}$ (CHIP SELECT)

A LOW on this input enables the 82C59A-2. No reading or writing of the chip will occur unless the device is selected.

$\overline{\text{WR}}$ (WRITE)

A LOW on this input enables the CPU to write control words (ICWs and OCWs) to the 82C59A-2.

$\overline{\text{RD}}$ (READ)

A LOW on this input enables the 82C59A-2 to send the status of the Interrupt Request Register (IRR), In Service Register (ISR), the Interrupt Mask Register (IMR), or the Interrupt level onto the Data Bus.

A_0

This input signal is used in conjunction with $\overline{\text{WR}}$ and $\overline{\text{RD}}$ signals to write commands into the various command registers, as well as reading the various status registers of the chip. This line can be tied directly to one of the address lines.

THE CASCADE BUFFER/COMPARATOR

This function block stores and compares the IDs of all 82C59A-2's used in the system. The associated three I/O pins (CAS0–2) are outputs when the 82C59A-2 is used as a master and are inputs when the 82C59A-2 is used as a slave. As a master, the 82C59A-2 sends the ID of the interrupting slave device onto the CAS0–2 lines. The slave thus selected will send its preprogrammed subroutine address onto the Data Bus during the next one or two consecutive $\overline{\text{INTA}}$ pulses. (See section "Cascading the 82C59A-2".)

INTERRUPT SEQUENCE

The powerful features of the 82C59A-2 in a microcomputer system are its programmability and the interrupt routine addressing capability. The latter allows direct or indirect jumping to the specific interrupt routine requested without any polling of the interrupting devices. The normal sequence of events during an interrupt depends on the type of CPU being used.

The events occur as follows in an MCS-80/85 system:

1. One or more of the INTERRUPT REQUEST Lines (IR7–0) are raised high, setting the corresponding IRR bit(s).

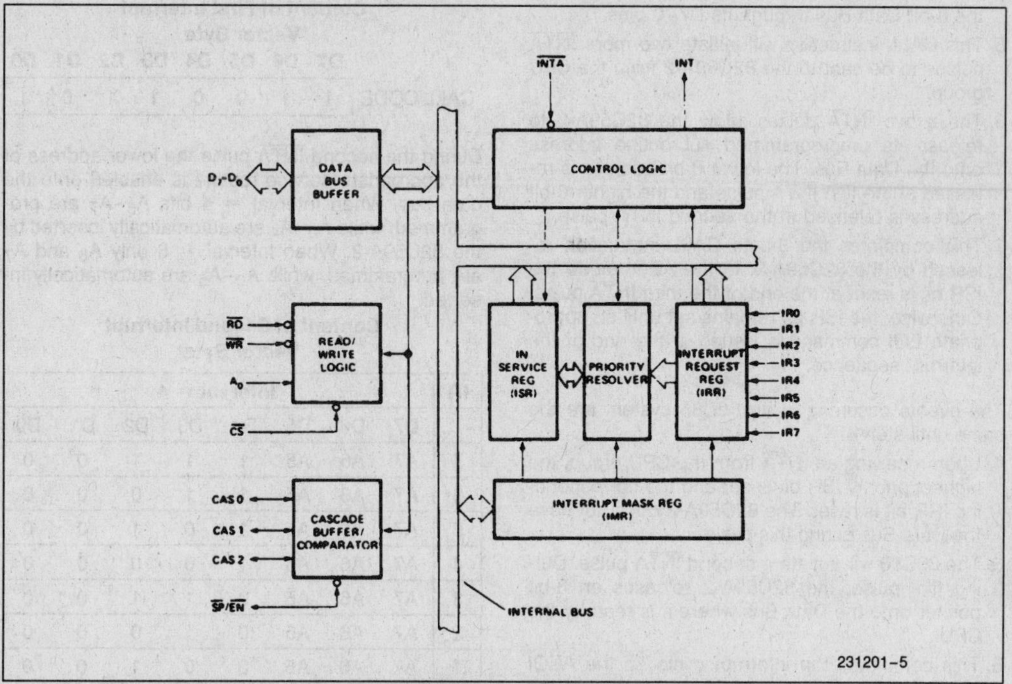

Figure 4. 82C59A-2 Block Diagram

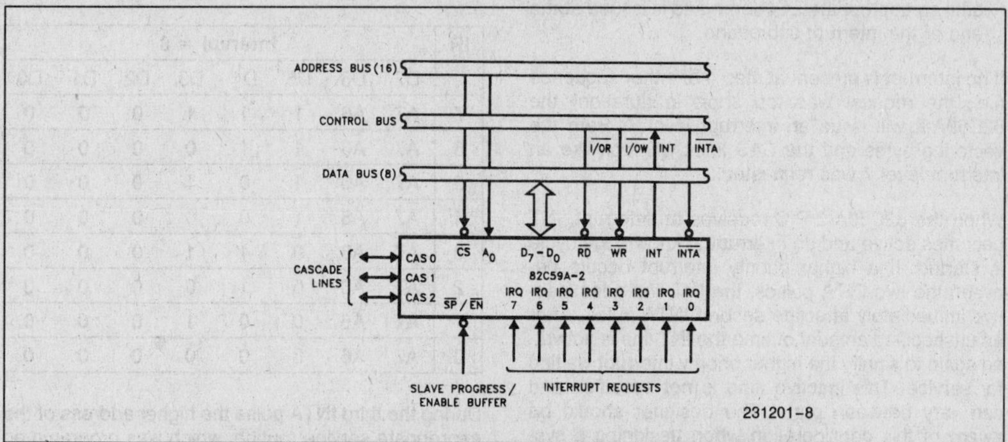

Figure 5. 82C59A-2 Interface to Standard System Bus

2. The 82C59A-2 evaluates these requests, and sends an INT to the CPU, if appropriate.
3. The CPU acknowledges the INT and responds with an $\overline{\text{INTA}}$ pulse.
4. Upon receiving an $\overline{\text{INTA}}$ from the CPU group, the highest priority ISR bit is set, and the corresponding IRR bit is reset. The 82C59A-2 will also release a CALL instruction code (11001101) onto the 8-bit Data Bus through its D7–0 pins.
5. This CALL instruction will initiate two more $\overline{\text{INTA}}$ pulses to be sent to the 82C59A-2 from the CPU group.
6. These two $\overline{\text{INTA}}$ pulses allow the 82C59A-2 to release its preprogrammed subroutine address onto the Data Bus. The lower 8-bit address is released at the first $\overline{\text{INTA}}$ pulse and the higher 8-bit address is released at the second $\overline{\text{INTA}}$ pulse.
7. This completes the 3-byte CALL instruction released by the 82C59A-2. In the AEOI mode the ISR bit is reset at the end of the third $\overline{\text{INTA}}$ pulse. Otherwise, the ISR bit remains set until an appropriate EOI command is issued at the end of the interrupt sequence.

The events occurring in an 80C86 system are the same until step 4.

4. Upon receiving an $\overline{\text{INTA}}$ from the CPU group, the highest priority ISR bit is set and the corresponding IRR bit is reset. The 82C59A-2 does not drive the Data Bus during this cycle.
5. The 80C86 will initiate a second $\overline{\text{INTA}}$ pulse. During this pulse, the 82C59A-2 releases an 8-bit pointer onto the Data Bus where it is read by the CPU.
6. This completes the interrupt cycle. In the AEOI mode the ISR bit is reset at the end of the second $\overline{\text{INTA}}$ pulse. Otherwise, the ISR bit remains set until an appropriate EOI command is issued at the end of the interrupt subroutine.

If no interrupt is present at step 4 of either sequence (i.e., the request was too short in duration) the 82C59A-2 will issue an interrupt level 7. Both the vectoring bytes and the CAS lines will look like an interrupt level 7 was requested.

When the 82C59A-2 PIC receives an interrupt, INT becomes active and an interrupt acknowledge cycle is started. If a higher priority interrupt occurs between the two INTA pulses, the INT line goes inactive immediately after the second INTA pulse. After an unspecified amount of time the INT line is activated again to signify the higher priority interrupt waiting for service. This inactive time is not specified and can vary between parts. The designer should be aware of this consideration when designing a system which uses the 82C59A-2. It is recommended that proper asynchronous design techniques be followed.

INTERRUPT SEQUENCE OUTPUTS

MCS®-80, MCS-85

This sequence is timed by three $\overline{\text{INTA}}$ pulses. During the first $\overline{\text{INTA}}$ pulse the CALL opcode is enabled onto the data bus.

Content of First Interrupt Vector Byte

	D7	D6	D5	D4	D3	D2	D1	D0
CALL CODE	1	1	0	0	1	1	0	1

During the second $\overline{\text{INTA}}$ pulse the lower address of the appropriate service routine is enabled onto the data bus. When Interval = 4 bits A_5–A_7 are programmed, while A_0–A_4 are automatically inserted by the 82C59A-2. When Interval = 8 only A_6 and A_7 are programmed, while A_0–A_5 are automatically inserted.

Content of Second Interrupt Vector Byte

IR	Interval = 4							
	D7	D6	D5	D4	D3	D2	D1	D0
7	A7	A6	A5	1	1	1	0	0
6	A7	A6	A5	1	1	0	0	0
5	A7	A6	A5	1	0	1	0	0
4	A7	A6	A5	1	0	0	0	0
3	A7	A6	A5	0	1	1	0	0
2	A7	A6	A5	0	1	0	0	0
1	A7	A6	A5	0	0	1	0	0
0	A7	A6	A5	0	0	0	0	0

IR	Interval = 8							
	D7	D6	D5	D4	D3	D2	D1	D0
7	A7	A6	1	1	1	0	0	0
6	A7	A6	1	1	0	0	0	0
5	A7	A6	1	0	1	0	0	0
4	A7	A6	1	0	0	0	0	0
3	A7	A6	0	1	1	0	0	0
2	A7	A6	0	1	0	0	0	0
1	A7	A6	0	0	1	0	0	0
0	A7	A6	0	0	0	0	0	0

During the third INTA pulse the higher address of the appropriate service routine, which was programmed as byte 2 of the initialization sequence (A_8 – A_{15}), is enabled onto the bus.

Content of Third Interrupt Vector Byte

D7	D6	D5	D4	D3	D2	D1	D0
A15	A14	A13	A12	A11	A10	A9	A8

80C86, 80C88

80C86, 80C88 mode is similar to MCS-80 mode except that only two Interrupt Acknowledge cycles are issued by the processor and no CALL opcode is sent to the processor. The first interrupt acknowledge cycle is similar to that of MCS-80, 85 systems in that the 82C59A-2 uses it to internally freeze the state of the interrupts for priority resolution and as a master it issues the interrupt code on the cascade lines at the end of the INTA pulse. On this first cycle it does not issue any data to the processor and leaves its data bus buffers disabled. On the second interrupt acknowledge cycle in 80C86, 80C88 mode the master (or slave if so programmed) will send a byte of data to the processor with the acknowledged interrupt code composed as follows (note the state of the ADI mode control is ignored and A_5–A_{11} are unused in 80C86, 80C88 mode):

Content of Interrupt Vector Byte for 80C86, 80C88 System Mode

	D7	D6	D5	D4	D3	D2	D1	D0
IR7	T7	T6	T5	T4	T3	1	1	1
IR6	T7	T6	T5	T4	T3	1	1	0
IR5	T7	T6	T5	T4	T3	1	0	1
IR4	T7	T6	T5	T4	T3	1	0	0
IR3	T7	T6	T5	T4	T3	0	1	1
IR2	T7	T6	T5	T4	T3	0	1	0
IR1	T7	T6	T5	T4	T3	0	0	1
IR0	T7	T6	T5	T4	T3	0	0	0

PROGRAMMING THE 82C59A-2

The 82C59A-2 accepts two types of command words generated by the CPU:

1. *Initialization Command Words (ICWs)*: Before normal operation can begin, each 82C59A-2 in the system must be brought to a starting point — by a sequence of 2 to 4 bytes timed by $\overline{WR}$ pulses.
2. *Operation Command Words (OCWs)*: These are the command words which command the 82C59A-2 to operate in various interrupt modes. These modes are:
   a. Fully nested mode
   b. Rotating priority mode
   c. Special mask mode
   d. Polled mode

The OCWs can be written into the 82C59A-2 anytime after initialization.

INITIALIZATION COMMAND WORDS (ICWS)

GENERAL

Whenever a command is issued with A0 = 0 and D4 = 1, this is interpreted as Initialization Command Word 1 (ICW1). ICW1 starts the initialization sequence during which the following automatically occur.

a. The edge sense circuit is reset, which means that following initialization, an interrupt request (IR) input must make a low-to-high transition to generate an interrupt.

b. The Interrupt Mask Register is cleared.

c. IR7 input is assigned priority 7.

d. The slave mode address is set to 7.

e. Special Mask Mode is cleared and Status Read is set to IRR.

f. If IC4 = 0, then all functions selected in ICW4 are set to zero. (Non-Buffered mode*, no Auto-EOI, MCS-80, 85 system).

***NOTE:**
Master/Slave in ICW4 is only used in the buffered mode.

5

INITIALIZATION COMMAND WORDS 1 AND 2 (ICW1, ICW2)

A_5–A_{15}: *Page starting address of service routines.* In an MCS 80/85 system, the 8 request levels will generate CALLs to 8 locations equally spaced in memory. These can be programmed to be spaced at intervals of 4 or 8 memory locations, thus the 8 routines will occupy a page of 32 or 64 bytes, respectively.

The address format is 2 bytes long (A_0–A_{15}). When the routine interval is 4, A_0–A_4 are automatically inserted by the 82C59A-2, while A_5–A_{15} are programmed externally. When the routine interval is 8, A_0–A_5 are automatically inserted by the 82C59A-2, while A_6–A_{15} are programmed externally.

The 8-byte interval will maintain compatibility with current software, while the 4-byte interval is best for a compact jump table.

In an 80C86, 80C88 system A_{15}–A_{11} are inserted in the five most significant bits of the vectoring

byte and the 82C59A-2 sets the three least significant bits according to the interrupt level. A_{10}–A_5 are ignored and ADI (Address Interval) has no effect:

LTIM: If LTIM = 1, then the 82C59A-2 will operate in the level interrupt mode. Edge detect logic on the interrupt inputs will be disabled.

ADI: CALL address interval. ADI = 1 then interval = 4; ADI = 0 then interval = 8.

SNGL: Single. Means that this is the only 82C59A-2 in the system. If SNGL = 1 no ICW3 will be issued.

IC4: If this bit is set — ICW4 has to be read. If ICW4 is not needed, set IC4 = 0.

INITIALIZATION COMMAND WORD 3 (ICW3)

This word is read only when there is more than one 82C59A-2 in the system and cascading is used, in which case SNGL = 0. It will load the 8-bit slave register. The functions of this register are:

a. In the master mode (either when SP = 1, or in buffered mode when M/S = 1 in ICW4) a "1" is set for each slave in the system. The master then will release byte 1 of the call sequence (for MCS-80/85 system) and will enable the corresponding slave to release bytes 2 and 3 (for 80C86, 80C88 only byte 2) through the cascade lines.

b. In the slave mode (either when $\overline{SP}$ = 0, or if BUF = 1 and M/S = 0 in ICW4) bits 2-0 identify the slave. The slave compares its cascade input with these bits and, if they are equal, bytes 2 and 3 of the call sequence (or just byte 2 for 80C86, 80C88 are released by it on the Data Bus.

INITIALIZATION COMMAND WORD 4 (ICW4)

SFNM: If SFNM = 1 the special fully nested mode is programmed.

BUF: If BUF = 1 the buffered mode is programmed. In buffered mode $\overline{SP}/\overline{EN}$ becomes an enable output and the master/slave determination is by M/S.

M/S: If buffered mode is selected: M/S = 1 means the 82C59A-2 is programmed to be a master, M/S = 0 means the 82C59A-2 is programmed to be a slave. If BUF = 0, M/S has no function.

AEOI: If AEOI = 1 the automatic end of interrupt mode is programmed.

μPM: Microprocessor mode: μPM = 0 sets the 82C59A-2 for MCS-80, 85 system operation, μPM = 1 sets the 82C59A-2 for 80C86 system operation.

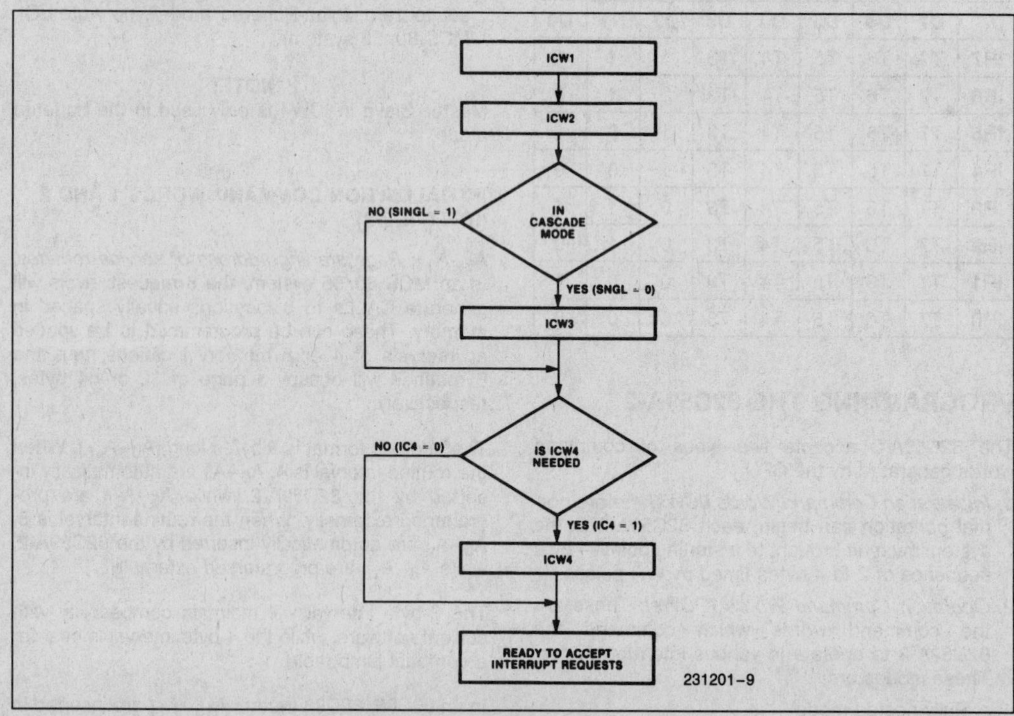

Figure 6. Initialization Sequence

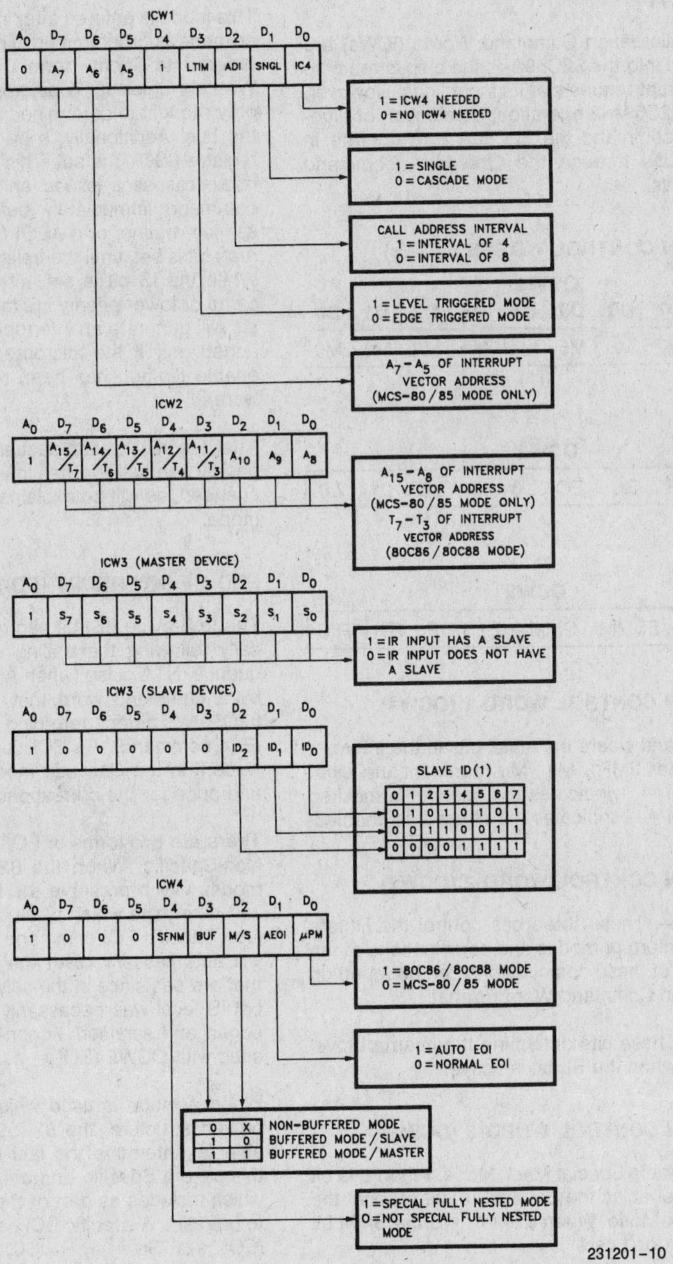

ICW1

A_0	D_7	D_6	D_5	D_4	D_3	D_2	D_1	D_0
0	A_7	A_6	A_5	1	LTIM	ADI	SNGL	IC4

1 = ICW4 NEEDED
0 = NO ICW4 NEEDED

1 = SINGLE
0 = CASCADE MODE

CALL ADDRESS INTERVAL
1 = INTERVAL OF 4
0 = INTERVAL OF 8

1 = LEVEL TRIGGERED MODE
0 = EDGE TRIGGERED MODE

$A_7 - A_5$ OF INTERRUPT VECTOR ADDRESS (MCS-80/85 MODE ONLY)

ICW2

A_0	D_7	D_6	D_5	D_4	D_3	D_2	D_1	D_0
1	A_{15}/T_7	A_{14}/T_6	A_{13}/T_5	A_{12}/T_4	A_{11}/T_3	A_{10}	A_9	A_8

$A_{15} - A_8$ OF INTERRUPT VECTOR ADDRESS (MCS-80/85 MODE ONLY)
$T_7 - T_3$ OF INTERRUPT VECTOR ADDRESS (80C86/80C88 MODE)

ICW3 (MASTER DEVICE)

A_0	D_7	D_6	D_5	D_4	D_3	D_2	D_1	D_0
1	S_7	S_6	S_5	S_4	S_3	S_2	S_1	S_0

1 = IR INPUT HAS A SLAVE
0 = IR INPUT DOES NOT HAVE A SLAVE

ICW3 (SLAVE DEVICE)

A_0	D_7	D_6	D_5	D_4	D_3	D_2	D_1	D_0
1	0	0	0	0	0	ID_2	ID_1	ID_0

SLAVE ID (1)

0	1	2	3	4	5	6	7
0	1	0	1	0	1	0	1
0	0	1	1	0	0	1	1
0	0	0	0	1	1	1	1

ICW4

A_0	D_7	D_6	D_5	D_4	D_3	D_2	D_1	D_0
1	0	0	0	SFNM	BUF	M/S	AEOI	μPM

1 = 80C86/80C88 MODE
0 = MCS-80/85 MODE

1 = AUTO EOI
0 = NORMAL EOI

BUF	M/S	
0	X	NON-BUFFERED MODE
1	0	BUFFERED MODE/SLAVE
1	1	BUFFERED MODE/MASTER

1 = SPECIAL FULLY NESTED MODE
0 = NOT SPECIAL FULLY NESTED MODE

231201-10

NOTE:
Slave ID is equal to the corresponding master IR input.

Figure 7. Initialization Command Word Format

OPERATION COMMAND WORDS (OCWs)

After the initialization Command Words (ICWs) are programmed into the 82C59A-2, the chip is ready to accept interrupt requests at its input lines. However, during the 82C59A-2 operation, a selection of algorithms can command the 82C59A-2 to operate in various modes through the Operation Command Words (OCWs).

OPERATION CONTROL WORDS (OCWs)

OCW1

A0	D7	D6	D5	D4	D3	D2	D1	D0
1	M7	M6	M5	M4	M3	M2	M1	M0

OCW2

A0	D7	D6	D5	D4	D3	D2	D1	D0
0	R	SL	EOI	0	0	L2	L1	L0

OCW3

A0	D7	D6	D5	D4	D3	D2	D1	D0
0	0	ESMM	SMM	0	1	P	RR	RIS

OPERATION CONTROL WORD 1 (OCW1)

OCW1 sets and clears the mask bits in the interrupt Mask Register (IMR). $M_7 - M_0$ represent the eight mask bits. M = 1 indicates the channel is masked (inhibited), M = 0 indicates the channel is enabled.

OPERATION CONTROL WORD 2 (OCW2)

R, SL, EOI — These three bits control the Rotate and End of Interrupt modes and combinations of the two. A chart of these combinations can be found on the Operation Command Word Format.

L_2, L_1, L_0—These bits determine the interrupt level acted upon when the SL bit is active.

OPERATION CONTROL WORD 3 (OCW3)

ESMM — Enable Special Mask Mode. When this bit is set to 1 it enables the SMM bit to set or reset the Special Mask Mode. When ESMM = 0 the SMM bit becomes a "don't care".

SMM — Special Mask Mode. If ESMM = 1 and SMM = 1 the 82C59A-2 will enter Special Mask Mode. If ESMM = 1 and SMM = 0 the 82C59A-2 will revert to normal mask mode. When ESMM = 0, SMM has no effect.

FULLY NESTED MODE

This mode is entered after initialization unless another mode is programmed. The interrupt requests are ordered in priority form 0 through 7 (0 highest). When an interrupt is acknowledged the highest priority request is determined and its vector placed on the bus. Additionally, a bit of the Interrupt Service register (ISO-7) is set. This bit remains set until the microprocessor issues an End of Interrupt (EOI) command immediately before returning from the service routine, or if AEOI (Automatic. End of Interrupt) bit is set, until the trailing edge of the last INTA. While the IS bit is set, all further interrupts of the same or lower priority are inhibited, while higher levels will generate an interrupt (which will be acknowledged only if the microprocessor internal interrupt enable flip-flop has been re-enabled through software).

After the initialization sequence, IR0 has the highest priority and IR7 the lowest. Priorities can be changed, as will be explained, in the rotating priority mode.

END OF INTERRUPT (EOI)

The In Service (IS) bit can be reset either automatically following the trailing edge of the last in sequence $\overline{\text{INTA}}$ pulse (when AEOI bit in ICW4 is set) or by a command word that must be issued to the 82C59A-2 before returning from a service routine (EOI command). An EOI command must be issued twice if in the Cascade mode, once for the master and once for the corresponding slave.

There are two forms of EOI command: Specific and Non-Specific. When the 82C59A-2 is operated in modes which preserve the fully nested structure, it can determine which IS bit to reset on EOI. When a Non-Specific EOI command is issued the 82C59A-2 will automatically reset the highest IS bit of those that are set, since in the fully nested mode the highest IS level was necessarily the last level acknowledged and serviced. A non-specific EOI can be issued with OCW2 (EOI = 1, SL = 0, R = 0).

When a mode is used which may disturb the fully nested structure, the 82C59A-2 may no longer be able to determine the last level acknowledged. In this case a Specific End of Interrupt must be issued which includes as part of the command the IS level to be reset. A specific EOI can be issued with OCW2 (EOI = 1, SL = 1, R = 0, and L0-L2 is the binary level of the IS bit to be reset).

It should be noted that an IS bit that is masked by an IMR bit will not be cleared by a non-specific EOI if the 82C59A-2 is in the Special Mask Mode.

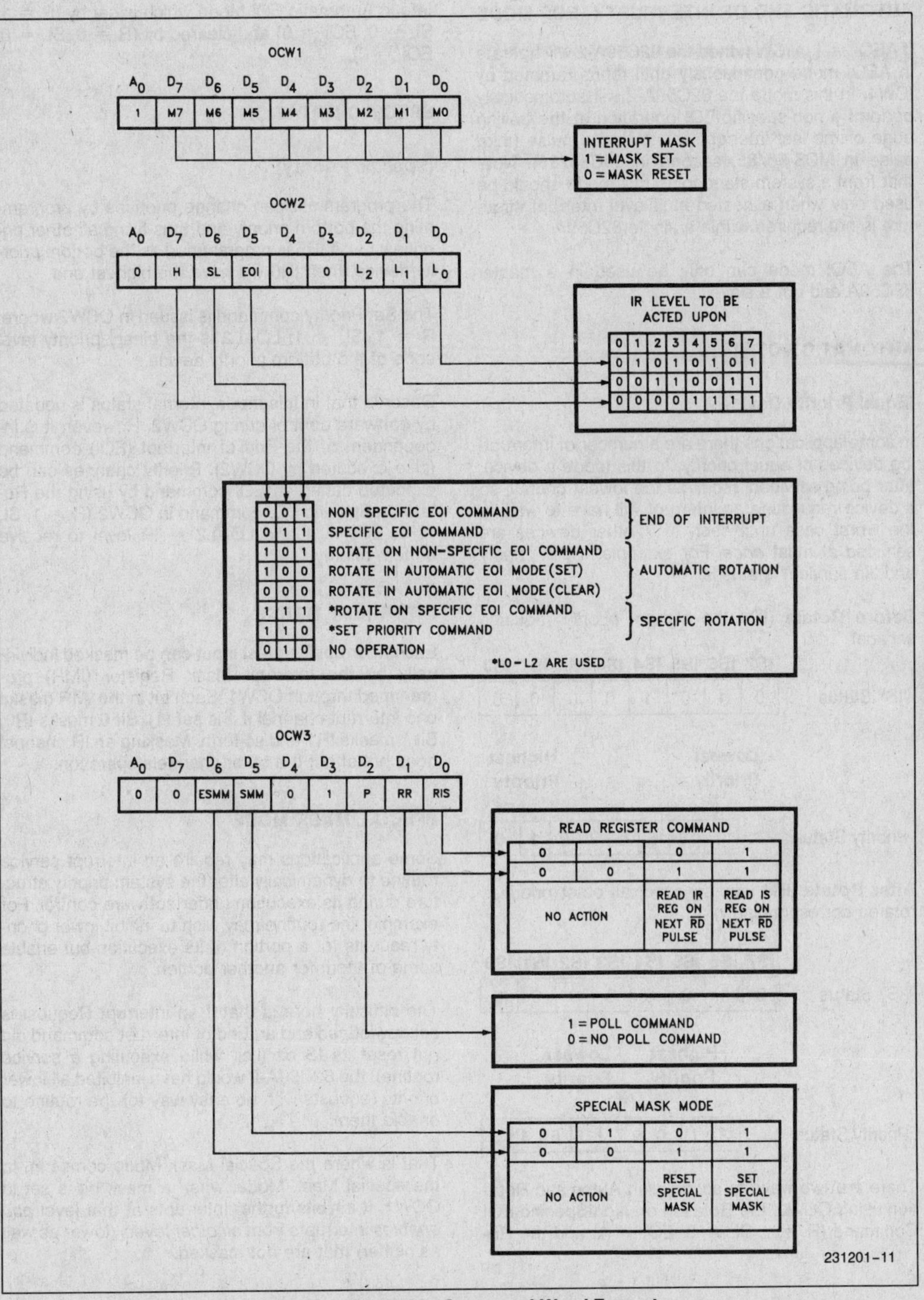

OCW1

A_0	D_7	D_6	D_5	D_4	D_3	D_2	D_1	D_0
1	M7	M6	M5	M4	M3	M2	M1	M0

INTERRUPT MASK
1 = MASK SET
0 = MASK RESET

OCW2

A_0	D_7	D_6	D_5	D_4	D_3	D_2	D_1	D_0
0	R	SL	EOI	0	0	L_2	L_1	L_0

IR LEVEL TO BE ACTED UPON

0	1	2	3	4	5	6	7
0	1	0	1	0	1	0	1
0	0	1	1	0	0	1	1
0	0	0	0	1	1	1	1

R	SL	EOI	Command	
0	0	1	NON SPECIFIC EOI COMMAND	END OF INTERRUPT
0	1	1	SPECIFIC EOI COMMAND	END OF INTERRUPT
1	0	1	ROTATE ON NON-SPECIFIC EOI COMMAND	AUTOMATIC ROTATION
1	0	0	ROTATE IN AUTOMATIC EOI MODE (SET)	AUTOMATIC ROTATION
0	0	0	ROTATE IN AUTOMATIC EOI MODE (CLEAR)	AUTOMATIC ROTATION
1	1	1	*ROTATE ON SPECIFIC EOI COMMAND	SPECIFIC ROTATION
1	1	0	*SET PRIORITY COMMAND	SPECIFIC ROTATION
0	1	0	NO OPERATION	

*L0–L2 ARE USED

OCW3

A_0	D_7	D_6	D_5	D_4	D_3	D_2	D_1	D_0
0	0	ESMM	SMM	0	1	P	RR	RIS

READ REGISTER COMMAND

RIS	0	1	0	1
RR	0	0	1	1
	NO ACTION		READ IR REG ON NEXT $\overline{RD}$ PULSE	READ IS REG ON NEXT $\overline{RD}$ PULSE

1 = POLL COMMAND
0 = NO POLL COMMAND

SPECIAL MASK MODE

SMM	0	1	0	1
ESMM	0	0	1	1
	NO ACTION		RESET SPECIAL MASK	SET SPECIAL MASK

231201–11

Figure 8. Operation Command Word Format

AUTOMATIC END OF INTERRUPT (AEOI) MODE

If AEOI = 1 in ICW4, then the 82C59A-2 will operate in AEOI mode continuously until reprogrammed by ICW4. In this mode the 82C59A-2 will automatically perform a non-specific EOI operation at the trailing edge of the last interrupt acknowledge pulse (third pulse in MCS-80/85, second in 80C86/88). Note that from a system standpoint, this mode should be used only when a nested multilevel interrupt structure is not required within a single 82C59A.

The AEOI mode can only be used in a master 82C59A and not a slave.

AUTOMATIC ROTATION

(Equal Priority Devices)

In some applications there are a number of interrupting devices of equal priority. In this mode a device, after being serviced, receives the lowest priority, so a device requesting an interrupt will have to wait, in the worst case until each of 7 other devices are serviced at most *once*. For example, if the priority and "in service" status is:

Before Rotate (IR4 the highest priority requiring service)

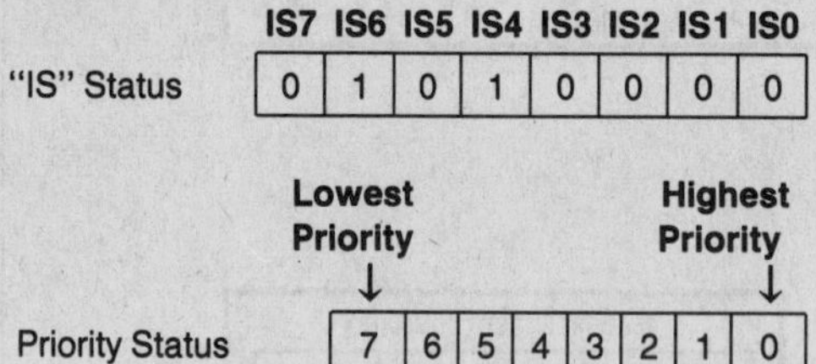

	IS7	IS6	IS5	IS4	IS3	IS2	IS1	IS0
"IS" Status	0	1	0	1	0	0	0	0

Priority Status	7	6	5	4	3	2	1	0

After Rotate (IR4 was serviced, all other priorities rotated correspondingly)

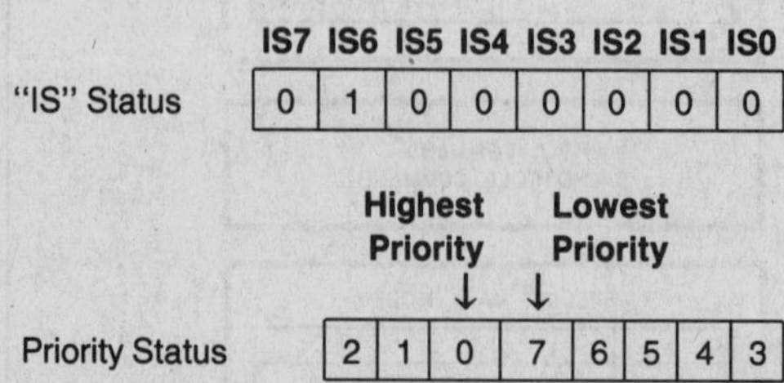

	IS7	IS6	IS5	IS4	IS3	IS2	IS1	IS0
"IS" Status	0	1	0	0	0	0	0	0

Priority Status	2	1	0	7	6	5	4	3

There are two ways to accomplish Automatic Rotation using OCW2, the Rotation on Non-Specific EOI Command (R = 1, SL = 0, EOI = 1) and the Rotate in Automatic EOI Mode which is set by (R = 1, SL = 0, EOI = 0) and cleared by (R = 0, SL = 0, EOI = 0).

SPECIFIC ROTATION

(Specific Priority)

The programmer can change priorities by programming the bottom priority and thus fixing all other priorities; i.e., if IR5 is programmed as the bottom priority device, then IR6 will have the highest one.

The Set Priority command is issued in OCW2 where: R = 1, SL = 1; LO–L2 is the binary priority level code of the bottom priority device.

Observe that in this mode internal status is updated by software control during OCW2. However, it is independent of the End of Interrupt (EOI) command (also executed by OCW2). Priority changes can be executed during an EOI command by using the Rotate on Specific EOI command in OCW2 (R = 1, SL = 1, EOI = 1 and LO–L2 = IR level to receive bottom priority).

INTERRUPT MASKS

Each Interrupt Request input can be masked individually by the Interrupt Mask Register (IMR) programmed through OCW1. Each bit in the IMR masks one interrupt channel if it is set (1). Bit 0 masks IR0, Bit 1 masks IR1 and so forth. Masking an IR channel does not affect the other channels operation.

SPECIAL MASK MODE

Some applications may require an interrupt service routine to dynamically alter the system priority structure during its execution under software control. For example, the routine may wish to inhibit lower priority requests for a portion of its execution but enable some of them for another portion.

The difficulty here is that if an interrupt Request Is acknowledged and an End of Interrupt command did not reset its IS bit (i.e., while executing a service routine), the 82C59A-2 would have inhibited all lower priority requests with no easy way for the routine to enable them.

That is where the Special Mask Mode comes in. In the special Mask Mode, when a mask bit is set in OCW1, it inhibits further interrupts at that level *and enables* interrupts from *all other* levels (lower as well as higher) that are not masked.

Thus, any interrupts may be selectivity enabled by loading the mask register.

The special Mask Mode is set by OCW3 where: SSMM = 1, SMM = 1, and cleared where SSMM = 1, SMM = 0.

POLL COMMAND

In Poll mode the INT output functions as it normally does. The microprocessor should ignore this output. This can be accomplished either by not connecting the INT output or by masking interrupts within the microprocessor, thereby disabling its interrupt input. Service to devices is achieved by software using a Poll command.

The Poll command is issued by setting P = "1" in OCW3. The 82C59A-2 treats the next $\overline{RD}$ pulse to the 82C59A-2 (i.e., $\overline{RD}$ = 0, $\overline{CS}$ = 0) as an interrupt acknowledge, sets the appropriate IS bit if there is a request, and reads the priority level. Interrupt is frozen from $\overline{WR}$ to $\overline{RD}$.

The word enabled onto the data bus during $\overline{RD}$ is:

D7	D6	D5	D4	D3	D2	D1	D0
I	—	—	—	—	W2	W1	W0

WO–W2:

Binary code of the highest priority level requesting service.

I: Equal to a "1" if there is an interrupt.

This mode is useful if there is a routine command common to several levels so that the $\overline{INTA}$ sequence is not needed (saves ROM space). Another application is to use the poll mode to expand the number of priority levels to more than 64.

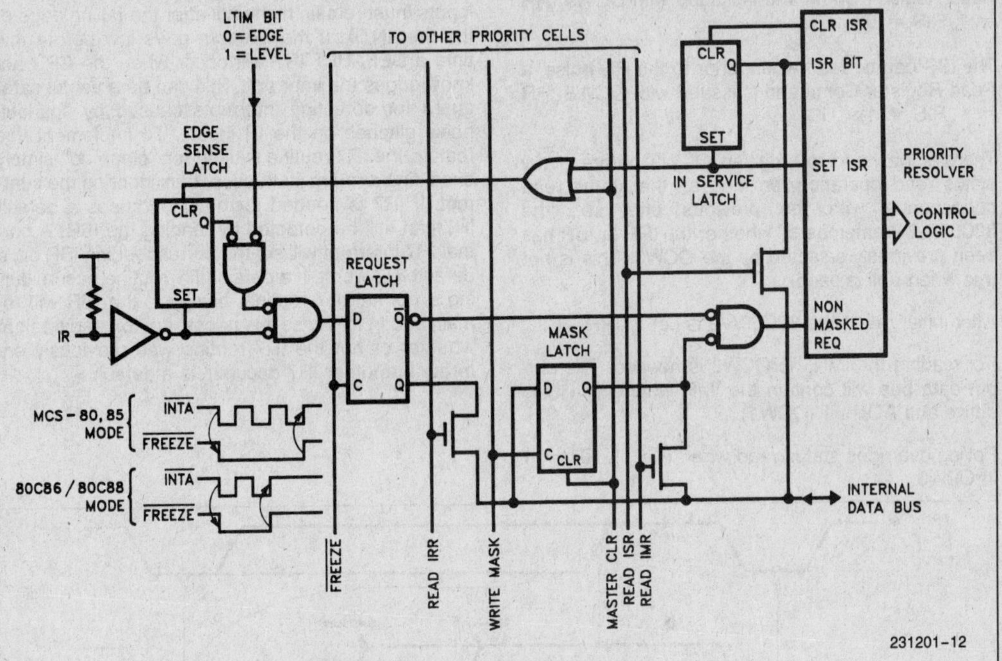

231201-12

NOTES:
1. Master Clear active only during ICW1
2. Freeze/ is active during $\overline{INTA}$/and poll sequences only
3. Truth Table for D-Latch

C	D	Q	OPERATION
1	Di	Di	FOLLOW
0	X	Qn-1	HOLD

Figure 9. Priority Cell—Simplified Logic Diagram

READING THE 82C59A-2 STATUS

The input status of several internal registers can be read to update the user information on the system. The following registers can be read via OCW3 (IRR and ISR or OCW1 [IMR]).

Interrupt Request Register (IRR): 8-bit register which contains the levels requesting an interrupt to be acknowledged. The highest request level is reset from the IRR when an interrupt is acknowledged. (Not affected by IMR).

In-Service Register (ISR): 8-bit register which contains the priority levels that are being serviced. The ISR is updated when an End of Interrupt Command is issued.

Interrupt Mask Register: 8-bit register which contains the interrupt request lines which are masked.

The IRR can be read when, prior to the RD pulse, a Read Register Command is issued with OCW3 (RR = 1, RIS = 0.)

The ISR can be read when, prior to the RD pulse, a Read Register Command is issued with OCW3 (RR = 1, RIS = 1):

There is no need to write an OCW3 before every status read operation, as long as the status read corresponds with the previous one; i.e., the 82C59A-2 "remembers" whether the IRR or ISR has been previously selected by the OCW3. This is not true when poll is used.

After initialization the 82C59A-2 is set to IRR.

For reading the IMR, no OCW3 is needed. The output data bus will contain the IMR whenever $\overline{RD}$ is active and AO = 1 (OCW1).

Polling overrides status read when P = 1, RR = 1 in OCW3.

EDGE AND LEVEL TRIGGERED MODES

This mode is programmed using bit 3 in ICW1.

If LTIM = '0', an interrupt request will be recognized by a low to high transition on an IR input. The IR input can remain high without generating another interrupt.

If LTIM = '1', an interrupt request will be recognized by a 'high' level on IR Input, and there is no need for an edge detection. The interrupt request must be removed before the EOI command is issued or the CPU interrupt is enabled to prevent a second interrupt from occurring.

The priority cell diagram shows a conceptual circuit of the level sensitive and edge sensitive input circuitry of the 82C59A-2. Be sure to note that the request latch is a transparent D type latch.

In both the edge and level triggered modes the IR inputs must remain high until after the falling edge of the first INTA. If the IR input goes low before this time a DEFAULT IR7 will occur when the CPU acknowledges the interrupt. This can be a useful safeguard for detecting interrupts caused by spurious noise glitches on the IR inputs. To implement this feature the IR7 routine is used for "clean up" simply executing a return instruction, thus ignoring the interrupt. If IR7 is needed for other purposes a default IR7 can still be detected by reading the ISR. A normal IR7 interrupt will set the corresponding ISR bit, a default IR7 won't. If a default IR7 routine occurs during a normal IR7 routine, however, the ISR will remain set. In this case it is necessary to keep track of whether or not the IR7 routine was previously entered. If another IR7 occurs it is a default.

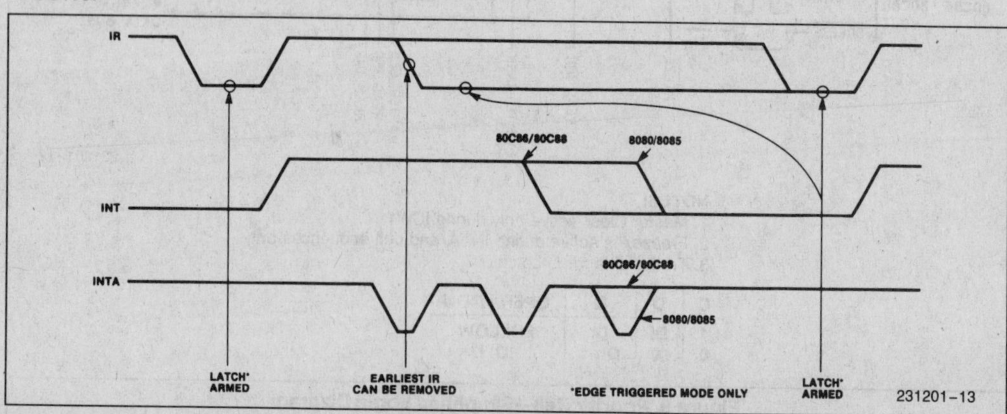

Figure 10. IR Triggering Timing Requirements

THE SPECIAL FULLY NESTED MODE

This mode will be used in the case of a big system where cascading is used, and the priority has to be conserved within each slave. In this case the fully nested mode will be programmed to the master (using ICW4). This mode is similar to the normal nested mode with the following exceptions:

a. When an interrupt request from a certain slave is in service this slave is not locked out from the master's priority logic and further interrupt requests from higher priority IR's within the slave will be recognized by the master and will initiate interrupts to the processor. (In the normal nestled mode a slave is masked out when its request is in service and no higher requests from the same slave can be serviced.)

b. When exiting the Interrupt Service routine the software has to check whether the interrupt serviced was the only one from that slave. This is done by sending a non-specific End of Interrupt (EOI) command to the slave and then reading its In-Service register and checking for zero. If it is empty, a non-specific EOI can be sent to the master too. If not, no EOI should be sent.

BUFFERED MODE

When the 82C59A-2 is used in a large system where bus driving buffers are required on the data bus and the cascading mode is used, there exists the problem of enabling buffers.

The buffered mode will structure the 82C59A-2 to send an enable signal on $\overline{SP}/\overline{EN}$ to enable the buffers. In this mode, whenever the 82C59A-2's data bus outputs are enabled, the $\overline{SP}/\overline{EN}$ output becomes active.

This modification forces the use of software programming to determine whether the 82C59A-2 is a master or a slave. Bit 3 in ICW4 programs the buffered mode, and bit 2 in ICW3 determines whether it is a master or a slave.

CASCADE MODE

The 82C59A-2 can be easily interconnected in a system of one master with up to eight slaves to handle up to 64 priority levels.

The master controls the slaves through the 3 line cascade bus. The cascade bus acts like chip selects to the slaves during the $\overline{INTA}$ sequence.

In a cascade configuration, the slave interrupt outputs are connected to the master interrupt request inputs. When a slave request line is activated and afterwards acknowledged, the master will enable the corresponding slave to release the device routine address during bytes 2 and 3 of INTA. (Byte 2 only for 80C86/80C88).

The cascade bus lines are normally low and will contain the slave address code from the trailing edge of the first INTA pulse to the trailing edge of the third pulse. Each 82C59A-2 in the system must follow a separate initialization sequence and can be programmed to work in a different mode. An EOI command must be issued twice: once for the master and once for the corresponding slave. An address decoder is required to activate the Chip Select (CS) input of each 82C59A-2.

The cascade lines of the Master 82C59A-2 are activated only for slave inputs, non slave inputs leave the cascade line inactive (low).

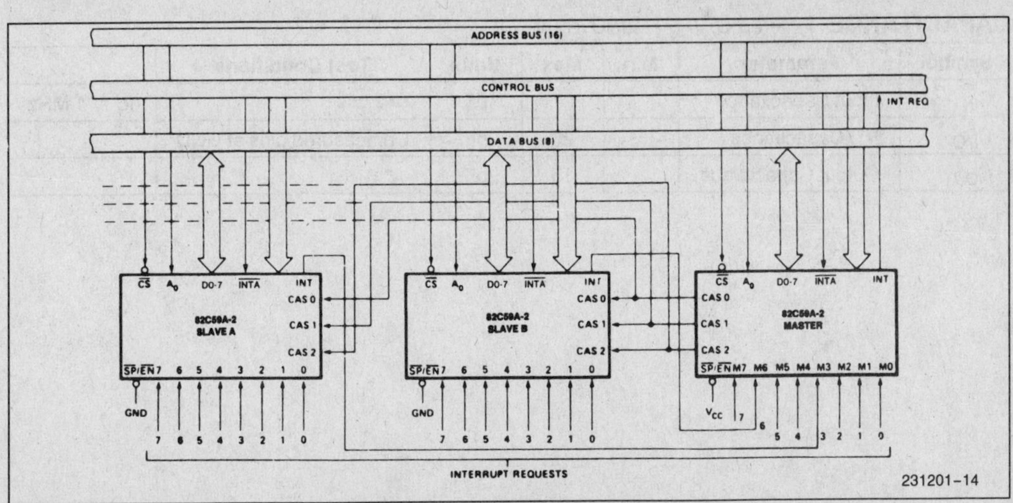

Figure 11. Cascading the 82C59A-2

NOTICE: This is a production data sheet. The specifications are subject to change without notice.

ABSOLUTE MAXIMUM RATINGS*

Ambient Temperature Under Bias ...... 0°C to 70°C
Storage Temperature .... −65°C to + 150°C
Supply Voltage (w.r.t. ground) .... −0.5 to 7.0V
Input Voltage (w.r.t. ground) ... −0.5 to V_{CC} + 0.5V
Output Voltage (w.r.t. ground) .. −0.5 to V_{CC} + 0.5V
Power Dissipation .... 0.9 Watt

**WARNING: Stressing the device beyond the "Absolute Maximum Ratings" may cause permanent damage. These are stress ratings only. Operation beyond the "Operating Conditions" is not recommended and extended exposure beyond the "Operating Conditions" may affect device reliability.*

D.C. CHARACTERISTICS T_A = 0°C to 70°C, V_{CC} = 5V ±10%

Symbol	Parameter	Min	Max	Units	Test Conditions
I_{CCS}	Standby Supply Current		10	μA	V_{IN} = V_{CC} or GND All IR = GND Outputs Unloaded V_{CC} = 5.5V
I_{CC}	Operating Supply Current		5	mA	(Note)
V_{IH}	Input High Voltage	2.2	V_{CC} + 0.5	V	
V_{IL}	Input Low Voltage	−0.5	0.8	V	
V_{OL}	Output Low Voltage		0.4	V	I_{OL} = 2.5 mA
V_{OH}	Output High Voltage	3.0 V_{CC} −0.4		V	I_{OH} = −2.5 mA I_{OH} = −100 μA
I_{LI}	Input Leakage Current		±1.0	μA	0V ≤ V_{IN} ≤ V_{CC}
I_{LO}	Output Leakage Current		±10	μA	0V ≤ V_{OUT} ≤ V_{CC}
I_{LIR}	IR Input Leakage Current		−300 +10	μA	V_{IN} = 0 V_{IN} = V_{CC}

NOTE:
Repeated data input with 80C86-2 timings.

CAPACITANCE T_A = 25°C; V_{CC} = GND = 0V

Symbol	Parameter	Min	Max	Units	Test Conditions	
C_{IN}	Input Capacitance		7	pF		fc = 1 MHz
$C_{I/O}$	I/O Capacitance		20	pF	Unmeasured pins at GND	
C_{OUT}	Output Capacitance		15	pF		

A.C. CHARACTERISTICS $T_A = 0°C$ to $70°C$, $V_{CC} = 5V \pm 10\%$

TIMING REQUIREMENTS

Symbol	Parameter	82C59A-2		Units	Test Conditions
		Min	Max		
TAHRL	AO/$\overline{CS}$ Setup to $\overline{RD}$/$\overline{INTA}$ ↓	10		ns	
TRHAX	AO/$\overline{CS}$ Hold after $\overline{RD}$/$\overline{INTA}$ ↑	5		ns	
TRLRH	$\overline{RD}$/$\overline{INTA}$ Pulse Width	160		ns	
TAHWL	AO/$\overline{CS}$ Setup to $\overline{WR}$ ↓	0		ns	
TWHAX	AO/$\overline{CS}$ Hold after $\overline{WR}$ ↑	0		ns	
TWLWH	$\overline{WR}$ Pulse Width	190		ns	
TDVWH	Data Setup to $\overline{WR}$ ↑	160		ns	
TWHDX	Data Hold after $\overline{WR}$ ↑	0		ns	
TJLJH	Interrupt Request Width (Low)	100		ns	(See Note)
TCVIAL	Cascade Setup to Second or Third $\overline{INTA}$ ↓ (Slave Only)	40		ns	
TRHRL	End of $\overline{RD}$ to next $\overline{RD}$ End of $\overline{INTA}$ to next $\overline{INTA}$ within an $\overline{INTA}$ sequence only	160		ns	
TWHWL	End of $\overline{WR}$ to next $\overline{WR}$	190		ns	
*TCHCL	End of Command to next Command (Not same command type) End of $\overline{INTA}$ sequence to next $\overline{INTA}$ sequence.	400		ns	

*Worst case timing for TCHCL in an actual microprocessor system is typically much greater than 400 ns (i.e. 8085A = 1.6 μs, 8085-A2 = 1 μs, 80C86 = 1 μs, 80C86-2 = 625 ns)

NOTE:
This is the low time required to clear the input latch in the edge triggered mode.

5

TIMING RESPONSES

Symbol	Parameter	8259A-2		Units	Test Conditions**
		Min	Max		
TRLDV	Data Valid from $\overline{RD}/\overline{INTA}$ ↓		120	ns	1
TRHDZ	Data Float after $\overline{RD}/\overline{INTA}$ ↑	10	85	ns	2
TJHIH	Interrupt Output Delay		300	ns	1
TIALCV	Cascade Valid from First $\overline{INTA}$ ↓ (Master Only)		360	ns	1
TRLEL	Enable Active from $\overline{RD}$ ↓ or $\overline{INTA}$ ↓		110	ns	1
TRHEH	Enable Inactive from $\overline{RD}$ ↑ or $\overline{INTA}$ ↑		150	ns	1
TAHDV	Data Valid from Stable Address		200	ns	1
TCVDV	Cascade Valid to Valid Data		200	ns	1

**Test Condition Definition Table

TEST CONDITION	V1	R1	R2	C1
1	1.7V	523Ω	OPEN	100 pf
2	4.5V	1.8 kΩ	1.8 kΩ	30 pf

A.C. TESTING INPUT, OUTPUT WAVEFORM

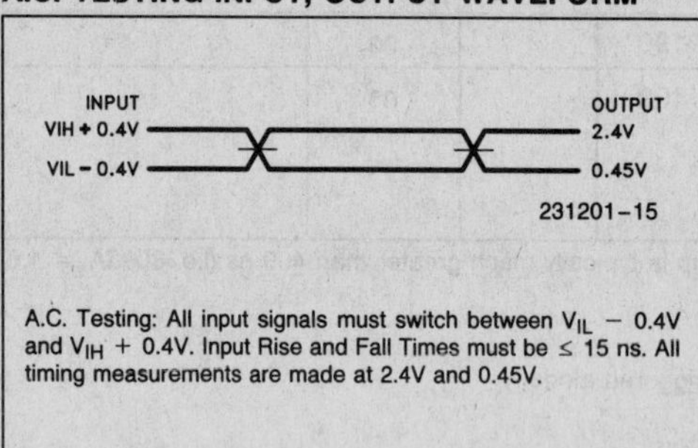

A.C. Testing: All input signals must switch between $V_{IL} - 0.4V$ and $V_{IH} + 0.4V$. Input Rise and Fall Times must be ≤ 15 ns. All timing measurements are made at 2.4V and 0.45V.

A.C. TESTING LOAD CIRCUIT

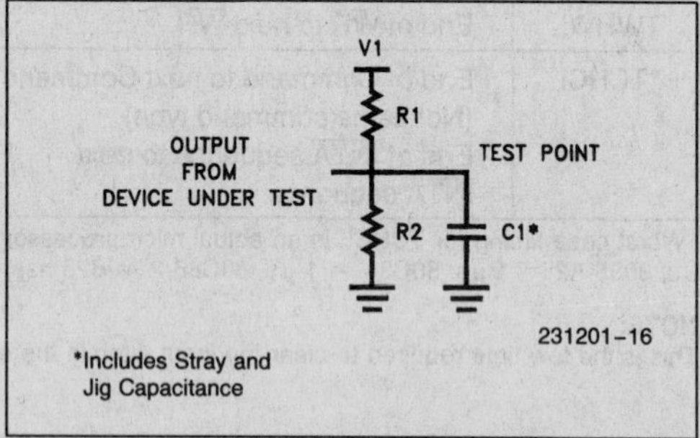

*Includes Stray and Jig Capacitance

WAVEFORMS

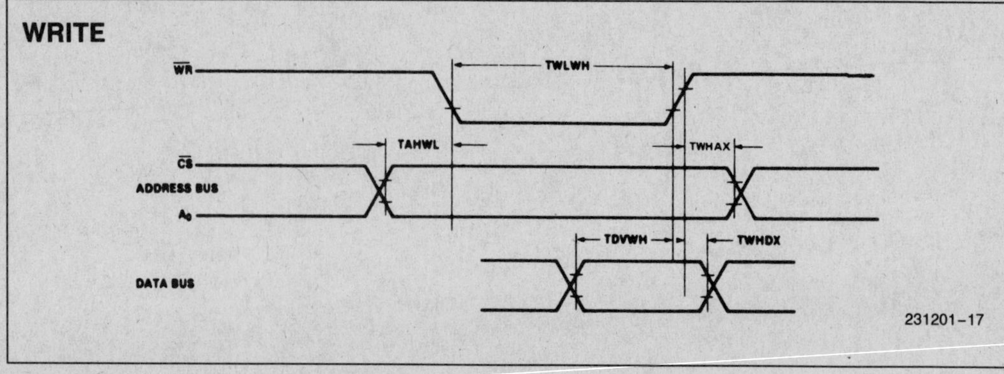

WAVEFORMS (Continued)

READ/INTA

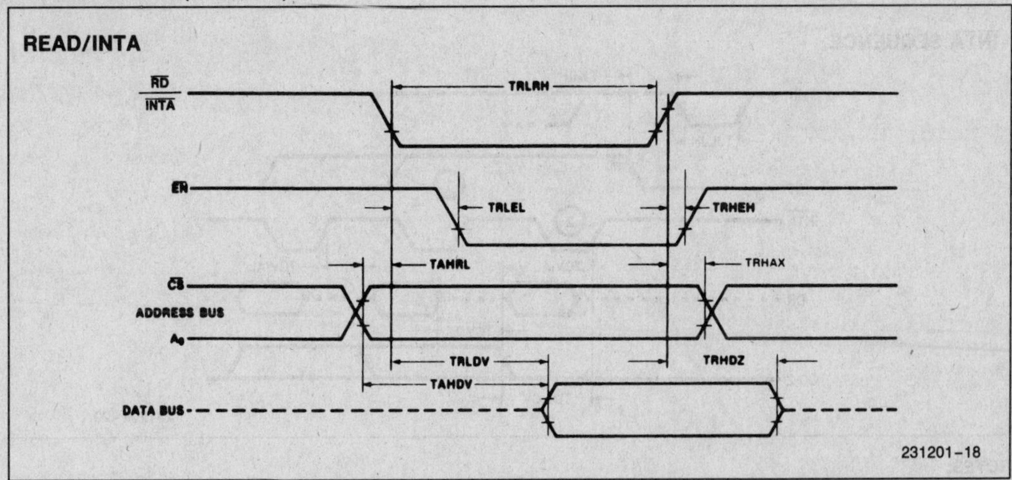

231201–18

OTHER TIMING

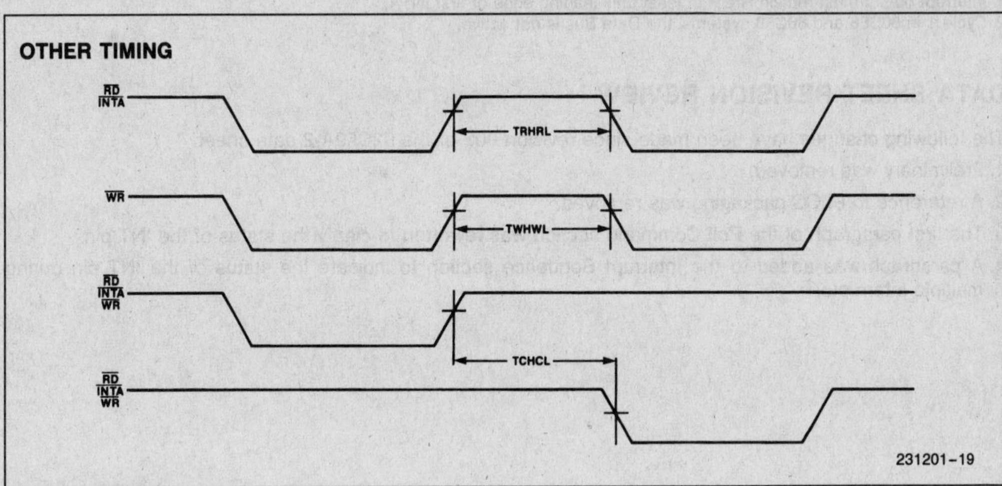

231201–19

5

WAVEFORMS (Continued)

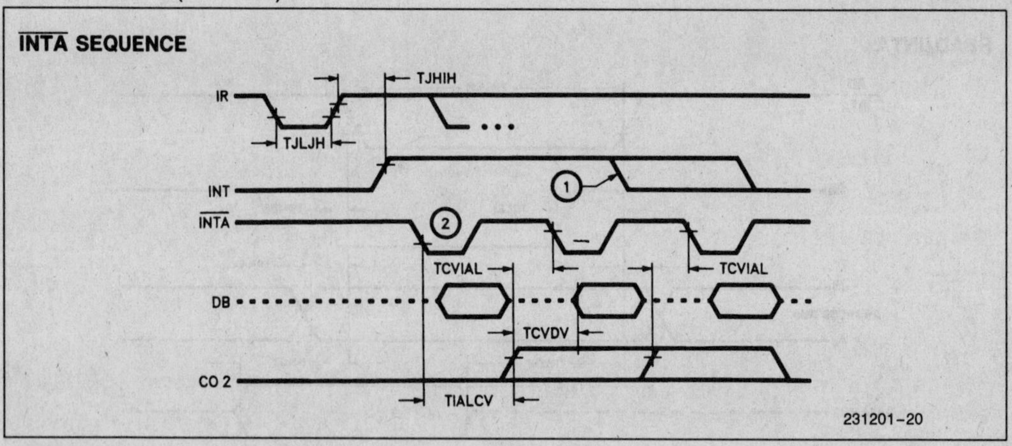

NOTES:
1. Interrupt output must remain HIGH at least until leading edge of first INTA.
2. Cycle 1 in 80C86 and 80C88 systems, the Data Bus is not active.

DATA SHEET REVISION REVIEW

The following changes have been made since revision 003 of the 82C59A-2 data sheet.

1. Preliminary was removed.
2. A reference to PLCC packaging was removed.
3. The first paragraph of the Poll Command section was rewritten to clarify the status of the INT pin.
4. A paragraph was added to the Interrupt Sequence section to indicate the status of the INT pin during multiple interrupts.

8279/8279-5
PROGRAMMABLE KEYBOARD/DISPLAY INTERFACE

- **Simultaneous Keyboard Display Operations**
- **Scanned Keyboard Mode**
- **Scanned Sensor Mode**
- **Strobed Input Entry Mode**
- **8-Character Keyboard FIFO**
- **2-Key Lockout or N-Key Rollover with Contact Debounce**
- **Dual 8- or 16-Numerical Display**
- **Single 16-Character Display**
- **Right or Left Entry 16-Byte Display RAM**
- **Mode Programmable from CPU**
- **Programmable Scan Timing**
- **Interrupt Output on Key Entry**
- **Available in EXPRESS**
  - **—Standard Temperature Range**
  - **—Extended Temperature Range**

The Intel 8279 is a general purpose programmable keyboard and display I/O interface device designed for use with Intel microprocessors. The keyboard portion can provide a scanned interface to a 64-contact key matrix. The keyboard portion will also interface to an array of sensors or a strobed interface keyboard, such as the hall effect and ferrite variety. Key depressions can be 2-key lockout or N-key rollover. Keyboard entries are debounced and strobed in an 8-character FIFO. If more than 8 characters are entered, overrun status is set. Key entries set the interrupt output line to the CPU.

The display portion provides a scanned display interface for LED, incandescent, and other popular display technologies. Both numeric and alphanumeric segment displays may be used as well as simple indicators. The 8279 has 16x8 display RAM which can be organized into dual 16x4. The RAM can be loaded or interrogated by the CPU. Both right entry, calculator and left entry typewriter display formats are possible. Both read and write of the display RAM can be done with auto-increment of the display RAM address.

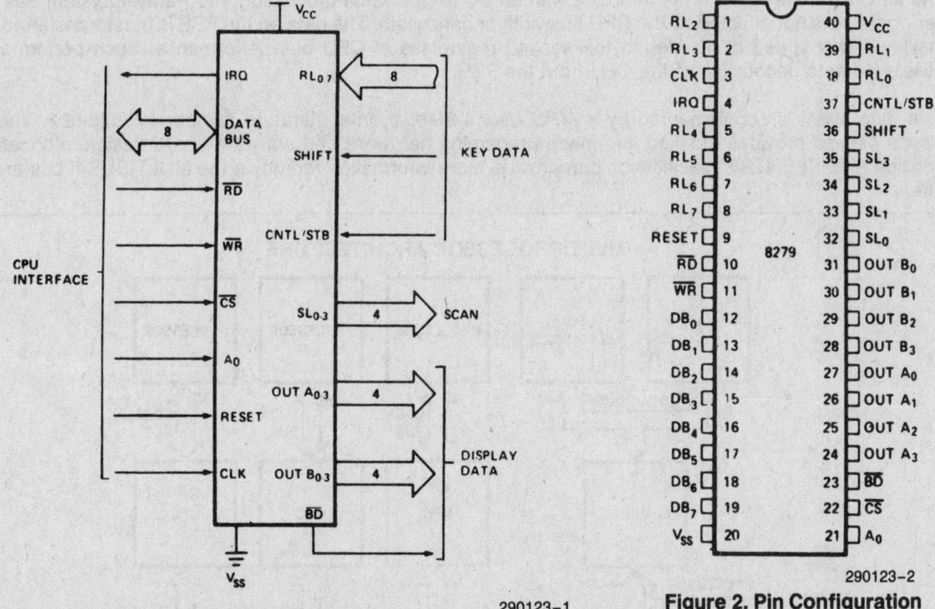

Figure 1. Logic Symbol

Figure 2. Pin Configuration

The complete document for this product is available on Intel's "Data-on-Demand" CD-ROM system. To obtain a copy, contact your local Intel field sales office, Intel technical distributor or call 1-800-548-4725.

September 1987
Order Number: 290123-002

82389 MESSAGE PASSING COPROCESSOR A MULTIBUS II BUS INTERFACE CONTROLLER

- **Highly Integrated VLSI Device**
  - **—Single-Chip Interface for the Parallel System Bus (IEEE 1296)**
  - **—Interrupt Handling/Bus Arbitration Functions**
  - **—Dual-Buffer Input and Output DMA Capabilities**
  - **—Nine 32-Byte High Speed FIFOs**
- **Multiple Interface Support**
  - **—Complete Protocol Support of the PSB Bus (Message Passing)**
  - **—Processor Independent Interface (8-, 16-, or 32-Bit CPU)**
  - **—Low-Cost 8-Bit Microcontroller Interface**
  - **—Dual-Port Memory Interface**
- **High Performance Coprocessing Functions**
  - **—Offloads CPU for Communication and Bus Interfacing**
  - **—40 Megabytes/sec Burst Transfer Speed**
  - **—Optimized for Real-Time Response (Max. 900 ns for 32-Byte Interrupt Packet)**
- **CMOS Technology**
- **149-Pin PGA Package (15 x 15 Grid)**

The MPC 82389 is a highly integrated VLSI device that maximizes the performance of a Multibus II based multiprocessor system. It integrates the functions of bus arbitration, data transmit packetizing, error handling and interrupt control. Because of these integrated functions, the host CPU can be offloaded to utilize the maximum bus performance and subsequently increase the system throughput. The MPC 82389 also supports geographic addressing by providing access to the local interconnect registers for reference and control.

The MPC 82389 is designed to interface with an 8-, 16-, or 32-bit processor. The Parallel System Bus (PSB) performance is not affected by the CPU buswidth or bandwidth. The data on the PSB is burst transferred at the maximum bus speed of 40 Megabytes/second regardless of CPU bus performance. Such performance is possible due to decoupling of the CPU from the PSB.

This data sheet is supplemented by a *MPC User's Manual*, Intel literature number 176526-002. The *MPC User's Manual* provides detailed information regarding hardware and software board design information. In addition, the IEEE 1296 specification can provide more information regarding the MULTIBUS II bus architecture.

MULTIPROCESSOR ARCHITECTURE

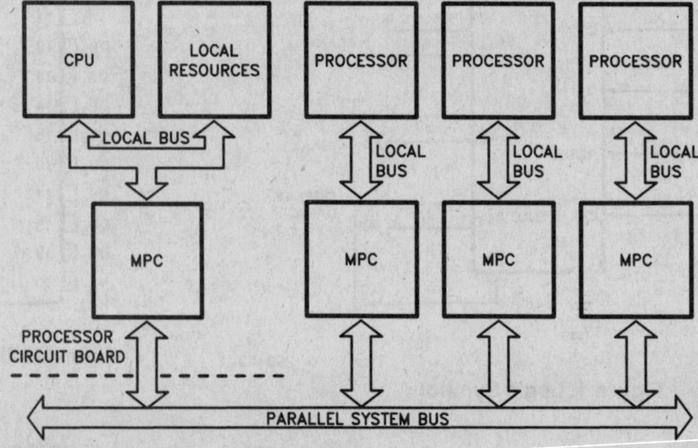

290145–1

November 1991
Order Number: 290145-004

1.0 MPC 82389 INTRODUCTION

The 82389 Message Passing Coprocessor (MPC) is a highly integrated CMOS VLSI device which interfaces any microprocessor to the MULTIBUS II Parallel System Bus (PSB). The PSB is defined for easy access and sharing of resources in a processing environment which allows the existence of both intelligent and non-intelligent add-in boards. The MPC complements the MULTIBUS II environment by providing an optimized interface for the PSB at its maximum bandwidth. The MPC also offloads the host CPU, thus increasing system throughput, by providing the necessary bus arbitration, message passing protocol, error handling and interrupt control for a MULTIBUS II system. Figure 1-1 shows an example of the MPC's message passing performance.

1.1 Functional Overview

The MPC 82389 is a bus interface controller which offloads the host CPU for interprocessor communication on the PSB. The MPC 82389 features four interfaces which support a variety of data transfer operations.

1.1.1 MPC 82389 INTERFACES

The three primary interfaces to the MPC (PSB Interface, Host CPU Interface and Interconnect Interface) all function asynchronously to one another. This is accomplished through the use of internal latches and FIFOs that allow references to occur simultaneously on all interfaces. In addition to the three primary interfaces, the MPC contains a Dual-Port Interface which provides compatibility with past system implementations and software.

—PSB Interface
The PSB Interface is the synchronized, shared data pathway in the MULTIBUS II system.

—Host CPU Interface
The Host CPU Interface is a set of addressable registers and ports that is the private pathway for the local microprocessor on the MULTIBUS II board.

—Interconnect Interface
The Interconnect Interface provides a path for added board functionality that is independent from the host CPU.

—Dual-Port Interface
The Dual-Port Interface supports shared memory references.

1.1.2 MAJOR OPERATIONS

—Unsolicited and Solicited Message Passing
The unsolicited and solicited message passing protocol is an interprocessor communication protocol which allows an intelligent agent* on the PSB to communicate with another agent without any CPU intervention at full PSB speed.

—PSB Memory and I/O Single Cycle Access
The MPC performs single cycle read/write transfers from the host to memory and I/O locations across the PSB. The MPC handles bus arbitration, parity generation and error detection without CPU intervention.

—Local Interconnect Access
The host CPU and other agents on the PSB can access local interconnect space via the MPC.

*An agent is any device with an interface to the PSB.

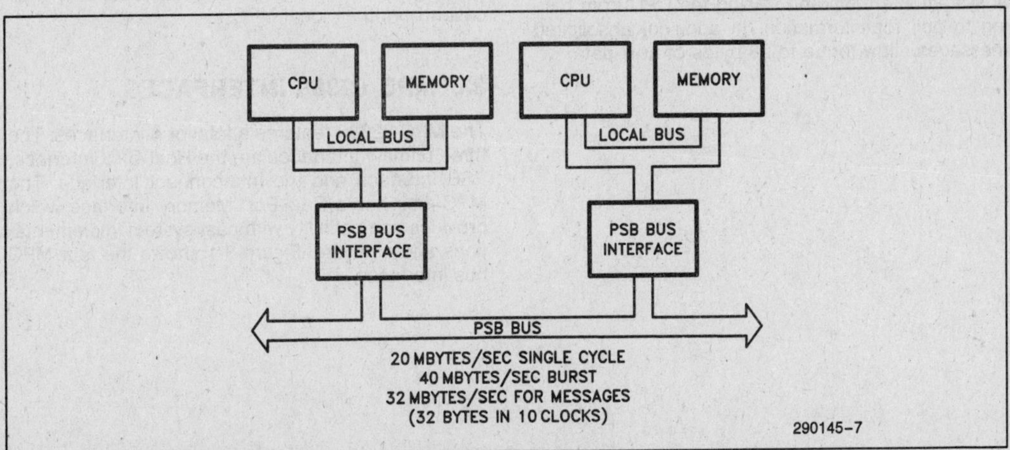

Figure 1-1. Message Passing Performance Example

—Remote Interconnect Access
The MPC enables the host CPU to access remote interconnect locations assigned to other PSB agents.

—Dual-Port Memory Access Support
Other PSB agents can access dual-port memory via the MPC.

—Central Services Module (CSM) support
The MPC has a minimal set of built-in CSM support features which allow the CSM to be incorporated into any MULTIBUS II board design.

2.0 MESSAGE PASSING PROTOCOL

The MULTIBUS II architecture designates the data transfer protocol between agents on the PSB as message passing. Message passing allows agents to transfer variable amounts of data at maximum PSB speed. The MPC fully supports the PSB's standardized message passing protocol. The entire handshaking procedure between agents on the PSB is handled by the MPC without CPU intervention.

There are two types of messages that can be transmitted from one agent to another: Unsolicited Messages and Solicited Messages.

2.1 Unsolicited Messages

Unsolicited messages are short, fixed-length messages that can arrive unexpectedly. Unsolicited messages can be transmitted without explicit buffer allocation and without synchronization between sending and receiving agents on the PSB. Unsolicited messages are often referred to as intelligent or virtual interrupts, since they can be used as a signaling mechanism between boards, replacing traditional system interrupts and freeing the CPU from having to poll for information. In addition, unsolicited messages allow for up to 28 bytes of user data.

2.2 Solicited Messages

Solicited messages are used to transfer large amounts of data. Up to 16 Mbytes (less 1 byte) of data can be transferred in a single solicited message transmission sequence. Solicited message transfers require the receiving agent to explicitly allocate a buffer. Buffer negotiation between sending and receiving agents is handled using unsolicited messages as follows:

— A buffer request message initiates a solicited message transfer. It requests the receiving agent to allocate a buffer large enough to hold the solicited data.

— A buffer grant message must be returned by the receiving agent before the solicited data can be transferred. The buffer grant informs the sending agent's MPC that a buffer has been allocated and indicates that the receiving agent's MPC is ready to begin the data transfer.

— A buffer reject message is returned by the receiving agent if a buffer for the solicited data cannot be provided. In this case, the rejection is final, and no further action is required.

If a DMA controller handles the solicited message transfer, DMA controller setup is also needed. Typically, the sending agent programs its DMA controller immediately before sending a buffer request, and the receiving agent programs its DMA controller immediately before sending a buffer grant.

Once solicited buffer negotiation is complete (the sending agent's MPC has received a buffer grant), the agents transfer the data without further intervention. The data is sent as a series of solicited packets on the sending agent's local bus. The MPCs perform transfer and routing across the PSB automatically. At the end of the solicited data transfer, both the sending and receiving agents get a completion indication from their local MPC.

3.0 MPC 82389 INTERFACES

The MPC 82389 features a total of 4 interfaces. The three primary interfaces are the Host CPU Interface, PSB Interface and the Interconnect Interface. The MPC also has a Dual-Port Memory Interface which provides compatibility with past system implementations and software. Figure 3-1 shows the four MPC bus interfaces.

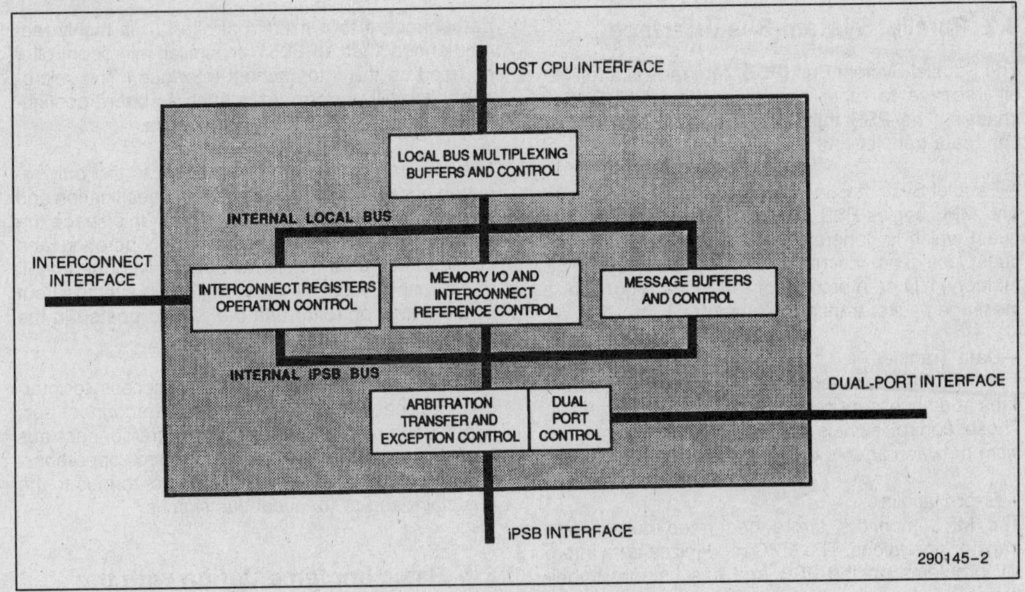

Figure 3-1. MPC Bus Interfaces

3.1 Host CPU Interface

The Host CPU Interface connects an 8-, 16-, or 32-bit processor to the MPC. The Host CPU Interface supports direct references to memory, I/O, and interconnect address space on the PSB. The entire Host CPU Interface is composed of three sub-interfaces: Register Sub-Interface, Reference Sub-Interface and DMA Sub-Interface.

—Register Sub-Interface
The Register Sub-Interface is composed of a bank of 8-bit registers on the Host CPU Interface. These registers provide the configuration, status and command interface for the host CPU. A host register operation is independent from operations which may be in progress at the MPC's other interfaces. However, some host register operations are dependent on the internal state of the MPC. In host register operations, the maximum duration is decided by the strobe width. Thus, the number of wait states required at the local interface is under the control of the host CPU.

—Reference Sub-Interface
The Reference Sub-Interface supports direct references to memory, I/O, and interconnect address space on the PSB. Memory and I/O references are initiated by the CPU to the MPC. The MPC responds to a memory or I/O reference by putting the CPU on hold while arbitrating for the PSB. The CPU is held in wait states until the reference is complete or until a bus exception condition occurs on the PSB. The Reference Sub-Interface supports both read and write operations to the registers. The local interconnect address space is differentiated from the interconnect address on the PSB by the bit pattern stored in the MPC's slot address register.

—DMA Sub-Interface
The DMA Sub-Interface supports data transfers between the local memory and the MPC during solicited message operations. The DMA Interface is designed to support either two-cycle or fly-by (single-cycle) read/write transfers. For two-cycle operations, the DMA controller performs one cycle into memory and another cycle to the MPC; a read command is used to get data from the MPC and a write command is used to put data into the MPC. Fly-by operations allow data to be transferred during a single bus cycle; a fly-by transfer will use a write command to get data from the MPC (corresponding to a memory write) and a read command to put data into the MPC (corresponding to a memory read). The higher performance possible with fly-by transfers mandates the alignment of data on 4-byte boundaries.

3.2 Parallel System Bus Interface

The Parallel System Bus (PSB) Interface is a full 32-bit interface to other boards in the MULTIBUS II chassis. The PSB Interface supports PSB arbitration, data transfer and error handling.

—Parallel System Bus Arbitration
The MPC begins PSB access arbitration upon a request which is generated inside the MPC. This request could be the result of a synchronized PSB memory, I/O or interconnect reference request or a message packet transmit request from the CPU.

—Data Transfer
The PSB Interface contains all the address/data lines and necessary control signals for data transfer. These control signals provide the control mechanism between agents during transfer operations.

—Error Handling
The MPC monitors errors generated during data transfer operations. The MPC recognizes data integrity problems on the PSB and bus timeout conditions.

3.3 Interconnect Interface

The Interconnect Interface is an independent 8-bit communication interface which allows the MPC to be connected to a microcontroller. (It is highly recommended that an 8051 or similar microcontroller be used on the Interconnect Interface.) This microcontroller will perform tasks such as board configuration at startup and local diagnostics.

The interconnect space of an agent is the only required bus space by the IEEE 1296 specification and has a 512-byte register range. Within this space the microcontroller can store the local operating and configuration parameters associated with the agent. For example, local diagnostics can be executed out of the microcontroller and the results posted in the interconnect space.

Local resources on an agent gain access to interconnect space through the MPC's interconnect bus. A microcontroller connects to the interconnect bus for intelligent handling of interconnect operations. All interconnect bus signals are asynchronous to the bus clock and to the local bus signals.

3.4 Basic Implementation with the MPC 82389

Figure 3-2 shows a basic implementation of the MPC 82389. Included in this implementation is the Interconnect Interface, the Host CPU Interface and the PSB Interface.

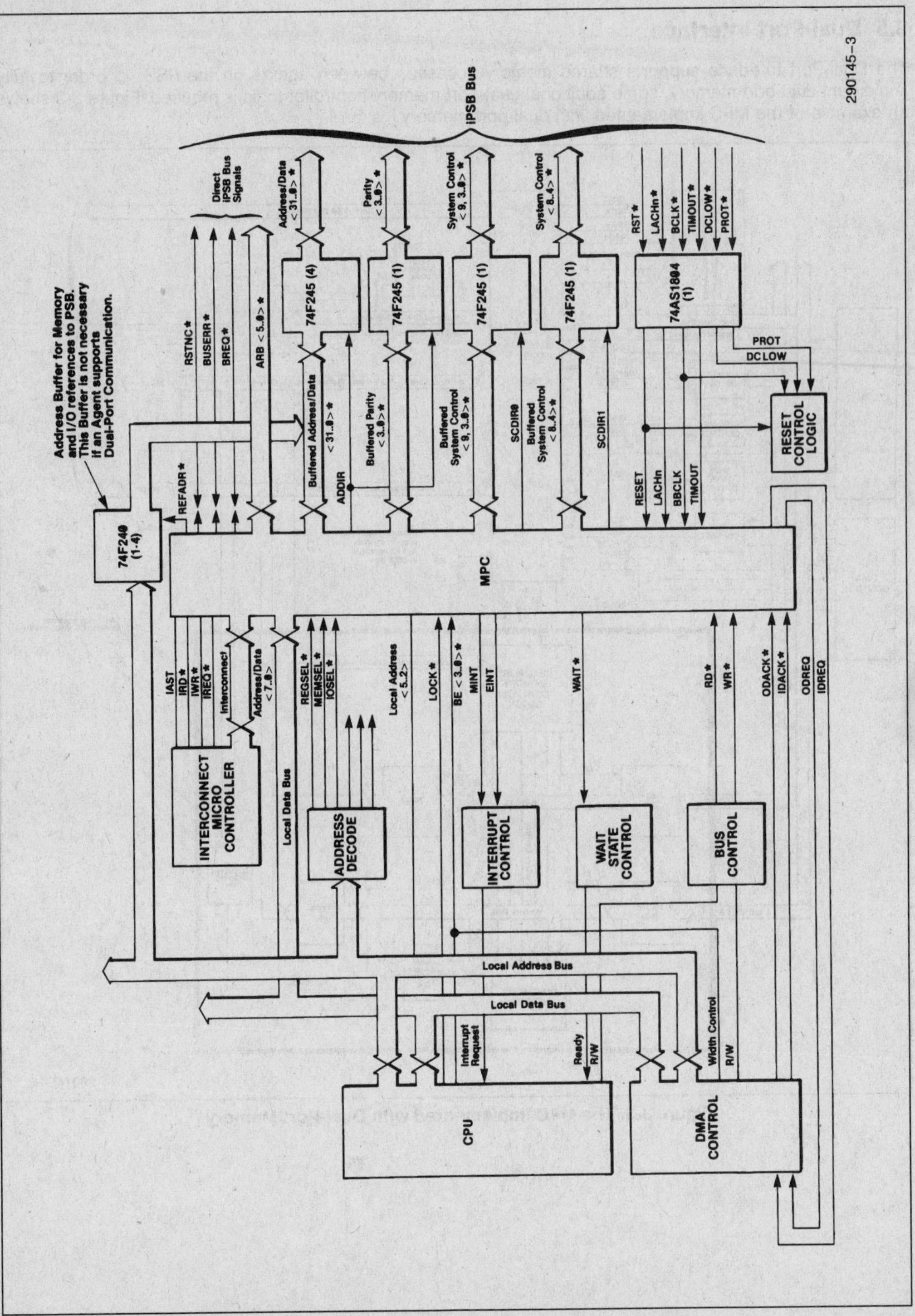

290145-3

Figure 3-2. MPC Implementation to Support References

3.5 Dual-Port Interface

The Dual-Port Interface supports shared memory accesses between agents on the PSB. In order to fully implement dual-port memory, some additional dual-port memory controller logic is required. Figure 3-3 shows an example of the MPC implemented with dual-port memory.

290145–4

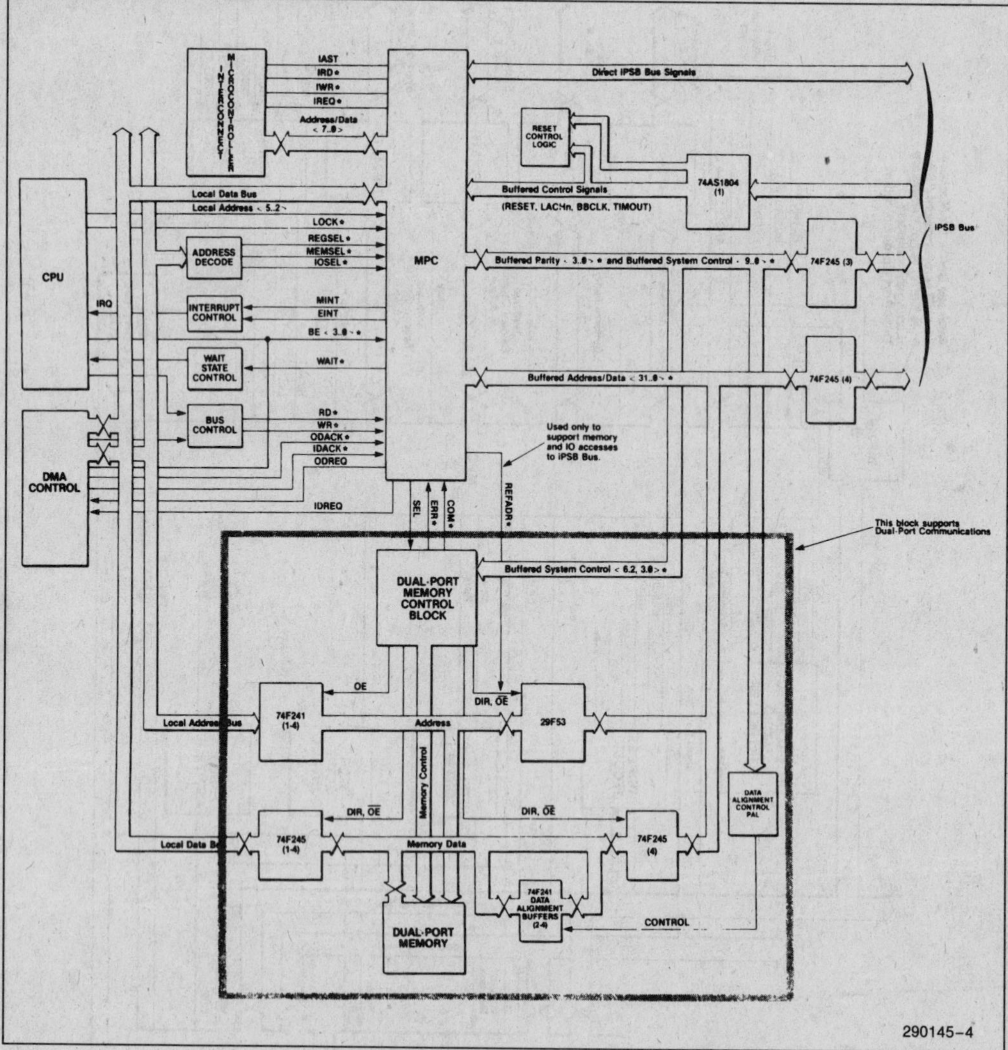

Figure 3-3. The MPC Implemented with Dual-Port Memory

4.0 MPC 82389 OPERATIONS

The primary function of the MPC 82389 is MULTIBUS II message passing. In addition to message passing, the MPC performs the following functions:

— Memory and I/O Reference

— Local Interconnect Reference

— Remote Interconnect Reference

— Interconnect Replier Operations

— Dual-Port Replier Operations

— Central Services Module Support

4.1 MULTIBUS II Message Passing

The MPC manages the routing of message packets as they flow between the interfaces of each MULTIBUS II agent in the system. For message traffic on the PSB, message decode logic on the PSB input bus determines message routing through the MPC. For the Host CPU Interface and Interconnect Interface, the MPC defines a signal protocol for message passing.

MULTIBUS II messages, both unsolicited and solicited, are transferred through nine dedicated internal FIFO buffers between the Host CPU Interface and PSB Interface. Unsolicited messages are intelligent (also called virtual) interrupts which notify the receiving agent to prepare for the receipt of solicited messages. Unsolicited messages use the Transmit/Error FIFO and the Receive FIFO. The Transmit FIFO holds a 32-byte packet for transmittal across the PSB. If there is an error in transmission, the Transmit FIFO becomes the Error FIFO, where the errant message can be read back along with error status. The Receive FIFO is a circular queue of four 32-byte buffers from which unsolicited messages are received from the PSB by the host CPU.

Solicited messages consist of information data packets which are transmitted between agents. Solicited messages use the Solicited Input FIFO and Solicited Output FIFO. These FIFOs are dual 32-byte buffers which are used for the temporary storage of solicited data packets as they travel between the Host CPU Interface and the PSB Interface. The solicited output header logic attaches header information to the solicited data packet before sending it onto the PSB. All FIFOs are able to operate independently and concurrently, thus creating a true multitasking message passing environment. Figure 4-1 shows the nine dedicated internal FIFO buffers.

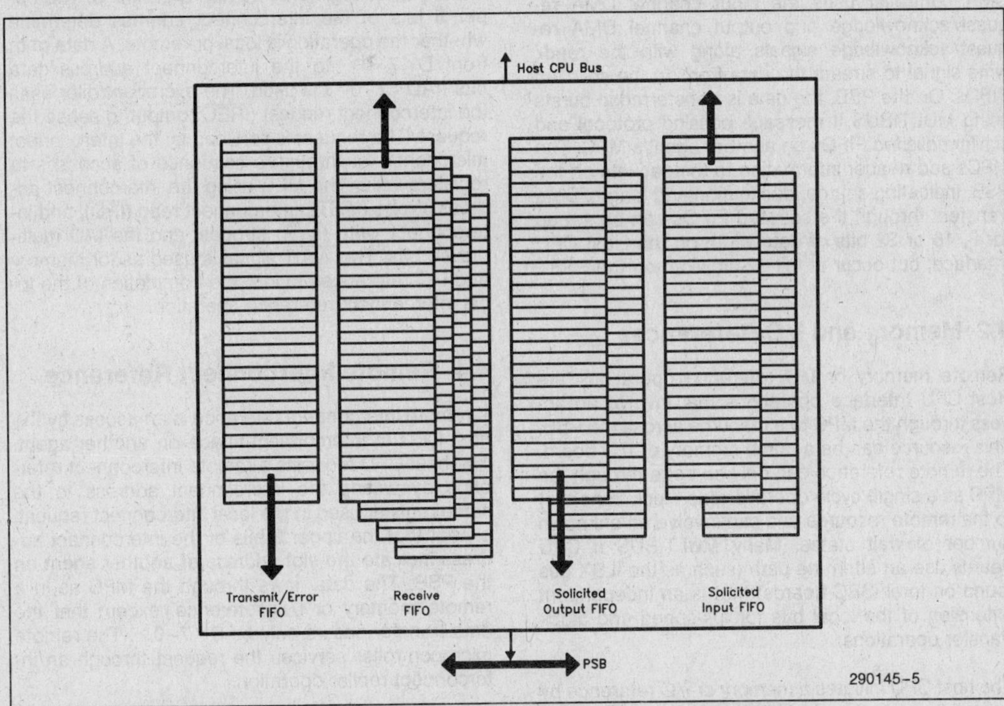

Figure 4-1. The MPC Uses Nine Dedicated Internal 32-Byte FIFO Buffers

4.1.1 UNSOLICITED TRANSMIT/RECEIVE

Unsolicited message passing sequences occur between the Host CPU Interface and the PSB Interface using FIFOs internal to the MPC. FIFO status is available on the Host CPU Interface and in state machines internal to the MPC. On the Host CPU Interface, host register operations write bytes to the Transmit FIFO and read bytes from the Receive FIFO. On the PSB, the MPC manages the emptying and filling of the Transmit and Receive FIFOs using MULTIBUS II message passing protocol and the Transmit and Receive FIFOs on another agent's MPC. For detailed information about message passing protocol across the PSB, see the *IEEE 1296 High Performance Synchronous 32-bit Bus Standard.*

4.1.2 SOLICITED INPUT/OUTPUT

Solicited transfers are pre-negotiated using unsolicited message sequences. Dedicated FIFOs (Solicited Input FIFO and Solicited Output FIFO) are then used for the transfer of solicited data packets. This allows large amounts of data to be moved between agents independently of unsolicited messages. In most cases, the solicited transfer occurs under DMA control, freeing the host CPU to handle other activities. The DMA controller uses the input channel DMA request/acknowledge and output channel DMA request/acknowledge signals along with the read/write signal to stream the data from/to the solicited FIFOs. On the PSB, the data is transferred in bursts using MULTIBUS II message passing protocol and similar solicited FIFOs on another agent's MPC. The MPCs add header information to the packets on the PSB, indicating source, destination and length. Data transfers through the solicited FIFOs can be set up for 8, 16 or 32 bits of data width on the Host CPU Interface, but occur at full 32-bit width on the PSB.

4.2 Memory and I/O References

Remote memory or I/O reference operations are Host CPU Interface operations that involve an access through the MPC to a resource across the PSB. This resource can be a dumb memory or I/O board. The remote reference can only be done through the MPC as a single cycle operation (no block transfers) to the remote resource and can involve an unknown number of wait states. Many MULTIBUS II CPU boards use an alternate path (such as the iLBX bus found on Intel iSBC boards) that is an independent extension of the local bus for full-speed and block transfer operations.

The host CPU initiates a memory or I/O reference by activating memory select ($\overline{\text{MEMSEL}}$†) or I/O select ($\overline{\text{IOSEL}}$), A<5-2>, $\overline{\text{BE}}$<3-0>, with a $\overline{\text{RD}}$ or $\overline{\text{WR}}$ strobe. If necessary, $\overline{\text{LOCK}}$ is activated to allow back-to-back accesses across the PSB, holding all other agents off the memory or I/O resource. The MPC activates its $\overline{\text{WAIT}}$ output to indicate that the operation is in progress.

The data for reference operation proceeds through the MPC and PSB to a memory or I/O address on another agent. A data path from D<31-0> through the buffered address/data bus ($\overline{\text{BAD}}$<31-0>) is used for the data transfer. Data is latched internally in a reference data latch. Parity is generated to the PSB on BPAR <3-0> for the data on each write operation and checked on data read. Completion of the operation is indicated when the MPC deactivates the $\overline{\text{WAIT}}$ output.

The memory or I/O address for the reference operation is routed around the MPC through an external reference address latch. This latch is controlled by the REFADR signal from the MPC.

4.3 Local Interconnect Reference

A local interconnect reference operation is an access by the host CPU to the interconnect records maintained by the local interconnect microcontroller. The geographic interconnect address is preloaded into a pair of registers internal to the MPC. The upper 5 bits of the interconnect address determine whether the operation is local or remote. A data path from D<7-0> to the interconnect address/data bus (IAD<7-0>) is used. The microcontroller uses the interconnect request ($\overline{\text{IREQ}}$) output to sense the request. The request is serviced by the interconnect microcontroller through a sequence of accesses to registers within the MPC using the interconnect address strobe ($\overline{\text{IAST}}$), interconnect read ($\overline{\text{IRD}}$), and interconnect write ($\overline{\text{IWR}}$) strobes, and the IAD multiplexed bus. The $\overline{\text{WAIT}}$ signal is used as for memory and I/O references to indicate completion of the local interconnect reference operation.

4.4 Remote Interconnect Reference

A remote interconnect reference is an access by the host CPU to interconnect space on another agent. The host CPU requests a remote interconnect reference by writing the interconnect address to the same register used in the local interconnect request, except that the upper 5 bits of the interconnect address indicate the slot address of another agent on the PSB. The data flows through the MPC as in a remote memory or I/O reference, except that the data transfer occurs only on D<7-0>. The remote microcontroller services the request through an interconnect replier operation.

†* indicates that the signal is active low.

4.5 Interconnect Replier Operations

When another agent performs a remote interconnect reference request, it gains access to local interconnect space through the MPC. The MPC decodes an interconnect request on the PSB for a slot ID match and signals the interconnect microcontroller independently of the local bus interface. The microcontroller then handles the request in the same way as a local interconnect request.

4.6 Dual-Port Replier Operations

Other agents can access dual-port memory via the MPC. A memory access request on the PSB is decoded by the MPC for an address range match and serviced by the dual-port controller (external circuitry must be provided). The MPC provides only the handshaking path. Data transfer occurs directly on the $\overline{BAD}$ bus. If a bus exception occurs while a dual-port memory reference is in progress, the MPC will signal the dual-port controller to terminate the operation.

4.7 Central Services Modular Support

The IEEE 1296 specification defines the Central Services Module (CSM) that resides in Slot 0 of a MULTIBUS II system. The CSM is responsible for these functions:

— reset sequencing (generates reset signal on the PSB)

— assignment of card slot and arbitration IDs during reset initialization

— generation of system wide clocks for all agents (bus clocks and time of day)

— generation of bus timeout

— battery back-up of system constants (host ID, time of day, etc.)

The MPC has a minimal set of built-in CSM support features that allow the incorporation of CSM into any MULTIBUS II board design. The MPC, interconnect microcontroller, and a small amount of external circuitry can fully implement the CSM automatically when the board is inserted into Card Slot 0.

4.7.1 ADDITIONAL CSM REQUIREMENTS

In addition to the interconnect microcontroller and the MPC, the following functions must be provided through external logic:

— clock generation

— PSB reset generation

— cold/warm start detection

— PSB timeout generation

The clock generator provides the bus clock ($\overline{BCLK}$) and central clock ($\overline{CCLK}$) signals to the PSB. The reset generator provides the hardware reset line ($\overline{RESET}$) to all agents on the PSB. Cold/warm start detection circuitry distinguishes between a power-up reset and a warm-start reset; on power-up the CSM assigns arbitration and slot IDs. The PSB timeout function determines when the PSB is hung.

See the *MPC User's Manual* (Intel literature number 176526-002) and the *CSM\002 Hardware Reference Manual* (Intel literature number 459706-001) for more information about the CSM.

5.0 MPC 82389 PIN DESCRIPTIONS

This section describes each signal pin (or group of pins) on the MPC. Emphasis is placed on giving as much information as possible to ease the task of designing hardware associated with the MPC signal pins. The pins are described in terms of these functional groups:

- PSB interface
- local bus (host CPU) interface
- dual-port memory control
- interconnect bus interface

5.1 PSB Signals

The PSB signals provide the interface to other boards in the MULTIBUS II chassis. Very little support circuitry is required for this part of the board. Only high-current drivers and reset control logic is needed. Some MPC signal pins have built-in open collector high-current drivers that allow connection directly to the PSB. For complete information on the PSB, see the *IEEE 1296 High Performance Synchronous 32-bit Bus Standard* document.

PSB signals fall into five groups, depending on function:

- arbitration operation signal group
- address/data bus signal group
- system control signal group
- central control signal group
- exception operation signal group

Unless otherwise stated, all PSB signals are synchronous to the bus clock.

5

NOTE:
High current drivers used to drive the buffered address/data (BAD) bus should be controlled with minimal logic. This is to limit propagation delays and avoid possible bus contention problems. Ensure that the placement of these drivers and the MPC is done as close to the PSB (the P1 connector on a MULTIBUS II board) as possible to minimize signal stub lengths and capacitive loading.

5.1.1 ARBITRATION OPERATION SIGNAL GROUP

These MPC pins are used by an agent to obtain exclusive access to the PSB. They are all high-current drive, open-collector signals. Below is a description of each signal.

BREQ (Bus Request). BREQ is a bidirectional open-collector signal that connects directly to the PSB. As an input to the MPC, it indicates that agents are awaiting access to the bus. As an output, the MPC asserts BREQ to request PSB access.

ARB<5-0> (Arbitration). ARB<5-0> are bidirectional, open-collector signals that connect directly to the PSB. ARB<5-0> are used (during normal operation) to identify the mode and arbitration priority of an agent during an arbitration cycle. During system initialization (while reset is active), the central services module (CSM) drives these signals to initialize slot and arbitration IDs.

5.1.2 ADDRESS/DATA BUS SIGNAL GROUP

This signal group includes a 32-bit multiplexed address/data path (BAD<31-0>) and the byte parity signals (BPAR<3-0>). These signals require buffering through bus transceivers before connection to the PSB. This signal group also includes the bus transceiver control signals (ADDIR and REFADR).

BAD<31-0> (Buffered Address/Data). BAD<31-0> are the 32 bidirectional, multiplexed address/data signals that provide the interface to the PSB address/data bus (AD) when buffered through 74F245 or equivalent bus transceivers.

NOTE:
Do not use pull-up resistors to drive the BAD bus high. If pull-up resistors are present, the MPC cannot guarantee valid logic states with proper timing.

BPAR<3-0> (Buffered Parity). BPAR are four signals that provide parity for the 32-bit BAD bus. These bidirectional lines connect to the PSB PAR<3-0> signals through a 74F245 or equivalent transceiver. These signals are used to receive byte parity for incoming data and to drive byte parity for outgoing data.

ADDIR (Address/Data Direction). ADDIR is an output that provides direction control over the bus transceivers buffering the BAD<31-0> and BPAR<3-0> signals. In the high state, this signal causes the transceivers to drive address/data information along with parity onto the PSB. In the low state, this signal causes address/data information and parity to be received from the PSB.

REFADR (Reference Address Enable). REFADR is an output used to enable external reference address buffers during reference operations. Asserting this signal places the reference address onto the BAD bus. The address path enabled by this signal is only used for memory and I/O reference operations to the PSB. It is not used during message passing or for PSB references to interconnect space.

5.1.3 SYSTEM CONTROL SIGNAL GROUP

The system control signal group on the PSB provides a control mechanism between agents during transfer operations.

BSC<9-0> (Buffered System Control). BSC<9-0> is a group of ten bidirectional signals that connect to the PSB through 74F245 or equivalent transceivers. Agents on the PSB use these signals for commands or status, depending on the phase of the operation. The function of each of these lines during request and reply phases of transfer operations is summarized in Table 5-1.

Table 5-1. Summary of $\overline{\text{BSC}}$ Signal Functions

Signal	Request Phase	Reply Phase
$\overline{\text{BSC0}}$	Bus Owner in Request Phase	Bus Owner in Reply Phase
$\overline{\text{BSC1}}$	LOCK	LOCK
$\overline{\text{BSC2}}$	Data Width	End-of-Transfer
$\overline{\text{BSC3}}$	Data Width	Bus Owner Ready
$\overline{\text{BSC4}}$	Address Space	Replying Agent Ready
$\overline{\text{BSC5}}$	Address Space	Agent Status
$\overline{\text{BSC6}}$	Read/Write Data Transfer	Agent Status
$\overline{\text{BSC7}}$	Reserved	Agent Status
$\overline{\text{BSC8}}$	Even Parity on BSC<7-4>	Even Parity on BSC<7-4>
$\overline{\text{BSC9}}$	Even Parity on BSC<3-0>	Even Parity on BSC<3-0>

NOTE:
The end-of-transfer (EOT) handshake in single-cycle operations is indicated by BSC<4,3,2> as follows: the requesting MPC drives $\overline{\text{BSC}}$<3,2> and waits for the replier to drive $\overline{\text{BSC4}}$; when the replier responds, the EOT handshake is complete.

SCDIR<1,0> (System Control Direction). SCDIR<1,0> are output signals that provide direction control of the 74F245 transceivers driving and receiving $\overline{\text{BSC}}$<9-0>. SCDIR0 provides control for $\overline{\text{BSC}}$<9,3-0>, while SCDIR 1 provides control for $\overline{\text{BSC}}$<8-4>. When either signal is high, the bus transceiver drives $\overline{\text{BSC}}$ signals onto the PSB. When either signal is low, signals on the PSB are driven onto the $\overline{\text{BSC}}$ lines.

5.1.4 CENTRAL CONTROL SIGNAL GROUP

The central control signal group provides bus status and control information for devices operating on the PSB. The CSM, residing in slot 0 of the MULTIBUS II backplane, generates $\overline{\text{BCLK}}$, LACHn, and RESET.

BBCLK (Buffered Bus Clock). BBCLK is received by the MPC to synchronize all operations on the PSB. This input should be connected to $\overline{\text{BCLK}}$ (on the PSB) using a 74AS1804 or equivalent inverting buffer. The falling edge of $\overline{\text{BCLK}}$ provides all system timing references. BBCLK normally has a fixed operating frequency of 10 MHz.

NOTE:
$\overline{\text{BCLK}}$ can be varied from DC to 10 MHz. You may use this feature for single-stepping on the PSB during debugging.

LACHn (ID Latch). LACHn is an input signal used during initialization of slot and arbitration IDs (where "n" is the slot number). When the RESET signal is active, LACHn indicates when a slot or arbitration ID is available and should be latched. LACHn is an active high input and should be connected to the $\overline{\text{LACHn}}$ signal on the PSB with a 74AS1804 or equivalent inverting buffer.

RESET. Reset is an input that places the MPC in a known state. Only the parts of the MPC involved with initialization of slot and arbitration IDs remain unaffected. RESET is an active high input and should be connected to the $\overline{\text{RST}}$ signal on the PSB with a 74AS1804 or equivalent inverting buffer.

If the MPC is used in a CSM implementation, the interconnect microcontroller and some external logic controls RESET. On power up, the CSM generates the RESET signal to the backplane. Within a few clock cycles, receiving MPCs complete their internal reset. Table 5-2 summarizes the states of MPC signal outputs while the RESET signal is active.

Table 5-2. Signal States During Reset

Signal	Reset State	Signal	Reset State
BREQ	Z(H)	ARB<5-0>	Z(H)
BAD<31-0>	Z	D<31-0>	Z
ADDIR	L	SEL	H
REFADR	H	WAIT	H
BSC<9-0>	Z	ODREQ, IDREQ	L
SCDIR<1,0>	L	MINT, EINT	L
BUSERR	Z(H)	RSTNC	L

NOTE:
H = Electrical high state.
L = Electrical low state.
Z = High impedance (tri-state).

RSTNC (Reset Not Complete). Agents assert RSTNC during reset to extend the initialization time period beyond the time that RESET allows. RSTNC is a bidirectional OR-tied signal on the PSB that is low when one or more agents have not completed their reset requirements. Agents cannot perform bus operations while RSTNC is asserted. However, agents may access local interconnect space if your firmware implementation allows such access. RSTNC is an open-collector signal with high-current drive that connects directly to the PSB.

5.1.5 Exception Operation Signal Group

The exception operation signal group indicates exception errors on the PSB.

BUSERR (Bus Error). The MPC asserts BUSERR when a data integrity problem on the PSB is detected during a transfer operation. Possible problems are: detection of a parity error on the BAD bus or BSC lines, or a protocol error associated with the BSC lines. BUSERR is a bidirectional, open-collector signal with high current drive that connects directly to the PSB.

TIMOUT (Timeout). TIMOUT, as an input from the PSB, is used to detect a bus timeout condition. The CSM activates this signal when it determines that an agent is taking too much time asserting a handshake signal, or if a bus owner has maintained bus ownership for an excessive length of time. The exact amount of time is a fixed value relative to BBCLK that is approximately 10,000 clock cycles (1 ms @ 10 MHz). TIMOUT is an active high input to the MPC and must be connected to the TIMOUT signal of the PSB through a 74AS1804 or equivalent inverting buffer.

When the MPC is configured for CSM operation, TIMOUT becomes an output, generating the timeout condition to all agents on the PSB. In this case, the TIMOUT pin should be connected to the PSB by a 74F242 driver or equivalent.

5.2 Dual-Port Memory Control Signals

The MPC provides these signals (SEL, COM, ERR) to support dual-port memory. In order to fully implement dual-port memory, some additional dual-port memory controller logic is required.

SEL (Select). The SEL output indicates that a dual-port memory access is in progress. SEL initiates dual-port operations and may be used to enable the dual-port data buffers onto the BAD bus. When the MPC receives the EOT handshake, or if the MPC detects an exception, it deactivates SEL.

COM (Complete). COM is an input to the MPC. The dual-port memory controller asserts COM to indicate completion of a dual-port access. COM is assumed to be synchronous to the bus clock. After the memory controller has asserted COM, the MPC asserts the replier ready (BSC4) signal on the next bus clock. The memory controller cannot deassert COM until the EOT handshake is complete on the PSB. This requires that the memory controller monitor the PSB for the EOT handshake.

ERR (Error). ERR, an input to the MPC, is asserted by the dual-port memory controller to signal a memory data parity error. ERR must be stable (high or low) whenever COM is asserted. The MPC responds to this signal by completing the replier handshake on the PSB using a *data error* agent error code. This signal may be asynchronous to the bus clock since it is qualified by the COM signal.

5.3 Local Bus Signals

The MPC local bus allows many types of microprocessors, perhaps with differing data widths, byte alignment, and bit ordering, to connect to the MULTIBUS II PSB. This microprocessor is often referred to as the *host CPU* on the MULTIBUS II processor board. The MPC has five signal groups on the local bus:

- data bus
- address/status signals
- transfer control
- interrupt signals
- DMA control lines

5.3.1 DATA BUS

The local data bus is the signal path for data transfers between the host CPU and the MPC.

D<31–0>. D<31–0> is the 32-bit local data bus. Although this is a 32-bit interface, the MPC allows operation with processors using 8-, 16-, or 32-bit data busses.

NOTE:
Intel CPU architecture defines bit 0 and byte 0 as least significant. When connecting non-Intel processors to the MPC local data bus, it is important that this bit and byte ordering be maintained across the PSB. This allows agents of differing CPU types to work together in a single chassis. If byte-swapping is needed, see the discussion of the *byte enable* (BE<3–0>) signal pins.

5.3.2 ADDRESS/STATUS SIGNALS

The address/status signals select or identify all MPC operations over the local bus.

A<5–2> (Address). The address inputs select MPC registers for message and interconnect space operations. A1 and A0 are omitted to provide a consistent register address for all data bus width options. A <5–2> are qualified by $\overline{RD}$ or $\overline{WR}$ and therefore must be stable within the specified set-up and hold window.

$\overline{MEMSEL}$ (Memory Select). This MPC input signal tells the MPC that the current operation is a memory reference across the PSB. $\overline{MEMSEL}$ is qualified by $\overline{RD}$ or $\overline{WR}$ and therefore must be stable within the specified set-up and hold window.

NOTE:
$\overline{MEMSEL}$, $\overline{IOSEL}$, $\overline{REGSEL}$ $\overline{IDACK}$, and $\overline{ODACK}$ are mutually exclusive. In order to be valid, no more than one should be active during the same set-up and hold window.

$\overline{IOSEL}$ (I/O Select). This input signal tells the MPC that the current operation is an I/O reference to the PSB. $\overline{IOSEL}$ is qualified by $\overline{RD}$ or $\overline{WR}$ and therefore must be stable within the specified set-up and hold window.

$\overline{REGSEL}$ (Register Select). This input signal is used to identify MPC register operations. $\overline{REGSEL}$ is qualified by $\overline{RD}$ or $\overline{WR}$ and therefore must be stable within the specified set-up and hold window.

$\overline{LOCK}$. This input signal allows back-to-back operations to be performed on the PSB or local interconnect space. When the bus owner activates $\overline{LOCK}$, all other agents are held off the PSB or local resource until $\overline{LOCK}$ is deactivated.

$\overline{BE}$<3–0> (Byte Enable). These input signals, generated by the host CPU or DMA controller, validate bytes on the data bus. $\overline{BE}$<3–0> are qualified by $\overline{RD}$ or $\overline{WR}$ and therefore must be stable within the specified set-up and hold window. $\overline{BE}$<3–0> correspond to data bytes 3 through 0 on the data bus (where byte 3 is D<31–24>). For remote reference operations, only combinations supported by the IEEE 1296 specification are valid.

A 32-bit local bus requires that all byte enable and data signals are used. For 16-bit local buses, $\overline{BE1}$ and $\overline{BE2}$ are used to indicate which of the two bytes will contain valid data, and only D<15–0> are used. For 8-bit local bus operations, $\overline{BE1}$ and $\overline{BE0}$ are used to select which byte of the PSB will carry the valid data byte. This mode uses ony D<7–0> (on the local bus). Note that during all read operations, the MPC drives all data lines (D<31–0>). Consecutive accesses to message FIFOs must be in ascending byte sequence 0, 1, 2, 3 in any non-overlapping combination.

Table 5-3 shows the valid byte enable combinations for both the local data bus (D<31–0>) and the PSB ($\overline{AD}$<31–0>):

Table 5-3. Valid Byte Enable Combinations

$\overline{\text{BE3}}$	$\overline{\text{BE2}}$	$\overline{\text{BE1}}$	$\overline{\text{BE0}}$	D31–24	D23–16	D15–8	D7–0	AD31–24	AD23–16	AD15–8	AD7–0
L	L	L	L	V3	V2	V1	V0	V3	V2	V1	V0
L	L	L	H	V3	V2	V1	X	V3	V2	V1	X
H	L	L	L	X	V2	V1	V0	X	V2	V1	V0
L	L	H	H	V3	V1	X	X	X	X	V3	V2
H	L	L	H	X	V2	V1	X	X	V2	V1	X
H	H	L	L	X	X	V1	V0	X	X	V1	V0
L	H	H	H	V3	X	X	X	X	X	V3	X
H	L	H	H	X	V2	X	X	X	X	X	V2
H	H	L	H	X	X	V1	X	X	X	V1	X
H	H	H	L	X	X	X	V0	X	X	X	V0
L	H	L	H	X	X	X	V0	X	X	V0	X
L	H	H	L	X	X	X	V0	X	X	X	V0

NOTES:
L = Electrical low state (active)
H = Electrical high state (inactive)
Vn = Valid data bytes
X = Active bytes with undefined data

For the 32-bit host interface, legal combinations of byte enables form *byte lanes:* the paths where valid data bytes are present during a single transfer on the local data bus (as well as in the MULTIBUS II environment). Non-Intel Microprocessors can use byte lanes to perform byte-swapping or other data manipulations in hardware. The figure below illustrates the legal byte lanes as they relate to byte enable combinations:

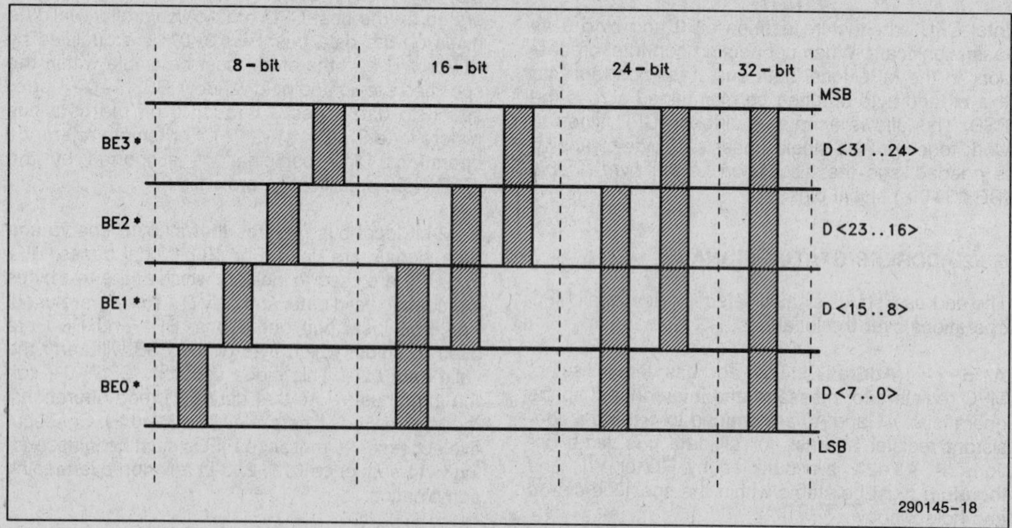

Figure 5-4. Byte Lanes

Each shaded box in Figure 5-4 represents a valid byte lane for a given combination of $\overline{BE}$ during a single read or write operation. There are four types of byte lanes: 8-bit, 16-bit, 24-bit and 32-bit. Bit and byte ordering follow the Intel standard of bit or byte 0 as least significant. Assume that invalid byte lanes contain any value of data (i.e. non-constant). Take precautions (masking in software, etc.) to ensure that invalid data does not cause problems.

When using a DMA controller to handle solicited data transfers to/from local memory, misalignment of data in memory and resulting partial packets are handled using the $\overline{BE}$ lines. The DMA interface of the MPC provides support by only incrementing internal pointers (or detecting completion) when the proper byte-enable signal is active. Table 5-4 shows which $\overline{BE}$ line the MPC recognizes for partial packets:

Table 5-4. Byte Enable Usage for DMA Control

DMA Width	Bytes Remaining	Byte Enable Recognized
32-bit	>3	$\overline{BE3}$
32-bit	3	$\overline{BE2}$
32-bit	2	$\overline{BE1}$
32-bit	1	$\overline{BE0}$
16-bit	>1	$\overline{BE1}$
16-bit	1	$\overline{BE0}$
8-bit	>0	$\overline{BE0}$

5.3.3 TRANSFER CONTROL SIGNALS

Transfer operation control to the MPC over the local bus is provided by two command signals and a wait signal. This handshake provides fully interlocked (two-sided handshake) operation.

$\overline{RD}$ (Read). This input signal starts a read operation. $\overline{RD}$ must transition cleanly, since it is used to qualify other signals in the read operation.

$\overline{WR}$ (Write). This input signal starts a write operation. $\overline{WR}$ must transition cleanly, since it is used to qualify other signals in the write operation.

$\overline{WAIT}$. $\overline{WAIT}$ is an MPC output signal used to extend a transfer operation. The signal will be used by the MPC for all accesses that require synchronization to another resource. It is activated when a command goes active and deactivated when the operation is completed.

5.3.4 INTERRUPT SIGNALS

Interrupt signals are used to inform the host CPU that the MPC requires service. The MPC generates two signals: one for message operations and one for reference errors.

MINT (Message Interrupt). The MINT output signal is used for all message-related signaling to the host CPU. This includes the arrival of an unsolicited message, the availability of the transmit FIFO, the completion of a solicited transfer, and an error-on message transfer.

EINT (Error Interrupt). The EINT output signal is used to signal all errors related to memory, I/O, or interconnect space operations. Internal registers in the MPC provide exact details of the error via interconnect space.

5.3.5 DMA CONTROL SIGNALS

The MPC provides four DMA control signals that connect with an external DMA controller.

ODREQ (Output Channel DMA Request). ODREQ is an output signal that enables DMA transfers to the MPC (i.e., output to the PSB). This signal behaves as a normal DMA request line during solicited message output operations. ODREQ is activated during the transfer phase of a solicited message operation when the solicited output FIFO is empty. The DMA controller responds to ODREQ by moving data from local memory to the FIFO for transfer to a receiving agent on the PSB.

IDREQ (Input Channel DMA Request). IDREQ is an output signal that enables DMA transfers from the MPC (i.e. input from the PSB). This signal behaves as a normal DMA request line during solicited message input operations. IDREQ is activated during the transfer phase of a solicited message operation when the solicited input FIFO is full. The DMA controller responds to ODREQ by moving data from the FIFO to local memory. When the FIFO is emptied, IDREQ is deactivated.

$\overline{ODACK}$ (Output Channel DMA Acknowledge). $\overline{ODACK}$ is generated by the DMA controller in response to an output channel DMA request. $\overline{ODACK}$ is qualified by $\overline{RD}$ or $\overline{WR}$ and therefore must be stable within the specified set-up and hold window.

NOTE:
$\overline{MEMSEL}$, $\overline{IOSEL}$, $\overline{REGSEL}$ $\overline{IDACK}$, and $\overline{ODACK}$ are mutually exclusive. In order to be valid, no more than on should be active during the same set-up and hold window.

$\overline{IDACK}$ (Input Channel DMA Acknowledge). $\overline{IDACK}$ is generated by the DMA controller in response to an input channel DMA request. $\overline{IDACK}$ is qualified by $\overline{RD}$ or $\overline{WR}$ and therefore must be stable within the specified set-up and hold window.

5.4 Interconnect Bus Signals

Brief descriptions of the interconnect bus signal pins are given here. For more information on using the interconnect microcontroller, see the *MPC User's Manual*, Chapter 5, "Interconnect Programming" (Order number 176526-002).

IAD<7–0> (Interconnect Address/Data). IAD<7–0> is an 8-bit, bidirectional, multiplexed address and data bus intended to interface directly to a microcontroller. In addition to the MPC, other interconnect accessible local resources can be connected to this bus.

$\overline{\text{IREQ}}$ (Interconnect Request). The MPC asserts this output signal when an interconnect operation has been requested from either the local bus or the PSB. The MPC asserts $\overline{\text{IREQ}}$ to the interconnect microcontroller at different times for read and write operations. For a read operation, $\overline{\text{IREQ}}$ is asserted immediately after detecting an address match between the requested address and an internal register. For a write operation, $\overline{\text{IREQ}}$ is delayed until valid data is available (i.e., $\overline{\text{BSC3}}$ is asserted). In either case, if the local bus interface has locked the local interconnect space, $\overline{\text{IREQ}}$ is inhibited.

IAST (Interconnect Address Strobe). IAST is a signal from the microcontroller that tells the MPC that a valid address is on the interconnect bus. IAST may be directly connected to the ALE (Address Latch Enable or equivalent) output of most microcontrollers. IAST must provide clean transitions.

$\overline{\text{IRD}}$ (Interconnect Bus Read). The microcontroller asserts $\overline{\text{IRD}}$ to perform a read operation to one of the MPC interconnect interface registers. $\overline{\text{IRD}}$ must provide clean transitions.

NOTE:
When $\overline{\text{IRD}}$ and $\overline{\text{IWR}}$ are activated at the same time, *all* MPC outputs are disabled. Use this feature to disable the MPC in board test applications.

$\overline{\text{IWR}}$ (Interconnect Write). The microcontroller asserts $\overline{\text{IWR}}$ to perform a write operation to one of the MPC interconnect interface registers. $\overline{\text{IWR}}$ must provide clean transitions.

6.0 Package Dimensions

The MPC 82389 is packaged in a 149-pin Ceramic Pin Grid Array (PGA). The pins are arranged 0.100 inch (2.54 mm) center-to-center, in a 15 x 15 matrix. Please refer to Figure 6-3 for case outlines.

A wide variety of sockets are available including the zero-insertion force socket for prototyping.

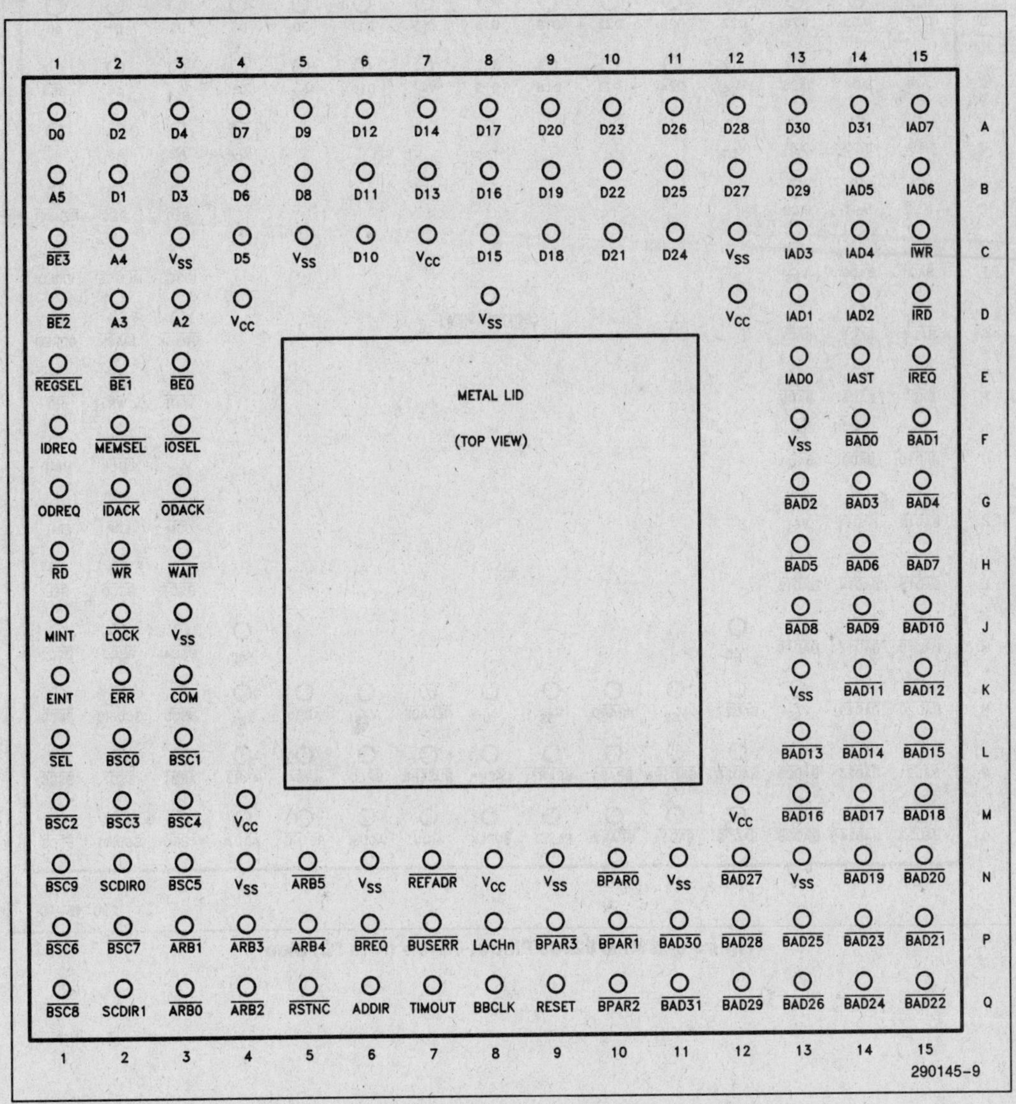

	1	2	3	4	5	6	7	8	9	10	11	12	13	14	15
A	D0	D2	D4	D7	D9	D12	D14	D17	D20	D23	D26	D28	D30	D31	IAD7
B	A5	D1	D3	D6	D8	D11	D13	D16	D19	D22	D25	D27	D29	IAD5	IAD6
C	$\overline{BE3}$	A4	V_{SS}	D5	V_{SS}	D10	V_{CC}	D15	D18	D21	D24	V_{SS}	IAD3	IAD4	$\overline{IWR}$
D	$\overline{BE2}$	A3	A2	V_{CC}				V_{SS}				V_{CC}	IAD1	IAD2	$\overline{IRD}$
E	$\overline{REGSEL}$	$\overline{BE1}$	$\overline{BE0}$										IAD0	IAST	$\overline{IREQ}$
F	IDREQ	$\overline{MEMSEL}$	$\overline{IOSEL}$										V_{SS}	$\overline{BAD0}$	$\overline{BAD1}$
G	ODREQ	$\overline{IDACK}$	$\overline{ODACK}$										$\overline{BAD2}$	$\overline{BAD3}$	$\overline{BAD4}$
H	$\overline{RD}$	$\overline{WR}$	$\overline{WAIT}$										$\overline{BAD5}$	$\overline{BAD6}$	$\overline{BAD7}$
J	MINT	$\overline{LOCK}$	V_{SS}										$\overline{BAD8}$	$\overline{BAD9}$	$\overline{BAD10}$
K	EINT	$\overline{ERR}$	$\overline{COM}$										V_{SS}	$\overline{BAD11}$	$\overline{BAD12}$
L	$\overline{SEL}$	$\overline{BSC0}$	$\overline{BSC1}$										$\overline{BAD13}$	$\overline{BAD14}$	$\overline{BAD15}$
M	$\overline{BSC2}$	$\overline{BSC3}$	$\overline{BSC4}$	V_{CC}								V_{CC}	$\overline{BAD16}$	$\overline{BAD17}$	$\overline{BAD18}$
N	$\overline{BSC9}$	SCDIR0	$\overline{BSC5}$	V_{SS}	$\overline{ARB5}$	V_{SS}	$\overline{REFADR}$	V_{CC}	V_{SS}	$\overline{BPAR0}$	V_{SS}	$\overline{BAD27}$	V_{SS}	$\overline{BAD19}$	$\overline{BAD20}$
P	$\overline{BSC6}$	$\overline{BSC7}$	$\overline{ARB1}$	$\overline{ARB3}$	$\overline{ARB4}$	$\overline{BREQ}$	$\overline{BUSERR}$	LACHn	$\overline{BPAR3}$	$\overline{BPAR1}$	BAD30	BAD28	BAD25	BAD23	BAD21
Q	$\overline{BSC8}$	SCDIR1	ARB0	$\overline{ARB2}$	$\overline{RSTNC}$	ADDIR	TIMOUT	BBCLK	RESET	$\overline{BPAR2}$	BAD31	BAD29	BAD26	BAD24	BAD22

METAL LID

(TOP VIEW)

290145-9

Figure 6-1. MPC 82389 Pinout—View from Top Side

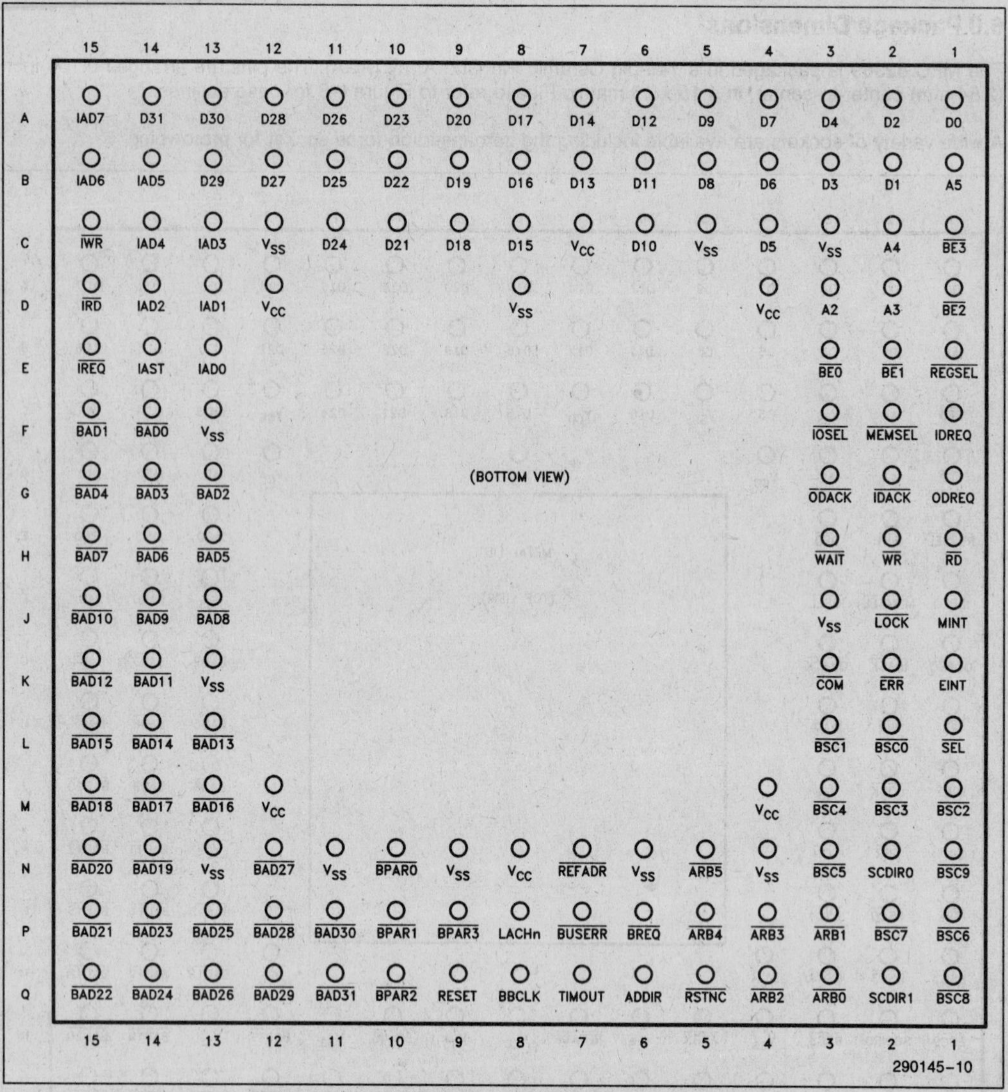

	15	14	13	12	11	10	9	8	7	6	5	4	3	2	1
A	IAD7	D31	D30	D28	D26	D23	D20	D17	D14	D12	D9	D7	D4	D2	D0
B	IAD6	IAD5	D29	D27	D25	D22	D19	D16	D13	D11	D8	D6	D3	D1	A5
C	$\overline{IWR}$	IAD4	IAD3	V_{SS}	D24	D21	D18	D15	V_{CC}	D10	V_{SS}	D5	V_{SS}	A4	$\overline{BE3}$
D	$\overline{IRD}$	IAD2	IAD1	V_{CC}				V_{SS}				V_{CC}	A2	A3	$\overline{BE2}$
E	$\overline{IREQ}$	IAST	IAD0										$\overline{BE0}$	$\overline{BE1}$	$\overline{REGSEL}$
F	$\overline{BAD1}$	$\overline{BAD0}$	V_{SS}										$\overline{IOSEL}$	$\overline{MEMSEL}$	IDREQ
G	$\overline{BAD4}$	$\overline{BAD3}$	$\overline{BAD2}$					(BOTTOM VIEW)					$\overline{ODACK}$	$\overline{IDACK}$	ODREQ
H	$\overline{BAD7}$	$\overline{BAD6}$	$\overline{BAD5}$										$\overline{WAIT}$	$\overline{WR}$	$\overline{RD}$
J	$\overline{BAD10}$	$\overline{BAD9}$	$\overline{BAD8}$										V_{SS}	$\overline{LOCK}$	MINT
K	$\overline{BAD12}$	$\overline{BAD11}$	V_{SS}										$\overline{COM}$	$\overline{ERR}$	EINT
L	$\overline{BAD15}$	$\overline{BAD14}$	$\overline{BAD13}$										$\overline{BSC1}$	$\overline{BSC0}$	$\overline{SEL}$
M	$\overline{BAD18}$	$\overline{BAD17}$	$\overline{BAD16}$	V_{CC}								V_{CC}	$\overline{BSC4}$	$\overline{BSC3}$	$\overline{BSC2}$
N	$\overline{BAD20}$	$\overline{BAD19}$	V_{SS}	$\overline{BAD27}$	V_{SS}	$\overline{BPAR0}$	V_{SS}	V_{CC}	$\overline{REFADR}$	V_{SS}	$\overline{ARB5}$	V_{SS}	$\overline{BSC5}$	SCDIR0	$\overline{BSC9}$
P	$\overline{BAD21}$	$\overline{BAD23}$	$\overline{BAD25}$	$\overline{BAD28}$	$\overline{BAD30}$	$\overline{BPAR1}$	$\overline{BPAR3}$	LACHn	$\overline{BUSERR}$	$\overline{BREQ}$	$\overline{ARB4}$	$\overline{ARB3}$	$\overline{ARB1}$	$\overline{BSC7}$	$\overline{BSC6}$
Q	$\overline{BAD22}$	$\overline{BAD24}$	$\overline{BAD26}$	$\overline{BAD29}$	$\overline{BAD31}$	$\overline{BPAR2}$	RESET	BBCLK	TIMOUT	ADDIR	$\overline{RSTNC}$	$\overline{ARB2}$	$\overline{ARB0}$	SCDIR1	$\overline{BSC8}$

290145–10

Figure 6-2. MPC 82389 Pinout—View from Pin Side

Table 6-1. MPC Signal Summary

Mnemonic	Type	Pin #	Mnemonic	Type	Pin #	Mnemonic	Type	Pin #
V_{CC}		D4	REFADR	O	N7	IAST	I	E14
A5	I	B1	ADDIR	O	Q6	$\overline{IRD}$	I	D15
A4	I	C2	$\overline{BPAR3}$	I/O	P9	$\overline{IWR}$	I	C15
A3	I	D2	$\overline{BAD31}$	I/O	Q11	IAD7	I/O	A15
A2	I	D3	$\overline{BAD30}$	I/O	P11	IAD6	I/O	B15
$\overline{BE3}$	I	C1	$\overline{BAD29}$	I/O	Q12	IAD5	I/O	B14
$\overline{BE2}$	I	D1	$\overline{BAD28}$	I/O	P12	IAD4	I/O	C14
$\overline{BE1}$	I	E2	$\overline{BAD27}$	I/O	N12	IAD3	I/O	C13
$\overline{BE0}$	I	E3	$\overline{BAD26}$	I/O	Q13	IAD2	I/O	D14
$\overline{IOSEL}$	I	F3	$\overline{BAD25}$	I/O	P13	IAD1	I/O	D13
$\overline{MEMSEL}$	I	F2	$\overline{BAD24}$	I/O	Q14	IAD0	I/O	E13
$\overline{REGSEL}$	I	E1	$\overline{BAD23}$	I/O	P14	V_{CC}		D12
$\overline{IDACK}$	I	G2	$\overline{BAD22}$	I/O	Q15	V_{SS}		C12
$\overline{ODACK}$	I	G3	$\overline{BAD21}$	I/O	P15	D31	I/O	A14
IDREQ	O	F1	$\overline{BAD20}$	I/O	N15	D30	I/O	A13
ODREQ	O	G1	$\overline{BAD19}$	I/O	N14	D29	I/O	B13
$\overline{WR}$	I	H2	$\overline{BAD18}$	I/O	M15	D28	I/O	A12
$\overline{RD}$	I	H1	$\overline{BAD17}$	I/O	M14	D27	I/O	B12
$\overline{WAIT}$	O	H3	$\overline{BAD16}$	I/O	M13	D26	I/O	A11
V_{SS}		J3	$\overline{BAD15}$	I/O	L15	D25	I/O	B11
MINT	O	J1	$\overline{BAD14}$	I/O	L14	D24	I/O	C11
EINT	O	K1	$\overline{BAD13}$	I/O	L13	D23	I/O	A10
$\overline{LOCK}$	I	J2	$\overline{BAD12}$	I/O	K15	D22	I/O	B10
$\overline{ERR}$	I	K2	$\overline{BAD11}$	I/O	K14	D21	I/O	C10
$\overline{SEL}$	O	L1	$\overline{BAD10}$	I/O	J15	D20	I/O	A9
$\overline{COM}$	I	K3	$\overline{BAD9}$	I/O	J14	D19	I/O	B9
$\overline{BSC9}$	I/O	N1	$\overline{BAD8}$	I/O	J13	D18	I/O	C9
$\overline{BSC8}$	I/O	Q1	$\overline{BAD7}$	I/O	H15	D17	I/O	A8
$\overline{BSC7}$	I/O	P2	$\overline{BAD6}$	I/O	H14	D16	I/O	B8
$\overline{BSC6}$	I/O	P1	$\overline{BAD5}$	I/O	H13	D15	I/O	C8
$\overline{BSC5}$	I/O	N3	$\overline{BAD4}$	I/O	G15	D14	I/O	A7
$\overline{BSC4}$	I/O	M3	$\overline{BAD3}$	I/O	G14	D13	I/O	B7
$\overline{ARB3}$	I/O, OC	P4	V_{SS}		N13	D2	I/O	A2

Table 6-1. MPC Signal Summary (Continued)

Mnemonic	Type	Pin#	Mnemonic	Type	Pin#	Mnemonic	Type	Pin#
$\overline{BSC3}$	I/O	M2	$\overline{BAD2}$	I/O	G13	D12	I/O	A6
$\overline{BSC2}$	I/O	M1	$\overline{BAD1}$	I/O	F15	D11	I/O	B6
$\overline{BSC1}$	I/O	L3	$\overline{BAD0}$	I/O	F14	D10	I/O	C6
$\overline{BSC0}$	I/O	L2	$\overline{BPAR2}$	I/O	Q10	D9	I/O	A5
SCDIR1	O	Q2	$\overline{BPAR1}$	I/O	P10	D8	I/O	B5
SCDIR0	O	N2	$\overline{BPAR0}$	I/O	N10	D7	I/O	A4
V_{CC}		M4	V_{CC}		N8	D6	I/O	B4
V_{SS}		N4	V_{SS}		N9	D5	I/O	C4
$\overline{ARB5}$	I/O, OC	N5	V_{SS}		N11	D4	I/O	A3
$\overline{ARB4}$	I/O, OC	P5	V_{CC}		M12	D3	I/O	B3
$\overline{ARB2}$	I/O, OC	Q4	V_{SS}		F13	D1	I/O	B2
$\overline{ARB1}$	I/O, OC	P3	V_{SS}		K13	D0	I/O	A1
$\overline{ARB0}$	I/O, OC	Q3	BBCLK	I	Q8	V_{CC}		C7
V_{SS}		N6	LACHn	I	P8	V_{SS}		D8
$\overline{BREQ}$	I/O, OC	P6	RESET	I	Q9	V_{SS}		C5
TIMOUT	I/O	Q7	$\overline{RSTNC}$	I/O, OC	Q5	$\overline{BUSERR}$	I/O, OC	P7
$\overline{IREQ}$	O	E15	V_{SS}		C3			

NOTES:
I = input
O = output
I/O = input/output
OC = open-collector
* = active-low

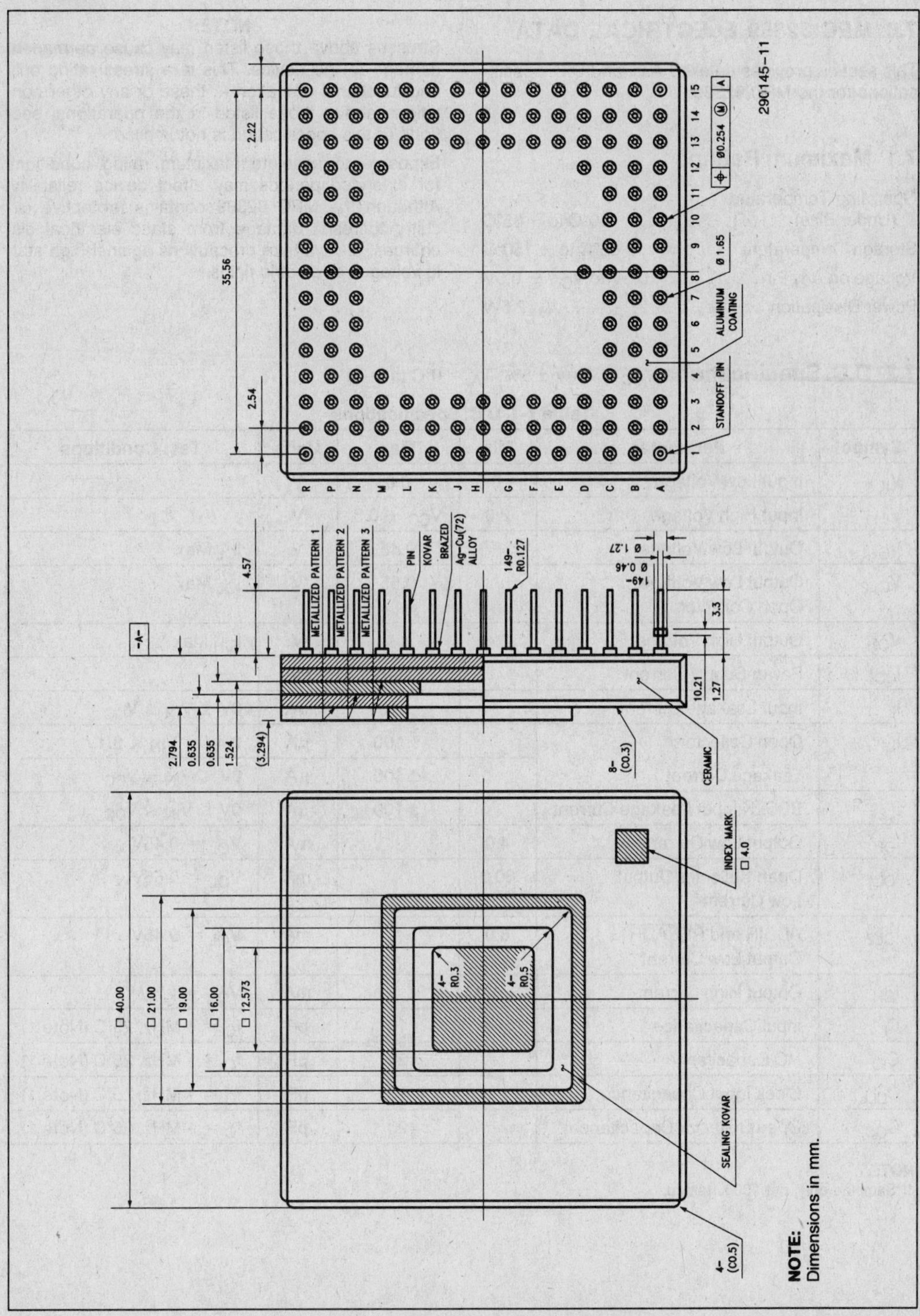

NOTE:
Dimensions in mm.

290145-11

Figure 6-3. 149-Pin PGA Package Dimensions

7.0 MPC 82389 ELECTRICAL DATA

This section provides detailed A.C. and D.C. specifications for the MPC 82389.

7.1 Maximum Ratings

Operating Temperature
(Under Bias) .... −10°C to +85°C

Storage Temperature .... −65°C to +150°C

Voltage on Any Pin.......... −0.5V to V_{CC} + 0.5V

Power Dissipation.......................... 2.5W

NOTE:
Stresses above those listed may cause permanent damage to the device. This is a stress rating only and functional operation at these or any other conditions above those listed in the operational sections of this specification is not implied.

Exposure to absolute maximum rating conditions for extended periods may affect device reliability. Although the MPC 82389 contains protective circuitry to resist damage from static electrical discharges, always take precautions against high static voltages or electric fields.

7.2 D.C. Specifications V_{CC} = 5.0V ±5%, T_A = 0°C to +70°C

Table 7-1. D.C. Specifications

Symbol	Parameter	Min	Max	Units	Test Conditions
V_{IL}	Input Low Voltage	−0.5	0.8	V	
V_{IH}	Input High Voltage	2.0	V_{CC} + 0.5	V	
V_{OL1}	Output Low Voltage		0.45	V	I_{OL} Max
V_{OL2}	Output Low Voltage Open Collector		0.55	V	I_{OL} Max
V_{OH}	Output High Voltage	2.4		V	I_{OH} Max
I_{CC}	Power Supply Current		400	mA	
I_L	Input Leakage Current		±10	μA	0V ≤ V_{IN} ≤ V_{CC}
I_{L1}	Open Collector		±100	μA	0.4V ≤ V_{IN} ≤ 2.4V
	Leakage Current		±400	μA	0V ≤ V_{IN} ≤ V_{CC}
I_{L2}	BBCLK Input Leakage Current		±100	μA	0V ≤ V_{IN} ≤ V_{CC}
I_{OL}	Output Low Current	4.0		mA	V_{OL} = 0.45V
I_{OL1}	Open Collector Output Low Current	60.0		mA	V_{OL} = 0.55V
I_{OL2}	ADDIR and $\overline{\text{REFADR}}$ Output Low Current	8.0		mA	V_{OL} = 0.45V
I_{OH}	Output High Current	−1.0		mA	V_{OH} = 2.4V
C_I	Input Capacitance		10	pF	f_C = 1 MHz, 25°C (Note 1)
C_{IO}	I/O Capacitance		20	pF	f_C = 1 MHz, 25°C (Note 1)
C_{CLK}	Clock Input Capacitance		15	pF	f_C = 1 MHz, 25°C (Note 1)
C_{OC}	Open Collector Capacitance		20	pF	f_C = 1 MHz, 25°C (Note 1)

NOTE:
1. Sampled only, not 100% tested.

7.3 A.C. Specifications

The A.C. specifications for the MPC 82389 are specified in Tables 7-2, 7-3 and 7-4 and Figures 7-2, 7-3, 7-4 and 7-5. Figure 7-1 specifies the test points for measuring the A.C. parameters. Table 7-2 and Figures 7-2 and 7-3 specify the A.C. parameters for the host CPU bus. Table 7-3 and Figure 7-4 specify the A.C. parameters for the interconnect bus. Table 7-4 and Figure 7-5 specify the A.C. parameters for the PSB. Figure 7-6 defines the test load for the A.C. specifications.

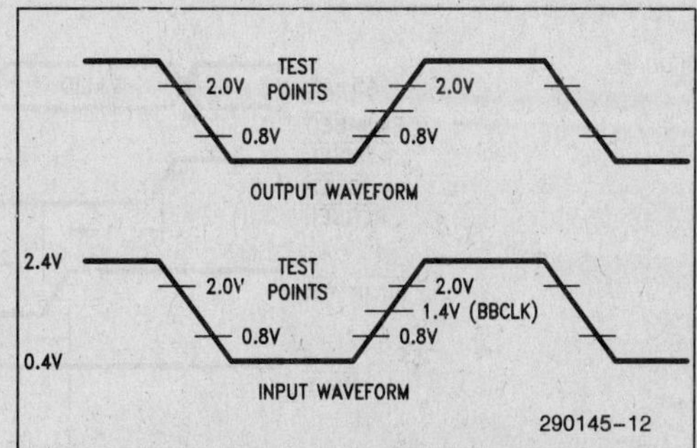

Figure 7-1. A.C. Test Waveforms

Table 7-2. Host CPU Bus A.C. Specifications (V_{CC} = 5V ±5%, T_A = 0°C to +70°C)

Symbol	Parameter	Min	Max	Units	Test Conditions
t_1	Address and $\overline{BE}$ Setup to Command Active	20		ns	
	Select and DACK Setup to Command Active	18		ns	
t_2	Address, $\overline{BE}$, Select and DACK Hold from Command Active	5		ns	
t_3	Time between Commands	24		ns	
t_4	Command Inactive to Read Data Disable (Note 5)		15	ns	
t_5	Read Data Hold from Command Inactive	3		ns	
t_6	Read Data Enable from Command Active	0		ns	
t_7	$\overline{WAIT}$ Active from Command Active		20	ns	C_L = 50 pF
t_8	Command Inactive from $\overline{WAIT}$ Inactive	0		ns	
t_9	$\overline{WAIT}$ Inactive to Read Data Valid		25	ns	C_L = 90 pF
t_{10}	Command Active to Write Data Valid		200	ns	
t_{11}	Write Data Hold from $\overline{WAIT}$ Inactive	0		ns	
t_{12}	Command Active to $\overline{LOCK}$ Active (Note 1)		100	ns	
t_{13}	$\overline{LOCK}$ Hold from $\overline{WAIT}$ Inactive (Note 2)	0		ns	
t_{14}	Command Active Time	42		ns	
t_{15}	Read Data Valid from Command Active		42	ns	C_L = 90 pF
t_{16}	Write Data Setup to Command Inactive —Registers —DMA	 20 20		 ns ns	
t_{17}	Write Data Hold from Command Inactive	3		ns	
t_{18}	Command Active to MINT or DREQ Inactive (Notes 3, 4)		42	ns	C_L = 50 pF
t_{19}	Command Active to DREQ Inactive (Note 4)		25	ns	C_L = 50 pF

NOTES:
1. Required to guarantee locking of resource.
2. Required to guarantee resource remains locked.
3. MINT deassertion only if no other sources are pending.
4. For DREQ inactive timing, t_{19} applies to a normal last transfer deassert condition and t_{18} to an error deassert condition.
5. Disable condition occurs when the output current becomes less than the input leakage specification.

5

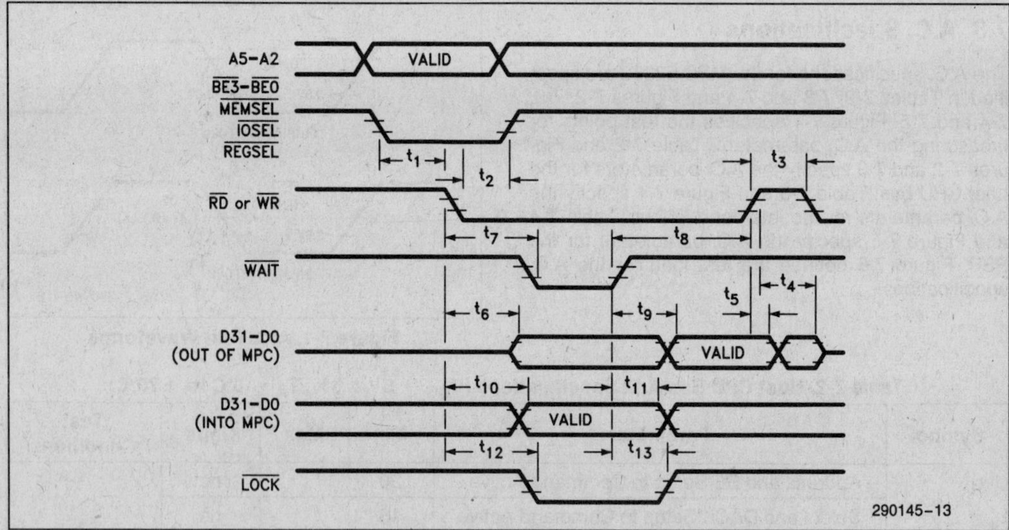

Figure 7-2. Host CPU Interface Reference Operation Timing

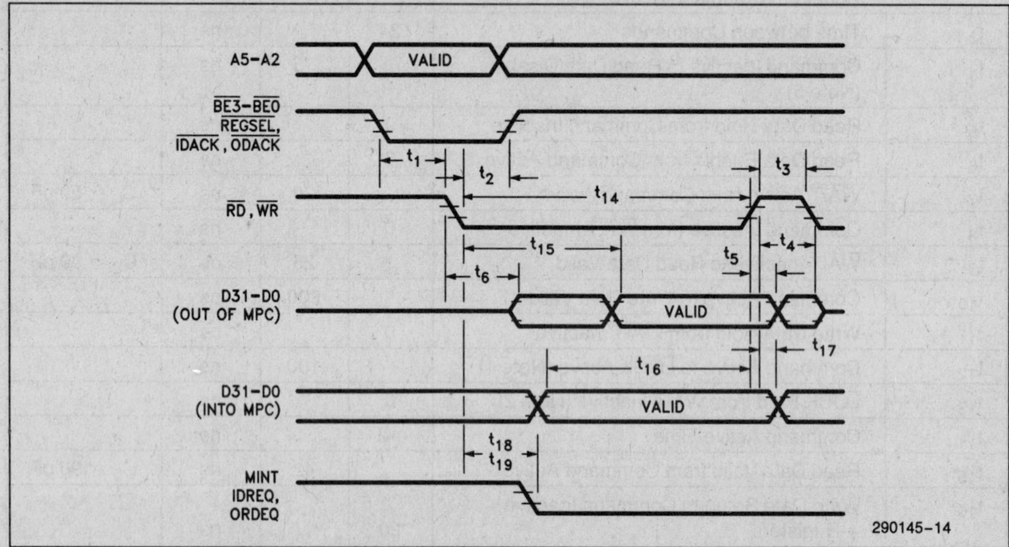

Figure 7-3. Host CPU Interface Register and DMA Operation Timing

Table 7-3. Interconnect Bus A.C. Specifications (V_{CC} = 5V ±5%, T_A = 0°C to +70°C)

Symbol	Parameter	Min	Max	Units	Test Conditions
t_{31}	IAST Active Time	85		ns	
t_{32}	Command Active Time	250		ns	
t_{33}	Command Inactive to IAST Active	25		ns	
t_{33A}	IAST Inactive to Command Active	120		ns	
t_{34}	Address Setup to IAST Inactive	40		ns	
t_{35}	Address Hold from IAST Inactive	20		ns	
t_{36}	Write Data Setup to Command Inactive	120		ns	
t_{37}	Write Data Hold from Command Inactive	5		ns	
t_{38}	Read Data Enable from Command Active	0		ns	
t_{39}	Read Data Valid from Command Active		120	ns	C_L = 150 pF
t_{40}	Read Data Hold from Command Inactive	0		ns	
t_{41}	Read Data Disable from Command Inactive (Note 2)		30	ns	
t_{42}	EINT, $\overline{IREQ}$ Inactive from Command Active (Note 1)		100	ns	C_L = 150 pF

NOTES:
1. EINT inactive only on write to error register. $\overline{IREQ}$ inactive only on write to arbitration register.
2. Disable condition occurs when the output current becomes less than the input leakage specification.

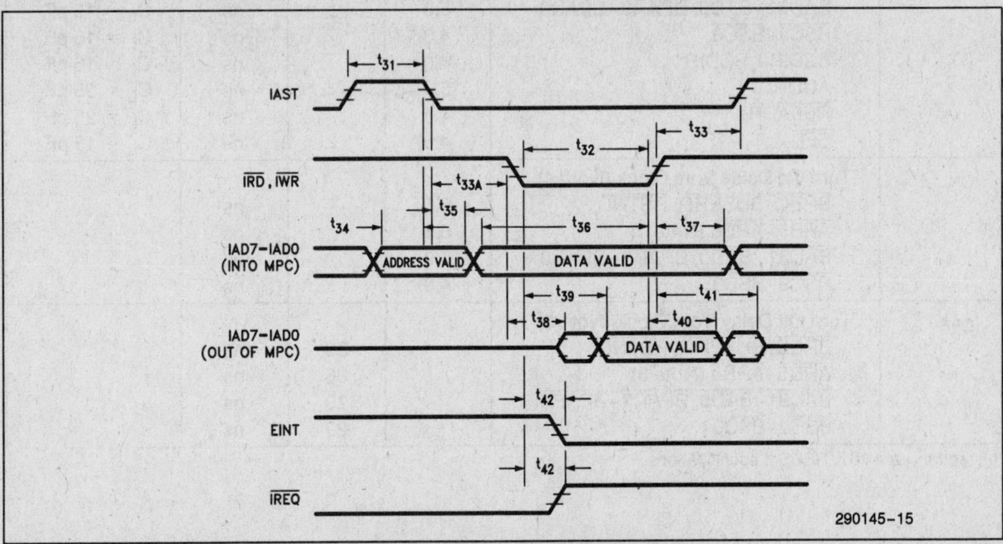

Figure 7-4. Interconnect Bus Timing

5

Table 7-4. PSB Interface A.C. Specifications (V_{CC} = 5V ±5%, T_A = 0°C to +70°C)

Symbol	Parameter		Min	Max	Units	Test Conditions
t_{CP}	Clock Period		99.9		ns	
*t_{CL}	$\overline{\text{BCLK}}$ Low Time		40		ns	
*t_{CH}	$\overline{\text{BCLK}}$ High Time		40		ns	
t_{BCL}	BBCLK Low Time		38		ns	
t_{BCH}	BBCLK High Time		38		ns	
t_{RB}	$\overline{\text{BCLK}}$ Rise Time		1	5	ns	
t_{FB}	$\overline{\text{BCLK}}$ Fall Time		1	2	ns	
t_R	BBCLK Rise Time		0.5	1	ns	
t_F	BBCLK Fall Time		0.5	1	ns	
t_{SK}	$\overline{\text{BCLK}}$ to BBCLK Skew (Note 1)		−0.5	4.0	ns	
t_{CD}	Clock to Output Delay					
	$\overline{\text{BREQ}}$, $\overline{\text{BUSERR}}$, $\overline{\text{RSTNC}}$ (Note 2)			36	ns	C_L = 500 pF
	$\overline{\text{ARB5}}$–$\overline{\text{ARB0}}$ (Notes 2, 3)			36	ns	C_L = 500 pF
	$\overline{\text{BAD31}}$–$\overline{\text{BAD0}}$, $\overline{\text{BSC7}}$–$\overline{\text{BSC0}}$			29	ns	C_L = 75 pF
	$\overline{\text{BPAR3}}$–$\overline{\text{BPAR0}}$, $\overline{\text{BSC9}}$, $\overline{\text{BSC8}}$			29	ns	C_L = 50 pF
	SCDIR0, SCDIR1	(H to L)		19	ns	C_L = 25 pF
		(L to H)		21	ns	C_L = 25 pF
	ADDIR	(L to H)		21	ns	C_L = 50 pF
		(H to L)		27	ns	C_L = 50 pF
	$\overline{\text{REFADR}}$			29	ns	C_L = 75 pF
	$\overline{\text{SEL}}$			29	ns	C_L = 50 pF
t_H	Hold Time from Clock					
	$\overline{\text{BREQ}}$, $\overline{\text{BUSERR}}$, $\overline{\text{RSTNC}}$		6.5		ns	C_L = 25 pF
	$\overline{\text{ARB5}}$–$\overline{\text{ARB0}}$ (Note 3)		6.5		ns	C_L = 25 pF
	$\overline{\text{BAD31}}$–$\overline{\text{BAD0}}$, $\overline{\text{BPAR3}}$–$\overline{\text{BPAR0}}$		5.0		ns	C_L = 15 pF
	$\overline{\text{BSC9}}$–$\overline{\text{BSC0}}$		4.0		ns	C_L = 15 pF
	SCDIR0, SCDIR1		4.0		ns	C_L = 15 pF
	ADDIR		5.0		ns	C_L = 25 pF
	$\overline{\text{REFADR}}$		4.0		ns	C_L = 25 pF
	$\overline{\text{SEL}}$		4.0		ns	C_L = 15 pF
t_{ON}	Turn On Delay from Clock (Note 4)					
	$\overline{\text{BREQ}}$, $\overline{\text{BUSERR}}$, $\overline{\text{RSTNC}}$		6.5		ns	
	$\overline{\text{ARB5}}$–$\overline{\text{ARB0}}$ (Note 1)		6.5		ns	
	$\overline{\text{BAD31}}$–$\overline{\text{BAD0}}$, $\overline{\text{BPAR3}}$–$\overline{\text{BPAR0}}$		5.0		ns	
	$\overline{\text{BSC9}}$–$\overline{\text{BSC0}}$		4.0		ns	
t_{OFF}	Turn Off Delay from Clock (Note 5)					
	$\overline{\text{BREQ}}$, $\overline{\text{BUSERR}}$, $\overline{\text{RSTNC}}$			36	ns	
	$\overline{\text{ARB5}}$–$\overline{\text{ARB0}}$ (Note 3)			36	ns	
	$\overline{\text{BAD31}}$–$\overline{\text{BAD0}}$, $\overline{\text{BPAR3}}$–$\overline{\text{BPAR0}}$			29	ns	
	$\overline{\text{BSC9}}$–$\overline{\text{BSC0}}$			29	ns	

*t_{CL} and t_{CH} are MULTIBUS II specifications.

Table 7-4. PSB Interface A.C. Specifications (V_{CC} = 5V ±5%, T_A = 0°C to +70°C) (Continued)

Symbol	Parameter	Min	Max	Units	Test Conditions
t_{SU}	Input Setup Time to Clock				
	$\overline{\text{BREQ}}$, $\overline{\text{BUSERR}}$, $\overline{\text{RSTNC}}$	22		ns	
	$\overline{\text{ARB5}}$–$\overline{\text{ARB0}}$ (Note 3)	40		ns	
	$\overline{\text{BAD31}}$–$\overline{\text{BAD0}}$, $\overline{\text{BPAR3}}$–$\overline{\text{BPAR0}}$	24		ns	
	$\overline{\text{BSC9}}$–$\overline{\text{BSC0}}$	24		ns	
	TIMEOUT, LACHn, RESET	24		ns	
	$\overline{\text{COM}}$, $\overline{\text{ERR}}$	40		ns	
t_{IH}	Input Hold Time from Clock				
	$\overline{\text{BREQ}}$, $\overline{\text{BUSERR}}$, $\overline{\text{RSTNC}}$	0		ns	
	$\overline{\text{ARB5}}$–$\overline{\text{ARB0}}$ (Note 3)	0		ns	
	$\overline{\text{BAD31}}$–$\overline{\text{BAD0}}$, $\overline{\text{BPAR3}}$–$\overline{\text{BPAR0}}$	3		ns	
	$\overline{\text{BSC9}}$–$\overline{\text{BSC0}}$	2		ns	
	TIMEOUT, LACHn, RESET	2		ns	
	$\overline{\text{COM}}$, $\overline{\text{ERR}}$	3		ns	

NOTES:

1. The clock timings are provided to reference the MPC specification to the PSB specifications. These specifications assume a 74AS1804 or equivalent buffer.
2. The 500 pF load is a distributed load as defined in the PSB specification. The open drain signals are designed such that the output delay and bus loss meets the PSB specification requirement.
3. The $\overline{\text{ARB5}}$–$\overline{\text{ARB0}}$ signal timings are with respect to the first and last clock of the arbitration period. Details can be found in the PSB specification. Also, the arbitration logic has been designed to meet the loop delay specification accounting for the full path of input to output plus bus loss.
4. Minimum turn on times are measured the same way as hold times. Specifically, the logic level driven by another device on the previous clock cycle must not be disturbed.
5. Maximum turn off times are measured to the condition where the output leakage current becomes less than the input leakage specification.
6. All stated capacitances are based on design requirements. Production test limitations may require some parameters to be tested under a different condition.

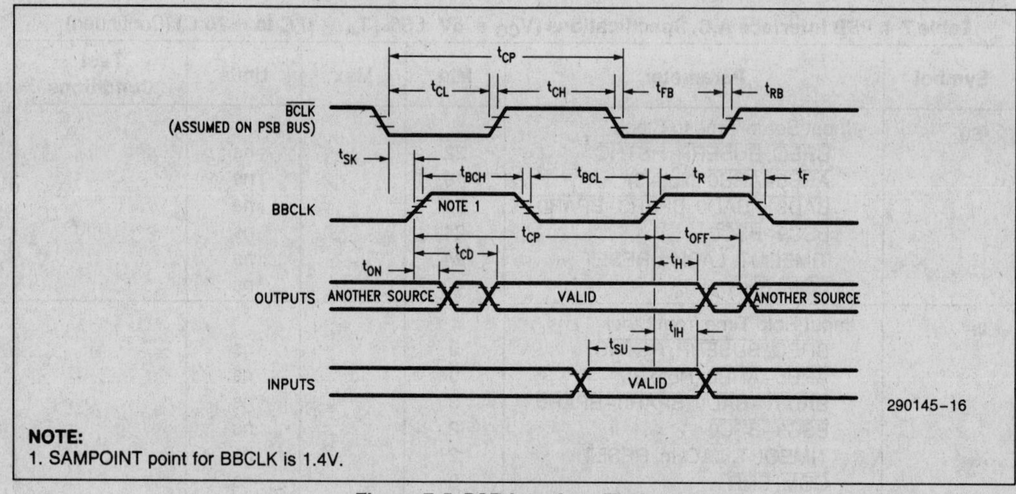

Figure 7-5. PSB Interface Timing

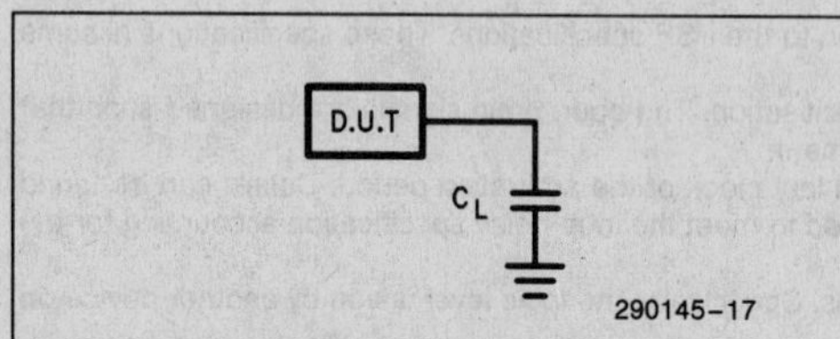

Figure 7-6. A.C. Test Load

8.0 REFERENCE DOCUMENTS

Part Number	Title Description
176526-002	MPC User's Manual
146077	MULTIBUS II Architecture Specifications
149299	Interconnect Interface Specifications
149300	MULTIBUS II MPC External Product Specifications
149247	MULTIBUS II Transport Protocol Specifications
459706-001	CSM/002 Hardware Reference Manual

NORTH AMERICAN SALES OFFICES

ALABAMA

Intel Corp.
600 Boulevard South
Suite 104-I
Huntsville 35802
Tel: (800) 628-8686
FAX: (205) 883-3511

ARIZONA

†Intel Corp.
410 North 44th Street
Suite 500
Phoenix 85008
Tel: (800) 628-8686
FAX: (602) 244-0446

CALIFORNIA

Intel Corp.
3550 Watt Avenue
Suite 140
Sacramento 95821
Tel: (800) 628-8686
FAX: (916) 488-1473

†Intel Corp.
9655 Granite Ridge Dr.
3rd Floor, Suite 4A
San Diego 92123
Tel: (800) 628-8686
FAX: (619) 467-2460

Intel Corp.
1781 Fox Drive
San Jose 95131
Tel: (800) 628-8686
FAX: (408) 441-9540

*†Intel Corp.
1551 N. Tustin Avenue
Suite 800
Santa Ana 92701
Tel: (800) 628-8686
TWX: 910-595-1114
FAX: (714) 541-9157

†Intel Corp.
15260 Ventura Boulevard
Suite 360
Sherman Oaks 91403
Tel: (800) 628-8686
FAX: (818) 995-6624

COLORADO

*†Intel Corp.
600 S. Cherry St.
Suite 700
Denver 80222
Tel: (800) 628-8686
TWX: 910-931-2289
FAX: (303) 322-8670

CONNECTICUT

†Intel Corp.
103 Mill Plain Road
Danbury 06811
Tel: (800) 628-8686
FAX: (203) 794-0339

FLORIDA

†Intel Corp.
800 Fairway Drive
Suite 160
Deerfield Beach 33441
Tel: (800) 628-8686
FAX: (305) 421-2444

Intel Corp.
2250 Lucien Way
Suite 100, Room 8
Maitland 32751
Tel: (800) 628-8686
FAX: (407) 660-1283

GEORGIA

†Intel Corp.
20 Technology Parkway
Suite 150
Norcross 30092
Tel: (800) 628-8686
FAX: (404) 605-9762

IDAHO

Intel Corp.
9456 Fairview Ave., Suite C
Boise 83704
Tel: (800) 628-8686
FAX: (208) 377-1052

ILLINOIS

*†Intel Corp.
Woodfield Corp. Center III
300 N. Martingale Road
Suite 400
Schaumburg 60173
Tel: (800) 628-8686
FAX: (708) 706-9762

INDIANA

†Intel Corp.
8910 Purdue Road
Suite 350
Indianapolis 46268
Tel: (800) 628-8686
FAX: (317) 875-8938

MARYLAND

*†Intel Corp.
10010 Junction Dr.
Suite 200
Annapolis Junction 20701
Tel: (800) 628-8686
FAX: (410) 206-3678

MASSACHUSETTS

*†Intel Corp.
Westford Corp. Center
5 Carlisle Road
2nd Floor
Westford 01886
Tel: (800) 628-8686
TWX: 710-343-6333
FAX: (508) 692-7867

MICHIGAN

†Intel Corp.
7071 Orchard Lake Road
Suite 100
West Bloomfield 48322
Tel: (800) 628-8686
FAX: (313) 851-8770

MINNESOTA

†Intel Corp.
3500 W. 80th St.
Suite 360
Bloomington 55431
Tel: (800) 628-8686
TWX: 910-576-2867
FAX: (612) 831-6497

NEW JERSEY

Intel Corp.
2001 Route 46, Suite 310
Parsippany 07054-1315
Tel: (800) 628-8686
FAX: (201) 402-4893

*†Intel Corp.
Lincroft Office Center
125 Half Mile Road
Red Bank 07701
Tel: (800) 628-8686
FAX: (908) 747-0983

NEW YORK

*Intel Corp.
850 Crosskeys Office Park
Fairport 14450
Tel: (800) 628-8686
TWX: 510-253-7391
FAX: (716) 223-2561

†Intel Corp.
300 Westage Business Center
Suite 230
Fishkill 12524
Tel: (800) 628-8686
FAX: (914) 897-3125

*†Intel Corp.
2950 Express Dr., South
Suite 130
Islandia 11722
Tel: (800) 628-8686
TWX: 510-227-6236
FAX: (516) 348-7939

OHIO

*Intel Corp.
56 Milford Dr., Suite 205
Hudson 44236
Tel: (800) 628-8686
FAX: (216) 528-1026

*†Intel Corp.
3401 Park Center Drive
Suite 220
Dayton 45414
Tel: (800) 628-8686
TWX: 810-450-2528
FAX: (513) 890-8658

OKLAHOMA

Intel Corp.
6801 N. Broadway
Suite 115
Oklahoma City 73162
Tel: (800) 628-8686
FAX: (405) 840-9819

OREGON

†Intel Corp.
15254 N.W. Greenbrier Pkwy.
Building B
Beaverton 97006
Tel: (800) 628-8686
TWX: 910-467-8741
FAX: (503) 645-8181

PENNSYLVANIA

*†Intel Corp.
925 Harvest Drive
Suite 200
Blue Bell 19422
Tel: (800) 628-8686
FAX: (215) 641-0785

SOUTH CAROLINA

Intel Corp.
7403 Parklane Rd., Suite 3
Columbia 29223
Tel: (800) 628-8686
FAX: (803) 788-7999

Intel Corp.
100 Executive Center Drive
Suite 109, B183
Greenville 29615
Tel: (800) 628-8686
FAX: (803) 297-3401

TEXAS

†Intel Corp.
8911 N. Capital of Texas Hwy.
Suite 4230
Austin 78759
Tel: (800) 628-8686
FAX: (512) 338-9335

*†Intel Corp.
5000 Quorum Drive
Suite 750
Dallas 75240
Tel: (800) 628-8686

*†Intel Corp.
20515 SH 249
Suite 401
Houston 77070
Tel: (800) 628-8686
TWX: 910-881-2490
FAX: (713) 988-3660

UTAH

†Intel Corp.
428 East 6400 South
Suite 135
Murray 84107
Tel: (800) 628-8686
FAX: (801) 268-1457

WASHINGTON

†Intel Corp.
2800 156th Avenue S.E.
Suite 105
Bellevue 98007
Tel: (800) 628-8686
FAX: (206) 746-4495

WISCONSIN

Intel Corp.
400 N. Executive Dr.
Suite 401
Brookfield 53005
Tel: (800) 628-8686
FAX: (414) 789-2746

CANADA

BRITISH COLUMBIA

Intel Semiconductor of
Canada, Ltd.
999 Canada Place
Suite 404, #11
Vancouver V6C 3E2
Tel: (800) 628-8686
FAX: (604) 844-2813

ONTARIO

†Intel Semiconductor of
Canada, Ltd.
2650 Queensview Drive
Suite 250
Ottawa K2B 8H6
Tel: (800) 628-8686
FAX: (613) 820-5936

†Intel Semiconductor of
Canada, Ltd.
190 Attwell Drive
Suite 500
Rexdale M9W 6H8
Tel: (800) 628-8686
FAX: (416) 675-2438

QUEBEC

†Intel Semiconductor of
Canada, Ltd.
1 Rue Holiday
Suite 320
Tour East
Pt. Claire H9R 5N3
Tel: (800) 628-8686
FAX: 514-694-0064

†Sales and Service Office
*Field Application Location

NORTH AMERICAN DISTRIBUTORS

ALABAMA

Arrow/Schweber Electronics
1015 Henderson Road
Huntsville 35806
Tel: (205) 837-6955
FAX: (205) 721-1581

Hamilton Hallmark
4890 University Square, #1
Huntsville 35816
Tel: (205) 837-8700
FAX: (205) 830-2565

MTI Systems
4950 Corporate Dr., #120
Huntsville 35805
Tel: (205) 830-9526
FAX: (205) 830-9557

Pioneer Technologies Group
4835 University Square, #5
Huntsville 35805
Tel: (205) 837-9300
FAX: (205) 837-9358

Wyle Laboratories
7800 Governers Drive
Tower Building, 2nd Floor
Huntsville 35806
Tel: (205) 830-1119
FAX: (205) 830-1520

ARIZONA

Anthem Electronics
1555 W. 10th Place, #101
Tempe 85281
Tel: (602) 966-6600
FAX: (602) 966-4826

Arrow/Schweber Electronics
2415 W. Erie Drive
Tempe 85282
Tel: (602) 431-0030
FAX: (602) 252-9109

Avnet Computer
1626 S. Edwards Drive
Tempe 85281
Tel: (602) 902-4600
FAX: (602) 902-4640

Hamilton Hallmark
4637 S. 36th Place
Phoenix 85040
Tel: (602) 437-1200
FAX: (602) 437-2348

Wyle Laboratories
4141 E. Raymond
Phoenix 85040
Tel: (602) 437-2088
FAX: (602) 437-2124

CALIFORNIA

Anthem Electronics
9131 Oakdale Ave.
Chatsworth 91311
Tel: (818) 775-1333
FAX: (818) 775-1302

Anthem Electronics
1 Oldfield Drive
Irvine 92718-2809
Tel: (714) 768-4444
FAX: (714) 768-6456

Anthem Electronics
580 Menlo Drive, #8
Rocklin 95677
Tel: (916) 624-9744
FAX: (916) 624-9750

Anthem Electronics
9369 Carroll Park Drive
San Diego 92121
Tel: (619) 453-9005
FAX: (619) 546-7893

Anthem Electronics
1160 Ridder Park Drive
San Jose 95131
Tel: (408) 452-2219
FAX: (408) 441-4504

Arrow Commercial Systems Group
1502 Crocker Avenue
Hayward 94544
Tel: (510) 489-5371
FAX: (510) 489-9393

Arrow Commercial Systems Group
14242 Chambers Road
Tustin 92680
Tel: (714) 544-0200
FAX: (714) 731-8438

Arrow/Schweber Electronics
26707 W. Agoura Road
Calabasas 91302
Tel: (818) 880-9686
FAX: (818) 772-8930

Arrow/Schweber Electronics
48834 Kato Road, Suite 103
Fremont 94538
Tel: (510) 490-9477

Arrow/Schweber Electronics
6 Cromwell #100
Irvine 92718
Tel: (714) 838-5422
FAX: (714) 454-4206

Arrow/Schweber Electronics
9511 Ridgehaven Court
San Diego 92123
Tel: (619) 565-4800
FAX: (619) 279-8062

Arrow/Schweber Electronics
1180 Murphy Avenue
San Jose 95131
Tel: (408) 441-9700
FAX: (408) 453-4810

Avnet Computer
3170 Pullman Street
Costa Mesa 92626
Tel: (714) 641-4150
FAX: (714) 641-4170

Avnet Computer
1361B West 190th Street
Gardena 90248
Tel: (800) 426-7999
FAX: (310) 327-5389

Avnet Computer
755 Sunrise Boulevard, #150
Roseville 95661
Tel: (916) 781-2521
FAX: (916) 781-3819

Avnet Computer
1175 Bordeaux Drive, #A
Sunnyvale 94089
Tel: (408) 743-3454
FAX: (408) 743-3348

Avnet Computer
21150 Califa Street
Woodland Hills 91376
Tel: (818) 594-8301
FAX: (818) 594-8333

Hamilton Hallmark
3170 Pullman Street
Costa Mesa 92626
Tel: (714) 641-4100
FAX: (714) 641-4122

Hamilton Hallmark
1175 Bordeaux Drive, #A
Sunnyvale 94089
Tel: (408) 435-3500
FAX: (408) 745-6679

Hamilton Hallmark
4545 Viewridge Avenue
San Diego 92123
Tel: (619) 571-7540
FAX: (619) 277-6136

Hamilton Hallmark
21150 Califa St.
Woodland Hills 91367
Tel: (818) 594-0404
FAX: (818) 594-8234

Hamilton Hallmark
580 Menlo Drive, #2
Rocklin 95762
Tel: (916) 624-9781
FAX: (916) 961-0922

Pioneer Standard
5850 Canoga Blvd., #400
Woodland Hills 91367
Tel: (818) 883-4640

Pioneer Standard
217 Technology Dr., #110
Irvine 92718
Tel: (714) 753-5090

Pioneer Technologies Group
134 Rio Robles
San Jose 95134
Tel: (408) 954-9100
FAX: (408) 954-9113

Wyle Laboratories
15370 Barranca Pkwy.
Irvine 92713
Tel: (714) 753-9953
FAX: (714) 753-9877

Wyle Laboratories
15360 Barranca Pkwy., #200
Irvine 92713
Tel: (714) 753-9953
FAX: (714) 753-9877

Wyle Laboratories
2951 Sunrise Blvd., #175
Rancho Cordova 95742
Tel: (916) 638-5282
FAX: (916) 638-1491

Wyle Laboratories
9525 Chesapeake Drive
San Diego 92123
Tel: (619) 565-9171
FAX: (619) 365-0512

Wyle Laboratories
3000 Bowers Avenue
Santa Clara 95051
Tel: (408) 727-2500
FAX: (408) 727-5896

Wyle Laboratories
17872 Cowan Avenue
Irvine 92714
Tel: (714) 863-9953
FAX: (714) 263-0473

Wyle Laboratories
26010 Mureau Road, #150
Calabasas 91302
Tel: (818) 880-9000
FAX: (818) 880-5510

Zeus Arrow Electronics
6276 San Ignacio Ave., #E
San Jose 95119
Tel: (408) 629-4789
FAX: (408) 629-4792

Zeus Arrow Electronics
22700 Savi Ranch Pkwy.
Yorba Linda 92687-4613
Tel: (714) 921-9000
FAX: (714) 921-2715

COLORADO

Anthem Electronics
373 Inverness Drive South
Englewood 80112
Tel: (303) 790-4500
FAX: (303) 790-4532

Arrow/Schweber Electronics
61 Inverness Dr. East, #105
Englewood 80112
Tel: (303) 799-0258
FAX: (303) 373-5760

Hamilton Hallmark
12503 E. Euclid Drive, #20
Englewood 80111
Tel: (303) 790-1662
FAX: (303) 790-4991

Hamilton Hallmark
710 Wooten Road, #102
Colorado Springs 80915
Tel: (719) 637-0055
FAX: (719) 637-0088

Wyle Laboratories
451 E. 124th Avenue
Thornton 80241
Tel: (303) 457-9953
FAX: (303) 457-4831

CONNECTICUT

Anthem Electronics
61 Mattatuck Heights Road
Waterburg 06705
Tel: (203) 575-1575
FAX: (203) 596-3232

Arrow/Schweber Electronics
12 Beaumont Road
Wallingford 06492
Tel: (203) 265-7741
FAX: (203) 265-7988

Avnet Computer
55 Federal Road, #103
Danbury 06810
Tel: (203) 797-2880
FAX: (203) 791-9050

Hamilton Hallmark
125 Commerce Court, Unit 6
Cheshire 06410
Tel: (203) 271-2844
FAX: (203) 272-1704

Pioneer Standard
2 Trap Falls Road
Shelton 06484
Tel: (203) 929-5600

FLORIDA

Anthem Electronics
598 South Northlake Blvd., #1024
Altamonte Springs 32701
Tel: (813) 797-2900
FAX: (813) 796-4880

Arrow/Schweber Electronics
400 Fairway Drive, #102
Deerfield Beach 33441
Tel: (305) 429-8200
FAX: (305) 428-3991

Arrow/Schweber Electronics
37 Skyline Drive, #3101
Lake Mary 32746
Tel: (407) 333-9300
FAX: (407) 333-9320

Avnet Computer
3343 W. Commercial Boulevard
Bldg. C/D, Suite 107
Ft. Lauderdale 33309
Tel: (305) 730-9110
FAX: (305) 730-0368

Avnet Computer
3247 Tech Drive North
St. Petersburg 33716
Tel: (813) 573-5524
FAX: (813) 572-4324

Hamilton Hallmark
3350 N.W. 53rd St., #105-107
Ft. Lauderdale 33309
Tel: (305) 484-5482
FAX: (305) 484-2995

Hamilton Hallmark
10491 72nd St. North
Largo 34647
Tel: (813) 541-7440
FAX: (813) 544-4394

Hamilton Hallmark
7079 University Boulevard
Winter Park 32792
Tel: (407) 657-3300
FAX: (407) 678-4414

Pioneer Technologies Group
337 Northlake Blvd., #1000
Alta Monte Springs 32701
Tel: (407) 834-9090
FAX: (407) 834-0865

Pioneer Technologies Group
674 S. Military Trail
Deerfield Beach 33442
Tel: (305) 428-8877
FAX: (305) 481-2950

Pioneer Technologies Group
8031-2 Phillips Highway
Jacksonville 32256
Tel: (904) 730-0065

Wyle Laboratories
1000 112 Circle North
St. Petersburg 33716
Tel: (813) 530-3400
FAX: (813) 579-1518

GEORGIA

Arrow Commercial Systems Group
3400 C. Corporate Way
Duluth 30136
Tel: (404) 623-8825
FAX: (404) 623-8802

Arrow/Schweber Electronics
4250 E. Rivergreen Pkwy., #E
Duluth 30136
Tel: (404) 497-1300
FAX: (404) 476-1493

Avnet Computer
3425 Corporate Way, #G
Duluth 30136
Tel: (404) 623-5452
FAX: (404) 476-0125

Hamilton Hallmark
3425 Corporate Way, #G & #A
Duluth 30136
Tel: (404) 623-5475
FAX: (404) 623-5490

Pioneer Technologies Group
4250 C. Rivergreen Parkway
Duluth 30136
Tel: (404) 623-1003
FAX: (404) 623-0665

Wyle Laboratories
6025 The Corners Pkwy., #111
Norcross 30092
Tel: (404) 441-9045
FAX: (404) 441-9086

ILLINOIS

Anthem Electronics
1300 Remington Road, Suite A
Schaumberg 60173
Tel: (708) 884-0200
FAX: (708) 885-0480

Arrow/Schweber Electronics
1140 W. Thorndale Rd.
Itasca 60143
Tel: (708) 250-0500

Avnet Computer
1124 Thorndale Avenue
Bensenville 60106
Tel: (708) 860-8572
FAX: (708) 773-7976

Hamilton Hallmark
1130 Thorndale Avenue
Bensenville 60106
Tel: (708) 860-7780
FAX: (708) 860-8530

MTI Systems
1140 W. Thorndale Avenue
Itasca 60143
Tel: (708) 250-8222
FAX: (708) 250-8275

Pioneer Standard
2171 Executive Dr., #200
Addison 60101
Tel: (708) 495-9680
FAX: (708) 495-9831

Wyle Laboratories
2055 Army Trail Road, #140
Addison 60101
Tel: (800) 853-9953
FAX: (708) 620-1610

INDIANA

Arrow/Schweber Electronics
7108 Lakeview Parkway West Dr.
Indianapolis 46268
Tel: (317) 299-2071
FAX: (317) 299-2379

Avnet Computer
485 Gradle Drive
Carmel 46032
Tel: (317) 575-8029
FAX: (317) 844-4964

Hamilton Hallmark
4275 W. 96th
Indianapolis 46268
Tel: (317) 872-8875
FAX: (317) 876-7165

Pioneer Standard
9350 Priority Way West Dr.
Indianapolis 46250
Tel: (317) 573-0880
FAX: (317) 573-0979

NORTH AMERICAN DISTRIBUTORS (Contd.)

KANSAS

Arrow/Schweber Electronics
9801 Legler Road
Lenexa 66219
Tel: (913) 541-9542
FAX: (913) 541-0328

Avnet Computer
15313 W. 95th Street
Lenexa 61219
Tel: (913) 541-7989
FAX: (913) 541-7904

Hamilton Hallmark
10809 Lakeview Avenue
Lenexa 66215
Tel: (913) 888-4747
FAX: (913) 888-0523

KENTUCKY

Hamilton Hallmark
1847 Mercer Road, #G
Lexington 40511
Tel: (800) 235-6039
FAX: (606) 288-4936

MARYLAND

Anthem Electronics
7168A Columbia Gateway Drive
Columbia 21046
Tel: (410) 995-6640
FAX: (410) 290-9862

Arrow Commercial Systems Group
200 Perry Parkway
Gaithersburg 20877
Tel: (301) 670-1600
FAX: (301) 670-0188

Arrow/Schweber Electronics
9800J Patuxent Woods Dr.
Columbia 21046
Tel: (301) 596-7800
FAX: (301) 995-6201

Avnet Computer
7172 Columbia Gateway Dr., #G
Columbia 21045
Tel: (301) 995-3571
FAX: (301) 995-3515

Hamilton Hallmark
10240 Old Columbia Road
Columbia 21046
Tel: (410) 988-9800
FAX: (410) 381-2036

North Atlantic Industries
Systems Division
7125 River Wood Dr.
Columbia 21046
Tel: (301) 312-5800
FAX: (301) 312-5850

Pioneer Technologies Group
15810 Gaither Road
Gaithersburg 20877
Tel: (301) 921-0660
FAX: (301) 670-6746

Wyle Laboratories
7180 Columbia Gateway Dr.
Columbia 21046
Tel: (410) 312-4844
FAX: (410) 312-4953

MASSACHUSETTS

Anthem Electronics
36 Jonspin Road
Wilmington 01887
Tel: (508) 657-5170
FAX: (508) 657-6008

Arrow/Schweber Electronics
25 Upton Dr.
Wilmington 01887
Tel: (508) 658-0900
FAX: (508) 694-1754

Avnet Computer
10 D Centennial Drive
Peabody 01960
Tel: (508) 532-9886
FAX: (508) 532-9660

Hamilton Hallmark
10 D Centennial Drive
Peabody 01960
Tel: (508) 531-7430
FAX: (508) 532-9802

Pioneer Standard
44 Hartwell Avenue
Lexington 02173
Tel: (617) 861-9200
FAX: (617) 863-1547

Wyle Laboratories
15 Third Avenue
Burlington 01803
Tel: (617) 272-7300
FAX: (617) 272-6809

MICHIGAN

Arrow/Schweber Electronics
19880 Haggerty Road
Livonia 48152
Tel: (800) 231-7902
FAX: (313) 462-2686

Avnet Computer
2876 28th Street, S.W., #5
Grandville 49418
Tel: (616) 531-9607
FAX: (616) 531-0059

Avnet Computer
41650 Garden Brook Rd. #120
Novi 48375
Tel: (313) 347-1820
FAX: (313) 347-4067

Hamilton Hallmark
44191 Plymouth Oaks Blvd., #1300
Plymouth 48170
Tel: (313) 416-5800
FAX: (313) 416-5811

Hamilton Hallmark
41650 Garden Brook Rd., #100
Novi 49418
Tel: (313) 347-4271
FAX: (313) 347-4021

Pioneer Standard
4505 Broadmoor S.E.
Grand Rapids 49512
Tel: (616) 698-1800
FAX: (616) 698-1831

Pioneer Standard
13485 Stamford
Livonia 48150
Tel: (313) 525-1800
FAX: (313) 427-3720

MINNESOTA

Anthem Electronics
7646 Golden Triangle Drive
Eden Prairie 55344
Tel: (612) 944-5454
FAX: (612) 944-3045

Arrow/Schweber Electronics
10100 Viking Drive, #100
Eden Prairie 55344
Tel: (612) 941-5280
FAX: (612) 942-7803

Avnet Computer
10000 West 76th Street
Eden Prairie 55344
Tel: (612) 829-0025
FAX: (612) 944-2781

Hamilton Hallmark
9401 James Ave South, #140
Bloomington 55431
Tel: (612) 881-2600
FAX: (612) 881-9461

Pioneer Standard
7625 Golden Triange Dr., #G
Eden Prairie 55344
Tel: (612) 944-3355
FAX: (612) 944-3794

Wyle Laboratories
1325 E. 79th Street, #1
Bloomington 55425
Tel: (612) 853-2280
FAX: (612) 853-2298

MISSOURI

Arrow/Schweber Electronics
2380 Schuetz Road
St. Louis 63141
Tel: (314) 567-6888
FAX: (314) 567-1164

Avnet Computer
741 Goddard Avenue
Chesterfield 63005
Tel: (314) 537-2725
FAX: (314) 537-4248

Hamilton Hallmark
3783 Rider Trail South
Earth City 63045
Tel: (314) 291-5350
FAX: (314) 291-0362

NEW HAMPSHIRE

Avnet Computer
2 Executive Park Drive
Bedford 03102
Tel: (800) 442-8638
FAX: (603) 624-2402

NEW JERSEY

Anthem Electronics
26 Chapin Road, Unit K
Pine Brook 07058
Tel: (201) 227-7960
FAX: (201) 227-9246

Arrow/Schweber Electronics
4 East Stow Rd., Unit 11
Marlton 08053
Tel: (609) 596-8000
FAX: (609) 596-9632

Arrow/Schweber Electronics
43 Route 46 East
Pine Brook 07058
Tel: (201) 227-7880
FAX: (201) 538-4962

Avnet Computer
1-B Keystone Ave., Bldg. 36
Cherry Hill 08003
Tel: (609) 424-8961
FAX: (609) 751-2502

Hamilton Hallmark
1 Keystone Ave., Bldg. 36
Cherry Hill 08003
Tel: (609) 424-0110
FAX: (609) 751-2552

Hamilton Hallmark
10 Lanidex Plaza West
Parsippani 07054
Tel: (201) 515-5300
FAX: (201) 515-1601

MTI Systems
43 Route 46 East
Pinebrook 07058
Tel: (201) 882-8780
FAX: (201) 539-6430

Pioneer Standard
14-A Madison Rd.
Fairfield 07006
Tel: (201) 575-3510
FAX: (201) 575-3454

Wyle Laboratories
20 Chapin Road, Bldg. 10-13
Pinebrook 07058
Tel: (201) 882-8358
FAX: (201) 882-9109

NEW MEXICO

Alliance Electronics, Inc.
10510 Research Ave.
Albuquerque 87123
Tel: (505) 292-3360
FAX: (505) 275-6392

Avnet Computer
7801 Academy Rd.
Bldg. 1, Suite 204
Albuquerque 87109
Tel: (505) 828-9725
FAX: (505) 828-0360

NEW YORK

Anthem Electronics
47 Mall Drive
Commack 11725
Tel: (516) 864-6600
FAX: (516) 493-2244

Arrow/Schweber Electronics
3375 Brighton Henrietta
Townline Rd.
Rochester 14623
Tel: (716) 427-0300
FAX: (716) 427-0735

Arrow/Schweber Electronics
20 Oser Avenue
Hauppauge 11788
Tel: (516) 231-1000
FAX: (516) 231-1072

Avnet Computer
933 Motor Parkway
Hauppauge 11788
Tel: (516) 434-7443
FAX: (516) 434-7426

Avnet Computer
2060 Townline Rd.
Rochester 14623
Tel: (716) 272-9110
FAX: (716) 272-9685

Hamilton Hallmark
933 Motor Parkway
Hauppauge 11788
Tel: (516) 434-7470
FAX: (516) 434-7491

Hamilton Hallmark
1057 E. Henrietta Road
Rochester 14623
Tel: (716) 475-9130
FAX: (716) 475-9119

Hamilton Hallmark
3075 Veterans Memorial Hwy.
Ronkonkoma 11779
Tel: (516) 737-0600
FAX: (516) 737-0838

MTI Systems
1 Penn Plaza
250 W. 34th Street
New York 10119
Tel: (212) 643-1280
FAX: (212) 643-1288

Pioneer Standard
68 Corporate Drive
Binghamton 13904
Tel: (607) 722-9300
FAX: (607) 722-9562

Pioneer Standard
60 Crossway Park West
Woodbury, Long Island 11797
Tel: (516) 921-8700
FAX: (516) 921-2143

Pioneer Standard
840 Fairport Park
Fairport 14450
Tel: (716) 381-7070
FAX: (716) 381-5955

Zeus Arrow Electronics
100 Midland Avenue
Port Chester 10573
Tel: (914) 937-7400
FAX: (914) 937-2553

NORTH CAROLINA

Arrow/Schweber Electronics
5240 Greensdairy Road
Raleigh 27604
Tel: (919) 876-3132
FAX: (919) 878-9517

Avnet Computer
2725 Millbrook Rd., #123
Raleigh 27604
Tel: (919) 790-1735
FAX: (919) 872-4972

Hamilton Hallmark
5234 Greens Dairy Road
Raleigh 27604
Tel: (919) 878-0819
FAX: (919) 878-8729

Pioneer Technologies Group
2200 Gateway Ctr. Blvd, #215
Morrisville 27560
Tel: (919) 460-1530
FAX: (919) 460-1540

OHIO

Arrow Commercial Systems Group
284 Cramer Creek Court
Dublin 43017
Tel: (614) 889-9347
FAX: (614) 889-9680

Arrow/Schweber Electronics
6573 Cochran Road, #E
Solon 44139
Tel: (216) 248-3990
FAX: (216) 248-1106

Arrow/Schweber Electronics
8200 Washington Village Dr.
Centerville 45458
Tel: (513) 435-5563
FAX: (513) 435-2049

Avnet Computer
7764 Washington Village Dr.
Dayton 45459
Tel: (513) 439-6756
FAX: (513) 439-6719

Avnet Computer
30325 Bainbridge Rd., Bldg. A
Solon 44139
Tel: (216) 349-2505
FAX: (216) 349-1894

Hamilton Hallmark
7760 Washington Village Dr.
Dayton 45459
Tel: (513) 439-6735
FAX: (513) 439-6711

Hamilton Hallmark
5821 Harper Road
Solon 44139
Tel: (216) 498-1100
FAX: (216) 248-4803

Hamilton Hallmark
777 Dearborn Park Lane, #L
Worthington 43085
Tel: (614) 888-3313
FAX: (614) 888-0767

MTI Systems
23404 Commerce Park Rd.
Beachwood 44122
Tel: (216) 464-6688
FAX: (216) 464-3564

Pioneer Standard
4433 Interpoint Boulevard
Dayton 45424
Tel: (513) 236-9900
FAX: (513) 236-8133

Pioneer Standard
4800 E. 131st Street
Cleveland 44105
Tel: (216) 587-3600
FAX: (216) 663-1004

OKLAHOMA

Arrow/Schweber Electronics
12101 E. 51st Street, #106
Tulsa 74146
Tel: (918) 252-7537
FAX: (918) 254-0917

Hamilton Hallmark
5411 S. 125th E. Ave., #305
Tulsa 74146
Tel: (918) 254-6110
FAX: (918) 254-6207

Pioneer Standard
9717 E. 42nd St., #105
Tulsa 74146
Tel: (918) 665-7840
FAX: (918) 665-1891

NORTH AMERICAN DISTRIBUTORS (Contd.)

OREGON

Almac Arrow Electronics
1885 N.W. 169th Place
Beaverton 97006
Tel: (503) 629-8090
FAX: (503) 645-0611

Anthem Electronics
9090 S.W. Gemini Drive
Beaverton 97005
Tel: (503) 643-1114
FAX: (503) 626-7928

Avnet Computer
9750 Southwest Nimbus Ave.
Beaverton 97005
Tel: (503) 627-0900
FAX: (502) 526-6242

Hamilton Hallmark
9750 S.W. Nimbus Ave.
Beaverton 97005
Tel: (503) 526-6200
FAX: (503) 641-5939

Wyle Laboratories
9640 Sunshine Court
Bldg. G, Suite 200
Beaverton 97005
Tel: (503) 643-7900
FAX: (503) 646-5466

PENNSYLVANIA

Anthem Electronics
355 Business Center Dr.
Horsham 19044
Tel: (215) 443-5150
FAX: (215) 675-9875

Avnet Computer
213 Executive Drive, #320
Mars 16046
Tel: (412) 772-1888
FAX: (412) 772-1890

Pioneer Technologies Group
259 Kappa Drive
Pittsburgh 15238
Tel: (412) 782-2300
FAX: (412) 963-8255

Pioneer Technologies Group
500 Enterprise Road
Keith Valley Business Center
Horsham 19044
Tel: (713) 530-4700

Wyle Laboratories
1 Eves Drive, #111
Marlton 08053-3185
Tel: (609) 985-7953
FAX: (609) 985-8757

TEXAS

Anthem Electronics
651 N. Plano Road, #401
Richardson 75081
Tel: (214) 238-7100
FAX: (214) 238-0237

Arrow/Schweber Electronics
11500 Metric Blvd., #160
Austin 78758
Tel: (512) 835-4180
FAX: (512) 832-5921

Arrow/Schweber Electronics
3220 Commander Dr.
Carrollton 75006
Tel: (214) 380-6464
FAX: (214) 248-7208

Arrow/Schweber Electronics
10899 Kinghurst Dr., #100
Houston 77099
Tel: (713) 530-4700

Avnet Computer
4004 Beltline, Suite 200
Dallas 75244
Tel: (214) 308-8181
FAX: (214) 308-8129

Avnet Computer
1235 North Loop West, #525
Houston 77008
Tel: (713) 867-8572
FAX: (713) 861-6851

Hamilton Hallmark
12211 Technology Blvd.
Austin 78727
Tel: (512) 258-8848
FAX: (512) 258-3777

Hamilton Hallmark
11420 Page Mill Road
Dallas 75243
Tel: (214) 553-4300
FAX: (214) 553-4395

Hamilton Hallmark
8000 Westglen
Houston 77063
Tel: (713) 781-6100
FAX: (713) 953-8420

Pioneer Standard
1826-D Kramer Lane
Austin 78758
Tel: (512) 835-4000
FAX: (512) 835-9829

Pioneer Standard
13765 Beta Road
Dallas 75244
Tel: (214) 263-3168
FAX: (214) 490-6419

Pioneer Standard
10530 Rockley Road, #100
Houston 77099
Tel: (713) 495-4700
FAX: (713) 495-5642

Wyle Laboratories
1810 Greenville Avenue
Richardson 75081
Tel: (214) 235-9953
FAX: (214) 644-5064

Wyle Laboratories
4030 West Braker Lane, #330
Austin 78758
Tel: (512) 345-8853
FAX: (512) 345-9330

Wyle Laboratories
11001 South Wilcrest, #100
Houston 77099
Tel: (713) 879-9953
FAX: (713) 879-6540

UTAH

Anthem Electronics
1279 West 2200 South
Salt Lake City 84119
Tel: (801) 973-8555
FAX: (801) 973-8909

Arrow/Schweber Electronics
1946 W. Parkway Blvd.
Salt Lake City 84119
Tel: (801) 973-6913
FAX: (801) 972-0200

Avnet Computer
1100 E. 6600 South, #150
Salt Lake City 84121
Tel: (801) 266-1115
FAX: (801) 266-0362

Hamilton Hallmark
1100 East 6600 South, #120
Salt Lake City 84121
Tel: (801) 266-2022
FAX: (801) 263-0104

Wyle Laboratories
1325 West 2200 South, #E
West Valley 84119
Tel: (801) 974-9953
FAX: (801) 972-2524

WASHINGTON

Almac Arrow Electronics
14360 S.E. Eastgate Way
Bellevue 98007
Tel: (206) 643-9992
FAX: (206) 643-9709

Anthem Electronics
19017 - 120th Ave., N.E. #102
Bothell 98011
Tel: (206) 483-1700
FAX: (206) 486-0571

Avnet Computer
17761 N.E. 78th Place
Redmond 98052
Tel: (206) 867-0160
FAX: (206) 867-0161

Hamilton Hallmark
8630 154th Avenue
Redmond 98052
Tel: (206) 881-6697
FAX: (206) 867-0159

Wyle Laboratories
15385 N.E. 90th Street
Redmond 98052
Tel: (206) 881-1150
FAX: (206) 881-1567

WISCONSIN

Arrow/Schweber Electronics
200 N. Patrick, #100
Brookfield 53045
Tel: (414) 792-0150
FAX: (414) 792-0156

Avnet Computer
20875 Crossroads Circle, #400
Waukesha 53186
Tel: (414) 784-8205
FAX: (414) 784-6006

Hamilton Hallmark
2440 S. 179th Street
New Berlin 53146
Tel: (414) 797-7844
FAX: (414) 797-9259

Pioneer Standard
120 Bishop Way #163
Brookfield 53005
Tel: (414) 784-3480
FAX: (414) 780-3613

Wyle Laboratories
W226 N555 Eastmound Drive
Waukesha 53186
Tel: (414) 521-9333
FAX: (414) 521-9498

ALASKA

Avnet Computer
1400 West Benson Blvd., #400
Anchorage 99503
Tel: (907) 274-9899
FAX: (907) 277-2639

CANADA

ALBERTA

Avnet Computer
2816 21st Street Northeast
Calgary T2E 6Z2
Tel: (403) 291-3284
FAX: (403) 250-1591

Zentronics
6815 8th Street N.E., #100
Calgary T2E 7H
Tel: (403) 295-8838
FAX: (403) 295-8714

BRITISH COLUMBIA

Almac Arrow Electronics
8544 Baxter Place
Burnaby V5A 4T8
Tel: (604) 421-2333
FAX: (604) 421-5030

Hamilton Hallmark
8610 Commerce Court
Burnaby V5A 4N6
Tel: (604) 420-4101
FAX: (604) 420-5376

Zentronics
11400 Bridgeport Rd., #108
Richmond V6X 1T2
Tel: (604) 273-5575
FAX: (604) 273-2413

ONTARIO

Arrow/Schweber Electronics
1093 Meyerside, Unit 2
Mississauga L5T 1M4
Tel: (416) 670-7769
FAX: (416) 670-7781

Arrow/Schweber Electronics
36 Antares Dr., Unit 100
Nepean K2E 7W5
Tel: (613) 226-6903
FAX: (613) 723-2018

Avnet Computer
Canada System Engineering Group
151 Superior Blvd.
Mississuaga L5T 2L1
Tel: (416) 795-3835
FAX: (416) 677-5091

Avnet Computer
190 Colonade Road
Nepean K2E 7J5
Tel: (613) 727-2000
FAX: (613) 226-1184

Hamilton Hallmark
151 Superior Blvd., Unit 1-6
Mississauga L5T 2L1
Tel: (416) 564-6060
FAX: (416) 564-6033

Hamilton Hallmark
190 Colonade Road
Nepean K2E 7J5
Tel: (613) 226-1700
FAX: (613) 226-1184

Zentronics
5600 Keaton Crescent, #1
Mississauga L5R 3S5
Tel: (416) 507-2600
FAX: (416) 507-2831

Zentronics
155 Colonnade Rd., South
#17
Nepean K2E 7K1
Tel: (613) 226-8840
FAX: (613) 226-6352

QUEBEC

Arrow/Schweber Electronics
1100 St. Regis Blvd.
Dorval H9P 2T5
Tel: (514) 421-7411
FAX: (514) 421-7430

Arrow/Schweber Electronics
500 Boul. St.-Jean-Baptiste Ave.
Quebec H2E 5R9
Tel: (418) 871-7500
FAX: (418) 871-6816

Avnet Computer
2795 Reu Halpern
St. Laurent H4S 1P8
Tel: (514) 335-2483
FAX: (514) 335-2481

Hamilton Hallmark
7575 Transcanada Highway
#600
St. Laurent H4T 2V6
Tel: (514) 335-1000
FAX: (514) 335-2481

Zentronics
520 McCaffrey
St. Laurent H4T 1N3
Tel: (514) 737-9700
FAX: (514) 737-5212